With the aid of the alphabetical thumb index at the edge of the page you can quickly locate the letter you need to find in the French-English and English-French dictionary. Once you have located the letter you need on the thumb index, simply flip to the correspondingly marked part of the dictionary.

If you are left-handed, you can use the thumb index at the end of this book.

A l'aide de l'index alphabétique en bord de page, vous pouvez rapidement trouver la lettre que vous cherchez dans les parties français-anglais et anglais-français du dictionnaire. Après avoir localisé la lettre dans l'index, il vous suffit de faire basculer les pages jusqu'à la partie du dictionnaire que vous avez repérée.

Si vous êtes gaucher, vous pouvez utiliser l'index qui se trouve à la fin de ce dictionnaire.

W9-CDD-958

A
B
C
D
E
F
G
H
I
J
K
L
M
N
O
P
Q
R
S
T
U
V
W
X
Y
Z

## Comment utiliser le dictionnaire

Toutes les entrées (mots, abréviations, composés, variantes orthographiques, renvois) sont présentées dans l'ordre alphabétique et imprimées en caractères gras. Les abréviations sont suivies de leur forme développée.

**ADN** [adɛɛn] *m abr de* **acide désoxyribonucléique** DNA
**ado** [ado] *mf inf abr de* **adolescent**
**adolescence** [adɔlesɑ̃s] *f* adolescence

Les verbes anglais à particule viennent directement après le verbe de base et sont introduits par le signe ◆.

Les exposants en chiffre arabe indiquent qu'il s'agit de mots identiques avec des sens différents (homographes).

**cor**[1] [kɔʀ] *m* MUS horn
**cor**[2] [kɔʀ] *m* MED corn

La transcription de la phonétique est faite d'après l'alphabet phonétique international. Pour la transcription phonétique de l'anglais, la division en syllabes est indiquée avec des points.

**décalage** [dekalaʒ] *m* ➊ (*action: d'un horaire*) pushing back …

On trouvera entre chevrons les formes irrégulières au pluriel, un numéro renvoyant aux tableaux de conjugaison française se trouvant en annexe ou les formes irrégulières des verbes et adjectifs anglais.

**eau** [o] <x> *f* water; …
**ébahir** [ebaiʀ] <8> *vt* to astonish

La forme du féminin est toujours indiquée lorsqu'elle diffère du masculin. Les substantifs français sont toujours suivis de l'indication du genre.

**fondateur, -trice** [fɔ̃datœʀ, -tʀis] *m, f* founder

Les chiffres romains subdivisent une entrée en différentes catégories grammaticales, les chiffres arabes en ses différents sens.

**gauche** [goʃ] **I.** *adj* ➊ (*opp: droit*) left ➋ (*maladroit*) uneasy; (*geste*) jerky **II.** *m* **un crochet du ~** a left hook …

Le tilde remplace l'entrée dans les exemples et tournures idiomatiques. Le signe ▶ introduit le bloc des expressions figées, des idiomes et des proverbes. Les <u>mots soulignés</u> permettent une meilleure orientation.

**hors** [´ɔʀ] *prep* ➊ (*à l'extérieur de*) **~ de** outside ➋ (*au-delà de*) **~ d'atteinte** [o de portée] out of reach ▶ **~ de <u>danger</u>** out of danger; **~ de <u>prix</u>** exorbitant

## How to use the dictionary

**atlas** ['æt·ləs] <-es> *n* atlas *m*
**ATM** [ˌeɪˈtiˈem] *n abbr of* **automated teller machine** DAB *m*
**atmosphere** ['æt·məs·fɪr] *n* atmosphère *f;* ...

All entries (including words, abbreviations, compounds, variant spellings and cross-references) appear in alphabetical order and are printed in bold type. Abbreviations are followed by their full form.

**build** [bɪld] **I.** *n* charpente *f* ...
◆ **build in** *vt* (*cupboard*) encastrer; (*security, penalty*) introduire
◆ **build on** *vt* ❶ (*add*) ajouter ...

English phrasal verbs come directly after the base verb and are marked with a diamond (◆).

**console¹** [kən·'soʊl] *vt* consoler
**console²** ['kan·soʊl] *n* (*switch panel*) console *f*

Superscript, or raised numbers, indicate identically spelled words with different meanings (so-called homographs).

**disadvantage** [ˌdɪs·əd·'væn·tɪdʒ] **I.** *n* inconvénient *m;* ...

The International Phonetic Alphabet is used for all phonetic transcriptions. Transcriptions of English are divided into syllables by means of centered dots.

**eat** [it] **I.**<ate, eaten> *vt* manger; ...
**empty** ['em(p)·ti] **I.**<-ier, -iest> *adj* ❶ (*with nothing inside*) vide; ...

Irregular plural forms, numbers referring to the French conjugation tables in the appendix and forms of English irregular verbs and adjectives are given in angle brackets.

French feminine forms are shown unless they are identical to the masculine form. French nouns are followed by their gender.

**gossip** ['ga·səp] **I.** *n* ❶ (*rumor*) potins *mpl* ❷ *pej* (*person who gossips*) commère *f* **II.** *vi* cancaner; ...

Roman numerals are used for the parts of speech of a word, and Arabic numerals for sense divisions.

**hot** [hat] <-ter, -test> *adj* ❶ (*very warm*) chaud(e); **it's** ~ il fait chaud ❷ (*spicy*) fort(e) ... ▸ **to get into** ~ <u>water</u> se fourrer dans le pétrin

The swung dash represents the entry word in examples and idioms.
The ▸ sign introduces a block of set expressions, idioms and proverbs. Key words are <u>underlined</u> as a guide.

# FRENCH–ENGLISH

## Pocket Dictionary

---

## Dictionnaire de poche
# FRANÇAIS–ANGLAIS

**Second Edition**

**BARRON'S Foreign Language Guides**
**French-English Pocket Dictionary**
**Dictionnaire de poche Français-Anglais**

Second edition for the United States and Canada published in 2015 by Barron's Educational Series, Inc.
First edition for the United States and Canada published in 2008 by Barron's Educational Series, Inc.

**Editorial Management:** Gabriela Neumann
**Contributors:** Frédéric Auvrai, Ruth Urbom, Dr. Christiane Wirth

**Typesetting:** Dörr + Schiller GmbH, Stuttgart

*All inquiries should be addressed to:*
Barron's Educational Series, Inc.
250 Wireless Boulevard
Hauppauge, New York 11788
**www.barronseduc.com**

ISBN: 978-1-4380-0607-9
Library of Congress Control No.: 2015939109

Printed in China
9 8 7 6 5 4 3 2 1

# Table des matières
# Contents

# La transcription phonétique du français

## French phonetic symbols

### Voyelles
### Vowels

| | | | | |
|---|---|---|---|---|
| [a] | bac | | [o] | auto |
| [ɑ] | classe | | [ɔ] | obtenir |
| [e] | état | | [ø] | Europe |
| [ɛ] | caisse | | [œ] | cœur |
| [ə] | menace | | [u] | coup |
| [i] | diplôme | | [y] | nature |

### Nasales
### Nasal Vowels

| | |
|---|---|
| [ã] | chanson |
| [ɛ̃] | afin |
| [ɔ̃] | bonbon |
| [œ̃] | aucun |

### Semi-consonnes
### Semiconsonants

| | |
|---|---|
| [j] | pièce |
| [w] | boîte |
| [ɥ] | huile |

## Consonnes
## Consonants

| | | | | |
|---|---|---|---|---|
| [b] | beau | | [ɲ] | digne |
| [d] | du | | [ŋ] | camping |
| [f] | feu | | [p] | page |
| [g] | gant | | [ʀ] | règle |
| [ʒ] | jour | | [s] | sel |
| [k] | cœur | | [ʃ] | chef |
| [l] | loup | | [t] | timbre |
| [m] | marché | | [v] | vapeur |
| [n] | nature | | [z] | zèbre |

## Signe
## Sign

| | |
|---|---|
| [´] | héros (h aspiré/aspirate h) |

# English phonetic symbols
## La transcription phonétique de l'anglais

**Vowels**
**Voyelles**

| | | | | |
|---|---|---|---|---|
| [a] | farm, father, not | | [i] | beat, bee, belief, me |
| [æ] | man, plant, sad | | [ɪ] | it, near, wish |
| [e] | hed, get, hair | | [ɔ] | all, law, long |
| [ə] | actor, ago, better | | [u] | do, soon, you |
| [ə] | nation, sudden, wonderful | | [ʊ] | look, push, sure |
| [ɜ] | bird, her | | [ʌ] | but, son |

**Diphthongs**
**Diphtongues**

| | | | | |
|---|---|---|---|---|
| [aɪ] | buy, by, life | | [ɔɪ] | boy, oil |
| [aʊ] | growl, house | | [oʊ] | road, rope, show |
| [eɪ] | lame, name | | [ju] | abuse, pupil |

## Consonants
## Consonnes

| | | | | |
|------|-------------------|---|------|-------------------------|
| [b] | been, blind | | [ŋ] | long, prank, string |
| [d] | do, had | | [p] | happy, paper |
| [ð] | father, this | | [r] | dry, red |
| [dʒ] | jam, object | | [s] | sand, stand, yes |
| [f] | father, wolf | | [ʃ] | fish, ship, station |
| [g] | beg, go | | [t] | fat, tell |
| [h] | house | | [t̬] | butter, water |
| [j] | youth | | [θ] | death, thank |
| [ʒ] | pleasure | | [tʃ] | catch, church |
| [k] | keep, milk | | [v] | live, voice |
| [l] | ill, lamp, oil | | [w] | water, we, which |
| [m] | am, man | | [z] | gaze, these, zeal |
| [n] | manner, no | | | |

## Signs
## Signes

| | |
|------|--------------------|
| ['] | primary stress |
| [,] | secondary stress |
| [·] | syllable division |

# Aa

**A, a** [ɑ] *m inv* A, a; **~ comme Anatole** (*au téléphone*) a as in Alpha

**a¹** [a] *indic prés de* **avoir**

**a²** [a] *m* INFORM **a commercial** at sign

**à** [a] <à + le = au, à la, à + les = aux> *prep* ❶ (*introduit un complément de temps*) at; **à 8 heures/Noël** at 8 o'clock/Christmas; **à quelle heure?** what time?, when?; **le cinq juin au matin** on the morning of June fifth ❷ (*indique une époque*) in; **au printemps** in (the) spring; **aux premiers beaux jours** with the first days of nice weather; **nous te reverrons à Pâques** we will see you again at Easter ❸ (*indique une date ultérieure*) **on se verra aux prochaines vacances** we will see each other next vacation; **à mon retour** when I get back ❹ (*pour prendre rendez-vous*) **à demain!** see you tomorrow! ❺ (*jusque*) until; **je serai absent de lundi à jeudi** I will be away from Monday to Thursday ❻ (*pour indiquer une direction*) to); **aller à l'école/aux États-Unis** to go to school/to the United States; **s'asseoir à son bureau** to sit down at one's desk ❼ (*indique le lieu où l'on est*) **être à la piscine/poste** to be at the swimming pool/the post office; **habiter à Paris/aux États-Unis** to live in Paris/in the United States; **habiter au troisième étage** to live on the second floor; **être assis à son bureau** to be at one's desk; **au coin de la rue** at the corner of the street; **à cinq minutes/trois kilomètres d'ici** five minutes/three kilometers from here; **à la télévision/la page 36/l'épaule** on television/page 36/the shoulder; **avoir mal à la tête** to have a headache ❽ (*indique le nombre de personnes*) **nous travaillons à 2/3/12 sur ce projet** there are 2/3/12 of us working on this project; **on peut tenir à 50 dans cette salle** this room can hold 50 people ❾ (*par*) **à l'heure** by the hour; **à la journée** on a daily basis; **7 litres aux 100 (kilomètres)** 7 liters per 100 (kilometers); **acheter au poids** to buy by weight ❿ (*cause*) **à sa démarche, on voit qu'il a mal** you can tell from the way he walks that he is in pain ⓫ (*conséquence*) to); **à ma plus grande surprise** to my complete surprise ⓬ (*d'après*) **à la demande de qn** at sb's request ⓭ (*indique une appartenance*) **c'est à moi/lui** it's mine/his; **un ami à eux** a friend of theirs ⓮ (*indique le moyen*) **coudre qc à la machine** to sew sth by machine; **cuisiner au beurre** to cook with butter; **au microscope** under the microscope; **boire à la bouteille** to drink from the bottle ⓯ (*introduit un superlatif*) **elle est au plus mal** she is very ill ⓰ (*au point de*) **s'ennuyer à mourir** to be bored to death; **c'est à rendre fou** it's enough to drive you crazy ⓱ (*complément indirect*) **donner qc à qn** to give sth to sb, give sth sth; **jouer aux cartes** to play cards; **penser à qn/qc** to think about [*o of*] sth/sb; **parler à qn** to speak to sb; **téléphoner à qn** to (tele)phone sb; **participer à qc** to take part in sth ⓲ (*locution verbale*) **elle prend plaisir à cuisiner** she enjoys cooking; **il se met à pleuvoir** it's beginning to rain; **c'est facile à faire** it's easy to do; **maison à vendre** house for sale

**abaissement** [abɛsmɑ̃] *m* (*d'une vitre, d'un niveau, des prix*) lowering

**abaisser** [abese] <1> I. *vt* ❶ (*rideau, température, prix*) to lower ❷ (*avilir*) to humble II. *vpr* **s'~** ❶ (*descendre: vitre, rideau*) to be lowered ❷ (*s'humilier*) to humble oneself

**abajoue** [abaʒu] *f* (*d'un hamster, singe*) cheek pouch

**A**

**abandon** [abãdɔ̃] *m* ❶ (*désertion, délaissement*) abandonment ❷ (*fait de renoncer à*) giving up ❸ SPORT withdrawal

**abandonné(e)** [abãdɔne] *adj* abandoned; (*chat*) stray

**abandonner** [abãdɔne] <1> I. *vt* ❶ (*déserter, quitter*) to abandon ❷ (*laisser derrière soi: déchets*) to leave behind ❸ (*renoncer à: hypothèse, méthode*) to discard; (*pouvoir, fonction*) to relinquish; (*piste, combat, études*) to give up II. *vi* to give up

**abasourdir** [abazuʀdiʀ] <8> *vt* ❶ (*stupéfier*) to stun ❷ (*assourdir*) to deafen

**abat-jour** [abaʒuʀ] *m inv* lampshade

**abats** [aba] *mpl* (*de porc, mouton*) offal; (*de volaille*) giblets

**abattoir** [abatwaʀ] *m* slaughterhouse

**abattre** [abatʀ] *irr* I. *vt* ❶ (*faire tomber*) ~ qc (*mur, maison, quille*) to knock sth down; (*cloison*) to break sth down; (*arbre*) to fell sth; (*forêt*) to chop sth down; (*avion*) to shoot sth down ❷ (*tuer: animal de boucherie*) to slaughter; ~ un animal blessé to put down an injured animal ❸ (*assassiner*) to kill ❹ (*affaiblir*) ~ qn (*fièvre, maladie*) to knock sb out II. *vpr* s'~ ❶ (*tomber*) to fall down; s'~ sur le sol to collapse on the ground ❷ (*tomber brutalement: pluie*) to come pouring down; (*grêle*) to pelt down

**abattu(e)** [abaty] I. *part passé de* **abattre** II. *adj* ❶ (*physiquement*) exhausted ❷ (*moralement*) despondent

**abbaye** [abei] *f* abbey

**abbé** [abe] *m* ❶ (*prêtre*) priest ❷ (*supérieur d'une abbaye*) abbot

**abcès** [apsɛ] *m* abscess

**abdication** [abdikasjɔ̃] *f* abdication

**abdiquer** [abdike] <1> *vi* (*roi*) to abdicate

**abdomen** [abdɔmɛn] *m* abdomen

**abdominal(e)** [abdɔminal, -o] <-aux> *adj* abdominal

**abdominaux** [abdɔmino] *mpl* ANAT abdominal muscles

**abeille** [abɛj] *f* bee

**aberrant(e)** [abeʀɑ̃, ɑ̃t] *adj* deviant; (*idée*) preposterous

**aberration** [abeʀasjɔ̃] *f* aberration

**abîmer** [abime] <1> I. *vt* (*détériorer*) to ruin II. *vpr* ❶ (*se gâter*) s'~ to spoil ❷ (*détériorer*) s'~ les yeux to ruin one's eyes

**aboiement** [abwamã] *m* bark; les ~s d'un chien a dog's barking

**abolir** [abɔliʀ] <8> *vt* (*esclavage, loi*) to abolish

**abolition** [abɔlisjɔ̃] *f* abolition

**abominable** [abɔminabl] *adj* ❶ (*horrible*) appalling; (*action*) heinous ❷ (*très mauvais, insupportable*) abominable

**abomination** [abɔminasjɔ̃] *f* (*acte particulièrement répugnant*) abomination

**abondamment** [abɔ̃damã] *adv* (*servir*) plentifully; (*fleurir*) abundantly

**abondance** [abɔ̃dɑ̃s] *f* ❶ (*profusion*) abundance ❷ (*richesse*) wealth

**abondant(e)** [abɔ̃dɑ̃, ɑ̃t] *adj* (*nourriture*) copious; (*réserves*) plentiful; des pluies ~es heavy rainfall

**abonder** [abɔ̃de] <1> *vi* ❶ (*exister en grande quantité*) to be plentiful ❷ (*avoir en quantité*) ~ en qc to be full of sth ❸ (*être de même avis*) ~ dans le sens de qn to agree wholeheartedly with sb

**abonné(e)** [abɔne] I. *adj* (*qui a un abonnement*) être ~ à un journal to subscribe to a newspaper; être ~ au téléphone to have a telephone II. *m(f)* (*théâtre*) season ticket holder; (*d'un journal, service*) subscriber

**abonnement** [abɔnmã] *m* (*au bus*) pass; ~ téléphonique telephone service; ~ mensuel monthly subscription; prendre un ~ à un journal to subscribe to a newspaper

**abonner** [abɔne] <1> I. *vpr* s'~ à un journal to subscribe to a newspaper; s'~ à un club to join a club II. *vt* ~ qn au théâtre to buy sb a season ticket for the theater; ~ qn à un journal to buy sb a subscription to a newspaper

**abord** [abɔʀ] *m* ❶ (*alentours*) les ~s d'une ville the area around a town

**A**

❷(*attitude*) être d'un ~ **facile** to be approachable ▸ (**tout**) **d'** ~ (*temporel*) at first; (*avant tout*) first of all; **d'** ~ **inf d'** ~ **tu n'avais qu'à demander!** for one thing, all you had to do was ask!

**abordable** [abɔʀdabl] *adj* (*bon marché*) affordable

**aborder** [abɔʀde] <1> I. *vt* ❶(*accoster, évoquer*) to tackle ❷(*appréhender, amorcer: auteur, texte, virage*) to approach II. *vi* NAUT to land

**aboutir** [abutiʀ] <8> *vi* ❶(*réussir*) to succeed *inf*; (*projet*) to be a success; **ne pas** ~ not to turn out well ❷(*conduire à*) ~ **à/dans qc** (*rue*) to lead to/into sth ❸(*se terminer par*) ~ **à qc** (*démarche*) to lead to sth

**aboyer** [abwaje] <6> *vi* (*chien*) to bark

**abrégé** [abʀeʒe] <1> I. *vt* ❶(*texte réduit*) summary; **mot en** ~ abbreviated form of a word ❷(*ouvrage*) handbook

**abréger** [abʀeʒe] <2a, 5> *vt* ~ **qc** (*souffrances, rencontre*) to cut sth short; (*mot, texte*) to abbreviate sth

**abreuver** [abʀœve] <1> I. *vt* (*donner à boire: animal*) to water II. *vpr* (*boire*) **s'** ~ (*animal*) to drink

**abréviation** [abʀevjasjɔ̃] *f* abbreviation

**abri** [abʀi] *m* ❶(*protection naturelle*) shelter; **être à l'** ~ **des intempéries** to be sheltered from bad weather; **mettre qc à l'** ~ to put sth under cover ❷(*souterrain*) (underground) shelter ❸(*lieu aménagé*) shelter; ~ **de jardin** garden shed; **être à l'** ~ (*personne*) to be under cover ▸ **être à l'** ~ **du besoin** to be protected from hardship

**abribus**® [abʀibys] *m* bus shelter

**abricot** [abʀiko] *adj, m* apricot

**abriter** [abʀite] <1> I. *vt* ❶(*protéger*) to shelter ❷(*héberger*) to harbor II. *vpr* ❶(*se protéger*) **s'** ~ **de qc** to take shelter from sth ❷(*se protéger des intempéries*) **s'** ~ to take shelter

**abrupt** [abʀypt] *m* steep slope

**abrupt(e)** [abʀypt] *adj* (*raide: pente*) steep

**abruti(e)** [abʀyti] *m(f)* *inf* idiot

**abrutir** [abʀytiʀ] <8> *vt* to exhaust

**abrutissant(e)** [abʀytisɑ̃, ɑ̃t] *adj* (*travail*) mind-numbing; (*musique*) deafening

**A.B.S.** [abeɛs] *m abr de* **Antilock Braking System** ABS

**absence** [apsɑ̃s] *f* ❶(*opp: présence*) absence; **en l'** ~ **de qn** in the absence of sb ❷(*manque*) lack; **en l'** ~ **de preuves** in the absence of proof

**absent(e)** [apsɑ̃, ɑ̃t] I. *adj* ❶(*opp: présent*) absent; **les élèves** ~**s** absentees; **être** ~ **à une réunion** to be absent from a meeting ❷(*qui manque*) **être** ~ **de qc** to be absent from sth; **il était** ~ **de la réunion** he was not at the meeting ❸(*distrait: air, regard*) vacant II. *m(f)* absentee

**absentéisme** [apsɑ̃teism] *m* absenteeism; (*d'un élève*) truancy

**absenter** [apsɑ̃te] <1> *vpr* **s'** ~ (*ne pas venir*) not to attend; (*être absent*) to be absent; (*partir*) to leave

**absolu(e)** [apsɔly] *adj* ❶(*total: silence*) utter; (*confiance*) absolute; (*amour*) perfect ❷POL, LING absolute

**absolument** [apsɔlymɑ̃] *adv* ❶(*à tout prix*) without fail ❷(*totalement*) entirely; ~ **pas/rien** absolutely not/nothing ▸ ~! absolutely!; **vous êtes sûr? –** ~! are you sure? positive!

**absorbant(e)** [apsɔʀbɑ̃, ɑ̃t] *adj* (*tissu*) absorbent

**absorber** [apsɔʀbe] <1> *vt* ❶(*consommer*) to consume; (*médicament*) to take ❷(*s'imbiber*) to absorb ❸(*accaparer: travail*) to occupy

**absorption** [apsɔʀpsjɔ̃] *f* ❶(*action de manger, de boire*) swallowing ❷(*action d'avaler un médicament*) taking ❸(*pénétration*) absorption ❹ECON takeover

**abstenir** [apstəniʀ] <9> *vpr* ❶(*éviter*) **s'** ~ **de faire qc** to refrain from doing sth ❷POL **s'** ~ to abstain

**abstention** [apstɑ̃sjɔ̃] *f* abstention

**abstinence** [apstinɑ̃s] *f* abstinence

**abstraction** [apstʀaksjɔ̃] *f* ❶(*action d'abstraire*) abstraction; **faire** ~ **de qc** to disregard sth ❷(*idée*) abstraction

**A**

**abstrait** [apstrɛ] *m* (*abstraction*) abstract ideas *pl*

**abstrait(e)** [apstrɛ, ɛt] *adj* abstract

**absurde** [apsyrd] *adj* absurd

**absurdité** [apsyrdite] *f* absurdity

**abus** [aby] *m* ❶ (*consommation excessive, usage abusif*) abuse ❷ (*injustice*) injustice ❸ JUR ~ **de biens sociaux** misuse of corporate assets

**abuser** [abyze] <1> I. *vi* ❶ (*consommer avec excès*) to overindulge; ~ **de l'alcool** to drink too much ❷ (*profiter de qn*) to go too far ❸ (*exploiter*) ~ **de la crédulité de qn** to take advantage of sb's credulity II. *vpr* (*se tromper*) **si je ne m'abuse** if I'm not mistaken

**abusif, -ive** [abyzif, -iv] *adj* ❶ (*exagéré*) excessive; **consommation abusive d'alcool** alcohol abuse ❷ (*injuste: licenciement*) wrongful

**acacia** [akasja] *m* acacia

**académicien(ne)** [akademisjɛ̃, jɛn] *m(f)* ❶ (*membre d'une académie*) academician ❷ (*membre de l'Académie française*) member of the French Academy

**académie** [akademi] *f* ❶ (*société savante*) academy ❷ (*école*) ~ **de danse** dance academy ❸ ECOLE, UNIV ≈ regional board of education

**Académie** [akademi] *f* academy; **l'~ française** the French Academy

**académique** [akademik] *adj* ❶ *a.* ECOLE, UNIV academic ❷ (*de l'Académie française*) of the French Academy ❸ *Belgique, Québec, Suisse* (*universitaire*) **année ~** academic year

**acajou** [akaʒu] *m, adj inv* mahogany

**accablant(e)** [akɑblɑ̃, ɑ̃t] *adj* ❶ (*psychiquement pénible: chaleur*) oppressive; (*douleur*) excruciating; (*travail*) exhausting ❷ (*psychologiquement pénible: nouvelle*) devastating ❸ (*accusateur: témoignage*) damning

**accabler** [akɑble] <1> *vt* ❶ (*abattre: douleur, travail*) to overwhelm; (*nouvelle*) to devastate ❷ (*confondre: témoignage*) to damn

**accalmie** [akalmi] *f a.* METEO lull

**accaparer** [akapare] <1> *vt* ❶ (*monopoliser*) to monopolize; (*poste-clé, attention*) to grab ❷ (*occuper complètement*) ~ **qn** (*travail*) to leave sb with no time for anything else

**accéder** [aksede] <5> *vt* ❶ (*parvenir*) **on accède à la cuisine par la salle à manger** you get to the kitchen through the dining room ❷ (*atteindre*) ~ **à un poste** to obtain a post; ~ **en finale** to get through to the finals ❸ (*consentir: souhait, requête*) to grant

**accélérateur** [akseleratœr] *m* accelerator

**accélération** [akselerasjɔ̃] *f* acceleration

**accélérer** [akselere] <5> I. *vt, vi* to accelerate *inf* II. *vpr* **s'~** (*pouls*) to quicken

**accent** [aksɑ̃] *m* ❶ (*signe sur les voyelles*) accent; **e ~ aigu** e acute ❷ (*manière de prononcer*) accent ❸ (*accentuation*) stress ❹ (*intonation expressive*) tone ▶ **mettre l'~ sur qc** to stress sth

**accentuation** [aksɑ̃tɥasjɔ̃] *f* ❶ (*augmentation: du chômage*) rise; (*des symptômes*) worsening ❷ LING accentuation

**accentué(e)** [aksɑ̃tɥe] *adj* ❶ LING (*voyelle*) stressed ❷ (*prononcé: traits*) marked

**accentuer** [aksɑ̃tɥe] <1> I. *vt* ❶ (*prononcer un accent*) to stress ❷ (*intensifier: effet, action*) to intensify; (*force, risque, efforts*) to increase II. *vpr* **s'~** to become more pronounced

**acceptable** [akseptabl] *adj* acceptable; (*repas*) decent; (*prix*) reasonable

**acceptation** [akseptasjɔ̃] *f* acceptance

**accepter** [aksepte] <1> *vt* ❶ (*prendre, se soumettre à*) to accept ❷ (*être d'accord*) ~ **qc** to agree to sth; ~ **de** +*infin* to agree to +*infin* ❸ (*tolérer*) ~ **qn** to put up with sb ❹ (*relever: défi*) to accept

**accès** [aksɛ] *m* ❶ (*entrée*) access; ~ **interdit** no entrance ❷ (*action d'accéder à une position*) ~ **à un club** admission

to a club ❸ (*crise: de fièvre*) bout ❹ IN-
FORM access

**accessible** [aksesibl] *adj* (*compréhensible, où l'on peut accéder*) accessible

**accessoire** [akseswaʀ] **I.** *adj* incidental
**II.** *m* ❶ (*pièce complémentaire*) accessory ❷ THEAT, CINE **les ~s** props

**accident** [aksidã] *m* accident

**accidenté(e)** [aksidãte] *adj* ❶ (*inégal:
terrain*) uneven; (*région*) undulating
❷ (*qui a eu un accident*) injured; (*voiture*) damaged

**accidentel(le)** [aksidãtɛl] *adj* ❶ (*dû à
un accident*) accidental ❷ (*dû au hasard*) fortuitous

**accidentellement** [aksidãtɛlmã] *adv*
❶ (*dans un accident*) **mourir ~** to die
accidentally ❷ (*par hasard*) by accident

**acclamation** [aklamasjɔ̃] *f* cheering

**acclamer** [aklame] <1> *vt* to cheer

**acclimatation** [aklimatasjɔ̃] *f* acclima-
tion

**acclimater** [aklimate] <1> *vpr* (*s'adapter*) **s'~** to adapt

**accolade** [akɔlad] *f* embrace

**accommodant(e)** [akɔmɔdã, ãt] *adj*
(*camarade, patron, directeur*) accom-
modating

**accommoder** [akɔmɔde] <1> **I.** *vt*
(*adapter*) to adapt **II.** *vpr* ❶ (*s'arranger*)
**s'~** to come to an agreement
with sb ❷ (*se contenter de*) **s'~ de qc**
to make do with sth

**accompagnateur, -trice** [akɔ̃paɲa-
tœʀ, -tʀis] *m, f* ❶ (*guide*) guide ❷ MUS
accompanist ❸ ECOLE leader

**accompagnement** [akɔ̃paɲmã] *m a.*
MUS, CULIN accompaniment

**accompagner** [akɔ̃paɲe] <1> **I.** *vt*
❶ (*aller avec, être joint à*) *a.* MUS to accompany; **du vin accompagne le plat**
the dish is accompanied by wine ❷ (*survenir en même temps*) **~ qc** to go (together) with sth **II.** *vpr* ❶ MUS **s'~ à la
guitare** to accompany oneself on the
guitar ❷ (*aller avec*) **s'~ de qc** to come
with sth

**accompli(e)** [akɔ̃pli] *adj* (*parfait*) accomplished

**accomplir** [akɔ̃pliʀ] <8> *vt* ❶ (*s'acquitter de*) **~ qc** (*travail, devoir*) to carry sth
out; (*promesse*) to fulfill sth ❷ (*exécuter, réaliser: ordre, miracle*) to perform

**accord** [akɔʀ] *m* ❶ (*consentement,
convention*) agreement; **donner son ~
à qn** to give one's agreement to sb
❷ (*bonne intelligence*) harmony ❸ MUS
(*association de plusieurs sons*) chord;
(*réglage*) tuning ❹ LING **faute d'~** mistake in agreement ▸ **être d'~** to agree;
**être d'~ avec qn sur qc** to agree with
sb about sth; **être en ~ avec soi-
-même** to be in harmony with oneself;
**se mettre d'~** to come to an
agreement with sb; (*c'est*) **d'~!** OK! *inf*

**accordéon** [akɔʀdeɔ̃] *m* accordion

**accordéoniste** [akɔʀdeɔnist] *mf* accor-
dionist

**accorder** [akɔʀde] <1> **I.** *vt* ❶ (*donner:
crédit, délai, faveur*) to grant; (*confiance*) to give ❷ (*attribuer*) **~ de la valeur
à qc** to value sth; **~ de l'importance à
qc** to attach importance to sth ❸ MUS to
tune ❹ LING **~ l'adjectif avec le nom**
to make the adjective agree with the
noun **II.** *vpr* ❶ (*se mettre d'accord*) **s'~
avec qn sur une solution** to agree on
a solution with sb ❷ (*s'octroyer*) **s'~
une journée de congé** to give oneself
a day off ❸ LING **s'~ avec qc** (*verbe, adjectif*) to agree with sth

**accoster** [akɔste] <1> **I.** *vi* NAUT to dock
**II.** *vt* ❶ (*aborder*) to accost ❷ NAUT
(*quai*) to come alongside

**accouchement** [akuʃmã] *m* MED birth

**accoucher** [akuʃe] <1> *vi* ❶ MED to give
birth; **~ d'une fille** to give birth to
[*o* have] a girl ❷ *inf* (*parler*) **allez, ac-
couche!** come on, spit it out!

**accouder** [akude] <1> *vpr* **s'~ à qc** to
lean on sth; **elle était accoudée au
comptoir** she had her elbows on the
counter

**accoudoir** [akudwaʀ] *m* armrest

**accoupler** [akuple] <1> **I.** *vpr* ZOOL **s'~**
to couple **II.** *vt* ❶ ZOOL to mate ❷ (*mettre par deux: chevaux*) to yoke ❸ TECH
to couple; ELEC to connect (up)

**A**  **accourir** [akuRiR] *vi irr avoir o être (personne)* to come running, to rush *fig*

**accoutrement** [akutRəmã] *m* outfit

**accoutumance** [akutymãs] *f* ❶ *(adaptation)* familiarization ❷ *(besoin)* addiction

**accoutumé(e)** [akutyme] *adj* usual

**accro** [akRo] *mf inf abr de* **accroché** ❶ *(drogué)* addict ❷ *(passionné)* fanatic

**accroc** [akRo] *m* ❶ *(déchirure)* tear ❷ *(incident)* hitch

**accrochage** [akRɔʃaʒ] *m* ❶ *(action d'accrocher: d'un tableau)* hanging; *(d'un wagon)* coupling ❷ *(collision)* crash ❸ *(altercation)* quarrel

**accrocher** [akRɔʃe] <1> I. *vt* ❶ *(suspendre)* to hang ❷ *(déchirer)* to snag ❸ *(entrer en collision)* to hit ❹ *(attirer: regards)* to catch II. *vpr (se retenir)* **s'~ à qc** to cling to sth ❷ *(se faire un accroc)* **s'~ à qc** to get caught on sth ❸ *(persévérer)* **s'~** to stick it out ❹ *inf (mettre ses espoirs dans)* **s'~ à qc** to cling to sth ❺ *inf (se disputer)* **s'~ avec qn** to clash with sb III. *vi* ❶ *inf (bien établir le contact)* to click ❷ *(plaire)* to catch on

**accroissement** [akRwasmã] *m (du chômage)* rise; *(du chiffre d'affaires)* increase; **~ de la population** population growth

**accroître** [akRwɑtR] *irr* I. *vt* to increase; *(patrimoine)* to add to; *(pouvoir, chances)* to increase II. *vpr* **s'~** to grow

**accroupir** [akRupiR] <8> *vpr* **s'~** to squat (down)

**accru(e)** [akRy] *adj* enhanced

**accueil** [akœj] *m* ❶ *(fait de recevoir)* welcome ❷ *(lieu)* reception

**accueillant(e)** [akœjã, ãt] *adj (hôte)* hospitable; *(sourire)* warm; *(maison)* welcoming

**accueillir** [akœjiR] *vt irr* ❶ *(recevoir)* to welcome ❷ *(héberger)* **~ qn** to accommodate sb ❸ *(réagir à: nouvelle)* to greet; *(projet, idée)* to receive

**accumulateur** [akymylatœR] *m* ❶ *(pile rechargeable)* storage battery ❷ INFORM accumulator

**accumulation** [akymylasjɔ̃] *f* accumulation; *(de marchandises)* stockpiling; *(de preuves)* mass; *(d'énergie)* storage

**accumuler** [akymyle] <1> I. *vt* to accumulate; *(énergie)* to store; *(preuves, erreurs)* to amass; *(marchandises)* to stockpile II. *vpr* **s'~** to accumulate; *(dettes, vaisselle)* to pile up

**accusateur, -trice** [akyzatœR, -tRis] *adj (regard)* accusing; *(document)* incriminating

**accusatif** [akyzatif] *m* LING accusative

**accusation** [akyzasjɔ̃] *f* ❶ *(reproche)* accusation ❷ JUR charge

**accusé** [akyze] *m* **~ de réception** acknowledgement of receipt

**accusé(e)** [akyze] *m(f)* JUR defendant

**accuser** [akyze] <1> I. *vt (déclarer coupable)* to accuse; **~ qn d'un vol** to accuse sb of theft; *(police)* to charge sb with theft ❷ *vpr* **s'~ de qc** ❶ *(se déclarer coupable)* to confess to sth ❷ *(se rendre responsable)* to take the blame for sth

**acharné(e)** [aʃaRne] *adj (travailleur)* hard; *(joueur)* tenacious; *(combat)* fierce

**acharnement** [aʃaRnəmã] *m (d'un combattant)* relentlessness; *(d'un joueur)* tenacity

**acharner** [aʃaRne] <1> *vpr* ❶ *(persévérer)* **s'~ sur un projet** to work away at a project ❷ *(ne pas lâcher prise)* **s'~ sur une victime** to hound a victim

**achat** [aʃa] *m* ❶ *(action)* buying ❷ *(chose achetée)* purchase; **faire des ~s** to shop

**acheminer** [aʃ(ə)mine] <1> *vt* ❶ *(transporter: courrier)* to deliver; *(voyageurs, marchandises)* to transport ❷ *(conduire)* **~ un convoi** to route a convoy

**acheter** [aʃ(ə)te] <4> I. *vt* to buy; **~ qc à qn** to buy sth from sb II. *vpr* **s'~ qc** to buy oneself sth

**acheteur, -euse** [aʃtœR, -øz] *m, f*

**①** (*client*) buyer; JUR purchaser **②** (*de profession*) buyer

**achever** [aʃ(ə)ve] <4> I. vt **①** (*accomplir: discours*) to end; (*œuvre, bouteille*) to finish; ~ **un livre** to reach the end of a book **②** (*tuer*) ~ **qn** to finish sb off **③** (*épuiser*) **cette journée m'a achevé!** today almost finished me off! II. vpr (*se terminer*) **s'**~ (*vie, journée*) to draw to an end

**acide** [asid] I. adj **①** (*aigre: fruit, saveur*) sour; (*remarque*) cutting **②** CHIM acidic II. m CHIM acid

**acidité** [asidite] f **①** (*aigreur: d'un fruit*) sourness **②** CHIM acidity

**acidulé(e)** [asidyle] adj sour

**acier** [asje] m (*métal*) steel

**acné** [akne] f acne

**acompte** [akɔ̃t] m **①** (*engagement d'achat*) deposit **②** (*avance*) advance

**à-côté** [akote] <à-côtés> m **①** (*détail*) side issue **②** (*gain occasionnel*) extra

**à-coup** [aku] <à-coups> m (*saccade: d'un moteur*) sputter

**acoustique** [akustik] adj acoustic

**acquéreur** [akerœr] m buyer

**acquérir** [akerir] irr vt **①** (*devenir propriétaire*) to acquire; (*obtenir: compétence*) to acquire; (*faveur*) to win; (*expérience, importance*) to gain

**acquiescer** [akjese] <2> vi (*approuver*) to approve

**acquis** [aki] mpl **①** (*savoir*) experience **②** **les ~ sociaux** social benefits

**acquis(e)** [aki, iz] I. part passé de **acquérir** II. adj **①** (*obtenu: fortune, expérience*) acquired; (*droit, avantages*) established **②** (*reconnu*) accepted

**acquisition** [akizisjɔ̃] f acquisition

**acquittement** [akitmɑ̃] m **①** JUR (*d'un accusé*) acquittal **②** (*règlement: d'une dette*) paying off; (*d'une facture*) payment

**acquitter** [akite] <1> I. vt **①** (*déclarer non coupable: accusé*) to acquit **②** (*payer*) to pay; (*dette*) to settle **③** (*signer: livraison*) to receipt II. vpr **s'**~ **d'une dette** to pay off a debt

**âcre** [ɑkr] adj (*irritant: odeur, saveur*) acrid

**A**

**acrobate** [akrɔbat] mf acrobat

**acrobatie** [akrɔbasi] f **①** (*discipline*) acrobatics + vb sing **②** (*tour*) acrobatic feat

**acrylique** [akrilik] m CHIM acrylic

**acte** [akt] m **①** (*action*) act; **passer à l'**~ to act **②** JUR (*manifestation de volonté*) act; (*document*) certificate; (*contrat*) deed; ~ **de vente** bill of sale; **prendre** ~ **de qc** to note sth; (*prendre connaissance de*) to bear sth in mind **③** THEAT act

**acteur, -trice** [aktœr, -tris] m, f **①** THEAT, CINE actor, actress m, f **②** (*participant*) **les ~s d'un événement** those involved in an event

**actif** [aktif] m LING active voice

**actif, -ive** [aktif, -iv] I. adj **①** (*dynamique, productif*) a. ELEC, LING active **②** FIN (*marché*) buoyant **③** ECON (*population*) working **④** (*efficace*) active; (*poison*) potent II. m, f (*travailleur*) working person

**action** [aksjɔ̃] f **①** (*acte*) action; **faire une bonne** ~ to do a good deed **②** sans pl (*fait d'agir, démarche*) action; **passer à l'**~ to take action **③** (*effet*) effect; **l'**~ **de qc sur qc** the effect of sth on sth; (*intervention: du gouvernement*) action **④** (*péripéties, intrigue*) action **⑤** (*mesure ponctuelle*) ~ **syndicale** labor union action **⑥** JUR lawsuit **⑦** FIN share

**actionnaire** [aksjɔnɛr] mf shareholder

**actionner** [aksjɔne] <1> vt (*mettre en mouvement: levier*) to move; (*moteur*) to start

**activer** [aktive] <1> I. vt **①** (*accélérer: circulation sanguine, travaux*) to speed up; (*feu*) to stoke **②** CHIM, INFORM to activate II. vi inf to get a move on III. vpr **s'**~ **①** (*s'affairer*) to be very busy **②** inf (*se dépêcher*) to hurry up

**activité** [aktivite] f **①** sans pl (*fait d'être actif*) activity; (*d'une personne*) energy **②** (*occupation*) activity; **pratiquer une** ~ **sportive** to take part in a sport

**A**

❸ (*profession*) employment ❹ *sans pl* (*ensemble d'actes*) activity

**actrice** [aktʀis] *f v.* **acteur**

**actualiser** [aktɥalize] <1> *vt* (*mettre à jour*) to update

**actualité** [aktɥalite] *f* ❶ *sans pl* (*modernité: d'un sujet*) topicality ❷ *sans pl* (*événements*) current events; l'~ **politique** political events *pl*; l'~ **sportive** the sports news ❸ *pl* TV, RADIO the news + *vb sing*; CINE newsreel + *vb sing*

**actuel(le)** [aktɥɛl] *adj* ❶ (*présent*) current ❷ (*d'actualité*) topical

**actuellement** [aktɥɛlmã] *adv* at present

**acuponcture** [akypɔ̃ktyʀ] *f* acupuncture

**acupuncture** [akypɔ̃ktyʀ] *f v.* **acuponcture**

**adaptateur** [adaptatœʀ] *m* TECH adapter

**adaptation** [adaptasjɔ̃] *f* ❶ *sans pl* (*action de s'adapter*) adaptation ❷ CINE, THEAT adaptation

**adapter** [adapte] <1> I. *vt* ❶ (*poser: embout*) to fix ❷ (*accorder*) *a.* CINE, THEAT to adapt II. *vpr* ❶ (*s'habituer à*) s'~ **à qn/qc** to adapt to sb/sth ❷ (*s'ajuster à*) s'~ **à qc** (*clé*) to fit sth

**addition** [adisjɔ̃] *f* ❶ (*somme*) addition; (*de problèmes*) sum ❷ (*facture*) check, bill

**additionner** [adisjɔne] <1> I. *vt* ❶ (*faire l'addition de*) ~ **qc** to add sth up ❷ (*ajouter*) ~ **qc à qc** to add sth to sth II. *vpr* s'~ (*erreurs, problèmes*) to accumulate; (*chiffres*) to add up

**adepte** [adɛpt] *mf* (*d'une secte*) follower; (*d'un sport*) fan

**adéquat(e)** [adekwa, at] *adj* appropriate; (*tenue*) suitable

**adhérence** [adeʀãs] *f* adhesion; (*d'un pneu, d'une semelle*) grip

**adhérent(e)** [adeʀã, ãt] I. *adj* adherent II. *m(f)* member

**adhérer** [adeʀe] <5> *vi* ❶ (*coller*) ~ **à qc** to stick to sth; ~ **à la route** to grip the road ❷ (*approuver*) ~ **à un point de vue** to share a view ❸ (*reconnaître*)

~ **à un idéal** to subscribe to an ideal ❹ (*devenir membre de*) ~ **à un parti** to join a party

**adhésif** [adezif] *m* (*substance*) adhesive

**adhésif, -ive** [adezif, -iv] *adj* adhesive

**adhésion** [adezjɔ̃] *f* ❶ (*approbation*) ~ **à qc** support for sth ❷ (*inscription*) ~ **à l'OTAN** joining NATO ❸ (*fait d'être membre*) membership

**adieu** [adjø] <x> I. *m* (*prise de congé*) farewell *soutenu*; **dire** ~ **à qn** to say goodbye to sb; **faire ses** ~**x à qn** to bid farewell to sb II. *interj* goodbye

**adjectif** [adʒɛktif] *m* adjective

**adjoint(e)** [adʒwɛ̃, wɛ̃t] *m(f)* assistant; ~ **au maire** deputy mayor

**adjudant** [adʒydã] *m* MIL warrant officer

**adjuger** [adʒyʒe] <2a> I. *vt* (*attribuer aux enchères*) to auction; ~ **un tableau à qn** to knock a painting down to sb II. *vpr* ❶ (*obtenir*) s'~ **une grosse part du marché** to grab a large market share ❷ (*s'approprier*) s'~ **qc** to take sth for oneself

**admettre** [admɛtʀ] *vt irr* ❶ (*laisser entrer*) to admit ❷ (*recevoir*) ~ **qn à sa table** to invite sb to eat with you ❸ (*accueillir, accepter: excuse*) to accept ❹ ECOLE, UNIV (*à un concours*) to pass ❺ (*reconnaître*) to admit to; **il est admis que ...** it is an accepted fact that ... ❻ (*supposer*) to assume; **admettons que** +*subj* let's suppose that; **en admettant que** +*subj* supposing that; ❼ (*permettre*) to allow

**administrateur** [administʀatœʀ] *m* ~ **de site** webmaster

**administrateur, -trice** [administʀatœʀ, -tʀis] *m, f* (*gestionnaire: d'organisme, de théâtre*) administrator

**administratif, -ive** [administʀatif, -iv] *adj* (*bâtiment, autorités*) administrative ❷ (*officiel*) **langue administrative** official language

**administration** [administʀasjɔ̃] *f* ❶ *sans pl* (*gestion: d'une entreprise*) management; ~ **d'un pays** government of a country ❷ (*secteur du service pu-*

*blic*) department; **~ pénitentiaire** prison authorities *pl* ❸ *sans pl* (*action de donner: d'un médicament*) administering

**Administration** [administʀasjɔ̃] *f sans pl* **l'~** ≈ the Civil Service

**administrer** [administʀe] <1> *vt* ❶ (*gérer: entreprise*) to manage; (*pays*) to govern ❷ (*donner*) **~ un remède à qn** to administer a remedy to sb

**admirable** [admiʀabl] *adj* admirable

**admirateur, -trice** [admiʀatœʀ, -tʀis] *m, f* admirer

**admiratif, -ive** [admiʀatif, -iv] *adj* admiring

**admiration** [admiʀasjɔ̃] *f sans pl* admiration; **être en ~ devant qc/qn** to be lost in admiration for sth/sb

**admirer** [admiʀe] <1> *vt* (*apprécier*) to admire

**admissible** [admisibl] *adj* ❶ (*tolérable, concevable*) acceptable ❷ (*accepté: à un examen*) eligible

**admission** [admisjɔ̃] *f* ❶ *sans pl* (*accès*) **~ dans à l'Union européenne** admission to the European Union; **~ dans une discothèque** entry to a (night)club ❷ ECOLE, UNIV admission

**ADN** [ɑdeɛn] *m abr de* **acide désoxyribonucléique** DNA

**ado** [ado] *mf inf abr de* **adolescent**

**adolescence** [adɔlesɑ̃s] *f* adolescence

**adolescent(e)** [adɔlesɑ̃, ɑ̃t] *adj, m(f)* adolescent, teen

**adopter** [adɔpte] <1> *vt* ❶ (*prendre comme son enfant*) to adopt ❷ (*s'approprier: point de vue*) to take; (*cause*) to take up ❸ POL (*motion, loi*) to pass

**adoptif, -ive** [adɔptif, -iv] *adj* (*enfant*) adopted; (*parents*) adoptive

**adoption** [adɔpsjɔ̃] *f* ❶ adoption ❷ (*approbation*) approval; (*d'une loi*) passing

**adorable** [adɔʀabl] *adj* ❶ (*joli: enfant*) adorable; (*endroit, objet*) beautiful ❷ (*gentil: enfant*) delightful; (*personne*) charming; (*sourire*) lovely

**adoration** [adɔʀasjɔ̃] *f sans pl* ❶ REL adoration

**adorer** [adɔʀe] <1> *vt* (*aimer*) ❶ REL to adore; **~ faire qc** to love doing sth

**adosser** [adose] <1> *vt* **~ qc contre un mur** to put sth against a wall; **être adossé au mur** (*personne*) to be leaning against the wall

**adoucir** [adusiʀ] <8> **I.** *vt* (*linge, eau, peau*) to soften; (*voix*) to moderate; (*contraste*) to tone down; (*chagrin, épreuve*) to ease; (*personne*) to mellow; (*boisson*) to sweeten **II.** *vpr* **s'~** (*personne, saveur*) to mellow; (*voix, couleur, peau*) to soften; **la température s'est adoucie** the weather has gotten milder

**adoucissant** [adusisɑ̃] *m* softener; (*pour le linge*) fabric softener

**adrénaline** [adʀenalin] *f* adrenaline

**adresse¹** [adʀɛs] *f* ❶ (*domicile*) *a.* INFORM address; **~ électronique** e-mail address ❷ (*discours*) speech

**adresse²** [adʀɛs] *f sans pl* ❶ (*dextérité*) skill ❷ (*tact*) tact

**adresser** [adʀese] <1> **I.** *vt* ❶ (*envoyer*) to address; (*lettre, colis*) to send ❷ (*émettre*) **~ un compliment à qn** to pay sb a compliment; **~ la parole à qn** to speak to sb **II.** *vpr* **s'~ à qn** to speak to sb; **adressez-vous à l'office de tourisme** ask at the tourist office

**adroit(e)** [adʀwa, wat] *adj* ❶ (*habile*) dexterous ❷ (*subtil*) shrewd

**adulte** [adylt] **I.** *adj* (*opp: jeune: personne*) adult; (*animal*) full-grown **II.** *mf* adult

**adultère** [adyltɛʀ] **I.** *adj* adulterous **II.** *m* adultery

**advenir** [advəniʀ] <9> **I.** *vi* to happen **II.** *vi impers* ❶ (*arriver*) **quoi qu'il advienne** come what may ❷ (*devenir*) **que va-t-il ~ de moi?** what will become of me?

**adverbe** [advɛʀb] *m* adverb

**adversaire** [advɛʀsɛʀ] *mf* adversary, opponent

**adverse** [advɛʀs] *adj* ❶ (*forces, équipe*) opposing; (*parti, camp*) opposite ❷ JUR **la partie ~** the other side

**aération** [aeʀasjɔ̃] *f sans pl* ❶ (*action*

**A**

*d'aérer: d'une pièce*) airing ② (*circulation d'air*) ventilation

**aérer** [aere] <5> I. *vt* ① (*ventiler: pièce, literie*) to air; (*terre*) to aerate ② (*alléger*) to lighten II. *vpr* **s'~** to get some fresh air

**aérien(ne)** [aerjɛ̃, jɛn] *adj* ① AVIAT **transport ~** air transportation; **compagnie ~ne** airline (company) ② (*en l'air: câble*) overhead

**aérobic** [aerɔbik] *f* aerobics + *vb sing*

**aérodrome** [aerodrom] *m* aerodrome

**aérodynamique** [aerodinamik] *adj* aerodynamic, streamlined

**aérogare** [aerogar] *f* (airport) terminal

**aéroglisseur** [aeroglisœr] *m* hovercraft

**aéronautique** [aeronotik] I. *adj* aeronautical II. *f sans pl* aeronautics + *vb sing*

**aéroport** [aeropɔr] *m* airport

**aérosol** [aerɔsɔl] *m* ① aerosol ② (*pulvérisateur*) **déodorant en ~** deodorant spray

**aérospatial(e)** [aerospasjal, -jo] <-aux> *adj* aerospace

**aérospatiale** [aerospasjal] *f* (*industrie*) aerospace industry

**affable** [afabl] *adj* affable

**affaiblir** [afeblir] <8> I. *vt* ① a. POL, MIL to weaken ② (*diminuer l'intensité: sentiments*) to dull; (*bruit*) to muffle II. *vpr* **s'~** to weaken; (*personne, sens d'un mot*) to become weaker; (*vent*) to die down; (*autorité, économie*) to be weakened

**affaiblissement** [afeblismɑ̃] *m* weakening; (*d'un bruit*) fading

**affaire** [afer] *f* ① (*préoccupation*) business; **ce n'est pas mon/ton ~** it's none of your/my business ② *sans pl* (*problème*) matter; **se tirer d'~** to manage ③ (*scandale*) affair; **sale ~** nasty business ④ JUR case ⑤ (*transaction*) transaction ⑥ *sans pl* (*entreprise*) concern ⑦ *pl* (*commerce*) **être dans les ~s** to be in business ⑧ *pl* POL affairs; **~ d'État** affair of state ⑨ *pl* (*effets personnels*) **prendre toutes ses ~s** to take all one's

belongings ▶ **avoir ~ à qn/qc** to be dealing with sb/sth

**affaissement** [afɛsmɑ̃] *m* subsidence

**affaisser** [afese] <1> *vpr* **s'~** (*baisser de niveau*) to subside; (*poutre*) to sag; (*tête*) to droop

**affaler** [afale] <1> *vpr* **être affalé dans un fauteuil** to be slumped in an armchair

**affamé(e)** [afame] *adj* starving

**affectation** [afɛktasjɔ̃] *f* (*nomination*) ADMIN appointment; MIL posting

**affecté(e)** [afɛkte] *adj* (*feint: sentiment*) feigned

**affecter** [afɛkte] <1> *vt* ① (*feindre: sentiment, attitude*) to feign ② (*nommer*) **~ qn à un poste** to appoint sb to a post; **~ qn dans une région** to post sb to a region ③ (*émouvoir*) to move ④ (*concerner: épidémie, événement*) to affect ⑤ (*mettre à disposition*) **~ une somme à qc** to allocate a sum to sth

**affectif, -ive** [afɛktif, -iv] *adj* ① emotional ② PSYCH affective

**affection** [afɛksjɔ̃] *f* ① (*tendresse*) a. PSYCH affection ② MED ailment

**affectionner** [afɛksjɔne] <1> *vt* (*préférer*) **~ qc** to be fond of sth

**affectueusement** [afɛktɥøzmɑ̃] *adv* affectionately; **bien ~** with fond regards

**affectueux, -euse** [afɛktɥø, -øz] *adj* affectionate

**affichage** [afiʃaʒ] *m* ① *sans pl* (*action de poser des affiches*) posting ② INFORM display

**affiche** [afiʃ] *f* ① (*feuille imprimée*) a. ADMIN notice ② (*avis officiel*) public notice ③ (*poster*) poster ④ *sans pl* (*programme théâtral*) bill; **être à l'~** to be on

**afficher** [afiʃe] <1> I. *vt* ① (*placarder*) **~ qc** to stick sth up; (*résultat d'un examen*) to post sth ② (*montrer publiquement*) a. CINE to show ③ THEAT **~ complet** to be sold out ④ INFORM, TECH to display II. *vi* **défense d'~** post no bills III. *vpr* (*s'exhiber*) **s'~** (*quelque chose*) to be displayed; (*personne*) to flaunt oneself

**A**

**affilée** [afile] **d'~** (*sans interruption*) at a stretch; (*l'un après l'autre*) one after the other

**affiner** [afine] <1> I. *vt* ❶ (*purifier, rendre plus fin: métal, verre, style*) to refine; (*odorat, ouïe*) to sharpen ❷ (*fromage*) to mature II. *vpr* **s'~** (*style, goût*) to refine; (*odorat, ouïe*) to sharpen

**affinité** [afinite] *f* affinity

**affirmatif** [afiʀmatif] *interj inf a.* TEL affirmative

**affirmatif, -ive** [afiʀmatif, -iv] *adj* (*opp: négatif*) *a.* LING affirmative; (*ton*) assertive

**affirmation** [afiʀmasjɔ̃] *f* ❶ (*déclaration, opp: négation*) affirmation ❷ *sans pl* (*manifestation*) *a.* LING assertion

**affirmer** [afiʀme] <1> *vt* ❶ (*soutenir*) to maintain ❷ (*manifester: autorité, position*) to assert ❸ (*proclamer*) to affirm

**affluent** [aflyɑ̃] *m* tributary

**affluer** [aflye] <1> *vi* ❶ (*arriver en grand nombre: foule*) to flock ❷ (*couler en abondance: sang*) to rush ❸ (*apparaître en abondance: argent*) to flow

**afflux** [afly] *m sans pl* (*arrivée massive: de clients*) influx; (*de fluide*) inrush; **~ de visiteurs** flood

**affolé(e)** [afɔle] *adj* (*paniqué: personne, animal*) panic-stricken

**affolement** [afɔlmɑ̃] *m sans pl* panic

**affoler** [afɔle] <1> I. *vt* ❶ (*effrayer*) **~ qn** (*nouvelle*) to throw sb into turmoil ❷ (*inquiéter*) **~ qn** to throw sb into a panic II. *vpr* **s'~** to panic

**affranchir** [afʀɑ̃ʃiʀ] <8> *vt* ❶ (*avec des timbres*) to stamp; (*machine*) to frank ❷ HIST (*esclave*) to set free

**affranchissement** [afʀɑ̃ʃismɑ̃] *m* ❶ (*mettre des timbres*) stamping ❷ (*frais de port*) postage ❸ (*libération: d'un pays*) liberation; (*d'un esclave*) freeing

**affréter** [afʀete] <5> *vt* ❶ AVIAT, NAUT to charter ❷ AUTO to rent

**affreusement** [afʀøzmɑ̃] *adv* (*horriblement*) horribly; (*en retard*) dreadfully

**affreux, -euse** [afʀø, -øz] *adj* ❶ (*laid*) hideous ❷ (*horrible: cauchemar*) horri-

ble; (*mort*) terrible ❸ (*désagréable*) awful; (*temps*) terrible

**affrontement** [afʀɔ̃tmɑ̃] *m* ❶ MIL, POL confrontation ❷ (*conflit*) conflict

**affronter** [afʀɔ̃te] <1> I. *vt* ❶ (*combattre*) *a.* SPORT to face ❷ (*faire face à: situation difficile, hiver*) to confront II. *vpr* **s'~** to confront one another

**affûter** [afyte] <1> *vt* to grind; (*crayon*) to sharpen

**afin** [afɛ̃] *prep* (in order) to; **~ de gagner la course** (so as) to win the race; **~ qu'on puisse vous prévenir** so that we can let you know

**africain(e)** [afʀikɛ̃, ɛn] I. *adj* African II. *m(f)* African

**afrikans** [afʀikɑ̃s] *m* Afrikaans; *v.a.* **français**

**Afrique** [afʀik] *f* l'~ Africa; l'~ **australe/du Nord** Southern/North Africa; l'~ **noire** Black Africa; l'~ **du Sud** South Africa

**afro-américain(e)** [afʀoameʀikɛ̃, ɛn] <atro-américains> *adj* African-American

**Afro-Américain(e)** [afʀoameʀikɛ̃, ɛn] <Afro-Américains> *m(f)* African-American

**afterwork** [aftœʀwœʀk] *m* |**soirée**| **~** after-work get-together

**agaçant(e)** [agasɑ̃, ɑ̃t] *adj* irritating

**agacer** [agase] <2> *vt* ❶ (*énerver*) to irritate ❷ (*taquiner*) to tease

**âge** [ɑʒ] *m* ❶ (*temps de vie*) age; **avoir l'~ de** +*infin* to be old enough to +*infin*; **à l'~ de 8 ans** at the age of eight; **quel ~ as-tu/a-t-il?** how old are you/is he? ❷ (*ère*) age ▸ **le troisième ~** (*la vieillesse*) old age; (*les personnes*) senior citizens

**âgé(e)** [ɑʒe] *adj* old; **les personnes ~es** the elderly; **être ~ de 10 ans** to be 10 years old

**agence** [aʒɑ̃s] *f* ❶ (*bureau*) agency ❷ (*représentation commerciale*) sales office ❸ (*succursale*) branch

**agencer** [aʒɑ̃se] <2> *vt* ❶ (*ordonner: éléments*) to arrange ❷ (*structurer, combiner: phrase, mots*) to put togeth-

**A**

er; (*roman*) to structure; (*couleurs*) to harmonize ❸ (*aménager: local*) to lay out

**agenda** [aʒɛ̃da] *m* ❶ diary ❷ INFORM ~ **électronique** electronic organizer ❸ POL agenda

**agenouiller** [aʒ(ə)nuje] <1> *vpr* (*poser les genoux sur*) **s'~** to kneel down

**agent** [aʒɑ̃] *m* ❶ (*policier*) police officer, policeman, policewoman *m, f;* ~ **de la circulation** ≈ traffic officer ❷ ECON, POL, CHIM, ART agent; ~ **commercial** sales representative; ~ **immobilier** real estate agent; ~ **technique** technician ❸ (*employé*) employee; ~ **administratif** official

**agent(e)** [aʒɑ̃, ɑ̃t] *m(f)* (*espion*) agent

**agglomération** [aglɔmeʁasjɔ̃] *f* ❶ (*zone urbaine*) urban [*o* metropolitan] area; **l'~ bordelaise** Bordeaux and its suburbs ❷ (*ville et banlieue*) town

**aggravation** [agʁavasjɔ̃] *f* (*d'une crise*) worsening; (*du chômage*) increase

**aggraver** [agʁave] <1> **I.** *vt* ❶ (*faire empirer: situation, crise*) to aggravate; (*risque, chômage*) to increase ❷ (*renforcer: peine*) to increase **II.** *vpr* **s'~** (*pollution, chômage*) to increase; (*conditions sociales, difficultés*) to get worse

**agile** [aʒil] *adj* agile

**agilité** [aʒilite] *f sans pl* (*aisance*) agility

**agir** [aʒiʁ] <8> **I.** *vi* ❶ (*faire, être actif*) to act; ~ **bien** to do the right thing ❷ (*exercer une influence*) ~ **sur qc** to act on sth; ~ **sur qn** to bring pressure to bear on sb ❸ (*opérer: médicament, poison*) to take effect **II.** *vpr impers* ❶ (*il est question de*) **il s'agit de qn/qc** it concerns sb/sth; **de quoi s'agit-il?** what is it about? ❷ (*il faut*) **il s'agit de faire qc** sth must be done

**agitateur, -trice** [aʒitatœʁ, -tʁis] *m, f* POL agitator

**agitation** [aʒitasjɔ̃] *f* ❶ (*animation*) activity ❷ (*excitation*) excitement ❸ (*troubles*) agitation ❹ (*malaise social*) unrest

**agité(e)** [aʒite] *adj* ❶ (*animé de mouve-*

*ments: mer*) rough ❷ (*nerveux*) agitated ❸ (*excité*) excited ❹ (*troublé: situation*) hectic; (*époque*) turbulent

**agiter** [aʒite] <1> **I.** *vt* ❶ (*secouer: bouteille*) to shake; (*drapeau, mouchoir, main*) to wave ❷ (*inquiéter*) to upset **II.** *vpr* **s'~** ❶ (*bouger*) to move around ❷ (*s'exciter*) to fidget ❸ (*s'énerver*) to get worked up

**agneau, agnelle** [aɲo, aɲɛl] <x> *m, f* lamb

**agonie** [agɔni] *f* death throes *pl*

**agoniser** [agɔnize] <1> *vi* to be dying

**agrafe** [agʁaf] *f* ❶ COUT hook ❷ (*pour papiers*) staple

**agrafer** [agʁafe] <1> *vt* ❶ (*attacher: feuilles*) to staple (together) ❷ (*fermer: jupe*) to fasten

**agrafeuse** [agʁaføz] *f* stapler

**agraire** [agʁɛʁ] *adj* (*politique*) agrarian; (*réforme*) land

**agrandir** [agʁɑ̃diʁ] <8> **I.** *vt* ❶ (*rendre plus grand*) to enlarge ❷ (*rendre plus large*) to widen ❸ (*développer: entreprise*) to expand ❹ PHOT to enlarge **II.** *vpr* **s'~** ❶ (*se creuser, s'élargir*) to get bigger; (*passage*) to get wider; (*écart*) to widen ❷ (*se développer: entreprise, ville*) to expand ❸ (*devenir plus nombreux: famille*) to grow

**agrandissement** [agʁɑ̃dismɑ̃] *m* ❶ (*extension: d'une maison*) extension; (*d'une entreprise*) expansion ❷ PHOT enlargement

**agréable** [agʁeabl] *adj* ❶ (*gentil: personne*) pleasant ❷ (*qui plaît, agrée*) nice

**agréablement** [agʁeabləmɑ̃] *adv* pleasantly

**agréé(e)** [agʁee] *adj* JUR (*expert*) registered; **fournisseur ~** authorized dealer

**agréer** [agʁee] <1> *vt soutenu* (*remerciements*) to accept; **veuillez ~, Madame/Monsieur, mes salutations distinguées** very sincerely yours

**agresser** [agʁese] <1> *vt* ❶ (*attaquer, insulter*) to attack; **se faire ~** to be assaulted ❷ (*avoir un effet nocif sur*) to damage

**agresseur** [agʀɛsœʀ] *m* (*État, pays*) aggressor

**agresseur, -euse** [agʀɛsœʀ, -øz] *m, f* (*personne*) assailant

**agressif, -ive** [agʀesif, -iv] *adj* (*personne, comportement*) aggressive; (*pays*) hostile

**agression** [agʀesjɔ̃] *f* (*attaque, coups*) attack; **être victime d'une ~** to be attacked; (*être volé*) to be mugged

**agressivité** [agʀesivite] *f* aggression

**agricole** [agʀikɔl] *adj* agricultural; (*produit*) farm; (*peuple*) farming; **ouvrier ~** farm hand

**agriculteur, -trice** [agʀikyltœʀ, -tʀis] *m, f* farmer

**agriculture** [agʀikyltyʀ] *f* agriculture, farming

**agripper** [agʀipe] <1> I. *vt* to grab II. *vpr* **s'~ à qn/qc** to cling on to sb/sth

**agroalimentaire** [agʀoalimɑ̃tɛʀ] I. *adj* food-processing II. *m* **l'~** the food-processing industry

**ah** [ˈɑ] I. *interj* ❶ (*de joie, sympathie, déception, d'admiration*) ~! oh! ❷ *iron* ~ ~, **tu l'as écrit toi-même?** so you wrote it yourself, did you? ❸ (*rire*) ~! ~! ha! ha! ▸~ **bon** oh well; ~ **bon?** really?; ~ **non** oh no; ~ **non alors!** certainly not!; ~ **oui** oh yes; ~ **oui, je vois ...** oh, I see... II. *m* ❶ (*d'admiration*) gasp ❷ (*de soulagement*) sigh

**ahuri(e)** [ayʀi] I. *adj* ❶ (*stupéfait*) stunned ❷ (*stupide*) stupefied II. *m(f)* péj, *inf* halfwit

**ahurissant(e)** [ayʀisɑ̃, ɑ̃t] *adj* stupefying; (*personne*) incredible; (*chiffre*) staggering

**ai** [e] *indic prés de* **avoir**

**aide** [ɛd] I. *f* ❶ (*assistance*) help; ~ **médicale** health care; **à l'~!** help!; **appeler qn à l'~** to call on sb's help; **apporter son ~ à qn** to help sb ❷ *fig* **à l'~ d'un couteau** with a knife ❸ (*secours financier*) aid; ~ **sociale** ≈ welfare II. *mf* (*assistant*) assistant; ~ **familiale** helper

**aide-ménagère** [ɛdmenaʒɛʀ] <aides--ménagères> *f* home helper

**aider** [ede] <1> I. *vt* ❶ (*seconder*) to help ❷ (*donner de l'argent*) to aid ❸ (*prêter assistance*) to assist II. *vi* ❶ (*être utile: personne, conseil*) to be useful ❷ (*contribuer*) ~ **à qc** to help towards sth III. *vpr* ❶ (*utiliser*) **s'~ de qc** to use sth ❷ (*s'entraider*) **s'~** to help each other

**aie** [ɛ] *subj prés de* **avoir**

**aïe** [aj] *interj* ❶ (*douleur*) ~! ouch! ❷ (*de surprise*) ~, **les voilà!** oh no, here they come!

**aigle** [ɛgl] I. *mf* ZOOL eagle II. *f* MIL eagle

**aigre** [ɛgʀ] *adj* (*acide: odeur, lait*) sour

**aigre-doux, -douce** [ɛgʀədu, -dus] <aigres-doux> *adj* sweet and sour

**aigreur** [ɛgʀœʀ] *f* ❶ (*acidité*) sourness ❷ (*saveur aigre*) acidity ❸ (*animosité: d'une remarque*) sharpness

**aigri(e)** [egʀi] *adj* embittered

**aigrir** [egʀiʀ] <8> *vpr* **s'~** ❶ (*devenir acide: lait, vin*) to turn sour ❷ (*devenir amer: personne*) to become embittered

**aigu(ë)** [egy] *adj* ❶ (*pointu*) sharp; (*pointe*) pointed ❷ (*coupant*) cutting ❸ (*strident: voix, note*) high-pitched ❹ (*vif: intelligence, perception*) keen ❺ (*violent, pénétrant: douleur*) acute ❻ (*à son paroxysme: crise*) severe

**aiguillage** [egɥijaʒ] *m* CHEMDFER (*dispositif*) switch; (*manœuvre*) shunting

**aiguille** [egɥij] *f* ❶ COUT, MED (*d'une seringue*) needle; ~ **à coudre** sewing needle ❷ (*petite tige pointue: d'une montre*) hand; (*d'une balance*) pointer; ~ **de pin** pine needle ❸ GEO peak

**aiguiller** [egɥije] <1> *vt* ❶ CHEMDFER to shunt ❷ (*orienter*) ~ **qn vers/sur qc** to steer sb toward/onto sth

**aiguiser** [egize] <1> *vt* ❶ (*affiler: couteau, intelligence*) to sharpen ❷ (*stimuler: curiosité, désir*) to rouse

**ail** [aj] *m* garlic

**aile** [ɛl] *f* wing; (*d'un moulin*) sail

**aileron** [ɛlʀɔ̃] *m* ❶ ANAT, CULIN, NAUT (*de l'oiseau*) wing tip; (*du requin*) fin ❷ AVIAT (*d'un avion, aéronef*) aileron

**ailier** [elje] *m* winger

**aille** [aj] *subj prés de* **aller**

**A**

**ailleurs** [ajœʀ] *adv* (*autre part*) elsewhere; **regarder ~** to look somewhere else; **nulle part ~** nowhere else ▶**d'~ ...** moreover ...; **par ~** (*sinon*) otherwise; (*en outre*) moreover

**ailloli** [ajɔli] *m* aioli

**aimable** [ɛmabl] *adj* ❶(*attentionné*) kind ❷(*agréable, souriant*) pleasant

**aimant** [ɛmɑ̃] *m* magnet

**aimer** [eme] <1> **I.** *vt* ❶(*éprouver de l'amour*) to love; **je t'aime** I love you ❷(*éprouver de l'affection*) **~ qc** to be fond of sth ❸(*apprécier, trouver bon: nourriture, boisson, nature*) to like ❹(*désirer, souhaiter*) **j'aimerais + infin** I would like to +*infin* ❺(*préférer*) **~ mieux le football que le tennis** to prefer soccer to tennis; **j'aime autant m'en aller** I'd rather leave; **j'aimerais mieux que tu viennes** I'd rather you came **II.** *vpr* ❶(*d'amour*) **s'~** to love each other ❷(*d'amitié*) **s'~** to like each other ❸(*se plaire*) **s'~ dans une robe** to think one looks good in a dress ❹(*faire l'amour*) **s'~** to make love

**aine** [ɛn] *f* ANAT groin

**aîné(e)** [ene] **I.** *adj* ❶(*plus âgé de deux*) elder ❷(*plus âgé de plusieurs*) eldest **II.** *m(f)* ❶(*plus âgé de deux*) **l'~** the elder boy; **l'~e** the elder girl ❷(*plus âgé parmi plusieurs*) **l'~** the eldest boy; **l'~e** the eldest girl **III.** *mpl Québec* **les ~s** (*le troisième âge*) senior citizens

**ainsi** [ɛ̃si] *adv* ❶(*de cette manière*) this [*o* that] way; **c'est mieux ~** it's better this [*o* that] way; **et ~ de suite** and so on (and so forth); **pour ~ dire** (*presque*) virtually; (*si l'on peut le dire*) so to speak ❷REL **~ soit-il!** amen; *fig* so be it! ❸(*par exemple*) for instance

**air¹** [ɛʀ] *m* ❶ *sans pl* (*gaz*) air; **~ conditionné** air conditioning; **en plein ~** (*concert*) open-air; (*piscine*) outdoor ❷ *sans pl* (*brise dans une pièce*) air ❸ *pl* (*ciel*) **voler dans les ~s** to fly through the skies ❹(*haut*) **les mains en l'~!** hands up!

**air²** [ɛʀ] *m* ❶(*apparence*) air; **avoir l'~ distingué/d'une reine** to look dis-

tinguished/like a queen; **avoir l'~ (d'être) triste** to look sad; **cette proposition m'a l'~ idiote** that suggestion seems stupid to me; **il a l'~ de faire froid** it looks cold ❷(*ressemblance*) **elle a un faux ~ de ma femme** she looks a little like my wife ❸(*expression*) look; **d'un ~ décidé** in a resolute manner ▶**de quoi aurais-je l'~?** I'd look like a fool!

**air³** [ɛʀ] *m* ❶(*mélodie*) tune ❷(*aria*) aria

**airbag**® [ɛʀbag] *m* air bag

**airbus**® [ɛʀbys] *m* Airbus®

**aire** [ɛʀ] *f* ❶(*emplacement*) *a.* MATH area; **~ de repos** rest area

**airelle** [ɛʀɛl] *f* ❶(*à baies noires*) blueberry ❷(*à baies rouges*) cranberry

**aisance** [ɛzɑ̃s] *f* ❶(*richesse*) affluence ❷(*facilité, naturel*) ease

**aise** [ɛz] *f* **se sentir à l'~** to feel at ease; **se mettre à l'~** (*s'installer confortablement*) to make oneself at home; (*enlever sa veste*) to make oneself comfortable

**aisé(e)** [eze] *adj* (*fortuné*) wealthy

**aisselle** [ɛsɛl] *f* armpit

**ajourner** [aʒuʀne] <1> *vt* (*reporter*) to postpone; (*paiement*) to delay; (*procès, séance*) to adjourn

**ajout** [aʒu] *m* addition

**ajouter** [aʒute] <1> **I.** *vt* (*mettre en plus, additionner, dire en plus*) to add; **~ 3 à 4** to add 3 and 4 (together) **II.** *vpr* **s'~ à qc** to add to sth

**ajuster** [aʒyste] <1> *vt* (*régler: vêtement*) to alter; (*ceinture de sécurité*) to adjust

**alarmant(e)** [alaʀmɑ̃, ɑ̃t] *adj* alarming

**alarme** [alaʀm] *f* (*signal, dispositif*) alarm

**alarmer** [alaʀme] <1> **I.** *vt* (*personne*) to alarm; (*bruit*) to startle **II.** *vpr* **s'~ de qc** to become alarmed about sth

**album** [albɔm] *m* album; (*volume illustré*) illustrated book

**alcool** [alkɔl] *m* ❶CHIM alcohol; **~ à 90°** ≈ rubbing alcohol; **~ à brûler** denatured alcohol ❷(*spiritueux*) spirit

**alcoolémie** [alkɔlemi] *f* **taux d'~** (blood) alcohol level

**alcoolique** [alkɔlik] *adj, mf* alcoholic

**alcoolisé(e)** [alkɔlize] *adj* alcoholic

**Alcootest®** [alkɔtɛst] *m* ❶ (*appareil*) Breathalyzer® ❷ (*test*) Breathalyzer® test

**alémanique** [alemanik] *adj* Alemannic; **la Suisse ~** German-speaking Switzerland

**alentours** [alɑ̃tuʀ] *mpl* ❶ (*abords*) surroundings; **les ~ de la ville** the area around the town; **dans les ~** in the vicinity ❷ *fig* **aux ~ de minuit** around midnight; **aux ~ de 500 gens** about 500 people

**alerte** [alɛʀt] **I.** *adj* alert; (*style*) lively; (*démarche*) brisk **II.** *f* ❶ (*alarme*) alert; **~ à la bombe** bomb scare; **donner l'~** to raise the alarm ❷ (*signes inquiétants*) warning signs *pl*

**alerter** [alɛʀte] <1> *vt* ❶ (*donner l'alarme*) to alert ❷ (*informer*) to notify ❸ (*prévenir*) to warn

**algèbre** [alʒɛbʀ] *f* algebra

**Algérie** [alʒeʀi] *f* **l'~** Algeria

**algérien** [alʒeʀjɛ̃] *m* Algerian; *v.a.* **français**

**algérien(ne)** [alʒeʀjɛ̃, jɛn] *adj* Algerian

**Algérien(ne)** [alʒeʀjɛ̃, jɛn] *m(f)* Algerian

**algue** [alg] *f* **les ~s** algae; (*sur la plage*) seaweed + *vb sing*

**alibi** [alibi] *m* JUR alibi

**aliéné(e)** [aljene] *m(f)* insane person

**alignement** [aliɲ(ə)mɑ̃] *m* (*action d'aligner, rangée, mise en conformité*) alignment

**aligner** [aliɲe] <1> **I.** *vt* ❶ (*mettre en ligne*) **~ des soldats** to line up soldiers; **~ des chiffres** to align figures ❷ (*rendre conforme*) **~ une politique sur qc** to bring a policy into line with sth **II.** *vpr* ❶ (*se mettre en ligne*) **s'~** to line up; (*soldats*) to fall into line ❷ (*être en ligne*) to be in a line ❸ (*se conformer*) **s'~ sur qn/qc** to fall into line with sb/sth ❹ POL **s'~ sur qn/qc** to align oneself with sb/sth

**aliment** [alimɑ̃] *m* ❶ (*pour une personne*) food; **des ~s** food + *vb sing* ❷ (*pour un animal d'élevage*) feed

**alimentaire** [alimɑ̃tɛʀ] *adj* **industrie ~** food industry

**alimentation** [alimɑ̃tasjɔ̃] *f* ❶ (*action: d'une personne, d'un animal*) feeding ❷ (*produits pour une personne, un animal*) diet ❸ (*commerce*) food retailing; **magasin d'~** grocery store ❹ (*industrie*) food industry; **~ animale** animal nutrition ❺ (*approvisionnement*) **l'~ d'une usine en charbon** the supply of coal to a factory

**alimenter** [alimɑ̃te] <1> **I.** *vt* ❶ (*nourrir: personne, animal*) to feed ❷ (*approvisionner*) **~ une ville en eau** to supply water to a town; **~ un compte** to deposit money into an account ❸ (*entretenir*) **~ la conversation** (*personne*) to keep the conversation going; (*événement*) to fuel conversation **II.** *vpr* **s'~** ❶ (*bébé*) to feed oneself ❷ (*manger*) to eat

**aliter** [alite] <1> *vt* **être alité** to be bedridden

**allaitement** [alɛtmɑ̃] *m* **~ maternel** (*d'un bébé*) breastfeeding; (*d'un animal*) suckling

**allaiter** [alete] <1> *vt* ❶ (*pour un bébé*) to breastfeed ❷ (*pour un animal*) to suckle

**alléchant(e)** [aleʃɑ̃, ɑ̃t] *adj* (*odeur, plat*) mouthwatering; (*proposition, promesse*) tempting

**allécher** [aleʃe] <5> *vt* ❶ (*mettre en appétit*) **~ qn** to give sb an appetite ❷ (*tenter en faisant miroiter qc: personne*) to entice

**allée** [ale] *f* ❶ (*chemin dans une forêt, un jardin*) path ❷ (*rue*) road ❸ (*passage*) **~ centrale** aisle ❹ *Suisse* (*couloir d'entrée d'un immeuble*) hall

**allégé(e)** [aleʒe] *adj* low-fat

**alléger** [aleʒe] <2a, 5> *vt* ❶ (*rendre moins lourd*) to lighten ❷ (*réduire: impôts, dettes*) to reduce; (*programmes scolaires*) to cut down

**Allemagne** [almaɲ] *f* **l'~** Germany; **l'~**

**A**

de l'Est/de l'Ouest HIST East/West Germany; **la République fédérale d'~** the Federal Republic of Germany

**allemand** [almɑ̃] *m* German; *v.a.* **français**

**allemand(e)** [almɑ̃, ɑ̃d] *adj* German

**Allemand(e)** [almɑ̃, ɑ̃d] *m(f)* German

**aller**[1] [ale] *irr* **I.** *vi* **être ❶** (*se déplacer à pied*) to go; **on a sonné; peux-tu y ~?** there is someone at the door; can you get it?; **y ~ en courant/en nageant** to run/swim there; **~ et venir** (*de long en large*) to pace up and down; (*entre deux destinations*) to come and go; **pour ~ à l'hôtel de ville?** how do I get to city hall? **❷** (*se déplacer à cheval*) to ride; (*se déplacer à vélo*) to cycle **❸** (*pour faire quelque chose*) **~ à la boulangerie** to go to the bakery; **~ se coucher/se promener** to go to bed/ for a walk; **~ voir qn** to go and see sb; **je vais voir ce qui se passe** I'm going to see what's going on; **~ chercher les enfants à l'école** to go and pick up the children from school **❹** (*rouler*) to drive **❺** (*voler*) **j'irai en avion** I'll fly **❻** (*être acheminé*) **~ à Paris** to go to Paris **❼** (*mener*) **cette rue va vers la plage** this road leads to the beach **❽** (*s'étendre, atteindre*) **~ de ... à ...** (*étendue*) to stretch from... to...; **~ jusqu'à la mer** to reach the sea; **mon congé maternité va jusqu'à la fin de l'année** my maternity leave runs until the end of the year **❾** (*avoir sa place quelque part*) **~ à la cave** to belong in the cellar **❿** (*être conçu pour*) **ce plat ne va pas au micro-ondes** this dish cannot go in the microwave **⓫** (*oser*) **jusqu'à +infin** to go so far as to +infin **⓬** (*progresser*) **~ vite** (*personne, chose*) to go fast; (*nouvelles*) to travel fast **⓭** (*se porter*) **il va bien/mal/mieux** he's well/ not well/better; **comment ça va/vas-tu/allez-vous?** how are you?; **comment va ta santé?** *inf* how are you doing?; **ça va pas(, la tête)?** *inf* are you crazy! **⓮** (*fonctionner, évoluer*) **ça va les études ?** how are your studies?;

**tout va bien/mal** everything's going well/wrong; **quelque chose ne va pas** something's wrong **⓯** (*connaître bientôt*) **~ au-devant de difficultés** to be asking for problems **⓰** (*prévenir*) **~ au-devant des désirs de qn** to anticipate sb's wishes **⓱** (*pour donner un âge approximatif*) **il va sur la quarantaine** he's pushing forty **⓲** (*convenir à qn*) **ça va** that's fine; **ça ira** (*suffire*) that'll do; (*faire l'affaire*) that'll be fine; **ça peut ~** it's not too bad; **~ à qn** to suit sb; **ça (te) va?** is that all right with you?; **ça me va!** that's fine by me! **⓳** (*être seyant*) **~ bien à qn** to suit sb **⓴** (*être coordonné, assorti*) **~ avec qc** to go with sth; **~ ensemble** to go together; **~ bien avec qc** to go well with sth **㉑** (*convenir, être adapté à*) **cet outil va en toute circonstance** this tool can be used in any situation **㉒** (*se dérouler*) **les choses vont très vite** things are moving very quickly; **plus ça va, plus j'aime le théâtre** I'm loving the theater more and more **㉓** (*pour commencer, démarrer*) **on y va?** (*pour initier un départ*) shall we go?; (*pour initier un commencement*) shall we start? **㉔** *impers* (*être en jeu*) **il y va de notre vie** our lives are at stake **㉕** (*ne rien faire*) **se laisser ~** (*se négliger*) to let oneself go; (*abandonner, se décontracter*) to let go **㉖** (*être*) **il en va de même pour toi** the same goes for you ▶ **cela va de soi** it goes without saying; **ça va** (**comme ça**)! *inf* OK; **où allons-nous?** what's the world coming to! **II.** *aux être* **❶** (*pour exprimer le futur proche*) **~ +infin** to be going to +infin **❷** (*pour exprimer la crainte*) **et s'il allait tout raconter?** what if he told everything? **III.** *vpr être* **s'en ~ ❶** (*partir à pied*) to go away; (*en voiture, à vélo, en bateau, en avion*) to drive/cycle/sail away/fly away; **s'en ~ en vacances** to go on vacation **❷** (*disparaître: années*) to pass; (*forces*) to fail; (*cicatrice, tache, fatigue*) to fade (away) **IV.** *interj* **❶** (*invitation à agir*) **vas-y/allons-y/allez-y!**

(*en route!*) let's go!; (*au travail!, pour encourager*) come on!; **vas-y/allez-y!, allons!** go on!; **allez, presse-toi un peu!** come on, hurry up!; **allez, au revoir!** okay, bye then!; **allons/allez donc!** *iron, inf* (*c'est évident!*) oh come on!; (*vraiment?*) no, really? ❷ (*voyons!*) **un peu de calme, allons!** come on, let's have some quiet! ❸ (*pour exprimer la résignation, la conciliation*) **je le sais bien, va!** I know!; **va/allez savoir!** who knows! ❹ (*non!?*) **allez!** *inf* you're joking! ❺ (*d'accord!*) **alors, va pour le ciné!** the movies it is then!

**aller²** [ale] *m* ❶ (*trajet*) outbound journey; **après deux ~s et retours** after two roundtrips ❷ (*billet*) **~** (**simple**) one-way ticket; **un ~ pour Grenoble, s'il vous plaît** a one-way ticket to Grenoble, please; **~ retour** roundtrip ticket ❸ *inf* (*gifle*) **un ~ et retour** a slap

**allergie** [alɛrʒi] *f* allergy

**allergique** [alɛrʒik] *adj* MED allergic

**alliage** [aljaʒ] *m* alloy

**alliance** [aljɑ̃s] *f* ❶ (*engagement mutuel*) alliance; REL covenant ❷ (*union*) **par ~** by marriage ❸ (*combinaison*) combination ❹ (*anneau*) wedding ring

**allié(e)** [alje] I. *adj* ❶ POL allied ❷ **être ~ à qn** to be related to sb by marriage II. *m(f)* ❶ POL ally ❷ (*ami*) supporter

**allier** [alje] <1> I. *vt* ❶ (*associer*) **~ la grâce à la force** to combine grace and power ❷ CHIM **~ l'or à l'argent** to alloy gold with silver II. *vpr* ❶ POL **s'~** to become allies ❷ POL (*conclure une alliance avec*) **s'~ à un pays** to form an alliance with a country

**allô** [alo] *interj* hello

**allocation** [alɔkasjɔ̃] *f* (*somme*) allowance; **~ chômage** unemployment compensation; **~ vieillesse** ≈ social security; **~s familiales** ≈ welfare

**allocution** [alɔkysjɔ̃] *f* speech

**allonger** [alɔ̃ʒe] <2a> I. *vi* (*devenir plus long*) **les jours allongent à partir du 21 décembre** the days start to get longer on December 21 II. *vt* ❶ (*rendre*

*plus long*) to lengthen ❷ (*étendre: bras*) to stretch out ❸ (*coucher: blessé*) to lay down; **être allongé** to be lying down III. *vpr* **s'~** ❶ (*devenir plus long: personne*) to grow taller; (*ombres*) to lengthen ❷ (*se prolonger: jours*) to get longer; (*durée moyenne de la vie*) to increase ❸ (*se coucher*) to lie down

**allumage** [alymaʒ] *m* ❶ lighting ❷ AUTO ignition

**allumer** [alyme] <1> I. *vt* ❶ (*faire brûler, mettre en marche: feu, cigarette, four, poêle*) to light; **être allumé** (*feu, cigarette*) to be lit ❷ (*faire de la lumière: feu*) to light; (*lampe, projecteur*) to switch on; **~ le couloir** to turn the light on in the hallway; **la cuisine est allumée** the light is on in the kitchen II. *vpr* **s'~** ❶ (*s'enflammer: bûche, bois, papier*) to catch fire; (*briquet*) to light ❷ (*devenir lumineux*) **sa fenêtre vient de s'~** a light has just come on at her window ❸ (*se mettre en marche automatiquement*) **s'~** (*appareil*) to turn itself on ❹ (*être mis en marche*) **s'~** (*moteur*) to start

**allumette** [alymɛt] *f* match

**allure** [alyr] *f* ❶ *sans pl* (*vitesse*) speed; **à toute ~** at full speed ❷ *sans pl* (*apparence*) look ❸ *pl* (*airs*) ways

**allusion** [a(l)lyzjɔ̃] *f* (*sous-entendu*) allusion; **faire ~ à qn/qc** to allude to sb/sth

**alors** [alɔr] I. *adv* ❶ (*à ce moment-là*) then; **jusqu'~** until then ❷ (*par conséquent*) so ❸ (*dans ce cas*) so; **~, je comprends!** in that case, I understand! ❹ *inf* (*impatience, indignation*) **~, tu viens?** so are you coming or not? ▶ **ça ~!** my goodness!; **et ~?** (*suspense*) and then what happened?; (*perplexité*) so what?; **~, là, je ne sais pas!** well, I really don't know about that!; **non, mais ~!** honestly! II. *conj* **~ que ... +indic** ❶ (*pendant que*) **il s'est mis à pleuvoir ~ que nous étions encore en train de manger** it started to rain while we were still eating ❷ (*tandis que*) **il part en Californie ~ que je**

**A**

reste à Paris he's going to California while I stay in Paris ❸ (*bien que*) **elle a allumé une cigarette ~ que c'était interdit de fumer** she lit a cigarette even though smoking was forbidden

**alouette** [alwɛt] *f* lark

**alourdir** [aluʀdiʀ] <8> **I.** *vt* (*rendre plus lourd*) ~ **qc** to weigh sth down **II.** *vpr* **s'~** (*paupières*) to droop; (*démarche*) to slow down

**Alpes** [alp] *fpl* **les ~** the Alps

**alphabet** [alfabɛ] *m* alphabet

**alphabétique** [alfabetik] *adj* alphabetical

**alpinisme** [alpinism] *m* mountaineering

**alpiniste** [alpinist] *mf* mountaineer

**Alsace** [alzas] *f* **l'~** Alsace

**alsacien** [alzasjɛ̃] *m* Alsatian; *v.a.* **français**

**alsacien(ne)** [alzasjɛ̃, jɛn] *adj* Alsatian

**Alsacien(ne)** [alzasjɛ̃, jɛn] *m(f)* Alsatian

**altercation** [altɛʀkasjɔ̃] *f* altercation, dispute

**altérer** [alteʀe] <5> **I.** *vt* ❶ (*détériorer*) to spoil; (*couleur*) to alter; (*qualité*) to lower; (*caractère, métal*) to affect ❷ (*décomposer: visage, traits*) to distort; (*voix*) to strain **II.** *vpr* **s'~** (*se détériorer: qualité*) to deteriorate; (*aliment*) to go bad; (*vin*) to become spoiled; (*relations*) to break down; (*couleur, matière*) to change

**altermondialiste** [altɛʀmɔ̃djalist] *mf* opponent of globalization

**alternance** [altɛʀnɑ̃s] *f* ❶ (*succession*) alternation ❷ POL changeover

**alternatif, -ive** [altɛʀnatif, -iv] *adj* ❶ TECH, ELEC alternating ❷ (*qui offre un choix: solution*) alternative

**alternative** [altɛʀnativ] *f* alternative

**alterner** [altɛʀne] <1> *vt, vi* to alternate

**altitude** [altityd] *f* ❶ GEO altitude; **l'~ de ce mont est de 400 m** this mountain is 400 m high; **avoir une faible ~** (*ville*) to be low-lying ❷ AVIAT **voler à haute ~** to fly at high altitude

**alto** [alto] *m* ❶ (*instrument*) viola ❷ (*musicien*) violist

**alu** *inf*, **aluminium** [alyminjɔm] *m* aluminum

**alunir** [alyniʀ] <8> *vi* to land (on the moon)

**amabilité** [amabilite] *f* ❶ (*gentillesse*) kindness; **ayez l'~ de m'apporter un café** be so kind as to bring me a coffee ❷ *pl* (*politesses*) polite remarks

**amaigrir** [ameɡʀiʀ] <8> *vpr* **s'~** to lose weight

**amaigrissant(e)** [ameɡʀisɑ̃, ɑ̃t] *adj* slimming

**amalgame** [amalɡam] *m* ❶ (*alliage de métaux, matière obturatrice*) *a.* MED amalgam ❷ (*mélange: de matériaux*) mixture; **un ~ d'idées** a hodgepodge of ideas

**amande** [amɑ̃d] *f* ❶ (*fruit*) almond ❷ (*graine*) kernel

**amandier** [amɑ̃dje] *m* almond tree

**amant** [amɑ̃] *m* lover

**amas** [ama] *m* (*de pierres*) heap; (*de papiers*) pile; (*de souvenirs*) mass

**amasser** [amase] <1> *vt* (*objets, fortune*) to amass; (*preuves, données*) to gather together

**amateur, -trice** [amatœʀ, -tʀis] **I.** *m, f* ❶ (*opp: professionnel*) amateur ❷ **sans art** (*connaisseur*) ~ **d'art** art lover; **être ~ de bons vins** to be a connoisseur of fine wines ❸ *péj* (*dilettante*) **je ne le fais qu'en ~** I only do it as an amateur **II.** *adj* pas de forme féminine amateur

**ambassade** [ɑ̃basad] *f* (*institution, bâtiment*) embassy; **l'~ de France** the French embassy

**ambassadeur, -drice** [ɑ̃basadœʀ, -dʀis] *m, f* ambassador

**ambiance** [ɑ̃bjɑ̃s] *f* ❶ (*climat*) atmosphere; **d'~** (*lumière*) subdued; (*musique*) mood ❷ (*gaieté*) **la musique met de l'~** music livens things up

**ambiant(e)** [ɑ̃bjɑ̃, jɑ̃t] *adj* (*température*) ambient; (*idées, influences*) prevailing

**ambigu(ë)** [ɑ̃biɡy] *adj* ambiguous

**ambiguïté** [ɑ̃biɡuite] *f* ambiguity

**ambitieux, -euse** [ɑ̃bisjø, -jøz] **I.** *adj*

ambitious **II.** *m, f* man, woman *m, f* with ambition

**ambition** [ãbisjɔ̃] *f* **①** (*désir de réussite*) ambition **②** (*prétention*) aspiration

**ambre** [ãbʀ] *m* (*résine*) ~ (**jaune**) amber

**ambulance** [ãbylãs] *f* ambulance

**ambulancier, -ière** [ãbylãsje, -jɛʀ] *m, f* **①** (*conducteur*) ambulance driver **②** (*infirmier*) emergency medical technician, paramedic

**âme** [ɑm] *f* soul

**amélioration** [ameljɔʀasjɔ̃] *f* **①** *pl* (*travaux*) **apporter des ~s à une maison** to carry out improvements on a house **②** (*progrès*) improvement; (*de la conjoncture*) upturn **③** METEO improvement

**améliorer** [ameljɔʀe] <1> **I.** *vt* (*rendre meilleur: conditions de travail, vie*) to improve; (*qualité, production, budget*) to increase **II.** *vpr* **s'~** to improve; (*temps*) to get better

**amen** [amɛn] *interj* amen

**aménagement** [amenaʒmã] *m* **①** (*équipement*) equipment **②** ARCHIT (*modification*) conversion; (*installation*) setting up; (*construction*) construction **③** (*création: d'un quartier, d'une usine*) construction; (*d'un jardin*) laying out **④** (*adaptation*) improvement **⑤** (*réorganisation*) ~ **du temps de travail** (*réforme*) restructuring of working hours; (*gestion*) flexible time management **⑥** ADMIN development

**aménager** [amenaʒe] <2a> *vt* **①** (*équiper: pièce*) to arrange; (*étagère, placard*) to build **②** (*modifier par des travaux*) ~ **un grenier en atelier** to convert a loft into a studio **③** (*créer: parc, quartier*) to lay out **④** (*adapter: finances, horaires*) to arrange **⑤** ADMIN (*ville*) to develop

**amende** [amãd] *f* (*p.-v.*) parking ticket; (*à payer*) fine

**amener** [am(ə)ne] <4> **I.** *vt* **①** *inf* (*apporter, mener*) to bring **②** (*acheminer: gaz, liquide*) to transport **③** (*provoquer*) to bring about **④** (*entraîner*) **son**

**métier l'amène à voyager** his job involves traveling **⑤** (*introduire: thème, plaisanterie*) to introduce **⑥** (*diriger*) ~ **la conversation sur un sujet** to lead the conversation on to a subject **⑦** (*convaincre*) ~ **qn à** + *infin* to lead sb to + *infin* **II.** *vpr inf* (*se rappliquer*) **s'~** to show up; **amène-toi!** come on!

**amenuiser** [amənɥize] <1> **I.** *vt* **①** (*amincir*) to thin down **②** (*réduire: chances, espoir*) to fade **II.** *vpr* **s'~** (*espoir, forces*) to dwindle; (*ressources*) to run low; (*temps*) to run out

**amer, -ère** [amɛʀ] *adj* bitter

**américain** [ameʀikɛ̃] *m* American (English); *v.a.* **français**

**américain(e)** [ameʀikɛ̃, ɛn] *adj* American

**Américain(e)** [ameʀikɛ̃, ɛn] *m(f)* American

**Amérique** [ameʀik] *f* **l'~** America; **l'~ centrale/latine/du Nord/du Sud** Central/Latin/North/South America

**amerrir** [ameʀiʀ] <8> *vi* to land (in the sea)

**amertume** [amɛʀtym] *f* bitterness

**ameublement** [amœbləmã] *m* **①** (*meubles*) furniture **②** (*action de meubler*) furnishing

**ameuter** [amøte] <1> *vt* (*alerter*) to bring out

**ami(e)** [ami] **I.** *m(f)* **①** (*opp: ennemi*) friend; ~ **des bêtes** animal lover; **se faire des ~s** to make friends **②** (*amant*) boyfriend; **petite ~e** girlfriend **II.** *adj* (*regard, parole*) friendly; **être très ~ avec qn** to be very good friends with sb

**amiable** [amjabl] *adj* (*décision, constat*) amicable

**amiante** [amjãt] *m* asbestos

**amical(e)** [amikal, -o] <-aux> *adj* a. SPORT friendly

**amicale** [amikal] *f* (*association*) club

**amicalement** [amikalmã] *adv* **①** in a friendly manner; (*recevoir*) warmly **②** (*formule de fin de lettre*) **bien ~** best wishes

**amincir** [amɛ̃siʀ] <8> **I.** *vt* ~ **qn/qc** to

**A**

make sb/sth look thinner **II.** *vi inf* to lose weight **III.** *vpr* **s'~** (*personne*) to get slimmer

**amiral** [amiʀal, -o] <-aux> *m* admiral

**amitié** [amitje] *f* ❶ *a.* POL friendship; **se lier d'~ avec qn** to strike up a friendship with sb; **avoir de l'~ pour qn** to be fond of sb ❷ *pl* (*formule de fin de lettre*) **~s, Bernadette** kind regards, Bernadette; **faire toutes ses ~s à qn** to send one's best wishes to sb

**ammoniaque** [amɔnjak] *f* (*liquide*) ammonia

**amnésie** [amnezi] *f* amnesia

**amnésique** [amnezik] **I.** *adj* amnesic **II.** *mf* amnesiac

**amnistie** [amnisti] *f* amnesty

**amnistier** [amnistje] <1> *vt* to amnesty

**amocher** [amɔʃe] <1> *vt inf* ❶ (*abîmer*) to ruin; (*voiture*) to smash up ❷ *inf* (*blesser*) **~ qn** to mess sb up

**amoindrir** [amwɛ̃dʀiʀ] <8> **I.** *vt* (*autorité*) to weaken; (*importance*) to dwindle **II.** *vpr* **s'~** (*facultés*) to slip away; (*forces, fortune*) to dwindle

**amont** [amɔ̃] *m* (*partie supérieure: d'un cours d'eau*) upstream water ▸ **en ~ de St. Louis** upriver from St. Louis

**amoral(e)** [amɔʀal, -o] <-aux> *adj* amoral

**amorcer** [amɔʀse] <2> *vt* ❶ (*garnir d'une amorce: explosif*) to arm ❷ (*pour la pêche*) to bait ❸ (*ébaucher un mouvement*) **~ un virage** to take a bend ❹ (*engager: conversation*) to start up; (*réforme*) to initiate ❺ INFORM to boot

**amortir** [amɔʀtiʀ] <8> *vt* ❶ (*affaiblir: choc, chute*) to cushion; (*bruit, douleur*) to deaden ❷ (*rembourser*) to redeem; (*dette, emprunt*) to pay off ❸ (*rentabiliser: coût*) to recoup

**amortisseur** [amɔʀtisœʀ] *m* AUTO shock absorber

**amour** [amuʀ] **I.** *m* ❶ (*sentiment*) love ❷ (*acte*) lovemaking; **faire l'~** to make love ❸ (*personne*) love ❹ (*attachement, altruisme, goût pour*) **~ de la justice** love of justice; **~ du sport** love of sports ❺ (*terme d'affection*) **mon ~**

my darling **II.** *mpl* **f si** *poétique* loves ▸ **à tes/vos ~s!** *iron* cheers!

**amoureusement** [amuʀøzmã] *adv* (*avec amour, soin*) lovingly

**amoureux, -euse** [amuʀø, -øz] **I.** *adj* (*personne, regard*) loving; **la vie amoureuse de qn** sb's love life; **être/ tomber ~ de qn** to be/fall in love with sb **II.** *m, f* ❶ (*soupirant*) sweetheart; (*sentiment plus profond*) lover ❷ (*passionné*) **~ de la musique** music lover

**amour-propre** [amuʀpʀɔpʀ] <amours-propres> *m* self-esteem

**amovible** [amɔvibl] *adj* detachable; (*disque*) removable

**ampère** [ãpɛʀ] *m* ampere

**amphithéâtre** [ãfiteatʀ] *m* ❶ ARCHIT amphitheater ❷ UNIV lecture hall ❸ THEAT (upper) gallery

**ample** [ãpl] *adj* ❶ (*large*) loose ❷ (*d'une grande amplitude: mouvement*) sweeping; (*voix*) sonorous ❸ (*abondant: provisions*) plentiful ❹ (*opp: restreint: projet, sujet*) vast

**amplement** [ãpləmã] *adv* fully; **être ~ suffisant** to be more than enough

**ampleur** [ãplœʀ] *f* ❶ (*largeur: d'un vêtement*) looseness; (*d'une voix*) sonorousness ❷ (*étendue: d'un récit*) opulence; (*d'un sujet*) scope; (*d'une catastrophe*) extent; **prendre de l'~** (*épidémie*) to spread; (*manifestation*) to grow considerably

**ampli** *inf*, **amplificateur** [ãplifikatœʀ] *m* amplifier

**amplifier** [ãplifje] <1> **I.** *vt* ❶ (*augmenter*) to increase; (*image*) to enlarge ❷ (*développer: échanges, coopération, idée*) to develop ❸ (*exagérer*) **~ qc** to build sth up **II.** *vpr* **s'~** (*bruit*) to grow; (*échange, mouvement, tendance*) to increase; (*scandale*) to intensify

**ampoule** [ãpul] *f* ❶ ELEC bulb ❷ (*cloque*) blister

**amputation** [ãpytasjɔ̃] *f* ❶ ANAT amputation ❷ (*diminution: d'un texte, du territoire national*) truncation

**amputer** [ãpyte] <1> *vt* ❶ ANAT to amputate; **être amputé d'un bras** to have one's arm amputated ❷*fig* (*texte, budget*) **~ qc** to hack sth down

**amusant(e)** [amyzɑ̃, ɑ̃t] *adj* ❶ (*divertissant: jeu, vacances*) fun ❷ (*drôle, curieux*) funny

**amuse-gueule** <amuse--gueule(s)> *m inf* appetizer; (*petit sandwich*) snack

**amusement** [amyzmɑ̃] *m* ❶ (*divertissement*) entertainment ❷ (*jeu*) game

**amuser** [amyze] <1> I. *vt* ❶ (*divertir*) to entertain ❷ (*faire rire*) **~ qn** to make sb laugh ❸ (*détourner l'attention*) to divert II. *vpr* **s'~** ❶ (*jouer*) to play ❷ (*se divertir*) **bien s'~** to have a very good time; (*à une soirée*) to enjoy oneself; **amuse-toi/amusez-vous bien!** have fun! ❸ (*batifoler*) to frolic

**amygdale** [amidal] *f* tonsil

**an** [ɑ̃] *m* year; **avoir cinq ~s** to be five (years old); **homme de cinquante ~s** a fifty-year-old (man); **fêter ses vingt ~s** to celebrate one's twentieth birthday; **l'~ dernier/prochain** last/next year; **tous les ~s** every year; **par ~** per year; **en l'~ 200 avant Jésus-Christ** in (the year) 200 BC; **le nouvel ~, le premier de l'~** New Year's Day

**anal(e)** [anal, -o] <-aux> *adj* anal

**analogie** [analɔʒi] *f* analogy

**analphabète** [analfabɛt] *adj, mf* illiterate

**analyse** [analiz] *f* ❶ (*opp: synthèse*) *a.* MATH analysis ❷ MED **~ de sang** blood test

**analyser** [analize] <1> *vt* ❶ LING (*mot*) to parse ❷ MATH, MED, PSYCH to analyze

**analyste** [analist] *mf* ❶ (*technicien*) analyst ❷ PSYCH (psycho)analyst

**ananas** [anana(s)] *m* pineapple

**anarchie** [anaʀʃi] *f* anarchy

**anarchique** [anaʀʃik] *adj* anarchic

**anarchiste** [anaʀʃist] *adj, mf* anarchist

**anatomie** [anatɔmi] *f a. inf* (*science*) anatomy

**ancêtre** [ɑ̃sɛtʀ] I. *mf* ❶ (*aïeul, à l'origine d'une famille*) ancestor ❷ (*précurseur: d'un genre artistique*) forerunner

❸ *inf* (*vieillard*) oldster II. *mpl* HIST forebears

**anchois** [ɑ̃ʃwa] *m* anchovy

**ancien(ne)** [ɑ̃sjɛ̃, jɛn] I. *adj* ❶ (*vieux: bâtiment, coutume*) old; (*objet d'art*) antique; (*livre*) antiquarian ❷ *antéposé* (*ex-*) old ❸ (*antique: culture, peuple*) ancient ❹ (*qui a de l'ancienneté*) **être ~ dans le métier** to have been doing a job for a long time II. *m(f)* (*personne*) **les ~s** the elderly; SOCIOL the elders

**ancienneté** [ɑ̃sjɛnte] *f* ❶ (*dans une entreprise*) length of service ❷ (*avantages acquis*) seniority

**ancre** [ɑ̃kʀ] *f* anchor ▶ **jeter l'~** to drop anchor

**Andorre** [ɑ̃dɔʀ] *f* **l'~** Andorra

**andouillette** [ɑ̃dujɛt] *f* andouillette (sausage)

**âne** [ɑn] *m* ❶ ZOOL donkey; *v.a.* **ânesse** ❷ (*imbécile*) **quel ~!** what a fool!

**anéantir** [aneɑ̃tiʀ] <8> *vt* ❶ (*détruire: ennemi*) to annihilate; (*armée, ville, effort*) to wipe out; (*espoir*) to dash ❷ (*déprimer, accabler*) to overwhelm; (*mauvaise nouvelle*) to crush

**anecdote** [anɛkdɔt] *f* anecdote

**anémie** [anemi] *f* ❶ MED anemia ❷ (*crise*) slump

**ânerie** [ɑnʀi] *f* ❶ (*caractère stupide*) stupidity ❷ (*parole*) silly remark ❸ (*acte*) stupid mistake

**ânesse** [ɑnɛs] *f* she-ass; *v.a.* **âne**

**anesthésie** [anɛstezi] *f* MED (*état*) anesthesia; (*drogue*) anesthetic

**anesthésiste** [anɛstezist] *mf* anesthesiologist

**ange** [ɑ̃ʒ] *m* angel

**angine** [ɑ̃ʒin] *f* sore throat

**anglais** [ɑ̃glɛ] *m* English; *v.a.* **français**

**anglais(e)** [ɑ̃glɛ, ɛz] *adj* English

**Anglais(e)** [ɑ̃glɛ, ɛz] *m(f)* ❶ (*personne d'Angleterre*) Englishman, Englishwoman *m, f;* **les ~** the English ❷ *Québec* (*anglophone*) English speaker

**angle** [ɑ̃gl] *m* ❶ (*coin*) corner ❷ MATH, PHOT angle; **~ mort** blind spot ❸ (*point de vue*) angle

**Angleterre** [ɑ̃glətɛʀ] *f* **l'~** England

**A** **anglophone** [ãglɔfɔn] I. *adj* English-speaking; **être ~** to be an English speaker II. *mf* English speaker

**Anglo-Saxon(ne)** [ãglosaksɔ̃, ɔn] <Anglo-Saxons> *m(f)* Anglo-Saxon

**angoissant(e)** [ãgwasã, ãt] *adj* agonizing; (*moment, jour*) harrowing

**angoisse** [ãgwas] *f* ❶ (*peur, malaise*) anxiety ❷ (*douleur*) agony ❸ PHILOS angst

**angoissé(e)** [ãgwase] I. *adj* anxious II. *m(f)* worrier

**angoisser** [ãgwase] <1> *vt* (*inquiéter*) to worry; (*situation, nouvelle, silence*) to distress

**angora** [ãgɔʀa] I. *adj* **laine ~** angora wool II. *m* (*chat, lapin, laine*) angora

**anguille** [ãgij] *f* eel

**animal** [animal, -o] <-aux> *m* (*bête*) animal

**animal(e)** [animal, -o] <-aux> *adj* ❶ ZOOL, BIO (*matières, fonctions*) animal ❷ (*rapporté à l'homme: instinct*) animal; (*comportement, confiance*) instinctive ❸ *péj* (*bestial*) brutish

**animateur, -trice** [animatœʀ, -tʀis] *m, f* ❶ (*spécialiste de l'animation: d'un groupe*) leader; (*d'un club de vacances*) camp counselor; (*d'un club de sport*) coach; (*d'une fête*) entertainer ❷ (*présentateur*) RADIO, TV host

**animation** [animasjɔ̃] *f* ❶ (*grande activité: d'un bureau*) activity; (*d'un quartier*) life ❷ (*vivacité: d'une discussion*) liveliness; **mettre de l'~** to liven things up ❸ (*excitation*) excitement ❹ (*conduite de groupe*) leadership

**animé(e)** [anime] *adj* (*discussion*) animated; (*rue*) busy; (*personne*) lively; **dessin ~** cartoon

**animer** [anime] <1> I. *vt* ❶ (*mener: débat, groupe, entreprise*) to lead; (*émission*) to host ❷ (*mouvoir*) to drive ❸ (*égayer*) ~ **qc** to liven sth up ❹ (*ressusciter*) to revive II. *vpr* **s'~** (*yeux*) to light up; (*conversation, rue*) to liven up

**animosité** [animozite] *f* animosity

**anis** [anis] *m* ❶ BOT anise ❷ CULIN aniseed

**anisette** [anizɛt] *f* anisette

**annales** [anal] *fpl* annals

**anneau** [ano] <x> *m* ❶ (*cercle, bague*) *a.* ASTR ring ❷ (*maillon*) link ❸ *pl* SPORT racetrack

**année** [ane] *f* ❶ (*durée*) year; **au cours des dernières ~s** over the last years; **bien des ~s après** many years later; **dans les ~s à venir** in the years to come; **tout au long de l'~** the whole year round ❷ (*âge*) year ❸ (*date*) year; **l'~ prochaine/dernière/passée** next/last year; **~ de naissance** year of birth; **en début/en fin d'~** at the beginning/end of the year; **les ~s trente** the (nineteen) thirties; **bonne ~, bonne santé!** health and happiness in the New Year!; **souhaiter la bonne ~ à qn** to wish sb a happy New Year ▶ **les ~s folles** the Roaring Twenties

**année-lumière** [anelymjɛʀ] <années-lumière> *f* light year

**annexe** [anɛks] *f* annex; **joindre en ~** to attach

**annexer** [anɛkse] <1> *vt* (*territoire, pays*) to annex

**anniversaire** [anivɛʀsɛʀ] I. *adj* (*jour, cérémonie*) anniversary II. *m* (*d'une personne*) birthday; (*d'un événement*) anniversary; **bon ~!** Happy birthday!; (*à un couple*) Happy anniversary!

**annonce** [anɔ̃s] *f* ❶ (*avis: d'un événement imminent*) announcement ❷ (*information officielle*) ~ **de qc** notice of sth; (*transmise par les médias*) announcement of sth ❸ (*petite annonce*) classified advertisements; **les petites ~s** classified ads; **passer une ~ dans un journal** to place an ad in the paper ❹ (*présage*) sign; (*indice*) indication ❺ JEUX declaration

**annoncer** [anɔ̃se] <2> I. *vt* ❶ (*communiquer: fait, décision*) to announce ❷ (*prédire*) to predict ❸ (*être le signe de: printemps*) to be the harbinger of; (*signal*) to give ❹ JEUX to declare II. *vpr* (*se présenter*) **bien/mal s'~** to seem promising/unpromising

**annotation** [anɔtasjɔ̃] *f* annotation

**annoter** [anɔte] <1> *vt* to annotate

**annuaire** [anɥɛʀ] *m* directory

**annuel(le)** [anɥɛl] *adj* ❶ (*périodique*) annual ❷ (*qui dure un an*) yearlong

**annulaire** [anɥlɛʀ] **I.** *m* ring finger **II.** *adj* ring-shaped

**annulation** [anylasjɔ̃] *f* ❶ (*suppression: d'une commande, d'un rendez-vous*) cancellation ❷ JUR (*d'un examen, contrat*) cancellation; (*d'un jugement*) overturning

**annuler** [anyle] <1> **I.** *vt* ❶ (*supprimer*) *a.* INFORM to cancel ❷ JUR (*jugement*) to overturn; (*mariage*) to annul **II.** *vpr* s'~ to cancel each other out

**anodin(e)** [anɔdɛ̃, in] *adj* (*personne*) insignificant; (*critique, détail, propos*) trivial; (*blessure*) superficial

**anonymat** [anɔnima] *m* anonymity

**anonyme** [anɔnim] *adj* anonymous

**anorak** [anɔʀak] *m* anorak

**anorexie** [anɔʀɛksi] *f* (*refus de s'alimenter*) anorexia

**anorexique** [anɔʀɛksik] *adj, mf* anorexic

**anormal(e)** [anɔʀmal, -o] <-aux> *adj* ❶ (*inhabituel*) unusual ❷ (*non conforme à la règle*) abnormal; (*comportement*) perverse ❸ (*injuste*) unfair

**ANPE** [aɛnpeø] *f abr de* **Agence nationale pour l'emploi** ❶ (*organisme national*) National Employment Agency (*government agency managing employment legislation and job searches*) ❷ (*agence locale*) employment office

**anse** [ɑ̃s] *f* ❶ (*d'un panier*) handle ❷ (*petite baie*) cove

**antarctique** [ɑ̃taʀktik] *adj* Antarctic

**Antarctique** [ɑ̃taʀktik] *m* l'~ the Antarctic (Ocean); (*continent*) Antarctica

**antécédent** [ɑ̃tesedɑ̃] *m* ❶ LING, PHILOS antecedent ❷ *pl* MED (*medical*) history + *vb sing* ❸ *pl* (*actes du passé: d'une personne*) past record + *vb sing*; (*d'une affaire*) antecedents

**antécédent(e)** [ɑ̃tesedɑ̃, ɑ̃t] *adj* ~ **à qc** preceding sth

**antenne** [ɑ̃tɛn] *f* ❶ (*pour capter*) antenna ❷ RADIO, TV **une heure d'~** an hour of airtime; **à l'~** on the air ❸ ZOOL antenna ❹ MIL (*poste avancé*) outpost

**antérieur(e)** [ɑ̃teʀjœʀ] *adj* ❶ (*précédent*) previous; **être ~ à qc** to be prior to sth ❷ ANAT **patte ~e** forefoot ❸ LING anterior

**antériorité** [ɑ̃teʀjɔʀite] *f* ❶ (*dans le temps*) precedence ❷ LING anteriority

**anthologie** [ɑ̃tɔlɔʒi] *f* anthology

**anti-âge** [ɑ̃tiaʒ] *adj inv* anti-aging; **crème ~** anti-aging cream

**antibiotique** [ɑ̃tibjɔtik] *adj, m* antibiotic

**antibrouillard** [ɑ̃tibʀujaʀ] **I.** *adj* fog **II.** *m* fog light

**anticipation** [ɑ̃tisipasjɔ̃] *f* (*prévision*) anticipation

**anticiper** [ɑ̃tisipe] <1> **I.** *vi* ❶ (*devancer les faits*) to look too far ahead ❷ (*se représenter à l'avance*) to think ahead; (*prévoir*) to plan **II.** *vt* ❶ (*prévoir: avenir, événement*) to predict ❷ FIN, SPORT to anticipate

**anticorps** [ɑ̃tikɔʀ] *m* antibody

**anticyclone** [ɑ̃tisiklon] *m* METEO anticyclone

**antidépresseur** [ɑ̃tidepʀɛsœʀ] *adj, m* antidepressant

**antidote** [ɑ̃tidɔt] *m* MED antidote

**anti-effraction** [ɑ̃tiefʀaksjɔ̃] *adj inv* (*porte, fenêtre*) burglarproof

**antigel** [ɑ̃tiʒɛl] *m* antifreeze

**anti-inflammatoire** [ɑ̃tiɛ̃flamatwaʀ] <anti-inflammatoires> *adj* anti-inflammatory

**antillais(e)** [ɑ̃tijɛ, jɛz] *adj* West Indian

**Antillais(e)** [ɑ̃tijɛ, ɛz] *m(f)* West Indian

**Antilles** [ɑ̃tij] *fpl* **les ~** the West Indies

**antimite** [ɑ̃timit] *adj* mothproof

**antimondialiste** [ɑ̃timɔ̃djalist] *mf* anti-globalization activist

**antioxydant** [ɑ̃tiɔksidɑ̃] *m* CHIM antioxidant

**antipathie** [ɑ̃tipati] *f* antipathy

**antipathique** [ɑ̃tipatik] *adj* unpleasant, (*comportement*) antisocial

**anti-piratage** [ɑ̃tipiʀataʒ] *adj inv* INFORM (*document, fichier*) copy-protected; **protection ~** copy protection

**A** antiquaire [ãtikɛʀ] mf antique dealer

antique [ãtik] adj antique; (lieu) ancient

Antiquité [ãtikite] f sans pl HIST l'~ antiquity

antireflet [ãtiʀəflɛ] adj (verre) nonglare

antirides [ãtiʀid] adj anti-wrinkle

antirouille [ãtiʀuj] I. adj inv rustproof II. m rustproofer

antisémite [ãtisemit] I. adj anti-Semitic II. mf anti-Semite

antiseptique [ãtisɛptik] I. adj antiseptic II. m antiseptic

anti-spam [ãtispam] <anti-spams> I. adj spam; **filtre ~** spam filter II. m spam protection

antitabac [ãtitaba] adj inv anti-smoking

antivol [ãtivɔl] I. adj inv anti-theft II. m (d'un vélo) bicycle lock

anus [anys] m anus

anxiété [ãksjete] f ❶ MED, PSYCH anxiety ❷ (trait de caractère) worry

anxieusement [ãksjøzmã] adv anxiously

anxieux, -euse [ãksjø, -jøz] I. adj worried; (attente) anxious II. m, f worrier

AOC [aɔse] abr de appellation d'origine contrôlée (regional quality control label for wine, cheese, etc.)

aorte [aɔʀt] f aorta

août [u(t)] m ❶ August; **~ est un mois d'été** August is a summer month ❷ (pour indiquer la date, un laps de temps) **en ~** in August; **début/fin ~** at the beginning/end of August; **pendant tout le mois d'~** for the whole of August; **le 15 ~, c'est l'Assomption** the Assumption is on August 15

apaiser [apeze] <1> I. vt to calm; (douleur) to soothe; (faim, désir) to satisfy; (soif) to slake; (protestations) to quell; (colère) to pacify; (scrupules, craintes) to allay; (dieux) to appease II. vpr s'~ (personne) to calm down; (douleur) to die down; (colère, tempête) to abate

apartheid [apaʀtɛd] m apartheid

apercevoir [apɛʀsəvwaʀ] <12> I. vt ❶ (entrevoir) to see ❷ (remarquer) to

notice ❸ (distinguer) to distinguish; (percevoir) to perceive ❹ (prévoir) to see II. vpr ❶ (se voir) s'~ to notice each other ❷ (se rendre compte) s'~ d'une erreur de qn to notice an error; **sans s'en ~** without noticing

aperçu [apɛʀsy] m ❶ (idée générale) overview ❷ INFORM preview

apéritif [apeʀitif] m aperitif

apéro [apeʀo] m inf abr de **apéritif**

apeuré(e) [apœʀe] adj frightened

aphone [afon] adj voiceless

aphte [aft] m MED canker sore

apiculteur, -trice [apikyltœʀ, -tʀis] m, f beekeeper

apitoyer [apitwaje] <6> vpr s'~ sur qn/qc to feel sorry for sb/sth

aplati(e) [aplati] adj flat

aplatir [aplatiʀ] <8> I. vt to flatten; ~ qc (voûte) to flatten sth down; (pli) to smooth sth out II. vpr ❶ (se plaquer) s'~ sur la table to lie flat on the table; s'~ contre le mur to flatten oneself against the wall ❷ (devenir plat) s'~ to become flatter ❸ (être rendu plat) s'~ to be flattened ❹ (s'écraser) s'~ contre qc to smash into sth

à plus [aplys] interj inf see you

apnée [apne] f SPORT diving without oxygen

apocalypse [apɔkalips] f (désastre) apocalypse

apogée [apɔʒe] m summit

a posteriori [a pɔstɛʀjɔʀi] adv, adj after the event

apostrophe [apɔstʀɔf] f ❶ (signe) apostrophe ❷ (interpellation) insult

apostropher [apɔstʀɔfe] <1> vt ~ qn to shout at sb

apothéose [apɔteoz] f ❶ (consécration) apotheosis ❷ (sommet) summit ❸ (partie finale) grand finale

apôtre [apotʀ] m ❶ REL, HIST apostle ❷ (propagateur d'une idée) advocate

apparaître [apaʀɛtʀ] vi irr être ❶ (se montrer) to appear ❷ (surgir: fièvre) to break out; (difficulté, idée, vérité) to arise; (obstacle) to loom ❸ (se révéler) ~ à qn (vérité) to reveal itself to sb ④(*sembler*) ~ **grand à qn** to appear big to sb ⑤(*se présenter*) ~ **comme qc à qn** to appear to sb to be sth

**appareil** [aparɛj] *m* ❶(*machine, instrument*) device; (*radio, télévision*) set; **à l'~** on the telephone; **qui est à l'~?** who is speaking?; ~ **photo(graphique)** camera; ~**s ménagers** household appliances ❷(*prothèse*) appliance; (*dentaire*) brace; (*dentier*) denture; ~ **auditif** hearing aid ❸(*avion*) aircraft ❹ANAT system ❺POL machinery ❻*pl* SPORT apparatus

**appareiller** [apareje] <1> **I.** *vi* ❶ to get under way **II.** *vt* ❶NAUT to fit out ❷(*assortir*) to match

**apparemment** [aparamɑ̃] *adv* apparently; (*vraisemblablement*) probably

**apparence** [aparɑ̃s] *f* ❶(*aspect*) appearance ❷(*ce qui semble être*) outward appearance

**apparent(e)** [aparɑ̃, ɑ̃t] *adj* ❶(*visible*) apparent ❷(*évident, manifeste*) obvious ❸(*supposé, trompeur*) apparent

**apparenté(e)** [aparɑ̃te] *adj* ❶(*ressemblant*) ~ **à qc** resembling sth ❷(*parent*) ~ **à qn/qc** related to sb/sth

**apparition** [aparisjɔ̃] *f* ❶(*action de paraître: d'une personne*) appearance ❷*sans pl* (*fait de devenir visible*) appearance ❸(*d'un être surnaturel*) apparition

**appart** *inf*, **appartement** [apartəmɑ̃] *m* ❶(*habitation*) apartment ❷(*dans un hôtel*) suite

**appartenance** [apartənɑ̃s] *f* (*dépendance*) **mon ~ à un parti** my membership in a party; **mon ~ à une famille** my belonging to a family

**appartenir** [apartəniʀ] <9> **I.** *vi* ❶(*être la propriété de*) ~ **à qn** to belong to sb ❷(*faire partie de*) *a.* MATH ~ **à qc** to be a member of sth **II.** *vi impers* **il appartient à qn de** +*infin* it is up to sb to +*infin*

**appât** [apa] *m* bait; **l'~ du gain** the lure of gain

**appauvrir** [apovʀiʀ] <8> **I.** *vt* (*personne, pays*) to impoverish **II.** *vpr* **s'~** to become impoverished

**appauvrissement** [apovʀismɑ̃] *m* impoverishment

**appel** [apɛl] *m* ❶(*cri, signal*) *a.* INFORM call ❷(*demande*) appeal; **faire ~ à qn/qc** to call on sb/sth ❸(*exhortation*) ~ **à qc** to call to sth; **lancer un ~ à qn** to make an appeal to sb ❹(*vérification de présence*) register; MIL roll call; **faire l'~** to take attendance; MIL to do roll call ❺TEL ~ **téléphonique** telephone call ❻SPORT takeoff ▶ ~ **d'offres** call for bids

**appeler** [aple] **I.** *vt* ❶(*interpeller, nommer*) to call ❷(*faire venir*) to call; **faire ~ qn** to send for sb ❸(*téléphoner à*) to call ❹(*réclamer*) **les affaires m'appellent** business calls ❺(*désigner*) ~ **qn à une charge/un poste** to appoint sb to a duty/job ❻(*se référer à*) **en ~ à qc** to appeal to sth ❼INFORM ~ **qc** to call up sth **II.** *vi* (*héler, téléphoner*) to call **III.** *vpr* ❶(*porter comme nom*) **s'~** to be called; **comment t'appelles-tu/s'appelle cette plante?** what's your/this plant's name?; **je m'appelle** my name is ❷(*être équivalent à*) **cela s'appelle faire qc** *inf* that's what you call doing sth

**appellation** [apelasjɔ̃, apɛllasjɔ̃] *f* appellation; ~ **d'origine** label of origin

**appendicite** [apɛ̃disit] *f* MED appendicitis

**appétissant(e)** [apetisɑ̃, ɑ̃t] *adj* ❶(*alléchant*) appetizing ❷*inf* (*attirant*) attractive

**appétit** [apeti] *m* ❶(*faim*) appetite; **avoir de l'~** to have an appetite; **donner de/couper l'~ à qn** to give sb an/to ruin sb's appetite; **bon ~!** enjoy your meal! ❷*fig* ~ **de vengeance** thirst for revenge

**applaudir** [aplodiʀ] <8> *vt, vi* to applaud

**applaudissements** [aplodismɑ̃] *mpl* applause + *vb sing*

**appli** [apli] *f inf* TEL, INET (*d'un portable*) app

**application** [aplikasjɔ̃] *f* ❶(*pose, uti-*

**A**

*lisation*) application; **lancer une ~** to start a program ❷ (*mise en pratique: d'une idée*) putting into practice; (*d'une décision, mesure*) implementation; **mettre qc en ~** apply ❸ TEL, INFORM application; (*d'un portable*) app

**appliqué(e)** [aplike] *adj* ❶ (*attentif et studieux*) conscientious ❷ (*soigné*) careful ❸ (*mis en pratique*) applied

**appliquer** [aplike] <1> I. *vt* ❶ (*poser*) **~ de la peinture sur qc** to paint sth ❷ (*mettre en pratique*) to implement; (*remède*) to administer; (*mode d'emploi, règlement*) to follow II. *vpr* ❶ (*se poser*) **s'~ sur qc** to be applied to sth ❷ (*correspondre à*) **s'~ à qn/qc** to apply to sb/sth ❸ (*s'efforcer*) **s'~ à faire qc** to apply oneself to doing sth

**appoint** [apwɛ̃] *m* (*complément*) extra contribution; (*aide*) extra help

**apport** [apɔʀ] *m* ❶ (*contribution*) **l'~ de qn/qc à qc** the contribution of sb/sth to sth ❷ (*source*) **~ de vitamines** supply of vitamins ❸ FIN financial contribution

**apporter** [apɔʀte] <1> *vt* ❶ (*porter*) to bring ❷ (*fournir*) **~ une preuve à qc** to supply proof for sth; **~ sa contribution/son concours à qc** to contribute to/support sth ❸ (*procurer*) to supply; (*consolation, soulagement*) to give; (*ennuis*) to bring ❹ (*produire*) **~ une modification à qc** to make a modification to sth ❺ (*mettre*) **~ du soin à qc** to exercise care in doing sth ❻ (*profiter à*) **~ beaucoup à qn/qc** to give a lot to sb/sth

**appréciable** [apʀesjabl] *adj* appreciable; (*changement*) noticeable

**appréciation** [apʀesjasjɔ̃] *f* ❶ *sans pl* (*évaluation: d'une distance*) estimation; (*d'une situation*) appraisal; (*d'un objet de valeur*) valuation ❷ (*commentaire*) evaluation ❸ (*jugement*) assessment

**apprécier** [apʀesje] <1> I. *vt* ❶ (*évaluer: distance, vitesse*) to estimate; (*objet, valeur*) to value; (*importance*) to as-

sess ❷ (*aimer*) to like II. *vi* infil **n'a pas apprécié!** he didn't take kindly to that!

**appréhender** [apʀeɑ̃de] <1> *vt* ❶ (*redouter*) **~ de faire qc** to dread doing sth ❷ (*arrêter*) to apprehend

**appréhension** [apʀeɑ̃sjɔ̃] *f* apprehension

**apprendre** [apʀɑ̃dʀ] <13> I. *vt* ❶ (*être informé de*) **~ qc** to hear sth; (*événement*) to learn of sth ❷ (*annoncer*) **~ une chose à qn** to announce sth to sb ❸ (*étudier: leçon, langue, métier*) to learn ❹ (*devenir capable de*) **~ à** +*infin* to learn to +*infin* ❺ (*enseigner*) **~ qc à qn** to teach sth to sb II. *vi* to learn III. *vpr* **s'~ facilement** (*langue*) to be easy to learn

**apprenti(e)** [apʀɑ̃ti] *m(f)* ❶ (*élève*) apprentice ❷ (*débutant*) novice

**apprentissage** [apʀɑ̃tisaʒ] *m* (*formation*) training; **il fait son ~ de menuisier** he is doing his apprenticeship as a carpenter

**apprêter** [apʀete] <1> *vpr* **s'~ à** +*infin* (*se préparer*) to get ready to +*infin*; (*être sur le point de*) to be just about to +*infin*

**apprivoiser** [apʀivwaze] <1> *vt* to tame

**approbation** [apʀɔbasjɔ̃] *f* ❶ (*accord*) approval ❷ (*jugement favorable*) approbation; (*du public*) approval

**approche** [apʀɔʃ] *f* ❶ (*arrivée, manière d'aborder un sujet*) approach; **à l'~ de la ville** near the town; **mon ~ du problème** my approach to the problem ❷ (*proximité*) **l'~ d'un événement** the approaching event; **à l'~ du printemps** at the onset of spring

**approcher** [apʀɔʃe] <1> I. *vi* (*personne*) to approach; (*moment, date, saison, orage, jour*) to draw near; (*nuit*) to close in II. *vt* ❶ (*mettre plus près*) **~ une chose de qn/qc** to move a thing closer to sb/sth; **elle approcha son visage du sien** she brought her face close to his ❷ (*venir plus près*) to approach; **ne m'approche pas!** don't come near me! **III.** *vpr* **s'~ de qn/qc** to approach sb/sth

**approfondir** [apʀɔfɔ̃diʀ] <8> *vt* to deepen

**approprié(e)** [apʀɔpʀije] *adj* **~ à qc** suitable for sth; (*réponse, style*) appropriate for sth

**approprier** [apʀɔpʀije] <1> *vpr* **s'~ un bien** to appropriate property; **s'~ un droit** to assume a right

**approuver** [apʀuve] <1> *vt* **①** (*agréer*) to approve; **~ que qn fasse qc** (*subj*) to approve of sb doing sth **②** JUR (*contrat*) to ratify; (*projet de loi*) to pass; (*nomination, procès verbal*) to approve

**approvisionnement** [apʀɔvizjɔnmɑ̃] *m* **①** (*ravitaillement*) **~ en qc** supplying of sth **②** (*réserve*) **~ en qc** supplies of sth

**approvisionner** [apʀɔvizjɔne] <1> **I.** *vt* **~ une ville en qc** to supply a town with sth; **~ un magasin en qc** to stock a store with sth; **~ un compte en qc** to deposit sth into an account **II.** *vpr* **s'~ en qc** to stock up with sth

**approximatif, -ive** [apʀɔksimatif, -iv] *adj* approximate; (*valeur*) rough; (*terme*) imprecise

**approximation** [apʀɔksimasjɔ̃] *f* estimate; MATH approximation

**appui** [apɥi] *m* **①** (*support*) support **②** (*aide*) help **③** (*justification*) **à l'~ de qc** in support of sth

**appuie-tête** [apɥitɛt] <appuie-tête(s)> *m* headrest

**appuyer** [apɥije] <6> **I.** *vi* **①** (*presser*) **~ sur qc** to press on sth **②** (*insister sur*) **~ sur qc** (*prononciation*) to stress sth; (*argumentation*) to emphasize sth **II.** *vt* **①** (*poser*) **~ qc contre/sur qc** to lean sth against/on sth **②** (*presser*) **~ sa main/son pied sur qc** to press on sth with one's hand/foot **③** (*soutenir*) to support **III.** *vpr* **①** (*prendre appui*) **s'~ contre/sur qn/qc** to lean against/on sb/sth **②** (*compter sur*) **s'~ sur qn/qc** to rely on sb/sth **③** (*se fonder sur*) **s'~ sur qc** (*preuves*) to be based on sth

**après** [apʀɛ] **I.** *prep* **①** (*plus loin/tard*

*que*) after; **bien/peu ~ qc** a long/short time after sth; **~ avoir fait qc** after doing sth **②** (*derrière*) after; **~ toi/vous!** after you! **③** *inf* (*contre*) **être furieux ~ qn** to be furious with sb; **en avoir ~ qn** to have it in for sb **④** (*chaque*) **jour ~ jour** day after day **⑤** (*selon*) **d'~ qn/qc** according to sb/sth; **d'~ moi** in my opinion **II.** *adv* **①** (*plus tard/loin, ensuite/derrière*) later; (*par la suite*) after; **aussitôt ~** straight afterwards; **longtemps/peu ~** a long time/slightly after **②** (*dans un classement*) behind **③** (*qui suit*) **d'~** following ▶ **et ~?** *inf* and then?; **~ tout** after all **III.** *conj* **~ que qn a fait qc** after sb did sth

**après-demain** [apʀɛdmɛ̃] *adv* the day after tomorrow

**après-guerre** [apʀɛɡɛʀ] <après-guerres> *m* **l'~** (*période*) the postwar years *pl*; (*situation*) the postwar situation

**après-midi** [apʀɛmidi] **I.** *m o f inv* afternoon; **cet(te) ~** this afternoon; **(dans) l'~** in the afternoon; **4 heures de l'~** 4 o'clock in the afternoon **II.** *adv* **mardi/demain ~** Tuesday/tomorrow afternoon

**après-rasage** [apʀɛʀazaʒ] *m inv* after-shave

**après-ski** [apʀɛski] *m inv* après-ski

**après-vente** [apʀɛvɑ̃t] *adj inv* **service ~** after sales service

**a priori** [apʀijɔʀi] **I.** *adv* **①** (*au premier abord*) at first sight **②** (*en principe*) in theory **II.** *m inv* preconception

**apte** [apt] *adj* **①** (*capable*) able **②** MIL. **être ~ au service** to be fit for duty

**aptitude** [aptityd] *f* aptitude

**aquarelle** [akwaʀɛl] *f* watercolor

**aquarium** [akwaʀjɔm] *m* aquarium

**aquatique** [akwatik] *adj* aquatic

**Aquitaine** [akitɛn] *f* **l'~** Aquitaine

**arabe** [aʀab] **I.** *adj* Arab; **les Émirats ~s** (*unis*) the (United) Arab Emirates **II.** *m* Arabic; *v.a.* **français**

**Arabe** [aʀab] *mf* Arab

**Arabie** [aʀabi] *f* **l'~ (Saoudite)** (Saudi) Arabia

**arachide** [aʀaʃid] *f* **①** (*plante*) peanut

**A**

@ *Québec* (*cacahouète*) **des ~s salées** salted peanuts

**araignée** [aʀeɲe] *f* spider

**arbitrage** [aʀbitʀaʒ] *m* ❶ (*fonction*) refereeing; (*au tennis, base-ball*) umpiring; ❷ (*juridiction, médiation*) arbitration; FIN arbitrage ❸ (*sentence*) arbitrament

**arbitraire** [aʀbitʀɛʀ] *adj* arbitrary

**arbitre** [aʀbitʀ] *mf* ❶ SPORT referee; (*au tennis, base-ball*) umpire ❷ (*conciliateur*) arbitrator

**arbitrer** [aʀbitʀe] <1> *vt* ❶ (*servir de conciliateur*) to arbitrate ❷ SPORT to referee; (*tennis, cricket*) to umpire

**arbre** [aʀbʀ] *m* ❶ BOT tree ❷ TECH shaft

**arbuste** [aʀbyst] *m* bush

**arc** [aʀk] *m* ❶ (*arme*) bow ❷ MATH arc ❸ ARCHIT arch; **~ de triomphe** triumphal arch

**arcade** [aʀkad] *f* ❶ ARCHIT archway ❷ ANAT **~ sourcilière** arch of the eyebrows

**arc-en-ciel** [aʀkɑ̃sjɛl] <arcs-en-ciel> *m* rainbow

**archaïque** [aʀkaik] *adj* archaic

**arche** [aʀʃ] *f* ❶ (*forme*) arch ❷ REL **~ de Noé** Noah's Ark

**archéologie** [aʀkeɔlɔʒi] *f* archaeology

**archéologique** [aʀkeɔlɔʒik] *adj* archaeological

**archéologue** [aʀkeɔlɔg] *mf* archaeologist

**archet** [aʀʃɛ] *m* bow

**archevêque** [aʀʃəvɛk] *m* archbishop

**archipel** [aʀʃipɛl] *m* archipelago

**architecte** [aʀʃitɛkt] *mf* architect

**architecture** [aʀʃitɛktyʀ] *f* ARCHIT, INFORM architecture; (*style*) design

**archiver** [aʀʃive] <1> *vt* to archive

**archives** [aʀʃiv] *fpl* ❶ (*documents publics*) archives ❷ (*documents personnels*) records

**Arctique** [aʀktik] *m* **l'~** the Arctic

**ardent(e)** [aʀdɑ̃, ɑ̃t] *adj* ❶ (*brûlant*) burning; ❷ (*violent: désir, passion*) burning; (*amour, lutte, haine*) passionate; (*imagination*) fervent

**ardeur** [aʀdœʀ] *f* ❶ (*chaleur*) ardor; (*force vive*) keenness; (*de la foi,*

*conviction*) fervor; (*de la jeunesse, d'une passion*) ardor ❸ (*zèle*) zeal

**ardoise** [aʀdwaz] I. *f sans pl* slate II. *adj inv* (*couleur*) slate gray

**arène** [aʀɛn] *f* (*piste, amphithéâtre romain*) arena

**arête** [aʀɛt] *f* ❶ ZOOL (*d'un poisson*) (fish)bone ❷ (*bord saillant*) edge; (*du nez*) bridge

**argent** [aʀʒɑ̃] I. *m* ❶ FIN money; **~ de poche** pocket money ❷ (*métal*) silver II. *adj inv* (*couleur*) silver

**argenté(e)** [aʀʒɑ̃te] *adj* ❶ (*ton*) silvery; (*couleur, cheveux*) silver ❷ (*recouvert d'argent*) silver-plated

**argenterie** [aʀʒɑ̃tʀi] *f sans pl* ❶ (*vaisselle*) silverware ❷ (*couverts*) silver

**argentin(e)** [aʀʒɑ̃tɛ̃, in] *adj* Argentinean

**Argentin(e)** [aʀʒɑ̃tɛ̃, in] *m(f)* Argentinean

**Argentine** [aʀʒɑ̃tin] *f* **l'~** Argentina

**argile** [aʀʒil] *f* clay

**argot** [aʀgo] *m* ❶ *sans pl* (*langue verte*) slang ❷ (*langage particulier*) jargon

**argument** [aʀgymɑ̃] *m* (*raisonnement, preuve*) argument

**argumentation** [aʀgymɑ̃tasjɔ̃] *f* argumentation

**argumenter** [aʀgymɑ̃te] <1> *vi* **~ contre qn/qc** to argue with sb/sth

**aride** [aʀid] *adj* dry

**aridité** [aʀidite] *f sans pl* dryness

**aristocrate** [aʀistɔkʀat] *mf* aristocrat

**aristocratie** [aʀistɔkʀasi] *f* aristocracy

**arithmétique** [aʀitmetik] I. *f* arithmetic II. *adj* arithmetical

**armateur** [aʀmatœʀ] *m* ship owner

**armature** [aʀmatyʀ] *f* (*charpente*) armature; (*d'une tente, parapluie*) frame; (*d'un soutien-gorge*) underwire

**arme** [aʀm] *f* ❶ (*instrument*) weapon ❷ (*corps de l'armée*) branch (of the armed services)

**armé(e)** [aʀme] *adj* armed

**armée** [aʀme] *f* ❶ (*institution, troupes*) **l'~** the armed services *pl*; **~ de terre** the Army; **être à l'~** to be in the army ❷ (*foule*) crowd

**armement** [aʀməmɑ̃] *m* ❶ *sans pl* (*action: d'un pays, d'une armée, d'un soldat*) arming; (*d'un navire*) fitting out; (*d'un fusil*) cocking ❷ (*armes: d'un soldat, d'une troupe*) weapons *pl*; (*d'un pays, avion, bateau*) arms *pl*

**armer** [aʀme] <1> **I.** *vt* ❶ (*munir d'armes: soldat, pays*) to arm ❷ (*équiper: soldat*) to equip; (*bateau*) to fit out ❸ (*aguerrir*) ~ **qn contre qc** to arm against sth ❹ (*charger: fusil*) to cock ❺ (*renforcer: béton*) to reinforce **II.** *vpr* ❶ (*se munir d'armes*) **s'~ contre qn/ qc** to arm oneself against sb/sth ❷ (*se munir de*) **s'~ de patience** to call upon all one's patience

**armistice** [aʀmistis] *m* armistice

**armoire** [aʀmwaʀ] *f* cupboard

**armure** [aʀmyʀ] *f* ❶ MIL armor ❷ *fig* defense

**armurier** [aʀmyʀje] *m* ❶ (*marchand, fabricant*) gunsmith ❷ HIST, MIL armorer

**arnaque** [aʀnak] *f inf* con

**arnaquer** [aʀnake] <1> *vt inf* (*escroquer*) to con

**aromate** [aʀɔmat] *m* **les ~s** herbs and spices

**aromatiser** [aʀɔmatize] <1> *vt* (*aliment*) to flavor; (*savon*) to perfume

**arome, arôme** [aʀom] *m* ❶ (*odeur: du café*) aroma; (*d'un vin*) nose ❷ (*additif alimentaire*) flavoring

**arracher** [aʀaʃe] <1> **I.** *vt* ❶ (*extraire: herbes*) to pull up; (*arbre*) to uproot; (*légumes*) to dig up; (*clou, poil, page*) to pull out; (*dent*) to pull ❷ (*déchirer: affiche*) to rip down; ~ **un bras à qn** (*personne*) to rip sb's arm off; (*chien*) to bite sb's arm off ❸ (*prendre*) ~ **qn à qn** to rescue sb from sb; ~ **qn/qc des mains de qn** to grab sb/sth from sb's hands ❹ (*obtenir*) ~ **de l'argent à qn** to extract money from sb ❺ (*soustraire*) ~ **qn à la mort** to snatch sb from death **II.** *vi fig, inf* (*sauce*) to have a kick **III.** *vpr* ❶ (*se déchirer*) **s'~ les cheveux** to tear one's hair out ❷ (*se disputer*) **s'~ qn/qc** to fight over sb/sth ❸ *inf* (*partir*) **s'~** to tear oneself away

**arrangement** [aʀɑ̃ʒmɑ̃] *m* arrangement

**arranger** [aʀɑ̃ʒe] <2a> **I.** *vt* ❶ (*disposer*) to arrange; (*coiffure*) to fix; (*vêtement*) to straighten ❷ (*organiser: voyage, réunion, rencontre*) to arrange ❸ (*régler*) to sort out ❹ (*contenter*) to suit; **si ça vous arrange** if it's convenient for you; **ça l'arrange que qn fasse qc** (*subj*) it suits him for sb to do sth ❺ (*réparer*) to fix ❻ *inf* (*malmener*) to fix **II.** *vpr* ❶ (*se mettre d'accord*) **s'~ avec qn pour** +*infin* to arrange with sb to +*infin* ❷ (*s'améliorer*) **s'~** (*problème*) to be settled; (*situation, état de santé*) to improve ❸ (*se débrouiller*) **s'~ pour que qn fasse qc** (*subj*) to see to it that sb does sth

**arrestation** [aʀɛstasjɔ̃] *f* arrest

**arrêt** [aʀɛ] *m* ❶ (*interruption: d'une machine, d'un moteur, de la production*) stopping; (*d'une centrale*) shutdown; (*des négociations, essais*) cessation; ~ **cardiaque** cardiac arrest; **sans ~** (*sans interruption*) nonstop; (*fréquemment*) continually ❷ (*halte, station: d'un train, automobiliste*) stop; **dix minutes d'~** à **Nancy** a ten-minute stop in Nancy; ~ **d'autobus** bus stop ❸ JUR (*jugement*) ruling ❹ MIL (*sanction*) **mettre qn aux ~s** to put sb under arrest ▸ ~ **de jeu** stop; ~ **de maladie** (*congé*) sick leave; (*certificat*) doctor's certificate; **être en ~ de maladie** to be on sick leave

**arrêté** [aʀete] *m* order

**arrêté(e)** [aʀete] *adj* (*décision*) firm; (*idée*) fixed

**arrêter** [aʀete] <1> **I.** *vi* to stop; ~ **de faire qc** to stop doing sth **II.** *vt* ❶ (*stopper, interrompre*) to stop; (*télé, machine*) to switch off ❷ **au voleur, arrêtez-le!** stop thief! ❸ (*terminer*) to end ❹ (*bloquer*) to block ❺ (*abandonner*) to give up ❻ (*faire prisonnier*) to arrest ❼ (*fixer: détails, date*) to fix **III.** *vpr* ❶ (*s'immobiliser, s'interrompre*) **s'~** to stop; **s'~ de faire qc** to stop doing sth ❷ (*séjourner*) to stop off ❸ (*cesser*) **s'~**

**A**

to cease; (*épidémie*) to end; (*pluie, travail*) to stop; **s'~ de fumer** to quit smoking

**arrêt-maladie** [aʀɛmaladi] <arrêts--maladie> *m* (*congé*) sick leave; (*certificat*) doctor's certificate

**arrhes** [aʀ] *fpl* deposit

**arrière** [aʀjɛʀ] **I.** *m* **①** *sans pl* (*queue: d'un train*) rear; (*d'un bateau*) stern; (*d'une voiture, avion*) back **②** (*pour une indication spatiale, temporelle*) **être en ~ de qn/qc** to be behind sb/sth; **se pencher/aller en ~** to lean/go backwards; **regarder en ~** (*derrière soi*) to look behind one [*o* back]; (*vers le passé*) to look back; **rester en ~** to stay behind **③** SPORT fullback; **jouer ~ centre** to play center back **II.** *adj inv* **roue/siège ~** back wheel/seat

**arrière-cour** [aʀjɛʀkuʀ] <arrière--cours> *f* backyard

**arrière-grand-mère** [aʀjɛʀgʀɑ̃mɛʀ] <arrière-grands-mères> *f* great-grandmother

**arrière-grand-père** [aʀjɛʀgʀɑ̃pɛʀ] <arrière-grands-pères> *m* great-grandfather

**arrière-grands-parents** [aʀjɛʀgʀɑ̃paʀɑ̃] *mpl* great-grandparents

**arrière-petite-fille** [aʀjɛʀpətitfij] <arrière-petites-filles> *f* great-grand-daughter

**arrière-petit-fils** [aʀjɛʀpətifis] <arrière-petits-fils> *m* great-grandson

**arrière-petits-enfants** [aʀjɛʀpətizɑ̃fɑ̃] *mpl* great-grandchildren

**arrière-plan** [aʀjɛʀplɑ̃] <arrière-plans> *m a. fig* background

**arrivage** [aʀivaʒ] *m* **①** (*arrivée: de marchandises*) delivery **②** (*marchandises*) consignment

**arrivée** [aʀive] *f* **①** (*action, halle d'arrivée*) arrival **②** (*endroit: d'une course*) finish **③** TECH (*robinet*) inlet

**arriver** [aʀive] <1> **I.** *vi* être **①** (*venir*) to arrive; **comment arrive-t-on chez eux?** how do we get to their place? **②** (*approcher*) to come; (*nuit*) to close in **③** (*terminer une compétition*)

~ (**le**) **premier** to come in first; ~ **avant/après qn, ~ devant/derrière qn** to come in in front of/behind sb **④** (*aller jusque*) ~ **aux mollets** (*robe*) to come down to one's calves; ~ **jusqu'à la maison** (*conduite, câble*) to reach the house; **il m'arrive à l'épaule** he comes up to my shoulder **⑤** (*réussir*) ~ **à** +*infin* to manage to +*infin* **⑥** (*réussir socialement*) **être arrivé** to have arrived **⑦** (*survenir*) **qu'est-ce qui est arrivé?** what's happened? **⑧** (*aboutir*) **en ~ à faire qc** to end up doing sth **II.** *vi impers* **être ①** (*survenir*) **qu'est-ce qu'il t'est arrivé?** what happened to you? **②** (*se produire de temps en temps*) **il m'arrive de faire qc** sometimes I do sth

**arrogance** [aʀɔgɑ̃s] *f* arrogance

**arrogant(e)** [aʀɔgɑ̃, ɑ̃t] *adj* arrogant

**arrondir** [aʀɔ̃diʀ] <8> *vt* **①** (*rendre rond*) ~ **qc** to round sth off **②** (*accroître: fortune*) to increase **③** (*simplifier*) ~ **qc à qc** (*en augmentant*) to round sth up to sth; (*en diminuant*) to round sth down to sth

**arrondissement** [aʀɔ̃dismɑ̃] *m* district (*administrative division of major French cities*)

**arroser** [aʀoze] <1> *vt* **①** (*à l'arrosoir, couler à travers*) to water **②** (*au jet, avec un produit*) to spray **③** (*mouiller: pluie*) to drench **④** CULIN (*rôti*) to baste; (*gâteau*) to soak **⑤** *inf* (*fêter*) to celebrate

**arrosoir** [aʀozwaʀ] *m* watering can

**arsenal** [aʀsənal, -o] <-aux> *m* arsenal

**art** [aʀ] *m* **①** ART art; ~ **de vivre** art of living **②** *sans pl* (*style*) **③** *sans pl* (*technique, talent*) skill **④** *Québec* (*lettre*) **faculté des ~s** arts faculty

**artère** [aʀtɛʀ] *f* **①** ANAT artery **②** (*voie de communication en ville*) main road **③** (*voie de communication dans un pays*) main highway

**arthrose** [aʀtʀoz] *f* MED osteoarthritis

**artichaut** [aʀtiʃo] *m* artichoke

**article** [aʀtikl] *m* **①** (*marchandise*) item

❷ (*écrit*) *a.* JUR, LING article ❸ INFORM ~ **de forum** news item

**articulation** [aʀtikylasjɔ̃] *f* ❶ ANAT, TECH joint ❷ (*enchaînement*) linking phrase ❸ (*combinaison*) joining ❹ (*prononciation*) articulation

**articuler** [aʀtikyle] <1> I. *vt* (*prononcer: son*) to articulate; (*mot, phrase*) to pronounce II. *vpr* ANAT, TECH **s'~ sur qc** to articulate on sth; **s'~ à qc** (*os*) to articulate with sth

**artifice** [aʀtifis] *m* ❶ (*moyen ingénieux*) device ❷ *souvent pl* (*tromperie*) trick

**artificiel(le)** [aʀtifisjɛl] *adj* ❶ (*fabriqué*) artificial; (*parfum*) synthetic ❷ (*factice*) forgery

**artillerie** [aʀtijʀi] *f* artillery

**artisan(e)** [aʀtizɑ̃, an] *m(f)* craftsman *m*, craftswoman *f*; ~ **boulanger** traditional baker

**artisanal(e)** [aʀtizanal, -o] <-aux> *adj* traditional; (*produit*) homemade

**artisanat** [aʀtizana] *m* ❶ (*métier*) craft industry ❷ (*les artisans*) craftspeople

**artiste** [aʀtist] *mf* artist

**artistique** [aʀtistik] *adj* artistic

**as¹** [a] *indic prés de* **avoir**

**as²** [ɑs] *m* (*champion*) *a.* JEUX ace

**ascendance** [asɑ̃dɑ̃s] *f sans pl* ❶ (*origine*) ancestry ❷ ASTR ascent

**ascenseur** [asɑ̃sœʀ] *m* elevator

**ascension** [asɑ̃sjɔ̃] *f* ascent; **faire l'~ d'une montagne** to climb a mountain

**asiatique** [azjatik] *adj* Asian

**Asiatique** [azjatik] *mf* Asian

**Asie** [azi] *f* **l'~** Asia; **l'~ centrale** Central Asia; **l'~ Mineure** Asia Minor

**asile** [azil] *m* ❶ REL, JUR, POL asylum ❷ (*refuge*) refuge

**asocial(e)** [asɔsjal, -jo] <-aux> I. *adj* antisocial II. *m(f)* (*social*) misfit

**aspect** [aspɛ] *m* ❶ *sans pl* (*apparence*) appearance ❷ (*trait de caractère*) side ❸ (*point de vue*) aspect

**asperge** [aspɛʀʒ] *f* (*légume*) asparagus + *vb sing*

**asperger** [aspɛʀʒe] <2a> I. *vt* ~ **qn/qc d'eau** to spray sb/sth with water II. *vpr*

**s'~ de parfum** to spray oneself with perfume

**asphyxie** [asfiksi] *f sans pl* (*suffocation*) asphyxiation

**asphyxier** [asfiksje] <1> *vpr* (*ne plus pouvoir respirer*) **s'~** to suffocate

**aspic** [aspik] *m* ❶ CULIN aspic ❷ ZOOL asp

**aspirateur** [aspiʀatœʀ] *m* vacuum cleaner; **passer l'~** to vacuum

**aspiration** [aspiʀasjɔ̃] *f* ❶ *sans pl* (*inspiration*) inhalation ❷ TECH drawing up; (*d'un liquide, de poussières*) sucking up ❸ (*avec la bouche*) sucking up ❹ LING, MED aspiration ❺ *sans pl* (*élan*) ambition ❻ *pl* (*désirs*) aspirations

**aspirer** [aspiʀe] <1> I. *vt* ❶ (*inspirer*) to breathe in ❷ (*inhaler: air, odeur*) to inhale ❸ (*avec la bouche*) to suck in ❹ LING to aspirate ❺ TECH to suck up II. *vi* (*désirer*) ~ **à qc** to aspire to sth ❷ (*chercher à obtenir*) ~ **à qc** to long for sth

**aspirine** [aspiʀin] *f* aspirin

**assagir** [asaʒiʀ] <8> I. *vt* (*passions*) to calm; ~ **qn** to calm sb down II. *vpr* **s'~** (*personne*) to settle down; (*passion*) to calm down

**assainir** [aseniʀ] <8> *vt* ARCHIT, FIN to stabilize

**assaisonnement** [asɛzɔnmɑ̃] *m sans pl* (*action, ingrédient*) seasoning; (*d'une salade*) dressing

**assaisonner** [asɛzɔne] <1> *vt* ❶ (*épicer*) to season; ~ **la salade** to dress a salad ❷ (*agrémenter*) ~ **qc de qc** to embellish sth with sth

**assassin** [asasɛ̃] *m* murderer; POL assassin

**assassin(e)** [asasɛ̃, in] *adj* ❶ (*séducteur: regard*) provocative ❷ (*qui tue: main*) deadly; (*regard*) murderous

**assassinat** [asasina] *m* murder; POL assassination

**assassiner** [asasine] <1> *vt* to murder; POL to assassinate

**assaut** [aso] *m a. fig* assault

**assécher** [aseʃe] <5> *vt* ❶ (*mettre à sec*) to dry ❷ (*vider*) to drain

**ASSEDIC** [asedik] *fpl abr de* **Associa-**

**A**

tion pour l'emploi dans l'industrie et le commerce ❶ *(organisme)* organization managing unemployment insurance ❷ *(indemnités)* benefits

**assemblage** [asɑ̃blaʒ] *m* ❶ AUTO, CINE *(action)* assembly; COUT sewing together; *(d'une charpente, de pièces de bois)* joining; *(de feuilles)* binding ❷ *(résultat: de couleurs, formes)* collection

**assemblée** [asɑ̃ble] *f (réunion)* meeting; POL assembly

**assembler** [asɑ̃ble] <1> I. *vt* ❶ *(monter: pièces)* to assemble ❷ *(réunir: couleurs)* to put together; *(vêtement, pièces d'étoffe)* to sew together ❸ *(recueillir: pièces)* to assemble; *(idées, données)* to gather II. *vpr* **s'~** to gather

**asseoir** [aswar] *irr* I. *vt* ❶ to sit; **faire ~ qn** to make sb sit down; **être/rester assis** to remain seated; **assis!** sit! II. *vpr* **s'~** to sit; **asseyez-vous!** sit down!

**assermenté(e)** [asɛrmɑ̃te] *adj* on oath; **être ~** to be under oath

**assez** [ase] *adv* ❶ *(suffisamment)* enough; **il y a ~ de place** there is enough room; **être ~ riche** to be rich enough ❷ *(plutôt)* rather; **aimer ~ les films de Bergman** to like Bergman's films quite a bit ❸ *(quantité suffisante)* **c'est ~** it's enough [*o* sufficient] ❹ *(de préférence, dans l'ensemble)* **être ~ content de soi** to be quite pleased with oneself ❺ ECOLE **~ bien** satisfactory ❻ *(exprimant la lassitude)* **~!** enough!; **en avoir plus qu'~ de qn/qc** to have more than enough of sb/sth

**assidu(e)** [asidy] *adj (régulier: présence, travail)* regular; *(élève, employé, lecteur)* assiduous

**assiéger** [asjeʒe] <2a, 5> *vt* ❶ MIL *(place, population)* to lay siege to; *(armée)* to besiege ❷ *(prendre d'assaut: guichet)* to besiege; *(personne, hôtel)* to mob

**assiette** [asjɛt] *f* ❶ CULIN plate; **~ plate** plate; **~ creuse** bowl; **~ à dessert** dessert plate; **~ à soupe** soup bowl

❷ *(base de calcul)* base for mortgage calculations

**assimilation** [asimilasjɔ̃] *f* ❶ *(comparaison)* **~ à qc** comparison with sth ❷ *(amalgame)* **~ de qc à qc** equating of sth and sth ❸ BIO assimilation; BOT photosynthesis

**assimiler** [asimile] <1> I. *vt* ❶ *(confondre)* **~ qn/qc à qn/qc** to equate sb/sth with sb/sth ❷ BIO to assimilate; BOT to photosynthesize ❸ *(apprendre: connaissances)* to take in ❹ *(intégrer)* to integrate II. *vi* to assimilate III. *vpr* ❶ *(s'identifier)* **s'~ à qn** to identify with sb ❷ *(s'apprendre)* to be taken in ❸ *(s'intégrer)* **s'~ à qc** to integrate into sth

**assis(e)** [asi, iz] I. *part passé de* **asseoir** II. *adj (position)* sitting

**assises** [asiz] *fpl* JUR assizes

**assistanat** [asistana] *m* UNIV, ECOLE assistantship

**assistance** [asistɑ̃s] *f* ❶ *(public)* audience ❷ *(secours)* assistance; **demander ~ à qn** to ask sb for help; **prêter ~ à qn** to help sb ❸ *(aide organisée)* **~ médicale** medical care; **~ technique** technical support

**assistant** [asistɑ̃] *m* INFORM **~ pages web** web page wizard

**assistant(e)** [asistɑ̃, ɑ̃t] *m(f) (aide)* assistant; MED medical assistant; **~ social** social worker

**assisté(e)** [asiste] I. *adj* ❶ SOCIOL *(enfant)* in care; *(famille)* on welfare ❷ AUTO **direction ~e** power steering II. *m(f)* person on welfare

**assister** [asiste] <1> I. *vi* ❶ *(être présent)* **~ à qc** to be present at sth ❷ *(regarder)* **~ à qc** to watch sth ❸ *(être témoin de)* **~ à qc** to be a witness to sth ❹ *(participer)* **~ à qc** to take part in sth II. *vt* ❶ *(aider)* **~ qn dans qc** to help sb with sth ❷ *(être aux côtés de)* to comfort

**association** [asɔsjasjɔ̃] *f* association

**associé(e)** [asɔsje] I. *m(f)* associate II. *adj (gérant)* associate

**associer** [asɔsje] <1> I. *vt* ❶ *(faire parti-*

*ciper*) **~ qn à sa joie** to share one's joy with sb; **~ qn à un travail** to involve sb in a job ② (*unir, lier: choses, personnes*) to associate; (*couleurs*) to combine **II.** *vpr* ① (*s'allier*) **s'~ avec qn** to join with sb ② (*s'accorder*) **s'~** (*choses*) to go together ③ (*participer à*) **s'~ à la joie de qn** to share in sb else's happiness

**assoiffé(e)** [aswafe] *adj* (*qui a soif*) parched

**assombrir** [asɔ̃bʀiʀ] <8> **I.** *vt* ① (*obscurcir*) to darken ② (*rembrunir, peser sur: personne*) to sadden **II.** *vpr* **s'~** to darken; (*horizon, visage*) to cloud over; (*personne*) to grow sad

**assommer** [asɔme] *vt* ① (*étourdir*) to knock out; (*animal*) to stun ② (*abrutir*) **le soleil m'a assommé** the sun drained me

**Assomption** [asɔ̃psjɔ̃] *f* **l'~** the Assumption

**assorti(e)** [asɔʀti] *adj* (*couleurs, vêtements*) matching; **des personnes/ choses sont bien/mal ~es** people/ things are well/badly matched

**assortiment** [asɔʀtimɑ̃] *m* ① (*mélange*) selection ② (*arrangement*) **~ de couleurs** color arrangement

**assortir** [asɔʀtiʀ] <8> *vt* ① (*harmoniser: couleurs, fleurs*) to match ② (*réunir: personnes*) to mix

**assoupi(e)** [asupi] *adj* ① (*somnolent*) sleepy ② (*affaibli: passion*) calmed; (*douleur*) dulled

**assoupir** [asupiʀ] <8> *vpr* **s'~** to fall asleep

**assouplir** [asupliʀ] <8> **I.** *vt* ① (*rendre plus souple: cheveux, linge*) to soften; **~ le cuir** to make leather supple; **~ les muscles** to exercise the muscles ② (*rendre moins rigoureux: règlement*) to relax **II.** *vpr* **s'~** ① (*devenir plus souple: chaussures*) to soften; (*cuir*) to become supple ② (*devenir moins rigide*) to relax

**assouplissant** [asuplisɑ̃] *m* fabric softener

**assumer** [asyme] <1> **I.** *vt* ① (*exercer,*

*supporter: risque, responsabilité*) to take on; (*tâche, fonction*) to undertake; (*poste*) to take up; (*douleur*) to accept ② (*accepter: condition*) to accept; (*instincts*) to trust **II.** *vpr* (*s'accepter*) **s'~** to accept oneself **III.** *vi inf* to accept one's situation

**assurance** [asyʀɑ̃s] *f* ① *sans pl* (*aplomb*) self-confidence ② (*garantie*) insurance ③ (*contrat*) insurance policy ④ (*société*) insurance company

**assuré(e)** [asyʀe] *adj* ① (*opp: hésitant: démarche*) confident; (*regard*) knowing ② (*garanti*) guaranteed

**assurer** [asyʀe] <1> **I.** *vt* ① (*garantir par un contrat d'assurance*) to insure ② (*se charger de*) **~ qc** (*protection*) to deal with sth ③ (*rendre sûr: avenir, fortune*) to insure ④ (*accorder*) **~ une retraite à qn** to provide a pension for sb **II.** *vpr* ① (*contracter une assurance*) **s'~ à la compagnie X contre qc** to insure against sth with company X ② (*vérifier*) **s'~ de qc** to make sure of sth **III.** *vi inf* to cope

**assureur** [asyʀœʀ] *m* insurer

**astérisque** [asteʀisk] *m* asterisk

**asthmatique** [asmatik] *adj, mf* asthmatic

**asthme** [asm] *m* asthma

**asticot** [astiko] *m inf* (*ver*) maggot

**astiquer** [astike] <1> *vt* to polish; (*meubles, pomme*) to shine

**astre** [astʀ] *m* star

**astrologie** [astʀɔlɔʒi] *f* astrology

**astrologique** [astʀɔlɔʒik] *adj* astrological

**astrologue** [astʀɔlɔg] *mf* astrologer

**astronaute** [astʀonot] *mf* astronaut

**astronome** [astʀɔnɔm] *mf* astronomer

**astronomie** [astʀɔnɔmi] *f* astronomy

**astronomique** [astʀɔnɔmik] *adj* ① ASTR astronomic ② (*faramineux*) astronomical

**astuce** [astys] *f* ① *sans pl* (*qualité*) astuteness ② *souvent pl* (*truc*) trick ③ *gén pl, inf* (*plaisanterie*) joke

**astucieux, -euse** [astysjø, -jøz] *adj* clever

**A**

**asymétrique** [asimetʀik] *adj* asymmetrical

**atchoum** [atʃum] *interj* kerchoo

**atelier** [atəlje] *m* ① (*lieu de travail*) workshop; (*d'un artiste*) studio ② ECON (*d'une usine*) factory floor ③ (*ensemble des ouvriers*) workshop ④ (*groupe de réflexion*) workshop

**athée** [ate] I. *adj* atheistic II. *mf* atheist

**athlète** [atlɛt] *mf* athlete

**athlétique** [atletik] *adj* athletic

**athlétisme** [atletism] *m* track and field

**atlantique** [atlɑ̃tik] *adj* Atlantic; **côte ~** Atlantic coast

**Atlantique** [atlɑ̃tik] *m* l'~ the Atlantic

**atlas** [atlas] *m* GEO, ANAT atlas

**atmosphère** [atmɔsfɛʀ] *f* atmosphere

**atmosphérique** [atmɔsferik] *adj* atmospheric

**atome** [atom] *m* PHYS atom

**atomique** [atɔmik] *adj* atomic

**atout** [atu] *m* ① asset; JEUX trump card ② (*qualité*) asset

**atroce** [atʀɔs] *adj* ① (*horrible: crime, image*) appalling; (*vengeance, peur*) terrible ② *inf* (*affreux: musique, film*) appalling; (*temps, repas*) terrible; (*personne*) awful

**atrocité** [atʀɔsite] *f* ① (*cruauté*) atrocity ② *pl* (*action*) atrocities

**atrophier** [atʀɔfje] <1> *vpr* (*diminuer*) s'~ to waste away

**attachant(e)** [ataʃɑ̃, ɑ̃t] *adj* (*personne, roman, région*) captivating; (*enfant, animal*) endearing

**attache** [ataʃ] *f* ① (*lien*) link ② (*pour attacher les animaux*) leash ③ (*pour attacher des plantes, des arbres*) tie ④ (*pour attacher un cadre*) clip ⑤ *gén pl* (*relations*) tie

**attaché(e)** [ataʃe] I. *adj* ① (*lié par l'affection, l'habitude*) **être ~ à qn/qc** to be attached to sb/sth ② (*ligoté*) **être ~ à qn/qc** to be tied to sb/sth II. *m(f)* attaché

**attaché-case** [ataʃekɛz] <attachés-cases> *m* attaché case

**attachement** [ataʃmɑ̃] *m* (*affection*) a. INFORM attachment

**attacher** [ataʃe] <1> I. *vt* ① (*fixer*) **~ qc à qc** to fasten sth to sth ② (*fixer avec une corde, ficelle*) **~ qn/qc sur qc** to tie sb/sth to sth ③ (*fixer avec des clous*) **~ qc sur qc** to nail sth to sth ④ (*mettre ensemble*) to attach; (*feuilles de papier*) to staple; **~ les mains à qn** to tie sb's hands ⑤ (*fermer: lacets, tablier*) to tie; (*montre, collier*) to fasten; **~ sa ceinture de sécurité** to put on one's seat belt ⑥ (*faire tenir*) **~ ses cheveux avec un élastique** to tie one's hair back with a rubber band; **~ un paquet avec de la ficelle** to wrap a package with string ⑦ (*enchaîner*) **~ qn à qn/qc** to bind sb to sb/sth ⑧ (*attribuer*) **~ de l'importance à qc** to attach importance to sth; **~ de la valeur à qc** to value sth II. *vi inf* (*aliment, gâteau*) to stick III. *vpr* ① (*mettre sa ceinture de sécurité*) **s'~** to belt up ② (*être attaché*) **s'~ à qc** to become attached to sth ③ (*s'encorder*) **s'~ à une corde** to tie oneself on to a rope ④ (*se fermer*) **s'~ avec/par qc** to fasten with sth ⑤ (*se lier d'affection*) **s'~ à qn/qc** to become attached to sb/sth

**attaquant(e)** [atakɑ̃, ɑ̃t] *m(f)* attacker

**attaque** [atak] *f* ① (*acte de violence*) a. MIL, MED, SPORT attack ② (*critique acerbe*) **~ contre qn/qc** attack on sb/sth ③ MUS attack

**attaquer** [atake] <1> I. *vt* ① (*assaillir*) a. SPORT to attack ② (*pour voler: personne*) to mug ③ (*critiquer*) **~ qn sur qc** to attack sb about sth ④ JUR (*jugement, testament*) to contest; **~ qn en justice** to sue sb ⑤ (*ronger: organe, fer*) to attack; (*falaise*) to erode ⑥ (*commencer*) to begin; (*sujet*) to launch into; (*travail*) to start ⑦ *inf* (*commencer à manger*) **~ un plat** to dig into a meal ⑧ (*chercher à surmonter: difficulté*) to tackle II. *vpr* ① (*affronter*) **s'~ à qn/qc** to attack sb/sth ② (*chercher à résoudre*) **s'~ à un problème** to tackle a problem ③ (*commencer*) **s'~ à qc** to launch into sth

**attarder** [ataʀde] <1> *vpr* **s'~** to linger

**atteindre** [atɛ̃dʀ] *vt irr* ❶ (*toucher, parvenir à, joindre par téléphone*) to reach ❷ (*rattraper*) ~ **qn/qc** to catch up with sb/sth ❸ (*blesser moralement*) to wound ❹ (*troubler intellectuellement*) to impair ❺ (*émouvoir*) to affect

**atteinte** [atɛ̃t] *f* (*dommage causé*) **c'est une ~ à ma réputation** it is an attack on my reputation

**atteler** [at(ə)le] <3> I. *vt* (*voiture, animal*) to hitch up II. *vpr* **s'~ à un travail** to get down to work

**attendre** [atɑ̃dʀ] <14> I. *vt* ❶ (*patienter*) ~ **qn/qc** to wait for sb/sth ❷ (*ne rien faire avant de*) ~ **qn/qc pour faire qc** to wait for sb/sth before doing sth ❸ (*compter sur*) to expect; **n'~ que ça** to expect just that; **en attendant mieux** until something better comes along ❹ (*être préparé*) ~ **qn** (*voiture, surprise*) to be waiting for sb; (*sort, déception*) to lay in wait for sb ❺ *inf* (*se montrer impatient avec*) ~ **après qn** *inf* to wait for ever for sb ❻ *inf* (*avoir besoin de*) ~ **après qc** to be waiting on sth ❼ (*jusqu'à*) **mais en attendant** but in the meantime; **en attendant que qn fasse qc** (*subj*) while waiting for sb to do sth ❽ (*toujours est-il*) **en attendant** all the same II. *vi* ❶ (*patienter*) to wait; **faire ~ qn** to make sb wait ❷ (*retarder*) **sans ~ plus longtemps** without waiting any longer ❸ (*interjection*) **attends!** (*pour interrompre, pour réfléchir*) wait!; (*pour menacer*) just you wait! III. *vpr* **s'~ à qc** to expect sth; (*en cas de chose désagréable*) to dread sth; **comme il fallait s'y ~** as you might have expected

**attendrir** [atɑ̃dʀiʀ] <8> I. *vt* ❶ (*émouvoir*) to move ❷ (*apitoyer: cœur*) to melt; ~ **qn** to move sb to pity ❸ CULIN to tenderize II. *vpr* (*s'émouvoir*) **se laisser ~** to be moved; (*changer d'avis*) to relent

**attendrissant(e)** [atɑ̃dʀisɑ̃, ɑ̃t] *adj* moving

**attendu(e)** [atɑ̃dy] I. *part passé de* **attendre** II. *adj* (*espéré*) expected

**attentat** [atɑ̃ta] *m* ~ **contre qn** assassination attempt on sb; ~ **contre qc** attack on sth

**attente** [atɑ̃t] *f* ❶ (*expectative*) **l'~ de qn/qc** the wait for sb/sth; **salle d'~** waiting room ❷ (*espoir*) **contre toute ~** against all expectations; **dans l'~ de qc** in the hope of sth

**attenter** [atɑ̃te] <1> *vi* ~ **à ses jours** to attempt suicide; ~ **à la vie de qn** to make an attempt on sb's life

**attentif, -ive** [atɑ̃tif, -iv] *adj* (*vigilant, prévenant*) attentive

**attention** [atɑ̃sjɔ̃] *f* ❶ (*concentration, intérêt*) attention; **avec ~** attentively; **à l'~ de qn** for sb's attention; **prêter ~ à qn/qc** to pay attention to sb/sth ❷ *souvent pl* (*prévenance*) attention ❸ (*soin*) **faire ~ à qn/qc** to be careful with sb/sth; **fais ~!** be careful! ❹ (*avertissement*) **~!** watch out!; ~ **à la marche!** watch your step!; **alors là, ~** (**les yeux**)! *inf* watch out!

**attentionné(e)** [atɑ̃sjɔne] *adj* ~ **envers qn** considerate toward sb

**attentivement** [atɑ̃tivmɑ̃] *adv* attentively

**atténuer** [atenɥe] <1> I. *vt* (*douleur*) to relieve; (*bruit, amertume*) to lessen; (*passion*) to soothe; (*couleur*) to soften II. *vpr* **s'~** to subside; (*bruit, douleur*) to die down; (*amertume*) to ease; (*secousse sismique*) to die away

**atterré(e)** [ateʀe] *adj* appalled

**atterrir** [ateʀiʀ] <8> *vi* ❶ AVIAT, NAUT (*avion*) to land; (*bateau*) to dock ❷ *inf* (*se retrouver*) to end up

**atterrissage** [ateʀisaʒ] *m* landing

**attestation** [atɛstasjɔ̃] *f* certificate

**attester** [atɛste] <1> *vt* ❶ (*certifier*) ~ **qc/que qn a fait qc** to attest that sb/sth has done sth ❷ (*certifier par écrit*) ~ **qc/que qn a fait qc** to certify that sb/sth has done sth ❸ (*être là preuve*) ~ **qc/que qn a fait qc** to prove that sb/sth has done sth

**attirail** [atiʀaj] *m inf* gear

**attirance** [atiʀɑ̃s] *f* attraction

**attirant(e)** [atiʀɑ̃, ɑ̃t] *adj* (*personne, physionomie*) attractive

**attirer** [atiʀe] <1> **I.** *vt* ❶ (*tirer à soi, retenir*) *a.* PHYS **le regard/l'attention** to make people look/pay attention ❷ (*faire venir: personne*) to attract; (*animal*) to lure ❸ (*allécher*) to entice ❹ (*intéresser: projet, pays*) to draw ❺ (*procurer*) **~ des ennuis à qn** to cause sb problems **II.** *vpr* ❶ (*se plaire*) **s'~** to attract each other; PHYS to attract ❷ (*obtenir, susciter*) **s'~ de nombreux ennemis** to make many enemies

**attitude** [atityd] *f* ❶ (*du corps*) bearing ❷ (*disposition*) attitude ❸ *souvent pl* (*affectation*) façade

**attouchement** [atuʃmɑ̃] *m* ❶ (*toucher*) touch ❷ (*caresse légère*) stroke ❸ *souvent pl* (*caresse sexuelle*) fondling + *vb sing*

**attractif, -ive** [atʀaktif, -iv] *adj* (*séduisant*) attractive

**attraction** [atʀaksjɔ̃] *f* (*séduction, divertissement*) *a.* PHYS, LING attraction

**attrait** [atʀɛ] *m* appeal

**attrape** [atʀap] *f* trick

**attraper** [atʀape] <1> **I.** *vt* ❶ (*capturer, saisir*) **~ qn/un animal par qc** to catch sb/an animal with sth ❷ (*saisir, atteindre, avoir*) to catch; **~ qn à faire qc** to catch sb doing sth; **~ le bus/une maladie** to catch the bus/a disease; **attrape!** catch! ❸ (*tromper*) **~ qn** to catch sb out; **être bien attrapé** to be caught out ❹ (*comprendre: bribes, paroles*) to catch ❺ (*savoir reproduire: comportement, style, accent*) to pick up ❻ (*recevoir: punition, amende*) to get **II.** *vpr* **s'~** (*se transmettre: maladie contagieuse*) to get caught

**attrayant(e)** [atʀɛjɑ̃, jɑ̃t] *adj* (*paysage, personne*) attractive

**attribuer** [atʀibɥe] <1> **I.** *vt* ❶ (*donner*) **~ un prix à qn** to award a prize to sb ❷ (*considérer comme propre à*) **~ un mérite à qn** to give sb credit; **~ de l'importance à qc** to attach importance to sth **II.** *vpr* ❶ (*s'approprier*)

**s'~ qc** to give oneself sth ❷ (*s'adjuger, revendiquer*) **s'~ qc** to claim sth

**attribut** [atʀiby] **I.** *m* ❶ (*propriété, symbole*) attribute ❷ LING **~ du sujet** noun complement **II.** *adj* LING (*adjectif*) predicative

**attribution** [atʀibysjɔ̃] *f* ❶ (*action*) awarding; (*d'une indemnité*) allocation ❷ *pl* (*compétences*) attributions

**attristant(e)** [atʀistɑ̃] *adj* ❶ (*désolant, triste*) saddening ❷ (*déplorable*) deplorable

**attrister** [atʀiste] <1> **I.** *vt* to sadden **II.** *vpr* **s'~ devant qc** to be saddened by sth

**attroupement** [atʀupmɑ̃] *m* gathering

**au** [o] = **à + le** *v.* à

**aubaine** [obɛn] *f* ❶ (*avantage*) godsend ❷ Québec (*solde*) sale

**aube** [ob] *f* (*point du jour*) dawn; **à l'~** at dawn

**aubépine** [obepin] *f* hawthorn

**auberge** [obɛʀʒ] *f* inn; **~ de jeunesse** youth hostel

**aubergine** [obɛʀʒin] **I.** *f* (*légume*) eggplant **II.** *adj inv* (*couleur*) eggplant

**aubergiste** [obɛʀʒist] *mf* innkeeper

**aucun(e)** [okœ̃, yn] **I.** *adj antéposé* ❶ (*nul*) **~ ... ne ...**, **ne ... ~ ...** no; **n'avoir ~e preuve** to have no proof; **en ~e façon** in no way; **sans faire ~ bruit** without making any noise ❷ (*dans une question*) any **II.** *pron* **~ ne ...**, **ne ... ~** not ... any; **n'aimer ~ de ces romans** to not like any of these books

**aucunement** [okynmɑ̃] *adv* in no way

**audace** [odas] *f* ❶ (*témérité*) daring; **avoir de l'~** to be daring ❷ (*effronterie*) audacity

**audacieux, -euse** [odasjø, -jøz] *adj* ❶ (*hardi*) daring ❷ (*effronté*) audacious ❸ (*risqué, osé: projet*) risky; (*mode*) daring

**au-dedans** [odədɑ̃] **I.** *adv* inside **II.** *prep* **~ de qc** inside sth

**au-dehors** [odəɔʀ] **I.** *adv* outside **II.** *prep* **~ de qc** outside sth

**au-delà** [od(ə)la] **I.** *adv* beyond **II.** *prep* beyond sth **III.** *m* beyond

**au-dessous** [od(ə)su] **I.** *adv* underneath **II.** *prep* ❶ (*plus bas*) ~ **de qn/qc** under sb/sth ❷ (*au sud de, inférieur à*) below

**au-dessus** [od(ə)sy] **I.** *adv* ❶ (*plus haut*) above ❷ (*mieux*) **il n'y a rien** ~ there's nothing better **II.** *prep* ~ **de qn/ qc** above sb/sth

**au-devant** [od(ə)vɑ̃] *prep* **aller** ~ **des désirs de qn** to anticipate sb's wishes

**audible** [odibl] *adj* (*qu'on peut entendre*) audible

**audience** [odjɑ̃s] *f* ❶ (*entretien*) audience ❷ JUR hearing ❸ MEDIA (*public*) audience; TV (*audimat*) viewership

**audimat** [odimat] *m* **l'**~ the ratings *pl* (*monitoring device used for television ratings*)

**audiovisuel** [odjovisɥɛl] *m* (*procédés*) audio-visual methods *pl*

**audiovisuel(le)** [odjovisɥɛl] *adj* audio-visual

**auditeur, -trice** [oditœʀ, -tʀis] *m, f* (*de médias*) listener; (*d'une télévision*) viewer

**auditif, -ive** [oditif, -iv] *adj* (*mémoire*) auditive; **appareil** ~ hearing aid

**audition** [odisjɔ̃] *f* ❶ (*sens, écoute*) a. JUR hearing ❷ THEAT, CINE, MUS audition

**auditoire** [oditwaʀ] *m* ❶ (*assistance*) audience ❷ *Belgique, Suisse* (*amphithéâtre, salle de cours d'une université*) lecture hall

**augmentation** [ɔgmɑ̃tasjɔ̃] *f* ~ **du chômage** rise in unemployment; ~ **d'une production** growth in production

**augmenter** [ɔgmɑ̃te] <1> **I.** *vt* ❶ (*accroître*) to increase ❷ (*accroître le salaire*) ~ **qn de 1000 dollars** to give sb a 1000-dollar rise **II.** *vi* ❶ (*s'accroître*) to increase; (*salaire*) to go up; (*douleur*) to get worse ❷ (*devenir plus cher, im pôts, prix*) to rise; (*marchandise, vie*) to become more expensive

**aujourd'hui** [oʒuʀdɥi] *adv* ❶ (*opp: hier, demain*) today; **quel jour sommes-nous** ~? what day is it today?; **à partir d'**~ as of today; **dès** ~ from today; **il y a** ~ **huit mois que qn a fait qc** eight months ago today sb did sth ❷ (*actuellement*) today; **au jour d'**~ *inf* as of now

**aumône** [omon] *f* (*don*) alms *pl*

**auparavant** [opaʀavɑ̃] *adv* before

**auprès de** [opʀɛ də] *prep* ❶ (*tout près, à côté de*) **être** ~ **qn** to be near sb; **viens t'asseoir** ~ **moi** come and sit down next to me ❷ (*en comparaison de*) ~ **qn/qc** compared to sb/sth ❸ (*aux yeux de*) in the opinion of

**auquel** [okɛl] = **à + lequel** *v.* lequel

**aura** [ɔʀa] *f* aura

**aurai** [ɔʀe] *fut de* avoir

**auréole** [ɔʀeɔl] *f* ❶ (*tache*) ring ❷ (*halo: d'un astre*) aureole ❸ (*cercle doré: d'un saint*) halo

**auriculaire** [ɔʀikylɛʀ] *m* little finger

**aurore** [ɔʀɔʀ] *f* (*aube*) daybreak; (*heure du jour*) dawn

**auscultation** [ɔskyltasjɔ̃] *f* auscultation

**ausculter** [ɔskylte] <1> *vt* to auscultate

**aussi** [osi] **I.** *adv* ❶ (*élément de comparaison*) **elle est** ~ **grande que moi** she is as tall as I am ❷ (*également*) too; **c'est** ~ **mon avis** that's my opinion too; **bon appétit! — merci, vous** ~! enjoy your meal! — thank you, and you too! ❸ (*en plus*) also; **non seulement ..., mais** ~ not only ..., but also ❹ *inf* (*non plus*) **moi** ~, **je ne suis pas d'accord** me too, I don't agree ❺ (*bien que*) ~ **riche soit-il** no matter how rich he may be ❻ (*autant (que)*) **Paul** ~ **bien que son frère** Paul as much as his brother ❼ (*d'ailleurs*) **mais** ~ **...?** and ...? **II.** *conj* ~ (**bien**) so

**aussitôt** [osito] **I.** *adv* ❶ (*tout de suite*) right away; ~ **après** straight after ❷ (*sitôt*) immediately; ~ **dit,** ~ **fait** no soon er said than done **II.** *conj* ~ **que qn a fait qc** as soon as sb has done sth

**austère** [ostɛʀ] *adj* austere

**austérité** [osteʀite] *f* austerity

**Australie** [ostʀali] *f* **l'**~ Australia

**A**

**australien** [ostʀaljɛ̃] *m* Australian; *v.a.* **français**

**australien(ne)** [ostʀaljɛ̃, jɛn] *adj* Australian

**Australien(ne)** [ɔstʀaljɛ̃, jɛn] *m(f)* Australian

**autant** [otɑ̃] *adv* ❶ *(tant)* as much; **comment peut-il dormir ~?** how can he sleep that much?; **~ d'argent** as much money ❷ *(relation d'égalité)* **~ que** as much as; **en faire ~** to do as much; **d'~** accordingly; **il n'y a pas ~ de neige que l'année dernière** there is not as much snow as last year ❸ *(cela revient à)* you might as well ❹ *(sans exception)* **tous ~ que vous êtes** each and every one of you ❺ *(pour comparer)* **~ j'aime la mer, ~ je déteste la montagne** I dislike the mountains as much as I like the sea ❻ *(dans la mesure où)* **(pour) ~ que qn fasse qc** *(subj)* as much as sb does sth ❼ *(encore plus/moins (pour la raison que))* **d'~ moins ... que qn a fait qc** even less so ... since sb has done sth; **d'~ (plus) que qn a fait qc** even more so, given that sb has done sth; **d'~ mieux/moins/plus** that much better/less/more

**autel** [otɛl] *m* altar

**auteur** [otœʀ] *m* ❶ *(écrivain, créateur)* author ❷ *(responsable)* author; *(d'un attentat)* perpetrator ❸ *(compositeur)* composer

**authenticité** [otɑ̃tisite] *f* ❶ *(véracité: d'un document)* authenticity ❷ *(sincérité: d'une interprétation)* faithfulness

**authentique** [otɑ̃tik] *adj* ❶ *(véritable)* authentic ❷ *(sincère: personne)* sincere; *(émotion)* genuine

**autiste** [otist] **I.** *adj* autistic **II.** *mf* autistic person

**auto** [oto] *f abr de* **automobile** car

**autobiographie** [otobjɔɡʀafi] *f* autobiography

**autobiographique** [otobjɔɡʀafik] *adj* autobiographical

**autobus** [otobys] *m* bus; **~ scolaire** *Québec* *(car de ramassage scolaire)* school bus

**autocar** [otokaʀ] *m* coach

**autochtone** [otokton] *mf* native

**autocollant** [otokɔlɑ̃] *m* sticker

**autocollant(e)** [otokɔlɑ̃, ɑ̃t] *adj* self-adhesive

**autocuiseur** [otokɥizœʀ] *m* pressure cooker

**autodéfense** [otodefɑ̃s] *f* self-defense; *(prévention)* self-protection

**autodidacte** [otodidakt] **I.** *adj* self-taught **II.** *mf* autodidact

**autoécole, auto-école** [otoekɔl] <auto-écoles> *f* driving school

**autogestion** [otoʒɛstjɔ̃] *f* self-management

**autographe** [otoɡʀaf] *m* autograph

**automate** [otomat] *m* automaton

**automatique** [otomatik] **I.** *adj* automatic **II.** *m* ❶ TEL direct dialing ❷ *(pistolet)* automatic **III.** *f* AUTO automatic

**automatiquement** [otomatikmɑ̃] *adv* automatically

**automatiser** [otomatize] <1> *vt* to automate

**automne** [otɔn] *m* fall, autumn; **cet ~** this fall; **en ~** in the fall; **l'~, ...** in (the) fall, ...

**automobile** [otomɔbil] **I.** *adj* ❶ TECH **voiture ~** motor car ❷ *(relatif à la voiture)* car; **sport ~** car [*o* auto] racing **II.** *f* ❶ *(voiture, industrie)* automobile, car ❷ *(sport)* driving

**automobiliste** [otomɔbilist] *mf* motorist

**autonome** [otonom] *adj* ❶ *(indépendant)* autonomous; **travailleur ~** *Québec* *(freelance)* freelance ❷ *(responsable: vie)* autonomous; *(personne, existence)* self-sufficient ❸ INFORM offline

**autonomie** [otonomi] *f* ❶ autonomy; *(d'une personne)* independence ❷ TECH battery life

**autoportrait** [otopɔʀtʀɛ] *m* self-portrait

**autopsie** [otɔpsi] *f* MED autopsy

**autoradio** [otoʀadjo] *m* car stereo

**autorisation** [otoʀizasjɔ̃] *f* ❶ *(permission)* permission ❷ JUR authorization ❸ *(permis)* permit

**A**

**autorisé(e)** [otoʀize] *adj* authorized; (*tournure*) official

**autoriser** [otoʀize] <1> *vt* ❶ (*permettre, habiliter*) to authorize; **~ qn à +***infin* to authorize sb to +*infin* ❷ (*rendre licite: stationnement*) to permit; (*manifestation, sortie*) to authorize ❸ (*donner lieu à: abus, excès*) to permit

**autoritaire** [otoʀitɛʀ] *adj* authoritarian

**autorité** [otoʀite] *f* authority

**autoroute** [otoʀut] *f* ❶ AUTO highway; **~ à péage** turnpike, toll road ❷ INFORM **~s de l'information** information (super)highway

**autoroutier, -ière** [otoʀutje, -jɛʀ] *adj* highway

**autostop, auto-stop** [otostɔp] *m sans pl* hitchhiking; **faire de l'~** to hitchhike

**autour** [otuʀ] I. *adv* around II. *prep* ❶ (*entourant, environ*) **~ de qn/des 1000 dollars** around sb/1000 dollars; **~ des 15 heures** around 3 p.m. ❷ (*à proximité de*) **~ de qn/qc** around sb/sth

**autre** [otʀ] I. *adj antéposé* ❶ (*différent*) other; **~ chose** something else; **d'une ~ manière** in another way ❷ (*supplémentaire*) other; **il nous faut une ~ chaise** we need another chair ❸ (*second des deux*) **l'~ ...** the other ... ► **nous** ~s ..., **vous** ~s ... US/WE ..., YOU ... II. *pron indéf* ❶ other; **un ~/ une ~** (*que*) someone other (than); **quelqu'un d'~** someone other than; **qui d'~ ?** who else? ❷ (*chose différente, supplé mentaire*) other; **d'~s** others; **quelques ~s** some others; **quelque chose d'~** something else; **rien d'~** nothing else; **quoi d'~ ?** what else? ❸ (*personne supplémentaire*) another ❹ (*opp: l'un*) **l'un l'~/l'une l'~/les uns les ~s** one another ► **entre ~s** among others; **un/ une ~ !** same again!

**autrefois** [otʀəfwɑ] *adv* in the past

**autrement** [otʀəmɑ̃] *adv* ❶ (*différemment*) differently; **tout ~** altogether differently; **je ne pouvais pas faire ~** I couldn't do otherwise [*o* anything else]

❷ (*sinon, sans quoi, à part cela*) otherwise ► **~ dit** in other words

**Autriche** [otʀiʃ] *f* l'~ Austria

**autrichien(ne)** [otʀiʃjɛ̃, jɛn] *adj* Austrian

**Autrichien(ne)** [otʀiʃjɛ̃, jɛn] *m(f)* Austrian

**autruche** [otʀyʃ] *f* ostrich

**autrui** [otʀɥi] *pron inv* someone else; (*les autres*) others; **pour le compte d'~** for a third party

**auvent** [ovɑ̃] *m* canopy

**aux** [o] = **à + les** *v.* **à**

**auxiliaire** [ɔksiljɛʀ] I. *adj* ❶ (*troupe, verbe, moteur, armée*) auxiliary ❷ (*non titulaire*) auxiliary II. *mf* auxiliary III. *m* LING auxiliary

**avachi(e)** [avaʃi] *adj* ❶ (*amorphe: personne*) out of shape; (*attitude, air*) sloppy ❷ (*déformé: chaussures*) misshapen; (*sac, vêtement*) baggy

**avais** [avɛ] *imparf de* **avoir**

**aval** [aval] *m* ❶ (*partie inférieure: d'un cours d'eau*) downstream water; **en ~** downstream ❷ (*soutien*) authorization

**avalanche** [avalɑ̃ʃ] *f* avalanche

**avaler** [avale] <1> *vt* ❶ (*absorber, manger, encaisser*) to swallow ❷ *fig* (*roman, livre*) to devour; (*kilomètre, route*) to eat up

**avance** [avɑ̃s] *f* ❶ (*progression*) advance ❷ (*opp: retard*) **être en ~** (*personne, train*) to be early; **être en ~ dans son programme** to be running ahead of schedule ❸ (*précocité*) **être en ~ pour son âge** to be advanced for one's age; **être en ~ sur qn** to be ahead of sb ❹ (*distance*) **avoir de l'~ sur qn/qc** to be ahead of sth/sb ❺ (*somme sur un achat*) advance payment; (*somme sur le salaire*) advance ❻ *pl* (*approche amoureuse*) **faire des ~s à qn** to make advances on sb ► **à l'~, d'~** in advance

**avancé(e)** [avɑ̃se] *adj* ❶ (*en avant dans l'espace*) ahead ❷ (*en avance dans le temps*) advanced; **être ~ dans son travail** to be ahead in one's work

**avancement** [avɑ̃smɑ̃] *m* ❶ (*progrès:*

**A**

*des travaux, des technologies*) progress ❷ (*promotion*) promotion

**avancer** [avɑ̃se] <2> I. *vt* ❶ (*opp: retarder*) ~ *qc* (*rendez-vous, départ*) to bring sth forward ❷ (*pousser en avant*) ~ *qc* (*chaise, table*) to move sth forward; (*voiture*) to drive sth forward; ~ **de huit cases** JEUX move forward eight squares ❸ (*affirmer*) to suggest; (*idée, thèse*) to put forward ❹ (*faire progresser: travail*) to speed up ❺ (*payer par avance: argent*) to pay in advance ❻ (*prêter: argent*) to lend II. *vi* ❶ (*approcher: armée*) to advance; (*personne, conducteur, voiture*) to move forward; **avance vers moi!** come toward me! ❷ (*être en avance*) ~ **de 5 minutes** (*montre*) to be 5 minutes fast ❸ (*former une avancée: rocher, balcon*) to overhang ❹ (*progresser: personne, travail*) to progress; (*nuit, jour*) to get longer III. *vpr* ❶ **s'~** (*pour sortir d'un rang, en s'approchant*) to move forward; (*pour continuer sa route*) to advance; **s'~ vers qn/qc** to move toward sb/sth ❷ (*prendre de l'avance*) **s'~ dans son travail** to progress in one's work ❸ (*se risquer, anticiper*) **là, tu t'avances trop!** you're going too far there!

**avant** [avɑ̃] I. *prep* ❶ (*temporel*) before; **bien/peu** ▸ ~ **qc** well/shortly before sth; ~ **de faire qc** before doing sth ❷ (*devant*) in front of; **en** ~ **de qn/qc** in front of sb/sth ▸ ~ **tout** above all II. *adv* ❶ (*devant*) in front; **passer** ~ to go in front; **en** ~ in front ❷ *après compl* (*plus tôt*) before; **plus/trop** ~ earlier/too early; **le jour/l'année d'**~ the day/year before ▸ **en** ~ (**marche**)! forward (march)! III. *conj* ~ **que qn ne fasse qc** (*subj*) before sb does sth IV. *m* ❶ (*partie antérieure*) front; **à/vers l'**~ at/to the front; **à l'**~ **du bateau** in the bow of the boat ❷ SPORT (*joueur*) forward V. *adj inv* (*opp: arrière*) front; **le clignotant** ~ **droit** the front right turn signal

**avantage** [avɑ̃taʒ] *m* ❶ (*intérêt*) advantage; **à son** ~ to his advantage; **être à son** ~ to be at one's best; **tirer** ~ **de** to benefit from sth; **qc présente l'**~ **de faire qc** sth has the advantage of doing sth ❷ *souvent pl* (*gain*) benefit ❸ (*supériorité*) *a.* SPORT advantage

**avantager** [avɑ̃taʒe] <2a> *vt* ❶ (*favoriser*) ~ **qn par rapport à qn** to favor sb over sb ❷ (*mettre en valeur*) to flatter

**avantageux, -euse** [avɑ̃taʒø, -ʒøz] *adj* ❶ (*intéressant: investissement*) profitable; (*rendement*) attractive ❷ (*favorable: portrait*) flattering; (*termes*) favorable

**avant-bras** [avɑ̃brɑ] <avant-bras> *m* forearm

**avant-centre** [avɑ̃sɑ̃tʀ] <avants-centres> *m* center-forward

**avant-dernier, -ière** [avɑ̃dɛʀnje, -jɛʀ] <avant-derniers> *adj, m, f* penultimate

**avant-hier** [avɑ̃tjɛʀ] *adv* the day before yesterday

**avant-midi** [avɑ̃midi] *m o f inv, Québec* (*matinée*) morning

**avant-première** [avɑ̃pʀəmjɛʀ] <avant-premières> *f* preview

**avant-propos** [avɑ̃pʀɔpo] <avant-propos> *m* foreword

**avare** [avaʀ] I. *adj* miserly; **être ~ de qc** to be sparing with sth II. *mf* miser

**avarie** [avaʀi] *f* damage

**avarié(e)** [avaʀje] *adj* ❶ (*en panne: bateau*) damaged ❷ (*pourri: nourriture*) rotten

**avec** [avɛk] I. *prep* ❶ (*ainsi que, contre, au moyen de, grâce à, envers*) with; **être gentil/poli** ~ **qn** to be kind/polite towards sb ❷ (*à cause de*) because of ❸ (*en ce qui concerne*) ~ **moi, vous pouvez avoir confiance** with me, you've got nothing to worry about ❹ (*d'après*) ~ **ma sœur, il faudrait ...** according to my sister, we should ... ▸ **et** ~ **ça ...** *inf* on top of that; ~ **tout ça** *inf* with all that; **et** ~ **cela** (**Madame/Monsieur**)? anything else, (Sir/

Ma'am)? **II.** *adv inf* **tu viens ~?** *Belgique* are you coming along?

**avenir** [av(ə)niʀ] *m* future; **à l'~** in the future; **d'~** of the future

**aventure** [avɑ̃tyʀ] *f* ❶ (*histoire*) adventure; **il m'est arrivé une ~** something happened to me ❷ (*liaison*) affair

**aventurer** [avɑ̃tyʀe] <1> **I.** *vt* (*argent, réputation*) to risk **II.** *vpr* **s'~ sur la route** to venture onto the road; **s'~ dans une affaire risquée** to get involved in a risky business

**aventureux, -euse** [avɑ̃tyʀø, -øz] *adj* ❶ (*audacieux*) adventurous ❷ (*risqué: entreprise, projet*) risky

**aventurier, -ière** [avɑ̃tyʀje, -jɛʀ] *m, f* adventurer

**avenue** [av(ə)ny] *f* avenue

**avérer** [aveʀe] <5> *vpr* **s'~ exact** to turn out to be true

**averse** [avɛʀs] *f a. fig* shower; **~ de grêle** hailstorm

**avertir** [avɛʀtiʀ] <8> *vt* ❶ (*informer*) to inform ❷ (*mettre en garde*) to warn

**avertissement** [avɛʀtismɑ̃] *m* ❶ (*mise en garde, signal*) warning ❷ SPORT (*sanction*) caution

**avertisseur** [avɛʀtisœʀ] *m* alarm

**aveu** [avø] <x> *m* confession

**aveuglant(e)** [avœglɑ̃, ɑ̃t] *adj* ❶ (*éblouissant: lumière, soleil*) dazzling; **être ~** (*lumière*) to be blinding ❷ (*évident*) blindingly obvious

**aveugle** [avœgl] **I.** *adj* blind **II.** *mf* blind person ▸ **en ~** blind

**aveuglement** [avœgləmɑ̃] *m* blindness

**aveuglément** [avœglemɑ̃] *adv* blindly

**aveugler** [avœgle] <1> *vt* (*éblouir*) to dazzle

**avez** [ave] *indic prés de* **avoir**

**aviateur, -trice** [avjatœʀ, -tʀis] *m, f* aviator

**aviation** [avjasjɔ̃] *f* ❶ aviation; (*sport*) flying; **compagnie d'~** aviation company ❷ MIL air force

**avide** [avid] *adj* (*personne, yeux, curiosité*) avid; (*lèvres*) greedy; **~ de vengeance** hungry for revenge

**avion** [avjɔ̃] *m* plane, airplane; **~ à héli-**ce/**à réaction** propeller/jet plane; **~ de ligne** airliner; **aller/voyager en ~** to go/travel by plane; **il est malade en ~** he gets airsick; **par ~** (*sur les lettres*) airmail

**aviron** [aviʀɔ̃] *m* ❶ (*rame*) oar ❷ (*sport*) rowing, crew; **faire de l'~** to row

**avis** [avi] *m* ❶ (*opinion*) opinion; **donner son ~ sur qc** to give one's opinion on sth; **être d'~ de faire qc** to think that sth should be done; **je suis d'~ qu'il vienne** I think he should come; **être de l'~ de qn** to share sb's opinion ❷ (*notification*) notice; **~ au lecteur** foreword; **~ de décès** announcement of death; **~ de recherche** (*écrit*) wanted notice; (*radiodiffusé/télédiffusé*) missing persons notice

**avocat** [avɔka] *m* avocado

**avocat(e)** [avɔka, at] *m(f)* (*profession*) lawyer; **~ général/de la défense** counsel for the prosecution/for the defense; **~ de la partie civile** counsel for the plaintiff

**avoine** [avwan] *f* oats *pl*

**avoir** [avwaʀ] *irr* **I.** *vt* ❶ (*devoir, recevoir, assister à*) have. MFD to have; **ne pas ~ à** +*infin* to not have to +*infin*; **tu n'as pas à t'occuper de ça** you don't have to take care of that ❷ (*obtenir, attraper: train*) to catch; (*examen*) to pass; (*logement, aide, renseignement*) to get; **pouvez-vous m'~ ce livre?** could you get me this book?; **j'ai eu des vertiges** I felt dizzy ❸ (*porter sur ou avec soi: canne, pipe*) to have; (*chapeau, vêtement*) to wear ❹ (*être doté de*) **quel âge as-tu?** how old are you?; **~ 15 ans** to be 15 years old; **~ 2 mètres de haut/large** to be 2 meters tall/wide ❺ (*éprouver*) **~ faim/soif/peur** to be hungry/thirsty/afraid ❻ *inf* (*rouler*) **vous m'avez bien eu!** you had me there! ▸ **en ~ après qn** *inf* to have it in for sb; **en ~ jusque-là de qc** *inf* to have had it up to there with sth; **j'en ai pour deux minutes** I'll be two minutes; **vous en avez pour 100 dollars**

it'll cost around \$100; **j'ai!** JEUX, SPORT mine!; **on les aura!** we'll get them!; **qu'est-ce qu'il/elle a?** what's the matter with him/her? II. *aux* **il n'a rien dit** he didn't say anything; **il n'a toujours rien dit** he still hasn't said anything; **elle a couru/marché deux heures** (*hier*) she ran/walked for two hours; (*vient de*) she has run/walked for two hours; **l'Italie a été battue par le Brésil** Italy was beaten by Brazil III. *vt impers* ❶ (*exister*) **il y a du beurre sur la table** there's butter on the table; **il y a des verres dans le placard** there are glasses in the cupboard; **il n'y a pas que l'argent dans la vie** there's more to life than money; **qu'y a-t-il? – il y a que j'ai faim!** what's the matter? – I'm hungry, that's what!; **il n'y a pas à discuter** there's no two ways about it; **il n'y a qu'à partir plus tôt** we'll just have to leave earlier; **il n'y a que toi pour faire cela!** only you would do that! ❷ (*temporel*) **il y a 3 jours** 3 days ago ▶ **il n'y a plus rien à faire** there's nothing else that can be done; **il n'y a**

**pas de quoi!** don't mention it! IV. *m* ❶ (*crédit*) credit ❷ (*bon d'achat*) credit note

**avons** [avɔ̃] *indic prés de* **avoir**

**avortement** [avɔʀtəmɑ̃] *m* abortion; (*spontané*) miscarriage

**avorter** [avɔʀte] <1> *vi* (*de façon volontaire*) to abort; (*de façon spontanée*) to miscarry; **se faire ~** to have an abortion

**avouer** [avwe] <1> I. *vt* to admit; **~ faire qc** to admit to doing sth; **je dois vous ~ que** I have to confess to you that II. *vi* ❶ (*confesser*) to confess ❷ (*admettre*) to admit

**avril** [avʀil] *m* April ▶ **poisson d'~** April Fool; *v.a.* **août**

**axe** [aks] *m* ❶ *a.* MATH axis; **dans l'~ de qc** in line with sth ❷ (*tige, pièce: d'une roue, pédale*) axle ❸ (*ligne directrice: d'un discours, d'une politique*) theme ❹ (*voie de circulation*) main road

**axer** [akse] <1> *vt* **~ qc sur qc** to center sth around sth else

**ayant** [ɛjɑ̃] *part prés de* **avoir**

**azote** [azɔt] *m* nitrogen

**azur** [azyʀ] *m* **ciel d'~** azure sky

# Bb

**B**

**B, b** [be] *m inv* B, b; **~ comme Berthe** (*au téléphone*) b as in Bravo
**babines** [babin] *fpl* (*d'un animal*) chops
**bâbord** [babɔʀ] *m* port
**babouin** [babwɛ̃] *m* ZOOL baboon
**baby-foot®** [babifut] *m inv* foosball
**baby-sitting** [bebisitiŋ, babisitiŋ] *m sans pl* babysitting; **faire du ~** to babysit
**bac¹** [bak] *m* ❶ (*récipient*) tank; (*cuvette*) basin; (*d'un évier*) sink; (*d'un réfrigérateur*) tray ❷ (*bateau*) ferry
**bac²** [bak] *m inf abr de* **baccalauréat** baccalaureate
**baccalauréat** [bakalɔʀea] *m* ❶ (*examen à la fin de la terminale*) baccalaureate (*secondary school examinations*) ❷ *Québec* (*études universitaires du premier cycle, ≈ DEUG en France*) ≈ associate's degree
**bâche** [baʃ] *f* tarpaulin, tarp
**bachelier, -ière** [baʃɔlje, -jɛʀ] *m, f*: person with the baccalaureate
**bachelor** [baʃ(ə)lɔʀ] *m* bachelor's [degree]; **passer un ~ en communication** get a bachelor's [degree] in communications
**bâcler** [bakle] <1> *vt inf* (*devoir, travail*) to botch
**bactérie** [bakteʀi] *f* bacterium
**badaud(e)** [bado, -od] *m(f)* onlooker
**badge** [badʒ] *m* badge
**baffle** [bafl] *m* speaker
**bafouer** [bafwe] <1> *vt* (*sentiment*) to ridicule; (*règlement*) to defy
**bafouiller** [bafuje] <1> *vt, vi inf* to stammer
**bagage** [bagaʒ] *m* ❶ *pl* baggage + *vb sing*, luggage + *vb sing* ❷ (*connaissances*) baggage + *vb sing*; (*pour assumer une tâche*) qualifications
**bagarre** [bagaʀ] *f* ❶ (*pugilat*) fighting ❷ (*lutte*) fight ❸ (*compétition*) battle

**bagatelle** [bagatɛl] *f* ❶ (*somme*) trifling sum ❷ (*vétille*) trifle
**bagne** [baɲ] *m* (*prison*) penal colony; **quel ~!** it's slavery!
**bagnole** [baɲɔl] *f inf* car
**bague** [bag] *f a.* TECH ring
**baguette** [bagɛt] *f* ❶ (*pain*) baguette ❷ (*bâton*) stick; (*d'un tambour*) drumstick; (*d'un chef d'orchestre*) baton ❸ (*couvert chinois*) chopstick ❹ TECH beading
**bahut** [bay] *m* ❶ (*buffet*) sideboard ❷ (*coffre*) chest ❸ *inf* (*lycée*) school ❹ *inf* (*camion*) truck
**baie** [bɛ] *f* ❶ GEO bay ❷ (*fenêtre*) **~ vitrée** bay window ❸ BOT berry
**baignade** [beɲad] *f* ❶ (*action*) swim; (*activité*) swimming ❷ (*lieu*) swimming place
**baigner** [beɲe] <1> I. *vt* to bathe II. *vi* **~ dans qc** to be swimming in sth III. *vpr* **se ~** to take a bath; (*dans une piscine*) to go swimming
**baignoire** [beɲwaʀ] *f* (*pour prendre un bain*) (bath)tub
**bail** [baj, bo] <-aux> *m* (*contrat: d'un local commercial*) lease
**bâillement** [bajmɑ̃] *m* yawn
**bâiller** [baje] <1> *vi* ❶ (*action: personne*) to yawn ❷ (*être entrouvert: porte*) to be ajar; (*col*) to gape
**bâillonner** [bajɔne] <1> *vt* ❶ (*action*) to gag ❷ *fig* (*opposition, presse*) to stifle
**bain** [bɛ̃] *m* ❶ (*action*) bath ❷ (*eau*) bath(water) ❸ **prendre un ~ de soleil** to sunbathe
**bain-marie** [bɛ̃maʀi] <bains-marie> *m* double boiler, bain-marie
**baiser¹** [beze] *m* ❶ (*bise*) kiss ❷ (*en formule*) **bons ~s** (*with*) love
**baiser²** [beze] <1> I. [beze] *vt* ❶ *soutenu* to kiss ❷ *inf* (*coucher avec*) to screw ❸ *inf* (*tromper*) to have II. *vi inf* to screw

**B**

**baisse** [bɛs] f ❶ (*le fait de baisser*) lowering; (*de pouvoir, d'influence*) decline; (*de popularité*) decrease; (*de pression*) drop ❷ FIN fall ▶ **~ de tension** ELEC drop in voltage; MED drop in pressure

**baisser** [bese] <1> I. vt ❶ (*faire descendre: store, rideau*) to lower; (*vitre de voiture*) to wind down; (*col*) to turn down ❷ (*fixer plus bas, réviser à la baisse*) to lower ❸ (*orienter vers le bas: tête*) to bow; (*yeux*) to lower ❹ (*rendre moins fort: son*) to turn down; (*voix*) to lower II. vi ❶ (*diminuer de niveau, d'intensité: forces, vue*) to fail; (*vent, niveau, rivière*) to go down; (*baromètre*) to fall; (*température*) to drop ❷ ECON, FIN to drop; (*prix*) to fall ❸ (*s'affaiblir: personne*) to weaken III. vpr **se ~** to stoop; (*pour esquiver*) to duck

**bal** [bal] m (*réunion populaire*) dance; (*réunion d'apparat*) ball

**balade** [balad] f inf ❶ (*promenade à pied*) walk; (*promenade en voiture*) drive ❷ (*excursion*) jaunt

**balader** [balade] <1> I. vt inf **~ qn** to take sb for a walk II. vpr **se ~** inf (*se promener à pied*) to go for a walk; (*se promener en voiture*) to go for a drive

**baladeur** [baladœr] m Walkman®

**balai** [balɛ] m ❶ (*ustensile*) broom ❷ ELEC (*d'une dynamo*) brush ❸ AUTO **~ d'essuie-glace** windshield wiper blade

**balance** [balãs] f ❶ (*instrument*) scales pl ❷ POL, ECON balance

**Balance** [balãs] f Libra; **être (du signe de la) ~** to be a Libra

**balancer** [balãse] <2> I. vt ❶ (*ballotter: personne*) to swing; **~ les bras/ses jambes** to swing one's arms/legs ❷ (*tenir en agitant: sac, encensoir, lustre*) to swing; (*branche, bateau*) to rock ❸ inf (*envoyer: objet*) to throw ❹ inf (*se débarrasser: objet*) to throw ❺ (*employé*) to fire II. vpr **se ~** ❶ (*bouger: bateau*) to rock; (*branches*) to sway ❷ (*sur une balançoire*) to swing

**balançoire** [balãswar] f swing

**balayage** [balɛjaʒ] m ❶ (*action*) sweeping ❷ INFORM scanning

**balayer** [baleje] <7> vt ❶ (*ramasser*) to sweep up ❷ (*nettoyer*) to sweep ❸ (*passer sur*) **~ qc** (*faisceau lumineux*) to sweep over sth; (*vent*) to sweep across sth ❹ INFORM to scan ❺ (*chasser: doute*) to sweep away; (*obstacle, objection, argument*) to brush aside

**balayette** [balɛjɛt] f brush (*for a dustpan*), whiskbroom

**balayeur, -euse** [balɛjœr, -jøz] m, f street sweeper

**balbutier** [balbysje] <1> vi (*bredouiller*) to stammer; (*bébé*) to babble

**balcon** [balkɔ̃] m ❶ (*balustrade*) balcony ❷ THEAT circle

**baleine** [balɛn] f ZOOL whale

**balisage** [balizaʒ] m ❶ (*action*) marking out; (*d'une piste d'atterrissage*) beaconing ❷ (*signaux: d'une cheminé, piste de ski*) markers pl; (*d'une route*) signs pl ❸ INFORM tagging

**balise** [baliz] f ❶ AVIAT, NAUT beacon ❷ (*de sentier*) marker ❸ INFORM tag

**baliser** [balize] <1> vt ❶ (*signaliser*) **~ qc** a. AVIAT, NAUT to mark sth out; (*sentier*) to mark the way ❷ INFORM (*texte*) to highlight

**baliverne** [balivɛrn] f nonsense

**ballade** [balad] f ballad

**ballant(e)** [balɑ̃, ɑ̃t] adj (*jambes*) dangling; (*bras*) loose

**balle** [bal] f ❶ JEUX, SPORT ball ❷ (*projectile*) bullet ❸ pl, inf HIST (*francs*) **100 ~s** 100 francs

**ballerine** [balrin] f ❶ (*danseuse*) ballerina ❷ (*chaussure*) ballet shoe

**ballet** [balɛ] m ballet

**ballon** [balɔ̃] m ❶ JEUX, SPORT ball ❷ (*baudruche, aérostat*) balloon ❸ GEO round-topped mountain ❹ (*appareil*) **~ d'eau chaude** (hot) water heater ❺ (*test*) **~ d'essai** feeler

**balluchon** [balyʃɔ̃] m bundle

**balnéaire** [balneɛr] adj **station ~** seaside resort

**balourd** [balur] m (*maladroit*) clumsy person

**balourd(e)** [balur, urd] adj clumsy

**Baltique** [baltik] *f* **la** (**mer**) ~ the Baltic (Sea)

**baluchon** [balyʃɔ̃] *m v.* **balluchon**

**balustrade** [balystrad] *f* balustrade

**bambin(e)** [bɑ̃bɛ̃] *m(f)* infant

**bambou** [bɑ̃bu] *m* bamboo

**ban** [bɑ̃] *m pl* (*publication: de mariage*) banns

**banal(e)** [banal] <s> *adj* banal; (*idée, affaire*) conventional; (*propos*) commonplace; (*personne, choses*) ordinary

**banaliser** [banalize] <1> *vt* ~ **qc** to make sth commonplace

**banalité** [banalite] *f* ❶(*platitude*) triteness; (*de la vie*) ordinariness; (*d'un propos*) banality ❷(*propos*) platitude

**banane** [banan] *f* ❶(*fruit*) banana ❷(*pochette*) fanny pack

**banc** [bɑ̃] *m* ❶(*meuble*) bench ❷GEO layer ❸(*colonie: de poissons*) school ❹(*amas*) ~ **de sable** sandbank ❺ *Québec* ~ **de neige** (*congère*) snowdrift ❻JUR ~ **des accusés** dock

**bancaire** [bɑ̃kɛʀ] *adj* bank

**bancal(e)** [bɑ̃kal] <s> *adj* ❶(*instable: meuble*) rickety; (*personne*) lame ❷*fig* (*raisonnement*) lame

**bande¹** [bɑ̃d] *f* ❶(*long morceau étroit: de métal*) strip; (*d'un magnétophone*) tape; CINE film ❷MED bandage ► ~ **dessinée** cartoon

**bande²** [bɑ̃d] *f* ❶(*groupe: de personnes*) bunch; (*de loups, chiens*) pack; (*d'oiseaux*) flock ❷(*groupe constitué*) gang; ~ **de copains** band of friends

**bande-annonce** [bɑ̃dɑnɔ̃s] <bandes--annonces> *f* trailer

**bandeau** [bɑ̃do] <x> *m* ❶(*dans les cheveux*) coiled hairstyle ❷(*serre-tête*) headband ❸(*sur les yeux*) blindfold

**bander** [bɑ̃de] <1> I. *vt* ❶(*panser*) to bandage ❷(*tendre*) to tense II. *vi inf* to have a hard-on

**banderole** [bɑ̃dʀɔl] *f* ❶(*petite bannière*) streamer ❷(*bande avec inscription*) banner

**bande-son** [bɑ̃dsɔ̃] <bandes-son> *f* soundtrack

**bande-vidéo** [bɑ̃dvideo] <bandes-vi-déo> *f* videotape

**bandit** [bɑ̃di] *m* ❶(*malfaiteur*) bandit ❷(*personne malhonnête*) crook

**bandoulière** [bɑ̃duljɛʀ] *f* shoulder strap

**bang** [bɑ̃g] I. *interj* bang II. *m inv* bang

**banlieue** [bɑ̃ljø] *f* (*d'une ville*) suburb; **la** ~ the suburbs

**banlieusard(e)** [bɑ̃ljøzaʀ, aʀd] *m(f)* suburbanite

**banni(e)** [bani] I. *adj* (*personne*) exiled II. *m(f)* ❶(*exilé*) exile ❷(*exclu*) outcast

**bannière** [banjɛʀ] *f* streamer, REL banner

**bannir** [baniʀ] <8> *vt* ❶(*mettre au ban*) ~ **qn d'un pays** to banish sb from a country ❷(*supprimer*) to ban

**banque** [bɑ̃k] *f* FIN, INFORM bank; ~ **de données** databank, database

**banqueroute** [bɑ̃kʀut] *f* bankruptcy

**banquet** [bɑ̃kɛ] *m* banquet

**banquette** [bɑ̃kɛt] *f* ❶(*siège*) seat; ~ **avant/arrière** AUTO front/back seat ❷ARCHIT window seat ❸(*chemin*) path; (*d'une voie*) bank

**banquier, -ière** [bɑ̃kje, -jɛʀ] *m, f* FIN, JEUX banker

**baptême** [batɛm] *m* baptism

**baptiser** [batize] <1> *vt* (*appeler*) ~ **qn Pierre** to christen [*o* baptize] sb Pierre

**baquet** [bakɛ] *m* tub

**bar¹** [baʀ] *m* bar

**bar²** [baʀ] *m* ZOOL bass

**bar³** [baʀ] *m* PHYS bar

**baraque** [baʀak] *f* ❶(*cabane*) hut; (*pour les outils de jardinage*) (tool) shed ❷*inf* (*maison*) pad; (*maison délabrée*) shack

**baraquement** [baʀakmɑ̃] *m* camp

**baratiner** [baʀatine] <1> I. *vt inf* ❶(*bonimenter*) ~ **qn** to give sb a (sales) spiel ❷(*essayer de persuader*) to sweet-talk ❸(*draguer*) qn to hit on sb II. *vi inf* to chatter

**barbare** [baʀbaʀ] I. *adj* ❶(*cruel*) barbaric ❷(*grossier*) barbarous II. *m* barbarian

**B** **barbarie** [baʀbaʀi] *f* ❶ (*opp: civilisation*) barbarism ❷ (*cruauté*) barbarity

**barbe** [baʀb] *f* ❶ (*poils*) a. ZOOL beard; (*d'un chat*) whiskers *pl* ❷ CULIN - **à papa** cotton candy

**barbecue** [baʀbəkju] *m* barbecue; **faire un ~** to have a cookout

**barbelé(e)** [baʀbəle] I. *adj* **fil de fer ~** barbed wire II. *m* barbed wire

**barbiturique** [baʀbityʀik] *m* BIO barbiturate

**barboter** [baʀbɔte] <1> I. *vi* **~ dans qc** to be mixed up in sth II. *vt inf* to pinch

**barbouiller** [baʀbuje] <1> *vt* ❶ (*enduire*) **~ qn/qc de qc** to smear sb/sth with sth ❷ (*peindre*) **~ qc** to daub paint on sth; (*mur*) to daub sth

**barbu** [baʀby] *m* bearded man

**barbu(e)** [baʀby] *adj* bearded

**barder** [baʀde] <1> I. *vt* (*garnir*) **~ qn de décorations** to cover sb with medals II. *vi inf* **ça barde** the sparks are flying

**barème** [baʀɛm] *m* scale; (*tableau*) table; ECOLE grading scale

**baril** [baʀil] *m* barrel

**bariolé(e)** [baʀjɔle] *adj* multicolored

**barman** [baʀman, -mɛn] <s *o* -men> *m* barman, bartender

**baromètre** [baʀɔmɛtʀ] *m* barometer

**baron(ne)** [baʀɔ̃, ɔn] *m(f)* baron, baroness *m, f*

**baroque** [baʀɔk] I. *adj* ❶ ARCHIT, MUS baroque ❷ (*bizarre*) weird II. *m* Baroque

**barque** [baʀk] *f* boat

**barquette** [baʀkɛt] *f* ❶ (*tartelette*) tartlet ❷ (*récipient: de fraises*) basket

**barrage** [baʀaʒ] *m* ❶ (*barrière*) barrier ❷ ELEC dam

**barre** [baʀ] *f* ❶ (*pièce*) bar; **~ de chocolat** chocolate bar ❷ JUR (*au tribunal*) **~ des témoins** witness stand ❸ (*trait*) slash ❹ SPORT (*pour la danse*) barre; (*en athlétisme*) bar ❺ NAUT helm ❻ INFORM **~ de défilement** scroll bar; **~ de menu** menu toolbar; **~ de titre** title bar

**barré(e)** [baʀe] *adj* (*rue*) blocked; (*porte*) barred

**barreau** [baʀo] <x> *m* ❶ JUR bar

❷ (*tube, barre: d'une échelle*) rung; (*d'une grille*) bar

**barrer** [baʀe] <1> I. *vt* ❶ (*bloquer: route*) to block; (*porte*) to bar; **~ le chemin** (*personne*) to stand in the way; (*voiture*) to block the road ❷ (*biffer*) **~ qc** to cross sth out ❸ NAUT to steer ❹ *Québec* (*fermer à clé*) to lock II. *vi* to steer III. *vpr inf* **se ~** to take off

**barrette** [baʀɛt] *f* ❶ (*pince*) barrette ❷ (*bijou*) brooch

**barricade** [baʀikad] *f* barricade

**barricader** [baʀikade] <1> I. *vt* (*porte, rue*) to barricade II. *vpr* ❶ (*derrière une barricade*) **se ~** to barricade oneself ❷ (*s'enfermer*) **se ~ dans sa chambre** to lock oneself in one's room

**barrière** [baʀjɛʀ] *f* ❶ (*fermeture*) gate; CHEMDFER (*grade crossing*) gate ❷ (*clôture*) fence ❸ (*séparation*) a. SPORT barrier

**barrique** [baʀik] *f* barrel

**barrir** [baʀiʀ] <8> *vi* (*éléphant*) to trumpet

**bar-tabac** [baʀtaba] <bars-tabac> *m*: *café selling tobacco*

**bas¹** [ba] *m* (*partie inférieure*) bottom; (*d'une maison*) downstairs

**bas²** [ba] *m* stocking

**bas(se)** [ba, bas] I. *adj* ❶ (*de peu de/à faible hauteur*) low; (*stature*) short ❷ (*peu intense*) mild ❸ (*dans la hiérarchie sociale*) lowly II. *adv* ❶ (*à faible hauteur*) low ❷ (*au-dessous*) **loger en ~** to live downstairs ❸ (*ci-dessous*) **voir plus ~** see below ❹ (*au pied de*) **en ~ de la colline** at the bottom of the hill ❺ (*opp: aigu*) low ❻ (*doucement*) softly; **parler (tout) ~** to speak in a low voice

**bas-côté** [bakote] <bas-côtés> *m* ❶ (*bord: d'une route, autoroute*) shoulder ❷ ARCHIT (*d'une église*) side aisle

**bascule** [baskyl] *f* ❶ (*balançoire*) seesaw ❷ (*balance*) scale

**basculer** [baskyle] <1> I. *vi* (*tomber*) to fall over II. *vt* (*faire pivoter*) **~ qc** to tip sth over

**base** [baz] *f* ❶ (*pied*) a. LING base ❷ (*principe, composant principal*) basis ❸ (*connaissances élémentaires*) la ~, les ~s the basics ❹ MIL, MATH, CHIM, INFORM base; ~ **de données** database

**baser** [baze] <1> I. *vt* (*fonder*) ~ **qc sur qc** to base sth on sth II. *vpr* **se ~ sur qc** to base oneself on sth

**bas-fond** [bafɔ̃] <bas-fonds> *m* ❶ (*endroit*) shoal ❷ *pl* (*d'une ville*) slums; (*d'une société*) dregs

**basilic** [bazilik] *m* basil

**basilique** [bazilik] *f* basilica

**basket**[1] [baskɛt] *f souvent pl* (*chaussure*) tennis shoe

**basket**[2] [baskɛt], **basket-ball** [baskɛtbol] <basket-balls> *m* basketball

**basketteur, -euse** [basketœr, -øz] *m, f* basketball player

**basque**[1] [bask] I. *adj* Basque; **Pays ~** Basque Country II. *m* Basque; *v.a.* **français**

**basque**[2] [bask] *f* basque

**Basque** [bask] *mf* Basque

**basse** [bɑs] *f* bass

**bassin** [basɛ̃] *m* ❶ (*récipient*) bowl ❷ (*pièce d'eau: d'une fontaine, piscine*) pool; (*d'un jardin*) pond ❸ (*dans un port*) dock ❹ GEO basin ❺ ANAT pelvis

**bassine** [basin] *f* bowl

**bastille** [bastij] *f* (*château fort*) fortress

**bastion** [bastjɔ̃] *m* ❶ (*fortification*) stronghold ❷ (*haut lieu*) bastion

**bas-ventre** [bavɑ̃tr] <bas-ventres> *m* stomach

**bataille** [bataj] *f* ❶ (*pendant une guerre*) battle ❷ (*épreuve de force*) struggle ❸ (*bagarre*) fight ❹ (*jeu*) strip-jack-naked

**batailler** [bataje] <1> *vi* ❶ (*se battre*) ~ **pour qc** to fight for sth ❷ (*argumenter*) to argue

**bataillon** [batajɔ̃] *m* ❶ MIL battalion ❷ (*grand nombre*) army

**bâtard(e)** [batar, ard] *m(f)* ❶ (*enfant*) bastard ❷ (*chien*) mutt

**bateau** [bato] <x> I. *adj inv* ute II. *m* (*embarcation*) boat

**bateau-mouche** [batomuʃ] <bateaux-mouches> *m: sightseeing boat on the River Seine in Paris*

**batelier, -ière** [batalje, -jɛr] *m, f* boatman *m*, boatwoman *f*

**bâti** [bati] *m* ❶ COUT tacking ❷ TECH frame

**bâti(e)** [bati] *adj* **être bien ~** to be well-built

**bâtiment** [batimɑ̃] *m* ❶ (*édifice*) building ❷ ECON building [*o* construction] industry

**bâtir** [batir] <8> *vt* ❶ (*construire*) to build ❷ (*fonder*) ~ **une théorie sur qc** to build a theory on sth

**bâton** [batɔ̃] *m* ❶ (*canne, stick*) stick ❷ (*trait vertical*) vertical line

**bâtonnet** [batɔnɛ] *m* short stick; (*pour examiner la gorge*) tongue depressor

**battant** [batɑ̃] *m* ❶ (*pièce métallique: d'une cloche*) clapper ❷ (*panneau mobile: d'une fenêtre*) opener; (*d'une porte*) door (*right or left part of a double door*)

**battant(e)** [batɑ̃, ɑ̃t] *m(f)* fighter

**battement** [batmɑ̃] *m* ❶ (*bruit*) banging; (*de la pluie*) beating ❷ (*mouvement*) ~ **des cils** flutter of one's eyelashes ❸ (*rythme: du pouls, cœur*) beating ❹ (*intervalle de temps*) break

**batterie** [batri] *f* ❶ (*groupe*) a. AUTO, MIL battery ❷ MUS percussion ❸ (*ensemble d'ustensiles*) ~ **de cuisine** kitchen utensils *pl*

**batteur** [batœr] *m* ❶ (*mixeur*) whisk ❷ MUS drummer

**battre** [batr] *irr* I. *vt* ❶ (*frapper, vaincre*) to hit ❷ (*travailler en tapant: blé*) to thresh; (*fer, tapis, matelas*) to beat ❸ (*mélanger, mixer: blanc d'œuf, œuf entier*) to beat; (*crème*) to whip ❹ (*frapper*) **faire ~ les volets** (*vent, tempête*) to make the shutters bang ❺ (*parcourir en cherchant: campagne, région*) to scour ❻ MUS (*mesure, tambour*) to beat II. *vi* ❶ (*cogner*) to bang; (*porte, volet*) to slam ❷ (*frapper*) ~ **contre qc** to knock against sth; (*pluie*) to beat against sth ❸ (*agiter*) ~ **des ailes** to flap one's wings; ~ **des cils** to flutter one's eyelashes III. *vpr* ❶ (*se bagarrer*) **se ~ contre qn** to fight

**B**

sb ❷ (*se disputer*) **se ~ avec qn pour qc** to fight with sb over sth ❸ (*militer*) **se ~ pour qc** to fight for sth
**battu(e)** [baty] **I.** *part passé de* **battre II.** *adj* (*vaincu*) beaten
**baume** [bom] *m* balm
**baux** [bo] *v.* **bail**
**bavard(e)** [bavaʀ, aʀd] **I.** *adj* ❶ (*loquace*) talkative ❷ (*indiscret*) gossipy **II.** *m(f)* ❶ (*qui parle beaucoup*) chatterbox *inf* ❷ (*indiscret*) gossip
**bavardage** [bavaʀdaʒ] *m* ❶ (*papotage*) chatting ❷ (*propos vides*) twaddle ❸ (*commérages*) gossip
**bavarder** [bavaʀde] <1> *vi* ❶ (*papoter*) **~ avec qn** to chat with sb ❷ (*divulguer un secret*) to blab *inf*
**bave** [bav] *f* ❶ (*salive*) drool; (*d'un animal enragé*) foam ❷ (*liquide gluant: des gastéropodes*) slime
**baver** [bave] <1> *vi* ❶ (*saliver*) to drool; (*escargot, limace*) to leave a trail ❷ (*couler: stylo, porte-plume*) to leak ❸ (*médire*) **~ sur qn/qc** to malign sb/sth
**bavoir** [bavwaʀ] *m* bib
**bavure** [bavyʀ] *f* ❶ (*tache*) smudge ❷ (*erreur*) blunder
**bazar** [bazaʀ] *m* ❶ (*magasin*) general store ❷ (*souk*) bazaar ❸ *inf* (*désordre*) mess; (*amas d'objets hétéroclites*) junk
**bazarder** [bazaʀde] <1> *vt inf* **~ qc** to get rid of sth; (*vendre*) to sell sth off
**B.D.** [bede] *f abr de* **bande dessinée** comic strip; (*livre*) comic book
**béant(e)** [beã, ãt] *adj* (*yeux*) wide open; (*blessure, gouffre, trou*) gaping
**béat(e)** [bea, at] *adj* ❶ (*heureux*) blissful ❷ (*content de soi*) smug ❸ (*niais*) beatific
**béatitude** [beatityd] *f* beatitude
**beau** [bo] <x> *m* ❶ (*beauté*) **le ~** the beautiful ❷ METEO **le temps se met au ~** the weather's getting nice
**beau, belle** [bo, bɛl] <*devant un nom masculin commençant par une voyelle ou un h muet* bel, x> *adj antéposé* ❶ (*opp: laid*) beautiful; (*homme*) handsome ❷ (*qui plaît à l'esprit*) fine; **c'est**

**du ~ travail** that's nice work ❸ (*agréable*) fine; (*voyage*) lovely; **la mer est belle** the sea is calm ❹ (*intensif*) excellent ❺ (*sacré*) terrible ▶ **il a ~ faire qc** although he does sth; **il fait ~** the weather's good
**beaucoup** [boku] *adv* ❶ (*en grande quantité*) **boire ~** to drink a lot ❷ (*intensément*) **ce film m'a ~ plu** I liked this movie a lot ❸ (*fréquemment*) **aller ~ au cinéma** to go to the movies often [*o a lot*] ❹ (*plein de*) **~ de neige** a lot of snow ❺ (*de nombreux*) **~ de voitures** many cars ❻ (*beaucoup de personnes*) **~ pensent la même chose** many (people) think the same (thing) ❼ (*beaucoup de choses*) **il y a encore ~ à faire** there is still much to be done ❽ *avec un comparatif* **~ plus rapide/petit** much [*o a lot*] faster/smaller ❾ *avec un adverbe* **c'est ~ trop** it's way too much
**beau-fils** [bofis] <beaux-fils> *m* ❶ (*gendre*) son-in-law ❷ (*fils du conjoint*) stepson
**beau-frère** [bofʀɛʀ] <beaux-frères> *m* brother-in-law
**beau-père** [bopɛʀ] <beaux-pères> *m* ❶ (*père du conjoint*) father-in-law ❷ (*conjoint de la mère*) stepfather
**beauté** [bote] *f* (*a. personne*) beauty
**beaux-arts** [bozaʀ] *mpl* **les ~** the fine arts
**beaux-parents** [bopaʀã] *mpl* in-laws
**bébé** [bebe] *m* baby
**bébé-éprouvette** [bebeepʀuvɛt] <bébés-éprouvette> *m* test-tube baby
**bec** [bɛk] *m* ❶ (*chez un oiseau*) beak ❷ *inf* (*bouche*) mouth ❸ (*extrémité pointue: d'une plume*) nib; (*d'une clarinette, flûte*) mouthpiece ❹ *Belgique, Québec, Suisse, Nord, inf* **donner un ~** (*faire un bisou*) to kiss
**bécasse** [bekas] *f* (*oiseau*) woodcock
**béchamel** [beʃamɛl] *f* béchamel (sauce)
**bêche** [bɛʃ] *f* spade
**bêcher** [beʃe] <1> *vt, vi* AGR to dig
**bédé** [bede] *f inf* comic strip; (*livre*) comic book
**bédo** [bedo] *m inf* joint; **fumer le ~**

smoke a joint; (*habituellement*) smoke pot

**bée** [be] *adj v.* **bouche**

**beefsteak** [biftɛk] *v.* **bifteck**

**bégaiement** [begɛmɑ̃] *m* stuttering

**bégayer** [begeje] <7> **I.** *vi* to stutter **II.** *vt* to stutter (out)

**bégonia** [begɔnja] *m* begonia

**bègue** [bɛg] **I.** *adj* stuttering **II.** *mf* stutterer

**beige** [bɛʒ] *adj, m* beige

**beignet** [bɛɲɛ] *m* fritter

**bêler** [bele] <1> *vi* to bleat

**belette** [bəlɛt] *f* ZOOL weasel

**belge** [bɛlʒ] *adj* Belgian

**Belge** [bɛlʒ] *mf* Belgian

**Belgique** [bɛlʒik] *f* **la ~** Belgium

**bélier** [belje] *m* ❶ ZOOL ram ❷ MIL battering ram

**Bélier** [belje] *m* Aries; *v.a.* **Balance**

**belle** [bɛl] **I.** *adj v.* **beau II.** *f* ❶ SPORT tie-breaker ❷ (*conquête*) beauty; (*petite amie*) girlfriend

**belle-fille** [bɛlfij] <belles-filles> *f* ❶ (*bru*) daughter-in-law ❷ (*fille du conjoint*) stepdaughter

**belle-mère** [bɛlmɛr] <belles-mères> *f* ❶ (*mère du conjoint*) mother-in-law ❷ (*conjointe du père*) stepmother

**belle-sœur** [bɛlsœr] <belles-sœurs> *f* sister-in-law

**belliqueux, -euse** [belikø, -øz] *adj* (*guerrier*) warlike; (*discours*) aggressive

**belote** [bəlɔt] *f:* popular card game

**belvédère** [bɛlvedɛr] *m* (*édifice*) belvedere

**bémol** [bemɔl] *m* MUS flat

**bénédiction** [benediksjɔ̃] *f* ❶ (*grâce*) grace ❷ (*action: d'un(e) fidèle, d'un navire*) blessing

**bénéfice** [benefis] *m* ❶ COM profit ❷ (*avantage*) benefit

**bénéficiaire** [benefisjɛr] **I.** *mf* ❶ beneficiary ❷ *Suisse* (*d'une retraite*) pensioner **II.** *adj* (*entreprise, opération*) profitable

**bénéficier** [benefisje] <1> *vi* **~ de qc**

(*avoir*) to have sth; (*avoir comme avantage*) to benefit from sth

**bénéfique** [benefik] *adj* beneficial

**Benelux** [benelyks] *m* **le ~** the Benelux countries

**bénévolat** [benevɔla] *m* volunteering; (*activité*) volunteer work

**bénévole** [benevɔl] **I.** *adj* ❶ (*volontaire*) voluntary ❷ (*gratuit*) unpaid; (*fonction*) voluntary **II.** *mf* volunteer; (*dans une fonction*) volunteer worker

**bénin, bénigne** [benɛ̃, beniɲ] *adj* harmless; (*tumeur*) benign; (*punition*) mild

**bénir** [benir] <8> *vt a.* REL to bless

**bénit(e)** [beni, it] *adj* blessed; (*eau*) holy

**bénitier** [benitje] *m* font

**benjamin(e)** [bɛ̃ʒamɛ̃, in] *m(f)* youngest child

**benne** [bɛn] *f* ❶ TECH (*de charbon, minerai*) tub ❷ (*container*) Dumpster®; (*d'un camion*) dump truck bed

**B.E.P.C.** [beøpese] *m abr de* **brevet d'études du premier cycle** *general exams taken at age 16*

**béquille** [bekij] *f* ❶ (*canne*) crutch ❷ (*support: d'une moto, d'un vélo*) stand

**berceau** [bɛrso] <x> *m* (*couffin*) cradle

**bercer** [bɛrse] <2> *vt* (*personne, canot, navire*) to rock

**berceuse** [bɛrsøz] *f* (*chanson*) lullaby

**béret** [bere] *m* **~ basque** beret

**berge** [bɛrʒ] *f* ❶ (*rive*) bank ❷ *plé, inf* (*années*) years

**berger** [bɛrʒe] *m* (*chien*) sheepdog

**berger, -ère** [bɛrʒe, -ɛr] *m, f* shepherd, shepherdess *m, f*

**bergerie** [bɛrʒəri] *f* sheepfold

**berlingot** [bɛrlɛ̃go] *m* ❶ (*bonbon*) hard candy ❷ (*emballage*) carton

**bermuda** [bɛrmyda] *m* (pair of) Bermuda shorts

**berner** [bɛrne] <1> *vt* to fool

**besogne** [bəzɔɲ] *f* work

**besoin** [bəzwɛ̃] *m* ❶ (*nécessité*) **le ~ de sommeil de qn** sb's need for sleep ❷ *pl* (*nécessités*) **les ~s financiers de**

**B**

**qn** sb's financial requirements ❸(*né-cessité d'uriner*) ~ **naturel** call of nature ▶**avoir ~ de qc** to need sth; **dans le ~** in need

**bestial(e)** [bɛstjal, -jo] <-aux> *adj* beastly; (*instinct, avidité*) animal

**bestialité** [bɛstjalite] *f* bestiality

**bestiaux** [bɛstjo] *mpl* livestock

**best-seller** [bɛstsɛlœʀ] <best-sellers> *m* bestseller

**bétail** [betaj] *m sans pl* livestock

**bête** [bɛt] **I.** *f* ❶(*animal*) animal ❷(*insecte*) bug ❸(*qui a du talent*) star **II.** *adj* (*personne, histoire, question*) stupid

**bêtement** [bɛtmã] *adv* ❶stupidly ❷(*malencontreusement*) foolishly

**bêtise** [betiz] *f* ❶(*manque d'intelligence*) stupidity ❷(*parole*) nonsense ❸ **faire une ~** to do something silly

**béton** [betɔ̃] *m* concrete

**bétonner** [betɔne] <1> *vt* to concrete

**bétonnière** [betɔnjɛʀ] *f* ❶(*machine*) cement mixer ❷(*camion*) cement truck

**betterave** [bɛtʀav] *f* beet

**beugler** [bøgle] <1> *vi* (*meugler: vache, veau*) to moo; (*taureau, bœuf*) to bellow

**beur(e)** [bœʀ] *m(f) inf:* person born in France of North African parents

**beurre** [bœʀ] *m* butter

**beurré(e)** [bœʀe] *adj inf:* tanked-up

**beurrer** [bœʀe] <1> *vt* to butter

**beurrier** [bœʀje] *m* butter dish

**biais** [bjɛ] *m* ❶(*device*); (*échappatoire*) way; **par le ~ de** through

**bibelot** [biblo] *m* trinket

**biberon** [bibʀɔ̃] *m* (baby) bottle

**bible** [bibl] *f* bible

**bibliographie** [biblijɔgʀafi] *f* bibliography

**bibliothécaire** [biblijɔtekɛʀ] *mf* librarian

**bibliothèque** [biblijɔtɛk] *f* ❶(*salle, collection*) library ❷(*étagère*) bookshelf; (*armoire*) bookcase

**biblique** [biblik] *adj* biblical

**bicéphale** [bisefal] *adj* ❶(*à deux têtes*) two-headed, double-headed; **l'aigle ~** the double-headed eagle ❷(*à deux chefs*) with two leaders

**biceps** [bisɛps] *m* biceps

**biche** [biʃ] *f* doe

**bicolore** [bikɔlɔʀ] *adj* bicolored

**bicyclette** [bisiklɛt] *f* bicycle; **faire de la ~** to go cycling

**bidet** [bidɛ] *m* (*cuvette*) bidet

**bidon** [bidɔ̃] **I.** *m* ❶(*récipient*) can; (*de lait*) milk-churn ❷ *inf* (*ventre*) belly **II.** *adj inv, inf* (*attentat, attaque*) phony

**bidonville** [bidɔ̃vil] *m* slum; (*du tiers-monde*) shantytown

**bien** [bjɛ̃] **I.** *adv* ❶(*beaucoup*) ~ **des gens** many people; **il a ~ du mal à** +*infin* he finds it very hard to +*infin* ❷(*très*) very ❸(*au moins*) at least ❹(*plus*) **c'est ~ mieux** it's much better; ~ **assez** more than enough ❺(*de manière satisfaisante*) well; **tu ferais ~ de me le dire** you should tell me ❻(*comme il se doit: agir, se conduire, se tenir*) well; (*s'asseoir*) properly ❼(*vraiment: avoir l'intention*) really; (*rire, boire*) a lot; (*imaginer, voir*) clearly; **aimer ~ qn/qc** to really like sb/sth; **je veux ~ t'aider** I'm happy to help you; **j'y compte ~!** I'm counting on it! ❽(*à la rigueur*) **il a ~ voulu nous recevoir** he was kind enough to see us; **je vous prie de ~ vouloir faire qc** I would be grateful if you could do sth; **j'espère ~!** I should hope so! ❾(*pourtant*) however ❿(*en effet*) **il faut ~ s'occuper** you have to keep busy(, don't you?) ⓫(*aussi*) **tu l'as ~ fait, toi!** YOU did it, didn't you! ⓬(*effectivement*) really ⓭(*sans le moindre doute*) definitely ⓮(*typiquement*) **c'est ~ toi** that's just like you ⓯(*probablement*) probably; (*sûrement*) surely ▶**aller ~** to be fine; **comment allez-vous? – ~ merci** how are you? – fine, thank you; **ou ~** or; ~ **plus** much more; ~ **que tu sois trop jeune** although you are too young **II.** *adj inv* ❶(*satisfaisant*) **être ~** to be good ❷(*en forme*) **être ~** to be in shape; **se**

**B**

**sentir** ~ to feel good ❸ (*à l'aise*) **être** ~ to be OK; **être** ~ **avec qn** to be comfortable with sb ❹ (*joli*) pretty; (*homme*) good-looking ❺ (*sympathique, qui présente bien*) nice ❻ (*comme il faut*) fine **III.** *m* ❶ (*capital physique ou moral*) good; **le** ~ **et le mal** good and evil ❷ (*capital matériel*) *a.* JUR possessions ❸ ECON ~**s de consommation** consumer goods

**bien-être** [bjɛ̃nɛtʀ] *m sans pl* ❶ well-being ❷ (*confort*) comfort

**bienfaisance** [bjɛ̃fəzɑ̃s] *f* charity

**bienfait** [bjɛ̃fɛ] *m* ❶ (*action généreuse*) kindness; (*du ciel, des dieux*) godsend ❷ *pl* (*de la science, d'un traitement*) benefits

**bienfaiteur, -trice** [bjɛ̃fɛtœʀ, -tʀis] *m, f* ❶ (*sauveur*) savior ❷ (*mécène*) benefactor

**bienheureux, -euse** [bjɛ̃nœʀø, -øz] *m, f* blessed one

**bienséance** [bjɛ̃seɑ̃s] *f* decorum

**bientôt** [bjɛ̃to] *adv* ❶ (*prochainement*) soon; **à** ~ **!** see you soon! ❷ (*rapidement*) quickly

**bienveillance** [bjɛ̃vɛjɑ̃s] *f* kindness

**bienveillant(e)** [bjɛ̃vɛjɑ̃, jɑ̃t] *adj* kindly; (*comportement*) kind

**bienvenu(e)** [bjɛ̃v(ə)ny] **I.** *adj* welcome **II.** *m(f)* **être le/la ~(e) pour qn/ qc** to be very welcome to sb/sth

**bienvenue** [bjɛ̃v(ə)ny] **I.** *f* **souhaiter la ~ à qn** to welcome sb **II.** *interj Québec, inf* ~ **!** (*de rien! je vous en prie!*) you're welcome!

**bière¹** [bjɛʀ] *f* beer; ~ **blonde** lager beer; ~ **brune** dark ale; ~ **(à la) pression** draft beer

**bière²** [bjɛʀ] *f* coffin, casket

**bifteck** [biftɛk] *m* steak

**bifurcation** [bifyʀkasjɔ̃] *f* (*embranchement*) fork

**bifurquer** [bifyʀke] <1> *vi* ❶ (*se diviser*) to divide ❷ (*changer de direction*) to turn off

**bigorneau** [bigɔʀno] <x> *m* ZOOL winkle

**bigoudi** [bigudi] *m* curler

**bijou** [biʒu] <x> *m* (*joyau*) jewel; **des** ~**x** jewelry

**bijouterie** [biʒutʀi] *f* ❶ (*boutique*) jeweler's shop ❷ (*art*) jewelry making ❸ (*commerce*) jewelry trade ❹ (*objets*) jewelry

**bijoutier, -ière** [biʒutje, -jɛʀ] *m, f* jeweler

**bilan** [bilɑ̃] *m* ❶ FIN balance sheet ❷ (*résultat*) final result; (*d'un accident*) final toll; **faire un** ~ **de qc** to assess sth ❸ MED checkup ❹ COM, ECON **déposer le** ~ to file for bankruptcy

**bilatéral(e)** [bilateʀal, -o] <-aux> *adj* (*des deux côtés*) bilateral

**bile** [bil] *f* ❶ ANAT bile ❷ (*amertume*) bitterness

**bilingue** [bilɛ̃g] **I.** *adj* bilingual **II.** *mf* bilingual person

**billard** [bijaʀ] *m* ❶ (*jeu*) pool, billiards + *vb sing* ❷ (*lieu*) pool hall ❸ (*table*) pool table

**bille¹** [bij] *f* ❶ (*petite boule*) marble ❷ (*au billard*) pool ball ❸ TECH **stylo à** ~ ballpoint pen

**bille²** [bij] *f inf* face

**billet** [bijɛ] *m* ❶ (*entrée, titre de transport*) ticket; ~ **aller/aller-retour** one-way/roundtrip ticket ❷ (*numéro*) ticket ❸ (*argent*) bill ❹ (*message*) note

**billetterie** [bijɛtʀi] *f* ❶ (*caisse*) ticket office ❷ (*distributeur de billets*) ~ **automatique** ATM, cash machine

**bimensuel(le)** [bimɑ̃sɥɛl] *adj* semimonthly

**bimestriel(le)** [bimɛstʀijɛl] *adj* **être** ~ bimonthly

**biocarburant** [bjokaʀbyʀɑ̃] *m* biofuel

**biodégradable** [bjodegʀadabl] *adj* ECOL biodegradable

**biodégrader** [bjodegʀade] *vpr* ECOL **se** ~ to biodegrade

**biographie** [bjɔgʀafi] *f* biography

**biographique** [bjɔgʀatik] *adj* biographical

**biologie** [bjɔlɔʒi] *f* biology

**biologique** [bjɔlɔʒik] *adj* (*conditions, agriculture*) biological; **aliments** ~**s** organic food + *vb sing*

**B**

**biologiste** [bjɔlɔʒist] *mf* biologist
**biomasse** [bjomas] *f* biomass
**biotechnologie** [bjotɛknɔlɔʒi] *f* biotechnology
**biotope** [bjɔtɔp] *m* biotope
**bip** [bip] *m* (*son*) beep
**bis** [bis] **I.** *adv* **①** n° **12** ~ n° 12 a **②** MUS repeat **II.** *m* encore
**bis(e)** [bi, biz] *adj* gray-brown
**biscotte** [biskɔt] *f* melba toast
**biscuit** [biskɥi] *m* **①** (*gâteau sec*) cookie **②** (*pâtisserie*) sponge **③** (*céramique*) biscuit
**bise¹** [biz] *f* (*vent du Nord*) north wind
**bise²** [biz] *f inf* kiss; **se faire la ~** to kiss each other on the cheek; **grosses ~s!** hugs and kisses!
**bisexuel(le)** [bisɛksɥɛl] *adj* bisexual
**bison** [bizɔ̃] *m* American buffalo; (*d'Europe*) bison
**bisou** [bizu] *m inf* kiss
**bissextile** [bisɛkstil] *adj* **année ~** leap year
**bistouri** [bisturi] *m* lancet
**bit** [bit] *m* INFORM *abr de* **B**Inary digi**T**, **chiffre binaire** bit
**bitume** [bitym] *m* **①** (*asphalte*) asphalt **②** *inf* (*trottoir*) sidewalk
**bizarre** [bizaʀ] *adj* strange
**bizarrement** [bizaʀmɑ̃] *adv* strangely
**blafard(e)** [blafaʀ, aʀd] *adj* pale
**blague** [blag] *f inf* **①** (*histoire drôle*) joke **②** (*farce*) trick **③** (*tabatière*) tobacco pouch
**blaguer** [blage] <1> *vi* to be kidding
**blagueur, -euse** [blagœʀ, -øz] **I.** *adj* (*sourire, air*) teasing **II.** *m, f* joker
**blaireau** [blɛʀo] <x> *m* **①** ZOOL badger **②** (*pour la barbe*) shaving brush
**blâme** [blɑm] *m* (*sanction*) reprimand
**blâmer** [blɑme] <1> *vt* **①** (*désapprouver*) to disapprove **②** (*condamner moralement*) to blame **③** (*sanctionner*) to reprimand
**blanc** [blɑ̃] *m* **①** (*couleur, vin, linge*) white **②** TYP, INFORM space **③** (*espace vide dans un devoir*) blank **④** (*espace vide sur une cassette*) space **⑤** (*fard blanc*) white powder **⑥** CULIN **~ d'œuf**

egg white; **~ de poulet** white meat **⑦** BOT (*maladie*) powdery mildew
**blanc(he)** [blɑ̃, blɑ̃ʃ] *adj* **①** (*de couleur blanche*) white **②** (*non écrit: bulletin de vote, feuille*) blank **③** (*propre: draps*) clean **④** (*pâle, non bronzé: personne, peau*) white **⑤** (*innocent*) pure **⑥** (*fictif: mariage*) unconsummated; (*examen*) practice
**Blanc(he)** [blɑ̃, blɑ̃ʃ] *m(f)* White
**blanche** [blɑ̃ʃ] *adj v.* **blanc**
**blancheur** [blɑ̃ʃœʀ] *f* whiteness; (*du visage, teint*) paleness
**blanchir** [blɑ̃ʃiʀ] <8> **I.** *vt* **①** (*rendre blanc*) to whiten; (*mur*) to whitewash; (*linge, draps, cheveux*) to bleach **②** (*nettoyer: linge*) to launder **③** (*disculper*) **~ qn** to exonerate sb **④** (*légaliser: argent*) to launder **⑤** CULIN (*légumes*) to blanch **II.** *vi* to turn white
**blanchisserie** [blɑ̃ʃisʀi] *f* laundry
**blasé(e)** [blɑze] *adj* blasé
**blason** [blɑzɔ̃] *m* coat of arms
**blasphémer** [blasfeme] <5> *vt, vi* to blaspheme
**blazer** [blazɛʀ, blazœʀ] *m* blazer
**blé** [ble] *m* **①** (*plante*) wheat **②** (*grain*) grain **③** *inf* (*argent*) dough
**bled** [blɛd] *m péj, inf* (godforsaken) hole
**blême** [blɛm] *adj* (*visage*) sallow; (*lumière*) pale
**blessant(e)** [blɛsɑ̃, ɑ̃t] *adj* hurtful
**blessé(e)** [blese] **I.** *adj* **①** MED injured; (*soldat*) wounded **②** (*offensé*) hurt **II.** *m(f) a.* MIL casualty; **les ~s** the injured
**blesser** [blese] <1> **I.** *vt* **①** MED to injure; MIL to wound **②** (*meurtrir*) **~ les pieds** (*chaussures*) to hurt one's feet **③** (*offenser*) to hurt; (*oreille, vue*) to offend **II.** *vpr* **se ~** to hurt oneself; (*sérieusement*) to injure oneself
**blessure** [blesyʀ] *f* (*lésion, plaie*) *a.* MIL wound
**bleu** [blø] *m* **①** (*couleur*) blue; **~ ciel** sky-blue; **~ clair/foncé** light/dark blue **②** (*marque*) bruise **③** (*vêtement*) (pair of) overalls **④** (*fromage*) blue cheese **⑤** *pl* SPORT **les ~s** the blues (*the French*

*national soccer team, which wears blue*)

**bleu(e)** [blø] *adj* ❶ (*de couleur bleue*) blue ❷ CULIN (*steak*) very rare

**bleuet** [bløɛ] *m* (*fleur*) cornflower

**blindé** [blɛ̃de] *m* armored

**blindé(e)** [blɛ̃de] *adj* (*renforcé: porte*) reinforced; (*voiture*) armored

**bloc** [blɔk] *m* ❶ (*masse de matière*) block ❷ (*cahier, carnet*) pad ❸ (*ensemble, pâté de maisons, immeuble*) block ❹ (*union*) group

**blocage** [blɔkaʒ] *m* ❶ (*action: des roues, freins*) locking; (*d'une pièce mobile, porte, d'un boulon*) jamming; (*d'un écrou, d'une vis*) over tightening; (*avec une cale*) wedging ❷ ECON (*des prix, salaires*) freezing ❸ PSYCH block

**bloc-notes** [blɔknɔt] <blocs-notes> *m* notepad

**blocus** [blɔkys] *m* blockade

**blogosphère** [blɔɡɔsfɛʀ] *f* INET blogo-sphère

**blond** [blɔ̃] *m* (*couleur*) blond

**blond(e)** [blɔ̃, blɔ̃d] I. *adj* blond; (*tabac, cigarettes*) mild; (*bière*) lager II. *m(f)* (*personne*) blond; (*femme*) blonde

**blonde** [blɔ̃d] *f* ❶ (*bière*) lager beer ❷ (*cigarette*) mild cigarette ❸ *Québec* (*maîtresse, fiancée*) **la ~ d'un homme** a man's girlfriend

**blondir** [blɔ̃diʀ] <8> *vi* (*cheveux*) to become lighter

**bloquer** [blɔke] <1> I. *vt* ❶ (*immobiliser*) to jam; (*passage, route, porte*) to block; (*vis, écrou*) to over tighten; (*pièce mobile, boulon*) to tighten; **être bloqué dans l'ascenseur** to be trapped in the elevator ❷ ECON (*a. négociations*) to freeze ❸ (*regrouper: jours de congé*) to group together; (*paragraphes*) to combine ❹ SPORT (*balle*) to block ❺ *Québec* (*coller, échouer*) to fail II. *vpr* **se ~** ❶ (*s'immobiliser*) to jam; (*roues, freins*) to lock ❷ PSYCH **se ~** (*programme*) to seize up III. *vi* ❶ *inf* PSYCH **~ qc** to block sth (out) ❷ INFORM (*programme*) to block

**blottir** [blɔtiʀ] <8> *vpr* **se ~ contre qn** to snuggle up against sb

**blouse** [bluz] *f* ❶ (*tablier*) overall ❷ (*corsage*) blouse

**blouson** [bluzɔ̃] *m* jacket

**blues** [blus] *m inv* ❶ (*musique*) blues ❷ (*cafard*) **avoir un coup de ~** to have the blues

**bob** [bɔb] *m* SPORT bobsled

**bobine** [bɔbin] *f* ❶ (*cylindre*) reel; (*de fil*) bobbin ❷ ELEC **~ d'allumage** coil ❸ *inf* (*mine*) face

**bobsleigh** [bɔbslɛg] *m v.* **bob**

**bocal** [bɔkal, -o] <-aux> *m* jar

**bœuf** [bœf, bø] I. *m* ❶ ZOOL ox ❷ (*opp: taureau, vache*) bullock ❸ (*viande*) beef II. *adj Suisse, inf* (*bête*) **c'est ~** that's silly

**bogue** [bɔg] *m o f* INFORM bug

**bohème** [bɔɛm] I. *adj* bohemian II. *f* Bohemia

**bohémien(ne)** [bɔemjɛ̃, jɛn] *m(f)* Bohemian

**boire** [bwaʀ] *irr* I. *vt* ❶ (*avaler un liquide*) to drink ❷ (*s'imprégner de*) to absorb II. *vi* to drink; **~ à la santé de qn** to drink (to) sb's health III. *vpr* **se ~ à l'apéritif** to be drunk as an aperitif

**bois** [bwa] I. *m* ❶ (*forêt*) woods *pl* ❷ (*matériau*) wood; (*en planches, sur pied*) lumber ❸ (*gravure*) woodcut II. *mpl* ❶ MUS woodwind ❷ (*cornes: des cervidés*) antlers

**boisé(e)** [bwaze] *adj* wooded

**boiserie** [bwazʀi] *f* woodwork

**boisson** [bwasɔ̃] *f* (*liquide buvable*) drink

**boîte** [bwat] *f* ❶ (*récipient*) box; **~ à lunch** *Québec* (*gamelle*) lunch box; **~ aux lettres** mailbox ❷ (*conserve*) can; **~ de conserves** can (of food); **en ~** canned ❸ *inf* (*discothèque*) club; **~ de nuit** nightclub ❹ *inf* (*entreprise*) company ❺ MED **~ crânienne** cranium ❻ AVIAT **~ noire** black box ❼ AUTO **~ de vitesses** transmission ❽ INFORM **~ aux lettres (électronique)** (electronic) mailbox; **~ de réception** in box

**boiter** [bwate] <1> *vi* ❶ (*clopiner*) to

**B**

limp ②*fig* (*raisonnement, comparaison*) to fall down

**boiteux, -euse** [bwatø, -øz] *adj* (*bancal: meuble*) wobbly; (*personne*) lame

**boîtier** [bwatje] *m* (*boîte*) box; (*pour des instruments, cassettes*) case

**bol** [bɔl] *m* ①(*récipient*) bowl ②*inf* (*chance*) luck; **avoir du ~** to be lucky ③*Québec* (*cuvette*) **~ de toilette** toilet bowl ▶ **en avoir ras le ~** *inf* to be fed up

**bolet** [bɔlɛ] *m* BOT boletus

**bolide** [bɔlid] *m* sports car

**bombardement** [bɔ̃baʀdəmɑ̃] *m* MIL bombing; **~ aérien** aerial bombardment

**bombarder** [bɔ̃baʀde] <1> *vt* MIL to bomb

**bombe** [bɔ̃b] *f* ①MIL bomb; **~ lacrymogène** teargas grenade ②(*atomiseur*) spray ③(*casquette*) riding hat

**bombé(e)** [bɔ̃be] *adj* bombé

**bomber** [bɔ̃be] <1> *vt* (*gonfler: poitrine, torse*) to stick out

**bon** [bɔ̃] I. *m* ①(*coupon d'échange*) coupon, voucher; **~ de caisse** cash voucher ②FIN **~ du Trésor** Treasury bill ③(*ce qui est bon*) good part ④(*personne*) good person II. *adv* **sentir ~** to smell good ▶ **il fait ~** the weather's nice

**bon(ne)** [bɔ̃, bɔn] <meilleur> *adj* antéposé ①(*opp: mauvais*) good; **être ~ en latin** to be good at Latin ②(*adéquat, correct*) right; (*remède, conseil a.*) good ③(*valable: billet, ticket*) valid ④(*agréable*) good; (*soirée, surprise, vacances*) nice; (*eau*) good ⑤(*délicieux*) good; (*comestible*) OK ⑥(*intensif de quantité, de qualité*) good ⑦(*être fait pour*) **c'est ~ à savoir** that's worth knowing ⑧(*être destiné à*) **être ~ pour qc** to be in for sth ▶ **c'est ~** (*a bon goût, fait du bien*) it's good; (*ça ira comme ça*) that's fine; (*tant pis*) that'll have to do; **pour de ~?** for good?

**bonbon** [bɔ̃bɔ̃] *m* ①(*friandise*) candy; **~ acidulé** sour drop ②*Belgique* (*biscuit*) cookie

**bond** [bɔ̃] *m* ①(*action: d'une personne, d'un animal*) leap; SPORT jump; (*d'une balle*) bounce ②ECON **~ en avant** leap forward

**bondé(e)** [bɔ̃de] *adj* jam-packed

**bondir** [bɔ̃diʀ] <8> *vi* (*sauter*) to jump; **~ à la porte** to leap to the door

**bonheur** [bɔnœʀ] *m* ①(*état*) happiness ②(*chance*) luck; **le ~ de vivre** the good fortune to be alive; **porter ~ à qn** to bring sb (good) luck ▶ **par ~** luckily

**bonhomme** [bɔnɔm, bɔ̃zɔm] <bonshommes> *m* ①*inf* (*homme*) man; (*plutôt négatif*) guy; **~ de neige** snowman ②(*petit garçon*) **petit ~** little fellow

**bonjour** [bɔ̃ʒuʀ] I. *interj* ①(*salutation*) hello; **dire ~ à qn** to say hello to sb ②*Québec* (*bonne journée*) have a nice day II. *m* **donner bien le ~ à qn de la part de qn** to pass on sb's regards to sb

**bonne** [bɔn] *f* maid; *v.a.* **bon**

**bonnet** [bɔnɛ] *m* ①(*coiffure*) hat; (*du nourrisson, du bébé*) bonnet; **~ de bain** shower cap ②(*poche: du soutien-gorge*) cup

**bonsoir** [bɔ̃swaʀ] *interj* (*en arrivant*) good evening; (*en partant*) good night

**bonté** [bɔ̃te] *f* kindness

**bonus** [bɔnys] *m* bonus

**bord** [bɔʀ] *m* side; (*d'une table*) edge; (*d'un trottoir*) curb; (*d'un lac, d'une rivière*) bank; (*de la mer*) shore; (*d'un chapeau*) brim; **au ~ de (la) mer** by the sea ▶ **à ~** on board; **au ~ du lac** by the lake

**bordeaux** [bɔʀdo] I. *m* Bordeaux (wine) II. *adj inv* burgundy

**bordel** [bɔʀdɛl] I. *m* ①*vulg* (*maison close*) brothel, whorehouse ②*inf* (*désordre*) chaos II. *interj inf* goddammit

**border** [bɔʀde] <1> *vt* (*longer*) **la route est bordée d'arbres** trees run alongside the road; **la place est bordée d'arbres** the square is surrounded by trees ②(*couvrir*) **~ qn** to tuck sb in

**bordereau** [bɔʀdəro] <x> *m* (*formulaire*) note

**bordier** [bɔʀdje] *m* *Suisse* (*riverain*) (local) resident

**bordure** [bɔʀdyʀ] *f* ①(*bord*) side; (*d'un*

*quai*) edge; (*du trottoir*) curb; (*empiè-cement*) surround ❷ (*rangée*) line

**boréal(e)** [bɔʀeal, -o] <s *o* -aux> *adj* northern

**borgne** [bɔʀɲ] *adj* (*éborgné: personne*) blind in one eye

**borne** [bɔʀn] *f* ❶ (*pierre*) marker ❷ (*protection*) post ❸ *pl* (*limite*) limits; **dépasser les ~s** (*personne*) to go too far ❹ *inf* (*distance de 1 km*) kilometer ❺ ELEC terminal

**borné(e)** [bɔʀne] *adj* limited; (*personne*) narrow-minded

**bosse** [bɔs] *f* ❶ (*déformation*) bump ❷ (*protubérance, difformité*) hump

**bosser** [bɔse] <1> **I.** *vi inf* to work; (*travailler dur*) to slave; (*bûcher*) to cram **II.** *vt inf* (*matière*) to cram (for)

**bossu(e)** [bɔsy] *m(f)* hunchback

**botanique** [bɔtanik] *adj* botanical

**botte** [bɔt] *f* ❶ (*chaussure*) boot ❷ (*paquet: de légumes, fleurs*) bunch; (*de foin, paille*) (*en gerbe*) sheaf; (*au carré*) bale

**bottin**® [bɔtɛ̃] *m* directory

**bouc** [buk] *m* ❶ ZOOL billy goat ❷ (*barbe*) goatee ▸ **~ émissaire** scapegoat

**bouche** [buʃ] *f* (*ouverture*) a. ANAT, ZOOL, GEO mouth; **les ~s du Rhône** the mouth of the River Rhone; **~ de métro** subway entrance ▸ **~ bée** open mouthed

**bouché(e)** [buʃe] *adj* ❶ METEO (*temps*) cloudy; (*ciel*) overcast ❷ (*sans avenir*) hopeless ❸ *inf* (*idiot: personne*) stupid

**bouche-à-bouche** [buʃabuʃ] *m sans pl* mouth-to-mouth; **faire du ~ à qn** to give sb the kiss of life

**bouchée** [buʃe] *f* ❶ (*petit morceau*) morsel ❷ (*ce qui est dans la bouche*) mouthful

**boucher** [buʃe] <1> **I.** *vt* (*bouteille*) to cork; (*trou, toilettes, évier*) to block, to fill in; (*fente*) to fill; **avoir le nez bouché** to have a stuffy nose **II.** *vpr* **se ~** (*évier*) to get blocked; **se ~ le nez** to hold one's nose; **se ~ les oreilles** to plug one's ears

**boucher, -ère** [buʃe, -ɛʀ] *m, f a. péj* butcher

**boucherie** [buʃʀi] *f* ❶ (*magasin*) butcher's (shop) ❷ (*métier*) butchery ❸ (*massacre*) slaughter ▸ **faire ~** *Suisse, Québec* (*tuer le cochon*) to slaughter the pig

**boucherie charcuterie** [buʃʀiʃaʀkytʀi] <*boucheries charcuteries*> *f* butcher's shop and delicatessen

**bouchon** [buʃɔ̃] *m* ❶ (*pour boucher: d'une bouteille*) stopper; (*de liège*) cork; (*d'une carafe, d'un évier*) plug; (*d'un bidon, tube, réservoir*) cap; **sentir le ~** (*vin*) to be corked ❷ (*à la pêche*) float ❸ (*embouteillage*) traffic jam

**boucle** [bukl] *f* ❶ (*objet en forme d'anneau: de soulier, ceinture*) buckle; **~ d'oreille** earring ❷ (*qui s'enroule*) curl ❸ (*de cheveux*) curl ❸ (*forme géométrique*) a. INFORM, AVIAT loop

**bouclé(e)** [bukle] *adj* (*cheveux, poils*) curly

**boucler** [bukle] <1> **I.** *vt* ❶ (*attacher*) to buckle; **~ la ceinture de sécurité** to put on one's seat belt ❷ *inf* (*fermer: magasin, porte*) to close ❸ (*terminer*) **~ qc** (*affaire, recherches*) to wrap sth up ❹ (*équilibrer: budget*) to balance ❺ POL, MIL (*encercler*) to surround; (*quartier*) to seal off **II.** *vt* ❶ (*friser*) **ses cheveux bouclent naturellement** her hair is naturally curly ❷ INFORM to loop

**bouclier** [buklije] *m* (*protection*) a. MIL shield

**bouddhisme** [budism] *m* Buddhism

**bouddhiste** [budist] *adj, mf* Buddhist

**bouder** [bude] <1> *vi* to sulk

**boudeur, -euse** [budœʀ, -øz] **I.** *adj* sulky **II.** *m, f* sulker

**boudin** [budɛ̃] *m* ❶ (*charcuterie*) blood sausage; **~ noir** black pudding ❷ *inf* (*fille grosse et disgracieuse*) dumpling

**boudiné(e)** [budine] *adj* (*en forme de boudin: doigt*) fat

**boue** [bu] *f* mud

**bouée** [bwe] *f* ❶ (*balise*) buoy ❷ (*protection gonflable*) float; **~ de sauvetage** life preserver; *fig* lifeline

**B**

**boueux, -euse** [bwø, -øz] *adj* (*chaussures, chemin*) muddy

**bouffe** [buf] *f inf* grub

**bouffée** [bufe] *f* ❶ (*souffle*) **tirer des ~s de sa pipe** to puff on one's pipe; **~ d'air frais** puff of cold air ❷ (*odeur*) whiff ❸ (*poussée*) **~ de chaleur** hot flash

**bouffer** [bufe] <1> *vt, vi inf* (*manger*) to eat

**bouffi(e)** [bufi] *adj* (*gonflé: visage*) bloated; (*yeux*) puffy; (*mains*) swollen

**bouffon(ne)** [bufɔ̃, ɔn] *m(f)* clown

**bougeoir** [buʒwaʀ] *m* candlestick

**bouger** [buʒe] <2a> **I.** *vi* ❶ (*remuer*) to move ❷ POL (*protester*) to kick up a fuss ❸ *inf* (*changer, s'altérer*) to change; (*couleur*) to fade; (*tissu*) to shrink ❹ (*se déplacer, voyager*) to move around; **je ne bouge pas d'ici!** I'm staying right here! **II.** *vt* to move **III.** *vpr inf* **se ~** ❶ (*se remuer*) to move ❷ (*faire un effort*) to put oneself out

**bougie** [buʒi] *f* ❶ (*chandelle*) candle ❷ AUTO spark plug

**bougon(ne)** [bugɔ̃, ɔn] *adj* grumpy

**bougonner** [bugɔne] <1> *vi* to mutter

**bouillant(e)** [bujɑ̃, jɑ̃t] *adj* (*qui bout, très chaud*) boiling

**bouille** [buj] *f inf* face

**bouillie** [buji] *f* baby food

**bouillir** [bujiʀ] *irr* **I.** *vi* ❶ (*être en ébullition*) to be boiling ❷ (*porter à ébullition*) to boil ❸ (*laver à l'eau bouillante, stériliser*) to boil, to wash in boiling water **II.** *vt* (*lait, viande, linge*) to boil

**bouilloire** [bujwaʀ] *f* kettle

**bouillon** [bujɔ̃] *m* ❶ (*soupe*) stock ❷ (*bouillonnement*) bubble

**bouillonner** [bujɔne] <1> *vi* (*produire des bouillons*) to bubble

**bouillotte** [bujɔt] *f* hot-water bottle

**boulanger, -ère** [bulɑ̃ʒe, -ɛʀ] *m, f* baker

**boulangerie** [bulɑ̃ʒʀi] *f* (*magasin, métier*) bakery

**boulangerie-pâtisserie** [bulɑ̃ʒʀipatisʀi] <boulangeries-pâtisseries> *f* bakery and pastry shop

**boulanger-pâtissier** [bulɑ̃ʒepatisje] <boulangers-pâtissiers> *m* baker-pastry chef

**boule** [bul] *f* ❶ (*sphère*) ball ❷ (*objet de forme ronde*) **~ de glace** scoop of ice cream; **~ de neige** snowball; **~ de coton** cotton ball ❸ *plé, inf* (*testicules*) balls ❹ *pl* JEUX **jeu de ~s** game of (lawn) bowls ❺ *inf* (*devenir fou*) **perdre la ~** to go crazy ❻ *Belgique* (*bonbon*) candy

**bouleau** [bulo] <x> *m* BOT birch (tree)

**bouledogue** [buldɔg] *m* ZOOL bulldog

**boulet** [bulɛ] *m* ❶ (*boule de métal pour charger les canons*) cannonball ❷ (*boule de métal attachée aux pieds des condamnés*) ball ❸ (*fardeau*) ball and chain

**boulette** [bulɛt] *f* (*petite boule*) pellet

**boulevard** [bulvaʀ] *m* boulevard

**bouleversement** [bulvɛʀsəmɑ̃] *m* distress; (*dans la vie d'une personne*) upheaval

**bouleverser** [bulvɛʀse] <1> *vt* ❶ (*causer une émotion violente: personne*) to shake ❷ (*apporter des changements brutaux*) ~ **qc** (*carrière, vie*) to turn sth upside down; (*emploi du temps*) to disrupt sth

**boulimie** [bulimi] *f* MED bulimia

**boulon** [bulɔ̃] *m* bolt

**boulot** [bulo] *m inf* ❶ (*travail*) work ❷ (*emploi*) job

**boum**[1] [bum] **I.** *interj* bang **II.** *m* (*bruit sonore*) boom

**boum**[2] [bum] *f inf* party

**bouquet** [bukɛ] *m* ❶ (*botte: de fleurs*) bunch; (*chez le fleuriste*) bouquet; (*de persil, thym*) bunch ❷ (*parfum: d'un vin*) bouquet

**bouquin** [bukɛ̃] *m inf* book

**bouquiner** [bukine] <1> *vi inf* to read

**bourdon** [buʀdɔ̃] *m* ❶ ZOOL bumblebee ❷ MUS drone; (*d'un orgue*) bourdon

**bourdonner** [buʀdɔne] <1> *vi* (*moteur, hélice*) to hum; (*insecte*) to buzz

**bourg** [buʀ] *m* village

**bourgeois(e)** [buʀʒwa, waz] **I.** *adj* ❶ (*relatif à la bourgeoisie*) bourgeois;

**classe ~e** middle-class ❷ *péj* (*étroitement conservateur*) bourgeois **II.** *m(f)* ❶ (*qui appartient à la bourgeoisie*) *a. péj* bourgeois ❷ HIST burgess ❸ *Suisse* (*personne possédant la bourgeoisie*) burgess

**bourgeoisie** [buʀʒwazi] *f* ❶ (*classe sociale*) bourgeoisie, middle-classes *pl* ❷ HIST burgesses *pl*

**bourgeon** [buʀʒɔ̃] *m* bud

**bourgmestre** [buʀgmɛstʀ] *m Belgique* (*maire*) burgomaster

**bourgogne** [buʀgɔɲ] *m* Burgundy (*wine*)

**Bourgogne** [buʀgɔɲ] *f* **la ~** Burgundy

**bourguignon(ne)** [buʀgiɲɔ̃, ɔn] *adj* ❶ (*de Bourgogne*) Burgundian ❷ CULIN **bœuf ~** beef bourguignon (*beef cooked in red wine*)

**Bourguignon(ne)** [buʀgiɲɔ̃, ɔn] *m(f)* Burgundian

**bourrasque** [buʀask] *f* METEO (*de vent*) gust; (*de neige*) flurry

**bourré(e)** [buʀe] *adj* ❶ (*plein à craquer*) jam-packed; (*portefeuille*) full ❷ *inf* (*ivre*) plastered

**bourreau** [buʀo] <x> *m* ❶ (*exécuteur*) executioner ❷ (*tortionnaire*) torturer; **~ des cœurs** *iron* lady-killer

**bourrelet** [buʀlɛ] *m* ❶ (*pour isoler*) weather strip ❷ ANAT (*de chair, graisse*) spare tire *inf*

**bourrer** [buʀe] <1> *vt* (*remplir*) to stuff; (*pipe*) to fill

**bourse¹** [buʀs] *f* ❶ (*porte-monnaie*) purse ❷ (*allocation*) **~ d'études** scholarship ❸ *pl* ANAT scrotum

**bourse²** [buʀs] *f* FIN **la Bourse** (*lieu*) the stock exchange; (*ensemble des cours*) the stock market

**boursier, -ière¹** [buʀsje, -jɛʀ] *m, f* scholarship student

**boursier, -ière²** [buʀsje, -jɛʀ] *adj* (*relatif à la Bourse*) stock market

**boursouflure** [buʀsuflyʀ] *f* (*de la peau, du visage*) puffiness; (*d'une surface, peinture*) blistering

**bousculade** [buskylad] *f* ❶ (*remous de foule*) crush ❷ (*précipitation*) rush

**bousculer** [buskyle] <1> *vt* ❶ (*heurter: personne*) to shove; **~ qc** (*livres, chaises*) to knock sth over ❷ (*mettre sens dessus dessous*) **~ qc** to turn sth upside down ❸ (*modifier brutalement*) **~ qc** (*conception, traditions*) to turn sth upside down; (*projet*) to turn sth around

**boussole** [busɔl] *f* compass

**bout** [bu] *m* ❶ (*extrémité: du doigt, nez*) tip; (*d'un objet*) end; **~ à ~** end to end; **jusqu'au ~** to the end ❷ (*limite*) end; **tout au ~** at the very end ❸ (*morceau*) bit; **~ d'essai** CINE screen test ❹ (*terme*) end; **au ~ d'un moment** after a while ▸ **être à ~ de souffle** to be out of breath; **venir à ~ de qc** to finish sth off

**bouteille** [butɛj] *f* **~ consignée/non consignée** refundable/non-refundable bottle; **boire à la ~** to drink from the bottle

**boutique** [butik] *f* ❶ (*magasin*) shop ❷ (*magasin de prêt-à-porter*) boutique

**bouton** [butɔ̃] *m* ❶ COUT (*de vêtement*) button ❷ (*commande d'un mécanisme: de la radio, télé, sonnette*) button; (*de porte*) doorknob; (*d'un interrupteur*) switch ❸ MED **~ de fièvre** cold sore; **~ d'acné** pimple ❹ BOT bud ❺ INFORM button; **~ Démarrer** Start button; **~ droit de la souris** right mouse button

**boutonner** [butɔne] <1> **I.** *vt, vi* to button **II.** *vpr* **se ~** (*personne*) to button oneself up

**boutonnière** [butɔnjɛʀ] *f* buttonhole

**bouture** [butyʀ] *f* cutting

**bovin(e)** [bɔvɛ̃, in] **I.** *adj* (*qui concerne le bœuf*) bovine **II.** *mpl* cattle

**box** [bɔks] <es> *m* ❶ (*dans une écurie*) (box) stall; (*dans un garage*) garage ❷ JUR **~ des accusés** dock

**boxe** [bɔks] *f* boxing

**boxer¹** [bɔkse] <1> **I.** *vi* to box **II.** *vt inf* **~ qn** to punch sb

**boxer²** [bɔksɛʀ] *m* (*short*) boxers *pl*

**boxeur, -euse** [bɔksœʀ, -øz] *m, f* boxer

**boyau** [bwajo] <x> *m* ❶ *pl* ANAT guts

**B**

② (*chambre à air*) inner tube ③ (*corde: d'une raquette, d'un violon*) catgut

**boycott** [bɔjkɔt] *m*, **boycottage** [bɔj-kɔtaʒ] *m* boycott

**boycotter** [bɔjkɔte] <1> *vt* to boycott

**boy-scout** [bɔjskut] <boy-scouts> *m* boy scout

**B.P.** [bepe] *abr de* **boîte postale** post office box

**bracelet** [bʀaslɛ] *m* bracelet; (*rigide*) bangle

**braconner** [bʀakɔne] <1> *vi* (*à la chasse, à la pêche*) to poach

**braconnier, -ière** [bʀakɔnje, -ijɛʀ] *m, f* (*à la chasse, à la pêche*) poacher

**brader** [bʀade] <1> *vt* ① COM ~ **qc** to sell sth cheaply ② (*se débarrasser de*) to sell sth off

**braderie** [bʀadʀi] *f* flea market

**braguette** [bʀagɛt] *f* fly

**braillard(e)** [bʀajaʀ, -jaʀd] *m(f) inf* bawler

**braille** [bʀaj] *m* Braille

**brailler** [bʀaje] <1> *vi* to bawl

**braise** [bʀɛz] *f* embers *pl*

**braiser** [bʀeze] <1> *vt* to braise

**bramer** [bʀame] <1> *vi* (*cerf, daim*) to bell

**brancard** [bʀɑ̃kaʀ] *m* (*civière*) stretcher

**brancardier, -ière** [bʀɑ̃kaʀdje, -jɛʀ] *m, f* stretcher bearer

**branche** [bʀɑ̃ʃ] *f* ① (*famille, domaine*) a. BOT branch ② (*tige: d'une paire de lunettes*) arm; (*d'un chandelier*) branch; (*de ciseaux*) blade; (*d'un compas*) leg

**branché(e)** [bʀɑ̃ʃe] *adj inf* cool; **être ~ cinéma** (*adorer*) to be a movie fan; (*s'y connaître*) to be a movie buff

**branchement** [bʀɑ̃ʃmɑ̃] *m* ① (*action*) connecting ② (*circuit*) connection ③ IN-FORM ~ **Internet** Internet access

**brancher** [bʀɑ̃ʃe] <1> I. *vt* (*raccorder*) ~ **le téléphone sur le réseau** to connect the telephone (to the network) II. *vpr* **se ~ sur qc** to tune into sth

**brandir** [bʀɑ̃diʀ] <8> *vt* (*arme*) to brandish; (*drapeau*) to wave

**branlant(e)** [bʀɑ̃lɑ̃, ɑ̃t] *adj* shaky

**branler** [bʀɑ̃le] <1> I. *vi* to wobble II. *vpr vulg* **se ~** to jerk [*o* whack] off

**braquer** [bʀake] <1> I. *vt* ① AUTO ~ **le volant à droite** to crank the (steering) wheel to the right ② (*diriger*) ~ **le regard sur qn** to look at sb; ~ **une arme sur qn** to aim a weapon at sb ③ *inf* (*attaquer: banque, magasin*) to rob II. *vpr* **se ~** to dig one's heels in

**bras** [bʀa] *m* ① (*membre*) arm; **se donner le ~** to lock arms; ~ **dessus - dessous** arm in arm ② (*main-d'œuvre*) worker ③ TECH (*d'un levier, électrophone*) arm; (*d'un fauteuil*) armrest; (*d'un brancard*) shaft ④ GEO inlet; ~ **de mer** sound

**brassard** [bʀasaʀ] *m* armband

**brasse** [bʀas] *f* breaststroke; ~ **papillon** butterfly

**brasser** [bʀase] <1> *vt* ① (*mélanger*) to mix; (*pâte*) to knead ② (*fabriquer: bière*) to brew

**brasserie** [bʀasʀi] *f* ① (*restaurant*) brasserie ② (*industrie*) brewing industry ③ (*entreprise*) brewery

**brasseur** [bʀasœʀ] *m* brewer

**brassière** [bʀasjɛʀ] *f* ① (*sous-vêtement*) undershirt (*for a baby*) ② Québec, *inf* (*soutien-gorge*) bra

**brave** [bʀav] *adj* ① (*courageux*) brave ② *antéposé* (*honnête*) decent ③ (*naïf*) naive

**braver** [bʀave] <1> *vt* ① (*défier*) ~ **un adversaire** to stand up to an opponent ② (*ne pas respecter: convenances, loi*) to flout

**bravo** [bʀavo] I. *interj* bravo! II. *m* cheer

**bravoure** [bʀavuʀ] *f* bravery

**break** [bʀɛk] *m* ① AUTO station wagon ② (*pause*) a. SPORT break

**brebis** [bʀǝbi] *f* ewe

**brèche** [bʀɛʃ] *f* (*dans une clôture, un mur*) gap; (*dans une coque*) hole; (*sur une lame*) notch; MIL (*sur le front*) breach

**bredouille** [bʀǝduj] *adj* (*sans rien, sans succès*) empty-handed

**bredouiller** [brəduje] <1> vt ~ **qc** to stammer sth out

**bref, brève** [brɛf, brɛv] **I.** adj brief; (concis) short; **soyez ~!** get on with it!; **d'un ton ~** sharply **II.** adv **en ~** in short; **enfin ~** in short

**Brésil** [brezil] m **le ~** Brazil

**brésilien(ne)** [breziljɛ̃, jɛn] adj Brazilian

**Brésilien(ne)** [breziljɛ̃, jɛn] m(f) Brazilian

**Bretagne** [brətaɲ] f **la ~** Brittany

**bretelle** [brətɛl] f ① COUT (de soutien-gorge) strap; (de sac) (shoulder) strap ② pl (de pantalon) suspenders ③ (bifurcation d'autoroute) on/off ramp; **~ d'accès** access road

**breton** [brətɔ̃] m Breton; v.a. **français**

**breton(ne)** [brətɔ̃, ɔn] adj Breton

**Breton(ne)** [brətɔ̃, -ɔn] m(f) Breton

**breuvage** [brœvaʒ] m ① (boisson) brew; péj potion ② Québec (boisson non alcoolisée) beverage

**brevet** [brəvɛ] m ① (diplôme) diploma ② (certificat) certificate; **~ d'invention** patent; **~ de pilot** pilot's license

**brevetable** [brəvətabl] adj patentable

**breveter** [brəv(ə)te] <3> vt to patent

**bribe** [brib] f souvent pl, fig (de conversation) fragment

**bric-à-brac** [brikabrak] m inv odds and ends; (d'un antiquaire) bric-a-brac

**bricolage** [brikɔlaʒ] m ① (travail d'amateur) do-it-yourself jobs ② (mauvais travail) makeshift job

**bricole** [brikɔl] f ① (objet de peu de valeur) trifle ② (petit événement) hassle

**bricoler** [brikɔle] <1> **I.** vi ① (effectuer des petits travaux) to do odd jobs; **savoir ~** to be a handyman ② péj (faire du mauvais travail) to rig a job ③ (ne pas avoir de travail fixe) to go from one job to the next **II.** vt ① (construire, installer) **~ qc** to fix sth up ② (réparer tant bien que mal) to fix

**bricoleur, -euse** [brikɔlœr, -øz] **I.** adj do-it-yourself **II.** m, f handyman, handywoman m, f

**bride** [brid] f ① (pièce de harnais) bridle ② TECH strap

**bridé(e)** [bride] adj **des yeux ~s** slanted eyes

**bridge** [bridʒ] m JEUX, MED bridge

**brièvement** [brijɛvmã] adv ① (de manière succincte) concisely ② (pour peu de temps) briefly

**brièveté** [brijɛvte] f ① (courte longueur) briefness ② (courte durée) brevity

**brigade** [brigad] f MIL brigade; **~ antidrogue** drug squad

**brigadier** [brigadje] m (de gendarmerie) sergeant; (d'artillerie, de cavalerie) corporal

**briguer** [brige] <1> vt (solliciter: emploi) to seek

**brillamment** [brijamã] adv brilliantly

**brillant** [brijã] m (diamant) brilliant

**brillant(e)** [brijã, jãt] adj ① (étincelant: meubles, yeux, cheveux) shining; (couleurs) brilliant; (plan d'eau) sparkling ② (qui a de l'allure) brilliant; (victoire) dazzling

**briller** [brije] <1> vi ① (rayonner) to shine; (diamant) to sparkle ② (se mettre en valeur) **~ par qc** to shine by sth

**brimade** [brimad] f bullying

**brimer** [brime] <1> vt ① (faire subir des vexations) to bully; (désavantager) to frustrate

**brin** [brɛ̃] m (mince tige) blade; **~ de paille** wisp of straw; **~ de muguet** sprig of lily of the valley

**bringue** [brɛ̃g] f ① inf (fête) binge ② Suisse (querelle) brawl

**brio** [brijo] m brio

**brioche** [brijɔʃ] f brioche

**brique¹** [brik] **I.** f ① (matériau) brick; **maison de ~** brick house ② (matière ayant cette forme) **~ de savon** bar of soap **II.** app inv (couleur) brick red

**brique®²** [brik] f (emballage) carton

**briquet** [brikɛ] m (cigarette) lighter

**brise** [briz] f breeze

**brise-glace** [brizglas] m inv icebreaker

**briser** [brize] <1> **I.** vt ① (casser) to break ② (mater: révolte) to quell; (grè-

**B**

*ve, blocus*) to break ❸ (*anéantir: espoir, illusions*) to shatter; (*amitié*) to break up; (*forces, volonté, silence*) to break ❹ (*fatiguer: voyage*) to exhaust ❺ (*interrompre: conversation*) to interrupt; (*monotonie, ennui, silence*) to break ▸ ~ **le cœur à qn** to break sb's heart; **être brisé** *Québec* (*être en panne*) to be broken II. *vpr* ❶ (*se casser*) **se ~** (*vitre, porcelaine*) to break ❷ (*échouer*) **se ~ contre/sur qc** (*résistance, assauts*) to break down against/on sth; (*vagues*) to break against/on sth

**britannique** [bʀitanik] *adj* British

**Britannique** [bʀitanik] I. *mf* British person II. *adj* **les Îles ~s** the British Isles

**brocante** [bʀɔkɑ̃t] *f* ❶ (*boutique*) secondhand store ❷ (*foire*) flea market

**brocanteur, -euse** [bʀɔkɑ̃tœʀ, -øz] *m, f* secondhand dealer

**broche** [bʀɔʃ] *f* ❶ (*bijou*) brooch ❷ CULIN skewer ❸ MED pin

**brochet** [bʀɔʃɛ] *m* pike

**brochette** [bʀɔʃɛt] *f* ❶ CULIN skewer ❷ *iron* (*groupe de personnes*) bunch

**brochure** [bʀɔʃyʀ] *f* brochure

**brocoli** [bʀɔkɔli] *m* broccoli

**broder** [bʀɔde] <1> *vt, vi* COUT to embroider

**broderie** [bʀɔdʀi] *f* embroidery

**bronchite** [bʀɔ̃ʃit] *f* MED bronchitis

**bronzage** [bʀɔ̃zaʒ] *m* tan

**bronze** [bʀɔ̃z] *m* bronze

**bronzé(e)** [bʀɔ̃ze] *adj* tanned

**bronzer** [bʀɔ̃ze] <1> I. *vi* to tan II. *vpr* to sunbathe

**brosse** [bʀɔs] *f* ❶ (*ustensile, pinceau*) brush; **~ à cheveux** hairbrush; **~ à dents** toothbrush ❷ (*coupe de cheveux*) crewcut

**brosser** [bʀɔse] <1> I. *vt* ❶ (*épousseter*) to brush ❷ (*esquisser: situation, portrait*) to paint II. *vpr* **se ~** to brush one's clothes; **se ~ les cheveux/les dents** to brush one's hair/teeth

**brouette** [bʀuɛt] *f* wheelbarrow

**brouhaha** [bʀuaa] *m* hubbub

**brouillard** [bʀujaʀ] *m* (*épais*) fog, smog

**brouille** [bʀuj] *f* argument, quarrel

**brouillé(e)** [bʀuje] *adj* ❶ (*fâché*) **être ~ avec qn** to be on bad terms with sb ❷ (*atteint*) **avoir le teint ~** to have a muddy complexion

**brouiller** [bʀuje] <1> I. *vt* ❶ (*rendre trouble*) to muddle ❷ (*embrouiller*) **~ l'esprit à qn** to confuse sb ❸ (*rendre inintelligible: émission, émetteur*) to scramble II. *vpr* (*se fâcher*) **se ~ avec qn** to fall out with sb

**brouillon** [bʀujɔ̃] *m* rough copy; (*pour une lettre, un discours*) (rough) draft

**brouillon(ne)** [bʀujɔ̃, jɔn] *adj* ❶ (*désordonné: élève*) careless ❷ (*peu clair*) muddled

**broussaille** [bʀusɑj] *f* undergrowth

**brouter** [bʀute] <1> I. *vt* **~ de l'herbe** to graze grass; (*cervidés*) to browse grass II. *vi* to graze; (*cervidés*) to browse

**broyer** [bʀwaje] <6> *vt* (*écraser, détruire: aliments, ordures*) to crush; (*céréales*) to grind

**Bruges** [bʀyʒ] Bruges

**bruissement** [bʀɥismɑ̃] *m* (*des feuilles, du vent, du papier*) rustling; (*d'un ruisseau*) murmur

**bruit** [bʀɥi] *m* ❶ (*son*) noise; (*de vaisselle*) clatter; (*de ferraille*) rattle ❷ (*vacarme*) racket ❸ (*rumeur*) rumor; **le ~ court que** there's a rumor going around that ▸ **faire du ~** to cause a sensation

**bruitage** [bʀɥitaʒ] *m* sound effects

**brûlant(e)** [bʀylɑ̃, ɑ̃t] *adj* ❶ (*très chaud*) burning; (*liquide*) boiling ❷ (*passionné*) passionate; (*regard*) fiery ❸ (*délicat: sujet, question*) burning

**brûlé** [bʀyle] *m* **ça sent le ~** there's a smell of burning

**brûlé(e)** [bʀyle] *adj* (*a. plat*) burnt

**brûler** [bʀyle] <1> I. *vi* ❶ (*se consumer*) *a.* CULIN to burn ❷ (*être très chaud*) to be burning ❸ (*être irrité: bouche, gorge, yeux*) to burn ❹ (*être dévoré*) **~ de** +*infin* to be longing to +*infin* ❺ (*être proche du but*) **tu brûles!** you're getting hot! II. *vt* ❶ (*détruire par le feu: forêt*) to burn; **~ une maison** to burn down a house ❷ (*pour* *chauffer, éclairer: bois, allumette*) to burn ❸ (*endommager*) ~ **un tissu** (*bougie, cigarette, fer à repasser*) to burn some fabric ❹ (*ne pas respecter: stop, signal*) to run; (*étape*) to skip ❺ (*consommer*) a. CULIN to burn III. *vpr* **se** ~ to burn oneself; **se** ~ **les doigts** to burn one's fingers

**brûlure** [bʀylyʀ] *f* (*blessure, plaie, tache*) burn

**brume** [bʀym] *f* (*brouillard*) mist

**brumeux, -euse** [bʀymø, -øz] *adj* ❶ MÉTÉO misty ❷ (*confus*) hazy

**brumisateur**® [bʀymizatœʀ] *m* spray

**brun** [bʀœ̃] *m* (*couleur*) brown

**brun(e)** [bʀœ̃, bʀyn] I. *adj* ❶ (*opp: blond: cheveux, peau, tabac*) dark; **bière** ~ **e** dark ale; **être** ~ to have dark hair ❷ (*bronzé*) tanned II. *m(f)* man with dark hair, brunette *f*

**brunante** [bʀynãt] *f* Québec (*crépuscule*) dusk

**brune** [bʀyn] I. *adj v.* **brun** II. *f* ❶ (*cigarette*) cigarette made from dark tobacco ❷ (*bière*) dark ale

**brunir** [bʀyniʀ] <8> I. *vi* to tan; (*cheveux*) to go darker II. *vt* to tan; (*boiserie*) to polish

**brushing**® [bʀœʃiŋ] *m* blow-dry

**brusque** [bʀysk] *adj* ❶ (*soudain*) abrupt ❷ (*sec: personne, ton, manières*) blunt; (*geste*) abrupt

**brusquer** [bʀyske] <1> *vt* to rush

**brut(e)** [bʀyt] *adj* ❶ (*naturel*) raw, crude; (*champagne*) (extra) dry, brut; (*diamant*) uncut, rough; (*toile*) unbleached ❷ *fig* (*fait*) hard; (*idée*) raw ❸ ÉCON gross

**brutal(e)** [bʀytal, -o] <-aux> *adj* ❶ (*violent*) brutal; (*manières*) rough; (*instinct*) savage ❷ (*qui choque: langage, réponse*) blunt; (*réalisme, vérité*) stark ❸ (*soudain: choc, mort*) sudden; (*coup, décision*) brutal

**brutalement** [bʀytalmã] *adv* ❶ (*violemment*) violently ❷ (*sans ménagement*) brutally ❸ (*soudainement*) suddenly

**brutaliser** [bʀytalize] <1> *vt* to bully

**brutalité** [bʀytalite] *f* ❶ *sans pl* (*violence*) violence; (*de paroles, d'un jeu*) brutality ❷ *sans pl* (*soudaineté*) suddenness

**brute** [bʀyt] *f* ❶ (*violent*) brute ❷ (*rustre*) oaf

**Bruxelles** [bʀy(k)sɛl] Brussels

**bruyamment** [bʀyjamã, bʀyijamã] *adv* (*avec bruit*) noisily

**bruyant(e)** [bʀyjã, bʀyijã, jãt] *adj* (*a. réunion, foule*) noisy

**bruyère** [bʀyjɛʀ, bʀyijɛʀ] *f* heather

**bu(e)** [by] *part passé de* **boire**

**buanderie** [byɑ̃dʀi] *f* ❶ (*dans une maison*) laundry (room) ❷ Québec (*blanchisserie*) laundry

**bûche** [byʃ] *f* ❶ (*bois*) log ❷ CULIN ~ **de Noël** Yule log

**bûcheron(ne)** [byʃʀɔ̃, ɔn] *m(f)* lumberjack

**budget** [bydʒɛ] *m* FIN budget

**budgétaire** [bydʒetɛʀ] *adj* budgetary

**buée** [bye] *f* **se couvrir de** ~ to mist up

**buffet** [byfɛ] *m* ❶ CULIN buffet ❷ (*meuble*) ~ **de cuisine** kitchen cabinet

**buffle** [byfl] *m* buffalo

**bug** [bœg] *m* INFORM bug

**buisson** [bɥisɔ̃] *m* bush

**bulbe** [bylb] *m* BOT, ANAT bulb

**bulle** [byl] *f* ❶ PHYS, MÉD bubble ❷ (*dans une bande dessinée*) speech bubble

**bulletin** [byltɛ̃] *m* ❶ (*communiqué, rubrique*) bulletin; ~ **d'information** news bulletin ❷ POL ~ **de vote** ballot ❸ ÉCOLE ~ **scolaire** report card ❹ (*certificat*) certificate; ~ **de paye** paycheck stub

**buraliste** [byʀalist] *mf* tobacconist

**bureau** [byʀo] <x> *m* ❶ (*meuble*) desk ❷ (*pièce, lieu de travail*) office ❸ (*service*) center ❹ (*comité*) ~ **exécutif** executive committee ❺ (*établissement réservé au public*) ~ **de change** currency exchange; ~ **de poste** post office; ~ **de tabac** tobacco shop; ~ **de vote** polling place ❻ INFORM **ordinateur de** ~ desktop

**bureaucratique** [byʀokʀatik] *adj* bureaucratic

**bureautique®** [byʀotik] *f* office automation

**burin** [byʀɛ̃] *m* ❶ (*outil*) burin, graver ❷ (*ciseau*) chisel

**bus¹** [bys] *m abr de* **autobus** bus

**bus²** [bys] *m* INFORM ~ **de données** data bus

**bus³** [by] *passé simple de* **boire**

**buste** [byst] *m* ❶ (*torse*) chest ❷ (*poitrine de femme, sculpture*) bust

**bustier** [bystje] *m* ❶ (*sous-vêtement*) strapless bra ❷ (*vêtement*) bustier

**but** [by(t)] *m* ❶ (*destination*) *a.* SPORT goal ❷ (*objectif*) aim

**butane** [bytan] *m* butane

**buter** [byte] <1> I. *vi* ~ **contre qc** ❶ (*heurter*) to stumble over sth ❷ (*faire face à une difficulté*) to come up against sth II. *vt* ~ **qn** *inf* (*tuer*) to knock sb off III. *vpr* **se** ~ **sur qc** to come up against sth

**butin** [bytɛ̃] *m* spoils

**butte** [byt] *f* hill

**buvable** [byvabl] *adj* (*potable*) drinkable

**buvais** [byvɛ] *imparf de* **boire**

**buvant** [byvɑ̃] *part prés de* **boire**

**buvard** [byvaʀ] *m* blotter

**buvette** [byvɛt] *f* (*local*) café; (*en plein air*) refreshment stand

**buveur, -euse** [byvœʀ, -øz] *m, f* ❶ (*alcoolique*) drinker ❷ (*consommateur: d'un restaurant*) customer

**buvez** [byve], **buvons** [byvɔ̃] *indic prés et impératif de* **boire**

**byte** [bajt] *m* INFORM byte

# Cc

**C, c** [se] *m inv* C, c; **c cédille** c cedilla; ~ **comme Célestin** (*au téléphone*) c as in Charlie

**c'** <*devant "a"* ç> *pron dém v.* **ce**

**ça** [sa] *pron dém* ❶ *inf* (*pour désigner ou renforcer*) that; **qu'est-ce que c'est que** ~? what's that?; **ah** ~ **non!** definitely not!; ~ **est** *Belgique* (*c'est*) it's; *v.a.* **cela** ❷ *inf* (*répétitif*) **les haricots? si, j'aime** ~ beans? yes, I do like them; **le fer,** ~ **rouille** iron simply rusts ❸ *péj* (*personne*) **et** ~ **vote!** and people like that vote! ▶~ **par exemple!**, ~ **alors!** (my) goodness!; **c'est** ~ that's right; **c'est comme** ~ that's how it is; ~ **va?** how are things?; **pas de** ~! that's out of the question!; *v.a.* **cela**

**çà** [sa] ~ **et là** here and there

**cabane** [kaban] *f* ❶ (*abri*) hut; *péj* shack ❷ *inf* (*prison*) clink ❸ *Québec* maple syrup shed ❹ *Suisse* (*refuge de haute montagne*) (mountain) refuge

**cabaret** [kabaʀɛ] *m* ❶ (*boîte de nuit*) nightclub ❷ *Québec* (*plateau*) tray

**cabillaud** [kabijo] *m* cod

**cabine** [kabin] *f* ❶ (*poste de commande: d'un camion*) cab; (*d'un avion, véhicule spatial*) cockpit ❷ (*petit local*) cabin; ~ **téléphonique** (tele)phone booth; ~ **d'essayage** fitting room

**cabinet** [kabinɛ] *m* ❶ *pl* (*toilettes*) toilet ❷ (*bureau: d'un médecin, d'un avocat*) office ❸ POL cabinet ❹ (*endroit isolé*) ~ **de toilette** bathroom

**câble** [kɑbl] *m* ❶ (*corde*) cable; ~ **du téléphone** telephone line ❷ TV cable television

**câbler** [kɑble] <1> *vt* ❶ (*transmettre*) to cable ❷ TV to link up to the cable network

**cabosser** [kabɔse] <1> *vt* to dent

**caca** [kaka] *m enfantin, inf* **faire** ~ to go number two

**cacahouète**, **cacahuète** [kakawɛt] *f* peanut

**cacao** [kakao] *m* cocoa

**cache** [kaʃ] *m* ❶ PHOT, CINE mask; **mettre un ~ sur qc** mask sth ❷ INFORM cache; **sauvegarder qc en ~** cache sth

**cache-cache** [kaʃkaʃ] *m inv* hide-and-seek

**cachemire** [kaʃmir] *m* cashmere

**cache-nez** [kaʃne] *m inv* scarf

**cache-pot** [kaʃpo] <cache-pots> *m* flowerpot holder

**cacher¹** [kaʃe] <1> I. *vt* to hide; **~ qc à qn** to hide sth from sb II. *vpr* ❶ (*se dissimuler*) **se ~** to hide ❷ (*tenir secret*) **ne pas se ~ de qc** to make no secret of sth

**cacher²** [kaʃɛr] *adj v.* casher

**cachet** [kaʃɛ] *m* ❶ MED tablet ❷ (*tampon*) stamp ❸ (*rétribution*) fee

**cachette** [kaʃɛt] *f* hiding place ►**en ~** on the sly

**cachot** [kaʃo] *m* (*cellule*) dungeon

**cachottier, -ière** [kaʃɔtje, -jɛr] I. *adj* secretive II. *m, f* secretive person

**cacophonie** [kakɔfɔni] *f* cacophony

**cactus** [kaktys] *m* cactus

**c.-à-d.** *abr de* **c'est-à-dire** i.e.

**cadastre** [kadastr] *m* (*registre*) land register

**cadavre** [kadavr] *m* (*d'une personne*) corpse; (*d'un animal*) carcass

**cadeau** [kado] <x> *m* present; **faire ~ de qc à qn** to give sth as a present to sb; **en ~** as a present

**cadenas** [kadna] *m* padlock

**cadence** [kadãs] *f* ❶ (*rythme*) rhythm; **en ~** in time ❷ (*vitesse*) rate

**cadet(te)** [kadɛ, ɛt] I. *adj* ❶ (*le plus jeune*) youngest ❷ (*plus jeune que qn*) younger II. *m(f)* ❶ (*dernier-né*) youngest child ❷ (*plus jeune que qn*) younger child; **c'est ma ~te** that's my younger sister ❸ SPORT *15–17 year-old* athlete ❹ MIL, HIST cadet

**cadran** [kadrã] *m* ❶ (*affichage*) dial; (*d'un baromètre*) face, **~ solaire** sundial ❷ *Québec*, *inf* (*réveil*) alarm (clock)

**cadre** [kadr] I. *m* ❶ (*encadrement*) a. INFORM frame ❷ (*environnement*) surroundings *pl;* **dans un ~ de verdure** in a rural setting ❸ (*limites*) scope; **dans le ~ de qc** within the context of sth II. *mf* executive; **~ supérieur** senior manager

**cafard** [kafar] *m* ❶ (*insecte*) cockroach ❷ (*spleen*) depression; **avoir le ~** to be down in the dumps

**café** [kafe] *m* ❶ (*boisson*) coffee; **~ crème** coffee with milk; **~ liégeois** coffee ice cream; **~ au lait** café au lait ❷ (*établissement*) café; **~ avec terrasse** street café ❸ (*plante*) coffee bush; **~ en grains** coffee beans ❹ *Suisse* (*dîner*) **un ~ complet** dinner

**caféine** [kafein] *f* caffeine

**café-tabac** [kafetaba] <cafés-tabacs> *m: café and tobacco shop in one*

**cafétéria** [kafeterja] *f* cafeteria

**cafetière** [kaftjɛr] *f* coffee pot; **~ électrique** coffee machine

**cage** [kaʒ] *f* ❶ (*pour enfermer*) cage; **~ à lapin** (rabbit) hutch ❷ SPORT goal ❸ ANAT **~ thoracique** rib cage ❹ TECH **~ d'ascenseur** elevator shaft; **~ d'escalier** stairwell

**cageot** [kaʒo] *m* ❶ (*emballage*) crate ❷ *inf* (*fille*) dog

**cahier** [kaje] *m* ❶ ECOLE notebook; **~ d'exercices** workbook; **~ de textes** homework notebook ❷ TYP section

**caille** [kaj] *f* (*oiseau*) quail

**cailler** [kaje] <1> *vi* ❶ (*coaguler: lait*) to curdle; (*sang*) to coagulate ❷ *inf* (*avoir froid*) to be freezing

**caillou** [kaju] <x> *m* (*pierre*) pebble

**caisse** [kɛs] *f* ❶ (*boîte*) box ❷ FIN (*dans un magasin*) cashier; (*dans un supermarché*) checkout; (*dans une banque*) teller's window; **~ enregistreuse** cash register; **~ noire** slush fund; **tenir la ~** to be the cashier; **passer à la ~** to go to the cashier; **~ d'épargne** savings bank ❸ (*organisme de gestion*) fund; **~ d'assurance maladie** medical insurance company ❹ (*boîtier d'une horloge*) casing; (*d'un tambour*) sound box; (*d'une voiture*) body; **grosse ~** bass drum ❺ *inf* (*voiture*) car

**caissier, -ière** [kesje, -jɛr] *m, f* cashier

**C**

**cajoler** [kaʒɔle] <1> vt (*câliner*) to cuddle

**calamar** [kalamaʀ] m v. **calmar**

**calamité** [kalamite] f calamity

**calanque** [kalɑ̃k] f rocky inlet

**calcaire** [kalkɛʀ] I. adj chalky; (*roche, relief*) limestone II. m GEO limestone

**calciné(e)** [kalsine] adj charred

**calcium** [kalsjɔm] m calcium

**calcul¹** [kalkyl] m ❶ (*opération*) calculation; ~ **mental** mental arithmetic ❷ (*arithmétique*) ~ **algébrique** algebra ❸ pl (*estimation*) calculations

**calcul²** [kalkyl] m MED stone

**calculatrice** [kalkylatʀis] f calculator

**calculer** [kalkyle] <1> I. vi ❶ MATH ~ **mentalement** to calculate in one's head ❷ (*compter ses sous*) to economize II. vt ❶ (*déterminer par le calcul*) to calculate ❷ (*évaluer, prévoir: risque*) to gauge; (*chances*) to weigh up ❸ (*étudier: attitude*) to study; (*geste*) to calculate

**calculette** [kalkylɛt] f pocket calculator

**cale¹** [kal] f NAUT hold; **être/mettre en ~ sèche** to be in/put into dry dock

**cale²** [kal] f (*coin*) wedge

**caleçon** [kalsɔ̃] m ❶ (*pour homme*) boxer shorts pl; ~ **de bain** swimming trunks pl; **des ~s longs** long johns pl ❷ (*pour femme*) leggings pl

**calendrier** [kalɑ̃dʀije] m ❶ (*almanach*) calendar ❷ (*programme*) schedule

**calepin** [kalpɛ̃] m ❶ notebook ❷ *Belgique* (*cartable porté à la main*) briefcase; (*sur le dos*) satchel

**caler** [kale] <1> I. vi ❶ AUTO to stall ❷ inf (*être rassasié*) to be full II. vt ❶ (*fixer avec une cale*) to wedge; (*roue*) to chock ❷ AUTO to stall

**calfeutrer** [kalføtʀe] <1> I. vt to stop up II. vpr se ~ to shut oneself away; (*rester au chaud*) to make oneself cozy

**calibre** [kalibʀ] m a. fig caliber; (*des fruits, œufs*) grade

**câlin** [kalɛ̃] m cuddle

**câlin(e)** [kalɛ̃, in] adj ❶ (*qui aime les caresses*) cuddly ❷ (*caressant*) tender

**câliner** [kaline] <1> vt ~ **qn** to cuddle sb

**calmant(e)** [kalmɑ̃, ɑ̃t] I. adj ❶ (*tranquillisant*) tranquilizing ❷ (*antidouleur*) painkilling II. m ❶ (*tranquillisant*) tranquilizer ❷ (*antidouleur*) painkiller

**calmar** [kalmaʀ] m ❶ ZOOL squid ❷ CULIN calamari pl

**calme** [kalm] I. adj calm; (*lieu*) quiet II. m ❶ (*sérénité*) calmness; **rester ~** to remain calm; **du ~!** calm down! ❷ (*tranquillité*) quietness; **du ~!** quiet! ❸ METEO calm

**calmement** [kalməmɑ̃] adv calmly

**calmer** [kalme] <1> I. vt ❶ (*apaiser: personne, esprits*) to calm (down); (*discussion*) to tone down ❷ (*soulager: douleur*) to soothe; (*colère, nerfs*) to calm; (*fièvre*) to bring down; (*impatience*) to curb; **~ la faim de qn** to take the edge off sb's hunger II. vpr se ~ to calm down; (*discussion*) to quiet down; (*tempête*) to die down; (*crainte*) to subside

**calomnie** [kalɔmni] f calumny

**calorie** [kalɔʀi] f calorie

**calvaire** [kalvɛʀ] m ❶ (*épreuve*) ordeal ❷ (*croix*) wayside cross ❸ (*peinture*) Calvary

**calvitie** [kalvisi] f (*tonsure*) bald spot

**camarade** [kamaʀad] mf ❶ (*collègue*) colleague; ~ **d'études** fellow student ❷ POL comrade

**camaraderie** [kamaʀadʀi] f companionship

**Camargue** [kamaʀg] f **la ~** the Camargue

**Cambodge** [kɑ̃bɔdʒ] m **le ~** Cambodia

**cambouis** [kɑ̃bwi] m dirty grease

**cambriolage** [kɑ̃bʀijɔlaʒ] m burglary

**cambrioler** [kɑ̃bʀijɔle] <1> vt ~ **qc** to burglarize

**cambrioleur, -euse** [kɑ̃bʀijɔlœʀ, -øz] m, f burglar

**camélia** [kamelja] m camellia

**camembert** [kamɑ̃bɛʀ] m (*fromage*) Camembert

**caméra** [kameʀa] f camera

**caméraman** [kameraman, -mɛn] <s o -men> *m* cameraman

**caméscope** [kameskɔp] *m* camcorder

**camion** [kamjɔ̃] *m* truck

**camionnette** [kamjɔnɛt] *f* van, pickup (truck)

**camionneur** [kamjɔnœʀ] *m* trucker

**camomille** [kamɔmij] *f* ① (*fleur*) chamomile ② (*tisane*) chamomile tea

**camoufler** [kamufle] <1> *vt* ① MIL to camouflage ② (*tenir secret*) to conceal

**camp** [kɑ̃] *m* ① camp ② Québec (*chalet, villa*) ~ (**d'été**) cottage ▶ **foutre** le ~ *inf* to take off; **fiche-moi** le ~! *inf* beat it!

**campagnard(e)** [kɑ̃paɲaʀ, aʀd] I. *adj* (*vie*) country; (*manières*) rustic II. *m(f)* countryman, countrywoman *m, f*

**campagne** [kɑ̃paɲ] *f* ① (*opp: ville*) country; **à la** ~ in the country; **en pleine** ~ in the countryside ② (*paysage*) countryside ③ *a.* MIL campaign

**campement** [kɑ̃pmɑ̃] *m* ① (*résultat*) camp ② (*action*) camping

**camper** [kɑ̃pe] <1> *vi* to camp

**campeur, -euse** [kɑ̃pœʀ, -øz] *m, f* camper

**camping** [kɑ̃piŋ] *m* ① (*action de camper*) camping; **faire du** ~ to go camping ② (*lieu*) (**terrain de**) ~ campsite, campground

**camping-car** [kɑ̃piŋkaʀ] <camping-cars> *m* motor home, RV

**camping-gaz®** [kɑ̃piŋgaz] *m inv* camping stove

**Canada** [kanada] *m* le ~ Canada

**Canadair®** [kanadɛʀ] *m* firefighting aircraft

**canadien(ne)** [kanadjɛ̃, jɛn] *adj* Canadian

**Canadien(ne)** [kanadjɛ̃, jɛn] *m(f)* Canadian

**canadienne** [kanadjɛn] *f* ① (*veste*) sheepskin-lined jacket ② (*tente*) ridge tent

**canaille** [kanɑj] I. *adj* (*air, manière*) coarse II. *f a.* iron rascal

**canal** [kanal, -o] <-aux> *m* ① canal

② Québec (*chaîne*) ~ **de télévision** television channel

**canalisation** [kanalizasjɔ̃] *f* ① (*réseau*) mains *pl* ② (*tuyau*) pipe

**canaliser** [kanalize] <1> *vt* (*centraliser: énergie, foule*) to channel

**canapé** [kanape] *m* ① (*meuble*) sofa; ~ **convertible** sofa bed ② CULIN canapé

**canapé-lit** [kanapeli] <canapés-lits> *m* sofa bed

**canard** [kanaʀ] *m* ① (*oiseau*) duck ② (*opp: cane*) drake ③ *inf* (*journal*) rag

**canari** [kanaʀi] *m* canary

**cancer** [kɑ̃sɛʀ] *m* cancer

**Cancer** [kɑ̃sɛʀ] *m* Cancer; *v.a.* **Balance**

**cancéreux, -euse** [kɑ̃seʀø, -øz] *adj* cancerous

**cancre** [kɑ̃kʀ] *m inf* dunce

**candidat(e)** [kɑ̃dida, at] *m(f)* ① (*à un examen, aux élections*) candidate ② (*à un poste*) applicant

**candidature** [kɑ̃didatyʀ] *f* ① (*aux élections*) candidacy; **poser sa** ~ **aux élections** to stand in an election ② (*à un poste, un jeu*) application; **poser sa** ~ **à un poste** to apply for a job

**canette** [kanɛt] *f* (*bouteille*) small bottle

**canevas** [kanva] *m* (*toile*) canvas

**caniche** [kaniʃ] *m* poodle

**canicule** [kanikyl] *f* ① (*période*) dog days ② (*chaleur*) scorching heat

**canif** [kanif] *m* penknife

**caniveau** [kanivo] <x> *m* gutter

**canne** [kan] *f* ① (*bâton*) (walking) stick ② (*tige*) ~ **à sucre** sugar cane ③ (*gaule*) ~ **à pêche** fishing rod

**cannelle** [kanɛl] *f* cinnamon

**cannibale** [kanibal] *adj, mf* cannibal

**canoë** [kanɔe] *m* ① (*embarcation*) canoe ② (*sport*) canoeing

**canoë-kayak** [kanɔekajak] <canoës-kayaks> *m* canoeing

**canon** [kanɔ̃] I. *adj inv, inf* **super** ~ fantastic II. *m* ① (*arme*) gun; HIST cannon ② (*tube: d'un fusil*) barrel ③ (*machine*) ~ **à neige** snow cannon

**canot** [kano] *m* ① (*small*) boat; ~ **pneumatique/de sauvetage** rubber dinghy/lifeboat ② Québec (*canoë*) canoe

**cantatrice** [kãtatʀis] *f* opera singer

**cantine** [kãtin] *f* canteen

**canton** [kãtɔ̃] *m* ❶ (*en France*) ≈ district ❷ (*en Suisse*) canton

**cantonner** [kãtɔne] <1> *vt* (*reléguer*) ~ **qn dans qc** to confine sb to sth

**C.A.O.** [seao] *abr de* **conception assistée par ordinateur** CAD

**caoutchouc** [kautʃu] *m* ❶ (*matière*) rubber ❷ (*élastique*) rubber band ❸ (*plante*) rubber plant

**cap** [kap] *m* ❶ (*pointe de terre*) cape ❷ (*direction*) course

**C.A.P.** [seape] *m abr de* **certificat d'aptitude professionnelle** *vocational training certificate*

**capable** [kapabl] *adj* capable

**capacité** [kapasite] *f* ❶ (*contenance, puissance*) capacity *a.* INFORM capacity ❷ (*faculté*) ability

**cape** [kap] *f* (*vêtement*) cape

**capillaire** [kapilɛʀ] *adj* ❶ (*pour les cheveux*) **lotion** ~ hair lotion ❷ ANAT **vaisseau** ~ capillary vessel

**capitaine** [kapitɛn] *m* ❶ MIL, NAUT, SPORT captain; ~ **des pompiers** fire chief ❷ AVIAT flight captain

**capital** [kapital, -o] <-aux> *m* ❶ (*somme d'argent*) capital ❷ *pl* FIN capital ❸ (*richesse*) ~ **intellectuel** intellectual wealth

**capital(e)** [kapital, -o] <-aux> *adj* fundamental

**capitale** [kapital] *f* (*ville*) capital (city)

**capitalisme** [kapitalism] *m* capitalism

**capitulation** [kapitylasjɔ̃] *f a.* MIL capitulation

**capituler** [kapityle] <1> *vi* to capitulate

**caporal** [kapɔʀal, -o] <-aux> *m* corporal

**capot** [kapo] *m* AUTO hood

**capote** [kapɔt] *f* ❶ AUTO (*d'une voiture*) top ❷ *inf* (*préservatif*) ~ (**anglaise**) rubber

**câpre** [kɑpʀ] *f* caper

**caprice** [kapʀis] *m* ❶ (*fantaisie*) whim ❷ (*amourette*) passing fancy ❸ *pl* (*changement*) vagaries ❹ (*exigence*

*d'un enfant*) **faire un** ~ to throw a tantrum

**capricieux, -euse** [kapʀisjø, -jøz] *adj* ❶ (*instable: personne*) capricious ❷ (*irrégulier: chose*) unreliable; (*temps*) unpredictable

**Capricorne** [kapʀikɔʀn] *m* Capricorn; *v.a.* **Balance**

**capsule** [kapsyl] *f* ❶ (*bouchon: d'une bouteille*) cap ❷ (*médicament*) capsule

**capter** [kapte] <1> *vt* ❶ (*canaliser: source*) to harness; (*énergie*) to capture ❷ (*recevoir: émission, message*) to get ❸ (*chercher à obtenir*) ~ **l'attention de qn** to catch sb's attention

**captivant(e)** [kaptivã, ãt] *adj* captivating

**captiver** [kaptive] <1> *vt* to captivate

**captivité** [kaptivite] *f* captivity

**capturer** [kaptyʀe] <1> *vt* to capture

**capuche** [kapyʃ] *f* hood

**capuchon** [kapyʃɔ̃] *m* ❶ (*capuche*) hood ❷ (*bouchon*) cap

**capucine** [kapysin] *f* BOT nasturtium

**car¹** [kaʀ] *m* bus; ~ **de ramassage scolaire** school bus

**car²** [kaʀ] *conj* because, for

**carabine** [kaʀabin] *f* rifle

**caractère** [kaʀaktɛʀ] *m* ❶ (*tempérament, nature*) nature; **avoir un** ~ **de cochon** *inf* to have a foul temper ❷ (*fermeté, personne, symbole*) character; **en** ~**s gras/italiques** in bold type/italics

**caractériel(le)** [kaʀakteʀjɛl] *adj* (*personne*) emotionally disturbed

**caractériser** [kaʀakteʀize] <1> **I.** *vt* ❶ (*être typique de qn*) to be characteristic of sb ❷ (*définir*) to characterize **II.** *vpr* **se** ~ **par qc** to be characterized by sth

**caractéristique** [kaʀakteʀistik] **I.** *adj* **être** ~ **de qn/qc** to be characteristic of sb/sth **II.** *f* characteristic; ~**s techniques** design features

**carafe** [kaʀaf] *f* carafe

**Caraïbes** [kaʀaib] *fpl* **les** ~ the Caribbean

**carambolage** [kaʀãbɔlaʒ] *m* pileup

**caramel** [kaʁamɛl] *m* caramel

**caraméliser** [kaʁamelize] <1> **I.** *vt* ❶ (*recouvrir*) to coat with caramel ❷ (*cuire: sucre*) to caramelize **II.** *vi, vpr* to caramelize

**carapace** [kaʁapas] *f* ❶ (*d'un crabe, d'une tortue*) shell ❷ (*protection morale*) shield

**caravane** [kaʁavan] *f* trailer

**carburant** [kaʁbyʁɑ̃] *m* fuel

**carburateur** [kaʁbyʁatœʁ] *m* carburetor

**carcasse** [kaʁkas] *f* ❶ (*squelette*) carcass ❷ (*charpente: d'un bateau*) skeleton; (*d'un édifice*) frame

**cardiaque** [kaʁdjak] *adj* **malaise ~** heart trouble

**cardinal** [kaʁdinal, -o] <-aux> *m* cardinal

**cardinal(e)** [kaʁdinal, -o] <-aux> *adj* MATH cardinal

**cardiologue** [kaʁdjɔlɔg] *mf* cardiologist

**carême** [kaʁɛm] *m* ❶ (*jeûne*) fast ❷ (*période*) Lent

**carence** [kaʁɑ̃s] *f* ❶ MED deficiency ❷ PSYCH **~ affective** emotional deprivation

**caressant(e)** [kaʁesɑ̃, ɑ̃t] *adj* (*personne*) affectionate; (*voix*) tender

**caresse** [kaʁɛs] *f* caress

**caresser** [kaʁese] <1> *vt* (*effleurer*) to caress

**car-ferry** [kaʁfeʁi] <car-ferries> *m* car ferry

**cargaison** [kaʁgɛzɔ̃] *f* (*chargement*) cargo

**cargo** [kaʁgo] *m* freighter

**caricature** [kaʁikatyʁ] *f* caricature

**caricaturer** [kaʁikatyʁe] <1> *vt* to caricature

**caricaturiste** [kaʁikatyʁist] *mf* caricaturist

**carie** [kaʁi] *f* MED caries; **avoir une ~** to have a cavity

**carié(e)** [kaʁje] *adj* decayed; **avoir une dent ~e** to have a bad tooth

**carillon** [kaʁijɔ̃] *m* ❶ (*d'une église*) bells *pl* ❷ (*sonnerie: d'une horloge*) chimes *pl*

**carnage** [kaʁnaʒ] *m a. fig* carnage

**carnassier, -ière** [kaʁnasje, -jɛʁ] *m* carnivore

**carnaval** [kaʁnaval] <s> *m* carnival

**carnet** [kaʁnɛ] *m* ❶ (*calepin*) notebook; **~ d'adresses** address book; **~ de notes** report card; **~ d'épargne** *Suisse* (*livret*) savings book; **~ de santé** health chart ❷ (*paquet*) **~ de timbres** book of stamps; **~ de chèques** checkbook

**carotte** [kaʁɔt] *f* ❶ carrot; **~ rouge** *Suisse* (*betterave*) beet

**carpe** [kaʁp] *f* carp

**carré(e)** [kaʁe] **I.** *adj* ❶ (*rectangulaire*) square ❷ (*robuste*) **~ d'épaules** broad-shouldered ❸ MATH **kilomètre ~** square kilometer **II.** *m* ❶ MATH square ❷ JEUX **un ~ d'as** four aces

**carreau** [kaʁo] <x> *m* ❶ (*vitre*) window(pane); **faire les ~x** to clean the windows ❷ (*carrelage*) tiled floor ❸ (*motif*) **tissu à grands ~x** large-checked fabric; **papier à petits ~x** small-squared paper ❹ JEUX diamond; **as de ~** ace of diamonds

**carrefour** [kaʁfuʁ] *m a. fig* crossroads

**carrelage** [kaʁlaʒ] *m* ❶ (*action*) tiling ❷ (*revêtement*) tiles *pl*

**carreler** [kaʁle] <3> *vt* to tile

**carreleur, -euse** [kaʁlœʁ, -øz] *m, f* tiler

**carrière¹** [kaʁjɛʁ] *f* career

**carrière²** [kaʁjɛʁ] *f* **~ de pierres** stone quarry; **~ de sable** sandpit

**carrosserie** [kaʁɔsʁi] *f* ❶ AUTO body ❷ (*métier*) vehicle body building

**carrure** [kaʁyʁ] *f* ❶ (*largeur du dos*) breadth across the shoulders ❷ (*envergure*) stature

**cartable** [kaʁtabl] *m* ❶ ECOLE school bag ❷ *Québec* (*classeur à anneaux*) ring binder

**carte** [kaʁt] *f* ❶ GEO map; **~ routière** road map ❷ JEUX **~ à jouer** playing card; **tirer les ~s à qn** to read sb's cards ❸ (*dans le domaine postal*) **~ postale** postcard ❹ CULIN menu ❺ (*bristol*) **~ de visite** business card ❻ (*moyen de paiement*) **~ à mémoire/à puce** smart card; **~ bancaire/de**

**C**

**crédit** bank/credit card; **~ de téléphone** phone card ➐ *(document)* **~ (nationale) d'identité** ID card; **~ de sécurité sociale** ≈ social security card; **~ grise** car registration papers ➑ INFORM **~ enfichable/réseau/son/vidéo** plug-in/network/sound/video card; **~ graphique/mère** graphics card/motherboard

**carton** [kaʀtɔ̃] *m* ➊ *(matière)* cardboard ➋ *(emballage)* (cardboard) box ▸ **~ jaune/rouge** yellow/red card

**cartouche** [kaʀtuʃ] *f* ➊ *(munition: d'un fusil)* cartridge ➋ *(emballage)* **~ de cigarettes** carton of cigarettes ➌ *(recharge)* **~ d'encre** ink cartridge

**cas** [kɑ] *m* ➊ *a.* MED, JUR, LING case; **~ d'urgence** emergency; **c'est bien le ~** it is the case; **dans ce ~** in that case; **dans le ~ contraire** otherwise; **dans le ~ présent** in this particular case; **dans tous les ~** in any case; **en aucun ~** on no account ➋ *(hypothèse)* **au ~/dans le ~/pour le ~ où qn ferait qc** in case sb does sth; **en ~ de qc** in case of sth; **en ~ de besoin** if necessary; **en ~ de pluie** in case it rains

**cascade** [kaskad] *f* ➊ *(chute d'eau)* waterfall ➋ CINE stunt

**cascadeur, -euse** [kaskadœʀ, -øz] *m, f* CINE stuntman, stuntwoman *m, f*

**case** [kɑz] *f* ➊ *(carré: d'un formulaire)* box; *(d'un damier)* square; **~ départ** start; *fig* square one ➋ *(casier)* compartment ➌ *(hutte)* hut ➍ *Suisse, Québec (boîte)* **~ postale** post office box

**caser** [kaze] <1> I. *vt* ➊ *(loger)* to put up ➋ *(marier)* to marry off II. *vpr* **se ~** ➊ *(se loger)* to find a place to stay ➋ *(se marier)* to get married

**caserne** [kazɛʀn] *f* barracks *pl*

**casher** [kaʃɛʀ] *adj inv* kosher

**casier** [kazje] *m* ➊ *(case)* compartment; **~ à bouteilles** bottle rack ➋ JUR **~ judiciaire** police record

**casino** [kazino] *m* casino

**casque** [kask] *m* ➊ *(protection)* helmet; *(d'un motocycliste)* crash helmet ➋ *(séchoir)* hair dryer ➌ MUS headphones *pl*

▸ **~ bleu** blue helmet *(member of the U.N. peacekeeping force)*

**casquette** [kaskɛt] *f* cap

**cassant(e)** [kasɑ̃, ɑ̃t] *adj* ➊ *(fragile: substance)* brittle ➋ *(sec: ton)* curt

**cassation** [kasasjɔ̃] *f* JUR cassation

**casse** [kɑs] I. *f* ➊ *(dégât)* damage ➋ *(bagarre)* **il va y avoir de la ~** *inf* things are going to get rough ➌ *(commerce du ferrailleur)* junkyard II. *m inf* break-in

**cassé(e)** [kase] *adj (voix)* hoarse

**casse-cou** [kasku] *m inv, inf* daredevil

**casse-croûte** [kaskʀut] *m inv* ➊ *(collation)* snack ➋ *Québec (café, restaurant où l'on sert des repas rapides)* snack bar

**casse-noix** [kasnwa] *m inv* nutcracker

**casser** [kase] <1> I. *vt* ➊ *(briser: objet)* to break; *(branche)* to snap; *(noix)* to crack ➋ *(troubler: ambiance)* to disturb; **~ le moral à qn** *inf* to break sb's spirit ➌ ECON *(croissance)* to stop; **~ les prix** to slash prices ➍ POL, SOCIOL *(grève)* to break ➎ JUR *(jugement)* to quash; *(mariage)* to annul ➏ MIL to demote ▸ **~ les pieds à qn** *inf* to annoy sb II. *vi* *(objet)* to break; *(branche, fil)* to snap III. *vpr* ➊ *(se rompre)* **se ~** to break; *(branche)* to snap ➋ *(être fragile)* **se ~** to be fragile ➌ *(se briser)* **se ~ un bras** to break one's arm; **se ~ une dent** to break off a tooth ➍ *inf (se fatiguer)* **ne pas se ~** not to strain oneself ➎ *inf (s'en aller)* to split

**casserole** [kasʀɔl] *f* saucepan

**cassette** [kasɛt] *f* cassette

**casseur, -euse** [kasœʀ, -øz] *m, f* ➊ *(ferrailleur)* scrap (metal) dealer ➋ *(au cours d'une manifestation)* rioter

**cassis** [kasis] *m (fruit)* blackcurrant

**cassoulet** [kasulɛ] *m* cassoulet *(meat and bean stew)*

**cassure** [kasyʀ] *f* ➊ *(brisure)* break ➋ *(rupture: d'une amitié)* rupture

**castor** [kastɔʀ] *m* beaver

**castrer** [kastʀe] <1> *vt* to castrate

**catacombes** [katakɔ̃b] *fpl* catacombs

**catalogue** [katalɔg] *m* catalogue

**cataloguer** [katalɔge] <1> vt (classer) to catalog

**cataracte** [kataʀakt] f MED cataract

**catastrophe** [katastʀɔf] f catastrophe; **faire qc en ~** to do sth in a mad rush

**catastrophique** [katastʀɔfik] adj catastrophic

**catch** [katʃ] m wrestling

**catéchisme** [kateʃism] m ❶ (enseignement, livre) catechism ❷ (dogme) dogma

**catégorie** [kategɔʀi] f ❶ (groupe) category ❷ SPORT class ❸ (qualité) de **1ère ~** (produit alimentaire) premium food product; (hôtel) first-class hotel

**catégorique** [kategɔʀik] adj categoric(al); **être ~ sur qc** to be adamant about sth

**cathédrale** [katedʀal] f cathedral

**catholique** [katɔlik] I. adj REL (Roman) Catholic II. mf (Roman) Catholic

**cauchemar** [koʃmaʀ] m a. fig nightmare

**causant(e)** [kozã, ãt] adj talkative

**cause** [koz] I. f ❶ (raison, ensemble d'intérêts) cause; **fermé pour ~ de maladie** closed because of illness; **pour la bonne ~** for a good cause ❷ JUR lawsuit ▸ **mettre qn en ~** to implicate sb II. prep **à ~ de** because of

**causer**[1] [koze] <1> vt (provoquer) to cause

**causer**[2] [koze] <1> vt, vi (parler) to talk; (sans façon) to chat; **je te/vous cause!** inf I'm talking to you!

**caution** [kosjɔ̃] f ❶ FIN guarantee; **se porter ~ pour qn** to stand as guarantor for sb ❷ JUR bail; **être libéré sous ~** to be released on bail ❸ (appui) support

**cavalerie** [kavalʀi] f MIL cavalry

**cavalier, -ière** [kavalje, -jɛʀ] I. adj péj (impertinent) offhand II. m, f ❶ SPORT horseman, horsewoman m, f ❷ (au bal) partner III. m ❶ MIL cavalryman ❷ JEUX knight

**cave** [kav] f (local souterrain, provision de vins) cellar; **~ voûtée** vault

**caveau** [kavo] <x> m (tombeau) vault

**caverne** [kavɛʀn] f cavern

**caviar** [kavjaʀ] m CULIN caviar

**cavité** [kavite] f cavity

**CD** [sede] m abr de **Compact Disc** CD

**C.D.D.** [sedede] m abr de **contrat à durée déterminée** fixed-term contract

**C.D.I.** [sedei] m ❶ abr de **contrat à durée indéterminée** permanent employment contract ❷ abr de **centre de documentation et d'information** learning resources center

**CD-ROM** [sederɔm] m abr de **Compact Disc Read Only Memory** CD-ROM

**ce**[1] [sə] <devant "en" et formes de "être" commençant par une voyelle c', devant "a" ç'> pron dém ❶ (pour désigner) **c'est un beau garçon** he's a handsome boy; **~ sont de bons souvenirs** they're happy memories; **c'est beau, la vie** life is beautiful; **c'est moi/ lui/nous** it's me/him/us; **à qui est ce livre? – c'est à lui** whose book is this? – it's his ❷ (dans une question) **qui est-ce?, c'est qui?** inf (sur un homme) who is he?; (sur une femme) who is she?; (sur plusieurs personnes) who are they?; (au téléphone) who is speaking?; **qui est-ce qui/que** who/whom; **qu'est-ce (que c'est)?, c'est quoi?** inf what is it?; **qu'est-ce qui/que** what; **c'est qui** [o **qui c'est**] **ce Monsieur?** inf who is this man?; **est-ce vous?, c'est vous?** inf is it you? ❸ (pour insister) **c'est plus tard qu'elle y songea** she didn't think about it until later; **c'est maintenant qu'on en a besoin** right now is when we need it; **c'est en tombant que l'objet a explosé** the thing exploded when it fell; **c'est vous qui le dites!** that's what you say!; **c'est un scandale de voir cela** it's scandalous to see that; **c'est à elle de** +infin (c'est à son tour) it's her turn to +infin; (c'est son rôle) she has to +infin; **c'est à vous de prendre cette décision** you have to make this decision ❹ (pour expliquer) **c'est que ...** you see ...; (dans une réponse) actually ...; (pour préciser la raison) it's because ... ❺ (devant une relative) **voilà tout ~**

**que je sais** that's all I know; **dis-moi ~ dont tu as besoin** tell me what you need; **~ à quoi je ne m'attendais pas** what I wasn't expecting; **~ à quoi j'ai pensé** what I thought; **~ que c'est idiot!** how stupid it is!; **~ que** [*o* **qu'est--ce que**] **ce paysage est beau!** how beautiful this landscape is!; **qu'est-ce qu'on s'amuse!** *inf* what a good time we're having!; **~ qu'il parle bien** *inf* how well he speaks ►**et ~** and that; **à ~ qu'on dit, qn a fait qc** it is said that sb has done sth; **sur ~** whereupon

**ce²** [sə] *adj dém* ①(*pour désigner*) this; *v.a.* **cette** ②(*intensif, péjoratif*) **comment peut-il raconter ~ mensonge!** how can he tell such a lie! ③(*avec étonnement*) what (a); **~ toupet!** what nerve! ④(*en opposition*) **~ livre-ci … ~ livre-là** this book … that book ⑤(*temporel*) **~ jour-là** that day; **~ mois-ci** this month

**ceci** [səsi] *pron dém* this; **~ explique cela** one thing explains another; **il a ~ d'agréable qu'il est gai** what is pleasant about him is that he is cheerful; **à ~ près qu'il ment** except that he's lying; *v.a.* **cela**

**cécité** [sesite] *f* blindness

**céder** [sede] <5> **I.** *vt* ①(*abandonner au profit de qn*) **~ qc à qn** to let sb have sth ②(*vendre*) to sell **II.** *vi* ①(*renoncer*) to give up ②(*capituler*) to give in; (*troupes*) to withdraw ③(*succomber*) **~ à qc** to give way to sth ④(*se rompre*) to give (way)

**CEDEX** [sedɛks] *m abr de* **courrier d'entreprise à distribution exceptionnelle** postal code for official use

**cédille** [sedij] *f* cedilla

**cèdre** [sɛdʀ] *m* cedar

**ceinture** [sɛ̃tyʀ] *f* ① *a.* AUTO, AVIAT, SPORT belt; **attacher sa ~ de sécurité** to fasten one's seatbelt ②(*partie d'un vêtement*) waistband

**ceinturon** [sɛ̃tyʀɔ̃] *m* MIL belt

**cela** [s(ə)la] *pron dém* ①(*pour désigner*) that; **~ te plaît?** do you like that?; **après ~** after that; **je ne pense qu'à ~** that's all I think about ②(*pour renforcer*) **qui/quand/où ~?** who/when/where is/was that?; **comment ~?** what do you mean?; **~ fait dix jours que j'attends** I've been waiting for ten days ►**c'est ~** même exactly; **et avec ~?** anything else?; **sans ~** otherwise; *v.a.* **ça, ceci**

**célébration** [selebʀasjɔ̃] *f* celebration

**célèbre** [selɛbʀ] *adj* famous

**célébrer** [selebʀe] <5> *vt* ①(*fêter*) to celebrate ②(*vanter: exploit*) to praise

**célébrité** [selebʀite] *f* fame; **qn est une ~** sb is a celebrity

**céleri** [sɛlʀi] *m* celery

**céleri-rave** [sɛlʀiʀav] <céleris-raves> *m* celeriac

**célibat** [seliba] *m* single status; (*d'un prêtre*) celibacy

**célibataire** [selibatɛʀ] **I.** *adj* single **II.** *mf* single person

**celle, celui** [sɛl] <s> *pron dém* ① + *prép* **~ de Paul est plus jolie** Paul's is more beautiful ② + *pron rel* **~ que tu as achetée est moins chère** the one you bought is cheaper ③ + *adj, part passé, part prés, infin* (*en opposition*) the one; **cette marchandise est meilleure que ~ que vous vendez** these goods are better than the ones you sell

**celle-ci, celui-ci** [sɛlsi] <celles-ci> *pron dém* ①(*en désignant: chose*) this one; (*personne*) she ②(*référence à un antécédent*) the latter; **il écrit à sa sœur – ~ ne répond pas** he writes to his sister but she doesn't answer (*en opposition*) **~ est moins chère que celle-là** this one is cheaper than that one; (*avec un geste*) this one here; *v.a.* **celle-là**

**celle-là, celui-là** [sɛlla] <celles-là> *pron dém* ①(*en désignant: chose*) that one; (*personne*) she ②(*référence à un antécédent*) **ah! je la retiens – alors!** *inf* I'll remember her all right!; **elle est bien bonne ~!** that's a good one! ③(*en opposition*) *v.* **celle-ci**

**celles, ceux** [sɛl] *pl pron dém* ① + *prép*

those; **~ d'entre vous** those of you
**②** + *pron rel* **~ qui ont fini peuvent**
**sortir** those who have finished may leave **③** + *adj, part passé, part prés, infin*
those; *v.a.* **celle**
**celles-ci, ceux-ci** [sɛlsi] *pl pron dém*
**①** (*pour distinguer*) these (ones) **②** (*référence à un antécédent*) the latter; *v.a.*
**celle-ci ③** (*en opposition*) **~ sont**
**moins chères que celles-là** these are
cheaper than those; (*avec un geste*)
these here; *v.a.* **celle-là**
**celles-là, ceux-là** [sɛlla] *pl pron dém*
**①** (*en désignant*) those (ones) **②** (*référence à un antécédent*) **ah! je les retiens ~ alors!** *inf* I'll remember them
all right! **③** (*en opposition*) *v.* **celles-là**
**cellier** [selje] *m* storeroom (*for food and
wine*)
**cellophane®** [selɔfan] *f* cellophane®
**cellulaire** [selylɛʀ] **I.** *adj* **①** BIO **divi-**
**sion ~** cell division **②** (*relatif à la prison*) **fourgon ~** prison van **II.** *m* Québec (*téléphone portable*) cell phone
**cellule** [selyl] *f* cell
**cellulite** [selylit] *f* MED cellulite
**celte** [sɛlt] *adj* Celtic
**celtique** [sɛltik] **I.** *adj* Celtic **II.** *m* Celtic; *v.a.* **français**
**celui, celle** [səlɥi] <ceux> *pron dém*
the one; *v.a.* **celle**
**celui-ci, celle-ci** [səlɥisi] <ceux-ci>
*pron dém* (*chose*) this one; (*personne*)
he; *v.a.* **celle-ci, celui-là**
**celui-là, celle-là** [səlɥila] <ceux-là>
*pron dém* **①** (*en désignant: chose*) that
one; (*personne*) he **②** (*avec un geste*)
**~ est meilleur** that one is better **③** (*référence à un antécédent*) *v.* **celle-là**
**④** (*en opposition*) *v.* **celui-ci, celle-ci**
**cendre** [sɑ̃dʀ] *f* ash
**cendrier** [sɑ̃dʀije] *m* (*d'un fumeur*) ashtray
**censé(e)** [sɑ̃se] *adj* **①** (*présumé en train
de faire qc*) **être ~** +*infin* to be supposed to +*infin* **②** (*présumé capable de
faire qc*) **je suis ~ connaître la réponse** I'm supposed to know the answer
**censeur** [sɑ̃sœʀ] *mf* **①** CINE, PRESSE cen-

sor **②** ECOLE *person responsible for discipline in a school*
**censure** [sɑ̃syʀ] *f* **①** CINE, PRESSE censorship **②** POL censure
**censurer** [sɑ̃syʀe] <1> *vt* CINE, PRESSE to
censor
**cent¹** [sɑ̃] **I.** *adj* a [*o* one] hundred; **cinq**
**~ euros** five hundred euros; **~ un** a
[*o* one] hundred and one ▸ **avoir ~ fois**
**raison** to be absolutely right; **pour ~**
percent; **~ pour ~** a [*o* one] hundred
percent **II.** *m inv* hundred; *v.a.* **cinq,**
**cinquante**
**cent²** [sɛnt] *m* FIN cent
**centaine** [sɑ̃tɛn] *f* **①** (*environ cent*)
**une ~ de personnes** about a hundred
people; **des ~s de personnes** hun-
dreds of people **②** (*cent unités*) hundred
**centenaire** [sɑ̃tnɛʀ] **I.** *adj* hun-
dred-year-old; **être ~** to be a hundred
years old **II.** *mf* centenarian **III.** *m* centennial
**centième** [sɑ̃tjɛm] **I.** *adj antéposé* hundredth **II.** *mf* **le/la ~** the hundredth
**III.** *m* (*fraction*) fraction **IV.** *f* THEAT hundredth performance; *v.a.* **cinquième**
**centilitre** [sɑ̃tilitʀ] *m* centiliter
**centime** [sɑ̃tim] *m* **①** HIST centime
**②** **~ d'euro** cent; **une pièce de 50 ~s**
a 50-cent coin ▸ **ne pas avoir un ~ sur**
**soi** not to have a cent
**centimètre** [sɑ̃timɛtʀ] *m* **①** (*unité*) centimeter **②** (*ruban*) tape measure
**central** [sɑ̃tʀal, -o] <-aux> *m* TEL
switchboard
**central(e)** [sɑ̃tʀal, -o] <-aux> *adj* (*situé
au centre, important*) central; **partie**
**~e** main part
**centrale** [sɑ̃tʀal] *f* **①** ELEC power plant
**②** COM head office **③** (*prison*) prison
**centraliser** [sɑ̃tʀalize] <1> *vt* to central-
ize
**centre** [sɑ̃tʀ] *m* **①** (*milieu, organisme*)
center; **~ hospitalier régional** regional
hospital complex; **~ universitaire** university; **~ d'achats** Québec (*centre
commercial*) shopping center; **~ éques-**
**tre** riding school **②** SPORT (*terrain*) mid-

field; (*joueur*) midfielder; (*passe*) center pass

**centrer** [sɑ̃tʀe] <1> *vt* to center

**centuple** [sɑ̃typl] *m a. fig* hundredfold

**cep** [sɛp] *m* vine stock

**cépage** [sepaʒ] *m* varietal

**cèpe** [sɛp] *m* cep

**cependant** [s(ə)pɑ̃dɑ̃] *adv* however

**céramique** [seʀamik] **I.** *adj* ceramic **II.** *f* ❶ (*objet*) ceramic ❷ (*art*) ceramics *pl*

**cercle** [sɛʀkl] *m* ❶ (*forme géométrique, groupe*) circle ❷ (*groupe sportif*) club

**cercueil** [sɛʀkœj] *m* coffin, casket

**céréale** [seʀeal] *f:* cereal

**cérébral(e)** [seʀebʀal, -o] <-aux> *adj* ❶ ANAT cerebral ❷ (*intellectuel*) intellectual

**cérémonie** [seʀemɔni] *f* ceremony

**cerf** [sɛʀ] *m* ZOOL stag

**cerfeuil** [sɛʀfœj] *m* chervil

**cerf-volant** [sɛʀvɔlɑ̃] <cerfs-volants> *m* ❶ (*jouet*) kite ❷ ZOOL stag beetle

**cerise** [s(ə)ʀiz] *f* cherry

**cerisier** [s(ə)ʀizje] *m* ❶ (*arbre*) cherry (tree) ❷ (*bois*) cherry (wood)

**cerner** [sɛʀne] <1> *vt* ❶ *a. fig* (*entourer d'un trait*) to outline ❷ (*encercler: ennemi*) to surround ❸ (*évaluer: problème*) to define; (*difficulté*) to assess; **~ qn** *inf* to figure sb out

**certain(e)** [sɛʀtɛ̃, ɛn] **I.** *adj* certain; **être sûr et ~** to be absolutely certain **II.** *adj indéf* ❶ *pl antéposé* (*quelques*) some ❷ (*bien déterminé*) **un ~ endroit** a certain place **III.** *pron pl* some; **~s d'entre vous** some of you; **aux yeux de ~s** in some people's eyes

**certainement** [sɛʀtɛnmɑ̃] *adv* ❶ (*selon toute apparence*) most probably ❷ (*sans aucun doute*) certainly

**certes** [sɛʀt] *adv* (*pour exprimer une réserve*) **c'est le plus doué, ~! mais ...** he's the most talented, admittedly, but ...; **il n'est ~ pas doué** he's certainly not talented

**certificat** [sɛʀtifika] *m* (*attestation*) cer-

tificat; **~ de scolarité** proof of attendance

**certifier** [sɛʀtifje] <1> *vt* ❶ (*assurer*) to assure ❷ JUR to certify

**certitude** [sɛʀtityd] *f* certainly

**cerveau** [sɛʀvo] <x> *m* ❶ *a.* ANAT brain ❷ (*esprit*) mind ❸ (*organisateur*) brains *pl*

**cervelle** [sɛʀvɛl] *f* ❶ *inf* (*esprit*) brain ❷ CULIN brains *pl*

**cervical(e)** [sɛʀvikal, -o] <-aux> *adj* ANAT **les vertèbres ~es** the cervical vertebrae

**ces** [se] *adj dém pl* ❶ (*pour désigner*) these; *v.a.* **cette** ❷ *inf* (*intensif, péjoratif*) **il a de ~ idées!** he has some crazy ideas; **comment peut-il raconter ~ mensonges** how can he tell such lies ❸ (*avec étonnement*) **~ mensonges!** what lies! ❹ (*en opposition*) **~ gens-ci ... ~ gens-là** these people ... those people ❺ (*temporel*) **~ nuits-ci** these last few nights; **dans ~ années-là** during those years

**C.E.S.** [seøɛs] *m* ECOLE *abr de* **collège d'enseignement secondaire** junior high school

**césarienne** [sezaʀjɛn] *f* MED Caesarean (section)

**cesser** [sese] <1> **I.** *vt* to stop; **cessez ces cris!** stop shouting!; **faire ~ qc** to put an end to sth; **~ de fumer** to stop smoking **II.** *vi* to stop; (*conflit*) to come to an end; (*fièvre*) to pass

**cessez-le-feu** [sesel(e)fø] *m inv* cease-fire

**c'est-à-dire** [sɛtadiʀ] *conj* ❶ (*à savoir*) that is (to say) ❷ (*justification*) **~ que ...** which means that ... ❸ (*rectification*) **~ que ...** well, actually ...

**cet** [sɛt] *adj dém v.* **ce**

**cette** [sɛt] *adj dém* ❶ (*pour désigner*) this; **alors, ~ grippe, comment ça va?** well then, how's your flu? ❷ (*intensif, péjoratif*) **comment peut-il raconter ~ histoire!** how can he tell such a story! ❸ (*avec étonnement*) **~** what (a); **~ chance!** what luck! ❹ (*en opposition*) **~ version-ci ... ~ version-là** this

version … that version ❺ (*temporel*)
~ **nuit** (*la nuit dernière*) last night; (*la
nuit qui vient*) tonight; ~ **semaine** this
week; ~ **semaine-là** that week

**ceux, celles** [sø] *pl pron dém* those; *v.a.*
**celles**

**ceux-ci, celles-ci** [søsi] *pl pron dém*
❶ (*pour distinguer*) these (ones) ❷ (*référence à un antécédent*) the latter; *v.a.*
**celle-ci** ❸ (*en opposition*) *v.* **ceux-là,
celles-ci**

**ceux-là, celles-là** [søla] *pl pron dém*
❶ (*en désignant*) those ❷ (*référence à
un antécédent*) *v.* **celle-là** ❸ (*en opposition*) those; *v.a.* **ceux-ci, celles-ci**

**Cévennes** [seven] *fpl* **les** ~ the Cévennes

**cf., Cf.** [kɔfɛr] *abr de* **confer** cf.

**chacun(e)** [ʃakœ̃, ʃakyn] *pron* ❶ (*chose
ou personne dans un ensemble défini*)
each (one); ~/~**e de nous** each (one)
of us; ~ (**à**) **son tour** each in turn ❷ (*de
deux personnes*) ~ **des deux** both of
them ❸ (*toute personne*) everyone

**chagrin** [ʃagrɛ̃] *m* (*peine*) grief

**chagriner** [ʃagrine] <1> *vt* ~ **qn** (*causer de la peine*) to grieve sb; (*contrarier*) to bother sb

**chahut** [ʃay] *m* uproar; (*bruit*) racket

**chahuter** [ʃayte] <1> **I.** *vi* (*élèves*) to
create a ruckus; (*enfants*) to romp
around; (*faire du bruit*) to make a racket
**II.** *vt* (*professeur*) to rag; **ce professeur est toujours chahuté** this teacher always loses control of his class

**chaîne** [ʃɛn] *f* ❶ (*bijou, dispositif métallique, suite d'éléments*) chain ❷ *pl*
AUTO ~ **à neige** snow chains ❸ ECON assembly line ❹ RADIO, TV (*émetteur*)
channel; (*programme*) program; ~ **câ-
blée** cable channel; **sur la 3e** ~ on
channel 3 ❺ (*appareil stéréo*) ~ **hi-fi**
stereo system ❻ COM (*groupement*)
~ **de magasins** chain of stores

**chair** [ʃɛr] **I.** *f* ❶ (*viande, pulpe*) flesh;
~ **à saucisse** ground meat ❷ *a.* REL, LIT
(*corps opposé à esprit*) flesh ▸ **avoir la
~ de poule** to have goose bumps **II.** *adj
inv* **couleur** ~ flesh-colored

**chaire** [ʃɛr] *f* UNIV chair

**chaise** [ʃɛz] *f* chair

**châle** [ʃɑl] *m* shawl

**chalet** [ʃalɛ] *m* ❶ (*maison de bois en
montagne*) chalet ❷ *Québec* (*maison
de campagne située près d'un lac ou
d'une rivière*) cabin (*near water*)

**chaleur** [ʃalœr] *f* ❶ (*température élevée*) warmth; (*très élevée*) *a.* PHYS heat
❷ *fig* heat; (*d'un accueil*) warmth

**chaleureux, -euse** [ʃalœrø, -øz] *adj*
warm; (*soirée*) pleasant

**chalutier** [ʃalytje] *m* (*bateau*) trawler

**chamailler** [ʃamaje] <1> *vpr inf* **se** ~ to
squabble

**chambre** [ʃɑ̃br] *f* ❶ (*pièce où l'on couche*) bedroom; ~ **individuelle/double**
single/double room; ~ **d'amis** guest
room ❷ (*pièce spéciale*) ~ **forte** strong
room; ~ **froide** cold (storage) room
❸ POL house ❹ JUR division ❺ COM ~ **de
commerce et d'industrie** chamber of
commerce ❻ (*tuyau*) ~ **à air** inner tube

**chambrer** [ʃɑ̃bre] <1> *vt* ❶ (*tempérer*)
to bring to room temperature ❷ *inf* (*se
moquer de*) to tease

**chameau** [ʃamo] <x> *m* ❶ ZOOL camel
❷ *inf* (*femme*) beast ❸ *inf* (*homme*)
heel

**champ** [ʃɑ̃] *m* ❶ *a.* AGR, PHYS, MIL field
❷ *pl* (*campagne*) country(side); **fleurs
des** ~**s** wild flowers

**champagne** [ʃɑ̃paɲ] *m* champagne

**champignon** [ʃɑ̃piɲɔ̃] *m* ❶ BOT, CULIN
mushroom ❷ *a.* MED fungus ❸ *inf* (*accélérateur*) accelerator

**champion(ne)** [ʃɑ̃pjɔ̃, -jɔn] **I.** *adj inf*
**être** ~ to be great **II.** *m(f)* (*vainqueur*)
*a. fig* champion

**championnat** [ʃɑ̃pjɔna] *m* championship

**chance** [ʃɑ̃s] *f* ❶ (*bonne fortune, hasard*) (good) luck; **coup de** ~ stroke of
luck; **avoir de la** ~ to be lucky; **avoir
de la** ~ **de** +*infin* to be lucky enough to
+*infin*; **porter** ~ **à qn** to bring sb (good)
luck; **par** ~ luckily; **bonne** ~! good
luck!; **quelle** ~! what a stroke of (good)
luck! ❷ (*probabilité, possibilité de suc-*

cès) chance; **tenter sa ~** to try one's luck

**chancelier** [ʃãsəlje] *m* HIST chancellor

**chanceux, -euse** [ʃãsø, -øz] *adj* lucky

**Chandeleur** [ʃãd(ə)lœʀ] *f* REL **la ~** Candlemas

**chandelier** [ʃãdəlje] *m* candelabra; (*bougeoir*) candlestick

**chandelle** [ʃãdɛl] *f* ❶ (*bougie*) candle; **dîner aux ~s** candlelight dinner ❷ SPORT **faire la ~** to do a shoulder stand

**change** [ʃãʒ] *m* ❶ (*échange d'une monnaie*) (foreign) exchange; **bureau de ~** currency exchange ❷ (*taux du change*) exchange rate

**changement** [ʃãʒmã] *m* ❶ (*modification*) change; **~ en bien/mal** change for the better/worse; **~ de temps** change in the weather; **il n'y a aucun ~** there's been no change ❷ CHEMDFER **vous avez un ~ à Francfort** you have to change in Frankfurt ❸ TECH **~ de vitesse** (*dispositif*) gears *pl*; (*mouvement*) change of gear(s)

**changer** [ʃãʒe] <2a> I. *vt* ❶ (*modifier, remplacer*) to change ❷ (*déplacer*) **~ qc de place** to move sth to a different spot; **~ qn de poste** to move sb to a different job ❸ (*échanger*) **~ pour** [*o* **contre**] **qc** to exchange for sth ❹ FIN (*convertir*) **~ contre qc** to change for sth ❺ (*divertir*) **~ qn de qc** to be a change for sb from sth; **cela m'a changé les idées** that took my mind off things II. *vi* ❶ (*se transformer, substituer*) to change; **~ de chemise** to change one's shirt; **~ de voiture** to trade in one's car ❷ (*déménager*) **~ de ville** to move to another town ❸ AUTO **~ de vitesse** to change gears ❹ (*faire un échange*) **~ de place avec qn** to change (places) with sb ❺ CHEMDFER **à Paris** to change in Paris; **~ de train** to change trains ❻ (*pour exprimer le franchissement*) **~ de trottoir** to cross over to the other side of the road; **~ de file** to change lanes III. *vpr* **se ~** to get changed

**chanson** [ʃãsɔ̃] *f* ❶ MUS song ❷ *inf* (*rengaine*) old story

**chant** [ʃã] *m* ❶ (*action de chanter, musique vocale*) singing; **apprendre le ~** to learn how to sing ❷ (*chanson*) song; **~ de Noël** (Christmas) carol ❸ (*bruits harmonieux: du coq*) crow(ing); (*du grillon*) chirp(ing); (*des oiseaux*) singing

**chantage** [ʃãtaʒ] *m* blackmail; **faire du ~ à qn** to blackmail sb

**chanter** [ʃãte] <1> I. *vi* ❶ (*produire des sons*) to sing; (*coq*) to crow; (*poule*) to cackle; (*insecte*) to chirp ❷ (*menacer*) **faire ~ qn** to blackmail sb II. *vt* (*interpréter*) to sing

**chanterelle** [ʃãtʀɛl] *f* (*champignon*) chanterelle

**chanteur, -euse** [ʃãtœʀ, -øz] *m, f* singer

**chantier** [ʃãtje] *m* ❶ (*lieu*) construction site; (*travaux*) building work; **être en ~** (*immeuble*) to be under construction ❷ *inf* (*désordre*) mess ❸ *Québec* (*exploitation forestière*) lumber camp

**chantilly** [ʃãtiji] *f* whipped cream

**chaos** [kao] *m* chaos

**chaotique** [kaɔtik] *adj* chaotic

**chapeau** [ʃapo] <x> *m* (*couvre-chef*) hat; **~ de sécurité** *Québec* (*casque*) safety helmet ▶ **~!** *inf* well done!

**chapelle** [ʃapɛl] *f* chapel

**chapelure** [ʃaplyʀ] *f* bread crumbs *pl*

**chapiteau** [ʃapito] <x> *m* ❶ (*tente de cirque, le cirque*) big top ❷ (*tente pour une manifestation*) marquee ❸ ARCHIT (*couronnement*) capital

**chapitre** [ʃapitʀ] *m* chapter

**chaque** [ʃak] *adj inv* ❶ (*qui est pris séparément*) each, every ❷ *inf* (*chacun*) each; **un peu de ~** a little of everything ❸ (*tous/toutes les*) every

**char** [ʃaʀ] *m* ❶ MIL tank ❷ (*voiture décorée*) float

**charbon** [ʃaʀbɔ̃] *m* ❶ (*combustible*) coal; **~ de bois** charcoal ❷ MED anthrax

**charcuterie** [ʃaʀkytʀi] *f* ❶ (*boutique*) pork butcher (shop) ❷ (*spécialité*) cooked pork meats *pl*

**charcutier, -ière** [ʃaʁkytje, -jɛʁ] *m, f* pork butcher

**chardon** [ʃaʁdɔ̃] *m* thistle

**charge** [ʃaʁʒ] *f* **❶** (*fardeau*) burden; (*d'un camion*) load **❷** (*responsabilité*) responsibility; **avoir la ~ de qn/qc** to be responsible for sb/sth; **être à** (**la**) **~ de qn** (*personne*) to be dependent on sb; **personnes à ~** dependents; **prendre qc en ~** to take care of sth; **à ~ pour qn de** +*infin* it's up to sb to +*infin* **❸** (*fonction*) office **❹** *souvent pl* (*obligations financières*) expenses *pl* **❺** JUR, MIL charge

**chargé(e)** [ʃaʁʒe] *adj* **❶** (*qui porte une charge*) **~ de qc** loaded with sth; **voyageur très ~** traveler laden down with luggage **❷** (*plein: programme, journée*) full **❸** (*responsable*) **~ de qn/qc** to be in charge of sb/sth **❹** (*garni: fusil*) loaded; (*batterie*) charged **❺** (*lourd: conscience*) troubled **⑥** MED (*estomac*) overloaded; (*langue*) coated **❼** (*rempli*) **le ciel restera ~** the sky will remain overcast **❽** (*exagéré: style*) intricate

**chargement** [ʃaʁʒəmɑ̃] *m* (*action*) *a.* INFORM loading **❷** (*marchandises*) load **❸** (*fret*) freight

**charger** [ʃaʁʒe] <2a> **I.** *vt* **❶** (*faire porter une charge: marchandise*) to load; **~ qn/qc de qc** to load sb/sth up with sth; **~ sur/dans qc** to load onto/into sth **❷** (*attribuer une mission à*) **~ qn de qc** to make sb responsible for sth; **être chargé de qc** to be in charge of sth **❸** (*accuser*) **~ qn de qc** to charge sb with sth **❹** (*attaquer*) to charge (at) **❺** TECH (*arme, appareil photo*) to load; (*batterie*) to charge **⑥** INFORM to load **II.** *vi* (*attaquer*) to charge **III.** *vpr* (*s'occuper de*) **se ~ de qn/qc** to take care of sb/sth; **se ~ de** +*infin* to undertake to +*infin*

**chariot** [ʃaʁjo] *m* **❶** (*plate-forme tractée*) wagon **❷** (*petit engin de transport*) cart; **~ élévateur** forklift **❸** (*caddy à bagages*) luggage cart **❹** COM shopping cart

**charisme** [kaʁism] *m* charisma

**charitable** [ʃaʁitabl] *adj* charitable

**charité** [ʃaʁite] *f* (*amour du prochain, action*) charity

**charlatan** [ʃaʁlatɑ̃] *m* **❶** (*escroc*) con man **❷** (*mauvais médecin*) quack (doctor)

**charmant(e)** [ʃaʁmɑ̃, ɑ̃t] *adj a. iron* **❶** (*agréable*) charming **❷** (*ravissant*) delightful

**charme** [ʃaʁm] *m* **❶** (*attrait: d'une personne, d'un lieu*) charm; **faire du ~ à qn** to use one's charms on sb **❷** *souvent pl* (*beauté*) charms *pl* **❸** (*envoûtement*) spell

**charmer** [ʃaʁme] <1> *vt* **❶** (*enchanter*) to charm **❷** (*envoûter*) to enchant

**charmeur, -euse** [ʃaʁmœʁ, -øz] **I.** *adj* (*sourire*) winning; (*air*) charming **II.** *m, f* (*séducteur*) charmer

**charnel(le)** [ʃaʁnɛl] *adj* **❶** (*corporel*) physical **❷** (*sexuel*) carnal

**charnière** [ʃaʁnjɛʁ] **I.** *f* (*gond*) hinge **II.** *adj* (*de transition*) transitional

**charnu(e)** [ʃaʁny] *adj* fleshy

**charogne** [ʃaʁɔɲ] *f* **❶** (*cadavre: d'un animal*) decaying carcass; (*d'une personne*) decaying corpse **❷** *péj, inf* bastard

**charpente** [ʃaʁpɑ̃t] *f* (*bâti*) frame(work); **~ du toit** roof structure

**charpentier** [ʃaʁpɑ̃tje] *m* carpenter

**charrette¹** [ʃaʁɛt] *f* cart

**charrette²** [ʃaʁɛt] *f Suisse* (*coquin, canaille*) so-and-so

**charrier** [ʃaʁje] <1> **I.** *vt* (*transporter*) **~ qc** to cart sth (along); (*rivière*) to carry sth (along) **II.** *vi inf* to go too far

**charrue** [ʃaʁy] *f* plow

**charte** [ʃaʁt] *f* charter

**charter** [ʃaʁtɛʁ] **I.** *m* **❶** (*vol*) charter flight **❷** (*avion*) chartered plane **II.** *app inv* charter

**chasse¹** [ʃas] *f* **❶** (*action*) hunting; **~ au trésor** treasure hunt; **la ~ est ouverte** it's open season; **faire la ~ aux souris** to chase mice **❷** (*poursuite*) **~ aux sorcières** witch-hunt; **prendre qn/qc en ~** to give chase to sb/sth **❸** (*lieu*) hunting ground; **~ gardée** private hunting ground ❹ AVIAT **pilote de ~** fighter pilot

**chasse²** [ʃas] f inf (chasse d'eau) (toilet) flush; **tirer la ~** to flush the toilet

**chasse-neige** [ʃasnɛʒ] m inv ❶ (véhicule) snowplow ❷ (en ski) **descendre en ~** to snowplow down

**chasser** [ʃase] <1> I. vi ❶ (aller à la chasse) to go hunting ❷ (déraper) to skid II. vt ❶ (aller à la chasse) to hunt ❷ (faire partir) **~ qn/qc de qc** to drive sb/sth out [o away] from sth ❸ fig (idées noires) to dispel

**chasseur** [ʃasœʀ] m ❶ MIL chasseur ❷ (avion) fighter ❸ (groom) bellhop ❹ fig **~ de têtes** headhunter

**chasseur, -euse** [ʃasœʀ, -øz] m, f hunter

**châssis** [ʃasi] m TECH, AUTO chassis

**chasteté** [ʃastəte] f chastity

**chat¹** [ʃa] m (animal) cat; (mâle) tomcat; v.a. **chatte** ▸ **avoir un ~ dans la gorge** to have a frog in one's throat; **il n'y a pas un ~ dans la rue** there's not a soul in the street

**chat²** [tʃat] m INFORM chat

**châtaigne** [ʃatɛɲ] f (fruit) (sweet) chestnut

**châtain** [ʃatɛ̃] adj pas de forme féminine chestnut brown

**château** [ʃato] <x> m ❶ (palais) palace ❷ (forteresse) **~ fort** castle ❸ (belle maison) manor (house) ❹ fig **~ d'eau** water tower; **~ de sable** sand castle

**châtiment** [ʃatimã] m punishment

**chatouiller** [ʃatuje] <1> vt (faire des chatouilles) to tickle; **elle lui chatouille le bras** she is tickling his arm

**chatouilleux, -euse** [ʃatujø, -jøz] adj (sensible aux chatouilles) ticklish

**châtrer** [ʃatʀe] <1> vt to castrate

**chatroom** [tʃatʀum] m INET chat room

**chatte** [ʃat] f (female) cat; v.a. **chat**

**chatter** [tʃate] <1> vi INFORM to chat

**chaud** [ʃo] m (chaleur) warmth; (chaleur extrême) heat; **il fait ~** it's warm [o hot]; **tenir ~ à qn** to keep sb warm; **crever de ~** inf to be sweltering; **garder qc au ~** to keep sth warm [o hot]; **il**

**a assez/trop ~** he is warm enough/too warm ▸ **il/elle a eu ~** inf he/she had a narrow escape

**chaud(e)** [ʃo, ʃod] adj ❶ (opp: froid) warm; (très chaud) hot; **repas ~** hot meal; **vin ~** mulled wine ❷ antéposé (intense: discussion) heated ❸ (chaleureux: couleur, ton) warm ❹ inf (sensuel) hot

**chaudement** [ʃodmã] adv ❶ (contre le froid) warmly ❷ (vivement: féliciter) warmly; (recommander) heartily

**chaudière** [ʃodjɛʀ] f boiler

**chaudron** [ʃodʀɔ̃] m cauldron

**chauffage** [ʃofaʒ] m ❶ (installation) heating ❷ (appareil) heater

**chauffant(e)** [ʃofɑ̃, ɑ̃t] adj heating; (brosse) heated

**chauffard** [ʃofaʀ] m reckless driver

**chauffe-eau** [ʃofo] m inv water heater; (à accumulation) hot-water heater

**chauffer** [ʃofe] <1> I. vi ❶ (être sur le feu) to be warming up; (très chaud) to be heating up ❷ (devenir chaud) to warm up; (très chaud) to heat up ❸ (devenir trop chaud: moteur) to overheat ▸ **ça va ~** inf there's going to be trouble II. vt ❶ (rendre plus chaud: personne) to warm [o to heat] up; (pièce, maison) to heat; (eau) to heat (up); **faire ~** to warm [o to heat] (up) ❷ TECH to heat; **~ à blanc** to make white-hot ❸ (mettre dans l'ambiance) to warm up III. vpr **se ~ au gaz** to use natural gas for heating

**chauffeur** [ʃofœʀ] m ❶ (conducteur) driver; **~ routier** long-distance truck driver; **~ de taxi** taxi driver ❷ (personnel) chauffeur

**chaume** [ʃom] m ❶ (partie des tiges) stubble ❷ (toiture) thatch

**chaumière** [ʃomjɛʀ] f (à toit de chaume) thatched cottage

**chaussée** [ʃose] f road ▸ **~ glissante** slippery surface

**chausser** [ʃose] <1> I. vt ❶ (mettre: chaussures) to put on; (skis) to clip on; **être chaussé de bottes** to be wearing boots ❷ (aller) **bien/mal ~** (chaussu-

*re*) well/poorly shod **II.** *vi* **du 40/44** to wear size 7/10 (*in US sizes*); **du combien chaussez-vous?** what size do you wear? **III.** *vpr* **se ~** to put one's shoes on

**chaussette** [ʃosɛt] *f* ❶ (*socquette*) sock ❷ (*mi-bas*) knee-highs

**chausson** [ʃosõ] *m* ❶ (*chaussure*) slipper; **des ~s pour bébés** bootees; **~ de danse** ballet shoe ❷ CULIN **~ aux pommes** apple turnover

**chaussure** [ʃosyR] *f* ❶ (*soulier*) shoe; **~s à talons** high-heeled shoes; **~s à crampons** (*d'athlète*) spikes ❷ (*industrie*) shoe industry ❸ (*commerce*) shoe trade

**chauve** [ʃov] **I.** *adj* bald **II.** *m* bald(-headed) man

**chauve-souris** [ʃovsuRi] <chauves--souris> *f* bat

**chauvin(e)** [ʃovɛ̃, in] **I.** *adj* chauvinistic **II.** *m(f)* chauvinist

**chaux** [ʃo] *f* lime, whitewash

**chavirer** [ʃaviRe] <1> *vt, vi* to capsize

**chef** [ʃɛf] *m* ❶ (*responsable*) boss; (*d'une tribu*) chief(tain); **ingénieur en ~ à qn** chief engineer; **~ d'État** head of state; **~ d'entreprise** company head; **~ d'orchestre** conductor ❷ (*meneur*) leader ❸ MIL (*sergent-chef*) sergeant ❹ (*cuisinier*) chef

**chef-d'œuvre** [ʃɛdœvR] <chefs-d'œuvre> *m* masterpiece

**chef-lieu** [ʃɛfljø] <chefs-lieux> *m* county seat

**chemin** [ʃ(ə)mɛ̃] *m* ❶ way; **demander son ~ à qn** to ask sb the way; **prendre le ~ de la gare** to head for the station; **rebrousser ~** to turn back; **~ faisant, en ~** on the way; **se tromper de ~** to go the wrong way; **faire tout le ~ à pied/en voiture** to walk/drive all the way; **le ~ de la réussite** the road to success ❷ INFORM path ▸ **ne pas y aller par quatre ~s** not to beat around the bush

**chemin de fer** [ʃ(ə)mɛdəfɛR] <chemins de fer> *m* railroad

**cheminée** [ʃ(ə)mine] *f* ❶ (*à l'exté-*

*rieur*) chimney (stack); (*de locomotive*) smokestack ❷ (*dans une pièce*) fireplace ❸ (*conduit*) chimney

**cheminer** [ʃ(ə)mine] <1> *vi fig* (*pensée*) to progress

**chemise** [ʃ(ə)miz] *f* ❶ (*vêtement*) shirt; **~ de nuit** (*de femme*) nightgown; (*d'homme*) nightshirt ❷ (*dossier*) folder

**chemisier** [ʃ(ə)mizje] *m* blouse

**chêne** [ʃɛn] *m* ❶ (*arbre*) oak (tree) ❷ (*bois*) oak

**chenille** [ʃ(ə)nij] *f* caterpillar

**chèque** [ʃɛk] *m* (*pièce bancaire*) check; **faire un ~ de 100 dollars à qn** to write sb a check for 100 dollars

**chéquier** [ʃekje] *m* checkbook

**cher, chère** [ʃɛR] **I.** *adj* ❶ (*coûteux*) expensive, dear ❷ (*aimé*) dear; **c'est mon plus ~ désir** it's my greatest desire ❸ *antéposé* (*estimé*) dear; **~ Monsieur** dear Sir; **chère Madame** dear Madam; **~s tous** dear all **II.** *m, f appellatif* **mon ~/ma chère** my dear **III.** *adv* ❶ (*opp: bon marché*) a lot (of money); **acheter qc trop ~** to pay too much for sth; **avoir pour pas ~** *inf* to get cheap; **coûter/valoir ~** to cost/to be worth a lot ❷ *fig* **coûter ~ à qn** to cost sb dearly; **payer ~ qc** to pay dearly for sth

**chercher** [ʃɛRʃe] <1> **I.** *vt* ❶ (*rechercher: personne, objet, compromis*) to look for; **~ qn des yeux** to look around for sb ❷ (*ramener, rapporter*) **aller/venir ~ qn/qc** to go/to come and get sb/sth; **envoyer un enfant ~ qn/qc** to send a child for sb/sth ▸ **tu l'as (bien) cherché!** you asked for it! **II.** *vi* ❶ (*s'efforcer de*) **~ à** +*infin* to try to +*infin*; **~ à ce que qn fasse qc** (*subj*) to try to make sb do sth ❷ (*fouiller*) **~ dans qc** to look in sth ❸ (*réfléchir*) to think

**chercheur, -euse** [ʃɛRʃœR, -øz] *m, f* ❶ (*savant*) researcher ❷ (*aventurier*) **~ d'or** gold digger

**chéri(e)** [ʃeRi] **I.** *adj* beloved **II.** *m(f)* ❶ (*personne aimée*) darling ❷ *péj* (*favori*) **le ~/la ~e de qn** sb's darling

**chétif, -ive** [ʃetif, -iv] *adj* (*arbre*) stunted; (*personne*) puny

**cheval** [ʃ(ə)val, -o] <-aux> I. *m* ❶ ZOOL horse ❷ SPORT **faire du ~** to go horseback riding; **monter à ~** to ride a horse; **promenade à ~** horseback ride ❸ AUTO, FIN **~ fiscal** *horsepower, used to determine vehicle registration tax* ❹ JEUX knight; **~ à bascule** rocking horse II. *adv* **être à ~ sur les principes** to be a stickler for principles

**chevalerie** [ʃ(ə)valʀi] *f* chivalry

**chevalet** [ʃ(ə)valɛ] *m* (*de peintre*) easel; (*d'un violon*) bridge

**chevalier** [ʃ(ə)valje] *m* knight

**cheval-vapeur** [ʃ(ə)valvapœʀ] <chevaux-vapeur> *m* horsepower

**chevauchée** [ʃ(ə)voʃe] *f* (*promenade*) ride

**chevaucher** [ʃ(ə)voʃe] <1> I. *vt* **~ qc** to sit astride sth II. *vpr* **se ~** to overlap

**chevelu(e)** [ʃəvly] *adj* hairy

**chevelure** [ʃəvlyʀ] *f* (*cheveux*) hair

**chevet** [ʃ(ə)vɛ] *m* headboard; **table de ~** bedside table; **être au ~ de qn** to be at sb's bedside

**cheveu** [ʃ(ə)vø] <x> *m* hair; **avoir les ~x longs** to have long hair ▸ **avoir un ~ sur la langue** to have a lisp

**cheville** [ʃ(ə)vij] *f* ❶ ANAT ankle ❷ (*tige pour assembler*) peg ❸ (*tige pour boucher*) dowel

**chèvre** [ʃɛvʀ] I. *f* ❶ (*animal*) goat ❷ (*femelle*) nanny goat II. *m* (*fromage*) goat cheese

**chevreau** [ʃəvʀo] <x> *m* kid

**chèvrefeuille** [ʃɛvʀəfœj] *m* honeysuckle

**chevreuil** [ʃəvʀœj] *m* ❶ (*animal*) roe deer ❷ (*mâle*) roebuck ❸ CULIN venison ❹ *Québec* (*cerf de Virginie*) deer

**chevronné(e)** [ʃəvʀɔne] *adj* experienced

**chewing-gum** [ʃwiŋɡɔm] <chewing-gums> *m* (chewing) gum

**chez** [ʃe] *prep* ❶ (*au logis de qn*) **~ qn** at sb's place; **~ soi** at home; **je rentre ~ moi** I'm going home; **je viens ~ toi** I'll come to your place; **passer ~ qn** to stop by sb's place; **aller ~ le coiffeur** to go to the hairdresser's; **faites comme ~ vous!** make yourself at home!; **à côté** [*o* près] **de ~ moi** near my place ❷ (*dans le pays de qn*) **ils rentrent ~ eux, en Italie** they're going back home to Italy; **une coutume bien de ~ nous** *inf* a good old local custom ❸ (*dans la personne*) **~ les Durand** at the Durand's; **~ Corneille** in Corneille

**chez-moi** [ʃemwa] *m inv*, **chez-soi** [ʃeswa] *m inv* (own) home

**chiant(e)** [ʃjɑ̃, ʃjɑ̃t] *adj inf* damn annoying

**chic** [ʃik] I. *m sans pl* chic II. *adj inv* ❶ (*élégant*) chic; (*allure*) stylish ❷ (*sélect*) smart ▸ **bon ~ bon genre** *iron* chic and conservative

**chicane** [ʃikan] *f* ❶ (*morceau de route*) chicane ❷ (*querelle*) squabble

**chicaner** [ʃikane] <1> I. *vi* **~ sur qc** to squabble about sth II. *vt* ❶ (*chercher querelle à*) **~ qn sur qc** to quibble with sb over sth ❷ *Québec* (*ennuyer, tracasser*) to bother

**chiche** [ʃiʃ] I. *adj* (*capable*) **t'es pas ~ de faire ça!** *inf* you couldn't do that! II. *interj inf* **~ que je le fais!** (*capable*) I bet you I can do it!; **~!** (*pari accepté*) you're on

**chicorée** [ʃikɔʀe] *f* ❶ (*plante*) chicory ❷ (*café*) chicory coffee

**chien** [ʃjɛ̃] I. *m* ❶ (*animal*) dog; (**attention**) **~ méchant!** beware of the dog!; *v.a.* **chienne** ❷ (*pièce coudée: d'un fusil*) hammer ▸ **vie de ~** dog's life; **temps de ~** foul weather; **il a un mal de ~ pour finir son travail** he has great difficulty finishing his work II. *adj inv* (*avare*) mean; **ne pas être ~ avec qn** to be quite generous toward sb

**chienne** [ʃjɛn] *f* bitch; *v.a.* **chien**

**chiffon** [ʃifɔ̃] *m* ❶ (*tissu*) rag ❷ (*vêtement de femme*) **parler ~s** *inf* to talk (about) clothes

**chiffonné(e)** [ʃifɔne] *adj* (*froissé*) crumpled

**chiffonner** [ʃifɔne] <1> I. *vt* ❶ (*froisser*) to crumple ❷ (*chagriner*) to bother II. *vpr* **se ~** to crumple

**chiffre** [ʃifʀ] *m* ❶ (*caractère*) figure; ~ **romain** roman numeral; **un numéro à trois ~s** a three-figure number ❷ (*montant*) total; ~ **d'affaires** sales ❸ (*nombre: des naissances*) number ❹ (*statistiques*) **les ~s** the figures; **les ~s du chômage** the unemployment statistics ❺ (*code: d'un coffre-fort*) combination; (*d'un message*) code

**chiffrer** [ʃifʀe] <1> I. *vt* ❶ (*numéroter*) to number ❷ (*évaluer*) to assess ❸ (*coder*) to encode II. *vpr* **se ~ à qc** to amount to sth

**chignon** [ʃiɲɔ̃] *m* bun

**Chili** [ʃili] *m* **le ~** Chile

**chilien(ne)** [ʃiljɛ̃, jɛn] *adj* Chilean

**Chilien(ne)** [ʃiljɛ̃, jɛn] *m(f)* Chilean

**chimère** [ʃimeʀ(ə)] *f* (*utopie*) wild dream

**chimie** [ʃimi] *f* chemistry

**chimique** [ʃimik] *adj* chemical

**chimiste** [ʃimist] *mf* chemist

**chimpanzé** [ʃɛ̃pɑ̃ze] *m* chimpanzee

**Chine** [ʃin] *f* **la ~** China

**chinois(e)** [ʃinwa, waz] I. *adj* Chinese II. *m* (*langue*) Chinese; *v.a.* **français** ❷ CULIN (*conical*) strainer

**Chinois(e)** [ʃinwa, waz] *m(f)* Chinese

**chiot** [ʃjo] *m* pup(py)

**chipoter** [ʃipɔte] <1> *vi* (*ergoter*) ~ **sur qc** to quibble about sth

**chips** [ʃips] *f gén pl* chips

**chique** [ʃik] *f* ❶ (*tabac*) plug ❷ *Belgique* (*bonbon*) candy

**chirurgical(e)** [ʃiʀyʀʒikal, -o] <-aux> *adj* surgical

**chirurgie** [ʃiʀyʀʒi] *f* surgery; ~ **esthétique** cosmetic surgery

**chirurgien(ne)** [ʃiʀyʀʒjɛ̃, jɛn] *m(f)* surgeon; ~ **dentiste** oral surgeon

**chlore** [klɔʀ] *m* chlorine

**chloroforme** [klɔʀɔfɔʀm] *m* chloroform

**chlorophylle** [klɔʀɔfil] *f* chlorophyll

**choc** [ʃɔk] *m* ❶ (*émotion brutale, coup*) shock ❷ *fig* (*des idées*) clash; ~ **culturel** culture shock ❸ (*heurt*) impact ❹ (*collision*) crash

**chocolat** [ʃɔkɔla] I. *m* chocolate; ~ **en**

**poudre** hot chocolate mix II. *adj inv* (*couleur*) chocolate(-colored)

**chœur** [kœʀ] *m* ❶ (*chanteurs*) choir ❷ (*groupe*) chorus

**choisi(e)** [ʃwazi] *adj* (*sélectionné: morceau*) selected

**choisir** [ʃwaziʀ] <8> I. *vi* to choose II. *vt* to choose III. *vpr* **se ~ qn/qc** to choose sb/sth

**choix** [ʃwa] *m* ❶ (*action de choisir: d'un ami, cadeau*) choice; **un dessert au ~** a choice of dessert; **laisser le ~ à qn** to let sb decide ❷ (*décision*) **c'est un ~ à faire** it's a choice to be made; **porter son ~ sur qc** to decide on sth ❸ (*variété*) selection ❹ (*qualité*) **de ~** choice; **de premier/second ~** top grade/grade two

**cholestérol** [kɔlɛsteʀɔl] *m* cholesterol

**chômage** [ʃomaʒ] *m* unemployment; **être au ~** to be unemployed; **toucher le ~** *inf* to get unemployment compensation

**chômer** [ʃome] <1> *vi* ❶ (*être sans travail*) to be unemployed ❷ (*ne pas travailler*) to be idle

**chômeur, -euse** [ʃomœʀ, -øz] *m, f* unemployed person

**chope** [ʃɔp] *f* ❶ (*verre*) beer mug ❷ (*contenu*) pint

**choquant(e)** [ʃɔkɑ̃, ɑ̃t] *adj* shocking

**choquer** [ʃɔke] <1> *vt* ❶ (*scandaliser*) to shock ❷ (*offusquer: pudeur*) to offend (against) ❸ (*commotionner*) ~ **qn** to shake sb (up)

**chorale** [kɔʀal] *f* choir

**chorégraphie** [kɔʀegʀafi] *f* choreography

**choriste** [kɔʀist] *mf* (*d'église*) choir member; (*d'opéra*) member of the chorus

**chose** [ʃoz] I. *f* ❶ (*objet*) thing; **appeler les ~s par leur nom** to call a spade a spade; **ne pas faire les ~s à moitié** not to do things by halves; **chaque ~ en son temps** everything in its own time; **les meilleures ~s ont une fin** all good things come to an end; **c'est la moindre des ~s** it's the least I could do

**②** (*ensemble d'événements, de circonstances*) les ~s things; **au point où en sont les ~s** at the point we've got to **③** (*ce dont il s'agit*) matter; **comment a-t-il pris la ~?** how did he take it?; **encore une ~** something else; **c'est ~ faite** it's done; **mettre les ~s au point** to clear things up; **c'est tout autre ~** that's completely different **④** (*paroles*) **j'ai plusieurs ~s à vous dire** I have several things to tell you; **parler de ~s et d'autres** to talk about one thing or another; **passer à autre ~** to talk about something else ▶ **voilà autre ~!** *inf* that's something else; **pas grand-~** nothing much; **avant toute ~** above all (else); **à peu de ~s près** more or less **II.** *adj inv, inf* **être/se sentir tout ~** to be/feel not quite oneself

**chou** [ʃu] <x> *m* **①** (*légume*) cabbage; **~ de Bruxelles** Brussels sprouts **②** CULIN **~ à la crème** cream puff

**chouchou** [ʃuʃu] *m* (*élastique*) scrunchie

**chouchou(te)** [ʃuʃu, ut] *m(f)* *inf* pet; **~ de qn** sb's darling

**choucroute** [ʃukʀut] *f* sauerkraut

**chouette** [ʃwɛt] **I.** *adj inf* great **II.** *f* (*oiseau*) owl

**chou-fleur** [ʃuflœʀ] <choux-fleurs> *m* cauliflower

**chou-rave** [ʃuʀav] <choux-raves> *m* kohlrabi

**choyer** [ʃwaje] <6> *vt* **~ qn** to pamper sb

**chrétien(ne)** [kʀetjɛ̃, jɛn] **I.** *adj* Christian **II.** *m(f)* Christian

**christ** [kʀist] *m* (*crucifix*) crucifix

**christianisme** [kʀistjanism] *m* Christianity

**chrome** [kʀom] *m* (*métal*) chromium

**chromosome** [kʀomozom] *m* chromosome

**chronique** [kʀɔnik] **I.** *adj* chronic **II.** *f* **①** LIT chronicle **②** TV, RADIO program; **~ littéraire** literary feature section

**chronologie** [kʀɔnɔlɔʒi] *f* chronology

**chronologique** [kʀɔnɔlɔʒik] *adj* chronological

**chronomètre** [kʀɔnɔmɛtʀ] *m* SPORT stopwatch

**chrysanthème** [kʀizɑ̃tɛm] *m* chrysanthemum

**C.H.U.** [seaʃy] *m abr de* **centre hospitalier universitaire** ≈ university hospital

**chuchoter** [ʃyʃɔte] <1> *vt, vi* to whisper

**chut** [ʃyt] *interj* sh

**chute** [ʃyt] *f* **①** (*action: d'une personne, des feuilles*) fall; **~ des cheveux** hair loss; **faire une ~ de 5 m** to fall 5 m; **en ~ libre** in a free fall **②** (*effondrement: d'un gouvernement, du dollar*) fall **③** GEO **~ d'eau** waterfall; **les ~s du Niagara** Niagara Falls **④** METEO **~ de neige** snowfall **⑤** (*baisse rapide*) **~ de pression/température** drop in pressure/temperature **⑥** (*déchets: de tissu, papier*) scrap **⑦** (*fin: d'une histoire*) punch line

**chuter** [ʃyte] <1> *vi* **①** *inf* (*tomber*) to fall **②** *inf* (*échouer: candidat*) to fail **③** (*baisser*) to fall

**ci** [si] *adv* **comme ~ comme ça** *inf* soso; **~ et ça** this and that; **à cette heure-~** (*à une heure précise*) at this time; *v.a.* **ceci, celui**

**ci-après** [siapʀɛ] *adv* below

**cibiste** [sibist] *mf* CB enthusiast

**cible** [sibl] **I.** *f* **①** SPORT target **②** COM, CINE, TV target group **II.** *adj* **langue ~** target language

**cibler** [sible] <1> *vt* to target

**ciboulette** [sibulɛt] *f* **①** BOT chive **②** CULIN chives *pl*

**cicatrice** [sikatʀis] *f* scar

**cicatrisation** [sikatʀizasjɔ̃] *f* scarring

**cicatriser** [sikatʀize] <1> **I.** *vt a. fig* to heal **II.** *vi, vpr* to heal (up)

**ci-contre** [sikɔ̃tʀ] *adv* opposite

**ci-dessous** [sid(ə)su] *adv* below

**ci-dessus** [sid(ə)sy] *adv* above

**cidre** [sidʀ] *m* cider

**ciel** [sjɛl, sjø] <cieux *o* s> *m* **①** <s> (*firmament*) sky **②** REL heaven ▶ **au nom du ~!** for heaven's sake

**cierge** [sjɛʀʒ] *m* (*chandelle*) candle

**cieux** [sjø] *pl de* **ciel**

**cigale** [sigal] *f* cicada

**cigare** [sigaʀ] *m* ❶ cigar ❷ *Belgique (remontrance)* rocket
**cigarette** [sigaʀɛt] *f* cigarette
**ci-gît** [siʒi] here lies
**cigogne** [sigɔɲ] *f* stork
**ci-inclus** [siɛ̃kly] enclosed
**ci-joint** [siʒwɛ̃] enclosed
**cil** [sil] *m* eyelash
**cime** [sim] *f* (*d'un arbre*) top; (*d'une montagne*) summit
**ciment** [simã] *m* cement
**cimenter** [simãte] <1> *vt a. fig* to cement
**cimetière** [simtjɛʀ] *m* cemetery
**ciné** [sine] *m inf abr de* **cinéma**
**ciné-club** [sineklœb] <ciné-clubs> *m* film club
**cinéma** [sinema] *m* (*art, salle*) cinema; ~ **muet** silent movies *pl*; **faire du** ~ to be in the movies ▶ **arrête ton** ~ *inf* cut out the games
**cinémathèque** [sinematɛk] *f* (*archives*) film archive(s)
**cinématographique** [sinematɔgʀafik] *adj* film, movie
**cinglé(e)** [sɛ̃gle] I. *adj inf* crazy II. *m(f) inf* **quel** ~ what a nut case!
**cinq** [sɛ̃k, *devant une consonne* sɛ̃] I. *adj* ❶ five; **en** ~ **exemplaires** in quintuplicate; **dans** ~ **jours** in five days; **faire qc un jour sur** ~ to do sth once every five days; **un Français/ foyer sur** ~ one in five Frenchmen/ households; **vendre qc par** ~ to sell sth in fives; **rentrer** ~ **par** ~ to come in [*o to go in*] five at a time; **ils sont venus à** ~ five of them came ❷ (*dans l'indication de l'âge, la durée*) **avoir** ~ **ans** to be five (years old); **à** ~ **ans** at the age of five; **période de** ~ **ans** five-year period ❸ (*dans l'indication de l'heure*) **il est** ~ **heures** it's five o'clock; **il est dix heures** ~/**moins** ~ it's five past ten/five to ten; **toutes les** ~ **heures** every five hours ❹ (*dans l'indication de la date*) **le** ~ **mars** the fifth of March, March fifth; **arriver le** ~ **mars** to arrive (on) March fifth; **arriver le** ~ to arrive on the fifth; **nous sommes** [*o on est*] **le** ~

**mars** it's the fifth of March; **le vendredi** ~ **mars** (on) Friday, the fifth of March; **Aix, le** ~ **mars** Aix, March fifth; **tous les** ~ **du mois** on the fifth of each month ❺ (*dans l'indication de l'ordre*) **arriver** ~ **ou sixième** to come in fifth or sixth ❻ (*dans les noms de personnages*) **Charles V** Charles V, Charles the Fifth II. *m inv* ❶ five; **deux et trois font** ~ two and three make five; **compter de** ~ **en** ~ to count by fives ❷ (*numéro*) five; **habiter (au) 5, rue de l'église** to live at 5 Church Street ❸ (*bus*) **le** ~ the (number) five ❹ JEUX **le** ~ **de cœur** the five of hearts ❺ ECOLE **avoir** ~ **sur dix** ≈ to get a grade of D ▶ ~ **sur** ~ perfectly III. *f* (*table/chambre/... numéro cinq*) five IV. *adv* fifthly
**cinquantaine** [sɛ̃kãtɛn] *f* ❶ (*environ cinquante*) **une** ~ **de personnes/pages** about fifty people/pages ❷ (*âge approximatif*) **avoir la** ~ [*o* **une** ~ **d'années**] to be about fifty (years old); **approcher de la** ~ to be pushing fifty; **avoir (largement) dépassé la** ~ to be (well) over fifty (years old)
**cinquante** [sɛ̃kãt] I. *adj* ❶ fifty; **à** ~ (**à l'heure**) at fifty kilometers an hour (*around 30 miles an hour*) ❷ (*dans l'indication des époques*) **les années** ~ the fifties II. *m inv* ❶ (*cardinal*) fifty ❷ (*taille de confection*) **faire du** ~ (*homme*) to wear a size forty; (*femme*) to wear a size sixteen; *v.a.* **cinq**
**cinquantenaire** [sɛ̃kãtnɛʀ] *m* fiftieth anniversary
**cinquantième** [sɛ̃kãtjɛm] I. *adj antéposé* fiftieth II. *mf* **le/la** ~ the fiftieth III. *m* (*fraction*) fiftieth; *v.a.* **cinquième**
**cinquième** [sɛ̃kjɛm] I. *adj antéposé* fifth; **la** ~ **page avant la fin** the fifth to last page; **arriver** ~/**obtenir la** ~ **place** to finish fifth/to get fifth place; **le** ~ **centenaire** the fifth anniversary II. *mf* **le/la** the fifth, **être le/la** ~ **de la classe** to be fifth in the class III. *m* ❶ (*fraction*) fifth; **les trois** ~**s du gâteau** three fifths of the cake ❷ (*étage*) fifth; **habiter au** ~ to live on the fifth

**C**

floor ❸ (*arrondissement*) **habiter dans le ~** to live in the fifth arrondissement ❹ (*dans une charade*) fifth syllable **IV.** *f* ❶ (*vitesse*) fifth gear; **passer en ~** to shift into fifth gear ❷ ECOLE seventh grade

**cinquièmement** [sɛ̃kjɛmmɑ̃] *adv* fifthly

**cintre** [sɛ̃tʀ] *m* ❶ (*portemanteau*) (coat) hanger ❷ ARCHIT curve

**cirage** [siʀaʒ] *m* (*produit*) (shoe) polish

**circoncis(e)** [siʀkɔ̃si, iz] *adj* circumcised

**circoncision** [siʀkɔ̃sizjɔ̃] *f* circumcision

**circonférence** [siʀkɔ̃feʀɑ̃s] *f* circumference

**circonscription** [siʀkɔ̃skʀipsjɔ̃] *f* ❶ ADMIN district ❷ POL constituency, district

**circonscrire** [siʀkɔ̃skʀiʀ] *vt irr* ❶ (*délimiter*) to delimit ❷ (*borner*) **~ les recherches à un secteur** to limit the search to one area ❸ (*empêcher l'extension de: incendie*) to contain ❹ (*cerner: sujet*) to define

**circonstance** [siʀkɔ̃stɑ̃s] *f* ❶ *souvent pl* (*conditions*) circumstance; **en toutes ~s** in any case ❷ (*occasion*) occasion; **air de ~** apt expression

**circuit** [siʀkɥi] *m* ❶ (*itinéraire touristique*) tour ❷ (*parcours*) roundabout route ❸ SPORT, ELEC circuit ❹ (*jeu*) **~ électrique** electric track ❺ ECON **~ de distribution** distribution network

**circulaire** [siʀkylɛʀ] **I.** *adj* circular **II.** *f* circular

**circulation** [siʀkylasjɔ̃] *f* ❶ (*trafic*) traffic; **~ interdite** (*aux piétons*) closed to pedestrians; (*aux voitures*) closed to traffic; **la ~ est difficile** traffic conditions are bad ❷ ECON, MED circulation

**circuler** [siʀkyle] <1> *vi* ❶ (*aller et venir*) to get around; **~ en voiture** to travel (around) by car; **circulez!** move along! ❷ (*passer de main en main, couler*) to circulate ❸ (*se renouveler*) **l'air circule dans la pièce** the air circulates in the room ❹ (*se répandre: nouvelle*) to circulate; **faire ~ qc** to circulate sth

**cire** [siʀ] *f* wax

**ciré** [siʀe] *m* oilskin

**cirer** [siʀe] <1> *vt* to polish ▸**j'en ai**

rien à ~, moi, de toutes tes histoires! *inf* I don't give a damn about all that!

**cirque** [siʀk] *m* circus

**ciseau** [sizo] <x> *m* ❶ *pl* (*instrument*) (pair of) scissors *pl* ❷ (*outil*) chisel

**citadelle** [sitadɛl] *f* citadel

**citadin(e)** [sitadɛ̃, in] **I.** *adj* **la vie ~e** city [*o* town] life **II.** *m(f)* city dweller

**citation** [sitasjɔ̃] *f* ❶ (*extrait*) quotation ❷ JUR **~ d'un accusé** summons *pl* + *vb sing*; **~ d'un témoin** subpoena

**cité** [site] *f* ❶ (*ville moyenne*) town ❷ (*grande ville*) *a.* HIST city ❸ (*immeubles*) housing project; **~ universitaire** student residence halls *pl*

**cité-dortoir** [sitedɔʀtwaʀ] <cités-dortoirs> *f* bedroom community

**citer** [site] <1> *vt* ❶ (*rapporter*) to quote ❷ (*énumérer*) to name ❸ (*reconnaître les mérites*) to commend; **~ en exemple** to hold up as an example ❹ JUR (*accusé*) to summon; (*témoin*) to subpoena

**citerne** [sitɛʀn] *f* ❶ (*réservoir*) tank ❷ (*pour l'eau de pluie*) water tank

**citoyen(ne)** [sitwajɛ̃, jɛn] *m(f)* citizen

**citron** [sitʀɔ̃] **I.** *m* ❶ (*fruit*) lemon; **~ pressé** fresh lemon juice ❷ *inf* (*tête*) noggin **II.** *adj inv* (*jaune*) **~** lemon yellow

**citrouille** [sitʀuj] *f* BOT pumpkin

**civet** [sivɛ] *m* stew

**civière** [sivjɛʀ] *f* stretcher

**civil** [sivil] *m* ❶ (*personne*) civilian ❷ (*vie civile*) **dans le ~** in civilian life

**civil(e)** [sivil] *adj* ❶ (*relatif au citoyen*) *a.* JUR civil; **année ~e** calendar year; **responsabilité ~e** personal liability; **se porter partie ~e** to take civil action ❷ (*opp: religieux*) **mariage ~** civil wedding

**civilisation** [sivilizasjɔ̃] *f* civilization

**civiliser** [sivilize] <1> **I.** *vt* to civilize **II.** *vpr inf* **se ~** to become civilized

**civique** [sivik] *adj* civic; **instruction ~** civics *pl* + *vb sing*

**clafoutis** [klafuti] *m*: sweet dish made of cherries baked in pancake batter

C

**clair** [klɛʀ] **I.** *adv* (*distinctement, sans ambiguïté*) clearly; **voir ~ dans qc** *fig* to see through sth, to get to the bottom of sth **II.** *m* (*clarté*) **~ de lune** moonlight ▶ **le plus ~ de mon/son temps** most of my/his time; **tirer qc au ~** to clarify sth, to clear sth up; **en ~** in clear; (*dire sans ambiguïté*) to put it clearly

**clair(e)** [klɛʀ] *adj* ❶ (*lumineux*) light; (*flamme, pièce*) bright ❷ (*opp: foncé*) light ❸ (*peu consistant*) thin ❹ (*intelligible, transparent, évident*) clear ▶ **ne pas être ~** *inf* (*être saoul*) to be tipsy; (*être suspect*) to be a bit dubious; (*être fou*) to be a bit crazy

**clairière** [klɛʀjɛʀ] *f* clearing

**claironner** [klɛʀɔne] <1> **I.** *vt iron* to shout from the rooftops **II.** *vi* to play the bugle

**clairsemé(e)** [klɛʀsəme] *adj* ❶ (*dispersé*) scattered ❷ (*peu dense*) thin

**clairvoyance** [klɛʀvwajɑ̃s] *f* perceptiveness

**clan** [klɑ̃] *m a.* HIST clan

**clandestin(e)** [klɑ̃dɛstɛ̃, in] **I.** *adj* clandestine; **passager ~** stowaway **II.** *m(f)* (*immigrant*) illegal immigrant

**clandestinité** [klɑ̃dɛstinite] *f* ❶ (*fait de ne pas être déclaré*) secrecy ❷ (*vie cachée*) **entrer dans la ~** to go underground

**clapoter** [klapɔte] <1> *vi* to lap

**clapotage** [klapataʒ] *m* MED ❶ (*action*) pulling of a muscle ❷ (*résultat*) pulled muscle

**claque¹** [klak] *f* ❶ (*tape sur la joue*) slap ❷ *Québec* (*protection de chaussure, en caoutchouc*) tip

**claque²** [klak] *m* opera hat

**claquer** [klake] <1> **I.** *vt* ❶ (*jeter violemment*) to slam ❷ *inf* (*dépenser*) to blow ❸ *inf* (*fatiguer*) to wear out **II.** *vi* ❶ (*produire un bruit sec: drapeau*) to flap; (*porte, volet*) to bang; (*fouet*) to crack; **il claque des dents** his teeth are chattering ❷ *inf* (*mourir*) to kick the bucket ❸ *inf* (*se casser: élastique*) to snap; (*verre*) to shatter **III.** *vpr inf* MED **se ~ un muscle** to pull a muscle

**claquettes** [klakɛt] *fpl* (*danse*) tap dancing; **faire des ~** to tap-dance

**clarifier** [klaʀifje] <1> **I.** *vt a. fig* to clarify **II.** *vpr* **se ~** (*fait*) to become clarified

**clarinette** [klaʀinɛt] *f* MUS clarinet

**clarté** [klaʀte] *f* ❶ (*lumière: d'une bougie*) light; (*d'une étoile, du ciel*) brightness ❷ (*transparence: d'eau*) clearness ❸ (*opp: confusion*) clarity; **s'exprimer avec ~** to express oneself clearly

**classe** [klas] *f* ❶ (*groupe*) class; **~s moyennes** middle classes; **~ ouvrière** working class; **~ d'âge** age group ❷ (*rang*) **de grande/première ~** first class; **billet de deuxième ~** second class ticket ❸ *inf* (*élégance*) **être ~** to be classy; **c'est ~!** that's chic! ❹ ECOLE class; (*salle*) classroom; **en ~** in class; **~ de cinquième/seconde** seventh/tenth grade; **~ terminale** twelfth grade; **passer dans la ~ supérieure** to move up a year; **faire (la) ~** to teach; **être en ~, avoir ~** to be teaching; **aller en ~** to go to school ❺ (*séjour*) **~ verte** school (*field*) trip to the country ❻ MIL class; **faire ses ~s** to do one's basic training; *fig* to make a start

**classé(e)** [klase] *adj* ❶ (*protégé: bâtiment*) listed (*in the national register of historic places*) ❷ (*réglé: affaire*) closed ❸ (*de valeur*) classified

**classement** [klasmɑ̃] *m* ❶ (*rangement*) filing ❷ (*classification: d'un élève*) grading; (*d'un joueur*) ranking; (*d'un hôtel*) rating ❸ (*place sur une liste*) classification

**classer** [klase] <1> **I.** *vt* ❶ (*ordonner*) to classify ❷ (*répartir*) to class ❸ (*ranger selon la performance*) to rank ❹ (*régler*) to close ❺ (*mettre dans le patrimoine national: monument*) to list **II.** *vpr* (*obtenir un certain rang*) **se ~ premier** to rank first

**classeur** [klasœʀ] *m* ❶ (*dossier*) file ❷ INFORM folder

**classicisme** [klasisism] *m* ART classicism

**classification** [klasifikasjɔ̃] *f* classification

**classifier** [klasifje] <1> *vt* to classify

**classique** [klasik] **I.** *adj* ❶ ART, ECOLE classical ❷ (*habituel*) classic; (*produit*) standard **II.** *m* ❶ (*auteur, œuvre*) classic ❷ (*musique*) classical music

**clause** [kloz] *f* clause

**claustrophobe** [klostʀɔfɔb] **I.** *adj* claustrophobic **II.** *mf*: person suffering from claustrophobia

**clavecin** [klavsɛ̃] *m* MUS harpsichord

**clavicule** [klavikyl] *f* ANAT collarbone

**clavier** [klavje] *m* keyboard

**clé** [kle] *f* ❶ (*instrument*) key; **~ de contact** ignition key; **fermer à ~** to lock ❷ (*moyen d'accéder à*) **la ~ du succès** the key to success ❸ (*outil*) wrench; **~ anglaise** crescent wrench ❹ MUS (*signe*) key; (*pièce*) peg; **~ de sol** treble clef ❺ SPORT lock

**clef** [kle] *f v.* **clé**

**clémence** [klemɑ̃s] *f* clemency

**clément(e)** [klemɑ̃, ɑ̃t] *adj* clement; (*temps*) mild

**clémentine** [klemɑ̃tin] *f* clementine

**clergé** [klɛʀʒe] *m* clergy

**clic** [klik] **I.** *interj* click **II.** *m* click; **~ sur la souris** mouse click; **à portée de ~** a click away

**cliché** [kliʃe] *m* ❶ (*banalité*) cliché ❷ (*photo*) shot

**client(e)** [klijɑ̃, jɑ̃t] *m(f)* ❶ (*acheteur*) customer ❷ (*bénéficiaire d'un service: d'un restaurant*) diner; (*d'un avocat*) client; (*d'un médecin*) patient ❸ ECON buyer

**clientèle** [klijɑ̃tɛl] *f* (*d'un magasin, restaurant*) clientele; (*d'un avocat*) clients *pl*; (*d'un médecin*) patients *pl*

**cligner** [kliɲe] <1> **I.** *vt* ❶ (*fermer à moitié*) to squint ❷ (*ciller*) **~ des yeux** to blink; **~ de l'œil** to wink **II.** *vi* to blink

**clignotant** [kliɲɔtɑ̃] *m* AUTO turn signal; **mettre le/son ~** to signal

**clignotant(e)** [kliɲɔtɑ̃, ɑ̃t] *adj* blinking

**clignoter** [kliɲɔte] <1> *vi* ❶ (*ciller*) **ses yeux clignotaient** he/she was blinking ❷ (*éclairer*) to go on and off

**climat** [klima] *m a.* METEO climate

**climatisation** [klimatizasjɔ̃] *f* air conditioning

**climatiser** [klimatize] <1> *vt* to air-condition

**clin d'œil** [klɛ̃dœj] <clins d'œil *o* clins d'yeux> *m* wink; **faire un ~ à qn** to wink at sb ► **en un ~** in a flash

**clinique** [klinik] **I.** *adj* clinical **II.** *f* clinic

**clip** [klip] *m* ❶ TV (video) clip ❷ (*bijou*) clip

**clique** [klik] *f* péj, inf clique

**cliquer** [klike] <1> *vi* INFORM to click; **~ sur un symbole avec la souris** to click on an icon with the mouse; **~ deux fois de suite sur l'icône** double-click on the icon

**cliquetis** [klik(ə)ti] *m* (*de la monnaie, clés*) jangling; (*de verres*) clinking

**clochard(e)** [klɔʃaʀ, aʀd] *m(f)* bum

**cloche¹** [klɔʃ] *f* bell

**cloche²** [klɔʃ] **I.** *adj* inf ❶ (*maladroit*) clumsy ❷ (*stupide*) stupid **II.** *f* inf ❶ (*maladroit*) clumsy thing ❷ (*idiot*) dope ❸ (*clochards*) bums *pl*

**cloche-pied** [klɔʃpje] **à ~** hopping

**clocher** [klɔʃe] *m* (*church*) tower

**cloison** [klwazɔ̃] *f* partition

**cloître** [klwatʀ] *m* cloister

**cloîtrer** [klwatʀe] <1> *vpr* **se ~ dans sa maison** to shut oneself away at home

**clone** [klɔn] *m* BIO clone

**clope** [klɔp] *m o f* inf ❶ (*cigarette*) smoke ❷ (*mégot*) butt

**cloque** [klɔk] *f* blister

**cloquer** [klɔke] <1> *vi* to blister

**clore** [klɔʀ] *vt irr* ❶ (*terminer*) to conclude; **~ un discours** (*conclusion, remerciements*) to bring a speech to a close ❷ (*entourer: terrain, propriété*) to enclose ❸ FIN (*compte*) to close

**clos** [klo] *m* (*vignoble*) garden

**clos(e)** [klo, kloz] **I.** *part passé de* **clore** **II.** *adj* ❶ (*fermé*) close ❷ (*achevé*) closed

**clôture** [klotyʀ] *f* ❶ (*enceinte*) fence; (*d'arbustes, en ciment*) wall ❷ (*fin: d'un festival*) close; (*d'un débat*) conclusion; (*d'un compte*) closure ❸ INFORM **~ de session** sign off

**clôturer** [klotyʀe] <1> *vt* ❶ (*entourer*) to enclose ❷ (*finir*) to conclude

**clou** [klu] *m* ❶ (*pointe*) nail ❷ (*attraction*) highlight ❸ *pl, inf* (*passage*) crossing + *vb sing* CULIN **~ de girofle** clove

**clouer** [klue] <1> *vt* ❶ (*fixer*) to nail; (*planches, caisse*) to nail down ❷ *inf* (*immobiliser*) **~ qn au lit** to keep sb stuck in bed

**clouté(e)** [klute] *adj* (*chaussures, pneus*) studded

**clown** [klun] *m* clown

**club** [klœb] *m* club

**C.N.R.S.** [seɛnɛrɛs] *m abr de* **Centre national de la recherche scientifique** ≈ NSF (*government institution sponsoring research*)

**coaguler** [kɔagyle] <1> *vi, vi, vpr* (**se**) **~** to coagulate

**coalition** [kɔalisjɔ̃] *f* coalition

**cobaye** [kɔbaj] *m* guinea pig

**cobra** [kɔbra] *m* cobra

**coca(-cola)®** [kɔka(kɔla)] *m* Coca-Cola®

**cocaïne** [kɔkain] *f* cocaine

**cocarde** [kɔkard] *f* rosette

**cocasse** [kɔkas] *adj inf* comical

**coccinelle** [kɔksinɛl] *f* ❶ ZOOL ladybug ❷ AUTO Beetle®

**coccyx** [kɔksis] *m* ANAT coccyx

**cocher¹** [kɔʃe] <1> *vt* to check off

**cocher²** [kɔʃe] *m* coachman

**cochon** [kɔʃɔ̃] *m* ❶ (*animal*) pig ❷ CULIN pork ❸ (*cobaye*) **~ d'Inde** guinea pig

**cochon(ne)** [kɔʃɔ̃, ɔn] **I.** *adj inf* ❶ (*sale*) dirty ❷ (*obscène*) smutty **II.** *m(f) péj, inf* ❶ (*personne sale*) pig ❷ (*vicieux*) swine

**cochonnerie** [kɔʃɔnri] *f inf* ❶ (*nourriture*) slop ❷ (*toc*) junk *souvent pl, inf* ❸ (*obscénités*) smut ❹ *pl* (*saletés*) mess

**cochonnet** [kɔʃɔnɛ] *m* ❶ ZOOL piglet ❷ (*aux boules*) jack

**cocker** [kɔkɛr] *m* cocker spaniel

**cocktail** [kɔktɛl] *m* ❶ (*boisson, mélange*) cocktail ❷ (*réunion*) cocktail party

**coco** [koko] *m péj* (*type*) dude

**cocon** [kɔkɔ̃] *m* cocoon

**cocorico** [kɔkɔriko] *m* cock-a-doodle-doo

**cocotier** [kɔkɔtje] *m* coconut palm

**cocotte** [kɔkɔt] *f* ❶ (*marmite*) casserole dish ❷ *enfantin* (*poule*) hen; **~ en papier** paper bird

**cocotte-minute®** [kɔkɔtminyt] <cocottes-minute> *f* pressure cooker

**cocu(e)** [kɔky] **I.** *adj inf* deceived; **faire qn ~** to be unfaithful to sb **II.** *m(f) inf* deceived husband, wife *m, f*

**code** [kɔd] *m* ❶ (*chiffrage*) code; **~ postal** Zip Code ❷ (*permis*) written test ❸ (*feux*) low beams ❹ JUR civil code; **~ de la route** traffic code

**coder** [kɔde] <1> *vt* to encode

**codifier** [kɔdifje] <1> *vt* to codify

**coefficient** [kɔefisjɑ̃] *m* MATH, PHYS coefficient

**coéquipier, -ière** [koekipje, -jɛr] *m, f* teammate

**cœur** [kœr] *m* heart; **en plein ~ de l'hiver** in the dead of winter ► **avoir le ~ sur la main** to be openhanded; **avoir un ~ d'or/de pierre** to have a heart of gold/stone; **si le ~ vous en dit** if you feel like it; **fendre le ~** to break one's heart; **prendre qc à ~** to take sth to heart; **tenir à ~** to mean a lot to one; **apprendre/connaître/réciter par ~** to learn/know/recite sth by heart; **sans ~** heartless

**coexister** [kɔɛgziste] <1> *vi* to coexist

**coffre** [kɔfr] *m* ❶ (*meuble*) chest ❷ AUTO boot ❸ (*coffre-fort*) safe

**coffre-fort** [kɔfrəfɔr] <coffres-forts> *m* safe

**coffret** [kɔfrɛ] *m* case; **~ à bijoux** jewel box

**cognac** [kɔnak] *m* cognac

**cogner** [kɔne] <1> **I.** *vt* (*heurter*) to bang on **II.** *vi* (*taper*) **~ à/sur/contre qc** to bang at/on/against sth ❷ (*heurter*) **~ contre qc** (*volet, caillou*) to bang against sth ❸ *inf* (*chauffer: soleil*) to beat down **III.** *vpr* **se ~ la tête contre qc** to bang one's head against sth

**cohabitation** [koabitasjɔ̃] f cohabitation

**cohabiter** [koabite] <1> vi to cohabit

**cohérent(e)** [koeʀɑ̃, ɑ̃t] adj (ensemble) coherent; (conduite, texte) consistent

**cohésion** [koezjɔ̃] f (solidarité) cohesion

**cohue** [kɔy] f ❶ (foule) crowd ❷ (bousculade) crush

**coiffé(e)** [kwafe] adj ❶ (peigné) **être ~** to have done one's hair ❷ (chapeauté) **être ~ de qc** to be crowned with sth

**coiffer** [kwafe] <1> I. vt ❶ (peigner) **~ qn** to do sb's hair ❷ (mettre un chapeau) to put a hat on ❸ (dépasser) to nose out II. vpr ❶ (se peigner) **se ~** to do one's hair ❷ (mettre un chapeau) **se ~ de qc** to put sth on (one's head)

**coiffeur, -euse** [kwafœʀ, -øz] m, f hairdresser

**coiffeuse** [kwaføz] f dressing table

**coiffure** [kwafyʀ] f ❶ (façon d'être peigné) hairstyle ❷ (chapeau) hat ❸ (métier) hairdressing

**coin** [kwɛ̃] m ❶ (angle) corner; **au ~ de la rue** at the corner of the street; **sourire en ~** half-smile ❷ (petit espace) spot; **~ cuisine/repas** kitchen/dining area ▸ **aux quatre ~s du <u>monde</u>** all over the world

**coincé(e)** [kwɛ̃se] adj inf hung-up

**coincer** [kwɛ̃se] <2> I. vt ❶ (caler) **~ entre deux chaises** to wedge between two chairs ❷ (immobiliser) **~ qc** (personne) to jam sth; (grain de sable, panne) to jam sth up ❸ (acculer) **~ qn contre un mur** to pin sb against a wall ❹ inf (attraper) to grab ❺ inf (coller) to catch out II. vi (poser problème) to get sticky III. vpr **se ~ le doigt** to pinch one's finger

**coïncidence** [kɔɛ̃sidɑ̃s] f coincidence

**coïncider** [kɔɛ̃side] <1> vi ❶ (être concomitant) to coincide ❷ (correspondre) to match up

**coing** [kwɛ̃] m quince

**col** [kɔl] m ❶ cout (d'un vêtement) collar; **~ roulé** polo neck ❷ geo pass ❸ (goulot) neck ❹ anat (du fémur) neck; **~ de l'utérus** cervix

**colère** [kɔlɛʀ] f ❶ (irritation) anger ❷ (accès d'irritation) fit of rage; **être/ se mettre en ~ contre qn** to be/get angry with sb; **en ~** angry

**coléreux, -euse** [kɔleʀø, -øz], **colérique** [kɔleʀik] adj quick-tempered

**colin** [kɔlɛ̃] m coalfish

**colique** [kɔlik] f ❶ (diarrhée) diarrhea ❷ gén pl (douleurs) stomachache

**colis** [kɔli] m parcel

**collabo** [ko(l)labo] mf péj, inf (pendant une guerre) collaborator

**collaborateur, -trice** [ko(l)labɔʀatœʀ, -tʀis] m, f ❶ (membre du personnel) staff member ❷ (intervenant occasionnel) associate ❸ (pendant une guerre) collaborator

**collaboration** [ko(l)labɔʀasjɔ̃] f ❶ (coopération, pendant une guerre) collaboration; **en ~ avec** in collaboration with ❷ (contribution) contribution

**collaborer** [ko(l)labɔʀe] <1> vi ❶ (coopérer) to collaborate; **~ à qc** to work on sth ❷ (pendant une guerre) to collaborate

**collant** [kɔlɑ̃] m ❶ (bas) tights pl ❷ (body pour la gymnastique) body suit ❸ (body pour la danse, l'acrobatie) leotard

**collant(e)** [kɔlɑ̃, ɑ̃t] adj ❶ (moulant) clinging ❷ (poisseux) sticky ❸ inf (importun: enfant) clingy

**collation** [kɔlasjɔ̃] f light meal

**colle** [kɔl] f ❶ (matière) glue ❷ (masse) sticky mass ❸ (punition) detention

**collecte** [kɔlɛkt] f (quête) collection

**collecter** [kɔlɛkte] <1> vt (dons) to collect

**collectif, -ive** [kɔlɛktif, -iv] adj ❶ (commun) common; (travail) collective; **équipements ~s** shared facilities ❷ ling collective

**collection** [kɔlɛksjɔ̃] f collection; **faire la ~ de qc** to collect sth

**collectionner** [kɔlɛksjɔne] <1> vt to collect

**collectionneur, -euse** [kɔlɛksjɔnœr, -øz] *m, f* collector

**collectivité** [kɔlɛktivite] *f* ❶(*société*) community ❷JUR organization; **~s locales** local authorities ❸(*communauté*) group

**collège** [kɔlɛʒ] *m* ECOLE school

**collégien(ne)** [kɔleʒjɛ̃, jɛn] *m(f)* (*élève*) pupil

**collègue** [kɔ(l)lɛg] *mf* colleague

**coller** [kɔle] <1> **I.** *vt* ❶(*fixer*) to stick; (*enveloppe*) to stick down; (*pièces*) to stick together; (*timbre, étiquette*) to stick on; (*affiche, papier peint*) to stick up ❷(*presser*) **~ à qc** to stick sth on sth ❸*inf* (*donner*) **~ un devoir à qn** to give sb some homework; **~ une baffe à qn** to slap sb ❹*inf* (*embarrasser par une question*) to catch out ❺*inf* (*suivre*) to tail ❻*inf* (*planter*) to stick ❼*inf* (*rester*) **être collé quelque part** to be stuck somewhere **II.** *vi* ❶(*adhérer*) to stick; **qc qui colle** sth sticky ❷(*mouiller*) to cling ❸*inf* (*suivre*) **~ à qc** to hang on to sth ❹(*s'adapter*) **~ à la route** to hug the road; **~ au sujet** to stick (close) to the subject ❺*inf* (*bien marcher*) **entre eux, ça ne colle pas** they're not getting along **III.** *vpr* ❶(*s'accrocher*) **se ~ à qn** to cling to sb ❷(*se presser*) **se ~ à qc** to snuggle up to sb

**collier** [kɔlje] *m* ❶(*bijou*) necklace; (*rigide*) chain ❷(*courroie: d'un chien, cheval*) collar

**colline** [kɔlin] *f* hill

**collision** [kɔlizjɔ̃] *f* collision

**colloque** [kɔ(l)lɔk] *m* conference

**colmater** [kɔlmate] <1> *vt* (*fuite*) to stop; (*fissure*) to fill; (*brèche*) to close

**colocataire** [kɔlɔkatɛr] *mf* cotenant; (*d'appartement*) roommate

**colombage** [kɔlɔ̃baʒ] *m* half-timbering; **maison à ~** half-timbered house

**colombe** [kɔlɔ̃b] *f* dove

**colon** [kɔlɔ̃] *m* ❶(*opp: indigène*) colonist ❷(*enfant*) child (*at a summer camp*) ❸(*pionnier*) settler

**colonel** [kɔlɔnɛl] *m* colonel

**colonial(e)** [kɔlɔnjal, -jo] <-aux> *adj* colonial

**colonie** [kɔlɔni] *f* ❶(*territoire, communauté*) colony ❷(*centre*) **~ de vacances** summer camp

**coloniser** [kɔlɔnize] <1> *vt* to colonize

**colonne** [kɔlɔn] *f* ❶ARCHIT, MIL, PRESSE column ❷ANAT **~ vertébrale** spinal column

**colorant** [kɔlɔrɑ̃] *m* coloring

**colorant(e)** [kɔlɔrɑ̃, ɑ̃t] *adj* coloring; **shampooing ~** hair dye

**coloration** [kɔlɔrasjɔ̃] *f* ❶(*processus*) coloring ❷(*teinte*) tint ❸(*nuance*) color

**coloré(e)** [kɔlɔre] *adj* (*en couleurs*) colored

**colorer** [kɔlɔre] <1> **I.** *vt* to color **II.** *vpr* **se ~** (*visage*) to turn red

**colorier** [kɔlɔrje] <1> *vt* ❶(*jeu*) to color (in) ❷ART to color

**coloris** [kɔlɔri] *m* ❶(*teinte*) shade ❷(*couleur*) color

**colossal(e)** [kɔlɔsal, -o] <-aux> *adj* colossal

**colosse** [kɔlɔs] *m* ❶(*géant*) colossus ❷*fig* giant

**colporter** [kɔlpɔrte] <1> *vt* ❶(*vendre*) to peddle ❷*péj* (*répandre*) to hawk

**colporteur, -euse** [kɔlpɔrtœr, -øz] *m, f* peddler

**colza** [kɔlza] *m* rape

**coma** [kɔma] *m* coma; **être dans le ~** to be in a coma

**combat** [kɔ̃ba] *m* combat

**combatif, -ive** [kɔ̃batif, -iv] *adj* combative

**combattant(e)** [kɔ̃batɑ̃, ɑ̃t] *m(f)* combatant; **ancien ~** veteran

**combattre** [kɔ̃batr] *irr* **I.** *vt, vi* to fight **II.** *vpr* **se ~** to fight each other

**combien** [kɔ̃bjɛ̃] **I.** *adv* ❶(*concernant la quantité*) how much; **~ de temps** how long; **depuis ~ de temps** for how long; **~ coûte cela?** how much does that cost?; **ça fait ~?** *inf* how much is that?; **je vous dois ~?** what do I owe you? ❷(*concernant le nombre*) how many; **~ de personnes** how many people; **~ de fois** how often **II.** *m inf* **①** (*en parlant de la date*) **nous sommes le ~?** what's the date today? **②** (*en parlant d'un intervalle*) **le bus passe tous les ~?** how often does the bus come? **III.** *mf* **c'est le/la ~?** what number is he/she?

**combinaison** [kɔ̃binɛz] *f* **①** (*assemblage*) *a.* CHIM combination **②** (*chiffres*) code **③** (*mot*) password **④** (*sous-vêtement*) slip **⑤** (*vêtement*) suit **⑥** (*stratagème*) scheme

**combine** [kɔ̃bin] *f inf* scheme; **connaître la ~** to know the way

**combiné** [kɔ̃bine] *m* **①** TEL handset **②** (*épreuve de ski*) **~ nordique** Nordic combined competition

**combiner** [kɔ̃bine] <1> **I.** *vt* **①** (*réunir*) *a.* CHIM **~ qc avec qc** to combine sth with sth **②** (*organiser: plan*) to think up; (*mauvais coup*) to cook up **II.** *vpr* **①** (*s'assembler*) *a.* CHIM **se ~ avec qc** to combine with sth **②** (*s'arranger*) **bien/mal se ~** to work out all right/all wrong

**comble¹** [kɔ̃bl] *m* **①** (*summum: de la bêtise*) height; **c'est le ~!** that beats everything! **②** *souvent pl* (*grenier*) eaves

**comble²** [kɔ̃bl] *adj* packed

**combler** [kɔ̃ble] <1> *vt* **①** (*boucher*) to fill in **②** (*rattraper: déficit*) to make up for; (*lacune*) to fill; **~ un retard** to catch up **③** (*satisfaire: personne, vœu*) to satisfy

**combustible** [kɔ̃bystibl] **I.** *adj* combustible **II.** *m* fuel

**combustion** [kɔ̃bystjɔ̃] *f* combustion

**comédie** [kɔmedi] *f* **①** (*pièce*) play; **~ musicale** musical (comedy) **②** (*film*) comedy **③** (*simulation*) performance

**comédien(ne)** [kɔmedjɛ̃, jɛn] *m(f)* **①** (*acteur*) actor **②** (*hypocrite*) phony

**comestible** [kɔmɛstibl] *adj* edible

**comète** [kɔmɛt] *f* comet

**comique** [kɔmik] **I.** *adj* **①** (*amusant*) funny **②** THEAT, CINE, LIT comic **③** (*auteur*) comic author **③** (*interprète*) comic actor **③** (*genre*) comedy

**comité** [kɔmite] *m* (*réunion*) committee; **~ d'entreprise** ≈ workers' council (*dealing with welfare and cultural matters*)

**commandant(e)** [kɔmɑ̃dɑ̃, ɑ̃t] *m(f)* **①** MIL (*chef*) commander; (*grade*) major; (*dans l'armée de l'air*) major; **~ en chef** commander-in-chief **②** AVIAT, NAUT captain

**commande** [kɔmɑ̃d] *f* **①** (*achat, marchandise*) order; **passer une ~** to place an order **②** TECH **à distance** remote control **③** INFORM command; **message d'attente de ~** command prompt ▶ **prendre les ~s** to take control

**commandement** [kɔmɑ̃dmɑ̃] *m* **①** (*direction*) control **②** (*état-major*) **le haut ~** the High Command **③** (*ordre*) command **④** REL commandment

**commander** [kɔmɑ̃de] <1> *vt* **①** (*passer commande*) **~ qc à qn** to order sth from sb **②** (*exercer son autorité*) to command **③** (*ordonner*) **~ qc à qn** to command sth from sb **④** (*diriger*) to direct **⑤** (*faire fonctionner*) to control **II.** *vi* **①** (*passer commande*) to order **②** (*exercer son autorité*) to command **III.** *vpr* **①** (*être actionné*) **se ~ de l'extérieur** to be controlled from the outside **②** (*se contrôler*) **ne pas se ~** (*sentiments*) to be beyond one's control

**comme** [kɔm] **I.** *conj* **①** (*au moment où, étant donné que*) as **②** (*de même que*) (just) like; **hier ~ aujourd'hui** yesterday just like today **③** (*exprimant une comparaison*) **il était ~ mort** it was as if he was dead; **grand/petit ~ ça** this big/small; **~ si** as if **④** (*en tant que*) as; **~ plat principal** as the main course **⑤** (*tel que*) like; **je n'ai jamais vu un film ~ celui-ci** I've never seen a film like this **⑥** (*quel genre de*) in the way of; **qu'est-ce que tu fais ~ sport?** what sports do you play? ▶ **... ~ tout** *inf* **il est mignon ~ tout!** he's so sweet! **II.** *adv* **①** (*exclamatif*) **~ c'est gentil!** isn't that kind! **②** (*manière*) how; **~ ça** like that; **c'est ~ ça** that's the way it is; **il n'est pas ~ ça** he's not like that

**►~ ci ~ ça** so-so; **~ quoi** (*disant que*) to the effect that; (*ce qui prouve*) which goes to show

**commémorer** [kɔmemɔʀe] <1> *vt* to commemorate

**commencement** [kɔmɑ̃smɑ̃] *m* beginning

**commencer** [kɔmɑ̃se] <2> **I.** *vt* to begin **II.** *vi* ❶ (*débuter: événement*) to begin ❷ (*faire en premier*) **~ par qc/par faire qc** to begin with sth/by doing sth **►ça commence bien** *iron* that's a good start; **ça commence à bien faire** it's getting to be a little bit too much; **pour ~** to start with

**comment** [kɔmɑ̃] *adv* ❶ (*de quelle façon*) how; **~ ça va?** how are things?; **et toi, ~ tu t'appelles?** and what's your name?; **~ est-ce que ça s'appelle en français?** what's the word for that in French? ❷ (*invitation à répéter*) ~? what? **►~ cela?** how come?; **et ~!** and how!

**commentaire** [kɔmɑ̃tɛʀ] *m* ❶ RADIO, TV commentary ❷ *péj* (*remarque*) comment; **sans ~!** no comment!

**commentateur, -trice** [kɔmɑ̃tatœʀ, -tʀis] *m, f* commentator

**commenter** [kɔmɑ̃te] <1> *vt* (*événement*) to comment on; (*texte*) to give an interpretation of

**commerçant(e)** [kɔmɛʀsɑ̃, ɑ̃t] **I.** *adj* ❶ (*avec des magasins: rue*) shopping ❷ (*habile*) **être ~** to have business sense **II.** *m(f)* (*personne*) storekeeper

**commerce** [kɔmɛʀs] *m* ❶ (*activité*) business; **faire du ~** to be in business; **dans le ~** in business; **chambre de ~** chamber of commerce; **employé de ~** shop assistant; **~ électronique** e-commerce ❷ (*magasin*) shop, store; **~ de détail** retailing; **~ en gros** wholesaling

**commercial(e)** [kɔmɛʀsjal, -jo] <-aux> **I.** *adj* ❶ COM commercial; **centre ~** shopping center ❷ *péj* (*film*) commercial; (*sourire*) mercenary **II.** *m(f)* sales representative

**commercialiser** [kɔmɛʀsjalize] <1> *vt*

❶ (*vendre*) to market ❷ (*lancer*) to put on the market

**commettre** [kɔmɛtʀ] *vt irr* (*délit, attentat*) to commit; (*faute*) to make

**commissaire** [kɔmisɛʀ] *mf* ❶ (*policier*) superintendent; **madame le/la ~** madam; **monsieur le ~** sir ❷ (*membre d'une commission*) commissioner

**commissaire-priseur, -euse** [kɔmisɛʀpʀizœʀ, -øz] <commissaires-priseurs> *m, f* auctioneer

**commissariat** [kɔmisaʀja] *m* police station

**commission** [kɔmisjɔ̃] *f* ❶ ADMIN, COM commission ❷ (*message*) message ❸ (*mission*) commission ❹ *pl* (*courses*) shopping

**commode¹** [kɔmɔd] *adj* ❶ (*pratique*) practical ❷ *souvent négatif* (*facile*) convenient ❸ (*d'un caractère facile*) **ses parents n'ont pas l'air ~** her parents don't look easy to get along with

**commode²** [kɔmɔd] *f* commode

**commodité** [kɔmɔdite] *f* ❶ (*agrément*) comfort ❷ (*simplification*) convenience ❸ *pl* (*éléments de confort*) conveniences

**commotion** [kɔmosjɔ̃] *f* shock; **~ cérébrale** concussion

**commun** [kɔmœ̃] *m* **hors du ~** out of the ordinary; **en ~** in common; **faire qc en ~** to do sth together

**commun(e)** [kɔmœ̃, yn] *adj* ❶ (*comparable, général, courant, trivial*) common; **n'avoir rien de ~ avec qn/qc** to have nothing in common with sb/sth ❷ (*collectif*) communal

**communal(e)** [kɔmynal, -o] <-aux> *adj* ❶ (*fonds*) communal; (*du village*) village; (*de la ville*) city ❷ *Belgique* **conseil ~** (*conseil municipal*) city council; **maison ~e** (*mairie*) city hall

**communautaire** [kɔmynotɛʀ] *adj* ❶ (*commun*) common ❷ (*de l'UE*) Community

**communauté** [kɔmynote] *f* ❶ (*groupe*) *a.* REL community ❷ (*identité*) sharing

**Communauté économique euro-péenne** f European Economic Community

**Communauté européenne** f European Community

**commune** [kɔmyn] f commune

**communiant(e)** [kɔmynjā, jāt] m(f) communicant

**communicatif, -ive** [kɔmynikatif, -iv] adj ❶ (contagieux) transmissible ❷ (expansif) communicative

**communication** [kɔmynikasjɔ̃] f ❶ (transmission) communication ❷ TEL (jonction) connection; (conversation) call; **être en ~ avec qn** to be on the phone with sb ❸ (message) message ❹ (relation) public relations ❺ (liaison) **moyen de ~** means of communication

**communion** [kɔmynjɔ̃] f communion

**communiqué** [kɔmynike] m communiqué; **~ de presse** press release

**communiquer** [kɔmynike] <1> I. vt ❶ (faire connaître) **~ une demande à qn** to convey a request to sb ❷ (transmettre) **~ un dossier à qn** to pass a file on to sb II. vi **~ avec qn** to communicate with sb

**communisme** [kɔmynism] m communism

**communiste** [kɔmynist] I. adj communist II. mf communist

**compact** [kɔpakt] m CD

**compact(e)** [kɔpakt] adj ❶ (dense) dense ❷ (petit) compact

**compagne** [kɔpaɲ] f partner

**compagnie** [kɔpaɲi] f company ▸ **tenir ~ à qn** to keep sb company; **en ~ de qn** in sb's company

**compagnon** [kɔpaɲɔ̃] m ❶ (concubin) partner ❷ (ouvrier) journeyman

**comparable** [kɔparabl] adj comparable

**comparaison** [kɔparεzɔ̃] f comparison; **en ~ de/par ~ avec** in comparison with; **sans ~** far and away

**comparaître** [kɔparεtr] vi irr **~ devant qn** to appear before sb

**comparer** [kɔpare] <1> I. vt, vi to compare II. vpr **se ~ à qn** to compare oneself to sb

**compartiment** [kɔpartimā] m compartment

**compas** [kɔpa] m compass

**compatibilité** [kɔpatibilite] f compatibility

**compatible** [kɔpatibl] adj compatible

**compatriote** [kɔpatrijɔt] mf compatriot

**compensation** [kɔpāsasjɔ̃] f ❶ (dédommagement) compensation ❷ (équilibre) balance ❸ FIN (d'une dette) offsetting ▸ **en ~** in compensation

**compenser** [kɔpāse] <1> vt ❶ (équilibrer) **~ qc par qc** to offset sth with sth ❷ (dédommager) **pour ~** to compensate ❸ (remercier) **pour ~** to make up

**compétence** [kɔpetās] f ❶ (capacité) competence ❷ (responsabilité) domain

**compétent(e)** [kɔpetā, āt] adj competent; **être ~ en qc** to be competent at sth

**compétitif, -ive** [kɔpetitif, -iv] adj competitive

**compétition** [kɔpetisjɔ̃] f competition

**compilateur** [kɔpilatœr] m INFORM compiler

**compilation** [kɔpilasjɔ̃] f compilation

**compiler** [kɔpile] <1> vt INFORM to compile

**complaisant(e)** [kɔplεzā, āt] adj ❶ (obligeant) obliging ❷ (indulgent) kindly ❸ (satisfait) self-satisfied

**complément** [kɔplemā] m ❶ (ce qui s'ajoute) **un ~ d'information** further information ❷ LING complement; **~ du verbe** verb complement; **~ circonstanciel de temps/lieu** adverbial phrase of time/place; **~ du nom** noun phrase; **~ d'objet direct** direct object

**complémentaire** [kɔplemātεr] adj complementary; (renseignement) additional

**complet, -ète** [kɔplε, -εt] adj ❶ complete; (pain) whole-wheat ❷ (achevé) utter ❸ (plein: autobus, hôtel, parking) full; **afficher ~** to play to full houses

**complètement** [kɔplεtmā] adv completely

**compléter** [kɔplete] <5> I. vt to complete **II.** *vpr* **se ~** to complement each other

**complexe** [kɔ̃plɛks] *adj, m* complex

**complexé(e)** [kɔ̃plɛkse] *adj inf* ① PSYCH neurotic ② (*coincé*) uptight

**complexité** [kɔ̃plɛksite] *f* complexity

**complication** [kɔ̃plikasjɔ̃] *f* complication

**complice** [kɔ̃plis] **I.** *adj* ① (*acolyte*) **être ~ d'un vol** to be party to a theft ② (*de connivence*) knowing **II.** *mf* accomplice

**complicité** [kɔ̃plisite] *f* ① (*participation*) complicity; **~ de vol** JUR aiding and abetting a theft ② (*connivence*) complicity

**compliment** [kɔ̃plimɑ̃] *m* ① (*éloge*) compliment ② (*félicitations*) congratulations

**complimenter** [kɔ̃plimɑ̃te] <1> *vt* ① (*congratuler*) **~ qn pour qc** to congratulate sb on sth ② (*faire l'éloge*) **~ qn pour** [*o* **sur**] **qc** to compliment sb on sth

**compliqué(e)** [kɔ̃plike] *adj* complicated; **c'est pas ~** *inf* it's easy enough

**compliquer** [kɔ̃plike] <1> **I.** *vt* to complicate **II.** *vpr* ① (*devenir plus compliqué*) **se ~** (*choses, situation*) to get complicated; **ça se complique** *inf* things are getting complicated ② (*rendre plus compliqué*) **se ~ la vie** to make one's life complicated

**complot** [kɔ̃plo] *m* conspiracy

**comploter** [kɔ̃plɔte] <1> **I.** *vt* to conspire **II.** *vi* **~ contre qn** to conspire against sb

**comportement** [kɔ̃pɔrtəmɑ̃] *m* behavior

**comporter** [kɔ̃pɔrte] <1> **I.** *vt* ① (*être constitué de*) to consist of ② (*inclure*) to have **II.** *vpr* **se ~** ① (*se conduire*) to behave ② (*réagir*) to respond

**composant** [kɔ̃pozɑ̃] *m* ① CHIM constituent ② ELEC component

**composant(e)** [kɔ̃pozɑ̃, ɑ̃t] *adj* component

**composé** [kɔ̃poze] *m* compound

**composé(e)** [kɔ̃poze] *adj* compound

**composer** [kɔ̃poze] <1> **I.** *vt* ① (*constituer*) to form; (*équipe*) to select ② (*créer: plat*) to devise; (*musique*) to compose; (*texte*) to write ③ (*former*) to make up **II.** *vi* MUS to compose **III.** *vpr* **se ~ de qc** to be composed of sth

**compositeur,  -trice** [kɔ̃pozitœr, -tris] *m, f* composer

**composition** [kɔ̃pozisjɔ̃] *f* ① (*organisation*) make-up ② ART, LIT, MUS (*d'une musique*) composition; (*d'un texte*) writing ③ (*œuvre, structure*) composition; **une œuvre de ma ~** a work composed by me

**composter** [kɔ̃pɔste] <1> *vt* to date-stamp

**compote** [kɔ̃pɔt] *f* compote; **~ de pommes** applesauce

**compréhensible** [kɔ̃preɑ̃sibl] *adj* comprehensible

**compréhensif, -ive** [kɔ̃preɑ̃sif, -iv] *adj* understanding

**compréhension** [kɔ̃preɑ̃sjɔ̃] *f* ① (*clarté*) intelligibility ② (*tolérance*) understanding ③ (*intelligence*) comprehension

**comprendre** [kɔ̃prɑ̃dr] <13> **I.** *vt* ① (*saisir, concevoir, s'apercevoir de*) to understand; **faire ~ qc à qn** (*expliquer*) to get sb to understand sth; (*dire indirectement*) to drop sb a hint about sth ② (*comporter*) to comprise ③ (*inclure*) to include **II.** *vi* to understand; **se faire ~** (*par un étranger*) to make oneself understood; (*dire carrément*) to make oneself clear **III.** *vpr* **se ~** ① (*être compréhensible*) to be comprehensible ② (*communiquer*) to understand each other ③ (*s'accorder: personnes*) to reach an understanding

**compresse** [kɔ̃prɛs] *f* compress

**compression** [kɔ̃presjɔ̃] *f* ① PHYS, INFORM compression ② (*réduction*) reduction

**comprimé** [kɔ̃prime] *m* tablet

**comprimé(e)** [kɔ̃prime] *adj* PHYS **air ~** compressed air

**comprimer** [kɔ̃prime] <1> *vt* (*presser*) *a.* INFORM to compress

C

**compris(e)** [kɔ̃pʀi, iz] **I.** *part passé de* **comprendre II.** *adj* ❶ (*inclus*) included; **T.V.A. ~e** including VAT; (**la**) **T.V.A. non ~e** VAT not included ❷ (*situé*) **être ~ entre cinq et sept pourcent** to be between five and seven percent; **période ~e entre 1920 et 1930** period from 1920 to 1930

**compromettant(e)** [kɔ̃pʀɔmetɑ̃, ɑ̃t] *adj* compromising

**compromettre** [kɔ̃pʀɔmɛtʀ] *irr* **I.** *vt* ❶ (*impliquer*) to compromise ❷ (*menacer*) to put at risk **II.** *vpr* **se ~ avec qn/dans qc** to compromise oneself with sb/in sth

**compromis** [kɔ̃pʀɔmi] *m* compromise

**comptabiliser** [kɔ̃tabilize] <1> *vt* FIN to list

**comptabilité** [kɔ̃tabilite] *f* ❶ (*discipline*) accounting ❷ (*comptes, service*) accounts *pl*

**comptable** [kɔ̃tabl] *mf* accountant

**comptant** [kɔ̃tɑ̃] **I.** *m sans pl* cash **II.** *adv* (*payer*) (in) cash

**compte** [kɔ̃t] *m* ❶ *sans pl* (*calcul*) calculation; (*des points*) scoring; **~ à rebours** countdown ❷ *sans pl* (*résultat*) total; **avez-vous le bon ~ de chaises?** (*suffisamment*) do you have enough chairs?; (*le même nombre*) do you have all the chairs?; **le ~ est bon** (*en payant*) that's right; (*rien ne manque*) everything's there; **le ~ y est** *inf* it's all there ❸ (*note*) bill; **faire le ~** to add up ❹ (*écritures comptables*) account; **faire/tenir les ~s** to do/to keep the accounts ❺ (*compte en banque*) bank account; **~ chèque** checking account; **~ chèque postal** *post office checking account* ▶ **en fin de ~** when all is said and done; **tout ~ fait** all things considered; **rendre ~ de qc à qn** (*pour se justifier*) to justify sth to sb; (*avertir*) to report sth to sb; **se rendre ~ de qc** to realize sth; **tu te rends ~!** (*imagine*) just think!; **tenir ~ de qc** to take account of sth; **à son ~** (*travailler*) for oneself; **pour le ~ de qn/qc** for sb/sth

**compte-gouttes** [kɔ̃tgut] *m inv* dropper ▶ **au ~** bit by bit

**compter** [kɔ̃te] <1> **I.** *vt* ❶ (*chiffrer, ajouter*) to count; **dix personnes sans ~ les enfants** ten people, not counting the children ❷ (*totaliser*) to count up ❸ (*facturer*) **~ 100 euros à qn pour le dépannage** to charge sb 100 euros for the repair ❹ (*prévoir*) **~ 200 g/20 euros par personne** to allow 200 grams/20 euros per head ❺ (*prendre en compte*) to allow for ❻ (*ranger parmi*) **~ qn/qc parmi ...** to place sb/sth among ... ❼ (*comporter*) to have ❽ (*avoir l'intention de*) **~ +infin** to intend to +*infin*; (*espérer*) to expect to +*infin* **II.** *vi* ❶ (*énumérer, calculer*) to count ❷ (*être économe*) **dépenser sans ~** to spend without thinking of the cost ❸ (*tenir compte de*) **~ avec qn/qc** to take sth into account ❹ (*s'appuyer*) **~ sur qn/qc** to count on sb/sth ❺ (*avoir de l'importance*) to count; **~ pour qn** to mean a lot to sb **III.** *vpr* (*s'inclure*) **se ~** to include oneself

**compte rendu** [kɔ̃tʀɑ̃dy] *m* account; TV, RADIO report

**compteur** [kɔ̃tœʀ] *m* ❶ AUTO odometer ❷ (*enregistreur: électricité*) meter ❸ INFORM **~ de visites** hit counter

**comptoir** [kɔ̃twaʀ] *m* counter

**comte** [kɔ̃t] *m* count

**comté** [kɔ̃te] *m* county

**comtesse** [kɔ̃tɛs] *f* countess

**con(ne)** [kɔ̃, kɔn] *inf* **I.** *adj parfois inv* stupid **II.** *m(f)* fool; **pauvre ~!** *péj* you stupid prick! *vulg;* **pauvre ~ne!** *péj* stupid bitch!; **faire le ~** to fool around

**concentration** [kɔ̃sɑ̃tʀasjɔ̃] *f* concentration

**concentré** [kɔ̃sɑ̃tʀe] *m* CULIN concentrate

**concentré(e)** [kɔ̃sɑ̃tʀe] *adj* ❶ (*condensé*) concentrated; (*lait*) condensed ❷ (*attentif*) **être ~** to be concentrating

**concentrer** [kɔ̃sɑ̃tʀe] <1> **I.** *vt* (*rassembler*) to concentrate **II.** *vpr* **se ~ sur qn/qc** to concentrate on sb/sth

**concept** [kɔ̃sɛpt] *m* concept

**conception** [kɔ̃sɛpsjɔ̃] f ① *sans pl* (*idée*) a. BIO conception ② *sans pl* (*élaboration*) design; ~ **assistée par ordinateur** computer-aided design ▶**Immaculée Conception** Immaculate Conception

**concernant** [kɔ̃sɛʀnɑ̃] *prep* (*quant à*) concerning

**concerner** [kɔ̃sɛʀne] <1> *vt* to concern; **en** [*o* **pour**] **ce qui concerne qn/qc** as far as sb/sth is concerned

**concert** [kɔ̃sɛʀ] *m* concert

**concertation** [kɔ̃sɛʀtasjɔ̃] f consultation

**concerter** [kɔ̃sɛʀte] <1> *vpr* **se ~ sur qc** to consult about sth

**concession** [kɔ̃sesjɔ̃] f ① (*compromis, terrain*) a. ADMIN concession ② COM dealership

**concessionnaire** [kɔ̃sesjɔnɛʀ] *mf* COM dealer

**concevable** [kɔ̃s(ə)vabl] *adj* conceivable

**concevoir** [kɔ̃s(ə)vwaʀ] <12> I. *vt* ① *soutenu* (*engendrer*) to conceive ② (*se représenter*) to imagine; (*solution*) to think of; ~ **qc comme qc** to think of sth as sth ③ (*élaborer*) to design II. *vpr* (*se comprendre*) **cela se conçoit facilement** that is easily understandable

**concierge** [kɔ̃sjɛʀʒ] *mf* concierge

**concilier** [kɔ̃silje] <1> *vt* (*harmoniser*) to reconcile

**concis(e)** [kɔ̃si, iz] *adj* concise; **soyez ~** be brief

**concitoyen(ne)** [kɔ̃sitwajɛ̃, jɛn] *m(f)* fellow citizen

**concluant(e)** [kɔ̃klyã, ãt] *adj* conclusive

**conclure** [kɔ̃klyʀ] *irr* I. *vt* ① (*signer: marché, pacte*) to sign; (*accord*) to reach ② (*terminer: discours*) to conclude; (*repas*) to finish (off) ③ (*déduire*) ~ **qc de qc** to conclude sth from sth II. *vi* (*terminer*) ~ **par qc** to conclude with sth; **pour ~** in conclusion III. *vpr* **se ~ par qc** to end with sth

**conclusion** [kɔ̃klyzjɔ̃] f ① (*signature: d'un accord*) signing; (*d'un mariage*) conclusion ② (*fin, déduction*) conclu-

sion; **en ~** in conclusion; **~, ...** the upshot is, ...

**concombre** [kɔ̃kɔ̃bʀ] *m* cucumber

**concorder** [kɔ̃kɔʀde] <1> *vi* to agree

**concourir** [kɔ̃kuʀiʀ] *vi irr* ① *soutenu* (*contribuer*) ~ **à qc** to work toward sth ② (*être en compétition*) ~ **à qc** to compete in sth

**concours** [kɔ̃kuʀ] *m* ① (*compétition, jeu*) a. SPORT competition ② ECOLE, UNIV (*pour une école*) entrance examination; (*pour un prix*) prize competition ③ (*aide*) support

**concret** [kɔ̃kʀɛ] *m sans pl* concrete

**concret, -ète** [kɔ̃kʀɛ, -ɛt] *adj* concrete

**concrétiser** [kɔ̃kʀetize] <1> I. *vt* ① (*réaliser: rêve, projet*) to realize ② (*matérialiser*) to bring to fruition II. *vpr* **se ~** to be realized

**conçu(e)** [kɔ̃sy] *part passé de* **concevoir**

**concubin(e)** [kɔ̃kybɛ̃, in] *m(f)* partner

**concubinage** [kɔ̃kybinaʒ] *m* cohabitation

**concurrence** [kɔ̃kyʀãs] f *sans pl* (*compétition, les concurrents*) a. COM competition

**concurrencer** [kɔ̃kyʀãse] <2> *vt* to be in competition with

**concurrent(e)** [kɔ̃kyʀã, ãt] I. *adj* competing II. *m(f)* competitor

**condamnation** [kɔ̃danasjɔ̃] f ① *sans pl* JUR (*action*) conviction; (*peine*) sentence; ~ **avec sursis** suspended sentence ② (*réprobation*) condemnation ③ (*fermeture*) closing

**condamné(e)** [kɔ̃dane] *m(f)* (*convicted*) prisoner; ~ **à mort** prisoner sentenced to death

**condamner** [kɔ̃dane] <1> *vt* ① JUR (*déclarer coupable*) to convict; ~ **qn à 10 ans de prison** to sentence sb to ten years in prison ② (*obliger*) ~ **qn à** +*infin* to condemn sb to +*infin* ③ (*fermer avec des pierres*) to wall up; (*avec du bois*) to board up; (*rue*) to seal off; (*à clé*) to lock

**condenser** [kɔ̃dãse] *vt, vpr* (**se**) ~ **to** condense

**condiment** [kɔ̃dimɑ̃] *m* condiment; *fig* spice

**condition** [kɔ̃disjɔ̃] *f* condition; **à ~ que** +*subj* on condition that; **à ~ de faire qc** provided that sth is done; **se mettre en ~ pour qc** SPORT, PSYCH to get oneself into condition for sth; **dans ces ~s** in that case

**conditionnel** [kɔ̃disjɔnɛl] *m* conditional

**conditionnel(le)** [kɔ̃disjɔnɛl] *adj* conditional

**condoléances** [kɔ̃dɔleɑ̃s] *fpl form* condolences; **(toutes) mes ~!** my deepest sympathy

**conducteur, -trice** [kɔ̃dyktœʀ, -tʀis] I. *adj* PHYS conducting II. *m, f* driver

**conduire** [kɔ̃dɥiʀ] *irr* I. *vi* ❶ (*piloter*) to drive ❷ (*aboutir*) **~ à la catastrophe** to lead to disaster II. *vt* ❶ (*guider, diriger*) to lead ❷ (*en voiture*) **~ qn en ville** to take sb into town ❸ (*mener*) **~ qn à** +*infin* to lead sb to +*infin* III. *vpr* ❶ (*se comporter*) **se ~** to behave ❷ AUTO **se ~ facilement** to drive nicely

**conduit** [kɔ̃dɥi] *m* pipe; ANAT duct

**conduite** [kɔ̃dɥit] *f* ❶ *sans pl* AUTO **~ à droite/à gauche** right-/left-hand drive ❷ (*façon de conduire*) driving ❸ *sans pl* (*responsabilité*) management ❹ (*comportement*) conduct ❺ (*tuyau*) pipe

**cône** [kon] *m* cone

**confection** [kɔ̃fɛksjɔ̃] *f* ❶ CULIN preparation ❷ *sans pl* (*prêt-à-porter*) ready-to-wear

**confectionner** [kɔ̃fɛksjɔne] <1> *vt* ❶ CULIN to prepare ❷ (*fabriquer*) to make

**confédération** [kɔ̃federasjɔ̃] *f* ❶ POL confederation ❷ (*syndicat, groupement*) union

**conférence** [kɔ̃feʀɑ̃s] *f* ❶ (*exposé*) lecture ❷ (*réunion*) a. POL conference

**conférencier, -ière** [kɔ̃feʀɑ̃sje, -jɛʀ] *m, f* lecturer

**confesser** [kɔ̃fese] <1> I. *vi* to go to confession II. *vt* (*péché, erreur*) to confess III. *vpr* **se ~ à qn** to confess to sb; **aller se ~** to go to confession

**confession** [kɔ̃fesjɔ̃] *f* ❶ (*sacrement, aveu*) confession ❷ (*religion*) denomination

**confessionnal** [kɔ̃fesjɔnal, -o] <-aux> *m* confessional

**confetti** [kɔ̃feti] *m* confetti

**confiance** [kɔ̃fjɑ̃s] *f sans pl* confidence, trust; **perdre/reprendre ~ (en soi)** to lose/get back one's self-confidence

**confiant(e)** [kɔ̃fjɑ̃, jɑ̃t] *adj* ❶ (*sans méfiance*) trusting; **~ en qn/qc** trusting in sb/sth ❷ (*sûr de soi*) confident

**confidence** [kɔ̃fidɑ̃s] *f* confidence; **mettre qn dans la ~** to let sb in on the secret

**confidentiel(le)** [kɔ̃fidɑ̃sjɛl] *adj* ❶ (*secret*) confidential ❷ (*restreint: tirage*) limited

**confier** [kɔ̃fje] <1> I. *vt* ❶ (*dévoiler*) to confide ❷ (*remettre*) **~ une mission à qn** to entrust sb with a mission II. *vpr* (*se confesser*) **se ~ à qn** to confide in sb

**confirmation** [kɔ̃firmasjɔ̃] *f* confirmation

**confirmer** [kɔ̃firme] <1> I. *vt* to confirm II. *vpr* (*être exact*) **se ~** to prove correct

**confiserie** [kɔ̃fizri] *f* (*sucrerie*) sweet

**confisquer** [kɔ̃fiske] <1> *vt* to confiscate

**confit** [kɔ̃fi] *m* **~ d'oie** goose confit

**confit(e)** [kɔ̃fi, it] *adj* (*fruits*) candied; (*condiments*) pickled

**confiture** [kɔ̃fityʀ] *f* jam

**conflit** [kɔ̃fli] *m* conflict

**confluent** [kɔ̃flyɑ̃] *m* confluent

**confondre** [kɔ̃fɔ̃dʀ] <14> I. *vi* to make a mistake II. *vt* (*mêler*) to confuse

**conforme** [kɔ̃fɔʀm] *adj* ❶ (*correspondant*) **être ~ à qc** (*normes*) to comply with sth; **copie certifiée ~** certified copy ❷ (*en accord avec*) **être ~ à qc** to be in accordance with sth ❸ (*conformiste*) conventional

**conformité** [kɔ̃fɔʀmite] *f* conformity

**confort** [kɔ̃fɔʀ] *m* ❶ *sans pl* (*luxe*) comfort ❷ (*commodité*) **offrir un grand ~ d'utilisation** to be designed for easy

use ❸ *sans pl* (*bien-être*) well-being; **aimer son ~** to like to feel at ease
**confortable** [kɔ̃fɔʀtabl] *adj* comfortable
**confortablement** [kɔ̃fɔʀtabləmɑ̃] *adv* ❶ (*commodément*) comfortably ❷ (*largement*) **vivre ~** to live in comfort
**confrère** [kɔ̃fʀɛʀ] *m* colleague
**confrontation** [kɔ̃fʀɔ̃tasjɔ̃] *f* confrontation
**confronter** [kɔ̃fʀɔ̃te] <1> I. *vt* ❶ JUR to confront ❷ (*mettre en face de*) to compare II. *vpr* **se ~ à qc** to be confronted with sth
**confus(e)** [kɔ̃fy, yz] *adj* ❶ (*indistinct*) vague ❷ (*embrouillé*) confused ❸ (*embarrassé*) ashamed
**confusion** [kɔ̃fyzjɔ̃] *f* ❶ *sans pl* (*embarras*) embarrassment ❷ (*erreur*) confusion ❸ *sans pl* (*agitation*) confusion; (*désordre*) chaos
**congé** [kɔ̃ʒe] *m* ❶ (*vacances*) vacation; **~s payés** paid vacation; **avoir 2 jours de ~** to have two days off; **être en ~ de maladie** to be on sick leave; **~ (de) maternité** maternity leave ❷ (*licenciement*) **donner son ~ à qn** to dismiss sb ❸ (*salutation*) **prendre ~ de qn/qc** to take (one's) leave of sb/sth
**congédier** [kɔ̃ʒedje] <1> *vt* (*employé*) to dismiss; (*visiteur*) to send away
**congélateur** [kɔ̃ʒelatœʀ] *m* freezer
**congeler** [kɔ̃ʒ(ə)le] <4> *vt, vpr* (**se**) to freeze
**congère** [kɔ̃ʒɛʀ] *f* snowdrift
**congrès** [kɔ̃gʀɛ] *m* congress
**conique** [kɔnik] *adj* conical
**conjoint(e)** [kɔ̃ʒwɛ̃, wɛ̃t] *m(f)* *form* spouse
**conjonction** [kɔ̃ʒɔ̃ksjɔ̃] *f* conjunction
**conjoncture** [kɔ̃ʒɔ̃ktyʀ] *f sans pl* ECON economic situation
**conjugaison** [kɔ̃ʒygɛzɔ̃] *f* conjugation
**conjugal(e)** [kɔ̃ʒygal, -o] <-aux> *adj* conjugal
**conjuguer** [kɔ̃ʒyge] <1> I. *vt* ❶ LING to conjugate ❷ (*unir*) to combine II. *vpr* LING **se ~** to conjugate
**connaissance** [kɔnɛsɑ̃s] *f* ❶ *sans pl* (*fait de connaître*) knowledge; **pren-**

**dre ~ de qc** to learn of sth; **à ma ~** to my knowledge; **en ~ de cause** knowingly ❷ *pl* (*choses apprises*) knowledge; **avoir une bonne ~ des langues** to have a good command of languages; **approfondir ses ~s** to deepen one's knowledge ❸ (*personne*) acquaintance; **faire la ~ de qn** to make sb's acquaintance; **je suis enchanté de faire votre ~** I'm delighted to make your acquaintance ❹ (*lucidité*) consciousness; **perdre ~** to faint; MED to lose consciousness
**connaisseur, -euse** [kɔnɛsœʀ, -øz] I. *adj* knowledgeable II. *m, f* ART, CULIN connoisseur
**connaître** [kɔnɛtʀ] *irr* I. *vt* ❶ (*savoir*) know; **on connaît les meurtriers?** do we know the murderers?; **vous connaissez la nouvelle?** have you heard the news?; **comme je te connais, ...** knowing you the way I do, ... ❷ (*comprendre*) **~ son métier** to know one's job; **ne rien ~ à qc** to know nothing about sth ❸ (*rencontrer*) to get to know; **faire ~ qn à qn** to introduce sb to sb ❹ (*éprouver*) to have; **~ un succès fou** to be a huge success II. *vpr* ❶ (*se fréquenter*) **se ~ depuis longtemps** to have known each other a long time ❷ (*être capable de se juger*) **se ~** to know oneself ❸ (*être spécialiste*) **s'y ~** to be an expert; **s'y ~ en ordinateurs** to know all about computers
**connard** [kɔnaʀ] *m inf* stupid ass
**connasse** [kɔnas] *f inf* stupid bitch
**connecter** [kɔnɛkte] <1> I. *vt* to connect; **~ des ordinateurs en réseau** to network computers; **connecté** online; **non connecté** offline II. *vpr* **se ~ au réseau** to get onto the network; **se ~ à Internet** to get on the Internet
**connerie** [kɔnʀi] *f* ❶ *sans pl, inf* (*stupidité*) stupidity ❷ (*acte*) idiocy
**connexion** [kɔnɛksjɔ̃] *f* ❷ INFORM connection
**connu(e)** [kɔny] I. *part passé de* **connaître** II. *adj* known
**conquérant(e)** [kɔ̃keʀɑ̃, ɑ̃t] I. *adj* (*es-*

**C**

*prit*) dominating; (*air*) swaggering
II. *m(f)* conqueror

**conquérir** [kɔ̃keRiR] *vt irr* to conquer; (*cœur, personne*) to win

**conquête** [kɔ̃kɛt] *f* conquest

**conquis(e)** [kɔ̃ki, iz] *part passé de* **conquérir**

**consacrer** [kɔ̃sakRe] <1> I. *vt* (*donner*) to devote II. *vpr* **se ~ à qn/qc** to devote oneself to sth

**consciemment** [kɔ̃sjamã] *adj* consciously

**conscience** [kɔ̃sjɑ̃s] *f* ① *sans pl* PSYCH consciousness; **avoir/prendre ~ de qc** to be/become conscious of sth; **perdre/reprendre ~** to lose/regain consciousness ② *sans pl* (*connaissance*) **la ~ de qc** the knowledge of sth ③ *sans pl* (*sens moral*) conscience; **donner bonne ~ à qn** to put sb's conscience at ease; **donner mauvaise ~ à qn** to give sb a guilty conscience

**consciencieux, -euse** [kɔ̃sjɑ̃sjø, -jøz] *adj* conscientious

**conscient(e)** [kɔ̃sjɑ̃, jɑ̃t] *adj* ① (*informé*) aware ② (*lucide*) conscious

**consécration** [kɔ̃sekRasjɔ̃] *f sans pl* (*confirmation*) crowning (point)

**consécutif, -ive** [kɔ̃sekytif, -iv] *adj* ① (*à la file*) consecutive ② (*résultant de*) **~ à qc** following sth

**conseil** [kɔ̃sɛj] *m* ① (*recommandation*) piece of advice; **donner des ~s à qn** to give sb advice; **demander ~ à qn** to ask sb for advice; **faire qc sur le ~ de qn** to do sth on sb's advice ② (*personne*) adviser ③ (*assemblée*) council; **~ municipal** city council; **~ de classe** staff meeting (*to discuss a particular class*); **~ de l'Europe** Council of Europe

**conseiller** [kɔ̃seje] <1> I. *vt* ① (*recommander: vin*) to recommend; **~ la prudence à qn** to advise sb to be careful ② (*inciter*) **~ à qn de** +*infin* to advise sb to +*infin* ③ (*guider*) **~ qn dans qc** to advise sb on sth II. *vt impers* **il est conseillé à qn de** +*infin* sb is advised to +*infin*

**conseiller, -ère** [kɔ̃seje, -ɛR] *m, f* ① (*qui donne des conseils*) adviser ② (*expert*) **~ en entreprise** business consultant ③ ADMIN, POL councilor; **~ municipal** city councilor; **~ fédéral** *Suisse* federal councilor ④ ECOLE **~ d'orientation** career counselor

**consensus** [kɔ̃sɛ̃sys] *m* consensus

**consentement** [kɔ̃sɑ̃tmɑ̃] *m* consent

**consentir** [kɔ̃sɑ̃tiR] <10> I. *vi* (*accepter*) **~ à qc** to consent to sth; **~ à ce que qn fasse qc** (*subj*) to consent to sb doing sth II. *vt* (*accorder*) to grant

**conséquence** [kɔ̃sekɑ̃s] *f* consequence; **avoir qc pour** [*o* **comme**] **~** to result in sth; **sans ~** of no consequence; **en ~** (*donc*) consequently; (*conformément à cela*) accordingly; **en ~ de qc** as a consequence of sth

**conséquent(e)** [kɔ̃sekɑ̃, ɑ̃t] *adj* ① (*cohérent*) consistent; **par ~** in consequence ② *inf* (*considérable*) sizeable

**conservateur, -trice** [kɔ̃sɛRvatœR, -tRis] I. *adj* ① POL conservative ② CULIN **agent ~** preservative II. *m, f* ① (*directeur: d'un musée*) curator ② POL conservative III. *m* preservative

**conservation** [kɔ̃sɛRvasjɔ̃] *f* (*action: d'un aliment*) preserving; (*d'un monument*) conservation; (*garde: d'un aliment*) keeping; (*des archives*) conservation

**conservatoire** [kɔ̃sɛRvatwaR] *m* ① MUS conservatory ② THEAT academy

**conserve** [kɔ̃sɛRv] *f* tin; **des petits pois en ~** canned peas; **mettre qc en ~** (*industriellement*) to can; (*à la maison*) to preserve

**conserver** [kɔ̃sɛRve] <1> I. *vt* ① (*garder: papiers, aliments*) to keep; (*monument*) to maintain ② CULIN to preserve ③ (*ne pas perdre*) to keep; **~ son calme** to stay calm II. *vi inf* **qc/ça conserve** sth/that keeps you young III. *vpr* **se ~** (*aliment*) to keep

**considérable** [kɔ̃sideRabl] *adj* considerable; (*travail*) sizable

**considération** [kɔ̃sideRasjɔ̃] *f* ① *pl* (*raisonnement*) consideration ② (*estime*) respect ❸ (*attention*) **en ~ de qc** in consideration of sth; **prendre qn/qc en ~** to take sb/sth into consideration

**considérer** [kɔ̃sidere] <5> **I.** *vt* ❶ (*étudier*) to consider; **considérant que** considering (that) ❷ (*estimer*) **être considéré** to be respected ❸ (*contempler*) to stare at ❹ (*penser*) **~ que ...** to think that ... ❺ (*tenir pour*) **~ qn comme un traître** to consider sb a traitor **II.** *vpr* (*se tenir pour*) **se ~ comme le responsable** to consider oneself responsible

**consigne** [kɔ̃siɲ] *f* ❶ *sans pl* baggage check ❷ *sans pl* COM deposit ❸ (*instructions*) orders *pl*

**consigné(e)** [kɔ̃siɲe] *adj* returnable

**consigner** [kɔ̃siɲe] <1> *vt* ❶ (*facturer*) **la bouteille est consignée** there is a deposit on the bottle ❷ (*enregistrer*) to record

**consistance** [kɔ̃sistɑ̃s] *f* consistency

**consistant(e)** [kɔ̃sistɑ̃, ɑ̃t] *adj* ❶ (*épais*) thick ❷ *inf* (*substantiel*) substantial

**consister** [kɔ̃siste] <1> *vi* **~ en qc** to consist of sth; **~ à faire qc** to consist in doing sth

**consœur** [kɔ̃sœʀ] *f* colleague; *v.a.* **confrère**

**consolation** [kɔ̃sɔlasjɔ̃] *f* consolation

**console** [kɔ̃sɔl] *f* ❶ (*meuble*) console (table) ❷ TECH console

**consoler** [kɔ̃sɔle] <1> **I.** *vt* to console **II.** *vpr* **se ~** to console each other

**consolider** [kɔ̃sɔlide] <1> *vt* (*rendre solide*) to strengthen; (*mur, table*) to brace

**consommateur, -trice** [kɔ̃sɔmatœʀ, -tʀis] *m, f* consumer

**consommation** [kɔ̃sɔmasjɔ̃] *f* ❶ *sans pl* (*usage*) a. ECON **~ de qc** consumption of sth ❷ (*boisson*) drink

**consommer** [kɔ̃sɔme] <1> **I.** *vi* (*boire*) to drink ❶ (*acheter*) to consume **II.** *vt* ❶ CULIN (*plat*) to eat; (*vin*) to drink ❷ (*user*) to consume **III.** *vpr* **se ~ chaud** to be eaten hot; (*boisson*) to be drunk hot; **à ~ avant le ...** use by ...

**consonne** [kɔ̃sɔn] *f* consonant

**conspiration** [kɔ̃spiʀasjɔ̃] *f* **~ contre qn/qc** conspiracy against sb/sth

**conspirer** [kɔ̃spiʀe] <1> *vi* to conspire

**constamment** [kɔ̃stamɑ̃] *adv* constantly

**constance** [kɔ̃stɑ̃s] *f* constancy

**constant(e)** [kɔ̃stɑ̃, ɑ̃t] *adj* constant

**constat** [kɔ̃sta] *m* report; **~ à l'amiable** joint accident report

**constatation** [kɔ̃statasjɔ̃] *f* observation; **arriver à la ~ que ...** to reach the conclusion that ...

**constater** [kɔ̃state] <1> *vt* to observe

**constellation** [kɔ̃stelasjɔ̃] *f* ASTR constellation

**consterné(e)** [kɔ̃stɛʀne] *adj* dismayed

**consterner** [kɔ̃stɛʀne] <1> *vt* to dismay

**constipation** [kɔ̃stipasjɔ̃] *f* constipation

**constipé(e)** [kɔ̃stipe] *adj* MED constipated

**constituer** [kɔ̃stitɥe] <1> **I.** *vt* ❶ (*composer*) to make up ❷ (*former: gouvernement*) to form; (*dossier*) to build up; (*société*) to set up ❸ (*représenter*) to constitute **II.** *vpr* ❶ JUR (*s'instituer*) **se ~ témoin** to come forward as a witness ❷ (*accumuler*) **se ~** to build up

**constitution** [kɔ̃stitysjɔ̃] *f* ❶ POL constitution ❷ *sans pl* (*élaboration: d'un groupe*) formation; (*d'une bibliothèque*) creation; (*d'un dossier*) putting together ❸ *sans pl* (*composition*) make-up

**constitutionnel(le)** [kɔ̃stitysjɔnɛl] *adj* constitutional

**constructeur** [kɔ̃stʀyktœʀ] *m* builder

**constructif, -ive** [kɔ̃stʀyktif, -iv] *adj* constructive

**construction** [kɔ̃stʀyksjɔ̃] *f* ❶ *sans pl* (*action*) building ❷ (*secteur*) construction; **être en ~** to be under construction ❸ (*édifice*) building

**construire** [kɔ̃stʀɥiʀ] *irr vt* ❶ (*bâtir*) to build ❷ (*fabriquer*) to make ❸ (*élaborer*) to construct

**consul** [kɔ̃syl] *m* consul

**consulat** [kɔ̃syla] *m* consulate

**consultant(e)** [kɔ̃syl/tɑ̃, ɑ̃t] I. *adj* consultant II. *m(f)* consultant

**consultation** [kɔ̃syltasjɔ̃] *f* ❶ *sans pl* (*examen: d'un ouvrage*) consulting; (*d'un agenda, d'un horaire*) checking ❷ (*séance*) consultation ❸ *Suisse* (*prise de position*) consultation

**consulter** [kɔ̃sylte] <1> I. *vi* to consult II. *vt* ❶ (*demander avis*) to consult ❷ (*regarder: montre, agenda, ouvrage*) to check ❸ POL ~ **l'opinion** to poll public opinion III. *vpr* **se** ~ to confer

**consumer** [kɔ̃syme] <1> I. *vt* (*brûler*) to consume II. *vpr* **se** ~ to waste away; (*cigarette*) to burn away

**contact** [kɔ̃takt] *m* ❶ *sans pl* (*toucher*) contact; **au** ~ **de l'air** in contact with air ❷ (*rapport*) contact; **au** ~ **de qn** through contact with sb; **prendre** ~ **avec qn/qc** to get in contact with sb/ sth ❸ ELEC, AUTO connection; **couper/ mettre le** ~ to turn the engine off/on

**contacter** [kɔ̃takte] <1> *vt* to contact

**contagieux, -euse** [kɔ̃taʒjø, -jøz] *adj* contagious

**contagion** [kɔ̃taʒjɔ̃] *f* contagion

**container** [kɔ̃tɛnɛʀ] *m* container

**contaminer** [kɔ̃tamine] <1> *vt* (*personne, virus*) to infect; (*milieu*) to contaminate

**conte** [kɔ̃t] *m* tale

**contemplation** [kɔ̃tɑ̃plasjɔ̃] *f sans pl* contemplation

**contempler** [kɔ̃tɑ̃ple] <1> I. *vt* to contemplate II. *vpr* **se** ~ to gaze at oneself

**contemporain(e)** [kɔ̃tɑ̃pɔʀɛ̃, ɛn] *adj, m(f)* contemporary

**contenance** [kɔ̃t(ə)nɑ̃s] *f* ❶ (*capacité*) capacity ❷ (*attitude*) attitude

**conteneur** [kɔ̃t(ə)nœʀ] *m* container

**contenir** [kɔ̃t(ə)niʀ] <9> I. *vt* ❶ (*renfermer*) to contain ❷ (*maîtriser: foule*) to restrain II. *vpr* **se** ~ to contain oneself

**content(e)** [kɔ̃tɑ̃, ɑ̃t] *adj* ❶ (*heureux*) ~ **de qc** happy about sth; **être** ~ **pour qn** to be glad for sb; **être** ~ **que** +*subj* to be glad that ❷ (*satisfait*) ~ **de qn/qc** pleased with sb/sth; **être** ~ **de soi** to be pleased with oneself

**contenter** [kɔ̃tɑ̃te] <1> I. *vt* (*personne*) to please; (*besoin*) to satisfy II. *vpr* **se** ~ **de qc** to satisfy oneself with sth

**contenu** [kɔ̃t(ə)ny] *m* content

**contenu(e)** [kɔ̃t(ə)ny] *adj* restrained

**contestable** [kɔ̃tɛstabl] *adj* questionable

**contestataire** [kɔ̃tɛstatɛʀ] I. *adj* **être** ~ to call things into question; (*mouvement*) to protest II. *mf* protester

**contestation** [kɔ̃tɛstasjɔ̃] *f* protest

**contester** [kɔ̃tɛste] <1> I. *vi* to call things into question II. *vt* (*discuter*) to dispute; **je ne conteste pas que** +*subj* I don't dispute that; **être contesté** to be questioned

**contexte** [kɔ̃tɛkst] *m* ❶ LING context ❷ (*situation*) background

**continent** [kɔ̃tinɑ̃] *m* ❶ GEO continent ❷ (*opp: île*) mainland

**continu** [kɔ̃tiny] *m sans pl* **en** ~ continuously

**continu(e)** [kɔ̃tiny] *adj* (*ligne*) unbroken; (*effort, bruit*) continuous

**continuation** [kɔ̃tinɥasjɔ̃] *f* continuation

**continuel(le)** [kɔ̃tinɥɛl] *adj* ❶ (*fréquent*) constant ❷ (*ininterrompu*) continual

**continuellement** [kɔ̃tinɥɛlmɑ̃] *adv* ❶ (*fréquemment*) constantly ❷ (*sans s'arrêter*) continually

**continuer** [kɔ̃tinɥe] <1> I. *vi* ❶ (*se poursuivre*) to continue; (*bruit, pluie*) to go on ❷ (*poursuivre*) to carry on; (*à pied*) to walk on; (*en voiture*) to drive on; ~ **à lire** to carry on reading ❸ (*persister*) ~ **à croire que ...** to continue to believe that ...; ~ **à faire qc** to continue doing sth II. *vt* ❶ (*poursuivre*) to continue; (*politique*) to pursue ❷ (*prolonger*) to extend

**contour** [kɔ̃tuʀ] *m* outline; (*appréciation esthétique*) *a.* GEO contour

**contourner** [kɔ̃tuʀne] <1> *vt* ❶ (*faire le tour*) ~ **qc** (*route, voiture*) to bypass sth; (*personne*) to go around sth ❷ (*éluder*) to get around

**contraceptif** [kɔ̃trasɛptif] *m* contraceptive

**contraceptif, -ive** [kɔ̃trasɛptif, -iv] *adj* contraceptive

**contraception** [kɔ̃trasɛpsjɔ̃] *f* contraception

**contracter** [kɔ̃trakte] <1> *vpr* se ~ to contract; (*visage*) to tense

**contractuel(le)** [kɔ̃traktɥɛl] **I.** *adj* (*obligation*) contractual; (*employé*) contract **II.** *m(f)* (*auxiliaire de police*) traffic policeman

**contradiction** [kɔ̃tradiksjɔ̃] *f sans pl* contradiction; **être en ~ avec qn** to be in disagreement with sb; **être en ~ avec qc** to be inconsistent with sth

**contradictoire** [kɔ̃tradiktwar] *adj* (*incompatible*) contradictory; (*influences*) conflicting

**contraignant(e)** [kɔ̃trɛɲɑ̃, ɑ̃t] *adj* restricting

**contraindre** [kɔ̃trɛ̃dr] *irr vt* ~ **qn à l'économie/à l'action** to force sb to be economical/to act

**contraint(e)** [kɔ̃trɛ̃, ɛ̃t] *adj* forced

**contrainte** [kɔ̃trɛ̃t] *f* constraint; **sous la ~** under pressure

**contraire** [kɔ̃trɛr] **I.** *adj* ❶ (*opposé*) opposite; (*preuve*) opposing; (*opinions*) conflicting ❷ (*incompatible*) ~ **à l'usage** contrary to general practice; ~ **à la loi** against the law ❸ (*défavorable*) contrary **II.** *m* contrary; **bien au ~** on the contrary

**contrairement** [kɔ̃trɛrmɑ̃] *adv* ~ **à qn/qc** contrary to sb/sth; ~ **à ce que je croyais** contrary to what I thought

**contrariant(e)** [kɔ̃trarjɑ̃, jɑ̃t] *adj* ❶ (*opp: docile*) annoying ❷ (*fâcheux*) upsetting

**contrarier** [kɔ̃trarje] <1> *vt* ❶ (*fâcher*) to annoy ❷ (*gêner: projets*) to thwart

**contrariété** [kɔ̃trarjete] *f sans pl* annoyance

**contraste** [kɔ̃trast] *m* contrast

**contraster** [kɔ̃traste] <1> *vt* ~ **avec qc** to contrast with sth

**contrat** [kɔ̃tra] *m* contract; ~ **à durée déterminée/indéterminée** fixed-term/open contract; ~ **de location** rental agreement; ~ **de travail** work contract

**contravention** [kɔ̃travɑ̃sjɔ̃] *f* ❶ (*procès-verbal*) parking ticket ❷ (*amende*) fine

**contre** [kɔ̃tr] **I.** *prep* ❶ (*opposition, contact*) against; **serrés les uns ~ les autres** squashed up against each other; **avoir qc ~ qn/qc** to have sth against sb/sth; **être furieux ~ qn** to be furious with sb ❷ (*échange*) for; **échanger un sac ~ une montre** to exchange a bag for a watch ❸ (*proportion*) **ils se battaient à dix ~ un** they were fighting ten against one; **le projet de loi a été adopté à 32 voix ~ 24** the bill passed by 32 votes to 24 **II.** *adv* (*opposition*) **être/voter ~** to be/vote against (it); **je n'ai rien ~** I have no objection; **par ~** on the other hand **III.** *m* SPORT counter

**contrebalancer** [kɔ̃trəbalɑ̃se] <2> *vt* ❶ (*équilibrer*) to counterbalance ❷ (*compenser*) to offset

**contrebande** [kɔ̃trəbɑ̃d] *f* ❶ (*activité*) smuggling ❷ (*marchandise*) contraband

**contrebandier, -ière** [kɔ̃trəbɑ̃dje, -jɛr] *m, f* smuggler

**contrebas** [kɔ̃trəba] *adv* **en ~ de qc** below sth

**contrebasse** [kɔ̃trəbas] *f* double bass

**contrecarrer** [kɔ̃trəkare] <1> *vt* to thwart

**contrecœur** [kɔ̃trəkœr] *adv* **à ~** reluctantly

**contrecoup** [kɔ̃trəku] *m* repercussion

**contre-courant** [kɔ̃trəkurɑ̃] <contre-courants> *m* countercurrent; **à ~** against the current

**contredire** [kɔ̃trədir] *irr* **I.** *vt* to contradict **II.** *vpr* se ~ to contradict oneself

**contrefaçon** [kɔ̃trəfasɔ̃] *f* ❶ (*action*) forging ❷ (*abus.*) forgery

**contrefaire** [kɔ̃trəfɛr] *vt irr* ❶ (*imiter*) to forge ❷ (*déguiser*) to imitate

**contrefait(e)** [kɔ̃trəfɛ, ɛt] *adj* (*imité*) counterfeit

**contre-jour** [kɔ̃trəʒuʀ] *m* back light; **à ~** into the light

**contremaître, -maîtresse** [kɔ̃trəmɛtr, -mɛtrɛs] *m, f* foreman, forewoman *m, f*

**contrepartie** [kɔ̃trəparti] *f* compensation ▸**en ~** in compensation; (*par contre*) on the other hand

**contrepoids** [kɔ̃trəpwa] *m* counterweight; (*d'une horloge*) balance weight; **faire ~** to act as a counterbalance

**contrepoison** [kɔ̃trəpwazɔ̃] *m* antidote

**contrer** [kɔ̃tre] <1> I. *vi* JEUX to counter II. *vt* to block

**contresens** [kɔ̃trəsɑ̃s] *m* misinterpretation; (*dans une traduction*) mistranslation

**contretemps** [kɔ̃trətɑ̃] *m* mishap; **à ~** at the wrong moment; MUS off the beat

**contribuable** [kɔ̃tribɥabl] *mf* taxpayer

**contribuer** [kɔ̃tribɥe] <1> *vi* **~ à qc** to contribute to sth

**contribution** [kɔ̃tribysjɔ̃] *f* **①** (*participation*) **~ à qc** contribution to sth; **mettre qn à ~ pour qc** to make use of sb for sth **②** *pl* (*impôts*) local tax **③** *pl* (*service*) tax office **④** INFORM news item

**contrôle** [kɔ̃trol] *m* **①** (*vérification: des passeports*) control; (*douane*) check **②** *sans pl* (*surveillance*) monitoring; **exercer un ~ sur qc** to monitor sth **③** ECOLE test; **~ de géographie** geography test; **~ continu** UNIV continuous assessment **④** (*maîtrise*) **garder/perdre le ~ de qc** to keep/lose control of sth

**contrôler** [kɔ̃trole] <1> I. *vt* **①** (*vérifier: liste, affirmation*) to check; (*comptes*) to audit **②** (*surveiller: opération*) to supervise; (*prix*) to monitor **③** (*maîtriser*) to control II. *vpr* **se ~** to control oneself

**contrôleur** [kɔ̃trolœr] *m* INFORM controller

**contrôleur, -euse** [kɔ̃trolœr, -øz] *m, f* **①** (*dans le train*) inspector **②** FIN auditor

**controversé(e)** [kɔ̃trɔvɛrse] *adj* controversial

**contusion** [kɔ̃tyzjɔ̃] *f* contusion

**convaincant(e)** [kɔ̃vɛ̃kɑ̃, ɑ̃t] *adj* convincing

**convaincre** [kɔ̃vɛ̃kr] *irr* I. *vt* (*persuader*) **~ qn de qc** (*par des arguments*) to convince sb of sth; **~ qn de +infin** to persuade sb to +infin II. *vpr* **se ~ de qc** to convince sb of sth

**convaincu(e)** [kɔ̃vɛ̃ky] I. *part passé de* **convaincre** II. *adj* **être ~ de qc** to be convinced of sth

**convalescence** [kɔ̃valesɑ̃s] *f* convalescence

**convalescent(e)** [kɔ̃valesɑ̃, ɑ̃t] I. *adj* convalescent II. *m(f)* convalescent

**convenable** [kɔ̃vnabl] *adj* **①** (*adéquat*) suitable; (*distance*) reasonable **②** (*correct*) appropriate **③** (*acceptable: salaire, vin*) decent

**convenablement** [kɔ̃vnabləmɑ̃] *adv* **①** (*de manière adéquate: habillé, être équipé*) suitably **②** (*décemment: se tenir, s'exprimer, s'habiller*) properly **③** (*de manière acceptable*) reasonably

**convenance** [kɔ̃vnɑ̃s] *f* **①** *pl* (*bon usage*) suitability **②** (*agrément*) **trouver qc à sa ~** to find sth to one's liking

**convenir¹** [kɔ̃vnir] <9> I. *vi* **①** (*aller*) **~ à qn** (*climat, nourriture*) to suit sb **②** (*être approprié*) **~ à qc** to suit sth II. *vi impers* **il convient de +infin** it is advisable to +infin; **comme il convient** as is right

**convenir²** [kɔ̃vnir] <9> I. *vi* **①** (*s'entendre*) **~ de qc** to agree on sth **②** (*reconnaître*) **~ de qc** to admit sth II. *vt impers* **il est convenu que +subj** it is agreed that; **comme convenu** as agreed III. *vt* (*reconnaître*) **~ que …** to agree that …

**convention** [kɔ̃vɑ̃sjɔ̃] *f* **①** (*accord*) agreement **②** (*règle*) convention

**conventionné(e)** [kɔ̃vɑ̃sjɔne] *adj* (*établissement, médecin*) recognized (*by French Social Security*)

**conventionnel(le)** [kɔ̃vɑ̃sjɔnɛl] *adj* conventional

**convenu(e)** [kɔ̃vny] I. *part passé de* **convenir** II. *adj* agreed

**convergence** [kɔ̃vɛrʒɑ̃s] *f* convergence

**converger** [kɔvɛʀʒe] <2a> vi (intérêts, efforts) to converge

**conversation** [kɔvɛʀsasjɔ̃] f ❶ (discussion) conversation; **~ téléphonique** telephone conversation; **faire la ~ à qn** to make conversation with sb; **changer de ~** to change the subject ❷ (manière de discuter) **avoir de la ~** inf to be a good conversationalist

**conversion** [kɔvɛʀsjɔ̃] f **~ de qc en qc** conversion of sth into sth

**convertir** [kɔvɛʀtiʀ] <8> I. vt to convert II. vpr (adopter) **se ~ au catholicisme** to convert to Catholicism

**conviction** [kɔviksjɔ̃] f conviction; **avoir la ~ de qc** to be convinced of sth

**convier** [kɔvje] <1> vt (inviter) to invite

**convive** [kɔviv] mf gén pl guest

**convivial(e)** [kɔvivjal, -jo] <-aux> adj ❶ (sociable) convivial ❷ INFORM user-friendly

**convocation** [kɔvɔkasjɔ̃] f ❶ (avant une réunion) convening; (d'une personne) invitation ❷ JUR summons ❸ ECOLE notification (of examinees) ❹ MIL call-up

**convoi** [kɔvwa] m ❶ (véhicules) convoy ❷ (personnes) column ❸ CHEMDFER train ❹ (cortège funèbre) funeral procession

**convoiter** [kɔvwate] <1> vt to long for; péj to covet

**convoitise** [kɔvwatiz] f lust

**convoquer** [kɔvɔke] <1> vt ❶ (faire venir) to invite; (assemblée) to convene; **être convoqué pour l'examen** date to be notified of an examination date ❷ MIL to call up ❸ JUR to summons

**convulsion** [kɔvylsjɔ̃] f gén pl MED convulsion

**cool** [kul] adj inv, inf cool

**coopérant(e)** [kɔɔpeʀɑ̃, ɑ̃t] I. m(f) aid worker II. adj (coopératif) cooperative

**coopératif, -ive** [kɔ(ɔ)peʀatif, -iv] adj cooperative

**coopération** [kɔɔpeʀasjɔ̃] f ❶ (collaboration) **~ de qn à un projet** sb's co-operation on a project ❷ POL overseas development ❸ sans pl MIL community

work, often done abroad, as national service

**coopérative** [kɔ(ɔ)peʀativ] f ❶ (groupement) cooperative ❷ (local) co-op

**coopérer** [kɔɔpeʀe] <5> vi (collaborer) **~ à qc** to cooperate on sth

**coordination** [kɔɔʀdinasjɔ̃] f sans pl coordination

**coordonné(e)** [kɔɔʀdɔne] adj coordinated

**coordonnées** [kɔɔʀdɔne] fpl ❶ inf (renseignements) **les ~ de qn** sb's details ❷ MATH coordinates

**coordonner** [kɔɔʀdɔne] <1> vt (harmoniser) to coordinate

**copain, copine** [kɔpɛ̃, kɔpin] m, f inf friend; **être très ~/copine avec qn** to be very close to sb; **petit ~/petite copine** boyfriend/girlfriend

**copie** [kɔpi] f ❶ (double, produit) a. PRESSE copy ❷ INFORM **~ de sécurité** backup (copy) ❸ (feuille double) sheet ❹ (devoir) paper

**copier** [kɔpje] <1> I. vt ❶ (transcrire) **~ qc dans un livre** to copy sth from a book ❷ (photocopier) to (photo)copy ❸ (imiter, plagier) to copy II. vi ECOLE **~ sur qn** to copy off sb

**copieur** [kɔpjœʀ] m (appareil) copier

**copieur, -euse** [kɔpjœʀ, -jøz] m, f ECOLE copycat

**copieux, -euse** [kɔpjø, -jøz] adj copious

**copilote** [kɔpilɔt] mf ❶ AVIAT copilot ❷ AUTO navigator

**copine** [kɔpin] f v. copain

**coproduction** [kɔpʀɔdyksjɔ̃] f coproduction

**copropriétaire** [kɔpʀɔpʀijetɛʀ] mf joint owner

**copyright** [kɔpiʀajt] m inv copyright

**coq** [kɔk] m ❶ (mâle) cock ❷ CULIN **~ au vin** coq au vin ❸ SPORT **poids ~** bantamweight

**coque** [kɔk] f ❶ TECH (d'un navire) hull; (d'une voiture) body ❷ ZOOL cockle

**coquelicot** [kɔkliko] m poppy

**coqueluche** [kɔklyʃ] f MED whooping cough

**coquet(te)** [kɔkɛ, ɛt] adj ❶ (élégant)

**être ~** to be smart ② (*charmant*) charming ③ *inf* (*important*) tidy

**coquetier** [kɔktje] *m* egg cup

**coquetterie** [kɔkɛtRi] *f* ① (*souci d'élégance*) smartness ② (*désir de plaire*) charm

**coquillage** [kɔkijaʒ] *m* shell

**coquille** [kɔkij] *f* ① ZOOL shell; **~ Saint-Jacques** scallop shell; CULIN scallop ② TYP misprint ③ CULIN (*récipient*) shell ④ ART shell motif

**coquin(e)** [kɔkɛ̃, in] **I.** *adj* ① (*espiègle*) mischievous ② (*grivois*) naughty **II.** *m(f)* rascal

**cor¹** [kɔR] *m* MUS horn

**cor²** [kɔR] *m* MED corn

**corail¹** [kɔRaj, -o] <-aux> **I.** *m* coral **II.** *app inv* coral

**corail®²** [kɔRaj] *adj inv* CHEMDFER **train ~** ≈ express train

**Coran** [kɔRɑ̃] *m* **le ~** the Koran

**corbeau** [kɔRbo] <x> *m* ① (*oiseau*) crow ② *inf* (*dénonciateur*) poison-pen letter writer

**corbeille** [kɔRbɛj] *f* (*panier*) basket; **~ à papier/à pain** wastepaper/bread basket

**corbillard** [kɔRbijaR] *m* hearse

**corde** [kɔRd] *f* ① (*lien, câble*) rope; (*plus fine*) cord; **~ à linge** clothesline; **~ à sauter** jump rope ② (*d'un instrument, d'une raquette*) string; **les (instruments à) cordes** the strings; **grimper à la ~** to go up the climbing rope ③ *sans pl* (*bord de piste*) rail ④ ANAT **~s vocales** vocal cords **► il pleut des ~s** it's raining cats and dogs

**cordialement** [kɔRdjalmɑ̃] *adv* cordially

**cordon** [kɔRdɔ̃] *m* ① (*petite corde*) cord; (*d'un tablier*) string ② (*décoration*) sash ③ GEO **~ littoral** offshore bar ④ ANAT **~ ombilical** umbilical cord

**cordon-bleu** [kɔRdɔ̃blø] <cordons--bleus> *m inf* cordon bleu cook

**cordonnier, -ière** [kɔRdɔnje, -jɛR] *m, f* ① (*réparateur*) shoe repairer ② (*fabricant*) shoemaker

**Corée** [kɔRe] *f* **la ~** Korea; **la ~ du Nord/du Sud** North/South Korea

**coréen** [kɔReɛ̃] *m* Korean; *v.a.* **français**

**coréen(ne)** [kɔReɛ̃, ɛn] *adj* Korean

**Coréen(ne)** [kɔReɛ̃, ɛn] *m(f)* Korean

**coriace** [kɔRjas] *adj* tough; (*personne*) hard-headed

**corne** [kɔRn] *f* ① ZOOL horn; **les ~s** (*d'un cerf*) the antlers ② *sans pl* (*callosité*) calluses *pl*

**cornée** [kɔRne] *f* ANAT cornea

**cornemuse** [kɔRnəmyz] *f* MUS bagpipes *pl*

**corner¹** [kɔRne] <1> *vt* **~ une page** to bend down the corner of a page

**corner²** [kɔRnɛR] *m* SPORT corner kick

**cornet** [kɔRnɛ] *m* ① CULIN cone ② Suisse (*sachet, poche* (*en papier, en plastique*)) bag

**corniche** [kɔRniʃ] *f* ① ARCHIT cornice ② (*escarpement*) ledge ③ (*route*) corniche

**cornichon** [kɔRniʃɔ̃] *m* ① CULIN gherkin ② *inf* (*personne*) nitwit

**corporation** [kɔRpɔRasjɔ̃] *f* ① (*association*) corporate body ② HIST guild

**corporel(le)** [kɔRpɔRɛl] *adj* (*physique*) bodily; (*soins*) personal

**corps** [kɔR] *m* ① ANAT, CHIM body; **~ et âme** body and soul; **~ à corps** man to man ② (*groupe*) **~ diplomatique** diplomatic corps; **~ médical** medical profession; **~ de métier** building trade; (*des artisans*) builders; **~ d'armée** army corps ③ ASTR **~ céleste** celestial body

**corpulence** [kɔRpylɑ̃s] *f* build

**corpulent(e)** [kɔRpylɑ̃, ɑ̃t] *adj* corpulent

**correct(e)** [kɔRɛkt] *adj* ① (*exact*) correct; **c'est ~** Québec (*ça va bien*) everything's OK ② (*convenable*) decent ③ *inf* (*acceptable*) OK

**correctement** [kɔRɛktəmɑ̃] *adv* correctly; (*se conduire, s'habiller*) properly

**correcteur** [kɔRɛktœR] *m* corrector; **~ orthographique** INFORM spell checker

**correcteur, -trice** [kɔRɛktœR, -tRis] **I.** *adj* (*ruban*) correction; (*mesure*) corrective **II.** *m, f* ECOLE examiner; TYP proofreader

**correction** [kɔʀɛksjɔ̃] *f* ❶ (*action*) correction; ECOLE to grade sth; **faire la ~ de qc** to correct sth ❷ (*châtiment*) beating ❸ (*justesse*) accuracy ❹ (*bienséance*) good manners

**correctionnel(le)** [kɔʀɛksjɔnɛl] *adj* correctional; (*tribunal*) criminal

**corres** [kɔʀɛs] *mf inf abr de* **correspondant**

**correspondance** [kɔʀɛspɔ̃dɑ̃s] *f* ❶ (*échange de lettres*) *a.* COM correspondence ❷ (*en voyage*) connection

**correspondant(e)** [kɔʀɛspɔ̃dɑ̃, ɑ̃t] **I.** *adj* corresponding **II.** *m(f)* ❶ (*contact*) correspondent; (*d'un jeune*) pen pal ❷ (*au téléphone*) **votre ~** the person you are calling ❸ COM associate ❹ CINE, TV correspondent

**correspondre** [kɔʀɛspɔ̃dʀ] <14> *vi* ❶ (*être en contact*) **~ avec qn** to write to sb; **~ par fax/courrier électronique** to send messages by fax/e-mail ❷ (*en voyage*) **~ avec qc** to connect with sth ❸ (*aller avec*) **~ à qc** to correspond to sth ❹ (*s'accorder avec*) **sa version des faits ne correspond pas à la réalité** his version of the facts does not match up with reality ❺ (*être typique*) **~ à qn** to be very like sb ❻ (*être l'équivalent de*) **ce mot correspond exactement au terme anglais** this word corresponds exactly to the English term

**corridor** [kɔʀidɔʀ] *m* corridor

**corrigé** [kɔʀiʒe] *m* ECOLE answer key

**corriger** [kɔʀiʒe] <2a> *vt* ❶ (*relever les fautes*) to grade ❷ (*supprimer les fautes*) to correct; (*rectifier: théorie*) to correct; (*prévisions*) to adjust; (*mauvaise habitude*) to break ❹ (*punir*) to beat

**corrompre** [kɔʀɔ̃pʀ] *vt irr* (*acheter*) to bribe

**corrompu(e)** [kɔʀɔ̃py] **I.** *part passé de* **corrompre II.** *adj* ❶ (*malhonnête*) corrupt ❷ (*perverti*) depraved

**corrosif, -ive** [kɔʀozif, -iv] *adj* corrosive

**corrosion** [kɔʀozjɔ̃] *f* corrosion

**corruptible** [kɔʀyptibl] *adj* venal

**corruption** [kɔʀypsjɔ̃] *f* ❶ (*délit*) bribery ❷ *sans pl* (*moral*) corruption

**corsage** [kɔʀsaʒ] *m* blouse; (*d'une robe*) bodice

**corse** [kɔʀs] **I.** *adj* Corsican **II.** *m* Corsican; *v.a.* **français**

**Corse** [kɔʀs] **I.** *f* **la ~** Corsica **II.** *mf* Corsican

**corsé(e)** [kɔʀse] *adj* ❶ (*épicé*) spicy; (*vin*) full-bodied; (*café*) strong-flavored ❷ (*scabreux*) spicy ❸ (*compliqué*) tough

**corset** [kɔʀsɛ] *m* corset

**cortège** [kɔʀtɛʒ] *m* procession

**cortisone** [kɔʀtizɔn] *f* cortisone

**corvée** [kɔʀve] *f* ❶ (*obligation pénible*) chore; **quelle ~!** what a pain! ❷ MIL fatigue ❸ HIST corvée ❹ *Suisse, Québec* (*travail non payé, fait de plein gré*) voluntary community work

**cosmétique** [kɔsmetik] *adj* cosmetic

**cosmonaute** [kɔsmɔnot] *mf* cosmonaut

**cosmopolite** [kɔsmɔpɔlit] *adj* cosmopolitan

**cosmos** [kɔsmos] *m* cosmos

**costaud(e)** [kɔsto, od] *adj inf* ❶ (*fort*) tough ❷ (*solide*) sturdy

**costume** [kɔstym] *m* ❶ (*complet*) suit ❷ (*tenue: d'époque, de théâtre, d'un pays*) costume

**cote** [kɔt] *f* ❶ FIN share price ❷ (*popularité*) popularity; **avoir la ~ avec qn** *inf* to be popular with sb ❸ SPORT (*d'un cheval*) odds

**côte** [kot] *f* ❶ (*littoral*) coast ❷ (*pente, colline*) hill; **les ~s du Rhône** the Rhone hills ❸ ANAT rib ❹ CULIN chop; **~ de bœuf** beef rib ▸ **à ~** side by side

**côté** [kote] **I.** *m* ❶ (*partie latérale*) side; **des deux ~s de qc** from both sides of sth; **sauter de l'autre ~ du ruisseau** to jump across the stream; **du ~ de ...** from the ... side ❷ (*aspect*) side; **par certains ~s** in some ways ❸ (*direction*) way; **de quel ~ allez-vous?** which way are you going?; **du ~ de la mer** by the sea; **du ~ opposé** on the opposite side ❹ (*parti*) side; **du ~ de qn**

**C**

on sb's side; **aux ~s de qn** at sb's side; **de mon ~** for my part; **du ~ paternel** on the father's side ▶ **d'un ~ ..., de l'autre** (~) on the one hand ..., on the other; **de ce ~** *inf* in that respect; **mettre l'argent de ~** to put some money away; **laisser qn/qc de ~** to leave sb/sth aside II. *adv* ❶ (*à proximité*) **chambre à ~** next room ❷ (*en comparaison*) **à ~** in comparison ❸ (*en plus*) **à ~** on the side ❹ (*voisin*) **les gens (d')à ~** the people next door; **nos voisins (d')à ~** our next-door neighbors ▶ **passer à ~ de qc** to miss sth III. *prep* ❶ (*à proximité de*) **à ~ de qn/qc** next to sb/sth; **à ~ de Paris** near Paris; **juste à ~ de qc** just by sth ❷ (*en comparaison de*) **à ~ de qn/qc** next to sb/sth ❸ (*hors de*) **répondre à ~ de la question** to miss the point of the question; (*intentionnellement*) to avoid the question

**coté(e)** [kɔte] *adj* reputed

**coteau** [kɔto] <x> *m* ❶ (*versant*) hill ❷ (*vignoble*) vineyard

**Côte d'Azur** [kotdazyʀ] *f* **la ~** the Côte d'Azur, the French Riviera

**Côte d'Ivoire** [kotdivwaʀ] *f* **la ~** Côte d'Ivoire, the Ivory Coast

**côtelé(e)** [kot(ə)le] *adj* ribbed

**côtelette** [kotlɛt] *f* CULIN cutlet

**coter** [kɔte] <1> *vt* ❶ FIN to list ❷ (*apprécier*) **être coté** to be listed ❸ SPORT **être coté à 5 contre 1** to have odds of 5 to 1

**côtier, -ière** [kotje, -jɛʀ] *adj* coastal

**cotillons** [kɔtijɔ̃] *mpl* petticoat + *vb sing*

**cotisation** [kɔtizasjɔ̃] *f* subscription; **~ ouvrière** worker contributions

**cotiser** [kɔtize] <1> I. *vi* **à qc** to contribute to sth II. *vpr* **se ~ pour** +*infin* to club together to +*infin*

**coton** [kɔtɔ̃] *m* ❶ (*matière, fil*) cotton ❷ (*ouate*) cotton (wadding)

**coton-tige®** [kɔtɔ̃tiʒ] <cotons-tiges> *m* Q-Tip®

**côtoyer** [kotwaje] <6> *vt* (*fréquenter*) to frequent

**cou** [ku] *m* neck

**couchant** [kuʃɑ̃] I. *adj* setting; **au soleil ~** at sunset II. *m* sunset

**couche** [kuʃ] *f* ❶ (*épaisseur*) *a.* GEO, METEO layer; **passer deux ~s de peinture sur qc** to put two coats of paint on sth ❷ SOCIOL level ❸ (*lange*) diaper ❹ *pl* MED confinement; **faire une fausse ~** to have a miscarriage

**couché(e)** [kuʃe] *adj* ❶ (*étendu*) lying down ❷ (*au lit*) **être déjà ~** to be already in bed

**couche-culotte** [kuʃkylɔt] <couches--culottes> *f* disposable diaper

**coucher** [kuʃe] <1> I. *vi* ❶ (*dormir*) to sleep; **~ à l'hôtel** to spend the night at a hotel ❷ *inf* (*avoir des relations sexuelles*) **~ avec qn** to sleep with sb II. *vt* ❶ (*mettre au lit*) to put to bed ❷ (*étendre*) to lay down; (*bouteille*) to lay on its side; (*blés*) to flatten III. *vpr* ❶ (*aller au lit*) **se ~** to go to bed; **envoyer qn se ~** to send sb to bed ❷ (*s'allonger*) **se ~** to lie down ❸ (*se courber sur*) **se ~ sur qc** to lean over sth ❹ (*disparaître*) **le soleil se couche** the sun is setting IV. *m* ❶ (*fait d'aller au lit*) going to bed ❷ (*crépuscule*) setting; **au ~ du soleil** at sunset

**couchette** [kuʃɛt] *f* couchette

**coucou** [kuku] I. *m* ❶ (*oiseau*) cuckoo ❷ (*pendule*) cuckoo clock II. *interj* peekaboo

**coude** [kud] *m* ❶ ANAT elbow ❷ (*courbure*) bend ▶ **se serrer les ~s** to stick together

**coudre** [kudʀ] *irr* I. *vi* to sew II. *vt* ❶ (*assembler*) to sew together ❷ (*fixer*) **~ un bouton à qc** to sew a button on sth

**couette** [kwɛt] *f* ❶ (*édredon*) duvet ❷ *gén pl* (*coiffure*) bunches

**couffin** [kufɛ̃] *m* basket

**couiner** [kwine] <1> *vi* (*lièvre, porc*) to squeal; (*rat*) to squeak; (*personne*) to whine; (*porte*) to creak

**coulant(e)** [kulɑ̃, ɑ̃t] *adj* ❶ *inf* (*indulgent*) easygoing ❷ (*fluide: pâte, fromage*) runny ❸ (*léger: style*) free-flowing

**coulée** [kule] *f* **~ de lave** lava flow

C

**couler** [kule] <1> **I.** *vi* ❶ (*s'écouler*) to flow; (*faiblement*) to ooze; (*fortement*) to pour ❷ (*préparer*) **faire ~ un bain à qn** to run a bath for sb ❸ (*fuir*) to leak ❹ (*goutter*) to drip; (*œil*) to run ❺ (*sombrer*) to sink **II.** *vt* ❶ (*verser*) **~ du plomb dans un moule** to cast lead in a mold ❷ (*sombrer, faire échouer*) to sink

**couleur** [kulœʀ] **I.** *f* ❶ (*teinte, peinture*) *a.* POL color; **reprendre des ~s** to get one's color back ❷ (*linge*) colored **II.** *adj sans pl* **~ rose** rose-colored

**couleuvre** [kulœvʀ] *f* grass snake

**coulis** [kuli] *m* CULIN (*de légumes, fruits*) coulis

**coulissant(e)** [kulisɑ̃, ɑ̃t] *adj* sliding

**coulisse** [kulis] *f* ❶ *souvent pl* THEAT wings ❷ (*rainure: d'un tiroir*) runner

**coulisser** [kulise] <1> *vi* **~ sur qc** to slide along sth

**couloir** [kulwaʀ] *m* ❶ (*corridor*) *a.* CHEMDFER corridor ❷ AVIAT aisle ❸ SPORT lane ❹ GEO gully ❺ **~ aérien** air traffic lane; **~ d'autobus** bus lane

**coup** [ku] *m* ❶ (*agression*) blow; **donner un ~ à qn** to hit sb; **~ de bâton** blow with a stick; **~ de poing/de pied** punch/kick; **~ de couteau** stab; **d'un ~ de dent** with a bite ❷ (*bruit*) knock; **frapper trois ~s** to knock three times; **~ de sifflet** blast of the whistle ❸ (*heurt*) knock ❹ (*décharge*) **~ de feu** shot ❺ (*choc moral*) blow; **porter un ~ à qn** to deal sb a blow; **c'est un ~ rude pour elle** it's a hard blow for her ❻ (*action rapide*) **d'un ~ de crayon** with the stroke of a pencil; **passer un ~ d'éponge sur qc** to sponge sth down; **se donner un ~ de peigne** to give one's hair a quick comb; **donner un ~ de frein** to brake; **~ de téléphone** phone call ❼ SPORT shot; **le ~ droit** forehand; **~ franc** (*au foot*) free kick; (*au basket*) free throw; **donner le ~ d'envoi à qc** to kick sth off ❽ JEUX ❾ (*manifestation brusque*) **~ de tonnerre** roll of thunder; **~ de vent** gust of wind; **~ de foudre** lightning flash; (*pour qn*)

love at first sight; **~ de soleil** sunstroke ❿ (*accès*) **avoir un ~ de cafard** to be down in the dumps ⓫ (*action*) **~ d'État** coup d'état; **~ de maître** masterstroke; **être sur un ~** to be on to sth ⓬ (*action désagréable*) **il nous fait le ~ (à) chaque fois** he pulls the same trick on us every time; **faire/mijoter un mauvais ~** to play/plan a dirty trick ⓭ (*quantité bue*) drink; **boire un ~** *inf* to have a drink ⓮ (*événement*) **~ de chance** [*o* **veine**] bit of luck ▶ **prendre un ~ de froid** to catch cold; **donner un ~ de main à qn** to give sb a hand; **jeter un ~ d'œil sur le feu** to keep an eye on the fire; **avoir un ~ de barre** *inf* to suddenly feel tired; **~ de tête** impulse; **tenir le ~** *inf* (*personne*) to cope; (*objet, voiture*) to withstand the strain; **ça vaut le ~ de faire qc** it's worth doing sth; **du même ~** at the same time; **du premier ~** at the first go; **d'un seul ~** in one go; **tout à ~** suddenly; **après ~** afterwards; **du ~** *inf* as a result; **sur le ~** (*aussitôt*) instantly; (*au début*) straightaway; **à tous les ~s** every time; (*à tout propos*) all the time

**coupable** [kupabl] **I.** *adj* (*fautif, condamnable*) guilty **II.** *mf* ❶ (*responsable*) guilty party ❷ (*malfaiteur*) culprit

**coupant(e)** [kupɑ̃, ɑ̃t] *adj* sharp

**coupe** [kup] *f* ❶ (*verre*) glass ❷ (*récipient*) dish ❸ SPORT cup; **la ~ du monde de football** the World Cup

**coupe-feu** [kupfø] <coupe-feu(x)> **I.** *m* firebreak; (*mur*) fireguard **II.** *app inv* **porte ~** fire door

**coupe-ongle** [kupɔ̃gl] <coupe-ongles> *m* nail clippers

**coupe-papier** [kuppapje] *m inv* paper cutter

**couper** [kupe] <1> **I.** *vi* ❶ (*être tranchant*) to cut; **attention, ça coupe!** careful, it's sharp! ❷ (*prendre un raccourci*) to take a short cut ❸ TEL **ne coupez pas!** hold the line! ❹ CINE **coupez!** cut! ❺ JEUX to cut ❻ (*être mordant*) to bite **II.** *vt* ❶ (*trancher*) to cut;

(*tête, branche*) to cut off; (*volaille*) to cut up; (*arbre*) to cut down; **~ les cheveux à qn** to cut sb's hair ❷ (*isoler*) to cut off ❸ (*raccourcir: texte*) to cut ❹ (*interrompre: ligne téléphonique*) to cut; (*communication*) to cut off; **~ l'eau à qn** to cut off sb's water ❺ (*mettre un terme: fièvre*) to bring down; **~ les ponts avec qn** to cut oneself off from sb ❻ (*bloquer: route*) to cut off; **~ la respiration à qn** to wind sb ❼ (*diluer*) to dilute ❽ JEUX to cut ❾ (*scinder: mot, paragraphe*) to break **III.** *vpr* ❶ (*se blesser*) **se ~** to cut oneself; **se ~ la main** to cut one's hand ❷ (*trancher*) **se ~ les ongles** to cut one's nails; **se ~ du pain** to cut (oneself) some bread ❸ (*se contredire*) **se ~** to contradict oneself ❹ (*être coupé*) **bien se ~** to give oneself a nasty cut

**couper-coller** [kupekɔle] INFORM **I.** *vt* cut and paste **II.** *m* cutting and pasting

**couperose** [kupʁoz] *f* blotches *pl* (*on the face*)

**coupe-vent** [kupvɑ̃] <coupe-vent(s)> *m* ❶ (*vêtement*) Windbreaker® ❷ (*abri*) windbreak

**couple** [kupl] **I.** *m* couple **II.** *f* Québec, *inf* **une ~ de qc** (*quelques*) a couple of sth

**couplet** [kuplɛ] *m* couplet

**coupole** [kupɔl] *f* dome

**coupon** [kupɔ̃] *m* ❶ COUT roll ❷ (*bon*) voucher ❸ FIN coupon

**coupon-réponse** [kupɔ̃ʁepɔ̃s] <coupons-réponse> *m* reply form

**coupure** [kupyʁ] *f* ❶ (*blessure*) cut ❷ PRESSE **~ de journal** press clipping ❸ LIT, CINE CUT ❹ (*interruption*) **~ d'électricité** (*involontaire*) power failure; (*volontaire*) power outage ❺ (*billet*) **petites ~s** small bills

**cour** [kuʁ] *f* ❶ (*espace clos: d'un bâtiment*) courtyard; **~ de l'école** playground ❷ (*courtisans*) court ❸ (*cercle de personnes: d'un puissant*) courtiers *pl* ❹ JUR **d'assises** Assize Court ❺ *Belgique* (*toilettes*) toilet ▸ **faire la ~ à qn** to court sb

**courage** [kuʁaʒ] *m* ❶ (*bravoure*) courage; **perdre ~** to lose heart; **bon ~!** best of luck! ❷ (*ardeur*) spirit; **avec ~** with determination

**courageusement** [kuʁaʒøzmɑ̃] *adv* courageously

**courageux, -euse** [kuʁaʒø, -ʒøz] *adj* ❶ (*opp: lâche*) courageous ❷ (*travailleur*) willing

**couramment** [kuʁamɑ̃] *adv* ❶ (*aisément: parler*) fluently ❷ (*souvent*) commonly

**courant** [kuʁɑ̃] *m* ❶ (*cours d'eau, d'air*) *a.* ELEC current; **~ d'air** air current; (*gênant*) draft ❷ (*mouvement*) movement; **un ~ de pensée** a school of thought ❸ (*cours*) **dans le ~ de la journée** during the day ▸ **être au ~ de qc** to be aware of sth; **mettre qn au ~ de qc** to keep sb up to date on sth

**courant(e)** [kuʁɑ̃, ɑ̃t] *adj* ❶ (*habituel*) usual; (*dépenses, procédé, langue*) everyday ❷ (*en cours: année, affaires, prix*) current

**courbature** [kuʁbatyʁ] *f souvent pl* ache

**courbe** [kuʁb] **I.** *adj* curved; (*ligne, trajectoire, surface*) curving **II.** *f* GEO, FIN curve; (*d'une route, d'un fleuve*) bend; (*des reins*) line

**courbé(e)** [kuʁbe] *adj* bowed down

**courber** [kuʁbe] <1> **I.** *vi* **~ sous qc** (*personne, bois*) to bend under sth **II.** *vt* ❶ (*plier*) to bend ❷ (*pencher*) **~ le dos** to stoop; **la tête devant qn** to give in to sb **III.** *vpr* **se ~** ❶ (*se baisser*) to bend down; (*à cause de l'âge*) to be bent; (*pour saluer*) to bow ❷ (*ployer*) to bend

**coureur** [kuʁœʁ] *m Québec* **~ des bois** (*chasseur et trappeur*) trapper

**coureur, -euse** [kuʁœʁ, -øz] *m, f* ❶ SPORT (*athlète, cheval*) runner; (*voiture, cycliste*) entrants ❷ (*coureur de jupons*) womanizer

**courge** [kuʁʒ] *f* marrow

**courgette** [kuʁʒɛt] *f* zucchini

**courir** [kuʁiʁ] *irr* **I.** *vi* ❶ (*se mouvoir, se dépêcher*) *a.* SPORT to run; (*plus vite*) to dash; **~ partout** to run all over the place; **~ faire qc** to run and do sth; **~ chercher le médecin** to run and get the doctor; **bon, j'y cours** OK, I'm off ❷ (*se répandre*) to go around; **faire ~ le bruit que qn est mort** to spread the rumor that sb is dead ❸ (*se diriger vers*) **~ à la faillite** to be headed for bankruptcy **II.** *vt* ❶ (*participer à une course*) to run (in) ❷ (*parcourir: campagne, monde*) to roam; (*magasins*) to do ❸ (*fréquenter*) **~ les filles** to chase women

**couronne** [kuʀɔn] *f* ❶ BOT, MED, FIN, POL crown ❷ (*pain*) ring

**couronné** [kuʀɔne] *adj* crowned

**couronnement** [kuʀɔnmɑ̃] *m* coronation

**couronner** [kuʀɔne] <1> *vt* ❶ (*coiffer d'une couronne, consacrer*) to crown ❷ (*récompenser*) to award a prize to

**courrier** [kuʀje] *m* ❶ (*lettres*) mail; **faire son ~** to go through one's mail ❷ PRESSE **le ~ du cœur** advice column ❸ (*personne*) courier ❹ INFORM **~ électronique** electronic mail; **~ "arrivée"/"départ"** incoming/outgoing mail

**courroie** [kuʀwa] *f* belt

**cours** [kuʀ] *m* ❶ (*déroulement*) course; **au ~ de qc** in the course of sth; **le mois en ~** the current month ❷ (*leçon*) lesson; UNIV lecture; **~ particuliers** private lessons; **suivre un ~** [*o* des ~] to take a course; **~ de maths** *inf* math lessons ❸ (*école*) school ❹ FIN (*d'une monnaie*) rate; (*de produits*) price; **avoir ~** to be legal tender ❺ (*courant*) **~ d'eau** stream; (*rivière*) river

**course** [kuʀs] *f* ❶ (*action de courir*) running; **c'est la ~!** *inf* it's a mad rush! ❷ (*épreuve*) race; **vélo de ~** racing bike; **faire la ~ avec qn** to race (with) sb; **~ contre la montre** *a. fig* race against the clock; **~ à pied** race; **~ de vitesse** speed trial ❸ JEUX **les ~s** the races ❹ (*déplacement*) trip; **~ en taxi** taxi ride ❺ (*commission*) **les ~s** the shopping; **faire les ~s** to do the shop-

ping; **faire une ~** (*régler qc*) to go and do sth; (*faire un achat*) to go and buy sth ❻ (*ruée*) **la ~ aux armements** the arms race ❼ Suisse (*excursion, voyage organisé*) excursion

**court** [kuʀ] *m* **~ de tennis** tennis court

**court(e)** [kuʀ, kuʀt] **I.** *adj* ❶ (*opp: long*) short **II.** *adv* ❶ (*opp: long*) short ❷ (*concis*) **faire ~** to be brief; **tout ~** simply ▸ **être à ~ de qc** to be short of sth

**court-bouillon** [kuʀbujɔ̃] <courts-bouillons> *m* stock

**court-circuit** [kuʀsiʀkyi] <courts-circuits> *m* short-circuit

**courtier, -ière** [kuʀtje, -jɛʀ] *m, f* broker

**courtois(e)** [kuʀtwa, waz] *adj* courteous

**courtoisie** [kuʀtwazi] *f* courtesy

**couru(e)** [kuʀy] **I.** *part passé de* **courir** **II.** *adj* **c'est ~ d'avance** it's a foregone conclusion

**couscous** [kuskus] *m* couscous

**cousin(e)** [kuzɛ̃, in] *m(f)* cousin; **~s germains** first cousins

**coussin** [kusɛ̃] *m* ❶ (*objet moelleux, rembourré*) cushion ❷ Belgique (*oreiller*) pillow

**cousu(e)** [kuzy] **I.** *part passé de* **coudre** **II.** *adj* sewn; **~ main** handsewn

**coût** [ku] *m* cost

**coûtant** [kutɑ̃] *adj* **prix ~** cost price

**couteau** [kuto] <x> *m* ❶ (*ustensile*) knife; **~ de cuisine/suisse** kitchen/Swiss Army knife ❷ (*coquillage*) razor clam ▸ **remuer le ~ dans la plaie** to twist the knife in the wound

**coûter** [kute] <1> *vt* to cost; **ça m'a coûté 10 euros** it cost me 10 euros; **ça coûte cher** it's expensive; **ça coûte combien?** how much does it cost?

**coûteux, -euse** [kutø, -øz] *adj* expensive

**coutume** [kutym] *f* custom; **avoir ~ de** +*infin* to be accustomed to +*infin*

**couture** [kutyʀ] *f* ❶ (*action, ouvrage*) sewing ❷ (*suite de points*) seam

**couturier** [kutyʀje] *m* (**grand**) **~** (fashion) designer

**couturière** [kutyʀjɛʀ] *f* (*à son compte*) dressmaker

**couvée** [kuve] *f* ❶ (*œufs*) clutch ❷ (*poussins*) brood

**couvent** [kuvɑ̃] *m* convent

**couver** [kuve] <1> **I.** *vi* (*feu*) to smolder; (*émeute*) to be brewing **II.** *vt* ❶ ZOOL to sit on ❷ (*materner*) to cocoon

**couvercle** [kuvɛʀkl] *m* lid

**couvert** [kuvɛʀ] *m* ❶ (*ustensiles*) cutlery; **mettre le ~** to set the table ❷ (*place*) place setting

**couvert(e)** [kuvɛʀ, ɛʀt] **I.** *part passé de* **couvrir II.** *adj* ❶ (*habillé*) **être trop ~** to be wearing too much ❷ (*protégé*) **être ~** to be covered ❸ (*assuré*) **être ~ par une assurance** to be covered by insurance ❹ (*opp: en plein air*) indoor ❺ METEO (*ciel, temps*) overcast ❻ (*recouvert*) **~ de poussière** covered in dust ❼ (*plein de*) **être ~ de sang** to be covered in blood

**couverture** [kuvɛʀtyʀ] *f* ❶ (*tissu: d'un lit*) blanket ❷ (*page*) cover ❸ PRESSE (*d'un événement*) coverage ❹ ADMIN, FIN cover ❺ (*prétexte*) front

**couvre-feu** [kuvʀəfø] <couvre-feux> *m* curfew

**couvre-lit** [kuvʀəli] <couvre-lits> *m* bedspread

**couvreur, -euse** [kuvʀœʀ, -øz] *m, f* roofer

**couvrir** [kuvʀiʀ] <11> **I.** *vt* ❶ (*mettre sur*) to cover; (*récipient*) to put the lid on; (*livre*) to cover; **~ un toit (de tuiles)** to tile a roof ❷ (*recouvrir*) **~ qc (couverture, toile)** to cover sth up; **qc couvre qn** sb is covered in sth; **~ de qc** to cover in sth ❸ (*habiller*) to dress ❹ (*cacher: visage*) to cover up; (*son*) to drown ❺ (*protéger, garantir, parcourir*) to cover ❻ (*combler*) **~ qn de cadeaux** to shower sb with gifts **II.** *vpr* ❶ **se ~** (*s'habiller*) to dress; (*mettre un chapeau*) to put one's hat on; **couvre-toi, il fait froid!** cover up warmly, it's cold! ❷ (*se protéger*) **se ~** to cover oneself ❸ METEO **le ciel se couvre (de nuages)** the sky is becoming overcast ❹ (*se rem-*

*plir de*) **se ~ de taches** to get stains all over oneself

**covoiturage** [kovwatyʀaʒ] *m* carpooling

**crabe** [kʀab] *m* crab

**crac** [kʀak] *interj* crack

**crachat** [kʀaʃa] *m* spit

**cracher** [kʀaʃe] <1> **I.** *vi* ❶ (*expectorer*) to spit ❷ (*baver*) to blot **II.** *vt* ❶ (*rejeter*) to spit ❷ (*émettre: fumée, lave*) to spit out

**crachin** [kʀaʃɛ̃] *m* drizzle

**craie** [kʀɛ] *f* chalk

**craindre** [kʀɛ̃dʀ] *irr* **I.** *vt* ❶ (*redouter*) to be afraid of ❷ (*pressentir*) to fear ❸ (*être sensible à*) **~ la chaleur** to dislike the heat **II.** *vi* **~ pour qn/qc** to fear for sb/sth; **il n'y a rien à ~** there's nothing to be afraid of; **ça ne craint rien** *inf* don't sweat it; (*ce n'est pas fragile*) it can take anything ▸ **ça craint!** *inf* that's dicey!

**crainte** [kʀɛ̃t] *f* ❶ (*peur*) **~ de qn/qc** fear of sb/sth; **soyez sans ~(s)!** never fear!; **de [o par] ~ de qc** for fear of sth ❷ (*pressentiment*) worry

**craintif, -ive** [kʀɛ̃tif, -iv] *adj* timid

**crampe** [kʀɑ̃p] *f* cramp

**crampon** [kʀɑ̃pɔ̃] *m* SPORT crampons; (*de foot*) spike

**cramponner** [kʀɑ̃pɔne] <1> **I.** *vt inf* to pester **II.** *vpr* (*se tenir*) **se ~ à qn/qc** to cling on to sb/sth

**cran¹** [kʀɑ̃] *m* ❶ (*entaille: d'une arme*) notch ❷ (*trou*) hole

**cran²** [kʀɑ̃] *m inf* **avoir du ~** to have guts

**crâne** [kʀɑn] *m* skull ▸ **ne rien <u>avoir</u> dans le ~** to be a total numskull

**crâneur, -euse** [kʀɑnœʀ, -øz] *m, f* showoff

**crapaud** [kʀapo] *m* toad

**crapule** [kʀapyl] *f* villain

**crapuleux, -euse** [kʀapylø, -øz] *adj* villainous; (*vie*) dissolute

**craquant(e)** [kʀakɑ̃, ɑ̃t] *adj inf* gorgeous

**craqueler** [kʀakle] <3> *vpr* **se ~** to craze

**craquer** [kʀake] <1> I. *vi* ❶ (*faire un bruit: bonbon*) to be crunchy; (*chaussures, bois, parquet*) to squeak; (*feuilles mortes, neige*) to crunch; (*disque*) to crackle; **faire ~ une allumette** to strike a match; **faire ~ ses doigts** to crack one's knuckles ❷ (*céder: branche*) to snap; (*glace*) to crack; (*se déchirer: vêtement*) to tear; (*aux coutures*) to come apart ❸ (*s'effondrer: personne*) to crack up; (*nerfs*) to crack ❹ (*s'attendrir*) **~ pour qc** to go for sth ▶ **plein à ~** full to bursting II. *vt* (*allumette*) to strike

**crash** [kʀaʃ] <(e)s> *m* crash

**crasse** [kʀas] *f* (*saleté*) filth

**crasseux, -euse** [kʀasø, -øz] *adj* filthy

**cratère** [kʀatɛʀ] *m* crater

**cravache** [kʀavaʃ] *f* whip

**cravate** [kʀavat] *f* tie

**crawl** [kʀol] *m* crawl

**crayon** [kʀejɔ̃] *m* pencil; **~ feutre** felt-tip; **~ de couleur** colored pencil

**créancier, -ière** [kʀeɑ̃sje, -jɛʀ] *m, f* FIN creditor

**créateur, -trice** [kʀeatœʀ, -tʀis] I. *adj* creative II. *m, f* ART designer

**créatif, -ive** [kʀeatif, -iv] *adj* creative

**création** [kʀeasjɔ̃] *f* creation; **~ d'entreprise** start of a company

**créativité** [kʀeativite] *f* creativity

**créature** [kʀeatyʀ] *f* creature

**crèche** [kʀɛʃ] *f* ❶ REL crib ❷ (*pouponnière*) nursery

**crédibilité** [kʀedibilite] *f* credibility

**crédible** [kʀedibl] *adj* credible

**crédit** [kʀedi] *m* ❶ (*paiement échelonné*) credit; **acheter à ~** to buy on credit ❷ (*prêt*) loan ❸ (*banque*) bank ❹ (*opp: débit*) credit ❺ *pl* POL funds

**créditer** [kʀedite] <1> *vt* **~ un compte de 100 euros** to credit 100 euros to an account

**créditeur, -trice** [kʀeditœʀ, -tʀis] *adj* **compte ~** account in credit

**crédule** [kʀedyl] *adj* credulous

**crédulité** [kʀedylite] *f* credulity

**créer** [kʀee] <1> I. *vt* ❶ (*emploi, œuvre, problèmes*) to create; (*entreprise*) to

start ❷ THEAT **~ une pièce** to put on the first performance of a play II. *vi* to create III. *vpr* **se ~ des problèmes** to create problems for oneself

**crémaillère** [kʀemajɛʀ] *f* **pendre la ~** to have a housewarming (party)

**crématoire** [kʀematwaʀ] *adj* **four ~** crematorium

**crème** [kʀɛm] I. *adj inv* cream II. *f* ❶ (*produit laitier, de soins, entremets*) cream ❷ (*liqueur*) **~ de cassis** crème de cassis ❸ (*le meilleur*) **la ~ de ...** the best of ... III. *m* coffee with milk or cream

**crémerie** [kʀemʀi] *f* dairy

**crémeux, -euse** [kʀemø, -øz] *adj* creamy

**créneau** [kʀeno] <x> *m* ❶ AUTO parking space; **faire un ~** to parallel park ❷ COM opening

**créole** [kʀeɔl] I. *adj* Creole II. *m* Creole; *v.a.* français

**Créole** [kʀeɔl] *mf* Creole

**crêpe** [kʀɛp] *f* ❶ CULIN crêpe

**crêperie** [kʀepʀi] *f* crêpe restaurant

**crépi** [kʀepi] *m* roughcast

**crépiter** [kʀepite] <1> *vi* (*feu*) to crackle; (*arme*) to rattle

**crépu(e)** [kʀepy] *adj* frizzy

**crépuscule** [kʀepyskyl] *m* twilight

**cresson** [kʀesɔ̃, kʀasɔ̃] *m* watercress

**crête** [kʀɛt] *f* ❶ ZOOL crest; (*de coq*) comb ❷ (*sommet: d'une montagne, d'un toit*) ridge; (*d'une vague*) crest

**crétin(e)** [kʀetɛ̃, in] I. *adj inf* cretinous II. *m(f) inf* cretin

**creuser** [kʀøze] <1> I. *vt* ❶ (*excaver*) to dig; (*sillon*) to plow ❷ (*évider: tombe*) to dig; (*pomme, falaise*) to hollow out II. *vi* to dig III. *vpr* **se ~** to grow hollow; (*roche*) to be hollowed out ▶ **se ~ la tête** to rack one's brains

**creux** [kʀø] *m* ❶ (*cavité*) cavity; (*dans un terrain, de la main*) hollow; (*d'une vague*) trough ❷ ANAT **le ~ des reins** the small of the back ❸ (*manque d'activité*) slack period ❹ *inf* (*faim*) **avoir un ~** to be a bit hungry

**creux, -euse** [kʀø, -øz] *adj* ❶ (*vide*)

hollow; (*ventre, tête*) empty ❷(*vain: paroles*) empty ❸(*concave*) hollow ❹(*rentré: visage*) gaunt ❺(*sans activité*) slack; **les heures creuses** off-peak hours

**crevaison** [kʀəvɛzɔ̃] *f* flat

**crevant(e)** [kʀəvɑ̃, ɑ̃t] *adj inf* exhausting

**crevasse** [kʀəvas] *f* ❶(*fissure*) crevice ❷(*gerçure*) crack

**crevé(e)** [kʀəve] *adj inf* (*fatigué*) dead

**crever** [kʀəve] <4> **I.** *vi* ❶(*éclater: ballon, sac*) to burst ❷AUTO to have a flat ❸(*être plein de*) ~ **de jalousie** to be dying of jealousy ❹*inf* (*souffrir*) ~ **de froid** to be freezing; ~ **de faim** to be starving; ~ **d'envie de qc** to be dying for sth **II.** *vt* ❶(*percer: abcès, ballon, pneu*) to burst ❷*inf* (*exténuer*) to kill **III.** *vpr inf* **se ~ à faire qc** to kill oneself doing sth

**crevette** [kʀəvɛt] *f* prawn

**cri** [kʀi] *m* (*d'une personne*) cry, shout; (*d'un animal*) cry; **pousser un** ~ to cry out

**criant(e)** [kʀijɑ̃, jɑ̃t] *adj* ❶(*révoltant: injustice*) screaming ❷(*manifeste: preuve*) striking

**criard(e)** [kʀijaʀ, jaʀd] *adj* ❶(*braillard: personne*) squealing; (*voix*) piercing ❷(*tapageur*) loud

**cric** [kʀik] *m* jack

**crier** [kʀije] <1> **I.** *vi* ❶(*hurler*) to cry (out); (*bébé*) to scream ❷*inf* (*se fâcher*) ~ **contre/après qn** to yell at sb ❸(*émettre des sons: mouette*) to cry; (*oiseau*) to call; (*cochon*) to squeal; (*souris*) to squeak **II.** *vt* ❶(*à voix forte*) ~ **qc à qn** to yell sth to sb ❷(*proclamer*) ~ **son innocence** to proclaim one's innocence ▶ **sans** ~ **gare** without warning

**crime** [kʀim] *m* ❶(*meurtre*) a. JUR crime ❷(*faute morale*) **c'est un** ~! it's criminal!

**criminalité** [kʀiminalite] *f sans pl* criminality

**criminel(le)** [kʀiminɛl] **I.** *adj* criminal

**II.** *m(f)* ❶(*assassin*) murderer ❷(*coupable*) criminal

**crinière** [kʀinjɛʀ] *f* mane

**crique** [kʀik] *f* creek

**criquet** [kʀikɛ] *m* cricket; ~ **pèlerin** desert locust

**crise** [kʀiz] *f* ❶MED attack; ~ **cardiaque/d'appendicite** heart/appendicitis attack; **faire une** ~ **de nerfs** to have an attack of nerves ❷ECON, POL, FIN crisis ▶ **piquer une** ~ *inf* to burst into a fit of rage

**crispé(e)** [kʀispe] *adj* tense; (*poing*) clenched

**crisper** [kʀispe] <1> **I.** *vt* ❶(*contracter*) to tense ❷(*agacer*) ~ **qn** to get on sb's nerves **II.** *vpr* **se** ~ ❶(*se contracter*) to tense ❷(*se serrer: main*) to tighten; (*poing*) to clench

**crisser** [kʀise] <1> *vi* (*pneus, freins*) to squeal

**cristal** [kʀistal, -o] <-aux> *m* ❶(*en minéralogie, verre*) crystal ❷*pl* (*cristallisation*) crystals

**cristallin** [kʀistalɛ̃] *m* (*de l'œil*) crystalline lens

**cristallin(e)** [kʀistalɛ̃, in] *adj* ❶(*voix, son*) crystal; (*eau*) crystal-clear ❷MIN crystalline

**critère** [kʀitɛʀ] *m* criterion

**critique** [kʀitik] **I.** *adj* critical **II.** *f* (*reproche*) criticism; (*revue*) review; **faire la** ~ **d'un livre** to review a book **III.** *mf* critic

**critiquer** [kʀitike] <1> *vt* ❶(*condamner*) to criticize ❷(*juger*) to review

**croasser** [kʀɔase] <1> *vi* to croak

**croche-pied** [kʀɔʃpje] <croche-pieds> *m* **faire un** ~ **à qn** to trip sb up

**crochet** [kʀɔʃɛ] *m* ❶(*pour accrocher*) a. SPORT hook ❷(*aiguille*) crochet hook ❸*pl* TYP square brackets

**crochu(e)** [kʀɔʃy] *adj* (*bec, doigts*) clawlike; **avoir le nez** ~ to have a hooknose

**croco** *inf*, **crocodile** [kʀɔkɔdil] *m* (*cuir*) crocodile

**crocus** [kʀɔkys] *m* crocus

**croire** [kʀwaʀ] *irr* **I.** *vt* ❶(*tenir pour vrai*) to believe; **faire** ~ **qc à qn** to make sb think sth ② (*avoir confiance en*) to believe ③ (*s'imaginer*) to think ④ (*supposer*) **c'est à ~ qu'il va pleuvoir** you'd think it was going to rain; **il faut ~ que le patron a raison** it seems the boss is right; **il croit que je suis bête?** does he think I'm stupid? ⑤ (*estimer*) ~ **qn capable** to think sb capable; **on l'a crue morte** we thought she was dead ▶ **il n'en croyait pas ~ ses <u>oreilles</u>/<u>yeux</u>** he couldn't believe his ears/eyes II. *vi* ~ **en qn/qc** to believe in sb/sth ▶ **veuillez ~ à mes <u>sentiments</u> les meilleurs** *form* ≈ Yours sincerely III. *vpr* **se ~ intelligent** to think oneself clever; **se ~ tout permis** to think one can get away with anything

**croisé(e)** [kʀwaze] *adj* **les bras ~s** with one's arms crossed ▶ **rester les <u>bras</u> ~s** to sit and do nothing; <u>**mots**</u> **~s** crossword

**croisement** [kʀwazmɑ̃] *m* ① *sans pl* AUTO **feux de ~** low beams ② (*intersection*) crossroads ③ (*mélange*) cross

**croiser** [kʀwaze] <1> I. *vt* ① (*mettre en croix: bras*) to fold; (*jambes, mains*) to cross ② (*couper: route, regard*) to cross; (*véhicule*) to pass ③ (*passer à côté de qn*) ~ **qn** to meet sb; ~ **qc** (*regard*) to fall on sth; **son regard a croisé le mien** our eyes crossed ④ BIO, ZOOL to cross II. *vpr* **se ~** ① (*passer l'un à côté de l'autre: personnes, regards*) to meet ② (*se couper*) to cross

**croiseur** [kʀwazœʀ] *m* cruiser

**croisière** [kʀwazjɛʀ] *f* cruise

**croissance** [kʀwasɑ̃s] *f sans pl* growth

**croissant** [kʀwasɑ̃] *m* ① CULIN croissant ② *sans pl* (*forme*) ~ **de lune** crescent

**croissant(e)** [kʀwasɑ̃, ɑ̃t] *adj* growing

**croître** [kʀwatʀ] *vi irr* ① (*grandir*) to grow ② (*augmenter: choses, colère*) to increase; (*chômage*) to go up

**croix** [kʀwa] *f a.* REL cross; **mettre une ~ dans la case qui convient** to put an X in the appropriate box; ~ **de la Légion d'honneur** Cross of the Legion of Honor ▶ **faire une ~ sur qc** *inf* to kiss sth goodbye

**Croix-Rouge** [kʀwaʀuʒ] *f* **la ~** the Red Cross

**croquant(e)** [kʀɔkɑ̃, ɑ̃t] *adj* crisp; (*biscuit*) crunchy

**croque-monsieur** [kʀɔkməsjø] *m inv* toasted ham and cheese sandwich

**croquer** [kʀɔke] <1> I. *vt* ① (*manger*) to munch ② (*dessiner*) to sketch II. *vi* ① (*être croustillant: salade*) to be crisp; (*bonbons*) to be crunchy ② (*mordre*) ~ **dans une pomme** to bite into an apple

**croquis** [kʀɔki] *m* sketch

**cross** [kʀɔs] *m* ① (*course à pied*) cross-country race ② (*sport*) cross-country running

**crotte** [kʀɔt] *f* ① *inf* (*excrément: de chien*) turd *vulg*; (*de cheval, lapin*) droppings *pl*; (*de nez*) booger ② CULIN ~ **en chocolat** chocolate drop

**crotté(e)** [kʀɔte] *adj* covered in mud

**crottin** [kʀɔtɛ̃] *m* ① (*excrément*) droppings *pl* ② (*fromage*) round goat cheese

**crouler** [kʀule] <1> *vi* ① (*s'écrouler*) to collapse ② *fig* ~ **sous le travail** to be going under with work ③ (*s'effondrer*) to fall in

**croupe** [kʀup] *f* rump

**croupier, -ière** [kʀupje, -jɛʀ] *m, f* croupier

**croupir** [kʀupiʀ] <8> *vi* ① (*se corrompre: eau*) to stagnate; (*détritus*) to rot ② (*végéter*) ~ **en prison** to rot away in jail

**croustillant(e)** [kʀustijɑ̃, jɑ̃t] *adj* ① (*pain*) crusty; (*biscuit*) crunchy ② (*grivois*) tasty

**croustille** [kʀustij] *f Québec* chips *pl*

**croustiller** [kʀustije] <1> *vi* (*pain*) to be crusty; (*biscuit*) to be crunchy

**croûte** [kʀut] *f* ① *sans pl* (*couche externe: de pain, fromage*) crust ② CULIN pastry ③ *sans pl* (*couche*) layer; MED scab ④ (*sédiment*) scale ⑤ GEO **~ terrestre** earth's crust ▶ **casser** la **~** *inf* to have something to eat

**croûton** [kʀutɔ̃] *m* ① (*extrémité*) crust ② (*pain frit*) crouton

**croyance** [kʀwajãs] f ① *sans pl* (*le fait de croire*) **la ~ dans/en qc** belief in sth ② (*ce que l'on croit*) ~ **religieuse** religious belief

**croyant** [kʀwajã] *part prés de* **croire**

**croyant(e)** [kʀwajã, jãt] **I.** *adj* believing **II.** *m(f)* believer

**C.R.S.** [seeʀɛs] *m abr de* **compagnie républicaine de sécurité** security police; (*policier*) security policeman

**cru** [kʀy] *m* ① (*terroir*) vineyard ② (*vin*) **un grand ~** a great vintage

**cru(e)** [kʀy] **I.** *part passé de* **croire II.** *adj* ① (*opp: cuit: aliments*) raw ② (*direct*) blunt

**crû(e)** [kʀy] *part passé de* **croître**

**cruauté** [kʀyote] f *sans pl* cruelty

**cruche** [kʀyʃ] f ① (*récipient*) jug ② *inf* (*sot*) dumb

**crucial(e)** [kʀysjal, -jo] <-aux> *adj* crucial

**crucifier** [kʀysifje] <1> *vt* to crucify

**crucifix** [kʀysifi] *m* crucifix

**crue** [kʀy] f ① (*montée*) rise in the water level ② (*inondation*) flood

**cruel(le)** [kʀyɛl] *adj* ① (*méchant*) cruel ② (*douloureux: sort*) cruel; (*épreuve*) harsh

**crus** [kʀy] *passé simple de* **croire**

**crûs** [kʀy] *passé simple de* **croître**

**crustacé** [kʀystase] *m* ① crustacean ② CULIN ~**s** seafood

**crypter** [kʀipte] <1> *vt* to encrypt

**cube** [kyb] *m* ① (*mesure volumétrique*) **mètre ~** cubic meter ② (*jouet*) block

**cubique** [kybik] *adj* (*en forme de cube*) cubic

**cueillette** [kœjɛt] f *sans pl* ① (*action*) picking ② (*récolte*) harvest

**cueillir** [kœjiʀ] *vt irr* ① (*ramasser*) to pick ② *inf* (*arrêter*) to nab ③ *inf* (*prendre au passage*) to snatch

**cuiller, cuillère** [kɥijɛʀ] f ① (*ustensile*) spoon; ~ **à café**, ~ **à thé** *Québec* teaspoon; ~ **à soupe**, ~ **à table** *Québec* tablespoon ② (*contenu: d'huile*) spoonful

**cuillerée, cuillérée** [kɥijeʀe] f ~ **à café** teaspoonful; ~ **à soupe** tablespoonful

**cuir** [kɥiʀ] *m sans pl* leather ► ~ **chevelu** scalp

**cuire** [kɥiʀ] *irr* **I.** *vt* ① CULIN to cook; (*à la vapeur*) to steam; (*à l'étouffée*) to braise; (*au four: viande*) to roast; (*pain, gâteau*) to bake; (*à la poêle*) to fry; **faire ~ qc au four** to cook sth in the oven ② TECH to fire **II.** *vi* ① CULIN (*viande, légumes*) to cook; (*pain, gâteau*) to bake ② *inf* (*avoir très chaud*) to roast

**cuisine** [kɥizin] f ① (*pièce*) kitchen ② (*art culinaire*) cuisine; (*nourriture*) cooking; **recette de ~** recipe; **faire la ~** to cook

**cuisiner** [kɥizine] <1> **I.** *vi* (*faire la cuisine*) to cook **II.** *vt* ① (*préparer des plats*) to cook ② *inf* (*interroger*) to grill

**cuisinier, -ière** [kɥizinje, -jɛʀ] *m, f* cook

**cuisinière** [kɥizinjɛʀ] f cooker

**cuisse** [kɥis] f ① ANAT thigh ② CULIN leg

**cuisson** [kɥisõ] *m* ① *sans pl* CULIN cooking ② (*durée*) cooking time

**cuit(e)** [kɥi, kɥit] **I.** *part passé de* **cuire II.** *adj* ① CULIN cooked; **ne pas être assez ~** to be undercooked; **être trop ~** to be overcooked ② TECH fired; **terre ~e** terracotta ► **c'est ~** *inf* so much for that!; **c'est du tout ~** *inf* it's as good as done; **être ~** *inf* to be done for

**cuivre** [kɥivʀ] *m* ① (*métal et ustensiles*) copper ② *pl* MUS **les ~s** the brass

**cul** [ky] *m sans pl, inf* ass ► **boire ~ sec** *inf* to down a drink

**culasse** [kylas] f ① AUTO cylinder head ② (*d'un fusil*) breech

**culbute** [kylbyt] f (*galipette*) **faire une ~** to do a somersault

**culbuter** [kylbyte] <1> **I.** *vi* (*tomber*) to tumble **II.** *vt* (*faire tomber*) to knock over

**cul-de-sac** [kydsak] <culs-de-sac> *m* cul-de-sac

**culinaire** [kylinɛʀ] *adj* **art ~** art of cooking

**culminant(e)** [kylminã, ãt] *adj* (*point d'une montagne*) highest

**culot** [kylo] *m* ① (*fond*) base ② *inf* (*assurance*) nerve

**culotte** [kylɔt] *f* **❶** (*slip*) panties *pl* **❷** (*short*) shorts *pl* **❸** SPORT pants; **~s de cheval** riding breeches; *fig* big thighs

**culotté(e)** [kylɔte] *adj inf* **❶** (*effronté*) sassy **❷** (*audacieux*) daring

**culpabiliser** [kylpabilize] <1> I. *vt* to make feel guilty II. *vi* to feel guilty III. *vpr* **se ~** to make oneself feel guilty

**culpabilité** [kylpabilite] *f sans pl* guilt

**culte** [kylt] *m* **❶** *sans pl* (*vénération*) cult **❷** *sans pl* (*cérémonie chrétienne*) worship; (*païenne*) cult; (*religion*) religion **❸** (*office protestant*) service **❹** *fig* **vouer un ~ à qn** to worship sb

**cultivateur, -trice** [kyltivatœʀ, -tʀis] *m, f* farmer

**cultivé(e)** [kyltive] *adj* cultivated

**cultiver** [kyltive] <1> I. *vt* **❶** AGR (*terres*) to farm; (*blé, fruits*) to grow **❷** (*exercer: mémoire*) to exercise; (*don*) to cultivate **❸** (*entretenir: relation*) to cultivate; (*langue*) to keep up II. *vpr* **se ~ en faisant qc** to improve oneself doing sth

**culture** [kyltyʀ] *f* **❶** *sans pl* (*agriculture*) farming; **~ de la vigne** wine growing **❷** *pl* (*terres cultivées*) fields **❸** BIO culture **❹** *sans pl* (*savoir*) learning; (*connaissances spécialisées*) culture; **~ générale** general knowledge **❺** (*civilisation*) culture **❻** SPORT **~ physique** exercises

**culturel(le)** [kyltyʀɛl] *adj* cultural

**culturisme** [kyltyʀism] *m sans pl* bodybuilding

**cumin** [kymɛ̃] *m* cumin

**cumul** [kymyl] *m sans pl* **~ de mandats** holding of several offices

**cumuler** [kymyle] <1> *vt* (*accumuler*) to accumulate

**curatif, -ive** [kyʀatif, -iv] *adj* curative

**cure** [kyʀ] *f* treatment; **~ thermale** spa cure

**curé** [kyʀe] *m* priest

**cure-dent** [kyʀdɑ̃] <cure-dents> *m* toothpick

**curer** [kyʀe] <1> I. *vt* to clean out II. *vpr* **se ~ les ongles** to clean one's nails

**curieux** [kyʀjø] *mpl* (*badauds*) onlookers

**curieux, -euse** [kyʀjø, -jøz] I. *adj* **❶** (*indiscret, étrange*) curious; **ce qui est ~, c'est que ..., chose curieuse, ...** the odd thing is, ... **❷** (*intéressé*) **être ~ de qc** to be keen on sth; **être ~ de faire qc** to be keen on doing sth; **être ~ d'apprendre qc** to be keen to learn sth; **être ~ de savoir** to be interested in knowing II. *m, f sans pl* (*indiscret*) inquisitive person

**curiosité** [kyʀjozite] *f* curiosity

**curiste** [kyʀist] *mf* patient having spa therapy

**curriculum (vitæ)** [kyʀikylɔm(vite)] *m inv* curriculum vitae, resumé

**curry** [kyʀi] *m sans pl* curry

**curseur** [kyʀsœʀ] *m* cursor

**cuve** [kyv] *f* **❶** (*pour vin*) vat **❷** (*pour pétrole, eau*) tank

**cuvée** [kyve] *f* vintage

**cuvette** [kyvɛt] *f* **❶** (*récipient*) bowl **❷** (*partie creuse: d'un évier*) basin **❸** GEO basin

**CV** *abr de* **cheval fiscal** hp

**C.V.** *abr de* **curriculum vitæ**

**cyanure** [sjanyʀ] *m* cyanide

**cybercafé** [sibɛʀkafe] *m* cybercafé

**cyberespace** [sibɛʀɛspas] *m* cyberspace

**cyberguerre** [sibɛʀgɛʀ] *m* INFORM cyberwar

**cyclamen** [siklamɛn] *m* cyclamen

**cycle** [sikl] *m* **❶** BIO, MED, ASTR, ECON cycle **❷** ECOLE **premier ~** middle school, **deuxième ~** high school **❸** UNIV **premier ~** first two years (*leading to "DEUG" or equivalent*); **deuxième ~** final year (*leading to the "licence"*); **troisième ~** postgraduate study

**cyclique** [siklik] *adj* cyclic

**cyclisme** [siklism] *m sans pl* cycling

**cycliste** [siklist] I. *adj* **course ~** cycle race; **coureur ~** racing cyclist II. *mf* cyclist

**cyclomoteur** [siklomotœʀ] *m* scooter

**cyclone** [siklon] *m* **❶** (*tempête*) hurricane **❷** METEO cyclone

**cygne** [siɲ] *m* swan

**cylindre** [silɛ̃dʀ] *m* cylinder

**cylindrée** [silɛ̃dʀe] *f* **①** *sans pl* (*volume*) capacity **②** (*voiture*) **petite ~** small engine; **une grosse ~** (*moto*) high-powered bike

**cylindrique** [silɛ̃dʀik] *adj* cylindrical

**D**

## Dd

**D, d** [de] *m inv* D, d; **~ comme Désiré** (*au téléphone*) e as in Delta

**d'** *v.* **de**

**d'abord** [dabɔʀ] *v.* **abord**

**d'accord** [dakɔʀ] *v.* **accord**

**dactylo** [daktilo] **I.** *mf* typist **II.** *f abr de* **dactylographie: apprendre la ~** to learn to type

**dahlia** [dalja] *m* dahlia

**daim** [dɛ̃] *m* **①** ZOOL deer **②** (*cuir*) suede

**dalle** [dal] *f* (*plaque*) slab ► **avoir la ~** *inf* to be ravenous; **je(n')y comprenais que ~** *inf* I couldn't understand a damn thing

**dame** [dam] **I.** *f* **①** (*femme*) lady; **la première ~ de France** the First Lady of France **②** *pl* (*jeu*) checkers **③** JEUX queen **II.** *interj inf* **~!** my word!

**damné(e)** [dane] **I.** *adj antéposé, inf* damned **II.** *m(f)* damned man, woman *m, f*

**Danemark** [danmaʀk] *m* **le ~** Denmark

**danger** [dɑ̃ʒe] *m* danger; **les ~s de la route** road hazards; **pas de ~!** no way!; **~ de mort!** risk of death!; **mettre qc en ~** to put sth in danger

**dangereusement** [dɑ̃ʒʀøzmɑ̃] *adv* dangerously

**dangereux, -euse** [dɑ̃ʒʀø, -øz] *adj* dangerous; **zone dangereuse** danger zone

**danois** [danwa] *m* Danish; *v.a.* **français**

**danois(e)** [danwa, waz] *adj* Danish

**Danois(e)** [danwa, waz] *m(f)* Dane

**dans** [dɑ̃] *prep* **①** (*à l'intérieur de*) in; **jouer ~ la cour** to play in the playground **②** (*à travers*) through; (*dedans*) in; **regarder ~ une longue vue** to look through a telescope; **rentrer ~ un arbre** to run into a tree **③** (*contenant*) **boire ~ un verre** to drink from a glass **④** (*futur, dans un délai de, état, manière, cause*) in; **~ une heure** in an hour; **~ combien de temps?** when? **⑤** (*dans le courant de*) during **⑥** (*environ*) around

**danse** [dɑ̃s] *f* dance ► **mener la ~** to run the show

**danser** [dɑ̃se] <1> *vt, vi* to dance

**danseur, -euse** [dɑ̃sœʀ, -øz] *m, f* dancer

**Danube** [danyb] *m* **le ~** the Danube

**date** [dat] *f* date; **~ limite d'envoi** deadline for submission; **à quelle ~?** on what date?; **amitié de longue ~** long-standing friendship

**dater** [date] <1> **I.** *vt* to date; **être daté du ...** to be dated ... **II.** *vi* **①** (*remonter à*) **~ du XIV^e siècle** (*objet, maison*) to date from the fourteenth century; **à ~ d'aujourd'hui** from [*o* as of] today **②** (*être démodé*) to date ► **ne pas ~ d'hier** to go back a long way

**datif** [datif] *m* dative

**datte** [dat] *f* date

**dauphin** [dofɛ̃] *m* ZOOL dolphin

**daurade** [dɔʀad] *f* ZOOL sea bream

**davantage** [davɑ̃taʒ] *adv* **①** (*plus: gagner, travailler, manger*) more; (*bien*)

---

**cymbale** [sɛ̃bal] *f sans pl* MUS cymbal

**cynique** [sinik] **I.** *adj* (*brutal*) cynical **II.** *mf a.* PHILOS cynic

**cynisme** [sinism] *m a.* PHILOS cynicism

**cyprès** [sipʀɛ] *m* cypress

**~ de ...** a lot more of ... ❷ (*plus long-temps*) any longer

**de**¹ [də, dy, de] <d', de la, du, des> *prep* ❶ (*point de départ*) from; **~ ... à ...** from ... to ... ❷ (*origine*) from; **venir ~ Paris/d'Angleterre** to be from Paris/England, **le vin d'Italie** Italian wine; **tu es d'où?** where are you from?; **le train ~ Paris** (*provenance*) the train from Paris; (*destination*) the train to Paris ❸ (*appartenance, partie*) of; **la femme d'Antoine** Antoine's wife; **la majorité des Français** the majority of French people ❹ (*matière*) **~ bois/verre** wooden/glass ❺ (*spécificité*) **roue ~ secours** spare tire ❻ (*contenu*) **un sac ~ pommes de terre** a bag of potatoes; **combien ~ kilos?** how many kilograms?; **un billet ~ cent dollars** a hundred-dollar bill; **une jeune fille ~ 20 ans** a twenty-year old girl; **gagner 30 euros ~ l'heure** to earn 30 euros an hour ❼ (*qualification*) **cet idiot ~ Durand** that idiot Durand ❽ (*qualité*) **ce film est d'un ennui/d'un triste!** this film is so boring/so sad ❾ (*particule nobiliaire*) de; **le général ~ Gaulle** General de Gaulle ❿ (*agent, temporel*) by; **~ quoi ...?** by what?; **~ nuit** by night; **~ temps en temps** from time to time ⓫ (*manière*) **~ mémoire** from memory ⓬ (*moyen*) with; **faire signe ~ la main** to wave ⓭ (*introduction d'un complément*) **c'est à toi ~ jouer** it's up to you now

**de²** [də, dy, de] <d', de la, du, des> *art partitif, parfois non traduit* **du vin/~ la bière/des gâteaux** (some) wine/beer/cakes

**dé¹** [de] *m* ❶ (*jeu*) die; **jeter les ~s** to throw the dice ❷ (*cube*) **couper qc en ~s** to dice sth

**dé²** [de] *m* **~ à coudre** thimble

**dealer** [dilœʀ] *m inf* dealer

**dealeur, -euse** [dilœn, øz] *m, f v.* **dealer**

**déambulateur** [deɑ̃bylatøʀ] *m* walker, *a light portable frame used to support a*

handicapped person; (*muni de roulettes*) rollator

**déballer** [debale] <1> *vt* ❶ (*sortir*) to unpack ❷ *inf* (*raconter: secrets*) come out with

**débarbouiller** [debaʀbuje] <1> **I.** *vt* **~ qn** to clean sb up (quickly) **II.** *vpr* **se ~** to clean oneself up (quickly)

**débarcadère** [debaʀkadɛʀ] *m* landing stage

**débardeur** [debaʀdœʀ] *m* ❶ (*pull sans bras*) sweater vest ❷ (*t-shirt sans bras*) tank top ❸ (*ouvrier*) docker

**débarquement** [debaʀkəmɑ̃] *m* ❶ (*opp: embarquement: des marchandises*) unloading; (*des voyageurs*) landing ❷ (*descente: des troupes*) landing

**débarquer** [debaʀke] <1> **I.** *vt* NAUT (*marchandises*) to unload; (*passagers*) to land **II.** *vi* ❶ (*opp: embarquer: passager*) to land; NAUT to disembark; (*troupes*) to land ❷ *inf* (*arriver*) **~ chez qn** to turn up at sb's place ❸ *inf* (*ne pas être au courant*) to have no idea what's going on

**débarras** [debaʀɑ] *m* junk room ▸ **bon ~!** good riddance!

**débarrasser** [debaʀɑse] <1> **I.** *vt* (*pièce, grenier*) to clear out; (*table*) to clear **II.** *vpr* ❶ (*ôter*) **se ~ de son manteau** to take off one's coat ❷ (*donner ou vendre*) **se ~ de vieux livres** to get rid of old books ❸ (*liquider*) **se ~ d'une affaire** to finish a matter ❹ (*éloigner*) **se ~ de qn** to get rid of sb

**débat** [deba] *m* ❶ (*discussion*) discussion ❷ (*discussion entre deux candidats*) debate ❸ JUR proceedings, hearing

**débattre** [debatʀ] *irr* **I.** *vt* to discuss; (*de façon formelle*) to debate ▸ **à ~** negotiable **II.** *vi* **~ de qc** to discuss sth **III.** *vpr* **se ~** to struggle

**débauche** [deboʃ] *f* ❶ (*vice*) debauchery ❷ (*abondance, excès*) abundance

**débaucher** [deboʃe] <1> **I.** *vt* ❶ (*détourner d'un travail*) to lure away ❷ (*licencier*) to lay off **II.** *vpr* **se ~** to take to a life of debauchery

**débile** [debil] **I.** *adj* ❶ *inf* (*stupide*) cra-

**D**

zy ② (*atteint de débilité*) feeble-minded ③ (*frêle: corps*) feeble; (*enfant*) sickly; (*santé*) poor **II.** *mf* ① MED person with a weak constitution; ~ **mental** feeble-minded person ② *péj, inf* (*imbécile*) cretin

**débilité** [debilite] *f* ① MED (*de l'esprit*) feebleness; (*du corps*) weakness ② *inf* (*stupidité*) idiocy

**débit** [debi] *m* ① COM turnover ② (*écoulement: d'un tuyau, d'une rivière*) rate of flow ③ (*élocution*) delivery ④ FIN debit

**débiter** [debite] <1> *vt* ① FIN ~ **un compte de 100 euros** to debit 100 euros from an account ② (*vendre*) to sell ③ *péj* (*dire: discours, poème*) to spew out; (*banalités, sottises*) to come out with ④ (*produire*) to produce

**débiteur, -trice** [debitœʀ, -tʀis] **I.** *m, f* debtor; **être le ~ de qn** to be in debt to sb **II.** *adj* (*compte*) in debit

**déblayer** [debleje] <7> *vt* (*débarrasser*) to clear

**débloquer** [deblɔke] <1> **I.** *vt* ① TECH (*frein*) to release; (*écrou, vis*) to loosen; (*serrure, porte*) to unjam ② ECON (*crédit, marchandise*) to release ③ (*trouver une issue à: crise*) to ease **II.** *vi inf* to be crazy **III.** *vpr* TECH **se ~** (*vis*) to loosen; (*serrure, porte*) to unjam

**déboiser** [debwaze] <1> *vt* to deforest

**déboîter** [debwate] <1> **I.** *vt* ① MED **sa chute lui a déboîté une épaule** he dislocated his shoulder when he fell ② (*démonter: porte*) to take off its hinges; (*tuyaux*) to disconnect **II.** *vpr* **se ~ une épaule** to dislocate a shoulder **III.** *vi* AUTO to pull out

**débordant(e)** [debɔʀdɑ̃, ɑ̃t] *adj* (*activité*) frenzied; (*enthousiasme, imagination, joie*) unbridled

**débordé(e)** [debɔʀde] *adj* ① (*submergé*) overwhelmed ② (*détaché du bord: drap*) untucked; (*lit*) unmade

**débordement** [debɔʀdəmɑ̃] *m* ① (*inondation: d'un liquide, d'une rivière*) overflowing ② (*flot, explosion*) ~ **de paroles** flood of words ③ *gén pl*

(*désordres*) uncontrolled behavior ④ *pl* (*excès*) excess

**déborder** [debɔʀde] <1> **I.** *vi* ① (*sortir: liquide, récipient*) to overflow; (*lac, rivière*) to burst its banks ② (*être plein de*) ~ **de joie** to be overflowing with joy ③ (*dépasser les limites*) ~ **sur le terrain voisin** to grow out onto the neighboring land **II.** *vt* ① (*dépasser*) ~ **les autres** to stand out from the others ② (*être dépassé*) **être débordé par qn/qc** to be overwhelmed by sb/sth

**débouché** [debuʃe] *m* ① (*marché*) outlet ② *pl* (*perspectives*) prospects ③ (*issue*) opening; (*d'une rue*) end

**déboucher** [debuʃe] <1> **I.** *vt* ① (*désobstruer: nez, lavabo*) to unclog ② (*ouvrir*) to open; (*bouteille*) to uncork; (*tube*) to take the top off **II.** *vpr* **se ~** (*tuyau, lavabo, nez*) to unclog **III.** *vi* ① (*sortir: piéton*) to step out; (*véhicule*) to move out ② (*sortir à grande vitesse: véhicule*) to hurtle out ③ (*aboutir*) ~ **dans/sur une rue** (*personne, voie*) to come out into/onto a road ④ (*aboutir à*) ~ **sur qc** to lead onto sth

**déboucler** [debukle] <1> *vt* (*ceinture*) to undo

**débourser** [debuʀse] <1> *vt* to pay (out)

**debout** [d(ə)bu] *adj, adv inv* ① (*en position verticale: personne*) standing (up); **être ~** to be standing up; **se mettre ~** to get up ② (*levé*) **être/rester ~** to be/stay up ③ (*opp: malade, fatigué*) **je ne tiens plus ~** I'm ready to drop ④ (*en bon état*) **tenir encore ~** (*construction, institution*) to be still standing

**déboutonner** [debutɔne] <1> **I.** *vt* (*chemise, gilet*) to unbutton; (*bouton*) to undo **II.** *vpr* **se ~** (*personne*) to undo one's buttons; (*vêtement*) to come undone

**débrancher** [debʀɑ̃ʃe] <1> *vt* to unplug

**débrayer** [debʀeje] <7> *vi* ① AUTO to release the clutch ② (*faire grève*) to stop work

**débris** [debʀi] *m* ① *gén pl* (*fragment*)

bits; (*d'une explosion*) debris ❷ *pl* (*restes*) remains

**débrouillard(e)** [debʀujaʀ, jaʀd] **I.** *adj inf* resourceful **II.** *m(f) inf* shrewd operator

**débrouiller** [debʀuje] <1> **I.** *vt* ❶ (*démêler: écheveau, fil*) to unravel ❷ (*élucider: affaire*) to sort out ❸ *inf* (*former*) ~ **qn** to show sb the basics **II.** *vpr inf* **se ~** (*s'en sortir*) to manage; (*réussir*) to sort things out; **se ~ pour** +*infin* to fix it to +*infin*

**début** [deby] *m* ❶ (*commencement*) beginning; **au ~ de qc** at the beginning of sth ❷ *pl* (*tentatives, apparitions*) **les ~s de qn dans/à qc** sb's early days in sth

**débutant(e)** [debytã, ãt] **I.** *adj* (*joueur, footballeur*) novice **II.** *m(f)* ❶ (*élève, ouvrier*) beginner; SPORT novice ❷ (*acteur*) actor making his debut

**débuter** [debyte] <1> *vt, vi* to start

**décacheter** [dekaʃte] <3> *vt* (*lettre*) to open; (*document scellé*) to break open

**décadence** [dekadãs] *f* ❶ (*état*) decadence ❷ (*déclin*) decline

**décadent(e)** [dekadã, ãt] *adj* (*art, civilisation*) decadent

**décaféiné** [dekafeine] *m* decaffeinated

**décalage** [dekalaʒ] *m* ❶ (*action: d'un horaire*) pushing back ❷ (*écart temporel*) time difference; (*entre événements*) time lag; (*après un vol*) jet lag ❸ (*écart spatial*) staggering ❹ (*différence*) discrepancy

**décalé(e)** [dekale] *adj* ❶ (*non aligné*) **la maison est ~e** the house is set back/forward ❷ (*bancal*) wobbly ❸ (*inattendu: humour, ton*) off-key ❹ (*déphasé*) **être ~** (*dans le temps*) out of sync; (*dans une société*) out of step

**décaler** [dekale] <1> **I.** *vt* ❶ (*avancer/retarder*) ~ **qc d'un jour** to bring sth forward/push sth back a day ❷ (*déplacer: meuble, appareil*) to move forward/back **II.** *vpr* **se ~ en arrière/vers la droite** to move back/to the right

**décanter** [dekãte] <1> **I.** *vt* (*liquide, vin*) to allow to settle **II.** *vi* (*liquide, vin*) to settle **III.** *vpr* **se ~** (*liquide*) to settle; (*idées, réflexions*) to get clearer

**décapant** [dekapã] *m* ❶ (*pour métal*) abrasive ❷ (*pour peinture*) stripper

**décapant(e)** [dekapã, ãt] *adj* ❶ (*abrasif: produit*) stripping; (*pouvoir*) abrasive ❷ (*article, humour*) caustic

**décaper** [dekape] <1> *vt* (*métal*) to clean; (*bois, meuble*) to strip

**décapiter** [dekapite] <1> *vt* ❶ (*étêter: condamné*) to behead; (*fleur*) to take the head off ❷ *fig* (*parti, réseau*) to leave without a leader

**décapotable** [dekapɔtabl] **I.** *adj* convertible **II.** *f* convertible

**décapsuleur** [dekapsylœʀ] *m* bottle opener

**décéder** [desede] <5> *vi être form* to pass away

**déceler** [des(ə)le] <4> *vt* ❶ (*découvrir*) to detect; (*cause, raison, intrigue*) to discover; (*sentiment, fatigue*) to discern ❷ (*être l'indice de*) to reveal

**décembre** [desãbʀ] *m* December; *v.a.* **août**

**décence** [desãs] *f* decency

**décennie** [deseni] *f* decade

**décent(e)** [desã, ãt] *adj* decent

**décentralisation** [desãtʀalizasjɔ̃] *f* decentralization

**décentraliser** [desãtʀalize] <1> **I.** *vt* to decentralize **II.** *vpr* **se ~** to be decentralized

**déception** [desɛpsjɔ̃] *f* disappointment

**décerner** [desɛʀne] <1> *vt* to award

**décès** [desɛ] *m form* (*mort*) death

**décevant(e)** [des(ə)vã, ãt] *adj* disappointing

**décevoir** [des(ə)vwaʀ] <12> *vt* to disappoint

**déchaîné(e)** [deʃene] *adj* (*passions, vent, mer*) raging; (*instincts*) unbridled; (*foule, enfant*) wild

**déchaîner** [deʃene] <1> **I.** *vt* (*passions*) to unleash; (*enthousiasme, conflit, indignation*) to arouse **II.** *vpr* **se ~ contre qn/qc** to blow up at sb/sth

**D**

**décharge** [deʃaʀʒ] f ❶ (dépôt) dump ❷ (salve: de carabine) shot; (de plombs) volley ❸ ELEC, JUR discharge

**déchargement** [deʃaʀʒəmɑ̃] m unloading

**décharger** [deʃaʀʒe] <2a> I. vt ❶ (voiture) to unload ❷ (passagers) to land ❸ (libérer) ~ qn d'un travail to relieve sb of a job ❹ (soulager) to vent ❺ ELEC, JUR to discharge II. vpr ❶ (se libérer) se ~ du travail sur qn to pass work off onto sb ❷ ELEC (batterie) se ~ to go flat III. vi inf (éjaculer) to come

**déchausser** [deʃose] <1> I. vt (skis) to take off II. vpr se ~ ❶ (enlever ses chaussures) se ~ to take one's shoes off ❷ MED (dent) to come loose

**déchéance** [deʃeɑ̃s] f ❶ (déclin) degeneration; (d'une civilisation) decline ❷ JUR (d'un souverain) deposition

**déchetterie** [deʃɛtʀi] f waste collection center

**déchiffrer** [deʃifʀe] <1> I. vt ❶ (décrypter: message, code, hiéroglyphes) to decipher ❷ MUS ~ un morceau to sight-read a piece ❸ (déceler: intentions) to work out; (sentiments) to make out II. vi MUS to sight-read

**déchiré(e)** [deʃiʀe] adj torn

**déchirement** [deʃiʀmɑ̃] m ❶ (déchirure: d'un muscle, d'un tissu) tearing ❷ (souffrance) heartache ❸ (divisions) splits

**déchirer** [deʃiʀe] <1> I. vt ❶ (déchirer) to tear ❷ (couper: enveloppe) to tear (open) ❸ (troubler: silence) to tear through ❹ (faire souffrir) ~ qn to tear sb apart ❺ (diviser: parti, pays) to split II. vpr ❶ (rompre) se ~ (sac) to tear (open); (vêtement) to get torn; (nuage) to break up; (cœur) to break ❷ MED se ~ un muscle to tear a muscle ❸ (se quereller) se ~ to tear each other apart

**déchirure** [deʃiʀyʀ] f ❶ (accroc: d'un vêtement) tear ❷ MED ~ ligamentaire/musculaire torn ligament/muscle ❸ (trouée: du ciel) break

**décibel** [desibɛl] m decibel

**décidé(e)** [deside] adj (air, personne) decisive; **c'est ~, ...** it's (all) settled

**décidément** [desidemɑ̃] adv ❶ (après répétition d'une expérience désagréable) well! ❷ (après hésitation ou réflexion) **oui, ~, c'est bien lui le meilleur!** yes, he's the best, definitely!

**décider** [deside] <1> I. vt ❶ (prendre une décision) to decide on; ~ de +infin to decide to +infin ❷ (persuader) ~ qn à +infin to convince sb to +infin II. vi ~ de qc to determine sth III. vpr ❶ (être fixé) se ~ (chose, événement) to be decided ❷ (prendre une décision) se ~ to decide; **se ~ à +infin** to make a decision to +infin

**décisif, -ive** [desizif, -iv] adj (moment, bataille) critical; (argument, preuve, ton) decisive; (intervention, rôle) crucial

**décision** [desizjɔ̃] f ❶ (choix) decision; **prendre une ~** to make a decision ❷ (fermeté) decisiveness

**déclaration** [deklaʀasjɔ̃] f ❶ (discours, témoignage) statement ❷ (propos) declaration ❸ (aveu d'amour) ~ d'amour declaration of love ❹ ADMIN (enregistrement: d'un décès, changement de domicile) registration ❺ (formulaire) ~ d'accident accident report

**déclarer** [deklaʀe] <1> I. vt ❶ (annoncer) ~ que ... to say that ...; ~ qn coupable to find sb guilty; ~ la guerre to declare war ❷ (enregistrer: employé, marchandise) to declare; (décès, naissance) to register II. vpr ❶ (se manifester) se ~ (incendie, orage) to break out; (fièvre, maladie) to set in ❷ (se prononcer) se ~ pour/contre qn/qc to declare oneself for/against sb/sth ❸ (se dire) se ~ l'auteur du crime to admit to having committed the crime ❹ (faire une déclaration d'amour) se ~ à qn to declare oneself to sb

**déclenchement** [deklɑ̃ʃmɑ̃] m (d'un mécanisme) activation; (d'un conflit) setting off; (d'une offensive) launch

**déclencher** [deklɑ̃ʃe] <1> I. vt ❶ TECH (ressort) to release; (mécanisme) to activate ❷ (*provoquer: conflit, réaction*) to set off; (*offensive*) to launch **II.** *vpr* **se ~** (*mécanisme*) to be set off; (*attaque, grève*) to be launched

**déclic** [deklik] *m* ❶ (*mécanisme*) release mechanism ❷ (*bruit*) click

**déclin** [deklɛ̃] *m* (*des forces physiques et mentales*) decline; (*de la popularité*) falling off; (*du jour*) closing; (*du soleil*) setting

**déclinaison** [deklinɛzɔ̃] *f* LING declension ❷ ASTR declination

**décliner** [dekline] <1> **I.** *vt* ❶ (*refuser*) a. LING to decline ❷ (*dire*) to state **II.** *vi* ❶ (*baisser: jour*) to draw to a close; (*forces, prestige*) to decline ❷ ASTR to set **III.** *vpr* **se ~** LING to decline

**décoder** [dekɔde] <1> *vt* (*message*) to decode

**décodeur** [dekɔdœʀ] *m* decoder

**décollage** [dekɔlaʒ] *m* ❶ (*envol*) a. ECON takeoff ❷ (*décollement: d'un papier peint, timbre-poste*) removal

**décoller** [dekɔle] <1> **I.** *vt* (*timbre*) to unstick **II.** *vi* ❶ AVIAT, ECON to take off ❷ *inf* (*partir, sortir*) **ne pas ~ de devant la télé** to be glued to the TV ❸ *inf* (*maigrir*) to slim down **III.** *vpr* **se ~** (*timbre*) to peel off; (*carrelage*) to come off; (*rétine*) to become detached

**décolleté** [dekɔlte] *m* décolleté

**décolleté(e)** [dekɔlte] *adj* ❶ (*échancré: vêtement*) low-cut ❷ (*dénudé: personne*) décolleté

**décoloniser** [dekɔlɔnize] <1> *vt* (*pays, habitants*) to decolonize

**décolorant** [dekɔlɔʀɑ̃] *m* bleaching agent

**décolorant(e)** [dekɔlɔʀɑ̃, ɑ̃t] *adj* (*action, pouvoir*) bleaching

**décoloration** [dekɔlɔʀasjɔ̃] *f* decolorization; (*des cheveux*) bleaching; (*des rideaux, de la tapisserie, d'une matière*) fading

**décoloré(e)** [dekɔlɔʀe] *adj* (*cheveux, poils*) bleached; (*couleur*) washed-out; (*papier, affiches*) faded; (*lèvres*) pale

**décolorer** [dekɔlɔʀe] <1> **I.** *vt* **~ des tissus/vêtements avec qc** to take the

color out of cloth/clothes with sth **II.** *vpr* ❶ (*perdre sa couleur*) **se ~** (*cheveux*) to lose its color; (*étoffe*) to fade ❷ (*enlever la couleur*) **se ~ les cheveux** to bleach one's hair

**décombres** [dekɔ̃bʀ] *mpl* rubble; *fig* ruins

**décommander** [dekɔmɑ̃de] <1> **I.** *vt* (*rendez-vous, réunion*) to call off; (*marchandise*) to cancel; **~ qn** to put sb off **II.** *vpr* **se ~** to cancel

**décomposé(e)** [dekɔ̃poze] *adj* ❶ (*putréfié: substance organique*) rotting; (*cadavre*) decomposed ❷ (*altéré: visage, traits*) distorted

**décomposer** [dekɔ̃poze] <1> **I.** *vt* ❶ (*détailler, diviser*) a. CHIM, MATH, LING to break down ❷ PHYS to resolve ❸ MATH to factor ❹ LING to parse ❺ (*analyser: idée, problème, savoir*) to analyze ❻ (*altérer: substance*) to rot; (*morale*) to shake; (*visage, trait*) to unsettle **II.** *vpr* ❶ (*se diviser, se détailler*) **se ~ en qc** CHIM to break down into sth; PHYS, MATH to resolve into sth; MATH to factor into sth; LING to be analyzable as ❷ (*pouvoir s'analyser*) **se ~ en qc** (*problème, idée, savoir*) to break down into sth ❸ (*s'altérer*) **se ~** (*substance organique*) to rot; (*cadavre*) to decompose; (*visage, traits*) to collapse; (*société*) to break down

**décomprimer** [dekɔ̃pʀime] <1> *vt* TECH (*air*) to decompress

**décompte** [dekɔ̃t] *m* ❶ (*compte: des bulletins de vote*) counting; (*des points*) reckoning ❷ (*facture*) statement ❸ (*déduction*) deduction

**déconcentré(e)** [dekɔ̃sɑ̃tʀe] *adj* decentralized

**déconcerter** [dekɔ̃sɛʀte] <1> *vt* to disconcert

**décongeler** [dekɔ̃ʒ(ɔ)le] <4> *vt, vi* to defrost

**déconnecter** [dekɔnɛkte] <1> **I.** *vt* ELEC, INFORM to disconnect **II.** *vi* *inf* to take a break **III.** *vpr* **se ~ de son travail** get away from one's work

**D**

**déconseillé(e)** [dekɔ̃seje] *adj* unadvisable

**déconseiller** [dekɔ̃seje] <1> *vt* ~ **qc à qn** to advise sb against sth

**décontaminer** [dekɔ̃tamine] <1> *vt* (*lieu, personne, rivière*) to decontaminate; INFORM (*disquettes*) to repair

**décontracté(e)** [dekɔ̃trakte] I. *adj* ❶ (*détendu: partie du corps, personne*) relaxed ❷ *inf* (*sûr de soi*) laid-back; *péj* cocksure ❸ *inf* (*non guindé: atmosphère, situation, style, ton*) relaxed; (*tenue*) casual II. *adv inf* (*s'habiller*) casually; (*conduire*) in a relaxed way

**décontracter** [dekɔ̃trakte] <1> I. *vt* to relax II. *vpr* **se** ~ to relax

**décor** [dekɔr] *m* ❶ (*agencement, art de la décoration*) decoration ❷ THEAT scenery; CINE set ❸ (*cadre*) scenery; (*arrière-plan*) setting ❹ (*style*) decor ▶ **envoyer qn dans le** ~ *inf* to push sb off the road

**décorateur, -trice** [dekɔratœr, -tris] *m, f* ❶ (*designer*) decorator ❷ CINE, THEAT designer

**décoratif, -ive** [dekɔratif, -iv] *adj* decorative; **motifs** ~**s** ornamental motifs

**décoration** [dekɔrasjɔ̃] *f* ❶ (*fait de décorer, résultat, distinction*) decoration ❷ (*art*) decorative art

**décorer** [dekɔre] <1> *vt* to decorate; ~ **une vitrine de qc** to dress a window with sth

**décortiquer** [dekɔrtike] <1> *vt* ❶ (*enlever l'enveloppe: arbre, tige*) to take the bark off; (*noix, noisettes, graines*) to shell ❷ (*détailler: texte*) to dissect; (*affaire*) to examine from every angle

**découpage** [dekupaʒ] *m* ❶ (*fait de trancher avec un couteau: d'un gâteau*) cutting (up); (*d'une viande*) (*par le boucher*) cutting up; (*pour servir*) carving; (*d'une volaille*) jointing ❷ (*fait de couper suivant un contour, tracé*) cutout ❸ ADMIN, POL division ❹ CINE (*d'un film*) division into scenes

**découper** [dekupe] <1> I. *vt* ❶ (*trancher: gâteau*) to cut (up); (*volaille*) joint; (*tranche de saucisson*) to slice ❷ (*cou-*

per suivant un contour, tracé: tissu, moquette*) to cut out II. *vpr* (*se profiler*) **se** ~ **dans/sur qc** to stand out against sth

**découragé(e)** [dekuraʒe] *adj* discouraged

**décourageant(e)** [dekuraʒɑ̃, ʒɑ̃t] *adj* discouraging; (*nouvelle, résultats, travail*) disheartening

**découragement** [dekuraʒmɑ̃] *m* discouragement

**décourager** [dekuraʒe] <2a> I. *vt* to discourage II. *vpr* **se** ~ to get discouraged

**décousu** [dekuzy] *m sans pl* disjointed/rambling nature

**décousu(e)** [dekuzy] *adj* ❶ COUT unstitched ❷ (*dépourvu de logique: conversation, récit, devoir*) disjointed; (*idées*) incoherent

**découvert** [dekuvɛr] *m* ❶ FIN deficit; (*d'un compte*) overdraft ❷ MIL (*terrain*) exposed terrain

**découvert(e)** [dekuvɛr, ɛrt] *adj* ❶ (*nu*) bare ❷ (*dégagé: lieu, zone*) open

**découverte** [dekuvɛrt] *f* discovery; **faire la** ~ **de qc** to discover sth

**découvrir** [dekuvrir] <11> I. *vt* ❶ (*trouver, deviner, percer, déceler*) to discover; ~ **que qc est vrai** to find out that sth is true ❷ (*enlever la couverture, mettre à jour*) to uncover ❸ (*ouvrir*) ~ **une casserole** to take the lid off a saucepan ❹ (*enlever ce qui couvre*) to take the cover off; (*statue*) to unveil ❺ (*apercevoir: panorama*) to get a view of; (*personne*) to see ❻ (*laisser voir: jambes, épaules, ciel*) to reveal; (*racines, terre*) to uncover II. *vpr* ❶ (*enlever sa couverture*) **se** ~ (*au lit*) to push back the covers; (*enlever son vêtement*) to remove one's clothing; (*enlever son chapeau*) to take one's hat off ❷ (*s'exposer aux attaques*) **se** ~ (*armée*) to expose itself ❸ (*se confier*) **se** ~ **à qn** to confide in sb ❹ (*apprendre*) **se** ~ **des dons/un goût pour qc** to discover a gift/a taste for sth ❺ (*apparaître*) **se** ~ (*panorama, paysage*) to come into view; (*secret*) to come into the open; (*vérité*) to become known ⑥(*s'éclaircir*) **le ciel se découvre** the sky is clearing

**décrédibiliser** [dekʀedibilize] <1> *vt* discredit

**décret** [dekʀɛ] *m* POL decree

**décréter** [dekʀete] <5> **I.** *vt* ①POL to decree; (*mesures*) to order; (*état d'urgence*) to declare ②*fig* ~ **que qc doit se faire** to decree that sth must be done **II.** *vpr* **qc/ça ne se décrète pas** sth/that can't be legislated (for)

**décrire** [dekʀiʀ] *vt irr* to describe

**décrocher** [dekʀɔʃe] <1> **I.** *vt* ①(*dépendre: linge, rideaux, tableau*) to take down; (*laisse, sangle, volets*) to undo; ~ **le téléphone** (*pour répondre*) to pick up the phone; (*pour ne pas être dérangé*) to take the phone off the hook ②*inf* (*obtenir: prix*) to win ③SPORT (*concurrents, peloton*) to pull away from, to leave behind **II.** *vpr* **se** ~ (*personne, poisson*) to get off the hook; (*vêtement, tableau*) to come down **III.** *vi* ①(*au téléphone*) answer; **tu peux ~?** Can you get it? ②*inf* (*décompresser*) to take a break; (*se désintéresser*) to give up; (*arrêter le travail*) to call a halt; (*abandonner une activité, course*) to drop out ③(*ne plus écouter*) to switch off ④(*se détacher: armée, troupes*) to pull back ⑤AVIAT (*avion*) to stall ⑥RADIO (*émetteur*) to break off

**décroître** [dekʀwɑtʀ] *vi irr* avoir o être to decrease; (*jours*) to draw in; (*vitesse*) to go down

**décrue** [dekʀy] *f* (*des eaux*) fall

**déçu(e)** [desy] **I.** *part passé de* **décevoir II.** *adj* disappointed **III.** *m(f) souvent pl* **les ~s** the disillusioned

**dédaigneux, -euse** [dedɛɲø, -øz] *adj* contemptuous

**dedans** [d(ə)dã] **I.** *adv* + *verbe de mouvement* in; + *verbe d'état* inside; **en** ~ (*on*) inside; *fig* (*deep*) inside ► **rentrer** (**en plein**) ~ *inf* (*heurter en voiture*) to crash right into sb; (*heurter à pied*) to bump right into sb **II.** *m sans pl* inside

**dédicace** [dedikas] *f* ①(*sur une photo, un livre*) dedication; (*sur un monument*) inscription ②(*consécration: d'une église, d'un temple*) dedication

**dédicacer** [dedikase] <2> *vt* ~ **un roman à qn** to dedicate a novel to sb

**dédier** [dedje] <1> *vt* ~ **une œuvre à qn** to dedicate a work to sb

**dédommagement** [dedɔmaʒmã] *m* compensation

**dédommager** [dedɔmaʒe] <2a> **I.** *vt* ~ **une victime de qc** to compensate a victim for sth **II.** *vpr* **se** ~ **de qc** to make it up to oneself for sth

**déduction** [dedyksjɔ̃] *f* deduction

**déduire** [dedɥiʀ] *irr* **I.** *vt* ①(*retrancher: acompte, frais*) to deduct ②(*conclure*) to deduce **II.** *vpr* **se** ~ **de qc** to be deductible from sth

**déesse** [deɛs] *f* goddess

**défaillance** [defajãs] *f* ①(*faiblesse: d'une personne*) (*physique*) faint spell; (*morale*) weakness; (*intellectuelle*) lapse of memory ②(*dysfonctionnement: d'un moteur, système*) failure; (*d'une loi*) deficiency ③JUR (*d'un témoin*) failure to appear ► **tomber** **en** ~ to feel faint

**défaire** [defɛʀ] *irr* **I.** *vt* ①(*détacher*) to undo ②(*enlever ce qui est fait*) to undo; (*ourlet, rangs d'un tricot*) to unpick; (*construction*) to take down ③(*mettre en désordre*) to spoil ④(*déballer*) to unpack ⑤(*rompre: contrat*) to break; (*plan, projet*) to finish off; (*mariage*) to break up ⑥(*battre: armée*) to defeat ⑦(*débarrasser*) ~ **qn d'une habitude** to rid sb of a habit **II.** *vpr* ①(*se détacher*) **se** ~ (*paquet, ourlet, bouton, lacets*) to come undone; (*coiffure*) to get messed up ②*fig* **se** ~ (*amitié, relation*) to come to an end ③(*se séparer*) **se** ~ **de qn/qc** to get rid of sb/sth

**défait(e)** [defɛ, defɛt] **I.** *part passé de* **défaire II.** *adj* (*mine, visage, air*) weary

**défaite** [defɛt] *f* defeat

**défaut** [defo] *m* ①(*travers*) fault ②(*imperfection physique*) blemish; (*d'une*

**D**

*matière*) flaw ❸ (*faiblesse, inconvénient*) problem ❹ (*manque*) ~ **de preuves** insufficient evidence ▸ **faire** ~ to be lacking; **par** ~ by default

**défavorable** [defavɔʀabl] *adj* ❶ (*difficile: conditions, temps*) unfavorable ❷ (*opp: en faveur de*) **être** ~ **à un projet** to be against a project ❸ (*qui ne convient pas*) **le climat est** ~ **à l'agriculture** the climate isn't suitable for agriculture

**défavorisé(e)** [defavɔʀize] *adj* underprivileged

**défavoriser** [defavɔʀize] <1> *vt* ~ **Jean par rapport à Paul** to favor Paul over Jean

**défectueux, -euse** [defɛktɥø, -øz] *adj* (*appareil, prononciation*) faulty; (*organisation*) inadequate

**défendre¹** [defɑ̃dʀ] <14> I. *vt* to defend; ~ **une cause** to stand up for a cause II. *vpr* ❶ (*se protéger*) **se** ~ **contre un agresseur** to defend oneself against an attacker ❷ (*se préserver*) **se** ~ **de la chaleur** to protect oneself from the heat ❸ (*se débrouiller*) **se** ~ **en qc** to get by in sth ❹ *inf* (*être défendable*) **se** ~ (*idée, projet*) to have something to be said for it

**défendre²** [defɑ̃dʀ] <1> I. *vt* (*interdire*) to forbid II. *vpr* (*s'interdire*) **se** ~ **tout plaisir** to refuse all pleasures

**défendu(e)** [defɑ̃dy] I. *part passé de* **défendre** II. *adj* forbidden

**défense¹** [defɑ̃s] *f* ❶ (*fait de défendre*) defense; **légitime** ~ self-defense; **sans** ~ defenseless ❷ SPORT defense

**défense²** [defɑ̃s] *f* (*interdiction*) prohibition; ~ **de fumer** no smoking

**défense³** [defɑ̃s] *f* ZOOL tusk

**défenseur** [defɑ̃sœʀ] *mf* defender; JUR defense attorney; ~ **des droits de l'Homme/de l'environnement** human rights/environmental activist

**défensif, -ive** [defɑ̃sif, -iv] *adj* defensive

**défensive** [defɑ̃siv] *f* **être sur la** ~ to be on the defensive

**déferlement** [defɛʀləmɑ̃] *m* (*des vagues*) breaking; (*de la mer*) surging

**défi** [defi] *m* (*provocation, challenge*) challenge

**déficience** [defisjɑ̃s] *f* (*faiblesse*) deficiency

**déficient(e)** [defisjɑ̃, jɑ̃t] I. *adj* (*intelligence, forces, personne*) feeble; (*raisonnement*) weak II. *m(f)* ~ **mental** mentally disabled person

**déficit** [defisit] *m* ❶ FIN deficit; ~ **de la balance des paiements** balance of payments deficit; **combler le** ~ to make up the deficit ❷ (*perte*) *a.* MED ~ **de qc** deficiency in sth

**déficitaire** [defisitɛʀ] *adj* (*budget, entreprise*) in deficit; (*année, récolte*) poor

**défier** [defje] <1> I. *vt* ❶ (*provoquer*) ~ **qn aux échecs** to challenge sb at chess ❷ (*parier, braver*) **je te défie de faire ça** I dare you to do it ❸ (*soutenir l'épreuve de*) ~ **la raison/le bon sens** to defy reason/common sense II. *vpr* **se** ~ **de qn/qc** to distrust sb/sth

**défigurer** [defigyʀe] <1> *vt* ❶ (*abîmer le visage de qn*) to disfigure; (*rendre moins beau*) to spoil ❷ (*enlaidir: monument*) to deface; (*paysage*) to spoil ❸ (*travestir: faits, vérité*) to distort; (*article, texte*) to mar

**défilé** [defile] *m* ❶ (*cortège de manifestants*) march; (*cortège de fête*) parade; ~ **de mode** fashion show ❷ (*succession*) ~ **d'images** stream of images ❸ (*gorge*) pass

**défiler** [defile] <1> I. *vi* ❶ (*marcher en colonne, file: soldats, armée, manifestants*) to march; (*pour une cérémonie*) to parade; (*cortège*) to file past; (*mannequins*) to parade past ❷ (*se succéder: clients, visiteurs*) to come and go one after the other; (*voitures, rames*) to come by in a constant stream; (*souvenirs, images*) to keep coming in succession; (*jours*) to come and go endlessly ❸ (*passer en continu: bande, film*) to unreel; (*texte*) to scroll; (*paysage*) to pass by ❹ INFORM **faire** ~ **qc vers le haut/bas** to scroll sth up/down II. *vpr* *inf* (*se dérober*) **se** ~ to wriggle out of; (*s'éclipser*) to slip away

**défini(e)** [defini] *adj* ❶ (*déterminé: chose*) precise ❷ LING (*article*) definite

**définir** [definiʀ] <8> *vt* to define

**définitif** [definitif] *m inf* **c'est du** ~ this is for good

**définitif, -ive** [definitif, -iv] *adj* ❶ (*opp: provisoire*) definitive; (*refus, décision, victoire*) final ❷ (*sans appel: argument*) conclusive; (*jugement*) final ▸ **en définitive** when all is said and done

**définition** [definisjɔ̃] *f* definition; **par** ~ by definition

**définitivement** [definitivmɑ̃] *adv* definitely; (*s'installer, quitter*) for good

**défoncer** [defɔ̃se] <2> **I.** *vt* ❶ (*casser en enfonçant: porte, vitre*) to smash in ❷ (*enlever le fond*) to knock the bottom out of ❸ *inf* (*droguer*) ~ **qn** (*drogue*) to get sb high; *fig* to give sb a high **II.** *vpr* **se** ~ ❶ (*se détériorer: sol*) to get broken up ❷ *inf* (*se droguer*) to get high ❸ *inf* (*se donner du mal*) to knock oneself out

**déformation** [defɔʀmasjɔ̃] *f* ❶ (*altération*) putting out of shape; (*qui plie*) bending (out of shape); (*qui tord*) twisting (out of shape); (*qui comprime*) crushing; (*d'un nom*) corruption; (*de pensées, faits*) deformation; (*d'un caractère*) warping ❷ MED malformation ▸ ~ **professionnelle** occupational obsession

**déformer** [defɔʀme] <1> **I.** *vt* ❶ (*altérer*) to put out of shape; (*en pliant*) to bend (out of shape); (*en tordant*) to twist (out of shape); (*en comprimant*) to crush (out of shape); (*jambes, doigts*) to deform; (*chaussures*) to ruin the shape of; (*bouche*) to twist ❷ (*fausser: faits, pensées, voix*) to distort; (*goût*) to pervert **II.** *vpr* **se** ~ (*chaussures, vêtements*) to lose their shape; (*étagère*) to get twisted

**défouler** [defule] <1> **I.** *vpr* **se** ~ to let off steam **II.** *vt* ❶ (*libérer son agressivité*) ~ **son ressentiment sur qn/une voiture** to take one's resentment out on

sb/a car ❷ (*décontracter*) **la course me défoule** running helps me to relax

**dégagé(e)** [degaʒe] *adj* ❶ (*opp: encombré: ciel, vue, route*) clear; (*sommet*) clearly visible ❷ (*découvert*) **elle avait le front** ~ her hair was gathered back from her forehead ❸ (*décontracté: allure, air, ton, manière*) casual

**dégager** [degaʒe] <2a> **I.** *vt* ❶ (*libérer: objet enfoui*) to unearth; (*objet couvert*) to uncover; (*objet coincé*) to loosen ❷ (*bronches, nez, rue, couloir*) to free ❸ (*faire apparaître: cou, épaules*) to bare ❹ (*soustraire à une obligation*) ~ **sa responsabilité** to deny responsibility ❺ (*produire: odeur, parfum, gaz, fumée*) to give off ❻ SPORT to clear ❼ ECON, FIN (*crédits*) to free; (*profits, bénéfices*) to produce ❽ (*extraire*) ~ **une idée de qc** to bring out an idea from sth **II.** *vpr* ❶ (*se libérer*) **se** ~ (*passage, voie d'accès*) to be cleared; (*voie respiratoire*) to clear ❷ *fig* **se** ~ **de ses obligations** to free oneself from one's obligations ❸ (*émaner*) **se** ~ **de qc** (*fumée, odeur*) to come from sth; (*gaz, vapeur*) to be given off by sth ❹ (*ressortir*) **se** ~ **de qc** (*idée, vérité*) to emerge from sth; (*impression, mystère*) to be created by sth **III.** *vi inf* ❶ (*sentir mauvais*) to reek ❷ (*déguerpir*) to clear out; (*s'écarter*) to get out of the way; **dégage de là!** out of the way!

**dégât** [dega] *m* damage; ~**s matériels** structural damage ▸ **faire des** ~**s** to wreak havoc

**dégel** [deʒɛl] *m* ❶ (*fonte des glaces*) a. POL thaw ❷ ECON revival ❸ FIN unfreezing

**dégeler** [deʒ(ə)le] <4> **I.** *vt* ❶ (*faire fondre*) to thaw ❷ (*réchauffer détendre*) to thaw out ❸ (*débloquer: crédits, dossier*) to unfreeze **II.** *vi* ❶ (*fondre*) to thaw ❷ *impers* **il dégèle** it's thawing out **III.** *vpr* ❶ (*être moins réservé*) se to warm up ❷ (*se réchauffer*) **se** ~ **les pieds/mains** to warm one's feet/hands

**dégénérer** [deʒenere] <5> *vi* ❶ (*per-*

dre ses qualités, se changer en) to degenerate ② (se dégrader) to deteriorate

**dégivrer** [deʒivʀe] <1> vt (réfrigérateur) to defrost; (vitres, avion) to de-ice

**dégonfler** [degɔ̃fle] <1> I. vt ① (décompresser: enflure) to bring down; (ballon, pneu) to let the air out of ② (diminuer: prix, budget) to slim down ③ (minimiser: importance) to play down II. vpr se ~ ① (se décompresser: ballon, pneu) to deflate; (enflure) to go down ② inf (avoir peur) to chicken out; (reculer) to back down III. vi (enflure) to go down

**dégouliner** [deguline] <1> vi (liquide, confiture) (goutte à goutte) to drip; (en filet) to trickle

**dégourdi(e)** [degurdi] I. adj smart II. m(f) smart kid

**dégourdir** [degurdir] <8> I. vt (affranchir) to wake up II. vpr (se donner de l'exercice) se ~ to warm up; se ~ les jambes to stretch one's legs

**dégoût** [degu] m ① (écœurement) disgust; ~ du fromage strong dislike of cheese ② (aversion) son ~ pour qn/qc the disgust he felt for sb/sth ③ (lassitude) weariness

**dégoûtant(e)** [degutɑ̃, ɑ̃t] I. adj disgusting II. m(f) inf ① (personne sale) filthy person ② (vicieux) revolting person

**dégoûté(e)** [degute] adj (écœuré: personne, mine) disgusted; **je suis** ~ (scandalisé) I'm disgusted; (lassé) I'm sick and tired of it all; **être** ~ **de la vie/de vivre** to be sick of life/of living

**dégoûter** [degute] <1> I. vt ① (répugner physiquement) to disgust ② (ôter l'envie de) ~ qn to turn sb off II. vpr se ~ de qc/qn to get sick of sb/sth

**dégradant(e)** [degradɑ̃, ɑ̃t] adj degrading

**dégradation** [degradasjɔ̃] f ① (dégâts) damage; (de l'environnement) damaging ② (détérioration) deterioration ③ (avilissement) a. MIL degradation

**dégradé** [degrade] m ① (camaïeu: de couleurs) gradation ② (coupe de cheveux) layered cut

**dégrader** [degrade] <1> I. vt ① (détériorer: édifice, route) to damage; (situation, climat social) to worsen ② (faire un dégradé) to layer ③ MIL to degrade II. vpr se ~ ① (s'avilir) to degrade oneself ② (se détériorer: édifice) to deteriorate; (situation, climat social, temps) to worsen

**dégraisser** [degrese] <1> vt ① (nettoyer: métal, laine) to degrease ② (enlever la graisse: cheveux) to make less greasy ③ inf ECON (effectifs, entreprise) to slim down

**degré** [dəgre] m ① (intensité) a. MED degree; (de l'échelle de Richter) point; **jusqu'à un certain** ~ up to a point ② (dans la hiérarchie) level ③ ECOLE **l'enseignement du premier/second** ~ primary/secondary education ④ MATH, GEO, MUS degree; **20** ~**s Celsius** 20 degrees Celsius; ~ **en alcool** alcohol content

**dégriffé(e)** [degrife] adj without the designer label

**déguisé(e)** [degize] adj ① (pour tromper) disguised ② (costumé) dressed up; (pour le carnaval) in fancy dress

**déguisement** [degizmɑ̃] m ① (travestissement) disguise ② (costume) fancy dress

**déguiser** [degize] <1> I. vt ① (costumer) ~ **un enfant en pirate** to dress up a child as a pirate ② (contrefaire: voix, écriture, vérité) to disguise II. vpr se ~ en qc (pour tromper) to disguise oneself as sth; (pour s'amuser) to dress up as sth

**dégustation** [degystasjɔ̃] f (de fruits de mer, fromage) sampling; (de vin, café) tasting

**déguster** [degyste] <1> I. vt ① (goûter) to taste ② (savourer) to savor II. vi ① (savourer) to savor ② inf (subir des coups) to get done over; (subir des douleurs) to go through hell; (subir des réprimandes) to get bawled out

**dehors** [dəɔʀ] I. adv ① (à l'extérieur)

outside; (*en plein air*) outdoors ❷ (*pas chez soi*) out ▶ **mettre qn ~** to throw sb out; **au ~** outside; **de ~** from outside; **rester en ~** to stay outside; **~!** out! **II.** *m* ❶ (*extérieur*) **les bruits du ~** the noises from outside ❷ *gén pl* (*apparences: d'une personne*) (outward) appearances

**déjà** [deʒa] **I.** *adv* ❶ (*dès maintenant*) already ❷ (*auparavant*) before; **à cette époque ~** even at this time; **tu as ~ vu le film?** have you (ever) seen the film? ❸ (*à la fin d'une question*) **comment vous appelez-vous ~?** what's your name again? **II.** *conj inf* **~ qu'elle a fait ça** well, at least she's done that

**déjeuner** [deʒœne] <1> **I.** *vi* ❶ (*à midi*) to have lunch ❷ (*le matin*) to have breakfast **II.** *m* (*repas de midi*) lunch; **au ~** at lunch(time)

**délabré(e)** [delabre] *adj* (*maison, mur*) dilapidated

**délabrer** [delabre] <1> **I.** *vt* (*santé*) to ruin **II.** *vpr* ❶ (*se dégrader*) **se ~** (*maison, mur*) to become dilapidated; (*santé*) to ruin; (*affaires*) to fall apart ❷ (*se ruiner*) **se ~ qc** to ruin

**délai** [delɛ] *m* ❶ (*temps accordé*) time limit; (*date butoir*) deadline; **~ de livraison** COM delivery time ❷ (*sursis*) more time; (*pour un contrat*) extension ▶ **dans les ~s** on time; **dans un ~ de** within

**délaisser** [delese] <1> *vt* ❶ (*négliger*) to neglect ❷ (*abandonner: enfant*) to abandon; (*activité*) to give up

**délasser** [delase] <1> *vt, vi, vpr* (**se**) to relax

**délavé(e)** [delave] *adj* ❶ (*pâle: couleur*) faded; (*yeux*) watery ❷ (*couleur, tissu, jeans*) faded ❸ (*détrempé: terre*) waterlogged

**délégation** [delegasjɔ̃] *f* ❶ (*groupe, agence d'État*) delegation ❷ (*mandat*) proxy ❸ COM **~ commerciale** (*filiale*) bureau; (*représentants*) trade delegation

**délégué(e)** [delege] **I.** *adj* delegated

**II.** *m(f)* (*d'une association, d'un parti*) delegate

**déléguer** [delege] <5> **I.** *vt* ❶ **~ qn à un congrès/une négociation** to assign sb to attend a congress/handle negotiations ❷ (*transmettre*) **~ sa responsabilité à qn** to delegate one's responsibility to sb **II.** *vi* to delegate

**délibération** [deliberasjɔ̃] *f* ❶ (*débat: de l'assemblée*) debate; **les ~s du jury** UNIV the jury deliberations ❷ (*décision*) resolution ❸ (*réflexion*) deliberation

**délibérément** [deliberemɑ̃] *adv* deliberately

**délibérer** [delibere] <5> *vi* ❶ (*débattre*) **~ sur qc** to deliberate on sth ❷ (*décider*) **~ sur** [*o de*] **qc** to resolve on sth ❸ (*réfléchir*) **~ sur qc** to consider sth

**délicat(e)** [delika, at] *adj* ❶ (*fin, fragile*) delicate ❷ (*léger*) **d'un geste** delicately ❸ (*difficile*) **c'est une question/situation ~e** it's a delicate matter/situation ❹ (*raffiné, sensible*) refined; (*palais*) discerning ❺ (*plein de tact: personne, geste*) thoughtful

**délicatesse** [delikatɛs] *f* ❶ (*finesse, difficulté: d'un objet, travail*) delicacy ❷ (*douceur*) gentleness ❸ (*raffinement*) refinement ❹ (*tact*) consideration; **manque de ~** tactlessness

**délice** [delis] **I.** *m* (*jouissance*) delight **II.** *fpl* delights

**délicieux, -euse** [delisjø, -jøz] *adj* ❶ (*exquis: mets*) delicious; (*sensation, sentiment*) delightful ❷ (*charmant: personne*) delightful

**délimitation** [delimitasjɔ̃] *f* delimitation

**délimiter** [delimite] <1> *vt* ❶ (*borner*) **~ qc** to mark sth out ❷ *fig* (*responsabilités, sujet*) to define

**délinquance** [delɛ̃kɑ̃s] *f* crime, criminality; **~ juvénile** juvenile delinquency

**délinquant(e)** [delɛ̃kɑ̃, ɑ̃t] **I.** *adj* delinquent **II.** *m(f)* delinquent

**délirant(e)** [delirɑ̃, ɑ̃t] *adj* (*histoire, idée*) hilarious; (*enthousiasme, joie*) frenzied

**délire** [delir] *m* ❶ (*divagation*) delirium

**D**

**D**

② (*exaltation*) frenzy; **une foule en ~** a frenzied crowd ► **c'est le ~ total!** *inf* it's complete madness!

**délirer** [delire] <1> *vi* ① MED to be delirious ② (*être exalté*) **~ de joie/d'enthousiasme** to be wild with joy/enthusiasm ③ (*dérailler*) to be out of one's mind ④ (*dire des bêtises*) to talk nonsense

**délit** [deli] *m* crime, misdemeanor; **~ mineur** petty offense; **prendre qn en flagrant ~ de qc** to catch sb doing sth red-handed

**délivrance** [delivrãs] *f* ① (*soulagement, libération*) relief ② ADMIN issue ③ MED delivery

**délivrer** [delivre] <1> **I.** *vt* ① (*libérer*) **~ l'otage de qc** to free the hostage from sth ② ADMIN (*certificat, passeport*) to issue **II.** *vpr* **se ~ de ses liens** to free oneself from one's bonds

**délocaliser** [delɔkalize] <1> *vt* to relocate

**déloger** [delɔʒe] <2a> **I.** *vt* to get out; (*locataire, habitant*) to evict; (*animal*) to start **II.** *vi* Belgique (*découcher*) to spend the (entire) night out

**déloyal(e)** [delwajal, -jo] <-aux> *adj* unfair

**deltaplane®** [dɛltaplan] *m* ① (*appareil*) hang-glider ② (*sport*) hang-gliding

**déluge** [delyʒ] *m* ① (*averse*) downpour ② *fig* **recevoir un ~ de protestations** to be inundated with protests

**démagogie** [demagɔʒi] *f* demagogy

**demain** [dəmɛ̃] *adv* tomorrow; **à ~!** see you tomorrow!

**demande** [d(ə)mãd] *f* ① (*souhait, prière*) request; **~ en mariage** proposal ② ADMIN request; **~ d'emploi** job application ③ PSYCH **~ de qc** need for sth ④ ECON **~ en qc** demand for sth ⑤ (*formulaire*) claim form ► **sur** (**simple**) **~** by request

**demander** [d(ə)mãde] <1> **I.** *vt* ① (*solliciter*) **~ conseil** to ask advice; **~ un renseignement à qn** to ask sb for information; **~ pardon à qn** to apologize to sb ② (*appeler: médecin, plombier*)

to call (for) ③ (*vouloir parler à*) **~ un employé/poste** to ask for an employee/sb's extension ④ (*s'enquérir de*) **~ à qn** to ask sb ⑤ (*nécessiter: soin, eau, travail*) to require ⑥ (*exiger*) **en ~ beaucoup/trop à qn** to ask a lot/too much of sb ⑦ (*rechercher*) **~ du personnel qualifié** to look for qualified staff ⑧ (*exiger un prix*) **~ un prix pour qc** to ask a price for sth **II.** *vi* **~ à qn si** to ask sb if ► **il n'y a qu'à ~** all you have to do is ask **III.** *vpr* **se ~ ce que/comment** to wonder what/how

**demandeur, -euse** [d(ə)mãdœr, -øz] *m, f* ① TEL caller ② (*requérant*) claimant; **~ d'emploi/d'asile** job/asylum seeker

**démangeaison** [demãʒɛzɔ̃] *f* gén pl (*irritation*) itch

**démanger** [demãʒe] <2a> **I.** *vt* to itch **II.** *vi* (*avoir envie*) **ça me/le démange de le faire** *inf* I'm/he's (just) itching to do it

**démanteler** [demãt(ə)le] <4> *vt* to dismantle

**démaquillant** [demakijã] *m* makeup remover

**démaquillant(e)** [demakijã, jãt] *adj* cleansing; **lait ~** cleansing lotion

**démaquiller** [demakije] <1> **I.** *vt* **~ qn** to take sb's makeup off **II.** *vpr* **se ~ le visage** to take one's makeup off

**démarcation** [demarkasjɔ̃] *f a. fig* demarcation; **ligne de ~** boundary (line); MIL demarcation line

**démarche** [demarʃ] *f* ① (*allure*) walk ② (*cheminement: d'une argumentation*) approach; (*d'une personne*) (line of) approach ③ (*intervention*) step; **faire des ~s** to take steps

**démarquer** [demarke] <1> **I.** *vt* ① (*dégriffer*) to sell designer brands in a discount store ② (*solder*) to mark down **II.** *vpr* ① SPORT **se ~** to get open ② (*prendre ses distances*) **se ~ de qn/qc** to distinguish oneself from sb/sth

**démarrage** [demaraʒ] *m* ① (*mise en marche*) start-up ② (*départ*) moving off ③ SPORT burst of speed ④ (*lancement*) launch ⑤ INFORM **~ à chaud/à froid** warm/cold boot ▸ **au** ~ upon starting the engine; *fig* at the start

**démarrer** [demaʀe] <1> I. *vi* ❶ (*mettre en marche*) to start up ❷ (*se mettre en marche: voiture*) to move off; (*machine*) to start up ❸ (*partir*) to leave ❹ (*débuter: campagne, exposition*) to launch; (*conversation*) to start up; (*industrie, économie*) to take off ⑤ SPORT to pull away ❻ INFORM **~ un logiciel** [*o* **un programme**] to start a program II. *vt* ❶ (*mettre en marche*) to start up ❷ *inf* (*lancer*) to start up; (*mouvement*) to launch; (*processus*) to get under way ❸ *inf* (*commencer*) **~ le travail/les peintures** to get the work/the painting started ❹ INFORM **~ un logiciel** to start up software

**démarreur** [demaʀœʀ] *m* starter

**démasquer** [demaske] <1> I. *vt* (*voleur, traître, espion*) to unmask; (*plan, fraude, trahison*) to expose II. *vpr* **se ~** to drop one's mask

**démêlé** [demele] *m* trouble

**démêler** [demele] <1> *vt* ❶ (*défaire: fil, cheveux*) to untangle ❷ (*éclaircir: affaire*) to sort out; (*intentions, plans*) to penetrate

**déménagement** [demenaʒmɑ̃] *m* ❶ (*changement de domicile, départ d'un logement*) move ❷ (*fait de quitter le logement, déplacement de meubles*) removal ❸ (*fait de vider une pièce*) emptying

**déménager** [demenaʒe] <2a> I. *vi* ❶ (*changer de domicile, quitter un logement*) to move; **~ à Paris/rue de …** to move to Paris/ … Street ❷ *inf* (*partir*) **faire ~ qn** to kick sb out II. *vt* ❶ (*transporter ailleurs: meubles*) to move; (*pour débarrasser: meubles, objet*) to clear out ❷ (*vider: maison, pièce*) to clear (out)

**déménageur** [demenaʒœʀ] *m* ❶ (*déménageur*) mover ❷ (*entrepreneur*) (furniture) mover

**démener** [dem(ə)ne] <4> *vpr* ❶ (*se débattre*) **se ~** to struggle ❷ (*faire des efforts*) **se ~ pour** +*infin* to put in a lot of effort to +*infin*

**dément(e)** [demɑ̃, ɑ̃t] I. *adj* ❶ (*aliéné*) demented ❷ *inf* (*insensé, super*) brilliant II. *m(f)* person with dementia

**démentir** [demɑ̃tiʀ] <10> I. *vt* ❶ (*contredire*) **~ qn** to deny sb's claim ❷ (*nier*) to deny ❸ (*infirmer*) to contradict II. *vi* to issue a denial III. *vpr* **un succès qui ne se dément pas** an ongoing success

**démesuré(e)** [deməzyʀe] *adj* enormous; (*importance, proportions*) excessive; (*orgueil*) immoderate

**démettre** [demɛtʀ] *irr* I. *vt* ❶ (*luxer: bras, poignet*) to wrench; (*épaule*) to dislocate ❷ (*révoquer*) **~ qn de ses fonctions** to relieve sb of their duties II. *vpr* ❶ (*se luxer*) **se ~ le bras** to wrench one's arm ❷ (*renoncer à*) **se ~ de qc** to resign from sth

**demeure** [d(ə)mœʀ] *f* home

**demeuré(e)** [dəmœʀe] I. *adj* half-witted II. *m(f)* half-wit

**demeurer** [dəmœʀe] <1> *vi* ❶ *avoir* (*habiter*) to reside ❷ *avoir* (*subsister*) to remain ❸ *être* (*rester*) to remain ❹ *impers* **il demeure que c'est arrivé** it still happened

**demi** [d(ə)mi] *m* ❶ (*fraction*) **un ~** a half; **trois ~s** three halves ❷ (*bière*) glass of beer

**demi(e)** [d(ə)mi] I. *m(f)* (*moitié*) half II. *adj* **une heure et ~e** an hour and a half; **avoir quatre ans et ~** to be four and a half; **un verre/une bouteille à ~ plein(e)** a half-full glass/bottle

**demi-bouteille** [d(ə)mibutɛj] <demi-bouteilles> *f* half-bottle

**demi-douzaine** [d(ə)miduzɛn] <demi-douzaines> *f* half a dozen

**demie** [d(ə)mi] *f* (*heure*) **neuf heures et ~** nine thirty; **partir à la ~** to leave at half past

**demi-finale** [d(ə)mifinal] <demi-finales> *f* semifinal

**demi-frère** [d(ə)mifʀɛʀ] <demi-frères> *m* half brother

**D**

**demi-heure** [d(ə)mijœʀ] <demi-heures> f half-hour

**démilitariser** [demilitaʀize] <1> vt to demilitarize

**demi-litre** [d(ə)militʀ] <demi-litres> m ①(contenu) half a liter ②(contenant) half-liter

**demi-pension** [d(ə)mipɑ̃sjɔ̃] <demi-pensions> f ①(hôtel) hotel providing one meal for guests; **en ~** on half board ②ECOLE half board

**demi-pensionnaire** [d(ə)mipɑ̃sjɔnɛʀ] <demi-pensionnaires> mf day student

**démis(e)** [demi, iz] I. part passé de **démettre** II. adj dislocated

**demi-sœur** [d(ə)misœʀ] <demi-sœurs> f half sister

**démission** [demisjɔ̃] f ①(action) resignation ②(renoncement) abdication (of responsibility)

**démissionner** [demisjɔne] <1> vi (se démettre) **~ de sa fonction** to give up one's duties; **~ de son poste** to resign from one's position

**demi-tarif** [d(ə)mitaʀif] <demi-tarifs> m half-price

**demi-tour** [d(ə)mituʀ] <demi-tours> m (d'une personne) about-face; (de manivelle) half-turn; **faire ~** (à pied, en voiture) to make a U-turn; MIL to about face

**démocrate** [demɔkʀat] I. adj democratic II. mf democrat

**démocratie** [demɔkʀasi] f democracy

**démocratique** [demɔkʀatik] adj democratic

**démocratiser** [demɔkʀatize] <1> I. vt to make more democratic; (sport) to popularize II. vpr **se ~** to become more democratic; (sport) to be popularized

**démodé(e)** [demɔde] adj old-fashioned; (procédé, théorie) outdated

**démographique** [demɔgʀafik] adj (données, étude) demographic; **croissance ~** population growth

**démolir** [demɔliʀ] <8> I. vt ①(détruire) to demolish; (mur) to knock down ②inf (frapper) to beat the living daylights out of ③inf (critiquer) to tear to shreds ④inf (saper le moral: événement, nouvelle) to shatter II. vpr inf **se ~ l'estomac/la santé** to do terrible things to one's stomach/health

**démolition** [demɔlisjɔ̃] f ①(opp: construction: d'une maison, d'un mur) demolition ②fig destruction

**démon** [demɔ̃] m demon; (enfant) devil

**démonstration** [demɔ̃stʀasjɔ̃] f ①(preuve, argumentation) a. MATH demonstration; **voiture de ~** demo car ②gén pl (manifestation) **~s de joie** show of joy

**démontable** [demɔ̃tabl] adj **les meubles sont ~s** the furniture can be taken apart

**démonter** [demɔ̃te] <1> I. vt ①(défaire: meuble) to take apart; (appareil) to dismantle; (auvent, tente) to take down; (pneu, porte) to take off ②(déconcerter) to take aback II. vpr **se ~** ①(être démontable) **l'appareil se démonte** the machine can be dismantled ②(se troubler) to be taken aback

**démontrer** [demɔ̃tʀe] <1> I. vt to demonstrate II. vpr **cela se démontre** that can be demonstrated

**démoralisant(e)** [demɔʀalizɑ̃, ɑ̃t] adj demoralizing

**démoraliser** [demɔʀalize] <1> I. vt to demoralize II. vi to be demoralizing III. vpr **se ~** to become demoralized

**démotiver** [demɔtive] <1> vt to cause to lose motivation

**démuni(e)** [demyni] adj ①(pauvre) destitute ②(impuissant) **~ devant qn/qc** powerless in the face of sb/sth ③(privé de) **être ~ de qc** to be without sth; **~ d'intérêt** devoid of interest

**dénicher** [denife] <1> vt (bistrot, objet rare) to discover; (personne) to track down

**dénombrer** [denɔ̃bʀe] <1> vt to count

**dénomination** [denɔminasjɔ̃] f denomination

**dénommé(e)** [denɔme] adj antéposé **un/une ~ Durand** a certain Durand; **le/la ~ Durand** the (afore)said Durand

**dénommer** [denɔme] <1> vt to call

**dénoncer** [denɔ̃se] <2> **I.** *vt* ❶ (*trahir: criminel, complice*) to denounce ❷ (*s'élever contre: abus, injustice*) to denounce **II.** *vpr* **se ~ à la police** to turn oneself in to the police

**dénonciation** [denɔ̃sjasjɔ̃] *f* ❶ (*délation*) denunciation; (*dans une dictature*) informing ❷ (*accusation*) denunciation

**dénouement** [denumɑ̃] *m* (*d'une intrigue*) dénouement; (*de l'enquête*) outcome

**dénouer** [denwe] <1> **I.** *vt* (*ficelle, lacets, nœud*) to untie; (*intrigue, affaire*) to clear up **II.** *vpr* **se ~** to conclude

**dénoyauter** [denwajote] <1> *vt* to pit

**denrée** [dɑ̃ʁe] *f* commodity; **~s alimentaires** foodstuffs

**dense** [dɑ̃s] *adj* ❶ *a.* PHYS dense ❷ (*condensé: œuvre, film*) condensed; (*style*) compact

**densité** [dɑ̃site] *f* density

**dent** [dɑ̃] *f* ❶ ANAT (*de l'homme, animal*) tooth; **~ de devant/de lait** front/baby tooth; **se laver les ~s** to brush one's teeth; **brosse à ~s** toothbrush ❷ *fig* (*d'une fourchette*) tine; (*d'un peigne, engrenage*) tooth ❸ (*sommet de montagne*) peak ▶ **avoir une ~ contre qn** to hold a grudge against sb; **grincer des ~s** to grind one's teeth

**dentaire** [dɑ̃tɛʁ] *adj* dental

**dentelle** [dɑ̃tɛl] *f* lace

**dentier** [dɑ̃tje] *m* denture

**dentifrice** [dɑ̃tifʁis] *m* toothpaste

**dentiste** [dɑ̃tist] *mf* dentist

**dénudé(e)** [denyde] *adj* bare

**dénuder** [denyde] <1> **I.** *vt* ❶ (*dévêtir*) to bare ❷ (*laisser voir: dos, bras*) to show (off) ❸ ELEC (*câble*) to strip **II.** *vpr* **se ~** (*personne*) to take one's clothes off; (*arbre*) to lose its leaves

**dénué(e)** [denye] *adj* **être ~ d'intérêt** to be devoid of interest

**déodorant** [deɔdɔʁɑ̃] *m* deodorant

**déodorant(e)** [deɔdɔʁɑ̃, ɑ̃t] *adj* deodorant

**dépannage** [depanaʒ] *m* ❶ (*réparation: d'une machine, voiture*) fixing;

**service de ~** emergency road service ❷ (*solution provisoire*) stopgap

**dépanner** [depane] <1> *vt* ❶ (*réparer: machine, voiture*) to fix; ~ **qn** to help out sb who's broken down; (*remorquer*) to give sb a tow ❷ *inf* (*aider*) ~ **qn** to help sb out

**dépanneuse** [depanøz] *f* tow truck

**départ** [depaʁ] *m* ❶ (*action de partir*) departure; **après leur ~** after they left ❷ SPORT start; ~ **en flèche** flying start ❸ (*lieu*) **quai de ~ des grandes lignes** the main line departure platform ❹ (*d'un poste*) leaving; ~ **à la retraite** retirement ❺ (*début, origine*) start; **point de ~** starting point; **au/dès le ~** at/from the outset ▶ **prendre un bon/mauvais ~** to get off to a good/bad start; **prendre un nouveau ~ (dans la vie)** to make a fresh start (in life)

**département** [depaʁtəmɑ̃] *m* ❶ ADMIN department (*one of the main administrative divisions of France*); ~ **d'outre-mer** overseas department ❷ (*secteur*) *a.* UNIV department ❸ *Suisse* (*subdivision du pouvoir exécutif, fédéral ou cantonal*) department (*administrative division in Switzerland*) ❹ *Québec* ~ **d'État** (*ministère des Affaires étrangères*) State Department

**départemental(e)** [depaʁtəmɑ̃tal, -o] <-aux> *adj* departmental; **route ~e** secondary road

**dépassé(e)** [depase] *adj* ❶ (*démodé*) outdated ❷ (*désorienté*) **Je suis ~ par tout ça** I'm out of my depth in all this

**dépasser** [depase] <1> **I.** *vt* ❶ (*doubler*) to pass ❷ (*aller plus loin que*) to go past ❸ (*outrepasser: limite*) to go beyond ❹ (*aller plus loin en quantité: dose*) to exceed; ~ **qn de dix centimètres** to be ten centimeters taller than sb ❺ (*surpasser*) to outdo; ~ **l'attente de qn** to exceed sb's expectations **II.** *vi* ❶ (*doubler*) to pass ❷ (*être trop haut, trop long: bâtiment, tour*) to tower above; (*vêtement*) to show **III.** *vpr* **se ~** to surpass oneself

**dépaysé(e)** [depeize] *adj* **être ~** to be out of one's natural environment

**dépaysement** [depeizmã] *m* ❶ (*désorientation*) disorientation ❷ (*changement*) change of surroundings ❸ (*changement salutaire*) change of scenery

**dépayser** [depeize] <1> *vt* ❶ (*désorienter*) to disorientate ❷ (*changer les idées*) ~ **qn** to give sb a change of scenery

**dépêche** [depɛʃ] *f* dispatch

**dépêcher** [depeʃe] <1> I. *vpr* **se ~** to hurry (up) II. *vt form* ~ **qn auprès de qn** to dispatch sb to sb

**dépeindre** [depɛ̃dʀ] *vt irr* to depict

**dépendance** [depãdãs] *f* (*assujettissement*) dependency; (*d'un drogué*) addiction

**dépendant(e)** [depãdã, ãt] *adj* dependent; **être ~ de la drogue** to be addicted to drugs

**dépendre** [depãdʀ] <14> I. *vi* ❶ (*être sous la dépendance de*) ~ **de qn/qc** to be dependent on sb/sth ❷ (*faire partie de*) ~ **de qc** (*terrain*) to belong to sth ❸ (*relever de*) ~ **de qn/qc** to be answerable to sb/sth ❹ (*être conditionné par*) ~ **de qc/qn** to depend on sb/sth; **ça dépend** *inf* that depends II. *vt* (*décrocher*) to take down

**dépens** [depã] **aux ~ de qn** at sb's expense

**dépense** [depãs] *f* ❶ (*frais*) expense; **~s publiques/de l'État** public/state spending ❷ (*usage*) expenditure; **~ physique** physical exercise

**dépenser** [depãse] <1> I. *vt* ❶ (*débourser*) to spend ❷ (*consommer: électricité, énergie*) to consume II. *vpr* **se ~** to expend energy; (*enfants*) to use up their energy

**dépensier, -ière** [depãsje, -jɛʀ] I. *adj* extravagant II. *m, f* spendthrift

**dépeupler** [depœple] <1> I. *vt* (*pays, région*) to depopulate II. *vpr* **se ~** to be depopulated

**dépilatoire** [depilatwaʀ] *adj* hair remover

**dépistage** [depistaʒ] *m* (*d'un malfaiteur*) tracking down; (*d'une maladie*) detection; **test de ~ du Sida** AIDS test

**déplacé(e)** [deplase] *adj* ❶ (*inopportun: intervention, présence*) inappropriate ❷ (*inconvenant: geste, propos*) uncalled for

**déplacement** [deplasmã] *m* ❶ (*changement de place: d'un objet*) moving; (*d'un os*) dislocation ❷ (*voyage*) trip; **être en ~** to be on a trip ❸ (*mouvement*) movement ❹ (*mutation*) transfer

**déplacer** [deplase] <2> I. *vt* ❶ (*changer de place: objet, meuble*) to move ❷ MED (*articulation*) to dislocate ❸ (*muter: fonctionnaire*) to transfer ❹ (*réinstaller*) *a.* TECH to displace II. *vpr* ❶ (*être en mouvement, se décaler*) **se ~** to move ❷ (*voyager*) **se ~ en avion/voiture** to travel by plane/car, fly/drive ❸ MED **se ~ une articulation** to dislocate a joint

**déplaire** [deplɛʀ] *irr* I. *vi* (*ne pas plaire*) ~ **à qn** to displease sb; (*irriter*) to annoy sb II. *vpr* **se ~ en ville/dans un emploi** not to be happy in town/with a job

**dépliant** [deplijã] *m* leaflet; **~ touristique** travel brochure

**déplier** [deplije] <1> I. *vt* (*drap, vêtement, plan, journal*) to unfold; (*sur une table*) to spread out; (*jambes*) to stretch out II. *vpr* **se ~** to fold out

**déployer** [deplwaje] <7> I. *vt* ❶ (*déplier: ailes, carte*) to spread out; (*voile, drapeau*) to unfurl ❷ (*mettre en œuvre: énergie, ingéniosité, courage*) to display ❸ (*étaler: charmes, richesses*) to show off II. *vpr* ❶ (*se déplier*) **se ~** (*ailes, tissu*) to spread out; (*voile, drapeau*) to be unfurled ❷ (*se disperser: soldats, troupes*) to be deployed; (*cortège*) to spread out

**dépopulation** [depɔpylasjɔ̃] *f* depopulation

**déportation** [depɔʀtasjɔ̃] *f* HIST deportation; **en ~** in the (concentration) camps

**déporter** [depɔʀte] <1> I. *vt* ❶ (*exiler, bannir*) to deport ❷ HIST (*interner*) to send to a concentration camp ❸ (*faire dévier: voiture, vélo*) to push off course **II.** *vpr* AUTO **se ~** to swerve

**déposer** [depoze] <1> **I.** *vt* ❶ (*poser*) to place ❷ (*se débarrasser*) to put down ❸ (*conduire, livrer: personne*) to drop off; (*ordures*) to dump ❹ (*confier: bagages, lettre, carte de visite*) to leave ❺ FIN (*argent, chèque, valeur*) to deposit ❻ (*faire enregistrer: brevet, rapport*) to file; (*marque*) to register; (*projet de loi*) to bring up for discussion; (*réclamation, plainte*) to lodge ❼ (*démonter: appareil*) to take down; (*moteur*) to strip down ❽ (*abdiquer: couronne*) to abdicate ❾ (*destituer*) to depose **II.** *vi* ❶ (*témoigner*) to give evidence ❷ (*laisser un dépôt: vin, eau*) to settle **III.** *vpr* **se ~** (*lie, poussière*) to settle

**déposition** [depozisjɔ̃] *f* ❶ (*témoignage*) statement; **faire/recueillir/signer une ~** to make/take/sign a statement ❷ (*destitution: d'un souverain*) deposition

**déposséder** [deposede] <5> *vt* (*personne*) to dispossess

**dépôt** [depo] *m* ❶ (*présentation: d'un projet de loi*) introduction ❷ (*enregistrement: d'une plainte*) lodging; (*d'une marque déposée*) registration; (*d'un brevet*) filing ❸ FIN (*d'un chèque, d'argent, de titres*) depositing; (*somme déposée*) deposit; **~ de bilan** bankruptcy filing ❹ (*fait de poser: d'une gerbe*) laying ❺ (*sédiment*) deposit ❻ (*entrepôt: d'autobus*) depot; **~ d'ordures** dump

**dépouillé(e)** [depuje] *adj* ❶ (*sobre: décor*) bare; (*style, texte*) unadorned ❷ (*exempt*) **être ~ de qc** devoid of sth

**dépouillement** [depujmɑ̃] *m* (*examen*) **~ du scrutin** counting the votes

**dépouiller** [depuje] <1> **I.** *vt* ❶ (*ouvrir*) **~ le scrutin** to count the votes; **~ le courrier** to go through the mail ❷ (*dévaliser*) to rob; **~ qn de ses biens** to strip sb of their possessions **II.** *vpr* (*se déshabiller*) **se ~ de ses vêtements** to take off one's clothes

**dépourvu(e)** [depuʀvy] *adj* ❶ (*privé*)

**être ~** to have nothing; **être ~ de bon sens** to have no common sense ❷ (*ne pas être équipé*) **être ~ de chauffage** to be without heating ▸ **prendre qn au ~** to take sb unawares

**dépoussiérer** [depusjeʀe] <5> *vt* ❶ (*nettoyer*) to dust ❷ (*rajeunir*) to blow the dust off

**dépressif, -ive** [depʀesif, -iv] **I.** *adj* depressive **II.** *m, f* depressive

**dépression** [depʀesjɔ̃] *f* ❶ (*découragement*) *a.* PSYCH, METEO depression; **faire une ~ nerveuse** to have a nervous breakdown ❷ ECON slump

**déprimant(e)** [depʀimɑ̃, ɑ̃t] *adj* (*démoralisant*) depressing

**déprimé(e)** [depʀime] *adj* (*personne*) depressed

**déprimer** [depʀime] <1> **I.** *vt* (*démoraliser*) to depress **II.** *vi inf* to be depressed

**déprivatisation** [depʀivatizasjɔ̃] *f* nationalization

**déprogrammer** [depʀɔgʀame] <1> *vt* ❶ CINE, TV (*émission, spectacle*) to take off ❷ INFORM (*robot*) to deprogram

**depuis** [dəpɥi] **I.** *prep* ❶ (*à partir d'un moment*) since; (*à partir d'un lieu*) from; **~ quelle date?** since when?; **~ Paris, ...** from Paris; **~ mon plus jeune âge** since my childhood ❷ (*durée*) for; **je la connais ~ peu** I've (only) known her a short while; **~ cela** since then **II.** *adv* since

**député(e)** [depyte] *m(f)* deputy

**déraciner** [deʀasine] <1> *vt* ❶ (*arracher: arbre, peuple*) to uproot ❷ (*éliminer: préjugé*) to root out

**déraillement** [deʀajmɑ̃] *m* (*d'un train*) derailing

**dérailler** [deʀaje] <1> *vi* ❶ (*sortir des rails: train*) to be derailed ❷ *inf* (*déraisonner*) to talk nonsense ❸ (*mal fonctionner: machine, appareil*) to play up

**dérailleur** [deʀajœʀ] *m* derailleur

**dérangement** [deʀɑ̃ʒmɑ̃] *m* ❶ (*gêne*) trouble ❷ (*incident technique*) **être en ~** (*ligne, téléphone*) to be out of order

**déranger** [deʀɑ̃ʒe] <2a> **I.** *vt* ❶ (*gê-*

ner) to disturb ❷ (*mettre en désordre*) to untidy; (*objets, affaires, coiffure*) to mess up ❸ (*perturber: projets*) to spoil **II.** *vi* ❶ (*arriver mal à propos*) to be a nuisance ❷ (*mettre mal à l'aise*) to upset people **III.** *vpr* ❶ (*se déplacer*) **se ~** to go/come out ❷ (*interrompre ses occupations*) **se ~ pour qn** to go to trouble for sb; **ne vous dérangez pas pour moi!** don't put yourself out for me!

**déraper** [deʀape] <1> *vi* ❶ (*glisser: personne, semelles*) to slip; (*voiture*) to skid ❷ (*dévier: personne, conversation*) to veer off ❸ ECON (*prix, politique économique*) to get out of control

**dératiseur, -euse** [deʀatizœʀ, -øz] *m, f* rat catcher

**déréglé(e)** [deʀegle] *adj* ❶ (*dérangé: estomac*) upset; (*pouls, appétit*) unsettled; **le mécanisme est ~** the mechanism isn't working right ❷ (*désordonné: habitudes*) unsettled; (*vie, existence*) disordered; (*mœurs*) dissolute

**dérégler** [deʀegle] <5> *vt* ❶ (*déranger: mécanisme*) to disturb; (*climat, appétit*) to unsettle ❷ (*pervertir: mœurs*) to corrupt **II.** *vpr* ❶ (*mal fonctionner*) **se ~** (*machine*) to go wrong; (*climat, estomac*) to become unsettled ❷ (*se pervertir: mœurs*) to be corrupted

**dérive** [deʀiv] *f* ❶ (*déviation: d'un avion, bateau*) drift; **~ des continents** continental drift; **être à la ~** (*bateau*) to be adrift ❷ AVIAT fin; NAUT centerboard ❸ FIN (*d'une monnaie, de l'économie*) slump ► **partir à la ~** (*projets*) to go awry

**dériver** [deʀive] <1> **I.** *vt* (*détourner*) to divert **II.** *vi* ❶ LING **~ de qc** to derive from sth ❷ (*s'écarter: barque*) to drift

**dernier** [dɛʀnje] *m Belgique* **le ~ de tout** (*la fin de tout*) the last straw

**dernier, -ière** [dɛʀnje, -jɛʀ] **I.** *adj* ❶ *antéposé* (*ultime*) last; **être ~ en classe** to be at the bottom of the class ❷ *antéposé* (*le plus récent: œuvre, mode, nouvelle, édition*) latest; **ces ~s temps** just recently ❸ *postposé* (*antérieur: an,*

*mois, semaine, siècle*) last **II.** *m, f* **le ~(-ière)** the last; **en ~** lastly

**dernièrement** [dɛʀnjɛʀmɑ̃] *adv* lately

**dérober** [deʀɔbe] <1> *vt* (*voler*) to steal

**dérogation** [deʀɔgasjɔ̃] *f* ❶ (*exception*) exemption; **par ~** by way of exemption ❷ (*violation*) breach

**déroulant(e)** [deʀulɑ̃, ɑ̃t] *adj* INFORM drop-down; **menu ~** drop-down

**déroulement** [deʀulmɑ̃] *m* ❶ (*processus: d'une cérémonie*) course; (*suite des faits: d'un crime*) stages ❷ (*fait de dérouler*) unwinding

**dérouler** [deʀule] <1> **I.** *vt* (*dévider: tuyau, rouleau*) to unroll; (*store*) to wind down **II.** *vpr* ❶ (*s'écouler*) **se ~** (*vie, manifestation, crime, cérémonie, concert*) to take place ❷ (*se dévider*) **se ~** (*bobine, cassette*) to unwind

**déroute** [deʀut] *f* rout; (*effondrement*) collapse

**dérouter** [deʀute] <1> *vt* ❶ (*écarter de sa route*) to reroute ❷ (*déconcerter*) to take aback

**derrière** [dɛʀjɛʀ] **I.** *prep* behind; **être ~ qn** (*dans un classement*) to be behind sb; (*soutenir qn*) to be (right) behind sb; **faire qc ~ qn** *fig* to do sth behind sb's back; **par ~ qc** at the back of sth **II.** *adv* behind **III.** *m* ❶ (*partie arrière: d'une maison*) back ❷ *inf* (*postérieur: d'un animal*) rump; (*d'une personne*) bottom

**des¹** [de] **I.** *art déf pl contracté* **les pages ~ livres** (*ces livres*) the pages of the books; (*livres en général*) the pages of books; *v.a.* **de II.** *art partitif, parfois non traduit* **je mange ~ épinards** I eat spinach

**des²** [de, də] <*devant adjectif* **de**> *art indéf pl, parfois non traduit* **j'ai acheté ~ pommes et de beaux citrons** I bought (some) apples and some nice lemons

**dès** [dɛ] *prep* (*à partir de*) as from; **~ lors** (*à partir de ce moment-là*) from then on; (*par conséquent*) in which case; **~ maintenant** from now on;

~ **mon retour je ferai ...** as soon as I get back I will do ...; ~ **Valence** after Valence

**désaccord** [dezakɔʀ] *m* ❶(*mésentente*) discord ❷(*divergence, désapprobation*) disagreement; ~ **d'idées** difference of opinion ❸(*contradiction*) discrepancy

**désaffecté(e)** [dezafɛkte] *adj* (*église, école, usine*) disused

**désagréable** [dezagʀeabl] *adj* unpleasant

**désaltérant(e)** [dezalteʀɑ̃, ɑ̃t] *adj* thirst-quenching

**désaltérer** [dezalteʀe] <5> I. *vt* ~ **qn** to quench the thirst of sb II. *vpr* **se** ~ to quench one's thirst

**désapprouver** [dezapʀuve] <1> I. *vt* ~ **qn/qc** to disapprove of sb/sth II. *vi* to disapprove

**désarmement** [dezaʀməmɑ̃] *m* (*d'une personne, population*) disarmament; (*d'un navire*) laying up

**désastre** [dezastʀ] *m* disaster

**désastreux, -euse** [dezastʀø, -øz] *adj* ❶(*catastrophique*) disastrous ❷(*nul*) terrible; **c'était** ~ it was a disaster

**désavantage** [dezavɑ̃taʒ] *m* disadvantage; (*physique*) handicap; **c'est à son** ~ it's against him

**désavantageux, -euse** [dezavɑ̃taʒø, -jøz] *adj* disadvantageous

**descendance** [desɑ̃dɑ̃s] *f* ❶(*postérité*) descendants *pl* ❷(*origine*) descent

**descendant(e)** [desɑ̃dɑ̃, ɑ̃t] I. *adj* (*chemin*) going down; (*gamme*) descending II. *m(f)* descendant

**descendre** [desɑ̃dʀ] <14> I. *vi être* ❶(*aller du haut vers le bas: vu d'en haut/d'en bas: avion*) to go/come down; (*oiseau*) to fly down; (*parachutiste*) to float down; ~ **à la cave/par l'escalier** to go down to the basement/by the stairs; ~ **en voiture/en avion** to drive/fly down ❷(*quitter, sortir*) ~ **du bateau/du train** to get off the boat/the train; ~ **de la voiture** to get out of the car ❸(*aller, se rendre*) ~ **en ville** to go into town ❹(*faire irruption*) ~ **dans un**

bar (*police, voyous*) to burst into a bar ❺(*loger*) ~ **à l'hôtel/chez qn** to stay at a hotel/at a friend's place ❻(*être issu de*) ~ **de qn** to descend from sb ❼(*aller en pente*) ~ **en pente douce** (*route, chemin*) to go down; (*vignoble, terrain*) to slope downwards ❽(*baisser: marée*) to go out; (*niveau de l'eau, prix, taux*) to go down; (*baromètre, thermomètre*) to fall ❾(*atteindre*) *a.* mus ~ **à/ jusqu'à** (*robe, cheveux, puits*) to go down to/as far as ▶~ **dans la rue** to take to the streets II. *vt avoir* ❶(*se déplacer à pied: vu d'en haut: escalier, colline*) to go down; (*vu d'en bas*) to come down ❷(*se déplacer en véhicule: vu d'en haut/d'en bas: rue, route*) to drive down ❸(*porter en bas: vu d'en haut*) to take down; (*vu d'en bas*) to bring down ❹(*baisser: stores, rideaux*) to lower; (*tableau, étagère*) to take down ❺ *inf* (*abattre: avion*) to shoot down; (*personne*) to do in ❻ *inf* (*critiquer: film, auteur*) to slam

**descente** [desɑ̃t] *f* ❶(*opp: montée: d'une pente*) way down; (*à pied*) walk down; (*en voiture*) drive down; (*en escalade*) climb down; (*à ski*) ski down; (*d'un fleuve*) sail down ❷ AVIAT descent ❸(*arrivée*) **à la ~ d'avion/de bateau** as the passengers disembarked ❹(*action de descendre au fond de*) ~ **dans qc** descent into sth ❺(*attaque brusque*) **une ~ de police** a police raid ❻(*pente*) downward slope ❼(*action de porter en bas, déposer: vu d'en haut*) taking down; (*vu d'en bas*) bringing down ▶~ **aux enfers** descent into Hell

**descriptif** [dɛskʀiptif] *m* specifications *pl*

**descriptif, -ive** [dɛskʀiptif, -iv] *adj* descriptive

**description** [dɛskʀipsjɔ̃] *f* description; (*d'un événement*) account

**désemparé(e)** [dezɑ̃paʀe] *adj* (*personne*) distraught

**désenfler** [dezɑ̃fle] <1> I. *vt* ~ **qc** to bring down the swelling in sth II. *vi, vpr* (**se**) ~ to go down

**D**

**déséquilibre** [dezekilibʀ] *m* ❶ (*instabilité, inégalité: des forces, valeurs*) imbalance; (*d'une construction, personne*) instability ❷ PSYCH **~ mental** mental instability

**déséquilibré(e)** [dezekilibʀe] **I.** *adj* (*personne*) off balance; PSYCH unstable; (*balance*) badly adjusted; (*quantités*) unbalanced **II.** *m(f)* (*personne*) unbalanced person

**déséquilibrer** [dezekilibʀe] <1> *vt* (*personne*) to throw off balance; *fig* to unbalance; (*objet*) to make unsteady; (*budget*) to unbalance

**désert** [dezɛʀ] *m* ❶ GEO desert ❷ (*lieu dépeuplé*) wilderness

**désert(e)** [dezɛʀ, ɛʀt] *adj* ❶ (*sans habitant: pays, région, maison*) deserted; (*île*) desert ❷ (*peu fréquenté: plage, rue*) deserted

**déserter** [dezɛʀte] <1> **I.** *vt* ❶ (*quitter: lieu, son poste*) to abandon ❷ (*abandonner, renier: cause, syndicat, parti*) to desert; (*réunions*) to forsake **II.** *vi* MIL to desert

**déserteur** [dezɛʀtœʀ] **I.** *m* MIL deserter **II.** *adj* deserting

**désertique** [dezɛʀtik] *adj* (*climat, plante, région*) desert

**désespérant(e)** [dezɛspeʀɑ̃, ɑ̃t] *adj* (*décourageant*) **être ~** (*notes, comportement*) to be hopeless

**désespéré(e)** [dezɛspeʀe] **I.** *adj* (*personne*) desperate; (*cas, situation*) (*critique*) desperate; (*sans espoir*) hopeless **II.** *m(f)* person in despair

**désespérer** [dezɛspeʀe] <5> **I.** *vi* to despair **II.** *vt* ❶ (*affliger*) **~ qn** to drive sb to despair ❷ (*décourager*) **~ qn** to make sb despair **III.** *vpr* **se ~** to despair

**désespoir** [dezɛspwaʀ] *m* despair ▶ **en ~ de <u>cause</u>** in desperation

**déshabiller** [dezabije] <1> **I.** *vt* (*personne*) to undress **II.** *vpr* **se ~** (*se dévêtir*) to get undressed

**déshabituer** [dezabitɥe] <1> **I.** *vt* **~ qn de qc** to get sb out of the habit of doing sth **II.** *vpr* **se ~ de qc** (*exprès*) to rid

oneself of a habit; (*sans essayer*) to lose the habit of doing sth

**déshérité(e)** [dezeʀite] **I.** *adj* ❶ (*privé d'héritage*) disinherited ❷ (*désavantagé*) underprivileged **II.** *mpl* **les ~s** the underprivileged

**déshériter** [dezeʀite] <1> *vt* ❶ JUR to disinherit ❷ (*priver d'avantages*) to deprive

**déshonorant(e)** [dezɔnɔʀɑ̃, ɑ̃t] *adj* shameful

**déshonorer** [dezɔnɔʀe] <1> **I.** *vt* ❶ (*porter atteinte à l'honneur de*) to dishonor ❷ (*défigurer: monument, paysage*) to disfigure **II.** *vpr* **se ~** to bring shame on oneself

**designer** [dizajnœʀ, dezajnœʀ] *mf* designer

**désigner** [deziɲe] <1> *vt* ❶ (*montrer, indiquer*) to indicate; **~ qn/qc du doigt** to point at sb/sth ❷ (*choisir*) **~ qn comme qc** to designate sb as sth ❸ (*qualifier*) **être tout désigné pour qc** to be ideal for sth

**désillusion** [dezi(l)lyzjɔ̃] *f* disillusionment

**désinfectant** [dezɛ̃fɛktɑ̃] *m* disinfectant

**désinfectant(e)** [dezɛ̃fɛktɑ̃, ɑ̃t] *adj* disinfectant

**désinfecter** [dezɛ̃fɛkte] <1> *vt* to disinfect

**désintégrer** [dezɛ̃tegʀe] <5> **I.** *vt* ❶ GEO, PHYS to disintegrate ❷ *fig* (*famille, parti*) to split up **II.** *vpr* **se ~** ❶ (*se désagréger*) to split up ❷ GEO, PHYS to disintegrate

**désintéressé(e)** [dezɛ̃teʀese] *adj* disinterested

**désintéresser** [dezɛ̃teʀese] <1> **I.** *vt* (*dédommager: créancier*) to pay off; (*partenaire*) to buy out **II.** *vpr* **se ~ de qn/qc** to take no interest in sb/sth; (*perdre intérêt*) to lose interest in sb/sth

**désintérêt** [dezɛ̃teʀe] *m* lack of interest

**désintoxication** [dezɛ̃tɔksikasjɔ̃] *f* MED detoxification

**désintoxiquer** [dezɛ̃tɔksike] <1> **I.** *vt* ❶ MED (*drogué, alcoolique*) to detoxify;

**se faire ~** to get detoxified ② (*purifier l'organisme: citadin, fumeur*) to clean out the system of **II.** *vpr* **se ~ ①** MED (*alcoolique, toxicomane*) to get detoxified ② (*s'oxygéner*) to clean out the system

**désir** [dezir] *m* ① (*souhait*) **~ de qc** wish for sth ② (*appétit sexuel*) desire

**désirable** [deziRabl] *adj* desirable

**désirer** [dezire] <1> *vt* ① (*souhaiter*) to want ② (*convoiter*) to desire ► **laisser à ~** to leave a lot to be desired

**désobéir** [dezɔbeiʀ] <8> *vi* **~ à qn/un ordre** to disobey sb/an order; **~ à la loi** to break the law

**désobéissant(e)** [dezɔbeisɑ̃, ɑ̃t] *adj* disobedient

**désodorisant** [dezɔdɔʀizɑ̃] *m* deodorizer

**désodorisant(e)** [dezɔdɔʀizɑ̃, ɑ̃t] *adj* deodorizing

**désœuvré(e)** [dezœvʀe] *adj* idle

**désœuvrement** [dezœvʀəmɑ̃] *m* idleness; **faire qc par ~** to do sth for want of better

**désolé(e)** [dezɔle] *adj* ① (*éploré*) disconsolate ② (*navré*) sorry ③ (*désert et triste: lieu, paysage*) desolate

**désoler** [dezɔle] <1> **I.** *vt* ① (*affliger*) to sadden ② (*contrarier*) to upset **II.** *vpr* (*être navré*) **se ~** to be sorry

**désordonné(e)** [dezɔʀdɔne] *adj* ① (*qui manque d'ordre*) untidy ② (*qui manque d'organisation: esprit, personne*) disorganized ③ (*incontrôlé: gestes, mouvements*) uncoordinated ; (*élans*) wild; (*fuite, combat*) disorderly

**désordre** [dezɔʀdʀ] *m* ① *sans pl* (*absence d'ordre: d'une personne, d'un lieu*) untidiness ② (*confusion: de l'esprit, des idées*) lack of organization ③ (*absence de discipline*) disorder ④ *gén pl* POL riots

**désorienté(e)** [dezɔʀjɑ̃te] *adj* disoriented

**désorienter** [dezɔʀjɑ̃te] <1> *vt* ① (*égarer: personne*) to disorient ; (*avion*) to throw off course ② (*déconcerter*) to confuse

**désormais** [dezɔʀmɛ] *adv* ① (*au passé*)

from then on ② (*au présent*) from now on

**desquels, desquelles** [dekɛl] *pron v.* **lequel**

**dessécher** [deseʃe] <1> **I.** *vt* ① (*rendre sec: terre, peau, bouche*) to dry (out); (*végétation, plantes*) to wither; (*fruits*) to dry up ② (*rendre maigre: personne, corps*) to wither ③ (*rendre insensible: personne*) to harden **II.** *vpr* **se ~ ①** (*devenir sec: bouche, lèvres*) to get parched; (*terre, peau*) to dry up; (*végétation*) to wither ② (*maigrir*) to shrivel ③ (*devenir insensible*) to grow hardened

**desserrer** [desere] <1> **I.** *vt* ① (*dévisser*) to unscrew ② (*relâcher: étau, cravate, ceinture*) to loosen; (*frein à main*) to let off ③ (*écarter: poing*) to unclench **II.** *vpr* **se ~** (*vis, étau, nœud*) to work loose; (*frein à main*) to come off; (*personnes, rangs*) to break up

**dessert** [desɛʀ] *m* CULIN (*mets, moment*) dessert

**desservir** [desɛʀviʀ] *vt irr* ① (*débarrasser: table*) to clear ② (*nuire à*) to do a disservice to ③ (*s'arrêter*) **le train dessert cette gare/ce village** the train stops at this station/in this village

**dessin** [desɛ̃] *m* ① (*image*) drawing; **~(s) animé(s)** cartoon ② (*activité*) drawing ③ (*motif*) design ④ (*ligne: du visage*) line; (*des veines*) pattern

**dessinateur, -trice** [desinatœʀ, -tʀis] *m, f* ① ART draftsman ② ECON designer

**dessiner** [desine] <1> **I.** *vi* to draw **II.** *vt* ① ART to draw ② TECH (*plan d'une maison*) to draw (up); (*meuble, véhicule, jardin*) to design ③ (*souligner: contours, formes*) to show off ④ (*former: courbe, virages*) to form

**dessous** [d(ə)su] **I.** *adv* ① (*sous: passer, regarder, être (placé)*) underneath ② *fig* **agir (par) en ~** to act deceitfully **II.** *prep* ① (*sous*) **en ~ de qc** under ② (*plus bas que*) **en ~ de qc** under sth **III.** *m* ① (*face inférieure, de ce qui est plus bas: d'une assiette, langue*) under-

D

side; (*d'une étoffe*) wrong side; (*des pieds, chaussures*) sole ② pl (*sous-vêtements*) underwear ③ pl (*aspects secrets: d'une affaire, de la politique*) underside

**dessous-de-plat** [d(ə)sud(ə)pla] *m inv* table mat (*to go under hot dishes*)

**dessus** [d(ə)sy] **I.** *adv* (*sur qn/qc*) on top; (*là-haut*) above; (*marcher, appuyer*) on it; (*voler*) over it **II.** *prep* **enlever qc de ~ qc** to take sth off (the top of) sth **III.** *m* (*partie supérieure, ce qui est au-dessus: de la tête, du pied*) top; (*de la main*) back ▸ **avoir le ~** to have the upper hand

**dessus-de-lit** [d(ə)syd(ə)li] *m inv* bedspread

**déstabiliser** [destabilize] <1> *vt* to destabilize

**destin** [dɛstɛ̃] *m* fate

**destinataire** [dɛstinatɛʀ] *mf* addressee; (*d'un mandat*) payee

**destination** [dɛstinasjɔ̃] *f* ① (*lieu*) destination; **le train/les voyageurs à ~ de Paris** the train/passengers for Paris ② (*utilisation prévue, vocation*) purpose

**destiner** [dɛstine] <1> **I.** *vt* ① (*réserver à, attribuer*) **~ un poste à qn** to mean for sb to have a job ② (*prévoir un usage*) **~ un local à qc** to intend that a place should be used for sth ③ (*vouer*) **elle le destine à être avocat/son successeur** she plans for him to be a lawyer/her successor **II.** *vpr* **se ~ à la politique** to intend to go into politics

**destituer** [dɛstitɥe] <1> *vt* (*ministre, fonctionnaire*) to remove from office; (*souverain*) to depose; (*officier*) to break; **~ qn de ses fonctions** to relieve sb of their duties

**destructif, -ive** [dɛstryktif, -iv] *adj* destructive

**destruction** [dɛstryksjɔ̃] *f* ① (*action, dégât*) destruction ② (*extermination*) extermination ③ (*altération: des tissus organiques*) destruction

**désunir** [dezynir] <8> *vt* (*couple, famille*) to divide; (*équipe*) to split up

**détachable** [detaʃabl] *adj* (*amovible: partie, capuche*) removable; (*feuilles*) tear-out

**détachant** [detaʃɑ̃] *m* stain remover

**détacher¹** [detaʃe] <1> **I.** *vt* ① (*délier, libérer: prisonnier*) to unchain; (*chien*) to let loose; (*en enlevant un lien*) to let off the leash ② (*défaire: cheveux, nœud*) to untie; (*lacet, ceinture*) to undo ③ (*arracher, retirer: timbre*) to take off; (*feuille, pétale*) to pull off ④ ADMIN **~ qn à Paris** to send sb to Paris on temporary assignment ⑤ (*ne pas lier: lettres, notes*) to keep separate ⑥ (*détourner*) **être détaché de qn** to have broken off with sb **II.** *vpr* ① (*se libérer*) **se ~** to untie oneself ② (*se séparer*) **se ~ de qc** (*bateau, satellite*) to detach itself from sth; (*par accident*) to come away from sth ③ (*se défaire*) **se ~** (*chaîne*) to come off; (*lacet*) to come undone ④ (*prendre ses distances*) **se ~ de qn** to break off with sb

**détacher²** [detaʃe] <1> *vt* **~ qc** to remove a stain from sth

**détail** [detaj] <s> *m* ① (*particularité, élément d'un ensemble*) detail; **dans les moindres ~s** down to the last detail ② *sans pl* (*énumération: des dépenses, d'un compte*) breakdown ③ *sans pl* COM **commerce de ~** retail business; **vente au ~** retail sale ④ (*accessoire*) detail

**détaillant(e)** [detajɑ̃, jɑ̃t] *m(f)* retailer

**détaillé(e)** [detaje] *adj* detailed

**détailler** [detaje] <1> *vt* ① COM (*articles*) to sell separately; (*marchandise*) to (sell) retail ② (*couper en morceaux: tissu*) to sell lengths of ③ (*faire le détail de: plan, raisons*) to set out in detail; (*histoire*) to tell in detail ④ (*énumérer: défauts, points*) to list

**détartrer** [detartre] <1> *vt* (*chaudière, conduit*) to descale

**détecter** [detɛkte] <1> *vt* to detect

**détective** [detɛktiv] *mf* detective

**déteindre** [detɛ̃dr] *irr* **I.** *vi* ① to run ② (*influencer*) **~ sur qn/qc** to rub off on sb/sth II. *vt* (*soleil*) to fade; ~ **qc à qc** to bleach sth with sth

**détendre** [detɑ̃dʀ] <14> I. *vt* (*relâcher: arc, ressort, corde*) to slacken; (*personne, muscle, atmosphère*) to relax; (*situation*) to ease II. *vpr* **se ~** (*se relâcher: ressort*) to be released; (*arc*) to unbend; (*corde*) to slacken; (*muscle, personne, atmosphère*) to relax; (*situation*) to ease

**détendu(e)** [detɑ̃dy] *adj* (*personne*) relaxed; (*relâché: corde*) slack

**détenir** [det(ə)niʀ] <9> *vt* ❶ (*posséder: objet, pouvoir, preuve, majorité, secret*) to have; (*objets volés, document*) to have (in one's possession); (*poste, position*) to occupy; (*record, titre*) to hold ❷ (*retenir prisonnier*) to detain

**détente** [detɑ̃t] *f* ❶ (*relâchement: d'un ressort*) release; (*d'une corde*) slackening ❷ (*délassement*) relaxation

**détenteur, -trice** [detɑ̃tœʀ, -tʀis] *m, f* (*d'un objet, d'un document*) possessor; (*d'un compte, d'un brevet*) holder

**détention** [detɑ̃sjɔ̃] *f* ❶ (*possession: d'un document, d'une somme, d'un secret, d'armes*) possession ❷ (*incarcération*) detention; ~ **provisoire** temporary custody

**détenu(e)** [det(ə)ny] *m(f)* prisoner

**détergent** [detɛʀʒɑ̃] *m* detergent

**détergent(e)** [detɛʀʒɑ̃, ʒɑ̃t] *adj* detergent

**détérioration** [deteʀjɔʀasjɔ̃] *f* (*d'un appareil, de marchandises*) deterioration; (*des conditions de vie, des relations*) worsening

**détériorer** [deteʀjɔʀe] <1> I. *vt* ❶ (*endommager: appareil, marchandise*) to damage ❷ (*nuire à: climat social, relations*) to worsen; (*santé*) to deteriorate II. *vpr* **se ~** ❶ (*s'abîmer: appareil, marchandise*) to be damaged ❷ (*se dégrader: temps, conditions, santé*) to worsen

**déterminant(e)** [detɛʀminɑ̃, ɑ̃t] *adj* (*action, rôle, événement*) decisive; (*argument, raison*) deciding

**détermination** [detɛʀminasjɔ̃] *f* ❶ (*fixation: d'une grandeur, de l'heure, du lieu, de la cause*) determining ❷ (*décision*) resolution ❸ (*fermeté*) a. PHILOS determination

**déterminé(e)** [detɛʀmine] *adj* ❶ (*précis: idée, lieu, but*) specific ❷ (*défini: moment, heure, quantité*) precise ❸ (*décidé: personne, air*) determined

**déterminer** [detɛʀmine] <1> I. *vt* ❶ (*définir, préciser: sens, inconnue, distance*) to determine; (*adresse, coupable, cause*) to discover ❷ (*convenir de: date, lieu*) to set; (*détails*) to settle ❸ (*décider*) ~ **qn à qc/à faire qc** to decide sb on sth ❹ (*motiver, entraîner: retards, crise, phénomène, révolte*) to bring about II. *vpr* (*se décider*) **se ~ à** +*infin* to determine to +*infin*

**déterrer** [detere] <1> *vt* ❶ (*exhumer: arbre, trésor, personne*) to dig up; (*mine, obus*) to dig out ❷ (*dénicher: vieux manuscrit, loi*) to uncarth

**détester** [detɛste] <1> I. *vt* to hate II. *vpr* **se ~** to hate oneself

**détonation** [detɔnasjɔ̃] *f* (*d'une arme à feu*) shot; (*d'une bombe, d'un obus*) explosion; (*d'un canon*) boom

**détour** [detuʀ] *m* ❶ (*sinuosité*) bend; **au ~ du chemin** at the bend in the path ❷ (*trajet plus long*) detour ❸ (*biais*) roundabout phrases ▶ **au ~ d'une conversation** in the course of a conversation

**détournement** [detuʀnəmɑ̃] *m* ❶ (*déviation*) diversion; ~ **d'avion** hijacking ❷ (*vol*) misappropriation; (*de fonds*) misappropriation; ~ **de mineur** corruption of a minor

**détourner** [detuʀne] <1> I. *vt* ❶ (*changer la direction de: rivière, circulation*) to divert; (*par la contrainte: avion*) to hijack; (*coup*) to ward off; (*tir*) to push away ❷ (*tourner d'un autre côté: tête, visage*) to turn away; ~ **son regard** to look away ❸ (*dévier: colère, fléau*) to avert; (*texte*) to twist ❹ (*distraire*) ~ **qn de qc** to take sb's mind off sth ❺ (*soustraire: somme, fonds*) to misappropriate

**II.** *vpr* ❶ (*tourner la tête*) **se ~** to look away ❷ (*se détacher*) **se ~ de qn/qc** to turn away from sb/sth ❸ (*s'égarer*) **se ~ de sa route** to wander from one's route; (*prendre une autre route*) to take a detour

**D détraqué(e)** [detʀake] **I.** *adj* ❶ (*déréglé: appareil, mécanisme*) broken down ❷ (*dérangé: estomac*) upset ❸ *inf* (*dérangé*) cracked **II.** *m(f) inf* weirdo

**détraquer** [detʀake] <1> **I.** *vt* ❶ (*abîmer: appareil*) to upset the workings of ❷ *inf* (*déranger: santé*) to weaken; (*estomac, nerfs*) to upset; (*personne*) to unhinge **II.** *vpr* **se ~** ❶ (*être abîmé: montre*) to go wrong ❷ (*être dérangé: estomac*) to be upset ❸ METEO (*temps*) (*se gâter*) to turn bad; (*se dérégler*) to become unsettled

**détresse** [detʀɛs] *f* (*sentiment, situation*) distress

**détriment** [detʀimã] **au ~ de qn** to the detriment of sb

**détroit** [detʀwa] *m* strait; **~ de Gibraltar** straits of Gibraltar

**détromper** [detʀɔ̃pe] <1> **I.** *vt* **~ qn** to set sb straight **II.** *vpr* **détrompe-toi/détrompez-vous!** think again!

**détrôner** [detʀone] <1> *vt* ❶ (*destituer: souverain*) to dethrone ❷ (*supplanter: rival, chanteur*) to oust

**détruire** [detʀɥiʀ] *irr* **I.** *vt* ❶ (*démolir*) to destroy; (*clôture, mur*) to knock down ❷ (*anéantir: armes, population*) to wipe out; (*déchets, machine*) to destroy ❸ (*ruiner, anéantir: personne, illusions*) to shatter; (*santé, réputation*) to ruin; (*plans, espoirs*) to wreck; (*capitalisme, dictature*) to destroy **II.** *vi* to destroy **III.** *vpr* **se ~** (*effets contraires, mesures*) to cancel each other out

**dette** [dɛt] *f a. fig* debt

**deuil** [dœj] *m* ❶ (*affliction*) grief ❷ (*décès*) bereavement ❸ (*signes, durée du deuil*) mourning; **porter/quitter le ~** to be in/come out of mourning

**deux** [dø] **I.** *adj* ❶ two; **tous les ~** both of them; **à ~** together ❷ (*quelques*)

j'habite à **~ pas d'ici** I live just down the road from here **II.** *m inv* (*cardinal*) two ▸**à nous ~!** here we go!; **en moins de ~** *inf* in two secs; **entre les ~** between the two; *v.a.* **cinq**

**deuxième** [døzjɛm] **I.** *adj antéposé* second **II.** *mf* **le/la ~** the second **III.** *f* (*vitesse*) second (gear); *v.a.* **cinquième**

**deuxièmement** [døzjɛmmã] *adv* secondly

**deux-pièces** [døpjɛs] *m inv* ❶ (*appartement*) two-room apartment ❷ (*maillot de bain, vêtement féminin*) two-piece

**deux-points** [døpwɛ̃] *mpl inv* LING colon

**deux-roues** [døʀu] *m inv* two-wheeled vehicle (*bicycle or motorbike*)

**dévaliser** [devalize] <1> *vt* ❶ (*voler*) to rob ❷ *inf* (*vider: réfrigérateur, magasin*) to raid

**dévaloriser** [devalɔʀize] <1> **I.** *vt* ❶ (*dévaluer*) to devalue; (*pouvoir d'achat*) to fall ❷ (*déprécier: mérite, talent, personne*) to depreciate **II.** *vpr* **se ~** ❶ (*se déprécier: monnaie, marchandise*) to lose value ❷ (*se dénigrer: personne*) to undervalue oneself

**dévaluation** [devalɥasjɔ̃] *f* FIN devaluation

**dévaluer** [devalɥe] <1> **I.** *vt* FIN to devalue **II.** *vpr* **se ~** ❶ FIN to be devalued ❷ (*se dévaloriser*) to undervalue oneself

**devancer** [d(ə)vãse] <2> *vt* ❶ (*distancer*) **~ qn de cinq secondes/mètres** to be five seconds/meters ahead of sb ❷ (*être le premier: rival, concurrent*) to lead ❸ (*précéder*) **~ qn** to go on ahead of sb ❹ (*aller au devant de: personne, question*) to anticipate

**devant** [d(ə)vã] **I.** *prep* ❶ (*en face de: être, se trouver, rester*) in front of; (*avec mouvement: aller, passer*) past ❷ (*en avant de*) in front of; (*à une certaine distance*) ahead of ❸ (*face à, en présence de*) **~ qn** (*s'exprimer*) to; (*pleurer*) in front of **II.** *adv* ❶ (*en face*) in front ❷ (*en avant*) in front; (*avec mouvement*) forward; **être loin ~** to be way

out in front **III.** *m* (*partie avant: d'un vêtement, d'une maison*) front; (*d'un bateau*) prow; (*d'un objet*) front (part)
▶ **prendre les ~s** to take the initiative

**dévaster** [devaste] <1> *vt* ❶ (*détruire: pays, terres, récoltes*) to devastate ❷ *fig* (*âme*) to ravage

**développé(e)** [dev(ə)lɔpe] *adj* developed; (*odorat*) acute; (*vue*) keen

**développement** [devlɔpmã] *m* ❶ BIO (*croissance*) development; (*multiplication: de bactéries, d'une espèce*) growth ❷ ECON (*de l'industrie, d'une affaire, de la production*) growth; **pays en voie de ~** developing country ❸ (*extension: des relations, des connaissances*) growth; (*d'une maladie*) development; (*d'une épidémie, d'une crise*) spread ❹ (*évolution: de l'intelligence, de la civilisation*) growth ❺ (*exposition détaillée*) *a.* ECOLE, MUS development ❻ PHOT developing

**développer** [dev(ə)lɔpe] <1> **I.** *vt* ❶ (*faire progresser, croître, mette au point*) *a.* MUS, MED to develop ❷ (*exposer en détail: thème, pensée, plan*) to elaborate on; (*chapitre*) to develop ❸ MATH (*fonction*) to develop; (*calcul*) to carry out ❹ PHOT **faire ~ une pellicule** to get film developed **II.** *vpr* **se ~** ❶ *a.* ECON, TECH to develop; (*personnalité*) to evolve; (*plante, tumeur*) to grow ❷ (*s'intensifier: échanges, haine, relations*) to grow ❸ (*se propager*) to develop; (*usage*) to grow up

**devenir** [dəv(ə)niʀ] <9> **I.** *vi* être **~ riche/ingénieur** to become rich/an engineer; **qu'est-ce que tu deviens?** *inf* what are you up to? **II.** *m* soutenu ❶ (*évolution*) evolution ❷ (*avenir*) future

**déverser** [devɛʀse] <1> **I.** *vt* ❶ (*verser: liquide*) to pour ❷ (*décharger: sable, ordures*) to dump; (*bombes*) to shower **II.** *vpr* **se ~ dans une rivière** to pour into a river

**dévêtir** [devetiʀ] *vt, vpr irr* (**se**) **~** to undress

**déviation** [devjasjõ] *f* ❶ (*action/résultat: de la circulation*) diversion; (*d'un projectile, d'une aiguille aimantée*) deviation; (*d'un rayon lumineux*) deflection ❷ (*chemin*) diversion ❸ (*déformation: de la colonne vertébrale*) curvature ❹ (*attitude différente*) deviation

**dévier** [devje] <1> **I.** *vi* (*véhicule*) to swerve; (*bateau*) to go off course; (*aiguille magnétique*) to deviate **II.** *vt* (*circulation*) to divert; (*coup, balle, rayon lumineux*) to deflect; (*conversation*) to steer away

**deviner** [d(ə)vine] <1> **I.** *vt* ❶ (*trouver: réponse, secret, énigme*) to guess ❷ (*pressentir: sens, pensée*) to guess; (*menace, danger*) to see ❸ (*entrevoir*) to make out **II.** *vpr* ❶ (*se trouver*) **la réponse se devine facilement** the answer is easy to guess ❷ (*transparaître*) **se ~** (*tendance, goût*) to be apparent

**devinette** [d(ə)vinɛt] *f* riddle

**devis** [d(ə)vi] *m* estimate

**dévisager** [devizaʒe] <2a> *vt* to stare at

**devise** [d(ə)viz] *f* ❶ (*formule, règle de conduite*) motto ❷ (*monnaie*) currency

**dévisser** [devise] <1> **I.** *vi* SPORT to fall **II.** *vt* (*écrou, couvercle, tube*) to unscrew; (*roue*) to unbolt **III.** *vpr* **se ~** ❶ (*pouvoir être enlevé/ouvert*) to screw off ❷ (*se desserrer*) to come loose

**dévoiler** [devwale] <1> **I.** *vt* ❶ (*découvrir: statue, plaque*) to unveil; (*charmes, rondeurs*) to reveal ❷ (*révéler*) to reveal; (*scandale, perfidie*) to bring to light **II.** *vpr* **se ~** (*mystère, fourberie*) to be revealed

**devoir** [d(ə)vwaʀ] *irr* **I.** *vt* (*argent*) to owe **II.** *aux* ❶ (*nécessité*) **~ +infin** to have to +infin; **tu ne dois pas mentir** you mustn't lie ❷ (*obligation exprimée par autrui*) **tu aurais dû rentrer** you should have gone home ❸ (*fatalité*) **cela devait arriver un jour** that was bound to happen one day ❹ (*prévision*) **normalement, il doit arriver ce soir** if all goes well, he should ar-

**D**

rive tonight **III.** *vpr* **se ~ de** +*infin* to owe it to oneself to +*infin* **IV.** *m* ❶ (*obligation morale*) duty ❷ ECOLE test; (*devoir surveillé*) in-class test ❸ *pl* (*devoirs à la maison*) homework ▶ **manquer** **à son ~** to fail in one's duty

**dévorer** [devɔʀe] <1> **I.** *vi* (*personne*) to have a voracious appetite **II.** *vt* ❶ *a. fig* (*avaler*) to devour ❷ (*regarder*) **~ des yeux** to look voraciously at ❸ (*tourmenter*) **~ qn** (*tâche*) to eat up sb's time; (*remords, peur, soif*) to eat away at sb

**dévoué(e)** [devwe] *adj* devoted

**dévouement** [devumã] *m* devotion

**dévouer** [devwe] <1> *vpr* **se ~** to make a sacrifice; **se ~ à qn/qc** to devote oneself to sb/sth

**diabète** [djabɛt] *m* diabetes

**diabétique** [djabetik] **I.** *adj* diabetic **II.** *mf* diabetic

**diable** [djɑbl] *m* ❶ (*démon, personne*) devil ❷ (*chariot*) cart ❸ (*marmite*) pot ▶ **allez au ~**! get lost!

**diabolique** [djabɔlik] *adj* ❶ (*venant du diable*) diabolic ❷ (*très méchant*) diabolical

**diagnostic** [djagnɔstik] *m* MED *a. fig* diagnosis

**diagnostiquer** [djagnɔstike] <1> *vt* MED *a. fig* to diagnose

**diagonale** [djagɔnal] *f* diagonal line

**dialecte** [djalɛkt] *m* dialect

**dialogue** [djalɔg] *m* dialogue; (*en tête-à-tête*) conversation

**dialoguer** [djalɔge] <1> **I.** *vi* ❶ (*converser*) **~ avec qn** to talk with sb ❷ (*négocier*) **~ avec qn** to have a dialogue with sb ❸ INFORM **~ avec qc** to interact with sth **II.** *vt* to turn into dialogue

**diamant** [djamã] *m* diamond; **~ brut** rough diamond; **~s de sang** blood diamonds

**diamètre** [djamɛtʀ] *m* diameter

**diaphragme** [djafʀagm] *m* *a.* ANAT diaphragm

**diapositive** [djapozitiv] *f* slide

**diarrhée** [djaʀe] *f* diarrhea

**dictateur, -trice** [diktatœʀ, -tʀis] *m, f* dictator

**dictature** [diktatyʀ] *f* ❶ POL dictatorship ❷ (*autoritarisme*) tyranny

**dictée** [dikte] *f a.* ECOLE dictation

**dicter** [dikte] <1> *vt* ❶ (*faire écrire*) to dictate ❷ (*imposer*) **~ ses volontés** (*personne*) to dictate one's will; (*circonstance, événement*) to impose its own terms

**dictionnaire** [diksjɔnɛʀ] *m* dictionary

**dicton** [diktɔ̃] *m* saying

**didacticiel** [didaktisjɛl] *m* INFORM courseware

**dièse** [djɛz] *m* sharp

**diesel** [djezɛl] *m* diesel

**diète** [djɛt] *f* diet; **mettre qn/être à la ~** to put sb/to be on a diet

**diététique** [djetetik] **I.** *adj* healthy **II.** *f* dietetics

**dieu** [djø] <x> *m* (*divinité*) god

**diffamation** [difamasjɔ̃] *f* defamation

**différence** [difeʀãs] *f* difference; **à la ~ de qn/qc** unlike sb/sth

**différencier** [difeʀãsje] <1> **I.** *vt* to differentiate **II.** *vpr* ❶ (*se distinguer*) **se ~ de qn par qc** to be unlike sb in sth ❷ BIO **se ~** to differentiate

**différend** [difeʀã] *m* dispute

**différent(e)** [difeʀã, ãt] *adj* different; **~ de** different from

**différer** [difeʀe] <5> **I.** *vi* ❶ (*être différent*) to differ ❷ (*avoir une opinion différente*) **~ sur qc** to differ over sth **II.** *vt* to postpone; (*échéance, paiement*) to defer

**difficile** [difisil] *adj* ❶ (*ardu*) difficult ❷ (*incommode: sentier, escalade*) hard; **~ d'accès** hard to get to ❸ (*qui donne du souci: moment*) difficult ❹ (*contrariant, exigeant: personne, caractère*) difficult; **~ à vivre** hard to live with ▶ **être ~ sur la nourriture** to be finicky about food

**difficilement** [difisilmã] *adv* ❶ (*péniblement*) with difficulty ❷ (*à peine*) barely

**difficulté** [difikylte] *f* difficulty; **se**

**heurter à des ~s** to come up against problems

**difforme** [difɔʀm] *adj* (*membre, bête*) deformed; (*arbre*) twisted

**diffus(e)** [dify, yz] *adj* ❶(*disséminé: douleur*) diffuse; (*lumière, chaleur*) diffused ❷(*sans netteté*) vague; (*sentiments, souvenirs*) dim ❸(*verbeux: écrivain, style*) nebulous

**diffuser** [difyze] <1> I. *vt* ❶(*répandre: lumière, bruit*) to give out; (*idée*) to spread ❷(*retransmettre*) to broadcast ❸(*commercialiser*) to distribute ❹(*distribuer: tract, photo*) to distribute; (*pétition, document*) to circulate II. *vpr* se ~ (*bruit, chaleur, odeur*) to emanate

**diffusion** [difyzjɔ̃] *f* ❶(*propagation: de la chaleur, lumière*) diffusion ❷(*d'un concert, d'une émission*) broadcasting ❸(*commercialisation, distribution*) distribution ❹(*action de se diffuser: d'un poison, gaz*) spreading

**digérer** [diʒeʀe] <5> I. *vi* to digest II. *vt* ❶(*assimiler*) a. ANAT to digest ❷ *inf* (*accepter: affront*) to stomach III. *vpr* **bien/mal se ~** to be easy/hard to stomach

**digeste** [diʒɛst] *adj* digestible

**digestif** [diʒɛstif] *m* (after dinner) liqueur

**digestif, -ive** [diʒɛstif, -iv] *adj* digestive

**digestion** [diʒɛstjɔ̃] *f* digestion

**digital(e)** [diʒital, -o] <-aux> *adj* digital

**digne** [diɲ] *adj* (*qui mérite*) **~ de ce nom** worthy of the name

**dignité** [diɲite] *f* ❶(*noblesse, titre*) dignity ❷(*amour-propre*) (sense of) dignity

**digue** [dig] *f* ❶dike ❷(*rempart*) sea wall

**dilapider** [dilapide] <1> *vt* to waste; (*fortune, patrimoine*) to squander

**dilater** [dilate] <1> I. *vt* ❶(*augmenter le volume de*) to expand ❷(*agrandir un conduit, orifice*) to dilate; (*narines*) to flare II. *vpr* se ~ (*métal, corps*) to expand; (*pupille, cœur, poumons*) to dilate; (*narines*) to flare

**dilemme** [dilɛm] *m* dilemma

**diluer** [dilɥe] <1> I. *vt* ❶(*étendre, délayer*) ~ **avec de l'eau/dans de l'eau** to dilute with water/in water ❷(*affaiblir*) **~ qc** to water sth down II. *vpr* se ~ ❶(*se délayer*) to be diluted ❷ *fig* (*identité, personnalité*) to be lost

**dimanche** [dimɑ̃ʃ] *m* ❶(*veille de lundi*) Sunday; **le ~** on Sunday(s); **tous les ~s** every Sunday; **~ matin** on Sunday morning ❷(*jour férié*) **promenade du ~** Sunday walk

**dimension** [dimɑ̃sjɔ̃] *f* ❶(*taille*) size ❷ *pl* (*mesures*) measurements; (*géométriques*) dimensions ❸(*importance*) proportions; **prendre la ~ de qn/qc** to get the measure of sb/sth; **à la ~ de qc** corresponding to sth ❹(*aspect*) dimension

**diminuer** [diminɥe] <1> I. *vi* to diminish; (*bruit, vent, lumière, niveau de l'eau, fièvre*) to go down; (*nombre, forces*) to dwindle; (*brouillard*) to clear; (*jours*) to shorten II. *vt* ❶(*réduire*) to reduce; (*impôts, prix*) to lower; (*durée, rideau*) to shorten; (*gaz, chauffage*) to turn down ❷(*affaiblir: autorité, mérite, joie, souffrance*) to diminish; (*violence*) to reduce; (*forces*) to decrease ❸(*discréditer*) to depreciate III. *vpr* se ~ (*se rabaisser*) to depreciate oneself

**diminutif** [diminytif] *m* diminutive

**diminutif, -ive** [diminytif, -iv] *adj* diminutive

**diminution** [diminysjɔ̃] *f* ❶(*baisse, affaiblissement: de l'appétit, de la chaleur*) loss; (*des forces, des chances*) dwindling; (*de la circulation, du nombre*) decrease; (*des impôts, prix*) reduction; (*de la température, de la fièvre*) fall; **en ~** (*nombre, température*) falling ❷(*réduction: de la consommation, des prix, impôts, salaires*) reduction; (*d'une durée*) shortening

**dinde** [dɛ̃d] *f* turkey

**dindon** [dɛ̃dɔ̃] *m* a. *inf* turkey (cock)

**dindonneau** [dɛ̃dɔno] <x> *m* (turkey) poult

**dîner** [dine] <1> I. *vi* ❶to have dinner ❷ *Belgique, Québec* (*prendre le repas de midi*) to have lunch II. *m* ❶dinner;

**au ~** at dinner ② *Belgique, Québec (repas de midi, déjeuner)* lunch

**dingue** [dɛ̃g] **I.** *adj inf* ① *(fou)* loony ② *(fan)* **~ du foot** soccer fanatic **II.** *mf inf*

**diode** [djɔd] *f* diode; **~ électroluminescente** light-emitting diode, LED

**diphtérie** [difteʀi] *f* diphtheria

**diplomate** [diplɔmat] **I.** *adj* diplomatic **II.** *mf* diplomat

**diplomatie** [diplɔmasi] *f* ① *(relations extérieures, carrière, habileté)* diplomacy ② *(personnel)* diplomatic corps

**diplôme** [diplom] *m* degree, diploma; **~ de fin d'études** graduation diploma

**diplômé(e)** [diplome] **I.** *adj* qualified **II.** *m(f)* **~ d'une université** graduate of a university

**dire** [diʀ] *irr* **I.** *vt* ① *(exprimer, prétendre, traduire)* to say; *(peur)* to put into words; **dis voir** hey, ...; **qu'est-ce que tu dis de ça?** what do you say to that?; **que ~?** what can you say?; ..., **comment ~,** ... ..., how can I put it, ... ② *(ordonner)* **à qn de venir** to tell sb to come ③ *(plaire)* **cela me dit** I'd like that ④ *(croire, penser)* **on dirait que...** anyone would think ... ⑤ *(reconnaître)* **il faut ~ qu'elle a raison** it must be said that she's right ⑥ *(réciter: chapelet, messe, prière)* to say; *(poème)* to recite ⑦ *(signifier)* **vouloir ~** to mean ⑧ *(évoquer)* to tell ⑨ JEUX **~** to call ▶**eh ben dis/dites donc!** *inf* well then! **II.** *vpr* ① *(penser)* **se ~ que qn a fait qc** to think that sb's done sth ② *(se prétendre)* **se ~ médecin/malade** to claim to be a doctor/ill ③ *(l'un(e) à l'autre)* **se ~ qc** to tell each other sth ④ *(s'employer)* **ça se dit/ne se dit pas en français** you say that/don't say that in French ⑤ *(être traduit: nom)* to be called; **ça se dit ... en français** the French for that is ...; **comment se dit ... en français?** how do you say ... in French? **III.** *m gén pl* claims; *(d'un témoin)* statement

**direct** [diʀɛkt] *m* ① TV **le ~** live TV; **en ~** live ② CHEMDFER nonstop train ③ SPORT jab

**direct(e)** [diʀɛkt] *adj* direct

**directement** [diʀɛktəmɑ̃] *adv* ① *(tout droit)* straight ② *(sans transition ou intermédiaire)* directly

**directeur, -trice** [diʀɛktœʀ, -tʀis] **I.** *adj* *(idée, ligne)* main; *(principe)* guiding; *(rôle)* leading; *(roue)* front **II.** *m, f* director; *(d'une école primaire)* head

**direction** [diʀɛksjɔ̃] *f* ① *(orientation)* direction ② *(action)* management; *(d'un groupe, pays)* running; **avoir/prendre la ~ de qc** to be in/take charge of sth ③ *(fonction, bureau)* management ④ AUTO steering

**directive** [diʀɛktiv] *f gén pl* directives

**directrice** [diʀɛktʀis] *v.* **directeur**

**dirigeant(e)** [diʀiʒɑ̃, ɑ̃t] **I.** *adj* *(parti)* ruling; *(fonction, pouvoir, rôle)* executive **II.** *m(f)* leader; **les ~s** *(dans une entreprise)* the management; *(dans un parti)* the leadership; *(dans un pays)* the executive

**diriger** [diʀiʒe] <2a> **I.** *vi* to lead **II.** *vt* ① *(gouverner: administration, journal, entreprise)* to run; *(syndicat, personnes)* to lead; *(musicien, orchestre)* to conduct; *(mouvement, manœuvre, instincts)* to direct ② *(être le moteur de)* **~ le cours de la vie de qn** to direct the course of sb's life ③ *(piloter: voiture)* to drive; *(avion)* to fly; *(bateau)* to steer ④ *(faire aller)* **~ qn vers la gare** to direct sb to the station ⑤ *(orienter)* **~ une arme contre qn/qc** to aim a gun at sb/sth **III.** *vpr* ① *(aller)* **se ~ vers qn/qc** to head toward sb/sth ② *(s'orienter)* **se ~ vers le nord** *(aiguille)* to point north ③ ECOLE, UNIV **se ~ vers la médecine** to head toward a career in medicine

**dis** [di] *indic prés et passé simple de* **dire**

**discerner** [disɛʀne] <1> *vt* ① *(percevoir)* to make out ② *(saisir)* to perceive; *(mobile)* to see ③ *(différencier)* **~ qc de qc** to distinguish sth from sth

**disciple** [disipl] *m* disciple

**disciplinaire** [disiplinɛʀ] *adj* disciplinary

**discipline** [disiplin] *f* discipline

**discipliné(e)** [disipline] *adj* disciplined

**disco** [disko] I. *m* disco II. *adj inv* disco

**discontinu(e)** [diskɔ̃tiny] *adj* (*ligne*) broken; (*effort*) intermittent

**discothèque** [diskɔtɛk] *f* ❶ (*boîte de nuit*) discotheque ❷ (*collection*) record library ❸ (*meuble*) disc rack ❹ (*organisme de prêt*) record library

**discours** [diskuʀ] *m* ❶ (*allocution*) speech ❷ (*propos*) **leur ~ sur l'immigration** the way they talk about immigration ❸ (*bavardage*) talk

**discret** [diskʀɛ, -ɛt] *adj* ❶ (*réservé, sobre*) discreet ❷ (*retiré*) secluded

**discrètement** [diskʀɛtmã] *adv* discreetly; (*s'habiller*) quietly

**discrétion** [diskʀesjɔ̃] *f* ❶ (*réserve, silence*) discretion; **~ assurée** confidentiality guaranteed ❷ (*sobriété*) discreetness; (*d'une toilette, d'un maquillage*) simplicity; (*des décors*) unobtrusiveness

**discrimination** [diskʀiminasjɔ̃] *f* (*ségrégation*) discrimination

**discriminatoire** [diskʀiminatwaʀ] *adj* discriminatory

**disculper** [diskylpe] <1> I. *vt* **~ qn de qc** to find sb not guilty of sth II. *vpr* **se ~** to clear oneself

**discussion** [diskysjɔ̃] *f* ❶ (*conversation, débat*) discussion ❷ POL **~ du budget** budget debate ❸ (*querelle*) argument

**discutable** [diskytabl] *adj* (*théories*) debatable; (*goût*) questionable

**discuté(e)** [diskyte] *adj* controversial

**discuter** [diskyte] <1> I. *vt* ❶ (*débattre*) to discuss ❷ (*contester: ordre, autorité*) to question; **~ le prix** to argue over the price II. *vi* ❶ (*bavarder*) **~ de qc avec qn** to talk to sb about sth ❷ (*négocier*) **~ avec qn** to discuss with sb ❸ (*contester*) **on ne discute pas!** no arguments! III. *vpr* **ça se discute** that's debatable

**disent** [diz] *indic et subj prés de* **dire**

**disjoncter** [disʒɔ̃kte] <1> I. *vi inf* ❶ ELEC **ça a disjoncté!** a fuse has blown!

❷ (*débloquer*) to be off one's head II. *vt* ELEC to blow

**disjoncteur** [disʒɔ̃ktœʀ] *m* circuit breaker

**disloquer** [dislɔke] <1> I. *vt* ❶ (*démolir*) to smash; (*parti, famille, domaine*) to break up; (*empire*) to dismantle ❷ (*disperser: manifestation*) to break up II. *vpr* ❶ (*se défaire*) **se ~** (*meuble, voiture, jouet*) to fall to pieces; (*empire*) to dismantle; (*famille, manifestation, assemblée, parti, société*) to break up ❷ MED **se ~ qc** to dislocate sth

**disons** [dizɔ̃] *indic prés et impératif de* **dire**

**disparaître** [dispaʀɛtʀ] *vi irr avoir* ❶ (*ne plus être là*) to disappear ❷ (*passer, s'effacer: trace, tache*) to disappear; (*douleur, espoir, crainte, soucis*) to vanish (*away*); (*colère*) to evaporate ❸ (*ne plus exister: obstacle*) to disappear; (*s'éteindre: culture, espèce, mode, dialecte, coutume*) to die out; (*mourir: personne*) to pass away; (*dans un naufrage*) to be lost

**disparition** [dispaʀisjɔ̃] *f* ❶ (*opp: apparition*) disappearance; (*d'une coutume, d'une culture*) passing; (*du soleil*) (*le soir*) setting; (*par mauvais temps*) disappearance ❷ (*mort*) death

**disparu(e)** [dispaʀy] I. *part passé de* **disparaître** II. *adj* **être porté ~** to be reported missing III. *m(f)* ❶ (*défunt*) deceased ❷ (*porté manquant*) missing person

**dispense** [dispãs] *f* exemption

**dispenser** [dispãse] <1> I. *vt* ❶ (*exempter*) **~ qn de qc** to exempt sb from sth ❷ (*distribuer*) **~ qc à qn** to give sth to sb; **~ des soins à un malade** to care for a sick person II. *vpr* **se ~ de qc** (*tâche*) to excuse oneself from sth; (*commentaire*) to refrain from sth

**disperser** [dispɛʀse] <1> I. *vt* ❶ (*éparpiller: papiers, cendres*) to scatter; (*troupes*) to disperse ❷ (*répartir*) to spread out II. *vpr* **se ~** ❶ (*partir dans tous les sens*) to scatter ❷ (*se décon-*

*centrer*) **elle se disperse** she bites off more than she can chew

**dispersion** [dispɛʀsjɔ̃] *f* (*des graines, cendres*) scattering; (*d'un attroupement*) dispersal; (*de l'esprit*) overstretching

**D disponibilité** [dispɔnibilite] *f sans pl* availability

**disponible** [dispɔnibl] *adj* available

**disposé(e)** [dispoze] *adj* **être bien/mal** ~ to be in a good/bad mood; **être** ~ **à** +*infin* to be inclined to +*infin*

**disposer** [dispoze] <1> I. *vt* ❶ (*arranger, placer: fleurs*) to arrange; (*objets*) to lay out; (*joueurs, soldats*) to position ❷ (*engager*) ~ **qn à** +*infin* to incline sb to +*infin* II. *vi* ❶ (*avoir à sa disposition*) ~ **de qc** to have sth ❷ *soutenu* (*aliéner*) ~ **de qc** to dispose of sth III. *vpr* **se** ~ **à** +*infin* to be preparing to +*infin*

**dispositif** [dispozitif] *m* ❶ (*mécanisme*) device ❷ (*ensemble de mesures*) measures *pl*

**disposition** [dispozisjɔ̃] *f* ❶ *sans pl* (*agencement*) arrangement; (*d'un article, texte*) structure ❷ (*clause*) provision ▶ **prendre des ~s pour qc** to make arrangements for sth

**disproportion** [dispʀɔpɔʀsjɔ̃] *f* lack of proportion

**disproportionné(e)** [dispʀɔpɔʀsjɔne] *adj* (*corps*) disproportionate; (*réactions*) exaggerated

**dispute** [dispyt] *f* quarrel; (*entre adversaires*) dispute

**disputer** [dispyte] <1> I. *vt* ❶ *inf* (*gronder*) ~ **qn** to tell sb off ❷ (*contester*) ~ **qc à qn** to fight with sb over sth ❸ SPORT (*match*) to fight II. *vpr* ❶ (*se quereller*) **se** ~ **avec qn** to quarrel with sb ❷ (*lutter pour*) **se** ~ **qc** to fight for sth ❸ SPORT **se** ~ (*match*) to be held

**disqualifier** [diskalifje] <1> I. *vt* to disqualify II. *vpr* **se** ~ to be disqualified

**disque** [disk] *m* ❶ (*objet rond*) disc ❷ MUS record; ~ **compact** compact disc ❸ SPORT discus ❹ INFORM ~ **dur** hard disk

**disquette** [diskɛt] *f* floppy disk; ~ **d'installation** installation disk

**disséminer** [disemine] <1> I. *vt* (*graines*) to scatter; (*idées*) to disseminate II. *vpr* **se** ~ ❶ (*se disperser*) to be scattered ❷ (*se répandre*) to spread out

**disséquer** [diseke] <5> *vt* to dissect

**dissertation** [disɛʀtasjɔ̃] *f* ECOLE essay

**dissident(e)** [disidɑ̃, ɑ̃t] I. *adj* dissident II. *m(f)* dissident

**dissimulation** [disimylasjɔ̃] *f* ❶ *sans pl* (*duplicité*) dissimulation ❷ (*action de cacher*) concealment

**dissimuler** [disimyle] <1> I. *vt* ❶ (*cacher*) *a.* FIN to conceal ❷ (*taire*) ~ **qc à qn** to hide sth from sb II. *vi* **elle sait** ~ she can put on a good act III. *vpr* **se** ~ to conceal oneself

**dissipation** [disipasjɔ̃] *f* (*morale*) dissipation; (*du patrimoine*) waste; (*de la brume*) lifting

**dissipé(e)** [disipe] *adj* undisciplined

**dissiper** [disipe] <1> I. *vt* ❶ (*faire disparaître*) to dissipate ❷ (*lever: soupçons, doutes*) to dissipate; (*illusions*) to scatter; (*malentendu*) to clear up ❸ (*dilapider*) to squander ❹ ECOLE to distract II. *vpr* **se** ~ (*brume*) to lift; (*doutes, craintes, soupçons, inquiétude*) to vanish; ECOLE to be distracted

**dissocier** [disɔsje] <1> *vt* (*envisager séparément*) ~ **qc de qc** to dissociate sth from sth

**dissolution** [disɔlysjɔ̃] *f* ❶ (*action*) dissolution ❷ (*liquide*) solution

**dissolvant** [disɔlvɑ̃] *m* solvent; (*pour les ongles*) nail polish remover

**dissolvant(e)** [disɔlvɑ̃, ɑ̃t] *adj* solvent

**dissoudre** [disudʀ] *irr* I. *vt* to dissolve II. *vpr* **se** ~ to be dissolved

**dissuader** [disɥade] <1> *vt* ~ **qn de qc** to dissuade sb from sth

**dissuasif, -ive** [disɥazif, -iv] *adj* dissuasive

**dissuasion** [disɥazjɔ̃] *f* dissuasion

**distance** [distɑ̃s] *f* ❶ (*éloignement*) *a.* MATH, SPORT distance; **à une** ~ **de 500 m** 500 meters away ❷ (*écart*) gap ▶ **pren-**

dre ses ~s à l'égard de qn to distance oneself from sb

**distancer** [distɑ̃se] <2> vt ❶ SPORT to outdistance ❷ (*surpasser*) to outdo

**distant(e)** [distɑ̃, ɑ̃t] adj ❶ (*réservé: personne, attitude*) distant ❷ (*éloigné*) separated

**distillation** [distilasjɔ̃] f distillation

**distiller** [distile] <1> vt to distill

**distinct(e)** [distɛ̃, ɛ̃kt] adj distinct

**distinctement** [distɛ̃ktəmɑ̃] adv distinctly

**distinctif, -ive** [distɛ̃ktif, -iv] adj distinctive; *signe* ~ distinguishing mark

**distinction** [distɛ̃ksjɔ̃] f distinction

**distingué(e)** [distɛ̃ge] adj (*élégant, éminent*) distinguished

**distinguer** [distɛ̃ge] <1> I. vt ❶ (*percevoir, différencier*) to distinguish ❷ (*caractériser*) **sa grande taille le distingue** he is distinguished by his height ❸ (*honorer*) to honor II. vi (*faire la différence*) ~ **entre qn et qn/entre qc et qc** to distinguish sb from sb else/sth from sth else III. vpr ❶ (*différer*) **se ~ de qn/qc par qc** to be distinguished from sb/sth by sth ❷ (*s'illustrer*) **se ~ par qc** to distinguish oneself by sth

**distraction** [distraksjɔ̃] f ❶ sans pl (*inattention*) lack of concentration ❷ (*étourderie*) absent-mindedness ❸ sans pl (*dérivatif*) distraction ❹ gén pl (*passe-temps*) pastime

**distraire** [distrɛr] irr I. vt ❶ (*délasser*) to amuse ❷ (*déranger*) ~ **qn de qc** to distract sb from sth II. vpr **se ~** to enjoy oneself

**distrait(e)** [distrɛ, ɛt] I. part passé de **distraire** II. adj absent-minded

**distrayant(e)** [distrɛjɑ̃, jɑ̃t] adj entertaining

**distribanque®** [distribɑ̃k] m cash machine, ATM

**distribuer** [distribɥe] <1> vt ❶ (*donner*) à FIN, COM to distribute; (*cartes*) to deal; ~ **le courrier** to deliver the mail ❷ (*arranger, répartir: éléments, mots*) to arrange; (*joueurs de foot*) to position

**distributeur** [distribytœr] m (slot) machine; ~ **de billets/boissons** ATM/drink machine

**distributeur, -trice** [distribytœr, -tris] m, f ❶ (*personne*) ~ **de prospectus** sb who distributes fliers ❷ COM, CINE distributor; (*entreprise*) dealer; (*diffuseur*) distributor

**distribution** [distribysjɔ̃] f ❶ (*répartition*) distribution; (*du courrier*) delivery; (*des cartes*) dealing ❷ FIN (*des dividendes*) distribution; (*des actions*) issue; ~ **des prix** prize-giving ❸ COM supply ❹ CINE, THEAT cast ❺ (*arrangement: des éléments, mots*) arrangement; (*des pièces, de l'appartement*) layout; (*des joueurs*) positioning

**district** [distrikt] m district

**dît** |di| indic prés de **dire**

**dit(e)** [di, dit] I. part passé de **dire** II. adj (*touristique, socialiste*) so-called

**dites** [dit] indic prés de **dire**

**divaguer** [divage] <1> vi ❶ (*délirer: malade*) to be delirious ❷ inf (*déraisonner*) to talk nonsense

**divan** [divɑ̃] m couch, sofa

**divergent(e)** [divɛrʒɑ̃, ʒɑ̃t] adj divergent

**diverger** [divɛrʒe] <2a> vi to diverge

**divers(e)** [divɛr, ɛrs] I. adj ❶ (*différent, varié*) various ❷ (*inégal, contradictoire: mouvements, intérêts*) diverse ❸ toujours au pl (*plusieurs*) various; **à ~es reprises** on several occasions II. mpl sundries

**diversifier** [divɛrsifje] <1> vt to diversify

**diversité** [divɛrsite] f diversity

**divertir** [divɛrtir] <8> I. vt ❶ (*délasser*) to amuse ❷ (*changer les idées de qn*) ~ **qn** to take sb's mind off things II. vpr **se ~** to enjoy oneself

**divertissant(e)** [divɛrtisɑ̃, ɑ̃t] adj entertaining

**divertissement** [divɛrtismɑ̃] m ❶ ou au pl (*action*) amusement; (*passe-temps*) pastime ❷ MUS divertissement

**divinité** [divinite] f ❶ sans pl (*caractère divin*) divinity ❷ (*dieu*) deity

**diviser** [divize] <1> I. vt (*fractionner,*

**D**

**D**

*désunir*) *a.* MATH ~ **qc en qc** to divide sth into sth **II.** *vpr* ➊ (*se séparer*) **se ~ en qc** (*cellule, route*) to divide into sth; (*parti*) to split into sth ➋ (*être divisible*) **se ~** (*nombre*) to divide; (*ouvrage*) to divide (up)

**division** [divizjɔ̃] *f* ➊ division ➋ *Québec* (*service intermédiaire entre la direction et la section d'une entreprise*) division (*of a company*)

**divorce** [divɔʀs] *m* divorce

**divorcé(e)** [divɔʀse] **I.** *adj* ~ **de qn** divorced from sb **II.** *m(f)* divorcee

**divorcer** [divɔʀse] <2> *vi* ~ **de qn** to divorce sb

**divulguer** [divylge] <1> *vt* to disclose; ~ **un secret à qn** to tell sb a secret

**dix** [dis, *devant une voyelle* diz, *devant une consonne* di] **I.** *adj* ten **II.** *m inv* ten; *v.a.* **cinq**

**dix-huit** [dizɥit, *devant une consonne* dizɥi] **I.** *adj* eighteen **II.** *m inv* eighteen; *v.a.* **cinq**

**dix-huitième** [dizɥitjɛm] <dix-huitièmes> **I.** *adj antéposé* eighteenth **II.** *mf* **le/la ~** the eighteenth **III.** *m* (*fraction*) eighteenth; *v.a.* **cinquième**

**dixième** [dizjɛm] **I.** *adj antéposé* tenth **II.** *mf* **le/la ~** the tenth **III.** *m* (*fraction*) tenth; **les neuf ~s des gens** nine out of ten people; *v.a.* **cinquième**

**dix-neuf** [diznœf] **I.** *adj* nineteen **II.** *m inv* nineteen; *v.a.* **cinq**

**dix-neuvième** [diznœvjɛm] <dix-neuvièmes> **I.** *adj antéposé* nineteenth **II.** *mf* **le/la ~** the nineteenth **III.** *m* (*fraction*) nineteenth; *v.a.* **cinquième**

**dix-sept** [dissɛt] **I.** *adj* seventeen **II.** *m inv* seventeen; *v.a.* **cinq**

**dix-septième** [dissɛtjɛm] <dix-septièmes> **I.** *adj antéposé* seventeenth **II.** *mf* **le/la ~** the seventeenth **III.** *m* (*fraction*) seventeenth; *v.a.* **cinquième**

**dizaine** [dizɛn] *f* ➊ (*environ dix*) **une ~ de personnes/pages** ten people/pages or so ➋ (*âge approximatif*) **avoir une ~ d'années** to be around ten

**djeuns, djeun's, djeunz** [dʒœns] *mpl inf* kids, teens

**do** [do] *m inv* C; ~ **dièse/bémol** C sharp/flat

**docile** [dɔsil] *adj* docile

**docker** [dɔkɛʀ] *m* docker

**docteur** [dɔktœʀ] *mf* doctor

**doctrine** [dɔktʀin] *f* doctrine

**document** [dɔkymɑ̃] *m* ➊ document ➋ (*preuve*) piece of evidence

**documentaire** [dɔkymɑ̃tɛʀ] **I.** *adj* documentary **II.** *m* documentary

**documentation** [dɔkymɑ̃tasjɔ̃] *f* documentation

**documenter** [dɔkymɑ̃te] <1> **I.** *vt* ~ **qn sur qn/qc** to provide sb with full information on sb/sth **II.** *vpr* **se ~ sur qn/qc** to inform oneself fully on sb/sth

**dodo** [dodo] *m enfantin, inf* **faire ~** (*s'endormir*) to go night-night; (*dormir*) to be in dreamland

**doigt** [dwa] *m* ANAT (*de la main, d'un gant*) finger ▸ **je suis à un ~ de le faire** I'm this close to doing it

**doigté** [dwate] *m* ➊ MUS fingering ➋ (*savoir-faire*) adroitness

**dois** [dwa] *indic prés de* **devoir**

**doit** [dwa] **I.** *indic prés de* **devoir II.** *m* debit

**doivent** [dwav] *indic et subj prés de* **devoir**

**dollar** [dɔlaʀ] *m* dollar

**dolmen** [dɔlmɛn] *m* dolmen, portal tomb

**D.O.M.** [dɔm] *m abr de* **département d'outre-mer** French overseas department

**domaine** [dɔmɛn] *m* ➊ (*terre*) estate ➋ (*sphère*) field ➌ INFORM domain

**domestique** [dɔmɛstik] **I.** *adj* ➊ (*ménager: vie, affaires, ennuis*) domestic; **animal ~** pet ➋ ECON (*marché*) domestic **II.** *mf* servant

**domicile** [dɔmisil] *m* ➊ (*demeure*) home ➋ ADMIN residence ➌ **travail-/visite à ~** home working/visit

**domicilier** [dɔmisilje] <1> *vt form* **être domicilié à Paris** to reside in Paris

**dominant(e)** [dɔminɑ̃, ɑ̃t] *adj* (*position, nation*) dominant; (*opinion, vent*) prevailing

**dominateur, -trice** [dɔminatœʀ, -tʀis] *adj* dominating

**domination** [dɔminasjɔ̃] *f* (*suprématie*) domination

**dominer** [dɔmine] <1> **I.** *vt* ❶ (*être le maître de*) to dominate ❷ (*contrôler: larmes, chagrin*) to suppress; (*sujet*) to be master of ❸ (*surpasser*) to outclass ❹ (*surplomber*) to look over ❺ (*être plus fort que*) ~ **le tumulte** (*orateur, voix*) to make oneself heard above the commotion **II.** *vi* ❶ (*prédominer, commander*) a. SPORT to dominate ❷ (*commander sur les mers*) to rule **III.** *vpr* **se** ~ to take hold of oneself

**dommage** [dɔmaʒ] *m* ❶ (*préjudice*) harm; ~ **et intérêts** damages ❷ *pl* (*dégâts*) damage ► **c'est bien** ~! it's such a shame!; **quel** ~! what a shame!

**dompter** [dɔ̃(p)te] <1> *vt* (*cheval, fauve*) to tame; (*rebelles, imagination, passions, peur*) to subdue

**dompteur, -euse** [dɔ̃(p)tœʀ, -øz] *m, f* tamer

**D.O.M.-T.O.M.** [dɔmtɔm] *mpl abr de* **départements et territoires d'outre- -mer** French overseas departments and territories

**don** [dɔ̃] *m* (*action, cadeau, aptitude*) gift; (*charitable*) donation; ~ **d'organe** organ donation

**donateur, -trice** [dɔnatœʀ, -tʀis] *m, f* donor

**donation** [dɔnasjɔ̃] *f* donation

**donc** [dɔ̃k] *conj* so

**donné(e)** [dɔne] *adj* (*déterminé*) given ► **étant** ~ **qc** given that

**donnée** [dɔne] *f gén pl* ❶ (*élément d'appréciation*) given ❷ ECOLE ~**s du problème** details of the problem ❸ *pl* INFORM, ADMIN data

**donner** [dɔne] <1> **I.** *vt* ❶ (*remettre*) ~ **qc à qn** to give sth to sb, to give sb sth ❷ (*communiquer*) ~ **le bonjour à qn** to say hello to sb ❸ (*causer*) **ça donne faim/soif** it makes you hungry/thirsty ❹ (*conférer*) **cette couleur te donne un air sévère** that color makes you look strict ❺ (*attribuer*) ~ **de l'impor-**

tance à qn/qc to give importance to sb/sth ❻ (*produire*) ~ **des résultats** (*recherches*) to give results ❼ (*faire passer pour*) ~ **qc pour certain** to say sth is a certainty **II.** *vi* (*s'ouvrir sur*) ~ **sur qc** (*pièce, fenêtre*) to look (out) onto sth; (*porte*) to open out to sth **III.** *vpr* ❶ (*se dévouer*) **se** ~ **à qn/qc** to devote oneself to sb/sth ❷ (*faire l'amour*) **se** ~ **à qn** to give oneself to sb

**donneur, -euse** [dɔnœʀ, -øz] *m, f* a. MED donor

**dont** [dɔ̃] *pron rel* ❶ *compl d'un subst* **cet acteur,** ~ **le dernier film** that actor, whose latest film ❷ *compl d'un ver* **la femme** ~ **vous me parlez** the woman you are telling me about ❸ (*partie d'un tout*) including

**dopage** [dɔpaʒ] *m* drug use

**doper** [dɔpe] <1> **I.** *vt* ❶ (*stimuler*) to stimulate; (*économie*) to boost; (*ventes*) to beef up *inf* ❷ SPORT to give drugs to **II.** *vpr* **se** ~ to use drugs

**doré** [dɔʀe] *m Québec* (*poisson d'eau douce à chair estimée*) yellow pike

**doré(e)** [dɔʀe] *adj* ❶ (*avec de l'or*) gilded ❷ (*de couleur ressemblant à de l'or, agréable*) golden; **prison** ~**e** gilded cage

**dorénavant** [dɔʀenavɑ̃] *adv* henceforth

**dorer** [dɔʀe] <1> **I.** *vt* ❶ (*recouvrir d'or, colorer*) to gild ❷ CULIN (*gâteau*) to brown **II.** *vi* CULIN to brown **III.** *vpr* **se faire** ~ **au soleil** to sunbathe

**dormeur, -euse** [dɔʀmœʀ, -øz] *m, f* sleeper

**dormir** [dɔʀmiʀ] *vi irr* ❶ (*sommeiller*) to sleep ❷ (*être négligé: capitaux, affaire*) to lie dormant ❸ (*être calme, sans bruit: maison, nature*) to be asleep

**dortoir** [dɔʀtwaʀ] *m* dormitory

**doryphore** [dɔʀifɔʀ] *m* Colorado potato beetle

**dos** [do] *m* (*d'une personne, d'un objet*) back ► **en avoir plein le** ~ *inf* to be fed up; **faire qc dans le** ~ **de qn** to do sth behind sb's back

**dosage** [dozaʒ] *m* MED dosage; *fig* mixture

**dose** [doz] f ❶ BIO dose ❷ CULIN part

**doser** [doze] <1> vt ❶ BIO (médicament) to measure a dose of; (ingrédients) to measure out; (cocktail) to mix in the right proportions ❷ (mesurer) to use just the right amount of

**dosette** [dozɛt] f (sachet, minidose) pod; ~ **de café** coffee pod

**dossier** [dosje] m ❶ (appui pour le dos) back ❷ (classeur) a. ADMIN file; ~ **de candidature** application

**douane** [dwan] f ❶ (administration, poste) customs pl ❷ (droit) (customs) duty

**douanier, -ière** [dwanje, -jɛʀ] I. adj customs II. m, f customs officer

**doublage** [dublaʒ] m ❶ CINE (en langue étrangère) dubbing; (pour les cascades) doubling ❷ COUT lining

**double** [dubl] I. adj double; ~ **personnalité** split personality II. adv (voir) double III. m ❶ (quantité) twice the amount ❷ (copie, exemplaire identique) copy; (personne) double; **un ~ de clé** a spare key ❸ SPORT doubles pl

**doublé(e)** [duble] adj ❶ COUT (vêtement) lined ❷ CINE (en langue étrangère) dubbed

**doubler** [duble] <1> I. vt ❶ (multiplier par deux) to double ❷ (mettre en double: papier) to fold (in two); (fil) to double ❸ (garnir intérieurement) to line ❹ Belgique (redoubler) ~ **une classe** to repeat a year ❺ CINE (en langue étrangère) to dub; (pour les cascades) to double ❻ THEAT ~ **qn** to stand in for ❼ (dépasser: véhicule) to pass II. vi (être multiplié par deux: nombre, prix) to double III. vpr **se** ~ **de qc** to be coupled with sth

**doublure** [dublyʀ] f ❶ COUT (d'un vêtement) lining ❷ CINE stand-in ❸ THEAT understudy

**douce** [dus] v. **doux**

**doucement** [dusmɑ̃] adv ❶ (avec précaution) carefully ❷ (sans bruit) quietly ❸ (avec délicatesse, graduellement) gently ❹ (faiblement) softly ❺ (médiocrement) not so well

**douceur** [dusœʀ] f ❶ (sensation: d'une étoffe, musique, de la lumière) softness; (d'un fruit) sweetness; (de la température) mildness ❷ (sentiment: d'un caractère, de la vie) sweetness ❸ gén pl (friandises) sweets; (plat sucré) desserts ❹ pl (amabilités) sweet words

**douche** [duʃ] f shower

**doucher** [duʃe] <1> I. vt ❶ (tremper) to shower ❷ (décevoir: enthousiasme) to drown II. vpr **se** ~ to have a shower

**doué(e)** [dwe] adj gifted

**douillet(te)** [dujɛ, jɛt] adj ❶ (sensible) (over)sensitive ❷ (pleurnicheur) susceptible ❸ (confortable: logis, nid, lit) cozy

**douleur** [dulœʀ] f ❶ (physique) pain ❷ (moral) sorrow

**douloureux, -euse** [duluʀø, -øz] adj (qui fait mal, qui fait de la peine) painful

**doute** [dut] m doubt ► **mettre qc en** ~ to put sth in doubt

**douter** [dute] <1> I. vi ❶ (être incertain) ~ **de qc** to doubt sth ❷ (se méfier) ~ **de qn/qc** to have doubts about sb/sth II. vpr (pressentir) **se** ~ **de qc** to suspect sth

**douteux, -euse** [dutø, -øz] adj ❶ (incertain) doubtful ❷ péj (goût, mœurs) dubious; (vêtement) none too clean

**doux** [du] m (temps) the mild weather

**doux, douce** [du, dus] adj ❶ (au toucher, à l'oreille, à la vue) soft ❷ (au goût: fruit, saveur, vin) sweet; (piment, moutarde, tabac) mild; **les drogues douces** soft drugs ❸ (à l'odorat: odeur, parfum) sweet ❹ (clément: climat, temps) mild ❺ (gentil, patient: personne) kind ❻ (modéré: peine) mild; (croissance) gradual; (fiscalité) moderate; (gestes, pente) gentle; **à feu** ~ on moderate heat ❼ (agréable: vie, souvenir, visage) sweet ► **en douce** inf on the quiet

**douzaine** [duzɛn] f ❶ (douze) dozen ❷ (environ douze) **une** ~ **de personnes/choses** twelve or so people/things

**douze** [duz] **I.** *adj inv* twelve **II.** *m inv* twelve; *v.a.* **cinq**

**douzième** [duzjɛm] **I.** *adj antéposé* twelfth **II.** *mf* **le/la** ~ the twelfth **III.** *m* twelfth; *v.a.* **cinquième**

**doyen(ne)** [dwajɛ̃, jɛn] *m(f)* ❶ (*aîné*) doyen ❷ UNIV dean

**dragée** [dʀaʒe] *f* sugared almond

**dragon** [dʀagɔ̃] *m* dragon

**draguer** [dʀage] <1> **I.** *vt* ❶ (*pêcher*) to use a dragnet to fish for ❷ (*dégager: chenal, sable*) to dredge; (*mines*) to sweep ❸ *inf* (*racoler*) to hit on sb **II.** *vi inf* (*racoler*) to try to pick people up

**dragueur** [dʀagœʀ] *m* dredger

**drainer** [dʀene] <1> *vt* ❶ MED, AGR to drain ❷ (*rassembler: capitaux*) to tap

**dramatique** [dʀamatik] *adj* dramatic

**dramatiser** [dʀamatize] <1> **I.** *vt* to dramatize **II.** *vi* to overdramatize

**drame** [dʀam] *m a. fig* (*pièce*) drama; **tourner au** ~ to take a tragic turn

**drap** [dʀa] *m* ❶ (*linge: de lit*) sheet ❷ *Belgique* (*serviette*) towel

**drapeau** [dʀapo] <x> *m* flag

**draper** [dʀape] <1> **I.** *vt* (*envelopper, plisser*) ~ **qc/qn de qc** to drape sb/sth in sth **II.** *vpr* **se** ~ **dans une cape** to drape oneself in a cloak

**dressage** [dʀesaʒ] *m* ❶ (*domptage: d'un animal*) taming; (*pour un concours hippique*) dressage ❷ (*montage*) putting up

**dresser** [dʀese] <1> **I.** *vt* ❶ (*établir: bilan, liste, carte, procuration*) to draw up ❷ (*ériger: barrière, monument*) to raise; (*échafaudage, tente*) to put up ❸ (*lever: buste*) to draw up; (*menton, tête*) to lift up; (*oreilles*) to prick up ❹ (*disposer: plat*) to lay out; (*piège*) to set; (*autel*) to raise ❺ (*dompter: animal*) to tame; (*chien*) to train; *péj* (*enfant, soldat*) to break in ❻ (*mettre en opposition*) ~ **qn contre qn/qc** to set sb against sb/sth **II.** *vpr* ❶ (*se mettre droit*) **se** ~ to draw oneself up ❷ (*s'élever*) **se** ~ (*bâtiment, statue*) to rise ❸ (*s'insurger*) **se** ~ **contre qn/qc** to rise against sb/sth

**dresseur, -euse** [dʀesœʀ, -øz] *m, f* trainer

**drogue** [dʀɔg] *f a. fig* drug

**drogué(e)** [dʀɔge] *m(f)* (drug) addict

**droguer** [dʀɔge] <1> **I.** *vt* to drug **II.** *vpr* **se** ~ to take drugs

**droguerie** [dʀɔgʀi] *f* hardware store

**droit** [dʀwa] **I.** *adv* straight ▶ **tout** ~ straight ahead **II.** *m* ❶ (*prérogative*) right; **avoir le** ~ **de** +*infin* to be entitled to +*infin* ❷ JUR (*règles*) law; ~ **civil/public** civil/public law ❸ *pl* (*taxe*) tax ❹ (*à la boxe*) right

**droit(e)** [dʀwa, dʀwat] *adj* ❶ (*opp: gauche*) right ❷ (*non courbe, non penché: chemin, ligne, nez*) straight; **angle** ~ right angle ❸ (*honnête, loyal: personne*) upright

**droite** [dʀwat] *f* ❶ MATH straight line ❷ (*côté droit*) *a.* POL right; **un parti de** ~ a right-wing party; **à** ~ on the right

**droitier, -ière** [dʀwatje, -jɛʀ] **I.** *m, f* (*personne*) right handed person **II.** *adj inf* POL right-wing

**drôle** [dʀol] *adj* funny

**drôlement** [dʀolmɑ̃] *adv* ❶ (*bizarrement*) in a funny way ❷ *inf* (*rudement*) really

**D.R.O.M.** [dʀɔm] *mpl v.* **départements et régions d'outre-mer** overseas departments and regions

**dru(e)** [dʀy] *adj* (*barbe, herbe*) thick

**du** [dy] = **de + le** *v.* **de**

**dû** [dy] <dus> *m* due

**dû, due** [dy] <dus> **I.** *part passé de* **devoir II.** *adj* ❶ (*que l'on doit*) owed ❷ (*imputable*) **être** ~ **à qc** to be due to sth ❸ (*mérité*) **être** ~ **à qn** to be sb's due

**duc** [dyk] *m* duke

**duchesse** [dyʃɛs] *f* duchess

**duel** [dɥɛl] *m a. fig* duel

**dune** [dyn] *f* dune

**duo** [dɥo, dyo] *m* MUS duct

**duper** [dype] <1> *vt* to fool

**duplex** [dyplɛks] *m* ❶ ARCHIT **appartement en** ~ duplex ❷ CINE, TV linkup

**duquel, de laquelle** [dykɛl] <desquel(le)s> = **de + lequel** *v.* **lequel**

**dur(e)** [dyʀ] **I.** *adj* ❶ (*ferme*) hard; (*porte, serrure*) stiff; (*viande*) tough; (*sommeil*) heavy ❷ (*difficile, pénible: travail, obligation, vie, climat*) hard ❸ (*sévère: regard, critique*) harsh **II.** *adv* (*travailler*) hard **III.** *m(f)* ❶ (*personne inflexible*) hard man, woman *m, f* ❷ *inf* (*personne sans peur*) hard case ❸ TECH **maison en ~** traditionally built house

**durable** [dyʀabl] *adj* (*chose, construction*) durable; (*souvenir, effet, influence*) lasting

**durant** [dyʀɑ̃] *prep* ❶ (*au cours de*) during ❷ (*tout au long de*) **travailler sa vie ~** to work all one's life

**durcir** [dyʀsiʀ] <8> **I.** *vt* to harden; (*acier*) to temper **II.** *vi* (*aliment, pâte*) to harden; (*colle, peinture*) to set **III.** *vpr* **se ~** to harden; (*colle*) to set

**durée** [dyʀe] *f* ❶ duration; **les chômeurs de longue ~** the long-term unemployed ❷ (*permanence*) durability

**durer** [dyʀe] <1> *vi* ❶ + *compl de temps* (*avoir une certaine durée, se prolonger*) to last ❷ (*se conserver: personne*) to endure; (*matériel, vêtement*) to last ▸ **pourvu que ça dure!** let's hope it lasts!

**dureté** [dyʀte] *f* ❶ (*fermeté*) hardness ❷ (*rigueur*) harshness

**dus** [dy] *passé simple de* **devoir**

**duvet** [dyvɛ] *m* ❶ (*plumes, poils*) down ❷ (*sac de couchage*) sleeping bag

**DVD** [devede] *m inv* INFORM *abr de* **Digital Versatile Disc** DVD

**dynamique** [dinamik] **I.** *adj* dynamic **II.** *f* dynamic

**dynamiser** [dinamize] <1> *vt* to inject dynamism into

**dynamisme** [dinamism] *m* dynamism

**dynamite** [dinamit] *f* dynamite

**dynamiter** [dinamite] <1> *vt* to dynamite

**dynamo** [dinamo] *f* dynamo

**dynastie** [dinasti] *f* dynasty

# Ee

**E, e** [ø] *m inv* E, e; **~ comme Eugène** (*au téléphone*) e as in Echo

**eau** [o] <x> *f* water; **~ minérale/de source** mineral/spring water; **~ du robinet** tap water

**eau-de-vie** [od(ə)vi] <eaux-de-vie> *f* brandy

**ébahir** [ebaiʀ] <8> *vt* to astonish

**ébauche** [eboʃ] *f* (*d'une œuvre*) outline; (*d'un tableau*) sketch; (*d'un sourire*) flicker

**ébéniste** [ebenist] *mf* cabinetmaker

**éberlué(e)** [ebɛʀlye] *adj inf* dumbfounded

**éblouir** [ebluiʀ] <8> *vt* to dazzle

**éblouissant(e)** [ebluisɑ̃, ɑ̃t] *adj* ❶ (*aveuglant*) dazzling ❷ (*merveilleux: forme*) stunning

**éboueur** [ebuœʀ] *m* garbage man

**ébouillanter** [ebujɑ̃te] <1> *vpr* **s'~ qc** to scald sth

**ébouriffé(e)** [eburife] *adj* disheveled

**ébranler** [ebʀɑ̃le] <1> **I.** *vt* to shake **II.** *vpr* **s'~** (*convoi*) to set off; (*train*) to move off

**ébréché(e)** [ebʀeʃe] *adj* chipped

**ébriété** [ebʀijete] *f form* drunkenness

**ébruiter** [ebʀɥite] <1> *vt, vpr* (**s'**)**~** to spread

**ébullition** [ebylisjɔ̃] *f* (*d'un liquide*) boiling; **porter à ~** to bring to a boil

**écaille** [ekaj] *f* ❶ ZOOL scale ❷ (*petite particule*) **se détacher par ~s** (*peinture*) to flake off ❸ (*matière*) tortoiseshell

**écarquiller** [ekaʀkije] <1> *vt* **~ les**

**yeux devant qc** to stare wide-eyed at sth

**écart** [ekaʀ] *m* ❶(*distance*) gap ❷(*différence: de prix, cours*) difference ❸(*contradiction*) discrepancy ❹(*mouvement brusque*) **faire un ~** (*personne*) to move out of the way ▸ **mettre qn à l'~** to keep sb out of the way

**écarté(e)** [ekaʀte] *adj* ❶(*isolé: lieu*) out of the way ❷(*distant: bras*) spread out; (*dents*) spaced; (*jambes*) wide apart

**écartement** [ekaʀtəmã] *m* spread; (*des rails*) gauge

**écarter** [ekaʀte] <1> I. *vt* ❶(*séparer: objets*) to move apart; (*rideaux*) to pull open; (*bras*) to open; (*doigts, jambes*) to spread out ❷(*exclure: plan*) to rule out; (*objection*) to overrule; (*idée*) to brush aside; (*danger*) to remove; **~ qn de qc** to exclude sb from sth ❸(*éloigner*) **~ qn de qc** to move sb away from sth; *fig* to keep sb away from sth ❹*Québec* (*perdre*) to mislay II. *vpr* ❶(*se séparer*) **s'~** (*foule*) to move aside ❷(*s'éloigner*) **s'~ de qc** to move out of the way of sth ❸*Québec* (*s'égarer*) to get lost

**ecclésiastique** [eklezjastik] I. *adj* ecclesiastical; (*vie*) religious II. *m* clergyman

**échafaudage** [eʃafodaʒ] *m* ❶(*construction*) scaffolding ❷(*empilement*) pile

**échalote** [eʃalɔt] *f* shallot

**échancré(e)** [eʃãkʀe] *adj* (*robe*) with a low neckline

**échancrure** [eʃãkʀyʀ] *f* (*d'une robe*) low neckline

**échange** [eʃãʒ] *m* ❶(*action d'échanger*) **~ de qc contre qc** exchanging sth for sth; **en ~ de qc** in exchange for sth ❷*gén pl* ECON trade ❸ECOLE **~s scolaires** (school) exchange programs

**échanger** [eʃãʒe] <2a> *vt* (*adresses, idées, anneaux*) to exchange; (*timbres*) to swap; (*marchandises*) to trade

**échangeur** [eʃãʒœʀ] *m* interchange

**échantillon** [eʃãtijõ] *m* sample

**échappatoire** [eʃapatwaʀ] *f* ❶(*subterfuge*) loophole ❷(*issue*) way out

**échapper** [eʃape] <1> I. *vi* ❶(*s'enfuir*) **~ à qn** to escape from sb; **~ à un danger** to escape danger ❷(*se soustraire à*) **~ à qc** to avoid sth ❸(*être oublié*) **son nom m'échappe** his/her name escapes me ❹(*ne pas être remarqué*) **~ à** [*o* **à l'attention de**] **qn** to escape sb's attention ❺(*ne pas être compris*) **le problème lui échappe** he doesn't grasp the problem ❻(*glisser des mains*) **laisser ~ qc** to drop sth ❼(*dire par inadvertance*) **~ à qn** (*gros mot, paroles*) to slip out II. *vpr* ❶(*s'évader*) **s'~ de qc** to escape from sth ❷(*s'esquiver*) **s'~ de qc** to get away from sth ❸(*sortir*) **s'~ de qc** (*fumée, cri*) to come from sth; (*gaz*) to escape from sth; (*flammes*) to rise from sth III. *vt Québec* (*laisser tomber involontairement*) to drop

**écharde** [eʃaʀd] *f* splinter

**écharpe** [eʃaʀp] *f* ❶(*vêtement*) scarf ❷(*étoffe servant d'insigne: du maire*) sash ❸(*bandage*) sling

**échasse** [eʃɑs] *f* stilt

**échauffer** [eʃofe] <1> *vpr* **s'~** ❶SPORT to warm up ❷(*s'énerver*) to get heated

**échéance** [eʃeãs] *f* ❶(*date limite*) **date d'~** (*pour une dette*) due date; (*d'un bon*) maturity date; (*pour un travail*) deadline ❷(*délai*) time; FIN term ❸(*règlement*) payment due

**échec**[1] [eʃɛk] *m* failure

**échec**[2] [eʃɛk] *m pl* (*jeu*) chess + *vb sing*; **jouer aux ~s** to play chess ▸ (*être*) **~ et mat** to be checkmate

**échelle** [eʃɛl] *f* ❶(*escabeau, hiérarchie*) ladder ❷(*proportion, rapport, graduation*) scale; **à l'~ de 1:100 000** on a scale of 1 to 100,000; **à l'~ nationale/communale** on a national/local level

**échelon** [eʃlõ] *m* ❶(*barreau*) rung ❷ADMIN (*de la hiérarchie*) grade; **gravir un ~** to go up a grade

**échelonner** [eʃ(ə)lɔne] <1> I. *vt* ❶(*étaler: paiements*) to spread out ❷(*graduer: difficultés*) to graduate; **~ les sa-**

E

**laires** to set up a salary scale ❸ (*disposer à intervalles réguliers*) to space out II. *vpr* s'~ **sur deux ans** to be spread out over two years

**échine** [eʃin] *f* ❶ (*colonne vertébrale*) spine ❷ CULIN chine

**échiquier** [eʃikje] *m* chess board

**écho** [eko] *m* ❶ (*réflexion sonore: d'une montagne*) echo ❷ (*rubrique*) gossip column ❸ (*effet*) reaction; (*dans la presse*) coverage

**échographie** [ekɔgrafi] *f* (ultrasound) scan

**échouer** [eʃwe] <1> I. *vi* to fail II. *vt* **faire ~ qc** to wreck sth

**éclabousser** [eklabuse] <1> *vt* to splash

**éclair** [eklɛʀ] I. *m* ❶ METEO lightning flash ❷ PHOT flash ❸ CULIN éclair ❹ (*bref moment*) ~ **de lucidité** lucid moment ▸ **en un ~** in a flash II. *app inv* **visite ~** flying visit

**éclairage** [eklɛʀaʒ] *m* lighting

**éclaircie** [eklɛʀsi] *f* METEO sunny spell

**éclaircir** [eklɛʀsiʀ] <8> I. *vt* ❶ (*rendre clair*) to lighten ❷ (*élucider: situation*) to clarify; (*meurtre, énigme*) to solve; (*affaire*) to clear up II. *vpr* ❶ (*se dégager*) s'~ (*temps*) to brighten up ❷ (*rendre plus distinct*) s'~ **la gorge** [*o* **la voix**] to clear one's throat ❸ (*devenir compréhensible*) s'~ (*idée*) to become clear; (*mystère*) to be cleared up

**éclairer** [eklere] <1> I. *vt* ❶ (*fournir de la lumière*) to light (up) ❷ (*laisser passer la lumière*) ~ **une pièce** to give light to a room ❸ (*expliquer: texte*) to clarify ❹ (*instruire*) ~ **un collègue sur qn/qc** to enlighten a colleague about sb/sth II. *vi* to give light III. *vpr* ❶ (*se fournir de la lumière*) s'~ **à l'électricité/au gaz** to have electric/gas lighting ❷ (*devenir lumineux*) s'~ (*visage*) to light up ❸ (*se clarifier*) s'~ (*situation*) to become clear

**éclat** [ekla] *m* ❶ (*fragment*) splinter ❷ (*bruit*) ~ **de joie** joyful outburst ❸ (*scandale*) fuss ❹ (*luminosité: d'un métal*) shine; (*d'un astre*) brightness; (*d'une couleur*) brilliance; (*d'un dia-*

*mant*) sparkle ▸ **rire aux ~s** to laugh out loud

**éclatant(e)** [eklatɑ̃, ɑ̃t] *adj* ❶ (*radieux: beauté, santé*) radiant ❷ (*remarquable: exemple*) shining; (*succès*) brilliant; (*victoire*) resounding; (*revanche*) spectacular

**éclater** [eklate] <1> I. *vi* ❶ (*exploser: bombe*) to explode ❷ (*déborder, crever: tête, pneu*) to burst ❸ (*se fragmenter: structure*) to break up; (*verre*) to shatter ❹ (*commencer: orage*) to break out ❺ (*survenir brusquement: nouvelle*) to break ❻ (*retentir: cris*) to go up; (*coup de feu, détonation*) to ring out; ~ **de rire** to burst out laughing ❼ (*se manifester*) **laisser ~ sa colère** to explode with anger ❽ (*s'emporter*) to explode II. *vpr inf* (*se défouler*) s'~ to have a great time

**éclipse** [eklips] *f* eclipse

**écluse** [eklyz] *f* lock

**écœurant(e)** [ekœʀɑ̃, ɑ̃t] *adj* ❶ (*trop sucré*) cloying ❷ (*trop gras*) heavy ❸ (*physiquement*) revolting ❹ (*moralement*) disgusting ❺ (*décourageant: facilité, injustice*) sickening ▸ **en ~** Québec (*très, beaucoup*) fantastically

**écœurement** [ekœʀmɑ̃] *m* ❶ (*nausée*) nausea ❷ (*dégoût*) disgust ❸ (*découragement*) **ressentir un immense ~** to feel thoroughly sick

**écœurer** [ekœʀe] <1> I. *vi* (*dégoûter*) to be sickening II. *vt* ❶ (*dégoûter*) ~ **qn** to make sb feel sick ❷ (*indigner*) to revolt ❸ (*décourager: injustice, déception*) to sicken

**école** [ekɔl] *f* school; ~ **primaire** [*o* **élémentaire**]/**secondaire** elementary/secondary school; ~ **publique** public school; **aller à l'~** to go to school; **renvoyer qn de l'~** to expel sb from school

**écolier, -ière** [ekɔlje, -jɛʀ] *m, f* schoolboy, schoolgirl *m, f*

**écolo** [ekɔlo] I. *m, f inf abr de* **écologiste** tree-hugger II. *adj inf abr de* **écologique**

**écologie** [ekɔlɔʒi] *f* ecology

**écologique** [ekɔlɔʒik] *adj* (*catastrophe,*

*solution*) ecological; (*société*) environmentally friendly

**écologiste** [ekɔlɔʒist] **I.** *m, f* ❶ (*ami de la nature, spécialiste de l'écologie*) ecologist ❷ POL environmentalist **II.** *adj* (*pratique*) environmentally friendly; (*politique, mouvement, groupe*) environmental; (*parti*) green

**économe** [ekɔnɔm] *adj* **être ~** to be thrifty

**économie** [ekɔnɔmi] *f* ❶ (*vie économique*) economy; **~ de marché** market economy ❷ (*science*) economics ❸ (*gain*) saving ❹ *pl* (*épargne*) savings

**économique** [ekɔnɔmik] *adj* ❶ (*bon marché*) economical ❷ (*qui a rapport à l'économie*) economic

**économiser** [ekɔnɔmize] <1> **I.** *vi* (*mettre de l'argent de côté*) to save; (*dépenser moins*) to economize **II.** *vt* to save

**économiseur** [ekɔnɔmizœr] *m* INFORM **~ d'écran** screen saver

**écorce** [ekɔrs] *f* ❶ BIO (*d'un arbre*) bark; (*d'un fruit*) rind ❷ GEO **~ terrestre** earth's crust

**écorcher** [ekɔrʃe] <1> **I.** *vt* ❶ (*égratigner*) **être écorché** (*genou*) to be grazed; (*visage*) to be scratched ❷ (*faire mal*) **~ les oreilles** to grate on one's ears ❸ (*déformer: nom*) to mispronounce; (*vérité*) to distort **II.** *vpr* (*s'égratigner*) **s'~** to get scratched

**écorchure** [ekɔrʃyr] *f* scratch

**écossais** [ekɔsɛ] *m* ❶ (*gaélique*) Gaelic ❷ (*du sud*) Scots; *v.a.* **français**

**écossais(e)** [ekɔsɛ, ɛz] *adj* Scottish; **jupe ~e** kilt

**Écossais(e)** [ekɔsɛ, ɛz] *m(f)* Scot; **un ~ a** Scotsman; **une ~ e** a Scotswoman

**Écosse** [ekɔs] *f* **l'~** Scotland

**écotourisme** [ekɔturism] *m* ecotourism

**écoulement** [ekulmã] *m* ❶ (*évacuation: d'un liquide*) outflow ❷ (*mouvements du temps*) passing ❸ COM (*des stocks*) movement; (*des produits*) sale

**écouler** [ekule] <1> **I.** *vt* ❶ COM (*marchandises*) to sell ❷ (*mettre en circulation: faux billets*) to circulate **II.** *vpr* **s'~**

❶ (*s'épancher: liquide*) to flow ❷ (*passer: temps*) to pass ❸ (*disparaître: fonds*) to get spent ❹ (*se vendre: marchandises*) to be sold

**écourter** [ekurte] <1> *vt* ❶ (*raccourcir*) to shorten ❷ (*abréger: séjour, attente*) to cut short ❸ (*tronquer*) **être écourté** (*citation*) to be curtailed

**écouter** [ekute] <1> **I.** *vt* ❶ (*prêter l'oreille*) **~ qn/qc** to listen to sb/sth; **~ qn chanter** to listen to sb sing ❷ (*tenir compte de*) **~ qn/qc** to take notice of sb/sth ❸ (*obéir*) **~ qn** to listen to sb **II.** *vi* to listen **III.** *vpr* (*s'observer avec complaisance*) **trop s'~** to take a bit too much care of oneself

**écouteur** [ekutœr] *m* ❶ (*récepteur: du téléphone*) handset ❷ *pl* (*casque*) earphones *pl*

**écran** [ekrã] *m* ❶ (*protection*) shield ❷ TV, CINE, INFORM screen; **à l'~** TV on TV; CINE on the screen; **~ à cristaux liquides** liquid crystal display

**écrasant(e)** [ekrazã, ãt] *adj* (*accablant: poids*) unbearable; (*nombre*) overwhelming; (*défaite*) crushing

**écraser** [ekraze] <1> **I.** *vt* ❶ (*broyer*) to crush; (*légumes*) to mash; (*cigarette*) to stub out ❷ (*appuyer fortement sur*) **~ la pédale d'accélérateur** to step hard on the accelerator ❸ (*tuer*) **~ qn/qc** (*conducteur*) to run sb/sth over; (*avalanche*) to crush sb/sth ❹ (*accabler*) **~ qn** (*douleur*) to weigh sb down; (*impôt*) to overburden sb **II.** *vi inf* (*ne pas insister*) to shut up **III.** *vpr* ❶ (*heurter de plein fouet*) **s'~ au** [*o* **sur le**] **sol/contre un arbre** to crash into the ground/a tree ❷ (*se crasher*) **s'~** to crash ❸ (*se serrer*) **s'~ dans qc** to be crushed in sth; **s'~ contre le mur/sur le sol** to be crushed up against the wall/on the ground ❹ *inf* (*se taire*) **s'~ devant qn** to shut up in front of sb ❺ (*ne pas protester*) to keep one's mouth shut

**écrevisse** [ekrəvis] *f* crayfish

**écrier** [ekrije] <1> *vpr* **s'~** to cry out

**écrire** [ekrir] *irr* **I.** *vt* ❶ (*tracer, inscrire,*

*rédiger*) ~ **qc dans/sur qc** to write sth in/on sth ❷ (*orthographier*) **comment écrit-on ce mot?** how do you spell that word? **II.** *vi* (*tracer, rédiger*) to write **III.** *vpr* **s'~** to be spelt

**écrit** [ekʀi] *m* ❶ (*document*) written document ❷ (*ouvrage*) text ❸ (*épreuve, examen*) written paper

**écriteau** [ekʀito] <x> *m* sign

**écriture** [ekʀityʀ] *f* ❶ (*façon d'écrire*) handwriting ❷ (*alphabet, style*) writing

**écrivain** [ekʀivɛ̃] *m* writer

**écrou** [ekʀu] *m* nut

**écrouer** [ekʀue] <1> *vt* to imprison

**écrouler** [ekʀule] <1> *vpr* **s'~** ❶ (*tomber: maison*) to collapse; (*arbre, rocher*) to fall down ❷ (*baisser brutalement: cours de la bourse*) to collapse ❸ (*prendre fin brutalement: empire, projet, gouvernement, théorie*) to collapse; (*fortune*) to vanish ❹ (*s'affaler*) to collapse

**écumer** [ekyme] <1> **I.** *vt* ❶ (*enlever l'écume*) to skim ❷ (*piller: région*) to plunder **II.** *vi* ❶ (*se couvrir d'écume*) to foam ❷ (*baver*) to foam at the mouth ❸ (*suer*) to lather ❹ (*être furieux*) ~ **de colère** [*o* **rage**] to foam at the mouth

**écureuil** [ekyʀœj] *m* squirrel

**écurie** [ekyʀi] *f* stable

**édenté(e)** [edɑ̃te] *adj* toothless

**EDF** [ødeɛf] *f abr de* **Électricité de France** French electricity company

**édifice** [edifis] *m* ❶ (*bâtiment*) building ❷ (*ensemble organisé*) edifice

**éditer** [edite] <1> *vt* to publish

**éditeur** [editœʀ] *m* INFORM editor

**éditeur, -trice** [editœʀ, -tʀis] **I.** *adj* **maison éditrice** publishing house **II.** *m, f* publisher

**édition** [edisjɔ̃] *f* ❶ (*publication: d'un disque*) issue; (*d'un livre*) edition ❷ (*livre*) edition ❸ (*métier*) **l'~** publishing ❹ (*établissement*) **les ~s** publishers *pl* ❺ PRESSE (*tirage*) edition ❻ INFORM editing

**éditique** [editik] *m* INFORM desktop publishing

**éditorial** [editɔʀjal, -jo] <-aux> *m* editorial

**édredon** [edʀədɔ̃] *m* eiderdown

**éducateur, -trice** [edykatœʀ, -tʀis] **I.** *adj* (*fonction*) educational **II.** *m, f* educator

**éducatif, -ive** [edykatif, -tiv] *adj* (*jeu, méthode*) educational; (*système*) education

**éducation** [edykasjɔ̃] *f* ❶ (*pédagogie*) education ❷ (*bonnes manières*) (good) manners

**éduquer** [edyke] <1> *vt* (*former*) to educate

**effacé(e)** [efase] *adj* ❶ (*estompé: couleur*) faded ❷ (*discret: rôle, personne*) self-effacing; (*manière*) retiring

**effacer** [efase] <2> **I.** *vt* ❶ (*faire disparaître: trace*) to erase; (*tache*) to remove; (*avec du correcteur*) to white out ❷ (*supprimer une information: tableau noir*) to clean; (*disquette*) to wipe; (*texte sur écran*) to delete ❸ (*faire oublier*) to erase; (*crainte*) to dispel; (*faute*) to wipe away **II.** *vpr* **s'~** ❶ (*s'estomper: crainte*) to be dispelled ❷ (*se laisser enlever: tache*) to go ❸ (*se faire petit*) to be unobtrusive

**effaceur** [efasœʀ] *m* eraser pen

**effectif** [efɛktif] *m* (*d'une armée, d'un parti*) strength; (*d'une entreprise*) staff

**effectif, -ive** [efɛktif, -iv] *adj* (*aide*) real; (*pouvoir*) effective; (*travail*) actual

**effectivement** [efɛktivmɑ̃] *adv* ❶ (*concrètement: aider, travailler*) effectively ❷ (*réellement*) actually

**effectuer** [efɛktɥe] <1> **I.** *vt* (*faire: investissement*) to make; (*parcours*) to do; (*réforme*) to carry out **II.** *vpr* **s'~** (*mouvement, paiement*) to be made; (*parcours*) to be done; (*transaction*) to be carried out

**effervescence** [efɛʀvesɑ̃s] *f* ❶ (*bouillonnement*) effervescence ❷ (*agitation*) agitation

**effervescent(e)** [efɛʀvesɑ̃, ɑ̃t] *adj* ❶ (*pétillant: liquide, comprimé*) effervescent ❷ (*tumultueux*) turbulent

**effet** [efɛ] *m* ❶ (*résultat*) effect ❷ (*im-*

*pression*) impression ❸ (*phénomène*) effect; **~ de serre** greenhouse effect ▶ **en** ~ indeed; (*pour justifier ses propos*) as a matter of fact; (*pour confirmer le propos d'un tiers*) that's right

**efficace** [efikas] *adj* effective; (*personne*) efficient

**efficacité** [efikasite] *f* (*d'une méthode*) effectiveness; (*d'une personne, machine*) efficiency

**effleurer** [eflœʀe] <1> *vt* ❶ (*toucher*) to brush against; (*aborder: sujet*) to touch on ❷ (*passer par la tête*) ~ **qn** to occur to sb

**effondrement** [efɔ̃dʀəmɑ̃] *m* ❶ (*écroulement*) collapse ❷ (*fin brutale: d'une civilisation, d'un projet*) collapse; (*des prix*) slump; (*d'une fortune*) melting away

**effondrer** [efɔ̃dʀe] <1> *vpr* **s'~** ❶ (*s'écrouler: pont*) to collapse; (*plancher, sol*) to cave in ❷ (*être anéanti: empire, civilisation, preuve, argumentation*) to collapse; (*projet*) to fall through; (*fortune*) to melt away ❸ (*baisser brutalement: cours de la bourse*) to slump ❹ (*craquer: personne*) to break down ❺ INFORM (*ordinateur*) to crash

**efforcer** [efɔʀse] <2> *vpr* **s'~ de** +*infin* to endeavor to +*infin*

**effort** [efɔʀ] *m* effort ▶ **faire un ~ sur soi-même pour** +*infin* to force oneself to +*infin*

**effraction** [efʀaksjɔ̃] *f* ❶ (*cambriolage*) break-in ❷ (*accusation*) breaking and entering

**effrayant(e)** [efʀεjɑ̃, ɑ̃t] *adj* ❶ (*qui fait peur*) frightening; (*silence*) dreadful ❷ *inf* (*extrême: prix*) terrifying

**effrayer** [efʀeje] <7> I. *vt* (*faire très peur à*) to terrify II. *vpr* (*craindre*) **s'~ de qc** to be scared of sth

**effréné(e)** [efʀene] *adj* wild

**effronté(e)** [efʀɔ̃te] I. *adj* impudent II. *m(f)* impudent individual

**effroyable** [efʀwajabl] *adj* ❶ (*épouvantable*) appalling ❷ *inf* (*incroyable*) dreadful

**égal(e)** [egal, -o] <-aux> I. *adj* ❶ (*de même valeur*) equal; **de prix ~** at the same price ❷ (*sans variation*) **être d'humeur ~e** to be even-tempered II. *m(f)* equal; **considérer qn comme son ~** to consider sb as one's equal ▶ **négocier d'~ à ~** to negotiate on equal terms

**également** [egalmɑ̃] *adv* ❶ (*pareillement*) equally ❷ (*aussi*) also

**égaler** [egale] <1> *vt* ❶ MATH **deux plus deux égale(nt) quatre** two plus two is four ❷ (*être pareil*) to equal

**égalisation** [egalizasjɔ̃] *f* ❶ (*nivellement*) leveling (out) ❷ SPORT tying

**égaliser** [egalize] <1> I. *vt* ❶ (*rendre égal*) to equal (out); (*revenus*) to level (out); (*cheveux*) to trim II. *vi* to equalize III. *vpr* **s'~** to level (out)

**égalité** [egalite] *f* ❶ (*absence de différences*) equality; (*des adversaires*) even match ❷ (*absence de variations*) **~ d'humeur** even temper ❸ MATH equality

**égard** [egaʀ] *m pl* consideration ▶ **à l'~ de qn** towards sb

**égaré(e)** [egaʀe] *adj* ❶ (*perdu*) lost ❷ (*troublé*) distraught

**égarer** [egaʀe] <1> I. *vt* ❶ (*induire en erreur*) to mislead ❷ (*perdre*) to misplace ❸ (*faire perdre la raison*) ~ **qn** to make sb distraught II. *vpr* (*se perdre*) **s'~** to get lost ❷ (*divaguer*) **s'~** to wander

**églantine** [eglɑ̃tin] *f* dog rose

**églefin** [egləfɛ̃] *m* haddock

**église** [egliz] *f* ❶ (*édifice*) church ❷ (*communauté*) **l'Église protestante/catholique** the Protestant/Catholic Church

**égoïsme** [egɔism] *m* selfishness

**égoïste** [egɔist] I. *adj* selfish II. *mf* selfish person

**égorger** [egɔʀʒe] <2a> I. *vt* ❶ (*couper la gorge*) ~ **qn/un animal avec qc** to cut sb's/an animal's throat ❷ *inf* (*ruiner*) to bleed dry II. *vpr* **s'~** to cut each other's throats

E

**égout** [egu] *m* sewer; **bouche d'**~ manhole

**égoutter** [egute] <1> **I.** *vt* (**faire**) ~ **qc** to drain sth **II.** *vpr* **s'**~ (*feuilles, linge*) to drip; (*vaisselle*) to drain

**égouttoir** [egutwar] *m* ~ **à vaisselle** dish drainer

**égratigner** [egratiɲe] <1> **I.** *vt* to scratch **II.** *vpr* **s'**~ **le genou** to scratch one's knee

**égratignure** [egratiɲyr] *f* scratch

**égyptien** [eʒipsjɛ̃] *m* Egyptian Arabic; *v.a.* **français**

**égyptien(ne)** [eʒipsjɛ̃, jɛn] *adj* Egyptian

**Égyptien(ne)** [eʒipsjɛ̃, jɛn] *m(f)* Egyptian

**eh** [e, ɛ] *interj* hey; ~ **bien!** *inf* well well!

**éjecter** [eʒɛkte] <1> *vt* ❶ (*rejeter: machine*) to eject ❷ *inf* (*expulser*) to kick out

**élaboration** [elabɔrasjɔ̃] *f* (*composition: d'un plan*) working out

**élaborer** [elabɔre] <1> **I.** *vt* (*composer: plan*) to work out **II.** *vpr* **s'**~ to develop

**élan** [elɑ̃] *m* ❶ (*mouvement*) **prendre son** ~ to build up speed; (*en courant*) to take a run up ❷ (*accès: de tendresse*) surge; (*d'enthousiasme*) burst

**élancé(e)** [elɑ̃se] *adj* slender

**élancement** [elɑ̃smɑ̃] *m* shooting [*o* sharp] pain

**élancer**[1] [elɑ̃se] <2> *vi* **ma jambe m'élance** I have shooting pains in my leg

**élancer**[2] [elɑ̃se] <2> *vpr* ❶ (*se précipiter*) **s'**~ **vers qn/qc** to rush up to sb/sth ❷ (*prendre son élan*) **s'**~ to take a run-up

**élargir** [elarʒir] <8> **I.** *vt* ❶ (*rendre plus large*) to widen ❷ cout (*jupe*) to let out ❸ (*développer: horizon, débat*) to broaden **II.** *vpr* **s'**~ (*fleuve*) to widen; (*chaussures*) to give; (*horizon*) to broaden (out) **III.** *vi* (*pull*) to stretch out

**élargissement** [elarʒismɑ̃] *m* ❶ (*action: d'une route, de chaussures*) widening; (*d'une jupe*) letting out; (*d'un débat*) broadening out; (*d'une majorité, de l'Union européenne*) enlargement ❷ (*fait de s'élargir: d'un canal, d'une route*) widening; (*de l'Union européenne*) enlargement

**élasticité** [elastisite] *f* elasticity

**élastique** [elastik] **I.** *adj* elastic; (*pas*) springy; (*loi*) flexible **II.** *m a.* cout elastic; (*bracelet*) rubber band

**électeur, -trice** [elɛktœr, -tris] *m, f* voter

**élection** [elɛksjɔ̃] *f* ❶ election ❷ (*choix*) **patrie/pays d'**~ adopted homeland/country

**électoral(e)** [elɛktɔral, -o] <-aux> *adj* electoral

**électorat** [elɛktɔra] *m* electorate

**électricien(ne)** [elɛktrisjɛ̃, jɛn] *m(f)* electrician

**électricité** [elɛktrisite] *f* electricity

**électrique** [elɛktrik] *adj* (*cuisinière, moteur*) electric; **centrale** ~ power plant

**électriser** [elɛktrize] <1> *vt* to electrify

**électrocardiogramme** [elɛktrokardjɔgram] *m* electrocardiogram

**électrocuter** [elɛktrɔkyte] <1> **I.** *vt* **être électrocuté** to be electrocuted **II.** *vpr* **s'**~ **avec qc** to get electrocuted with sth

**électroménager** [elɛktromenaʒe] **I.** *adj* **appareil** ~ (household) appliance **II.** *m* ❶ (*appareils*) household appliances *pl* ❷ (*commerce*) household appliances *pl*

**électronicien(ne)** [elɛktrɔnisjɛ̃, jɛn] *m(f)* electrical engineer

**électronique** [elɛktrɔnik] **I.** *adj* electronic **II.** *f* electronics + *vb sing*

**élégance** [elegɑ̃s] *f sans pl* elegance

**élégant(e)** [elegɑ̃, ɑ̃t] *adj* elegant

**élément** [elemɑ̃] *m* ❶ (*composant, donnée, groupe*) *a.* chim element ❷ (*mobilier*) unit ❸ *pl* (*rudiments*) ~**s de composition** elementary composition

**élémentaire** [elemɑ̃tɛr] *adj* elementary

**éléphant** [elefɑ̃] *m* elephant

**élevage** [el(ə)vaʒ] *m* ❶ (*action*) breed-

ing ❷ (*ensemble d'animaux*) animals *pl*
❸ (*exploitation*) farm
**élève** [elɛv] *mf* pupil
**élevé(e)¹** [el(ə)ve] *adj* ❶ (*haut*) high
❷ (*noble: conversation*) elevated; (*opinion*) high
**élevé(e)²** [el(ə)ve] **I.** *adj* (*éduqué*)
**bien/mal ~** well/badly brought up
**II.** *m(f)* **mal ~** rude individual
**élever¹** [el(ə)ve] <4> **I.** *vt* ❶ (*ériger: monument, mur*) to erect ❷ (*porter vers le haut*) to raise up ❸ (*porter plus haut: niveau, voix*) to raise ❹ (*promouvoir*) **~ qn au rang de ...** to elevate sb to the rank of ... ❺ (*susciter: critique, doute*) to express; (*objection*) to raise **II.** *vpr* ❶ (*être construit*) **s'~** (*mur, édifice*) to go up ❷ (*se dresser*) **s'~ à 10/100 mètres** (*plateau*) to rise to 10/100 meters ❸ (*se faire entendre*) **s'~** to rise up ❹ (*surgir*) **s'~** (*discussion, doutes*) to arise ❺ (*se chiffrer*) **s'~ à 1000 euros** to come to 1000 euros ❻ (*s'opposer à*) **s'~ contre qc** to protest against sth
**élever²** [el(ə)ve] <4> *vt* ❶ (*prendre soin de: personne*) to bring up, to raise ❷ (*éduquer*) to educate ❸ (*faire l'élevage de: vaches*) to breed; (*volaille*) to farm
**éleveur, -euse** [el(ə)vœʀ, -øz] *m, f* breeder
**éliminatoire** [eliminatwaʀ] **I.** *adj* ❶ ECOLE, UNIV (*note, faute*) failing; **épreuve ~** qualifying exam ❷ SPORT preliminary **II.** *f souvent pl* preliminary (heat)
**éliminer** [elimine] <1> **I.** *vt* ❶ (*supprimer*) to eliminate; (*tartre*) to remove; (*pièces défectueuses*) to get rid of ❷ (*tuer*) to liquidate ❸ SPORT **~ qn de la course** to eliminate sb from the race; (*pour dopage*) to disqualify sb from the race ❹ ECON (*déchets*) to dispose of **II.** *vpr* **s'~ facilement** (*tache*) to be easy to remove
**élire** [eliʀ] *vt irr* to elect
**élite** [elit] *f* elite; **université d'~** elite university

**elle** [ɛl] *pron pers* ❶ (*personne*) she; (*chose*) it; **~ est grande** (*femme*) she's tall; (*objet*) it's big ❷ *interrog, non traduit* **Sophie a-t-~ ses clés?** does Sophie have her keys? *v.a.* **il** ❸ (*répétitif*) **regarde la lune comme ~ est ronde** look how big the moon is; *v.a.* **il** ❹ *inf* (*pour renforcer*) **c'est ~ qui l'a dit** she's the one who said so ❺ *avec une préposition* **avec/sans ~** with/without her; **à ~ seule** on her own; **c'est à ~!** it's hers! ❻ *dans une comparaison* her; **il est comme ~** he is like her ❼ (*soi*) herself; *v.a.* **lui**
**elle-même** [ɛlmɛm] *pron pers* (*elle en personne*) herself; (*chose*) itself; *v.a.* **lui-même**
**elles** [ɛl] *pron pers* ❶ (*fém pl*) they; **~ sont grandes** (*personnes*) they're tall; (*choses*) they're big ❷ *interrog, non traduit* **les filles, sont-~ venues?** have the girls come? ❸ (*répétitif*) **regarde les fleurs comme ~ sont belles** look how pretty the flowers are; *v.a.* **il** ❹ *inf* (*pour renforcer*) **~, elles n'ont pas ouvert la bouche** THEY didn't open their mouths; **il veut les aider, ~?** he wants to help THEM? ❺ *avec une préposition* **avec/sans ~** with/without them ❻ *dans une comparaison* them; **ils sont comme ~** they're like them ❼ (*soi*) themselves; *v.a.* **elle**
**elles-mêmes** [ɛlmɛm] *pron pers* (*elles en personne*) themselves; *v.a.* **moi-même, nous-même**
**elliptique** [eliptik] *adj* elliptic; (*tournure, formule*) elliptical; **vélo ~** elliptical machine
**éloge** [elɔʒ] *m* (*louange*) praise
**élogieux, -euse** [elɔʒjø, -jøz] *adj* (*paroles*) complimentary
**éloigné(e)** [elwaɲe] *adj* ❶ (*dans l'espace*) **~ de qc** a long way from sth ❷ (*isolé*) remote ❸ (*dans le temps, la parenté*) distant ❹ (*différent*) **~ de qc** far (removed) from sth
**éloignement** [elwaɲmã] *m* ❶ (*distance*) **l'~** distance ❷ (*séparation d'avec*)

**E**

l'~ **de qn** removal of sb ❸ *(fait de se te-nir à l'écart)* ~ **de qc** keeping away from sth

**éloigner** [elwaɲe] <1> **I.** *vt* ❶ *(mettre à distance: objet)* to move away; *(person-ne)* to take away ❷ *(détourner)* ~ **qn du sujet** to move sb away from the subject ❸ *(dans le temps)* **chaque jour qui passe nous éloigne de notre jeunesse** every passing day takes us further away from our youth ❹ *(écarter: soupçons)* to dispel; *(danger)* to ward off ❺ *(détacher)* ~ **qn de qn** to estrange sb from sb **II.** *vpr* ❶ *(devenir de plus en plus lointain)* **s'~** *(nuages)* to go away; *(bruit)* to fade into the distance; *(vent, tempête)* to pass over ❷ *(aller ailleurs)* **s'~** to move away ❸ *(aller plus loin)* **ne t'éloigne pas trop, s'il te plaît!** don't go too far away, please! ❹ *(dans le temps)* **s'~ de qc** to get further away from sth ❺ *(s'estomper)* **s'~** *(souvenir)* to fade; *(danger)* to pass ❻ *(s'écarter de qc)* **s'~ du sujet** to wander off the subject

**élu(e)** [ely] **I.** *part passé de* **élire II.** *adj* elected **III.** *m(f)* ❶ POL elected representative ❷ REL **les ~s** the elect

**élucider** [elyside] <1> *vt* to elucidate

**Élysée** [elize] *m* **l'~** the Élysée (Palace) *(the official residence of the French President)*

**e-mail** [imel] <e-mails> *m* e-mail

**émail** [emaj, emo] <-aux> *m* a. ANAT enamel; **en ~** enameled

**émaillé(e)** [emaje] *adj (revêtu d'émail)* enameled

**émancipé(e)** [emɑ̃sipe] *adj* emancipated

**émanciper** [emɑ̃sipe] <1> *vpr* **s'~** to become emancipated

**emballage** [ɑ̃balaʒ] *m* ❶ *(en papier)* wrapping ❷ *(conditionnement)* packaging

**emballer** [ɑ̃bale] <1> **I.** *vt* ❶ *(empaqueter avec du papier)* to wrap; *(empaqueter dans un conditionnement rigide)* to package ❷ *inf (enthousiasmer)* **être emballé par qc** to be turned on by sth

❸ AUTO *(moteur)* to race ❹ *inf (séduire)* to pull **II.** *vpr* ❶ *inf (s'enthousiasmer)* **s'~ pour qc** to get turned on by sth ❷ *inf (s'emporter)* **s'~** to get worked up ❸ *(partir à une allure excessive)* **s'~** *(animal)* to bolt; *(moteur)* to race

**embarcadère** [ɑ̃baʁkadɛʁ] *m* pier

**embarcation** [ɑ̃baʁkasjɔ̃] *f* boat, craft

**embarquement** [ɑ̃baʁkəmɑ̃] *m* ❶ *(chargement: des marchandises)* loading ❷ NAUT embarkation ❸ AVIAT ~ **immédiat, porte 5!** immediate boarding, gate 5!

**embarquer** [ɑ̃baʁke] <1> **I.** *vi* ❶ ~ **dans l'avion** to board the plane ❷ *Québec (monter)* ~ **dans l'auto-bus/dans une voiture** to get on the bus/into a car **II.** *vt* ❶ *(prendre à bord d'un bateau)* to embark; *(marchandises)* to load ❷ *(à bord d'un véhicule: passagers)* to take on board; *(animaux)* to load ❸ *(voler)* to swipe ❹ *inf (arrêter: voleur)* to cart off **III.** *vpr* ❶ *(monter à bord d'un bateau)* **s'~** to board ❷ *(s'engager)* **s'~ dans qc** to get involved in sth

**embarras** [ɑ̃baʁa] *m* ❶ *(gêne)* embarrassment ❷ *(tracas)* trouble

**embarrassant(e)** [ɑ̃baʁasɑ̃, ɑ̃t] *adj* ❶ *(délicat)* awkward ❷ *(ennuyeux: situation)* uncomfortable ❸ *(encombrant)* cumbersome

**embarrassé(e)** [ɑ̃baʁase] *adj* ❶ *(gêné: personne)* self-conscious; *(air, sourire)* embarrassed ❷ *(encombré)* ~ **de qc** *(personne)* burdened with sth; *(couloir)* cluttered with sth

**embarrasser** [ɑ̃baʁase] <1> **I.** *vt* ❶ *(déconcerter)* ~ **qn** to put sb in an awkward position ❷ *(tracasser)* to bother ❸ *(gêner dans ses mouvements)* to hamper ❹ *(encombrer: couloir)* to clutter **II.** *vpr* ❶ *(s'encombrer)* **s'~ de qn/qc** to burden oneself with sb/sth ❷ *(se soucier)* **s'~ de qc** to trouble oneself with sth

**embaucher** [ɑ̃boʃe] <1> **I.** *vt* ECON ~ **qn** to hire sb, to take sb on **II.** *vi* to hire workers, to take on workers

**embellir** [ābeliʀ] <8> I. *vi* to grow more attractive II. *vt* (*personne*) to make more attractive; (*maison, ville*) to beautify; (*réalité*) to embellish

**embêtant** [ābɛtã] *m inf* **l'~, c'est qu'il est sourd** the trouble is he's deaf

**embêtant(e)** [ābɛtã, ãt] *adj inf* ❶ (*agaçant: personne*) annoying ❷ (*fâcheux*) awkward

**embêter** [ābete] <1> I. *vt inf* ❶ (*importuner, contrarier*) to bother ❷ (*casser les pieds*) to pester II. *vpr inf* ❶ (*s'ennuyer*) **s'~** to be bored ❷ (*se démener*) **s'~ à faire qc** to go to the trouble of doing sth

**emboîter** [ābwate] <1> I. *vt* to fit together II. *vpr* **des choses s'emboîtent les unes dans les autres** things fit into each other

**embouchure** [ābuʃyʀ] *f* ❶ GEO mouth ❷ MUS embouchure ❸ (*mors*) mouthpiece

**embourber** [ābuʀbe] <1> I. *vt* **~ qc** to get sth stuck II. *vpr* ❶ (*s'enliser*) **s'~** to get stuck ❷ (*s'empêtrer*) **s'~ dans qc** to get bogged down in sth ❸ (*s'enfoncer*) **s'~ dans qc** to sink into sth

**embouteillage** [ābutɛjaʒ] *m* AUTO traffic jam

**emboutir** [ābutiʀ] <8> *vt* AUTO to bang into

**embranchement** [ābʀãʃmã] *m* ❶ (*point de jonction*) junction ❷ (*ramification*) fork

**embrasser** [ābʀase] <1> I. *vt* ❶ (*donner un baiser*) to kiss ❷ (*saluer*) **je t'/ vous embrasse** (with) love ❸ (*prendre dans les bras*) to embrace II. *vpr* **s'~** ❶ (*donner un baiser*) to kiss (each other) ❷ (*prendre dans ses bras*) to embrace

**embrayage** [ābʀɛjaʒ] *m* clutch

**embrayer** [ābʀeje] <7> *vi* ❶ AUTO (*conducteur*) to put into gear ❷ (*commencer à parler*) **~ sur qn/qc** to get started on sb/sth

**embrouillé(e)** [ābʀuje] *adj* muddled

**embrouiller** [ābʀuje] <1> I. *vt* ❶ (*rendre confus: chose*) to tangle ❷ (*faire perdre le fil: personne*) to muddle II. *vpr* **s'~** to get muddled

**embûches** [ābyʃ] *fpl* pitfall

**embuer** [ābɥe] <1> *vt* **~ qc** to mist sth up

**éméché(e)** [emeʃe] *adj inf* tipsy

**émeraude** [emʀod] I. *adj inv* emerald (green) II. *f* emerald

**émerger** [emɛʀʒe] <2a> *vi* ❶ (*sortir*) **~ de qc** (*plongeur*) to come up from sth; (*soleil*) to come out from sth ❷ (*être apparent*) to stand out ❸ *inf* (*se réveiller*) to emerge ❹ (*sortir du stress*) to get one's head above water

**émerveiller** [emɛʀveje] <1> I. *vt* **~ qn** to make sb marvel II. *vpr* **s'~ de** [*o* **devant**] **qc** to marvel at sth

**émetteur** [emetœʀ] *m* CINE, TV transmitter; LING speaker

**émetteur, -trice** [emetœʀ, -tʀis] I. *adj* ❶ CINE, TV **poste ~** transmitter ❷ FIN issuing II. *m, f* FIN (*d'un chèque*) drawer

**émettre** [emɛtʀ] *irr* I. *vi* CINE, TV to broadcast II. *vt* ❶ (*produire: son, lumière*) to give out; (*odeur*) to give off; (*radiations*) to emit ❷ (*formuler: opinion*) to express; (*hypothèse*) to put forward ❸ FIN to issue; (*chèque*) to write

**émeute** [emøt] *f* riot

**émietter** [emjete] <1> *vt, vpr* **s'~** to crumble

**émigrant(e)** [emigʀã, ãt] *m(f)* emigrant

**émigration** [emigʀasjõ] *f* emigration

**émigré(e)** [emigʀe] *m(f)* emigrant

**émigrer** [emigʀe] <1> *vi* to emigrate

**émincer** [emɛ̃se] <2> *vt* to slice thinly

**émission** [emisjõ] *f* ❶ CINE, TV program ❷ PHYS emission ❸ FIN issuing; (*d'un chèque*) writing ❹ (*à la poste: d'un timbre-poste*) issue

**emmêler** [āmele] <1> I. *vt* ❶ (*enchevêtrer*) to tangle II. *vpr* ❶ (*s'enchevêtrer*) **o'** to get tangled ❷ (*s'embrouiller*) **s'~ dans un récit** to muddle up a story

**emménagement** [āmenaʒmã] *m* **après l'~** after moving in

**emménager** [āmenaʒe] <2a> *vi*

~ **dans un appartement** to move into an apartment

**emmener** [ɑ̃m(ə)ne] <4> vt ❶(*conduire*) ~ **qn au cinéma** to take sb to the movies ❷ *inf* (*prendre avec soi, emporter*) to take ❸(*comme prisonnier*) to take away

**emmerdeur, -euse** [ɑ̃mɛʀdœʀ, -øz] *m, f inf* pain in the ass

**emmitoufler** [ɑ̃mitufle] <1> I. *vt* **être emmitouflé dans qc** to be all wrapped up in sth II. *vpr* **s'~ dans qc** to wrap oneself up in sth

**émotif, -ive** [emɔtif, -iv] *adj* (*personne*) emotional

**émotion** [emosjɔ̃] *f* ❶(*surprise, chagrin*) shock ❷(*joie*) joy ❸(*sentiment*) emotion ►~**s fortes** strong sensations

**émoustiller** [emustije] <1> *vt* to titillate

**émouvant(e)** [emuvɑ̃, ɑ̃t] *adj* moving

**émouvoir** [emuvwaʀ] *irr* I. *vt* ❶(*bouleverser*) to move ❷(*changer de sentiment*) **se laisser ~ par qn/qc** to be moved by sb/sth II. *vpr* **s'~ de qc** to be moved by sth

**empaillé(e)** [ɑ̃paje] *adj* (*rempli de paille: animal*) stuffed; (*siège*) straw-bottomed

**empaqueter** [ɑ̃pak(ə)te] <3> *vt* to pack

**emparer** [ɑ̃paʀe] <1> *vpr* ❶(*saisir*) **s'~ de qc** (*pour le tenir*) to take hold of sth; (*pour l'emporter*) to grab sth ❷(*conquérir*) **s'~ d'un marché** to take over a market ❸(*envahir*) **s'~ de qn** to take hold of sb

**empêchement** [ɑ̃pɛʃmɑ̃] *m* **j'ai eu un ~** sth came up

**empêcher** [ɑ̃peʃe] <1> I. *vt* (*faire obstacle à, ne pas permettre*) to prevent; ~ **que qn fasse qc** (*subj*), ~ **qn de faire qc** to prevent sb from doing sth II. *vpr* **je ne peux pas m'~ de le faire** I can't help myself from doing it

**empereur** [ɑ̃pʀœʀ] *m* emperor; *v.a.* **impératrice**

**empester** [ɑ̃pɛste] <1> I. *vi* to stink II. *vt* ❶(*empuantir*) to stink out ❷(*répandre une mauvaise odeur de*) ~ **qc** to stink of sth

**empêtrer** [ɑ̃petʀe] <1> *vpr* **s'~ dans qc** to get tangled up in sth

**empiéter** [ɑ̃pjete] <5> *vi* ❶(*usurper, déborder dans l'espace*) ~ **sur qc** to encroach on sth ❷(*déborder dans le temps*) to overlap

**empiffrer** [ɑ̃pifʀe] <1> *vpr inf* **s'~ de qc** to stuff oneself with sth

**empiler** [ɑ̃pile] <1> *vt, vpr* (**s'**)~ to pile up

**empire** [ɑ̃piʀ] *m* POL empire

**empirer** [ɑ̃piʀe] <1> *vi* to worsen

**emplacement** [ɑ̃plasmɑ̃] *m* ❶(*endroit*) site ❷(*place*) position; (*d'un tombeau*) site ❸(*dans un parking*) space

**emplettes** [ɑ̃plɛt] *fpl* **faire des ~** to do some shopping

**emploi** [ɑ̃plwa] *m* ❶(*poste*) job; ~ **à mi-temps/à plein temps** part-time/full-time job ❷ ECON l'~ employment; **être sans ~** to be unemployed ❸(*utilisation*) *a.* LING use ► ~ **du temps** schedule; ECOLE timetable

**employé(e)** [ɑ̃plwaje] *m(f)* employee; ~ **de banque/de bureau** bank/office worker

**employer** [ɑ̃plwaje] <6> I. *vt* ❶(*faire travailler*) to employ ❷(*utiliser*) *a.* LING to use II. *vpr* ❶ LING **s'~** to be used ❷(*se consacrer*) **s'~ à faire qc** to apply oneself to do sth

**employeur, -euse** [ɑ̃plwajœʀ, -jøz] *m, f* employer

**empocher** [ɑ̃pɔʃe] <1> *vt* (*argent*) to pocket

**empoigner** [ɑ̃pwaɲe] <1> I. *vt* (*personne*) to grab II. *vpr* **s'~** to exchange blows

**empoisonnement** [ɑ̃pwazɔnmɑ̃] *m* ❶(*intoxication*) food poisoning ❷ *sans pl* (*crime*) poisoning ❸(*meurtre*) poisoning ❹ *gén pl, inf* (*tracas*) nuisance

**empoisonner** [ɑ̃pwazɔne] <1> I. *vt* ❶(*intoxiquer*) to poison ❷(*contenir du poison*) **être empoisonné** to be poisoned ❸(*être venimeux*) **être empoi-**

**sonné** (*propos*) to be venomous ④ (*gâter*) **elle m'empoisonne la vie** she makes my life miserable ⑤ (*empuantir*) **~ l'air** to make a stench ⑥ *inf* (*embêter*) **~ qn avec qc** to drive sb crazy with sth II. *vpr* ① (*s'intoxiquer*) **s'~ avec qc** to poison oneself with sth ② *inf* (*s'ennuyer*) **qu'est-ce qu'on s'empoisonne ici!** what a drag this is!

**emporter** [ɑ̃pɔʀte] <1> I. *vt* ① (*prendre avec soi*) to take away ② (*enlever*) to take away; (*blessé*) to carry away ③ (*transporter*) **~ qn vers qc** to take sb off to sth ④ (*entraîner, arracher*) **~ qc** (*vent*) to carry sth off ▸ **l'~ sur qn** to beat sb II. *vpr* **s'~ contre qn/qc** to get angry with sth

**empreinte** [ɑ̃pʀɛ̃t] *f* ① (*trace*) prints; **~s digitales** fingerprints ② (*marque durable*) mark

**empressement** [ɑ̃pʀɛsmɑ̃] *m* attentiveness

**empresser** [ɑ̃pʀese] <1> *vpr* ① (*se hâter de*) **s'~ de** +*infin* to hasten to +*infin* ② (*faire preuve de zèle*) **s'~ auprès de qn** to make a fuss over sb

**emprisonner** [ɑ̃pʀizɔne] <1> *vt* ① (*incarcérer*) to imprison ② (*enfermer*) **~ qn/un animal dans qc** to lock sb/an animal up in sth ③ (*serrer fermement*) to hold; (*main, bras*) to grip ④ (*enlever toute liberté*) **~ qn/qc par qc** to trap sb/sth in sth

**emprunt** [ɑ̃pʀœ̃] *m* ① (*somme, objet*) loan ② (*emprunt public*) borrowing

**emprunter** [ɑ̃pʀœ̃te] <1> I. *vi* FIN to borrow II. *vt* ① (*se faire prêter, imiter*) to borrow ② (*prendre: passage souterrain, autoroute*) to take

**ému(e)** [emy] *adj* moved

**émulation** [emylasjɔ̃] *f a.* INFORM emulation

**émuler** [emyle] <1> *vt* INFORM to emulate

**en** [ɑ̃] I. *prep* ① (*lieu*) in; **~ mer** at sea; **~ bateau** in a boat; **être ~ 5e** to be in the seventh grade ② (*direction*) to; **aller ~ ville/France** to go to town/France ③ (*date, moment*) in; **~ semaine** during the week; **de jour ~ jour** from day to day ④ (*manière d'être, de faire*) **être ~ bonne/mauvaise santé** to be in good/bad health; **être parti ~ voyage** to be away on a trip ⑤ (*transformation: changer, convertir*) into; (*se déguiser*) as ⑥ (*en tant que*) as ⑦ *gérondif* (*simultanéité*) **~ sortant** on one's way out ⑧ *gérondif* (*condition*) by ⑨ *gérondif* (*concession*) while ⑩ *gérondif* (*manière*) **~ chantant/courant** singing/running ⑪ (*état, forme*) in; **du café ~ grains**/**poudre** coffee beans/instant coffee ⑫ (*fait de*) **c'est ~ laine/bois** it's wool/wood ⑬ (*moyen de transport*) by; **~ train**/**voiture** by train/car ⑭ (*partage, division*) in ⑮ (*pour indiquer le domaine*) in ⑯ *après certains verbes* **croire ~ qn** to believe in sb; **parler ~ son nom** to speak in sb's name ▸ **s'~ aller** to go away; **~ plus** besides II. *pron* ① *non traduit* (*pour des indéfinis, des quantités*) **as-tu un stylo? – oui, j'~ ai un/non, je n'~ ai pas** do you have a pen? – yes, I do/no I don't ② *tenant lieu de subst* **j'~ connais qui feraient mieux de ...** some people would do well to ... ③ (*de là*) **j'~ viens** I've just been there ④ (*de cela*) **j'~ ai besoin** I need it ⑤ (*à cause de cela*) **elle ~ est malade** it has made her sick

**encadré** [ɑ̃kadʀe] *m* box

**encadrement** [ɑ̃kadʀəmɑ̃] *m* ① (*cadre*) frame ② (*prise en charge*) training

**encadrer** [ɑ̃kadʀe] <1> *vt* ① (*mettre dans un cadre*) to frame ② (*entourer*) to put a border around; (*annonce, éditorial*) to (put in a) box; (*visage*) to frame; (*cible*) to draw a circle around ③ (*s'occuper de*) to supervise; (*diriger*) to lead ④ MIL to straddle ⑤ *inf* (*dans un carambolage*) **~ qc** to smash into sth

**encaisser** [ɑ̃kese] <1> I. *vi* ① (*toucher de l'argent*) to get one's money ② *inf* (*savoir prendre des coups*) to take it II. *vt* ① (*percevoir*) to receive; (*chèque*) to cash ② *inf* (*recevoir, supporter*) to take; **c'est dur à ~** it's hard to take ▸ **je**

E

**ne peux <u>pas</u> les ~** *inf* I can't stand them

**en-cas** [ɑ̃ka] *m inv* snack

**encastrable** [ɑ̃kastRabl] *adj* built-in

**encastrer** [ɑ̃kastRe] <1> I. *vt* **~ qc dans/sous qc** to build sth in/under sth II. *vpr* **s'~ dans/sous qc** to be fitted in/under sth; (*automobile*) to jam under sth

**enceinte**¹ [ɑ̃sɛ̃t] *adj* **être ~ de qn** to be pregnant by sb; **être ~ de trois mois** to be three months pregnant

**enceinte**² [ɑ̃sɛ̃t] *f* **①** (*fortification, rempart*) (surrounding) wall **②** (*espace clos*) enclosure; (*d'une foire, d'un parc naturel*) area **③** (*haut-parleur*) speaker

**encens** [ɑ̃sɑ̃] *m* incense

**encercler** [ɑ̃sɛRkle] <1> *vt* **①** (*entourer, être disposé autour de*) to surround **②** (*cerner*) to encircle

**enchaînement** [ɑ̃ʃɛnmɑ̃] *m* **①** (*succession, structure logique*) sequence **②** (*transition*) **~ entre qc et qc** progression from one thing to another

**enchaîner** [ɑ̃ʃene] <1> I. *vt* **①** (*attacher avec une chaîne*) **~ des personnes l'une à l'autre** to chain people to each other **②** (*mettre bout à bout: idées*) to link up II. *vpr* **①** (*s'attacher avec une chaîne*) **des personnes s'enchaînent à qc/l'une à l'autre** people chain themselves to sth/to each other **②** (*se succéder*) **s'~** to connect III. *vi* (*continuer*) **~ sur qc** to carry on and talk about sth

**enchanté(e)** [ɑ̃ʃɑ̃te] *adj* **①** (*ravi*) **être ~ de qc** to be delighted with sth **②** (*magique*) enchanted **▶ ~!** delighted!; **~ de faire votre <u>connaissance</u>** delighted to meet you

**enchanter** [ɑ̃ʃɑ̃te] <1> *vt* **①** (*ravir*) to delight **②** (*ensorceler*) to enchant

**enchère** [ɑ̃ʃɛR] *f gen pl* (*offre d'achat*) bid; **les ~s sont ouvertes** the bidding is open; **acheter aux ~s** to buy at auction

**enchérir** [ɑ̃ʃeRiR] <8> *vi* **~ sur qn/qc** to bid more than sb/sth

**enchevêtrer** [ɑ̃ʃ(ə)vetRe] <1> *vpr* **s'~** (*branches*) to grow in a tangle; (*fils*) to get tangled; (*pensées*) to get muddled

**enclencher** [ɑ̃klɑ̃ʃe] <1> I. *vt* **①** TECH (*vitesse*) to engage **②** (*engager*) to set in motion II. *vpr* **s'~** to engage

**enclos** [ɑ̃klo] *m* **①** (*espace*) enclosure; (*pour le bétail*) pen; (*pour des chevaux*) paddock **②** (*clôture*) wall

**encolure** [ɑ̃kɔlyR] *f* **①** (*cou: d'un animal, d'une personne*) neck **②** (*col: d'une robe*) neck(line) **③** (*tour de cou*) neck size

**encombrant(e)** [ɑ̃kɔ̃bRɑ̃, ɑ̃t] *adj* **①** (*embarrassant*) cumbersome **②** (*importun*) burdensome **③** *iron* (*compromettant: personne, passé*) troublesome

**encombre** [ɑ̃kɔ̃bR] **sans ~** without incident

**encombré(e)** [ɑ̃kɔ̃bRe] *adj* **①** (*embouteillé: route*) congested **②** (*trop plein: pièce, table*) cluttered **③** (*surchargé: lignes téléphoniques*) busy

**encombrement** [ɑ̃kɔ̃bRəmɑ̃] *m* **①** (*sans passage possible: d'une rue*) congestion; (*des lignes téléphoniques*) overloading **②** (*embouteillage*) traffic jam

**encombrer** [ɑ̃kɔ̃bRe] <1> I. *vt* **①** (*bloquer: passage*) to obstruct **②** (*s'amonceler sur*) to clutter up **③** (*surcharger*) to overload II. *vpr* (*s'embarrasser de*) **ne pas s'~ de qn/qc** not to burden oneself with sb/sth

**encontre** [ɑ̃kɔ̃tR] **aller à l'~ de qc** to run counter to sth

**encore** [ɑ̃kɔR] I. *adv* **①** (*continuation*) still; **hier/ce matin ~** just yesterday/this morning **②** (*répétition*) again; **je peux essayer ~ une fois?** can I try again?; **c'est ~ moi!** it's me again! **③** + *nég* **pas ~/~ pas** not yet **④** + *comp* **~ mieux/moins/plus** even better/less/more **⑤** (*renforcement*) **non seulement ..., mais ~** not only ..., but besides **⑥** (*objection*) **~ faut-il le savoir!** you've got to know that though! **⑦** (*restriction*) **~ heureux qu'elle l'ait fait** thank goodness she did it; **si ~ on avait son adresse!** if we only had her address ▶ **et puis** <u>**quoi**</u> **~!** whatever next! **II.** *conj* **il acceptera, ~ que, avec lui, on ne sait jamais** *inf* he'll agree, although you never know with him

**encouragement** [ãkuʀaʒmã] *m* ❶ encouragement ❷ ECOLE praise

**encourager** [ãkuʀaʒe] <2a> *vt* to encourage

**encrasser** [ãkʀase] <1> **I.** *vt* to soil; (*suie, fumée*) to soot up; (*calcaire*) to scale up **II.** *vpr* **s'~** to get dirty; (*chaudière*) to get scaled up; (*cheminée*) to clog up with soot

**encre** [ãkʀ] *f* (*pour écrire*) ink; **à l'~ in** ink; **~ d'imprimerie** printer's ink ▶ **il a fait** <u>**couler**</u> **de l'~** to cause a lot of ink to flow

**encyclopédie** [ãsiklɔpedi] *f* encyclopedia

**endetté(e)** [ãdete] *adj* **~ de 2000 euros** 2000 euros in debt

**endettement** [ãdɛtmã] *m* indebtedness; **~ public** national debt

**endetter** [ãdete] <1> **I.** *vt* **~ qn** to get sb into debt **II.** *vpr* **s'~** to get into debt; **s'~ de 2000 euros auprès de qn** to borrow 2000 euros from sb

**endiablé(e)** [ãdjable] *adj* (*danse, rythme*) frenzied; (*vitalité*) boisterous

**endive** [ãdiv] *f* endive, chicory

**endoctriner** [ãdɔktʀine] <1> *vt* to indoctrinate

**endolori(e)** [ãdɔlɔʀi] *adj* painful; (*personne*) in pain

**endommager** [ãdɔmaʒe] <2a> *vt* to damage

**endormant(e)** [ãdɔʀmã, ãt] *adj* dreary

**endormi(e)** [ãdɔʀmi] **I.** *adj* ❶ (*opp: éveillé*) asleep; (*passion*) dormant ❷ (*engourdi*) **j'ai la main/jambe ~e** my hand/leg has gone to sleep ❸ *inf* (*apathique: personne, esprit*) sluggish; (*regard*) sleepy **II.** *m(f)* *inf* sluggard

**endormir** [ãdɔʀmiʀ] *irr* **I.** *vt* ❶ (*faire dormir, ennuyer*) **~ qn** to put sb to sleep ❷ (*anesthésier*) **~ qn** to put sb under ❸ (*faire disparaître: douleur*) to deaden; (*soupçons*) to lull; (*vigilance*)

to dupe **II.** *vpr* **s'~** ❶ (*s'assoupir*) to fall asleep ❷ (*devenir très calme: ville*) to go to sleep ❸ (*s'atténuer: sensation*) to die down; (*faculté, sens*) to go to sleep

**endosser** [ãdose] <1> *vt* (*responsabilité*) to take on; **~ les conséquences** to take responsibility for the consequences

**endroit¹** [ãdʀwa] *m* place; **à plusieurs ~s** in several places; **par ~s** in places

**endroit²** [ãdʀwa] *m* (*opp: envers, tapis: d'un vêtement*) right side; (*vêtement*) **être à l'~** to be the right way out; (*feuille*) to be the right way up

**enduire** [ãdɥiʀ] *irr* **I.** *vt* **~ de qc** to coat with sth **II.** *vpr* **s'~ de qc** to cover oneself with sth

**enduit** [ãdɥi] *m* coating

**endurance** [ãdyʀãs] *f* endurance

**endurant(e)** [ãdyʀã, ãt] *adj* tough

**endurci(e)** [ãdyʀsi] *adj* ❶ (*insensible: cœur, criminel*) hardened; (*personne*) hard-hearted ❷ (*invétéré: célibataire*) confirmed; (*fumeur*) hardened; (*joueur*) seasoned ❸ (*résistant*) **~ au froid/aux privations** inured to cold/privation

**endurcir** [ãdyʀsiʀ] <8> **I.** *vt* ❶ (*physiquement*) **~ qn à qc** to inure sb to sth ❷ (*moralement*) to harden **II.** *vpr* ❶ (*physiquement*) **s'~ à qc** to inure oneself to sth ❷ (*moralement*) **s'~** to harden one's heart

**endurer** [ãdyʀe] <1> *vt* (*insulte*) to bear; (*privations*) to endure

**énergétique** [enɛʀʒetik] *adj* ❶ ECON **les besoins ~s** energy needs ❷ ANAT **valeur ~** energy value

**énergie** [enɛʀʒi] *f* energy; (*d'un style*) vigor; **avec ~** vigorously

**énergique** [enɛʀʒik] *adj* energetic

**énervant(e)** [enɛʀvã, ãt] *adj* irritating; (*travail, attente*) annoying

**énervé(e)** [enɛʀve] *adj* ❶ (*agacé*) irritated ❷ (*excité*) restless ❸ (*nerveux*) edgy

**énerver** [enɛʀve] <1> **I.** *vt* ❶ (*agacer*) to irritate ❷ (*exciter*) to make restless **II.** *vpr* **s'~ après qn/qc** to get annoyed at sb/sth; **ne nous énervons pas!** let's stay calm!

**enfance** [ãfãs] *f* ❶ (*période*) childhood; **petite** ~ infancy ❷ *sans pl* (*les enfants*) children ▶ **(re)tomber en** ~ to fall into one's second childhood

**enfant** [ãfã] *mf* ❶ (*garçon, fille*) child; **faire un** ~ to have a child; ~ **unique** only child ❷ *pl* (*descendants*) children ▶ ~ **de chœur** (*qui chante*) choirboy; (*à la messe*) altar boy; **ne pas être un** ~ **de chœur** *fig* to be no angel; ~ **gâté/pourri** spoiled child; ~ **prodige** (*child*) prodigy; **l'**~ **prodigue** the prodigal son

**enfantin(e)** [ãfãtɛ̃, in] *adj* ❶ (*relatif à l'enfant: rires*) childish ❷ (*simple*) childishly simple

**enfer** [ãfɛʀ] *m* ❶ (*situation*) *a.* REL hell; **c'est l'**~ it's hell on earth ❷ *pl* HIST underworld ▶ **d'**~ excellent; **bruit d'**~ hell of a commotion

**enfermer** [ãfɛʀme] <1> I. *vt* ❶ (*mettre dans un lieu fermé: enfant, prisonnier*) to lock up; (*animal*) to pen up ❷ (*maintenir*) ~ **qn/qc dans le rôle de ...** to confine sb/sth in the role of ... ❸ (*entourer*) to enclose ▶ **être/rester enfermé chez soi** to be/stay shut away at home II. *vpr* ❶ (*s'isoler*) **s'**~ **dans qc** to shut oneself away in sth ❷ (*se cantonner*) **s'**~ **dans le silence** to retreat into silence

**enfiler** [ãfile] <1> I. *vt* ❶ (*traverser par un fil: aiguille, perles*) to thread ❷ (*passer: pull-over*) to pull on II. *vpr* ❶ *inf* (*s'envoyer*) **s'**~ **une boisson** to knock back a drink ❷ *inf* (*se taper*) **s'**~ **tout le travail** to be stuck with all the work

**enfin** [ãfɛ̃] *adv* ❶ (*fin d'une attente*) at last ❷ (*fin d'une énumération*) finally ❸ (*pour corriger ou préciser*) anyway ❹ (*marquant la gêne*) well ❺ (*bref*) after all ❻ (*pour clore la discussion*) ~, ... anyway, ... ❼ (*tout de même*) really ❽ (*marque l'irritation*) come on ▶ ~ **bref** in short; ~ **passons** anyway, let's move on

**enflammer** [ãflame] <1> I. *vt* ❶ (*mettre le feu à*) to set on fire ❷ (*exalter*)

to set alight; (*imagination*) to fire II. *vpr* ❶ (*prendre feu*) **s'**~ to catch fire ❷ (*s'animer: personne*) to come alive

**enflé(e)** [ãfle] *adj* MED swollen

**enfler** [ãfle] <1> I. *vt* ❶ (*faire augmenter: rivière*) to swell; (*voix*) to raise; ~ **les doigts** to make the fingers swell up II. *vi, vpr* (**s'**)~ to swell up

**enfoncer** [ãfɔ̃se] <2> I. *vt* ❶ (*planter: clou*) to knock in; (*punaise*) to press in; (*couteau*) to push in; (*coude*) to dig in ❷ (*mettre*) ~ **ses mains dans qc** to put one's hands down into sth ❸ (*briser en poussant: porte*) to break down ❹ (*aggraver la situation de*) ~ **qn dans la dépendance** to push sb further into dependence II. *vi* ~ **dans qc** to sink into sth III. *vpr* ❶ (*aller vers le fond*) **s'**~ **dans la neige** to sink into the snow ❷ (*se creuser*) **s'**~ (*mur, maison*) to subside; (*sol, matelas*) to sink ❸ (*se planter*) **s'**~ **une aiguille dans le bras** to stick a needle into one's arm ❹ (*pénétrer*) **s'**~ **dans qc** (*vis*) to work its way into sth ❺ (*s'engager*) **s'**~ **dans l'obscurité** to plunge into the darkness ❻ *inf* (*se perdre*) **s'**~ to get oneself into more trouble

**enfoui(e)** [ãfwi] I. *part passé de* **enfouir** II. *adj* ❶ (*recouvert*) ~ **dans/sous qc** buried in/under sth ❷ (*caché: village*) tucked away

**enfouir** [ãfwiʀ] <8> I. *vt* (*mettre en terre, cacher*) to bury II. *vpr* ❶ (*se blottir*) **s'**~ **sous ses couvertures** to snuggle down under the covers ❷ (*se réfugier*) **s'**~ **dans un trou/terrier** to dive into a hole/burrow

**enfourcher** [ãfuʀʃe] <1> *vt* (*cheval, vélo*) to mount; (*chaise*) to sit down astride

**enfourner** [ãfuʀne] <1> *vt* ❶ (*mettre au four*) to put in the oven ❷ *inf* (*ingurgiter*) to put away

**enfreindre** [ãfʀɛ̃dʀ] *vt irr* to infringe

**enfuir** [ãfɥiʀ] *vpr irr* (*fuir*) **s'**~ to run away

**engagé(e)** [ãgaʒe] I. *adj* ~ **dans qc**

committed to sth **II.** *m(f)* ❶ MIL volunteer ❷ SPORT entrants

**engageant(e)** [ãgaʒã, ãt] *adj* (*aspect, avenir*) inviting; (*paroles*) winning; (*mine*) appealing; (*sourire*) engaging

**engagement** [ãgaʒmã] *m* ❶ (*promesse, dépense*) *a.* POL commitment ❷ (*embauche*) taking on ❸ (*bataille*) engagement ❹ THEAT, CINE contract ❺ SPORT (*coup d'envoi*) kickoff; (*inscription*) entry

**engager** [ãgaʒe] <2a> **I.** *vt* ❶ (*mettre en jeu: parole*) to give; (*honneur, vie*) to put at stake; (*responsabilité*) to accept ❷ (*lier*) to commit ❸ (*embaucher: représentant*) to hire; (*comédien*) to engage ❹ (*commencer: débat*) to open ❺ (*faire prendre une direction à*) **être mal engagé** to be badly positioned **II.** *vpr* ❶ (*promettre*) **s'~ à** +*infin* to undertake to +*infin* ❷ (*louer ses services*) **s'~** MIL to volunteer; **s'~ dans la marine** to join the navy ❸ (*pénétrer*) **s'~ dans une rue** to enter a street ❹ (*se lancer*) **s'~ dans qc** to get involved in sth ❺ (*prendre position*) **s'~ dans la lutte contre qc** to get involved in the struggle against sth

**engin** [ãʒɛ̃] *m* ❶ *inf* (*machin*) thingamajig ❷ TECH machine ❸ MIL weaponry; (*de guerre*) engine; **~ atomique** atomic device ❹ *inf* (*objet encombrant*) contraption ❺ (*véhicule*) heavy vehicle

**englober** [ãglɔbe] <1> *vt* to encompass

**engloutir** [ãglutiʀ] <8> **I.** *vi* to devour **II.** *vt* ❶ (*dévorer*) to wolf down ❷ (*dilapider: personne*) to run through; (*entreprise*) to swallow up; **~ sa fortune dans qc** to sink one's fortune into sth ❸ (*faire disparaître: inondation, vagues, brume*) to swallow up; (*éruption*) to engulf **III.** *vpr* **s'être englouti dans la mer** to be swallowed up by the sea

**engouffrer** [ãgufʀe] <1> **I.** *vt* ❶ (*entraîner: tempête*) to engulf ❷ *inf* (*dévorer*) to wolf down ❸ (*dilapider*) **~ de l'argent dans qc** to sink money into sth **II.** *vpr* **elles s'engouffrèrent dans le couloir** they plunged into the corridor

**engourdi(e)** [ãguʀdi] *adj* (*doigts*) numb; (*esprit*) sluggish

**engourdir** [ãguʀdiʀ] <8> **I.** *vt* ❶ (*ankyloser: doigts, mains*) to numb ❷ (*affaiblir: personne*) to make drowsy; (*volonté, esprit*) to numb **II.** *vpr* **s'~** ❶ (*s'ankyloser*) to go numb; (*bras*) to go to sleep ❷ (*s'affaiblir: personne*) to become drowsy; (*esprit, facultés, sentiment*) to be numbed

**engrais** [ãgʀɛ] *m* fertilizer

**engraisser** [ãgʀese] <1> **I.** *vt* ❶ (*rendre plus gras*) to fatten ❷ (*fertiliser*) to fertilize **II.** *vi* to fatten up **III.** *vpr* **s'~ de qc** to grow fat on sth

**engrenage** [ãgʀənaʒ] *m* gears *pl* ▸ **être pris dans un/l'~** to be caught in a downward spiral

**engueuler** [ãgœle] <1> **I.** *vt inf* to bawl out **II.** *vpr inf* ❶ (*se crier dessus*) **s'~** to have a shouting match ❷ (*se disputer*) **s'~ avec qn** to have an argument

**énième** [ɛnjɛm] *adj* **le/la ~** the umpteenth; **pour la ~ fois** for the umpteenth time

**énigmatique** [enigmatik] *adj* enigmatic

**énigme** [enigm] *f* enigma

**enivrant(e)** [ãnivʀã, ãt] *adj* intoxicating; (*parfum*) heady

**enivrer** [ãnivʀe] <1> *vpr* ❶ (*se soûler*) **s'~** to get drunk ❷ *fig* **s'~ de qc** to be intoxicated by sth

**enjamber** [ãʒãbe] <1> *vt* (*franchir: mur*) to straddle

**enjeu** [ãʒø] <x> *m* ❶ (*argent*) stake ❷ *fig* **être l'~ de qc** to be at stake in sth

**enjoliveur** [ãʒɔliveœʀ] *m* hubcap

**enlacer** [ãlase] <2> **I.** *vt* to embrace **II.** *vpr* ❶ (*s'étreindre*) **s'~** to embrace ❷ (*entourer*) **s'~ autour de qc** to twine around sth

**enlaidir** [ãlediʀ] <8> **I.** *vi* (*devenir laid*) to become ugly **II.** *vt* (*rendre laid: personne*) to make ugly; (*paysage*) to disfigure

**enlèvement** [ãlɛvmã] *m* abduction

**enlever** [ãlve] <4> **I.** *vt* ❶ (*déplacer de par-dessus*) to take off; (*débarrasser*) to

**E**

take away ❷ (*faire disparaître: tache*) to remove; (*mot*) to cut out ❸ (*ôter*) ~ **l'envie/le goût à qn de faire qc** to discourage sb from doing sth ❹ (*retirer: chapeau, montre, vêtement*) to take off ❺ (*kidnapper*) to abduct II. *vpr* s'~ ❶ (*disparaître: tache*) to go ❷ (*se détacher*) to come off ❸ *inf* (*se pousser*) **enlève-toi de là!** get out of here!

**enliser** [ɑ̃lize] <1> *vpr* s'~ ❶ (*s'enfoncer*) to sink ❷ (*stagner*) to get bogged down

**enneigé(e)** [ɑ̃neʒe] *adj* snow-covered; (*village, voiture*) snowed in

**ennemi(e)** [en(ə)mi] I. *adj* enemy; (*frères*) rival II. *m(f)* enemy; ~ **public numéro un** public enemy number one; ~ **héréditaire/juré** traditional/sworn enemy

**ennui** [ɑ̃nɥi] *m* ❶ (*désœuvrement*) boredom ❷ (*lassitude*) ennui ❸ *souvent pl* (*problème*) trouble ▶ **l'~, c'est que ...** the problem is that ...

**ennuyé(e)** [ɑ̃nɥije] *adj* bothered; **être bien ~** to feel really awkward; (*avoir un problème*) to be in a real mess; **il est ~ de devoir le faire** it bothers him to have to do it

**ennuyer** [ɑ̃nɥije] <6> I. *vt* ❶ (*lasser*) to bore ❷ (*être peu attrayant*) ~ **qn** to be a nuisance to sb ❸ (*être gênant*) **ça m'ennuie de devoir le faire** it bothers me to have to do it ❹ (*irriter*) ~ **qn avec qc** to trouble sb with sth ❺ (*déplaire*) to annoy II. *vpr* s'~ to be bored

**ennuyeux, -euse** [ɑ̃nɥijø, -jøz] *adj* ❶ (*lassant*) boring; ~ **à mourir** deadly boring ❷ (*contrariant*) bothersome

**énorme** [enɔʀm] *adj* ❶ (*très gros*) enormous ❷ (*incroyable*) tremendous

**énormément** [enɔʀmemɑ̃] *adv* (*difficile, riche*) tremendously; (*aimer, boire*) an awful lot; ~ **d'argent/de gens** an awful lot of money/people

**enquête** [ɑ̃kɛt] *f* ❶ (*étude*) ~ **sur qc** survey on sth ❷ (*sondage d'opinions*) survey ❸ ADMIN, JUR inquiry

**enquêter** [ɑ̃kete] <1> *vi* ❶ (*s'informer*) *a.* ADMIN, JUR ~ **sur qn/qc** to investigate

sb/sth ❷ (*faire une enquête, un sondage*) *a.* COM, SOCIOL ~ **sur qc** to conduct a survey on sth

**enragé(e)** [ɑ̃ʀaʒe] I. *adj* ❶ (*atteint de la rage*) rabid ❷ (*passionné: chasseur, joueur*) fanatical ❸ (*furieux*) livid II. *m(f)* fanatic

**enrager** [ɑ̃ʀaʒe] <2a> *vi* to be livid

**enrayer** [ɑ̃ʀeje] <7> I. *vt* ❶ (*juguler: chômage, hausse des prix, épidémie, maladie*) to check ❷ (*stopper*) to stop II. *vpr* s'~ to jam

**enregistrement** [ɑ̃ʀ(ə)ʒistʀəmɑ̃] *m* ❶ CINE, TV recording ❷ INFORM (*action*) logging; (*document*) record ❸ AUTO registration

**enregistrer** [ɑ̃ʀ(ə)ʒistʀe] <1> I. *vt* ❶ CINE, TV to record ❷ (*mémoriser*) to register ❸ (*noter par écrit: déclaration*) to register; (*commande*) to take ❹ AUTO to register; **faire ~ ses bagages** to check in one's baggage ❺ (*constater: phénomène*) to show ❻ INFORM to save; ~ **sous ...** to save as ... II. *vi* CINE, TV, INFORM to record

**enrhumer** [ɑ̃ʀyme] <1> I. *vt* **être enrhumé** to have a cold II. *vpr* s'~ to catch (a) cold

**enrichir** [ɑ̃ʀiʃiʀ] <8> I. *vt* to enrich II. *vpr* s'~ **de qc** ❶ (*devenir riche*) to get rich with sth ❷ (*s'améliorer, augmenter*) to be enriched with sth

**enrôler** [ɑ̃ʀole] <1> I. *vt* ❶ (*recruter*) ~ **qn dans qc** to recruit sb into sth ❷ MIL to enlist II. *vpr* s'~ **dans qc** to join sth

**enroué(e)** [ɑ̃ʀwe] *adj* hoarse

**enrouler** [ɑ̃ʀule] <1> I. *vt* (*câble*) to coil II. *vpr* s'~ **autour de/sur qc** to wind around/on sth

**enseignant(e)** [ɑ̃sɛɲɑ̃, ɑ̃t] I. *adj* **le corps ~** teachers *pl* II. *m(f)* teacher

**enseigne** [ɑ̃sɛɲ] *f* sign

**enseignement** [ɑ̃sɛɲ(ə)mɑ̃] *m* ❶ (*activité, profession*) teaching; **l'~ des langues vivantes** modern language teaching ❷ (*institution*) education; ~ **public** public education; ~ **secondaire/supérieur/technique/universitaire** sec-

ondary/higher/technical/university
education ❸ (*leçon*) lesson; **tirer un ~
de qc** to learn a lesson from sth
**enseigner** [ɑ̃seɲe] <1> *vt* to teach
**ensemble** [ɑ̃sɑ̃bl] I. *adv* together ▸**aller bien/mal ~** to go well/badly together; **aller ~** to match II. *m* ❶ (*totalité*) **l'~ du personnel/des questions**
all the staff/questions ❷ (*unité*) whole
❸ (*groupement*) **~ de lois** set of laws
❹ MUS ensemble ❺ MATH set ❻ (*vêtement*) outfit ❼ (*groupe d'habitations*)
**grand ~** large development ▸**impres-
sion/vue d'~** overall impression/view;
**dans l'~** on the whole
**ensevelir** [ɑ̃səvliʀ] <8> *vt* (*recouvrir*)
**~ qn/qc sous qc** to bury sb/sth under
sth
**ensoleillé(e)** [ɑ̃sɔleje] *adj* sunny
**ensommeillé(e)** [ɑ̃sɔmeje] *adj* (*personne*) drowsy; (*paysage, ville*) sleepy
**ensorceler** [ɑ̃sɔʀsəle] <3> *vt* ❶ (*envoûter*) to enchant ❷ (*fasciner*) to bewitch
**ensuite** [ɑ̃sɥit] *adv* ❶ (*par la suite*)
afterwards ❷ (*derrière en suivant*) then
❸ (*en plus*) what is more
**ensuivre** [ɑ̃sɥivʀ] *vpr irr, défec* **s'~** to
ensue
**entaille** [ɑ̃taj] *f* ❶ (*encoche*) notch
❷ (*coupure*) gash
**entailler** [ɑ̃taje] <1> I. *vt* ❶ (*faire une
entaille*) to notch ❷ (*blesser*) **~ la joue
à qn** to gash sb's cheek II. *vpr* **s'~ la
joue avec qc** to gash one's cheek on sth
**entamer** [ɑ̃tame] <1> *vt* ❶ (*prendre le
début de: bouteille*) to open; (*fromage*)
to start (on) ❷ (*attaquer*) **~ qc** to cut
into sth ❸ (*amorcer*) to start; (*négociations*) to open; (*poursuites*) to institute
**entartrer** [ɑ̃taʀtʀe] <1> I. *vt* **~** to scale up;
**~ les dents** to cover the teeth in plaque
II. *vpr* **s'~** (*chaudière, conduite*) to scale up
**entassement** [ɑ̃tasmɑ̃] *m* ❶ (*action:
d'objets*) piling up ❷ (*pile*) pile ❸ (*encombrement*) crowding
**entasser** [ɑ̃tase] <1> I. *vt* ❶ (*amonceler*) to pile up; (*argent*) to amass ❷ (*serrer*) to cram II. *vpr* ❶ (*s'amonceler*) **s'~**

to pile up ❷ (*se serrer*) **s'~ dans une
pièce** to cram into a room
**entendre** [ɑ̃tɑ̃dʀ] <14> I. *vi* to hear; **se
faire ~** to make oneself heard II. *vt*
❶ (*percevoir*) to hear; **je l'ai entendu
dire** I've heard it said ❷ (*écouter*)
**~ qn/qc** to listen to sb/sth ❸ (*comprendre*) to understand; **laisser ~
que ...** (*faire savoir*) to make it known
that ...; (*faire croire*) to give the impression that ...; **qu'est-ce que vous en-
tendez par là?** what do you mean by
that? ❹ (*vouloir*) **~** +*infin* to intend to
+*infin*; **faites comme vous l'enten-
dez!** do as you see fit! ▸**~ parler de
qn/qc** to hear of sb/sth; **je ne veux
rien ...** ! I'm not listening!; **à ~ les gens**
to hear people talk III. *vpr* ❶ (*avoir de
bons rapports*) **s'~ avec qn** to get
along with sb ❷ (*se mettre d'accord*)
**s'~ sur qc** to agree on sth; **s'~ pour**
+*infin* to agree to +*infin* ❸ (*s'y connaître*) **s'y ~ en qc** to know about sth
▸**on ne s'entend plus parler** you
can't hear yourself speak; **entendons-
-nous bien!** let's get this straight!
**entendu(e)** [ɑ̃tɑ̃dy] I. *part passé de* **entendre** II. *adj* ❶ (*convenu*) agreed
❷ (*complice: regard*) knowing
▸**bien ~** of course
**entente** [ɑ̃tɑ̃t] *f* ❶ (*amitié*) friendship
❷ (*fait de s'accorder*) understanding
❸ (*accord*) a. ECON agreement; **arriver
[***o* **parvenir] à une ~** to come to an
agreement ❹ POL entente
**enterrement** [ɑ̃tɛʀmɑ̃] *m* burial
**enterrer** [ɑ̃teʀe] <1> I. *vt* ❶ to bury;
**~ un scandale** to hush up a scandal
❷ (*renoncer à*) to put (sth) behind one
II. *vpr* **s'~ à la campagne** to hide oneself away in the country
**en-tête** [ɑ̃tɛt] <en-têtes> *f* (*d'un journal*) headline; (*d'un papier à lettres*)
letterhead
**entêté(e)** [ɑ̃tete] I. *adj* (*personne*) obstinate II. *m(f)* stubborn individual
**entêtement** [ɑ̃tɛtmɑ̃] *m* stubbornness
**entêter** [ɑ̃tete] <1> *vpr* **s'~ dans qc/à
faire qc** to persist in sth/in doing sth

**E**

**enthousiasme** [ɑ̃tuzjasm] *m* enthusiasm

**enthousiasmer** [ɑ̃tuzjasme] <1> I. *vt* ~ **qn** to fill sb with enthusiasm II. *vpr* **s'~ pour** qn/qc to get enthusiastic about sb/sth

**enthousiaste** [ɑ̃tuzjast] I. *adj* enthusiastic II. *mf* enthusiast

**entier** [ɑ̃tje] *m* whole number ▶ **le livre/l'orchestre en ~** the whole book/ orchestra

**entier, -ière** [ɑ̃tje, -jɛʀ] *adj* ❶ (*dans sa totalité*) whole; **dans le monde ~** in the whole world ❷ (*absolu*) complete ❸ (*intact: personne*) safe and sound; (*objet, collection*) intact ❹ (*non réglé*) **la question reste entière** the question is still unsolved ❺ (*sans concession: personne*) strong-minded ▶ **tout ~** entire

**entièrement** [ɑ̃tjɛʀmɑ̃] *adv* entirely

**entonnoir** [ɑ̃tɔnwaʀ] *m* funnel

**entorse** [ɑ̃tɔʀs] *f* sprain

**entortiller** [ɑ̃tɔʀtije] <1> I. *vt* ❶ (*enrouler*) ~ **qc autour de qc** to twine sth around sth ❷ (*enjôler*) to cajole II. *vpr* ❶ (*s'enrouler*) **s'~ autour de qc** to twine around sth ❷ (*s'envelopper*) **s'~ dans qc** to wrap oneself up in sth ❸ (*s'embrouiller*) **s'~ dans qc** to get in a muddle over sth

**entourage** [ɑ̃tuʀaʒ] *m* entourage

**entourer** [ɑ̃tuʀe] <1> I. *vt* ❶ (*être autour*) to surround ❷ (*mettre autour*) ~ **un mot** to circle a word ❸ (*soutenir*) ~ **qn** to rally around sb ❹ *fig* ~ **qc de mystère** to surround sth in mystery II. *vpr* **s'~ de bons amis** to surround oneself with good friends; **s'~ de précautions** to take every precaution

**entracte** [ɑ̃tʀakt] *m* THEAT, CINE intermission

**entraide** [ɑ̃tʀɛd] *f* mutual support

**entraider** [ɑ̃tʀede] <1> *vpr* **s'~** to help each other

**entrain** [ɑ̃tʀɛ̃] *m* spirit

**entraînement** [ɑ̃tʀɛnmɑ̃] *m* ❶ (*pratique*) practice ❷ SPORT training

**entraîner** [ɑ̃tʀene] <1> I. *vt* ❶ (*empor-*

*ter*) ~ **qc** to carry sth along ❷ (*emmener*) ~ **qn** to take sb off ❸ (*inciter*) ~ **qn à** [*o* **dans**] **qc** to drag sb into sth; ~ **qn à faire qc** to push sb into doing sth ❹ (*causer*) ~ **qc** to lead to sth ❺ (*stimuler*) ~ **qn** (*éloquence, musique*) to carry sb along ❻ SPORT (*exercer: joueur*) to train II. *vpr* **s'~ à** [*o* **pour**] **qc/à faire qc** to practice sth/doing sth

**entraîneur, -euse** [ɑ̃tʀɛnœʀ, -øz] *m, f* SPORT coach

**entre** [ɑ̃tʀ] *prep* ❶ between ❷ (*parmi des personnes*) among; **la plupart d'eux/elles** the majority of them; ~ **autres** among others; ~ **nous** between us ❸ (*à travers*) through; **passer ~ les mailles du filet** to slip through the net ❹ (*dans*) into ❺ (*indiquant une relation*) **ils se sont disputés ~ eux** they had an argument

**entrecroiser** [ɑ̃tʀəkʀwaze] <1> I. *vt* to intertwine II. *vpr* **s'~** (*routes*) to intersect

**entrée** [ɑ̃tʀe] *f* ❶ (*arrivée: d'une personne*) coming in; (*d'un acteur*) entrance; (*d'un train*) arrival; **faire une ~ triomphale** to make a triumphant entry ❷ (*accès*) entrance; ~ **de service** service entrance ❸ (*droit d'entrer*) entry; ~ **interdite** no entry ❹ (*vestibule: d'un appartement, d'une maison*) hall; (*d'un hôtel, immeuble*) entrance hall ❺ (*billet*) ticket ❻ (*somme perçue*) receipt ❼ (*adhésion*) **son ~ dans le parti** his joining the party ❽ (*admission*) ~ **dans un club** admission to a club ❾ (*commencement*) ~ **en action** coming into play; ~ **en vigueur** coming into force ❿ CULIN first course ⓫ TYP (*d'un dictionnaire*) headword ⓬ INFORM input

**entrelacer** [ɑ̃tʀəlase] <2> I. *vt* to intertwine II. *vpr* **s'~** to intertwine

**entremêler** [ɑ̃tʀəmele] <1> I. *vt fig* ~ **qc de qc** to intermingle sth with sth II. *vpr* **s'~** (*doigts*) to intertwine; (*lèvres*) to intermingle; **s'~ à** [*o* **avec**] **qc** to mingle with sth

**entremets** [ɑ̃tʀəmɛ] *m* dessert

**entreposer** [ɑ̃tʀəpoze] <1> *vt* (*meubles*) to put into storage

**entrepôt** [ɑ̃tʀəpo] *m* warehouse

**entreprenant(e)** [ɑ̃tʀəpʀənɑ̃, ɑ̃t] *adj* ❶ (*dynamique*) enterprising ❷ (*galant*) forward

**entreprendre** [ɑ̃tʀəpʀɑ̃dʀ] <13> *vt* (*commencer*) **~ une étude/une carrière** to embark on a study/a career

**entrepreneur, -euse** [ɑ̃tʀəpʀənœʀ, -øz] *m, f* ❶ (*créateur d'entreprise*) entrepreneur ❷ TECH contractor

**entreprise** [ɑ̃tʀəpʀiz] *f* ❶ (*firme*) business; **petites et moyennes ~s** small and medium-sized businesses; **~ privée/publique** private/state enterprise; **~ de construction/transports** construction/transportation firm ❷ (*opération*) undertaking

**entrer** [ɑ̃tʀe] <1> I. *vi* être ❶ (*pénétrer*) to enter; (*vu de l'intérieur*) to come in; (*vu de l'extérieur*) to go in; **défense d'~!** no entry!; **faire/laisser ~ qn** to show/let sb in ❷ (*pénétrer dans un lieu*) **~ dans qc** to enter sth; (*vu de l'intérieur*) to come into sth; (*vu de l'extérieur*) to go into sth ❸ (*aborder*) **~ dans les détails** to go into detail ❹ *inf* (*heurter*) **~ dans qc** to slam into sth ❺ (*s'engager dans*) **~ dans un club/un parti/la police** to join a club/a party/the police; **~ dans la vie active** to embark on working life ❻ (*être admis*) **~ à l'hôpital** to go into the hospital; **~ à l'école/en sixième** to start school/sixth grade ❼ (*s'enfoncer*) **la clé n'entre pas dans le trou de la serrure** the key won't go into the lock ❽ (*s'associer à*) **~ dans la discussion** to join the discussion ❾ (*comme verbe support*) **~ en application** to come into force; **~ en contact avec qn** to make contact with sb; **~ en guerre** to go to war; **~ en scène** to enter; **~ en ligne de compte** to be taken into consideration; **~ en fonction** to take up office II. *vt* avoir ❶ (*faire pénétrer*) **~ qc dans qc** to bring/take sth into sth ❷ INFORM to enter

**entre-temps** [ɑ̃tʀətɑ̃] *adv* meanwhile

**entretenir** [ɑ̃tʀət(ə)niʀ] <9> I. *vt* ❶ (*maintenir en bon état: machine, voiture*) to maintain; (*beauté, vêtement*) to look after ❷ (*faire vivre*) to support; (*maîtresse*) to keep ❸ (*faire durer: correspondance*) to carry on; (*espoir, illusions*) to foster; (*souvenirs*) to keep alive; **~ sa forme** to keep in shape ❹ (*parler à*) **~ qn de qn/qc** to converse with sb about sb/sth II. *vpr* ❶ (*converser*) **s'~ avec qn de qn/qc** to speak with sb about sb/sth ❷ (*se conserver en bon état*) **s'~** (*personne*) to keep in shape

**entretenu(e)** [ɑ̃tʀət(ə)ny] I. *part passé de* **entretenir** II. *adj* ❶ (*tenu en bon état*) well maintained; (*maison*) well kept ❷ (*pris en charge*) **c'est une femme ~e/un homme ~** she's/he's a kept woman/man

**entretien** [ɑ̃tʀətjɛ̃] *m* ❶ (*maintien en bon état: de la peau, d'un vêtement*) care; (*d'une maison*) upkeep; (*d'une machine*) maintenance ❷ (*discussion en privé*) discussion; (*pour un emploi*) interview

**entrevoir** [ɑ̃tʀəvwaʀ] *vt irr* ❶ (*voir indistinctement*) **~ qc** to make sth out; (*voir brièvement*) to catch a glimpse of sth ❷ (*pressentir*) to foresee

**entrevue** [ɑ̃tʀəvy] *f* interview

**entrouvert(e)** [ɑ̃tʀuvɛʀ, ɛʀt] *adj* ajar

**entrouvrir** [ɑ̃tʀuvʀiʀ] <11> *vt, vpr* (**s'**)**~** to open halfway

**énumération** [enymeʀasjɔ̃] *f* enumeration; **faire une ~ de qc** to list sth

**énumérer** [enymeʀe] <5> *vt* to list

**envahir** [ɑ̃vaiʀ] <8> *vt* ❶ MIL (*pays*) to invade ❷ (*se répandre, infester*) **~ les rues** to swarm into the streets; **~ le terrain de football** to invade the playing field; **~ le marché** (*nouveau produit*) to flood the market ❸ (*gagner*) **le doute/la terreur envahit qn** sb is seized by doubt/terror ❹ (*importuner*) to intrude on

**envahissant(e)** [ɑ̃vaisɑ̃, ɑ̃t] *adj* (*importun: personne*) intrusive

**envahisseur, -euse** [ãvaisœʀ, -øz] *m, f* invader

**enveloppe** [ãvlɔp] *f* ❶ (*pour le courrier*) envelope; ~ **autocollante** [*o* **autoadhésive**] self-adhesive envelope ❷ (*protection*) covering ❸ (*budget*) budget; ~ **budgétaire** budget allocation

**envelopper** [ãvlɔpe] <1> I. *vt* (*verre*) to wrap up II. *vpr* **s'~ dans son manteau** to wrap oneself up in one's coat

**envenimer** [ãv(ə)nime] <1> I. *vt* (*aggraver*) to inflame II. *vpr* (*se détériorer*) **s'~** (*situation, conflit*) to aggravate

**envers** [ãvɛʀ] I. *prep* ~ **qn/qc** towards sb/sth; **son mépris** ~ **qn/qc** her contempt for sb/sth II. *m* (*d'une feuille de papier*) other side; (*d'une étoffe, d'un vêtement*) wrong side; (*d'une assiette, feuille d'arbre*) underside ▶ **l'~ du décor** the other side of the coin; **à l'~** (*dans le mauvais sens*) the wrong way; (*à rebours*) the wrong way around; (*de bas en haut*) upside down; (*à reculons*) backwards; (*en désordre*) upside down; **tout marche à l'~** everything's upside down

**enviable** [ãvjabl] *adj* enviable

**envie** [ãvi] *f* ❶ (*désir, besoin*) desire; **ses ~s de voyage** his/her wish to travel; **avoir ~ de faire qc** to feel like doing sth; **mourir d'~ de** +*infin* to be dying to +*infin*; **ça me donne ~ de partir en vacances** it makes me want to take a vacation; **l'~ lui en est passée** [*o* **lui a passé**] he didn't feel like it anymore ❷ (*convoitise, jalousie, péché capital*) envy ▶ **faire ~ à qn** (*personne, réussite*) to make sb envious; (*nourriture*) to tempt sb; **ça fait ~** it's very tempting; (*met en appétit*) it's very appealing

**envier** [ãvje] <1> *vt* ~ **qn pour sa richesse/d'être riche** to envy sb for their wealth/for being rich

**envieux, -euse** [ãvjø, -jøz] I. *adj* ~ **de qn/qc** envious of sb/sth II. *m, f* envious person

**environ** [ãviʀɔ̃] I. *adv* around II. *mpl* (*d'une ville*) surroundings; **Reims et ses ~s** Reims and the surrounding area; **dans les ~s du château** in the area around the castle; **aux ~s de Pâques** around Easter; **aux ~s de 100 euros** in the neighborhood of 100 euros

**environnement** [ãviʀɔnmã] *m* ❶ (*milieu écologique*) environment ❷ (*environs*) surroundings ❸ (*milieu social*) background

**environner** [ãviʀɔne] <1> I. *vt* to surround II. *vpr* **s'~ de qn/qc** to surround oneself with sb/sth

**envisager** [ãvizaʒe] <2a> *vt* ❶ (*considérer: question, situation*) to consider; (*avenir, mort*) to contemplate ❷ (*projeter*) ~ **un voyage pour qn** to envisage a journey for sb; ~ **de faire qc** to envisage doing sth ❸ (*prévoir: orage, visite*) to foresee

**envoi** [ãvwa] *m* ❶ (*expédition: d'un paquet, d'une lettre*) sending; (*d'une marchandise, commande, de vivres*) dispatch ❷ (*colis*) package; (*courrier*) letter; ~ **recommandé** registered mail

**envol** [ãvɔl] *m* (*d'un oiseau*) taking flight; **prendre son ~** (*oiseau*) to take flight

**envoler** [ãvɔle] <1> *vpr* **s'~** ❶ (*quitter le sol*) to fly away; (*avion*) to take off; **s'~ dans le ciel** (*ballon*) to fly off into the sky ❷ (*augmenter: monnaie, prix*) to soar ❸ (*disparaître: peur, paroles*) to vanish; (*temps*) to fly

**envoûter** [ãvute] <1> *vt* to bewitch

**envoyé(e)** [ãvwaje] *m(f)* ❶ PRESSE correspondent; ~ **spécial** special correspondent ❷ POL, REL envoy

**envoyer** [ãvwaje] *irr* I. *vt* ❶ (*expédier*) to send; (*démission*) to put in ❷ (*lancer: ballon*) to throw; (*avec le pied*) to kick; (*balle de tennis*) to serve; (*coup de pied, gifle, signal*) to give; ~ **un baiser à qn** to blow sb a kiss ▶ ~ **balader qn** *inf* to send sb packing; ~ **tout promener** *inf* to throw everything up II. *vpr* (*se transmettre*) **s'~ des vœux** to send each other greetings

**éolienne** [eɔljɛn] *f* (*machine*) windmill

**épagneul(e)** [epaɲœl] *m(f)* spaniel

**épais(se)** [epɛ, ɛs] I. *adj* thick II. *adv* il

**n'y en a pas ~** *inf* there's not much of it

**épaisseur** [epɛsœʀ] *f* (*dimension*) thickness; (*de la neige*) depth; (*d'une couche, couverture*) layer; **avoir une ~ de 7 cm, avoir 7 cm d'~** to be 7 cm thick

**épaissir** [epesiʀ] <8> **I.** *vi* (*liquide*) to thicken **II.** *vpr* **s'~** (*devenir plus consistant: liquide, air*) to thicken; (*forêt, brouillard*) to get thicker

**épanoui(e)** [epanwi] *adj* ❶(*ouvert: fleur*) in bloom ❷(*radieux: sourire, visage*) radiant ❸(*développé harmonieusement: corps*) glowing with health ❹(*équilibré: caractère, personne*) fulfilled

**épanouir** [epanwiʀ] <8> *vpr* **s'~** ❶(*s'ouvrir: fleur*) to bloom ❷(*devenir joyeux: visage*) to light up ❸(*trouver le bonheur, prendre des formes*) to blossom ❹(*se développer: personne, compétence*) to develop; **s'~ dans un travail** to be fulfilled in a job

**épanouissement** [epanwismɑ̃] *m* (*d'une fleur*) blooming; *fig* blossoming

**épargnant(e)** [epaʀɲɑ̃, ɑ̃t] *m(f)* saver

**épargne** [epaʀɲ] *f* ❶(*action*) saving ❷(*sommes*) savings *pl*

**épargner** [epaʀɲe] <1> **I.** *vt* ❶(*par économie*) to save ❷(*compter, ménager: forces*) to conserve; (*peine*) to spare ❸(*éviter*) ~ **un discours à qn** to spare sb a speech ❹(*laisser vivre*) to spare **II.** *vpr* **s'~ qc** to spare oneself sth

**éparpiller** [epaʀpije] <1> **I.** *vt* ❶(*disséminer: personnes*) to disperse; (*miettes*) to scatter ❷(*disperser inefficacement: forces, talent*) to dissipate **II.** *vpr* **s'~** ❶(*se disséminer: foule*) to scatter; (*maisons*) to be scattered ❷(*se disperser: personne*) to fail to focus oneself

**épaté(e)** [epate] *adj inf* staggering

**épater** [epate] <1> *vt inf* (*stupéfier*) to amaze; **ça l'épate, hein?** amazing, isn't it?

**épaule** [epol] *f* ANAT shoulder; **hausser les ~s** to shrug one's shoulders

**épauler** [epole] <1> **I.** *vt* ❶(*aider*) ~ **qn** to help sb (out) ❷(*appuyer: arme*) to raise (to one's shoulder) **II.** *vi* to raise one's gun (to one's shoulder) **III.** *vpr* ❶(*s'entraider*) **s'~** to help each other out ❷(*s'appuyer*) **s'~ contre qn/qc** to lean against sb/sth

**épave** [epav] *f* ❶(*débris*) wreckage ❷(*véhicule, personne*) wreck

**épée** [epe] *f* sword

**épeler** [ep(ə)le] <3> *vt, vi* to spell

**épervier** [epɛʀvje] *m* ❶ZOOL sparrow hawk ❷(*filet de pêche*) cast net

**éphémère** [efemɛʀ] *adj* (*bonheur*) short-lived; (*beauté*) transient; (*instant, vie*) fleeting

**épice** [epis] *f* spice

**épicé(e)** [epise] *adj* ❶CULIN spicy ❷(*grivois: histoire*) juicy

**épicer** [epise] <2> *vt* ❶(*assaisonner*) to spice ❷(*corser*) ~ **une histoire de qc** to spice up a story with sth

**épicerie** [episʀi] *f* (*magasin*) grocery store; **~ fine** delicatessen

**épicier, -ière** [episje, -jɛʀ] *m, f* ❶(*tenant d'épicerie*) grocer ❷*péj* shopkeeper

**épidémie** [epidemi] *f* epidemic

**épiderme** [epidɛʀm] *m* skin

**épier** [epje] <1> **I.** *vt* ~ **qn** to spy on sb **II.** *vpr* **s'~** to watch each other closely

**épileptique** [epilɛptik] **I.** *adj* epileptic **II.** *mf* **être ~** to be (an) epileptic

**épiler** [epile] <1> **I.** *vt* ~ **les jambes** to remove leg hair; (~ **les sourcils**) to pluck one's eyebrows **II.** *vpr* **s'~ les jambes** to remove the hair on one's legs; (*avec de la cire*) to wax one's legs

**épinard** [epinaʀ] *m* spinach

**épine** [epin] *f* thorn

**épingle** [epɛ̃gl] *f* pin; **~ à cheveux** hairpin; **~ à nourrice** safety pin ▶ **tirer son ~ du jeu** (*s'en sortir*) to get out in time; (*réussir*) to do nicely for oneself

**épingler** [epɛ̃gle] <1> *vt* ❶(*accrocher avec des épingles*) ~ **des photos au mur** to pin photos to the wall ❷*inf* (*attraper*) to nab

**épisode** [epizɔd] *m* episode ▶ **par ~s** episodically

**épisodique** [epizɔdik] *adj* occasional

**épisodiquement** [epizɔdikmɑ̃] *adv* occasionally

**éploré(e)** [eplɔʀe] *adj* tearful

**éplucher** [eplyʃe] <1> *vt* ① (*nettoyer: fruits, légumes, crevettes*) to peel ② *fig* (*comptes*) to dissect

**épluchure** [eplyʃyʀ] *f souvent pl* peelings; **une ~** a peeling

**éponge** [epɔ̃ʒ] *f* sponge ▸ **jeter l'~** to throw in the towel; **passer l'~ sur qc** to forget about sth

**éponger** [epɔ̃ʒe] <2a> **I.** *vt* (*table*) to wipe down; (*sol*) to mop; (*liquide*) to mop up **II.** *vpr* **s'~ le front** to wipe one's brow

**époque** [epɔk] *f* (*moment*) time; (*ère*) age; **l'~ glaciaire/moderne** the ice/modern age; **la Belle Époque** the Belle Époque; **à l'~** [*o* **à cette ~**] in those days; **à l'~ de qc** at the time of sth; **à cette ~ de l'année** at this time of year ▸ **vivre avec son ~** to be of one's time

**épouser** [epuze] <1> *vt* ① (*se marier avec*) to marry ② (*partager: idées, cause*) to espouse; (*intérêts*) to take up ③ (*s'adapter à*) **~ les formes du corps** (*robe*) to cling to the body

**épousseter** [epuste] <3> *vt* to dust

**épouvantable** [epuvɑ̃tabl] *adj* terrible; (*temps*) appalling

**épouvantail** [epuvɑ̃taj] <s> *m* scarecrow

**épouvante** [epuvɑ̃t] *f* horror; **film d'~** horror film

**épouvanter** [epuvɑ̃te] <1> **I.** *vt* ① (*horrifier*) to terrify ② (*inquiéter*) to frighten **II.** *vpr* ① (*prendre peur*) **s'~** to be terrified ② (*redouter*) **il s'épouvante de qc** sth frightens him

**époux, -ouse** [epu, -uz] *m, f form* spouse; **les ~** the bride and groom; **Mme Dumas, épouse Meyers** Mme. Dumas, married name Meyers

**épreuve** [epʀœv] *f* ① (*test*) test; **mettre qn/qc à l'~/à rude ~** to put sb/sth to the test/to a tough test ② ÉCOLE (*examen*) examination ③ SPORT event ④ (*moment difficile, malheur*) trial;

**dure ~** severe trial ▸ **~ de force** showdown; **résister à l'~ du temps** to stand the test of time; **à l'~ des balles** bulletproof; **à toute ~** (*nerfs, santé*) rock-solid; (*courage*) indomitable; (*patience, optimisme*) unfailing; (*énergie*) unflagging

**éprouvant(e)** [epʀuvɑ̃, ɑ̃t] *adj* trying; (*climat, chaleur*) testing

**éprouver** [epʀuve] <1> *vt* ① (*ressentir: besoin, sentiment*) to feel ② (*subir: malheur, désagréments*) to suffer ③ (*tester*) to put to the test ④ (*ébranler physiquement, moralement*) to distress ⑤ (*ébranler matériellement*) to strike

**éprouvette** [epʀuvɛt] *f* test tube

**épuisant(e)** [epɥizɑ̃, ɑ̃t] *adj* exhausting

**épuisé(e)** [epɥize] *adj* ① (*éreinté*) tired-out; **être ~ de fatigue** to be exhausted ② (*tari: filon, réserves, gisement*) exhausted ③ (*totalement vendu: édition, livre*) out of print

**épuisement** [epɥizmɑ̃] *m* ① (*fatigue, tarissement*) exhaustion ② (*vente totale*) **jusqu'à ~ du stock** while stocks last

**épuiser** [epɥize] <1> **I.** *vt* ① (*fatiguer*) **~ qn** to tire sb out ② (*tarir, venir à bout de: économies, réserves, sujet*) to exhaust ③ (*vendre totalement*) **les stocks sont épuisés** the stocks have run out **II.** *vpr* ① (*se tarir*) **s'~** (*réserves*) to run out; (*sol*) to be worked out; (*source*) to dry up; (*forces*) to be exhausted ② (*se fatiguer*) **s'~ à faire qc/ sur qc** to tire oneself out doing sth/ over sth

**équateur** [ekwatœʀ] *m* equator

**équation** [ekwasjɔ̃] *f* equation; **~ du premier/second degré** first-/second-degree equation

**équatorial(e)** [ekwatɔʀjal, -jo] <-aux> *adj* equatorial

**équerre** [ekɛʀ] *f* square

**équilibre** [ekilibʀ] *m* ① *a.* POL, ÉCON balance; **en ~** balanced; **mettre qc en ~** to balance sth ② PSYCH equilibrium

**équilibré(e)** [ekilibʀe] *adj* ① (*en équili-*

*bre*) balanced ❷ (*stable: personne, esprit*) stable

**équilibrer** [ekilibʀe] <1> **I.** *vt* ❶ (*mettre en équilibre*) to balance; **bien ~ ses repas** to eat well-balanced meals ❷ (*stabiliser*) to bring into balance ❸ (*contrebalancer*) to counterbalance **II.** *vpr* **s'~** to balance out

**équipage** [ekipaʒ] *m* (*d'un avion, bateau*) crew

**équipe** [ekip] *f a.* SPORT team; **faire ~ avec qn** to team up with sb; **l'~ de jour/nuit/du matin/soir** (*à l'usine*) the day/night/morning/evening shift; **en ~** in a team

**équipement** [ekipmɑ̃] *m* ❶ (*action: d'un hôtel, hôpital*) fitting; **l'~ industriel de la région** the regional industrial plant ❷ (*matériel*) equipment; (*d'une voiture*) fittings ❸ *souvent pl* (*installations*) facilities

**équiper** [ekipe] <1> *vpr* **s'~ en qc** to equip oneself with sth

**équipier, -ière** [ekipje, -jɛʀ] *m, f* team member; NAUT crew member

**équitable** [ekitabl] *adj* fair

**équitation** [ekitasjɔ̃] *f* horseback riding; **faire de l'~** to go horseback riding

**équivalence** [ekivalɑ̃s] *f* ❶ (*valeur égale*) equivalence ❷ UNIV recognition of a foreign degree; **elle a obtenu une ~ pour son diplôme** her diploma has been recognized

**équivalent** [ekivalɑ̃] *m* equivalent; **sans ~** without an exact equivalent

**équivalent(e)** [ekivalɑ̃, ɑ̃t] *adj* equivalent

**équivaloir** [ekivalwaʀ] *vi irr* **~ à qc** to be equivalent to sth

**équivoque** [ekivɔk] **I.** *adj* ❶ (*ambigu: expression, terme*) ambiguous; (*attitude*) equivocal ❷ (*louche: personne, relation, passé*) dubious; (*regard*) questionable **II.** *f* (*ambiguïté*) ambiguity; (*malentendu*) misunderstanding; (*incertitude*) doubt; **sans ~** unambiguous; **rester dans l'~** to remain in a state of uncertainty

**érable** [eʀabl] *m* maple

**érafler** [eʀafle] <1> **I.** *vt* to graze **II.** *vpr* **s'~ le genou** to scrape one's knee

**éraflure** [eʀaflyʀ] *f* scratch

**ère** [ɛʀ] *f* ❶ era; **~ industrielle** industrial age; **avant notre ~** B.C. ❷ GEO period; **~ tertiaire/quaternaire** Tertiary/Quaternary (period)

**érémiste** [eʀemist] *mf* recipient of the RMI (*welfare payments*)

**ériger** [eʀiʒe] <2a> **I.** *vt form* ❶ (*dresser, élever: monument*) to erect ❷ (*élever au rang de*) **~ qn en martyr** to make sb into a martyr **II.** *vpr form* **s'~ en juge** to set oneself up as a judge

**ermite** [ɛʀmit] *m* hermit

**érosion** [eʀozjɔ̃] *f* ❶ GEO erosion ❷ (*affaiblissement*) weakening

**érotique** [eʀɔtik] *adj* erotic

**errant(e)** [eʀɑ̃, ɑ̃t] *adj* (*personne, regard, vie*) wandering; (*animal*) stray

**errer** [eʀe] <1> *vi* to wander

**erreur** [eʀœʀ] *f* error, mistake; **~ de jugement** error of judgment; **~ judiciaire** miscarriage of justice; **~ médicale** medical error; **j'ai commis une ~** I've made a mistake; **être dans l'~** to be wrong; **faire ~** to be mistaken; **induire qn en ~** to mislead sb; **par ~** by mistake; **sauf ~ de ma part** unless I'm mistaken ▶ **~ de jeunesse** error of youth; **l'~ est humaine** *prov* to err is human

**erroné(e)** [eʀɔne] *adj* wrong

**éruption** [eʀypsjɔ̃] *f* ❶ MED outbreak ❷ GEO eruption; **en ~** (*volcan*) erupting

**es** [ɛ] *indic prés de* **être**

**escabeau** [ɛskabo] <x> *m* ❶ (*échelle*) steps *pl* ❷ (*tabouret*) stool

**escalade** [ɛskalad] *f* ❶ (*ascension*) climb ❷ (*sport*) climbing; **faire de l'~** to go climbing ❸ (*surenchère*) escalation

**escalader** [ɛskalade] <1> *vt* ❶ (*monter: montagne*) to climb ❷ (*franchir*) **~ un mur** to scale a wall

**escalator** [ɛskalatɔʀ] *m* escalator

**escale** [ɛskal] *f* ❶ NAUT port of call ❷ AVIAT (*arrêt*) stop; **~ technique** refueling stop; **le vol s'effectue sans ~** it

**E**

is a nonstop flight; (*lieu*); **une ~ à To-kyo** a stopover in Tokyo

**escalier** [ɛskalje] *m sing o pl* stairs *pl*; **~ roulant** escalator; **~ de service** back stairs; **tomber dans les ~s** to fall down the stairs

**escalope** [ɛskalɔp] *f* scallop

**escargot** [ɛskaʀɡo] *m* ❶ ZOOL, CULIN snail ❷ (*personne, véhicule*) slowpoke; **rouler comme un ~** to drive at a snail's pace

**escarpé(e)** [ɛskaʀpe] *adj* steep

**escarpin** [ɛskaʀpɛ̃] *m* pump

**esclave** [ɛsklav] **I.** *adj* enslaved **II.** *mf* slave

**escompte** [ɛskɔ̃t] *m* COM, FIN discount

**escorte** [ɛskɔʀt] *f* escort

**escorter** [ɛskɔʀte] <1> *vt* to escort

**escroc** [ɛskʀo] *m* crook

**escroquer** [ɛskʀɔke] <1> *vt* to con; **se faire ~ par qn de 500 euros** to get conned out of 500 euros by sb

**escroquerie** [ɛskʀɔkʀi] *f* fraud

**espace** [ɛspas] **I.** *m* space; **~ publicitaire** advertising space; **~ aérien** airspace; **dans l'~ d'un été/moment** in (the space of) a summer/a moment **II.** *f* TYP, INFORM space

**espacement** [ɛspasmɑ̃] *m* ❶ (*distance*) space; TYP (*des lignes, mots*) spacing ❷ (*action d'espacer*) **l'~ de mes visites** the time between my visits

**espacer** [ɛspase] <2> **I.** *vt* (*séparer*) to space out; **il espace ses visites** he's making less frequent visits **II.** *vpr* (*devenir plus rare*) **s'~** to become less frequent

**espadon** [ɛspadɔ̃] *m* ZOOL swordfish

**espadrille** [ɛspadʀij] *f* ❶ espadrille ❷ *Québec* (*basket*) sneaker; **~s de tennis** tennis shoes

**Espagne** [ɛspaɲ] *f* **l'~** Spain

**espagnol** [ɛspaɲɔl] *m* Spanish; *v.a.* **français**

**espagnol(e)** [ɛspaɲɔl] *adj* Spanish

**Espagnol(e)** [ɛspaɲɔl] *m(f)* Spaniard

**espèce** [ɛspɛs] *f* ❶ BIO (*catégorie*) species; **~ animale** species of animal; **~ canine** dog species; **l'~ (humaine)** the

human race ❷ (*sorte*) *a. péj* sort; **~ d'imbécile!** *inf* you damn idiot!; **de ton ~** like you; **de cette/de la pire ~** *inf* of that/the worst sort ❸ *pl* (*argent liquide*) cash; **régler** [*o* **payer**] **en ~s** to pay cash

**espérance** [ɛspeʀɑ̃s] *f* ❶ (*espoir*) hope; (*attente*) expectation; **donner de grandes ~s** to show great promise; **fonder de grandes ~s sur qn/qc** to have high expectations of sb/sth; **contre toute ~** against all expectations ❷ (*durée*) **~ de vie** life expectancy

**espérer** [ɛspeʀe] <5> **I.** *vt* ❶ (*souhaiter*) to hope; **je l'espère bien** I hope so; **nous espérons vous revoir bientôt** we hope to see you again soon ❷ (*compter sur*) **~ qc** to hope for sth; **espères-tu qu'il te vienne en aide?** are you hoping he'll help you out? **II.** *vi* to hope; **espérons!** let's just hope!; **~ en l'avenir** to have faith in the future

**espiègle** [ɛspjɛɡl] *adj* (*enfant, sourire*) roguish

**espièglerie** [ɛspjɛɡləʀi] *f* mischievousness

**espion(ne)** [ɛspjɔ̃, jɔn] **I.** *m(f)* spy **II.** *app* spy

**espionnage** [ɛspjɔnaʒ] *m* espionage; **les services d'~** the intelligence services; **film/roman d'~** spy film/novel

**espionner** [ɛspjɔne] <1> *vt* **~ qn** to spy on sb; **~ une conversation** to eavesdrop on a conversation

**espoir** [ɛspwaʀ] *m* hope; **sans ~** hopeless; **conserver l'~** to keep hoping; **ne pas perdre ~** not to lose hope; **enlever tout ~ à qn** to take away all hope from sb; **fonder** [*o* **placer**] **de grands ~s sur** [*o* **en**] **qn/qc** to have high hopes for sb/sth; **dans l'~ de faire qc** in the hope of doing sth ▶ **l'~ fait** <u>vivre</u> *prov* one must live in hope

**esprit** [ɛspʀi] *m* ❶ (*pensée*) mind; **avoir l'~ étroit/large** to be narrow-/broad-minded ❷ (*tête*) **avoir qn/qc à l'~** to have sb/sth on one's mind; **une idée me traverse l'~** an idea has crossed my mind; **une idée/un mot me**

**vient à l'~** an idea/word has come into my head; **dans mon/son ~** (*souvenir*) as I/she remembers it; (*opinion*) in my/her mind; (*opinion*) in miles away ❸ (*humour*) wit; **plein d'~** witty; **faire de l'~** to try to be witty ❹ (*personne*) **~ fort** [o **libre**] rationalist; **~ retors** devious mind ❺ (*caractère*) **avoir bon/mauvais ~** to be helpful/unhelpful ❻ (*intention, prédisposition, être spirituel*) spirit; **il a l'~ à qc** his mind is on sth; **dans cet ~** in this spirit; **avoir l'~ de compétition/de contradiction** to be competitive/argumentative; **avoir l'~ de famille** to be a family person; **avoir l'~ d'organisation** to be an organizer; **avoir l'~ d'entreprise** to be enterprising ▶ **faire du** <u>mauvais</u> **~** to make trouble; **avoir l'~ mal <u>tourné</u>** to have a dirty mind

**esquimau**[1] [ɛskimo] *m* (*langue*) *a. péj* Eskimo; *v.a.* **français**

**esquimau®2** [ɛskimo] <x> *m* CULIN Eskimo Pie®

**esquimau(de)** [ɛskimo, od] <x> *adj a. péj* Eskimo

**Esquimau(de)** [ɛskimo, od] *m(f) a. péj* Eskimo

**esquisse** [ɛskis] *f* ❶ ART, ECON sketch ❷ (*amorce: d'un sourire, regret*) hint ❸ (*présentation rapide*) outline

**esquisser** [ɛskise] <1> **I.** *vt* ❶ ART to sketch ❷ (*amorcer*) **~ un sourire** to give a hint of a smile ❸ (*présenter rapidement*) to outline **II.** *vpr* **s'~** (*silhouette, solution*) to begin to emerge; **s'~ sur le visage de qn** (*sourire*) to flicker across sb's face

**esquiver** [ɛskive] <1> **I.** *vt* (*éviter*) to dodge **II.** *vpr* **s'~** to slip away

**essai** [ese] *m* ❶ *gén pl* (*test*) test; (*d'un appareil, médicament*) trial; **faire l'~ de qc** to try sth out; **être à l'~** to undergo testing; **mettre qn à l'~** to put sb to the test ❷ (*tentative*) attempt ❸ SPORT attempt, try, (*en sport automobile*) trial ❹ LIT essay ▶ **marquer/transformer un ~** SPORT to score/convert a try

**essaim** [esɛ̃] *m* swarm; **un ~ d'abeilles/de moustiques** a swarm of bees/mosquitos

**essayer** [eseje] <7> **I.** *vt* ❶ (*tester: chaussures, vêtement*) to try on; (*nourriture, médicament, méthode*) to try out; (*boucher, coiffeur*) to try ❷ (*tenter*) to try **II.** *vi* to try; **~ de** +*infin* to try to +*infin*; **ça ne coûte rien d'~** it costs nothing to try **III.** *vpr* **s'~ à une chose/activité** to try one's hand at sth/an activity

**essence** [esɑ̃s] *f* ❶ (*carburant*) gas, gasoline; **prendre de l'~** to get some gas ❷ (*nature profonde*) essence; **l'~ du livre** the essence of the book; **par ~** essentially

**essentiel** [esɑ̃sjɛl] *m* ❶ (*le plus important*) **l'~** the main thing; **emporter l'~** to take the bare essentials; **pour l'~** essentially; **aller à l'~** to get straight to the point ❷ (*la plus grande partie*) **l'~ de qc** the best part of sth

**essentiel(le)** [esɑ̃sjɛl] *adj a.* PHILOS essential

**essentiellement** [esɑ̃sjɛlmɑ̃] *adv* essentially

**essieu** [esjø] <x> *m* AUTO, TECH axle; **rupture d'~** broken axle

**essor** [esɔR] *m* (*développement*) rise; (*d'un art, d'une civilisation*) high point; **être en plein ~** to be thriving; (*ville*) to be booming ▶ **prendre son ~** (*industrie, secteur, entreprise*) to take off; (*oiseau*) to soar

**essorer** [esɔRe] <1> *vt, vi* (*à la main*) to wring, (*à la machine*) to spin dry

**essouffler** [esufle] <1> **I.** *vt* **~ qn** to leave sb out of breath **II.** *vpr* **s'~ à faire qc** to get out of breath doing sth; *fig* to wear oneself out doing sth

**essuie-glace** [esɥiglas] <essuie-glaces> *m* windshield wiper

**essuie-mains** [esɥimɛ̃] *m inv* hand towel

**essuie-tout** [esɥitu] *m inv* paper towel

**essuyer** [esɥije] <6> **I.** *vt* ❶ (*sécher*) to dry; (*larmes*) to wipe away ❷ (*éponger: surface*) to mop; (*de l'eau par terre*) to mop up ❸ (*nettoyer: meubles*) to clean;

E

**E**

(*chaussures*) to wipe ❹ (*subir: échec, perte*) to suffer; **~ des reproches/des coups** to be blamed/beaten; **~ un refus** to meet with a refusal **II.** *vpr* ❶ (*se sécher*) **s'~** to dry oneself ❷ (*se nettoyer*) **s'~ les pieds** to wipe one's feet

**est¹** [ɛ] *indic prés de* **être**

**est²** [ɛst] **I.** *m sans al* east; **l'~/l'Est** the east/East; **l'autoroute de l'Est** the eastern highway; **les régions de l'~** eastern regions; **l'Europe de l'~** Eastern Europe; **les pays de l'Est** the eastern countries; **le bloc de l'Est** the Eastern Bloc; **le conflit entre l'Est et l'Ouest** the East/West conflict; **à l'~** (*vers le point cardinal*) eastward; (*dans/vers la région*) to the east; **à l'~ de qc** east of sth; **dans l'~ de** in the east of; **vers l'~** (*direction*) eastward; (*position*) toward the east; **d'~ en ouest** from east to west **II.** *adj inv* east

**est-allemand(e)** [ɛstalmɑ̃, ɑ̃d] *adj* HIST East German

**est-ce que** [ɛskə] *adv* ne se traduit pas **où ~ tu vas?** where are you going?

**esthétique** [ɛstetik] **I.** *adj* aesthetic **II.** *f* ❶ (*beauté*) aesthetic ❷ (*théorie*) aesthetics + *vb sing*

**estimable** [ɛstimabl] *adj* ❶ (*digne d'estime: personne*) estimable; (*travail*) respectable ❷ (*assez bon, honnête: résultats*) respectable ❸ (*évaluable*) calculable

**estimatif, -ive** [ɛstimatif, -iv] *adj* (*bilan, coûts*) estimated; **devis ~** estimate

**estimation** [ɛstimasjɔ̃] *f* assessment

**estime** [ɛstim] *f* esteem; **digne d'~** worthy of esteem; **l'~ de soi-même** self-esteem; **avoir de l'~ pour qn** to esteem sb

**estimer** [ɛstime] <1> **I.** *vt* ❶ (*évaluer*) to estimate ❷ (*considérer*) **~ qc inutile** to consider sth unnecessary ❸ (*respecter*) **~ qn pour ses qualités humaines** to esteem sb for their human qualities; **savoir ~ un service à sa juste valeur** to recognize the true value of a favor **II.** *vpr* **s'~ trahi** to consider oneself betrayed; **s'~ heureux d'avoir été sé-**

lectionné to consider oneself lucky to have been selected

**estival(e)** [ɛstival, -o] <-aux> *adj* (*mode, période*) summer

**estomac** [ɛstɔma] *m* stomach; **avoir mal à l'~** to have a stomachache ▶ **il a l'~ dans les talons** he is starving; **avoir l'~ noué** to have a knot in one's stomach; **peser** [*o* **rester** *inf*] **sur l'~ à qn** to weigh on sb's stomach

**Estonie** [ɛstɔni] *f* **l'~** Estonia

**estonien** [ɛstɔnjɛ̃] *m* Estonian; *v.a.* **français**

**estonien(ne)** [ɛstɔnjɛ̃, jɛn] *adj* Estonian

**Estonien(ne)** [ɛstɔnjɛ̃, jɛn] *m(f)* Estonian

**estrade** [ɛstʀad] *f* platform

**estropier** [ɛstʀɔpje] <1a> **I.** *vt* to cripple; (*langue, nom*) to mangle **II.** *vpr* **s'~** to be crippled

**estuaire** [ɛstɥɛʀ] *m* estuary

**esturgeon** [ɛstyʀʒɔ̃] *m* sturgeon

**et** [e] *conj* and; **à quatre heures ~ demie** at four thirty; **son mari ~ son amant ...** both her husband and her lover ...; **~ alors!** so what!

**étable** [etabl] *f* cowshed

**établi(e)** [etabli] *adj* ❶ (*en place: ordre*) established; (*pouvoir*) ruling ❷ (*sûr: vérité, fait*) established ❸ *Suisse* (*installé*) settled

**établir** [etabliʀ] <8> **I.** *vt* ❶ (*édifier*) to set up ❷ (*fixer: liste, emploi du temps*) to draw up; (*prix*) to set ❸ (*rédiger: facture, chèque*) to make out; (*constat*) to draw up ❹ (*faire: comparaison*) to draw up ❺ (*déterminer: circonstances, identité*) to establish ❻ SPORT (*record*) to set **II.** *vpr* **s'~** ❶ (*s'installer*) to settle ❷ (*professionnellement*) to set up (in business); **s'~ à son compte** to set up (in business) on one's own ❸ (*s'instaurer: usage*) to become customary; (*relations*) to develop; (*régime*) to become established ❹ (*se rendre indépendant*) to settle (down); **tous mes enfants se sont établis** all my children are settled

**établissement** [etablismɑ̃] *m* ❶ (*insti-*

tution) setting up; **les ~s Dupond** Dupond Ltd.; **~ scolaire** school ❷(*hôtel*) establishment

**étage** [etaʒ] *m* (*d'une maison*) floor; **immeuble à** [*o* **de**] **trois/quatre ~s** three/four-story building; **à l'~** upstairs

**étagère** [etaʒɛʀ] *f* ❶(*tablette*) shelf ❷(*meuble*) shelves *pl*

**étain** [etɛ̃] *m* pewter

**étais** [etɛ] *imparf de* **être**

**étalage** [etalaʒ] *m* ❶ COM (*action*) window dressing ❷(*devanture*) display; (*tréteaux*) stall ❸(*déploiement*) show; **faire ~ de qc** to put on a show [*o* display] of sth

**étaler** [etale] <1> **I.** *vt* ❶(*éparpiller*) to strew ❷(*déployer: carte, journal*) to spread out; (*tapis*) to unroll ❸(*exposer pour la vente*) to set out ❹(*étendre: peinture, gravier*) to spread ❺(*dans le temps*) to spread out ❻(*exhiber: connaissances*) to parade; (*luxe*) to flaunt **II.** *vpr* ❶(*s'étendre*) **bien/mal s'~** (*beurre*) to spread with ease/difficulty; (*peinture*) to go on with ease/difficulty ❷(*dans l'espace*) **s'~** (*plaine, ville*) to spread out ❸(*s'afficher*) **s'~** (*inscription, nom*) to be written ❹(*s'exhiber*) **s'~** (*luxe*) to flaunt itself ❺(*se vautrer*) **s'~** to sprawl ❻ *inf* (*tomber*) **s'~** to go sprawling ❼(*dans le temps*) **s'~ dans le temps** to be spread out over time

**étanche** [etɑ̃ʃ] *adj* (*montre*) waterproof; (*compartiment*) watertight

**étang** [etɑ̃] *m* pond

**étant** [etɑ̃] *part prés de* **être**

**étape** [etap] *f* ❶(*trajet, période*) stage; **~ de la vie** stage in life; **d'~ en ~** step by step; **faire qc par ~s** to do sth in steps; **il ne faut pas brûler les ~s!** one mustn't take short cuts! ❷(*lieu d'arrêt, de repos*) stopping point; **faire ~** to stop off

**état** [eta] *m* ❶(*manière d'être*) state; **~ d'urgence** state of emergency; **dans l'~ actuel des choses** as things stand (at the present); **~ mental/physique** physical/mental condition; **être en ~**

(*stylo*) to work; (*machine, appareil*) to be in (good) working order; (*appartement, maison*) to be in good condition; **être en ~ de marche** (*voiture, bicyclette*) to be in (good) working condition; (*appareil, machine*) to be in (good) working order; **être en ~ de** +*infin* to be in a good state to +*infin* ❷(*liste: des recettes, dépenses*) statement ▶**en tout ~ de cause** in any event; **~ d'esprit** state of mind; **~ civil** civil status; (*service*) ≈ county clerk's office; **ne pas être dans son ~ normal** not to be one's usual self; **être dans un ~ second** (*drogué*) to be high; **avoir des ~s d'âme** to be in the grips of anxiety; **être dans tous ses ~s** to be (all) worked up; **être en ~ de choc** MED to be in a state of shock

**État** [eta] *m* POL state; **~s membres de l'UE** member states of the EU

**États-Unis** [etazyni] *mpl* **les ~ d'Amérique** the United States of America

**etc.** [ɛtsetera] *abr de* **et cætera, et cetera** etc.

**été¹** [ete] *m* summer; **l'~ indien** *Québec*(*bref retour du beau temps en octobre*) Indian summer; (*volcan*) extinct *v.a.* **automne**

**été²** [ete] *part passé de* **être**

**éteindre** [etɛ̃dʀ] *irr* **I.** *vt* ❶(*lumière, radio, chauffage*) to turn off; (*bougie*) to blow out; (*feu, cigarette*) to put out ❷(*éteindre la lumière de*) **~ la pièce/l'escalier** to turn the light off in the room/on the stairs **II.** *vi* to turn the light out **III.** *vpr* **s'~** (*cesser de brûler*) to go out

**éteint(e)** [etɛ̃, ɛ̃t] **I.** *part passé de* **éteindre** **II.** *adj* (*bougie, cigarette*) extinguished; (*volcan*) extinct

**étendre** [etɑ̃dʀ] <14> **I.** *vt* ❶(*coucher*) to lay out ❷(*poser à plat: tapis*) to unroll; **~ une couverture sur qn** to pull a blanket over sb ❸(*faire sécher*) to hang out ❹(*déployer: bras, jambes*) to stretch; (*ailes*) to spread ❺ *inf* (*faire tomber*) to floor ❻ *inf* (*coller à un examen*) to fail **II.** *vpr* ❶(*se reposer*) **s'~** to lie down ❷(*s'allonger*) to stretch oneself out ❸ (*s'appesantir*) **s'~ sur qc** to expand on sth ❹ (*occuper*) **s'~** to stretch out ❺ (*augmenter*) **s'~** (*épidémie, incendie, tache*) to spread; (*ville, pouvoir, connaissances, cercle*) to grow

**étendu(e)** [etɑ̃dy] **I.** *part passé de* **étendre II.** *adj* ❶ (*déployé: corps, jambes*) outstretched; (*ailes*) outspread ❷ (*vaste: plaine, vue*) wide; (*ville*) sprawling ❸ (*considérable: connaissances, vocabulaire*) extensive; (*pouvoir*) wide-ranging; (*signification*) broad

**étendue** [etɑ̃dy] *f* ❶ (*dimension: d'un pays*) area ❷ (*espace*) expanse ❸ (*ampleur: d'une catastrophe*) scale; **l'~ des connaissances de qn** the extent of sb's knowledge

**éternel(le)** [etɛʀnɛl] *adj* ❶ (*qui dure longtemps*) eternal; (*regrets*) endless; (*recommencement*) constant ❷ *antéposé* (*inévitable*) inevitable ❸ *antéposé, péj* (*sempiternel*) perpetual

**éternellement** [etɛʀnɛlmɑ̃] *adv* eternally; (*depuis toujours*) always; (*sans arrêt*) constantly

**éterniser** [etɛʀnize] <1> **I.** *vt* (*faire traîner*) ~ **qc** to drag sth out **II.** *vpr* ❶ (*traîner*) to drag on ❷ *inf* (*s'attarder*) to take forever; **s'~ sur un sujet** to dwell endlessly on a subject

**éternité** [etɛʀnite] *f* eternity

**éternuement** [etɛʀnymɑ̃] *m gén pl* sneeze; **des ~s** sneezing + *vb sing*

**éternuer** [etɛʀnɥe] <1> *vi* to sneeze

**êtes** [ɛt] *indic prés de* **être**

**Éthiopie** [etjɔpi] *f* **l'~** Ethiopia

**éthiopien** [etjɔpjɛ̃] *m* Ethiopian; *v.a.* **français**

**éthiopien(ne)** [etjɔpjɛ̃, jɛn] *adj* Ethiopian

**Éthiopien(ne)** [etjɔpjɛ̃, jɛn] *m(f)* Ethiopian

**éthique** [etik] **I.** *adj* ethical **II.** *f* ethics *pl*

**étincelant(e)** [etɛ̃s(ə)lɑ̃, ɑ̃t] *adj* ❶ (*scintillant*) sparkling ❷ (*éclatant: couleurs*) brilliant

**étinceler** [etɛ̃s(ə)le] <3> *vi* ❶ (*à la lumière: diamant*) to sparkle; (*or, cou-*

*teau, lame*) to gleam; (*étoile*) to twinkle ❷ (*de propreté: vitre*) to gleam

**étincelle** [etɛ̃sɛl] *f* ❶ (*parcelle incandescente*) spark ❷ (*lueur*) **des ~s s'allument dans ses yeux** fire flashed in her eyes ❸ (*un petit peu de*) **une ~ de génie/d'intelligence** a spark of genius/intelligence

**étiqueter** [etikte] <3> *vt* to label

**étiquette** [etikɛt] *f* ❶ (*marque*) *a.* INFORM label; **~ de réseau** netiquette ❷ (*adhésif*) sticker; (*de prix*) ticket ❸ (*protocole*) **l'~** etiquette

**étirer** [etiʀe] <1> *vpr* **s'~** ❶ (*s'allonger*) to stretch out ❷ (*se distendre: textile*) to stretch

**étoffe** [etɔf] *f* material

**étoile** [etwal] *f* star; **~ filante/du berger** shooting/evening star; **restaurant cinq ~s** five-star restaurant ▸ **coucher** [*o* **dormir**] **à la belle ~** to sleep under the stars; **avoir foi** [*o* **être confiant**] **en son ~** to follow one's star

**étoilé(e)** [etwale] *adj* (*nuit*) starry

**étonnant(e)** [etɔnɑ̃, ɑ̃t] *m* **l'~ est qu'elle reste** the amazing thing is that she's staying

**étonnant(e)** [etɔnɑ̃, ɑ̃t] *adj* ❶ (*surprenant*) amazing; **ce n'est pas ~** it's no surprise ❷ (*remarquable: personne, ouvrage*) astonishing

**étonné(e)** [etɔne] *adj* astonished

**étonnement** [etɔnmɑ̃] *m* astonishment

**étonner** [etɔne] <1> **I.** *vt* to astonish **II.** *vpr* **s'~ de qc** to be surprised at sth

**étouffant(e)** [etufɑ̃, ɑ̃t] *adj* stifling

**étouffé(e)** [etufe] *adj* (*bruit, son*) muffled; (*rires*) stifled

**étouffer** [etufe] <1> **I.** *vt* ❶ (*priver d'air*) to stifle; (*tuer*) to suffocate; **cette chaleur m'étouffe** I'm stifled by this heat ❷ (*arrêter: feu*) to smother ❸ (*atténuer: bruit*) to muffle ❹ (*dissimuler: bâillement*) to stifle; (*sanglot*) to strangle; (*scandale*) to hush up ❺ (*faire taire: rumeur, opposition*) to stifle ❻ (*réprimer: révolte*) to put down **II.** *vi* to suffocate; **on étouffe ici!** it's suffocating in here! **III.** *vpr* **s'~** to choke

**étourderie** [eturdəri] *f* ❶ *sans pl* (*caractère*) absent-mindedness ❷ (*acte*) careless mistake

**étourdi(e)** [eturdi] **I.** *adj* scatterbrained **II.** *m(f)* scatterbrain

**étourdir** [eturdir] <8> **I.** *vt* ❶ (*assommer*) to stun ❷ (*abrutir*) ~ **qn** (*bruit*) to deafen sb; (*mouvement*) to make sb dizzy; (*paroles*) to daze sb ❸ (*enivrer*) ~ **qn** (*parfum, vin*) to go to sb's head **II.** *vpr* **s'**~ to make oneself numb

**étourdissant(e)** [eturdisã, ãt] *adj* (*bruit*) deafening; (*succès, personne*) stunning; (*rythme*) dizzying

**étourdissement** [eturdismã] *m* dizzy spell

**étrange** [etrãʒ] *adj* strange

**étrangement** [etrãʒmã] *adv* ❶ (*de façon étrange*) strangely ❷ (*beaucoup, très*) surprisingly

**étranger** [etrãʒe] *m* **l'**~ foreign countries; **séjourner à l'**~ to live abroad

**étranger, -ère** [etrãʒe, -ɛr] **I.** *adj* ❶ (*d'un autre pays*) foreign ❷ (*d'un autre groupe*) outside ❸ (*non familier: usage, notion*) unfamiliar ❹ (*extérieur*) **être** ~ **au sujet** to be irrelevant to the subject **II.** *m, f* ❶ (*d'un autre pays*) foreigner ❷ (*d'une autre région*) outsider

**étrangeté** [etrãʒte] *f sans pl* (*originalité*) strangeness

**étrangler** [etrãgle] <1> **I.** *vt* ❶ (*tuer*) to strangle ❷ (*serrer le cou*) ~ **qn** (*cravate*) to choke sb ❸ (*empêcher qn de parler*) **l'émotion/la fureur l'étranglait** she was choking with emotion/fury **II.** *vpr* **s'**~ **avec qc** ❶ (*mourir*) to strangle oneself with sth ❷ (*en mangeant*) to choke on sth

**être** [ɛtr] *irr* **I.** *vi* ❶ (*pour qualifier, indiquer le lieu*) to be; ~ **professeur/infirmière** to be a teacher/a nurse ❷ (*pour indiquer la date, la période*) **on est le 2 mai/mercredi** it's May 2/Wednesday ❸ (*appartenir*) ~ **à qn** to belong to sb ❹ (*travailler*) ~ **dans l'enseignement/le textile** to be in teaching/textiles ❺ (*pour indiquer l'activité en cours*) ~ **toujours à faire qc** to be al-

ways doing sth ❻ (*pour exprimer une étape d'une évolution*) **où en es-tu de tes maths?** how are you doing in math?; **j'en suis à me demander si …** I'm beginning to wonder if … ❼ (*être absorbé par, attentif à*) ~ **tout à son travail** to be completely wrapped up in one's work ❽ (*pour exprimer l'obligation*) **qc est à faire** sth must be done ❾ (*provenir*) ~ **de qn** (*enfant*) to be sb's; (*œuvre*) to be by sb; ~ **d'une région/famille** to be from a region/family ❿ (*être vêtu/chaussé de*) ~ **en costume/pantoufles** to be in a suit/slippers ⓫ *au passé* (*aller*) **avoir été faire/acheter qc** to have gone to do/buy sth ⓬ (*exister*) to be ▸ **je n'y suis pour rien** it has nothing to do with me; **ça y est** (*c'est fini*) that's it; (*je comprends*) I see; (*je te l'avais dit*) there you are; (*pour calmer qn*) there, there; **c'est vrai, n'est-ce pas?** it's true, isn't it? **II.** *vi impers* **il est impossible/étonnant que qn ait fait qc** (*subj*) it's impossible/surprising that sb did sth; **il est dix heures/midi/minuit** it's ten o'clock/noon/midnight **III.** *aux* ❶ (*comme auxiliaire du passé actif*) ~ **venu** to have come ❷ (*comme auxiliaire du passif*) **le sol est lavé chaque jour** the floor is washed every day **IV.** *m* being

**étrier** [etrije] *m* stirrup

**étroit(e)** [etrwa, wat] *adj* ❶ (*opp: large: rue*) narrow; (*chaussures*) tight; **il est à l'**~ **dans cette veste** that jacket is rather tight on him ❷ (*opp: lâche, relâché: lien, surveillance*) tight

**étude** [etyd] **I.** *f* ❶ (*apprentissage*) study ❷ (*recherches, ouvrage: de la nature, d'un dossier, projet*) study; ~ **de marché** market research; ~ **sur qc** study on sth ❸ (*bureau: d'un notaire*) office ❹ ÉCOLE (*moment*) prep **II.** *fpl* study; ~**s primaires/secondaires/supérieures** primary/secondary/higher education; **faire des** ~**s** to go to college

**étudiant(e)** [etydjã, jãt] **I.** *adj* student **II.** *m(f)* student

**étudier** [etydje] <1> **I.** *vt, vi* to study **II.** *vpr* **s'~** ❶ (*s'analyser*) to analyze oneself ❷ (*s'observer mutuellement*) to study each other

**étui** [etɥi] *m* case

**eu(e)** [y] *part passé de* **avoir**

**eucalyptus** [økaliptys] *m* eucalyptus

**euh** [ø] *interj* er

**euphorique** [øfɔrik] *adj* euphoric

**EUR** *m abr de* **euro** EUR

**eurasien(ne)** [ørazjɛ̃, jɛn] *adj* Eurasian

**Eurasien(ne)** [ørazjɛ̃, jɛn] *m(f)* Eurasian

**euro** [øro] *m* (*monnaie*) euro

**Europe** [ørɔp] *f* l'~ Europe; l'~ **centrale/de l'Est/l'Ouest** Central/Eastern/Western Europe

**européanisation** [ørɔpeanizasjɔ̃] *f* Europeanization

**européaniser** [ørɔpeanize] <1> **I.** *vt* to Europeanize **II.** *vpr* **s'~** to be Europeanized

**européen(ne)** [ørɔpeɛ̃, ɛn] **I.** *adj* ❶ GEO **le continent ~** the European continent ❷ POL, ECON European; **l'Union ~ne** the European Union **II.** *fpl* (*élections*) the European elections

**Européen(ne)** [ørɔpeɛ̃, ɛn] *m(f)* European

**eurosignal** [ørosiɲal] *m* pager

**eus** [y] *passé simple de* **avoir**

**eux** [ø] *pron pers, pl masc ou mixte* ❶ *inf* (*pour renforcer*) ~, **ils n'ont pas ouvert la bouche** THEY didn't open their mouths; **c'est ~ qui l'ont dit** THEY said it ❷ *avec une préposition* **avec/sans** ~ with/without them; **à ~ seuls** by themselves; **c'est à ~!** it's theirs! ❸ *dans une comparaison* them; **plus fort qu'~** stronger than them ❹ (*soi*) them; *v.a.* **lui**

**eux-mêmes** [ømɛm] *pron pers* (*eux en personne*) themselves; *v.a.* **moi--même, nous-même**

**évacuation** [evakɥasjɔ̃] *f* ❶ (*opération organisée: des habitants, blessés*) evacuation; (*d'une salle de tribunal*) clearing ❷ (*écoulement*) draining; **système d'~** drainage system ❸ *Suisse* (*ac-*

*tion de vider*) ~ **des ordures** waste disposal

**évacuer** [evakɥe] <1> *vt* ❶ *a.* MIL (*ville, habitants, blessés*) to evacuate ❷ (*vider: eaux usées*) to drain away

**évadé(e)** [evade] *m(f)* escapee

**évader** [evade] <1> *vpr* ❶ (*s'échapper*) **s'~ d'une prison** to escape from prison ❷ (*fuir*) **s'~ du réel** to escape reality

**évaluation** [evalɥasjɔ̃] *f* ❶ (*estimation approximative: des coûts, risques, chances*) assessment; (*d'une fortune*) valuation ❷ (*par expertise: des dégâts*) appraisal; ~ **des connaissances** ECOLE aptitude test

**évaluer** [evalɥe] <1> *vt* (*poids, distance*) to estimate; (*chances*) to assess

**évanoui(e)** [evanwi] *adj* ❶ (*sans conscience: personne*) unconscious; **tomber ~** to faint ❷ (*disparu: bonheur, rêve*) vanished

**évanouir** [evanwir] <8> *vpr* ❶ (*perdre connaissance*) **s'~ de qc** to faint with sth ❷ (*disparaître*) **s'~** (*image, fantôme*) to vanish; (*illusions, espoirs*) to fade away

**évanouissement** [evanwismɑ̃] *m* ❶ (*syncope*) faint; **avoir un ~** to faint ❷ (*disparition*) disappearance; (*d'une illusion, d'un rêve*) vanishing

**évaporation** [evapɔrasjɔ̃] *f* evaporation

**évaporer** [evapɔre] <1> *vpr* **s'~** (*eau, parfum*) to evaporate

**évasif, -ive** [evazif, -iv] *adj* evasive

**évasion** [evazjɔ̃] *f* escape

**éveil** [evɛj] *m* ❶ (*état éveillé*) **tenir qn en ~** to keep sb on the alert ❷ (*réveil*) ~ **des sens/d'un sentiment chez qn** the awakening of the senses/of a feeling in sb

**éveillé(e)** [eveje] *adj* ❶ (*en état de veille*) awake ❷ (*alerte*) alert; **esprit ~** lively mind

**éveiller** [eveje] <1> **I.** *vt* ❶ (*faire naître: attention*) to attract; (*désir, soupçons*) to arouse ❷ (*développer: intelligence*) to stimulate **II.** *vpr* ❶ (*naître*) **s'~ chez** [*o* **en**] **qn** (*amour*) to awaken in sb; (*soupçon*) to be aroused in sb's mind

**❷** (*éprouver pour la première fois*) **s'~ à l'amour** (*personne*) to awaken to love **❸** (*se mettre à fonctionner*) **s'~** (*esprit*) to come to life

**événement, évènement** [evɛnmɑ̃] *m* event ► **elle est dépassée par les ~s** she's been overtaken by the events

**éventail** [evɑ̃taj] <s> *m* **❶** fan; **en ~** fan-shaped **❷** (*choix*) range

**éventualité** [evɑ̃tɥalite] *f* **❶** (*caractère*) **dans l'~ d'une guerre** in the event of a war **❷** (*possibilité*) possibility

**éventuel(le)** [evɑ̃tɥɛl] *adj* possible

**éventuellement** [evɑ̃tɥɛlmɑ̃] *adv* possibly

**évêque** [evɛk] *m* bishop

**évidemment** [evidamɑ̃] *adv* **❶** (*en tête de phrase, en réponse*) of course **❷** (*comme on peut le voir*) obviously

**évidence** [evidɑ̃s] *f* **❶** *sans pl* (*caractère*) obviousness; **de toute** [*o* à l'] ~ obviously **❷** (*fait*) obvious fact; **c'est une ~** it's obvious; **se rendre à l'~** to accept the obvious **❸** (*vue*) **être bien en ~** (*objet*) to be there for all to see

**évident(e)** [evidɑ̃, ɑ̃t] *adj* obvious; (*signe*) clear; (*bonne volonté*) evident; **il est ~ que qn a fait qc** it's obvious sb did sth ► **c'est pas ~!** *inf* it's no simple matter!

**évier** [evje] *m* sink

**évitable** [evitabl] *adj* avoidable

**éviter** [evite] <1> I. *vt* **❶** (*se soustraire à, fuir: erreur, endroit, regard, conflit*) to avoid; **~ de faire qc** to avoid doing sth; **~ que qn (ne) fasse qc** (*subj*) to prevent sb from doing sth; **il m'évite** he's avoiding me **❷** (*se dérober à: sort, corvée*) to evade; **~ de faire qc** to get out of doing sth **❸** (*épargner*) **~ qc à qn** to spare sb sth II. *vpr* **❶** (*essayer de ne pas se rencontrer*) **s'~** to avoid each other **❷** (*ne pas avoir*) **s'~ des soucis/ tracas** to avoid worries/trouble

**évolué(e)** [evɔlɥe] *adj* (*pays, société*) advanced; (*idées, personne*) progressive

**évoluer** [evɔlɥe] <1> *vi* **❶** (*changer: chose, monde*) to change; (*sciences*) to

evolve, to advance; (*goûts, situation*) to develop **❷** (*se transformer: personne, maladie*) to develop; **~ vers qc** to develop into sth

**évolution** [evɔlysjɔ̃] *f* **❶** (*développement: d'une personne, maladie, d'un phénomène*) development; (*des goûts, comportements*) change; (*des sciences*) advance; **l'~ des techniques** technical progress **❷** BIO evolution; **théorie de l'~** theory of evolution

**évoquer** [evɔke] <1> *vt* **❶** (*rappeler à la mémoire: fait, enfance, souvenirs*) to recall; **~ qn** to call sb to mind **❷** (*décrire*) to conjure up **❸** (*faire allusion à: problème, sujet*) to bring up **❹** (*faire penser à*) **ce mot n'évoque rien pour moi** the word doesn't bring anything to mind

**ex¹** [ɛks] *mf inf* ex

**ex², ex.** [ɛks] *abr de* **exemple** e.g.

**exact(e)** [ɛgzakt] *adj* **❶** (*précis: description, valeur, mots*) exact **❷** (*correct: calculs, réponse*) right; **c'est ~ qu'elle l'a fait** it is true that she did it **❸** (*ponctuel: personne*) punctual

**exactement** [ɛgzaktəmɑ̃] *adv* exactly

**exactitude** [ɛgzaktityd] *f* **❶** (*précision*) accuracy; **avec ~** accurately **❷** (*ponctualité*) punctuality; **arriver avec ~** to arrive right on time

**ex æquo** [ɛgzeko] I. *adj inv* **être premier ~ en qc** to be tied for first in sth II. *adv* (*classer*) equal; **arriver en troisième place ~** to finish tied for third place

**exagération** [ɛgzaʒerasjɔ̃] *f* exaggeration

**exagéré(e)** [ɛgzaʒere] *adj* exaggerated; (*prix*) inflated

**exagérer** [ɛgzaʒere] <5> I. *vt* to exaggerate II. *vi* **❶** (*amplifier en parlant*) to exaggerate **❷** (*abuser*) to go too far

**exalté(e)** [ɛgzalte] I. *adj* excited; (*personne*) elated; (*imagination*) fevered II. *m(f) péj* hothead

**examen** [ɛgzamɛ̃] *m* **❶** examination; **~ d'entrée/de passage** entrance/final exam **❷** JUR **mise en ~** charging

**examinateur, -trice** [ɛgzaminatœʀ, -tʀis] *m, f* examiner

**examiner** [ɛgzamine] <1> I. *vt* to examine; (*maison*) to look over II. *vpr* **s'~ dans un miroir** to examine oneself in a mirror

**exaspérant(e)** [ɛgzaspeʀɑ̃, ɑ̃t] *adj* exasperating

**exaspérer** [ɛgzaspeʀe] <5> *vt* ~ **qn avec qc** to exasperate sb with sth

**exaucer** [ɛgzose] <2> *vt* ❶ (*écouter: Dieu*) to hear ❷ (*réaliser: désir, souhait*) to grant

**excédent** [ɛksedɑ̃] *m* surplus; ~ **de bagages** excess baggage

**excellence** [ɛkselɑ̃s] *f* excellence ▶ **par** ~ par excellence

**excellent(e)** [ɛkselɑ̃, ɑ̃t] *adj* excellent

**excentricité** [ɛksɑ̃tʀisite] *f sans pl* eccentricity

**excentrique** [ɛksɑ̃tʀik] I. *adj* eccentric II. *mf* eccentric

**excepté** [ɛksɛpte] *prep* except; ~ **que/ si qn fait qc** except that/if sb does sth; **avoir tout prévu, ~ ce cas** to have foreseen everything but this situation

**exception** [ɛksɛpsjɔ̃] *f* exception; **régime d'~** special treatment; **faire ~ à la règle** to be an exception to the rule; **à l'~ de qn/qc** with the exception of sb/ sth; **sauf ~** allowing for exceptions

**exceptionnel(le)** [ɛksɛpsjɔnɛl] *adj* ❶ (*extraordinaire: personne*) exceptional; (*occasion*) unique; **cela n'a rien d'~** there's nothing remarkable about that ❷ (*occasionnel: prime, congé, mesure*) special; **à titre ~** exceptionally

**exceptionnellement** [ɛksɛpsjɔnɛlmɑ̃] *adv* exceptionally

**excès** [ɛksɛ] *m* ❶ (*surplus*) ~ **de vitesse** speeding; ~ **de zèle** overzealousness ❷ *pl* (*abus, violences*) excesses ▶ **tomber dans l'~ inverse** to go to the opposite extreme

**excessif, -ive** [ɛksesif, -iv] *adj* ❶ excessive ❷ (*immodéré: tempérament*) extreme

**excitant(e)** [ɛksitɑ̃, ɑ̃t] *adj* ❶ exciting ❷ (*stimulant: café*) stimulating

**excitation** [ɛksitasjɔ̃] *f* excitement

**excité(e)** [ɛksite] I. *adj* excited II. *m(f)* hothead

**exciter** [ɛksite] <1> I. *vt* ❶ (*provoquer: désir, curiosité*) to arouse ❷ (*aviver: imagination*) to excite; (*douleur*) to increase ❸ (*passionner*) ~ **qn** (*idée, travail*) to excite sb; (*sensation*) to give sb a thrill ❹ (*mettre en colère*) ~ **qn** (*personne*) to irritate sb; (*alcool, chaleur*) to make sb irritable ❺ (*troubler sexuellement*) to arouse II. *vpr* **s'~ sur qc** ❶ (*s'énerver*) to get worked up about sth ❷ *inf* (*s'acharner*) to go hard at sth

**exclamation** [ɛksklamasjɔ̃] *f* exclamation; **point d'~** exclamation point

**exclu(e)** [ɛkskly] I. *part passé de* **exclure** II. *adj* ❶ (*impossible*) **il n'est pas ~ que** +*subj* it is not impossible that ❷ (*non compris*) **mardi** ~ except (for) Tuesday III. *m(f)* **les ~s** the excluded

**exclure** [ɛksklyʀ] *irr* I. *vt* ❶ (*sortir*) ~ **qn d'un parti/d'une école** to expel sb from a party/a school ❷ (*écarter: possibilité, hypothèse*) to rule out; (*élément*) to ignore II. *vpr* **s'~** to be mutually exclusive

**exclusif, -ive** [ɛksklyzif, -iv] *adj* exclusive

**exclusion** [ɛksklyzjɔ̃] *f* exclusion; (*du lycée*) expulsion

**exclusivement** [ɛksklyzivmɑ̃] *adv* ❶ (*seulement, uniquement*) exclusively ❷ (*exclu*) exclusive

**exclusivité** [ɛksklyzivite] *f* exclusive rights *pl;* **une ~ XY** an XY exclusive, a scoop ▶ **en** ~ exclusively

**excursion** [ɛkskyʀsjɔ̃] *f* excursion

**excuse** [ɛkskyz] *f* ❶ (*raison, prétexte*) excuse ❷ *pl* (*regret*) **faire des ~s** to apologize for; **mille ~s!** I'm so sorry!

**excuser** [ɛkskyze] <1> I. *vt* ❶ (*pardonner: faute, retard*) to forgive; **excuse-moi/excusez-moi!** forgive me! ❷ (*défendre: personne, conduite*) to excuse II. *vpr* **s'~ de qc** to apologize for sth ▶ **je m'excuse de vous déranger** forgive me for bothering me

**exécuter** [ɛgzekyte] <1> *vt* ❶ (*effec-*

*tuer: projet*) to carry out; (*travail*) to do; **~ les dernières volontés de qn** to grant sb's last wishes ❷ INFORM (*fichier*) to run ❸ (*tuer*) to execute

**exécution** [ɛgzekysjɔ̃] *f* ❶ (*d'un travail*) doing; (*d'un projet*) carrying out; (*d'un programme*) implementation; (*d'une commande*) fulfillment; **mettre une loi à ~** to enforce a law; **mettre une menace à ~** to carry out a threat ❷ JUR (*d'un jugement*) enforcement ❸ (*mise à mort*) execution

**exemplaire** [ɛgzɑ̃plɛʀ] **I.** *adj* exemplary **II.** *m* ❶ (*copie: d'un livre*) copy; **en deux ~s** in duplicate ❷ (*spécimen*) specimen

**exemple** [ɛgzɑ̃pl] *m* (*modèle, illustration*) example; **donner l'~** to show an example; **prendre ~ sur qn** to follow sb's example; **par ~** for example

**exercer** [ɛgzɛʀse] <2> **I.** *vt* ❶ (*pratiquer: fonction*) to fulfill; **~ le métier de professeur/d'infirmière** to work as a teacher/nurse ❷ (*mettre en usage: pouvoir, droit*) to exercise; (*talent*) to use; (*pression, autorité*) to exert ❸ (*entraîner: oreille, goût, mémoire*) to train; (*jugement*) to exercise **II.** *vi* to practice **III.** *vpr* ❶ (*s'entraîner*) **s'~** to practice; SPORT to train; **s'~ à la trompette** to practice the trumpet ❷ (*se manifester*) **s'~ dans un domaine** (*habileté, influence*) to be put to use in a field

**exercice** [ɛgzɛʀsis] *m* ❶ ÉCOLE, MUS, SPORT exercise; **~ à trous** fill-in-the blank exercise ❷ *sans pl* (*activité physique*) exercise; **faire** [*o* **prendre**] **de l'~** to exercise ❸ (*pratique: d'un droit, du pouvoir*) practice; **dans l'~ de ses fonctions** in the exercise of one's duties ▸ **en ~** practicing; POL in office

**ex-femme** [ɛksfam] <ex-femmes> *f* **mon ~** my ex-wife

**exhibitionniste** [ɛgzibisjɔnist] **I.** *m/f* exhibitionist **II.** *adj* exhibitionistic

**exigeant(e)** [ɛgziʒɑ̃, ʒɑ̃t] *adj* demanding; **être ~ à l'égard de qn** to demand a lot of sb

**exigence** [ɛgziʒɑ̃s] *f* ❶ (*caractère*) demanding attitude ❷ *pl* (*prétentions*) demands ❸ *pl* (*impératifs*) **~s de la mode** (fashion) dictates

**exiger** [ɛgziʒe] <2a> *vt* ❶ (*réclamer*) to demand ❷ (*nécessiter: personne, animal, plante*) to require; (*travail, circonstances*) to demand

**exil** [ɛgzil] *m* exile; **condamner qn à l'~** to exile sb

**exilé(e)** [ɛgzile] **I.** *adj* exiled **II.** *m(f)* exile

**exiler** [ɛgzile] <1> **I.** *vt* to exile **II.** *vpr* **s'~** to go into exile; **s'~ en France** to go off to France in exile

**existence** [ɛgzistɑ̃s] *f* existence

**exister** [ɛgziste] <1> *vi* to exist

**ex-mari** [ɛksmaʀi] <ex-maris> *m* **mon ~** my ex-husband

**exotique** [ɛgzɔtik] *adj* exotic

**expansion** [ɛkspɑ̃sjɔ̃] *f* ÉCON expansion; **~ démographique** population growth; **être en pleine ~** to be booming; **secteur en pleine ~** boom sector

**expatrier** [ɛkspatʀije] <1> **I.** *vt* (*personne*) to expatriate **II.** *vpr* **s'~** to leave one's own country

**expédier** [ɛkspedje] <1> *vt* (*envoyer*) to send; **~ qc par bateau** to send sth by sea

**expéditeur, -trice** [ɛkspeditœʀ, -tʀis] **I.** *m, f* sender **II.** *adj* **bureau ~** forwarding office

**expéditif, -ive** [ɛkspeditif, -iv] *adj* ❶ (*rapide: solution, méthode*) expeditious; **justice expéditive** rough justice ❷ (*trop rapide*) hasty

**expédition** [ɛkspedisjɔ̃] *f* ❶ (*envoi*) dispatching; (*par la poste*) sending ❷ (*mission*) expedition ❸ (*exécution: des affaires courantes*) dispatching

**expérience** [ɛkspeʀjɑ̃s] *f* ❶ *sans pl* (*pratique*) experience; **par ~** from experience ❷ (*événement*) experience; **~ amoureuse** love affair ❸ (*essai*) experiment; **~s sur les animaux** animal experiments

**expérimenté(e)** [ɛkspeʀimɑ̃te] *adj* experienced

**expérimenter** [ɛkspeʀimɑ̃te] <1> vt ~ **un médicament sur qn/un animal** to test a drug on sb/an animal

**expert(e)** [ɛkspɛʀ, ɛʀt] I. adj (cuisinière) expert; (médecin) specialist; (technicien) trained II. m(f) ❶ (spécialiste) expert ❷ JUR (pour évaluer un objet, des dommages) assessor

**expert-comptable, experte-comptable** [ɛkspɛʀkɔ̃tabl, ɛkspɛʀtkɔ̃tabl] <experts-comptables> m, f accountant

**expertise** [ɛkspɛʀtiz] f ❶ (estimation de la valeur) valuation ❷ (examen) appraisal

**expertiser** [ɛkspɛʀtize] <1> vt ❶ (étudier l'authenticité) to appraise ❷ (estimer) to assess

**expiration** [ɛkspiʀasjɔ̃] f ❶ ANAT exhalation ❷ (fin: d'un délai, mandat) expiry

**expirer** [ɛkspiʀe] <1> I. vt to exhale II. vi (s'achever: mandat, délai) to expire

**explicatif, -ive** [ɛksplikatif, -iv] adj explanatory

**explication** [ɛksplikasjɔ̃] f ❶ (indication, raison) explanation ❷ (commentaire, annotation) commentary; ~ **de texte** critical analysis ❸ (discussion) discussion ❹ pl (mode d'emploi) instructions

**explicitement** [ɛksplisitmɑ̃] adv explicitly

**expliquer** [ɛksplike] <1> I. vt ❶ (faire connaître) to explain; ~ **à qn pourquoi/comment qn a fait qc** to explain to sb why/how sb did sth ❷ (faire comprendre: fonctionnement) to explain; (texte) to comment on II. vpr ❶ (se faire comprendre) s'~ to explain ❷ (justifier) s'~ **sur son choix** to explain one's choice ❸ (rendre des comptes à) s'~ **devant le tribunal/la police** to explain to the court/the police ❹ (avoir une discussion) s'~ **avec son fils sur qc** to clear the air with one about sth ❺ (comprendre) s'~ **qc** to explain sth ❻ (être compréhensible) s'~ to become clear

**exploit** [ɛksplwa] m ❶ (prouesse) feat ❷ iron exploit

**exploitant(e)** [ɛksplwatɑ̃, ɑ̃t] m(f) ~ **agricole** farmer

**exploitation** [ɛksplwatasjɔ̃] f ❶ (action: d'une ferme, mine) working; (de ressources naturelles) exploitation ❷ (entreprise) concern; ~ **agricole** farm ❸ (utilisation: d'une situation, idée) exploitation; (de données) utilization ❹ (abus) exploitation

**exploiter** [ɛksplwate] <1> vt ❶ (faire valoir: terre, mine) to work; (ressources) to exploit ❷ (utiliser: situation) to exploit; ~ **une idée/les résultats** to make use of an idea/the results ❸ (abuser) to exploit

**explorateur** [ɛksplɔʀatœʀ] m INFORM browser; ~ **de réseau** network explorer

**explorateur, -trice** [ɛksplɔʀatœʀ, -tʀis] m, f explorer

**explorer** [ɛksplɔʀe] <1> vt to explore

**exploser** [ɛksploze] <1> vi to explode

**explosif** [ɛksplozif] m explosive

**explosif, -ive** [ɛksplozif, -iv] adj explosive; **obus** ~ explosive shell

**explosion** [ɛksplozjɔ̃] f ❶ (éclatement: d'une bombe) explosion ❷ (manifestation soudaine) ~ **de joie/colère** outburst of joy/anger; ~ **démographique** population explosion

**exportateur** [ɛkspɔʀtatœʀ] m (pays) exporting

**exportateur, -trice** [ɛkspɔʀtatœʀ, -tʀis] I. adj exporting II. m, f (personne) exporter

**exportation** [ɛkspɔʀtasjɔ̃] f ❶ (action) export(ation) ❷ pl (biens) exports ❸ INFORM export

**exporter** [ɛkspɔʀte] <1> vt a. INFORM to export

**exposé** [ɛkspoze] m ❶ (discours) talk; **faire un** ~ **sur qc** to give a talk on sth ❷ (description) account

**exposer** [ɛkspoze] <1> I. vt ❶ (montrer: tableau) to exhibit; (marchandise) to display ❷ (décrire) ~ **qc** to set sth out ❸ (mettre en péril: vie, honneur) to risk

**④** (*disposer*) **~ qc au soleil** to expose sth to the sun; **une pièce bien exposée** a well-lit room **II.** *vpr* **s'~ à qc** to expose oneself to sth

**exposition** [ɛkspozisjɔ̃] *f* **①** (*étalage: de marchandise*) display **②** (*présentation, foire*) *a.* ART exhibition **③** (*orientation*) **~ au sud** southern exposure **④** (*action de soumettre à qc*) *a.* PHOT exposure

**exprès** [ɛksprɛ] *adv* **①** (*intentionnellement*) on purpose **②** (*spécialement*) (**tout**) **~** specially

**express** [ɛksprɛs] **I.** *adj* **café ~** espresso coffee; **train ~** express train **II.** *m* **①** (*café*) espresso **②** (*train*) express train

**expressif, -ive** [ɛksprɛsif, -iv] *adj* expressive

**expression** [ɛksprɛsjɔ̃] *f* expression; **~ familière/figée** colloquial/set expression ▶ **veuillez agréer l'~ de mes sentiments distingués** yours truly

**exprimer** [ɛksprime] <1> **I.** *vt* **①** (*faire connaître*) to express **②** (*indiquer*) **~ qc** (*signe*) to indicate sth **II.** *vpr* **①** (*parler*) to express oneself; **s'~ en français** to speak in French; **ne pas s'~** to say nothing **②** (*se manifester*) **s'~ sur un visage** to show on a face

**expulser** [ɛkspylse] <1> *vt* **①** (*élève, étranger*) to expel; (*joueur*) to eject

**expulsion** [ɛkspylsjɔ̃] *f* (*d'un élève, étranger*) expulsion; (*d'un locataire*) eviction; (*d'un joueur*) ejection

**exquis(e)** [ɛkski, iz] *adj* (*goût, manières, plat, parfum*) exquisite; (*personne, journée*) delightful

**extensible** [ɛkstɑ̃sibl] *adj* extending

**extension** [ɛkstɑ̃sjɔ̃] *f* **①** (*allongement: d'un ressort*) stretching; (*d'un bras*) extension **②** (*accroissement: d'une ville*) growth; (*d'un incendie, d'une épidémie*) spreading **③** INFORM **~ de mémoire** memory expansion ▶ **par ~** by extension

**extérieur** [ɛksterjœʁ] *m* **①** (*monde extérieur*) outside world **②** (*dehors*) outside; **aller à l'~** to go outside; **à l'~ de**

la ville outside the town; **de l'~** from outside

**extérieur(e)** [ɛksterjœʁ] *adj* **①** (*décor*) exterior; (*bruit*) from outside; (*activité*) outside **②** (*objectif: réalité*) external **③** (*visible*) outward **④** POL. COM **politique ~e** foreign policy **⑤** *Québec* (*étranger(-ère)*) **ministère des affaires ~es** foreign affairs ministry

**extérioriser** [ɛksterjɔʁize] <1> **I.** *vt* (*sentiment*) to express; PSYCH to externalize **II.** *vpr* **s'~** (*personne*) to express oneself; (*colère, joie*) to be (outwardly) expressed

**extermination** [ɛkstɛʁminasjɔ̃] *f* extermination

**exterminer** [ɛkstɛʁmine] <1> *vt* exterminate

**externe** [ɛkstɛʁn] **I.** *adj* (*surface*) outer **II.** *mf* ECOLE day student

**extincteur** [ɛkstɛ̃ktœʁ] *m* extinguisher

**extinction** [ɛkstɛ̃ksjɔ̃] *f* **①** (*action: d'un incendie*) extinction; (*des lumières*) turning out **②** (*disparition*) extinction **③** *fig* **~ de voix** loss of voice

**extorquer** [ɛkstɔʁke] <1> *vt* to extort

**extorsion** [ɛkstɔʁsjɔ̃] *f* extortion

**extra** [ɛkstʁa] **I.** *adj inv* **①** (*qualité*) super **②** *inf* (*formidable*) great **II.** *m* (*gâterie*) **un ~** treat

**extraire** [ɛkstʁɛʁ] *vt irr* **①** (*sortir: charbon, pétrole, dent*) to extract; (*marbre*) to quarry; **passage extrait d'un livre** passage from a book **②** (*séparer*) to extract

**extrait** [ɛkstʁɛ] *m* **①** extract; (*fragment*) excerpt; **~ de compte** bank statement; **~ de naissance** birth certificate **②** (*concentré*) extract; **~ de lavande** lavender extract

**extraordinaire** [ɛkstʁaɔʁdinɛʁ] *adj* **①** (*opp: ordinaire: réunion, budget*) extraordinary; (*dépenses*) exceptional **②** (*insolite: nouvelle, histoire*) extraordinary **③** (*exceptionnel*) remarkable

**extravagance** [ɛkstʁavagɑ̃s] *f* **①** (*caractère*) eccentricity **②** (*action*) extravagance **③** (*idée*) extravagant idea

E

**extravagant(e)** [ɛkstravagɑ̃, ɑ̃t] **I.** *adj* extravagant **II.** *m(f)* eccentric

**extrême** [ɛkstrɛm] **I.** *adj* ❶ *(au bout d'un espace)* farthest; *(au bout d'une durée)* latest ❷ *(excessif)* extreme **II.** *m* ❶ *(dernière limite)* extreme ❷ *pl (opposé)* a. MATH extremes ❸ POL l'~ **gauche/droite** the far right/left ▶ **pousser** qc à l'~ to take sth to extremes

**extrêmement** [ɛkstrɛmmɑ̃] *adv* extremely; *(jaloux)* insanely

**Extrême-Orient** [ɛkstrɛmɔrjɑ̃] *m* l'~ the Far East

**extrémiste** [ɛkstremist] **I.** *adj* POL extremist **II.** *mf* POL extremist

**extrémité** [ɛkstremite] *f* ❶ *(bout)* end; ~ **de la forêt/d'une ville** edge of the forest/town ❷ *pl (mains, pieds)* extremities

**F**

# Ff

**F, f** [ɛf] *m inv* F, f; ~ **comme François** *(au téléphone)* f as in Foxtrot

**F** ❶ HIST *abr de* **franc** F ❷ *abr de* **fluor** F ❸ *(appartement)* **F2/F3** one/two-bedroom apartment

**fa** [fa] *m inv* ❶ MUS F ❷ *(solfège)* fa; *v.a.* **do**

**fable** [fabl] *f* LIT fable

**fabricant(e)** [fabrikɑ̃, ɑ̃t] *m(f)* manufacturer

**fabrication** [fabrikasjɔ̃] *f* manufacturing; *(artisanale)* making; **défaut/secret de** ~ manufacturing defect/secret

**fabrique** [fabrik] *f* factory

**fabriquer** [fabrike] <1> **I.** *vt* ❶ *(produire)* to manufacture ❷ *inf (faire)* **mais qu'est-ce que tu fabriques?** what on earth are you up to?; *(avec impatience)* what do you think you're doing? ❸ *(inventer)* to fabricate **II.** *vpr* ❶ *(se produire)* to be mass-produced ❷ *(se construire)* **se ~ une table avec** qc to make a table out of sth ❸ *(s'inventer)* **se ~ une histoire** to think up a story

**fabuler** [fabyle] <1> *vi* to tell stories; PSYCH to fantasize

**fabuleux, -euse** [fabylø, -øz] *adj* ❶ *inf (fantastique)* fabulous ❷ *inf (incroyable)* incredible ❸ LIT mythical; *(animal)* fabulous; **récit** ~ myth

**fac** [fak] *f inf abr de* **faculté** university

**façade** [fasad] *f* ❶ *(devant: d'un édifice)* façade; *(d'un magasin)* front ❷ *(région côtière)* coast ❸ *(apparence trompeuse)* façade

**face** [fas] *f* ❶ *(visage, côté, aspect)* face ❷ *(côté d'une monnaie, disquette, d'un disque)* a. MATH, MIN side; **pile ou ~?** heads or tails? ❸ *(indiquant une orientation)* **attaquer de** ~ to attack from the front; **être en** ~ **de** qn/qc to be across from sb/sth; **le voisin d'en** ~ the neighbor across the street ▶ **être/se trouver** ~ **à** ~ **avec** qn to be face to face with sb; **faire** ~ to confront the situation; ~ **à cette crise …** faced with this crisis …

**face-à-face** [fasafas] *m inv* encounter

**facétie** [fasesi] *f* joke

**facette** [fasɛt] *f* facet

**fâché(e)** [faʃe] *adj* ❶ *(en colère)* angry ❷ *(navré)* **il est** ~ **de tout ceci** he's sorry about all this ❸ *(en mauvais termes)* **être** ~ **avec** qn to be at odds with sb

**fâcher** [faʃe] <1> **I.** *vt (irriter)* to annoy **II.** *vpr* ❶ *(se mettre en colère)* **se** ~ **contre** qn to get angry with sb ❷ *(se brouiller)* **se** ~ **avec** qn to fall out with sb

**fâcheux, -euse** [faʃø, -øz] *adj* ❶ *(regrettable: idée)* regrettable; *(contre-*

*temps*) unfortunate ② (*déplaisant: nou-velle*) unpleasant

**facile** [fasil] **I.** *adj* ① (*simple*) easy; **c'est plus ~ de** +*infin* it's easier to +*infin* ② *péj* (*sans recherche: plaisanterie*) facile; **c'est un peu ~!** that's a little bit cheap ③ (*conciliant*) easygoing **II.** *adv inf* ① (*sans difficulté*) easy ② (*au moins*) easily

**facilement** [fasilmɑ̃] *adv* easily

**facilité** [fasilite] *f* ① (*opp: difficulté*) ease; **~ d'emploi** ease of use; **être d'une grande ~** to be very easy; **pour plus de ~, ...** for greater simplicity ... ② (*aptitude*) gift; **~ de caractère** easy-going character; **avoir des ~s** to be gifted ③ *sans pl, péj* facility; **céder à la ~** to take the easy way out ④ *pl* (*occasion*) opportunities ⑤ (*possibilité*) chance

**faciliter** [fasilite] <1> *vt* to facilitate

**façon** [fasɔ̃] *f* ① (*manière*) **~ de faire qc** way of doing sth; **de** [*o* **d'une**] **~ très impolie** very impolitely ② *pl* (*comportement*) manners; **faire des ~s** to put on airs; (*faire le difficile*) to make a fuss ③ (*travail*) tailoring ④ (*forme*) cut ⑤ +*subst* (*imitation*) **un sac ~ croco** an imitation crocodile skin bag ▶ **en aucune ~** not at all; **d'une ~ générale** in a general way; **de toute ~, ...** anyway, ...; **de toutes les ~s** at any rate; **dire à qn sa ~ de penser** to give sb a piece of one's mind; (**c'est une**) **~ de parler** in a manner of speaking; **à ma ~** in my own way; **faire qc de ~ à ce que** +*subj* to do sth so that ...; **repas sans ~** simple meal; **personne sans ~** an easygoing person

**façonner** [fasɔne] <1> **I.** *vt* ① (*travailler*) to shape; (*pierre*) to work ② (*faire*) to make; (*statuette de bois*) to carve ③ (*usiner*) to shape **II.** *vpr* **se ~** ① (*travailler: bois, métal*) to be worked ② (*se fabriquer*) to be made

**facteur** [faktœʀ] *m* factor

**facteur, -trice** [faktœʀ, -tʀis] *m, f* ① (*livreur de courrier*) mailman, postman,

-woman *m, f* ② (*fabricant*) **~ d'orgues** organ builder

**factice** [faktis] *adj* ① (*faux*) artificial; (*livres, bouteilles*) dummy ② (*affecté: voix*) artificial; (*sourire*) feigned; (*gaieté*) sham

**factrice** [faktʀis] *f v.* **facteur**

**facture** [faktyʀ] *f* COM bill

**facturer** [faktyʀe] <1> *vt* ① (*établir une facture*) **~ une réparation à qn** to invoice sb for a repair ② (*faire payer*) **~ une réparation à qn** to put a repair on sb's bill

**facultatif, -ive** [fakyltatif, -iv] *adj* optional

**faculté**[1] [fakylte] *f* UNIV (*université*) university; (*département*) faculty; **~ de droit** faculty of law

**faculté**[2] [fakylte] *f* ① (*disposition*) faculty ② (*possibilité*) **la ~ de faire qc** the facility of doing sth; (*droit*) the right to do sth

**fada** [fada] **I.** *adj inf* cracked **II.** *m, f inf* nut

**fadaise** [fadɛz] *f gén pl* ① (*balivernes*) nonsense ② (*propos*) drivel

**fade** [fad] *adj* ① (*sans saveur: plat, goût*) bland; **c'est ~** it's tasteless ② (*sans éclat: ton*) dull ③ (*sans intérêt: personne, propos*) dreary; (*traits*) bland ④ *Belgique* (*lourd*) **il fait ~** it's muggy

**fadeur** [fadœʀ] *f* ① (*manque de saveur*) blandness ② (*manque d'éclat*) dullness ③ *fig* (*d'un roman*) dreariness

**fagoter** [fagɔte] <1> *vt péj* to dress up

**faible** [fɛbl] **I.** *adj* ① (*sans force, défense*) weak; **sa vue est ~** he has poor eyesight ② (*influençable, sans volonté*) **être ~ de caractère** to have a weak character ③ (*trop indulgent*) **être ~ avec qn** to be soft on sb ④ *antéposé* (*restreint: rapport*) faint; (*protestation, résistance*) feeble; **à une ~ majorité** by a narrow majority; **à ~ altitude** at low altitude ⑤ (*peu perceptible*) faint ⑥ (*médiocre: élève*) weak; (*devoir*) poor; **le terme est ~** that's putting it mildly ⑦ ECON **économiquement ~**

with a low income ⑥ (*bête*) ~ **d'esprit**
feeble-minded **II.** *m, f* ❶ weak person
❷ (*personne sans volonté*) weakling
❸ ECON **les économiquement** ~**s**
low-income groups **III.** *m sans pl* (*défaut*) weak point; **avoir un** ~ **pour qn**
to have a soft spot for sb

**faiblement** [fɛblǝmã] *adv* ❶ (*mollement*) weakly ❷ (*légèrement*) slightly;
**bière** ~ **alcoolisée** low-alcohol beer

**faiblesse** [fɛblɛs] *f* ❶ (*manque de force, grande indulgence, insuffisance*) weakness; **sa** ~ **de constitution** his/her
weak constitution; ~ **pour** [*o* **à l'égard de**] **qn/qc** weakness towards sb/sth;
**par** ~ out of weakness ❷ (*manque d'intensité*) **la** ~ **du bruit** the faintness of
the noise ❸ (*médiocrité: d'un élève*)
weakness; (*d'un devoir*) feebleness
❹ *souvent pl* (*défaillance*) dizzy spell
❺ (*syncope*) fainting fit

**faiblir** [feblir] <8> *vi* (*personne, pouls, résistance*) to weaken; (*cœur, force*) to
fail; (*espoir, lumière*) to fade; (*ardeur*)
to wane; (*revenu, rendement*) to fall;
(*chances, écart*) to lessen; (*vent*) to
drop

**faïence** [fajɑ̃s] *f* earthenware

**faille¹** [faj] *subj prés de* **falloir**

**faille²** [faj] *f* ❶ GEO fault ❷ (*crevasse*) rift
❸ (*défaut*) flaw; **volonté sans** ~ iron
will; **détermination sans** ~ utter determination

**faillir** [fajiʀ] *vi irr* ❶ (*manquer*) **il a failli acheter ce livre** he almost bought that
book ❷ (*manquer à*) ~ **à son devoir** to
fail in one's duty ❸ (*faire défaut*) **ma mémoire n'a pas failli** my memory
did not fail me

**faillite** [fajit] *f* ❶ COM, JUR bankruptcy;
**faire** ~ to go bankrupt ❷ (*échec*) failure

**faim** [fɛ̃] *f* ❶ hunger; **avoir** ~ to be hungry; **avoir une** ~ **de loup** to be starving
❷ (*famine*) famine ❸ (*désir ardent*)
**avoir** ~ **de qc** to hunger for sth ▸ **laisser qn sur sa** ~ to leave sb wanting
more

**fainéant(e)** [fɛneɑ̃, ɑ̃t] **I.** *adj* idle
**II.** *m(f)* idler

**fainéantise** [fɛneɑ̃tiz] *f* idleness

**faire** [fɛʀ] *irr* **I.** *vt* ❶ (*fabriquer: objet, vêtement, produit, gâteau*) to make; (*maison, nid*) to build ❷ (*mettre au monde*)
~ **un enfant/des petits** to have a
child/young ❸ (*évacuer*) ~ **ses besoins** to do one's business ❹ (*être l'auteur de: faute, offre, discours, loi, prévisions*) to make; (*livre, chèque*) to write;
(*conférence, cadeau*) to give; ~ **une promesse à qn** to make sb a promise;
~ **la guerre contre qn** to make war
against sb; ~ **la paix** to make peace;
~ **l'amour à qn** to make love to sb;
~ **une farce à qn** to play a trick on sb;
~ **la bise à qn** to kiss sb on the cheek;
~ **du bruit** to make noise; *fig* to cause a
sensation; ~ **l'école buissonnière** to
play hooky; ~ **étape** to stop off; ~ **grève**
to strike; ~ **sa toilette** to wash ❺ (*avoir une activité: travail, métier, service militaire*) to do; **je n'ai rien à** ~ I've nothing to do; ~ **du théâtre** (*acteur de cinéma*) to act in the theater; (*étudiants*) to
do some acting; (*comme carrière*) to go
on the stage; ~ **du violon/du piano/ du jazz** to play the violin/the piano/
jazz; ~ **de la politique** to be involved
in politics; ~ **du sport** to do sports;
~ **du tennis** to play tennis; ~ **du vélo/ canoë** to go cycling/canoeing; ~ **du cheval** to go horseback riding; ~ **du patin à roulettes** to roller-skate; ~ **du camping** to go camping; ~ **des photos**
to take pictures; ~ **du cinéma** to be in
films; **ne** ~ **que bavarder** to do nothing
but talk; **que faites-vous dans la vie?**
what do you do in life? ❻ (*étudier*)
~ **des études** to go to college; ~ **son droit/de la recherche** to do law/research ❼ (*préparer*) ~ **un café à qn** to
make sb a coffee; ~ **ses bagages** to
pack (one's bags); ~ **la cuisine** to cook
❽ (*nettoyer, ranger: argenterie, chaussures, chambre*) to clean; (*lit*) to make;
~ **la vaisselle** to do the dishes ❾ (*accomplir: mouvement*) to make; ~ **une promenade** to go for a walk; ~ **un pansement à qn** to put a bandage on

sb; ~ **le plein (d'essence)** to fill up; ~ **un bon score** to get a high score; ~ **les courses** to do the shopping; ~ **la manche** *inf* to beg, to panhandle; ~ **bon voyage** to have a good trip ➓ *inf* MED ~ **de la fièvre** to have a fever ➊ (*parcourir: distance, trajet, pays, magasins*) to do; ~ **des zigzags/du stop** to zigzag/hitchhike ➋ (*offrir à la vente: produit*) to sell; **ils/elles font combien?** how much are they going for? ➌ (*cultiver*) to grow ➍ (*feindre, agir comme*) ~ **le pitre** [*o* **le clown**] to clown around; **il a fait comme s'il ne me voyait pas** he pretended not to see me ➎ (*donner une qualité, transformer*) **il a fait de lui une star** he made him a star ➏ (*causer*) ~ **plaisir à qn** (*personne*) to please sb; ~ **le bonheur de qn** to make sb happy; ~ **du bien à qn** to do sb good; ~ **du mal à qn** to harm sb; **ça ne fait rien** it doesn't matter; ~ **honte à qn** to shame sb; **qu'est-ce que ça peut bien te ~?** what's it got to do with you? ➐ (*servir de*) **cet hôtel fait aussi restaurant** the hotel has a restaurant too ➑ (*laisser quelque part*) **qu'ai-je bien pu ~ de mes lunettes?** what can I have done with my glasses? ➒ (*donner comme résultat*) to make; **deux et deux font quatre** two and two make [*o* are] four ➓ (*habituer*) ~ **qn à qc** to get sb used to sth ㉑ (*devenir*) **il fera un excellent avocat** he'll make an excellent lawyer ㉒ (*dire*) ~ **comprendre qc à qn** to explain sth to sb ㉓ (*avoir pour conséquence*) ~ **que qn a été sauvé** to mean that sb was saved ㉔ (*être la cause de*) ~ **chavirer un bateau** to make a boat capsize ㉕ (*aider à*) ~ **faire pipi à un enfant** to help a child go potty ㉖ (*inviter à*) ~ **venir un médecin** to call a doctor; ~ **entrer/sortir le chien** to let the dog in/put the dog out; ~ **voir qc à qn** to show sb sth ㉗ (*charger de*) ~ **réparer/changer qc par qn** to (o have] sth repaired/changed by sb; ~ **faire qc à qn** to get sb to do sth ㉘ (*forcer, inciter à*)

~ **ouvrir qc** to have sth opened; ~ **payer qn** to make sb pay ㉙ (*pour remplacer un verbe déjà énoncé*) **elle le fait/l'a fait** she is doing so/has done so **II.** *vi* ➊ (*agir*) ~ **vite** to be quick; ~ **attention à qc** to be careful about sth; ~ **de son mieux** to do one's best; **tu peux mieux ~** you can do better; **tu fais bien de me le rappeler** it's a good thing you reminded me; **tu ferais mieux/bien de te taire** you should keep quiet; ~ **comme si de rien n'était** as if there was nothing the matter ➋ (*dire*) to say; **"sans doute", fit-il** "no doubt", he said ➌ *Inf* (*durer*) **ce manteau me fera encore un hiver** this coat will last me another year ➊ (*paraître, rendre*) ~ **vieux/paysan** to look old/like a peasant; ~ **bon/mauvais effet** to look good/bad; ~ **désordre** (*pièce*) to look messy ➎ (*mesurer, peser*) ~ **1,2 m de long/de large/de haut** to be 1.2 meters long/wide/high; ~ **trois kilos** to be [*o* weigh] three kilograms; ~ **8 euros** to come to 8 euros; **ça fait peu** that's not much ➏ (*être incontinent*) ~ **dans sa culotte** to wet one's pants ▶ ~ **partie de qc** to be part of sth; ~ **la queue** *inf* to line up; ~ **la une** *inf* to make the front page; ~ **manger qn** to help sb eat; **il fait bon vivre** life is sweet; **faites comme chez vous!** *iron* make yourself at home!; **ne pas s'en** ~ *inf* not to worry; **se** ~ **mal** to hurt oneself; **ça ne se fait pas** you just don't do that; **tant qu'à** ~, **allons-y** let's go, we might as well **III.** *vi impers* ➊ METEO **il fait chaud/froid/jour/nuit** it's hot/cold/light/dark; **il fait beau/mauvais** the weather's nice/awful; **il fait (du) soleil** the sun's shining; **il fait dix degrés** it's ten degrees ➋ (*temps écoulé*) **cela fait bien huit ans** it's a good eight years ago now ➌ (*pour indiquer l'âge*) **ça me fait 40 ans** *inf* I'll be 40 **IV.** *vpr* ➊ **se** ~ **une robe** to make oneself a dress; **se** ~ **des illusions** to have illusions; **se** ~ **une raison de qc** to resign oneself to sth; **se** ~ **des amis**

**F**

to make friends ❷ (*action réciproque*)
**se ~ des caresses** to stroke each other;
**se ~ des politesses** to exchange cour-
tesies ❸ *inf* (*se taper*) **il faut se le ~
celui-là!** he's a real pain; **je vais me le
~ celui-là!** I'm going to do him over!
❹ (*se former*) **se ~** (*fromage, vin*) to
mature; **se ~ tout seul** (*homme politique*) to make it on one's own ❺ (*devenir*) **se ~ vieux** to get on in years; **se ~
beau** to make oneself up; **se ~ rare** to
be a stranger ❻ (*s'habituer à*) **se ~ à la
discipline** to get used to discipline
❼ (*être à la mode*) **se ~** (*activité, look,
vêtement*) to be popular; **ça se fait
beaucoup de ~ qc** doing sth is very
popular ❽ (*arriver, se produire*) **se ~** to
happen; (*film*) to get made ❾ *impers*
**comment ça se fait?** how come?; **il se
fait tard** it's getting late ❿ (*agir en vue
de*) **se ~ vomir** to make oneself sick
⓫ (*sens passif*) **se ~ opérer** to have an
operation; **il s'est fait retirer son permis** he lost his license; **il s'est fait
voler son permis** he had his license
stolen ► **ne pas s'en ~** *inf* (*ne pas s'inquiéter*) not to worry; (*ne pas se gêner*)
not to bother oneself

**faire-part** [fɛʀpaʀ] *m inv* announcement; (*pour inviter*) invitation

**fair-play** [fɛʀplɛ] *inv* I. *m* fair play II. *adj*
fair

**faisable** [fəzabl] *adj* (*en principe*) feasible; (*en pratique*) possible

**faisan(e)** [fəzɑ̃, an] *m(f)* pheasant

**faisandé(e)** [fəzɑ̃de] *adj* gamey

**faisceau** [fɛso] <x> *m* ❶ (*rayon*) beam
❷ (*fagot*) bundle ❸ (*ensemble*) **~ de
faits** set of facts

**fait** [fɛ] *m* ❶ fact ❷ (*événement*) event;
(*phénomène*) phenomenon; **les ~s se
sont passés à minuit** the incident occurred at midnight ❸ JUR **les ~s** (*action criminelle, délit*) crime; (*éléments
constitutifs*) acts amounting to a crime;
(*état des choses*) evidence; **~s de
guerre** acts of war ❹ (*conséquence*)
**être le ~ de qc** to be the result of sth;
**c'est le ~ du hasard si** it's pure chance

if ❺ RADIO, PRESSE **~ divers** PRESSE news
story; (*événement*) incident; **~s divers**
(*rubrique*) news in brief ► **les ~s et
gestes de qn** sb's every action; **aller**
(*droit*) **au ~** to get straight to the point;
**mettre qn au ~ de qc** to inform sb
about sth; **prendre qn sur le ~** to
catch sb red-handed; **en venir au ~** to
get to the point; **au ~** by the way; **tout
à ~** quite; (*comme réponse*) absolutely;
**gouvernement de ~** de facto government; **de ce ~** thereby; **du ~ de qc** by
the very fact of sth; **du ~ que qn fait
toujours qc** as sb always does sth; **en ~**
actually

**fait(e)** [fɛ, fɛt] I. *part passé de* **faire**
II. *adj* ❶ (*propre à*) **être ~ pour qc** to
be made for sth; **c'est ~ pour** *inf* that's
what it's for ❷ (*constitué*) **avoir la
jambe bien ~e** to have good legs;
**c'est une femme bien ~e** she's a
good-looking woman ❸ (*arrangé: ongles*) varnished; (*yeux*) made up
❹ (*mûr: fromage*) ready ❺ *inf* (*pris*)
**être ~** to be done for ❻ (*tout prêt*) **expression toute ~e** set expression
► **c'est bien ~ pour toi/lui** serves
you/him right; **c'est toujours ça de ~**
that's one thing done; **vite ~ bien ~**
quickly and efficiently; **c'est comme si
c'était ~** consider it done

**faîte** [fɛt] *m* (*de l'arbre*) top; (*d'une
montagne*) summit; **~ du toit** rooftop

**faitout, fait-tout** [fɛtu] *m inv* stewpot

**falaise** [falɛz] *f* ❶ (*paroi*) cliff face
❷ (*côte, rocher*) cliff

**falbalas** [falbala] *mpl* ❶ *péj* (*colifi-
chets*) frills ❷ (*grandes toilettes*) finery

**falloir** [falwaʀ] *irr* I. *vi impers* ❶ (*besoin*) **il faut qn/qc pour** +*infin* sb/sth
is needed to +*infin;* **il me faudra du
temps** I'll need time ❷ (*devoir*) **il faut
faire qc** sth must be done; **que faut-il
faire?** what must be done?; (*moi/toi/
il*) what must I/you/he do?; **il faut que**
+*subj* sb has (got) to +*infin* ❸ (*être probablement*) **il faut être fou pour parler ainsi** you have to be crazy to talk
like that ❹ (*se produire fatalement*) **il**

**fallait que ça arrive** that (just) had to happen ⑤ (*faire absolument*) **il fallait me le dire** you should have told me; **il ne faut surtout pas lui en parler** you really must not talk about it to him ▶ **(il) faut se le/la faire** [o **farcir**] *inf* he's/ she's a real pain; **il le faut** it has to be done; **comme il faut** properly; **une vieille dame très comme il faut a** very proper old lady; **il ne fallait pas!** you shouldn't have! II. *vpr impers* **il s'en faut de peu** to come very close (to happening)

**falsification** [falsifikasjɔ̃] *f* (*d'un document, d'une monnaie, signature*) forgery; (*de la vérité*) altering; (*d'une marchandise*) adulteration

**falsifier** [falsifje] <1> *vt* (*document, signature*) to falsify; (*monnaie*) to forge; (*vérité, histoire*) to alter

**famé(e)** [fame] *adj* **mal ~** of ill repute

**famélique** [famelik] *adj* starved-looking

**fameux, -euse** [famø, -øz] *adj* ① (*excellent: mets, vin*) superb; (*idée, travail*) excellent; **ce n'est pas ~** *inf* it's not too good ② *antéposé, a. iron* (*énorme: problème, erreur*) terrible; (*raclée*) terrific ③ (*célèbre*) famous

**familial(e)** [familjal, -jo] <-aux> *adj* family

**familiariser** [familjaʀize] <1> **I.** *vt* **~ qn avec qc** to familiarize sb with sth **II.** *vpr* **se ~ avec une méthode** to familiarize oneself with a method; **se ~ avec qn** to become acquainted with sb

**familiarité** [familjaʀite] *f* ① (*bonhomie, amitié, comportement*) familiarity ② (*habitude de*) **~ avec qc** knowledge of sth ③ *pl, péj* (*paroles*) overfamiliar remarks

**familier** [familje] *m* regular

**familier, -ière** [familje, -jɛʀ] *adj* ① familiar ② (*routinier: comportement, tâche*) usual ③ (*simple, bonhomme, conduite, entretien*) informal; (*personne*) casual ④ (*non recherché: expression, style*) informal ⑤ *péj* (*cavalier*) **~ avec qn** offhand with sb ⑥ (*domestique*) **des animaux ~s** pets

**familièrement** [familjɛʀmɑ̃] *adv* ① (*en langage courant*) in (ordinary) conversation ② (*simplement: s'exprimer*) informally ③ (*amicalement*) in a familiar way ④ *péj* (*cavalièrement*) offhandedly

**famille** [famij] *f* ① family; **~ d'accueil** host family; **~ proche** close family; **en ~** we're a family here ② *Belgique, Suisse* **attendre de la ~** (*être enceinte*) to be in the family way ③ *Suisse* **grande ~** (*famille nombreuse*) large family

**famine** [famin] *f* famine

**fan** [fan] *mf* fan

**fana** [fana] *inf abr de* **fanatique I.** *adj* **être ~ de qn/qc** to be crazy [o nuts] about sb/sth **II.** *mf* fanatic; **~ d'ordinateur** computer geek [o nerd]

**fanatique** [fanatik] **I.** *adj* fanatical **II.** *mf* fanatic; **~ de football** soccer fanatic

**fanatiser** [fanatize] <1> *vt* to fanaticize

**fanatisme** [fanatism] *m* fanaticism; **avec ~** fanatically

**fané(e)** [fane] *adj* (*fleur*) wilted; (*couleur, étoffe, beauté*) faded

**faner** [fane] <1> **I.** *vpr* **se ~** (*fleur*) to wilt; (*couleur*) to fade **II.** *vt* ① (*ternir: couleur, étoffe, beauté*) to fade ② (*flétrir*) **~ une plante** to make a plant wilt ③ (*retourner: foin*) to toss **III.** *vi* to make hay

**fanes** [fan] *fpl* (*de carottes*) top; (*de radis*) leaves *pl*

**fanfare** [fɑ̃faʀ] *f* ① (*orchestre*) band ② (*air*) fanfare ▶ **arriver en ~** to arrive in a blaze of glory

**fanfaron(ne)** [fɑ̃faʀɔ̃, ɔn] **I.** *adj* (*personne*) boastful; (*air, attitude*) swaggering **II.** *m(f)* braggart; **faire le ~** to crow

**fanfaronner** [fɑ̃faʀɔne] <1> *vi* to brag

**fanfreluche** [fɑ̃fʀəlyʃ] *f gén pl, a. péj* frills

**fanion** [fanjɔ̃] *m* ① (*petit drapeau servant d'emblème*) pennant ② (*sur un terrain de sport*) flag

**fantaisie** [fɑ̃tezi] *f* ① (*caprice*) whim; **à** [o **selon**] **sa ~** as the fancy takes him ② (*extravagance*) extravagance ③ (*délire, idée*) fantasy ④ (*imagination, originalité*) imagination; **être dépourvu**

**F**

**F**

de ~ to lack imagination ❺ (qui sort de la norme, original) bijoux/bouton ~ novelty jewelry/button

**fantaisiste** [fɑ̃tezist] **I.** adj ❶ (peu sérieux: explication, hypothèse) fanciful ❷ (peu fiable) unreliable ❸ (anticonformiste) eccentric ❹ (bizarre) odd **II.** mf ❶ (personne peu sérieuse) joker ❷ (anticonformiste) eccentric

**fantasme** [fɑ̃tasm] m fantasy

**fantasmer** [fɑ̃tasme] <1> vi to fantasize

**fantasque** [fɑ̃task] adj fanciful; (bizarre) odd; (excentrique) eccentric

**fantassin** [fɑ̃tasɛ̃] m foot soldier

**fantastique** [fɑ̃tastik] **I.** adj fantastic; (atmosphère) uncanny; (événement, rêve) from the realms of fantasy **II.** m le ~ the fantastic

**fantôme** [fɑ̃tom] **I.** m ❶ (spectre) ghost ❷ (illusion, souvenir) phantom; les ~s du passé the ghosts of the past **II.** app (sans réalité: administration, cabinet) shadow; (société) bogus ▸ **train** ~ ghost train

**faon** [fɑ̃] m fawn

**faramineux, -euse** [faraminø, -øz] adj inf amazing

**farandole** [farɑ̃dɔl] f (danse) farandole

**farce¹** [fars] f ❶ (tour) trick ❷ (plaisanterie) joke ❸ (chose peu sérieuse) a. THEAT farce ❹ (objet) ~s et attrapes tricks

**farce²** [fars] f CULIN stuffing

**farceur, -euse** [farsœr, -øz] **I.** m, f practical joker **II.** adj être ~ to be a practical joker

**farci(e)** [farsi] adj CULIN stuffed

**farcir** [farsir] <8> **I.** vt ❶ CULIN ~ qc de qc to stuff sth with sth ❷ péj (bourrer) ~ qc de qc to stuff sth full of sth **II.** vpr péj, inf ❶ (supporter) se ~ qn/qc to put up with sb/sth; il faut se le ~! it's a pain in the neck ❷ (se payer) se ~ la vaisselle to do the dishes

**fard** [far] m makeup; ~ à joues blusher; ~ à paupières eye shadow ▸ **piquer** un ~ inf to turn red

**fardeau** [fardo] <x> m burden; plier

sous le ~ de qc to bend under the burden of sth

**farder** [farde] <1> **I.** vt to make up **II.** vpr se ~ to make up

**farfelu(e)** [farfəly] **I.** adj inf crazy **II.** m(f) inf crank

**farfouiller** [farfuje] <1> vi inf ~ dans qc to rummage around

**farine** [farin] f flour

**farineux** [farinø] m floury

**farineux, -euse** [farinø, -øz] adj ❶ (couvert de farine) floury ❷ (abîmé, sec: pomme, pomme de terre) starchy; (fromage) chalky

**farniente** [farnjɛnte, farnjɑ̃t] m lazing around

**farouche** [faruʃ] adj ❶ (timide) shy ❷ (peu sociable) unsociable; (air) standoffish; ne pas être ~ (animal) to be quite tame ❸ (violent, hostile: air, regard) fierce; (opiniâtre: volonté, résistance) ferocious; (énergie) frenzied

**farouchement** [faruʃmɑ̃] adv fiercely

**fart** [fart] m wax

**farter** [farte] <1> vt to wax

**fascicule** [fasikyl] m ❶ (livret) part ❷ (fascicule d'information) information booklet

**fascinant(e)** [fasinɑ̃, ɑ̃t] adj fascinating

**fascination** [fasinasjɔ̃] f fascination

**fasciner** [fasine] <1> vt ❶ (hypnotiser) to fascinate ❷ (séduire) to beguile

**fascisme** [faʃism, fasism] m fascism

**fasciste** [faʃist, fasist] **I.** adj fascist(ic) **II.** mf fascist

**fasse** [fas] subj prés de faire

**faste¹** [fast] m splendor

**faste²** [fast] adj ❶ (favorable) lucky ❷ (couronné de succès) good; jour ~ lucky day

**fast-food** [fastfud] <fast-foods> m fast food place

**fastidieux, -euse** [fastidjø, -jøz] adj tedious

**fastueux, -euse** [fastɥø, -øz] adj (cadre, décor) sumptuous; (fête) magnificent; (vie) luxurious

**fatal(e)** [fatal] adj ❶ (malheureux, irrésistible) fatal; être ~ à qn to be fatal for sb; **porter un coup ~ à qn/qc** to deal sb/sth a fatal blow ❷ *(inévitable)* inevitable ❸ *(marqué par le destin: moment, jour, air, regard)* fateful

**fatalement** [fatalmã] *adv (blessé)* fatally

**fataliste** [fatalist] **I.** *adj* fatalistic **II.** *mf* fatalist

**fatalité** [fatalite] *f* ❶ *(destin hostile)* fate ❷ *(inévitabilité)* inevitability

**fatidique** [fatidik] *adj* fateful

**fatigant(e)** [fatigã, ãt] *adj* ❶ *(épuisant: études, travail)* tiring ❷ *(assommant: personne)* tiresome

**fatigue** [fatig] *f* ❶ *(diminution des forces: d'une personne)* tiredness; *(des yeux)* strain ❷ *(état d'épuisement)* exhaustion ❸ *(usure: d'un mécanisme, moteur)* wear

**fatigué(e)** [fatige] *adj* ❶ *(personne, cœur)* tired; *(foie)* upset ❷ *(usé: chaussures, vêtement)* worn-out ❸ *(excédé)* **être ~ de qn/qc** to be tired of sb/sth

**fatiguer** [fatige] <1> **I.** *vt* ❶ *(causer de la fatigue)* **~ qn** *(travail, marche)* to tire sb (out); *(personne)* to overwork sb ❷ *(déranger)* **~ le foie/l'organisme** to put a strain on one's liver/body ❸ *(excéder)* **~ qn** to get on sb's nerves ❹ *(ennuyer)* **~ qn** to wear sb out **II.** *vi* ❶ *(peiner: machine, moteur)* to labor; *(cœur)* to get tired ❷ *(s'user: pièce, joint)* to get worn; *(poutre)* to show the strain ❸ *inf (en avoir assez)* to be fed up **III.** *vpr* ❶ *(peiner)* **se ~** *(personne, cœur)* to get tired ❷ *(se lasser)* **se ~ de qc** to get tired of sth; **se ~ à faire qc** to get tired of doing sth ❸ *(s'évertuer)* **se ~ à faire qc** to wear oneself out doing sth

**fatras** [fatrɑ] *m* clutter; *(choses sans valeurs, inutiles)* junk

**faubourg** [fobuʀ] *m* suburb

**fauche** [foʃ] *f sans pl, inf* thieving

**fauché(e)** [foʃe] *adj inf* **être ~** to be broke

**faucher** [foʃe] <1> *vt* ❶ *(couper)* to reap ❷ *(abattre)* **~ qn** *(véhicule)* to mow sb

down; *(mort)* to cut sb down ❸ *inf (voler)* **~ qc à qn** to pinch sth off sb

**faucheuse** [foʃøz] *f* reaper

**faucille** [fosij] *f* sickle

**faucon** [fokõ] *m* ❶ *(oiseau)* falcon ❷ POL hawk

**faudra** [fodra] *fut de* **falloir**

**faufiler** [fofile] <1> *vpr* **se ~ parmi la foule** to slip through the crowd

**faune**[1] [fon] *f* ZOOL fauna

**faune**[2] [fon] *m* HIST faun

**faussaire** [foseʀ] *mf* forger

**fausser** [fose] <1> *vt* ❶ *(altérer)* to distort; *(intentionnellement)* to falsify ❷ *(déformer: bois)* to warp; *(mécanisme)* to damage

**faut** [fo] *indic prés de* **falloir**

**faute** [fot] *f* ❶ *(erreur)* mistake ❷ *(mauvaise action)* misdeed ❸ *(manquement à des lois, règles)* offense; **~ de goût** lapse of taste; **commettre une ~** to do something wrong; **sans ~** without fail ❹ *(responsabilité)* **faire retomber** [*o* **rejeter**] **la ~ sur qn** to put the blame on sb; **c'est (de) ma ~** it's my fault ❺ SPORT fault; *(agression)* foul ❻ JUR **~ pénale** criminal offense ❼ *(par manque de)* **~ de** for lack of time; **~ de mieux** for lack of anything better ▶ **~ de quoi** failing which

**fauteuil** [fotœj] *m* ❶ *(siège)* armchair; **~ roulant** wheelchair ❷ *(place dans une assemblée)* seat

**fauteur** [fotœʀ] *m* **~ de désordre/troubles** troublemaker

**fautif, -ive** [fotif, -iv] **I.** *adj* ❶ *(coupable)* at fault; **être ~** to be in the wrong ❷ *(avec des fautes: texte)* faulty; *(citation, calcul)* inaccurate; *(mémoire)* defective **II.** *m, f* guilty party

**fauve** [fov] **I.** *adj* ❶ *(couleur)* fawn ❷ *(sauvage)* wild **II.** *m* ❶ *(couleur)* fawn ❷ *(animal)* big cat

**fauvette** [fovɛt] *f* warbler

**faux** [fo] **I.** *f (outil)* scythe **II.** *m* ❶ false; **discerner le vrai du ~** to tell truth from falsehood ❷ *(falsification, imitation)* forgery **III.** *adv (chanter)* out of tune

**F**

**faux, fausse** [fo, fos] *adj* ❶ *antéposé* (*imité: marbre, perle, meuble*) imitation; (*papiers, signature, tableau*) forged; (*monnaie*) counterfeit ❷ *antéposé* (*postiche: barbe, dents, nom*) false ❸ *antéposé* (*simulé: dévotion, humilité*) feigned; (*modestie, pudeur*) false ❹ *antéposé* (*mensonger: promesse, réponse, serment*) false ❺ *antéposé* (*pseudo: col*) detachable; (*fenêtre, porte, plafond*) false ❻ *postposé* (*fourbe: air, caractère, personne*) deceitful; (*attitude*) dishonest ❼ *antéposé* (*imposteur: ami, prophète*) false ❽ (*erroné: raisonnement, résultat, numéro*) wrong; (*affirmation, thermomètre*) inaccurate ❾ *antéposé* (*non fondé: espoir, principe*) false; (*crainte, soupçon*) groundless ❿ *postposé* (*ambigu: atmosphère, situation*) awkward ⓫ *antéposé* (*maladroit*) **une fausse manœuvre** a clumsy move; (*au volant*) a steering error; **faire fausse route** to go the wrong way ⓬ MUS (*note*) wrong

**faux-filet** [fofilɛ] <faux-filets> *m* sirloin

**faux-monnayeur** [fomɔnɛjœʀ] <faux-monnayeurs> *m* counterfeiter

**faux-sens** [fosɑ̃s] *m inv* mistranslation

**faveur** [favœʀ] *f* ❶ (*bienveillance, bienfait*) favor ❷ (*considération*) **gagner la ~ du public** to win public approval; **voter en ~ de qn** to vote for sth; **se déclarer** [*o* **se prononcer**] **en ~ de qn/qc** to come out in favor of sth

**favorable** [favɔʀabl] *adj* favorable; **donner un avis ~** to give a positive response; **être ~ à qn/qc** to feel favorable to sb/sth; (*circonstances, suffrages, opinion*) to favor sb/sth

**favorablement** [favɔʀabləmɑ̃] *adv* favorably

**favori(te)** [favɔʀi, it] **I.** *adj* favorite **II.** *m(f) a.* SPORT favorite

**favoris** [favɔʀi] *mpl* side whiskers

**favoriser** [favɔʀize] <1> *vt* ❶ to favor; **les familles les plus favorisées** the most fortunate families ❷ (*aider*) to further

**favoritisme** [favɔʀitism] *m* POL, ECON favoritism

**fax** [faks] *m abr de* **téléfax** fax

**faxer** [fakse] <1> *vt* to fax

**fayot** [fajo] *m inf* (*haricot*) bean

**FB** *m abr de* **franc belge** *v.* **franc**

**fébrile** [febʀil] *adj* feverish

**fébrilité** [febʀilite] *f* ❶ (*activité débordante*) fevered activity ❷ (*excitation*) fevered state

**fécal(e)** [fekal, -o] <-aux> *adj* fecal; **matières ~es** feces

**fécond(e)** [fekɔ̃, ɔ̃d] *adj* ❶ (*productif: esprit*) fertile; (*idée, conversation, sujet*) fruitful; (*écrivain, siècle*) prolific ❷ (*prolifique*) rich

**fécondation** [fekɔ̃dasjɔ̃] *f* fertilization; (*des fleurs*) pollination

**féconder** [fekɔ̃de] <1> *vt* to fertilize; (*fleur*) to pollinate

**fécondité** [fekɔ̃dite] *f* fertility

**fécule** [fekyl] *f* starch; CULIN cornstarch

**féculent** [fekylɑ̃] *m* starchy food

**fédéral(e)** [federal, -o] <-aux> *adj* federal

**fédéralisme** [federalism] *m* federalism

**fédéraliste** [federalist] **I.** *adj* federalist **II.** *mf* federalist

**fédération** [federasjɔ̃] *f* federation

**fédérer** [federe] <5> *vt* to federate

**fée** [fe] *f* fairy

**feeling** [filiŋ] *m* feeling

**féerie** [fe(e)ʀi] *f* ❶ (*ravissement*) enchantment ❷ THEAT, CINE extravaganza

**féerique** [fe(e)ʀik] *adj* magical

**feignant(e)** [fɛɲɑ̃, ɑ̃t] *v.* **fainéant**

**feindre** [fɛ̃dʀ] *vt irr* to feign; **~ d'être malade** to pretend to be ill

**feint(e)** [fɛ̃, fɛ̃t] **I.** *part passé de* **feindre** **II.** *adj* feigned; (*maladie*) sham

**feinte** [fɛ̃t] *f* ❶ (*ruse*) pretense ❷ SPORT dummy

**feinter** [fɛ̃te] <1> *vt* ❶ SPORT to dummy ❷ *inf* (*rouler*) to take in

**fêlé(e)** [fele] *adj* ❶ (*fendu*) cracked ❷ *inf* (*dérangé*) **tu es complètement ~!** you're off your head!

**fêler** [fele] <1> **I.** *vt* **son opération à la gorge a fêlé sa voix** his throat operation left him with a cracked voice **II.** *vpr* **se ~** to crack

**félicitations** [felisitasjɔ̃] *fpl* congratulations; **avec les ~ du jury** with the commendation of the examiners

**féliciter** [felisite] <1> **I.** *vt* **~ qn pour qc** to congratulate sb on sth **II.** *vpr* **se ~ de qc** to feel pleased (with oneself) about sth

**félin** [felɛ̃] *m* cat

**félin(e)** [felɛ̃, in] *adj* (*race*) of cats; (*démarche, grâce*) feline

**fêlure** [felyʀ] *f* crack

**femelle** [fəmɛl] **I.** *adj* (*animal, organe*) female **II.** *f* femelle

**féminin** [feminɛ̃] *m* LING feminine

**féminin(e)** [feminɛ̃, in] *adj* ❶ (*opp: masculin: population, sexe*) female ❷ (*avec un aspect féminin*) a. LING feminine ❸ (*de femmes: voix*) woman's; (*vêtements, mode, revendications, football*) women's; (*condition*) female

**féminisation** [feminizasjɔ̃] *f* **~ de l'enseignement** (*action*) the growing number of women teachers; (*résultat*) the predominance of women in teaching

**féminiser** [feminize] <1> **I.** *vt* (*homme*) to make effeminate; (*femme*) to make more feminine **II.** *vpr* **se ~** ❶ (*se faire femme*) to become effeminate ❷ (*comporter de plus en plus de femmes: parti politique*) to be taken over by women

**féminisme** [feminism] *m* feminism

**féministe** [feminist] **I.** *adj* feminist; **mouvement ~** women's movement **II.** *mf* feminist

**féminité** [feminite] *f* femininity

**femme** [fam] *f* ❶ (*opp: homme*) woman; **vêtements de** [*o* **pour**] **~s** women's clothes ❷ (*épouse*) wife ❸ (*adulte*) (grown) woman ❹ (*profession*) **une ~ ingénieur/médecin** a female engineer/doctor; **~ d'État** stateswoman; **~ au foyer** housewife; **~ de chambre** chambermaid; **~ de ménage** cleaning lady; **~ d'intérieur** housewife

**femme-enfant** [famɑ̃fɑ̃] <femmes-enfants> *f* woman-child

**femmelette** [famlɛt] *f péj* ❶ (*homme*) weakling ❷ (*femme*) frail female

**fémur** [femyʀ] *m* femur, thighbone

**fendiller** [fɑ̃dije] <1> *vpr* **se ~** to craze

**fendre** [fɑ̃dʀ] <14> **I.** *vt* ❶ (*couper en deux: bois*) to split ❷ (*fissurer: glace*) to crack open; (*pierre, rochers*) to split **II.** *vpr* ❶ (*se fissurer*) **se ~** to crack ❷ (*se blesser*) **se ~ la lèvre** to cut one's lip open

**fendu(e)** [fɑ̃dy] *adj* ❶ (*ouvert: crâne*) cracked; (*lèvre*) cut ❷ (*fissuré*) cracked ❸ (*avec une fente d'aisance: jupe, veste*) slashed

**tenêtre** [f(ə)nɛtʀ] *f* window

**fennec** [fenɛk] *m* ZOOL fennec

**fenouil** [fənuj] *m* fennel

**fente** [fɑ̃t] *f* ❶ (*fissure: d'un mur, rocher*) crack ❷ (*interstice*) slit; (*pour une lame, lettre*) slot; (*dans une veste*) vent

**féodal** [feɔdal] <-aux> *m* HIST feudal lord

**féodal(e)** [feɔdal, -o] <-aux> *adj* feudal

**féodalité** [feɔdalite] *f* HIST feudalism

**fer** [fɛʀ] *m* ❶ (*métal, sels de fer*) iron; **en ~** [*o* **de**] iron ❷ (*pièce métallique: d'une lance, flèche*) head; **~ à cheval** horseshoe ❸ (*appareil*) **~ à friser** curling iron; **~ à repasser** iron ▶ **tomber les quatre ~s en l'air** *inf* to fall flat on one's back; **santé de ~** robust health

**ferai** [f(ə)ʀe] *fut de* **faire**

**fer-blanc** [fɛʀblɑ̃] <fers-blancs> *m* tin (plate)

**férié(e)** [feʀje] *adj* **jour ~** public holiday

**fermage** [fɛʀmaʒ] *m* tenant farming

**ferme¹** [fɛʀm] **I.** *adj* ❶ (*consistant, résolu*) firm ❷ (*assuré: écriture, voix, main*) firm; (*pas*) steady ❸ (*définitif: achat, commande, prix*) firm; (*cours, marché*) steady **II.** *adv* ❶ (*beaucoup: boire, travailler*) hard ❷ (*avec ardeur: discuter*) passionately; (*pour acheter*) hard ❸ (*définitivement: acheter, vendre*) firm ❹ (*avec opiniâtreté*) **tenir ~** to hold firm

**ferme²** [fɛʀm] *f* ❶ (*bâtiment*) farmhouse ❷ (*exploitation*) farm

F

**ferme³** [fɛʀm] **la ~!** *inf* shut up!

**fermé(e)** [fɛʀme] *adj* ❶ (*opp: ouvert: magasin, porte*) closed; (*à clé*) locked; (*vêtement*) fastened up; (*robinet*) turned off; (*mer*) enclosed ❷ (*privé: milieu, monde*) closed; (*club, cercle*) exclusive ❸ (*peu communicatif: personne*) uncommunicative; (*air, visage*) impassive ❹ (*insensible à*) **être ~ à qc** to be untouched by sth

**fermement** [fɛʀməmã] *adv* firmly

**fermentation** [fɛʀmãtasjɔ̃] *f* BIO fermentation

**fermenter** [fɛʀmãte] <1> *vi* (*jus*) to ferment; (*pâte*) to leaven

**fermer** [fɛʀme] <1> **I.** *vi* ❶ (*être, rester fermé*) to close ❷ (*pouvoir être fermé*) **bien/mal ~** (*vêtement*) to fasten up/not fastened up properly; (*boîte, porte*) to close/not close properly **II.** *vt* ❶ (*opp: ouvrir: porte, yeux, école, passage, compte*) to close; (*rideau*) to draw; **~ une maison à clé** to lock up a house ❷ (*boutonner*) to button up ❸ (*cacheter: enveloppe*) to seal ❹ (*arrêter: robinet, appareil*) to turn off ❺ (*rendre inaccessible*) **cette carrière m'est fermée** this career is closed to me **III.** *vpr* ❶ (*se refermer*) **se ~** (*porte, yeux*) to close; (*plaie*) to close up ❷ (*passif*) **se ~** (*boîte, appareil*) to close ❸ (*refuser l'accès à*) **se ~** (*personne*) to close up

**fermeté** [fɛʀməte] *f* ❶ (*solidité, autorité*) firmness ❷ (*courage*) steadfastness ❸ (*concision: d'un style*) sureness ❹ FIN (*d'un cours, marché, d'une monnaie*) stability

**fermeture** [fɛʀmətyʀ] *f* ❶ (*dispositif: d'un sac, vêtement*) fastening; **~ automatique** automatic closing ❷ (*action: d'une porte, d'un magasin, guichet*) closing; (*d'une école, frontière, entreprise*) closure; **après la ~ des bureaux/du magasin** after office/store hours

**fermier, -ière** [fɛʀmje, -jɛʀ] **I.** *adj* (*de ferme: beurre*) dairy; (*poulet, canard*) free-range **II.** *m, f* farmer

**fermoir** [fɛʀmwaʀ] *m* clasp

**féroce** [feʀɔs] *adj* ❶ (*sauvage: animal*) ferocious ❷ (*impitoyable: personne*) ferocious; (*critique, satire*) savage; (*air, regard*) fierce ❸ (*irrésistible: appétit*) voracious; (*envie*) raging

**férocité** [feʀɔsite] *f* ❶ (*sauvagerie: d'un animal*) ferocity ❷ (*barbarie: d'un dictateur*) savagery ❸ (*violence: d'un combat*) savagery; (*d'un regard*) fierceness ❹ (*ironie méchante: d'une critique, attaque*) savagery

**ferraille** [feʀaj] *f* ❶ (*vieux métaux*) scrap (iron) ❷ *inf* (*monnaie*) small change

**ferrailleur, -euse** [feʀajœʀ, -jøz] *m, f* scrap dealer

**ferré(e)** [feʀe] *adj* (*cheval*) shod; (*bâton, soulier*) steel-tipped

**ferrer** [feʀe] <1> *vt* (*cheval*) to shoe

**ferreux, -euse** [feʀø, -øz] *adj* ferrous

**ferronnerie** [feʀɔnʀi] *f* (*objets*) ironwork; **en ~** iron; **~ d'art** wrought iron work

**ferroviaire** [feʀɔvjɛʀ] *adj* railway

**ferry** [feʀi] <ferries> *m abr de* **ferry-boat, car-ferry**

**ferry-boat** [feʀibot] <ferry-boats> *m* ferry (boat)

**fertile** [fɛʀtil] *adj* fertile

**fertiliser** [fɛʀtilize] <1> *vt* to fertilize

**fertilité** [fɛʀtilite] *f* ❶ (*richesse: d'une région, terre*) fertility ❷ (*créativité*) **~ d'esprit/d'imagination** fertile mind/imagination

**fervent(e)** [fɛʀvã, ãt] **I.** *adj* fervent **II.** *m(f)* **~ de football** soccer enthusiast

**ferveur** [fɛʀvœʀ] *f* fervor

**fesse** [fɛs] *f* buttock

**fessée** [fese] *f* **donner une ~ à qn** to smack sb's bottom

**fessier** [fesje] **I.** *adj* (*muscle*) gluteal **II.** *m iron, inf* rear end

**festin** [fɛstɛ̃] *m* feast

**festival** [fɛstival] <s> *m* festival

**festivalier, -ière** [fɛstivalje, -jɛʀ] *m, f* festival-goer

**festivités** [fɛstivite] *fpl* festivities

**festoyer** [fɛstwaje] <6> *vi* to feast

**fête** [fɛt] *f* ❶ (*religieuse*) feast; (*civile*) holiday ❷ (*jour férié*) ~ **des Mères/Pères** Mother's/Father's Day; ~ **du travail** Labor Day ❸ (*jour du prénom*) name day ❹ *pl* (*congé*) holidays ❺ (*kermesse*) ~ **foraine** fair ❻ (*réception*) party; **un jour de** ~ holiday ▶ **ambiance/air/atmosphère de** ~ (*solennel*) feast day feeling/air/atmosphere; (*gai*) festive feeling/air/atmosphere

**Fête-Dieu** [fɛtdjø] <Fêtes-Dieu> *f* **la** ~ Corpus Christi

**fêter** [fete] <1> *vt* ❶ (*célébrer*) to celebrate ❷ (*faire fête à*) ~ **qn** to put on a celebration for sb

**fétiche** [fetiʃ] **I.** *m* ❶ (*amulette*) fetish ❷ (*mascotte*) mascot **II.** *app* (*film*) cult; **objet** ~ lucky charm

**fétichisme** [fetiʃism] *m* fetishism

**fétichiste** [fetiʃist] **I.** *adj* fetishistic **II.** *mf* fetishist

**fétide** [fetid] *adj* fetid

**feu** [fø] <x> *m* ❶ (*source de chaleur, incendie*) fire; ~ **de camp** campfire; **mettre le** ~ **à qc** to set sth on fire ❷ *souvent pl* (*lumière*) **être sous le** ~ **des projecteurs** to be in the spotlight ❸ *souvent pl* AVIAT, AUTO, NAUT lights ❹ AUTO ~ **tricolore/de signalisation** traffic lights; **passer au** ~ **rouge** to run a red light ❺ (*brûleur d'un réchaud à gaz*) burner; **à** ~ **doux/vif** on low/high heat ❻ *soutenu* (*ardeur*) heat; **dans le** ~ **de l'action** in the heat of the action ❼ (*spectacle*) ~ **d'artifice** fireworks *pl* ▶ **ne pas faire long** ~ not to last long; ~ **vert** (*permission*) green light; **péter le** ~ to be full of life; **n'y voir que du** ~ to be completely taken in; **tempérament de** ~ fiery temperament

**feuillage** [fœjaʒ] *m* ❶ (*ensemble de feuilles*) foliage ❷ (*rameaux coupés*) greenery

**feuille** [fœj] *f* ❶ BOT (*d'un arbre, d'une fleur, salade*) leaf ❷ (*plaque mince: d'aluminium, or*) leaf; (*de carton, contreplaqué*) sheet ❸ (*page*) ~ **de papier** sheet of paper ❹ (*formulaire*) ~ **de maladie/soins** form issued by

doctor for claiming medical expenses; ~ **de paie** pay stub [*o* slip]; ~ **d'impôt** (*déclaration d'impôt*) tax return; (*avis d'imposition*) tax notice ❺ IN-FORM sheet ❻ (*journal*) ~ **de chou** *péj* rag

**feuilleté** [fœjte] *m* CULIN puff pastry

**feuilleté(e)** [fœjte] *adj* ❶ (*triplex*) **verre** ~ laminated glass ❷ CULIN **pâte** ~**e** puff pastry

**feuilleter** [fœjte] <3> *vt* ❶ (*tourner les pages*) ~ **un livre** to leaf through a book ❷ (*parcourir*) ~ **un livre** to glance through a book

**feuilleton** [fœjtɔ̃] *m* ❶ PRESSE serial ❷ TV ~ **télévisé** soap (opera) ❸ (*événement à rebondissements*) saga

**feuillu** [fœjy] *m* broad-leaved tree

**feuillu(e)** [fœjy] *adj* ❶ (*chargé de feuilles*) leafy ❷ (*opp: résineux*) broad-leaved

**feutre** [føtʀ] *m* ❶ (*étoffe*) felt ❷ (*stylo*) felt-tip (pen) ❸ (*chapeau*) felt hat

**feutré(e)** [føtʀe] *adj* ❶ (*fait de feutre*) felt ❷ (*discret: bruit, pas*) muffled; **marcher à pas** ~**s** to pad along

**feutrer** [føtʀe] <1> *vi, vpr* (**se**) ~ to felt

**fève** [fɛv] *f* ❶ broad bean ❷ *Québec* (*haricot*) bean

**février** [fevʀije] *m* February; *v.a.* **août**

**FF** [ɛfɛf] **I.** *m* HIST *abr de* **franc français** *v.* **franc II.** *f* SPORT *abr de* **Fédération française** French Federation

**fiabilité** [fjabilite] *f* (*d'un appareil de mesure*) accuracy; (*d'un mécanisme, d'une personne*) reliability

**fiable** [fjabl] *adj* (*appareil de mesure*) accurate; (*mécanisme, personne*) reliable

**fiacre** [fjakʀ] *m* (hackney) carriage

**fiançailles** [fjɑ̃saj] *fpl* engagement

**fiancé(e)** [fjɑ̃se] **I.** *adj* engaged **II.** *m(f)* fiancé, fiancée *m, f*

**fiancer** [tjɑ̃se] <2> **I.** *vt* ~ **qn avec** [*o* **à**] **qn** to betroth sb to sb **II.** *vpr* **se** ~ **avec** [*o* **à**] **qn** to get engaged to sb

**fiasco** [fjasko] *m* fiasco

**fibre** [fibʀ] *f* ❶ (*substance filamenteuse: d'un bois, muscle, d'une plante, vian-*

*de)* fiber ② *(sensibilité)* **avoir la ~ sensible** to be a sensitive soul

**fibreux, -euse** [fibʀø, -øz] *adj* fibrous

**ficelé(e)** [fis(ə)le] *adj inf* **être mal ~** *inf (personne, intrigue, travail)* to be a mess

**ficeler** [fis(ə)le] <3> *vt* to tie up

**ficelle** [fisɛl] *f* ① *(corde)* string ② *(pain)* ficelle *(stick of French bread)* ▶ **connaître toutes les ~s du métier** to know the tricks of the trade

**fiche** [fiʃ] *f* ① *(piquet)* pin ② *(carte)* card ③ *(feuille, formulaire)* form; **~ de paie** pay stub [*o* slip]; **~ d'état civil** attestation of civil status; **~ technique** specifications *pl* ▶ **~ Suisse** *(dossier)* file

**ficher¹** [fiʃe] <1> **I.** *vt part passé:* fichu, *inf* ① *(faire)* to do; **ne rien ~** to do not a damn thing ② *(donner: claque, coup)* to give ③ *(mettre)* **~ qn dehors/à la porte** to kick sb out ④ *(se désintéresser)* **j'en ai rien à fiche!** I couldn't care less! ▶ **~ un coup à qn** to belt sb **II.** *vpr part passé:* fichu, *inf* ① *(se mettre)* **fiche-toi ça dans le crâne!** get that into your (thick) head! ② *(se flanquer)* **se ~ un coup de marteau** to do oneself with a hammer ③ *(se moquer)* **se ~ de qn** to pull sb's leg ④ *(se désintéresser)* **je m'en fiche** I don't care

**ficher²** [fiʃe] <1> **I.** *vt (inscrire)* **~ qn/qc** to put sb/sth on file **II.** *vpr* **se ~ dans qc** *(arête)* to get stuck in sth; *(flèche, pieu, piquet)* to stick in sth

**fichier** [fiʃje] *m a.* INFORM file

**fichu** [fiʃy] *m* (head)scarf

**fichu(e)** [fiʃy] **I.** *part passé de* **ficher** **II.** *adj inf* ① *antéposé (sale: caractère, métier, temps)* lousy ② *antéposé (sacré: habitude, idée)* damn; **un ~ problème** one hell of a problem ③ *(en mauvais état)* **la voiture est ~e** the car's totaled ④ *(gâché)* **être ~** *(vacances, soirée)* to be completely ruined ⑤ *(perdu, condamné)* **être ~** *(personne)* to be done for ⑥ *(capable)* **être/n'être pas ~ de faire qc** to be perfectly capable of doing/not up to doing sth ▶ **être bien/mal ~** *(bien bâti)* to have

a good/lousy body; *(habillé)* to look good/a mess

**fictif, -ive** [fiktif, -iv] *adj* ① *(imaginaire: personnage, récit)* imaginary ② *(faux: adresse, nom)* false; *(concurrence)* artificial; *(vente, contrat)* bogus

**fiction** [fiksjɔ̃] *f* ① *(imagination)* imagination ② *(fait imaginé)* invention; **film de ~** film that tells a story ③ *(œuvre d'imagination)* work of fiction

**fidèle** [fidɛl] **I.** *adj* ① *(constant)* faithful ② *(qui ne trahit pas qc)* **être ~ à une habitude** to stick to a habit ③ *(exact: récit, reproduction, traduction)* faithful; *(souvenir, historien, narrateur)* accurate ④ *(fiable: mémoire)* reliable; *(montre)* accurate **II.** *mf (personne: d'un homme politique)* follower; *(d'un magasin)* regular (customer) **III.** *mpl* REL faithful

**fidèlement** [fidɛlmɑ̃] *adv* ① *(loyalement: servir, obéir)* faithfully ② *(régulièrement: suivre une émission)* regularly ③ *(d'après l'original: reproduire, traduire)* faithfully; *(décrire)* accurately

**fidéliser** [fidelize] <1> *vt* **~ ses clients** to establish customer loyalty

**fidélité** [fidelite] *f* ① *(dévouement)* **~ à** [*o* **envers**] **qn** faithfulness to sb; *(dans le couple)* fidelity to sb ② *(attachement)* **~ à une habitude** adherence to a habit ③ *(exactitude: d'une copie, traduction, d'un portrait)* fidelity

**fiel** [fjɛl] *m* gall

**fiente** [fjɑ̃t] *f* droppings *pl*

**fier** [fje] <1> *vpr* **se ~ à qn** to put one's trust in sb

**fier, fière** [fjɛʀ] **I.** *adj* **~ de qn/qc** proud of sb/sth **II.** *m, f* **faire le ~ avec qn** *(crâner)* to act big in front of sb; *(être méprisant)* to lord it over sb

**fièrement** [fjɛʀmɑ̃] *adv* proudly

**fierté** [fjɛʀte] *f* pride

**fièvre** [fjɛvʀ] *f* ① MED fever ② *(vive agitation)* excitement ③ *(désir ardent)* burning desire

**fiévreusement** [fjevʀøzmɑ̃] *adv* feverishly

**fiévreux, -euse** [fjevʀø, -øz] *adj* feverish

**figé(e)** [fiʒe] *adj* fixed; (*attitude*) rigid

**figer** [fiʒe] <2a> I. *vt* ① (*durcir: graisse, sauce*) to congeal ② (*horrifier*) ~ **qn** (*surprise, terreur*) to root sb to the spot II. *vpr* (*durcir*) **se ~** (*graisse, huile, sauce*) to congeal; (*sang*) to clot; (*visage*) to harden; (*sourire*) to set

**fignoler** [fiɲɔle] <1> I. *vi inf* to polish things up II. *vt inf* to polish up

**figue** [fig] *f* fig

**figuier** [figje] *m* fig tree

**figurant(e)** [figyʀɑ̃, ɑ̃t] *m(f)* ① CINE extra ② THEAT walk-on ③ (*potiche*) puppet

**figuratif, -ive** [figyʀatif, -iv] *adj* figurative

**figure** [figyʀ] *f* ① (*visage, mine*) face ② (*personnage*) a. MATH figure ③ (*image*) illustration ④ SPORT figure skating ▶ **casser la ~ à qn** *inf* to smash sb's face in; **se casser la ~** *inf* to have a bad fall; (*projet*) to fail miserably

**figuré(e)** [figyʀe] *adj* ① (*opp: concret: sens*) figurative ② (*riche en figures: langage*) full of imagery

**figurer** [figyʀe] <1> I. *vi* ① THEAT to have a walk-on part ② CINE to be an extra ③ SPORT, POL **ne faire que ~** to play a minor role; (*dans un classement*) to be an also-ran ④ (*être mentionné*) to appear II. *vt* (*représenter*) to represent III. *vpr* **se ~ qn/qc** to imagine sb/sth

**figurine** [figyʀin] *f* figurine

**fil** [fil] *m* ① (*pour coudre*) thread; (*pour tricoter*) yarn; (*de haricot*) string; **~ de fer** wire; **~ de fer barbelé** barbed wire ② (*câble: d'un téléphone, d'une lampe*) wire ③ (*conducteur électrique*) line ④ (*corde à linge*) clothesline ⑤ (*enchaînement*) **suivre le ~ de la conversation** to follow the thread of the conversation ▶ **de ~ en aiguille** one thing leading to another; **donner du ~ à retordre à qn** to be a headache for sb; **au ~ des ans** over the years

**filament** [filamɑ̃] *m* ① ELEC filament ② (*fil: d'une bave, glu*) thread

**filandreux, -euse** [filɑ̃dʀø, -øz] *adj* ① (*rempli de filandres: viande*) stringy ② (*long: discours*) long-winded

**filature** [filatyʀ] *f* ① (*usine*) mill ② (*action*) spinning ③ (*surveillance*) tailing; **prendre qn en ~** to tail sb

**file** [fil] *f* ① (*colonne*) line; (*d'attente*) queue; **se mettre à** [*o* **prendre**] **la ~** to get into line ② (*voie de circulation*) lane ▶ **en ~ indienne** in single file [*o* Indian file]

**filer** [file] <1> I. *vi* ① (*s'abîmer: maille, collant*) to run ② (*s'écouler lentement: essence*) to run; (*sable, sirop*) to trickle ③ (*aller vite: personne, voiture, temps*) to fly by; (*étoile*) to shoot down; (*argent*) to disappear ④ *inf* (*partir vite: personne pressée*) to dash (off); (*voleur*) to make off; **~ à l'anglaise** to take French leave; **laisser ~ qn** to let sb get away II. *vt* ① (*tisser*) to spin ② (*surveiller*) to tail ③ *inf* (*donner*) **~ de l'argent à qn** to slip sb some money

**filet** [file] *m* ① (*réseau de maille*) net ② CULIN fillet ③ (*petite quantité*) **~ d'huile/de sang/d'eau** trickle of oil/blood/water

**filial(e)** [filjal, -jo] <-aux> *adj* (*amour, piété*) filial

**filiale** [filjal] *f* subsidiary company

**filiation** [filjasjɔ̃] *f* ① (*descendance*) filiation ② (*relation: des idées, mots*) relation

**filière** [filjɛʀ] *f* ① (*suite de formalités*) channel ② UNIV course option ③ (*réseau: de la drogue, du trafic*) network

**filiforme** [filifɔʀm] *adj* (*jambes, personne*) spindly; (*antennes*) filiform

**filigrane** [filigʀan] *m* (*d'un billet de banque, timbre*) watermark ▶ **apparaître en ~** to be apparent beneath the surface

**fille** [fij] *f* ① (*opp: garçon*) girl ② (*opp: fils*) daughter ③ (*prostituée*) whore

**fillette** [fijɛt] *f* little girl

**filleul(e)** [fijœl] *m(f)* godson, goddaughter *m, f*

**film** [film] *m* ① (*pellicule, couche*) film ② (*œuvre*) movie; **~ vidéo** video film; **~ d'action** action movie

**filmer** [filme] <1> *vt, vi* to film

**filon** [filɔ̃] *m* ❶ (*en minéralogie*) vein ❷ *inf* (*travail*) cushy job

**filou** [filu] *m inf* ❶ (*personne malhonnête*) rogue ❷ (*enfant, chien espiègle*) rascal

**fils** [fis] *m* (*opp: fille*) son; Dupont ~ Dupont junior ▶ **de père en ~** from father to son; **être bien le ~ de son père** to be one's father's son

**filtre** [filtʀ] *m* filter

**filtrer** [filtʀe] <1> I. *vi* to filter through II. *vt* ❶ (*pénétrer: liquide, lumière, son*) to filter ❷ (*contrôler: informations*) to screen

**fin** [fɛ̃] *f* ❶ (*issue, mort*) end; ~ **de série** oddment; **la ~ du monde** the end of the world; **mettre ~ à qc** to put an end to sth; **à la ~** at the end; **sans ~** endless ❷ (*but*) ~ **en soi** end in itself; **arriver** [*o* **parvenir**] **à ses ~s** to achieve one's ends ❸ *Québec* ~ **de semaine** (*week-end*) weekend ▶ **en ~ de compte** at the end of the day; **arrondir ses ~s de mois** to make a bit extra

**fin(e)** [fɛ̃, fin] I. *adj* ❶ (*opp: épais*) fine; (*couche, étoffe, tranche*) thin ❷ (*gracieux: traits, visage*) delicate; (*jambes, taille*) slender ❸ (*recherché: mets, vin*) choice ❹ (*de qualité supérieure: mets, vin, lingerie*) fine ❺ (*subtil: personne, remarque*) astute; (*humour, nuance*) witty; (*esprit, observation*) sharp ❻ *antéposé* (*très habile: cuisinier, tireur*) expert; ~ **gourmet** gourmet ❼ *Québec* (*aimable, gentil*) kind II. *adv* ❶ (*complètement: soûl*) blind; (*prêt*) absolutely ❷ (*finement: écrire*) small

**final(e)** [final, -o] <s *o* -aux> *adj* (*qui vient à la fin: consonne, résultat*) final; (*discours, accord*) closing; **point ~** period

**finale**¹ [final] *m* MUS finale

**finale**² [final] *f* SPORT final

**finalement** [finalmɑ̃] *adv* ❶ (*pour finir*) finally ❷ (*en définitive*) in the end

**finance** [finɑ̃s] *f* ❶ *pl* (*ressources pécuniaires: d'une personne, d'un pays*) finances ❷ (*ministère*) **les Finances** Ministry of Finance ▶ **moyennant** ~ for a consideration

**financement** [finɑ̃smɑ̃] *m* financing

**financer** [finɑ̃se] <2> I. *vi iron* to cough up II. *vt* to finance

**financier** [finɑ̃sje] *m* financier

**financier, -ière** [finɑ̃sje, -jɛʀ] *adj* (*problèmes, crise, politique, soucis*) financial; **établissement** ~ finance company

**financièrement** [finɑ̃sjɛʀmɑ̃] *adv* financially

**finasser** [finase] <1> *vi* to scheme

**finaud(e)** [fino, od] I. *adj* crafty II. *m(f)* crafty son of a gun

**finement** [finmɑ̃] *adv* ❶ (*délicatement: brodé, ciselé*) delicately ❷ (*astucieusement: manœuvrer, agir*) astutely; (*faire remarquer, observer*) shrewdly

**finesse** [finɛs] *f* ❶ (*minceur: des cheveux, d'une pointe de stylo*) fineness; (*d'une tranche*) thinness ❷ (*délicatesse: d'un visage*) delicacy; (*des mains, de la taille*) slenderness ❸ (*raffinement: d'une broderie, porcelaine*) delicacy; (*d'un aliment*) refinement ❹ (*sensibilité: d'un goût*) keenness; (*d'une ouïe, de l'odorat*) acuteness ❺ (*subtilité: d'une personne*) shrewdness; (*d'une allusion*) subtlety; **sa ~ d'esprit** his shrewd mind ❻ *pl* (*difficultés: d'une langue, d'un art*) subtleties

**fini** [fini] *m* ❶ (*perfection: d'un produit*) finish ❷ MATH, PHILOS **le ~** the finite

**fini(e)** [fini] *adj* ❶ (*terminé*) **être** ~ to be finished; (*jour, spectacle*) to be over ❷ (*opp: infini*) finite ❸ *péj* (*complet: menteur, voleur*) accomplished ❹ (*cousu*) **bien/mal** ~ well/badly finished

**finir** [finiʀ] <8> I. *vi* ❶ (*s'arrêter: rue, propriété*) to end; (*vacances, spectacle, contrat*) to (come to an) end; **tout ça n'en finit pas** all that takes for ever ❷ (*terminer*) to finish; **avoir fini** to have [*o* be] finished; **laissez-moi ~ (de parler)!** let me finish!; **en ~ avec qc** to get sth over with ❸ SPORT ~ **à la quatrième place** to finish fourth ❹ (*en venir à*) ~ **par faire qc** (*choix final*) to end up doing sth; (*après des retards*) to finally do sth ❺ (*se retrouver*) ~ **en prison** to end up in prison **II.** *vt* ❶ (*arriver au bout de*) *a.* SPORT to finish; ~ **de manger/de s'habiller** to finish eating/getting dressed ❷ (*consommer, utiliser jusqu'au bout: plat, assiette, bouteille*) to finish (off); (*vêtement*) to wear out ❸ (*passer la fin de*) ~ **ses jours à la campagne** to end one's days in the country ❹ (*cesser: dispute*) to stop; **on n'a pas fini de parler d'elle** we haven't heard the last of her ❺ (*être le dernier élément de*) to complete ❻ (*fignoler*) ~ **un ouvrage** to finish off a job

**finition** [finisjɔ̃] *f* ❶ (*action: d'un meuble, d'une œuvre d'art*) finishing ❷ (*résultat*) finish ❸ *gén pl* TECH finishing touches

**finlandais(e)** [fɛ̃lɑ̃dɛ, ɛz] *adj* Finnish

**Finlandais(e)** [fɛ̃lɑ̃dɛ, ɛz] *m(f)* Finn

**Finlande** [fɛ̃lɑ̃d] *f* **la** ~ Finland

**finnois** [finwa] *m* Finnish; *v.a.* **français**

**finnois(e)** [finwa, waz] *adj* Finnish

**Finnois(e)** [finwa, waz] *m(f)* Finn

**fiord** [fjɔrd] *m* fjord

**fioriture** [fjɔrityr] *f* flourish; **sans** ~**s** plain (and unadorned)

**firent** [fir] *passé simple de* **faire**

**firmament** [firmamɑ̃] *m* firmament

**firme** [firm] *f* firm

**fis** [fi] *passé simple de* **faire**

**fisc** [fisk] *m* **le** ~ the taxman

**fiscal(e)** [fiskal, -o] <-aux> *adj* fiscal

**fiscalité** [fiskalite] *f* tax regime

**fission** [fisjɔ̃] *f* fission

**fissure** [fisyr] *f* crack

**fissurer** [fisyre] <1> **I.** *vt* (*éclair*) to fork **II.** *vpr* **se** ~ to crack

**fit** [fi] *passé simple de* **faire**

**fîtes** [fit] *passé simple de* **faire**

**fixation** [fiksasjɔ̃] *f* ❶ (*pose*) settling ❷ (*détermination*) fixing ❸ (*obsession*) fixation; **faire une** ~ **sur qn/qc** to have a fixation on sb/sth ❹ (*dispositif*) fastening

**fixe** [fiks] **I.** *adj* fixed; **idée** ~ idée fixe **II.** *m* basic (salary) **III.** *interj* ~! attention!

**fixé(e)** [fikse] *adj* ❶ PSYCH (*personne*)

fixated ❷ (*renseigné*) **être** ~ **sur le compte de qn** to have sb sized up ❸ (*décidé*) **ne pas encore être** ~ to have not yet decided

**fixement** [fiksəmɑ̃] *adv* **regarder qn/qc** ~ to give sb/sth a fixed stare

**fixer** [fikse] <1> **I.** *vt* ❶ (*attacher, conserver, arranger*) *a.* CHIM, PHOT to fix ❷ (*retenir: population*) to settle ❸ (*regarder*) ~ **qn/qc** to look hard at sb/sth ❹ (*arrêter*) ~ **son attention sur qc** to focus one's attention on sth ❺ (*définir: règle, conditions, limites*) to set **II.** *vpr* ❶ (*s'accrocher*) **se** ~ **au mur** to hang on the wall ❷ (*se déposer*) **se** ~ to be deposited ❸ (*s'établir*) **se** ~ **à Paris** to settle in Paris ❹ (*se poser*) **se** ~ **sur qn/qc** (*attention*) to settle on sb/sth; (*choix*) to fall on sb/sth ❺ (*se définir*) **se** ~ **un but** to set oneself a target

**fjord** [fjɔrd] *m* **v.** **fiord**

**flac** [flak] *interj* splash

**flacon** [flakɔ̃] *m* bottle; (*de parfum*) perfume bottle

**flagada** [flagada] *adj inv, inf* **être** ~ to be washed-out

**flagellation** [flaʒelasjɔ̃, flaʒɛllasjɔ̃] *f* flagellation

**flageller** [flaʒele] <1> **I.** *vt* to flog **II.** *vpr* **se** ~ to scourge oneself

**flageoler** [flaʒɔle] <1> *vi* to shake; (*jambes*) to tremble

**flagrant(e)** [flagrɑ̃, ɑ̃t] *adj* blatant; (*injustice*) flagrant

**flair** [flɛr] *m* (*du chien*) (sense of) smell ▶ **avoir du** ~ (*odorat*) to have a good nose; (*idées*) to have a sixth sense

**flairer** [flere] <1> *vt* ❶ (*renifler*) to sniff ❷ (*sentir: animal*) to scent ❸ (*pressentir: animal, personne*) to sense

**flamand** [flamɑ̃] *m* Flemish; *v.a.* **français**

**flamand(e)** [flamɑ̃, ɑ̃d] *adj* Flemish

**Flamand(e)** [flamɑ̃, ɑ̃d] *m(f)* Fleming

**flamant** [flamɑ̃] *m* flamingo

**flambé(e)** [flɑ̃be] *adj* ❶ CULIN flambéd; **tarte** ~**e** Alsatian onion tart ❷ *inf* (*fichu*) **être** ~ (*personne*) done for; (*affaire*) down the drain

**F**

**flambeau** [flɑ̃bo] <x> m torch

**flambée** [flɑ̃be] f ❶ (feu) blaze ❷ (brusque accès, montée: de violence) flare-up ❸ (du dollar) upward surge; (de terrorisme) outbreak

**flamber** [flɑ̃be] <1> I. vi to blaze; (maison) to burn down II. vt ❶ (cheveux, volaille) to singe ❷ CULIN to flambé

**flamboyant(e)** [flɑ̃bwajɑ̃, jɑ̃t] adj ❶ (étincelant: feu, soleil) blazing; (couleur) flaming; (chrome) gleaming; (source de lumière) flashing ❷ ART flamboyant

**flamboyer** [flɑ̃bwaje] <6> vi (soleil) to blaze; (couleur) to flame; (source de lumière) to flash; (chrome) to gleam

**flamenco** [flamɛnko] I. m flamenco II. adj flamenco

**flamme** [flam] f ❶ flame ❷ pl (brasier) flames; **être en ~s** to be ablaze ❸ (éclat: des yeux) fire ❹ (pavillon) pennant ❺ (tampon de la poste) slogan ❻ (ampoule) candle (bulb) ▶ **descendre qn/qc en ~s** to shoot sb/sth down in flames

**flan** [flɑ̃] m flan, custard tart

**flanc** [flɑ̃] m ❶ (partie latérale: du corps, d'un navire, d'une montagne) side; (d'un cheval) flank ❷ MIL flank ▶ **tirer au ~** inf to skive

**flancher** [flɑ̃ʃe] vi inf (personne) to waver; (son cœur/sa mémoire a flanché) his heart/his memory let him down

**Flandre** [flɑ̃dʀ] f la ~/les ~s Flanders

**flanelle** [flanɛl] f flannel

**flâner** [flɑne] <1> vi ❶ (se promener) to stroll ❷ (musarder) to hang around

**flânerie** [flɑnʀi] f ❶ (promenade) stroll ❷ (musardise) idling; (au lit) lying around

**flanquer** [flɑ̃ke] <1> I. vt inf ❶ (envoyer) ~ **des objets à la figure de qn** to fling things in sb's face ❷ (mettre) ~ **qn à la porte/dehors** to kick sb out ❸ (donner) ~ **la frousse à qn** to frighten sb II. vpr inf ❶ (s'envoyer) **se ~ des objets à la figure** to fling things at each other ❷ (se mettre) **se**

**~ dans une situation délicate** to get oneself into an awkward situation ❸ (tomber) **se ~ par terre** to hit the deck

**flaque** [flak] f puddle; (de sang) pool

**flash** [flaʃ] <es> m ❶ PHOT, CINE flash ❷ RADIO, TV ~ **info** [o **d'information**] newsflash

**flash-back** [flaʃbak] m inv flashback

**flasque** [flask] I. adj flabby II. f flask III. m flange; (de mécanique) cheek

**flatter** [flate] <1> I. vt ❶ (louer) ~ **qn/la vanité de qn** to flatter sb/sb's vanity; **être flatté de qc** to be flattered about sth ❷ (caresser: animal) to stroke ❸ (être agréable à) ~ **le palais** to appeal to the palate II. vpr ❶ (se féliciter) **se ~ de qc** to pride oneself on sth ❷ (aimer à croire) **se ~ de faire qc** to like to think one can do sth

**flatterie** [flatʀi] f flattery

**flatteur, -euse** [flatœʀ, -øz] I. adj flattering II. m, f flatterer

**fléau** [fleo] <x> m ❶ (calamité) scourge ❷ (partie d'une balance) beam ❸ AGR flail

**flèche**[1] [flɛʃ] f ❶ (arme, signe) arrow ❷ (sur une église) spire

**flèche**[2] [flɛʃ] f ~s **de lard** flitch of bacon

**flécher** [fleʃe] <5> vt to signpost

**fléchette** [fleʃɛt] f ❶ (petite flèche) dart ❷ pl (jeu) darts

**fléchir** [fleʃiʀ] <8> I. vt ❶ (plier: bras, genoux) to bend ❷ (faire céder: personne) to sway II. vi ❶ (se plier) to bend ❷ (diminuer) to fall; (exigences, sévérité) to be tempered; (volonté) to weaken; (prix, cours) to slip ❸ (céder) to yield

**fléchissement** [fleʃismɑ̃] m ❶ (flexion: du bras, de la jambe) bending; (d'une poutre, planche) sagging ❷ (diminution: de la production, natalité) falling off; (des prix) fall ❸ (renoncement: de la volonté) yielding

**flegmatique** [flɛgmatik] I. adj phlegmatic II. mf phlegmatic person

**flegme** [flɛgm] m composure

**flemme** [flɛm] f inf laziness; **j'ai la ~ de**

**faire la vaisselle** I can't be bothered doing the dishes

**flétri(e)** [fletʀi] *adj* ❶ (*plante*) withered; (*fleur*) wilted

**flétrir** [fletʀiʀ] <8> I. *vt* ❶ (*faner: fleur*) to wilt ❷ (*rider: visage*) to wither ❸ HIST to brand II. *vpr* **se ~** ❶ (*se faner: plante*) to wither; (*fleur*) to wilt ❷ (*se rider: visage*) to wither

**fleur** [flœʀ] *f* ❶ flower; (*d'un cerisier, pommier*) blossom; **en ~(s)** in flower ❷ (*partie du cuir*) grain side ❸ *gén pl* BIO (*de vin*) flowers ❹ (*compliment*) **jeter des ~ à qn** *inf* to lavish praise on sb ❺ *sans pl, soutenu* (*ce qu'il y a de meilleur*) **la** (*fine*) **~ de la ville** the town's high society ▶ **à** [*o* **dans**] **la ~ de l'âge** in one's prime; **~ bleue** sentimental; **avoir une sensibilité à ~ de peau** to be highly susceptible

**fleuri(e)** [flœʀi] *adj* ❶ (*en fleurs*) in bloom ❷ (*couvert, garni de fleurs*) decorated with flowers ❸ (*avec des motifs floraux*) flowered ❹ (*coloré: teint*) florid ❺ (*qui sent les fleurs*) flower-scented ❻ (*orné: style*) flowery

**fleurir** [flœʀiʀ] <8> I. *vi* ❶ (*mettre des fleurs*) to flower ❷ (*s'épanouir: amitié*) to blossom ❸ *iron* (*se couvrir de poils*) to sprout hair II. *vt* (*orner, décorer: table, tombe*) to put flowers on

**fleuriste** [flœʀist] *mf* florist

**fleuve** [flœv] *m* ❶ (*rivière*) river ❷ (*flot*) **~ de lave/de boue** torrent of lava/mud

**flexibilité** [flɛksibilite] *f* flexibility

**flexible** [flɛksibl] I. *adj* ❶ (*souple: tige en bois*) pliable; (*en plastique, métal*) flexible ❷ (*adaptable*) flexible; *péj* pliable II. *m* hose

**flexion** [flɛksjɔ̃] *f* ❶ (*mouvement corporel*) bending ❷ LING inflection ❸ PHYS flexion

**flexitarien(ne)** [flɛksitaʀjɛ̃, jɛn] *m* flexitarian

**flic** [flik] *m inf* cop

**flingue** [flɛ̃g] *m inf* gun

**flinguer** [flɛ̃ge] <1> I. *vt inf* ❶ (*tuer*) to

waste ❷ (*critiquer*) to shoot to pieces II. *vpr inf* **se ~** to put a bullet in oneself

**flipper¹** [flipœʀ] *m* pinball machine

**flipper²** [flipe] <1> *vi* ❶ *inf* (*être angoissé*) to be on a downer ❷ *inf* (*être excité*) to be high

**flirt** [flœʀt] *m* ❶ (*amourette*) flirtation ❷ (*petite histoire d'amour*) affair ❸ (*personne*) flirt

**flirter** [flœʀte] <1> *vi* to flirt

**flocon** [flɔkɔ̃] *m* ❶ (*petite masse peu dense: de neige*) flake ❷ (*petite touffe: de coton, bourre*) tuft ❸ CULIN flake; **~s de maïs** cornflakes

**floconneux, -euse** [flɔkɔnø, -øz] *adj* fluffy

**flopée** [flɔpe] *f inf* **une ~ de gamins/touristes** a crowd of kids/tourists

**floraison** [flɔʀɛzɔ̃] *f* ❶ (*fait de fleurir*) flowering ❷ (*fleurs*) blooms *pl* ❸ (*époque*) heyday ❹ (*épanouissement*) blossoming; (*de talents*) flowering

**floral(e)** [flɔʀal, -o] <-aux> *adj* floral

**flore** [flɔʀ] *f* flora

**florilège** [flɔʀilɛʒ] *m* anthology

**florin** [flɔʀɛ̃] *m* HIST (*monnaie*) florin

**florissait** [flɔʀisɛ] *imparf de* **fleurir**

**florissant(e)** [flɔʀisɑ̃, ɑ̃t] *adj* ❶ (*prospère*) flourishing ❷ (*resplendissant: santé, teint*) blooming

**flot** [flo] *m* ❶ (*vague*) wave ❷ *soutenu* (*quantité importante: d'images, de souvenirs, larmes*) flood; (*de personnes, sang*) stream; (*de paroles*) torrent; **couler à ~s** to flow freely; **entrer à ~s** (*lumière*) to flood in ❸ *sans pl* (*marée montante*) rising tide

**flottant(e)** [flɔtɑ̃, ɑ̃t] *adj* ❶ *a.* FIN floating ❷ (*dans l'air: foulard, drapeaux*) streaming; (*crinière, chevelure*) flowing ❸ (*instable*) irresolute

**flotte¹** [flɔt] *f* fleet

**flotte²** [flɔt] *f inf* ❶ (*eau*) water ❷ (*pluie*) rain

**flottement** [flɔtmɑ̃] *m* ❶ (*ondulation: d'un drapeau*) fluttering ❷ (*hésitation*) undecidedness

**flotter** [flɔte] <1> I. *vi* ❶ (*être porté sur un liquide*) to float ❷ (*être en suspen*-

sion dans l'air: brouillard) to drift; (parfum) to float ❸ (onduler) to flutter ❹ (être ample) **sa jupe flotte autour d'elle** her skirt flaps around her ❺ (hésiter) to waver II. *vi impers, inf* (pleuvoir) to pour down III. *vt* (bois) to float

**flotteur** [flɔtœʀ] *m* TECH float

**flou** [flu] I. *m* ❶ (opp: netteté) vagueness ❷ CINE, PHOT blur ❸ (non ajustement: d'une coiffure, d'une mode) looseness ❹ (imprécision: d'une pensée) haziness; (d'une argumentation) woolliness II. *adv* in a blur

**flou(e)** [flu] *adj* ❶ blurred; (photo) out of focus ❷ (non ajusté: vêtement, coiffure) loose ❸ (imprécis: idée, pensée) hazy; (relation, rôle) vague

**fluctuation** [flyktɥasjɔ̃] *f* fluctuation; (de l'opinion) swing

**fluctuer** [flyktɥe] <1> *vi* to fluctuate

**fluet(te)** [flɥɛ, ɛt] *adj* ❶ (frêle) slender ❷ (peu sonore: voix) reedy

**fluide** [flɥid, flɥid] I. *adj* ❶ (qui s'écoule facilement) fluid ❷ (ample: style, vêtement) flowing ❸ (difficile à saisir: pensée) elusive II. *m* ❶ CHIM fluid ❷ (force occulte) aura

**fluidifier** [flɥidifje] <1> *vt* to liquefy

**fluidité** [flɥidite] *f* ❶ (liquidité: du sang) fluidity ❷ AUTO **~ du trafic** free-flowing traffic ❸ ECON (d'un marché) flexibility ❹ *fig* (d'un style) flow; (d'une pensée) elusiveness

**fluo** [flyɔ] *adj sans pl abr de* **fluorescent**

**fluor** [flyɔʀ] *m* fluorine

**fluoré(e)** [flyɔʀe] *adj* (eau) fluoridated; (dentifrice) fluoride

**fluorescence** [flyɔʀesɑ̃s] *f* fluorescence

**fluorescent(e)** [flyɔʀesɑ̃, ɑ̃t] *adj* fluorescent

**flûte** [flyt] I. *f* ❶ (instrument) flute ❷ (pain) loaf of French bread ❸ (verre) flute (glass) II. *interj inf* darn it

**fluvial(e)** [flyvjal, -jo] <-aux> *adj* GEO fluvial; (port, transport) river

**flux** [fly] *m* ❶ (marée) ebb [o incoming] tide; **le ~ et le reflux** the ebb and flow ❷ MED, PHYS, ECON flow

**fluxion** [flyksjɔ̃] *f* **~ de poitrine** pneumonia

**F.M.** [ɛfɛm] *f abr de* **Frequency Modulation** FM

**FMI** [ɛfɛmi] *m abr de* **Fonds monétaire international** IMF

**focaliser** [fɔkalize] <1> I. *vt* to focus II. *vpr* ❶ PHYS **se ~** to be focussed ❷ (se concentrer) **se ~ sur qn/qc** to focus on sb/sth

**fœtal(e)** [fetal, -o] <-aux> *adj* fetal

**fœtus** [fetys] *m* fetus

**foi** [fwa] *f* ❶ (croyance) **~ en qn** faith in sb; **avoir la ~** to have faith ❷ (confiance) **avoir ~ en qn/qc** soutenu to have faith [o confidence] in sb/sth ▸ **être de bonne/mauvaise ~** to be in good/bad faith; **faire ~** to be valid; **ma ~** well

**foie** [fwa] *m* ❶ ANAT liver ❷ CULIN **~ gras** foie gras

**foin** [fwɛ̃] *m sans pl* hay

**foire** [fwaʀ] *f* ❶ (marchée, exposition, fête) fair ❷ *inf* (endroit bruyant) madhouse ❸ INFORM **~ aux questions** frequently asked questions (file) ▸ **faire la ~** *inf* to live it up

**foirer** [fwaʀe] <1> *vi* ❶ *inf* (rater) to come to grief ❷ *inf* (être défectueux: écrou, vis) to slip; (obus, fusée) to misfire

**foireux, -euse** [fwaʀø, -øz] I. *adj inf* ❶ (qui a peur) chicken-hearted ❷ (mauvais) lousy II. *m, f inf* chicken

**fois** [fwa] *f* ❶ (fréquence) time; **une ~** once; *Belgique* (donc) then; **une ~ par an** [o **l'an**] once a year; **deux ~** twice; **(à) chaque ~** each time; **il était une ~ ...** once upon a time ❷ dans un comparatif **cinq ~ plus élevé que** five times higher than; **cinq ~ plus d'argent/de personnes** five times more money/people ❸ (comme multiplicateur) **9 ~ 3 font 27** 9 times 3 is 27 ▸ **neuf ~ sur dix** nine times out of ten; **trois ~ rien** absolutely nothing; **un seul enfant/bateau à la ~** just one child/boat at a time; **tout à la ~** at one and the same time; **des ~** inf sometimes

**foison** [fwazɔ̃] **à ~** in plenty

**foisonner** [fwazɔne] <1> *vi* to abound

**fol** [fɔl] *adj v.* **fou**

**folâtrer** [fɔlɑtre] <1> *vi* to play about

**folichon(ne)** [fɔliʃɔ̃, ɔn] *adj inf* **ne pas être ~** not to be a lot of fun

**folie** [fɔli] *f* ❶ (*démence, déraison*) madness ❷ (*passion*) **~ de qc** mad passion for sth; **aimer qn/qc à la ~** to love sb/sth madly ❸ (*conduite/paroles*) foolish deed/word ❹ HIST folly

**folio** [fɔljo] *m* TYP folio

**folklore** [fɔlklɔʀ] *m* ❶ (*traditions populaires*) folklore ❷ *péj* (*cinéma*) nonsense

**folklorique** [fɔlklɔʀik] *adj* ❶ (*relatif au folklore*) folk ❷ *péj, inf* (*farfelu*) weird

**folle** [fɔl] **I.** *adj v.* **fou II.** *f péj, inf* (*homosexuel*) queen, queer *sl*

**follement** [fɔlmɑ̃] *adv* wildly; (*amoureux*) madly; (*comique*) uproariously

**foncé(e)** [fɔ̃se] *adj* dark

**foncer** [fɔ̃se] <2> **I.** *vt* ❶ (*rendre plus foncé*) to darken ❷ (*creuser*) to dig; (*puits*) to sink ❸ CULIN to line **II.** *vi* ❶ *inf* (*aller très vite en courant*) **~ sur qn/qc** to rush at sb/sth; (*en voiture*) to charge at sb/sth ❷ *inf* (*aller très vite en agissant rapidement*) to show drive ❸ (*devenir plus foncé*) to go darker

**fonceur, -euse** [fɔ̃sœʀ, -øz] *m, f inf* (*personne dynamique*) dynamic individual ❷ (*audacieux*) go-getter

**foncier, -ière** [fɔ̃sje, -jɛʀ] *adj* ❶ land; (*revenus*) from land ❷ (*fondamental: défaut, erreur, problème*) fundamental; (*qualité, gentillesse*) innate

**foncièrement** [fɔ̃sjɛʀmɑ̃] *adv* fundamentally

**fonction** [fɔ̃ksjɔ̃] *f* ❶ *a.* CHIM, LING, MATH, INFORM function; **elle a pour ~ de +*infin*** her function is to +*infin* ❷ (*activité professionnelle*) post ❸ (*charge*) duty ▶ **la ~ publique** public service (*state sector employment*); **en ~ de qc** in accordance with sth; **en ~ du temps** depending on the weather

**fonctionnaire** [fɔ̃ksjɔnɛʀ] *mf* state employee; (*dans l'administration*) civil servant

**fonctionnalité** [fɔ̃ksjɔnalite] *f* ❶ *sans pl* practicality ❷ *gén pl* INFORM functionality

**fonctionnel(le)** [fɔ̃ksjɔnɛl] *adj* functional

**fonctionnement** [fɔ̃ksjɔnmɑ̃] *m* working

**fonctionner** [fɔ̃ksjɔne] <1> *vi* to work; (*organe, administration*) to function

**fond** [fɔ̃] *m* ❶ (*partie inférieure*) bottom; **au ~ du sac** at the bottom of the bag ❷ TECH, ARCHIT base ❸ (*partie la plus éloignée: d'une pièce, d'un couloir*) far end; (*d'une armoire*) back; **au ~ du jardin** at the back of the garden ❹ (*partie intime*) **avoir un bon ~** to be a good person deep down; **du ~ du cœur** from the bottom of one's heart ❺ (*degré le plus bas*) **être au ~ de l'abîme** to be in the depths of despair ❻ (*ce qui est essentiel: des choses, d'un problème*) heart; **aller au ~ des choses** to get to the heart of the matter ❼ (*opp: forme*) content ❽ (*dans une bouteille, un verre*) **il reste un ~** there's a drop left ❾ (*hauteur d'eau*) depth ❿ (*pièce rapportée*) patch ⓫ (*arrière-plan*) background ⓬ CULIN base ⓭ SPORT (*résistance*) staying power; (*course*) long-distance race; **ski de ~** cross-country skiing ⓮ (*base*) **~ de teint** foundation ▶ **connaître qc comme le ~ de sa poche** to know sth like the back of one's hand; **à ~** thoroughly; (*respirer*) deeply; (*connaître*) in depth; **à ~ de train** at full tilt; **au** [*o* **dans le**] **~, ...** *inf* when it comes down to it; **article de ~** a feature article; **de ~ en comble** from top to bottom

**fondamental(e)** [fɔ̃damɑ̃tal, -o] <-aux> *adj* ❶ basic; (*élément, propriété, loi*) fundamental ❷ (*essentiel*) vital ❸ (*en science: recherche*) basic ❹ MUS fundamental ❺ LING **l'anglais ~** basic English

**fondamentalement** [fɔ̃damɑ̃talmɑ̃] *adv* fundamentally

**fondamentaliste** [fɔ̃damɑ̃talist] **I.** *adj* fundamentalist **II.** *mf* fundamentalist

F

**fondant(e)** [fɔ̃dɑ̃, ɑ̃t] *adj* ❶ (*qui fond: glace, neige*) melting ❷ (*mûr: poire*) that melts in the mouth ❸ (*tendre*) tender

**fondateur, -trice** [fɔ̃datœʀ, -tʀis] *m, f* founder

**fondation** [fɔ̃dasjɔ̃] *f* ❶ (*fait de fonder, institution*) foundation ❷ (*création par don ou legs*) establishment ❸ *pl* ARCHIT (*d'un bâtiment*) foundations

**fondé(e)** [fɔ̃de] **I.** *adj* **être bien ~** (*crainte, critique, confiance*) to be fully justified; (*opinion*) to be well-founded; (*pressentiment*) to be well-grounded **II.** *m(f)* **~ de pouvoir** proxy

**fondement** [fɔ̃dmɑ̃] *m* ❶ *pl* foundations ❷ (*motif, raison*) grounds; **ne reposer sur aucun ~** to have no foundation ❸ PHILOS fundament

**fonder** [fɔ̃de] <1> **I.** *vt* ❶ to found ❷ (*financer: prix*) to found; (*dispensaire, institution*) to set up ❸ (*faire reposer*) **~ une décision sur qc** to base a decision on sth **II.** *vpr* **se ~ sur qc** (*personne*) to base oneself on; (*attitude, raisonnement*) to be based on

**fondeur** [fɔ̃dœʀ] *m* smelter

**fondeur, -euse** [fɔ̃dœʀ, -øz] *m, f* (*au ski*) cross-country skier

**fondre** [fɔ̃dʀ] <14> **I.** *vi* ❶ to melt ❷ (*se dissoudre*) **~ dans un liquide/sous la langue** to dissolve in a liquid/under the tongue ❸ (*s'attendrir*) **~ en larmes** to break into tears ❹ *inf* (*maigrir*) **~ de 10 kilos** to shed 10 kilograms ❺ (*diminuer rapidement: argent, muscles*) to vanish; (*diminuer partiellement*) to dwindle ❻ (*dissiper*) **faire ~ sa colère** to melt away one's anger ❼ (*se précipiter*) **~ sur qn/qc** (*oiseau, ennemi*) to bear down on sb/sth **II.** *vt* ❶ to melt; (*bijoux, argenterie*) to melt down ❷ (*fabriquer*) to cast ❸ (*fusionner*) **~ qc dans qc** to combine sth into sth ❹ (*incorporer*) **~ qc dans qc** to merge sth with sth **III.** *vpr* ❶ (*former un tout avec*) **se ~ dans qc** to merge into sth ❷ (*disparaître*) **se ~ dans le brouillard** to vanish into the mist; (*appel*) to be lost in the mist

**fonds** [fɔ̃] *m* ❶ (*commerce*) business ❷ (*terrain*) land ❸ (*organisme, capital*) fund; **~ publics** [*o* **d'État**] public funds; **gérer les ~** to manage the money ❹ (*ressources*) assets *pl*; (*d'une langue*) resources *pl* ❺ (*œuvres: d'une bibliothèque*) collection ❻ (*qualités physiques ou intellectuelles*) resources

**fondu** [fɔ̃dy] *m* CINE **~ enchaîné** fade-in fade-out

**fondu(e)** [fɔ̃dy] **I.** *part passé de* **fondre** **II.** *adj* (*couleurs, tons*) blending; (*fromage*) melted; **neige ~e** melted snow; (*au sol*) slush

**fondue** [fɔ̃dy] *f* fondue

**font** [fɔ̃] *indic prés de* **faire**

**fontaine** [fɔ̃tɛn] *f* ❶ (*construction*) fountain ❷ (*source*) spring ❸ CULIN (*creux dans la farine*) well

**fonte** [fɔ̃t] *f* ❶ (*fusion: d'un métal*) smelting ❷ (*fabrication*) founding ❸ (*métal*) cast iron

**footballeur, -euse** [futbolœʀ, -øz] *m, f* soccer player

**footing** [futiŋ] *m* jogging; **faire du/son ~** to go/be jogging

**forage** [fɔʀaʒ] *m* drilling

**forain(e)** [fɔʀɛ̃, ɛn] **I.** *adj* (*attraction, baraque*) fairground; **fête ~e** carnival **II.** *m(f)* carny

**force** [fɔʀs] *f* ❶ ANAT strength ❷ PHYS force ❸ (*courage*) strength ❹ (*niveau intellectuel*) intellect ❺ (*pouvoir*) force; **~ de dissuasion** deterrent; **employer la ~** to use force; **l'union fait la ~** unity is strength ❻ *gén pl* (*ensemble de personnes*) force ❼ MIL **~ de frappe** strike force; **~s de l'ordre** police; **~(s) armée(s)/militaire(s)** armed forces ❽ (*autorité: de l'habitude, de la loi*) force; (*d'un argument, préjugé*) power; **par la ~ des choses** in the way of things ❾ (*degré d'intensité: d'un choc, coup, tremblement de terre, du vent*) force; (*d'une carte, passion, d'un désir, sentiment*) strength; (*de l'égoïsme, de la haine*) intensity ❿ TECH (*d'un câble,* mur, d'une barre) strength ⑪ (puissance, efficacité: d'un moteur) power; (d'un médicament, poison) strength ⑫ (vigueur: d'un style, terme) strength ⑬ sans pl (électricité) three-phase current ▸ **être dans la ~ de l'âge** to be in the prime of life; **à ~ de pleurer** by dint of crying; **faire qc de ~** to do sth by force

**forcé(e)** [fɔʀse] adj ❶ (imposé: atterrissage, mariage) forced; (bain) unintended; **travaux ~s** forced labor ❷ (artificiel: attitude) affected; (rire, sourire) forced; (amabilité, gaieté) false ❸ inf (inévitable: conséquence, suite) inevitable ❹ LIT, ART (style, trait) unnatural; (comparaison, effet) strained ▸ **c'était ~!** inf bound to happen!

**forcément** [fɔʀsemɑ̃] adv inevitably; **pas ~** not necessarily; **~!** of course!

**forcené(e)** [fɔʀsəne] I. adj ❶ (très violent) frenzied ❷ (démesuré) wild; (partisan) fanatical II. m(f) maniac; **être un ~ du boulot** inf to be a workaholic

**forcer** [fɔʀse] <2> I. vt ❶ (obliger) **~ qn à** +infin to force sb to +infin ❷ (tordre: sens) to distort ❸ (enfoncer: porte, serrure) to force; (coffre) to force open; (barrage) to force one's way through ❹ (susciter: admiration, estime, sympathie, confiance) to compel; (attention) to demand; (respect) to command ❺ (vouloir obtenir plus de qc: cheval) to override ❻ (vouloir infléchir: conscience, destin, succès) to force; (consentement) to exact ❼ (intensifier: voix) to strain ❽ (exagérer: dépense, note) to push up II. vi ❶ to force ❷ (agir avec force) **~ sur qc** to put force on sth ❸ inf (abuser) **~ sur les pâtisseries** to overdo the pastries ❹ (supporter un effort excessif: moteur) to labor III. vpr **se ~ à** +infin to force oneself to +infin

**forcir** [fɔʀsiʀ] <8> vi ❶ (devenir plus fort) to get stronger ❷ (grossir) to fill out

**forer** [fɔʀe] <1> vt ❶ (former en creu-

sant: trou, puits) to dig ❷ (faire un trou dans: roche) to drill through

**forestier, -ière** [fɔʀɛstje, -jɛʀ] I. adj forest II. m, f forester

**foret** [fɔʀɛ] m drill

**forêt** [fɔʀɛ] f ❶ (bois) forest ❷ (grande quantité) mass

**forêt-noire** [fɔʀɛnwaʀ] <forêts-noires> f (gâteau) Black Forest cake

**Forêt-Noire** [fɔʀɛnwaʀ] f GEO **la ~** the Black Forest

**forfait** [fɔʀfɛ] m ❶ (prix fixé) set price ❷ FIN estimated tax ❸ SPORT **~ de neige** ski pass ▸ **déclarer ~** to scratch

**forfaitaire** [fɔʀfɛtɛʀ] adj (indemnité) lump; (montant, prix) all-inclusive

**forge** [fɔʀʒ] f ❶ (fourneau) forge ❷ pl (usine) ironworks

**forger** [fɔʀʒe] <2a> I. vt ❶ (façonner) to forge ❷ (inventer: excuse, prétexte) to think up II. vpr ❶ (se fabriquer) **~ une réputation** to forge oneself a reputation ❷ (s'inventer) **se ~ un prétexte** to dream up an excuse

**forgeron** [fɔʀʒəʀɔ̃] m blacksmith

**formaliser** [fɔʀmalize] <1> I. vpr **se ~ de qc** to take offense at sth II. vt to formalize

**formalité** [fɔʀmalite] f formality

**format** [fɔʀma] m format

**formatage** [fɔʀmataʒ] m INFORM formatting

**formater** [fɔʀmate] <1> vt INFORM to format

**formateur, -trice** [fɔʀmatœʀ, -tʀis] I. adj training; (expérience, influence) formative II. m, f trainer

**formation** [fɔʀmasjɔ̃] f ❶ LING, GEO, BOT formation ❷ MATH (d'un cercle, cylindre) describing ❸ (action de se former: du monde, des dunes, d'une couche) formation; (du capitalisme, d'un embryon, os, système nerveux) development ❹ (apprentissage professionnel) training; **~ professionnelle** vocational training; **~ continue** [o **permanente**] continuing education ❺ (éducation morale et intellectuelle) upbringing; (du caractère, goût) forming ❻ (groupe de *personnes*) *a.* MIL, SPORT formation; (*dans le domaine politique*) grouping **⑦** (*puberté*) puberty

**forme** [fɔʀm] *f* **①** (*aspect extérieur: en deux dimensions*) shape; (*en trois dimensions*) form; **en ~ de croix/de cœur** cross-/heart-shaped; **sous la ~ de qn/qc** in the shape of sb/sth **②** (*silhouette*) shape **③** *pl* (*galbe du corps*) figure **④** (*variante, condition physique, intellectuelle*) *a.* ART, LIT, LING, JUR form **⑤** *pl* (*bienséance*) conventions ►**en bonne** (**et due**) **~** in due form

**formel(le)** [fɔʀmɛl] *adj* **①** (*explicite: déclaration, engagement*) definite; (*refus, ordre*) clear; (*preuve*) positive; **être ~ sur qc** to be categorical about sth **②** ART, LING, PHILOS formal **③** (*de pure forme*) outward

**formellement** [fɔʀmɛlmɑ̃] *adv* **①** (*expressément*) categorically **②** (*concernant la forme*) formally

**former** [fɔʀme] <1> I. *vt* **①** (*façonner, constituer, produire*) to form **②** (*créer, organiser: association, parti, coalition*) to form; (*complot*) to organize **③** (*assembler des éléments: équipes, collection*) to build; (*cortège, armée*) to form **④** (*concevoir: idée, pensée*) to have; **~ le projet/dessein de** +*infin* to plan/intend to +*infin* **⑤** (*instruire: personne*) to train; (*caractère*) to form; **~ qn** (*voyage, épreuve*) to form sb's character **⑥** (*prendre l'aspect, la forme de: cercle*) to describe; (*boucle*) to form II. *vpr* **①** (*naître*) **se ~** (*images*) to form **②** (*se disposer*) **se ~ en colonne** to draw up in a column **③** (*s'instruire*) **se ~** to educate oneself

**formica®** [fɔʀmika] *m* Formica®

**formidable** [fɔʀmidabl] *adj* **①** *inf* (*très bien: film, type*) terrific **②** (*hors du commun: volonté*) remarkable; (*dépense, détonation*) tremendous; **c'est ~!** it's incredible!

**formidablement** [fɔʀmidabləmɑ̃] *adv* incredibly

**formulaire** [fɔʀmylɛʀ] *m* **①** (*papier*) form **②** (*recueil de formules*) formulary

**formulation** [fɔʀmylasjɔ̃] *f* formulation

**formule** [fɔʀmyl] *f* **①** (*en science, chimie*) formula **②** (*paroles rituelles*) phrase; **~ de politesse** letter ending **③** (*choix, possibilité*) option; **~ à 10 euros** 10-euro menu **④** (*façon de faire*) method **⑤** AUTO, SPORT **~ I** Formula 1

**formuler** [fɔʀmyle] <1> *vt* **①** (*exprimer: pensée*) to formulate; (*demande, requête*) to make **②** (*mettre en formule*) to formulate

**forsythia** [fɔʀsisja] *m* forsythia

**fort** [fɔʀ] I. *adv* **①** (*intensément: frapper*) hard; (*parler, crier*) loudly; (*sentir*) powerfully; **respirez ~!** breathe in deeply! **②** (*beaucoup*) **avoir ~ à faire** to have much to do; **j'en doute ~** I very much doubt it **③** *antéposé* (*très: intéressant, mécontent*) very **④** *inf* (*bien*) **toi, ça ne va pas ~** you're in a bad way ►**y aller un peu/trop ~** *inf* you're going a little/way too far II. *m* **①** (*forteresse*) fort **②** (*spécialité*) **la cuisine, ce n'est pas mon ~** cooking is not my forte **③** (*milieu, cœur*) **au plus ~ de la bataille** in the thick of battle

**fort(e)** [fɔʀ, fɔʀt] I. *adj* **①** (*robuste, puissant*) strong **②** (*de grande intensité: averse, mer*) heavy; (*lumière, rythme, goût*) strong; (*battement*) loud; (*chaleur*) intense **③** (*pour les sensations/sentiments*) strong; (*colère, dégoût, douleur, émotion*) deep; (*rhume*) heavy; (*désir, ferveur*) intense; (*fièvre*) high **④** MUS, LING (*temps*) strong **⑤** (*important qualitativement: œuvre, phrase, geste politique*) powerful; (*présomption*) strong; **dire qc haut et ~** to say sth out loud **⑥** (*important quantitativement: somme, baisse, hausse*) large; (*différence*) great; (*mortalité, consommation de gaz*) high; **faire payer le prix ~** to pay full price **⑦** (*doué*) good; **être très ~ sur un sujet** to be well up in a subject **⑧** (*excessif: plaisanterie*) off; (*terme*) strong **⑨** (*gros: chevilles, jambes*) thick; (*personne*) stout; (*poitrine*) large **⑩** *postposé* (*courageux*) brave; (*âme*) brave ►**c'est plus ~ que**

**moi** I can't help it; **c'est trop** [o un peu] ~! it's a little bit too much! **II.** *m(f)* (*personne*) strong person

**fortement** [fɔʀtəmɑ̃] *adv* ❶ (*vigoureusement*) strongly; (*secouer*) hard; **s'exprimer** ~ to express oneself forcefully ❷ (*vivement*) **insister** ~ **sur qc** to insist strongly on sth ❸ (*beaucoup*) very much

**forteresse** [fɔʀtəʀɛs] *f* fortress

**fortifiant** [fɔʀtifjɑ̃] *m* (*remède*) tonic

**fortifiant(e)** [fɔʀtifjɑ̃, jɑ̃t] *adj* (*remède*) fortifying

**fortification** [fɔʀtifikasjɔ̃] *f* fortification

**fortifier** [fɔʀtifje] <1> **I.** *vt* ❶ (*rendre vigoureux*) a. MIL to fortify ❷ (*affermir: volonté, amitié*) to strengthen **II.** *vi* (*tonifier*) to fortify **III.** *vpr* **se** ~ ❶ (*devenir fort: santé, personne*) to grow stronger ❷ (*s'affermir: amitié, croyance*) to be strengthened ❸ MIL to be fortified

**fortuit(e)** [fɔʀtɥi, it] *adj* fortuitous; (*remarque*) chance; **cas** ~ fortuitous case

**fortuitement** [fɔʀtɥitmɑ̃] *adv* fortuitously

**fortune** [fɔʀtyn] *f* ❶ (*richesse*) wealth; **avoir de la** ~ to be rich; **faire** ~ to make a fortune ❷ *inf* (*grosse somme*) fortune ❸ (*magnat*) **les grandes** ~**s** large private fortunes ❹ (*chance*) luck; **la bonne** ~ good luck ▶ **de** ~ makeshift

**fortuné(e)** [fɔʀtyne] *adj* (*riche*) wealthy

**forum** [fɔʀɔm] *m* ❶ forum ❷ INFORM newsgroup; ~ **de discussion sur Internet** chatroom

**fosse** [fos] *f* ❶ (*cavité*) a. MUS pit ❷ GEO trench ❸ (*tombe, charnier*) grave ❹ ANAT ~**s nasales** nasal fossae

**fossé** [fose] *m* ❶ (*tranchée*) ditch ❷ (*écart*) gap; ~ **des générations** generation gap

**fossette** [fosɛt] *f* dimple

**fossile** [fɔsil] **I.** *adj* ❶ GEO fossil(ized) ❷ *péj, inf* (*démodé*) fossilized **II.** *m/f* GEO a. *fig* fossil

**fossiliser** [fɔsilize] <1> **I.** *vt* GEO (*rendre fossile*) to fossilize **II.** *vpr* **se** ~ ❶ GEO (*devenir fossile*) to fossilize ❷ *fig, inf*

(*personne*) to become a fossil; (*idée*) to become fossilized

**fossoyeur** [foswajœʀ] *m* gravedigger

**fou, folle** [fu, fɔl] <*devant un nom masculin commençant par une voyelle ou un h muet*fol> **I.** *adj* ❶ (*dément*) crazy, mad ❷ (*dérangé*) **être** ~ **à lier** to be raving mad; **devenir** ~ to go crazy; **c'est à devenir** ~, **il y a de quoi devenir** ~ it would drive you crazy ❸ (*idiot*) **il faut être** ~ **pour faire cela** only a madman would do that ❹ (*insensé: idée, projet, tentative*) crazy; (*imagination, jeunesse, désir, rires*) wild; (*joie*) insane; (*regard*) crazed; **c'est l'amour** ~ they're head over heels (in love); **passer une folle nuit** to have a wild night; **avoir le** ~ **rire** to have (a fit of) the giggles [o laugh attack] ❺ (*éperdu*) **être** ~ **de chagrin** to be mad with grief; **être** ~ **de désir** to be wild with desire; **être** ~ **de colère** to be blazing with anger ❻ (*amoureux*) **être** ~ **de qn** to be wild about sb; **être** ~ **de jazz** to be crazy about jazz ❼ (*énorme, incroyable: courage, énergie, mal*) unbelievable; **un argent** ~ an unbelievable amount of money; **il y avait un monde** ~ the place was packed ❽ (*exubérant*) **être tout** ~ to be beside oneself with excitement ❾ (*en désordre, incontrôlé: cheveux, mèche*) untidy **II.** *m, f* ❶ (*dément*) madman, madwoman *m, f* ❷ (*écervelé*) **jeune** ~ young fool; **vieux** ~ crazy old fool; **crier/travailler comme un** ~ to yell/work like crazy ❸ (*personne exubérante*) **faire le** ~ (*faire, dire des bêtises*) to talk like an idiot; (*se défouler*) to act the fool ❹ JEUX bishop ❺ (*bouffon*) jester

**foudre**[1] [fudʀ] *f* METEO lightning

**foudre**[2] [fudʀ] *m* (*tonneau*) tun

**foudroyant(e)** [fudʀwajɑ̃, jɑ̃t] *adj* ❶ (*soudain: mort*) instant; (*succès*) overnight; (*vitesse, progrès, attaque*) lightning; (*nouvelle*) devastating ❷ (*mortel: maladie, poison*) devastating ❸ (*réprobateur*) **jeter un regard** ~ **sur qn** to look daggers at sb

F

**F**

**foudroyer** [fudʀwaje] <6> vt ❶ (frapper par la foudre) **être foudroyé** to be struck by lightning ❷ (électrocuter) **être foudroyé** to be electrocuted ❸ (tuer) to strike down ❹ (abattre, rendre stupéfait) ~ **qn** (malheur) to devastate sb; (surprise) to knock sb flat

**fouet** [fwɛ] m ❶ (verge) whip ❷ CULIN whisk ❸ (châtiment) **donner le ~ à qn** to whip sb ▸ **de plein ~** head-on

**fouetter** [fwete] <1> **I.** vt ❶ (frapper: personne, animal) to whip; **le vent me fouette au visage** the wind is whipping my face ❷ CULIN (blanc d'œufs) to whisk; (crème) to whip ❸ (stimuler: amour-propre, orgueil) to sting; (désir) to whip up; (imagination) to stir **II.** vi (frapper) **la pluie fouette contre les vitres** the rain is lashing the windows

**fougère** [fuʒɛʀ] f BOT fern

**fougue** [fug] f ardor

**fougueux, -euse** [fugø, -øz] adj (réponse, intervention, attaque, cheval) spirited; (tempérament, personne, orateur, discours) fiery

**fouille** [fuj] f ❶ (inspection) search; ~ **corporelle** body search ❷ pl (en archéologie) dig ❸ (excavation) excavation

**fouiller** [fuje] <1> **I.** vt ❶ (inspecter: lieu, poches) to search; (horizon) to scan; (dossier) to examine; ~ **un problème** to go into a problem; ~ **la vie de qn** to delve into sb's life ❷ (creuser) ~ **qc** (animal) to dig sth; (archéologue) to excavate sth **II.** vi ❶ (inspecter) ~ **dans qc** to look through sth; ~ **dans ses souvenirs** to dig among one's memories ❷ (creuser) to dig **III.** vpr **se** ~ to go through one's pockets

**fouillis** [fuji] m muddle

**fouiner** [fwine] <1> vi inf to snoop around

**fouineur, -euse** [fwinœʀ, -øz] m, f busybody

**foulard** [fulaʀ] m ❶ (fichu) (head)scarf ❷ (écharpe) scarf ❸ (tissu) foulard

**foule** [ful] f ❶ (multitude de personnes) crowd; **il y a/n'y a pas** ~ there are lots of/not a lot of people ❷ (grand nombre) **une** ~ **de gens/questions** masses of people/questions ❸ (peuple) **la** ~ the mob

**foulée** [fule] f SPORT stride ▸ **dans la** ~ **de qc** in the wake of sth

**fouler** [fule] <1> **I.** vt (écraser: raisin) to tread; TECH (cuir, peau) to tan **II.** vpr ❶ (se tordre) **se** ~ **la cheville** to sprain one's ankle ❷ iron, inf (se fatiguer) **se** ~ to kill oneself

**foulure** [fulyʀ] f MED sprain

**four** [fuʀ] m ❶ (à) **~**; (à) **micro-ondes** microwave (oven) ❷ TECH furnace; (pour la poterie) kiln; ~ **électrique** electric furnace ❸ inf (échec) flop ▸ **il fait noir comme dans un** ~ it's as dark as night

**fourbe** [fuʀb] adj deceitful; (gentillesse) guileful

**fourberie** [fuʀbəʀi] f guile

**fourbu(e)** [fuʀby] adj exhausted

**fourche** [fuʀʃ] f ❶ (outil, de bicyclette, branchement) fork ❷ COUT (d'un pantalon) crotch ❸ Belgique (temps libre d'une ou deux heures dans un horaire de cours) break

**fourcher** [fuʀʃe] <1> vi (cheveux) to split; (c'est) **ma langue** (qui) **a fourché** it was a slip of the tongue

**fourchette** [fuʀʃɛt] f ❶ CULIN fork ❷ (marge) range; **se situer dans une** ~ **de 41 à 47%** to lie in the 41 to 47% range

**fourgon** [fuʀgɔ̃] m ❶ CHEMDFER coach ❷ (voiture); MIL wagon; ~ **de police** police van; ~ **funéraire** hearse

**fourgonnette** [fuʀgɔnɛt] f van

**fourmi** [fuʀmi] f ❶ ZOOL ant ❷ (symbole d'activité) busy bee ▸ **avoir des** ~**s dans les jambes** to have pins and needles in one's legs

**fourmilière** [fuʀmiljɛʀ] f ❶ ZOOL anthill ❷ (foule grouillante) hive of activity

**fourmillement** [fuʀmijmã] m ❶ (agitation) swarming ❷ (foisonnement) teeming ❸ (picotement) tingling

**fourmiller** [fuʀmije] <1> vi ❶ (abonder) **les moustiques/fautes fourmil-**

**lent** it's swarming with mosquitoes/ mistakes ② (*picoter*) **j'ai les pieds qui** (**me**) **fourmillent** I've got pins and needles in my feet

**fournaise** [fuʀnɛz] *f* ① (*foyer ardent*) blaze ② (*lieu surchauffé*) **c'est une ~ ici** it's like an oven in here ③ (*lieu de combat*) battleground ④ *Québec* (*appareil de chauffage central*) boiler

**fourneau** [fuʀno] <x> *m* ① (*cuisinière*) stove; **~ à charbon** coal-burning stove ② (*chaufferie*) furnace; **haut ~** blast furnace

**fournée** [fuʀne] *f* **~ de pains** batch of loaves; **par ~s** in bunches

**fourni(e)** [fuʀni] *adj* ① (*épais: chevelure, cheveux*) lush; (*barbe, sourcils*) bushy ② (*approvisionné*) stocked; **être bien ~** (*magasin*) to be well-stocked; (*table*) to be well-supplied

**fournil** [fuʀni] *m* bakery

**fournir** [fuʀniʀ] <8> **I.** *vt* ① (*approvisionner*) **~ un client/un commerce en qc** to supply a customer/a business with sth ② (*procurer*) **~ qc à des réfugiés** to provide refugees with sth; **~ un logement/travail à qn** to find sb a place to live/a job; **~ un renseignement à qn** to provide sb with some information; **~ des précisions** to give details ③ (*présenter: alibi, preuve*) to provide; (*autorisation*) to give; (*pièce d'identité*) to produce ④ (*produire*) to produce; **les abeilles fournissent du miel** bees produce honey; **~ un gros effort** to put in a lot of effort **II.** *vi* (*subvenir à*) **le magasin n'arrivait plus à ~** the store couldn't cope **III.** *vpr* **se ~ en charbon chez qn** to get one's coal from sb

**fournisseur** [fuʀnisœʀ] *m* INFORM provider; **~ d'accès Internet** Internet service provider

**fournisseur, -euse** [fuʀnisœʀ, -øz] **I.** *m, f* supplier **II.** *adj* **les pays ~s de l'Espagne** countries supplying Spain

**fourniture** [fuʀnityʀ] *f* ① (*livraison*) supply ② *pl* (*accessoires*) supplies

**fourrage** [fuʀaʒ] *m* fodder

**fourré** [fuʀe] *m* thicket

**fourré(e)** [fuʀe] *adj* ① (*doublé de fourrure: gants, manteau*) fur-lined ② CULIN (*bonbons, gâteau*) filled

**fourreau** [fuʀo] <x> *m* ① (*gaine: d'une épée*) sheath; (*d'un parapluie*) cover ② (*robe moulante*) sheath

**fourrer** [fuʀe] <1> **I.** *vt* ① *inf* (*mettre*) **~ qc dans qc** to put sth in sth ② (*garnir*) **~ qc avec du lapin** to trim sth with rabbit fur ③ CULIN **~ qc au chocolat** to put a chocolate filling in sth **II.** *vpr inf* (*se mettre*) **se ~ sous les couvertures** to dive under the covers; **quelle idée s'est-il fourré dans la tête?** what's this idea he's got into his head?

**fourre-tout** [fuʀtu] *m inv* ① *péj* (*local*) junk room ② (*sac*) carryall

**fourreur, -euse** [fuʀœʀ, -øz] *m, f* furrier

**fourrière** [fuʀjɛʀ] *f* (*pour voitures, animaux*) pound

**fourrure** [fuʀyʀ] *f* fur

**foutaise** [futɛz] *f inf* ① (*chose sans valeur*) bit of garbage ② (*futilité*) bull; **quelle ~!** what a load of bull!

**foutu(e)** [futy] **I.** *part passé de* **foutre II.** *adj inf* ① (*perdu: chose*) bust; **être ~** (*chose*) to be bust; (*personne*) to have had it; (*malade*) to be a goner ② *antéposé* (*maudit*) damned ③ (*vêtu*) **comment es-tu encore ~ ce matin?** what on earth are you wearing this morning? ④ (*capable*) **être/ne pas être ~ de faire qc** to be capable of/not up to doing sth ▶ **être bien/mal ~** (*personne*) to have a good/lousy body; (*travail, appareil*) to be a good/lousy job; **être mal ~** to feel lousy

**foyer** [fwaje] *m* ① (*famille*) family; (*maison*) home; **~ paternel** paternal home; **les jeunes ~s** young families; **fonder un ~** to start a family ② (*résidence*) hostel ③ (*salle de réunion*) hall ④ THEAT foyer ⑤ (*âtre*) hearth ⑥ (*cheminée*) fireplace ⑦ (*centre: d'une civilisation*) center; **~ lumineux** light source; **le ~ de la crise/de l'épidémie** the epicenter of the crisis/the epidemic ⑧ (*incen-*

*die*) heart ⑥ (*chambre de combustion*) firebox ⑩ (*en optique*) MATH, PHYS focus

**frac** [fʀak] *m* tailcoat

**fracas** [fʀaka] *m* (*bruit de choses qui se heurtent*) crash; (*bruit sourd*) roar; ~ **du tonnerre** crash of thunder; **à grand** ~ making a great stir

**fracasser** [fʀakase] <1> *vt, vpr* (**se**) ~ **to** smash

**fracking** [fʀekiŋ] *m* GEOL fracking

**fraction** [fʀaksjɔ̃] *f* ❶ MATH, REL fraction ❷ (*partie d'un tout: d'un groupe, d'une somme*) part; **une** ~ **de seconde** a fraction of a second

**fractionnement** [fʀaksjɔnmɑ̃] *m* CHIM fractionation; (*d'un patrimoine, paiement*) division

**fractionner** [fʀaksjɔne] <1> **I.** *vt* ❶ (*diviser*) to divide up ❷ (*partager*) to share out ❸ CHIM to fractionate **II.** *vpr* **se ~ en plusieurs groupes** to divide up into (several) groups

**fracture** [fʀaktyʀ] *f* ❶ MED fracture ❷ *fig* ~ **sociale** social breakdown

**fracturer** [fʀaktyʀe] <1> **I.** *vt* ❶ (*briser: porte, voiture*) to break open ❷ MED to fracture **II.** *vpr* MED **se ~ le bras** to fracture one's arm

**fragile** [fʀaʒil] *adj* ❶ (*cassant*) fragile ❷ (*délicat, faible: personne, santé, organisme*) delicate; (*estomac, cœur*) weak ❸ (*précaire: paix, bonheur, gloire*) fragile; (*argument, preuve, hypothèse*) flimsy; (*équilibre, économie*) shaky ❹ (*peu solide: bâtiment*) flimsy

**fragilisé(e)** [fʀaʒilize] *adj* (*santé*) weakened

**fragiliser** [fʀaʒilize] <1> *vt* to weaken; (*au niveau psychologique*) to destabilize

**fragilité** [fʀaʒilite] *f* ❶ (*facilité à se casser*) fragility ❷ (*faiblesse*) weakness ❸ (*précarité: des arguments, d'une hypothèse, d'une preuve*) flimsiness; (*d'un équilibre, d'une économie*) instability; (*de la paix*) fragility

**fragment** [fʀagmɑ̃] *m* ❶ (*débris*) bit ❷ (*extrait d'une œuvre*) extract ❸ (*œu-*

*vre incomplète*) fragment ❹ (*partie: d'une vie*) episode

**fragmentaire** [fʀagmɑ̃tɛʀ] *adj* (*connaissance, exposé*) sketchy; (*effort, travail*) patchy

**fragmentation** [fʀagmɑ̃tasjɔ̃] *f* BIO, GEO fragmentation; (*d'un pays*) breaking up; (*d'un problème*) breaking down

**fragmenter** [fʀagmɑ̃te] <1> **I.** *vt* ~ **qc en qc** to split sth up into sth **II.** *vpr* **se ~** to fragment

**fraîche** [fʀɛʃ] **I.** *adj v.* **frais II.** *f* **à la ~** (*le matin*) in the cool of the early morning; (*le soir*) in the cool of the evening

**fraîchement** [fʀɛʃmɑ̃] *adv* (*récemment: cueilli, labouré*) freshly; (*arrivé*) newly

**fraîcheur** [fʀɛʃœʀ] *f* ❶ (*sensation agréable*) coolness; (*sensation désagréable*) chilliness ❷ (*froideur: d'un accueil*) coolness ❸ (*éclat: d'une fleur, couleur, d'un teint*) freshness; (*d'une robe*) crispness; (*d'un livre*) originality ❹ (*bonne forme*) vitality; (*d'une équipe*) freshness ❺ (*qualité d'une production récente: d'un produit alimentaire*) freshness ❻ (*pureté, vivacité: d'un sentiment*) freshness; (*d'une idée*) originality

**fraîchir** [fʀeʃiʀ] <8> *vi* (*air, temps*) to turn cool; (*eau*) to cool; (*vent*) to freshen

**frais¹** [fʀɛ] *mpl* ❶ costs; ~ **de scolarité** tuition; **faux** ~ overheads; **tous ~ compris** all inclusive ❷ COM, ECON ~ **d'entretien** upkeep ▸ **faire des** ~ to spend money

**frais²** [fʀɛ] *m* (*fraîcheur*) cool; **mettre au** ~ (*bouteille*) to chill; **à conserver au** ~ keep cool

**frais, fraîche** [fʀɛ, fʀɛʃ] *adj* ❶ (*légèrement froid: endroit, eau, vent*) cool; **servir qc très** ~ to serve sth chilled ❷ (*opp: avarié, sec, en conserve*) fresh; (*œuf*) fresh-laid ❸ (*peu cordial*) cool ❹ (*agréable: fleur, teint, couleur, parfum*) fresh; (*son, voix*) bright ❺ (*en forme: personne*) lively; (*reposé, sain*) refreshed; **être ~ et dispos** to be fresh as a daisy ❻ (*récent: peinture*) wet; (*bles-*

_sure, souvenir_) fresh; **des nouvelles fraîches** some fresh news ⑦ (_pur: âme, joie_) pure; (_sentiment_) untainted

**fraise** [fʀɛz] **I.** _f_ ① (_fruit_) strawberry; **confiture de ~(s)** strawberry jam; **à la ~** strawberry ② (_collerette_) ruff ③ (_chez le dentiste_) drill ④ _inf_ (_figure_) mug; **ramener sa ~** _inf_ to horn in **II.** _adj inv_ strawberry

**fraisier** [fʀezje] _m_ strawberry plant

**framboise** [fʀɑ̃bwaz] _f_ ① (_fruit_) raspberry ② (_eau-de-vie_) raspberry liqueur

**framboisier** [fʀɑ̃bwazje] _m_ raspberry bush

**franc** [fʀɑ̃] _m_ ① HIST (_monnaie_) franc; **~ français/belge** French/Belgian franc ② (_monnaie_) **~ suisse** Swiss franc

**franc, franche** [fʀɑ̃, fʀɑ̃ʃ] _adj_ ① (_loyal, sincère: personne, contact_) straightforward; (_rire, gaieté_) open; (_regard_) candid; **être ~ avec qn** to be frank with sb ② (_net: couleur_) strong; (_hostilité_) open; (_situation_) clear-cut ③ _antéposé_ (_véritable_) utter; (_succès_) complete ④ (_libre_) free; **port ~** free port

**franc, franque** [fʀɑ̃, fʀɑ̃k] _adj_ Frankish; **les rois ~s** the Frankish kings

**Franc, Franque** [fʀɑ̃, fʀɑ̃k] _m, f_ Frank

**français** [fʀɑ̃sɛ] _m_ ① **le ~** French; **le ~ familier/standard** everyday/standard French; **parler (le) ~** to speak French; **traduire en ~** to translate into French ② THEAT **le Français** the "Comédie française" ▸ **je parle (le) ~ pourtant** I'm not speaking Chinese, am I?

**français(e)** [fʀɑ̃sɛ, ɛz] _adj_ French

**Français(e)** [fʀɑ̃sɛ, ɛz] _m(f)_ Frenchman, Frenchwoman _m, f_; **les ~** the French

**française** [fʀɑ̃sɛz] _f_ **à la ~** in the French style

**France** [fʀɑ̃s] _f_ **la ~** France

**franchement** [fʀɑ̃ʃmɑ̃] _adv_ ① (_sincèrement_) frankly ② (_sans hésiter_) **entrer ~ dans** to go straight to the point ③ (_clairement_) plainly ④ (_vraiment_) really

**franchir** [fʀɑ̃ʃiʀ] <8> _vt_ ① (_passer par-dessus_) **~ un fossé** to step over a ditch; **~ un obstacle** to clear an obstacle; **~ la voie** to cross the line; **~ des pas décisifs** to take decisive steps ② (_aller au-delà_) to cross; (_barrage_) to get past; (_seuil_) to step across; (_limite_) to go beyond; **~ la ligne d'arrivée** to cross the finishing line ③ (_surmonter: examen, épreuve_) to get through; (_difficulté_) to get over ④ (_parcourir; traverser: col_) to go across; **une étape importante vient d'être franchie** an important stage has been achieved

**franchise** [fʀɑ̃ʃiz] _f_ ① (_sincérité: d'une personne_) frankness; (_d'un regard_) openness; **en toute ~** in all honesty ② (_des assurances_) excess ③ (_exonération_) allowance; **~ de bagages** baggage allowance; **en ~** duty-free ④ (_montant_) tax allowance ⑤ COM franchise

**franchissable** [fʀɑ̃ʃisabl] _adj_ (_obstacle_) clearable; **la limite est ~** the limit can be exceeded; **la rivière est ~** the river can be crossed

**francilien(ne)** [fʀɑ̃siljɛ̃, ɛn] _adj_ of the Île-de-France

**franciser** [fʀɑ̃size] <1> _vt_ **~ un mot** to turn into a French word

**franc-maçon(ne)** [fʀɑ̃masɔ̃, ɔn] <francs-maçons> _m(f)_ Freemason

**franco** [fʀɑ̃ko] _adv_ ① COM postage paid ② _inf_ (_carrément_) **y aller ~** to get right on with it

**franco-allemand(e)** [fʀɑ̃koalmɑ̃, ɑ̃d] <franco-allemands> _adj_ Franco-German

**francophile** [fʀɑ̃kɔfil] **I.** _adj_ Francophile **II.** _mf_ Francophile

**francophobe** [fʀɑ̃kɔfɔb] **I.** _adj_ Francophobic **II.** _mf_ Francophobe

**francophone** [fʀɑ̃kɔfɔn] **I.** _adj_ (_pays, région_) francophone; (_personne_) French-speaking; **être ~** to be a French speaker **II.** _mf_ French-speaker

**francophonie** [fʀɑ̃kɔfɔni] _f_ **la ~** the French-speaking world

**franc-parler** [fʀɑ̃paʀle] <francs-parlers> _m_ forthrightness; **avoir son ~** to be outspoken

**frange** [fʀɑ̃ʒ] _f_ fringe

**frangin(e)** [fʀɑ̃ʒɛ̃, ʒin] _m(f)_ _inf_ brother

**F**

**frangipane** [fʀãʒipan] *f* frangipane

**franglais** [fʀãglɛ] *m* Franglais

**franque** [fʀãk] *adj v.* **franc**

**franquiste** [fʀãkist] **I.** *adj* pro-Franco; **l'Espagne ~** Franco's Spain **II.** *mf* Franco supporter

**frappant(e)** [fʀapã, ãt] *adj* striking

**frappe** [fʀap] *f* ❶ TECH (*d'une monnaie*) minting ❷ (*façon de frapper: d'une dactylo, pianiste*) touch; (*d'un boxeur*) punch; (*d'un footballeur*) kick ❸ (*exemplaire dactylographié*) typescript

**frappé(e)** [fʀape] *adj* ❶ (*saisi*) **~ de stupeur** thunderstruck; **~ de panique** panic-stricken ❷ (*refroidi*) chilled; **café ~** iced coffee ❸ *inf* (*fou*) screwy

**frapper** [fʀape] <1> **I.** *vt* ❶ (*heurter, cogner*) **~ qn au visage** to hit sb in the face ❷ (*avec un couteau*) to stab ❸ (*saisir*) **~ qn d'horreur** to fill sb with horror; **~ qn de stupeur** to leave sb thunderstruck ❹ (*affliger*) **~ qn** (*maladie, malheur*) to strike sb; (*mesure, impôt*) to affect sb; (*sanction*) to hit sb; **être frappé d'amnésie** to be affected by amnesia ❺ (*étonner*) to strike; (*imagination*) to fire; **être frappé de la ressemblance** to be struck by the resemblance ❻ TECH (*médaille*) to strike; (*monnaie*) to mint ❼ (*glacer: champagne*) to chill; (*café*) to ice **II.** *vi* ❶ (*donner des coups*) to knock; **~ à la porte** to knock on the door ❷ (*taper*) **~ dans ses mains** to clap one's hands **III.** *vpr* (*se donner des coups*) **se ~ le front** to slap one's forehead

**fraternel(le)** [fʀatɛʀnɛl] *adj* ❶ (*de frère: amour*) brotherly ❷ (*de sœur: amour*) sisterly ❸ (*affectueux*) fraternal

**fraternellement** [fʀatɛʀnɛlmã] *adv iron* fraternally

**fraternisation** [fʀatɛʀnizasjɔ̃] *f* fraternization

**fraterniser** [fʀatɛʀnize] <1> *vi* ❶ to fraternize ❷ (*sympathiser*) to get along

**fraternité** [fʀatɛʀnite] *f* brotherhood

**fraude** [fʀod] *f* ❶ fraud; **~ douanière** customs fraud; **~ fiscale** tax evasion ❷ (*aux examens*) cheating ▶ **en ~** (*illégalement*) fraudulently; (*en secret*) in secret, on the quiet; **passer des marchandises à la frontière en ~** to smuggle in goods

**frauder** [fʀode] <1> **I.** *vt* (*tromper*) to defraud; **~ le fisc** [*o* **les impôts**] to cheat the taxman; **~ la douane** to defraud customs **II.** *vi* (*tricher*) **~ à un examen** to cheat on an exam

**fraudeur, -euse** [fʀodœʀ, -øz] *m, f* ❶ (*escroc*) crook ❷ (*à la frontière*) smuggler ❸ (*aux examens*) cheat(er)

**frauduleusement** [fʀodyløzmã] *adv* fraudulently

**frauduleux, -euse** [fʀodylø, -øz] *adj* (*concurrence, moyen, dossier, trafic*) fraudulent; (*banquier*) dishonest

**frayer** [fʀeje] <7> **I.** *vt* (*ouvrir*) **~ à qn un passage dans la foule** to clear a way through the crowd for sb **II.** *vi* ❶ ZOOL (*se reproduire*) to spawn ❷ (*fréquenter*) **~ avec qn** to associate with sb **III.** *vpr* **se ~ un passage/une voie/un chemin** to get through; *fig* to make one's way

**frayeur** [fʀejœʀ] *f* fright

**fredonner** [fʀədɔne] <1> *vt* to hum

**free-lance** [fʀilãs] <free-lances> **I.** *mf* freelance(r) **II.** *adj inv* (*journaliste, styliste*) freelance

**freezer** [fʀizœʀ] *m* freezer

**frégate** [fʀegat] *f* (*bateau*) frigate

**frein** [fʀɛ̃] *m* ❶ (*dispositif*) brake ❷ (*entrave, limite*) **être/mettre un ~ à qc** to be/put a curb on sth; **sans ~** unchecked

**freinage** [fʀɛnaʒ] *m* ❶ (*action*) braking ❷ (*ralentissement: de la hausse des prix*) curbing

**freiner** [fʀene] <1> **I.** *vi* to brake **II.** *vt* ❶ (*ralentir, entraver*) to slow down ❷ (*modérer: personne, ambitions*) to curb; (*hausse des prix, offre*) to check; (*production*) to slow down **III.** *vpr inf* (*se modérer*) **se ~** to restrain oneself

**frelater** [fʀəlate] <1> *vt* to adulterate

**frêle** [fʀɛl] *adj* (*personne, corps, tige*) frail; (*bateau*) fragile; (*silhouette*) slim

**frelon** [fʀəlɔ̃] *m* ZOOL hornet

**frémir** [fʀemiʀ] <8> *vi* **①** *soutenu* (*frissonner*) ~ **d'impatience/de colère** to seethe with impatience/anger; ~ **d'horreur** to shudder with horror; **faire ~ qn** (*récit, criminel*) to make sb shudder **②** (*s'agiter légèrement: feuillage*) to tremble; (*ailes*) to quiver **③** (*être sur le point de bouillir: eau*) to shiver

**frémissant(e)** [fʀemisɑ̃, ɑ̃t] *adj* (*voix*) trembling; (*eau*) simmering

**frémissement** [fʀemismɑ̃] *m* **①** *soutenu* (*frisson d'émotion: des lèvres*) tremble; (*du corps, d'une personne*) shiver; ~ **d'horreur** shudder; ~ **de fièvre** feverish tremble **②** (*mouvement léger: d'une corde, des ailes*) vibration; (*de l'eau*) ripple; (*du feuillage*) trembling **③** (*murmure: des feuilles*) rustling **④** ECON, POL slight upturn

**french cancan** [fʀɛnʃkɑ̃kɑ̃] <french cancans> *m* cancan

**frêne** [fʀɛn] *m* BOT ash

**frénésie** [fʀenezi] *f* frenzy; ~ **de consommation** frenzied consumption; **avec ~** wildly

**frénétique** [fʀenetik] *adj* **①** (*passionné: sentiment, personne*) frenzied; (*enthousiasme*) wild **②** (*au rythme déchaîné*) frenetic; (*applaudissements*) wild; (*personne*) frenzied

**frénétiquement** [fʀenetikmɑ̃] *adv* wildly

**fréon®** [fʀeɔ̃] *m* Freon®

**fréquemment** [fʀekamɑ̃] *adv* frequently

**fréquence** [fʀekɑ̃s] *f* **①** frequency **②** INFORM ~ **de rafraîchissement d'image** screen refresh rate

**fréquent(e)** [fʀekɑ̃, ɑ̃t] *adj* frequent

**fréquentable** [fʀekɑ̃tabl] *adj* (*lieu*) where one can safely go; (*personne*) that you can safely be seen with; **un type peu ~** not a nice sort of guy

**fréquentation** [fʀekɑ̃tasjɔ̃] *f* **①** (*action*) ~ **d'une personne** seeing a person **②** *gén pl* (*relation*) acquaintance; **avoir de bonnes/mauvaises ~s** to keep good/bad company

**fréquenté(e)** [fʀekɑ̃te] *adj* (*établissement, lieu, rue*) busy; (*promenade*) popular

**fréquenter** [fʀekɑ̃te] <1> **I.** *vt* **①** (*aller fréquemment dans: bars, théâtres*) to frequent; ~ **l'école** to go to school **②** (*avoir des relations avec*) to see **II.** *vpr* **①** (*par amitié*) **se ~** to see each other **②** (*par amour*) **se ~** to be dating

**frère** [fʀɛʀ] *m* **①** REL brother; ~ **siamois** Siamese twin brother; **se ressembler comme des ~s jumeaux** to be like two peas in a pod **②** *inf* (*objet*) twin

**frérot** [fʀeʀo] *m inf* kid brother

**fresque** [fʀɛsk] *f* (*peinture*) fresco

**fret** [fʀe(t)] *m* NAUT, AVIAT (*prix*) freight charge **②** (*chargement*) freight

**frétillant(e)** [fʀetijɑ̃, jɑ̃t] *adj* **①** (*remuant: poisson*) wriggling; (*queue*) wagging **②** *fig* **être ~ de joie** to be quivering with joy

**frétiller** [fʀetije] <1> *vi* **①** (*remuer: poisson*) to wriggle; **le chien frétille de la queue** the dog was wagging its tail **②** *fig* ~ **d'impatience** to quiver with impatience

**friable** [fʀijabl] *adj* (*pâte*) crumbly; (*roche, sol*) friable

**friand** [fʀijɑ̃] *m* **①** (*pâté*) ≈ meat pie **②** (*gâteau*) almond cake

**friand(e)** [fʀijɑ̃, jɑ̃d] *adj* ~ **de chocolat/nouveautés** fond of chocolate/novelties

**friandise** [fʀijɑ̃diz] *f* sweet(s)

**fric** [fʀik] *m inf* (*argent*) dough

**fricassée** [fʀikase] *f* fricassee

**friche** [fʀiʃ] *f* AGR fallow; **être en ~** to lie fallow

**friction** [fʀiksjɔ̃] *f* **①** (*frottement*) massage **②** PHYS friction **③** *gén pl* (*désaccord*) friction

**frictionner** [fʀiksjɔne] <1> **I.** *vt* to rub down **II.** *vpr* **se ~** to rub oneself down

**frigidaire®** [fʀiʒidɛʀ] *m* fridge

**frigide** [fʀiʒid] *adj* frigid

**frigidité** [fʀiʒidite] *f* frigidity

**frigo** [fʀigo] *m inf abr de* **frigidaire**

**frigorifier** [fʀigɔʀifje] <1> *vt* **①** *inf*

(*avoir très froid*) **être frigorifié** to be frozen stiff ❷ (*congeler*) to freeze

**frigorifique** [fʀigɔʀifik] *adj* refrigerated; (*machine*) refrigerating

**frileux, -euse** [fʀilø, -øz] *adj* ❶ (*sensible au froid: personne*) that feels the cold ❷ (*craintif*) timid

**frimer** [fʀime] <1> *vi inf* ❶ (*fanfaronner*) to show off ❷ (*se vanter*) to make oneself look big

**frimeur, -euse** [fʀimœʀ, -øz] *m, f inf* show-off

**frimousse** [fʀimus] *f inf* ❶ (*visage*) sweet little face ❷ INFORM smiley

**fringale** [fʀɛ̃gal] *f* ❶ *inf* (*faim*) **avoir la ~** to be hungry ❷ (*envie*) **~ de lectures** craving to read

**fringant(e)** [fʀɛ̃gɑ̃, ɑ̃t] *adj* (*personne*) dashing; (*personne âgée*) spry; (*cheval*) frisky

**fringuer** [fʀɛ̃ge] <1> *vt, vpr inf* (**se**) **~** to dress (oneself) up

**fringues** [fʀɛ̃g] *fpl inf* clothes

**fripe** [fʀip] *f gén pl* ❶ (*vieux vêtements*) old clothes ❷ (*vêtements d'occasion*) secondhand clothes

**fripé(e)** [fʀipe] *adj* crumpled

**friper** [fʀipe] <1> **I.** *vt* to crease **II.** *vpr* **se ~** to get creased

**fripier, -ière** [fʀipje, -jɛʀ] *m, f* second-hand clothes dealer

**fripouille** [fʀipuj] *f inf* rascal

**frire** [fʀiʀ] *vt, vi irr* to fry

**frisbee®** [fʀizbi] *m* Frisbee®

**frise** [fʀiz] *f* ARCHIT frieze

**frisé(e)** [fʀize] *adj* (*cheveux*) curly; (*fille*) curly-haired

**frisée** [fʀize] *f* (*salade*) curly endive

**friser** [fʀize] <1> **I.** *vt* ❶ (*mettre en boucles: cheveux, moustache*) to curl ❷ (*frôler*) **~ le ridicule** (*situation, remarque*) to border on the ridiculous; **~ la soixantaine** to be pushing sixty **II.** *vi* (*cheveux*) to curl **III.** *vpr* (*se faire des boucles*) **se faire ~** to have one's hair curled

**frisotter** [fʀizɔte] <1> *vi* (*cheveux*) to go curly

**frisquet(te)** [fʀiskɛ, ɛt] *adj inf* nippy

**frisson** [fʀisɔ̃] *m* shiver; **~ de dégoût** shudder of disgust; **avoir des ~s** to shiver ▸ **le grand ~** a big thrill; **j'en ai le ~** it gives me the shivers

**frissonner** [fʀisɔne] <1> *vi* (*avoir des frissons*) **~ de désir/plaisir** to tremble with desire/pleasure; **~ de froid/peur** to shiver with cold/fear

**frit(e)** [fʀi, fʀit] **I.** *part passé de* **frire II.** *adj inf* (*fichu*) damn

**frite** [fʀit] *f* **des ~s** French fries ▸ **avoir la ~** *inf* to be in (top) form

**friterie** [fʀitʀi] *f* ❶ (*baraque à frites*) French fry stand ❷ (*atelier de friture*) establishment selling fried foods

**friteuse** [fʀitøz] *f* CULIN deep fryer

**friture** [fʀityʀ] *f* ❶ (*aliments*) fried food ❷ *Belgique* (*baraque à frites*) French fry stand ❸ (*graisse*) fat ❹ (*action*) frying ❺ RADIO, TEL interference

**frivole** [fʀivɔl] *adj* (*personne, spectacle*) frivolous; (*discours*) shallow; (*occupation, lecture*) trivial

**frivolité** [fʀivɔlite] *f* (*d'une personne*) frivolousness; (*d'une conversation, d'une occupation*) triviality; (*d'un discours*) shallowness

**froc** [fʀɔk] *m inf* (*pantalon*) pants *pl*

**froid** [fʀwa] *m.* **I.** *m* ❶ (*température*) cold; **il fait ~** it's cold; **avoir ~** to be cold; **j'ai ~ aux pieds** my feet are cold; **attraper** [*o* **prendre**] (**un coup de**) **~** to catch (a) cold ❷ (*brouille*) **être en ~ avec qn** to be on bad terms with sb ▸ **il fait un ~ de canard** [*o* **loup**] *inf* it's freezing out; **j'en ai ~ dans le dos** it makes my blood run cold **II.** *adv* **à ~** TECH cold; (*sans préparation*) (from) cold; (*sans émotion*) cold-bloodedly; (*avec insensibilité*) coolly; **démarrage à ~** cold start

**froid(e)** [fʀwa, fʀwad] *adj* cold; **rester ~ comme le marbre** to remain as cold as ice

**froidement** [fʀwadmɑ̃] *adv* ❶ (*sans chaleur*) coldly; (*accueillir, recevoir*) coolly ❷ (*avec sang-froid: raisonner*) with a cool head; (*réagir*) coolly ❸ (*avec insensibilité*) coolly

**froideur** [fʀwadœʀ] *f* (*d'un comporte-*

*ment*) coldness; (*d'un accueil, d'une réaction*) coolness; **accueillir qc avec ~** to give sth a cool reception

**froissable** [fʀwasabl] *adj* **être ~** to crease easily

**froissement** [fʀwasmɑ̃] *m* ❶ (*bruit*) rustle ❷ (*claquage*) **~ d'un muscle** strain(ing) ❸ (*blessure*) bad feeling

**froisser** [fʀwase] <1> **I.** *vt* ❶ (*chiffonner: tôles, papier*) to crumple; (*tissu*) to crease ❷ (*blesser: personne, orgueil*) to hurt **II.** *vpr* ❶ (*se chiffonner*) **se ~** (*tissu*) to crease; (*papier*) to get crumpled ❷ (*se claquer*) **se ~ un muscle** to strain a muscle ❸ (*se vexer*) **se ~** to get offended; **être froissé** to be offended

**frôlement** [fʀolmɑ̃] *m* ❶ (*contact léger*) touch ❷ (*frémissement*) swish

**frôler** [fʀole] <1> **I.** *vt* ❶ (*effleurer*) to brush against ❷ (*passer très près*) to graze; **~ le ridicule** (*remarque, situation*) to border on the ridiculous ❸ (*éviter de justesse*) **~ la mort** to narrowly escape death **II.** *vpr* **se ~** (*avec contact*) to brush against each other; (*sans contact*) to pass by each other

**fromage** [fʀomaʒ] *m* cheese; **~ blanc** quark

**fromager, -ère** [fʀomaʒe, -ɛʀ] **I.** *adj* (*industrie, production*) cheese **II.** *m, f* (*marchand*) cheese merchant; (*fabricant*) cheesemaker

**fromagerie** [fʀomaʒʀi] *f* ❶ (*industrie*) cheesemaking industry ❷ (*lieu de fabrication*) dairy

**froment** [fʀomɑ̃] *m* wheat

**froncement** [fʀɔ̃smɑ̃] *m* (*du nez*) wrinkling; **~ des sourcils** frown

**froncer** [fʀɔ̃se] <2> *vt* ❶ COUT to gather ❷ (*plisser: nez*) to wrinkle; **~ les sourcils** to frown

**fronces** [fʀɔ̃s] *fpl* gathers; **à ~** gathered

**fronde**[1] [fʀɔ̃d] *f* ❶ (*arme*) sling ❷ (*jouet*) slingshot

**fronde**[2] [fʀɔ̃d] *f* (*insurrection*) revolt

**fronde**[3] [fʀɔ̃d] *f* BOT frond

**front** [fʀɔ̃] *m* ❶ ANAT forehead ❷ (*façade*) façade; (*d'une montagne*) face; **~ de mer** seafront ❸ MIL, METEO, POL

front; **Front populaire** Popular Front (*leftwing government coalition elected in 1936*) ▸ **relever le ~** to lift one's head high; **de ~** (*côte à côte*) side by side; **attaquer un problème de ~** to tackle a problem head on; **se heurter de ~** to collide head on

**frontal** [fʀɔ̃tal, -o] <-aux> *m* MED frontal bone

**frontal(e)** [fʀɔ̃tal, -o] <-aux> *adj* ❶ MED frontal ❷ (*de face: attaque, collision*) head-on

**frontalier, -ière** [fʀɔ̃talje, -jɛʀ] **I.** *adj* border **II.** *m, f* border dweller

**frontière** [fʀɔ̃tjɛʀ] **I.** *f* border **II.** *app inv* border

**fronton** [fʀɔ̃tɔ̃] *m* pediment

**frottement** [fʀɔtmɑ̃] *m* ❶ (*bruit*) rubbing (noise) ❷ (*contact*) rubbing; **étoffe usée par les ~s** fabric that has been worn thin ❸ PHYS friction ❹ *pl* (*frictions*) friction

**frotter** [fʀɔte] <1> **I.** *vi* **~ contre qc** to rub against sth; (*porte*) to scrape against sth **II.** *vt* ❶ (*astiquer: chaussures, meubles*) to polish ❷ (*nettoyer*) to rub; (*avec une brosse*) to scrub; **~ ses semelles sur le paillasson** to wipe one's soles on the doormat ❸ (*cirer: parquet*) to polish ❹ (*frictionner pour laver*) to scrub; (*frictionner pour sécher*) to rub down; (*frictionner pour réchauffer*) to rub ❺ (*gratter: allumette*) to strike; **~ qc contre/sur qc** to rub sth against/on sth ❻ (*enduire*) **~ qc d'ail** to rub sth with garlic **III.** *vpr* ❶ (*se laver*) **se ~** to give oneself a scrub ❷ (*se sécher*) **se ~** to rub oneself down ❸ (*se nettoyer*) **se ~ les ongles** to scrub one's nails ❹ (*se gratter*) **se ~ les yeux/le nez** to rub one's eyes/nose ❺ (*entrer en conflit*) **se ~ à qn** to cross sb

**frottis** [fʀɔti] *m* MED Pap smear

**froufrou** [fʀufʀu] *m* ❶ (*bruit*) rustling ❷ *pl* (*dentelles*) frills

**froussard(e)** [fʀusaʀ, aʀd] **I.** *adj inf* chicken **II.** *m(f) inf* chicken

**frousse** [fʀus] *f inf* fright; **avoir la ~** to be scared out of one's wits

**fructifier** [fʀyktifje] <1> vi ❶ (*produire: arbre, idée*) to bear; (*terre*) to yield ❷ (*rapporter: capital*) to yield a profit; **faire ~ qc** to make sth yield a profit

**fructueux, -euse** [fʀyktɥø, -øz] adj (*collaboration*) fruitful; (*lecture*) rewarding; (*recherches, efforts, essai, travaux*) productive; (*opération financière, commerce*) profitable

**frugal(e)** [fʀygal, -o] <-aux> adj frugal

**fruit** [fʀɥi] m ❶ pl fruit; **jus de ~(s)** fruit juice; **~s rouges/confits** summer/glacé fruit ❷ (*crustacés*) **~s de mer** seafood ❸ (*résultat: de l'expérience, de la réflexion, d'un effort*) fruits; (*d'une union, de l'amour*) fruit; **être le ~ du hasard** to come about by chance; **le ~ d'une imagination délirante** the child of a fevered imagination; **porter ses ~s** to bear fruit ►**~ défendu** forbidden fruit

**fruité(e)** [fʀɥite] adj fruity

**fruitier, -ière** [fʀɥitje, -jɛʀ] I. adj (*arbre*) fruit II. m, f fruit seller

**fruste** [fʀyst] adj (*personne*) rough-mannered; (*manières*) rough

**frustrant(e)** [fʀystʀɑ̃, ɑ̃t] adj frustrating

**frustration** [fʀystʀasjɔ̃] f frustration

**frustré(e)** [fʀystʀe] I. adj frustrated II. m(f) inffrustrated individual

**frustrer** [fʀystʀe] <1> vt ❶ a. PSYCH to frustrate ❷ (*priver*) **~ qn de qc** to deprive sb of sth

**FS** [ɛfɛs] m abr de **franc suisse** SF

**fuchsia** [fyʃja, fyksja] I. m a. BOT fuchsia II. adj inv fuchsia

**fuel** [fjul] m ❶ (*combustible*) **~ domestique** heating oil ❷ (*carburant*) diesel

**fugace** [fygas] adj transient; (*beauté*) fleeting

**fugitif, -ive** [fyʒitif, -iv] I. adj ❶ (*en fuite*) runaway ❷ (*éphémère*) fleeting II. m, f (*de sa famille*) runaway; (*de la justice*) fugitive

**fugue** [fyg] f ❶ (*fuite*) **un mineur en ~** a runaway minor; **faire une ~/des ~s** to run away ❷ MUS fugue

**fuguer** [fyge] <1> vi infto run away

**fugueur, -euse** [fygœʀ,-øz] I. m, f runaway II. adj **enfant ~** young runaway

**fuir** [fɥiʀ] irr I. vi ❶ (*s'enfuir*) **~ d'un pays** to flee a country ❷ (*détaler*) **~ devant qn/qc** to run away from sb/sth; **faire ~ qn** to make sb run away ❸ (*se dérober*) **~ devant qc** to run away from sth ❹ (*ne pas être étanche*) to leak ❺ (*s'échapper: liquide*) to leak (out); (*gaz*) to escape II. vt (*éviter: danger*) to evade; **~ ses responsabilités** to try to escape one's responsibilities; **~ la présence de qn** to keep away from sb

**fuite** [fɥit] f ❶ flight; **prendre la ~** to take flight; (*chauffeur accidenté*) to drive away; **être en ~** (*accusé*) to be on the run ❷ (*dérobade*) **~ devant qc** to run away from sth ❸ (*trou*) **avoir une ~** to have a leak ❹ (*perte*) leak; **il y a une ~** there's a leak ❺ (*indiscrétion: d'une information*) leak; **l'auteur de la ~** the leaker

**fulgurant(e)** [fylgyʀɑ̃, ɑ̃t] adj ❶ (*rapide: vitesse, réplique*) lightning; (*progrès*) staggering ❷ (*violent: douleur*) shooting ❸ (*éblouissant: lueur*) dazzling; (*regard*) blazing

**fumant(e)** [fymɑ̃, ɑ̃t] adj ❶ (*qui dégage de la fumée*) smoking ❷ (*qui dégage de la vapeur*) steaming ❸ inf (*sensationnel*) dazzling

**fumé(e)** [fyme] adj smoked; (*verres de lunettes*) smoke-tinted

**fume-cigarette** [fymsigaʀɛt] <fume-cigarettes> m cigarette holder

**fumée** [fyme] f ❶ smoke; (*polluante*) fumes ❷ (*vapeur légère*) steam ❸ (*vapeur épaisse*) fumes pl

**fumer** [fyme] <1> I. vi ❶ (*aspirer de la fumée de tabac, dégager de la fumée*) to smoke ❷ (*dégager de la vapeur*) to steam; (*acide*) to give off fumes II. vt to smoke

**fumet** [fymɛ] m ❶ (*odeur*) aroma ❷ (*bouquet: d'un vin*) bouquet

**fumeur, -euse** [fymœʀ, -øz] I. m, f smoker II. app **zone ~** smoking area

F

**fumier** [fymje] *m* ❶ (*engrais naturel*) manure ❷ *inf* (*salaud*) bastard

**fumigation** [fymigasjɔ̃] *f* a. MED fumigation

**fumigène** [fymiʒɛn] *adj* **grenade/ bombe** ~ smoke grenade/bomb; **engin/appareil** ~ smoke machine

**fumiste** [fymist] **I.** *adj péj, inf* lazy **II.** *mf* ❶ *péj, inf* joker ❷ (*ouvrier*) chimney sweep

**fumoir** [fymwar] *m* smoking room

**funambule** [fynãbyl] *mf* tightrope walker

**funboard** [fœnbɔrd] *m* ❶ (*planche à voile*) sailboard ❷ (*sport*) sailboarding

**funèbre** [fynɛbr] *adj* ❶ (*funéraire*) funeral; **veillée** ~ wake ❷ (*lugubre: silence*) funereal; (*idées, mine*) gloomy

**funérailles** [fyneraj] *fpl* funeral; ~ **nationales** state funeral

**funéraire** [fynerɛr] *adj* (*monument*) funerary; **dalle** ~ tombstone

**funeste** [fynɛst] *adj* ❶ (*fatal: coup*) fatal; (*jour*) fateful; (*suites*) tragic; **être à qn/qc** to have dire consequences for sb/sth ❷ (*de mort: pressentiment, vision*) deathly; **de ~s pressentiments** a premonition of death ❸ (*triste: récit*) sad

**funiculaire** [fynikylɛr] *m* funicular

**funk** [fœnk] *adj inv* funky; **musique** ~ funk(y music)

**fur** [fyr] **au ~ et à mesure** as one goes along; **passe-moi les photos au ~ et à mesure** pass me the photos as you look at them

**furax** [fyraks] *adj inf* (*furieux*) livid

**furet** [fyrɛ] *m* ferret

**fureter** [fyr(ə)te] <4> *vi* to ferret around

**fureteur** [fyr(ə)tœr] *m Québec* INFORM browser

**fureteur, -euse** [fyr(ə)tœr, -øz] **I.** *m, f* pry **II.** *adj* (*regard*) prying

**fureur** [fyrœr] *f* ❶ rage; **mettre qn en ~** to infuriate sb; **être en ~ contre qn** to be furious at sb; **avec ~** furiously ❷ (*violence*) fury ▶ **faire ~** to be (all) the rage

**furibond(e)** [fyribɔ̃, 5d] *adj* (*regard, ton*) enraged; (*personne*) livid

**furie** [fyri] *f* ❶ (*violence*) fury; **mer en ~** raging sea; **personne/animal en ~** enraged person/animal; **être en ~** to be in a rage ❷ *péj* (*femme déchaînée*) fury

**furieux, -euse** [fyrjø, -jøz] *adj* ❶ (*en colère, violent*) furious ❷ *iron* (*extrême: envie*) overwhelming; (*appétit*) furious

**furoncle** [fyrɔ̃kl] *m* boil

**furtif, -ive** [fyrtif, -iv] *adj* furtive

**furtivement** [fyrtivmã] *adv* furtively

**fus** [fy] *passé simple de* **être**

**fusain** [fyzɛ̃] *m* ❶ (*dessin*) charcoal drawing ❷ (*crayon*) charcoal pencil ❸ BOT spindle tree

**fuseau** [fyzo] <x> *m* ❶ (*instrument*) spindle ❷ (*pantalon*) ski pants *pl* ❸ GEO ~ **horaire** time zone

**fusée** [fyze] *f* rocket

**fuselage** [fyz(ə)laʒ] *m* fuselage

**fuselé(e)** [fyz(ə)le] *adj* tapering

**fuser** [fyze] <1> *vi* (*liquide, vapeur*) to spurt out; (*étincelles*) to fly (up); (*lumière*) to shine out; (*rires, cris*) to go up; (*coups de feu*) to ring out

**fusible** [fyzibl] *m* fuse

**fusil** [fyzi] *m* ❶ (*à chevrotines*) shotgun; (*à balles*) rifle ❷ (*aiguisoir*) steel ▶ **changer son ~ d'épaule** (*changer de méthode/d'opinion*) to have a change of heart; (*retourner sa veste*) to switch sides

**fusillade** [fyzijad] *f* ❶ (*coups de feu*) gunfire ❷ (*exécution*) shooting

**fusiller** [fyzije] <1> *vt* to shoot

**fusil-mitrailleur** [fyzimitrajœr] <fusils-mitrailleurs> *m* machine gun

**fusion** [fyzjɔ̃] *f* ❶ (*fonte: des atomes*) fusion; (*d'un métal*) melting; (*de la glace*) thawing; **en ~** molten ❷ ECON, POL merger ❸ (*union: de cœurs, corps, d'esprits*) union ❹ INFORM (*de fichiers*) merging

**fusionner** [fyzjɔne] <1> *vt, vi a.* INFORM to merge

**fût** [fy] *m* cask

**F**

**futaie** [fytɛ] *f* forest
**futé(e)** [fyte] **I.** *adj* smart **II.** *m(f)* **petit ~** clever son of a gun
**futile** [fytil] *adj* ❶ (*inutile, creux: choses, occupation*) pointless; (*conversation, propos*) empty; (*prétexte, raison*) trivial ❷ (*frivole: personne, esprit*) trivial
**futilité** [fytilite] *f* ❶ *sans pl* (*inutilité, insignifiance: d'une occupation*) pointlessness; (*d'une conversation, d'un propos, d'une vie*) emptiness ❷ *sans pl* (*frivolité: d'une personne, d'un esprit*) triviality; (*d'un raisonnement*) vacuity ❸ *pl* (*bagatelles*) trivialities

**futur** [fytyʀ] *m* future
**futur(e)** [fytyʀ] **I.** *adj* future; **une ~e maman** a mother-to-be **II.** *m(f) inf* (*fiancé*) fiancé, fiancée *m, f*
**futuriste** [fytyʀist] *adj* futuristic
**fuyais** [fɥijɛ] *imparf de* **fuir**
**fuyant** [fɥijɑ̃] *part prés de* **fuir**
**fuyant(e)** [fɥijɑ̃, ɑ̃t] *adj* ❶ (*évasif: attitude*) evasive; (*regard*) shifty; **être ~** (*personne*) to be hard to grasp ❷ (*incurvé: menton, front*) receding
**fuyard(e)** [fɥijaʀ, aʀd] *m(f)* ❶ (*fugitif*) runaway ❷ (*déserteur*) deserter
**fuyez** [fɥije], **fuyons** [fɥijɔ̃] *indic prés et impératif de* **fuir**

# Gg

**G, g** [ʒe] *m inv* G, g; **~ comme Gaston** (*au téléphone*) g as in Golf
**gabarit** [gabaʀi] *m* ❶ (*dimension*) size ❷ *inf* (*stature*) build
**gabegie** [gabʒi] *f* chaos
**Gabon** [gabɔ̃] *m* **le ~** Gabon
**gabonais(e)** [gabɔnɛ, ɛz] *adj* Gabonese
**gâcher** [gɑʃe] <1> *vt* (*plaisir, vacances*) to ruin; (*vie*) to fritter away; (*temps, argent*) to waste
**gâchette** [gɑʃɛt] *f* (*d'une arme*) trigger ▶ **avoir la ~ <u>facile</u>** to be trigger-happy
**gâchis** [gɑʃi] *m* ❶ (*gaspillage*) waste ❷ (*mauvais résultat*) mess
**gadget** [gadʒɛt] *m* ❶ (*bidule*) thingamajig ❷ (*innovation*) gadget
**gadoue** [gadu] *f* mud
**gaffe¹** [gaf] *f inf* blunder; **faire une ~** to put one's foot in it
**gaffe²** [gaf] *f inf* <u>faire</u> **~** to be careful
**gaffer** [gafe] <1> *vi inf* to blunder; (*en parole*) to put one's foot in one's mouth
**gag** [gag] *m* gag
**gaga** [gaga] **I.** *adj inf* ❶ (*gâteux*) gaga ❷ (*fou*) **être ~ de qn** to be crazy about sb **II.** *m inf* **vieux ~** old fool

**gage** [gaʒ] *m* ❶ (*garantie*) guarantee; (*témoignage*) proof ❷ (*dépôt*) security; **mettre qc en ~** to pawn sth ❸ JEUX forfeit ❹ *pl* (*salaire*) wages
**gagnant(e)** [gaɲɑ̃, ɑ̃t] **I.** *adj* winning **II.** *m(f)* winner
**gagne-pain** [gaɲpɛ̃] *m inv* meal ticket
**gagner** [gaɲe] <1> **I.** *vi* ❶ (*vaincre*) **~ à qc** to win at sth ❷ (*trouver un avantage*) **est-ce que j'y gagne?** what do I get out of this? ❸ (*avoir une meilleure position*) **~ à être connu** to improve on acquaintance **II.** *vt* ❶ (*s'assurer: argent, récompense*) to earn; (*prix*) to win ❷ (*remporter: lot, argent*) to win ❸ (*économiser: place, temps*) to save ❹ (*obtenir comme résultat: réputation*) to gain ❺ (*conquérir: ami, confiance*) to win over ❻ (*atteindre: lieu*) to reach ❼ (*avancer*) **~ qc** (*incendie, épidémie*) to overtake sth ❽ (*envahir*) **~ qn** (*maladie*) to spread to sb; (*fatigue, peur*) to overcome sb; **le froid la gagnait** the cold was overcoming her ▶ **c'est <u>toujours</u> ça de gagné** that's always something

**gagneur, -euse** [gaɲœʀ, -øz] *m, f* winner

**gai(e)** [ge, gɛ] *adj* cheerful; (*personne*) happy; (*événement*) cheerful; (*ambiance*) lively; (*vêtement, pièce, couleur*) bright ▸ **c'est ~!** *iron* that's great!; **ça va être ~!** it's going be a load of fun!

**gaiement** [gemɑ̃, gɛmɑ̃] *adv* cheerfully ▸ **allons-y ~!** *iron* come on, then!

**gaieté** [gete] *f* gaiety; (*d'une personne*) cheerfulness ▸ **ne pas faire qc de ~ de cœur** to do sth with great reluctance

**gaillard** [gajaʀ] *m* ① (*costaud*) hefty fellow ② *inf* (*lascar*) guy

**gaillard(e)** [gajaʀ, aʀd] *adj* (*personne*) lively

**gaîment** [gemɑ̃, gɛmɑ̃] *adv* v. **gaiement**

**gain** [gɛ̃] *m* ① (*profit*) profit ② (*économie*) saving ▸ **obtenir ~ de cause** to be proven right; JUR to win one's case

**gaine** [gɛn] *f* ① (*ceinture*) girdle ② (*étui*) sheath; (*d'un pistolet*) holster

**gaîté** [gete] *f* v. **gaieté**

**gala** [gala] *m* gala; **~ de bienfaisance** charity gala

**galant(e)** [galɑ̃, ɑ̃t] *adj* ① (*courtois*) gallant ② (*d'amour*) **rendez-vous ~** romantic engagement

**galanterie** [galɑ̃tʀi] *f* gallantry

**galaxie** [galaksi] *f* galaxy

**galbé(e)** [galbe] *adj* (*objet*) curved; (*jambe*) shapely

**gale** [gal] *f* ① (*chez les hommes*) scabies ② (*chez les animaux*) mange ▸ **ne pas avoir la ~** to not have the plague

**galère** [galɛʀ] *f* ① *inf* (*corvée*) mess; **quelle ~!** what a drag! ② HIST galley

**galerie** [galʀi] *f* ① (*souterrain*) tunnel; (*d'une mine*) level ② ~ **marchande** shopping mall ③ (*balcon*) circle ④ ART gallery; ~ **de peinture** art gallery ⑤ AUTO roof rack ▸ **amuser la ~** to clown around

**galet** [galɛ] *m* pebble

**galette** [galɛt] *f* (*crêpe*) (*savory*) crepe

**galeux, -euse** [galø, -øz] *adj* (*mur*) flaking

**galipette** [galipɛt] *f inf* somersault

**gallicisme** [ga(l)lisism] *m* Gallicism

**gallois** *m* Welsh; *v.a.* **français**

**gallois(e)** [galwa, az] *adj* Welsh

**Gallois(e)** [galwa, az] *m(f)* Welshman, Welshwoman *m, f*

**gallo-romain(e)** [ga(l)lɔʀɔmɛ̃, ɛn] <gallo-romains> *adj* Gallo-Roman

**galon** [galɔ̃] *m* ① *pl* MIL stripes ② COUT braid ③ *Québec* (*ruban gradué en pieds, en pouces et en lignes*) tape measure

**galop** [galo] *m* gallop; **au ~** at a gallop ▸ **arriver au (triple) ~** to arrive at top speed

**galoper** [galɔpe] <1> *vi* to gallop

**galopin** [galɔpɛ̃] *m inf* (*gamin des rues*) urchin

**galvaniser** [galvanize] <1> *vt* to galvanize

**galvaudé(e)** [galvode] *adj* trite

**gambader** [gɑ̃bade] <1> *vi* to leap; (*animal*) to gambol

**gambas** [gɑ̃bas] *fpl* gambas

**gamelle** [gamɛl] *f* (*d'un campeur*) billy; (*d'un soldat*) mess kit; (*d'un ouvrier*) lunch box; (*d'un chien*) bowl

**gamin(e)** [gamɛ̃, in] **I.** *adj* childish; (*air*) playful **II.** *m(f) inf* kid

**gaminerie** [gaminʀi] *f* playfulness

**gamme** [gam] *f* range; MUS scale

**gang** [gɑ̃g] *m* gang

**ganglion** [gɑ̃glijɔ̃] *m* ganglion

**gangster** [gɑ̃gstɛʀ] *m* gangster

**gant** [gɑ̃] *m a.* INFORM glove; **~ de toilette** washcloth ▸ **aller à qn comme un ~** (*vêtement*) to fit sb like a glove; **prendre des ~s avec qn** to handle sb with kid gloves

**garage** [gaʀaʒ] *m* garage; **~ à vélos** bicycle shed

**garagiste** [gaʀaʒist] *mf* ① (*qui tient un garage*) garage owner ② (*mécanicien*) mechanic

**garant(e)** [gaʀɑ̃, ɑ̃t] *m(f)* guarantor; **se porter ~ de qc** to guarantee sth; JUR to be responsible for sth

**garantie** [gaʀɑ̃ti] *f* ① (*bulletin de garantie*) warranty (card); **qc est encore sous ~** sth is still under warranty

**②** (*gage, caution*) security; (*de paiement*) guarantee **③** (*sûreté*) **sans ~** without guarantee **④** (*assurance*) **~ contre les risques** risk insurance **⑤** (*certitude*) **pouvez-vous me donner votre ~ que ...** can you assure me that ... **⑥** (*précaution*) **prendre des ~s** to take precautions

**garantir** [garɑ̃tir] <8> *vt* **①** (*répondre de, par contrat*) **~ qc à qn** to guarantee sth to sb; **être garanti un an** to be guaranteed (for) one year **②** (*assurer*) to assure **► iron je te garantis que ...** I guarantee that ...

**garçon** [garsɔ̃] *m* **①** (*enfant*) boy **②** (*jeune homme*) young man; **être beau ~** to be good-looking; **~ d'honneur** best man **③** (*fils*) son **④** (*serveur*) waiter **► c'est un véritable ~ manqué** she is a real tomboy; **vieux ~** bachelor

**garde¹** [gard] *f* **①** *sans pl* (*surveillance*) **avoir la ~ de qn** to be in charge of looking after sb; **confier qn à la ~ de qn** to put sb in sb's care **②** JUR (*d'enfants*) custody; **~ à vue** police custody **③** (*veille*) guard duty **④** (*permanence le week-end*) weekend duty; (*permanence de nuit*) night duty; **infirmière de ~** duty nurse; **être de ~** (*médecin, pharmacie*) to be on duty **⑤** (*patrouille*) patrol **► être sur ses ~s** to be on one's guard; **mettre qn en ~ contre qn/qc** to warn sb about sb/sth; **monter la ~** to be on guard; (*soldat*) to mount guard; **sans y prendre ~** without realizing it

**garde²** [gard] *m* **①** (*surveillant: d'une propriété*) guard; **~ forestier** forest ranger; **~ du corps** bodyguard **②** (*sentinelle*) guard; (*soldat*) guardsman

**garde-à-vous** [gardavu] *m inv* **~!** attention!

**garde-barrière** [gard(ə)barjɛr] <gardes-barrières> *mf* railroad crossing keeper

**garde-boue** [gard(ə)bu] *m inv* fender

**garde-chasse** [gardə∫as] <gardes--chasse(s)> *mf* gamekeeper

**garde-fou** [gard(ə)fu] <garde-fous> *m* railing

**garde-malade** [gard(ə)malad] <gardes-malades> *mf* home nurse

**garde-manger** [gard(ə)mɑ̃ʒe] *m inv* cooler

**garder** [garde] <1> **I.** *vt* **①** (*surveiller*) to watch; (*maison, enfant, animal*) to look after; (*personne âgée*) to care for; **donner qc à ~ à qn** to give sth to sb to look after **②** (*stocker*) to keep; (*marchandises*) to stock **③** (*ne pas perdre*) to keep; (*espoir, défaut, manie*) to still have **④** (*réserver*) to reserve; (*place*) to save **⑤** (*tenir, ne pas dévoiler*) to keep **⑥** (*retenir*) to detain **⑦** (*conserver sur soi*) **~ qc** to keep sth on **⑧** (*ne pas quitter: lit, chambre*) to stay in **II.** *vpr* **①** (*se conserver*) **se ~** (*aliment*) to keep **②** (*s'abstenir*) **se ~ de** +*infin* to be careful not to +*infin*

**garderie** [gardəri] *f* (day) nursery

**garde-robe** [gardərɔb] <garde-robes> *f* wardrobe

**gardien(ne)** [gardjɛ̃, jɛn] **I.** *m(f)* **①** (*surveillant*) warden; (*d'un immeuble*) building manager; (*d'un entrepôt*) guard; (*d'un zoo, cimetière*) keeper; **~ de musée** museum attendant; **~ de nuit** night watchman **②** (*défenseur*) protector; **~ de la paix** policeman **II.** *adj* Belgique (*maternelle*) **école ~ne** nursery

**gardiennage** [gardjenaʒ] *m* **①** (*d'immeuble*) caretaking **②** (*de locaux*) guarding; **société de ~** security company

**gare¹** [gar] *f* station; **~ centrale** central station; **~ routière** bus station; **entrer en ~** to approach the platform

**gare²** [gar] *interj* **~ à toi!** watch it! **► sans crier ~** without warning

**garer** [gare] <1> **I.** *vt* to park **II.** *vpr* **se ~ ①** (*parquer*) to park **②** (*se ranger*) to pull over

**gargariser** [gargarize] <1> *vpr* **①** (*se rincer*) **se ~** to gargle **②** *péj, inf* (*savourer*) **se ~ de qc** to delight in sth

**gargarisme** [gargarizm] *m* gargle

**gargouiller** [gaʁguje] <1> *vi* to gurgle; (*estomac*) to growl

**garni(e)** [gaʁni] *adj* ① CULIN garnished ② (*rempli*) **portefeuille bien ~** fat wallet

**garnir** [gaʁniʁ] <8> *vt* ① (*orner*) to garnish ② (*équiper*) **~ qc de qc** to equip sth with sth ③ (*renforcer*) to reinforce ④ (*remplir*) **être garni de qc** to be filled with sth

**garnison** [gaʁnizɔ̃] *f* garrison

**garniture** [gaʁnityʁ] *f* ① (*ornement*) trimming ② CULIN vegetables ③ (*renfort*) covering ④ AUTO lining

**garrigue** [gaʁig] *f* scrubland; (*dans le Midi*) garrigue (*heathland in Provence*)

**garrot** [gaʁo] *m* ① MED tourniquet ② (*partie du corps: d'un cheval*) withers

**gars** [ga] *m inf* lad; **salut les ~!** hi guys!

**gasoil, gas-oil** [gazwal] *m* diesel oil

**gaspillage** [gaspijaʒ] *m* waste

**gaspiller** [gaspije] <1> *vt* (*fortune*) to squander; (*eau, temps, talent*) to waste

**gastronome** [gastʁɔnɔm] *mf* gourmet

**gastronomie** [gastʁɔnɔmi] *f* gastronomy

**gastronomique** [gastʁɔnɔmik] *adj* (*restaurant*) gourmet; (*guide*) food

**gâteau** [gato] <x> I. *m* cake; **~ sec** cookie; **~ au chocolat/à la crème** chocolate/cream cake ▶ **c'est pas du ~!** *inf* it is not easy! II. *app inv, inf* (*maman, papa*) indulgent

**gâter** [gate] <1> I. *vt* (*combler: personne*) to spoil ▶ **nous sommes gâtés** just our luck II. *vpr* **se ~** (*viande*) to go bad; (*fruits*) to spoil; (*choses, temps*) to turn bad; (*situation, ambiance*) to go sour

**gâteux, -euse** [gatø, -øz] I. *adj* ① *péj* (*sénile*) senile ② (*fou de*) besotted II. *m, f péj* senile old fool

**gauche** [goʃ] I. *adj* ① (*opp: droit*) left ② (*maladroit*) uneasy; (*geste*) jerky II. *m* **un crochet du ~** a left hook III. *f* ① left; **à ~** on the left; **de ~ à droite** from left to right ② POL **la ~** the Left; **idées/partis de ~** left-wing ideas/parties

**gaucher, -ère** [goʃe, -ɛʁ] I. *adj* left-handed II. *m, f* left-hander, southpaw

**gaucherie** [goʃʁi] *f* awkwardness

**gauchiste** [goʃist] *mf* leftist

**gaufre** [gofʁ] *f* waffle

**gaufrette** [gofʁɛt] *f* wafer

**gaufrier** [gofʁije] *m* waffle iron

**Gaule** [gol] *f* **la ~** Gaul

**gaullisme** [golism] *m* Gaullism

**gaulliste** [golist] *mf* Gaullist

**gaulois(e)** [golwa, waz] *adj* Gallic

**Gaulois(e)** [golwa, waz] *m(f)* Gaul

**gaver** [gave] <1> I. *vt* ① (*engraisser: oie*) to force-feed ② (*bourrer*) **~ qn de qc** to cram sb with sth II. *vpr* **se ~ de qc** to gorge oneself on sth

**gay** [gɛ] I. *adj inv* gay II. *m* gay

**gaz** [gaz] *m* ① (*vapeur invisible*) gas; **~ lacrymogène** teargas; **~ d'échappement** exhaust fumes *pl* ② *pl* (*flatulence*) gas

**gaze** [gaz] *f* gauze

**gazelle** [gazɛl] *f* gazelle

**gazer** [gaze] <1> *vt* to gas

**gazeux, -euse** [gazø, -øz] *adj* ① (*relatif au gaz*) gaseous ② (*qui contient du gaz*) sparkling

**gazinière** [gazinjɛʁ] *f* gas stove

**gazoduc** [gazɔdyk] *m* gas pipeline

**gazole** [gazɔl] *m* diesel oil

**gazon** [gazɔ̃] *m* lawn

**gazouiller** [gazuje] <1> *vi* (*bébé*) to gurgle; (*oiseau*) to chirp

**geai** [ʒɛ] *m* jay

**géant(e)** [ʒeɑ̃, ɑ̃t] I. *adj* giant II. *m(f)* a. COM giant

**gel** [ʒɛl] *m* ① METEO ice ② (*blocage*) freeze; **~ des salaires** salary freeze ③ (*crème*) gel

**gélatine** [ʒelatin] *f* gelatin

**gélatineux, -euse** [ʒelatinø, -øz] *adj* gelatinous

**gelée** [ʒ(ə)le] *f* ① METEO frost ② CULIN Jell-O®

**geler** [ʒ(ə)le] <4> I. *vt* to freeze; (*bourgeons*) to nip II. *vi* ① METEO to freeze; (*rivière*) to freeze over; (*fleurs*) to be nipped ② (*avoir froid*) to be cold; **on**

**gèle ici!** we're freezing in here! ❸ *impers* **il gèle** it is freezing

**gélule** [ʒelyl] *f* capsule

**Gémeaux** [ʒemo] *mpl* Gemini; *v.a.* **Balance**

**gémir** [ʒemiʀ] <8> *vi* to moan

**gémissement** [ʒemismɑ̃] *m* moaning

**gênant(e)** [ʒɛnɑ̃, ɑ̃t] *adj* irritating; (*question, situation*) embarrassing

**gencive** [ʒɑ̃siv] *f* gum

**gendarme** [ʒɑ̃daʀm] *m* ❶ (*policier*) police officer ❷ *inf* (*personne autoritaire*) bossy person

**gendarmerie** [ʒɑ̃daʀməʀi] *f* ❶ (*corps militaire*) police force ❷ (*bâtiment*) police station

**gendre** [ʒɑ̃dʀ] *m* son-in-law

**gène** [ʒɛn] *m* gene

**gêne** [ʒɛn] *f* ❶ (*malaise*) discomfort ❷ (*ennui*) **devenir une ~ pour qn** to become a problem for sb ❸ (*trouble*) trouble ▶ **être sans ~** to be thoughtless

**généalogie** [ʒenealɔʒi] *f* genealogy; (*d'une personne*) ancestry

**gêner** [ʒene] <1> **I.** *vt* ❶ (*déranger*) to bother ❷ (*entraver: piétons*) to disrupt ❸ (*mettre mal à l'aise*) to cause to feel ill at ease; **être gêné** to feel ill at ease; **ça me gêne de vous dire ça** I feel uneasy about telling you that **II.** *vpr* ❶ **se ~ pour** +*infin* to put oneself out to +*infin* ❷ (*être intimidé, avoir honte*) **se ~** to feel awkward

**général** [ʒeneʀal, -o] <-aux> *m* general

**général(e)** [ʒeneʀal, -o] <-aux> *adj* ❶ (*commun, collectif*) general; **en règle ~** generally (speaking) ❷ (*vague*) vague ❸ (*qui embrasse l'ensemble*) **directeur ~** director general; **quartier ~** headquarters ❹ (*total*) **atteint de paralysie ~e** affected by overall paralysis ▶ **en ~** in general; **d'une façon ~e** generally; (*dans l'ensemble*) as a whole

**générale** [ʒeneʀal] *f* THEAT dress rehearsal

**généralement** [ʒeneʀalmɑ̃] *adv* ❶ (*habituellement*) usually ❷ (*opp: en détail*) generally

**généralisation** [ʒeneʀalizasjɔ̃] *f* (*d'un conflit*) spread; (*d'une mesure*) generalization

**généraliser** [ʒeneʀalize] <1> **I.** *vt* ❶ (*rendre général*) to make general ❷ (*répandre: méthode, mesure*) to generalize **II.** *vpr* **se ~** (*procédé*) to become widespread

**généraliste** [ʒeneʀalist] *adj* **médecin ~** general practitioner

**généralité** [ʒeneʀalite] *f* gén pl (*idées générales*) general points; *péj* generalities

**générateur, -trice** [ʒeneʀatœʀ, -tʀis] **I.** *adj* **~ de qc** generative of sth **II.** *m, f* generator

**génération** [ʒeneʀasjɔ̃] *f* generation

**générer** [ʒeneʀe] <5> *vt* ❶ (*produire*) to produce ❷ INFORM to generate

**généreusement** [ʒeneʀøzmɑ̃] *adv* generously

**généreux, -euse** [ʒeneʀø, -øz] *adj* ❶ (*libéral*) generous ❷ (*riche: terre*) rich; (*vin*) generous ❸ *iron* (*plantureux: formes, poitrine*) ample; (*décolleté*) generous

**générique** [ʒeneʀik] **I.** *m* credits *pl* **II.** *adj* generic

**générosité** [ʒeneʀozite] *f* ❶ (*libéralité*) generosity ❷ (*magnanimité*) magnanimity ❸ *pl* (*cadeau*) kindnesses

**genèse** [ʒənɛz] *f* (*production*) genesis

**Genèse** [ʒənɛz] *f* REL **la ~** Genesis

**genêt** [ʒənɛ] *m* broom

**génétique** [ʒenetik] **I.** *adj* genetic **II.** *f* genetics

**Genève** [ʒ(ə)nɛv] Geneva

**génial(e)** [ʒenjal, -jo] <-aux> *adj* ❶ (*ingénieux*) inspired ❷ *inf* (*formidable*) great

**génie** [ʒeni] *m* ❶ (*esprit*) genius ❷ (*don*) **avoir le ~ de dire qc** to have the gift for saying sth ❸ HIST genie ❹ MIL Engineers *pl* ❺ (*art*) **~ civil/génétique** civil/genetic engineering

**genièvre** [ʒənjɛvʀ] *m* juniper

**génital(e)** [ʒenital, -o] <-aux> *adj* genital

**génitif** [ʒenitif] *m* genitive

**génocide** [ʒenɔsid] *m* genocide

**génoise** [ʒenwaz] *f* (*gâteau*) sponge cake

**genou** [ʒ(ə)nu] <x> *m* knee; **sur les ~x de qn** on sb's knees; **à ~x** kneeling

**genouillère** [ʒənujɛr] *f* kneeler; MED knee support

**genre** [ʒɑ̃r] *m* ❶(*sorte*) type ❷(*allure*) appearance ❸ART genre ❹(*espèce*) **~ humain** mankind ❺LING gender ▶ **ça fait mauvais ~** that looks bad; **ce n'est pas mon ~** it is not my style

**gens** [ʒɑ̃] *mpl*, *fpl* people; **~ du monde** society people

**gentiane** [ʒɑ̃sjan] *f* gentian

**gentil(le)** [ʒɑ̃ti, ij] *adj* ❶(*aimable*) kind; **~ avec qn** kind to sb ❷(*joli*) pretty ❸(*sage*) good ❹iron (*coquet*) **~le somme** tidy sum

**gentilhomme** [ʒɑ̃tijɔm, ʒɑ̃tizɔm] <gentilshommes> *m* gentleman

**gentillesse** [ʒɑ̃tijɛs] *f* ❶(*qualité*) kindness ❷(*action, parole*) favor

**gentiment** [ʒɑ̃timɑ̃] *adv* ❶(*aimablement*) kindly ❷(*sagement*) clearly

**géographe** [ʒeɔgraf] *mf* geographer

**géographie** [ʒeɔgrafi] *f* geography

**géographique** [ʒeɔgrafik] *adj* geographical

**géologie** [ʒeɔlɔʒi] *f* geology

**géologique** [ʒeɔlɔʒik] *adj* geological

**géologue** [ʒeɔlɔg] *mf* geologist

**géomètre** [ʒeɔmɛtr] *mf* surveyor

**géophysicien(ne)** [ʒeofizisjɛ̃, jɛn] *m(f)* geophysicist

**gérance** [ʒerɑ̃s] *f* (*gestion*) management

**géranium** [ʒeranjɔm] *m* geranium

**gérant(e)** [ʒerɑ̃, ɑ̃t] *m(f)* manager

**gerbe** [ʒɛrb] *f* (*de blé*) sheaf; (*de fleurs, d'eau, d'écume*) spray

**gercer** [ʒɛrse] <2> *vi* to crack

**gerçure** [ʒɛrsyr] *f* **avoir des ~s aux mains** to have chapped hands

**gérer** [ʒere] <5> *vt* ❶(*diriger*) to manage ❷(*coordonner: crise*) to handle; (*temps libre*) to manage

**gériatrie** [ʒerjatri] *f* geriatrics + *vb sing*

**Germain(e)** [ʒɛrmɛ̃, ɛn] *m(f)* German

**germanique** [ʒɛrmanik] *adj* Germanic

**germaniste** [ʒɛrmanist] *mf* German scholar

**germanophile** [ʒɛrmanɔfil] *adj* Germanophile

**germanophobe** [ʒɛrmanɔfɔb] *adj* Germanophobe

**germanophone** [ʒɛrmanɔfɔn] **I.** *adj* German-speaking; **être ~** to be a German speaker **II.** *mf* German speaker

**germe** [ʒɛrm] *m* ❶(*semence*) seed ❷MED germ

**germer** [ʒɛrme] <1> *vi* to sprout; (*idée, sentiment*) to form

**gérondif** [ʒerɔ̃dif] *m* gerund

**gésier** [ʒezje] *m* gizzard

**gestation** [ʒɛstasjɔ̃] *f* ❶(*grossesse*) gestation ❷(*genèse*) preparation

**geste** [ʒɛst] *m* ❶(*mouvement*) gesture; **~ de la main** wave of the hand ❷(*action*) act; **~ d'amour** gesture of love

**gesticuler** [ʒɛstikyle] <1> *vi* to gesticulate

**gestion** [ʒɛstjɔ̃] *f* management; **~ d'entreprise** business management

**gestionnaire** [ʒɛstjɔnɛr] **I.** *mf* management **II.** *m* INFORM **~ de fichiers** file manager

**geyser** [ʒɛzɛr] *m* (*source*) geyser

**ghetto** [geto] *m* ghetto

**gibier** [ʒibje] *m* ❶(*animaux de chasse*) game ❷fig **~ de potence** gallows bird

**giboulée** [ʒibule] *f* sudden shower

**gicler** [ʒikle] <1> **I.** *vi* (*eau*) to squirt; (*boue*) to spurt **II.** *vt* Suisse (*asperger, éclabousser*) to splash

**gicleur** [ʒiklœr] *m* jet

**gifle** [ʒifl] *f* slap

**gifler** [ʒifle] <1> *vt* ❶(*battre*) to slap ❷(*fouetter*) **la pluie me giflait la figure** the rain lashed my face

**gigantesque** [ʒigɑ̃tɛsk] *adj* gigantic

**gigot** [ʒigo] *m* leg

**gigoter** [ʒigɔte] <1> *vi* inf to wriggle around

**gilet** [ʒilɛ] *m* ❶(*vêtement sans manches*) vest; **~ de sauvetage** life jacket ❷(*lainage*) cardigan

**gingembre** [ʒɛ̃ʒɑ̃br] *m* ginger

**girafe** [ʒiraf] *f* giraffe

G

**giratoire** [ʒiʀatwaʀ] *adj* **sens ~** roundabout

**giroflée** [ʒiʀɔfle] *f* wallflower

**girolle** [ʒiʀɔl] *f* chanterelle

**girouette** [ʒiʀwɛt] *f* ❶ (*plaque placée au sommet d'un édifice*) weather vane ❷ *inf* (*personne*) waverer

**gisement** [ʒizmɑ̃] *m* deposit

**gitan(e)** [ʒitɑ̃, an] *m(f)* gypsy

**gîte** [ʒit] *m* shelter; **~ rural** cabin

**givrant(e)** [ʒivʀɑ̃, ɑ̃t] *adj* freezing

**givre** [ʒivʀ] *m* frost

**givré(e)** [ʒivʀe] *adj* ❶ (*couvert de givre*) covered in frost; (*fenêtre*) frosted ❷ *inf* (*fou*) **être ~** to be crazy [*o* mad]

**glace** [glas] *f* ❶ (*eau congelée*) ice ❷ CULIN ice cream ❸ (*miroir*) mirror ❹ (*vitre*) plate glass

**glacé(e)** [glase] *adj* ❶ (*très froid*) freezing; (*personne*) frozen ❷ CULIN (*fruit, marrons*) glacé; (*gâteau*) iced ❸ (*recouvert d'un apprêt brillant*) **papier ~** gloss paper ❹ (*inimical: accueil, regard*) icy

**glacer** [glase] <2> I. *vt* ❶ (*refroidir*) to ice ❷ (*impressionner*) to chill II. *vpr* **se ~** to freeze

**glaciaire** [glasjɛʀ] *adj* ice

**glacial(e)** [glasjal, -jo] <s *o* -aux> *adj* ❶ (*très froid*) freezing ❷ (*inimical*) icy

**glacier** [glasje] *m* ❶ GEO glacier ❷ (*métier*) ice cream maker

**glacière** [glasjɛʀ] *f* ❶ (*coffre*) cooler, ice chest ❷ *inf* (*lieu*) fridge

**glaçon** [glasɔ̃] *m* ❶ (*petit cube*) ice cube ❷ *inf* (*personne*) cold fish ❸ *pl* (*pieds, mains*) blocks of ice

**glaïeul** [glajœl] *m* gladiolus

**glaise** [glɛz] *f* clay

**gland** [glɑ̃] *m* acorn

**glande** [glɑ̃d] *f* gland

**glaner** [glane] <1> *vt* to glean

**glapir** [glapiʀ] <8> *vi* to yap

**glauque** [glok] *adj* ❶ (*verdâtre*) bluegreen ❷ (*lugubre*) dreary

**glissant(e)** [glisɑ̃, ɑ̃t] *adj* ❶ (*qui glisse*) slippery ❷ (*dangereux*) dangerous

**glisse** [glis] *f* ❶ (*aptitude à glisser*) glide ❷ Suisse (*traîneau, luge*) sled

**glissement** [glismɑ̃] *m* **~ de terrain** landslide

**glisser** [glise] <1> I. *vi* ❶ (*être glissant*) to be slippery ❷ (*se déplacer*) to slide **~ sur l'eau/sur la neige** to glide over the water/snow ❸ (*tomber*) **se laisser ~** to slide ❹ (*déraper*) to skid ❺ (*échapper de*) **ça m'a glissé des mains** it slipped out of my hands ❻ (*ne faire qu'une impression faible*) **~ sur qn** (*critique, remarque*) to wash over sb II. *vt* to slide; (*regard*) to sneak III. *vpr* ❶ (*pénétrer*) **se ~ dans la maison** to slip into the house ❷ (*s'insinuer*) **se ~ dans qc** to creep into sth

**glissière** [glisjɛʀ] *f* **~ de sécurité** crash barrier

**global(e)** [glɔbal, -o] <-aux> *adj* global; (*somme*) total

**globalement** [glɔbalmɑ̃] *adv* globally

**globalité** [glɔbalite] *f* global nature

**globe** [glɔb] *m* globe; **~ oculaire** eyeball

**globule** [glɔbyl] *m* globule

**globuleux, -euse** [glɔbylø, -øz] *adj* (*yeux*) protruding

**gloire** [glwaʀ] *f* ❶ (*célébrité*) fame ❷ (*mérite*) distinction ❸ (*personne*) celebrity ▶ **à la ~ de qn/qc** in praise of sb/sth

**glorieux, -euse** [glɔʀjø, -jøz] *adj* glorious

**glorification** [glɔʀifikasjɔ̃] *f* glorification

**glorifier** [glɔʀifje] <1> I. *vt* to glorify II. *vpr* **se ~ de qc** to glory in sth

**glossaire** [glɔsɛʀ] *m* glossary

**glouton(ne)** [glutɔ̃, ɔn] I. *adj* greedy II. *m(f)* glutton

**glu** [gly] *f* ❶ (*colle*) birdlime ❷ *inf* (*personne*) leech

**gluant(e)** [glyɑ̃, ɑ̃t] *adj* sticky

**glucide** [glysid] *m* carbohydrate

**gluten** [glytɛn] *m* gluten; **sans ~** gluten-free

**glycémie** [glisemi] *f* MED glycemia

**glycine** [glisin] *f* wisteria

**Go** *abr de* **giga-octet** GB

**GO** [ʒeo] *fpl abr de* **grandes ondes** LW

**gobelet** [gɔblɛ] *m* beaker

**gober** [gɔbe] <1> *vt* ❶ (*avaler en aspirant: huître, œuf*) to swallow whole ❷ *inf* (*croire*) to swallow

**godasse** [gɔdas] *f inf* shoe

**goéland** [gɔelɑ̃] *m* seagull

**goélette** [gɔelɛt] *f* schooner

**gogo** [gogo] **à ~** *inf* plenty of

**goguenard(e)** [gɔg(ə)naʀ, aʀd] *adj* mocking

**goinfre** [gwɛ̃fʀ] **I.** *adj* piggish **II.** *mf péj* greedy pig

**goinfrerie** [gwɛ̃fʀəʀi] *f péj* piggery

**goitre** [gwatʀ] *m* goiter

**golf** [gɔlf] *m* golf; (*terrain*) golf course

**golfe** [gɔlf] *m* gulf

**golfeur, -euse** [gɔlfœʀ, -øz] *m, f* golfer

**gomme** [gɔm] *f* ❶ (*bloc de caoutchouc*) eraser ❷ (*substance*) gum

**gommer** [gɔme] <1> *vt* to rub out; (*de sa mémoire*) to erase

**gond** [gɔ̃] *m* hinge ▶ **sortir de ses ~s** to fly off the handle

**gondoler** [gɔ̃dɔle] <1> *vi* to crinkle; (*planche*) to warp

**gonflable** [gɔ̃flabl] *adj* inflatable

**gonflé(e)** [gɔ̃fle] *adj* ❶ (*rempli*) swollen; (*yeux, visage*) puffy ❷ *inf* (*culotté*) cheeky

**gonflement** [gɔ̃fləmɑ̃] *m* ❶ (*d'un pneu*) inflation; (*d'un ballon*) blowing up; (*d'une plaie, d'un organe, du visage*) swelling ❷ (*augmentation: des effectifs*) expansion; (*de l'épargne*) build-up ❸ (*surestimation: d'une facture, note de frais*) inflation; (*d'un incident*) exaggeration

**gonfler** [gɔ̃fle] <1> **I.** *vt* (*pneus*) to inflate; (*ballon*) to blow up; (*voiles*) to fill **II.** *vi* to swell; (*pâte*) to rise **III.** *vpr* **se ~** (*poitrine*) to expand; (*voiles*) to fill

**gonzesse** [gɔ̃zɛs] *f péj, inf* chick

**gorge** [gɔʀʒ] *f* ❶ (*partie du cou*) throat ❷ GEO gorge

**gorgée** [gɔʀʒe] *f* mouthful

**gorille** [gɔʀij] *m* gorilla

**gosier** [gozje] *m* throat

**gosse** [gɔs] *mf inf* kid; **sale ~** brat

**gothique** [gɔtik] **I.** *adj* Gothic **II.** *m* Gothic

**gouda** [guda] *m* gouda

**goudron** [gudʀɔ̃] *m* tar

**goudronné(e)** [gudʀɔne] *adj* tarred

**gouffre** [gufʀ] *m* ❶ (*abîme*) abyss ❷ (*chose ruineuse*) bottomless pit

**goulache** [gulaʃ] *m o f* goulash

**goulet** [gulɛ] *m* **~ d'étranglement** bottleneck

**goulot** [gulo] *m* ❶ (*col d'une bouteille*) neck; **boire au ~** to drink from the bottle ❷ (*goulet*) **~ d'étranglement** bottleneck

**goulu(e)** [guly] *adj* greedy

**goulûment** [gulymɑ̃] *adv* greedily

**gourde** [guʀd] *f* ❶ (*bouteille*) flask ❷ *inf* (*personne*) clot

**gourmand(e)** [guʀmɑ̃, ɑ̃d] **I.** *adj* **être ~** to be greedy **II.** *m(f)* gourmand; (*de sucreries*) a person with a sweet tooth

**gourmandise** [guʀmɑ̃diz] *f* fondness for good food; (*défaut*) greediness

**gourmet** [guʀmɛ] *m* gourmet

**gousse** [gus] *f* **~ de vanille** vanilla pod; **~ d'ail** garlic clove

**goût** [gu] *m* ❶ *sans pl* (*sens, saveur, jugement*) taste; **avoir bon ~** (*plat*) to taste good; (*personne*) to have good taste; **être de mauvais ~** to be in bad taste; **avec ~** tastefully ❷ *sans pl* (*envie*) inclination; **prendre ~ à qc** to get a taste for sth ❸ *sans pl* (*penchant*) **~ pour les maths** gift for math ❹ *pl* (*préférences*) taste ❺ (*avis*) **à mon ~** in my opinion

**goûter** [gute] <1> **I.** *vi* ❶ (*prendre le goûter: enfant*) to have an afternoon snack ❷ (*essayer*) **~ à qc** to try sth ❸ (*toucher*) **~ aux plaisirs de la vie** to sample life's pleasures ❹ *Belgique, Québec* (*plaire par le goût*) to be tasty **II.** *vt* ❶ (*essayer*) to try ❷ (*savourer*) to savor ❸ *Belgique, Québec* (*avoir le goût de*) **~ qc** to taste of sth **III.** *m* afternoon snack

**goutte** [gut] *f* drop; **~ à ~** drop by drop ▶ **se ressembler comme deux ~s d'eau** to be like two peas in a pod

**goutte-à-goutte** [gutagut] *m inv* drip
**goutter** [gute] <1> *vi* to drip; (*canalisation*) to leak
**gouttière** [gutjɛʀ] *f* gutter
**gouvernail** [guvɛʀnaj] *m* ① (*barre*) helm ② *fig* **tenir le ~** to be at the helm
**gouvernement** [guvɛʀnəmã] *m* government
**gouvernemental(e)** [guvɛʀnəmãtal, -o] <-aux> *adj* (*journal*) pro-government; (*parti, politique*) governing
**gouverner** [guvɛʀne] <1> I. *vi* to govern II. *vt* ① (*diriger*) to govern ② (*maîtriser*) to control
**gouverneur** [guvɛʀnœʀ] *m* governor
**G.P.L.** [ʒepeɛl] *m abr de* **gaz de pétrole liquéfié** L.P.G.
**G.R.** [ʒeɛʀ] *m abr de* (**sentier de**) **grande randonnée** main hiking trail
**grâce** [gʀɑs] *f* ① *sans pl* (*charme*) grace; **avec ~** gracefully; (*parler*) charmingly ② *sans pl* (*faveur*) favor ③ *sans pl* (*clémence*) mercy ④ JUR pardon ▸ **~ à qn/qc** thanks to sb/sth
**gracier** [gʀasje] <1> *vt* to pardon
**gracieusement** [gʀasjøzmã] *adv* ① (*charmant*) charmingly ② (*gratuitement*) free of charge
**gracieux, -euse** [gʀasjø, -jøz] *adj* ① (*charmant*) charming ② (*aimable*) kindly ③ (*gratuit*) free of charge
**gradation** [gʀadasjɔ̃] *f* gradation
**grade** [gʀad] *m* grade; UNIV status; (*de capitaine*) rank; **monter en ~** to be promoted
**gradé(e)** [gʀade] *m(f)* officer
**gradins** [gʀadɛ̃] *mpl* terraces
**graduation** [gʀaduasjɔ̃] *f* gradation
**graduel(le)** [gʀaduɛl] *adj* gradual
**graduer** [gʀadue] <1> *vt* ① (*augmenter graduellement*) to increase in difficulty ② (*diviser en degrés*) to graduate
**graffiti** [gʀafiti] <(s)> *m* graffiti
**grain** [gʀɛ̃] *m* ① *sing o pl* (*petite chose arrondie*) spot ~ **de beauté** beauty spot ② (*graine*) grain; (*d'une grenade*) seed; ~ **de café** coffee bean; ~ **de raisin** grape ③ (*particule*) speck ④ (*texture*) texture; (*d'un cuir*) grain ⑤ *sans pl* (*petite quantité*) touch ⑥ MÉTÉO heavy shower

**graine** [gʀɛn] *f* seed
**graisse** [gʀɛs] *f* ① (*matière grasse*) fat ② (*lubrifiant*) grease
**graisser** [gʀese] <1> *vt* to grease
**graisseux, -euse** [gʀesø, -øz] *adj* greasy; (*cahier, nappe*) grease-stained
**grammaire** [gʀa(m)mɛʀ] *f* grammar
**grammatical(e)** [gʀamatikal, -o] <-aux> *adj* (*analyse*) grammatical; (*exercice*) grammar
**gramme** [gʀam] *m* gram
**grand(e)** [gʀã, ãd] I. *adj* ① (*dont la taille dépasse la moyenne*) big; (*arbre*) tall; (*jambe, avenue*) long; (*format, entreprise*) large; ~ **magasin** department store ② (*extrême, fameux*) great; (*buveur, fumeur*) heavy; (*travailleur*) hard; (*collectionneur*) great ③ (*intense*) great; (*bruit, cri*) loud; (*vent*) strong; (*coup*) hard; (*soupir*) heavy ④ (*respectable: dame, monsieur*) great; ~**es écoles** France's prestigious graduate level schools ⑤ (*généreux: sentiment*) noble ⑥ (*exagéré: mots*) big; (*gestes*) sweeping; **prendre de ~s airs** to take on airs II. *adv* **voir** ~ to see things on a large scale III. *m(f)* ① (*personne/objet grands*) big person/thing ② (*personne importante*) **un ~ du football** a soccer legend
**grand-angle** [gʀãtãgl] <grands-angles> *m* wide-angle lens
**grand-chose** [gʀãʃoz] **pas** ~ not much
**Grande-Bretagne** [gʀãdbʀətaɲ] *f* **la ~** Great Britain
**grandeur** [gʀãdœʀ] *f* ① (*dimension*) size; **de même** ~ of the same size ② (*puissance*) greatness ③ (*générosité*) generosity
**grandiose** [gʀãdjoz] *adj* imposing
**grandir** [gʀãdiʀ] <8> I. *vi* ① (*devenir plus grand*) to grow; ~ **de dix centimètres** to grow ten centimeters ② (*devenir plus mûr*) to grow up ③ (*augmenter*) to increase; (*foule*) to get bigger ④ *fig* **sortir grandi de qc** to come out of sth a better person

**II.** *vt* ❶ (*rendre plus grand: personne*) to make taller; (*chose*) to make bigger ❷ (*ennoblir*) **qc grandit qn** sth makes sb a better person **III.** *vpr* ❶ (*se rendre plus grand*) **se ~** to get bigger ❷ (*s'élever*) **se ~ par qc** to grow up through sth

**grand-mère** [gʀɑ̃mɛʀ] <grands-mères> *f* grandmother

**grand-peine** [gʀɑ̃pɛn] **avoir ~ à faire qc** to have great difficulty in doing sth

**grand-père** [gʀɑ̃pɛʀ] <grands-pères> *m* grandfather

**grands-parents** [gʀɑ̃paʀɑ̃] *mpl* grandparents

**grange** [gʀɑ̃ʒ] *f* barn

**granule** [gʀanyle] *m* granule

**granulé(e)** [gʀanyle] *adj* granular

**granuleux, -euse** [gʀanylø, -øz] *adj* granular; (*cuir*) textured; (*peau, roche*) grainy

**graphique** [gʀafik] **I.** *adj* graphic **II.** *m* graph

**graphisme** [gʀafism] *m* ❶ (*écriture*) handwriting ❷ (*aspect d'une lettre*) script ❸ ART graphics; (*d'un artiste*) drawing style

**graphiste** [gʀafist] *mf* graphic designer

**graphite** [gʀafit] *m* graphite

**graphologue** [gʀafɔlɔg] *mf* graphologist

**grappe** [gʀap] *f* cluster; **~ de raisin** bunch of grapes

**gras** [gʀɑ] **I.** *m* ❶ CULIN fat ❷ (*graisse*) grease ❸ (*partie charnue de la jambe*) fleshy part **II.** *adv* coarsely

**gras(se)** [gʀɑ, gʀɑs] *adj* ❶ (*formé de graisse*) fatty; **40% de matières ~ses** 40% fat ❷ (*gros*) fat ❸ (*graisseux*) greasy; (*chaussée*) slippery; (*terre, boue*) slimy ❹ (*imprimé*) **en (caractère) ~** bold ❺ BOT **plante ~se** succulent ❻ (*épais: voix*) deep; (*rire*) throaty; (*toux*) loose

**grassement** [gʀɑsmɑ̃] *adv* (*payer*) generously

**gratification** [gʀatifikasjɔ̃] *f* bonus

**gratifier** [gʀatifje] <1> *vt* **~ qn d'une récompense** to give sb a reward

**gratin** [gʀatɛ̃] *m* ❶ CULIN gratin ❷ *sans pl, inf* (*haute société*) upper crust

**gratiné(e)** [gʀatine] *adj* ❶ CULIN au gratin ❷ *inf* (*extraordinaire: raclée*) harsh; (*aventure*) wild

**gratiner** [gʀatine] <1> **I.** *vi* to brown **II.** *vt* (**faire**) **~ qc** to brown sth under the broiler

**gratis** [gʀatis] *adj, adv inf* free

**gratitude** [gʀatityd] *f* gratitude

**gratte-ciel** [gʀatsjɛl] *m inv* skyscraper

**grattement** [gʀatmɑ̃] *m* scratching

**gratter** [gʀate] <1> **I.** *vi* ❶ (*racler*) to scratch ❷ (*récurer*) to scrape off ❸ (*démanger*) to itch **II.** *vt* (*racler*) to scratch; (*mur, table, carottes, sol*) to scrape; (*allumette*) to strike **III.** *vpr* **se ~ qc** to scratch sth

**gratuit(e)** [gʀatɥi, ɥit] *adj* ❶ (*gratis*) free ❷ (*arbitraire: affirmation, supposition*) unwarranted; (*accusation*) unfounded; (*acte*) unmotivated; (*cruauté*) gratuitous

**gratuitement** [gʀatɥitmɑ̃] *adv* ❶ (*gratis*) free ❷ (*sans motif: affirmer*) wantonly; (*agir*) without motivation; (*commettre un crime*) gratuitously

**gravats** [gʀava] *mpl* rubble

**grave** [gʀav] **I.** *adj* ❶ (*sérieux*) serious; (*nouvelles*) bad; **ce n'est pas ~** it doesn't matter ❷ (*digne: assemblée*) solemn ❸ LING **accent ~** grave accent ❹ (*profond*) low; (*voix a.*) deep **II.** *m* **les ~s et les aigus** the low and the high registers

**gravement** [gʀavmɑ̃] *adv* ❶ (*dignement*) gravely; (*marcher*) solemnly ❷ (*fortement*) seriously

**graver** [gʀave] <1> **I.** *vt* ❶ (*tracer en creux*) to engrave **qc sur/dans qc** to engrave sth on/in sth ❷ (*à l'eau-forte*) **~ qc sur cuivre/sur bois** to etch sth on copper/wood ❸ (*fixer*) **~ qc dans sa mémoire** to imprint sth into one's memory ❹ INFORM to burn **II.** *vpr* **se ~ dans la mémoire de qn** to be engraved into sb's memory

**graveur** [gʀavœʀ] *m* INFORM burner; **~ de CD-ROM/DVD** CD-ROM/DVD writer

**G**

**graveur, -euse** [gravœr, -øz] *m, f* ART engraver

**gravier** [gravje] *m* gravel

**gravillon** [gravijɔ̃] *m* bit of gravel

**gravir** [gravir] <8> *vt* to climb

**gravitation** [gravitasjɔ̃] *f* gravitation

**gravité** [gravite] *f* ❶ (*sévérité*) solemnity; **avec ~** seriously; (*regarder*) solemnly ❷ (*importance: d'une situation*) seriousness; (*d'une catastrophe, sanction, d'un problème*) gravity ❸ PHYS gravity

**graviter** [gravite] <1> *vi* **~ autour de qn/qc** to revolve around sb/sth

**gravure** [gravyr] *f* ❶ *sans pl* (*technique*) engraving; (*à l'eau-forte*) etching ❷ (*œuvre*) engraving; (*sur cuivre*) copperplate engraving; (*sur bois*) woodcutting; (*à l'eau-forte*) etching ❸ (*reproduction*) plate

**gré** [gre] **de bon ~** willingly; **de mon/son plein ~** of my/his own free will; <u>au</u> **~ de qn** (*de l'avis de*) according to sb's opinion; (*selon les désirs de*) according to sb's wishes

**grec** [grɛk] *m* **le ~ ancien/moderne** ancient/modern Greek; *v.a.* **français**

**grec, grecque** [grɛk] *adj* Greek

**Grec, Grecque** [grɛk] *m, f* Greek

**Grèce** [grɛs] *f* **la ~** Greece

**gréco-romain(e)** [grekorɔmɛ̃, ɛn] <gréco-romains> *adj* Greco-Roman

**greffe** [grɛf] *f* ❶ MED transplant ❷ BOT grafting; (*greffon*) graft

**greffier, -ière** [grefje, -jɛr] *m, f* clerk of the court

**grêle** [grɛl] **I.** *adj* spindly; (*apparence*) lanky; (*son, voix*) thin **II.** *f* hail

**grêler** [grele] <1> *vi impers* **il grêle** it is hailing

**grelotter** [grɛlɔte] <1> *vi* **~ de fièvre** to shiver with fever

**grenade** [grənad] *f* ❶ MIL grenade ❷ BOT pomegranate

**grenadine** [grənadin] *f* grenadine

**grenat** [grəna] *adj inv* dark red

**grenier** [grənje] *m* (*d'une maison*) attic; (*d'une ferme*) loft

**grenouille** [grənuj] *f* ❶ (*rainette*) frog ❷ *fig, inf* **~ de bénitier** Holy Roller

**grès** [grɛ] *m* ❶ (*roche*) sandstone ❷ (*poterie*) stoneware

**grésil** [grezil] *m* fine hail

**grésillement** [grezijmɑ̃] *m* crackling; (*de la friture*) sizzling

**grésiller** [grezije] <1> *vi* to sizzle

**grève** [grɛv] *f* strike; **~ sur le tas/de la faim** sit-down/hunger strike; **être en ~, faire ~** to be on strike

**gréviste** [grevist] *mf* striker

**gribouiller** [gribuje] <1> *vt, vi* to scribble

**grief** [grijɛf] *m* **avoir des ~s contre qn** to have grievances against sb

**grièvement** [grijɛvmɑ̃] *adv* seriously

**griffe** [grif] *f* ❶ (*ongle pointu*) claw ❷ (*marque*) stamp ❸ (*signature*) signature ❹ *Belgique* (*égratignure, éraflure*) scratch ▸ **porter la ~ de qn** to carry the stamp of sb; **tomber entre les ~s de qn** to fall into sb's clutches

**griffé(e)** [grife] *adj* (*vêtement*) designer

**griffer** [grife] <1> *vt* to scratch

**griffonner** [grifɔne] <1> *vt, vi* to scribble

**griffure** [grifyr] *f* scratch

**grignoter** [griɲɔte] <1> **I.** *vi* (*personne*) to nibble; (*animal*) to gnaw **II.** *vt* ❶ (*manger du bout des dents*) **~ qc** (*personne*) to nibble sth; (*animal*) to gnaw at sth; (*entièrement*) to eat away at sth ❷ (*restreindre: capital, libertés*) to erode; (*espaces*) to eat away at

**gril** [gril] *m* griddle

**grillade** [grijad] *f* grill; **faire des ~s** to grill some meat

**grillage** [grija3] *m* ❶ (*treillis métallique*) wire netting ❷ (*clôture*) wire fencing

**grille** [grij] *f* ❶ (*clôture*) railings ❷ (*porte*) gate ❸ (*treillis*) grille; (*d'un château fort*) portcullis; (*d'un four*) grate ❹ (*tableau*) **~ d'horaires** schedule; **~ de mots croisés** crossword puzzle

**grille-pain** [grijpɛ̃] *m inv* toaster

**griller** [grije] <1> **I.** *vi* ❶ (*cuire: viande, poisson*) to grill; (*pain*) to toast; **faire ~**

to grill; (*café, châtaignes*) to roast; (*pain*) to toast ② *inf* (*avoir chaud*) to boil II. *vt* ① (*faire cuire*) to cook; (*café, châtaignes*) to roast; (*pain*) to toast ② (*détruire*) ~ **qc** (*soleil, feu*) to burn sth ③ ELEC **être grillé** to have blown ④ (*brûler: feu rouge*) to run ⑤ *inf* (*fumer*) to smoke

**grillon** [gʀijɔ̃] *m* cricket

**grimace** [gʀimas] *f* grimace; **faire des ~s** to make funny faces

**grimacer** [gʀimase] <2> *vi* to grimace

**grimpant(e)** [gʀɛ̃pɑ̃, ɑ̃t] *adj* **rosier ~** climbing rose

**grimper** [gʀɛ̃pe] <1> I. *vi* ① (*escalader, monter*) ~ **sur le toit/à** [*o* **dans**] **l'arbre/à l'échelle** to climb on the roof/up the tree/up the ladder ② (*augmenter*) to soar II. *vt* (*escalier*) to climb

**grimpeur, -euse** [gʀɛ̃pœʀ, -øz] *m, f* ① (*alpiniste*) climber ② (*cycliste*) hill specialist

**grinçant(e)** [gʀɛ̃sɑ̃, ɑ̃t] *adj* (*ton*) squeaky; (*humour*) darkly humorous

**grincement** [gʀɛ̃smɑ̃] *m* (*d'une roue, porte*) squeaking; (*de dents*) grinding

**grincer** [gʀɛ̃se] <2> *vi* to grate; (*parquet*) to creak; (*craie*) to scrape

**grippe** [gʀip] *f* flu; ~ **aviaire** bird flu ▶ **prendre qn en ~** to take a dislike to sb

**grippé(e)** [gʀipe] *adj* flu-ridden; **être ~** to have the flu

**gripper** [gʀipe] <1> *vi, vpr* (**se**) ~ to jam; (*moteur, système*) to seize up

**gris-vert** [gʀivɛʀ] *adj inv* green-gray

**gris(e)** [gʀi, gʀiz] *adj* gray

**grisaille** [gʀizɑj] *f* ① (*monotonie*) dullness; (*de la vie quotidienne*) monotony ② (*caractère terne: de l'aube, du paysage*) grayness

**grisant(e)** [gʀizɑ̃, ɑ̃t] *adj* (*succès*) exhilarating; (*parfum, vin*) intoxicating

**grisâtre** [gʀizɑtʀ] *adj* grayish

**gris-bleu** [gʀiblø] *adj inv* blue-gray

**grisé** [gʀize] *m* gray tint

**griser** [gʀize] <1> I. *vt, vi* to intoxicate; (*flatteries, succès, bonheur*) to overwhelm II. *vpr* (*s'étourdir*) **se ~ de qc** to get drunk on sth

**grisonnant(e)** [gʀizɔnɑ̃, ɑ̃t] *adj* graying

**Grisons** [gʀizɔ̃] *mpl* **les ~** the Graubünden (*Swiss canton*)

**gris-vert** [gʀivɛʀ] *adj inv* green-gray

**grive** [gʀiv] *f* thrush

**grognement** [gʀɔɲmɑ̃] *m* (*du cochon*) grunting; (*de l'ours, du chien*) growl; (*d'une personne*) grunt

**grogner** [gʀɔɲe] <1> *vi* ① (*pousser son cri: chien, ours*) to growl; (*cochon*) to grunt ② (*ronchonner*) ~ **contre** [*o* **après**] **qn** to grumble about sb

**grognon(ne)** [gʀɔɲɔ̃, ɔn] *adj* grumpy; (*enfant*) grouchy

**groin** [gʀwɛ̃] *m* (*du porc*) snout

**grommeler** [gʀɔmle] <3> I. *vi* to mutter II. *vt* ~ **des injures contre qn** to mutter insults about sb

**grondement** [gʀɔ̃dmɑ̃] *m* (*d'un canon, du tonnerre*) rumbling; (*d'un torrent, d'un moteur*) roar; (*d'un chien*) growl

**gronder** [gʀɔ̃de] <1> I. *vi* ① (*émettre un son menaçant*) to roar; (*canon*) to rumble; (*chien*) to growl ② (*être près d'éclater: révolte*) to brew II. *vt* to scold

**groom** [gʀum] *m* bellboy

**gros** [gʀo] I. *m* ① COM bulk; **commerçant en ~** wholesale merchant; **prix de ~** wholesale price ② (*la plus grande partie*) **le ~ du travail** the bulk of the work ▶ **en ~** COM in bulk; (*à peu près*) more or less; (*dans l'ensemble*) on the whole II. *adv* ① (*beaucoup*) a lot; (*jouer, parier*) for high stakes ② (*grand-écrire*) big

**gros(se)** [gʀo, gʀos] I. *adj* ① (*épais*) thick; (*manteau, couverture*) heavy; (*poitrine, lèvres*) big; (*foie*) enlarged ② (*de taille supérieure*) big ③ (*corpulent*) fat ④ (*intense: fièvre*) high; (*sécheresse*) serious; (*appétit*) large; (*soupir, averse*) heavy; (*voix*) loud; (*bises*) big ⑤ (*important: dépenses, dégâts*) heavy; (*client*) important; (*faute, opération*) big; (*récolte*) large ⑥ (*extrême: buveur, mangeur*) big; (*joueur*) heavy; (*fainéant*) great ⑦ (*peu raffiné*) crude ⑧ (*exagéré: histoire*) exaggerated

**⑨**(*pénible: travaux*) difficult **II.** *m(f)* fat person

**groseille** [gʀozɛj] *f* currant

**grossesse** [gʀosɛs] *f* pregnancy

**grosseur** [gʀosœʀ] *f* ❶(*dimension*) size; (*d'un fil*) thickness ❷(*boule*) lump

**grossier, -ière** [gʀosje, -jɛʀ] *adj* ❶(*imparfait: instrument*) crude; (*réparation*) superficial; (*imitation*) poor; (*manières, mensonge*) bad; (*personne*) crass; (*ruse, plaisanterie*) unsubtle; (*erreur*) stupid ❷(*malpoli: personne*) rude ❸ *postposé*(*vulgaire*) vulgar

**grossièrement** [gʀosjɛʀmɑ̃] *adv* ❶(*de façon imparfaite*) crudely; (*emballer, réparer, exécuter, imiter*) clumsily; (*se tromper*) grossly; (*calculer*) roughly ❷(*de façon impolie*) impolitely; (*répondre*) rudely; (*insulter*) grossly

**grossièreté** [gʀosjɛʀte] *f* ❶ *sans pl* (*qualité*) coarseness ❷(*remarque*) coarse comment

**grossir** [gʀosiʀ] <8> **I.** *vi* ❶(*devenir plus gros: personne, animal*) to become fatter; (*point, nuage*) to get bigger; (*fruit*) to swell; (*ganglions, tumeur*) to grow ❷(*augmenter en nombre: foule, nombre*) to get bigger ❸(*augmenter en intensité: bruit faible*) to get louder **II.** *vt* ❶(*rendre plus gros*) to make fatter ❷(*augmenter en nombre: foule, nombre de chômeurs*) to swell; (*équipe*) to get bigger ❸(*exagérer: événement, fait*) to exaggerate

**grossissant(e)** [gʀosisɑ̃, ɑ̃t] *adj* ❶(*flot*) swelling; (*foule, nombre*) growing ❷(*qui fait paraître plus gros: miroir, verre*) enlarging

**grossiste** [gʀosist] *mf* wholesaler

**grosso modo** [gʀosomɔdo] *adv* more or less; (*expliquer, décrire*) in rough terms; (*calculer, estimer*) roughly

**grotesque** [gʀɔtɛsk] *adj* grotesque

**grotte** [gʀɔt] *f* cave

**grouiller** [gʀuje] <1> **I.** *vi* (*foule*) to mill around; **la place grouille de touristes** the square was teeming with tourists **II.** *vpr inf* **se ~** to hurry up

**groupe** [gʀup] *m* ❶group; **~ de rock** rock band; **~ sanguin** blood group [*o* type] ❷(*ensemble de choses*) **~ électrogène** generating set

**groupement** [gʀupmɑ̃] *m* **~ syndical/ professionnel** union/professional organization

**grouper** [gʀupe] <1> **I.** *vt* ❶(*réunir: personnes, objets, idées*) to group together; (*ressources*) to pool ❷(*classer*) to categorize **II.** *vpr* **se ~** to gather; (*personnes, partis*) to form a group; **se ~ autour de qn** to gather around sb

**gruau** [gʀyo] *m* groats *pl*

**grue** [gʀy] *f* crane

**gruger** [gʀyʒe] <2a> *vt* ❶(*duper*) to swindle ❷ *Québec* (*grignoter*) to nibble

**grumeau** [gʀymo] <x> *m* lump

**grutier, -ière** [gʀytje, -jɛʀ] *m, f* crane driver

**gruyère** [gʀyjɛʀ] *m* Gruyère cheese

**Guadeloupe** [gwadlup] *f* **la ~** Guadeloupe

**gué** [ge] *m* ford; **traverser à ~** to ford a river

**guenilles** [gənij] *fpl* rags

**guenon** [gənɔ̃] *f* female monkey; *v.a.* singe

**guépard** [gepaʀ] *m* cheetah

**guêpe** [gɛp] *f* wasp

**guêpier** [gepje] *m* wasps' nest ▸ **se fourrer dans un ~** to land oneself in trouble

**guère** [gɛʀ] *adv* ❶(*pas beaucoup*) **ne ~ manger** to hardly eat anything ❷(*pas souvent*) **cela ne se dit ~** that is not often said ❸(*pas longtemps*) **ça ne dure ~** it doesn't last long ❹(*seulement*) **je ne peux ~ demander qu'à mes parents** I can only ask my parents

**guérir** [geʀiʀ] <8> **I.** *vt* **~ qn de qc** to cure sb of sth **II.** *vi* to get better; (*plaie, blessure*) to heal; (*rhume*) to get better **III.** *vpr* ❶ MED **se ~** to be cured; (*tout seul*) to cure oneself ❷(*se débarrasser*) **se ~ de qc** to be cured of sth

**guérison** [geʀizɔ̃] *f* (*processus, résultat*) recovery; (*d'une blessure*) healing;

**être en voie de ~** to be on the road to recovery

**guérisseur, -euse** [gerisœr, -øz] *m, f* healer; (*rebouteux*) quack

**guerre** [gɛr] *f* ❶ (*lutte armée entre groupes/États*) war; **la Grande ~, la ~ de 14** the First World War, the Great War; **ministre de la ~** Minister for War ❷ *fig* **déclarer la ~ à qn** to declare war on sb; **faire la ~ à qc** to wage war on sth

**guerrier, -ière** [gɛrje, -jɛr] **I.** *adj* warlike **II.** *m, f* warrior

**guet** [gɛ] **faire le ~** to be on watch

**guet-apens** [gɛtapã] *m inv* ambush

**guetter** [gete] <1> *vt* ❶ (*épier*) to watch ❷ (*attendre: occasion, signal*) to watch for; (*personne*) to wait for ❸ (*menacer*) ~ **qn** (*maladie, danger, mort*) to threaten sb

**gueulante** [gœlãt] *f* **pousser une ~ contre qn** *inf* to shout one's head off at sb

**gueule** [gœl] *f* ❶ (*bouche d'un animal*) mouth ❷ *inf* (*figure*) face ❸ *inf* (*bouche humaine*) (**ferme**) **ta ~!** shut it! ▶ **casser la ~ à qn** *inf* to smash sb's face in; **se casser la ~** *inf* (*personne*) to fall flat on one's face; **faire la ~ à qn** *inf* to be in a bad mood with sb

**gueuler** [gœle] <1> **I.** *vi inf* ❶ (*crier*) to yell ❷ (*protester*) to kick up a fuss **II.** *vt inf* to bellow

**guichet** [giʃɛ] *m* counter

**guide** [gid] **I.** *mf* ❶ (*cicérone*) guide ❷ (*conseiller*) advisor **II.** *m* guidebook; **~ touristique/gastronomique** tourist/restaurant guide **III.** *fpl* reins

**guider** [gide] <1> *vt* ❶ (*indiquer le chemin, diriger, accompagner*) to guide ❷ (*conseiller*) to advise

**guidon** [gidɔ̃] *m* handlebars *pl*

**guignol** [giɲɔl] *m* puppet; **faire le ~** to clown around

**guillemets** [gijmɛ] *mpl* quotation marks; **entre ~** in quotation marks

**guillotine** [gijɔtin] *f* guillotine

**guindé(e)** [gɛ̃de] *adj* starchy

**Guinée** [gine] *f* **la ~** Guinea

**guinguette** [gɛ̃gɛt] *f* dance hall

**guirlande** [girlãd] *f* garland; **~ lumineuse** string of lights

**guise** [giz] **à ma/sa ~** as I like/he/she/it likes; **en ~ de** by way of

**guitare** [gitar] *f* guitar

**Guyane** [gɥijan] *f* **la ~** Guiana

**gym** [ʒim] *f inf abr de* **gymnastique**

**gymnase** [ʒimnɑz] *m* ❶ (*halle*) gymnasium ❷ *Suisse* (*école secondaire, lycée*) secondary school

**gymnastique** [ʒimnastik] *f* gymnastics + *vb sing*

**gynécologie** [ʒinekɔlɔʒi] *f* gynecology

**gynécologue** [ʒinekɔlɔg] *mf* gynecologist

**gyrophare** [ʒirofar] *m* revolving light

G

# Hh

**H, h** [aʃ, ´aʃ] *m inv* H, h; **~ comme Henri** (*au téléphone*) h as in Hotel

**h** *abr de* **heure**

**ha** [´a] *abr de* **hectare** ha

**habile** [abil] *adj* ❶ (*adroit: personne, mains*) skillful ❷ (*malin*) clever

**habileté** [abilte] *f* ❶ *sans pl* (*adresse*) skill ❷ (*ruse*) trick

**habiliter** [abilite] <1> *vt* JUR to authorize

**habillé(e)** [abije] *adj* ❶ (*vêtu: personne*) dressed ❷ (*de fête: vêtement*) smart

**habillement** [abijmɑ̃] *m* (*ensemble des vêtements*) clothing

**habiller** [abije] <1> **I.** *vt* ❶ (*vêtir*) to dress ❷ (*déguiser*) **~ qn en qc** to dress sb up as sth ❸ (*fournir en vêtements*) to clothe ❹ (*recouvrir, décorer*) to cover **II.** *vpr* ❶ (*se vêtir*) **s'~** to dress (oneself); (*mettre des vêtements de cérémonie*) to dress up ❷ (*se déguiser*) **s'~ en fée/homme** to dress up as a fairy/a man ❸ (*acheter ses vêtements*) **s'~ de neuf** to buy new clothes

**habit** [abi] *m* ❶ *pl* (*vêtements*) clothes *pl* ❷ (*costume de fête*) dress; (*de fée, de soldat*) costume ❸ (*uniforme*) dress

**habitable** [abitabl] *adj* (in)habitable

**habitacle** [abitakl] *m* ❶ AUTO (*de voiture*) passenger compartment ❷ (*poste de pilotage: de petit avion, d'avion de chasse*) cockpit; (*d'avion de ligne*) flight deck

**habitant(e)** [abitɑ̃, ɑ̃t] *m(f)* ❶ (*occupant: d'un pays, d'une ville*) resident, inhabitant; (*d'un immeuble, d'une maison*) occupant ❷ *Québec* (*paysan*) farmer

**habitat** [abita] *m* ❶ BOT, ZOOL habitat ❷ GEO settlement ❸ (*conditions de logement*) housing conditions

**habitation** [abitasjɔ̃] *f* ❶ (*demeure*) home ❷ (*logis*) house; **~ à loyer modéré** public housing unit

**habiter** [abite] <1> **I.** *vi* to live; **~ à la campagne/en ville/à Bordeaux** to live in the country/in town/in Bordeaux **II.** *vt* ❶ (*occuper*) **~ une maison/caravane** to live in a house/a trailer; GEO (*île, région*) to inhabit; **~ (le) 17, rue Leblanc** to live at (number) 17, rue Leblanc ❷ *fig, soutenu* **~ qn/qc** (*passion, sentiment*) to abide in sb/sth

**habitude** [abityd] *f* ❶ (*pratique*) habit; **avoir l'~ de qc** to get used to sth; (*s'y connaître*) to be used to sth; **avoir l'~ de faire qc** to be in the habit of doing sth; **d'~** usually ❷ (*coutume*) custom

**habitué(e)** [abitye] *m(f)* (*d'un magasin, restaurant*) regular (customer)

**habituel(le)** [abityɛl] *adj* usual

**habituer** [abitye] <1> **I.** *vt* ❶ (*accoutumer*) **~ qn/un animal à qc** to get sb/an animal used to sth ❷ (*avoir l'habitude*) **être habitué à qc** to be used to sth **II.** *vpr* **s'~ à qn/qc** to get used to sb/sth

**hache** [´aʃ] *f* (*à manche long*) ax; (*à manche court*) hatchet

**haché(e)** [´aʃe] *adj* ❶ (*coupé menu: fines herbes, légume*) chopped; (*viande*) ground ❷ (*entrecoupé*) jerky

**hacher** [´aʃe] <1> *vt* ❶ (*couper: fines herbes, légumes*) to chop; (*viande*) to grind ❷ (*entrecouper: phrase, discours*) to interrupt

**hachis** [´aʃi] *m* ❶ (*chair à saucisse*) hamburger (meat), ground meat ❷ (*plat*) **~ de légumes** chopped vegetables

**hachoir** [´aʃwaʀ] *m* ❶ (*couteau*) cleaver; (*avec lame courbe*) chopping knife ❷ (*machine*) **~ à viande** meat grinder

**hachurer** [´aʃyʀe] <1> *vt* (*diagramme, chaussée*) to hatch

**hachures** [´aʃyʀ] *fpl* (*d'un diagramme, de la chaussée*) hatching

**hagard(e)** [´agaʀ, aʀd] *adj* wild

**haie** [´ɛ] f ❶ (*clôture*) hedge ❷ SPORT hurdle; (*équitation*) fence ❸ (*rangée: de personnes*) row

**haine** [´ɛn] f hatred

**haineux, -euse** [´ɛnø, -øz] adj ❶ (*plein de haine*) full of hatred ❷ (*plein de méchanceté*) malevolent

**haïr** [´aiʀ] vt irr to hate

**hâle** [´ɑl] m tan

**hâlé(e)** [´ale] adj (sun)tanned

**haleine** [alɛn] f sans pl (*souffle*) breath
► **travail de longue ~** long and demanding job

**haletant(e)** [´al(ə)tã, ãt] adj (*personne, animal, respiration*) panting

**haleter** [´al(a)te] <4> vt to pant

**hall** [´ol] m (*d'immeuble*) (entrance) hall; (*d'hôtel*) foyer; (*de gare*) concourse

**halle** [´al] f ❶ (*partie d'un marché*) covered market ❷ HIST **les Halles** *former central food market in Paris* ❸ Suisse **~ de gymnastique** (*gymnase*) gym(nasium)

**hallucinant(e)** [a(l)lysinã, ãt] adj staggering, incredible

**hallucination** [a(l)lysinasjɔ̃] f MED hallucination

**halluciner** [alysine] <1> vi inf **j'hallucine!** I'm seeing things!

**halogène** [alɔʒɛn] I. m CHIM halogen II. app halogen

**halte** [´alt] I. f ❶ (*pause*) stop; (*repos*) break ❷ CHEMDFER halt II. interj ~! stop!

**haltère** [altɛʀ] m dumbbell

**hamac** [´amak] m hammock

**hamburger** [´ãbuʀɡœʀ, ´ãbœʀɡœʀ] m CULIN hamburger

**hameau** [´amo] <x> m hamlet

**hameçon** [amsɔ̃] m fishhook

**hamster** [´amstɛʀ] m ZOOL hamster

**han** [´ã] I. m grunt II. interj ~! oof!

**hanche** [´ãʃ] f ANAT hip

**handball, hand-ball** [´ãdbal] m sans pl SPORT handball

**handballeur, -euse** [´ãdbalœʀ, -øz] m, f SPORT handball player

**handicap** [´()ãdikap] m handicap

**handicapé(e)** [´ãdikape] I. adj handi-

capped II. m(f) MED disabled person; **~ physique** physically disabled person

**handicaper** [´ãdikape] <1> vt to handicap

**hangar** [´ãɡaʀ] m ❶ AGR, CHEMDFER shed ❷ (*entrepôt*) warehouse ❸ AVIAT **~ à avions** aircraft hangar ❹ NAUT **~ à bateaux** boathouse ❺ Québec (*abri de bois pour le chauffage*) wood shed

**hanneton** [´an(ə)tɔ̃] m ZOOL (*en Amérique du Nord*) June beetle [o bug]; (*en Europe*) cockchafer

**hanter** [ãte] <1> vt ❶ (*fréquenter*) to haunt ❷ (*obséder*) **~ qn** (*idée, souvenir*) to haunt sb

**happer** [´ape] <1> vt ❶ (*saisir brusquement*) **~ qn/qc** (*train, voiture*) to hit sb/sth ❷ (*attraper*) **~ qc** (*animal, oiseau*) to snap sth up

**haras** [´aʀɑ] m stud farm

**harassant(e)** [aʀasã, ãt] adj exhausting

**harcèlement** [´aʀsɛlmã] m ❶ MIL **guerre de ~** war of harassment ❷ (*tracasserie*) harassment

**harceler** [´aʀsəle] <4> vt ❶ a. MIL to harass, to harry; (*poursuivre*) to pursue ❷ (*importuner*) to harass, to plague

**hardware** [´aʀdwɛʀ] m INFORM hardware

**harem** [´aʀɛm] m harem

**hareng** [´aʀã] m ❶ (*poisson*) herring ❷ CULIN **~ saur** smoked herring

**hargne** [´aʀɲ] f ❶ (*comportement agressif*) aggressiveness ❷ (*méchanceté*) spite

**hargneux, -euse** [´aʀɲø, -øz] adj ❶ (*agressif: personne, caractère, ton*) bad-tempered; (*chien*) vicious ❷ (*méchant*) spiteful

**haricot** [´aʀiko] m (*légume*) bean

**harmonica** [aʀmɔnika] m MUS harmonica

**harmonie** [aʀmɔni] f a. MUS harmony

**harmonieux, -euse** [aʀmɔnjø, -jøz] adj harmonious; (*instrument, voix*) melodious

**harmonisation** [aʀmɔnizasjɔ̃] f harmonization

**harmoniser** [aʀmɔnize] <1> I. *vt* to harmonize II. *vpr* s'~ to harmonize

**harnacher** [´aʀnaʃe] <1> *vt* (*mettre le harnais à: animal*) to harness

**harnais** [´aʀnɛ] *m* ❶ (*équipement: d'un cheval*) harness ❷ (*sangles: d'un pilote*) harness; (*d'un plongeur*) gear

**harpe** [´aʀp] *f* MUS harp

**harpon** [´aʀpɔ̃] *m* harpoon

**hasard** [´azaʀ] *m* ❶ (*évènement fortuit, fatalité*) chance ❷ *pl* (*aléas, risque*) les ~s de la guerre the hazards of war ▶ à **tout** ~ just in case; **au** ~ at random; **par** ~ (*se rencontrer*) by chance; (*laisser tomber un verre*) by accident

**hasarder** [´azaʀde] <1> I. *vt* (*tenter, avancer: démarche, remarque, question*) to hazard II. *vpr* ❶ (*s'aventurer*) se ~ dans un quartier/la rue to venture (out) into a district/the street ▶ à (*risquer à*) se ~ à faire qc to risk doing sth

**hasardeux, -euse** [´azaʀdø, -øz] *adj* ❶ hazardous; (*affirmation*) rash

**hasch** [´aʃ] *m abr de* **haschich** *inf* hash

**haschich, haschisch** [´aʃiʃ] *m* hashish

**hâte** [´at] *f* haste

**hâter** [´ate] <1> I. *vt* to hasten II. *vpr* se ~ to hurry

**hâtif, -ive** [´atif, -iv] *adj* ❶ (*trop rapide: décision, réponse*) hasty; (*travail*) hurried ❷ (*précoce: croissance, développement*) precocious; (*fruit, légume*) early

**hausse** [´os] *f* ❶ (*action: des prix, salaires*) increase ❷ (*processus*) rise; **être en nette** ~ to be rising sharply ❸ FIN **jouer à la** ~ to speculate on a rising market

**haussement** [´osmã] *m* ~ d'épaules shrug (of the shoulders)

**hausser** [´ose] <1> I. *vt* ❶ (*surélever: mur*) to raise ❷ (*amplifier*) ~ le ton [*o* la voix] to raise one's voice ❸ (*augmenter: prix*) to raise ❹ (*soulever: sourcils*) to raise; ~ les épaules to shrug (one's shoulders) II. *vpr* se ~ sur la pointe des pieds to stand (up) on tip-toe

**haut** [´o] I. *adv* ❶ (*opp: bas: sauter*) high ❷ (*ci-dessus*) voir plus ~ see above ❸ (*fort, franchement*) out loud ❹ (*à un haut degré*) viser trop ~ to aim too high ❺ MUS chanter trop ~ to sing sharp ▶ regarder [*o* traiter] qn de ~ to look down on sb; **en** ~ de at the top of II. *m* ❶ (*hauteur*) height; avoir un mètre de ~ to be one meter high ❷ (*altitude*) top; du ~ de ... from the top of ... ❸ (*sommet, opp: bas*) top; l'étagère du ~ the top shelf ▶ des ~s et des bas ups and downs

**haut(e)** [´o, ´ot] *adj* ❶ (*grand*) high; le plus ~ étage the top floor ❷ (*en position élevée: nuage*) high ❸ GÉO (*montagne, plateau*) high; (*région, Rhin*) upper; marée ~e high tide ❹ (*intense, fort*) a. ELEC high; à voix ~e out loud ❺ (*élevé: prix*) high ❻ (*supérieur: fonctionnaire*) senior ❼ (*très grand*) great

**hautain(e)** [´otɛ̃, ɛn] *adj* haughty

**hautbois** [´obwa] *m* MUS oboe

**haut-de-forme** [´od(ə)fɔʀm] *m inv* top hat

**haute-fidélité** [´otfidelite] <hautes-fidélités> I. *adj inv* (*chaîne*) hi-fi II. *f* hi-fi

**hautement** [´otmã] *adv* highly

**hauteur** [´otœʀ] *f* ❶ (*grandeur, altitude*) height; la ~ est de 3 mètres the height is 3 meters ❷ SPORT saut en ~ high jump ❸ (*même niveau*) à la ~ de qc (*au même niveau que*) (on a) level with sth; (*dans les environs de*) in the area of sth ❹ (*colline*) hill(top) ❺ (*noblesse*) loftiness ❻ (*arrogance*) haughtiness

**haut-le-cœur** [´ol(ə)kœʀ] *m inv* avoir un ~ to feel sick

**haut-parleur** [´opaʀlœʀ] <haut-parleurs> *m* loudspeaker

**Havane** [´avan] *f* la ~ Havana

**hé** [he, ´e] *interj* (*pour appeler*) hey!

**hebdo** *m inf v.* **hebdomadaire**

**hebdomadaire** [ɛbdɔmadɛʀ] I. *adj* (*réunion, revue*) weekly II. *m* (*journal, magazine*) weekly

**hébergement** [ebɛʀʒəmã] *m* lodging; (*d'un réfugié*) taking in

**héberger** [ebɛʁʒe] <2a> *vt* ❶ (*loger provisoirement: ami*) to put up ❷ (*accueillir: réfugié*) to take in
**hébété(e)** [ebete] *adj* dazed
**hébraïque** [ebʁaik] *adj* Hebrew
**hébreu** [ebʁø] <x> I. *adj féminin: israélite, juive* Hebrew II. *m* Hebrew; *v.a.* **français** ❷ *inf* **c'est de l'~** it's all Greek to me
**Hébreux** [ebʁø] *mpl* **les ~** the Hebrews
**HEC** [ˈaʃøse] *f abr de* (**école des**) **hautes études commerciales** *prestigious French business school*
**hectare** [ɛktaʁ] *m* hectare (*equal to 100 ares or 2.471 acres*)
**hectolitre** [ɛktɔlitʁ] *m* hectoliter (*equal to 100 liters*)
**hégémonie** [eʒemɔni] *f* hegemony
**hein** [ˈɛ̃] *interj inf* ❶ (*comment?*) huh ❷ (*renforcement de l'interrogation*) **que vas-tu faire, ~ ?** what are you going to do (then), eh? ❸ (*marque l'étonnement*) **~? qu'est-ce qui se passe?** hey, what's going on here? ❹ (*n'est-ce pas?*) **il fait froid, ~ ?** it's cold, isn't it?
**hélas** [elɑs] *interj soutenu* alas
**hélice** [elis] *f* ❶ TECH (*d'avion, de bateau*) propeller ❷ MATH helix
**hélicoptère** [elikɔptɛʁ] *m* helicopter
**héliport** [elipɔʁ] *m* heliport
**helvétique** [ɛlvetik] *adj* Swiss; **la Confédération ~** the Swiss Federal Republic
**hématome** [ematom] *m* MED bruise; (*sérieux*) hematoma
**hémicycle** [emisikl] *m* ❶ (*demi-cercle*) semicircle; (*d'un théâtre, parlement*) hemicycle ❷ (*salle d'une assemblée nationale*) **l'~** the chamber ❸ (*bancs d'une assemblée nationale*) **l'~** ≈ the House floor
**hémiplégique** [emipleʒik] *adj, mf* MED hemiplegic
**hémisphère** [emisfɛʁ] *m* GEO, ANAT hemisphere
**hémoglobine** [emɔglɔbin] *f* MED hemoglobin
**hémophile** [emɔfil] MED I. *adj* hemophilic II. *mf* hemophiliac

**hémophilie** [emɔfili] *f* MED hemophilia
**hémorragie** [emɔʁaʒi] *f* ❶ MED hemorrhage ❷ (*perte en hommes*) **~ démographique** hemorrhage of the population
**hémorroïde** [emɔʁɔid] *f gén pl* MED hemorrhoid
**henné** [ˈene] *m* (*arbuste, colorant*) henna
**hennir** [ˈeniʁ] <8> *vi* to neigh, to whinny
**hep** [ˈɛp, hɛp] *interj* hey!
**hépatite** [epatit] *f* MED **~ virale** viral hepatitis
**herbage** [ɛʁbaʒ] *m* (*herbe, pré*) pasture
**herbe** [ɛʁb] *f* ❶ BOT grass; **mauvaise ~** weed ❷ MED, CULIN herb; **fines ~s** mixed herbs
**herbicide** [ɛʁbisid] I. *adj* herbicidal II. *m* herbicide
**herboriser** [ɛʁbɔʁize] <1> *vi* to collect plants
**herboriste** [ɛʁbɔʁist] *mf* herbalist
**héréditaire** [eʁeditɛʁ] *adj* hereditary
**hérédité** [eʁedite] *f* ❶ BIO heredity ❷ JUR right of inheritance
**hérésie** [eʁezi] *f* heresy
**hérétique** [eʁetik] I. *adj* heretical II. *mf* heretic
**hérissé(e)** [ˈeʁise] *adj* ❶ (*dressé*) (standing) on end; (*barbe*) bristly ❷ (*piquant: cactus*) prickly
**hérisser** [ˈeʁise] <1> I. *vt* ❶ (*dresser: poils, piquants*) to bristle; (*plumes*) to ruffle ❷ (*faire dresser*) **la peur lui a hérissé les poils** fear made its fur stand on end ❸ (*remplir*) **~ qc de qc** to spike sth with sth ❹ (*irriter*) **~ qn** to ruffle sb's feathers II. *vpr* **se ~** ❶ (*se dresser: cheveux, poils*) to stand on end ❷ (*dresser ses poils, plumes: chat*) to bristle; (*oiseau*) to ruffle its feathers ❸ (*se fâcher*) to bristle
**hérisson** [ˈeʁisɔ̃] *m* ZOOL (*en Europe, Afrique, Asie*) hedgehog
**héritage** [eʁitaʒ] *m* ❶ (*succession, biens*) inheritance ❷ *fig* (*d'une civilisation, de coutumes*) heritage

**hériter** [eʀite] <1> *vt, vi* ~ (**qc**) **de qn** to inherit (sth) from sb

**héritier, -ière** [eʀitje, -jɛʀ] *m, f* ❶ heir *m*, heiress *f* ❷ (*fils*) **son** ~ *inf* his son and heir

**hermaphrodite** [ɛʀmafʀɔdit] *m* BIO hermaphrodite

**hermétique** [ɛʀmetik] *adj* ❶ (*étanche: fermeture, joint*) hermetic; (*à l'air*) airtight; (*à l'eau*) watertight; (*impénétrable: poésie, secret*) impenetrable; (*écrivain*) obscure

**hernie** [ˈɛʀni] *f* MED hernia

**héroïne**¹ [eʀɔin] *f* (*drogue*) heroin

**héroïne**² [eʀɔin] *f v.* **héros**

**héroïque** [eʀɔik] *adj* ❶ (*digne d'un héros*) heroic ❷ (*légendaire*) **les temps** ~**s du cinéma** the great days of cinema

**héroïsme** [eʀɔism] *m* heroism

**héron** [ˈeʀɔ̃] *m* heron

**héros, héroïne** [ˈeʀo, eʀɔin] *m, f* hero *m*, heroine *f*

**herpès** [ɛʀpɛs] *m* MED herpes

**herse** [ˈɛʀs] *f* ❶ AGR harrow ❷ (*grille d'entrée: d'une forteresse*) portcullis

**hertz** [ɛʀts] *m inv* ELEC hertz

**hésitant(e)** [ezitã, ãt] *adj* (*personne, pas, voix*) hesitant; (*électeur*) wavering

**hésitation** [ezitasjɔ̃] *f* ❶ (*incertitude*) hesitation ❷ (*arrêt*) **sans** ~ without hesitation

**hésiter** [ezite] <1> *vi* to hesitate

**hétéro** [eteʀo] *inf* I. *adj abr de* **hétérosexuel(le)** straight II. *mf abr de* **hétérosexuel(le)** straight

**hétéroclite** [eteʀɔklit] *adj* (*collection, ensemble*) motley; (*objets*) sundry; (*œuvre, bâtiment*) heterogeneous

**hétérogène** [eteʀɔʒɛn] *adj* heterogeneous

**hétérosexuel(le)** [eteʀosɛksɥɛl] *adj, m(f)* heterosexual

**hêtre** [ˈɛtʀ] *m* ❶ (*arbre*) beech (tree) ❷ (*bois*) beech (wood)

**heu** [ˈø] *interj* ❶ (*pour ponctuer à l'oral*) hmm! ❷ (*embarras*) uh!; ~ ... **comment dirais-je?** uh … how can I put it?

**heure** [œʀ] *f* ❶ (*mesure de durée*) hour;

**une** ~ **et demie** an hour and a half; **une** ~ **de retard** an hour's delay ❷ (*indication chiffrée*) **dix** ~**s du matin/du soir** ten o'clock in the morning/in the evening; **à trois** ~**s** at three o'clock ❸ (*point précis du jour*) **il est quelle** ~? *inf* what time is it?; **à quelle** ~? (at) what time? ❹ (*distance*) **être à deux** ~**s de qc** to be two hours (away) from sth ❺ (*moment dans la journée*) ~ **de fermeture** closing time; **à l'**~ on time ❻ (*moment dans le cours des événements*) **l'**~ **est grave** these are difficult times ▸**l'**~ **H** zero hour; **de bonne** ~ early; **être/ne pas être à l'**~ (*personne*) to be/not to be on time; (*montre*) to be right/wrong; **à tout à l'**~! (*bientôt*) see you (soon)!; (*plus tard*) see you (later)!

**heureusement** [øʀøzmã] *adv* ❶ (*par bonheur*) fortunately ❷ (*favorablement*) **se terminer** ~ to have a happy ending

**heureux, -euse** [øʀø, -øz] I. *adj* ❶ (*rempli de bonheur: personne, vie, souvenir*) happy; **être** ~ **de qc** to be happy with sth; **être** ~ **de** +*infin* to be happy to +*infin* ❷ (*chanceux*) fortunate ❸ (*favorable: issue, coïncidence, résultat*) happy; (*circonstances, réponse*) favorable II. *m, f* **faire un** ~ *inf* to make somebody very happy

**heurt** [ˈœʀ] *m* ❶ (*conflit*) clash ❷ (*soutenu* (*impact, coup: d'un portail*) slam

**heurter** [ˈœʀte] <1> I. *vi* ~ **à la porte** to knock on the door II. *vt* ❶ (*entrer rudement en contact*) ~ **qn** (*à pied*) to bump into sb; (*en voiture*) to hit sb ❷ (*choquer: personne, sentiments*) to offend III. *vpr* ❶ (*se cogner contre*) **se** ~ to bump into each other ❷ (*buter contre*) **se** ~ **à qc** (*problème, refus*) to come up against sth ❸ (*entrer en conflit*) **se** ~ **avec qn** (*personne*) to clash with sb

**hexagonal(e)** [ɛgzagɔnal, -o] <-aux> *adj* ❶ hexagonal ❷ (*concerne l'Hexagone français: problème, frontières*) French

**hexagone** [ɛgzagɔn, ɛgzagɔ̃] *m* hexagone

**Hexagone** [ɛgzagɔn, ɛgzagɔ̃] *m* l'~ ≈ France (*because of its geographical shape*)

**hibernation** [ibɛʀnasjɔ̃] *f* hibernation

**hiberner** [ibɛʀne] <1> *vi* to hibernate

**hibou** [´ibu] <x> *m* owl

**hic** [´ik] *m inf* snag

**hideux, -euse** [´idø, -øz] *adj* hideous

**hier** [jɛʀ] *adv* ❶ (*la veille*) yesterday ❷ (*passé récent*) **vous ne vous connaissez que d'~** you've hardly known each other any time at all

**hiérarchie** [jeʀaʀʃi] *f* hierarchy

**hiérarchique** [´jeʀaʀʃik] *adj* hierarchic(al)

**hi-fi** [´ifi] *inv abr de* **High Fidelity** I. *adj* hi-fi; **chaîne ~** stereo (system) II. *f* hi-fi

**hilarant(e)** [ilaʀɑ̃, ɑ̃t] *adj* hilarious

**hindi** [´indi, indi] *m* Hindi; *v.a.* **français**

**hindouisme** [ɛ̃duism] *m* Hinduism

**hip** [´ip] *interj* ~ ~ ~! **hourra!** hip, hip, hooray!

**hippie** [´ipi] <hippies> I. *adj* hippie II. *mf* hippie

**hippique** [ipik] *adj* equine; **concours ~** horse show

**hippisme** [ipism] *m* horseback riding

**hippodrome** [ipodʀom] *m* racetrack

**hippopotame** [ipɔpɔtam] *m* ZOOL hippopotamus

**hirondelle** [iʀɔ̃dɛl] *f* swallow

**hirsute** [iʀsyt] *adj* (*tête*) tousled; (*barbe*) shaggy

**hispanique** [ispanik] *adj* Hispanic

**hispano-américain(e)** [ispanoameʀikɛ̃, ɛn] <hispano-américains> *adj* Spanish-American

**hisser** [´ise] <1> I. *vt* (*drapeau, voile*) to hoist II. *vpr* (*grimper*) **se ~ sur le mur** to heave oneself (up) onto the wall

**histoire** [istwaʀ] *f* ❶ *sans pl* (*science, événements*) history ❷ (*récit, conte, blague, propos mensonger*) story ❸ *inf* (*suite d'événements*) story; (*affaire*) business ❹ *gén pl, inf* (*complications*) fuss; (*problèmes*) trouble

**historien(ne)** [istɔʀjɛ̃, jɛn] *m(f)* historian

**historique** [istɔʀik] I. *adj* (*événement, monument*) historic; (*document, roman*) historical II. *m* (*d'un mot, d'une institution*) history; (*d'une affaire*) review

**hitlérien(ne)** [itleʀjɛ̃, jɛn] *adj* HIST Hitlerian

**HIV** [´aʃive] *m* MED *abr de* **Human Immunodeficiency Virus** HIV

**hiver** [ivɛʀ] *m* winter; *v.a.* **automne**

**hivernal(e)** [ivɛʀnal, -o] <-aux> *adj* ❶ (*de l'hiver*) winter ❷ (*comme en hiver*) wintry

**H.L.M.** [´aʃɛlɛm] *m o f inv abr de* **habitation à loyer modéré** ≈ public housing (project); (*appartement*) ≈ public housing unit (*low-rent, government-owned housing*)

**hobby** [´ɔbi] <hobbies> *m* hobby

**hochement** [´ɔʃmɑ̃] *m* ~ **de tête** (*pour approuver*) nod (of the head); (*pour désapprouver*) shake of the head

**hocher** [´ɔʃe] <1> *vt* ~ **la tête** (*pour approuver*) to nod (one's head); (*pour désapprouver*) to shake one's head

**hockey** [´ɔkɛ] *m* hockey

**holà** [´ɔla] I. *interj* ~! **pas si vite!** hold on! not so fast! II. *m* **mettre le ~ à qc** to put a stop to sth

**hold-up** [´ɔldœp] *m inv* hold-up

**hollandais** [´ɔllɑ̃dɛ] *m* Dutch; *v.a.* **français**

**hollandais(e)** [´ɔllɑ̃dɛ, ɛz] *adj* Dutch

**Hollandais(e)** [´ɔllɑ̃dɛ, ɛz] *m(f)* Dutchman, Dutchwoman *m, f*

**Hollande** [´ɔllɑ̃d] *f* **la ~** Holland

**holocauste** [olokost] *m* (*génocide*) holocaust

**homard** [´ɔmaʀ] *m* CULIN, ZOOL lobster

**homéopathie** [ɔmeɔpati] *f* homeopathy

**homicide** [ɔmisid] *m* JUR murder, homicide; ~ **involontaire** manslaughter; ~ **volontaire** (first-degree) murder

**hommage** [ɔmaʒ] *m* ❶ (*témoignage de respect, œuvre ou manifestation en*

H

*l'honneur de qn*) tribute ② *pl, soutenu* (*compliments*) respects

**homme** [ɔm] *m* man; **vêtements d'~** [o **pour ~s**] menswear; **~ politique** politician; **~ d'État** statesman

**homme-grenouille** [ɔmgʀənuj] <hommes-grenouilles> *m* frogman

**homme-sandwich** [ɔmsɑ̃dwitʃ] <hommes-sandwichs> *m* sandwich man

**homo** [omo] I.*adj abr de* **homosexuel(le)** *inf* gay II.*mf abr de* **homosexuel(le)** *inf* gay man, woman *m, f*

**homogène** [ɔmɔʒɛn] *adj* homogeneous

**homogénéiser** [ɔmɔʒeneize] <1> *vt* CULIN, CHIM to homogenize

**homologue** [ɔmɔlɔg] *adj* (*équivalent*) homologous

**homologuer** [ɔmɔlɔge] <1> *vt* ① (*reconnaître officiellement: prix*) to authorize; (*record*) to ratify ② (*déclarer conforme aux normes: siège-auto*) to license

**homosexualité** [ɔmɔsɛksɥalite] *f* homosexuality

**homosexuel(le)** [ɔmɔsɛksɥɛl] I.*adj* homosexual II.*m(f)* homosexual

**Hongrie** [ˈɔ̃gʀi] *f* **la ~** Hungary

**hongrois** [ˈɔ̃gʀwa] *m* Hungarian; *v.a.* **français**

**hongrois(e)** [ˈɔ̃gʀwa, waz] *adj* Hungarian

**Hongrois(e)** [ˈɔ̃gʀwa, waz] *m(f)* Hungarian

**honnête** [ɔnɛt] *adj* ① (*probe: personne*) honest; (*commerçant, entreprise*) respectable ② (*franc: personne*) honest ③ (*honorable: conduite, intention, propos*) honorable; (*méthode*) fair

**honnêtement** [ɔnɛtmɑ̃] *adv* ① (*convenablement: payer, gagner sa vie*) honestly ② (*loyalement, avec probité: gérer une affaire*) honorably

**honnêteté** [ɔnɛtte] *f* ① (*probité, franchise: d'une personne*) honesty ② (*honorabilité: d'une conduite, intention, d'un propos*) decency

**honneur** [ɔnœʀ] *m* ① *sans pl* (*principe moral*) honor ② *sans pl* (*réputation*)

credit ③ (*privilège*) honor; **nous avons l'~ de vous faire part de ...** *form* we are pleased to inform you of ... ④ *pl* (*marques de distinctions*) honors ⑤ (*considération*) **faire un grand ~ à qn en faisant qc** to do sb a great honor by doing sth ► **en quel ~?** *iron* what for?

**honorable** [ɔnɔʀabl] *adj* ① (*estimable: personne, profession*) honorable ② (*respectable, suffisant*) respectable

**honorer** [ɔnɔʀe] <1> I.*vt* ① (*traiter avec considération, respecter, célébrer*) a. COM to honor ② (*faire honneur à*) **~ qn** (*sentiments, conduite*) to be a credit to sb II.*vpr* **s'~ d'être qc** to pride oneself on being sth

**honorifique** [ɔnɔʀifik] *adj* honorary

**honte** [ˈɔ̃t] *f* ① (*déshonneur*) disgrace; (**c'est**) **la ~!** *inf* it's a disgrace! ② *sans pl* (*sentiment d'humiliation*) shame; **avoir ~ de qn/qc** to be ashamed of sb/sth

**honteux, -euse** [ˈɔ̃tø, -øz] *adj* (*acte, défaite, sentiment*) shameful; **être ~ de qc** to be ashamed of sth

**hop** [ˈɔp] *interj* ① (*pour faire sauter*) come on, jump! ② (*pour marquer une action brusque*) **allez ~!** come on, off you go!

**hôpital** [ɔpital, -o] <-aux> *m* hospital

**hoquet** [ˈɔkɛ] *m* hiccup

**horaire** [ɔʀɛʀ] I.*adj* hourly II.*m* ① (*répartition du temps*) timetable; **~ de travail** hours of work ② (*tableau: des cours, trains, bus*) timetable; (*des vols*) schedule

**horde** [ˈɔʀd] *f* horde

**horizon** [ɔʀizɔ̃] *m* ① *sans pl* (*ligne*) horizon ② (*étendue*) view ③ (*perspective*) horizon

**horizontal(e)** [ɔʀizɔ̃tal, -o] <-aux> *adj* horizontal

**horizontale** [ɔʀizɔ̃tal] *f* ① MATH horizontal ② (*position*) **être à l'~** to be horizontal

**horloge** [ɔʀlɔʒ] *f* (*appareil*) clock

**horloger, -ère** [ɔʀlɔʒe, -ɛʀ] I.*adj* watch-making II.*m, f* watchmaker

**horlogerie** [ɔRlɔʒRi] *f* ❶ (*secteur économique*) watchmaking; (*commerce*) watchmaking business ❷ (*magasin*) ~ **bijouterie** jewelry store (*specializing in clocks and watches*)

**hormonal(e)** [ɔRmɔnal, -o] <-aux> *adj* hormonal

**hormone** [ɔRmɔn] *f* hormone

**horodateur** [ɔRɔdatœR] *m* (*au parking*) ticket machine

**horoscope** [ɔRɔskɔp] *m* horoscope

**horreur** [ɔRœR] *f* ❶ (*sensation d'épouvante, de dégoût*) horror ❷ (*atrocité: d'un crime, supplice*) horror ❸ (*aversion*) **avoir ~ de qn/qc** (*haïr*) to hate sb/sth ❹ *pl* (*grossièretés, actions infâmes*) terrible things

**horrible** [ɔRibl] *adj* ❶ (*abominable: spectacle, meuble*) horrible; (*acte, accident, cris*) terrible ❷ (*extrême, très mauvais*) terrible

**horrifier** [ɔRifje] <1> *vt* to horrify

**hors** [ˈɔR] *prep* ❶ (*à l'extérieur de*) ~ **de** outside ❷ (*au-delà de*) ~ **d'atteinte** [*o* **de portée**] out of reach ▸ ~ **de danger** out of danger; ~ **de prix** exorbitant

**hors-bord** [ˈɔRbɔR] *m inv* ❶ (*moteur*) outboard ❷ (*bateau*) speedboat

**hors-d'œuvre** [ˈɔRdœvR] *m inv* CULIN starter

**hors-jeu** [ˈɔRʒø] *m inv* SPORT offside

**hortensia** [ɔRtɑ̃sja] *m* BOT hydrangea

**horticulteur, -trice** [ɔRtikyltœR, tRis] *m, f* horticulturist

**horticulture** [ɔRtikyltyR] *f* horticulture

**hospice** [ɔspis] *m* (*hôpital*) home

**hospitalier, -ière** [ɔspitalje, -jɛR] *adj* ❶ (*à l'hôpital*) hospital ❷ (*accueillant*) hospitable

**hospitaliser** [ɔspitalize] <1> *vt* to hospitalize

**hospitalité** [ɔspitalite] *f* hospitality

**hostie** [ɔsti] *f* REL host

**hostile** [ɔstil] *adj* **être ~ à qn/qc** to be hostile to(ward) sb/sth

**hostilité** [ɔstilite] *f* hostility

**hôte** [ot] **I.** *mf* (*d'une personne, d'un*

*hôtel*) guest **II.** *m* INFORM host (computer)

**hôte, hôtesse** [ot, otɛs] *m(f)* ❶ soutenu (*maître de maison*) host, hostess *m, f* ❷ COM ~**sse de caisse** cashier

**hôtel** [ɔtɛl, otɛl] *m* ❶ (*hôtellerie*) hotel ❷ (*riche demeure*) mansion ▸ ~ **de ville** city [*o* town] hall

**hôtelier, -ière** [otalje, ɔtalje, -jɛR] **I.** *adj* hotel; **industrie hôtelière** hotel business **II.** *m, f* hotelier

**hôtellerie** [otɛlRi, ɔtɛlRi] *f* (*profession*) hotel business

**hôtesse** [otɛs] *f* ❶ *v.* **hôte** ❷ (*profession*) flight attendant, stewardess

**hotte** [ˈɔt] *f* ❶ (*appareil d'aspiration: d'une cheminée*) hood ❷ (*panier*) basket

**hou** [ˈu] *interj* ❶ (*pour faire honte*) tut-tut!; (*pour conspuer*) boo! ❷ (*pour faire peur*) boo!

**houblon** [ˈublɔ̃] *m* ❶ (*plante*) hop ❷ (*ingrédient de la bière*) hops *pl*

**houe** [ˈu] *f* hoe

**houleux, -euse** [ˈulø, -øz] *adj* ❶ (*agité par la houle: mer*) stormy ❷ (*troublé: séance*) stormy; (*assemblée*) tumultuous

**houppe** [ˈup] *f* ~ **de cheveux** tuft of hair

**hourra** [ˈuRa] **I.** *interj* hurray! **II.** *m* cheer

**houspiller** [ˈuspije] <1> *vt* ~ **qn** to tell sb off

**housse** [ˈus] *f* cover; ~ **de siège/couette** seat/duvet cover

**hovercraft** [ˈɔvœRkRaft] *m* hovercraft

**H.S.** [aʃɛs] *abr de* **hors service: être ~** *inf* (*personne*) to be beat, to be out of it

**hublot** [ˈyblo] *m* (*d'un bateau*) porthole; (*d'un avion, appareil ménager*) window

**hue** [ˈy] *interj* ❶ (*avancer*) giddyup! ❷ (*tourner à droite*) gee!

**huées** [ˈɥe] *fpl* (*cris de réprobation*) boos

**huer** [ˈɥe] <1> *vt* to boo

**huguenot(e)** [ˈygno, ɔt] *m(f)* Huguenot

H

**huile** [ɥil] f oil; **~ d'olive/de tournesol** olive/sunflower oil

**huiler** [ɥile] <1> vt (mécanisme) to oil; (moule) to grease

**huis** [ɥi] à **~ clos** behind closed doors; JUR in camera

**huissier** [ɥisje] m ❶ JUR (officier ministériel) bailiff ❷ (appariteur) usher

**huit** [ɥit, devant une consonne ´ɥi] I. adj eight II. m inv eight ▸ **le grand ~** the roller coaster; v.a. **cinq**

**huitaine** [´ɥitɛn] f ❶ (ensemble d'environ huit éléments) **une ~ de personnes/pages** about eight people/pages ❷ (une semaine) **dans une ~** in a week or so

**huitante** [´ɥitɑ̃t] adj Suisse (quatre-vingts) eighty; v.a. **cinq, cinquante**

**huitième** [´ɥitjɛm] I. adj antéposé eighth II. mf **le/la ~** the eighth III. m ❶ (fraction) eighth ❷ SPORT **~ de finale** round of sixteen; v.a. **cinquième**

**huître** [ɥitʀ] f oyster

**hum** [´œm] interj (pour exprimer le doute, la gêne, une réticence) hmm!

**humain(e)** [ymɛ̃, ɛn] adj ❶ (propre à l'homme: chair, dignité, vie) human; **les êtres ~s** human beings ❷ (compatissant, sensible) humane

**humainement** [ymɛnmɑ̃] adv ❶ (avec humanité: traiter) humanely ❷ (avec les capacités humaines) **faire tout ce qui est ~ possible** to do all that is humanly possible

**humaniser** [ymanize] <1> I. vt (conditions de vie, travail) to humanize II. vpr **s'~** to become more human

**humaniste** [ymanist] I. adj humanistic II. mf humanist

**humanitaire** [ymanitɛʀ] adj (aide, organisation) humanitarian

**humanité** [ymanite] f humanity

**humanoïde** [ymanɔid] adj, m humanoid

**humble** [œ̃bl] adj humble

**humecter** [ymɛkte] <1> I. vt (doigts, timbre, linge) to moisten II. vpr **s'~ les lèvres** to moisten one's lips

**humer** [´yme] <1> vt (plat) to smell

**humeur** [ymœʀ] f ❶ (état d'âme) mood; **être de bonne/mauvaise ~** to be in a good/bad mood ❷ (tempérament) temper ❸ (irritation) (bad) temper

**humide** [ymid] adj ❶ (qui a pris l'humidité) damp ❷ METEO (climat, temps) humid

**humidifier** [ymidifje] <1> vt to humidify

**humidité** [ymidite] f humidity

**humiliant(e)** [ymiljɑ̃, jɑ̃t] adj humiliating

**humiliation** [ymiljasjɔ̃] f humiliation

**humilier** [ymilje] <1> I. vt to humiliate II. vpr **s'~ devant qn** to humble oneself before sb

**humilité** [ymilite] f humility

**humoriste** [ymɔʀist] mf humorist

**humoristique** [ymɔʀistik] adj humorous

**humour** [ymuʀ] m humor

**huppe** [´yp] f (d'oiseau) crest

**huppé(e)** [´ype] adj ❶ ZOOL crested ❷ inf (de haut rang: personne, restaurant) classy

**hurlement** [´yʀləmɑ̃] m (d'un animal, d'une personne, du vent) howl(ing); (de la foule) roar(ing); (de freins) squeal(ing)

**hurler** [´yʀle] <1> I. vi ❶ (pousser des hurlements: animal, personne) to howl; (foule) to roar; **~ de douleur/rage** to howl with pain/rage ❷ (produire un son semblable à un hurlement: vent) to howl; (freins) to squeal II. vt (injures) to yell; (menaces) to scream

**hurrah** [´uʀa] interj v. **hourra**

**hutte** [´yt] f hut

**hydratant(e)** [idʀatɑ̃, ɑ̃t] adj moisturizing

**hydrater** [idʀate] <1> I. vt ❶ (en cosmétique) to moisturize ❷ CHIM to hydrate II. vpr CHIM **s'~** to become hydrated

**hydraulique** [idʀolik] I. adj hydraulic II. f sans pl hydraulics

**hydravion** [idʀavjɔ̃] m seaplane

**hydrocarbure** [idʀɔkaʀbyʀ] *m* CHIM hydrocarbon

**hydrocution** [idʀɔkysjɔ̃] *f* MED immersion syncope

**hydroélectrique, hydro-électrique** [idʀoelɛktʀik] *adj* hydroelectric; **centrale ~** hydroelectric power station [*o* plant]

**hydrogène** [idʀɔʒɛn] *m* CHIM hydrogen

**hydroglisseur** [idʀogliscœʀ] *m* jetfoil

**hydrophile** [idʀɔfil] *adj* **coton ~** cotton (wadding)

**hyène** [jɛn, ´jɛn] *f* ZOOL hyena

**hygiène** [iʒjɛn] *f sans pl* ❶ (*bonnes conditions sanitaires*) hygiene ❷ (*soin: des cheveux, d'un bébé*) care

**hygiénique** [iʒjenik] *adj* ❶ (*de propreté*) hygienic; **papier ~** toilet paper ❷ (*sain*) healthy

**hymne** [imn] *m* MUS hymn

**hyperlien** [ipɛʀljɛ̃] *m* INFORM hyperlink

**hypermarché** [ipɛʀmaʀʃe] *m* superstore

**hypermétrope** [ipɛʀmetʀɔp] I. *adj* far-sighted II. *mf* far-sighted person

**hypertension** [ipɛʀtɑ̃sjɔ̃] *f* MED high blood pressure

**hypertexte** [ipɛʀtɛkst] *m* INFORM hypertext

**hyperthermie** [ipɛʀtɛʀmi] *f* MED hyperthermia

**hypnose** [ipnoz] *f* hypnosis

**hypnotiser** [ipnɔtize] <1> *vt* to hypnotize

**hypocalorique** [ipokalɔʀik] *adj* low-calorie

**hypocondriaque** [ipɔkɔ̃dʀijak] *adj péj* (*personne*) hypochondriac

**hypocrisie** [ipɔkʀizi] *f* hypocrisy

**hypocrite** [ipɔkʀit] I. *adj* hypocritical II. *mf* hypocrite

**hypotension** [ipotɑ̃sjɔ̃] *f* MED low blood pressure

**hypothéquer** [ipoteke] <5> *vt* ❶ FIN (*maison*) to mortgage; (*créance*) to secure (by mortgage) ❷ (*engager*) **~ l'avenir** to sign away one's future

**hypothèse** [ipɔtɛz] *f* ❶ (*supposition*) hypothesis ❷ (*éventualité, cas*) **dans l'~ où ...** on the assumption that ...

**hypothétique** [ipɔtetik] *adj* hypothetical

**hystérie** [isteʀi] *f* hysteria

**hystérique** [isteʀik] I. *adj* hysterical II. *mf* hysterical person

H

# l i

**l, i** [i] *m inv* l, i; **~ comme Irma** (*au téléphone*) i as in India

**iceberg** [ajsbɛʀg, isbɛʀg] *m* iceberg

**ici** [isi] *adv* ❶ (*lieu*) here; **~ et là** here and there; (**à partir**) **d'~** from here; **les gens d'~** the people (from around) here; **par ~ on croit ...** around here people think ...; **d'~ à Paris/au musée** from here to Paris/the museum; **près/loin d'~** near/a long way from here; **sortez d'~!** get out of here!; **viens ~ immédiatement!** come here right now!; **je suis venu jusqu'~** I came (all the way) here; **viens par ~** come over here; (*monter*) come up here; (*descendre*) come down here ❷ (*temporel*) **jusqu'~** up till now; **d'~** from now; **d'~ peu** very soon; **d'~ là** between now and then; **d'~ (à) 2010/(à) demain** between now and 2010/tomorrow; **d'~ (à) la semaine prochaine** between now and next week; **d'~ une semaine** a week from now

**icône** [ikon] *f* INFORM icon

**idéal** [ideal, -o] <-**aux** *o s*> *m* ❶ (*modèle*) ideal ❷ *sans pl* (*le mieux*) **l'~ serait qu'elle revienne** the ideal thing would be for her to come back

**idéal(e)** [ideal, -o] <-**aux** *o s*> *adj inf* (*rêvé, imaginaire: femme, société, beauté*) ideal; **des vacances ~es** a perfect vacation

**idéaliste** [idealist] *mf* idealist

**idée** [ide] *f* ❶ (*projet, inspiration, suggestion, opinion*) idea; **~ de génie** brain wave; **donner l'~ à qn de faire qc** to give sb the idea of doing sth; **~ fixe** obsession; **~s noires** gloomy thoughts; **se faire à l'~ que qn est mort** to get used to the idea of sb being dead; **il faut te changer les ~s** you should put everything out of your mind; **se faire une ~ de qc** to have a (particular) idea of sth; **ne pas avoir la moin-** **dre ~ de qc** to have absolutely no idea of sth; **aucune ~!** no idea!; **on n'a pas ~!, a-t-on ~!** you have no idea! ❷ (*esprit*) **cela m'est venu à l'~** it occurred to me ▶ **se faire des ~s** (*s'imaginer des choses*) to imagine things; (*se faire des illusions*) to have another thing coming

**identifier** [idɑ̃tifje] <1> **I.** *vt* to identify **II.** *vpr* **s'~ à qn/qc** to identify oneself with sb/sth

**identique** [idɑ̃tik] *adj* identical

**identité** [idɑ̃tite] *f* (*d'une personne*) identity

**idéologie** [ideɔlɔʒi] *f* ideology

**idiot(e)** [idjo, idjɔt] **I.** *adj* idiotic **II.** *m(f)* idiot; **tu me prends pour un ~?** do you take me for some kind of idiot?

**idole** [idɔl] *f* idol

**if** [if] *m* yew

**ignoble** [iɲɔbl] *adj* disgraceful; (*taudis*) sordid

**ignorance** [iɲɔʀɑ̃s] *f* ignorance

**ignorant(e)** [iɲɔʀɑ̃, ɑ̃t] **I.** *adj* (*inculte*) ignorant; **être ~ en qc** to know nothing about sth **II.** *m(f)* ignoramus

**ignorer** [iɲɔʀe] <1> **I.** *vt* ❶ (*opp: savoir*) not to know; **ne pas ~ qc** to be aware of sth; **n'~ rien de qc** to know all about sth ❷ (*négliger*) to ignore **II.** *vpr* **s'~** (*feindre de ne pas se connaître*) to ignore each other

**il** [il] *pron pers* ❶ (*masc, personne*) he ❷ (*masc, objet*) it ❸ *interrog, non traduit* **Louis a-t-il ~ ses clés?** does Louis have his keys? ❹ (*répétitif*) **~ est beau, ce costume** this suit's nice; **regarde le soleil, ~ se couche** look at the sun - it's setting; **l'oiseau, ~ fait cui-cui** birds go tweet-tweet ❺ *impers* it; **~ est possible qu'elle vienne** it's possible she may come; **~ pleut** it's raining; **~ faut que je parte** I've got to go; **~ y a deux ans** two years ago; **~ paraît qu'elle vit**

**là-bas** apparently she lives there; *v.a.* **avoir**

**île** [il] *f* island; **les ~s Hawaï** the Hawaiian Islands; **les ~s Britanniques** the British Isles; **l'~ de Pâques** Easter Island

**Île-de-France** [ildəfʀɑ̃s] *f* **l'~** the Île-de-France (*the area surrounding Paris*)

**illégal(e)** [i(l)legal, -o] <-aux> *adj* illegal

**illégitime** [i(l)leʒitim] *adj* (*enfant, demande*) illegitimate

**illimité(e)** [i(l)limite] *adj* ❶ (*sans bornes: confiance, pouvoirs*) unlimited; (*reconnaissance*) boundless ❷ (*indéterminé: durée, congé*) indefinite

**illisible** [i(l)lizibl] *adj* (*indéchiffrable: écriture*) illegible

**illumination** [i(l)lyminasjɔ̃] *f* ❶ (*action d'éclairer: d'une rue, d'un quartier*) lighting; (*au moyen de projecteurs*) floodlighting ❷ *pl* (*lumières festives*) illuminations *pl*

**illuminer** [i(l)lymine] <1> I. *vt* (*éclairer*) **~ un endroit** (*lustre*) to light up a place II. *vpr* **s'~** (*s'éclairer vivement: vitrine*) to be lit up; (*monument*) to be floodlit

**illusion** [i(l)lyzjɔ̃] *f* (*erreur*) illusion

**illusionniste** [i(l)lyzjɔnist] *mf* illusionist

**illustration** [i(l)lystrasjɔ̃] *f* illustration

**illustre** [i(l)lystʀ] *adj* illustrious

**illustré** [i(l)lystʀe] *m* magazine

**illustré(e)** [i(l)lystʀe] *adj* illustrated

**îlot** [ilo] *m* ❶ (*petite île*) islet ❷ (*pâté de maisons*) block ❸ (*groupe isolé*) island

**ils** [il] *pron pers* ❶ (*pl masc ou mixte*) they ❷ *interrog, non traduit* **les enfants sont-~ là?** are the children here? ❸ (*répétitif*) **regarde les paons comme ~ sont beaux** look how beautiful the peacocks are; *v.a.* **il**

**image** [imaʒ] *f* ❶ (*dessin*) picture; **~ de marque** (brand) image ❷ (*reflet*) *a. fig* image ▶ **à l'~ de qn/qc** in the image of sb/sth

**imaginaire** [imaʒinɛʀ] I. *adj* imaginary II. *m* **l'~** the imagination

**imagination** [imaʒinasjɔ̃] *f* imagination

**imaginer** [imaʒine] <1> I. *vt* ❶ (*se représenter, supposer*) to imagine; **~ de faire qc** to imagine doing sth ❷ (*inventer*) to think up II. *vpr* ❶ (*se représenter*) **s'~ qn/qc autrement** to imagine sb/sth differently ❷ (*se voir*) **s'~ à la plage/dans vingt ans** to imagine oneself at the beach/in twenty years ❸ (*croire faussement*) **s'~ qc** to imagine sth

**imbattable** [ɛ̃batabl] *adj* unbeatable

**imbécile** [ɛ̃besil] I. *adj* idiotic II. *mf* cretin; **faire l'~** (*vouloir paraître stupide*) to act stupid; (*se conduire stupidement*) to act like a fool

**imbiber** [ɛ̃bibe] <1> I. *vt* to soak II. *vpr* **s'~ de qc** to become soaked with sth

**imbuvable** [ɛ̃byvabl] *adj* ❶ (*boisson*) undrinkable ❷ *inf* (*détestable*) appalling

**IME** [iɛmø] *m abr de* **Institut monétaire européen** EMI

**imitateur, -trice** [imitatœʀ, -tʀis] *m, f* ❶ (*personne qui imite*) imitator ❷ (*comédien*) impressionist

**imitation** [imitasjɔ̃] *f* ❶ (*action*) imitation ❷ (*plagiat*) copy ❸ (*contrefaçon: d'une signature*) forgery

**imiter** [imite] <1> *vt* ❶ (*reproduire*) to imitate; (*pour amuser*) to mimic ❷ (*prendre pour modèle*) to imitate ❸ (*singer, reproduire*) to mimic; (*signature*) to forge ❹ (*avoir l'aspect de*) **~ qc** to look like sth

**immangeable** [ɛ̃mɑ̃ʒabl] *adj* inedible

**immatriculation** [imatrikylasjɔ̃] *f* (*d'un étudiant, d'une voiture*) registration

**immatriculer** [imatrikyle] <1> *vt* to register

**immédiat** [imedja] *m* immediate future

**immédiat(e)** [imedja, jat] *adj* ❶ (*très proche*) immediate; (*contact*) direct, (*soulagement, effet*) instantaneous ❷ (*sans intermédiaire*) direct

**immédiatement** [imedjatmɑ̃] *adv* ❶ (*tout de suite*) immediately ❷ (*sans intermédiaire*) directly

**immense** [i(m)mɑ̃s] *adj* immense

**immergé(e)** [imɛʀʒe] *adj* (*rocher, terres*) submerged

**immeuble** [imœbl] *m* building

**immigrant(e)** [imigʀɑ̃, ɑ̃t] I. *adj* immigrant II. *m(f)* immigrant

**immigré(e)** [imigʀe] I. *adj* immigrant II. *m(f)* immigrant

**immigrer** [imigʀe] <1> *vi* to immigrate

**imminent(e)** [iminɑ̃, ɑ̃t] *adj* imminent; (*conflit, danger*) impending

**immobile** [i(m)mɔbil] *adj* ❶ (*fixe*) still; (*personne*) motionless; (*partie, pièce*) fixed ❷ (*qui n'évolue pas*) immovable

**immobilier** [imɔbilje] *m* l'~ real estate

**immobilier, -ière** [imɔbilje, -jɛʀ] *adj* (*annonce, société, ensemble*) property; (*saisie*) of property; (*crise, placement*) in property; (*revenus*) from property; **agent** ~ real estate agent

**immobiliser** [imɔbilize] <1> I. *vt* ❶ (*stopper: camions*) to stop; (*circulation*) to bring to a standstill ❷ (*paralyser: personne*) to paralyze ❸ MED, SPORT to immobilize II. *vpr* s'~ (*personne, machine, train*) to come to a halt

**immobilité** [imɔbilite] *f* ❶ (*inertie*) stillness ❷ (*immuabilité*) immovability

**immonde** [i(m)mɔ̃d] *adj* ❶ (*d'une saleté extrême*) foul ❷ (*répugnant: crime, action*) sordid; (*personne*) squalid; (*propos*) vile

**immoral(e)** [i(m)mɔʀal, -o] <-aux> *adj* immoral

**immoralité** [i(m)mɔʀalite] *f* immorality

**immortalité** [imɔʀtalite] *f* immortality

**immortel(le)** [imɔʀtɛl] *adj* REL immortal

**impact** [ɛ̃pakt] *m* (*heurt, influence*) impact; **avoir de l'**~ **sur qn/qc** to have an impact on sb/sth; (*intervention, nouvelle*) to make an impact on sb/sth

**impair** [ɛ̃pɛʀ] *m* ❶ (*opp: pair*) odd numbers ❷ (*gaffe*) blunder

**impair(e)** [ɛ̃pɛʀ] *adj* odd

**impardonnable** [ɛ̃paʀdɔnabl] *adj* (*erreur, faute*) inexcusable

**imparfait** [ɛ̃paʀfɛ] *m* imperfect

**impasse** [ɛ̃pɑs] *f* (*rue*) dead end ▸ **être dans l'**~ to be in an impasse

**impassible** [ɛ̃pasibl] *adj* (*personne, visage*) impassive

**impatience** [ɛ̃pasjɑ̃s] *f* impatience

**impatient(e)** [ɛ̃pasjɑ̃, jɑ̃t] I. *adj* impatient; **je suis** ~ **de te voir** I can't wait to see you II. *m(f)* impatient person

**impatienter** [ɛ̃pasjɑ̃te] <1> *vpr* s'~ **de qc** to get impatient with sth

**impensable** [ɛ̃pɑ̃sabl] *adj* unthinkable

**impératif** [ɛ̃peʀatif] *m* ❶ *souvent pl* (*nécessité*) constraint ❷ LING imperative

**impératrice** [ɛ̃peʀatʀis] *f* empress; *v.a.* **empereur**

**imperceptible** [ɛ̃pɛʀsɛptibl] *adj* (*indécelable*) imperceptible; **être** ~ **à l'oreille** to be too faint to hear

**imperfection** [ɛ̃pɛʀfɛksjɔ̃] *f* ❶ *sans pl* (*opp: perfection*) imperfection ❷ *souvent pl* (*défaut: d'une matière, d'un roman, plan*) flaw; (*d'un visage, de la peau*) blemish

**impérialiste** [ɛ̃peʀjalist] I. *adj* imperialist(ic) II. *mf* imperialist

**imperméable** [ɛ̃pɛʀmeabl] I. *adj* (*sol*) impermeable; (*tissu, toile*) waterproof II. *m* raincoat

**impertinence** [ɛ̃pɛʀtinɑ̃s] *f* impertinence

**impertinent(e)** [ɛ̃pɛʀtinɑ̃, ɑ̃t] I. *adj* impertinent II. *m(f)* impertinent person

**imperturbable** [ɛ̃pɛʀtyʀbabl] *adj* imperturbable

**impitoyable** [ɛ̃pitwajabl] *adj* (*personne*) pitiless; (*critique, jugement*) merciless; (*haine*) unrelenting; (*regard*) without pity

**implanter** [ɛ̃plɑ̃te] <1> I. *vt* (*introduire*) a. MED to implant; **être implanté** (*industrie*) to be implanted; (*personne*) to be settled in II. *vpr* s'~ (*se fixer*) to be implanted; (*immigrants*) to settle; (*parti politique*) to become established

**implicite** [ɛ̃plisit] *adj* implicit

**impliquer** [ɛ̃plike] <1> *vt* ❶ (*signifier, avoir pour conséquence*) to imply ❷ (*demander*) ~ **de la concentration**

to involve concentration ❸ (*mêler*) ~ **qn dans qc** to involve sb in sth
**implorer** [ɛ̃plɔʀe] <1> *vt* to implore
**impoli(e)** [ɛ̃pɔli] **I.** *adj* ~ **envers qn** impolite to sb **II.** *m(f)* impolite person
**impolitesse** [ɛ̃pɔlitɛs] *f* impoliteness
**impopulaire** [ɛ̃pɔpylɛʀ] *adj* unpopular
**importance** [ɛ̃pɔʀtɑ̃s] *f* ❶ (*rôle*) importance; **accorder de l'~ à qc** to grant importance to sth; **prendre de l'~** to take on some importance; **sans ~** of no importance ❷ (*ampleur*) size
**important** [ɛ̃pɔʀtɑ̃] *m* important thing
**important(e)** [ɛ̃pɔʀtɑ̃, ɑ̃t] *adj* ❶ (*considérable*) important; **quelque chose d'~** something important ❷ (*gros*) considerable; (*dégâts*) large-scale; (*somme, quantité*) large
**importateur, -trice** [ɛ̃pɔʀtatœʀ, -tʀis] **I.** *adj* **un pays ~ de blé** a wheat-importing country **II.** *m, f* importer
**importation** [ɛ̃pɔʀtasjɔ̃] *f* ❶ (*commerce*) importing ❷ (*produit*) import
**importer¹** [ɛ̃pɔʀte] <1> *vt* to import
**importer²** [ɛ̃pɔʀte] <1> *vi* ❶ (*être important*) **la seule chose qui importe, c'est que ...** the only thing that matters is that ...; **cela importe peu/ beaucoup** that's very/not very important; **peu importe que** +*subj* it doesn't matter if; **qu'importe qc** who cares about sth; **qu'importe si qn fait qc** what does it matter if sb does sth ❷ (*intéresser*) ~ **fort peu à qn** to be of very little importance to sb; **ce qui m'importe, c'est ...** the important thing for me is ... ▸ **n'importe comment** no matter how; **n'importe lequel/laquelle** any; (*des deux*) either; **n'importe** (*cela m'est égal*) it doesn't matter; (*néanmoins*) even so; **n'importe où** anywhere; **n'importe quand** any time; **n'importe quel** +*subst* any; **acheter à n'importe quel prix** to buy at any price; **n'importe qui** anybody; **n'importe quoi** anything; **dire n'importe quoi** to talk nonsense
**import-export** [ɛ̃pɔʀɛkspɔʀ] <im-

ports-exports> *m* import-export (business)
**imposable** [ɛ̃pozabl] *adj* taxable
**imposant(e)** [ɛ̃pozɑ̃, ɑ̃t] *adj* ❶ (*majestueux*) imposing ❷ (*considérable*) impressive; (*somme*) hefty
**imposé(e)** [ɛ̃poze] *adj* (*prix, date*) fixed
**imposer** [ɛ̃poze] <1> **I.** *vt* ❶ (*exiger: décision*) to impose; (*repos*) to order; ~ **qc à qn** to impose sth on sb ❷ (*prescrire: date*) to set; ~ **qc à qn** to impose sth on sb; ~ **à qn de** +*infin* to force sb to +*infin* ❸ (*faire accepter de force*) ~ **le silence à qn** to impose silence on sb ❹ (*faire reconnaître: produit*) to establish ❺ FIN (*personne, revenu, marchandise*) to tax **II.** *vpr* ❶ (*devenir indispensable*) **s'~ à qn** (*repos*) to be vital for sb; (*solution*) to force itself on sb; (*prudence*) to be required of sb; **ça s'impose** that's a matter of course ❷ (*être importun*) **s'~** to impose oneself ❸ (*se faire reconnaître*) **s'~** to stand out
**impossibilité** [ɛ̃pɔsibilite] *f* impossibility; **être dans l'~ de** +*infin* to be unable to +*infin*; **mettre qn dans l'~ de** +*infin* to make it impossible for sb to +*infin*
**impossible** [ɛ̃pɔsibl] **I.** *adj* ❶ (*irréalisable, insupportable*) impossible ❷ *inf* (*invraisemblable*) ridiculous **II.** *m* impossible
**imposteur** [ɛ̃pɔstœʀ] *m* impostor
**impôt** [ɛ̃po] *m* tax; ~ **sur le revenu** income tax; ~ **foncier** property tax
**impotent(e)** [ɛ̃pɔtɑ̃, ɑ̃t] **I.** *adj* crippled **II.** *m(f)* cripple
**imprécision** [ɛ̃pʀesizjɔ̃] *f* vagueness
**imprégner** [ɛ̃pʀeɲe] <5> **I.** *vt* ❶ (*imbiber: bois*) to impregnate; (*étoffe*) to soak; ~ **un tampon de qc** to soak a wad of cloth in sth ❷ (*marquer*) ~ **qn** (*atmosphère*) to leave its mark on sb; (*sentiment*) to fill sb **II.** *vpr* **s'~ d'eau** to soak up water; **s'~ d'une odeur** to be filled with a smell
**impression** [ɛ̃pʀesjɔ̃] *f* (*sentiment*) im-

pression; **avoir l'~ que ...** to have the impression that ..

**impressionnant(e)** [ɛ̃pʀesjɔnɑ̃, ɑ̃t] *adj* ❶ (*imposant*) impressive ❷ (*considérable*) remarkable

**impressionner** [ɛ̃pʀesjɔne] <1> *vt* ~ **qn** to impress sb; (*films d'horreur*) to upset sb; **se laisser ~ par qn/qc** to feel intimidated by sb/sth

**impressionnisme** [ɛ̃pʀesjɔnism] *m* Impressionism

**imprévisible** [ɛ̃pʀevizibl] *adj* unforeseeable; (*personne*) unpredictable

**imprévu** [ɛ̃pʀevy] *m* ❶ (*ce à quoi on ne s'attend pas*) **l'~** the unexpected; **des vacances pleines d'~s** a vacation with lots of surprises ❷ (*fâcheux*) unexpected incident; **en cas d'~** in the event of any (unexpected) problem

**imprévu(e)** [ɛ̃pʀevy] *adj* unexpected

**imprimante** [ɛ̃pʀimɑ̃t] *f* INFORM printer

**imprimé** [ɛ̃pʀime] *m* ❶ (*formulaire*) form ❷ (*tissu*) print ❸ (*ouvrage imprimé*) printed matter

**imprimé(e)** [ɛ̃pʀime] *adj* printed

**imprimer** [ɛ̃pʀime] <1> *vt* to print

**imprimerie** [ɛ̃pʀimʀi] *f* ❶ (*technique*) printing ❷ (*établissement*) print shop

**improbable** [ɛ̃pʀɔbabl] *adj* improbable

**imprononçable** [ɛ̃pʀɔnɔ̃sabl] *adj* unpronounceable

**improviser** [ɛ̃pʀɔvize] <1> I. *vt, vi* ❶ improvise II. *vpr* ❶ (*opp: se préparer*) **s'~** to be improvised ❷ (*devenir subitement*) **s'~ infirmière** to take on the role of nurse

**improviste** [ɛ̃pʀɔvist] **à l'~** unexpectedly; **arriver à l'~** to arrive without warning

**imprudence** [ɛ̃pʀydɑ̃s] *f* carelessness; (*en prenant des risques*) rashness; **avoir l'~ de** +*infin* to be foolish enough to +*infin*

**imprudent(e)** [ɛ̃pʀydɑ̃, ɑ̃t] I. *adj* ❶ (*négligent*) foolish ❷ (*dangereux*) rash II. *m(f)* careless fool

**impuissance** [ɛ̃pɥisɑ̃s] *f* ❶ (*faiblesse*) powerlessness ❷ (*sur le plan sexuel*) impotence

**impuissant** [ɛ̃pɥisɑ̃] *m* impotent man

**impuissant(e)** [ɛ̃pɥisɑ̃, ɑ̃t] *adj* ❶ (*faible*) powerless; (*effort*) hopeless ❷ (*sexuellement*) impotent

**impulsif, -ive** [ɛ̃pylsif, -iv] I. *adj* impulsive II. *m, f* man, woman *m, f* of impulse

**in** [in] *adj inv, inf* hip

**inabordable** [inabɔʀdabl] *adj* **des loyers ~s** rents people can't afford

**inacceptable** [inaksɛptabl] *adj* unacceptable

**inaccessible** [inaksesibl] *adj* ❶ (*hors d'atteinte: sommet*) inaccessible; **~ à qn/qc** out of reach to sb/sth ❷ (*inabordable: personne*) unapproachable ❸ (*insensible*) **être ~ à qc** to be impervious to sth ❹ (*trop cher*) beyond one's means

**inachevé(e)** [inaʃ(ə)ve] *adj* unfinished

**inactif, -ive** [inaktif, -iv] I. *adj* ❶ (*oisif*) idle; **être ~** (*personne*) to be out of work ❷ (*inefficace*) ineffective II. *m, f* **les ~s** the non-working population

**inadmissible** [inadmisibl] *adj* unacceptable

**inaperçu(e)** [inapɛʀsy] *adj* **passer ~** to pass unnoticed

**inapte** [inapt] *adj* ❶ **~ à qc** unsuitable for sth ❷ MIL unfit

**inattaquable** [inatakabl] *adj* unassailable

**inattendu** [inatɑ̃dy] *m* **l'~** the unexpected

**inattendu(e)** [inatɑ̃dy] *adj* unexpected

**inattentif, -ive** [inatɑ̃tif, -iv] *adj* (*distrait*) inattentive

**inattention** [inatɑ̃sjɔ̃] *f* (*distraction*) lack of attention

**inauguration** [inogyʀasjɔ̃] *f* (*d'une exposition, route, de locaux*) opening; (*d'une statue, d'un monument*) unveiling; (*d'une ligne aérienne*) inauguration

**inaugurer** [inogyʀe, inɔgyʀe] <1> *vt* ❶ (*ouvrir solennellement: exposition, bâtiment, locaux, route*) to open; (*monument*) to unveil; (*ligne aérienne*) to inaugurate ❷ (*utiliser pour la première* *fois: maison, machine, voiture*) to christen

**inavoué(e)** [inavwe] *adj* (*sentiment, amour*) unavowed; (*acte, crime*) unconfessed

**incalculable** [ɛ̃kalkylabl] *adj* (*considérable*) incalculable; (*nombre*) countless

**incapable** [ɛ̃kapabl] I. *adj* incapable II. *mf* incompetent

**incapacité** [ɛ̃kapasite] *f* ❶(*inaptitude*) incapacity; ~ **de** +*infin* inability to +*infin*; **être dans l'**~ **de** +*infin* to be unable to +*infin* ❷(*convalescence*) disability; ~ **de travail** work disability

**incarcérer** [ɛ̃kaʀseʀe] <5> *vt* to incarcerate

**incassable** [ɛ̃kasabl] *adj* unbreakable

**incendie** [ɛ̃sɑ̃di] *m* fire ▶ ~ **criminel** arson

**incendier** [ɛ̃sɑ̃dje] <1> *vt* ❶(*mettre en feu*) to set on fire ❷ *inf* (*engueuler*) **se faire** ~ **par qn** to catch hell from sb

**incertain(e)** [ɛ̃sɛʀtɛ̃, ɛn] *adj* ❶(*opp: assuré, décidé*) uncertain ❷(*douteux*) doubtful; (*temps*) unsettled

**incertitude** [ɛ̃sɛʀtityd] *f* uncertainty

**incessant(e)** [ɛ̃sesɑ̃, ɑ̃t] *adj* (*bruit, pluie*) incessant; (*réclamations, critiques, coups de fil*) unending; (*efforts*) ceaseless

**inceste** [ɛ̃sɛst] *m* incest

**incident** [ɛ̃sidɑ̃] *m* ❶(*anicroche*) incident; ~ **technique** technical hitch; **sans** ~ without incident ❷(*péripétie*) episode ▶ **l'**~ **est clos** the matter is closed

**incinérer** [ɛ̃sineʀe] <5> *vt* (*cadavre*) to cremate; (*ordures ménagères*) to incinerate

**inciter** [ɛ̃site] <1> *vt* ~ **qn à l'action** to spur sb on to act; ~ **qn à l'achat** to push sb to buy

**inclinaison** [ɛ̃klinɛzɔ̃] *f* (*déclivité: d'une pente, route*) incline; (*d'un toit, mur*) slope

**incliné(e)** [ɛ̃kline] *adj* ❶(*pentu: pente, terrain*) sloping; (*toit*) pitched ❷(*penché*) leaning; (*tête*) bending

**incliner** [ɛ̃kline] <1> I. *vt* (*buste, corps*)

to bow; (*bouteille*) to tilt; (*dossier d'une chaise*) to lean; ~ **la tête** to bow one's head; (*pour acquiescer*) to nod one's head II. *vpr* ❶(*se courber*) **s'**~ **devant qn/qc** to bow to sb/sth ❷(*céder*) **s'**~ **devant qn/qc** to yield to sb/sth

**inclus(e)** [ɛ̃kly, ɛ̃klyz] *adj* included; **jusqu'au dix mars** ~ up to and including March 10, through March 10

**incognito** [ɛ̃kɔɲito] I. *adv* incognito II. *m* anonymity; **garder l'**~ to remain anonymous

**incohérence** [ɛ̃kɔeʀɑ̃s] *f* ❶(*caractère illogique, contradictoire*) inconsistency ❷(*inintelligibilité*) incoherence

**incohérent(e)** [ɛ̃kɔeʀɑ̃, ɑ̃t] *adj* ❶(*contradictoire*) inconsistent ❷(*bizarre*) incoherent

**incolore** [ɛ̃kɔlɔʀ] *adj* colorless

**incomparable** [ɛ̃kɔ̃paʀabl] *adj* incomparable

**incompatible** [ɛ̃kɔ̃patibl] *adj* incompatible

**incompétence** [ɛ̃kɔ̃petɑ̃s] *f* lack of competence; *péj* incompetence; ~ **en qc** ignorance where sth is concerned

**incompétent(e)** [ɛ̃kɔ̃petɑ̃, ɑ̃t] *adj* ignorant; *péj* incompetent

**incomplet, -ète** [ɛ̃kɔ̃plɛ, -ɛt] *adj* incomplete; (*œuvre, travail*) unfinished

**incompréhensible** [ɛ̃kɔ̃pʀeɑ̃sibl] *adj* incomprehensible; (*paroles*) unintelligible

**incompréhensif, -ive** [ɛ̃kɔ̃pʀeɑ̃sif, -iv] *adj* unsympathetic

**incompris(e)** [ɛ̃kɔ̃pʀi, iz] I. *adj* misunderstood II. *m(f)* misunderstood person

**inconcevable** [ɛ̃kɔ̃svabl] *adj* ❶(*inimaginable*) inconceivable ❷(*incroyable*) incredible

**inconfortable** [ɛ̃kɔ̃fɔʀtabl] *adj* ❶(*sans confort*) uncomfortable ❷(*déplaisant: situation*) awkward

**inconnu** [ɛ̃kɔny] *m* **l'**~ the unknown

**inconnu(e)** [ɛ̃kɔny] I. *adj* ❶(*ignoré*) unknown ❷(*nouveau: émotion*) (hitherto) unknown; (*odeur, parfum*) strange

**II.** m(f) ❶ (étranger) stranger ❷ (qui n'est pas célèbre) unknown

**inconsciemment** [ɛ̃kɔ̃sjamɑ̃] adv ❶ (sans s'en rendre compte) unconsciously ❷ PSYCH subconsciously

**inconscience** [ɛ̃kɔ̃sjɑ̃s] f ❶ (légèreté) thoughtlessness ❷ (irresponsabilité) recklessness ❸ (évanouissement) unconsciousness

**inconscient** [ɛ̃kɔ̃sjɑ̃] m PSYCH unconscious

**inconscient(e)** [ɛ̃kɔ̃sjɑ̃, jɑ̃t] **I.** adj ❶ (évanoui) unconscious ❷ (machinal, irréfléchi) automatic; (effort, élan) unconscious **II.** m(f) (irresponsable) thoughtless person

**inconsolable** [ɛ̃kɔ̃sɔlabl] adj ❶ (désespéré) disconsolate ❷ (déchirant: chagrin, peine) inconsolable

**incontestable** [ɛ̃kɔ̃tɛstabl] adj indisputable; (principe, réussite, droit) unquestionable; (fait, preuve, qualité) undeniable

**incontesté(e)** [ɛ̃kɔ̃tɛste] adj undoubted; (champion, leader) undisputed

**incontournable** [ɛ̃kɔ̃turnabl] adj (fait, exigence) unavoidable

**incontrôlable** [ɛ̃kɔ̃trolabl] adj ❶ (invérifiable) unverifiable ❷ (irrépressible: besoin, envie) uncontrollable; (passion) ungovernable; (attirance) irresistible ❸ (ingouvernable) out of control

**inconvénient** [ɛ̃kɔ̃venjɑ̃] m ❶ (opp: avantage) disadvantage; (d'une situation) drawback ❷ gén pl (conséquence fâcheuse) consequences ❸ (obstacle) l'~, c'est que c'est cher the problem is that it's expensive ▸ il n'y a pas d'~ à faire qc/à ce que qc soit fait (subj) there is no problem about doing sth/sth being done; ne pas voir d'~ à qc/à ce que qn fasse qc (subj) to have no objection to sth/to sb doing sth

**incorrect(e)** [ɛ̃kɔrɛkt] adj ❶ (défectueux: expression, style) inappropriate; (montage) incorrect; (réponse) wrong ❷ (inconvenant) improper; (langage, ton) impolite ❸ (impoli) impolite

**incorrigible** [ɛ̃kɔriʒibl] adj incorrigible

**increvable** [ɛ̃krəvabl] adj ❶ inf (infatigable: personne) tireless; (appareil, voiture) everlasting ❷ (qui ne peut être crevé: pneu, ballon) puncture-proof

**incroyable** [ɛ̃krwajabl] adj (extraordinaire, bizarre) incredible

**incrustation** [ɛ̃krystasjɔ̃] f INFORM pop-up window

**inculpé(e)** [ɛ̃kylpe] m(f) JUR accused

**incurable** [ɛ̃kyrabl] adj ❶ MED incurable ❷ (incorrigible) incorrigible; (ignorance) hopeless

**Inde** [ɛ̃d] f l'~ India; de l'~ Indian

**indécent(e)** [ɛ̃desɑ̃, ɑ̃t] adj ❶ indecent ❷ (déplacé) out of place

**indéchiffrable** [ɛ̃deʃifrabl] adj (illisible) indecipherable

**indécis(e)** [ɛ̃desi, iz] adj ❶ (hésitant) undecided ❷ (douteux: question) undecided; (résultat, victoire) uncertain; (temps) unsettled

**indécision** [ɛ̃desizjɔ̃] f (doute) uncertainty; péj indecision

**indéfini(e)** [ɛ̃defini] adj (indéterminé) ill-defined

**indéfiniment** [ɛ̃definimɑ̃] adv indefinitely

**indéfinissable** [ɛ̃definisabl] adj indefinable

**indélébile** [ɛ̃delebil] adj (ineffaçable, perpétuel) indelible; (couleur, encre) permanent

**indemne** [ɛ̃dɛmn] adj unscathed

**indemniser** [ɛ̃dɛmnize] <1> vt ❶ (rembourser) to reimburse ❷ (compenser) ~ qn pour qc to compensate sb for sth

**indemnité** [ɛ̃dɛmnite] f ❶ (réparation) compensation ❷ (forfait) indemnity ❸ (prime) allowance; (d'un maire, conseiller régional) salary; ~ de chômage unemployment benefit

**indépendamment** [ɛ̃depɑ̃damɑ̃] adv (en dehors de cela) apart from everything else ▸ ~ de qc (outre) apart from sth; (abstraction faite de) disregarding sth; (sans dépendre de) independently of sth

**indépendance** [ɛ̃depɑ̃dɑ̃s] f (liberté, autonomie) independence

**indépendant(e)** [ɛ̃depɑ̃dɑ̃, ɑ̃t] *adj*
❶ (*libre, souverain, indocile*) independent ❷ (*à son compte*) self-employed;
(*artiste, architecte, journaliste*) free-
lance ❸ (*séparé: chambre*) self-contained; (*systèmes*) separate ❹ (*sans liaison avec*) ~ **de qn/qc** independent of
sb/sth

**indescriptible** [ɛ̃dɛskʁiptibl] *adj* indescribable

**indésirable** [ɛ̃deziʁabl] *adj* undesirable

**indestructible** [ɛ̃dɛstʁyktibl] *adj* (*personne, construction*) indestructible;
(*foi, solidarité*) steadfast; (*liaison,
amour*) enduring; (*impression*) indelible

**indéterminé(e)** [ɛ̃detɛʁmine] *adj*
❶ (*non précisé*) indeterminate; (*date*)
unspecified ❷ (*incertain*) uncertain;
(*sens, termes*) vague ❸ (*indistinct*) vague

**index** [ɛ̃dɛks] *m* ❶ (*doigt*) index finger
❷ (*table alphabétique*) index

**indicatif** [ɛ̃dikatif] *m* ❶ TEL prefix; **l'~
de la France** the code for France
❷ LING indicative

**indicatif, -ive** [ɛ̃dikatif, -iv] *adj* (*qui
renseigne*) indicative; (*vote*) straw poll;
(*prix*) suggested

**indication** [ɛ̃dikasjɔ̃] *f* ❶ (*information*)
information; **une ~ sur qc** (some) information about sth ❷ (*signalisation:
d'une adresse, d'un numéro, prix*) indication; (*d'un virage dangereux*) sign
❸ (*prescription*) direction ❹ (*indice*)
~ **de qc** indicator of sth

**indice** [ɛ̃dis] *m* ❶ (*signe*) indication
❷ (*trace*) clue ❸ (*preuve*) evidence; JUR
piece of evidence ❹ ECON, FIN index
❺ TV ~ **d'écoute** ratings *pl*

**indien(ne)** [ɛ̃djɛ̃, jɛn] *adj* Indian

**Indien(ne)** [ɛ̃djɛ̃, jɛn] *m(f)* Indian

**indifférence** [ɛ̃difeʁɑ̃s] *f* ❶ (*insensibilité, apathie*) indifference ❷ (*détache-
ment*) disinterest

**indifférent(e)** [ɛ̃difeʁɑ̃, ɑ̃t] *adj* ❶ (*insensible: attitude, personne*) indifferent; (*mère*) unfeeling; **laisser qn ~** to
leave sb unmoved ❷ (*égal*) **être ~ à qn**

(*personne*) to be of no importance to
sb; (*choix, sort, avis*) not to matter to sb

**indigeste** [ɛ̃diʒɛst] *adj* (*cuisine, nourriture*) indigestible

**indigestion** [ɛ̃diʒɛstjɔ̃] *f* indigestion

**indignation** [ɛ̃diɲasjɔ̃] *f* indignation

**indigne** [ɛ̃diɲ] *adj* ❶ (*qui ne mérite
pas*) **être ~ de qn/qc** to be unworthy
of sb/sth; **être ~ de +**infin to be unworthy to **+**infin ❷ (*inconvenant*) **être
~ de qn** (*action, attitude, sentiment*)
to be unworthy of sb ❸ (*odieux*) disgraceful; (*époux, fils*) unworthy

**indigner** [ɛ̃diɲe] <1> *vpr* **s'~ contre
qn/qc** to get indignant with sb/over
sth

**indiqué(e)** [ɛ̃dike] *adj* ❶ (*conseillé*) advisable ❷ (*adéquat*) right ❸ (*fixé*) appointed; (*date*) agreed

**indiquer** [ɛ̃dike] <1> *vt* ❶ (*désigner*)
~ **qc à qn** to show sb sth; (*écriteau, flèche*) to indicate sth to sb; ~ **qn/qc de
la main** to point to sb/sth ❷ (*recommander*) ~ **qn/qc à qn** to suggest sb/
sth to sb ❸ (*dire*) ~ **à qn qc** to tell sb
about sth; (*expliquer*) to explain sth to
sb; ~ **à qn comment y aller** to tell sb
how to get there ❹ (*révéler*) ~ **qc/que
qn est passé** to show sth/that sb has
been here ❺ (*marquer: adresse*) to
write down; (*lieu*) to mark

**indirectement** [ɛ̃diʁɛktəmɑ̃] *adv* indirectly

**indiscipliné(e)** [ɛ̃disipline] *adj* undisciplined

**indiscret, -ète** [ɛ̃diskʁɛ, ɛt] **I.** *adj*
❶ (*curieux: personne*) inquisitive;
(*yeux*) prying ❷ (*bavard*) indiscreet
❸ (*inconvenant*) indiscreet; (*démarche*) intrusive; (*présence*) uncalled for
**II.** *m, f* (*personne bavarde*) gossip; (*personne curieuse*) inquisitive person

**indiscrétion** [ɛ̃diskʁesjɔ̃] *f* ❶ (*curiosité,
tendance à divulguer*) indiscretion;
**sans ~, peut-on savoir si ...** without
wishing to pry, could I ask if ... ❷ (*acte*)
indiscretion; (*bavardage*) indiscreet
word

**indiscutable** [ɛ̃diskytabl] *adj* (*fait*) undeniable; (*succès, supériorité, réalité*) undoubted; (*personne, crédibilité*) unquestionable; (*témoignage*) irrefutable

**indispensable** [ɛ̃dispɑ̃sabl] *adj* indispensable; (*précautions*) vital; (*devoir*) unavoidable; **il est ~ de** +*infin*/**que qc soit fait** (*subj*) it is essential to +*infin*/ that sth be done; **être ~ à qn/qc** [*o* **pour qc**] to be indispensable to sb/ for sth

**indissociable** [ɛ̃disɔsjabl] *adj* indissociable

**indistinct(e)** [ɛ̃distɛ̃, ɛ̃kt] *adj* (*murmure, vision, voix*) indistinct; (*couleur*) vague; (*objet*) unclear

**individu** [ɛ̃dividy] *m* individual

**individualiser** [ɛ̃dividɥalize] <1> *vt* (*personnaliser: appartement, voiture*) to personalize

**individualiste** [ɛ̃dividɥalist] *adj* ❶ PHILOS individualist ❷ *péj* self-centered

**individualité** [ɛ̃dividɥalite] *f* individuality; (*nouveauté*) originality

**individuel(le)** [ɛ̃dividɥɛl] *adj* individual; (*propriété, initiative*) personal; (*maison*) private

**individuellement** [ɛ̃dividɥɛlmɑ̃] *adv* individually

**indivisible** [ɛ̃divizibl] *adj* indivisible

**induction** [ɛ̃dyksjɔ̃] *f* induction; **cuisinière à ~** induction stove

**indulgent(e)** [ɛ̃dylʒɑ̃, ʒɑ̃t] *adj* indulgent; (*en punissant*) lenient

**industrialiser** [ɛ̃dystʀijalize] <1> **I.** *vt* (*région, pays, agriculture*) to industrialize; (*découverte*) to commercialize **II.** *vpr* **s'~** (*pays, région*) to be industrialized

**industrie** [ɛ̃dystʀi] *f* industry

**industriel(le)** [ɛ̃dystʀijɛl] **I.** *adj* industrial; (*pain*) factory-produced **II.** *m(f)* industrialist

**inédit** [inedi] *m* ❶ (*ouvrage*) unpublished work ❷ (*chose nouvelle*) novelty

**inédit(e)** [inedi, it] *adj* ❶ (*non publié*) unpublished ❷ (*nouveau*) novel

**inefficace** [inefikas] *adj* (*démarche*) ineffective; (*employé, machine*) inefficient

**inégal(e)** [inegal, -o] <-aux> *adj* ❶ (*différent*) unequal ❷ (*changeant*) uneven

**inégalé(e)** [inegale] *adj* unequalled

**inégalité** [inegalite] *f* ❶ (*différence*) disparity ❷ (*disproportion*) unevenness; (*des forces*) imbalance; **~ des chances** inequality of opportunity

**inépuisable** [inepɥizabl] *adj* ❶ (*intarissable*) inexhaustible ❷ (*infini: indulgence, patience*) endless; (*curiosité*) boundless

**inespéré(e)** [inɛspeʀe] *adj* unexpected

**inestimable** [inɛstimabl] *adj* incalculable; (*objet*) priceless

**inévitable** [inevitabl] *adj* ❶ (*certain, fatal*) inevitable; (*accident*) unavoidable ❷ (*nécessaire*) inescapable; (*opération*) unavoidable ❸ *antéposé, iron* (*habituel*) inevitable

**inexact(e)** [inɛgzakt] *adj* ❶ (*erroné: renseignement, résultat*) inaccurate; (*calcul, théorie*) incorrect ❷ (*déformé: traduction, citation, récit*) inaccurate; **non, c'est ~** no, that's wrong; **il est ~ de** +*infin* it is incorrect to +*infin*

**inexcusable** [inɛkskyzabl] *adj* inexcusable; (*personne*) unforgivable

**inexistant(e)** [inɛgzistɑ̃, ɑ̃t] *adj* ❶ (*qui n'existe pas, imaginaire*) nonexistent ❷ *péj* (*nul*) nonexistent; (*résultat*) appalling; (*aide*) not worth speaking of

**inexpérimenté(e)** [inɛkspeʀimɑ̃te] *adj* inexperienced

**inexplicable** [inɛksplikabl] *adj* inexplicable

**inexploité(e)** [inɛksplwate] *adj* (*gisement, richesses*) untapped; (*talent*) unexploited

**inexploré(e)** [inɛksplɔʀe] *adj* unexplored

**infaisable** [ɛ̃fəzabl] *adj* impracticable

**infatigable** [ɛ̃fatigabl] *adj* tireless; (*amour, patience*) untiring

**infect(e)** [ɛ̃fɛkt] *adj* ❶ (*répugnant*) vile; (*nourriture*) foul; (*lieu, logement*) sordid ❷ *inf* (*ignoble*) lousy

**infecter** [ɛ̃fɛkte] <1> *vpr* MED **s'~** to get infected

**infectieux, -euse** [ɛ̃fɛksjø, -jøz] *adj* infectious

**infection** [ɛ̃fɛksjɔ̃] *f* infection

**inférieur(e)** [ɛ̃ferjœr] **I.** *adj* ❶ (*dans l'espace*) lower; **les étages ~s** the lower floors ❷ (*en qualité*) inferior; **être ~ à qn/qc** to be inferior to sb/sth ❸ (*en quantité*) ~ **à qn/qc** less than sb/sth; **~ en nombre** smaller in number **II.** *m(f)* inferior

**infériorité** [ɛ̃ferjɔrite] *f* ❶ (*en qualité, rang*) inferiority; **en position d'~** in a position of weakness ❷ (*moindre quantité*) smaller number

**infidèle** [ɛ̃fidɛl] **I.** *adj* ❶ (*perfide*) unfaithful; **être ~ à qn** to be unfaithful to sb; **être ~ à sa parole** to be untrue to one's word ❷ (*inexact: récit*) inaccurate; (*traduction*) unfaithful ❸ REL infidel **II.** *mf* REL infidel

**infidélité** [ɛ̃fidelite] *f* ❶ sans pl (*déloyauté*) disloyalty ❷ (*action: d'un conjoint*) infidelity; (*d'un ami*) betrayal

**infini** [ɛ̃fini] *m* MATH **tendre vers l'~** to tend toward infinity ▶ **à l'~** for ever and ever

**infini(e)** [ɛ̃fini] *adj* ❶ (*qui n'a pas de limite*) a. MATH infinite ❷ (*immense: distance, nombre*) vast; (*étendue, longueur*) immense ❸ (*extrême*) infinite; (*reconnaissance*) deepest; (*richesses*) immeasurable ❹ (*interminable: lutte*) never-ending; (*propos, temps*) endless

**infiniment** [ɛ̃finimɑ̃] *adv* ❶ (*sans borne*) infinitely ❷ (*extrêmement*) immensely; (*regretter*) deeply ❸ (*beaucoup de*) ~ **de tendresse** the utmost tenderness

**infinité** [ɛ̃finite] *f* ❶ (*caractère de ce qui est infini*) infinity ❷ (*très grand nombre*) **une ~ de choses** an infinite number of things

**infinitif** [ɛ̃finitif] *m* infinitive

**infinitif, -ive** [ɛ̃finitif, -iv] *adj* **proposition infinitive** infinitive clause

**infirme** [ɛ̃firm] **I.** *adj* ❶ (*à la suite d'un accident*) disabled; (*pour cause de vieillesse*) infirm **II.** *mf* disabled person

**infirmerie** [ɛ̃firməri] *f* infirmary; (*d'une école*) sick bay

**infirmier, -ière** [ɛ̃firmje, -jɛr] *m, f* nurse

**infirmité** [ɛ̃firmite] *f* ❶ disability ❷ (*imperfection*) weakness

**inflammable** [ɛ̃flamabl] *adj* inflammable

**inflammation** [ɛ̃flamasjɔ̃] *f* inflammation

**inflation** [ɛ̃flasjɔ̃] *f* inflation

**infliger** [ɛ̃fliʒe] <2a> *vt* ❶ (*donner*) ~ **une amende à qn pour qc** to fine sb for sth; ~ **un châtiment à qn** to punish sb ❷ (*faire subir: coups, récit*) to inflict; (*politique*) to impose

**influençable** [ɛ̃flyɑ̃sabl] *adj* easy to influence

**influence** [ɛ̃flyɑ̃s] *f* (*effet, autorité*) influence; (*des mesures, d'un médicament*) effect; **sous l'~ de la colère** in the grip of anger; **sous ~** under influence

**influencer** [ɛ̃flyɑ̃se] <2> *vt* ~ **qn** to influence sb; (*mesures*) to have an effect on sb

**info** [ɛ̃fo] *f inf abr de* **information** piece of news; **les ~s** the news

**infogroupe** [ɛ̃fogrup] *m* INFORM newsgroup

**informateur, -trice** [ɛ̃fɔrmatœr, -tris] *m, f* informer

**informaticien(ne)** [ɛ̃fɔrmatisjɛ̃, jɛn] *m(f)* computer scientist

**informatif, -ive** [ɛ̃fɔrmatif, -iv] *adj* ❶ (*riche en informations*) informative ❷ (*destiné à informer: publicité*) informational

**information** [ɛ̃fɔrmasjɔ̃] *f* ❶ (*renseignement*) piece of information; **prendre des ~s sur qn/qc** to obtain information about sb/sth; **une réunion d'~** a briefing session ❷ souvent pl (*nouvelles*) news; **les ~s de vingt heures** the eight o'clock news; **~s sportives** sports news; **magazine d'~** news magazine ❸ sans pl (*fait d'informer*) information; **faire de l'~** to give out information ❹ pl INFORM, TECH information

**informatique** [ɛ̃fɔrmatik] I. *adj* **industrie ~** computer industry; **saisie ~** data capture II. *f* computer science

**informatisation** [ɛ̃fɔrmatizasjɔ̃] *f* (*d'une entreprise*) computerization

**informatisé(e)** [ɛ̃fɔrmatize] *adj* (*poste de travail*) computerized; **système ~** computer-based system

**informatiser** [ɛ̃fɔrmatize] <1> I. *vt* to computerize II. *vpr* **s'~** to be computerized

**informer** [ɛ̃fɔrme] <1> I. *vt* to inform; **des personnes bien informées** well-informed people II. *vi* to inform III. *vpr* **s'~ de qc** (*poser des questions*) to inquire about sth; (*se renseigner*) to inform oneself about sth; **s'~ sur qn** (*sa santé*) to ask after sb; (*son caractère*) to find out about sb

**infraction** [ɛ̃fraksjɔ̃] *f* offense; **~ au code de la route** traffic offense

**infranchissable** [ɛ̃frɑ̃ʃisabl] *adj* impassible

**infrastructure** [ɛ̃frastryktyr] *f* infrastructure

**infusion** [ɛ̃fyzjɔ̃] *f* infusion

**ingénieur** [ɛ̃ʒenjœr] *mf* engineer

**ingrat(e)** [ɛ̃gra, at] I. *adj* ❶ (*opp: reconnaissant*) **~ envers qn** ungrateful to sb ❷ (*infructueux: métier; sujet*) thankless; (*vie*) unrewarding ❸ (*dépourvu de charme: visage*) unlovely II. *m(f)* ungrateful wretch

**ingratitude** [ɛ̃gratityd] *f* (*d'une personne*) ingratitude; (*d'une tâche*) thanklessness

**ingrédient** [ɛ̃gredjɑ̃] *m* ingredient

**inguérissable** [ɛ̃gerisabl] *adj* (*maladie*) incurable

**ingurgiter** [ɛ̃gyrʒite] <1> *vt* (*avaler: nourriture*) to wolf down; (*boisson*) to gulp down; **faire ~ qc à qn** to force sth down sb

**inhabitable** [inabitabl] *adj* (*région*) uninhabitable; (*maison*) unfit for habitation

**inhabituel(le)** [inabityɛl] *adj* unusual

**inhaler** [inale] <1> *vt* MED to inhale

**inhumain(e)** [inymɛ̃, ɛn] *adj* inhuman

**inimaginable** [inimaʒinabl] *adj* unimaginable

**ininterrompu(e)** [inɛ̃terɔ̃py] *adj* uninterrupted; (*série*) unbroken; (*spectacle*) nonstop

**initial(e)** [inisjal, -jo] <-aux> *adj* (*cause, choc, lettre*) initial; (*état, position*) original

**initiale** [inisjal] *f* initial

**initialisation** [inisjalizasjɔ̃] *f* INFORM initialization

**initiation** [inisjasjɔ̃] *f* initiation; **cours d'~** introductory course

**initiative** [inisjativ] *f* (*idée première, dynamisme*) initiative; **avoir l'~ de qc** to have the idea for sth

**initié(e)** [inisje] I. *adj* experienced II. *m* insider; **délit d'~** FIN insider trading

**injecter** [ɛ̃ʒɛkte] <1> *vt* to inject

**injection** [ɛ̃ʒɛksjɔ̃] *f* injection

**injure** [ɛ̃ʒyr] *f* insult

**injurier** [ɛ̃ʒyrje] <1> I. *vt* to insult II. *vpr* **s'~** to insult each other

**injurieux, -euse** [ɛ̃ʒyrjø, -jøz] *adj* offensive

**injuste** [ɛ̃ʒyst] *adj* unfair

**injustice** [ɛ̃ʒystis] *f* injustice

**inné(e)** [i(n)ne] *adj* innate

**innocence** [inɔsɑ̃s] *f* ❶ (*naïveté*) innocence ❷ (*caractère inoffensif*) harmlessness

**innocent(e)** [inɔsɑ̃, ɑ̃t] I. *adj* ❶ (*opp: coupable*) innocent; **être ~ de qc** to be not guilty of sth ❷ (*inoffensif*) **ce n'est pas ~ si qn fait qc** it is no accident if sb does sth II. *m(f)* innocent

**innombrable** [i(n)nɔ̃brabl] *adj* innumerable

**innovation** [inɔvasjɔ̃] *f* innovation

**innover** [inɔve] <1> I. *vt* to create II. *vi* **~ en** (**matière de**) **qc** to innovate in the field of sth

**inoccupé(e)** [inɔkype] *adj* ❶ (*vide: place, terrain*) vacant; (*maison*) unoccupied ❷ (*oisif*) unoccupied

**inodore** [inɔdɔr] *adj* odorless

**inoffensif, -ive** [inɔfɑ̃sif, -iv] *adj* (*personne*) inoffensive; (*piqûre, remède*) harmless

**inondation** [inɔ̃dasjɔ̃] *f* (*débordement d'eaux*) flood; (*d'un fleuve*) flooding

**inonder** [inɔ̃de] <1> *vt* ❶ (*couvrir d'eaux*) to flood; **être inondé** (*personnes*) to be flooded (out) ❷ (*tremper*) ~ **qn/qc de qc** to soak sb/sth with sth; ~ **qn/qc** (*chose*) to pour down sb/sth ❸ (*submerger*) ~ **qn de qc** to swamp sb with sth

**inoubliable** [inublijabl] *adj* unforgettable

**inouï(e)** [inwi] *adj* ❶ (*inconnu*) unheard of ❷ *inf* (*formidable*) **être ~** (*personne*) to be beyond belief

**inoxydable** [inɔksidabl] *adj* stainless

**inquiet, -ète** [ɛ̃kjɛ, -ɛt] *adj* ❶ (*anxieux*) worried; **ne sois pas ~!** don't worry!; **être ~ de qc** to be worried about sth ❷ (*qui dénote l'appréhension: regard, attente*) anxious

**inquiétant(e)** [ɛ̃kjetɑ̃, ɑ̃t] *adj* ❶ (*alarmant*) worrying; **devenir ~** to cause anxiety ❷ (*patibulaire*) disturbing

**inquiéter** [ɛ̃kjete] <5> I. *vt* to worry II. *vpr* ❶ (*s'alarmer*) **s'~** to be disturbed ❷ (*se soucier de*) **s'~ au sujet de la maison** to worry about the house; **s'~ de savoir si/qui** to be anxious to know if/who

**insalubre** [ɛ̃salybʀ] *adj* (*climat*) unhealthy; (*quartier*) insalubrious

**insanité** [ɛ̃sanite] *f* (*d'une personne*) insanity; (*d'un propos, d'un acte*) absurdity

**insatisfait(e)** [ɛ̃satisfɛ, ɛt] *adj* ❶ (*mécontent*) **~ de qn/qc** dissatisfied with sb/sth ❷ (*inassouvi*) unsatisfied

**inscription** [ɛ̃skʀipsjɔ̃] *f* ❶ (*texte*) inscription; (*d'un poteau indicateur*) words ❷ (*immatriculation*) registration; **~ d'un élève à une école** enrollment of a pupil in a school; **~ de qn à un concours** sb's entry in a competition; **~ de qn à un club** sb's joining a club

**inscrire** [ɛ̃skʀiʀ] *irr* I. *vt* ❶ (*noter*) ~ **qc dans un carnet** to write sth down in a notebook; ~ **qc à l'ordre du jour** to put sth on the agenda; **être inscrit dans ma mémoire** to be etched in my memory ❷ (*immatriculer*) ~ **qn à une école/dans un club** to enroll sb in a school/in a club; ~ **qn sur une liste** to put sb on a list; (*pour prendre rendez-vous*) to put sb on a waiting list; **être inscrit à la faculté** to be in college; **être inscrit dans un club** to be a member of a club II. *vpr* ❶ (*s'immatriculer*) **s'~ à une école** to enroll in a school; **s'~ à une faculté** to register at a university, college; **s'~ à un parti/club** to join a party/club; **s'~ sur une liste** to put one's name down on a list ❷ (*s'insérer dans*) **s'~ dans le cadre de qc** (*décision, mesure, projet*) to come within the context of sth ❸ (*apparaître*) **s'~ sur l'écran** to appear on the screen

**inscrit(e)** [ɛ̃skʀi, it] I. *part passé de* **inscrire** II. *adj* (*candidat, électeur*) registered III. *m(f)* person (registered); (*à un examen*) (registered) candidate; (*à un parti*) (registered) member; (*sur une liste électorale*) (registered) voter; (*à une faculté*) (registered) student

**insecte** [ɛ̃sɛkt] *m* insect

**insecticide** [ɛ̃sɛktisid] *m* insecticide

**insécurité** [ɛ̃sekyʀite] *f* insecurity

**insensé(e)** [ɛ̃sɑ̃se] *adj* insane ▸ **c'est ~!** it's sheer madness!

**insensible** [ɛ̃sɑ̃sibl] *adj* ❶ (*physiquement*) **être ~** (*personne*) to be unconscious; (*lèvres, membre*) to be numb; **~ à la douleur** to be insensitive to pain ❷ (*moralement*) insensitive

**inséparable** [ɛ̃sepaʀabl] *adj* (*amis, idées*) inseparable

**insérer** [ɛ̃seʀe] <5> I. *vt* to insert II. *vpr* **s'~ dans qc** (*personne*) to integrate with sth

**insertion** [ɛ̃sɛʀsjɔ̃] *f* **~ dans qc** integration into sth; **centre d'~** rehabilitation center

**insignifiant(e)** [ɛ̃siɲifjɑ̃, jɑ̃t] *adj* insignificant; (*paroles*) trivial

**insistance** [ɛ̃sistɑ̃s] *f* insistence; **avec ~** insistently

**insistant(e)** [ɛ̃sistɑ̃, ɑ̃t] *adj* (*ton, regard*) insistent; (*rumeur*) persistent

**insister** [ɛ̃siste] <1> *vi* ❶ (*pour persua-*

*der*) ~ **sur qc** to insist on sth ❷ (*persé-vérer*) to keep on trying ❸ (*mettre l'accent sur*) ~ **sur qc** to stress sth

**insolation** [ɛ̃sɔlasjɔ̃] *f* sunstroke

**insolence** [ɛ̃sɔlɑ̃s] *f* (*impertinence*) insolence

**insolent(e)** [ɛ̃sɔlɑ̃, ɑ̃t] **I.** *adj* ❶ (*impertinent*) insolent ❷ (*arrogant*) arrogant **II.** *m(f)* insolent person

**insoluble** [ɛ̃sɔlybl] *adj* insoluble

**insomniaque** [ɛ̃sɔmnjak] **I.** *adj* insomniac; **être ~** to have insomnia **II.** *mf* insomniac

**insomnie** [ɛ̃sɔmni] *f* insomnia

**insonoriser** [ɛ̃sɔnɔʀize] <1> *vt* to soundproof

**insouciant(e)** [ɛ̃susjɑ̃, jɑ̃t] *adj* (*heureux*) carefree; (*imprévoyant*) unconcerned

**insoutenable** [ɛ̃sutnabl] *adj* (*insupportable*) unbearable

**inspecter** [ɛ̃spɛkte] <1> *vt* to inspect

**inspecteur, -trice** [ɛ̃spɛktœʀ, -tʀis] *m, f* inspector; **~ de police** police detective; **~ des finances** state auditor (*auditing public finances*)

**inspection** [ɛ̃spɛksjɔ̃] *f* ❶ (*contrôle*) inspection ❷ (*corps de fonctionnaires*) board of inspectors

**inspiration** [ɛ̃spiʀasjɔ̃] *f a.* MED inspiration; **prendre une grande ~** to breathe in deeply ▸ **d'~ orientale** of oriental inspiration

**inspirer** [ɛ̃spiʀe] <1> **I.** *vt* ❶ ANAT to breathe in ❷ (*susciter*) ~ **du dégoût** to make one feel disgust; ~ **de la confiance** (*personne*) to inspire confidence ❸ (*suggérer*) ~ **une idée à qn** to give sb an idea; ~ **un roman à qn** to give sb the idea for a novel ❹ (*être à l'origine de: œuvre, personnage de roman*) to inspire; (*décision*) to prompt; **être inspiré par qc/qn** to be inspired by sth/sb ❺ (*rendre créatif*) ~ **qn** to inspire sb **II.** *vpr* **s'~ de qn/qc** to be inspired by sb/sth; **un film qui s'inspire d'un roman** a film inspired by a novel **III.** *vi* to breathe in

**instabilité** [ɛ̃stabilite] *f* instability

**instable** [ɛ̃stabl] *adj* unstable; (*temps*) unsettled; (*personne*) restless

**installation** [ɛ̃stalasjɔ̃] *f* ❶ (*mise en place*) installation; (*d'un meuble*) assembly; (*d'un campement*) setting up; ~ **de l'eau/du gaz** installation of water/gas ❷ *gén pl* (*équipement*) equipment; ~**s électriques/sanitaires** (*fils/tuyaux*) wiring/plumbing; (*prises/lavabos*) electrical/bathroom fixtures ❸ (*emménagement*) moving in

**installé(e)** [ɛ̃stale] *adj* ❶ (*aménagé: appartement*) furnished; (*atelier*) equipped ❷ (*qui jouit d'une situation confortable*) well-off; **être ~** to be set up in life

**installer** [ɛ̃stale] <1> **I.** *vt* ❶ (*mettre en place sous terre: câbles, tuyaux*) to lay ❷ (*mettre en place chez qn: câbles, tuyaux, électricité*) to put in; (*eau courante, électricité*) to install; (*meuble*) to assemble; (*barrage*) to build ❸ (*caser, loger*) ~ **qn/qc quelque part** to put sb/sth somewhere; **être installé en Bretagne** to live in Brittany ❹ (*établir officiellement*) to install **II.** *vpr* ❶ (*s'asseoir*) **s'~** to sit (down); (*commodément*) to settle (oneself) ❷ (*se loger*) **s'~** to settle; **s'~ chez qn** to move in with sb ❸ (*s'établir*) **s'~** to set up; (*commerçant*) to open up

**instant** [ɛ̃stɑ̃] *m* moment; **à chaque ~** (*d'ici peu*) at any moment; (*constamment*) all the time; **au même ~** at the same moment; **à l'~ (même)** at that (very) moment; (*tout de suite*) right away; **à l'~ où qn a fait qc** at the moment when sb did sth; **dans un ~** in a moment; **d'un ~ à l'autre** from one minute to the next; **pour l'~** for the moment; (*pendant*) **un ~** for a moment; **un ~!** one moment!

**instantané(e)** [ɛ̃stɑ̃tane] *adj* ❶ (*immédiat: réaction, réponse*) instant; (*mort*) instantaneous; **être ~** (*réponse*) to come instantly; (*mort*) to be immediate ❷ CULIN (*café*) instant; **soupe ~e** instant soup

**instauration** [ɛ̃stɔʀasjɔ̃] *f* (*d'un gouver-*

*nement*) establishment; (*d'un processus*) starting

**instaurer** [ɛ̃stɔʀe] <1> I. *vt* (*gouvernement*) to establish; (*mode*) to start; (*liens*) to create; (*processus*) to set up II. *vpr* **s'~** to be established; (*état d'esprit*) to be created; (*doute*) to be raised; **s'~ entre des personnes** (*collaboration*) to be set up; (*débat*) to open up

**instinct** [ɛ̃stɛ̃] *m* (*tendance innée*) instinct; **d'[o par] ~** by instinct

**instinctif, -ive** [ɛ̃stɛ̃ktif, -iv] *adj* instinctive

**institut** [ɛ̃stity] *m* institute; **Institut universitaire de technologie** technical school; **~ de beauté** beauty salon

**instituteur, -trice** [ɛ̃stitytœʀ, -tʀis] *m, f* (elementary school) teacher

**institution** [ɛ̃stitysjɔ̃] *f* ❶ (*établissement d'enseignement*) school ❷ (*création, fondation*) creation; (*d'un régime*) founding; (*d'une mesure, d'un usage*) institution ❸ (*chose instituée*) a. POL institution

**Institut monétaire européen** *m* European Monetary Institute

**instructif, -ive** [ɛ̃stʀyktif, -iv] *adj* instructive

**instruction** [ɛ̃stʀyksjɔ̃] *f* ❶ (*enseignement*) education; **~ civique** civics ❷ (*prescription*) a. MIL, ADMIN instruction ❸ *gén pl* (*mode d'emploi*) instructions

**instruit(e)** [ɛ̃stʀyi, it] *adj* educated

**instrument** [ɛ̃stʀymɑ̃] *m* ❶ (*outil*) instrument; **~ de travail** tool ❷ MUS **~ de musique** musical instrument; **jouer d'un ~** to play an instrument ❸ (*moyen*) tool

**insuffisant(e)** [ɛ̃syfizɑ̃, ɑ̃t] *adj* ❶ (*en quantité*) insufficient; (*moyens, personnel*) inadequate; (*nombre, dimension*) too small; **être ~** to not be enough; (*nombre, dimension*) to be too small ❷ (*en qualité*) inadequate; (*candidat, élève*) weak; (*travail*) poor

**insuline** [ɛ̃sylin] *f* insulin

**insulte** [ɛ̃sylt] *f* insult; **~ à la mémoire de qn** insult to the memory of sb

**insulter** [ɛ̃sylte] <1> I. *vt* to insult II. *vpr* **s'~** (*personnes*) to insult each other

**insupportable** [ɛ̃sypɔʀtabl] *adj* ❶ (*intolérable*) unbearable ❷ (*désagréable: caractère*) insufferable

**insurmontable** [ɛ̃syʀmɔ̃tabl] *adj* insurmountable

**insurrection** [ɛ̃syʀɛksjɔ̃] *f* insurrection

**intact(e)** [ɛ̃takt] *adj* intact

**intégral(e)** [ɛ̃tegʀal, -o] <-aux> *adj* (*audition, texte*) full; (*horreur*) utter

**intégration** [ɛ̃tegʀasjɔ̃] *f* ❶ (*union: économique, européenne, politique*) integration ❷ (*assimilation*) **~ dans qc** integration into sth ❸ *inf* (*admission*) **~ à qc** admission to sth

**intègre** [ɛ̃tɛgʀ] *adj* (*vie, juge*) honest; (*personne*) upright

**intégrer** [ɛ̃tegʀe] <5> *vpr* **s'~ à** [*o* **dans**] **qc** (*personne, chose*) to integrate into sth

**intégriste** [ɛ̃tegʀist] I. *adj* fundamentalist II. *mf* fundamentalist

**intellectuel(le)** [ɛ̃telɛktɥɛl] I. *adj* ❶ (*mental*) mental ❷ (*sollicitant l'intelligence*) intellectual II. *m(f)* intellectual

**intelligence** [ɛ̃teliʒɑ̃s] *f* (*entendement*) a. INFORM intelligence; **avec ~** intelligently

**intelligent(e)** [ɛ̃teliʒɑ̃, ʒɑ̃t] *adj* intelligent; **c'est ~!** *iron* that's clever!

**intempéries** [ɛ̃tɑ̃peʀi] *fpl* bad weather

**intenable** [ɛ̃t(ə)nabl] *adj* ❶ (*intolérable*) unbearable ❷ (*indéfendable*) untenable ❸ (*insupportable: adulte, enfant*) unruly; (*classe*) rowdy; **être ~** to be out of control

**intense** [ɛ̃tɑ̃s] *adj* ❶ (*fort*) intense ❷ (*dense: activité*) intense; (*circulation*) heavy

**intensif, -ive** [ɛ̃tɑ̃sif, -iv] *adj* intensive

**intensifier** [ɛ̃tɑ̃sifje] <1> I. *vt* to intensify; (*efforts, production*) to step up, (*chute des cours*) to accelerate II. *vpr* **s'~** to intensify; (*production*) to be stepped up

**intensité** [ɛ̃tɑ̃site] *f* (*d'un regard, sentiment, de la chaleur, lumière*) intensity;

~ **lumineuse** brightness; ~ **du courant** current

**intention** [ɛ̃tɑ̃sjɔ̃] f ❶(*volonté*) intention; **avoir de bonnes/mauvaises ~s à l'égard de qn** to be well-intentioned/ill-intentioned toward sb; **c'est l'~ qui compte** it's the thought that counts; **sans ~** unintentionally ❷(*but*) **à cette ~** to that end ▸ **à l'~ de qn** for sb

**intentionné(e)** [ɛ̃tɑ̃sjɔne] *adj* **être bien/mal ~ à l'égard de qn** to be well-intentioned/ill-intentioned toward sb

**intentionnel(le)** [ɛ̃tɑ̃sjɔnɛl] *adj* intentional; **être ~** to be deliberate; JUR to be premeditated

**interactif, -ive** [ɛ̃tɛʀaktif, -iv] *adj* interactive

**interaction** [ɛ̃tɛʀaksjɔ̃] f a. INFORM interaction

**intercepter** [ɛ̃tɛʀsɛpte] <1> *vt* to intercept

**interchangeable** [ɛ̃tɛʀʃɑ̃ʒabl] *adj* interchangeable

**interdiction** [ɛ̃tɛʀdiksjɔ̃] f prohibition; ~ **de stationner/de fumer** no parking/smoking

**interdire** [ɛ̃tɛʀdiʀ] *irr* **I.** *vt* ❶(*défendre*) ~ **à qn de** +*infin* to forbid sb to +*infin* ❷(*empêcher*) to preclude; ~ **à qn de faire qc** to stop sb from doing sth; **qc interdit le sport/le travail à qn** sth stops sb from playing sports/working ❸(*empêcher l'accès de*) ~ **sa porte à qn** to bar sb from one's door **II.** *vpr* **s'~ qc** to deny oneself sth; **s'~ qc/de faire qc** to abstain from doing sth

**interdit** [ɛ̃tɛʀdi] m taboo

**interdit(e)** [ɛ̃tɛʀdi, it] *adj* forbidden; (*film*) banned; ~ **aux moins de 16 ans** under 16 not admitted; ~ **aux chiens** no dogs allowed; ~ **au public** do not enter; **il est ~ à qn de** +*infin* sb is not allowed to +*infin;* **être ~ de séjour** to be banned from certain premises

**intéressant(e)** [ɛ̃teʀesɑ̃, ɑ̃t] **I.** *adj* ❶(*digne d'intérêt*) interesting; **chercher à se rendre ~** to seek attention;

**ne pas être/être peu ~** *péj* to be of no/little interest ❷(*avantageux: prix, affaire*) attractive; ~ **pour qn** worth sb's while; **il est ~ pour qn de** +*infin* it's worth sb's while to +*infin;* **être ~ à faire** to be worth doing **II.** *m(f)* **faire l'~** *péj* to show off

**intéressé(e)** [ɛ̃teʀese] **I.** *adj* ❶(*captivé*) interested ❷(*concerné*) concerned ❸(*égoïste*) self-interested **II.** *m(f)* ❶(*personne concernée*) person concerned ❷(*personne qui s'intéresse à qc*) interested person

**intéresser** [ɛ̃teʀese] <1> **I.** *vt* ❶(*captiver*) to interest; **être intéressé à faire qc** to be interested in doing sth; **rien ne l'intéresse** she's not interested in anything ❷(*concerner*) to concern **II.** *vpr* **s'~ à qn/qc** to be interested in sb/sth

**intérêt** [ɛ̃teʀɛ] m ❶(*attention, importance, attrait*) ~ **pour qn/qc** interest in sb/sth; **avec ~** with interest; **sans ~** without any interest; **un film/livre sans (aucun) ~** a film/book of no interest ❷(*importance*) significance ❸(*souvent pl (cause)* interest; **défendre les ~s de qn** to defend sb's interests ❹(*avantage*) **par ~** out of self-interest; **dans l'~ de qn** in sb's (own) interest; **dans l'~ de qc** in the interests of sth; **ne pas voir l'~ de faire qc** to see no point in doing sth ❺(*souvent pl (rendement)* interest; **7% d'~** 7% interest ▸ **il promet de revenir et (il) y a ~!** *inf* he's promised to come back and he'd better!

**interface** [ɛ̃tɛʀfas] f INFORM interface

**intérieur** [ɛ̃teʀjœʀ] m ❶(*opp: extérieur: d'un bâtiment*) interior; (*d'un objet*) inside; **à l'~** (*dedans*) inside; (*opp: en plein air*) indoors; **à l'~ de** inside; **à l'~ du magasin** inside the store; **à l'~ de la ville** within the city ❷(*aménagement: d'une maison, d'un magasin*) interior (design) ❸(*logement*) home; **femme d'~** house-proud woman ❹(*espace, pays*) interior; **à l'~ des terres** inland ❺(*ministère*) **à l'Intérieur** at the Ministry of the Interior

**intérieur(e)** [ɛ̃teRjœR] *adj* ① (*opp: extérieur*) interior ② (*concernant un pays*) domestic ③ PSYCH inner

**intermédiaire** [ɛ̃teRmedjɛR] **I.** *adj* (*couleur, ton*) intermediate; (*espace, niveau, époque*) intervening; (*solution*) compromise **II.** *mf* ① (*médiateur*) intermediary ② COM middleman **III.** *m* par l'~ de qn/qc through

**interminable** [ɛ̃teRminabl] *adj* interminable

**intermittence** [ɛ̃teRmitɑ̃s] *f* intermittence; (*sans la continuité voulue*) irregularity

**international(e)** [ɛ̃teRnasjɔnal, -o] <-aux> **I.** *adj* international **II.** *m(f)* SPORT international

**internaute** [ɛ̃teRnot] **I.** *adj* Internet **II.** *mf* Internet surfer

**interne** [ɛ̃teRn] **I.** *adj* internal **II.** *mf* ① ECOLE boarding student ② MED intern

**Internet** [ɛ̃teRnɛt] *m* Internet; **accéder à ~** to access the Internet; **commercer sur ~** to engage in e-commerce

**interpeller** [ɛ̃teRpəle] <1> *vt* ① (*arrêter*) **~ qn** (*police*) to detain sb (for questioning) ② (*sommer de s'expliquer*) **~ un témoin sur un accident** to question a witness about an accident ③ (*apostropher*) **~ qn** to call out to sb; (*avec brusquerie*) to yell at sb

**interphone®** [ɛ̃teRfɔn] *m* intercom; **parler à qn par l'~** to speak to sb over the intercom

**interposer** [ɛ̃teRpoze] <1> *vpr* ① **s'~ dans qc** to intervene in sth ② (*se placer*) **s'~** to interpose; **s'~ entre deux personnes** to put oneself between two people

**interprétation** [ɛ̃teRpRetasjɔ̃] *f* interpretation

**interprète** [ɛ̃teRpRɛt] *mf* ① MUS player ② CINE, THEAT actor ③ (*traducteur*) interpreter ④ (*porte-parole*) spokesman, spokeswoman *m*, *f*

**interpréter** [ɛ̃teRpRete] <5> *vt* ① MUS, CINE, THEAT to play; (*de façon personnelle*) to interpret ② (*expliquer, traduire*) to interpret ③ (*comprendre*) **~ qc en**

**bien/mal** to take sth the right/wrong way

**interrogation** [ɛ̃teRɔgasjɔ̃] *f* ① (*question*) question ② ECOLE test ③ (*action de questionner*) interrogation

**interrogatoire** [ɛ̃teRɔgatwaR] *m* (*de la police*) questioning

**interroger** [ɛ̃teRɔʒe] <2a> **I.** *vt* ① (*questionner*) **~ qn sur un sujet** to question sb on a subject; (*pour un sondage*) to poll sb on a subject; **40% des personnes interrogées** 40% of those questioned ② (*consulter: répondeur*) to check ③ (*examiner: conscience*) to examine **II.** *vpr* **s'~ sur qn/qc** to wonder about sb/sth

**interrompre** [ɛ̃teRɔ̃pR] *irr* **I.** *vt* ① (*couper la parole, déranger*) to interrupt ② (*arrêter: activité*) to interrupt; (*grossesse*) to terminate; (*silence*) to break; **être interrompu** (*trafic*) to be disrupted **II.** *vpr* **s'~** (*personne*) to break off; (*discussion, film*) to close; (*conversation*) to stop

**interrupteur** [ɛ̃teRyptœR] *m* switch

**interruption** [ɛ̃teRypsjɔ̃] *f* ① (*arrêt définitif*) end; **~ (volontaire) de grossesse** termination of pregnancy ② (*arrêt provisoire*) interruption; **sans ~** continuously; **~ de deux heures/trois mois** two-hour/three-month break

**intersection** [ɛ̃teRsɛksjɔ̃] *f* ① (*de routes*) intersection; (*de voies ferrées*) crossing ② MATH intersection

**intervalle** [ɛ̃teRval] *m* ① (*écart*) gap; (*espace de temps*); **~ de temps** interval; **à huit jours d'~** (*après huit jours*) a week later; (*séparés de huit jours*) a week apart ② MUS interval

**intervenir** [ɛ̃teRvəniR] <9> *vi* ① (*entrer en action: police, pompiers*) to intervene; **~ dans un débat/une affaire** to intervene in a debate/an affair ② (*prendre la parole*) to speak ① (*survenir: accord*) to be reached; (*contretemps*) to occur; (*fait*) to happen

**intervention** [ɛ̃teRvɑ̃sjɔ̃] *f* ① (*action*) intervention ② (*prise de parole*) speech ③ MED operation

**interview** [ɛ̃tɛʀvju] *f* interview

**intestin** [ɛ̃tɛstɛ̃] *m souvent pl* intestine

**intestinal(e)** [ɛ̃tɛstinal, -o] <-aux> *adj* intestinal; **transit** ~ digestion

**intime** [ɛ̃tim] *adj* ❶ (*secret*) intimate; (*hygiène, toilette*) personal; (*vie, chagrin*) private; **journal** ~ personal diary ❷ (*privé: cérémonie, dîner*) quiet ❸ (*confortable: atmosphère, lieu*) intimate ❹ (*étroit, proche: ami, rapports*) close; **être** ~ **avec qn** to be on close terms with sb

**intimider** [ɛ̃timide] <1> *vt* to intimidate

**intimité** [ɛ̃timite] *f* ❶ (*vie privée*) privacy; **dans l'**~ (*se marier*) in a private ceremony; (*déjeuner*) with friends ❷ (*relation étroite*) intimacy ❸ (*confort: d'un salon*) comfort

**intituler** [ɛ̃tityle] <1> I. *vt* ~ **un livre "Mémoires"** to title a book "Memoirs"; **être intitulé "Mémoires"** to be entitled "Memoirs" II. *vpr* **s'**~ **"Mémoires"** to be entitled "Memoirs"

**intolérable** [ɛ̃tɔleʀabl] *adj* intolerable

**intolérance** [ɛ̃tɔleʀɑ̃s] *f* (*sectarisme*) intolerance

**intolérant(e)** [ɛ̃tɔleʀɑ̃, ɑ̃t] *adj* intolerant

**intoxication** [ɛ̃tɔksikasjɔ̃] *f* ❶ (*empoisonnement*) poisoning; ~ **alimentaire** food poisoning ❷ (*influence*) brainwashing

**intoxiquer** [ɛ̃tɔksike] <1> I. *vt* (*empoisonner*) to poison; **être légèrement intoxiqué** (*pompier*) to be suffering from smoke inhalation II. *vpr* **s'**~ to poison oneself

**intramusculaire** [ɛ̃tʀamyskylɛʀ] *adj* intramuscular

**intransigeant(e)** [ɛ̃tʀɑ̃ziʒɑ̃, ʒɑ̃t] *adj* uncompromising

**intrépide** [ɛ̃tʀepid] *adj* ❶ (*courageux*) intrepid ❷ (*audacieux*) unashamed

**intrigant(e)** [ɛ̃tʀigɑ̃, ɑ̃t] I. *adj* scheming II. *m(f)* schemer

**intrigue** [ɛ̃tʀig] *f* ❶ CINE, LIT, THEAT plot ❷ (*manœuvre*) intrigue ❸ (*liaison*) ~ **amoureuse** love affair

**intriguer** [ɛ̃tʀige] <1> I. *vt* ❶ (*travail-* *ler*) to puzzle ❷ (*piquer la curiosité*) to intrigue II. *vi* to scheme

**introduction** [ɛ̃tʀɔdyksjɔ̃] *f* introduction; **chapitre d'**~ introductory chapter; **en** ~ by way of introduction

**introduire** [ɛ̃tʀɔdɥiʀ] *irr* I. *vt* ❶ (*personne*) to show in; (*objet*) to insert; (*liquide, gaz*) to introduce; ~ **qn dans une pièce** to show sb into a room; ~ **qn chez une famille** to introduce sb to a family; ~ **une clé dans qc** to insert a key into sth; ~ **du tabac en contrebande** to smuggle in tobacco ❷ (*faire adopter: mode*) to introduce II. *vpr* ❶ (*se faire admettre*) **s'**~ **dans une famille/un milieu** to gain entry to a family/a circle ❷ (*s'infiltrer*) **s'**~ **dans une maison** to get into a house; **s'**~ **dans qc** (*eau, fumée*) to seep into sth; (*impureté*) to get into sth ❸ (*se mettre*) **s'**~ **qc dans le nez/les oreilles** to put sth in one's nose/ears

**introuvable** [ɛ̃tʀuvabl] *adj* (*perdu: chose, personne*) nowhere to be found

**intrus(e)** [ɛ̃tʀy, yz] I. *adj* intruding; (*visiteur*) unwelcome II. *m(f)* intruder
▶ **cherchez** l'~ find the one that doesn't belong

**intuition** [ɛ̃tɥisjɔ̃] *f* intuition

**intuitivement** [ɛ̃tɥitivmɑ̃] *adv* intuitively

**inusable** [inyzabl] *adj* durable

**inutile** [inytil] *adj* useless; (*effort, mesure*) pointless; **être** ~ **à qn** to be no use to sb; **se sentir** ~ to feel useless; **il est/ n'est pas** ~ **de faire qc/que qn fasse qc** (*subj*) it's pointless/worthwhile doing sth/for sb to do sth; ~ **d'insister!** it's no good insisting!

**inutilement** [inytilmɑ̃] *adv* ❶ (*sans utilité*) uselessly ❷ (*en vain*) pointlessly

**inutilisable** [inytilizabl] *adj* ❶ (*qui n'offre aucune utilité*) useless ❷ (*dont on ne peut se servir*) unusable

**inutilité** [inytilite] *f* pointlessness

**invalide** [ɛ̃valid] I. *adj* disabled II. *mf* disabled person

**invariable** [ɛ̃vaʀjabl] *adj* ❶ (*qui ne*

*change pas*) *a.* LING invariable ② (*qu'on ne peut changer*) unchangeable

**invasion** [ɛ̃vazjɔ̃] *f* MIL *a. fig* invasion

**invendable** [ɛ̃vɑ̃dabl] *adj* nonmarketable; **il est ~** it can't be sold

**inventaire** [ɛ̃vɑ̃tɛʀ] *m* ① JUR (*des biens*) inventory ② COM inventory

**inventer** [ɛ̃vɑ̃te] <1> *vt* to invent

**invention** [ɛ̃vɑ̃sjɔ̃] *f* ① invention ② (*imagination*) inventiveness ③ (*mensonge*) lie

**invérifiable** [ɛ̃veʀifjabl] *adj* unverifiable

**inverse** [ɛ̃vɛʀs] I. *adj* opposite; MATH inverse II. *m* opposite; **c'est l'~ qui est vrai** the opposite is true; **à l'~ de qn/qc** contrary to sb/sth

**inversement** [ɛ̃vɛʀsəmɑ̃] *adv* conversely; **et/ou ~** and/or vice-versa

**inverser** [ɛ̃vɛʀse] <1> I. *vt* (*mots, phrases*) to turn around; (*évolution, mouvement, rôles*) to reverse II. *vpr* **s'~** (*mouvement, tendance*) to be reversed

**investir** [ɛ̃vɛstiʀ] <8> I. *vt* ① FIN ~ **son argent dans qc** to invest one's money in sth ② *fig* ~ **du temps/du travail dans qc** to invest time/work in sth II. *vi* ECON, FIN to invest III. *vpr* **s'~ dans qc** to involve oneself deeply in sth

**investissement** [ɛ̃vɛstismɑ̃] *m* ① ECON, FIN investment ② (*engagement*) ~ **de qn dans une activité** sb's involvement in an activity

**invincible** [ɛ̃vɛ̃sibl] *adj* (*personne, armée*) invincible; (*courage, détermination*) insuperable; (*charme, envie*) irresistible

**invisible** [ɛ̃vizibl] *adj* invisible

**invitation** [ɛ̃vitasjɔ̃] *f* invitation; ~ **à une manifestation/au restaurant/à déjeuner** invitation to a demonstration/a meal out/to lunch

**invité(e)** [ɛ̃vite] *m(f)* guest

**inviter** [ɛ̃vite] <1> *vt* ① (*convier*) ~ **qn à** + *infin* to invite sb to + *infin*; ~ **qn à danser** to ask sb to dance; ~ **qn à un anniversaire** to invite sb to a birthday party; ~ **qn chez soi** to invite sb over (to one's place) ② (*prier*) ~ **qn à** + *infin* to ask sb to + *infin*; ~ **qn à entrer** to ask

sb in; **être invité à** + *infin* to be requested to + *infin* ③ (*inciter à*) ~ **qn à une discussion** to invite sb to take part in a discussion; ~ **qn à** + *infin* to call on sb to + *infin*

**in vitro** [invitʀo] *adj, adv inv* in vitro

**invivable** [ɛ̃vivabl] *adj* unbearable

**involontaire** [ɛ̃vɔlɔ̃tɛʀ] *adj* (*erreur, mouvement, réflexion*) involuntary; (*spectateur, témoin*) unwitting; (*offense*) unintended

**involontairement** [ɛ̃vɔlɔ̃tɛʀmɑ̃] *adv* (*sursauter*) involuntarily; (*voir*) unwittingly; (*offenser*) unintentionally

**invraisemblable** [ɛ̃vʀɛsɑ̃blabl] *adj* ① (*qui ne semble pas vrai: histoire, argument*) improbable ② (*incroyable*) incredible

**invulnérable** [ɛ̃vylneʀabl] *adj* invulnerable

**Irak** [iʀak] *m* l'~ Iraq

**irakien(ne)** [iʀakjɛ̃, jɛn] *adj* Iraqi

**Iran** [iʀɑ̃] *m* l'~ Iran

**iranien(ne)** [iʀanjɛ̃, jɛn] *adj* Iranian

**iris** [iʀis] *m* ANAT, BOT iris

**irlandais** [iʀlɑ̃dɛ] *m* Irish; **l'~ gaélique** Irish Gaelic; *v.a.* **français**

**irlandais(e)** [iʀlɑ̃dɛ, ɛz] *adj* Irish

**Irlandais(e)** [iʀlɑ̃dɛ, ɛz] *m(f)* Irishman, Irishwoman *m, f*; **les ~** the Irish

**Irlande** [iʀlɑ̃d] *f* l'~ Ireland; **la république** [*o* **l'État libre**] **d'~** Republic of Ireland, Irish Republic; **l'~ du Nord** Northern Ireland

**ironie** [iʀɔni] *f* irony

**ironique** [iʀɔnik] *adj* ironic

**irradier** [iʀadje] <1a> I. *vi* (*douleur, lumière*) to radiate II. *vt* to irradiate

**irrationnel** [iʀasjɔnɛl] *m* l'~ the irrational

**irrationnel(le)** [iʀasjɔnɛl] *adj* irrational

**irréalisable** [iʀealizabl] *adj* unrealizable

**irréaliste** [iʀealist] *adj* unrealistic

**irréel(le)** [iʀeɛl] *adj* unreal

**irrégularité** [iʀegylaʀite] *f* ① (*inégalité*) irregularity; *pl* (*d'une surface, d'un terrain*) unevenness ② (*manque de régularité: d'un élève, d'une équi-*

*pe*) uneven performance ❸ *gén pl* (*illégalité*) irregularity; (*d'une situation*) illegality

**irrégulier, -ère** [iʀegylje, -ɛʀ] *adj* ❶ (*inégal*) irregular; (*écriture, terrain*) uneven ❷ (*discontinu: rythme, vitesse*) irregular; (*sommeil*) fitful; (*effort, travail, élève, sportif, résultats*) erratic ❸ (*illégal: absence, opération, procédure*) unauthorized; (*situation*) irregular ❹ LING (*pluriel, verbe*) irregular

**irrémédiable** [iʀemedjabl] *adj* (*aggravation*) irreversible; (*défaite*) irretrievable; (*erreur, défaut*) irreparable; (*mal*) incurable; (*malheur*) beyond remedy; (*situation*) irremediable

**irremplaçable** [iʀɑ̃plasabl] *adj* irreplaceable; (*instant*) unrepeatable

**irréparable** [iʀepaʀabl] **I.** *adj* (*objet, machine*) beyond repair; (*dommage, perte*) irreparable; (*erreur*) irretrievable **II.** *m* l'~ the irreparable

**irréprochable** [iʀepʀɔʃabl] *adj* (*vie, mère*) beyond reproach; (*travail*) faultless

**irrésistible** [iʀezistibl] *adj* ❶ (*impérieux*) irresistible ❷ (*qui fait rire*) uproarious

**irrésolu(e)** [iʀezɔly] *adj* (*personne, caractère*) irresolute; (*problème, question*) unresolved

**irrespirable** [iʀɛspiʀabl] *adj* stifling

**irresponsable** [iʀɛspɔ̃sabl] **I.** *adj* (*comportement, personne*) irresponsible; JUR incapable **II.** *mf* irresponsible person

**irréversible** [iʀevɛʀsibl] *adj* irreversible

**irriguer** [iʀige] <1> *vt* AGR to irrigate

**irritation** [iʀitasjɔ̃] *f* ❶ (*énervement*) irritation ❷ MED inflammation

**irriter** [iʀite] <1> *vt* to irritate

**irruption** [iʀypsjɔ̃] *f* faire ~ (*personne*) to burst in; (*eau*) to flood in

**islam** [islam] *m* l'~ Islam

**islamique** [islamik] *adj* Islamic

**Islande** [islɑ̃d] *f* l'~ Iceland

**isolé(e)** [izɔle] *adj* ❶ (*éloigné, unique: endroit, maison*) isolated ❷ (*seul: personne, maison*) lonely; (*bâtiment, arbre*) solitary ❸ TECH, ELEC insulated

**isolement** [izɔlmɑ̃] *m* ❶ (*solitude*) isolation ❷ ELEC, TECH insulation

**isoler** [izɔle] <1> **I.** *vt* ❶ (*séparer des autres*) *a.* BIO, CHIM to isolate; **être isolé du reste du monde** (*village*) to be cut off from the rest of the world ❷ TECH, ELEC ~ **qc de l'humidité** to insulate sth from dampness ❸ (*considérer à part*) ~ **qc** to take sth on its own **II.** *vpr* **s'~ de qn/qc** to isolate oneself from sb/sth

**isotherme** [izɔtɛʀm] *adj* **bouteille/sac ~** insulated flask/bag

**Israël** [isʀaɛl] *m* l'~ Israel

**israélien(ne)** [isʀaeljɛ̃, jɛn] *adj* Israeli

**israélite** [isʀaelit] **I.** *adj* Israelite **II.** *mf* Israelite

**issu(e)** [isy] *adj* ❶ (*né de*) **être ~ d'une famille modeste** to be from a modest family ❷ (*résultant de*) **être ~ de qc** to arise from sth

**issue** [isy] *f* ❶ (*sortie*) exit; **~ de secours** emergency exit; **chemin/route/voie sans ~** dead end; (*signalisation*) no through road ❷ (*solution*) outcome; **sans ~** (*problème*) with no solution; (*situation*) at a standstill; (*avenir*) with no prospects ❸ (*fin*) end; **avoir une ~ fatale/heureuse** to end in tragedy/happily

**Italie** [itali] *f* l'~ Italy

**italien** [italjɛ̃] *m* Italian; *v.a.* **français**

**italien(ne)** [italjɛ̃, jɛn] *adj* Italian

**Italien(ne)** [italjɛ̃, jɛn] *m(f)* Italian

**italique** [italik] **I.** *m* **en ~(s)** in italics **II.** *adj* italic

**itinéraire** [itineʀɛʀ] *m* ❶ (*parcours*) itinerary ❷ *fig* path

**ivoire** [ivwaʀ] *m* ivory

**ivoirien(ne)** [ivwaʀjɛ̃, jɛn] *adj* Ivorian

**ivre** [ivʀ] *adj* drunk

**ivrogne** [ivʀɔɲ] *mf* drunk

# J j

**J, j** [ʒi] *m inv* J, j; **~ comme Joseph** (*au téléphone*) j as in Juliet

**j'** [ʒ] *pron v.* **je**

**jacasser** [ʒakase] <1> *vi* (*pie, personne*) to chatter

**jacinthe** [ʒasɛ̃t] *f* hyacinth

**jade** [ʒad] *m* jade

**jadis** [ʒadis] *adv* formerly

**jaguar** [ʒagwaʀ] *m* jaguar

**jaillir** [ʒajiʀ] <8> *vi* ❶(*gicler: eau*) to gush out; (*sang*) to spurt out; (*flammes*) to shoot up; (*éclair*) to flash ❷(*fuser: rires*) to burst out ❸(*surgir: personne*) to spring up [*o* out] ❹(*se manifester: vérité, idée*) to emerge

**jalon** [ʒalɔ̃] *m* ❶(*piquet*) marker ❷*souvent pl* (*repère*) landmark

**jalonner** [ʒalɔne] <1> *vt* ❶(*tracer: terrain*) to mark out ❷(*marquer*) **~ une carrière** (*succès*) to punctuate

**jalousie** [ʒaluzi] *f* ❶(*en amour, amitié*) jealousy ❷(*envie*) envy

**jaloux, -ouse** [ʒalu, -uz] **I.** *adj* ❶(*en amour, amitié*) **~ de qn** jealous of sb ❷(*envieux*) **~ de qn/qc** envious of sb/sth **II.** *m, f* ❶(*en amour, amitié*) jealous person ❷(*envieux*) envious person

**Jamaïque** [ʒamaik] *f* **la ~** Jamaica

**jamais** [ʒamɛ] *adv* ❶*avec construction négative* (*en aucun cas*) never; **~ plus** [*o* **plus ~**] never again ❷(*seulement*) only; **ça ne fait ~ que deux heures qu'il est parti** he left just two hours ago ❸*avec construction positive ou interrogative* (*un jour*) ever; **si ~ elle donne de l'argent** if ever she should give money

**jambe** [ʒɑ̃b] *f* leg; **les ~s croisées** with one's legs crossed

**jambière** [ʒɑ̃bjɛʀ] *f* legging

**jambon** [ʒɑ̃bɔ̃] *m* ham; **~ de Paris** cooked ham

**jambonneau** [ʒɑ̃bɔno] <x> *m* ham knuckle

**jante** [ʒɑ̃t] *f* rim

**janvier** [ʒɑ̃vje] *m* January; *v.a.* **août**

**Japon** [ʒapɔ̃] *m* **le ~** Japan

**japonais** [ʒapɔnɛ] *m* Japanese; *v.a.* **français**

**japonais(e)** [ʒapɔnɛ, ɛz] *adj* Japanese

**japper** [ʒape] <1> *vi* to yap

**jardin** [ʒaʀdɛ̃] *m* garden; **~ public** (*public*) park

**jardinage** [ʒaʀdinaʒ] *m* gardening

**jardiner** [ʒaʀdine] *vi* to do some gardening

**jardinier, -ière** [ʒaʀdinje, -jɛʀ] **I.** *adj* (*plante*) garden **II.** *m, f* gardener

**jardinière** [ʒaʀdinjɛʀ] *f* ❶CULIN mixed vegetables ❷(*bac à plantes*) window box

**jargon** [ʒaʀgɔ̃] *m* *péj* ❶(*charabia*) gibberish ❷(*langue technique*) jargon

**jarret** [ʒaʀɛ] *m* (*chez l'homme*) back of the leg; (*chez l'animal*) hock

**jauge** [ʒoʒ] *f* **~ d'essence** gas gauge

**jaunâtre** [ʒonɑtʀ] *adj* yellowish

**jaune** [ʒon] **I.** *adj* yellow **II.** *m* ❶(*couleur*) yellow ❷(*partie d'un œuf*) (egg) yolk **III.** *adv* **rire ~** to give a forced laugh

**jaunir** [ʒoniʀ] <8> **I.** *vi* to turn yellow; (*papier*) to yellow **II.** *vt* **~ un tissu** (*lumière*) to turn a material yellow; (*nicotine*) to stain a material yellow

**jaunisse** [ʒonis] *f* jaundice

**javel** [ʒavɛl] *f sans pl* bleach

**javelot** [ʒavlo] *m* javelin

**jazz** [dʒaz] *m* jazz

**je** [ʒə, ʒ] <j'> *pron pers* I; **moi, ~ m'appelle Jean** my name is Jean; **que vois-~?** what do I see there?

**jean** [dʒin] *m* ❶(*tissu*) denim ❷*sing o pl* (*pantalon*) (pair of) jeans

**jeep®** [dʒip] *f* Jeep®

**jersey** [ʒɛʀzɛ] *m* jersey

**jet** [ʒɛ] *m* ❶(*giclée: d'un tuyau*) jet; **~ d'eau** fountain ❷(*action*) throwing;

(*d'un filet*) casting ❸ (*résultat*) throw ▶ **le premier** ~ the first draft

**jetable** [ʒ(ə)tabl] *adj* disposable

**jetée** [ʒ(ə)te] *f* jetty

**jeter** [ʒ(ə)te] <3> **I.** *vt* ❶ (*lancer*) to throw; ~ **un ballon/une pierre à qn** to throw a ball to sb/a stone at sb ❷ (*lâcher: pistolet*) to drop; (*sonde*) to cast; (*bouée*) to throw ❸ (*se débarrasser de*) to throw away; (*liquide*) to pour out; (*lest*) to jettison ❹ *inf* (*vider: importun*) to chuck out; (*employé*) to fire ❺ (*pousser*) ~ **qn à terre** to throw sb to the ground ❻ (*mettre rapidement*) ~ **qc sur ses épaules** to fling sth over one's shoulders ❼ (*mettre en place: passerelle*) to set up ❽ (*émettre: étincelles*) to throw out ❾ (*répandre: trouble*) to stir up; (*désordre*) to spread ❿ (*dire: remarque*) to throw in ▶ ~ **un regard/(coup d')œil à qn** to glance at sb; (*pour surveiller*) to keep an eye on sb; **en** ~ *inf* to be really something **II.** *vpr* ❶ (*s'élancer*) **se** ~ to throw oneself; **se** ~ **en arrière** to jump back; **se** ~ **à plat ventre/sous un train** to throw oneself down/in front of a train; **se** ~ **au cou de qn** to fling oneself around sb's neck; **se** ~ **contre un arbre** to crash into a tree; **se** ~ **à l'eau** to jump into the water; *fig* to take the plunge ❷ (*s'engager*) **se** ~ **à l'assaut de qc** to launch into sth ❸ (*déboucher*) **se** ~ **dans qc** to flow into sth ❹ (*être jetable*) **se** ~ to be disposable

**jeton** [ʒ(ə)tɔ̃] *m* ❶ JEUX counter ❷ (*plaque à la roulette*) chip ❸ TEL token ▶ **faux** ~ *inf* phony; **avoir les** ~**s** *inf* to be scared stiff

**jeu** [ʒø] <x> *m* ❶ (*fait de s'amuser*) play, playing; ~ **de dés** game of dice; ~ **de rôle(s)** role play; ~ **d'équipe** team game; ~ **de piste** treasure hunt; **jouer le** ~ to play the game ❷ (*boîte, partie*) game; ~ **vidéo/de construction** video/building game ❸ SPORT (*manière de jouer*) game ❹ (*lieu du jeu*) ~ **de boules** bowling ground without grass; **terrain de** ~**x** playground; SPORT

playing field; **le ballon est hors** ~ the ball is out of bounds; **remettre le ballon en** ~ to put the ball back into play ❺ (*jeu d'argent*) ~ **de hasard** game of chance ❻ (*série*) ~ **de clés** set of keys ❼ (*interaction*) ~ **des alliances** interplay of alliances ❽ (*manège: du destin*) game; ~ **de l'amour** love-play ❾ (*habileté*) **jouer double** ~ to play a double game ❿ (*action facile*) **c'est un** ~ **d'enfant** it's child's play ▶ **être vieux** ~ to be old-fashioned; **faire le** ~ **de qn** to play into sb's hands; **mettre sa vie en** ~ to risk one's life

**jeudi** [ʒødi] *m* Thursday; ~ **saint** Maundy Thursday; *v.a.* **dimanche**

**jeun** [ʒœ̃] **venez à** ~ come without having eaten or drunk anything

**jeune** [ʒœn] **I.** *adj* ❶ (*opp: vieux*) young ❷ *antéposé* (*cadet*) **ma** ~ **sœur** my younger sister; **le** ~ **Durandol** Durandol junior ❸ (*inexpérimenté*) inexperienced; **être** ~ **dans le métier** to be new to the trade ❹ *postposé* (*comme un jeune*) **faire** ~ to look young ❺ *antéposé* (*d'enfance*) **dès son plus** ~ **âge** from his/her earliest years ❻ *postposé* (*nouveau: vin*) young **II.** *mf* ❶ (*personne*) young man/girl ❷ *pl* (*jeunes gens*) young people

**jeûne** [ʒøn] *m* REL, MED fast, fasting; **la rupture du** ~ breaking one's fast; (*fêtes de la fin du ramadan*) Eid al-Fitr

**jeûner** [ʒøne] <1> *vi* to fast

**jeunesse** [ʒœnɛs] *f* ❶ (*état*) youthfulness ❷ (*période*) youth ❸ (*personnes jeunes*) young people ❹ (*nouveauté, fraîcheur*) youthfulness

**JO** [ʒio] *mpl abr de* **jeux Olympiques** Olympics

**joaillerie** [ʒɔajʀi] *f* ❶ (*bijouterie*) jewelry store ❷ (*art, métier*) jewelry making ❸ (*marchandises*) jewelry

**job** [dʒɔb] *m inf* job

**jockey** [ʒɔkɛ] *m* jockey

**jogging** [(d)ʒɔgiɲ] *m* ❶ (*footing*) jogging; **faire du** ~ to go jogging ❷ (*survêtement*) sweatsuit

**joie** [ʒwa] *f* ❶ (*bonheur*) joy; **cri de** ~

cry of joy; **avec ~** with delight; **~ de vi-vre** joie de vivre; **je m'en fais une (tel-le) ~** I'm (really) looking forward to it; **pleurer/sauter de ~** to weep/jump for joy ② *pl (plaisirs)* pleasures *pl*; **sans ~s** joyless ►**c'est pas la ~** *inf* things could be better

**joindre** [ʒwɛ̃dR] *irr* **I.** *vt* ① *(faire se tou-cher)* to join; *(mains)* to clasp; *(talons)* to put together ② *(relier)* to link ③ *(rassembler)* **~ des efforts** to com-bine efforts ④ *(ajouter)* **~ qc à un dos-sier** to add sth to a file; **~ le geste à la parole** to suit the action to the word ⑤ *(atteindre: personne)* to reach **II.** *vi (fenêtre)* to shut properly; *(lattes)* to fit properly **III.** *vpr* ① *(s'associer)* **se ~ à qn/qc** to join sb/sth; **joignez-vous à nous** come (over) and join us ② *(partici-per à)* **se ~ à une conversation** to join in a conversation **se ~** to touch

**joint** [ʒwɛ̃] *m* ① *(espace)* joint ② *(garni-ture: d'un couvercle)* seal; *(d'un robi-net)* washer

**joint(e)** [ʒwɛ̃, ɛ̃t] **I.** *part passé de* **join-dre** **II.** *adj* ① *(adhérent)* **mains ~es** clasped hands; **pieds ~s** feet together ② *(commun: efforts, compte)* joint ③ *(ajouté)* enclosed; **pièce ~e** enclo-sure ④ *(sans jeu)* fitting tightly together ⑤ *(bien assemblés: planches)* fitted flush

**jointure** [ʒwɛ̃tyR] *f* joint

**joli(e)** [ʒɔli] *adj* ① *(agréable: voix)* pleas-ant; *(intérieur, vêtement d'homme)* nice; *(chanson, vêtement de femme)* nice, pretty ② *(considérable)* nice; *(po-sition)* good ③ *iron* **un ~ gâchis** a fine mess; **c'est du ~!** that's great!

**joncher** [ʒɔ̃ʃe] <1> *vt* to strew

**jonction** [ʒɔ̃ksjɔ̃] *f* ① *(liaison)* a. TECH, ELEC junction; *(de routes)* (road) junc-tion; *(de fleuves)* confluence; *(de voies ferrées)* points *pl* ② *(action)* linkup

**jongler** [ʒɔ̃gle] <1> *vi* to juggle

**jonquille** [ʒɔ̃kij] **I.** *f* daffodil **II.** *adj inv* (bright) yellow

**Jordanie** [ʒɔRdani] *f* **la ~** Jordan

**jouable** [ʒwabl] *adj* ① MUS playable ② *(faisable)* feasible

**joual** [ʒwal] <s> *m Québec* joual; *v.a.* **français**

**joue** [ʒu] *f* ① ANAT cheek; **avoir les ~s creuses** to be hollow-cheeked ② *pl (parois latérales: d'un fauteuil)* side panels ►**en ~!** take aim!

**jouer** [ʒwe] <1> **I.** *vi* ① *(s'amuser)* a. SPORT, MUS to play; **~ au foot** to play soc-cer; **~ du piano** to play the piano; **faire ~ qn** to organize a game for sb; **à toi/vous de ~!** it's your turn! ② *fig* **~ avec les sentiments de qn** to play with sb's feelings; **c'est pour ~** I'm only joking ③ THEAT, CINE to play; **~ dans qc** to act in sth ④ *(affecter d'être)* **~ à qn** to play at be-ing sb ⑤ FIN **~ à la bourse** to speculate on the stock market ⑥ *(risquer)* **~ avec sa santé** to gamble with one's health ⑦ *(intervenir: mesure)* to apply; *(rela-tions)* to count; **~ de son influence** to use one's influence ►**ça a joué en ma faveur** that has worked in my favor; **bien joué!** *(au jeu)* well played!; *fig* well done! **II.** *vt* ① JEUX, MUS *(carte, re-vanche)* to play; *(pion)* to move; **je joue atout cœur** hearts are trumps ② *(miser)* to back ③ *(risquer: sa tête)* to risk; *(sa réputation)* to stake ④ THEAT, CINE *(pièce)* to stage; *(rôle)* to play ⑤ *(feindre)* **~ la comédie** to put on an act ►**rien n'est encore joué** nothing is settled yet **III.** *vpr* ① *(se moquer)* **se ~ de qn** to deceive sb; **se ~ des lois** to scoff at the law ② *(être joué)* **se ~** *(film)* to be shown; *(spectacle)* to be on ③ *(se dérouler)* **se ~** *(crime)* to happen ④ *(se décider)* **se ~** *(avenir)* to be at stake

**jouet** [ʒwɛ] *m (jeu)* toy; **marchand de ~s** toy store owner

**joueur, -euse** [ʒwœR, -øz] **I.** *adj (ani-mal, enfant, tempérament)* playful **II.** *m, f* JEUX, SPORT player; **être mau-vais ~** to be a bad loser

**joufflu(e)** [ʒufly] *adj* chubby-cheeked

**jouir** [ʒwiR] <8> *vi* ① *(apprécier)* **~ de la vie** to enjoy life ② *(disposer de)* **~ de**

**privilèges/d'une bonne santé** to enjoy privileges/good health; **~ d'un bien** to own a property ③(*sexuellement*) to have an orgasm

**jouissance** [ʒwisɑ̃s] *f* ①(*plaisir*) pleasure; **être avide de ~s** to be pleasure-loving ②(*usage*) **la ~ d'un immeuble** the use of a building ③(*orgasme*) orgasm

**jour** [ʒuʀ] *m* ①(*24 heures*) day; **par ~** daily; **tous les ~** a day, daily; **tous les ~s** every day ②(*opp: nuit*) day; **dormir le ~** to sleep during the day; **être de ~** MIL to be on day duty ③(*opp: obscurité*) daylight; **faux ~** deceptive light; **il fait (grand) ~** it's (broad) daylight; **le ~ baisse/se lève** it's getting dark/light; **au petit ~** at dawn ④(*jour précis*) day; **le ~ J** (on) D-day; **~ de Noël** (on) Christmas Day; **~ des Rois** Twelfth Night; **~ du Seigneur** Sabbath; **les ~s de marché/de pluie** (on) market/rainy days; **plat du ~** today's special; **goût du ~** current tastes *pl*; **notre entretien de ce ~** our discussion today ⑤(*période vague*) **à ce ~** to date; **un de ces ~s** one of these days; **de nos ~s** these days; **l'autre ~** the other day; **un ~ ou l'autre** someday; **habit de tous les ~s** workaday clothes *pl*; **tous les ~s que (le bon) Dieu fait** day in day out ⑥*pl*, *soutenu* (*vie*) **finir ses ~s à l'hospice** to end one's days in a home; **vieux ~s** old age ▶**d'un ~ à l'autre** (*soudain*) from one day to the next; (*sous peu*) any day now; **au grand ~** for all to see; **se montrer sous son vrai ~** to show one's true colors; **demain, il fera ~** tomorrow is another day; **mettre qc à ~** to update sth; **se mettre à ~ dans qc** to bring oneself up to date on sth; **voir le ~** (*personne*) to come into the world; (*projet*) to see the light of day; **au ~ le ~** one day at a time; (*précairement*) from hand to mouth

**journal** [ʒuʀnal, -o] <-aux> *m* ①PRESSE newspaper; **~ de mode** fashion magazine ②(*bureaux*) newspaper office ③(*mémoire*) **~ intime** personal diary;

**~ de bord** NAUT (ship's) logbook ④(*média non imprimé*) **~ télévisé** television news *pl*

**journalier, -ière** [ʒuʀnalje, -jɛʀ] **I.** *adj* daily **II.** *m, f* AGR day laborer

**journalisme** [ʒuʀnalism] *m* journalism

**journaliste** [ʒuʀnalist] *mf* journalist

**journée** [ʒuʀne] *f* ①(*durée du jour, temps de travail*) day; **pendant la ~** during the day; **~ de grève** day of strike action; **~ de 8 heures** 8-hour day ②(*salaire*) day's wages *pl* ③(*recette*) day's takings *pl*; **faire une ~/des ~s** to work as a day laborer; **être payé à la ~** to be paid by the day ④(*distance*) **à une ~ de marche/voyage** a day's walk/journey away

**jovial(e)** [ʒɔvjal, -jo] <*s o* -aux> *adj* jovial

**jovialité** [ʒɔvjalite] *f* joviality

**joyau** [ʒwajo] <x> *m a. fig* jewel

**joyeusement** [ʒwajøzmɑ̃] *adv* happily

**joyeux, -euse** [ʒwajø, -jøz] *adj* (*chant*) joyful; (*personne*) cheerful; (*compagnie*) merry; **joyeuse fête!** many happy returns!; **~ anniversaire!** happy birthday!

**jubilation** [ʒybilasjɔ̃] *f* jubilation

**jubiler** [ʒybile] <1> *vi* to be jubilant

**jucher** [ʒyʃe] <1> *vpr* **se ~ sur qc** to perch on sth

**judaïque** [ʒydaik] *adj* Jewish; (*loi*) Judaic

**judaïsme** [ʒydaism] *m* Judaism

**judiciaire** [ʒydisjɛʀ] *adj* judicial; (*casier*) police [*o* criminal] record; **police ~** ≈ Criminal Investigation Department

**judicieux, -euse** [ʒydisjø, -jøz] *adj* judicious

**judo** [ʒydo] *m* judo

**juge** [ʒyʒ] *mf* ①(*magistrat*) judge; **~ d'instruction** examining magistrate ②(*arbitre*) referee; **je vous laisse ~** I'll let you be the judge ③SPORT **~ de touche** linesman

**juge-arbitre** [ʒyʒaʀbitʀ] <juges-arbitres> *m* referee

**jugement** [ʒyʒmɑ̃] *m* ①(*action de ju-*

*ger, opinion*) judgment ② (*sentence*) sentence

**juger** [ʒyʒe] <2a> I. *vt* ① JUR ~ **qn pour vol** to try sb for theft; ~ **qn coupable** to find sb guilty ② (*arbitrer*) ~ **un différend** to arbitrate in a dispute ③ (*évaluer: livre, situation*) to judge ④ (*estimer*) to consider II. *vi* ① JUR to judge ② (*estimer*) ~ **de qc** to assess sth; **à en** ~ **par qc** judging by sth

**juif, -ive** [ʒɥif, -iv] *adj* Jewish

**Juif, -ive** [ʒɥif, -iv] *m, f* Jew; **le ~ errant** the Wandering Jew

**juillet** [ʒɥijɛ] *m* July; *v.a.* **août**

**juin** [ʒɥɛ̃] *m* June; *v.a.* **août**

**jumeau, -elle** [ʒymo, -ɛl] <x> I. *adj* twin II. *m, f* ① (*besson*) twin; **vrais/ faux ~x** identical/fraternal twins ② (*frère*) twin brother ③ (*sœur*) twin sister ④ (*sosie*) double

**jumelage** [ʒymlaʒ] *m* pairing

**jumeler** [ʒymle] <3> *vt* POL (*deux villes*) to pair up

**jumelles** [ʒymɛl] *fpl* (*en optique*) binoculars *pl*

**jument** [ʒymɑ̃] *f* mare

**jumping** [dʒœmpiŋ] *m* show jumping

**jungle** [ʒɑ̃gl, ʒɔ̃gl] *f* jungle

**junior** [ʒynjɔr] I. *adj* (*catégorie*) junior II. *mf* junior

**jupe** [ʒyp] *f* skirt

**Jura** [ʒyra] *m* **le ~** the Jura (Mountains)

**jurassien(ne)** [ʒyrasjɛ̃, jɛn] *adj* of the Jura (Mountains)

**juré(e)** [ʒyre] I. *adj a. fig* sworn II. *m(f)* JUR juror

**jurer** [ʒyre] <1> I. *vt* ① (*promettre, affirmer*) ~ **à ses parents de** +*infin* to swear to one's parents to +*infin*; **faire ~ à un collègue de** +*infin* to make a colleague swear to +*infin*; **je te** [*o* **vous**] **jure!** *inf* honestly! ② (*se promettre*) ~ **de se venger** to swear vengeance ③ (*croire*) **j'aurais juré que c'était toi** I could have sworn that it was you; **ne ~ que par qn/qc** to swear by sb/sth II. *vi* ① (*pester*) ~ **contre qn/qc** to swear at sb/sth ② (*détonner*) ~ **avec qc** to clash with sth ③ (*affirmer*) ~ **de**

**qc** to swear to sth ④ (*croire*) **il ne faut ~ de rien** you never can tell III. *vpr* ① (*se promettre mutuellement*) **se ~ qc** to swear sth to one another ② (*décider*) **se ~ de** +*infin* to vow to +*infin*

**juridique** [ʒyridik] *adj* ① (*judiciaire*) judicial ② (*qui a rapport au droit*) legal

**jurisprudence** [ʒyrisprydɑ̃s] *f* case law

**juriste** [ʒyrist] *mf* lawyer

**juron** [ʒyrɔ̃] *m* swear word

**jury** [ʒyri] *m* ① JUR jury ② ART, SPORT panel of judges ③ ECOLE, UNIV board of examiners

**jus** [ʒy] *m* ① (*suc: d'un fruit, d'une viande*) juice ② *inf* (*café*) coffee ③ *inf* (*courant*) juice

**jusque** [ʒysk] <*jusqu'>* I. *prep* ① (*limite de lieu*) as far as; **grimper jusqu'à 3000 m** to climb up to 3,000 meters; **jusqu'aux genoux** up to one's knees; **viens jusqu'ici!** come up to here!; **jusqu'où?** how far? ② (*limite de temps*) until; **jusqu'à midi/au soir** until noon/the evening; **jusqu'à/en mai** until now/May ③ (*y compris*) even; **tous jusqu'au dernier** every last one; ~ **dans** even in ④ (*au plus*) **jusqu'à dix personnes** up to ten people ⑤ (*limite*) **jusqu'à un certain point** up to a (certain) point; **jusqu'où** as far as ⑥ (*assez pour*) **manger jusqu'à en être malade** to eat to the point of being sick; **il va jusqu'à prétendre que c'est moi** he goes so far as to claim that it's me II. *conj* **jusqu'à ce qu'il vienne** until he comes

**justaucorps** [ʒystokɔr] *m* SPORT body stocking

**juste** [ʒyst] I. *adj* ① (*équitable*) just; (*condition*) fair; **ce n'est pas ~** it's not fair ② *antéposé* (*fondé*) justified ③ (*trop court: vêtement*) too short ④ (*trop étroit*) too tight; (*ouverture*) narrow ⑤ (*à peine suffisant*) barely enough ⑥ (*exact*) correct; (*heure*) right; **c'est ~!** that's (quite) right!; **à 8 heures ~(s)** at 8 o'clock on the dot; **apprécier qc à sa ~ valeur** to appreciate the true worth of sth ⑦ (*pertinent*) pertinent

**⑧** MUS (*note*) true; (*voix, instrument*) in tune **II.** *m* REL just man **III.** *adv* **①** (*avec exactitude*) accurately; (*penser*) logically; (*raisonner*) soundly; **parler ~** to find the right words; **dire ~** to be right; **deviner ~** to guess right(ly) **②** (*exactement, seulement*) just; **il habite ~ à côté** he lives right next door **③** (*à peine: mesurer*) exactly; **au plus ~** just enough; **cela entre ~** that barely fits in; **tout ~** hardly ▶ **être un peu ~** *inf* (*avoir peu d'argent*) to be short of cash; **au ~** exactly

**justement** [ʒystəmɑ̃] *adv* **①** (*à bon droit*) rightly **②** (*pertinemment: remarquer*) correctly; (*penser*) logically; (*raisonner*) soundly **③** (*exactement*) exactly **④** (*précisément*) precisely

**justesse** [ʒystɛs] *f* **①** (*précision*) accuracy **②** (*pertinence*) aptness; (*d'un raisonnement*) soundness ▶ **de ~** only just

**justice** [ʒystis] *f* **①** (*principe*) justice **②** (*loi*) law; **rendre la ~** to dispense justice; **obtenir ~** to obtain justice **③** (*juridiction*) jurisdiction; **en ~** in court; **assigner qn en ~** to summon sb to court ▶ **se faire ~** (*se venger*) to take the law into one's own hands

**justicier, -ière** [ʒystisje, -jɛʀ] *m, f* **①** (*redresseur de torts*) righter of wrongs **②** (*vengeur*) avenger

**justifiable** [ʒystifjabl] *adj* justifiable

**justificatif** [ʒystifikatif] *m* (*preuve*) documentary evidence

**justification** [ʒystifikasjɔ̃] *f* **①** (*explication: d'un acte, d'une conduite*) justification **②** (*preuve*) proof; (*d'un paiement*) receipt

**justifier** [ʒystifje] <1> **I.** *vt* **①** (*donner raison à, expliquer*) a. TYP, INFORM to justify **②** (*disculper*) to vindicate **③** (*prouver*) **~ une créance** to justify a claim **II.** *vi* **~ d'un paiement/de son identité** to give proof of payment/of one's identity **III.** *vpr* (*se disculper*) **se ~ de qc auprès de qn** to justify oneself to sb about sth

**juteux, -euse** [ʒytø, -øz] *adj* **①** (*opp: sec: fruit*) juicy **②** *inf* (*lucratif*) lucrative

**juvénile** [ʒyvenil] *adj* youthful

**juxtaposer** [ʒykstapoze] <1> *vt* to juxtapose

# Kk

**K, k** [kɑ] *m inv* K, k; **~ comme Kléber** (*au téléphone*) k as in Kilo
**kangourou** [kɑ̃guʀu] *m* kangaroo
**karaoké** [kaʀaɔke] *m* karaoke
**karaté** [kaʀate] *m* karate
**karting** [kaʀtiŋ] *m* go-carting
**képi** [kepi] *m* kepi
**kermesse** [kɛʀmɛs] *f* ❶ (*fête de bienfaisance*) charity carnival ❷ *Belgique, Nord* (*fête patronale*) fair
**kidnapper** [kidnape] <1> *vt* to kidnap
**kilo** [kilo] *m abr de* **kilogramme** kilo
**kilogramme** [kilɔgram] *m* kilogram
**kilométrage** [kilɔmetraʒ] *m* (*d'une voiture*) mileage
**kilomètre** [kilɔmɛtʀ] *m* kilometer; **140 ~s à l'heure** 140 kilometers an hour; **~ carré** square kilometer
**kilomètre-heure** [kilɔmɛtʀœʀ] <kilomètres-heure> *m* kilometer per hour
**kiné** [kine], **kinési** [kinezi] *mf inf v.* **kinésithérapeute** physio
**kinésithérapeute** [kineziteʀapøt] *mf* physiotherapist

**kiosque** [kjɔsk] *m* (*lieu de vente*) kiosk; **~ à journaux** newsstand
**kir®** [kiʀ] *m* kir; **~ royal** kir royal (*champagne with blackcurrant liqueur*)
**kit** [kit] *m* ❶ (*prêt-à-monter*) kit ❷ (*pour un téléphone portable*) **~ piéton** hands-free kit; **~ auto** [*o* **mains libres**] car kit
**kiwi** [kiwi] *m* kiwi
**klaxon®** [klaksɔn] *m* horn; **donner un coup/petit coup de ~** to honk the horn
**klaxonner** [klaksɔne] <1> *vi* to honk (one's horn)
**kleenex®** [klinɛks] *m* Kleenex®, tissue
**km** *abr de* **kilomètre** km
**Ko** [kao] *m abr de* **kilo-octet** kb
**K.-O.** [kao] *adj inv, inf abr de* **knock-out** (*assommé*) knocked out; SPORT KO'd; **mettre qn ~** to KO sb
**Koweït** [kɔwɛt] *m* **le ~** Kuwait
**krach** [kʀak] *m* FIN crash
**Kuwait** [kɔwɛt] *m v.* **Koweït**
**kyste** [kist] *m* cyst

**L, l** [ɛl] *m inv* L, l; **~ comme Louis** (*au téléphone*) l as in Lima

**l** *abr de* **litre** liter

**l'** *art, pron v.* **le, la**

**la¹** [la] <*devant voyelle ou h muet* **l'**> **I.** *art déf* the **II.** *pron pers, fém* ① (*personne*) her; **il ~ voit/l'aide** he sees/helps her ② (*animal ou objet*) it; **là-bas, il y a une mouche/ma ceinture, ~ vois-tu?** there's a fly/my belt over there, can you see it? ③ *avec un présentatif* **~ voici!** here it/she is!

**la²** [la] *m inv* MUS A, la; **donner le ~ to** set the tone; *v.a.* **do**

**là¹** [la] *adv* ① (*avec déplacement à distance*) (over) there ② (*avec/sans déplacement à proximité/distance*) there; **passer par ~** to go that way; **de ~** from there; **quelque part par ~** (*en montrant du doigt*) somewhere over there; (*dans une région*) somewhere around there ③ (*ici, avec une personne à qui on parle*) here; **je suis ~** here I am; **peux-tu être ~ à six heures?** can you be here [o come] at six o'clock? ④ (*à ce moment-là*) **à partir de ~** from then on ⑤ (*alors*) then

**là²** [la] *interj* now

**là-bas** [labɑ] *adv* ① (*avec déplacement à distance*) over there ② (*avec l'endroit précisé*) over; **à Paris** in Paris

**label** [labɛl] *m* (*marque de qualité*) brand (name); (*vêtements*) label

**labo** [labo] *m inf* lab

**laboratoire** [labɔʀatwaʀ] *m* (*salle*) laboratory

**laborieux, -euse** [labɔʀjø, -jøz] *adj* ① (*pénible*) laborious; (*recherche*) painstaking; **eh bien, c'est ~!** *inf* it's tough going! ② (*travailleur: classes, masses*) working; (*personne*) industrious; (*vie*) hardworking

**labourer** [labuʀe] <1> *vt* ① AGR to plow ② (*creuser*) to slash into

**labyrinthe** [labiʀɛ̃t] *m* ① (*dédale*) labyrinth ② (*complication*) maze

**lac** [lak] *m* lake; **~ Léman** Lake Geneva; **les Grands ~s** the Great Lakes

**lacer** [lase] <2> *vt* to tie (up)

**lacet** [lasɛ] *m* ① (*cordon*) (shoe)lace; **à ~s** with laces ② (*virage*) bend

**lâche** [laʃ] **I.** *adj* ① (*poltron, méprisable*) cowardly ② (*détendu: corde*) slack **II.** *mf* coward

**lâcher** [laʃe] <1> **I.** *vt* ① (*laisser aller involontairement*) to let go of ② (*laisser aller délibérément*) to release; **~ une bêtise/un mot** to come out with something silly/a word ③ *inf* (*abandonner*) to abandon; **tout ~** *inf* to drop everything **II.** *vi* to give way; (*corde*) to break

**lâcheté** [laʃte] *f* ① (*couardise*) cowardice ② (*bassesse*) lowness

**laconique** [lakɔnik] *adj* laconic; (*réponse*) concise

**lacrymogène** [lakʀimɔʒɛn] *adj* **gaz ~** tear gas

**lactose** [laktoz] *m o f* CHIM, MED lactose; **suivre un régime sans ~** eat a lactose-free diet

**lacune** [lakyn] *f* gap

**là-dedans** [lad(ə)dɑ̃] *adv* ① (*lieu*) inside; **je ne reste pas ~** I am not staying in there ② (*direction*) into ③ (*en parlant d'une affaire*) **n'avoir rien à voir ~** to have nothing to do with it

**là-dessous** [lad(ə)su] *adv* ① (*dessous*) underneath ② *fig* behind; **qu'y a-t-il ~?** what's the story?

**là-dessus** [lad(ə)sy] *adv* ① (*direction, ici*) on here ② (*direction, là-bas*) on there ③ (*à ce sujet*) about that; **compte ~** count on it ④ (*sur ce*) on that matter

**lagune** [lagyn] *f* lagoon

**là-haut** [lao] *adv* ① (*au-dessus: direction, dans le ciel*) up there ② (*au-dessus: lieu*) on top

**laïcité** [laisite] *f* secularity; *(de l'enseignement)* secular stance

**laid(e)** [lɛ, lɛd] *adj* **①***(opp: beau)* ugly **②***(moralement: action, défaut)* mean

**laideur** [lɛdœr] *f* ugliness

**lainage** [lɛnaʒ] *m* **①***(étoffe)* wool **②***(vêtement)* wool(en)

**laine** [lɛn] *f* **①***(fibre)* wool **②***(vêtement)* **une petite ~** a light cardigan **③***(laine minérale)* ~ **de verre** glass wool

**laïque** [laik] *adj* layperson, layman *m,* laywoman *f*

**laisse** [lɛs] *f* *(lanière)* leash

**laisser** [lese] <1> **I.** *vt* **①***(faire rester)* to leave; ~ **qn perplexe** to puzzle sb; ~ **qn tranquille** to leave sb alone **②***(accorder: choix)* to give; ~ **la parole à qn** to let sb speak **③***(ne pas prendre)* to leave **④***(réserver: part de tarte)* to reserve; ~ **qc à qn** to leave sth for sb **⑤***(quitter)* **je te/vous laisse!** I'm off! **⑥***(déposer: personne)* to drop **⑦***(oublier)* to leave **⑧***(produire: traces, auréoles)* to leave **⑨***(remettre)* to leave **⑩***(léguer)* ~ **qc à qn** to bequeath sth to sb **II.** *aux (permettre)* ~ **qn/qc** +*infin* to allow sb/sth to +*infin* ► **~ faire** to do nothing; **se ~ faire** *(subir)* not to put up a fight

**laisser-aller** [leseale] *m inv* carelessness

**lait** [lɛ] *m* **①***(aliment)* milk; ~ **en poudre** powdered milk; ~ **longue conservation** long-life milk **②***(liquide laiteux)* lotion; ~ **de toilette** *(pour le corps)* body lotion; *(pour le visage)* beauty lotion

**laitage** [lɛtaʒ] *m* milk products

**laiton** [lɛtɔ̃] *m* brass

**laitue** [lety] *f* lettuce

**lambeau** [lɑ̃bo] <x> *m* scrap; **en ~x** in rags

**lame** [lam] *f* blade

**lamelle** [lamɛl] *f* **①***(petite lame)* strip **②***(tranche fine)* slice

**lamentable** [lamɑ̃tabl] *adj* **①***(pitoyable: état, mine, salaire)* pitiful; *(ton,*

*voix)* miserable; *(résultats, travail)* appalling **②***(honteux)* shameful

**lamenter** [lamɑ̃te] <1> *vpr* **se ~ sur qc** to moan about sth

**lampadaire** [lɑ̃padɛr] *m* **①***(lampe sur pied)* floor lamp **②***(réverbère)* streetlight

**lampe** [lɑ̃p] *f* **①***(appareil)* lamp; ~ **de poche** flashlight; ~ **témoin** warning light **②***(ampoule)* bulb

**lampion** [lɑ̃pjɔ̃] *m* Chinese lantern

**lance** [lɑ̃s] *f* **①***(arme)* spear **②***(tuyau)* hose

**lancée** [lɑ̃se] *f* way; **sur ma/sa ~** in my/his/her/its stride

**lancement** [lɑ̃smɑ̃] *m* **①***(envoi)* a. COM launch **②**INFORM start-up

**lance-pierre** [lɑ̃spjɛr] <lance-pierres> *m* slingshot

**lancer** [lɑ̃se] <2> **I.** *vt* **①***(projeter: jambe)* to fling; *(fusée)* to launch; *(coup)* to throw **②***(faire connaître: mode, mouvement)* to launch **③***(donner de l'élan: moteur, voiture)* to start; *(marque, produit, entreprise)* to launch **④***(inaugurer: programme, campagne, projet)* to launch **⑤***(envoyer: nouvelle)* to send; *(ultimatum)* to give **⑥***(émettre: accusation, menace)* to hurl; ~ **un appel à qn** to (launch an) appeal to sb **⑦**INFORM to start up **II.** *vpr* **①***(se précipiter)* **se ~ à la poursuite de qn** to dash after sb; **allez, lance-toi!** go on, go for it! *inf* **②***(s'engager)* **se ~ dans qc** to embark on sth; **se ~ dans le cinéma** to get into the movies **III.** *m* SPORT throw; *(du poids)* shot put

**landau** [lɑ̃do] <s> *m* *(pour enfant)* baby carriage

**lande** [lɑ̃d] *f* moor

**Landes** [lɑ̃d] *fpl* **les ~** the Landes *(region in the southwest of France)*

**langage** [lɑ̃gaʒ] *m* **①***(idiome)* a. INFORM language **②***(jargon)* jargon

**langer** [lɑ̃ʒe] <2a> *vt* ~ **un bébé** to change a baby's diaper

**langouste** [lɑ̃gust] *f* rock lobster, spiny lobster

**langoustine** [lɑ̃gustin] *f* langoustine

**langue** [lãg] f ❶ ANAT tongue; **tirer la ~ à qn** to stick one's tongue out at sb ❷ (*langage*) language; **~ étrangère/ maternelle** foreign/native language ▸ **~ de bois** political double talk; **donner sa ~ au chat** to give up; **tenir sa ~** to hold one's tongue

**Languedoc** [lãg(ə)dɔk] m le ~ Languedoc

**languette** [lãgɛt] f (*patte: d'une chaussure*) tongue; (*d'une boîte*) strip

**languir** [lãgir] <8> I. vi ❶ (*s'enliser: conversation*) to flag ❷ (*patienter*) **faire ~ qn** to make sb wait II. vpr **se ~ de qn** to pine for sb

**lanière** [lanjɛr] f strip

**lanterne** [lãtɛrn] f lantern

**laper** [lape] <1> vt to lap up

**lapin** [lapɛ̃] m ZOOL, CULIN rabbit; **~ de garenne** wild rabbit; v.a. **lapine** ▸ **poser un ~ à qn** *inf* to stand sb up

**lapine** [lapin] f ZOOL rabbit; v.a. **lapin**

**laps** [laps] m **~ de temps** time lapse

**laque** [lak] f ❶ (*pour les cheveux*) hair spray ❷ (*peinture*) lacquer

**laqué(e)** [lake] adj ❶ (*peint*) lacquered ❷ CULIN **canard ~** Peking duck

**laquelle** [lakɛl] pron v. **lequel**

**lard** [lar] m bacon ▸ **gros ~** fat slob

**lardon** [lardɔ̃] m CULIN bacon bit

**large** [larʒ] I. adj ❶ (*opp: étroit*) wide; (*cercle*) large; **être ~ d'épaules** to have broad shoulders; **~ de 10 mètres** 10 meters wide ❷ (*ample: vêtement*) loose ❸ (*important*) big; (*champ d'action, diffusion*) wide; **de ~s extraits** extensive extracts ❹ (*ouvert: acception, sens*) broad; **avoir les idées ~s** to be open-minded; **~ d'esprit** broad-minded II. adv (*calculer*) on the generous side; **voir ~** to think big III. m ❶ (*haute mer*) open sea ❷ (*largeur*) **un champ de 30 mètres de ~** a field 30 meters wide ▸ **au ~ de la côte** off the coast

**largement** [larʒəmã] adv ❶ (*opp: étroitement*) wide ❷ (*amplement*) **vous avez ~ le temps** you have plenty of time; **~ assez** more than enough

❸ (*généreusement*) generously ❹ (*au minimum*) at least ❺ *inf* (*assez*) **c'est ~ suffisant** it is more than enough

**largeur** [larʒœr] f ❶ (*dimension*) width ❷ (*opp: mesquinerie*) **~ d'esprit** generosity of spirit

**larguer** [large] <1> vt ❶ NAUT (*ancre*) to slip; (*voile*) to unfurl ❷ AVIAT (*parachutistes, troupes*) to release; ❸ *inf* (*laisser tomber: projets, travail*) to give up; **~ un ami** to dump a friend

**larme** [larm] f ❶ (*pleur*) tear; **en ~s** in tears ❷ *inf* (*goutte*) drop ▸ **avoir les ~s aux yeux** to have tears in one's eyes; **fondre en ~s** to dissolve into tears

**larve** [larv] f ❶ ZOOL larva ❷ (*personne déchue*) worm *inf*

**larynx** [larɛ̃ks] m larynx

**las(se)** [la, las] adj (*personne*) tired; (*geste*) weary

**laser** [lazɛr] I. m laser II. app compact disc

**lasser** [lase] <1> I. vt to tire II. vpr **se ~ de qc** to tire of sth

**lassitude** [lasityd] f ❶ (*fatigue physique*) fatigue ❷ (*fatigue morale*) weariness

**latéral(e)** [lateral, -o] <-aux> adj (*de côté*) lateral; **porte ~e** side door

**latex** [latɛks] m latex

**latin** [latɛ̃] m Latin; v.a. **français**

**latin(e)** [latɛ̃, in] adj ❶ Latin ❷ (*opp: anglo-saxon, orthodoxe*) Latin

**latino-américain(e)** [latinoamerikɛ̃, ɛn] <latino-américains> adj Latin-American

**latitude** [latityd] f GEO latitude; **être à 45° de ~ nord** to be at latitude 45° north

**latte** [lat] f (*planche*) slat

**lauréat(e)** [lɔrea, at] I. adj award-winning; **les élèves/étudiants ~s** prize-winning students II. m(f) award-winner; **~ du prix Nobel** Nobel prize winner

**laurier** [lɔrje] m ❶ BOT bay tree ❷ CULIN bay ❸ pl (*gloire*) praise

**lavable** [lavabl] *adj* washable; **~ uniquement à la main** hand wash only

**lavabo** [lavabo] *m* ① (*cuvette*) bathroom sink ② *pl* (*toilettes*) toilets

**lavage** [lavaʒ] *m* washing ►**~ d'estomac** stomach pumping

**lavande** [lavɑ̃d] *f* lavender

**lave** [lav] *f* lava

**lave-glace** [lavglas] <lave-glaces> *m* windshield washer

**lave-linge** [lavlɛ̃ʒ] *m inv* washing machine

**laver** [lave] <1> **I.** *vt* ① (*nettoyer*) to clean; (*vaisselle, sol*) to wash; (*mur*) to wash (down); **~ qc à la machine** to machine-wash sth; **~ qc à l'éponge** to sponge sth (down); **~ qc à la main** to hand-wash sth ② (*disculper*) **~ qn d'un soupçon** to clear sb of a suspicion **II.** *vpr* ① (*se nettoyer*) **se ~** to wash (oneself); **se ~ les dents** to brush one's teeth ② (*être lavable*) **se ~** to be washable

**laverie** [lavʀi] *f* laundry

**laveuse** [lavøz] *f Québec* (*lave-linge*) washing machine

**lave-vaisselle** [lavvɛsɛl] *m inv* dishwasher

**lavoir** [lavwaʀ] *m* wash house

**laxatif** [laksatif] *m* laxative

**laxatif, -ive** [laksatif, -iv] *adj* laxative

**layette** [lɛjɛt] *f* layette

**le** [lə] <*devant voyelle ou h muet* l'> **I.** *art déf* the **II.** *pron pers, masc* ① (*personne*) **elle ~ voit/l'aide** she sees/helps him ② (*animal ou objet*) **là-bas, il y a un cochon/sac, ~ vois-tu?** there's a pig/bag over there · can you see it? ③ (*valeur neutre*) **je ~ comprends** I understand; **je l'espère!** I hope so! ④ *avec un présentatif* **~ voici/voilà!** here/there he [*o* it] is!

**leader** [lidœʀ] **I.** *m* leader **II.** *adj inv* leader

**leasing** [liziŋ] *m* leasing

**lécher** [leʃe] <5> **I.** *vt* (*assiette, cuillère, bol, plat*) to lick (clean); (*visage, glace*) to lick; (*lait*) to lap up **II.** *vpr* **se ~ les lèvres** to lick one's lips

**leçon** [l(ə)sɔ̃] *f a.* ECOLE lesson

**lecteur** [lɛktœʀ] *m* ① MEDIA player ② INFORM drive; **~ de CD-ROM/disquettes/DVD** CD-ROM/disk/DVD drive; **~ optique** optical character reader

**lecteur, -trice** [lɛktœʀ, -tʀis] *m, f* ① (*liseur, personne qui fait la lecture*) reader ② UNIV, ECOLE teaching assistant

**lecture** [lɛktyʀ] *f* ① (*action de lire*) reading ② (*action de lire à haute voix*) reading out loud; **faire la ~ de qc à qn** to read sth to sb; **donner ~ de qc** to read sth out ③ (*qc qui se lit*) *a.* CINE, TV, INFORM reading; **~ optique** optical character reading

**légal(e)** [legal, -o] <-aux> *adj* legal; (*fête*) public; (*heure*) standard

**légaliser** [legalize] <1> *vt* ① (*autoriser*) to legalize ② (*authentifier*) to authenticate

**légalité** [legalite] *f* (*respect de la loi*) legality; **sortir de la ~** to step beyond the law

**légendaire** [leʒɑ̃dɛʀ] *adj* ① (*mythique: animal*) mythical; (*figure, histoire*) legendary ② (*célèbre*) famous

**légende** [leʒɑ̃d] *f* ① (*mythe*) legend ② (*explication: d'une carte, d'un plan*) key; (*d'une photo*) caption

**léger, -ère** [leʒe, -ɛʀ] *adj* ① (*opp: lourd*) light; (*vêtement*) light(weight) ② (*de faible intensité*) slight; (*peine*) mild; (*doute, soupçon*) faint; (*couche de neige*) thin; **blessures ~s** slight injuries ③ (*insouciant*) **d'un cœur ~** with a light heart ④ *péj* (*superficiel*) thoughtless ►**à la légère** thoughtlessly

**légèrement** [leʒɛʀmɑ̃] *adv* ① (*un peu, vraiment*) slightly ② (*avec des choses légères*) lightly ③ (*avec grâce, délicatement*) nimbly

**légèreté** [leʒɛʀte] *f* ① (*faible poids*) lightness ② (*insouciance*) frivolity

**Légion** [leʒjɔ̃] *f* ① MIL **~ etrangère** Foreign Legion ② (*décoration*) **~ d'honneur** Legion of Honor

**législateur, -trice** [leʒislatœʀ, -tʀis] *m, f* legislator

**législatif, -ive** [leʒislatif, -iv] *adj* legislative

**législation** [leʒislasjɔ̃] *f* legislation

**légitime** [leʒitim] *adj a.* JUR legitimate; **femme ~** lawful wife

**légitimer** [leʒitime] <1> *vt* ❶ (*justifier*) to justify ❷ JUR to legitimate

**léguer** [lege] <5> *vt* JUR ~ **qc à qn** to bequeath sth to sb

**légume** [legym] *m* vegetable; **~s secs** pulses

**lendemain** [lɑ̃dmɛ̃] *m* ❶ *sans pl* (*jour suivant*) **le ~** the following day; **le ~ soir** the following evening; **du jour au ~** from one day to the next ❷ (*temps qui suit*) **au ~ du mariage** after the wedding ❸ (*avenir*) future

**lent(e)** [lɑ̃, lɑ̃t] *adj* slow; (*esprit*) slow-witted

**lentement** [lɑ̃tmɑ̃] *adv* slowly

**lenteur** [lɑ̃tœʀ] *f* slowness

**lentille** [lɑ̃tij] *f* ❶ BOT, CULIN lentil ❷ (*en optique*) lens

**léopard** [leɔpaʀ] *m* ❶ ZOOL leopard ❷ (*fourrure*) leopard skin

**lèpre** [lɛpʀ] *f* MED leprosy

**lequel, laquelle** [ləkɛl, lakɛl, lekɛl] <lesquels, lesquelles> I. *pron interrog* which; **regarde cette fille! – laquelle?** look at that girl! – which one?; **~/laquelle d'entre vous ...?** which of you ...?; **auxquels de ces messieurs devrai-je m'adresser?** to which of these gentlemen should I speak?; **demandez à l'un de vos élèves, n'importe ~!** ask any of your students, doesn't matter which!; **je ne sais lesquels prendre!** I don't know which ones to take! II. *pron rel* ❶ (*se rapportant à une personne*) who(m); **la concierge, laquelle ...** the caretaker, who ...; **la personne à laquelle je fais allusion** the person to whom I am referring; **les grévistes, au nombre desquels il se trouve** the strikers, among whom there is ❷ (*se rapportant à un animal, un objet*) which; **la situation délicate dans laquelle nous nous trouvons** the delicate situation in which we find our-

selves; **la liberté, au nom de laquelle ...** freedom, in whose name ...

**les** [le] I. *art déf* the II. *pron pers, pl* ❶ (*personnes, animaux, objets*) them ❷ *avec un présentatif* they; **~ voici/ voilà !** here/there they are!

**lesbien(ne)** [lɛzbjɛ̃, jɛn] *adj* lesbian

**lesbienne** [lɛzbjɛn] *f* lesbian

**léser** [leze] <5> *vt* ❶ (*désavantager*) to damage ❷ (*nuire*) **~ les intérêts de qn** to be against sb's interests

**lésiner** [lezine] <1> *vi* **~ sur qc** to skimp on sth

**lésion** [lezjɔ̃] *f* lesion

**lessive** [lesiv] *f* ❶ (*détergent*) detergent ❷ (*lavage, linge à laver*) laundry; **faire la ~** to do the laundry

**lessiver** [lesive] <1> *vt* ❶ (*nettoyer: pièce, sol*) to wash; (*murs*) to wash (down) ❷ *inf* (*épuiser*) **être lessivé** to be worn out

**lest** [lɛst] *m* ballast

**léthargie** [letaʀʒi] *f* lethargy

**lettre** [lɛtʀ] *f* ❶ (*missive, signe graphique*) letter; **~ de candidature** letter of application; **mettre une ~ à la poste** to mail a letter; **par ~** by mail ❷ *pl* UNIV (*opp: sciences*) arts; **professeur de ~s** French teacher ❸ *sans pl* (*sens strict*) **à la ~** to the letter; **prendre qc à la ~** to take sth literally

**leucémie** [løsemi] *f* MED leukemia

**leur¹** [lœʀ] *pron pers, inv* ❶ (*personnes, animaux, objets*) them ❷ (*avec un sens possessif*) **le cœur ~ battait fort** their hearts were beating fast; *v.a.* **me**

**leur²** [lœʀ] <leurs> I. *dét poss* their; *v.a.* **ma, mon** II. *pron poss* ❶ **le/la ~** their; **les ~s** theirs; *v.a.* **mien** ❷ *pl* (*ceux de leur famille*) **les ~s** their family; (*leurs partisans*) their people; **vous êtes des ~s** you are with them; *v.a.* **mien** ▸ **ils y mettent du ~** they pull their weight

**leurs** [lœʀ] *v.* **leur**

**levain** [ləvɛ̃] *m* (*pour pain, pour gâteau*) leaven

**levant** [ləvɑ̃] *m* (*est*) east

**levée** [l(ə)ve] *f* collection

**lever** [l(ə)ve] <4> I. *vt* ❶ (*soulever*) to

lift; *(jambe, tête, visage)* to raise; ~ **la main** to raise one's hand; ~ **les yeux vers qn** to look up at sb ② *(sortir du lit)* ~ **un enfant/un malade** to get a child/a sick person out of bed; **faire ~ qn** to make sb get up ③ *(faire cesser)* **être levé** *(séance)* to come to an end **II.** *vpr* **se ~** ① *(se mettre debout, sortir du lit)* to get up; **se ~ de table** to leave the table ② *(commencer à paraître: lune, soleil)* to rise; *(jour, aube)* to break ③ *(se soulever: rideau, main)* to go up ④ *(commencer à s'agiter: mer)* to rise; *(vent)* to get up ⑤ *(devenir meilleur: temps, brouillard)* to clear **III.** *vi* ① *(gonfler: pâte)* to rise ② *(pousser)* to come up **IV.** ~ **au** ~ **du soleil** at sunrise; ~ **du jour** daybreak

**lève-tard** [lɛvtaʀ] *mf inv, inf* late riser

**lève-tôt** [lɛvto] *mf inv, inf* early riser

**levier** [ləvje] *m (tige de commande, pour lever)* lever; ~ **de (changement de) vitesse** stick shift, gearshift; **faire ~ sur qc** to lever sth up

**lèvre** [lɛvʀ] *f* ① ANAT lip; ~ **inférieure/supérieure** lower/upper lip ② *pl (parties de la vulve)* labia

**lévrier** [levʀije] *m* greyhound

**levure** [l(ə)vyʀ] *f a.* CHIM yeast

**lexique** [lɛksik] *m* ① *(dictionnaire bilingue)* lexicon ② *(en fin d'ouvrage)* glossary ③ *(vocabulaire)* lexis

**lézard** [lezaʀ] *m* lizard

**lézarde** [lezaʀd] *f* crack

**lézarder¹** [lezaʀde] <1> *vi inf* to bask in the sun

**lézarder²** [lezaʀde] <1> *vt, vpr* **(se)** ~ to crack

**liaison** [ljɛzɔ̃] *f* ① *(contact)* contact; ~ **radio/téléphonique** radio/telephone link; **mettre qn en ~ avec qn** to put sb in contact with sb; **travailler en ~ étroite avec qn** to work in close contact with sb ② *(enchaînement)* connection ③ LING liaison ④ *(relation amoureuse)* affair

**liasse** [ljas] *f (de documents)* bundle; *(de billets)* wad

**Liban** [libɑ̃] *m* **le** ~ Lebanon

**libeller** [libele] <1> *vt (chèque)* to make out; *(contrat)* to draw up

**libellule** [libelyl] *f* dragonfly

**libéral(e)** [liberal, -o] <-aux> **I.** *adj* liberal **II.** *m(f)* POL Liberal

**libéralisme** [liberalism] *m* ① ECON, POL free market philosophy ② *(tolérance)* liberalism

**libérateur, -trice** [liberatœʀ, -tʀis] **I.** *adj* liberating **II.** *m, f* liberator

**libération** [liberasjɔ̃] *f* ① *(mise en liberté)* release ② *(délivrance) a. fig* liberation

**libéré(e)** [libeʀe] *adj (émancipé)* liberated

**libérer** [libeʀe] <5> **I.** *vt* ① *(relâcher)* to discharge ② *(délivrer)* to free ③ *(décharger)* ~ **qn de sa dette** to relieve sb of his/her debt ④ *(dégager: voie)* to unblock ⑤ *(rendre disponible: chambre)* to free; **cela me libérerait un peu de temps** that will give me some time **II.** *vpr* ① *(se délivrer)* **sc ~ de ses soucis** to relieve oneself of one's worries ② *(se rendre libre)* **se ~** to get away ③ *(devenir vacant)* **se ~** *(poste, place)* to become free

**liberté** [libɛʀte] *f* ① *sans pl (opp: oppression, emprisonnement)* freedom, liberty; **en ~** *(opp: en captivité)* in the wild; *(opp: en prison)* free; **être en ~ provisoire/surveillée** to be on bail/probation; **rendre la ~ à qn** to give someone back his/her freedom ② *sans pl (loisir)* leisure; **quelques heures/jours de** ~ a few hours/days off ③ *(droit, indépendance, absence de contrainte)* freedom; **laisser toute ~ à qn** to give sb complete freedom; **parler en toute ~** to speak freely ▸ **Liberté, Égalité, Fraternité** Liberty, Equality, Fraternity

**libraire** [libʀɛʀ] *mf* bookseller

**librairie** [libʀeʀi] *f* bookstore

**librairie-papeterie** [libʀɛʀipapɛtʀi] <librairie-papeteries> *f* book and stationery store

**libre** [libʀ] *adj* ① *a.* POL free; **elle est ~ de ses choix** she's free to make her own choices; **ne pas être ~** (*personne*) not to be available ❷ (*opp: marié: personne*) single ❸ (*sans contrainte: discussion, esprit*) open; **être ~ de tout engagement** to be free of any commitment ❹ (*opp: entravé: cheveux*) loose ❺ (*autorisé*) **entrée ~** please come in ❻ ECOLE, UNIV independent ❼ SPORT **exercices/figures ~s** freestyle

**librement** [librəmɑ̃] *adv* freely

**libre-service** [librəsɛrvis] <libres-services> *m* ❶ (*magasin*) self-service shop ❷ (*restaurant*) self-service restaurant ❸ *sans pl* (*système de vente*) self-service

**Libye** [libi] *f* **la ~** Libya

**licence** [lisɑ̃s] *f* ❶ UNIV degree; **~ ès sciences** science degree; **faire une ~ d'allemand** to do a German degree ❷ COM, JUR license ❸ SPORT permit; **joueur titulaire d'une ~** authorized player

**licenciement** [lisɑ̃simɑ̃] *m* dismissal; **~ collectif** mass layoffs; **~ économique** layoff

**licencier** [lisɑ̃sje] <1> *vt* to fire

**lie** [li] *f* (*dépôt*) deposit; **~ de vin** wine sediment

**lié(e)** [lje] *adj* (*proche*) **être ~ avec qn** to be friendly with sb

**liège** [ljɛʒ] *m* cork; **bouchon de ~** cork

**Liège** [ljɛʒ] Liège

**lien** [ljɛ̃] *m* ❶ (*attache*) tie; (*chaîne*) link ❷ (*rapport*) a. INFORM link ❸ (*ce qui unit*) **~ de parenté** family ties; **nouer des ~s avec qn** to tighten a bond with sb

**lier** [lje] <1> I. *vt* ❶ (*attacher*) **~ qn/qc à qc** to tie sb/sth to sth ❷ (*assembler*) **~ les mots** to join words up ❸ (*mettre en relation*) **être lié à qc** to be linked to sth ❹ (*unir*) **~ qn/qc à qn/qc** to bind sb/sth to sb/sth ❺ (*astreindre*) **être lié par un serment** to be bound by an oath II. *vpr* **se ~ avec qn** to make friends with sb

**lierre** [ljɛr] *m* ivy

**lieu¹** [ljø] <x> *m* ❶ (*endroit*) place; **~ de séjour** place of residence; **~ de nais-**

**sance/travail** place of birth/work; **~ de rencontre** meeting place ❷ *pl* (*endroit précis*) **sur les ~x de l'accident** at the scene of the accident ❸ (*endroit particulier*) **en haut ~** in high places; **en ~ sûr** (*à l'abri*) in a safe place; (*en prison*) in prison ❹ (*dans une succession*) **en premier/second ~** in the first/second place; **en dernier ~** finally ❺ (*place*) **avoir ~** to take place; **tenir ~ de qc à qn** to serve as sth for sb; **au ~ de qc** instead of sth ❻ (*raison*) **il n'y a pas ~ de s'inquiéter** there is no reason to worry; **donner ~ à qc** (*provoquer*) to cause sth; (*fournir l'occasion de*) to give rise to sth

**lieu²** [ljø] <s> *m* ZOOL **~ noir** coalfish

**lieu commun** [ljøkɔmœ̃] <lieux communs> *m* commonplace

**lieue** [ljø] *f* (*mesure*) a. NAUT league ▶ **nous étions à mille ~s de penser que ...** it never crossed our minds that ...

**lieutenant** [ljøt(ə)nɑ̃] *m* ❶ MIL lieutenant ❷ (*adjoint*) second in command

**lièvre** [ljɛvr] *m* ZOOL hare

**lifting** [liftiŋ] *m* facelift

**ligament** [ligamɑ̃] *m* ANAT ligament

**ligne** [liɲ] *f* ❶ (*trait, limite réelle, forme*) a. CHEMDFER, ELEC, TEL line; **~ de départ/d'arrivée** starting/finish line; **~ de but** goal line; **une ~ de métro** a subway line; **être en ~** TEL to be on the phone; INFORM to be on line; **gardez la ~!** Québec (*ne quittez pas*) hold the line! ❷ (*limite imaginaire*) **~ de tir** line of fire ❸ (*suite de mots*) a. INFORM line; **de huit ~s** eight lines long; **à la ~!** new line!; **~ commentaire/de commande** comment/command line; **en/hors online/offline** ❹ *sans pl* (*silhouette*) figure; **avoir/garder la ~** to have/keep a slim figure ❺ (*ensemble de produits cosmétiques*) line ❻ (*point*) **les grandes ~s de l'ouvrage** the main outline of the work ❼ (*direction*) **~ droite** straight line ❽ (*à la pêche*) (fishing) line ❾ (*rangée*) a. MIL row; **se mettre en ~** to line up ❿ (*filiation*) **en ~ directe** in a direct line ▶ **entrer en ~ de** <u>compte</u> to have to be taken into account; **prendre qc en ~ de** <u>compte</u> to take sth into account

**lignée** [liɲe] *f* (*descendance*) lineage

**ligoter** [ligɔte] <1> *vt* ❶ (*attacher*) to tie up ❷ (*priver de liberté*) **être ligoté** to be imprisoned

**ligue** [lig] *f* league

**liguer** [lige] <1> *vpr* **se ~ contre qn** to conspire together against sb

**lilas** [lila] *adj inv, m* lilac

**limace** [limas] *f* slug

**lime** [lim] *f* (*outil*) file; **~ à ongles** nail file

**limer** [lime] <1> I. *vt* (*ongles, clé, métal*) to file; (*bois*) to plane II. *vpr* **se ~ les ongles** to file one's nails

**limitation** [limitasjɔ̃] *f* limitation; **~ de vitesse** speed limit

**limite** [limit] I. *app* ❶ (*extrême: âge, poids, prix, vitesse*) maximum; (*cas*) borderline ❷ (*presque impossible*) very difficult; **ce cas me paraît ~** this case seems nearly impossible to me ❸ *inf* (*pas terrible*) **être ~** to be borderline II. *f* ❶ (*démarcation*) boundary ❷ (*dans le temps*) deadline ❸ (*borne*) *a.* MATH limit; **sans ~s** (*ambition, vanité*) boundless; (*pouvoir*) limitless; **être à la ~ du supportable** to be barely tolerable; **il y a des ~s** there are limits; **dans les ~s du possible** subject to what is possible ▶ **à la ~** in a pinch; **à la ~, je ferais mieux de ...** in a way, I'd be better off ...; **à la ~, on croirait que ...** one would almost think that ...

**limité(e)** [limite] *adj* limited

**limiter** [limite] <1> I. *vt* ❶ (*délimiter*) to limit ❷ (*restreindre*) **~ qc à l'essentiel** to restrict sth to what is essential; **~ les dégâts** to limit the damage II. *vpr* **se ~ dans qc** (*en mangeant, buvant, dans son comportement*) to be careful when it comes to sth

**limonade** [limɔnad] *f* lemonade

**limousine** [limuzin] *f* limousine

**limpide** [lɛ̃pid] *adj* ❶ (*pur*) limpid; (*re-*

*gard*) lucid; (*air*) clear ❷ (*intelligible*) clear

**limpidité** [lɛ̃pidite] *f* (*pureté*) limpidity; (*de l'air*) clearness

**lin** [lɛ̃] *m* ❶ BOT flax ❷ (*fibre textile*) linen

**linge** [lɛ̃ʒ] *m* ❶ *sans pl* (*vêtements*) clothing; **du ~ de rechange/de toilette** clean/bathroom linen; **avoir du ~ à laver** to have clothes to wash ❷ (*morceau de tissu*) cloth ▶ **blanc comme un ~** as white as a sheet

**lingerie** [lɛ̃ʒʀi] *f* ❶ *sans pl* (*dessous*) **~ féminine** lingerie ❷ (*local*) linen room

**lingot** [lɛ̃go] *m* ❶ (*lingot d'or*) gold ingot ❷ (*masse de métal*) ingot

**linguistique** [lɛ̃gɥistik] I. *adj* ❶ (*relatif à la science du langage*) linguistic ❷ (*relatif à la langue*) **communauté/famille ~** speech community/family II. *f* linguistics + *vb sing*

**lion** [ljɔ̃] *m* lion; *v.a.* **lionne**

**Lion** [ljɔ̃] *m* Leo; *v.a.* **Balance**

**lionne** [ljɔn] *f* lioness; *v.a.* **lion**

**liquéfier** [likefje] <1> I. *vt* to liquefy II. *vpr* **se ~** (*gaz*) to condense; (*solide*) to melt

**liqueur** [likœʀ] *f* liqueur

**liquidation** [likidasjɔ̃] *f* ❶ (*solde*) sale; **~ totale du stock** going-out-of-business sale ❷ JUR (*d'une succession, d'un compte*) liquidation

**liquide** [likid] I. *adj* ❶ (*fluide*) liquid; **être trop ~** (*sauce*) to be too thin ❷ (*disponible*) **argent ~** cash II. *m* ❶ (*fluide*) liquid; **~ vaisselle** dish soap; **~ de frein(s)** brake fluid ❷ *sans pl* (*argent*) cash

**liquider** [likide] <1> *vt* ❶ COM (*marchandise*) to sell off; (*stock*) to liquidate ❷ *inf* (*se débarrasser: adversaire*) to eliminate; (*dossier*) to get rid of ❸ *inf* (*tuer*) to eliminate ❹ *inf* (*finir: boisson, nourriture*) to clear ❺ JUR (*société*) to liquidate; (*compte*) to settle

**lire**[1] [liʀ] irr I. *vi* to read; **elle sait ~** she can read; **~ à haute voix** to read aloud; **~ dans les lignes de la main de qn** to read sb's palm; **~ dans les pensées de qn** to read sb's thoughts **II.** *vt* to read; **en espérant vous/te ~ bientôt** hoping to hear from you soon **III.** *vpr* ❶ *(se déchiffrer)* **l'hébreu se lit de droite à gauche** Hebrew reads from right to left ❷ *(se comprendre)* **ce texte se ~ de deux manières** this text can be interpreted in two ways ❸ *(se deviner)* **la surprise se lisait sur son visage** surprise was written all over his face

**lire²** [liʀ] *f* HIST *(monnaie)* lira

**lis¹** [lis] *m* lily

**lis²** [li] *indic prés de* **lire**

**liseuse** [lizøz] *f* ❶ *(vêtement)* bed jacket ❷ INFORM e-reader

**lisible** [lizibl] *adj* legible

**lisiblement** [lizibləmɑ̃] *adv* legibly

**lisière** [lizjɛʀ] *f* ❶ COUT selvage ❷ *(limite)* edge; *(d'un champ)* boundary

**lisse** [lis] *adj* smooth

**lisser** [lise] <1> **I.** *vt* to smooth; *(papier)* to smooth (out) **II.** *vpr* **se ~ les cheveux** to smooth down one's hair

**liste** [list] *f* *(nomenclature)* list; **~ électorale** electoral roll; **~ de mariage** wedding list; **faire la ~ de qc** to list sth

**lister** [liste] <1> *vt* to list

**listing** [listiŋ] *m* listing

**lit¹** [li] *m* ❶ *(meuble)* bed; **~ pour deux personnes** double bed; **aller au ~** to go to bed; **mettre qn au ~** to put sb to bed; **au ~!** bedtime!; **être cloué au ~** to be bedridden ❷ *(creux: d'une rivière)* bed; **sortir de son ~** to burst its banks

**lit²** [li] *indic prés de* **lire**

**litchi** [litʃi] *m* litchi

**literie** [litʀi] *f* ❶ *(sommier et matelas)* bed ❷ *(linge)* bedding

**litière** [litjɛʀ] *f* litter; *(d'un cheval, d'une vache)* bedding; **~ pour chats** kitty litter

**litige** [litiʒ] *m* ❶ *(contestation)* dispute ❷ JUR lawsuit

**litre** [litʀ] *m* ❶ *(mesure)* liter ❷ *(bouteille)* liter bottle

**littéraire** [liteʀɛʀ] **I.** *adj* literary **II.** *mf* ❶ *(opp: scientifique)* literary type ❷ *(étudiant, professeur)* student/teacher of literature

**littéral(e)** [literal, -o] <-aux> *adj* *(traduction, sens)* literal; *(copie)* exact

**littéralement** [literalmɑ̃] *adv* literally

**littérature** [literatyʀ] *f* literature

**littoral** [litɔʀal, -o] *m* coast

**littoral(e)** [litɔʀal, -o] <-aux> *adj* coastal

**livide** [livid] *adj* livid; *(lèvres)* blue-tinged; *(lumière)* pale

**living** [liviŋ] *m*, **living-room** [liviŋʀum] <living-rooms> *m* living room

**livrable** [livʀabl] *adj* which can be delivered

**livraison** [livʀɛzɔ̃] *f* delivery; **~ à domicile** home delivery

**livre¹** [livʀ] *m* ❶ *(ouvrage)* book; **~ de poche** paperback; **~ de cuisine** cookbook; **~ scolaire** schoolbook ❷ *sans pl (industrie)* **le ~** the book trade; **salon du ~** book fair ❸ *(registre)* **~ d'or** visitors' book

**livre²** [livʀ] *f* ❶ *(unité monétaire anglaise)* pound; **~ sterling** pound sterling ❷ *Québec (unité de masse valant 0,453 kg)* pound

**livrer** [livʀe] <1> **I.** *vt* ❶ *(fournir)* to deliver; **se faire ~ qc** to have sth delivered ❷ *(remettre)* **~ qn à la police** to hand sb over to the police ❸ *(dénoncer)* to give away ❹ *(abandonner)* **être livré à soi-même** to be left alone ❺ *(dévoiler)* to reveal **II.** *vpr* ❶ *(se rendre)* **se ~ à qn** to give oneself up to sb ❷ *(se confier)* **se ~ à qn** to confide in sb ❸ *(se consacrer)* **se ~ à ses occupations habituelles** to immerse oneself in one's usual occupations

**livret** [livʀɛ] *m* *(registre)* booklet; **~ (de caisse) d'épargne** bankbook; **~ de famille** family record book; **~ scolaire** report card

**livreur, -euse** [livʀœʀ, -øz] *m, f* delivery person

**lobe** [lɔb] *m* ANAT, BOT lobe

**local** [lɔkal, -o] <-aux> *m* **des locaux** *(salles)* premises *pl*; *(bureaux)* offices *pl*

**local(e)** [lɔkal, -o] <-aux> *adj* local; **1 h 30 heure ~e** 1:30 a.m. local time

**localiser** [lɔkalize] <1> **I.** *vt* ① (*situer*) **~ qc sur la carte** to locate sth on the map ② (*circonscrire*) to localize **II.** *vpr* **se ~** (*conflit, épidémie*) to be confined

**localité** [lɔkalite] *f* town

**locataire** [lɔkatɛʀ] *mf* tenant; **être ~** to rent

**location** [lɔkasjɔ̃] *f* ① (*bail: d'une habitation, d'un terrain, d'une voiture*) renting; **voiture de ~** rental car; **prendre/donner un appartement en ~** to rent an apartment ② (*maison à louer*) **prendre une ~ pour les vacances** to rent a house during vacation

**locomotion** [lɔkɔmosjɔ̃] *f* locomotion

**locomotive** [lɔkɔmɔtiv] *f* TECH locomotive

**locution** [lɔkysjɔ̃] *f* phrase

**loge** [lɔʒ] *f* ① (*pièce: d'un concierge*) lodge; (*d'un acteur*) dressing room ② THEAT box ▶ **être aux premières ~s** to be in the front row

**logement** [lɔʒmɑ̃] *m* ① (*habitation*) accommodation; (*appartement*) apartment; (*maison*) house; MIL quarters *pl*; (*chez un civil*) billet ② (*secteur*) **le ~** housing; **crise du ~** housing crisis

**loger** [lɔʒe] <2a> **I.** *vi* (*séjourner: personne*) to live **II.** *vt* ① (*héberger*) **~ qn** to put sb up ② (*contenir: hôtel*) to accommodate **III.** *vpr* ① (*trouver un logement*) **se ~ chez un ami** to stay at a friend's house ② (*se placer*) **se ~ entre deux vertèbres** (*balle*) to lodge between two vertebrae

**logeur, -euse** [lɔʒœʀ, -ʒøz] *m, f* landlord, landlady *m, f*

**logiciel** [lɔʒisjɛl] *m* software; **~ gratuit** freeware; **~ anti-virus** anti-virus software; **~ de courrier électronique** e-mail software; **~ de traitement de texte** word processing software; **~ de navigation** browser

**logique** [lɔʒik] **I.** *adj* logical **II.** *f* PHILOS, MATH logic; **en toute ~** logically

**logiquement** [lɔʒikmɑ̃] *adv* ① (*normalement*) logically ② (*rationnellement*) rationally

**loi** [lwa] *f* ① (*prescription légale*) a. PHYS, MATH law; **j'ai la ~ pour moi** I have the law on my side ② (*ordre imposé*) rules; (*par Dieu*) law; **faire la ~** to lay down the law

**loin** [lwɛ̃] *adv* ① (*distance*) far; **~ d'ici** a long way from here; **au ~** in the distance; **de ~** from a distance; **plus ~** farther ② *fig* far; **il ira ~** he will go far; **j'irais même plus ~** I would go even further; **voir plus → page 28** see below page 28; **elle revient de ~** she had a close call ③ (*dans le temps*) far; **il n'est pas très ~ de minuit** it's close to midnight; **de ~ en ~** here and there ④ (*au lieu de*) **~ de faire qc** far from doing sth; **~ de cela** far from that ▶ **de ~** by far; **~ de là** far from it

**lointain(e)** [lwɛ̃tɛ̃, ɛn] *adj* ① (*dans l'espace*) faraway ② (*dans le temps: avenir*) far off; (*époque, souvenir*) distant ③ (*indirect*) distant ④ (*détaché, absent: personne*) remote; (*regard*) faraway

**loir** [lwaʀ] *m* dormouse

**loisir** [lwaziʀ] *m* ① *sing o pl* (*temps libre*) leisure; **heures de ~** free time ② (*passe-temps*) hobby

**lombaire** [lɔ̃bɛʀ] *f* lumbar vertebra *pl*

**londonien(ne)** [lɔ̃dɔnjɛ̃, jɛn] *adj* Londoner

**Londres** [lɔ̃dʀ] London; **le Grand ~** Greater London

**long** [lɔ̃] **I.** *adv* **en dit ~ sur qc** speaks volumes about sth; **en savoir ~ sur qc** to know a lot about sth **II.** *m* **en ~** lengthways; **de ~ en large** to and fro; **en ~ et en large** in great detail; **tout au ~ du parcours** all along the way; **tout au ~ de sa vie** throughout his life; **tout le ~ du mur** all along the wall

**long, longue** [lɔ̃, lɔ̃ɡ] *adj* long; **~ de 5 km** 5 km long; **ce sera ~** it'll take a long time; **être ~ à faire qc** to be slow in doing sth

**longer** [lɔ̃ʒe] <2a> *vt* ① (*border*) **~ qc**

**L**

(*mur*) to border sth; (*sentier, rivière*) to run alongside sth ❷ (*se déplacer le long de*) ~ **qc** (*bateau, véhicule*) to travel along sth; (*personne*) (*à pied*) to walk along sth; (*en voiture*) to travel along sth

**longévité** [lɔ̃ʒevite] *f* ❶ (*longue durée de vie*) longevity ❷ (*durée de vie*) life expectancy

**longitude** [lɔ̃ʒityd] *f* longitude; **43° de ~ est/ouest** longitude 43° east/west

**longtemps** [lɔ̃tɑ̃] *adv* (*un temps long*) for a long time; **il y a ~** a long time ago; **j'en ai pour ~** it'll take me a long time; **je n'en ai pas pour ~** I won't be long; **elle n'est pas là pour ~** she's not here for long; **aussi ~ que ...** as long as ...; **~ avant/après qc** long before/after sth

**longue** [lɔ̃g] **I.** *adj v.* **long II.** *f* **à la ~** eventually

**longuement** [lɔ̃gmɑ̃] *adv* at length; (*s'étendre sur un sujet*) in detail; (*étudier*) for a long time

**longueur** [lɔ̃gœʀ] *f* length; **avoir 10 cm de ~** to be 10 cm in length; **plier en ~** to fold lengthwise; **~ d'onde** wavelength ▸ **traîner en ~** to drag on; **à ~ d'année/de journée** all day/day

**longue-vue** [lɔ̃gvy] ‹longues-vues› *f* telescope

**look** [luk] *m* (*d'une personne*) appearance ▸ **avoir un ~ d'enfer** *inf* to look great

**lopin** [lɔpɛ̃] *m* **~ de terre** plot of land

**loque** [lɔk] *f* ❶ (*vêtement*) rags; **en ~s** in rags ❷ *péj* (*personne*) wreck

**loquet** [lɔkɛ] *m* latch

**lorgner** [lɔʀɲe] ‹1› *vt* ❶ (*reluquer*) to eye *inf* ❷ (*convoiter*) **~ qc** to have one's eye on sth

**lorrain(e)** [lɔʀɛ̃, ɛn] *adj* of Lorraine

**Lorraine** [lɔʀɛn] *f* **la ~** Lorraine

**lors** [lɔʀ] *adv* **~ de notre arrivée** at the time of our arrival; **~ d'un congrès** during a conference; **depuis ~** since then; **dès ~** (*à partir de ce moment-là*) from then on; (*de ce fait*) in that case; **dès ~ que qn a fait qc** once sb does sth

**lorsque** [lɔʀsk(ə)] ‹lorsqu'› *conj* when

**losange** [lɔzɑ̃ʒ] *m* lozenge; **en** (**forme de**) **~** diamond-shaped

**lot** [lo] *m* ❶ (*prix*) prize; **gagner le gros ~** to hit the jackpot ❷ (*assortiment*) batch; (*aux enchères*) lot ❸ (*parcelle*) parcel ❹ INFORM **traitement par ~s** batch processing ❺ JUR (*part*) share

**loterie** [lɔtʀi] *f* ❶ (*jeu*) lottery; **gagner à la ~** to win the lottery ❷ (*hasard*) chance

**lotion** [losjɔ̃] *f* lotion

**lotissement** [lɔtismɑ̃] *m* (*ensemble immobilier*) housing development

**loto** [lɔto] *m* (*jeu de société*) lotto

**lotte** [lɔt] *f* monkfish

**louable** [lwabl] *adj* (*digne de louange*) praiseworthy

**loubard(e)** [lubaʀ, aʀd] *m(f) inf* hooligan

**louche¹** [luʃ] *adj* (*douteux, suspect*) dubious; (*passé*) shady; (*affaire, histoire, personne*) suspicious

**louche²** [luʃ] *f* (*ustensile*) ladle

**loucher** [luʃe] ‹1› *vi* ❶ MED to squint ❷ *inf* (*lorgner*) **~ sur qn** to eye sb; **~ sur l'héritage** to have one's eye on an inheritance

**louer¹** [lwe] ‹1› *vt* to praise

**louer²** [lwe] ‹1› **I.** *vt* to rent; **à ~** for rent **II.** *vpr* **se ~** (*appartement, voiture, chambre*) to be rented (out)

**loueur, -euse** [lwœʀ, -øz] *m, f* **~ de chambres** landlord *m*, landlady *f*; **~ de voitures** car rental agent

**loup** [lu] *m* ❶ (*mammifère*) wolf; *v.a.* **louve** ❷ (*poisson*) **~** (**de mer**) sea bass ❸ (*masque*) eye mask

**loupe** [lup] *f* magnifying glass

**louper** [lupe] ‹1› **I.** *vt inf* ❶ (*ne pas réussir: examen*) to fail; **être loupé** (*soirée*) to be ruined; (*mayonnaise, gâteau*) to be spoiled ❷ (*manquer*) to miss **II.** *vi inf* (*échouer: projet, tentative*) to fail

**lourd(e)** [luʀ, luʀd] **I.** *adj* ❶ *a.* antéposé (*de grand poids*) heavy ❷ (*pesant: jambes, paupières, tête*) heavy; **avoir l'estomac ~** to feel bloated; **avoir le cœur ~** to have a heavy heart ❸ *a.* an-

*téposé* (*oppressant: chaleur*) sultry; **il fait ~** it is sultry ❹ *a. antéposé* (*important: impôts, dettes*) heavy ❺ *a. antéposé* (*pénible: tâche*) serious; **emploi du temps très ~** very busy schedule ❻ (*chargé*) **~ de signification** full of meaning ❼ (*gauche*) heavy; (*compliment, plaisanterie*) heavy-handed ❽ (*opp: fin, délicat*) heavy ❾ *a. antéposé* (*grave*) serious ❿ *a. antéposé* (*sévère: défaite, peine*) severe ⓫ (*profond: sommeil*) deep ⓬ (*dense: terre, liquide*) dense **II.** *adv* **peser ~** to be heavy ▶ **pas ~** *inf* not much

**lourdement** [luʀdəmɑ̃] *adv* heavily; (*se tromper*) seriously; (*insister*) strenuously

**lourdeur** [luʀdœʀ] *f* ❶ (*pesanteur*) **des ~s d'estomac** a bloated feeling ❷ (*caractère massif*) heaviness

**loutre** [lutʀ] *f* ZOOL otter

**louve** [luv] *f* she-wolf; *v.a.* **loup**

**louveteau** [luvto] <x> *m* ❶ ZOOL wolf cub ❷ (*jeune scout*) Cub Scout

**lover** [lɔve] <1> *vpr* **se ~** to coil up

**loyal(e)** [lwajal, -jo] <-aux> *adj* (*ami*) loyal; (*services*) faithful; (*conduite, procédés*) fair; (*adversaire*) honest

**loyauté** [lwajote] *f* loyalty; (*d'un adversaire, d'un procédé*) honesty

**loyer** [lwaje] *m* rent

**lubrifiant** [lybʀifjɑ̃] *m* lubricant

**lubrifier** [lybʀifje] <1a> *vt* to lubricate

**lucarne** [lykaʀn] *f* (*petite fenêtre*) dormer window; (*d'une entrée, d'un cachot*) small window

**lucide** [lysid] *adj* ❶ (*clairvoyant: intelligence, jugement*) clear-sighted ❷ (*conscient*) conscious

**lucratif, -ive** [lykʀatif, -iv] *adj* lucrative

**ludiciel** [lydisjɛl] *m* INFORM computer game, videogame

**lueur** [lɥœʀ] *f* ❶ (*faible clarté, signe passager*) glimmer; (*des braises*) flicker; **~ d'espoir** glimmer of hope ❷ (*éclat fugitif dans le regard*) **~ de colère/joie** gleam of anger/joy

**luge** [lyʒ] *f* sled; **faire de la ~** to sled

**lugubre** [lygybʀ] *adj* lugubrious; (*per-*

*sonne, pensée*) gloomy; (*paysage*) dismal

**lui** [lɥi] **I.** *pron pers* ❶ (*personne masc ou fém*) **je ~ ai demandé s'il/si elle venait** I asked him/her if he/she was coming ❷ (*animal, objet masc ou fém*) it ❸ (*avec un sens possessif*) **le cœur ~ battait fort** his/her heart was beating hard; *v.a.* **me II.** *pron pers, masc* ❶ him; **tu veux l'aider, ~?** do you want to help HIM?; **à ~ seul** him alone ❷ (*soi*) himself; **il ne pense qu'à ~** he only thinks of himself

**lui-même** [lɥimɛm] *pron pers* himself; **~ n'en savait rien** he himself did not know anything about it; **il est venu de ~** he came by his own choice; **M. X? – ~!** Mr. X? – himself!

**luire** [lɥiʀ] *vi irr* ❶ (*briller*) to shine ❷ (*réfléchir la lumière: feuilles*) to glimmer; (*lac, rosée*) to glisten

**luisant(e)** [lɥizɑ̃, ɑ̃t] *adj* shining; (*yeux*) (*de joie*) shining; (*de colère*) gleaming

**lumbago** [lœbago] *m* lumbago

**lumière** [lymjɛʀ] *f* ❶ (*clarté naturelle, éclairage*) light; **~ du soleil** sunlight; **~ du jour** daylight; **~ de la lune** moonlight ❷ *pl* (*connaissances*) knowledge ❸ (*personne intelligente*) **être une ~** to be a bright spark; **ne pas être une ~** not to be too bright ❹ (*ce qui permet de comprendre*) **faire la ~ sur une affaire** to get to the bottom of a matter

**luminaire** [lyminɛʀ] *m* (*lampe*) lamp

**lumineux, -euse** [lyminø, -øz] *adj* ❶ (*qui répand la lumière*) luminous; (*enseigne, rayon*) neon ❷ (*brillant, éclatant: couleur, yeux*) bright; (*regard*) luminous; (*teint*) translucent ❸ (*clair: pièce, appartement*) light

**luminosité** [lyminozite] *f* ❶ (*éclat lumineux: du ciel, d'une couleur*) luminosity ❷ (*clarté: d'une pièce, d'un appartement*) brightness

**lunatique** [lynatik] *adj* (*personne*) lunatic; (*humeur*) quirky

**lundi** [lœdi] *m* Monday; **~ de Pâques/Pentecôte** Easter/Whitmonday; *v.a.* **dimanche**

**L**

**lune** [lyn] *f* moon

**lunette** [lynɛt] *f* ❶ *pl* (*verres*) glasses; ~s **noires** dark glasses; ~ **de plongée** goggles; ~s **de soleil** sunglasses; **mettre ses** ~s to put one's glasses on ❷ (*instrument*) sight ❸ (*petite fenêtre: d'un toit*) skylight; ~ **arrière** AUTO rear window ❹ (*anneau: des WC*) toilet seat

**lustre** [lystʀ] *m* (*lampe*) ceiling light

**lustrer** [lystʀe] <1> *vt* (*faire briller: voiture*) to shine

**luthier** [lytje] *m* (stringed-)instrument maker

**lutin** [lytɛ̃] *m* elf

**lutte** [lyt] *f* ❶ (*combat*) fight; ~ **contre/pour qn/qc** fight against/for sb/sth; ~ **antidrogue** war on drugs; ~ **des classes** class struggle ❷ SPORT wrestling

**lutter** [lyte] <1> *vi* ❶ (*combattre*) to fight; (*se démener*) to struggle; ~ **contre la mort** to fight death; ~ **contre le sommeil/le vent** to fight against sleep/the wind ❷ (*mener une action*) ~ **contre qc** to fight against sth

**lutteur, -euse** [lytœʀ, -øz] *m, f* ❶ SPORT wrestler ❷ (*battant*) fighter

**luxation** [lyksasjɔ̃] *f* (*de l'épaule, de la hanche*) dislocation

**luxe** [lyks] *m* ❶ (*opp: nécessité*) luxury; **ce n'est pas du** ~ *inf* it's a necessity ❷ (*coûteux*) **de** ~ luxury

**Luxembourg** [lyksɑ̃buʀ] *m* ❶ (*ville*) Luxembourg ❷ (*pays*) **le** (**grand-duché du**) ~ (the grand duchy of) Luxembourg ❸ (*à Paris*) **le** (**palais du**) ~ *the seat of the French Senate in Paris*; **le** (**jardin du**) ~ *the Luxembourg Gardens*

**luxembourgeois(e)** [lyksɑ̃buʀʒwa, waz] *adj* Luxembourg

**luxer** [lykse] <1> *vpr* **se** ~ **l'épaule** to dislocate one's shoulder

**luxueux, -euse** [lyksɥø, -øz] *adj a.* antéposé luxurious

**luxuriant(e)** [lyksyʀjɑ̃, jɑ̃t] *adj* (*végétation*) lush

**lycée** [lise] *m* ❶ high school; ~ **d'enseignement général et technologique** technology school; ~ **professionnel** vocational school; **être prof au** ~ to be a high school teacher; **aller au** ~ to go to high school ❷ *Belgique* (*établissement secondaire pour filles*) girls' school

**lycéen(ne)** [liseɛ̃, ɛn] *m(f)* high school student

**lycra**® [likʀa] *m* Lycra®

**lymphatique** [lɛ̃fatik] *adj* MED **système** ~ lymphatic system

**lyncher** [lɛ̃ʃe] <1> *vt* to lynch

**lynx** [lɛ̃ks] *m* lynx

**lys** [lis] *m v.* **lis**

# Mm

**M, m** [ɛm] *m inv* M, m; ~ **comme Marcel** (*au téléphone*) m as in Mike

**m** [ɛm] *abr de* **mètre** m

**M.** <MM.> *m abr de* **Monsieur** Mr.

**m'** *pron v.* **me**

**ma** [ma, me] <mes> *dét poss* my
► ~ **pauvre!** you poor thing!

**macabre** [makabʀ] *adj* macabre

**macadam** [makadam] *m* (*revêtement routier*) tarmac

**macaron** [makaʀɔ̃] *m* CULIN macaroon

**macérer** [maseʀe] <5> *vt, vi* CULIN to macerate

**mâcher** [maʃe] <1> *vt* (*mastiquer*) to chew; (*ronger*) to gnaw

**machin** [maʃɛ̃] *m inf* (*truc*) whatchamacallit

**machination** [maʃinasjɔ̃] *f* plot

**machine** [maʃin] *f* (*appareil*) appliance; ~ **à café** coffee machine; ~ **à coudre/à sous** sewing/slot machine; ~ **à laver** washing machine, washer; **écrire/taper à la** ~ to type

**machiste** [mat(t)ʃist] **I.** *adj* chauvinist **II.** *m* chauvinist

**macho** [matʃo] *m inf* macho

**mâchoire** [maʃwaʀ] *f* ❶ ANAT (*d'un mammifère*) jaw; (*d'un insecte*) mandible ❷ *pl* TECH jaws

**maçon(ne)** [masɔ̃, ɔn] *m(f)* (*ouvrier*) bricklayer

**Madagascar** [madagaskaʀ] *f* Madagascar

**madame** [madam, medam] <mesdames> *f* ❶ *souvent non traduit* (*femme à qui on s'adresse*) Madam *iron;* **bonjour** ~ good morning; **bonjour Madame Larroque** good morning, Mrs. Larroque; **bonjour mesdames** good morning, ladies; **Mesdames, mesdemoiselles, messieurs!** Ladies and Gentlemen! ❷ (*profession*) **Madame la Duchesse/le juge/le professeur/la Présidente** Madam ❸ (*sur une enveloppe*) **Madame Dupont** Mrs. Dupont ❹ (*en-tête*) (**Chère**) **Madame,** Dear Madam,; **Madame, Monsieur,** Sir, Madam,; **Madame, Mademoiselle, Monsieur,** Mr., Mrs., Miss

**mademoiselle** [mad(ə)mwazɛl, med(ə)mwazɛl] <mesdemoiselles> *f* ❶ *souvent non traduit* (*jeune femme à qui on s'adresse*) Miss; **bonjour** ~ good morning; **bonjour Mademoiselle Larroque** good morning, Miss Larroque; **bonjour mesdemoiselles** good morning, ladies; **Mesdames, mesdemoiselles, messieurs!** Ladies and Gentlemen! ❷ (*sur une enveloppe*) **Mademoiselle Aporé** Miss Aporé ❸ (*en-tête*) (**Chère**) **Mademoiselle,** Dear Madam,; **Madame, Mademoiselle, Monsieur,** Mr., Mrs., Miss

**Madrid** [madʀid] Madrid

**mag** [mag] *m inf v.* **magazine** news; **le** ~ **de vingt heures** the eight o'clock news

**magasin** [magazɛ̃] *m* ❶ (*boutique*) store, shop; ~ **spécialisé** specialty store; **grand** ~ department store; ~ **d'alimentation/d'usine** food/factory store; **tenir un** ~ to run a store ❷ (*entrepôt: d'un port*) warehouse; MIL arsenal; **en** ~ in stock ❸ TECH, PHOT magazine

**magazine** [magazin] *m* PRESSE, CINÉ, TV magazine; ~ **électronique** e-zine

**mage** [maʒ] **I.** *m* magus **II.** *app* **les Rois** ~**s** the Three Wise Men

**Maghreb** [magʀɛb] *m* **le** ~ the Maghreb

**maghrébin(e)** [magʀebɛ̃, in] *adj* North African

**magicien(ne)** [maʒisjɛ̃, jɛn] *m(f)* ❶ (*sorcier*) wizard ❷ (*illusionniste*) magician

**magie** [maʒi] *f* ❶ (*pratiques occultes*) witchcraft ❷ (*séduction*) magic

**magique** [maʒik] *adj* ❶ (*surnaturel*)

**M**

**baguette** ~ magic wand ②(*merveilleux*) magical

**magnétique** [manetik] *adj* magnetic

**magnétisme** [manetism] *m* PHYS magnetism

**magnéto** *inf*, **magnétophone** [manetɔfɔn] *m* ①(*à cassettes*) cassette recorder ②(*à bandes*) tape recorder

**magnétoscope** [manetɔskɔp] *m* video, VCR

**magnifique** [manifik] *adj* a. antéposé ①(*très beau*) attractive; (*temps*) magnificent ②(*somptueux*) magnificent; (*femme*) gorgeous

**magnolia** [manɔlja] *m* magnolia

**magrébin(e)** [magʀebɛ̃, in] *adj v.* **maghrébin**

**mai** [mɛ] *m* May; *v.a.* **août**

**maigre** [mɛgʀ] I. *adj* ①(*opp: gros*) thin ②CULIN lean; (*bouillon*) clear ③antéposé (*faible*) poor; (*chance*) slim; (*profit*) meager ④a. antéposé (*peu abondant: végétation*) sparse; (*récolte*) poor; (*repas*) light II. *mf* thin person

**maigreur** [mɛgʀœʀ] *f* ①(*opp: embonpoint*) thinness ②(*pauvreté: d'un sol*) poorness ③(*opp: abondance: d'un profit, des revenus*) meagerness

**maigrir** [megʀiʀ] <8> *vi* to lose weight; **il a maigri de figure** his face has slimmed down; ~ **de cinq kilos** to lose five kilograms

**maille** [maj] *f* ①COUT stitch; ~ **filée** run ②(*maillon: d'une chaîne, armure*) link

**maillon** [majɔ̃] *m* (*anneau*) link ▸ **être un ~ de la chaîne** to be a link in the chain

**maillot** [majo] *m* ①(*pour se baigner*) ~ **de bain** (*de femme*) swimsuit; (*d'homme*) swimming trunks; ~ **de bain une pièce/deux pièces** one-/two-piece swimsuit ②SPORT soccer shirt ③(*sous-vêtement*) ~ **de corps** undershirt

**main** [mɛ̃] *f* ①ANAT, SPORT hand; **battre des ~s** to clap one's hands; **se donner la ~** to hold hands; (*aider*) to help one another out; **prendre qn par la ~** to take sb by the hand; **serrer la ~ à qn** to shake sb's hand; **tendre la ~ à qn** to reach out to sb; **être fait (à la) ~** to be handmade; **sac à ~** purse, handbag; **frein à ~** emergency brake, hand brake; **écrire à la ~** to write (by hand); (*la*) ~ **dans la ~** hand in hand; **les ~s en l'air!, haut les ~s!** hands up! ②(*style: d'un artiste, maître*) style; **de ~ de maître** with a master's hand ③ JEUX lead; **avoir la ~** to be in the lead ▸ **donner un coup de ~ à qn** to give sb a hand; **j'en mettrais ma ~ au feu** I would stake my life on it; **prendre qn la ~ dans le sac** to catch sb red-handed; **gagner qc haut la ~** to win sth hands down; **voter à ~ levée** to vote by a show of hands; **avoir les ~s libres** to have a free hand; **à ~s nues** with bare fists; **de première/seconde ~** first-hand/secondhand; **avoir qc sous la ~** to have sth on hand; **il se fait la ~** he's getting the knack of it; **passer la ~** (*transmettre ses pouvoirs*) to step down; **il perd la ~** he's losing his touch; **en venir aux ~s** to come to blows; **de la ~ à la ~** directly

**main-d'œuvre** [mɛ̃dœvʀ] <mains-d'œuvre> *f* workforce

**maintenance** [mɛ̃tnãs] *f* maintenance

**maintenant** [mɛ̃t(ə)nã] *adv* ①a. en tête de phrase (*en ce moment, cela dit*) now; **dès** ~ as of now ②(*actuellement*) today ③(*désormais*) henceforth

**maintenir** [mɛ̃t(ə)niʀ] <9> I. *vt* ①(*conserver: ordre, offre, contrat, politique*) to maintain; (*tradition*) to preserve ②(*soutenir*) to keep ③(*contenir*) to hold; ~ **les prix** to hold prices ④(*affirmer*) to claim II. *vpr* **se** ~ to persist; (*institution*) to live on; (*paix*) to hold; (*santé, prix*) to remain steady

**maintien** [mɛ̃tjɛ̃] *m* ①(*conservation*) upholding; (*des libertés, traditions*) preservation; (*d'un contrat*) maintenance ②(*attitude*) bearing ③(*soutien*) support

**maire** [mɛʀ] *mf* mayor

**mairie** [meʀi] *f* ①(*hôtel de ville*) city [*o* town] hall ②(*administration*) city council ❸ (*fonction de maire*) mayoralty

**mais** [mɛ] I. *conj* but II. *adv* ❶ (*pourtant, renforcement, impatience*) but; **tu ne m'aimes pas ~ ~ si!** you don't love me – of course I do!; **~ encore** but besides ❷ *inf* (*indignation*) **non ~, tu me prends pour ...** for goodness sake, do you take me for ... III. *m* but

**maison** [mɛzɔ̃] I. *f* ❶ (*habitation*) house ❷ (*famille*) family; **être de la ~** to be part of the family ❸ (*entreprise*) company; **~ mère** parent company; **~ de couture** fashion house; **~ de disques** record shop; **~ d'édition** publishing house; **avoir quinze ans de ~** to have worked in the company for fifteen years ❹ (*bâtiment*) **~ de maître** family mansion; **~ d'arrêt** prison; **~ de repos/retraite** convalescent/retirement home ▶ **~ close** brothel II. *app inv* ❶ (*particulier à une maison*) in-house; (*esprit, genre*) house ❷ (*opp: industriel: pâté*) homemade

**Maison-Blanche** [mɛzɔ̃blɑ̃ʃ] *f sans pl* **la ~** the White House

**maître** [mɛtʀ] I. *m* ART, LIT master; **~ à penser** intellectual guide II. *mf* UNIV **~ de conférences** assistant professor

**maître, maîtresse** [mɛtʀ, mɛtʀɛs] I. *adj* ❶ (*principal*) **œuvre maîtresse** master work ❷ (*qui peut disposer de*) **être ~ de soi** to be in control of oneself II. *m, f* ❶ (*chef*) master; **~ des lieux** master of the house; **~ de maison** host ❷ (*patron*) instructor; **~ nageur** swimming instructor ❸ ÉCOLE (*à l'école primaire*) teacher ❹ (*propriétaire: d'un chien*) master

**maître chanteur, -euse** [mɛtʀəʃɑ̃tœʀ, -øz] *m, f* blackmailer

**maîtresse** [mɛtʀɛs] I. *adj v.* maître II. *f* (*liaison*) mistress

**maîtrise** [mɛtʀiz] *f* ❶ (*contrôle*) control; **~ d'une langue** mastery of a language ❷ (*habileté*) mastery ❸ (*sang-froid*) **~ de soi** self-control ❹ UNIV master's degree ❺ (*grade*) supervisors *pl*

**maîtriser** [mɛtʀize] <1> I. *vt* ❶ (*domi-*

ner, dompter: *situation, sujet*) to master; **~ qn/qc** to bring sb/sth under control ❷ (*contenir: émotion, passion*) to suppress; (*réactions*) to control; (*larmes*) to force back II. *vpr* **se ~** to control oneself

**majeur** [maʒœʀ] *m* ANAT middle finger

**majeur(e)** [maʒœʀ] I. *adj* ❶ (*très important: difficulté, intérêt, événement*) major ❷ (*le plus important*) main ❸ *antéposé* (*la plupart*) **la ~e partie du temps** most of the time ❹ JUR **être ~** to be of age II. *m(f)* JUR adult

**majorité** [maʒɔʀite] *f* ❶ (*majeure partie*) majority; **en ~** mostly ❷ JUR majority

**majuscule** [maʒyskyl] *adj, f* capital

**mal¹** [mal] I. *adv* ❶ badly; **ça va ~ finir!** it will end badly!; **le moment est vraiment ~ choisi** this really is not the best moment ❷ (*pas dans le bon ordre, de la bonne façon, de manière immorale*) **il s'y prend ~** he is going about it the wrong way; **il a ~ tourné** he's gone wrong ❸ (*de manière inconvenante*) **~ répondre** to reply rudely ❹ (*de manière défavorable*) **être ~ vu** to be frowned upon ▶ **pas ~** *avec ou sans nég* (*assez bien*) not bad; (*passablement, assez*) enough; *sans nég, inf* (*opp: très peu*) quite a few; **je m'en fiche pas ~** I couldn't care less II. *adj inv* ❶ (*mauvais, immoral*) **faire quelque chose/ne rien faire de ~** to do something/nothing bad; **j'ai dit quelque chose de ~?** did I say something wrong? ❷ (*malade: se sentir*) ill ❸ (*pas à l'aise*) **être ~** to be uncomfortable

**mal²** [mal, mo] <maux> *m* ❶ *a.* REL **le ~** evil ❷ *sans pl* (*action, parole, pensée mauvaise*) harm; **faire du ~ à qn** to harm sb; **dire du ~ de qn** to say bad things about sb; **il n'y a pas de ~ à qc** there is no harm in sth ❸ *sans pl* (*maladie, malaise*) illness; **~ de mer** seasickness ❹ (*souffrance physique*) **~ de tête** headache; **~ de ventre** stomachache; **il a ~ à la main** his hand hurts; **avoir ~ à la jambe** to have a sore leg; **(se) faire ~**

**M**

to hurt (oneself); **ces chaussures me font ~ aux pieds** these shoes hurt my feet ⑤ (*souffrance morale*) **faire ~** to hurt; **~ de vivre** depression; **~ du pays** homesickness; **qn/qc me fait ~ au cœur** sb/sth makes me feel sick ⑥ (*calamité*) disaster ⑦ *sans pl* (*peine*) difficulty ⑧ *sans pl* (*dégât*) damage; **le travail ne fait pas de ~ à qn** hard work never hurt anyone ⑨ (*manque*) **un peintre en ~ d'inspiration** a painter suffering from a lack of inspiration ▶ **le ~ est fait** the damage is done

**malade** [malad] **I.** *adj* ① (*souffrant*) ill; **tomber ~** to fall sick; **être ~ du sida** to suffer from AIDS ② (*bouleversé*) **~ de jalousie/d'inquiétude** to be sick with jealousy/worry ③ *inf* (*cinglé*) **être ~** to be crazy ④ (*en mauvais état: économie, entreprise*) in a bad way **II.** *mf* ① (*personne souffrante*) invalid; **grand ~** seriously ill person; **~ mental** mentally ill person ② (*patient*) patient

**M maladie** [maladi] *f* ① (*affection*) illness; **~ de cœur/peau** heart/skin condition; **~ infantile/mentale** childhood/mental illness; **être en ~** to be off work sick ② (*manie*) mania ▶ **faire une ~ de qc** *inf* to make a mountain out of sth

**maladif, -ive** [maladif, -iv] *adj* ① (*souffreteux: personne*) sickly; (*air, pâleur*) unhealthy ② (*maniaque: besoin, peur*) pathological

**maladresse** [maladʀɛs] *f* ① (*gaucherie: d'un comportement, geste*) clumsiness; (*d'un style*) awkwardness ② (*bévue, gaffe*) blunder

**maladroit(e)** [maladʀwa, wat] **I.** *adj* ① (*opp: habile, leste: geste, personne*) clumsy; (*caresses, style, personne*) awkward ② *fig* (*parole, remarque*) tactless **II.** *m(f)* ① (*personne malhabile*) butterfingers ② (*gaffeur*) blunderer

**malaise** [malɛz] *m* ① MED faintness; **avoir un ~** to feel faint ② (*crise*) discontent; **~ social** social unrest

**malchance** [malʃɑ̃s] *f* misfortune

**malchanceux, -euse** [malʃɑ̃sø, -øz] *adj* (*personne*) unlucky

**mâle** [mɑl] *adj, m* male

**malédiction** [malediksjɔ̃] *f* ① (*fatalité, action de maudire*) malediction ② (*malheur*) curse

**malentendant(e)** [malɑ̃tɑ̃dɑ̃, ɑ̃t] *m(f)* person with hearing problems; **les ~s** the hard of hearing

**malentendu** [malɑ̃tɑ̃dy] *m* misunderstanding

**malfaiteur, -trice** [malfɛtœʀ, -tʀis] *m, f* criminal

**malformation** [malfɔʀmasjɔ̃] *f* malformation

**malgré** [malgʀe] *prep* ① (*en dépit de*) despite; **~ tout** despite everything ② (*contre le gré de*) **~ moi/elle/lui** against my/her/his will

**malheur** [malœʀ] *m* ① (*événement pénible*) misfortune; **si jamais il m'arrivait ~** if ever anything bad happened to me ② *sans pl* (*malchance*) bad luck; **par ~** through bad luck ③ (*tort*) **avoir le ~ de** +*infin* to be foolish enough to +*infin* ▶ **faire un ~** *inf* (*avoir un gros succès*) to be a big hit

**malheureusement** [malœʀøzmɑ̃] *adv* (*hélas*) unfortunately

**malheureux, -euse** [malœʀø, -øz] **I.** *adj* ① (*qui souffre: personne, air*) unhappy ② *a. antéposé* (*regrettable, fâcheux*) regrettable; (*incident, suites, initiative, parole*) unfortunate ③ (*malchanceux: candidat, joueur*) unlucky ④ *antéposé* (*insignifiant*) wretched ⑤ *antéposé* (*infortuné: victime*) unfortunate **II.** *m, f* ① (*indigent*) needy person ② (*infortuné*) poor soul

**malhonnête** [malɔnɛt] *adj* ① (*indélicat, déloyal*) dishonest ② *iron* rude

**malhonnêteté** [malɔnɛtte] *f* dishonesty

**malice** [malis] *f* ① (*espièglerie*) mischief ② (*méchanceté*) spite

**malicieux, -euse** [malisjø, -jøz] *adj* (*espiègle*) mischievous; (*méchant*) malicious

**malin, maligne** [malɛ̃, malin] **I.** *adj* ① (*astucieux: personne*) shrewd; (*sourire*) cunning; (*air*) smart ② *a. antéposé* (*méchant*) sly; (*influence*) malicious

**❸** MED (*tumeur*) malignant **II.** *m, f* (*personne astucieuse*) crafty person; **faire le ~** to show off

**malle** [mal] *f* trunk

**mallette** [malɛt] *f* (*porte-documents*) briefcase

**malmener** [malməne] <4> *vt* **❶** (*rudoyer*) to manhandle **❷** (*critiquer*) to criticize **❸** MIL, SPORT (*bousculer*) **~ qn** to give sb a hard time

**malpoli(e)** [malpɔli] **I.** *adj inf* (*mal élevé*) discourteous; (*enfant*) rude **II.** *m(f)* *inf* rude person

**malsain(e)** [malsɛ̃, ɛn] *adj* unhealthy

**malt** [malt] *m* malt

**maltraiter** [maltʀete] <1> *vt* **❶** (*brutaliser*) to mistreat **❷** (*critiquer*) to slam

**maman** [mamɑ̃] *f* **❶** (*mère*) mother **❷** (*appellation*) mommy

**mamie** [mami] *f inf* granny

**mammifère** [mamifɛʀ] *mf* mammal

**manager¹** [manadʒɛʀ, manadʒœʀ] *m* ECON, SPORT manager; THEAT agent

**manager²** [mana(d)ʒe] <2a> *vt* to manage

**manche¹** [mɑ̃ʃ] *f* **❶** COUT (*d'un vêtement*) sleeve **❷** (*aux courses*) round **❸** (*au ski*) leg **❹** JEUX game ► **faire la ~** to panhandle

**manche²** [mɑ̃ʃ] *m* **❶** (*poignée*) handle **❷** MUS (*d'une guitare, d'un violon*) neck

**Manche** [mɑ̃ʃ] *f* **la ~** the English Channel

**manchette** [mɑ̃ʃɛt] *f* **❶** (*poignet: d'une chemise*) cuff **❷** SPORT forearm blow **❸** COUT false sleeve **❹** TECH headline

**manchot** [mɑ̃ʃo] *m* (*pingouin*) penguin

**manchot(e)** [mɑ̃ʃo, ɔt] **I.** *adj* (*amputé d'un bras*) one-armed **II.** *m(f)* (*personne*) person with one arm

**mandarine** [mɑ̃daʀin] *f* mandarin

**mandat** [mɑ̃da] *m* **❶** (*mission*) mandate **❷** JUR **~ d'arrêt** arrest warrant **❸** COM, FIN money order

**manège** [manɛʒ] *m* **❶** (*attraction foraine*) merry-go-round **❷** (*agissements*) ruse

**manette** [manɛt] *f* INFORM **~ de jeu** joystick

**mangeable** [mɑ̃ʒabl] *adj* edible

**manger** [mɑ̃ʒe] <2a> **I.** *vt* **❶** (*se nourrir de, absorber*) to eat **❷** (*ronger: mites, rouille, lèpre*) to eat away **❸** *iron* (*dévorer*) to devour **❹** (*dilapider: capital, héritage, temps*) to swallow up **❺** (*consommer: essence*) to guzzle **❻** *inf* (*ne pas articuler: mots*) to mumble **II.** *vi* (*personne, animal*) to eat; **inviter qn à ~** to invite sb to dinner; **donner à ~ à un bébé/aux vaches** to feed a baby/the cows **III.** *vpr* **qc se mange chaud** sth is eaten hot

**mangue** [mɑ̃g] *f* mango

**maniabilité** [manjabilite] *f* (*d'une voiture*) maneuverability; (*d'un appareil, d'une machine*) ease of use; (*d'un livre, outil*) handiness

**maniaque** [manjak] **I.** *adj* **❶** (*pointilleux: soin*) fanatical; (*personne*) fussy **❷** MED, PSYCH (*euphorie*) maniacal **II.** *mf* **❶** (*personne trop méticuleuse*) fanatic **❷** MED, PSYCH maniac

**manie** [mani] *f* **❶** (*tic*) habit **❷** (*obsession*) mania

**maniement** [manimɑ̃] *m* **❶** (*manipulation*) handling; (*d'un appareil*) use **❷** (*gestion: des affaires*) management **❸** (*maîtrise: d'une langue*) use

**manier** [manje] <1> *vt* **❶** (*se servir de, utiliser, maîtriser*) to use; (*appareil*) to handle **❷** (*manipuler, avoir entre les mains*) **~ qn/qc** to manipulate sb/sth

**manière** [manjɛʀ] *f* **❶** (*façon*) way; **~ de faire qc** way of doing sth; **avoir la ~** to have the knack; **à la ~ de qn/qc** like sb/sth; **à ma/sa ~** in my/his/her own way; **de ~ brutale/rapide** brutally/quickly; **d'une certaine ~** in a way; **d'une ~ générale** generally; **d'une ~ ou d'une autre** in one way or another; **de toute ~** in any case; **de ~ à** +*infin* so as to +*infin*; **de ~ (à ce) qu'il soit satisfait** (*subj*) so that he's satisfied; **de quelle ~?** how!, **en aucune ~** not at all **❷** *pl* (*comportement*) manners; **faire des ~s** to put on airs; **en voilà des ~s!** what a way to behave! **❸** (*style: d'un artiste, écrivain*) manner **❹** LING

**M**

adverbe/**complément de** ~ adverb/complement of manner

**maniéré(e)** [manjere] *adj* mannered; (*ton, personne*) affected

**manifestant(e)** [manifɛstɑ̃, ɑ̃t] *m(f)* demonstrator

**manifestation** [manifɛstasjɔ̃] *f* ❶ POL demonstration ❷ (*événement*) event ❸ (*expression: d'un sentiment*) expression; (*d'une humeur*) show; (*de joie, amitié*) demonstration

**manifester** [manifɛste] <1> I. *vt* to show II. *vi* to demonstrate III. *vpr* **se** ~ ❶ (*se révéler*) to appear; (*crise*) to arise ❷ (*se faire connaître*) to make oneself known; (*candidat*) to put oneself forward ❸ (*s'exprimer*) to express oneself ❹ (*se montrer: personne*) to appear

**manigance** [manigɑ̃s] *f gén pl* scheme

**manipulation** [manipylasjɔ̃] *f* ❶ (*maniement: d'une machine, d'un ordinateur*) use; (*d'un outil, produit, d'une substance*) handling ❷ *pl* (*expériences*) experiments ❸ *péj* (*manœuvre: de la foule, l'opinion*) manipulation

**manipuler** [manipyle] <1> *vt* ❶ (*manier: outil*) to use; (*substance*) to handle ❷ *péj* (*fausser*) to manipulate; (*écritures, résultats*) to fiddle ❸ (*influencer*) to manipulate

**manivelle** [manivɛl] *f* AUTO starting crank

**mannequin** [mankɛ̃] *m* ❶ (*pour le tailleur, la vitrine*) dummy ❷ (*pour le peintre, sculpteur, de mode*) model

**manœuvre** [manœvʀ] I. *f* ❶ (*maniement: d'une machine*) operation; (*d'un véhicule*) handling; **fausse** ~ error; *fig* wrong move ❷ (*action, exercice*) *a.* MIL maneuver; ~ **de diversion** diversion ❸ *péj* (*agissement, machination*) ploy II. *m* laborer

**manœuvrer** [manœvʀe] <1> I. *vt* ❶ (*faire fonctionner: machine*) to operate; (*outil*) to use ❷ (*conduire: véhicule*) to drive ❸ *péj* (*manipuler*) to manipulate II. *vi* ❶ (*agir habilement*) *a.* MIL to maneuver ❷ AUTO to maneuver the car

**manquant(e)** [mɑ̃kɑ̃, ɑ̃t] *adj* (*pièce, somme, article*) missing; (*personne*) absent

**manque** [mɑ̃k] *m* ❶ (*carence*) lack; **un enfant en** ~ **d'affection** a child lacking affection ❷ *pl* (*lacunes*) failings ❸ (*défauts*) faults ❹ (*vide*) gap ❺ MED (*privation*) withdrawal

**manquer** [mɑ̃ke] <1> I. *vt* ❶ (*rater, laisser passer: but, bus, train, marche*) to miss; **une occasion à ne pas** ~ a chance not to be missed ❷ (*se venger*) **ne pas** ~ **qn** to not let sb get away with it ❸ (*opp: réussir: examen*) to fail ❹ (*opp: assister à: film, réunion*) to miss; (*cours, école*) to skip II. *vi* ❶ (*être absent*) to be missing ❷ (*faire défaut, être insuffisant, ne pas avoir assez de*) **commencer à** ~ to start to run out; **qc te manque pour** +*infin* you don't have sth to +*infin*; **qn manque de qc** sb is lacking sth ❸ (*regretter de ne pas avoir*) **mes enfants/les livres me manquent** I miss my children/books ❹ (*rater: attentat, tentative*) to fail ❺ (*ne pas respecter*) **il manque à sa parole** he fails to keep his word; ~ **à ses obligations** to neglect one's obligations ❻ (*faillir*) ~ (**de**) **faire qc** to almost do sth ❼ (*ne pas omettre*) **ne pas** ~ **de** +*infin* to be sure to +*infin* ▸ **il ne manquait plus que ça** that's all we needed III. *vpr* ❶ (*rater son suicide*) **se** ~ to botch one's suicide bid ❷ (*ne pas se rencontrer*) **se** ~ **de 5 minutes** to miss each other by 5 minutes

**manteau** [mɑ̃to] <x> *m* coat

**manucure** [manykyʀ] *mf* manicurist

**manuel** [manɥɛl] *m* ❶ (*livre didactique*) handbook; ~ **scolaire** textbook ❷ (*manuel d'utilisation*) manual

**manuel(le)** [manɥɛl] I. *adj* manual II. *m(f)* ❶ (*personne qui travaille de ses mains*) manual worker ❷ (*personne douée de ses mains*) person good with their hands

**manuscrit** [manyskʀi] *m* manuscript

**manuscrit(e)** [manyskʀi, it] *adj* (*écrit à la main*) handwritten

**maquillage** [makijaʒ] *m* ❶ (*se maquiller, produits de beauté*) makeup ❷ (*d'une voiture*) disguising

**maquiller** [makije] <1> **I.** *vt* ❶ (*farder*) ~ **qn** to make sb up ❷ (*falsifier*) to forge; (*vérité*) to doctor; (*voiture*) to disguise **II.** *vpr* (*se farder*) **se** ~ to put on one's makeup

**marais** [mare] *m* marsh

**marbre** [marbr] *m* ❶ (*pierre, objet, statue*) marble ❷ (*plateau: d'une cheminée*) marble mantel; (*d'une commode*) marble top ❸ *fig* **être/rester de** ~ to be/remain indifferent

**marchand(e)** [marʃɑ̃, ɑ̃d] **I.** *adj* ❶ (*qui transporte des marchandises: marine, navire*) merchant ❷ (*où se pratique le commerce*) **rue** ~**e** market street; **galerie** ~**e** shopping arcade ❸ (*dans le commerce*) **valeur** ~**e** market value **II.** *m(f)* ❶ (*commerçant*) tradesman; ~ **ambulant** traveling salesman ❷ *fig* ~ **de sable** sandman; ~ **de tapis** *péj* tough bargainer

**marchander** [marʃɑ̃de] <1> **I.** *vt* ~ **le prix/un tapis** to bargain over the price/a carpet **II.** *vi* to bargain

**marchandise** [marʃɑ̃diz] *f* merchandise

**marche**[1] [marʃ] *f* ❶ (*action*) *a.* sport walking; **se mettre en** ~ (*personnes*) to make a move; (*cortège, caravane*) to set off; ~ **à suivre** procedure ❷ (*allure*) gait; (*d'un navire*) sailing ❸ (*trajet*) walk ❹ MIL, POL march ❺ (*mouvement continu: d'une étoile*) course; (*d'une caravane, d'un véhicule*) movement; **en** ~ **arrière** in reverse ❻ (*fonctionnement: d'une entreprise, horloge*) working; (*d'une machine*) functioning; **mettre un appareil en** ~ to start up a device ❼ MUS march ▸ **faire** ~ **arrière** to backpedal; AUTO to reverse

**marche**[2] [marʃ] *f* (*d'un escalier*) stair; (*d'un véhicule, devant une maison*) step

**marché** [marʃe] *m* ❶ (*lieu de vente, opérations financières, l'offre et la demande, clientèle potentielle*) market ❷ (*contrat*) bargain; **conclure un** ~ **avec qn/qc** to strike a deal with sb/sth; ~ **conclu!** it's a deal! ▸ **bon** ~ *inv* cheap

**marcher** [marʃe] <1> *vi* ❶ (*se déplacer*) to walk ❷ MIL ~ **sur la ville/Paris** to march on the town/Paris ❸ (*poser le pied*) ~ **sur/dans qc** to step on/in sth ❹ *fig* ~ **sur/dans qc** to tread on/in sth ❺ (*être en activité: métro, bus*) to run ❻ (*fonctionner*) to function; (*montre, télé, machine*) to work ❼ (*réussir: affaire, film*) to be a success; (*études*) to go well; (*procédé*) to work ❽ *inf* (*croire naïvement*) to be taken for a ride; **faire** ~ **qn** to take sb for a ride ❾ *inf* (*être d'accord*) **je marche (avec vous)** OK!

**mardi** [mardi] *m* Tuesday; *v.a.* **dimanche** ▸ ~ **gras** Shrove Tuesday; (*carnaval*) Mardi Gras

**mare** [mar] *f* ❶ (*eau stagnante*) pond ❷ (*après la pluie*) puddle ❸ (*flaque*) ~ **de sang/d'huile** pool of blood/oil

**marécage** [marekaʒ] *m* marsh

**maréchal-ferrant** [mareʃalferɑ̃] <maréchaux-ferrants> *m* blacksmith

**marée** [mare] *f* ❶ (*mouvements de la mer*) tide; **à** ~ **basse/haute** at low/high tide ▸ ~ **noire** oil slick

**margarine** [margarin] *f* margarine

**marge** [marʒ] *f* ❶ (*espace blanc, délai*) margin ❷ *fig* **vivre en** ~ **de la société** to live cut off from society

**marginal(e)** [marʒinal, -o] <-aux> **I.** *adj* ❶ (*accessoire*) marginal ❷ (*en marge de la société, peu orthodoxe*) **être** ~ to be on the fringes (of society) **II.** *m(f)* ❶ (*asocial*) dropout ❷ (*en marge de la société*) fringe member of society

**marguerite** [margərit] *f* daisy

**mari** [mari] *m* husband

**mariage** [marjaʒ] *m* ❶ (*institution, union*) marriage; **demander qn en** ~ to ask sb's hand in marriage ❷ (*cérémonie*) wedding ❸ (*vie conjugale*) married life; **fêter les 25/10 ans de** ~ to celebrate 25/10 years of marriage

**M**

❹ (*de plusieurs choses*) marriage ❺ (*combinaison*) combination

**marié(e)** [maʀje] **I.** *adj* **être ~** to be married **II.** *m(f)* ❶ (*le jour du mariage*) **les ~ s** the married couple ❷ (*marié depuis peu*) **jeune ~** newlywed

**marier** [maʀje] <1> **I.** *vt* ❶ (*procéder au mariage de, donner en mariage*) **~ qn avec qn** to marry sb to sb ❷ *Belgique, Nord, Québec* (*épouser*) to marry ❸ (*combiner*) to combine; (*couleurs, goûts, parfums*) to marry **II.** *vpr* ❶ (*contracter mariage*) **se ~ avec qn** to marry sb ❷ (*s'harmoniser*) **se ~ (ensemble)** to blend; **se ~ avec qc** to marry with sth

**marin** [maʀɛ̃] *m* sailor

**marin(e)** [maʀɛ̃, in] *adj* ❶ (*relatif à la mer*) sea ❷ (*relatif au marin: costume*) sailor

**marine** [maʀin] **I.** *f* navy **II.** *adj gén inv* navy (blue)

**mariner** [maʀine] <1> *vi* CULIN (*aliment*) to marinate

**marionnette** [maʀjɔnɛt] *f* puppet

**maritime** [maʀitim] *adj* ❶ (*du bord de mer*) seaside; (*région, ville*) coastal ❷ (*relatif au commerce par mer*) maritime; (*transport, compagnie*) shipping

**marketing** [maʀkɛtiŋ] *m* marketing

**marmelade** [maʀməlad] *f* (*de pommes, d'abricots*) jam, jelly; (*d'oranges*) marmalade

**marmotte** [maʀmɔt] *f* marmot

**Maroc** [maʀɔk] *m* **le ~** Morocco

**marocain(e)** [maʀɔkɛ̃, ɛn] *adj* Moroccan

**marquant(e)** [maʀkɑ̃, ɑ̃t] *adj* (*important: fait, événement*) outstanding; (*personnage, œuvre*) striking; (*souvenir*) vivid

**marque** [maʀk] *f* ❶ (*trace, repère*) a. LING mark; (*de coups de fouet*) wound ❷ (*tache*) stain ❸ SPORT marker; **à vos ~ s!** on your marks! ❹ (*témoignage*) **~ de confiance** sign of trust; **~ de respect** mark of respect ❺ (*signe distinctif*) sign; (*au fer rouge*) signal ❻ COM brand; **~ déposée** registered trademark; **produit de ~** branded product ❼ (*insigne*) badge ❽ (*score*) score ► **invité de ~** distinguished visitor

**marqué(e)** [maʀke] *adj* ❶ (*net: curiosité, traits du visage*) marked; (*préférence, différence*) distinct; (*trait*) pronounced ❷ (*traumatisé*) **être ~** to be marked

**marquer** [maʀke] <1> **I.** *vt* ❶ (*indiquer, distinguer, laisser une trace sur, représenter*) to mark; (*heure, degré*) to show; **~ qc d'un trait/d'une croix** to mark a line/cross on sth; **il a marqué son époque** (*personne, événement*) he/it left his/its mark ❷ (*souligner: rythme*) to beat; (*paroles*) to stress ❸ (*respecter: feu rouge*) to respect; **~ un temps d'arrêt** (*dans un discours, dans un mouvement*) to pause ❹ (*inscrire, noter*) to write ❺ SPORT to mark; (*but*) to score **II.** *vi* (*jouer un rôle important*) **~ dans qc** to have an impact on sth

**marqueur** [maʀkœʀ] *m* ❶ (*crayon*) a. INFORM marker ❷ (*marqueur fluorescent*) highlighter

**marraine** [maʀɛn] *f* godmother

**marrant(e)** [maʀɑ̃, ɑ̃t] *adj inf* funny

**marre** [maʀ] *adv inf* **en avoir ~ de qn/ qc** to be fed up with sb/sth

**marrer** [maʀe] <1> **I.** *vpr* **se ~** *inf* to laugh **II.** *vi* **faire ~ qn** to make sb laugh

**marron** [maʀɔ̃] **I.** *m* (*fruit*) chestnut **II.** *adj inv* brown

**mars** [maʀs] *m* (*mois*) March; *v.a.* **août**

**marseillais(e)** [maʀsɛjɛ, jɛz] *adj* from/ of Marseille; (*accent, banlieue*) Marseille; (*restaurants*) in Marseille

**Marseillaise** [maʀsɛjɛz] *f* **la ~** the Marseillaise (*the French national anthem*)

**marteau** [maʀto] <x> **I.** *m* hammer; **~ piqueur** pneumatic drill **II.** *adj inf* loopy

**marteler** [maʀtəle] <4> *vt* ❶ (*frapper*) to hammer ❷ (*scander*) to hammer out

**Martinique** [maʀtinik] *f* **la ~** Martinique

**martyr(e)** [maʀtiʀ] **I.** *adj* (*enfant*) battered; (*mère*) stricken; (*pays, peuple*) martyred **II.** *m(f)* (*personne sacrifiée*) martyr

**martyre** [maʀtiʀ] *m* **①** REL martyr **②** (*grande douleur*) agony

**martyriser** [maʀtiʀize] <1> *vt* (*faire souffrir*) to bully

**mascara** [maskaʀa] *m* mascara

**mascotte** [maskɔt] *f* mascot

**masculin** [maskylɛ̃] *m* LING masculine

**masculin(e)** [maskylɛ̃, in] *adj* male

**masochiste** [mazɔʃist] **I.** *adj* masochistic **II.** *mf* masochist

**masque** [mask] *m* **①** (*objet*) mask **②** (*air, face*) front

**masqué(e)** [maske] *adj* (*recouvert d'un masque*) masked

**masquer** [maske] <1> **I.** *vt* (*dissimuler, recouvrir d'un masque*) to conceal; MIL to camouflage; (*odeur, visage*) to mask; (*lumière*) to obscure; (*vérité*) to hide **II.** *vpr* (*mettre un masque*) **se ~** to put on a mask; **se ~ le visage** to hide one's face

**massacre** [masakʀ] *m* **①** (*tuerie*) massacre **②** (*travail mal fait*) mess

**massacrer** [masakʀe] <1> **I.** *vt* **①** (*tuer sauvagement: peuple*) to massacre; (*animaux*) to slaughter **②** *inf* (*démonter, mettre à mal*) **~ qn** to make mincemeat out of sb **③** *inf* (*détériorer*) **~ qc** to make a mess of sth **II.** *vpr* **se faire ~** to be massacred

**massage** [masaʒ] *m* massage

**masse** [mas] *f* **①** (*volume*) mass; **les ~s populaires** the working classes; **ce genre de films, ça me plaît pas des ~s** *inf* I don't really go for this type of film **②** ECON **~ salariale** payroll

**masser¹** [mase] <1> **I.** *vt* (*grouper*) to gather together; (*troupes*) to mass **II.** *vpr* (*se grouper*) **se ~** to assemble

**masser²** [mase] <1> *vt* (*faire un massage à*) to massage

**masseur, -euse** [masœʀ, -øz] *m, f* masseur, masseuse *m, f*

**massif** [masif] *m* **①** BOT clump **②** GEO massif

**massif, -ive** [masif, -iv] *adj* **①** (*lourd: carrure, meuble*) heavy; (*esprit*) strong;

(*bâtiment, visage*) huge **②** (*pur: argent, bois*) solid **③** (*important*) massive; (*doses*) huge

**master** [mastœʀ, mastɛʀ] *m* UNIV (*diplôme*) master's [degree]

**masturber** [mastyʀbe] <1> *vt, vpr* (**se**) **~** to masturbate

**mat** [mat] *adj inv* JEUX checkmated

**mât** [mɑ] *m* **①** NAUT mast **②** (*poteau*) pole

**mat(e)** [mat] *adj* **①** (*sans reflet, sourd: bruit, son*) dull; (*or, argent*) mat **②** (*opp: pâle: peau, teint*) dark

**match** [matʃ] <(e)s> *m* match; **~ nul** draw, tie

**matelas** [matla] *m* (*pièce de literie*) mattress

**matelot** [matlo] *m* sailor

**mater¹** [mate] <1> *vt* **①** (*faire s'assagir*) to subdue **②** (*réprimer, vaincre*) to bring under control; (*révolte, rébellion*) to quash

**mater²** [mate] <1> *vt inf* (*regarder*) to eye

**matérialiser** [mateʀjalize] <1> **I.** *vt* **①** (*concrétiser*) to realize **②** (*signaliser*) to mark **II.** *vpr* **se ~** to materialize

**matérialiste** [mateʀjalist] **I.** *adj a.* PHILOS materialistic **II.** *mf a.* PHILOS materialist

**matériau** [mateʀjo] <x> *m* **①** (*matière*) material **②** *pl, fig* equipment

**matériel** [mateʀjɛl] *m* **①** (*équipement, assortiment d'un magasin*) equipment **②** INFORM hardware

**matériel(le)** [mateʀjɛl] *adj* **①** (*concret, qui concerne des objets*) material **②** (*qui concerne l'argent: ennui, conditions*) financial; (*civilisation*) materialistic **③** PHILOS materialist

**maternel(le)** [matɛʀnɛl] *adj* **①** (*de/ pour la mère*) motherly; (*tendresse, instinct*) maternal **②** (*du côté de la mère: grand-père*) maternal; (*biens*) mother's **③** ECOLE **école ~le** nursery school

**maternelle** [matɛʀnɛl] *f* nursery school

**materner** [matɛʀne] <1> *vt péj* to baby

**maternité** [matɛʀnite] **I.** *f* **①** (*bâti-*

**M**

*ment*) maternity hospital ❷ (*faculté d'engendrer*) pregnancy ❸ (*condition de mère*) motherhood **II.** *app* maternity

**mathématicien(ne)** [matematisjɛ̃, jɛn] *m(f)* mathematician

**mathématique** [matematik] **I.** *adj* mathematical **II.** *fpl* mathematics

**matière** [matjɛʀ] *f* ❶ (*substance*) material; **~ première** raw material ❷ PHILOS, PHYS, ART matter ❸ (*sujet, thème*) a. ECOLE subject; (*d'une discussion*) theme; **en ~ de sport/d'impôts** in the matter of sports/tax

**matin** [matɛ̃] **I.** *m* (*début du jour, matinée*) morning; **le ~** in the morning; **un ~ de juillet** a July morning; **du ~ au soir** from morning until night; **ce ~** this morning; **chaque ~, tous les ~s** every morning; **au petit ~** early in the morning; **6/11 heures du ~** 6/11 o'clock in the morning; **l'équipe du ~** the morning shift ▸**être du ~** (*être en forme le matin*) to be a morning person; (*être de l'équipe du matin*) to be on the morning shift **II.** *adv* **mardi ~** Tuesday morning; **~ et soir** morning and evening; (*tout le temps*) from morning till night

**matinal(e)** [matinal, -o] <-aux> *adj* ❶ (*du matin*) morning ❷ (*qui se lève tôt*) **être ~** to be an early bird; (*ponctuellement*) to be up early

**matinée** [matine] *f* ❶ (*matin*) morning ❷ CINE, THEAT, MUS matinee ▸**faire la grasse ~** to sleep in

**mature** [matyʀ] *adj* mature

**maturité** [matyʀite] *f* ❶ a. BOT, BIO maturity; **venir à ~** to come to maturity ❷ Suisse (*examen correspondant au baccalauréat*) baccalaureate (secondary school examinations)

**maudit(e)** [modi, it] **I.** *adj* ❶ antéposé (*fichu*) blasted ❷ postposé (*réprouvé: poète, écrivain*) accursed ❸ postposé (*funeste*) disastrous; (*lieu*) cursed **II.** *m(f)* (*rejeté*) damned soul

**maussade** [mosad] *adj* sullen; (*ciel*) dark; (*humeur*) morose; (*temps, paysage*) gloomy

**mauvais** [movɛ] **I.** *adv* bad; **il fait ~** the

weather is bad **II.** *m* (*ce qui est mauvais*) bad part

**mauvais(e)** [movɛ, ɛz] *adj* ❶ antéposé bad; (*action*) wrong; **la balle est ~e** the ball is out; **être ~ en qc** to be bad at sth; **c'est ~ pour la santé** it is bad for your health ❷ (*méchant: intention, regard*) spiteful; (*sujet*) bad; (*sourire*) nasty ❸ (*agité*) **la mer est ~e** the sea is rough

**mauve** [mov] *adj, m* (*couleur*) mauve

**maximal(e)** [maksimal, -o] <-aux> *adj* maximum

**maximum** [maksimɔm, maksima] <s *o* maxima> **I.** *adj* maximum **II.** *m* maximum; JUR maximum sentence; **il fait le ~** he's doing everything he can; **s'amuser/travailler un ~** *inf* to have great fun/work incredibly hard

**mayonnaise** [majɔnɛz] *f* mayonnaise

**mazout** [mazut] *m* heating oil

**mdr** [ɛmdeɛʀ] *interj v.* **mort de rire** INFORM lol

**me** [mə] <*devant voyelle ou h muet* m'> *pron pers* ❶ me; **il m'explique le chemin** he's explaining the way to me ❷ *avec être, devenir, sembler, soutenu* to me; **cela ~ semble bon** that seems fine to me; **son amitié m'est chère** his/her/its friendship is dear to me; **ça m'est bon de rentrer au pays** it does me good to return to my home country; **le café m'est indispensable** I can't do without coffee ❸ *avec les verbes pronominaux* **je ~ nettoie** I'm cleaning myself up; **je ~ nettoie les ongles** I'm cleaning my nails; **je ~ fais couper les cheveux** I'm having my hair cut ❹ (*avec un sens possessif*) **le cœur ~ battait fort** my heart was beating hard ❺ *avec un présentatif* **~ voici** [*o* **voilà**]! here I am!

**mec** [mɛk] *m inf* guy

**mécanicien(ne)** [mekanisjɛ̃, jɛn] *m(f)* mechanic

**mécanique** [mekanik] **I.** *adj* ❶ (*automatique*) mechanical ❷ *inf* (*technique: difficulté*) technical **II.** *f* mechanics

**mécanisme** [mekanism] *m* mechanism

**méchanceté** [meʃɑ̃ste] f ❶ sans pl (cruauté) cruelty ❷ (acte, parole) spiteful

**méchant(e)** [meʃɑ̃, ɑ̃t] I. adj ❶ (opp: gentil) nasty; (enfant) naughty; (animal) vicious; **être ~ avec qn** to be nasty to sb; (enfant) to be disobedient to sb; **attention, chien ~!** beware of the dog! ❷ antéposé (sévère) harsh; (soleil, mer) nasty ❸ antéposé, inf (extraordinaire) serious II. m(f) bad person

**mèche** [mɛʃ] f ❶ (cordon: d'une bougie) wick ❷ (touffe) **~ de cheveux** lock of hair

**méconnaissable** [mekɔnɛsabl] adj unrecognizable

**méconnu(e)** [mekɔny] adj unrecognized

**mécontent(e)** [mekɔ̃tɑ̃, ɑ̃t] I. adj **~ de qn/qc** dissatisfied with sb/sth II. m(f) malcontent

**médaille** [medaj] f badge; (décoration) medal

**médecin** [medsɛ̃] m ❶ doctor; **~ légiste** medical examiner ❷ Suisse (chirurgien) **~ dentiste** oral surgeon

**médecine** [medsin] f medicine

**média** [medja] m medium; **les ~s** the media

**médiateur, -trice** [medjatœʀ, -tʀis] I. adj ❶ (de conciliation) mediatory ❷ MATH mediating II. m, f mediator

**médiathèque** [medjatɛk] f multimedia library

**médiation** [medjasjɔ̃] f (d'un conflit) mediation

**médiatique** [medjatik] adj (image, sport, personne, campagne) media

**médiatisation** [medjatizasjɔ̃] f mediatization

**médiatiser** [medjatize] <1> vt to mediatize; (excessivement) to hype

**médical(e)** [medikal, -o] <-aux> adj medical

**médicament** [medikamɑ̃] m medicine

**médiocre** [medjɔkʀ] I. adj ❶ (petit: salaire) meager ❷ (minable) mediocre; (sol) poor; (vie) sad ❸ (faible: élève) poor ❹ péj (peu intelligent) thick;

(mesquin) mean II. mf second-rater III. m nonentity

**médiologie** [medjɔlɔʒi] f media studies

**méditation** [meditasjɔ̃] f ❶ (réflexion) thought ❷ REL meditation

**méditer** [medite] <1> I. vi ❶ (réfléchir) **~ sur qc** to think about sth ❷ REL to meditate II. vt ❶ (réfléchir sur) **~ qc** to meditate on sth ❷ (projeter) to contemplate

**Méditerranée** [mediteʀane] f **la (mer) ~** the Mediterranean (Sea)

**méditerranéen(ne)** [mediteʀaneɛ̃, ɛn] I. adj Mediterranean II. m(f) sb from the Mediterranean region

**médium** [medjɔm] m medium

**méduse** [medyz] f jellyfish

**meeting** [mitiŋ] m meeting

**méfait** [mefɛ] m ❶ (faute) wrongdoing ❷ gén pl (conséquence néfaste) **les ~s de l'alcool** the harm caused by alcohol

**méfiance** [mefjɑ̃s] f distrust

**méfier** [mefje] <1> vpr ❶ (être soupçonneux) **se ~ de qn/qc** to be wary of sb/sth ❷ (faire attention) **se ~** to watch out

**meilleur** [mɛjœʀ] I. adv better; **il fait ~** the weather is better II. m **le ~** the best

**meilleur(e)** [mɛjœʀ] I. adj ❶ comp de bon better; **acheter qc ~ marché** to buy sth cheaper ❷ superl **le/la ~(e) élève** the best student II. m(f) **le/la ~(e) de la classe** the top of the class

**mélancolie** [melɑ̃kɔli] f melancholy

**mélancolique** [melɑ̃kɔlik] adj melancholy

**mélange** [melɑ̃ʒ] m ❶ (action) mixing ❷ (résultat) blend

**mélanger** [melɑ̃ʒe] <2a> I. vt ❶ (mêler) **~ du café et du lait** to mix coffee and milk ❷ (mettre en désordre) to mix up ❸ (confondre) to muddle II. vpr **se ~** to mix

**mêlé(e)** [mele] adj ❶ (mélangé, composite) mixed ❷ (impliqué) **être ~ à une affaire** to be caught up in an affair

**mêlée** [mele] f ❶ (corps à corps) brawl; (dans un débat d'idées) fray ❷ (conflit) **entrer/se jeter dans la ~** to launch

**M**

oneself into the fray ❸ (*personnes mê-lées*) mixture; (*choses mêlées*) muddle ❹ SPORT scrum

**mêler** [mele] <1> I. *vt* ❶ (*mélanger, allier*) to mix; (*voix*) to mingle; (*ingrédients*) to blend ❷ (*ajouter*) ~ **des détails pittoresques à un récit** to add colorful details to a story ❸ (*mettre en désordre*) (*fils*) to mix up ❹ (*impliquer*) ~ **qn à qc** to involve sb in sth II. *vpr* ❶ (*se mélanger*) **se ~ à qc** to mix with sth ❷ (*joindre*) **se ~ à la foule** to mingle with the crowd ❸ (*participer*) **se ~ à la conversation** to join in the conversation ❹ *péj* (*s'occuper*) **se ~ de qc** to meddle with sth

**mélodie** [melɔdi] *f* melody

**mélodieux, -euse** [melɔdjø, -jøz] *adj* melodious

**melon** [m(ə)lɔ̃] *m* melon

**membre** [mɑ̃bʀ] I. *m* ❶ ANAT, ZOOL limb ❷ (*adhérent*) a. MATH member II. *app* **État ~/pays ~** member state/country

**même** [mɛm] I. *adj* ❶ (*identique, simultané*) same ❷ (*semblable*) same; **c'est la ~ chose** it's the same thing ❸ (*en personne*) **être la gaieté/la bonne humeur ~** to be happiness/good humor personified ❹ (*pour renforcer*) **c'est cela ~ qui ...** it is that very thing which ... II. *pron indéf* **le/la ~** the same ❶ (*de plus, jusqu'à*) even; ~ **pas** not even ❷ (*précisément*) **ici ~** at this very place; **je le ferai aujourd'hui ~** I will do it this very day ❸ *inf* (*en plus*) ~ **que c'est vrai** and what's more, it's true ▸ **être à ~ de** +*infin* to be able to +*infin*; **il en est de ~ pour qn/qc** it is the same for sb/sth; **tout de ~** all the same

**mémé** [meme] *f inf* granny

**mémoire**[1] [memwaʀ] *f* ❶ (*capacité*) memory; **avoir la ~ des chiffres/dates** to have a good memory for figures/dates; **si j'ai bonne ~** if my memory serves me; **il se remet qc en ~** he reminds himself of sth; **pour ~** for the record ❷ INFORM memory; ~ **cache/centrale** cache/core memory; ~ **morte**

read-only memory; ~ **RAM** random-access memory; ~ **ROM** read-only memory; ~ **tampon** buffer; ~ **virtuelle** virtual storage; ~ **vive** random-access memory

**mémoire**[2] [memwaʀ] *m* ❶ *pl* (*journal*) memoir ❷ (*dissertation*) dissertation ❸ (*exposé*) paper

**mémorable** [memɔʀabl] *adj* ❶ (*qui fait date*) memorable ❷ (*inoubliable*) unforgettable

**mémoriser** [memɔʀize] <1> *vt* ❶ (*apprendre*) to memorize ❷ INFORM to store

**menaçant(e)** [mənasɑ̃, ɑ̃t] *adj* menacing; (*décision, ciel, geste*) threatening

**menace** [mənas] *f* (*parole, geste, danger*) threat

**menacer** [mənase] <2> I. *vt* ❶ (*faire peur avec, faire des menaces de*) ~ **qn d'une arme** to threaten sb with a weapon; ~ **qn de mort/de faire qc** to threaten sb with death/doing sth ❷ (*constituer une menace pour*) to menace; (*santé*) to threaten II. *vi* to threaten

**ménage** [menaʒ] *m* ❶ (*entretien de la maison*) housework; **faire le ~** (*nettoyer*) to do the housework; (*réorganiser*) to sort things out ❷ (*vie commune*) **être/se mettre en ~ avec qn** to live with/move in with sb ❸ (*couple*) married couple ❹ (*famille*) family

**ménager** [menaʒe] <2a> I. *vt* ❶ (*employer avec mesure: revenus*) to economize; (*forces*) to conserve; ~ **ses paroles** to use words sparingly ❷ (*traiter avec égards pour raisons de santé*) ~ **qn** to be gentle with sb ❸ (*traiter avec égards par respect ou intérêt*) ~ **qn** to handle sb with care II. *vpr* ❶ (*prendre soin de soi*) **se ~** to take care of oneself ❷ (*se réserver*) **se ~ du temps** to keep some time for oneself

**ménager, -ère** [menaʒe, -ɛʀ] *adj* household

**ménagère** [menaʒɛʀ] *f* (*service de couverts*) cutlery set

**mendiant(e)** [mɑ̃djɑ̃, jɑ̃t] *m(f)* beggar

**mendier** [mɑ̃dje] <1> I. *vi* to beg II. *vt*

**~ de l'argent/du pain** to beg for money/bread

**mener** [məne] <4> I. vt ❶ (amener) to take; **~ un enfant à l'école/chez le médecin** to take a child to school/the doctor ❷ (conduire, faire agir) to lead; **~ une entreprise à la ruine** to lead a company into ruin ❸ (diriger) to direct; (négociations) to lead ❹ (administrer) to manage II. vi to lead; **~ (par) deux à zéro** to lead two to nothing

**méninge** [menɛ̃ʒ] f ANAT brain

**mensonge** [mɑ̃sɔ̃ʒ] m ❶ (opp: vérité) lie; **raconter un ~ à qn** to (tell a) lie to sb ❷ sans pl (action, habitude) lying

**mensuel** [mɑ̃sɥɛl] m monthly publication

**mensuel(le)** [mɑ̃sɥɛl] adj monthly

**mental** [mɑ̃tal] m sans pl spirit

**mental(e)** [mɑ̃tal, -o] <-aux> adj (psychique, intellectuel, de tête) mental; (prière) silent

**mentalité** [mɑ̃talite] f mentality

**menteur, -euse** [mɑ̃tœʀ, -øz] I. adj (personne) lying II. m, f liar

**menthe** [mɑ̃t] f mint

**mention** [mɑ̃sjɔ̃] f ❶ (fait de signaler) mention ❷ (indication) comment; **rayer les ~s inutiles** delete as appropriate ❸ ECOLE, UNIV grade; **avec (la) ~ bien** ≈ with a B average

**mentionner** [mɑ̃sjɔne] <1> vt to mention

**mentir** [mɑ̃tiʀ] <10> vi to lie; **~ à qn** to lie to sb

**menton** [mɑ̃tɔ̃] m chin

**menu** [məny] m ❶ a. INFORM menu; **barre de ~** menu-bar ❷ (repas) meal

**menu(e)** [məny] adj postposé ❶ (frêle: personne) slender; (jambes, bras) slim; (taille) thin ❷ antéposé (qui a peu d'importance: détails, occupations) minor; (soucis, dépenses) petty ❸ souvent antéposé (qui a peu de volume) fine; (souliers) thin; (bruits) slight

**menuiserie** [mənɥizʀi] f ❶ sans pl (métier) carpentry ❷ (atelier) carpenter's workshop

**menuisier** [mənɥizje] m carpenter

**mépris** [mepʀi] m ❶ (opp: estime) contempt ❷ (opp: prise en compte) disregard

**méprise** [mepʀiz] f mistake

**mépriser** [mepʀize] <1> vt ❶ (opp: estimer) to look down on ❷ (opp: prendre en compte: insultes) to ignore

**mer** [mɛʀ] f ❶ (étendue d'eau, littoral) sea; **en haute ~** on the high seas; **~ Noire/Rouge** Black/Red Sea; **~ des Caraïbes** Caribbean Sea; **prendre la ~** to put out to sea; **passer ses vacances à la ~** to spend one's vacation by the sea ❷ (eau de mer) seawater ❸ (marée) **quand la ~ est basse/haute** when the tide is low/high

**mercenaire** [mɛʀsənɛʀ] m, f mercenary

**mercerie** [mɛʀsəʀi] f ❶ (magasin) notions store ❷ (commerce, marchandises) notions

**merci** [mɛʀsi] I. interj ❶ (pour remercier) thank you; **~ bien** thank you very much; **~ à vous pour tout** thank you for everything ❷ (pour exprimer l'indignation, la déception) thanks II. m thank you; **un grand ~ à vous de nous avoir aidés** a big thanks to you for having helped us III. f **être à la ~ de qn/qc** to be at the mercy of sb/sth

**mercredi** [mɛʀkʀədi] m Wednesday; **~ des Cendres** Ash Wednesday; v.a. **dimanche**

**mercure** [mɛʀkyʀ] m mercury

**Mercure** [mɛʀkyʀ] f ASTR, HIST Mercury

**mercurochrome®** [mɛʀkyʀokʀom] m Mercurochrome®

**merde** [mɛʀd] I. f ❶ vulg shit ❷ inf (ennui) problem ❸ inf (saleté) crap ❹ inf (personne, chose sans valeur) shit; **ne pas se prendre pour une ~** inf he thinks the sun shines out of his ass vulg; **c'est de la ~, ce stylo** this pen's a piece of shit ▸ **foutre la ~** inf to wreak havoc; **temps/boulot de ~** inf crappy weather/job II. interj inf **~ alors!** shit!

**merder** [mɛʀde] <1> vi inf to screw up

**mère** [mɛʀ] I. f ❶ (femme) mother; **~ au foyer** housewife (and mother); **~ porteuse** surrogate mother ❷ REL

~ **supérieure** Mother Superior **II.** *app* **maison** ~ parent company; **fille** ~ single mother

**merguez** [mɛʀgɛz] *f: spicy sausage from North Africa*

**meringue** [məʀɛ̃g] *f* meringue

**mérite** [meʀit] *m* ❶(*qualité, vertu de qn*) merit; **elle a bien du** ~ all credit to her ❷*sans pl* (*valeur*) worth ❸(*avantage: d'un appareil, d'une organisation*) advantage

**mériter** [meʀite] <1> *vt* ❶(*avoir droit à qc*) to deserve; ~ **de réussir/d'être récompensé** to deserve to succeed/to be reimbursed ❷(*valoir*) to be worth; **cela mérite réflexion** that deserves some thought

**merveille** [mɛʀvɛj] *f* wonder; (*d'une création*) marvel; **à** ~ beautifully

**merveilleux, -euse** [mɛʀvɛjø, -jøz] **I.** *adj* ❶(*exceptionnel*) marvelous; (*très beau*) beautiful ❷*postposé* (*surnaturel, magique*) **monde** ~ magic world **II.** *m* **le** ~ the supernatural

**mes** [me] *dét poss v.* **ma, mon**

**mésaventure** [mezavɑ̃tyʀ] *f* misadventure

**mesdames** [medam] *fpl v.* **madame**

**mesdemoiselles** [medmwazɛl] *fpl v.* **mademoiselle**

**message** [mesaʒ] *m* ❶(*nouvelle*) news; ~ **publicitaire** advertisement ❷(*note écrite, communication solennelle*) *a.* INFORM, TEL message

**messager, -ère** [mesaʒe, -ɛʀ] *m, f* messenger

**messagerie** [mesaʒʀi] *f* message service; ~ **électronique** INFORM electronic mail; ~ **instantanée** INFORM instant messaging

**messe** [mɛs] *f* mass

**messie** [mesi] *m* messiah

**messieurs** [mesjø] *mpl v.* **monsieur**

**mesure** [m(ə)zyʀ] *f* ❶(*action: d'une surface*) measurement ❷(*dimension*) measurement; (*de la température*) measure; ~**s de qn** sb's measurements ❸(*unité, récipient, contenu, limite, disposition*) measure; **outre** ~ beyond

measure; **par** ~ **de sécurité** as a safety precaution; **prendre des** ~**s** to take steps ❹MUS tempo ▸ **à** ~ **as**; **dans la** ~ **du possible** as far as possible; **être en** ~ **de** +*infin* to be able to +*infin*

**mesuré(e)** [məzyʀe] *adj* (*ton*) steady; (*pas*) measured; (*personne*) moderate

**mesurer** [məzyʀe] <1> **I.** *vi* (*avoir pour mesure*) to measure; ~ **5 m de large/ de long** to be 5 meters wide/long; **combien mesures-tu?** how tall are you? **II.** *vt* ❶(*déterminer les dimensions*) to measure ❷(*évaluer*) to assess; (*conséquences, risque*) to measure ❸(*modérer: paroles, propos*) to weigh **III.** *vpr* ❶(*se comparer à*) **se** ~ **à qn** to compare oneself with sb ❷(*être mesurable*) **se** ~ **en mètres** to be measured in meters

**métal** [metal, -o] <-aux> *m* metal

**métallique** [metalik] *adj* metallic; **fil** ~ metal wire

**métallisé(e)** [metalize] *adj* metallic

**métamorphose** [metamɔʀfoz] *f* metamorphosis

**météo** [meteo] *inv abr de* **météorologie, météorologie**

**météorologie** [meteɔʀɔlɔʒi] *f* meteorology

**météorologique** [meteɔʀɔlɔʒik] *adj* meteorological

**méthode** [metɔd] *f* ❶(*technique*) method ❷(*manuel*) ~ **de piano** piano manual ❸*sans pl, inf*(*manière de faire, logique*) way

**méticuleux, -euse** [metikylø, -øz] *adj* meticulous

**métier** [metje] *m* ❶(*profession*) occupation; **apprendre/exercer un** ~ to learn/practice a profession; **être du** ~ to be in the trade; **qu'est-ce que vous faites comme** ~?, **quel** ~ **faites-vous?** what is your job? ❷*pl* (*ensemble de métiers*) **les** ~**s du bois/de la restauration** the wood/catering trades ❸*sans pl* (*secteur d'activité: d'une entreprise*) business ❹*sans pl* (*rôle*) **il fait son** ~ he is doing his job ❺*sans pl* (*technique*) technique; (*habileté*) skill;

**avoir du ~** to have practical experience; **connaître son ~** to know what one is doing ⑥TECH **~ à tisser** weaving loom

**métis(se)** [metis] **I.** *adj* (*personne*) half-caste **II.** *m(f)* (*personne*) half-caste

**mètre** [mɛtʀ] *m* ❶(*unité de mesure*) meter; **~ cube/carré** cubic/square meter; **par 500 ~s de fond** 500 meters down; **à cinquante ~s d'ici** fifty meters from here ❷(*instrument*) meter ruler ❸SPORT **piquer un cent ~s** *inf* to sprint

**métro** [metʀo] *m* subway; **~ souterrain/aérien** subway system/elevated railway; **en ~** by subway ❷(*station*) subway station

**metteur** [metœʀ] *m* TV, THEAT, CINE **~ en scène** director

**mettre** [mɛtʀ] *irr* **I.** *vt* ❶(*placer, poser*) to put; (*à plat, couché, horizontalement*) to lay; (*debout, verticalement*) to stand; (*assis*) to sit; (*suspendre*) to hang; **~ les mains en l'air** to put one's hands up ❷(*déposer, entreposer*) **~ à la fourrière** to impound; **~ qc à l'abri** to leave sth in the shade ❸(*jeter*) **~ qc à la poubelle/au panier** to throw sth in the trash/basket ❹(*ajouter, conditionner*) **~ trop de sel dans la soupe** to put too much salt in the soup; **~ du vin en bouteilles** to bottle wine ❺(*répandre*) **~ du beurre sur une tartine** to butter some bread; **~ de la crème sur ses mains** to put lotion on one's hands ❻(*ajuster, adapter*) **~ un nouveau moteur** to break in a new motor ❼(*coudre*) **~ un bouton à une veste** to sew [*o* put] a button on a jacket ❽(*introduire*) to insert; **~ une lettre dans une enveloppe** to put a letter into an envelope ❾(*écrire*) **~ un nom sur une liste** to put a name on a list ❿(*nommer, inscrire, classer*) **~ qn au service clients** to put sb in customer service; **~ ses enfants à l'école privée** to put one's children in private school; **~ au-dessus/en dessous de qn/qc** to put above/below sb/sth ⓫(*revêtir*)

**~ qc** (*vêtement, chaussures, chapeau, lunettes, bijou, bague, maquillage*) to put sth on; (*lentilles de contact*) to put sth in; (*broche*) to pin sth on ⓬(*consacrer*) **~ deux heures/une journée à faire un travail** to take two hours/a day to do a job ⓭(*investir*) **~ beaucoup d'argent dans un projet** to put a lot of money in a project ⓮(*transformer*) **~ qc au propre** to copy sth out neatly; **~ qc en forme** to get sth into shape ⓯(*faire fonctionner*) **~ qc** to turn sth on; **~ la radio/télé plus fort** to turn up the radio/television ⓰(*régler*) **~ une montre à l'heure** to set a watch to the right time ⓱(*installer: rideaux, papier peint*) to hang; (*moquette*) to lay; (*électricité*) to install ⓲(*faire*) **~ qc à cuire/à chauffer** to cook/heat sth ⓳(*envoyer*) **~ le ballon dans les buts** to put the ball in the goal; **je lui ai mis mon poing dans la figure** *inf* I punched him in the face ⓴INFORM **~ à jour** to update ㉑*fig* **~ un peu de fantaisie dans sa vie** to bring a bit of fantasy into one's life **II.** *vpr* ❶(*se placer*) **se ~ debout/assis** to get up/sit down; **se ~ à genoux** to kneel down; **se ~ à la disposition de qn/qc** to put oneself at sb's/sth's disposal ❷(*placer sur soi*) **il se met les doigts dans le nez** he put his fingers in his nose ❸(*se ranger*) **se ~ dans l'armoire/à droite** to go in the cupboard/on the right ❹(*porter*) **se ~ en pantalon/rouge** to put on a pair of pants/red clothes; **se ~ du parfum** to put on some perfume ❺(*commencer à*) **se ~ au travail** to get down to work; **bon, je m'y mets**, I'll get down to it ❻(*pour exprimer le changement d'état*) **se ~ en colère** to get angry; **se ~ en route** to set off; **se ~ en place** (*réforme, nouvelle politique*) to be put in place ❼(*se coincer*) **se ~ dans qc** to get caught in sth ❽*inf* **se ~ avec qn** (*coéquipiers*) to get together with sb ❾*fig* **mets-toi bien ça dans le crâne!** get that into your head!

**meuble** [mœbl] *m* (*mobilier*) piece of

M

furniture; **~s** furniture + *vb sing;* **~s de jardin** garden furniture

**meublé** [mœble] *m* ❶ (*chambre*) furnished room ❷ (*appartement*) furnished apartment

**meublé(e)** [mœble] *adj* furnished

**meubler** [mœble] <1> **I.** *vt* ❶ (*garnir de meubles*) to furnish ❷ (*remplir: silence, conversation*) to fill **II.** *vpr* **se ~** to buy furniture

**meurtre** [mœrtr] *m* murder

**meurtrier, -ière** [mœrtrije, -ijɛr] **I.** *adj* murderer (*accident, coup*) fatal; (*carrefour, route*) lethal **II.** *m, f* murderer

**Meuse** [mœz] *f* **la ~** the Meuse (river)

**mexicain(e)** [mɛksikɛ̃, ɛn] *adj* Mexican

**Mexique** [mɛksik] *m* **le ~** Mexico

**mi** [mi] *m inv* E; (*dans la gamme*) mi; *v.a.* do

**mi-août** [miut] *f sans pl* **à la ~** in mid-August

**miauler** [mjole] <1> *vi* to meow

**mi-chemin** [miʃmɛ̃] **à ~** midway

**micro** [mikro] *abr de* **microphone, micro-ordinateur, micro-informatique**

**microbe** [mikrɔb] *m* ❶ BIO germ ❷ *inf* (*avorton*) runt

**microclimat** [mikroklima] *m* microclimate

**micro-informatique** [mikroɛ̃fɔrmatik] *f sans pl* computer science

**micro-ondes** [mikroɔ̃d] *m inv* (*four*) microwave

**micro-ordinateur** [mikroɔrdinatœr] <micro-ordinateurs> *m* PC

**microphone** [mikrɔfɔn] *m* microphone, mike *inf*

**microscope** [mikrɔskɔp] *m* microscope

**midi** [midi] *m* ❶ *inv, sans art ni autre dét* (*heure*) twelve o'clock; (*mi-journée*) noon, midday; **à ~** at noon; **entre ~ et deux** between twelve and two o'clock; **mardi/demain ~** Tuesday/tomorrow at noon ❷ (*moment du déjeuner*) lunchtime; **ce ~** today at lunchtime; **le repas de ~** lunch ❸ (*sud*) south

**Midi** [midi] *m* **le ~** the South of France

**mie** [mi] *f sans pl* (*de pain*) soft part

**miel** [mjɛl] *m* honey

**mien(ne)** [mjɛ̃, mjɛn] *pron poss* ❶ **le/ la ~(ne)** mine; **les ~s** mine; **cette maison est la ~ne** this house is mine ❷ *pl* (*ceux de ma famille*) **les ~s** my family; (*mes partisans*) my circle ►**j'y mets du ~** I pull my weight

**miette** [mjɛt] *f* ❶ (*aliment: de pain, gâteau*) crumb ❷ (*petit fragment*) **être réduit en ~s** (*verre, porcelaine*) to be smashed to smithereens

**mieux** [mjø] **I.** *adv comp de* **bien** ❶ better; **qn va ~** sb is better; **pour ~ dire** in other words; **on ferait ~ de réfléchir avant de parler** one would do better to think before speaking; **aimer ~** +*infin* to prefer to +*infin;* **plus il s'entraîne, ~ il joue** the more he trains, the better he plays; **qn n'en fait que ~ qc** sb just does sth better ❷ *en loc conjonctive* **d'autant ~ que qn fait qc** all the better that sb does sth ❸ *en loc adverbiale* **de ~ en ~** better and better; **tant ~ pour qn!** so much the better for sb ►**il vaut ~ qu'elle fasse qc** (*subj*) it would be better if she did sth **II.** *adv superl de* **bien** ❶ +*vb* **c'est lui qui travaille le ~** he is the one who works the hardest; **c'est ce qu'on fait de ~** it is what we do best ❷ + *adj* **il est le ~ disposé à nous écouter** he is the most prepared to listen to us; **un exemple des ~ choisis** a perfectly chosen example ❸ *en loc verbale* **le ~ serait de ne rien dire** the best thing would be to say nothing; **elle fait du ~ qu'elle peut** she does her best ❹ *en loc adverbiale* **il travaille de son ~** he is working his hardest **III.** *adj comp de* **bien** ❶ (*en meilleure santé*) **il la trouve ~** he thinks she is better ❷ (*plus agréable d'apparence*) **elle est ~ les cheveux courts** she looks better with short hair ❸ (*plus à l'aise*) **vous serez ~ dans le fauteuil** you would be more comfortable in the armchair ❹ (*préférable*) **c'est ~ ainsi** it is better this way **IV.** *adj superl de* **bien** ❶ (*le plus réussi*) **c'est avec les cheveux courts qu'elle est**

le ~ she looks best with her hair short ❷ *en loc verbale* **il est au ~ avec qn** he's well in with sb **V.** *m* ❶ (*une chose meilleure*) **trouver ~** to find (something) better ❷ (*amélioration*) **un lé-ger** ~ a slight improvement

**mignon(ne)** [miɲɔ̃, ɔn] **I.** *adj* ❶ (*agréable à regarder*) cute ❷ *inf* (*gentil*) kind **II.** *m(f)* **mon/ma ~(ne)** sweetheart

**migraine** [migʀɛn] *f* MED migraine

**migrateur, -trice** [migʀatœʀ, -tʀis] *adj* migratory

**migration** [migʀasjɔ̃] *f* migration

**mi-hauteur** [mi'otœʀ] **à ~** halfway up

**milice** [milis] *f* ❶ (*police*) militia ❷ *Belgique* (*service militaire*) national [*o* military] service

**milieu** [miljø] <x> *m* ❶ *sans pl* (*dans l'espace, dans le temps*) a. SPORT middle; **le bouton du ~** the middle button; **~ de terrain** midfield ❷ *sans pl* (*moyen terme*) medium ❸ (*environnement*) *a.* BIO, SOCIOL environment; **les ~x populaires** the working class ❹ *sans pl* (*criminels*) **le ~** the underworld

**militaire** [militɛʀ] **I.** *adj* army; (*opération, discipline, service*) military **II.** *mf* (*personne*) serviceman

**militant(e)** [militɑ̃, ɑ̃t] **I.** *adj* militant **II.** *m(f)* militant

**militer** [milite] <1> *vi* ❶ (*être militant*) to be a militant ❷ (*lutter*) **~ pour/contre qc** to fight for/against ❸ (*plaider*) **~ en faveur de/contre qn/qc** (*argument, comportement*) to militate for/against sb/sth

**mille¹** [mil] **I.** *adj* (*chiffre*) thousand; **~ un** a thousand and one **II.** *m inv* ❶ (*cardinal*) one thousand ❷ (*cible*) bull's-eye ▸ **des ~ et des** <u>cents</u> *inf* tons of money; *v.a.* **cinq, cinquante**

**mille²** [mil] *m* NAUT **~ marin** nautical mile

**millénaire** [milenɛʀ] **I.** *adj* thousand-year old; (*très vieux*) ancient **II.** *m* millennium

**milliard** [miljaʀ] *m* billion

**milliardaire** [miljaʀdɛʀ] *mf* billionaire

**millième** [miljɛm] **I.** *adj antéposé* thousandth **II.** *mf* **le/la ~** the thousandth **III.** *m* (*fraction*) thousandth; *v.a.* **cin-quième**

**millier** [milje] *m* **un/deux ~(s) de personnes/choses** one/two thousand people/things; **des ~s de personnes/choses** thousands of people/things; **des ~s et des ~s** thousands and thou-sands; **par ~s** by thousands

**millimètre** [milimɛtʀ] *m* millimeter

**million** [miljɔ̃] *m* **un/deux ~(s) de per-sonnes/choses** one/two million peo-ple/things; **des ~s de personnes/choses** millions of people/things; **des ~s de bénéfices** millions in profits; **des ~s et des ~s** millions and mil-lions; *v.a.* **cinq, cinquante**

**millionnaire** [miljɔnɛʀ] *mf* millionaire

**mi-long, -longue** [milɔ̃, -lɔ̃g] <mi-longs> *adj* mid-length

**mime** [mim] *mf* ❶ (*acteur*) mime ❷ (*imitateur*) mimic

**mimer** [mime] <1> *vt* ❶ THEAT to mime ❷ (*imiter*) to mimic **M**

**mimosa** [mimoza] *m* mimosa

**minable** [minabl] **I.** *adj* ❶ (*misérable: lieu*) shabby; (*aspect*) run-down ❷ (*mé-diocre*) pathetic **II.** *mf* loser

**mince** [mɛ̃s] **I.** *adj* ❶ (*fin*) thin ❷ (*élan-cé*) slim ❸ (*modeste*) slender; (*preuve, résultat*) slim; **ce n'est pas une ~ af-faire** it's no easy task **II.** *adv* thinly **III.** *interj inf* (*pour exprimer le mécon-tentement*) **~ (alors)!** rats!

**minceur** [mɛ̃sœʀ] *f sans pl* ❶ (*finesse: d'une feuille, couverture*) thinness ❷ (*sveltesse: d'une personne, de la tail-le*) slimness

**mincir** [mɛ̃siʀ] <8> *vi* to get slimmer

**mine¹** [min] *f* ❶ *sans pl* (*aspect du visa-ge*) expression; **avoir bonne ~** to look well; *iron, inf* (*avoir l'air ridicule*) to look stupid; **avoir mauvaise/une peti-te ~** to look ill/off-color; **ne pas payer de ~** to be not much to look at ❷ *sans pl* (*allure*) appearance ▸ **~** <u>de rien</u> *inf* (*sans se gêner*) all casually; (*malgré les apparences*) you'd never think it, but

**mine²** [min] *f* ❶ (*gisement*) mine ❷ *a. fig* (*souterraine, lieu aménagé, source*) mine

**mine³** [min] *f* (*d'un crayon*) lead

**mine⁴** [min] *f* MIL mine

**minerai** [minʀɛ] *m* ore

**minéral** [mineʀal, -o] <-aux> *m* minéral

**minéral(e)** [mineʀal, -o] <-aux> *adj* mineral

**mineur** [minœʀ] *m* miner

**mineur(e)** [minœʀ] I. *adj* (*peu important*) *a.* JUR, MUS minor II. *m(f)* JUR minor; **interdit aux ~s** under 18 years old not permitted

**miniature** [minjatyʀ] *f* miniature

**minigolf** [minigɔlf] *m* miniature golf; (*terrain*) miniature golf course

**minijupe** [miniʒyp] *f* miniskirt

**minimal(e)** [minimal, -o] <-aux> *adj* minimal

**minime** [minim] *adj* minor; (*dégâts, dépenses*) minimal

**minimiser** [minimize] <1> *vt* to minimize

**minimum** [minimɔm, minima] <s *o* minima> I. *adj* minimum II. *m* ❶ *sans pl* (*plus petite quantité, somme la plus faible, niveau le plus bas, valeur la plus basse*) minimum; **un ~ de risques** the fewest possible risks ❷ *sans pl* JUR minimum sentence

**ministère** [ministɛʀ] *m* ❶ (*bâtiment, portefeuille*) department, ministry; **~ de la Défense** ≈ Department of Defense; (*en Europe*) Ministry of Defense; **~ des Affaires étrangères** ≈ State Department; (*en Europe*) Ministry of Foreign Affairs ❷ (*cabinet, gouvernement*) government

**ministre** [ministʀ] *mf* POL secretary; (*en Europe*) minister; **Premier ~** Prime Minister, Premier; **~ des Affaires étrangères** ≈ Secretary of State; (*en Europe*) Minister of Foreign Affairs; **~ d'Etat** Minister without Portfolio

**minitel®** [minitɛl] *m* minitel® (*viewdata service giving access to a partially free*

*electronic telephone directory as well as numerous pay services*)

**minoritaire** [minɔʀitɛʀ] *adj* minority

**minorité** [minɔʀite] *f* minority

**minuit** [minɥi] *m sans pl ni dét* midnight; **à ~ et demi** at half past midnight

**minuscule** [minyskyl] I. *adj* ❶ (*très petit*) minute ❷ (*en écriture*) small II. *f* (*lettre*) small letter

**minute** [minyt] *f* minute; **d'une ~ à l'autre** from one moment to another; **information de dernière ~** last-minute information

**minuter** [minyte] <1> *vt* (*organiser*) to time

**minutieux, -euse** [minysjø, -jøz] *adj* meticulous; (*personne, examen*) thorough; (*exposé, description*) detailed

**miracle** [miʀakl] I. *m* miracle; **par ~** miraculously II. *app inv* miracle

**miraculeux, -euse** [miʀakylø, -øz] *adj* miraculous

**mirage** [miʀaʒ] *m* (*vision*) mirage

**miroir** [miʀwaʀ] *m* mirror

**mise** [miz] *f* ❶ JEUX bet ❷ FIN outlay ❸ *sans pl* (*habillement*) clothing ❹ (*fait de mettre*) **~ à feu** (*d'une fusée*) launch; **~ à jour** updating; **~ à la retraite** retirement; **~ à prix** upset [*o* reserve] price; **~ en garde** warning; **~ en marche** switching on; **~ en œuvre** implementation; **~ en pratique** putting into practice; **~ en scène** CINE production; *a.* THEAT staging; (*dans la vie privée*) performance ❺ INFORM **~ à jour** update; **~ en page** page layout ❻ *Suisse* (*vente aux enchères*) auction

**miser** [mize] <1> I. *vi* ❶ (*parier sur*) **~ sur un animal/sur le rouge** to bet on an animal/the red; **~ 8 contre 1** to place a bet at odds of 8 to 1 ❷ *inf* (*compter sur*) **~ sur qn/qc pour +*infin*** to rely on sb/sth to +*infin* II. *vt* (*jouer*) **~ 100 dollars sur un cheval** to bet 100 dollars on a horse

**misérable** [mizeʀabl] *adj* ❶ (*pauvre: personne, famille*) poverty-stricken; (*logement, aspect*) shabby ❷ (*pitoyable*) pitiful ❸ *antéposé* (*malheureux*) miserable

**misère** [mizɛʀ] *f* ❶ (*détresse*) misery ❷ *gén pl* (*souffrances*) woes ▸ **salaire de** ~ starvation wage

**missile** [misil] *m* missile

**mission** [misjɔ̃] *f* ❶ (*tâche culturelle, dangereuse, officielle*) a. MIL mission ❷ (*délégation*) delegation ❸ (*vocation*) mission

**mite** [mit] *f* moth

**mi-temps** [mitɑ̃] I. *f inv* SPORT halftime II. *m inv* (*travail*) part-time; **travailler à** ~ to work part-time

**mitigé(e)** [mitiʒe] *adj* (*réaction, sentiments*) mixed; (*accueil, zèle, impression*) lukewarm

**mi-voix** [mivwa] **à** ~ in an undertone

**mixage** [miksaʒ] *m* mixing

**mixer** [mikse] <1> *vt* to mix

**mixeur** [miksœʀ] *m* mixer

**mixte** [mikst] *adj* ❶ (*pour les deux sexes: chorale, classe*) mixed ❷ (*formé d'éléments différents: mariage, végétation, salade*) mixed; (*commission*) joint; (*cuisinière*) combination

**mixture** [mikstyʀ] *f* ❶ CHIM, MED mixture ❷ *péj* (*boisson*) concoction

**MJC** [ɛmʒise] *f abr de* **maison des jeunes et de la culture** community youth and arts center

**Mlle** [madmwazɛl] <s> *f abr de* **Mademoiselle** Miss

**MM.** [mesjø] *mpl abr de* **Messieurs** Messrs.

**Mme** [madam] <s> *f abr de* **Madame** Mrs.

**Mo** [ɛmo] *m abr de* **méga-octet** MB

**mobile** [mɔbil] I. *adj* ❶ (*opp: fixe*) moving ❷ (*non sédentaire: forces de police, population*) mobile ❸ (*changeant: regard*) changing; (*yeux*) darting II. *m* ❶ (*motif*) motive ❷ PHYS moving body ❸ ART mobile

**mobilier** [mɔbilje] *m* (*ameublement*) furniture

**mobilier, -ière** [mɔbilje, -jɛʀ] *adj* moveable; (*crédit, saisie*) transferable; (*vente*) personal property

**mobilisation** [mɔbilizasjɔ̃] *f* a. MIL mobilization

**mobiliser** [mɔbilize] <1> I. *vt* ❶ (*rassembler*) to assemble ❷ MIL to mobilize; (*réservistes*) to call up II. *vi* MIL to mobilize III. *vpr* **se** ~ to take action

**moche** [mɔʃ] *adj inf* (*laid*) ugly

**modalité** [mɔdalite] *f* ❶ *pl* (*procédure*) methods *pl* ❷ MUS modality ❸ JUR clause

**mode¹** [mɔd] I. *f* ❶ (*goût du jour*) style, fashion; **à la** ~ in style ❷ (*métier*) fashion industry ❸ CULIN **à la** ~ **de qc** in the style of sth II. *app* fashion

**mode²** [mɔd] *m* ❶ (*méthode*) ~ **d'emploi** directions for use; ~ ~ **de production** production method; ~ **de transport** mode of transportation; ~ **de paiement** method of payment ❷ LING mood ❸ MUS mode ❹ INFORM ~ **paysage** (*orientation d'une page*) landscape

**modèle** [mɔdɛl] I. *m* ❶ (*référence, maquette*) a. LING, TYP model; **prendre qn sur** ~ to model oneself after sb; ~ **réduit** scale model ❷ COUT, ART pattern II. *adj* (*exemplaire*) model

**modeler** [mɔd(ə)le] <4> *vt* ❶ (*pétrir: poterie*) to model; (*pâte*) to mold ❷ (*façonner: caractère, relief*) to shape

**modélisme** [mɔdelism] *m* modeling

**modération** [mɔdeʀasjɔ̃] *f* moderation

**modéré(e)** [mɔdeʀe] I. *adj* ❶ (*raisonnable: vent, froid, opinion*) moderate; (*prix*) reasonable ❷ (*médiocre: désir, résultat*) average; (*enthousiasme, succès*) moderate; (*optimisme*) restrained II. *m(f)* POL moderate

**modérer** [mɔdeʀe] <5> *vt* (*tempérer: personne*) to restrain; (*ambitions, colère, dépenses*) to control; (*passion*) to curb; (*vitesse*) to reduce; (*désirs*) to temper

**moderne** [mɔdɛʀn] I. *adj* up-to-date; (*pays*) progressive; (*idée, histoire*) modern II. *m* modern style

**moderniser** [mɔdɛʀnize] <1> I. *vt* to modernize II. *vpr* **se** ~ (*ville, pays*) to modernize; (*personne*) to bring oneself up to date

**M**

**modernité** [mɔdɛʀnite] *f* modernity; (*d'une pensée*) progressiveness

**modeste** [mɔdɛst] *adj* modest

**modestie** [mɔdɛsti] *f* modesty

**modification** [mɔdifikasjɔ̃] *f* modification

**modifier** [mɔdifje] <1> I. *vt a.* LING to modify II. *vpr* **se** ~ to be modified

**modique** [mɔdik] *adj* modest

**modulation** [mɔdylasjɔ̃] *f* modulation

**moelle** [mwal, mwɛl] *f* ANAT, BOT marrow; ~ **épinière** spinal chord

**moelleux** [mwɛlø] *m* ❶ (*d'un lit, d'un tapis*) softness ❷ (*d'un vin*) mellowness

**moelleux, -euse** [mwɛlø, -øz] *adj* ❶ (*au toucher*) soft ❷ (*au goût, agréable: vin, son, voix*) mellow

**mœurs** [mœʀ(s)] *fpl* ❶ (*coutumes: d'une personne, société*) customs; (*d'un animal*) habits; **entrer dans les** ~ to become common ❷ (*règles morales*) morals; **une personne de bonnes/mauvaises** ~ a person of high/low moral standards ❸ (*façon de vivre*) ways

**moi** [mwa] I. *pron pers* ❶ *inf* (*pour renforcer*) ~, **je n'ai pas ouvert la bouche** I never opened my mouth; **c'est ~ qui l'ai dit** I'm the one who said it; **il veut m'aider,** ~? he wants to help ME? ❷ *avec un verbe à l'impératif* **regarde~** look at me; **donne-~ ça!** give me that! ❸ *avec une préposition* **avec/ sans** ~ with/without me; **à** ~ **seul** by myself; **la maison est à** ~ the house is mine; **c'est à** ~ **de décider** it is for me to decide; **c'est à** ~! it's mine! ❹ *dans une comparaison* me; **tu es comme** ~ you're like me; **plus fort que** ~ stronger than me ❺ (*emphatique*) **c'est** ~! (*me voilà, je suis le responsable*) it's me; **et** ~(, **alors**)? *inf* and what about me? ▸ **à** ~! help! II. *m* PHILOS, PSYCH ego

**moignon** [mwaɲɔ̃] *m* stump

**moi-même** [mwamɛm] *pron pers* myself; **je suis venu de** ~ I came of my own accord

**moindre** [mwɛ̃dʀ] *adj antéposé* ❶ (*inférieur: inconvénient, degré, étendue*) lesser; (*prix, qualité*) lower ❷ (*le plus petit*) **le** ~ **bruit** the slightest noise; **le** ~ **mal** the lesser evil; **ce serait la** ~ **des choses/des politesses** it would be the least you could do/be common courtesy

**moine** [mwan] *m* monk

**moineau** [mwano] <x> *m* sparrow

**moins** [mwɛ̃] I. *adv* ❶ less; **rouler** ~ **vite** to drive slower; **les enfants de** ~ **de 13 ans** children under 13; ~ ... ~ ... the less ... the less ...; ~ ..., **plus** ... the less ..., the more ...; ❷ *superl* **le** ~ the least ▸ **à** ~ **de faire qc** unless you do sth; **à** ~ **que qn ne fasse qc** (*subj*) unless sb does sth; **au** ~ at least; (**tout**) **au** ~ at the very least; (**tout**) ~ the less so because; **de** ~, **en** ~ (*argent*) less; (*enfants*) fewer; **il a un an de** ~ **que moi** he is one year younger than me; **de** ~ **en** ~ less and less; **du** ~ at least; ~ **que rien** (*gagner, payer*) next to nothing II. *prep* ❶ (*soustraction*) less ❷ (*heure*) to; **il est midi** ~ **vingt** it's twenty to twelve ❸ (*température*) minus; **il fait** ~ **3** it is minus 3 degrees, it is 3 degrees below (zero) III. *m* ❶ (*minimum*) least ❷ (*signe*) minus

**mois** [mwa] *m* month; **le** ~ **de janvier/ mars** the month of January/March; **les** ~ **en r** the months with an r in them; **au** ~ monthly; **au** ~ **de janvier/d'août** in January/August; **elle est dans son deuxième** ~ she is in her second month (of pregnancy); **le premier/ cinq/dernier du/de ce** ~ the first/fifth/last day of/this month

**moisi** [mwazi] *m* mold

**moisi(e)** [mwazi] *adj* moldy

**moisir** [mwaziʀ] <8> *vi* ❶ (*se gâter*) to mold ❷ (*être inutilisé: voiture, meuble*) to rot; (*argent, capital*) to stagnate; (*talent*) to go to waste ❸ *inf* (*croupir: personne*) to stagnate

**moisissure** [mwazisyʀ] *f* mold

**moisson** [mwasɔ̃] *f* AGR harvest

**moite** [mwat] *adj* sticky

**moitié** [mwatje] *f* ❶ (*partie, milieu*) half; **la** ~ **du temps/de l'année** half the time/year; **~ moins/plus** half less/ more; **à ~ ivre** half drunk; **à ~ prix** half--price; **ne jamais rien faire à ~** to do nothing by halves; **de ~** by half; **pour ~** half to blame ❷ *iron (épouse)* other half

**molaire** [mɔlɛʀ] *f* ANAT molar

**molécule** [mɔlekyl] *f* molecule

**mollet** [mɔlɛ] *m* ANAT calf

**mollusque** [mɔlysk] *m* ZOOL mollusk

**moment** [mɔmɑ̃] *m* ❶ *(instant)* moment; **au dernier/même ~** at the last/ same moment; **à ce ~-là** at that moment; **à [o pour] un ~** for a moment; **à tout/aucun ~** at any/no time; **attendre qn/qc à tout ~** to be expecting sb/ sth at any moment; **au ~ de la chute du mur de Berlin** at the time of the fall of the Berlin Wall; **au ~ de partir, je me suis aperçu ...** as I was about to leave, I noticed ...; **à partir du ~ où qn a fait qc** from the moment sb did sth; **dans un ~** in a moment; **du ~ que qn fait qc** the moment sb does sth; **d'un ~ à l'autre** from one moment to another; **en ce ~** at the moment; **pour le ~** for the moment; **par ~s** from time to time; **sur le ~** at the time; **un ~!** one moment!; **au bon ~** at the right time; **le présent ~** the present time; **passer un bon ~** to have a good time ❷ *(occasion)* opportunity; **le bon/mauvais ~** the right/wrong time; **le ~ venu** when the time comes; **c'est le ~ ou jamais** it's now or never; **c'est le ~ de** +*infin* this is the moment to +*infin*; **ce n'est pas le ~** this is not the right time

**momentané(e)** [mɔmɑ̃tane] *adj (désir, ennui)* short-lived; *(effort)* brief; *(arrêt, espoir, gêne)* momentary

**momentanément** [mɔmɑ̃tanemɑ̃] *adv* for a moment

**momie** [mɔmi] *f* mummy

**mon** [mɔ̃, me] <mes> *dét poss* my; **~ Dieu!** my God!; **~ Père** Father; **~ colonel** Sir; **à ~ avis** in my opinion; **à ~ approche** as I approach(ed) ▶ **~ œil!** I bet!; **~ pauvre!** you poor thing!

**Monaco** [mɔnako] Monaco

**monarchie** [mɔnaʀʃi] *f* monarchy

**monarque** [mɔnaʀk] *m* monarch

**monastère** [mɔnastɛʀ] *m* monastery

**mondain(e)** [mɔ̃dɛ̃, ɛn] I. *adj* society II. *m(f)* socialite

**monde** [mɔ̃d] *m* ❶ *(univers)* world; **~ du rêve** realm of dreams; **le ~ des vivants** the land of the living; **plaisirs du ~** worldly pleasures ❷ *(groupe social)* **le ~ rural** the rural community; **~ du travail/des affaires** world of work/business ❸ *(foule)* crowd; **peu/ beaucoup de ~** not many/a lot of people; **un ~ fou** crowds of people; **pas grand ~** not many people ❹ *(société)* **tout le ~ en parle** everyone is talking about it; **c'est à tout le ~** it belongs to everyone ▶ **l'autre ~** the afterworld; **pas le moins du ~** not in the least; **mettre qn au ~** to give birth to sb; **pour rien au ~** for anything

**mondial** [mɔ̃djal] *m* SPORT world championship

**mondial(e)** [mɔ̃djal, -jo] <-aux> *adj* worldwide; *(économie, politique)* world

**mondialisation** [mɔ̃djalizasjɔ̃] *f* globalization

**monégasque** [mɔnegask] *adj* Monacan

**Monégasque** [mɔnegask] *mf* Monacan

**monétaire** [mɔnetɛʀ] *adj (marché, politique)* financial; *(union, unité)* monetary

**mongolien(ne)** [mɔ̃gɔljɛ̃, jɛn] I. *adj* MED Down Syndrome II. *m(f)* MED person with Down syndrome

**moniteur** [mɔnitœʀ] *m (écran)* monitor

**moniteur, -trice** [mɔnitœʀ, -tʀis] *m, f* **~ de colonies** camp counselor; **~ d'auto-école** driving instructor

**monnaie** [mɔnɛ] *f* ❶ ECON, FIN money; **fausse ~** counterfeit money; **~ électronique** e-cash ❷ *(devise)* currency; **~ nationale/unique** national/single currency ❸ *(petites pièces)* **la ~ de 100 dollars** change for 100 dollars; **faire la ~ sur qc à qn** to give sb change for sth ❹ *(argent rendu)* change ❺ *(pièce)* coin

**M**

**monologue** [mɔnɔlɔg] *m* monologue

**monoparental(e)** [monopaʀɑtal, -o] <-aux> *adj* (*famille, autorité*) single parent

**monopole** [mɔnɔpɔl] *m* ❶ ECON monopoly ❷ (*exclusivité*) **avoir le ~ de qc** to have a monopoly on sth

**monopoliser** [mɔnɔpɔlize] <1> *vt* to monopolize

**monotone** [mɔnɔtɔn] *adj* monotonous; (*style, vie*) dreary

**monsieur** [məsjø, mesjø] <messieurs> *m* ❶ *souvent non traduit* (*homme à qui on s'adresse*) Sir; **bonjour ~** good morning; **bonjour Monsieur Larroque** good morning, Mr. Larroque; **bonjour messieurs** good morning, gentlemen; **Mesdames, mesdemoiselles, messieurs!** Ladies and Gentlemen!; **messieurs et chers collègues ...** gentlemen and colleagues ...; **Monsieur le Professeur Dupont/le Président François** Professor Dupont/President François; **Monsieur Untel** Mister So-and-so ❷ (*sur une enveloppe*) **Monsieur Pujol** Mr. Pujol ❸ (*en-tête*) (**Cher**) **Monsieur,** Dear Sir,; **Madame, Monsieur,** Sir, Madam,; **Madame, Mademoiselle, Monsieur,** Mr., Mrs., Miss; **messieurs dames** Ladies and Gentlemen ❹ (*un homme*) **un ~** a gentleman

**monstre** [mɔ̃stʀ] **I.** *m* ❶ (*animal fantastique*) monster ❷ (*personne laide*) freak ❸ (*personne moralement abjecte*) brute ❹ BIO, ZOOL freak of nature **II.** *adj inf* gigantic

**monstrueux, -euse** [mɔ̃stʀyø, -øz] *adj* ❶ (*difforme*) freakish ❷ (*colossal*) massive ❸ (*ignoble*) monstrous

**monstruosité** [mɔ̃stʀyozite] *f* (*caractère ignoble*) monstrousness

**mont** [mɔ̃] *m* GEO mount; **le ~ Sinaï** Mount Sinai

**montage** [mɔ̃taʒ] *m* ❶ (*assemblage: d'un appareil, d'une pièce de vêtement*) assembly; (*d'un bijou*) mounting; (*d'une tente*) pitching ❷ CINE, TV, THEAT, TYP editing; (*d'une maquette*) as-

sembly; (*d'une opération*) organization; (*d'une page*) layout; (*d'une pièce de théâtre*) production; (*d'une exposition*) setting up

**montagnard(e)** [mɔ̃taɲaʀ, aʀd] **I.** *adj* mountain **II.** *m(f)* mountain dweller

**montagne** [mɔ̃taɲ] *f a. fig* mountain; **en haute ~** high up in the mountains; **habiter la ~** to live in the mountains ▶ **~s** <u>russes</u> roller coaster; (**se**) <u>faire</u> **une ~ de qc/rien** to make a mountain out of sth/a molehill

**montagneux, -euse** [mɔ̃taɲø, -øz] *adj* mountainous

**montant** [mɔ̃tɑ̃] *m* ❶ (*somme*) sum; (*total*) total ❷ (*pièce verticale: d'un lit*) post; (*d'une porte*) jamb

**montant(e)** [mɔ̃tɑ̃, ɑ̃t] *adj* (*chemin*) uphill; (*col*) high; (*mouvement*) upward; **marée ~e** rising tide

**montée** [mɔ̃te] *f* ❶ (*fait de croître: des eaux*) rising; (*de la colère, de l'islam, d'un parti*) rise; (*d'un danger, du mécontentement, de la violence*) increase; **la ~ des prix/de la température** the rise in prices/in temperature ❷ (*poussée: de la sève*) rise ❸ (*côte, pente*) hill ❹ (*action de monter*) climb; (*d'un avion, ballon*) ascent

**monter** [mɔ̃te] <1> **I.** *vi* ❶ *être* (*grimper*) to go up; (*vu d'en haut*) to come up; (*alpiniste*) to climb up; **~ sur une échelle** to climb a ladder; **~ dans sa chambre** to go (up) to one's room; **~ jusqu'à qc** (*eau, robe*) to reach sth; **~ à 200 km/h** to go up to 200 km/h ❷ (*chevaucher*) **~ à cheval/bicyclette/moto** to ride a horse/bike/motorcycle ❸ *être* (*prendre place dans*) **~ dans une voiture** to get into a car; **~ dans un train/avion/bus** to get on a train/plane/bus ❹ *être* (*aller vers le nord*) to go up ❺ *être* (*s'élever: avion, flammes, soleil*) to rise; (*route, chemin*) to go up ❻ *avoir o être* (*augmenter de niveau: baromètre, mer, sève*) to rise; (*lait*) to come; (*impatience, bruits*) to increase ❼ *avoir o être* (*augmenter: actions, croissance*) to increase; (*pression*) to grow ⑤ *être (passer à l'aigu: ton, voix)* to get higher ⑥ *avoir o être (faire une ascension sociale)* to move up in the world **II.** *vt avoir* ❶ *(gravir: personne)* to go up; *(vu d'en haut)* to come up; *(échelle)* to climb ❷ *(porter en haut, vu d'en bas)* ~ **qc** to take sth up; *(porter en haut, vu d'en haut)* to bring sth up ❸ CULIN ~ **qc** to whisk sth up ❹ *(chevaucher)* to mount ❺ *(couvrir)* to mount ❻ *(augmenter: prix)* to increase; ~ **le son** to turn up the volume ❼ *(organiser: affaire)* to organize; *(association, projet)* to set up; *(opération)* to mount; *(pièce de théâtre)* to stage; *(film)* to make; *(spectacle)* to put together ❽ *(fomenter: coup, complot)* to organize; *(histoire)* to make up ❾ TECH *(assembler, installer: échafaudage)* to erect; *(tente)* to pitch; *(maison)* to set up; *(mur)* to build; *(pneu)* to fit **III.** *vpr (atteindre)* **se ~ à 2000 dollars** to come to 2000 dollars

**monteur, -euse** [mɔ̃tœʀ, -øz] *m, f* ❶ TECH installer ❷ CINE editor

**montgolfière** [mɔ̃gɔlfjɛʀ] *f* hot air balloon

**montre** [mɔ̃tʀ] *f* watch ▸ **course contre** la ~ race against the clock

**montréalais(e)** [mɔ̃ʀealɛ, ɛz] *adj* from Montreal

**Montréalais(e)** [mɔ̃ʀealɛ, ɛz] *m(f)* person from Montreal

**montre-bracelet** [mɔ̃tʀəbʀaslɛ] <montres-bracelets> *f* wristwatch

**montrer** [mɔ̃tʀe] <1> **I.** *vt* ❶ *(prouver)* **il se ~ qc** he proves himself to be sth ❷ *(apparaître)* **se ~** to appear

**monture** [mɔ̃tyʀ] *f* ❶ *(animal)* mount ❷ *(en optique)* frame ❸ *(bijou)* setting

**monument** [mɔnymɑ̃] *m* ❶ *(mémorial)* memorial; ~ **funéraire** funeral monument ❷ *(édifice)* monument

**monumental(e)** [mɔnymɑ̃tal, -o] <-aux> *adj* ❶ *(imposant)* monumental ❷ *inf (énorme: erreur)* colossal; *(orgueil)* monumental

**moquer** [mɔke] <1> *vpr* ❶ *(ridiculiser)*

**se ~ de qn/qc** to make fun of sb/sth ❷ *(dédaigner)* **se ~ de faire qc** to not care about doing sth; **je m'en moque pas mal** I really couldn't care less ❸ *(tromper)* **se ~ du monde** to have (some) nerve

**moquerie** [mɔkʀi] *f* jeer; **les ~s** mockery

**moquette** [mɔkɛt] *f* (fitted) carpet

**moqueur, -euse** [mɔkœʀ, -øz] **I.** *adj (air)* mocking; **être très ~** to always make fun of people **II.** *m, f* mocker

**moral** [mɔʀal, -o] <-aux> *m (état psychologique)* morale ▸ **avoir le ~** to be in good spirits; **ne pas avoir le ~** to be in low spirits; **remonter le ~ à qn** to cheer sb up

**moral(e)** [mɔʀal, -o] <-aux> *adj* moral

**morale** [mɔʀal] *f* ❶ *(principes)* morality ❷ *(éthique)* ethic ▸ **faire la ~ à qn** to lecture sb

**moralité** [mɔʀalite] *f* ❶ *(valeur morale)* morality ❷ *(leçon)* moral

**morbide** [mɔʀbid] *adj (malsain: goût, littérature)* morbid; *(imagination)* gruesome

**morceau** [mɔʀso] <x> *m* ❶ *(fragment)* piece; **sucre en ~x** cube sugar; ~ **par ~** bit by bit ❷ *(viande)* cut ❸ ART piece ▸ **manger un ~** to have a bite (to eat)

**morceler** [mɔʀsəle] <3> **I.** *vt* ~ **qc** to divide sth up; *(terrain, héritage)* to parcel sth up **II.** *vpr* **se ~** *(propriété, terrain)* to be split up

**mordant(e)** [mɔʀdɑ̃, ɑ̃t] *adj* ❶ *(incisif)* incisive; *(personne, trait d'esprit)* sharp; *(ton, voix)* cutting; *(vent)* biting ❷ *(qui entame: corrosif)* destructive; *(lime)* sharp

**mordre** [mɔʀdʀ] <14> **I.** *vi* ❶ *(attaquer)* to bite ❷ *(se laisser prendre)* ~ **à l'appât** to bite; *fig* to take the bait ❸ *(prendre goût)* ~ **à qc** to take to sth ❹ *(enfoncer les dents)* ~ **dans qc** to bite into sth ❺ *(pénétrer)* ~ **dans qc** to eat into sth ❻ *(empiéter)* ~ **sur qc** to go past sth **II.** *vt* ❶ *(serrer avec les dents)* to bite; ~ **qn à l'oreille/la jambe** to bite sb's ear/leg ❷ *(empiéter sur: démarcation)*

**M**

to go past **III.** *vpr* **se ~ la langue** to bite one's tongue

**morfondre** [mɔʀfɔdʀ] <14> *vpr* **se ~** ①(*s'ennuyer*) to fret ②(*languir*) to mope

**morgue** [mɔʀg] *f* ①(*institut médico-légal*) morgue ②(*salle d'hôpital*) mortuary

**morne** [mɔʀn] *adj* bleak; (*vie, paysage*) dismal; (*regard*) sullen

**morose** [mɔʀoz] *adj* (*personne, situation*) morose; (*temps, air*) sullen

**morphologie** [mɔʀfɔlɔʒi] *f* morphology

**morse¹** [mɔʀs] *m* ZOOL walrus

**morse²** [mɔʀs] *m* Morse code

**morsure** [mɔʀsyʀ] *f* ①(*action de mordre, plaie*) bite ②(*d'un insecte*) sting

**mort** [mɔʀ] *f* (*décès, destruction*) death ▶**tu vas <u>attraper</u> la ~** *inf* you will catch your death; **se <u>donner</u> la ~** to take one's own life; **en vouloir <u>à</u> ~ à qn** to hate sb (with a vengeance)

**mort(e)** [mɔʀ, mɔʀt] **I.** *part passé de* **mourir II.** *adj* ①(*décédé, sans animation, hors d'usage*) dead ②(*inf* (*épuisé*) **être ~** to be stone tired ③(*avec un fort sentiment de*) **être ~ de honte/peur** to be mortified/scared stiff ④(*éteint: yeux, regard*) lifeless; (*feu*) out ⑤(*qui n'existe plus: langue*) dead ▶**<u>tomber</u> raide ~** to drop stone dead **III.** *m/f* ①(*défunt*) dead person ②(*dépouille*) dead body ▶**<u>faire</u> le ~** (*comme si on était mort*) to play dead; (*ne pas répondre*) to lie low

**mortalité** [mɔʀtalite] *f* mortality

**mortel(le)** [mɔʀtɛl] **I.** *adj* ①(*sujet à la mort*) mortal ②(*causant la mort*) fatal ③(*extrême, pénible: frayeur, haine*) mortal; (*froid, chaleur*) deathly; (*pâleur, ennemi, silence*) deadly ④*inf* (*ennuyeux*) deadly **II.** *m/f souvent pl* mortal

**morue** [mɔʀy] *f* ①ZOOL **~ séchée/fraîche** dried/fresh cod ②*vulg* (*prostituée*) whore

**mosaïque** [mɔzaik] *f* (*image*) mosaic

**Moselle** [mozɛl] *f* **la ~** the Moselle river

**mosquée** [mɔske] *f* mosque

**mot** [mo] *m* ①(*moyen d'expression*) word; **gros ~** swear word; **~ composé** compound; **chercher ses ~s** to look for the right words; **c'est le ~ juste** it is the right word; **à ces ~s** with these words; **~ pour ~** word for word ②(*message*) message; **~ d'excuse** excuse note; **~ d'ordre** slogan; **laisser un ~ à qn** to leave a message for sb ③(*parole mémorable*) saying ④*a.* INFORM **~ de passe** password ⑤JEUX **faire des ~s croisés** to do crosswords puzzles ▶**le fin ~ de l'<u>affaire</u>** the real story; **dire <u>deux</u> ~s à qn** to give sb a piece of one's mind; **expliquer/raconter qc en <u>deux</u> ~s** to explain/tell sth briefly; **avoir son ~ à dire** to have something to say

**motard(e)** [mɔtaʀ] *m(f) inf* ①(*motocycliste*) motorcyclist, biker ②(*policier*) motorcycle cop

**mot-clé** [mokle] <mots-clés> *m* keyword

**moteur** [mɔtœʀ] **I.** *m* ①TECH motor; **~ à explosion** internal combustion engine; **~ diesel** diesel engine ②(*cause*) **être le ~ de qc** (*concurrence*) to be the catalyst for sth; (*personne*) to be the driving force behind sth ③INFORM **~ de recherche** search engine **II.** *app* **bloc ~** engine block; **frein ~** engine braking

**moteur, -trice** [mɔtœʀ, -tʀis] *adj* (*muscle, nerf*) motor; (*force, roue*) driving

**motif** [mɔtif] *m* ①(*raison*) motive ②*pl* (*dans un jugement*) grounds ③(*ornement*) motif ④(*modèle*) pattern

**motivation** [mɔtivasjɔ] *f* ①(*justification*) **~ de qc** motivation for sth ②ECON **lettre de ~** application letter

**motivé(e)** [mɔtive] *adj* ①(*justifié*) justified ②(*stimulé: personne*) motivated

**motiver** [mɔtive] <1> *vt* ①(*justifier*) to justify ②(*causer*) to cause ③(*stimuler*) to motivate

**moto** [moto] *f abr de* **motocyclette** motorbike

**motocross, moto-cross** [motokʀɔs] *m inv* motocross

**motocycliste** [motosiklist] **I.** *adj* motorcycling **II.** *mf* motorcyclist

**motoriser** [motorize] <1> *vt* to motorize

**mou** [mu] *m* ❶ *inf* (*personne*) sluggish person ❷ (*qualité*) softness

**mou, molle** [mu, mɔl] *<devant un nom masculin commençant par une voyelle ou un h muet* mol*>* **I.** *adj* ❶ (*opp: dur*) soft ❷ (*flasque*) flabby ❸ (*amorphe, faible: personne, geste*) feeble; (*résistance, protestations*) weak **II.** *adv* (*jouer*) tiredly

**mouchard(e)** [muʃar, ard] *m(f)* ❶ (*rapporteur*) informer ❷ *péj* (*indicateur de police*) snitch

**mouche** [muʃ] *f* ❶ (*animal, a. pour la pêche*) fly ❷ (*centre: d'une cible*) bull's-eye

**moucher** [muʃe] <1> **I.** *vt* ~ (**le nez à**) **qn** to blow sb's nose **II.** *vpr* **se** ~ (**le nez**) to blow one's nose

**mouchoir** [muʃwar] *m* ~ **en papier** tissue, Kleenex®; ~ **en tissu** handkerchief

**moudre** [mudr] *vt irr* to grind

**mouette** [mwɛt] *f* seagull

**mouillé(e)** [muje] *adj* ❶ (*trempé*) wet ❷ (*plein d'émotion: voix*) emotional ❸ (*plein de larmes: regard, yeux*) tearful

**mouiller** [muje] <1> **I.** *vt* ❶ (*humecter*) to wet ❷ (*tremper*) to soak; **se faire** ~ to get soaked ❸ CULIN ~ **un rôti avec du bouillon** to baste a roast with stock ❹ NAUT (*ancre*) to cast; (*mines*) to lay ❺ *inf* (*compromettre*) ~ **qn dans qc** to implicate sb in sth **II.** *vi* (*jeter l'ancre*) to cast anchor **III.** *vpr* ❶ (*passer sous l'eau*) **se** ~ to get wet; **se** ~ **les mains** to get one's hands wet ❷ (*se tremper*) **se** ~ to get soaked ❸ (*s'humecter: yeux*) to brim with tears ❹ *inf* (*se compromettre*) **se** ~ **dans qc** to get involved in sth ❺ *inf* (*s'engager*) **se** ~ **pour qn/pour** +*infin* to put oneself on the line for sb/to +*infin*

**moulage** [mulaʒ] *m* ❶ (*action de mouler*) molding ❷ (*empreinte, objet*) cast

**moule¹** [mul] *m* ❶ (*forme*) a. CULIN mold ❷ (*empreinte*) cast

**moule²** [mul] *f* mussel

**mouler** [mule] <1> *vt* ❶ (*fabriquer*) to mold ❷ (*coller à*) **des vêtements qui moulent le corps** clothes that hug the body

**moulin** [mulɛ̃] *m* mill; ~ **à vent** windmill

**moulu(e)** [muly] **I.** *part passé de* **moudre II.** *adj* (*en poudre*) ground

**mourant(e)** [murɑ̃, ɑ̃t] **I.** *adj* (*musique, son*) faint; (*personne, feu, lumière*) dying **II.** *m(f)* dying person

**mourir** [murir] *vi irr* être ❶ (*cesser d'exister: personne, animal, plante*) to die; (*fleuve*) to dry up; ~ **de chagrin/soif** to die of grief/thirst; ~ **de faim** to starve to death; ~ **de froid** to freeze to death; **il est mort assassiné/empoisonné** he was murdered/poisoned ❷ (*venir de mourir*) **être mort** to have died ❸ (*tuer*) to kill ❹ (*disparaître peu à peu*) to die out; (*voix, bruit, feu*) to die down ▸ **c'est à** ~ **de** *rire* you'd die laughing; **s'ennuyer à** ~ to be bored to death

**mousse¹** [mus] **I.** *f* ❶ (*écume*) froth; ~ **à raser** shaving cream ❷ BOT moss ❸ CULIN mousse ❹ (*matière*) foam **II.** *app inv* **vert** ~ moss green

**mousse²** [mus] *m* cabin boy

**mousseline** [muslin] *f* muslin

**mousser** [muse] <1> *vi* ❶ (*produire de la mousse*) to foam; **faire** ~ to lather ❷ *inf* (*vanter*) **faire** ~ **qn/qc** to sing the praises of sb/sth

**mousseux** [musø] *m* sparkling wine

**moustache** [mustaʃ] *f* ❶ mustache ❷ (*du chat*) whiskers

**moustiquaire** [mustiker] *f* ❶ (*rideau*) mosquito net ❷ (*à la fenêtre, à la porte*) mosquito screen

**moustique** [mustik] *m* ❶ ZOOL mosquito ❷ *péj* (*enfant*) little squirt

**moutarde** [mutard] **I.** *f* mustard **II.** *app inv* mustard

**mouton** [mutɔ̃] *m* ❶ ZOOL sheep

M

②*(peau)* sheepskin ③*(viande)* mutton ④*(poussière)* bit of fluff

**mouvement** [muvmɑ̃] *m* ①*(action, partie de l'œuvre)* movement ②*(impulsion)* reaction; **~ de colère/d'humeur** burst of anger/bad temper; **~ d'impatience** impatient gesture; ③*(animation)* activity ④ECON *(de marchandises, capitaux, fonds)* movement ⑤ADMIN *(changement d'affectation)* move ⑥*(évolution)* trend; **~ d'opinion** movement of public opinion; **~ d'idées** intellectual movement ⑦MUS *(tempo)* movement ▸**il est libre de ses ~s** he is free to come and go as he pleases

**moyen** [mwajɛ̃] *m* ①*(procédé, solution)* means; **essayer par tous les ~s de +*infin*** to try everything to +*infin*; **par le ~ de** by means of; **au ~ de qc** using sth ②*(manière)* way ③*pl (capacités physiques)* strength ④*pl (capacités intellectuelles)* faculties; **par ses propres ~s** by himself ⑤*pl (ressources financières)* means; **il/elle a les ~s!** inf he/she can afford it! ⑥*souvent pl (instruments)* **~ de transport/contrôle** means of transport/control ▸**se débrouiller avec les ~s du bord** to make do; **pas ~!** no way!

**moyen(ne)** [mwajɛ̃, jɛn] *adj* ①*(intermédiaire, en proportion)* medium; *(classe)* middle; **à ~ terme** in the medium term; *v.a.* **moyenne** ②*(ni bon, ni mauvais)* average ③*(du type courant)* standard; **le Français ~** the average Frenchman

**Moyen Âge, Moyen-Âge** [mwajɛnɑʒ] *m* Middle Ages *pl*

**moyennant** [mwajɛnɑ̃] *prep* **~ une récompense/un petit service** in return for a reward/small favor; **~ 2000 dollars** for 2000 dollars

**moyenne** [mwajɛn] *f* ①MATH, ECOLE average; **la ~ d'âge** the average age; **en ~** on average; **avoir la ~ en qc** to get a passing grade in sth ②*(type le plus courant)* standard

**Moyen-Orient** [mwajɛnɔʀjɑ̃] *m* **le ~** the Middle East

**mue** [my] *f* ①ZOOL *(de l'oiseau)* molting; *(du serpent)* sloughing; *(d'un mammifère)* shedding ②ANAT changing

**muesli** [mysli] *m* muesli

**muet(te)** [mɥɛ, mɥɛt] **I.** *adj* silent **II.** *m(f)* mute

**muguet** [mygɛ] *m* lily of the valley

**mule**[1] [myl] *f* ZOOL (she) mule ▸**être têtu comme une ~** to be as stubborn as a mule

**mule**[2] [myl] *f (pantoufle)* mule

**mulet** [mylɛ] *m* ZOOL (he) mule

**mulot** [mylo] *m* field mouse

**multicolore** [myltikɔlɔʀ] *adj* multicolored

**multiculturel(le)** [myltikyltyʀɛl] *adj* multicultural

**multimédia** [myltimedja] **I.** *adj inv* CINE, TV, INFORM multimedia **II.** *m* **le ~** multimedia

**multinationale** [myltinasjɔnal] *f (entreprise)* multinational

**multiple** [myltipl] *adj* ①*(nombreux)* numerous ②*(maints, varié: occasions, raisons, cas)* many; **à de ~s reprises** on many occasions ③*(complexe)* a. MATH, TECH multiple

**multiplexe** [myltiplɛks] **I.** *adj* multiplex **II.** *m* multiplex

**multiplication** [myltiplikasjɔ̃] *f* BOT, MATH multiplication

**multiplicité** [myltiplisite] *f* multiplicity

**multiplier** [myltiplije] **I.** *vt* ①MATH, BOT to multiply; **~ sept par trois** to multiply seven by three ②*(augmenter le nombre de: efforts, attaques)* to increase **II.** *vpr* **se ~** to multiply

**multiracial(e)** [myltiʀasjal, -jo] <-aux> *adj* multiracial

**multitude** [myltityd] *f* ①*(grand nombre)* mass ②*(foule)* multitude

**municipal(e)** [mynisipal, -o] <-aux> *adj* ①*(communal)* municipal; *(élections)* local; **conseil ~** city council ②*(de la ville)* town

**municipalité** [mynisipalite] *f* ①*(administration)* city council ②*(commune)* municipality

**munir** [myniʀ] <8> **I.** *vt* **~ qn/qc de pi-**

**les** to provide sb/sth with batteries **II.** *vpr* **se ~ de qc** to provide oneself with sth; *fig* to arm oneself with sth

**munitions** [mynisjɔ̃] *fpl* ammunition

**muqueuse** [mykøz] *f* mucous membrane

**mur** [myʀ] *m* wall

**mûr(e)** [myʀ] *adj* (*fruit*) ripe; (*pays*) mature; (*pour qc*) ready

**mûre** [myʀ] *f* ❶ (*fruit de la ronce*) blackberry ❷ (*fruit du mûrier*) mulberry

**mûrement** [myʀmã] *adv* at length

**murer** [myʀe] <1> *vt* ❶ TECH to block up ❷ (*isoler: avalanche*) to block; **être muré dans le silence** to be immured in silence

**mûrir** [myʀiʀ] <8> **I.** *vi* to ripen; (*projet, idée*) to develop **II.** *vt* ❶ (*rendre mûr: fruit*) to ripen ❷ (*rendre sage*) to mature ❸ (*méditer*) to nurture

**murmure** [myʀmyʀ] *m* ❶ (*chuchotement*) murmur ❷ *pl* (*protestation*) murmurings

**murmurer** [myʀmyʀe] <1> **I.** *vi* (*chuchoter, protester*) to murmur **II.** *vt* **~ qc à qn** to murmur sth to sb

**muscle** [myskl] *m* muscle

**musclé(e)** [myskle] *adj* ❶ (*athlétique*) muscular ❷ *fig, inf* (*gouvernement, discours, politique*) tough ❸ (*vif: style*) vigorous

**muscler** [myskle] <1> *vt* **~ qn** to develop sb's muscles; **~ le dos/les jambes** to develop the back/leg muscles

**musculaire** [myskylɛʀ] *adj* muscular

**musculation** [myskylasjɔ̃] *f* body building

**musculature** [myskylatyʀ] *f* muscle structure

**museau** [myzo] <x> *m* (*du chien*) muzzle; (*du porc, poisson*) snout

**musée** [myze] *m* museum

**museler** [myzle] <3> *vt* ❶ (*mettre une muselière*) to muzzle ❷ (*bâillonner*) to silence

**muselière** [myzəljɛʀ] *f* muzzle

**musical(e)** [myzikal, -o] <-aux> *adj* musical; **comédie ~e** musical

**music-hall** [myzikol] <music-halls> *m* ❶ (*spectacle*) variety show ❷ (*établissement*) music hall

**musicien(ne)** [myzisjɛ̃, jɛn] **I.** *adj* musical **II.** *m(f)* musician

**musique** [myzik] *f* (*art, harmonie*) music; **mettre qc en ~** to set sth to music ▸ **connaître la ~** *inf* to know the story

**musulman(e)** [myzylmã, an] *adj* Muslim

**Musulman(e)** [myzylmã, an] *m(f)* Muslim

**mutilation** [mytilasjɔ̃] *f* mutilation

**mutilé(e)** [mytile] *m(f)* disabled person

**mutiler** [mytile] <1> **I.** *vt a. fig* to mutilate **II.** *vpr* **se ~** to mutilate oneself

**mutin(e)** [mytɛ̃, in] **I.** *adj* mischievous **II.** *m(f)* rebel

**mutisme** [mytism] *m* silence

**mutuel(le)** [mytɥɛl] *adj* (*réciproque*) mutual

**myope** [mjɔp] **I.** *adj* shortsighted **II.** *mf* shortsighted person

**myosotis** [mjɔzɔtis] *m* forget-me-not

**myrtille** [miʀtij] *f* blueberry

**mystère** [mistɛʀ] *m* ❶ (*secret*) secret ❷ (*énigme*) mystery; **être un ~ pour qn** to be a mystery to sb

**mystérieusement** [misterjøzmã] *adv* ❶ (*en secret*) secretively ❷ (*inexplicablement, d'une façon mystérieuse*) mysteriously

**mystérieux** [misterjø] *m* **le ~** mysterious

**mystérieux, -euse** [misterjø, -jøz] *adj* mysterious

**mystifier** [mistifje] <1> *vt* to fool

**mystique** [mistik] *adj* ❶ (*religieux*) mystical ❷ (*exalté, fervent*) mystic

**mythe** [mit] *m* myth

**mythique** [mitik] *adj* mythical; (*imaginaire*) imaginary; **récit ~** myth

**mythomane** [mitɔman] *adj, mf* mythomaniac

**M**

# Nn

**N, n** [ɛn] **I.** *m inv* N, n; **~ comme Nicolas** (*au téléphone*) n as in November **II.** *f*: road equivalent to a state highway **n'** *v.* **ne**

**NAC** [nak] *mpl v.* **nouveaux animaux de compagnie** [new types of] exotic pets

**nacre** [nakʀ] *f* mother of pearl

**nacré(e)** [nakʀe] *adj* pearly

**nage** [naʒ] *f* swimming; (*façon de nager*) stroke; **libre/sur le dos** freestyle/backstroke ▶ **à la ~** swimming; **être en ~** to be in a sweat

**nageoire** [naʒwaʀ] *f* fin

**nager** [naʒe] <2a> **I.** *vi* ❶ (*se mouvoir dans l'eau, baigner*) to swim ❷ *fig* **~ dans le bonheur** to be overjoyed ❸ (*flotter*) **~ sur qc** to float in sth ❹ *inf* (*ne pas comprendre*) to be lost **II.** *vt* to swim; (*crawl*) to do

**nageur, -euse** [naʒœʀ, -ʒøz] *m, f* swimmer

**naïf, naïve** [naif, naiv] *adj* ❶ *péj* (*crédule*) gullible ❷ (*naturel*) naïve

**nain(e)** [nɛ̃, nɛn] **I.** *adj* (*personne*) dwarf **II.** *m(f)* dwarf

**naissance** [nɛsɑ̃s] *f* ❶ (*venue au monde, apparition*) birth; **à la ~** at birth ❷ (*origine*) source ▶ **donner ~ à un enfant** to give birth to a child

**naître** [nɛtʀ] *vi vir être* ❶ (*venir au monde*) to be born; **être né musicien** to be a born musician ❷ (*apparaître: crainte, désir, soupçon, difficulté*) to arise; (*idée*) to be born ❸ (*être destiné à*) **être né pour qn/qc** to be made for sb/sth

**naïveté** [naivte] *f* innocence; **avoir la ~ de** +*infin* to be naïve enough to +*infin*

**nana** [nana] *f inf* chick

**nanti(e)** [nɑ̃ti] **I.** *adj* rich **II.** *m(f)* rich person

**nappe** [nap] *f* ❶ (*linge*) tablecloth ❷ (*vaste étendue: d'eau*) sheet; (*de brouillard*) blanket; **~ de pétrole** oil slick

**napper** [nape] <1> *vt* CULIN **~ qc de chocolat** to cover sth in chocolate

**narcisse** [naʀsis] *m* BOT narcissus

**narcissisme** [naʀsisism] *m* narcissism

**narcose** [naʀkoz] *f* narcosis

**narguer** [naʀge] <1> *vt* to flout; (*agacer*) to laugh at

**narine** [naʀin] *f* nostril

**narrateur, -trice** [naʀatœʀ, -tʀis] *m, f* narrator

**narration** [naʀasjɔ̃] *f* (*activité*) narration; (*histoire*) narrative

**nasal(e)** [nazal, -o] <-aux> *adj* LING nasal

**naseau** [nazo] <x> *m* nostril

**natal(e)** [natal] <s> *adj* (*langue, terre*) native

**natalité** [natalite] *f* birthrate

**natation** [natasjɔ̃] *f* swimming

**Natel®** [natɛl] *m Suisse* (*téléphone portable*) cell phone

**natif, -ive** [natif, -iv] **I.** *adj* **être ~ de Toulouse** to be a native of Toulouse **II.** *m, f* native

**nation** [nasjɔ̃] *f* ❶ (*peuple*) nation ❷ (*pays*) country; **les Nations unies** the United Nations

**national(e)** [nasjɔnal, -o] <-aux> *adj* ❶ (*de l'État*) national; **fête ~e** national holiday ❷ (*opp: local, régional: entreprise*) state-owned; **route ~e** road equivalent to a state highway

**nationaliser** [nasjɔnalize] <1> *vt* to nationalize

**nationaliste** [nasjɔnalist] **I.** *adj* nationalist **II.** *mf* nationalist

**nationalité** [nasjɔnalite] *f* nationality

**natte** [nat] *f* ❶ (*cheveux*) braid; **se faire une ~** to braid one's hair ❷ (*tapis*) (straw) mat

**naturalisation** [natyʀalizasjɔ̃] *f* POL naturalization

**naturalisé(e)** [natyralize] **I.** *adj* naturalized **II.** *m(f)* naturalized citizen

**naturaliser** [natyralize] <1> *vt* ~ **qn français** to grant sb French citizenship

**naturaliste** [natyralist] **I.** *adj* ART, LIT, PHILOS naturalistic **II.** *mf* naturalist

**nature** [natyr] **I.** *f* ❶ (*environnement, caractère*) nature ❷ ART ~ **morte** still life ▸ **petite** ~ *inf* delicate flower; **de** [*o* **par**] ~ naturally; **plus vrai que** ~ larger than life **II.** *adj inv* ❶ (*sans assaisonnement: café, thé*) black; (*yaourt*) plain ❷ *inf* (*simple*) simple

**naturel** [natyrɛl] *m* ❶ (*caractère*) nature ❷ (*spontanéité*) naturalness

**naturel(le)** [natyrɛl] *adj* ❶ (*opp: artificiel, inné*) natural; (*père*) biological; (*produit*) organic ❷ (*simple: manières, personne, style*) simple

**naturellement** [natyrɛlmɑ̃] *adv* ❶ (*bien entendu*) of course; ~! naturally! ❷ (*opp: artificiellement, de façon innée, aisément*) naturally ❸ (*spontanément*) easily ❹ (*automatiquement*) automatically

**naturisme** [natyrism] *m* naturism

**naturiste** [natyrist] **I.** *adj* naturist **II.** *mf* naturist

**naufrage** [nofraʒ] *m* NAUT wreck ▸ **faire** ~ (*bateau, projet*) to be wrecked

**naufragé(e)** [nofraʒe] *m(f)* shipwrecked person

**nausée** [noze] *f* ❶ (*haut-le-cœur*) bout of nausea; **j'ai la** ~ [*o* **des ~s**] I feel nauseous ❷ (*dégoût*) disgust ▸ **cette personne/cette odeur me donne la** ~ this person/smell makes me feel sick

**nautique** [notik] *adj* **ski** ~ waterskiing; **sport** ~ watersports *pl*

**naval(e)** [naval] <s> *adj* naval; **chantier** ~ shipyard

**navet** [navɛ] *m* ❶ BOT turnip ❷ *péj, inf* (*œuvre sans valeur*) piece of garbage; (*mauvais film*) flop

**navette** [navɛt] *f* shuttle

**navigant(e)** [navigɑ̃, ɑ̃t] *adj* AVIAT **personnel** ~ flying personnel; NAUT seagoing personnel

**navigateur** [navigatœr] *m* INFORM browser; ~ **Web** Web browser

**navigateur, -trice** [navigatœr, -tris] *m, f* ❶ NAUT sailor ❷ AUTO, AVIAT navigator

**naviguer** [navige] <1> *vi* ❶ AVIAT to fly ❷ NAUT to sail ❸ INFORM ~ **sur le Web** to surf the Web

**navire** [navir] *m* ship; ~ **de commerce** merchantman; ~ **pétrolier** oil tanker

**navrant(e)** [navrɑ̃, ɑ̃t] *adj* **c'est** ~! it is a shame!

**navré(e)** [navre] *adj* **être** ~ **de qc** to be (terribly) sorry about sth

**nazi(e)** [nazi] *abr de* **national-socialiste I.** *adj* Nazi **II.** *m(f)* Nazi

**nazisme** [nazism] *m abr de* **national--socialisme** Nazism

**N.B.** [ɛnbe] *abr de* **nota bene** N.B.

**ne** [nə] <*devant voyelle ou h muet* n'> *adv* <*avec autre mot négatif*> **il** ~ **mange pas le midi** he doesn't eat at lunchtime; **elle n'a guère d'argent** she has hardly any money; **je** ~ **fume plus** I don't smoke anymore; **je** ~ **me promène jamais** I never go for walks; **je** ~ **vois personne** I can't see anyone; **personne** ~ **vient** nobody comes; **je** ~ **vois rien** I can't see anything; **rien** ~ **va plus** no more bets; **il n'a ni frère ni sœur** he has no brothers or sisters; **tu n'as aucune chance** you have no chance ⬩ <*sans autre mot négatif, soutenu*> **je n'ose le dire** I dare not say it ❸ (*seulement*) **je** ~ **vois que cette solution** this is the only solution I can see; **il n'y a pas que vous qui le dites** you're not the only one to say so

**né(e)** [ne] **I.** *part passé de* **naître II.** *adj souvent écrit avec un trait d'union* (*de naissance*) née; **Madame X, ~e Y** Mrs. X, née Y

**néant** [neɑ̃] **I.** *m* nothingness **II.** *pron* (*rien*) **signes particuliers:** ~ distinguishing marks: none

**nécessaire** [neseser] **I.** *adj a.* PHILOS, MATH (*indispensable*) **être** ~ **à qc** to be necessary for sth **II.** *m* ❶ (*opp: super-*

**N**

*flu)* **le ~** what is required ❷ *(étui)* **~ à ongles** nail kit

**nécessairement** [nesesɛrmɑ̃] *adv* necessarily

**nécessité** [nesesite] *f* necessity ►**de première ~** absolutely essential

**nécessiter** [nesesite] <1> *vt* to require

**nectar** [nɛktaʀ] *m* nectar

**nectarine** [nɛktaʀin] *f* nectarine

**néerlandais** [neɛʀlɑ̃dɛ] *m* Dutch; *v.a.* **français**

**néerlandais(e)** [neɛʀlɑ̃dɛ, ɛz] *adj* Dutch

**Néerlandais(e)** [neɛʀlɑ̃dɛ, ɛz] *m(f)* Dutchman, Dutchwoman *m, f*

**nef** [nɛf] *f* ARCHIT nave

**négatif** [negatif] *m* PHOT negative

**négatif, -ive** [negatif, -iv] *adj* negative

**négation** [negasjɔ̃] *f* LING negation

**négligé(e)** [negliʒe] *adj* neglected; *(intérieur)* neglected; *(style, travail)* careless; *(tenue)* sloppy

**négligeable** [negliʒabl] *adj* negligible; *(élément, facteur)* inconsiderable; *(détail, moyens)* insignificant

**négligent(e)** [negliʒɑ̃, ʒɑ̃t] *adj (élève)* careless; *(employé)* negligent

**négliger** [negliʒe] <2a> I. *vt* ❶ *(se désintéresser de, délaisser)* to neglect; *(occasion)* to miss; *(conseil, détail, fait)* to disregard ❷ *(omettre de faire)* **~ de** +*infin* to fail to +*infin* II. *vpr* **se ~** to neglect oneself

**négociant(e)** [negɔsjɑ̃, ʒɑ̃t] *m(f)* trader; **~ en gros** wholesaler

**négociation** [negɔsjasjɔ̃] *f gén pl* negotiation

**négocier** [negɔsje] <1> I. *vi* POL **~ avec qn** to negotiate with sb II. *vt* ❶ COM, JUR, POL **~ la capitulation avec qn** *(discuter)* to discuss surrender with sb; *(obtenir après discussion)* to negotiate surrender with sb ❷ COM, FIN, AUTO to negotiate

**nègre** [nɛgʀ] *m péj* Negro

**neige** [nɛʒ] *f* ❶ METEO snow ❷ CULIN **battre les blancs (d'œufs) en ~** to beat the egg whites until they become stiff

► **être blanc comme ~** to be a white as snow

**neiger** [neʒe] <2a> *vi impers* **il neige** it's snowing

**nénuphar** [nenyfaʀ] *m* water lily

**néon** [neɔ̃] *m* ❶ CHIM neon ❷ *(tube fluorescent)* neon light

**néonazi(e)** [neonazi] I. *adj* neo-Nazi II. *m(f)* neo-Nazi

**nerf** [nɛʀ] *m* ❶ ANAT, MED nerve ❷ *pl* PSYCH nerves; **avoir les ~s fragiles** to be highly strung; **être sur les ~s** *inf* to be keyed up; **être malade des ~s** to suffer from nerves ►**taper sur les ~s à qn** *inf* to get on sb's nerves; **un peu de ~!**, **du ~!** *inf* buck up!

**nerveux, -euse** [nɛʀvø, -øz] I. *adj* ❶ ANAT, MED *(spasme, troubles)* nervous ❷ *(irritable)* irritable; *(animal, personne)* touchy ❸ *(émotif)* emotional ❹ *(vigoureux: animal, personne)* energetic; *(style)* vigorous; *(moteur, voiture)* responsive II. *m, f* highly-strung person

**nervosité** [nɛʀvozite] *f* nervousness

**n'est-ce pas** [nɛspa] *adv* ❶ *(invitation à acquiescer)* **c'est vrai, ~?** it's true, isn't it?; **vous viendrez, ~?** you'll come, won't you? ❷ *(renforcement)* of course

**net(te)** [nɛt] I. *adj* ❶ postposé *(propre)* clean; *(copie, intérieur)* neat ❷ postposé *(précis)* precise; *(position, réponse)* exact ❸ *a.* antéposé *(évident)* clear; *(amélioration, différence, tendance)* distinct ❹ postposé *(distinct: dessin, écriture, souvenir)* clear; *(contours, image)* sharp; *(cassure, coupure)* clean ❺ *inf (opp: cinglé)* sharp ❻ postposé COM, FIN **salaire ~** net salary; **être ~ d'impôt** to be net of taxes II. *adv* ❶ *(brusquement: se casser)* cleanly; *(s'arrêter)* dead ❷ *(franchement: dire, refuser)* straight out ❸ COM net

**Net** [nɛt] *m* **le ~** the Net

**nettement** [nɛtmɑ̃] *adv* ❶ *(sans ambiguïté)* clearly ❷ *(distinctement)* distinctly; *(se détacher)* sharply; *(se souvenir)* clearly ❸ *(largement)* markedly

**netteté** [nɛtte] *f* ❶ *(précision)* neatness

**②**(*caractère distinct, franc*) clearness; (*des contours, d'une image*) cleanness
**nettoyage** [netwajaʒ] *m* **①**(*lavage*) cleaning **②**MIL, POL cleaning up
**nettoyer** [netwaje] <6> I. *vt* (*laver*) to clean II. *vpr* se ~ (*personne, animal*) to wash oneself
**nettoyeur** [netwajœʁ] *m* (*appareil*) cleaner; ~ **vapeur** steam cleaner; ~ **à haute pression** pressure washer
**neuf¹** [nœf] *adj* nine; *v.a.* **cinq**
**neuf²** [nœf] *m* new ▸ **il y a du** ~ something new has happened
**neuf, neuve** [nœf, nœv] *adj* new; **flambant** ~ brand new ▸ **quelque chose/rien de** ~ something/nothing new
**neurochirurgien(ne)** [nøʁoʃiʁyʁʒjɛ̃, jɛn] *m(f)* neurosurgeon
**neurologie** [nøʁɔlɔʒi] *f* neurology
**neurologue** [nøʁɔlɔg] *mf* neurologist
**neurone** [nøʁon] *m* **①**BIO, INFORM neuron **②***pl* (*cerveau*) brain
**neutraliser** [nøtʁalize] <1> *vt* **①**(*empêcher d'agir: concurrent, système*) to neutralize **②**(*mettre hors d'état de nuire: ennemi, gang*) to overpower
**neutralité** [nøtʁalite] *f* **①**(*impartialité*) neutrality; (*d'un livre, rapport, enseignement*) impartiality **②**POL, CHIM, ELEC neutrality
**neutre** [nøtʁ] I. *adj* **①**(*impartial*) neutral **②**(*qui ne choque pas*) *a.* POL, CHIM, ELEC neutral **③**(*asexué*) *a.* LING, ZOOL neuter II. *m* LING neuter noun
**neuvième** [nœvjɛm] *adj* antéposé ninth; *v.a.* **cinquième**
**neveu** [n(ə)vø] <x> *m* nephew
**névrose** [nevʁoz] *f* neurosis
**nez** [ne] *m* nose; **saigner du** ~ to have a nosebleed ▸ **avoir le** ~ **fin** to have a flair for business; **avoir du** ~ **pour qc** *inf* to have an instinct for sth; **avoir le** ~ **dans les livres** *inf* to have one's nose stuck in a book; **se bouffer le** ~ *inf* to be at each other's throats; **fourrer son** ~ **dans qc** *inf* to poke one's nose into sth; **(re)tomber sur le** ~ **de qn** *inf* to backfire on sb; ~ **à** ~ face to face; **rire**

**au** ~ **de qn** to laugh in sb's face; **devant [o sous] le** ~ **de qn** *inf* under sb's nose
**ni** [ni] *conj* **①***après une autre nég* **il ne sait pas dessiner** ~ **peindre** he can't draw or paint; **il n'a rien vu** ~ **personne** he didn't see anything or anybody; **rien de fin** ~ **de distingué** nothing elegant or distinguished **②***entre deux négations* **je ne l'aime** ~ **ne l'estime** I neither like nor respect him **③**(*alternative négative*) ~ **l'un** ~ **l'autre** neither one nor the other; ~ **plus** ~ **moins que** neither more nor less than
**niais(e)** [njɛ, njɛz] I. *adj* foolish; (*style*) inane II. *m(f)* fool
**niche** [niʃ] *f* **①**(*abri*) kennel **②**(*alcôve*) niche
**nicher** [niʃe] <1> I. *vi* **①**(*nidifier*) to nest **②***inf* (*habiter*) to settle II. *vpr* se ~ **dans un arbre** to nest in a tree
**nickel** [nikɛl] I. *m* nickel II. *adj inv, inf* (*impeccable*) spotless
**nicotine** [nikɔtin] *f* nicotine
**nid** [ni] *m* ZOOL nest; ~ **d'aigle** aerie
**nièce** [njɛs] *f* niece
**nier** [nje] <1> I. *vt* (*contester, refuser l'idée de*) to deny II. *vi* to deny the claim(s)
**Nil** [nil] *m* **le** ~ **the** Nile
**n'importe** [nɛ̃pɔʁt] *v.* **importer**
**nippon, -o(n)ne** [nipɔ, -ɔn] *adj* Japanese
**nitouche** [nituʃ] *f* **sainte** ~ goody-goody
**nitrate** [nitʁat] *m* nitrate
**niveau** [nivo] <x> *m* **①**(*hauteur*) *a.* TECH level **②**(*degré*) level; ~ **de vie** standard of living ▸ **au plus haut** ~ at the highest level; **au** ~ **de qn/qc** (*hauteur*) at the level of sb/sth; (*près de*) by sb/sth; (*valeur*) on the level of sb/sth; **au niveau (de la) sécurité** as for security
**niveler** [nivle] <3> *vt* to even out; (*sol, terrain*) to level
**noble** [nɔbl] I. *adj* noble II. *mf* nobleman, noblewoman *m, f*
**noblesse** [nɔblɛs] *f* nobility
**noce** [nɔs] *f a. pl* wedding ▸ **faire la** ~ *inf* to live it up

**N**

**nocif, -ive** [nɔsif, -iv] *adj* harmful

**nocturne** [nɔktyrn] **I.** *adj* nocturnal **II.** *f* (*manifestation nocturne*) evening demonstration

**Noël** [nɔɛl] *m* ❶ REL Christmas; **arbre de ~** Christmas tree; **nuit de ~** Christmas Eve; **joyeux ~** Merry Christmas ❷ (*période de Noël*) Christmas time

**nœud** [nø] *m* ❶ (*boucle, vitesse, protubérance*) *a.* NAUT, BOT knot; **~ papillon** bow tie ❷ (*point essentiel: d'une pièce, d'un roman, d'un débat*) crux

**noir** [nwar] *m* ❶ (*couleur, vêtement*) black; (*de deuil*) mourning ❷ (*obscurité*) dark ❸ *inf* (*café*) espresso ❹ PHOT **~ et blanc** black and white ►**~ sur blanc** in black and white; **broyer du ~** to be all gloom and doom; **au ~** on the black market; **travail au ~** moonlighting

**noir(e)** [nwar] *adj* ❶ (*opp: blanc; illégal, satanique*) black; (*ciel*) dark ❷ (*foncé: lunettes*) dark; (*raisin*) black; **la rue est ~e de monde** the street is teeming with people ❸ (*propre à la race*) black; **l'Afrique ~e** black Africa ❹ (*obscur*) dark ❺ (*sinistre*) dark; (*humour*) black ❻ LIT, CINE **film ~** film noir; **série ~e** thriller series

**Noir(e)** [nwar] *m(f)* black (person)

**noircir** [nwarsir] <8> **I.** *vt* ❶ (*salir*) to dirty ❷ (*colorer: étoffe*) to blacken ❸ (*dénigrer*) **~ la réputation de qn** to blacken sb's reputation ❹ (*couvrir d'écriture: cahier, feuille*) to cover **II.** *vi* (*façade, fruit*) to go black; (*ciel, peau*) to darken; (*bois, couleur*) to discolor **III.** *vpr* **se ~** (*façade*) to turn black; (*ciel*) to darken; (*bois, couleur*) to discolor

**noisetier** [nwaztje] *m* hazel tree

**noisette** [nwazɛt] **I.** *f* ❶ (*fruit*) hazelnut ❷ CULIN **une ~ de beurre** a pat of butter **II.** *adj inv* hazel

**noix** [nwa] *f* ❶ (*fruit*) walnut ❷ *péj* (*individu stupide*) idiot ❸ (*viande*) fillet ❹ (*quantité*) **une ~ de beurre** a pat of butter

**nom** [nɔ̃] *m* ❶ (*dénomination*) name;

**quel est le ~ de ...?** what's the name of ...?; **je ne le connais que de ~** I only know him by name; **donner son ~ à qn/qc** to give one's name to sb/sth ❷ LING noun; **~ composé** compound noun ►**~ d'un chien!**, **~ d'une pipe!** heavens!; **~ de Dieu** (**de ~ de Dieu**)! my God!; **porter bien/mal son ~** to suit/not suit one's name; **au ~ du Père, du Fils et du Saint-Esprit** in the name of the Father, the Son, and the Holy Spirit

**nomade** [nɔmad] **I.** *adj* ❶ (*opp: sédentaire*) nomadic; ZOOL migratory ❷ (*errant*) wandering **II.** *mf* nomad

**nombre** [nɔ̃br] *m* number

**nombreux, -euse** [nɔ̃brø, -øz] *adj* numerous; (*foule, clientèle, famille*) large; **ils sont ~ à faire qc** many of them do sth

**nombril** [nɔ̃bril] *m* navel

**nomenclature** [nɔmɑ̃klatyr] *f* ❶ (*entrées: d'un dictionnaire*) word list ❷ (*terminologie*) nomenclature

**nominal(e)** [nɔminal, -o] <-aux> *adj* nominal

**nominatif, -ive** [nɔminatif, -iv] *m* LING nominative

**nomination** [nɔminasjɔ̃] *f* (*désignation*) nomination

**nominé(e)** [nɔmine] **I.** *adj* nominated **II.** *m* nominee

**nommer** [nɔme] <1> *vt* ❶ (*appeler: chose*) to call; **une femme nommée Laetitia** a woman named Laetitia ❷ (*citer*) to name; **quelqu'un que je ne nommerai pas** somebody who will remain anonymous ❸ (*désigner*) to designate; (*avocat, expert*) to appoint; **~ qn à un poste/à une fonction** to appoint sb to a job/position

**non** [nɔ̃] **I.** *adv* ❶ (*réponse*) no; **je pense que ~** I don't think so, I think not; **moi ~, mais** not me, but; **ah ~!** no!; **ça ~!** certainly not!; **mais ~!** (*atténuation*) of course not!; (*insistance*) definitely not!; (**oh**) **que ~!** *inf* definitely not! ❷ (*opposition*) not; **je n'y vais pas – moi ~ plus** I'm not going – nor am I; **il n'en est pas question ~ plus** it's also out of the question; **~ seulement ..., mais (encore)** not only ..., but also ❸ *inf (sens interrogatif)* **vous venez, ~?** you're coming, aren't you?; **~, pas possible!** no, I don't believe it! ❹ *(sens exclamatif)* **~, par exemple!** for goodness sake!; **~ mais (alors)!** *inf* honestly!; **~, mais dis donc!** *inf* really! ❺ *(qui n'est pas)* **~ polluant** non-polluting **II.** *m inv* no; **48% de ~** 48% noes

**nonante** [nɔnãt] *adj Belgique, Suisse (quatre-vingt-dix)* ninety; *v.a.* **cinq, cinquante**

**non-assistance** [nɔ̃nasistãs] <non-assistances> *f* **~ à personne en danger** failure to assist a person in danger

**non-croyant(e)** [nɔ̃kʀwajã, jãt] <non-croyants> **I.** *adj* non-believing **II.** *m(f)* nonbeliever

**non-fumeur, -euse** [nɔ̃fymœʀ, -øz] <non-fumeurs> **I.** *adj (espace)* non-smoking; **zone ~** no-smoking [*o* smoke-free] area **II.** *m, f* nonsmoker

**nonne** [nɔn] *f* nun

**non-sens** [nɔ̃sãs] *m inv* ❶ *(absurdité)* nonsense ❷ ECOLE meaningless word

**non-stop** [nɔnstɔp] *adj inv* nonstop

**non-violence** [nɔ̃vjɔlãs] <non-violences> *f* non-violence

**non-violent(e)** [nɔ̃vjɔlã, ãt] <non-violents> **I.** *adj* non-violent **II.** *m(f)* supporter of non-violence

**non-voyant(e)** [nɔ̃vwajã, jãt] <non-voyants> *m(f)* visually impaired person

**nord** [nɔʀ] **I.** *m (point cardinal)* north; **au ~ de qc** to the north of sth; **être exposé au ~** to have northerly exposure; **dans le ~** de in the north of; **du ~** from the north; **vers le ~** towards the north
▶ **perdre le ~** *(perdre son calme)* to blow one's top; *(perdre la raison)* to go crazy **II.** *adj inv* north; *(banlieue, latitude)* northern

**Nord** [nɔʀ] **I.** *m* Nord; **le grand ~** the far North; **l'Europe du ~** Northern Europe; **le ~ canadien** the North of Canada; **dans le ~** *(dans la région)* in the North;

*(vers la région)* to the North **II.** *adj inv* **l'hémisphère ~** the Northern hemisphere; **le pôle ~** the North Pole

**nord-africain(e)** [nɔʀafʀikɛ̃, ɛn] <nord-africains> *adj* North African

**nord-coréen(ne)** [nɔʀkɔʀeɛ̃, ɛn] <nord-coréens> *adj* North Korean

**nord-est** [nɔʀɛst] *m inv* northeast

**nordique** [nɔʀdik] *adj* Nordic

**nord-ouest** [nɔʀwɛst] *m inv* northwest

**normal(e)** [nɔʀmal, -o] <-aux> *adj* ❶ *(ordinaire)* normal ❷ *(compréhensible)* normal; **il est/n'est pas ~ que +subj/de +infin** it is/is not all right for sb to +infin ❸ *(sain)* normal

**normale** [nɔʀmal] *f* ❶ *(état habituel)* normal situation ❷ *(norme)* norm; **des capacités au-dessus de la ~** above-normal capacities ❸ METEO **~s saisonnières** seasonal norms

**normalement** [nɔʀmalmã] *adv* ❶ *(conformément aux normes)* normally ❷ *(selon toute prévision)* all being well

**normaliser** [nɔʀmalize] <1> **I.** *vt* ❶ *(standardiser)* to standardize ❷ *(rendre normal)* to normalize **II.** *vpr* **la situation se normalise** the situation is getting back to normal

**normand(e)** [nɔʀmã, ãd] *adj* Norman

**Normand(e)** [nɔʀmã, ãd] *m(f)* Norman

**Normandie** [nɔʀmãdi] *f* **la ~** Normandy

**norme** [nɔʀm] *f* norm

**Norvège** [nɔʀvɛʒ] *f* **la ~** Norway

**nos** [no] *dét poss v.* **notre**

**nostalgie** [nɔstalʒi] *f* nostalgia

**nostalgique** [nɔstalʒik] *adj* nostalgic

**notable** [nɔtabl] **I.** *adj* notable **II.** *mf* worthy

**notaire** [nɔtɛʀ] *m* notary

**notamment** [nɔtamã] *adv* ❶ *(particulièrement)* notably ❷ *Belgique (nommément)* specifically

**note** [nɔt] *f* ❶ *(communication, annotation)* a. ECOLE, MUS note; **~ de bas de page** footnote ❷ *(facture)* bill
▶ **fausse ~** MUS wrong note; *(maladresse)* sour note; **prendre qc en ~**

(*inscrire*) to take a note of sth; (*prendre conscience*) to take note of sth

**noter** [nɔte] <1> *vt* ① (*inscrire*) to write down ② (*remarquer*) to note ③ ADMIN, ECOLE to grade; (*employé*) to rate; ~ **qn/ qc 6 sur 10** to grade sb/sth 6 out of 10

**notice** [nɔtis] *f* ① (*mode d'emploi*) ~ (*explicative*) instructions ② (*préface*) note

**notion** [nosjɔ̃] *f* ① (*idée, conscience*) **la ~ de l'heure** [*o* **du temps**] the notion of time ② *pl* (*connaissances*) basic knowledge

**notoriété** [nɔtɔʀjete] *f* ① (*renommée: d'une personne, œuvre*) fame ② (*caractère connu*) notoriety; **être de ~ publique** to be common knowledge

**notre** [nɔtʀ, no] <nos> *dét poss* ① our; *v.a.* **ma, mon** ② REL **Notre Père qui êtes aux cieux** Our Father, who art in heaven

**nôtre** [notʀ] *pron poss* ① **le/la/les ~s** our; *v.a.* **mien** ② *pl* (*ceux de notre famille*) **les ~s** our folks; (*nos partisans*) our people; **il est des ~s** he's one of us; *v.a.* **mien**

**Notre-Dame** [nɔtʀədam] *f inv* ① REL Our Lady ② (*à Paris*) Notre Dame

**nouer** [nwe] <1> **I.** *vt* ① (*faire un nœud avec*) to knot ② (*entourer d'un lien*) to do up; (*paquet, bouquet*) to tie up ③ (*établir: alliance*) to form; (*contact, relation, amitié*) to strike up ④ (*paralyser*) **l'émotion/les sanglots lui a/ont noué la gorge** emotion/sobs choked him **II.** *vpr* ① (*se serrer*) **sa gorge se noua en voyant cela** he felt a lump in his throat when he saw it ② (*s'attacher*) **se ~ autour du cou** to be tied around the neck; (*accidentellement*) to get tied around one's neck

**nougat** [nuga] *m* nougat

**nougatine** [nugatin] *f* nougatine

**nouille** [nuj] **I.** *f* ① CULIN noodle ② *inf* oaf **II.** *adj* ① *inf* (*empoté*) clumsy ② *inf* (*tarte*) idiot

**nourrice** [nuʀis] *f* ① (*gardienne*) nanny ② (*bidon*) jerry can

**nourrir** [nuʀiʀ] <8> **I.** *vt* ① (*donner à*

*manger à: personne, animal*) to feed; ~ **qn au biberon/à la cuillère** to bottle-feed/spoon-feed sb; ~ **qn au sein** to breastfeed sb; **être bien/mal nourri** to be well-/under-fed ② (*faire vivre*) ~ **qn** to provide for sb ▸ **être nourri et logé** to have room and board **II.** *vpr* (*s'alimenter*) **se ~ de qc** to feed on sth; **bien se ~** to eat well

**nourrisson** [nuʀisɔ̃] *m* infant

**nourriture** [nuʀityʀ] *f* (*produits*) food

**nous** [nu] *pron pers* ① *sujet* we; **vous avez fini, mais pas ~** you've finished but we haven't; ~ **autres** the rest of us ② *complément d'objet direct et indirect us* ③ *avec être, devenir, sembler, soutenu* **cela ~ semble bon** that seems fine to us; *v.a.* **me** ④ *avec les verbes pronominaux* **nous ~ punissons** we're punishing ourselves; **nous ~ voyons souvent** we see each other often; **nous ~ nettoyons les ongles** we're cleaning our nails ⑤ *inf* (*pour renforcer*) ~, ~ **n'avons pas** [*o* **on n'a pas** *inf*] **ouvert la bouche** we never opened our mouths; **c'est ~ qui l'avons dit** we're the ones who said it; **il veut ~ aider, ~?** he wants to help US? ⑥ (*avec un sens possessif*) **le cœur ~ battait fort** our hearts were beating fast ⑦ *avec un présentatif* ~ **voici** [*o* **voilà**]! here we are! ⑧ *avec une préposition* **avec/sans ~** with/ without us; **à ~ deux** between the two of us; **la maison est à ~** the house is ours; **c'est à ~ de décider** it's for us to decide; **c'est à ~!** it's our turn! ⑨ *dans une comparaison* us; **vous êtes comme ~** you're like us; **plus fort que ~** stronger than us ⑩ *inf* (*signe d'intérêt*) **comment allons-~?** how are we?

**nous-même** [numɛm] <nous-mêmes> *pron pers* ① (*nous en personne*) ~**s n'en savions rien** we know nothing; **nous sommes venus de ~s** we came of our own accord ② (*j'ai froid – nous aussi*) I'm cold – so are we; *v.a.* **moi-même**

**nouveau** [nuvo] <x> *m* **du ~** new ▸ **à** [*o* **de**] **~** again

**nouveau, nouvelle** [nuvo, nuvɛl, nu-vɛl] <*devant un nom masculin commençant par une voyelle ou un h muet* **nouvel, x**> I. *adj* ❶ (*récent*) new; **rien de ~** nothing new ❷ *antéposé* (*répété*) another; **une nouvelle fois** another time ❸ *antéposé* (*de fraîche date*) **les ~x venus** the newcomers ▸ **c'est ~** (**ça**)! *inf* that's new! II. *m, f* new man, new woman *m, f*

**nouveau-né(e)** [nuvone] <nouveau--nés> I. *adj* newborn II. *m(f)* newborn

**nouveauté** [nuvote] *f* ❶ (*en librairie*) new book; (*en salle*) new film; (*voiture, avion*) new model ❷ (*innovation*) novelty

**nouvelle** [nuvɛl] *f* ❶ (*événement*) piece of news; (*information*) piece of information; **connaissez-vous la ~?** have you heard the news? ❷ *pl* (*renseignements sur qn*) **avoir des ~s de qn** to have news from sb; **donner de ses ~s** to tell sb one's news ❸ *pl* CINE, TV news + *vb sing* ❹ LIT short story ▸ **pas de ~s, bonnes ~s** *prov* no news is good news; **aux dernières ~** the last I heard; *v.a.* **nouveau**

**Nouvelle-Calédonie** [nuvɛlkaledoni] *f* **la ~** New Caledonia

**Nouvelle-Zélande** [nuvɛlzelãd] *f* **la ~** New Zealand

**novembre** [nɔvãbʀ] *m* November; *v.a.* **août**

**novice** [nɔvis] I. *adj* **être dans qc** to be a novice at sth II. *mf* ❶ (*débutant*) beginner ❷ REL novice

**noyau** [nwajo] <x> *m* ❶ BOT pit ❷ PHYS, BIO nucleus; GEO core ❸ (*groupe humain*) nucleus

**noyer**[1] [nwaje] *m* ❶ (*arbre*) walnut tree ❷ (*bois*) walnut

**noyer**[2] [nwaje] <6> I. *vt* ❶ (*tuer, oublier*) to drown ❷ (*inonder*) to flood ❸ CULIN to water down ❹ AUTO to flood II. *vpr* (*mourir*) **se ~** to drown

**nu** [ny] *m* ART nude

**nu(e)** [ny] *adj* ❶ (*sans vêtement*) naked;

**les pieds ~s** barefoot; **se mettre torse ~** to strip to the waist ❷ (*non protégé: fil électrique, lame*) bare

**nuage** [nɥaʒ] *m* ❶ (*nébulosité, amas*) cloud ❷ (*très petite quantité*) **un ~ de lait** a drop of milk ▸ **être dans les ~s** to be in the clouds; **ciel sans ~(s)** cloudless sky

**nuageux, -euse** [nɥaʒø, -ʒøz] *adj* METEO cloudy

**nuance** [nɥãs] *f* ❶ (*gradation de couleur*) shade; (*détail de couleur*) nuance ❷ (*légère différence*) nuance; POL shade of opinion

**nucléaire** [nykleɛʀ] I. *adj* nuclear II. *m* nuclear technology

**nudisme** [nydism] *m* nudism

**nudiste** [nydist] I. *adj* nudist II. *mf* nudist

**nuée** [nɥe] *f* (*grand nombre*) horde

**nuire** [nɥiʀ] *vi irr* **à qn/qc** to damage sb/sth

**nuisance** [nɥizãs] *f* environmental nuisance; **~s sonores** noise pollution

**nuisant(e)** [nɥizã, ãt] *adj* (*bruit, odeur*) noxious

**nuisible** [nɥizibl] *adj* (*influence, habitude*) harmful; (*gaz*) noxious; **animaux/ insectes ~s** pests; **être ~ à qc** to be harmful to sth

**nuit** [nɥi] *f* ❶ (*espace de temps, nuitée*) night; **bonne ~!** good night!; **mardi, dans la ~** in the course of Tuesday night ❷ (*obscurité*) darkness; **la ~ tombe** night is falling; **il fait/commence à faire ~** it is dark/beginning to get dark ❸ (*temps d'activité*) **de ~** night; **être de ~** to be on nights; **faire la ~** to be the night watchman ▸ **~ blanche** sleepless night; **~ de noces** wedding night

**nul(le)** [nyl] I. *adj* ❶ (*mauvais: discours, film, devoir*) lousy; **il est ~ en physique** (*médiocre*) he's no good at physics; (*incompétent*) he's hopeless at physics ❶ (*ennuyeux, raté*) **c'était ~, cette fête** that party was awful ❸ *inf* (*crétin*) **c'est ~/t'es ~ d'avoir fait qc** it's/ you're stupid to do sth ❹ SPORT nil; (*égalité*) drawn; **match ~** draw ❺ (*minime:*

N

*risque, différence*) non-existent ⑥MATH zero ⑦JUR, POL (*élection, testament*) null and void II. *m(f)* idiot

**nullement** [nylmã] *adv* (*aucunement*) not at all; (*en aucun cas*) in any way

**nullité** [nylite] *f* ①(*manque de valeur, incompétence*) uselessness ②(*personne*) nonentity ③JUR nullity

**numérique** [nymerik] *adj* ①(*exprimé en nombre*) numerical ②INFORM, TEL digital; **des données ~s** digital data

**numériser** [nymerize] <1> *vt* INFORM to digitize

**numéro** [nymero] *m* ①(*nombre*) number; **~ de téléphone** telephone number; **faire un ~** to dial a number; **~ vert** toll-free number ②PRESSE issue ③(*spec-*

*tacle*) number ④*inf* (*personne*) character ▶**faire son ~ à qn** *inf* to put on one's act for sb; **~ un** number one

**numérotation** [nymerɔtasjɔ̃] *f* numbering; **~ à 10 chiffres** 10-digit phone numbering

**numéroter** [nymerɔte] <1> *vt* to number

**nuque** [nyk] *f* nape of the neck

**nutritif, -ive** [nytritif, -iv] *adj* ①(*nourricier*) nourishing; (*qualité, valeur, substance*) nutritional ②MED **besoins ~s** nutritive requirements

**nutrition** [nytrisjɔ̃] *f* nutrition

**nylon®** [nilɔ̃] *m* nylon®

**nymphomane** [nɛ̃fɔman] I. *adj* nymphomaniac II. *f* nymphomaniac

# Oo

**O, o** [o] *m inv* O, o; **~ comme Oscar** (*au téléphone*) o as in Oscar

**ô** [o] *interj* oh

**oasis** [ɔazis] *f* oasis

**obéir** [ɔbeir] <8> *vi* ①(*se soumettre*) **~ à qn** to obey sb; **~ à une loi/un ordre** to obey a law/an order ②(*céder à*) **~ à son instinct** to follow one's instinct

**obèse** [ɔbɛz] I. *adj* obese II. *mf* obese person

**obésité** [ɔbezite] *f* obesity

**objecter** [ɔbʒɛkte] <1> *vt* to object; **~ qc à qn** to advance sth to sb as an objection

**objecteur** [ɔbʒɛktœr] *m* **~ de conscience** conscientious objector

**objectif** [ɔbʒɛktif] *m* ①(*but*) objective ②(*en optique*) a. PHYS, PHOT lens

**objectif, -ive** [ɔbʒɛktif, -iv] *adj* objective

**objection** [ɔbʒɛksjɔ̃] *f* objection

**objectivité** [ɔbʒɛktivite] *f* objectivity

**objet** [ɔbʒɛ] *m* ①(*chose*) a. LING object; **~ d'art** objet d'art ②(*but*) purpose;

**avoir qc pour ~** to have the aim of sth ▶**~s trouvés** lost and found

**obligation** [ɔbligasjɔ̃] *f* ①(*nécessité*) a. JUR obligation; **~ de** +*infin* obligation to +*infin*; **être dans l'~ de** +*infin* to be obliged to +*infin* ②*pl* (*devoirs*) obligations; (*devoirs civiques, scolaires*) duties; **ses ~s de citoyen/de père de famille** his duties as a citizen/father ③FIN bond ▶**sans ~ d'achat** with no obligation to buy

**obligatoire** [ɔbligatwar] *adj* ①(*exigé*) compulsory; **présence ~** mandatory attendance ②*inf* (*inévitable*) inevitable

**obligé(e)** [ɔbliʒe] *adj* ①(*nécessaire*) vital; (*inévitable*) inevitable ②(*reconnaissant*) **être ~ à qn de qc** to be obliged to sb for sth

**obliger** [ɔbliʒe] <2a> I. *vt* ①(*forcer*) to force; **~ qn à** +*infin* to force sb to +*infin*; **on était bien obligés!** we had to! ②(*contraindre moralement, rendre service à*) to oblige II. *vpr* (*s'engager*)

**s'~ à faire qc** to commit oneself to doing sth

**oblique** [ɔblik] *adj* oblique

**oblitérer** [ɔblitere] <5> *vt* to obliterate

**obnubiler** [ɔbnybile] <1> *vt* ❶ (*obscurcir: esprit, pensée*) to cloud ❷ (*obséder*) to obsess

**obscène** [ɔpsɛn] *adj* obscene

**obscur(e)** [ɔpskyr] *adj* ❶ (*sombre*) dark ❷ (*incompréhensible, inconnu*) obscure

**obscurément** [ɔpskyremɑ̃] *adv* ❶ (*vaguement*) obscurely; (*deviner, sentir*) in an obscure way ❷ (*de façon peu claire*) vaguely

**obscurité** [ɔpskyrite] *f* ❶ (*absence de lumière*) darkness ❷ (*manque de clarté: d'une affaire*) obscurity

**obsédé(e)** [ɔpsede] *m(f)* ❶ (*par le sexe*) sex maniac ❷ (*fanatique*) obsessive

**obséder** [ɔpsede] <5> *vt* to obsess; (*souci, remords*) to haunt

**obsèques** [ɔpsɛk] *fpl* funeral

**observateur, -trice** [ɔpsɛrvatœr, -tris] I. *adj* (*personne, regard, esprit*) observant II. *m, f* observer

**observation** [ɔpsɛrvasjɔ̃] *f* observation; **être en ~** to be under observation

**observatoire** [ɔpsɛrvatwar] *m* ❶ GEO, ASTR, METEO observatory ❷ MIL observation post ❸ ECON economic research institute

**observer** [ɔpsɛrve] <1> I. *vt* ❶ (*regarder attentivement*) **~ qn faire qc** to watch sb doing sth ❷ (*surveiller*) to observe ❸ (*remarquer*) to notice; **faire ~ qc à qn** to point sth out to sb ❹ (*respecter: coutume, attitude*) to respect; (*discrétion, règle*) to observe; (*jeûne*) to keep II. *vi* to observe III. *vpr* **s'~** ❶ (*se surveiller*) to watch each other ❷ (*s'épier*) to spy on each other

**obsession** [ɔpsesjɔ̃] *f* obsession

**obstacle** [ɔpstakl] *m* obstacle; **faire ~ à qn/qc** to hinder sb/sth

**obstiné(e)** [ɔpstine] *adj* ❶ (*entêté*) obstinate ❷ (*persévérant*) persistent ❸ (*incessant: toux*) stubborn

**obstiner** [ɔpstine] <1> *vpr* **s'~ dans qc** to persist in sth

**obtenir** [ɔptənir] <9> *vt* ❶ (*recevoir*) to get; (*avantage*) to obtain; **~ de qn que** +*subj* to get sb to +*infin* ❷ (*parvenir à*) to obtain; (*examen*) to pass; (*majorité, total*) to achieve

**obtus(e)** [ɔpty, yz] *adj a.* MATH obtuse

**occasion** [ɔkazjɔ̃] *f* ❶ (*circonstance favorable*) opportunity; **c'est l'~ ou jamais** it's now or never; **à la première ~** at the earliest opportunity ❷ COM (*offre avantageuse*) bargain; **voiture d'~** used car ❸ (*cause*) **être l'~ de qc** to be the cause of sth ▸ **à l'~** on occasion; **à l'~ de qc** on the occasion of sth

**occasionnel(le)** [ɔkazjɔnɛl] *adj* occasional; (*travail*) casual

**occasionner** [ɔkazjɔne] <1> *vt* to cause

**occident** [ɔksidɑ̃] *m* (*opp: orient*) west

**occidental(e)** [ɔksidɑtal, -o] <-aux> *adj* ❶ GEO, POL Western ❷ (*opp: oriental*) western

**occulte** [ɔkylt] *adj* ❶ (*ésotérique*) occult ❷ (*secret*) secret

**occupant(e)** [ɔkypɑ̃, ɑ̃t] I. *adj* MIL occupying II. *m(f)* ❶ MIL **l'~** the occupier ❷ (*habitant: d'une chambre, d'une voiture*) occupant; (*des lieux*) occupier

**occupation** [ɔkypasjɔ̃] *f* ❶ (*activité*) occupation ❷ (*métier*) job ❸ MIL, HIST occupation; **l'armée d'~** the occupying army

**occupé(e)** [ɔkype] *adj* ❶ (*opp: inoccupé: personne*) busy; (*place, toilettes, ligne téléphonique*) engaged; (*chambre d'hôtel*) occupied; **être ~ à qc** to be busy doing sth ❷ MIL, POL (*pays, usine*) occupied

**occuper** [ɔkype] <1> I. *vt* ❶ (*remplir: place*) to occupy; (*temps*) to spend ❷ (*habiter: appartement*) to occupy ❸ (*exercer: emploi, poste*) to hold; (*fonction*) to occupy ❹ (*employer*) **~ qn à qc** to occupy sb with sth ❺ MIL, POL (*pays, usine*) to occupy II. *vpr* ❶ (*s'employer*) **s'~ de littérature/politique** to be involved in literature/politics ❷ (*prendre en charge*) **s'~ de qn/**

**O**

**qc** to take care of sb/sth; **occupe-toi de tes affaires!** mind your own business!

**océan** [ɔseã] m ocean; **l'~ Atlantique/ Indien/Pacifique** the Atlantic/Indian/ Pacific Ocean

**océanologie** [ɔseanɔlɔʒi] f oceanology

**ocre** [ɔkʀ] I. f (colorant) ocher II. adj inv ocher

**octane** [ɔktan] m octane

**octante** [ɔktãt] adj Belgique, Suisse eighty; v.a. **cinq, cinquante**

**octet** [ɔktɛ] m byte

**octobre** [ɔktɔbʀ] m October; v.a. **août**

**octroyer** [ɔktʀwaje] <6> I. vt ~ **qc à qn** to grant sb sth; ~ **une faveur à qn** to do sb a favor II. vpr **s'~ qc** to claim sth

**oculiste** [ɔkylist] mf eye specialist

**odeur** [ɔdœʀ] f smell; **sans ~** odorless

**odieux, -euse** [ɔdjø, -jøz] adj ❶ (ignoble: personne) obnoxious; (caractère) odious ❷ (insupportable: personne) unbearable

**odorat** [ɔdɔʀa] m sense of smell

**œcuménisme** [ekymenism] m ecumenism

**œdème** [ødɛm, edɛm] m edema

**œil** [œj, jø] <yeux> m ❶ ANAT eye; **lever/baisser les yeux** to raise/lower one's eyes; **se maquiller les yeux** to put on eye makeup ❷ (regard) look; **il la cherche/suit des yeux** his eyes seek her out/follow her ❸ (regard averti) eye; **avoir l'~ à tout** to keep an eye on everything ❹ (regard rapide) **jeter un coup d'~ au journal/à l'heure** to glance at the newspaper/time; **au premier coup d'~** at first glance ❺ (vision, vue) **regarder qn d'un ~ envieux/ méchant** to give someone a jealous/ malicious look ❻ (jugement) **d'un ~ critique** with a critical eye; **ne plus voir les choses du même ~** to no longer see things in the same way ❼ (judas) spyhole ► **avoir un ~ au beurre noir** to have a black eye; **loin des yeux, loin du cœur** prov out of sight, out of mind; **ne pas avoir les yeux dans sa poche** not to miss a thing;

**coûter les yeux de la tête** to cost an arm and a leg; **qn a les yeux plus grands que le ventre** inf sb has eyes bigger than his stomach; **pour les beaux yeux de qn** inf to be nice to sb; **ne pas avoir froid aux yeux** to have a sense of adventure; **à l'~ nu** to the naked eye; **cela crève les yeux** inf it's staring you in the face; **ne dormir que d'un ~** to sleep with one eye open; **fermer les yeux sur qc** to turn a blind eye to sth; **ouvrir l'~** to keep one's eyes open; **ouvrir les yeux à qn sur qc** to open sb's eyes about sth; **se rincer l'~** inf to get an eyeful; **cela saute aux yeux** it's staring you in the face; **taper dans l'~ de qn** inf to catch sb's eye; **avoir qn à l'~** inf to have an eye on sb; **aux yeux de qn** in sb's eyes; **sous l'~ de qn** under sb's eye; **mon ~!** inf my foot!

**œil-de-bœuf** [œjdəbœf] <œils-de- -bœuf> m bull's-eye

**œillade** [œjad] f (clin d'œil) wink

**œillère** [œjɛʀ] f eyecup ► **avoir des ~s** to have blinders on

**œillet**[1] [œjɛ] m BOT carnation; ~ **d'Inde** French marigold

**œillet**[2] [œjɛ] m ❶ (petit trou: d'une chaussure) eyelet ❷ (renfort métallique) grommet

**œsophage** [ezɔfaʒ] m esophagus

**œuf** [œf, ø] m ❶ ZOOL, CULIN egg; ~**s de poisson** spawn; ~**s brouillés/à la coque** scrambled/boiled eggs; ~ **au plat** fried egg; ~ **à la neige** floating island ❷ (qui a la forme d'un œuf) ~ **de Pâques** Easter egg ► **mettre tous ses ~s dans le même panier** to put all one's eggs in one basket; **va te faire cuire un ~!** inf go jump off a cliff!; **dans l'~** in the bud; **quel ~!** inf what an idiot!

**œuvre** [œvʀ] I. f ❶ ART, LIT, TECH work; ~ **d'art** work of art; **les ~s complètes d'un auteur** the complete works of an author ❷ (résultat: de l'érosion, du temps) work ❸ pl (actes) deeds ❹ (organisation caritative) ~ **de bienfaisance** charity; **les bonnes ~s** charities

▶ **être** à l'~ to be at work; **mettre en** ~ to implement; **se mettre** à l'~ to get down to work II. *m* **être à pied d'**~ to be ready to start working; **le gros** ~ the shell

**offense** [ɔfɑ̃s] *f* (*affront*) offense

**offenser** [ɔfɑ̃se] <1> I. *vt* (*outrager*) to offend II. *vpr* (*se vexer*) **s'~ de qc** to take offense at sth

**offensive** [ɔfɑ̃siv] *f* offensive; **passer à l'~** to go on the offensive

**office** [ɔfis] *m* ❶ (*agence, bureau*) office; **du tourisme** tourist information office ❷ REL service ❸ (*fonction, charge*) office ❹ (*pièce*) kitchen ▶ **d'~** (*par voie d'autorité*) officially; (*en vertu d'un règlement*) automatically; (*sans demander*) without any consultation

**officiel(le)** [ɔfisjɛl] I. *adj* official II. *m(f)* official

**officier** [ɔfisje] *m* ❶ ADMIN, JUR **d'état civil** registrar ❷ MIL officer ❸ (*titulaire d'une distinction*) **~ de la Légion d'honneur** Officer of the Legion of Honor

**offrande** [ɔfʁɑ̃d] *f* REL offering

**offrant** [ɔfʁɑ̃] *m* **le plus** ~ the highest bidder

**offre** [ɔfʁ] *f* ❶ (*proposition*) offer; ECON supply; **~ d'emplois** help wanted ads ❷ (*aux enchères*) bid

**offrir** [ɔfʁiʁ] <11> I. *vt* ❶ (*faire un cadeau*) **~ qc à qn** to give sb sth ❷ (*proposer*) **~ le bras à qn** to offer sb one's arm; **~ à qn de faire qc** to offer to do sth for sb; **il nous a offert le déjeuner** he gave us lunch ❸ (*comporter: avantages, inconvénients*) to have; (*difficulté*) to present II. *vpr* ❶ (*se présenter*) **s'~ à qn/qc** to reveal oneself to sb/sth ❷ (*s'accorder*) to treat oneself; **s'~ des vacances** to treat oneself to a vacation

**offusquer** [ɔfyske] <1> I. *vt* to offend II. *vpr* **s'~ de qc** to take offense at sth

**oie** [wa] *f* ❶ (*oiseau*) goose ❷ *inf* (*personne niaise*) silly goose

**oignon** [ɔɲɔ̃] *m* ❶ CULIN onion ❷ BOT bulb ▶ **occupe-toi de tes ~s!** *inf* mind your own business!

**oiseau** [wazo] <x> *m* ❶ (*en ornithologie*) bird ❷ *péj* (*type*) character

**oisif, -ive** [wazif, -iv] I. *adj* idle II. *m, f* idler

**olive** [ɔliv] I. *f* olive II. *adj inv* olive

**olivier** [ɔlivje] *m* ❶ (*arbre*) olive tree ❷ (*bois*) olive wood

**olympiade** [ɔlɛ̃pjad] *f* Olympiad

**olympique** [ɔlɛ̃pik] *adj* Olympic

**ombragé(e)** [ɔ̃bʁaʒe] *adj* shady

**ombre** [ɔ̃bʁ] *f* ❶ (*opp: soleil*) shade; **à l'~** in the shade; **~s chinoises** shadowgraphs ❷ (*soupçon*) **il n'y a pas l'~ d'un doute** there is not a shadow of a doubt; **sans l'~ d'une hésitation** without a hint of hesitation ▶ **faire de l'~ à qn** to overshadow sb; **mettre qn à l'~** *inf* to lock sb up

**ombrelle** [ɔ̃bʁɛl] *f* parasol

**omelette** [ɔmlɛt] *f* CULIN omelet

**omnibus** [ɔmnibys] I. *m* CHEMDFER local train II. *app* (*train*) local

**omnivore** [ɔmnivɔʁ] *adj* omnivorous

**omoplate** [ɔmɔplat] *f* shoulder blade

**on** [ɔ̃] *pron pers* ❶ (*tout le monde*) people; (*toute personne*) one, you; **~ dit qu'elle l'a fait** they say that she did it; **en France, ~ boit du vin** in France, people drink wine; **après un moment, on n'y pense plus** after a while you don't think about it anymore; **on peut imaginer une autre solution** another solution can be envisaged ❷ (*quelqu'un*) somebody; **~ vous demande au téléphone** somebody wants to speak to you on the telephone; **j'attends qu'~** [*o que l'~*] **apporte le dessert** I'm waiting for the dessert to come ❸ *inf* (*nous*) we; **~ s'en va!** off we go!; **nous, ~ veut bien!** we would love to!; **~ fait ce qu'~** [*o que l'~*] **peut** we're doing what we can ❹ *inf* (*tu, vous*) you; **alors Marie, ~ s'en va déjà?** so Marie, are you off already? ❺ *inf* (*il s, elle s*) qu' [*o que l'~*] **est jolie aujourd'hui!** aren't they pretty today! ❻ (*je, moi*) **oui, oui, ~ va le faire!** yeah, yeah, I'll do it!

**oncle** [ɔ̃kl] *m* uncle

**onctueux, -euse** [ɔ̃ktɥø, -øz] *adj* ①(*moelleux, lisse: potage, sauce*) smooth ②(*doux au toucher*) smooth; (*crème*) creamy

**onde** [ɔ̃d] *f* ①PHYS, RADIO wave; **petites/ grandes ~s** short/long wave ②*pl* (*ondulation: blé, foule*) waves

**ondée** [ɔ̃de] *f* shower

**on-dit** [ɔ̃di] *m inv* hearsay

**ondulation** [ɔ̃dylasjɔ̃] *f* ①(*mouvement onduleux, ligne sinueuse: du blé, des vagues*) undulation ②(*vagues: des cheveux*) waves *pl*

**onduler** [ɔ̃dyle] <1> **I.** *vi* ①(*ondoyer: blé, vague*) to undulate; (*serpent*) to slither ②(*être sinueux: route*) to snake; (*cheveux*) to wave **II.** *vt* (*cheveux*) to wave

**onéreux, -euse** [ɔneʁø, -øz] *adj* expensive; (*loyer, marchandise*) costly; **à titre ~** against payment

**ongle** [ɔ̃gl] *m* ANAT nail; **~s des pieds et des mains** fingernails and toenails; **se faire les ~s** to do one's nails

**onglet** [ɔ̃glɛ] *m* ①(*entaille: d'un canif, d'une règle*) notch ②(*encoche, échancrure*) thumb index ③INFORM tab

**O**

**onze** [ɔ̃z] **I.** *adj* eleven **II.** *m inv* eleven; *v.a.* **cinq**

**onzième** [ɔ̃zjɛm] **I.** *adj antéposé* eleventh **II.** *mf* **le/la ~** the eleventh **III.** *m* (*fraction*) eleventh; *v.a.* **cinquième**

**opaque** [ɔpak] *adj* ①(*opp: transparent*) opaque ②(*dense: brouillard*) thick; (*obscurité*) impenetrable

**opéra** [ɔpeʁa] *m* opera

**opérateur** [ɔpeʁatœʁ] *m* INFORM, MATH operator; **~ de téléphonie numérique mobile** digital mobile telephone network operator

**opérateur, -trice** [ɔpeʁatœʁ, -tʁis] *m, f* ①TECH, TEL operator ②FIN dealer

**opération** [ɔpeʁasjɔ̃] *f* ①MED, MATH, MIL operation; **l'~ ville propre** anti-litter campaign ②(*transaction*) deal; **~s boursières** stock transactions

**opérer** [ɔpeʁe] <5> **I.** *vt* ①MED **~ qn de qc** to operate on sb for sth; **~ qn du rein** to operate on sb's kidney ②(*provo-*

*quer*) **~ un changement** to bring about a change ③(*réaliser: choix*) to make; (*réforme*) to achieve **II.** *vi* ①(*produire: charme, médicament*) to work ②(*procéder*) to act **III.** *vpr* **s'~** ①(*se réaliser*) to happen ②MED to be operated on

**opinion** [ɔpinjɔ̃] *f* ①(*avis*) opinion; **avoir une ~ sur un sujet** to have an opinion on a subject; **se faire une ~** to form an opinion ②(*jugement collectif*) **l'~ publique** public opinion ③*gén pl* (*convictions*) (**à**) **chacun ses ~s** to each his own; **liberté d'~** freedom of opinion

**opportun(e)** [ɔpɔʁtœ̃, yn] *adj* (*démarche, intervention*) timely; **au moment ~** at the right moment

**opportunité** [ɔpɔʁtynite] *f* ①(*bien-fondé*) timeliness ②(*occasion*) opportunity

**opposé** [ɔpoze] *m* opposite ▸**à l'~** (*dans l'autre direction*) the other way; (*au contraire*) directly opposite; **à l'~ de qn/qc** unlike sb/qc

**opposé(e)** [ɔpoze] *adj* ①(*d'en face*) *a.* PHYS opposing; MATH opposite ②(*contraire: avis, intérêt*) conflicting; (*caractère, goût*) opposing ③(*hostile*) **être ~ à qc** to be opposed to sth

**opposer** [ɔpoze] <1> **I.** *vt* ①(*comparer*) **~ qn/qc et** [*o* à] **qn/qc** to compare sb/sth with sb/sth ②MIL **le conflit oppose les deux nations** the conflict opposes the two nations ③SPORT **ce match oppose l'équipe X à** [*o* et] **l'équipe Y** this match pits team X against team Y ④(*répondre par*) **~ un refus à qn** to refuse sb ⑤(*objecter*) **~ des arguments/raisons à qn/qc** to submit arguments/reasons against sb/ sth **II.** *vpr* ①(*faire obstacle*) **s'~ à qn/ qc** to oppose sb/sth ②(*faire contraste*) **s'~** to contrast

**opposition** [ɔpozisjɔ̃] *f* ①(*résistance*) **~ à qc** opposition to sth; **faire ~ à qc** to oppose sth ②(*différence: des opinions, caractères*) clash ③(*combat*) **~ de deux adversaires** opposition of two adversaries ④POL the opposition ▸**faire**

**~ à un chèque** to stop payment on a check; **en ~** at odds; **par ~** in contrast; **par ~ à qn/qc** (*contrariété*) in contrast to sb/sth; (*par défi*) as opposed to sb/sth

**oppresser** [ɔpʀese] <1> vt ❶ (*angoisser: sentiment, souvenir*) to oppress ❷ (*suffoquer: chaleur, temps*) to stifle

**oppression** [ɔpʀesjɔ̃] f ❶ (*tyrannie, angoisse*) oppression ❷ (*suffocation*) stifling feeling

**opprimer** [ɔpʀime] <1> vt to oppress

**opter** [ɔpte] <1> vi **~ pour qc** to opt for sth

**opticien(ne)** [ɔptisjɛ̃, jɛn] m(f) optician

**optimal(e)** [ɔptimal, -o] <-aux> adj optimum

**optimiste** [ɔptimist] **I.** adj optimistic **II.** mf optimist

**option** [ɔpsjɔ̃] f ❶ (*choix*) choice ❷ ECOLE elective ❸ (*promesse d'achat*) **prendre une ~ sur une maison** to take out an option on a house ❹ AUTO optional extra

**optique** [ɔptik] **I.** adj (*nerf*) optic; (*verre, centre*) optical **II.** f ❶ (*science, lentille*) optics + vb sing ❷ (*point de vue*) perspective

**opulent(e)** [ɔpylɑ̃, ɑ̃t] adj ❶ (*très riche: personne, pays*) rich; (*vie*) opulent ❷ (*plantureux: formes, poitrine*) ample

**or¹** [ɔʀ] m gold; **d'~/en ~** made of gold ▶ **rouler sur l'~** to be rolling in money; **affaire en ~** a bargain

**or²** [ɔʀ] conj ❶ (*dans un syllogisme*) now ❷ (*transition*) but

**orage** [ɔʀaʒ] m ❶ METEO storm; **le temps est à l'~** there's a storm coming ❷ (*dispute*) upset ▶ **il y a de l'~ dans l'air** inf there's a storm brewing

**orageux, -euse** [ɔʀaʒø, -ʒøz] adj ❶ METEO stormy; (*pluie*) thundery; (*nuage*) thunder ❷ (*agité, houleux: adolescence, époque*) turbulent; (*discussion*) stormy

**oral** [ɔʀal, -o] <-aux> m oral (exam)

**oral(e)** [ɔʀal, -o] <-aux> adj ❶ (*opp: écrit*) oral ❷ (*buccal: cavité*) oral;

**prendre par voie ~e** take by mouth ❸ PSYCH (*stade*) oral

**orange** [ɔʀɑ̃ʒ] **I.** f orange; **~ amère/ sanguine** bitter/blood orange **II.** m ❶ (*couleur*) orange ❷ AUTO yellow; **le feu passe/est à l'~** the lights are changing to/are on yellow **III.** adj inv orange

**orangé** [ɔʀɑ̃ʒe] m orangy color

**orangé(e)** [ɔʀɑ̃ʒe] adj orangy

**orangeade** [ɔʀɑ̃ʒad] f orangeade

**orateur, -trice** [ɔʀatœʀ, -tʀis] m, f speaker

**orbite** [ɔʀbit] f ❶ ANAT (eye-)socket ❷ ASTR orbit

**orchestre** [ɔʀkɛstʀ] m ❶ MUS orchestra; **~ de cuivres** brass band ❷ (*emplacement*) stalls pl; **fosse d'~** orchestra pit ❸ THEAT, CINE (*place de devant*) orchestra (section) seat; (*public assis devant*) orchestra section pl

**orchestrer** [ɔʀkɛstʀe] <1> vt ❶ MUS to orchestrate ❷ (*organiser: campagne de presse, de publicité*) to orchestrate; (*manifestation*) to organize

**orchidée** [ɔʀkide] f orchid

**ordinaire** [ɔʀdinɛʀ] **I.** adj ❶ (*habituel: événement, fait*) ordinary; (*réaction, geste*) usual ❷ (*courant: produit*) everyday ❸ péj (*médiocre*) average **II.** m ❶ (*banalité, habitude*) ordinary; **ça change de l'~** that's a change; **d'~** ordinarily ❷ (*menu habituel*) everyday menu

**ordinairement** [ɔʀdinɛʀmɑ̃] adv ordinarily

**ordinal(e)** [ɔʀdinal, -o] <-aux> adj ordinal

**ordinateur** [ɔʀdinatœʀ] m computer; **~ portable** laptop computer; **assisté par ~** computer-assisted; **travailler sur ~** to work on the computer

**ordonnance** [ɔʀdɔnɑ̃s] f ❶ MED prescription; **médicament délivré sur ~** prescription medicine ❷ JUR order

**ordonner** [ɔʀdɔne] <1> vt ❶ (*arranger*) to arrange; MATH to arrange in order ❷ (*commander*) **~ qc à qn** to order sth for sb; MED to prescribe sth for sb; **~ que**

+*subj* to order sb to +*infin* ❸ REL to ordain

**ordre¹** [ɔʀdʀ] *m* ❶ (*caractère ordonné: d'une pièce, personne*) tidiness; **avoir de l'~** to be tidy ❷ (*classement, organisation, stabilité sociale, association honorifique, congrégation*) *a.* BOT, ZOOL, HIST order; **par ~ alphabétique** in alphabetical order; **rappeler qn à l'~** to call sb to order; **rentrer dans l'~** to return to normal ❸ (*genre*) nature; **d'~ politique/économique** of a political/economic nature ❹ (*association*) association; REL order ▸ **de l'~ de** of roughly; **de premier/deuxième ~** first-/second-rate; **en ~** in order

**ordre²** [ɔʀdʀ] *m* ❶ (*commandement*) order; **donner l'~ à qn de** +*infin* to give sb the order to +*infin*; **être sous les ~s de qn** to be under sb's command; **à vos ~s!** yes sir! ❷ (*directives*) order; **sur ~ du médecin** on doctor's orders; **~ de grève** strike call ❸ (*commande*) order; **par ~** by order ▸ **~ du jour** agenda; **jusqu'à nouvel ~** until further instructions; **à l'~ de** payable to

**O ordure** [ɔʀdyʀ] *f* ❶ *pl* (*détritus, objets usés*) garbage; **jeter/mettre qc aux ~s** to throw sth away ❷ *inf* (*personne*) swine ❸ *pl* (*propos obscènes*) filth

**ordurier, -ière** [ɔʀdyʀje, -jɛʀ] *adj* filthy

**oreille** [ɔʀɛj] *f* ❶ ANAT ear; **des ~s décollées** protruding ears ❷ (*ouïe*) **avoir l'~ fine** (*entendre bien*) to have a good sense of hearing; (*percevoir les nuances*) to have a sharp ear ▸ **être dur d'~** to be hard of hearing; **casser les ~s à qn** to deafen sb; **dormir sur ses deux ~s** to sleep soundly; **je ne l'entends pas de cette ~** I'm not having it; **se faire tirer l'~** to need a lot of persuading

**oreiller** [ɔʀeje] *m* pillow

**orfèvrerie** [ɔʀfevʀəʀi] *f* ❶ (*travail*) gold work ❷ (*art*) goldsmithing ❸ (*objet*) gold plate

**organe** [ɔʀgan] *m* ❶ ANAT organ ❷ (*porte-parole*) mouthpiece ❸ (*instrument*) instrument ❹ (*voix*) organ ❺ ADMIN **les**

**~s dirigeants d'un parti** the leadership of a party

**organigramme** [ɔʀganigʀam] *m* ❶ ADMIN organizational chart ❷ INFORM flow chart

**organique** [ɔʀganik] *adj* organic

**organisateur** [ɔʀganizatœʀ] *m* INFORM organizer

**organisateur, -trice** [ɔʀganizatœʀ, -tʀis] I. *adj* organizing II. *m, f* organizer; (*d'une manifestation, d'un voyage*) leader

**organisation** [ɔʀganizasjɔ̃] *f* organization

**organiser** [ɔʀganize] <1> I. *vt* ❶ (*préparer, planifier*) to organize ❷ (*structurer*) to set up II. *vpr* **s'~ pour qc** to get organized for sth

**organisme** [ɔʀganism] *m* ❶ BIO organism ❷ ADMIN organization; **~ de crédit/tourisme** credit/tourist company

**orgasme** [ɔʀgasm] *m* orgasm

**orge** [ɔʀʒ] *f* barley

**orgue** [ɔʀg] I. *m* organ; **~ de Barbarie** barrel organ II. *fpl* organ + *vb sing*

**orgueil** [ɔʀgœj] *m* ❶ (*fierté*) pride ❷ (*prétention*) arrogance

**orgueilleux, -euse** [ɔʀgøjø, -jøz] I. *adj* ❶ (*fier*) proud ❷ (*prétentieux*) arrogant II. *m, f* proud person

**Orient** [ɔʀjɑ̃] *m* **l'~** the Orient

**orientable** [ɔʀjɑ̃tabl] *adj* swiveling; (*lampe*) adjustable; (*antenne, bras*) movable

**oriental(e)** [ɔʀjɑ̃tal, -o] <-aux> *adj* ❶ (*situé à l'est d'un lieu*) eastern ❷ (*relatif à l'Orient*) oriental

**orientation** [ɔʀjɑ̃tasjɔ̃] *f* ❶ (*position: d'une maison*) aspect; (*du soleil, d'un phare, d'une antenne, d'un avion, navire*) direction ❷ (*tendance, direction: d'une enquête, d'un établissement*) tendency; (*d'une campagne, d'un parti politique*) trend ❸ PSYCH, ECOLE guidance

**orienté(e)** [ɔʀjɑ̃te] *adj* oriented

**orienter** [ɔʀjɑ̃te] <1> I. *vt* ❶ (*diriger: carte, plan*) to turn; **~ une antenne/ un phare vers** [*o* **sur**] **qc** to position [o turn] an antenna/headlight toward sth ❷ (*guider*) ~ **une activité/conversation vers qc** to turn an activity/conversation toward sth; ~ **un visiteur vers qc** to direct a visitor toward sth ❸ PSYCH, ECOLE to guide ❹ MATH (*droite, grandeur*) to orient **II.** *vpr* ❶ *a. fig* **s'**~ to find one's bearings ❷ (*se tourner vers*) **s'**~ **vers qc** to turn toward sth; **s'**~ **au nord** (*vent*) to move around to the north

**origan** [ɔʀigɑ̃] *m* oregano

**originaire** [ɔʀiʒinɛʀ] *adj* **être** ~ **d'une ville/d'un pays** to originally come from a town/country

**original** [ɔʀiʒinal, -o] <-aux> *m* original

**original(e)** [ɔʀiʒinal, -o] <-aux> **I.** *adj* ❶ (*premier: édition, titre*) first ❷ (*inédit, personnel, authentique: texte, version, gravure, idée*) original ❸ *péj* (*bizarre*) eccentric **II.** *m(f)* eccentric

**originalité** [ɔʀiʒinalite] *f* ❶ (*nouveauté*) novelty ❷ (*élément original*) originality ❸ *péj* (*bizarrerie: d'une personne*) eccentricity

**origine** [ɔʀiʒin] *f* ❶ (*commencement*) beginning; **à l'**~ in the beginning ❷ (*cause: d'un échec*) cause; **quelle est l'**~ **de …?** what caused this …? ❸ (*ascendance, provenance*) origin ▶ **être à l'**~ **de qc** (*personne*) to be behind sth; **être à l'**~ **d'un mal** (*chose*) to be the cause of an evil; **appellation d'**~ label of origin; **être d'**~ **française/ouvrière** to have French origins/a working-class background; **d'**~ **paysanne/noble** from peasant/noble stock

**O.R.L.** [ɔɛʀɛl] **I.** *mf abr de* **oto-rhino-laryngologiste** E.N.T. specialist **II.** *f abr de* **oto-rhino-laryngologie** E.N.T.

**ornement** [ɔʀnəmɑ̃] *m* ❶ (*chose décorative*) ornament; **arbre/plante d'**~ ornamental tree/plant ❷ (*décoration*) adornment; ARCHIT, ART embellishment

**orner** [ɔʀne] <1> **I.** *vt* ❶ (*parer*) to adorn; (*style, vérité*) to embellish ❷ (*servir d'ornement*) to decorate; **être orné de qc** (*objet, vêtements*) to be decorated with sth; (*mur, pièce, salle*)

to be adorned with sth **II.** *vpr* **s'**~ **de qc** (*personne*) to adorn oneself with sth; (*chose*) to be decorated with sth

**ornière** [ɔʀnjɛʀ] *f* rut

**orphelin(e)** [ɔʀfəlɛ̃, in] **I.** *adj* orphan; ~ **de père** fatherless; ~ **de mère** motherless **II.** *m(f)* orphan

**orphelinat** [ɔʀfəlina] *m* orphanage

**orteil** [ɔʀtɛj] *m* toe

**orthographe** [ɔʀtɔgʀaf] *f* spelling; **quelle est l'**~ **de votre nom?** how do you spell your name?; **les fautes d'**~ spelling mistakes

**orthopédique** [ɔʀtɔpedik] *adj* orthopedic

**orthopédiste** [ɔʀtɔpedist] *mf* orthopedist

**orthophoniste** [ɔʀtɔfɔnist] *mf* speech therapist

**ortie** [ɔʀti] *f* (stinging) nettle

**os** [ɔs, -o] <os> *m* ❶ (*matière*) *a.* ANAT bone; ~ **à moelle** marrowbone; **en** ~ bone ❷ *pl* (*ossements, restes*) bones ▶ **il y a un** ~ *inf* there's a snag; **tomber sur un** ~ *inf* to come across a snag

**osciller** [ɔsile] <1> *vi* (*balancer*) to oscillate; (*personne*) to rock; (*tête*) to shake; (*flamme*) to flicker; (*pendule*) to swing

**osé(e)** [oze] *adj* ❶ (*téméraire*) daring; (*démarche, expédition*) risky ❷ (*choquant*) bold

**oseille** [ozɛj] *f* ❶ BOT sorrel ❷ *inf* (*argent*) bread, dough

**oser** [oze] <1> **I.** *vt* ❶ (*risquer*) to dare ❷ (*se permettre de*) **j'ose espérer que …** I hope that …; **si j'ose dire** if I may say so **II.** *vi* to dare

**osier** [ozje] *m* willow; **panier/meubles en** ~ wicker basket/furniture

**osseux, -euse** [ɔsø, -øz] *adj* ❶ (*relatif aux os*) bone ❷ (*maigre: corps, main*) bony

**ostentatoire** [ɔstɑ̃tatwaʀ] *adj* soutenu (*luxe, consommation*) ostentatious

**otage** [ɔtaʒ] *m* hostage

**ôter** [ote] <1> **I.** *vt* ❶ (*retirer*) to remove; ~ **sa chemise/ses gants** to take one's shirt/gloves off ❷ (*faire disparaî-*

**O**

*tre*) ~ **un goût/une odeur** to get rid of a taste/smell ➌ (*débarrasser*) ~ **qc** (*menottes, pansements*) to take sth off; (*prendre: objet, envie*) to take sth away; (*illusion*) to dispel ➍ (*retrancher*) ~ **un nom d'une liste** to take a name out of a list II. *vpr* (*s'écarter*) **s'~** to get out of the way ▶ **ôte-toi de là que je m'y mette!** *iron, inf* move out of the way!

**otite** [ɔtit] *f* ear infection

**oto-rhino-laryngologiste** [ɔtɔʀinolaʀɛ̃gɔlɔʒist] <oto-rhino-laryngologistes> *mf* ear, nose and throat specialist

**ou** [u] *conj* ➊ (*alternative, approximation, en d'autres termes*) or; ~ (**bien**) or; ~ (**bien**) ... ~ (**bien**) ... either ... or ...; **c'est l'un ~ l'autre** it's one or the other ➋ (*sinon*) (*alors*) otherwise; **tu m'écoutes, ~ alors tu ...** listen to me, or out you ...

**où** [u] **I.** *pron* ➊ (*spatial*) where; **là ~** where; **je le suis partout ~ il va** I follow him everywhere he goes; **d'~ il vient** where he comes from; (*duquel*) which it comes from; **jusqu'~** how far; **par ~ il faut aller** the way to go; **le chemin par ~ nous sommes passés** the way we came ➋ (*temporel: jour, matin, soir*) when, on which; (*moment*) when, at which; (*année, siècle*) in which ➌ (*abstrait*) **à l'allure ~ il va** at the speed he's going; **au prix ~ j'ai acheté cet appareil** at the price I paid for this camera; **dans l'état ~ tu es** in the state you're in **II.** *adv interrog* ➊ (*spatial*) where; ~ **s'arrêter?** where does one stop?; ~ **aller?** where can we go?; **d'~ êtes-vous?** where are you from?; **jusqu'~** *a. fig* how far; **par ~** which way ➋ (*abstrait*) ~ **en étais-je?** where was I?; ~ **voulez-vous en venir?** what are you leading up to? **III.** *adv indéf* ➊ (*là où*) where; **par ~ que vous passiez** wherever you went ➋ (*de là*) **d'~ que vienne le vent** wherever the wind comes from; **d'~ l'on peut conclure que ...** from which one can

conclude that ...; **d'~ mon étonnement** hence my surprise

**ouate** [wat] *f* ~ (**hydrophile**) cotton (wadding)

**oubli** [ubli] *m* ➊ (*perte du souvenir*) forgetfulness; ~ **de son nom** forgetting her name; **tomber dans l'~** to be forgotten ➋ (*étourderie*) oversight; **réparer un ~** to make up for an oversight; **par ~** due to an oversight ➌ (*lacune*) lapse (of memory) ➍ (*manquement à: du devoir filial, d'une promesse, règle*) neglect

**oublier** [ublije] <1> **I.** *vt* ➊ (*ne plus se rappeler*) to forget; **être oublié par qn/qc** to be forgotten by sb/sth; **qc ne doit pas faire ~ que ...** sth must not let us forget that ... ➋ (*négliger*) to forget; **se sentir oublié** to feel forgotten; **il ne faudrait pas ~ que** one must not forget that; **sans ~ le patron/les accessoires** without forgetting the boss/the accessories ➌ (*omettre*) to omit; (*mot, virgule*) to leave out ➍ (*évacuer de son esprit: injure, querelle*) to forget ➎ (*manquer à*) to neglect ➏ (*laisser par inadvertance*) ~ **qc** to leave sth behind ▶ **se faire** ~ to keep out of sight **II.** *vpr* ➊ (*sortir de l'esprit*) **qn/qc s'oublie** sb/sth is forgotten ➋ (*ne pas penser à soi*) **s'~** not to think of oneself; **ne pas s'~** to remember number one ➌ (*se laisser aller*) **s'~** to forget oneself ➍ (*faire ses besoins*) **s'~** (*personne, animal*) to have an accident

**ouest** [wɛst] **I.** *m* **l'~** the west; **à** [*o* **dans**] **l'~** in the west; **à** [*o* **vers**] **l'~** to the west; **à l'~ de qc** west of sth; **vent d'~** westerly wind; **les régions de l'~** the western regions **II.** *adj inv* westerly; (*banlieue, longitude, partie*) western

**Ouest** [wɛst] *m* West; **les pays de l'~** the West; **les gens de l'~** Westerners

**oui** [´wi] **I.** *adv* ➊ (*opp: non*) yes; ~ **ou non?** yes or no?; **répondre par** ~ **ou par non** to give a yes or no reply ➋ (*intensif*) yes indeed; **ah** [*o* **ça**] ~, (**alors**)! oh yes!; **hé** ~**!** oh yes!; **alors, tu arri-**

**ves, ~?** *inf* so are you coming then?; **que ~!** *inf* I should say so! ③(*substitut d'une proposition*) **croire/penser que ~** to believe/think so; **craindre/dire que ~** to fear/say so; **je dirais que ~** I would think so II. *m inv* ①(*approbation*) yes; **~ à qn/qc** yes to sb/sth ②(*suffrage*) aye ▶**pour un ~ (ou) pour un non** at the least thing

**ouïe** [wi] *f* (*sens*) hearing; zool gill

**ouragan** [uʀaɡɑ̃] *m* ①(*tempête*) hurricane ②(*déchaînement*) storm ③(*personne déchaînée*) whirlwind

**ours** [uʀs] I. *m* ①zool bear; **~ blanc [o polaire]/brun** polar/brown bear; *v.a.* **ourse** ②(*jouet d'enfant*) **un ~ en peluche** a teddy bear ③*inf* (*misanthrope*) old bear II. *adj inv, inf* gruff

**ourse** [uʀs] *f* she-bear; *v.a.* **ours** ▶**la Grande/Petite Ourse** the Big/Little Dipper

**oursin** [uʀsɛ̃] *m* sea urchin

**outil** [uti] *m* (*instrument, moyen*) a. inform tool

**outrage** [utʀaʒ] *m* insult; **~ à agent** insulting a police officer; **~ à magistrat** contempt of court

**outrance** [utʀɑ̃s] *f* extravagance; **à ~** to excess

**outre¹** [utʀ] *f* (*sac*) goatskin

**outre²** [utʀ] I. *prep* (*en plus de*) as well as; **~ le fait que cela est connu** besides the fact that it is known II. *adv* **en ~** moreover

**outré(e)** [utʀe] *adj* ①(*indigné*) outraged ②(*excessif*) overdone

**outremer** [utʀəmeʀ] I. *m* ①(*en minéralogie*) lapis lazuli ②(*bleu*) ultramarine II. *adj inv* ultramarine

**outre-mer** [utʀəmeʀ] *adv* overseas

**outrepasser** [utʀəpɑse] <1> *vt* (*droits, limites, pouvoir*) to overstep; (*ordre*) to exceed

**ouvert(e)** [uveʀ, ɛʀt] I. *part passé de* **ouvrir** II. *adj* open; (*robinet*) on; **être ~ à qn/qc** to be open to sb/sth

**ouverture** [uveʀtyʀ] *f* ①(*action d'ouvrir; fait de rendre accessible au public, inauguration*) opening; (*d'un robinet*)

turning on; **les jours/heures d'~** opening days/times; **l'~ au public** opening to the public ②(*commencement*) opening ③(*orifice*) opening; (*d'un volcan*) mouth ④(*attitude ouverte*) openness; **~ d'esprit** open-mindedness ⑤*pl* (*avance, proposition: de négociations, paix*) overtures ⑥mus overture ⑦phot aperture ⑧com, jur (*d'un compte, d'une information judiciaire*) reading; (*d'un crédit*) setting up; (*d'une succession*) reading ⑨inform **~ d'une session** login

**ouvrable** [uvʀabl] *adj* working

**ouvrage** [uvʀaʒ] *m* ①(*objet fabriqué*) work; **~ de sculpture** sculpture ②(*livre*) **~ d'histoire** historical work ③(*travail*) piece of work; cout work; **se mettre à l'~** to start work

**ouvre-boîte** [uvʀəbwat] <ouvre-boîtes> *m* can opener

**ouvre-bouteille** [uvʀ(ə)butɛj] <ouvre-bouteilles> *m* bottle opener

**ouvrier, -ière** [uvʀije, -ijɛʀ] I. *adj* (*classe, mouvement, quartier*) working-class; (*conflit, législation, condition*) industrial; (*militant*) labor II. *m, f* (*travailleur manuel*) worker; **~ d'usine/spécialisé** factory/unskilled worker; **~ qualifié** skilled worker

**ouvrir** [uvʀiʀ] <11> I. *vt* ①(*opp: fermer, écarter, déployer, rendre accessible, fonder, créer, inaugurer, commencer, percer*) a. sport, jur, fin to open; (*à clé*) to unlock; **~ un crédit à qn** to set up a loan for sb ②*inf* (*faire fonctionner: chauffage, télé, robinet, gaz*) to turn on ③(*débloquer, frayer*) **~ une issue/un passage à qn/qc** to open up a way out/way through for sb/sth ④(*être en tête de: marche, procession*) to lead; **~ une liste** to head a list ⑤(*provoquer une blessure*) **~ qc** (*jambe, ventre, crâne*) to cut sth open ▶**l'~** *inf* to open one's mouth II. *vi* ①(*donner sur*) **~ sur qc** to open on to sth ②(*être accessible au public, être rendu ac-*

O

*cessible au public*) ~ **le lundi** to open on Mondays; ~ **à 15 h** to open at 3 p.m. ❸ (*commencer*) ~ **par qc** to begin with sth III. *vpr* ❶ (*opp: se fermer*) **s'~** to open; (*vêtement*) to unfasten; (*foule*) to part; **mal s'~** to open wrongly ❷ (*devenir accessible à*) **s'~ au commerce** to open up for trade ❸ (*commencer*) **s'~ par qc** to begin with sth; (*exposition, séance*) to open with sth ❹ (*se blesser*) **s'~ les veines** to slash one's wrists; **s'~ la lèvre** to split one's lip; **s'~ la jambe/le crâne** to cut one's leg/one's head open

**ovale** [ɔval] I. *adj* oval II. *m* oval
**ovation** [ɔvasjɔ̃] *f* ovation
**OVNI** [ɔvni] *m abr de* objet volant non identifié UFO
**oxyde** [ɔksid] *m* oxide; ~ **de carbone** carbon monoxide
**oxyder** [ɔkside] <1> *vt, vpr* (**s'**)~ to oxidize
**oxygène** [ɔksiʒɛn] *m* ❶ CHIM oxygen ❷ (*air pur*) fresh air ❸ (*souffle nouveau*) new lease on life
**oxygéné(e)** [ɔksiʒene] *adj* (*cheveux*) bleached; **eau ~e** hydrogen peroxide
**oxygéner** [ɔksiʒene] <5> *vpr* **s'~** to bleach one's hair
**ozone** [ozon, ɔzɔn] *f* ozone

# Pp

**P, p** [pe] *m inv* P, p; ~ **comme Pierre** (*au téléphone*) p as in Papa
**pacifique** [pasifik] *adj* peaceful; (*personne, pays, peuple*) peace-loving
**Pacifique** [pasifik] *m* **le ~** the Pacific
**pacifiste** [pasifist] I. *adj* pacifist II. *mf* pacifist
**pack** [pak] *m* pack
**pacotille** [pakɔtij] *f* ❶ (*mauvaise marchandise*) garbage; **de ~** cheap; *fig* worthless ❷ (*bijoux*) cheap jewelry
**PACS** [paks] *m abr de* pacte civil de solidarité *formal civil contract between a non-married heterosexual or homosexual couple*
**pacte** [pakt] *m* pact; ~ **d'alliance** treaty of alliance; **le ~ de Varsovie** HIST the Warsaw Pact
**pagaïe, pagaille** [pagaj] *f inf* mess ► **en** ~ in a mess; (*en quantité*) by the ton
**page** [paʒ] *f* ❶ (*feuillet*) page; **la ~ des sports d'un journal** the sports page in a newspaper; (**en**) ~ **20** on page 20; **la ~ de publicité** the ads page ❷ RADIO,

TV **la ~ de publicité** commercials ❸ INFORM ~ **d'accueil/personnelle** home page; **bas de ~** page bottom; **pied/haut de ~** footer/header ► **tourner la ~** to let bygones be bygones; (*pour recommencer*) to turn over a new leaf
**paie¹** [pɛ] *f* (*d'un ouvrier, salarié*) pay
**paie²** [pɛ] *indic et subj prés de* **payer**
**paiement** [pɛmɑ̃] *m* payment
**paillasson** [pajasɔ̃] *m* doormat
**paille** [paj] *f* ❶ *inv* (*chaume, tiges tressées*) straw ❷ (*pour boire*) (drinking) straw ► **tirer à la courte ~** to draw straws
**pain** [pɛ̃] *m* ❶ *inv* (*aliment*) bread; ~ **de seigle** rye bread ❷ (*miche*) loaf; ~ **de seigle** loaf of rye bread; ~ **au chocolat** *chocolate croissant* ❸ CULIN (*de poisson, légumes*) loaf ► **avoir du ~ sur la planche** *inf* to have a lot on one's plate; **petit ~** roll; **gagner son ~** to earn one's bread; **elle ne mange pas de ce ~-là** she won't have any of that
**pair** [pɛʀ] *m* **une jeune fille au ~** an au

pair (girl); **un jeune homme au** ~ a male au pair; **hors (de)** ~ unrivaled

**pair(e)** [pɛʀ] *adj* ❶ (*divisible par deux*) even ❷ (*au nombre de deux*) in pairs

**paire** [pɛʀ] *f* ❶ (*de chaussures, gants, lunettes*) pair; **donner une** ~ **de claques à qn** to slap sb's face ❷ (*aux cartes*) pair ►**les deux font la** ~ *inf* they're two of a kind

**paisible** [pezibl] *adj* peaceful

**paix** [pɛ] *f* ❶ (*opp: guerre, entente*) peace; **les manifestations en faveur de la** ~ peace demonstrations ❷ (*traité*) peace treaty ❸ (*tranquillité*) **la** ~**!** peace and quiet!; **avoir la** ~ to have some peace (and quiet); **laisser qn en** ~ to leave sb in peace ►**faire la** ~ **avec qn** to make (one's) peace with sb

**Pakistan** [pakistɑ̃] *m* **le** ~ Pakistan

**palais**[1] [palɛ] *m* palace; ~ **de l'Élysée** Élysée Palace (*residence of the French President*); ~ **des sports** sports stadium

**palais**[2] [palɛ] *m* ANAT palate

**pâle** [pɑl] *adj* pale

**Palestine** [palɛstin] *f* **la** ~ Palestine

**palestinien(ne)** [palɛstinjɛ̃, jɛn] *adj* Palestinian

**palette** [palɛt] *f* ❶ (*plateau de chargement*) pallet ❷ (*ensemble de couleurs, ustensile du peintre*) palette ❸ (*gamme*) ~ **de produits** range of products ❹ (*raquette*) ~ **de ping-pong** *Québec* Ping-Pong® paddle

**palier** [palje] *m* (*plateforme d'escalier*) landing; **habiter sur le même** ~ to live on the same floor

**pâlir** [paliʀ] <8> *vi* (*devenir pâle*) to turn pale ►~ **d'envie** to turn green with envy

**palissade** [palisad] *f* fence

**palpitant(e)** [palpitɑ̃, ɑ̃t] *adj* thrilling

**pamplemousse** [pɑ̃pləmus] *m* CULIN grapefruit

**panaché** [panaʃe] *m* shandy

**pancarte** [pɑ̃kaʀt] *f* notice; (*d'un manifestant*) placard; ~ **électorale/publicitaire** election/publicity poster

**panier** [panje] *m* ❶ (*corbeille*) basket; ~ **à provisions** shopping basket; ~ **à salade** salad shaker ❷ (*contenu*) ~ **de cerises** basket of cherries ❸ (*au basket-ball*) basket

**panique** [panik] **I.** *f* panic; **être pris de** ~ to panic; **pas de** ~**!** don't panic! **II.** *adj* (*peur, terreur*) panic-stricken

**paniquer** [panike] <1> **I.** *vt inf* ~ **qn** to scare the daylights out of sb; **être paniqué de devoir** +*infin* to be panicking about having to +*infin* **II.** *vi inf* to panic **III.** *vpr* **se** ~ to panic

**panne** [pan] *f* ❶ (*arrêt de fonctionnement*) breakdown; ~ **de courant** power failure; ~ **de moteur** engine failure; **tomber en** ~ to break down; **être en** ~ (*automobiliste, voiture, moteur*) to have broken down; (*machine*) to be out of order ❷ *inf* (*manque*) **je suis en** ~ **de café** I am out of coffee

**panneau** [pano] <x> *m* ❶ AUTO ~ **de signalisation** road sign ❷ AVIAT, CHEMDFER ~ **horaire** (*des arrivées*) arrivals board; (*des départs*) departures board ❸ (*pancarte*) board; ~ **d'affichage** (*pour petites annonces, résultats*) bulletin board; (*pour publicité*) billboard ❹ (*au basket-ball*) backboard ❺ TECH ~ **solaire** solar panel

**panoramique** [panɔʀamik] *adj* panoramic; (*restaurant*) with a panoramic view; **écran** ~ CINE wide screen

**pansement** [pɑ̃smɑ̃] *m* ❶ (*action*) **faire un** ~ **à qn** to bandage sb up ❷ (*compresse*) dressing; ~ **adhésif** Band-Aid®

**pantalon** [pɑ̃talɔ̃] *m* (*pair of*) pants

**panthère** [pɑ̃tɛʀ] *f* ZOOL panther

**pantin** [pɑ̃tɛ̃] *m* (*marionnette*) jumping jack

**pantomime** [pɑ̃tɔmim] *f* ❶ *sans pl* (*jeu du mime*) mime ❷ (*pièce mimée*) mime (show) ❸ (*comédie*) scene

**pantouflard(e)** [pɑ̃tuflaʀ, aʀd] *inf* **I.** *adj* stay-at-home **II.** *m(f)* stay-at-home

**pantoufle** [pɑ̃tufl] *f* slipper

**paon** [pɑ̃] *m* ZOOL peacock

**papa** [papa] *m* dad(dy)

**papauté** [papote] *f* papacy

**pape** [pap] *m* REL pope

**P**

**paperasse** [papʀas] *f péj* ❶(*papiers inutiles à lire*) (useless) papers *pl*; (*papiers à remplir*) forms *pl* ❷(*grosse quantité de papiers*) stack of paper(s)

**papeterie** [papɛtʀi] *f* ❶(*magasin*) stationery store ❷(*fabrication*) paper-making (industry) ❸(*usine*) paper mill

**papi** [papi] *m enfantin, inf* v. **papy**

**papier** [papje] *m* ❶*sans pl* (*matière*) paper; **bout/feuille/morceau de ~** bit/sheet/piece of paper; **~ hygiénique** toilet paper; **~ peint** wallpaper ❷(*feuille*) piece of paper; (*à remplir*) form ❸(*article*) article ❹(*document*) paper ❺*pl* (*papiers d'identité*) papers

**papier-filtre** [papjefiltʀ] <papiers-filtres> *m* filter paper

**papier-toilette** [papjetwalɛt] <papiers-toilette> *m* toilet paper

**papillon** [papijɔ̃] *m* ❶zool butterfly; **~ de nuit** moth ❷sport (*nage*) ~ butterfly (stroke)

**papillonner** [papijɔne] <1> *vi* to flit around

**papillote** [papijɔt] *f* ❶(*pour les bonbons*) candy wrapper ❷culin **en ~** cooked wrapped in greaseproof paper or foil

**papoter** [papɔte] <1> *vi* to chatter

**paprika** [papʀika] *m* culin paprika

**papy** [papi] *m enfantin, inf* grandpa

**paquebot** [pakbo] *m* naut liner

**pâquerette** [pɑkʀɛt] *f* bot daisy

**Pâques** [pɑk] **I.** *m* Easter; **lundi/œuf/vacances de ~** Easter Monday/egg/vacation **II.** *fpl* Easter; **joyeuses ~!** Happy Easter!

**paquet** [pakɛ] *m* ❶(*boîte*) packet; (*de café, sucre*) bag; (*de cigarettes*) pack; (*de linge, vêtements*) bundle ❷(*colis*) parcel ❸*inf* (*grande quantité: de billets*) wad; (*d'eau*) torrent; (*de neige*) heap ❹inform packet ▶ **être un ~ de nerfs** *inf* to be a bundle of nerves; **mettre le ~** *inf* to pull out all the stops; (*payer beaucoup*) to spare no expense

**paquet-cadeau** [pakɛkado] <paquets-cadeaux> *m* gift-wrapped package

**par** [paʀ] *prep* ❶(*grâce à l'action de, au moyen de*) by; **tout faire ~ soi-même** to do everything by oneself; **~ chèque/carte bancaire** by check/debit card; **~ tous les moyens** using all possible means ❷(*origine*) **un oncle ~ alliance** an uncle by marriage; **descendre de qn ~ sa mère** to descend from sb on one's mother's side ❸*gén sans art* (*cause, motif*) through; **~ sottise/devoir** out of stupidity/duty ❹(*à travers, via*) **regarder ~ la fenêtre** to look out the window; **venir ~ le chemin le plus court** to come (by) the shortest way; **est-il passé ~ ici?** did he come this way? ❺(*localisation*) **habiter ~ ici/là** to live around here/there (somewhere); **~ 5 mètres de fond** at a depth of 5 meters; **être assis ~ terre** to be sitting on the ground; **tomber ~ terre** to fall to the ground ❻(*distribution, mesure*) by; **un ~ un** one by one; **heure ~ heure** hour by hour; **~ moments** at times; **~ centaines/milliers** in their hundreds/thousands ❼(*durant, pendant*) **~ temps de brouillard** in fog; **~ temps de pluie** in wet weather; **~ les temps qui courent** these days; **~ le passé** in the past ▶ **~ contre** on the other hand

**parabole** [paʀabɔl] *f* ❶rel parable ❷math parabola ❸(*antenne*) satellite dish

**parabolique** [paʀabɔlik] *adj* parabolic; **antenne ~** tel satellite dish

**parachute** [paʀaʃyt] *m* parachute; **sauter en ~** to parachute

**parachutiste** [paʀaʃytist] **I.** *adj* mil unité ~ paratroop unit **II.** *mf* ❶mil paratrooper ❷sport parachutist

**paradis** [paʀadi] *m* paradise ▶ **tu ne l'emporteras pas au ~** you won't get away with that

**paradisiaque** [paʀadizjak] *adj* heavenly

**paradoxal(e)** [paʀadɔksal, -o] <-aux> *adj* paradoxical

**paragraphe** [paʀagʀaf] *m a.* typ (*alinéa: d'un devoir, texte*) paragraph

**paraître** [paʀɛtʀ] *irr* **I.** *vi* ❶(*sembler*)

~ +*infin* to appear to +*infin;* **cela me paraît** (**être**) **une erreur** it looks like a mistake to me ② (*apparaître: personne*) to appear ③ (*être publié: journal, livre*) to come out; **faire ~ qc** (*maison d'édition*) to bring sth out; (*auteur*) to have sth published ④ (*être visible: sentiment*) to show ⑤ (*se mettre en valeur*) **aimer ~** to like to show off; **désir de ~** to want to be noticed **II.** *vi impers* **il me paraît difficile de** +*infin* it strikes me as difficult to +*infin;* **il lui paraît impossible que** +*subj* it seems impossible to him that ▶**il paraît que qn va** +*infin* it seems that sb is going to +*infin;* (*soi-disant*) sb is apparently going to +*infin;* **il paraîtrait que ...** it would seem that ...; **il paraît que oui!** so it seems!; **sans qu'il y paraisse** without it showing

**parallèle** [paralɛl] **I.** *adj* ❶ (*en double*) *a.* MATH parallel ❷ (*non officiel: marché, police*) unofficial **II.** *f* MATH parallel (líne) **III.** *m* parallel

**parallèlement** [paralɛlmɑ̃] *adv* ❶ (*dans l'espace*) in parallel ❷ (*dans le temps*) at the same time

**paralysé(e)** [paralize] **I.** *adj* (*bras, personne*) paralyzed **II.** *m(f)* paralytic

**paralyser** [paralize] <1> *vt* to paralyze

**paralysie** [paralizi] *f* paralysis

**paramètre** [paramɛtR] *m* parameter

**parapente** [parapɑ̃t] *m* ❶ (*parachute rectangulaire*) parachute ❷ (*sport*) paragliding

**parapluie** [paraplɥi] *m* umbrella

**parasite** [parazit] **I.** *adj* parasitic(al) **II.** *m* ❶ (*profiteur*) *a.* BIO parasite ❷ *pl* RADIO, TV interference

**parasol** [parasɔl] *m* parasol

**paratonnerre** [paratɔnɛR] *m* lightning rod

**paravent** [paravɑ̃] *m* screen

**parc** [paRk] *m* ❶ (*jardin*) park; **~ botanique** botanic(al) garden(s); **~ d'attractions** amusement park ❷ (*région protégée*) **~ naturel** nature reserve; **~ national** national park ❸ (*bassin d'élevage*) **~ à huîtres/moules** oyster/mussel

bed ❹ (*pour bébé*) playpen ❺ (*emplacement*) **~ des expositions** exhibition hall

**parcelle** [paRsɛl] *f* (*terrain*) parcel of land

**parce que** [paRskə] *conj* because

**par-ci** [paRsi] **~, par-là** here and there

**parcmètre** [paRkmɛtR] *m* parking meter

**parcourir** [paRkuRiR] *vt irr* ❶ (*accomplir: trajet, distance*) to cover ❷ (*traverser, sillonner: ville, rue*) to go through; (*en tous sens: ville, rue*) to go all over; (*rue*) to go up and down; (*région, pays*) to travel through; (*en tous sens: région, pays*) to travel the length and breadth of; **~ une région** (*navire*) to sail through a region; (*ruisseau*) to run through a region; (*objet volant*) to fly through a region ❸ (*examiner rapidement: journal, lettre, texte*) to glance through; **~ qc des yeux** to run one's eye over sth

**parcours** [paRkuR] *m* ❶ (*trajet: d'un véhicule*) trip; (*d'un fleuve*) course ❷ SPORT (*piste*) course; (*épreuve*) round

**par-derrière** [paRdɛRjɛR] *adv* ❶ (*opp: par-devant: attaquer, emboutir*) from behind ❷ (*dans le dos de qn*) **~ qn** behind sb; *fig* (*raconter, critiquer*) behind sb's back

**par-dessous** [paRdəsu] *prep, adv* under(neath)

**par-dessus** [paRdəsy] **I.** *prep* over (the top of) **II.** *adv* over (the top)

**pardessus** [paRdəsy] *m* overcoat

**pardon** [paRdɔ̃] *m* forgiveness, REL pardon; **demander ~ à qn** to apologize to sb ▶**~?** (I beg your) pardon?

**pardonner** [paRdɔne] <1> **I.** *vt* (*absoudre*) **~ qc à qn** to forgive sb for sth ▶**pardonne-moi/pardonnez-moi** excuse [*o* pardon] me **II.** *vi* ❶ (*être fatal*) **ne pas ~** (*maladie, poison, erreur*) to be very unforgiving ❷ (*absoudre*) to forgive

**paré(e)** [paRe] *adj* **être ~ contre qc** to be prepared for sth

**pare-brise** [paRbRiz] *m inv* AUTO windshield

P

**pare-chocs** [paʀʃɔk] *m inv* AUTO ~ **ar-rière/avant** rear/front bumper

**pareil(le)** [paʀɛj] **I.** *adj* ❶ *(identique)* the same; **être ~ à** [*o* **que**] **qn/qc** to be the same as sb/sth ❷ *(tel)* **une voitu-re/idée/vie ~le** a car/an idea/a life like that, such a car/an idea/a life **II.** *m/f* **c'est du ~ au même** *inf* it makes no difference; **sans ~** unparalleled **III.** *adv inf (s'habiller)* the same

**pareillement** [paʀɛjmɑ̃] *adv* ❶ *(également)* likewise; **Bonne Année! – à vous ~!** Happy New Year! – (and) the same to you! ❷ *(de la même façon)* the same

**parent** [paʀɑ̃] *m* parent

**parent(e)** [paʀɑ̃, ɑ̃t] *m/f (personne de la famille)* relative

**parenté** [paʀɑ̃te] *f* ❶ *(lien familial, ana-logie)* relationship ❷ *(ensemble des pa-rents)* relatives *pl*

**parenthèse** [paʀɑ̃tɛz] *f* ❶ TYP, MATH bracket ❷ *(digression)* parenthesis ❸ *(incident)* interlude ▸ **mettre qc en-tre ~s** to put sth in brackets; *(oublier provisoirement)* to set sth aside

**paresse** [paʀɛs] *f* laziness

**paresser** [paʀese] <1> *vi* ~ **au lit** to laze around in bed

**paresseux, -euse** [paʀesø, -øz] **I.** *adj* lazy; *(attitude)* casual **II.** *m, f* lazy per-son

**parfait** [paʀfɛ] *m* ❶ LING perfect ❷ CULIN parfait

**parfait(e)** [paʀfɛ, ɛt] *adj* ❶ *(sans dé-faut)* perfect; *(beauté)* flawless ❷ *(qui répond exactement à un concept)* per-fect; *(discrétion)* absolute; *(ignorance)* complete ❸ *antéposé (modèle: gentle-man, idiot)* perfect; *(crapule, filou)* ut-ter

**parfaitement** [paʀfɛtmɑ̃] *adv* ❶ *(de fa-çon parfaite)* perfectly; **parler ~ fran-çais** to speak perfect French ❷ *(tout à fait: idiot, ridicule)* perfectly ❸ *(oui, bien sûr)* absolutely

**parfois** [paʀfwa] *adv* sometimes

**parfum** [paʀfɛ̃] *m* ❶ *(substance)* per-fume ❷ *(odeur)* scent ❸ CULIN flavor

**parfumerie** [paʀfymʀi] *f* ❶ *(magasin)* perfume shop ❷ *(usine, fabrication)* perfumery ❸ *(produits)* perfumes *pl*

**pari** [paʀi] *m* bet

**parier** [paʀje] <1> **I.** *vt* ❶ ~ **qc à qn** to bet sb sth; ~ **qc sur qn/qc** to bet sth on sb/sth; **tu paries que j'y arrive!** you bet I'll do it! **II.** *vi* to bet; ~ **sur qn/qc** to bet on sb/sth

**Paris** [paʀi] *m* Paris

**parisien(ne)** [paʀizjɛ̃, jɛn] *adj (ban-lieue, métro, mode)* Paris *avant subst; (personne, société, vie)* Parisian

**Parisien(ne)** [paʀizjɛ̃, jɛn] *m/f* Parisian

**parka** [paʀka] *m o f* parka, anorak

**parking** [paʀkiŋ] *m* AUTO parking lot

**Parlement** [paʀləmɑ̃] *m* ~ **européen** European Parliament

**parlementaire** [paʀləmɑ̃tɛʀ] **I.** *adj* par-liamentary **II.** *mf* ❶ *(député)* Member of Parliament; *(aux Etats-Unis)* Con-gressman, -woman *m, f* ❷ *(médiateur)* mediator

**parler** [paʀle] <1> **I.** *vi* ❶ *(prendre la parole)* to talk ❷ *(exprimer)* to speak; ~ **avec les mains** to use one's hands when talking; ~ **par gestes** to use sign language ❸ *(converser, discuter)* ~ **de qn/qc avec qn** to talk about sb/sth with sb ❹ *(entretenir)* ~ **de qn/qc à qn** *(dans un but précis)* to talk about sb/sth to sb; *(raconter)* to tell sb about sb/sth ❺ *(adresser la parole)* ~ **à qn** to speak to sb ❻ *(avoir pour sujet)* ~ **de qn/qc** *(article, film, journal, livre)* to be about sb/sth; *(brièvement)* to men-tion sb/sth ❼ *(en s'exprimant de telle manière)* **généralement/légalement parlant** generally/legally speaking ▸ **faire ~ de soi** to get oneself talked about; **sans ~ de qn/qc** not to mention sb/sth **II.** *vt* ❶ *(être bilingue: langue)* to speak ❷ *(aborder un sujet)* ~ **affai-res/politique** to talk business/politics **III.** *vpr* ❶ *(être employé)* **se ~** *(langue)* to be spoken ❷ *(s'entretenir: person-nes)* to talk to each other; **se ~ à soi--même** to talk to oneself ❸ *(s'adresser la parole)* **ne plus se ~** to not speak to each other anymore **IV.** *m* ❶ (*manière*) speech ❷ (*langue régionale*) dialect

**parlophone**® [paʀlɔfɔn] *m Belgique* intercom

**parmi** [paʀmi] *prep* (*entre*) among(st); ~ **la foule** in the crowd

**parodie** [paʀɔdi] *f* parody

**paroisse** [paʀwas] *f* parish

**parole** [paʀɔl] *f* ❶ *souvent pl* (*mot*) word; **une ~ célèbre** a famous saying; **la ~ de Dieu** the word of God ❷ (*promesse*) ~ **d'honneur** word of honor; **c'est un homme de ~** he's a man of his word; **tu peux la croire sur ~** you can take her word for it ❸ *sans pl* (*faculté de parler*) speech; **perdre/retrouver la ~** to lose/regain one's speech ❹ *sans pl* (*fait de parler*) **ne plus adresser la ~ à qn** to not speak to sb anymore; **couper la ~ à qn** to cut sb short ❺ *sans pl* (*droit de parler*) **demander/prendre la ~** to ask/begin to speak; **avoir la ~** to be speaking; **donner la ~ à qn** to invite sb to speak; **temps de ~** speaking time ❻ *pl* MUS (*de chanson classique*) words; (*de chanson populaire*) lyrics ▶ **ma ~!** (*je le jure!*) cross my heart!; (*exprimant l'étonnement*) my word!

**parquet** [paʀkɛ] *m* ❶ (*plancher*) parquet (floor) ❷ JUR public prosecutor's office

**parrain** [paʀɛ̃] *m* ❶ REL godfather ❷ (*celui qui parraine qn/qc: d'un athlète, festival, théâtre*) sponsor; (*d'un artiste, projet, d'une fondation*) patron; (*d'une entreprise, initiative*) promoter ❸ *fig* (*de la mafia*) godfather

**parrainer** [paʀɛne] <1> *vt* ❶ (*apporter son soutien à: athlète, festival, théâtre*) to sponsor; (*artiste, projet, fondation*) to support; (*entreprise, initiative*) to promote ❷ (*introduire*) to sponsor

**parsemer** [paʀsəme] <4> *vt* ❶ (*répandre*) ~ **un gâteau de qc** to sprinkle a cake with sth; ~ **son devoir/son discours de qc** to pepper one's homework/one's speech with sth ❷ (*être répandu sur*) ~ **le sol** to be strewn around on the ground

**part** [paʀ] *f* ❶ (*portion*) share; (*de gâteau*) piece; (*de légumes*) helping, portion ❷ (*partie*) part ❸ (*participation*) ~ **dans qc** part in sth; **avoir ~ à qc** to be involved in sth; **prendre ~ à qc** to take part in sth; **prendre ~ aux frais** to make a contribution toward the costs ❹ FIN share ▶ **faire la ~ des choses** to take everything into account; **autre ~** *inf* somewhere else; **d'autre ~** moreover; **d'une ~ ..., d'autre ~ ...** on the one hand ..., on the other (hand) ...; **de ~ et d'autre de qn/qc** on both sides of sb/sth; **citoyen à ~ entière** full citizen; **nulle ~** nowhere; **de toute(s) ~(s)** from all sides; **faire ~ de qc à qn** to inform sb of sth; **prendre qn à ~** to take sb aside; **cas/place à ~** unique case/place; **mettre qc à ~** to put sth aside; **à ~ lui/cela** apart from him/that; **à ~ que qn a fait qc** *inf* apart from the fact that sb has done sth; **de ma/sa ~** from me/him; **de la ~ de qn** (*au nom de*) on behalf of sb; **donner à qn le bonjour de la ~ de qn** to give sb sb's regards; **pour ma/sa ~** as far as I'm/he's concerned

**partage** [paʀtaʒ] *m* ❶ (*division: d'un terrain, gâteau, butin*) dividing up ❷ (*répartition: d'un trésor, d'aliments*) sharing out; (*d'un appartement*) sharing; (*des voix*) distribution ▶ **régner sans ~** to rule absolutely

**partager** [paʀtaʒe] <2a> **I.** *vt* ❶ (*diviser: gâteau, pièce, terrain*) to divide (up); ~ **qc en qc** to divide sth (up) into sth ❷ (*répartir*) ~ **qc entre des personnes/choses/qc et qc** to share sth between people/things/sth and sth ❸ (*avoir en commun: appartement, frais, bénéfices, passions, goûts, responsabilité*) to share ❹ (*s'associer à*) ~ **l'avis de qn** to share sb's point of view; ~ **la surprise de qn** to be just as surprised as sb; **être partagé** (*frais*) to be shared, (*avis*) to be divided, (*plaisir, amour*) to be mutual ❺ (*donner une part de ce que l'on possède*) ~ **qc avec qn** to share sth with sb ❻ (*hésiter*) **être partagé entre qc et qc** to be torn between sth and sth ❼ (*être d'opinion différente*) **ils sont partagés sur qc/en ce qui concerne qc** they are divided on sth/as far as sth is concerned II. *vpr* ❶ (*se diviser*) **se ~ en qc** to be divided into sth ❷ (*se répartir*) **se ~ qc** to share sth between themselves; **se ~ entre** (*voix*) to be divided between

**partagiciel** [paʀtaʒisjɛl] *m Québec* IN-FORM shareware

**partance** [paʀtɑ̃s] **être en ~** (*avion*) to be about to take off; (*train*) to be about to depart; (*bateau*) to be about to set sail

**partant(e)** [paʀtɑ̃, ɑ̃t] I. *adj inf* **être ~ pour qc** to be ready for sth; **je suis ~!** count me in! II. *m(f)* ❶ (*opp: arrivant*) person leaving ❷ SPORT starter

**partenaire** [paʀtənɛʀ] *mf* partner

**parti** [paʀti] *m* ❶ POL party; **~ de droite/gauche** right-wing/left-wing party ❷ (*camp*) **se ranger du ~ de qn** to side with sb ❸ (*personne à marier*) match ▸ **~ pris** prejudice; **prendre ~ pour qn** to take sb's side; **prendre ~ contre qn** to side against sb; **prendre le ~ de** +*infin* to make up one's mind to +*infin*

**parti(e)** [paʀti] *part passé de* **partir**

**partial(e)** [paʀsjal, -jo] <-aux> *adj* (*juge*) biased; (*critique*) prejudiced

**participant(e)** [paʀtisipɑ̃, ɑ̃t] I. *adj* **personnes ~es** participants II. *m(f)* (*à une débat*) participant; (*à un concours*) entrant

**participation** [paʀtisipasjɔ̃] *f* ❶ (*présence, contribution*) participation; **~ électorale** voter turnout ❷ (*partage*) **~ aux bénéfices** profit sharing ❸ (*droit de regard*) involvement

**participe** [paʀtisip] *m* LING participle

**participer** [paʀtisipe] <1> *vi* ❶ (*prendre part*) **~ à une réunion/à un colloque** to take part in a meeting/in a seminar ❷ (*collaborer*) **~ à la conversation** to join in the conversation ❸ (*payer*) **~ aux frais** to contribute to the costs

**particularité** [paʀtikylaʀite] *f* ❶ (*caractère*) particularity ❷ (*caractéristique*)

distinctive feature; **qn/qc a la ~ de ...** a distinctive feature of sb/sth is that ...

**particulier** [paʀtikylje] *m* ❶ (*personne privée*) individual ❷ ADMIN, COM private individual

**particulier, -ière** [paʀtikylje, -jɛʀ] *adj* ❶ (*spécifique: aspect, exemple*) particular; (*trait*) characteristic; **"signes ~s (néant)"** "distinguishing features (none)" ❷ (*spécial*) particular; (*aptitude, cas*) special ❸ (*privé: conversation, leçon, secrétaire*) private ❹ (*étrange*) peculiar; **être d'un genre ~** to be a little strange ▸ **en ~** (*en privé*) in private; (*notamment*) in particular; (*séparément*) separately

**particulièrement** [paʀtikyljɛʀmɑ̃] *adv* particularly; **je n'y tiens pas ~** I'm not very particular

**partie** [paʀti] *f* ❶ (*part*) part; **la majeure ~ du temps** most of the time; **en ~** partly; **en grande ~** largely; **faire ~ de qc** to be part of sth ❷ *pl, inf* (*les parties sexuelles masculines*) a man's private parts ❸ JEUX, SPORT game ❹ (*divertissement*) **~ de chasse/pêche** hunting/fishing trip ▸ **ce n'est pas une ~ de plaisir** it's no picnic; **la ~ est jouée** the die is cast; **être de la ~** to join in; (*s'y connaître*) to know a thing or two

**partir** [paʀtiʀ] <10> *vi* **être** ❶ (*s'en aller*) to go; (*voiture, train, avion*) to leave; (*lettre*) to go (off); **~ en courant** to run away; **~ en ville** to go into town; **être parti pour (ses) affaires** to be away on business; **~ en vacances** to take a vacation; **~ en voyage** to go (away) on a trip; **~ à la recherche de qn/qc** to go (off) looking for sb/sth; **~ chercher qn** to go and get sb ❷ (*après un séjour*) to leave ❸ (*démarrer: coureur, moteur*) to start; **c'est parti!** *inf* we're off! ❹ (*sauter, exploser: fusée, coup de feu*) to go off ❺ (*se mettre à*) **~ dans de grandes explications** to launch into long explanations ❻ (*disparaître: douleur*) to go (away); (*odeur*) to go; (*tache*) to come out ❼ (*mourir*) to pass away ❽ (*venir de*)

P

**ce train part de Berlin** this train leaves from Berlin; **la deuxième personne en partant de la gauche** the second person from the left ❾ (*commencer une opération*) ~ **d'un principe/d'une idée** to start from a principle/from an idea ▸ **à ~ de** from

**partisan(e)** [paʀtizɑ̃, an] **I.** *adj* (*favorable à*) **être ~ de qc** to be in favor of sth **II.** *m(f)* supporter; (*d'une idée*) advocate

**partout** [paʀtu] *adv* ❶ (*en tous lieux*) everywhere; **un peu ~** here and there; **~ où ...** wherever ... ❷ SPORT **on en est à trois** ~ it's three all

**parution** [paʀysjɔ̃] *f* publication

**parvenir** [paʀvəniʀ] <9> *vi être* ❶ (*atteindre*) ~ **à une maison/au sommet** to reach a house/the summit ❷ (*arriver*) ~ **à qn** (*colis, lettre*) to reach sb; (*bruit*) to reach sb's ears; **faire ~ une lettre à qn** to get a letter to sb ❸ (*réussir à obtenir*) ~ **à la gloire** to attain glory; ~ **à convaincre qn** to manage to persuade sb ❹ (*atteindre naturellement*) **être parvenu au terme de sa vie** to have reached the end of one's life

**pas**[1] [pɑ] *m* ❶ (*enjambée*) step; **au ~ de charge** on the double; **au ~ de course/de gymnastique** at a run/a jog trot; **marcher d'un bon ~** to walk at a good pace ❷ *pl* (*trace*) footprints; **revenir sur ses** ~ to retrace one's steps ❸ (*allure: d'une personne*) pace; (*d'un cheval*) walk; **marcher au ~** to march ❹ (*pas de danse*) dance step ❺ (*entrée*) ~ **de la porte** doorstep; **sur le ~ de la porte** on the doorstep ▸ **faire les** <u>cent</u> ~ to pace up and down; **à** <u>deux</u> ~ a stone's throw away; **faux** ~ faux pas; **faire un** <u>faux</u> ~ to make a silly mistake; (*par indiscrétion*) to commit a faux pas; **se sortir d'un** <u>mauvais</u> ~ to get oneself out of a tight spot; **céder le** ~ **à qn** to give precedence to sb; ~ **à ~** step by step; **de ce** ~ right away

**pas**[2] [pɑ] *adv* ❶ (*négation*) **ne ~ croire** not to believe; (**ne**) ~ **de ... no ...**; **il ne fait ~ son âge** he doesn't look his age;

**j'ai ~ le temps** *inf* I don't have (the) time; (**ne**) ~ **beaucoup/assez de ...** not a lot of/enough ... ❷ *sans verbe* ~ **de réponse** no reply; ~ **bête!** *inf* not a bad idea!; ~ **absolument** ~! absolutely not!; ~ **encore** not again; ~ **du tout** not at all; ~ **que je sache** not as far as I know; ~ **toi?** aren't you? ❸ *avec un adj* not; **une histoire ~ ordinaire** an unusual story; **c'est vraiment ~ banal!** that's really something unusual!

**passage** [pasaʒ] *m* ❶ (*venue*) **observer le ~ des voitures** to watch the cars go by; **observer le ~ des oiseaux** to watch the birds fly by; **"~ interdit"** "do not enter"; **personne de ~** someone who is passing through; **il y a du ~** *inf* (*personnes*) there are a lot of comings and goings; (*circulation*) there's a lot of traffic ❷ (*court séjour*) **lors de son dernier ~ chez X** when he was last at X's ❸ (*avancement*) **lors du ~ d'un élève en classe supérieure** when a student moves up to the next grade; ~ **au grade de capitaine** promotion to captain ❹ (*transformation*) transition; ~ **de l'enfance à l'adolescence** passage from childhood to adolescence ❺ (*voie pour piétons*) passage(way); ~ **clouté** pedestrian crossing; **les valises encombrent le ~** the suitcases are blocking the way ❻ CHEMDFER ~ **à niveau** grade crossing ❼ (*galerie marchande*) (shopping) arcade ❽ (*fragment: d'un roman, morceau musical*) passage ▸ **céder le ~ à qn/qc** to let sb go first; **au ~** (*en chemin*) on the way past; (*soit dit en passant*) by the way

**passager, -ère** [pasaʒe, -ɛʀ] **I.** *adj* ❶ (*de courte durée*) fleeting; (*beauté, bonheur*) passing; (*pluies*) occasional ❷ (*très fréquenté: lieu, rue*) busy **II.** *m, f* passenger

**passant** [pɑsɑ̃] *m* (*d'une ceinture*) (belt) loop

**passant(e)** [pɑsɑ̃, ɑ̃t] *m(f)* passerby

**passe** [pɑs] *f* SPORT pass ▸ **être dans une** <u>mauvaise</u> ~ to be going through a

**P**

bad patch; **être en ~ de faire qc** to be on one's way to do sth

**passé** [pɑse] **I.** m ❶ (*temps révolu*) past; **par le ~** in the past; **tout ça c'est du ~** *inf* that's all in the past (now) ❷ LING past tense; **~ simple** simple past; **~ composé** present perfect **II.** *prep* (*après*) ~ **minuit** after midnight; ~ **la frontière** once past the border

**passé(e)** [pɑse] *adj* ❶ (*dernier*) last ❷ (*révolu*) past; (*angoisse*) former ❸ (*délavé: couleur*) faded ❹ (*plus de*) **il est midi ~/deux heures ~ es** it's past noon/two o'clock

**passeport** [pɑspɔʀ] *m* passport

**passer** [pɑse] <1> **I.** *vi avoir ou être* ❶ (*se déplacer*) to pass; (*aller*) to go past; (*venir*) to come past; **laisser ~ qn/une voiture** to let sb/a car past ❷ (*desservir: bus, métro, train*) to stop; **le bus va bientôt ~** the bus will be here soon ❸ (*s'arrêter un court instant*) ~ **chez qn** to call (in) on sb; ~ **à la poste** to go to the post office ❹ (*avoir un certain trajet*) ~ **au bord de qc** (*route, train*) to go around the edge of sth; ~ **dans une ville** (*automobiliste, voiture*) to go through a town; (*rivière*) to flow through a town; ~ **devant qn/qc** to go past sb/qc; ~ **entre deux maisons** (*personne*) to pass between two houses; (*route*) to run between two houses; ~ **par San Francisco** (*automobiliste, route*) to go through San Francisco; (*avion*) to go via San Francisco; ~ **sous qc** to go under sth; ~ **sur un pont** to go over a bridge; ~ **sur l'autre rive** to cross (over) to the other bank ❺ (*traverser en brisant*) ~ **à travers le pare-brise** to go through the windshield; ~ **à travers la glace** to fall through the ice ❻ (*réussir à franchir: personne, animal, véhicule*) to get through; (*objet, meuble*) to fit through ❼ (*s'infiltrer par, filtrer*) ~ **à travers qc** (*eau, lumière*) to go through sth ❽ (*se trouver*) **où est passée ta sœur/la clé?** where's your sister/the key gone? ❾ (*changer*) ~ **de la salle à manger au salon** to go from

the dining room into the living room; ~ **de maison en maison** to go from house to house; ~ **en seconde** AUTO to shift into second; **le feu passe au rouge** the light is changing to red; **le feu passe du vert à l'orange** the light is changing from green to yellow ❿ (*aller définitivement*) ~ **dans le camp ennemi** to go over to the enemy camp ⓫ (*être consacré à*) **60% du budget passent dans les traitements** 60% of the budget goes to salaries ⓬ (*faire l'expérience de*) ~ **par des moments difficiles** to go through some hard times ⓭ (*utiliser comme intermédiaire*) ~ **par qn** to go through sb ⓮ (*être plus/moins important*) ~ **avant/après qn/qc** to come before/after sb/sth ⓯ (*avoir son tour, être présenté*) to go; **faire ~ qn avant/après les autres** to let sb go before/after the others; ~ **à un examen** to go for a test; ~ **à la radio/télé** to be on the radio/TV; **le film passe au Rex** the movie is showing at the Rex ⓰ (*être accepté*) ECOLE ~ **en sixième** to go into the seventh grade; **la plaisanterie est bien/mal passée** the joke went over/ didn't go over well ⓱ (*ne pas tenir compte de, oublier*) ~ **sur les détails** to pass over the details; **passons!** let's say no more! ⓲ JEUX to pass ⓳ (*s'écouler: temps*) to pass; **on ne voyait pas le temps ~** we didn't see the time go by ⓴ (*disparaître*) to go; (*colère*) to die down; (*chagrin*) to pass (off); (*mode*) to die out; (*pluie*) to pass over; (*orage*) to blow over; (*couleur*) to fade; **ça te passera** you'll get over it ㉑ (*devenir*) ~ **capitaine/directeur** to become a captain/director ㉒ ~ **pour qc** (*être pris pour*) to be taken for sth; (*avoir la réputation de*) to be regarded as sth ㉓ (*présenter comme*) **faire ~ qn pour qc** to make sb out to be sth ▶ **ça passe ou ça casse!** *inf* (it's) all or nothing! **II.** *vt avoir* ❶ (*donner: sel, photo*) to pass; (*consigne, travail, affaire*) to pass on; ~ **un message à qn** to give sb a message; ~ **la grippe/un virus à qn** to give sb the flu/a virus ❷(*prêter*) ~ **un livre à qn** to lend sb a book ❸SPORT ~ **la balle à qn** to pass the ball ❹(*au téléphone*) ~ **qn à qn** to put sb through to sb ❺ECOLE, UNIV (*examen*) to take; ~ **un examen avec succès** to pass an exam ❻(*vivre, occuper*) ~ **ses vacances à Rome** to vacation in Rome; **des nuits passées à boire** nights spent drinking ❼(*présenter: film, diapositives*) to show; (*disque, cassette*) to put on ❽(*franchir: rivière, seuil, montagne*) to cross; (*obstacle*) to overcome; (*en sautant: obstacle*) to jump over; (*tunnel, écluse, mur du son*) to go through, (*frontière*) to cross (over); **faire ~ la frontière à qn** to get sb over the border ❾(*faire mouvoir*) ~ **sa tête à travers le grillage/par la portière** to stick one's head through the railings/around the door; ~ **le chiffon sur l'étagère** to dust the bookshelf ❿(*étaler, étendre*) ~ **une couche de peinture sur qc** to give sth a coat of paint ⓫(*faire subir une action*) ~ **qc sous le robinet** to rinse sth under the faucet ⓬CULIN (*sauce, soupe, thé*) to strain ⓭(*calmer*) ~ **sa colère sur qn/qc** to take out one's anger on sb/sth ⓮(*sauter* (*volontairement*): *chapitre, page*) to skip; (*son tour*) to miss ⓯(*oublier*) leave out; ~ **les détails** to leave out the details ⓰(*permettre*) ~ **tous ses caprices à qn** to indulge sb's every whim ⓱(*enfiler*) ~ **un pull** to pull on a sweater ⓲AUTO (*vitesse*) ~ **la seconde** to shift into second ⓳COM, JUR (*accord, convention*) to reach; (*contrat*) to sign; ~ **un marché** to make a deal **III.** *vpr* ❶(*s'écouler*) **le temps/le jour se passe** time/the day goes by ❷(*avoir lieu*) to happen; **que s'est-il passé?** what (has) happened?; **que se passe-t-il?** what's going on? ❸(*se dérouler*) **se ~** (*action, histoire, manifestation*) to take place; **l'accident s'est passé de nuit** the accident happened at night; **si tout se passe bien** if everything goes well ❹(*se débrouiller sans*) **se ~ de**

**qn/qc** to do without sb/sth ❺(*renoncer à*) **se ~ de faire qc** to go without doing sth ❻(*se mettre*) **se ~ de la crème sur le visage** to put cream on one's face; **se ~ la main sur le front/dans les cheveux** to wipe one's brow/run one's hand through one's hair ▸ **ça ne se passera pas** <u>comme</u> **ça!** *inf* not if I have anything to do with it!

**passerelle** [pasʀɛl] *f* ❶(*pont*) footbridge ❷NAUT gangway; (*pont supérieur*) bridge ❸AVIAT (*passerelle télescopique*) Jetway®; (*amovible*) boarding stairs ❹INFORM gateway

**passe-temps** [pastɑ̃] *m inv* pastime

**passif** [pasif] *m* ❶LING passive ❷FIN liabilities *pl*

**passif, -ive** [pasif, -iv] *adj* passive

**passion** [pasjɔ̃] *f* passion; ~ **du sport** passion for sports; **vivre une ~ avec qn** to have a passionate affair with sb

**passionnant(e)** [pasjɔnɑ̃, ɑ̃t] *adj* fascinating

**passionné(e)** [pasjɔne] **I.** *adj* passionate; **être ~ de qc** to have a passion for sth **II.** *m(f)* enthusiast; ~ **de cinéma** movie buff

**passionner** [pasjɔne] <1> **I.** *vt* to fascinate **II.** *vpr* **se ~ pour qc** to be fascinated by sth

**passivement** [pasivmɑ̃] *adv* passively

**passivité** [pasivite] *f* passivity

**passoire** [paswaʀ] *f* sieve

**pastel** [pastɛl] *m, app inv* (*couleur*) pastel

**pastèque** [pastɛk] *f* watermelon

**pasteur** [pastœʀ] *mf* ❶(*prêtre*) pastor ❷(*berger*) shepherd

**pastille** [pastij] *f* ❶MED lozenge; ~ **de menthe** (pepper)mint ❷(*gommette*) ~ **autocollante** sticker ❸INFORM button

**pastis** [pastis] *m* pastis (*anise-flavored alcoholic aperitif*)

**patate** [patat] *f* ❶*inf* (*pomme de terre*) spud, potato; ~ **douce** sweet potato ❷Québec (*pomme frite*) ~**s frites** (French) fries ❸*inf* (*imbécile*) dope

**patauger** [patoʒe] <2a> *vi* ❶(*marcher*) to squelch around ❷(*barboter*) to paddle ③ (*ne pas suivre: élève*) not to follow

**pâte** [pɑt] *f* ① CULIN (*à tarte*) pastry; (*à pain*) dough; ~**s alimentaires** pasta; **fromage à ~ molle/dure** soft/hard cheese ② (*substance molle*) paste; ~ **à modeler** ≈ Playdough®

**pâté** [pɑte] *m* ① CULIN pâté ② (*tache d'encre*) (ink) blot ③ (*sable moulé*) ~ **de sable** sand [*o* mud] pie ④ (*ensemble*) ~ **de maisons** block (of houses)

**paternel(le)** [patɛʀnɛl] *adj* paternal

**paternité** [patɛʀnite] *f* paternity

**pâteux, -euse** [pɑtø, -øz] *adj* (*sauce*) thickish; (*pain, masse*) stodgy; (*langue*) furry

**patience** [pasjɑ̃s] *f* patience; **n'avoir aucune patience** to be extremely impatient; **prendre ~** to be patient; ~**!** don't be so impatient!

**patient(e)** [pasjɑ̃, ɑ̃t] **I.** *adj* patient **II.** *m(f)* MED patient

**patienter** [pasjɑ̃te] <1> *vi* to wait; **faire ~ qn** to ask sb to wait; (*au téléphone*) to ask sb to hold (on)

**patin** [patɛ̃] *m* ~ **à glace** ice skate; ~ **à roulettes** roller skate; ~**s en ligne** inline skates, in-line skates ▸ **rouler un ~ à qn** *inf* to French-kiss sb

**patinage** [patinaʒ] *m* ~ **sur glace** ice-skating; ~ **à roulettes** roller-skating

**patineur, -euse** [patinœʀ, -øz] *m, f* skater

**patinoire** [patinwaʀ] *f* ① (*piste de patinage*) skating rink ② (*endroit glissant*) ice rink

**pâtisserie** [pɑtisʀi] *f* ① (*magasin*) pastry shop ② (*métier*) confectionery ③ (*gâteaux*) cakes and pastries *pl* ④ (*préparation de gâteaux*) cake and pastry making

**pâtissier, -ère** [pɑtisje, -ɛʀ] *m, f* pastry cook

**patois** [patwa] *m* patois

**patrie** [patʀi] *f* ① (*nation*) homeland; **mourir pour la ~** to die for one's country ② (*lieu de naissance*) birthplace

**patrimoine** [patʀimwan] *m* ① (*biens de famille*) *a.* BIO inheritance ② (*bien commun*) heritage

**patriote** [patʀijɔt] **I.** *adj* patriotic **II.** *mf* patriot

**patriotique** [patʀijɔtik] *adj* patriotic

**patron(ne)** [patʀɔ̃, ɔn] *m(f)* ① (*employeur*) employer; **les grands ~s de l'industrie** the industry tycoons ② (*chef*) boss ③ (*propriétaire*) owner ④ (*gérant*) manager ⑤ (*artisan*) ~ **boulanger** master baker ⑥ (*leader: d'une organisation*) head ⑦ REL patron

**patronage** [patʀɔnaʒ] *m* patronage

**patrouille** [patʀuj] *f* patrol

**patte¹** [pat] *f* ① *a.* infleg ② (*d'un chien, chat, ours*) paw ③ *inf* (*main*) hand ▸ **à quatre ~s** *inf* on all fours

**patte²** [pat] *f Suisse* ① (*chiffon*) duster ② (*torchon*) dishtowel

**pâturage** [pɑtyʀaʒ] *m* (*herbage*) pasture

**paume** [pom] *f* ① ANAT (*de la main*) palm ② SPORT **jeu de ~** real tennis

**paumé(e)** [pome] *inf* **I.** *adj* ① (*perdu: lieu, village*) godforsaken ② (*désorienté*) mixed up ③ (*socialement inadapté*) **être complètement ~** to be completely screwed up **II.** *m(f)* **c'est un ~** he's completely screwed up

**paumer** [pome] <1> **I.** *vt inf* to lose **II.** *vpr infse* ~ to get lost

**paupière** [popjɛʀ] *f* ANAT eyelid

**paupiette** [popjɛt] *f* ~ **de veau** stuffed scallop of veal

**pause** [poz] *f* ① (*interruption*) break ② MUS intermission ③ SPORT halftime

**pauvre** [povʀ] **I.** *adj* ① (*opp: riche*) poor; (*mobilier, vêtement*) shabby; (*végétation*) sparse; (*style*) weak; **être ~ en graisse/oxygène** to be low in fat/ oxygen ② antéposé (*médiocre: argument, salaire*) poor ③ antéposé (*digne de pitié*) poor; (*sourire*) weak ④ *inf* ~ **type** (*malheureux*) poor guy; (*minable*) loser **II.** *mf* (*sans argent*) poor man *m*, poor woman *f*

**pauvreté** [povʀəte] *f* poverty; (*du sol*) poorness; (*d'une habitation, du mobilier*) shabbiness

**pavé** [pave] *m* ❶ (*dalle*) paving stone ❷ (*revêtement*) paving ❸ *péj, inf* (*livre*) weighty tome ❹ (*morceau de viande*) ~ **de bœuf** thick steak ❺INFORM ~ **numérique** numeric keypad

**pavillon** [pavijõ] *m* ❶ (*maison particulière*) house; ~ **de banlieue** house in the suburbs ❷ (*petite maison dans un jardin*) summerhouse; ~ **de chasse** hunting lodge ❸ (*bâtiment: d'un hôpital*) block; (*d'un château*) wing ❹NAUT flag

**pavoiser** [pavwaze] <1> *vi inf* (*se réjouir*) to rejoice

**payable** [pɛjabl] *adj* payable; ~ **fin juillet** (*somme*) payable by the end of July; (*objet*) that must be paid for by the end of July

**payant(e)** [pɛjã, ãt] *adj* ❶ (*opp: gratuit*) where you have to pay; **c'est** ~ you have to pay ❷ (*rentable: entreprise, coup*) profitable

**paye** [pɛj] *v.* **paie**

**payer** [peje] <7> **I.** *vt* ❶ (*acquitter, rétribuer*) to pay; ~ **par chèque/en espèces** to pay by check/in cash; ~ **qn à l'heure** to pay sb by the hour ❷ (*verser de l'argent pour: maison, service*) to pay for; **faire** ~ **qc à qn mille euros** to charge sb a thousand euros for sth ❸ (*récompenser*) to reward ❹ (*offrir*) ~ **qc à qn** to buy sth for sb; ~ **un coup à qn** *inf* to treat sb ❺ (*expier*) ~ **qc de qc** to pay for sth with sth; **tu me le paieras!** you'll pay for this! **II.** *vi* ❶ (*régler*) to pay ❷ (*être rentable*) to pay; (*politique, tactique*) to pay off ❸ (*expier*) ~ **pour qn/qc** to pay for what sb did/sth **III.** *vpr* ❶ *inf* (*s'offrir*) **se** ~ **qc** to buy oneself sth ❷ *inf* (*se prendre*) **se** ~ **un arbre** to wrap one's car around a tree ❸ (*passif*) **la commande se paie à la livraison** orders are to be paid for on delivery ▸ **se** ~ **la tête de qn** *inf* (*tourner en ridicule*) to make fun of sb; (*tromper*) to pull sb's leg

**pays** [pei] *m* ❶ (*nation, État*) country; ~ **membres de l'UE** member countries of the EU; ~ **en voie de développement** developing country ❷ *sans pl* (*région*) region; **mon** ~ **natal** the area where I was born; **les gens du** ~ the local people; **saucisson/vin de** ~ local sausage/wine ❸ *sans pl* (*patrie*) native country ❹ *sans pl* (*terre d'élection*) **c'est le** ~ **du vin** it's wine country ❺GEO area; **plat** ~ flat country(side) ❻ (*village*) village; **un petit** ~ **perdu** a small isolated town ▸ **voir du** ~ to get around

**paysage** [peizaʒ] *m* landscape

**paysan(ne)** [peizã, an] **I.** *adj* ❶ (*agricole: monde, problème*) farming; (*revendication*) farmers' ❷ (*rural: mœurs, vie*) country ❸ *péj* (*rustre: air, manières*) rustic **II.** *m(f)* (*agriculteur*) farmer

**Pays-Bas** [peiba] *mpl* **les** ~ the Netherlands

**P.C.** [pese] *m* ❶ *abr de* **personal computer** INFORM PC; ~ **de poche** handheld ❷ *abr de* **poste de commandement** MIL headquarters

**P.D.G.** [pedeʒe] *m inf abr de* **Président-directeur général** chairman and chief executive officer

**péage** [peaʒ] *m* ❶ (*lieu*) tollbooth ❷ (*taxe*) toll; **route à** ~ toll road, turnpike

**peau** [po] <x> *f* ❶ (*épiderme; d'une personne*) skin ❷ *pl* (*morceaux desséchés*) ~**x autour des ongles** cuticles; ~**x mortes** dead skin ❸ (*cuir*) hide ❹ (*enveloppe, pellicule: d'une tomate, du lait*) skin; (*d'une orange, pomme, banane*) peel ▸ **coûter la** ~ **des fesses** *inf* to cost an arm and a leg; **n'avoir que la** ~ **sur les os** to be nothing but skin and bone(s); **vieille** ~ *péj, inf* old hag; **j'aurai ta/leur** ~ **!** *inf* I'll get you/them!; **avoir qc dans la** ~ *inf* to have sth in one's blood; **être bien/mal dans sa** ~ to feel good/bad about oneself; **faire la** ~ **à qn** *inf* to bump sb off; **y laisser sa** ~ *inf* to get killed; **risquer sa** ~ **pour qn/qc** *inf* to risk one's neck for sb/sth

**pêche¹** [pɛʃ] *f* peach; ~ **Melba** peach Melba ▸ **avoir la** ~ *inf* to be full of pep

**pêche**[2] [pɛʃ] *f sans pl* ① (*profession*) fishing; ~ **au saumon** salmon fishing; **produit de la** ~ catch ② (*loisir*) fishing; (*à la ligne*) angling, fishing ③ (*prises*) catch

**péché** [peʃe] *m* sin

**pêcher**[1] [peʃe] <1> I. *vi* to go fishing; (*avec une canne*) to go angling [*o* fishing] II. *vt* ① (*être pêcheur de*) ~ **qc** to fish for sth ② (*attraper: poisson, crustacé, grenouille*) to catch ③ *inf* (*chercher*) ~ **qc** (*idée, histoire*) to dig sth up; (*costume, vieux meuble*) to pick sth up

**pêcher**[2] [peʃe] *m* peach (tree)

**pécheur, pécheresse** [peʃœʀ, peʃʀɛs] *m, f* sinner

**pêcheur, -euse** [peʃœʀ, -øz] *m, f* ① (*professionnel*) fisherman *m*, fisherwoman *f* ② (*à la ligne*) fisher, angler

**pédagogie** [pedagɔʒi] *f* ① (*science*) education ② (*méthode d'enseignement*) educational methods *pl* ③ *sans pl* (*qualité*) teaching ability

**pédagogique** [pedagɔʒik] *adj* educational; (*matériel*) teaching; (*exposé, résumé*) well-presented

**pédagogue** [pedagɔg] I. *mf* ① (*enseignant*) teacher ② (*spécialiste*) educator II. *adj* **être** ~ to be a good teacher

**pédale** [pedal] *f* ① (*levier pour le pied: d'une bicyclette, voiture, poubelle*) pedal ② *péj, inf* (*homosexuel*) queer ▶ **perdre les** ~**s** *inf* to lose it

**pédalo**® [pedalo] *m* pedal boat; **faire du** ~ to go out in a pedal boat

**pédant(e)** [pedɑ̃, ɑ̃t] I. *adj péj* pedantic II. *m(f) péj* pedant

**pédéraste** [pederast] *m* ① (*homosexuel*) homosexual ② (*pédophile*) pederast

**pédestre** [pedɛstʀ] *adj* **randonnée** ~ ramble; **sentier** ~ footpath

**peigne** [pɛɲ] *m* comb; ~ **fin** fine-tooth comb; **se donner un coup de** ~ to run a comb through one's hair

**peigner** [peɲe] <1> I. *vt* (*cheveux, chien*) to comb; ~ **qn** to comb sb's hair II. *vpr* **se** ~ to comb one's hair

**peignoir** [pɛɲwaʀ] *m* robe

**peindre** [pɛ̃dʀ] *irr* I. *vi* (*au pinceau*) to paint II. *vt* ~ **qc en rouge/jaune** to paint sth red/yellow

**peine** [pɛn] I. *f* ① (*chagrin, douleur*) sorrow; **des** ~**s de cœur** heartaches; **avoir de la** ~/**beaucoup de** ~ to be upset/very upset; **faire de la** ~ **à qn** to upset sb ② JUR sentence; ~ **de mort** death penalty ③ (*effort, difficulté*) trouble; **avoir de la** ~/**beaucoup de** ~ **à faire qc** to have trouble/a lot of trouble doing sth; **ne vous donnez pas cette** ~ please don't bother; **avec** ~ with difficulty; **sans** ~ without (any) difficulty; **pour la/sa** ~ (*en récompense*) for one's trouble; (*en punition*) as a punishment ▶ **c'est bien la** ~ **de faire qc** *iron* what's the point of doing sth; **sous** ~ **de ...** on pain of ...; **roule doucement sous** ~ **de glisser** drive slowly or you'll skid II. *adv* ① (*très peu*) à ~ hardly ② (*tout au plus*) à ~ only just; **il y a à** ~ **huit jours** barely a week ago ③ (*juste*) **avoir à** ~ **commencé/fini** to have just started/finished ④ (*aussitôt*) à ~ ... no sooner ... ▶ **à** ~! *iron* you don't say!

**peiner** [pene] <1> I. *vi* ① (*avoir des difficultés*) ~ **à/pour faire qc** to have trouble doing sth; ~ **sur un problème** to struggle with a problem ② (*avoir des problèmes: moteur, voiture*) to labor II. *vt* ~ **qn** (*nouvelle, refus*) to upset sb; (*décevoir*) to disappoint sb; (*faire de la peine à*) to hurt sb

**peintre** [pɛ̃tʀ] *m* painter

**peinture** [pɛ̃tyʀ] *f* ① (*couleur*) paint; ~ **à l'eau** watercolor; ~ **à l'huile** oil paint ② (*couche, surface peinte*) paintwork; ~ **fraîche!** wet paint! ③ *sans pl* (*action*) painting ④ *sans pl* ART painting; **musée de** ~ art gallery ⑤ (*toile*) painting; ~ **murale** mural; ~ **à l'huile** oil painting ⑥ *sans pl* (*description, évocation*) portrayal; **faire la** ~ **de qc** to portray sth ▶ **je ne peux pas le voir en** ~ *inf* I can't stand (the sight of) him

**pelage** [pəlaʒ] *m* (*d'un animal*) coat

**pelé** [pəle] *m Belgique* (*partie du gîte à la noix*) bottom round of beef

**P**

**pelé(e)** [pəle] *adj* (*personne*) bald(-headed)

**pêle-mêle** [pɛlmɛl] *adv* all jumbled up; **les choses sont ~** everything's all over the place

**peler** [pəle] <4> I. *vi* ➊ (*perdre sa peau*) to peel ➋ *inf* (*avoir froid*) to be freezing (cold) II. *vt* to peel III. *vpr* **se ~ facilement** to peel easily

**pèlerin** [pɛlʀɛ̃] *m* REL pilgrim

**pèlerinage** [pɛlʀinaʒ] *m* ➊ (*voyage*) pilgrimage ➋ (*lieu*) place of pilgrimage

**pelle** [pɛl] *f* shovel; (*d'un jardinier*) spade; **~ à tarte** cake server ▶ **rouler une ~ à qn** *inf* to give sb a French kiss

**pellicule** [pelikyl] *f* ➊ PHOT, CINE film ➋ (*mince couche: de poussière, givre, crème, pétrole*) film ➌ *souvent pl* (*peau morte*) dandruff

**pelote** [p(ə)lɔt] *f* ➊ (*boule de fils*) ball ➋ SPORT **~ basque** pelota, jai alai

**pelouse** [p(ə)luz] *f* lawn

**peluche** [p(ə)lyʃ] *f* ➊ (*matière*) plush; **ours en ~** teddy (bear) ➋ (*jouet*) soft toy; (*animal en peluche*) stuffed animal ➌ (*poil*) fluff ➍ (*poussière*) piece of fluff ➎ (*d'un pull*) pill

**pénal(e)** [penal, -o] <-aux> *adj* (*code*) penal; **affaire ~e** criminal matter *pl*; **droit ~** criminal law

**pénaliser** [penalize] <1> *vt* ➊ SPORT to penalize ➋ (*désavantager: classe, religion*) to discriminate against; **~ qn/qc de qc** to penalize sb/sth by sth ➌ (*sanctionner*) to punish ➍ (*sanctionner d'une amende*) to fine

**pénalité** [penalite] *f a.* SPORT penalty

**penchant** [pɑ̃ʃɑ̃] *m* **~ à qc** tendency towards sth; **~ pour qc** liking for sth

**pencher** [pɑ̃ʃe] <1> I. *vi* ➊ (*perdre l'équilibre*) to tip (over); (*arbre*) to tilt; (*bateau*) to list; **le vent fait ~ l'arbre** the tree is bending over in the wind ➋ (*ne pas être droit*) to bend sideways; **~ à droite** to lean to the right ➌ (*se prononcer pour*) **~ pour qc** to be inclined to favor sth II. *vt* (*bouteille, carafe*) to tip; (*table, chaise*) to tilt; **~ la tête** (*en avant, sur qc*) to bend one's

head (forward); (*de honte*) to hang one's head; (*sur le côté*) to put one's head to one side; **~ la tête en arrière** to tip one's head back III. *vpr* ➊ (*baisser*) **se ~** to bend down; **se ~ par la fenêtre** to lean out (of) the window ➋ (*examiner*) **se ~ sur un problème** to look into a problem

**pendant** [pɑ̃dɑ̃] I. *prep* ➊ (*pour indiquer une durée*) for; **~ trois jours/des kilomètres et des kilomètres** for three days/miles and miles ➋ (*au cours de, simultanément à*) during; **~ ce temps** meanwhile; **~ longtemps** for a long time II. *conj* ➊ (*tandis que*) **~ que** while ➋ (*aussi longtemps que*) **~ que** as long as ▶ **~ que tu y es** *iron* while you're at it; **~ que j'y pense** while I think of it

**pendant(e)** [pɑ̃dɑ̃, ɑ̃t] *adj* ➊ (*tombant*) hanging; (*langue*) hanging out ➋ (*ballant: jambes*) dangling ➌ JUR (*procès, affaire*) pending

**pendentif** [pɑ̃dɑ̃tif] *m* (*bijou*) pendant

**penderie** [pɑ̃dʀi] *f* ➊ (*garde-robe*) wardrobe ➋ (*placard mural*) closet ➌ (*armoire*) cupboard

**pendre** [pɑ̃dʀ] <14> I. *vi* être ➊ (*être suspendu*) to hang; **~ à qc** to be hanging on sth; **~ de qc** to be hanging from sth ➋ (*tomber: cheveux, guirlande*) to hang down; (*joues*) to sag II. *vt* ➊ (*accrocher*) **~ qc au portemanteau/dans l'armoire** to hang sth (up) on the coat rack/in the wardrobe ➋ (*mettre à mort*) **~ qn à un arbre** to hang sb from a tree; **être pendu** to be hanged III. *vpr* ➊ (*s'accrocher*) **se ~ à une branche** to hang from a branch; **se ~ au cou de qn** to throw one's arms around sb's neck; (*par crainte*) to cling to sb ➋ (*se suicider*) **se ~** to hang oneself

**pendule** [pɑ̃dyl] I. *f* clock II. *m* (*d'un sourcier*) pendulum

**pénétrant(e)** [penetʀɑ̃, ɑ̃t] *adj* ➊ (*qui transperce: froid*) bitter; (*air*) bitterly cold; (*pluie*) penetrating ➋ (*fort: odeur*) strong, penetrating ➌ (*aigu: regard*) penetrating

P

**pénétrer** [penetʀe] <5> I. vi ①(entrer) ~ **dans qc** (personne, véhicule, armée) to enter sth; (par la force, abusivement) to break into sth; (balle) to penetrate sth; ~ **sur un marché** to break into a market ②(prendre place) ~ **dans qc** (idée) to sink into sth; (habitude) to establish itself in sth ③(s'insinuer) ~ **dans qc** (odeur, liquide, crème, vent) to get into sth; (soleil) to shine into sth II. vt ①(transpercer) ~ **qc** to penetrate sth; ~ **qn** (froid, humidité) to go right through sb; (regard) to penetrate sb ②(imprégner: mode, habitude) to become established in sth ③(découvrir: mystère, secret) to penetrate; (intentions, sens) to fathom

**pénible** [penibl] adj ①(fatigant, difficile) hard; (chemin) rough; (respiration) labored; **il est ~ à qn de** +infin it's very hard for sb to +infin ②(douloureux: heure, moment) painful; (circonstance, événement) distressing; **être ~ à qn** to be painful for sb ③(désagréable: sujet, circonstance) unpleasant; **il m'est ~ de constater que ...** I am sorry to find that ... ④(agaçant: personne, caractère) tiresome; **c'est ~!** isn't it awful!; **il est vraiment ~** inf he's a real pain (in the neck)

**péniblement** [peniblǝmɑ̃] adv ①(difficilement) with difficulty ②(tout juste) just about

**pénis** [penis] m penis

**pensée¹** [pɑ̃se] f ①(idée) thought ②sans pl (opinion) thinking ③sans pl PHILOS thought; (chrétienne, marxiste) thinking

**pensée²** [pɑ̃se] f BOT pansy

**penser** [pɑ̃se] <1> I. vi ①(réfléchir) to think; **faculté de ~** capacity for thought; ~ **à qc** to think of sth ②(juger) ~ **différemment sur qc** to think differently about sth ③(songer à) ~ **à qn/qc** to think about sb/sth ④(ne pas oublier) ~ **à qn/qc** to remember sb/sth; ~ **à** +infin to remember to +infin; **faire ~ à qn/qc** to remind one of sb/sth ⑤(s'intéresser à) ~ **aux autres** to

think of others ▸ **laisser à ~ que ...** to let it be thought that ...; **mais j'y pense ...** but I was just thinking ...; **tu n'y penses pas!** inf you don't mean it! II. vt ①to think; ~ **qn intelligent/sincère** to consider sb intelligent/sincere; **c'est bien ce que je pensais** that's exactly what I was thinking; **je pense que oui/que non** I think/don't think so; **vous pensez bien que ...** inf you can well imagine that ... ②(avoir l'intention de) ~ **faire qc** to be thinking of doing sth ▸ **cela me fait ~ que ...** that reminds me that ...; **pensez que ...** (tenez compte) to think that ...; (imaginez) you can well imagine that ...

**pensif, -ive** [pɑ̃sif, -iv] adj thoughtful

**pension** [pɑ̃sjɔ̃] f ①(allocation) pension; ~ **alimentaire** (en cas de divorce) alimony; (à un enfant naturel) child support ②ECOLE boarding school ③(petit hôtel) guesthouse, inn ④(hébergement) room and board; ~ **complète** full board; **être en ~ chez qn** to be boarding with sb

**pensionnaire** [pɑ̃sjɔnɛʀ] mf ①ECOLE boarder ②(dans un hôtel) guest ③(dans une famille) lodger

**pente** [pɑ̃t] f (d'une route, colline, d'un terrain) slope; (d'un toit) pitch; **monter la ~** to climb (up) the hill; **en ~** sloping; **descendre/monter en ~ douce/raide** to slope gently/steeply downwards/upwards ▸ **être sur une mauvaise ~** to be going downhill; **remonter la ~** to get back on one's feet again

**Pentecôte** [pɑ̃tkot] f Pentecost; **les vacances de (la) ~** Pentecost break

**pénurie** [penyʀi] f (pauvreté) penury; (manque) shortage; ~ **d'eau/vivres** water/food shortage; ~ **d'argent/de capitaux** lack of money/capital; ~ **de personnel** staff shortage; ~ **de logements** housing shortage

**people** [pipœl] inv I. adj (journaliste, magazine) celebrity; **presse ~** celebrity magazines II. mpl celebs

**pépé** [pepe] m inf grandpa

**pépin** [pepɛ̃] m ①(graine: d'un raisin,

*d'une pomme*) pip; **sans ~s** seedless ❷ *inf* (*ennui, difficulté*) hitch; **j'ai eu un gros ~** I've had big trouble ❸ *inf* (*parapluie*) umbrella

**perçant(e)** [pɛʀsɑ̃, ɑ̃t] *adj* (*cri, regard, voix*) piercing; (*froid*) bitter; (*esprit*) penetrating

**perceptible** [pɛʀsɛptibl] *adj* (*détail, mouvement, son, amélioration*) perceptible

**perception** [pɛʀsɛpsjɔ̃] *f* perception; (*des couleurs, odeurs*) sense

**percer** [pɛʀse] <2> I. *vi* ❶ (*apparaître: dent*) to come through; **le soleil perce à travers les nuages** the sun is breaking through the clouds ❷ (*transparaître*) **~ dans qc** (*sentiment, ironie*) to show in sth ❸ (*devenir populaire: artiste*) to make a name for oneself II. *vt* ❶ (*forer: trou*) to make; (*avec une perceuse*) to drill ❷ (*faire des trous dans*) **~ qc d'un trou/de trous** to make a hole/holes in sth; (*avec une perceuse*) to drill a hole/holes in sth ❸ (*perforer: mur, tôle*) to make a hole in; (*coffre-fort*) to break open; (*abcès, ampoule*) to burst; (*avec une lame*) to lance; (*pneu, tympan*) to burst; (*oreille, narine*) to pierce; (*tonneau*) to broach; **être percé** (*chaussette, chaussure, poche*) to have holes in; (*d'un seul trou*) to have a hole in ❹ (*creuser une ouverture dans: mur, rocher*) to make an opening in ❺ (*traverser: ligne, front*) to break through ❻ (*déchirer: nuages*) to break through; (*obscurité, silence*) to pierce; **~ les oreilles à qn** (*bruit*) to make sb's ears ring ❼ (*découvrir: mystère, secret*) to penetrate

**perceuse** [pɛʀsøz] *f* drill

**perche¹** [pɛʀʃ] *f* ZOOL perch

**perche²** [pɛʀʃ] *f* ❶ pole; (*d'un téléski*) rod; MEDIA boom ❷ SPORT **la ~, le saut à la ~** (*épreuve*) pole vault; (*sport*) pole vaulting ▸ **tendre la ~ à qn** to throw sb a line

**percher** [pɛʀʃe] <1> I. *vi* (*oiseau*) to perch II. *vt inf* (*mettre*) **~ qc sur qc** to stick sth on sth III. *vpr* **se ~** to perch

**percuter** [pɛʀkyte] <1> I. *vi* **~ contre qc** to crash into sth II. *vt* to strike; **~ qn** (*avec la voiture*) to crash into sb

**perdant(e)** [pɛʀdɑ̃, ɑ̃t] I. *adj* (*billet, numéro, cheval*) losing; **être ~** to lose out II. *m(f)* loser

**perdre** [pɛʀdʀ] <14> I. *vi* **~ au jeu/au loto/aux élections** to lose at the tables/in the lottery/in the elections ▸ **y ~** COM to take a loss II. *vt* ❶ to lose; (*date, nom*) to forget ❷ (*cesser d'avoir: réputation, estime, vitesse*) to lose; (*habitude*) to get out of; **~ de son prestige** to lose some of one's prestige; **n'avoir rien à ~ dans qc** to have nothing to lose by sth ❸ (*se voir privé d'une partie de soi*) to lose; **il perd la vue/l'ouïe** his sight/hearing is failing; **~ le goût de qc** to lose one's taste for sth ❹ (*laisser s'échapper: sang*) to lose; **tu perds ton pantalon** your pants are falling down; **elle perdait une de ses chaussures** one of her shoes was coming off ❺ (*gaspiller: du temps, une heure*) to waste; **~ une occasion** to miss an opportunity; **faire ~ une heure à qn** to waste an hour of sb's time ❻ (*rater*) **~ qc en ne faisant pas qc** to miss sth by not doing sth; **tu n'y perds rien!** you haven't missed anything! ❼ (*ruiner*) **~ qn** to be the ruin of sb ▸ **tu ne perds rien pour attendre!** you're not getting off so lightly! III. *vpr* ❶ (*s'égarer*) **se ~ dans la/en forêt** to get lost in the/a forest; **se ~ en route** (*colis, lettre*) to get lost in the mail ❷ (*s'attarder à*) **se ~ dans des explications** to get bogged down in explanations ❸ (*se plonger*) **se ~ dans ses pensées** to be lost in thought ❹ (*disparaître*) **se ~** (*sens, bonnes habitudes*) to be lost; (*coutume, tradition, métier*) to be dying out ❺ (*se gâter*) **se ~** (*fruits, légumes*) to go bad; (*récolte*) to be lost ❻ (*rester inutilisé*) **se ~** (*ressources*) to go to waste; (*initiative, occasion*) to be lost ▸ **je m'y perds** I can't make heads or tails of it

**perdrix** [pɛʀdʀi] *f* partridge

**perdu(e)** [pɛʀdy] I. *part passé de* **per-**

P

**dre II.** adj ① lost ②(qui a été égaré: objet) lost; (chien) stray; (sans propriétaire) abandoned ③(gaspillé, manqué) **soirée/temps/argent de ~** waste of an evening/of time/of money; **occasion de ~** wasted opportunity ④(de loisir) **à mes heures ~es** in my spare time ⑤(isolé: pays, coin, endroit) out-of-the-way ⑥(mourant) dying

**père** [pɛʀ] m ①(géniteur) father; **Durand ~** Durand senior; **de ~ en fils** from father to son ②(créateur, fondateur: d'une idée, théorie, d'un projet) father; (d'une institution) founder ③inf (monsieur) **le ~ Dupont** old (man) Dupont ▶**tel ~, tel fils** like father, like son; **~** Fouettard bogeyman; **~** Noël Santa Claus

**perfection** [pɛʀfɛksjɔ̃] f sans pl perfection; **à la ~** to perfection

**perfectionné(e)** [pɛʀfɛksjɔne] adj (machine, dispositif) advanced; **très ~** sophisticated

**perfectionner** [pɛʀfɛksjɔne] <1> **I.** vt to improve; (système, technique, appareil) to develop; (mettre au point) to perfect **II.** vpr **se ~** to improve; (système, technique, appareil) to be developed; (être mis au point) to be perfected; **se ~ en français** (personne) to improve one's French; **se ~ dans/en qc** (personne) to increase one's knowledge of/in sth

**perfectionniste** [pɛʀfɛksjɔnist] mf, adj perfectionist

**perforatrice** [pɛʀfɔʀatʀis] f card punch

**perforer** [pɛʀfɔʀe] <1> vt to pierce; (percer d'un trou) to punch; (percer de trous réguliers) to perforate

**perforeuse** [pɛʀfɔʀøz] f card punch

**performance** [pɛʀfɔʀmɑ̃s] f a. SPORT performance; **~s** (d'une machine, voiture) performance + vb sing

**performant(e)** [pɛʀfɔʀmɑ̃, ɑ̃t] adj (appareil, technique) high-performance; (entreprise, industrie, produit) successful; (cadre, manager) effective

**péridurale** [peʀidyʀal] f epidural

**périmé(e)** [peʀime] adj ①(carte, visa, garantie) expired; **médicament/ yaourt ~** medicine/yogurt past its expiration date ②(démodé, dépassé: conception, institution) outdated; **être ~** to be outdated [o out of date]

**période** [peʀjɔd] f ①(époque) time; **la ~ classique** the classical period ②(espace de temps) period; **une ~ d'un an** a period of a year; **~ électorale** election time; **~ de (la) vie** period of one's life; **~ d'essai** trial period; **par ~(s)** from time to time

**périodique** [peʀjɔdik] **I.** adj ①(cyclique) a. PRESSE periodical ②(hygiénique) **serviette ~** sanitary napkin, pad **II.** m PRESSE periodical

**périodiquement** [peʀjɔdikmɑ̃] adv periodically

**péripétie** [peʀipesi] f event

**périphérique** [peʀifeʀik] **I.** adj (extérieur) **quartier ~** outlying area **II.** m ①(boulevard) **le ~ de Paris** the Paris beltway; **~ intérieur/extérieur** inner/outer beltway ②INFORM peripheral; **~ d'entrée/de sortie** input/output device

**périssable** [peʀisabl] adj (denrée) perishable

**perle** [pɛʀl] f ①(pearl; (boule) bead ②inf (erreur) howler ③(chose de grande valeur) jewel ▶**c'est une ~ rare** she is a gem

**permanence** [pɛʀmanɑ̃s] f ①ADMIN, MED duty; **assurer la ~/être de ~** to be on duty ②(bureau) duty office ③ÉCOLE study room ▶**en ~** (siéger) permanently; (surveiller) continuously

**permanent(e)** [pɛʀmanɑ̃, ɑ̃t] adj ①(constant, continu) permanent; (contrôle, collaboration, liaison, formation) ongoing; (tension, troubles) continuous ②(opp: spécial, extraordinaire: envoyé, représentant, personnel) permanent; (armée, commission) standing

**permanente** [pɛʀmanɑ̃t] f perm

**permettre** [pɛʀmɛtʀ] irr **I.** vt impers ①(être autorisé) **il est permis à qn de** +infin sb is authorized to +infin ②(être possible) **il est permis à qn**

**de** +*infin* sb is able to +*infin;* **est-il permis d'être aussi bête!** nobody has a right to be that stupid! II. *vt* **①** (*autoriser*) ~ **à qn de** +*infin* to authorize sb to +*infin;* (*donner droit à*) to entitle sb to +*infin;* ~ **que qn** +*subj* to authorize sb to +*infin;* **c'est permis par la loi** it is permitted by law; **vous permettez?** may I?; **vous permettez que je fasse qc?** (*subj*) may I do sth? **②** (*rendre possible*) ~ **à qn de** +*infin* (*chose*) to allow sb to +*infin;* **si le temps le permet** weather/time permitting ▸ **permettez!/tu permets!** sorry! III. *vpr* **①** (*s'accorder*) **se** ~ **une fantaisie** to indulge oneself **②** (*oser*) **se** ~ **bien des choses** to take a lot of liberties

**permis** [pɛʀmi] *m* **①** (*document du permis de conduire*) driver's license; (*examen du permis de conduire*) driving test; **échouer au** ~ to fail one's driving test **②** (*licence*) ~ **de chasse/pêche** hunting/fishing permit; ~ **de construire** building permit **③** (*autorisation*) ~ **de séjour** residence permit

**permis(e)** [pɛʀmi, z] *part passé de* **permettre**

**permission** [pɛʀmisjɔ̃] *f* **①** *sans pl* (*autorisation*) ~ **de** +*infin* permission to +*infin;* ~ **de minuit** late pass **②** MIL leave

**perpendiculaire** [pɛʀpɑ̃dikylɛʀ] *adj* **être** ~ **à qc** to be perpendicular to sth

**perpétuel(le)** [pɛʀpetɥɛl] *adj* (*angoisse, difficultés*) perpetual; (*murmure, lamentations*) incessant

**perpétuer** [pɛʀpetɥe] <1> I. *vt* (*tradition, souvenir*) to perpetuate; (*nom*) to carry on II. *vpr* **se** ~ (*abus, injustices, tradition*) to be perpetuated; (*espèce*) to survive

**perpétuité** [pɛʀpetɥite] *f* **à** ~ in perpetuity; (*condamnation*) for life; **être condamné à** ~ to receive a life sentence

**perplexe** [pɛʀplɛks] *adj* (*personne, mine*) perplexed; **rendre qn** ~ to puzzle sb

**perroquet** [pɛʀɔke] *m* (*oiseau, personne*) parrot

**perruche** [peʀyʃ, peʀyʃ] *f* parakeet

**perruque** [peʀyk, peʀyk] *f* wig

**persécuter** [pɛʀsekyte] <1> *vt* to persecute

**persécution** [pɛʀsekysjɔ̃] *f* persecution

**persévérance** [pɛʀseveʀɑ̃s] *f* perseverance

**persévérant(e)** [pɛʀseveʀɑ̃, ɑ̃t] *adj* persevering

**persévérer** [pɛʀseveʀe] <5> *vi* to persevere; ~ **dans ses efforts** to persevere in one's efforts; ~ **à faire qc** to persist in doing sth

**persienne** [pɛʀsjɛn] *f* shutter

**persil** [pɛʀsi] *m* parsley

**persister** [pɛʀsiste] <1> *vi* (*persévérer*) ~ **dans qc** to persist in sth; ~ **dans un projet** to persevere in a project; ~ **à faire qc** to persist in doing sth

**personnage** [pɛʀsɔnaʒ] *m* **①** ART, LIT character; CINE part; **les** ~**s de Walt Disney** Walt Disney characters; **jouer le** ~ **d'un voleur** to play the part of a thief **②** (*rôle*) image **③** (*individu*) individual; **un grossier** ~ an uncouth individual **④** (*personnalité*) celebrity; ~**s politiques** political figures

**personnalisé(e)** [pɛʀsɔnalize] *adj* personalized

**personnaliser** [pɛʀsɔnalize] <1> *vt* **①** (*adapter*) to personalize **②** (*rendre personnel*) ~ **qc** to give a personal touch to sth

**personnalité** [pɛʀsɔnalite] *f* (*caractère, personne*) personality

**personne¹** [pɛʀsɔn] *f* **①** (*individu, être humain*) *a.* LING person; **dix** ~**s** ten people; ~ **âgée** elderly person; **les** ~**s âgées** the elderly; **la** ~ **qui/les** ~**s qui** the person/people who; **je respecte sa** ~ I respect his/her dignity **②** (*femme*) woman; (*jeune fille*) girl ▸ **à charge** dependent; **grande** ~ grown-up; **tierce** ~ third party; **en** ~ in person

**personne²** [pɛʀsɔn] *pron indéf* **①** (*opp: quelqu'un*) nobody, no one; **il n'y a** ~ there's nobody there; ~ **d'autre** nobody

**P**

else ② (*quelqu'un*) anybody, anyone; **une place sans presque ~** a place with practically no one ▸ **plus rapide que ~** faster than anyone

**personnel** [pɛʀsɔnɛl] *m* staff; (*d'une entreprise*) personnel; **~ enseignant** faculty

**personnel(le)** [pɛʀsɔnɛl] *adj* ① (*individuel*) personal ② LING (*forme, pronom*) personal

**personnellement** [pɛʀsɔnɛlmɑ̃] *adv* personally

**perspective** [pɛʀspɛktiv] *f* ① MATH, ART perspective ② (*éventualité, horizon*) **une ~ réjouissante** a joyful prospect; **~s d'avenir** prospects for the future; **ouvrir des ~s** to widen one's horizons; **à la ~ de qc** at the prospect of sth; **dans cette ~** with this in mind ③ (*panorama*) view ④ (*point de vue*) point of view ▸ **en ~** ART in perspective; (*en vue*) in prospect

**perspicace** [pɛʀspikas] *adj* ① (*sagace*) perspicacious ② (*très capable d'apercevoir*) clear-sighted; (*observation*) observant

**persuader** [pɛʀsɥade] <1> I. *vt* **~ qn de qc** to persuade sb of sth; **~ qn de +infin** (*intellectuellement*) to convince sb to +*infin*; (*sentimentalement*) to persuade sb to +*infin*; **~ qn que qn a fait qc** to convince sb that sb did sth II. *vpr* **se ~ de qc** to convince oneself of sth; **se ~ que qn a fait qc** to convince oneself that sb did sth

**persuasif, -ive** [pɛʀsɥazif, -iv] *adj* persuasive

**perte** [pɛʀt] *f* ① (*privation*) *a.* COM loss; **en cas de ~** if lost; **~ du sommeil** lack of sleep; **~ de mémoire** memory loss; **~ de temps/d'argent** waste of time/money; **~ d'autorité/de prestige** loss of authority/prestige ② (*ruine, financière*) ruin ③ (*déchet*) waste ④ *pl* (*morts*) losses ▸ **à ~ de vue** (*très loin*) as far as the eye can see; (*interminablement*) interminably; **en pure ~** fruitlessly; **courir à sa ~** to be on the road to ruin; **à ~** at a loss

**pertinence** [pɛʀtinɑ̃s] *f* pertinence; (*d'un argument, raisonnement*) relevance; **parler avec ~** to speak pertinently

**pertinent(e)** [pɛʀtinɑ̃, ɑ̃t] *adj* pertinent

**perturbation** [pɛʀtyʀbasjɔ̃] *f* disruption

**perturbé(e)** [pɛʀtyʀbe] *adj* ① (*troublé: personne*) perturbed ② (*dérangé: service*) interrupted; (*monde*) upside down; (*trafic*) disrupted

**perturber** [pɛʀtyʀbe] <1> *vt* (*service*) to disrupt; (*personne*) to disturb

**pervers(e)** [pɛʀvɛʀ, ɛʀs] I. *adj* perverse II. *m(f)* pervert

**pesant(e)** [pəzɑ̃, ɑ̃t] *adj* heavy

**peser** [pəze] <4> I. *vt* (*mesurer le poids, estimer*) to weigh; (*marchandises, ingrédients*) to weigh out ▸ **tout bien pesé** all things considered II. *vi* ① (*avoir un certain poids*) to weigh; **ne rien ~** to weigh nothing; **~ lourd** to be heavy; **~ 2 milliards d'euros** *inf* to cost 2 billion euros ② (*être lourd*) to be heavy ③ (*exercer une pression*) **~ sur/contre qc** to lean on sth ④ (*accabler*) **des soupçons pèsent sur lui** worries weigh him down; **des remords pesaient sur elle** remorse weighed her down ⑤ (*influencer*) **~ sur qn/qc** to influence sb/sth III. *vpr* **se ~** to weigh oneself

**pessimiste** [pesimist] I. *adj* pessimistic II. *m, f* pessimist

**peste** [pɛst] *f* ① MED plague ② (*personne ou chose*) pain ▸ **se méfier de qn/qc comme de la ~** to be highly suspicious of sb/sth

**pester** [pɛste] <1> *vi* **~ contre qn/qc** to curse sb/sth

**pétanque** [petɑ̃k] *f* petanque

**pétard** [petaʀ] *m* ① (*explosif*) firecracker ② *inf* (*cigarette de haschich*) joint ③ *inf* (*postérieur*) ass ▸ **être/se mettre en ~** *inf* to be/get in a rage

**péter** [pete] <5> I. *vi inf* ① (*faire un pet*) to fart ② (*éclater*) to explode; (*verre, assiette*) to smash; (*ampoule*) to blow II. *vt inf* to bust; **j'ai pété la cou-**

ture de mon pantalon I've split the
seam of my pants

**pète-sec** [pɛtsɛk] **I.** *adj inv, inf* (*air*)
highhanded **II.** *m, f inv, inf* tyrant

**pétillant(e)** [petijɑ̃, jɑ̃t] *adj* (*gazeux,
brillant*) sparkling; **des yeux ~s de
malice** eyes shining with evil

**pétiller** [petije] <1> *vi* (*faire des bulles*)
to fizz; (*champagne*) to sparkle

**petit(e)** [p(ə)ti, it] **I.** *adj* ❶ (*opp:
grand*) small; (*lumière*) faint; **au ~
jour** in the early morning; **à ~e vitesse** slowly ❷ (*de courte durée*) short;
**faire un ~ salut/sourire** give a little
wave/smile ❸ (*de basse extraction*) **le
~ peuple** the lower classes ❹ (*jeune*)
young; **les ~es classes** the lower
grades ❺ (*terme affectueux*) little;
(*mots*) sweet; **ton ~ mari** your darling
husband; **~ copain** [*o* **ami**] boyfriend
❻ (*condescendant*) **jouer au ~ chef**
to play the boss ❼ (*mesquin, bas, vil:
esprit*) mean; (*intérêts*) petty ❽ (*médiocre: vin, année, cru*) average; (*santé*) poor ❾ (*pour atténuer*) little; **une
~e heure** a bit less than an hour
❿ (*miniature*) **~(e)s soldats/voitures**
toy soldiers/cars ▸ **se faire tout ~** to
keep out of sight **II.** *m(f)* ❶ (*enfant*)
child ❷ ZOOL **les ~s du lion** the lion's
young ▸ **mon ~/ma ~e** my friend; **~,
~, ~!** kitty, kitty, kitty! **III.** *adv* **voir ~**
to think small ▸ **~ à ~** little by little;
**en ~** in miniature; (*écrire*) in small letters

**petite-fille** [p(ə)titfij] <petites-filles>
*f* granddaughter

**petit-fils** [p(ə)tifis] <petits-fils> *m*
grandson

**petit-four** [p(ə)tifuʀ] <petits-fours>
*m* petit four

**pétition** [petisjɔ̃] *f* petition

**petits-enfants** [p(ə)tizɑ̃fɑ̃] *mpl* grand-
children

**pétrin** [petʀɛ̃] *m inf* (*difficultés*) mess

**pétrir** [petʀiʀ] <8> *vt* (*malaxer*) to
knead

**pétrole** [petʀɔl] **I.** *m* oil **II.** *app* (*bleu,
vert*) dark blue-green

**pétrolier** [petʀɔlje] *m* (*navire*) oil
tanker

**pétrolier, -ière** [petʀɔlje, -jɛʀ] *adj* oil

**peu** [pø] **I.** *adv* ❶ (*opp: beaucoup, très*)
not ... much; *avec un adj ou un adv* not
very; **je lis ~** I don't read much; **j'y
vais ~** I don't go there often [*o* much];
**être ~ aimable** to be unfriendly;
**~ avant/après** shortly before/after;
**avant** [*o* **d'ici**] [*o* **sous**] **~** soon; **il est
parti depuis ~** he's only recently left;
**bien/trop ~** very little/too little; **~ de
temps/d'argent** little time/money;
**~ de voitures/jours** few cars/days; **en
~ de temps** in a very short time ❷ (*rarement*) **~ souvent** rarely ▸ **à ~** bit
by bit; **à ~ près** more or less; **de ~** just
**II.** *pron indéf* (*peu de personnes, peu
de choses*) few; **~ importe** it doesn't
really matter **III.** *m* **le ~ de temps/
d'argent qu'il me reste** the little
time/money that I have left; **le ~ de
personnes/choses** the few people/
things; **le ~ que j'ai vu** the little I've
seen; **un ~ de beurre/bonne volonté**
a little butter/good will; **un ~ de monde** a few people ▸ **un ~ partout** all over
the place; (**et**) **pas qu'un ~!** not half!;
**pour un ~ elle partait** she was almost
leaving; **pour si ~** for so little; **pour ~
que** ₁ *subj* so long as; **tant soit ~** slightly; **attends un ~ que je t'attrape** *inf*
just you wait

**peuple** [pœpl] *m* people; **le ~ chrétien**
the Christian people

**peuplé(e)** [pœple] *adj* populated; (*région*) inhabited

**peuplier** [pøplije] *m* poplar tree

**peur** [pœʀ] *f* fear; **la ~ du ridicule** fear
of ridicule; **avoir ~ de faire qc** to be
afraid of doing sth; **avoir ~ pour qn** to
be afraid for sb; **avoir ~ pour sa vie/
santé** to fear for one's life/health; **avoir
~ que qn fasse qc** (*subj*) to be afraid
that sb might do sth; **faire ~ à qn** to
scare sb ▸ **avoir une ~ bleue** to be
scared stiff; **j'ai bien ~ que qn ait fait
qc** (*subj*) I am really afraid that sb has
done sth; **à faire ~** frighteningly; **pren-**

**P**

<u>dre</u> ~ to get scared; **par** ~ **du ridicule/ des critiques** for fear of ridicule/criticism; **de** ~ **de faire qc/que qn fasse qc** (*subj*) for fear of doing sth/that sb might do sth

**peureux, -euse** [pœʀø, -øz] **I.** *adj* fearful **II.** *m, f* fearful person

**peut-être** [pøtεtʀ] *adv* ❶ (*éventuellement*) maybe, perhaps; ~ **que qn va faire qc** maybe sb will do sth; ~ **bien** could be ❷ (*environ*) maybe ❸ (*marque de doute*) perhaps; **ce médicament est ~ efficace, mais ...** this medicine may well be effective, but ...

**phare** [faʀ] *m* ❶ (*projecteur*) headlight; ~ **antibrouillard** fog light ❷ (*tour*) lighthouse

**pharmacie** [faʀmasi] *f* ❶ (*boutique*) drugstore; ~ **de garde** pharmacy on duty (*open for night or weekend service*) ❷ (*science*) pharmacy ❸ (*armoire*) medicine cabinet

**pharmacien(ne)** [faʀmasjɛ̃, jεn] *m(f)* pharmacist

**phase** [faz] *f* phase; (*d'une maladie*) stage

**phénomène** [fenɔmεn] *m* ❶ (*fait*) phenomenon ❷ *inf* (*individu*) freak

**philatélie** [filateli] *f* ❶ (*science*) philately ❷ (*hobby*) stamp collecting

**philatéliste** [filatelist] *mf* philatelist

**philosophe** [filɔzɔf] **I.** *mf* philosopher **II.** *adj* philosophical

**philosopher** [filɔzɔfe] <1> *vi* to philosophize

**philosophie** [filɔzɔfi] *f* philosophy

**philosophique** [filɔzɔfik] *adj* philosophical

**phonétique** [fɔnetik] **I.** *f* phonetics + *vb sing* **II.** *adj* phonetic

**phoque** [fɔk] *m* seal

**photo** [fɔto] *f abr de* **photographie** ❶ (*cliché*) photo, picture; ~ **de famille/d'identité** family/passport photo; **faire une** ~ to take a picture; **prendre qn/qc en** ~ to take a picture of sb/sth ❷ (*art*) photography; **faire de la** ~ to be a photographer

**photocopie** [fɔtɔkɔpi] *f* photocopy

**photocopier** [fɔtɔkɔpje] <1> *vt* to photocopy

**photocopieur** [fɔtɔkɔpjœʀ] *m*, **photocopieuse** [fɔtɔkɔpjøz] *f* photocopier

**photographe** [fɔtɔgʀaf] *mf* photographer

**photographie** [fɔtɔgʀafi] *f* ❶ (*activité*) photography ❷ (*image*) photograph

**photographier** [fɔtɔgʀafje] <1> *vt* ❶ PHOT to photograph ❷ (*mémoriser*) to memorize

**photomaton®** [fɔtɔmatɔ̃] *m* photo booth

**phrase** [fʀaz] *f* sentence

**physicien(ne)** [fizisjɛ̃, jεn] *m(f)* physicist

**physique** [fizik] **I.** *adj* physical **II.** *m* ❶ (*aspect extérieur*) physical appearance; **avoir un beau** ~ to be good looking ❷ (*constitution*) **grâce à son** ~ **robuste** thanks to his robust physique ▶**il/elle a le** ~ **de l'emploi** he/she looks the part **III.** *f* physics

**physiquement** [fizikmɑ̃] *adv* physically; **être très bien** ~ to be physically attractive

**piailler** [pjaje] <1> *vi* (*animal*) to chirp; (*enfant*) to whine

**piano** [pjano] **I.** *m* MUS piano; ~ **à queue** grand piano; **jouer du** ~ to play the piano **II.** *adv* softly; (**y**) **aller** ~ *inf* to go easy

**pianoter** [pjanɔte] <1> *vi* ❶ (*jouer sans talent*) ~ **sur un piano** to tinkle away at the piano ❷ (*taper comme un débutant*) to tap at the keyboard; ~ **sur un ordinateur** to tap away on a computer

**piaule** [pjol] *f inf* room

**P.I.B.** [peibe] *m abr de* **produit intérieur brut** GDP

**pic** [pik] *m* (*sommet*) peak ▶**à** ~ steeply; **couler à** ~ to sink to the bottom

**pickpocket** [pikpɔkεt] *m* pickpocket

**picorer** [pikɔʀe] <1> **I.** *vi* (*becqueter: animal*) to peck **II.** *vt* (*becqueter: animal*) ~ **qc** to peck at sth

**picoter** [pikɔte] <1> *vt* **la fumée (me) picote les yeux** the smoke is stinging my eyes; **les orties picotent la peau**

the nettles burn your skin; **ça me pico-te le nez** that tickles my nose
**pie** [pi] *f* ❶ (*oiseau*) magpie ❷ *inf* (*femme*) chatterbox
**pièce** [pjɛs] *f* ❶ (*salle*) room ❷ (*monnaie*) **~ de monnaie** coin; **~ d'un euro** one euro coin; **~s (en) euro** euro coins ❸ THEAT **~ de théâtre** play ❹ MUS piece ❺ (*document*) paper; **~ d'identité** proof of identity, identification; **les ~s documents**; **~ justificative** proof; **~ à conviction** exhibit ❻ (*élément constitutif*) part; (*d'une collection, d'un trousseau*) piece; **~ de mobilier** piece of furniture; **~ de musée** museum piece ❼ (*quantité*) **~ de viande** cut of meat ❽ (*pour rapiécer*) patch ❾ (*unité*) **acheter/vendre à la ~** buy/sell separately ▸ **~ de rechange** [*o* **détachée**] spare part; **créer qc de toutes ~s** to make sth out of bits and pieces; **construire qc de toutes ~s** to build sth from nothing; **être inventé de toutes ~s** to be a lie from start to finish; **mettre/tailler qn/qc en ~s** to pull/hack sb/sth to pieces; **être payé aux ~s** to be paid piecework
**pied** [pje] *m* ❶ (*opp: tête*) foot; **~ plat** flat foot; **à ~** on foot; **au ~!** heel! ❷ (*support: d'un lit*) leg; (*microphone*) stand ❸ (*partie inférieure: d'une chaussette, d'un bas*) foot ❹ (*base*) foot; (*d'un champignon*) stalk; **au ~ d'une colline/d'un mur** at the foot of a hill/against a wall; **mettre qc au ~ de qc** to put sth at the foot of sth; **être au ~ de qc** to be at the foot of sth ❺ (*plant*) **~ de salade/poireau** lettuce/leek; **~ de vigne** vine ❻ (*pas*) **marcher d'un ~ léger** to walk with a spring in one's step; **ils s'en vont/marchent du même ~** they are leaving/walking in step ▸ **mettre qn au ~ du mur** to put sb's back to the wall; **avoir bon ~ bon œil** to be as fit as a fiddle; **avoir/rouler le ~ au plancher** to have/drive with a lead foot; **mettre les ~s dans le plat** (*commettre une gaffe*) to goof up; **mettre ~ à terre** to set foot on land; **avoir/**

**garder les ~s sur terre** to have/keep both feet on the ground; **des ~s à la tête** from head to toe; **partir du bon/mauvais ~** to get off to a good/bad start; **se lever du ~ gauche** to get up on the wrong side of the bed; **remplacer qn au ~ levé** to stand in for sb at the last minute; **~s nus** barefoot; **avoir ~** to have a footing in; **casser les ~s à qn** *inf* to get on sb's nerves; **être sur ~** to be up and about; **ça lui fait les ~s** *inf* that serves him/her right; **lever le ~** (*ralentir*) to ease off the accelerator; **marcher sur les ~s de qn** (*faire mal*) to tread on sb's feet; **mettre les ~s quelque part** to set foot somewhere; **mettre un projet sur ~** to set up a project; **perdre ~** (*se noyer, ne plus comprendre*) to get out of one's depth; **remettre qn/qc sur ~** to stand sb/sth up again; **traîner les ~s** to drag one's feet; **tomber** [*o* **se jeter**] **aux ~s de qn** to fall at sb's feet; **faire un ~ de nez à qn** to thumb one's nose at sb
**pied-noir** [pjenwaʀ] <pieds-noirs> **I.** *mf inf* pied-noir (*person of European descent living in Algeria during French rule*) **II.** *adj* pied-noir
**piège** [pjɛʒ] *m* trap; **~ à souris** mousetrap; **prendre un animal au ~** to catch an animal in a trap; **prendre qn au ~** to trap sb; **tendre un ~ à qn** to set a trap for sb; **tomber dans le/un ~** to fall into the/a trap
**piéger** [pjeʒe] <2a, 5> *vt* ❶ (*attraper: animal*) to trap ❷ (*tromper*) **~ qn** to catch sb out; **se faire ~ par qn** to be caught out by sb; **se laisser ~** to get caught out; (*par de bonnes paroles*) to be taken in
**pierre** [pjɛʀ] *f* ❶ (*caillou*) stone ❷ (*pierre précieuse*) gem(stone) ▸ **faire d'une ~ deux coups** to kill two birds with one stone; **~ tombale** tombstone; **poser la première ~ de qc** to lay the first stone of sth
**piétiner** [pjetine] <1> **I.** *vi* ❶ (*trépigner*) **~ de colère/d'impatience** to stamp one's feet in anger/with impa-

tience ❷ (*avancer péniblement*) to be at a standstill; ~ **sur place** to stand around ❸ (*ne pas progresser*) to mark time **II.** *vt* (*marcher sur: sol, neige*) to tread on; ~ (*pelouse*) to trample; **qc de rage** to trample on sth in rage

**piéton(ne)** [pjetɔ̃, ɔn] **I.** *adj* (*zone, rue*) pedestrian **II.** *m(f)* pedestrian

**piétonnier, -ière** [pjetɔnje, -jɛʀ] *adj v.* **piéton(ne) I.**

**pigeon** [piʒɔ̃] *m* ❶ ZOOL pigeon; ~ **voyageur** homing pigeon ❷ *inf* (*dupe*) **être le ~ dans l'affaire** to be the sucker in the whole thing

**piger** [piʒe] <2a> *vt, vi inf* to get it; **ne rien ~** not to get anything

**pile¹** [pil] *f* ❶ (*tas*) pile ❷ ELEC battery; **fonctionner à ~s** to be battery-operated ❸ *Midi* (*évier*) sink

**pile²** [pil] *adv* ❶ (*avec précision: arriver*) on the dot; ((*s'*)*arrêter*) dead ❷ (*brusquement:* (*s'*)*arrêter*) suddenly ❸ (*au bon moment: arriver*) right on time; **ça tombe ~!** that's perfect timing! ❹ (*exactement*) **à 10 heures ~** at 10 o'clock on the dot ▶ **~ poil** *inf* exactly

**pile³** [pil] *f* **le côté ~** tails; ~ **ou face?** heads or tails?; **on va jouer ça à ~ ou face!** let's flip for it!

**piler** [pile] <1> **I.** *vt* to crush **II.** *vi inf* (*voiture*) to slam on the brakes

**pilier** [pilje] *m* ❶ ARCHIT pillar ❷ SPORT prop forward

**piller** [pije] <1> *vt* (*mettre à sac*) to loot

**pilote** [pilɔt] **I.** *adj* ❶ (*qui ouvre la voie: projet, essai*) pilot ❷ (*expérimental*) test ❸ (*exemplaire*) model ❹ NAUT (*bateau, navire*) pilot **II.** *mf* ❶ AVIAT pilot; ~ **de ligne** airline pilot ❷ AUTO driver; ~ **de course** racecar driver; ~ **d'essai** test pilot **III.** *m* ❶ (*dispositif*) ~ **automatique** automatic pilot ❷ INFORM driver

**piloter** [pilɔte] <1> *vt* ❶ AUTO (*avion, navire*) to pilot; (*voiture*) to drive ❷ INFORM to drive

**pilule** [pilyl] *f* MED pill

**piment** [pimɑ̃] *m* ❶ CULIN pepper; ~ **en**

**poudre** chili powder ❷ (*piquant*) spice; **donner du ~ à qc** to spice sth up

**pimenter** [pimɑ̃te] <1> *vt* ❶ CULIN ~ **qc** to add chili to sth ❷ *fig* ~ **qc** to add spice to sth

**pince** [pɛ̃s] *f* ❶ TECH pair of pliers ❷ ZOOL claw ❸ COUT **pantalon à ~s** front-pleated slacks ❹ (*épingle*) ~ **à linge** clothespin ❺ (*instrument d'épilation*) ~ **à épiler** tweezers *pl*

**pincé(e)** [pɛ̃se] *adj* ❶ (*hautain*) starchy; (*sourire, ton*) stiff ❷ (*serré: nez, narines*) thin; (*lèvres*) tight

**pinceau** [pɛ̃so] <x> *m* brush ▶ **se mélanger les ~x** *inf* to get mixed up

**pincée** [pɛ̃se] *f* pinch

**pincer** [pɛ̃se] <2> **I.** *vt* ❶ (*faire mal: personne*) to pinch; (*crabe, écrevisse*) to nip; ~ **la joue/le bras à qn** to pinch sb's cheek/arm; (*crabe, écrevisse*) to nip sb's cheek/arm ❷ (*serrer fortement*) ~ **la bouche** to clamp one's mouth shut; ~ **les lèvres** to pucker one's lips ❸ *inf* (*arrêter*) to catch; **se faire ~ par qn** to get caught by sb **II.** *vpr* ❶ (*se blesser, se serrer la peau*) **se ~** to pinch oneself; **se ~ le doigt** to get one's finger caught ❷ (*boucher*) **se ~ le nez** to hold one's nose **III.** *vi* **pince-moi, je rêve!** pinch me, I'm dreaming!; **en ~ pour qn** *inf* to be gone on sb

**pincette** [pɛ̃sɛt] *f* pair of tongs

**ping-pong** [piŋpɔ̃g] *m inv* Ping-Pong®, table tennis

**pinotte** [pinɔt] *f Québec, inf* (*cacahuète*) peanut

**pinson** [pɛ̃sɔ̃] *m* chaffinch

**pion** [pjɔ̃] *m* JEUX pawn

**pion(ne)** [pjɔ̃, pjɔn] *m(f)* ECOLE supervisor

**pipe** [pip] *f* pipe

**piquant** [pikɑ̃] *m* ❶ (*épine*) thorn; (*de ronce*) prickle ❷ (*agrément*) **avoir du ~** (*récit, livre*) to be spicy

**piquant(e)** [pikɑ̃, ɑ̃t] *adj* ❶ (*pointu: joue, plante*) prickly; (*rose*) thorny ❷ CULIN (*moutarde, radis*) hot; (*odeur*) pungent; (*goût, sauce*) spicy

**P**

**pique** [pik] *m* JEUX spade; **valet de ~** jack of spades

**pique-nique** [piknik] <pique-niques> *m* picnic

**pique-niquer** [piknike] <1> *vi* to picnic

**piquer** [pike] <1> I. *vt* ❶ (*faire une piqûre: personne, guêpe, moustique*) to sting; (*serpent, puce*) to bite ❷ (*donner la mort*) **~ un animal** to put an animal to sleep ❸ (*prendre/fixer avec un objet pointu: olive, papillon*) to stick ❹ (*enfoncer par le bout*) **~ une aiguille dans qc** to jab a needle into sth ❺ (*picoter: yeux, visage*) to sting; **~ la peau** to prickle; **~ la langue** to tingle on one's tongue ❻ *inf* (*faire brusquement*) **~ un cent mètres** to do a hundred meter sprint; **~ une colère/une crise** to fly into a rage/have a fit; **~ un fard** to turn red; **~ un roupillon** to take a nap ❼ *inf* (*voler*) to pinch ❽ *inf* (*arrêter, attraper*) to catch II. *vi* ❶ (*faire une piqûre: moustique, aiguille*) to sting; (*serpent, puce*) to bite ❷ (*descendre*) **~ sur qc** to swoop down on sth ❸ (*se diriger*) **~ sur qn/qc** to head for sb/sth ❹ (*irriter un sens: fumée, ortie*) to sting; (*moutarde, radis*) to be hot; (*barbe, pull*) to prickle; (*froid, vent*) to bite; (*eau gazeuse*) to fizz III. *vpr* ❶ (*se blesser*) **se ~ avec une aiguille/à un rosier** to prick oneself with a needle/on a rosebush; **se ~ avec des orties** to get stung by (stinging) nettles ❷ (*se faire une injection*) **se ~** to inject oneself; (*drogué*) to shoot up; **se ~ à qc** to inject oneself with sth; (*drogué*) to shoot up with sth

**piquet** [pikɛ] *m* (*pieu: de parc, jardin*) post; (*de tente*) peg ▸ **être/rester planté comme un ~** *inf* to stand around doing nothing; **aller au ~** ÉCOLE to go into time-out; **~ de grève** picket line

**piqûre** [pikyʀ] *f* ❶ (*blessure: d'épingle*) stab; (*de guêpe*) sting; (*de moustique*) bite ❷ MED shot, injection; **faire une ~ à qn** to give sb a shot

**pirate** [piʀat] I. *m* ❶ NAUT pirate ❷ AVIAT **~ de l'air** hijacker ❸ AUTO **~ de la route** carjacker II. *adj* pirate

**pirater** [piʀate] <1> *vt* to pirate; **~ un ordinateur** INFORM to hack a computer

**pire** [piʀ] I. *adj* ❶ (*plus mauvais*) worse; **rien de ~ que** nothing worse than; **de ~ en ~** worse and worse ❷ (*le plus mauvais*) **le/la ~ élève** the worst student II. *m* **le ~** the worst; **s'attendre au ~** to expect the worst; **au ~** if worst comes to worst

**pirouette** [piʀwɛt] *f* ❶ (*culbute: d'un acrobate, danseur, cheval*) pirouette ❷ (*volte-face*) about-face

**pis** [pi] *m* udder

**piscine** [pisin] *f* swimming pool

**pissenlit** [pisɑ̃li] *m* dandelion

**pisser** [pise] <1> *vi inf* to (take a) piss

**pistache** [pistaʃ] *f, adj inv* pistachio

**piste** [pist] *f* ❶ (*trace: d'un cambrioleur, suspect*) trail; (*d'un animal*) tracks *pl* ❷ (*indice*) clue ❸ AVIAT runway; **~ d'atterrissage/de décollage** landing/takeoff runway ❹ AUTO **~ cyclable** bicycle path ❺ (*au ski*) slope; **~ de ski de fond** cross-country ski track ❻ (*grand ovale à l'hippodrome*) track, course; (*grand ovale au vélodrome/circuit automobile*) track; **~ d'essai** test track; **cyclisme sur ~/épreuve sur ~** course cycling/course test ❼ (*espace pour le patinage*) rink; (*espace pour la danse*) floor; (*espace au cirque*) ring ❽ (*chemin dans le désert*) track; (*chemin à la montagne*) path ❾ CINE, TV track ▸ **brouiller les ~s** to confuse the issue; **entrer en ~** to come on to the scene

**pistolet** [pistolɛ] *m* ❶ (*arme*) pistol, gun ❷ (*pulvérisateur*) spray ❸ *Belgique* (*petit pain rond*) bread roll

**piston** [pistɔ̃] *m inf* (*favoritisme*) string pulling, wirepulling

**pistonner** [pistɔne] <1> *vt inf* **~ qn** to pull strings for sb; **se faire ~ par qn** to have sb pull strings

**piteux, -euse** [pitø, -øz] *adj* (*air, apparence*) pitiful; (*état*) pathetic; (*résultat*) miserable

**pitié** [pitje] *f* (*compassion*) pity; (*miséri-*

*corde*) mercy; **par ~** for pity's sake; **agir/combattre sans ~** to act/fight mercilessly; **être sans ~** to be merciless; **avoir/prendre ~ de qn** to have/take pity on sb; **faire ~ à qn** to make sb feel sorry for oneself; *péj* to be pitiful; **prendre qn/qc en ~** to take pity on sb/sth

**piton** [pitɔ̃] *m* ❶ (*crochet*) hook; SPORT piton ❷ GEO peak ❸ *Québec* (*bouton*) button ❹ *Québec* (*touche: d'un ordinateur, téléphone*) key; (*d'une télécommande*) button

**pitoyable** [pitwajabl] *adj* ❶ (*qui inspire la pitié: aspect, état, état, personne*) pitiful ❷ (*piteux*) pitiful; (*niveau de vie, résultat*) miserable

**pitre** [pitʀ] *m* clown

**pittoresque** [pitɔʀɛsk] *adj* picturesque

**pivoter** [pivɔte] <1> *vi* **~ sur qc** to revolve around sth; **faire ~ qc** to pivot sth

**pixel** [piksɛl] *m* INFORM pixel

**pizza** [pidza] *f* pizza; **morceau de ~ au fromage** slice of cheese pizza

**placard** [plakaʀ] *m* (*armoire*) cupboard; **~ à balais** broom cupboard

**placarder** [plakaʀde] <1> *vt* **~ un mur** to plaster a wall with posters

**place** [plas] *f* ❶ (*lieu public*) square; **~ de l'église/du marché** church/market square; **sur la ~ publique** in public ❷ (*endroit approprié*) place; **à la ~ de qc** in place of sth; **sur ~** on the spot; **être à sa ~** to be in the right place; **être en ~** (*installé*) to be installed; (*en fonction*) to be in place; **mettre une machine en ~** to install a machine; **mettre les meubles en ~** to set up furniture; **se mettre en ~** to be set up; **se mettre à la ~ de qn** to put oneself in sb else's shoes ❸ (*endroit quelconque*) spot; **être/rester cloué sur ~** to be/remain rooted to the spot; **prendre la ~ de qc** to take the place of sth; **il ne reste pas** [o **tient**] **en ~** he can't keep still ❹ (*espace*) room; **tenir/prendre de la ~** to take up room; **gagner de la ~** to gain some space ❺ (*emplacement réservé*) space; **~ assise** seat; **~ debout**

standing room; **~ de stationnement** parking space; **y a-t-il encore une ~ (de) libre?** is there another seat free? ❻ (*billet*) seat; **~ de cinéma/concert** cinema/concert ticket; **louer des ~s** to book seats ❼ (*emploi*) position ❽ *Belgique, Nord* (*pièce*) room ❾ *Québec* (*endroit, localité*) place ▶ **les ~s sont chères** *inf* there is a lot of competition; **faire ~ à qn/qc** to give way to sb/sth; **remettre qn à sa ~** to put sb in their place; **être/figurer en bonne ~ pour** +*infin* to be/look in a good position to +*infin;* **laisser qn sur ~** to leave sb behind

**placé(e)** [plase] *adj* ❶ (*situé*) **être bien/mal ~** (*objet*) to be well/awkwardly placed; (*terrain*) to be well/badly situated; (*spectateurs*) to be well/badly seated; **c'est de la fierté mal ~e!** it's misplaced pride!; **être bien/mal ~ pour répondre** to be in a good/bad position to reply; **tu es mal ~ pour me faire des reproches!** you're in no position to criticize me! ❷ SPORT placed; **être bien/mal ~** to be placed high/low ❸ (*dans une situation*) **être haut ~** to be high up

**placer** [plase] <2> I. *vt* ❶ (*mettre*) **~ qc sur l'étagère** to put sth on the shelf ❷ (*installer: sentinelle*) to place; **~ les spectateurs/les invités** to seat the spectators/guests; **~ un enfant dans une famille d'accueil** to place a child with a foster family ❸ (*introduire: anecdote, remarque*) to put in; **~ une idée dans qc** to put an idea in sth; **ne pas pouvoir ~ un mot** to not be able to get a word in ❹ (*mettre dans une situation professionnelle*) **~ un ami dans une entreprise comme qc** to get a friend a job in a company as sth ❺ FIN (*argent, capitaux, économies*) to invest II. *vpr* ❶ (*s'installer*) **se ~** to take up a position; (*debout*) **se ~** to stand ❷ (*se situer*) **se ~ dans le cas où ...** to suppose that ... ❸ (*avoir sa place désignée*) **se ~ devant/à côté de qc** (*meuble, objet, obstacle*) to belong in front of/next to sth

**④**(*prendre un certain rang*) **se ~ deuxième** to be placed second

**plafond** [plafɔ̃] *m* **①**(*opp: plancher*) ceiling **②**(*limite supérieure*) ceiling; (*d'un crédit*) limit ▸ **sauter au ~** *inf* to hit the roof

**plage** [plaʒ] *f* **①**(*rivage*) beach; **~ de galets/sable** pebble/sandy beach; **serviette de ~** beach towel; **sur la ~** on the beach; **être/aller à la ~** to be at/go to the beach **②**(*station balnéaire*) resort **③**AUTO **~ arrière** back shelf

**plaie** [plɛ] *f* **①**(*blessure*) wound **②**(*malheur*) bad luck **③** *inf* (*personne*) nuisance

**plaindre** [plɛ̃dʀ] *irr* **I.** *vt* (*s'apitoyer sur*) **~ qn** to pity sb; **je te plains vraiment** I really feel sorry for you **II.** *vpr* **①**(*se lamenter*) **se ~ de qc** to moan about sth **②**(*protester*) **se ~ de qn/qc à l'arbitre** to complain about sb/sth to the referee

**plaine** [plɛn] *f* plain

**plainte** [plɛ̃t] *f* **①**(*gémissement*) moan; **des ~s** moaning **②**(*récrimination*) *a.* JUR complaint; **porter ~ contre qn auprès du tribunal pour le vacarme** to press charges against sb for disturbing the peace

**plaire** [plɛʀ] *irr* **I.** *vi* **①**(*être agréable*) **qc plaît à qn** sb likes sth; **~ aux spectateurs** to please the audience **②**(*charmer*) **il lui plaît** she likes him; **les brunes me plaisent davantage** I like brunettes better **③**(*convenir*) **~ à qn** (*idée, projet*) to suit sb **④**(*être bien accueilli: chose*) to be appreciated **II.** *vi impers* (*être agréable*) **vous plairait-il de venir dîner?** would you like to come to dinner?; **comme il te/vous plaira** as you like; **quand ça te/vous plaira** whenever you like ▸ **s'il te/vous plaît** please; *Belgique* (*voici*) here you are **III.** *vpr* **①**(*se sentir à l'aise*) **se ~ avec qn** to enjoy sb's company, ou *au* Canada to like being in Canada **②**(*s'apprécier*) **se ~** (*personnes*) to like each another; **se ~ avec qc** to en-

joy being with sth **③**(*prendre plaisir*) **il se plaît à faire qc** he likes doing sth

**plaisanter** [plɛzɑ̃te] <1> *vi* **①**(*blaguer*) to joke; **je ne plaisante pas!** I'm not joking!; **~ sur qc** to joke about sth **②**(*dire par jeu*) **ne pas ~ sur la discipline/avec l'exactitude** to be strict about discipline/punctuality; **tu plaisantes!** you're joking!

**plaisanterie** [plɛzɑ̃tʀi] *f* (*blague*) joke; **~ de mauvais goût** tasteless joke; **par ~** for fun; **aimer la ~** to like jokes; **dire qc sur le ton de la ~** to say sth laughingly ▸ **les ~s les plus courtes sont les meilleures** brevity is the soul of wit

**plaisir** [pleziʀ] *m* **①**(*joie, distraction*) pleasure; **~ de faire qc** pleasure of doing sth; **il a ~ à faire qc** he enjoys doing sth; **prendre un malin ~ à faire qc** to get a kick out of doing sth; **faire ~ à qn** to please sb; (*rendre service à qn*) to do sb a favor; **maintenant fais-moi le ~ de te taire!** now, do me a favor and shut up!; **elle prend (du) ~ à qc** she takes pleasure in sth; **souhaiter à qn bien du ~** *iron* to wish sb joy; **faire ~ à voir** to be a pleasure to see; **par** [*o pour le*] **~** for the pleasure of it **②**(*jouissance sexuelle*) **se donner du ~** to pleasure each other **③** *pl* (*sentiment agréable*) **menus ~s** entertainment; **les ~s de la table** the pleasures of the table ▸ **faire durer le ~** to make the pleasure last; **au ~!** *inf* see you soon!; **avec grand ~** with great pleasure

**P**

**plan** [plɑ̃] *m* **①**(*représentation graphique, projet*) plan; **~ de travail** work plan; **~ d'action** plan of action **②**(*canevas: d'un devoir, livre, d'une dissertation*) plan **③**CINE, TV shot; (*cadrage*) frame; **~ fixe** static shot; **gros ~, ~ rapproché** close-up; **au premier ~** in the foreground **④** *inf* (*projet de sortie*) **j'ai un ~ d'enfer!** I have a great idea! **⑤**(*niveau*) **sur le ~ national/régional** on a national/regional level; **passer au second ~** to drop into the background; **de premier ~** leading; **de second ~**

second-rate; **sur le ~ moral** morally (speaking); **sur le ~ de qc** as regards sth ⑥(*surface*) **~ d'eau** stretch of water; **~ de travail** (*dans une cuisine*) work surface ▶ **laisser qn en** ~ *inf* to leave sb high and dry; **laisser qc en** ~ to drop sth

**planche** [plɑ̃ʃ] *f* ①(*pièce de bois*) plank; **~ à dessin/à repasser** drawing/ironing board ②(*scène*) **les ~s** the boards; **monter sur les ~s** to tread the boards ③SPORT **~ à roulettes** skateboard; **~ à voile** (*objet*) sailboard; (*sport*) windsurfing

**plancher** [plɑ̃ʃe] *m* floor ▶ **débarrasser le** ~ *inf* to beat it

**planer** [plane] <1> *vi* ①(*voler*) *a.* AVIAT to glide ②(*peser*) **~ sur qn/qc** (*danger, soupçons*) to hang over sb/sth; **laisser ~ le doute sur qc** to leave lingering doubt about sth ③ *inf* (*rêver*) to have one's head in the clouds ④ *inf* (*être sous effet euphorisant*) to be spaced out; (*sous l'effet d'une drogue*) to be high

**planétarium** [planetarjɔm] *m* planetarium

**planète** [planɛt] *f* planet; **la ~ Terre** the planet Earth

**planifier** [planifje] <1> *vt* to plan

**planning** [planiŋ] *m* ①(*calendrier*) calendar ②(*planification*) planning; **~ familial** family planning

**planque** [plɑ̃k] *f inf* ①(*cachette*) hiding place ②(*travail tranquille*) easy job; **c'est la ~ !** it's a cushy gig! ③(*lieu protégé*) hideout

**planquer** [plɑ̃ke] <1> *vt, vpr inf* (**se**) **~** to hide

**plantaire** [plɑ̃tɛʀ] *adj* plantar; **voûte ~** arch of the foot

**plantation** [plɑ̃tasjɔ̃] *f* ①(*exploitation agricole*) plantation ②(*action*) planting

**plante** [plɑ̃t] *f* plant

**planter** [plɑ̃te] <1> **I.** *vt* ①(*mettre en terre*) to plant ②(*garnir de*) **~ un jardin de/en qc** to plant a garden with sth; **avenue plantée d'arbres** tree-lined avenue ③(*enfoncer: pieu, pi-*

*quet*) to drive in; **~ un clou dans le mur** to hammer a nail into the wall; **~ ses griffes dans le bras à qn** (*chat*) to sink one's claws into sb's arm ④(*dresser: tente*) to pitch; (*échelle, drapeau*) to put up ⑤ *inf* (*abandonner*) **~ qn là** to drop sb; *fig* to dump sb **II.** *vpr* ① *inf* (*se tromper*) **se ~ dans qc** to screw up over sth; **se ~ à un examen** to screw up (on) an exam ②(*se mettre*) **se ~ une aiguille dans la main** to stick a needle in one's hand; **se ~ dans le mur** (*couteau, flèche*) to stick in the wall ③ *inf* (*se poster*) **se ~ dans le jardin** to take up one's position in the garden; **se ~ devant qn** to position oneself in front of sb ④ *inf* (*avoir un accident*) *a.* INFORM **se ~** to crash

**plaque** [plak] *f* ①(*matériau plat*) sheet ②(*présentation*) **~ de beurre** stick of butter ③(*couche*) **~ de verglas** sheet of ice ④MED patch ⑤(*pièce de métal: d'une porte, rue*) plaque; (*d'un policier*) badge; **~ minéralogique** license plate ⑥(*décoration*) plaque ⑦CULIN (*d'une cuisinière*) burner; **~ électrique** hotplate ⑧GEO plate ▶ **être à côté de la ~** *inf* to have (got) it all wrong; **mettre à côté de la ~** *inf* to be off target

**plaqué** [plake] *m* (*bois*) veneer; (*métal*) plate; **c'est du ~ chêne** it's oak-veneered; **bijoux en ~ or** gold-plated jewelry

**plaqué(e)** [plake] *adj* **~ (en) argent/or** silver/gold-plated; **~ chêne** oak-veneered

**plaquer** [plake] <1> **I.** *vt* ① *inf* (*abandonner: conjoint*) to dump; **~ un emploi** to ditch a job; **tout ~** to pack it all in; **~ son petit ami/fiancé** to dump one's boyfriend/fiancé ②(*aplatir*) **~ ses cheveux** to plaster one's hair down ③(*serrer contre*) **~ qn contre le mur/au mur** to pin sb up against/to the wall ④SPORT to tackle **II.** *vpr* (*se serrer*) **se ~ contre qc** to hold oneself against sth

**plastique** [plastik] **I.** *m* plastic; **en ~** plastic **II.** *adj inv* plastic

**plat** [pla] *m* ①(*récipient creux*) dish;

(*récipient plat*) plate; ~ **à viande** meat dish ❷(*contenu*) **un ~ de lentilles** a dish of lentils ❸(*mets, élément d'un repas*) course; ~ **principal** [*o de résistance*] main course; ~ **du jour** daily special; ~ **de poisson/légumes** fish/vegetable dish ▸ **faire tout un ~ de qc** *inf* to make a song and dance about sth

**plat(e)** [pla, plat] *adj* ❶(*égal, opp: arrondi*) flat; (*mer*) smooth ❷(*peu profond, peu haut: assiette, chaussure, talon*) flat; **mettre/poser qc à ~** to lay sth down flat ❸(*fade: conversation*) dull ❹(*obséquieux*) **faire de ~es excuses** to make an abject apology ❺(*vidé de son contenu*) **être à ~** (*pneu*) to be flat; (*batterie*) dead; *inf* (*épuisé*) to be run-down

**platane** [platan] *m* plane tree

**plateau** [plato] <x> *m* ❶(*support*) tray; ~ **à fromages** cheeseboard ❷CULIN ~ **de fruits de mer** seafood platter; ~ **de fromages** cheeseboard ❸(*partie plate: d'une balance*) pan ❹GEO plateau; ~ **continental** continental shelf ❺CINE, TV set; (*invités*) lineup; **sur le ~/hors du ~** on the set/off the set

**plâtre** [platʀ] *m* (*matériau*) *a.* MED plaster; **mur en ~** dry wall; **avoir un bras dans le ~** to have one arm in a cast

**plâtrer** [platʀe] <1> *vt* ❶(*couvrir de plâtre*) to plaster; (*trou, fissure*) to fill ❷(*mettre dans le plâtre*) to plaster

**plausible** [plozibl] *adj* plausible

**plein** [plɛ̃] **I.** *adv* ❶ *inf* (*beaucoup*) **avoir ~ d'argent/d'amis** to have loads of money/friends ❷(*exactement*) **en ~ dans l'œil/sur la table/dans la soupe** right in the eye/on the table/in the soup; **en ~ devant** straight ahead ▸ **mignon/gentil tout ~** *inf* just too cute/kind **II.** *prep* **de l'argent ~ les poches** tons of money **III.** *m* (*de carburant*) fill-up; **faire le ~** to fill the tank; **le ~, s'il vous plaît!** fill it up, please

**plein(e)** [plɛ̃, plɛn] *adj* ❶(*rempli*) full; (*journée, vie*) busy; **à moitié ~** half-full; **être ~ de bonne volonté/de joie** to be full of goodwill/joy; **être ~ de santé** to be bursting with health; **être ~ à craquer** to be full to bursting ❷(*rond: joues, visage*) round ❸(*sans réserve*) **à ~es mains** in handfuls; **mordre à ~es dents dans une pomme** to bite right down into an apple; **respirer à ~s poumons** to breathe deeply ❹(*au maximum de*) **à ~ régime**, **à ~e vapeur** at full power ❺(*au plus fort de*) **en ~ été/hiver** in the middle of summer/winter; **en ~ jour** in broad daylight; **en ~ nuit** in the middle of the night; **en ~ soleil** in full sun ❻(*au milieu de*) **être en ~ travail** to be in the middle of work; **viser en ~ cœur** to aim right for the heart; **en ~e rue** out in the road; **en ~e obscurité** in complete darkness; **en ~e lumière** in full sunlight; **en ~ vol** in full flight; **en ~ essor** booming; **en ~ boum** to be going full blast ❼(*sans vide: trait*) continuous; (*bois, porte*) solid ❽ *antéposé* (*total: victoire*) total; (*succès, confiance*) complete ❾(*entier: jour, mois*) whole ❿(*gravide*) pregnant

**pleinement** [plɛnmɑ̃] *adv* fully

**pleurer** [plœʀe] <1> **I.** *vi* ❶(*verser des larmes, crier: personne, bébé*) to cry; (*œil*) to water; **faire ~ qn** to make sb cry; **la poussière me fait ~** the dust makes my eyes water; ~ **de rage** to laugh so hard one cries ❷(*se lamenter*) ~ **sur qn/qc** to lament over sb/sth; ~ **sur son sort** to bemoan one's lot ❸(*réclamer*) to whine; **aller ~ auprès de qn** to go moaning to sb; ~ **après qc** *inf* to go begging for sth ❹(*extrêmement*) **triste à** (*faire*) ~ so sad you could cry; **maigre à** (*faire*) ~ pitifully thin; **bête à** ~ painfully stupid **II.** *vt* ❶(*regretter*) ~ **qn** to mourn for sb; ~ **sa jeunesse** to mourn one's youth ❷(*verser*) ~ **des larmes de joie/sang** to cry tears of joy/blood

**pleuvoir** [plœvwaʀ] *irr* **I.** *vi impers* **il pleut de grosses gouttes** it's raining heavily ▸ **qu'il pleuve ou qu'il vente** come rain or shine **II.** *vi* ❶(*s'abattre: coups, reproches*) to rain down ❷(*arri-*

**P**

*ver en abondance*) **les mauvaises nouvelles pleuvent en ce moment** there's no end to bad news at the moment

**Plexiglas®** [plɛksiglas] *m* Plexiglas®

**pli** [pli] *m* ❶ (*pliure*) pleat; (*du papier*) fold; **faire le ~ d'un pantalon** to put a crease in a pair of pants; **jupe à ~s** pleated skirt ❷ (*mauvaise pliure*) (**faux**) ~ crease; **cette veste fait des ~s/un ~** this jacket creases ❸ *sans pl* (*forme*) **avoir un beau ~** to have a nice shape ❹ JEUX **faire un ~** to win a trick ► **ça ne fait pas un ~** *inf* there is no doubt (about it)

**pliant(e)** [plijɑ̃, jɑ̃t] *adj* folding

**plier** [plije] <1> **I.** *vt* ❶ (*replier: papier, tissu*) to fold; (*linge, tente*) to fold up; **un papier plié en quatre** a piece of paper folded into four ❷ (*refermer*) to close; (*journal, carte routière*) to fold up ❸ (*fléchir: bras, jambe*) to flex ❹ (*courber*) **être plié par l'âge** to be bent over by age; **être plié par la douleur** to be doubled up in pain **II.** *vi* ❶ (*se courber*) **~ sous le poids de qc** to bend with the weight of sth ❷ (*céder*) to yield; **~ devant l'autorité du chef** to yield to the leader's authority **III.** *vpr* ❶ (*être pliant*) **se ~** to fold ❷ (*se soumettre*) **se ~ à la volonté de qn** to yield to sb's will

**plisser** [plise] <1> **I.** *vt* ❶ (*couvrir de faux plis*) to crease ❷ (*froncer: front*) to crease; (*yeux*) to screw up; (*nez*) to wrinkle; (*bouche*) to pucker **II.** *vi* to wrinkle; (*lin, tissu*) to crease

**plomb** [plɔ̃] *m* ❶ (*métal*) lead; **lourd comme du ~** as heavy as lead; **sans ~** (*essence*) unleaded ❷ (*fusible*) fuse ❸ (*pour la chasse*) lead shot; **du ~** shot ❹ (*à la pêche*) sinker ► **sommeil de ~** deep sleep; **par un soleil de ~** under a blazing sun

**plombier** [plɔ̃bje] *m* plumber

**plongé(e)** [plɔ̃ʒe] **I.** *part passé de* plonger **II.** *adj* ❶ (*absorbé*) immersed ❷ (*entouré*) **être ~ dans l'obscurité** to be surrounded by darkness

**plongeant(e)** [plɔ̃ʒɑ̃, ʒɑ̃t] *adj* (*décolleté*) plunging; **une vue ~e sur le parc** a view from above over the park

**plongée** [plɔ̃ʒe] *f* ❶ (*action de plonger*) diving ❷ SPORT **~ sous-marine** scuba diving

**plongeoir** [plɔ̃ʒwaʀ] *m* diving board

**plongeon** [plɔ̃ʒɔ̃] *m* ❶ SPORT dive ❷ (*chute*) fall; **faire un ~** to take a nose-dive

**plonger** [plɔ̃ʒe] <2a> **I.** *vi* ❶ (*s'immerger*) to plunge; **~ à la recherche de qc** to plunge into [*o* immerse oneself in] the search for sth ❷ (*faire un plongeon*) **~ dans l'eau** (*personne, oiseau*) to dive into the water; (*voiture*) to plunge into the water ❸ (*sombrer*) **~ dans le désespoir/la dépression** to plunge into despair/depression **II.** *vpr* **se ~ dans ses pensées** to immerse oneself in one's thoughts

**plongeur, -euse** [plɔ̃ʒœʀ, -ʒøz] *m, f* ❶ SPORT diver ❷ (*dans un restaurant*) dishwasher

**plouc** [pluk] **I.** *mf péj, inf* **être un ~** to be a hick **II.** *adj péj, inf* vulgar, hick

**pluie** [plɥi] *f* ❶ METEO rain; **saison des ~s** rainy season; **jours/temps de ~** rainy days/weather; **sous la ~** in the rain; **le temps est à la ~** it's going to rain ❷ *sans pl* (*grande quantité*) shower ► **après la ~ le beau temps** *prov* every cloud has a silver lining; **faire la ~ et le beau temps** to call the shots

**plume** [plym] *f* ❶ (*penne*) feather ❷ (*pour écrire*) quill

**plumer** [plyme] <1> *vt* (*animal*) to pluck; (*personne*) to rip off

**plupart** [plypaʀ] *f sans pl* **la ~ des élèves/femmes mariées** most students/married women; **la ~ d'entre nous/eux/elles** most of us/them; **la ~ sont venus** most of them came; **dans la ~ des cas** in most cases; **la ~ du temps** most of the time ► **pour la ~** for the most part

**pluriel** [plyʀjɛl] *m* plural

**plus¹** [ply] *adv* ❶ (*opp: encore*) **il n'est ~ très jeune** he's no longer very young;

il ne l'a ~ jamais vu he has never seen him since; **il ne pleut ~ du tout** it's completely stopped raining; **il ne neige presque ~** it has nearly stopped snowing; **il n'y a ~ personne** there's nobody left; **nous n'avons ~ rien à manger** we have nothing left to eat; **il ne dit ~ un mot** he didn't say another word; **elle n'a ~ un sou** she doesn't have a penny left; **ils n'ont ~ d'argent/de beurre** they have no more money/butter; **nous n'avons ~ du tout de pain** we have no bread left at all ❷ (*seulement encore*) **on n'attend ~ que vous** we're only waiting for you now; **il ne manquait ~ que ça** that was all we needed ❸ (*pas plus que*) **non ~** neither

**plus²** [ply(s)] **I.** *adv* ❶ (*davantage*) **être ~ dangereux/bête que lui** to be more dangerous/stupid than him; **deux fois ~ âgé/cher qu'elle** twice as old/expensive as her; **~ tard/tôt/près/lentement qu'hier** later/earlier/nearer/slower than yesterday ❷ (*dans une comparaison*) **je lis ~ que toi** I read more than you; **ce tissu me plaît ~ que l'autre** I like this fabric more than the other one ❸ (*très*) **il est ~ qu'intelligent** he is extremely intelligent; **elle est ~ que contente** she is more than happy ► **~ que jamais** more than ever; **~ ou moins** more or less; **le vin est bon, ni ~ ni moins** the wine is good, nothing more nothing less **II.** *adv emploi superl* **le/la ~ rapide/important(e)** the fastest/most important; **le ~ intelligent des élèves** the most intelligent student; **c'est le ~ intelligent d'eux** he is the most intelligent of all of them; **le ~ vite/souvent** the fastest/most often; **le ~ tard possible** as late as possible; **c'est lui qui lit le ~** he reads the most; **le ~ d'argent/de pages** the most money/pages; **le ~ possible de choses/personnes** as many things/people as possible; **il a pris le ~ de livres/d'argent qu'il pouvait** he took as many books/much money as he

could ► **au ~ tôt/vite** as soon as possible; **tout au ~** at the very most

**plus³** [plys, ply] *adv* more; **pas ~** no more; **~ d'une heure/de 40 ans** more than one hour/40 years; **les enfants de ~ de 12 ans** children over 12 years old; **il est ~ de minuit** it's after midnight; **tu as de l'argent? – ~ qu'il n'en faut** do you have any money? – more than enough; **~ de la moitié** more than half; **j'ai dépensé ~ d'argent que je ne le pensais** I have spent more money than I thought; **~ le temps passe, ~ l'espoir diminue** as time passes, hope fades ► **il réfléchit, (et) moins il a d'idées** the more he thinks, the fewer ideas he has; **de ~** furthermore; **un jour/une assiette de ~** another day/plate; **une fois de ~** once more; **boire de ~ en ~** to drink more and more; **de ~ en ~ beau** more and more beautiful; **de ~ en ~ vite** faster and faster; **en ~** as well; **il est moche, et il est stupide en ~** he is ugly, and he is stupid too; **être en ~** (*en supplément*) to be extra; (*de trop*) to be surplus; **en ~ de qc** as well as sth; **sans ~** and no more

**plus⁴** [plys] **I.** *conj* ❶ (*et*) and; **2 ~ 2 font 4** 2 and 2 make 4; **le loyer ~ les charges** rent plus expenses ❷ (*quantité positive*) **~ quatre degrés** plus four degrees **II.** *m* ❶ MATH plus sign ❷ (*avantage*) plus

**plus⁵** [ply] *passé simple de* **plaire**

**plusieurs** [plyzjœʀ] **I.** *adj antéposé, pl* several **II.** *pron pl* people; **~ m'ont raconté cette histoire** several people have told me this story; **~ d'entre nous/de ces journaux** several of us/of these newspapers ► **à ~ ils ont pu ...** several of them together were able to ...

**plus-que-parfait** [plyskapaʀfɛ] <plus-que-parfaits> *m* pluperfect

**plutôt** [plyto] *adv* ❶ (*de préférence*) **prendre ~ l'avion que le bateau** to take the plane rather than the boat; **cette maladie affecte ~ les enfants** this disease affects mainly children ❷ (*au*

**P**

*lieu de*) ~ **que de parler, il vaudrait mieux que vous écoutiez** rather than speaking, it would be better if you listened ❸ (*mieux*) ~ **mourir que** (**de**) **fuir** better to die than flee ❹ (*et pas vraiment*) **elle n'est pas méchante, ~ lunatique** she is not bad, just temperamental ❺ (*assez*) **être ~ gentil** to be quite kind; **c'est ~ bon signe** it is a pretty good sign; ~ **mal/lentement** fairly badly/slowly ❻ *inf* (*très*) very ❼ (*plus exactement*) **ou** ~ or rather

**P.M.E.** [peɛmø] *f abr de* **petites et moyennes entreprises** SME

**P.M.U.** [peɛmy] *m abr de* **Pari mutuel urbain** ≈ OTB (*horse betting system*)

**P.N.B.** [peɛnbe] *m abr de* **produit national brut** GNP

**pneu** [pnø] *m* tire; **avoir un ~ crevé** to have a flat tire

**pneumatique** [pnømatik] *adj* inflatable

**poche**[1] [pɔʃ] *f* ❶ (*cavité, sac*) bag; ~ **de thé** *Québec* (*sachet de thé*) teabag ❷ (*compartiment*) pocket ▸ **connaître qn/qc comme sa** ~ to know sb/sth like the back of one's hand; **se remplir les ~s** to fill one's pockets; **lampe de ~** flashlight

**poche**[2] [pɔʃ] *m inf* paperback

**poche**[3] [pɔʃ] *f Suisse* (*cuillère à pot, louche*) ladle

**pochette** [pɔʃɛt] *f* ❶ (*étui: de disque*) sleeve ❷ (*mouchoir de veste*) pocket handkerchief ❸ (*petit sac*) clutch bag

**poêle**[1] [pwal] *f* CULIN frying pan

**poêle**[2] [pwal] *m* stove

**poème** [pɔɛm] *m* poem

**poésie** [pɔezi] *f* poetry

**poète** [pɔɛt] *m* ❶ (*écrivain*) poet ❷ (*rêveur*) dreamer

**poétique** [pɔetik] *adj* poetic

**poids** [pwa] *m* ❶ (*mesure, objet, charge, responsabilité*) weight; **quel ~ faites-vous?** how much do you weigh?; **acheter/vendre au ~** to buy/sell by weight; **perdre/prendre du ~** to lose/gain weight; **surveiller son ~** to watch one's weight; **être un grand ~ pour qn** to be a heavy weight for sb; **se sentir**

**délivré d'un grand ~** to feel relieved of a great burden ❷ *sans pl* (*importance*) force; **un argument de ~** a forceful argument; **le ~ économique d'un pays** the economic force of a country; **donner du ~ à qc** to give weight to sth ❸ *sans pl* (*influence*) influence; **un homme de ~** a man of influence ❹ AUTO **~ lourd** freight vehicle ▸ **faire le ~** COM to make up the weight; **faire le ~ devant qn/qc** to be a match for sb/sth

**poignard** [pwaɲaʀ] *m* dagger

**poignarder** [pwaɲaʀde] <1> *vt* to stab

**poigne** [pwaɲ] *f* grip ▸ **avoir de la ~** to have a strong grip; *fig* to have an iron fist; **homme/femme à ~** strong man/woman

**poignée** [pwaɲe] *f* ❶ (*manche*) a. INFORM handle; (*d'une épée*) hilt; (*dans le bus, la baignoire*) grab-handle ❷ (*quantité*) handful; **une ~ de riz/de jeunes gens** a handful of rice/young people ▸ **à** [*o* **par**] (**pleines**) ~**s** in handfuls; **~ de main** handshake

**poignet** [pwaɲɛ] *m* wrist

**poil** [pwal] *m* ❶ ANAT hair; **les ~s de la barbe** the bristles [*o* hairs] of a beard; **il n'a pas de ~ sur le chest** he doesn't have any hair on his chest ❷ ZOOL coat; **à ~ ras/long** smooth-/long-haired; **manteau en ~ de lapin/renard** rabbit skin/fox fur coat; **le chat perd ses ~s** the cat's shedding ❸ (*filament*) bristle; (*d'un tapis, d'une moquette*) pile ❹ *inf* (*un petit peu*) **un ~ de gentillesse** an ounce of kindness ▸ **être de bon/mauvais ~** *inf* to be in a good/bad mood; **à ~** *inf* stark naked; **se mettre à ~** to strip off; **au ~!** *inf* great!

**poing** [pwɛ̃] *m* fist ▸ **envoyer** [*o* **mettre**] **son ~ dans la figure à qn** *inf* to punch sb in the face; **taper du ~ sur la table** to bang one's fist on the table; **dormir à ~s fermés** to sleep like a log

**point** [pwɛ̃] *m* ❶ (*ponctuation*) period; **~s de suspension** suspension points; **~ d'exclamation/d'interrogation** exclamation point/question mark ❷ (*lieu*) **~ de départ** point of departure; **~ de repère** landmark; *fig* reference; **~ de vente** sales point ❸MATH point; **~ d'intersection** point of intersection ❹(*dans une notation*) point ❺(*partie: d'ordre du jour*) point; **~ de détail** point of detail; **être d'accord sur tous les ~s** to agree on all points; **~ par ~** point by point ❻GEO **les quatre ~s cardinaux** the four points of the compass; **~ culminant** peak ❼POL **~ chaud** trouble spot ▸ **qn se fait un ~ d'honneur** [o **met un/son ~ d'honneur à** +*infin*] sb makes it a point (of honor) to +*infin;* **mettre les ~s sur les i à qn** to dot the i's and cross the t's; **~ de vue** viewpoint; (*opinion*) point of view; **à mon ~ de vue** in my opinion; **d'un certain ~ de vue** from a certain point of view; **au** [o **du**] **~ de vue de qc** from the point of view of sth; **au ~ de vue scientifique** from a scientific perspective; **c'est un bon/mauvais ~ pour qn/qc** it is a plus/minus for sb/sth; **jusqu'à un certain ~** (*relativement*) to a certain extent; **avoir raison jusqu'à un certain ~** to be right up to a point; **ça va jusqu'à un certain ~** *inf* it's OK up to a certain point; **~ commun** something in common; **n'avoir aucun ~ commun avec qn** to have nothing in common with sb; **~ faible/fort** weak/strong point; **au plus haut ~** extremely; **être mal en ~** to be unwell; **être toujours au même ~** to still be in the same situation; **~ noir** (*comédon*) blackhead; (*grave difficulté*) problem; (*lieu d'accidents*) (traffic) trouble spot; **à** (**un**) **tel** [o **à un ~ tel**] **que qn fait qc** to such an extent that sb did sth; **être au ~** (*procédé*) to be perfected; (*voiture*) to be tuned; **être sur le ~ de** +*infin* to be just about to +*infin;* **faire le ~ de la situation** (*journal*) to give an update on the situation; **mettre au ~** (*régler*) to tune; (*préparer dans les détails*) to develop; **mettre une technique au ~** to perfect a technique; **mettre qc au ~ avec qn** (*s'en-*

tendre avec qn sur qc) to settle sth with sb; (*éclaircir*) to clear sth up with sb; **je voudrais ma viande à ~** I would like my meat cooked medium; **arriver à ~** to arrive at the right time; **comment a-t-il pu en arriver à ce ~(-là)?** how could he have gotten to this state?; **au ~ qu'on a dû faire qc** [o **que qn fait** [o **fasse** (*subj*)] **qc** to the point where we had to do sth/that sb does sth; **le ~ sur qn/qc** (*dans un journal télévisé*) the update on sb/sth

**pointe** [pwɛt] *f* ❶(*extrémité*) point; **la ~ de l'île** the point of the island ❷(*objet pointu*) spike ❸(*clou*) tack ❹(*de danse*) pointe; **faire des ~s** to dance on pointes ❺(*petite quantité de*) **une ~ de cannelle** a pinch of cinnamon; **une ~ de méchanceté** a touch of evil; **une ~ d'ironie** a hint of irony ▸ **être à la ~ de qc** to be at the forefront of sth; **vitesse de ~** top speed; **heures de ~** rush hour; **de** [o **en**] **~** leading; **technologie/équipe de ~** leading-edge technology/team; **notre société est en ~/reste une entreprise de ~** our company is/remains at the cutting edge; **marcher sur la ~ des pieds** to tiptoe; **se mettre sur la ~ des pieds** to stand on one's tiptoes

**pointer** [pwɛte] <1> I. *vi* ❶ECON (*aller*) **~** (*ouvrier, employé*) to clock in; (*chômeur*) to sign on ❷(*au jeu de boules*) to aim for the jack ❸INFORM **~ sur une icône** to point on a icon II. *vt* (*diriger vers*) **~ qc sur/vers** to aim sth at sb/sth; **~ son/le doigt sur qn** to point one's finger at sb III. *vpr inf* **se ~** to show up

**pointeur** [pwɛtœʀ] *m* INFORM **~ de la souris** mouse pointer

**pointillé** [pwɛtije] *m* dotted line; **être en ~(s)** to appear in outline

**pointilleux, -euse** [pwɛtijø, -jøz] *adj* **être ~ sur qc** to be particular about sth

**pointu(e)** [pwɛty] *adj* ❶(*acéré*) razor sharp ❷(*grêle et aigu*) shrill ❸(*très poussé: formation*) intensive; (*analyse*) in-depth; (*sujet*) specialized

**P**

**pointure** [pwɛ̃tyʀ] f (shoe) size; **quelle est votre ~?** what size are you?

**point-virgule** [pwɛ̃viʀgyl] <points-virgules> m semicolon

**poire** [pwaʀ] f pear

**poireau** [pwaʀo] <x> m leek

**pois** [pwa] m pea; **~ cassés** split peas; **~ chiche** chick pea; **petit ~** peas ▶ **à ~** spotted

**poison** [pwazɔ̃] I. m poison II. mf inf ❶ (personne) nuisance ❷ (enfant insupportable) horror

**poisse** [pwas] f inf bad luck; **porter la ~ à qn** inf to be a jinx on sb; **quelle ~!** what bad luck!

**poisseux, -euse** [pwaso, -øz] adj sticky

**poisson** [pwasɔ̃] m ZOOL fish; **~ rouge** goldfish ▶ **être comme un ~ dans l'eau** to be in one's element; **~ d'avril** April Fool's Day; ▶ **~ d'avril!** April fool!

**poissonnerie** [pwasɔnʀi] f (boutique) fish shop

**Poissons** [pwasɔ̃] m Pisces; v.a. **Balance**

**Poitou** [pwatu] m **le ~** Poitou

**poitrine** [pwatʀin] f ❶ (d'un homme) chest; (d'une femme) breast; **le tour de ~** (d'un homme) chest measurement; (d'une femme) bust measurement ❷ CULIN breast

**poivre** [pwavʀ] m sans pl pepper

**poivrer** [pwavʀe] <1> I. vt **~ qc** to add pepper to sth II. vi to add pepper

**poivrière** [pwavʀijɛʀ] f pepper pot; (moulin) pepper mill

**poivron** [pwavʀɔ̃] m bell pepper

**polaire** [pɔlɛʀ] adj GEO polar

**polaroïd®** [pɔlaʀɔid] m ❶ (appareil) Polaroid® (camera) ❷ (photo) Polaroid® (picture)

**pôle** [pol] m GEO pole; **~ Nord/Sud** North/South Pole

**poli(e)** [pɔli] adj polite

**police¹** [pɔlis] f sans pl police; **~ judiciaire** ≈ Criminal Investigations Department; **~ municipale/nationale** local/national police force; **~ de l'air et des frontières** border patrol; **~ de la route** traffic police; **~ des mœurs** vice squad;

**~ secours** ≈ emergency services ▶ **faire la ~** to keep order

**police²** [pɔlis] f ❶ (contrat) **~ d'assurance** insurance policy ❷ INFORM **~ de caractères** font

**policier, -ière** [pɔlisje, -jɛʀ] I. adj **chien/état ~** police dog/state; **roman/film ~** detective novel/movie; **femme ~** policewoman II. m, f police officer

**poliment** [pɔlimɑ̃] adv politely

**politesse** [pɔlitɛs] f ❶ sans pl (courtoisie) politeness; **faire qc par ~** to do sth out of politeness ❷ pl (propos) polite remarks; (comportements) gestures of politeness; **se faire des ~s** to exchange polite remarks

**politicien(ne)** [pɔlitisjɛ̃, jɛn] m(f) politician

**politique** [pɔlitik] I. adj political II. f ❶ POL politics + vb sing; **~ économique/intérieure/sociale** economic/domestic/social politics; **~ de droite/gauche** right-/left-wing politics; **faire de la ~** to be involved in politics ❷ (ligne de conduite) policy; **pratiquer la ~ du moindre effort** to take the easy way out III. mf ❶ (gouvernant) politician ❷ (prisonnier politique) political prisoner ❸ (domaine politique) politics

**polluant** [pɔlɥɑ̃] m pollutant

**polluant(e)** [pɔlɥɑ̃, ɑ̃t] adj polluting

**polluer** [pɔlɥe] <1> vt, vi to pollute

**pollution** [pɔlysjɔ̃] f pollution

**polo** [pɔlo] m ❶ (chemise) polo shirt ❷ SPORT polo

**Pologne** [pɔlɔɲ] f la ~ Poland

**polonais** [pɔlɔnɛ] m Polish; v.a. **français**

**polonais(e)** [pɔlɔnɛ, ɛz] adj Polish

**Polynésie française** [pɔlinezifʀɑ̃sɛz] f la ~ French Polynesia

**pommade** [pɔmad] f ointment

**pomme** [pɔm] f ❶ (fruit) apple ❷ (pomme de terre) **~s dauphines** pommes [o potatoes] dauphine ❸ ANAT **~ d'Adam** Adam's apple ❹ BOT **~ de pin** pinecone ▶ **être/tomber dans les ~s** to have fainted/faint; **pour ma ~**

*inf* down to yours truly; **la vaisselle, ça va encore être pour ma ~!** yours truly is going to get stuck with the dishes again!

**pomme de terre** [pɔmdətɛʀ] <pommes de terre> *f* potato

**pommier** [pɔmje] *m* apple tree

**pompe** [pɔ̃p] *f* **①** (*machine*) pump; **~ à essence** gas pump; **~ à incendie** fire engine **②** *inf* (*chaussure*) shoe **③** *inf* SPORT pushups; **faire des ~s** to do push-ups ▶ **avoir un coup de ~** *inf* to feel suddenly exhausted; **être à côté de ses ~s** *inf* to be out of it

**pomper** [pɔ̃pe] <1> *vi* **①** (*puiser*) to pump **②** *inf* ECOLE **~ sur qn** to copy from sb

**pompier** [pɔ̃pje] *m* fireman ▶ **fumer comme un ~** to smoke like a chimney

**pompiste** [pɔ̃pist] *mf* gas station attendant

**poncer** [pɔ̃se] <2> *vt* to sand down

**ponctualité** [pɔ̃ktɥalite] *f* punctuality

**ponctuation** [pɔ̃ktɥasjɔ̃] *f* punctuation; **signes de ~** punctuation marks

**ponctuel(le)** [pɔ̃ktɥɛl] *adj* **①** (*exact*) punctual **②** (*momentané*) occasional; (*unique*) one-time

**pondre** [pɔ̃dʀ] <14> *vt, vi* to lay

**poney** [pɔnɛ] *m* pony

**pont** [pɔ̃] *m* **①** ARCHIT, NAUT bridge; **~ basculant/suspendu/routier** bascule/suspension/road bridge **②** (*vacances*) **faire le ~** to make it a long weekend (*by taking extra days off before or after a public holiday*) ▶ **couper les ~s avec qn/qc** to burn one's bridges with sb/sth

**populaire** [pɔpylɛʀ] *adj* **①** (*du peuple*) **république ~** people's republic **②** (*destiné à la masse*) popular; **bal ~** local dance **③** (*plébéien: goût*) common; **quartier ~** working-class area; **classes ~s** working classes **④** (*qui plaît*) well-liked; (*personne*) popular

**popularité** [pɔpylaʀite] *f* popularity

**population** [pɔpylasjɔ̃] *f* population

**porc** [pɔʀ] *m* **①** ZOOL pig **②** (*chair*) pork **③** *péj, inf* (*personne*) swine

**porcelaine** [pɔʀsəlɛn] *f* **①** (*matière*) porcelain **②** (*vaisselle*) china

**porcherie** [pɔʀʃəʀi] *f* pigsty

**porno** [pɔʀno] *inf abr de* **pornographie, pornographique**

**pornographie** [pɔʀnɔgʀafi] *f* pornography

**pornographique** [pɔʀnɔgʀafik] *adj* pornographic

**port¹** [pɔʀ] *m* NAUT, INFORM port; **~ fluvial/maritime** river/sea port; **~ de pêche** fishing port; **~ jeu/parallèle/série/imprimante** game/parallel/serial/printer port

**port²** [pɔʀ] *m* **①** (*fait de porter: d'un vêtement, casque, objet*) wearing; **~ obligatoire de la ceinture de sécurité** seatbelts must be worn **②** COM shipping; (*d'une lettre*) postage; **~ dû/payé** postage due/paid **③** (*allure: d'une personne*) bearing

**portable** [pɔʀtabl] **I.** *adj* portable **II.** *m* **①** TEL cell phone **②** INFORM laptop [*o* notebook] (computer)

**portail** [pɔʀtaj] <s> *m* **①** (*porte*) gate **②** INFORM portal

**portant(e)** [pɔʀtɑ̃, ɑ̃t] *adj* **être bien/mal ~** to be in good/poor health

**portatif, -ive** [pɔʀtatif, -iv] *adj* portable

**porte** [pɔʀt] *f* **①** (*ouverture, panneau mobile*) door; (*plus grand*) gate; **~ de garage** garage door; **~ du four/de la maison** oven/front door; **~ de devant/derrière** front/back door; **~ de secours** emergency exit; **~ de service** service entrance; **~ d'embarquement** departure gate; **à la ~** at the door; *Belgique* (*dehors, à l'extérieur*) outside; **de ~ en ~** from door to door; **forcer la ~** to force the door open; **claquer** [*o* **fermer**] **la ~ au nez de qn** to slam the door in sb's face **②** (*entrée: d'un château, d'une ville*) gate; **~ de Clignancourt** Porte de Clignancourt; **~ de Bourgogne** gateway to Burgundy ▶ **être aimable/poli comme une ~ de prison** to be like a bear with a sore head; **entrer par la grande/petite ~** to start at the top/bottom; **toutes les**

**P**

~s lui sont <u>ouvertes</u> every door is open to him; (**journée**) ~s <u>ouvertes</u> open house (day); **écouter** aux ~s to eavesdrop; <u>fermer</u>/<u>ouvrir</u> sa ~ à qn to close/open the door to sb; <u>forcer</u> la ~ de qn to force one's way into sb's home; <u>frapper</u> à la ~ de qn to knock at sb's door; <u>mettre</u> qn à la ~ to kick sb out; <u>prendre</u> la ~ to leave; **à** la ~ ! get out!; **à** [o <u>devant</u>] ma ~ nearby; **ce n'est pas la ~ à côté!** it's a way's away!

**porte-bagages** [pɔʀtbagaʒ] *m inv* ❶ (*sur un deux-roues*) rack ❷ (*dans un train*) luggage rack

**porte-bonheur** [pɔʀtbɔnœʀ] *m inv* good-luck charm

**porte-clés** [pɔʀtəkle] *m inv* key chain

**porte-documents** [pɔʀtdɔkymɑ̃] *m inv* briefcase

**portée** [pɔʀte] *f* ❶ (*distance*) range; **à ~ de vue** within sight; **à ~ de voix/de la main** within earshot/reach; **à la ~ de qn** within sb's reach; **hors de la ~ de qn** out of sb's reach ❷ (*effet: d'un acte, événement*) consequences *pl*; (*d'un argument, de paroles*) impact ❸ MUS staff ❹ ZOOL litter ❺ (*aptitude, niveau*) **être à la ~ de qn** (*livre, discours*) to be suitable for sb; **cet examen est à votre ~** this exam is within your abilities; **mettre qc à la ~ de qn** to make sth accessible to sb ❻ (*accessibilité*) **être à la ~ de qn** to be available to everyone; **à la ~ de toutes les bourses** suitable for all budgets

**portefeuille** [pɔʀtəfœj] *m* wallet

**portemanteau** [pɔʀtmɑ̃to] <x> *m* coat tree; (*mobile*) hat stand; (*crochets au mur*) coat rack

**porte-monnaie** [pɔʀtmɔnɛ] *m inv* purse

**porte-parapluies** [pɔʀtpaʀaplɥi] *m inv* umbrella stand

**porte-parole** [pɔʀtpaʀɔl] *m inv* ❶ (*personne*) spokesperson ❷ (*journal*) mouthpiece

**porter** [pɔʀte] <1> **I.** *vt* ❶ (*tenir*) to carry ❷ (*endosser: responsabilité, faute*) to shoulder; **faire ~ qc à qn** to make sb

shoulder sth ❸ *a. fig* (*apporter: en allant*) to take; (*en venant*) to bring; (*lettre, colis*) to deliver; (*attention*) to attract; (*assistance, secours*) to give; **la nuit porte conseil** it's best to sleep on it ❹ (*diriger*) **~ son regard/ses yeux sur qn/qc** to turn towards/one's eyes towards sb/sth; **~ son choix sur qc** to choose sth; **~ ses pas vers la porte** to turn one's feet towards the door; **~ le verre à ses lèvres** to bring the glass to one's lips; **~ la main au chapeau** to touch one's hat with one's hand; **~ la main à sa poche** to put one's hand in one's pocket; **~ qn quelque part** to take sb somewhere ❺ (*avoir sur soi: vêtement, lunettes*) to wear; (*nom, titre*) to carry; **~ la barbe/les cheveux longs** to have a beard/long hair ❻ (*révéler: traces*) to reveal; (*marque de fabrique*) to carry ❼ (*ressentir*) **~ de l'intérêt à qn/qc** to show an interest in sb/sth ❽ (*inscrire*) **être porté malade** to be called in sick; **être porté disparu** to be reported missing; **se faire ~ absent** to go missing ❾ (*avoir en soi*) **~ de la haine en soi** to feel hatred inside **II.** *vi* ❶ (*avoir pour objet*) **~ sur qc** (*action, effort*) to be concerned with sth; (*discours*) to be about sth; (*revendications, divergences, étude*) to concern sth; (*question, critique*) to revolve around sth ❷ (*avoir telle étendue*) **~ sur qc** to concern sth; (*préjudice*) to extend to sth ❸ (*faire effet: coup, critique*) to hit home; (*conseil*) to have its effect ❹ (*avoir une certaine portée: voix*) to carry ❺ (*reposer sur*) **~ sur qc** (*édifice, poids*) to be supported by sth; (*accent*) to fall on sth **III.** *vpr* ❶ (*aller*) **se ~ bien/mal** to be well/not well ❷ (*se présenter comme*) **se ~ acquéreur de qc** to offer to buy sth; **se ~ candidat** to come forward as a candidate; **se ~ volontaire** to volunteer ❸ (*se diriger*) **se ~ sur qn/qc** (*regard, choix, soupçon*) to fall on sb/sth; **se ~ vers qc** (*personne*) to go toward sb/sth ❹ (*être porté*) **se ~ en été/hiver** (*vête-*

*ments*) to be worn in summer/winter; **se ~ beaucoup en ce moment** to be fashionable at the moment

**porteur, -euse** [pɔʀtœʀ, -øz] *m, f* messenger

**portier, -ière** [pɔʀtje, -jɛʀ] *m, f* porter

**portière** [pɔʀtjɛʀ] *f* CHEMDFER, AUTO door

**portion** [pɔʀsjɔ̃] *f* CULIN portion, helping

**portoricain(ne)** [pɔʀtɔʀikɛ̃, -ɛn] *adj* Puerto Rican

**portrait** [pɔʀtʀɛ] *m* ❶ ART, PHOT portrait; **~ fidèle** good likeness; **faire le ~ de qn** (*peindre*) to paint a portrait of sb; (*faire une photo*) to take a portrait of sb ❷ (*description: d'une personne*) profile; (*d'une société*) portrait; **faire le ~ de qn** to paint a picture of sb ▸ **être tout le ~ de qn** to be the spitting image of sb

**portrait-robot** [pɔʀtʀɛʀɔbo] <portraits-robots> *m* ❶ police sketch ❷ (*caractéristiques*) profile

**portugais** [pɔʀtygɛ] *m* Portuguese; *v.a.* **français**

**portugais(e)** [pɔʀtygɛ, ɛz] *adj* Portuguese

**Portugais(e)** [pɔʀtygɛ, ɛz] *m(f)* Portuguese

**Portugal** [pɔʀtygal] *m* **le ~** Portugal

**pose** [poz] *f* ❶ (*attitude*) posture; ART, PHOT pose ❷ PHOT (*exposition*) exposure; (*photo*) photo

**poser** [poze] <1> **I.** *vt* ❶ (*mettre: livre, main, bagages*) to put down; (*échelle*) to lean; (*pieds*) to place; **~ qc par terre** to put sth down on the ground ❷ MATH (*opération*) to write; (*équation*) to set down ❸ (*installer: moquette*) to lay; (*rideau, tapisserie*) to hang; (*serrure*) to install ❹ (*énoncer: définition, principe*) to set out; (*devinette*) to set; (*question*) to ask; (*condition*) to lay down ❺ (*soulever: problème, question*) to put ❻ *Belgique, Québec* (*commettre, accomplir un acte*) **~ un acte** to carry out an act **II.** *vi* **~ pour qn/qc** to pose for sb/sth **III.** *vpr* **1** (*exister*) **se ~** (*question, difficulté, problème*) to arise; **se ~ des problèmes** to think about

problems; **il se pose la question si ...** he's wondering if ... ❷ (*cesser de voler*) **se ~ dans/sur qc** (*insecte, oiseau, avion*) to land in/on sth ❸ (*se fixer*) **se ~ sur qc** (*regard, yeux*) to turn towards sth; (*main*) to touch sth ❹ (*s'appliquer*) **se ~ facilement** (*moquette*) to be easy to install; (*papier peint, rideau*) to be easy to hang

**positif, -ive** [pozitif, -iv] *adj* positive

**position** [pozisjɔ̃] *f* (*emplacement, posture, en danse, situation*) position; (*dans une course*) place; **arriver en première/dernière ~** (*coureur, candidat*) to come in first/last place; **la ~ debout** standing; **en ~ allongée** lying down; **se mettre en ~ allongée/assise** to lie/sit down ▸ **être en ~ de force** to be in a position of strength

**positivement** [pozitivmɑ̃] *adv* positively

**positiver** [pozitive] <-> *vi* (*montrer sa confiance*) think positive

**posologie** [pozɔlɔʒi] *f* dosage

**posséder** [pɔsede] <5> *vt* ❶ (*avoir*) to possess ❷ (*disposer de: expérience, talent, mémoire, réflexes*) to have ❸ *inf* (*rouler*) to take in

**possessif** [pɔsesif] *m* possessive

**possessif, -ive** [pɔsesif, -iv] *adj* possessive

**possession** [pɔsesjɔ̃] *f* possession; **avoir qc en sa ~** to have sth in one's possession; **entrer en ~ de qc** to take possession of sth

**possibilité** [pɔsibilite] *f* ❶ (*éventualité*) possibility ❷ *pl* (*moyens matériels*) means; (*moyens intellectuels*) abilities

**possible** [pɔsibl] **I.** *adj* ❶ (*faisable, éventuel, indiquant une limite: cas, mesures*) possible; (*projet*) feasible; **il est ~ qu'il vienne** he may come; **les tomates les plus grosses ~s** the largest possible tomatoes; **autant que ~** as much as possible ❷ *inf* (*supportable*) **ne pas être ~** (*personne*) to be impossible ▸ **et imaginable** possible; (**c'est**) **pas ~!** *inf* I don't believe it! **II.** *m* **faire** (**tout**) **son ~ pour faire qc/**

**P**

**pour que** qn +*subj* to do everything one can to make sth happen/for sb to +*infin*

**postal(e)** [pɔstal, -o] <-aux> *adj* **carte ~e** postcard; **code ~** zip code

**poste¹** [pɔst] *f* (*bâtiment, administration*) post office; **mettre à la ~** to mail; **par la ~** by mail ► **~ aérienne** airmail; **~ restante** general delivery

**poste²** [pɔst] *m* ❶ (*emploi*) job; **~ de diplomate/de directeur** diplomatic/managerial post; **~ de professeur** teaching job; **être en ~ à New York/au ministère** to have a position in New York/at the ministry ❷ (*lieu de travail*) workplace ❸ (*appareil*) set; **~ de radio/de télévision** radio/television set ❹ (*lieu*) **~ de douane/de contrôle** customs/control post; **~ de police** police station; **~ frontière/de secours** border/first-aid post ❺ MIL post; **~ de commandement** command post; **~ d'observation** observation post ❻ INFORM **~ de travail** work station

**poster¹** [pɔste] <1> *vt* to post

**poster²** [pɔstɛʀ] *m* poster

**postillon** [pɔstijɔ̃] *m* spit; **envoyer des ~s à** qn to splutter at sb

**pot** [po] *m* ❶ (*en terre, en plastique*) pot; (*en verre*) jar; (*en métal*) can; **~ à eau/à lait** water/milk jug; **~ de confiture/miel** jar of jam/honey; **petit ~ pour bébé** jar of baby food; **mettre des plantes en ~** to pot plants ❷ *inf* (*chance*) **c'est pas de ~!** tough luck!; **avoir du ~/ne pas avoir de ~** to be lucky/unlucky ❸ *inf* (*consommation*) drink; (*réception*) cocktail party; (*d'adieu*) farewell party; **payer un ~ à** qn to buy sb a drink; **prendre un ~** to have a drink ❹ (*pot de chambre*) chamber pot; (*pour enfant*) potty ► **~ de colle** *inf* leech; **~ catalytique** catalytic converter; **~ d'échappement** exhaust pipe; **être sourd comme un ~** to be as deaf as a doorknob; **tourner autour du ~** to beat around the bush

**potable** [pɔtabl] *adj* potable; (*eau*) drinking

**potage** [pɔtaʒ] *m* soup

**potager** [pɔtaʒe] *m* vegetable garden

**potager, -ère** [pɔtaʒe, -ɛʀ] *adj* vegetable

**pote** [pɔt] *m inf* buddy

**poteau** [pɔto] <x> *m* post; **~ d'arrivée/départ** finishing/starting post; **~ électrique/télégraphique** electricity/telephone pole

**potelé(e)** [pɔtle] *adj* chubby; (*bras*) plump

**poterie** [pɔtʀi] *f* pottery

**potier, -ière** [pɔtje, -jɛʀ] *m, f* potter

**potimarron** [pɔtimaʀɔ̃] *m* BOT, GASTR red kuri squash

**potion** [posjɔ̃] *f* potion

**potiron** [pɔtiʀɔ̃] *m* pumpkin

**pou** [pu] <x> *m* louse ► **chercher des ~x à** qn to be out to make trouble for sb; **laid comme un ~** *inf* as ugly as sin

**poubelle** [pubɛl] *f* ❶ (*dans la cuisine*) trash (can) ❷ (*devant la porte*) garbage can

**pouce** [pus] *m* ❶ (*doigt: de la main*) thumb; (*du pied*) big toe ❷ (*mesure*) inch ❸ *Québec* (*auto-stop*) **faire du ~** to hitchhike ► **donner un coup de ~ à** qc to give sth a boost; **se tourner les ~s** *inf* to twiddle one's thumbs; **ne pas avancer d'un ~** to make no progress; **ne pas reculer d'un ~** to not back down an inch

**poudre** [pudʀ] *f* ❶ (*fines particules*) powder; **sucre en ~** caster sugar ❷ (*produit cosmétique*) face powder ► **prendre la ~ d'escampette** to hightail it; **jeter de la ~ aux yeux à** qn to try to impress sb; **il n'a pas inventé la ~** *inf* he's no rocket scientist

**poudrier** [pudʀije] *m* powder compact

**pouffer** [pufe] <1> *vi* **~ (de rire)** to burst out laughing

**poulailler** [pulaje] *m* henhouse

**poulain** [pulɛ̃] *m* foal

**poule** [pul] *f* ❶ (*femelle du coq*) hen ❷ (*poulet*) chicken ► **quand les ~s auront des dents** when pigs fly; **~ mouillée** wimp

**poulet** [pulɛ] *m* chicken

**poumon** [pumɔ̃] *m* lung; **à pleins ~s** at the top of one's voice; (*respirer*) deeply

**poupée** [pupe] *f* doll; **jouer à la ~** to play dolls

**pour** [puʀ] **I.** *prep* ❶ for; **j'en ai ~ une heure!** I'll be an hour!; **être grand ~ son âge** to be tall for one's age ❷ (*en direction de*) for; **partir ~ Paris/l'étranger** to leave for Paris/to go abroad; **~ où?** where to? ❸ (*en faveur de*) **~ qn/qc** for sb/sth; **être ~ faire qc** to be for doing sth ❹ (*quant à*) as for; **~ moi** as for me ❺ (*à cause de*) for; **merci ~ votre cadeau!** thank you for your gift; **remercier qn ~ avoir fait qc** to thank sb for having done sth ❻ (*à la place de*) for ❼ (*comme*) **prendre ~ femme** to take as sb's wife; **j'ai ~ principe de faire** it's a principle with me to do; **avoir ~ effet** to have as an effect ❽ (*pour ce qui est de*) **~ être furieux, je le suis!** I am so furious!; **~ autant que je sache** as far as I know ❾ (*dans le but de*) **~** +*infin* (in order) to +*infin*; **ce n'est pas ~ me déplaire** it's something I'm very pleased about; **~ que tu comprennes** so that you understand; **il est trop jeune ~** +*infin* he's too young to +*infin* ▸ **œil ~ œil, dent ~ dent** an eye for an eye, a tooth for a tooth **II.** *m* **le ~ et le contre** the pros and cons

**pourboire** [puʀbwaʀ] *m* tip

**pourcentage** [puʀsɑ̃] *m* ❶ *a.* COM **~ sur qc** markup on sth; **travailler/ être payé au ~** to work/be paid on commission ❷ (*proportion pour cent*) percentage

**pourchasser** [puʀʃase] <1> *vt* to pursue

**pourpre** [puʀpʀ] *adj* purple

**pourquoi** [puʀkwa] **I.** *conj* (*pour quelle raison, à quoi bon*) why; **~ continuer/ chercher?** why go on/look? ▸ **c'est ~** that's why; **c'est ~?** *inf* why's that? **II.** *adv* why; **je me demande bien ~** I wonder why; **voilà ~** that's why; **~ pas? [ó non?]** why not? **III.** *m inv* ❶ (*raison*) **le ~ de qc** the reason for sth; **chercher le ~ et le comment** to look for the how and why ❷ (*question*) question why

**pourri** [puʀi] *m* ❶ (*pourriture*) **ça sent le ~ dans cette pièce!** there's a rotten smell in this room! ❷ *péj* (*homme corrompu*) crook

**pourri(e)** [puʀi] *adj* ❶ (*putréfié: fruit, œuf, arbre, planche*) rotten; (*poisson, viande*) bad; (*cadavre*) rotting ❷ (*infect*) rotten; **quel temps ~!** what rotten weather! ❸ (*corrompu: personne, société*) corrupt ❹ (*gâté: enfant*) spoiled

**pourriel** [puʀjɛl] *m Can* INET spam

**pourrir** [puʀiʀ] <8> **I.** *vi* (*se putréfier: œuf, arbre, planche, fruit*) to rot; (*poisson*) to go bad; (*cadavre*) to decompose **II.** *vt* (*aliment*) to go bad; (*bois, végétaux, fruit*) to rot; (*enfant*) to become spoiled (rotten)

**poursuivre** [puʀsɥivʀ] *irr* **I.** *vt* ❶ (*courir après*) to pursue ❷ (*harceler*) **~ qn** (*personne*) to harass sb; (*souvenir, images, remords*) to hound sb ❸ (*rechercher: bonheur, gloire, idéal*) to seek; (*but*) to aim for; (*vérité*) to pursue ❹ (*continuer*) to continue; (*combat, enquête*) to pursue **II.** *vi* (*continuer*) to continue a story ❷ (*persévérer*) to persevere **III.** *vpr* **se ~** to continue; (*enquête, grève*) to carry on

**pourtant** [puʀtɑ̃] *adv* ❶ (*marque l'opposition, le regret*) however ❷ (*marque l'étonnement*) all the same; **c'est ~ facile!** it's easy though!

**pourvu** [puʀvy] *conj* ❶ (*souhait*) just so long as; **~ que nous ne manquions pas le train!** let's hope we don't miss the train! ❷ (*condition*) **~ que cela vous convienne** provided that it suits you

**poussé(e)** [puse] *adj* (*étude, technique*) advanced; (*discussion, enquête*) extensive; (*travail*) intensive; (*précision*) exhaustive

**pousser** [puse] <1> **I.** *vt* ❶ (*déplacer*) to push; (*troupeau*) to drive ❷ (*pour ouvrir*) **~ la porte/la fenêtre** to push the door/window open; (*pour fermer*);

P

~ **la porte/la fenêtre** to shut the door/window ❸ (*ouvrir en claquant*) ~ **la porte/la fenêtre** to fling the door/window open; (*fermer en claquant*); ~ **la porte/la fenêtre** to slam the door/window shut ❹ (*bousculer*) ~ **qn/qc du coude/pied** to nudge sb/sth with one's elbow/foot ❺ (*entraîner: courant, vent*) to push ❻ (*stimuler: candidat, élève, cheval*) to urge on; ~ **un moteur/une machine** to work an engine/a machine hard; **l'intérêt/l'ambition le pousse** he's driven by self-interest/ambition ❼ (*inciter à*) ~ **qn à** +*infin* to push sb to +*infin*; (*envie, intérêt, ambition*) to drive sb to +*infin*; ~ **qn à la consommation** to encourage sb to consume; ~ **qn au crime** to drive sb to crime ❽ (*diriger*) ~ **qn vers qc/qn** to push sb towards sth/sb ❾ (*émettre: cri, soupir*) to let out; ~ **des cris de joie** to shout with joy; ~ **des gémissements** to whimper ❿ (*exagérer*) ~ **qc à l'extrême/trop loin** to push sth to extremes/too far; ~ **la jalousie/la gentillesse jusqu'à faire qc** to carry jealousy/kindness to the point of doing sth ⓫ (*approfondir*) ~ **plus loin les études/recherches** to further study/research ⓬ (*poursuivre: enquête, recherches*) to pursue ⓭ (*cultiver*) **faire ~ des salades/légumes** to grow lettuce/vegetables; **faire ~ des fleurs** to grow flowers ⓮ (*grandir*) **se laisser ~ les cheveux/la barbe** to let one's hair/beard grow **II.** *vi* ❶ (*croître*) to grow; **sa première dent a poussé** his/her first tooth has grown ❷ (*faire un effort pour accoucher, pour aller à la selle*) to push ❸ (*aller*) ~ **jusqu'à Toulon** to press on as far as Toulon ❹ *inf* (*exagérer*) to overdo it **III.** *vpr* **se ~** ❶ (*s'écarter*) to shift; **pousse-toi un peu!** (*sur un banc*) move up a bit!; (*pour laisser un passage*) out of the way! ❷ (*se bousculer*) to jostle each other

**poussette** [pusɛt] *f* (*voiture d'enfant*) stroller

**poussière** [pusjɛʀ] *f* dust; **faire la ~** to do the dusting; **avoir une ~ dans l'œil** to have something in one's eye ▶ **réduire qn/qc en ~** to reduce sb/sth to dust; **tomber en ~** to crumble into dust; **2000 dollars et des ~s** *inf* 2,000 dollars and change

**poussiéreux, -euse** [pusjeʀø, -øz] *adj* dusty

**poussin** [pusɛ̃] *m* chick

**poutre** [putʀ] *f* ❶ ARCHIT (*de bois*) beam ❷ ARCHIT (*de métal*) girder ❸ SPORT beam

**pouvoir¹** [puvwaʀ] *irr* **I.** *aux* ❶ (*être autorisé*) can, may; **tu peux aller jouer** you may go and play; **il ne peut pas venir** he can't come; **puis-je fermer la fenêtre?** may I close the window? ❷ (*être capable de*) can, to be able to; **j'ai fait ce que j'ai pu** I did what I could; **je ne peux pas m'empêcher de tousser** I can't stop coughing ❸ (*éventualité*) **quel âge peut-il bien avoir?** how old can he be? ❹ (*suggestion*) **tu peux me prêter ton vélo?** could you please lend me your bike?; **tu aurais pu nous le dire plus tôt!** you could have told us sooner! **II.** *aux impers* **il peut/pourrait pleuvoir** it could/might rain; **il aurait pu y avoir un accident** there could have been an accident; **cela peut arriver** that may happen; **il peut se faire que** +*subj* it could happen that **III.** *vt* (*être capable de*) ~ **quelque chose pour qn** to be able to do something for sb; **ne rien faire pour qn** not to be able to do anything for sb ▶ **n'en plus ~ de qc** not to be able to take any more of sth; **je n'y peux rien** (*ne suis pas responsable*) it's got nothing to do with me; **on peut dire que qn a bien fait qc** sb certainly did sth well; **le moins qu'on puisse dire** the least that can be said; **qu'est-ce que cela peut te faire?** what's that got to do with you?; **ne rien ~ (y) faire** not to be able to do anything about it **IV.** *vpr impers* **cela se peut/pourrait** that is/could be possible; **non, ça ne se**

**peut pas** no, that's impossible; **il se pourrait qu'elle vienne** she might come

**pouvoir²** [puvwaʀ] m ①POL power; **prendre le** ~ to seize power ②(*autorité, influence*) ~ **sur qn** power over sb ③ECON ~ **d'achat** purchasing power

**prairie** [pʀeʀi] f meadow

**praline** [pʀaline] f ① ~ **grillée** caramelized peanut ②*Belgique* (*bonbon au chocolat*) chocolate

**pratique** [pʀatik] I. *adj* ①(*commode*) handy; (*solution*) practical; (*emploi du temps*) convenient ②(*réaliste*) practical; **n'avoir aucun sens** ~ to be not at all practical; **dans la vie** ~ in real life ③(*opp: théorique*) practical; **travaux** ~**s** lab work II. f ①(*opp: théorie, procédé*) practice; **dans la** [o **en**] ~ in practice; **mettre en** ~ to put into practice ②(*expérience*) practical experience; **avoir la** ~ **du métier** to be experienced in a profession; ~ **de la conduite** driving experience ③(*coutume*) practice

**pratiquement** [pʀatikmɑ̃] *adv* ①(*en réalité*) in practice ②(*presque*) practically

**pratiquer** [pʀatike] <1> I. *vt* ①(*exercer, mettre en pratique*) to practice; ~ **le tennis/golf** to play tennis/golf; **les prix qu'ils pratiquent** their prices ②(*faire: trou*) to make; (*opération*) to carry out II. *vi* MED, REL to practice

**pré** [pʀe] m field

**préalable** [pʀealabl] I. *adj* (*entretien, question*) preliminary; **je voudrais votre accord/avis** ~ I'd like your prior agreement/opinion II. m preliminary; **sans** (**aucun**) ~ without any preliminaries ► **au** ~ previously

**précaution** [pʀekosjɔ̃] f ①(*disposition*) precaution ②(*prudence*) caution; **par** ~ as a precaution; **s'entourer de** ~**s** to take every possible precaution

**précédent(e)** [pʀesedɑ̃, ɑ̃t] *adj* previous; **le jour** ~ the day before

**précéder** [pʀesede] <5> I. *vt* ①(*dans le temps, dans l'espace*) to precede; **le**

**jour qui précédait leur départ** the day preceding their departure; **l'article précède le nom** the article precedes the noun ②(*devancer*) ~ **qn** to go in front of sb ③(*devancer en voiture*) ~ **qn** to be in front of sb; **je vais vous** ~ **pour …** I am going to drive on ahead of you to …; **elle m'a précédé de quelques minutes** she was ahead of me by a few minutes II. *vi* to precede; **les jours qui précédaient** the preceding days

**prêcher** [pʀeʃe] <1> I. *vt* (*l'Évangile, croisade*) to preach; (*fraternité, haine*) to advocate II. *vi* REL to preach

**précieusement** [pʀesjøzmɑ̃] *adv* carefully

**précieux, -euse** [pʀesjø, -jøz] *adj* precious

**précipice** [pʀesipis] m precipice

**précipitamment** [pʀesipitamɑ̃] *adv* hurriedly; (*partir, s'enfuir*) in a rush

**précipitation** [pʀesipitasjɔ̃] f ①(*hâte*) haste; (*d'un départ, une décision*) hurry; **sans** ~ unhurriedly; **avec** ~ in haste; **partir avec** ~ to rush off ② *pl* METEO rainfall

**précipité(e)** [pʀesipite] *adj* ①(*hâtif: fuite, départ*) hurried; (*décision*) rushed ②(*accéléré: pas, rythme, respiration*) rapid

**précipiter** [pʀesipite] <1> I. *vt* ①(*jeter*) ~ **qn de l'escalier** to throw sb down the stairs; ~ **la voiture contre un arbre** to smash the car into a tree ②(*plonger*) ~ **qn dans le malheur** to plunge sb into misery; ~ **qn dans les bras de qn** to throw sb into sb's arms ③(*accélérer: pas, démarche*) to quicken ④(*brusquer: départ, décision*) to hasten; **il ne faut rien** ~ we must not be hasty ⑤ CHIM to precipitate II. *vi* CHIM to precipitate III. *vpr* (*s'élancer*) **se** ~ **de qc** to jump from sth; **se** ~ **dans le vide** to throw oneself into the void ②(*se jeter*) **se** ~ **à la porte/dans la rue** to dash to the door/into the street; **se** ~ **sur qn/dans les bras de qn** to rush up to sb/into sb's arms; **il s'est**

**précipité à mon secours** he raced to my rescue ❸(*s'accélérer*) **se** ~ to speed up; **les événements se précipitent** the pace of events quickened ❹(*se dépêcher*) **se** ~ to hurry

**précis(e)** [pʀesi, iz] *adj* ❶(*juste*) precise; **à 10 heures ~es** at exactly [*o* precisely] 10 o'clock ❷(*net*) particular

**précisément** [pʀesizemã] *adv* precisely

**préciser** [pʀesize] <1> **I.** *vt* ❶(*donner des précisions: point, fait*) to state; (*intention, idée*) to make clear; (*date, lieu*) to specify ❷(*souligner*) to point out **II.** *vpr* **se** ~ to take shape; (*menace, idée, situation*) to become clear

**précision** [pʀesizjɔ̃] *f* ❶(*justesse*) preciseness; (*d'un geste, d'un instrument*) precision; **être/ne pas être d'une grande** ~ to be/not be very precise ❷(*netteté: des contours, d'un trait*) distinctness ❸ *souvent pl* (*détail*) detail

**prédécesseur** [pʀedesesœʀ] *mf* predecessor

**prédestiné(e)** [pʀedɛstine] *adj* **être ~ à qc** to be predestined for sth

**prédiction** [pʀediksjɔ̃] *f* prediction

**prédire** [pʀediʀ] *vt irr* to predict

**préface** [pʀefas] *f* preface

**préfecture** [pʀefɛktyʀ] *f* prefecture; ~ **de police** police headquarters

**préféré(e)** [pʀefeʀe] **I.** *adj* (*ami*) best; (*chanteur*) favorite **II.** *m(f)* favorite

**préférence** [pʀefeʀãs] *f* preference; **avoir une** ~ [*o* **des** ~**s**] **pour qn/qc** to have a preference for sb/sth ▸ **de** ~ preferably; **de** ~ **à qc** in preference to sth

**préférer** [pʀefeʀe] <5> *vt* ~ **qn/qc à qn/qc** to prefer sth/sb to sth/sb else; **je préfère que tu le fasses** (*subj*) I would prefer you do it

**préfet** [pʀefɛ] *m* ❶ prefect; ~ **de police** chief of police ❷ *Belgique* (*directeur d'athénée, de lycée*) principal

**préfixe** [pʀefiks] *m* prefix

**préhistoire** [pʀeistwaʀ] *f* prehistory

**préjugé** [pʀeʒyʒe] *m* prejudice; **avoir un** ~ **contre qn** to be prejudiced against sb

**prélever** [pʀel(ə)ve] <4> *vt* (*somme, pourcentage*) to take off; (*taxe*) to deduct; (*organe, tissu*) to remove; (*sang*) to take; ~ **de l'argent sur le compte** to withdraw money from the account

**premier** [pʀəmje] *m* first ▸ **jeune** ~ romantic male lead; **en** ~ (*avant les autres*) first; (*pour commencer*) firstly

**premier, -ière** [pʀəmje, -jɛʀ] *adj* ❶ antéposé (*opp: dernier*) first; (*page*) front; **le** ~ **venu** the first to arrive; (*n'importe qui*) anybody; **en** ~ **lieu** in the first place; **dans les** ~**s temps** in the beginning; *v.a.* **cinquième** ❷(*principal: besoins, rudiments*) basic; (*objectif, rôle*) main; (*qualité*) primary; **au** ~ **plan** in the foreground; **marchandises de** ~ **choix** top quality products

**première** [pʀəmjɛʀ] *f* ❶(*vitesse*) first gear ❷ ECOLE eleventh grade ❸(*manifestation sans précédent*) first; ~ **mondiale** world first ❹ THEAT, CINE première; **grande** ~ grand première ❺ AUTO first class; **billet de** ~ first class ticket ▸ **être de** ~ to be first class

**premièrement** [pʀəmjɛʀmã] *adv* ❶(*en premier lieu*) in the first place ❷(*et d'abord*) firstly

**prenant(e)** [pʀənã, ãt] *adj* ❶(*captivant: film, livre*) absorbing ❷(*absorbant: travail, activité*) time-consuming

**prendre** [pʀãdʀ] <13> **I.** *vt avoir* ❶ to take; ~ **qc dans qc** to take sth from sth; ~ **qn par le bras** to take sb by the arm ❷(*absorber: boisson, café, sandwich*) to have; (*médicament*) to take; **vous prendrez quelque chose?** would you like something? ❸(*aller chercher*) ~ **qn chez lui/à la gare** to pick sb up at their house/the station ❹(*emporter: manteau, parapluie*) to take ❺ AUTO (*train, métro, ascenseur, avion*) to take; ~ **le volant** to drive ❻(*capturer: gibier*) to shoot; (*poisson, mouches*) to catch; (*forteresse, ville*) to take; **se faire** ~ to be captured; **être pris dans qc** to be caught in sth ❼(*se laisser séduire*) **se laisser** ~ **par qn/à qc** to be taken in by sb/sth ❽(*surprendre*) to catch; ~ **qn sur le fait** to catch sb red-handed; **on ne m'y prendra plus!** next time I won't get caught! ❾ (*acheter*) to buy; (*chambre, couchette*) to take; ~ **de l'essence** to get gas ❿ (*accepter*) ~ **qn comme locataire** to take sb as a tenant; ~ **qn comme cuisinier** to take on sb as a chef ⓫ (*noter, enregistrer: empreintes, notes*) to take; (*adresse, nom*) to take in; ~ **un rendez-vous** to make an appointment; ~ **des nouvelles de qn** to ask about sb; ~ **sa température** to take one's temperature ⓬ (*adopter: décision*) to make; (*précautions, mesure*) to take; (*air innocent*) to put on; (*ton menaçant*) to adopt; ~ **l'apparence/la forme de qc** to take on the appearance/form of sth ⓭ (*acquérir: couleur, goût de rance*) to acquire; (*nouveau sens*) to take on; ~ **du courage** to take courage; ~ **du poids** to gain weight; ~ **du ventre** to get a gut ⓮ MED - **froid** to catch cold; **être pris d'un malaise** to feel faint ⓯ (*s'accorder: plaisir, repos*) to have; (*des congés, vacances*) to take; ~ **sa retraite** to retire ⓰ (*coûter*) **ce travail me prend tout mon temps** this work takes up all my time ⓱ (*prélever, faire payer: argent, pourcentage*) to take; (*commission, cotisation*) to charge; **être pris sur le salaire** to be deducted from one's salary ⓲ *inf* (*recevoir, subir*) ~ **une averse** to get caught in a downpour; ~ **des coups/des reproches** to be on the wrong end of a beating/criticism; ~ **la balle/porte en pleine figure** to get hit right in the face by the ball/by the door ⓳ (*traiter: personne*) to handle; (*problème*) to deal with; ~ **qn par les sentiments** to appeal to sb's feelings ⓴ (*considérer comme*) ~ **qc pour prétexte** to use sth as an excuse; **pour qui me prends-tu?** who do you take me for? ㉑ (*assaillir: doute, faim, panique*) to strike; (*colère, envie*) to come over; **être pris par le doute/la panique** to be seized by doubt/panic

㉒ LING (*s'écrire*) **ce mot prend deux l** there are two l's in this word ㉓ **c'est à ~ ou à** **laisser** take it or leave it; ~ **qc sur soi** to take sth upon oneself; ~ **sur soi de** +*infin* to take it upon oneself to +*infin*; **qu'est-ce qui te/lui prend?** what's gotten into you/him? **II.** *vi* ❶ (*réussir*) **avec moi, ça ne prend pas!** *inf* it won't wash with me! ❷ *avoir* (*s'enflammer: feu*) to start ❸ *avoir o être* (*durcir: ciment, mayonnaise*) to set ❹ *avoir* (*se diriger*) ~ **à gauche/droite** (*personne*) to go left/right; (*chemin*) to turn left/right ❺ *avoir* (*faire payer*) ~ **beaucoup/peu** to charge a lot/little; ~ **cher** to be expensive; ~ **cher de l'heure** to be expensive by the hour **III.** *vpr* ❶ (*s'accrocher*) **se ~ le doigt dans la porte** to catch one's finger in the door ❷ (*se considérer*) **se ~ trop au sérieux** to take oneself too seriously ❸ (*procéder*) **s'y ~ bien/mal avec qn** to deal with sb the right/wrong way; **s'y ~ bien/mal avec qc** to handle sth well/badly; **s'y ~ à trois reprises** to have three tries at sth ❹ (*en vouloir*) **s'en ~ à qn/qc** to blame sb/sth ❺ (*s'attaquer*) **s'en ~ à qn/qc** to lay into sb/sth ❻ (*être pris*) **se ~** (*médicament*) to be taken ❼ (*se tenir*) **se ~ par le bras** to take each other's arm

**prénom** [pren5] *m* first name

**préoccupation** [preɔkypasjɔ̃] *f* ❶ (*souci*) worry ❷ (*occupation*) preoccupation

**préoccupé(e)** [preɔkype] *adj* preoccupied; **avoir l'air ~** to look worried

**préoccuper** [preɔkype] <1> **I.** *vt* ❶ (*inquiéter*) to worry; **l'avenir/la situation me préoccupe** I'm concerned about the future/the situation ❷ (*absorber: problème, affaire*) to preoccupy **II.** *vpr* **se ~ de qn/qc** to worry about sb/sth; **se ~ de faire qc** to worry about doing sth

**préparatifs** [preparatif] *mpl* preparations

**préparation** [preparasjɔ̃] *f* ❶ (*mise au point*) *a.* CHIM, MED preparation; (*d'un*

P

*discours, plan*) drafting; (*d'un complot*) hatching; **avoir qc en** ~ to have sth in the pipeline ❷ (*entraînement*) ~ **au Tour de France** training for the Tour de France ❸ ECOLE **classe de** ~ preparation class; **la** ~ **à l'examen** preparation for the exam

**préparer** [pʀepaʀe] <1> I. *vt* ❶ (*confectionner*) to prepare; **plat préparé** ready-made meal ❷ (*apprêter: affaires, bagages, terre*) to prepare; (*chambre, voiture*) to get ready; (*gibier, poisson, volaille*) to dress ❸ (*mettre au point: fête, plan, voyage*) to plan; ~ **un piège à qn** to lay a trap for sb ❹ (*travailler à: cours, discours, leçon*) to prepare; (*nouvelle édition, roman, thèse*) to work on; (*bac, concours*) to prepare for ❺ (*réserver*) **que nous prépare-t-il?** what has he got in store for us? ❻ (*entraîner*) **j'y étais préparé** I was prepared [*o* ready] for it II. *vpr* ❶ (*se laver, se coiffer, s'habiller*) **se** ~ to get ready ❷ (*faire en sorte d'être prêt*) **se** ~ **à un examen/une compétition** to prepare for an exam/a competition ❸ *soutenu* (*être sur le point de*) **se** ~ **à** +*infin* to be getting ready to +*infin* ❹ (*approcher*) **se** ~ (*événement*) to near; (*orage*) to brew; (*grandes choses, tragédie*) to approach

**préposition** [pʀepozisjɔ̃] *f* preposition

**près** [pʀɛ] I. *adv* ❶ (*à une petite distance, dans peu de temps*) near ▶ **de** ~ **ou de loin** either way you look at it; **ni de** ~ **ni de loin** in no way, shape, or form; **qn n'en est pas/plus à qc** ~ it's not going to make any difference to sb now/at this stage; **à cela** ~ **que qn a fait qc** if it wasn't for the fact that sb did sth; **à la minute** ~ to the minute; **à peu** (**de choses**) ~ approximately; (*ressembler*) nearly; **l'hôtel était à peu** ~ **vide/calme** the hotel was nearly empty/fairly quiet; **rater le bus à quelques secondes** ~ to miss the bus by a few seconds; **à une exception/quelques détails** ~ apart from one exception/some details; **au centimètre** ~ to the centimeter; re-

**garder de** ~ to watch closely; **voir qc de** ~ to see sth close up; **frôler qc de (tout/très)** ~ to come within an inch of sth; **(se) suivre de** ~ (*événements*) to happen close together II. *prep* ❶ (*à côté de*) ~ **d'une personne/un lieu** near a person/place; **habiter** ~ **de chez qn** to live near sb; ~ **du bord** near the edge ❷ (*à peu de temps de*) **être** ~ **du but** to be near one's goal; **être** ~ **de la retraite** to be close to retirement ❸ (*presque*) ~ **de** nearly ▶ **ne pas être** ~ **de faire qc** to have no intention of doing sth

**présence** [pʀezɑ̃s] *f* (*opp: absence, personnalité*) presence ▶ ~ **d'esprit** presence of mind

**présent** [pʀezɑ̃] *m* present ▶ **à** ~ at present; **à** ~ **qu'il est parti** now that he's gone; **dès à** ~ here and now; **jusqu'à** ~ until now

**présent(e)** [pʀezɑ̃, ɑ̃t] I. *adj* ❶ (*opp: absent: personne*) present; **les personnes** ~**es** those present ❷ (*qui existe*) **avoir qc** ~ **à l'esprit/à la mémoire** to have sth in one's mind/memory ❸ (*actuel: circonstances, état, temps*) current II. *m(f)* (*personne*) person present

**présentable** [pʀezɑ̃tabl] *adj* presentable

**présentateur, -trice** [pʀezɑ̃tatœʀ, -tʀis] *m, f* (*des informations, du journal télévisé*) newscaster; (*d'un programme*) presenter; (*d'une émission, discussion*) host

**présentation** [pʀezɑ̃tasjɔ̃] *f* ❶ presentation; (*d'un programme*) presentation ❷ (*fait d'introduire qn*) **les** ~**s** the introductions

**présenter** [pʀezɑ̃te] <1> I. *vt* ❶ (*faire connaître*) to introduce; (*cheval, troupe*) to present; ~ **qn à un juge** to present sb to a judge ❷ RADIO, TV (*émission*) to present; (*programme*) to introduce; ~ **le journal télévisé** to present the news ❸ (*décrire*) ~ **qn/qc comme qn/qc** to portray sb/sth as sb/sth ❹ (*montrer: billet, carte d'identité, document*) to present ❺ (*soumettre: pro-*

*blème, théorie, travail*) to submit; (*exprimer: critique, condoléances, félicitations*) to offer; **~ ses excuses à qn** to offer one's excuses to sb ⑥ (*donner une apparence*) to present; **c'est bien présenté** it is well presented ⑦ (*avoir*) to have; **~ un danger** to present a danger; **~ un aspect rugueux/humide** to look rough/damp ⑧ (*offrir*) to offer; (*plat, rafraîchissement, fleurs, bouquet*) to present ⑨ (*proposer: devis, dossier, projet de loi*) to present; (*addition, facture*) to submit; (*motion, demande*) to propose **II.** *vi* **~ bien/mal** *inf* to look good/awful **III.** *vpr* ❶ (*décliner son identité*) **se ~ à qn** to introduce oneself to sb ❷ (*se rendre, aller, venir*) **se ~ chez qn** to go to sb's house; **se ~ chez un employeur** to go to see an employer ❸ (*être candidat*) **se ~ à un examen** to take an exam; **se ~ pour un emploi** to apply for a job ❹ (*apparaître, exister, surgir*) **se ~** (*problème, difficulté, obstacle*) to arise; **se ~ à l'esprit de qn** to come to sb's mind ❺ (*paraître, avoir un certain aspect*) **se ~ sous forme de cachets** to be in tablet form; **ça se présente bien!** that bodes well!

**présentoir** [pʀezɑ̃twaʀ] *m* display

**préservatif** [pʀezɛʀvatif] *m* condom

**présidence** [pʀezidɑ̃s] *f* presidency

**président(e)** [pʀezidɑ̃, ɑ̃t] *m(f)* ❶ (*personne qui dirige: d'une association, d'un comité, jury, congrès*) chair; (*d'une université*) president; (*d'un tribunal*) presiding judge; (*d'une entreprise*) president; (*d'une assemblée*) speaker ❷ (*chef de l'État*) **le Président** the President; **le ~ de la République française** the President of the French Republic ❸ *Suisse* (*maire dans les cantons de Valais et de Neuchâtel*) mayor

**président-directeur général, présidente-directrice générale** [pʀezidɑ̃diʀɛktœʀʒeneʀal, pʀezidɑ̃tdiʀɛktœʀʒeneʀal] <présidents-directeurs généraux> *m, f* chief executive officer

**presque** [pʀɛsk] *adv* nearly; **tout le monde ou ~** everyone or almost every-

one; **je ne l'ai ~ pas entendu** I could hardly hear him; **je ne connais ~ personne** I know hardly anyone; **il pleurait ~** he was nearly crying

**presqu'île** [pʀɛskil] *f* peninsula

**presse** [pʀɛs] *f* (*journaux*) press; **~ écrite** press; **~ féminine** women's magazines; **~ quotidienne** daily newspapers

**pressé(e)**[1] [pʀese] *adj* (*qui se hâte*) **d'un pas ~** in a hurry; **être ~ d'arriver** to be in a hurry to arrive

**pressé(e)**[2] [pʀese] *adj* (*citron, orange*) freshly squeezed

**pressentiment** [pʀesɑ̃timɑ̃] *m* presentiment; **avoir le ~ de qc** to have a premonition of sth; **avoir le ~ qu'il va pleuvoir** to have a feeling that it will rain

**presse-papiers** [pʀɛspapje] *m inv* paperweight; INFORM clipboard

**presser**[1] [pʀese] <1> **I.** *vt* (*cadence, pas*) to speed up **II.** *vi* (*affaire*) to be urgent; **le temps presse** time is short ▶ **ça presse!** *inf* it's urgent! **III.** *vpr* **se ~** to hurry

**presser**[2] [pʀese] <1> **I.** *vt* (*fruit, éponge*) to squeeze; (*raisin*) to press **II.** *vpr* ❶ (*se serrer*) **se ~ contre qn/qc** to squash up against sb/sth ❷ (*se bousculer*) **se ~ vers la sortie** to rush for the exit

**pression** [pʀesjɔ̃] *f* ❶ (*contrainte*) *a.* MED, METEO, PHYS pressure; **subir des ~s** to be under pressure ❷ (*bouton*) snap fastener ❸ (*bière*) **bière (à la) ~** draft beer ▶ **être sous ~** to be under pressure

**prestige** [pʀɛstiʒ] *m* prestige

**prestigieux, -euse** [pʀɛstiʒjø, -jøz] *adj* (*lieu, événement, carrière, métier, école*) prestigious; (*objet, produits, artiste, scientifique*) renowned

**présumé(e)** [pʀezyme] *adj* (*auteur*) presumed

**prêt** [pʀɛ] *m* ❶ (*action de prêter*) lending ❷ (*crédit, chose prêtée*) loan; **~ à intérêt** interest-bearing loan

**prêt(e)** [pʀɛ, pʀɛt] *adj* ❶ (*préparé*) **~ à cuire** ready to cook; **fin ~** *inf* all set; **à vos marques; ~s? partez!** on your mark, get set, go! ❷*(disposé)* ~ **à** +*infin* ready to +*infin*

**prêt-à-porter** [pʀɛtapɔʀte] *m sans pl* ready-to-wear

**prétendre** [pʀetɑ̃dʀ] <14> *vt* ❶*(affirmer)* to claim; **à ce qu'on prétend, il est ...** according to what people say, he is ... ❷*(avoir la prétention de)* to seek

**prétentieux, -euse** [pʀetɑ̃sjø, -jøz] I. *adj (personne, ton)* pretentious II. *m, f* pretentious individual

**prétention** [pʀetɑ̃sjɔ̃] *f* ❶*sans pl (vanité)* pretentiousness; **maison sans ~** unpretentious house; **repas sans ~** simple meal; **avoir/ne pas avoir la ~ de** +*infin* to claim/not claim to +*infin*; **ce diplôme n'a pas la ~ de remplacer ...** this certificate does not seek to replace ... ❷*gén pl (ce à quoi on prétend)* expectation

**prêter** [pʀete] <1> I. *vt* ❶*(avancer pour un temps: livre, voiture, parapluie)* to lend ❷*(attribuer)* **~ une intention à qn** to claim sb has an intention II. *vi* ❶*(donner matière à)* **~ à équivoque** to be ambiguous; **~ à rire** to be laughable ❷*(consentir un prêt)* **~ à 8%** to lend at 8% III. *vpr* ❶*(consentir)* **se ~ à un jeu** to get involved in a game ❷*(être adapté à)* **se ~ à qc** to lend itself to sth

**prétexte** [pʀetɛkst] *m (raison apparente)* pretext; *(excuse)* excuse; **mauvais ~** lame excuse; **sous aucun ~** on no account; **sous ~ de manque de temps, elle est ...** using lack of time as an excuse, she is ...

**prétexter** [pʀetɛkste] <1> *vt* to give as an excuse; **elle prétexte qu'elle n'a pas le temps** she says that she hasn't got the time

**prêtre** [pʀɛtʀ] *m* REL priest

**preuve** [pʀœv] *f (indice probant, démonstration)* **~ de qc** proof of sth; **~ en main** concrete proof; **jusqu'à ~ du contraire** until there is proof to the contrary ▶ **faire ~ de bonne volonté/ courage** to show good will/courage;

**faire ses ~s** *(élève)* to prove oneself; *(méthode)* to prove itself

**prévenir** [pʀev(ə)niʀ] <9> I. *vt* ❶*(aviser)* to tell; *(médecin, police)* to inform; **~ qn de qc** to inform sb of sth ❷*(avertir)* to warn; **tu es prévenu!** you have been warned! II. *vi* to warn; **arriver sans ~** *(événement)* to happen without warning

**préventif, -ive** [pʀevɑ̃tif, -iv] *adj* preventative

**prévention** [pʀevɑ̃sjɔ̃] *f (mesures préventives)* prevention

**prévisible** [pʀevizibl] *adj* predictable

**prévision** [pʀevizjɔ̃] *f (d'un comportement, événement, phénomène)* prediction; *(des dépenses, recettes)* forecast; **les ~s météorologiques** the weather forecast; **en ~ du départ** in anticipation of one's departure

**prévoir** [pʀevwaʀ] *vt irr* ❶*(envisager ce qui va se passer)* to foresee; **il faut ~ les conséquences de ses actes** one must consider the consequences of one's actions; **plus beau/ moins cher que prévu** more beautiful/cheaper than expected ❷*(projeter)* to plan; **leur arrivée est prévue pour 3 heures** they are expected to arrive at 3 o'clock ❸*(envisager)* to arrange for; *(casse-croûte, couvertures)* to provide; **c'est prévu** it is planned; **tout est prévu pour ton arrivée** everything is set up for your arrival

**prier** [pʀije] <1> I. *vt* ❶REL to pray ❷*(inviter, solliciter)* **~ qn de** +*infin* to ask sb to +*infin;* **se faire ~** to have people beg; **sans se faire ~** without waiting to be asked twice ❸*(ordonner)* **~ qn de** +*infin* to order sb to +*infin* ▶ **je vous prie d'agréer mes sincères salutations/sentiments les meilleurs** yours sincerely; **je t'en/vous prie** *(fais/faites donc)* go ahead; *(s'il te/vous plaît)* please; *(il n'y a pas de quoi, après un remerciement)* you're welcome; *(il n'y a pas de quoi, après une excuse)* it's nothing; **je te/vous**

**prie!** please! **II.** vi REL **~ pour qn/qc** to pray for sb/sth

**prière** [pʀijɛʀ] f ❶ REL prayer; **faire sa ~** to say one's prayers ❷ (demande) plea; **~ d'essuyer ses pieds!** please wipe your feet! ▶ **tu peux faire ta ~!** iron say your prayers!

**primaire** [pʀimɛʀ] **I.** adj primary **II.** m ECOLE elementary school

**primauté** [pʀimote] f (supériorité) **~ de qc sur qc** primacy of sth over sth

**prime** [pʀim] f ❶ (allocation, en complément du salaire) bonus; (subvention payée par l'État) subsidy; **~ de fin d'année** Christmas bonus; **~ de risque** hazard pay; **~ de transport** transportation allowance ❷ (somme à payer) **~ d'assurance** insurance premium ▶ **en ~** on top

**primer** [pʀime] <1> vt to award a prize; **film/livre primé** award-winning film/book

**primevère** [pʀimvɛʀ] f primrose

**prince, princesse** [pʀɛ̃s, pʀɛ̃sɛs] m, f prince, princess m, f; **~ charmant** prince charming; **~ héritier** crown prince

**principal** [pʀɛ̃sipal, -o] <-aux> m (l'important) **le ~** the main thing

**principal(e)** [pʀɛ̃sipal, -o] <-aux> **I.** adj ❶ (le plus important) principal ❷ (premier dans une hiérarchie) **les principaux intéressés dans cette histoire** the ones most directly involved in this business; **les raisons ~es** the main reasons; **rôle ~ d'un film** leading role in a film ❸ LING **proposition ~e** main clause **II.** m(f) ECOLE principal

**principalement** [pʀɛ̃sipalmɑ̃] adv mainly

**principauté** [pʀɛ̃sipote] f principality

**principe** [pʀɛ̃sip] m ❶ (règle de conduite) a. PHYS, MATH principle; **avoir des ~s** to have scruples; **qn a pour ~ de** +infin it's a principle with sb to +infin ❷ (hypothèse) assumption; **poser des ~s** to make working assumptions ▶ **en ~** in principle [o theory]; **par ~** on principle; **pour le ~** on principle

**printanier, -ière** [pʀɛ̃tanje, -jɛʀ] adj (atmosphère, tenue) spring; **robe printanière** summer dress

**printemps** [pʀɛ̃tɑ̃] m spring

**prioritaire** [pʀijɔʀitɛʀ] **I.** adj ❶ (qui passe en premier); **être ~** to have priority ❷ AUTO **être ~** (automobiliste, route) to have the right of way **II.** mf (personne) person with priority; AUTO person who has the right of way

**priorité** [pʀijɔʀite] f priority; **~ sur qn/qc** priority over sb/sth; **en ~** as a priority; **avoir la ~** to have priority; AUTO to have the right of way

**pris** [pʀi] passé simple de **prendre**

**pris(e)** [pʀi, pʀiz] **I.** part passé de **prendre II.** adj ❶ (occupé) **être ~** (place) to be taken; **avoir les mains ~es** to have one's hands full ❷ (emploi du temps complet: personne) busy ❸ (en proie à) **être ~ de peur/de panique** to be stricken with fear/panic; **être ~ d'envie de** +infin to get an urge to +infin

**prise** [pʀiz] f ❶ (action de prendre avec les mains) hold ❷ (poignée, objet que l'on peut empoigner) grip; **lâcher ~** to let go; fig to loosen one's grip ❸ (animal capturé) catch ❹ ELEC **~ de courant** electrical socket; **~ multiple** adaptor ❺ CINE shooting ❻ (pincée: de tabac) pinch; (de drogue) snort ❼ MED **~ de sang** blood sample; **se faire faire une ~ de sang** to have a blood sample taken ❽ (action d'assumer) **~ en charge** ADMIN reimbursement of medical costs by insurance ❾ fig **~ de conscience** realization

**prison** [pʀizɔ̃] f prison

**prisonnier, -ière** [pʀizɔnje, -jɛʀ] **I.** adj (en détention) **être ~** to be held prisoner; (soldat) to be held captive **II.** m, f prisoner; **faire qn ~** to take sb prisoner

**privé** [pʀive] m ❶ (vie privée) private life; **dans le ~** in private ❷ ECON private sector

**privé(e)** [pʀive] **I.** adj (opp: public) private; **il est ici à titre ~** he is here in a private capacity **II.** m(f) inf (détective) private detective

P

**priver** [pʀive] <1> **I.** *vt* ① (*refuser à*) ~ **qn de liberté** to deprive sb of their freedom ② (*faire perdre à*) ~ **qn de tous ses moyens** to leave sb completely helpless; **être privé d'électricité** to be without electricity ③ (*frustrer*) ~ **qn de qc** to deprive sb of sth; **je ne veux pas vous** ~ I don't want to deprive you **II.** *vpr* (*se restreindre*) **se** ~ **pour qn** to make sacrifices for sb ▸ **ne pas se** ~ **faire qc** to make sure one does sth

**privilège** [pʀivilɛʒ] *m* privilege

**privilégié(e)** [pʀivileʒje] **I.** *adj* (*avantagé*) privileged **II.** *m(f)* privileged person

**privilégier** [pʀivileʒje] <1> *vt* ① (*avantager*) to favor ② (*donner la priorité*) ~ **qc** to lay great stress on sth

**prix** [pʀi] *m* ① (*coût, contrepartie*) price; ~ **d'ami** special price; ~ **coûtant** cost price; **dernier** ~ final offer; ~ **d'achat/de détail** purchase/retail price; ~ **de gros** wholesale price; **à** ~ **d'or** for a small fortune; **à bas** ~ cheaply; **à moitié** ~ half-price; **hors de** ~ outrageously expensive; **vendre au** ~ **fort** to charge the full price; **le** ~ **de la gloire/du succès** the price of glory/success; **à tout/aucun** ~ at any/not at any price ② (*valeur*) ~ **valuable**; **ne pas avoir de** ~ to be priceless ③ (*distinction, lauréat*) *a.* SPORT prize; ~ **Nobel** Nobel Prize ▸ **c'est le même** ~ *inf* it comes down to the same thing; **payer le** ~ **fort** to pay the full price; **y mettre le** ~ to pay what it costs

**pro** [pʀo] *mf inf abr de* **professionnel** pro

**probabilité** [pʀɔbabilite] *f* probability; **selon toute** ~ in all probability

**probable** [pʀɔbabl] *adj* probable

**probablement** [pʀɔbabləmɑ̃] *adv* probably

**problématique** [pʀɔblematik] **I.** *adj* (*qui pose problème*) problematic **II.** *f* issues *pl*

**problème** [pʀɔblɛm] *m* problem; **enfant/peau à** ~**s** *inf* problem child/skin; **ça me pose un** ~ [*o* **des** ~**s**] that's a bit of a problem for me; (**y a**)

**pas de** ~! *inf* no problem!; **les** ~**s de circulation/stationnement** traffic/parking problems; ~ **du logement/chômage** housing/unemployment problems; ~ **de géométrie** geometry problem

**procédé** [pʀɔsede] *m* ① (*méthode*) process; ~ **de fabrication** manufacturing process ② *souvent pl* (*façon d'agir*) behavior; **user de bons/mauvais** ~**s à l'égard de qn** to behave well/badly towards sb

**procéder** [pʀɔsede] <5> *vi* (*agir*) to proceed; ~ **par ordre** to do things in order

**procès** [pʀɔsɛ] *m* JUR (*civil*) lawsuit; (*criminel*) trial; **être en** ~ **avec qn** to be involved in a lawsuit with sb ▸ **faire le** ~ **de qn/qc** to put sb/sth on trial

**prochain** [pʀɔʃɛ̃] *m* (*être humain*) neighbor

**prochain(e)** [pʀɔʃɛ̃, ɛn] **I.** *adj* ① (*suivant*) next; **en août** ~ next August ② *postposé* (*proche: arrivée, départ*) impending; (*mort*) imminent; (*avenir*) near **II.** *m(f)* (*personne ou chose suivante*) next one

**prochaine** [pʀɔʃɛn] *f inf* ① (*station*) next station ② (*fois*) **à la** ~! see you soon!

**prochainement** [pʀɔʃɛnmɑ̃] *adv* soon

**proche** [pʀɔʃ] **I.** *adj* ① (*à proximité: lieu*) near; **être** ~ **de qc** to be near sth; **un restaurant tout** ~ a nearby restaurant; **la ville la plus** ~ the nearest town; ~**s l'une de l'autre** near to one another ② *antéposé* (*d'à côté: voisin*) next-door ③ (*imminent*) imminent ④ (*récent: événement, souvenir*) recent ⑤ *antéposé* (*de parenté étroite: cousin, parent*) close; **être** ~ **de qn** (*par la pensée*) to be close to sb ⑥ (*voisin*) **être** ~ **de qc** (*langue*) to be closely related to sth; (*prévision, attitude*) to be not far removed from sth **II.** *mf* ① (*ami intime*) close friend ② *mpl* (*parents*) **les** ~**s de qn** sb's close relatives [*o* family]

**Proche-Orient** [pʀɔʃɔʀjã] *m* **le ~** the Near East

**proclamer** [pʀɔklame] <1> I. *vt* ❶ (*affirmer, désigner comme: conviction, vérité*) to proclaim; (*innocence*) to declare ❷ (*annoncer publiquement*) to announce; (*état de siège, république*) to declare II. *vpr* (*se déclarer*) **se ~ indépendant** to declare one's independence; **se ~ république autonome** to proclaim autonomy as a republic

**procurer** [pʀɔkyʀe] <1> I. *vt* ❶ (*faire obtenir*) **~ qc à qn** to obtain sth for sb ❷ (*apporter: joie, ennuis*) to bring II. *vpr* (*obtenir*) **se ~ un travail** to get (oneself) a job

**prodige** [pʀɔdiʒ] *m* ❶ (*miracle*) miracle ❷ (*merveille*) marvel; **faire des ~s** to work wonders ❸ (*personne très douée*) prodigy

**producteur, -trice** [pʀɔdyktœʀ, -tʀis] I. *adj* COM producing; **~ de blé** wheat-growing; **les pays ~s de pétrole** the oil-producing countries II. *m, f* ❶ AGR grower ❷ (*fabricant*) manufacturer ❸ CINE, RADIO, TV producer

**productif, -ive** [pʀɔdyktif, -iv] *adj* productive

**production** [pʀɔdyksjɔ̃] *f* ❶ (*fait de produire*) production ❷ (*fabrication: de produits manufacturés*) production; **~ de voitures** automobile production; **~ d'électricité/énergie** electricity/energy generation ❸ (*exploitation*) **~ de blé/fruits** wheat-/fruit-growing; **~ de viande** meat production ❹ (*quantité produite*) production; (*d'énergie*) generation; AGR yield ❺ CINE, RADIO, TV production

**productivité** [pʀɔdyktivite] *f* ❶ (*rendement: d'une usine, d'un employé, ouvrier*) productivity ❷ (*rentabilité: d'un service, impôt*) profitability

**produire** [pʀɔdɥiʀ] *irr* I. *vt* ❶ ECON (*matières premières, produits manufacturés*) to produce; (*électricité*) to generate ❷ AGR, GEO (*cultivateur, arbre*) to grow; (*pays, région, terre*) to yield II. *vi* FIN to return III. *vpr* **se ~** ❶ (*survenir*)

to happen; (*changement*) to take place ❷ (*se montrer en public*) to appear in public ❸ (*se montrer sur la scène*) to appear on stage

**produit** [pʀɔdɥi] *m* ❶ ECON, CHIM, BIO, MATH product; **~ alimentaire** foodstuff; **~ s de beauté** cosmetics; **~ de première nécessité** vital commodities ❷ (*rapport, bénéfice*) **~ brut/net** gross/net profit; **~ intérieur brut** gross domestic product; **~ national brut** gross national product

**pro-européen(ne)** [pʀoøʀɔpeɛ̃, ɛn] *m(f)* pro-European

**prof** *inf v.* **professeur**

**professeur** [pʀɔfesœʀ] *mf* ❶ ECOLE teacher; **~ de lycée** schoolteacher; **~ des écoles** elementary school teacher; **~ de français/de piano** French/piano teacher ❷ UNIV (*avec chaire*) professor; (*sans chaire*) lecturer

**profession** [pʀɔfesjɔ̃] *f* profession; **exercer la ~ de qc** to practice the profession of sth

**professionnel(le)** [pʀɔfesjɔnɛl] I. *adj* ❶ (*relatif à un métier: conscience, qualification, vie*) professional; (*cours, enseignement*) vocational; **lycée ~** vocational school ❷ (*opp: amateur: écrivain, journaliste*) professional ❸ (*compétent*) adept II. *m(f)* ❶ (*homme de métier, personne compétente*) professional; **~ du tourisme** tourism professional ❷ SPORT **passer ~** *inf* to turn professional

**profil** [pʀɔfil] *m* ❶ (*relief*) outline; **de ~** in outline ❷ (*silhouette, aptitudes*) *a.* INFORM profile; **~ utilisateur** user profile ▶ **montrer son meilleur ~** to show one's best side

**profit** [pʀɔfi] *m* ❶ COM, FIN profit ❷ (*avantage*) advantage; **mettre à ~ une situation pour** +*infin* to take advantage of a situation to +*infin;* **au ~ de qn/qc** (*concert*) in aid of sb/sth; (*activités*) for sb/sth

**profiter** [pʀɔfite] <1> *vi* ❶ (*tirer avantage de*) **~ d'une situation/d'une occasion** to take advantage of a situation/an opportunity ❷ (*être utile à*) ~ **à qn** to benefit sb; (*repos, vacances*) to do sb good ❸ *inf* (*se fortifier*) to thrive; (*enfant*) to grow

**profond(e)** [pʀɔfɔ̃, ɔ̃d] **I.** *adj* ❶ (*qui s'enfonce loin*) deep; ~ **de 50 m** 50 meters deep ❷ (*très grand*) great; (*révérence, sommeil, nuit*) deep; (*sentiment*) profound; **dans la nuit ~ e** in the dark of night ❸ *postposé* (*caché: cause*) underlying; (*signification*) deep; (*tendance*) deep-rooted; **la France ~ e** rural France ❹ (*opp: superficiel, léger: esprit, penseur, regard*) profound; (*pensée, réflexion, soupir, voix*) deep ❺ *postposé* MED (*arriéré, débile*) seriously; **handicapé ~** severely handicapped **II.** *adv* (*creuser, planter*) deep

**profondément** [pʀɔfɔ̃demɑ̃] *adv* ❶ (*d'une manière profonde: s'incliner*) deeply; (*creuser, pénétrer*) deep ❷ (*beaucoup: respirer, aimer, réfléchir*) deeply; (*dormir*) soundly; (*influencer, ressentir*) profoundly; (*souhaiter*) sincerely; **se tromper ~** to be profoundly mistaken ❸ *antéposé* (*très, tout à fait: choqué, ému, touché, vexé*) deeply, greatly; (*convaincu, différent*) profoundly

**profondeur** [pʀɔfɔ̃dœʀ] *f* ❶ (*distance*) depth; **50 m de ~** a depth of 50 meters ❷ (*intensité: d'une voix*) deepness; (*d'un regard*) depth ► **en ~** (*connaissance*) in-depth

**programmable** [pʀɔgʀamabl] *adj* INFORM, TECH programmable

**programmation** [pʀɔgʀamasjɔ̃] *f* CINE, RADIO, TV, INFORM programming; **langage de ~** programming language

**programme** [pʀɔgʀam] *m* ❶ (*objectif planifié*) plan; (*étapes*) program; ~ **d'action** plan of action; ~ **de recherches** research program ❷ (*livret*) program; CINE, TV guide; **être au ~** to be on ❸ ECOLE syllabus ❹ UNIV course ► **être au ~** to be on the program; CINE, TV to be on; **être hors ~** not to be on the program; ECOLE not to be on the syllabus; **c'est tout un ~** that's quite a business

**programmer** [pʀɔgʀame] <1> *vt* ❶ CINE, TV to schedule ❷ THEAT to show ❸ (*établir à l'avance: journée, réjouissances, vacances*) to plan; **être programmé à dix heures** to be planned for ten o'clock ❹ TECH (*calculatrice*) to program; ~ **une machine à laver sur qc** to set a washing machine with sth

**progrès** [pʀɔgʀɛ] *m a.* ECOLE progress; **faire des ~ en qc** to make progress in sth ► **il y a du ~** *inf* there's progress; **on n'arrête pas le ~** *inf* progress never stops

**progresser** [pʀɔgʀese] <1> *vi* ❶ (*s'améliorer*) to progress; (*conditions de vie*) to improve ❷ (*augmenter: difficultés*) to increase; (*prix, salaires*) to rise ❸ (*s'étendre: épidémie, incendie, inondation, idées*) to spread ❹ (*avancer: armée, sauveteur, véhicule*) to advance

**progressif, -ive** [pʀɔgʀesif, -iv] *adj* (*amélioration, évolution, transformation*) gradual; (*développement, difficulté, amnésie, paralysie*) progressive

**progression** [pʀɔgʀesjɔ̃] *f* ❶ (*amélioration*) progress; (*des conditions de vie, du bien-être*) improvement ❷ (*augmentation: du chômage, de l'alcoolisme*) increase; (*des prix, salaires*) rise ❸ (*extension, développement*) spread ❹ (*marche en avant: d'un explorateur, sauveteur, véhicule, d'une armée*) progress

**progressivement** [pʀɔgʀesivmɑ̃] *adv* progressively; (*procéder*) gradually

**proie** [pʀwa] *f* (*opp: prédateur, victime*) prey ► **être en ~ à qc** to be plagued by sth

**projet** [pʀɔʒɛ] *m* ❶ (*intention*) plan; (*programme*) project; ~ **de vacances** vacation plans; ~ **de film** plan for a film; ~ **de construction** building project ❷ (*ébauche, esquisse*) draft; ~ **de loi** bill

**projeter** [pʀɔʒ(ə)te] <3> **I.** *vt* ❶ (*faire un projet*) to plan ❷ (*éjecter*) to throw; (*fumée*) to give off; (*étincelles*) to throw off **II.** *vpr* (*se refléter*) **se** ~ (*ombre, silhouette*) to be outlined

**prolétaire** [pʀɔletɛʀ] **I.** *adj* working-class, proletarian *form* **II.** *mf* proletarian

**prolétariat** [pʀɔletaʀja] *m* proletariat

**prolongation** [pʀɔlɔ̃gasjɔ̃] *f* ❶ (*allongement: d'un congé, délai, d'une trêve*) extension ❷ SPORT overtime ▶ **jouer les** ~**s** SPORT to play in overtime; *iron* to hang around

**prolonger** [pʀɔlɔ̃ʒe] <2a> **I.** *vt* ❶ (*faire durer davantage*) to prolong ❷ (*rendre plus long*) to extend; (*rue*) to continue **II.** *vpr* **se** ~ ❶ (*durer: débat, séance*) to go on; (*trêve*) to hold out; (*effet, séjour*) to last; (*maladie*) to continue ❷ (*s'étendre en longueur: chemin, rue*) to continue

**promenade** [pʀɔm(ə)nad] *f* ❶ (*balade à pied*) walk; (*balade en bateau*) sail; (*balade à cheval*) ride; ~ **en voiture** drive; ~ **à/en vélo** bike ride ❷ (*lieu où l'on se promène en ville*) promenade ❸ (*lieu où l'on se promène à la campagne*) walk

**promener** [pʀɔm(ə)ne] <4> **I.** *vt* ❶ (*accompagner*) ~ **qn/un animal** to take sb/an animal for a walk ❷ (*laisser errer*) ~ **ses doigts sur le clavier** to run one's fingers over the keyboard; ~ **son regard sur la plaine** to cast one's eyes over the plain **II.** *vpr* (*faire une promenade*) (**aller**) **se** ~ (*animal, personne*) to go for a walk; (*à cheval*) to go for a ride; (*en bateau*) to go for a sail; **se** ~ **en voiture** to go for a drive; **se** ~ **à vélo** [*o* **en**] to go for a bike ride

**promeneur, -euse** [pʀɔm(ə)nœʀ, -øz] *m, f* walker

**promesse** [pʀɔmɛs] *f* (*engagement*) promise ▶ ~ **en l'air** empty promise

**prometteur, -euse** [pʀɔmɛtœʀ, -øz] *adj* promising

**promettre** [pʀɔmɛtʀ] *irr* **I.** *vt* (*s'engager à, laisser présager*) to promise; ~ **une visite à qn** to promise to visit sb; ~ **le secret à qn** to promise to keep sb's secret; **ça je te le promets!** that I can

promise you! ▶ **c'est promis juré** *inf* it's a promise **II.** *vi* ❶ (*faire une promesse*) to promise ❷ (*être prometteur*) to be promising ▶ **ça promet!** *iron* that's promising! **III.** *vpr* (*prendre la résolution de*) **se** ~ **de** +*infin* to promise oneself to +*infin*

**promis(e)** [pʀɔmi, iz] *adj* **être** ~ **à qn/qc** to be destined for sb/sth

**promotion** [pʀɔmosjɔ̃] *f* ❶ (*avancement*) promotion ❷ (*progression*) ~ **sociale** social advancement ❸ ECOLE class ❹ (*produit en réclame*) special offer

**pronom** [pʀɔnɔ̃] *m* pronoun

**pronominal** [pʀɔnɔminal, o] <-aux> *m* reflexive verb

**pronominal(e)** [pʀɔnɔminal, -o] <-aux> *adj* pronominal; (*verbe*) reflexive

**prononcer** [pʀɔnɔ̃se] <2> **I.** *vt* ❶ (*articuler*) to pronounce ❷ (*dire, exprimer: parole*) to say; (*souhait*) to express; (*discours, plaidoyer*) to give **II.** *vpr* ❶ (*être articulé*) **se** ~ (*lettre, mot, nom*) to be pronounced ❷ (*prendre position*) **se** ~ **pour/contre qn/qc** to pronounce oneself for/against sb/sth ❸ (*formuler son point de vue, diagnostic*) **se** ~ **sur qc** to give an opinion on sth

**pronostic** [pʀɔnɔstik] *m* forecast

**propagande** [pʀɔpagɑ̃d] *f* propaganda ▶ **faire de la** ~ **à/pour qn/qc** to push sb/sth; POL to campaign for sb/sth

**propagation** [pʀɔpagasjɔ̃] *f* ❶ (*extension*) propagation ❷ (*diffusion: d'une idée, nouvelle*) spreading

**propager** [pʀɔpaʒe] <2a> **I.** *vt* (*diffuser: idée, nouvelle*) to spread **II.** *vpr* **se** ~ to spread

**propice** [pʀɔpis] *adj* favorable

**proportion** [pʀɔpɔʀsjɔ̃] *f* ❶ (*rapport*) proportion; **en** ~ **de qc** in proportion to sth ❷ *pl* (*taille, volume: d'une personne, d'un texte, édifice*) proportions; (*d'une recette*) quantities ▶ **toutes** ~**s gardées** relatively speaking

**proportionnellement** [pʀɔpɔʀsjɔnɛlmɑ̃] *adv* proportionally

P

**propos** [pʀɔpo] *m gén pl* (*paroles*) words; **tenir des ~ inacceptables** to say unacceptable things ▶**bien/mal à ~** at the right/wrong time; **à tout ~** constantly; **à ~ de tout et de rien** for no reason; **juger à ~ de** +*infin* to think it appropriate to +*infin*; **à ce ~** in this connection; **hors de ~** irrelevant; **à quel ~?** on what subject?; **à ~** well-timed; **à ~ de qc** about sth

**proposer** [pʀɔpoze] <1> I. *vt* ① (*soumettre: plan, projet*) to propose, to suggest; (*devoir, question, sujet*) to set; (*idée*) to suggest; (*décret, loi*) to put forward; **~ une nouvelle loi** (*gouvernement*) to propose a new law ② (*offrir: marchandise, paix, récompense, activité*) to offer; (*spectacle*) to propose ③ (*présenter*) **~ qn pour un poste/comme collaborateur** to suggest sb for a job/as a partner II. *vpr* (*offrir ses services*) **se ~ à qn comme chauffeur** to offer sb one's services as a driver

**proposition** [pʀɔpozisjɔ̃] *f* ① (*offre*) offer; **~ d'emploi** job offer; **~ de loi** private bill ② *pl* (*avances*) **des ~s propositions** ③ LING clause

**propre**[1] [pʀɔpʀ] I. *adj* ① (*opp: sale*) clean ② (*soigné: travail, intérieur, personne, tenue*) neat ③ (*opp: incontinent: enfant*) potty-trained; (*animal*) housebroken ④ (*honnête: affaire, argent*) honest ⑤ (*non polluant*) environmentally-friendly ▶**me/le voilà ~!** *inf* I'm/he's in a real mess! II. *m* **c'est du ~!** *inf* what a mess!; **mettre qc au ~** to copy sth neatly

**propre**[2] [pʀɔpʀ] I. *adj* ① antéposé (*à soi*) own ② postposé (*exact: mot, terme*) proper; (*sens*) literal; **le sens ~ d'un mot** the literal sense of a word ③ (*particulier: biens, capitaux*) separate II. *m* ① (*particularité*) particularity ② LING **au ~ et au figuré** literally and figuratively

**proprement** [pʀɔpʀəmɑ̃] *adv* ① (*avec soin*) cleanly; (*manger*) properly ② (*avec honnêteté*) honestly

**propreté** [pʀɔpʀəte] *f* ① (*opp: saleté*) cleanliness ② (*caractère non polluant*) cleanness

**propriétaire** [pʀɔpʀijetɛʀ] *mf* ① (*possesseur*) owner; (*d'un animal*) master ② (*opp: locataire*) landlord ③ (*bailleur*) lessor

**propriété** [pʀɔpʀijete] *f* ① (*domaine, immeuble*) ownership ② (*chose possédée*) property

**prospectus** [pʀɔspɛktys] *m* prospectus

**prostitué(e)** [pʀɔstitɥe] *m(f)* prostitute

**protecteur, -trice** [pʀɔtɛktœʀ, -tʀis] I. *adj* ① (*défenseur*) protective; ECON, POL protectionist ② (*condescendant: air, ton*) patronizing II. *m, f* ① (*défenseur*) guardian ② (*mécène*) patron

**protection** [pʀɔtɛksjɔ̃] *f* ① (*défense*) **~ contre qc** protection against sth; **~ de l'enfance** child welfare; **~ de l'environnement** environmental protection ② (*élément protecteur*) safety device ▶**~ sociale** social welfare; **mesures de ~** protective measure

**protégé(e)** [pʀɔteʒe] I. *adj* (*site, territoire*) protected; (*passage*) priority II. *m(f)* (*favori*) protégé

**protéger** [pʀɔteʒe] <2a, 5> I. *vt* ① (*défendre*) **~ qn/qc de/contre qn/qc** to protect sb/sth from sb/sth ② (*patronner: arts, carrière, sport*) to patronize; (*carrière, sport*) to sponsor II. *vpr* **se défendre**) **se ~ contre qn/qc** to protect oneself from sb/sth

**protestant(e)** [pʀɔtɛstɑ̃, ɑ̃t] *adj, m(f)* Protestant

**protestation** [pʀɔtɛstasjɔ̃] *f* (*plainte*) protest; **~ écrite** written complaint

**protester** [pʀɔtɛste] <1> *vi* (*s'opposer à*) to protest

**prouver** [pʀuve] <1> I. *vt* ① (*démontrer*) to prove; **il est prouvé que c'est vrai** it's been proven to be true; **il n'est pas prouvé que ce soit vrai** (*subj*) it hasn't been proven to be true ② (*montrer: amour*) to prove; (*reconnaissance*) to demonstrate; (*réponse, conduite*) to show II. *vpr* **se ~** ① (*se convaincre: personne*) to prove oneself ② (*être* *démontrable: chose*) to be demonstrated

**provenance** [pʀɔv(ə)nɑ̃s] *f* (*origine*) origin ▸ **être en ~ de ...** to be from; **de même ~** (*marchandises*) from the same source; **de toute ~** from everywhere

**provençal** [pʀɔvɑ̃sal] *m* Provençal; *v.a.* **français**

**provençal(e)** [pʀɔvɑ̃sal, -o] <-aux> *adj* Provençal

**Provençal(e)** [pʀɔvɑ̃sal, -o] <-aux> *m(f)* Provençal

**Provence** [pʀɔvɑ̃s] *f* **la ~** Provence

**proverbe** [pʀɔvɛʀb] *m* proverb; **comme dit le ~** according to the proverb

**province** [pʀɔvɛ̃s] *f* province ▸ **la Belle Province** Quebec; **faire très ~** *inf* to be very provincial

**provincial(e)** [pʀɔvɛ̃sjal, -jo] <-aux> **I.** *adj* ❶ (*opp: parisien: air, manières, rythme, vie*) provincial ❷ *Québec* (*opp: fédéral: mesures, décision*) Provincial **II.** *m(f)* Provincial

**proviseur** [pʀɔvizœʀ] *mf* ❶ principal ❷ *Belgique* (*adjoint du préfet* (*directeur de lycée*)) vice principal

**provision** [pʀɔvizjɔ̃] *f* ❶ *pl* (*vivres*) provisions ❷ (*réserve*) **~ d'eau** water reserves; **faire ~ de qc** to stock up on sth

**provisoire** [pʀɔvizwaʀ] **I.** *adj* ❶ (*opp: définitif*) *a.* JUR provisional; (*solution, mesure, installation*) temporary; (*bonheur, liaison*) fleeting ❷ (*intérimaire: gouvernement*) interim **II.** *m* **c'est du ~** it's temporary

**provocant(e)** [pʀɔvɔkɑ̃, ɑ̃t] *adj* provocative

**provocateur, -trice** [pʀɔvɔkatœʀ, -tʀis] **I.** *adj* provocative **II.** *m, f* agitator

**provocation** [pʀɔvɔkasjɔ̃] *f* (*défi*) provocation; **faire de la ~** to be provocative

**provoquer** [pʀɔvɔke] <1> **I.** *vt* ❶ (*causer*) to prompt; (*changement*) to bring about; (*colère, gaieté*) to provoke; (*mort, accident, explosion, révolte, désordre*) to cause ❷ (*énerver, agui-*

*cher*) to provoke **II.** *vpr* **se ~** to provoke each other

**prudemment** [pʀydamɑ̃] *adv* ❶ (*avec précaution*) carefully ❷ (*par précaution*) wisely

**prudence** [pʀydɑ̃s] *f* caution; **avoir la ~ de** +*infin* to have the good sense to +*infin*

**prudent(e)** [pʀydɑ̃, ɑ̃t] *adj* (*personne*) careful; (*précaution*) prudent; (*pas*) cautious

**prune** [pʀyn] *f* (*fruit*) plum ▸ **pour des ~s** *inf* for nothing

**pruneau** [pʀyno] <x> *m* ❶ CULIN prune ❷ *Suisse* (*quetsche*) plum

**prunier** [pʀynje] *m* plum tree ▸ **secouer qn comme un ~** *inf* to shake sb hard

**P.-S.** [peɛs] *m abr de* **post-scriptum** PS

**pschitt** [pʃit] *interj* fzzzt; **faire ~** make a fizzing sound

**pseudonyme** [psødɔnim] *m* pseudonym

**psy** [psi] *mf inf abr de* **psychanalyste, psychiatre, psychologue** shrink

**psychiatre** [psikjatʀ] *mf* psychiatrist

**psychiatrique** [psikjatʀik] *adj* psychiatric

**psychique** [psiʃik] *adj* psychic

**psychologique** [psikɔlɔʒik] *adj* psychological

**psychologue** [psikɔlɔɡ] **I.** *adj* perceptive **II.** *mf* psychologist

**pub¹** [pyb] *f inf abr de* **publicité**

**pub²** [pœb] *m* (*bar*) pub

**puberté** [pybɛʀte] *f* puberty

**public** [pyblik] *m* ❶ (*assistance*) audience; (*spectateurs*) public; (*lecteurs*) readership; (*auditeurs*) listeners; **être bon ~** to be easy to please; **le grand ~** the general public ❷ (*tous*) public; **en ~** (*en présence de personnes*) in public

**public, publique** [pyblik] *adj* (*commun, de l'État*) public; (*école*) state

**publication** [pyblikasjɔ̃] *f* publication

**publicitaire** [pyblisitɛʀ] *adj* **pancarte ~** billboard; **vente ~** promotional sale

**publicité** [pyblisite] *f* ❶ CINE, TV (*dans la presse*) advertising; (*à la radio, télé*)

**P**

commercial; **une page de ~** (*dans la presse*) a page of advertisements; (*à la radio, télé*) a commercial break ❷ (*réclame*) advertisement ❸ *sans pl* (*métier*) advertising ❹ *sans pl* (*action de rendre public*) publicity

**publier** [pyblije] <1> *vt* ❶ (*faire paraître: auteur, éditeur*) to publish ❷ (*rendre public*) to publicize; (*nouvelle*) to publish; (*communiqué*) to release

**publiquement** [pyblikmã] *adv* publicly

**puce** [pys] *f* ❶ ZOOL flea; **le marché aux ~s** the flea market ❷ INFORM chip; **ordinateur à ~ unique** single chip computer ❸ (*terme d'affection*) **viens, ma ~!** come here, dear! ▶ **mettre la ~ à l'oreille de qn** to get sb thinking; **secouer les ~s à qn** *inf* (*réprimander*) to tell sb off; (*dégourdir*) to wake sb up; **se secouer les ~s** to wake up

**puceron** [pys(ə)Rɔ̃] *m* greenfly

**pudeur** [pydœR] *f* ❶ (*décence*) modesty ❷ (*délicatesse*) decency

**pudique** [pydik] *adj* ❶ (*chaste: comportement, personne, geste*) modest ❷ (*plein de réserve: personne*) discreet

**puer** [pɥe] <1> I. *vi péj* to stink; **il pue des pieds** his feet stink II. *vt* ❶ *péj* (*empester*) **~ le renfermé** to smell musty ❷ *péj, inf* (*porter l'empreinte de*) **~ le fric** to stink of money

**puis**¹ [pɥi] *adv* then; **et ~ après** [*o quoi*]**?** *inf* so what?; **et ~ quoi encore!?** *inf* and what now?; **et ~** (*en outre*) and anyway

**puis**² [pɥi] *indic prés de* **pouvoir**

**puisque** [pɥisk(ə)] <puisqu'> *conj* since; **mais puisqu'elle est malade!** but she's sick, for heaven's sake!; **puisqu'il le faut!** if we have to!

**puissance** [pɥisãs] *f* power; (*des éléments, du vent*) strength; **grande ~** major power; **dix ~ deux** ten to the power of two

**puissant(e)** [pɥisã, ãt] I. *adj* ❶ (*d'une grande force*) strong ❷ (*qui a du pouvoir, qui a un grand potentiel économique ou militaire*) powerful ❸ (*très efficace*) potent II. *mpl* **les ~s** the powers

**puits** [pɥi] *m* ❶ (*pour l'eau*) well ❷ (*pour l'exploitation d'un gisement: d'une mine*) shaft; **~ de pétrole** oil well

**pull** [pyl] *m inf*, **pull-over** [pylɔvɛR, pylɔvœR] <pull-overs> *m* sweater

**punaise** [pynɛz] *f* ❶ ZOOL bug ❷ (*petit clou*) thumbtack

**punch** [pœnʃ] *m inv* (*dynamisme*) drive, **avoir du ~** *inf* to have drive

**punir** [pyniR] <8> *vt* ❶ (*châtier*) **~ qn d'une peine d'emprisonnement** to punish sb with a prison sentence ❷ (*sévir*) **être puni de mort** to be punishable by death

**punition** [pynisjɔ̃] *f* punishment

**punk** [pœ̃k, pœnk] *adj inv*, *mf* (*personne*) punk

**pupitre** [pypitR] *m* ❶ INFORM console ❷ MUS (*d'un musicien, choriste*) music stand; (*d'un chef d'orchestre*) rostrum; (*d'un piano*) music rest ❸ (*meuble à plan incliné*) desk

**pur(e)** [pyR] *adj* ❶ (*non altéré: air, eau*) pure ❷ (*non mélangé*) neat ❸ (*authentique: vérité*) plain; (*hasard, méchanceté*) sheer; **mais c'est de la folie ~e!** but it's sheer madness! ❹ (*opp: appliqué: recherche, science, mathématiques*) pure ❺ (*innocent: cœur, amour*) innocent; (*regard*) clear; (*jeune fille*) pure; (*intentions*) honorable ❻ (*harmonieux: ligne, son*) flowing; (*profil*) flawless; (*langue, style*) pure ▶ **~ et simple** pure and simple; **un "non" ~ et simple** a flat out "no"

**purée** [pyRe] *f* purée; **~ de pommes de terre** mashed potatoes

**purement** [pyRmã] *adv* purely; **~ et simplement** purely and simply

**pureté** [pyRte] *f* ❶ (*opp: souillure*) purity ❷ (*perfection*) flawlessness ❸ (*innocence: des intentions*) honorableness; (*d'un regard, de l'enfance*) innocence

**purger** [pyRʒe] <2a> I. *vt* ❶ (*vidanger: conduite, tuyauterie, chaudière, huile*) to drain; (*radiateur*) to bleed; **~ qc d'eau** to drain the water from sth ❷ JUR (*peine*) to serve ❸ MED **~ qn** to purge;

**être purgé** to take a purge **II.** *vpr* se ~ to take a purge; (*animal*) to purge itself
**purifier** [pyʀifje] <1> **I.** *vt* to purify **II.** *vpr* se ~ **de qc** to cleanse oneself of sth
**purin** [pyʀɛ̃] *m* slurry
**pur-sang** [pyʀsɑ̃] <pur(s)-sang(s)> *m* thoroughbred
**pus**[1] [py] *m* pus
**pus**[2] [py] *passé simple de* **pouvoir**

**putsch** [putʃ] *m* putsch
**puzzle** [pœzl, pœzœl] *m* jigsaw puzzle
**pyjama** [piʒama] *m* pajama; **en ~(s)** in pajamas
**pyramide** [piʀamid] *f* pyramid; **~ des âges** population pyramid
**Pyrénées** [piʀene] *fpl* **les ~** the Pyrenees
**pyrex**® [piʀɛks] *m* Pyrex®

# Q q

**Q, q** [ky] *m inv* Q, q; **~ comme Quintal** (*au téléphone*) q as in Quebec
**Q.I.** [kyi] *m abr de* **quotient intellectuel** *inv* IQ
**qu'** [k] *v.* **que**
**quai** [ke] *m* ❶ (*d'une gare, station de métro*) platform ❷ (*pour accoster*) quay ❸ (*voie publique*) embankment; **les ~s de la Seine** the banks of the Seine
**qualification** [kalifikasjɔ̃] *f* ❶ SPORT qualification; **match de ~** qualifier ❷ (*expérience*) ~ **professionnelle** professional qualification
**qualifié(e)** [kalifje] *adj* ❶ (*compétent: personne*) qualified ❷ (*formé*) skilled
**qualifier** [kalifje] <1> *vpr* SPORT **se ~ pour qc** to qualify for sth
**qualitatif, -ive** [kalitatif, -iv] *adj* (*analyse*) qualitative
**qualité** [kalite] *f* quality; **~s morales** moral qualities
**quand** [kɑ̃] **I.** *adv* when; **depuis/jusqu'à ~?** since/till when?; **de ~ date ce livre?** when did this book come out? **II.** *conj* ❶ when; **quand elle arrivera** when she arrives ❷ *inf* (*le moment où, le fait que*) when ❸ (*exclamatif*) ~ **je pense que ...!** when I think that ...!
▶ **~ même** (*malgré cela*) still; *inf* (*tout de même*) all the same; **tu aurais ~**

**même pu avertir** you could still have let us know
**quant** [kɑ̃t] *prep* (*pour ce qui concerne*) **~ à qn/qc** as for sb/sth
**quantitatif, -ive** [kɑ̃titatif, -iv] *adj* quantitative
**quantité** [kɑ̃tite] *f* ❶ (*nombre*) quantity; (*au sujet d'objets dénombrables, de personnes*) number ❷ (*grand nombre*) **(une) ~ de personnes/choses** a large number of people/things; **(des) ~s de personnes/de choses** a great many people/things; **(des) ~s a** great many; **en ~** in large numbers
**quarantaine** [kaʀɑ̃tɛn] *f* ❶ (*environ quarante*) **une ~ de personnes/pages** about forty people/pages ❷ (*âge approximatif*) **avoir la ~, approcher de la ~** to be pushing forty ❸ MED quarantine; *v.a.* **cinquantaine**
**quarante** [kaʀɑ̃t] **I.** *adj* forty; **~ et un** forty-one; **semaine de ~ heures** forty-hour week **II.** *m inv* ❶ (*cardinal*) forty ❷ (*taille de confection*) **faire du ~** to wear a size forty; *v.a.* **cinq, cinquante**
**quarantième** [kaʀɑ̃tjɛm] **I.** *adj antéposé* fortieth **II.** *mf* **le/la ~** the fortieth **III.** *m* (*fraction*) fortieth; *v.a.* **cinquième**
**quart** [kaʀ] *m* ❶ (*quatrième partie d'un tout*) quarter; **trois ~s** three quarters;

**~ de finale** quarterfinal ❷ CULIN (25 cl) quarter liter ❸ (15 minutes) quarter; **un ~ d'heure** quarter of an hour; (dans le décompte des heures) quarter; **il est 3 heures et/un ~** it's a quarter past three; **il est 4 heures moins le ~** it's a quarter to four ❹ (partie appréciable) quarter; **je n'ai pas fait le ~ de ce que je voulais faire** I haven't done half of what I wanted to; **les trois ~s de qc** the best part of sth; **les trois ~s du temps** most of the time ▶ **au ~ de tour** straight off; **passer un mauvais ~ d'heure** to have a miserable time

**quartier** [kaʀtje] m ❶ (partie de ville) district; **~ résidentiel** residential area ❷ (lieu où l'on habite, habitants) neighborhood; **les gens du ~** the people living here ❸ Suisse (banlieue) **~ périphérique** suburb

**quart-monde** [kaʀmɔ̃d] <quarts-mondes> m (pays les plus pauvres) the Fourth World

**quasi** [kazi] adv nearly; **~ mort** as good as dead

**quatorze** [katɔʀz] I. adj (cardinal) fourteen II. m inv fourteen; v.a. **cinq**

**quatorzième** [katɔʀzjɛm] I. adj antéposé fourteenth II. mf **le/la ~** the fourteenth III. m (fraction) fourteenth; v.a. **cinquième**

**quatre** [katʀ(ə)] I. adj (cardinal) four ▶ **manger comme ~** to eat like a wolf; **un de ces ~** (matins) inf one of these days II. m inv four; v.a. **cinq**

**quatre-heures** [katʀœʀ] m inv, inf snack

**quatre-quatre** [katkatʀə] m o f inv AUTO four-wheel drive

**quatre-vingt** [katʀəvɛ̃] <quatre-vingts> I. adj ~s eighty; **~ mille** eighty thousand II. m ~s eighty; v.a. **cinq, cinquante**

**quatre-vingt-dix** [katʀəvɛ̃dis] I. adj ninety II. m inv ninety; v.a. **cinq, cinquante**

**quatre-vingt-dixième** [katʀəvɛ̃dizjɛm] <quatre-vingt-dixièmes> I. adj antéposé ninetieth II. mf **le/la ~** the ninetieth III. m (fraction) ninetieth; v.a. **cinquième**

**quatre-vingtième** [katʀəvɛ̃tjɛm] <quatre-vingtièmes> I. adj antéposé eightieth II. mf **le/la ~** the eightieth III. m (fraction) eightieth; v.a. **cinquième**

**quatre-vingt-onze** [katʀəvɛ̃ɔ̃z] I. adj ninety-one II. m inv ninety-one; v.a. **cinq, cinquante**

**quatre-vingt-un, -une** [katʀəvɛ̃œ̃, -yn] adj, m inv eighty-one; v.a. **cinq, cinquante**

**quatre-vingt-unième** [katʀəvɛ̃ynjɛm] I. adj antéposé eighty-first II. mf **le/la ~** the eighty-first III. m (fraction) eighty-first; v.a. **cinquième**

**quatrième** [katʀijɛm] I. adj antéposé fourth II. mf **le/la ~** the fourth III. f ECOLE eighth grade; v.a. **cinquième**

**que** [kə] <qu'> I. conj ❶ (introduit une complétive) that; **je ne crois pas qu'il vienne** I don't think (that) he'll come ❷ (dans des formules de présentation) **peut-être** ~ perhaps ❸ (dans des questions) **qu'est-ce ~ c'est?** what is it?; **qu'est-ce que c'est ~ ça?** inf what's that?; **quand/où est-ce ~ tu pars?** when/where are you going? ❹ (reprend une conjonction de subordination) **si tu as le temps et qu'il fait beau** if you've got the time and the weather's nice ❺ (introduit une proposition de temps) **ça fait trois jours qu'il est là** he's been here for four days now ❻ (introduit une proposition de but) so (that); **taisez-vous qu'on entende l'orateur!** keep quiet so we can hear the speaker! ❼ (pour comparer) **plus/moins/autre ...** ~ more/less/other than; **(tout) aussi ...** ~ as ... as; **autant de ...** ~ as many (o much) ... as; **tel ~** such as ❽ (seulement) only; **il ne fait ~ travailler** all he does is work; **il n'est arrivé qu'hier** he only arrived yesterday; **la vérité, rien ~ la vérité** the truth and nothing but the truth II. adv (comme) (qu'est-ce) ~ **c'est beau!** how lovely it is! III. pron rel

❶ (*complément direct se rapportant à un substantif*) which, that; **ce ~** what; **chose ~** which; **quoi ~ tu dises** whatever you (may) say ❷ (*après une indication de temps*) **un jour qu'il faisait beau** one day when it was fine; **toutes les fois qu'il vient** every time he comes; **le temps ~ la police arrive, ...** by the time the police arrive, ... **IV.** *pron interrog* ❶ (*quelle chose?*) what?; **qu'est-ce ~ ...?** what ...?; **ce ~** what ❷ (*attribut du sujet*) what; **~ deviens-tu?** what are you up to?; **qu'est-ce ~ ...?** what ...?; **ce ~** what ❸ (*quoi*) what ▸ **qu'est-ce qui vous prend?** what's the matter with you?

**Québec** [kebɛk] *m* ❶ (*ville*) Quebec ❷ (*région*) **le ~** Quebec

**quel(le)** [kɛl] **I.** *adj* ❶ (*dans une question*) what; (*lequel*) which; **~ temps fait-il?** what's the weather like?; **~ le heure est-il?** what time is it?; **~ est le plus grand des deux?** which (one) is bigger?; **je me demande ~le a pu être sa réaction** I wonder what his reaction was; **~ que soit son choix** (*subj*) whatever he chooses; **~ les que soient les conséquences, ...** whatever the consequences (may be), ... ❷ (*exclamation*) what; **~ dommage!** what a shame!; **~ talent!** what talent! **II.** *pron* which; **de nous deux, ~ est le plus grand?** which of us is taller?

**quelconque** [kɛlkɔ̃k] *adj* ❶ (*n'importe quel*) **un ... ~** any ❷ (*ordinaire*) run-of-the-mill; (*médiocre*) indifferent

**quelque** [kɛlk] **I.** *adj indéf, antéposé* ❶ *pl* (*plusieurs*) some, a few; **à ~s pas d'ici** not far from here ❷ *pl* (*petit nombre*) **les ~s fois où ...** the few times that ... **II.** *adv* **~ peu** somewhat; **et ~(s)** *inf,* **10 kg et ~s** just over ten kilograms; **cinq heures et ~(s)** just after five o'clock

**quelque chose** [kɛlkəʃoz] *pron* something; **~ de beau** something beautiful; **c'est déjà ~!** that's something ▸ **prendre un petit ~** *inf* (*une collation*) to have a bite (to eat); (*un petit verre*) to

have a quick drink; **être pour ~ dans qc** to have something to do with sth; **~ comme** something like

**quelquefois** [kɛlkəfwa] *adv* sometimes

**quelque part** [kɛlkəpaʀ] *adv* somewhere

**quelques-uns, -unes** [kɛlkəzœ̃, -yn] *pron indéf* ❶ (*un petit nombre de personnes*) a few ❷ (*certaines personnes*) some people ❸ (*certains*) **quelques-unes des personnes/choses** some of the people/things; **j'en ai mangé ~/ quelques-unes** I ate some

**quelqu'un** [kɛlkœ̃] *pron indéf* (*une personne*) somebody, someone; **~ d'autre** somebody else

**qu'est-ce que** [kɛskə] *pron interrog* what

**qu'est-ce qui** [kɛski] *pron interrog* who

**question** [kɛstjɔ̃] *f* ❶ (*demande*) a. INFORM question; **poser une ~ à qn** to ask sb a question; **sans poser de ~s** without asking questions; **(re)mettre qc en ~** to call sth into question ❷ (*problème*) **c'est une ~ de temps** it's a question [*o* matter] of time; **c'est (toute) la ~** that's the big question; **ce n'est pas la ~** that's not the question [*o* issue] ❸ (*ensemble de problèmes soulevés*) question; **la ~ du chômage/pétrole** the unemployment/oil question [*o* issue] ▸ **il est ~ de qn/qc** (*il s'agit de*) it's a matter of sb/sth; (*on parle de*) people are talking about sb/sth; **il n'est pas ~ de qc** there's no question of sth; **hors de ~** out of the question; **pas ~!** *inf* no way!; **~ qc, ...** *inf* as for sth, ...

**questionnaire** [kɛstjɔnɛʀ] *m* questionnaire

**questionner** [kɛstjɔne] <1> *vt* (*interroger*) **~ qn sur qc** to question sb about sth

**quête** [kɛt] *f* (*collecte d'argent*) collection; **faire la ~** (*dans la rue: association*) to take a collection; (*chanteur des rues*) to pass the hat around

**queue** [kø] *f* ❶ ZOOL tail ❷ BOT stalk ❸ (*manche: d'une casserole, poêle*) handle; **~ de billard** pool cue ❹ AUTO (*d'un train, métro*) rear ❺ *inf* (*pénis*) cock ⑤ (*file de personnes*) line; **faire la ~** to line up; **se mettre à la ~** to get in line ▸ **faire une ~ de** <u>poisson</u> **à qn** to cut sb up; **n'avoir ni ~ ni** <u>tête</u> to make no sense

**qui** [ki] **I.** *pron rel* ❶ (*comme sujet se rapportant à une chose*) which, that; (*comme sujet se rapportant à une personne*) who, that; **toi ~ sais tout** you who think you know it all; **le voilà ~ arrive** here he comes; **j'en connais ~ ...** I know someone who ...; **c'est lui/elle ~ a fait cette bêtise** he/she was the one who did this stupid thing; **ce ~ ...** (*servant de sujet*) what; (*se rapportant à une phrase principale*) which; **ce ~ se passe est grave** what's going on is serious; **chose ~ ...** something which ... ❷ (*comme complément, remplace une personne*) **la dame à côté de ~ tu es assis/tu t'assois** the lady you're sitting/you sit next to; **l'ami dans la maison de ~ ...** the friend in whose house ...; **la dame à ~ c'est arrivé** the lady this happened to ❸ (*celui qui*) whoever; **~ fait qc ...** (*introduisant un proverbe, dicton*) he who does sth ... ▸ **~ que tu sois** (*subj*) whoever you are; **je ne veux être dérangé par ~ que ce soit** (*subj*) I don't want to be disturbed by anybody **II.** *pron interrog* ❶ (*qu'est-ce que*) **~ ...?** who ...?; **~ ça?** who's that ...?; **c'est qui est là?** who's there? ❷ (*question portant sur la personne complément direct*) **~ ...?** who, whom *form;* **~ as-tu parlé?** who did you see?; **~ croyez-vous?** who do you believe? ❸ (*question portant sur la personne complément indirect*) **à/avec ~ as-tu parlé?** who did you speak to/with?; **pour ~ as-tu voté?** who did you vote for?; **chez ~ est la réunion?** whose house is the meeting at? ❹ (*marque du sujet, personne ou chose*) **qui est-ce ~ ...?** who ...?; **qu'est-ce ~ ...?** what ...?

**quiche** [kiʃ] *f* **~** (**lorraine**) quiche (Lorraine)

**quiconque** [kikɔ̃k] **I.** *pron rel* (*celui qui*)

**~ veut venir** anyone who wants to come **II.** *pron indéf* (*personne*) **hors de question que ~ sorte** there's no question of anyone leaving; **elle ne veut recevoir d'ordres de ~** she won't take orders from anyone

**qui est-ce que** [kiɛskə] *pron interrog* (*question portant sur une personne en position complément*) **~ ...?** who, whom *form;* **avec/pour ~ tu l'as fait?** who did you do it with/for?

**qui est-ce qui** [kiɛski] *pron interrog* (*question portant sur une personne en position sujet*) **~ ...?** who ...?

**quille** [kij] *f* ❶ JEUX ninepin ❷ *inf* (*fin du service militaire*) end of military service

**quincaillerie** [kɛ̃kajʀi] *f* hardware store

**quinquennat** [kɛ̃kena] *m* five-year term

**quinte** [kɛ̃t] *f* MED **~ de toux** coughing fit

**quinzaine** [kɛ̃zɛn] *f* ❶ (*environ quinze*) **une ~ de personnes/pages** around fifteen people/pages ❷ (*deux semaines*) **revenir dans une ~ (de jours)** to come back in two weeks; **la première ~ de janvier** the first half [*o* two weeks] of January

**quinze** [kɛ̃z] **I.** *adj* fifteen; **tous les ~ jours** every two weeks **II.** *m inv* ❶ (*cardinal*) fifteen ❷ SPORT **le ~ d'Irlande** Ireland's team; *v.a.* **cinq**

**quinzième** [kɛ̃zjɛm] **I.** *adj antéposé* fifteenth **II.** *mf* **le/la ~** the fifteenth **III.** *m* (*fraction*) fifteenth; *v.a.* **cinquième**

**quitter** [kite] <1> *vt* ❶ (*prendre congé de, rompre avec, sortir de, partir de*) to leave; **ne quittez pas** TEL hold the line; **~ l'école** to leave school ❷ (*ne plus rester sur*) **la voiture a quitté la route** the car went off the road ❸ INFORM **~ un programme** to exit a program

**quoi** [kwa] **I.** *pron rel* ❶ (*annexe d'une phrase principale complète*) **..., ce à ~ il ne s'attendait pas** ..., which he didn't expect; **ce en ~ elle se trompait** ..., but she was mistaken there ❷ (*dans une question indirecte*) **elle ne comprend pas ce à ~** on fait allusion she doesn't understand what they're alluding to; **ce sur ~ je veux que nous discutons** what I want us to discuss ❸ *(comme pronom relatif)* **à/ de ~ ...** to/about which ...; **voilà de ~ je voulais te parler** that's what I wanted to talk to you about; **voilà à ~ je pensais** that's what I was thinking about ❹ *(cela)* **...**, **après ~ ...** ..., after which ... ❺ *(ce qui est nécessaire pour)* **de ~ faire qc** things needed to do sth; **as-tu de ~ écrire?** do you have something to write with?; **elle n'a pas de ~ vivre** she has nothing to live on; **il y a de ~ s'énerver, non?** it's enough to drive you crazy, isn't it?; **il est très fâché – il y a de ~!** he's really angry – he has every reason to be!; **il n'y a pas de ~ rire** it's nothing to laugh about ▸ **il n'y <u>a</u> pas de ~!** you're welcome; **~ que ce <u>soit</u>** *(subj)* anything; **si tu as besoin de ~ que ce soit, ...** *(subj)* if there's anything you need, ...; **elle n'a jamais dit ~ que ce soit** *(subj)* she never said anything (at all); **~ qu'il en <u>soit</u>** *(subj)* be that as it may; **~ <u>comme</u>** *inf (pour dire)* saying; **comme ~ on peut se tromper!** which just goes to show you can make mistakes!; **~ <u>que</u>** whatever **II.** *pron* **Interrog** ❶ + *prép* **à ~ penses-tu** *[o est-ce que tu penses]?* what are you thinking about?; **di-**

**tes-nous à ~ cela sert** tell us what it's for; **de ~ n'est-elle pas capable/ a-t-elle besoin?** is there anything she's not capable of/she needs?; **cette chaise est en ~?** *inf* what's this chair made of?; **par ~ commençons-nous?** where do we begin? ❷ *inf (qu'est-ce que)* what?; **c'est ~, ce truc?** what is this thing?; **tu sais ~?** you know what?; **~ encore?** what's that?; **tu es idiot, ou ~?** *inf* are you stupid or what? ❸ *(qu'est-ce qu'il y a de ...?)* **~ de neuf?** what's new?; **~ de plus facile/ beau que ...?** is there anything easier/ more beautiful than ...? ❹ *inf (comment?)* what? **III.** *interj* ❶ *(marque la surprise: comment!)* **~!** what! ❷ *inf (en somme)* **...**, **~!** ..., eh!; **il n'est pas bête, il manque un peu d'intelligence, ~!** he's not stupid, he's just not very bright, you know!

**quoique** [kwak(ə)] *conj* although

**quota** [k(w)ɔta] *m* quota

**quotidien** [kɔtidjɛ̃] *m* ❶ *(journal)* daily (paper) ❷ *(vie quotidienne)* daily life; *(train-train)* everyday life

**quotidien(ne)** [kɔtidjɛ̃, jɛn] *adj* ❶ *(journalier)* daily; **vie ~ne** daily life; *(train-train)* everyday life ❷ *(banal: tâches)* everyday

**quotient** [kɔsjɑ̃] *m* quotient

**Q**

# Rr

**R, r** [ɛʀ] *m inv* R, r; **rouler les ~** to roll one's R's; **~ comme Raoul** (*au téléphone*) r as in Romeo

**rab** [ʀab] *m inf* **il y a du ~** there's some left over

**rabaisser** [ʀabese] <1> *vt* (*dénigrer*) to belittle

**rabbin** [ʀabɛ̃] *m* REL rabbi

**raccommoder** [ʀakɔmɔde] <1> **I.** *vt* (*réparer: linge*) to mend; (*chaussettes*) to darn **II.** *vpr inf* **se ~** to get back together

**raccompagner** [ʀakɔ̃paɲe] <1> *vt* **~ qn à la maison** (*à pied*) to walk sb home; (*en voiture*) to drive sb home

**raccourci** [ʀakuʀsi] *m* a. INFORM shortcut; **~ clavier** keyboard shortcut

**raccourcir** [ʀakuʀsiʀ] <8> **I.** *vt* (*rendre plus court: texte, vêtement*) to shorten **II.** *vi* ❶ (*devenir plus court*) to get shorter ❷ (*au lavage: vêtement*) to shrink

**raccrocher** [ʀakʀɔʃe] <1> **I.** *vi* ❶ TEL to hang up ❷ *inf* SPORT (*renoncer: professionnel*) to retire **II.** *vpr* (*se cramponner*) **se ~ à qn/qc** to grab ahold of sb/sth

**R**  **race** [ʀas] *f* ❶ (*groupe ethnique*) race ❷ (*espèce zoologique, sorte*) breed; **chien/chat de ~** purebred dog/cat

**racheter** [ʀaʃte] <4> **I.** *vt* ❶ (*acheter en plus*) **~ du vin** to buy some more wine ❷ (*acheter d'autrui*) **~ une table à qn** to buy a table from sb ❸ (*se libérer de*) **~ une dette** to redeem a debt **II.** *vpr* **se ~ d'un crime** to make amends for a crime

**racine** [ʀasin] *f* (*origine*) a. BOT root ▸ **prendre ~** to take root

**racisme** [ʀasism] *m* (*théorie des races, hostilité*) racism; **~ anti-jeunes** prejudice against young people

**raciste** [ʀasist] *adj, mf* racist

**racketter** [ʀakete] <1> *vt* to run a pro-

tection racket; **~ qn** to extort money from sb

**raclée** [ʀakle] *f inf* ❶ (*volée de coups*) hiding ❷ (*défaite*) thrashing

**racler** [ʀakle] <1> **I.** *vt* ❶ (*nettoyer, frotter*) to scrape; (*casserole*) to scrape; (*boue, croûte*) to scrape off ❷ (*ratisser: sable*) to rake **II.** *vpr* **se ~ la gorge** to clear one's throat

**raclette** [ʀaklɛt] *f* ❶ CULIN (*spécialité, fromage*) raclette (*cheese melted and served on potatoes*) ❷ (*grattoir*) scraper

**raconter** [ʀakɔ̃te] <1> *vt* ❶ (*narrer*) **~ une histoire à qn** to tell sb a story; **~ un voyage** to relate a journey ❷ (*dire à la légère*) **~ des histoires** to talk nonsense ▸ **~ sa vie à qn** *inf* to tell sb one's life story

**radar** [ʀadaʀ] **I.** *m* radar **II.** *app* **contrôle-~** speed trap

**radiateur** [ʀadjatœʀ] *m* (*de chauffage central*) a. AUTO radiator

**radical** [ʀadikal, -o] <-aux> *m* LING root

**radical(e)** [ʀadikal, -o] <-aux> *adj* ❶ (*total*) drastic; (*refus*) total ❷ (*énergique*) radical ❸ (*foncier*) fundamental; **islam ~** radical Islam

**radicaliser** [ʀadikalize] <1> **I.** *vt* (*conflit*) to intensify; (*position*) to harden **II.** *vpr* **se ~** (*parti, régime, théorie*) to become more radical; (*conflit*) to intensify; (*position*) to harden

**radier** [ʀadje] <1> *vt* (*candidat, nom*) to remove; **~ un médecin** to revoke a doctor's license

**radieux, -euse** [ʀadjø, -jøz] *adj* radiant

**radin(e)** [ʀadɛ̃, in] **I.** *adj inf* (*avare*) tightfisted **II.** *m(f) inf* tightwad

**radio** [ʀadjo] *f* ❶ (*poste*) radio; **allumer/éteindre la ~** to turn the radio on/off ❷ (*radiodiffusion*) radio (broadcasting); **passer à la ~** (*personne*) to be on the radio; (*chanson*) to get played on the radio ❸ (*station*) radio station ❹ MED X-ray; **passer une ~** to have an X-ray

**radioactif, -ive** [ʀadjoaktif, -iv] *adj* radioactive

**radioactivité** [ʀadjoaktivite] *f* radioactivity

**radiographie** [ʀadjɔgʀafi] *f* MED ❶ (*procédé*) radiography ❷ (*cliché*) X-ray

**radiologue** [ʀadjɔlɔg] *mf* radiologist

**radio-réveil** [ʀadjoʀevɛj] <radios-réveils> *m* clock radio

**radis** [ʀadi] *m* radish ▸ **ça ne vaut pas un ~** *inf* it's not worth a penny [*o* red cent]

**radoucir** [ʀadusiʀ] <8> *vpr* se ~ ❶ (*se calmer: personne*) to soften ❷ METEO (*température, temps*) to get milder

**rafale** [ʀafal] *f* METEO gust; **~ de neige** snow flurry; **~ de vent/pluie** gust of wind/rain

**raffermir** [ʀafɛʀmiʀ] <8> *vpr* se ~ (*devenir ferme: voix*) to steady; (*peau, muscles*) to tone up; (*chair*) to firm up

**raffiné(e)** [ʀafine] *adj* (*délicat*) subtle; (*goût, cuisine, personne*) refined; (*esprit*) discriminating

**raffinerie** [ʀafinʀi] *f* **~ de pétrole/sucre** oil/sugar refinery

**raffoler** [ʀafɔle] <1> *vi* **~ de qn/qc** to be wild about sb/sth

**rafle** [ʀafl] *f* (*arrestation*) raid

**rafler** [ʀafle] <1> *vt* *inf* ❶ (*voler: bijoux*) to run off with ❷ (*remporter: prix*) to walk off with

**rafraîchir** [ʀafʀeʃiʀ] <8> *vpr* se ~ ❶ (*devenir plus frais: air, temps, température*) to get colder ❷ (*boire*) to have a cool drink ❸ (*se laver, arranger sa toilette, son maquillage*) to freshen up

**rafraîchissement** [ʀafʀeʃismɑ̃] *m* (*boisson*) cold drink

**rafting** [ʀaftiŋ] *m* **faire du ~** to go white-water rafting

**rage** [ʀaʒ] *f* ❶ (*colère*) rage; **être fou de ~** to be absolutely furious ❷ (*passion*) passion ❸ MED **la ~** rabies

**ragot** [ʀago] *m* *inf* piece of gossip; **des ragots** gossip

**ragoût** [ʀagu] *m* stew

**raide** [ʀɛd] **I.** *adj* ❶ (*rigide: personne, corps, membre*) stiff; (*cheveux*) straight ❷ (*escarpé: chemin, escalier, pente*) steep ❸ *inf* (*ivre*) plastered **II.** *adv* (*brusquement*) **tomber ~ mort** to drop stone dead

**raie**[1] [ʀɛ] *f* (*ligne*) line

**raie**[2] [ʀɛ] *indic et subj prés de* **rayer**

**rail** [ʀaj] *m* CHEMDFER, TECH rail

**raisin** [ʀɛzɛ̃] *m* grape; **~s secs** raisins

**raison** [ʀɛzɔ̃] *f* ❶ (*motif, sagesse*) reason; **~ d'être** raison d'être; **~ de vivre** reason for living; **avoir de bonnes/mauvaises ~s** to have good/bad reasons; **avoir de fortes ~s de penser que** to have good reason to think that; **ce n'est pas une ~ pour faire qc** that's no excuse for doing sth; **ramener qn à la ~** to bring sb back to their senses ❷ (*facultés intellectuelles*) mind; **avoir toute sa ~** to be in one's right mind; **perdre la ~** to lose one's mind ▸ **à plus forte ~, je ne le ferai pas** all the more reason why I won't do it; **à tort ou à ~** rightly or wrongly; **avoir ~** to be right; **donner ~ à qn** to agree that sb is right; **entendre ~** to listen to reason; **se faire une ~** to resign oneself; **pour quelle ~?** why?; **pour une ~ ou pour une autre** for one reason or another

**raisonnable** [ʀɛzɔnabl] *adj* (*sage*) reasonable

**raisonnement** [ʀɛzɔnmɑ̃] *m* (*façon de penser, argumentation*) reasoning

**raisonner** [ʀɛzɔne] <1> *vi* ❶ (*penser*) to think ❷ (*enchaîner des arguments*) to reason

**rajeunir** [ʀaʒœniʀ] <8> **I.** *vt* ❶ (*rendre plus jeune*) to rejuvenate ❷ (*donner moins que son âge à*) **ça ne nous rajeunit pas!** *hum* doesn't make us any younger, does it! **II.** *vi* ❶ (*se sentir plus jeune*) to feel younger ❷ (*sembler plus jeune*) to seem younger

**rajouter** [ʀaʒute] <1> *vt* **~ une phrase**

**à qc** to add a sentence to sth; **il faut ~ du sel/sucre** it needs salt/sugar ▶ **en** ~ *inf* to lay it on a bit thick

**rajuster** [Raʒyste] <1> *vt* (*remettre en place: vêtement, lunettes*) to adjust

**ralenti** [Ralɑ̃ti] *m* ❶ CINE, TV **au** ~ in slow motion; **l'entreprise fonctionne au** ~ the company is running under capacity ❷ AUTO idling speed; **tourner au** ~ (*moteur*) to idle

**ralentir** [Ralɑ̃tiʀ] <8> I. *vt* to slow down; (*zèle, activité*) to slacken II. *vi* (*marcheur, véhicule, croissance*) to slow down III. *vpr* **se** ~ ❶ (*devenir plus lent: allure, mouvement*) to slow down ❷ (*diminuer: ardeur, effort, zèle*) to flag; (*production, croissance*) to slacken off

**râler** [Rɑle] <1> *vi* (*grogner*) ~ **contre qn/qc** to moan about sb/sth; **faire** ~ **qn** to make sb angry

**râleur, -euse** [Rɑlœʀ, -øz] I. *adj inf* grouchy II. *m, f inf* moaner

**rallonge** [Ralɔ̃ʒ] *f* ❶ (*d'une table*) leaf ❷ ELEC extension cord

**rallonger** [Ralɔ̃ʒe] <2a> *vt* to lengthen

**rallumer** [Ralyme] <1> *vt* (*allumer: feu, cigarette*) to relight; (*lampe, lumière*) to switch on again; (*électricité*) to turn on again

**rallye** [Rali] *m* rally

**RAM** [Ram] *f abr de* **Random Access Memory** RAM

**ramasser** [Ramɑse] <1> I. *vt* ❶ (*collecter: bois mort, coquillages*) to gather; (*champignons*) to pick; (*ordures, copies*) to collect ❷ *inf* (*embarquer*) **se faire** ~ **par la police** to get nabbed by the police ❸ (*relever une personne qui est tombée*) ~ **qn qui est ivre mort** to pick up sb who's dead drunk ❹ (*prendre ce qui est tombé par terre*) to pick up II. *vpr* **se** ~ *inf* (*tomber*) to fall flat on one's face

**ramener** [Ramne] <4> I. *vt* ❶ (*reconduire*) ~ **qn chez soi** to take sb back home ❷ (*faire revenir, amener avec soi: beau temps*) to bring back; ~ **qn à la vie** to bring sb back to life; ~ **qn à la**

raison to bring sb back to their senses; ~ **qn/qc de Paris** to bring sb/sth back from Paris ❸ (*rétablir*) ~ **la paix** to restore peace ▶ **la** ~ *inf* (*être prétentieux*) to show off; (*vouloir s'imposer*) to butt in II. *vpr inf* (*arriver*) **se** ~ to show up

**rameur** [Ramœʀ] *m* rower

**rami** [Rami] *m* rummy

**rancard** [Rɑ̃kaʀ] *m inf* (*rendez-vous*) meeting

**rance** [Rɑ̃s] *adj* rancid

**rancœur** [Rɑ̃kœʀ] *f soutenu* rancor

**rançon** [Rɑ̃sɔ̃] *f* ❶ (*rachat*) ransom ❷ (*prix*) **la** ~ **de la gloire/du succès/progrès** the price of fame/success/progress

**rancune** [Rɑ̃kyn] *f* **garder** ~ **à qn de qc** to hold a grudge against sb for sth ▶ **sans** ~! no hard feelings!

**randonnée** [Rɑ̃dɔne] *f* **faire une** ~ **à pied/skis/bicyclette** to go for a hike/cross-country skiing/for a bicycle ride

**rang** [Rɑ̃] *m* ❶ (*suite de personnes ou de choses*) line; **en** ~ **par deux** in rows of two; **mettez-vous en** ~! line up! ❷ (*rangée de sièges*) row; **se placer au premier** ~ to sit in the front row ❸ (*position dans un ordre ou une hiérarchie*) rank ❹ (*condition*) station; **le** ~ **social** social standing

**rangée** [Rɑ̃ʒe] *f* row

**ranger** [Rɑ̃ʒe] <2a> I. *vt* ❶ (*mettre en ordre: maison, tiroir*) to straighten up ❷ (*mettre à sa place: objet, vêtements*) to put away ❸ (*classer: dossiers, fiches*) to file (away); **il passe son temps à** ~ he spends his time neatening up III. *vpr* **se** ~ (*s'écarter: piéton*) to stand aside; (*véhicule*) to pull over

**ranimer** [Ranime] <1> *vt* ❶ (*ramener à la vie: noyé, personne évanouie*) to revive ❷ (*revigorer: amour, feu*) to rekindle; (*espoir, forces*) to renew

**rap** [Rap] *m* rap

**rapace** [Rapas] I. *adj* ❶ (*avide*) rapacious; **oiseau** ~ bird of prey ❷ (*cupide: homme d'affaires, usurier*) money-grubbing II. *m* (*oiseau*) bird of prey

**rapatrier** [Rapatrije] <1> *vt* (*ramener:*

*personne*) to repatriate; (*objet*) to send home

**râpé(e)** [ʀɑpe] *adj* (*carotte, fromage*) grated ▶ **c'est** ► *inf* so much for that!

**râper** [ʀɑpe] <1> *vt* (*fromage, betteraves, carottes*) to grate

**rapide** [ʀapid] **I.** *adj* ❶ (*d'une grande vitesse*) fast; (*manière, progrès, réponse*) rapid; (*geste, intelligence, personne*) quick; **une réaction ~** a speedy reaction ❷ (*expéditif: décision, démarche*) hasty; (*visite*) hurried **II.** *m* ❶ (*train*) express train ❷ (*cours d'eau*) rapid

**rapidement** [ʀapidmɑ̃] *adv* quickly

**rapidité** [ʀapidite] *f* (*vitesse*) speed

**rappel** [ʀapɛl] *m* ❶ (*remise en mémoire, panneau de signalisation*) reminder ❷ (*admonestation*) **~ à l'ordre** call to order; POL naming ❸ FIN (*d'une facture, cotisation*) reminder ❹ THEAT curtain call ❺ MED booster

**rappeler** [ʀap(ə)le] <3> **I.** *vt* ❶ (*remémorer, évoquer: souvenir*) to remind; **~ une date à qn** to remind sb of a date ❷ (*appeler pour faire revenir*) to call back ❸ TEL **~ qn** to call sb back **II.** *vi* TEL to call back **III.** *vpr* **se ~ qn/qc** to remember sb/sth; **elle se rappelle que nous étions venus** she remembers that we had come

**rapport** [ʀapɔʀ] *m* ❶ (*lien*) link; **~ entre deux ou plusieurs choses** connection between two or several things; **~ de cause à effet** cause and effect relation; **~ qualité-prix** value for money ❷ (*relations*) relationship; **~s d'amitié/de bon voisinage** friendly/neighborly relations ❸ *pl* (*relations sexuelles*) (sexual) relations; **avoir des ~s avec qn** to have sex with sb ❹ (*compte rendu*) report; **rédiger un ~ sur qn/qc** to draw up a report on sb/sth ▶ **avoir ~ à qc** to be about sth; **en ~ avec** (*qui correspond à*) in keeping with; **mettre qc en ~ avec** (*en relation avec*) to relate sth to; **par ~ à qn/qc** (*en ce qui concerne*) regarding sb/sth;

(*proportionnellement*) compared to sb/sth

**rapporté(e)** [ʀapɔʀte] *adj* (*poche*) sewn-on; (*élément*) added

**rapporter** [ʀapɔʀte] <1> **I.** *vt* ❶ (*ramener, rendre*) **~ un livre à qn** to bring a book back to sb; **~ un livre à la bibliothèque** to return a book to the library ❷ (*être profitable*) **~ qc** (*action, activité*) to yield sth; (*métier*) to bring in sth ❸ *péj* (*répéter pour dénoncer*) to report **II.** *vpr* (*être relatif à*) **se ~ à qc** to relate to sth

**rapprocher** [ʀapʀɔʃe] <1> **I.** *vt* ❶ (*avancer: objets, chaises*) to bring closer; **rapproche ta chaise de la table/de moi!** move your chair closer to the table/me! ❷ (*réconcilier*) to reconcile; **ce drame nous a beaucoup rapprochés** this tragedy brought us closer together ❸ (*mettre en parallèle: idées, thèses*) to compare **II.** *vpr* ❶ (*approcher*) **se ~ de qn/qc** to approach sb/sth; **l'orage/le bruit se rapproche de nous** the storm/noise is getting closer (to us) ❷ (*sympathiser*) **se ~** to be reconciled

**raquette** [ʀakɛt] *f* ❶ SPORT paddle; **~ de tennis** tennis racket ❷ (*semelle pour la neige*) snowshoe

**rare** [ʀɑʀ] *adj* ❶ (*opp: fréquent: animal, édition, variété, objet, mot*) rare; **il est ~ qu'elle fasse des erreurs** (*subj*) she rarely makes mistakes ❷ (*exceptionnel*) unusual ❸ (*peu nombreux*) few ▶ **se faire ~** to become scarce

**rarement** [ʀaʀmɑ̃] *adv* rarely

**raser** [ʀɑze] <1> **I.** *vt* ❶ (*tondre*) to shave; (*cheveux*) to shave off; **être rasé de près** to be close-shaved ❷ (*effleurer*) **~ les murs** to hug the walls ❸ (*détruire: bâtiment, quartier*) to raze ❹ *inf* (*ennuyer*) to bore **II.** *vpr* (*se couper ras*) **se ~** to shave; **se ~ la barbe/la tête** to shave one's beard/hair off

**ras-le-bol** [ʀɑl(ə)bɔl] *m inv, inf* **en avoir ~ de qc** to be sick and tired of sth; **~!** I've had it up to here!

**rasoir** [ʀɑzwaʀ] **I.** *m* razor **II.** *adj inf* **qu'il est ~!** what a bore he is!

**R**

**rassembler** [ʀasɑ̃ble] <1> I. vt ① (réunir: documents, objets épars) to collect; (troupeau) to gather ② (regrouper: troupes, soldats) to rally; **~ des personnes** (personne) to gather together ③ (faire appel à: forces, idées) to gather; (courage) to summon ④ (remonter: charpente, mécanisme) to reassemble II. vpr se ~ (foule, participants) to gather; (écoliers, soldats) to assemble

**rasseoir** [ʀaswaʀ] vpr irr se ~ to sit down again; **va te ~!** go back to your seat!

**rassis, rassie** [ʀasi] adj (pain, pâtisserie) stale

**rassurant(e)** [ʀasyʀɑ̃, ɑ̃t] adj (nouvelle) reassuring; (visage) comforting

**rassurer** [ʀasyʀe] <1> I. vt to reassure; **ne pas être rassuré** to feel worried II. vpr se ~ to reassure oneself; **rassurez-vous!** don't worry!

**rasta** [ʀasta] I. adj inv, inf Rasta II. mf inf Rasta

**rat** [ʀa] m ZOOL rat ▶ **s'ennuyer comme un ~ mort** to be bored stiff

**rate** [ʀat] f ANAT spleen

**raté(e)** [ʀate] m(f) failure

**rater** [ʀate] <1> I. vt ① (manquer: cible, occasion, train) to miss ② (ne pas réussir) **~ sa vie** to make a mess of one's life; **j'ai raté la mayonnaise** I messed up the mayonnaise; **~ son examen** to flunk one's test; **être raté** to be ruined; (photos) to be spoiled ③ **il n'en rate pas une!** he's always making a fool of himself; **ne pas ~ qn** to fix sb II. vi (affaire, coup, projet) to fail III. vpr (mal se suicider) **il s'est raté** he bungled his suicide attempt

**ratifier** [ʀatifje] <1> vt (loi, traité) to ratify

**ration** [ʀasjɔ̃] f ration; **vous avez tous eu la même** ~ you've all had the same

**rationalité** [ʀasjɔnalite] f rationality

**rationner** [ʀasjɔne] <1> vt to ration; **~ qn** to put sb on rations

**R.A.T.P.** [ɛʀatepe] f abr de Régie autonome des transports parisiens Paris public transportation system

**rattacher** [ʀataʃe] <1> vt (renouer: lacet) to retie; (ceinture, jupe) to do up again

**rattraper** [ʀatʀape] <1> I. vt ① (rejoindre) **~ qn** to catch up to sb ② (regagner: temps perdu, retard) to make up for; (sommeil) to catch up on; (pertes) to recover ③ (retenir) to catch hold of; **~ qn par le bras/le manteau** to grab ahold of sb's arm/coat II. vpr ① (se raccrocher) **se ~ à une branche** to grab ahold of a branch ② (compenser, corriger une erreur) **se ~** to make up

**raturer** [ʀatyʀe] <1> vt to cross out; (corriger) to make a modification

**rauque** [ʀok] adj (son, toux) throaty; (cri, voix) hoarse

**ravagé(e)** [ʀavaʒe] adj inf nuts

**ravager** [ʀavaʒe] <2a> vt (pays, ville) to lay waste; (cultures) to devastate

**ravaler** [ʀavale] <1> vt ① (retenir: larmes, émotion) to hold back ② (nettoyer: façade) to restore

**rave** [ʀɛv] f rave

**ravi(e)** [ʀavi] adj delighted; **avoir l'air** ~ to look pleased; **être ~ de** +infin to be delighted to +infin

**ravin** [ʀavɛ̃] m ravine

**ravir** [ʀaviʀ] <8> vt to delight; **ta visite me ravit** I'm delighted by your visit; **ces vacances me ravissent** this vacation is delightful

**raviser** [ʀavize] <1> vpr se ~ to change one's mind

**ravissant(e)** [ʀavisɑ̃, ɑ̃t] adj beautiful; (femme) ravishingly beautiful

**ravisseur, -euse** [ʀavisœʀ, -øz] m, f kidnapper

**ravitaillement** [ʀavitajmɑ̃] m ① (approvisionnement: de la population, des troupes) supplying ② (denrées alimentaires) food supplies ③ MED **~ d'urgence** emergency feeding

**ravitailler** [ʀavitaje] <1> I. vt **~ qn en essence** to supply sb with gas; **~ les avions en vol** to refuel planes in flight II. vpr se **~ en qc** to get (fresh) supplies of sth

**rayé(e)** [ʀeje] adj ① (zébré) striped; (pa-

*pier*) lined ❷ (*éraflé: disque, vitre*) scratched

**rayer** [Reje] <7> *vt* ❶ (*érafler: disque, vitre*) to scratch ❷ (*biffer: mot, nom*) to cross out ❸ (*supprimer*) ~ **qn/qc de la liste** to strike sb's name/sth off the list

**rayon** [Rɛjɔ̃] *m* ❶ (*faisceau*) ray; ~ **laser** laser beam ❷ *pl* (*radiations*) radiation; ~**s X** X-rays; ~**s ultraviolets/infrarouges** ultraviolet/infrared rays ❸ (*étagère: d'une armoire*) shelf ❹ COM department; **c'est tout ce qu'il me reste en ~** that's all we have left in stock ❺ (*distance*) **dans un ~ de plus de 20 km** within a radius of more than 20 km ❻ (*d'une roue*) spoke ► ~ **de soleil** ray of sunshine

**rayonner** [Rɛjɔne] <1> *vi* (*irradier*) ~ **de joie** to be radiant with joy; ~ **de santé** to be glowing with health

**raz-de-marée** [Rɑdəmaʀe] *m inv* GEO tidal wave

**razzia** [Ra(d)zja] *f* raid; **faire une ~ sur qc** to raid sth

**ré** [Re] *m inv* MUS (*note*) D; (*en solfiant*) re; *v. a.* **do**

**réacteur** [Reaktœʀ] *m* ❶ AVIAT jet engine ❷ PHYS, CHIM reactor

**réaction** [Reaksjɔ̃] *f* reaction; **en ~ contre qn/qc** as a reaction against sb/ sth; **avoir des ~s rapides/un peu lentes** to have good/bad reflexes

**réactualiser** [Reaktɥalize] <1> *vt* to update; (*débat*) to relaunch

**réadapter** [Readapte] <1> *vt* (*réaccoutumer*) ~ **qn à la vie professionnelle** to help sb readjust to working life

**réaffirmer** [Reafiʀme] <1> *vt* (*intention, volonté*) to reassert; **je réaffirme que les choses se sont passées ainsi** I reaffirm that that's how things happened

**réagir** [Reaʒiʀ] <8> *vi* ❶ (*répondre spontanément*) **à qc** to react to sth; ~ **mal aux antibiotiques** to react badly to antibiotics ❷ *a.* MED (*s'opposer à*) to react against

**réajuster** [Reaʒyste] <1> *vt v.* **rajuster**

**réalisable** [Realizabl] *adj* feasible; (*rêve*) attainable

**réalisateur, -trice** [Realizatœʀ, -tʀis] *m, f* CINE, TV director

**réalisation** [Realizasjɔ̃] *f* ❶ (*exécution*) carrying out ❷ CINE, RADIO, TV directing

**réaliser** [Realize] <1> **I.** *vt* ❶ (*accomplir: ambition*) to achieve; (*projet, menace, travail, réforme*) to carry out; (*rêve, désir*) fulfill; (*effort*) to make; (*exploit*) to perform ❷ (*effectuer: plan, maquette, achat, vente, progrès*) to make; ~ **des bénéfices** to make a profit ❸ (*se rendre compte de*) ~ **l'ampleur de son erreur** to realize the extent of one's mistake ❹ CINE, RADIO, TV (*faire*) to direct **II.** *vi* to realize; **est-ce que tu réalises vraiment?** do you really understand? **III.** *vpr* **se** ~ (*projet*) to be carried out; (*rêve, vœu*) to come true; (*ambition*) to be achieved

**réalisme** [Realism] *m* realism

**réaliste** [Realist] **I.** *adj* realistic; ART, LIT realist **II.** *m, f* realist

**réalité** [Realite] *f* (*réel, chose réelle*) reality; **devenir ~** to become reality; (*rêve, souhait*) to come true; **la ~ dépasse la fiction** truth is stranger than fiction ► **en ~** in fact

**réaménager** [Reamenaʒe] <2a> *vt* (*site*) to redevelop

**réanimation** [Reanimasjɔ̃] *f* ❶ (*technique*) resuscitation ❷ (*service*) **service de ~** intensive care unit

**réanimer** [Reanime] <1> *vt* to resuscitate

**rebondir** [R(ə)bɔ̃diʀ] <8> *vi* ~ **contre qc** (*balle, ballon*) to bounce off sth

**rebondissement** [R(ə)bɔ̃dismɑ̃] *m* **nouveau ~ dans l'affaire X!** new development in the X case!

**rebours** [R(ə)buʀ] MIL **compte à ~** countdown

**rébus** [Rebys] *m* rebus; (*casse tête*) puzzle

**recaler** [R(ə)kale] <1> *vt inf* ECOLE to fail

**récapituler** [Rekapityle] <1> *vt* to recapitulate

**récemment** [Resamɑ̃] *adv* recently

**récent(e)** [Re$\tilde{a}$, $\tilde{a}$t] *adj* (*événement, période, passé*) recent

**récepteur** [ReseptœR] *m* ❶ RADIO receiver ❷ TEL ~ (**téléphonique**) receiver

**réception** [Resepsjɔ̃] *f* ❶ a. TV, RADIO (*fête*) reception; **donner une** ~ to hold a reception ❷ (*accueil*) welcome ❸ (*guichet d'accueil*) reception; (*hall d'accueil*) reception area ❹ SPORT (*de ballon*) catching; (*d'un sauteur*) landing

**réceptionniste** [Resepsjɔnist] *mf* receptionist

**récession** [Resesjɔ̃] *f* recession

**recette** [Rə(ə)set] *f* ❶ CULIN a. *fig* recipe ❷ *sans pl* COM proceeds *pl* ❸ *pl* COM (*opp: dépenses*) receipts; ~**s budgétaires** budgetary revenue

**recevoir** [Rəs(ə)vwaR, R(ə)səvwaR] <12> **I.** *vt* ❶ (*obtenir en récompense, bénéficier de, accepter*) to receive; **être bien/mal reçu** to be well/badly received; **recevez, cher Monsieur/ chère Madame, l'expression de mes sentiments distingués/mes sincères salutations** *form* yours truly ❷ (*obtenir en cadeau*) to get, be given; ~ **une décoration** to receive a decoration; ~ **une poupée en cadeau** to be given a doll as a present ❸ (*percevoir*) to be paid; ~ **un bon salaire** to get a good salary ❹ (*accueillir*) to welcome; ~ **qn à dîner** to have sb over for dinner; **j'ai reçu la visite de ma sœur** I received a visit from my sister ❺ (*subir: coup, projectile*) to get; **c'est moi qui ai tout reçu** (*coups*) I got the worst of it; ~ **une correction** to get a beating; **elle a reçu le ballon sur la tête** she got hit on the head by the ball ❻ (*admettre*) ~ **qn dans un club/une école** to admit sb into a club/school; **être reçu à un examen** to pass a test; **les candidats reçus** the successful candidates ❼ (*contenir*) **pouvoir ~ des personnes** (*salle*) to hold people; **cet hôtel peut ~ 80 personnes** this hotel can accommodate 80 people **II.** *vi* ❶ (*donner une réception*) to entertain ❷ SPORT

(*jouer sur son terrain*) **Lyon reçoit Montpellier** Lyon is playing Montpellier at home

**rechange** [Rə(ə)ʃɑ̃ʒ] *m* **prendre un** ~ to take a change of clothes ▶ **solution de** ~ alternative

**recharge** [R(ə)ʃaRʒ] *f* ❶ ELEC (*processus*) recharging ❷ (*cartouche: d'arme*) reload; (*d'un stylo à bille*) refill

**rechargeable** [R(ə)ʃaRʒabl] *adj* (*briquet, stylo*) refillable; **briquet/rasoir non** ~ disposable lighter/razor

**recharger** [R(ə)ʃaRʒe] <2a> **I.** *vt* (*arme*) to reload; (*briquet, stylo*) to refill; (*accumulateurs, batterie*) to recharge **II.** *vpr* ELEC **se** ~ to recharge

**réchaud** [Reʃo] *m* stove

**réchauffé(e)** [Reʃofe] *adj* hackneyed

**réchauffement** [Reʃofmɑ̃] *m* warming up; (*des relations, d'une amitié*) improvement; ~ **de la planète** global warming

**réchauffer** [Reʃofe] <1> **I.** *vt* ❶ CULIN (**faire**) ~ **qc** to heat sth up (again) ❷ (*donner de la chaleur à: corps, membres*) to warm up; **ce bouillon m'a bien réchauffé** this broth has warmed me up **II.** *vpr* ❶ (*devenir plus chaud*) **se** ~ (*temps, température, eau, planète*) to get warmer ❷ (*retrouver sa chaleur*) **se** ~ (*pieds, mains*) to warm up

**recherche** [R(ə)ʃeRʃ] *f* ❶ (*quête*) a. IN-FORM search; **la** ~ **d'un livre** the search for a book; **être à la** ~ **d'un appartement/de qn** to be looking for an apartment/sb; **la** ~ **du bonheur** the pursuit of happiness ❷ *gén pl* (*enquête*) investigation; **abandonner les** ~**s** to give up the search; **faire des** ~**s sur qc** to carry out an investigation into sth; **la** ~ **d'un criminel** the hunt for a criminal ❸ *sans pl* MED, ECOLE, UNIV research; **faire de la** ~ **scientifique** to do scientific research

**recherché(e)** [R(ə)ʃeRʃe] *adj* ❶ (*demandé: acteur, produit*) in great demand; (*livre*) highly sought-after ❷ (*raffiné: style*) mannered; (*expression*) studied; (*plaisir*) exquisite

**rechercher** [R(ə)ʃeRʃe] <1> *vt* ❶ (*cher-*

*cher à trouver*) ~ **un nom/une amie** to look for a name/a friend; ~ **un terroriste** to hunt for a terrorist; ~ **où/quand/comment/si c'est arrivé** to try to determine where/when/how/if it happened; **être recherché pour meurtre/vol** to be wanted for murder/theft ❷ (*reprendre*) **aller ~ qn/qc** to go and get sb/sth

**rechute** [R(ə)ʃyt] *f* MED relapse

**récidiver** [Residive] <1> *vi* MED to relapse

**récidiviste** [Residivist] **I.** *adj* recidivist; **être ~** to be a repeat offender **II.** *mf* JUR (*au second délit*) second offender; (*après plusieurs délits*) habitual offender

**récipient** [Resipjɑ̃] *m* container

**réciproque** [Resiprɔk] **I.** *adj* mutual; (*accord, aide*) reciprocal **II.** *f* ❶ reverse; **la ~ n'est pas toujours vraie** the converse is not always true ❷ MATH reciprocal

**réciproquement** [Resiprɔkmɑ̃] *adv* ❶ (*mutuellement*) **ils s'admirent ~** they admire each other ❷ (*inversement*) **et ~** and vice versa

**récit** [Resi] *m* story; (*narration*) account; ~ **d'aventures** adventure story

**récital** [Resital] <s> *m* recital

**réciter** [Resite] <1> *vt* (*leçon, poème*) to recite

**réclamation** [Reklamasjɔ̃] *f* ❶ (*plainte*) complaint; **déposer une ~** to lodge a complaint ❷ (*demande*) claim ❸ (*service*) **les ~s** complaints department ❹ TEL **téléphoner aux ~s** to call the repairs department

**réclame** [Reklam] *f* (*publicité*) advertising ▶ **en ~** on special offer

**réclamer** [Reklame] <1> **I.** *vt* ❶ (*solliciter: argent*) to ask for; (*aide, silence*) to call for ❷ (*demander avec insistance*) to demand; **je réclame la parole!** I ask to speak! ❸ (*revendiquer*) to demand; ~ **une augmentation à qn** to ask sb for a raise ❹ (*nécessiter: patience, soin, temps*) to require **II.** *vi* to complain

**récolte** [Rekɔlt] *f* ❶ (*activité*) harvest

❷ (*produits récoltés*) ~ **des abricots/pommes de terre** apricot/potato crop

**récolter** [Rekɔlte] <1> *vt* ❶ AGR to harvest ❷ (*recueillir: argent*) to collect; (*contraventions, coups, ennuis*) to get; (*points, voix*) to pick up

**recommandation** [R(ə)kɔmɑ̃dasjɔ̃] *f* ❶ (*appui*) recommendation ❷ (*conseil*) advice; **faire des ~s à qn** to give sb some advice

**recommandé** [R(ə)kɔmɑ̃de] *m* (*lettre, paquet*) ≈ registered; **en ~** ≈ by registered mail

**recommander** [R(ə)kɔmɑ̃de] <1> *vt* ❶ (*conseiller*) to advise; ~ **à qn de +** *infin* to advise sb to + *infin*; **être recommandé** to be advisable; **je recommande ce film** I recommend this film; **il est recommandé de +** *infin* it is advisable to + *infin* ❷ (*appuyer: candidat*) to recommend

**recommencer** [R(ə)kɔmɑ̃se] <2> **I.** *vt* ❶ (*reprendre*) to start again; (*combat, lutte*) to resume; ~ **un récit depuis le début** to begin a story (all over) again at the beginning ❷ (*refaire*) ~ **sa vie** to make a fresh start; **tout est à ~** everything has to be done over again; **si c'était à ~, ...** if I could do it all over again... ❸ (*répéter: erreur*) to make again; (*expérience*) to have again; **ne recommence jamais ça!** don't ever do that again! **II.** *vi* (*reprendre, se remettre à*) to start again; **la pluie recommence (à tomber)** it's starting to rain again; ~ **à espérer/marcher** to begin to hope/walk again ▶ (**et voilà que**) **ça recommence!** here we go again!

**récompense** [Rekɔ̃pɑ̃s] *f* ❶ *vt* (*matérielle*) reward ❷ ECOLE, SPORT (*prix*) award; **en ~ de qc** in return for sth

**récompenser** [Rekɔ̃pɑ̃se] <1> *vt* (*personne*) to reward

**recomposer** [R(ə)kɔ̃poze] <1> **I.** *vt* to reconstruct; (*numéro de téléphone*) to redial **II.** *vpr* **se ~** POL to re-form

**réconcilier** [Rekɔ̃silje] <1> **I.** *vt* (*personnes, choses*) to reconcile **II.** *vpr* **se ~** (*personnes*) to make up; (*pays*) to be

**R**

reconciled; **se ~ avec qn/qc** to be reconciled with sb/sth; **se ~ avec soi--même** to learn to live with oneself

**reconduire** [ʀ(ə)kɔ̃dɥiʀ] *vt irr* ❶ **~ qn chez lui** to see someone (back) home; **~ à la frontière** to escort sb back to the border; **~ qn en voiture à la gare** to drive sb back to the station

**réconfortant(e)** [ʀekɔ̃fɔʀtɑ̃, ɑ̃t] *adj* ❶ (*rassurant*) reassuring; (*consolant*) comforting; (*stimulant*) invigorating ❷ (*fortifiant*) fortifying

**réconforter** [ʀekɔ̃fɔʀte] <1> *vt* ❶ (*consoler*) to comfort; (*rassurer*) to reassure; (*stimuler*) to cheer up ❷ (*fortifier*) to fortify

**reconnaissance** [ʀ(ə)kɔnɛsɑ̃s] *f* ❶ a. POL (*gratitude*) gratitude; (*fait d'admettre les mérites de qn*) recognition; **en ~ de qc** (*pour remercier*) in appreciation of; (*pour honorer*) in recognition of ❷ JUR, ADMIN **~ de dette** acknowledgement of a debt; **~ d'enfant** (*par le père*) legal recognition of a child ❸ (*exploration, prospection: d'un pays, terrain*) reconnaissance; **faire une ~** to go on reconnaissance ❹ INFORM **~ optique de caractères/vocale** optical character/voice recognition

**reconnaissant(e)** [ʀ(ə)kɔnɛsɑ̃, ɑ̃t] *adj* grateful

**reconnaître** [ʀ(ə)kɔnɛtʀ] *irr* I. *vt* ❶ (*identifier*) to recognize; **je reconnais bien là ta paresse** that's just typical of you, you're so lazy; **~ qn à son style** to recognize sb by their style; **savoir ~ un faucon d'un aigle** to be able to tell a falcon from an eagle ❷ (*admettre: innocence, qualité*) to recognize; (*erreur, faute*) to admit; **~ la difficulté de la tâche** to acknowledge the difficulty of the task; **il faut ~ que nous sommes allés trop loin** we have to admit that we have gone too far ❸ (*admettre comme légitime: droit*) to recognize; **~ qn comme chef** to recognize sb as a leader ❹ JUR **~ qn innocent** to recognize sb's innocence ❺ (*être reconnaissant de: service, bienfait*) to recognize

II. *vpr* ❶ (*se retrouver*) **se ~ dans sa ville** to know one's way around one's town; **je me reconnais dans le comportement de mon fils** I can see myself in the way my son behaves ❷ (*être reconnaissable*) **se ~ à qc** to be recognizable by sth

**reconnu(e)** [ʀakɔny] I. *part passé de* **reconnaître** II. *adj* ❶ (*admis: chef*) acknowledged; (*fait*) accepted ❷ (*de renom*) **~ pour qc** well-known for sth

**reconsidérer** [ʀ(ə)kɔ̃sideʀe] <5> *vt* to reconsider

**reconstituer** [ʀ(ə)kɔ̃stitɥe] <1> I. *vt* ❶ (*remettre dans l'ordre: texte*) to restore; (*faits*) to reconstruct; (*puzzle*) to piece together; (*scène, bataille*) to recreate ❷ (*reformer, réorganiser*) to reform ❸ (*restaurer*) to reconstruct; (*vieux quartier, édifice*) to restore ❹ BIO to regenerate II. *vpr* **se ~** (*armée, parti*) to re-form; (*organe*) to regenerate

**reconstruction** [ʀ(ə)kɔ̃stʀyksjɔ̃] *f* reconstruction

**reconversion** [ʀ(ə)kɔ̃vɛʀsjɔ̃] *f* ❶ (*recyclage*) **suivre un stage de ~ en informatique** to do an IT-retraining course ❷ ECON **~ industrielle** industrial redevelopment

**reconvertir** [ʀ(ə)kɔ̃vɛʀtiʀ] <8> I. *vt* ❶ (*adapter*) **~ un entrepôt en usine** to convert a warehouse into a factory ❷ (*recycler*) **~ le personnel à l'informatique** to retrain the staff in IT II. *vpr* **se ~** (*personne*) to retrain; (*usine*) to be put to a new use; **se ~ dans la médecine** to retrain as a doctor

**recopier** [ʀ(ə)kɔpje] <1> *vt* ❶ (*transcrire*) to copy out ❷ (*mettre au propre*) to write up ❸ INFORM **~ un fichier sur une disquette à qn** to copy a file onto a floppy disk for sb

**record** [ʀ(ə)kɔʀ] I. *m* a. SPORT (*performance*) record; **~ d'affluence/de production** record attendance/production II. *app inv* **vitesse ~** record speed; **en un temps ~** in record time

**recoudre** [ʀ(ə)kudʀ] *vt irr* ❶ COUT to sew up (again); **~ un bouton** to sew a button back on ❷ MED to restitch; (*opéré*) to stitch up again

**recouper** [R(ə)kupe] <1> **I.** *vt* (*couper de nouveau: vêtement*) to recut; ~ **un morceau à qn** to cut another piece for sb **II.** *vpr* **se** ~ (*coïncider: chiffres*) to add up; (*faits*) to tie

**recours** [R(ə)kuR] *m* ❶ (*utilisation*) ~ **à qc** recourse to sth; **avoir** ~ **à qn** to turn to sb; **avoir** ~ **à la violence** to resort to violence ❷ (*ressource, personne*) resort; **c'est sans** ~ there's nothing we can do about it; **en dernier** ~ as a last resort

**recouvrir** [R(ə)kuvRiR] <11> *vt* ❶ (*couvrir entièrement*) to cover; ~ **un mur de papier peint** to put up wallpaper on a wall; **être recouvert de buée/crépi/neige** to be covered in condensation/roughcast/snow ❷ (*couvrir à nouveau*) ~ **un fauteuil** to reupholster an armchair; ~ **le toit de tuiles** to re-tile the roof ❸ (*inclure*) **une étude qui recouvre partiellement des domaines très divers** a study which touches on a wide range of fields

**recracher** [R(ə)kRaʃe] <1> **I.** *vi* to spit again **II.** *vt* (*expulser*) ~ **qc** to spit sth back out

**récrire** [RekRiR] *vt irr* ❶ (*rewriter*) to rewrite ❷ (*répondre*) ~ **une lettre à qn** to write another letter to sb

**recroqueviller** [R(ə)kRɔk(ə)vije] <1> *vpr* ❶ (*se rétracter*) **se** ~ to hunch up; (*fleur*) to curl up ❷ (*se tasser*) **se** ~ to shrink; (*avec l'âge*) to shrivel up; **se** ~ **sur un objet** to hunch over an object

**recrudescence** [R(ə)kRydesɑ̃s] *f* (*épidémie*) further outbreak; (*fièvre*) new bout

**recruter** [R(ə)kRyte] <1> **I.** *vt a.* MIL, POL to recruit; ~ **qn comme technicien** to hire sb as a technician **II.** *vi a.* MIL to recruit

**rectangle** [Rɛktɑ̃gl] **I.** *m* rectangle **II.** *adj* (*triangle, trapèze*) right-angled

**rectangulaire** [Rɛktɑ̃gylɛR] *adj* rectangular

**rectificatif** [Rɛktifikatif] *m* correction

**rectifier** [Rɛktifje] <1> *vt* ❶ (*corriger*) to correct ❷ (*redresser: route, tracé*) to straighten; (*position*) to correct ❸ (*rendre conforme: cravate*) to adjust; ~ **la position** to correct one's stance

**rectiligne** [Rɛktiliɲ] *adj* rectilinear; **parfaitement** ~ perfectly straight

**recto** [Rɛkto] *m* front; **voir au** ~ see other side; ~ **verso** on both sides (of the page)

**reçu** [R(ə)sy] *m* (*quittance*) receipt

**reçu(e)** [R(ə)sy] **I.** *part passé de* **recevoir II.** *adj* ❶ (*couramment admis*) accepted; **idée** ~**e** commonplace idea ❷ ÉCOLE **14 candidats sont** ~**s sur les 131 qui se sont présentés** of the 131 candidates who took the exam, 14 passed **III.** *m(f)* ~ **à un examen** successful candidate in an exam

**recueil** [Rəkœj] *m* (*ensemble*) collection; ~ **de poèmes** anthology of poems

**recueillement** [R(ə)kœjmɑ̃] *m* contemplation; (*religieux*) meditation

**recueillir** [R(ə)kœjiR] *irr* **I.** *vt* ❶ (*réunir: documents*) to collect ❷ (*obtenir: signatures*) to obtain; ~ **tous les suffrages** to win everybody's approval ❸ (*accueillir*) to welcome; **des réfugiés** to take in refugees ❹ (*enregistrer: déposition*) to take down; (*opinion*) to record **II.** *vpr* **se** ~ to gather one's thoughts; **se** ~ **sur la tombe d'un ami** to spend a moment in silence at a friend's grave

**recuire** [R(ə)kɥiR] *vt irr* to recook; (*cuire plus*) to cook longer

**recul** [R(ə)kyl] *m* ❶ (*éloignement dans le temps, l'espace*) distance; (*d'une voiture*) reversing ❷ (*réflexion*) **avec le** ~ with the benefit of hindsight; **prendre du** ~ to step back ❸ FIN fall

**reculer** [R(ə)kyle] <1> **I.** *vi* ❶ (*opp: avancer: véhicule*) to back up, to reverse; (*personne*) to step back; (*involontairement*) to draw back; ~ **devant le danger** to retreat in the face of danger; **faire** ~ **qn** to force sb back; **faire** ~ **un animal** to move an animal back; ~ **de deux pas** to take two steps back ❷ (*renoncer*) to shrink back; **faire** ~ **qn**

**R**

to make sb back down; **rien ne me fera ~** nothing will stop me; **ne ~ devant rien** not to flinch at anything ❸ (*diminuer: chômage*) to come down; (*influence*) to be on the decline; **faire ~ le chômage** to bring unemployment down ▸ **~ pour mieux sauter** to put off the inevitable **II.** *vt* (*meuble*) to move back; (*mur*) to push back; (*frontière*) to extend; (*véhicule*) to back up, to reverse; (*rendez-vous*) to postpone; (*décision, échéance*) to put off **III.** *vpr* **se ~** to take a step back; **recule-toi!** get back!

**reculons** [ʀ(ə)kylɔ̃] **à ~** backwards; **aller à l'école à ~** to plod unwillingly to school; **avancer à ~** to be getting nowhere

**récupération** [ʀekypeʀasjɔ̃] *f* ❶ (*reprise de possession: des biens, des forces*) recovery ❷ (*réutilisation: de la ferraille*) salvage; (*des chiffons*) reprocessing; (*du verre*) recycling ❸ (*recouvrement: des heures de cours, d'une journée de travail*) making up ❹ POL (*d'un mouvement politique, d'idées*) hijacking

**récupérer** [ʀekypeʀe] <5> **I.** *vi* to recuperate **II.** *vt* ❶ (*reprendre: argent, biens*) to recover ❷ *inf* (*retrouver: stylo prêté*) to get back ❸ *inf* (*aller chercher*) to pick up ❹ (*recouvrer: journée de travail*) to make up for; (*des forces de congés*) to get back ❺ POL (*mouvement, idée*) to hijack

**recyclage** [ʀ(ə)siklaʒ] *m* ❶ ECOL (*d'une entreprise*) reorientation; (*d'une personne*) retraining ❷ (*nouveau traitement: de l'air, l'eau*) recycling

**recycler** [ʀ(ə)sikle] <1> **I.** *vt* ❶ ECOL (*déchets, verre, eau*) to recycle ❷ (*reconvertir*) to retrain; (*mettre à jour*) to send on a refresher course; (*élève*) to reorient **II.** *vpr* (*se reconvertir*) **se ~** to retrain; (*entreprise*) to readapt itself; **se ~ dans l'enseignement** to retrain as a teacher

**rédacteur, -trice** [ʀedaktœʀ, -tʀis] *m, f* writer; **~ en chef** editor

**rédaction** [ʀedaksjɔ̃] *f* ❶ (*écriture: d'un article*) writing; (*d'une encyclopédie*) compilation ❷ PRESSE (*lieu*) editorial office; (*équipe*) editorial staff ❸ ECOLE composition

**redécouvrir** [ʀ(ə)dekuvʀiʀ] <11> *vt* to rediscover

**redémarrer** [ʀ(ə)demaʀe] <1> *vi* ❶ (*repartir*) to start again ❷ *fig* (*entreprise*) to relaunch; (*production, machines*) to start up again

**redescendre** [ʀ(ə)desɑ̃dʀ] <14> **I.** *vt avoir* ❶ (*vu d'en haut*) to go down; (*échelle*) to climb down; (*en courant: escalier*) to run down; (*en escaladant: escalier, échelle*) to climb down; (*voiture*) to drive down; (*vu d'en bas*) to come down ❷ (*porter vers le bas*) **~ qn/qc au marché** to take sb/sth down to the market; **~ qn/qc d'un arbre** to get sb/sth back down from a tree **II.** *vi être* (*baromètre, fièvre*) to fall again; (*marée*) to go out again; (*rue*) to go back down

**redevenir** [ʀ(ə)dəv(ə)niʀ] <9> *vi* to become again

**redire** [ʀ(ə)diʀ] *vt irr* (*répéter: histoire*) to tell again; (*rapporter*) to repeat

**redistribuer** [ʀ(ə)distʀibɥe] <1> *vt* (*répartir*) to redistribute; (*cartes*) to deal again

**redonner** [ʀ(ə)dɔne] <1> *vt* ❶ (*rendre*) to give back; **~ de l'espoir/des forces/courage** to restore hope/strength/courage ❷ (*donner à nouveau: cours*) to give again; **~ du travail à qn** to give sb more work; **ça m'a redonné soif** it made me thirsty again; **ça m'a redonné envie de jouer du piano** it made me want to play the piano again ❸ (*resservir*) **~ des légumes à qn** to give sb another helping of vegetables; **~ à boire à qn** to give sb more to drink ❹ (*refaire*) **~ forme à une chose** to give sth back its shape; **~ une couche (de peinture) à qc** to give sth another coat of paint

**redormir** [ʀ(ə)dɔʀmiʀ] *vi irr* (*plus longtemps*) to go back to sleep; **je ne pourrai pas ~ de la nuit** I'll never be able to get back to sleep

**redoubler** [ʀ(ə)duble] <1> **I.** vt **1** ECOLE ~ **une année** to repeat a grade **2** (*accroître*) ~ **d'efforts** to step up one's efforts; (*douleur*) to intensify **II.** vi to increase

**redresser** [ʀ(ə)dʀese] <1> **I.** vt **1** (*remettre droit: buste, corps*) to straighten; (*tête*) to lift up **2** (*rétablir*) to put right; ~ **le pays/l'économie** to get the country/the economy back on its feet again; ~ **une entreprise déficitaire** to turn a company around **3** (*rediriger: voiture*) to straighten **II.** vpr **se ~ 1** (*se mettre droit*) to stand up straight; (*se mettre assis*) to sit up straight; **redresse-toi!** (*personne assise*) sit up straight!; (*personne debout*) stand up straight! **2** (*se relever: pays, ville, économie*) to recover; (*avion*) to flatten out

**réduction** [ʀedyksjɔ̃] f **1** (*diminution*) reduction; **du personnel** layoff; ~ **d'impôts** tax cut **2** (*rabais*) ~ **de 5% sur un manteau** 5% off a coat; ~**s étudiants** student concessions; ~ **de prix** price cut

**réduire** [ʀedɥiʀ] irr **I.** vt **1** (*diminuer*) a. CULIN to reduce; (*salaire, texte, personnel*) to cut; (*temps de travail, peine*) to shorten; (*risques*) to lessen; (*chômage*) to bring down **2** (*transformer*) ~ **qc en bouillie** to reduce sth to a pulp **II.** vpr **se ~ à qc** to boil down to; (*montant*) to amount to sth

**réduit(e)** [ʀedɥi, it] adj **1** (*miniaturisé: échelle, modèle*) small-scale **2** (*diminué: prix*) cut; (*tarif*) reduced; (*vitesse*) low

**réel** [ʀeɛl] m **le ~** reality

**réel(le)** [ʀeɛl] adj **1** (*véritable*) real; (*danger*) genuine **2** FIN (*salaire*) actual

**réellement** [ʀeɛlmɑ̃] adv really

**refaire** [ʀ(ə)fɛʀ] vt irr **1** (*faire de nouveau*) to do again; (*plat, lit*) to make again; (*article*) to rewrite; (*addition*) to add up again; (*nœud*) to retie; ~ **du bruit** to make more noise **2** (*recommencer: travail, dessin*) to redo; ~ **la même faute** to repeat the same mistake; ~ **du sport** to play sports again; **si**

c'était à ~, **je ne ferais pas médecine** if I could start all over again, I wouldn't do medicine **3** (*remettre en état: meuble*) to restore; (*toit*) to redo; (*chambre*) to redecorate; ~ **la peinture de qc** to repaint sth; **se faire ~ le nez** to have one's nose redone

**référence** [ʀefeʀɑ̃s] f **1** (*renvoi*) reference; (*en bas de page*) footnote; ADMIN, COM reference number; **faire ~ à qn/qc** to refer to sb/sth; **en ~ à qc** in reference to sth **2** (*modèle*) **être une ~ to** be a recommendation; **il n'est pas une ~** iron he's nothing to go by; **ouvrage de ~** reference book

**référendum** [ʀefeʀɑ̃dɔm] m referendum

**refermer** [ʀ(ə)fɛʀme] <1> **I.** vt **1** (*opp: ouvrir*) to close; (*porte*) to shut **2** (*verrouiller*) ~ **qc à clé** to lock sth **II.** vpr **se ~** (*opp: s'ouvrir*) to close; (*plaie*) to heal up; **se ~ sur qn** (*porte*) to close on sb

**refiler** [ʀ(ə)file] <1> vt inf ~ **un objet sans valeur à qn** to palm off a worthless object on sb; **il m'a refilé la grippe** he gave me the flu

**réfléchi(e)** [ʀefleʃi] adj **1** (*raisonnable: action*) well thought-out; (*jugement*) well-considered **2** LING reflexive

**réfléchir** [ʀefleʃiʀ] <8> vi **1** (*penser*) to think; **donner à ~** (*chose*) to give food for thought; **demander à ~** (*personne*) to need time to think things over **2** (*cogiter*) ~ **à qc** to think about sth; **réfléchissez à ce que vous faites** think about what you're doing ▸ **c'est tout réfléchi** my mind is made up

**reflet** [ʀ(ə)flɛ] m **1** (*représentation, image réfléchie*) reflection **2** (*éclat: d'une étoffe*) shimmer; (*du soleil*) reflection

**réflexe** [ʀeflɛks] m **1** ANAT reflex **2** (*réaction rapide*) reaction; **avoir de bons ~s** to have good reflexes; **manquer de ~** to be slow to react

**réflexion** [ʀeflɛksjɔ̃] f **1** (*analyse*) thought; **après mûre ~** after careful consideration; **son idée demande ~** his idea deserves thought **2** (*remarque*)

**R**

remark; **faire des ~s à qn sur un su-jet** to make comments to sb about a subject ▸ ~ **faite** (*en fin de compte*) on reflection; (*changement d'avis*) on second thought

**réforme** [Refɔʀm] *f* ❶ ADMIN, POL reform ❷ MIL discharge ❸ HIST **la Réforme** the Reformation

**réformer** [Refɔʀme] <1> *vt* ❶ (*modifier*) to reform ❷ MIL to discharge; (*appelé*) to declare unfit for service

**refouler** [ʀ(ə)fule] <1> *vt* ❶ (*repousser: attaque, envahisseur*) to push back; (*foule*) to drive back; (*intrus*) to turn back; (*demande*) to reject ❷ (*réprimer*) to hold back; (*pulsion*) to repress; (*souvenir*) to suppress

**refrain** [ʀ(ə)fʀɛ̃] *m* ❶ MUS chorus ❷ (*rengaine*) song; **c'est toujours le même ~** it's always the same old story

**réfrigérateur** [Refriʒeʀatœʀ] *m* refrigerator; **~-congélateur combiné** refrigerator-freezer

**refroidir** [ʀ(ə)fʀwadiʀ] <8> **I.** *vt* ❶ (*faire baisser la température de*) to cool down ❷ (*décourager*) **~ qn** to dampen sb's spirits **II.** *vi* (*devenir plus froid: moteur, aliment*) to cool down; (*devenir trop froid*) to get cold; **mettre qc à ~** to leave sth to cool down **III.** *vpr* **se ~** (*devenir plus froid: chose*) to cool off; (*devenir trop froid*) to get cold

**refuge** [ʀ(ə)fyʒ] *m* ❶ (*abri, échappatoire*) refuge; **chercher/trouver ~ quelque part** to seek/find shelter somewhere; **chercher/trouver (un) ~ dans la drogue** to seek/find refuge in drugs ❷ (*pour animaux*) sanctuary ❸ (*dans une rue*) traffic island

**réfugié(e)** [Refyʒje] *m(f)* refugee

**réfugier** [Refyʒje] <1> *vpr* **se ~ chez qn** to take refuge with sb

**refus** [ʀ(ə)fy] *m* (*résistance*) refusal; **~ de priorité** refusal to give way; **ce n'est pas de ~** *inf* I wouldn't say no

**refuser** [ʀ(ə)fyze] <1> **I.** *vt* ❶ (*opp: accepter*) to refuse; (*invitation*) to decline; (*manuscrit*) to reject; **~ qc en bloc/tout net** to refuse sth outright/

flatly ❷ (*opp: accorder: objet, permission, entrée*) to refuse; (*compétence*) to deny **II.** *vi* to resist **III.** *vpr* ❶ (*se priver de*) **se ~ un plaisir** to deny oneself a pleasure; **elle ne se ~ rien!** *iron* she certainly does herself well! ❷ (*être décliné*) **se ~** (*une offre qui ne se refuse pas*) an offer you can't refuse; **ça ne se refuse pas** you can't say no to that

**régal** [Regal] *m* delight

**régaler** [Regale] <1> *vpr* ❶ (*savourer*) **se ~** to have a delicious meal; **on va se ~** we'll really enjoy this ❷ (*éprouver un grand plaisir*) **se ~ en faisant qc** to have a great time doing sth

**regard** [ʀ(ə)gaʀ] *m* look; **avec un ~ convoitise** with a greedy stare; **adresser un ~ à qn** to look at sb; **attirer les ~s de qn sur qc** to draw sb's attention to sth; **dévorer qn/qc du ~** to look hungrily at sb; **lancer un ~/des ~s à qn** to look at sb

**regarder** [ʀ(ə)gaʀde] <1> **I.** *vt* ❶ (*contempler*) to look at; (*observer, suivre des yeux avec attention*) to watch; **~ la télévision** to watch television; **as-tu regardé le match?** did you watch the game? ❷ (*consulter rapidement*) to look over; (*courrier*) to look through; (*numéro, mot*) to look up; **~ sa montre** to check one's watch ❸ (*vérifier: mécanisme*) to check ❹ (*envisager, considérer: situation, être*) to consider ❺ (*concerner*) **ça ne te regarde pas!** *iron* that's none of your business!; (*être l'affaire de qn*) this doesn't concern you!; **je fais ce qui me regarde** that is my business ▸ **regardez-moi ça!** *inf* just look at that! **II.** *vi* (*s'appliquer à voir*) to look; **tu n'as pas bien regardé** you didn't look closely enough; **~ dans un livre** to look up in a book **III.** *vpr* ❶ (*se contempler*) **se ~ dans qc** to look at oneself in sth ❷ (*se mesurer du regard*) **se ~** (*personnes*) to look at each other ▸ **tu (ne) t'es (pas) regardé!** *inf* you should take a good look at yourself!

**régie** [Reʒi] *f* ❶ CINE, THEAT, TV production team **②** TV, RADIO (*local*) control room

**régime** [ʀeʒim] *m* **①** (*système*) system of government; ~ **capitaliste/militaire** capitalist/military regime; **opposants au** ~ opponents of the regime **②** MED diet; **être au** ~ to be dieting; **se mettre au** ~ to go on a diet

**région** [ʀeʒjɔ̃] *f a.* ADMIN (*contrée*) region; ~ **frontalière** border zone; **la** ~ **parisienne** the area around Paris, Greater Paris

**régional(e)** [ʀeʒjɔnal, -o] <-aux> *adj* (*relatif à une région*) regional

**régisseur, -euse** [ʀeʒisœʀ, -øz] *m, f* CINE, TV assistant director; THEAT stage manager

**registre** [ʀeʒistʀ] *m* **①** *a.* LING (*livre*) register; ~ **d'état civil** ≈ register of births, marriages and deaths; ~**s de comptabilité** ledger **②** MUS range **③** INFORM **base de** ~**s** system registry

**règle** [ʀɛɡl] *f* **①** (*loi*) rule; **être en** ~ to be in order; **se faire une** ~ **de** +*infin* to make it a rule to +*infin*; **en** ~ **générale** as a rule **②** (*instrument*) ruler

**règlement** [ʀɛɡləmɑ̃] *m* **①** (*discipline*) regulations *pl*; ~ **intérieur** (*d'une entreprise*) company procedure; (*d'une organisation, assemblée*) house rules; (*d'une école*) school rules; ~ **de police** police regulation **②** (*différend*) ~ **de compte(s)** settling of scores; (*meurtre*) gangland slaying **③** (*paiement*) payment

**réglementer** [ʀɛɡləmɑ̃te] <1> *vt* to regulate

**régler** [ʀeɡle] <5> I. *vt* **①** (*résoudre*) to settle; (*problème*) to sort out; (*conflit, différend*) to resolve; **c'est une affaire réglée** it's all settled now **②** (*payer: facture*) to pay **③** (*réguler*) to regulate; (*circulation*) to control; (*montre*) to set **④** (*fixer: modalités, programme*) to decide on II. *vi* to pay III. *vpr* **①** (*se résoudre*) **l'affaire se règle** it's sorting itself out **②** (*être mis au point*) **se** ~ to be adjusted

**réglisse** [ʀeɡlis] I. *f* (*plante*) licorice

II. *m o f* (*bonbon*) licorice; (*bâton*) stick of licorice

**régner** [ʀeɲe] <5> *vi* ~ **sur qc** (*prince, roi*) to reign over sth

**regonfler** [ʀ(ə)ɡɔ̃fle] <1> *vt* **①** (*gonfler à nouveau: ballon, chambre à air*) to reinflate; (*avec la bouche: ballon*) to blow up again; ~ **un pneu** to pump a tire back up **②** *inf* (*tonifier*) ~ **qn** to strengthen sb's spirits; **être regonflé (à bloc)** to be back in top form

**régresser** [ʀeɡʀese] <1> *vi* to regress

**regret** [ʀ(ə)ɡʀɛ] *m* **①** (*nostalgie*) **le(s)** ~**(s) de qc** missing sth; ~**s éternels** sorely missed **②** (*contrariété*) **avoir le** ~ **de faire qc** to regret to (have to) do sth; **ne pas avoir de** ~**s** to have no regrets; **je suis au** ~ **de faire qc** I regret to (have to) do sth **③** (*remords*) ~ **de qc** regret over sth; **ne manifester aucun** ~ to show no regrets ▶ **à** ~ (*partir*) regretfully; (*accepter*) reluctantly; **allez, sans** ~**!** come on now, no looking back!

**regrettable** [ʀ(ə)ɡʀetabl] *adj* regrettable

**regretter** [ʀ(ə)ɡʀete] <1> I. *vt* **①** (*se repentir de, déplorer*) to regret; **je regrette de ne pas être venu avec vous** I'm sorry that I didn't come with you **②** (*déplorer l'absence de*) ~ **sa jeunesse** to be nostalgic for one's youth II. *vi* **je regrette** I'm sorry

**regrouper** [ʀ(ə)ɡʀupe] <1> I. *vt* (*mettre ensemble*) to bring together; (*personnes*) to gather together II. *vpr* **se** ~ **autour de qn** to group together around sb; (*se regrouper dans un but commun*) to join forces to a common objective

**régulariser** [ʀeɡylaʀize] <1> *vt* **①** (*mettre en ordre*) to sort out; (*acte administratif*) to put in order; (*situation (de couple)*) to regularize **②** (*ajuster*) to regulate

**régulier, -ière** [ʀeɡylje, -jɛʀ] *adj* **①** *a.* LIT, LING (*équilibré: vie, habitudes*) regular **②** (*constant: effort*) steady; (*résultats, vitesse*) consistent **③** (*à périodicité fixe: avion, train, ligne*) scheduled;

**R**

**manger à des heures régulières** to eat at regular times ④ (*légal: gouvernement*) legitimate; (*tribunal*) official; **être en situation régulière** to have one's papers in order

**régulièrement** [ʀegyljɛʀmɑ̃] *adv* (*périodiquement*) regularly

**réhabiliter** [ʀeabilite] <1> *vt* ❶ JUR to clear; **~ qn dans ses fonctions** to reinstate sb ❷ (*réinsérer*) to rehabilitate ❸ (*remettre à l'honneur*) **~ qc** to bring sth back into favor

**rein** [ʀɛ̃] *m* ❶ (*organe*) kidney ❷ *pl* (*bas du dos*) (lower) back

**réincarnation** [ʀeɛ̃kaʀnasjɔ̃] *f* reincarnation

**reine** [ʀɛn] *f a.* JEUX queen

**réinscription** [ʀeɛ̃skʀipsjɔ̃] *f* re-enrollment

**réinscrire** [ʀeɛ̃skʀiʀ] *irr* I. *vt* (*mettre à nouveau sur une liste*) (**faire**) **~ qn/qc sur une liste** to put sb/sth back on a list; (**faire**) **~ qn dans une nouvelle école** to put sb in a new school II. *vpr* se (**faire**) **~ sur une liste** to put oneself back on a list; **se** (**faire**) **~ à l'université** ADMIN to re-enroll in college; (*reprendre ses études*) to go back to college

**réinsertion** [ʀeɛ̃sɛʀsjɔ̃] *f* (*d'un délinquant*) rehabilitation

**réintégrer** [ʀeɛ̃tegʀe] <5> *vt* ❶ (*revenir dans*) **~ une place** to return to a seat; **~ sa cellule/maison** to return to one's cell/house ❷ (*rétablir*) **~ qn dans un groupe** to bring sb back into a group; **~ qn dans la société** to reintegrate sb into society

**rejeter** [ʀəʒ(ə)te] <3> I. *vt* ❶ (*refuser*) to reject; (*circonstances atténuantes*) to disregard; **être rejeté** to be rejected; (*exclu d'une communauté*) to be cast out ❷ (*évacuer*) **~ qc** (*déchets*) to throw sth out; (*épaves*) to cast sth up; (*nourriture*) to vomit sth ❸ (*se décharger de*) **~ une responsabilité sur qn/qc** to push a responsibility off on sb; **~ une faute sur qn/qc** to put the blame on sb/sth II. *vpr* (*s'accuser*) **se ~ la faute** (l'un l'autre) to blame each other

**rejoindre** [ʀ(ə)ʒwɛ̃dʀ] *irr* I. *vt* ❶ (*regagner: personne*) to meet again; **~ son domicile/un lieu** to return to one's home/a place ❷ (*déboucher*) **~ une route** (*route*) to rejoin a road; (*automobiliste*) to get back onto a road ❸ (*rattraper*) **~ qn** to catch up with sb; **vas-y, je te rejoins** go on, I'll catch up with you II. *vpr* **se ~** (*se réunir: personnes*) to meet up; (*choses*) to meet

**réjouir** [ʀeʒwiʀ] <8> *vpr* **se ~ de faire qc** to be delighted to do sth; (*à l'avance*) to look forward to doing sth; **se ~ à l'idée de ...** to be thrilled at the idea of ...

**relâcher** [ʀ(ə)lɑʃe] <1> *vt* ❶ (*desserrer*) to loosen; (*muscles*) to relax ❷ (*libérer*) to free ❸ (*cesser de tenir*) **~ qc** to let go of sth

**relais** [ʀ(ə)lɛ] *m* SPORT relay ▸ **prendre le ~ de qn/qc** to take over from sb/sth

**relancer** [ʀ(ə)lɑ̃se] <2> *vt* ❶ (*donner un nouvel essor à: mouvement, idée*) to revive; (*économie, production, immobilier*) to boost ❷ *inf* (*harceler*) to badger; (*client, débiteur*) to chase after

**relatif** [ʀ(ə)latif] *m* LING relative pronoun

**relatif, -ive** [ʀ(ə)latif, -iv] *adj* ❶ (*opp: absolu*) relative ❷ (*partiel*) relative ❸ (*en liaison avec*) **être ~ à qn/qc** to relate to sb/sth; **~ à qn/qc** concerning sb/sth ❹ *postposé* LING relative

**relation** [ʀ(ə)lasjɔ̃] *f* ❶ (*rapport, lien logique*) relation ❷ *pl* (*rapport entre personnes*) relationship; **avoir une ~ amoureuse avec qn** to be romantically involved with sb; **par ~s** through connections ❸ (*personne de connaissance*) contact ▸ **~s publiques** public relations; **en ~** in contact

**relativement** [ʀ(ə)lativmɑ̃] *adv* (*dans une certaine mesure: facile, honnête, rare*) relatively

**relativiser** [ʀ(ə)lativize] <1> *vt* **~ qc** to put sth into perspective

**relaxer** [ʀ(ə)lakse] <1> I. *vt* ❶ (*décontracter*) to relax ❷ JUR to free II. *vpr* **se ~** to relax

**relayer** [ʀ(ə)leje] <7> **I.** vt (*remplacer*) ~ **qn** to take over from sb; **se faire** ~ **par qn** (*personne*) to hand over to sb **II.** vpr **se** ~ **pour faire qc** to do sth in turns

**relent** [ʀ(ə)lɑ̃] m (*mauvaise odeur*) stink

**relève** [ʀ(ə)lɛv] f relief; **assurer la** ~ (*assurer la succession*) to take over

**relevé** [ʀəl(ə)ve, ʀ(ə)ləve] m ❶ FIN ~ **de compte** (bank) account statement; ~ **d'identité bancaire** slip giving bank account details ❷ (*liste, facture détaillée*) statement; ~ **de notes** ECOLE report card

**relevé(e)** [ʀəl(ə)ve, ʀ(ə)ləve] adj CULIN spicy

**relever** [ʀəl(ə)ve] <4> **I.** vt ❶ (*redresser: chaise, objet tombé*) to pick up; (*blessé*) to lift; ~ **qn** to help sb back up ❷ (*remonter*) ~ **qc** (*col, siège, strapontin, cheveux*) to put sth up; (*store, chaussettes*) to pull sth up; ~ **sa voile** to lift one's veil ❸ (*noter: adresse, renseignement, observation*) to note; (*compteur*) to read **II.** vi (*dépendre de*) ~ **de la compétence de qn** to fall in sb's sphere of competence); ~ **du miracle** to be miraculous **III.** vpr **se** ~ (*se remettre debout*) to get up

**relief** [ʀəljɛf] m ❶ GEO, ART, ARCHIT relief ❷ (*saillie*) **sans** ~ flat; **motif/caractères en** ~ raised design/characters ▶ **mettre qc en** ~ to accentuate sth

**relier** [ʀəlje] <1> vt ❶ (*réunir: personnes, choses*) to connect ❷ LING (*préposition*) to link ❸ TECH (*livre*) to bind

**religieuse** [ʀ(ə)liʒjøz] **I.** adj v. **religieux II.** f ❶ REL nun ❷ CULIN cream puff

**religieux** [ʀ(ə)liʒjø] m religious; (*moine*) monk

**religieux, -euse** [ʀ(ə)liʒjø, -jøz] adj REL (*personne, habit, vie, tradition, ordre*) religious; (*cérémonie, mariage, chant*) church

**religion** [ʀ(ə)liʒjɔ̃] f religion

**relire** [ʀ(ə)liʀ] irr **I.** vt (*lettre, roman*) to reread; (*pour vérifier une référence*:

*passage*) to check **II.** vpr **se** ~ to read over one's work

**reloger** [ʀ(ə)lɔʒe] <2a> vt to rehouse

**remake** [ʀimɛk] m remake

**remarier** [ʀ(ə)maʀje] <1> vpr **se** ~ **avec qn** to get remarried to sb

**remarquable** [ʀ(ə)maʀkabl] adj remarkable

**remarquablement** [ʀ(ə)maʀkabləmɑ̃] adv (*beau, intelligent*) remarkably; (*jouer, se porter, réussir*) brilliantly

**remarque** [ʀ(ə)maʀk] f remark; **faire une** ~ **à qn sur qc** to remark on sth to sb

**remarquer** [ʀ(ə)maʀke] <1> **I.** vt ❶ (*apercevoir*) to notice ❷ (*distinguer*) ~ **qn/qc par qc** to notice sb/sth because of sth ❸ (*noter*) to notice; **faire** ~ **qc à qn** to draw sb's attention to sb; **se faire** ~ *péj* to draw attention to oneself; **sans se faire** ~ without being noticed; **remarque, je m'en fiche!** listen, I couldn't care less! **II.** vpr **se** ~ to be noticeable

**rembarrer** [ʀɑ̃baʀe] <1> vt inf ~ **qn** to tell sb where to get off

**rembobiner** [ʀɑ̃bɔbine] <1> vt, vi to rewind

**remboursement** [ʀɑ̃buʀsəmɑ̃] m (*d'un emprunt, d'une dette*) repayment; (*des frais*) reimbursement; **contre** ~ cash with order

**rembourser** [ʀɑ̃buʀse] <1> vt to repay; **ce médicament n'est pas remboursé** insurance will not reimburse this medication; **je te rembourserai demain!** I'll pay you back tomorrow!

**remède** [ʀ(ə)mɛd] m (*moyen de lutte*) remedy; (*d'un problème*) cure; ~ **contre l'inflation** cure for inflation

**remerciement** [ʀ(ə)mɛʀsimɑ̃] m (*activité*) thanking; **des** ~**s** thanks pl; **adresser ses** ~**s à qn** to express one's thanks to sb; **avec tous mes/nos** ~**s** with all my/our thanks

**remercier** [ʀ(ə)mɛʀsje] <1> vt (*dire merci à*) ~ **qn/qc de qc** to thank sb/sth for sth; ~ **qn/qc de faire qc** to thank sb/sth for doing sth

**R**

**remettre** [ʀ(ə)mɛtʀ] *irr* **I.** *vt* **①** (*replacer*) ~ **qc** to put sth back; ~ **un bouton** to sew a button back on; ~ **qc debout** to stand sth up again; ~ **à cuire** to leave sth to cook some more; ~ **qn sur la bonne voie** to put sb back on the right track **②** (*rétablir*) ~ **qn/faire** ~ **qn en liberté** to free sb; ~ **une machine/un moteur en marche** to restart a machine/an engine; ~ **qc en ordre** to sort sth out; ~ **sa montre à l'heure** to reset one's watch **③** (*donner*) ~ **qc** (*récompense, prix*) to give sth; (*démission, devoir*) to hand sth in; ~ **un paquet à qn** to give a package to sb **④** (*rajouter: ingrédient*) to add (more); ~ **de l'huile dans le moteur** to add oil to the engine; ~ **du sel dans les légumes** to put more salt on the vegetables **⑤** (*ajourner*) ~ **une décision à la semaine prochaine** to leave [*o* postpone] a decision until the following week; ~ **un jugement à l'année prochaine** to defer a judgment until the following year **⑥** (*porter de nouveau*) ~ **qc** to put sth back on **⑦** (*confier*) ~ **un enfant à qn** to entrust a child to sb **⑧** *Belgique* (*rendre la monnaie*) to give change; ~ **sur 100 euros** to give change for 100 euros ►~ **ça** *inf* to do it all over again; **en** ~ *inf* to overdo it **II.** *vpr* **①** (*recouvrer la santé*) **se** ~ **de qc** to get over sth **②** (*recommencer*) **se** ~ **au travail** to get back to work; **se** ~ **en mouvement** to start again; **se** ~ **à faire qc** to start doing sth again **③** METEO **il se remet à pleuvoir** the rain's starting again **④** (*se replacer*) **se** ~ **en tête du groupe** to return to the top of the group; **se** ~ **debout** to get back on one's feet again; **se** ~ **à table** to return to the table **⑤** (*se réconcilier*) **se** ~ **avec qn** *inf* to get back together with sb

**remise** [ʀ(ə)miz] *f* **①** (*dépôt, attribution: d'une clé, d'une rançon*) handing over; (*d'une décoration, d'un cadeau*) presentation; (*d'une lettre, d'un paquet*) delivery; (*en mains propres*) handing over **②** (*dispense, grâce*) reduction; ~ **de peine** reduction of sentence **③** (*rabais*) discount; **faire une** ~ **de 5% à qn** to give sb a 5% discount **④** (*local*) shed ►~ **en état** restoration; ~ **en forme** getting back in shape; **centre de** ~ **en forme** health resort; ~ **à jour** updating

**remonte-pente** [ʀ(ə)mɔ̃tpɑ̃t] <remonte-pentes> *m* ski lift

**remonter** [ʀ(ə)mɔ̃te] <1> **I.** *vi* **①** *être* (*monter à nouveau*) ~ **dans une chambre/de la cuisine** to go back up to a bedroom/from the kitchen; ~ **à Paris** to go back to Paris; ~ **en bateau/à la nage** to sail/swim back up; ~ **sur l'échelle** to get back on the ladder; ~ **sur scène** to return to the stage; ~ +*infin* (*vu d'en bas*) to go back up to +*infin*; (*vu d'en haut*) to come back up to +*infin* **②** *être* (*reprendre place*) ~ **à bicyclette** to get back on one's bicycle; ~ **en voiture** to get back in the car; ~ **à bord** to go back on board **③** *avoir* (*s'élever de nouveau*) to go back up **④** *avoir* (*s'améliorer*) ~ **dans l'estime de qn** to rise in sb's esteem **⑤** *être* (*glisser vers le haut: jupe, vêtement*) to ride up; (*col*) to stand up **⑥** *avoir* (*dater de*) ~ **au mois dernier/à l'année dernière** (*événement, fait*) to have occurred last month/last year; **cela remonte au siècle dernier** that goes back to the last century; **cet incident remonte à quelques jours** this incident happened a few days ago **II.** *vt avoir* **①** ~ **qc** (*parcourir à pieds*) to go up sth; (*parcourir dans un véhicule*) to drive up sth; (*à la nage: fleuve, rivière*) to swim up sth **②** (*relever*) ~ **qc** (*col*) to turn sth up; (*chaussettes, pantalon, manches*) to pull sth up; (*bas du pantalon*) to hitch sth up; (*étagère, tableau, mur*) to raise sth; ~ **une note** ECOLE to increase a grade **③** (*rapporter du bas*) ~ **une bouteille de la cave à son père** to bring a bottle up from the cellar to one's father **④** (*porter vers le haut*) ~ **la valise au grenier** to take the suitcase up to the attic **⑤** (*faire marcher*) ~ **qc** (*mécanisme,* *montre*) to wind sth up; **être remonté contre qn** (*fâché*) to be mad with sb ❻ (*opp: démonter*) ~ **qc** (*appareil*) to put sth back together; (*roue, robinet*) to put sth back on ❼ (*remettre en état: affaires*) to boost; (*mur*) to rebuild; ~ **le moral de qn** to cheer sb up

**remords** [ʀ(ə)mɔʀ] *m* remorse; **des ~s** remorse; **avoir des ~** to feel remorse

**remorque** [ʀ(ə)mɔʀk] *f* (*d'un véhicule*) trailer

**remorquer** [ʀ(ə)mɔʀke] <1> *vt* (*voiture*) to tow; **se faire ~** to get a tow

**rempart** [ʀɑ̃paʀ] *m* MIL rampart; (*d'une ville*) wall

**remplaçant(e)** [ʀɑ̃plasɑ̃, ɑ̃t] *m(f)* MED locum tenens; ECOLE substitute teacher; SPORT substitute

**remplacement** [ʀɑ̃plasmɑ̃] *m* (*intérim*) **faire des ~s** to be a replacement

**remplacer** [ʀɑ̃plase] <2> I. *vt* ❶ (*changer, tenir lieu de*) to replace ❷ (*prendre la place de*) ~ **qn** to take over from sb II. *vpr* **se ~** to be replaced

**rempli(e)** [ʀɑ̃pli] *adj* ❶ (*plein*) full; **tasse ~ de thé** cup full of tea ❷ (*rond*) plump ❸ (*occupé: journée, vie*) full; (*emploi du temps*) busy

**remplir** [ʀɑ̃pliʀ] <8> I. *vt* ❶ (*rendre plein*) ~ **un carton de choses** to fill a box with things; ~ **une valise de vêtements** to pack a suitcase full of clothes ❷ (*occuper*) to fill ❸ (*compléter*) ~ **un formulaire** to fill out a form; ~ **un chèque** to write out a check ❹ (*réaliser, répondre à: mission, contrat, conditions*) to fulfill II. *vpr* **se ~ de personnes/liquide** to fill with people/liquid

**remporter** [ʀɑ̃pɔʀte] <1> *vt* ❶ (*reprendre*) ~ **qc** to take sth back ❷ (*gagner*) to win

**remuer** [ʀəmɥe] <1> I. *vi* (*bouger*) to move (around) II. *vt* ❶ (*bouger*) to move; (*hanches*) to sway; ~ **la queue** to wag its tail ❷ (*mélanger: mayonnaise, sauce, café*) to stir; (*salade*) to toss ❸ (*émouvoir*) to move III. *vpr* **se ~** ❶ (*bouger*) to move ❷ (*faire des efforts*) to go to a lot of trouble

**renaissance** [ʀ(ə)nɛsɑ̃s] *f* ❶ (*vie nouvelle*) rebirth ❷ HIST, ART **la Renaissance** the Renaissance

**renard** [ʀ(ə)naʀ] *m* (*animal, fourrure*) fox

**rencontre** [ʀɑ̃kɔ̃tʀ] *f* ❶ (*fait de se rencontrer*) meeting ❷ (*entrevue*) meeting ❸ SPORT fixture; ~ **de football/boxe** soccer/boxing match; ~ **d'athlétisme** track and field meet ▶ **faire une <u>mauvaise</u> ~** to have an unpleasant encounter; <u>aller</u>/<u>venir</u> **à la ~ de qn** to go/come to meet sb; <u>faire</u> **la ~ de qn** to meet sb

**rencontrer** [ʀɑ̃kɔ̃tʀe] <1> I. *vt* ❶ (*croiser, avoir une entrevue, faire la connaissance de*) a. SPORT to meet ❷ (*être confronté à*) to encounter II. *vpr* **se ~** to meet; **il les a fait se ~** they met through him

**rendez-vous** [ʀɑ̃devu] *m inv* ❶ (*rencontre officielle*) appointment; **avoir ~ avec qn** to have an appointment with sb; **donner un ~ à qn** to give sb an appointment; **prendre ~ avec qn** to make an appointment with sb; **sur ~** by appointment ❷ (*rencontre avec un ami*) meeting; **avoir ~ avec qn** to be meeting sb; **se donner ~** to arrange to meet; **donner un ~ à qn** to arrange to meet sb; ~ **à 8 heures/à la gare** see you at 8 o'clock/at the station ❸ (*rencontre entre amoureux*) date ❹ (*lieu de rencontre*) meeting place

**rendre** [ʀɑ̃dʀ] <14> I. *vt* ❶ (*restituer*) ~ **qc** to give sth back ❷ (*donner en retour*) to return; ~ **la monnaie sur 100 euros** to give the change from 100 euros ❸ (*rapporter*) ~ **qc** (*article défectueux*) to take sth back ❹ (*donner*) ~ **son devoir** to hand [*o* turn] in one's homework ❺ (*redonner*) ~ **la liberté/ la vue à qn** to give sb back their freedom/their sight; ~ **l'espoir/le courage à qn** to give sb new hope/courage ❻ (*faire devenir*) ~ **qc plus facile** to make sth easier; ~ **qn triste/joyeux** to make sb sad/happy; ~ **qc public** to make sth public; **c'est à vous ~ fou!**

it'd drive you crazy! **⑦** JUR (*jugement, verdict, arrêt*) to give **⑧** (*vomir*) ~ **qc** to throw sth back up **II.** *vi* (*vomir*) to vomit **III.** *vpr* **①** (*capituler*) **se** ~ to surrender; **se** ~ **à l'évidence** *fig* to accept the obvious **②** (*aller*) **se** ~ **chez qn/à son travail** to go to see sb/to work

**rêne** [ʀɛn] *f* rein

**renfermé** [ʀɑ̃fɛʀme] *m* **sentir le** ~ to smell musty

**renfermé(e)** [ʀɑ̃fɛʀme] *adj* withdrawn

**renfermer** [ʀɑ̃fɛʀme] <1> I. *vt* to hold **II.** *vpr* **se** ~ **sur soi-même** to withdraw into oneself

**renforcer** [ʀɑ̃fɔʀse] <2> I. *vt* **①** (*consolider*) to reinforce **②** (*intensifier*) to strengthen; (*couleur*) to enliven **③** (*affermir: paix*) to consolidate; (*position, sentiment, soupçon*) to strengthen **④** (*confirmer*) ~ **qn dans son opinion** to reinforce sb's opinion **II.** *vpr* (*s'affermir*) **se** ~ to be reinforced; (*popularité*) to increase

**renfort** [ʀɑ̃fɔʀ] *m* **①** *souvent pl* (*personnes*) helpers *pl* **②** (*supplément*) ~**s en nourriture/matériel** supplies of food/material **③** COUT lining **④** ARCHIT reinforcement **⑤** AUTO ~ **latéral** (*de sécurité*) side impact bar

**renier** [ʀənje] <1> *vt* (*promesse*) to break; (*idée, passé*) to disown; ~ **sa foi** to renounce one's faith

**renifler** [ʀ(ə)nifle] <1> I. *vi* to sniff **II.** *vt* **①** (*sentir, aspirer*) to sniff **②** *inf* (*pressentir*) to smell

**renne** [ʀɛn] *m* reindeer

**renommée** [ʀ(ə)nɔme] *f* **①** *sans pl* (*célébrité*) renown **②** (*réputation*) fame; **de** ~ **mondiale** world-famous

**renoncer** [ʀ(ə)nɔ̃se] <2> *vi* **①** (*abandonner*) ~ **à qc** to give sth up; ~ **au monde/aux plaisirs** to renounce the world/pleasure; ~ **à fumer/boire** to give up smoking/drinking **②** (*refuser un droit*) ~ **à qc** to renounce sth

**renouveler** [ʀ(ə)nuv(ə)le] <3> I. *vt* **①** (*remplacer*) to renew; ~ **des députés/un parlement** to elect new representatives/a new parliament; ~ **sa gar-**

**de-robe** to buy new clothes **②** (*répéter*) ~ **une offre/une promesse à qn** to renew an offer/a promise to sb; ~ **une question à qn** to ask sb a question again; ~ **sa candidature** (*à un emploi*) to reapply; POL to run again **③** (*prolonger: bail, passeport*) to renew **II.** *vpr* **se** ~ **①** (*être remplacé*) BIO to be renewed; POL to be re-elected **②** (*se reproduire*) to happen again **③** (*innover: artiste, style*) to renew oneself

**rénover** [ʀenɔve] <1> *vt* **①** (*remettre à neuf*) to renovate; (*meuble*) to restore **②** (*moderniser*) ~ **qc** to bring sth up to date

**renseignement** [ʀɑ̃sɛɲmɑ̃] *m* **①** (*information*) **un** ~ some [*o* a piece of] information; **à titre de** ~ for your information; **de plus amples** ~**s** further information [*o* details] **②** TEL **les** ~**s** information **③** MIL intelligence

**renseigner** [ʀɑ̃seɲe] <1> I. *vt* to inform; ~ **qn sur un élève** (*document*) to tell sb about a student **II.** *vpr* **se** ~ **sur qn/qc** to find out about sb/sth

**rentabilité** [ʀɑ̃tabilite] *f* ECON profitability

**rentrée** [ʀɑ̃tʀe] *f* **①** ECOLE new year; **le jour de la** ~ the day the schools go back **②** UNIV start of the new academic year **③** (*après les vacances d'été*) **à la** ~ after summer vacation; **la** ~ **politique** the return of congress; **la** ~ **théâtrale** the start of the new theater season **④** (*come-back*) comeback **⑤** (*fait de rentrer*) return; ~ **dans l'atmosphère** re-entry into the atmosphere **⑥** (*somme d'argent*) money coming in; ~**s** income

**rentrer** [ʀɑ̃tʀe] <1> I. *vi* **①** **être** (*retourner chez soi*) to go back, return; **comment rentres-tu?** how are you getting back?; ~ **au pays natal** to return to one's native country (*repartir chez soi*) to go home; (*revenir chez soi*) to come home; ~ **de l'école** to come home from school; **à peine rentré, il ...** the moment he got back home, he ...; **elle est déjà rentrée?** is she back already? **③** (*entrer à nouveau, vu* *de l'intérieur*) to come back in; (*vu de l'extérieur*) to go back in ❹ (*reprendre son travail: professeurs, députés, écoliers*) to go back; (*parlement*) to reconvene ❺ (*entrer*) **faire ~ qn** (*vu de l'intérieur*) to bring sb in; (*vu de l'extérieur*) to take sb in; **~ dans un café** to go into a café; **par la fenêtre** to get in through the window; **l'eau/le voleur rentre dans la maison** water/the thief is getting into the house ❻ (*s'insérer*) **~ dans une valise/un tiroir** to fit in a suitcase/a drawer; **~ les uns dans les autres** (*tubes*) to fit inside each other ❼ (*être inclus dans*) **~ dans qc** to go in sth; **faire ~ qn dans une catégorie** to put sth in a category ❽ (*devenir membre*) **~ dans la police/une entreprise** to join the police/a business, **faire ~ qn dans une entreprise** to take sb into a business ❾ (*commencer à étudier*) **~ en fac** to start college ❿ (*percuter*) **~ dans qc** to hit sth; (*conducteur*) to run into sth ⓫ COM, FIN (*article, créances*) to come in; **faire ~ des commandes/des impôts** to bring in orders/taxes ⓬ (*recouvrer*) **~ dans ses droits** to recover one's rights; **~ dans ses frais** to cover one's costs ▸ **elle lui est rentré dedans** *inf* she laid into him II. *vt avoir* ❶ (*ramener à l'intérieur: table, foin*) to bring in; (*tête, ventre*) to pull back; **~ son chemisier dans la jupe** to tuck one's blouse into one's skirt; **~ la voiture au garage** to put the car in the garage; **~ son cou dans les épaules** to hunch one's shoulders ❷ (*enfoncer*) **~ la clé dans la serrure** to put the key in the lock III. *vpr* **se ~ dedans** to lay into each other

**renversant(e)** [ʀɑ̃vɛʀsɑ̃, ɑ̃t] *adj inf* astonishing

**renverse** [ʀɑ̃vɛʀs] *f* **tomber à la ~** (*en arrière*) to fall backwards; (*de surprise*) to be staggered

**renversement** [ʀɑ̃vɛʀsəmɑ̃] *m* ❶ (*changement complet*) reversal; (*de tendance*) swing ❷ POL defeat; (*par un coup d'État*) overthrow

**renverser** [ʀɑ̃vɛʀse] <1> I. *vt* ❶ (*faire tomber*) **~ un vase** to knock over a vase; **~ un piéton** to run over a pedestrian; **~ des arbres** (*tempête*) to blow down trees ❷ (*répandre*) to spill ❸ (*réduire à néant: obstacles*) to scatter ❹ POL to defeat; (*ordre établi*) to overthrow ❺ (*pencher en arrière*) **~ le corps** to lean back; **~ la tête** to throw back one's head ❻ (*retourner*) **~ qc** to turn sth upside down ❼ (*inverser: ordre des mots, fraction*) to invert; (*situation, image*) to reverse II. *vpr* (*se retourner*) **se ~** to spill; (*bateau*) to capsize

**renvoi** [ʀɑ̃vwa] *m* ❶ (*réexpédition*) return ❷ SPORT return ❸ (*licenciement*) dismissal ❹ ECOLE, UNIV expulsion ❺ (*indication*) **~ à qc** reference to sth ❻ JUR, POL **~ devant qc/en qc** sending before/to sth ❼ (*ajournement*) **~ à qc** postponement until sth ❽ (*rot*) belch

**renvoyer** [ʀɑ̃vwaje] <6> *vt* ❶ (*envoyer à nouveau*) **~ une lettre à un client** to send a new letter to a customer ❷ SPORT to return ❸ (*retourner: compliment*) to return; **~ l'ascenseur** to send the elevator back ❹ (*réexpédier*) to return ❺ (*licencier*) to dismiss ❻ ECOLE, UNIV **~ un élève/étudiant** to expel a pupil/student ❼ (*éconduire*) **~ qn** to send sb away ❽ (*adresser*) **~ à qn** to send back to sb ❾ JUR **~ qn devant la cour d'assises** to send sb for trial at the court of assizes ❿ (*ajourner*) **~ qc à plus tard/à une date ultérieure** to leave sth until later/until a later date

**réorganisation** [ʀeɔʀɡanizasjɔ̃] *f* reorganization

**réorganiser** [ʀeɔʀɡanize] <1> *vt, vpr* (**se**) **~** to reorganize

**réorienter** [ʀeɔʀjɑ̃te] <1> I. *vt* ❶ (*changer d'orientation*) to reorient ❷ ECOLE **~ les élèves vers la littérature** to redirect students toward literature II. *vpr* **se ~ vers une branche** to turn to a new field

**réouverture** [ʀeuvɛʀtyʀ] *f* reopening

**repaire** [ʀ(ə)pɛʀ] *m* den

**répandre** [ʀepɑ̃dʀ] <14> I. *vt* ❶ (*laisser*

**R**

*tomber*) ~ **qc par terre/sur la table** to spread sth on the ground/the table; (*du liquide*) to pour sth on the ground/the table; (*par mégarde*) to spill sth on the ground/the table ❷ (*être source de*) ~ **qc** to give out sth ❸ (*épandre*) ~ **qc** (*gaz*) to give off sth ❹ (*faire connaître, susciter, verser*) to spread **II.** *vpr* ❶ (*s'écouler*) **se** ~ to spread; (*par accident*) to spill ❷ (*se disperser*) **se** ~ to spread out ❸ (*se dégager*) **se** ~ (*chaleur, fumée, odeur*) to spread; (*son*) to carry ❹ (*se propager*) **se** ~ (*épidémie*) to spread

**réparable** [ʀepaʀabl] *adj* (*panne, objet*) repairable

**reparaître** [ʀ(ə)paʀɛtʀ] *vi irr* ❶ *avoir* (*se montrer de nouveau*) to reappear ❷ *avoir o être* PRESSE (*journal, livre*) to reappear

**réparateur, -trice** [ʀepaʀatœʀ, -tʀis] **I.** *adj* (*sommeil*) refreshing **II.** *m, f* repairer; (*d'appareils*) repairman

**réparation** [ʀepaʀasjɔ̃] *f* ❶ *sans pl* (*remise en état*) repair; (*d'un accroc*) mending; (*d'une fuite*) stopping; **frais de** ~ repair costs; **être en** ~ to be under repair ❷ (*endroit réparé*) repair ❸ *pl* ARCHIT repair work ❹ *sans pl* (*correction*) correction ❺ *sans pl* (*compensation*) reparation ❻ (*dédommagement*) compensation ▸ **surface de** ~ SPORT penalty area

**réparer** [ʀepaʀe] <1> *vt* ❶ (*remettre en état: maison, route, dégât*) to repair; (*accroc, fuite*) to fix ❷ (*rattraper*) ~ **qc** to make up for sth

**reparler** [ʀ(ə)paʀle] <1> **I.** *vi* ~ **de qn/qc** to speak about sth again; **on reparlera bientôt de lui** you're going to hear more of him; ~ **à qn** to speak to sb again ▸ **on en reparlera** *inf* we'll talk about it another time **II.** *vpr* **se** ~ to talk to each other again

**repartir** [ʀ(ə)paʀtiʀ] <10> *vi être* ❶ (*se remettre à avancer*) to set off again ❷ (*s'en retourner*) to leave ❸ (*fonctionner à nouveau: moteur*) to start again; (*discussion, affaire*) to start up again

▸ **et c'est reparti** (**pour un tour**)**!** *inf* here we go again!

**répartir** [ʀepaʀtiʀ] <10> **I.** *vt* ❶ (*partager*) ~ **un butin/bénéfice/une somme** to divide up booty/profit/money; ~ **les touristes entre les deux bus** to divide the tourists between two buses ❷ (*diviser*) ~ **en groupes** to divide into groups ❸ (*disposer*) ~ **des troupes aux endroits stratégiques** to place troops at strategic positions; ~ **des choses sur les étagères** to spread things over the shelves ❹ (*étaler*) ~ **qc sur le corps/sur toute la semaine** to spread sth over the body/the whole week **II.** *vpr* ❶ (*se partager*) **ils se répartissent les élèves/la responsabilité** they divide the students/the responsibility among themselves ❷ (*être partagé*) **se** ~ to be distributed; **le travail se répartit comme suit** the work will be allocated as follows ❸ (*se diviser*) **se** ~ **en groupes** to be divided into groups

**répartition** [ʀepaʀtisjɔ̃] *f* ❶ (*partage*) distribution; ~ **des frais/rôles entre trois personnes** allocation of costs/roles among three people; **la** ~ **des élèves entre les classes et la suivante** the students are divided up between the classes as follows ❷ (*division*) **la** ~ **des touristes en groupes** the division of tourists into groups ❸ (*disposition: des troupes*) positioning ❹ (*étalement: d'une crème, lotion*) spreading; (*d'un programme*) scheduling ❺ (*localisation: de pièces, salles*) allocation

**repas** [ʀ(ə)pa] *m* (*nourriture, ensemble de plats, fait de manger*) meal; **cinq ~ par jour** five meals a day; **donner un grand** ~ to give a big dinner; **c'est l'heure du** ~ it's time to eat

**repasser¹** [ʀ(ə)pase] <1> **I.** *vi avoir* to iron **II.** *vt* ❶ (*défriper*) to iron ❷ (*aiguiser*) to sharpen **III.** *vpr* **se** ~ to iron

**repasser²** [ʀ(ə)pase] <1> **I.** *vi être* ❶ (*revenir*) to come by again; **ne pas** ~ **par la même route** not to go by the same way ❷ (*passer à nouveau: plat*) to be passed around again; (*film*) to be

showing again ❸ (*revoir le travail de*)
**~ derrière qn** to check sb's work
❹ (*retracer*) **~ sur qc** to go over sth
again **II.** *vt* avoir ❶ (*franchir de nouveau*) **~ qc** to cross sth again ❷ (*refaire: examen*) to retake ❸ (*remettre*) **~ une couche de peinture sur qc** to give sth another coat of paint ❹ (*redonner*)
**~ qc** (*plat, outil*) to hand sth back; **je te repasse papa** I'll give you back to Dad ❺ (*rejouer*) **~ qc** to put sth on again ❻ (*passer à nouveau*) **~ qc dans sa tête** to go back over sth in one's mind ❼ *inf* (*donner*) **~ un travail à qn** to hand a job to sb; **~ une maladie à qn** to give sb a disease

**repêcher** [ʀ(ə)peʃe] <1> *vt* ❶ (*retirer de l'eau*) **~ qc** to fish sth out ❷ *inf* ECOLE, UNIV **~ qn** to push sb through (*in borderline cases*); (*par examen complémentaire*) to give sb a second chance ❸ SPORT to let through by repechage

**repenser** [ʀ(ə)pɑ̃se] <1> *vi* **~ à qc** to think of sth again

**repentir** [ʀ(ə)pɑ̃tiʀ] **I.** *m* repentance **II.** <10> *vpr* **se ~ de qc/d'avoir fait qc** to repent sth/doing sth

**répercussion** [ʀepɛʀkysjɔ̃] *f* ❶ (*effet*) *a.* PHYS repercussion; **avoir peu de ~ s sur qc** to have little repercussion on sth ❷ ECON, FIN **~ de qc** passing on of sth

**répercuter** [ʀepɛʀkyte] <1> *vt* **I.** *vt* ❶ (*réfléchir*) to reflect; (*son*) to send back ❷ ECON, FIN **~ qc sur les prix des marchandises** to tack sth on to the cost of merchandise ❸ (*transmettre*) **~ qc** to pass sth on **II.** *vpr* ❶ (*être réfléchi*) **se ~** to be reflected ❷ (*se transmettre à*) **se ~ sur qc** to be passed on to sth

**repère** [ʀ(ə)pɛʀ] **I.** *m* ❶ (*signe*) marker ❷ (*trait*) mark **II.** *app* **des dates ~** landmark dates

**repérer** [ʀ(ə)peʀe] <5> **I.** *vt* ❶ *inf* (*découvrir*) to spot; **se faire ~ par qn** to be spotted by sb ❷ CINE (*lieux*) to scout for ❸ MIL (*localiser*) to locate **II.** *vpr inf* ❶ (*se retrouver, s'orienter*) **se ~ dans qc** to find one's way around ❷ (*se remarquer*) **se ~** to stand out

**répertoire** [ʀepɛʀtwaʀ] *m* ❶ index ❷ (*carnet*) address book ❸ THEAT repertoire ❹ INFORM directory ❺ *inf* (*grand nombre*) repertoire

**répertorier** [ʀepɛʀtɔʀje] <1> *vt* ❶ (*inscrire dans un répertoire*) to list ❷ (*classer*) **~ des personnes/choses** to classify people/things

**répéter** [ʀepete] <5> **I.** *vt* ❶ (*redire*) to repeat; **ne pas se faire ~ les choses deux fois** not to need telling twice; **~ à son fils de** +*infin* to keep telling one's son to +*infin*; **combien de fois vous ai-je répété que...?** how many times have I told you that...? ❷ (*rapporter*) to tell; (*propos*) to repeat ❸ (*refaire*) **~ qc** to do sth again ❹ (*mémoriser*) to learn ❺ THEAT, MUS to rehearse ❻ (*plagier*) to copy **II.** *vi* ❶ (*redire*) **répète un peu!** say that again! ❷ THEAT to rehearse **III.** *vpr* ❶ (*redire les mêmes choses*) **se ~** to repeat oneself ❷ (*se raconter*) **se ~** (*histoire*) to be told; **se ~ qc** to tell oneself sth ❸ (*se redire la même chose*) **se ~ qc/que** to keep telling oneself sth/that ❹ (*être reproduit, se reproduire*) **se ~** to happen again

**répétitif, -ive** [ʀepetitif, -iv] *adj* repetitive

**répétition** [ʀepetisjɔ̃] *f* ❶ (*redite*) repetition ❷ (*mémorisation: d'un rôle, morceau*) learning ❸ THEAT, MUS rehearsal; **~ générale** dress rehearsal ❹ (*renouvellement, reproduction: d'un accident*) recurrence; (*d'un exploit*) repeating

**répit** [ʀepi] *m* ❶ (*pause*) rest; **sans ~** nonstop ❷ (*délai supplémentaire*) breathing room

**replacer** [ʀ(ə)plase] <2> **I.** *vt* ❶ (*remettre à sa place*) to replace ❷ (*situer*) **~ un événement dans son époque** to put an event into its historical context **II.** *vpr* **se ~ dans qc** to take up one's position again in sth

**repli** [ʀəpli] *m* ❶ *pl* (*ondulations: d'un drapeau, de la peau*) fold; (*d'une rivière, d'un intestin*) bend ❷ (*retraite*) withdrawal ❸ FIN, ECON fall ❹ (*isole-*

R

*ment: d'un pays*) withdrawal ❺ COUT
fold

**replier** [R(ə)plije] <1> **I.** *vt* ❶ (*plier à nouveau*) to refold ❷ (*plier sur soi-même*) ~ **qc** (*bas de pantalon, manche, feuille*) to roll sth up; (*coin d'une page*) to fold sth down; (*mètre rigide*) to fold sth up ❸ (*rabattre*) ~ **qc** (*jambes, pattes*) to fold sth; (*ailes, couteau, lame*) to fold sth away; (*couverture, drap*) to fold sth down ❹ MIL to withdraw **II.** *vpr* ❶ (*faire retraite*) **se** ~ to fall back ❷ (*se protéger*) **se** ~ **sur qc** to fall back on sth ❸ (*se plier*) **se** ~ to fold ❹ (*se renfermer*) **se** ~ (*pays*) to withdraw; **se** ~ **sur soi-même** to withdraw into oneself

**réplique** [Replik] *f* ❶ (*réponse*) reply ❷ (*objection, réaction*) ~ **à qc** answer to sth ❸ THEAT cue ❹ ART replica ▸ **donner la** ~ **à qn** THEAT to give sb their cue; (*répondre*) to answer sb back; **être la vivante** ~ **de qn** to be the spitting image of sb

**répliquer** [Replike] <1> **I.** *vi* ❶ (*répondre*) to reply ❷ (*protester; répondre avec impertinence*) to retort **II.** *vt* ~ **la même chose à sa mère** to answer the same thing back to one's mother; ~ **qc à un argument** to reply sth to an argument

**répondant** [Repɔ̃dɑ̃] *m* **avoir du** ~ to have money; (*de la répartie*) to always have a ready reply

**répondeur** [Repɔ̃dœʀ] *m* answering machine

**répondeur, -euse** [Repɔ̃dœʀ, -øz] *adj* (*impertinent*) **un enfant** ~ a child that talks back

**répondre** [Repɔ̃dʀ] <14> **I.** *vi* ❶ (*donner une réponse*) to answer, to reply; ~ **par qc** to answer with sth; ~ **à une lettre** to reply to a letter; ~ **à une question** to reply to a [o answer] a question ❷ (*réagir*) **ne pas** ~ **au téléphone** not to answer the telephone ❸ (*être impertinent*) ~ **à qn** to answer [o talk] sb back **II.** *vt* ~ **qc à qn** to reply sth to sb; ~ **oui** to answer yes; **réponds-moi!** an-

swer me!; ~ **à qn de** +*infin* to reply by telling sb to +*infin*

**réponse** [Repɔ̃s] *f* ~ **à qc** reply [o answer] to sth; **rester sans** ~ to remain unanswered

**reportage** [R(ə)pɔʀtaʒ] *m* report

**reporter¹** [R(ə)pɔʀtɛʀ, R(ə)pɔʀtœʀ] *m* reporter

**reporter²** [R(ə)pɔʀte] <1> **I.** *vt* (*différer*) to postpone **II.** *vpr* (*se référer*) **se** ~ **à qc** to refer to sth; **se** ~ **à la page 13** see page 13

**repos** [R(ə)po] *m* ❶ (*détente*) rest; **prendre un peu de** ~ to have a little rest ❷ (*congé*) **une journée de** ~ a day off

**reposer¹** [R(ə)poze] <1> **I.** *vt* ❶ (*poser à nouveau*) ~ **qc** to put sth back ❷ (*répéter*) ~ **la question** to ask the question again **II.** *vi* (*être fondé sur*) ~ **sur une hypothèse** to be based on a hypothesis

**reposer²** [R(ə)poze] <1> **I.** *vt* (*délasser*) to relax **II.** *vpr* (*se délasser*) **se** ~ to rest

**repousser¹** [R(ə)puse] <1> **I.** *vt* ❶ (*attaque, ennemi*) to repel; ~ **des coups/un agresseur** to ward off blows/an attacker; ~ **la foule** to drive the crowd back ❷ (*écarter avec véhémence: des papiers*) to push away; ~ **qn sur le côté** to push sb aside ❸ (*refuser*) to ignore; (*demande*) to refuse ❹ (*remettre à sa place*) ~ **qc** to push sth back ❺ (*différer*) to postpone

**repousser²** [R(ə)puse] *vi* (*croître de nouveau*) to grow back; **laisser** ~ **sa barbe/ses cheveux** to let one's beard/hair grow

**reprendre** [R(ə)pʀɑ̃dʀ] <13> **I.** *vt* ❶ (*récupérer*) ~ **qc** (*objet prêté, parole, territoire, ville*) to take sth back; (*place*) to go back to sth; (*objet déposé*) to pick sth up; ~ **un employé** to rehire a worker; ~ **ses enfants à l'école** to pick up one's children after school; ~ **sa voiture et rentrer chez soi** to pick up one's car and go back home; ~ **la voiture/le volant après un accident** to get back in the car/go back to driving after an accident ❷ (*retrouver*) ~ **contact** to get back in touch; **~ ses habitudes** to get back into one's old habits; **~ son nom de jeune fille** to start using one's maiden name again; **~ confiance/espoir/courage** to get new confidence/ hope/courage; **~ conscience** to regain consciousness; **~ des forces** to get one's strength back ❸COM, ECON **~ qc** (*fonds de commerce, entreprise*) to take sth over; (*marchandise usagée*) to take sth back ❹(*continuer après une interruption: promenade*) to continue; **~ sa fonction** to return to one's job; **~ un travail** to go back to some work; **~ un récit** to go back to a story; **~ la route** to get back on the road; **~ (le chemin de) l'école** to set off for school; **~ son cours** (*conversation*) to pick up again; (*vie*) to go back to normal ❺(*recommencer*) **~ la lecture/le récit de qc** to begin reading/telling sth again ❻(*corriger: article, chapitre*) to rework; **~ un élève** to correct a student ❼COUT to alter; **~ qc** (*rétrécir*) to take sth in; (*raccourcir*) to take sth up; (*agrandir*) to let sth out; (*rallonger*) to let sth down ❽(*se resservir de*) **~ de la viande/du gâteau** to have some more meat/cake ❾(*s'approprier*) **~ une idée/suggestion** to take up an idea/ suggestion ▸ **que je ne t'y reprenne pas!** don't let me catch you doing that again! **II.** *vi* ❶(*se revivifier: affaires, convalescent*) to pick up; (*vie*) to return to normal ❷(*recommencer: douleurs, musique, pluie, conversation*) to start up again; (*classe, cours*) to start again ❸(*enchaîner*) to go on ❹(*répéter*) **je reprends: ...** to go back to what I was saying: ... **III.** *vpr* ❶(*se corriger*) **se ~** to correct oneself ❷(*s'interrompre*) **se ~** to stop ❸*soutenu* (*recommencer*) **s'y ~ à deux fois pour** +*infin* to have to try twice before one manages to +*infin* ❹(*se ressaisir*) **sc ~** to pull oneself together

**représentant(e)** [ʀ(ə)pʀezɑ̃tɑ̃, ɑ̃t] *m(f)* representative; **~ en papier/livres** paper/book salesperson; **~ de**

**commerce** sales representative; **la Chambre des ~s** *Belgique* the House of Representatives (*the lower house of the Belgian Parliament*)

**représentation** [ʀ(ə)pʀezɑ̃tasjɔ̃] *f* ❶(*description*) representation ❷THEAT performance

**représenter** [ʀ(ə)pʀezɑ̃te] <1> **I.** *vt* ❶(*décrire*) to represent; **~ qn comme qc** to make sb out to be sth ❷(*correspondre à: progrès, révolution, travail, autorité*) to represent ❸JUR, POL, COM to represent **II.** *vpr* ❶(*s'imaginer*) **se ~ qn/qc** to imagine sb/sth ❷(*survenir à nouveau*) **se ~** (*occasion, possibilité, problème*) to come up again ❸POL **se ~ à qc** to run for sth again

**répression** [ʀepʀesjɔ̃] *f* ❶JUR suppression ❷POL, PSYCH repression

**réprimer** [ʀepʀime] <1> *vt* ❶(*retenir*) to suppress; (*larmes*) to hold back ❷JUR, POL to suppress

**reproche** [ʀ(ə)pʀɔʃ] *m* reproach

**reprocher** [ʀ(ə)pʀɔʃe] <1> **I.** *vt* (*faire grief de*) **~ qc à qn** to reproach sb with sth; **~ à qn de faire qc** to reproach sb with doing sth; **avoir qc à ~ à qn** to have sth to reproach sb with **II.** *vpr* **se ~ qc/de faire qc** to blame oneself for sth/for doing sth; **avoir qc à se ~** to have done sth to feel guilty about

**reproduction** [ʀ(ə)pʀɔdyksjɔ̃] *f* (*copie*) reproduction

**reproduire** [ʀ(ə)pʀɔdɥiʀ] *vpr irr* **se ~** (*se répéter*) to happen again

**républicain(e)** [ʀepyblikɛ̃, ɛn] *adj, m(f)* republican

**république** [ʀepyblik] *f* republic; **République française** French Republic

**répugnant(e)** [ʀepyɲɑ̃, ɑ̃t] *adj* repulsive

**réputation** [ʀepytasjɔ̃] *f* ❶(*honneur*) repute ❷(*renommée*) reputation; **avoir bonne/mauvaise ~** to have a good/bad reputation

**réputé(e)** [ʀepyte] *adj* (*connu*) reputed; **ce professeur est ~ pour être sévère** that teacher has a reputation for being strict

**R**

**requête** [Rəkɛt] *f* INFORM search

**requin** [Rəkɛ̃] *m* ZOOL shark

**réquisitionner** [Rekizisjɔne] <1> *vt* (*requérir: biens, hommes*) to requisition

**R.E.R.** [ɛRøɛR] *m abr de* **réseau express régional** *express train service for the Paris region*

**rescapé(e)** [Rɛskape] *m(f)* survivor

**réseau** [Rezo] <x> *m* (*structure, organisation*) *a.* INFORM network; **le ~ Internet** the Internet

**réservation** [Rezɛʀvasjɔ̃] *f* reservation

**réserve** [Rezɛʀv] *f* ❶ (*provision*) reserve; **faire des ~s pour l'hiver** to build up reserves for the winter ❷ (*lieu protégé*) reserve; **~ indienne** Indian reservation; **~ de chasse** hunting preserve ▸ **avoir des ~s** *iron* to have reserves of fat to fall back on

**réservé(e)** [Rezɛʀve] *adj* ❶ (*discret*) reserved ❷ (*limité à certains*) **~ aux handicapés/autobus** reserved for the disabled/buses

**réserver** [Rezɛʀve] <1> I. *vt* ❶ (*garder: place*) to keep; **~ le meilleur pour la fin** to keep the best for the last ❷ (*retenir*) to reserve; (*voyage*) to book II. *vpr* (*se ménager*) **se ~ pour le dessert** to leave room for dessert; **se ~ pour plus tard** to save oneself for later

**résidence** [Rezidɑ̃s] *f* ❶ (*domicile*) residence; **~ principale** main residence ❷ (*appartement pour les vacances*) vacation apartment ❸ (*maison pour les vacances*) vacation home ❹ (*immeuble*) **~ universitaire** dormitory, residence hall; **~ pour personnes âgées** home for the elderly

**résident(e)** [Rezidɑ̃, ɑ̃t] *m(f)* (*étranger*) resident

**résider** [Rezide] <1> *vi* (*habiter*) to reside

**résigner** [Reziɲe] <1> *vpr* **se ~** to resign oneself; **se ~ à faire qc** to resign oneself to doing sth

**résilier** [Rezilje] <1> *vt* to cancel

**résistance** [Rezistɑ̃s] *f* (*opposition*) resistance; **la Résistance** HIST the French Resistance

**résistant(e)** [Rezistɑ̃, ɑ̃t] I. *adj* (*robuste: matériau*) resistant; (*étoffe*) heavy duty; (*personne, plante, animal*) tough; **l'acier est plus ~ que le fer** steel is stronger than iron II. *m(f)* HIST member of the French Resistance

**résister** [Reziste] <1> *vi* ❶ (*s'opposer*) **~ à qn** to resist sb; **~ à un désir/une tentation** to resist a desire/temptation ❷ (*supporter*) **résister à qc** to withstand sth; **~ au feu** to be fireproof

**résolu(e)** [Rezɔly] I. *part passé de* **résoudre** II. *adj* (*air, personne*) determined; (*ton*) resolute; **être ~ à qc** to be determined on sth; **être ~ à** +*infin* to be determined to +*infin*

**résolution** [Rezɔlysjɔ̃] *f* ❶ (*décision*) decision; **prendre une ~** to make a decision; **prendre la ~ de** +*infin* to resolve to +*infin* ❷ INFORM resolution

**résonance** [Rezɔnɑ̃s] *f* ❶ (*répercussion*) echo ❷ (*connotation*) overtones *pl*

**résonner** [Rezɔne] <1> *vi* (*salle*) to resonate

**résoudre** [Rezudʀ] *irr* I. *vt* ❶ (*trouver une solution: conflit, problème*) to resolve; (*mystère*) to solve ❷ (*décider*) **~ de** +*infin* to decide to +*infin*; **~ qn à** +*infin* to persuade sb to +*infin* II. *vpr* (*se décider*) **se ~ à faire qc** to make up one's mind to do sth

**respect** [Rɛspɛ] *m* (*égards*) respect; **~ de qn/qc** respect for sb/sth; **manquer de ~ à qn** to fail to show sb respect; **par ~ pour qn/qc** out of respect for sb/sth

**respecter** [Rɛspɛkte] <1> *vt* (*avoir des égards pour, observer*) to respect; **être respecté** to be respected; **se faire ~ par qn** to get sb's respect

**respiration** [Rɛspiʀasjɔ̃] *f* breathing; **~ artificielle** artificial respiration; **retenir sa ~** to hold one's breath

**respirer** [Rɛspiʀe] <1> *vi* ❶ (*inspirer*) to breathe ❷ (*se détendre*) to rest ❸ (*être rassuré*) to breathe easy

**responsabilité** [Rɛspɔ̃sabilite] *f* ❶ (*culpabilité*) responsibility; **avoir une ~**

**dans qc** to bear partial responsibility for sth ❷ JUR responsibility; **~ civile** civil liability; (*assurance*) civil liability insurance ❸ (*charge de responsable*) **~ de qc** responsibility for sth; **avoir/prendre des ~ s** to have/take on responsibilities; **avoir la ~ de qn/qc** to be responsible for sb/sth; **sous la ~ de qn** under sb ❹ (*conscience*) sense of responsibility

**responsable** [ʀɛspɔsabl] **I.** *adj* ❶ (*coupable, chargé de*) **être ~ de qc** to be responsible for sth ❷ JUR (*civilement, pénalement*) responsible; **être ~ de qn/ qc devant qn** to be answerable for sb/ sth to sb ❸ (*conscient: attitude, acte, personne*) responsible **II.** *mf* ❶ (*auteur*) person responsible; **les ~ s** those responsible ❷ (*personne compétente*) person in charge; (*d'une organisation, entreprise*) leader; **~ technique** technician

**ressaisir** [ʀ(ə)seziʀ] <8> *vpr* (*se maîtriser*) **se ~** to get ahold of oneself

**ressemblance** [ʀ(ə)sɑblɑs] *f* resemblance; **avoir une ~ avec qc** to bear a resemblance to sth

**ressembler** [ʀ(ə)sɑble] <1> **I.** *vi* ❶ (*être semblable*) **~ à qn** to resemble sb ❷ (*être semblable physiquement*) **~ à qn/qc** to look like [*o* resemble] sb/ sth ❸ *inf* (*être digne de*) **~ à qn** to be typical of [*o* just like] sb; **ça te ressemble de faire ça** it's just like you to do that ► **regarde un peu à quoi tu ressembles!** *inf* take a look at yourself! **II.** *vpr* ❶ (*être semblables*) **se ~** to be alike ❷ (*être semblables physiquement*) **se ~** to resemble each other

**ressentir** [ʀ(ə)sɑtiʀ] <10> *vt* to feel

**resserrer** [ʀ(ə)seʀe] <1> *vt* ❶ (*serrer plus fort: boulon, vis, ceinture*) to tighten ❷ (*fortifier: amitié, relations*) to strengthen

**ressortissant(e)** [ʀ(ə)sɔʀtisɑ, ɑt] *m(f)* national; **les ~ s étrangers résidant en France** foreign nationals residing in France

**ressource** [ʀ(ə)suʀs] *f pl* (*moyens*)

means; (*de l'État*) funds; **~ s naturelles** natural resources; **~ s personnelles** private income; **sans ~ s** with no means of support ► **avoir de la ~** to have strength in reserve

**ressusciter** [ʀesysite] <1> **I.** *vi* ❶ être REL **être ressuscité** to be risen ❷ *avoir* (*renaître: malade, nature*) to come back to life; (*pays, entreprise*) to revive **II.** *vt avoir* ❶ REL to raise ❷ **être ressuscité** (*malade, entreprise, pays*) to come back to life

**restant** [ʀɛstɑ] *m* rest; **~ de poulet/tissu** leftover chicken/cloth

**restaurant** [ʀɛstɔʀɑ] *m* restaurant; **aller au ~** to eat out; **~ universitaire** university cafeteria; **~ du cœur** soup kitchen run by volunteers for poor and homeless people during the winter

**restauration** [ʀɛstɔʀasjɔ] *f* ❶ ARCHIT, ART (*remise en état*) restoration ❷ (*hôtellerie*) catering; (*commerce*) restaurant business; **~ rapide** fast food ❸ INFORM restoration

**restaurer** [ʀɛstɔʀe] <1> **I.** *vt* ❶ (*remettre en état, rétablir*) **~/faire ~ qc** to restore sth ❷ POL (*ordre, paix, monarchie, régime*) to restore **II.** *vpr* **se ~** to have something to eat

**reste** [ʀɛst] *m* ❶ (*reliquat*) **le ~ de la journée/du temps/de ma vie** the rest of the day/the time/my life; **tout le ~** all the rest; **un ~ de tissu** a scrap of cloth ❷ MATH remainder ❸ *pl* (*reliefs: d'un repas*) leftovers; **ne pas laisser beaucoup de ~ s** not to leave much ► **faire le ~** to do the rest; **du ~** besides; **pour le ~** as for the rest

**rester** [ʀɛste] <1> **I.** *vi* être ❶ (*demeurer, ne pas s'en aller*) to stay; **~ chez soi** to stay at home; **~ (à) dîner** to stay for dinner; **~ sans parler/manger/ bouger** to stay silent/hungry/still ❷ (*continuer à être*) to stay; **~ debout/assis toute la journée** to stay standing/sitting all day; **~ immobile** to keep still ❸ (*subsister*) to remain; **ça m'est resté** (*dans ma mémoire*) I've never forgotten it; (*dans mes habitu-*

des) it has stuck with me; **beaucoup de choses restent à faire** much remains to be done ❹ (*ne pas se libérer de*) ~ **sur un échec** to never get over a failure ▸ **en ~ là** to stop there; **y ~** to meet one's end **II.** *vi impers* **être** ❶ (*être toujours là*) **il reste du vin** there's some wine left; **il n'est rien resté** there was nothing left; **il ne me reste** (**plus**) **que toi/cinquante euros** all I've got left is you/fifty euros ❷ (*ne pas être encore fait*) **je sais ce qu'il me reste à faire** I know what's left for me to do; **reste à savoir si …** it remains to be seen if …

**resto** [ʀɛsto] *m inf abr de* **restaurant**

**restoroute**® [ʀɛstoʀut] *f* roadside restaurant; (*de l'autoroute*) truck stop

**restreindre** [ʀɛstʀɛ̃dʀ] *irr* **I.** *vt* to restrict; (*champ d'action, crédit*) to limit; (*dépenses*) to cut **II.** *vpr* **se ~** (*s'imposer des restrictions*) to limit oneself; **se ~ dans ses dépenses** to cut down on one's spending; **se ~ sur la nourriture** to cut down on food

**restreint(e)** [ʀɛstʀɛ̃, ɛ̃t] **I.** *part passé de* **restreindre II.** *adj* limited

**restriction** [ʀɛstʀiksjɔ̃] *f* ❶ (*limitation: des libertés*) curtailment; (*des dépenses, de la consommation*) limiting; **mesures de ~** restrictions ❷ *pl* (*rationnement*) restrictions; **les ~s** rationing ❸ (*réserve*) reservation; **sans faire de ~s** unreservedly; **avec des ~s** with certain reservations; **sans ~** without reservation

**restructurer** [ʀɛstʀyktyʀe] <1> *vt* to restructure

**résultat** [ʀezylta] *m* ❶ MATH, SPORT, ECON, POL result; (*d'un problème*) solution; (*d'une intervention*) outcome ❷ (*conséquence, chose obtenue*) result; **avoir pour ~ une augmentation des prix** to result in price increases; **n'obtenir aucun ~** to achieve nothing; **obtenir quelques ~s** to get some results ▸ **sans ~** to no effect

**résumé** [ʀezyme] *m* summary ▸ **en ~** in short; **en ~: …** to put things briefly: …

**résumer** [ʀezyme] <1> *vt* (*récapituler*) to summarize

**rétablir** [ʀetabliʀ] <8> **I.** *vt* ❶ (*remettre en fonction: communication, courant*) to restore; (*contact, liaison*) to reestablish; **être rétabli** (*communication, contact*) to be reestablished; (*trafic*) to be moving again ❷ (*restaurer: confiance, équilibre, ordre*) to restore; (*monarchie, faits*) to reestablish; ~ **la vérité** to get back down to the truth ❸ MED ~ **qn** to bring sb back to health; **être rétabli** to be better **II.** *vpr* **se ~** ❶ (*guérir: personne, pays*) to recover ❷ (*revenir: calme, silence*) to return; (*trafic*) to return to normal

**rétablissement** [ʀetablismɑ̃] *m* (*d'un malade*) recovery; **bon ~!** get well soon!

**retaper** [ʀ(ə)tape] <1> **I.** *vt* (*remettre en état*) ~ **qc** (*maison, voiture*) to fix sth up; (*lit*) to straighten sth **II.** *vpr inf* **se ~ à la mer/la montagne** to retire to the sea/the mountains

**retard** [ʀ(ə)taʀ] *m* ❶ (*arrivée tardive*) late arrival; **un ~ d'une heure** being an hour late; **avec une heure/dix minutes de ~** an hour/ten minutes late; **arriver en ~** to arrive late; **avoir du ~/deux minutes de ~** to be late/two minutes late; **avoir du ~ sur son planning** to be behind schedule ❷ (*réalisation tardive*) **avoir du ~ dans un travail/paiement** to be behind on a job/with a payment; **être en ~ d'un mois pour** (**payer**) **le loyer** to be a month behind on the rent ❸ (*développement plus lent*) slow(er) progress; ECOLE lack of progress; **malgré leur retard** despite their being behind; **présenter un ~ de langage/de croissance** to be late developing in terms of language/growth

**retarder** [ʀ(ə)taʀde] <1> **I.** *vt* ❶ (*mettre en retard: personne, véhicule*) to delay; ~ **le départ du train** to hold up the departure of the train ❷ (*ralentir, empêcher*) ~ **qn** to delay sb; ~ **qn dans son travail** to hold up sb's work **II.** *vi*

~ **d'une heure** (*montre, horloge*) to be an hour slow

**retenir** [ʀ(ə)təniʀ, ʀət(ə)niʀ] <9> **I.** *vt* ❶ (*maintenir en place*) ~ **qn/qc** (*objet, bras, personne qui glisse*) to hold on to sb/sth; (*foule, personne*) to hold sb/sth back; ~ **qn par la manche** to hold on to sb's sleeve ❷ (*empêcher d'agir*) ~ **qn** to hold sb back; **retiens/retenez-moi, ou je fais un malheur** hold on to me or I'll do something I shouldn't ❸ (*empêcher de tomber*) to hold ❹ (*garder*) to keep; **je ne te retiens pas plus longtemps** I won't keep you any longer; ~ **qn prisonnier/en otage** to keep sb prisoner/hostage; **j'ai été retenu** I was held up ❺ (*requérir*) ~ **l'attention** to draw one's attention ❻ (*réserver: chambre, place*) to reserve; (*table*) to book ❼ (*se souvenir de*) to remember; **retenez bien la date** don't forget that date ❽ (*réprimer: colère, cri, geste*) to restrain; (*larmes, sourire*) to hold back; (*souffle*) to hold ❾ (*accepter, choisir: candidature*) to accept ❿ (*prélever*) ~ **un montant sur le salaire** to withhold some money from wages ▸ **je te/le/la retiens!** *inf* I won't forget you/him/her anytime soon! **II.** *vpr* ❶ (*s'accrocher*) **se ~ à qn/qc pour** +*infin* to hold on to sb/sth to +*infin* ❷ (*s'empêcher*) **se ~** to restrain oneself; **se ~ pour ne pas rire** to keep oneself from laughing ❸ (*contenir ses besoins naturels*) **se ~** to hold on

**retentissant(e)** [ʀ(ə)tãtisã, ãt] *adj* ❶ (*fort, sonore: cri, voix*) ringing; (*bruit, claque*) resounding ❷ (*fracassant: déclaration, succès*) resounding; (*scandale, discours*) sensational

**réticence** [ʀetisãs] *f* reluctance; **avec ~** reluctantly

**retiré(e)** [ʀ(ə)tiʀe] *adj* (*solitaire: lieu*) secluded

**retirer** [ʀ(ə)tiʀe] <1> **I.** *vt* ❶ (*enlever*) ~ **qc** (*vêtement, montre*) to take sth off; ~ **ses lunettes** to take one's glasses off; ~ **qc du commerce** to discontinue the sale of sth; ~ **qc du catalogue/pro-**

**gramme** to remove sth from the catalog/the program; ~ **le permis à qn** to take away sb's license ❷ (*faire sortir*) ~ **qc** to take sth out; ~ **la clé de la serrure** to take the key out of the lock ❸ (*prendre possession de: argent*) to withdraw; (*billet*) to collect; ~ **de l'argent à la banque/d'un compte** to withdraw money from the bank/an account ❹ (*ramener en arrière*) ~ **qc** (*main, tête*) to move sth away ❺ (*annuler: déclaration, paroles, candidature, offre*) to withdraw ❻ (*obtenir*) ~ **des avantages de qc** to get benefits from sth; ~ **un bénéfice de qc** to make a profit out of sth; ~ **qc d'une expérience** to get sth out of an experience ❼ (*extraire*) ~ **de l'huile d'une substance** to extract oil from a substance ❽ (*tirer de nouveau*) ~ **un coup de feu** to fire another shot ❾ (*faire un second tirage*) **faire ~ une photo** (*meilleur tirage*) to have a photo printed again; (*double*) to get a reprint of a photo **II.** *vi* to fire again **III.** *vpr* ❶ (*partir*) **se ~** to withdraw; **se ~ dans sa chambre** to withdraw to one's room; **se ~ à la campagne** to go off to live in the country ❷ (*annuler sa candidature*) **se ~** to withdraw ❸ (*reculer*) **se ~** (*armée, ennemi*) to withdraw; (*eau, mer*) to go out ❹ (*quitter*) **se ~ de la vie publique/des affaires** to leave public life/business

**retombée** [ʀ(ə)tɔ̃be] *f* ❶ *pl* (*répercussions*) fallout + *vb sing;* **les ~s médiatiques de qc** the media fallout from sth ❷ (*impact*) impact

**retomber** [ʀ(ə)tɔ̃be] <1> *vi* être ❶ (*tomber à nouveau*) to fall back; ~ **dans l'oubli/la misère** to fall back into oblivion/misery; ~ **dans la délinquance/la drogue** to relapse into delinquency/drugs ❷ (*tomber après s'être élevé*) to fall down again; (*ballon*) to come back down; (*capot*) to fall back down; (*fusée*) to fall back to earth ❸ (*baisser: curiosité, enthousiasme*) to dwindle; (*fièvre, cote de popularité*) to fall ❹ (*redevenir*) ~ **amoureux** to fall

**R**

in love again; ~ **malade/enceinte** to get ill/pregnant again ❺ (*échoir à*) ~ **sur qn** to fall on sb; **cela va me ~ dessus** it's all going to land on me; **faire ~ la faute sur qn** to give sb the blame for sth ❻ (*revenir, rencontrer*) ~ **au même endroit** to come back to the same place; ~ **sur qn** to come across sb again

**retoucher** [ʀ(ə)tuʃe] <1> I. vt ❶ (*corriger: vêtement*) to alter ❷ (*être remboursé*) ~ **mille dollars** to get a thousand dollars back II. vi ❶ (*toucher de nouveau*) ~ **à qc** to touch sth again ❷ (*regoûter à*) ~ **à l'alcool** to start drinking again

**retour** [ʀ(ə)tuʀ] I. m ❶ (*opp: départ*) return; (*chemin*) way back; (*à la maison*) way home; (*voyage*) return journey; (*à la maison*) journey home; **au ~** on the way back; (*en avion*) on the flight back; (*à l'arrivée*) when one gets back; **au ~ du service militaire** coming back from military service; **de ~ à la maison** back home; **être de ~** to be back ❷ (*à un état antérieur*) ~ **à la nature** return to nature; (*slogan*) back to nature; ~ **à la politique/terre** return to politics/the land; ~ **en arrière** flashback ❸ (*réapparition*) ~ **de la grippe** new outbreak of the flu; **la mode des années 60 est de ~** sixties fashions are back; ~ **en force** return in strength ❹ (*billet*) return (ticket); **un aller et ~ pour Paris** a roundtrip ticket for Paris ❺ CINE, TV rewind ~ **par ~ du courrier** by return mail; ~ **à l'expéditeur!** return to sender!; *inf* (*rendre la pareille*) same to you! II. app **match ~** return match

**retourner** [ʀ(ə)tuʀne] <1> I. vt avoir ❶ (*mettre dans l'autre sens*) ~ **qc** (*matelas, omelette, viande, cartes*) to turn sth over; (*caisse, tableau, verre*) to turn sth upside down ❷ (*mettre à l'envers*) ~ **qc** (*vêtement*) to turn sth inside out; (*manche, bas de pantalon*) to roll sth up; **être retourné** (*vêtement*) to be inside out; (*col*) to be turned up ❸ (*orien-*

*ter en sens opposé*) ~ **un compliment à qn** to return the compliment to sb; ~ **la situation en faveur de qn** to turn the situation back into sb's favor; ~ **l'opinion en sa faveur** to bring public opinion around ❹ (*faire changer d'opinion*) ~ **qn** to bring sb around ❺ (*renvoyer*) ~ **une lettre à l'expéditeur** to return a letter to the sender; ~ **des marchandises** to send goods back ❻ *inf* (*bouleverser: maison, pièce*) to turn upside down; (*personne*) to shake; **j'en suis tout retourné** I'm all shaken (up) II. vi être ❶ (*revenir*) to return; (*en partant*) to go back; (*en revenant*) to come back; (*en avion*) to fly back; ~ **sur ses pas** to retrace one's steps; ~ **chez soi** to go back home ❷ (*aller de nouveau*) ~ **à la montagne/chez qn** to go back to the mountains/to sb's house ❸ (*se remettre à*) ~ **à son travail** to get back to work; (*après une maladie, des vacances*) to go back [o return] to work III. vpr être ❶ (*se tourner dans un autre sens*) **se ~** (*personne*) to turn over; (*voiture, bateau*) to overturn; **se ~ sans cesse dans son lit** to toss and turn in one's bed ❷ (*tourner la tête*) **se ~** to look back; **se ~ vers qn/qc** to look back at sb/sth ❸ (*prendre parti*) **se ~ en faveur de/contre qn** to side with/turn against sb; **se ~ contre qn** JUR to take action against sb ❹ (*prendre un nouveau cours*) **se ~ contre qn** (*acte, action*) to backfire on sb ❺ (*repartir*) **s'en ~ dans son pays natal/en France** to go back to one's native country/to France

**retrait** [ʀ(ə)tʀɛ] m ❶ (*action de retirer: d'argent, d'un projet de loi, d'une candidature*) withdrawal; (*des bagages, d'un billet*) collection ❷ (*suppression: d'une autorisation*) withdrawal; ~ **du permis** (**de conduire**) revocation of driver's license

**retraite** [ʀ(ə)tʀɛt] f ❶ (*cessation du travail*) retirement; ~ **anticipée** early retirement; **être à la ~** to be retired; **par-**

**tir à la ~**, **prendre sa ~** to retire ❷ (*pension*) pension; **~ complémentaire** (*assurance*) pension (plan)

**retraité(e)** [ʀ(ə)tʀete] **I.** *adj* (*à la retraite*) retired **II.** *m(f)* retiree

**retransmettre** [ʀ(ə)tʀɑ̃smɛtʀ] *vt irr* to broadcast; (*émission*) to show

**retransmission** [ʀ(ə)tʀɑ̃smisjɔ̃] *f* broadcast

**rétrécir** [ʀetʀesiʀ] <8> **I.** *vt* (*rendre plus étroit*) to narrow; **~ une jupe** to take in a skirt; **~ une bague** to size a ring down **II.** *vi, vpr* (*laine, tissu*) to shrink

**rétro** [ʀetʀo] *abr de* **rétrograde I.** *adj inv* (*démodé*) old fashioned; (*mode*) retro **II.** *adv* (*s'habiller*) in retro clothing

**rétroéclairage** [ʀetʀoeklɛʀaʒ] *m* INFORM back lighting

**rétrolien** [ʀetʀɔljɛ̃] *m* INFORM trackback link

**rétroprojecteur** [ʀetʀopʀɔʒɛktœʀ] *m* overhead projector

**rétrospective** [ʀetʀɔspɛktiv] *f* ❶ ART retrospective ❷ CINE season ❸ *Québec* (*retour en arrière dans un film*) flashback

**retrousser** [ʀ(ə)tʀuse] <1> *vt* **~ qc** (*manche, bas de pantalon*) to roll sth up; (*moustache*) to curl sth

**retrouvailles** [ʀ(ə)tʀuvɑj] *fpl* reunion + *vb sing*

**retrouver** [ʀ(ə)tʀuve] <1> **I.** *vt* ❶ (*récupérer*) to find; **~ sa fonction/place** to return to one's post/seat; **j'ai retrouvé mon portefeuille** I've found my wallet ❷ (*rejoindre*) **~ qn** to meet (up with) sb ❸ (*recouvrer*) **~ l'équilibre** to get one's balance back; **~ son calme** to calm down again; **~ la santé** to return to health; **elle a retrouvé le sourire/le sommeil/l'espoir** she has been able to smile/sleep/hope again ❹ (*redécouvrir: situation, travail, marchandise*) to find **II.** *vpr* ❶ (*se réunir*) **se ~** (*personnes*) to meet; **j'espère qu'on se retrouvera bientôt** I hope we'll see each other again soon ❷ (*se présenter de nou-*

*veau*) **se ~** (*occasion, circonstance*) to turn up again ❸ (*être de nouveau*) **se ~ dans la même situation** to find oneself back in the same situation; **se ~ seul/désemparé** to find oneself alone/at a loss ❹ (*finir*) **se ~ en prison/dans le fossé** to end up in prison/in the ditch ❺ (*retrouver son chemin*) **se ~ dans une ville inconnue** to find one's way around a city one doesn't know ❻ (*voir clair*) **s'y ~** to make sense of it; **je n'arrive pas à m'y ~** I can't make any sense of all this

**rétroviseur** [ʀetʀɔvizœʀ] *m* rear view mirror; **~ extérieur/intérieur** sideview/interior mirror

**réunification** [ʀeynifikasjɔ̃] *f* (*de nations, d'États*) reunification

**réunifier** [ʀeynifje] <1> *vt* to reunify

**réunion** [ʀeynjɔ̃] *f* ❶ (*séance*) meeting; (*après une longue période*) reunion; (*rassemblement politique/public*) union; **~ de famille** family gathering; **~ de parents d'élèves** PTA meeting; **~ d'information** briefing session; **être en ~** to be in a meeting ❷ (*ensemble, rapprochement*) merging; (*d'États*) union; (*cercle d'amis*) gathering; (*convocation*) getting together

**Réunion** [ʀeynjɔ̃] *f* (**l'île de**) **la ~** Reunion (Island)

**réunir** [ʀeyniʀ] <8> **I.** *vt* ❶ (*mettre ensemble: objets, papiers*) to gather; (*faits, preuves, arguments*) to collect; **les conditions sont réunies pour que la tension baisse** conditions are right for the tension to lessen ❷ (*cumuler*) **~ toutes les conditions exigées** to meet all the requirements ❸ (*rassembler*) **~ des personnes** to bring people together; **~ des documents dans un classeur** to collect documents in a file **II.** *vpr* **se ~** (*se rassembler: personnes*) to gather

**réussi(e)** [ʀeysi] *adj* ❶ (*couronné de succès*) successful; (*examen*) with good results; **être vraiment ~** to be a real success ❷ (*bien exécuté*) successful; **ne pas être très réussi** to be somewhat of

R

a flop ► **c'est ~!** *iron* well done!, good job!

**réussir** [ʀeysiʀ] <8> **I.** *vi* ❶ *(aboutir à un résultat: chose)* to be a success; **~ bien/mal** to be/not be a success ❷ *(parvenir au succès)* **~ dans la vie/ dans les affaires** to succeed in life/ business; **~ à l'un examen** to pass the/a test ❸ *(être capable de)* **il réussit à** +*infin a. iron* he manages to +*infin*; **j'ai réussi à la convaincre** I managed to persuade him **II.** *vt* ❶ *(bien exécuter)* to manage; **~ son effet** to achieve the desired effect ❷ *(réaliser avec succès: épreuve, examen)* to pass; **~ sa vie** to make a success of one's life

**réussite** [ʀeysit] *f (bon résultat, succès)* success

**revaloriser** [ʀ(ə)valɔʀize] <1> *vt* ❶ *(opp: déprécier)* **~ qc** to raise the standing of sth ❷ FIN *(monnaie)* to revalue; *(rente, traitement, salaire)* to raise

**revanche** [ʀ(ə)vɑ̃ʃ] *f (vengeance)* revenge; JEUX, SPORT *(match)* return match; **j'ai gagné! tu veux qu'on fasse la ~?** *(subj)* I've won! do you want to even the score?; **prendre sa ~** SPORT to play a return match ► **en ~** *(par contre)* on the other hand; *(en contrepartie)* in exchange

**rêve** [ʀɛv] *m* dream; **beau/mauvais ~** nice/bad dream; **fais de beaux ~s!** sweet dreams! ► **c'est le ~** *inf* it's just perfect

**rêvé(e)** [ʀeve] *adj* perfect; *(solution)* ideal

**réveil** [ʀevɛj] *m* ❶ *(réveille-matin)* alarm clock; **mettre le ~ à 6 heures** to set the alarm for six o'clock ❷ *(retour à la réalité)* awakening

**réveiller** [ʀeveje] <1> **I.** *vt* ❶ *(sortir du sommeil, ramener à la réalité)* **~ qn** to wake sb up; **être réveillé** to be awake; **être bien réveillé** to be wide awake; **je suis mal réveillé** I haven't woken up properly ❷ *(raviver: curiosité, jalousie, cupidité)* to awaken; *(appétit)* to excite; *(rancune)* to reawaken **II.** *vpr*

**se ~** ❶ *(sortir du sommeil)* to wake up ❷ *(se raviver)* to reawaken; **dès que la douleur se réveillera** when the pain comes back ❸ *(volcan)* to awake

**réveillon** [ʀevɛjɔ̃] *m: Christmas or New Year's Eve, or the meal or party to celebrate them;* **fêter le ~ de Noël/du nouvel an** to celebrate Christmas Eve/ New Year's Eve

**réveillonner** [ʀevɛjɔne] <1> *vi (fêter Noël/le nouvel an)* to celebrate Christmas Eve/New Year's Eve

**révéler** [ʀevele] <5> *vt (divulguer)* to reveal; **~ de nouveaux faits/le scandale** *(enquête, journal)* to bring new facts/the scandal to light

**revendiquer** [ʀ(ə)vɑ̃dike] <1> *vt* ❶ *(réclamer: droit, augmentation de salaire)* to demand ❷ *(assumer: responsabilité)* to claim; **l'attentat a été revendiqué par la Maffia/n'a pas été revendiqué** the Mafia/nobody has claimed responsibility for the attack

**revendre** [ʀ(ə)vɑ̃dʀ] <14> *vt (vendre d'occasion)* **~ un piano à un collègue** to sell a piano to a colleague

**revenir** [ʀ(ə)vəniʀ, ʀəvniʀ] <9> *vi être* ❶ *(venir de nouveau: personne, lettre)* to come back; *(printemps)* to return; **~** +*infin* to come back to +*infin* ❷ *(rentrer)* to return; **~ en avion/en voiture/à pied** to fly/drive/walk back; **je reviens dans un instant** I'll be back in a moment ❸ *(recommencer)* **~ à un projet/sujet** to come back to a plan/ subject ❹ *(réexaminer)* **~ sur un sujet/le passé** to go back over a subject/ the past; **~ sur une affaire/un scandale** *péj* to rake over an affair/a scandal again ❺ *(se dédire de)* **~ sur une décision** to change a decision ❻ *(se présenter à nouveau à l'esprit)* **~ à qn** to come back to sb ❼ *(être déçu par)* **~ de ses illusions** to lose one's illusions ❽ *(équivaloir à)* **cela revient au même** it boils down to the same thing; **cela revient à dire que qn a fait qc** it's like saying sb did sth ❾ *(coûter au total)* **~ à 100 euros** to come to a 100 euros; **~ à 100**

**euros à qn** to cost sb a 100 euros; **~ cher** to work out to be expensive ⑩ CULIN **faire ~ les oignons/les légumes** to brown the onions/vegetables ► **je n'en reviens pas de son attitude** *inf* I can't get over his/her attitude; **elle revient de loin** it was a close call (for her)

**revenu** [R(ə)vəny, Rəvny] *m* income; **~ minimum d'insertion** *basic welfare benefit paid to the jobless*

**rêver** [Reve, Rɛve] <1> *vi* ① (*avoir un rêve*) **~ de qn/qc** to dream about sb/sth ② (*désirer*) **~ de qc/de faire qc** to dream of sth/of doing sth ③ (*divaguer*) **te prêter de l'argent? tu rêves!** lend you money? in your dreams!

**réviser** [Revize] <1> *vt, vi* ECOLE to revise

**révision** [Revizjɔ̃] *f* ① (*modification*) revision ② *pl* ECOLE revision

**revivre** [R(ə)vivR] *irr* **I.** *vi* (*être revigoré*) to come back to life **II.** *vt* (*vivre à nouveau*) to relive

**revoir** [R(ə)vwaR] *irr* **I.** *vt* ① (*voir à nouveau*) **~ qn/qc** to see sb/sth again; **au ~** goodbye ② (*regarder de nouveau*) **~ qn/qc** to look at sb/sth again ③ (*se souvenir*) **je la revois** I can see her now **II.** *vpr* **se ~** ① (*se retrouver*) to meet up ② (*se souvenir de soi*) **se ~ jeune** (*vieillard*) to see oneself as young man (again)

**révolte** [Revɔlt] *f* (*émeute*) revolt

**révolter** [Revɔlte] <1> **I.** *vt* (*individu*) to disgust; (*crime, injustice*) to revolt **II.** *vpr* **se ~ contre qn/qc** ① (*s'insurger*) to rebel against sb/sth ② (*s'indigner*) to be revolted by sb/sth

**révolution** [Revɔlysjɔ̃] *f* (*changement*) revolution

**Révolution** [Revɔlysjɔ̃] *f* HIST **la ~** the Revolution

**révolutionnaire** [RevɔlysjɔnɛR] *adj, mf* revolutionary

**revolver** [RevɔlvɛR] *m* revolver

**revue** [R(ə)vy] *f* (*magazine*) review

**rez-de-chaussée** [Red(ə)ʃose] *m inv* (*niveau inférieur*) first floor; **habiter au ~** to live on the first floor

**rhabiller** [Rabije] *vpr* **se ~** (*remettre ses vêtements*) to get dressed (again)

**Rhin** [Rɛ̃] *m* **le ~** the Rhine

**rhinocéros** [RinɔseRɔs] *m* rhinoceros

**Rhône** [Ron] *m* **le ~** the Rhone

**rhubarbe** [RybaRb] *f* rhubarb

**rhum** [Rɔm] *m* rum

**rhume** [Rym] *m* ① (*coup de froid*) cold; **attraper un ~** to catch a cold ② **~ des foins** hay fever

**R.I.B.** [Rib] *m abr de* **relevé d'identité bancaire** *bank account statement*

**ricaner** [Rikane] <1> *vi* ① (*avec mépris*) to snicker ② (*bêtement*) to giggle

**riche** [Riʃ] **I.** *adj* ① (*oppr. pauvre*) rich ② (*nourrissant: aliment, nourriture*) rich; **~ en calories** rich [*o* high] in calories **II.** *mf* rich person

**richesse** [Riʃɛs] *f* ① (*fortune*) wealth ② *pl* (*ressources*) wealth; (*d'un musée*) treasures ③ (*bien*) blessing

**ricocher** [Rikɔʃe] <1> *vi* **~ sur qc** to ricochet off sth

**ride** [Rid] *f* (*pli*) wrinkle

**ridé(e)** [Ride] *adj* wrinkled

**rideau** [Rido] <x> *m* ① (*voile*) curtain ② THEAT curtain ③ HIST **le ~ de fer** the Iron Curtain

**ridicule** [Ridikyl] **I.** *adj* (*personne, vêtement, conduite*) ridiculous **II.** *m* (*moqueries*) ridicule; (*absurdité*) ridiculousness; **couvrir qn/se couvrir de ~** to cover sb/oneself in ridicule

**ridiculiser** [Ridikylize] <1> **I.** *vt* to ridicule **II.** *vpr* **se ~** to make oneself ridiculous

**rien** [Rjɛ̃] **I.** *pron indéf* ① (*aucune chose*) nothing; **c'est ça ou ~** it's that or nothing; **ça ne vaut ~** it's worthless; **~ d'autre** nothing else; **~ de nouveau/mieux** nothing new/better; **il n'y a plus ~** there's nothing left ② (*seulement*) **~ que la chambre coûte 400 euros** the room alone costs 400 euros; **~ que d'y penser** just thinking about it ③ (*quelque chose*) anything; **être incapable de ~ dire** to be unable to say anything; **rester sans ~ faire** to do nothing ► **j'en ai ~ à ci-**

**R**

**rer** *inf* I couldn't care less; **ce n'est ~** it's nothing; **comme si de ~ n'était** as if there was nothing the matter; **elle n'est pour ~ dans ce problème** this problem has nothing to do with her; **de ~!** my pleasure!; **~ du tout** nothing at all; **~ que ça!** *iron* (*pas plus*) just that!; **c'est abuser** is that all? II. *m* ① (*très peu de chose*) trifle ② (*un petit peu*) tiny bit ▸ **en un ~ de temps** in no time

**rigolade** [Rigɔlad] *f inf* fun ▸ **c'est de la ~** (*c'est facile*) it's child's play; (*c'est pour rire*) it's just a bit of fun; (*ça ne vaut rien*) it's worthless; **prendre qc à la ~** to make a joke of sth; **prendre un examen à la ~** to treat a test like it was a joke

**rigoler** [Rigɔle] <1> *vi inf* ① (*rire*) to laugh; **faire ~ qn** to make sb laugh ② (*s'amuser*) to have fun ③ (*plaisanter*) **~ avec qn/qc** to have a laugh with sb/sth; **pour ~** for a laugh; **je (ne) rigole pas!** it's no joke!

**rigolo(te)** [Rigɔlo, ɔt] I. *adj inf* (*amusant*) funny II. *m(f) inf* (*homme amusant*) funny guy

**rigoureux, -euse** [RiguRø, -øz] *adj* ① (*sévère*) strict ② (*exact, précis*) rigorous ③ *antéposé* (*absolu: exactitude*) absolute; (*interdiction, authenticité*) total ④ (*dur: climat, hiver*) rigorous

**rigueur** [RigœR] *f* ① (*sévérité*) strictness; (*d'une punition*) harshness ② (*austérité*) austerity; **~ économique** economic rigor; **~ salariale** strict wage control ③ (*précision*) rigor ④ (*épreuve: d'un climat*) rigor ▸ **tenir ~ à qn de qc** to hold sth against sb; **à la ~** (*tout au plus*) at most; (*si besoin est*) in a pinch; **une tenue correcte est de ~** proper dress is essential

**rime** [Rim] *f* rhyme

**rimer** [Rime] <1> *vi* **~ avec qc** to rhyme with sth ▸ **ne ~ à rien** to make no sense

**rincer** [Rɛ̃se] <2> I. *vt* (*laver*) to rinse II. *vpr* **se ~ la bouche** to rinse one's mouth

**ringard(e)** [RɛgaR, aRd] *inf* I. *adj* uncool II. *m(f)* has-been

**rire** [RiR] *irr* I. *vi* ① (*opp: pleurer*) to laugh; **faire ~ qn** to make sb laugh; **laisse(z)-moi ~!** *iron* don't make me laugh! ② (*se moquer*) **~ de qn/qc** to laugh at sb/sth ③ (*s'amuser*) to have a laugh ④ (*plaisanter*) to joke; **tu veux ~!** you're joking! ▸ **sans ~?** no kidding? II. *m* ① (*action de rire*) laugh; **des ~s** laughter ② (*hilarité*) laughter; **fou ~** giggling

**ris¹** [Ri] *indic prés et passé simple de* **rire**

**ris²** [Ri] *m* CULIN **~ de veau** calf sweetbread

**risée** [Rize] *f* **être la ~ des voisins** to be the laughing stock of the neighbors

**risque** [Risk] *m* ① (*péril*) risk; **au ~ de déplaire** at the risk of upsetting you; **courir un ~/des ~s** to run a risk/risks ② *pl* (*préjudice possible*) risk ▸ **à mes/tes ~s et périls** at my/your own risk

**risqué(e)** [Riske] *adj* (*hasardeux*) risky

**risquer** [Riske] <1> *vt* ① (*mettre en danger*) to risk ② (*s'exposer à*) **~ le renvoi/la prison** to risk being fired/going to prison; **~ la mort** to risk death; **il ne risque rien** there's no risk ③ (*tenter, hasarder*) to chance; **~ le coup** to chance it ▸ **ça (ne) risque pas!** *inf* not likely; **ça ne risque pas de m'arriver** no fear of that happening to me

**rissoler** [Risɔle] <1> *vt* (*beignets*) to brown; (*pommes de terre*) to sauté

**rituel** [Ritɥɛl] *m* REL, SOCIOL ritual

**rituel(le)** [Ritɥɛl] *adj a.* REL, SOCIOL ritual

**rivage** [Rivaʒ] *m* shore

**rival(e)** [Rival, -o] <-aux> *adj, m(f)* rival

**rivaliser** [Rivalize] <1> *vi* (*soutenir la comparaison*) **~ avec qn** to vie with sb; **~ avec qc** to compare with sth

**rive** [Riv] *f* bank

**Riviera** [Rivjera] *f* **la ~** the Riviera

**rivière** [Rivjɛr] *f* (*cours d'eau*) river

**riz** [Ri] *m* rice; **~ au lait** ≈ rice pudding; **~ complet** brown rice

**R.M.I.** [ɛRɛmi] *m abr de* **revenu mini-**

**mum d'insertion** *basic welfare benefit paid to the jobless*

**RMIste, RMiste** [ɛʀɛmist] *v.* **érémiste**

**R.N.** [ɛʀɛn] *f abr de* **route nationale** ≈ state route

**R.N.I.S.** [ɛʀɛnies] *m abr de* **réseau de numérique à intégration de service** ISDN

**robe** [ʀɔb] *f* (*vêtement féminin*) dress; **se mettre en ~** to put on a dress

**robe de chambre** [ʀɔb də ʃɑ̃bʀ] *f* dressing gown

**robinet** [ʀɔbinɛ] *m* tap

**robot** [ʀɔbo] *m* ❶ (*machine automatique*) robot ❷ (*appareil ménager*) food processor

**robuste** [ʀɔbyst] *adj* (*personne, plante*) hardy; (*appétit*) hearty; (*foi*) robust

**roc** [ʀɔk] *m* (*pierre, personne*) rock
▸ **solide comme un ~** solid as a rock

**rocade** [ʀɔkad] *f* communications line

**roche** [ʀɔʃ] *f* GEO rock

**rocher** [ʀɔʃe] *m* rock

**roder** [ʀɔde] <1> *vt* AUTO, TECH **~ qc** (*moteur, voiture, engrenages*) to break sth in; (*cames, soupapes*) to grind

**rôder** [ʀode] <1> *vi* **~ dans les parages** to wander around

**rogner** [ʀɔɲe] <1> *vi* **~ sur qc** to cut down on sth

**rognon** [ʀɔɲɔ̃] *m* CULIN kidney

**roi** [ʀwa] *m* ❶ (*souverain, a. dans les jeux*) king ❷ (*premier*) **~ du pétrole** oil tycoon; **le ~ des imbéciles** the dumbest of the dumb ▸ **galette** [*o* **gâteau** *Midi*] **des Rois** Twelfth Night cake; **heureux comme un ~** happy as a king

**rôle** [ʀol] *m* ❶ THEAT, CINE role; **le premier ~** the main role; **~ de composition/de figurant** character/extra part ❷ (*fonction*) role ▸ **avoir le beau ~** to have it easy

**roller** [ʀɔlœʀ] *m* Rollerblade®; **faire du ~** to blade

**roller, -euse** [ʀɔlœʀ, -øz] *m, f* (*palineur*) rollerblader

**ROM** [ʀɔm] *f inv abr de* **Read Only Memory** ROM

**romain(e)** [ʀɔmɛ̃, ɛn] *adj* Roman

**roman** [ʀɔmɑ̃] *m* ❶ LIT novel ❷ ARCHIT, ART Romanesque

**roman(e)** [ʀɔmɑ̃, an] *adj* ARCHIT, ART Romanesque

**romanche** [ʀɔmɑ̃ʃ] I. *adj* **langue ~** Romansh II. *m* Romansh; *v.a.* **français**

**romancier, -ière** [ʀɔmɑ̃sje, -jɛʀ] *m, f* novelist

**romand(e)** [ʀɔmɑ̃, ɑ̃d] *adj* **la Suisse ~e** French-speaking Switzerland

**romantique** [ʀɔmɑ̃tik] *adj, mf* romantic

**romarin** [ʀɔmaʀɛ̃] *m* rosemary

**rompre** [ʀɔ̃pʀ] *irr* I. *vt* (*interrompre*) **~ qc** (*fiançailles, pourparlers, relations*) to break sth off II. *vi* (*se séparer*) **~ avec qn** to break it off with sb; **~ avec une tradition** to break with a tradition

**ronce** [ʀɔ̃s] *f pl* (*épineux*) brambles

**rond** [ʀɔ̃] I. *m* ❶ (*cercle*) ring ❷ (*trace ronde*) ring ❸ *inf* (*argent*) **n'avoir pas un ~** not to have a cent II. *adv* **ne pas tourner ~** *inf* (*personne*) to have sth the matter

**rond(e)** [ʀɔ̃, ʀɔ̃d] *adj* ❶ (*circulaire*) round ❷ (*rebondi*) round; (*personne*) plump ❸ (*net: chiffre, compte*) round ❹ *inf* (*ivre*) smashed

**rondelle** [ʀɔ̃dɛl] *f* CULIN slice

**rond-point** [ʀɔ̃pwɛ̃] <ronds-points> *m* traffic circle

**ronfler** [ʀɔ̃fle] <1> *vi* ❶ (*respirer: personne*) to snore ❷ *inf* (*dormir*) to snore away

**ronger** [ʀɔ̃ʒe] <2a> I. *vt* ❶ (*grignoter*) to gnaw ❷ (*miner*) to sap; **être rongé par la maladie** to be ravaged by illness; **être rongé de remords** to suffer the pangs of remorse II. *vpr* (*se grignoter*) **se ~ les ongles** to bite one's nails

**ronronner** [ʀɔ̃ʀɔne] <1> *vi* (*chat*) to purr

**rosbif** [ʀɔzbif] *m* CULIN roast beef

**rose**[1] [ʀoz] *f* BOT rose ▸ **envoyer qn sur les ~s** *inf* to send sb packing

**rose**[2] [ʀoz] I. *adj* ❶ (*rouge pâle*) pink ❷ (*érotique: messagerie*) sex II. *m* pink

R

▶**voir** la **vie/tout** en ~ to see life/things through rose-tinted glasses

**rosé** [ʀoze] *m* (*vin*) rosé (wine)

**rosé(e)** [ʀoze] *adj* rosé

**roseau** [ʀozo] <x> *m* reed

**rosée** [ʀoze] *f* dew

**rossignol** [ʀɔsiɲɔl] *m* ❶ (*oiseau*) nightingale ❷ *inf* COM piece of junk ❸ (*passepartout*) skeleton key

**rotation** [ʀɔtasjɔ̃] *f* ❶ (*mouvement*) rotation ❷ AVIAT, NAUT roundtrip

**roter** [ʀɔte] <1> *vi inf* to burp

**rôti** [ʀoti] *m* roast; ~ **de bœuf/porc/veau** roast beef/pork/veal

**rôtir** [ʀotiʀ, ʀɔtiʀ] <8> I. *vt a. inf* CULIN (*brûler*) to roast II. *vi* ❶ CULIN to roast; **faire** ~ **qc** to roast sth ❷ *inf* (*être exposé au soleil*) to fry in the sun

**rotule** [ʀɔtyl] *f* ANAT kneecap

**roucouler** [ʀukule] <1> I. *vi* ❶ ZOOL to coo ❷ *iron* (*tenir des propos tendres*) to bill and coo II. *vt iron* to murmur

**roue** [ʀu] *f* ❶ (*partie d'un véhicule*) wheel; ~ **arrière/avant** rear/front wheel; ~ **de secours** AUTO spare tire ❷ TECH wheel ▶ **être la cinquième** ~ **du** carrosse to be a fifth wheel

**rouge** [ʀuʒ] I. *adj* ❶ (*de couleur rouge*) red; **poisson** ~ goldfish ❷ (*congestionné*) red; ~ **de colère** red with anger ❸ (*incandescent*) red (hot) ❹ POL red ❺ (*délicat*) **journée classée** ~ **pour le trafic routier** peak traffic day II. *m* ❶ (*couleur*) red; **le feu est au** ~ the light has turned red ❷ *inf* (*vin*) red (wine); **un verre de** ~ a glass of red ❸ (*fard*) rouge; ~ **à lèvres** lipstick III. *adv* **voir** ~ to see red

**rougeole** [ʀuʒɔl] *f* measles

**rougir** [ʀuʒiʀ] <8> *vi* ❶ (*exprimer une émotion: personne*) to blush; ~ **de confusion/plaisir** to blush with embarrassment/pleasure; ~ **de colère** to get red with anger ❷ (*avoir honte*) **faire** ~ **qn** to make sb ashamed ❸ (*devenir rouge*) to go red

**rouille** [ʀuj] *f* rust

**rouillé(e)** [ʀuje] *adj* ❶ (*couvert de rouille*) rusty ❷ (*sclérosé*) rusty; (*muscles*) stiff

**rouiller** [ʀuje] <1> *vi* (*se couvrir de rouille*) to rust

**roulant(e)** [ʀulɑ̃, ɑ̃t] *adj* ❶ (*sur roues*) **fauteuil** ~ wheelchair ❷ CHEMDFER **personnel** ~ train crews *pl* ❸ (*mobile*) moving; **escalier** ~ escalator

**roulé(e)** [ʀule] *adj* **col** ~ polo neck ▶ **bien** ~ *inf* with a good figure

**rouler** [ʀule] <1> I. *vt* ❶ (*faire avancer*) to roll; (*brouette, poussette*) to push ❷ (*enrouler, enrober*) to roll; ~ **qc dans la farine** to roll sth in flour ❸ *inf* (*tromper*) to trick; **se faire** ~ **par qn** to get conned by sb ❹ (*faire tourner une partie du corps: épaules*) to sway; (*hanches*) to swing II. *vi* ❶ (*se déplacer sur roues: objet*) to roll; (*voiture*) to go; (*conducteur*) to drive; **on roulait vite** we were going fast; ~ **en Mercedes** to drive a Mercedes ❷ (*tourner sur soi*) to roll ▶ **ça roule** *inf* everything's fine! III. *vpr* (*se vautrer*) **se** ~ **par terre/dans l'herbe** to roll on the ground/in the grass

**roulette** [ʀulɛt] *f* ❶ (*petite roue*) wheel; **patins à** ~**s** roller skates ❷ (*jeu*) roulette

**roussi** [ʀusi] *m* **ça sent le** ~ (*sentir le brûlé*) there's a smell of burning; (*être suspect*) it smells fishy

**routard(e)** [ʀutaʀ, aʀd] *m(f)* backpacker

**route** [ʀut] *f* ❶ (*voie*) road; **la** ~ **de Paris** the Paris road; ~ **nationale/départementale** main/secondary highway ❷ (*voyage*) travel; **trois heures de** ~ (*en voiture*) three hours' driving; (*à pied*) three hours' walk; **être en** ~ **pour Paris** to be on the way to Paris; **bonne** ~! drive safely! ❸ (*itinéraire, chemin*) way; NAUT, AVIAT path; **demander sa** ~ to ask one's way ▶ **faire fausse** ~ to go the wrong way; (*se tromper*) to be on the wrong track; **faire de la** ~ to be out on the road a lot; **mettre qc en** ~ to get sth started; **en** ~! off we go!

**routier, -ière** [ʀutje, -jɛʀ] I. *adj* (*relatif à*

*la route*) road; **prévention routière** traffic safety **II.** *m, f* (*camionneur*) trucker

**routine** [ʀutin] *f* a. INFORM routine

**roux** [ʀu] *m* ➊ (*couleur*) reddish brown ➋ CULIN roux

**roux, rousse** [ʀu, ʀus] **I.** *adj* (*personne*) redheaded; (*cheveux*) red; (*barbe, feuillage*) reddish; (*pelage, robe de cheval*) chestnut **II.** *m, f* (*personne*) redhead

**royaume** [ʀwajom] *m* (*monarchie*) kingdom

**Royaume-Uni** [ʀwajomyni] *m* **le ~** the United Kingdom

**ruban** [ʀybã] *m* ➊ (*bande de tissu*) ribbon ➋ (*autres matériaux*) tape; **~ magnétique** *a.* INFORM magnetic tape; **~ adhésif** adhesive tape

**rubis** [ʀybi] *m* (*pierre précieuse*) ruby

**rubrique** [ʀybʀik] *f* ➊ PRESSE (*section*) page(s); (*article*) column; **~ littéraire/ sportive** the book/sports page; **~ des spectacles** the entertainment section ➋ (*titre, catégorie*) heading

**ruche** [ʀyʃ] *f* hive

**rude** [ʀyd] *adj* ➊ (*pénible: climat, montée*) hard ➋ (*rugueux: peau, surface, étoffe*) rough ➌ (*fruste: personne*) rough; (*manières*) rough and ready; (*traits*) rugged ➍ *antéposé* (*redoutable: gaillard*) hearty ➎ *antéposé, inf* (*sacré: appétit*) hearty

**rudement** [ʀydmã] *adv inf* (*sacrément*) awfully; **avoir ~ peur** to have the scare of one's life

**rudimentaire** [ʀydimãtɛʀ] *adj* (*sommaire: connaissances, installation*) basic

**rue** [ʀy] *f* ➊ (*artère*) street; **~ commerçante/à sens unique** shopping/one-way street; **~ piétonne** pedestrians only street; **dans la ~** in the street; **traîner dans les ~s** to hang around in the streets ➋ (*ensemble des habitants*) **toute la ~ la connaît** the whole street

knows her ▶ **courir les ~s** (*personne*) to wander through the streets; (*chose*) to be perfectly ordinary

**ruelle** [ʀyɛl] *f* lane

**rugby** [ʀygbi] *m* rugby

**rugueux, -euse** [ʀygø, -øz] *adj* rough

**ruine** [ʀɥin] *f* ➊ *pl* (*décombres*) ruins ➋ (*édifice délabré*) ruin ➌ (*personne*) wreck ➍ (*destruction*) **en ~(s)** in ruins; **tomber en ~(s)** to go to ruin ➎ (*perte de biens*) ruin

**ruiner** [ʀɥine] <1> **I.** *vt* ➊ (*dépouiller de sa richesse*) to ruin ➋ (*détruire*) to ruin; **~ tous les espoirs de qn** to dash all sb's hopes ➌ (*coûter cher*) **ça (ne) va pas te ~** *inf* it won't ruin you **II.** *vpr* **se ~ pour qn** to bankrupt oneself for sb

**ruisseau** [ʀɥiso] <x> *m* stream

**rumeur** [ʀymœʀ] *f* (*bruit qui court*) rumor; **faire courir une ~** to spread a rumor

**ruminer** [ʀymine] <1> **I.** *vt* ➊ (*ressasser*) to ponder ➋ ZOOL to ruminate **II.** *vi* to chew the cud

**rupture** [ʀyptyʀ] *f* ➊ (*cassure*) break ➋ (*déchirure: d'une corde*) breaking ➌ (*annulation: de fiançailles*) breaking off; **~ de contrat/traité** breach of contract/a treaty ➍ (*séparation*) breakup

**ruse** [ʀyz] *f* (*subterfuge*) ruse

**rusé(e)** [ʀyze] **I.** *adj* crafty **II.** *m(f)* crafty individual

**ruser** [ʀyze] <1> *vi* to use trickery

**russe** [ʀys] *adj, m* Russian; *v.a.* **français**

**Russe** [ʀys] *mf* Russian

**Russie** [ʀysi] *f* **la ~** Russia

**rustique** [ʀystik] *adj* (*mobilier, objets, outils*) rustic; (*personne, vie, coutumes*) country; (*arbre, plante*) hardy

**rythme** [ʀitm] *m* ➊ MUS rhythm ➋ (*allure, cadence*) rate; **ne pas pouvoir suivre le ~** not to be able to keep up ➌ (*mouvement régulier*) **~ cardiaque** cardiac rate

**R**

# Ss

**S, s** [ɛs] *m inv* S, s; **~ comme Suzanne** (*au téléphone*) s as in Sierra

**s** *f inv abr de* **seconde** s

**S** *abr de* **sud**

**s'** *v.* **se, si**

**sa** [sa, se] <ses> *dét poss* (*d'un homme*) his; (*d'une femme*) her; (*d'une chose, d'un animal*) its; *v.a.* **ma**

**sabbat** [saba] *m* REL Sabbath

**sabbatique** [sabatik] *adj* sabbatical

**sable** [sabl] **I.** *m* sand; **~s mouvants** quicksand **II.** *adj inv* sandy

**sablé(e)** [sable] *adj* CULIN **gâteau ~** ≈ shortbread cookie; **pâte ~e** sugar dough

**sabler** [sable] <1> *vt* (*couvrir de sable*) to sand

**sabot** [sabo] *m* ① (*chaussure*) clog ② ZOOL hoof

**sabotage** [sabotaʒ] *m* sabotage

**saboter** [sabɔte] <1> *vt* ① (*détruire volontairement*) *a. fig* to sabotage ② (*bâcler*) to botch

**sabrer** [sabʀe] <1> *vt* ① (*biffer*) to cross out ② (*raccourcir*) to hack at ③ (*ouvrir*) **~ le champagne** to open the champagne, (traditionally by removing the cork with a blow from a saber)

**sac¹** [sak] **I.** *m* ① bag; **~ congélation** freezer bag; **~ de couchage** sleeping bag; **~ à main** purse; **~ à provisions** shopping bag; **~ de plage/sport/voyage** beach/sport/travel bag; **~ à dos** backpack ② *inf* HIST (*dix francs ou mille anciens francs*) ten francs ▶ **l'affaire est/c'est dans le ~** – *inf* the thing's/it's in the bag **II.** *app inv* (*robe*) dress

**sac²** [sak] *m* (*pillage*) sack; **mettre à ~** to sack

**saccade** [sakad] *f* jolt

**saccager** [sakaʒe] <2a> *vt* (*dévaster*) to wreck; (*récolte*) to destroy

**sachet** [saʃɛ] *m* bag; (*petit emballage fermé*) sachet

**sacoche** [sakɔʃ] *f* ① (*sac*) bag; **~ de cycliste** saddlebag ② *Belgique* (*sac à main*) purse

**sac-poubelle** [sakpubɛl] <sacs-poubelles> *m* garbage bag

**sacquer** [sake] <1> *vt inf* ① (*renvoyer*) to fire; **se faire ~** to get fired ② (*noter sévèrement*) **~ qn** to give sb a lousy grade; **se faire ~** to get a lousy grade ③ (*détester*) **je ne peux pas la ~** I can't stand (the sight of) her

**sacre** [sakʀ] *m* ① (*d'un souverain, évêque*) consecration ② *Québec* (*jurement, formule de juron*) swearword

**sacré** [sakʀe] *m* sacred

**sacré(e)** [sakʀe] *adj* ① REL sacred; (*édifice*) holy ② *fig* (*horreur, terreur*) holy ③ (*inviolable: droits, lois*) sacred ④ *antéposé, inf* (*satané*) damned; (*farceur, gaillard, talent*) real; **avoir un ~ toupet** to have one hell of a nerve

**Sacré-Cœur** [sakʀekœʀ] *m sans pl* Sacred Heart

**sacrement** [sakʀəmɑ̃] *m* sacrament; **derniers ~s** last rites

**sacrer** [sakʀe] <1> *vt* ① (*introniser*) to consecrate ② (*déclarer*) **être sacré le meilleur roman de l'année** to be declared the best novel of the year

**sacrifice** [sakʀifis] *m* sacrifice; **faire le ~ de qc pour qc** to sacrifice sth for sth

**sacrifier** [sakʀifje] <1> **I.** *vt* ① (*renoncer à*) **~ qc pour** [*o* **à**] **qc** to sacrifice sth for sth ② (*négliger: personnage, rôle*) to neglect ③ COM (*marchandises*) to give away; (*prix*) to slash ④ REL to sacrifice **II.** *vpr* **se ~ pour ses enfants** to sacrifice oneself for one's children

**sadique** [sadik] **I.** *adj* sadistic **II.** *mf* sadist

**safari** [safaʀi] *m* safari

**safran** [safʀɑ̃] *m* CULIN, BOT saffron

**sage** [saʒ] **I.** *adj* ① (*avisé: conseil, personne*) wise ② (*docile: écolier, enfant*) well-behaved ③ (*décent, modéré: goût, vêtement*) restrained **II.** *m* wise man

**sage-femme** [saʒfam] <sages-femmes> *f* midwife

**sagement** [saʒmɑ̃] *adv* ① (*raisonnablement*) wisely ② (*modérément: user*) wisely ③ (*docilement*) quietly

**sagesse** [saʒɛs] *f* wisdom; **agir avec ~** to act wisely; **avoir la ~ de** +*infin* to have the good sense to +*infin*

**Sagittaire** [saʒitɛʀ] *m* Sagittarius; *v.a.* **Balance**

**Sahara** [saaʀa] *m* **le ~** the Sahara

**saharienne** [saaʀjɛn] *f* safari jacket

**saignant(e)** [sɛɲɑ̃, ɑ̃t] *adj* (*rouge: bifteck, viande*) rare

**saignement** [sɛɲmɑ̃] *m* bleeding

**saigner** [seɲe] <1> **I.** *vi* to bleed; **~ du nez** to have a nosebleed ▸ **ça va ~!** the fur will fly! **II.** *vt* (*tuer: animal*) to kill; (*personne*) to bleed

**sain(e)** [sɛ̃, sɛn] *adj* ① (*affaire, gestion*) healthy; (*constitution, politique, lectures*) sound ② (*non abîmé*) sound ▸ **~ et sauf** safe and sound

**saint(e)** [sɛ̃, sɛ̃t] **I.** *adj* REL holy; **jeudi ~** Maundy Thursday; **vendredi ~** Good Friday **II.** *m(f)* REL saint; **~ patron** patron saint; **le ~ des saints** the Holy of Holies

**Saint-Esprit** [sɛ̃tɛspʀi] *m sans pl* **le ~** the Holy Spirit

**Saint-Jean** [sɛ̃ʒɑ̃] *f sans pl* **la ~** Midsummer Day

**Saint-Père** [sɛ̃pɛʀ] <Saints-Pères> *m* Holy Father

**Saint-Sylvestre** [sɛ̃silvɛstʀ] *f sans pl* New Year's Eve

**saisie** [sezi] *f* ① JUR seizure; **~ mobilière** distress ② (*confiscation*) seizure ③ INFORM data entry; (*chez l'imprimeur*) keyboarding; **~ de données** data input

**saisir** [seziʀ] <8> **I.** *vt* ① (*prendre*) **~ qn par les épaules** to grab sb by the shoulders; **~ qn à bras le corps** to seize sb bodily ② (*attraper: ballon, corde*) to catch ③ (*mettre à profit: chance*) to grab; (*occasion*) to seize ④ (*comprendre*) to catch ⑤ CULIN (*viande*) to sear

⑥ (*confisquer*) to seize ⑦ JUR (*commission*) to submit a case to ⑧ INFORM to input **II.** *vpr* **se ~ de qc** to seize sth

**saison** [sɛzɔ̃] *f* season; **fruits de ~** fruit in season; **~ des amours** mating season; **en/hors ~** in/out of season

**saisonnier, -ière** [sɛzɔnje, -jɛʀ] **I.** *adj* (*propre à la saison, limité à la saison*) seasonal **II.** *m, f* seasonal worker

**salade** [salad] *f* ① BOT lettuce; CULIN salad ② *inf* (*confusion*) muddle ③ *pl, inf* (*mensonges*) fairy tales

**saladier** [saladje] *m* salad bowl

**salaire** [salɛʀ] *m* ① (*rémunération*) salary; (*d'un ouvrier*) pay ② (*récompense*) reward

**salami** [salami] *m* salami

**salarié(e)** [salaʀje] **I.** *adj* (*travail*) paid; (*personne*) salaried **II.** *m(f)* salaried worker

**salaud** [salo] **I.** *adj inf* **être ~** to be a bastard **II.** *m inf* bastard

**sale** [sal] **I.** *adj* ① (*opp: propre*) dirty ② *antéposé, inf* (*vilain, mauvais*) low; (*type, temps*) lousy; (*coup*) dirty; **il a une ~ gueule** (*il est malade*) he looks awful; (*il est méchant*) he looks nasty **II.** *m inf* **être au ~** to be in the wash

**salé** [sale] **I.** *m petit ~** salt pork **II.** *adv* **manger ~** to eat salty food

**salé(e)** [sale] *adj* ① (*contenant du sel: beurre, cacahuètes*) salted; (*eau*) salt; **être trop ~** (*soupe*) to be too salty ② (*opp: sucré*) savory ③ *inf* (*corsé: histoire*) juicy

**saler** [sale] <1> **I.** *vi* ① CULIN to add salt ② TECH to salt the roads **II.** *vt* ① CULIN to salt ② TECH (*route*) to salt ③ *inf* (*corser*) **~ l'addition** to bump up the bill

**saleté** [salte] *f* ① (*malpropreté*) dirtiness ② (*chose sale*) dirt; **faire des ~s partout** to make a mess everywhere ③ *sans pl* (*crasse*) filth ④ *inf* (*objet sans valeur*) piece of junk ⑤ *inf* (*maladie*) nasty bug ⑥ (*obscénité*) filthy name ▸ **faire des ~s** (*animal*) to mess; **~ d'ordinateur/de Maurice!** *inf* damn computer/Maurice!

**salir** [saliʀ] <8> **I.** *vt* **~ qc** to make sth

dirty **II.** *vpr* se ~ (*se souiller, devenir sale*) to get dirty; **se ~ les mains** to get one's hands dirty

**salive** [saliv] *f* saliva ▸ **avaler sa** ~ to keep one's mouth shut

**salle** [sal] *f* ❶ (*pièce*) room; ~ **à manger/de séjour** dining/living room; ~ **d'attente/de jeux** waiting/game room; ~ **de bains** bathroom; ~ **de cinéma** movie theater; ~ **de classe** classroom; ~ **des fêtes** community center; **faire du sport en** ~ to play indoor sports ❷ (*cinéma*) movie theater ❸ (*spectateurs*) audience

**salon** [salɔ̃] *m* ❶ (*salle de séjour*) living room ❷ (*mobilier*) living-room suite; ~ **de jardin** set of garden furniture ❸ (*salle d'hôtel pour les clients*) lounge ❹ (*salle d'hôtel pour des conférences*) function room ❺ (*commerce*) ~ **de coiffure** hairdresser's; ~ **de thé** tearoom

**salope** [salɔp] *f* ❶ *vulg* (*débauchée*) slut ❷ *inf* (*garce*) bitch

**saloper** [salɔpe] <1> *vt inf* ❶ (*bâcler*) to botch ❷ (*salir*) to mess up

**saloperie** [salɔpri] *f inf* ❶ (*objet sans valeur*) piece of crap ❷ *gén pl* (*saletés*) dirt ❸ (*mauvaise nourriture*) garbage ❹ (*maladie*) nasty bug ❺ (*méchanceté*) dirty trick ❻ (*obscénité*) filthy remark ▸ **c'est de la** ~ it's garbage; ~ **d'ordinateur/de bagnole** crappy computer/car

**salopette** [salɔpɛt] *f* (pair of) overalls

**saluer** [salɥe] <1> **I.** *vt* ❶ (*dire bonjour*) ~ **qn** to say hello to sb; ~ **qn de la main** to wave hello to sb ❷ (*dire au revoir*) ~ **qn** to say goodbye to sb ❸ (*rendre hommage*) to salute ❹ (*accueillir*) to welcome ❺ MIL ~ **un supérieur/le drapeau** to salute a superior/the flag **II.** *vi* ❶ THEAT to bow ❷ MIL to salute

**salut¹** [saly] **I.** *m* ❶ (*salutation*) greeting; **faire un** ~ **de la main** to wave a greeting ❷ MIL ~ **au drapeau** salute to one's flag **II.** *interj* ❶ *inf* (*bonjour*) ~**!** hi! ❷ *inf* (*au revoir*) ~**!** ciao!

**salut²** [saly] *m* ❶ (*sauvegarde*) safety ❷ REL salvation

**salutaire** [salytɛʀ] *adj* salutary; (*décision*) helpful; ~ **à qn/qc** (*avantageux*) beneficial to sb/sth; (*secourable*) helpful to sb/sth

**salutations** [salytasjɔ̃] *fpl form* salutations; **je vous prie/nous vous prions d'agréer, Madame/Monsieur, mes/nos ~s distinguées** sincerely yours

**samedi** [samdi] *m* Saturday; *v.a.* **dimanche**

**SAMU** [samy] *m abr de* **Service d'aide médicale d'urgence** ambulance service; (*médecin*) emergency doctor

**sanction** [sɑ̃ksjɔ̃] *f* ❶ (*punition*) penalty; ECOLE punishment ❷ ECON, POL sanction

**sanctionner** [sɑ̃ksjɔne] <1> **I.** *vt* (*punir*) to punish; ECON to levy sanctions on **II.** *vi* to punish

**sandwich** [sɑ̃dwitʃ] <(e)s> *m* CULIN sandwich

**sang** [sɑ̃] *m* ❶ ANAT blood; **être en** ~ to be covered in blood ❷ (*race*) blood ▸ **se faire du mauvais** ~ to fret

**sang-froid** [sɑ̃fʀwa] *m sans pl* ❶ (*maîtrise de soi*) sang-froid; **garder/perdre son** ~ to keep/to lose one's cool ❷ (*froideur*) cool; **agir avec** ~ to act coolly

**sanglant(e)** [sɑ̃glɑ̃, ɑ̃t] *adj* ❶ (*saignant*) bleeding ❷ (*violent*) cruel; (*rencontre, match*) bloody

**sanglier** [sɑ̃glije] *m* wild boar

**sangloter** [sɑ̃glɔte] <1> *vi* to sob

**sangsue** [sɑ̃sy] *f* leech

**sanguin(e)** [sɑ̃gɛ̃, in] *adj* ❶ ANAT plasma ~ blood plasma ❷ (*coloré*) red; **orange** ~**e** blood orange ❸ (*impulsif*) impulsive

**sanisette®** [sanizɛt] *f* coin operated toilet

**sanitaire** [sanitɛʀ] **I.** *adj* health; (*mesure*) sanitary **II.** *m gén pl* bathroom installations

**sans** [sɑ̃] **I.** *prep* without; ~ **arrêt** continually; ~ **but** aimless; **partir** ~ **fermer la porte/**~ **que tu le saches** to leave without closing the door/without you knowing ▸ ~ **plus** and that's all; ~ **quoi** otherwise **II.** *adv inf* without; **il va fal-**

**loir faire ~** we'll have to manage without

**sans-abri** [sɑ̃zabʀi] *m inv* homeless person

**sans-emploi** [sɑ̃zɑ̃plwa] *m inv* unemployed person

**sans-fil** [sɑ̃fil] *m inv* cordless phone

**sans-papiers** [sɑ̃papje] *mf inv:* illegal immigrant

**santé** [sɑ̃te] *f* ❶ (*opp: malade*) health; **être bon pour la ~** to be healthy; **être en bonne/mauvaise ~** to be in good/poor health ❷ ADMIN **la ~ publique** public health ▸ **à la ~ de qn** to sb's good health; **à ta ~!** to good health!

**santiag** [sɑ̃tjag] *f inv* cowboy boot

**saoudien(ne)** [saudjɛ̃, jɛn] *adj* Saudi Arabian

**saoul(e)** [su, sul] *adj v.* **soûl**

**saouler** [sule] <1> *vt v.* **soûler**

**saper** [sape] <1> *vpr inf* **se ~** to get dressed up

**sapeur-pompier** [sapœʀpɔ̃pje] <sapeurs-pompiers> *m* firefighter; **femme ~** firewoman

**sapin** [sapɛ̃] *m* fir tree; **~ de Noël** Christmas tree

**sarcasme** [saʀkasm] *m* sarcasm; (*remarque*) sarcastic remark

**sardine** [saʀdin] *f* sardine

**S.A.R.L.** [ɛsɑɛʀɛl] *f abr de* **société à responsabilité limitée** limited liability company

**sarrasin** [saʀazɛ̃] *m* buckwheat

**satanique** [satanik] *adj a.* REL satanic

**satellite** [satelit] *m* satellite

**satin** [satɛ̃] *m* satin

**satiné** [satine] *m* ❶ (*aspect luisant*) sheen ❷ (*douceur: de la peau*) silky-smoothness

**satiné(e)** [satine] *adj* satin-like

**satire** [satiʀ] *f* satire; **faire la ~ de qn/qc** (*pièce, texte*) to satirize sb/sth

**satisfaction** [satisfaksjɔ̃] *f* satisfaction ▸ **donner ~ à qn** to give sb satisfaction; **obtenir ~** to get satisfaction

**satisfaire** [satisfɛʀ] *irr* **I.** *vt* ❶ (*contenter: personne*) to satisfy ❷ (*assouvir: soif*) to slake; (*faim*) to satisfy ❸ (*donner droit à*) **~ une réclamation** to uphold a complaint **II.** *vi* **~ à une obligation** to fulfill an obligation **III.** *vpr* (*se contenter*) **se ~ de qc** to be satisfied with sth

**satisfait(e)** [satisfɛ, ɛt] *adj* **être ~ de qn/qc** to be satisfied with sb/sth

**saturer** [satyʀe] <1> *vt* ❶ (*soûler*) to swamp ❷ (*surcharger*) to overload

**Saturne** [satyʀn] *f* Saturn

**sauce** [sos] *f* CULIN sauce; **~ vinaigrette** salad dressing; **viande en ~** meat in a sauce

**saucée** [sose] *f inf* downpour

**saucisse** [sosis] *f* CULIN sausage

**saucisson** [sosisɔ̃] *m* CULIN sausage

**sauf** [sof] *prep* ❶ (*à l'exception de*) except; **~ que tu es trop jeune** except that you're too young ❷ (*à moins de*) **~ erreur de ma part** unless I am mistaken; **~ avis contraire** unless advised otherwise

**saumon** [somɔ̃] **I.** *m* salmon **II.** *adj inv* salmon **III.** *app* **rose ~** salmon pink

**saumure** [somyʀ] *f* brine

**sauna** [sona] *m* sauna

**saupoudrer** [sopudʀe] <1> *vt* CULIN **~ qc de sucre/sel** to sprinkle sth with sugar/salt; **~ qc de farine** to dust sth with flour

**saut** [so] *m* ❶ (*bond*) jump ❷ SPORT **~ à la perche** pole vaulting; **~ à la corde** jump roping; **~ en longueur** long jump; **~ de haies** hurdling; **~ d'obstacles** obstacle race ❸ INFORM break ▸ **au ~ du lit** on getting up, **faire un ~ chez qn** *inf* to drop [*o pop*] around to see sb

**sauté** [sote] *m* **~ de veau** sauté of veal

**sauter** [sote] <1> **I.** *vi* ❶ (*bondir*) to jump; (*sautiller*) to hop; (*sauter vers le haut*) to jump up; **~ du lit** to leap out of bed; **~ par la fenêtre/d'un train** to jump out of the window/a train ❷ SPORT to jump; **~ en parachute** to do a parachute jump; **~ à la corde** to jump rope ❸ (*se précipiter*) **~ sur l'occasion** to jump at the opportunity ❹ (*passer brusquement*) **~ d'un sujet à l'autre** to leap from one subject to another; **un**

**S**

**élève qui saute du CP en CE2** a student who jumps from first to third grade ❺(*jaillir: bouchon*) to pop (out); (*bouton*) to fly off; (*chaîne*) to snap ❻(*exploser: bâtiment, pont, bombe*) to blow up; **faire ~ qn/qc** to blow sb/sth up ❼ELEC (*fusibles, plombs*) to blow ❽*inf* (*ne pas avoir lieu: classe, cours*) to cancel ❾CULIN **faire ~ qc** to sauté sth; **des pommes de terre sautées** sautéed potatoes ❿(*clignoter: image*) to flicker ⓫(*annuler*) **faire ~ une contravention** to cancel a fine II. *vt* ❶(*franchir*) **~ un fossé/mur** to leap over a ditch/wall ❷(*omettre: étape, page, classe, repas*) to skip; (*mot*) to leave out ❸*inf* (*avoir des relations sexuelles*) to screw

**sauterelle** [sotʀɛl] *f* grasshopper

**sauteuse** [sotøz] *f* CULIN sauté pan

**sautiller** [sotije] <1> *vi* to hop

**sauvage** [sovaʒ] I. *adj* ❶(*hors norme: camping, vente*) unofficial; (*grève*) wildcat; (*concurrence*) unfair ❷(*opp: domestique*) wild ❸(*à l'état de nature: côte, lieu, pays*) wild ❹(*violent*) violent; (*haine, horde*) savage; (*cris*) wild II. *mf* ❶(*solitaire*) recluse ❷(*brute, indigène*) savage ▶ **comme un ~** *Québec* (*impoliment*) like a little savage

**sauvagement** [sovaʒmɑ̃] *adv* savagely; (*frapper, traiter*) brutally

**sauvegarde** [sovgaʀd] *f* ❶(*protection*) protection ❷INFORM backup; **faire la ~ d'un fichier** to save a file

**sauvegarder** [sovgaʀde] <1> *vt* ❶(*protéger*) to protect; (*relations, image de marque*) to maintain ❷INFORM to save

**sauver** [sove] <1> I. *vt* (*porter secours, sauvegarder*) *a.* INFORM to save; **~ qn/qc de qc** to save sb/sth from sth II. *vi* to save ▶ **sauve qui peut!** run for your life! III. *vpr* ❶(*s'enfuir*) **se ~** to escape ❷*inf* (*s'en aller*) **se ~** to dash

**sauvetage** [sov(ə)taʒ] *m* rescue

**sauveteur, -euse** [sov(ə)tœʀ, -øz] *m, f* rescuer

**sauveur, -euse** [sovœʀ, -øz] I. *adj* saving II. *m, f a.* REL savior

**savant(e)** [savɑ̃, ɑ̃t] I. *adj* ❶(*érudit*) learned ❷*antéposé, péj* (*discussion*) highbrow; (*calcul*) complex ❸(*habile*) skillful ❹(*dressé*) performing II. *m(f)* ❶(*lettré*) scholar ❷(*scientifique*) scientist

**saveur** [savœʀ] *f* ❶(*goût*) flavor; **sans ~** tasteless ❷(*attrait: d'une nouveauté, d'un interdit*) lure

**Savoie** [savwa] *f* **la ~** Savoy

**savoir** [savwaʀ] *irr* I. *vt* ❶(*être au courant, connaître, être conscient*) to know; **~ qc de** [*o* **sur**] **qn/qc** to know sth about sb/sth; **faire ~ à qn que tout va bien** to let sb know that everything is fine ❷(*être capable de*) **~ attendre/dire non** to be able to wait/say no ▶**~ y faire** *inf* to know how to handle things; **je ne veux rien ~** I just don't want to know; **à ~** that is; **on ne sait jamais** you never know; **n'en rien ~** to know nothing II. *vi* to know ▶**pas que je sache** not that I know; **pour autant que je sache!** for all I know III. *vpr* ❶(*être connu*) **se ~** to be known ❷(*avoir conscience*) **se ~ en danger/malade** to know that one is in danger/ill IV. *m* knowledge

**savoir-faire** [savwaʀfɛʀ] *m inv* savoir-faire

**savoir-vivre** [savwaʀvivʀ] *m inv* manners *pl*

**savon** [savɔ̃] *m* ❶(*savonnette*) soap ❷*inf* (*réprimande*) **passer un ~ à qn** to rake sb over the coals

**savonner** [savɔne] <1> *vt, vpr* (**se**) **~** to lather (oneself)

**savonnette** [savɔnɛt] *f* bar of soap

**savourer** [savuʀe] <1> *vt, vi* to savor

**saxo** [sakso] I. *m* sax II. *mf* sax player

**saxon** [saksɔ̃] *m* Saxon; *v.a.* **français**

**saxon(ne)** [saksɔ̃, ɔn] *adj* Saxon

**saxophone** [saksɔfɔn] *m* saxophone

**scandale** [skɑ̃dal] *m* ❶(*éclat*) scandal; **presse à ~** tabloids ❷(*indignation*) outrage ❸(*tapage*) disturbance ▶**faire ~** to cause a scandal

**scandaleux, -euse** [skɑ̃dalø, -øz] *adj*

(*honteux*) scandalous; (*prix, propos*) outrageous

**scandaliser** [skãdalize] <1> **I.** *vt* to shock **II.** *vpr* se ~ **de qc** to be shocked at sth

**Scandinavie** [skãdinavi] *f* la ~ Scandinavia

**scanner¹** [skane] <1> *vt* to scan

**scanner²** [skanɛʀ] *m*, **scanneur** [skanœʀ] *m* scanner

**sceau** [so] <x> *m* seal

**sceller** [sele] <1> *vt* ❶ TECH (*crochet*) to fix; (*pierre, barreaux, dalle*) to embed ❷ (*confirmer solennellement, fermer hermétiquement*) to seal; (*engagement*) to confirm ❸ (*authentifier par un sceau*) to seal

**scellés** [sele] *mpl* seals; **mettre les** ~ to fix seals; **sous** ~ under seal

**scénario** [senaʀjo, senaʀi] <s o scénarii> *m* ❶ (*script: d'un film*) screenplay; (*d'une pièce de théâtre*) script; (*d'un roman*) scenario ❷ (*déroulement prévu*) scenario

**scène** [sɛn] *f* ❶ (*spectacle*) scene; ~ **d'amour** love scene ❷ (*querelle*) scene; ~ **de jalousie** fit of jealousy; ~ **de ménage** domestic fight; **faire une** ~ **à qn** to have a big fight with sb ❸ (*estrade*) stage; **mettre une histoire en** ~ to stage a story; **mettre une pièce de théâtre en** ~ to direct a play; **en** ~ **!** on stage! ❹ (*décor, cadre: d'un crime, drame*) scene

**sceptique** [sɛptik] **I.** *adj* skeptical **II.** *mf* skeptic

**schéma** [ʃema] *m* ❶ (*abrégé*) outline ❷ (*dessin*) diagram

**schizophrène** [skizɔfʀɛn] *adj, mf* schizophrenic

**schizophrénie** [skizɔfʀeni] *f* schizophrenia

**scie** [si] *f* saw; ~ **circulaire/à bois** circular/wood saw

**sciemment** [sjamã] *adv* knowingly

**science** [sjãs] *f* ❶ (*domaine scientifique*) science ❷ (*disciplines scolaires*) **les** ~s the sciences; **faculté des** ~s college of science ❸ (*savoir faire*) expertise ❹ (*érudition*) knowledge

**science-fiction** [sjãsfiksjɔ̃] *f inv* science fiction

**scientifique** [sjãtifik] **I.** *adj* scientific **II.** *mf* ❶ (*savant*) scientist ❷ (*élève*) science student

**scier** [sje] <1> *vt* ❶ (*couper*) to saw; (*arbres*) to saw down ❷ *inf* (*estomaquer*) to bore; **être scié** to be bored stiff

**scinder** [sɛ̃de] <1> **I.** *vt* (*parti*) to split; (*question, problème*) to divide; **scindé en deux** split in two **II.** *vpr* se ~ **en qc** to split up into sth

**scintiller** [sɛ̃tije] <1> *vi* to sparkle

**scission** [sisjɔ̃] *f* split; **faire** ~ to split away

**sclérose** [skleʀoz] *f* ❶ (*encroûtement*) ossification ❷ MED sclerosis; ~ **en plaques** multiple sclerosis

**scolaire** [skɔlɛʀ] *adj* ❶ (*relatif à l'école: succès, année*) school; **échec** ~ failure at school ❷ *péj* (*livresque*) starchy

**scolarité** [skɔlaʀite] *f* schooling; (*période*) time at school

**scoliose** [skɔljoz] *f* scoliosis

**scoop** [skup] *m* scoop

**scooter** [skutœʀ, skutɛʀ] *m* scooter; ~ **des mers/des neiges** jet ski/snowmobile

**score** [skɔʀ] *m* score; **mener au** ~ to be ahead

**scorpion** [skɔʀpjɔ̃] *m* ZOOL scorpion

**Scorpion** [skɔʀpjɔ̃] *m* Scorpio; *v.a.* **Balance**

**scotch®** [skɔtʃ] *m sans pl* (*adhésif*) Scotch tape®

**scout(e)** [skut] **I.** *adj* scout **II.** *m(f)* boy scout, girl scout *m, f*

**script** [skʀipt] *m* ❶ CINE, THEAT script ❷ (*écriture*) printing

**scrupule** [skʀypyl] *m souvent pl* (*hésitation*) scruple; **avoir des** ~s **à faire qc** to have scruples about doing sth

**scrutin** [skʀytɛ̃] *m* ballot; ~ **majoritaire** election on majority basis

**sculpter** [skylte] <1> **I.** *vt* to sculpt; (*bois*) to carve **II.** *vi* to sculpt

**sculpteur, -euse** [skyltœʀ, -øz] *m, f* sculptor; **~ sur bois** woodcarver

**sculpture** [skyltyʀ] *f* la **~** sculpture; **la ~ sur bois** woodcarving

**S.D.F.** [ɛsdeɛf] *m, f abr de* **sans domicile fixe** homeless person

**se** [sə] <*devant voyelle ou h muet* s'> *pron pers* ❶ himself/herself; **il/elle ~ regarde dans le miroir** he/she looks at himself/herself in the mirror; **il/elle ~ demande s'il/si elle a raison** he/she asks if he's/she's right ❷ (*l'un/l'autre*) each other; **ils/elles ~ suivent/font confiance** they follow/trust each other ❸ *avec les verbes pronominaux* **ils/elles ~ nettoient** they clean themselves up; **il/elle ~ nettoie les ongles** he/she cleans his/her nails

**séance** [seɑ̃s] *f* ❶ CINE, THEAT showing ❷ (*période*) session; **~ de spiritisme** séance ❸ (*réunion*) meeting; **en ~** in session

**seau** [so] <x> *m* bucket, pail ▸ **il pleut à ~x** *inf* it's pouring down

**sec** [sɛk] **I.** *adv* ❶ (*fort: démarrer*) sharply; (*frapper*) hard ❷ (*abondamment: boire*) heavily ▸ **aussi ~** *inf* (*répondre*) straight off **II.** *m* **étang à ~** dried-up pond; **mettre qc à ~** to drain sth; **mettre qc au ~** to put sth in a dry place ▸ **être à ~** to be flat broke

**sec, sèche** [sɛk, sɛʃ] *adj* ❶ (*opp: humide*) dry ❷ (*déshydraté: figue*) dried; **légumes ~s** pulses; **raisins ~s** raisins ❸ (*opp: gras: bras*) lean; (*peau, cheveu, toux*) dry ❹ (*brusque: rire*) dry; **d'un coup ~** with a snap ❺ (*opp: aimable: refus*) curt; (*réponse, lettre, merci*) terse; (*ton, cœur*) cold ❻ (*pur: whisky, gin*) neat ❼ (*opp: doux: champagne, vin*) dry

**sèche-cheveux** [sɛʃʃəvø] *m inv* hair dryer

**sèche-linge** [sɛʃlɛ̃ʒ] *m inv* clothes dryer

**sécher** [seʃe] <5> **I.** *vt* ❶ (*rendre sec*) to dry ❷ *inf* (*ne pas assister à*) to skip **II.** *vi* ❶ (*devenir sec*) to dry; **mettre le linge à ~** to put the clothes out to dry ❷ (*se déshydrater: bois, plante, terre*) to dry out; (*fleur, fruits*) to dry up ❸ *inf* (*ne pas savoir*) to be stumped **III.** *vpr* **se ~** to dry oneself; **se ~ les mains/les cheveux** to dry one's hands/one's hair

**sécheresse** [seʃʀɛs] *f* dryness; METEO drought

**sèche-serviette** [sɛʃsɛʀvjɛt] <sèche-serviettes> *m inv* heated towel rack

**séchoir** [seʃwaʀ] *m* dryer

**second** [s(ə)gɔ̃] *m* (*dans une charade*) second

**second(e)** [s(ə)gɔ̃, ɔ̃d] *adj antéposé* ❶ (*deuxième, nouveau*) second ❷ (*qui n'a pas la primauté*) second; **au ~ plan** in the background; **de ~ ordre** second-rate; *v.a.* **cinquième**

**secondaire** [s(ə)gɔ̃dɛʀ] **I.** *adj* secondary **II.** *m* ECOLE **le ~** secondary education

**seconde** [s(ə)gɔ̃d] **I.** *adj v.* **second II.** *f* ❶ (*unité de temps*) *a.* MATH, MUS, AUTO second ❷ ECOLE tenth grade ❸ CHEMDFER second class; **billet de ~** second-class ticket

**seconder** [s(ə)gɔ̃de] <1> *vt* **~ qn dans son travail** to aid sb in his/her work; **être secondé par qn** to be helped by sb

**secouer** [s(ə)kwe] <1> **I.** *vt* ❶ (*agiter*) to shake ❷ (*ballotter: explosion, bombardement*) to rock; (*autobus, avion, personne*) to shake ❸ (*traumatiser: émotion*) to shake **II.** *vpr inf* **se ~** ❶ (*s'ébrouer*) to shake oneself ❷ (*réagir*) to get going

**secourir** [s(ə)kuʀiʀ] *vt irr* to help

**secourisme** [s(ə)kuʀism] *m* first aid

**secouriste** [s(ə)kuʀist] *mf* first aid worker

**secours** [s(ə)kuʀ] *m* ❶ (*sauvetage*) help; (*organisme*) aid organization; (*en montagne*) rescue service; **les ~** the rescue services; **donner les premiers ~ aux accidentés** to give first aid to accident victims ❷ (*aide*) help; **appeler qn à son ~** to call sb for help; **porter** [*o* **prêter**] **~ à qn** to help sb; **aller** [*o* **courir**]/**voler au ~ de qn/qc** to fly

to sb's/sth's aid; **sortie de ~** emergency exit; **au ~!** help! ❸ (*subvention*) grant
**secousse** [s(ə)kus] *f* ❶ (*choc*) jolt; **par ~s** bumpily ❷ POL upheaval
**secret** [sǝkʀɛ] *m* ❶ (*cachotterie, mystère*) secret; **garder un ~** to keep a secret; **ne pas avoir de ~ pour qn** to keep no secrets from sb ❷ *sans pl* (*confidentialité*) confidentiality; **garder le ~ sur qc** to maintain silence over sth ▸ **l'astrologie n'a plus de ~ pour elle** astrology holds no secrets for her; **en grand ~** in great secrecy
**secret, -ète** [sǝkʀɛ, -ɛt] *adj* (*caché*) secret; **garder qc ~** to keep sth secret
**secrétaire** [s(ə)kʀetɛʀ] I. *mf* secretary; **~ de direction** personal assistant; **~ de mairie** chief executive; **~ d'État aux Affaires étrangères** Secretary of State II. *m* secretary
**secrétariat** [s(ə)kʀetaʀja] *m* ❶ (*service administratif*) secretariat; **~ général des Nations Unies** general secretariat of the United Nations; **~ d'État** office of the Secretary of State ❷ (*fonction officielle*) post of secretary ❸ (*emploi de secrétaire*) secretarial work ❹ (*bureau*) secretary's office
**secrètement** [sǝkʀɛtmã] *adv* secretly
**secte** [sɛkt] *f* ❶ (*groupe organisé*) sect ❷ *péj* (*clan*) clan
**secteur** [sɛktœʀ] *m* ❶ (*domaine*) a. ECON sector ❷ (*coin*) a. ADMIN, POL, ELEC area; **panne de ~** area power outage
**section** [sɛksjɔ̃] *f* ❶ ADMIN, POL department; (*d'une voie ferrée*) section; (*d'un parcours*) stretch ❷ (*branche*) JUR branch; ECOLE course ❸ MIL section
**sectionner** [sɛksjɔne] <1> I. *vt* ❶ (*couper: artère, fil*) to sever ❷ (*subdiviser: circonscription, groupe*) to divide up II. *vpr* **se ~** (*câble, fil*) to be severed
**sécu** [seky] *f abr de* **Sécurité sociale** social security
**sécuriser** [sekyʀize] <1> *vt* **~ qn** to give sb a feeling of security
**sécurité** [sekyʀite] *f* ❶ (*opp: danger*) safety; (*au moyen de mesures organisées*) security; **règles/conseils de ~**

safety rules/advice; **être en ~** to be safe ❷ (*sentiment*) security; **se sentir en ~** to feel secure ❸ POL, ECON **~ de l'emploi** job security; **~ routière** road safety ▸ **en toute ~** in complete safety
**sédatif** [sedatif] *m* sedative; (*qui calme la douleur*) painkiller
**sédentaire** [sedãtɛʀ] *adj* sedentary
**séducteur, -trice** [sedyktœʀ, -tʀis] I. *adj* seductive II. *m, f* seducer, seductress *m, f*
**séduction** [sedyksjɔ̃] *f* ❶ (*pouvoir de séduire*) seduction; (*par le talent*) charm ❷ (*attrait*) appeal
**séduire** [seduiʀ] *irr* I. *vt* ❶ (*tenter*) to charm ❷ (*plaire à: personne*) to appeal to; **être séduit par une idée** to be won over by an idea II. *vi* to charm
**séduisant(e)** [sedɥizã, ãt] *adj* seductive; (*personne*) charming; (*projet, proposition*) attractive
**segmenter** [sɛgmãte] <1> *vt* (*sujet, surface*) to segment
**seigle** [sɛgl] *m* rye
**sein** [sɛ̃] *m* ANAT breast; **donner le ~ à un enfant** to breastfeed a child
**Seine** [sɛn] *f* **la ~** the Seine
**seize** [sɛz] *adj* sixteen; *v.a.* **cinq**
**seizième** [sɛzjɛm] I. *adj antéposé* sixteenth II. *m* ❶ (*fraction*) sixteenth ❷ SPORT **~ de finale** fourth round before the final of a competition; *v.a.* **cinquième**
**séjour** [seʒuʀ] *m* ❶ (*fait de séjourner*) stay; (*vacances*) vacation; **faire un ~ en Italie** to go to Italy; **mes ~s en Italie** my time in [*o* visits to] Italy ❷ (*salon*) living room
**séjourner** [seʒuʀne] <1> *vi* to stay
**sel** [sɛl] *m* ❶ CULIN, CHIM salt; **~ de cuisine/table** cooking/table salt; **gros ~** rock salt; **les ~s** smelling salts ❷ (*piquant*) spice; (*d'une histoire*) wit
**sélectif, -ive** [selɛktif, -iv] *adj* selective
**sélection** [selɛksjɔ̃] *f* ❶ SPORT, ZOOL, BIO (*fait de choisir, choix*) selection; **faire une ~** to choose ❷ (*choix avec règles et critères*) selection; **test de ~** trial

**S**

**sélectionner** [selɛksjɔne] <1> vt (*choisir*) a. INFORM to select

**self** [sɛlf] m inf self-service restaurant

**self-service** [sɛlfsɛʀvis] <self-services> m ❶ (*magasin*) self-service store ❷ (*restaurant*) self-service restaurant

**selle** [sɛl] f ❶ (*siège*) a. CULIN saddle ❷ pl (*matières fécales*) stool

**selon** [s(ə)lɔ̃] prep ❶ (*conformément à*) ~ **votre volonté** in accordance with your wishes ❷ (*en fonction de, d'après*) ~ **l'humeur/mes moyens** according to one's mood/my means; **c'est** ~ inf it depends; ~ **moi** in my opinion

**semaine** [s(ə)mɛn] f (*sept jours*) week; **à la** ~ weekly; **en** ~ during the week

**sémantique** [semãtik] I. adj semantic II. f semantics + vb sing

**semblable** [sãblabl] I. adj ❶ (*pareil*) similar; **rien de** ~ nothing like it ❷ antéposé (*tel*) such ❸ (*ressemblant*) like; ~ **à qn/qc** like sb/sth II. mf ❶ (*prochain*) fellow being ❷ (*congénère*) **lui et ses** ~**s** him and his kind

**semblant** [sãblã] m **retrouver un** ~ **de calme** to find some sort of calm ▸ **faire** ~ **de dormir** to pretend to be asleep; **elle ne pleure pas: elle fait juste** ~! she's not crying: she's just pretending!

**sembler** [sãble] <1> I. vi ~ **préoccupé** to seem preoccupied; **tu me sembles nerveux** you seem nervous (to me) II. vi impers ❶ (*paraître*) **il semble que ...** it seems that ...; **il semblerait que ...** it would appear that ... ❷ (*avoir l'impression de*) **il me semble bien vous avoir déjà rencontré** I have the feeling I've already met you ❸ (*paraître*) **il me semble, à ce qu'il me semble** it seems to me; **semble-t-il** it seems

**semelle** [s(ə)mɛl] f sole; ~ **intérieure** insole

**semer** [s(ə)me] <4> I. vi to sow II. vt ❶ AGR to sow ❷ (*joncher: confettis, fleurs*) to strew ❸ (*propager: discorde, zizanie*) to sow; (*terreur, panique*) to bring ❹ (*truffer*) **être semé de diffi-**

**cultés** to be strewn with difficulties ❺ (*se débarrasser de*) to get rid of ❻ inf (*égarer*) to lose

**semestriel(le)** [s(ə)mɛstʀijɛl] adj semi--annual

**séminaire** [seminɛʀ] m seminary

**semoule** [s(ə)mul] I. f CULIN semolina II. app (*sucre*) caster

**sénat** [sena] m POL, HIST senate

**sénateur, -trice** [senatœʀ, -tʀis] m, f senator

**Sénégal** [senegal] m **le** ~ Senegal

**sénégalais(e)** [senegalɛ, ɛz] adj Senegalese

**sénile** [senil] adj senile

**senior** [senjɔʀ] I. adj (*équipe*) senior II. mf ❶ (*sportif plus âgé*) senior ❷ (*vieillard*) **les** ~**s** senior citizens

**sens**¹ [sãs] m (*signification*) meaning; **au** ~ **large/figuré** in a broad/figurative sense; **n'avoir aucun** ~ to have no meaning

**sens**² [sãs] m ❶ (*direction*) direction; **dans le** ~ **de la longueur** lengthwise; **dans le** ~ **des aiguilles d'une montre** clockwise; **dans tous les** ~ all over the place; **en** ~ **inverse** the other way; **revenir en** ~ **inverse** to come back the other way around ❷ (*idée*) sense; **dans le** ~ **de qn/qc** along the same lines as sb/sth; **aller dans le même** ~ to go the same way ❸ AUTO ~ **giratoire** traffic circle; ~ **interdit** one-way street; (*panneau*) no entry; **rouler en** ~ **interdit** to drive the wrong way down a one-way street ▸ ~ **dessus dessous** upside down; **en ce** ~ **que ...** in the sense that ...; **en un** (*certain*) ~ in a way

**sens**³ [sãs] m sense; **avoir le** ~ **du rythme** to have a sense of rhythm; ~ **de la répartie** gift of repartee ▸ **tomber sous le** ~ to stand to reason; **à mon** ~ to my mind

**sensation** [sãsasjɔ̃] f sensation; (*émotion*) feeling ▸ **faire** ~ to create a sensation; **presse à** ~ tabloid press

**sensationnel** [sãsasjɔnɛl] m sensational

**sensationnel(le)** [sãsasjɔnɛl] adj sensational

**sensé(e)** [sɑ̃se] *adj* sensible

**sensibiliser** [sɑ̃sibilize] <1> *vt* ~ **qn à** *[o* **sur]** **qc** to make sb aware of sth

**sensibilité** [sɑ̃sibilite] *f* ❶ PSYCH (*d'une personne*) sensitiveness ❷ ANAT sensitivity

**sensible** [sɑ̃sibl] *adj* ❶ (*émotif, fragile, opp: indifférent, délicat*) sensitive; **être ~ aux attentions** to notice kindnesses; **être très ~ de la gorge** to have a very delicate throat ❷ (*perceptible*) noticeable ❸ (*fin: odorat, ouïe*) sensitive

**sensualité** [sɑ̃syalite] *f* sensuality

**sensuel(le)** [sɑ̃sɥɛl] *adj* sensual

**sentence** [sɑ̃tɑ̃s] *f* ❶ JUR sentence ❷ (*adage*) maxim

**sentier** [sɑ̃tje] *m* path

**sentiment** [sɑ̃timɑ̃] *m* ❶ (*émotion*) feeling ❷ (*sensibilité*) emotion ❸ (*conscience*) awareness of one's worth ❹ (*impression*) feeling; **le ~ d'être un raté** the feeling of being a loser ❺ *pl* (*formule de politesse*) **mes meilleurs ~s** my best wishes ❻ *pl* (*tendance*) disposition

**sentimental(e)** [sɑ̃timɑ̃tal, -o] <-aux> **I.** *adj* ❶ (*sensible: nature, personne*) romantic ❷ (*amoureux: problème, vie*) love (*opp: rationnel: attachement, réaction, valeur*) sentimental **II.** *m(f)* sentimentalist

**sentir** [sɑ̃tiʀ] <10> **I.** *vt* ❶ (*humer*) to smell ❷ (*goûter*) to taste ❸ (*ressentir*) to feel, I feel tiredness coming over me ❹ (*avoir une odeur*) ~ **la fumée** to smell of smoke; **ça sent le brûlé** there's a smell of burning ❺ (*avoir un goût*) ~ **l'ail/la vanille** to taste of garlic/vanilla ❻ (*annoncer*) **ça sent la neige** there's snow in the air ❼ (*pressentir*) to feel; ~ **qu'il va pleuvoir** to feel that it's going to rain ❽ (*rendre sensible*) **faire ~ son autorité à qn** to make sb feel one's authority ▸ **je ne peux pas la ~** I can't stand her **II.** *vi* ❶ (*avoir une odeur*) to smell; ~ **bon** to smell good ❷ (*puer*) to stink; **il sent des pieds** his feet stink **III.** *vpr* ❶ (*se trouver*) **se ~ fatigué** to feel tired ❷ (*être perceptible*) **qc se sent** (*amélioration, changement, effet*) sth can be felt ▸ **ne pas se ~ bien** *inf* not to feel well; **se ~ mal** to feel ill; **ils ne peuvent pas se ~** they can't stand each other

**séparation** [sepaʀasjɔ̃] *f* ❶ (*action de séparer*) separation; (*de convives*) parting; (*de manifestants*) dispersion ❷ JUR (*de biens*) separate ownership (*of property by married couples*) ❸ POL separation ❹ (*distinction*) dividing line ❺ (*cloison*) (**mur de**) ~ dividing wall

**séparé(e)** [sepaʀe] *adj* separate

**séparément** [sepaʀemɑ̃] *adv* (*examiner*) separately; (*vivre*) apart

**séparer** [sepaʀe] <1> **I.** *vt* ❶ (*désunir, détacher, diviser*) to separate; ~ **qc en deux groupes** to divide sth into two groups; ~ **un enfant de ses parents** to take a child away from his parents ❷ (*être interposé entre*) to separate ❸ (*différencier*) to distinguish between; ~ **la théorie de la pratique** to differentiate between theory and practice **II.** *vpr* ❶ (*se défaire de*) **se ~ de qc** to part with sth; **se ~ de qn** to let sb go ❷ (*se diviser*) **se ~ de qc** (*route*) to leave sth; **se ~ en qc** (*rivière, route*) to split into sth ❸ (*se détacher*) **se ~** to break up; **se ~ de qc** to break off from sth ❹ (*se disperser*) **se ~** to disperse

**sept** [sɛt] *adj* seven; *v.a.* **cinq**

**septante** [sɛptɑ̃t] *adj Belgique, Suisse* (*soixante-dix*) seventy; *v.a.* **cinq, cinquante**

**septantième** [sɛptɑ̃tjɛm] *adj antéposé, Belgique, Suisse* (*soixante-dixième*) seventieth; *v.a.* **cinquième**

**septembre** [sɛptɑ̃bʀ] *m* September; *v.a.* **août**

**septennat** [sɛptena] *m* seven-year period; POL seven-year (presidential) term

**septième** [sɛtjɛm] *adj antéposé* seventh; *v.a.* **cinquième**

**séquelle** [sekɛl] *f* (*d'un accident, d'une maladie*) aftereffect

**séquence** [sekɑ̃s] *f* ❶ CINE, TV, LING sequence ❷ INFORM string

**S**

**séquestrer** [sekɛstʀe] <1> vt (personne) to imprison; (otage) to hold

**serein(e)** [səʀɛ̃, ɛn] adj serene; (objectif) dispassionate

**sereinement** [səʀɛnmɑ̃] adv serenely; (agir, juger) dispassionately

**sérénité** [seʀenite] f serenity

**série** [seʀi] f ❶ (ensemble: de casseroles, volumes) set ❷ (succession) string ❸ CINE, TV series ❹ COM **véhicule de ~** mass-produced vehicle ►**~ noire** (roman) crime thriller; (succession de malheurs) string of disasters; **fabriquer qc en ~** to mass-produce sth; **tueur en ~** serial killer; **hors ~** (extraordinaire) outstanding; ECON custom-built

**sérieusement** [seʀjøzmɑ̃] adv ❶ (vraiment: croire, penser) seriously ❷ (avec sérieux: agir, travailler) conscientiously; **vous parlez ~?** are you serious? ❸ (gravement) seriously

**sérieux** [seʀjø] m ❶ (fiabilité, conscience) reliability; (d'une entreprise, d'un projet) seriousness; (d'un employé) conscientiousness ❷ (air grave, gravité: d'une situation, d'un état) seriousness; **garder son ~** to keep a straight face ►**prendre qc au ~** to take sth seriously; **se prendre au ~** to take oneself seriously

**sérieux, -euse** [seʀjø, -jøz] adj ❶ (opp: inconséquent) serious; **pas ~, s'abstenir** serious inquiries only ❷ (grave, opp: plaisantin) serious ❸ (digne de confiance) reliable; (promesse) genuine ❹ (consciencieux: élève, apprenti) conscientious ❺ (digne d'intérêt: problème) genuine; (renseignement) reliable ❻ (approfondi: études, recherches, travail) worthwhile ❼ a. antéposé (fort: différence, somme) considerable; (raison) good ❽ (sage) earnest

**seringue** [s(ə)ʀɛ̃g] f MED syringe

**serment** [sɛʀmɑ̃] m (engagement solennel) oath; **prêter ~** to take an oath; **sous ~** under oath

**séropositif, -ive** [seʀopozitif, -iv] I. adj seropositive; (en parlant du sida) HIV-positive II. m, f person who is sero-positive; (atteint du sida) person who is HIV positive

**serpent** [sɛʀpɑ̃] m (reptile) snake

**serpentin** [sɛʀpɑ̃tɛ̃] m (ruban) streamer

**serpillière** [sɛʀpijɛʀ] f floorcloth; **passer la ~** to clean up the floor

**serre** [sɛʀ] f AGR greenhouse; (serre chauffée) hothouse

**serré** [seʀe] adv ❶ (avec prudence) **jouer ~** to play a tight game; fig to play it tight ❷ (avec peu de moyens: vivre) on a tight budget

**serré(e)** [seʀe] adj ❶ (fort: café, alcool) strong ❷ (petit: budget, délai) tight ❸ (dense: forêt, foule) dense; **en rangs ~s** in serried ranks ❹ (rigoureux: combat, course) close ❺ (fauché: train de vie) impoverished; **être ~** to be pressed for cash

**serrer** [seʀe] <1> I. vt ❶ (tenir en exerçant une pression) to squeeze; **~ qn/qc dans ses bras/contre soi** to hold sb/sth in one's arms/against oneself; **~ qn à la gorge** to strangle sb ❷ (contracter: dents, mâchoires, poings) to clench; (lèvres) to tighten; **avoir la gorge serrée** to have a lump in one's throat; **~ les fesses** fig, inf to be scared stiff ❸ (rendre très étroit: ceinture, nœud) to tighten ❹ (se tenir près de) **~ qn/qc** to keep close behind sb/sth; **~ qn/qc contre un mur** to wedge sb/sth against a wall ❺ (rapprocher: invités) to squeeze up; **~ les rangs** to close ranks; **être serrés** (personnes, objets) to be squashed together ❻ (restreindre: budget) to cut back; (dépenses) to cut back on II. vi **~ à droite/ à gauche** to keep to the right/left III. vpr **se ~** ❶ (se rapprocher: personnes) to squeeze up; **se ~ contre qn** to squeeze up against sb ❷ (se contracter) **sa gorge se serre** his throat tightened ►**se ~ la ceinture** inf to tighten one's belt

**serrure** [seʀyʀ] f lock

**serrurier, -ière** [seʀyʀje, -jɛʀ] m, f locksmith

**serveur** [sɛrvœr] *m* INFORM server; **~ de courrier** mail server

**serveur, -euse** [sɛrvœr, -øz] *m, f* (*employé*) waiter

**serviable** [sɛrvjabl] *adj* helpful

**service** [sɛrvis] *m* ❶ (*au restaurant, bar, à l'hôtel, dans un magasin*) service; **manger au premier/second ~** to eat at the first/second sitting; **le ~ est assuré jusqu'à ...** (*au restaurant*) meals are served until ... ❷ (*pourboire*) service charge; (**le**) **~** (**est**) **compris** (the) service charge (is) included ❸ *pl* (*aide*) services; **se passer des ~s de qn** *form* to dispense with sb's services ❹ (*organisme officiel*) **~ administratif** (*d'État*) administrative department; (*d'une commune*) administrative service; **~s de l'immigration** immigration department; **~ du feu** *Suisse* fire department; **~ d'ordre** marshals *pl*; **le ~ public** the public services *pl*; **entreprise du ~ public** national utility company; **~ de santé** health service; **les ~s sociaux** social services; **~s spéciaux/secrets** special/secret services ❺ (*département*) department; **~ après-vente** after-sales service; **~s administratifs** (*d'une entreprise*) administration departments; **~ du personnel** personnel department ❻ MÉD department; **~ de cardiologie** cardiology department; **~ de réanimation** intensive care unit; **~ des urgences** emergency room ❼ MIL national service; **~ civil** non-military national service ❽ (*activité professionnelle*) duty; **heures de ~** hours on duty; **être de ~** to be on duty ❾ ÉCON (*prestations*) service ❿ (*action de servir*) service; **escalier de ~** service staircase ⓫ (*faveur*) favor; **demander un ~ à qn** to ask sb a favor; **rendre ~ à qn** to do sb a favor; **qu'y a-t-il pour votre ~?** how can I help you? ⓬ (*assortiment pour la table*) set; **~ à thé** tea set ⓭ (*engagement au tennis, au volley-ball*) service ⓮ REL **~** (**religieux**) (religious) service ▶ **à ton/votre ~!** at your service!; **~ en ligne** online service; **entrer en ~** (*unité*

*de production*) to come into service; **mettre qc en ~** to put sth into operation; **hors ~** out of order

**serviette** [sɛrvjɛt] *f* ❶ (*pour la toilette*) towel; **~ de plage /de bain** beach/bath towel; **~ hygiénique** sanitary napkin ❷ (*serviette de table*) napkin; **~ en papier** paper napkin ❸ (*attaché-case*) briefcase

**servir** [sɛrvir] *irr* **I.** *vt* to serve; **c'est servi!** *inf* ready!; **on vous sert, Madame/Monsieur?** are you being served Madam/Sir?; **qu'est-ce que je vous sers?** what would you like? **II.** *vi* ❶ (*être utile: voiture, outil, conseil, explication*) to be useful; **ça me sert à la réparation/à faire la cuisine** (*machine, outil*) I use it for doing repairs/for cooking; **à quoi cet outil peut-il bien ~?** what can this tool be used for? ❷ (*tenir lieu de*) **~ de guide à qn** to be a guide for sb; **ça te servira de leçon!** that'll teach you a lesson! ❸ (*être utilisable*) to be usable; **ce vélo peut encore/ne peut plus ~** this bike can still/ no longer be used ❹ SPORT (*au tennis, au volley-ball*) to serve ▶ **rien ne sert de courir, il faut partir à point** *prov* more haste, less speed **III.** *vpr* ❶ (*utiliser*) **se ~ d'un copain/article pour** +*infin* to use a friend/article to +*infin* ❷ (*prendre soi-même qc*) **se ~ des légumes** to help oneself to vegetables ❸ (*être servi*) **ce vin se sert frais** this wine should be served chilled

**ses** [se] *dét poss v.* **sa**, **son**

**session** [sesjɔ̃] *f* ❶ (*séance*) sitting; **~ d'examens** exam session ❷ INFORM session; **ouvrir/clore une ~** to log on/ off

**set** [sɛt] *m* SPORT set; **~ gagnant** winning set

**seuil** [sœj] *m* ❶ (*pas de la porte*) doorstep; **franchir le ~** to step through the door ❷ (*limite*) threshold; **~ de pauvreté** poverty line; **~ de rentabilité** break-even point

**seul(e)** [sœl] **I.** *adj* ❶ (*sans compagnie*) alone; **tout ~** all alone; **être ~ à ~** to be

S

alone with each other; **parler à qn ~ à ~** to speak to sb privately; **parler tout ~** to speak to oneself ② (*célibataire*) single ③ *antéposé* (*unique*) single; **~ et unique** one and only; **une ~ e fois** once; **être ~ de son espèce** to be unique ④ (*uniquement*) only; **il est ~ capable de le faire** he alone is able to do it; **~s les invités sont admis** only guests are admitted; **~ le résultat importe** only the result is important II. *m(f)* **le/la ~(e)** the only one; **vous n'êtes pas le ~ à ...** you're not the only one to ...; **un/une ~(e)** only one

**seulement** [sœlmɑ̃] *adv* just ▶ **non ~ ..., mais (encore)** not only ..., but; **pas ~** *soutenu* not just; **si ~** if only

**sève** [sɛv] *f* BOT sap

**sévère** [sevɛʀ] *adj* ① (*rigoureux: climat*) harsh; (*critique, jugement*) severe; (*concurrence, lutte*) strong; (*lutte*) hard; (*sélection*) rigorous ② (*grave: crise, pertes*) severe; (*échec*) terrible

**sévérité** [severite] *f* severity; (*d'une critique, d'un verdict*) harshness

**sexe** [sɛks] *m* ① (*catégorie, sexualité*) sex ② (*organe*) sex organs

**sexualité** [sɛksɥalite] *f* sexuality

**sexuel(le)** [sɛksɥɛl] *adj* ① (*relatif à la sexualité*) sexual; (*éducation*) sex ② (*relatif au sexe*) sex

**sexy** [sɛksi] *adj inv, inf* sexy

**shooter** [ʃute] <1> I. *vi* SPORT to shoot II. *vt* SPORT (*penalty, corner*) to take III. *vpr inf* (*se droguer*) **se ~ à qc** to shoot up with sth

**short** [ʃɔʀt] *m* shorts *pl*

**si¹** [si] <devant voyelle ou h muet s'> *conj* ① (*condition, hypothèse*) if; **~ je ne suis pas là, partez sans moi** if I'm not there, leave without me; **~ j'étais riche, ...** if I were rich, ...; **~ j'avais su!** if I'd only known! ② (*opposition*) if; **~ toi tu es mécontent, moi, je ne le suis pas!** even if you're unhappy, I'm not! ③ (*éventualité*) if; **~ nous profitions du beau temps?** how about taking advantage of the good weather? ④ (*désir, regret*) if only; **ah ~ je les te-**

nais! if only I'd got them!; **~ seulement tu étais venu hier!** if only you'd come yesterday! ▶ **~ ce n'est ...** if not ...; **~ ce n'est qn/qc** apart from sb/sth; **c'est ça** *inf* if that's how it is

**si²** [si] *adv* ① (*dénégation*) yes; **il ne vient pas – mais ~!** he's not coming – yes he is!; **tu ne peux pas venir – mais ~!** you can't come – yes I can! ② (*tellement*) so; **ne parle pas ~ bas!** don't speak so quietly; **une ~ belle fille** such a pretty girl; **elle était ~ impatiente qu'elle ne tenait plus en place** she was so impatient that she couldn't sit still ③ (*aussi*) **~ ... que** as ... as; **il n'est pas ~ intelligent qu'il le paraît** he's not as intelligent as he seems ▶ **~ bien que** so much so that; **j'en avais assez, ~ bien que je suis partie** I'd had enough, so much so that I left; **il viendra pas – oh que ~!** he won't come – oh yes he will!

**si³** [si] *adv* (*interrogation indirecte*) if

**si⁴** [si] *m inv* MUS ti; *v.a.* **do**

**Sicile** [sisil] *f* la ~ Sicily

**sidérer** [sidere] <5> *vt inf* to stagger

**sidérurgie** [sideʀyʀʒi] *f* steel industry

**siècle** [sjɛkl] *m* ① (*période de cent ans*) century; **au IIIᵉ ~ avant J.C.** in the 3rd century B.C. ② (*période remarquable*) **le ~ de Louis XIV** the age of Louis XIV ③ (*période très longue*) age; **depuis des ~s** for ages; **il y a des ~s que je ne t'ai vu** *inf* I haven't seen you for ages ▶ **du ~** *inf* (*combat, marché, inondation*) of the century

**siège** [sjɛʒ] *m* ① (*meuble, au Parlement*) *a.* POL seat; **~ avant/arrière** AUTO front/back seat; **~ pour enfant** child seat ② (*résidence: d'une organisation*) headquarters; **~ social** head office

**siéger** [sjeʒe] <2a, 5> *vi* ① (*avoir un siège: députés, procureur*) to sit ② (*tenir séance*) to be in session

**sien(ne)** [sjɛ̃, sjɛn] *pron poss* ① **le ~/la ~ne/les ~s** (*d'une femme*) hers; (*d'un homme*) his; *v.a.* **mien** ② *pl* (*ceux de sa famille*) **les ~s** his/her family; (*ses partisans*) his/her kind ▶ **faire des**

~**nes** *inf* to act up; **à la** (**bonne**) ~**ne!** *iron, inf* cheers!; **y mettre du** ~ to pull one's weight

**sieste** [sjɛst] *f* siesta

**sifflement** [sifləmɑ̃] *m* whistling; (*du serpent, de la vapeur*) hissing; ~ **d'oreilles** ringing in the ears

**siffler** [sifle] <1> **I.** *vi* to whistle; (*gaz, vapeur, serpent*) to hiss; **elle a les oreilles qui sifflent** there's a ringing in her ears **II.** *vt* ❶ (*appeler*) ~ **son co-pain/chien** to whistle for one's friend/dog; ~ **une fille** to whistle at a girl ❷ (*signaler en sifflant*) to blow the whistle; ~ **la fin du match** to blow the final whistle ❸ (*huer*) to boo; **se faire** ~ to be booed ❹ (*moduler: chanson, mélodie*) to whistle ❺ *inf* (*boire: verre*) to knock back

**sifflet** [siflɛ] *m* ❶ (*instrument*) whistle; **coup de** ~ blast of the whistle ❷ *pl* (*huées*) booing

**sigle** [sigl] *m* abbreviation

**signal** [siɲal, -o] <-aux> *m* a. INFORM signal; **donner le** ~ **du départ** to give the signal for departure; ~ **sonore** sound signal; ~ **d'alarme** alarm; **déclencher le** ~ **d'alarme** to set off the alarm

**signalement** [siɲalmɑ̃] *m* description

**signaler** [siɲale] <1> *vt* ❶ (*attirer l'attention sur*) to point out; ADMIN (*fait nouveau, perte, vol*) to report; ~ **une erreur à qn** to point out a mistake to sb ❷ (*marquer par un signal*) ~ **la direction à qn** (*carte, écriteau, balise*) to signpost the way for sb ❸ (*indiquer*) ~ **l'existence de qc** to show the existence of sth ▶ **rien à** ~ nothing to report

**signalisation** [siɲalizasjɔ̃] *f* (*d'un aéroport, port*) (*par lumière*) beaconing; (*d'une route*) (*par panneaux*) road signs *pl*; (*au sol*) markings *pl*; **feux de** ~ traffic lights

**signature** [siɲatyʀ] *f* ❶ (*action*) signing ❷ (*marque d'authenticité*) signature

**signe** [siɲ] *m* ❶ (*geste, indice*) sign; ~ **de** (**la**) **croix** sign of the cross; ~ **de la main** a gesture; (*pour saluer*) wave; ~ **de tête** (*pour dire oui*) nod; (*pour*

dire non) shake of the head; **faire** ~ **à qn** (*pour signaler qc*) to give sb a sign; (*pour contacter qn*) to get in touch with sb; **faire** ~ **à son fils de** +*infin* to gesture to one's son to +*infin;* **faire** ~ **que oui/non** (*de la tête*) to nod/shake one's head; (*d'un geste*) to say yes/no with one's hand ❷ (*trait distinctif*) mark; ~**s particuliers: néant** distinguishing marks: none ❸ LING, MATH ~ **de ponctuation** punctuation mark; ~ **d'égalité/de multiplication** equals/multiplication sign ❹ (*en astrologie*) sign; ~ **du zodiaque** sign of the zodiac ▶ **c'est bon/mauvais** ~ it's a good/bad sign

**signer** [siɲe] <1> *vt* ❶ (*apposer sa signature*) to sign; ~ **qc de son nom/de sa main** to sign one's name on sth/sth with one's own hand ❷ (*produire sous son nom: œuvre, pièce*) to produce; (*tableau*) to sign ▶ **c'est signé qn** *inf* it's got sb's fingerprints all over it

**signet** [siɲɛ] *m* INFORM bookmark

**significatif, -ive** [siɲifikatif, -iv] *adj* (*date, décision, fait*) significant; (*geste, silence, sourire*) meaningful; **être** ~ **de qc** to reflect sth

**signification** [siɲifikasjɔ̃] *f* (*sens*) meaning

**signifier** [siɲifje] <1> *vt* ❶ (*avoir pour sens*) to mean; **qu'est-ce que cela signifie?** what does that mean? ❷ (*faire connaître*) ~ **une intention à qn** to make an intention known to sb; ~ **une décision à qn** JUR to notify sb of a decision ▶ **qu'est-ce que ça signifie?** what's that supposed to mean?

**silence** [silɑ̃s] *m sans pl* (*absence de bruit, de paroles, d'information*) silence; (*calme*) stillness; **le** ~ **se fait dans la salle** a hush falls over the room; **quel** ~**!** how quiet it is!; **garder le** ~ **sur qc** to keep quiet about sth; **passer qc sous** ~ not to mention sth; **réduire qn au** ~ to reduce sb to silence; **rompre le** ~ to break the silence

**silencieux** [silɑ̃sjø] *m* muffler

**silencieux, -euse** [silɑ̃sjø, -jøz] *adj*

S

❶ (*opp: bruyant*) silent ❷ (*où règne le silence*) silent ❸ (*peu communicatif: personne*) quiet; (*majorité*) silent; **rester ~** to remain silent

**silhouette** [silwɛt] *f* ❶ (*allure, figure indistincte*) figure ❷ (*contour*) outline

**sillonner** [sijɔne] <1> *vt* (*traverser*) **~ une ville** (*personnes, touristes*) to go to and fro across a town; (*canaux, routes*) to crisscross a town; **~ le ciel** (*avions, éclairs*) to go back and forth across the sky

**similaire** [similɛʀ] *adj* similar

**simple** [sɛ̃pl] **I.** *adj* ❶ (*facile*) simple; **le plus ~, c'est ...** the simplest thing is to ... ❷ (*modeste*) unaffected; (*personne, revenus, famille*) modest ❸ (*non multiple: feuille, nœud*) single; **un aller ~ pour Paris, s'il vous plaît** a one-way ticket to Paris please ❹ *postposé* LING, CHIM simple ❺ *antéposé* (*rien d'autre que: formalité, remarque*) simple; **un simple regard/coup de téléphone** just a look/phone call; **"sur ~ appel"** "just call" ❻ (*naïf*) simple ▸ **c'est** (**bien**) **~** *inf* it's perfectly simple **II.** *m* ❶ SPORT singles ❷ (*personne naïve*) ~ **d'esprit** simple soul

**simplement** [sɛ̃pləmɑ̃] *adv* ❶ (*sans affectation: s'exprimer, se vêtir*) simply; (*recevoir, se comporter*) unpretentiously ❷ (*seulement*) simply; **tout ~** (*sans plus*) just; (*absolument*) quite simply

**simplicité** [sɛ̃plisite] *f* ❶ (*opp: complexité*) simplicity; **être d'une extrême ~** to be very simple; **être d'une ~ enfantine** to be child's play ❷ (*naturel*) plainness; **être resté d'une grande ~** to have stayed very simple; **parler avec ~** to speak plainly; **recevoir qn en toute ~** to give sb a simple welcome ❸ (*naïveté*) simpleness

**simplifier** [sɛ̃plifje] <1> **I.** *vt* to simplify **II.** *vpr* **se ~ la vie** to simplify life (for oneself)

**simulation** [simylasjɔ̃] *f* ❶ (*reconstitution*) simulation ❷ (*action de simuler un sentiment*) pretense ❸ (*action de simuler une maladie*) malingering

**simuler** [simyle] <1> *vt* ❶ (*feindre*) to feign ❷ (*reconstituer*) to simulate

**simultané(e)** [simyltane] *adj* simultaneous

**sincère** [sɛ̃sɛʀ] *adj* ❶ (*franc, loyal: aveu*) sincere; (*ami, repentir, réponse*) honest ❷ (*véritable: condoléances*) sincere; **veuillez agréer mes plus ~s salutations** sincerely yours

**sincérité** [sɛ̃seʀite] *f* (*franchise: des aveux, d'une personne, d'un sentiment*) sincerity; (*d'une explication, réponse*) frankness; **en toute ~** quite sincerely

**singe** [sɛ̃ʒ] *m* ❶ ZOOL monkey; **grand ~** great ape; **l'homme descend du ~** humankind is descended from the apes; *v.a.* **guenon** ❷ *inf* (*personne qui imite*) mimic; **faire le ~** *inf* to monkey around [*o* around]

**singulariser** [sɛ̃gylaʀize] <1> *vpr* **se ~ par qc** to distinguish oneself by sth

**singularité** [sɛ̃gylaʀite] *f* ❶ *sans pl* (*caractère original*) singularity ❷ *pl* (*excentricité*) peculiarity

**singulier** [sɛ̃gylje] *m* singular

**singulier, -ière** [sɛ̃gylje, -jɛʀ] *adj* ❶ (*bizarre*) strange ❷ (*étonnant*) singular ❸ LING singular

**singulièrement** [sɛ̃gyljɛʀmɑ̃] *adv* ❶ (*étrangement*) strangely ❷ (*fortement*) singularly

**sinistre** [sinistʀ] **I.** *adj* ❶ (*lugubre*) gloomy ❷ (*inquiétant: projet*) sinister ❸ (*terrible: nouvelle, spectacle*) gruesome **II.** *m* ❶ (*catastrophe*) disaster; (*réclamation*) claim

**sinistré(e)** [sinistʀe] **I.** *adj* (*bâtiment*) disaster-stricken; (*zone, région*) disaster; **personnes ~es à la suite des inondations** flood disaster victims **II.** *m(f)* victim

**sinon** [sinɔ̃] *conj* ❶ (*dans le cas contraire*) otherwise ❷ (*si ce n'est*) **que faire ~ attendre?** what shall we do but wait?; **à quoi sert la clé ~ à faire qc** what use is a key apart from doing sth; **aucun roman ~ "Madame Bovary"** no novel except "Madame Bovary"; **il**

ne s'intéresse à rien ~ à la musique he's not interested in anything apart from music; ~ ... du moins (en tout cas) if not ... at least

**sinusite** [sinyzit] *f* sinusitis

**sirène** [siʀɛn] *f* ❶ (*signal*) siren ❷ (*femme poisson*) mermaid

**sirop** [siʀo] *m* ❶ (*liquide sucré*) *a.* MED syrup; **pêches au** ~ peaches in syrup; ~ **contre la toux** cough syrup ❷ (*boisson diluée*) cordial

**siroter** [siʀɔte] <1> *vt inf* to sip

**sismique** [sismik] *adj* **secousse** ~ earth tremor

**site** [sit] *m* ❶ (*paysage*) place; (*région*) area; ~ **touristique** place of interest; ~ **historique/naturel** historical/natural site; ~ **sauvage** wild place ❷ (*lieu d'activité*) ~ **archéologique/olympique** archeological/Olympic site ❸ IN-FORM site; ~ (**sur**) **Internet**, ~ **Web** website

**sitôt** [sito] **I.** *adv* **pas de** ~ not for a while; **elle ne recommencera pas de** ~ *iron* she won't do that again in a hurry **II.** *conj* ~ **entré/arrivé** as soon as he came in/arrived ▸ ~ **dit**, ~ **fait** no sooner said than done

**situation** [situasjõ] *f* ❶ (*état: d'une personne*) position; ~ **de famille** marital status; **la** ~ **sociale de qn** sb's social standing; **dans ma** ~ in my situation; **remettre qc en** ~ to put sth back in context ❷ (*état conjoncturel*) *a.* ECON, FIN situation ❸ (*emploi*) post; **avoir une belle** ~ to have a good job

**situé(e)** [situe] *adj* situated

**situer** [situe] <1> **I.** *vt* ❶ (*localiser dans l'espace par la pensée*) ~ **son film à Paris** to set one's film in Paris; **je ne situe pas très bien ce lieu** I can't quite place this place; **pouvez-vous** ~ **l'endroit précis où ...?** can you locate the exact place where ...? ❷ (*localiser dans le temps*) ~ **qc en l'an ...** to place sth in the year ... ❸ *inf* (*définir: personne*) ~ **qn** to work sb out **II.** *vpr* **se** ~ ❶ (*se localiser dans l'espace*) to be situated ❷ (*se localiser dans le temps*) **se** ~ **en**

**l'an ...** to take place in the year ... ❸ (*se localiser à un certain niveau*) **se** ~ **entre 25 et 35%** to fall between 25 and 35%; **se** ~ **à un niveau inférieur** to be at a lower level ❹ (*se définir*) **se** ~ to be placed; **se** ~ **par rapport à qc** to be in relation to sth

**six** [sis, *devant une voyelle* siz, *devant une consonne* si] *adj* six; *v.a.* **cinq**

**sixième** [sizjɛm] **I.** *adj antéposé* sixth **II.** *f* ECOLE sixth grade; *v.a.* **cinquième**

**skate** [skɛt] *inf*, **skate-board** [skɛtbɔʀd] <skate-boards> *m* skateboard; **faire du** ~ to go skateboarding

**ski** [ski] *m* ❶ (*objet*) ski; **aller quelque part à** ~**s** to ski somewhere ❷ (*sport*) skiing; ~ **de fond** cross-country skiing; ~ **alpin** Alpine skiing; ~ **nautique** water-skiing; **faire du** ~ to go skiing; **des chaussures de** ~ ski boots; **station de** ~ ski resort

**skier** [skje] <1> *vi* to ski

**skieur, -euse** [skjœʀ, -jøz] *m, f* skier; ~ **de fond/hors piste** cross-country/off-piste skier

**slalom** [slalɔm] *m* (*épreuve de ski*) slalom

**slash** [slaʃ] *m* slash

**slave** [slav] *adj* Slavic

**Slave** [slav] *mf* Slav

**slip** [slip] *m* briefs *pl*; ~ (**de bain**) swimming trunks

**slogan** [slɔgã] *m* slogan

**slow** [slo] *m* slow dance

**smash** [sma(t)ʃ] *m* smash

**S.M.I.C.** [smik] *m abr de* **salaire minimum interprofessionnel de croissance** minimum wage

**smicard(e)** [smikaʀ, aʀd] *m(f) inf* minimum wage earner

**snack** [snak] *m*, **snack-bar** [snakbaʀ] <snack-bars> *m* snack bar

**snob** [snɔb] **I.** *adj* snobbish **II.** *mf* snob

**sociable** [sɔsjabl] *adj* ❶ (*aimable*) sociable ❷ SOCIOL social

**social** [sɔsjal, -jo] <-aux> *m* ❶ (*questions sociales*) social issues ❷ (*politique*) social policy

**social(e)** [sɔsjal, -jo] <-aux> *adj* social;

**aide** ~**e** ≈ welfare; **les logements sociaux** public housing

**socialisation** [sɔsjalizasjɔ̃] f ❶ POL collectivization ❷ PSYCH socialization

**socialiser** [sɔsjalize] <1> vt POL to collectivize; PSYCH to socialize

**socialisme** [sɔsjalism] m socialism

**socialiste** [sɔsjalist] adj, mf socialist

**société** [sɔsjete] f ❶ (communauté) society; ~ **de consommation** consumer society; **problème de** ~ social problem ❷ ECON company; ~ **à responsabilité limitée** limited liability company; ~ **anonyme** public limited company; ~ **civile** non-commercial company ❸ (ensemble de personnes) society; **la haute** ~ high society

**socioculturel(le)** [sɔsjokyltyʀɛl] adj sociocultural

**sociologie** [sɔsjɔlɔʒi] f sociology

**sociologue** [sɔsjɔlɔg] mf sociologist

**socquette** [sɔkɛt] f ankle sock

**soda** [sɔda] m (boisson aromatisée) soft drink

**sœur** [sœʀ] I. f ❶ (opp: frère, objet semblable) sister; ~ **de lait** foster sister; ~ **d'infortune** soutenu fellow sufferer ❷ REL nun; **ma** ~ Sister; **bonne** ~ inf nun; **se faire (bonne)** ~ to become a nun ▸ **et ta** ~(, **elle bat le beurre**)? inf get lost! II. adj ❶ (semblable: civilisation, âme) sister ❷ (apparentés) **être** ~**s** (choses) to be sisters

**sœurette** [sœʀɛt] f little sister

**SOFRES** [sɔfʀɛs] f abr de **Société française d'enquêtes par sondages** French public opinion poll company

**software** [sɔftwɛʀ, sɔftwaʀ] m software

**soi** [swa] pron pers avec une préposition oneself; **chez** ~ at home; **malgré** ~ despite oneself ▸ **en** ~ in itself; **un genre en** ~ a separate genre

**soi-disant** [swadizɑ̃] I. adj inv, antéposé so-called II. adv supposedly

**soie** [swa] f ❶ (tissu) silk ❷ (poils) bristle

**soif** [swaf] f ❶ (besoin de boire) thirst; **avoir** ~ to be thirsty; (plante) to need watering; **donner** ~ **à qn** to make sb

thirsty ❷ (désir) ~ **de vengeance** thirst for vengeance; ~ **de vivre** zest for life ▸ **mourir de** ~ to be dying of thirst

**soigner** [swaɲe] <1> I. vt ❶ (traiter: médecin) to treat; (infirmier) to look after; **se faire** ~ to get treatment ❷ (avoir soin de: animal, plante, personne) to look after; (mains, chevelure, plante) to take care of; (travail, repas, style, tenue) to take care over ❸ iron, inf (forcer l'addition: client) to swindle ▸ **va te faire** ~! inf you must be crazy II. vpr ❶ (essayer de se guérir) **se** ~ to treat oneself; **se** ~ **tout seul** to look after oneself ❷ iron (avoir soin de soi) **se** ~ to take good care of oneself ❸ (pouvoir être soigné) **se** ~ **par une thérapie** to be treatable by a therapy ▸ **ça se soigne!** inf there's a cure for that!

**soigneusement** [swaɲøzmɑ̃] adv (travailler, installer, éviter) carefully; (ranger) neatly

**soigneux, -euse** [swaɲø, -øz] adj (appliqué) meticulous; (ordonné) neat

**soi-même** [swamɛm] pron pers oneself; **le respect de** ~ self-respect

**soin** [swɛ̃] m ❶ sans pl (application) care; (ordre et propreté) tidiness; **avec beaucoup de** ~ with great care ❷ pl (traitement médical) treatment; ~**s à domicile** home treatment; **les premiers** ~**s** first aid ❸ pl (hygiène) ~**s du visage/corps** facial/body care + vb sing ❹ sans pl (responsabilité) **laisser à sa mère le** ~ **de** +infin to leave one's mother to +infin ❺ pl (attention) attention

**soir** [swaʀ] I. m evening; **le** ~ **tombe** evening is falling; **au** ~ in the evening; **hier au** ~ yesterday evening; **pour le repas de ce** ~ for this evening's meal; **8 heures du** ~ 8 o'clock in the evening; **le** ~ in the evening; **l'autre** ~ the other evening ▸ **du matin au** ~ from morning till night; **être du** ~ inf (être en forme le soir) to be a night owl; (être de l'équipe du soir) to be on the night shift II. adv evening; **hier** ~ yesterday evening; **mardi** ~ Tuesday evening

**soirée** [sware] f ❶ (*fin du jour*) evening; **en ~** in the evening; **demain en ~** tomorrow evening; **en fin de ~** at the end of the evening; **toute la ~** all evening; **dans la ~** in the evening; **lundi dans la ~, dans la ~ de lundi** on Monday evening ❷ (*fête*) party; **~ dansante/costumée** dance/fancy dress ball; **tenue de ~** evening dress ❸ THEAT, CINE evening performance; **en ~** in the evening

**soit** I. [swat] *adv* (*d'accord*) very well; **eh bien ~!** very well then! II. [swa] *conj* ❶ (*alternative*) **~ ..., ~ ...** either ..., or ...; **~ qu'il soit malade, ~ qu'il n'ait pas envie** (*subj*) either he's ill, or he doesn't want to ❷ (*c'est-à-dire*) that is

**soixantaine** [swasɑ̃tɛn] f ❶ (*environ soixante*) **une ~ de personnes/pages** about sixty people/pages ❷ (*âge approximatif*) **avoir la ~** [o **une ~ d'années**] about sixty years old; **approcher de la ~** to approach sixty; **avoir largement dépassé la ~** to be well past sixty

**soixante** [swasɑ̃t] *adj* sixty; **~ et un** sixty-one; **~ et onze** seventy-one; *v.a.* **cinq, cinquante**

**soixante-dix** [swasɑ̃tdis] *adj* seventy; *v.a.* **cinq, cinquante**

**soixante-dixième** [swasɑ̃tdizjɛm] <soixante-dixièmes> *adj antéposé* seventieth; *v.a.* **cinquième**

**soixantième** [swasɑ̃tjɛm] *adj antéposé* sixtieth; *v.a.* **cinquième**

**soja** [sɔʒa] *m* soya

**sol¹** [sɔl] *m* ❶ (*terre*) soil ❷ (*croûte terrestre*) ground; **personnel au ~** AVIAT ground crew ❸ (*plancher: d'une pièce, maison*) floor; **exercices au ~** SPORT floor exercises ❹ (*territoire*) soil

**sol²** [sɔl] *m inv* MUS so; *v.a.* **do**

**solaire** [sɔlɛʀ] *adj* ❶ (*utilisant la force du soleil*) a. ASTR solar; **cadran ~** sundial ❷ (*protégeant du soleil*) **huile ~** suntan oil

**soldat** [sɔlda] *m* soldier

**solde¹** [sɔld] *m* ❶ *pl* (*marchandises*) sale items; **dans les ~s de lainage** in

the woolen sales ❷ (*braderie*) sale; **~s d'été/d'hiver** summer/winter sales; **en ~** on sale ❸ (*balance*) balance

**solde²** [sɔld] f (*d'un soldat, matelot*) pay ▶ **être à la ~ de qn** to be in sb's pay

**solder** [sɔlde] <1> I. *vt* ❶ COM to sell at sale price; **~ tout son stock** to mark down prices on one's entire stock ❷ FIN (*dette*) to settle; (*fermer: compte*) to close II. *vpr* **se ~ par un échec/succès** (*conférence, tentative*) to end in success/failure

**soleil** [sɔlɛj] *m* ❶ ASTR sun; **~ couchant/levant** setting/rising sun; **au ~ levant** at sunrise ❷ (*rayonnement*) sunshine; (*temps ensoleillé*) sunny; **se mettre au ~** to go into the sunshine; **déteindre au ~** to fade in the sun; **il fait ~** it's sunny; **prendre le ~** to sunbathe ❸ (*fleur*) (*grand*) ~ sunflower

**solennel(le)** [sɔlanɛl] *adj* (*officiel, grave*) solemn

**solidaire** [sɔlidɛʀ] *adj* ❶ (*lié*) **être ~(s)** to stand together; **se montrer ~(s)** to show solidarity; **être ~ de** [o **avec**] **qn/de qc** to be behind sb/sth ❷ JUR (*cautionnement, obligation*) joint and several; (*contrat*) joint; **être ~ des actes de qn** to be liable for sb's acts

**solidarité** [sɔlidaʀite] f solidarity

**solide** [sɔlid] I. *adj* ❶ (*opp: liquide*) solid ❷ (*résistant: construction, outil*) sturdy; (*matériau*) strong; (*personne, santé*) robust ❸ (*sûr: connaissances, bon sens*) sound; (*amitié, base*) firm; (*source*) reliable; (*position*) strong ❹ (*robuste, vigoureux*) sturdy ❺ *antéposé, inf* (*substantiel: fortune, repas, coup de poing*) hefty; (*appétit*) hearty II. *m* ❶ MATH, PHYS solid ❷ (*aliments*) **du ~** solids ❸ *inf* (*chose sûre, résistante*) **c'est du ~!** it's good solid stuff!

**solidité** [sɔlidite] f ❶ (*robustesse: d'une machine, d'un meuble*) sturdiness; (*d'un tissu, vêtement*) strength; (*d'une personne*) robustness; (*d'un nœud*) tightness ❷ (*stabilité*) soundness ❸ (*sérieux: d'un argument, raisonnement*) soundness

S

**solitaire** [sɔlitɛʀ] **I.** *adj* ❶ (*seul: vie, caractère*) solitary; (*vieillard*) lonely ❷ (*isolé: maison*) isolated ❸ (*désert: parc, chemin*) deserted; (*demeure*) lonely **II.** *mf* solitary person; (*ermite*) recluse ▸ **en ~** alone; **un tour du monde en ~** a solo around-the-world trip **III.** *m* (*diamant, jeu*) solitaire

**solitude** [sɔlityd] *f* ❶ (*isolement*) loneliness ❷ (*tranquillité, lieu solitaire*) solitude

**solliciter** [sɔlisite] <1> *vt form* (*demander: audience, explication, emploi*) to seek

**solstice** [sɔlstis] *m* solstice

**soluble** [sɔlybl] *adj* ❶ (*pouvant être dissout: substance*) soluble; **~ dans l'eau** water soluble ❷ (*pouvant être résolu*) **être ~** (*problème*) to be solvable

**solution** [sɔlysjɔ̃] *f* ❶ (*issue, résultat*) *a.* CHIM, MED solution; **~ à un** [*o* **d'un**] **problème** solution to a problem; **~ de facilité** easy way out ❷ (*réponse: d'une énigme, d'un rébus*) answer

**solvable** [sɔlvabl] *adj* (*client, pays, demande, marché*) solvent; **client/pays non ~** insolvent customer/country

**sombre** [sɔ̃bʀ] *adj* ❶ (*obscur: lieu, nuit*) dark; **il fait ~** it's dark ❷ (*foncé*) **un bleu/rouge ~** dark blue/red ❸ (*sinistre: heure, année*) dark; (*avenir, réalité, tableau*) dismal; (*pensée*) gloomy ❹ (*triste: roman, visage*) grim; (*caractère, personne*) sombre ❺ *antéposé, inf* (*lamentable: histoire*) dark

**sombrer** [sɔ̃bʀe] <1> *vi* ❶ (*faire naufrage*) to sink ❷ (*personne*) **~ dans la folie** to sink into madness

**sommaire** [sɔmɛʀ] **I.** *adj* ❶ (*court*) brief ❷ (*élémentaire, rapide: examen*) cursory; (*réparation, repas*) quick ❸ (*expéditif: exécution, justice, procédure*) summary **II.** *m* ❶ (*table des matières*) table of contents ❷ (*résumé*) summary

**somme¹** [sɔm] *f* ❶ (*quantité d'argent*) sum ❷ (*total*) total; (*des angles*) sum; **faire la ~ de qc** to total sth ❸ (*ensemble*) amount; **la ~ des dégâts/des be-** soins the total damage/requirements ▸ **en ~, ~ toute** all in all

**somme²** [sɔm] *m* (*sieste*) nap; **piquer un ~** *inf* to take a nap

**sommeil** [sɔmɛj] *m* ❶ (*fait de dormir*) sleep; (*envie de dormir*) sleepiness; **avoir ~** to be sleepy; **tomber de ~** to be asleep on one's feet ❷ (*inactivité*) sleep; **être en ~** to be asleep; **laisser qc en ~** to leave sth in abeyance

**sommet** [sɔmɛ] *m* ❶ (*faîte: d'une montagne*) summit; (*d'une tour, hiérarchie, d'un arbre, toit*) top; (*d'une pente, vague*) crest; (*d'un crâne*) crown ❷ (*apogée*) height; **être au ~ de la gloire** to be at the height of one's fame ❸ POL summit

**somnambule** [sɔmnɑ̃byl] **I.** *adj* sleepwalking **II.** *mf* sleepwalker

**somnifère** [sɔmnifɛʀ] *m* soporific; (*cachet, pilule*) sleeping pill

**somnoler** [sɔmnɔle] <1> *vi* (*dormir à moitié*) to doze

**somptueux, -euse** [sɔ̃ptɥø, -øz] *adj* (*résidence, vêtement*) magnificent; (*repas*) sumptuous; (*cadeau*) lavish

**son¹** [sɔ̃] **I.** *m* sound; **au ~ de l'accordéon** to the accordion; **baisser le ~** to turn the volume down **II.** *app* (*spectacle*) **~ et lumière** sound-and-light (show)

**son²** [sɔ̃, se] <**ses**> *dét poss* ❶ (*d'une femme*) her; (*d'un homme*) his; (*d'un objet, animal*) its; *v.a.* **mon** ❷ *après un indéfini* one's, your; **c'est chacun ~ tour** everyone takes a turn

**sondage** [sɔ̃daʒ] *m* ❶ (*enquête*) poll ❷ (*contrôle rapide*) survey

**sonde** [sɔ̃d] *f* MED probe; (*cathéter*) catheter

**sonder** [sɔ̃de] <1> *vt* ❶ ADMIN (*personnes, intentions*) to poll ❷ (*interroger insidieusement: personne*) to sound out ❸ (*pénétrer: conscience, cœur, sentiments*) to probe

**songer** [sɔ̃ʒe] <2a> **I.** *vi* (*penser*) **~ à qn/qc** to think of sb/sth; (*réfléchir*) to think about sb/sth; **~ à faire qc** to think about doing sth **II.** *vt* **tout cela**

**est bien étrange, songeait-il** that is all very strange, he thought to himself

**songeur, -euse** [sɔ̃ʒœʀ, -øz] *adj* ➊ (*perdu dans ses pensées*) pensive ➋ (*perplexe*) **être ~** to be puzzled; **laisser qn ~** to leave sb wondering

**sonné(e)** [sɔne] *adj* ➊ *inf* (*cinglé*) crazy, mad ➋ *inf* (*groggy*) punch-drunk ▸ **avoir cinquante ans bien ~s** *inf* to be on the wrong side of fifty

**sonner** [sɔne] <1> I. *vt* ➊ (*tirer des sons de: cloche*) to ring; (*clairon*) to blow; **~ trois coups** to ring three times ➋ (*annoncer*) **~ l'alarme** (*personne, sirène*) to sound the alarm ➌ (*appeler*) **~ qn** to ring for sb ➍ *inf* (*étourdir, secouer*) to shake; (*coup, maladie, nouvelle*) to knock out; **être sonné** to be groggy ▸ **on (ne) t'a pas sonné** *inf* nobody asked you II. *vi* ➊ (*produire un son: cloche, réveil, téléphone*) to ring; (*angélus, trompette*) to sound ➋ (*produire un effet*) **~ bien** (*proposition*) to sound good; **~ faux** (*aveux*) to sound false ➌ (*être annoncé: heure*) to strike; (*fin*) to come; **midi/minuit sonne** noon/midnight strikes; **la récréation sonne** the recess bell rings; **quand sonne l'heure de qc** when it is time for sth ➍ (*s'annoncer*) to ring

**sonnerie** [sɔnʀi] *f* ➊ (*appel sonore*) ring ➋ (*mécanisme: d'un réveil*) ring; **~ électrique** electric alarm

**sonnette** [sɔnɛt] *f* (*d'une porte d'entrée*) doorbell; **~ d'alarme** alarm bell ▸ **tirer la ~ d'alarme** to sound the alarm bell

**sonore** [sɔnɔʀ] *adj* ➊ (*retentissant: voix, rire*) ringing; (*gifle, baiser*) loud ➋ (*relatif au son*) **onde ~** sound wave; **bande/piste ~** soundtrack; **ambiance/fond ~** background noise; **nuisances ~s** noise pollution ➌ LING (*consonne*) voiced

**sophistiqué(e)** [sɔfistike] *adj* sophisticated

**sorbet** [sɔʀbɛ] *m* sorbet

**sorcier, -ière** [sɔʀsje, -jɛʀ] I. *m, f* sorcerer *m*, witch *f* II. *adj* **ce n'est pas bien ~** it is not really difficult

**sordide** [sɔʀdid] *adj* ➊ (*répugnant: quartier, ruelle*) squalid ➋ (*ignoble*) sordid

**sort** [sɔʀ] *m* ➊ (*condition*) lot; (*situation*) situation ➋ (*destinée, hasard*) fate; **quel a été le ~ de ton ami?** what became of your friend?; **connaître le même ~ que** to suffer the same fate as; **tirer le vainqueur/les numéros au ~** to draw straws for the winner/the numbers

**sortant(e)** [sɔʀtɑ̃, ɑ̃t] I. *adj* ➊ (*en fin de mandat: coalition, député, ministre*) outgoing ➋ (*tiré au sort*) **les numéros ~s** the numbers which come up II. *m(f)* (*député*) incumbent; (*ministre*) outgoing minister

**sorte** [sɔʀt] *f* type, sort; **plusieurs ~s de pommes** several types of apples; **toutes ~s de personnes/choses** all sorts of people/things; **des disques de toutes ~s** all sorts of records; **ne plus avoir de marchandises d'aucune ~** to have no goods left at all ▸ **en quelque ~** in some way; **faire en ~ que tout se passe bien** to ensure that all goes well; **de la ~** of the sort

**sortie** [sɔʀti] *f* ➊ (*action de sortir: d'une personne*) exit; (*action de sortir: d'une personne*) departure; **~ de prison/d'hôpital** getting out of prison/hospital; **la ~ de piste** AUTO coming off the track ➋ (*promenade*) walk; (*en voiture, à bicyclette*) ride; (*excursion*) outing; **être de ~** (*personne*) to have a day off ➌ (*lieu par où l'on sort: d'un bâtiment, d'une autoroute, d'un garage*) exit; **~ de secours** emergency exit; **~ des artistes** stage door ➍ (*fin: d'un spectacle, d'une saison*) end; **~ de l'école/des bureaux** end of the school/working day; **à la ~ de l'usine** at the end of the factory day ➎ (*parution: d'une publication*) publication; (*d'un disque, d'un film*) release; (*d'un nouveau modèle, véhicule*) launch ➏ SPORT (*d'un ballon*) going out of bounds ⑦ (*exportation: de capitaux, devises*) export ⑧ INFORM (*output*) output; (*édition*); ~ (**sur imprimante**) printing ▶ **attendre** qn à la ~ *inf* to wait for sb outside

**sortir** [sɔʀtiʀ] <10> I. *vi* être ① (*partir*) to go out; (*venir*) to come out; ~ **par la fenêtre** to leave through the window; **faire** ~ **qn** to make sb leave; **faire** ~ **un animal** to get an animal out; **laisser** ~ **qn** to let sb out ② (*quitter*) ~ **du magasin** to leave the store; (*venir*) to come out of the store; ~ **du lit** to get out of bed; **d'où sors-tu?** where did you come from?; ~ **de chez ses amis** to come out of one's friends' house; **à quelle heure sors-tu du bureau?** what time do you leave the office?; ~ **de prison** to get out of prison; ~ **du garage** (*voiture*) to leave the garage ③ (*quitter son domicile*) to go out; ~ **de chez soi** to leave one's home; ~ **faire les courses** to go out shopping; **faire** ~ **un enfant/un animal** to get an animal/a child out; **laisser** ~ **un enfant/un animal** to let an animal/child out ④ (*se divertir*) to go out; ~ **en boîte/en ville** to go to a nightclub/into town ⑤ *inf* (*avoir une relation amoureuse avec*) ~ **avec qn** to go out with sb ⑥ (*en terminer avec*) ~ **d'une période difficile** to come through a difficult period ⑦ (*être tel après un événement*) ~ **indemne d'un accident** to come out of an accident unscathed; ~ **vainqueur/vaincu d'un concours** to emerge as the winner/loser in a competition ⑧ (*faire saillie*) ~ **de qc** to stick out of sth; **les yeux lui sortaient de la tête** *fig* his eyes were popping out of their sockets ⑨ COM (*capitaux, devises*) to leave ⑩ (*s'écarter*) ~ **du sujet** to get off the subject; **ça m'était complètement sorti de l'esprit** it had gone completely out of my head ⑪ SPORT ~ **en touche** to go out of bounds ⑫ (*être issu de*) ~ **de qc** to come from sth; ~ **de l'école de musique** to have studied at the music school ⑬ (*apparaître: bourgeons, plante*) to

come up; (*dent*) to come through; ~ **de terre** to come up out of the ground ⑭ (*paraître: livre*) to be published; (*film, disque*) to be released; (*nouveau modèle, voiture*) to be launched; **vient de** ~ just released; ~ **sur les écrans** to be released in the theaters ⑮ JEUX (*numéro*) to come up ▶ **(mais) d'où tu sors?** *inf* where've you been?; **ne pas en** ~ *inf* not to be able to cope II. *vt avoir* ① (*mener dehors*) to put out; (*porter dehors*) to take out ② (*expulser*) to get rid of ③ (*libérer*) ~ **qn d'une situation difficile** to get sb out of a difficult situation ④ (*retirer d'un lieu*) to get out; ~ **ses disques** to get out one's records; ~ **qc d'un sac/d'un tiroir** to get sth out of a bag/drawer; ~ **les mains de ses poches** to take one's hands out of one's pockets ⑤ COM (*des marchandises*) to take goods out; (*en fraude*) to smuggle goods out ⑥ (*lancer sur le marché: nouveau modèle, film, livre, disque*) to launch ⑦ *inf* (*débiter*) ~ **des âneries à qn** to come out with idiotic things in front of sb ⑧ *inf* (*éliminer*) to knock out; **se faire** ~ **par qn** to get knocked out by sb ⑨ *inf* (*tirer: numéro, carte*) to take III. *vpr* être ① (*se tirer*) **se** ~ **d'une situation/d'un piège** to get oneself out of a situation/trap ② (*réussir*) **s'en** ~ to manage; (*échapper à un danger, un ennui*) to get by; (*survivre*) to pull through IV. *m* **au** ~ **du lit** when one gets out of bed; **au** ~ **d'une réunion** at the end of a meeting

**sou** [su] *m pl, inf* money; **ça en fait des** ~**s!** *inf* that's a lot of money! ▶ **ne pas avoir un** ~ **en poche** *inf* to be flat broke; **être près de ses** ~**s** *inf* to be tightfisted

**souci** [susi] *m* ① *souvent pl* (*inquiétude*) worry; **se faire du** ~ **pour qn/qc** to worry about sb/sth; **sans** ~ free of worry ② (*préoccupation*) concern ③ (*respect*) **le** ~ **de la perfection** concern for perfection; **par** ~ **d'égalité** for equality's sake

**soucier** [susje] <1> *vpr* **se** ~ **de qn/de**

**la nourriture** to worry about sb/food; **se ~ de l'heure** to be worried about the time

**soucieux, -euse** [susjø, -jøz] *adj* ❶ (*inquiet: personne, air, ton*) worried ❷ (*préoccupé*) **être ~ de qn/de l'avenir** to be concerned about sb/the future

**soucoupe** [sukup] *f* saucer ▸ **~ volante** flying saucer

**soudain(e)** [sudɛ̃, ɛn] **I.** *adj* (*événement, geste*) sudden; (*sentiment*) unexpected **II.** *adv* suddenly

**soudainement** [sudɛnmɑ̃] *adv* suddenly

**souffle** [sufl] *m* ❶ (*respiration*) breathing; (*action, capacité pulmonaire*) breath; **~ au cœur** heart murmur; **avoir le ~ court** to be short of breath; **manquer de ~** to be short of breath; **perdre le ~** to get out of breath ❷ (*déplacement d'air: d'une explosion, d'un ventilateur*) blast ❸ (*vent*) puff; (*d'air*) breath ❹ (*vitalité*) energy; (*persévérance*) perseverance; **second ~** second wind ▸ **avoir du ~** to have a lot of breath; **être à couper le ~** to be breathtaking; **reprendre son ~** (*respirer*) to get one's breath back; (*se calmer*) to calm down; **dans un ~** in a breath

**soufflé** [sufle] *m* CULIN soufflé

**souffler** [sufle] <1> **I.** *vi* ❶ METEO (*vent*) to blow; **ça souffle** it's blowing hard ❷ (*insuffler de l'air*) **~ sur/dans qc** to blow on/into sth ❸ (*haleter*) to gasp ❹ (*se reposer*) to get one's breath back ❺ (*prendre du recul*) **laisser ~ qn** to give sb a rest **II.** *vt* ❶ (*éteindre*) to blow out ❷ (*déplacer en soufflant*) to blow away ❸ *inf* (*enlever*) **~ une affaire à qn** to steal a deal from sb; **~ un pion** JEUX to jump a checker ❹ (*détruire*) to blast ❺ (*dire discrètement*) **~ un secret à qn** to whisper a secret to sb ❻ THEAT to prompt ❼ *inf* (*stupéfier*) to stagger ❽ TECH **~ le verre** to blow glass

**souffrance** [sufʀɑ̃s] *f* suffering

**souffrir** [sufʀiʀ] <11> **I.** *vi* ❶ (*avoir mal, être malheureux*) to suffer; **faire ~ qn** to make sb suffer; **~ de la**

**tête/de l'estomac/des reins** to have a headache/stomach problems/kidney problems; **~ du froid/de la faim** to suffer from the cold/hunger; **ses dents le font ~** his teeth give him a lot of trouble ❷ (*être endommagé à cause de*) **~ du gel** (*cultures*) to suffer from frost-damage ❸ *inf* (*avoir des difficultés*) **il a souffert pour avoir l'examen** he had a hard time passing the exam **II.** *vt* ❶ (*endurer*) to bear ❷ (*admettre*) to allow

**soufre** [sufʀ] *m* sulfur ▸ **sentir le ~** to smack of heresy

**souhait** [swɛ] *m* ❶ (*désir*) wish; **exprimer le ~ de** +*infin* to express a desire to +*infin* ❷ (*très, très bien*) **joli à ~** extremely pretty; **paisible à ~** very peaceful ▸ **à tes/vos ~s!** bless you!

**souhaiter** [swete] <1> *vt* ❶ (*désirer*) **~ qc** to wish for sth; **~ que tout se passe bien** to hope that everything goes well; **nous souhaitons manger** we would like to eat; **je souhaiterais t'aider davantage** I would like to help you more ❷ (*espérer pour quelqu'un*) **~ bonne nuit à qn** to bid sb goodnight; **~ beaucoup de bonheur à qn** to wish sb lots of happiness; **~ un joyeux anniversaire à qn** to wish sb a happy birthday

**soûl(e)** [su, sul] *adj inf* (*ivre*) drunk

**soulagement** [sulaʒmɑ̃] *m* relief

**soulager** [sulaʒe] <2a> **I.** *vt* to relieve **II.** *vpr* ❶ (*se défouler*) **se ~ en faisant qc** to find relief by doing sth ❷ *inf* (*satisfaire un besoin naturel*) **se ~** to relieve oneself

**soûler** [sule] <1> **I.** *vt* ❶ (*enivrer*) **~ qn à la bière/au whisky** to get sb drunk on beer/whiskey ❷ (*tourner la tête*) **~ qn** to make sb's head spin **II.** *vpr* ❶ (*s'enivrer*) **se ~ à la bière/au whisky** to get drunk on beer/whiskey ❷ (*se griser*) **se ~ de musique** to get intoxicated by music

**soulever** [sul(ə)ve] <4> *vt* ❶ (*lever: poids*) to lift ❷ (*relever légèrement*) to lift up ③ (*susciter: problème, question*) to raise

**souligner** [suliɲe] <1> *vt* ① (*tirer un trait sous*) to underline ② (*accentuer, marquer*) to emphasize

**soumettre** [sumɛtʀ] *irr* **I.** *vt* ① (*asservir*) ~ **un joueur à qn/qc** to subject a player to sb/sth ② (*faire subir*) ~ **qn à des tests/analyses** to subject sb to tests/analyses ③ (*présenter*) ~ **une idée/un projet à qn** to submit an idea/project to sb **II.** *vpr* ① (*obéir*) **se ~ à la loi/à une décision** to submit to the law/a decision ② (*se plier à, suivre*) **se ~ à un entraînement spécial** to put oneself through special training

**soumis(e)** [sumi,-z] **I.** *part passé de* **soumettre II.** *adj* (*docile*) dutiful

**soupçon** [supsɔ̃] *m* ① (*suspicion*) suspicion ② (*très petite quantité: de sel, poivre*) pinch; (*d'ironie*) sprinkling

**soupçonner** [supsɔne] <1> *vt* (*suspecter*) ~ **qn de vol** to suspect sb of theft

**soupe** [sup] *f* ① (*potage*) soup; **assiette/cuillère à ~** soup dish/spoon ② (*neige fondue*) slush ③ (*organisme charitable*) ~ **populaire** soup kitchen ▶ **cracher dans la ~** *inf* to bite the hand that feeds you

**soupir** [supiʀ] *m* (*signe d'émotion*) sigh

**soupirer** [supiʀe] <1> *vi* to sigh

**souple** [supl] *adj* ① (*opp: rigide*) supple; (*tissu*) soft ② (*agile: bras, jambes, personne*) supple ③ (*adaptable*) flexible

**souplesse** [suplɛs] *f* (*adaptabilité*) flexibility; (*d'une personne*) suppleness

**source** [suʀs] **I.** *f* ① (*point d'eau*) spring; ~ **thermale/d'eau minérale** thermal/mineral water spring; **eau de ~** spring water ② (*naissance d'un cours d'eau*) source; **prendre sa ~ en Suisse** to rise in Switzerland ③ PHYS ~ **lumineuse/d'énergie** light/energy source ④ (*origine de l'information*) **de ~ sûre** from a reliable source ▶ **couler de ~** to come naturally **II.** *app* INFORM **langage/programme ~** source language/program

**sourcil** [suʀsi] *m* eyebrow ▶ **froncer les ~s** to knit one's brow

**sourd(e)** [suʀ, suʀd] **I.** *adj* ① (*qui n'entend pas*) deaf; ~ **d'une oreille** deaf in one ear ② (*étouffé: bruit*) muffled **II.** *m(f)* deaf person

**sourd-muet, sourde-muette** [suʀmɥɛ, suʀd(ə)mɥɛt] <sourds-muets> *m, f* deaf-mute

**souriant(e)** [suʀjɑ̃, jɑ̃t] *adj* smiling

**sourire** [suʀiʀ] **I.** *m* smile; **faire un ~** to give a smile; **faire un ~ à qn** to give sb a smile; **avoir le ~** *inf* to have a smile on one's face; **garder le ~** to keep smiling **II.** *vi irr* ① (*avoir un sourire*) to smile ② (*adresser un sourire*) ~ **à qn** to smile at sb

**souris** [suʀi] *f a.* INFORM mouse

**sous** [su] *prep* ① (*spatial, manière, dépendance, causal*) under ② (*temporel, pour exprimer un délai*) ~ **huitaine** within a week; ~ **peu** shortly ③ METEO in ④ MED on; **être ~ perfusion** to be on an IV

**sous-développé(e)** [sudev(ə)lɔpe] <sous-développés> *adj* underdeveloped

**sous-développement** [sudev(ə)lɔpmɑ̃] <sous-développements> *m* underdevelopment

**sous-directeur, -trice** [sudiʀɛktœʀ, -tʀis] <sous-directeurs> *m, f* deputy manager

**sous-entendre** [suzɑ̃tɑ̃dʀ] <14> *vt* (*dire implicitement*) to imply

**sous-entendu(e)** [suzɑ̃tɑ̃dy] <sous-entendus> *m* insinuation

**sous-estimer** [suzɛstime] <1> *vt* to underestimate

**sous-marin** [sumaʀɛ̃] <sous-marins> *m* submarine

**sous-préfecture** [supʀefɛktyʀ] <sous-préfectures> *f* sub-prefecture

**sous-sol** [susɔl] <sous-sols> *m* basement

**sous-tasse** [sutɑs] *f* Belgique, Suisse (*soucoupe*) saucer

**sous-titrer** [sutitʀe] <1> *vt* to subtitle

**soustraire** [sustʀɛʀ] *irr* **I.** *vi* to subtract

**II.** *vpr* **se ~ à une obligation** to shirk an obligation

**soutenir** [sut(ə)niʀ] <9> *vt* ❶ (*porter, aider, prendre parti pour*) to support ❷ (*maintenir debout, en bonne position*) to hold up ❸ ECON (*monnaie*) to prop up ❹ (*affirmer*) **~ que c'est la vérité** to maintain that it is the truth

**soutenu(e)** [sut(ə)ny] **I.** *part passé de* **soutenir II.** *adj* ❶ (*régulier: attention, effort*) sustained ❷ (*avec des effets de style: style, langue*) formal

**souterrain** [suteʀɛ̃] *m* underpass

**souterrain(e)** [suteʀɛ̃, ɛn] *adj* (*sous terre*) underground; **passage ~** underpass

**soutien** [sutjɛ̃] *m* ❶ (*aide, appui*) support; **apporter son ~ à qn** to support sb ❷ ECOLE **cours de ~** remedial lessons *pl*

**soutien-gorge** [sutjɛ̃ɡɔʀʒ] <soutiens-gorge(s)> *m* bra

**souvenir**[1] [suv(ə)niʀ] <9> *vpr* ❶ (*se rappeler, se remémorer*) **se ~ de qn/qc** to remember sb/sth; **il se souvient à qui il a parlé** he remembers who he spoke to ❷ (*se venger*) **je m'en souviendrai!** I'll remember this!

**souvenir**[2] [suv(ə)niʀ] *m* ❶ (*image dans la mémoire, ce qui rappelle qn/qc*) memory; **si mes ~s sont exacts, ...** if my memory is right, ...; **garder un bon/mauvais ~ de qn/qc** to have good/bad memories of sb/sth; **en ~ de qc/qn** in memory of sth/sb ❷ (*objet touristique*) souvenir

**souvent** [suvɑ̃] *adv* often; **le plus ~** most often

**souveraineté** [suv(ə)ʀɛnte] *f* (*d'un État, peuple*) sovereignty

**soviétique** [sɔvjetik] *adj* Soviet; **l'Union ~** the Soviet Union

**soyeux, -euse** [swajø, -jøz] *adj* ❶ (*doux*) silky ❷ (*brillant*) shiny

**spa** [spa] *m* health spa

**spacieux, -euse** [spasjø, -jøz] *adj* spacious

**spaghettis** [spaɡeti] *mpl* spaghetti + *vb sing*

**sparadrap** [spaʀadʀa] *m* Band-Aid®

**spatial(e)** [spasjal, -jo] <-aux> *adj* space

**spatule** [spatyl] *f* (*ustensile*) spatula

**spécial(e)** [spesjal, -jo] <-aux> *adj* ❶ (*opp: général*) special; **équipement ~** specialist equipment ❷ (*bizarre*) strange

**spécialement** [spesjalmɑ̃] *adv* ❶ (*en particulier*) especially ❷ (*tout exprès*) specially ❸ *inf* (*pas vraiment*) **tu as faim? – non, pas ~** are you hungry? – no, not particularly

**spécialiser** [spesjalize] <1> **I.** *vt* **~ qn dans un domaine précis** to train sb as a specialist in a particular field **II.** *vpr* **se ~ dans** [*o* **en**] **qc** to specialize in sth

**spécialiste** [spesjalist] *mf* ❶ (*expert*) expert ❷ (*technicien*) *a.* MED specialist

**spécification** [spesifikasjɔ̃] *f* specification

**spécifier** [spesifje] <1> *vt* to specify; (*loi*) to stipulate; **~ que ...** to specify that ...

**spécifique** [spesifik] *adj* specific

**spécimen** [spesimɛn] *m* (*exemplaire*) specimen

**spectacle** [spɛktakl] *m* ❶ (*ce qui s'offre au regard*) spectacle ❷ THEAT, CINE, TV show; **aller au ~** to go to a show ❸ (*show-business*) **le monde du ~** the entertainment world ❹ (*avec de gros moyens*) **à grand ~** spectacular

**spectaculaire** [spɛktakylɛʀ] *adj* spectacular

**spectateur, -trice** [spɛktatœʀ, -tʀis] *m, f* ❶ THEAT, SPORT spectator ❷ (*observateur*) onlooker

**spéculation** [spekylasjɔ̃] *f* speculation; **faire des ~s sur qc** to speculate about sth

**spéculer** [spekyle] <1> *vi* ❶ FIN, COM **~ sur qc** to speculate about sth ❷ (*compter sur*) **~ sur qc** to bank on sth

**spéléologie** [speleɔlɔʒi] *f* ❶ (*science*) speleology ❷ (*loisirs*) spelunking

**sperme** [spɛʀm] *m* sperm

**sphère** [sfɛʀ] *f* ❶ (*en science*) sphere ❷ (*domaine*) field; (*d'influence*) sphere

**S**

**spirale** [spiʀal] *f* spiral; **cahier à ~** spiral-bound notebook

**spirituel(le)** [spiʀityɛl] *adj* ❶ (*plein d'esprit*) witty ❷ (*qui se rapporte à l'esprit*) a. REL spiritual

**splendide** [splɑ̃did] *adj* splendid

**sponsor** [spɔ̃sɔʀ, spɔnsɔʀ] *m* sponsor

**sponsoriser** [spɔ̃sɔʀize] <1> *vt* to sponsor

**spontané(e)** [spɔ̃tane] *adj* spontaneous

**spontanément** [spɔ̃tanemɑ̃] *adv* spontaneously

**sport** [spɔʀ] **I.** *adj inv* (*coupe*) casual; **s'habiller ~** to dress casually **II.** *m* sport; **~ de combat/de compétition** combat/competitive sport; **faire du ~** to play sports; **chaussures de ~** sports shoes; **~s nautiques/d'hiver** water/winter sports ► **ça, c'est du ~** that's no fun

**sportif, -ive** [spɔʀtif, -iv] **I.** *adj* ❶ (*de sport*) **pages sportives d'un journal** sports pages of a newspaper ❷ (*de compétition*) **danse/natation sportive** competitive dancing/swimming ❸ (*qui fait du sport*) athletic ❹ (*typique de qui fait du sport: allure, démarche*) sporty **II.** *m, f* sportsman, sportswoman *m, f*

**spot** [spɔt] *m* ❶ (*lampe, projecteur*) light spot ❷ (*message publicitaire*) **~ publicitaire** commercial

**spray** [spʀɛ] *m* ❶ (*pulvérisation*) spray ❷ (*atomiseur*) aerosol

**sprint** [spʀint] *m* ❶ (*course sur petite distance*) sprint ❷ (*fin de course*) **~ final** final sprint

**square** [skwaʀ] *m* square

**squash** [skwaʃ] *m* squash

**squatter¹** [skwatœʀ] *m* squatter

**squatter²** [skwate] <1> *vt* to squat

**squelette** [skəlɛt] *m* ANAT, ARCHIT a. fig skeleton

**stabiliser** [stabilize] <1> **I.** *vt* ❶ (*consolider, équilibrer*) to consolidate ❷ (*rendre stable, éviter toute fluctuation*) to stabilize **II.** *vpr* (*devenir stable*) **se ~** to stabilize

**stable** [stabl] *adj* ❶ (*ferme, équilibré*) stable; (*terrain*) consolidated ❷ (*durable, qui ne varie pas*) stable

**stade** [stad] *m* ❶ SPORT stadium ❷ (*phase*) stage

**stage** [staʒ] *m* ❶ (*en entreprise*) **faire un ~** to do an internship; **~s** (*sur un CV*) work experience ❷ (*séminaire*) course; **~ d'initiation à qc** introductory course in sth ❸ (*période avant la titularisation*) probation

**stagiaire** [staʒjɛʀ] **I.** *adj* intern **II.** *mf* (*en entreprise*) intern

**stagner** [stagne] <1> *vi* to stagnate

**stand** [stɑ̃d] *m* ❶ (*dans une exposition*) stand ❷ (*dans une fête*) stall; **~ de tir** shooting range

**standard¹** [stɑ̃daʀ] *m* TEL switchboard

**standard²** [stɑ̃daʀ] **I.** *adj inv* standard **II.** *m* standard; **~ de vie** standard of living

**standardiser** [stɑ̃daʀdize] <1> *vt* to standardize

**station** [stasjɔ̃] *f* ❶ AUTO service station; **~ de taxis** taxi rank ❷ TV station ❸ TECH, REL station; **~ d'épuration** water-treatment plant; **~ (d')essence** gas station ❹ (*pour le tourisme*) **~ balnéaire/de sports d'hiver** sea/winter sports resort; **~ thermale** thermal spa

**stationnaire** [stasjɔnɛʀ] *adj* (*qui n'évolue pas*) stationary

**stationnement** [stasjɔnmɑ̃] *m* ❶ (*fait de stationner*) parking; **voitures en ~** parked cars; **ticket/disque de ~** parking ticket/permit; **~ payant** pay parking; **~ interdit** no parking ❷ Québec (*parc de stationnement*) parking lot

**station-service** [stasjɔ̃sɛʀvis] <stations-service(s)> *f* service station

**statistique** [statistik] **I.** *adj* statistical **II.** *f* (*science*) statistics + *vb sing*

**statue** [staty] *f* statue; **la ~ de la Liberté** the Statue of Liberty

**statut** [staty] *m* ❶ a. ADMIN status; **~ de fonctionnaire** civil servant status ❷ *pl* JUR (*d'une association, société*) statutes

**steak** [stɛk] *m* steak

**stéréophonie** [steʀeɔfɔni] *f* stereophony

**stéréotype** [steʀeɔtip] *m* stereotype

**stérile** [steʀil] *adj* sterile

**stérilet** [steʀilɛ] *m* IUD

**stériliser** [steʀilize] <1> *vt* to sterilize

**stérilité** [steʀilite] *f* ❶ AGR barrenness; BIO sterility ❷ (*absence de microbes*) sterility

**steward** [stiwaʀt] *m* steward

**stick** [stik] *m* stick

**stimulant** [stimylɑ̃] *m* ❶ (*médicament*) stimulant ❷ (*incitation*) stimulus

**stimulant(e)** [stimylɑ̃, ɑ̃t] *adj* stimulating

**stimulateur** [stimylatœʀ] *m* ~ **cardiaque** pacemaker

**stimuler** [stimyle] <1> *vt* ❶ (*activer, augmenter*) to stimulate ❷ (*encourager*) to encourage

**stock** [stɔk] *m* ❶ COM stock ❷ (*réserve*) supply; ~ **de sucre** supply of sugar

**stocker** [stɔke] <1> *vt* ❶ (*mettre en réserve*) to stock ❷ INFORM ~ **les données sur une disquette** to store data on a disk

**stop** [stɔp] **I.** *interj* (*halte, dans un télégramme*) stop; ~ **à l'inflation** end inflation **II.** *m* ❶ (*panneau*) stop sign; (*feu*) red light ❷ AUTO (*feu arrière*) brake light ❸ *inf* (*auto-stop*) **faire du** ~ to hitchhike; **en** ~ hitchhiking **III.** *app* **panneau** ~ stop sign

**stopper** [stɔpe] <1> *vt, vi* to stop

**store** [stɔʀ] *m* ❶ (*rideau à enrouler, à lamelles*) blind ❷ (*rideau de magasin*) awning

**stratagème** [strataʒɛm] *m* stratagem

**stratégie** [strateʒi] *f* strategy

**stratégique** [strateʒik] *adj* strategic

**streaming** [strimiŋ] *m* INET livestream, streaming

**stressant(e)** [stresɑ̃, ɑ̃t] *adj* stressful

**stresser** [strese] <1> **I.** *vt* to put under stress **II.** *vi* (*personne*) to stress

**strict(e)** [strikt] *adj* ❶ (*sévère*) strict; **être très** ~ **sur le règlement** to be very strict about the rules ❷ (*rigoureux: principe, observation, respect*) strict ❸ *antéposé* (*exact*) **c'est la** ~**e vérité** it's the exact truth ❹ *antéposé*

(*absolu*) minimum; **dans la plus** ~**e intimité** in the strictest privacy ❺ (*littéral*) **au sens** ~ in the strict sense (of the term) ❻ (*sobre: vêtement, tenue*) sober

**strictement** [striktəmɑ̃] *adv* strictly

**strophe** [strɔf] *f* verse

**structure** [stryktyʀ] *f* ❶ (*organisation*) structure ❷ (*lieu, service social*) ~ **d'accueil** welcome facilities

**structurer** [stryktyʀe] <1> **I.** *vt* to structure **II.** *vpr* **se** ~ to be structured

**studio** [stydjo] *m* (*logement*) *a.* CINE, TV studio

**stupéfaction** [stypefaksjɔ̃] *f* (*étonnement*) amazement

**stupéfait(e)** [stypefɛ, ɛt] *adj* (*étonné*) amazed

**stupéfiant** [stypefjɑ̃] *m* drug

**stupéfiant(e)** [stypefjɑ̃, jɑ̃t] *adj* amazing

**stupéfier** [stypefje] <1> *vt* (*étonner*) to amaze

**stupeur** [stypœʀ] *f* (*étonnement*) amazement; **être frappé de** ~ to be stunned

**stupide** [stypid] *adj* stupid

**style** [stil] *m* ❶ (*écriture*) *a.* ART, LIT, LING style ❷ (*genre*) type; (*d'un vêtement*) style; **des meubles de** ~ period furniture ❸ (*manière personnelle*) style; ~ **de vie** lifestyle

**styliste** [stilist] *mf* stylist

**stylo** [stilo] *m* pen; ~ (**à**) **plume/bille** fountain/ballpoint pen

**stylo-feutre** [stiloføtʀ] <stylos-feutres> *m* felt-tipped pen

**subir** [sybiʀ] <8> *vt* ❶ (*être victime de*) to suffer ❷ (*endurer*) to undergo; (*événements*) to go through; (*conséquences*) to suffer ❸ (*être soumis à*) ~ **le charme/l'influence** to be under the spell/influence; ~ **une opération/un interrogatoire** to undergo an operation/an interrogation ❹ (*être l'objet de*) ~ **des modifications** to be modified ❺ *inf* (*devoir supporter: personne*) to put up with

**subitement** [sybitmɑ̃] *adv* suddenly

**subjectif, -ive** [sybʒɛktif, -iv] *adj* subjective

**subjonctif** [sybʒɔ̃ktif] *m* subjunctive

**sublime** [syblim] *adj* ❶ (*admirable*) wonderful ❷ (*d'une haute vertu*) sublime

**submerger** [sybmɛʀʒe] <2a> *vt* ❶ (*inonder: digue, rives*) to submerge; (*plaine, terres*) to flood ❷ (*envahir*) ~ **qn de qc** to swamp sb with sth

**subordonné(e)** [sybɔʀdɔne] **I.** *m(f)* subordinate **II.** *adj* (*proposition*) subordinate

**subsidiaire** [sybzidjɛʀ, sypsidjɛʀ] *adj* subsidiary

**subsister** [sybziste] <1> *vi* ❶ (*subvenir à ses besoins*) to subsist ❷ (*demeurer: doute, erreur*) to remain; ~ **de qc** to live on sth

**substance** [sypstɑ̃s] *f* ❶ (*matière*) matter ❷ (*essentiel: d'un article, livre*) substance; **en** ~ in substance

**substantif** [sypstɑ̃tif] *m* noun

**substituer** [sypstitɥe] <1> **I.** *vt* ~ **un collègue/un mot à un autre** to substitute a colleague/one word for another **II.** *vpr* **se** ~ **à qn** to take sb's place

**subterfuge** [syptɛʀfyʒ] *m* subterfuge

**subtil(e)** [syptil] *adj* (*personne*) discerning; (*distinction, nuance, parfum*) subtle

**subtilité** [syptilite] *f soutenu* subtlety

**subvenir** [sybvəniʀ] <9> *vi* ~ **à qc** to provide for sth

**S** **subvention** [sybvɑ̃sjɔ̃] *f* grant

**succéder** [syksede] <5> **I.** *vi* ❶ (*venir après*) ~ **à qc** to follow sth ❷ (*assurer la succession*) ~ **à qn** to succeed sb ❸ (*hériter*) to succeed to **II.** *vpr* **se** ~ to follow one another

**succès** [syksɛ] *m* ❶ (*opp: échec*) ~ **en qc** success in sth; **avoir un** ~ **fou** *inf* to be a big hit; **avoir du** ~ **auprès de qn** to have success with sb; **être couronné de** ~ to be crowned with success; **remporter un** ~ to have a success; **à** ~ hit ❷ (*conquête amoureuse*) conquest ❸ SPORT, MIL victory

**successeur** [syksesœʀ] *mf* successor

**successif, -ive** [syksesif, -iv] *adj* successive

**succession** [syksesjɔ̃] *f* succession; **prendre la** ~ **de qn/qc** to succeed sb/sth; **droits de** ~ inheritance tax

**successivement** [syksesivmɑ̃] *adv* successively

**succomber** [sykɔ̃be] <1> *vi* ❶ (*mourir*) ~ **à qc** to die of sth ❷ (*être vaincu*) ~ **sous qc** to be overcome by sth; ~ **sous le poids de qc** to give way under the weight of sth ❸ (*céder à*) ~ **à la tentation/au charme de qn/qc** to give in to the temptation/charm of sb/sth

**succulent(e)** [sykylɑ̃, ɑ̃t] *adj* succulent

**succursale** [sykyʀsal] *f* branch

**sucer** [syse] <2> **I.** *vt* to suck **II.** *vpr* **se** ~ to be sucked

**sucette** [sysɛt] *f* (*bonbon*) lollipop

**sucre** [sykʀ] *m* sugar; (*morceau*) sugar lump; ~ **glace** powdered sugar; ~ **en morceaux/en poudre** lump/caster sugar; ~ **de canne** cane sugar

**sucré(e)** [sykʀe] *adj* sweet; (*par addition de sucre*) sugared

**sucrer** [sykʀe] <1> **I.** *vt* ❶ (*mettre du sucre*) to sugar; (*thé, café*) to put sugar in ❷ *inf* (*supprimer*) ~ **l'argent de poche à un enfant** to stop a child's allowance **II.** *vi* (*rendre sucré*) to sweeten

**sucrerie** [sykʀəʀi] *f* ❶ (*friandise*) sweet ❷ *Québec* (*fabrique de sucre d'érable*) maple sugar factory

**sucrette®** [sykʀɛt] *f* sweetener

**sud** [syd] **I.** *m* south; **au** ~ (*dans/vers la région*) in the south; (*vers le point cardinal*) to the south; **au** ~ **de qc** south of sth; **dans le** ~ **de** in the south of; **du** ~ southern; **vers le** ~ towards the south **II.** *adj inv* south; (*banlieue, latitude*) southern

**Sud** [syd] **I.** *m* South; **l'Europe du** ~ Southern Europe; **dans le** ~ (*dans la région*) in the South; (*vers la région*) to the South; **les gens du** ~ the Southerners **II.** *adj inv* **l'hémisphère** ~ the Southern hemisphere; **le pôle** ~ the South Pole

**sud-africain(e)** [sydafʀikɛ̃, ɛn] <sud--africains> *adj* South African

**sud-est** [sydɛst] *inv* **I.** *m* southeast **II.** *adj* southeast; **vent** ~ southeaster

**sud-ouest** [sydwɛst] *inv* **I.** *m* southwest **II.** *adj* southwest; **vent** ~ southwester

**Suède** [sɥɛd] *f* **la** ~ Sweden

**suer** [sɥe] <1> *vi* (*transpirer*) ~ **de qc** to sweat with sth

**sueur** [sɥœʀ] *f* sweat; **avoir des ~s** to be in a sweat; **être en** ~ to be bathed in sweat ▶ **avoir des ~s froides** to be in a cold sweat

**suffire** [syfiʀ] *irr* **I.** *vi* ❶ (*être assez*) to be enough ❷ (*satisfaire*) ~ **aux besoins de qn** to meet sb's needs; ~ **aux obligations** to meet the requirements **II.** *vi impers* **il suffit d'une fois** once is enough; **il suffit que vous soyez là pour qu'il se calme** you just have to be there for him to calm down; **ça suffit (comme ça)!** *inf* that's enough! **III.** *vpr* **se** ~ **à soi-même** to be self-sufficient

**suffisamment** [syfizamɑ̃] *adv* ~ **grand** big enough; ~ **de temps/livres** enough time/books; ~ **à boire** enough to drink

**suffisant(e)** [syfizɑ̃, ɑ̃t] *adj* (*nombre, techniques*) sufficient, enough; (*résultat, somme*) satisfactory; **ne pas être** ~ not to be enough; ~ **pour** +*infin* sufficient to +*infin*

**suffixe** [syfiks] *m* suffix

**suffoquer** [syfɔke] <1> **I.** *vt* ❶ (*étouffer*) to suffocate ❷ (*stupéfier*) to stun **II.** *vi* (*perdre le souffle*) to gasp for breath

**suffrage** [syfʀaʒ] *m* ❶ (*voix*) vote; ~ **universel** universal suffrage; **les ~s exprimés** valid votes ❷ *pl* (*approbation*) approval; **remporter tous les ~s** to meet with universal approval

**suggérer** [sygʒeʀe] <5> *vt* to suggest

**suggestion** [sygʒɛstjɔ̃] *f* suggestion

**suicide** [sɥisid] *m* (*mort volontaire*) suicide

**suicider** [sɥiside] <1> *vpr* **se** ~ to commit suicide

**suisse** [sɥis] **I.** *adj* Swiss; ~ **romand** Swiss French **II.** *m* ❶ (*gardien d'église*) beadle ❷ *Québec* (*écureuil rayé* (*sur la longueur*)) chipmunk ▶ **petit** ~ CULIN quark dish

**Suisse** [sɥis] **I.** *f* **la** ~ Switzerland **II.** *mf* Swiss; **c'est un** ~ **allemand/romand** he's a German-/French-speaking Swiss

**Suissesse** [sɥisɛs] *f* Swiss woman; ~ **romande** Swiss-French woman

**suite** [sɥit] *f* ❶ (*ce qui vient après: d'une lettre, d'un roman*) rest; **raconter la** ~ **de l'affaire** to tell what happened next; **attendre la** ~ to wait for what is to follow ❷ (*succession: d'événements, de nombres*) sequence; (*d'objets, de personnes*) series ❸ (*conséquence*) consequence; **sans** ~ with no repercussions ❹ (*nouvel épisode*) next episode; **la** ~ **au prochain numéro** to be continued in the next issue ❺ (*cohérence*) coherence ❻ (*appartement*) suite ❼ INFORM ~ **bureautique** office suite ▶ **tout de** ~ straightaway; **tout de** ~ **avant/après** immediately before/after; **donner** ~ **à qc** to follow up on sth; **faire** ~ **à qc** to follow up on sth; ~ **à qc** further to sth; **à la** ~ **de qc** following sth; **et ainsi de** ~ and so on; **de** ~ in a row; **par la** ~ afterwards; **par** ~ **de qc** as a result of sth

**suivant** [sɥivɑ̃] *prep* ❶ (*conformément à, en fonction de*) according to ❷ (*le long de*) along

**suivant(e)** [sɥivɑ̃, ɑ̃t] **I.** *adj* ❶ (*qui vient ensuite*) next ❷ (*ci-après*) following **II.** *m(f)* next one; **au** ~**!** next please!

**suivi** [sɥivi] *m* (*d'une affaire*) follow-up; (*d'un produit*) monitoring; ~ **médical** aftercare

**suivi(e)** [sɥivi] *adj* ❶ (*continu*) steady; (*effort*) sustained ❷ (*cohérent: conversation, raisonnement*) coherent; (*politique*) consistent

**suivre** [sɥivʀ] *irr* **I.** *vt* ❶ (*aller derrière, se conformer à*) to follow; **faire** ~ **qn** to have sb followed ❷ (*venir ensuite*) ~ **qn sur une liste** to come after sb on a list ❸ (*hanter*) to shadow ❹ ECOLE (*classe, cours*) to attend ❺ (*observer:*

S

*actualité, affaire, compétition*) to follow; **~ un élève/malade** to follow the progress of a pupil/patient ⑥ COM (*article, produit*) to keep in stock ⑦ (*comprendre*) to follow ▶ **être à ~** (*personne*) to be worth watching; (*exemple*) to be followed **II.** *vi* ① (*venir après*) to follow ② (*réexpédier*) **faire ~ qc** to forward sth ③ (*être attentif*) to follow ④ (*assimiler*) to copy **III.** *vi impers* **comme suit** as follows **IV.** *vpr* **se ~** ① (*se succéder*) to follow each other ② (*être cohérent*) to be in the right order

**sujet** [sуʒɛ] *m* ① (*thème*) a. LING, PHILOS subject; (*d'un examen*) question ② (*cause*) cause; **sans ~** without reason ③ (*individu*) subject ▶ **c'est à quel ~?** *inf* what is it about?; **à ce ~** on this subject; **au ~ de qn/qc** about sb/sth

**sujet(te)** [sуʒɛ, ʒɛt] *adj* **être ~ à qc/à** +*infin* to be prone to sth/to +*infin*

**super¹** [sуpɛʀ] *m abr de* **supercarburant** premium; **~ sans plomb/plombé** super unleaded/leaded gas

**super²** [sуpɛʀ] *adj inv, inf* super

**superbe** [sуpɛʀb] *adj* (*repas, vin, temps, résultat*) superb; (*corps, enfant*) magnificent

**superficie** [sуpɛʀfisi] *f* (*d'un terrain, pays*) area; (*d'un appartement*) surface area

**superficiel(le)** [sуpɛʀfisjɛl] *adj* superficial

**superflu(e)** [sуpɛʀfly] *adj* superfluous

**supérieur** [sуpeʀjœʀ] *m* higher education

**supérieur(e)** [sуpeʀjœʀ] **I.** *adj* ① (*plus haut dans l'espace: lèvre, mâchoire*) upper ② (*plus élevé dans la hiérarchie*) superior; (*animal, plante*) greater; (*cadre*) senior; **enseignement ~** higher education ③ (*de grande qualité*) superior ④ (*qui dépasse*) **être ~ à qn en vitesse** to be faster than sb; **~ en nombre** greater in number; **~ par la qualité** better quality; **être ~ à la moyenne** to be above average ⑤ (*prétentieux: air, regard, ton*) superior **II.** *m(f)* a. REL superior

**supériorité** [sуpeʀjɔʀite] *f* **~ sur qn/qc** superiority over sb/sth

**superlatif** [sуpɛʀlatif] *m* superlative

**supermarché** [sуpɛʀmaʀʃe] *m* supermarket

**superposé(e)** [sуpɛʀpoze] *adj* (*livres, pierres*) superimposed; **lits ~s** bunk beds

**superposer** [sуpɛʀpoze] <1> *vt* ① (*faire chevaucher*) to superimpose ② (*empiler*) to stack

**supersonique** [sуpɛʀsɔnik] *m* supersonic aircraft

**superstitieux, -euse** [sуpɛʀstisjø, -jøz] *adj* superstitious

**superviser** [sуpɛʀvize] <1> *vt* to supervise; (*travail*) to oversee

**superviseur** [sуpɛʀvizœʀ] *m* INFORM supervisor

**supplément** [syplemã] *m* ① (*surplus*) extra; **~ de salaire** bonus; **en ~** extra ② (*publication: d'un journal, d'une revue*) supplement ③ (*somme d'argent à payer*) surcharge; CHEMDFER upgrade charge; **un ~ de 100 euros** 100 euros extra

**supplémentaire** [syplemãtɛʀ] *adj* extra; **heures ~s** overtime + *vb sing*

**supplice** [syplis] *m* torture

**supplier** [syplije] <1> *vt* **~ qn de** +*infin* to beg sb to +*infin*

**support** [sуpɔʀ] *m* (*soutien*) support; (*d'un meuble, d'une statue*) stand

**supportable** [sуpɔʀtabl] *adj* bearable

**supporter¹** [sуpɔʀte] <1> **I.** *vt* ① (*psychiquement*) to bear; **~ de** +*infin* to bear to +*infin*; **il ne supporte pas qu'elle fasse qc** (*subj*) he can't bear her doing sth ② (*physiquement: alcool, chaleur*) to tolerate; (*douleur, opération*) to stand; **elle ne supporte pas l'avion** she can't stand planes ③ (*subir: affront, échec*) to suffer; **~ les conséquences de qc** to suffer [*o* endure] the consequences of sth ④ (*soutenir: pilier*) to support ⑤ SPORT **~ qn/qc** to support sb/sth **II.** *vpr* **se ~** to stand each other

**supporter²** [sypɔʁtɛʁ] *m*, **supporteur, -trice** [sypɔʁtœʁ, -tʁis] *m, f* supporter
**supposé(e)** [sypoze] *adj* supposed
**supposer** [sypoze] <1> *vt* ❶ (*imaginer*) to suppose; **je suppose qu'il va revenir** I suppose he'll come back; **supposons qu'elle dise non** +*subj* let's suppose she says no ❷ (*présumer*) to assume ❸ (*impliquer*) to presuppose
**supposition** [sypozisjɔ̃] *f* assumption
**supprimer** [sypʁime] <1> **I.** *vt* ❶ (*enlever*) **~ un avantage/emploi à qn** to take away sb's benefit/job ❷ (*abolir: libertés, peine de mort*) to abolish ❸ (*faire disparaître*) to get rid of ❹ (*tuer*) to eliminate **II.** *vpr* **se ~** to kill oneself
**suprême** [sypʁɛm] *adj* (*bonheur, cour, instance, pouvoir*) supreme; (*degré*) highest
**sur** [syʁ] *prep* ❶ (*position*) on; (*au-dessus de*) over; **marcher ~ la capitale** to march on the capital ❷ (*temporel*) **~ le soir** towards the evening; **~ ses vieux jours** in his later years; **~ le coup** (*immédiatement*) immediately; (*au début*) at first; **~ ce je vous quitte** and now I must leave you ❸ (*successif*) **coup ~ coup** shot after shot ❹ (*causal*) **~ sa recommandation** on his/her recommendation; **~ présentation d'une pièce d'identité** on presentation of a form of identification ❺ (*modal*) **ne me parle pas ~ ce ton!** don't speak to me like that!; **~ mesure** custom-made; **~ le mode mineur** in a minor key; **~ l'air de ...** to the tune of ... ❻ (*au sujet de*) about ❼ (*proportionnalité, notation, dimension*) **neuf fois ~ dix** nine times out of ten; **un enfant ~ deux** one child in two; **faire 5 mètres ~ 4** to measure 5 by four meters
**sûr(e)** [syʁ] *adj* ❶ (*convaincu, certain*) **~ de qn/qc** sure of sb/sth; **être ~ de faire qc/que ...** to be sure of doing sth/that ... ❷ (*sans danger*) safe; **en lieu ~** in a safe place ❸ (*digne de confiance*) trustworthy; (*temps*) reliable ❹ (*solide: arme*) sturdy; (*base, main*) steady; (*raisonnement, instinct*)

sound ▸ **bien** ~ of course; **bien** ~ **que oui** *inf* of course; **bien** ~ **que non** *inf* of course not; **être** ~ **et certain** to be absolutely sure; **c'est** ~ *inf* definitely; **pas** (**si**) ~! *inf* it's not so sure!
**surcharge** [syʁʃaʁʒ] *f* ❶ (*excès de charge*) overloading ❷ (*excédent de poids*) excess load
**surcharger** [syʁʃaʁʒe] <2a> *vt* to overload
**surdité** [syʁdite] *f* deafness
**surdoué(e)** [syʁdwe] **I.** *adj* (highly) gifted **II.** *m(f)* prodigy
**sûrement** [syʁmɑ̃] *adv* certainly
**surenchérir** [syʁɑ̃ʃeʁiʁ] <8> *vi* to bid higher; (*en rajouter*) to raise one's bid; **~ sur qn/qc** to top sb/sth
**surendettement** [syʁɑ̃dɛtmɑ̃] *m* excessive debt
**sûreté** [syʁte] *f* ❶ (*précision*) sureness ❷ (*sécurité*) safety; **mettre qn/qc en ~** to put sb/sth in a safe place
**surf** [sœʁf] *m* ❶ (*sport*) surfing; (*sur la neige*) snowboarding; **faire du ~** to go surfing; (*sur la neige*) to go snowboarding ❷ (*planche pour l'eau*) surfboard; (*planche pour la neige*) snowboard ❸ INFORM surfing
**surface** [syʁfas] *f* ❶ (*aire*) area; (*d'un appartement, d'une pièce*) surface area; **~ de réparation** SPORT penalty area ❷ (*couche superficielle*) surface; **à la ~** on the surface ❸ INFORM **~ de travail** user surface ▸ **grande** ~ superstore; **refaire ~** to resurface; **en** ~ on the surface
**surfer** [sœʁfe] <1> *vi* (*sur l'eau*) *a.* INFORM to surf; **~ sur le Web** to surf the Web
**surgelé(e)** [syʁʒəle] *adj* frozen
**surgelés** [syʁʒəle] *mpl* frozen foods
**surgir** [syʁʒiʁ] <8> *vi* to appear; (*arbres*) to rise up; (*difficulté*) to crop up
**surhumain(e)** [syʁymɛ̃, ɛn] *adj* superhuman
**surligner** [syʁliɲe] <1> *vt a.* INFORM to mark
**surmener** [syʁməne] <4> *vt* to overwork

**S**

**surmonter** [syʀmɔ̃te] <1> **I.** vt to surmount **II.** vpr se ~ (être maîtrisé: timidité) to be overcome

**surnaturel(le)** [syʀnatyʀɛl] adj a. REL supernatural

**surnom** [syʀnɔ̃] m ❶ (sobriquet) nickname ❷ (qualificatif) name

**surnombre** [syʀnɔ̃bʀ] m surplus

**surnommer** [syʀnɔme] <1> vt ~ qn **Junior** to nickname sb Junior

**surpasser** [syʀpɑse] <1> vpr se ~ to excel oneself

**surpeuplé(e)** [syʀpœple] adj (pays) over-populated; (salle) overcrowded

**surplomber** [syʀplɔ̃be] <1> vt ~ qc (étage, lumière) to overhang sth

**surplus** [syʀply] m (d'une somme, récolte) surplus ► **au** ~ moreover

**surpopulation** [syʀpɔpylasjɔ̃] f overpopulation

**surprenant(e)** [syʀpʀənɑ̃, ɑ̃t] adj surprising

**surprendre** [syʀpʀɑ̃dʀ] <13> **I.** vt ❶ (étonner) to surprise; **être surpris de qc/que** +subj to be surprised about sth/that ❷ (prendre sur le fait) ~ **qn à faire qc** to catch sb doing sth ❸ (découvrir: conversation) to overhear ❹ (prendre au dépourvu) ~ **qn dans son bureau** to surprise sb in their office **II.** vpr se ~ **à faire qc** to catch oneself doing sth

**surpris(e)** [syʀpʀi, iz] part passé de **surprendre**

**surprise** [syʀpʀiz] f (étonnement, chose inattendue) surprise; **faire la ~ à qn** to surprise sb; **à la grande ~ de qn** to everyone's great surprise; **avec/par ~** with/in surprise

**surproduction** [syʀpʀɔdyksjɔ̃] f overproduction

**surréaliste** [syʀʀealist] **I.** adj ❶ ART, LIT surrealist ❷ inf (extravagant) surreal **II.** mf surrealist

**sursaut** [syʀso] m ❶ (haut-le-corps) jump, start; **se réveiller en ~** to wake up with a start ❷ (élan: de colère) blaze; (d'énergie) burst

**sursauter** [syʀsote] <1> vi to jump

**sursis** [syʀsi] m ❶ (délai) extension; (pour payer) postponement ❷ JUR reprieve

**surtaxe** [syʀtaks] f surcharge

**surtout** [syʀtu] adv ❶ (avant tout) above all ❷ inf (d'autant plus) **j'ai peur de lui, ~ qu'il est si fort** I'm scared of him, with him being so strong ► ~ **pas** definitely not

**surveillance** [syʀvɛjɑ̃s] f (contrôle: de la police) surveillance; (des travaux, études) supervision

**surveillant(e)** [syʀvɛjɑ̃, jɑ̃t] m(f) supervisor; (de prison) prison guard; (de magasin) security guard

**surveiller** [syʀveje] <1> vt ❶ (prendre soin de) ~ **un enfant** to watch over a child; ~ **un malade** to care for a patient ❷ (suivre l'évolution) to watch; (éducation des enfants) to oversee ❸ (garder) to watch ❹ (assurer la protection de) to keep watch over ❺ CULIN to watch ❻ ECOLE (élèves) to supervise; (examen) to proctor

**survie** [syʀvi] f ❶ (maintien en vie) survival ❷ REL afterlife

**survivant(e)** [syʀvivɑ̃, ɑ̃t] **I.** adj surviving **II.** m(f) (rescapé) survivor

**survivre** [syʀvivʀ] vi irr ❶ (demeurer en vie) ~ **à qc** to survive sth ❷ (vivre plus longtemps que) ~ **à qn/qc** to survive sb/sth

**survoler** [syʀvɔle] <1> vt ❶ AVIAT to fly over ❷ (examiner: article) to skim through; (question) to skim over

**susceptible** [sysɛptibl] adj ❶ (ombrageux) touchy ❷ (en mesure de) **il est ~ de faire qc** he could do sth

**susciter** [sysite] <1> vt ❶ (faire naître) to arouse; (querelle) to provoke ❷ (provoquer: obstacle) to create; (troubles) to cause

**suspect(e)** [syspɛ, ɛkt] **I.** adj ❶ (louche) **être ~ à qn** to be suspicious to sb ❷ (soupçonné) **être ~ de qc** to be suspected of sth ❸ (douteux) suspect **II.** m(f) suspect

**suspecter** [syspɛkte] <1> vt (soupçonner) to suspect

**suspendre** [syspɑ̃dʀ] <14> *vt* ❶ (*accrocher*) ~ qc au **portemanteau/au mur** to hang sth on the coat rack/on the wall ❷ (*rester collé à*) **être suspendu aux lèvres de qn** to hang on sb's every word ❸ (*interrompre: séance, réunion, paiement*) to suspend ❹ (*remettre: décision*) to put off; (*jugement*) to defer ❺ (*destituer: fonctionnaire, joueur*) to suspend

**suspens** [syspɑ̃] **procès/dossier en ~** trial/file that is pending; **le projet est en ~** the project is in abeyance

**suspense** [syspɛns] *m* suspense

**suspicion** [syspisjɔ̃] *f* suspicion

**svelte** [svɛlt] *adj* svelte

**S.V.P.** [ɛsvepe] *abr de* **s'il vous plaît** please

**sweat-shirt** [switʃœʀt] <sweat-shirts> *m* sweatshirt

**syllabe** [sil(l)ab] *f* syllable

**symbole** [sɛ̃bɔl] *m* ❶ (*image*) a. CHIM, MATH symbol ❷ REL creed

**symbolique** [sɛ̃bɔlik] **I.** *adj* ❶ (*emblématique*) symbolic ❷ (*très modique*) nominal **II.** *f* symbology

**symboliser** [sɛ̃bɔlize] <1> *vt* to symbolize

**symétrie** [simetʀi] *f* a. MATH symmetry

**symétrique** [simetʀik] *adj* a. MATH symmetrical

**sympa** [sɛ̃pa] *adj inf abr de* **sympathique**

**sympathie** [sɛ̃pati] *f* ❶ (*inclination*) ~ **pour qn/qc** liking sb/sth; **inspirer la** ~ to be likeable ❷ (*lors d'un deuil*) sympathy

**sympathique** [sɛ̃patik] *adj* ❶ (*aimable: personne, animal*) friendly ❷ *inf* (*personne, plat*) nice; (*accueil*) warm; (*ambiance*) pleasant

**sympathiser** [sɛ̃patize] <1> *vi* ~ **avec qn** to get along well with sb

**symphonie** [sɛ̃fɔni] *f* symphony

**symptôme** [sɛ̃ptom] *m* ❶ (*indice*) sign ❷ MED symptom

**synagogue** [sinagɔg] *f* (*édifice*) synagogue

**synchroniser** [sɛ̃kʀɔnize] <1> *vt* to synchronize

**syncope** [sɛ̃kɔp] *f* blackout; **avoir une** ~ to faint

**syndicat** [sɛ̃dika] *m* ❶ (*syndicat de salariés*) labor union ❷ (*pour les touristes*) ~ **d'initiative** tourist office

**synonyme** [sinɔnim] **I.** *adj* **être** ~ **de qc** to be synonymous with sth **II.** *m* synonym

**syntaxe** [sɛ̃taks] *f* ❶ LING syntax ❷ *Belgique* (*première année du secondaire supérieur*) second-to-last year of secondary school

**synthèse** [sɛ̃tɛz] *f* synthesis; (*exposé d'ensemble*) summary; **faire la** ~ **de qc** to summarize sth ▸ **résine/produit de** ~ synthetic resin/product

**synthétique** [sɛ̃tetik] **I.** *adj* (*matériau*) artificial; (*fibres, caoutchouc*) synthetic **II.** *m* synthetic

**synthétiseur** [sɛ̃tetizœʀ] *m* MUS synthesizer

**systématique** [sistematik] *adj* systematic

**système** [sistɛm] *m* ❶ (*structure*) system; ~ **de vie** way of life ❷ *inf* (*combine*) way; **connaître le** ~ *inf* to know the system; ~ **D** *inf* resourcefulness ❸ (*institution*) system ❹ INFORM ~ **informatique/d'exploitation** computing/operating system; ~ **de gestion de base de données** database management system ❺ AUTO ~ **de guidage** guidance system ▸ **taper sur le** ~ **à qn** *inf* to get on sb's nerves

**Système monétaire européen** *m* European Monetary System

S

# Tt

**T, t** [te] *m inv* T, t; **en t** T-shaped; **~ com-me Thérèse** (*au téléphone*) t as in Tango

**t** *f abr de* **tonne** t.

**t'** *pron v.* te, tu

**ta** [ta, te] <tes> *dét poss* your; *v.a.* **ma**

**tabac** [taba] I. *m* ❶ (*plante, produit*) tobacco; **~ à priser** snuff ❷ *inf* (*magasin*) tobacco shop ▶ **faire un ~** *inf* to be a great success; **passer qn à ~** *inf* to beat sb up II. *adj inv* buff

**table** [tabl] *f* ❶ (*meuble, tablée, tableau*) table; (*d'autel*) altar stone; **mettre la ~** to set the table; **être à ~** to be having a meal; **à ~!** come and eat!; **service de ~** table linen; **~ des matières** table of contents ❷ (*nourriture*) food ▶ **se mettre à ~** (*aller manger*) to sit down to eat; *inf* (*avouer sa faute*) to own up

**tableau** [tablo] <x> *m* ❶ (*cadre*) picture; (*peinture*) painting ❷ (*scène, paysage*) scene ❸ ECOLE board ❹ (*panneau*) a. INFORM table; **~ de service** duty roster; **~ de bord** (*d'une voiture*) dashboard ❺ (*présentation graphique*) chart

**tablette** [tablɛt] *f* ❶ (*plaquette*) block ❷ *Québec* (*bloc de papier à lettres*) writing pad

**tableur** [tablœʀ] *m* INFORM spreadsheet

**tablier** [tablije] *m* (*vêtement*) apron

**tabou** [tabu] *m* taboo

**tabou(e)** [tabu] *adj* ❶ (*interdit*) taboo ❷ (*intouchable*) untouchable

**taboulé** [tabule] *m* tabbouleh

**tabouret** [taburɛ] *m* (*petit siège*) stool

**tache** [taʃ] *f* ❶ (*salissure*) stain; **~ de rousseur** freckle ❷ (*flétrissure*) blot ❸ (*impression visuelle*) patch; (*de couleur, peinture*) spot ▶ **faire ~** to stick out like a sore thumb

**tâche** [taʃ] *f* ❶ (*besogne*) work ❷ (*mission*) task ▶ **être dur à la ~** to be a hard worker

**tacher** [taʃe] <1> I. *vi* to stain II. *vt* ❶ (*faire des taches sur*) to stain ❷ (*moucheter*) **~ la peau de qc** to mark the skin of sth ❸ (*souiller*) to sully III. *vpr* **se ~** (*tissu*) to get stained; (*personne*) to get dirty

**tâcher** [taʃe] <1> *vi* ❶ (*s'efforcer*) **~ de** +*infin* to endeavor to +*infin* ❷ (*faire en sorte*) **~ que qc (ne) se produise (pas)** to ensure that sth (does not) happen

**tacite** [tasit] *adj* tacit

**taciturne** [tasityʀn] *adj* taciturn

**tact** [takt] *m* tact

**tactile** [taktil] *adj* tactile; (*écran*) touch-sensitive

**tactique** [taktik] I. *adj* tactical II. *f* tactic

**taffetas** [tafta] *m* taffeta

**taie** [tɛ] *f* (*d'un oreiller*) pillow case

**taille¹** [tɑj] *f* ❶ (*hauteur: d'une personne*) height ❷ (*dimension, importance, pointure*) size; **de ~** considerable; **la ~ en dessous** the next size down; **quelle ~ faites-vous?** what size are you? ❸ (*partie du corps, d'un vêtement*) waist ▶ **ne pas être à sa ~** (*vêtement*) to be the wrong size

**taille²** [tɑj] *f* ❶ (*d'un diamant, d'une pierre*) cut ❷ BOT coppice

**taille-crayon** [tɑjkʀɛjɔ̃] <taille--crayon(s)> *m* pencil sharpener

**tailler** [tɑje] <1> I. *vt* ❶ (*couper: arbre*) to prune; (*crayon*) to sharpen; (*ongles*) to trim; (*pierre*) to hew; (*diamant*) to cut; (*pièce de bois*) to carve ❷ (*découper: robe*) to cut out II. *vpr* ❶ (*conquérir*) **se ~ une place au soleil** to earn oneself a place in the sun ❷ (*se couper*) **se ~ la barbe** to trim one's beard

**tailleur** [tɑjœʀ] *m* ❶ (*couturier*) tailor ❷ (*tenue*) suit

**tailleur, -euse** [tɑjœʁ, -jøz] *m, f* (*ouvrier*) cutter

**taire** [tɛʁ] *irr* **I.** *vpr* ❶ (*être silencieux, faire silence*) **se ~** to be silent ❷ (*s'abstenir de parler*) **se ~ sur qc** to keep quiet about sth **II.** *vt* ❶ (*cacher*) to hush up ❷ (*refuser de dire: vérité*) to conceal **III.** *vi* **faire ~ qn** to shut sb up

**talent** [talɑ̃] *m* talent; **avoir du ~** to be talented

**talkie-walkie** [tokiwolki] <talkies-walkies> *m* walkie-talkie

**talon** [talɔ̃] *m* ❶ (*pièce de chaussure, chaussette*) *a.* ANAT heel; **~ aiguille** stiletto heel ❷ (*bout*) crust; (*d'un jambon, fromage*) heel ❸ (*d'un chèque*) stub ❹ JEUX talon

**talus** [taly] *m* embankment

**tambour** [tɑ̃buʁ] *m* ❶ (*d'un frein, lave-linge*) drum; (*d'une montre*) barrel ❷ (*musicien*) drummer ►**~ battant** briskly

**tamis** [tami] *m* ❶ (*crible*) sieve ❷ SPORT strings *pl*

**Tamise** [tamiz] *f* **la ~** the Thames

**tamiser** [tamize] <1> *vt* ❶ (*passer au tamis*) to sieve ❷ (*filtrer: lumière*) to filter

**tampon** [tɑ̃pɔ̃] **I.** *m* ❶ (*en coton*) wad ❷ (*périodique*) tampon ❸ (*à récurer*) scouring pad ❹ (*pansement*) pad ❺ (*cachet*) stamp ❻ (*bouchon*) plug ❼ CHEMDFER buffer **II.** *app inv* buffer

**tamponner** [tɑ̃pɔne] <1> *vt* ❶ (*heurter*) **~ qc** (*voiture*) to crash into sth ❷ (*timbrer*) to stamp

**tandis que** [tɑ̃diskə] *conj* ❶ *indic* while

**tanière** [tanjɛʁ] *f* ❶ (*repère: d'un animal*) den; (*d'un malfaiteur*) lair ❷ (*lieu retiré*) retreat

**tank** [tɑ̃k] *m* tank

**tanneur, -euse** [tanœʁ, -øz] *m, f* tanner

**tant** [tɑ̃] *adv* ❶ (*tellement*) so much ❷ (*une telle quantité*) **~ de choses/fois** so many things/times; **une voiture comme il y en a** **~** a perfectly ordinary car ❸ (*autant*) **~ qu'il peut** as much as he can; **ne pas en deman-**

**der ~** to not ask so much ❹ (*aussi longtemps que*) **~ que tu seras là** as long as you're there; **~ que j'y suis** while I'm here ❺ (*dans la mesure où*) **~ qu'à faire la vaisselle, tu peux aussi ...** since you're doing the dishes, you might as well... ►**~ qu'à <u>faire</u>** *inf* might as well; **en ~ que** as; **~ pis!** *inf* tough luck!

**tante** [tɑ̃t] *f* ❶ (*parente*) aunt ❷ *vulg* (*homosexuel*) queer

**tantôt** [tɑ̃to] *adv* ❶ (*en alternance*) **~ à pied ~ à vélo** sometimes on foot, sometimes by bike ❷ *Belgique* (*tout à l'heure*) later

**taon** [tɑ̃] *m* ZOOL horsefly

**tapage** [tapaʒ] *m* ❶ (*vacarme*) racket ❷ (*publicité*) talk

**tape-à-l'œil** [tapalœj] *inv* **I.** *adj* (*toilette*) flashy **II.** *m* show

**taper** [tape] <1> **I.** *vi* ❶ (*donner des coups*) to beat; **~ à la porte** to knock at the door; **~ sur qn** to beat sb ❷ (*frapper*) **~ de la main sur la table** to bang one's hand on the table; **~ dans le ballon** to kick the ball; **~ des mains** to clap ❸ (*dactylographier*) to type ❹ *inf* (*dire du mal de*) **~ sur qn** to run sb down ❺ *inf* (*cogner: soleil*) to beat down **II.** *vt* ❶ (*battre: tapis*) to beat; (*personne, animal*) to hit; (*amicalement*) to tap ❷ (*cogner*) **~ le pied contre qc** to stub one's foot on sth ❸ (*frapper de*) **~ la table du poing** to bang one's fist on the table ❹ (*produire en tapant*) **~ trois coups à la porte** to knock three times at the door ❺ (*dactylographier*) to type ❻ INFORM (*texte, code*) to enter **III.** *vpr* (*se frapper*) **c'est à se ~ la tête contre les murs!** it'd drive you up the wall! ►**je m'en tape** *inf* I couldn't care less

**tapir** [tapiʁ] <8> *vpr* **se ~ sous qc** (*animal, personne*) to hide away under sth

**tapis** [tapi] *m* ❶ (*textile protecteur*) rug ❷ JEUX baize ❸ (*vaste étendue*) carpet ❹ INFORM **~ (pour) souris** mouse pad ►**~ <u>roulant</u>** conveyor belt; (*pour baga-*

*ges*) carousel; **envoyer** qn au ~ SPORT to floor sb

**tapisser** [tapise] <1> vt ❶ (*revêtir: mur, pièce*) to wallpaper; (*fauteuil*) to upholster ❷ (*recouvrir: lierre, mousse*) to carpet

**tapisserie** [tapisʀi] f ❶ (*revêtement*) wallpaper ❷ (*pose du papier peint*) wallpapering ❸ ART (*activité*) tapestry-making; (*tapis*) tapestry

**tapoter** [tapɔte] <1> vt (*joues*) to pat

**taquiner** [takine] <1> vt ❶ (*s'amuser à agacer*) to tease ❷ (*faire légèrement souffrir: choses*) to bother

**tard** [taʀ] I. adv (*tardivement*) late; **le plus ~ possible** as late as possible; **au plus ~** at the latest; **pas plus ~ que ...** no later than ... ▸ **mieux vaut ~ que jamais** *prov* better late than never II. m **sur le ~** late in the day

**tarder** [taʀde] <1> vi ❶ (*traîner*) to be late; **sans ~** without delay; **~ à faire qc** to delay doing sth ❷ (*se faire attendre*) to take a long time

**tardif, -ive** [taʀdif, -iv] adj ❶ (*qui vient, qui se fait tard*) belated ❷ AGR (*fruits, fleurs*) late

**tare** [taʀ] f ❶ (*défaut: d'une personne, société*) flaw ❷ MED defect

**tari(e)** [taʀi] adj dried up

**tarif** [taʀif] m (*barème*) rate; (*d'une réparation*) cost

**tarir** [taʀiʀ] <8> I. vi (*cesser de couler*) to dry up II. vt (*assécher*) **~ qc** to dry sth up III. vpr **se ~** (*s'assécher*) to dry up

**tartare** [taʀtaʀ] adj ❶ HIST **les populations ~s** the Tartars ❷ CULIN **steak ~** steak tartare

**tarte** [taʀt] I. f ❶ CULIN tart ❷ *inf* (*gifle*) slap II. adj *inf* stupid

**tartine** [taʀtin] f ❶ CULIN **~ beurrée** piece of bread and butter; **~ grillée** piece of toast ❷ *péj, inf* (*long développement*) **écrire des ~s** to write reams

**tartiner** [taʀtine] <1> vt CULIN to spread

**tartre** [taʀtʀ] m fur; (*des dents*) tartar

**tas** [tɑ] m ❶ (*amas*) heap ❷ *inf* (*beau-*

*coup de*) **un ~ de choses/personnes** loads *pl* of things/people

**tasse** [tɑs] f ❶ (*contenu*) cup; **~ de thé** cup of tea ❷ (*récipient*) **~ à thé** teacup

**tasser** [tɑse] <1> I. vt ❶ (*comprimer*) to compress; (*paille, foin*) to pack ❷ (*en tapant: neige, sable, terre*) to pack down II. vpr **se ~** ❶ (*s'affaisser*) to settle ❷ *inf* (*s'arranger: difficulté, chose*) to sort itself out; (*ennui, querelle*) to settle down

**tâter** [tɑte] <1> I. vt to feel ▸ **le terrain** to find out the lay of the land II. vi (*faire l'expérience*) **~ de qc** to have a taste of sth III. vpr **se ~** *inf* (*hésiter*) to be of two minds

**tatillon(ne)** [tatijɔ̃, jɔn] adj finicky

**tâtonner** [tɑtɔne] <1> vi ❶ (*chercher en hésitant*) to grope around ❷ (*se déplacer sans voir*) to grope one's way along

**tatouage** [tatwaʒ] m ❶ (*action*) tattooing ❷ (*dessin sur la peau*) tattoo

**tatouer** [tatwe] <1> vt to tattoo

**taudis** [todi] m (*logement misérable*) slum

**taupe** [top] f ZOOL mole

**taureau** [tɔʀo] <x> m ZOOL bull

**Taureau** [tɔʀo] <x> m Taurus; *v.a.* **Balance**

**taux** [to] m ❶ (*pourcentage administrativement fixé*) rate ❷ (*mesure statistique*) a. MED level; (*en évolution*) rate; **~ de chômage** unemployment rate; **~ d'intérêt** interest rate; **~ de cholestérol** cholesterol level ❸ TECH **~ de compression** compression ratio

**taverne** [tavɛʀn] f ❶ (*gargote*) inn ❷ HIST tavern ❸ *Québec* (*débit de boissons réservé aux hommes*) tavern (*for men only*)

**taxation** [taksasjɔ̃] f FIN taxation

**taxe** [taks] f (*impôt*) tax; **~ à la valeur ajoutée** value added tax; **toutes ~s comprises** tax included; **hors ~s** duty free; (*sans T.V.A.*) VAT free

**taxi** [taksi] m ❶ (*véhicule*) taxi ❷ *inf* (*chauffeur*) cabby

**tchao** [tʃao] *interj inf* bye

**te** [tə] <*devant voyelle ou h muet* t'> *pron pers* you; *v.a.* **me**

**technicien(ne)** [tɛknisjɛ̃, jɛn] *m(f)* (*professionnel qualifié, expert*) technician

**technico-commercial(e)** [tɛknikokɔmɛrsjal, -jo] <technico-commerciaux> I. *adj* technical sales II. *m(f)* COM technical sales advisor

**technique** [tɛknik] I. *adj* (*ouvrage, revue, terme*) technical; **lycée ~** vocational-technical school II. *m* ECOLE vocational education III. *f* technique

**techno** [tɛkno] I. *adj* **musique ~** techno music II. *f* techno

**technologie** [tɛknɔlɔʒi] *f* technology; **~ de pointe** cutting edge technology

**tee-shirt** [tiʃœrt] <tee-shirts> *m* T-shirt

**teindre** [tɛ̃dʀ] *irr* I. *vt* to dye; (*bois*) to stain; **~ qc en rouge/noir** to dye sth red/black II. *vpr* (*se colorer les cheveux*) **se ~ en brun** to dye one's hair brown

**teint** [tɛ̃] *m* (*couleur de la peau*) complexion

**teint(e)** [tɛ̃, ɛ̃t] I. *part passé de* **teindre** II. *adj* dyed

**teinte** [tɛ̃t] *f* (*couleur*) shade

**teinter** [tɛ̃te] <1> *vt* (*colorer*) to dye

**teinture** [tɛ̃tyʀ] *f* ① (*colorant*) dye ② MED **~ d'arnica** tincture of arnica ③ (*fait de teindre*) dyeing

**tel(le)** [tɛl] I. *adj indéf* ① (*semblable, si fort/grand*) **un ~/une ~le ...** such a ...; **de ~(s) ...** such ... ② (*ainsi*) **~le n'est pas mon intention** that is not my intention; **~ père, ~ fils** like father, like son ③ (*comme*) **~ que qn/qc** such as [*o* like] sb/sth; **un homme ~ que lui** a man like him ④ (*un certain*) **~ jour et à ~ le heure** on such a day at such a time ▶ **en tant que ~** as such; **rendre qc ~ quel** *inf* to return sth as it is; **il n'y a rien de ~** there's nothing like it II. *pron indéf* **si ~ ou ~ le dit ...** if anybody tells you ...

**télé** [tele] *f inf abr de* **télévision** TV; **à la ~** on TV

**téléachat** [teleaʃa] *m* teleshopping

**téléboutique** [telebutik] *f* TEL phone center

**télécharger** [teleʃarʒe] *vt* **~ qc** (*vers l'aval*) to download sth; (*vers l'amont*) to upload sth

**télécommande** [telekɔmɑ̃d] *f* (*boîtier, procédé*) remote control

**télécommunication** [telekɔmynikasjɔ̃] *f gén pl* (*administration, technique*) telecommunication

**télécopie** [telekɔpi] *f* fax

**télécopieur** [telekɔpjœr] *m* fax machine

**téléfax** [telefaks] *m* fax

**télégramme** [telegram] *m* telegram

**télégraphier** [telegrafje] <1> *vt* ① (*envoyer un message en morse*) to wire ② NAUT to telegraph

**télégraphique** [telegrafik] *adj* ① TEL telegraph ② (*abrégé: style*) telegraphic

**téléguider** [telegide] <1> *vt* **~ qc** (*diriger à distance*) to operate sth by radio control

**téléobjectif** [teleɔbʒɛktif] *m* telephoto lens

**télépaiement** [telepɛmɑ̃] *m* electronic payment

**téléphérique** [teleferik] *m* cable car

**téléphone** [telefɔn] *m* telephone; **~ sans fil** cordless phone; **~ portable** cell phone; **~ arabe** *iron* grapevine; **appeler/avoir qn au ~** to call sb on the phone; **être au ~** to be on the phone

**téléphoner** [telefɔne] <1> I. *vt* (*transmettre par téléphone*) **~ une nouvelle à une amie** to tell a friend news over the phone II. *vi* (*parler au téléphone*) to telephone; **~ à qn** to (tele)phone sb III. *vpr* **se ~** to (tele)phone each other

**téléphonie** [telefɔni] *f* telephony; **~ mobile** mobile telephony

**télescope** [teleskɔp] *m* telescope

**télésiège** [telesjɛʒ] *m* chairlift

**téléski** [teleski] *m* ski lift

**téléspectateur, -trice** [telespɛktatœr, -tris] *m, f* (*television*) viewer

**télésurveillance** [telesyrvɛjɑ̃s] *f* remote surveillance

**Télétel®** [teletɛl] *m:* electronic telephone directory

**Télétex®** [teletɛks] *m* teletex

**télétravail** [teletʀavaj] *m* telecommuting

**téléviser** [televize] <1> *vt* to televise

**téléviseur** [televizœʀ] *m* television (set)

**télévision** [televizjɔ̃] *f* ① (*organisme, technique, programmes*) television; **regarder la ~** to watch television; **à la ~** on television; **~ par câble/satellite** cable/satellite television ② (*récepteur*) television (set) ③ *Québec* **~ communautaire** (*temps de télévision et moyens de réalisation mis à la disposition de collectivités, de groupes, pour la présentation de certaines émissions*) public access television

**télex** [telɛks] *m inv* telex

**tellement** [tɛlmɑ̃] *adv* ① (*si*) so; **ce serait ~ mieux** it'd be so much better ② (*tant*) so much ③ (*beaucoup*) **pas/plus ~** *inf* (*venir, aimer*) not much/much now; (*boire, manger, travailler*) not that much/much any more ④ *inf* (*tant de*) **avoir ~ d'amis/de courage** to have so many friends/so much courage ⑤ (*parce que*) because; **on le comprend à peine ~ il parle vite** you can hardly understand him, he speaks so fast

**téméraire** [temeʀɛʀ] *adj* ① (*audacieux*) daring ② (*imprudent: entreprise, jugement*) foolhardy

**témoignage** [temwaɲaʒ] *m* ① (*déposition*) testimony; **faire un faux ~** to lie under oath ② (*récit*) account; **selon divers ~s, ...** according to a number of witnesses, ... ③ (*manifestation*) expression; **~ d'affection** sign of affection

**témoigner** [temwaɲe] <1> **I.** *vi* ① (*déposer*) **~ en faveur de/contre qn** to testify in favor of/against sb ② (*faire un récit*) to give an account **II.** *vt* ① (*attester, jurer*) **~ avoir vu l'accusé** to testify that one saw the accused ② (*exprimer*) to express; **~ son attachement à qn** to show one's fondness for sb

**témoin** [temwɛ̃] **I.** *m* ① witness; **~ oculaire** eyewitness; **~ à charge/dé-**

charge prosecution/defense witness ② (*preuve*) **être (un) ~ de qc** to be proof of sth ③ SPORT baton ④ (*voyant lumineux*) warning light **II.** *app* **lampe ~** warning light; **appartement ~** model apartment

**tempe** [tɑ̃p] *f* temple

**tempérament** [tɑ̃peʀamɑ̃] *m* (*caractère*) temperament

**température** [tɑ̃peʀatyʀ] *f* ANAT, METEO, PHYS temperature; **~ ambiante** room temperature ▸ **avoir de la ~** to have a temperature; **prendre la ~ de qn** to take sb's temperature

**tempérer** [tɑ̃peʀe] <5> *vt* ① METEO to moderate ② (*modérer: enthousiasme*) to temper; (*ardeur*) to calm; (*douleur, peine*) to soothe

**tempête** [tɑ̃pɛt] *f a. fig* SPORT storm; **~ de neige** snowstorm

**temple** [tɑ̃pl] *m* temple; (*protestant*) church

**temporaire** [tɑ̃pɔʀɛʀ] *adj* temporary; **à titre ~** for the time being

**temporiser** [tɑ̃pɔʀize] <1> *vi* to delay

**temps¹** [tɑ̃] *m* ① (*durée, déroulement du temps, moment, période*) time; **passer tout son ~ à faire qc** to spend all one's time doing sth; **avoir tout son ~** to have plenty of time; **~ libre** free time; **à plein ~** full time; **emploi à ~ complet/partiel** full-time/part-time job ② *pl* (*époque*) times ③ (*saison*) **le ~ des cerises/moissons** the cherry/harvest season ④ LING tense ⑤ TECH **moteur à deux ~** two-stroke engine ⑥ MUS beat ▸ **le ~ c'est de l'argent** *prov* time is money; **la plupart du ~** most of the time; **ces derniers ~** lately; **~ mort** lull; SPORT time-out; **dans un premier ~** initially; **dans un second ~** subsequently; **tout le ~** all the time; **il est (grand) ~ de** +*infin* **qu'il parte** it is high time he that he left; **il était ~!** about time!; **mettre du ~ à faire qc** to take a (terribly) long time doing sth; **à ~** in time; **ces ~-ci** these days; **dans le ~** in the old days; **de ~ en ~** from time to time;

<u>depuis</u> le ~ it's been a such long time; <u>depuis</u> le ~ <u>que ...</u> considering how long ...; <u>depuis ce</u> ~-<u>là</u> since then; <u>en même</u> ~ at the same time; <u>en</u> ~ <u>de crise/guerre</u> in times of crisis/war; <u>en</u> ~ <u>de paix</u> in peacetime; <u>en</u> ~ <u>normal</u> [*o* ordinaire] under normal circumstances; <u>en peu de</u> ~ in a short time

**temps²** [tã] *m* METEO weather; **il fait beau/mauvais** ~ the weather is nice/bad; **quel** ~ **fait-il?** what's the weather like? ▸ <u>par tous les</u> ~ in all weather

**tenace** [tənas] *adj* ❶ (*persistant*) persistent; (*haine*) deep-seated; (*croyance*) deep-rooted ❷ (*obstiné: personne, résistance*) tenacious

**tenailler** [tənaje] <1> *vt* ~ **qn** (*faim*) to gnaw at sb

**tenailles** [t(ə)naj] *fpl* pliers

**tendance** [tãdãs] *f* ❶ (*propension*) tendency ❷ (*opinion*) leaning ❸ (*orientation*) trend ▸ <u>avoir</u> ~ **à** +*infin* to tend to +*infin*

**tendon** [tãdɔ̃] *m* tendon

**tendre¹** [tãdʀ] <14> I. *vt* ❶ (*raidir*) to tighten ❷ (*installer: tapisserie*) to hang ❸ (*présenter: bras*) to stretch out; (*cou*) to crane; (*joue*) to offer ▸ ~ <u>la main</u> **à qn** to give sb a hand II. *vpr* (*se raidir*) **se** ~ to tighten; (*relations*) to become strained III. *vi* ❶ (*aboutir à*) ~ **à** +*infin* to tend to +*infin*; ~ **vers zéro/l'infini** to tend towards zero/infinity ❷ (*viser à*) ~ **à** to aim for sth

**tendre²** [tãdʀ] I. *adj* ❶ (*opp: dur*) soft; (*peau, viande*) tender ❷ (*affectueux*) fond; (*ami*) loving ❸ (*jeune, délicat*) tender ❹ (*léger: couleur*) soft II. *mf* **c'est un** ~ he's tenderhearted

**tendresse** [tãdʀɛs] *f* ❶ *sans pl* (*affection*) affection; **avoir de la** ~ **pour qn** to feel affection for sb ❷ *sans pl* (*douceur*) tenderness; **regarder qn avec** ~ to look tenderly at sb ❸ *pl* (*marques d'affection*) affection

**ténèbres** [tenɛbʀ] *fpl* REL Tenebrae

**teneur** [tənœʀ] *f* ❶ (*contenu exact*) contents ❷ (*proportion*) content

**tenir** [t(ə)niʀ] <9> I. *vt* ❶ (*avoir à la main, dans les bras ...*) to hold ❷ (*maintenir dans la même position*) to keep ❸ (*rester dans un lieu*) ~ **la chambre/le lit** to stay in one's bedroom/in bed ❹ (*avoir: article, marchandise*) to have (in stock) ❺ MUS (*note*) to hold ❻ (*avoir sous son contrôle*) ~ **son cheval** to control one's horse ❼ (*s'occuper de: hôtel, magasin, maison*) to run; (*comptes*) to keep ❽ (*assumer: conférence, meeting*) to hold; (*rôle*) to have ❾ (*avoir reçu*) ~ **une information de qn** to have information from sb ❿ (*occuper: largeur, place*) to take up ⓫ (*être contraint*) **être tenu à qc** to be held to sth; **être tenu de** +*infin* to be obliged to +*infin* ⓬ (*respecter: parole, promesse*) to keep; (*pari*) to honor ⓭ (*énoncer*) ~ **des propos racistes** to make racist comments ▸ ~ <u>lieu de qc</u> to act as sth II. *vi* ❶ (*être attaché*) ~ **à qn** to care about sb ❷ (*vouloir absolument*) ~ **à faire qc/à ce que tout soit en ordre** (*subj*) to insist on doing sth/that everything be in order ❸ (*être fixé*) to stay up ❹ (*être cohérent: raisonnement, théorie, argument*) to stand up; (*histoire*) to hold water ❺ (*être contenu dans*) ~ **dans une voiture** to fit in a car ❻ (*se résumer*) ~ **en un mot** to come down to one word ❼ (*durer*) to last ❽ (*ressembler à*) ~ **de qn** to take after sb; ~ **de qc** to be reminiscent of sth ▸ ~ <u>bon</u> to hold out; **tiens/tenez!** well!; **tiens! il pleut** hey! it's raining III. *vpr* ❶ (*se prendre*) **se** ~ **par la main** to hold hands ❷ (*s'accrocher*) **se** ~ **à qc** to hold on to sth ❸ (*rester, demeurer*) **se** ~ **debout/assis/couché** to be standing/sitting/in bed ❹ (*se comporter*) **se** ~ to behave ❺ (*avoir lieu*) **se** ~ **dans une ville/le mois prochain** (*réunion, conférence*) to be held in a town/the following month ❻ (*être cohérent*) **se** ~ (*événements, faits*) to hold together ❼ (*se limiter à*) **s'en** ~ **à qc** to confine oneself to sth ❽ (*respecter*) **se** ~ **à qc** to respect sth

T

**IV.** vi impers (*dépendre de*) **ça tient à qn/qc** it depends on sb/sth

**tennis** [tenis] **I.** m ❶ SPORT tennis; **jouer au ~** to play tennis; **~ de table** table tennis ❷ (*court*) tennis court **II.** mpl (*chaussures*) tennis shoes

**ténor** [tenɔʀ] m (*soliste*) tenor

**tension** [tɑ̃sjɔ̃] f ❶ (*état tendu*) a. TECH, PHYS tension ❷ ELEC voltage ❸ MED pressure; **avoir de la ~** to have high blood pressure

**tentation** [tɑ̃tasjɔ̃] f a. REL temptation

**tentative** [tɑ̃tativ] f attempt; **~ de meurtre/vol** JUR attempted murder/robbery

**tente** [tɑ̃t] f tent; **monter une ~** to put up a tent

**tenter** [tɑ̃te] <1> vt ❶ (*allécher*) to tempt ❷ (*essayer*) to try; **~ de** +infin to try to +infin

**ténu(e)** [teny] adj ❶ (*peu perceptible: son, bruit*) faint; (*nuance, distinction*) fine ❷ (*fin: fil*) thin

**tenue** [t(ə)ny] f ❶ (*comportement*) behavior; **avoir de la ~/manquer de ~** to have good/no manners; **un peu de ~!** manners, please! ❷ (*vêtements*) outfit; **~ de soirée** evening dress ❸ MIL uniform; **~ de combat** combat dress ❹ (*gestion: d'une maison, restaurant*) running; **la ~ des livres de comptes** the bookkeeping ❺ (*réunion: d'un congrès, d'une assemblée*) holding ❻ AUTO **~ de route** road-handling

**tergal**® [tɛʀgal] m ≈ Dacron®

**terme**[1] [tɛʀm] m ❶ (*fin: d'un stage, voyage, travail*) end; **toucher à son ~** (*stage, soirée*) to come to an end ❷ (*date limite*) term; **à court/moyen/long ~** in the short/medium/long term; **naissance avant ~** premature birth ❸ (*échéance: due date* ▶ **mener qc à son ~** to bring sth to completion; **mettre un ~ à qc** to put an end to sth

**terme**[2] [tɛʀm] m ❶ (*mot*) term ❷ pl (*formule: d'un contrat, d'une loi*) terms ▶ **être en bons/mauvais ~s avec qn** to be on good/bad terms with sb; **en d'autres ~s** in other terms

**terminaison** [tɛʀminɛzɔ̃] f ending

**terminal** [tɛʀminal, -o] <-aux> m terminal

**terminal(e)** [tɛʀminal, -o] <-aux> adj (*phase*) final

**terminale** [tɛʀminal] f ECOLE senior year; **être en ~** to be in one's final year (of school)

**terminer** [tɛʀmine] <1> **I.** vt ❶ (*finir*) to finish ❷ (*passer la fin de, être le dernier élément de: soirée, vacances*) to end **II.** vi **~ de lire le journal** to finish reading the newspaper; **en ~ avec une tâche** to finish with a task; **pour ~, ...** to end with, ... **III.** vpr **se ~** (*année, vacances, stage*) to end

**terminus** [tɛʀminys] m terminus

**terne** [tɛʀn] adj ❶ (*sans éclat: œil, cheveux, regard*) lifeless; (*teint, visage*) pale; (*couleur*) drab; (*miroir, glace*) dull; (*métal*) tarnished ❷ (*monotone: personne, conversation, journée*) dull; (*vie, style*) drab

**terrain** [teʀɛ̃] m ❶ (*parcelle*) ground, piece of ground ❷ AGR land, piece of land; (*un terrain à bâtir*) a building site ❸ (*espace réservé*) **~ de camping** camping site; **~ de jeu** playground ❹ (*sol*) **un ~ plat/accidenté** (some) flat/undulating land; **un ~ vague** some wasteland; **véhicule tout ~** all-terrain vehicle ❺ gén pl GEO formation ❻ (*domaine*) field ❼ MIL terrain ▶ **aller sur le ~** to go into the field; **homme/femme de ~** man/woman with direct experience

**terrasse** [teʀas] f ❶ (*plateforme en plein air*) a. GEO terrace ❷ (*toit plat*) (**toit en**) **~** flat roof

**terrasser** [teʀase] <1> vt ❶ (*vaincre*) to bring down ❷ (*accabler, tuer*) **~ qn** (*mauvaise nouvelle*) to overwhelm sb; (*émotion, fatigue*) to strike sb down

**terre** [tɛʀ] f ❶ sans pl (*le monde*) **la ~** the earth ❷ sans pl (*croûte terrestre*) **la ~** the ground; **sous ~** underground ❸ (*matière*) soil ❹ (*terre cultivable*) land; **~ battue** packed earth ❺ gén pl (*propriété*) estate ❻ (*contrée, pays*) country ❼ (*continent*) ~ **ferme** terra firma ❽ *sans pl* (*argile*) clay; ~ **cuite** (*matière*) terracotta ❾ *sans pl* ELEC ground ❿ (*opp: ciel*) earth; **être sur** ~ to be on earth ▶ **par** ~ on the ground; **être par** ~ (*projet, plan*) to be in ruins

**terre à terre** [tɛratɛr] *adj inv* (*personne*) down-to-earth; (*préoccupations*) day-to-day

**terrer** [tere] <1> *vpr* **se** ~ (*se cacher: animal*) to crouch down; (*fuyard, criminel*) to lay low; (*soldat*) to lie flat

**terrestre** [terɛstr] *adj* ❶ (*de la Terre*) **la croûte/surface** ~ the earth's crust/surface ❷ (*sur la terre: espèce*) terrestrial; (*vie*) on earth ❸ (*opp: aquatique, marin*) **animal** ~ land animal ❹ (*opp: aérien, maritime*) ground ❺ (*de ce bas monde: plaisirs, séjour*) earthly

**terreur** [terœr] *f* ❶ (*peur violente, terrorisme*) terror ❷ (*personne terrifiante*) **être une** ~ *inf* (*personne*) to be a bully; (*enfant*) to be a terror

**terrible** [teribl] **I.** *adj* ❶ (*qui inspire de la terreur: crime*) terrible; (*catastrophe*) dreadful; (*jugement, année*) awful; (*personnage, arme*) fearsome ❷ (*très intense*) tremendous ❸ (*turbulent*) dreadful ❹ *inf* (*super*) terrific **II.** *adv inf* fantastically

**terrifiant(e)** [terifjɑ̃, ɑ̃t] *adj* incredible; (*nouvelle*) terrifying

**terrifier** [terifje] <1> *vt* to terrify

**territoire** [teritwar] *m* (*d'un animal, pays, d'une nation*) territory; (*d'une ville*) area; ~ **d'outre-mer** overseas territory

**territorial(e)** [teritɔrjal, -jo] <-aux> *adj* territorial

**terroir** [terwar] *m* soil; **vin/accent du** ~ country wine/accent; **écrivain du** ~ rural author

**terroriser** [terɔrize] <1> *vt* (*faire très peur*) to terrorize

**terrorisme** [terɔrism] *m* terrorism

**tertiaire** [tersjer] **I.** *adj* (*emploi, activité*) service **II.** *m* **le** ~ the service industry

**tertio** [tersjo] *adv* thirdly

**tes** [te] *dét poss v.* **ta, ton**

**test** [tɛst] *m* test; ~ **de grossesse** pregnancy test

**testament** [tɛstamɑ̃] *m* JUR will

**tester** [tɛste] <1> *vt* (*mettre à l'épreuve*) to test

**tétanos** [tetanos] *m* ❶ (*maladie*) tetanus ❷ (*contraction du muscle*) lockjaw

**tête** [tɛt] *f* ❶ ANAT, BOT head; **baisser/courber la** ~ to lower/bend one's head ❷ (*mémoire, raison*) **ne pas avoir de** ~ *inf* to be empty-headed; **perdre la** ~ (*devenir fou*) to lose one's mind; (*perdre son sang-froid*) to lose one's head ❸ (*mine, figure*) **avoir une bonne** ~ *inf* to have a friendly face; **avoir une sale** ~ *inf* (*avoir mauvaise mine*) to look awful; (*être antipathique*) to look unpleasant ❹ (*longueur*) **faire une** ~ **de moins/plus que qn** to be a head shorter/taller than sb ❺ (*vie*) **risquer sa** ~ to risk one's neck ❻ (*personne*) ~ **couronnée** crowned head; ~ **de mule** *inf* pain; ~ **de Turc** whipping boy ❼ (*chef*) **être la** ~ **de qc** *inf* to be the head of sth ❽ (*première place*) head; (*les premiers*) top; **wagon de** ~ front car; **prendre la** ~ **d'un gouvernement** to take over at the head of a government; **à la** ~ **de qc** at the top of sth ❾ (*début: d'un chapitre, d'une liste*) beginning ❿ (*extrémité: d'un clou, d'une épingle*) head; (*d'un champignon*) top ⓫ INFORM ~ **de lecture-écriture** read-write head ⓬ SPORT header ▶ **se jeter dans qc** ~ **baissée** to rush headlong into sth; **avoir la** ~ **dure** to be a blockhead; **garder la** ~ **froide** to keep a cool head; **avoir la grosse** ~ *inf* to be bigheaded; **avoir toute sa** ~ to have all one's wits about one; **en avoir par-dessus la** ~ *inf* to have had it up to here; **ne pas se casser la** ~ *inf* to not to go to much trouble; **faire la** ~ **à qn** *inf* to sulk at sb; **n'en faire qu'à sa** ~ to just suit oneself; **se mettre en** ~ **de** + *infin* to take it into one's head to + *infin*; **se mettre dans la** ~ **que ...** to get it into one's head that ...; **monter à la** ~ **de**

**qn** (*vin, succès*) to go to sb's head; **se payer la ~ de qn** *inf* to make fun of sb; **relever la ~** to lift up one's head up high

**tétine** [tetin] *f* ❶ (*biberon*) nipple ❷ (*sucette pour calmer*) pacifier

**têtu(e)** [tety] I. *adj* stubborn ▶ **être ~ comme une mule** to be as stubborn as a mule II. *m(f)* stubborn person

**texte** [tɛkst] *m* text ▶ **cahier de ~s** homework notebook

**textile** [tɛkstil] I. *adj* textile II. *m* ❶ (*matière*) textile ❷ *sans pl* (*industrie*) textiles

**texto®** [tɛksto] *adv* *inf* word for word

**texto®** [tɛksto] *m* text [message]; **envoyer un ~ à qn** text someone, send someone a text

**textuel(le)** [tɛkstɥɛl] *adj* (*copie, réponse, contenu*) exact; (*traduction*) literal

**TF1** [teɛfœ̃] *f abr de* **Télévision Française 1ère chaîne** private French television channel

**T.G.V.** [teʒeve] *m inv abr de* **train à grande vitesse** high speed train

**Thaïlande** [tajlɑ̃d] *f* **la ~** Thailand

**thé** [te] *m* tea

**théâtral(e)** [teatral, -o] <-aux> *adj* (*effet, geste*) theatrical

**théâtre** [teatr] *m* ❶ (*édifice, spectacle*) theater ❷ (*art dramatique, genre littéraire*) drama; **école de ~** drama school ❸ (*œuvres*) plays ❹ (*lieu: des combats, d'une dispute*) scene

**théière** [tejɛʁ] *f* teapot

**thème** [tɛm] *m* ❶ (*sujet: d'une discussion*) theme; (*d'une peinture*) subject ❷ ECOLE prose (*translation out of French*) ❸ MUS theme ❹ (*en astrologie*) **~ astral** birth chart

**théorie** [teɔʁi] *f* theory

**théorique** [teɔʁik] *adj* theoretical

**théoriquement** [teɔʁikmɑ̃] *adv* ❶ (*logiquement*) in theory ❷ (*par une théorie: fondé, justifié*) theoretically

**thérapeute** [teʁapøt] *mf* therapist

**thérapeutique** [teʁapøtik] *adj* therapeutic

**thérapie** [teʁapi] *f* therapy

**thermique** [tɛʁmik] I. *adj* thermal II. *f* heat sciences

**thermomètre** [tɛʁmɔmɛtʁ] *m* (*instrument*) thermometer

**thermos®** [tɛʁmos] *m o f* Thermos®

**thermostat** [tɛʁmɔsta] *m* thermostat

**thèse** [tɛz] *f* ❶ (*point de vue défendu*) argument ❷ UNIV (*recherches, ouvrage*) thesis; (*soutenance*) defense

**thon** [tɔ̃] *m* tuna

**thorax** [tɔʁaks] *m* thorax

**thuya** [tyja] *m* thuja, arborvitae

**thym** [tɛ̃] *m* thyme

**thyroïde** [tiʁɔid] I. *adj* **glande ~** thyroid gland II. *f* thyroid

**tibia** [tibja] *m* shin

**ticket** [tikɛ] *m* ticket; **~ de caisse** (*register*) receipt; **~ de cinéma/quai** movie/step-up ticket

**ticket-repas** [tikɛ-ʁəpa] <tickets-repas> *m*, **ticket-restaurant®** [tikɛ-ʁɛstɔʁɑ̃] *m* meal ticket

**tiède** [tjɛd] *adj* ❶ (*entre le chaud et le froid: gâteau, lit*) warm; (*eau, café, repas*) lukewarm ❷ (*de peu d'ardeur: engagement, accueil, soutien*) halfhearted

**tien(ne)** [tjɛ̃, ɛn] *pron poss* ❶ (*ce que l'on possède*) **le ~/la ~ne/les ~s** yours; *v.a.* **mien** ❷ *pl* (*ceux de ta famille*) **les ~s** your family; (*tes partisans*) your friends ▶ **à la ~ne(, Étienne)**! *inf* cheers!; **tu pourrais y mettre du ~**! you could put some effort into it!

**tiers** [tjɛʁ] *m* ❶ (*fraction*) third ❷ (*tierce personne*) **un ~** a third person; **assurance au ~** third party insurance

**tiers, tierce** [tjɛʁ, tjɛʁs] *adj* third

**tiers-monde** [tjɛʁmɔ̃d] *m sans pl* **le ~** the Third World

**tige** [tiʒ] *f* ❶ (*pédoncule: d'une fleur, feuille*) stem; (*d'une céréale, graminée*) stalk ❷ (*partie mince et allongée*) rod; (*d'une clé*) shank

**tigre** [tigʁ] *m* tiger; *v.a.* **tigresse**

**tigresse** [tigʁɛs] *f* tigress; *v.a.* **tigre**

**tilleul** [tijœl] *m* ❶ BOT linden tree ❷ (*infusion*) lime-blossom tea

**timbale** [tɛ̃bal] *f* ❶ (*gobelet*) tumbler ❷ (*contenu*) cup ❸ MUS kettledrum

**timbre¹** [tɛ̃br] *m* ❶ (*vignette, cachet*) stamp ❷ MED research stamp

**timbre²** [tɛ̃br] *m* (*qualité du son*) timbre; (*d'une flûte, voix*) tone

**timbré(e)¹** [tɛ̃bre] *adj* stamped

**timbré(e)²** [tɛ̃bre] *adj inf* (*un peu fou*) cracked

**timbre-poste** [tɛ̃brəpɔst] <timbres--poste> *m* postage stamp

**timbrer** [tɛ̃bre] <1> *vt* to stamp

**timide** [timid] **I.** *adj* ❶ (*timoré, de peu d'audace*) shy ❷ (*craintif: sourire, voix*) timid **II.** *mf* timid person

**tinter** [tɛ̃te] <1> *vi* (*cloche*) to ring; (*grelot, clochette*) to tinkle

**tique** [tik] *f* tick

**tir** [tiʀ] *m* ❶ MIL fire; (*prolongé*) firing; ~ **à blanc** firing blank rounds ❷ SPORT shot; ~ **au but** (*penalty*) penalty kick; ~ **à l'arc** archery ❸ (*projectile tiré*) shot ❹ (*stand*) **stand de** ~ rifle range ❺ (*forain*) **stand de** ~ shooting gallery

**tirade** [tiʀad] *f* ❶ (*paroles*) *a. péj* tirade ❷ THEAT monologue

**tirage** [tiʀaʒ] *m* ❶ (*action de tirer au sort*) ~ **au sort** draw ❷ FIN (*d'un chèque*) drawing ❸ TYP, ART, PHOT printing; (*ensemble des exemplaires*) impression

**tirailler** [tiʀaje] <1> *vt* ❶ (*tirer à petits coups*) to tug; (*pli*) to pull at ❷ (*harceler*) **être tiraillé entre deux choses** to be torn between two things

**tiré(e)** [tiʀe] *adj* (*fatigué*) drawn; **avoir les traits ~s** to look drawn

**tire-fesses** [tiʀfɛs] *m inv, inf* ski tow

**tirelire** [tiʀliʀ] *f* donation can; **casser sa** ~ **pour acheter qc** *inf* to break open the piggy bank to buy sth

**tirer** [tiʀe] <1> **I.** *vt* ❶ (*exercer une force de traction: signal d'alarme, chasse d'eau*) to pull; (*vers le bas: jupe, manche*) to pull down; (*vers le haut: chaussettes, collant*) to pull up; (*pour lisser: drap, collant*) to smooth; (*pour tendre/maintenir tendu: corde, toile*) to tighten; ~ **la sonnette** to ring the bell ❷ (*tracter: chariot, véhicule, charge*) to draw ❸ (*éloigner*) to draw away ❹ (*fermer: rideau*) to pull; (*ouvrir: ti-*

*roir, porte coulissante*) to pull open; ~ **la porte** to pull the door to; ~ **le verrou de qc** (*pour fermer*) to bolt sth; (*pour ouvrir*) to unbolt sth ❺ (*aspirer*) ~ **une longue bouffée** to take a deep breath ❻ (*lancer un projectile: balle, coup de fusil*) to fire ❼ (*toucher, tuer: perdrix, lièvre*) to shoot ❽ (*tracer, prendre au hasard: trait, carte, numéro, lettre*) to draw ❾ (*faire sortir*) ~ **qn du lit** to get sb out of bed; ~ **une citation d'un roman** to take a quote from a novel ❿ (*emprunter à*) ~ **son origine de qc** (*coutume*) to have its origins in sth ⓫ (*déduire*) ~ **une conclusion/leçon de qc** to draw a conclusion/learn a lesson from sth ⓬ FIN (*chèque*) to draw ⓭ PHOT, ART, TYP (*film, négatif, photo, lithographie*) to print ⓮ (*transvaser: vin*) to decant ▸ **on ne peut rien** ~ **de qn** you can get nothing out of sb **II.** *vi* ❶ (*exercer une traction*) ~ **sur les rênes de son cheval** to pull on the reins of one's horse ❷ (*aspirer*) ~ **sur sa cigarette** to puff on one's cigarette ❸ (*gêner: peau, cicatrice*) to pull ❹ (*à la chasse*) *a.* MIL to shoot ❺ (*au football*) to shoot ❻ (*avoir une certaine ressemblance avec*) ~ **sur qc** (*couleur*) to verge on sth ❼ TYP ~ **à 2000 exemplaires** to have a circulation of 2000 ❽ (*avoir du tirage: cheminée, poêle*) to draw well/badly **III.** *vpr* ❶ *inf* (*s'en aller*) **se** ~ to push off ❷ (*se sortir*) **se** ~ **d'une situation** to get out of a situation ❸ (*se blesser*) **se** ~ **une balle dans la tête** to put a bullet in one's head ▸ **il s'en tire bien** *inf* (*à la suite d'une maladie*) he's pulling through; (*à la suite d'un accident*) he's all right; (*à la suite d'un ennui*) he's out of the woods; (*réussir*) he's managing pretty well

**tiret** [tiʀe] *m* ❶ (*dans un dialogue, au milieu d'une phrase*) dash ❷ (*à la fin, au milieu d'un mot*) hyphen

**tireur, -euse** [tiʀœʀ, -øz] *m, f* ❶ MIL, SPORT (*avec une arme*) marksman *m*, markswoman *f* ❷ SPORT (*au football*) striker; (*au basket*) shooter; ~ **à l'arc** archer

**tiroir** [tiʀwaʀ] *m* drawer

**tiroir-caisse** [tiʀwaʀkɛs] <tiroirs-caisses> *m* cash register

**tisane** [tizan] *f* herbal tea; ~ **de verveine** verbena tea

**tisser** [tise] <1> *vt* ❶ (*tapis, laine*) to weave ❷ (*constituer*) ~ **sa toile** (*araignée*) to spin a web ❸ (*ourdir: intrigue*) to build

**tisserand(e)** [tisʀɑ̃, ɑ̃d] *m(f)* weaver

**tissu** [tisy] *m* ❶ (*textile*) fabric; ~ **éponge** toweling ❷ (*enchevêtrement: de contradictions, d'intrigues*) tissue; (*d'inepties*) catalog ❸ BIO tissue ❹ SOCIOL ~ **social** social fabric

**titre** [titʀ] *m* ❶ (*intitulé, qualité, trophée*) title; (*d'un chapitre*) heading; (*article de journal*) headline ❷ (*pièce justificative*) certificate; ~ **de transport** ticket ❸ (*valeur, action*) security ▸ **à** __juste__ ~ rightly; **à ce** ~ as such; **à** ~ **de qc** as sth

**tituber** [titybe] <1> *vi* ~ **d'ivresse** to stagger drunkenly

**titulaire** [titylɛʀ] **I.** *adj* ❶ (*en titre: professeur, instituteur*) with tenure ❷ (*détenteur*) **être** ~ **d'un poste/diplôme** to be the holder of a position/diploma **II.** *mf* ❶ ECOLE, UNIV, ADMIN incumbent ❷ (*détenteur*) ~ **de la carte/du poste** cardholder/post holder

**toast** [tost] *m* piece of toast

**toboggan** [tɔbɔgɑ̃] *m* ❶ TECH chute ❷ (*piste glissante*) slide ❸ *Québec* (*traîneau sans patins, fait de planches minces recourbées à l'avant*) toboggan

**toc** [tɔk] *m inf* (*imitation*) **du** ~ junk; **en** ~ fake

**toi** [twa] *pron pers* ❶ *inf* (*pour renforcer*) you; ~, **tu n'as pas ouvert la bouche** YOU haven't even opened your mouth; **c'est** ~ **qui l'as dit** you're the one who said it; **il veut t'aider,** ~? he wants to help YOU? ❷ *avec un verbe à l'impératif* **regarde-**~ look at yourself; **imagine-**~ **en Italie** imagine yourself in Italy; **lave-**~ **les mains** wash your

hands ❸ *avec une préposition* **avec/ sans** ~ with/without you; **à** ~ *seul* (*parler*) just to you ❹ *dans une comparaison* you; **je suis comme** ~ I'm like you; **plus fort que** ~? stronger than you; ❺ (*emphatique*) **c'est** ~? is that you?; **si j'étais** ~ if I were you; *v.a.* **moi**

**toile** [twal] *f* ❶ (*tissu*) cloth ❷ (*pièce de tissu*) piece of cloth ❸ ART, NAUT canvas ❹ INFORM ~ (**d'araignée**) **mondiale** World Wide Web ▸ ~ **d'araignée** spider web; (*poussière*) cobweb

**toilette** [twalɛt] *f* ❶ (*soins corporels*) washing; **faire sa** ~ (*personne*) to have a wash; (*animal*) to groom itself ❷ (*nettoyage: d'un édifice, monument*) cleaning ❸ (*vêtements*) outfit ❹ *pl* (*W.-C.*) toilet; **aller aux** ~**s** to go to the toilet

**toi-même** [twamɛm] *pron pers* (*toi en personne*) yourself; *v.a.* **moi-même**

**toit** [twa] *m* roof

**tôle** [tol] *f* ❶ (*en métallurgie*) sheet metal ❷ AUTO bodywork

**tolérable** [tɔleʀabl] *adj* tolerable; (*douleur*) bearable

**tolérance** [tɔleʀɑ̃s] *f* tolerance; ~ **à qc** tolerance of sth

**tolérant(e)** [tɔleʀɑ̃, ɑ̃t] *adj* tolerant

**tolérer** [tɔleʀe] <5> **I.** *vt* ❶ (*autoriser: infraction, pratique*) to tolerate ❷ (*supporter*) *a.* MED to tolerate; (*douleur*) to bear **II.** *vpr* (*se supporter*) **se** ~ to tolerate each other

**tomate** [tɔmat] *f* tomato

**tombe** [tɔ̃b] *f* grave

**tombeau** [tɔ̃bo] <x> *m* tomb

**tombée** [tɔ̃be] *f* ~ **de la nuit** |*o du* **jour**| nightfall

**tomber** [tɔ̃be] <1> *vi* être ❶ (*chuter, s'abattre*) to fall; ~ **en arrière/en avant** to fall backwards/forwards; ~ **dans les bras de qn** to fall into sb's arms; ~ (**par terre**) to fall; (*échafaudage*) to collapse ❷ (*être affaibli*) **je tombe de fatigue/sommeil** I'm ready to drop I'm so tired/sleepy ❸ (*se détacher: cheveux, dent*) to fall out; (*feuille, masque*) to fall ❹ (*arriver: nouvelle, télex*) to arrive; **qc tombe un lundi** sth falls on a Monday ❺ (*descendre: nuit, soir, neige, pluie, averse*) to fall; (*foudre*) to strike ❻ THEAT (*rideau*) to fall ❼ (*être vaincu*) to fall; (*dictateur, gouvernement*) to be brought down; (*record*) to be smashed ❽ MIL (*mourir*) to fall ❾ (*baisser: vent*) to drop; (*colère, enthousiasme, exaltation*) to fade ❿ (*disparaître, échouer: obstacle*) to disappear; (*plan, projet*) to fall through ⓫ (*pendre*) to hang; **bien/mal ~** (*vêtement*) to hang well/badly ⓬ inf (*se retrouver*) **~ enceinte** to become pregnant; **~ d'accord** to agree ⓭ (*être pris*) **~ dans un piège** to fall into a trap ⓮ (*être entraîné*) **~ dans l'oubli** to sink into oblivion ⓯ (*concerner par hasard*) **~ sur qn** to happen to sb; (*sort*) to choose sb ⓰ (*rencontrer, arriver par hasard*) **~ sur un article** to come across an article; **~ sur qn** to bump into sb ⓱ (*abandonner*) **laisser ~ un projet** to drop a project ⓲ (*se poser*) **~ sur qn/qc** (*conversation*) to come around to sb/sth; (*regard*) to light upon sb/sth ⓳ inf (*attaquer*) **~ sur qn** to lay into sb ▸ **bien/mal ~** to be a bit of good/bad luck; **ça tombe bien/mal** that's handy/a nuisance

**tome** [tɔm] *m* volume

**ton**¹ [tɔ̃] *m* ❶ (*manière de s'exprimer, couleur*) a. MUS tone ❷ (*timbre: d'une voix*) tone; **baisser/hausser le ~** to lower/raise one's voice

**ton**² [tɔ̃, te] <tes> *dét poss* (*à toi*) your; *v.a.* **mon** ▸ **ne fais pas ~ malin!** don't be smart!

**tonalité** [tɔnalite] *f* ❶ TEL dial tone ❷ (*timbre, impression d'ensemble*) a. LING tone

**tondeuse** [tɔ̃døz] *f* ❶ (*pour les cheveux, la barbe*) clippers *pl* ❷ (*pour le jardin*) **~ (à gazon)** lawnmower

**tondre** [tɔ̃dʀ] <14> *vt* to shear; (*gazon*) to mow

**tonifier** [tɔnifje] <1> I. *vt* (*cheveux, peau*) to condition; (*organisme, personne, muscles*) to tone up; (*esprit, personne*) to stimulate II. *vi* to tone up

**tonique** [tɔnik] *adj* ❶ (*revigorant: froid*) fortifying; (*boisson*) tonic ❷ (*stimulant: idée, lecture*) stimulating ❸ LING (*syllabe, voyelle*) accented

**tonne** [tɔn] *f* ❶ (*unité*) ton ❷ inf (*énorme quantité*) loads *pl* ▸ **en faire des ~s** inf to overdo it

**tonneau** [tɔno] <x> *m* ❶ (*récipient*) barrel ❷ (*accident de voiture*) somersault

**tonner** [tɔne] <1> *vi impers* **il tonne** it's thundering

**tonnerre** [tɔnɛʀ] *m* a. MÉTÉO thunder ▸ **fille/type/voiture du ~** inf awesome girl/guy/car

**top** [tɔp] I. *adj inv, antéposé* **~ model** supermodel II. *m* ❶ RADIO beep ❷ (*signal de départ*) starting signal ❸ SPORT get set ❹ inf (*niveau maximum*) **le ~** the best

**toqué(e)** [tɔke] *adj* inf (*cinglé*) cracked

**torche** [tɔʀʃ] *f* ❶ (*flambeau*) (flaming) torch ❷ (*lampe électrique*) flashlight

**torchon** [tɔʀʃɔ̃] *m* ❶ (*tissu*) cloth; **donner un coup de ~ sur/à qc** to dry/dust sth ❷ inf (*mauvais journal*) rag ❸ (*sale travail*) mess

**tordre** [tɔʀdʀ] <14> I. *vt* ❶ (*serrer en tournant: linge*) to wring; (*brins, fils*) to twist ❷ (*plier*) to bend; **être tordu** (*jambe, nez, règle*) to be twisted II. *vpr* ❶ (*faire des contorsions*) **se ~ de douleur/rire** to double up in pain/laughter ❷ (*se luxer*) **se ~ un membre** to dislocate a limb

**tordu(e)** [tɔʀdy] I. *part passé de* **tordre** II. *adj* inf (*esprit, personne, idée*) twisted III. *m(f)* inf weirdo

**tornade** [tɔʀnad] *f* tornado

**torréfier** [tɔʀefje] <1> *vt* to roast

**torrent** [tɔʀɑ̃] *m* (*cours d'eau, flot abondant*) torrent; **~ de larmes** flood of tears ▸ **il pleut à ~s** it's pouring down

**torrentiel(le)** [tɔʀɑ̃sjɛl] *adj* (*pluies*) torrential

**torride** [tɔʀid] *adj* ❶ (*brûlant*) burning; (*chaleur*) scorching ❷ (*passionné*) torrid

T

**torse** [tɔʀs] *m* ❶(*poitrine*) chest ❷ANAT, ART torso

**tort** [tɔʀ] *m* ❶(*erreur*) error; **avoir ~** to be wrong; **avoir grand ~ de** +*infin* to be very wrong to +*infin* ❷(*préjudice*) wrong; (*moral*) harm; **faire du ~ à qn/qc** to harm sb/sth ▶**à ~ ou à raison** rightly or wrongly; **parler à ~ et à travers** to talk complete nonsense

**tortiller** [tɔʀtije] <1> *vt* (*cheveux*) to twiddle; (*cravate, mouchoir*) to twiddle with

**tortue** [tɔʀty] *f* ZOOL tortoise; (*de mer*) turtle

**torture** [tɔʀtyʀ] *f* ❶(*supplice*) torture ❷(*souffrance*) torment

**tôt** [to] *adv* ❶(*de bonne heure*) early ❷(*à une date ou une heure avancée, vite*) soon; **plus ~** sooner; **le plus ~ possible** as soon as possible ▶**~ ou tard** sooner or later; **pas plus ~ ... que** no sooner ... than

**total** [tɔtal, -o] <-aux> *m* (*somme*) total ▶**faire le ~ de qc** to add sth up; **au ~** (*en tout*) all in all; (*somme toute*) in total

**total(e)** [tɔtal, -o] <-aux> *adj* ❶(*absolu: maîtrise, désespoir*) complete; (*obscurité, ruine*) total ❷FIN, MATH (*hauteur, somme*) total

**totaliser** [tɔtalize] <1> *vt* **~ qc** ❶(*additionner*) to add sth up ❷(*atteindre: nombre, voix, habitants*) to total sth up

**totalitaire** [tɔtalitɛʀ] *adj* totalitarian

**totalité** [tɔtalite] *f* whole

**touchant(e)** [tuʃɑ̃, ɑ̃t] *adj* (*émouvant*) moving; (*situation, histoire*) touching

**touche** [tuʃ] *f* ❶INFORM, MUS (*d'un accordéon, piano*) key; **~ "alternative"** Alt key; **~ "contrôle"** CTRL; **~ "échappement"** ESC; **~ "effacement"** BACKSPACE; **~ "entrée"** ENTER; **~ "espace"** SPACE; **~ (de) "fonction"** FUNCTION; **~ "majuscule"** SHIFT; **~ "retour"** RETURN; **~ "suppression"** DEL; **~ "tabulation"** TAB; **~ "verrouillage majuscule"** CAPS LOCK ❷(*coup de pinceau*) stroke ❸(*à la pêche*) bite ❹(*en escri-*

*me*) hit; (*au football, rugby: ligne*) touchline; (*au football: sortie du ballon*) throw-in; (*au rugby: sortie du ballon*) line-out ▶**faire une ~** *inf* to be a hit; **sur la ~** (*au bord du terrain*) on the bench; *inf* (*à l'écart*) on the sidelines

**toucher** [tuʃe] <1> I. *vt* ❶(*ballon, fond, plafond*) to touch ❷(*être contigu à*) to adjoin ❸(*frapper: balle, coup, explosion*) to hit; (*mesure, politique*) to affect ❹(*concerner*) to concern; (*histoire, affaire*) to involve ❺(*émouvoir: critique, reproche*) to affect; (*drame, deuil, scène*) to move ❻(*recevoir: argent, ration, commission, pension*) to receive; (*à la banque: chèque*) to cash ❼(*contacter, atteindre: personne, port, côte*) to reach II. *vi* ❶(*porter la main sur*) **~ à qc** to touch sth ❷(*se servir de*) **~ à ses économies** to use one's savings ❸(*tripoter*) **~ à qn** to lay a finger on sb ❹(*modifier*) **~ au règlement** to change the rules ❺(*concerner*) **~ à un domaine** to be connected with a field ❻(*aborder*) **~ à un problème/sujet** to broach a problem/subject ❼(*être proche de*) **~ à sa fin** to near its end III. *vpr* **se ~** (*personnes*) to touch; (*immeubles, localités*) to be next to each other IV. *m* ❶MUS, SPORT touch ❷(*impression*) feel ▶**au ~** by touch

**touffe** [tuf] *f* tuft

**toujours** [tuʒuʀ] *adv* ❶(*constamment*) always ❷(*encore*) still ❸(*en toutes occasions*) always ❹(*malgré tout*) still ▶**qn peut ~ faire qc** sb can always do sth; **depuis ~** always

**toupet** [tupɛ] *m* ❶(*touffe*) tuft of hair ❷ *inf* (*culot*) nerve

**tour¹** [tuʀ] *f* ❶(*monument*) *a.* MIL tower; **~ de forage** drilling rig ❷(*immeuble*) tower block ❸JEUX castle, rook

**tour²** [tuʀ] *m* ❶(*circonférence*) outline; **~ des yeux** eyeline; **~ de hanches/ poitrine** hip/chest measurement ❷(*brève excursion*) trip; **faire un ~** (*à pied*) to go for a walk; (*en voiture*) to go for a drive; (*à vélo*) to go for a ride; **~ d'horizon** survey ❸(*succession al-*

*ternée*) ~ **de garde** turn on duty; **c'est au ~ de qn de** +*infin* it's sb's turn to +*infin* ❹ (*rotation*) revolution ❺ (*duperie*) trick ❻ (*exercice habile*) stunt; ~ **de force** feat of strength; (*exploit moral*) achievement; ~ **de prestidigitation** [*o* **de magie**] magic trick ❼ (*séance*) performance; ~ **de chant** song recital ❽ POL round; ~ **de scrutin** round of voting ▶ **à ~ de rôle** in turn; **jouer un ~ à qn** to play a trick on sb

**tourbillon** [turbijɔ̃] *m* ❶ (*vent*) whirlwind; ~ **de neige** swirl of snow ❷ (*masse d'eau*) whirlpool

**tourisme** [turism] *m* tourism; **agence de** ~ travel agency; **office de** ~ tourist office

**touriste** [turist] *mf* tourist

**touristique** [turistik] *adj* tourist

**tourmenter** [turmɑ̃te] <1> I. *vt* (*tracasser:* ambition, envie, jalousie) to torment; (*doute, remords, scrupules*) to plague II. *vpr* **se** ~ to worry oneself sick

**tournant** [turnɑ̃] *m* ❶ (*virage*) bend ❷ (*changement*) turning point

**tournant(e)** [turnɑ̃, ɑ̃t] *adj* (*qui peut tourner:* plaque, pont, scène) revolving

**tourne-disque** [turnədisk] <tourne-disques> *m* record player

**tournée** [turne] *f* ❶ (*circuit: d'un artiste, conférencier*) tour; **être en** ~ to be on tour ❷ *inf* (*au café*) round

**tourner** [turne] <1> I. *vt* ❶ (*mouvoir en rond, orienter, détourner*) to turn; ~ **la lampe vers la gauche/le haut** to turn the lamp to the left/upwards; ~ **le dos à qn/qc** to turn one's back on sb/sth ❷ (*retourner:* page) to turn; (*disque, feuille*) to turn over ❸ (*contourner, en voiture, à vélo*) to round ❹ (*formuler*) to phrase ❺ (*transformer*) ~ **qn/qc en ridicule** to make a laughing stock of sb/sth; ~ **qc à son avantage** to turn sth to one's advantage ❻ CINE to shoot ❼ TECH to throw; (*bois*) to turn II. *vi* ❶ (*pivoter sur son axe*) to turn ❷ (*avoir un déplacement circulaire: personne, animal*) to turn; **la terre tourne autour du soleil** the earth revolves

around the sun ❸ (*fonctionner*) to run; ~ **à plein rendement** [*o régime*] to be working at full capacity; **faire ~ un moteur** to run an engine ❹ (*avoir trait à*) **la conversation tourne autour de qn/qc** the conversation centered on sb/sth ❺ (*bifurquer*) to turn off ❻ (*s'inverser*) to turn around; (*vent*) to change; **ma chance a tourné** my luck has changed [*o turned*] ~ **à/en qc** to change to/into sth; (*événement*) to turn into sth ❽ (*devenir aigre: crème, lait*) to turn ❾ CINE to shoot ❿ (*approcher*) ~ **autour de qc** (*prix, nombre*) to be around sth ▶ ~ **bien/mal** (*personne, chose*) to turn out well/badly III. *vpr* ❶ (*s'adresser à, s'orienter*) **se** ~ **vers qn/qc** to turn to sb/sth ❷ (*changer de position*) **se** ~ **vers qn/de l'autre côté** to turn towards sb/to the other side

**tournesol** [turnəsɔl] *m* sunflower

**tournevis** [turnəvis] *m* screwdriver

**tournoi** [turnwa] *m* tournament

**tournoyer** [turnwaje] <6> *vi* to whirl; (*plus vite*) to spin

**tournure** [turnyr] *f* ❶ (*évolution*) development ❷ LING form; (*idiomatique*) expression ❸ (*apparence*) bearing ▶ ~ **d'esprit** turn of mind; **prendre** ~ to take shape

**tour-opérateur** [turɔperatœr] <tour-opérateurs> *m* tour operator

**tourtereau** [turtəro] <x> *m* ❶ *pl, iron* (*amoureux*) lovebird ❷ (*oiseau*) young turtledove

**tourterelle** [turtərɛl] *f* turtledove

**tous** [tu, tus] *v.* **tout**

**Toussaint** [tusɛ̃] *f* **la** ~ All Saints' Day

**tousser** [tuse] <1> *vi* (*avoir un accès de toux*) to cough

**tout** [tu] I. *adv* ❶ (*totalement*) ~ **simple/bête** quite simple/easy; **le** ~ **premier/dernier** the very first/last; **c'est** ~ **autre chose** it's not the same thing at all ❷ (*très, vraiment*) very; ~ **près de** very near to; ~ **autour** (**de**) all around ❸ (*aussi*) ~**e maligne qu'elle soit, ...** (*subj*) as crafty as she may be ... ❹ *inv* (*en même temps*) ~ **en faisant qc** while doing sth ❺ (*en totalité*) completely; **tissu ~ laine/soie** pure wool/ silk material ►~ **d'un coup** (*en une seule fois*) in one go; (*soudain*) suddenly; ~ **à fait** exactly; **c'est ~ à fait possible** it is perfectly possible; ~ **de suite** straight away; **c'est ~ comme** *inf* it's the same thing; ~ **de même** all the same **II.** *m* ❶ (*totalité*) whole ❷ (*ensemble*) **le ~** everything ►**pas du ~!** not at all!; **elle n'avait pas du ~ de pain** she had no bread at all

**tout(e)** [tu, tut, *pl:* tu(s), tut] <tous, toutes> **I.** *adj indéf* ❶ *sans pl* (*entier*) ~ **le temps/l'argent** all the time/money; ~ **la journée** all day; ~ **ce bruit** all this noise ❷ *sans pl* (*tout à fait*) **c'est ~ le contraire** it's exactly the opposite ❸ *sans pl* (*seul, unique*) **c'est ~ l'effet que ça te fait?** is that all it does to you? ❹ *sans pl* (*complet*) **j'ai lu ~ Balzac** I have read all Balzac's works; ~ **Londres** the whole of London; **à ~ prix** at any price; **à ~e vitesse** at top speed ❺ *sans pl* (*quel qu'il soit*) ~ **homme** all men *pl*; **de ~e manière** in any case ❻ *pl* (*l'ensemble des*) ~**es les places** all the seats; **tous les jours** every day; **dans tous les cas** in any case ❼ *pl* (*chaque*) **tous les quinze jours/deux jours** every two weeks/two days ❽ *pl* (*ensemble*) **nous avons fait tous les cinq ce voyage** all five of us made the trip ❾ *pl* (*la totalité des*) **à tous égards** in all respects; **de tous côtés** (*arriver*) from everywhere; (*regarder*) from all around; **de ~es sortes** of all kinds **II.** *pron indéf* ❶ *sans pl* (*opp: rien*) everything ❷ *pl* (*opp: personne/aucun*) everybody/everything; **un film pour tous** a film for everyone; **nous tous** all of us; **tous/~es ensemble** all together ❸ *sans pl* (*l'ensemble des choses*) ~ **ce qui bouge** anything that moves ►**c(e n)'est pas ~ (que)** de +*infin* it's not enough just to +*infin*; ~ **ou rien** all or nothing; **en ~** (*au total*) in

all; (*dans toute chose*) in every respect; **en ~ et pour ~** all in all

**toutefois** [tutfwa] *adv* however

**tout-terrain** [tuterɛ̃] <tout-terrains> **I.** *adj* all-terrain, four-wheel drive; **vélo ~** mountain bike **II.** *m* (*véhicule*) all-terrain [*o* four-wheel drive] vehicle

**toux** [tu] *f* cough

**toxicité** [tɔksisite] *f* toxicity

**toxicomane** [tɔksikɔman] **I.** *adj* addicted to drugs **II.** *mf* drug addict

**toxique** [tɔksik] *adj* toxic; (*gaz*) poisonous

**tracasser** [trakase] <1> *vt* to worry; (*administration*) to harass

**trace** [tras] *f* ❶ (*empreinte*) tracks *pl* ❷ (*marque laissée, quantité minime*) trace; (*cicatrice*) mark; (*de fatigue*) sign ❸ (*voie tracée*) path; (*au ski*) track ►**suivre qn à la ~** to follow sb's trail

**tracer** [trase] <2> *vt* ❶ (*dessiner*) to draw; (*chiffre, mot*) to write ❷ (*frayer: piste, route*) to open up

**tract** [trakt] *m* handout; ~ **publicitaire** flier

**tracter** [trakte] <1> *vt* to tow

**tracteur** [traktœr] *m* tractor

**tradition** [tradisjɔ̃] *f* ❶ (*coutume*) tradition ❷ *sans pl a.* REL (*coutumes transmises*) tradition ❸ JUR transfer

**traditionnel(le)** [tradisjɔnɛl] *adj* ❶ (*conforme à la tradition*) traditional ❷ (*habituel*) usual

**traducteur** [tradyktœr] *m* INFORM translator

**traducteur, -trice** [tradyktœr, -tris] *m, f* (*interprète*) translator

**traduction** [tradyksjɔ̃] *f* ❶ (*dans une autre langue*) translation; ~ **en anglais** translation into English ❷ (*expression: d'un sentiment*) expression

**traduire** [tradɥir] *irr* **I.** *vt* ❶ (*dans une autre langue*) ~ **de l'anglais en français** to translate from English into French ❷ (*exprimer*) ~ **une pensée/un sentiment** (*chose*) to convey a thought/feeling; (*personne*) to express a thought/feeling ❸ JUR ~ **en justice** to bring sb up before the courts **II.** *vpr*

**①** (*être traduisible*) **se ~ en qc** to translate into sth **②** (*s'exprimer*) **se ~ par qc** (*sentiment*) to be conveyed by sth
**trafic** [tʀafik] *m* **①** (*circulation*) traffic **②** *péj* (*commerce*) trade; **~ de drogues** drug trafficking **③** *inf* (*activité suspecte*) funny business
**trafiquant(e)** [tʀafikɑ̃, ɑ̃t] *m(f)* trafficker
**trafiquer** [tʀafike] <1> *vt inf* **①** (*falsifier: comptes*) to fiddle; **~ un moteur/produit** to tamper with a product/engine **②** (*bricoler*) to fix **③** (*manigancer*) to plot
**tragédie** [tʀaʒedi] *f* tragedy
**tragique** [tʀaʒik] **I.** *adj* (*auteur, accident*) tragic **II.** *m sans pl* (*genre littéraire, gravité*) tragedy
**tragiquement** [tʀaʒikmɑ̃] *adv* tragically
**trahir** [tʀaiʀ] <8> **I.** *vt* **①** (*tromper*) to betray; (*femme*) to be unfaithful to **②** (*révéler*) to give away **③** (*dénaturer: auteur, pièce*) to be unfaithful to **④** (*lâcher: sens*) to misrepresent **II.** *vi* to be a traitor **III.** *vpr* **se ~ par une action** to give oneself away with an action
**train** [tʀɛ̃] *m* **①** CHEMDFER train; **~ express/omnibus/rapide** express/slow/fast train; **~ à grande vitesse** high speed train; **le ~ en direction/venant de Lyon** the train to/from Lyon; **prendre le ~** to take the train **②** (*allure*) pace; **à ce ~** at this rate; **~ de vie** lifestyle **③** (*jeu*) train; **~ d'atterrissage** landing gear **④** (*série: de textes, négociations*) batch **⑤** AUTO **~ avant/arrière** front/rear axle unit ▶ **être en ~ de faire qc** to be doing sth; **en ~** in shape; **mettre qc en ~** to get sth under way
**traîne** [tʀɛn] *f* COUT train
**traîneau** [tʀɛno] <x> *m* sleigh
**traîner** [tʀene] <1> **I.** *vt* **①** (*tirer*) to pull; (*jambe*) to drag **②** (*emmener de force*) to drag **③** (*être encombré de: personne*) to be unable to shake off; **~ qc avec soi** to carry sth around with one **II.** *vi* **①** (*lambiner: personne*) to lag behind; (*discussion, maladie, procès*)

to drag on **②** (*vadrouiller: personne*) to hang around **③** (*être en désordre*) to lie around **④** (*pendre à terre*) to drag **III.** *vpr* (*se déplacer difficilement*) **se ~** to drag oneself around
**train-train** [tʀɛ̃tʀɛ̃] *m sans pl, inf* boring routine
**traire** [tʀɛʀ] *vt irr, défec* to milk
**trait** [tʀɛ] *m* **①** (*ligne*) line **②** (*caractéristique*) trait; (*distinctif, dominant*) characteristic; (*d'une époque, d'un individu*) feature **③** *gén pl* (*lignes du visage*) feature **④** (*preuve*) act **⑤** MUS run **⑥** LING feature; **~ d'union** LING hyphen; (*lien*) link ▶ **avoir ~ à qc** to relate to sth; (*film, livre*) to deal with sth; **tirer un ~ sur qc** (*renoncer*) to draw a line under sth; **d'un ~** in one go
**traitant(e)** [tʀɛtɑ̃, ɑ̃t] *adj* (*shampoing, lotion*) medicated; **votre médecin ~** the doctor treating you
**traite** [tʀɛt] *f* **①** (*achat à crédit*) **~ de qc** installment for sth **②** AGR (*des vaches*) milking **③** (*trafic*) trade; **la ~ des noirs/blanches** the slave/white slave trade
**traité** [tʀɛte] *m* **①** POL treaty **②** (*ouvrage*) treatise
**traitement** [tʀɛtmɑ̃] *m* **①** MED, TECH treatment **②** (*façon de traiter: du chômage, d'un problème*) handling **③** (*comportement*) treatment; **~ de faveur** preferential treatment **④** (*de l'eau, de déchets radioactifs*) processing **⑤** INFORM **~ de l'information** [*o* **des données**] data processing; **~ de texte** word processing **⑥** (*rémunération*) salary
**traiter** [tʀɛte] <1> **I.** *vt* **①** (*se comporter envers, analyser*) *a.* MED to treat; **se faire ~ pour qc** to get treatment for sth **②** (*qualifier*) **~ qn de fou/menteur** to call sb crazy/a liar **③** (*régler: dossier*) to process; **~ une affaire/question** to deal with some business/an issue **④** TECH (*déchets*) to process; (*eaux*) to treat; **oranges non traitées** unwaxed oranges **⑤** INFORM (*données, texte*) to process **II.** *vi* **①** (*avoir pour sujet*) **~ de**

**qc** to deal with sth; (*film*) to be about sth ➁(*négocier*) ~ **avec qn** to negotiate with sb III. *vpr* (*être réglé*) **se** ~ to be dealt with

**traître, traîtresse** [tʀɛtʀ, tʀɛtʀɛs] I. *adj* ➀(*qui trahit*) treacherous ➁(*sournois*) underhand; (*escalier, virage*) treacherous; (*paroles*) threatening II. *m, f* traitor ▸ **en** ~ underhandedly

**trajectoire** [tʀaʒɛktwaʀ] *f* (*parcours: d'un véhicule*) path; (*d'un projectile*) trajectory; (*d'une planète*) orbit

**trajet** [tʀaʒɛ] *m* journey; (*d'une artère, d'un nerf*) course

**tram** [tʀam] *m inf abr de* **tramway**

**tramway** [tʀamwɛ] *m* tram

**tranchant(e)** [tʀɑ̃ʃɑ̃, ɑ̃t] *adj* (*coupant*) sharp

**tranche** [tʀɑ̃ʃ] *f* ➀(*portion*) slice ➁(*subdivision: de travaux*) section; (*de remboursement*) installment; ~ **d'âge** age group; ~ **de revenus** salary bracket ➂(*bord: d'une pièce de monnaie, d'une planche*) edge ➃(*viande*) piece

**tranchée** [tʀɑ̃ʃe] *f* (*fossé*) a. MIL trench

**trancher** [tʀɑ̃ʃe] <1> I. *vt* ➀(*couper au couteau*) to cut; (*mettre en tranches*) to slice; (*enlever*) to cut off; (*couper à l'épée*) to slash ➁(*résoudre: différend, débat*) to settle II. *vi* (*décider*) ~ **en faveur de qn/qc** to decide in favor of sb/sth

**tranquille** [tʀɑ̃kil] I. *adj* ➀(*calme, paisible*) quiet ➁(*en paix*) **être** ~ (*personne*) to have peace; **laisser qn** ~ to leave sb alone ➂(*rassuré*) at ease ➃(*assuré: conviction, courage*) quiet ➄*iron, inf* (*certain*) **là, je suis** ~ I'm sure of that ▸ **pouvoir** <u>dormir</u> ~ to be able to sleep easy; **se tenir** ~ to keep quiet II. *adv inf* ➀(*facilement*) easily ➁(*sans crainte*) with no worries

**tranquillement** [tʀɑ̃kilmɑ̃] *adv* ➀(*paisiblement, avec maîtrise de soi*) peacefully; (*vivre*) quietly ➁(*sans risque*) safely ➂(*sans se presser*) calmly

**tranquillisant** [tʀɑ̃kilizɑ̃] *m* tranquilizer

**tranquillité** [tʀɑ̃kilite] *f* ➀(*calme*) tranquility; (*d'un lieu, de la mer, rue*) calmness ➁(*sérénité*) peace; (*matérielle*) security ▸ **en toute** ~ with complete peace of mind

**transaction** [tʀɑ̃zaksjɔ̃] *f* COM transaction

**transat¹** [tʀɑ̃zat] *m abr de* **transatlantique** II.

**transat²** [tʀɑ̃zat] *f abr de* **transatlantique** transatlantic race

**transatlantique** [tʀɑ̃zatlɑ̃tik] I. *adj* transatlantic II. *m* ➀(*paquebot*) (transatlantic) liner ➁(*chaise*) deck chair

**transcrire** [tʀɑ̃skʀiʀ] *vt irr* ➀(*copier: manuscrit, texte*) to copy out; (*message oral*) to write down ➁ADMIN, LING, BIO, MUS to transcribe

**transe** [tʀɑ̃s] *f* ➀ *pl* (*affres*) agony + *vb sing* ➁(*état second*) trance

**transférer** [tʀɑ̃sfeʀe] <5> *vt* ➀(*déplacer*) *a.* FIN to transfer; (*cendres, dépouille*) to translate; **nos bureaux ont été transférés** we have moved offices ➁JUR to convey

**transfert** [tʀɑ̃sfɛʀ] *m* (*déplacement*) transfer

**transformable** [tʀɑ̃sfɔʀmabl] *adj* **être** ~ **en qc** to be convertible into sth; (*aspect*) to be transformable into sth

**transformation** [tʀɑ̃sfɔʀmasjɔ̃] *f* ➀(*changement*) change; (*d'une maison, pièce*) transformation; (*de matières premières*) conversion ➁(*métamorphose*) ~ **en qc** change into sth ➂SPORT conversion

**transformer** [tʀɑ̃sfɔʀme] <1> I. *vt* ➀(*modifier*) to change; (*entreprise*) to transform; (*vêtement*) to alter; (*matière première*) to convert ➁(*opérer une métamorphose*) ~ **une pièce en bureau** to convert a room into an office ➂SPORT (*essai, penalty*) to convert II. *vpr* ➀(*changer*) **se** ~ to change ➁(*changer de nature*) **se** ~ **en jeune homme sérieux** to turn into a serious young man ➂CHIM, PHYS **l'eau se transforme en glace** water is transformed into ice

**transfuser** [tʀɑ̃sfyze] <1> *vt* (*sang*) to transfuse

**transfusion** [tʀɑ̃sfyzjɔ̃] *f* transfusion

**transgresser** [tʀɑ̃sgʀese] <1> *vt* (*loi*) to break

**transistor** [tʀɑ̃zistɔʀ] *m* RADIO, ELEC transistor

**transit** [tʀɑ̃zit] *m* COM, ANAT transit ▶ **en** ~ in transit

**transition** [tʀɑ̃zisjɔ̃] *f* MUS, CINE, PHYS (*passage*) ~ **de l'enfance à qc** transition from childhood to sth; **sans** ~ suddenly ▶ **de** ~ transitional

**transitoire** [tʀɑ̃zitwaʀ] *adj* transitory; (*période*) provisional

**transmettre** [tʀɑ̃smɛtʀ] *irr* **I.** *vt* ① (*léguer*) to hand down ② (*faire parvenir: message*) to transmit; (*renseignement, ordre*) to pass on ③ (*en science*) *a.* RADIO, TEL, TV to transmit ④ BIO, MED ~ **une maladie à qn** to pass on a disease to sb **II.** *vpr* ① (*se passer*) **se** ~ **une maladie/des nouvelles** to pass a disease/some news on to each other ② (*se communiquer*) **se** ~ (*secret, maladie*) to be passed on; (*métier*) to be taught

**transmissible** [tʀɑ̃smisibl] *adj* MED transmittable

**transmission** [tʀɑ̃smisjɔ̃] *f* ① (*passation*) handing on; ~ **de l'autorité à qn** conferment of authority on sb ② (*diffusion*) *a.* INFORM ~ **d'une information à qn** passing on of information to sb; ~ **d'une lettre à qn** forwarding of a letter to sb; ~ **de données** data transmission ③ RADIO, TEL, TV broadcasting ④ BIO, MED, TECH, AUTO transmission

**transparence** [tʀɑ̃spaʀɑ̃s] *f* ① (*opp: opacité: du cristal, verre*) transparency; (*de l'air, de l'eau*) clearness ② (*absence de secret*) openness; (*d'une allusion*) transparency

**transparent** [tʀɑ̃spaʀɑ̃] *m* transparency; (*pour rétroprojecteur*) overhead

**transparent(e)** [tʀɑ̃spaʀɑ̃, ɑ̃t] *adj* ① (*opp: opaque*) transparent; (*air, eau*) clear; **papier** ~ see-through paper ② (*sans secret*) open; (*affaire, négocia-*

*tion*) transparent ③ (*limpide: regard, yeux*) limpid; (*personne*) open

**transpercer** [tʀɑ̃spɛʀse] <2> *vt* (*percer, passer au travers: regard, balle*) to pierce; ~ **qc** (*pluie*) to soak through sth; (*froid*) to go through sth

**transpiration** [tʀɑ̃spiʀasjɔ̃] *f* ① (*processus*) perspiring ② (*sueur*) perspiration; (*soudaine*) sweat

**transpirer** [tʀɑ̃spiʀe] <1> *vi* (*suer*) to perspire

**transplantation** [tʀɑ̃splɑ̃tasjɔ̃] *f* BIO, MED (*d'un organe*) transplant

**transplanter** [tʀɑ̃splɑ̃te] <1> *vt* BIO, MED, AGR to transplant

**transport** [tʀɑ̃spɔʀ] *m* ① (*acheminement*) transport; (*d'énergie*) carrying ② *pl* **les** ~**s** transportation ▶ **entreprise de** ~ trucking company; **moyens de** ~ means of transportation; ~**s en commun** public transportation

**transporter** [tʀɑ̃spɔʀte] <1> *vt* ① (*acheminer: voyageur, blessé, prisonnier*) to transport ② TECH (*énergie, son*) to carry

**transporteur** [tʀɑ̃spɔʀtœʀ] *m* ① TECH conveyor ② (*entreprise*) trucking company

**transposer** [tʀɑ̃spoze] <1> *vt* (*transférer*) to adapt

**transsexuel(le)** [tʀɑ̃(s)sɛksɥɛl] *adj, m/f* transsexual

**transvaser** [tʀɑ̃svaze] <1> *vt* to decant

**trappe** [tʀap] *f* (*ouverture*) hatch; (*dans le plancher*) *a.* THEAT trap door; ~ **d'évacuation** exit door

**traquer** [tʀake] <1> *vt* (*abus, injustices*) to hunt down; (*voleur*) to track down; (*vedette*) to hound

**traumatiser** [tʀomatize] <1> *vt* ① (*choquer*) to traumatize ② MED ~ **qn** to cause sb trauma

**traumatisme** [tʀomatism] *m* trauma

**travail** [tʀavaj, -o] <-aux> *m* ① (*activité*) work; **travaux dirigés** [*o* **pratiques**] ECOLE tutorial class; **un** ~ **d'amateur** piece of amateur workmanship; ~ **d'équipe** teamwork ② (*tâche*) task ③ (*activité professionnelle*) job; ~ (**au**)

**noir** illegal work; **se mettre au ~** to get down to work; **~ à la chaîne** assembly-line work; **~ à plein temps/à temps partiel** full-time/part-time work ④ *pl* (*ensemble de tâches*) **les travaux domestiques/ménagers** housework; **travaux d'urbanisme** urban planning ⑤ ECON labor ⑥ (*façonnage*) working; **~ de la pâte** working the dough ⑦ (*fonctionnement*) working ⑧ (*effet*) work; **~ de l'érosion** process of erosion ⑨ PHYS work ⑩ ADMIN **travaux publics** civil engineering; **ingénieur des travaux publics** civil engineer; **travaux!** work in progress! ⑪ HIST **travaux forcés** hard labor ▸ **se tuer au ~** to work oneself to death

**travailler** [tʀavaje] <1> **I.** *vi* ① (*accomplir sa tâche*) to work ② (*exercer un métier*) to work ③ (*s'exercer*) to practice; (*sportif*) to train ④ (*viser un but*) **~ à un reportage/sur un projet** to work on a report/project; **~ à satisfaire les clients** to work to satisfy the customers ⑤ (*fonctionner: esprit, muscle*) to work; **faire ~ sa tête** (*l'utiliser*) to use one's head; **~ de** (*réfléchir beaucoup*) to use one's mind ⑥ (*subir des modifications*) to work **II.** *vt* ① to work; (*phrase, style*) to work on; **travaillé à la main** handmade ② (*s'entraîner à*) to train ; (*morceau de musique*) to practice ③ (*tourmenter*) **~ qn** to worry sb; (*douleur, fièvre*) to torment sb; (*problème, question*) to preoccupy sb ④ (*opp: chômer*) **les jours travaillés** working days; **les jours non travaillés** holidays

**travailleur, -euse** [tʀavajœʀ, -jøz] **I.** *adj* hard-working **II.** *m, f* ① (*salarié*) worker; **~ indépendant** self-employed worker ② (*personne laborieuse*) hard worker

**travers** [tʀavɛʀ] *m* (*petit défaut*) failing ▸ **prendre qc de ~** to take sth the wrong way; **regarder qn de ~** (*avec animosité*) to give sb a dirty look; **à ~ qc, au ~ de qc** (*en traversant*) across sth; (*par l'intermédiaire de*) through sth; **à ~ les siècles** down the centuries;

**à ~ le monde** across the world; **de ~** (*en biais*) crooked; (*mal*) wrong; **en ~** across

**traversée** [tʀavɛʀse] *f* (*franchissement*) **la ~ d'une rue/d'un pont** crossing a road/bridge; **la ~ d'une région en voiture** driving through a region

**traverser** [tʀavɛʀse] <1> *vt* ① (*franchir*) to cross; **~ qc à pied/en voiture/à vélo/à la nage** to walk/drive/ride/swim across sth; **faire ~ qn** to help sb across ② (*se situer en travers de: route, fleuve, pont*) to cross ③ (*transpercer*) to pierce; (*clou*) to go through ④ (*subir*) to go through ⑤ (*se manifester dans*) **cette idée lui traverse l'esprit** the idea crosses her mind

**traversier** [tʀavɛʀsje] *m Québec* (*bac*) ferry

**traversin** [tʀavɛʀsɛ̃] *m* bolster

**travesti** [tʀavɛsti] *m* ① (*homosexuel*) transvestite ② (*artiste*) drag artist

**travesti(e)** [tʀavɛsti] *adj* fancy dress

**trébucher** [tʀebyʃe] <1> *vi* (*buter*) **~ sur une pierre** to stumble over a stone

**trèfle** [tʀɛfl] *m* ① BOT clover ② JEUX clubs *pl* ③ (*figure*) shamrock

**treize** [tʀɛz] **I.** *adj* thirteen **II.** *m inv* thirteen; *v.a.* **cinq**

**treizième** [tʀɛzjɛm] **I.** *adj antéposé* thirteenth **II.** *mf* **le/la ~** the thirteenth **III.** *m* (*fraction*) thirteenth; *v.a.* **cinquième**

**tréma** [tʀema] **I.** *m* dieresis **II.** *app* **e/i/u ~** e/i/u dieresis

**tremblement** [tʀɑ̃bləmɑ̃] *m* ① (*frissonnement*) shiver; (*des jambes*) shaking; (*d'une lumière, flamme*) flickering; **~ de terre** earthquake ② (*vibration*) shaking; (*des feuilles*) trembling

**trembler** [tʀɑ̃ble] <1> *vi* ① (*frissonner*) to shiver; (*flamme, lumière*) to flicker; **~ de colère** to shake with rage ② (*vibrer*) to tremble; (*voix*) to quaver ③ (*avoir peur*) to tremble; **faire ~ qn** to make sb tremble

**trempé(e)** [trɑ̃pe] *adj* ❶ (*mouillé*) soaked ❷ TECH (*acier, verre*) tempered

**tremper** [trɑ̃pe] <1> **I.** *vt* ❶ (*mouiller*) to soak; (*sol*) to wet ❷ (*humecter: grains, semence*) to soak ❸ (*plonger*) ~ **sa plume dans l'encre** to dip one's pen in the ink; ~ **son croissant dans son café au lait** to dunk one's croissant in one's coffee ❹ TECH (*acier*) to temper **II.** *vi* (*rester immergé*) **laisser** ~ **des légumes secs** to soak pulses

**tremplin** [trɑ̃plɛ̃] *m* ❶ SPORT diving board; (*au ski*) ski jump ❷ (*aide, soutien*) springboard

**trentaine** [trɑ̃tɛn] *f* ❶ (*environ trente*) **une** ~ **de personnes/pages** about thirty people/pages ❷ (*âge approximatif*) **avoir la** ~ to be about thirty years old; **approcher de la** ~ to be nearly thirty years old

**trente** [trɑ̃t] **I.** *adj* thirty **II.** *m inv* thirty; *v.a.* **cinq, cinquante**

**trentième** [trɑ̃tjɛm] **I.** *adj antéposé* thirtieth **II.** *mf* **le/la** ~ the thirtieth **III.** *m* (*fraction*) thirtieth; *v.a.* **cinquième**

**trépied** [trepje] *m* (*support*) trivet; (*d'un appareil photo*) tripod

**très** [trɛ] *adv* very; (*nécessaire*) extremely; **avoir** ~ **faim/peur** to be very hungry/frightened; **faire** ~ **attention** to be very careful

**trésor** [trezɔr] *m* ❶ (*richesse enfouie*) treasure ❷ *pl* (*richesses*) treasures ❸ ADMIN, FIN **Trésor (public)** (*moyens financiers*) Treasury; (*bureau*) Treasury Department

**trésorerie** [trezɔrri] *f* ❶ (*budget*) finances ❷ (*gestion: d'une entreprise*) accounts; (*budget*) budget ❸ ADMIN, FIN accounts; (*bureau*) accounts department

**trésorier, -ière** [trezɔrje, -jɛr] *m, f* treasurer

**tressaillir** [tresajir] *vi irr* to quiver; (*maison*) to shake; (*cœur*) to flutter

**tresse** [trɛs] *f* braid

**tresser** [trese] <1> *vt* to braid

**tréteau** [treto] <x> *m* (*support*) trestle

**trêve** [trɛv] *f* ❶ (*répit*) respite ❷ (*arrêt des hostilités*) truce ► ~ **de plaisanteries!** seriously now!

**tri** [tri] *m* (*choix, à la poste*) sorting; **faire le** ~ **de qc** to sort sth

**triangle** [trijɑ̃gl] *m* ❶ MATH, MUS triangle ❷ AUTO ~ **de présignalisation** warning triangle

**triangulaire** [trijɑ̃gylɛr] **I.** *adj* ❶ (*à trois côtés*) triangular ❷ (*à trois: accord, débat*) three-sided **II.** *f* POL three-way contest

**tribord** [tribɔr] *m* starboard

**tribu** [triby] *f* ❶ SOCIOL tribe ❷ *iron* (*grande famille*) clan

**tribunal** [tribynal, -o] <-aux> *m* ❶ (*juridiction*) court; ~ **correctionnel** criminal court; ~ **fédéral** *Suisse* (*cour suprême de la Suisse*) supreme court; ~ **de grande instance** ≈ superior court ❷ (*bâtiment*) courthouse

**tribune** [tribyn] *f* ❶ (*estrade*) platform; POL rostrum ❷ (*galerie surélevée*) gallery; SPORT (*d'un champ de courses, stade*) grandstand ❸ (*lieu d'expression*) forum; (*dans un journal*) opinion page

**tribut** [triby] *m* (*sacrifice*) price

**tricher** [trife] <1> *vi* (*frauder*) to cheat; ~ **aux cartes/à l'examen** to cheat at cards/on a test

**tricheur, -euse** [trifœr, -øz] **I.** *adj* **être** ~ to be a cheat **II.** *m, f* swindler; (*au jeu, à l'examen*) cheat; (*aux cartes*) cardsharp

**tricolore** [trikɔlɔr] *adj* ❶ (*bleu, blanc, rouge*) red, white and blue ❷ (*français: succès*) French ❸ (*de trois couleurs*) tricolored

**tricot** [triko] *m* ❶ (*vêtement*) sweater; (*gilet tricoté*) cardigan; ~ **de corps** undershirt ❷ TECH (*étoffe*) knitwear ❸ (*action*) knitting

**tricoter** [trikɔte] <1> **I.** *vt* to knit; **tricoté à la main/à la machine** hand-/machine-knitted **II.** *vi* (*faire du tricot*) to knit; **aiguille à** ~ knitting needle

**trier** [trije] <1> *vt* to sort; (*choisir*) to select

**trimestre** [trimɛstr] *m* ❶ (*période de*

*trois mois*) quarter; ECOLE term ❷ (*somme*) quarter

**trimestriel(le)** [trimɛstrijɛl] *adj* (*paiement, publication*) quarterly

**tringle** [trɛɡl] *f* rod

**trinquer** [trɛ̃ke] <1> *vi* ~ **à la santé de qn** to drink to sb's health

**trio** [trijo] *m a.* MUS trio

**triomphe** [trijɔ̃f] *m* triumph

**triompher** [trijɔ̃fe] <1> *vi* ❶ (*personne, vérité, mode*) to triumph ❷ (*crier victoire*) to rejoice

**triple** [tripl] **I.** *adj* triple **II.** *m* **le ~ du prix** three times the price; **le ~ de temps** three times as long

**tripoter** [tripɔte] <1> **I.** *vt* ❶ (*triturer: fruits*) to finger; ~ **des crayons/des pièces** to fiddle with pencils/coins ❷ (*toucher avec insistance*) ~ **qc** to fiddle with sth **II.** *vpr* ❶ (*se caresser*) **se ~** to play with oneself ❷ (*triturer*) **se ~ la barbe en parlant** to fiddle with one's beard while speaking

**trique** [trik] *f* (*gourdin*) cudgel

**triste** [trist] *adj* ❶ *a. antéposé* (*affligé, affligeant*) sad; **avoir l'air ~** to look sad; **avoir ~ mine** to be a sorry sight ❷ *a. antéposé* gloomy ❸ *antéposé, péj* (*déplorable: époque, mémoire*) dreadful; (*affaire*) sorry; (*résultats*) awful ▶ **ne pas être** ~ *inf* (*personne*) to be a laugh a minute; (*soirée, voyage*) to be eventful

**tristesse** [tristɛs] *f* ❶ (*état de mélancolie*) sadness ❷ (*chagrin*) sorrow

**trithérapie** [triterapi] *f* MED triple therapy

**trivial(e)** [trivjal, -jo] <-aux> *adj* ❶ (*vulgaire*) crude ❷ (*ordinaire*) mundane

**troc** [trɔk] *m* ❶ (*échange*) swap ❷ (*système économique*) **le ~** barter

**trognon** [trɔɲ5] *m* core; (*de chou*) stalk

**trois** [trwɑ] **I.** *adj* three ▶ **en ~ mots** in a word **II.** *m inv* three; *v.a.* **cinq**

**trois-étoiles** [trwɑzetwal] *adj inv* three-star

**troisième** [trwɑzjɛm] **I.** *adj antéposé* third; **le ~ âge** (*période de vie*) retire-

ment years *pl*; (*personnes âgées*) senior citizens *pl*; **le ~ cycle** graduate school **II.** *mf* **le/la ~** the third **III.** *f* ECOLE eighth grade; *v.a.* **cinquième**

**trombe** [trɔ̃b] *f* ❶ (*forte averse*) cloudburst ❷ METEO whirlwind ▶ **en ~** *inf* at top speed; **passer en ~** to race by

**trombone** [trɔ̃bɔn] **I.** *m* ❶ MUS trombone ❷ (*attache*) paper clip **II.** *mf* trombonist

**trompe** [trɔ̃p] *f* ❶ MUS trumpet ❷ ZOOL snout; (*d'un insecte*) proboscis ❸ *souvent pl* ANAT tube

**trompe-l'œil** [trɔ̃plœj] *m inv* ART trompe l'œil

**tromper** [trɔ̃pe] <1> **I.** *vt* ❶ (*duper*) to trick; ~ **qn sur le prix** to overcharge sb ❷ (*être infidèle à*) ~ **qn avec qn** to cheat on sb with sb ❸ (*décevoir*) ~ **l'attente/l'espoir de qn** to fall short of sb's expectations/hopes ❹ (*faire oublier*) ~ **qc** to keep sth at bay; (*faim, soif*) to stave off sth **II.** *vi* to deceive **III.** *vpr* ❶ (*faire erreur*) **se ~** to make a mistake; **se ~ dans son calcul** to get one's calculations wrong ❷ (*confondre*) **se ~ de direction** to take the wrong direction; **se ~ de numéro** to get the wrong number

**trompette** [trɔ̃pɛt] **I.** *f* MUS trumpet ▶ **nez en ~** turned-up nose **II.** *m* ❶ MUS trumpet player ❷ MIL bugler

**trompeur, -euse** [trɔ̃pœr, -øz] *adj* (*promesse*) empty; (*distance, résultats*) deceptive; (*ressemblance*) illusory; (*personne*) deceitful; (*discours*) misleading

**tronc** [trɔ̃] *m* ❶ BOT, ANAT trunk ❷ ECOLE ~ **commun** core curriculum

**tronçon** [trɔ̃sɔ̃] *m* ❶ (*partie*) section; (*d'une voie ferrée, autoroute*) stretch ❷ (*morceau coupé*) segment; (*d'une colonne*) section

**tronçonner** [trɔ̃sɔne] <1> *vt* ❶ (*diviser en tronçons*) to divide up ❷ (*découper*) to cut up ❸ (*scier*) to saw up

**trône** [tron] *m* throne

**tronquer** [trɔ̃ke] <1> *vt* (*détail*) to cut out; (*conclusion*) to shorten; (*texte, ci-*

*tation*) to abridge; (*données*) to cut down

**trop** [tʁo] *adv* ❶ (*de façon excessive*) too; (*manger, faire*) too much ❷ (*en quantité excessive*) ~ **de temps/travail** too much time/work ❸ (*pas tellement*) **ne pas ~ aimer qc** not to like sth much; **ne pas ~ savoir** not to be too sure; **je n'ai pas ~ envie** I don't really feel like it ▸ **c'est ~!** it's too much

**trophée** [tʁofe] *m* trophy

**tropical(e)** [tʁopikal, -o] <-aux> *adj* tropical

**tropique** [tʁopik] *m* ❶ GEO tropic ❷ (*région tropicale*) **les ~s** the tropics

**troquer** [tʁoke] <1> *vt* to swap

**trot** [tʁo] *m* (*allure*) trot

**trotter** [tʁote] <1> *vi* ❶ (*aller à petits pas: animal*) to scamper; (*personne*) to scurry ❷ (*aller au trot: cheval*) to trot

**trottiner** [tʁotine] <1> *vi* to jog along; (*enfant*) to toddle around

**trottinette** [tʁotinɛt] *f* toy scooter

**trottoir** [tʁotwaʁ] *m* sidewalk

**trou** [tʁu] *m* ❶ (*cavité*) hole; (*d'une aiguille*) eye; ~ **de la serrure** keyhole ❷ (*moment de libre*) gap ❸ (*déficit*) gap; ~ **(dans la couche) d'ozone** hole in the ozone layer ❹ (*vide: d'un témoignage, d'une œuvre*) gap; ~ **de mémoire** memory lapse

**troublant(e)** [tʁublɑ̃, ɑ̃t] *adj* ❶ (*déconcertant*) disconcerting; (*élément*) troubling ❷ (*inquiétant: événement, fait*) disturbing ❸ (*étrange: événement, mystère*) unsettling ❹ (*qui inspire le désir*) arousing

**trouble**[1] [tʁubl] **I.** *adj* ❶ (*opp: limpide: image, vue*) blurred; (*liquide*) cloudy; (*lumière*) dull ❷ (*équivoque: période*) dismal **II.** *adv* **voir ~** to have blurred vision

**trouble**[2] [tʁubl] *m* ❶ *pl* MED disorder; (*psychiques mentaux*) distress ❷ *pl* (*désordre: politiques, sociaux*) unrest ❸ (*désarroi*) confusion ❹ (*agitation*) turmoil

**troubler** [tʁuble] <1> **I.** *vt* ❶ (*gêner fortement*) to disrupt ❷ (*perturber*) to bother ❸ (*déranger*) to disturb ❹ (*émouvoir*) to unsettle; (*sexuellement*) to arouse ❺ MED (*digestion, facultés mentales*) to disturb ❻ (*altérer la clarté: atmosphère, ciel*) to cloud **II.** *vpr* **se ~** (*devenir trouble*) to become cloudy; (*mémoire*) to become blurred

**troué(e)** [tʁue] *adj* **chaussettes ~es** socks with holes in them

**trouer** [tʁue] <1> *vt* ~ **qc** ❶ (*faire un trou*) to make a hole in sth ❷ (*faire plusieurs trous*) to make holes in sth ❸ (*traverser: rayon de lumière*) to break through sth

**trouille** [tʁuj] *f inf* **ficher la ~ à qn** to scare the hell out of sb

**troupe** [tʁup] *f* ❶ MIL troop ❷ THEAT troupe

**troupeau** [tʁupo] <x> *m* herd

**trousse** [tʁus] *f* (*étui à compartiments*) case; ~ **d'écolier** pencil case; ~ **de toilette** [*o* **voyage**] toilet bag

**trousseau** [tʁuso] <x> *m* ❶ (*clés*) bunch of keys ❷ (*vêtements*) clothes *pl*; (*d'une mariée*) trousseau

**trouver** [tʁuve] <1> **I.** *vt* ❶ (*découvrir, avoir le sentiment*) to find; ~ **étrange qu'elle ait fait qc** (*subj*) to find it strange that she did sth ❷ (*voir*) ~ **du plaisir à faire qc** to take pleasure in doing sth; **aller/venir ~ qn** to go/come and find sb **II.** *vpr* ❶ (*être situé*) **se ~** to be ❷ (*être*) **se ~ bloqué/coincé** to find oneself stuck; **se ~ dans l'obligation de partir** to be compelled to leave ❸ (*se sentir*) **se ~ bien/mal** to feel good/uncomfortable ❹ (*exprime la coïncidence*) **ils se trouvent être nés le même jour** they turned out to have been born on the same day ❺ (*se rencontrer*) **un bon job se trouve toujours** one can always find a good job **III.** *vpr impers* ❶ (*par hasard*) **il se trouve que je suis libre** it so happens I'm free ❷ (*on trouve, il y a*) **il se trouve toujours un pour faire qc** there's always someone who'll do sth ▸ **si ça**

**se trouve, il va pleuvoir** *inf* it may well rain

**truand** [tʀɥɑ̃] *m* crook

**truc** [tʀyk] *m* ❶ *inf* (*chose*) thingamajig ❷ *inf* (*personne*) what's-his-name, what's-her-name *m, f* ❸ *inf* (*combine*) trick ❹ (*tour*) trick ▶ **c'est mon ~** *inf* it's my thing

**trucage** [tʀykaʒ] *m* ❶ (*falsification: de statistiques, de la réalité*) doctoring; (*des élections*) fixing ❷ CINE, PHOT effect

**truffe** [tʀyf] *f* ❶ BOT, CULIN truffle ❷ (*museau*) nose

**truie** [tʀɥi] *f* sow

**truite** [tʀɥit] *f* trout

**truquer** [tʀyke] <1> *vt* to fix; (*comptes*) to fiddle

**t-shirt** [tiʃœʀt] *m abr de* **tee-shirt**

**tsigane** [tsigan] **I.** *adj* **musique ~** Hungarian gypsy music **II.** *mf* Hungarian gypsy

**T.T.C.** [tetese] *abr de* **toutes taxes comprises** tax included

**tu** [ty] <*inf, devant voyelle ou h muet* t'> **I.** *pron pers* you **II.** *m* **dire ~ à qn** to use "tu" with sb

**tu(e)** [ty] *part passé de* **taire**

**tube¹** [tyb] *m* ❶ (*tuyau, emballage à presser*) a. ELEC tube ❷ ANAT **~ digestif** digestive tract

**tube²** [tyb] *m inf* (*chanson*) hit

**tuberculose** [tybɛʀkyloz] *f* tuberculosis

**tué(e)** [tɥe] *m(f)* **il y a eu deux blessés et un ~** there were two people injured and one person killed

**tuer** [tɥe] <1> **I.** *vt* ❶ (*donner la mort à*) to kill; (*gibier*) to shoot; **se faire ~** to get killed ❷ (*nuire à: espoir, environnement*) to ruin; (*initiative*) to kill off **II.** *vi* to kill **III.** *vpr* ❶ (*être victime d'un accident*) **se ~** to get killed ❷ (*se donner la mort*) **se ~** to kill oneself ❸ (*se fatiguer*) **se ~ à faire qc** to wear oneself out doing sth

**tuerie** [tyʀi] *f* slaughter

**tueur, -euse** [tɥœʀ, -øz] *m, f* killer

**tuile** [tɥil] *f* ❶ (*petite plaque: d'un toit*) tile ❷ *inf* (*événement fâcheux*) stroke of bad luck

**tulipe** [tylip] *f* tulip

**tuméfié(e)** [tymefje] *adj* swollen

**tumeur** [tymœʀ] *f* tumor

**tumulte** [tymylt] *m* (*d'une foule*) commotion; (*des flots, d'un orage*) tumult; (*des passions*) turmoil; (*de la rue, de la ville*) (*agitation*) hustle and bustle; (*bruit*) hubbub

**tuner** [tynœʀ] *m* tuner

**Tunisie** [tynizi] *f* **la ~** Tunisia

**tunisien(ne)** [tynizjɛ̃, jɛn] *adj* Tunisian

**tunnel** [tynɛl] *m* (*galerie*) tunnel

**turbine** [tyʀbin] *f* turbine

**turbo¹** [tyʀbo] *adj inv* turbo

**turbo², turbocompresseur** [tyʀbokɔ̃-pʀesœʀ] *m* turbocharger

**turbulent(e)** [tyʀbylɑ̃, ɑ̃t] *adj* (*agité*) turbulent

**turc** [tyʀk] *m* Turkish; *v.a.* **français**

**turc, turque** [tyʀk] *adj* Turkish

**Turc, Turque** [tyʀk] *m(f)* Turk

**Turquie** [tyʀki] *f* **la ~** Turkey

**turquoise** [tyʀkwaz] **I.** *f* (*pierre*) turquoise **II.** *m* (*couleur*) turquoise **III.** *adj inv* turquoise

**tutelle** [tytɛl] *f* ❶ (*protection abusive*) tutelage ❷ JUR (*d'un mineur, aliéné*) guardianship ❸ ADMIN, POL protection

**tuteur** [tytœʀ] *m* (*support*) stake

**tuteur, -trice** [tytœʀ, -tʀis] *m, f* ❶ JUR (*d'un mineur*) guardian ❷ ECOLE, UNIV tutor

**tutoyer** [tytwaje] <6> **I.** *vt* **~ qn** to use "tu" with sb **II.** *vpr* **se ~** to call each other "tu"

**tuyau** [tɥijo] <x> *m* ❶ (*tube rigide*) pipe; (*tube souple*) tube; **~ d'alimentation** supply pipe; **~ d'arrosage** garden hose ❷ *inf* (*conseil*) tip

**T.V.A.** [tevea] *f abr de* **taxe à la valeur ajoutée** VAT

**twitter** [twite] <1> *vi* TEL, INET tweet

**tympan** [tɛ̃pɑ̃] *m* ANAT eardrum

**type** [tip] **I.** *m* ❶ (*archétype, modèle*) type ❷ (*genre*) sort; **avoir le ~ chinois** to look Chinese ❸ (*individu quelconque*) guy ▶ **du troisième ~** of the third kind **II.** *app inv* typical

**typique** [tipik] *adj* typical

**tyran** [tiʀɑ̃] *m* tyrant
**tyrannie** [tiʀani] *f* (*despotisme, influence excessive*) tyranny

**tyranniser** [tiʀanize] <1> *vt* to bully
**tzigane** [tsigan] *adj v.* **tsigane**

# Uu

**U, u** [y] *m inv* U, u; ~ **comme Ursule** (*au téléphone*) u as in Uniform ▸ **en u** U-shaped
**UDF** [ydeɛf] *f abr de* **Union pour la démocratie française** *center-right* French political party
**UE** [yø] *f abr de* **Union Européenne** EU
**ulcère** [ylsɛʀ] *m* ulcer
**U.L.M.** [yɛlɛm] *m abr de* **ultra-léger motorisé** ultralight
**ultérieurement** [ylteʀjœʀmɑ̃] *adv* later; (*regretter*) subsequently
**ultime** [yltim] *adj a. antéposé* ultimate; (*ironie*) final
**ultra** [yltʀa] *mf* (*extrémiste de droite/ gauche*) right wing/left-wing extremist
**ultrason** [yltʀasɔ̃] *m* ultrasound
**ultraviolet** [yltʀavjɔlɛ] *m* ultraviolet
**ultraviolet(te)** [yltʀavjɔlɛ, ɛt] *adj* ultraviolet
**un** [œ̃] **I.** *adj* one ▸ **ne faire qu'~** to be as one; **elle n'a fait ni ~e ni deux, elle a refusé** she refused right off the bat **II.** *m inv* one **III.** *adv* firstly; **~, je suis fatigué, deux, j'ai faim** for one thing I'm tired, for another I'm hungry; *v.a.* **cinq**
**un(e)** [œ̃, yn] **I.** *art indéf* ❶ (*un certain*) a, an; **avec ~ grand courage** with great courage ❷ (*intensif*) **il y a ~ (de ces) bruit** it's so noisy; **ce type est d'~ culot!** this guy's got some nerve! **II.** *pron* ❶ (*chose/personne parmi d'autres*) one; **en connaître ~ qui ...** to know somebody who ...; **être l'~ de ceux qui ...** to be one of those who ... ❷ (*chose/personne opposée à une autre*) **les ~s ... et les autres ...** some

people ... and others ...; **ils sont assis en face l'~ de l'autre** they're sitting opposite each other; **ils sont aussi menteurs l'~ que l'autre** one's as big a liar as the other ▸ **l'~ dans l'autre** by and large; **l'~ ou l'autre** one or the other; **comme pas ~** extremely; **et d'~!** *inf* and that's that!; **~ par ~** one after the other
**unanime** [ynanim] *adj* unanimous
**unanimité** [ynanimite] *f* unanimity ▸ **à l'~** unanimously
**une** [yn] **I.** *art v.* **un II.** *f* ❶ (*première page du journal*) front page ❷ (*premier sujet*) main news ▸ **c'était moins ~!** *inf* it was a close call!
**uni(e)** [yni] *adj* ❶ (*sans motifs*) plain; (*unicolore*) self-colored ❷ (*en union*) **~ s par qc** united by sth
**unification** [ynifikasjɔ̃] *f* unification; (*des tarifs*) standardization
**unifier** [ynifje] <1> **I.** *vt* ❶ (*unir*) to unify; (*partis*) to unite ❷ (*uniformiser: programmes*) to standardize **II.** *vpr* **s'~** to unite
**uniforme** [ynifɔʀm] **I.** *adj* ❶ (*pareil*) uniform ❷ (*standardisé*) standardized ❸ (*invariable: vitesse*) steady; (*vie*) monotonous; (*mouvement, paysage*) uniform **II.** *m* uniform
**uniformiser** [ynifɔʀmize] <1> *vt* to standardize
**unilatéral(e)** [ynilateʀal, -o] <-aux> *adj* unilateral; **stationnement ~** parking on one side only
**union** [ynjɔ̃] *f* ❶ (*alliance, vie commune*) union; **en ~ avec qn** in union with sb ❷ (*juxtaposition: éléments*)

U

combination ❸ *(association)* association; **~ syndicale** federation of labor unions

**Union européenne** [ynjɔ̃ øʀɔpeɛn] f European Union

**Union monétaire** [ynjɔ̃ mɔnetɛʀ] f monetary union

**unique** [ynik] *adj* ❶ *(seul)* only; *(monnaie)* single; **un prix ~** one price; **enfant ~** only child; **rue à sens ~** one-way street ❷ *(exceptionnel)* unique

**unir** [yniʀ] <8> **I.** *vt* ❶ *(associer)* to unite ❷ *(marier)* **~ deux personnes** to join two people in matrimony ❸ *(combiner)* to combine ❹ *(relier)* **~ les gens** *(chemin de fer, langage)* to link people **II.** *vpr* ❶ *(s'associer)* **s'~** to unite ❷ *(se marier)* **s'~** to marry ❸ *(se combiner)* **s'~ à qc** to join with sth

**unisexe** [ynisɛks] *adj* unisex

**unitaire** [ynitɛʀ] *adj* ❶ *(simple)* a. MATH, PHYS unitary ❷ POL *(revendications)* common; *(mouvement)* unified

**unité** [ynite] f ❶ *(cohésion: d'une famille, classe)* unity; *(d'un texte)* cohesion ❷ MATH, MIL unit ❸ INFORM, TECH **~ centrale** central processing unit; **~ de sortie** output device ❹ COM **prix à l'~** unit price

**univers** [ynivɛʀ] m ❶ ASTRON universe; **~ parallèle** parallel universe ❷ *(milieu)* world

**universel(le)** [ynivɛʀsɛl] *adj* ❶ *(opp: particulier)* universal ❷ *(mondial)* world ❸ *(tous usages: remède)* all-purpose; **clé ~le** adjustable wrench

**universitaire** [ynivɛʀsitɛʀ] **I.** *adj* university; *(titre)* academic; **résidence ~** residence hall; **diplôme ~** degree; **restaurant ~** university cafeteria **II.** *mf* academic

**université** [ynivɛʀsite] f university; **~ d'été** summer school

**urbain(e)** [yʀbɛ̃, ɛn] *adj* urban

**urbanisme** [yʀbanism] m urban planning

**urgence** [yʀʒɑ̃s] f ❶ *(caractère urgent)* urgency; **il y a ~** it's urgent; **d'~** immediately ❷ *(cas urgent)* matter of urgency; MED emergency; **les ~s** the emergency room

**urgent(e)** [yʀʒɑ̃, ʒɑ̃t] *adj* urgent

**urgentiste** [yʀʒɑ̃tist] *mf* MED emergency physician

**urine** [yʀin] f urine

**uriner** [yʀine] <1> *vi* to urinate

**us** [ys] *mpl* **~ et coutumes** habits and customs

**usage** [yzaʒ] m ❶ *(utilisation)* use; **à l'~ de qn/qc** for sb/sth; **hors d'~** unusable; **méthode en ~** method in use; **être d'~ courant** to be in common use ❷ *(façon de se servir, consommation)* a. JUR use; **~ de faux** use of forged documents ❸ *(faculté)* **retrouver l'~ de la vue** to recover his/her sight; **perdre l'~ de la parole** to lose the power of speech ❹ *(coutume)* custom; **c'est contraire aux ~s** it's against common practice; **c'est l'~ de** +*infin* it's customary to +*infin* ▸ **à l'~** with use

**usager, -ère** [yzaʒe, -ɛʀ] *m, f* user

**usé(e)** [yze] *adj (détérioré)* worn; *(semelles)* worn-down

**user** [yze] <1> **I.** *vt* ❶ *(détériorer)* **~ qc** to wear sth out; *(roche)* to wear sth away ❷ *(épuiser)* **~ qn** to wear sb out ❸ *(consommer)* to use **II.** *vi* **~ d'un droit** to exercise a right **III.** *vpr* **s'~** to wear out; **s'~ à qc** to wear oneself out with sth

**usine** [yzin] f factory; **~ d'automobiles** car factory

**ustensile** [ystɑ̃sil] m *(de cuisine)* utensil; *(de jardinage)* tool

**usuel(le)** [yzɥɛl] *adj* usual; *(emploi)* normal; *(mot)* common; *(objet)* everyday

**usure** [yzyʀ] f ❶ *(détérioration)* wear and tear ❷ *(état)* wear ❸ *(érosion)* wearing away ❹ *(affaiblissement)* wearing out

**ut** [yt] m *inv* MUS C

**utérus** [yteʀys] m womb

**utile** [ytil] *adj (profitable)* useful

**utilisable** [ytilizabl] *adj* usable

**utilisation** [ytilizasjɔ̃] f use

**utiliser** [ytilize] <1> vt ❶ (se servir de) to use ❷ (recourir à: avantage) to make use of; (moyen, mot) to use ❸ (exploiter: personne) to use; (restes) to use up

**utilitaire** [ytilitɛʀ] I. adj (susceptible d'être utilisé) utilitarian; (objet) functional; (véhicule) commercial II. m ❶ INFORM utility ❷ AUTO commercial vehicle

**utilité** [ytilite] f ❶ (aide) use ❷ (caractère utile) usefulness; **je n'en ai pas l'~** I don't have any use for it

**U.V.** [yve] I. mpl abr de **ultraviolets** UV rays II. f abr de **unité de valeur** UNIV credit

# V v

**V, v** [ve] m inv V, v; **~ comme Victor** (au téléphone) v as in Victor ▶ **décolleté en V** V-neck

**vacancier, -ière** [vakɑ̃sje, -jɛʀ] m, f vacationer

**vacant(e)** [vakɑ̃, ɑ̃t] adj vacant

**vacarme** [vakaʀm] m racket

**vaccin** [vaksɛ̃] m vaccine

**vaccination** [vaksinasjɔ̃] f vaccination

**vacciner** [vaksine] <1> vt MED to vaccinate

**vache** [vaʃ] I. f ❶ ZOOL cow ❷ (cuir) cowhide ▶ **la ~!** inf damn! II. adj inf (méchant) mean

**vachement** [vaʃmɑ̃] adv inf damned

**vaciller** [vasije] <1> vi (personne) to stagger; (poteau) to sway; (lumière) to flicker

**vagabonder** [vagabɔ̃de] <1> vi (errer) to roam

**vagin** [vaʒɛ̃] m vagina

**vaginal(e)** [vaʒinal, -o] <-aux> adj vaginal

**vague¹** [vag] I. adj ❶ a. antéposé (indistinct) vague ❷ antéposé (lointain) faraway ❸ (ample: manteau) loose II. m (imprécision) vagueness

**vague²** [vag] f GEO, METEO (a. afflux) wave

**vaguement** [vagmɑ̃] adv ❶ (opp: précisément) vaguely ❷ (un peu) **avoir l'air ~ surpris** to seem slightly surprised

**vain(e)** [vɛ̃, vɛn] adj (inutile) vain ▶ **en ~** in vain

**vaincre** [vɛ̃kʀ] irr I. vi soutenu to prevail II. vt soutenu ❶ MIL (pays) to conquer ❷ MIL, SPORT (adversaire) to defeat ❸ (surmonter) to overcome

**vaincu(e)** [vɛ̃ky] I. part passé de **vaincre** II. adj defeated; **s'avouer ~** to admit defeat III. m(f) (perdant) **les ~s** the defeated; SPORT the losers

**vainqueur** [vɛ̃kœʀ] I. adj (victorieux) victorious II. mf ❶ MIL, POL victor ❷ SPORT winner

**vaisseau¹** [veso] <x> m ANAT vessel

**vaisseau²** [veso] <x> m ❶ NAUT vessel ❷ AVIAT **~ spatial** spacecraft ❸ ARCHIT nave

**vaisselle** [vɛsɛl] f ❶ (service de table) dishware, dishes pl ❷ (objets à nettoyer) dishes pl; **faire la ~** to do the dishes

**valable** [valabl] adj a. JUR, COM valid

**Valais** [valɛ] m **le ~** the Valais

**valeur** [valœʀ] f ❶ (prix) a. MATH, MUS, JEUX value; **de ~** of value ❷ FIN (cours) value; (titre) security ❸ ECON value; **~ ajoutée** value added ❹ (importance) value; **accorder de la ~ à qc** to value sth; **mettre qn en ~** to show sb to advantage; **mettre qc en ~** to show sth off ❺ (équivalent) **la ~ d'un litre** a liter's worth

**V**

**validation** [validasjɔ̃] f (*certification*) a. INFORM validation

**valide** [valid] adj ❶ (*bien portant: personne*) able-bodied ❷ (*valable: papier*) valid

**valider** [valide] <1> vt (*certifier*) a. INFORM to validate

**validité** [validite] f validity

**valise** [valiz] f suitcase; **faire sa ~** to pack one's bag

**vallée** [vale] f valley

**valoir** [valwaʀ] irr I. vi ❶ (*coûter*) to be worth; **combien ça vaut?** how much is it worth? ❷ (*mettre en avant*) **faire ~ un argument** to press an argument II. vt ❶ (*avoir de la valeur*) to be worth; **~ qc** to be worth sth; **ne pas ~ grand-chose** not to be worth much ❷ (*être valable*) to apply; **autant vaut** [o **vaudrait**] **faire qc** you might as well do sth ❸ (*être équivalent à*) a. JEUX to be worth; **rien ne vaut un bon lit quand on est fatigué** there's nothing like a good bed when you're tired ❹ (*mériter*) to deserve; **cette ville vaut le détour** this town is worth going out of your way to see ❺ (*avoir pour conséquence*) **~ qc à qn** to earn sb sth; **qu'est-ce qui nous vaut cet honneur?** to what do we owe this honor? III. vpr **se** ~ ❶ COM to be worth the same; **ces deux vases se valent** there's not much difference between these two vases ❷ (*être comparable: personnes, choses*) to be the same

**valoriser** [valɔʀize] <1> vt ECON (*région*) to develop; (*déchets*) to recover

**valse** [vals] f waltz

**van** [vɑ̃] m horse trailer

**vanille** [vanij] f CULIN, BOT vanilla

**vanité** [vanite] f vanity

**vanne** [van] f ❶ NAUT (*d'une écluse*) sluice ❷ inf (*plaisanterie*) **lancer des ~s à qn** to gibe at sb

**vannerie** [vanʀi] f ❶ (*fabrication*) basketry ❷ (*objets*) wickerwork

**vantard(e)** [vɑ̃taʀ, aʀd] I. adj boastful II. m(f) boaster

**vanter** [vɑ̃te] <1> I. vt to praise; **~ la**

**marchandise** to talk up the merchandise II. vpr **se ~ de qc** to boast of sth

**vapeur** [vapœʀ] f ❶ (*buée*) **~ d'eau** steam ❷ (*énergie*) **bateau à ~** steamboat; **machine à ~** steam-driven machine ❸ pl (*émanation*) fumes pl

**vaporeux, -euse** [vapɔʀø, -øz] adj (*tissu, cheveux*) gossamer

**vaporisateur** [vapɔʀizatœʀ] m spray

**vaporiser** [vapɔʀize] <1> I. vt (*pulvériser, imprégner*) to spray; **~ les cheveux avec de la laque** to put on some hair spray II. vpr **se ~ qc sur le visage** to spray sth on one's face

**varappe** [vaʀap] f rock climbing

**variable** [vaʀjabl] adj ❶ (*opp: constant*) variable ❷ METEO unsettled; **vent ~** variable wind

**variante** [vaʀjɑ̃t] f (*forme différente*) variant

**variateur** [vaʀjatœʀ] m **~ de lumière** dimmer; **~ de vitesse** speed variator

**variation** [vaʀjasjɔ̃] f ❶ (*changement*) change ❷ (*écart*) a. MATH, BIO, MUS variation

**varice** [vaʀis] f souvent pl varicose vein

**varicelle** [vaʀisɛl] f chickenpox

**varié(e)** [vaʀje] adj ❶ (*divers*) varied ❷ (*très différent: arguments*) various

**varier** [vaʀje] <1> I. vi ❶ (*évoluer*) to change ❷ (*être différent*) to vary II. vt (*diversifier, changer*) to vary

**variété** [vaʀjete] f ❶ (*diversité, changement*) a. ZOOL, BOT variety ❷ pl THEAT variety ❸ pl CINE, TV variety program

**variole** [vaʀjɔl] f smallpox

**vase¹** [vaz] m (*récipient*) vase

**vase²** [vaz] f mud

**vaseux, -euse** [vazø, -øz] adj ❶ (*boueux*) muddy ❷ inf (*confus*) muddled

**vasque** [vask] f basin

**vaste** [vast] adj antéposé ❶ (*immense*) immense; (*spacieux: appartement*) vast ❷ (*ample: vêtement*) huge

**Vatican** [vatikɑ̃] m **le ~** the Vatican

**vaurien(ne)** [voʀjɛ̃, jɛn] m(f) good-for-nothing

**V**

**veau** [vo] <x> *m* ❶ ZOOL calf; **~ marin** seal ❷ CULIN veal

**vécu** [veky] *m* **le ~** real life

**vécu(e)** [veky] **I.** *part passé de* **vivre** **II.** *adj* ❶ (*réel*) real-life ❷ (*éprouvé*) **bien ~** happy; **mal ~** traumatic

**vedette** [vədɛt] **I.** *f* ❶ (*rôle principal*) star; **avoir la ~** to play the starring role ❷ (*personnage connu*) star ❸ (*centre de l'actualité*) **avoir la ~** to be in the limelight **II.** *app* ❶ **mannequin ~** supermodel ❷ CINE, TV **émission ~** flagship program

**végétal** [veʒetal, -o] <-aux> *m* vegetable

**végétal(e)** [veʒetal, -o] <-aux> *adj* vegetable

**végétarien(ne)** [veʒetaʀjɛ̃, jɛn] **I.** *adj* vegetarian **II.** *m(f)* vegetarian

**végétation** [veʒetasjɔ̃] *f* ❶ BOT vegetation ❷ *pl* MED adenoids

**végéter** [veʒete] <5> *vi* (*plante*) to grow; (*personne*) to vegetate

**véhicule** [veikyl] *m* ❶ (*support*) a. AUTO vehicle ❷ (*agent de transmission: d'une maladie*) vector; (*d'une information*) medium

**veille** [vɛj] *f* ❶ day before; **la ~ au soir** the evening of the day before; **la ~ de Noël** Christmas Eve ❷ (*fait de ne pas dormir*) wakefulness ❸ (*garde de nuit*) night watch ▸ **à la ~ de qc** on the eve of sth; **en ~** in standby mode

**veillée** [veje] *f* ❶ (*soirée*) evening ❷ (*dans la nuit*) vigil

**veiller** [veje] <1> **I.** *vi* ❶ (*faire attention à*) **~ à qc** to attend to sth; **~ à** +*infin* to be sure to +*infin* ❷ (*surveiller*) to be on watch; **~ sur qn/qc** to watch over sb/sth ❸ (*ne pas dormir*) to stay awake **II.** *vt* **~ qn** to watch over sb

**veilleuse** [vɛjøz] *f* ❶ (*petite lampe*) night-light ❷ *pl* (*feu de position*) sidelights

**veinard(e)** [vɛnaʀ, aʀd] *m(f)* *inf* lucky dog

**veine** [vɛn] *f* ❶ ANAT vein ❷ (*inspiration*) vein ❸ *inf* (*chance*) luck ❹ (*veinure*) veining

**velcro®** [vɛlkʀo] *m* Velcro®

**vélo** [velo] *m* ❶ (*bicyclette*) bicycle; **à** [*o* **en** *inf*] **~** by bike ❷ (*activité*) cycling

**vélomoteur** [velomɔtœʀ] *m* moped

**velours** [v(ə)luʀ] *m* (*tissu*) velvet; **~ côtelé** corduroy

**velouté(e)** [vəlute] *adj* ❶ (*doux au toucher*) velvet-soft ❷ CULIN smooth

**velu(e)** [vəly] *adj* hairy

**vendange** [vɑ̃dɑ̃ʒ] *f souvent pl* (*récolte*) grape harvest + *vb sing*

**vendangeur, -euse** [vɑ̃dɑ̃ʒœʀ, -ʒøz] *m, f* grape-picker

**Vendée** [vɑ̃de] **f la ~** the Vendée

**vendeur, -euse** [vɑ̃dœʀ, øz] **I.** *m, f* ❶ (*opp: acheteur*) seller ❷ (*marchand dans un magasin*) sales assistant; **~ de légumes** vegetable merchant **II.** *adj* (*qui fait vendre*) **un argument ~** an argument that sells

**vendre** [vɑ̃dʀ] <14> **I.** *vi* COM to sell; **faire ~** to boost sales; **être à ~** to be for sale **II.** *vt* to sell; **~ qc aux enchères** to auction sth **III.** *vpr* ❶ COM **se ~** to be sold; **se ~ bien/mal** to sell well/badly ❷ *fig* **se ~** (*candidat*) to sell oneself

**vendredi** [vɑ̃dʀədi] *m* Friday; **~ saint** Good Friday; *v.a.* **dimanche**

**vénéneux, -euse** [venenø, -øz] *adj* poisonous

**vénérable** [veneʀabl] *adj* venerable

**vénérer** [veneʀe] <5> *vt* to revere

**vengeance** [vɑ̃ʒɑ̃s] *f* vengeance

**venger** [vɑ̃ʒe] <2a> **I.** *vt* to avenge **II.** *vpr* **se ~ de qn/qc** to take revenge on sb/for sth

**venimeux, -euse** [vənimø, -øz] *adj* poisonous

**venin** [vənɛ̃] *m* venom

**venir** [v(ə)niʀ] <9> **I.** *vi* être ❶ (*arriver, se situer dans un ordre*) to come; **faire ~ le médecin** to call for the doctor; **faire ~ les touristes** to bring in the tourists; **à ~** to come ❷ (*se présenter à l'esprit*) **l'idée m'est venue de chercher dans ce livre** I had the idea of looking in this book ❸ (*parvenir, étendre ses limites*) **~ jusqu'à qn/qc** to reach sb/sth ❹ (*arriver*) to arrive; (*nuit*) to fall;

**laisser ~ qn/qc** to let sb/sth come; **alors, ça vient?** *inf* ready yet? ❺ (*se développer: plante*) to grow ❻ (*provenir*) ~ **d'Angleterre** to come from England ❼ (*découler, être la conséquence*) ~ **de qc** to come from sth ❽ (*aboutir à*) **où veut-il en ~?** what is he getting at? II. *aux être* ❶ (*se déplacer pour*) **je viens manger** I'm coming for dinner ❷ (*avoir juste fini*) **je viens juste de finir** I've just finished ❸ (*être conduit à*) **s'il venait à passer par là** if he should go that way; **elle en vint à penser qu'il (le) faisait exprès** she got to the stage of thinking he was doing it on purpose III. *vi impers être* ❶ **il viendra un temps où** there will come a time when ❷ (*provenir*) **de là vient que qn a fait qc** the result of this is that sb did sth; **d'où vient que qn a fait qc?** how come sb did sth?

**vent** [vɑ̃] *m* ❶ (*courant d'air*) *a.* METEO, NAUT wind; **il y a du ~** it's windy; **instrument à ~** wind instrument ❷ (*tendance*) **dans le ~** fashionable

**vente** [vɑ̃t] *f* ❶ (*action*) sale; **~ par correspondance** mail order; **~ au détail** retail; **~ à distance** distance sales; **mettre qc en ~** to put sth on sale ❷ (*service*) sales ❸ *pl* (*chiffre d'affaires*) sales ❹ (*réunion où l'on vend*) **~ aux enchères** auction; (*action*) auctioning

**venteux, -euse** [vɑ̃tø, -øz] *adj* windy

**ventilateur** [vɑ̃tilatœʀ] *m* fan

**ventilation** [vɑ̃tilasjɔ̃] *f* (*aération*) ventilation

**ventiler** [vɑ̃tile] <1> *vt* (*aérer: pièce*) to ventilate

**ventre** [vɑ̃tʀ] *m* stomach; **avoir mal au ~** to have a stomach ache

**venu(e)** [v(ə)ny] I. *part passé de* venir II. *adj* **bien ~** (*conseil*) timely; **mal ~** unwelcome III. *m(f)* **nouveau ~** newcomer

**venue** [v(ə)ny] *f* arrival

**ver** [vɛʀ] *m* worm; **~ blanc** grub; **~ de terre** earthworm

**véracité** [veʀasite] *f* truth

**verbal(e)** [vɛʀbal, -o] <-aux> *adj* verbal

**verbaliser** [vɛʀbalize] <1> *vt* (*mettre une contravention*) to ticket

**verbe** [vɛʀb] *m* LING verb

**verdict** [vɛʀdikt] *m* verdict

**verdir** [vɛʀdiʀ] <8> *vi* (*nature*) to turn green

**verdure** [vɛʀdyʀ] *f* ❶ (*végétation*) greenery ❷ (*légumes*) greens *pl*

**véreux, -euse** [veʀø, -øz] *adj* ❶ (*gâté par les vers: fruit*) worm-eaten ❷ (*douteux: personne*) corrupt

**verger** [vɛʀʒe] *m* orchard

**verglaçant(e)** [vɛʀglasɑ̃, ɑ̃t] *adj* **pluie ~e** freezing rain

**verglacé(e)** [vɛʀglase] *adj* icy

**verglas** [vɛʀglɑ] *m* black ice

**vérificateur** [veʀifikatœʀ] *m* INFORM **~ orthographique** spell checker

**vérification** [veʀifikasjɔ̃] *f* ❶ (*contrôle*) verification ❷ (*confirmation*) confirmation

**vérifier** [veʀifje] <1> I. *vt* ❶ (*contrôler*) to verify ❷ (*confirmer*) to confirm II. *vpr* **se ~** (*soupçon*) to be confirmed

**véritable** [veʀitabl] *adj* ❶ *a. postposé* (*réel, authentique: cuir, perles*) real ❷ *antéposé* (*vrai*) true

**vérité** [veʀite] *f* ❶ (*opp: mensonge, connaissance du vrai*) truth ❷ *sans pl* (*réalisme*) realism ❸ *sans pl* (*sincérité*) truthfulness ▸ **il n'y a que la ~ qui blesse** *prov* the truth hurts; **à la ~** to tell the truth; **en ~** in fact

**vermeil(le)** [vɛʀmɛj] *adj* (*teint*) rosy

**vermine** [vɛʀmin] *f sans pl* (*parasites, racaille*) vermin

**vermoulu(e)** [vɛʀmuly] *adj* worm-eaten

**vernir** [vɛʀniʀ] <8> I. *vt* (*bois, peinture*) to varnish II. *vpr* **se ~ les ongles** to put on nail polish

**vernis** [vɛʀni] *m* ❶ (*laque*) varnish; **~ à ongles** nail polish ❷ (*aspect brillant*) shine

**verre** [vɛʀ] *m* ❶ (*matière, récipient, contenu*) glass; **~ à pied** stemmed glass; **prendre un ~** to have a drink ❷ (*objet: d'une montre*) glass; (*en optique*) lens

**verrier** [vɛʀje] *m* glass blower

**verrière** [vɛʀjɛʀ] f ❶ (toit) glass roof ❷ (paroi) glass wall

**verrou** [veʀu] m ❶ (loquet) bolt ❷ (serrure) lock

**verrouiller** [veʀuje] <1> vt (fermer) a. INFORM to lock

**verrue** [veʀy] f MED wart

**vers¹** [vɛʀ] prep ❶ (en direction de) ~ qn/qc toward sb/sth ❷ (aux environs de: lieu) around ❸ (aux environs de: temps) about

**vers²** [vɛʀ] m verse

**versant** [vɛʀsɑ̃] m (pente) slope; (d'un toit) side

**Verseau** [vɛʀso] <x> m Aquarius; v.a. **Balance**

**versement** [vɛʀsəmɑ̃] m payment; (sur un compte) deposit

**verser** [vɛʀse] <1> vt ❶ (faire couler) ~ de l'eau à qn to pour sb some water ❷ (payer) ~ une somme à qn to pay a sum to sb; ~ qc sur un compte to deposit sth in an account ❸ (ajouter) ~ qc au dossier to add sth to a file

**version** [vɛʀsjɔ̃] f ❶ (interprétation) a. MUS, THEAT, CINE version ❷ (modèle) model ❸ ECOLE unseen (translation into French)

**verso** [vɛʀso] m back

**vert** [vɛʀ] m green; passer au ~ (voiture) to go on a green light

**vert(e)** [vɛʀ, vɛʀt] I. adj ❶ (de couleur verte, écologiste) green ❷ (blême) ~ de peur white with fear; ~ de jalousie green with envy ❸ (de végétation) espaces ~s green spaces ❹ (à la campagne) classe ~e school camp ❺ (opp: mûr: fruit) unripe; (vin) young ❻ (opp: sec: bois, légumes) green ❼ (agricole) l'Europe ~e green Europe II. m(f) (écologiste) green

**vertébral(e)** [vɛʀtebʀal, -o] <-aux> adj colonne ~e spinal column

**vertèbre** [vɛʀtɛbʀ] f vertebra

**vertical(e)** [vɛʀtikal, -o] <-aux> adj vertical

**vertige** [vɛʀtiʒ] m ❶ sans pl (peur du vide) vertigo ❷ (malaise) dizzy spell; il a le ~ he's having a dizzy spell; donner

le ~ à qn (personne, situation) to make sb's head spin; (hauteur) to make sb dizzy

**vertu** [vɛʀty] f ❶ (qualité) virtue ❷ sans pl (moralité) virtue ❸ (pouvoir) power

**verve** [vɛʀv] f eloquence

**vessie** [vesi] f bladder

**veste** [vɛst] f ❶ (vêtement court, veston) jacket ❷ (gilet) cardigan

**vestiaire** [vɛstjɛʀ] m coat check

**vestibule** [vɛstibyl] m (d'une maison) hall; (d'un hôtel) lobby

**vestige** [vɛstiʒ] m souvent pl trace

**veston** [vɛstɔ̃] m jacket

**vêtement** [vɛtmɑ̃] m garment; des ~s clothes

**vétérinaire** [veteʀinɛʀ] I. adj veterinary II. mf veterinarian

**vêtir** [vetiʀ] vpr irr, soutenu se ~ to dress oneself

**vêtu(e)** [vety] I. part passé de **vêtir** II. adj dressed; ~ de qc wearing sth

**veuf, veuve** [vœf, vœv] I. adj widowed II. m, f widower, widow m, f

**vexer** [vɛkse] <1> I. vt to offend II. vpr se ~ de qc to be offended by sth

**via** [vja] prep via

**viable** [vjabl] adj viable

**viaduc** [vjadyk] m viaduct

**viager** [vjaʒe] m life annuity

**viager, -ère** [vjaʒe, -ɛʀ] adj life

**viande** [vjɑ̃d] f meat

**vibration** [vibʀasjɔ̃] f (d'une voix, corde) resonance; (d'un moteur) vibration

**vibrer** [vibʀe] <1> vi (trembler: voix, corde) to resonate; (mur, moteur) to vibrate

**vicaire** [vikɛʀ] m curate

**vice** [vis] m (anomalie) defect

**vice-président(e)** [vispʀezidɑ̃, ɑ̃t] <vice-présidents> m(f) vice president

**vice versa** [vis(e)vɛʀsa] adv et ~ and vice versa

**vicieux, -euse** [visjø, -jøz] I. adj ❶ (obsédé sexuel: personne, air) lecherous ❷ inf (vache, tordu: coup, personne) devious II. m, f (cochon) pervert

**victime** [viktim] f ❶ (blessé, mort) casualty ❷ (*personne/chose qui subit*) victim

**victoire** [viktwaʀ] *f* ~ **sur qn/qc** victory over sb/sth

**victorieux, -euse** [viktɔʀjø, -jøz] *adj* victorious

**victuailles** [viktyaj] *fpl* food + *vb sing*

**vidange** [vidãʒ] *f* ❶ (*action: d'un circuit*) emptying; AUTO oil change ❷ (*dispositif: d'un évier*) waste outlet

**vidanger** [vidãʒe] <2a> *vt* ❶ AUTO **faire ~ une voiture** to change the oil in a car ❷ (*vider*) to drain

**vide** [vid] **I.** *adj* ❶ (*opp: plein*) empty ❷ (*opp: riche: discussion*) empty; ~ **de qc** devoid of sth ❸ (*opp: occupé*) vacant **II.** *m* ❶ *sans pl* (*abîme*) void ❷ PHYS vacuum; **emballé sous ~** vacuum-packed ❸ (*espace vide*) gap ❹ (*néant*) void ▸ **faire le ~** (*évacuer ses soucis*) to clear one's mind

**vidéo** [video] **I.** *f* (*technique, film, émission*) video **II.** *adj inv* video

**vidéoclip** [videoklip] *m* video

**vidéoconférence** [videokɔ̃feʀãs] *f* videoconference

**vidéophone** [videofɔn] *m* videophone

**vide-ordures** [vidɔʀdyʀ] *m inv* waste disposal

**vidéotex®** [videotɛks] *m* videotex

**vider** [vide] <1> **I.** *vt* ❶ (*retirer, voler le contenu de*) to empty; ~ **un bassin de son eau** to empty the water out of a bowl ❷ (*verser: bouteille, boîte*) to empty ❸ (*faire s'écouler: substance liquide*) to drain; (*substance solide*) to empty ❹ (*consommer*) ~ **son verre** to drain one's glass ❺ *inf* (*expulser*) to throw out ❻ *inf* (*fatiguer*) **être vidé** to be exhausted ❼ CULIN (*poisson*) to clean **II.** *vpr* ❶ (*perdre son contenu*) **se ~** (*bouteille*) to be emptied; (*ville*) to empty ❷ (*s'écouler*) **se ~ dans le caniveau** (*eaux usées*) to drain into the gutter

**vie** [vi] *f* ❶ (*existence, biographie*) life; **être en ~** to be alive; **être sans ~** to be lifeless (*façon de vivre*) life; **la ~ active** work ▸ **gagner sa ~** to earn a living;

**refaire sa ~ avec qn** to make a new life with sb; **à ~** for life

**vieillard** [vjɛjaʀ] *m* old man

**vieillerie** [vjɛjʀi] *f* ~ **s** old-fashioned things; (*vêtements*) vintage clothing

**vieillesse** [vjɛjɛs] *f* ❶ (*opp: jeunesse*) old age ❷ *sans pl* (*personnes âgées*) **la ~** the elderly *pl*

**vieillir** [vjejiʀ] <8> **I.** *vi* ❶ (*prendre de l'âge: personne*) to grow old; (*chose*) to age; (*fromage, vin*) to mature ❷ *péj* (*diminuer: personne*) to age ❸ (*se démoder*) to become old-fashioned **II.** *vt* (*faire paraître plus vieux: coiffure, vêtements*) to date **III.** *vpr* **se ~** (*se faire paraître plus vieux*) to make oneself look older

**vieillissement** [vjejismã] *m* (*d'une personne, population*) aging

**viennoiserie** [vjɛnwazʀi] *f:* leavened dough pastries such as a croissants or brioche

**vierge** [vjɛʀʒ] *adj* ❶ (*non défloré: fille, garçon*) virgin ❷ (*intact: disquette, page*) blank; (*film*) unexposed ❸ (*inexploré: espace*) unexplored; **la forêt ~** virgin forest ❹ (*pur: laine*) new ❺ GEO **les Îles ~s** Virgin Islands

**Vierge** [vjɛʀʒ] *f* ❶ REL **la ~ Marie** the Virgin Mary; **la Sainte ~** the Blessed Virgin ❷ ASTR Virgo; *v.a.* **Balance**

**Vietnam, Viêt-nam** [vjɛtnam] *m* Vietnam; **le ~ du Nord/Sud** North/South Vietnam

**vieux** [vjø] **I.** *adv* (*faire, s'habiller*) old; **faire ~** (*coiffure, habits*) to look old **II.** *m* (*choses anciennes*) old stuff

**vieux, vieille** [vjø, vjɛj] <*devant un nom masculin commençant par une voyelle ou un h muet* vieil> **I.** *adj* ❶ *antéposé* old ❷ *antéposé, inf* (*sale: con, schnock*) old ▸ **vivre** ~ to live to a ripe old age **II.** *m, f* ❶ (*vieille personne*) old person; **un petit ~/une petite vieille** *inf* a little old man/woman ❷ *inf* (*mère/père*) old man *m*, old girl *f*; **mes ~** my folks ▸ **mon** ~! *inf* my friend!

V

**vif** [vif] *m* **le ~ du sujet** the heart of the matter; **sur le ~** from real life

**vif, vive** [vif, viv] *adj* ❶ (*plein de vie: personne*) lively ❷ (*rapide*) fast; **avoir l'esprit ~** to be quick-witted ❸ (*intense: douleur*) sharp; (*soleil*) brilliant; (*froid*) biting; (*couleur*) vivid; (*lumière*) bright ❹ *antéposé* (*profond: regret, intérêt*) deep; (*souvenir*) vivid; (*plaisir, chagrin*) intense; (*impression*) lasting

**vigile** [viʒil] *mf* security guard

**vigne** [viɲ] *f* ❶ BOT vine ❷ (*vignoble*) vineyard ❸ *sans pl* (*activité viticole*) winegrowing

**vigneron(ne)** [viɲ(ə)Rɔ̃, ɔn] *m(f)* winegrower

**vignette** [viɲɛt] *f* ❶ (*attestant un paiement*) label ❷ (*petite illustration*) vignette

**vignoble** [viɲɔbl] *m* ❶ (*terrain*) vineyard ❷ *sans pl* (*ensemble de vignobles*) vineyards *pl*

**vigoureux, -euse** [viguRø, -øz] *adj* ❶ (*fort*) strong ❷ (*ferme, énergique: coup, mesure*) vigorous

**vigueur** [vigœR] *f* ❶ (*énergie: d'une personne*) strength ❷ (*véhémence: d'un argument*) force; (*d'une réaction*) strength; **avec ~** vigorously ▸ **en ~** in force

**vilain(e)** [vilɛ̃, ɛn] *adj* ❶ (*laid*) ugly ❷ *antéposé* (*sale, inquiétant: mot, coup*) nasty ❸ *antéposé, enfantin* (*personne, animal*) naughty ❹ *antéposé* (*désagréable: temps*) lousy

**villa** [villa] *f* villa

**village** [vilaʒ] *m* village

**villageois(e)** [vilaʒwa, waz] *m(f)* villager

**village-vacances** [vilaʒvakɑ̃s] *m* vacation village

**ville** [vil] *f* ❶ (*agglomération*) town; **~ jumelée** sister city ❷ (*quartier*) area; **vieille ~** old town ❸ (*opp: la campagne*) **la ~** the city ❹ (*municipalité*) town; (*plus grande*) city ▸ **en ~** in town

**vin** [vɛ̃] *m* wine; **~ blanc/rosé/rouge** white/rosé/red wine; **~ de pays** local wine

**vinaigre** [vinɛgR] *m* vinegar

**vinaigrette** [vinɛgRɛt] *f* vinaigrette

**vingt** [vɛ̃] **I.** *adj* ❶ (*cardinal*) twenty; **~ et un** twenty-one ❷ (*dans l'indication des époques*) **les années ~** the twenties **II.** *m inv* twenty; *v.a.* **cinq**

**vingtaine** [vɛ̃tɛn] *f* ❶ (*environ vingt*) **une ~ de personnes/pages** about twenty people/pages ❷ (*âge approximatif*) **avoir une ~ d'années** to be about twenty

**vingt-et-un** [vɛ̃teœ̃] *inv m* JEUX blackjack

**vingtième** [vɛ̃tjɛm] **I.** *adj antéposé* twentieth **II.** *mf* **le/la ~** the twentieth **III.** *m* (*fraction, siècle*) twentieth; *v.a.* **cinquième**

**vinicole** [vinikɔl] *adj* **région ~** wine-producing region

**viol** [vjɔl] *m* rape

**violation** [vjɔlasjɔ̃] *f* ❶ (*trahison: d'un secret, serment*) violation ❷ (*effraction*) **~ de domicile** forced entry

**violemment** [vjɔlamɑ̃] *adv* violently

**violence** [vjɔlɑ̃s] *f* ❶ (*brutalité*) violence; **par la ~** violently ❷ (*acte*) act of violence; **se faire ~** to force oneself ❸ (*virulence: du comportement, d'une tempête*) violence

**violent(e)** [vjɔlɑ̃, ɑ̃t] *adj* violent

**violenter** [vjɔlɑ̃te] <1> *vt* **~ qn** to sexually assault sb

**violer** [vjɔle] <1> *vt* ❶ (*abuser de*) to rape; **se faire ~ par qn** to be raped by sb ❷ (*transgresser: droit, traité*) to violate; (*promesse*) to break; (*secret*) to betray

**violet** [vjɔlɛ] *m* purple

**violet(te)** [vjɔlɛ, ɛt] *adj* purple

**violette** [vjɔlɛt] *f* BOT violet

**violon** [vjɔlɔ̃] *m* violin

**violoncelle** [vjɔlɔ̃sɛl] *m* cello

**violoniste** [vjɔlɔnist] *mf* violinist

**V.I.P.** [veipe, viapi] *m inv abr de* **Very Important Person** *inf* VIP

**vipère** [vipɛR] *f* viper

**virage** [viRaʒ] *m* ❶ (*tournant*) turn ❷ (*changement: d'une politique*) U-turn

**V**

**virée** [viʀe] *f inf* spin

**virement** [viʀmɑ̃] *m* FIN transfer (of money)

**virer** [viʀe] <1> **I.** *vi* (*véhicule*) to turn; (*temps, visage, couleur*) to change; (*personne*) to turn around **II.** *vt* ❶ FIN ~ **une somme à qn/ sur le compte de qn** to transfer a sum to sb/sb's account ❷ *inf* (*renvoyer*) to fire ❸ *inf* (*se débarrasser de*) to get rid of

**virginité** [viʀʒinite] *f* virginity

**virgule** [viʀgyl] *f* comma

**viril(e)** [viʀil] *adj* (*mâle*) virile; (*attitude*) manly

**virilité** [viʀilite] *f* ❶ ANAT masculinity ❷ (*caractère viril*) virility

**virtuel(le)** [viʀtɥɛl] *adj* INFORM virtual

**virus** [viʀys] *m* MED, INFORM virus

**vis¹** [vis] *f* screw

**vis²** [vi] *indic prés de* **vivre**

**vis³** [vi] *passé simple de* **voir**

**visa** [viza] *m* (*autorisation de résider*) visa; ~ **d'entrée/de sortie** entry/exit visa

**visage** [vizaʒ] *m* face; **à ~ humain** with a human face; **Visage pâle** *péj* pale-face *sl*

**visagiste®** [vizaʒist] *mf* stylist

**vis-à-vis** [vizavi] *prep* ❶ (*en face de*) ~ **de l'église** opposite the church ❷ (*envers*) ~ **de qn/qc** towards sb/sth ❸ (*comparé à*) ~ **de qn/qc** next to sb/sth

**viscère** [viseʀ] *f* organ; **les ~s** the intestines

**viser** [vize] <1> **I.** *vi* ❶ (*avec une arme*) to take aim ❷ (*avoir pour but*) ~ **au succès** to aim for success; ~ **haut** to aim high **II.** *vt* ❶ (*mirer: tireur*) to aim ❷ (*ambitionner: carrière*) to aim at ❸ (*concerner*) ~ **qn/qc** (*remarque*) to be directed at sb/sth; (*mesure*) to be aimed at sb/sth ❹ (*chercher à atteindre*) to set one's sights on

**visibilité** [vizibilite] *f* visibility

**visible** [vizibl] *adj* ❶ (*qui peut être vu*) visible; **être ~** (*personne*) to be available ❷ (*évident*) obvious

**visiblement** [viziblemɑ̃] *adv* evidently

**visière** [vizjɛʀ] *f* eyeshade; (*d'une casquette*) peak

**vision** [vizjɔ̃] *f* ❶ (*faculté, action de voir qc*) sight ❷ (*conception, perception avec appareil*) view ❸ (*apparition*) a. REL vision

**visionnaire** [vizjɔnɛʀ] **I.** *adj* (*intuitif, halluciné*) visionary **II.** *mf* (*intuitif*) a. REL visionary

**visionner** [vizjɔne] <1> *vt* (*film, diapositives*) to view

**visionneuse** [vizjɔnøz] *f* (*appareil*) a. INFORM viewer

**visite** [vizit] *f* ❶ (*action de visiter*) visit; (*d'un musée*) tour; ~ **guidée** guided tour; **rendre ~ à qn** to visit sb; **en ~** on a visit ❷ MED (*d'un médecin*) consultation; ~ **médicale** medical checkup

**visiter** [vizite] <1> **I.** *vt* ❶ (*explorer*) a. COM, REL to visit ❷ MED (*malades*) to call on **II.** *vi* to visit **III.** *vpr* se ~ to visit each other

**visqueux, -euse** [viskø, -øz] *adj* (*liquide*) viscous; (*peau*) sticky

**visser** [vise] <1> **I.** *vt, vi* to screw on **II.** *vpr* se ~ to be screwed on

**visualisation** [vizɥalizasjɔ̃] *f* visualization; INFORM display

**visualiser** [vizɥalize] <1> *vt* to visualize; (*écran*) to display

**visuel** [vizɥɛl] *m* INFORM visual display unit

**visuel(le)** [vizɥɛl] *adj* (*mémoire, panneau*) visual

**vital(e)** [vital, -o] <-aux> *adj* vital

**vitamine** [vitamin] *f* vitamin

**vite** [vit] *adv* fast; **ce sera ~ fait** it'll soon be done; **faire ~** to hurry; **au plus ~** as quickly as possible

**vitesse** [vitɛs] *f* ❶ (*rapidité*) speed; **à la ~ de 100 km/h** at a speed of 100 km/h; ~ **maximale** AUTO speed limit ❷ (*promptitude*) quickness ❸ AUTO gear; (*d'un vélo*) speed; **changer de ~** to change gears ▸ **à toute ~** as fast as possible; **en (quatrième) ~** *inf* at top speed

**viticulteur, -trice** [vitikyltœʀ, -tʀis] *m, f* winegrower

**vitrage** [vitraʒ] *m* windows *pl*

**vitrail** [vitraj, -o] <-aux> *m* stained--glass window

**vitre** [vitr] *f* ❶ (*carreau*) pane of glass ❷ (*fenêtre*) window

**vitrine** [vitrin] *f* ❶ (*étalage*) (store) window ❷ (*armoire vitrée*) display cabinet

**vivable** [vivabl] *adj* (*personne*) that one can live with; (*monde*) fit to live in

**vivace** [vivas] *adj* ❶ BOT (*plante*) hardy ❷ (*tenace: foi*) steadfast; (*haine*) undying

**vivacité** [vivasite] *f* ❶ (*promptitude*) vivacity; ~ **d'esprit** quick-wittedness ❷ (*brusquerie: d'un langage*) sharpness

**vivant** [vivã] *m* ❶ (*personne en vie*) living person ❷ REL **les ~s** the living ► **du ~ de qn** when sb was alive; (*d'un mort*) in sb's lifetime

**vivant(e)** [vivã, ãt] *adj* ❶ (*en vie: personne, animal*) living; **être encore ~** to still be alive ❷ (*animé: souvenir*) clear; (*rue*) lively ❸ (*expressif*) lifelike

**vive** [viv] **I.** *adj v.* **vif II.** *interj* ~ **la mariée/la liberté!** long live the bride/freedom!

**vivement** [vivmã] **I.** *adv* ❶ (*intensément: intéresser*) keenly; (*regretter*) deeply ❷ (*brusquement: parler*) sharply ❸ (*avec éclat: briller*) brightly **II.** *interj* (*souhait*) ~ **les vacances!** I can't wait until vacation!

**vivier** [vivje] *m* ❶ (*étang*) fishpond ❷ (*bac*) fish tank

**vivifier** [vivifje] <1> *vt* (*stimuler*) to enliven

**vivre** [vivr] *irr* **I.** *vi* ❶ (*exister*) to live; **elle vit encore** she's still alive ❷ (*habiter, mener sa vie*) to live; ~ **bien/pauvrement** to live well/in poverty ❸ (*subsister*) ~ **de son salaire** to live on one's salary; **faire ~ qn** to support sb ❹ (*persister: coutume*) to live on ❺ (*être plein de vie: portrait*) to be alive; (*rue*) to be lively ► **qui vivra verra** *prov* what will be will be **II.** *vt* ❶ (*passer: moment*) to spend; (*vie*) to live ❷ (*être mêlé à: événement*) to live through ❸ (*éprouver intensément: épo-*

*que*) to live in **III.** *mpl* supplies ► **couper les ~s à qn** to cut off sb's allowance

**vocabulaire** [vɔkabylɛr] *m* vocabulary

**vocal(e)** [vɔkal, -o] <-aux> *adj* vocal

**vocalique** [vɔkalik] *adj* vowel

**vocation** [vɔkasjɔ̃] *f* ❶ (*disposition*) calling ❷ (*destination: d'une personne, d'un peuple*) destiny ❸ REL vocation

**vœu** [vø] <x> *m* ❶ (*désir*) wish ❷ *pl* (*souhaits*) wishes ❸ REL vow

**vogue** [vɔg] *f* vogue; **en ~** fashionable

**voici** [vwasi] **I.** *adv* here is/are; **mon père et voilà ma mère** here are my father and mother **II.** *prep soutenu* ❶ (*il y a*) ~ **quinze ans que son fils a fait qc** it's fifteen years (now) since his son did sth ❷ (*depuis*) ~ **bien des jours que j'attends** I've been waiting for several days now

**voie** [vwa] *f* ❶ (*passage*) way; ~ **d'accès** access road; ~ **sans issue** dead end ❷ (*file: d'une route*) lane; ~ **d'eau** NAUT (*brèche*) leak ❸ CHEMDFER ~ **ferrée** railroad track ❹ (*moyen de transport*) **par ~ aérienne** by air; **par ~ postale** by mail ❺ (*filière*) means; **la ~ de la réussite** the road to success ❻ (*ligne de conduite*) path; ~ **de fait** (*violence*) assault ❼ ANAT (*conduit*) tract; ~**s respiratoires** airways ❽ ASTR ~ **lactée** Milky Way ► **être en bonne ~** (*affaire*) to be well under way

**voilà** [vwala] **I.** *adv* ❶ (*opp: voici*) there; **voici ma maison, et ~ le jardin** here's my house and there's the garden ❷ (*pour désigner*) ~ **mes amis** there are my friends; ~ **pour toi** that's for you; ~ **pourquoi/où ...** that's why/where ...; **et ~ tout** and that's all; **la jeune femme que ~** the young woman over there; **en ~ une histoire!** what a story!; **me ~/te ~** here I am/you are ❸ (*explétif*) ~ **que la pluie se met à tomber** and then it starts to rain; **et le ~ qui recommence** there he goes again; **en ~ assez!** that's enough! ► **nous y ~** here we are **II.** *prep* ❶ (*il y a*) ~ **quinze ans que son enfant a fait**

**qc** it's been fifteen years since his/her child did sth ❷ (*depuis*) **~ bien une heure que j'attends** I've been waiting for over an hour now III. *interj* ❶ (*réponse*) there you are ❷ (*présentation*) this is ❸ (*naturellement*) **et ~!** so there!

**voile¹** [vwal] *m* ❶ (*foulard, léger écran*) *a. fig* veil ❷ (*tissu fin, pour cacher*) net

**voile²** [vwal] *f* ❶ NAUT sail ❷ SPORT **la ~** sailing

**voilé(e)¹** [vwale] *adj* (*femme, statue, allusion*) veiled

**voilé(e)²** [vwale] *adj* (*déformé: planche*) warped; **être ~** (*roue*) to be buckled

**voiler¹** [vwale] <1> I. *vpr* **se ~** ❶ (*se dissimuler*) to hide one's face; (*avec un voile*) to wear a veil ❷ (*perdre sa clarté: ciel, horizon*) to grow cloudy II. *vt* (*cacher: visage*) to veil

**voiler²** [vwale] <1> *vpr* (*se fausser*) **se ~** (*roue*) to buckle

**voilier** [vwalje] *m* NAUT sailboat

**voilure** [vwalyʀ] *f* NAUT sails *pl*

**voir** [vwaʀ] *irr* I. *vt* ❶ to see; **je l'ai vu comme je vous vois** I saw him as (clearly as) I can see you; **~ qn/qc faire qc** to see sb/sth do sth; **en ~** (*de dures*) *inf* to have some hard times; **faire ~ à qn qu'il se trompe** (*personne*) to show sb that he is mistaken ❷ (*montrer*) **fais-moi donc ~ ce que tu fais!** show me what you're doing! ❸ (*rencontrer, rendre visite à: personne*) to see; **aller/venir ~ qn** to go/come and see sb ❹ (*examiner: dossier, leçon*) to look at; **~ page 6** see page 6 ❺ (*se représenter*) **~ qc/qn sous un autre jour** to see sb/sth in a different light ❻ (*trouver*) **~ une solution à qc** to see a solution to sth ❼ (*apparaître*) **faire/ laisser ~ sa déception à qn** to show sb/let sb see one's disappointment ▸ **je voudrais bien t'y ~** *inf* I'd like to see you in the same position; **avoir quelque chose/n'avoir rien à ~ avec cette histoire** to be involved in/have nothing to do with this business; **~ qc venir** to see sth coming II. *vi* ❶ (*perce-*

*voir par la vue*) **tu vois sans tes lunettes?** can you see without your glasses? ❷ (*prévoir*) **~ grand/petit** to think big/small ❸ (*constater*) to see; **on verra bien** we'll see ❹ (*veiller*) **il faut ~ à ce que** +*subj* we have to see that ❺ *inf* (*donc*) **essaie/regarde ~!** just try/ look! ▸ **à toi de ~** it's up to you; **pour ~** to see (what happens); **vois-tu** you see III. *vpr* ❶ (*être visible*) **se ~ bien la nuit** (*couleur*) to stand out at night ❷ (*se rencontrer*) **se ~** to see each other ❸ (*se produire*) **se ~** (*phénomène*) to happen; **ça ne s'est jamais vu** it's unheard of ❹ (*se trouver*) **se ~ contraint de** +*infin* to find oneself obliged to +*infin* ❺ (*constater*) **se ~ mourir** to realize one is dying; **il s'est vu refuser l'entrée** he was turned away ❻ (*s'imaginer*) **se ~ faire qc** to see oneself doing sth

**voire** [vwaʀ] *adv* **~** (**même**) not to say

**voirie** [vwaʀi] *f* ❶ (*routes*) roads *pl* ❷ (*entretien des routes*) road maintenance; (*service administratif*) highway department

**voisin(e)** [vwazɛ̃, in] I. *adj* ❶ (*proche: maison*) neighboring; (*rue*) next; (*pièce*) adjoining; **région ~e de la frontière** border region; **être ~ de qc** to be next to sth ❷ (*analogue: sens*) similar; (*espèce animale*) related; **être ~ de qc** to be akin to sth II. *m(f)* (*dans une rue, un immeuble*) neighbor

**voisinage** [vwazinaʒ] *m* ❶ (*voisins*) neighborhood ❷ (*proximité*) nearness ❸ (*environs*) vicinity

**voiture** [vwatyʀ] *f* ❶ AUTO car; **~ de course** racecar; **~ de location/d'occasion** rental/used car ❷ CHEMDFER (*railroad*) car ❸ (*véhicule attelé*) cart; **~ à cheval** horse-drawn carriage ❹ (*véhicule utilitaire*) **~ de livraison/de dépannage** delivery/tow truck ▸ **en ~!** all aboard!

**voix** [vwa] *f* ❶ (*organe de la parole, du chant*) *a.* MUS voice; **à ~ basse** in a low voice; **à une/deux ~** in one/two parts ❷ (*son: d'un animal*) voice ❸ POL (*suf-*

*frage*) vote ❹ (*opinion: du peuple, de la conscience*) voice; **faire entendre la ~ de qn** to make sb's voice heard ❺ LING voice

**vol¹** [vɔl] *m* ZOOL, AVIAT flight; (*formation*) flock; **~ de nuit** night flight; **~ libre** hang-gliding ▸ **à ~ d'oiseau** as the crow flies; **rattraper qc au ~** to catch sth in midair

**vol²** [vɔl] *m* (*larcin*) theft; (*avec violence*) robbery

**volaille** [vɔlaj] *f* poultry

**volant** [vɔlã] *m* ❶ AUTO steering wheel; **être au ~** to be behind the wheel ❷ TECH flywheel ❸ (*garniture: d'un rideau*) flounce ❹ SPORT shuttlecock

**volant(e)** [vɔlã, ãt] *adj* flying

**volatiliser** [vɔlatilize] <1> *vpr* **se ~** (*disparaître*) to vanish

**volcan** [vɔlkã] *m* volcano

**volcanique** [vɔlkanik] *adj* volcanic

**volée** [vɔle] *f* ❶ (*groupe*) **une ~ de moineaux** a flock of sparrows ❷ (*décharge, raclée*) **une ~ de coups** a volley of blows ❸ SPORT volley; **monter à la ~** to come up to the net ❹ *Suisse* (*élèves d'une même promotion*) year

**voler¹** [vɔle] <1> *vi* ❶ (*se mouvoir dans l'air, être projeté*) to fly; **faire ~ des feuilles** to blow leaves around ❷ (*courir*) to fly along

**voler²** [vɔle] <1> **I.** *vt* ❶ (*dérober*) to steal ❷ (*tromper*) **~ qn sur la quantité** to cheat sb on the quantity ▸ **il ne l'a pas volé** *inf* he was asking for that **II.** *vi* to steal

**volet** [vɔlɛ] *m* ❶ (*persienne*) shutter ❷ (*feuillet: d'une pièce administrative*) section ❸ (*panneau: d'un triptyque*) wing ❹ AVIAT, TECH, AUTO flap ❺ (*partie: d'un plan*) point

**voleur, -euse** [vɔlœʀ, -øz] **I.** *adj* (*qui dérobe*) light-fingered **II.** *m, f* thief; **~ à la tire** pickpocket ▸ **au ~!** stop thief!

**volontaire** [vɔlɔ̃tɛʀ] **I.** *adj* ❶ (*voulu*) liberate; **incendie ~** arson ❷ (*non contraint*) voluntary ❸ (*décidé*) determined; *péj* (*personne*) willful **II.** *mf a.* MIL volunteer

**volontairement** [vɔlɔ̃tɛʀmã] *adv* ❶ (*exprès*) *a.* JUR deliberately ❷ (*de son plein gré*) voluntarily

**volonté** [vɔlɔ̃te] *f* ❶ (*détermination*) will ❷ (*désir*) wish ❸ (*énergie*) willpower ▸ **à ~** as desired

**volontiers** [vɔlɔ̃tje] *adv* ❶ (*avec plaisir*) willingly; (*réponse*) with pleasure ❷ (*souvent*) readily

**volt** [vɔlt] *m* volt

**voltage** [vɔltaʒ] *m* ELEC voltage

**voltiger** [vɔltiʒe] <2a> *vi* ❶ (*voler çà et là*) to flit about ❷ (*flotter légèrement*) **faire ~ qc** to make sth flutter

**volume** [vɔlym] *m* volume

**volumineux, -euse** [vɔlyminø, -øz] *adj* (*dossier*) voluminous; (*paquet*) bulky

**volupté** [vɔlypte] *f* ❶ (*plaisir sensuel*) sensual pleasure ❷ (*plaisir sexuel*) sexual pleasure ❸ (*plaisir intellectuel*) delight

**voluptueux, -euse** [vɔlyptyø, -øz] **I.** *adj* voluptuous **II.** *m, f* voluptuous person

**vomir** [vɔmiʀ] <8> *vt, vi* to vomit

**vomissement** [vɔmismã] *m* ❶ (*action*) vomiting ❷ (*vomissure*) vomit

**vorace** [vɔʀas] *adj* (*animal, personne*) voracious

**vos** [vo] *dét poss v.* **votre**

**Vosges** [voʒ] *fpl* **les ~** the Vosges

**votant(e)** [vɔtã, ãt] *m(f)* (*participant au vote, électeur*) voter

**vote** [vɔt] *m* ❶ (*adoption: des crédits*) voting; (*d'un projet de loi*) passing ❷ (*suffrage*) *a.* vote

**voter** [vɔte] <1> **I.** *vi* **~ contre/pour qn/qc** to vote against/for sb/sth; **~ sur qc** to vote on sth; **~ à main levée** to vote by a show of hands **II.** *vt* (*crédits*) to vote; (*loi*) to pass

**votre** [vɔtʀ] <**vos**> *dét poss* (*à une/plusieurs personne(s) vouvoyée(s), à plusieurs personnes tutoyées*) your; **à ~ avis** in your opinion; *v.a.* **ma, mon**

**vôtre** [votʀ] *pron poss* ❶ **le/la ~** yours; *v.a.* **mien** ❷ *pl* (*ceux de votre famille*) **les ~s** your family; (*vos partisans*) your friends; **il est des ~s?** is he

**V**

one of yours?; *v.a.* **mien** ►**à la** (**bon-ne**) ~! *inf* here's to you!

**vouer** [vwe] <1> I. *vt* ❶ (*condamner*) to doom; ~ **qn/qc à l'échec** to doom sb/sth to fail ❷ (*consacrer*) *a.* REL to devote ❸ (*ressentir*) ~ **de la haine à qn** to vow hatred toward sb II. *vpr* se ~ **à qn/qc** to dedicate oneself to sb/sth

**vouloir** [vulwar] *irr* I. *vt* ❶ (*exiger*) to want; **que lui voulez-vous?** what do you want from him? ❷ (*souhaiter*) **il veut/voudrait ce gâteau** he wants/would like this cake; **il voudrait être médecin** he would like to be a doctor ❸ (*consentir à*) **veux-tu/voulez-vous** [*o* **veuillez**] [*o* **voudriez-vous**] **prendre place** (*poli*) would you like to take a seat; (*impératif*) please take a seat ❹ (*attendre: décision, réponse*) to expect; **que veux-tu/voulez-vous que je te/vous dise?** what am I supposed to say? ❺ (*nécessiter: soins*) to require ❻ (*faire en sorte*) **le hasard a voulu qu'il parte ce jour-là** as fate would have it he left that day ❼ (*prétendre*) to claim; **la loi veut que tout délit soit puni** (*subj*) the law expects every crime to be punished ►**bien** ~ **que qn** +*subj* to be quite happy for sb to +*infin* II. *vi* ❶ (*être disposé*) to be willing ❷ (*souhaiter*) to wish ❸ (*accepter*) **ne plus** ~ **de qn** not to want anything more to do with sb; **ne plus** ~ **de qc** not to want sth anymore ❹ (*avoir des griefs envers*) **en** ~ **à un collègue de qc** to hold sth against a colleague ❺ (*avoir des visées sur*) **en** ~ **à qc/qn** to have designs on sth/sb ►(**moi,**) **je veux bien** (*volontiers*) I'd love to; (*concession douteuse*) I don't mind; **en** ~ *inf* to play to win; **de l'argent en veux-tu, en voilà!** money galore! III. *vpr* se ~ **honnête** to like to think of oneself as honest ► **s'en** ~ **de qc** to feel bad about sth

**voulu(e)** [vuly] I. *part passé de* **vouloir** II. *adj* ❶ (*requis: effet*) desired; (*moment*) required; **en temps** ~ in due course ❷ (*délibéré*) deliberate; **c'est** ~ *inf* it's all on purpose

**vous** [vu] I. *pron pers, 2. pers. pl, pers, forme de politesse* ❶ *sujet, complément d'objet direct et indirect* you ❷ *avec être, devenir, sembler, soutenu* **si cela** ~ **semble bon** if you approve; *v.a.* **me** ❸ *avec les verbes pronominaux* **vous** ~ **nettoyez** (**les ongles**) you clean your nails; **vous vous voyez dans le miroir** you see yourself in the mirror ❹ *inf* (*pour renforcer*) ~, **vous n'avez pas ouvert la bouche** YOU haven't opened your mouth; **c'est** ~ **qui l'avez dit** you're the one who said it; **il veut** ~ **aider**, ~? he wants to help YOU? ❺ (*avec un sens possessif*) **le cœur** ~ **battait fort** your heart was beating fast ❻ *avec un présentatif* you; ~ **voici** [*o* **voilà**]! here you are! ❼ *avec une préposition* **avec/sans** ~ with/without you; **à** ~ **deux** (*parler, donner*) to both of you; (*faire qc*) between the two of you; **la maison est à** ~? is the house yours?; **c'est à** ~ **de décider** it's for you to decide; **c'est à** ~! it's your turn! ❽ *dans une comparaison* you; **nous sommes comme** ~ we're like you; **plus fort que** ~ stronger than you II. *pron* ❶ (*on*) you; ~ **ne pouvez même pas dormir** you can't even sleep ❷ ((*à*) *quelqu'un*) **des choses qui** ~ **gâchent la vie** things which ruin your life III. *m* **dire** ~ **à qn** to call sb "vous"

**vous-même** [vumɛm] <vous-mêmes> *pron pers, 2. pers. pl, pers, forme de politesse* ❶ (*toi et toi en personne*) ~ **n'en saviez rien** YOU know nothing about it; **vous êtes venus de vous-mêmes** you came of your own free will ❷ (*toi et toi aussi*) yourself; **vous-mêmes** yourselves; *v.a.* **nous-même**

**voûte** [vut] *f* ❶ ARCHIT vault ❷ (*ciel*) ~ **étoilée** starry sky

**vouvoyer** [vuvwaje] <6> I. *vt* ~ **qn** to call sb "vous" II. *vpr* se ~ to call each other "vous"

**voyage** [vwajaʒ] *m* ❶ (*le fait de voyager*) travel; ~ **en avion/train** air/train travel ❷ (*trajet*) journey; ~ **aller/re-**

**tour** one-way/roundtrip journey ❸ *inf* (*trip*) trip

**voyager** [vwajaʒe] <2a> *vi* ❶ (*aller en voyage*) to travel ❷ COM **~ pour une entreprise** to travel for a company ❸ (*être transporté: marchandises*) to travel

**voyageur, -euse** [vwajaʒœʀ, -ʒøz] I. *adj* **être d'humeur voyageuse** to have a wayfaring nature II. *m, f* ❶ (*personne qui voyage*) traveler ❷ (*dans un avion/sur un bateau*) passenger

**voyagiste** [vwajaʒist] *m* tour operator

**voyant** [vwajɑ̃] *m* indicator light

**voyant(e)** [vwajɑ̃, jɑ̃t] I. *part prés de* **voir** II. *adj* ❶ (*qui se remarque*) garish III. *m(f)* ❶ (*devin*) visionary ❷ (*opp: aveugle*) sighted person

**voyelle** [vwajɛl] *f* vowel

**voyeur, -euse** [vwajœʀ, -jøz] *m, f* (*amateur de scènes lubriques*) voyeur

**voyou** [vwaju] I. *adj* **il/elle est un peu ~** he/she is a bit of a lout II. *m* ❶ (*délinquant*) lout ❷ (*garnement*) brat

**vrac** [vʀak] *m* **en ~** (*en grande quantité*) in bulk; (*non emballé*) loose; **des idées en ~** some ideas off the top of my head

**vrai** [vʀɛ] I. *m* **le ~** the truth; **être dans le ~** to be right; **il y a du ~** there's some truth ▸ **à dire ~** [*o* **à ~ dire**] in fact; **pour de ~** *inf* for real II. *adv* **dire ~** to speak the truth; **faire ~** to look real

**vrai(e)** [vʀɛ] *adj* ❶ (*véridique*) true; (*événement*) real ❷ *postposé* (*conforme à la réalité: personnage, tableau*) true to life ❸ *antéposé* (*authentique*) real; (*cause*) true ❹ *antéposé* (*digne de ce nom*) true ❺ *antéposé* (*convenable: méthode, moyen*) proper ▸ **pas ~?** *inf* right?; **~!** true!; **~?** is that true?

**vraiment** [vʀɛmɑ̃] *adv* really

**vraisemblable** [vʀɛsɑ̃blabl] *adj* ❶ (*plausible*) convincing ❷ (*probable*) likely

**vraisemblance** [vʀɛsɑ̃blɑ̃s] *f* ❶ (*crédibilité*) plausibility ❷ (*probabilité*) likelihood

**vrombir** [vʀɔ̃biʀ] <8> *vi* to throb

**V.R.P.** [veɛʀpe] *mf abr de* **voyageurs, représentants** *inv* rep

**VTT** [vetete] *m abr de* **vélo tout-terrain** ❶ (*vélo*) mountain bike ❷ (*sport*) mountain biking

**vu** [vy] I. *prep* in view of II. *conj* **~ qu'il est malade ...** since he's sick ... III. *m* **au ~ et au su de tous** publicly; **c'est du déjà ~** we've seen it all before; **c'est du jamais ~** it's unheard of IV. *adv* **ni ~ ni connu** with no one any the wiser

**vu(e)** [vy] I. *part passé de* **voir** II. *adj* ❶ *pas de forme féminine* (*compris*) all right; (*c'est*) **~?** *inf* (is it) OK? ❷ (*d'accord*) OK ❸ *form* (*lu*) read ❹ (*observé*) **la remarque est bien/mal ~e** it's a judicious/careless remark ❺ (*apprécié*) **être bien/mal ~ de qn** to be well-thought-of/disapproved of by sb ▸ **c'est tout ~!** *inf* it's a foregone conclusion

**vue** [vy] *f* ❶ (*sens*) eyesight *pl* ❷ (*regard, spectacle: d'une personne, du sang*) sight; **perdre qn/qc de ~** to lose sight of sb/sth ❸ (*panorama, photo, peinture, conception*) view; **~ d'ensemble** *fig* overview; **les ~s de qn** sb's views ❹ (*visées*) **avoir qn/qc en ~** to have sb/sth in one's sights ▸ **à ~ de nez** *inf* roughly; **à ~ d'œil** before one's eyes; **à la ~ de qn** (*sous le regard de qn*) with sb looking on; **en ~** (*visible*) in view; (*tout proche*) in sight; (*célèbre*) prominent; **en ~ de** (*faire*) qc with a view to (doing) sth

**vulgaire** [vylgɛʀ] I. *adj* ❶ (*grossier*) vulgar ❷ *antéposé* (*quelconque*) common ❸ *postposé* (*populaire*) popular II. *m* **tomber dans le ~** to lapse into vulgarity

**vulgariser** [vylgaʀize] <1> I. *vt* to popularize II. *vpr* **se ~** to become popularized

**vulnérable** [vylneʀabl] *adj* vulnerable; (*situation*) precarious

**vulve** [vylv] *f* **la ~** the vulva

V

# Ww

**W, w** [dubləve] *m inv* W, w; ~ **comme William** (*au téléphone*) w as in Whisky

**wagon** [vagɔ̃] *m* CHEMDFER car

**wagon-lit** [vagɔ̃li] <wagons-lits> *m* sleeping car

**wagon-restaurant** [vagɔ̃ʀɛstɔʀɑ̃] <wagons-restaurants> *m* restaurant car

**walkman®** [wɔkman] *m* Walkman®

**wallon(ne)** [walɔ̃] **I.** *adj* Walloon **II.** *m* **le** ~ Walloon; *v.a.* **français**

**Wallon(ne)** [walɔ̃] *m(f)* Walloon

**Wallonie** [walɔni] *f* **la** ~ Wallonia

**warning** [waʀniŋ] *m* warning

**water-polo** [watɛʀpɔlo] <water-polos> *m* water polo

**W.-C.** [vese] *mpl abr de* **water-closet(s)** WC

**Web, WEB** [wɛb] *m* INFORM **le** ~ the Web

**webcam** [wɛbkam] *f* webcam

**webnaute** [wɛbnot] *mf* (web) surfer

**week-end** [wikɛnd] <week-ends> *m* weekend

**welsch(e)** [vɛlʃ] *adj Suisse, iron* French-speaking (*from Switzerland*)

**World Wide Web** *m* INFORM World Wide Web

# Xx

**X, x** [iks] *m inv* ❶ (*lettre*) X, x; ~ **comme Xavier** (*au téléphone*) x as in X-ray ❷ *inf* (*plusieurs*) **x fois** Heaven knows how many times ❸ (*Untel*) X; **contre X** against persons unknown ❹ CINE **film classé X** X-rated movie

**xénophobe** [gzenɔfɔb] **I.** *adj* xenophobic **II.** *mf* xenophobe

**xylophone** [ksilɔfɔn] *m* xylophone

# Yy

**Y, y** [igRɛk] *m inv* Y, y; **~ comme Yvonne** (*au téléphone*) y as in Yankee

**y** [i] **I.** *adv* there **II.** *pron pers* (*à/sur cela*) **s'y entendre** to manage; **ne pas y tenir** not to be very keen

**yacht** [jɔt] *m* yacht

**yaourt** [jauRt] *m* yogurt

**Yémen** [jemɛn] *m* **le ~** Yemen

**yeux** [jø] *pl de* œil

# Zz

**Z, z** [zɛd] *m inv* Z, z; **~ comme Zoé** (*au téléphone*) z as in Zulu

**Zaïre** [zaiR] *m* HIST **le ~** Zaire

**zapper** [zape] <1> *vi* to zap

**zappette** [zapɛt] *f inf* remote

**zèbre** [zɛbR] *m* ZOOL zebra

**zèle** [zɛl] *m* zeal; **faire du ~** *péj* to go over the top

**zélé(e)** [zele] *adj* zealous

**zénith** [zenit] *m a. fig* zenith

**zéro** [zero] **I.** *num* ❶ *antéposé* (*aucun*) no ❷ *inf* (*nul*) useless **II.** *m* ❶ *inv* (*nombre*) naught ❷ *fig a.* METEO, PHYS zero ❸ ECOLE **avoir ~ sur dix/sur vingt** to have zero out of ten/twenty ❹ (*rien*) nothing ❺ (*personne incapable*) dead loss

**zeste** [zɛst] *m a. fig* zest

**zézayer** [zezeje] <7> *vi* to lisp

**zieuter** [zjøte] <1> *vt inf* to eye

**zinc** [zɛ̃g] *m* ❶ zinc ❷ *inf* (*comptoir*) counter ❸ *inf* (*avion*) plane

**zinzin** [zɛ̃zɛ̃] *adj inf* loopy

**zip®** [zip] *m* zipper

**zipper** [zipe] <1> *vt* INFORM *fichier, données* zip

**zodiaque** [zɔdjak] *m* zodiac

**zone** [zon] *f* ❶ *a.* GEO zone; **~ d'influence** sphere of influence ❷ (*monétaire*) area; **~ euro** eurozone ❸ INFORM **~ de dialogue** dialogue zone

**zoo** [z(o)o] *m* zoo

**zoologique** [zɔɔlɔʒik] *adj* zoological; **parc ~** zoo

**zut** [zyt] *interj inf* damn

# Aa

**A, a** [eɪ] <-'s *o* -s> *n* ❶ (*letter*) A *m*,
a *m*; ~ **as in Alpha** (*on telephone*) a
comme Anatole ❷ MUS la *m* ❸ SCHOOL
(*grade*) (très) bonne note *f* (*de 15 à 20
sur 20*) ❹ (*place, position*) **to go from
A to B** aller d'un point à un autre

**a** [ə] *indef art* (+ *consonant*) (*single, not
specified*) un(e); **a Ron Tyler phoned**
un certain Ron Tyler a téléphoné

**A** *n* ELEC *abbr of* **ampere** A *m*

**abandon** [ə·'bæn·dən] **I.** *vt* ❶ laisser
❷ (*give up*) abandonner; **to ~ a plan**
renoncer à un projet ❸ (*desert*) déserter ❹ (*lose self-control*) **to ~ oneself
to sth** s'abandonner à qc **II.** *n* abandon *m*

**abandoned** *adj* ❶ (*left*) abandonné(e)
❷ pej (*wicked*) dévergondé(e)

**abbey** ['æb·i] *n* abbaye *f*

**abbreviate** [ə·'bri·vi·eɪt] *vt* abréger

**abbreviation** [ə·ˌbri·vi·'eɪ·ʃən] *n* abréviation *f*

**ability** [ə·'bɪl·ə·ti] <-ies> *n* ❶ (*capability*) capacité *f* ❷ (*talent*) talent *m* ❸ *pl*
(*skills*) compétences *fpl*

**able** ['eɪ·bl] *adj* ❶ <more *o* better ~,
most *o* best ~> (*having the ability*) capable; **to be ~ to** +*infin* pouvoir +*infin*,
savoir +*infin* Belgique ❷ <more ~,
most ~ *o* abler, ablest> (*clever*) apte

**aboard** [ə·'bɔrd] **I.** *adv* à bord; **all ~!** RAIL
en voiture! **II.** *prep* à bord de

**abolish** [ə·'bal·ɪʃ] *vt* abolir; (*tax*) supprimer

**Aborigine** [ˌæb·ə·'rɪdʒ·ən·i] *n* Aborigène *mf*

**abort** [ə·'bɔrt] **I.** *vt* ❶ MED **to ~ a baby**
avorter d'un bébé ❷ (*call off*) annuler
**II.** *vi* MED avorter; (*miscarry*) faire une
fausse couche

**abortion** [ə·'bɔr·ʃən] *n* MED avortement *m*; **to have an ~** se faire avorter

**about** [ə·'baʊt] **I.** *prep* ❶ (*on subject of*)
à propos de; **book ~ sth** livre *m* sur qc;

**to talk ~ cinema** parler de cinéma; **to
talk ~ it** en parler ❷ (*characteristic of*)
**what I like ~ him** ce que j'aime en lui
❸ (*through, over*) **scattered ~ the
house** éparpillé dans la maison; **to go ~
a place** parcourir un lieu en tous sens
▶ **how** [*o* **what**] ~ **him?** et lui?; **how**
[*o* **what**] ~ **doing sth?** et si on faisait
qc?; **what ~ sth?** et qc? **II.** *adv* ❶ (*approximately*) **at ~ 3:00** vers 3 h; **~ 5
years ago** il y a environ 5 ans; **~ my
size** à peu près ma taille; **just ~
enough of sth** à peine assez de qc;
**that's ~ it** [*o* **all**] **for today** ça suffira
pour aujourd'hui ❷ (*almost*) presque;
**to be** (**just**) **~ ready to** +*infin* être
presque prêt à +*infin* ❸ (*around*) **all ~**
tout autour ❹ (*willing to*) **not to be ~
to** +*infin* ne pas être prêt à +*infin*; *s.a.*
**out, up**

**above** [ə·'bʌv] **I.** *prep* ❶ (*over*) au-dessus de; **~ suspicion** au-dessus de tout
soupçon ❷ (*greater than, superior to*)
**those ~ the age of 70** ceux de plus de
70 ans; **~ average** supérieur à la
moyenne; **~ (and beyond) sth** (très)
au-delà de qc ❸ (*more important than*)
**~ all** par-dessus tout; **he is not ~ begging** il irait jusqu'à mendier ❹ (*louder
than*) **to shout ~ the noise** crier par-
·dessus le bruit ❺ CEO (*upstream*) en
amont de; (*north of*) au nord de ▶ **to be
~ sb** [*o* **sb's head**] dépasser qn **II.** *adv*
(*on top of*) **up ~** ci-dessus; **from ~** *a.*
REL d'en haut **III.** *adj* (*previously mentioned*) précité(e); **the words ~** les
mots *mpl* ci-dessus **IV.** *n* **the ~** le(la)
susdit(e)

**abroad** [ə·'brɔd] *adv* ❶ à l'étranger
❷ *fig, form* **there is a rumor ~ that ...**
le bruit court que ...

**abrupt** [ə·'brʌpt] *adj* ❶ (*sudden*) sou-
dain(e); **~ end** fin *f* abrupte ❷ (*brusque*) brutal(e); **~ reply** réponse *f* brus-

**A**

que ❸ (*steep*) escarpé(e); **~ slope** pente *f* escarpée

**absence** ['æb·s⋅ⁿts] *n* ❶ (*not being there*) absence *f*; **~ from school** absence de l'école ❷ (*period away*) absence *f* ❸ (*lack*) manque *m*; **in the ~ of sth** faute de qc ▸ **~ makes the heart grow fonder** *prov* la distance renforce l'affection

**absent** ['æb·sⁿt] *adj* (*not there*) absent(e); **~ stare** regard *m* absent

**absentee ballot** *n* vote *m* par correspondance

**absent-minded** [ˌæb·sⁿt·'maɪn·dɪd] *adj* distrait(e)

**absolute** [ˌæb·sə·'lut] **I.** *adj a.* POL, MATH absolu(e) **II.** *n* PHILOS absolu *m*

**absolutely** *adv* absolument

**absorb** [əb·'sɔrb] *vt* ❶ (*take into itself*) absorber ❷ (*understand*) assimiler ❸ (*engross*) absorber

**abstain** [əb·'steɪn] *vi* s'abstenir

**abstract**[1] ['æb·strækt] **I.** *adj a.* ART abstrait(e) **II.** *n* ❶ PHILOS **the ~** l'abstrait *m* ❷ (*summary*) résumé *m* ❸ ART œuvre *f* abstraite

**abstract**[2] [əb·'strækt] *vt* (*summarize: book*) résumer

**absurd** [əb·'sɜrd] *adj* absurde

**abundance** [ə·'bʌn·dən(t)s] *n* abondance *f*; **in ~** à profusion

**abundant** [ə·'bʌn·dənt] *adj* abondant(e); **~ evidence/detail** abondance *f* de preuves/détails

**abuse** [ə·'bjus, *vb:* ə·'bjuz] **I.** *n* ❶ SOCIOL comportement *m* abusif; **child ~** sévices *mpl* sur les enfants ❷ (*insulting language*) injure *f*; **stream of ~** torrent *m* d'injures ❸ (*misuse*) abus *m*; **substance ~** abus de substances toxiques ❹ (*infringement*) violation *f* **II.** *vt* ❶ (*misuse*) abuser de ❷ (*infringe*) violer ❸ (*mistreat*) maltraiter; (*child*) exercer des sévices sur ❹ (*verbally*) injurier

**abusive** [ə·'bju·sɪv] *adj* injurieux(-euse); **~ to sb** grossier envers qn

**AC** [ˌeɪ·'si] *n* ELEC *abbr of* **alternating current** CA *m*

**academic** [ˌæk·ə·'dem·ɪk] **I.** *adj*

❶ SCHOOL scolaire ❷ UNIV universitaire; (*person*) studieux(-euse); **~ year** année *f* universitaire, année académique *Belgique, Québec, Suisse* ❸ (*theoretical*) théorique ❹ (*irrelevant*) hors de propos **II.** *n* UNIV universitaire *mf*

**academy** [ə·'kæd·ə·mi] <-ies> *n* ❶ (*institution*) école *f* ❷ (*school*) collège *m*

**accelerate** [ək·'sel·ə·reɪt] **I.** *vi* ❶ AUTO accélérer ❷ *fig* s'accélérer **II.** *vt* accélérer

**accent** ['æk·sent, *vb:* æk·'sent] **I.** *n* ❶ (*pronunciation*) accent *m*; **to have a strong ~** avoir un accent prononcé ❷ (*mark*) accent *m* ❸ LIT, MUS accentuation *f* **II.** *vt* ❶ LIT, MUS accentuer ❷ *fig* souligner

**accept** [ək·'sept] **I.** *vt* ❶ (*take*) accepter ❷ (*believe*) admettre ❸ (*resign oneself to*) se résigner; **to ~ one's fate** se soumettre à son destin ❹ (*welcome*) accepter **II.** *vi* (*say yes*) accepter

**acceptable** *adj* ❶ (*agreeable*) acceptable; **not ~ to sb** inadmissible pour qn ❷ (*welcome*) bienvenu(e) ❸ (*satisfactory*) satisfaisant(e)

**acceptance** [ək·'sep·(t)əns] *n* acceptation *f*; **~ speech** discours *m* de remerciement

**access** ['æk·ses] **I.** *n* ❶ (*way into*) accès *m*; **to deny sb ~ to sth** refuser à qn l'accès à qc ❷ COMPUT accès *m* ❸ LAW droit *m* de visite **II.** *vt* COMPUT accéder à; **to ~ a file** accéder à un dossier

**accessory** [ək·'ses·ər·i] <-ies> *n* ❶ (*for outfit, toy*) accessoire *m* ❷ *fig* fioriture *f* ❸ LAW complice *mf*

**accident** ['æk·sɪ·dənt] *n* accident *m*; **car ~** accident de voiture; **by ~** (*accidentally*) accidentellement; (*by chance*) par hasard; **it was no ~ that ...** ce n'était pas un hasard si ... ❷ **it was an ~ waiting to happen** cela devait forcément arriver

**accidental** [ˌæk·sɪ·'den·t̬ᵊl] **I.** *adj* accidentel(le); **~ discovery** découverte *f* fortuite **II.** *n* MUS accident *m*

**accidentally** *adv* accidentellement; (*by chance*) par hasard

**accommodate** [əˈkam‑ə‑deɪt] *vt form* ❶ (*store*) contenir ❷ (*help*) aider ❸ (*give place to stay*) héberger ❹ (*adapt*) **to ~ oneself to sth** s'accommoder de qc

**accommodation** [ə‚ka‑mə‑ˈdeɪ‑ʃən] *n* ❶ *pl* (*lodgings*) logement *m* ❷ *form* (*compromise*) compromis *m*

**accompany** [əˈkʌm‑pə‑ni] <‑ie‑> *vt* ❶ (*go with*) accompagner ❷ MUS **to ~ sb on the violin** accompagner qn au violon

**accomplice** [əˈkam‑plɪs] *n* complice *mf*

**accord** [əˈkɔrd] I. *n* ❶ (*treaty*) accord *m* ❷ (*agreement*) accord *m* ▸ **of one's own ~** de son plein gré II. *vt form* **to ~ sb sth** accorder qc à qn III. *vi* **to ~ with sth** s'accorder avec qc

**accordingly** [əˈkɔr‑dɪŋ‑li] *adv* ❶ (*appropriately*) de manière adéquate ❷ (*therefore*) donc

**according to** *prep* ❶ (*as told by*) **~ her/what I read** d'après elle/ce que j'ai lu ❷ (*as basis*) **~ the law** conformément à la loi ❸ (*as instructed by*) **~ the recipe** suivant la recette ❹ (*depending on*) en fonction de; **to classify ~ size** classer par taille

**account** [əˈkaʊnt] I. *n* ❶ FIN compte *m*; **checking ~** compte courant; **savings ~** compte épargne ❷ (*credit service*) **to put sth on one's ~** mettre qc sur son compte ❸ (*bill*) **to settle an ~** régler une facture ❹ *pl* (*financial records*) comptabilité *f* ❺ (*customer*) compte client ❻ (*description*) compte-rendu *m*; **to give an ~ of sth** faire le récit de qc; **by all ~s** au dire de tout le monde ❼ (*cause*) **on ~ of sth** en raison de qc; **on no ~** en aucun cas ❽ (*consideration*) **to take sth into ~** prendre qc en considération ❾ *form* (*importance*) **of little/no ~** sans grande/aucune importance ❿ (*responsibility*) **on one's own ~** de son propre chef ▸ **to be called to ~** devoir se justifier II. *vt form*

(*consider*) **to ~ sb sth** considérer qn comme qc

**accountant** [əˈkaʊn‑tənt] *n* comptable *mf*

**accounting** *n* comptabilité *f*

**accuracy** [ˈæk‑jər‑ə‑si] *n* ❶ (*correct aim*) précision *f* ❷ (*correctness: of report*) justesse *f*; (*of data*) exactitude *f*

**accurate** [ˈæk‑jər‑ət] *adj* ❶ (*on target*) précis(e) ❷ (*correct*) exact(e)

**accusation** [æk‑juˈzeɪ‑ʃən] *n* accusation *f*

**accuse** [əˈkjuz] *vt* accuser; **to be ~d of sth/doing sth** être accusé de qc/de faire qc

**accustomed** *adj* ❶ (*used*) habitué(e); **to be ~ to sth/doing sth** être habitué à qc/à faire qc; **to become ~ to sth** s'accoutumer à qc ❷ (*usual*) coutumier

**ace** [eɪs] I. *adj inf* (*very good*) fort(e); **~ driver** as du volant; **~ pilot** pilote *m* d'élite II. *n* ❶ (*card*) as *m*; **~ of hearts/clubs/spades/diamonds** as de cœur/trèfle/pique/carreau ❷ (*expert*) as *m* ❸ (*in tennis*) service *m* gagnant III. *vt* ❶ SPORTS **to ~ sb** écraser qn ❷ *sl* **to ~ a test** (*to get an excellent grade*) cartonner à un examen

**ache** [eɪk] I. *n* douleur *f*, *fig* peine *f*; **~s and pains** douleurs *fpl* II. *vi* ❶ (*have pain: patient*) souffrir; (*part of body*) faire mal ❷ *fig* **to be aching for sth/to** +*infin* mourir d'envie de qc/de +*infin*

**achievement** *n* ❶ (*feat*) exploit *m* ❷ (*achieving: of aim*) atteinte *f*; (*of ambition*) réalisation *f*

**acid** [ˈæs‑ɪd] I. *adj* ❶ CHEM acide; **~ rain** pluies *fpl* acides ❷ (*sour‑tasting*) acide ❸ (*sarcastic*) caustique; (*remark*) acerbe; (*voice*) aigre II. *n* ❶ CHEM acide *m* ❷ *inf* (*LSD*) acide *m*

**acknowledge** [əkˈnal‑ɪdʒ] *vt* ❶ (*admit*) admettre; (*mistake*) avouer; **to ~ that …** reconnaître que … ❷ (*show recognition of: admirers*) saluer ❸ (*thank for*) être reconnaissant(e) de; **to ~ one's sources** citer ses sources ❹ (*reply to*) répondre à; **to ~ receipt of sth** accuser réception de qc

**A**

**acknowledg(e)ment** n ❶ (*admission, recognition*) reconnaissance f; (*of guilt*) aveu m ❷ (*reply*) accusé m de réception ❸ (*greeting*) signe m ❹ pl (*in book*) remerciements mpl

**acquaint** [ə·'kweɪnt] vt **to ~ sb with sth** mettre qn au courant de qc; **to become ~ed with the facts** prendre connaissance des faits; **to get ~ed with sb** faire la connaissance de qn

**acquaintance** [ə·'kweɪn·tᵊn(t)s] n ❶ (*person*) connaissance f ❷ (*relationship*) relations fpl; **to make sb's ~** faire la connaissance de qn ❸ form (*knowledge*) **his ~ with the city** sa connaissance de la ville

**acquire** [ə·'kwaɪər] vt acquérir; **it's an ~d taste** c'est qc qu'on apprend à aimer

**acquisition** [ˌæk·wɪ·'zɪʃ·ᵊn] n acquisition f; **recent ~s** acquisitions récentes

**across** [ə·'krɑs] I. prep ❶ (*on other side of*) **~ sth** de l'autre côté de qc; **just ~ the street** juste en face; **~ from sb/sth** en face de qn/qc ❷ (*from one side to other*) **to walk ~ the bridge** traverser le pont; **to swim/drive/crawl ~ sth** traverser qc à la nage/en voiture/en rampant; **voters ~ America** les électeurs à travers l'Amérique ❸ (*on*) **surprise flashed ~ her face** la surprise passa sur son visage ❹ (*find unexpectedly*) **to come ~ sb/sth** tomber sur qn/qc ▸ **~ the board** (*increase taxes*) pour tous II. adv ❶ (*one side to other*) **to run/swim ~** traverser en courant/à la nage; **to be 2 m ~** avoir 2 mètres de large ❷ (*from one to another*) **to get sth ~ to sb** faire comprendre qc à qn

**act** [ækt] I. n ❶ (*action*) acte m; **~ of God** catastrophe f naturelle; **sexual ~** acte sexuel ❷ (*performance*) numéro m ❸ fig **it's all an ~** c'est du cinéma ❹ THEAT acte m ❺ LAW, POL loi f ▸ **to catch sb in the ~** prendre qn sur le fait; **get one's ~ together** inf se secouer II. vi ❶ (*take action*) agir; **to ~ as sth** servir de qc; **to ~ for sb** agir au nom de qn ❷ inf (*behave*) se comporter; **to ~ like sth** se conduire en qc ❸ THEAT jouer

❹ (*pretend*) jouer la comédie III. vt ❶ THEAT tenir le rôle de ❷ (*pretend*) **to ~ a part** jouer un rôle

◆**act out** vt **to ~ a dream** vivre un rêve

◆**act up** vi (*child*) mal se conduire; (*car, machine*) mal fonctionner, faire des siennes inf; **my knee is acting up on me** mon genou me joue des tours

**action** ['æk·ʃᵊn] n ❶ (*activeness*) action f; **plan of ~** plan m d'action; **to put a plan into ~** mettre un projet à exécution; **out of ~** hors service ❷ (*act*) action f; (*movement*) gestes mpl ❸ LIT, CINE action f ❹ MIL combat m; **to be killed/missing in ~** être tué/avoir disparu au combat ❺ (*battle*) combat m ❻ (*way of working*) effet m ❼ (*mechanism*) mécanisme m ❽ LAW procès m ❾ inf (*exciting events*) activité f; **there is a lot of ~ here** ça bouge beaucoup ici ▸ **to want a piece of the ~** inf vouloir une part du gâteau

**activate** ['æk·tɪ·veɪt] vt ❶ (*set going: system, machine*) actionner; **to ~ an alarm** déclencher une alarme ❷ CHEM activer

**active** ['æk·tɪv] adj actif(-ive); (*volcano*) en activité; **in the ~ voice** LING à la voix active; **to see ~ service** combattre

**activity** [æk·'tɪv·ə·ti] n ❶ (*opp: passivity*) activité f ❷ pl (*pursuit*) occupation f; **activities for children** des activités pour enfants

**actor** ['æk·tər] n acteur, actrice m, f

**actress** ['æk·trɪs] n actrice f

**actually** ['æk·tʃʊl·i] adv en fait, vraiment; **I wasn't ~ there** en fait, je n'étais pas là; **he ~ lied/fell asleep** il est allé jusqu'à mentir/s'endormir

**acute** [ə·'kjut] I. adj ❶ (*serious: illness, pain*) aigu(ë); (*difficulties*) grave; (*nervousness, anxiety*) vif(vive) f ❷ (*sharp: sense*) fin(e); (*observation*) perspicace ❸ (*intelligent*) avisé(e) ❹ MATH, LING (*angle, accent*) aigu(ë) II. n LING accent m aigu

**ad** [æd] n inf s. advertisement, adver-

**tising** pub *f*; (*in newspaper*) (petite) annonce *f*

**AD** [eɪ·ˈdi] *adj abbr of* **anno Domini** apr. J.-C.

**adapt** [ə·ˈdæpt] **I.** *vt* adapter; **to ~ sth for sth** adapter qc à qc **II.** *vi* s'adapter

**add** [æd] **I.** *vt* ajouter **II.** *vi* faire des additions

**addict** [ˈæd·ɪkt] *n* intoxiqué(e) *m(f)*; **drug ~** toxicomane *mf*; *fig* fana *mf*; **fitness/TV ~** accro *mf* de la forme/de la télé

**addicted** *adj* adonné(e); **to be ~ to sth** s'adonner à qc; *fig* ne pas pouvoir se passer de qc

**addiction** [ə·ˈdɪk·ʃ·ən] *n* ❶ dépendance *f*; **drug ~** toxicomanie *f* ❷ *fig* **~ to sth** passion *f* de qc

**addictive** [ə·ˈdɪk·tɪv] *adj* qui crée une dépendance ▶ **it's highly ~** c'est comme une drogue

**addition** [ə·ˈdɪʃ·ən] *n* ❶ *a.* MATH addition *f* ❷ (*added thing*) ajout *m* ▶ **in ~** de plus; **in ~ to sth** en plus de qc

**additional** [ə·ˈdɪʃ·ən·əl] *adj* additionnel(le)

**additive** [ˈæd·ə·tɪv] *n* additif *m*

**address** [ˈæd·res, *vb:* ə·ˈdres] **I.** *n* ❶ (*place of residence*) *a.* COMPUT adresse *f*; **home ~** adresse personnelle ❷ (*speech*) discours *m* ❸ (*title*) **form of ~** titre *m* **II.** *vt* ❶ (*write address on*) adresser ❷ (*speak to*) **to ~ sb** adresser la parole à qn ❸ (*use title*) **to ~ sb as 'Your Highness'** appeler qn 'Votre Altesse' ❹ (*give attention to: problem*) aborder

**adequate** [ˈæd·ɪ·kwət] *adj* ❶ (*supply*) suffisant(e); (*room*) convenable ❷ (*person*) compétent(e)

**adhere** [əd·ˈhɪr] *vi* adhérer; **to ~ to** (*surface, religion*) adhérer à; (*rules*) observer

**adhesive** [əd·ˈhi·sɪv] **I.** *adj* adhésif(-ive); **tape** sparadrap *m* **II.** *n* (*glue*) colle *f*

**adjust** [ə·ˈdʒʌst] **I.** *vt* ❶ TECH régler; (*salaries*) réajuster; (*size*) ajuster ❷ (*rearrange: clothes*) réajuster ❸ (*adapt*) **to ~ sth to sth** adapter qc en fonction

de qc **II.** *vi* **to ~ to sth** (*person*) s'adapter à qc; (*machine*) se régler sur qc

**adjustment** *n* ❶ (*mental*) adaptation *f* ❷ (*mechanical*) réglage *m*

**admin** [ˈæd·mɪn] *n inf abbr of* **administrator** administrateur, -trice *m, f*

**admiration** [ˌæd·mə·ˈreɪ·ʃ·ən] *n* admiration *f*

**admire** [əd·ˈmaɪər] *vt* admirer

**admirer** [əd·ˈmaɪər·ər] *n* admirateur, -trice *m, f*

**admission** [əd·ˈmɪʃ·ən] *n* ❶ (*entrance, entrance fee*) entrée *f*; (*into school, college*) inscription *f*; (*into a hospital*) admission *f* ❷ (*acknowledgment*) aveu *m*

**admit** [əd·ˈmɪt] <-tt-> *vt* ❶ (*acknowledge*) avouer; (*defeat, error*) reconnaître ❷ (*allow to enter: person*) admettre; (*air, water*) laisser passer

**admonish** [əd·ˈman·ɪʃ] *vt form* admonester; **to ~ sb for doing sth** reprocher à qn de faire qc

**ado** [ə·ˈdu] *n* **without further** [*o* **more**] **~** sans plus de cérémonie ▶ **much ~ about nothing** beaucoup de bruit pour rien

**adolescent** [ˌæd·ə·ˈles·ənt] **I.** *adj* ❶ (*teenage: boys, girls*) adolescent(e); (*behavior, fantasy*) d'adolescent ❷ *pej* puéril(e) **II.** *n* adolescent(e) *m(f)*

**adopt** [ə·ˈdapt] *vt* adopter; (*accent*) prendre; (*suggestion*) accepter

**adoption** [ə·ˈdap·ʃən] *n* LAW adoption *f*

**adorable** [ə·ˈdɔr·ə·bl] *adj* adorable

**adore** [ə·ˈdɔr] *vt a.* REL adorer

**adrenaline** [ə·ˈdren·ə·lɪn] *n* adrénaline *f*

**adult** [ə·ˈdʌlt] **I.** *n* adulte *mf* **II.** *adj* adulte; (*film*) pour adultes

**advance** [əd·ˈvæn(t)s] **I.** *adj* préalable **II.** *n* ❶ (*progress, forward movement*) progrès *m* ❷ FIN avance *f* ❸ *pl* (*sexual flirtation*) avances *fpl* ▶ **to do sth in ~** faire qc à l'avance **III.** *vt* ❶ (*develop: cause, interest*) faire avancer; **to ~ one's career** faire avancer sa carrière ❷ (*pay in advance*) avancer; **to ~ sb**

**A**

sth avancer qc à qn ❸ (*put forward: idea, suggestion*) avancer IV. *vi* avancer

**advanced** *adj* avancé(e); **~ search** recherche *f* avancée

**advantage** [əd·'væn·tɪdʒ] *n a.* SPORTS avantage *m*; **to give sb an ~ over sb** avantager qn par rapport à qn; **to take ~ of sb/sth** *a. pej* profiter de qn/qc

**adventure** [əd·'ven·tʃər] *n* aventure *f*

**adventurous** [əd·'ven·tʃər·əs] *adj* aventureux(-euse)

**adverse** ['æd·vɜrs] *adj* défavorable

**advertise** ['æd·vər·taɪz] I. *vt* ❶ (*publicize: product, event*) faire de la publicité pour; (*reduction, changes*) annoncer; (*in classified ads*) passer une annonce pour ❷ (*announce*) annoncer II. *vi* mettre une annonce

**advertisement** [æd·vər·'taɪz·mənt] *n* publicité *f*; (*in newspaper*) (petite) annonce *f*

**advertising** *n* publicité *f*

**advice** [əd·'vaɪs] *n* ❶ (*suggestion, opinion*) conseil *m*; **some** [*o* **a piece of**] **~** un conseil; **to ask for ~ on sth** demander conseil au sujet de qc; **to give sb ~** donner un conseil à qn ❷ ECON notification *f*

**advise** [əd·'vaɪz] I. *vt* ❶ (*give advice to*) **to ~ sb to** +*infin* conseiller à qn de +*infin*; **to ~ sb against sth** déconseiller qc à qn ❷ (*inform*) aviser qn de qc; **to ~ sb of sth** informer qn que ...; ❸ (*suggest*) recommander II. *vi* donner (un) conseil; **to ~ against sth** déconseiller qc

**advocate** ['æd·və·kət, *vb:* 'æd·və·keɪt] I. *n* ❶ POL partisan(e) *m(f)*; **~ of women's rights** défenseur *mf* des droits de la femme ❷ LAW avocat(e) *m(f)* II. *vt* préconiser

**aerial** ['er·i·əl] I. *adj* aérien(ne) II. *n* antenne *f*

**aerosol** ['er·ə·sɑl] *n* aérosol *m*

**affair** [ə·'fer] *n* ❶ (*matter, business*) affaire *f*; **the whole ~ was a disaster** ça a été un désastre ❷ (*sexual relationship*) liaison *f* ❸ (*event, occasion*) **it**

**was a quiet/grand ~** ça a été discret/grandiose

**affect** [ə·'fekt] *vt* ❶ (*change*) affecter; (*concern*) toucher; **to be ~ed by sth** être touché par qc ❷ (*move*) affecter; **to be very ~ed** être très affecté ❸ *pej, form* (*simulate*) feindre; (*accent*) prendre

**affection** [ə·'fek·ʃən] *n* affection *f*

**affectionate** [ə·'fek·ʃn·ət] *adj* affectueux(-euse)

**affirmative** [ə·'fɜr·mə·tɪv] I. *adj* affirmatif(-ive) II. *n* approbation *f*; **to answer** [*o* **reply**] **in the ~** répondre par l'affirmative

**afford** [ə·'fɔrd] *vt* ❶ (*have money or time for*) **to be able to ~** (**to do**) **sth** pouvoir se permettre (de faire) qc; **I can't ~ it** je n'en ai pas les moyens ❷ (*provide*) donner; **to ~ protection** offrir sa protection

**affordable** *adj* abordable

**Afghan** ['æf·gæn], **Afghani** [æf·'gæn·i] I. *adj* afghan(e) II. *n* ❶ (*person*) Afghan(e) *m(f)* ❷ LING afghan *m*; *s.a.* **English**

**Afghanistan** [æf·'gæn·ə·stæn] *n* l'Afghanistan *m*

**afraid** [ə·'freɪd] *adj* ❶ (*scared, frightened*) effrayé(e); **to feel** [*o* **to be**] **~** avoir peur; **to be ~ of doing** [*o* **to do**] **sth** avoir peur de faire qc; **to be ~ of sb/sth** avoir peur de qn/qc; **to be ~ that** craindre que +*subj* ❷ (*sorry*) **I'm so/not** je crains que oui/que non; **I'm ~ she's out** je suis désolé mais elle est sortie

**Africa** ['æf·rɪ·kə] *n* l'Afrique *f*

**African** ['æf·rɪ·kən] I. *adj* africain(e) II. *n* Africain(e) *m(f)*

**African American** ['æf·rɪ·kən·ə·'mer·ɪ·kən] *n* Afro-Américain(e) *m(f)*

**African-American** ['æf·rɪ·kən·ə·'mer·ɪ·kən] I. *adj* afro-américain(e) II. *n* *s.* **African American**

**after** ['æf·tər] I. *prep* ❶ après; **~ two days** deux jours plus tard; **~ meals** après manger; (**a**) **quarter ~ six** six heures et quart; **the day ~ tomorrow**

après-demain; **~ May 6** (*since then*) depuis le 6 mai; (*as of then*) à partir du 6 mai ❷ (*behind*) **to run ~ sb** courir après qn; **to go ~ one's goal** poursuivre son but ❸ (*following*) **D comes ~ C** le D suit le C; **to have fight ~ fight** avoir dispute sur dispute ❹ (*trying to get*) **to be ~ sb/sth** chercher qn/qc; **the police are ~ him** la police le recherche ❺ (*despite*) **~ all** après tout; **~ all this work** après tout ce travail ❻ (*similar to*) **to name sth/sb ~ sb** donner à qc/qn le nom de qn **II.** *adv* après; **soon ~** peu après; **the day ~** le lendemain **III.** *conj* après (que); **I'll call him ~ I've taken a shower** je l'appellerai quand j'aurai pris une douche

**aftermath** ['æf·tər·mæθ] *n* conséquences *fpl*; **in the ~ of sth** à la suite de qc

**afternoon** [ˌæf·tər·'nun] *n* après-midi *m o f inv*; **this ~** cet(te) après-midi; **4 o'clock in the ~** 4 heures de l'après-midi; **good ~!** bonjour!; **Monday ~s** tous les lundis après-midi

**afterthought** ['æf·tər·θɔt] *n sing* pensée *f* après coup ▶ **as an ~** après coup

**afterward(s)** ['æf·tər·wərd(z)] *adv* ❶ (*later*) après ❷ (*after something*) ensuite; **shortly ~** peu après

**again** [ə·'gen] *adv* ❶ (*as a repetition*) encore; (*one more time*) de nouveau; **never ~** plus jamais; **once ~** une fois de plus; **yet ~** encore une fois; **not ~!** encore!; **~ and ~** plusieurs fois ❷ (*anew*) **to start ~** recommencer à zéro ▶ **then ~** d'un autre côté

**against** [ə·'genst] **I.** *prep* ❶ (*in opposition to*) contre; **~ one's will** malgré soi; **to protect oneself ~ rain** se protéger de la pluie; **the odds are ~ sb/sth** les prévisions sont défavorables à qn/qc ❷ (*in contact with*) **to lean ~ a tree** s'adosser à un arbre; **to run ~ a wall** percuter un mur ❸ (*in contrast to*) **~ a green background** sur un fond vert ❹ (*in competition with*) **~ time/the clock** contre la montre; **the dollar rose/fell ~ the euro** le dollar a monté/a baissé par rapport à l'euro ❺ (*in ex-*

*change for*) contre **II.** *adv a.* POL **to be for or ~** être pour ou contre

**age** [eɪdʒ] **I.** *n* ❶ (*length of life*) âge *m*; **to be 16 years of ~** avoir 16 ans; **to be under ~** être mineur; **voting/retirement ~** âge du droit de vote/de la retraite; **old ~** vieillesse *f* ❷ (*long existence*) âge *m* ❸ (*era*) époque *f*; **digital ~** ère *f* informatique ❹ *pl* (*a long time*) des siècles *mpl* **II.** *vt, vi* vieillir

**aged** ['eɪ·dʒɪd] **I.** *adj* (*old*) vieux(vieille) **II.** *n* **the ~** *pl* les personnes âgées *fpl*

**agency** ['eɪ·dʒ°n(t)·si] <-ies> *n* ❶ agence *f*; **employment ~** agence pour l'emploi ❷ ADMIN organisme *m*

**agenda** [ə·'dʒen·də] *n* ❶ (*list*) ordre *m* du jour; **to be on the ~** être à l'ordre du jour ❷ (*program*) programme *m* d'action

**agent** ['eɪ·dʒ°nt] *n* agent *m;* **insurance ~** agent d'assurance

**aggravate** ['æg·rə·veɪt] *vt* ❶ (*make worse*) aggraver ❷ *inf* (*irritate*) exaspérer

**aggression** [ə·'gref·°n] *n* ❶ (*feelings*) agressivité *f* ❷ (*violence*) agression *f*

**aggressive** [ə·'gres·ɪv] *adj* agressif (ivc)

**aggressor** [ə·'gres·ər] *n* agresseur, -euse *m, f*

**agile** ['ædʒ·°l] *adj* ❶ (*in moving*) agile ❷ (*in thinking and acting*) habile; (*mind*) vif(vive)

**ago** [ə·'goʊ] *adv* **that was a long time ~** c'était il y a longtemps; **a minute/a year ~** il y a une minute/un an

**agonizing** *adj* ❶ (*painful*) atroce; **to die an ~ death** mourir d'une mort atroce ❷ (*causing anxiety*) angoissant(e)

**agony** ['æg·ə·ni] <-ies> *n* douleur *f* atroce; **to be in ~** souffrir le martyre

**agree** [ə·'gri] **I.** *vi* ❶ (*share, accept idea*) **to ~ with sb** être d'accord avec qn; **to ~ on sth** se mettre d'accord sur qc; **to ~ to sth** consentir à qc ❷ (*endorse*) **to ~ with sth** approuver qc ❸ (*be good for*) **to ~ with sb** être bon pour qn ❹ (*match up*) concorder ❺ LING s'accorder **II.** *vt* ❶ (*concur*) convenir de; **it is ~d that** il est convenu que

**A** +*subj;* **to be ~d on sth** être d'accord sur qc ❷ (*accept view, proposal*) **I ~ that it's expensive** c'est cher, je suis d'accord; **to ~ to** +*infin* (*when asked*) accepter de +*infin;* (*by mutual decision*) se mettre d'accord pour +*infin*

**agreement** *n* ❶ *a.* LING accord *m* ❷ (*state of accord*) **to be in ~ with sb** être d'accord avec qn; **to reach ~** se mettre d'accord ❸ (*pact*) accord *m* ❹ (*promise*) engagement *m; ~ to* +*infin* engagement à +*infin;* **America's ~ to send troops** l'engagement américain d'envoyer des troupes ❺ (*approval*) accord *m; ~* **to do/for sth** accord pour faire/pour qc

**agriculture** ['æg·rɪ·kʌl·tʃər] *n* agriculture *f*

**ahead** [ə·'hed] *adv* ❶ (*in front*) **straight ~** droit devant; **to be ~** *fig* (*party, team*) mener ❷ (*for the future*) à venir; **to look ~** penser à l'avenir

**aid** [eɪd] **I.** *n* aide *f;* **in ~ of sb/sth** au profit de qn/qc; **to come/go to the ~ of sb** venir/aller au secours de qn; **with the ~ of** (*person*) avec l'aide de; (*thing*) à l'aide de; **international ~** secours *m* international **II.** *vt* **to ~ sb with sth** aider qn à faire qc

**AIDS** [eɪdz] *n abbr of* **Acquired Immune Deficiency Syndrome** SIDA *m*

**ailment** ['eɪl·mənt] *n* maladie *f*

**aim** [eɪm] **I.** *vi* ❶ (*point a weapon*) viser; **to ~ at sb/sth** viser qn/qc ❷ (*plan to achieve*) **to ~ at** [*o* **for**] **sth** viser qc; **to ~ to do sth** avoir l'intention de faire qc **II.** *vt* ❶ (*point a weapon*) **to ~ sth at sb/sth** (*gun, launcher*) pointer qc sur qn/qc; (*spear, missile*) braquer; (*blow*) tenter de porter ❷ (*direct at*) **to ~ sth at sb** (*criticism, remark*) destiner qc à qn ❸ *fig* **to be ~ed at doing sth** viser à faire qc **III.** *n* ❶ (*plan to shoot*) pointage *m;* **to take ~** viser ❷ (*goal*) but *m;* **to do sth with the ~ of doing sth** faire qc dans le but de faire qc

**air** [er] **I.** *n* ❶ *a.* MUS air *m;* **by ~** par avion; **there was an ~ of menace/excitement** il y avait de la menace/de l'émotion dans l'air ❷ TV, RADIO **to be off/on** (**the**) **~** être hors antenne/à l'antenne ▸ **to be in the ~** se tramer; **to be up in the ~** être flou **II.** *vt* ❶ TV, RADIO diffuser ❷ (*expose to air*) aérer ❸ (*let know*) faire connaître **III.** *vi* ❶ TV, RADIO passer ❷ (*be exposed to air*) s'aérer

**air bag** *n* airbag *m*

**air-conditioned** ['er·kən·dɪʃ·ªnd] *adj* climatisé(e)

**air conditioner** ['er·kən·dɪʃ·ªn·ər] *n* climatiseur *m*

**air conditioning** ['er·kən·dɪʃ·ªn·ɪŋ] *n* climatisation *f*

**aircraft** ['er·kræft] <-> *n* avion *m*

**airfare** *n* tarif *m* des vols

**air force** *n* armée *f* de l'air

**airhead** ['er·hed] *n sl* bêta(sse) *m(f)*

**airlift** ['er·lɪft] **I.** *n* pont *m* aérien **II.** *vt* transporter par pont aérien

**airline** ['er·laɪn] *n* compagnie *f* aérienne; **budget** [*o* **no-frills**] **~** compagnie aérienne à bas coûts

**airmail** ['er·meɪl] *n* poste *f* aérienne; **to send sth (by) ~** envoyer qc par avion

**airplane** ['er·pleɪn] *n* avion *m*

**airport** ['er·pɔrt] *n* aéroport *m*

**airtight** ['er·taɪt] *adj* hermétique

**airway** ['er·weɪ] *n* ❶ ANAT voie *f* respiratoire ❷ (*route*) voie *f* aérienne ❸ (*airline*) compagnie *f* aérienne

**aisle** [aɪl] *n* allée *f;* (*of a church*) allée *f* centrale ▸ **to take sb down the ~** se marier avec qn

**ajar** [ə·'dʒar] *adj* entrouvert(e)

**AK** *n abbr of* **Alaska**

**AL** *n abbr of* **Alabama**

**Alabama** [ˌæl·ə·'bæm·ə] **I.** *n* l'Alabama *m* **II.** *adj* de l'Alabama

**alarm** [ə·'larm] **I.** *n* ❶ (*worry*) inquiétude *f;* (*fright*) frayeur *f* ❷ (*warning*) alarme *f;* **false ~** fausse alerte *f* ❸ (*warning device*) alarme *f;* **burglar ~** alarme antivol ❹ (*clock*) réveil *m,* cadran *m Québec* **II.** *vt* ❶ (*worry*) inquiéter ❷ (*cause fear*) effrayer

**Alaska** [ə·'læs·kə] **I.** *n* l'Alaska *m* **II.** *adj* de l'Alaska

**album** [ˈæl·bəm] *n* album *m*

**alcohol** [ˈæl·kə·hal] *n* alcool *m*

**alcoholic** [ˌæl·kə·ˈhal·ɪk] **I.** *n* alcoolique *mf* **II.** *adj* alcoolisé(e)

**alert** [əˈlɜrt] **I.** *adj* ❶ *(attentive)* alerte; *(watchful)* vigilant(e); *(wide-awake)* éveillé(e); **to be ~ to sth** être conscient de qc **II.** *n* ❶ *(alarm)* alerte *f* ❷ **to be on the ~ for sth** être en état d'alerte concernant qc *m* **III.** *vt* alerter; **to ~ sb to sth** avertir qn de qc

**alibi** [ˈæl·ɪ·baɪ] *n* alibi *m*

**alien** [ˈeɪ·li·ən] **I.** *adj* ❶ *(foreign)* étranger(-ère) ❷ *(strange)* étrange; **~ to sb** étranger à qn **II.** *n* ❶ *form (foreigner)* étranger, -ère *m, f*; **illegal ~** clandestin *m* ❷ *(extra-terrestrial creature)* extra-terrestre *m*

**alight**[1] [əˈlaɪt] *adj* ❶ *(on fire)* allumé(e); **to set sth ~** mettre le feu à qc; **to get sth ~** allumer qc ❷ *(shining brightly)* **to be ~ with sth** rayonner de qc

**alight**[2] [əˈlaɪt] *vi* ❶ *(land)* atterrir ❷ *(get out)* **to ~ from a vehicle** *form* descendre d'un véhicule

♦**alight on** *vi* **to ~ sth** tomber sur qc

**alignment** *n* alignement *m;* **to be out of ~** sortir de l'alignement

**alike** [əˈlaɪk] **I.** *adj* ❶ *(identical)* identique ❷ *(similar)* semblable **II.** *adv* de la même façon; **men and women ~** les hommes comme les femmes

**alive** [əˈlaɪv] *adj* ❶ *(not dead)* vivant(e); **to keep sb ~** maintenir qn en vie; **to keep hope ~** garder espoir ❷ *(active)* actif(-ive); **to come ~** *(city)* s'éveiller ❸ *(aware)* **to be ~ to sth** être conscient de qc

**all** [ɔl] **I.** *adj* tout(e) *m(f)*, tous *mpl*, toutes *fpl*; **~ the butter/my life** tout le beurre/toute ma vie; **~ the children/my cousins** tous les enfants/mes cousins; **~ children/animals** tous les enfants/les animaux **II.** *pron* ❶ *(everybody)* tous *mpl*, toutes *fpl*; **~ aboard!** tout le monde à bord!; **~ but one** tous sauf un(e); **they ~ refused** ils ont tous refusé; **he has four daughters, ~ blue-eyed** il a quatre filles, toutes aux

yeux bleus; **the kindest of ~** le plus gentil de tous; **once and for ~** une fois pour toutes ❷ *(everything)* tout; **most of ~** surtout; **the best of all** le meilleur; **for ~ I know** autant que je sache ❸ *(the whole quantity)* tout; **they took/drank it ~** ils ont tout pris/bu; **~ of France** toute la France; **it's ~ so different** tout est si différent; **it's ~ nonsense** c'est complètement absurde ❹ *(the only thing)* tout; **~ I want is ...** tout ce que je veux, c'est ... ▸**none at ~** *(people)* personne; *(of things)* aucun(e); *(of amount)* rien du tout; **not at ~** *(in no way)* pas du tout; **nothing at ~** rien du tout **III.** *adv* tout; **it's ~ wet/dirty** c'est tout mouillé/sale; **~ around** tout autour; **~ the same** quand même; **I'm ~ but finished** je suis à deux doigts d'avoir fini; **~ over the lawn** sur toute la pelouse; **~ over the country** dans tout le pays; **two ~** SPORTS deux partout

**all-American** [ˌɔl·ə·ˈmer·ɪ·kən] *adj* ❶ *(typically American)* typiquement américain(e); **~ boy** garçon *m* cent pour cent américain ❷ SPORTS **~ quarterback** quart-arrière nommé meilleur joueur de l'année

**allegation** [ˌæl·ɪ·ˈgeɪ·ʃən] *n* allégation *f*

**allege** [əˈledʒ] *vt* prétendre

**alleged** *adj form* LAW *(attacker/attack)* présumé(e)

**allegedly** *adv* prétendument; **he ~ did sth** il a fait qc à ce qu'il paraît

**allergic** [əˈlɜr·dʒɪk] *adj a. fig* allergique

**allergy** [ˈæl·ər·dʒɪ] <-ies> *n* allergie *f*

**all-important** [ˌɔl·ɪm·ˈpɔr·tənt] *adj* capital(e)

**allocate** [ˈæl·ə·keɪt] *vt* attribuer

**allot** [əˈlat] <-tt-> *vt* allouer

**allow** [əˈlaʊ] *vt* ❶ *(permit)* permettre; **photography is not ~ed** il est interdit de prendre des photos; **to ~ sb sth** *(officially)* autoriser qc à qn; **to ~ oneself a vacation** s'autoriser des vacances; **to ~ enough time** laisser suffisamment de temps ❷ *(allocate)* accorder; *(when planning)* prévoir ❸ *(plan)* prévoir

**A**

④ (*concede*) **to ~ that ...** reconnaître que ...

**allowance** [ə·ˈlaʊ·ən(t)s] *n* ① (*permitted amount*) allocation *f*; **baggage ~** franchise *f* de bagages ② (*money*) indemnité *f*; (*to child*) argent *m* de poche; (*to adult*) rente *f*; **cost-of-living/travel ~** indemnité *f* de logement/déplacement ③ (*prepare for*) **to make ~(s) for sth** prendre qc en considération

**all-purpose** [ɔl·ˈpɜr·pəs] *adj* multi-usage

**all right I.** *adj* ① (*o.k.*) d'accord; **that's [***o* **it's] ~** c'est bien; **will it be ~ if she comes?** c'est bon si elle vient? ② (*good*) pas mal; (*mediocre*) potable; **I feel ~** je me sens bien ③ (*normal*) **I feel ~** ça va; **is everything ~?** tout va bien?; **the driver was ~** (*safe*) le conducteur était sain et sauf **II.** *interj* ① (*expressing agreement*) d'accord; **~ calm down** ça va, du calme ② *inf* (*after thanks or excuse*) **it's ~** de rien **III.** *adv* ① (*well: work, progress*) comme il faut; **the party went ~** la fête s'est bien passée ② *inf* (*definitely*) **he saw us ~** il nous a vus, c'est sûr

**all-time** *adj* (*record*) absolu(e); **to be at an ~ high/low** être au plus haut/au plus bas

**almond** [ˈa·mənd] *n* ① (*nut*) amande *f* ② (*tree*) amandier *m*

**almost** [ˈɔl·moʊst] *adv* presque; **I ~ fell asleep** j'ai failli m'endormir

**aloe vera** [ˌal·oʊ·ˈvɪr·ə] *n* BOT aloès *m*

**alone** [ə·ˈloʊn] **I.** *adj* ① (*without others*) seul(e) ② (*only*) le(la) seul(e); **Paul ~ can do that** il n'y a que Paul qui puisse faire cela ▶ **not even sth, let ~ sth else** pas qc et encore moins qc d'autre **II.** *adv* tout(e) seul(e)

**along** [ə·ˈlɒŋ] **I.** *prep* ① (*on*) **all ~ sth** tout le long de qc; **sb walks ~ the road** qn marche le long de la route ② (*during*) **~ the way** en cours de route ③ (*beside*) **trees ~ the path** arbres *mpl* bordant le chemin ④ (*in addition to*) **~ with sth/sb** en plus de qc/qn

**II.** *adv* ① (*going forward*) **to walk ~** marcher ② (*to a place*) **to come ~** venir; **are you coming ~?** tu viens?, tu viens avec? ③ (*the whole time*) **all ~** depuis le début

**alongside** [ə·ˈlɒŋ·saɪd] **I.** *prep* ① (*next to*) **~ sth** à côté de qc ② *a.* NAUT **to stop ~ a quay** s'arrêter le long d'un quai ③ (*together with*) **to work ~ each other** travailler côte à côte; **to fight ~ sb** se battre aux côtés de qn; *s.a.* **along II.** *adv* ① (*next to*) côte à côte ② NAUT bord à bord; **to come ~** accoster

**aloof** [ə·ˈluf] *adj* distant(e)

**aloud** [ə·ˈlaʊd] *adv* (*read, think*) à voix haute; (*laugh*) fort

**alphabet** [ˈæl·fə·bet] *n* alphabet *m*

**alphabetical** [ˌæl·fə·ˈbet·ɪk· əl] *adj* alphabétique

**Alps** [ælps] *npl* **the ~** les Alpes

**already** [ɔl·ˈred·i] *adv* déjà

**also** [ˈɔl·soʊ] *adv* aussi

**altar** [ˈɔl·tər] *n* autel *m*

**alter** [ˈɔl·tər] **I.** *vt* changer; (*building*) faire des travaux sur; (*clothes*) retoucher **II.** *vi* changer

**alteration** [ˌɔl·tə·ˈreɪ·ʃən] *n* changement *m*; (*clothes*) retouches *fpl*; **an ~ to sth** une modification à qc

**alternate** [ˈɔl·ˈtɜr·nət] **I.** *vt, vi* alterner **II.** *adj* ① (*by turns*) alterné(e) ② (*different, alternative*) alternatif(-ive)

**alternative** [ɔl·ˈtɜr·nə·tɪv] **I.** *n* alternative *f* **II.** *adj* alternatif(-ive)

**alternative-fuel** *adj inv* qui fonctionne avec un carburant alternatif

**alternatively** *adv* sinon; (*as a substitute*) à défaut

**alt-fuel** *adj inv, inf abbr of* **alternative-fuel**

**although** [ɔl·ˈðoʊ] *conj* bien que +*subj*, quoique +*subj*; **~ it's snowing, ...** malgré la neige, ...; *s.a.* **though**

**altitude** [ˈæl·tə·tud] *n* altitude *f*

**altogether** [ˌɔl·tə·ˈgeð·ər] *adv* ① (*completely*) entièrement; **a different matter [***o* **thing] ~** une tout autre chose; **not ~** pas complètement ② (*in total*) globalement

**aluminum foil** n papier m d'aluminium

**always** ['ɔːl·weɪz] adv toujours

**am** [əm] 1st pers sing of **be**

**amaze** [ə·'meɪz] vt stupéfier; **to be ~d that sb comes** être très surpris que qn vienne

**amazement** n stupéfaction f

**amazing** adj stupéfiant(e); **it's (pretty) ~** c'est (vraiment) incroyable

**Amazon** ['æm·ə·zan] n ❶ GEO **the (river) ~** l'Amazone f; **the ~ rain forest** la forêt amazonienne ❷ (female warrior) amazone f

**ambassador** [æm·'bæs·ə·dər] n ambassadeur, -drice m, f

**ambiguous** [æm·'bɪg·juː·əs] adj ambigu(ë)

**ambition** [æm·'bɪʃ·ən] n ambition f

**ambulance** ['æm·bjuː·lən(t)s] n ambulance f

**ambush** ['æm·bʊʃ] I. vt tendre une embuscade à; **to be ~ed** être pris dans une embuscade II.<-es> n embuscade f

**amendment** n (change, changed words) modification f; (to a bill) amendement m

**America** [ə·'mer·ɪ·kə] n l'Amérique f

**American** [ə·'mer·ɪ·kən] I. adj américain(e) II. n ❶ (person) Américain(e) m(f) ❷ LING américain m; s.a. **English**

**American Indian** n s. **Native American**

**Americanism** [ə·'mer·ɪ·kə·nɪ·zəm] n américanisme m

**Americanize** [ə·'mer·ɪ·kə·naɪz] vt américaniser

**ammunition** [æm·jə·'nɪʃ·ən] n ❶ (for firearms) munitions fpl ❷ (in debate) armes fpl

**amnesia** [æm·'niː·ʒə] n amnésie f; **~ victim** amnésique mf

**amok** [ə·'mʌk] adv **to run ~** être pris de folie furieuse

**among** [ə·'mʌŋ] prep ❶ (between) **~ friends/yourselves** entre amis/vous; **to divide up sth ~ us** partager qc entre nous ❷ (as part of) (just) **one ~ many** un parmi tant d'autres; **~ my favorite artists** parmi mes artistes préfé-rés ❸ (in a group) **~ Texans** chez les Texans ❹ (in midst of) **~ the flowers/pupils** au milieu des [o parmi les] fleurs/élèves ❺ (in addition to) **~ other things** entre autres choses

**amount** [ə·'maʊnt] I. n quantité f; **any ~ of** inf des tas mpl de; **certain ~ of determination** certaine dose f de détermination II. vi ❶ (add up to) **to ~ to sth** s'élever à qc ❷ (mean) revenir à qc ❸ fig **sb will never ~ to much** qn n'ar-rivera jamais à rien

**amp** [æmp] n ❶ abbr of **ampere** A m ❷ inf abbr of **amplifier** ampli m

**ample** ['æm·pl] <-r, -st> adj ❶ (plentiful) largement assez de; **~ evidence** preuves fpl abondantes ❷ iron (large) gros(se); **~ bosom** poitrine opulente

**amplify** ['æm·plɪ·faɪ] <-ie-> vt ❶ MUS amplifier ❷ (enlarge upon) développer

**amuse** [ə·'mjuːz] vt ❶ amuser ❷ (occupy) divertir; **to keep sb ~d** occuper qn; **to ~ oneself** se divertir

**amusing** adj amusant(e); (situation) co-mique

**an** [ən] indef art (+ vowel) un(e); s.a. **a**

**anal** ['eɪ·nəl] adj ❶ ANAT anal(e) ❷ inf (too obsessed with details) maniaque

**analogy** [ə·'næl·ə·dʒi] <-ies> n analo-gie f; **to draw an ~** établir un paral-lèle m

**analysis** [ə·'næl·ə·sɪs] <-ses> n ❶ (detailed examination) analyse f ❷ (psychoanalysis) (psych)analyse f

**analytical** [ˌæn·ə·'lɪt·ɪk·əl] adj analy-tique; **~ mind** esprit m d'analyse

**analyze** ['æn·əl·aɪz] vt analyser; PSYCH (psych)analyser

**ancestor** ['æn·ses·tər] n ancêtre mf

**ancestry** ['æn·ses·tri] <-ies> n ascen-dance f; **to be of Polish ~** être d'ori-gine polonaise

**anchor** ['æŋ·kər] I. n ❶ (object) ancre f; **to drop/weigh ~** jeter/lever l'ancre ❷ fig point m d'ancrage; **to be sb's ~** être la planche de salut de qn ❸ TV, RA-DIO présentateur, -trice m, f II. vt ❶ (fasten firmly) ancrer ❷ TV, RADIO pré-senter III. vi mouiller

**A**

**ancient** ['eɪn(t)·ʃ°nt] **I.** *adj* ❶ (*old*) ancien(ne) ❷ HIST antique ❸ *inf* (*very old*) très vieux (vieille) **II.** *n pl* (*people*) **the ~s** les Anciens *mpl*

**and** [ənd] *conj* ❶ (*also*) et ❷ MATH plus ❸ (*then*) **to go ~ open the window** aller ouvrir la fenêtre ❹ (*increase*) **better ~ better** de mieux en mieux ▸ **wait ~ see** on verra; **~ so on** et ainsi de suite

**anesthesiologist** *n* anesthésiste *mf*

**anew** [ə·'nu] *adv* à [*o* de] nouveau; **to begin ~** recommencer

**angel** ['eɪn·dʒ°l] *n* ❶ *a.* REL ange *m* ❷ (*financial sponsor*) mécène *m*

**anger** ['æŋ·gər] **I.** *n* colère *f;* **~ at sb/sth** colère contre qn/qc **II.** *vt* mettre en colère; **to be ~ed by sth** être mis hors de soi par qc

**angle**¹ ['æŋ·gl] **I.** *n* MATH angle *m;* **at an ~ of 45 degrees** (*en*) formant un angle de 45 degrés; **at an ~ to sth** en biais par rapport à qc **II.** *vt* (*mirror, light*) orienter

**angle**² ['æŋ·gl] **I.** *n* (*perspective*) angle *m;* **new ~** nouvelle perspective *f* **II.** *vt* ❶ (*aim*) **to ~ sth at sb/sth** viser qn/qc par qc ❷ (*slant*) orienter

**Anglican** ['æŋ·glɪ·kən] **I.** *adj* anglican(e) **II.** *n* Anglican(e) *m(f)*

**Anglicism** *n* anglicisme *m*

**Anglicize** ['æŋ·glɪ·saɪz] *vt* angliciser

**Anglophile** ['æŋ·glə·faɪl] **I.** *n* anglophile *mf* **II.** *adj* anglophile

**Anglophobia** [ˌæŋ·glə·'fəʊ·bi·ə] *n* anglophobie *f*

**Anglophone** **I.** *n* anglophone *mf* **II.** *adj* anglophone

**angry** ['æŋ·gri] *adj* ❶ (*furious*) en colère; **to make sb ~** mettre qn en colère; **to be/get ~ with** [*o at*] **sb** être/se mettre en colère contre qn; **to be ~ about sth** être mis hors de soi par qc; **to be ~ that …** être furieux que … ❷ (*stormy: sky*) orageux (-euse) ❸ (*inflamed*) irrité(e)

**animal** ['æn·ɪ·m°l] **I.** *n* ❶ ZOOL animal *m;* **farm ~** animal de ferme ❷ (*person*) brute *f* ▸ **political ~** bête *f* de la politique **II.** *adj* animal(e)

**animated** *adj* ❶ (*lively*) animé(e); **~ dis-**

**cussion** vive discussion *f* ❷ CINE **~ cartoon** [*o* **film**] dessin *m* animé

**anime** ['æn·ə·me] *n* japanime *f*

**ankle** ['æŋ·kl] *n* cheville *f*

**ankle bracelet** *n* bracelet *m* de cheville

**annihilate** [ə·'naɪ·ə·leɪt] *vt* ❶ annihiler ❷ (*defeat*) anéantir

**anniversary** [ˌæn·ɪ·'vɜr·s°r·i] <-ies> *n* anniversaire *m; wedding ~* anniversaire de mariage; **golden ~** noces *fpl* d'or

**announce** [ə·'naʊn(t)s] *vt* annoncer

**announcement** *n* annonce *f*

**announcer** [ə·'naʊn(t)·sər] *n* présentateur, -trice *m,* f

**annoy** [ə·'nɔɪ] *vt* embêter; **it ~s me that/when …** ça me contrarie que/quand …

**annoyance** *n* ❶ (*state*) mécontentement *m; much to sb's ~* au grand déplaisir de qn; **to hide one's ~** dissimuler sa contrariété ❷ (*cause*) tracas *m*

**annoying** *adj* énervant(e); (*habit*) fâcheux(-euse); **the ~ thing about it is that …** ce qui m'agace, c'est que …

**annual** ['æn·ju·əl] **I.** *adj* annuel(le); **~ rainfall** hauteur *f* annuelle des précipitations **II.** *n* ❶ TYP publication *f* annuelle ❷ BOT plante *f* annuelle

**anonymous** [ə·'na·nə·məs] *adj* ❶ anonyme; **to remain ~** garder l'anonymat ❷ *fig* **rather ~ face** visage *m* assez banal

**anorexic I.** *adj* anorexique **II.** *n* anorexique *mf*

**another** [ə·'nʌð·ər] **I.** *pron* ❶ (*one more*) un(e) autre; **many ~** bien d'autres ❷ (*mutual*) **one ~** l'un l'autre **II.** *adj* un(e) autre; **~ piece of cake?** encore un morceau de gâteau?; **not that piece, ~ one** pas ce morceau-là, un autre; **~ $30** 30 dollars de plus

**answer** ['æn(t)·sər] **I.** *n* ❶ (*reply*) réponse *f;* **~ to a letter/question** réponse à une lettre/question; **there was no ~** (*at door*) il n'y avait personne; (*to letter, on phone*) il n'y a pas eu de réponse ❷ (*solution*) solution *f* **II.** *vt* ❶ (*respond to: question*) répondre à; **to ~ the telephone** répondre au téléphone;

**to ~ the door(bell)** ouvrir la porte (au coup de sonnette); **to ~ prayers** exaucer des prières ② (*fit, suit*) correspondre à; **to ~ a description** répondre à une description III. *vi* donner une réponse; **I called but nobody ~ed** j'ai téléphoné mais personne n'a répondu

◆**answer for** *vt* (*be responsible*) **to ~ sb/sth** répondre de qn/qc; **to have a lot to ~ to** *pej* avoir bien des comptes à rendre

**answering machine** *n* répondeur *m*

**ant** [ænt] *n* fourmi *f*

**Antarctica** [æn·'tark·tɪ·kə] *n* l'Antarctique *m*

**antenna¹** [æn·'tenə] <-nae> *n* ZOOL antenne *f*

**antenna²** [æn·'tenə] <-s> *n* (*aerial*) antenne *f*; **radio ~** antenne de radio

**anthem** ['æn(t)·θəm] *n a.* REL hymne *m* o *f*

**antibiotic** [ˌæn·tɪ·baɪ·'a·tɪk] I. *n* antibiotique *m* II. *adj* antibiotique

**anticipate** [æn·'tɪs·ə·peɪt] *vt* ① (*expect, foresee*) prévoir; **to ~ a lot of people** attendre beaucoup de monde; **to ~ trouble/that there will be trouble** je prévois des ennuis/qu'il y aura des ennuis; **~d victory** victoire *f* prévue ② (*look forward to*) savourer à l'avance ③ (*act in advance of*) anticiper

**anticipation** [æn·ˌtɪ·sə·'peɪ·ʃən] *n* ① plaisir *m* anticipé; **eager ~** attente *f* impatiente ② (*expectation*) attente *f*; **in ~ of sth** dans l'attente de qc ③ (*preemptive action*) sens *m* d'anticipation

**antidote** ['æn·tɪ·dout] *n* **~ for sth** antidote *m* à qc

**antifreeze** ['æn·tɪ·friz] *n* antigel *m*

**antilock braking system** *n* système *m* A.B.S

**antiperspirant** [ˌæn·tɪ·'pɜr·spər·ənt] I. *adj* anti-transpirant(e) II. *n* déodorant *m* anti-transpirant

**antique** [æn·'tik] I. *n* antiquité *f* II. *adj* ancien(ne)

**antiquity** [æn·'tɪk·wə·ti] *n* ① (*ancient times*) antiquité *f* ② (*great age*) ancienneté *f* ③ <-ies> (*relics*) antiquités *fpl*

**antisocial** [ˌæn·tɪ·'sou·ʃəl] *adj* ① (*harmful to society*) antisocial(e) ② (*not sociable*) asocial(e)

**antler** ['ænt·lər] *n* bois *mpl*

**antonym** ['æn·tən·ɪm] *n* antonyme *m*

**antsy** ['ænt·si] *adj inf* excité(e)

**anxiety** [æŋ·'zaɪ·ə·ti] *n* ① (*concern*) anxiété *f*; **to feel ~** être anxieux ② (*desire*) **~ to** +*infin* impatience à +*infin*

**anxious** ['æŋ(k)·ʃəs] *adj* ① (*concerned*) anxieux(-euse) ② (*eager*) **to be ~ for sth/for sth to happen** avoir un fort désir de qc/que qc arrive; **to be ~ to** +*infin* tenir (beaucoup) à +*infin*

**any** ['en·i] I. *adj* ① (*some*) **do they have ~ money/more soup?** ont-ils de l'argent/encore de la soupe?; **if we see ~ bears, ...** si jamais on voit des ours, ...; ② (*questions?*) des questions? ② (*not important which*) **~ glass will do** n'importe quel verre ira; **come at ~ time** viens/venez n'importe quand; **in ~ case** de toute façon ③ (*that may exist*) **~ trouble should be reported to me** tout incident doit m'être signalé II. *adv* ① (*not*) **I can't make it ~ simpler** je ne peux pas le simplifier davantage; **does he feel ~ better?** se sent-il mieux? ② (*at all*) **it doesn't help him ~** cela ne lui sert à rien III. *pron* ① (*some*) **do ~ of you know?** l'un d'entre vous connaît-il la réponse?; **I saw two cars, but he didn't see ~** j'ai vu deux voitures mais il n'en a vu aucune; **if you want ~, take some/one** si tu en veux, prends-en/prends-en un ② (*indefinite*) **buy ~ you see** achète ce que tu verras

**anybody** ['en·i·ba·di] *indef pron, sing* ① (*someone*) **if ~ knows** si quelqu'un sait; **I haven't seen ~ like that** je n'ai vu personne de tel ② (*whoever*) **~ can apply** n'importe qui peut postuler; **I can give them to ~ I want** je peux les donner à qui je veux; **~ else** n'importe qui d'autre; **~ but him** tout autre que lui ▸ **everybody who is ~** *iron*

**A**

tous les gens qui comptent; **it's ~'s guess** Dieu seul le sait; *s.a.* **somebody, nobody**

**anyhow** ['en·i·haʊ] *adv* ① (*in any case*) de toute façon; *s.a.* **anyway** ② (*in a disorderly way*) n'importe comment

**anymore** [en·i·'mɔr] *adv* ① (*any longer*) ne... plus; **she doesn't live here ~** elle n'habite plus ici ② (*from now on*) ne... plus; **I won't do it ~** je ne le referai plus

**anyone** ['en·i·wʌn] *pron s.* **anybody**

**anyplace** ['en·i·pleɪs] *adv inf s.* **anywhere**

**anything** ['en·i·θɪn] *indef pron, sing* ① (*something*) **does she know ~?** est-ce qu'elle sait quelque chose?; **I don't know ~** je ne sais rien; **hardly ~** presque rien; **is there ~ new?** quoi de neuf?; **~ else** quelque chose d'autre; **I didn't have ~ better** je n'ai rien trouvé de mieux ② (*whatever*) tout; **they can choose ~ they want** ils peuvent choisir ce qu'ils veulent; **~ and everything** tout et n'importe quoi; *s.a.* **something, nothing**

**anyway** ['en·i·weɪ] *adv* ① (*in any case*) de toute façon; **I bought it ~** je l'ai tout de même acheté ② (*well*) enfin

**anywhere** ['en·i·(h)wer] *adv* ① (*in any place*) n'importe où; **~ in France** partout en France ② (*some place*) **did you look ~ else?** est-ce que tu as cherché ailleurs?; **you won't hear this ~ else** tu n'entendras cela nulle part ailleurs ▸ **miles from ~** *inf* à des kilomètres de tout; **not to be ~ near as ...** *inf* être loin d'être aussi...; **doing sth doesn't get you ~** cela n'avance à rien de faire qc, il n'y a pas d'avance à faire qc *Belgique;* **~ between $5 and $50** *inf* quelque chose entre 5 dollars et 50 dollars

**apart** [ə·'part] *adv* ① (*separated*) écarté(e); **six km ~** à six km de distance ② (*separated from sb*) **when we're ~** lorsque nous sommes séparés ③ (*into pieces*) **to come ~** se démonter; **to take sth ~** démonter qc

**apartment** [ə·'part·mənt] *n* appartement *m*

**apartment building** *n,* **apartment house** *n* immeuble *m* (locatif), conciergerie *f Québec*

**ape** [eɪp] **I.** *n* ZOOL grand singe *m* ▸ **to go ~** *inf* être furax **II.** *vt* singer

**apiece** [ə·'pis] *adv* **to cost $2 ~** coûter 2 dollars pièce; **I gave them $2 ~** je leur ai donné 2 dollars chacun

**apologize** [ə·'pɑ·lə·dʒaɪz] *vi* **to ~ to sb for sth** s'excuser de qc auprès de qn; **to ~ profusely for doing sth** se confondre en excuses d'avoir fait qc

**apology** [ə·'pɑ·lə·dʒi] <-ies> *n* ① (*regret*) excuses *fpl;* **to be full of apologies** se confondre en excuses; **to owe sb an ~** devoir des excuses à qn ② *form* (*formal defense*) **~ for sth** apologie *f* de qc

**Appalachian Mountains** [ˌæp·ə·'leɪ·tʃən-] *npl* les (monts) Appalaches *mpl*

**appall** [ə·'pɔl] *vt* consterner

**appalling** *adj* ① (*shocking*) révoltant(e) ② (*terrible*) épouvantable

**apparatus** [ˌæp·ə·'ræt·əs] *n* ① (*equipment*) équipement *m;* **diving ~** SPORTS équipement de plongée ② (*machine*) appareil *m*

**apparel** [ə·'per·əl] *n form* (*clothing*) vêtements *mpl*

**apparent** [ə·'per·ənt] *adj* ① (*clear*) évident(e); **it is ~ that ...** il est clair que...; **for no ~ reason** sans raison apparente ② (*seeming*) apparent(e)

**apparently** *adv* apparemment

**appeal** [ə·'pil] **I.** *vi* ① (*attract*) **to ~ to sb/sth** plaire à qn/qc; **to ~ to the emotions/senses** faire appel aux émotions/sens ② LAW **to ~ against sth** faire appel contre qc; **~ against a verdict** contester un verdict ③ (*plead, call upon*) **to ~ to sb for sth** lancer un appel auprès de qn pour qc; **to ~ for advice/help** faire appel à des conseils/de l'aide **II.** *n* ① (*attraction*) attrait *m;* **sex ~** sex-appeal *m;* **to have ~** (*person*) avoir du charme; **it has little ~ for young people** ça a peu d'attrait pour les jeunes ② LAW appel *m;* **to file an ~ against sth** faire appel contre qc

❸ (*request*) demande *f*; (*by charity*) appel *m*; ~ **for calm** appel au calme

**appealing** *adj* ❶ (*attractive: idea, smile*) attrayant(e); **to be ~ to sb** attirer qn ❷ (*beseeching: eyes, look*) suppliant(e)

**appear** [əˈpɪr] *vi* ❶ (*become visible*) apparaître; (*on page, screen*) paraître ❷ (*seem*) paraître; **to ~ to be …** sembler être …; **it ~s to me that …** il me semble que … ❸ LAW (*as witness, defendant*) comparaître; **to ~ in court** comparaître en justice ❹ (*perform*) **to ~ in a film** jouer dans un film ❺ (*be published*) sortir

**appearance** [əˈpɪrˑən(t)s] *n* ❶ (*instance of appearing*) apparition *f*; **to put in** [o **make**] **an ~** faire acte de présence ❷ LAW comparution *f* ❸ (*looks*) apparence *f* ❹ (*aspect: of a place*) aspect *m*; (*of wealth*) apparence *f* ❺ (*performance*) entrée *f* en scène; ~ **on television** passage *m* à la télévision ❻ (*publication*) parution *f* ▶ **from all** ~**s** selon toute apparence; ~**s can be deceiving** *prov* il ne faut pas se fier aux apparences *prov*

**appendicitis** [əˌpen·dɪˈsaɪ·tɪs] *n* appendicite *f*

**appendix** [əˈpen·dɪks] *n* ❶ <-es> ANAT appendice *m* ❷ <-dices *o* -es> TYP (*of a book*) appendice *m*; (*of a report*) annexe *f*

**appetite** [ˈæp·əˌtaɪt] *n* appétit *m*; **to spoil one's ~** couper l'appétit de qn

**appetizer** [ˈæp·əˌtaɪ·zər] *n* ❶ (*food*) amuse-gueule *m* ❷ (*drink*) apéritif *m*

**applaud** [əˈplɔd] *vt, vi* applaudir

**applause** [əˈplɔz] *n* applaudissements *mpl*; **let's have a round of ~ for him** on l'applaudit bien fort

**apple** [ˈæp·l] *n* pomme *f* ▶ **the ~ of one's eye** la prunelle de ses yeux

**applesauce** *n* compote *f* de pommes

**appliance** [əˈplaɪ·ən(t)s] *n* appareil *m*; **household/electrical ~** appareil ménager/électrique

**applicant** [ˈæp·lɪ·kənt] *n* ❶ (*for job, admission*) candidat(e) *m(f)* ❷ ADMIN demandeur, -euse *m, f*

**application** [ˌæp·lɪˈkeɪ·ʃ⁽ə⁾n] *n* ❶ ADMIN demande *f*; (*for job, membership*) candidature *f*; **job ~** demande *f* d'emploi; **to submit an ~** faire une demande; (*for job, membership*) poser sa candidature ❷ (*relevance*) **to have particular ~ to sb/sth** s'appliquer particulièrement à qn/qc ❸ (*coating*) couche *f*; (*of ointment*) application *f* ❹ COMPUT application *f* ❺ (*perseverance*) application *f*

**apply** [əˈplaɪ] I. *vt* ❶ (*request*) **to ~ to sb/sth for a job** faire une demande d'emploi auprès de qn/qc ❷ (*submit an application*) **to ~ to Harvard** présenter une demande d'inscription à Harvard ❸ (*pertain*) s'appliquer; **to ~ to sb** concerner qn II. *vt* appliquer; **to ~ sth to sth** appliquer qc à qc; **to ~ pressure to sth** exercer une pression sur qc; **to ~ oneself** s'appliquer

**appointment** *n* ❶ (*meeting, arrangement*) rendez-vous *m*; **to make an ~ with sb** prendre rendez-vous avec qn; **dental ~** rendez-vous chez le dentiste; **by ~ only** uniquement sur rendez-vous ❷ (*selection*) **the ~ (of sb) as sth** la nomination (de qn) au poste de qc

**appreciate** [əˈpri·ʃiˌeɪt] I. *vt* ❶ (*be grateful for*) être reconnaissant(e) pour; **I would ~ if you didn't tell her** j'aimerais que tu ne le lui dises pas ❷ (*understand*) **to ~ the danger** être conscient du danger; **to ~ that …** se rendre compte que … ❸ (*value*) apprécier II. *vi* monter; **to ~ (in value) by 25%** prendre 25% de valeur

**appreciation** [əˌpri·ʃiˈeɪ·ʃ⁽ə⁾n] *n* ❶ (*gratitude*) appréciation *f* ❷ (*understanding*) compréhension *f*; **she has no ~ of the problem** elle ne comprend pas le problème ❸ FIN hausse *f*

**appreciative** [əˈpri·ʃəˌtɪv] *adj* ❶ (*appreciating*) sensible ❷ (*grateful*) reconnaissant(e)

**apprehensive** [ˌæp·rɪˈhen(t)·sɪv] *adj* d'appréhension; **to be ~ about sth** appréhender qc

**apprentice** [əˈpren·tɪs] *n* apprenti(e) *m(f)*

**A**

**approach** [ə'proʊtʃ] I. vt ❶ (get close(r) to) s'approcher de; **she's ~ing 60** elle n'a pas loin de soixante ans; **it was ~ing 3 o'clock** il était presque 3 heures ❷ (talk to) **to ~ sb/sth about sth** aborder qn/qc à propos de qc ❸ (deal with) aborder II. vi s'approcher III. n ❶ (coming, way of handling) approche f ❷ (onset) **the ~ of retirement/evening** l'approche de la retraite/de la soirée ❸ (access) accès m ❹ (proposition) proposition f

**appropriate** [ə'proʊ·pri·ət, vb: ə-'proʊ·pri·eɪt] I. adj (suitable) approprié(e); **~ to sth** approprié à qc; **to find the ~ words** trouver les mots justes; **the ~ time** le moment adéquat; **to be ~ for sth** convenir à qc II. vt form ❶ (take) s'approprier ❷ FIN **to ~ funds for sth** affecter des fonds à qc

**approval** [ə'pru·vəl] n approbation f; **nod of ~** signe m d'approbation ▶ **on ~** ECON à l'essai

**approve** [ə'pruv] I. vi (like) approuver; **to ~ of sb** apprécier qn II. vt approuver

**approximate** [ə'prak·sɪ·mət, vb: ə-'prak·sɪ·meɪt] I. adj approximatif(-ive) II. vt form s'approcher de III. vi form **to ~ to sth** s'approcher de qc

**approximately** [ə'prak·sɪ·mət·li] adv approximativement

**approximation** [ə,prak·sɪ·'meɪ·ʃən] n form ❶ (estimation) approximation f ❷ (semblance) semblant m

**apricot** ['eɪ·prɪ·kat] I. n ❶ BOT abricot m ❷ (color) abricot m II. adj abricot inv

**April** ['eɪ·prəl] n ❶ (month) avril m; **~ showers** giboulées fpl de mars ❷ (indication of a date or period) **during** [o **in**] **~** en avril; **at the beginning/end of** [o **in early/late**] **~** début/fin avril; **on ~ fourth, on the fourth of ~** le 4 avril ▶ **~ fool** (person) victime f d'un poisson d'avril

**apron** ['eɪ·prən] n ❶ (clothing) tablier m ❷ AVIAT **~ area** aire f de manœuvre ▶ **to be tied to one's mother's strings** être dans les jupes de sa mère

**apt** [æpt] adj ❶ (appropriate: remark) juste; (moment) bon(ne) ❷ (likely) **~ to +infin** enclin à +infin

**apt.** abbr of **apartment** appt

**aquarium** [ə'kwer·i·əm] <-s o -ria> n aquarium m

**Aquarius** [ə'kwer·i·əs] n Verseau m; **to be an ~** être (du) Verseau; **to be born under ~** être né sous le signe du Verseau

**aquatic** [ə'kwæt̬·ɪk] adj ❶ (water-related) aquatique ❷ SPORTS nautique

**aqueduct** ['æk·wɪ·dʌkt] n aqueduc m

**AR** n abbr of **Arkansas**

**Arab** ['er·əb] I. adj arabe; **the United ~ Emirates** les Émirats mpl arabes unis II. n (person) Arabe mf

**Arabian** [ə'reɪ·bi·ən] adj arabe; **the ~ peninsula** la péninsule arabique

**Arabic** ['er·ə·bɪk] n LING arabe m; s.a. **English**

**arbitration** [,ar·bə'treɪ·ʃən] n arbitrage m; **to go to ~** s'en remettre à un arbitrage

**arcade** [ar'keɪd] n ARCHIT arcade f; (for games) galerie f de jeux

**arch¹** [artʃ] I. n arche f; **~ of the foot** voûte f plantaire II. vi former une voûte; **sth ~es over sth** qc enjambe qc III. vt cintrer; **to ~ one's eyebrows** froncer les sourcils

**arch²** [artʃ] <-er, -est> adj narquois(e); **~ smile** sourire m railleur

**archaeologist** [,ar·ki·'a·lə·dʒɪst] n archéologue mf

**archaeology** [,ar·ki·'a·lə·dʒi] n archéologie f

**archenemy** [,artʃ·'en·ɪ·mi] <-ies> n ennemi(e) m(f) juré(e)

**archery** ['ar·tʃər·i] n tir m à l'arc

**architect** ['ar·kə·tekt] n a. fig architecte mf

**architecture** ['ar·kə·tek·tʃər] n architecture f

**Arctic** ['ark·tɪk] GEO I. adj arctique II. n **the ~** l'Arctique m

**arctic** ['ark·tɪk] adj fig (temperatures) glacial(e)

**Arctic Circle** n **the ~** le cercle polaire arctique

**A**

**are** [ar, ər] *2nd pers sing, pl of* **be**

**area** ['er·ɪ·ə] *n* ❶ (*place: in town*) zone *f*; (*in country*) région *f*; (*in office, home*) espace *m*; **in rural ~s** en zone(s) rurale(s); **the bar ~** le bar ❷ (*field*) domaine *m* ❸ (*land surface*) superficie *f* ❹ MATH aire *f*; (*of circle*) surface *f*

**area code** *n* TEL indicatif *m* de zone

**arena** [ə·'ri·nə] *n* ❶ SPORTS arène *f* ❷ (*for circus*) piste *f* ❸ *fig* scène *f*

**arguably** ['arg·ju·ə·bli] *adv* sans doute

**argue** ['arg·ju] I. *vi* ❶ (*have argument*) se disputer; **to ~ about sth with sb** se disputer avec qn au sujet de qc ❷ (*discuss*) **to ~ with sb about sth** débattre avec qn de qc ❸ (*reason*) argumenter II. *vt* ❶ (*debate*) discuter; **to ~ that …** alléguer que … ❷ (*persuade*) **to ~ sb into/out of doing sth** convaincre qn de faire/ne pas faire qc

**argument** ['arg·jə·mənt] *n* ❶ (*disagreement*) dispute *f*; **to have an ~** se disputer ❷ (*discussion*) débat *m* ❸ (*reasons*) argument *m*; **~ against/for sth** argument contre/pour qc; **the ~ that …** la thèse selon laquelle … ❹ CINE, LIT sujet *m*

**arid** ['er·ɪd] *adj* aride

**Aries** ['er·iz] *n* Bélier *m*; *s.a.* **Aquarius**

**arise** [ə·'raɪz] <arose, arisen> *vi* ❶ (*appear*) se produire; (*difficulty*) surgir; **to ~ from** provenir de ❷ *form* (*get up*) se lever

**arisen** [ə·'rɪz·ən] *pp of* **arise**

**aristocracy** [ˌer·ə·'sta·krə·si] <-ies> *n* + *sing/pl* aristocratie *f*

**aristocrat** [ə·'rɪ·stə·kræt] *n* aristocrate *mf*

**arithmetic** [ˌer·ɪθ·'me·tɪk] I. *n* arithmétique *f*; **to do the ~** faire le calcul II. *adj* arithmétique

**Arizona** I. *n* l'Arizona *m* II. *adj* de l'Arizona

**ark** [ark] *n* REL arche *f*; **Noah's ~** l'arche de Noé

**Arkansas** ['ar·kən·sɔ] I. *n* l'Arkansas *m* II. *adj* de l'Arkansas

**arm**[1] [arm] *n* ❶ a. *fig* ANAT, GEO bras *m*; **to hold/take sb in one's ~s** tenir/prendre qn dans ses bras; **~ in ~** bras dessus, bras dessous; **on sb's ~** au bras de qn ❷ (*sleeve*) manche *f* ❸ (*armrest*) accoudoir *m* ❹ (*division*) branche *f* ▶ **to keep sb at ~'s <u>length</u>** tenir qn à distance

**arm**[2] [arm] MIL I. *vt* ❶ armer ❷ *fig* **to ~ oneself for/against sth** s'armer pour/contre qc II. *n pl* armes *fpl* ▶ **take up ~s against sb/sth** partir en guerre contre qn/qc

**armchair** ['arm·ˌtʃer] *n* fauteuil *m*; **~ traveler** *fig* voyageur *m* en chambre

**armed** [armd] *adj a. fig* armé(e)

**armed forces** *npl* **the ~** les forces *fpl* armées

**armor** ['ar·mər] *n* ❶ MIL armure *f* ❷ ZOOL carapace *f*

**armored** *adj* (*ship*) cuirassé(e); (*vehicle, door*) blindé(e)

**armpit** ['arm·pɪt] *n* aisselle *f*

**army** ['ar·mi] <-ies> *n* armée *f*; **to join the ~** s'engager; **~ base** base *f* militaire

**aroma** [ə·'rou·mə] *n* arôme *m*

**aromatherapy** [ə·ˌrou·mə·'θer·ə·pi] *n* aromathérapie *f*

**aromatic** [ˌer·ə·'mæt·ɪk] *adj* aromatique

**arose** [ə·'rouz] *pt of* **arise**

**around** [ə·'raund] I. *prep* ❶ (*surrounding*) autour de; **all ~ sth** tout autour de qc; **to stand ~ sb** entourer qn; **to put sth ~ sb** envelopper qn de qc ❷ (*circling*) **to go ~ sth** faire le tour de qc [*o* contourner]; **the earth goes ~ the sun** la terre tourne autour du soleil; **to find a way ~ a problem** *fig* arriver à contourner un problème ❸ (*to other side of*) **to go ~ the corner** tourner au coin; **just ~ the corner** *fig* à deux pas d'ici ❹ (*visit*) **to show sb ~ a place** faire visiter un lieu à qn ❺ (*here and there*) **to wander ~ the world** errer de par le monde; **to drive ~ France** parcourir la France II. *adv* ❶ (*near*) autour; **all ~** tout autour ❷ (*in circumference*) **for 50 feet ~** dans un rayon de 50 pieds (*équivalant à 15,24 mètres*); **for miles ~** à des lieues à la ronde ❸(*aimlessly*) **to walk ~** se balader; **to stand** [*o* **hang**] **~** rester là sans but précis ❹(*nearby*) dans les parages; **is he ~?** est-il (par) là? ❺(*in existence*) **he's still ~** il est encore en vie; **how long have computers been ~?** depuis quand est-ce qu'il y a des ordinateurs? ▸ **the right/wrong** <u>way</u> **~** à l'endroit/l'envers; **to have** <u>been</u> **~** *inf* n'être pas né d'hier; *s.a.* **up**

**arouse** [əˈraʊz] *vt* exciter

**arr.** *n abbr of* **arrival** arr.

**arrange** [əˈreɪndʒ] *vt a.* MUS arranger; (*event*, *meeting*) organiser; (*deal*) convenir de; **to ~ with sb to** +*infin* s'organiser avec qn pour +*infin*; **to ~ for sb to** +*infin* faire en sorte que qn +*subj*; **I'll ~ everything** je m'occuperai de tout

**arrangement** *n a.* MUS arrangement *m*; (*placing*) disposition *f*; **to make ~s for sth** faire ce qui est nécessaire pour qc

**arrest** [əˈrest] I. *vt a.* LAW arrêter II. *n* LAW **to place under ~** mettre en état d'arrestation

**arrival** [əˈraɪvəl] *n* arrivée *f*; **on sb's/ sth's ~** à l'arrivée de qn/qc; **~s** AVIAT, RAIL arrivées *fpl*

**arrive** [əˈraɪv] *vi* arriver; **to ~ at a conclusion** parvenir à une conclusion

**arrogance** [ˈerəgən(t)s] *n* arrogance *f*

**arrogant** [ˈerəgənt] *adj* arrogant(e)

**arrow** [ˈerˈoʊ] *n* flèche *f*

**arsenal** [ˈarˈsənˈəl] *n* arsenal *m*

**arson** [ˈarˈsən] *n* incendie *m* criminel

**art** [art] *n* ❶ art *m* ❷ *pl* UNIV sciences *fpl* humaines

**artery** [ˈarˈtərˈi] <-ies> *n* artère *f*

**arthritis** [arˈθraɪˈtɪs] *n* arthrite *f*

**artichoke** [ˈarˈtəˈtʃoʊk] *n* artichaut *m*

**article** [ˈarˈtɪˈkl] *n a.* LING article *m*

**articulate** I. [arˈtɪkˈjəˈlət] *adj* ❶(*person*) éloquent(e) ❷(*speech*) clair(e) II. [arˈtɪkˈjəˈleɪt] *vt form* ❶(*express clearly*) exposer clairement; **to ~ an idea** formuler une idée ❷ *a.* LING articuler

**artifact** [ˈarˈtəˈfækt] *n* artefact *m*

**artificial** [arˈtəˈfɪʃˈəl] *adj a. pej* artificiel(le)

**artist** [ˈarˈtəst] *n* artiste *mf*

**artistic** [arˈtɪsˈtɪk] *adj* artistique

**artsy** [ˈarˈtsi] <-ier, -iest> *adj inf s.* **arty**

**artwork** [ˈarˈtwɜrk] *n* illustrations *fpl*

**arty** [ˈarˈti] <-ier, -iest> *adj inf* ❶(*person*) (du) genre artiste ❷(*style*) bohème

**as** [əz] I. *prep* comme; **I'm working/ speaking ~ her deputy** je travaille/ m'exprime en tant que son adjoint(e); **~ a baby, I was …** quand j'étais bébé, j'étais …; **to use sth ~ a lever** utiliser qc en guise de levier II. *conj* ❶(*in comparison*) que; **the same name ~ sb/ sb** le même nom que qc/qn ❷(*like*) comme; **~ it is** tel quel; **he's angry enough ~ it is** il est déjà assez furieux comme ça; **I came ~ promised** je suis venu comme promis; **~ if it were true** comme si c'était vrai ❸(*because*) puisque; **~ he's here, I'm going** étant donné qu'il est là, je pars ❹(*while*) pendant que; (*simultaneously*) au fur et à mesure que ❺(*although*) (~) **fine ~ the day is, …** si belle que soit la journée, … ▸ **~ far** (*to the extent that*) dans la mesure où; **~ far as I am concerned** en ce qui me concerne, pour moi III. *adv* **~ well** aussi; **~ simple/simply ~** aussi simple/simplement que; **~ long as** aussi longtemps que; **~ long ~ he's at home** (*provided*) tant qu'il est à la maison; **~ much as** (*same amount*) autant que; (~) **much ~ I'd like to go** bien que j'aie très envie d'y aller; **~ soon as** aussitôt que; **~ for you** quant à toi

**a.s.a.p.** [ˌeɪˈesˈeɪˈpi] *abbr of* **as soon as possible** dès que possible

**asbestos** [æzˈbesˈtəs] *n* amiante *f*

**ascend** [əˈsend] I. *vi* (*person*) monter; (*smoke*) s'élever II. *vt* (*stairs*, *cliff*) gravir ▸ **to ~** <u>the throne</u> monter sur le trône

**ascertain** [ˌæsˈərˈteɪn] *vt form* établir

**ash**[1] [æʃ] *n* (*powder*) cendre *f*

**ash**[2] [æʃ] *n* (*tree*) frêne *m*

**ashamed** [əˈʃeɪmd] *adj* **to feel ~** avoir

honte; **to be ~ of sb/sth** avoir honte de qn/qc; **to be ~ to** +*infin* avoir honte de +*infin*

**ashore** [ə'ʃɔr] *adv* ❶ (*on land*) à terre ❷ (*toward land*) vers le rivage

**ashtray** ['æʃˌtreɪ] *n* cendrier *m*

**Asia** ['eɪʒə] *n* l'Asie *f*; **~ Minor** l'Asie mineure

**Asian** ['eɪʒən], **Asiatic** [ˌeɪʒiˈætɪk] I. *adj* asiatique II. *n* Asiatique *mf*

**aside** [ə'saɪd] I. *n* aparté *m* II. *adv* ❶ (*to one side: put, move, look*) de côté ❷ (*thinking aloud*) en aparté ❸ (*ignoring*) **sth ~** qc mis(e) à part

**ask** [æsk] I. *vt* ❶ (*request*) demander; **~ your sister** demande à ta sœur; **to ~ sb a question about sth** poser à qn une question sur qc; **to ~ for advice** demander conseil; **to ~ sb to** +*infin* demander à qn de +*infin* ❷ (*expect*) **to ~ too much of sb** en demander trop à qn; **it's ~ing a lot** c'est demander beaucoup ❸ (*invite*) inviter; **to ~ sb out/home** inviter qn à sortir/chez soi ▶ **don't ~ me** qu'est-ce que j'en sais?; **if you ~ me** si tu veux/vous voulez mon avis II. *vi* ❶ (*request information*) se renseigner; **to ~ about sth** se renseigner sur qc ❷ (*make a request*) demander; **to ~ to** +*infin* demander à +*infin* ▶ **I ~ you!** je vous/t'en prie!

◆**ask for** vt (*food, object*) demander; **she's asking for you** (*person*) elle vous demande ❷ *inf* **to be asking for it** chercher qc; **you're asking for trouble** tu cherches les histoires

**asking** *n* **it's yours for the ~** tu n'as qu'à le demander pour l'avoir

**asleep** [ə'slip] *adj* endormi(e); **to be ~** dormir; **to fall ~** s'endormir

**asparagus** [ə'sper·ə·gəs] *n* asperge *f*

**aspect** ['æs·pekt] *n* ❶ (*point of view, feature*) aspect *m* ❷ (*appearance*) air *m*

**aspirin** ['æs·pər·ɪn] *n* aspirine *f*; **an ~** un cachet *m* d'aspirine

**ass**[1] [æs] <-es> *n* (*donkey*) âne *m*; **to make an ~ of oneself** se ridiculiser

**ass**[2] [æs] <-es> *n vulg* ANAT cul *m*

**assault** [ə'sɔlt] I. *n* ❶ MIL assaut *m*; **to make an ~ on sth** assaillir qc ❷ (*physical attack*) agression *f*; **indecent ~** attentat *m* à la pudeur; **sexual ~** violences *fpl* sexuelles ❸ (*attack*) attaque *f*; **~ on sb's reputation** *fig* attaque contre la réputation de qn II. *vt* ❶ MIL attaquer ❷ (*physically*) agresser; **to indecently ~ sb** se livrer à des violences sexuelles sur qn

**assemble** [ə'sem·bl] I. *vi* se rassembler II. *vt* assembler

**assembly** [ə'sem·bli] <-ies> *n* ❶ *a.* POL assemblée *f* ❷ (*meeting*) réunion *f* ❸ TECH assemblage *m*

**assent** [ə'sent] *n form* consentement *m*

**assertive** [ə'sɜr·tɪv] *adj* assuré(e); (*person*) qui a de l'assurance

**assertiveness** *n* assurance *f*

**assess** [ə'ses] *vt* (*amount, quantity*) évaluer; (*damage, situation*) faire le bilan de

**assessment** *n* évaluation *f*; (*of situation*) bilan *m*; (*of employee, student*) contrôle *m*

**asset** ['æs·et] *n* ❶ (*of value*) atout *m*; **~ to sth** atout pour qc ❷ FIN avoir *m*; **liquid ~s** liquidités *fpl*

**assign** [ə'saɪn] *vt* ❶ (*appoint*) **to ~ sb to duties, ~ duties to sb** assigner des responsabilités à qn ❷ (*send elsewhere*) **to ~ sb to a post** affecter qn à un poste ❸ (*set aside*) affecter ❹ (*give*) **to ~ the blame for sth to sth** rejeter la responsabilité de qc sur qc; **to ~ importance to sth** accorder de l'importance à qc ❺ (*allocate*) attribuer ❻ COMPUT transférer ❼ LAW **to ~ sth to sb** transmettre qc à qn

**assignment** *n* ❶ (*task*) mission *f* ❷ (*attribution*) affectation *f* ❸ SCHOOL, UNIV devoir *m*

**assist** [ə'sɪst] I. *vt* aider; (*process*) faciliter; **to ~ sb with sth** assister qn dans qc II. *vi* **to ~ with sth** aider dans qc

**assistance** [ə'sɪs·t²n(t)s] *n* aide *f*; **to be of ~ to sb/sth** être une aide pour qn/qc; **to come to sb's ~** venir à l'aide de qn

**A**

**assistant** [ə·ˈsɪs·tˀnt] I. *adj* ❶ adjoint(e) ❷ UNIV ~ **professor** ≈ maître *m* assistant II. *n* ❶ (*helper*) aide *mf* ❷ COMPUT assistant *m*

**association** [ə·ˌsoʊ·si·ˈeɪ·ʃˀn] *n* ❶ (*organization*) association *f* ❷ (*romantic relationship*) relation *f* ❸ (*involvement*) relations *mpl* ❹ (*mental connection*) association *f*

**assorted** [ə·ˈsɔr·t̬ɪd] *adj* (*mixed*) assorti(e)

**assortment** [ə·ˈsɔrt·mənt] *n* assortiment *m*

**assume** [ə·ˈsum] *vt* ❶ (*regard as true*) supposer; **you're assuming he's telling the truth** tu supposes qu'il dit la vérité ❷ (*adopt*) adopter; (*air, pose*) prendre; (*role*) endosser ❸ (*undertake*) **to ~ office/power** prendre ses fonctions/le pouvoir

**assumption** [ə·ˈsʌm(p)·ʃˀn] *n* ❶ (*supposition*) supposition *f*; **on the ~ that** en supposant que +*subj* ❷ (*hypothesis*) hypothèse *f* ❸ (*taking over*) ~ **of power** prise *f* de pouvoir

**assurance** [ə·ˈʃʊr·ˀn(t)s] *n* assurance *f*

**assure** [ə·ˈʃʊr] *vt* assurer; **let me ~ you that** je vous le garantis

**asthma** [ˈæz·mə] *n* asthme *m;* ~ **attack** crise *f* d'asthme

**asthmatic** [æz·ˈmæt̬·ɪk] I. *n* asthmatique *mf* II. *adj* asthmatique

**astonish** [ə·ˈstɑ·nɪʃ] *vt* étonner

**astonishing** *adj* étonnant(e)

**astonishment** *n* étonnement *m;* **to sb's ~ à** la surprise de qn; **to do sth in ~** faire qc avec étonnement

**astrology** [ə·ˈstrɑl·ə·dʒi] *n* astrologie *f*

**astronaut** [ˈæs·trə·nɔt] *n* astronaute *mf*

**astronomer** [ə·ˈstrɑ·nə·mər] *n* astronome *mf*

**astronomical** [ˌæs·trə·ˈnɑm·ɪk·əl] *adj* astronomique

**astronomy** [ə·ˈstrɑn·ə·mi] *n* astronomie *f*

**asylum** [ə·ˈsaɪ·ləm] *n* asile *m; fig* refuge *m*

**at¹** [ət] *prep* ❶ (*in location of*) à; ~ **home/school** à la maison/l'école;

~ **the office** au bureau; ~ **the window** devant la fenêtre; ~ **the dentist** chez le dentiste ❷ (*expressing time*) ~ **the same time** en même temps; ~ **the/no time** à ce moment-là/aucun moment; **to do one thing ~ a time** faire une chose à la fois; ~ **noon/midnight/3 o'clock** à midi/minuit/3 heures; ~ **night** (durant) la nuit; ~ **Easter** à Pâques ❸ (*toward*) **to point ~ people** montrer les gens du doigt; **to rush ~ sth/sb** se ruer sur qc/qn ❹ (*in reaction to*) ~ **the sight of sth** en voyant qc ❺ (*in an amount of*) ~ **all** en tout; **to sell sth ~ \$10 a pound** vendre qc 10 dollars la livre; ~ **65 mph** à 65 miles par heure ❻ (*in a state of*) **I'm not ~ my best/most alert** je ne suis pas vraiment en forme/très éveillé; ~ **war/peace** en guerre/paix; ~ **20** à l'âge de 20 ans; **a child ~ play** un enfant en train de jouer ❼ (*in ability to*) **to be good/bad ~ French** être bon/mauvais en français; **to be ~ an advantage** avoir l'avantage ❽ (*repetition, persistence*) **to tug ~ the rope** tirer sur la corde; **he's ~ it again** il recommence ▶~ **all** *often not translated* **do you know her husband ~ all?** est-ce que vous connaissez son mari?; **not angry ~ all** pas du tout fâché; **he said nothing at ~** il n'a rien dit du tout; **nobody ~ all** absolument personne; **to hardly work/talk ~ all** travailler/parler à peine; ~ **that** de surcroît; **that's where it's ~** *inf* c'est comme ça aujourd'hui; **let's see where we're ~** voyons où nous en sommes

**at²** [æt] *s.* **at sign**

**ate** [eɪt] *pt of* **eat**

**atheist** [ˈeɪ·θi·ɪst] I. *n* athée *mf* II. *adj* athée

**athlete** [ˈæθ·lit] *n* athlète *mf*

**athletic** [æθ·ˈlet̬·ɪk] *adj* ❶ SPORTS athlétique; (*club*) d'athlétisme ❷ (*physically fit*) sportif(-ive); (*body*) athlétique

**Atlantic** [ət·ˈlæn·t̬ɪk] I. *n* **the ~** l'Atlantique II. *adj* atlantique

**atlas** [ˈæt·ləs] <-es> *n* atlas *m*

**ATM** [ˌeɪ·tiˈem] *n abbr of* **automated teller machine** DAB *m*

**atmosphere** [ˈæt·məs·fɪr] *n* atmosphère *f*; **good working ~** bonne ambiance *f* de travail

**atrocious** [əˈtroʊ·ʃəs] *adj* atroce

**at sign** *n* COMPUT ar(r)obase *f*, a *m* commercial

**attach** [əˈtætʃ] *vt* ① (*fasten*) **to ~ sth to sth** attacher qc à qc ② (*connect*) **to ~ sth to sth** relier qc à qc ③ *form* (*send as enclosure*) **to ~ sth to sth** joindre qc à qc; **to ~ a file** COMPUT envoyer un fichier joint ④ (*join*) **to ~ oneself to sb** se coller à qn ⑤ (*assign*) **to be ~ed to sth** être affecté à qc ⑥ (*associate*) **to ~ importance to sth** attacher de l'importance à qc

**attachment** *n* ① (*fondness*) affection *f*; **to form an ~ to sb** se prendre d'affection pour qn ② (*support*) attachement *m* ③ COMPUT pièce *f* jointe ④ (*attached device*) accessoire *m* ⑤ LAW (*person*) arrestation *f*; (*property*) saisie *f*

**attack** [əˈtæk] I. *n* ① *a.* MIL, SPORTS attaque *f*; (*of person*) agression *f*; **terrorist/bomb ~** attentat *m* terroriste/à la bombe; **to be** [*o* **to go**] **on the ~** passer à l'attaque; **to be** [*o* **come**] **under ~** être attaqué ② MED crise *f*; **~ of giggles** crise de fou rire; **~ of hysteria** crise de nerfs II. *vt* ① attaquer; (*right*) porter atteinte à; **to ~ sb in the street** agresser qn dans la rue ② (*tackle: problem, food*) s'attaquer à III. *vi* attaquer

**attempt** [əˈtem(p)t] I. *n* (*try*) tentative *f*; **to make an ~ to +***infin* essayer de +*infin* ▸ **~ on sb's life** attentat *m* contre qn II. *vt* tenter

**attend** [əˈtend] I. *vt* ① (*be present at*) assister à; **to ~ church** aller à l'église ② (*accompany*) assister II. *vi* ① (*be present*) être présent ② *form* (*listen carefully*) être attentif

**attendance** [əˈten·dən(t)s] *n* ① (*being present*) présence *f*; **~ in classes** participation *f* aux cours; **to take ~** faire l'appel ② (*people*) assistance *f*; **~ was poor** il y avait peu de monde

**attendant** [əˈten·dənt] I. *n* ① (*official*) employé(e) *m(f)* ② (*servant*) serviteur *m* II. *adj* **~ on sth** résultant de qc

**attention** [əˈten·(t)ʃən] *n* ① attention *f*; **to attract sb's ~** attirer l'attention de qn; **it has been brought to my ~ that** on a attiré mon attention sur le fait que; **to call ~ to sth** signaler qc; **to pay ~** faire attention ② (*care*) soins *mpl*; **medical ~** soins *mpl* médicaux ③ MIL **to stand to ~** être au garde-à-vous; **~!** garde-à-vous!

**attic** [ˈæt·ɪk] *n* grenier *m*

**attitude** [ˈæt·ə·tud] *n* ① (*manner*) attitude *f* ② (*opinion*) opinion *f*; **I take the ~ that** ma position est que ③ (*position*) posture *f*; ART pose *f* ④ *inf* aplomb *m*

**attorney** [əˈtɜr·ni], **attorney-at-law** [əˌtɜr·ni·ət·ˈlɔ] *n* avocat(e) *m(f)*

**Attorney General** *n* ≈ ministre *mf* de la Justice

**attract** [əˈtrækt] *vt* attirer

**attraction** [əˈtræk·ʃən] *n* ① (*force, place of enjoyment*) attraction *f* ② (*appeal*) attrait *m*; **~ to sb** attirance *f* pour qn

**attractive** [əˈtræk·tɪv] *adj* ① (*good-looking*) *a. fig* séduisant(e) ② (*pleasant*) intéressant(e)

**attribute** [ˈæt·rɪ·bjut, *vb:* əˈtrɪ·bjut] I. *n* ① (*characteristic*) attribut *m* ② LING épithète *f* II. *vt* ① (*ascribe*) attribuer; **to ~ the blame to sb** attribuer la responsabilité à qn; **they ~d their success to being lucky** ils ont attribué leur réussite à la chance ② (*give credit for*) **to ~ sth to sb** accorder qc à qn

**at-will** *adj inv* LAW (*contract*) qui peut être cassé(e) sans motif ni préavis; (*employee*) licenciable sans motif ni préavis

**auction** [ˈɔk·ʃən] I. *n* vente *f* aux enchères, mise *f* Suisse; **to be sold at ~** être vendu aux enchères, être misé Suisse II. *vt* **to ~ sth** (**off**) vendre qc aux enchères

**audible** [ˈɔ·də·bl̩] *adj* audible; **barely ~** presque inaudible

**audience** [ˈɔ·dɪ·ən(t)s] *n* + *sing/pl vb*

**A**

① (*people*) public *m*; TV téléspectateurs *mpl*; RADIO auditeurs *mpl*; LIT lecteurs *mpl*; THEAT, CINE spectateurs *mpl*; **~ participation** participation *f* du public ② (*formal interview*) audience *f*

**audition** [ɔ·ˈdɪʃ·ən] **I.** *n* audition *f*; **to hold an ~ for a part** faire passer une audition pour un rôle **II.** *vt, vi* auditionner

**auditorium** [ɔ·də·ˈtɔr·iəm] <-s *o* auditoria> *n* ① auditorium *m* ② (*hall*) salle *f* (de spectacle) ③ UNIV amphithéâtre *m*

**August** [ˈɔg·əst] *n* août *m*; *s.a.* **April**

**aunt** [ænt] *n* tante *f*

**Australia** [ɔ·ˈstreɪ·ʒə] *n* l'Australie *f*; **South ~** l'Australie-Méridionale; **Western ~** l'Australie-Occidentale

**Australian** [ɔ·ˈstreɪ·ʒən] **I.** *adj* australien(ne) **II.** *n* ① (*person*) Australien(ne) *m(f)* ② LING australien *m*; *s.a.* **English**

**Austria** [ˈɔ·stri·ə] *n* l'Autriche *f*

**Austrian** [ˈɔ·stri·ən] **I.** *adj* autrichien(ne) **II.** *n* Autrichien(ne) *m(f)*

**authentic** [ɔ·ˈθen·tɪk] *adj* authentique

**authenticity** [ɔ·θən·ˈtɪs·ə· t̬i] *n* authenticité *f*

**author** [ˈɔ·θər] **I.** *n* auteur *m* **II.** *vt* rédiger

**authoritative** [ə·ˈθɔr·ə·təɪ·t̬ɪv] *adj* ① (*imperious*) autoritaire ② (*reliable*) qui fait autorité

**authority** [ə·ˈθɔr·ə·t̬i] <-ies> *n* ① (*right to control*) autorité *f*; **to be in ~** avoir l'autorité; **to have ~ over sb** avoir de l'autorité sur qn ② (*permission*) autorisation *f* ③ (*specialist*) autorité *f*; **to be an ~ on sth** être une autorité sur qc ④ (*organization*) administration *f*; **the authorities** les autorités ▶ **to have sth on good ~** savoir qc de source sûre

**authorization** [ɔ·θər·ɪ·ˈzeɪ·ʃən] *n* autorisation *f*

**authorize** [ˈɔ·θər·aɪz] *vt* autoriser

**autobiography** [ɔ·t̬ə·baɪ·ˈɑ·grə·fi] *n* autobiographie *f*

**autograph** [ˈɔ·t̬ə·græf] **I.** *n* autographe *m* **II.** *vt* signer

**automatic** [ɔ·t̬ə·ˈmæt̬·ɪk] **I.** *n* ① (*ma-*

*chine*) machine *f* automatique ② (*rifle*) automatique *m* **II.** *adj* automatique

**automobile** [ˈɔ·t̬ə·mou·bil] *n* automobile *f*; **~ accident** accident *m* de voiture; **~ industry** industrie *f* automobile

**autopsy** [ˈɔ·tɑp·si] <-ies> *n* ① MED autopsie *f*; **to perform an ~ on sb** pratiquer une autopsie sur qn ② *fig* analyse *f*

**autumn** [ˈɔ·t̬əm] *n* automne *m*; **in the ~** en automne

**autumnal** [ɔ·ˈtʌm·nəl] *adj* (*colors*) automnal(e); (*rain, equinox*) d'automne

**available** *adj* disponible; **this product is ~ in various colors** ce produit existe en plusieurs couleurs ② *fig* libre

**avalanche** [ˈæv·əl·æntʃ] *n a. fig* avalanche *f*

**avenue** [ˈæv·ə·nu] *n* ① (*street*) avenue *f* ② (*possibility*) possibilité *f*; **to explore all ~s** explorer toutes les possibilités

**average** [ˈæv·ər·ɪdʒ] **I.** *n* (*standard*) moyenne *f*; **by an ~ of 10%** de 10% en moyenne; **on ~** en moyenne; **well above/below** ~ bien au-dessus/en dessous de la moyenne **II.** *adj* (*typical: income, person, ability*) moyen(ne); **~ rainfall** taux *m* moyen de précipitations **III.** *vt* ① (*have a general value*) **to ~ 35 hours a week** travailler en moyenne 35 heures par semaine; **to ~ $45,000 per year** (*to earn*) gagner en moyenne 45 000 dollars par an; (*to cost*) coûter en moyenne 45 000 dollars par an ② (*calculate*) faire la moyenne de

**avg.** *n abbr of* **average**

**aviation** [ˌeɪ·vi·ˈeɪ·ʃən] *n* aviation *f*; **~ industry** industrie *f* aéronautique

**avid** [ˈæv·ɪd] *adj* (*reader, supporter*) passionné(e); (*desire*) ardent(e)

**avocado** [ˌæv·ə·ˈka·dou] <-s *o* -es> *n* BOT avocat *m*

**avoid** [ə·ˈvɔɪd] *vt* éviter; **to ~ sb/sth like the plague** éviter qn/qc comme la peste; **to ~ doing sth** éviter de faire qc; **you're ~ing the issue** tu esquives la question

**await** [ə·ˈweɪt] *vt* attendre; **eagerly/long ~ed** tant/longuement attendu

**awake** [ə·'weɪk] <awoke, awoken *o* awaked> I. *vi* ❶ se réveiller ❷ *fig* to ~ to sth prendre conscience de qc II. *vt* ❶ (*rouse from sleep: person*) réveiller ❷ (*restart: passion*) raviver III. *adj* ❶ éveillé(e); **wide** ~ complètement réveillé; **to keep sb** ~ empêcher qn de dormir ❷ *fig* **to be** ~ **to sth** être conscient de qc

**award** [ə·'wɔrd] I. *n* ❶ (*prize*) prix *m*; **to be presented with an** ~ recevoir un prix ❷ (*compensation*) dédommagement *m* II. *vt* (*prize*) décerner; (*damages, grant*) accorder

**aware** [ə·'wer] *adj* ❶ (*knowing*) **to be** ~ **that** ... être bien conscient que ...; **as far as I'm** ~ autant que je sache ❷ (*sense*) **to be** ~ **of sth** être conscient de qc ❸ (*well-informed*) **to be ecologically** ~ avoir une conscience écologique

**awareness** *n* conscience *f*; **to raise public** ~ **of a problem** sensibiliser le public à un problème; **environmental** ~ conscience *f* vis-à-vis de l'environnement

**away** [ə·'weɪ] *adv* ❶ (*elsewhere*) ~ **on vacation** parti en vacances ❷ (*in distance, opposite direction*) loin; **to be miles** ~ être très loin; **as far** ~ **as possible** aussi loin que possible; **to limp/ swim** ~ s'éloigner en boitant/en nageant ❸ (*in future time*) **it's a week** ~

c'est dans une semaine ❹ (*continuously*) **to write** ~ écrire sans s'arrêter

**awesome** ['ɔ·səm] *adj* ❶ (*impressive*) impressionnant(e) ❷ (*fearsome*) effrayant(e) ❸ *inf* (*good*) super; **to look** ~ avoir l'air super

**awful** ['ɔ·fəl] *adj* ❶ (*bad*) affreux(-euse); **it smells** ~ ça sent très mauvais; **you look** ~ tu as très mauvaise mine; **I felt** ~ **for saying that** je m'en suis voulu d'avoir dit ça ❷ (*great*) **an** ~ **lot (of)** énormément (de)

**awfully** *adv* ❶ (*badly*) affreusement ❷ (*very*) vraiment; ~ **long trip** trajet *m* interminable

**awkward** ['ɔ·kwərd] *adj* ❶ (*difficult*) difficile; **to make things** ~ **for sb** compliquer les choses pour qn ❷ (*not skillful*) maladroit(e) ❸ (*embarrassed: silence*) gêné(e); (*question*) gênant(e); **I feel so** ~ **asking her** je me sens mal à l'aise de lui demander

**awoke** [ə·'woʊk] *pt of* **awake**

**awoken** [ə·'woʊ·kən] *pp of* **awake**

**ax, axe** [æks] I. *n* hache *f* ▶ **to get the** ~ *inf* (*workers*) se faire virer; (*projects*) sauter; **to** have **an** ~ **to grind** agir par intérêt II.<axing> *vt* (*projects*) abandonner; (*job*) supprimer

**axle** ['æk·sl] *n* essieu *m*

**AZ** *n abbr of* **Arizona**

**B**

# Bb

**B, b** [biː] <-'s o -s> n ❶ *(letter)* B *m*,
b *m*; **~ as in Bravo** *(on telephone)* b
comme Berthe ❷ MUS si *m* ❸ SCHOOL
bonne note *f*, de 14 à 16 sur 20
**BA** [ˌbiːˈeɪ] *n abbr of* **Bachelor of Arts** ≈
licence *f* *(lettres et sciences humaines)*
**baby** [ˈbeɪ·bi] I. n ❶ *(child, childish person)* bébé *m* ❷ *(suckling)* nourrisson *m*
❸ *(youngest person)* benjamin(e) *m(f)*
❹ *inf* *(personal concern)* **it's your ~**
c'est ton bébé ❺ *inf* *(affectionate address)* chéri(e) *m(f)* II. adj ❶ *(young)*
bébé ❷ *(small)* tout(e) petit(e)
**baby carriage** *n* voiture *f* d'enfant
**baby-sit** [ˈbeɪ·sɪt] I. *vi* faire du baby-
-sitting II. *vt* garder
**babysitter** [ˈbeɪ·bɪ·ˌsɪt̬·ər] *n* baby-sitter
*mf*
**bachelor** [ˈbætʃ·əl·ər] *n* ❶ *(man)* célibataire *m* ❷ UNIV licencié(e) *m(f)*
**back** [bæk] I. n ❶ *(opp: front)* arrière *m*; *(of envelope)* dos *m*; *(of cupboard)* fond *m*; *(of paper)* verso *m*; **in
the ~ of a car** à l'arrière d'une voiture; **at the ~ of sth, in ~ of sth** derrière qc; **to look at the ~ of the book**
regarder à la fin du livre ❷ ANAT dos *m*;
**to be on one's ~** être étendu sur le
dos; **to turn one's ~ on sb/sth** *fig*
laisser qn/qc derrière soi ❸ SPORTS arrière *m* ▶ **to know sth like the ~ of
one's hand** connaître qc comme le
fond de sa poche; **behind sb's ~** dans
le dos de qn II. adj ❶ *(rear)* arrière; **on
the ~ page** sur la dernière page
❷ *(late)* **~ payments** paiements en retard; **~ tax** arriérés *mpl* d'impôt ❸ MED
*(pain)* dans le dos; *(problems)* de dos
III. adv ❶ *(to previous place, situation)* en arrière; **to bring ~ memories** rappeler des souvenirs; **to be ~**
être de retour; **to come ~** revenir;
**we're ~ where we started** nous retournons à la case départ; **to get there

and ~** y aller et revenir; **to put sth ~**
remettre qc à sa place; **to want sth ~**
vouloir que qc soit rendu *(subj)* ❷ *(to
the rear, behind)* vers l'arrière; **to go
~ and forth between A and B** aller
et venir entre A et B; **to lie ~** s'installer confortablement; **to sit ~** s'installer
(confortablement); **to stand ~** reculer
❸ *(in return)* en retour; **to hit sb ~**
rendre les coups à qn; **to read sth ~
to sb** relire qc à qn ❹ *(into past)* **a
few years ~** il y a quelques années;
**~ in 1980** en 1980; **to think ~** penser ▶ **to get ~ at sb** prendre sa revanche sur qn IV. vt ❶ *(support)* soutenir;
*(with money)* financer; *(with arguments, facts)* soutenir ❷ *(bet on:
horse)* parier sur ❸ *(reverse)* **to ~ a
car around the corner** faire marche
arrière dans le tournant
◆ **back away** *vi* **to ~ from sb/sth** reculer devant qn/qc
◆ **back down** *vi* ❶ descendre à reculons ❷ *fig* céder
◆ **back up** I. *vi* faire marche arrière
II. *vt* ❶ *(reverse)* faire reculer ❷ COMPUT
faire une sauvegarde de ❸ *(support)*
soutenir ❹ *(confirm)* confirmer
**backfire** [ˌbæk·ˈfaɪər] *vi* ❶ *(go wrong)*
mal tourner; **his plans ~d on him** ses
projets se sont retournés contre lui
❷ AUTO pétarader
**background** [ˈbæk·ɡraʊnd] I. n ❶ *(rear
view)* fond *m*; **in the ~** à l'arrière-plan
❷ *(to a situation)* contexte *m*; *(in society)* milieu *m* d'origine; *(of education,
work)* profil *m* II. adj *(information,
knowledge)* de base; *(noise)* de fond;
**background music** musique *f* d'ambiance
**backhand** [ˈbæk·hænd] *n* revers *m*
**backing** [ˈbæk·ɪŋ] *n* ❶ *(aid)* soutien *m*
❷ FASHION renfort *m* ❸ MUS accompagnement *m*

**backpack** ['bæk·pæk] I. *n* sac *m* à dos II. *vi* **to go ~ing** faire de la randonnée
**backpacker** *n* ❶ (*traveling*) adepte *mf* du trekking ❷ (*hiking*) randonneur, -euse *m, f*
**backside** ['bæk·saɪd] *n inf* postérieur *m* ▸ **to get off one's ~** bouger ses fesses
**backup** ['bæk·ʌp] *n* ❶ (*support*) renforts *mpl;* **~ team** renforts *mpl* ❷ (*serve*) **to have sth as a ~** avoir qc de secours ❸ COMPUT (fichier *m* de) sauvegarde *f*
**backward** ['bæk·wərd] I. *adj* ❶ (*directed to the rear*) rétrograde ❷ (*slow in learning*) lent(e) ❸ (*underdeveloped*) arriéré(e) II. *adv s.* **backward(s)**
**backward(s)** ['bæk·wərd(z)] *adv* ❶ (*toward the back*) en arrière; **to go ~ and forward(s)** (*machine part*) aller d'avant en arrière; (*person*) faire l'aller-retour ❷ (*in reverse*) à reculons ❸ (*into past*) **to look ~** remonter dans le passé ▸ **to bend over ~** se couper en quatre; **to know sth ~** connaître qc sur le bout des doigts
**backyard** *n* jardin *m* ▸ **in one's own ~** tout près de chez soi
**bacon** ['beɪ·kən] *n* lard *m* ▸ **to bring home the ~** faire bouillir la marmite
**bacteria** [bæk·'tɪr·i·ə] *n pl of* **bacterium**
**bacterium** [bæk·'tɪr·i·əm] <-ria> *n* bactérie *f*
**bad** [bæd] <worse, worst> I. *adj* ❶ (*opp: good*) mauvais(e); (*neighborhood*) mal fréquenté(e); **sb's ~ points** les défauts *mpl* de qn; **~ luck** malchance *f;* **~ check** chèque *m* en bois; **~ at history/tennis** mauvais en histoire/tennis; **to go from ~ to worse** aller de mal en pis; **not too ~** pas trop mal; **not ~!** pas mal!; **too ~** tant pis ❷ (*difficult*) **~ times** temps *mpl* difficiles ❸ (*harmful*) **to be ~ for sth/sb** ne pas être bon pour qc/qn ❹ (*spoiled*) pourri(e) ❺ MED grave; **to have a ~ cold** avoir un bon rhume; **I have a ~ leg/back** j'ai des problèmes avec ma jambe/mon dos ❻ (*unacceptable*) **to use ~**

**language** dire des gros mots II. *adv inf* mal; **to feel ~** se sentir mal; **to look ~** avoir l'air malade III. *n* mal *m;* **the ~** les méchants *mpl*
**badge** [bædʒ] *n* insigne *m;* (*with slogan*) badge *m*
**badger** ['bædʒ·ər] I. *n* blaireau *m* II. *vt* harceler
**badly** ['bæd·li] <worse, worst> *adv* ❶ (*poorly*) mal; **you didn't do too ~** tu ne t'es pas trop mal débrouillé ❷ (*critically*) **to think ~ of sb** penser du mal de qn ❸ (*very much: want*) vraiment ❹ (*severely: hurt, affected*) gravement
**badminton** ['bæd·mɪn·tən] *n* badminton *m*
**baffling** *adj* (*confusing*) déconcertant(e)
**bag** [bæg] I. *n* ❶ sac *m;* (*of candy*) sachet *m,* cornet *m Suisse* ❷ (*luggage*) sac *m* de voyage ❸ (*baggy skin*) poches *fpl* (sous les yeux) ❹ (*woman*) vieille grincheuse *f* ❺ (*game caught by hunter*) tableau *m* ▸ **it's in the ~** c'est du tout cuit II. *vt* <-gg-> ❶ (*put in bag*) mettre en sac ❷ *inf* (*obtain*) **to ~ sb sth** [*o* **sth for sb**] retenir qc pour qn ❸ (*hunt and kill*) abattre
**bagel** *n* petit pain en forme d'anneau
**baggage** ['bæg·ɪdʒ] *n* ❶ (*luggage*) bagages *mpl;* **~ claim** secteur *m* de retrait des bagages ❷ MIL équipement *m*
**baggage check** *n* bulletin *m* de consigne
**bagpipes** ['bæg·paɪps] *npl* cornemuse *f*
**bail** [beɪl] I. *n* caution *f;* **to jump ~** se dérober à la justice II. *vt* (*release*) libérer sous caution
**bait** [beɪt] I. *n* ❶ SPORTS appât *m* ❷ *fig* leurre *m* II. *vt* ❶ (*put bait on*) amorcer ❷ (*harass*) harceler ❸ (*annoy*) tourmenter
**bake** [beɪk] I. *n* gratin *m* II. *vi* ❶ (*cook: meat, cake*) cuire au four; **I hardly ever ~** je fais rarement des gâteaux ❷ *inf* (*be hot*) **to be baking** (*weather*) être torride; (*person*) crever de chaleur III. *vt* ❶ (*cook*) cuire; **~d potato** pomme *f* de terre en robe des champs ❷ (*harden by heat*) durcir

**baker** ['beɪ·kər] *n* boulanger, -ère *m, f*
**bakery** ['beɪ·kə·ri] *n* boulangerie *f*
**baking** I. *n* cuisson *f* II. *adj* cuit(e)
**baking powder** *n* levure *f* chimique
**baking soda** *n* bicarbonate *m* de soude
**balance** ['bæl·ən(t)s] I. *n* ❶ (*device*) balance *f* ❷ *a. fig* équilibre *m*; **to lose one's** ~ perdre l'équilibre ❸ (*state of equality*) équilibre *m*; **to strike a** ~ **between sth and sth** trouver le juste milieu entre deux choses ❹ FIN solde *m*; **a healthy bank** ~ un bon compte bancaire ▶ **to throw sb off** ~ déconcerter qn II. *vi* ❶ (*keep a steady position*) se tenir en équilibre ❷ (*be equal*) s'équilibrer III. *vt* ❶ (*compare*) **to** ~ **two things against each other** comparer les avantages de deux choses ❷ (*keep in a position*) maintenir en équilibre; **to** ~ **sth on sth** tenir qc en équilibre sur qc ❸ FIN (*books*) régler; (*budget*) équilibrer
**balcony** ['bæl·kə·ni] *n* balcon *m*
**bald** [bɔld] *adj* ❶ (*hairless*) chauve; **to go** ~ se dégarnir ❷ (*blunt*) simple ❸ (*plain: facts*) brut(e)
**bale** [beɪl] I. *n* ballot *m* II. *vt* mettre en ballot
**ball** [bɔl] *n* ❶ GAMES (*for tennis, golf*) balle *f*; (*for football, rugby*) ballon *m* ❷ (*round form*) boule *f*; ~ **of string/yarn** pelote *f* de ficelle/de laine ❸ ANAT éminence *f* ❹ (*dance*) bal *m* ▶ **to be on the** ~ avoir de la présence d'esprit; **to get the** ~ **rolling** mettre les choses en train; **to have a** ~ bien s'amuser; **to play** ~ jouer le jeu
**ballet** [bæl·'eɪ] *n* ballet *m*
**ballistic** [bə·'lɪs·tɪk] *adj* balistique ▶ **to go** ~ *sl* piquer une crise
**balloon** [bə·'lun] I. *n* ❶ GAMES ballon *m* ❷ (*for flying*) montgolfière *f* ❸ TYP (*in cartoons*) bulle *f* II. *vi* gonfler
**ballot** ['bæl·ət] I. *n* ❶ (*process*) scrutin *m* ❷ (*election*) vote *m* ❸ (*paper*) bulletin *m* de vote II. *vi* voter III. *vt* appeler à voter
**ballroom** ['bɔl·rʊm] *n* salle *f* de bal; ~ **dancing** danse *f* de salon

**balmy** ['ba·mi] <-ier, -iest> *adj* doux(douce)
**bamboo** [bæm·'bu] *n* bambou *m*
**ban** [bæn] I. *n* interdit *m*; **to place a** ~ **on sth** interdire II. *vt* <-nn-> (*person*) bannir; (*practice, guns*) interdire
**banana** [bə·'næn·ə] *n* banane *f*
**band¹** [bænd] *n* ❶ MUS orchestre *m*; (*pop group*) groupe *m*; **brass** ~ fanfare *f* ❷ (*group*) bande *f*
**band²** [bænd] I. *n* ❶ (*strip*) bande *f*; **head** ~ bandeau *m*; **waist** ~ ceinture *f* ❷ (*range*) tranche *f*; **tax** ~ tranche d'imposition ❸ (*ring*) anneau *m*; **wedding** ~ alliance *f* ❹ (*section*) série *f* II. *vt* grouper
**bandage** ['bæn·dɪdʒ] I. *n* pansement *m* II. *vt* mettre un pansement à
**bandit** ['bæn·dɪt] *n* bandit *m*
**bang** [bæŋ] I. *n* ❶ (*explosion*) bang *m* ❷ (*blow*) coup *m* violent ❸ *pl* (*hair*) frange *f* ❹ *vulg* (*sexual intercourse*) partie *f* de jambes en l'air ❺ (*drug dose*) dose *f* II. *adv* (*exactly*) **slap** ~ **into sth** en plein dans qc **to go** ~ exploser III. *interj* **bang!** bang! IV. *vi* (*hit*) claquer; **to** ~ **on the door** frapper à la porte V. *vt* ❶ (*hit*) **to** ~ **one's fist on the table** frapper du poing sur la table ❷ *vulg* (*have sex with*) baiser
**bank¹** [bæŋk] I. *n* banque *f*; **blood/data** ~ banque du sang/de données II. *vi* **to** ~ **with …** avoir un compte à … III. *vt* (*deposit*) **to** ~ **money/valuables** déposer de l'argent/des objets de valeur
   ◆**bank on** *vt* (*result, help*) compter sur; **to** ~ **sth happening** compter sur le fait que qc se passe (*subj*)
**bank²** [bæŋk] *n* (*row*) rangée *f*
**bank³** [bæŋk] I. *n* ❶ (*edge: of river*) bord *m*; (*of land*) talus *m* ❷ (*elevation in water*) banc *m* ❸ AVIAT virage *m* incliné ❹ (*mass*) massif *m*; (*of clouds*) amoncellement *m*; (*of fog*) couche *f* II. *vi* AVIAT virer (sur l'aile) III. *vt* AVIAT **to** ~ **an airplane** faire virer un avion sur l'aile
**banking** *n* banque *f*

**bankruptcy** ['bæŋk·rəp(t)·si] <-ies> *n* faillite *f*

**banner** ['bæn·ər] *n* ❶ (*flag*) bannière *f* ❷ (*slogan*) devise *f*

**bar** [bar] **I.** *n* ❶ (*elongated piece: of steel*) barre *f*; (*of chocolate*) tablette *f*; (*of gold*) lingot *m*; (*of soap*) savonnette *f* ❷ (*rod: of cage*) barreau *m* ❸ (*band: of light*) rai *m*; (*of color*) bande *f* ❹ CULIN bar *m*; (*counter*) comptoir *m* ❺ MUS mesure *f* ❻ SPORTS barre *f* ▸ *fig* obstacle *m* **II.** *vt* <-rr-> ❶ (*fasten*) verrouiller ❷ (*obstruct*) barrer; **to ~ the way** bloquer le passage ❸ (*prohibit*) **to ~ sb from sth/doing sth** défendre qc à qn/à qn de faire qc

**barb** [barb] *n* ❶ (*part of hook*) ardillon *m* ❷ (*insult*) pointe *f*

**barbecue** ['bar·bɪ·kju] **I.** *n* barbecue *m* **II.** *vt* griller au barbecue

**barbed** [barbd] *adj* ❶ (*with barbs*) barbelé(e) ❷ (*hurtful*) acéré(e)

**barber** ['bar·bər] *n* coiffeur *m*, barbier *m* Québec

**bare** [ber] **I.** *adj* ❶ (*uncovered*) nu(e); **with my ~ hands** à mains nues ❷ (*empty*) vide ❸ (*unadorned: fact*) brut(e); (*truth*) nu(e) ❹ (*little: minimum*) strict(e); **~ necessities of life** minimum *m* vital ▸ **the ~ bones of a story** l'essentiel d'une histoire **II.** *vt* **to ~ one's head** se découvrir la tête; **to ~ one's heart/soul to sb** dévoiler son cœur/son âme à qn

**barefoot** ['ber·fʊt] *adj, adv* pieds nus

**barely** ['ber·li] *adv* ❶ (*hardly*) à peine ❷ (*scantily: furnished*) pauvrement

**bargain** ['bar·gɪn] **I.** *n* ❶ (*agreement*) marché *m*; **to drive a hard ~** marchander dur; **to strike a ~** conclure un marché ❷ (*item*) affaire *f*; **a real ~** une bonne affaire **II.** *vi* ❶ (*negotiate*) **to ~ for sth** négocier pour qc ❷ (*exchange*) **to ~ away sth** brader qc

◆ **bargain for, bargain on** *vi* compter sur; **to get more than one bargained for** *fig* en avoir plus que son compte

**barge** [bardʒ] **I.** *n* péniche *f* **II.** *vt* **to ~**

**one's way to the front** foncer vers l'avant

**bark**[1] [bark] **I.** *n* ❶ ZOOL aboiement *m* ❷ (*cough*) toux *f* sèche **II.** *vt, vi* aboyer

**bark**[2] [bark] *n* BOT écorce *f*

**barley** ['bar·li] *n* orge *f*

**barman** ['bar·mən] *n* <-men> barman *m*

**barn** [barn] *n* grange *f*

**barometer** [bə·'ra·mə·ṭər] *n* baromètre *m*

**barrage** [bə·'ra(d)ʒ] *n* ❶ MIL tir *m* de barrage ❷ *fig* (*of questions*) déluge *m*

**barrel** ['ber·əl] **I.** *n* ❶ (*container*) tonneau *m* ❷ (*measure*) baril *m* ❸ (*part of gun*) canon *m* ❹ **I wouldn't say he's a ~ of laughs** c'est pas un marrant; **to have sb over a ~** tenir qn à sa merci **II.** *vi inf* (*drive fast*) foncer **III.** *vt* mettre en fût

**barrier** ['ber·i·ər] *n* barrière *f*

**barring** ['bar·ɪŋ] *prep* excepté; **~ error/the unexpected** sauf erreur/imprévu

**base**[1] [beɪs] **I.** *n* (*headquarters, supporting part*) base *f*; (*of statue*) socle *m*; (*of tree, post*) pied *m* ▸ **to be off** ▸ *inf* dérailler; **to touch ~** ▸ prendre contact **II.** *vt* ❶ (*place, support*) *a.* MIL baser; **a Boston-based firm** une société basée à Boston ❷ (*develop using sth*) **to ~ sth on sth** baser qc sur qc; **the theory is ~d on evidence** la théorie est construite sur des preuves; **to be ~d on a novel** être basé sur un roman

**base**[2] [beɪs] *adj* ❶ (*not honorable*) indigne; (*behavior*) ignoble ❷ (*not pure: metal*) vil(e)

**baseball** ['beɪs·bɔl] *n* ❶ (*game*) baseball *m* ❷ (*ball*) balle *f* de base-ball

**bash** [bæʃ] **I.** *n* ❶ (*blow*) coup *m* ❷ *inf* (*party*) fête *f* **II.** *vt* ❶ (*hit hard*) **to ~ sth against sth** cogner qc contre qc ❷ (*criticize*) démolir

**basic** *adj* ❶ (*fundamental*) fondamental(e), (*needs*) premier(-ère); **to be ~ to sth** être essentiel à qc; **the ~ idea is to ...** l'idée *f* essentielle est de; **~ facts** faits *mpl* principaux; **~ requirements**

**B**

minimum *m* requis ② (*lowest in level*) rudimentaire; ~ **vocabulary** vocabulaire *m* de base ③ CHEM basique

**basically** *adv* en fait

**basil** ['bæ·zəl] *n* basilic *m*

**basin** ['beɪ·sᵊn] *n* ① (*bowl*) cuvette *f* ② (*sink*) lavabo *m*

**basis** ['beɪ·sɪs] *n* <bases> base *f*; **to be the ~ for** (*agreement, discussion, progress, plan*) être le point de départ de; **on the ~ of sth** sur la base de qc

**basket** ['bæs·kət] *n* panier *m* ▸ **to be a ~ case** *pej* être un paumé

**basketball** ['bæs·kət·bɔl] *n* basket-ball *m*

**bastard** ['bæs·tərd] *n* ① bâtard *m* ② *fig, pej, vulg* salaud *m*; **to be a real ~ to sb** être un vrai salaud envers qn; **you ~!** salaud!

**bat¹** [bæt] *n* ZOOL chauve-souris *f* ▸ **to have ~s in the belfry** avoir une araignée au plafond; **like a ~ out of hell** comme un fou; (**as**) **blind as a ~** myope comme une taupe

**bat²** [bæt] *vt* **to ~ one's eyelids at sb** battre des paupières pour qn ▸ **she didn't ~ an eyelid when …** elle n'a pas bronché quand …

**bat³** [bæt] **I.** *n* batte *f* ▸ **right off the ~** sur le champ **II.** *vi* <-tt-> être à la batte **III.** *vt* <-tt-> **to ~ the ball** frapper la balle

**bath** [bæθ] *n* ① (*water, wash*) bain *m*; **to give sb/sth a ~** baigner qn/qc; **to take a ~** prendre un bain ② (*tub*) baignoire *f* ③ (*container*) cuvette *f*

**bathe** [beɪð] **I.** *vi* prendre un bain **II.** *vt* ① *a.* MED baigner; **to ~ one's eyes** se rincer les yeux; **to ~ one's feet** prendre un bain de pieds ② *fig* baigner; **to be ~d in sweat/tears** être en nage/baigné de larmes

**bathing suit** *n* maillot *m* de bain (une pièce)

**bathrobe** *n* peignoir *m* de bain

**bathroom** *n* ① (*room with bath*) salle *f* de bain ② (*lavatory*) toilettes *fpl*

**bathtub** *n* baignoire *f*

**batter** ['bæt·ər] **I.** *n* pâte *f* **II.** *vt* battre

**III.** *vi* **to ~ against the rocks** battre les rochers

**battery** ['bæt·ᵊr·i] <-ies> *n* ① ELEC pile *f*; **batteries not included** piles vendues séparément; **~-operated** (qui fonctionne) à piles ② (*large amount*) *a.* AUTO, MIL batterie *f*

**battle** ['bæt·l] **I.** *n* (*combat*) bataille *f*; **to be killed in ~** être tué au combat; **~ of wits/words** joute *f* d'esprit/oratoire; **to do ~** s'opposer; **~ against/for sth** lutte *f* contre/pour qc; **to fight a ~ for sth** se battre pour qc ▸ **it's half the ~** c'est la moitié du travail **II.** *vi* ① (*fight*) **to ~ over sth** se battre pour qc ② *fig* **to ~ against/for sth** lutter contre/pour qc **III.** *vt* combattre

**battlefield**, **battleground** *n a. fig* champ *m* de bataille

**battleship** ['bæt·l·ʃɪp] *n* cuirassé *m*

**bazaar** [bə·'zɑr] *n* ① bazar *m* ② (*event*) vente *f* de charité

**BC** [ˌbiˈsi] **I.** *n abbr of* British Columbia **II.** *adv abbr of* before Christ av JC

**be** [bi] <was, been> **I.** *vi + adj or n* ① (*expresses identity, position, place*) **he's American/a dentist** c'est un Américain/dentiste; **it's a key** c'est une clef; **to ~ in Spain** être en Espagne; **the statues are in the Louvre** les statues *fpl* se trouvent au Louvre ② (*expresses a state, situation*) **I'm cold/hungry** j'ai froid/faim; **my hands are cold** j'ai froid aux mains; **how are you? – I'm fine** comment vas-tu/allez-vous? – je vais bien; **~ quiet!** reste(z) tranquille!; **to ~ on a diet** faire un régime; **to ~ on the pill** prendre la pilule; **to ~ on welfare** toucher des allocations ③ (*expresses calculation/price*) **two and two is four** deux et deux font quatre; **this book is 50¢** ce livre fait 50 cents ④ (*indicates age*) **how old is he? – he's twenty** quel âge a-t-il? – il a vingt ans ⑤ (*take place*) **the meeting is next Tuesday** la réunion a lieu mardi prochain ⑥ (*exist*) **there is/are …** il y a …; **let her ~!** laisse-la tranquille! ⑦ (*impersonal use*) **what is it?** qu'est-

-ce que c'est?; **it's three** il est trois heures; **it's cold/windy** il fait froid/il y a du vent; **it's rainy** il pleut; **it's fair** c'est juste; **what's it to ~?** ce sera?; **as it were** pour ainsi dire ▶ **the ~-all and end-all** le but suprême; **so ~ it** soit; **far ~ it from sb to** +*infin* loin de qn l'idée de +*infin*; *s.a.* **off** II. *aux* ❶ (*expresses continuation*) **he's breathing** il respire; **she's still sleeping** elle est encore en train de dormir; **it's raining** il pleut ❷ (*expresses possibility*) **can it ~ that …?** *form* est-il possible que +*subj* ?; **what is he to do?** qu'est-il censé faire?; **may I ~ of service?** je peux vous aider? ❸ (*expresses passive*) **to ~ discovered by sb** être découvert par qn; **to ~ left speechless** rester bouche bée; **I'm asked to come at seven** on me demande de venir à sept heures ❹ (*expresses future*) **she's leaving tomorrow** elle part demain; **you are to wait here** vous devez attendre ici ❺ (*expresses future in past*) **she was never to see her brother again** elle n'allait jamais plus revoir son frère ❻ (*in conditionals*) **if sb were** [*o* **was**] **to** +*infin*, … si qn devait +*infin*, …; **if he were to work harder, he'd get better grades** s'il travaillait plus, il aurait de meilleures notes; **were sb to** +*infin*, … *form* si qn devait +*infin*, …

**beach** [biːtʃ] *n* plage *f*

**beacon** ['biːkən] *n* ❶ (*light*) signal *m* lumineux ❷ (*signal*) balise *f* ❸ (*lighthouse*) phare *m* ❹ (*guide*) flambeau *m*; **~ of hope** symbole *m* d'espoir

**bead** [biːd] *n a. fig* perle *f*

**beak** [biːk] *n* ❶ ZOOL bec *m* ❷ *inf* (*nose*) nez *m* crochu

**beam** [biːm] I. *n* ❶ (*stream of light*) rayon *m*; PHYS faisceau *m* (lumineux); **full ~** AUTO pleins phares *mpl* ❷ *a.* SPORTS poutre *f* ❸ (*big smile*) grand sourire *m* II. *vt* ❶ (*transmit*) diffuser ❷ (*send*) diriger III. *vi* ❶ **to ~ down on sth/sb** rayonner sur qc/qn ❷ (*smile*) sourire largement

**bean** [biːn] *n* ❶ (*seed*) haricot *m*, fève *f*

*Québec;* **green ~s** haricots verts; (Boston) **baked ~s** haricots blancs à l'étouffée de Boston, fèves au lard à la mélasse *Québec* ❷ (*pod*) cosse *f* ▶ **to spill the ~s to sb** (*vendre la mèche à qn*)

**bear**¹ [ber] *n* ZOOL ours *m*

**bear²** [ber] <bore, born(e)> I. *vt* ❶ (*carry, display*) porter ❷ (*bring: letter, news*) porter ❸ (*endure, deal with*) **to ~ the burden/the pain** supporter le poids/la douleur; **to ~ the blame** endosser la responsabilité; **I can't ~ the suspense** je ne supporte plus l'attente ❹ (*show*) **to ~ an** (**uncanny**) **likeness to sb** avoir une (troublante) ressemblance avec qn ❺ (*keep*) **to ~ sth/sb in mind** penser à qc/qn ❻ <born> *pp in passive* (*give birth to*) **to ~ sb a child** donner un enfant à qn; **animals ~ young** les animaux *mpl* se reproduisent ❼ (*generate*) **to ~ fruit** donner des fruits; *fig* porter ses fruits ❽ FIN, ECON **to ~ interest** rapporter un intérêt II. *vi* ❶ (*move*) **to ~ left/right** prendre à gauche/droite ❷ (*have influence*) **to bring pressure to ~ on sb** faire pression sur qn

♦ **bear up** *vi* ne pas se laisser abattre; **~!** courage!

**beard** [bɪrd] *n* ❶ (*hair*) barbe *f*; **to grow a ~** se laisser pousser une barbe; **to have a ~** porter la barbe ❷ ZOOL bouc *m*

**bearer** ['ber·ər] *n* ❶ (*messenger*) porteur, -euse *m, f* ❷ (*owner: of title, check*) porteur, -euse *m, f*; (*of passport, license*) titulaire *mf*

**bearing** ['ber·ɪŋ] *n* ❶ (*exact position*) position *f*; **to lose one's ~s** se désorienter; **to get one's ~s** *fig* s'orienter ❷ (*posture*) maintien *m* ❸ (*air*) allure *f* ❹ TECH **ball ~** roulement *m* à billes ❺ (*relevance*) influence *f*; **to have some ~ on sth** influer sur qc

**beat** [biːt] <beat, beaten> I. *n* ❶ (*pulsation*) battement *m* ❷ MUS temps *m*; (*rhythm*) rythme *m*; **strong ~** temps *m* fort ❸ (*sing* (*police working area*) secteur *m*; **he's on the ~** il fait une patrouille à pied II. *adj inf* épuisé(e) III. *vt*

**B**

❶(*strike*) battre; **to ~ sb to death** battre qn à mort; **to ~ sb black and blue** rouer qn de coups ❷(*mix food*) **to ~ eggs** battre des œufs ❸(*cut through*) **to ~ a path** se frayer un passage ❹(*defeat*) battre ❺ *inf* (*be better than*) **to ~ sth/sb** être meilleur que qc/qn; **nothing ~s sth** rien ne vaut qc ▶ **to ~ the living ~s daylights out of sb** *inf* tabasser qn; **to ~ sb at his/her own game** battre qn à son propre jeu; **to ~ the pants off sb** *inf* battre qn à plate(s) couture(s); **if you can't ~ them, join them** *prov* une alliance vaut mieux qu'une défaite; **it ~s me** ça me dépasse; ~ **it** dégage; **to ~ sb to it** devancer qn **IV.** *vi* battre
◆**beat back** *vt always sep* repousser; **the blaze was beaten back** les flammes *fpl* ont été repoussées
◆**beat down I.** *vi* (*hail, rain*) battre; (*sun*) taper; **the rain was beating down** il pleuvait à verse **II.** *vt always sep* faire baisser; **I managed to beat him down to $35** j'ai réussi à le faire descendre à 35 dollars
◆**beat off** *vt* repousser
◆**beat up I.** *vt always sep* passer à tabac **II.** *vi* **to ~ on sb** passer qn à tabac
**beaten** ['biːtˑən] *adj* (*metal*) martelé(e); **off the ~ path** hors des sentiers battus
**beating** ['biːtɪŋ] *n* ❶(*getting hit*) **to give sb a ~** rouer qn de coups ❷(*defeat*) **to take a ~** se faire battre à plate(s) couture(s); **sth will take some ~** qc est imbattable
**beautiful** ['bjuːˑtəˑfəl] *adj* ❶(*attractive*) beau(belle) ❷(*excellent*) magnifique ❸(*trendy*) **the ~ people** les beaux *mpl*
**beauty** ['bjuːˑtɪ] <-ies> *n* beauté *f*; **to be a** (**real**) ~ être d'une grande beauté; (*car*) être une (véritable) merveille
**beauty parlor** *n*, **beauty salon** *n*, **beauty shop** *n* institut *m* de beauté
**beaver** ['biːˑvər] **I.** *n* ZOOL castor *m* **II.** *vi inf* **to ~ away at sth** travailler d'arrache-pied à qc
**became** [bɪˈkeɪm] *pt of* **become**
**because** [bɪˈkɑz] **I.** *conj* parce que; ~ **I said that, I had to leave** j'ai dû partir

pour avoir dit cela; ~ **it's snowing** à cause de la neige; **not ~ I am sad, but …** non que je sois triste (*subj*), mais … **II.** *prep* ~ **of me** à cause de moi; ~ **of illness** pour cause de maladie; ~ **of the nice weather** en raison du beau temps
**beckon** ['bekˑən] **I.** *vt* **to ~ sb over** faire signe à qn de venir **II.** *vi* (*signal*) **to ~ to sb** faire signe à qn
**become** [bɪˈkʌm] <became, become> **I.** *vi* + *adj or n* devenir; **to ~ extinct** disparaître; **to ~ angry** s'énerver; **to ~ interested in sth/sb** commencer à s'intéresser à qc/qn; **I wonder what became of him** je me demande ce qu'il est devenu **II.** *vt* (*dress*) aller à; (*attitude*) convenir à
**bed** [bed] *n* ❶(*furniture*) lit *m*; **to get out of ~** se lever; **to go to ~** aller au lit; **to put sb to ~** mettre qn au lit; **in ~** au lit ❷(*related to sexuality*) **good in ~** bon(ne) au lit; **to go to ~ with sb** coucher avec qn ❸(*flower patch*) parterre *m* ❹(*bottom*) **sea ~** fond *m* de la mer; **river ~** lit *m* de la rivière ▶ **it's not a ~ of roses** ce n'est pas une partie de plaisir; **to get out of** [*o* **up on**] **the wrong side of the ~** se lever du mauvais pied
**bed and breakfast** *n* ≈ chambre *f* d'hôtes
**bedding** ['bedˑɪŋ] *n* ❶(*bed*) literie *f* ❷ZOOL litière *f*
**bedridden** ['bedˑˌrɪdˑən] *adj* alité(e)
**bedroom** ['bedˑrum] *n* chambre *f* à coucher; **guest ~** chambre d'amis; **three-~ house** maison *f* avec trois chambres; ~ **scene** scène *f* d'amour; **to have ~ eyes** avoir un regard troublant
**bedside table** *n* table *f* de chevet
**bedtime** ['bedˑtaɪm] *n* heure *f* du coucher; **it's** (**way**) **past my ~** je devrais déjà être au lit
**bee** [biː] *n* ❶ZOOL abeille *f*; **swarm of ~s** essaim *m* d'abeilles; **worker ~s** abeilles ouvrières ❷(*group*) cercle de personnes ayant une activité commune ▶ **to have a ~ in one's bonnet about sth**

**B**

faire une fixation sur qc; **to be a** <u>busy</u> ~
*iron* être débordant d'activité

**beech** [biːtʃ] *n* hêtre *m;* ~ **table** table *f*
en (bois de) hêtre; **made of** ~ en (bois
de) hêtre

**beef** [biːf] **I.** *n* ❶ (*meat*) bœuf *m;*
**ground** ~ bœuf haché; **roast** ~ rôti *m*
de bœuf ❷ *inf* (*complaint*) revendication *f;* **what's his** ~? qu'est qu'il veut?
**II.** *vi* **to** ~ **about sth** râler à cause de qc

**been** [bɪn] *pp of* **be**

**beeper** ['biː·pər] *n* récepteur *m* d'appel

**beer** [bɪr] *n* bière *f*

**beetle** ['biː·tl] *n* ❶ zoo scarabée *m*
❷ *inf* auto coccinelle *f*

**before** [bɪ·'fɔr] **I.** *prep* ❶ (*earlier*) avant;
~ **doing sth** avant de faire qc ❷ (*in
front of*) devant; ~ **our eyes** sous nos
yeux ❸ (*preceding*) avant; **C comes** ~
**D** le C précède le D ❹ (*having priority*)
**to put sth** ~ **sth else** donner la priorité
à qc sur qc d'autre ❺ (*facing sb*) **he has
sth** ~ **him** il a qc qui l'attend ►**business** ~ **pleasure** *prov* le travail
d'abord, le plaisir ensuite **II.** *adv* ❶ (*previously*) **I've seen it** ~ je l'ai déjà vu;
**I haven't seen it** ~ je ne l'ai jamais vu;
**the day** ~ la veille; **as** ~ comme par le
passé ❷ (*in front*) **this word and the
one** ~ ce mot et le précédent **III.** *conj*
❶ (*at previous time*) avant (que); **he
had a drink** ~ **he went** il a pris un verre avant de partir ❷ (*rather than*) **he'd
die** ~ **he'd tell the truth** il mourrait
plutôt que de dire la vérité ❸ (*until*) **it
was a week** ~ **he came** il s'est passé
une semaine avant qu'il ne vienne ❹ (*so
that*) **to have to do sth** ~ **sb would do
sth** devoir faire qc pour que qn fasse qc
(*subj*)

**beforehand** [bɪ·'fɔr·hænd] *adv* ❶ (*in
advance*) à l'avance ❷ (*earlier*) déjà

**beg** [beg] <-gg-> **I.** *vt* ❶ (*seek charity*)
quémander; **to** ~ **sb's pardon** s'excuser auprès de qn; **I** ~ **your pardon?** je
vous demande pardon? ❷ (*humbly re-
quest*) implorer; **to** ~ **sb to** +*infin* supplier qn de +*infin* ►**to** ~ **the** <u>question</u>
faire l'impasse sur l'essentiel **II.** *vi*

❶ (*seek charity*) mendier; **to** ~ **for sth**
mendier qc ❷ (*humbly request*) implo-
rer; **I** ~ **of you to** +*infin* je vous supplie
de +*infin;* **to** ~ **for mercy** demander
grâce; **I** ~ **to differ** *form* permettez-moi
d'être d'un autre avis ❸ (*sit up: dog*)
faire le beau

**began** [bɪ·'gæn] *pt of* **begin**

**beggar** ['beg·ər] **I.** *vt* **to** ~ **belief** dépasser l'imagination **II.** *n* ❶ (*poor person*)
mendiant(e) *m(f)* ❷ (*rascal*) voyou *m*
►~**s can't be** <u>choosers</u> *prov* faute de
grives on mange des merles *prov*

**begin** [bɪ·'gɪn] <-nn-, began, begun>
**I.** *vt* commencer; **to** ~ **work/a phase**
commencer le travail/une phase; **to** ~ **a
conversation** engager la conversation;
**to** ~ **to count** [*o* **counting**] commencer à compter **II.** *vi* (*start*) commencer;
**to** ~ **with** premièrement; **to** ~ **with a
song** commencer par une chanson

**beginner** [bɪ·'gɪn·ər] *n* débutant(e)
*m(f);* **absolute** ~ novice *mf*

**beginning** [bɪ·'gɪn·ɪŋ] **I.** *n* ❶ (*start*)
commencement *m; at* [*o in*] **the** ~ au début; **from**
~ **to end** du début à la fin; **to make a** ~
faire ses débuts ❷ (*origin*) origine *f;* **the**
~ **of humanity** l'aube *f* de l'humanité
**II.** *adj* initial(e)

**begun** [bɪ·'gʌn] *pp of* **begin**

**behalf** [bɪ·'hæf] *n* **on** ~ **of** au nom [*o* de
la part] **de sb** agir pour le
compte de qn

**behave** [bɪ·'heɪv] **I.** *vi* ❶ (*act: people*)
se comporter; (*object, substance*) réagir; **to** ~ **calmly in a crisis** garder son
calme pendant une crise; **to** ~ **strangely** se conduire bizarrement ❷ (*act in
proper manner*) bien se tenir; **to** ~
**well/badly** bien/mal se tenir; ~! tiens-
toi bien! ❸ (*function*) fonctionner **II.** *vt*
**to** ~ **oneself** se tenir bien

**behavior** [bɪ·'heɪ·vjər] *n* comportement *m; to be on one's best* ~ bien se
tenir

**behead** [bɪ·'hed] *vt* décapiter

**behind** [bɪ·'haɪnd] **I.** *prep* ❶ (*at the
back of*) derrière; **right** ~ **sb/sth** juste
derrière qn/qc; ~ **the wheel** au volant;

**B**

~ **the scenes** dans les coulisses ② (*hidden by*) **a face** ~ **a mask** un visage caché sous un masque ③ (*responsible for*) **who is** ~ **this?** qui se cache derrière ce projet?; **there is something** ~ **this** il y a quelque chose là-dessous ④ (*in support of*) **to be** ~ **sb/sth all the way** soutenir qn/qc à cent pour cent ⑤ (*late*) ~ **time** en retard; **to be/ get** ~ **schedule** être en/prendre du retard ⑥ (*less advanced than*) **to be** ~ **sb/the times** être en retard sur qn/son temps **II.** *adv* ① (*at the back*) derrière; **to stay** ~ rester en arrière; **to fall** ~ prendre du retard ② (*late*) en arrière; **to be** ~ **with sth** être en retard en qc; **to get** ~ **in sth** prendre du retard dans qc; **my watch is an hour** ~ ma montre retarde d'une heure ③ (*where one was*) **to leave one's bag** ~ oublier son sac; **to stay** ~ rester après les autres **III.** *n* ① (*buttocks*) postérieur *m*

**beige** [berʒ] *adj, n* beige; *s.a.* blue

**being** ['bi·ɪŋ] **I.** *present participle of* **be** **II.** *n* ① (*living thing*) être *m;* ~ **from another planet** créature *f* extraterrestre ② (*existence*) **to bring sth into** ~ concrétiser qc; **to come into** ~ prendre naissance **III.** *adj* **for the time** ~ pour l'instant

**Belgian** ['bel·dʒən] **I.** *adj* belge **II.** *n* Belge *mf*

**Belgium** ['bel·dʒəm] *n* la Belgique

**belief** [bɪ·'lif] *n* ① (*conviction*) conviction *f;* **to the best of my** ~ pour autant que je sache (*subj*); **in the** ~ **that …** convaincu que … ② REL foi *f;* **religious** ~**s** croyances *fpl* religieuses ③ (*trust*) foi *f;* **your** ~ **in yourself** ta confiance en toi-même

**believable** [bɪ·'li·və·bl] *adj* vraisemblable

**believe** [bɪ·'liv] *vt* ① (*presume true*) croire; ~ **you me!** *inf* crois-moi/croyez-moi!; **to make** ~ (**that**) … prétendre que … ② (*show surprise*) **not to** ~ **one's eyes/ears** ne pas en croire ses yeux/oreilles; **not to** ~ **one's luck** ne pas en revenir; **seeing is believing** il

faut le voir pour le croire ③ (*think*) croire

**bell** [bel] *n* ① (*object*) cloche *f;* (*bicycle, door*) sonnette *f* ② (*signal*) timbre *m* ▶ **alarm** [*o* **warning**] ~**s rang in sb's head** une petite lampe rouge s'est allumée dans la tête de qn; **that rings a** ~ ça me dit quelque chose

**bellboy** ['bel·bɔɪ] *n* groom *m*

**belligerent** [bɪ·'lɪdʒ·ᵊr·ənt] *adj* ① (*at war*) hostile; ~ **nation** pays belligérant ② (*aggressive*) querelleur(-euse)

**belly** ['bel·i] <-ies> *n inf* ventre *m;* (*of animal*) panse *f* ▶ **to go** ~ **up** *inf* tourner court

**belly flop** *n inf* SPORTS plat *m*

**belong** [bɪ·'lɔŋ] *vi* ① (*be the property*) **to** ~ **to sb** appartenir à qn ② (*be in right place*) se ranger; **to** ~ **together** aller ensemble; **to put sth back where it** ~**s** remettre qc à sa place; **this doesn't** ~ **here** cela n'a rien à faire ici; **to** ~ **to a club/church** appartenir à un club/une église

**belongings** *npl* affaires *fpl;* **personal** ~ effets *mpl* personnels

**below** [bɪ·'lou] **I.** *prep* ① (*lower than, underneath*) ~ **the table/surface** sous la table/surface; ~ **us/sea level** au-dessous de nous/du niveau de la mer; **the sun sinks** ~ **the horizon** le soleil disparaît à l'horizon ② (*less than*) ~ **freezing/average** au-dessous de zéro/de la moyenne; **it's 4 degrees** ~ **zero** il fait moins 4; **children** ~ **the age of twelve** les enfants de moins de douze ans ③ (*inferior to*) **to be** ~ **sb in rank** être d'un rang inférieur à qn; **to work** ~ **sb** être subordonné à qn **II.** *adv* ① (*lower down*) **there is sth** ~ en bas [*o* plus bas], il y a qc; **from** ~ venant d'en bas ② (*further in text*) **see** ~ voir ci-dessous ③ REL **here** ~ ici-bas; **down** ~ en enfer

**belt** [belt] **I.** *n* ① **a.** SPORTS, AUTO ceinture *f;* **blow below the** ~ coup *m* bas ② TECH sangle *f* ③ (*area*) zone *f* ④ *inf* (*punch*) gnon *m* ▶ **to tighten one's** ~ se serrer la ceinture **II.** *vt* ① (*secure*) sangler ② *inf* (*hit*) flanquer un coup à

III. *vi inf* se précipiter; **to ~ along** foncer

◆**belt out** *vt inf* chanter à pleine voix
◆**belt up** *vi* (*fasten*) attacher sa ceinture (de sécurité)

**bench** [ben(t)ʃ] *n* **①** (*seat*) banc *m* **②** SPORTS **the ~** la touche **③** LAW **the ~** [*o* **Bench**] (*judges*) la magistrature; (*judge trying a case*) la cour **④** (*workbench*) établi *m*

**bend** [bend] <bent, bent> I. *n* **①** (*curve*) courbe *f;* (*in pipe*) coude *m;* **to take a ~** AUTO prendre un virage **②** *pl, inf* (*illness*) mal *m* des caissons II. *vi* (*wood*) fléchir; (*path*) tourner; (*body*) courber; (*arm, leg*) se replier; (*frame*) se tordre III. *vt* (*make sth change direction*) **to ~ one's arms/knees** plier les bras/genoux ▸ **to ~ sb's ear** glisser un mot à l'oreille de qn; **to ~ the truth** déformer la vérité

◆**bend back** I. *vt* redresser II. *vi* se pencher en arrière
◆**bend down** *vi* s'incliner

**beneath** [bɪˈniːθ] I. *prep* sous, au-dessous de; *s.* **below** II. *adv* (*lower down*) (au-)dessous, en bas

**beneficial** *adj* profitable

**benefit** [ˈben·ɪ·fɪt] I. *n* **①** (*profit*) avantage *m,* bienfait *m;* **~ of independence** avantage de l'indépendance; **to derive** (**much**) **~ from sth** tirer profit *m* de qc; **for the ~ of sb** pour qn; **with the ~ of hindsight** avec le recul; **to the ~ of sth/sb** au profit de qc/qn; **to give sb the ~ of the doubt** accorder à qn le bénéfice du doute **②** (*perk from job*) avantage *m* **③** (*welfare payment*) prestations *fpl* sociales; **welfare ~s** avantages *mpl* sociaux II. <-t- *o* -tt-> *vi* **to ~ from sth** profiter de qc; **who do you think ~s from her death?** à qui croyez-vous que sa mort profiterait? III. <-t- *o* -tt-> *vt* profiter à

**bent** [bent] I. *pt, pp of* **bend** II. *n* **~ for sth** dispositions *fpl* pour qc III. *adj* **①** (*determined*) **to be ~ on sth** être déterminé à (faire) qc **②** (*twisted*) tordu(e) **③** (*stooped*) voûté(e)

**beret** [bəˈreɪ] *n* béret *m*
**berry** [ˈber·i] <-ies> *n* baies *fpl*
**berserk** [bərˈsɜrk] *adj* fou furieux (folle furieuse); **to go ~** être pris de folie furieuse

**berth** [bɜrθ] I. *n* **①** RAIL couchette *f* **②** NAUT (*for sailor*) bannette *f;* (*for ship*) mouillage *m* ▸ **to give sb/sth a wide ~** se tenir à l'écart de qn/qc II. *vt* (*ship*) amarrer

**beside** [bɪˈsaɪd] *prep* **①** (*next to*) auprès de; **right ~ sth/sb** juste à côté de qn/qc **②** (*together with*) **to work ~ sb** travailler aux côtés de qn **③** (*in comparison to*) **~ sth/sb** comparé à [*o* en comparaison de] qc/qn ▸ **to be ~ oneself with joy/worry** être comme fou de joie/d'inquiétude; **to be ~ the point** n'avoir rien à voir; *s.a.* **besides**

**besides** [bɪˈsaɪdz] I. *prep* **①** (*in addition to*) outre; **~ sth/sb** en plus de qc/sans compter qn **②** (*except for*) hormis; **~ sth/sb** à part qc/excepté qn II. *adv* **①** (*in addition*) en outre; **many more ~** bien d'autres encore [*else*] **nothing ~** rien de plus **③** (*moreover*) d'ailleurs

**best** [best] I. *adj superl of* **good** meilleur(e); **~ wishes** meilleurs vœux; **~ friend** meilleur(e) ami(e); **to want what is ~** vouloir ce qu'il y a de mieux; **it's ~ to** +*infin* il est préférable de +*infin* ▸ **the ~ part** la majeure partie; **to be sb's ~ bet** *inf* être ce que qn a de mieux à faire II. *adv superl of* **well** mieux; **we'd ~ be going now** on ferait mieux d'y aller; **to do as ~ one can** faire de son mieux III. *n* **①** (*the finest*) **the ~** le meilleur/la meilleure; **all the ~!** *inf* (*as toast*) santé!; (*saying goodbye*) à la prochaine!; (*wishing luck*) bonne chance!; **to be in the ~ of health** être en pleine santé; **to the ~ of my knowledge/power** autant que je sache/puisse (*subj*); **to be at one's ~** être au meilleur de sa forme; **to do/try one's best** [*o* **very**] **~** faire/essayer de son mieux; **to want the ~** vouloir ce qu'il y a de mieux; (*perspective*) **at ~**

**B**

au mieux; **this is journalism at its ~** ça c'est du vrai journalisme; **~ of luck with your exam!** bonne chance pour ton examen!; **at the ~ of times** même quand tout va bien ❸ SPORTS **to get the ~ of sb** *a. fig* triompher sur qn; **to play the ~ of three** jouer en trois sets **IV.** *vt form* battre

**bestseller** *n* best-seller *m*

**bet** [bet] <-tt-, bet *o* -ted, bet *o* -ted> **I.** *n* pari *m;* **to do sth for** [*o* on] **a ~** faire qc par défi; **to be the best ~** être ce qu'il y a de mieux à faire; **to place a ~ on sth** parier sur qc; **to make a ~ with sb** parier avec qn **II.** *vt* parier ▶ (**how much**) **do you want to ~?** tu paries (combien)?; **I'll ~!** *inf* et comment!; **you ~!** *inf* tu paries! **III.** *vi* parier; **to ~ on a horse** miser sur un cheval; **don't ~ on it!** *inf* ne compte pas dessus!

**betray** [bɪˈtreɪ] *vt* trahir

**better** [ˈbeɪ̯ər] **I.** *adj comp of* **good** ❶ (*finer, superior*) meilleur(e); **~ luck next time** plus de chance la prochaine fois; **it's ~ that way** c'est mieux comme ça; **much ~** beaucoup mieux; **to be ~ at sth** être meilleur à qc; **to be ~ at singing than sb** chanter mieux que qn ❷ (*healthier*) **to be ~** aller mieux; **to get ~** (*improve*) aller mieux; (*be cured*) être guéri ❸ (*most of*) **the ~ part** la majeure partie ▶ **discretion is the ~ part of valor** *prov* mieux vaut ne pas se faire remarquer; **~ late than never** *prov* mieux vaut tard que jamais *prov;* **~ safe than sorry** *prov* mieux vaut prévenir que guérir *prov;* **to go one ~** faire mieux **II.** *adv comp of* **well** ❶ (*manner*) **dressed/written** mieux habillé(e)/écrit(e); **to do much ~** faire beaucoup mieux; **to like sth much ~ than sth** aimer qc beaucoup plus que qc; **~ or still ...** mieux encore ... ❷ (*degree*) plus; **to be ~-known for sth than sth** être surtout connu pour qc plutôt que pour qc ❸ (*more advisably*) **you had ~ do sth** il faut que tu fasses qc (*subj*); **to think ~ of it** changer d'avis (après réflexion) **III.** *n*

❶ mieux *m;* **the more you do sth, the ~ it is** plus tu fais qc et meilleur c'est; **to change for the ~** changer en mieux; **the sooner, the ~** le plus tôt sera le mieux; **so much the ~** encore mieux ❷ *pl, fig* **sb's ~s** ceux qui sont supérieurs à qn ▶ **to get the ~ of sb** triompher de qn; **for ~ or** (**for**) **worse** pour le meilleur ou pour le pire **IV.** *vt* ❶ (*beat: time*) améliorer ❷ (*go further than*) renchérir sur ❸ (*in standing*) améliorer; **to ~ oneself** s'élever

**between** [bɪˈtwin] **I.** *prep* ❶ (*in middle of, within*) entre; **~ times** entre-temps ❷ (*in time*) **to eat ~ meals** manger entre les repas; **~ now and tomorrow** d'ici (à) demain ❸ (*interaction*) **a match ~ them** un match les opposant; **to do sth ~ the two of us** faire qc à nous deux; **~ ourselves** entre nous ❹ (*among*) **the 3 children have $10 ~ them** les 3 enfants *mpl* ont 10 dollars en tout; **nothing will come ~ them** rien ne les séparera; **~ you and me** entre nous ❺ (*combination of*) **the mule is a cross ~ a donkey and a horse** le mulet est un croisement entre l'âne et le cheval **II.** *adv* au milieu, dans l'intervalle ▶ **few and far** ~ rare, clairsemé; *s.a.* **in between**

**beverage** [ˈbevˈərˌɪdʒ] *n form* boisson *f,* breuvage *m Québec;* **alcoholic ~s** boissons alcoolisées

**beware** [bɪˈwer] **I.** *vi* être prudent; **~!** soyez prudents!; **~ of pickpockets!** méfiez-vous des pickpockets!; **beware of the dog** attention, chien méchant!; **to ~ of sb/sth** prendre garde à qn/qc **II.** *vt* se méfier de

**beyond** [bɪˈ(j)ɑnd] **I.** *prep* ❶ (*other side of*) **~ the mountain** au-delà de la montagne; **don't go ~ the line!** ne dépasse pas la ligne!; **from ~ the grave** d'outre-tombe ❷ (*after*) **~ the river/ 8 o'clock** après le fleuve/8 heures; **~ lunchtime** passé l'heure du repas ❸ (*further than*) **to see/go** (**way**) **~ sth** voir/aller (bien) au-delà de qc; **it goes ~ a joke** ça n'a plus rien de drôle;

**B**

~ **belief** incroyable; ~ **repair** irréparable; **he is** ~ **help** *iron, pej* on ne peut plus rien pour lui; ~ **the shadow of a doubt** sans le moindre doute ❹ (*too difficult for*) **to be** ~ **sb** dépasser qn; **it's** ~ **me** ça me dépasse; **it's** ~ **my abilities** c'est au-delà de mes compétences ❺ (*more than*) **to live** ~ **one's income** vivre au-dessus de ses moyens; **to go** ~ **just doing sth** ne pas se limiter à faire qc ❻ *with neg or interrog* (*except for*) ~ **sth** à part qc II. *adv* ❶ (*past*) ~ **the mountains** les montagnes *fpl* au loin ❷ (*future*) **the next ten years and** ~ la prochaine décennie et au-delà III. *n* **the** ~ REL l'au-delà *m*

**Bible** ['baɪ·bl] *n* Bible *f*

**bicycle** ['baɪ·sɪ·kl] *n* vélo *m;* ~ **ride** tour *m* de vélo; **to get on one's** ~ monter à vélo; **to ride a** ~ rouler à vélo; **by** ~ à vélo

**bid¹** [bɪd] <-dd-, bid *o* bade, bid *o* -den> *vt form* ❶ (*greet*) **to** ~ **sb good morning** dire bonjour à qn; **to** ~ **sb welcome** souhaiter la bienvenue à qn ❷ (*command*) **to** ~ **sb to** +*infin* ordonner à qn de +*infin*

**bid²** [bɪd] I. *n* ❶ (*offer*) offre *f* ❷ (*attempt*) tentative *f;* ~ **for power** tentative pour accéder au pouvoir II. <-dd-, bid, bid> *vi* faire une offre III. <-dd-, bid, bid> *vt* offrir

**bidder** ['bɪd·ər] *n* (*for auction lot*) offrant *m;* (*for contract*) candidat *m* à un appel d'offres; **the highest** ~ le plus offrant

**big** [bɪg] <-ger, -gest> *adj* ❶ (*large*) grand(e); (*oversized*) gros(se); ~ **game** gros gibier *m;* ~ **drop in prices** forte baisse *f* des prix; ~ **eater** *inf* gros mangeur *m;* **to be a** ~ **spender** *inf* dépenser beaucoup; ~ **tip** gros pourboire *m;* ~ **toe** gros orteil *m;* **the** ~**ger the better** plus c'est gros, mieux c'est; **the** ~**gest-ever egg** le plus grand œuf (jamais vu) ❷ (*grown-up*) *a. fig* grand(e); ~ **boy/brother** grand garçon/frère ❸ (*important*) grand(e); **he's** ~ **in his country** il est célèbre dans son pays;

~ **shot** *inf* gros bonnet *m;* ~ **day** grand jour *m;* **she's** ~ [*o* **a** ~ **name**] **in finance** elle est connue dans le monde de la finance ❹ *inf* (*great*) super; **in a** ~ **way** quelque chose de bien; **to be** ~ **on sth** être dingue de qc ❺ (*generous*) **it's really** ~ **of sb** *iron* c'est vraiment généreux de la part de qn ▸ **to be too** ~ **for one's boots** *inf* avoir la grosse tête; **the** ~ **boys** les gros bonnets *mpl;* ~ **deal!** *inf* et alors!; **no** ~ **deal** *inf* c'est rien; **what's the** ~ **idea?** *iron, inf* qu'est-ce que ça veux dire?; **to make it** ~ *inf* avoir du succès

**Big Apple** *n* **the** ~ *New York*

**big business** *n* les grandes entreprises *fpl;* **to be** ~ être du business

**Big Easy** *n* **the** ~ *La Nouvelle-Orléans*

**bike** [baɪk] I. *n* ❶ *inf* vélo *m,* **to get on a** ~ monter à vélo; **to ride a** ~ rouler à vélo ❷ (*motorcycle*) moto *f* II. *vi inf* rouler à vélo

**bikini** [bɪ·'ki·ni] *n* bikini *m*

**bilingual** [baɪ·'lɪŋ·gwəl] *adj* bilingue

**bill¹** [bɪl] I. *n* ❶ (*invoice*) facture *f;* (*for meal*) addition *f;* **to put it on sb's** ~ le mettre sur la note de qn; **to foot the** ~ payer la facture; *fig* payer les pots cassés ❷ (*paper money*) billet *m* ❸ LAW projet *m* de loi ❹ (*poster*) affiche *f* ▸ **to give sb/sth a clean** ~ **of health** trouver qn/qc en parfait état II. *vt* ❶ (*invoice*) facturer; **to** ~ **sb for sth** facturer qc à qn ❷ (*announce*) **to** ~ **sth as sth** déclarer qc comme qc

**bill²** [bɪl] *n* bec *m*

**billboard** ['bɪl·bɔrd] *n* panneau *m* d'affichage

**billiards** ['bɪl·jərdz] *n* billard *m*

**billion** ['bɪl·jən] I. *n* milliard *m* II. *adj* milliard *m*

**bimonthly** [,baɪ·'mʌn(t)θ·li] I. *adj* ❶ (*twice a month*) bimensuel(le) ❷ (*every two months*) bimestriel(le) II. *adv* ❶ (*twice a month*) deux fois par mois ❷ (*every two months*) tous les deux mois

**bin** [bɪn] *n* (*storage*) boîte *f*

**bind** [baɪnd] I. *n inf* **to be in some-**

**B**

**thing of a ~** *inf* être un peu dans le pétrin; **to put sb in a real ~** mettre qn dans le pétrin **II.**<bound, bound> *vi* lier **III.**<bound, bound> *vt* ❶ *(tie)* attacher; **to ~ sth/sb to sth** attacher qn/qc à qc; **to be bound hand and foot** être pieds et poings liés ❷ *(unite)* **to ~** *(together)* lier ensemble ❸ *(commit)* **to ~ sb to** +*infin* obliger qn à +*infin* ❹ TYP *(book)* relier ❺ *(when cooking)* lier

**binding** ['baɪnd·ɪŋ] **I.** *n* ❶ TYP reliure *f* ❷ FASHION ganse *f* **II.** *adj* obligatoire; **~ agreement** accord *m* qui engage

**bingo** ['bɪŋ·goʊ] **I.** *n* bingo *m* **II.** *interj inf* ~! et voilà!

**binoculars** [bɪ·'na·kjə·lərz] *npl* jumelles *fpl*

**biodegradable** [ˌbaɪ·oʊ·dɪ·'greɪ·də·bl] *adj* biodégradable

**biodiversity** [ˌbaɪ·oʊ·dɪ'vɜr·sə·t̬i] *n* biodiversité *f*

**biological** [ˌbaɪ·ə·'la·dʒɪ·kəl] *adj* biologique

**biologist** [baɪ·'a·lə·dʒɪst] *n* biologiste *mf*

**biology** [baɪ·'a·lə·dʒi] *n* biologie *f*

**birch** [bɜrtʃ] *n* ❶ *(tree)* bouleau *m* ❷ *(stick)* fouet *m*

**bird** [bɜrd] *n* ❶ *(animal)* oiseau *m*; **caged ~** oiseau en cage ❷ *inf (person)* type *m*; **strange ~** drôle *m* d'oiseau ▶ **to know about the ~s and bees** savoir que les bébés ne naissent pas dans les choux; **~s of a feather flock together** *prov* qui se ressemble s'assemble *prov*; **a ~ in the hand is worth two in the bush** *prov* un tiens vaut mieux que deux tu l'auras *prov*; **to kill two ~s with one stone** faire d'une pierre deux coups *prov*; **to feel free as a ~** se sentir libre comme l'air; **to be** *(strictly)* **for the ~s** *inf* être nul

**bird's-eye view** *n* vue *f* aérienne

**birth** [bɜrθ] *n* naissance *f*; **at/from ~** à la/de naissance; **date/place of ~** date *f*/lieu *m* de naissance; **to give ~ to sth** *a. fig* donner naissance à qc

**birth certificate** *n* acte *m* de naissance

**birth control** *n* contrôle *m* des naissances

**birthday** ['bɜrθ·deɪ] *n* anniversaire *m*; **happy ~!** joyeux anniversaire!

**biscuit** ['bɪs·kɪt] *n* petit pain *m*

**bishop** ['bɪʃ·əp] *n* ❶ REL évêque *m* ❷ *(chess piece)* fou *m*

**bit**¹ [bɪt] *n* ❶ *inf (fragment)* morceau *m*; **a ~ of meat/cloth/land** un bout de viande/tissu/terrain; **~ by ~** petit à petit; **to stay/wait for a ~** *inf* rester/attendre pendant un instant ❷ *(some)* **a** *(little)* **~** un peu; **a ~ of sth** un peu de qc; **not a ~** pas du tout; **quite a ~ of sth** assez de qc ▶ **a ~ of a** un peu; **we have a ~ of a problem** on a un petit problème

**bit**² [bɪt] *pt of* **bite**

**bit**³ [bɪt] *n* ❶ *(for horses)* mors *m* ❷ *(tool)* mèche *f*

**bit**⁴ [bɪt] *n* COMPUT *abbr of* **binary digit** bit *m*

**bitch** [bɪtʃ] **I.** *n* ❶ ZOOL chienne *f* ❷ *inf (woman)* garce *f* **II.** *vi inf* **to ~ about sb/sth** rouspéter contre qn/qc

**bite** [baɪt] **I.**<bit, bitten> *vt* mordre; *(insect)* piquer; **to ~ one's nails** se ronger les ongles; **to ~ sth off** arracher qc avec les dents **II.**<bit, bitten> *vi* ❶ *(when eating, attacking)* mordre; *(insect)* piquer; **to ~ into/through sth** mordre dans/à travers qc; **sb/sth won't** *(you)* *iron* qn/qc ne va pas te mordre ❷ *(in angling)* mordre ▶ **once bitten, twice shy** *prov* chat échaudé craint l'eau froide *prov* **III.** *n* ❶ *(of dog, snake)* morsure *f*; *(of insect)* piqûre *f*; *fig (of wind)* morsure *f*; *(of speech)* mordant *m*; *(of taste)* piquant *m* ❷ *(food)* bouchée *f*; **to have a ~ to eat** manger un morceau; **to take a big ~ of sth** prendre une grosse bouchée de qc; **to take a big ~ out of one's salary** *fig* prendre un gros morceau du salaire de quelqu'un ❸ *(in angling)* touche *f*

**bitten** ['bɪt·ən] *pp of* **bite**

**bitter** ['bɪt̬·ər] <-er, -est> *adj* ❶ *(acrid) a. fig* amer(-ère) ❷ *(intense: cold)* rude;

(*wind*) glacial(e); (*dispute*) âpre; (*tone*) acerbe; **to the ~ end** jusqu'au bout

**bitterly** *adv* ❶ (*painfully*) amèrement ❷ (*intensely*) extrêmement; **it's ~ cold** il fait rudement froid; (*suffer*) cruellement

**black** [blæk] **I.** *adj* noir(e); **Black American** Noir *m* américain; **~ arts** magie *f* noire; **~ coffee** café *m* noir; **Black Death** peste *f* noire ▸ **everything's ~ and white with her** pour elle tout est tout blanc ou tout noir **II.** *n* ❶ (*color*) noir *m* ❷ (*person*) Black Noir(e) *m(f)* ▸ **in ~ and white** écrit noir sur blanc; *s.a.* **blue**

**black-and-white** *adj* (*photo, television*) (en) noir et blanc

**blackberry** <-ies> *n* mûre *f*

**blackbird** *n* merle *m*

**blackboard** *n* tableau *m* noir

**black hat** *n* COMPUT chapeau *m* noir, pirate *m* informatique

**blacklist I.** *n* liste *f* noire **II.** *vt* mettre à l'index

**black market** *n* marché *m* noir

**black-marketer** *n* trafiquant(e) *m(f)*

**blackout** ['blæk·aʊt] *n* ❶ TV, RADIO interruption *f* ❷ (*censor, turning off of lights*) black-out *m* ❸ ELEC panne *f* de courant ❹ (*faint*) évanouissement *m* ❺ (*lapse of memory*) trou *m* de mémoire

**Black Sea** *n* **the ~** la Mer Noire

**blacksmith** *n* forgeron *m*

**blade**[1] [bleɪd] *n* lame *f*; (*on helicopter*) pale *f*; (*of wipers*) balai *m*; **~ of grass** brin *m* d'herbe

**blade**[2] [bleɪd] *vi inf* faire du roller

**blah-blah-blah** *interj inf* blablabla

**blame** [bleɪm] **I.** *vt* **to ~ sb/sth for sth** reprocher qc à qn/qc; **to ~ sth on sb/ sth** attribuer la responsabilité de qc à qn/qc; **I ~ myself** je m'en veux **II.** *n* reproches *mpl*; **to put the ~ on sb** mettre la faute sur le dos de qn

**bland** [blænd] *adj* insipide

**blank** [blæŋk] **I.** *adj* ❶ (*empty*) blanc(blanche); (*tape*) vierge; **~ check** chèque *m* en blanc; **~ page** page *f* blan-

che; **~ space** blanc *m;* **my mind's gone ~** j'ai la tête vide ❷ (*impassive: expression look*) absent(e) ❸ (*complete: refusal*) total(e) **II.** *n* ❶ (*space*) blanc *m* ❷ (*cartridge*) balle *f* à blanc ▸ **to draw a ~** faire chou blanc

**blanket** ['blæŋ·kɪt] **I.** *n* (*cover*) couverture *f*; *fig* (*of snow*) couche *f*; (*of fog*) nappe *f*; **II.** *vt* couvrir **III.** *adj* global(e); LING (*term*) général(e)

**blast** [blæst] **I.** *vt a. fig* faire sauter **II.** *vi* retentir **III.** *n* ❶ (*detonation*) détonation *f* ❷ (*gust of wind*) rafale *f* ❸ (*noise*) bruit *m* soudain; (*of whistle, horn*) coup *m* ❹ *inf* (*fun*) **it was a ~!** c'était génial! **IV.** *interj inf* **~ it!** merde alors!

**blaze** [bleɪz] **I.** *n* ❶ (*fire: for warmth*) feu *m*; (*out of control*) incendie *m* ❷ (*conflagration*) embrasement *m* ❸ *fig* **~ of color/light** déploiement *m* de couleurs/lumières; **in a ~ of publicity/glory** sous les trompettes de la publicité/de la gloire **II.** *vi* flamber **III.** *vt a. fig* **to ~ a trail** montrer la voie ◆ **blaze up** *vi* s'embraser

**bleach** [blitʃ] **I.** *vt* ❶ (*whiten*) blanchir; (*hair*) décolorer; (*spot*) javelliser ❷ (*disinfect*) javelliser **II.** *n* agent *m* blanchissant; (*cleaning product*) eau *m* de Javel

**bleachers** ['bli·tʃərz] *n pl* gradins *mpl*

**bleak** [blik] *adj* morne

**bled** [bled] *pt, pp of* **bleed**

**bleed** [blid] <bled, bled> **I.** *vi* saigner **II.** *vt* ❶ HIST saigner ❷ TECH, AUTO purger

**bleeding** *n* saignement *m*

**blend** [blend] **I.** *n* mélange *m* **II.** *vt* mélanger; (*wine*) couper **III.** *vi* se mélanger; (*colors*) s'harmoniser; **to ~ with sth** se marier avec qc

**blender** [blen·dər] *n* mixeur *m*

**bless** [bles] *vt* bénir; **~ you!** (*after sneeze*) à vos souhaits!; (*in thanks*) c'est tellement gentil!; **to be ~ed with sth** avoir le bonheur de posséder qc

**blessing** ['bles·ɪŋ] *n* bénédiction *f*

**blew** [blu] *pt of* **blow**

**blind** [blaɪnd] **I.** *n* ❶ (*window shade*)

**B**

store *m* ❷ (*subterfuge*) prétexte *m* ❸ *pl* (*people*) **the ~** les aveugles *mpl* ❹ (*in hunting*) affût *m* **II.** *vt a. fig* aveugler; **to ~ sb to sth** aveugler qn devant qc **III.** *adj* ❶ (*unable to see*) aveugle; **~ in one eye** borgne; **to be ~ to sth** *a. fig* être aveugle à qc ❷ (*hidden*) sans visibilité; (*door*) dérobé(e) **► as ~ as a bat** myope comme une taupe; **to turn a ~ eye** to sth fermer les yeux sur qc **IV.** *adv* à l'aveuglette; **~ drunk** *inf* complètement soûl

**blindfolded I.** *adj* aux yeux bandés **II.** *adv a. fig* les yeux fermés

**blind spot** *n* ❶ AUTO angle *m* mort ❷ *fig* point *m* faible

**bling** [blɪŋ] *sl* **I.** *n* bijoux *mpl* clinquants **II.** *adj* (*look, outfit*) flashy; (*person*) frimeur *inf*

**blink** [blɪŋk] **I.** *vt* ANAT **to ~ one's eyes** cligner des yeux **II.** *vi* cligner des yeux **III.** *n* (*act of blinking*) battement *m* des paupières; **in the ~ of an eye** *fig* en un clin d'œil **► sth is on the ~** *inf* qc est détraqué

**blister** ['blɪs·tər] **I.** *n* ❶ (*on skin*) ampoule *f* ❷ (*on paint*) cloque *f* ❸ (*in glass*) bulle *f* **II.** *vt* provoquer des cloques sur **III.** *vi* (*paint, metal*) cloquer; (*skin*) avoir des ampoules

**blizzard** ['blɪz·ərd] *n* tempête *f* de neige, poudrerie *f* *Québec*

**block** [blɑk] **I.** *n* ❶ (*solid lump of sth*) bloc *m*; (*of wood*) tronçon *m* ❷ COMPUT bloc *m* ❸ ARCHIT pâté *m* de maisons; **two ~s** away à deux rues d'ici ❹ (*barrier*) *a. fig* entrave *f*; **~ to sth** obstacle *m* à qc; **mental ~** PSYCH blocage *m* ❺ GAMES **building ~** cube *m* de construction **II.** *vt* (*road, passage*) bloquer; (*pipe*) boucher

  ◆**block off** *vt* (*road*) barrer

  ◆**block out** *vt* (*light*) bloquer; (*thoughts*) bloquer

  ◆**block up** *vt* boucher

**blockbuster** ['blɑk·ˌbʌs·tər] **I.** *n* grand succès *m*; (*book*) best-seller *m* **II.** *adj* à grand succès; (*film*) à grand spectacle

**blond(e)** [blɑnd] **I.** *adj* (*hair*) blond(e); (*complexion*) de blond(e) **II.** *n* blond(e) *m(f)*; **natural ~** vrai(e) blond(e)

**blood** [blʌd] *n a. fig* sang *m*; **to give ~** donner son sang **► to have ~ on one's hands** avoir du sang sur les mains; **~ is thicker than water** la voix du sang est la plus forte; **bad ~** animosité *f*; **in cold ~** de sang froid; **to have sth in one's ~** avoir qc dans le sang

**blood pressure** *n* tension *f* artérielle; **high ~** hypertension *f*; **low ~** hypotension *f*

**bloodshot** *adj* injecté(e) de sang

**blood test** *n* analyse *f* de sang

**bloody** ['blʌd·i] <-ier, -iest> *adj* ❶ (*with blood*) ensanglanté(e) ❷ *fig* sanglant(e)

**bloom** [blum] **I.** *n* fleur *f*; **to be in full ~** être en fleur(s) **II.** *vi a. fig* fleurir

**blossom** ['blɑs·əm] **I.** *n* fleur *f* **II.** *vi* ❶ (*flower*) fleurir ❷ *fig* s'épanouir; **to ~ into sth** se transformer en qc

**blouse** [blaʊs] *n* chemisier *m*

**blow**[1] [bloʊ] **I.** <blew, blown> *vi* (*expel air*) souffler; (*whistle*) retentir **► to ~ hot and cold** tergiverser **II.** *vt* ❶ (*expel air*) **to ~ air into a tube** souffler de l'air dans un tube; **the paper was ~n over the wall** le vent a soulevé le papier par-dessus le mur; **to ~ one's nose** se moucher; **to ~ sb a kiss** envoyer un baiser à qn ❷ (*play: trumpet*) souffler dans **► to ~ one's own trumpet** chanter ses propres louanges; **to ~ the whistle on sb** *inf* dénoncer qn **III.** *n* souffle *m*; (*wind*) coup *m* de vent

**blow**[2] [bloʊ] **I.** *n a. fig* coup *m*; **to come to ~s** en venir aux mains; **to soften the ~** amortir le choc; **to strike a ~ for sth** marquer un coup pour qc **II.** <blew, blown> *vi* (*explode*) exploser; (*tire*) éclater; (*fuse*) sauter; (*bulb*) griller **III.** *vt* ❶ (*destroy: fuse*) faire sauter; **to ~ sb's brains out** faire sauter la cervelle de qn ❷ *inf* (*spend*) claquer **► to ~ a fuse** *inf* péter les plombs; **to ~ sb's mind** *inf* époustoufler qn; **to ~ one's top** *inf* piquer une crise

  ◆**blow away I.** *vt* ❶ (*remove*) souffler;

(*wind*) emporter ② *inf* (*kill*) **to blow sb away** flinguer qn ③ *fig, inf* **to be blown away** être stupéfait ④ (*disappear*) s'envoler II. *vi* s'envoler

◆**blow down** I. *vi* s'abattre II. *vt* abattre

◆**blow off** I. *vt* emporter II. *vi* (*fly away*) s'envoler

◆**blow out** I. *vt* ① (*extinguish*) éteindre ② (*puff out*) gonfler II. *vi* ① (*be extinguished*) s'éteindre ② (*explode*) exploser; (*tire*) éclater; (*fuse*) sauter ③ (*fly*) s'envoler

◆**blow over** *vi* se calmer

◆**blow up** I. *vi* a. *fig* éclater; (*with anger*) s'emporter II. *vt* ① (*fill with air*) gonfler ② PHOT agrandir ③ (*destroy*) faire exploser ④ (*exaggerate*) gonfler

**blow-dry** ['bloʊˌdraɪ] I. *vt* **to ~ sb's hair** faire un brushing à qn II. *n* brushing *m*

**blown** [bloʊn] *pp of* **blow**

**blowtorch** ['bloʊˌtɔrtʃ] *n* chalumeau *m*

**blue** [blu] I. *adj* ① (*color*) bleu; **light/dark/bright ~ skirt** jupe *f* bleu clair/foncé/vif; **to turn ~** bleuir ② *fig* **to feel ~** broyer du noir ▶ **once in a ~ moon** tous les trente-six du mois; **out of the ~** sans crier gare II. *n* bleu *m*; **sky ~** bleu ciel; **to be a pale/deep ~** être d'un bleu pâle/profond

**blueberry** ['blu·ber·i] <-ies> *n* myrtille *f*

**blueprint** ['blu·prɪnt] *n a. fig* plan *m*

**blunder** ['blʌn·dɚ] I. *n* gaffe *f* II. *vi* ① (*make a mistake*) faire une gaffe ② (*move*) **to ~ around** tourner à l'aveuglette

**blunt** [blʌnt] I. *adj* ① (*blade*) émoussé(e); **~ instrument** instrument *m* contondant ② *fig* brusque II. *vt a. fig* émousser; **to ~ the impact of sth** atténuer l'impact de qc

**bluntly** *adv* brusquement; **to put it ~, ...** pour parler franchement, ...

**blurred** [blɜrd] *adj* flou(e)

**blush** [blʌʃ] I. *vi* rougir II. *n* rougeur *f*

**board** [bɔrd] I. *n* ① (*wood*) planche *f* ② (*blackboard*) tableau *m* ③ (*notice board*) panneau *m* d'affichage ④ GAMES (*for chess*) échiquier *m*; (*for checkers*) damier *m*; (*for other games*) jeu *m* ⑤ ADMIN conseil *m*; **~ of directors** conseil d'administration; **~ of education** conseil d'établissement ⑥ (*meals*) **room and ~** le gîte et le couvert ⑦ NAUT, AVIAT **to go on ~** monter à bord; (*bus, train*) monter dans, embarquer dans *Québec;* **to take on ~** embarquer; (*fact, situation*) prendre en compte ▶ **across the ~** à tous les niveaux; **to get sb on ~** s'assurer le soutien de qn II. *vt* ① (*cover*) **to ~ sth up** couvrir qc de planches; (*seal*) condamner qc ② (*lodge*) prendre [*o* avoir] en pension ③ (*get on: plane, boat*) monter à bord de; (*bus*) monter dans, embarquer dans *Québec* III. *vi* (*in school*) être pensionnaire; **to ~ with sb** être en pension chez qn

**boarding house** *n* pension *f*

**boast** [boʊst] I. *vi* se vanter; **to ~ about** [*o* of] **sth** se vanter de qc II. *vt* ① **to ~ that ...** se vanter que ... ② (*have: university, industry*) s'enorgueillir de; (*device, feature*) être équipé(e) de III. *n* **it's just a ~** c'est de la frime

**boastful** ['boʊst·fəl] *adj pej* vantard(e)

**boat** [boʊt] *n* bateau *m* ▶ **to be in the same ~** être dans la même galère; **to rock the ~** jouer les trouble-fêtes

**boating** ['boʊ·tɪŋ] *n* canotage *m*

**body** ['ba·di] <-ies> *n* ① (*physical structure*) corps *m*; *fig* (*of wine*) corps *m*; (*of hair*) volume *m* ② (*group*) organisme *m*; **legislative ~** corps législatif ③ (*amount*) masse *f*; (*of water*) étendue *f* ④ (*main part: car*) carrosserie *f*; (*plane*) fuselage *m* ▶ **over my dead ~**! plutôt mourir!; **just enough to keep ~ and soul together** tout juste de quoi subsister

**bodybuilding** *n* culturisme *m*

**bodyguard** *n* garde *mf* du corps

**body language** *n* langage *m* du corps

**bog** [bɔg] *n* (*wet ground*) marécage *m*; **peat ~** tourbière *f*

**bog down** <-gg-> vt to be/get bogged down in sth a. fig s'enliser dans qc

**B** **bogus** ['bou·gəs] adj faux(fausse)

**boil** [bɔɪl] I. n ① no art ébullition f; to bring sth to a ~ porter qc à ébullition ② MED furoncle m II. vi bouillir; to let sth ~ dry laisser le contenu de qc s'évaporer ▸to make sb's blood ~ mettre qn hors de lui III. vt ① (bring to boil) faire bouillir ② (cook in water) bouillir; ~ed potatoes pommes fpl de terre à l'eau; ~ed egg œuf m à la coque

◆**boil away** vi s'évaporer

◆**boil down** I. vi réduire II. vt faire réduire

◆**boil over** vi ① (rise and flow over) déborder ② (go out of control) exploser; to boil (over) with rage bouillir de rage

◆**boil up** I. vt faire bouillir II. vi fig (trouble, situation) surgir

**boiler** ['bɔɪ·lər] n chaudière f, fournaise f Québec

**boiling** adj bouillant(e); to be ~ with rage fig bouillir de rage

**boisterous** ['bɔɪ·st³r·əs] adj énergique

**bold**[1] [bould] <-er, -est> adj ① (brave, striking) audacieux(-euse) ② (aggressive) arrogant(e)

**bold**[2] [bould] n COMPUT, TYP in ~ en caractères gras

**bolt** [boult] I. vi décamper II. vt ① (lock) verrouiller ② (fasten) to ~ sth on(to) sth (with bolt) fixer qc à qc; fig plaquer qc sur qc III. n ① (for locking) verrou m ② (screw) boulon m ③ (lightning) éclair m; ~ of lightning coup m de foudre ④ (roll) rouleau m ⑤ (escape) to make a ~ for it décamper IV. adv to sit ~ upright s'asseoir bien droit

**bomb** [bam] I. n (explosive) bombe f; the Bomb la bombe atomique II. vt bombarder III. vi to ~ inf faire un flop

**bombard** [bam·'bard] vt ① MIL bombarder ② fig to ~ sb with sth bombarder qn de qc

**bone** [boun] I. n ① os m; (of fish) arête f

II. vt (meat) désosser; (fish) retirer les arêtes de

**bonfire** ['ban·faɪ·ər] n feu m de joie

**bonnet** ['ba·nɪt] n (hat) bonnet m

**bonus** ['bou·nəs] n ① (money) prime f; Christmas ~ prime f de fin d'année; productivity ~ prime f de rendement ② (advantage) avantage m ③ fig (sth extra) bonus m

**bony** ['bou·ni] adj <-ier, -iest> ① (with prominent bones) osseux(-euse) ② (full of bones: fish) plein d'arêtes

**boo** [bu] I. interj inf hou II. n, vt, vi <-s, -ing, -ed> huer

**booby trap** I. n piège m II. vt tendre un piège à

**book** [buk] I. n ① (for reading) livre m; (of stamps, tickets) carnet m; the ~s COM les livres mpl de compte; to do the ~s faire les comptes ▸to be in sb's bad ~s ne pas avoir la cote avec qn; to be in sb's good ~s être dans les petits papiers de qn; in my ~ d'après moi; to do things by the ~s faire les choses dans les règles II. vt ① (reserve) réserver ② FIN, COM inscrire; (police) dresser un P.V. à; SPORTS donner un avertissement à III. vi réserver

◆**book up** vt, vi réserver; to be booked up être complet

**booking** ['buk·ɪŋ] n (for room, seat) réservation f

**bookmark** n a. COMPUT signet m

**bookseller** n libraire mf

**bookshelf** n étagère f

**bookstore** n libraire f

**boom**[1] [bum] I. vi être en pleine croissance II. n essor m; construction ~ boom m dans la construction; ~ years années fpl glorieuses

**boom**[2] [bum] I. n grondement m II. vi to ~ (out) résonner; "come in", he ~ed "entrez", dit-il d'une voix sonore III. vt faire retentir

**boom**[3] [bum] n (for microphone) perche f de micro

**booster seat** n AUTO siège m pour enfant

**boot** [but] I. n ① (footwear: calf-length) botte f; (short) boot f ② COMPUT amorce f ► **to get the ~** se faire virer; **to put the ~ in** y aller fort **II.** vt ❶ inf (kick) **to ~ sth somewhere** envoyer qc quelque part (d'un coup de pied) ❷ COMPUT **to ~** amorcer

◆**boot out** vt inf flanquer à la porte

◆**boot up** COMPUT **I.** vt (system, program, computer) lancer **II.** vi démarrer

**booth** [buð] n ❶ (cubicle) cabine f; **voting ~** isoloir m ❷ (stand at fair) stand m

**bootleg** ['but·leg] <-gg-> **I.** adj ❶ (sold illegally) de contrebande ❷ (illegally copied) piraté(e) **II.** vt ❶ (sell illegally) vendre en contrebande ❷ (copy illegally) pirater **III.** vi faire de la contrebande; (media) faire du piratage

**booty**¹ ['bu·ti] n (stolen goods) butin m

**booty**² ['bu·ti] n sl (buttocks) cul m; **shake your ~!** bouge ton cul!

**booze** [buz] inf **I.** n alcool m **II.** vi picoler

**border** ['bɔr·dər] **I.** n ❶ (limit: of country) frontière f ❷ (decoration) bordure f **II.** vt border; **to be ~ed by Germany** avoir l'Allemagne pour pays limitrophe

**bore**¹ [bɔr] **I.** n ❶ (thing) barbe f ❷ (person) raseur, -euse m, f **II.** <-d> vt ennuyer

**bore**² [bɔr] **I.** n ❶ (caliber) calibre m ❷ (deep hole) forage m **II.** vt forer; **to ~ a hole** faire un trou

**boredom** ['bɔr·dəm] n ennui m

**boring** ['bɔr·ɪŋ] adj ennuyeux(-euse), ennuyant(e) Québec

**born** [bɔrn] adj a. fig né(e), **to be ~** naître

**borne** [bɔrn] pt of **bear**

**borough** ['bɜr·oʊ] n municipalité f

**borrow** ['bar·oʊ] vt emprunter

**bosom** ['bʊz·əm] n ❶ poitrine f ❷ fig cœur m

**boss**¹ [bas] **I.** n a. inf chef m **II.** vt pej, inf **to ~ sb around** donner des ordres à qn

**boss**² [bas] adj inf merveilleux(-euse)

**bossy** ['ba·si] <-ier, -iest> adj pej despotique

**botanical** [bə·'tæn·ɪk·əl] adj botanique

**botany** ['ba·t°n·i] n botanique f

**both** [boʊθ] **I.** adj, pron tous (les) deux; **~ of them** l'un et l'autre; **~ of us** nous deux; **on ~ sides** de part et d'autre; **I bought ~ the computer and the printer** j'ai acheté les deux, l'ordinateur et l'imprimante **II.** adv **to be ~ sad and pleased** être à la fois triste et content

**bother** ['ba·ðər] **I.** n ❶ (trouble) ennui m ❷ (annoyance) **it's no ~** il n'y a pas de problème; **I don't want to be a ~** je ne veux pas déranger **II.** vi **don't ~ to ring** ce n'est pas la peine de téléphoner **III.** vt ennuyer, chicaner Québec

**bottle** ['ba·tl] **I.** n (container) bouteille f; **baby ~** biberon m **II.** vt mettre en bouteilles

**bottled** ['ba·tld] adj en bouteille(s); **~ water** eau minérale

**bottom** ['ba·təm] **I.** n ❶ (lowest part) bas m; (of pajamas) pantalon m; (of the sea, a container) fond m; **from top to ~** de haut en bas ❷ (end: of street) bout m; **to be (at the) ~ of one's class** être le dernier de sa classe; **to start at the ~** commencer en bas de l'échelle ❸ (buttocks) derrière m ► **to mean sth from the ~ of one's heart** dire qc du fond du cœur; **to get to the ~ of sth** aller au fond des choses; **to be at the ~ of sth** être derrière qc **II.** adj (level) d'en bas; (jaw) inférieur(e); **bottom end** partie f inférieure; **~ of the table** bout m de la table

**bottom line** n ❶ FIN solde m final ❷ fig **the ~ is that ...** le fond du problème c'est que ...; **what's the ~?** c'est quoi l'essentiel?

**bought** [bɔt] pt of **buy**

**boulder** ['boʊl·dər] n bloc m de pierre

**bounce** [baʊn(t)s] **I.** n ❶ (springing action, rebound) rebond m ❷ (spring) bond m ❸ (bounciness: of hair, bed) ressort m ❹ (vitality, energy) vitalité f **II.** vi ❶ (spring into the air, rebound) rebondir ❷ (jump up and down) bondir ❸ inf COM (check) être refusé **III.** vt

**B**

❶ (*cause to rebound*) faire rebondir; **to ~ a baby on one's knee** faire sauter un bébé sur ses genoux ❷ *inf* COM **to ~ a check** refuser un chèque en bois

◆ **bounce back** *vi* ❶ rebondir ❷ *fig* se remettre

**bouncer** ['baʊn(t)·sər] *n* videur, -euse *m, f*

**bound**[1] [baʊnd] I. *vi* bondir II. *n* bond *m* ▸ **by leaps and ~s** à pas de géant

**bound**[2] [baʊnd] I. *vt* **to be ~ed by sth** être bordé par qc III. *n pl* limites *fpl*; **to be** [*o go*] **beyond the ~s of possibility** dépasser les limites du possible; **to be within the ~s of the law** être légal; **to keep sth within ~s** maintenir qc dans des limites acceptables; **to know no ~s** être sans limites ▸ **out of ~s** interdit

**bound**[3] [baʊnd] *adj* **~ for** en route pour

**bound**[4] [baʊnd] I. *pt, pp of* **bind** II. *adj* ❶ (*sure*) **he's ~ to come** c'est sûr qu'il viendra; **it was ~ to happen sooner or later** cela devait arriver tôt ou tard ❷ (*obliged*) **to be ~ to** +*infin* être obligé de +*infin*

**boundary** ['baʊn·dər·i] <-ies> *n* ❶ (*line, division*) limite *f* ❷ (*border: between countries*) frontière *f* ❸ SPORTS limites *fpl* du terrain ❹ *fig* **to blur the boundaries between sth and sth** estomper les différences entre qc et qc

**bouquet** [boʊ·'keɪ] *n* bouquet *m*

**bout** [baʊt] *n* ❶ (*period*) crise *f*; **~ of coughing** quinte *f* de toux ❷ SPORTS combat *m*

**bow**[1] [boʊ] *n* ❶ (*weapon*) arc *m* ❷ MUS archet *m* ❸ (*slip-knot*) nœud *m*

**bow**[2] [baʊ] *n* NAUT proue *f*

**bow**[3] [baʊ] I. *n* ❶ salut *m* ❷ *fig* **to take one's final ~** faire ses adieux II. *vi* **to ~ to sb/sth** saluer qn/qc; (*defer*) **to ~s** s'en remettre à III. *vt* (*one's head*) baisser

◆ **bow out** *vi* (*stop taking part*) tirer sa révérence

**bowl**[1] [boʊl] *n* ❶ bol *m*; (*for mixing*) saladier *m*; **~ of soup** assiette *f* de soupe ❷ SPORTS (*games*) championnat *m*; (*buil-*

*ding*); **The Hollywood Bowl** le Hollywood Bowl

**bowl**[2] [boʊl] SPORTS I. *vi* jouer au bowling II. *vt* faire rouler

**bowler** ['boʊ·lər] *n* SPORTS joueur, -euse *m, f* de bowling

**bowling** *n* bowling *m*

**bowling alley** *n* ❶ (*lane*) piste *f* de bowling ❷ (*building, room*) bowling *m*

**bow tie** *n* nœud *m* papillon

**box**[1] [baks] *n* ❶ (*container*) boîte *f*; (*of large format*) caisse *f*; (**cardboard**) ~ carton *m*; **tool ~** boîte à outils ❷ (*rectangular space*) case *f* ❸ THEAT loge *f* ❹ (*tree*) buis *m*

**box**[2] [baks] I. *vi* SPORTS faire de la boxe II. *vt* SPORTS boxer

◆ **box in** *vt* coincer

◆ **box up** *vt* mettre dans une boîte

**boxer** ['bak·sər] *n* ❶ (*dog*) boxer *m* ❷ (*person*) boxeur, -euse *m, f* ❸ *pl s.* **boxer shorts**

**boxer shorts** *n pl* boxer *m*

**boxing** ['bak·sɪŋ] *n* boxe *f*

**boxing gloves** *npl* gants *mpl* de boxe

**boxing match** *n* match *m* de boxe

**box number** *n* boîte *f* postale

**box office** *n* guichet *m*; **~ hit** succès *m* au box-office

**boy** [bɔɪ] *n* garçon *m* ▸ **a local ~** un jeune du coin; **to be one of the ~s** faire partie des copains; **~s will be ~s** *prov* il faut que jeunesse se passe *prov*; **the/our ~s** MIL les/nos gars *mpl* II. *interj* **oh ~!** bon sang!

**boyfriend** ['bɔɪ·frend] *n* petit ami *m*

**bra** [bra] *n* soutien-gorge *m*, brassière *f* Québec

**brace** [breɪs] I. *vt* ❶ (*prepare*) **to ~ oneself for sth** se préparer à qc ❷ (*support*) consolider II. *n* ❶ *pl* (*for teeth*) appareil *m* dentaire ❷ (*for leg*) appareil *m* orthopédique ❸ (*for back*) corset *m*

**bracelet** ['breɪs·lət] *n* bracelet *m*

**brag** [bræg] <-gg-> I. *vi pej, inf* **to ~ about sth** se vanter de qc II. *vt pej, inf* **to ~ that ...** se vanter que ...

**braid** [breɪd] **I.** n ❶ (*decoration*) galon m ❷ (*in hair*) tresse f **II.** vt tresser

**Braille** [breɪl] n braille m

**brain** [breɪn] **I.** n ❶ (*organ*) cerveau m; **use your ~(s)!** réfléchis!; ❷ (*intelligence*) intelligence f; **to have ~s** [o **a good ~**] être intelligent ❸ inf (*person*) cerveau m; **the best ~s** les meilleurs talents mpl ▸ **to** <u>blow</u> **sb's ~s out** faire sauter la cervelle à qn; **to** <u>pick</u> **sb's ~s** inf sonder les connaissances de qn **II.** adj cérébral(e)

**brain-dead** adj en état de coma dépassé; **to declare sb ~** conclure à la mort cérébrale de qn

**brain tumor** n tumeur f au cerveau

**brake** [breɪk] **I.** n ❶ AUTO frein m; **to apply** [o **put on**] **the ~s** freiner; **to slam on the ~(s)** inf piler ❷ fig **to put a ~** [o **the ~s**] **on** freiner **II.** vi freiner

**bran** [bræn] n (*of grain*) son m

**branch** [brɑːn(t)ʃ] **I.** n ❶ a. BOT branche f ❷ (*fork: of a river*) bras m; (*of a road*) embranchement m ❸ (*office: of bank*) agence f; (*of company, store*) succursale f ❹ (*division: of organization*) branche f **II.** vi ❶ se ramifier ❷ fig bifurquer

◆**branch off** vi ❶ (*fork*) bifurquer ❷ fig digresser

◆**branch out** vi ❶ (*enter a new field*) **to ~ into sth** étendre ses activités à qc; **to ~ on one's own** s'établir à son compte ❷ (*undertake new activities*) diversifier ses activités

**branch office** n succursale f

**brand** [brænd] **I.** n ❶ (*trade name*) marque f ❷ (*type*) genre m ❸ (*mark*) marque f (au fer) **II.** vt ❶ (*label*) **to be ~ed (as)** sth être catalogué comme qc ❷ (*mark*) **to ~ an animal** marquer un animal

**brand name** ['brænd·neɪm] n marque f

**brandy** ['bræn·di] n <-ies> n eau f de vie

**brass** [bræs] **I.** n ❶ (*metal*) laiton m ❷ + *sing/pl vb* MUS **the ~** les cuivres mpl **II.** adj en laiton

**brass band** n ≈ fanfare f

**brat** [bræt] n pej, inf sale gosse mf

**brave** [breɪv] **I.** adj courageux, -euse; **to give a ~ smile** sourire bravement ▸ **to put on a** <u>face</u> ne rien laisser paraître **II.** vt braver

**brawl** [brɔl] **I.** n bagarre f **II.** vi se bagarrer

**bray** [breɪ] vi braire

**bread** [bred] n pain m; **loaf of ~** pain m; **to bake ~** faire du pain ❷ inf (*money*) oseille f

**breadcrumb** n ❶ (*small fragment*) miette f ❷ pl CULIN panure f

**break** [breɪk] **I.** n ❶ (*gap*) trou m; (*crack*) fêlure f; (*into two parts*) fracture f; **a ~ in the clouds** une brèche dans les nuages ❷ (*interruption: in conversation, for snack*) pause f; (*in output*) interruption f; **commercial ~** pause de publicité; **to take a ~** prendre une pause; **to need a ~ from doing sth** avoir besoin de se reposer de qc ❸ SCHOOL récréation f ❹ (*escape*) évasion f; **to make a ~** s'évader ❺ (*opportunity*) chance f; **she got her big ~ in that film** elle a percé grâce à ce film ▸ **give me a ~!** fiche-moi la paix!; **to make a** <u>clean</u> **~** cesser complètement de se voir **II.** <broke, broken> vt ❶ (*shatter*) casser; **to ~ a nail/one's arm** se casser un ongle/le bras ❷ (*damage*) endommager ❸ fig **to ~ an alibi** écarter un alibi ❹ (*interrupt*) **to ~ (off) sth** rompre qc; **to ~ one's step** [o **stride**] ralentir; MIL rompre le pas; **to ~ sb's fall** arrêter la chute de qn ❺ (*put an end to: record*) battre; (*strike*) casser; **to ~ a habit** se débarrasser d'une habitude; **to ~ the suspense** [o **tension**] mettre fin au suspense; **to ~ sb's spirit** [o **will**] briser la résistance [o volonté] de qn ❻ SPORTS **to ~ a tie** prendre l'avantage; **to ~ sb's serve** (*in tennis*) faire le break ❼ (*violate: law*) enfreindre; (*treaty*) rompre; (*date*) annuler; **to ~ a promise to sb** ne pas tenir sa parole envers qn ❽ (*forcefully end*) **to ~ sb's hold** se dégager de l'emprise de qn ❾ (*decipher: code*) déchiffrer ❿ (*make public*) annoncer; **to ~ the news to sb** apprendre

**B**

la nouvelle à qn ⑪ (*make change for: bank note*) entamer ▶ **to ~ one's back** *inf* se briser le dos; **to ~ sb's back** être la fin de qn; **to ~ the bank** *iron* faire sauter la banque; **to ~ cover** quitter son abri; **to ~ fresh** [*o* **new**] **ground** innover; **to ~ sb's heart** briser le cœur de qn; **to ~ the ice** *inf* rompre la glace; **to ~ wind** lâcher un vent III. <broke, broken> *vi* ① (*shatter*) se casser; **she broke under torture/the strain** *fig* elle a craqué sous la torture/le stress ② (*separate*) se démonter ③ (*interrupt*) **shall we ~ for lunch?** si on faisait une pause pour le déjeuner? ④ (*strike*) se briser; **the wave broke on the shore** la vague s'est brisée sur le rivage ⑤ (*change sound: voice at puberty*) muer; (*with emotion*) se briser ⑥ (*begin: storm, scandal*) éclater; (*day*) se lever ⑦ SPORTS commencer ▶ **to ~ even** rentrer dans ses frais; **to ~ free** s'évader; **to ~ loose** s'échapper

◆ **break away** *vi* ① (*move*) **to ~ from sb** s'éloigner de qn; **old enough to ~** *fig* assez grand pour voler de ses propres ailes ② (*split off*) **to ~ from sb** se désolidariser de qn ③ (*separate*) **chunks of ice are breaking away from the iceberg** des blocs de glace se détachent de l'iceberg

◆ **break down I.** *vi* ① (*stop working*) tomber en panne; (*plan*) s'effondrer ② (*dissolve*) décomposer; (*marriage*) se détériorer ③ (*lose control emotionally*) craquer ④ (*be analyzed*) **to ~ into three parts** se décomposer en trois parties **II.** *vt* ① (*force to open*) enfoncer ② (*overcome: barrier*) faire tomber; (*resistance*) vaincre ③ CHEM dissoudre ④ (*separate*) **to ~ sth into sth** décomposer qc en qc

◆ **break in I.** *vi* ① (*enter*) entrer par effraction ② (*interrupt*) intervenir **II.** *vt* ① (*make comfortable*) **to break one's shoes in** faire ses chaussures ② AUTO roder ③ (*tame*) dompter

◆ **break into** *vi* ① (*enter*) **to ~ sth** s'introduire dans qc; **to ~ a car** forcer la portière d'une voiture ② (*start doing*) **to ~ applause/a run** se mettre à applaudir/courir; **to ~ laughter/tears** éclater de rire/en sanglots ③ (*get involved in*) **to ~ advertising/the youth market** percer dans la publicité/le marché des jeunes ④ (*start using: savings, new package*) entamer

◆ **break off I.** *vt* ① (*separate*) casser ② (*end*) rompre **II.** *vi* ① (*not stay attached*) se détacher ② (*stop speaking*) s'interrompre

◆ **break out** *vi* ① (*escape*) s'évader ② (*begin: epidemic, fire*) se déclarer; (*storm*) éclater ③ (*become covered with*) **to ~ in a rash** se couvrir de boutons; **to ~ in (a) sweat** se mettre à transpirer

◆ **break through** *vi* se frayer un chemin; (*army*) ouvrir une brèche; (*sun*) percer

◆ **break up I.** *vt* ① (*forcefully end*) **to ~ sth** interrompre ② (*split up: coalition*) disperser; (*family*) désunir; (*company, organization*) diviser; (*demonstrators*) disperser ③ (*dig up: ground*) retourner **II.** *vi* ① (*end a relationship*) se séparer ② (*come to an end: marriage*) se désagréger ③ (*fall apart*) s'effondrer ④ (*disperse*) se disperser ⑤ (*lose signal*) **you're breaking up** je ne t'entends plus

**breakable** ['breɪk·ə·bl] *adj* fragile

**breakdown** ['breɪk·daʊn] *n* ① (*collapse*) échec *m;* (*of ceasefire*) rupture *f* ② TECH panne *f* ③ (*division*) ventilation *f;* (*of expenses*) détail *m* ④ (*decomposition*) décomposition *f* ⑤ PSYCH dépression *f*

**breakfast** ['brek·fəst] *n* petit-déjeuner *m;* **to have ~** déjeuner; **to have sth for ~** prendre qc au petit-déjeuner

**breakthrough** ['breɪk·θru] *n* MIL percée *f;* (*in science, negotiations*) tournant *m*

**breast** [brest] *n* ① ANAT sein *m* ② (*bird's chest*) gorge *f* ③ CULIN blanc *m*

**breast cancer** *n* cancer *m* du sein

**breast-feed** *vt, vi* allaiter

**breaststroke** *n* brasse *f*

**breath** [breθ] *n* ❶ (*air*) souffle *m*; **to be out of ~** être à bout de souffle; **to be short of ~** être essoufflé; **to catch one's ~** reprendre son souffle; **to hold one's ~** retenir sa respiration; **to take a deep ~** respirer à fond ❷ (*air exhaled*) haleine *f* ❸ (*break*) **to go out for a ~ of fresh air** sortir prendre l'air ❹ *fig* **in the same ~** dans la foulée

**breathalyze** [ˈbreθ·əl·aɪz] *vt* faire subir un alcootest à

**breathe** [briđ] I. *vi* ❶ ANAT respirer; **to ~ through one's nose** respirer par le nez ❷ *fig* **to ~ more easily** respirer II. *vt* ❶ (*exhale*) **to ~ air into sb's lungs** insuffler de l'air dans les poumons de qn; **to ~ garlic fumes** souffler des relents d'ail ❷ (*whisper*) chuchoter ❸ (*let out*) **to ~ a sigh of relief** soupirer de soulagement ▶ **to ~ (new) _life_ into sth** redonner de la vie à qc; **to ~ down sb's _neck_** être sur le dos de qn; **not to ~ a _word_** ne pas souffler mot

**breathing** *n* respiration *f*

**breathing apparatus** *n* respirateur *m*

**breathless** *adj* à bout de souffle

**breathtaking** [ˈbreθ·teɪ·kɪŋ] *adj* stupéfiant(e)

**breath test** *n* alcootest *m*

**breed** [brid] I.<bred, bred> *vt* ❶ (*grow*) faire pousser ❷ (*raise*) élever ❸ (*engender*) engendrer II.<bred, bred> *vi* ZOOL se reproduire III. *n* ❶ ZOOL race *f* ❷ BOT espèce *f* ❸ *inf* (*type of person*) race *f*

**breeze** [briz] I. *n* ❶ (*wind*) brise *f* ❷ *inf* (*easy task*) **it's a ~** c'est un jeu d'enfant II. *vi* **to ~ in/past** entrer/passer avec nonchalance; **to ~ to victory** l'emporter haut la main

**brewery** [ˈbru·ər·i] <-ies> *n* brasserie *f*

**bribe** [braɪb] I. *vt* soudoyer II. *n* pot *m* de vin

**bribery** [ˈbraɪ·bər·i] *n* corruption *f*

**brick** [brɪk] *n* (*block*) brique *f*
   ◆ **brick in, brick up** *vt* murer

**bride** [braɪd] *n* ❶ (*fiancée*) future mariée *f* ❷ (*married*) jeune mariée *f;* **child ~** très jeune mariée

**bridegroom** *n* ❶ (*fiancé*) futur marié *m* ❷ (*married*) jeune marié *m*

**bridesmaid** *n* demoiselle *f* d'honneur

**bridge** [brɪdʒ] I. *n* ❶ ARCHIT, NAUT *a. fig* pont *m* ❷ MED bridge *m* ❸ ANAT arête *f* du nez ❹ (*part of glasses*) arcade *f* ❺ MUS chevalet *m* ❻ GAMES bridge *m* II. *vt* ❶ (*build bridge*) construire un pont sur ❷ (*bring together*) **to ~ the gap between sb/sth and sb/sth** rapprocher qn/qc de qn/qc

**bridle** [ˈbraɪ·dl] *n* bride *f*

**brief** [brif] I.<-er, -est> *adj* bref, brève II. *n* ❶ (*instructions*) instructions *fpl* ❷ (*case summary*) dossier *m* ❸ *pl* (*underpants*) slip *m* ▶ **in ~** en bref III. *vt* ❶ (*inform*) briefer; **to ~ sb on sth** mettre qn au courant de qc

**briefcase** [ˈbrif·keɪs] *n* serviette *f,* calepin *m Belgique*

**briefing** *n* briefing *m;* **to conduct a ~** tenir un briefing

**briefly** *adv* ❶ (*shortly*) brièvement ❷ (*in short*) en bref

**bright** [braɪt] *adj* ❶ (*light*) vif, vive; (*room*) clair(e); (*clothes*) de couleur(s) vive(s) ❷ (*shining*) brillant(e); (*day*) radieux, -euse ❸ (*sparkling*) éclatant(e) ❹ (*intelligent*) intelligent(e); (*idea*) bon(ne) ❺ (*cheerful*) jovial(e) ❻ (*promising*) brillant(e); **to look ~ for sb/sth** bien s'annoncer pour qn/qc ▶ **to look on the ~ _side_ of sth** prendre les choses du bon côté; **~ and _early_** de bon matin

**brilliant** [ˈbrɪl·jənt] *adj* ❶ (*shining*) éclatant(e) ❷ (*intelligent*) brillant(e)

**brilliantly** *adv* ❶ (*with great skill*) brillamment ❷ (*brightly*) **to shine ~** briller avec éclat; **~ _lit_** vivement éclairé

**bring** [brɪŋ] <brought, brought> *vt* ❶ (*come with, carry: things*) apporter; **I brought the box into the house** j'ai rentré la boîte dans la maison ❷ (*take, cause to come: people*) amener; **this ~s me to the question of money** cela me conduit au sujet de l'argent

**B**

**❸**(*cause to have or happen*) to ~ sth to sb, to ~ sb sth apporter qc à qn; to ~ sth on oneself s'attirer qc; to ~ sb luck porter chance à qn **❹** LAW rapporter; to ~ a charge against sb inculper qn; to ~ a complaint against sb porter plainte contre qn **❺**(*force*) to ~ oneself to +*infin* se résoudre à +*infin* **❻** FIN rapporter; to ~ a profit bien rapporter ▸ to ~ sth to sb's <u>attention</u> attirer l'attention de qn sur qc; to ~ sth to a <u>climax</u> porter qc à son paroxysme; to ~ sth to a <u>close</u> mettre fin à qc; to ~ sth under <u>control</u> maîtriser qc; to ~ sb up to <u>date</u> mettre qn au courant; to ~ sb <u>face</u> to face with sth confronter qn à qc; to ~ sb/sth to a <u>halt</u> faire arrêter qn/qc; to ~ sb back to <u>life</u> ramener qn à la vie; to ~ sth to <u>life</u> donner vie à qc; to ~ sth to <u>light</u> révéler; to ~ sth to <u>mind</u> rappeler qc

◆**bring about** *vt* **❶**(*cause to happen*) provoquer **❷**(*achieve*) amener

◆**bring along** *vt* (*food*) apporter; (*friend*) amener

◆**bring back** *vt* **❶**(*reintroduce*) ramener **❷**(*return*) rapporter **❸**(*call to mind: memories*) rappeler

◆**bring down** *vt* **❶**(*opp: bring up*) descendre **❷**(*topple*) renverser **❸**(*reduce*) faire baisser **❹**(*fell: trees, shelves*) faire tomber **❺**(*shoot down*) abattre **❻**(*make sad*) décourager ▸ to ~ the **house** (*with laughter*) faire rire tout le monde; (*by performance*) éblouir tout le monde

◆**bring forward** *vt* **❶** FIN reporter **❷**(*fix earlier time for*) avancer **❸**(*suggest*) proposer

◆**bring in** *vt* **❶**(*introduce*) introduire; to ~ a topic lancer un sujet **❷**(*call in, reap*) faire rentrer **❸**(*earn*) rapporter; to ~ a profit rapporter du bénéfice **❹**(*ask to participate*) faire intervenir **❺**(*produce*) rendre

◆**bring off** *vt* réussir

◆**bring on** *vt* **❶** MED causer **❷**(*cause to occur*) provoquer **❸**(*send in to play: reserve, actor*) faire entrer

◆**bring out** *vt* **❶** COM (*product*) lancer; (*book, film*) sortir **❷**(*stress*) faire ressortir **❸**(*utter*) to ~ a few words prononcer quelques mots

◆**bring over** *vt* amener

◆**bring up** *vt* **❶**(*opp: bring down*) monter **❷**(*rear*) to bring sb up élever qn **❸**(*mention*) parler de; to ~ sth for discussion aborder qc **❹** *inf* (*vomit*) rendre ▸ to ~ the <u>rear</u> fermer la marche

**brink** [brɪŋk] *n* bord *m;* to drive sb to the ~ pousser qn à bout; to drive sb to the ~ of tears pousser qn au bord des larmes; to be on the ~ of bankruptcy/war être au bord de la faillite/à deux doigts de la guerre

**briquette** [brɪˈket] *n* briquette *f*

**brisk** [brɪsk] <-er, -est> *adj* **❶**(*not sluggish*) vif, vive; (*walk, traffic*) rapide; business is ~ les ventes vont bon train **❷**(*refreshing*) vivifiant(e)

**Britain** [ˈbrɪtᵊn] *n s.* Great Britain

**British** [ˈbrɪtɪʃ] I. *adj* britannique II. *n pl* the ~ les Anglais *mpl;* (*as nationality*) les Britanniques *mpl*

**British Columbia** *n* la Colombie-Britannique

**Briton** [ˈbrɪtᵊn] *n* Britannique *mf*

**broad** [brɔd] <-er, -est> *adj* **❶**(*wide*) large **❷**(*spacious*) vaste **❸**(*general*) grand(e); (*description*) large **❹**(*wide-ranging: range, syllabus*) varié(e) **❺**(*strong*) fort(e) ▸ in ~ <u>daylight</u> en plein jour

**broadcaster** *n* RADIO, TV animateur, -trice *m, f*

**broadly** [ˈbrɔd·li] *adv* **❶**(*generally*) d'une manière générale **❷**(*widely*) largement; to smile [*o* grin] ~ avoir un large sourire

**broccoli** [ˈbrɑ·kᵊl·i] *n* brocoli *m*

**brochure** [broʊˈʃʊr] *n* brochure *f*

**broil** [brɔɪl] *vt* griller

**broke** [broʊk] I. *pt of* break II. *adj inf* fauché(e) ▸ to <u>go</u> ~ faire faillite; to <u>go</u> for ~ jouer le tout pour le tout

**broken** [ˈbroʊ·kᵊn] I. *pp of* break II. *adj* **❶**(*damaged*) cassé(e); the com-

**puter/fridge is** ~ l'ordinateur *m*/le frigidaire est en panne ②(*defeated, crushed*) brisé(e) ③(*interrupted*) interrompu(e) ④ LING ~ **Italian** mauvais italien ⑤(*weakened*) abattu(e); **to come from a ~ home** venir d'une famille désunie

**broken-down** *adj* ① TECH en panne, brisé(e) *Québec* ②(*dilapidated*) délabré(e)

**broken-hearted** *adj* **to be ~** avoir le cœur brisé

**bronze** [brɑnz] *n* bronze *m*

**brooch** [broʊtʃ] *n* broche *f*

**broom** [brum] *n* ①(*brush*) balai *m* ② BOT genêt *m*

**broomstick** ['brum·stɪk] *n* manche *m* à balai

**broth** [brɑθ] *n* bouillon *m*

**brother** ['brʌð·ər] *n* frère *m*

**brother-in-law** ['brʌð·ər·ɪn·lɔ] <brothers-in-law> *n* beau-frère *m*

**brotherly** ['brʌð·ər·li] *adv* fraternel(le); ~ **advice** conseil *m* d'ami

**brought** [brɔt] *pp, pt of* **bring**

**brown** [braʊn] I. *adj* brun(e), marron *inv*; (*hair*) châtain; *s.a.* **blue** II. *vi* (*leaves*) roussir, (*person*) bronzer III. *vt* brunir; (*meat*) faire dorer

**brown bear** *n* ours *m* brun

**brown rice** *n* riz *m* complet

**brown sugar** *n* sucre *m* brun

**browse** [braʊz] *vi* ①(*skim*) **to ~ through sth** feuilleter qc ②(*look around*) regarder ③(*graze*) brouter

**browser** ['braʊ·zər] *n* COMPUT ①(*software*) logiciel *m* de navigation, fureteur *m* *Québec* ②(*function*) explorateur *m*, navigateur *m*

**bruise** [bruz] I. *n* ① MED bleu *m* ②(*on fruit*) meurtrissure *m* II. *vt* ①(*injure outside of*) **to ~ one's arm** se faire un bleu au bras ②(*damage: fruit*) meurtrir ③(*hurt*) blesser III. *vi* se faire un bleu

**brush** [brʌʃ] I. *n* ①(*for hair*) brosse *f* ②(*broom*) balai *m* ③(*for painting*) pinceau *m* ④(*action*) **to give sth a ~** donner un coup de balai à qc ⑤(*encounter*) accrochage *m*; **to have a ~ with the** **law** avoir des démêlés avec la justice; **to have a ~ with death** frôler la mort ⑥(*brushwood*) broussailles *fpl* ⑦(*fox's tail*) queue *f* II. *vt* ①(*clean*) brosser; **to ~ one's teeth/hair** se brosser les dents/cheveux ②(*remove*) **to ~ sth off** enlever qc à la brosse/au balai ③(*graze, touch lightly in passing*) effleurer; **to ~ against sb** frôler qn

◆ **brush aside** *vt* ①(*move*) balayer (d'un seul geste) ②(*dismiss*) repousser

◆ **brush away** *vt* ①(*wipe*) essuyer ②(*push to one side*) écarter

◆ **brush off** *vt* ①(*rebuff, avoid*) repousser ②(*ignore*) écarter d'un geste

◆ **brush up** *vt* **to ~ on sth** se rafraîchir la mémoire en qc

**brush-off** ['brʌʃ·ɑf] *n* **to give sb the ~** envoyer qn sur les roses; **to get the ~ from sb** se faire envoyer sur les roses par qn

**Brussels** ['brʌs·əlz] *n* Bruxelles

**brutal** ['bru·t̬əl] *adj* ①(*savage*) violent(e) ②(*frank*) brutal(e)

**BS** [ˌbiˈes] *n* ① *abbr of* **Bachelor of Science** licencié(e) *m(f)* ès sciences ② *vulg abbr of* **bullshit** connerie(s) *f(pl)*

**bubble** ['bʌb·l] I. *n* bulle *f*; **to blow a ~** faire une bulle II. *vi* ①(*boil*) bouillonner ②(*sound*) glouglouter

**bubble bath** *n* bain *m* moussant

**bubble gum** *n* chewing-gum *m* (*qui fait des bulles*)

**bubbly** ['bʌb·li] *inf* I. *n* champagne *m* II. *adj* ①(*full of bubbles*) pétillant(e) ②(*lively*) plein(e) de vie

**bucket** ['bʌk·ɪt] *n* ①(*pail*) seau *m*; **champagne ~** seau à champagne ② *pl, inf* (*a lot*) beaucoup ▶ **to kick the ~** *inf* casser sa pipe

**bucketful** ['bʌk·ɪt·fʊl] <-s *o* bucketsful> *n* ① **a ~ of water** un plein seau d'eau ② *pl, fig* des masses *fpl*

**buckle** ['bʌk·l] I. *n* boucle *f* II. *vt* ①(*fasten*) boucler; (*belt*) attacher ②(*bend*) déformer III. *vi* ①(*fasten*) s'attacher ②(*bend*) se déformer

◆ **buckle down** *vi* s'y mettre; **to ~ to one's work** se mettre au travail

**B**

**bud¹** [bʌd] BOT **I.** n bourgeon m ▸ **to be in** ~ bourgeonner **II.**<-dd-> vi bourgeonner

**bud²** [bʌd] n inf pote m

**Buddha** ['buˑdə] n Bouddha m

**Buddhist I.** n bouddhiste mf **II.** adj bouddhiste

**buddy** ['bʌdˑi] n inf (pal) pote m; **calm down,** ~! du calme, coco! m

**budge** [bʌdʒ] **I.** vi ❶(move) bouger ❷(change opinion) changer d'avis **II.** vt faire bouger

**budget** ['bʌdʒ·ɪt] **I.** n budget m; **to draw up a** ~ établir un budget; ~ **deficit** déficit m budgétaire **II.** vt prévoir dans le budget ▸ **to** ~ **one's time** planifier son temps **III.** vi préparer un budget; **to** ~ **for sth** prévoir qc dans le budget **IV.** adj (cheap) à prix intéressant; ~ **airline** compagnie f aérienne pour budgets serrés

**budgetary** ['bʌdʒ·ɪ·ter·i] adj budgétaire

**buffalo** ['bʌf·ə·loʊ] <-(es)> n buffle m; (North American bison) bison m

**buffet¹** [bə·'feɪ] vt secouer

**buffet²** ['bʌf·ɪt] n buffet m

**bug** [bʌg] **I.** n ❶ZOOL punaise f ❷inf (insect) insecte m ❸MED microbe m; **there's a** ~ **going around** il y a un microbe qui circule ❹(fault) défaut m ❺COMPUT bogue m ❻TEL table f d'écoute ❼inf (enthusiasm) virus m **II.**<-gg-> vt ❶(tap) brancher sur table d'écoute ❷inf (annoy) casser les pieds à

**bugger** ['bʌg·ər] n inf ❶(person) salaud m ❷(thing) casse-pieds m

**buggy** ['bʌg·i] <-ies> n ❶(for baby) landau m ❷AUTO buggy m ❸(drawn by horses) boghei m

**build** [bɪld] **I.** n charpente f **II.**<built, built> vt ❶(construct) bâtir; (car, ship) construire; (memorial) édifier ❷fig (company) établir; (system) créer; (vocabulary) augmenter **III.**<built, built> vi ❶(construct) construire ❷(increase) augmenter

◆ **build in** vt (cupboard) encastrer; (security, penalty) introduire

◆ **build on** vt ❶(add) ajouter ❷(develop from) partir de

◆ **build up I.** vt ❶(accumulate: reserves, surplus) accumuler; (collection) développer; **to** ~ **speed** gagner de la vitesse ❷(strengthen) développer; **to** ~ **sb's hopes** donner de l'espoir à qn ❸(develop) développer ❹(hype) faire du battage autour de **II.** vi (increase) s'accumuler; (traffic) augmenter; (pressure) monter; (business) se développer

**builder** ['bɪl·dər] n entreprise f de bâtiment

**building** n ❶(place) bâtiment m; (for offices, apartments) immeuble m ❷(industry) le bâtiment ❸(process) construction f

**building site** n chantier m

**buildup** ['bɪld·ʌp] n ❶(increase, accumulation) montée f; (of waste, toxins) accumulation f; (of troops) rassemblement m; (of resentment, grievances) accumulation f; **traffic** ~ engorgement m ❷(hype) battage m publicitaire

**built** [bɪlt] **I.** pp, pt of **build II.** adj construit(e); **slightly** ~ fluet(te)

**built-in** ['bɪlt·ɪn] adj ❶encastré(e) ❷fig incorporé(e)

**bulb** [bʌlb] n ❶BOT bulbe m ❷ELEC ampoule f

**bulging** adj (eyes) globuleux(-euse); (forehead, wall) bombé(e)

**bulimia** [bju·'lɪm·i·ə], **bulimia nervosa** n boulimie f

**bulky** ['bʌl·ki] <-ier, iest> adj ❶(large) volumineux(-euse); (person) corpulent(e) ❷(awkwardly large) encombrant(e)

**bull¹** [bʊl] n ❶(male bovine) taureau m ❷(male animal) mâle m ▸ **like a** ~ **in a china shop** comme un éléphant dans un magasin de porcelaine

**bull²** [bʊl] n ❶inf (nonsense) foutaise f ❷FIN haussier m

**bulldog** ['bʊl·dɔg] n bouledogue m

**bulldozer** ['bʊl·doʊ·zər] n bulldozer m

**bullet** ['bʊl·ɪt] n ❶MIL balle f ❷TYP, COMPUT puce f ▸ **to bite the** ~ se forcer;

**B**

~ **train** train *m* à grande vitesse (*au Japon*)

**bulletin** ['bʊl·ə·tɪn] *n* ❶ TV, CINE (**news**) ~ actualités *fpl* télévisées; (*on one topic*) communiqué *m* spécial ❷ (*newsletter*) bulletin *m* d'informations; **church** ~ journal *m* paroissial

**bulletin board** *n* ❶ (*board*) tableau *m* d'affichage; ADMIN tableau *m* d'annonces ❷ COMPUT messagerie *f* électronique

**bulletproof** *adj* (*vest*) pare-balles *inv*; (*glass*) blindé(e)

**bullfight** ['bʊl·faɪt] *n* combat *m* de taureaux

**bullfrog** *n* grenouille-taureau *f*

**bull's-eye** *n* cible *f*; **to hit the** ~ *a. fig* faire mouche

**bully** ['bʊl·i] I. <-ies> *n* (*person*) tyran *m*; (*child*) brute *f* II. <-ie-> *vi* être une brute III. <-ie-> *vt* victimiser; **to** ~ **sb into doing sth** contraindre qn par la menace à faire qc IV. *interj* ~ **for you!** *inf* tant mieux pour toi/vous!; *iron* bravo!

**bum** [bʌm] I. *n* ❶ (*lazy person*) bon à rien, bonne *f* à rien ❷ (*tramp*) clochard(e) *m(f)* II. <-mm-> *vt* **to** ~ **a ride** faire de l'auto-stop; **to** ~ **a cigarette from sb** *inf* taper qn d'une cigarette

**bumblebee** ['bʌm·bl·bi] *n* bourdon *m*

**bump** [bʌmp] I. *n* ❶ (*swelling*) bosse *f* ❷ (*protrusion*) protubérance *f* ❸ *inf* (*blow*) léger coup *m* ❹ (*thud*) bruit *m* sourd ❺ (*collision*) léger accrochage *m* II. *vt* (*car*) tamponner; (*one's head*) se cogner III. *vi* **to** ~ **against sth** se cogner contre qc

**bumper**[1] ['bʌm·pər] *n* AUTO pare-chocs *m*; **back/front** ~ pare-chocs arrière/avant

**bumper**[2] ['bʌm·pər] *adj* (*crowd, crop*) record; (*packet*) géant(e); (*year, issue*) exceptionnel(le)

**bumpy** ['bʌm·pi] <-ier, iest> *adj* ❶ (*uneven*) inégal(e) ❷ (*jarring*) cahoteux(-euse); (*road*) défoncé(e) ❸ *fig* difficile; **to have a** ~ **ride** passer par des moments difficiles

**bun** [bʌn] *n* ❶ (*bread*) petit pain pour hot-dog ou hamburger ❷ (*pastry*) petit pain *m* au lait ❸ (*knot of hair*) chignon *m*

**bunch** [bʌn(t)ʃ] <-es> I. *n* ❶ (*group of similar objects*) ensemble *m*; (*of bananas*) régime *m*; (*of radishes*) botte *f*; (*of flowers*) bouquet *m*; (*of grapes*) grappe *f*; (*of keys*) trousseau *m* ❷ (*group of people*) groupe *m*; (*of idiots, thieves*) bande *f* ❸ (*lot*) **a** ~ **of problems** un tas de problèmes ❹ (*wad*) **in a** ~ en liasse ▶**the best of the** ~ le meilleur de tous II. *vt* **to be** ~**ed up** être serrés comme des sardines

**bundle** ['bʌn·dl] I. *n* ❶ (*pile*) tas *m*; (*wrapped up*) paquet *m*; (*of papers*) liasse *f*; **wrapped in a** ~ empaqueté ▶~ **of nerves** paquet *m* de nerfs; **to make a** ~ **on sth** faire son beurre sur qc II. *vt* (*put*) fourrer III. *vi* **to** ~ **into sth** (*people*) s'entasser dans qc

**bunk** [bʌŋk] *n* ❶ NAUT, RAIL couchette *f*; **bottom/top** ~ lit *m* supérieur/inférieur ❷ *inf* (*rubbish*) bêtises *fpl*

**bunk bed** *n* lit *m* superposé

**bunny** ['bʌn·i], **bunny rabbit** *n* childspeak Jeannot lapin *m*

**Bunsen burner** ['bʌ(t)·sᵊn·bɜr·nər] *n* bec *m* Bunsen

**buoy** [bɔɪ] *n* bouée *f*

**bureau** ['bjʊr·oʊ] <-s ou -x> *n* ❶ (*government department*) service *m* gouvernemental ❷ (*office*) bureau *m* ❸ (*dresser*) commode *f*

**bureaucracy** [bjʊ·ˈrɑ·krə·si] *n pej* bureaucratie *f*

**burger** ['bɜr·gər] *n inf* hamburger *m*

**burglar** ['bɜr·glər] *n* cambrioleur, -euse *m, f*

**burglary** ['bɜr·glᵊr·i] <-ies> *n* ❶ (*stealing*) cambriolage *m* ❷ LAW vol *m* avec effraction

**burn** [bɜrn] I. *n* brûlure *f* II. <-t *o* -ed, -t *o* -ed> *vi* ❶ (*be in flames*) brûler ❷ (*be overheated: meat, pan*) brûler ❸ (*be switched on: light*) être allumé(e) ❹ (*feel very hot: with fever, irritation*) brûler; I ~ **easily** je prends facilement des coups de soleil; **my eyes are** ~**ing**

mes yeux piquent ⑤ (*feel an emotion*)
**to be ~ing with desire** brûler de désir;
**his face was ~ing with shame/anger** son visage était rouge de honte/colère ⑥ *fig* **to ~ to** + *infin* se languir de
+ *infin* ▸ **my ears are ~ing** mes oreilles
sifflent III. <-t o -ed, -t o -ed> *vt*
① (*consume*) brûler; **to be ~ed to the
ground** être complètement détruit par
le feu; **to be burned at the stake** mourir sur le bûcher ② (*overheat: meat,
pan*) laisser brûler; **to ~ sth to a crisp**
carboniser qc ③ (*hurt, irritate: skin*)
brûler; **to ~ one's tongue** se brûler la
langue ④ (*consume as fuel*) **to ~ gas** se
chauffer au gaz ▸ **to ~ the <u>candle</u> at
both ends** brûler la chandelle par les
deux bouts; **money ~s a <u>hole</u> in her
pocket** l'argent lui brûle les doigts
◆**burn away** I. *vi* brûler; (*forest,
house*) être en feu; (*candle*) se consumer II. *vt* détruire par le feu
◆**burn down** I. *vt* incendier II. *vi* brûler complètement
◆**burn out** I. *vi* (*stop burning*) s'éteindre; (*fire, candle*) se consumer II. *vt*
① (*stop burning*) **the boat is burning
itself out** le bateau achève de brûler
② (*be destroyed*) **the factory was
burned out** le feu a détruit l'usine
③ (*become ill*) **she burned herself
out** elle s'est ruiné la santé
◆**burn up** I. *vt* *inf* griller II. *vi*
① (*be consumed*) se consumer ② (*feel
constantly*) **to be burned up with sth**
être dévoré par qc
**burner** ['bɜr·nər] *n* brûleur *m* ▸ **to put
sth on the <u>back</u> ~** laisser qc de côté
**burning** ['bɜr·nɪŋ] *adj* ① (*on fire: candle*) allumé(e); (*building, clothes*) en
feu; (*log*) qui brûle ② (*hot*) brûlant(e);
(*desire*) ardent(e) ③ (*controversial*)
controversé(e) ④ (*stinging*) cuisant(e);
**~ sensation** sensation *f* de brûlure
**burnt** [bɜrnt] *adj* ① (*scorched*) roussi(e)
② (*consumed*) calciné(e); **~ beyond
recognition** carbonisé
**burp** [bɜrp] I. *n* renvoi *m*; (*from baby*)
rot *m* II. *vi* roter; (*baby*) faire un rot

III. *vt* **to ~ a baby** faire faire son rot à
un bébé
**burrow** ['bɜr·oʊ] I. *n* terrier *m* II. *vt*
creuser III. *vi* ① ZOOL se terrer ② (*dig*)
**to ~ through sth** creuser un tunnel à
travers qc
**burst** [bɜrst] I. *n* ① (*hole in pipe*)
tuyau *m* éclaté ② (*brief period*) **~ of
laughter** éclat *m* de rire; **~ of activity**
regain *m* d'activité; **~ of applause** salve *f* d'applaudissement; **~ of gunfire**
rafale *f* de coups de feu II. <-, -> *vi*
① (*explode*) exploser; (*bag, balloon*)
éclater ② (*be eager*) **to be ~ing to** + *infin* mourir d'envie de + *infin*; **he is
~ing with happiness/confidence/
pride** il déborde de bonheur/de
confiance en lui/ de fierté ③ (*showing
movement*) **the door ~ open** la porte
s'est ouverte brusquement ▸ **to be
~ing at the <u>seams</u>** *inf* être plein à craquer, être paqueté *Québec*; (*room, movie theater*) être bondé III. <-, -> *vt*
faire éclater; **a river ~s its banks** une
rivière sort de son lit
◆**burst in** *vi* faire irruption; **to ~ on sb**
faire irruption chez qn
◆**burst out** *vi* ① (*speak*) s'écrier
② (*suddenly begin*) **to ~ laughing** éclater de rire
**bury** ['ber·i] <-ie-> *vt* ① (*put underground*) enterrer; **buried under the
snow** enseveli sous la neige ② (*attend a
burial*) **to ~ sb** assister à l'enterrement
de qn ③ (*hide*) dissimuler; **to ~ oneself
in one's work** fuir dans le travail ▸ **to
~ the <u>hatchet</u>** enterrer la hache de
guerre
**bus** [bʌs] I. <-es o -ses> *n* ① (*vehicle*)
autobus *m*; **school ~** car *m* de ramassage scolaire, autobus *m* scolaire *Québec*
② COMPUT bus *m* II. <-s- o -ss-> *vt*
transporter en car III. <-s- o -ss-> *vi*
voyager en car
**busboy** *n* aide-serveur *m*
**bus driver** *n* conducteur, -trice *m*, *f* de
bus
**bush** [bʊʃ] *n* ① <-es> BOT buisson *m*
② (*great amount*) **~ of hair** tignasse *f*

**B**

❸ (*land*) **the ~** la brousse ▸ **to beat around the ~** tourner autour du pot

**bushel** ['bʊʃ·əl] *n* (*unit of volume*) boisseau *m*

**bushy** ['bʊʃ·i] <-ier, -iest> *adj* broussailleux(-euse)

**business** ['bɪz·nɪs] *n* ❶ (*trade*) affaires *fpl*; **to be good for ~** être bon pour les affaires; **I'm here on ~** je suis ici pour affaires; **to do ~ with sb** faire des affaires avec qn ❷ (*commerce*) commerce *m*; (*revenue*) chiffre *m* d'affaires ❸ (*activity*) **to be in ~** avoir une activité commerciale; *inf* être fin prêt; **to put sb out of ~** faire fermer boutique à qn; **to set up in ~ as a baker** s'établir boulanger ❹ <-es> (*profession*) métier *m*; **what line of ~ are you in?** que faites-vous/fais-tu dans la vie? ❺ <-es> (*firm*) société *f*; **to start up a ~** créer une entreprise; **small ~es** les petites entreprises *fpl* ❻ (*matter, task*) affaire *f*; **unfinished ~** affaire pendante; **it's none of your ~** *inf* ça ne te/vous regarde pas; **he has no ~ doing this** il n'a aucun droit de faire cela ❼ (*process*) **to get on with the ~ of sth** s'occuper de qc ▸ **to mind one's own** *inf* se mêler de ses affaires; **to mean ~** ne pas plaisanter; **to get down to ~** passer aux choses sérieuses; **like nobody's ~** *inf* extrêmement vite

**business card** *n* carte *f* de visite

**business hours** *n* heures *fpl* de bureau

**businesslike** *adj* méthodique

**businessman** <-men> *n* homme *m* d'affaires; (*entrepreneur*) entrepreneur *m*

**business trip** *n* voyage *m* d'affaires

**businesswoman** <-women> *n* femme *f* d'affaires; (*entrepreneur*) entrepreneuse *f*

**bus station** *n* gare *f* routière

**bus stop** *n* arrêt *m* d'autobus

**bust¹** [bʌst] *n* ❶ (*statue*) buste *m* ❷ (*bosom*) poitrine *f* (de femme)

**bust²** [bʌst] **I.** *adj inf* (*bankrupt*) **to go ~** faire faillite **II.** *n* ❶ (*failure*) échec *m* ❷ *inf* (*punch*) coup *m* ❸ *sl* (*raid*) descente *f* de police; **drug ~** saisie *f* de drogue **III.** *vt sl* ❶ (*break*) casser ❷ (*arrest*) choper

**busty** ['bʌs·ti] *adj inf* (*woman*) fort(e) de poitrine

**busy¹** ['bɪz·i] <-ier, -iest> *adj* ❶ (*occupied*) occupé(e); **I'm very ~ this week** je suis très pris cette semaine; **to be ~ with sth** être occupé à faire qc; **to get ~** se mettre au travail ❷ (*full of activity: period, week, store*) très actif(-ive); (*street*) animé(e) ❸ (*hectic*) **a ~ time** une période mouvementée ❹ (*exhausting*) fatigant(e) ❺ *pej* (*overly decorated*) trop bariolé(e) ❻ TEL occupé(e) ▸ **she is as ~ as a bee** elle déborde d'activité

**busy²** ['bɪz·i] <-ie-> *vt* **to ~ oneself** s'occuper; **to ~ oneself with sth** s'appliquer à faire qc

**but** [bʌt] **I.** *conj* mais **II.** *prep* sauf; **he's nothing ~ a liar** il n'est rien d'autre qu'un menteur; **the last house ~ one** l'avant-dernière maison *f* **III.** *n* mais *m* ▸ **no ~s about it!** il n'y a pas de mais qui tienne! **IV.** *adv form* ❶ (*only*) seulement; **she's ~ a young girl** elle n'est qu'une petite fille ❷ (*really*) (mais) vraiment

**butcher** ['bʊtʃ·ər] **I.** *n* boucher *m* **II.** *vt* ❶ (*slaughter: animal*) abattre ❷ (*murder*) massacrer ❸ SPORTS **they ~ed the other team** ils ont écrasé l'autre équipe ❹ (*mangle: language*) estropier

**butler** ['bʌt·lər] *n* majordome *m*

**butt** [bʌt] **I.** *n* ❶ (*bottom part: of tree*) souche *f*; (*of rifle*) crosse *f* ❷ (*cigarette*) mégot *m* ❸ (*blow*) coup *m* de tête ❹ (*person*) **to be the ~ of sb's jokes** être la risée de qn ❺ (*container*) tonneau *m* ❻ *inf* (*bottom*) cul *m* **II.** *vt* donner un coup de tête à

**butter** ['bʌt·ər] **I.** *n* beurre *m* **II.** *vt* beurrer

**butterfly** ['bʌt·ər·flaɪ] <-ies> *n* ❶ ZOOL *a. fig* papillon *m* ❷ TECH écrou *m* à oreilles ❸ SPORTS nage *f* papillon ▸ **to have butterflies in one's stomach** avoir l'estomac noué

**butthead** *n sl* idiot(e) *m(f)*

**button** ['bʌt·ən] I. *n* ❶ FASHION, COMPUT bouton *m*, piton *m Québec* ❷ TECH sonnette *f* ▸ **to be right on the** ~ mettre dans le mille II. *vt* boutonner ▸ ~ **it!** *inf* la ferme!

**buy** [baɪ] I. *n* achat *m*; **it's quite a** ~ c'est plutôt une affaire II.<*bought*, bought> *vt* ❶ acheter; **to** ~ **a plane ticket** prendre un billet d'avion; **to** ~ **sb a present** acheter un cadeau à qn ❷ *inf* (*believe*) **I don't** ~ **that** je ne marche pas ▸ **to** ~ **the farm** *inf* partir les pieds devant; **to** ~ **time** gagner du temps

♦ **buy off** *vt* acheter

♦ **buy out** *vt* COM désintéresser; **to buy sb out** racheter les parts de qn

♦ **buy up** *vt* **to** ~ **houses/shares** acheter toutes les maisons/toutes les parts; **to** ~ **the whole store** *fig* dévaliser tout le magasin

**buyer** ['baɪ·ər] *n* acheteur, -euse *m, f*

**buzz** [bʌz] I. *vi* ❶ (*make a low sound*) vrombir; (*buzzer*) sonner; (*bee*) bourdonner ❷ *inf* (*be tipsy*) être éméché(e) ❸ *fig* **the room** ~ed **with conversation** la salle résonnait de brouhaha II. *vt* ❶ *inf* TEL appeler ❷ AVIAT raser III. *n* ❶ (*humming noise*) bourdonnement *m*; (*low noise*) vrombissement *m*; (*of doorbell*) sonnerie *f*; ~ **of conversation** brouhaha *m* ❷ *inf* TEL coup *m* de fil; **to give sb a** ~ passer un coup de fil à qn ❸ *inf* (*feeling*) **to get a** ~ **out of sth** prendre son pied avec qc

**buzzer** ['bʌz·ər] *n* avertisseur *m* sonore; **door** ~ sonnette *f*

**by** [baɪ] I. *prep* ❶ (*near*) **to stand/lie/be** ~ **sth/sb** se tenir/être étendu(e)/être près [*o* à côté de] de qc/qn; **close** [*o* **near**] ~ **sb/sth** tout près de qn/qc ❷ (*during*) ~ **day/night** le [*o* de] jour/la [*o* de] nuit; ~ **moonlight** au clair de lune; ~ **the way** en cours de route ❸ (*at latest time*) ~ **tomorrow** d'ici demain; ~ **midnight** avant minuit; **by now** à l'heure qu'il est; ~ **then** à ce mo-

ment-là; ~ **the time sb saw him ...** le temps [*o* avant] que qn le voie (*subj*) ... ❹ (*showing agent, cause*) **a novel** ~ **Joyce** un roman de Joyce; **killed** ~ **sth/sb** tué par qc/qn; **surrounded** ~ **dogs** entouré de chiens; **made** ~ **hand** fait (à la) main ❺ (*using*) ~ **rail/plane/tram** en train/par avion/avec le tram; ~ **means of sth** au moyen de qc; ~ **doing sth** en faisant qc; **to hold sb** ~ **the arm** tenir qn par le bras; **to go in** ~ **the door** entrer par la porte; **to call sb/sth** ~ **name** appeler qn/qc par son nom ❻ (*through*) ~ **chance/mistake** par hasard/erreur; **what does he mean** ~ **that?** que veut-il dire par là? ❼ (*past*) **to walk** ~ **the post office** passer devant la poste; **to run** ~ **sb** passer à côté de qn en courant ❽ (*alone*) **to do sth/to be** ~ **oneself** faire qc/être tout seul ❾ (*in measurement*) **paid** ~ **the hour** payé à l'heure; ~ **the day** par jour; **to buy** ~ **the kilo/dozen** acheter au kilo/à la douzaine; **to multiply/divide** ~ **4** multiplier/diviser par 4; **to increase** ~ **10%** augmenter de 10%; **4 feet** ~ **6** de 4 pieds sur 6 (*de 1,20 m sur 1,80 m environ*) ❿ (*from perspective of*) **to judge** ~ **appearances** juger d'après les apparences; **it's all right** ~ **me** *inf* moi, je suis d'accord II. *adv* ❶ (*in reserve*) **to put sth** ~ mettre/poser qc de côté ❷ (*gradually*) ~ **and** ~ peu à peu ❸ (*past*) **to go/pass** ~ passer ▸ ~ **and large** d'une façon générale

**bye** [baɪ] *interj inf* salut

**bye-bye** [,baɪ·'baɪ] *interj inf* au revoir; **to go** ~ *childspeak* s'en aller

**bylaw** ['baɪ·lɔ] *n* règlement *m*

**bypass** ['baɪ·pæs] I. *n* ❶ AUTO route *f* de contournement ❷ MED pontage *m* II. *vt* ❶ (*make a detour*) contourner ❷ (*ignore*) **to** ~ **sb** agir sans informer qn ❸ (*avoid*) laisser de côté

**by-product** ['baɪ·prə·dʌkt] *n* sous-produit *m*; *fig* effet *m* secondaire

**byte** [baɪt] *n* COMPUT octet *m*

# Cc

**C, c** [si] *n* ① (*letter*) C *m*, c *m*; **~ as in Charlie** (*on telephone*) c comme Célestin ② MUS do *m* ③ SCHOOL assez bien *m*

**C** *abbr of* **Celsius**

**CA** *n abbr of* **California**

**ca.** *prep abbr of* **circa**

**cab** [kæb] *n* taxi *m*; **by ~** en taxi

**cabbage** ['kæb·ɪdʒ] *n* chou *m*

**cabbie** *n*, **cabdriver** *n* chauffeur *m* de taxi

**cabin** ['kæb·ɪn] *n* ① (*area on a vehicle*) cabine *f* ② (*small house*) cabane *f*

**cabinet** ['kæb·ɪ·nət] *n* ① (*storage place*) meuble *m*; **file ~** classeur *m*; **medicine ~** armoire *f* à pharmacie ② (*glass-fronted*) vitrine *f* ③ + *sing/pl vb* (*group of advisers*) cabinet *m*

**cable** ['keɪ·bl] I. *n a.* TEL câble *m* II. *vt* câbler

**cable car** *n* ① (*car on track*) funiculaire *m* ② (*suspended transportation system*) téléphérique *m*

**cable television, cable TV** *n* télévision *f* par câble

**cacao** [kə·'ka·oʊ] *n* cacao *m*

**cache** [kæʃ] *n* ① (*storage place*) cachette *f*; (*of weapons*) cache *f* ② COMPUT cache *f*

**cactus** ['kæk·təs] <-es *o* cacti> *n* cactus *m*

**caddie, caddy** ['kæd·i] I. *n* SPORTS caddie® *m* II. <caddied, caddied, caddying> *vi* **to ~ for sb** être le caddie de qn

**cafe, café** [kæf·'eɪ] *n* café *m*, estaminet *m* Nord, Belgique, pinte *f* Suisse

**cafeteria** [ˌkæf·ə·'tɪr·i·ə] *n* cafétéria *f*

**caffeine** ['kæf·'in] *n* caféine *f*

**cage** [keɪdʒ] I. *n a. fig* cage *f* II. *vt* enfermer dans une cage

**cake** [keɪk] I. *n* ① (*sweet*) gâteau *m*; **a piece of ~** un morceau de gâteau ② (*other food: of fish, potato, soap*) pain *m* ▶ **a piece of ~** *inf* une part du gâteau; **to want to have one's ~ and eat it, too** vouloir le beurre et l'argent du beurre; **to sell like hot ~** se vendre comme des petits pains II. *vt* (*blood*) coaguler; **to be ~d with sth** être couvert de qc III. *vi* ① (*dry*) sécher ② (*harden*) durcir; (*blood*) se coaguler

**calcium** ['kæl·si·əm] *n* calcium *m*

**calculate** ['kæl·kjə·leɪt] I. *vt* calculer; **to ~ sth at sth** estimer qc à qc II. *vi* calculer; **to ~ on sth** compter sur qc

**calculation** *n* calcul *m*; **to make ~s** effectuer des calculs

**calculator** *n* calculatrice *f*

**calendar** ['kæl·ən·dər] *n* calendrier *m*

**calf¹** [kæf] <calves> *n* ZOOL veau *m*

**calf²** [kæf] <calves> *n* ANAT mollet *m*

**California** [ˌkæl·ə·'fɔr·njə] *n* la Californie

**Californian** I. *n* Californien(ne) *m(f)* II. *adj* californien(ne)

**call** [kɔl] I. *n* ① TEL appel *m*; **telephone ~** appel *m* téléphonique; **to return a ~** rappeler ② (*visit*) visite *f* ③ (*shout*) cri *m*; **~ for help** appel *m* au secours ④ (*animal cry*) cri *m* ⑤ (*summons*) convocation *f* ⑥ REL vocation *f* ⑦ POL appel *m*; **~ for sth** appel à qc ⑧ ECON demande *f* ⑨ *form* (*need*) *a. iron* besoin *m* ⑩ COMPUT appel *m* ▶ **the ~ of nature** un besoin pressant; **to be on ~** (*doctor*) être de garde II. *vt* ① (*address as*) appeler; **to be ~ed sth** s'appeler qc; **to ~ sb names** injurier qn ② (*telephone*) appeler ③ (*say out loud*) appeler ④ (*make noise to attract*) crier ⑤ (*summon*) appeler; **to ~ sb as a witness** appeler qn à témoin; **to ~ sth to mind** rappeler qc ⑥ (*regard as*) trouver; **to ~ sb/sth a liar** considérer qn/qc comme étant un menteur; **you ~ this a party?** tu appelles/vous appelez cela une fête? ⑦ (*wake by telephoning*) réveiller ⑧ (*decide to*

**C**

*have*) appeler ► **to ~ sb's bluff** mettre qn au pied du mur; **to ~ it a day** *inf* s'en tenir là; **to ~ it quits** en rester là; **to ~ the shots** mener la barque III. *vi* ❶ (*telephone*) téléphoner; **to ~ collect** appeler en PCV ❷ (*drop by*) passer ❸ (*shout*) crier ❹ (*summon*) appeler

◆ **call away** *vt* **to call sb away** appeler qn

◆ **call back** I. *vt* rappeler II. *vi* ❶ (*phone again*) rappeler ❷ (*return*) repasser

◆ **call for** *vt* ❶ (*make necessary*) appeler à; **to be called for** être nécessaire ❷ (*come to get: person*) appeler; (*object, doctor*) faire venir ❸ (*ask*) appeler; **to ~ help** appeler à l'aide ❹ (*demand, require: food, attention*) demander

◆ **call in** I. *vt* ❶ (*ask to come*) faire venir; **to call sb in to** +*infin* faire venir qn pour +*infin* ❷ (*withdraw: money, book*) retirer de la circulation; (*car*) rappeler; (*a loan*) exiger le remboursement de II. *vi* appeler

◆ **call off** *vt* ❶ (*cancel*) annuler ❷ (*order back*) rappeler

◆ **call on** *vt insep* ❶ (*appeal to*) demander à ❷ (*pay a short visit*) rendre visite à ❸ *fig* (*appeal to*) avoir recours à

◆ **call out** I. *vt* ❶ (*shout*) appeler; **to ~ names at sb** injurier qn ❷ (*yell*) crier II. *vi* ❶ (*shout*) appeler ❷ (*yell*) crier ❸ *fig* (*demand*) **to ~ for sth** exiger qc

◆ **call up** *vt* ❶ (*telephone*) appeler ❷ COMPUT (*find and display*) appeler ❸ (*ordered to join the military*) appeler ❹ (*conjure up: memories*) évoquer

**caller** *n* ❶ (*person on the telephone*) correspondant(e) *m(f)* ❷ (*visitor*) visiteur, -euse *m, f*

**calligraphy** [kə-'lɪg-rə-fi] *n* calligraphie *f*

**calm** [ka(l)m] I. *adj* calme; **to keep ~** rester tranquille II. *vt* calmer; **to ~ oneself** se calmer

**calmly** *adv* calmement

**calorie** ['kæl-ə-ri] *n* calorie *f*

**calorie-laden** *adj inv* hypercalorique

**camcorder** ['kæm-kɔr-dər] *n* caméscope *m*

**came** [keɪm] *pt of* **come**

**camel** ['kæm-əl] I. *n* ❶ (*animal*) chameau *m*; **she-~** chamelle *f* ❷ (*color*) fauve *m* II. *adj* ❶ (*camelhair*) en poil de chameau ❷ (*color*) fauve

**camera**[1] ['kæm-ər-ə] *n* ❶ (*photography*) appareil *m* photo ❷ (*television*) caméra *f*; **~ operator** cadreur *m*

**camera**[2] ['kæm-ər-ə] *n a. fig* **in ~** = LAW à huis clos

**camouflage** ['kæm-ə-flɑʒ] I. *n* camouflage *m* II. *vt* camoufler; **to ~ oneself** se camoufler

**camp**[1] [kæmp] I. *n a. fig a.* MIL camp *m*; **summer ~** camp de vacances; **refugee ~** camp de réfugiés II. *vi* camper; **to ~ out** camper; **to go ~ing** faire du camping

**camp**[2] [kæmp] THEAT, SOCIOL I. *n no art* (*theatrical style*) manières *fpl* II. *adj* ❶ (*theatrical*) affecté(e) ❷ (*effeminate*) efféminé(e)

**campaign** [kæm-'peɪn] I. *n* campagne *f*; **~ for/against sth** campagne en faveur de/contre qc ❷ (*advertising*) ~ ECON campagne de publicité II. *vi* faire campagne; **to ~ for sb/sth** faire campagne en faveur de qn/qc; **to ~ against sb/sth** faire campagne contre qn/qc

**camper** *n* ❶ (*person*) campeur, -euse *m, f* ❷ (*vehicle*) camping-car *m*

**campfire** *n* feu *m* de camp

**campground** *n* camping *m*

**camping** *n* camping *m*; **to go ~** faire du camping; **~ equipment** équipement *m* de camping

**campsite** *n* ❶ (*place to camp*) terrain *m* de camping ❷ (*place for a tent*) place *f* pour camper

**campus** ['kæm-pəs] *n* campus *m*; **to be on ~** être sur le campus

**can**[1] [kæn] I. *n* ❶ (*metal container*) boîte *f* de conserve ❷ (*container's contents*) bidon *m*; (*of beer, paint*) boîte *f* ❸ *inf* **the ~** (*prison*) la taule ❹ *inf* (*toilet*) **the ~** les chiottes *fpl* ► **a ~ of worms** un véritable guêpier; **to be in the ~** CINE être dans la boîte; *fig* être dans la poche II. *vt* ❶ (*put in cans*) mettre en boîte, canner *Québec* ❷ *inf* (*fire*) jeter

**can**[2] [kən] <could, could> *aux* ❶ (*be able to*) pouvoir; **sb ~ +**infin qn peut **+**infin; **I will do all I ~** je ferais de mon mieux ❷ (*have knowledge*) savoir; **I ~ swim/cook** je sais nager/cuisiner; **I ~ speak French** je parle le français ❸ (*be permitted to*) pouvoir; **~ do** aucun problème; **s. may** ❹ (*offering assistance*) pouvoir; **~ I help you?** puis-je vous aider?; **s. may** ❺ (*making a request*) pouvoir; **~ I come?** est-ce que je peux venir? ❻ (*be possible*) **sb ~ do sth** qn fait peut-être qc ❼ (*said to show disbelief*) **~ it be true?** est-ce que c'est possible?; **how ~ you?** comment peux-tu faire une chose pareille!

**Canada** [ˈkæn·ə·də] *n* le Canada

**Canadian I.** *adj* canadien(ne) **II.** *n* Canadien(ne) *m(f)*

**canal** [kə·ˈnæl] *n* canal *m*

**cancel** [ˈkæn(t)·səl] <-l- *o* -ll-> **I.** *vt* ❶ (*annul*) annuler; (*order*) décommander; (*contract*) résilier; (*check*) faire opposition à; **to ~ each other** s'annuler ❷ (*mark as being used: a stamp*) oblitérer; (*ticket*) composter **II.** *vi* se décommander

**cancellation** [ˌkæn(t)·səl·ˈeɪ·ʃən] *n* annulation *f*; (*of a contract*) résiliation *f*

**cancer** [ˈkæn(t)·sər] *n* MED cancer *m*

**cancerous** [ˈkæn(t)·sˑr·əs] *adj* cancéreux(-euse)

**candid** [ˈkæn·dɪd] *adj* franc(he); **~ picture** photo *f* instantanée

**candidacy** [ˈkæn·dɪ·də·si] *n* candidature *f*

**candidate** [ˈkæn·dɪ·dət] *n* candidat(e) *m(f)*; **to stand as ~ for sth** se porter candidat à qc

**candle** [ˈkæn·dl] *n* bougie *f* ▶ **to burn one's ~ at both ends** brûler la chandelle par les deux bouts; **to not hold a ~ to sb/sth** ne pas arriver à la cheville de qn/qc

**candlelight** *n* lueur *f* d'une bougie; **~ dinner** dîner *m* aux chandelles

**candlestick** *n* bougeoir *m*

**candy** [ˈkæn·di] **I.** *n* bonbon(s) *m(pl)* **II.** *vt* glacer

**cane** [keɪn] *n* ❶ (*dried plant stem*) canne *f*; (*for wickerwork, baskets*) rotin *m* ❷ (*stick*) canne *f*

**canine** [ˈkeɪ·naɪn] **I.** *n* canine *f* **II.** *adj* canin(e)

**canned** [kænd] *adj* ❶ (*preserved in metal containers: food*) en conserve; (*beer*) en boîte ❷ *pej* TV, MUS (*pre-recorded*) en boîte

**cannibal** [ˈkæn·ɪ·bəl] *n* cannibale *mf*

**cannon** [ˈkæn·ən] **I.** *n* MIL (*weapon*) canon *m*; **~ fire** tir *m* de canon **II.** *vi* **to ~ into sb/sth** percuter qn/qc

**cannot** [ˈkæn·ɑt] *aux* (*can not*) *s.* **can**

**canoe** [kə·ˈnu] *n* NAUT (*boat*) canot *m*

**canon** [ˈkæn·ən] *n* canon *m*

**can opener** *n* ouvre-boîtes *m*

**can't** [kænt] = **can + not** *s.* **can**

**canteen** [kæn·ˈtin] *n* MIL gourde *f*

**canyon** [ˈkæn·jən] *n* canyon *m*

**cap**[1] [kæp] **I.** *n* ❶ (*hat*) casquette *f*; **shower ~** bonnet *m* de douche ❷ UNIV **~ and gown** costume *m* académique; **iron ~** tenue *f* d'apparat ❸ (*cover*) couvercle *m*; (*of a bottle*) bouchon *m*; (*of a pen, lens*) capuchon *m*; (*of a mushroom*) chapeau *m*; (*of a tooth*) émail *m* ❹ (*limit*) plafond *m* ▶ **to put on one's thinking ~** *inf* cogiter **II.** <-pp-> *vt* ❶ (*limit*) limiter ❷ (*cover*) *a. fig* coiffer; (*bottle*) capsuler; (*a tooth*) recouvrir d'émail

**cap**[2] [kæp] *n* TYP, PUBL *abbr of* **capital** (**letter**) capitale *f*; **in ~s** en capitales

**capability** [ˌkeɪ·pə·ˈbɪl·ə·ti] *n* capacité *f*

**capable** [ˈkeɪ·pə·bl] *adj* ❶ (*competent*) compétent(e) ❷ (*able*) capable; **to be ~ of doing sth** être capable de faire qc

**capacity** [kə·ˈpæs·ə·ti] *n* ❶ <-ies> (*amount*) capacité *f*; (*of container*) contenance *f*; **seating ~** nombre *m* de places assises ❷ (*ability*) aptitude *f*; **to have a ~ for sth** avoir une aptitude à faire qc ❸ (*output*) rendement *m*; **at full ~** à plein rendement ❹ (*position*) fonction *f*; **in the ~ of sth** en qualité de qc

**cape¹** [keɪp] *n* GEO cap *m*

**cape²** [keɪp] *n* FASHION cape *f*

**Cape Canaveral** *n* Cap Canaveral *m*

**capital¹** ['kæp·ə·tļ] **I.** *n* ❶ (*principal city*) a. *fig* capitale *f* ❷ (*letter form*) lettre *f* capitale; **in ~ s** en capitales **II.** *adj* ❶ (*principal: city*) principal(e) ❷ (*letter form: letter*) capital(e) ❸ LAW (*punishable by death*) capital(e)

**capital²** ['kæp·ə·tļ] *n* FIN capital *m;* **to put ~ into sth** investir dans qc

**capitalist I.** *n* a. *pej* capitaliste *mf* **II.** *adj* capitaliste

**capital letter** *n* lettre *f* capitale; **in ~s** en lettres capitales

**capital punishment** *n* peine *f* capitale

**capitulate** [kə·'pɪtʃ·ə·leɪt] *vi* a. *fig* MIL capituler; **to ~ to sb/sth** capituler face à qn/qc

**cappuccino** [ˌkæp·ə·'tʃi·noʊ] *n* cappuccino *m*

**Capricorn** ['kæp·rə·kɔrn] *n* Capricorne *m; s.a.* **Aquarius**

**capsize** ['kæp·saɪz] NAUT **I.** *vt* ❶ (*make turn over*) faire chavirer ❷ *fig* (*ruin*) faire échouer **II.** *vi* (*turn over*) chavirer

**captain** ['kæp·tᵊn] **I.** *n* a. *fig* capitaine *m* **II.** *vt* ❶ (*be in charge of*) mener ❷ (*be officer*) être capitaine de

**captive** ['kæp·tɪv] **I.** *n* captif, -ive *m, f* **II.** *adj* captif(-ive); **to take sb ~** capturer qn; **to hold sb ~** maintenir qn captif

**captivity** [kæp·'tɪv·ə·ṭi] *n* captivité *f*

**capture** ['kæp·tʃər] **I.** *vt* ❶ (*take prisoner*) capturer ❷ (*take possession of: city, control*) prendre; **to ~ sth** s'emparer de qc ❸ (*gain*) gagner ❹ ECON (*the market*) s'accaparer ❺ ART, CINE (*atmosphere*) rendre; (*on film*) immortaliser; **to ~ the moment** saisir l'instant ❻ *fig* (*attention*) captiver; (*moment, moods*) saisir ❼ COMPUT saisir **II.** *n* ❶ (*act of capturing*) capture *f* ❷ (*captured person, thing*) prise *f* ❸ COMPUT saisie *f*

**car** [kar] *n* voiture *f;* **by ~** en voiture; **~ accident** accident *m* de voiture

**caravan** ['ker·ə·væn] *n* caravane *f*

**carbohydrate** [ˌkar·boʊ·'haɪ·dreɪt] *n* CHEM hydrate *m* de carbone

**carbon dioxide** *n* CHEM gaz *m* carbonique

**carbon footprint** *n* empreinte *f* carbone, bilan *m* carbone

**carbon monoxide** *n* CHEM oxyde *m* de carbone

**carcinogen** [kar·'sin·ə·ˌdʒen] *n* MED substance *f* cancérigène

**carcinogenic** *adj* MED cancérigène

**card¹** [kard] **I.** *n* ❶ (*piece of stiff paper*) carte *f;* **birthday ~** carte d'anniversaire; **Christmas ~** carte de Noël; **business ~** carte de visite; **index ~** fiche *f* ❷ (*means of payment*) carte *f;* **credit ~** carte de crédit ❸ GAMES carte *f;* **to play ~s** jouer aux cartes ❹ (*proof of identity*) pièce *f* d'identité; **ID ~** carte *f* d'identité; **membership ~** carte de membre ❺ COMPUT carte *f* ❻ (*cardboard*) carton *m* ▸ **to lay one's ~s on the table** mettre cartes sur table; **to be on the ~s** être très vraisemblable **II.** *vt* ❶ (*write an account*) ficher ❷ *inf* (*demand identification*) demander les papiers d'identité à

**card²** [kard] **I.** *n* (*in mechanics*) peigne *m* **II.** *vt* peigner

**cardboard** ['kard·bɔrd] *n* (*thick paper*) carton *m;* **~ box** boîte *f* en carton

**card catalog** *n* fichier *m*

**cardiac** ['kar·dɪ·æk] *adj* MED cardiaque

**cardigan** ['kar·dɪ·gən] *n* cardigan *m*

**care** [ker] **I.** *n* ❶ (*looking after*) soin *m;* **hair ~** soin capillaire; **to take good ~ of sb/sth** prendre bien soin de qn/qc; **to be in sb's ~** être sous la responsabilité de qn; **to take ~ of oneself** s'occuper de ses affaires; **to take ~ of sth** s'occuper de qc; **(in) ~ of sb** aux bons soins de qn; **take ~!** fais attention (à toi)!; (*goodbye*) salut! ❷ (*carefulness*) prudence *f;* **to do sth with ~** faire qc avec prudence; **to take ~ that** veiller à ce que +*subj* ❸ (*worry*) souci *m;* **to not have a ~ in the world** ne pas avoir le moindre souci **II.** *vi* ❶ (*be concerned*) se faire du souci; **to ~ about sb/sth** se soucier de qn/qc; **not to ~ about sb/sth** se moquer de qn/qc; **I don't ~** ça m'est égal; **I couldn't ~ less** je m'en fiche; **who ~s?** qu'est-ce que ça fait? ②(*feel affection*) aimer; **to ~ about sb** aimer qn ③(*want*) vouloir; **to ~ to ~** +*infin* vouloir +*infin*; **to ~ for sth** vouloir qc

**career** [kə·ˈrɪr] **I.** *n* carrière *f*; **~ politician** homme *m* politique de carrière **II.** *vi* aller à toute vitesse

**carefree** [ˈker·fri] *adj* insouciant(e)

**careful** *adj* ①(*cautious*) prudent(e); **to be ~ doing sth** être prudent en faisant qc; (**be**) **~!** attention! ②(*showing attention*) attentif(-ive); **to be ~ with/about sth** faire attention à qc; **to be ~** (**that**) veiller à ce que +*subj*; **to be ~ to** +*infin* veiller à +*infin* ③(*painstaking: worker*) soigneux (-euse); (*work*) soigné(e); **to pay ~ attention to sth** prêter une attention particulière à qc

**careless** *adj* ①(*lacking wisdom: driver*) imprudent(e) ②(*inattentive*) inattentif(-ive); **~ error** erreur *f* d'inattention ③(*not worried*) insouciant(e) ④(*unthinking: remark*) irréfléchi(e) ⑤(*lacking care: work*) négligé(e); **to be ~** manquer de soin

**carelessness** *n* négligence *f*

**caretaker** *n* ①(*custodian*) concierge *mf* ②POL **~ government** gouvernement *m* intérimaire

**cargo** [ˈkɑr·goʊ] *n* cargaison *f*

**carnival** [ˈkɑr·nə·vəl] *n* carnaval *m*

**carnivore** [ˈkɑr·nə·vɔr] *n a. iron* carnivore *m*

**carol** [ˈker·əl] **I.** *n* (**Christmas**) **~** chant *m* de Noël **II.** *vi* chanter joyeusement; (*for Christmas*) chanter des chants de Noël

**carpenter** [ˈkɑr·pən·tər] *n* menuisier *m*

**carpentry** [ˈkɑr·pən·tri] *n* menuiserie *f*

**carpet** [ˈkɑr·pət] **I.** *n* ①(*rug*) *a. fig* tapis *m*; **~ of flowers** tapis de fleurs ②(*wall-to-wall*) moquette *f*, tapis *m* plain *Belgique*; **wall-to-wall ~** moquette *f* ▸ **to sweep sth under the ~** essayer de dissimuler qc **II.** *vt* **to ~ sth** re-

couvrir qc d'un tapis; (*with wall-to-wall carpet*) moquetter qc

**carriage** [ˈker·ɪdʒ] *n* ①(*horse-drawn vehicle*) voiture *f* ②(*posture*) port *m* ③(*part of a typewriter*) chariot *m*

**carrier** [ˈkæ·ri·ər] *n* ①(*person*) porteur, -euse *m, f* ②MIL (*vehicle*) véhicule *m* blindé; (*aircraft*) **~** porte-avions *m* ③(*transportation company: for people*) entreprise *f* de transport de personnes; (*for freight*) entreprise *f* de transport de fret; (*by air*) compagnie *f* aérienne ④(*entrepreneur*) transporteur *m* ⑤MED porteur, -euse *m, f* ⑥TEL **wireless ~** opérateur *m* de téléphonie mobile

**carrot** [ˈker·ət] *n* ①(*vegetable*) carotte *f* ②*inf* (*reward*) carotte *f*; **to dangle a ~ for sb** agiter une carotte devant qn

**carry** [ˈker·i] <-ies, -ied> **I.** *vt* ①(*transport*) porter ②(*transport*) transporter ③(*have on one's person*) avoir sur soi ④(*remember: a tune*) se rappeler; **to ~ sth in one's head** retenir qc dans sa tête ⑤MED transmettre ⑥(*have*) **to ~ insurance** être assuré ⑦(*support*) supporter ⑧(*keep going*) continuer ⑨(*sell*) vendre ⑩(*win support*) gagner à sa cause ⑪(*approve a bill*) voter ⑫PUBL rapporter; **to ~ a headline** faire la une ⑬(*develop: argument*) développer; (*too far*) pousser ⑭MATH (*put into next column: a number*) retenir ⑮(*stand*) **to ~ oneself** se comporter ⑯(*be pregnant: child*) attendre **II.** *vi* ①(*be audible*) porter ②(*fly*) voler

◆**carry forward** *vt* ECON reporter

◆**carry off** *vt* ①(*take away*) enlever ②(*succeed*) réussir ③(*win*) remporter

◆**carry on I.** *vt* soutenir **II.** *vi* ①(*continue*) poursuivre; **to ~ doing sth** continuer à faire qc, perdurer à faire qc *Belgique*; **to ~ as if nothing had happened** faire comme si rien ne s'était passé ②*inf* (*make a fuss*) faire des histoires ③(*complain*) **to ~ at sb** se plaindre à bâtons rompus auprès de qn

◆**carry out** *vt* réaliser; (*threat, plan*) mettre à exécution; (*attack*) conduire;

C

(*reform, test*) effectuer; (*orders*) exécuter; **to ~ sth to the letter** suivre les ordres à la lettre

◆**carry over I.** *vt* ❶ ECON (*bring forward*) apporter ❷ FIN reporter ❸ (*postpone*) retarder; (*holiday*) reporter **II.** *vi* **to ~ into sth** avoir des répercussions sur qc

◆**carry through** *vt* ❶ (*support*) soutenir ❷ (*complete*) mener à bien

**carryover I.** *n* FIN report *m* **II.** *vt* reporter

**CARS** [ka:rz] *n no pl abbr of* **Car Allowance Rebate System** prime *f* à la casse

**carsick** *adj* **to be ~** être malade en voiture

**cart** [kart] **I.** *n* ❶ (*vehicle*) voiture *f* à bras; **horse ~** charrette *f* ❷ (*in supermarket*) chariot *m* ▶ **to put the ~ before the horse** mettre la charrue avant les bœufs *prov* **II.** *vt* ❶ (*transport*) charrier ❷ (*carry*) transporter par camion ❸ (*carry around*) trimballer

**carte blanche** [ˌkart·'bla(n)ʃ] *n* carte *f* blanche; **to be given ~** avoir carte blanche

**cartilage** ['kar·t̬əl·ɪdʒ] *n* MED cartilage *m*

**carton** ['kar·t̬ən] *n* ❶ (*box*) carton *m* ❷ (*packaging*) boîte *f*; (*of milk, juice*) brique *f*; (*of cigarettes*) cartouche *f*

**cartoon** [kar·'tun] *n* ❶ CINE dessin *m* animé ❷ (*critical*) dessin *m* satirique

**cartridge** ['kar·trɪdʒ] *n* ❶ (*ink, ammunition*) cartouche *f* ❷ (*cassette*) cassette *f* ❸ (*pick-up head*) cellule *f* de lecture

**cartwheel** ['kart·(h)wil] **I.** *n* ❶ (*wheel*) roue *f* de charrette ❷ (*sport*) **to do/turn a ~** faire une roue **II.** *vi* faire la roue

**carve** [karv] **I.** *vt* ❶ (*cut a figure*) sculpter; (*with a chisel*) ciseler ❷ (*cut*) tailler; (*meat*) découper; **to ~ sth out from sth** tailler qc dans qc ❸ *fig* (*establish*) **to ~ a niche for oneself** se tailler une place dans qc **II.** *vi* sculpter

**carving** *n* ❶ (*art*) sculpture *f* ❷ (*figure*) sculpture *f*; (*of wood*) figurine *f* en bois

**case**[1] [keɪs] *n* ❶ *a.* MED cas *m*; **in any ~**

en tout cas; **in ~ it rains** au cas où il pleuvrait; **~ in point** exemple *m* typique ❷ LING cas *m*; **in the genitive ~** au génitif ❸ LAW affaire *f*; **to lose one's ~** perdre son procès

**case**[2] [keɪs] *n* ❶ (*chest*) coffre *m* ❷ (*container*) boîte *f*; (*bottles*) caisse *f*; (*vegetables*) cageot *m*; (*silverware, jewels*) écrin *m*; (*glasses, cigarettes, flute*) étui *m*; **glass ~** vitrine *f* ❸ TYP *s.* **lower case, upper case**

**cash** [kæʃ] **I.** *n* liquide *m*; **to pay in ~** payer comptant; **to be strapped for ~** *inf* être à court d'argent **II.** *vt* (*exchange for money*) toucher; (*check*) encaisser

◆**cash in I.** *vt* se faire rembourser ▶ **to ~ (one's chips)** *inf* casser sa pipe **II.** *vi* **to ~ on sth** tirer profit de qc

**cashier** [kæʃ·'ɪr] *n* caissier, -ière *m, f*

**casino** [kə·'si·noʊ] *n* casino *m*

**casket** ['kæs·kɪt] *n* ❶ (*coffin*) cercueil *m* ❷ (*box*) coffret *m*

**casserole** ['kæs·ə·roʊl] *n* ❶ (*stew*) ragoût *m* (en cocotte) ❷ (*cooking pot*) cocotte *f*; **~ dish** marmite *f*

**cassette** [kə·'set] *n* cassette *f*; **audio/video ~** cassette audio/vidéo

**cassette recorder** *n* magnétophone *m* à cassettes

**cast** [kæst] **I.** *n* ❶ THEAT, CINE acteurs *mpl*; (*list*) distribution *f* ❷ (*molded object*) moule *m* ❸ MED plâtre *m* ❹ (*act of throwing: spear, line*) lancer *m* ❺ *fig* (*of mind*) tournure *f* **II.**<*cast, cast*> *vt* ❶ (*throw*) jeter; (*a line, spear*) lancer ❷ *fig* (*direct: doubt, a shadow*) jeter; **to ~ light on sth** éclaircir qc; **to ~ an eye over sth** balayer qc du regard ❸ (*allocate roles: play*) distribuer les rôles de; **to be ~ in the role of sb** jouer le rôle de qn; **to ~ sb as sb** donner le rôle de qn à qn ❹ (*give*) **to ~ one's vote** voter ❺ ART (*make in a mold*) fondre

◆**cast aside** *vt* ❶ (*rid oneself of*) se débarrasser de ❷ (*free oneself of*) se défaire de

◆**cast off I.** *vt* ❶ *s.* **cast aside** ❷ (*drop stitches*) **to ~ stitches** arrêter les mailles ③(*reject*) rejeter II. *vi* NAUT larguer les amarres

◆**cast out** *vt* ①(*reject*) rejeter ②(*exorcise: demons, ideas*) chasser

**castle** ['kæs·l] I. *n* ①(*building*) château *m* ②(*fortress*) château fort ③ *inf* (*chess piece*) tour *f* ► **a man's home is his** ~ charbonnier est maître chez lui II. *vi* GAMES roquer

**casual** ['kæʒ·u·əl] *adj* ①(*relaxed*) décontracté(e) ②(*not permanent*) occasionnel(le); (*relation*) de passage; (*sex*) sans lendemain ③(*careless, not serious*) désinvolte; (*attitude*) insouciant(e) ④ FASHION (*clothes*) sport *inv*

**casually** *adv* ①(*without premeditation: glance, remark*) en passant; (*meet*) par hasard ②(*informally: walk*) avec décontraction; (*dressed*) sport ③(*carelessly: treat*) avec désinvolture

**casualty** ['kæʒ·u·əl·ti] <-ies> *n* ①(*accident victim*) victime *f* d'un accident; (*injured person*) blessé(e) *m(f)*; (*dead person*) perte *f* (*victims*) *pl* (*victims*) victimes *fpl*; MIL pertes *fpl* ②*fig* (*negative result*) conséquence *f* néfaste

**casualwear** *n* vêtements *mpl* sport

**cat** [kæt] *n* ①(*feline*) chat(te) *m(f)*; **stray** ~ chat errant ②(*class of animal*) félin *m* ► **to fight like** ~ **and dog** se quereller comme chien et chat; **to play (a game of)** ~ **and mouse** jouer au chat et à la souris; **the** ~**'s got sb's tongue** avoir perdu sa langue; **to let the** ~ **out of the bag** vendre la mèche; **to look like something the** ~ **dragged in** être dégoûtant; **to rain** ~**s and dogs** pleuvoir à torrent

**catalog, catalogue** ['kæt̬·ə·lɔg] I. *n* ①(*book*) catalogue *m*; **mail order** ~ catalogue de vente par correspondance ②(*repeated events: of mistakes*) suite *f* II. *vt* cataloguer

**catalyst** ['kæt̬·ə·lɪst] *n* CHEM *a. fig* catalyseur *m*

**catalytic** [kæt̬·ə·'lɪt·ɪk] *adj* catalytique

**catastrophe** [kə·'tæs·trə·fi] *n* ①(*terrible thing*) catastrophe *f* ②*fig* fléau *m*

**catastrophic** *adj* catastrophique

**catch** [kætʃ] <-es> I. *n* ①SPORTS prise *f* au vol ②(*fishing*) prise *f* ③(*device*) loquet *m*; (*of window*) loqueteau *m*; (*of jewel*) fermoir *m* ④ *inf* (*suitable partner*) (bon) parti *m* ⑤(*trick*) truc *m*; ~**-22** (*situation*) cercle *m* vicieux II. <caught, caught> *vt* ①(*intercept and hold*) attraper ②(*grasp*) saisir ③(*capture*) attraper; *fig* (*atmosphere*) rendre ④(*attract*) attirer; (*attention*) retenir ⑤*fig* (*captivate*) captiver ⑥(*get*) prendre; **to** ~ **a few rays** prendre un peu le soleil ⑦(*not miss: train, bus*) attraper; (*be on time: train, bus*) prendre ⑧(*perceive, understand: sounds*) saisir; (*radio*) écouter; (*film*) voir; **to** ~ **sight of sb/sth** apercevoir qn/qc ⑨(*take by surprise*) surprendre; **to get caught** se faire prendre; **to** ~ **sb doing sth** surprendre qn en train de faire qc; **to** ~ **sb red-handed** prendre qn en flagrant délit ⑩(*become entangled*) **to get caught (up) in sth** être pris dans qc ⑪(*contract: habit*) prendre ⑫MED (*be infected*) attraper ⑬(*hit: missile, blow*) atteindre ⑭(*start burning*) **to** ~ **fire** prendre feu ⑮ *inf* (*fool*) avoir ► **to** ~ **one's breath** reprendre son souffle III. *vi* ①(*start: fire*) prendre ②(*be stuck*) **to** ~ **on sth** s'accrocher à qc

◆**catch on** *vi* ①(*be popular*) avoir du succès ②(*understand*) piger

◆**catch out** *vt* ①(*take by surprise*) surprendre; **to be caught out by sth** être surpris par qc ②(*trick*) piéger

◆**catch up** I. *vt* rattraper; **to be/get caught up in sth** être entraîné/se laisser entraîner dans qc II. *vi* rattraper son retard; **to** ~ **with sb/sth** rattraper qn/qc; **to** ~ **on work** rattraper son travail

**catcher** *n* SPORTS (*baseball player*) receveur *m*

**catching** *adj a. fig, inf* contagieux(-euse)

**categorize** ['kæ·t̬ə·gə·raɪz] *vt* classer

**category** ['kæ·t̬ə·gɔr·i] <-ies> *n* catégorie *f*

**catering** *n* ①(*providing of food and drink*) restauration *f* ②(*service*) (service) *m* traiteur *m*

**caterpillar** [ˈkæt̬·ər·pɪl·ər] n ZOOL chenille f

**catfish** n poisson-chat m

**cathedral** [kəˈθiːdrəl] n cathédrale f

**cattle** [ˈkæt̬·l] npl bétail m inv; **dairy ~** vaches fpl laitières

**cattle prod** n baguette f électrique

**caught** [kɔt] pt, pp of **catch**

**cauliflower** [ˈkɔ·lɪ·flaʊər] n chou-fleur m

**cause** [kɔz] I. n ❶(origin) cause f ❷(motive) raison f ❸(objective) cause f ❹(movement) cause f; **to act for the ~ of democracy** agir pour la démocratie ❺(court case) affaire f II. vt provoquer; (trouble, delay) causer; **to ~ sb harm** faire du tort à qn; **the teacher's remarks ~d the child to cry** les remarques fpl du maître ont fait pleurer l'enfant

**caustic** [ˈkɔ·stɪk] adj a. fig caustique; (humor) décapant(e)

**caution** [ˈkɔ·ʃən] I. n ❶(carefulness) prudence f ❷(warning) avertissement m; **~!** attention! ▸ **to treat sb/ sth with ~** prendre qn/qc avec des pincettes II. vt form mettre en garde; **to ~ sb against a danger** prévenir qn d'un danger; **to ~ sb against doing sth** déconseiller qn de faire qc

**cautious** [ˈkɔ·ʃəs] adj prudent(e); **to be ~** se montrer prévoyant

**cave** [keɪv] I. n ❶(hole) grotte f ❷MIN affaissement m II. vi faire de la spéléologie

**caveat** [ˈkæv·i·æt] n mise f en garde

**cave dweller** n troglodyte mf

**caveman** <-men> n ❶(prehistoric man) homme m des cavernes ❷pej (socially underdeveloped) sauvage m

**cavern** [ˈkæ·vərn] n caverne f

**cavity** [ˈkæ·və·t̬i] <-ties> n ❶ANAT cavité f ❷(hollow space) creux m ❸(in a tooth) carie f

**CD** [ˌsiˈdi] n abbr of **compact disc** CD m

**CD player** n abbr of **compact disc player** lecteur m de CD

**CD-ROM** n abbr of **compact disc read-only memory** COMPUT CD-ROM m, cédérom m

**cease** [sis] I. n **without ~** sans cesse II. vi cesser III. vt (aid) couper; (fire) cesser; (payment) interrompre

**ceiling** [ˈsi·lɪŋ] n ❶(opposite floor, upper limit) plafond m ❷METEO **cloud ~** couverture f nuageuse ❸AVIAT plafond m ▸ **he hit the ~** inf il explosa de colère

**celebrate** [ˈsel·ə·breɪt] I. vi faire la fête II. vt ❶(mark an event with festivities) célébrer; (anniversary of death) commémorer; (a deal) fêter ❷REL (Eucharist) célébrer ❸(revere publicly) **to ~ sb as a hero** élever qn au rang de héros

**celebration** n ❶(party) fête f; **this calls for a ~!** inf il faut marquer ça ! ❷(of an occasion) cérémonie f ❸(of a death) commémoration f ❹(religious ceremony) célébration f

**celebrity** [səˈleb·rə·t̬i] n <-ties> ❶(famous person) célébrité f ❷(of the entertainment industry) star f ❸(fame) célébrité f

**celery** [ˈsel·ər·i] n céleri m

**cell** [sel] n ❶(small room) cellule f ❷(compartments) case f ❸(part of honeycomb) alvéole m of ❹BIO, POL cellule f ❺ELEC **battery ~** élément m de pile

**cellar** [ˈsel·ər] n cave f

**cellist** n violoncelliste mf

**cello** [ˈtʃel·oʊ] <-s o -li> n violoncelle m

**cellophane®** [ˈsel·ə·feɪn] n cellophane® f

**cell phone** [ˈsel·foʊn] n téléphone m portable, mobile m, cellulaire m Québec, Natel® m Suisse

**cellular** [ˈsel·jʊ·lər] adj ❶(porous) a. BIO cellulaire ❷TECH alvéolaire ❸TEL **~ (tele)phone** téléphone m portable, cellulaire m Québec, Natel® m Suisse

**Celsius** [ˈsel·si·əs] adj (thermometer) de Celsius; **twenty degrees ~** vingt degrés Celsius

**cement** [sɪˈment] I. n ❶(used in construction) ciment m ❷(concrete) béton m ❸(binding material) mastic m

**❹** (*uniting idea*) ciment *m* **II.** *vt* cimenter ▸ **to ~ a friendship** sceller une amitié

**cemetery** ['sem·ə·ter·i] <-ries> *n* cimetière *m*

**censor** ['sen(t)·sər] **I.** *n* censeur *mf* **II.** *vt* censurer

**cent** [sent] *n* cent *m* ▸ **to put in your/his/her two ~s worth** *inf* mettre ton/son grain de sel

**centennial** [sen·'ten·i·əl] **I.** *adj* centenaire **II.** *n* centenaire *m*

**center** ['sen·tər] **I.** *n* centre *m;* **test ~** centre d'essai **II.** *vt* centrer

**centigrade I.** *n* METEO **ten degrees ~** dix degrés (Celsius) **II.** *adj* centigrade

**centigram** *n* centigramme *m*

**centiliter** *n* centilitre *m*

**centimeter** *n* centimètre *m*

**central** ['sen·trəl] *adj* ❶ (*close to the middle*) central(e) ❷ (*paramount*) primordial(e); (*issue*) essentiel(le) ❸ (*national: bank*) central(e)

**Central America** *n* l'Amérique *f* centrale

**century** ['sen·(t)ʃər·i] <-ies> *n* siècle *m;* **to be centuries old** avoir plusieurs siècles

**CEO** [ˌsi·i·'ou] *n abbr of* **chief executive officer**

**ceramics** *n + sing vb* céramique *f*

**cereal** ['sɪr·i·əl] *n* céréale *f*

**ceremony** ['ser·ə·moun·i] <-nies> *n* ❶ (*celebration*) cérémonie *f* ❷ (*required behavior*) cérémonial *m*

**certain** ['sɜr·tən] **I.** *adj* certain(e); **to be ~ about sth** être certain de qc; **please be ~ to turn out the lights** assurez-vous que vous avez éteint les lumières; **he no longer was ~ where they lived** il ne savait plus exactement où ils habitaient **II.** *pron + pl vb* **~ of her students have failed the exam** certain(e)s de ses étudiant(e)s ont raté l'examen

**certainly** *adv* ❶ (*surely*) certainement; **she ~ is right!** elle a raison, c'est sûr ! ❷ (*gladly*) bien sûr

**certainty** ['sɜr·tən·ti] *n* certitude *f*

**certificate** [sər·'tɪf·ɪ·kət] *n* ❶ (*document*) certificat *m;* **birth ~** extrait *m* de naissance; **death/marriage ~** acte *m* de décès/mariage; **~ of ownership** titre *m* de propriété ❷ SCHOOL diplôme *m;* **teaching ~** ≈ certificat *m* d'aptitude à l'enseignement

**certification** *n* ❶ (*state or process*) authentification *f* ❷ (*document*) certificat *m*

**certify** ['sɜr·tə·faɪ] <-ie-> *vt* certifier; **to ~ sb as insane** déclarer qn fou

**cessation** [ses·'eɪ·ʃən] *n form* ❶ (*end*) cessation *f* ❷ (*pause*) interruption *f;* (*of hostilities*) trêve *f*

**chagrin** [ʃə·'grɪn] *n* dépit *m*

**chain** [tʃeɪn] **I.** *n* ❶ (*set of related things*) chaîne *f;* **gold/silver ~** chaîne en or/en argent; **fast food ~** chaîne de fast-food; **~ of mishaps** série *f* de malheurs ❷ (*rings to hold captive*) entraves *fpl;* **ball and ~** boulet *m;* **~ gang** chaîne de forçats ❸ GEO chaîne *f* ❹ (*restrictions*) joug *m* **II.** *vt* enchaîner ▸ **to be ~ed to a desk** être rivé à son bureau

**chair** [tʃer] **I.** *n* ❶ (*seat*) chaise *f* ❷ (*chairman, chairwoman*) président(e) *m(f)* ❸ (*head*) présidence *f* ❹ (*head of an academic department*) chaire *f* ❺ (*place in an official body*) **to have a ~ on a board** être membre d'un comité ❻ **the ~** (*the electric chair*) la chaise électrique **II.** *vt* présider

**chairlift** *n* télésiège *m*

**chairman** <-men> *n* président *m*

**chairperson** *n* président(e) *m(f)*

**chairwoman** <-women> *n* présidente *f*

**chalk** [tʃɔk] **I.** *n* craie *f* **II.** *vt* écrire à la craie

**◆chalk up** *vt* ❶ inscrire ❷ (*achieve*) remporter ▸ **chalk sth up to experience** *inf* mettre qc sur le compte de l'expérience

**chalkboard** *n* tableau *m*

**challenge** ['tʃæl·ɪndʒ] **I.** *n* ❶ (*test, difficulty*) défi *m* ❷ LAW récusation *f* **II.** *vt* ❶ (*ask to compete*) défier; **to ~ sb to** +*infin* défier qn de +*infin* ❷ (*question*) contester ❸ (*stimulate*) stimuler ❹ MIL **to ~ sb** sommer qn d'indiquer son nom et le motif de sa présence ❺ LAW récuser

**challenger** *n* concurrent(e) *m(f)*

**challenging** *adj* (*book*) stimulant(e); (*idea*) provocateur(-trice); (*behavior*) de défi

**champ** [tʃæmp] *n* *inf* champion(ne) *m(f)*

**champagne** [ʃæmˈpeɪn] *n* champagne *m*

**champion** [ˈtʃæm·pi·ən] I. *n* ❶ SPORTS champion *m*; **defending ~** champion en titre ❷ (*supporter or defender*) défenseur *m* II. *vt* défendre

**championship** *n* ❶ (*competition*) championnat *m* ❷ (*supporting*) défense *f*

**chance** [tʃæn(t)s] I. *n* ❶ (*random*) hasard *m*; **by any ~** à tout hasard ❷ (*likelihood*) chance *f* ❸ (*opportunity*) occasion *f*; **to miss one's ~** laisser passer sa chance ❹ (*hazard*) risque *m*; **to take a ~** tenter le coup II. *vi* **they ~d to be there** il se trouve qu'ils étaient là III. *vt* tenter

**change** [tʃeɪndʒ] I. *n* ❶ (*alteration*) changement *m*; **it's a ~ for the worse** c'est changer pour le pire; **to have to make four ~s** devoir changer quatre fois; **for a ~** pour changer ❷ (*fluctuation*) évolution *f*; **there's no ~ in his condition** son état n'a pas évolué ❸ (*extra outfit: of clothes*) rechange *m* ❹ (*coins*) monnaie *f*; **small ~** petite monnaie; **do you have ~ for a twenty-dollar bill?** avez-vous/as-tu de la monnaie sur un billet de vingt dollars? II. *vi* ❶ (*alter*) passer; **the wind ~d to west** le vent a tourné à l'ouest ❷ (*get on different plane or train*) changer ❸ (*put on different clothes*) se changer; **I'll ~ into a dress** je me change pour mettre une robe; **the baby needs changing** le bébé a besoin d'être changé III. *vt* ❶ (*alter*) changer ❷ (*give coins for*) faire la monnaie de ❸ (*exchange currencies*) **to ~ money** changer de l'argent ❹ (*to swap*) échanger

**changeover** *n* *sing* passage *m*

**channel** [ˈtʃæn·əl] I. *n* ❶ TV chaîne *f*; **change the ~** changer de chaîne; **on ~ five** sur la cinq ❷ (*waterway*) canal *m*; **the English Channel** la Manche ❸ (*means*) moyen *m* de canaliser II. <-l- o -ll-> *vt* canaliser

**Channel Tunnel** *n* tunnel *m* sous la Manche

**Chanukah** *n* s. Hanukkah

**chaos** [ˈkeɪ·as] *n* ❶ (*confusion*) chaos *m* ❷ *fig* pagaille *f*; **the room was in a total ~** la pièce était sens dessus dessous

**chaotic** [keɪˈa·t̮ɪk] *adj* chaotique

**chap** [tʃæp] <-pp-> I. *vi* se gercer II. *vt* gercer III. *n* gerçure *f*

**chapel** [ˈtʃæp·əl] *n* chapelle *f*

**chapter** [ˈtʃæp·t̮ər] *n* ❶ (*of a book*) chapitre *m* ❷ (*episode*) épisode *m* ❸ (*of an organization*) branche *f*

**character** [ˈker·ək·t̮ər] *n* ❶ (*set of qualities*) *a.* COMPUT, TYP caractère *m* ❷ (*person in a book or play*) personnage *m* ❸ (*odd or different person*) personnage *m*

**characteristic** [ˌker·ək·təˈrɪs·tɪk] I. *n* caractéristique *f* II. *adj* caractéristique

**characterization** *n* caractérisation *f*

**charge** [tʃardʒ] I. *n* ❶ (*cost*) frais *mpl*; **free of ~** gratuit ❷ LAW accusation *f*; **to press ~s against sb** porter des accusations contre qn; **to drop the ~s against sb** retirer sa plainte contre qn ❸ MIL charge *f* ❹ (*authority*) **to be in ~** être responsable; **to take ~ of sth** prendre qc en charge; **I'm in ~ here** c'est moi le chef ici ❺ ELEC charge *f* II. *vi* ❶ (*ask a price*) faire payer ❷ (*lunge, attack*) charger; **to ~ at sb** charger qn ❸ ELEC (*battery*) se (re)charger III. *vt* ❶ (*ask a price*) faire payer ❷ (*interest, commission*) prélever ❷ (*accuse*) accuser; **to be ~d with sth** être accusé de qc ❸ (*order*) ordonner; **to ~ sb with sth** confier qc à qn ❹ ELEC, MIL (re)charger ❺ (*attack*) charger

**charge card** *n* carte *f* de crédit

**charging station** *n* chargeur *m*; (*for electric vehicles*) borne *f* de recharge

**charitable** [ˈtʃer·ɪ·t̮ə·bl] *adj* ❶ (*with*

*money*) généreux(-euse); (*with kind-ness*) altruiste ❷ (*concerning charity*) charitable; (*foundation*) caritatif(-ive); (*donations*) généreux(-euse)

**charity** ['tʃer·ə·t̬i] *n* ❶ (*generosity*) générosité *f* ❷ (*organization*) association *f* caritative; ~ **work** bonnes œuvres *fpl* <-**ties**> (*organization*) bonnes œuvres *fpl*

**charm** [tʃɑrm] **I.** *n* ❶ (*quality*) charme *m* ❷ (*characteristic*) attraits *mpl* ❸ (*pendant*) amulette *f* ❹ (*talisman*) talisman *m*; **lucky** ~ porte-bonheur *m* **II.** *vt* séduire; **to** ~ **sb into doing sth** obtenir qc de qn par le charme

**charming** *adj* ❶ (*likable*) *a. pej* charmant(e) ❷ *iron, pej* (*inconsiderate*) odieux(-euse)

**chart** [tʃɑrt] **I.** *n* ❶ (*table*) graphique *m*; **medical** ~ courbe *f* ❷ *pl* (*weekly list*) hit-parade *m* **II.** *vt* ❶ (*represent*) représenter; (*progress*) observer; **the map ~s the course of the river** la carte montre le cours de la rivière ❷ (*examine*) examiner ❸ (*plan*) planifier

**charter flight** *n* vol *m* charter

**chase** [tʃeɪs] **I.** *n* ❶ (*pursuit*) poursuite *f*; **to give** ~ **to sb** donner la chasse à qn ❷ (*hunt*) chasse *f* **II.** *vt* poursuivre ▸ **to** ~ **women** courir après les femmes

**chassis** ['tʃæs·i] <-> *n* châssis *m*

**chat** [tʃæt] **I.** *n* ❶ (*conversation*) conversation *f*; **to have a** ~ **with sb about sth** discuter avec qn au sujet de qc ❷ (*inconsequential talk*) bavardage *m* ❸ COMPUT chat *m* **II.** *vi* <-tt-> bavarder; **to** ~ **with** [*o* to] **sb about sb/sth** discuter avec qn de qn/qc

**chatter I.** *n* conversation *f*; (*of birds*) pépiements *mpl* **II.** *vi* ❶ (*converse*) **to** ~ **about sth** converser à propos de qc ❷ (*make clacking noises*) claquer; (*machines*) cliqueter; (*birds*) pépier ❸ COMPUT chatter

**cheap** [tʃip] *adj* ❶ (*inexpensive*) bon marché *inv*; (*ticket*) économique; **dirt** ~ très bon marché; ~ **labor** *pej* main-d'œuvre *f* sous-payée; **to be** ~ **to operate** être peu coûteux à l'utilisation

❷ *fig* (*worthless: joke*) facile; **to look** ~ avoir l'air vulgaire ❸ *pej* (*shoddy: goods*) de pacotille ❹ *pej, inf* (*miserly*) radin(e) ❺ *pej* (*mean: trick, liar*) sale ▸ **a** ~ **shot** un mauvais coup

**cheapen** ['tʃi·pən] *vt* ❶ (*lower price*) déprécier ❷ (*reduce morally*) rabaisser

**cheat** [tʃit] **I.** *n* ❶ (*trickster*) tricheur, -euse *m, f* ❷ (*deception*) tromperie *f* **II.** *vi* tricher; **to be caught** ~**ing** se faire surprendre en train de tricher **III.** *vt* tromper; **to** ~ **sb out of sth** escroquer qn de qc; **to feel** ~**ed** se sentir dupé

**check** [tʃek] **I.** *n* ❶ (*inspection*) vérification *f*; **security** ~ inspection *f* de sécurité; **spot** ~**s** inspections *fpl* ponctuelles ❷ (*search for information*) enquête *f*; **background** ~ investigation *f* de fond; **to run a** ~ **on sb** vérifier les antécédents de qn ❸ (*money*) chèque *m*; **a** ~ **for ...** un chèque pour la somme de ...; **to make a** ~ **out to sb** écrire un chèque à l'ordre de qn; **to pay by** [*o* **with a**] ~ payer par chèque ❹ (*receipt for deposit*) reçu *m* ❺ (*place for leaving items*) **coat** ~ vestiaire *m* ❻ (*pattern*) carreaux *mpl* ❼ (*check mark*) marque *f* ❽ (*intersection*) intersection *f* ❾ (*bill*) addition *f* ❿ GAMES échec *m* **II.** *adj* (*shirt*) à carreaux **III.** *vt* ❶ (*inspect*) vérifier; **to** ~ **through** [*o* **over**] **sth** passer qc en revue; **to double-**~ revérifier qc ❷ (*control: person, ticket, work*) contrôler ❸ (*make a mark*) marquer; (*answer, item*) cocher (sur une liste) ❹ (*halt*) faire échec à; (*crisis*) enrayer ❺ (*temporarily deposit*) mettre en consigne ❻ AVIAT enregistrer ❼ GAMES **to** ~ **sb's king** mettre le roi en échec **IV.** *vi* ❶ (*examine*) vérifier; **to** ~ **on sth** vérifier qc; **to** ~ **on sb** examiner qn; **to** ~ **with sb/sth** vérifier auprès de qn/qc ❷ (*ask*) demander; **to** ~ **with sb** demander à qn ❸ (*halt*) s'arrêter ❹ (*be in accordance with*) **to** ~ **with sth** être en harmonie avec qc

◆**check in I.** *vi* (*at airport*) se présenter à l'enregistrement; (*at hotel*) signer le registre **II.** *vt* enregistrer

◆**check off** *vt* cocher (sur une liste)

◆**check out** I. *vi* quitter l'hôtel; **to ~ of a room** payer la facture d'une chambre d'hôtel II. *vt* ❶ (*investigate*) enquêter sur ❷ (*verify*) vérifier ❸ *inf* (*look at*) jeter un œil à

◆**check up** *vi* vérifier

**checkbook** *n* carnet *m* de chèques

**checker** *n* (*in supermarket*) caissier, -ière *m, f*

**checkers** *n* GAMES jeu *m* de dames

**check-in desk** *n* bureau *m* d'enregistrement

**checking account** *n* compte *m* courant

**check-in time** *n* heure *f* d'enregistrement

**checklist** *n* liste *f* de contrôle

**check mark** *n* marque *f*

**checkmate** I. *n* ❶ (*in chess*) échec *m* et mat ❷ (*defeat*) défaite *f* II. *vt* ❶ (*in chess*) mettre en échec ❷ (*defeat*) vaincre

**checkout** *n* caisse *f*

**checkpoint** *n* point *m* de contrôle

**checkup** *n* bilan *m* de santé

**cheek** [tʃik] *n* (*face*) joue *f*

**cheeky** ['tʃi·ki] <-ier, -iest> *adj* effronté(e)

**cheer** [tʃɪr] I. *n* ❶ (*shout*) acclamation *f*; **three ~s for the champion!** trois hourras pour le champion! ❷ (*joy*) gaieté *f* II. *vi* pousser des acclamations III. *vt* ❶ (*applaud*) acclamer ❷ (*cheer up*) remonter le moral à

**cheerful** *adj* ❶ (*happy*) joyeux(-euse) ❷ (*positive in attitude*) optimiste ❸ (*bright*) lumineux(-euse); (*color*) vif(vive); (*tune*) gai(e) ❹ (*willing*) de bonne grâce

**cheese** [tʃiz] *n* fromage *m* ▸ **the big ~** *inf* grand chef *m*; **say ~** souriez, le petit oiseau va sortir

**cheeseburger** *n* hamburger *m* au fromage

**cheesecake** *n* gâteau *m* au fromage

**cheetah** ['tʃi·tə] *n* guépard *m*

**chef** [ʃef] *n* chef *m*; **pastry ~** chef pâtissier

**chemical** ['kem·ɪ·kəl] I. *n* ❶ (*atom*) atome *m* ❷ (*additive*) produit *m* chimique II. *adj* chimique

**chemist** ['kem·ɪst] *n* chimiste *mf*

**chemistry** ['kem·ɪ·stri] *n* ❶ (*study of chemicals*) chimie *f* ❷ *inf* (*attraction*) osmose *f*

**cherry** ['tʃer·i] I. <-ries> *n* ❶ (*fruit*) cerise *f* ❷ (*tree*) cerisier *m* II. *n* ❶ (*of cherry*) à la cerise ❷ (*made of wood*) en cerisier ❸ (*flavored*) parfumé(e) à la cerise ❹ (*red*) rouge cerise *inv*

**cherry blossom** *n* fleur *f* de cerisier

**chess** [tʃes] *n* échecs *mpl*

**chessboard** *n* échiquier *m*

**chest** [tʃest] *n* ❶ (*part of the torso*) poitrine *f*; **hairy ~** torse *m* velu ❷ (*breasts*) poitrine *f* ❸ (*trunk*) armoire *f*; **medicine ~** pharmacie *f* ▸ **to get sth off one's ~** se soulager le cœur

**chestnut** I. *n* ❶ (*brown nut*) marron *m*; **horse ~** châtaigne *f*; **hot ~** marrons chauds ❷ (*old joke*) vieille plaisanterie qui a perdu son effet II. *n* ❶ (*eyes*) marron; (*hair*) châtain

**chew** [tʃu] I. *n* ❶ (*bite*) bout *m* ❷ (*candy*) bonbon *m* mou II. *vt* mâcher

◆**chew out** *vt inf* engueuler

**chewing gum** ['tʃu·ɪŋ·ɡʌm] *n* chewing-gum *m*

**chewy** ['tʃu·i] *adj* caoutchouteux(-euse)

**chick** [tʃɪk] *n* ❶ (*chicken*) poussin *m* ❷ (*bird*) oiselet *m* ❸ *sl* (*young woman*) poulette *f*

**chicken** ['tʃɪk·ɪn] I. *n* poulet *m* ▸ **~ and egg problem** [*o* **situation**] éternel dilemme *m* de la poule ou de l'œuf; **to be a spring ~** être de première jeunesse II. *adj sl* (*cowardly*) dégonflé(e)

**chickenpox** *n* varicelle *f*

**chief** [tʃif] I. *n* chef *m*; **to be ~ of sth** être à la tête de qc II. *adj* ❶ (*top*) premier(-ère) ❷ (*major*) principal(e)

**chief executive officer** *n* président-directeur *m* général

**chiefly** *adv* principalement

**child** [tʃaɪld] <children> *n* enfant *m*; **unborn ~** enfant à naître; **two-year-old ~** enfant de deux ans ▸ **a flower ~** hippie *mf*

**child abuse** n mauvais traitements mpl à enfants; (sexual) sévices mpl sexuels

**childbirth** n accouchement m

**childhood** n enfance f

**childish** adj pej immature

**childless** adj sans enfant

**childproof** adj sans risque pour les enfants; (cap) cap de sécurité

**children** ['tʃɪl·drən] n pl of **child**

**chili** ['tʃɪl·i] <-es> n ❶(chili con carne) chili m ❷(hot pepper) piment m (rouge)

**chill** [tʃɪl] I. adj (cold) frais(fraîche) II. n ❶(coldness) fraîcheur f ❷(shivering) frisson m; **to send a ~ down someone's spine** faire frissonner qn de peur f ❸(cold) coup m de froid ❹fig froideur f; **to cast a ~ over sth** jeter un froid sur qc III. vt ❶(make cold) refroidir ❷CULIN mettre au frais ❸fig (frighten) faire frissonner IV. vi ❶(become cold) refroidir ❷sl **to ~ (out)** (calm down) se relaxer; (pass time) traîner

**chilling** adj ❶(cold) a. fig glacial(e) ❷(frightening) à vous donner la chair de poule

**chilly** ['tʃɪl·i] < ier, iest> adj ❶frais(fraîche); **to feel ~** avoir froid; **it's ~ out today** il fait un peu froid aujourd'hui ❷(unwelcoming: relationship) froid(e)

**chimney** ['tʃɪm·ni] n ❶(pipe) cheminée f; (of stove) tuyau m ❷(fireplace) âtre m de cheminée

**chimpanzee** [tʃɪm·ˈpæn·zi] n chimpanzé m

**chin** [tʃɪn] n menton m ▶ **to keep one's ~ up** garder la tête haute; **to take it on the ~** accepter sans se plaindre

**china** ['tʃaɪ·nə] n porcelaine f

**China** ['tʃaɪ·nə] n la Chine

**Chinese** I. adj chinois(e) II. n ❶(person) Chinois(e) m(f) ❷LING chinois m; s.a. **English**

**chip** [tʃɪp] I. n ❶(flake) fragment m ❷(place where piece is missing) ébréchure f; **the cup has a ~ in it** la tasse est ébréchée ❸ pl (potato snack) chips

fpl ❹COMPUT puce f électronique ❺(money token) jeton m ▶ **to be a ~ off the old block** inf tenir de ses ancêtres; **when the ~s are down** inf lorsque les ennuis arrivent II. vt <-pp-> fragmenter III. vi <-pp-> s'ébrécher

**chiropractor** n chiropraticien(ne) m(f)

**chit-chat** ['tʃɪt·tʃæt] I. n inf bavardage m II. vi inf bavarder

**chlorine** ['klɔr·in] n chlore m

**chocolate** ['tʃɔk·lət] n chocolat m; **~ bar** tablette f de chocolat

**choice** [tʃɔɪs] I. n ❶(selection) choix m; **to be of sb's ~** être choisi par qn; **he has no ~ but to ...** il n'a pas d'autre moyen que de... ❷(range) **wide ~** large sélection f ❸(selection) option f II. adj ❶(top quality) de choix ❷(angry) cinglant(e)

**choir** [kwaɪər] n chorale f; **church ~** chœurs mpl

**choke** [tʃoʊk] I. n starter m II. vi étouffer; **to ~ on sth** s'étouffer avec qc; **to ~ to death** mourir étouffé III. vt ❶(deprive of air) étouffer ❷(block) boucher; (with leaves) bloquer

◆**choke back** vt (tears) ravaler

◆**choke down** vt avaler

◆**choke off** vt étouffer

◆**choke up** vt ❶(block) boucher ❷fig **to be choked up** être bouleversé

**cholesterol** [kə·ˈles·tə·rɔl] n cholestérol m

**chomp** [tʃɑmp] vi **to ~ (down) on sth**, **to ~ into sth** mâchonner qc m ▶ **to be ~ing at the bit** ronger son frein

**choose** [tʃuz] <chose, chosen> I. vt choisir II. vi choisir; **to do as one ~s** faire comme on l'entend ▶ **little [o not much] to ~ between ...** pas beaucoup de choix entre ...

**choos(e)y** ['tʃu·zi] <-ier, -iest> adj **to be ~ about sth** être difficile quant à qc

**chop** [tʃɑp] I. vt <-pp-> ❶(cut) couper; (herbs) hacher ❷(reduce) réduire II. n ❶(meat) côtelette f ❷(blow) coup m

◆**chop down** vt abattre

◆**chop off** vt trancher

**chopper** n ❶(tool) hachette f ❷inf

**C**

(*helicopter*) hélico *m* ❸ *inf* (*motorcycle*) chopper *m*

**chopsticks** *npl* baguettes *fpl*

**chord** [kɔrd] *n* accord *m* ▸ **it strikes a ~ with me** ça me rappelle qc

**chore** [tʃɔr] *n* ❶ (*task*) travail *m* de routine; **household ~** tâche *f* ménagère ❷ (*tedious task*) corvée *f*

**choreograph** [ˈkɔr·i·ə·græf] *vt* faire la chorégraphie de

**chorus** [ˈkɔr·əs] **I.** *n* ❶ (*refrain*) refrain *m* ❷ + *sing/pl vb* (*singers*) chœur *m* ❸ *sing* (*utterance*) chœur *m* **II.** *vt* chanter en chœur

**chose** [tʃoʊz] *pt of* **choose**

**chosen** *pp of* **choose**

**Christ** [kraɪst] **I.** *n* Jésus Christ *m* **II.** *interj inf* bon Dieu!

**christen** [ˈkrɪs·ən] *vt* ❶ (*baptize*) baptiser ❷ (*use for first time*) étrenner

**Christian** [ˈkrɪs·tʃən] **I.** *n* chrétien(ne) *m(f)* **II.** *adj* chrétien(ne)

**Christianity** [ˌkrɪs·tʃi·ˈæn·ə·t̬i] *n* christianisme *m*

**Christmas** [ˈkrɪs·məs] <-es *o* -ses> *n* *no art* Noël *m*; **at ~** à (la) Noël; **Merry ~** Joyeux Noël

**Christmas carol** *n* chant *m* de Noël

**Christmas Day** *n* Noël *m*

**Christmas Eve** *n* soir *m* de Noël

**Christmas tree** *n* sapin *m* de Noël

**chronic** [ˈkrɑ·nɪk] *adj* ❶ (*long-lasting*) chronique ❷ (*having a chronic complaint: alcoholic*) invétéré(e) ❸ (*bad*) insupportable ❹ (*habitual*) **to be ~ liars** avoir pour habitude de mentir

**chronological** *adj* chronologique

**chuck** [tʃʌk] **I.** *n* ❶ (*touch*) petite tape *f* ❷ (*beef cut*) paleron *m* **II.** *vt* ❶ *inf* (*throw*) jeter ❷ *inf* (*end relationship*) plaquer ❸ *inf* (*stop*) abandonner ◆ **chuck out** *vt* ❶ (*throw away*) jeter ❷ (*make leave*) flanquer à la porte

**chuckle** [ˈtʃʌk·l] **I.** *n* gloussement *m* **II.** *vi* glousser

**Chunnel** [ˈtʃʌn·əl] *n inf* **the ~** le tunnel sous la Manche

**church** [tʃɜrtʃ] *n* ❶ (*building*) église *f*;

(*for Protestants*) temple *m* ❷ (*organization*) Eglise *f* ❸ (*service*) office *m*

**churchyard** *n* cimetière *m* situé autour d'une église

**CIA** [ˌsi·aɪ·ˈeɪ] *n abbr of* **Central Intelligence Agency** CIA *f*

**cider** [ˈsaɪ·dər] *n* *no art* jus *m* de pommes

**cigar** [sɪ·ˈgɑr] *n* cigare *m*

**cigar box** *n* boîte *f* à cigares

**cigarette** [ˌsɪg·ə·ˈret] *n* cigarette *f*

**cigarette butt** *n* mégot *m*

**cinema** [ˈsɪn·ə·mə] *n* cinéma *m*

**cinnamon** [ˈsɪn·ə·mən] *n* *no art* cannelle *f*; **~ stick** bâton *m* de cannelle

**circa** [ˈsɜr·kə] *prep* environ; (*date*) vers

**circle** [ˈsɜr·kl] **I.** *n* ❶ (*round*) cercle *m*; **to go around in ~s** faire des cercles ❷ (*group*) cercle *m* ❸ (*professionals*) milieu *m* ❹ (*under eyes*) cernes *fpl* ▸ **to come full ~** revenir au point de départ; **to run/go around in ~s** tourner en rond; **a vicious ~** un cercle vicieux **II.** *vt* ❶ (*move around*) tourner autour de ❷ (*surround*) entourer **III.** *vi* tourner

**circuit** [ˈsɜr·kɪt] *n* ❶ ELEC circuit *m* ❷ SPORTS circuit *m* ❸ (*circular route*) circuit *m*

**circular** [ˈsɜr·kjə·lər] **I.** *adj* circulaire **II.** *n* circulaire *f*; (*for advertisement*) prospectus *m*

**circulation** *n* ❶ (*blood flow*) circulation *f* sanguine ❷ (*copies sold*) tirage *m* ❸ (*currency*) circulation *f*

**circumstance** [ˈsɜr·kəm·stæn(t)s] *n* (*situation*) circonstance *f*; **in/under any ~s** en toutes circonstances; **in/under the ~s** dans ces conditions

**circus** [ˈsɜr·kəs] *n a. fig* cirque *m*; **traveling ~** cirque forain ▸ **it's a ~ here!** *inf* c'est le cirque ici!

**citation** [saɪ·ˈteɪ·ʃən] *n a.* MIL citation *f*

**citizen** [ˈsɪt̬·ɪ·zən] *n* ❶ (*national*) citoyen(ne) *m(f)*; **U.S. ~** citoyen *m* américain ❷ (*resident*) habitant(e) *m(f)*

**citizenship** *n* citoyenneté *f*; **to apply for ~ of a country** demander la nationalité d'un pays; **joint ~** double nationalité *f*; **good ~** civisme *m*

**citrus** ['sɪt·rəs] <citrus o citruses> n agrume m

**city** ['sɪt̬·i] <-ies> I. n ① (*town*) ville f; **capital ~** capitale f ② (*government*) **the ~** la municipalité II. adj urbain(e); (*life*) citadin(e)

**city council** n conseil m municipal

**city hall** n municipalité f; **City Hall** Hôtel m de Ville

**city slicker** n inf citadin(e) m(f) maniéré(e)

**citywide** adj à travers toute la ville

**civics** n + sing vb instruction f civique

**civil** ['sɪv·əl] adj ① <inv> (*of citizens*) civil(e) ② (*courteous*) poli(e)

**civil court** n tribunal m civil

**civil defense** n protection f civile

**civil disobedience** n désobéissance f civile

**civilian** [sɪ·'vɪl·jən] <inv> I. n civil(e) m(f) II. adj civil(e); **in ~ life** dans le civil

**civilization** n civilisation f

**civilize** ['sɪv·ə·laɪz] vt civiliser

**civil marriage** n mariage m civil

**civil rights** npl droits mpl civils

**civil servant** n fonctionnaire mf

**civil service** n fonction f publique

**civil union** n union f civile

**civil war** n guerre f civile; **the Civil War** la guerre de Sécession

**claim** [kleɪm] I. n ① (*demand*) revendication f; **to make no ~ to be sth** n'avoir aucune prétention à être qc; **~ to fame** chose f notable ② (*money demand*) réclamation f; (*for refund*) demande f de remboursement ③ (*assertion*) déclaration f; **his ~ to have sth** sa déclaration selon laquelle il possède qc ④ (*right*) droit m II. vt ① (*declare*) revendiquer; **to ~ that ...** déclarer que ... ② (*assert*) prétendre; **to ~ to be sth** prétendre être qc ③ (*demand: immunity*) réclamer; (*title, throne*) revendiquer ④ (*require*) demander, (*time*) prendre ⑤ (*collect: luggage*) récupérer ⑥ (*cause sb's death*) **to ~ sb's life** causer la mort de qn ► **to ~ the moral high ground** prétendre d'une moralité irréprochable III. vi **to ~ for damages** faire une demande de dommages et intérêts; **to ~ on the insurance** demander à être indemnisé

**clamp** [klæmp] I. n ① (*fastener*) agrafe f; ELEC attache f ② AUTO sabot m de Denver II. vt ① (*fasten*) fixer ② (*clench*) serrer; (*handcuffs*) resserrer ③ AUTO mettre un sabot à

◆**clamp down** I. vi **to ~ on sth** sévir contre qc II. vt fixer

**clap** [klæp] I. <-pp-> vt ① (*hit*) taper; **to ~ one's hands** (**together**) frapper dans ses mains; (*applaud*) applaudir ② (*applaud*) applaudir ③ (*place*) jeter; (*a lid*) remettre II. <-pp-> vi ① (*slap palms together*) frapper des mains ② (*applaud*) applaudir III. n ① (*act of clapping*) claquement m ② (*noise: of thunder*) coup m ③ sl **the ~** la chaude-pisse

**clarification** n (*explanation*) éclaircissement m

**clarify** ['kler·ɪ·faɪ] <-ie-> I. vt ① (*make clearer*) clarifier ② (*explain: sb's mind, opinion*) éclaircir; (*question*) élucider ③ (*skim*) clarifier II. vi se clarifier

**clarity** ['kler·ə·t̬i] n clarté f; (*of a photo*) netteté f; **~ of thought** lucidité f

**clash** [klæʃ] I. vi ① (*fight, argue*) s'affronter; **to ~ over sth** se disputer pour qc; **to ~ with sb/sth** se heurter à qn/qc ② (*compete*) s'opposer ③ (*contradict*) être incompatible ④ (*not match*) être opposé(e) ⑤ (*make harsh noise*) résonner bruyamment II. vt **to ~ sth together** faire résonner qc III. n ① (*hostile encounter*) affrontement m ② (*argument*) querelle f ③ (*contest*) opposition f ④ (*conflict*) conflit m ⑤ (*incompatibility*) incompatibilité f ⑥ (*harsh noise*) fracas m

**clasp** [klæsp] I. n ① (*grip*) serrement m ② (*device*) agrafe f; **~ of sth** fermeture f de qc II. vt étreindre; **to ~ one's hands** joindre les mains

**class** [klæs] I. n ① (*student group*) classe f ② (*lesson*) cours m ③ UNIV (*graduates*) promotion f; **the ~ of 2007** la promotion de 2007 ④ (*quality*) **the mid-**

**dle/working ~** la classe moyenne/ouvrière; **the upper ~** la haute société ⑤ (*grade*) classe *f* ▸ **to be in a ~ of one's own** être le meilleur dans sa catégorie II. <inv> *adj* de classe; **world~-champion** champion *m* hors pair III. *vt* classer; **to ~ sb as sth** considérer qn comme qc

**classic** ['klæs·ɪk] I. *adj* ① (*of excellence*) classique ② (*traditional*) traditionnel(le) ③ (*typical*) typique ④ *inf* (*foolish*) **that's ~!** que c'est stupide! II. *n* classique *m*

**classical** *adj* classique

**classics** *n* ① *pl* (*great literature*) grands classiques *mpl* ② (*Greek and Roman studies*) lettres *fpl* classiques

**classification** [ˌklæs·ə·fɪ·ˈkeɪ·ʃ°n] *n* ① *no art* (*categorization*) classification *f* ② (*group*) classe *f*

**classified** <inv> *adj* classé(e); **~ advertisements** petites annonces *fpl*

**classify** ['klæs·ɪ·faɪ] <-ie-> *vt* classer

**classmate** *n* camarade *mf* de classe

**classroom** *n* salle *f* de classe

**classy** ['klæs·i] <-ier, -iest> *adj* qui a de la classe

**clause** [klɔz] *n* ① (*part of sentence*) proposition *f* ② (*statement in law*) clause *f*

**claw** [klɔ] I. *n* ① (*nail*) griffe *f* ② (*pincer*) pince *f* ▸ **to get one's ~s into sb/sth** *inf* tenir qn/qc entre ses griffes II. *vt* griffer

**clay** [kleɪ] I. *n* ① (*earth*) terre *f* glaise; (*for pottery*) argile *f*; **modeling ~** pâte *f* à modeler ② SPORTS terre *f* battue II. *adj* ① (*of earth*) d'argile ② SPORTS en terre battue

**clean** [klin] I. *adj* ① (*free of dirt*) *a. fig* propre; **spotlessly ~** impeccable ② (*with no pollution: fuel*) propre; (*air*) pur(e) ③ (*fair: fight*) dans les règles ④ (*moral: life*) sain(e); (*joke*) décent(e) ⑤ (*clear, sharp*) net(te); **~ design** belle coupe *f* ⑥ (*inf*) (*straight*) clean *inv* ⑦ (*blank: sheet of paper, record*) vierge ⑧ (*complete*) définitif(-ive); **to make a ~ sweep of sth** remporter qc; **to make a ~ break** rompre une bonne fois pour

toute II. *n* nettoyage *m*, appropriation *f* Belgique III. <inv> *adv* complètement; **to ~ forget that ...** bel et bien oublier que ... IV. *vt* ① (*remove dirt*) nettoyer, approprier Belgique, poutser Suisse; **to ~ sth from [o off] sth** enlever qc de qc ② (*wash and gut: fish*) vider V. *vi* ① (*wash*) nettoyer ② (*can be washed*) se nettoyer ③ (*do the cleaning*) faire le ménage

◆ **clean out** *vt* ① (*clean*) nettoyer à fond ② *inf* (*leave penniless: person*) faucher ③ *inf* (*take all: house*) dévaliser

◆ **clean up** I. *vt* ① (*make clean*) *a. fig* nettoyer; **to clean oneself up** se laver ② (*make neat*) *a. fig* mettre de l'ordre dans II. *vi* ① (*make clean*) *a. fig* nettoyer ② (*make neat*) remettre tout en ordre ③ (*remove dirt from oneself*) se laver ④ *inf* (*make profit*) rapporter gros ⑤ SPORTS rafler tous les prix

**cleaner** *n* ① (*substance*) produit *m* d'entretien ② (*tool*) appareil *m* de nettoyage ③ (*person*) agent *m* de service

**cleaning lady** *n* femme *f* de ménage

**cleanliness** *n* propreté *f*

**clean-shaven** *adj* rasé(e) de près

**clean-up** *n* ① (*clean*) nettoyage *m*, appropriation *f* Belgique ② (*making legal*) épuration *f*

**clear** [klɪr] I. *adj* ① (*understandable*) clair(e); **to make oneself ~** bien se faire comprendre; **to make sth ~ to sb** bien faire comprendre qc à qn; **do I make myself ~?** me suis-je bien fait comprendre?; **let's get this ~** que les choses soient claires *subj* ② (*sure, obvious*) clair(e); (*lead, majority, advantage*) net(te); **to be ~ about sth** être sûr de qc ③ (*free from confusion*) clair(e); (*person*) lucide ④ (*free from guilt*) **to have a ~ conscience** avoir la conscience tranquille ⑤ (*empty*) dégagé(e); **on a ~ day** par temps clair ⑥ (*transparent*) transparent(e) ⑦ (*pure: skin*) net(te); (*sound*) cristallin(e); (*water*) limpide ⑧ (*cloudless*) dégagé(e) ⑨ <inv> (*distinct*) net(te); (*voice*) clair(e) ⑩ (*free*) libre ⑪ (*net: profit*) net(te) ⑫ <inv> (*not* *touching*) **to keep ~ of sb/sth** rester à l'écart de qn/qc **II.** *n* **to be in the ~** être au-dessus de tout soupçon **III.** *adv* **to stand ~ of sth** s'éloigner de qc **IV.** *vt* ❶(*remove blockage: road, area*) dégager; **to ~ one's throat** s'éclaircir la voix; **to ~ the way to sth** *fig* ouvrir la voie à qc ❷(*remove doubts*) clarifier ❸(*acquit*) disculper; **to ~ one's name** blanchir son nom; **to ~ a debt** s'acquitter d'une dette ❹(*empty: drawer, building*) vider; (*table, room*) débarrasser ❺(*disperse: crowd*) disperser; (*fog, smoke*) dissiper ❻(*clean*) nettoyer; **to ~ the air** aérer; *fig* détendre l'atmosphère ❼(*give permission*) approuver; **to ~ sth with sb** avoir l'accord de qn; **to ~ sb to do sth** donner le feu vert à qn; **to ~ customs** dédouaner ❽SPORTS (*ball*) dégager ❾(*jump over*) franchir ❿COMPUT effacer ▸ **to ~ the decks** déblayer le terrain **V.** *vi* ❶(*become transparent*) *a. fig* (*weather, face*) s'éclaircir ❷(*disappear: fog, smoke*) se dissiper ❸FIN être viré(e)

◆**clear away I.** *vt* débarrasser **II.** *vi* se dissiper

◆**clear off I.** *vi inf* filer **II.** *vt* retirer

◆**clear out I.** *vt* ❶(*empty*) vider ❷(*tidy*) ranger **II.** *vi inf* filer; **to ~ of somewhere** évacuer les lieux

◆**clear up I.** *vt* ❶(*tidy*) ranger ❷(*resolve*) dissiper **II.** *vi* ❶(*tidy*) ranger; **to ~ after sb** passer derrière qn ❷(*go away*) disparaître ❸(*stop raining*) s'éclaircir

**clearance** [ˈklɪr·ən(t)s] *n* ❶(*act of clearing*) dégagement *m* ❷(*space*) espace *m* libre ❸(*approval of bank check*) compensation *f* ❹(*permission*) autorisation *f*

**clearance sale** *n* liquidation *f*

**clearly** *adv* ❶(*distinctly*) clairement ❷(*well*) distinctement ❸(*obviously*) manifestement ❹(*unambiguously*) explicitement

**clench** [klen(t)ʃ] *vt* serrer dans les mains; **to ~ one's fist** serrer les poings

**clergy** [ˈklɜr·dʒi] *n + pl vb* clergé *m*

**cleric** [ˈkler·ɪk] *n* ecclésiastique *m*

**clerical staff** *n* personnel *m* de bureau

**clerical work** *n* travail *m* administratif

**clerk** [klɜrk] **I.** *n* (*receptionist*) réceptionniste *mf*; **sales ~** vendeur, -euse *m, f* **II.** *vi* travailler comme employé(e) de bureau

**clever** [ˈklev·ər] *adj* ❶(*skillful*) habile; (*trick*) astucieux(-euse); (*gadget*) ingénieux(-euse) ❷(*intelligent*) intelligent(e) ❸ *pej* (*quick-witted*) futé(e)

**cliché** [kliˈʃeɪ] *n* ❶(*platitude*) cliché *m* ❷ *no art* (*worn-out phrase*) phrase *f* toute faite

**client** [ˈklaɪənt] *n* client(e) *m(f)*

**cliff** [klɪf] *n* falaise *f*

**climate** [ˈklaɪ·mət] *n* climat *m* ▸ **the ~ of opinion** les courants *mpl* de l'opinion

**climax** [ˈklaɪ·mæks] **I.** *n* ❶(*highest point*) apogée *f*; **to reach a ~** atteindre son paroxysme ❷(*orgasm*) orgasme *m* **II.** *vi* ❶(*reach high point*) atteindre son paroxysme ❷(*orgasm*) jouir

**climb** [klaɪm] **I.** *n* ❶(*ascent*) montée *f*; (*of mountain*) ascension *f*; **~ up/down** montée *f*/descente *f* ❷(*steep part*) côte *f* ❸ *fig* ascension *f*; **~ to power** ascension au pouvoir **II.** *vt* grimper; (*mountain*) faire l'ascension de; (*wall*) escalader; (*tree*) grimper à; (*stairs*) monter ▸ **to ~ the walls** être dingue **III.** *vi* (*ascend*) grimper; **to ~ over a wall** escalader un mur ❷(*increase*) augmenter ❸(*rise*) monter ❹(*get into*) **to ~ into sth** monter dans qc ❺(*get out*) **to ~ out of sth** se hisser hors de qc

◆**climb down I.** *vi* ❶(*go down*) descendre ❷ *fig* revenir sur sa position **II.** *vt* descendre

**climber** *n* ❶(*mountains*) alpiniste *mf* ❷(*rock faces*) varappeur, -euse *m, f* ❸(*plant*) plante *f* grimpante ❹ *inf* (*striver*) **social ~** arriviste *mf*

**climbing I.** *n* ❶(*mountains*) alpinisme *m* ❷(*rock faces*) varappe *f* **II.**<inv> *adj* ❶(*of plants*) grimpant(e) ❷(*for going up mountains*) de montagne

**cling** [klɪŋ] <clung, clung> vi ❶(*hold tightly*) **to ~** (*together*) être collé l'un à l'autre; **to ~** (*on*) **to sth** se cramponner à qc; (*be dependent on*); **to ~** (*persist*) être tenace

**clinic** ['klɪnɪk] n ❶(*hospital*) clinique f ❷(*hospital department*) service m

**clinical** adj ❶ MED clinique n ❷(*hospital-like*) austère ❸ pej (*emotionless*) froid(e); **to be ~** être froidement objectif

**clip**[1] [klɪp] I. n ❶(*fastener*) trombone m ❷(*jewelry*) clip m ❸(*gun part*) chargeur m II. <-pp-> vt **to ~ sth together** attacher qc III. vi **to ~ on** s'attacher

**clip**[2] [klɪp] <-pp-> I. vt ❶(*trim*) couper; (*hedge*) tailler; (*sheep*) tondre ❷(*make hole in*) poinçonner ❸(*reduce*) diminuer ❹(*attach*) attacher ❺(*hit: curb*) accrocher II. n ❶(*trim*) coupe f d'entretien ❷(*extract*) clip m ❸(*sharp hit*) claque f ❹ inf (*fast speed*) **at a** (**fair/fast/good**) **~** à toute vitesse

**clipboard** n COMPUT presse-papiers m

**cloak** [kloʊk] I. n ❶(*outer garment*) grande cape f ❷(*covering*) manteau m; (*of mist*) nappe f II. vt masquer

**cloakroom** n (*coat deposit*) vestiaire m

**clock** [klak] I. n ❶(*pendule f*; **alarm ~** réveil m; **around the ~** 24 heures sur 24; **to work against the ~** travailler contre la montre; **to watch the ~** surveiller l'heure ❷(*speedometer*) compteur m II. vt ❶(*measure time or speed*) chronométrer ❷ inf (*hit*) coller un pain

◆**clock in** vi pointer

◆**clock out** vi pointer (à la sortie)

◆**clock up** vt insep **he clocked up 300 miles** il a fait 300 miles au compteur

**clock radio** n radio-réveil m

**clockwise** adj dans le sens des aiguilles d'une montre

**clockwork** n mécanisme m ▶ **to go like ~** aller comme sur des roulettes

**clog** [klɔg] n sabot m

**clone** [kloʊn] I. n clone m II. vt cloner

**close**[1] [kloʊs] I. adj ❶(*near*) proche; **at ~ range** à bout portant ❷(*intimate*)

proche; **to be ~ to sb** être proche de qn; (*ties*) étroit(e) ❸(*similar: resemblance*) fort(e); **to be ~ in sth** se ressembler dans qc ❹(*careful*) minutieux(-euse) ❺(*airless*) étouffant(e); (*weather*) lourd(e) ❻(*almost equal: contest*) serré(e) ❼(*dense*) serré(e) ▶ **to keep a ~ eye on sb/sth** surveiller qn/qc de très près II. adv ❶(*near in location*) près ❷(*near in time*) proche; **to get ~** (s')approcher ❸ fig proche

**close**[2] [kloʊz] I. n fin f; **to bring sth to a ~** conclure qc; **to come to a ~** prendre fin II. vt ❶(*shut*) fermer ❷(*end*) mettre fin à; (*bank account*) fermer; (*deal*) conclure ▶ **to ~ one's eyes to sth** fermer les yeux sur qc III. vi ❶(*shut*) fermer; (*eyes, door*) se fermer ❷(*end*) prendre fin

◆**close down** vt, vi fermer définitivement

◆**close in** vi ❶(*surround*) **to ~ on sth** se rapprocher de qc ❷(*get shorter*) se raccourcir

◆**close off** vt condamner

◆**close up** vt, vi fermer

**closed** adj fermé(e) ▶ **behind ~ doors** à l'abri des regards indiscrets

**closely** adv ❶(*intimately*) étroitement; **to be ~ linked** être très proche ❷(*carefully*) **~ guarded secret** secret m bien gardé

**close-up** n gros plan m

**closing** I. <inv> adj final(e); (*speech*) de clôture II. n ❶(*ending*) clôture f ❷(*end of business hours*) heure f de fermeture

**closing date** n date f limite

**closure** ['kloʊ-ʒər] n ❶ fermeture f ❷ PSYCH **to get ~** tourner la page

**clot** [klat] I. n (*lump*) caillot m II. <-tt-> vi coaguler

**cloth** [klɔθ] I. n ❶ no art (*material*) tissu m; **table~** nappe f ❷(*rag*) chiffon m ❸(*clergy*) clergé m II. <inv> adj en tissu

**clothe** [kloʊð] vt vêtir

**clothes** npl vêtements mpl, hardes fpl Québec; **to put one's ~ on** s'habiller

**clothesline** n corde f à linge

**clothespin** n pince f à linge

**clothing** n form vêtements mpl

**cloud** [klaʊd] I. n a. fig nuage m ► **to be on ~ nine** être au septième ciel; **to be under a ~** être l'objet de soupçons II. vt ❶ (darken) a. fig obscurcir ❷ (make less clear) rendre trouble III. vi ❶ (become overcast) se couvrir ❷ fig s'assombrir

**cloudburst** n averse f

**clouded** adj ❶ (cloudy) nuageux(-euse) ❷ (not transparent: liquid) trouble ❸ (confused: mind) troublé(e)

**cloudless** adj sans nuages

**cloudy** <-ier, -iest> adj ❶ (overcast) nuageux(-euse); **partly ~ skies** ciel m partiellement couvert ❷ (not transparent: liquid) trouble ❸ (unclear) nébuleux(-euse)

**clown** [klaʊn] I. n a. fig clown m II. vi to ~ **around** faire le clown

**club** [klʌb] I. n ❶ (group, team) club m; **to join a ~** adhérer à un club; **tennis ~** club de tennis; **join the ~!** bienvenue au club! ❷ SPORTS (stick) club m; **golf ~** club de golf ❸ (weapon) gourdin m ❹ GAMES (playing card) trèfle m; **queen of ~s** reine f de trèfle ❺ (disco) boîte f II. <-bb-> vt frapper avec un gourdin; **to ~ sb/an animal to death** frapper qn/un animal à mort

**clubbing** vi to go ~ aller en boîte

**clue** [klu] n ❶ (hint) indice m ❷ fig (secret) secret m ❸ (idea) idée f; **to not have a ~** ne pas avoir la moindre idée

**clueless** adj inf largué(e)

**clumsiness** n maladresse f

**clumsy** ['klʌmzi] <-ier, -iest> adj a. fig maladroit(e)

**clung** [klʌŋ] pp, pt of cling

**cluster** ['klʌstər] I. n ❶ (group) groupe m; (of fruit) grappe f; (of flowers, trees) bouquet m; (of persons) groupe m; (of bees) essaim m; (of stars) amas m ❷ LING groupe m II. vi to ~ **together** se regrouper

**clutch** [klʌtʃ] I. vi to ~ **at sth** se cramponner à qc II. vt saisir III. n ❶ sing

AUTO (transmission device) embrayage m ❷ fig (group) groupe m ❸ (claw) a. fig griffe f ► **to be in the ~es of sb/sth** être entre les griffes de qn/qc

**clutter** ['klʌtər] I. n encombrement m II. vt encombrer

**CO** [ˌsiːˈoʊ] n ❶ abbr of **Colorado** ❷ MIL abbr of **Commanding Officer** officier m commandant

**c/o** abbr of **care of** chez

**coach** [koʊtʃ] I. n ❶ SPORTS (professional coach) entraîneur m ❷ (teacher) professeur m particulier ❸ (in airplane) classe f économique ❹ (stagecoach) carrosse m II. vt ❶ (give private teaching) donner des cours de soutien à ❷ SPORTS entraîner ❸ (support professionally) coacher

**coaching** n ❶ (support) soutien m ❷ SPORTS entraînement m ❸ (professional support) coaching m

**coal** [koʊl] n charbon m ► **to drag sb over the ~s** réprimander qn sévèrement

**coal mine** n mine f de charbon

**coal miner** n mineur m

**coarse** [kɔrs] <-r, -st> adj a. fig grossier(-ère); (salt, sand) gros(se); (surface) rugueux(-euse); (features) rude

**coast** [koʊst] I. n côte f; **three miles off the ~** à trois miles de la côte; **from ~ to ~** d'un bout à l'autre du pays ► **the ~ is clear** la voie est libre II. vi ❶ (move easily) avancer en roue libre ❷ (make progress) avancer sans difficulté

**coastal** adj côtier(-ère)

**Coast Guard** n the ~ les garde-côtes mpl

**coastline** n littoral m

**coat** [koʊt] I. n ❶ (outer garment) manteau m; **leather ~** manteau en cuir ❷ (animal's outer covering) pelage m ❸ (layer) couche f II. vt couvrir; **to ~ sth with sth** couvrir qc de qc

**coat hanger** n cintre m

**coattails** npl queue f de pie ► **on sb's ~** dans le sillage de qn

**co-author** [koʊˈɔːθər] I. n coauteur m II. vt être le coauteur de

C

**coax** [kouks] *vt* enjôler; **to ~ sb to do sth** enjôler qn pour qu'il fasse qc (*subj*)

**cobblestone** *n* pavé *m*

**cobweb** ['kab·web] *n* (*web made by spider*) toile *f* d'araignée

**cock** [kak] **I.** *n* ① (*male chicken*) coq *m* ② *vulg* (*penis*) bit(t)e *f* **II.** *vt* (*ready gun*) armer

**cockiness** *n* suffisance *f*

**cockpit** ['kak·pɪt] *n* ① (*pilot's area*) cockpit *m* ② *sing* (*area of fighting*) arène *f*

**cockroach** ['kak·routʃ] *n* cafard *m*

**cockscomb** ['kak·skoum] *n* ZOOL crête *f* de coq

**cocktail** ['kak·teɪl] *n* cocktail *m*; **shrimp ~** cocktail de crevettes

**cocky** ['ka·ki] <-ier, -iest> *adj* culotté(e)

**cocoa** ['kou·kou] *n* cacao *m*

**coconut** ['kou·kə·nʌt] *n* noix *f* de coco

**coconut milk** *n* lait *m* de coco

**cod** [kad] <~(s)> *n* ① (*fish*) morue *f* ② (*fresh fish*) cabillaud *m*

**code** [koud] **I.** *n* code *m*; **to write sth in ~** coder qc; **~ of conduct** déontologie *f* **II.** *vt* coder

**code name** *n* nom *m* de code

**code word** *n* mot *m* de passe

**coed** *adj inf* (*school, team*) mixte; **to go ~** devenir mixte

**coeducational** *adj* (*school*) mixte

**coerce** [kou·'ɜrs] *vt form* contraindre

**coffee** ['kɔ·fi] *n* ① (*hot drink*) café *m*; **instant ~** café instantané; **cup of ~** tasse *f* de café; **black ~** café *m* noir ② *s.* **coffee-colored**

**coffee break** *n* pause *f* café

**coffee-colored** *adj* couleur café

**coffee cup** *n* tasse *f* à café

**coffee pot** *n* cafetière *f*

**coffee shop** *n* café *m*

**coffin** ['kɔ·fɪn] *n* cercueil *m*

**cognac** ['kou·njæk] *n* cognac *m*

**cohabit** [kou·'hæb·ɪt] *vi form* cohabiter

**cohabitation** *n* cohabitation *f*

**coherent** [kou·'hɪr·ənt] *adj* cohérent(e)

**coil** [kɔɪl] **I.** *n* ① (*wound spiral*) rouleau *m*; (*of rope*) pli *m* ② *inf* MED stéri-

let *m* **II.** *vi* (*snake*) **to ~ around sth** s'enrouler autour de qc **III.** *vt* enrouler; **to ~ oneself around sth** s'enrouler autour de qc

**coin** [kɔɪn] **I.** *n* pièce *f*; **gold ~** pièce en or **II.** *vt* inventer ▸ **to ~ a phrase ...** pour ainsi dire ...

**coincidence** *n* coïncidence *f*

**coincidentally** *adv* par coïncidence

**col.** [kal] *n* ① *abbr of* **column** ② *abbr of* **college** ③ *abbr of* **colony**

**Col.** *n abbr of* **colonel**

**cold** [kould] **I.** *adj* <-er, -est> (*not warm*) *a. fig* froid(e); **~ beer** bière *f* fraîche; **to be ~** (*weather*) faire froid; (*person*) avoir froid; **to get ~** (*soup, coffee*) se refroidir; **to get ~** (*person*) avoir froid ▸ **to have/get ~ feet** perdre son sang froid; **to pour ~ water on sth** démolir qc **II.** *n* ① (*low temperature*) froid *m* ② MED rhume *m*; **to catch a ~** attraper froid

**cold-blooded** *adj* ① ZOOL (*ectothermic: animal*) à sang froid ② (*extremely evil: murderer*) sans pitié

**cold cuts** *npl* assiette *f* anglaise

**cold feet** *n pl, inf* **to get ~** se défiler

**cold-hearted** *adj* sans cœur

**cold sore** *n* MED herpès *m*

**cold sweat** *n* sueur *f* froide; **to break out in a ~** commencer à avoir des sueurs froides

**coleslaw** ['koul·slɔ] *n* salade *f* de chou

**collaborate** [kə·'læb·ə·reɪt] *vi a. pej* collaborer

**collapse** [kə·'læps] **I.** *vi a. fig* s'effondrer; (*government*) tomber **II.** *n a. fig* effondrement *m*; (*of government*) chute *f*

**collapsible** *adj* pliant(e)

**collar** ['ka·lər] **I.** *n* ① (*piece around neck*) col *m* ② (*band*) collier *m* **II.** *vt* ① *inf* saisir au collet ② *fig* retenir

**colleague** ['ka·lig] *n* collègue *mf*

**collect** ['ka·lekt] **I.** *vi* ① (*gather: crowd*) se rassembler; (*dust, dirt*) s'amasser ② (*gather money*) faire la quête **II.** *vt* ① (*gather: money, taxes*) percevoir; (*water, news*) recueillir ② (*gather things as hobby: stamps, an-*

*tiques*) collectionner ❸ (*pick up*) aller chercher ❹ *form* (*regain control*) reprendre; **to ~ one's thoughts** rassembler ses idées ❺ (*receive*) recevoir **III.** *adv* TEL **to call ~** téléphoner en PCV

**collect call** *n* appel *m* en PCV

**collectible I.** *adj* ❶ (*worth collecting*) prisé(e) par les collectionneurs ❷ (*can be collected*) disponible **II.** *n* pièce *f* de collection

**collection** [kə·ˈlek·ʃən] *n* ❶ (*money gathered*) collecte *f*; **to have a ~ for sth** faire une collecte pour qc ❷ (*object collected*) collection *f* ❸ *fig* (*large number*) collection *f* ❹ (*range of designed clothes*) collection *f* ❺ (*act of getting: of garbage*) ramassage *m*

**collector** *n* ❶ (*one who gathers objects*) collectionneur, -euse *m, f*; **stamp ~** philatéliste *mf* ❷ (*one who collects payments*) collecteur, -trice *m, f*; **tax ~** percepteur, -trice *m, f*

**college** [ˈkal·ɪdʒ] *n* ❶ (*university*) université *f*; **to go to ~** aller à l'université; **~ education** études *fpl* supérieures ❷ (*part of university*) faculté *f*

**collegiate** [kə·ˈli·dʒɪt] *adj* universitaire

**collide** [kə·ˈlaɪd] *vi* **to ~ with sb/sth** se heurter à qn/qc

**collision** [kə·ˈlɪʒ·ən] *n* (*hit*) collision *f*

**colloquial** [kə·ˈloʊ·kwi·əl] *adj* familier(-ère)

**colonel** [ˈkɜr·nəl] *n* MIL colonel *m*

**colonize** [ˈka·lə·naɪz] *vt* coloniser

**colony** [ˈka·lə·ni] *n* colonie *f*

**color** [ˈkʌl·ər] **I.** *n* ❶ (*appearance*) a. *fig* couleur *f*; **to give sth ~, to give ~ to sth** colorer qc ❷ (*dye*) colorant *m*; (*for hair*) coloration *f* ❸ (*ruddiness*) teint *m* ❹ *pl* POL, GAMES couleurs *fpl* ❺ (*character*) **to show one's true ~s** se montrer tel que l'on est ▸**to pass with flying ~s** être reçu avec mention **II.** *vt* ❶ (*change color*) colorer; **to ~ one's hair** se teindre les cheveux ❷ (*distort*) déformer **III.** *vi* rougir

**Colorado** [ˌka·lə·ˈræd·oʊ] *n* le Colorado

**colorblind** *adj* daltonien(ne)

**colorblindness** *n* daltonisme *m*

**color-code** *vt* faire un code couleurs

**colored** *adj* ❶ (*having a color*) coloré(e); (*pencil*) de couleur ❷ *pej* (*person*) de couleur

**colorfast** *adj* **this shirt is ~ (when washed)** les couleurs de cette chemise résistent au lavage

**colorful** *adj* ❶ (*full of color*) coloré(e) ❷ (*lively*) gai(e); (*part of town*) pittoresque; (*description*) intéressant(e)

**coloring** *n* ❶ (*complexion*) complexion *f* ❷ (*chemical*) **artificial ~s** couleurs *fpl* artificielles

**colorless** *adj* ❶ (*having no color*) incolore ❷ (*bland*) fade; (*city*) ennuyeux(-euse)

**color scheme** *n* combinaison *f* de couleurs

**color television** *n* télévision *f* (en) couleur

**colossal** [kə·ˈla·səl] *adj* colossal(e)

**column** [ˈka·ləm] *n* ❶ (*pillar*) a. *fig* colonne *f*; **spinal ~** colonne vertébrale ❷ (*article*) rubrique *f*

**columnist** *n* chroniqueur, -euse *m, f*

**comb** [koʊm] **I.** *n* ❶ (*hair device*) peigne *m* ❷ ZOOL *s.* **cockscomb II.** *vt* ❶ (*groom with a comb*) **to ~ one's hair** se peigner ❷ (*search*) chercher minutieusement

**combination** [ˌkam·bə·ˈneɪ·ʃən] *n* ❶ (*mixture of things*) mélange *m* ❷ (*arrangement*) arrangement *m*; (*of circumstances*) concours *m* ❸ (*sequence of numbers*) combinaison *f* de nombres ▸**in ~** en association

**combine** [ˈkam·baɪn] **I.** *vt* mélanger, **to ~ business with pleasure** joindre l'utile à l'agréable **II.** *vi* s'unir; **to ~ against sb** se liguer contre qn

**combined** *adj* mélangé(e); (*efforts*) conjugué(e)

**come** [kʌm] <came, come, coming> *vi* ❶ (*arrive*) arriver; **to ~ toward sb** venir vers qn; **the year to ~** l'année *f* à venir; **to ~ from a place** venir d'un endroit ❷ (*happen*) arriver; **how ~?** comment ça se fait? ❸ (*exist*) **to ~ in a size/ color** être disponible en une taille/une couleur; **this shirt ~s with the pants** cette chemise est vendue avec le pantalon ④(*become*) **to ~ loose** se desserrer; **to ~ open** s'ouvrir ⑤ *inf* (*have an orgasm*) jouir ▶ **to ~ clean about sth** révéler qc; **to have it coming** n'avoir que ce que l'on mérite; **~ again?** comment?

◆**come about** *vi* arriver

◆**come across** I. *vt* (*photos*) tomber sur; (*problem, obstacle*) rencontrer II. *vi* faire une impression; **to ~ well/badly** bien/mal passer; **to ~ as sth** donner l'impression d'être qc

◆**come along** *vi* arriver; **~!** allez, viens!; **are you coming along?** tu viens?, tu viens avec? *Belgique*

◆**come apart** *vi* ①(*break*) tomber en morceaux ②(*detach*) se défaire

◆**come around** *vi* ①(*change one's mind*) changer d'avis; **to ~ sb's way of thinking** se rallier à l'opinion de qn ②(*regain consciousness*) revenir à soi ③(*visit*) passer ④(*recur*) arriver

◆**come at** *vt* ①(*attack*) attaquer ②(*arrive*) parvenir à

◆**come away** *vi* partir; **to ~ from sth** se détacher de qc

◆**come back** *vi* revenir; **it'll ~ to me** ça me reviendra

◆**come by** I. *vt insep* ① *s.* **come across** ②(*obtain by chance*) trouver II. *vi* passer

◆**come down** *vi* ①(*move down*) descendre; (*curtain*) baisser ②(*in rank: people*) descendre d'un rang ③(*land*) atterrir ④(*fall: rain, snow*) tomber ⑤(*visit southern place*) descendre; **he came down from Chicago** il est descendu de Chicago ⑥(*become less: prices, cost, inflation*) baisser ⑦(*be detached*) se décrocher ⑧*fig* (*to be a matter*) **to ~ to sth** se ramener à qc; **to ~ to the fact that …** en venir au fait que …

◆**come forward** *vi* ①(*advance*) **to ~ to sb** s'avancer vers qn ②(*offer assistance*) se présenter; **to ~ with sth** présenter qc; **to ~ with a suggestion** faire une suggestion

◆**come in** *vi* ①(*enter*) entrer; **~!** entrez! ②(*arrive*) arriver; (*tide, sea*) monter; (*news, results, call*) s'annoncer; (*money*) rentrer; **to ~ first** arriver premier; **when do grapes ~?** quand commence la saison du raisin? ③(*become fashionable*) faire son apparition ④(*be*) **to ~ handy/useful** être pratique/utile ⑤(*participate in*) intervenir ⑥(*receive*) **to ~ for criticism** faire l'objet de critiques

◆**come into** *vt* ①(*enter*) entrer dans; **to ~ office** entrer en fonction; **to ~ fashion** devenir à la mode; **to ~ power** arriver au pouvoir; **to ~ the world** venir au monde ②(*get involved in*) **to ~ sb's life** s'ingérer dans la vie de qn ③(*be relevant*) **to ~ it** entrer en ligne de compte; **anger doesn't ~ it** la colère n'a rien à voir là-dedans ④(*inherit*) hériter de

◆**come off** I. *vi* ① *inf* (*succeed*) réussir ②(*end up*) **to ~ well/badly** bien/mal s'en tirer ③(*become detached*) se détacher ④(*rub off: stain*) partir; (*ink*) s'effacer II. *vt* ①(*fall*) tomber de ②(*climb down*) descendre de ③(*detach*) se détacher de ④*MED* **to ~ one's medication** arrêter son traitement ⑤ *inf* (*expression of annoyance*) **~ it!** arrête ton char!

◆**come on** I. *vi* ①(*exhortation*) **~! you can do it!** allez! tu peux le faire!; **~! just stop it!** hé! ça suffit! arrête! ②(*improve*) faire des progrès; **he really came on with his tennis** il a fait de gros progrès au tennis ③(*start*) commencer; **to have a headache coming on** sentir venir un mal de tête ④(*start to work*) se mettre en route; (*lights*) s'allumer ⑤*THEAT, CINE* entrer en scène ⑥ *inf* (*express sexual interest*) **to ~ to sb** draguer qn II. *vt s.* **come upon**

◆**come out** *vi* ①(*appear, go out*) sortir; (*sun, star*) apparaître; (*flowers*) éclore ②(*express opinion*) se prononcer; **to ~ in favor of/against sth** se prononcer en faveur/contre qc ③(*emerge, result*) sortir; **to ~ of sth** se

**C**

sortir de qc; **to ~ first** sortir premier ④ (*become known*) être révélé; **to ~ that ...** s'avérer que ... ⑤ (*say*) **to ~ with sth** sortir qc ⑥ (*reveal one's homosexuality*) révéler son homosexualité ⑦ (*be removed*) partir; (*cork*) retirer; (*tooth, hair*) tomber ⑧ (*fade: shirt*) déteindre ⑨ (*be published: book, film*) sortir ⑩ PHOT **the pictures came out pretty nice** les photos *fpl* ont été réussies; **to not ~** ne rien donner ⑪ (*end up*) **to ~ at a price** s'élever à un prix ▶ **it will all ~ in the** <u>wash</u> *prov* on le saura tôt ou tard

◆**come over** I. *vi* ① (*come nearer*) se rapprocher ② (*visit*) passer; **why don't you ~ tomorrow?** pourquoi ne viens-tu pas me voir demain? ③ (*come, travel*) venir; **to ~ from France** venir de France ④ (*make impression*) **to ~ as sth** avoir l'air d'être qc; **to ~ well** bien passer II. *vt* (*person*) gagner; **what has ~ you?** qu'est-ce qui te prend?

◆**come round** *vi s.* **come around**

◆**come through** I. *vi* ① (*survive*) survivre ② (*penetrate*) percer II. *vt* (*war, injuries*) survivre à

◆**come to** I. *vt* ① (*reach*) atteindre; (*decision*) en venir à; (*conclusion*) arriver à; **this road comes to an end** cette route est sans issue; **to ~ rest** s'arrêter; **she will ~ no harm** il ne lui arrivera pas de mal; **to ~ nothing** n'aboutir à rien; **I can't ~ terms with his illness** je n'arrive pas à me faire à sa maladie ② (*amount to*) s'élever à II. *vi* revenir à soi

◆**come under** *vt* ① (*be listed under*) être classé sous; **the case came under his care** l'affaire *f* lui incombait ② (*be subjected to*) subir; **to ~ criticism** être sujet aux critiques; **to ~ suspicion** commencer à être soupçonné

◆**come up** I. *vi* ① (*go up*) monter; **to ~ for lunch** se manifester pour le déjeuner ② (*arise, be mentioned: problem, situation*) se présenter; **to ~ against a problem** se heurter à un problème; **he came up in the speech** il a été cité

dans le discours ③ (*appear*) apparaître; (*sun*) se lever; (*plant*) sortir; (*tide*) monter ④ (*approach*) (s')approcher; **the flood came up to the city** l'inondation *f* est arrivée jusqu'à la ville ⑤ LAW (*case*) passer au tribunal ⑥ (*shine*) retrouver de sa brillance ⑦ (*produce*) **to ~ with sth** (*solution*) trouver qc; (*idea*) proposer qc II. *vt* monter

◆**come upon** *vt* (*find*) tomber sur

**comeback** ['kʌm·bæk] *n* ① (*return*) retour *m*; **to make a ~** faire son retour; *fig* faire une rentrée (théâtrale) ② (*retort*) réplique *f*

**comedian** [kə·'mi·di·ən] *n* comique *mf*

**comedy** ['ka·mə·di] *n* ① CINE, THEAT, LIT comédie *f* ② (*funny situation*) farce *f*

**comet** ['ka·mɪt] *n* comète *f*

**comfort** ['kʌm(p)·fərt] I. *n* ① (*ease*) confort *m* ② (*consolation*) réconfort *m* ③ *pl* (*pleasurable things*) commodités *fpl* II. *vt* réconforter

**comfortable** *adj* ① (*offering comfort*) confortable ② (*pleasant: sensation*) agréable ③ (*at ease*) à l'aise; **to make oneself ~** se mettre à l'aise ④ (*having money*) aisé(e) ⑤ MED **to be ~** ne pas souffrir ⑥ (*substantial*) confortable; **he has a ~ lead over his opponent** il a une avance confortable sur son adversaire

**comfortably** *adv* ① (*in a comfortable manner: sit, lie*) confortablement ② (*in a pleasant way*) agréablement ③ (*financially stable*) **to live ~** mener une vie aisée ④ (*easily*) facilement ⑤ (*substantially*) **to lead ~** avoir une avance confortable

**comforter** *n* édredon *m*

**comforting** *adj* consolant(e)

**comfy** ['kʌm(p)·fi] <-ier, -iest> *adj inf* confortable

**comic** ['ka·mɪk] I. *n* ① (*comedian*) comique *mf* ② (*cartoon*) bande *f* dessinée II. *adj* comique

**comic book** *n* bande *f* dessinée

**comic strip** *n* bande *f* dessinée

**coming** I. *adj* ① (*next: year*) prochain(e); (*generation*) futur(e) ② (*ap-*

*proaching*) à venir; (*hurricane*) qui approche; (*difficulties*) qui s'annonce; **in the ~ weeks** dans les semaines à venir; **this ~ Sunday** ce dimanche II. *n* ➊ (*arrival*) venue *f* ➋ REL **the ~ of the Messiah** l'avènement *m* du Messie ▶**~s and goings** les allées et venues *fpl*

**comma** [ˈka·mə] *n* virgule *f*

**command** [kəˈmænd] I. *vt* ➊ (*order*) **to ~ sb** ordonner à qn; **I ~ that** j'ordonne que +*subj* ➋ (*have command over: regiment, ship*) commander ➌ (*have at one's disposal*) avoir à sa disposition ➍ *form* (*inspire: respect*) imposer ➎ *form* (*give*) **his house ~s a view of the beach** sa maison donne sur la plage II. *vi* commander III. *n* ➊ (*order*) ordre *m;* **to have sth at one's ~** avoir la responsabilité de qc ➋ (*control*) maîtrise *f;* **to be in ~ of sth** avoir le contrôle de qc ➌ MIL commandement *m;* **to take ~ of a force** prendre le commandement d'une troupe ➍ COMPUT commande *f* ➎ (*knowledge: of a language*) maîtrise *f* ➏ *form* (*view*) vue *f*

**commander** *n* MIL chef *m*

**commemorate** [kəˈmem·ə·reɪt] *vt* commémorer

**commemorative** [kəˈmem·ər·ə·tɪv] *adj* commémoratif(-ive)

**commendable** *adj* louable

**comment** [ˈka·ment] I. *n* commentaire *m;* **to make a ~ about sth** faire une observation à propos de qc; **no ~** sans commentaire II. *vi* faire un commentaire; **to ~ on sth** faire des commentaires sur qc III. *vt* **to ~ that ...** remarquer que ...

**commentary** [ˈka·mən·ter·i] *n* commentaire *m*

**commentate** [ˈka·mən·teɪt] *vi* TV, RADIO faire le commentaire; **to ~ on sth** commenter qc

**commentator** *n* TV, RADIO commentateur, -trice *m, f*

**commercial** I. *adj* ➊ (*relating to commerce*) commercial(e) ➋ *pej* (*profit-orientated: production, movie*) mer-

cantile ➌ (*available to public*) commercial(e) II. *n* publicité *f*

**commercialize** [kəˈmɜr·ʃə·laɪz] *vt* commercialiser

**commission** [kəˈmɪʃ·ən] I. *vt* ➊ (*order*) commander; **to ~ sb to** +*infin* charger qn de +*infin* ➋ MIL mettre en service; **to ~ sb as sth** nommer qn à qc II. *n* ➊ (*order*) commission *f;* **to carry out a ~** s'acquitter d'une commission ➋ (*system of payment*) commission *f;* **to be on ~** travailler à la commission ➌ (*investigative body*) commission *f;* **fact-finding ~** commission d'enquête ➍ MIL affectation *f* ➎ *form* (*perpetration: of a crime, murder*) perpétration *f* ▶**out of ~** hors de service

**commit** [kəˈmɪt] <-tt-> *vt* ➊ (*carry out*) commettre; **to ~ suicide** se suicider ➋ (*bind*) engager; **to ~ oneself to a relationship** s'engager dans une relation; **to ~ money to a project** mettre de l'argent dans un projet ➌ (*institutionalize: prisoner*) incarcérer; (*patient*) interner ➍ (*entrust*) confier; **to ~ to memory** apprendre par cœur; **to ~ to paper** rapporter sur papier

**committee** [kəˈmɪt̬·i] *n* comité *m;* **to be on a ~** être membre d'un comité

**commodity** [kəˈma·də·t̬i] <-ties> *n* ➊ (*product*) denrée *f* ➋ (*raw material*) matière *f* première

**common** [ˈka·mən] I. <-er, -est *o* more ~, most ~> *adj* ➊ (*ordinary: name*) courant(e); **in ~ use** d'un usage courant ➋ (*widespread*) (*disease*) répandu(e); **it is ~ knowledge that...** il est de notoriété publique que... ➌ *inv* (*shared*) commun(e); **the ~ good** le bien commun; **to have sth in ~ with sb/sth** avoir qc en commun avec qn/qc ➍ <-er, -est> *pej* (*low-class*) commun(e); (*criminal, thief*) de bas étage ➎ (*average*) ordinaire; **the ~ people** les gens *mpl* ordinaires; (*man*) du peuple; (*accent*) populaire II. *n* terrain *m* communal

**common-law marriage** *n* concubinage *m*

**common sense** n bon sens m

**commonsense** adj sensé(e)

**Commonwealth** n the ~ (of Nations) le Commonwealth

**commotion** [kə·'mou·ʃ³n] n agitation f

**communicate** [kə·'mju·nɪ·keɪt] I. vt communiquer; (illness) transmettre II. vi communiquer

**communication** n a. form communication f; **means of** ~ moyens mpl de communication

**communicative** [kə·'mju·nə·keɪ·ṭɪv] adj communicatif(-ive)

**communism** ['kam·jə·nɪ·z³m] n communisme m

**community center** n centre m culturel

**commute** [kə·'mjut] I. vi **to** ~ **to work** faire la navette entre son domicile et son travail II. vt form ⬤ (change) échanger; **to** ~ **sth for** [o **into**] **sth** changer qc en qc ⬤ LAW commuer III. n trajet m

**commuter** n banlieusard(e) m(f), navetteur, -euse m, f Belgique (personne qui fait la navette entre deux lieux); ~ **train** train m de banlieue

**compact¹** [kam·'pækt] I. adj compact(e) II. vt form compacter III. ['kam·pækt] n ⬤ AUTO voiture f de petit modèle ⬤ (cosmetic case) poudrier m

**compact²** ['kam·pækt] n form pacte m

**companion** [kəm·'pæn·jən] n ⬤ (accompanying person or animal) compagnon m, compagne f ⬤ (reference book) vade-mecum m

**company** ['kʌm·pə·ni] <-ies> n ⬤ compagnie f; **Duggan and Company** Duggan et Compagnie; **in (the)** ~ **of sb** en compagnie de qn

**comparable** ['kam·p³r·ə·bl] adj comparable; ~ **to** [o **with**] **sth** comparable à qc

**comparative** [kəm·'per·ə·ṭɪv] I. adj comparatif(-ive) II. n LING comparatif m

**comparatively** adv ⬤ (by comparison) en comparaison ⬤ (relatively) relativement

**compare** [kəm·'per] I. vt comparer II. vi être comparable ▸ **to** ~ **favorably with sth** faire le poids avec qc

**comparison** [kəm·'per·ɪ·s³n] n comparaison f; **by** [o **in**] ~ **with sb/sth** en comparaison avec qn/qc; **for** ~ en comparaison

**compartment** [kəm·'part·mənt] n a. RAIL compartiment m **C**

**compass** ['kʌm·pəs] <-es> n ⬤ (direction-finding device) boussole f; NAUT, TECH compas m ⬤ form (range) portée f ⬤ MUS registre m

**compassion** [kəm·'pæʃ·³n] n compassion f

**compassionate** [kəm·'pæʃ·³n·ət] adj compatissant(e)

**compatible** [kəm·'pæṭ·ə·bl] adj ⬤ (able to co-exist) a. COMPUT, MED compatible; **to be** ~ **with sb/sth** être compatible avec qn/qc; (suited for); **to be** ~ **with sb/sth** être bien assorti avec qn/qc ⬤ (consistent) cohérent(e)

**compel** [kəm·'pel] <-ll-> vt ⬤ form (force) contraindre ⬤ form (bring out) produire

**compensate** ['kam·pən·seɪt] I. vt dédommager qc II. vi **to** ~ **for sth** compenser qc

**compensation** n ⬤ (monetary amends) dédommagement m ⬤ (recompense) compensation f; **in** ~ en compensation

**compete** [kəm·'pit] vi ⬤ (strive) rivaliser; **to** ~ **for sth** se disputer qc; **to** ~ **in an event** participer à un évènement; **to** ~ **with sb** être en compétition avec qn ⬤ SPORTS être en compétition

**competent** ['kam·pɪ·t³nt] adj ⬤ (capable) compétent(e) ⬤ LAW (witness) autorisé(e)

**competition** [ˌkam·pə·'tɪʃ·³n] n ⬤ (state of competing) compétition f; **to be in** ~ **with sb** être en compétition avec qn ⬤ (rivalry) **I'm sure she's no** ~ je suis sûr qu'elle n'est pas une adversaire redoutable ⬤ (contest) **beauty/swimming/diving** ~ concours m de beauté/de natation/de plongée

**competitive** [kəm·'peṭ·ə·ṭɪv] adj compétitif(-ive); (spirit, sports) de compétition; (person) qui a l'esprit de compétition

**competitiveness** *n* compétitivité *f*

**competitor** *n* compétiteur, -trice *m, f*

**compile** [kəm·'paɪl] *vt a.* COMPUT compiler

**complain** [kəm·'pleɪn] *vi* se plaindre; **to ~ about/of sth** se plaindre de qc

**complaint** [kəm·'pleɪnt] *n* ❶(*expression of displeasure*) a. ECON réclamation *f*; **to have/make a ~ about sb/sth** avoir/faire une réclamation à propos de qn/qc ❷(*accusation, charge*) plainte *f* ❸(*illness*) souffrance *f*

**complete** [kəm·'plit] I. *vt* ❶(*add what is missing*) compléter ❷(*finish*) achever ❸(*fill out entirely*) remplir II. *adj* ❶(*whole*) complet(-ète) ❷(*total*) total(e); **the man's a ~ fool!** l'homme *m* est un parfait idiot!; **~ stranger** parfait étranger *m*

**completely** *adv* complètement

**completion** [kəm·'pli·ʃən] *n* achèvement *m*

**complex** ['kam·plɛks] I. *adj* complexe II. <-xes> *n* complexe *m*

**complexion** [kəm·'plɛk·ʃən] *n* ❶(*natural appearance of facial skin*) teint *m* ❷(*character*) complexion *f*

**complexity** [kəm·'plɛk·sə·t̬i] *n* complexité *f*

**compliance** *n* form conformité *f*; **in ~ with the law/regulations** conformément à la loi/aux dispositions (réglementaires); **to act** [*o* **be**] **in ~ with sth** se conformer à qc

**complicate** ['kam·plə·keɪt] *vt* compliquer

**complicated** *adj* compliqué(e)

**complication** *n a.* MED complication *f*

**compliment** ['kam·plə·mənt] I. *n* compliment *m*; **to pay sb a ~** adresser un compliment à qn ▸ **to be fishing for ~s** mendier les éloges II. *vt* **to ~ sb on sth** complimenter qn pour qc

**complimentary** [ˌkam·plə·'men·tər·i] *adj* ❶(*characterized by compliment*) élogieux(-euse); **to be ~ about sth** être élogieux à l'égard de qc ❷(*free, without charge*) gratuit(e)

**comply** [kəm·'plaɪ] *vi* form **to ~ with sth** se conformer à qc

**component** [kəm·'pou·nənt] *n* ❶(*part*) constituant *m*; (*of a system*) élément *m* ❷TECH composant *m*

**composer** *n* compositeur, -trice *m, f*

**composure** [kəm·'pou·ʒər] *n* calme *m*; **to lose/to regain one's ~** perdre/retrouver son sang froid

**compound** ['kam·paʊnd] I. *vt* ❶(*make worse: a problem*) aggraver ❷(*mix*) **to ~ sth with sth** mélanger qc avec qc ❸(*make up*) constituer II. *n* ❶(*enclosed area*) enceinte *f* ❷CHEM (*mixture*) composé *m* ❸LING mot *m* composé ❹(*combination: of feelings, thoughts*) composition *f* III. *adj* composé(e)

**comprehend** [ˌkam·prɪ·'hend] *vt, vi a.* form comprendre

**comprehension** [ˌkam·prɪ·'hen(t)·ʃən] *n* compréhension *f*; **listening ~ test** test *m* de compréhension orale; **reading ~ test** test de compréhension écrite; **beyond ~** au-delà de tout entendement; **he has no ~ of the size of the problem** il n'a aucune idée de l'ampleur du problème

**comprehensive** [ˌkam·prə·'hen(t)·sɪv] *adj* intégral(e); (*global: coverage*) total(e); (*list*) complet(-ète)

**compression** [kəm·'prɛʃ·ən] *n a.* COMPUT compression *f*

**compromise** ['kam·prə·maɪz] I. *n* compromis *m* II. *vi* transiger; **to ~ at** [*o* **on**] **sth** accepter une concession III. *vt pej* compromettre

**compulsion** [kəm·'pʌl·ʃən] *n* ❶(*irresistible desire/urge*) compulsion *f*; **to have a ~ to** +*infin* avoir un besoin compulsif de +*infin* ❷(*force*) contrainte *f*; **to be under ~ to** +*infin* être dans l'obligation de +*infin*

**compulsory** [kəm·'pʌl·sər·i] *adj* (*attendance, education*) obligatoire

**compute** [kəm·'pjut] *vt* calculer ▸ **it doesn't ~** *inf* cela ne cadre pas

**computer** *n* COMPUT ordinateur *m*

**computer-aided design** *n* conception *f* assistée par ordinateur

**computer game** n jeu m informatique; (on games console) jeu m vidéo

**computer graphics** n + sing/pl vb infographie f

**computerize** [kəm·'pju·tə·raɪz] I. vt ① (store on computer) stocker sur ordinateur ② (equip with computers) informatiser II. vi s'informatiser

**computer literacy** n connaissances fpl en informatique

**computer literate** adj initié(e) à l'informatique

**computer programmer** n (analyste-)programmeur (en informatique), -euse m, f

**con** [kan] <-nn-> I. vt to ~ sb into believing that … tromper qn en lui faisant croire que …; to ~ sb out of $10 escroquer qn de 10 dollars II. n inf arnaque f

**conceal** [kən·'sil] vt cacher; (evidence, surprise) dissimuler; to ~ sth from sb cacher qc à qn; to ~ the truth cacher la vérité

**concede** [kən·'sid] I. vt concéder; to ~ that … admettre que … II. vi céder

**conceited** adj pej suffisant(e)

**concentrate** ['kan(t)·sᵊn·treɪt] I. vi ① (focus one's thoughts) se concentrer; to ~ on sth se concentrer sur qc ② (gather, come together) se rassembler II. vt concentrer; to ~ one's thoughts se concentrer III. n (not diluted liquid) concentré m; fruit juice ~ jus m de fruit concentré

**concentrated** adj ① (focused) concentré(e); (effort) résolu(e) ② (not diluted: juice, solution) concentré(e)

**concentration** n concentration f; ~ on sth concentration f sur qc; to lose (one's) ~ se déconcentrer

**concept** ['kan·sept] n (idea, project) concept m

**concern** [kən·'sɜrn] I. vt ① (apply to, involve, affect) concerner; to ~ oneself about sth s'occuper de qc; to be ~ed with sth être concerné par qc ② (worry) inquiéter; to ~ oneself s'inquiéter ▶ to whom it may ~ ADMIN à qui de

droit II. n ① (interest) intérêt m; to be of ~ to sb intéresser qn ② (care) souci m ③ (worry) inquiétude f; ~ for sth inquiétude à propos de qc; it's that … ce qui l'inquiète c'est que … ④ (company, business) entreprise f; a going ~ une entreprise qui marche bien

**concerned** adj ① (involved) concerné(e); as far as I'm ~ en ce qui me concerne; the conference is something ~ with linguistics la conférence a à voir avec la linguistique ② (worried) inquiet(-ète); isn't he ~ that she finds out? il n'a pas peur qu'elle l'apprenne?; to be ~ about sth se faire du souci pour qc

**concerning** prep en ce qui concerne

**concert** ['kan·sərt] n concert m; ~ hall salle f de concert; in ~ fig de concert; in ~ with sb fig en accord avec qn

**concession** [kən·'seʃ·ᵊn] n (sth granted) concession f; to make a ~ to sb faire une concession à qn; to make a ~ to sth tenir compte de qc

**concise** [kən·'saɪs] adj (answer, letter) concis(e); (edition, dictionary) abrégé(e)

**conclude** [kən·'klud] I. vi conclure; to ~ from sth that … conclure à partir de qc que … II. vt conclure

**concluding** adj (chapter, episode) dernier(-ère); (remark, word) de conclusion

**conclusion** [kən·'klu·ʒᵊn] n conclusion f; in ~ en conclusion; to come to a ~ parvenir à une conclusion; to draw the ~ that … tirer la conclusion selon laquelle …; don't jump to ~s! ne va pas te faire de film!

**conclusive** [kən·'klu·sɪv] adj concluant(e)

**concoct** [kən·'kakt] vt concocter

**concrete** ['kan·krit] I. n ① béton m; reinforced ~ béton armé ② fig to be cast in ~ être fixe II. adj en béton

**concussion** [kən·'kʌʃ·ᵊn] n commotion f

**condemn** [kən·'dem] vt ① (reprove, denounce, sentence) condamner; to be ~ed to death être condamné à mort

**C**

(*formally pronounce unsafe*) **to ~ a building** déclarer un bâtiment insalubre ③ (*pronounce unsafe for consumption*) déclarer impropre à la consommation

**condensation** *n* ① (*process, on window*) condensation *f* ② (*reducing in size*) réduction *f*

**condescending** *adj* condescendant(e)

**condition** [kən·ˈdɪʃ·ən] I. *n* ① (*state*) état *m;* **in mint ~** en parfait état ② (*circumstance*) condition *f;* **weather ~s** conditions météorologiques; **working ~s** conditions de travail ③ (*term, stipulation*) condition *f;* **on the ~ that ...** à condition que ... ④ (*physical state*) forme *f;* **to be out of ~** ne pas être en forme; **to be in no ~ to** +*infin* ne pas être en état de +*infin* ⑤ (*disease*) maladie *f;* **heart ~** maladie cardiaque II. *vt* conditionner; **to ~ sb to sth/to** +*infin* habituer qn à qc/à +*infin;* **to ~ one's hair** utiliser de l'après-shampooing

**conditional** I. *adj* conditionnel(le); **to be ~ on sth** dépendre de qc II. *n* LING **the ~** le conditionnel

**conditioner** *n* ① (*for hair*) après-shampooing *m* ② (*for clothes*) adoucissant *m*

**condo** [ˌkan·doʊ] *n inf abbr of* **condominium**

**condom** [ˈkan·dəm] *n* préservatif *m*

**condominium** [ˌkan·də·ˈmɪn·i·əm] *n* ① (*apartment building with shared areas*) appartement *m* en copropriété ② (*unit of apartment building*) immeuble *m* en copropriété

**conduct** [kan·ˈdʌkt] I. *vt* ① (*carry out: negotiations, meeting, experiment*) mener ② (*direct: business, orchestra*) diriger; **to ~ one's life** mener sa vie ③ (*guide, lead*) conduire ④ (*behave*) **to ~ oneself** se comporter ⑤ ELEC, PHYS (*transmit*) être conducteur de II. *vi* MUS diriger III. *n* ① (*management*) gestion *f* ② (*behavior*) comportement *m*

**conductor** *n* ① (*director of musical performance*) chef *m* d'orchestre ② PHYS, ELEC conducteur *m* ③ (*fare collector: of train*) chef *m* de train

**cone** [koʊn] *n* ① MATH cône *m;* **traffic ~** balise *f* de signalisation ② (*holder for ice cream*) cornet *m;* **ice-cream ~** cornet de glace ③ (*oval shaped fruit of a conifer*) pomme *f* de pin

**conference** [ˈkan·fər·ən(t)s] *n* (*long meeting*) conférence *f*

**confess** [kən·ˈfes] I. *vi* ① (*admit*) **to ~ to sth** avouer qc ② REL **to ~ to a priest** se confesser à un prêtre II. *vt* ① (*admit*) avouer; **to ~ oneself sth** s'avouer qc ② REL (*sins*) confesser

**confession** [kən·ˈfeʃ·ən] *n* ① (*admission*) aveu *m;* **to have a ~ to make** avoir un aveu à faire ② (*admission of a crime*) aveux *mpl;* **to give a ~** faire des aveux ③ (*admission of sin*) confession *f;* **to go to ~** aller se confesser

**confide** [kən·ˈfaɪd] *vt* confier; **to ~ to sb that ...** confier à qn que ...

**confidence** [ˈkan·fə·dən(t)s] *n* ① (*secrecy*) confidence *f;* **in ~** en confidence ② (*complete trust*) confiance *f;* **to place one's ~ in sb/sth** faire confiance à qn/qc ③ *pl* (*secrets*) confidences *fpl* ④ (*self assurance*) confiance *f* en soi; **to lack ~** manquer de confiance en soi

**confident** [ˈkan·fə·dənt] *adj* ① (*sure*) sûr(e); **to be ~ about sth** être sûr de qc ② (*self-assured*) sûr(e) de soi; **she's a very ~ person** elle est très sûre d'elle

**confidential** *adj* confidentiel(le)

**confidentially** *adv* confidentiellement

**configuration** [kən·ˌfɪɡ·jə·ˈreɪ·ʃən] *n* configuration *f*

**confirm** [kən·ˈfɜrm] I. *vt* ① (*verify*) confirmer ② REL **to be ~ed** recevoir la confirmation II. *vi* confirmer

**confirmation** [ˌkan·fər·ˈmeɪ·ʃən] *n a.* REL confirmation *f*

**confiscate** [ˈkan·fə·skeɪt] *vt* **to ~ sth from sb** confisquer qc à qn

**conflict** [ˈkan·flɪkt] I. *n* conflit *m;* **~ of interests** conflit d'intérêts; **to come into ~ with sb** entrer en conflit avec qn II. *vi* (*do battle, be opposed to*) **to ~ with sb/sth** être en conflit avec qn/qc

**conflicting** *adj* (*ideas, claim, evidence*)

contradictoire; (*interest, advice*) contraire

**conform** [kən·'fɔrm] *vi* **to ~ to sth** être conforme à qc

**confront** [kən·'frʌnt] *vt* (*danger, enemy*) affronter; **to be ~d by a crowd of journalists** se retrouver face à une armée de journalistes

**confrontation** *n* ❶(*encounter*) confrontation *f* ❷(*direct clash*) affrontement *m*

**confuse** [kən·'fjuz] *vt* ❶(*perplex: person*) troubler; **you're confusing me!** tu m'embrouilles! ❷(*put into disarray: matters*) compliquer ❸(*mix up*) confondre

**confused** *adj* ❶(*perplexed*) embrouillé(e); **to be a bit ~ about what to do** ne plus savoir trop quoi faire ❷(*mixed up*) confus(e)

**confusing** *adj* confus(e)

**confusion** [kən·'fju·ʒ°n] *n* ❶(*mix up*) confusion *f* ❷(*disorder*) désordre *m*

**congested** *adj* ❶(*overcrowded: street, town*) encombré(e) ❷MED (*arteries*) congestionné(e)

**congestion** [kən·'dʒest·ʃ°n] *n* ❶(*overcrowding*) encombrement *m* ❷MED congestion *f*

**congratulate** [kən·'grætʃ·ə·leɪt] *vt* féliciter; **to ~ sb on sth** féliciter qn de qc

**congregation** *n* congrégation *f*

**congress** ['kɑn·grəs] *n* congrès *m*; **Congress** POL le Congrès

**congressional** *adj* du Congrès

**congressman** <-men> *n* membre *m* (masculin) du Congrès

**congresswoman** <-women> *n* membre *m* (féminin) du Congrès

**conifer** ['kɑ·nə·fər] *n* conifère *m*

**conjugate** ['kɑn·dʒə·geɪt] I. *vi* se conjuguer II. *vt* conjuguer

**conjure** ['kʌn·dʒər] I. *vi* faire des tours de passe-passe II. *vt* faire apparaître; (*spirits*) conjurer

  ◆**conjure up** *vt* évoquer; **to ~ the spirits of the dead** invoquer les esprits des morts

**conjurer** *n* prestidigitateur, -trice *m, f*

**conjuror** *n s.* **conjurer**

**conk** [kɑŋk] *vt iron, inf* **to ~ one's head on sth** flanquer un gnon à qn

  ◆**conk out** *vi inf* ❶(*break down: machine, vehicle*) tomber en panne ❷(*become exhausted*) s'écrouler

**con man** *n abbr of* **confidence man** escroc *m*

**connect** [kə·'nekt] I. *vi* être relié; (*cables, wires*) être connecté; (*rooms*) communiquer; (*train, plane*) assurer la correspondance; **to ~ to the Internet** se connecter sur Internet II. *vt* ❶(*join*) relier; **to ~ sth to sth** relier qc à qc; **to be ~ed** être joint ❷ELEC brancher ❸(*attach*) raccorder; (*train, wagon*) accrocher ❹*fig* (*link*) lier; **to be ~ed to sb/with sth** être lié à qn/qc; **to be well ~ed** avoir des relations; **to be ~ed** (*related*) être apparenté ❺(*associate*) associer qn/qc à qc ❻(*join by telephone*) mettre en communication; **to ~ sb with sb/sth** relier qn par téléphone avec qn/qc ❼(*in tourism*) **to ~ with sth** assurer la correspondance avec qc ❽COMPUT connecter; **to ~ sb to the Internet** connecter qn sur Internet

**Connecticut** [kə·'net̬·ɪ·kət] *n* le Connecticut

**connecting** *adj* de connexion; (*room*) communiquant(e); (*time*) de correspondance; **~ flight** correspondance *f*

**connection** *n* ❶(*association, logical link*) rapport *m*; **in ~ with sth** au sujet de qc; **to make the ~ between two things** faire le rapprochement entre deux choses ❷(*personal link*) lien *m*; **there is no ~ with the Dixons** il n'y a pas de lien *m* de parenté avec les Dixon ❸ *pl* (*contacts*) relations *fpl*; **to have useful ~s** avoir des relations ❹ELEC branchement *m* ❺TEL communication *f* ❻COMPUT (*to the Internet*) connexion *f* ❼TECH (*of pipes*) raccordement *m* ❽(*in travel*) correspondance *f* ► **in ~ with ...** à propos de ...

**conquer** ['kɑŋ·kər] *vt* conquérir; (*Mount*

C

*Everest*) faire l'ascension de; (*problem*) surmonter

**conquest** ['kɒn·kwəst] *n* ❶ MIL conquête *f* ❷ *iron* (*sexual adventure*) conquête *f* amoureuse

**conscience** ['kɒn·(t)ʃ³n(t)s] *n* conscience *f;* **matter of ~** cas *m* de conscience; **clear ~** conscience tranquille; **sth is on one's ~** avoir qc sur la conscience

**conscientious** *adj* consciencieux(-euse)

**conscious** ['kɒn(t)·ʃəs] *adj* ❶ (*deliberate*) conscient(e); (*decision*) délibéré(e) ❷ (*aware*) conscient(e); **fashion ~** qui suit la mode; **to be health ~** faire attention à sa santé; **to be ~ of sth** être conscient de qc

**consciousness** *n* ❶ MED connaissance *f;* **to lose ~** perdre connaissance; **to regain ~** revenir à soi ❷ (*awareness*) conscience *f;* **to raise one's ~** prendre conscience de qc

**conscription** [kən·ˈskrɪp·ʃ³n] *n* conscription *f*

**consecutive** [kən·ˈsek·jə·t̬ɪv] *adj* consécutif(-ive)

**consent** [kən·ˈsent] I. *n* form permission *f;* **to give one's ~** accorder son consentement II. *vi* **to ~ to** +*infin* consentir à +*infin*

**consequence** ['kɒn(t)·sɪ·kwən(t)s] *n* conséquence *f;* **to suffer the ~s** subir les conséquences; **as a ~** par conséquent

**consequently** *adv* par conséquent

**conservation** [ˌkɒn(t)·sər·ˈveɪ·ʃ³n] *n* conservation *f;* **wildlife ~** protection *f* de la vie sauvage

**conservative** [kən·ˈsɜr·və·t̬ɪv] *adj* conservateur(-trice); **to be a ~ dresser** s'habiller de façon traditionnelle; **at a ~ estimate** au minimum

**conserve** [kən·ˈsɜrv] *vt* conserver; (*one's strength*) économiser; **to ~ energy** faire des économies d'énergie

**consider** [kən·ˈsɪd·ər] *vt* ❶ (*think about*) considérer; **to ~ taking a trip** envisager de faire un voyage ❷ (*look attentively at*) examiner ❸ (*show regard for*) prendre en considération ❹ (*regard*

*as*) considérer; **to ~ sb as sth** considérer qn comme qc; **to ~ that ...** penser que ...

**considerable** *adj* considérable

**considerate** [kən·ˈsɪ·dᵊr·ət] *adj* prévenant(e)

**consideration** *n* ❶ (*careful thought*) considération *f;* **to take sth into ~** prendre qc en considération ❷ (*thoughtfulness*) égard *m;* **to show ~ for sb** montrer de la considération à qn; **for a small ~** *iron* moyennant finance

**considered** *adj* (*carefully thought out*) bien pensé(e)

**considering** I. *prep* étant donné; **~ the weather** vu le temps II. *adv inf* tout compte fait III. *conj* **~ (that)** étant donné que

**consist** [kən·ˈsɪst] *vi* **to ~ of sth** consister en qc

**consistent** [kən·ˈsɪs·t³nt] *adj* cohérent(e)

**console¹** [kən·ˈsoʊl] *vt* consoler

**console²** ['kɒn·soʊl] *n* (*switch panel*) console *f*

**consonant** I. *n* consonne *f* II. *adj* **to be ~ with sth** être en accord avec qc

**conspicuous** [kən·ˈspɪk·ju·əs] *adj* voyant(e); (*feature*) notable; **to be ~ by one's absence** *iron* briller par son absence

**constant** ['kɒn(t)·stənt] I. *n* constante *f* II. *adj* ❶ (*continuous*) constant(e); (*chatter*) ininterrompu(e); (*noise*) persistant(e); (*shelling*) permanent(e) ❷ (*unchanging: love*) durable; (*support*) inébranlable; (*temperature*) constant(e) ❸ (*frequent: use*) fréquent(e)

**constantly** *adv* constamment; (*bicker*) continuellement; (*complain*) tout le temps

**constellation** [ˌkɒn(t)·stə·ˈleɪ·ʃ³n] *n* ❶ ASTR constellation *f* ❷ (*group of famous people gathered together*) pléiade *f*

**constitution** *n* ❶ CHEM composition *f* ❷ POL, MED constitution *f;* **to have a**

**strong/weak ~** avoir une bonne/mauvaise constitution

**construction** n ① (*act of building, word arrangement*) construction f ② (*building*) bâtiment m ③ (*interpretation*) interprétation f; **to put a ~ on sth** interpréter qc d'une façon différente

**constructive** [kən·'strʌk·tɪv] *adj* constructif(-ive)

**consul** ['kan(t)·səl] n consul m

**consulate** ['kan(t)·sjʊ·lət] n consulat m

**consult** [kən·'sʌlt] I. *vi* consulter; **to ~ with sb** être en consultation avec qn II. *vt* ① (*seek information*) consulter ② (*examine*) examiner; (*one's feelings*) s'en référer à

**consultant** [kən·'sʌl·tənt] n ECON expert m conseil; **computer ~** expert conseil en informatique; **management ~** conseiller m en organisation

**consulting** *adj* consultant(e)

**consume** [kən·'sum] *vt* ① (*eat or drink*) consommer ② (*use up: fuel, energy*) consommer; (*money*) dilapider ③ (*destroy*) consumer ④ (*fill with*) **to be ~d** (*by anger, greed, hatred*) être dévoré; (*by jealousy*) être rongé; **to be ~d by passion for sb** brûler de passion pour qn

**consumer** n consommateur, -trice m, f; **~ advice/credit** conseils mpl/crédit m au consommateur; **~ rights** droits mpl du consommateur

**consumption** [kən·'sʌm(p)·ʃən] n no pl ① (*using up*) consommation f; **energy ~** consommation f d'énergie ② (*eating, drinking*) consommation f; **unfit for human ~** impropre à la consommation [humaine] ③ *fig* (*use*) **for internal ~** destiné(e) à l'usage interne ④ no pl HIST, MED phtisie f

**contact** ['kan·tækt] I. n ① (*state of communication*) contact m; **to have ~ with the** (**outside**) **world** être en contact avec le monde; **to lose ~ with sb** perdre le contact avec qn; **to make ~ with sb** prendre contact avec qn ② (*connection*) rapport m; **business ~s** relations fpl d'affaires ③ (*act of touching*) **physical ~** contact m physique; **to come into ~ with sth** entrer en contact avec qc ④ ELEC contact m électrique ▸ **they made eye ~** leurs regards se sont croisés II. *vt* contacter

**contact lens** n lentille f de contact

**contagious** *adj* ① contagieux(-euse) ② *fig* (*enthusiasm, laugh*) communicatif(-ive)

**contain** [kən·'teɪn] *vt* contenir; (*anger*) retenir; (*examples*) renfermer; **to ~ one's laugh** s'empêcher de rire

**container** n ① (*box*) récipient m ② (*for transport*) conteneur m

**contaminate** [kən·'tæm·ɪ·neɪt] *vt* contaminer

**contamination** n contamination f

**contemplate** ['kan·tem·pleɪt] I. *vi* méditer II. *vt* ① (*gaze at*) contempler ② (*consider*) considérer; **to ~ suicide** songer au suicide ③ (*intend*) **to ~ doing sth** penser faire qc; **suicide was never ~d** il n'a jamais été question de suicide

**contemporary** [kən·'tem·pə·rer·i] I. n contemporain(e) m(f) II. *adj* contemporain(e)

**contempt** [kən·'tem(p)t] n mépris m; **to hold sb/sth in ~** mépriser qn/qc; **to treat sb/sth with ~** traiter qn/qc avec dédain

**content¹** ['kan·tent] n ① (*all things inside*) contenu m; **to have a high/low fat ~** avoir une riche/pauvre teneur en matières grasses ② (*substance*) substance f

**content²** [kən·'tent] I. *vt* satisfaire; **to ~ oneself with sth** se contenter de qc II. *adj* satisfait(e); **to one's heart's ~** à souhait; **to be ~ with sth** se satisfaire de qc; **to be ~ to** + *infin* ne pas demander mieux que de + *infin*

**contented** *adj* satisfait(e)

**contentious** *adj* contesté(e)

**contentment** n contentement m

**contents** n pl ① (*things held in sth*) contenu m ② PUBL (**table of**) **~** table f des matières

**contest** ['kan·test, vb: kən·'test] I. n

**➊** (*competition*) concours *m;* **beauty ~** concours de beauté **➋** SPORTS compétition *f* **➌** (*dispute*) combat *m* II. *vt* **➊** (*challenge*) contester **➋** (*compete for*) disputer

**contestant** [kən·'tes·tənt] *n* concurrent(e) *m(f)*

**context** ['kan·tekst] *n* contexte *m*

**continent**[1] ['kan·tə·n·ənt] *n* continent *m*

**continent**[2] ['kan·tə·n·ənt] *adj* continent(e)

**continental** *adj* **➊** (*relating to a continent*) continental(e) **➋** (*of the mainland*) **~ Europe** Europe *f* continentale; **the ~ United States** les Etats-Unis *mpl* continentaux

**continental breakfast** *n* petit-déjeuner *m* continental (*comprenant café, pain et confiture*)

**contingency** *n form* contingence *f*

**continual** [kən·'tɪn·ju·əl] *adj* continuel(le)

**continually** *adv* continuellement

**continuation** *n* **➊** (*continuing, next stage*) continuation *f* **➋** (*extension*) prolongement *m*

**continue** [kən·'tɪn·ju] I. *vi* continuer; **to ~ doing sth** continuer à faire qc II. *vt* continuer; (*work*) poursuivre

**continuous** *adj* continu(e)

**contraception** [,kan·trə·'sep·ʃ°n] *n* contraception *f*

**contraceptive** [,kan·trə·'sep·tɪv] *n* contraceptif *m;* **~ pill** pilule *f* contraceptive

**contract**[1] ['kan·trækt] I. *n* contrat *m;* **to breach/to draw up a ~** rompre/établir un contrat; **to enter into a ~** passer un contrat II. *vi* **to ~ to** +*infin* s'engager à +*infin*

**contract**[2] [kən·'trækt] I. *vi* se contracter II. *vt* contracter

**contraction** *n* contraction *f*

**contractual** *adj* contractuel(le); (*conditions*) du contrat

**contradict** [,kan·trə·'dɪkt] I. *vi* contredire II. *vt* contredire

**contradiction** *n* contradiction *f*

**contradictory** [,kan·trə·'dɪk·tər·i] *adj* contradictoire

**contrary** ['kan·trer·i] I. *n* contraire *m;* **on the ~** au contraire II. *adj* contrariant(e)

**contrast** [kən·'træst] I. *n* contraste *m;* **in ~ to sth** en contraste avec qc II. *vt* comparer III. *vi* contraster

**contribute** [kən·'trɪ·bjut] I. *vi* **to ~ toward/to sth** contribuer à qc II. *vt* **➊** (*help toward an aim*) **to ~ sth to/toward sth** offrir qc à qc **➋** (*submit for publication*) **to ~ sth to sth** écrire qc pour qc

**contribution** *n* **➊** (*something contributed*) contribution *f* **➋** (*text for publication*) article *m*

**control** [kən·'troʊl] <-ll-> I. *n* **➊** (*power of command*) contrôle *m;* **to be in ~ of sth** contrôler qc; **to be under ~** être maîtrisé; **to go out of ~** perdre le contrôle; **to lose ~ over sth** perdre le contrôle de qc; **to have ~ over sb** avoir de l'autorité sur qn **➋** (*self-restraint*) maîtrise *f* **➌** ECON, FIN contrôle *m* **➍** (*place for checking*) **to go through customs ~** passer à la douane **➎** MED, PHYS (*person*) sujet *m* témoin; **~ group** groupe *m* témoin **➏** ELEC **~ board/panel** tableau *m* de bord/commande **➐** *pl* (*switches*) commandes *fpl* II. *vt* <-ll-> **➊** (*restrain, curb*) maîtriser **➋** (*run*) contrôler

**control tower** *n* tour *f* de contrôle

**controversial** [,kan·trə·'vɜr·ʃ°l] *adj* controversé(e)

**controversy** ['kan·trə·vɜr·si] <-sies> *n* controverse *f*

**convection oven** *n* four *m* à convection

**convenience** [kən·'vin·jən(t)s] *n* commodité *f;* **at your ~** comme cela te/vous convient

**convenience store** *n* épicerie *f* de quartier

**convenient** [kən·'vin·jənt] *adj* commode; (*moment*) opportun(e); **to be ~ for sth** (*within easy reach*) être bien situé pour qc

**convent** ['kan·vənt] *n* couvent *m*

**convention** [kən·'ven·(t)ʃⁿn] *n* convention *f*

**conventional** *adj* conventionnel(le)

**conversation** [ˌkan·vər·'seɪʃⁿn] *n* conversation *f*; **to hold a ~** tenir une conversation

**converse¹** [kən·'vɜrs] *vi form* converser

**converse²** ['kan·vɜrs] *form* I. *adj* inverse II. *n* inverse *m*

**conversion** [kən·'vɜr·ʒⁿn] *n* ① *(changing opinions)* conversion *f*; **~ sth** conversion à qc ② *(changing opinions)* **to undergo a ~** changer d'opinion ③ *(adoption for other purposes)* conversion *f*; *(of house, city)* aménagement *m* ④ FIN conversion *f*; **~ rate** taux *mpl* de conversion

**convert** ['kən·'vɜrt] I. *n* converti(e) *m(f)*; **to become a ~ to sth** se convertir à qc II. *vi* **to ~ to sth** se convertir à qc III. *vt* **to ~ sth into sth** convertir qc en qc

**convertible** I. *n* décapotable *f* II. *adj* convertible

**convict** ['kan·vɪkt, *vb:* kən·'vɪkt] I. *n* détenu(e) *m(f)* II. *vt* **to ~ sb of sth** reconnaître qn coupable de qc III. *vi* rendre un verdict de culpabilité

**conviction** [kən·'vɪk·ʃⁿn] *n* ① *(act of finding guilty)* condamnation *f*; **~ for sth** condamnation pour qc ② *(firm belief)* conviction *f*; **to have a deep ~ that…** avoir une conviction profonde que…

**convince** [kən·'vɪn(t)s] *vt* convaincre

**convincing** *adj* convaincant(e)

**convoy** ['kan·vɔɪ] I. *n* convoi *m*; **in ~** en convoi II. *vt* convoyer

**cook** [kʊk] I. *n* cuisinier, -ière *m, f* ► **too many ~s spoil the broth** *prov* trop de cuisiniers gâtent la sauce II. *vi* ① *(prepare food)* cuisiner ② *(be cooked)* cuire ③ *inf (do well)* se débrouiller pas mal ④ *inf (ready to go)* y aller ► **what's ~ing?** qu'est-ce qui se mijote là? III. *vt* ① *(prepare food)* cuisiner ② *(prepare food using heat)* cuire ► **to ~ the books** brouiller les comptes

**cookbook** *n* livre *m* de cuisine

**cooker** ['kʊ·kər] *n* ① *(stove)* cuisinière *f*; **induction ~** plaque [*o* table] *f* à induc-

tion; **rice ~** cuiseur *m* de riz ② *inf (cooking apple)* pomme *f* à cuire

**cookie** ['kʊk·i] *n* ① CULIN biscuit *m*; **chocolate-chip ~** cookie *m* aux pépites de chocolat ② *inf (person)* type *m*, nana *f*; **tough ~** dur(e) *m(f)* à cuire ③ COMPUT cookie *m* ► **that's the way the ~ crumbles!** c'est la vie!

**cooking** *n* cuisine *f*; **~ oil** huile *f* de cuisson

**cool** [kul] I. *adj* ① *(slightly cold)* frais(fraîche) ② *(calm)* tranquille; *inf* cool; **to keep a ~ head** garder la tête froide ③ *(unfriendly, cold)* froid(e); *(welcome)* glacial(e) ④ *(fresh: color)* froid(e) ⑤ *inf (fashionable)* cool ► **as a cucumber** tranquille II. *interj inf* cool! III. *n* ① *(coolness)* fraîcheur *f* ② *(calm)* sang-froid *m*; **to keep one's ~** garder son calme IV. *vi* se refroidir V. *vt* ① *(make cold)* refroidir ② *inf* **~ it!** reste cool!

**cooperate** [koʊ·'a·pə·reɪt] *vi* **to ~ in sth** coopérer à qc

**cooperation** *n* coopération *f*; **~ in sth** coopération à qc

**cooperative** [koʊ·'a·pər·ə·t̬ɪv] I. *n* coopérative *f* II. *adj* coopératif(-ive)

**coordinate** [ˌkoʊ·'ɔr·dⁿn·eɪt] I. *n* coordonnée *f* II. *vi* **to ~ with sth** aller avec qc III. *vt* coordonner IV. *adj* coordonné(e)

**coordination** *n* coordination *f*

**coordinator** *n* coordinateur, -trice *m, f*

**cop** [kap] *inf* I. *n* flic *m* II. <-pp-> *vt* ① *(grab)* saisir; **to ~ a feel** peloter rapidement ② LAW **to ~ a plea** plaider coupable

**cope** [koʊp] *vi* ① *(master a situation)* **to ~ with sth** faire face à qc ② *(deal with)* **to ~ with sth** supporter qc

**copier** ['ka·pi·ər] *n* photocopieuse *f*

**copper** ['ka·pər] I. *n (metal)* cuivre *m* II. *adj (color)* cuivre; **~-colored** cuivré(e)

**copy** ['ka·pi] I. <-pies> *n* ① *(facsimile)* copie *f*; **to make a ~ of sth** photocopier qc ② PHOT épreuve *f* ③ ART reproduction *f* ④ PUBL *(of a book)* exemplai-

re m; **carbon** ~ carbone m; **true** ~ copie f conforme ⑤ (*text to be published*) article m ⑥ (*topic for an article*) sujet m d'article ⑦ COMPUT copie f; **hard** ~ COMPUT impression f d'un fichier informatique ▶ **to be a** carbon ~ **of sb** être le sosie de qn II. <-ie-> vt a. fig copier III. vi pej (*cheat*) copier; **to ~ from/off sb** copier sur qn
◆ **copy down** vt recopier

**copycat** inf I. adj d'imitation; (*version*) copié(e) II. n childspeak, pej copieur, -euse m, f

**copyedited** n secrétaire mf de rédaction

**copy machine** n inf photocopieuse f

**copyright** I. n droits mpl d'auteur; **to hold the ~ on sth** avoir les droits d'auteur sur qc; **out of ~** dans le domaine public II. vt déposer

**coral** ['kɔr·əl] I. n corail m II. adj ① (*of reddish color*) corail inv ② (*of coral*) de corail

**coral reef** n récif m de corail

**cord** [kɔrd] n ① (*rope*) corde f; **spinal** ~ moelle f épinière; **umbilical** ~ cordon m ombilical ② (*string*) ficelle f ③ ELEC fil m électrique

**cordial** ['kɔr·dʒəl] I. adj ① (*friendly*) chaleureux(-euse); (*relations*) cordial(e) ② form (*strong*) fort(e); (*dislike*) profond(e) II. n liqueur f

**cordless** adj sans fil

**cordon** ['kɔr·dⁿn] I. n cordon m II. vt **to ~ sth off** établir un cordon de sécurité tout autour de qc

**corduroy** ['kɔr·də·rɔɪ] n ① (*material*) velours m côtelé ② pl (*pants*) pantalon m en velours côtelé

**core** [kɔr] I. n ① (*center*) partie f centrale ② (*center with seeds*) noyau m; **apple/pear** ~ trognon m de pomme/ poire ③ PHYS nucléon m; ~ **of a nuclear reactor** cœur m d'un réacteur nucléaire ④ (*most important part*) essentiel m; **to be at the ~ of a problem** être au centre du problème ⑤ ELEC mèche f ⑥ COMPUT mise f en mémoire des bits ▶ **to the ~** au cœur m; **to be rotten to**

the ~ être pourri jusqu'à la moelle II. adj (*issue*) central(e) III. vt évider

**cork** [kɔrk] I. n ① liège m ② (*stopper*) bouchon m II. vt (*put stopper in: bottle*) boucher

**corkscrew** ['kɔrk·skru] I. n tire-bouchon m II. adj en tire-bouchon

**corn¹** [kɔrn] n ① (*plant*) maïs m ② inf (*something trite*) banalité f

**corn²** [kɔrn] n MED cor m

**corn bread** n pain m de maïs

**corncob** n épi m de maïs

**corner** ['kɔr·nər] I. n ① (*intersection of two roads*) coin m; **just around the ~** à deux pas d'ici; **to cut ~s** prendre des raccourcis ② (*place*) coin m ③ SPORTS corner m ④ (*difficult position*) **to be in a tight ~** être dans le pétrin ⑤ (*domination*) **to have a ~ of the market** avoir le monopole du marché ⑥ (*periphery*) commissure f; **out of the ~ of one's eye** du coin de l'œil ⑦ fig **to be around the ~** être sur le point de; **to have turned the ~** avoir surmonté la crise II. vt ① (*hinder escape*) attraper; *iron* coincer ② ECON (*market*) accaparer III. vi (*auto*) virer; **to ~ well** prendre bien les virages

**cornerstone** n pierre f angulaire

**cornflakes** npl corn-flakes mpl

**cornmeal** n farine f de maïs

**cornrow** n (*hairstyle*) tresses fpl africaines

**cornstarch** n farine f de maïs

**cornucopia** [ˌkɔr·nə·'kou·pi·ə] n ① (*horn*) corne m ② (*abundance*) abondance f; ~ **of performances** profusion f de spectacles

**corny** ['kɔr·ni] <-ier, -iest> adj inf banal(e)

**coronary** ['kɔr·ə·ner·i] I. n inf infarctus m II. adj coronaire

**coronation** [ˌkɔr·ə·'neɪ·ʃən] n couronnement m

**corporal** ['kɔr·pər·əl] I. n MIL caporal m II. adj form corporel(le)

**corporate** ['kɔr·pər·ət] I. n société f II. adj ① (*of corporation*) d'entreprise; (*shared by group*) de l'entreprise;

(clients, workers) de la société; ~ **identity** image f de marque de l'entreprise; ~ **policy** stratégie f globale ❷ (collective) commun(e)

**corporation** n (business) société f; **multinational** ~ multinationale f

**corpse** [kɔrps] n cadavre m

**correct** [kə-'rekt] I. vt ❶ (put right) corriger; (watch) régler II. adj ❶ (accurate) juste; **that is** ~ **form** c'est exact ❷ (proper) correct(e)

**correction** [kə-'rek-ʃən] n ❶ (change) rectification f ❷ (improvement) correction f ❸ (improvement through punishment) punition f

**correction fluid** n correcteur m liquide

**correctly** adv correctement

**correlation** n ❶ (connection) corrélation f ❷ (relationship) lien m

**correspond** [ˌkɔr-ə-'spand] vi ❶ (be equal to) correspondre; **to** ~ **with** [o **to**] **sth** correspondre à qc; **to** ~ **closely/roughly to sth** être très/peu conforme à qc ❷ (write) correspondre; **to** ~ **with sb** correspondre avec qn

**correspondence** [ˌkɔr-ə-'span-dən(t)s] n correspondance f; **business** ~ courrier m d'affaires

**correspondent** n (writer of letters, journalist) correspondant(e) m(f); **special** ~ envoyé(e) m(f) spécial

**corridor** ['kɔr-ə-dər] n ❶ (passage) corridor m ❷ RAIL, AUTO, AVIAT couloir m

**corrugated** ['kɔr-ə-geɪ-tɪd] adj ❶ (furrowed) ridé(e) ❷ (rutted: road, iron) ondulé(e)

**corrupt** [kə-'rʌpt] I. vt ❶ (debase) dépraver ❷ (influence by bribes) corrompre ❸ COMPUT (file) altérer II. vi se corrompre III. adj (influenced by bribes) corrompu(e); (practice) malhonnête; ~ **morals** moralité f douteuse

**corruption** n ❶ (debasement) dépravation f ❷ (bribery) corruption f ❸ LING altération f

**cosine** ['koʊ-saɪn] n cosinus m

**cosmetic** [kaz-'met̬-ɪk] I. n cosmétique m; ~**s** produits mpl de beauté II. adj ❶ (related to beauty) cosméti-

que; (surgery) esthétique ❷ pej (superficial) superficiel(le); (change, improvement) de forme

**cosmonaut** ['kaz-mə-nɔt] n spationaute mf

**cost** [kast] I. vt ❶ <cost, cost> (amount to) coûter; **it** ~ **him dearly** ça lui est revenu cher ❷ <cost, cost> (cause the loss of) coûter; **to** ~ **sb dearly** coûter cher à qn ❸ <costed, costed> (calculate price) évaluer le coût de II. n ❶ (price) prix m; **at no extra** ~ sans dépense supplémentaire; **at huge** ~ à grands frais ❷ (sacrifice) renoncement m; **to learn sth to one's** ~ apprendre qc aux dépens de qn; **at all** ~(**s**) à n'importe quel prix ❸ pl LAW frais mpl d'instance et dépens mpl

**costar, co-star** I. n covedette f; **to be sb's** ~ avoir la vedette avec qn II. <-rr-> vi **to** ~ **with sb** partager la vedette avec qn

**costly** ['kast-li] <-ier, -iest> adj cher(chère); (mistake) qui coûte cher; **to prove** ~ s'avérer coûteux

**costume** ['ka-stum] n costume m; **to wear a clown** ~ porter un déguisement de clown

**cot** [kat] n lit m de camp

**cottage** n cottage m; **summer** ~ maison f de vacances (d'été)

**cottage cheese** n cottage m (fromage blanc à gros caillots, légèrement salé)

**cotton** ['ka-tən] I. n ❶ coton m ❷ (thread) fil m II. adj en coton

**cotton candy** n barbe f à papa

**cotton gin** n égreneuse f de coton

**cotton-picking** adj inf sacré(e); **keep your** ~ **hands off!** retire tes sales pattes de là!

**cottontail** n lapin m

**couch** [kaʊtʃ] I. n canapé m II. vt formuler

**couch potato** n inf **to be a** ~ passer sa vie devant la télé

**cough** [kɔf] I. n (loud expulsion of air) toux f II. vi ❶ (expel air loudly through lungs) tousser ❷ AUTO avoir des ratés III. vt tousser en crachant

**C**

**◆cough up I.** vt **①** (bring up) cracher **②** inf (pay reluctantly: money) cracher **II.** vi inf **①** (pay) casquer **②** (admit) cracher le morceau

**cough medicine** n médicament m contre la toux

**could** [kʊd] pt, subj of **can**

**council** ['kaʊn(t)·sǝl] n ADMIN conseil m; **Council of Europe** Conseil de l'Europe

**councilman** n ADMIN conseiller m

**councilwoman** n ADMIN conseillère f

**counsel** ['kaʊn(t)·sǝl] **I.** <-l- o -ll-> vt (advise) conseiller **II.** n **①** form (advice) conseil m **②** (lawyer) avocat(e) m(f)

**count¹** [kaʊnt] n (aristocrat) comte m

**count²** [kaʊnt] **I.** n **①** (totaling up) compte m; **final ~** décompte m définitif; **at the last ~** au dernier comptage **②** (measured amount) dénombrement m **③** (number) **to keep/to lose ~ of sth** tenir/perdre le compte de qc **④** LAW chef m d'accusation **⑤** (opinion) **to agree/disagree with sb on several ~s** être d'accord/en désaccord avec qn à plusieurs égards **⑥** (reason) **to fail on a number of ~s** échouer pour un certain nombre de raisons ▶ **to be out for the ~** être K.O. **II.** vt **①** (number) compter **②** (consider) **to ~ sb as a friend** considérer qn comme un ami ▶ **to ~ one's blessings** s'estimer heureux; **don't ~ your chickens before they're hatched!** prov il ne faut pas vendre la peau de l'ours avant de l'avoir tué; **to ~ the cost(s)** calculer ses dépenses **III.** vi **①** (number) compter **②** (be considered) **to ~ as sth** être considéré comme qc **③** (be of value) compter; **that's what ~s** c'est ce qui compte; **it ~s toward sth** ça compte pour qc

**◆count out** vt always sep **①** (number off aloud) compter pièce par pièce **②** SPORTS **to be counted out** (defeated) être mis K.O. **③** inf **count me out of this trip** ne comptez pas sur moi pour ce voyage

**counter** ['kaʊn·ţɚ] **I.** n **①** (service point) comptoir m **②** (machine) compteur m **③** (disc) jeton m **④** fig **under the ~** sous le manteau **II.** vt contrer **III.** vi **①** (oppose) riposter; **to ~ with sth** riposter par qc **②** (react by scoring) parer un coup **IV.** adv **to run ~ to sth** aller à l'encontre de qc; **to act ~ to sth** agir de façon contraire à qc

**counterattack I.** n contre-attaque f **II.** vt contre-attaquer **III.** vi **①** (attack in return) riposter **②** SPORTS contre-attaquer

**counterclockwise** adj dans le sens inverse des aiguilles d'une montre

**counterespionage** n contre-espionnage m

**counterfeit I.** adj faux(fausse) **II.** vt contrefaire **III.** n contrefaçon f

**counterintelligence** n contre-espionnage m

**counterintuitive** adj contraire à l'intuition

**countermeasure** n mesure f défensive

**counteroffer** n contre-proposition f

**counterproductive** adj contre-productif(-ive); **to prove ~** se révéler inefficace

**counterrevolution** n contre-révolution f

**counterterrorism** n contre-terrorisme m

**countertop** n plan m de travail

**counterweight** n contrepoids m

**countess** ['kaʊn·ţɪs] n comtesse f

**countless** adj innombrable

**country** ['kʌn·tri] **I.** n **①** (rural area) campagne f; **in the ~** dans la campagne **②** <-ies> (political unit) pays m; **native ~** patrie f **③** (area of land) région f; **open ~** rase campagne f; **rough ~** région f sauvage **④** (music style) country f **II.** adj **①** (rural) campagnard(e) **②** (in the countryside: people, manners) de la campagne; (road) de campagne; (life) à la campagne **③** (relating to music style) country inv; (singer) de country

**country club** n club m de loisirs

**country mile** n **not by a ~** inf pas de beaucoup

**countryside** n campagne f

**county** ['kaʊn·ti] <-ies> n comté m
**county fair** n foire f agricole
**coupe** ['ku·peɪ] n coupé m
**couple** ['kʌp·l] I. n ① (a few) quelque; **a ~ (of)** ... quelques ..., une couple de ... Québec; **another ~ (of)** ... encore un peu de ...; **every ~ of days** tous les deux jours ② + sing/pl vb (two people) couple m II. vt joindre; **sth ~d with sth** (in conjunction with) qc en supplément de qc; **sth is ~d to sth** (linked) qc est associé à qc III. vi s'accoupler
**coupon** ['ku·pɑn] n ① (voucher) bon m ② (order form) bulletin-réponse m
**courage** ['kɜr·ɪdʒ] n (bravery) courage m ▶ **Dutch ~** courage m pris dans l'alcool
**courageous** [kə·'reɪ·dʒəs] adj courageux(-euse)
**courier** ['kʊr·i·ər] n messager m; **motorcycle/bike ~** coursier, -ière m, f
**course** [kɔrs] I. n ① (direction) cours m; **to be on ~ for sth** être en route pour qc; fig être sur la voie de qc; **to change ~** changer de direction; fig prendre une autre voie ② (development: of time, event) cours m; **in due ~** dans les temps voulus; **during the ~ of sth** au cours de qc; **of ~** bien sûr, sans autre Suisse; **of ~ not** bien sûr que non ③ (series of classes) cours m; **to take a ~ in sth** prendre/suivre un cours de qc ④ MED (of treatment) traitement m ⑤ SPORTS (area) parcours m ⑥ (part of meal) plat m ⑦ CONSTR (layer) couche f II. vi (river, blood) couler
**court** [kɔrt] I. n ① (room for trials) tribunal m; **in ~** au tribunal ② (judicial body) tribunal m; **~ of law** cour f de justice; **to take sb to ~** poursuivre qn en justice ③ SPORTS terrain m; (tennis) court m; (for basketball) terrain m ④ (yard) cour f ⑤ (road) ruelle f ⑥ no indef art (ruling sovereign) cour f II. vt ① (try to attract) courtiser; (a woman) faire la cour à ② (seek) rechercher III. vi s'être fréquenter
**courteous** ['kɜr·ti·əs] adj courtois(e)
**courtesy** ['kɜr·tə·si] <-ies> n ① (politeness) politesse f ② (decency) courtoisie f ③ (permission) autorisation f; **~ of sth** avec l'autorisation de qc; (because of) grâce à qc
**courtesy bus** n bus m gratuit
**courtesy car** n voiture f mise à la disposition des clients
**courthouse** ['kɔrt·haʊs] <courthouses> n palais m de justice
**court-martial** <courts-martial> I. n cour f martiale II. vt traduire en cour martiale
**court reporter** n greffier, -ière m, f
**courtroom** n salle f d'audience
**courtyard** n cour f intérieure
**cousin** ['kʌz·ᵊn] n cousin(e) m(f)
**cover** ['kʌv·ər] I. n ① (top) couverture f; (on pot) couvercle m; (on furniture) housse f ② PUBL couverture f; **to read sth from ~ to ~** lire qc de la première à la dernière page ③ pl (sheets) **the ~s** les draps mpl ④ (means of concealing) couverture f; **under ~ of darkness** sous le couvert de la nuit; **to go under ~** prendre une identité d'emprunt ⑤ (shelter) abri m; **to run for ~** se mettre à l'abri ⑥ FIN couverture f ⑦ CULIN couvert m ⑧ MUS (recording) reprise f ▶ **never judge a book by its ~** il ne faut jamais juger sur les apparences II. vt ① (put over) couvrir; (surface, wall, sofa) recouvrir; **to ~ sth with sth** recouvrir qc de qc; **to ~ sth with sth** (re)couvrir qc de qc ② (hide) dissimuler ③ (pay: one's costs) couvrir ④ (extend over) s'étendre sur ⑤ (travel) parcourir ⑥ (deal with) traiter de ⑦ (include) inclure ⑧ (be enough for) couvrir ⑨ (report on) couvrir ⑩ (insure) a. fig couvrir; **to ~ sb for/against sth** couvrir qn contre qc ⑪ MIL, SPORTS couvrir ⑫ (do sb's job) remplacer ⑬ (adapt song) reprendre ▶ **to ~ your ass** [o **back**] inf se couvrir; **to ~ one's tracks** brouiller ses pistes
◆ **cover up** I. vt ① (conceal) dissimuler ② (protect) recouvrir; **to cover oneself up** s'emmitoufler; **to keep sth covered up** fig garder qc au chaud

C

**II.** *vi* ❶ (*wear sth*) se couvrir ❷ (*protect*) **to ~ for sb** couvrir qn

**coverage** [ˈkʌvˑərˑɪdʒ] *n* ❶ (*attention or inclusion*) a. *fig* couverture *f*; **to receive a lot of media ~** recevoir beaucoup d'attention de la presse ❷ (*insurance*) couverture *f*; **full ~** garantie *f* totale

**cover charge** *n* taxe *f* sur le couvert

**covered** *adj* ❶ (*roofed*) couvert(e) ❷ (*insured*) couvert(e)

**covering** *n* couverture *f*; **floor ~** revêtement *m* de sol

**cover letter** *n* lettre *f* de présentation

**cover-up** *n* couverture *f*

**cow**[1] [kaʊ] *n* ❶ (*female ox*) vache *f* ❷ (*female mammal*) femelle *f*; **elephant ~** femelle éléphant

**cow**[2] [kaʊ] *vt* intimider

**coward** [kaʊərd] *n pej* lâche *mf*

**cowboy** [ˈkaʊˑbɔɪ] **I.** *n* cow-boy *m* **II.** *adj* (*typical of western cattle hand*) de cow-boy

**cowgirl** *n* vachère *f*

**co-worker** *n* collègue *mf*

**coziness** *n* confort *m*

**cozy** [ˈkoʊˑzi] <-ier, -iest> *adj* ❶ (*comfortable*) a. *fig* douillet(te) ❷ *pej* (*convenient*) pépère ❸ (*intimate*) intime

**CPA** *n abbr of* **certified public accountant** expert-comptable *m*

**CPR** *n abbr of* **cardiopulmonary resuscitation** réanimation *f* cardio-pulmonaire

**CPU** [ˌsiˑpiˑˈju] *n* COMPUT *abbr of* **Central Processing Unit** UCT *f*

**crab**[1] [kræb] *n* ❶ (*sea animal*) crabe *m* ❷ *no indef art* (*flesh of sea animal*) crabe *m* ❸ (*in astrology*) Cancer *m*

**crab**[2] [kræb] *vi* gâcher

**crabgrass** *n* digitaire *f*

**crack** [kræk] **I.** *n* ❶ (*fissure*) fissure *f*; (*on skin*) gerçure *f*; *inf* (*between buttocks*) raie *f* ❷ (*opening: of door*) entrebâillement *m* ❸ (*sharp sound*) craquement *m*; (*of a rifle, whip*) claquement *m* ❹ (*form of cocaine*) crack *m* ❺ *inf* (*joke*) plaisanterie *f* ❻ *inf* (*attempt*) essai *m* ▸ **at the ~ of** <u>dawn</u> aux

aurores **II.** *adj* <inv> d'élite **III.** *vt* ❶ (*make a crack in*) fêler; (*nuts*) casser ❷ (*solve: a problem*) résoudre; (*a code*) déchiffrer ❸ (*make sound with*) faire claquer; **to ~ the whip** faire claquer le fouet; *fig* agir avec autorité ❹ (*hit*) frapper; (*one's knuckles*) craquer ▸ **to ~ a joke** dire une plaisanterie **IV.** *vi* ❶ (*have a crack*) se fêler; (*skin, lips*) se gercer; (*paint*) se craqueler; (*facade*) se fissurer ❷ *inf* (*fail: relationship*) casser ❸ (*break down*) craquer ❹ (*make a sharp noise*) craquer; (*whip*) claquer; (*voice*) se casser

◆**crack down** *vi* sévir; **to ~ on sb/sth** sévir contre qn/qc

◆**crack up I.** *vi* ❶ (*break*) se briser ❷ (*have a breakdown*) craquer ❸ *inf* (*laugh*) mourir de rire **II.** *vt* ❶ (*make laugh*) **to crack sb up** faire éclater qn de rire ❷ (*make claims about*) **sth is not all it's cracked up to be** *inf* qc n'est pas aussi fantastique qu'il n'y paraît

**crackdown** *n* mesure *f*; **to have a ~ on** sévir contre

**cracked** *adj* ❶ (*having fissures*) fissuré(e); (*lips*) gercé(e) ❷ (*crazy*) fêlé(e)

**cracker** *n* ❶ (*dry biscuit*) biscuit *m* sec ❷ (*device*) pétard *m* ❸ *pej* (*poor white Southerner*) pauvre blanc *m* du Sud

**crackhead** *n sl* accro *mf* au crack

**crack house** *n inf* repaire *m* de crack

**crackle** [ˈkræk·l] **I.** *vi* ❶ (*make sharp sounds*) craquer; (*fire, radio*) crépiter ❷ (*be tense*) se tendre **II.** *n* craquement *m*; (*of fire, radio*) crépitement *m*

**cradle** [ˈkreɪ·dl] **I.** *n* ❶ (*baby's bed*) berceau *m*, berce *f Belgique* ❷ (*framework*) structure *f* **II.** *vt* (*hold in one's arms*) bercer

**craft** [kræft] *inv* **I.** *n* ❶ (*means of transport*) embarcation *f* ❷ (*skill*) métier *m* ❸ (*trade*) artisanat *m*; (*of glass-blowing, acting*) art *m* ❹ (*ability*) capacité *f* **II.** *vt* créer; (*a poem*) écrire

**craftsman** <-men> *n* artisan *m*

**crafty** [ˈkræf·ti] <-ier, -iest> *adj* rusé(e)

**cram** [kræm] <-mm-> **I.** *vt* *inf* fourrer;

**to ~ sb's head with sth** *pej* bourrer la tête de qn de qc II. *vi* bûcher

**cramp** [kræmp] I. *vt* gêner ▶ **to ~ sb's style** *iron, inf* faire perdre les moyens à qn II. *n* crampe *f*; **menstrual ~s** règles *fpl* douloureuses

**crampon** ['kræm·pən] *n* crampon *m*

**crane** [kreɪn] I. *n* ❶ (*vehicle for lifting*) grue *f* ❷ (*bird*) grue *f* II. *vt* to ~ **one's neck** tendre le cou

**crank**[1] [kræŋk] I. *n* ❶ *pej, inf* farfelu(e) *m(f)* ❷ *pej, inf* (*crazy*) dingue *mf* II. *adj inf* dingue

**crank**[2] [kræŋk] *n* manivelle *f*

**crap** [kræp] *vulg* I. *n sing* merde *f;* **to take a ~** chier; **a bunch of ~** (*nonsense*) un tas de conneries II. <-pp-> *vi* chier

**crappy** <-ier, -iest> *adj inf* merdique

**crash** [kræʃ] I. *n* ❶ (*accident*) accident *m;* **train/plane ~** catastrophe *f* ferroviaire/aérienne ❷ (*noise*) fracas *m* ❸ ECON (*collapse*) krach *m* ❹ COMPUT plantage *m* II. *vi* ❶ (*have an accident*) avoir un accident; (*plane*) s'écraser; **to ~ into sb/sth** rentrer dans qn/qc ❷ (*make loud noise*) faire du fracas ❸ ECON (*collapse*) s'effondrer ❹ COMPUT se planter ❺ *inf* (*go to sleep*) **to ~ out** s'écrouler III. *vt* (*damage in accident*) **to ~ the car** avoir un accident de voiture ▶ **to ~ a party** *inf* s'incruster dans une fête

**crash course** *n* cours *m* intensif

**crash diet** *n* régime *m* draconien

**crash helmet** *n* casque *m* de protection

**crash-land** *vi* atterrir d'urgence

**crash landing** *n* atterrissage *m* d'urgence

**crate** [kreɪt] *n* (*open box*) caisse *f*

**crater** ['kreɪ·tər] *n* cratère *m;* **bomb ~** entonnoir *m*

**crave** [kreɪv] *vt* avoir des envies de; **to be craving for sth** avoir très envie de qc

**crawl** [krɔl] I. *vi* ❶ (*move slowly*) ramper; (*car*) rouler au pas; (*baby*) marcher à quatre pattes; **time ~s by** le temps passe lentement ❷ *inf* (*to be full of*) **~ with sth** grouiller de qc ▶ **to make sb's flesh ~** donner la chair de poule à qn II. *n* ❶ (*movement*) reptation *f* ❷ SPORTS crawl *m*

**crawlspace** *n* faux plafond *m;* (*underground space*) vide *m* sanitaire

**crayon** ['kreɪ·ɑn] I. *n* crayon *m* II. *vt* crayonner

**craze** [kreɪz] *n* engouement *m;* **the latest ~** la dernière folie

**crazy** <-ier, -iest> *adj* fou(folle); **to be ~ about sb/sth** être dingue de qn/qc *inf;* **to do sth like ~** *inf* faire qc comme un dératé

**crazy quilt** *n* édredon *m* en patchwork

**creak** [krik] I. *vi* grincer, (*bones, floor*) craquer II. *n* grincement *m;* (*of floor, bones*) craquement *m*

**creaky** <-ier, -iest> *adj* ❶ (*squeaky*) grinçant(e) ❷ (*unsafe*) dangereux(-euse)

**cream** [krim] I. *n* ❶ CULIN crème *f;* **whipped ~** crème fouettée ❷ (*cosmetic product*) crème *f* ❸ *fig* (*the best*) la crème; **the ~ of the crop** la fine fleur II. *adj* ❶ (*containing cream*) à la crème ❷ (*off-white color*) crème *inv* III. *vt* ❶ (*beat*) battre en crème; **~ed potatoes** purée *f* de pommes de terre ❷ (*remove cream*) écrémer ❸ (*add cream*) ajouter de la crème à ❹ (*apply lotion*) se mettre de la crème

**cream cheese** *n* crème *f* de fromage à tartiner

**cream-colored** *adj* crème *inv*

**creamy** <-ier, -iest> *adj* ❶ (*smooth, rich*) crémeux(-euse) ❷ (*off-white*) crème *inv*

**crease** [kris] I. *n* pli *m;* (*of a book*) pliure *f* II. *vt* (*wrinkle*) froisser III. *vi* se froisser

**create** [kri·'eɪt] I. *vt* ❶ (*produce, invent*) créer; **to ~ sth from sth** produire qc à partir de qc ❷ (*cause: problem, precedent, nuisance*) créer; (*a desire, a scandal, tension*) provoquer, (*a sensation, impression*) faire ❸ (*appoint*) nommer II. *vi* créer

**creationism** *n* créationnisme *m*

**creative** [kriˈeɪˌtɪv] *adj* ❶ (*inventive: person, activity*) créatif(-ive) ❷ (*which creates: power, artist*) créateur(-trice)

**creator** *n* créateur, -trice *m, f*; **the Creator** le Créateur

**creature** [ˈkriˑtʃər] *n a. fig, pej* créature *f*; **weak ~** *inf* pauvre créature

**credentials** [krɪˈden(t)ˌʃəlz] *npl* références *fpl*

**credibility** [ˌkred·əˈbɪl·əˌti] *n* crédibilité *f*

**credible** [ˈkred·ə·bl] *adj* crédible

**credit** [ˈkred·ɪt] I. *n* ❶ (*praise*) mérite *m*; **to sb's ~** à l'honneur de qn; **to do sb ~** faire honneur à qn; **to take (the) ~ for sth** s'attribuer le mérite de qc ❷ (*recognition*) reconnaissance *f*; **to give sb ~ for sth** reconnaître que qn a fait qc ❸ FIN crédit *m*; **to buy/sell sth on ~** acheter/vendre qc à crédit ❹ (*completed unit of student's work*) unité *f* de valeur ❺ *pl* (*list of participants*) générique *m* ❻ UNIV unité *f* de valeur II. *vt* ❶ FIN (*money*) virer; **to ~ sb/an account with a sum** créditer qn/un compte d'une somme ❷ (*believe*) croire ❸ (*give credit to*) attribuer

**credit card** *n* carte *f* de crédit

**credit union** *n* société *f* de crédit mutuel

**creditworthy** *adj* solvable

**credo** *n* credo *m inv*

**creep** [krip] I. *n inf* (*unpleasant person*) saligaud *m*, sale bête *f* ▸ **to give sb the ~s** donner la chair de poule à qn II.<crept, crept> *vi* ramper; **to ~ in/out** entrer/sortir à pas de loup ◆ **creep up** *vi* grimper; **to ~ on sb** prendre qn par surprise

**creepy** <-ier, -iest> *adj inf* qui donne la chair de poule

**cremate** [krɪˈmeɪt] *vt* incinérer

**cremation** *n* incinération *f*

**crematorium** [ˌkri·məˈtɔr·i·əm] <-s *o* -ria> *n* crématorium *m*

**crêpe** [kreɪp] *n* ❶ CULIN crêpe *f* ❷ (*fabric*) crêpe *m*

**crept** [krept] *pp, pt of* **creep**

**crest** [krest] I. *n* ❶ ZOOL crête *f* ❷ (*top*)

*a. fig* crête *f* ❸ (*insignia*) armoiries *fpl* II. *vt* atteindre le sommet de

**cretin** [ˈkri·tⁿ] *n a. pej* crétin(e) *m(f)*

**crew** [kru] I. *n* + *sing/pl vb* ❶ (*working team*) NAUT, AVIAT équipage *m*; RAIL équipe *f* ❷ SPORTS (*of rowing*) équipe *f* ❸ *pej, inf* (*gang*) bande *f* II. *vt* être membre de l'équipage de III. *vi* **to ~ for sb** être l'équipier de qn

**crewcut** *n* coupe *f* en brosse

**crew neck** *n* ❶ (*round neck*) encolure *f* ras du cou ❷ (*sweater with round neck*) pull *m* ras du cou

**crib** [krɪb] I. *n* ❶ (*baby's bed*) lit *m* d'enfant ❷ *sl* (*one's home*) piaule *f* II.<-bb-> *vt pej, inf* plagier III.<-bb-> *vi pej, inf* **to ~ from sb** copier sur qn

**cricket**[1] [ˈkrɪk·ɪt] *n, n* SPORTS cricket *m*

**cricket**[2] [ˈkrɪk·ɪt] *n* (*jumping insect*) criquet *m*

**crime** [kraɪm] *n* ❶ (*illegal act*) crime *m* ❷ (*shameful act*) délit *m*

**criminal** [ˈkrɪm·ɪ·nᵊl] I. *n* criminel(le) *m(f)* II. *adj* criminel(le)

**crimson** [ˈkrɪm·zᵊn] I. *n* cramoisi *m* II. *adj* cramoisi(e)

**cringe** [krɪndʒ] *vi* ❶ (*physically*) avoir un mouvement de recul ❷ *inf* (*embarrassment*) avoir envie de rentrer sous terre

**cripple** [ˈkrɪp·l] I. *n pej* infirme *mf* II. *vt* ❶ (*leave physically disabled*) estropier ❷ *fig* (*seriously disable*) endommager ❸ (*paralyze*) paralyser

**crisis** [ˈkraɪ·sɪs] <-ses> *n* crise *f*

**crisp** [krɪsp] <-er, -est> *adj* ❶ (*hard and brittle*) croustillant(e); (*snow*) craquant(e) ❷ (*firm and fresh*) croquant(e) ❸ (*bracing: air*) vif(vive) ❹ (*sharp*) tranchant(e) ❺ (*quick and precise*) nerveux(-euse)

**crisscross** [ˈkrɪs·krɑs] I. *vt* entrecroiser II. *vi* s'entrecroiser III. *adj* entrecroisé(e)

**critic** [ˈkrɪt̬·ɪk] *n* ❶ (*reviewer*) critique *mf* ❷ (*censurer*) détracteur, -trice *m, f*

**critical** *adj* critique

**critical mass** *n* ❶ PHYS masse *f* critique ❷ *fig* point *m* critique

**criticism** [ˈkrɪt·ɪ·sɪ·zᵊm] *n* critique *f*

**criticize** [ˈkrɪt·ɪ·saɪz] *vt, vi* critiquer

**critique** [krɪˈtik] I. *n* critique *f* II. *vt* se pencher de manière critique sur

**critter** [ˈkrɪt·ər] *n inf* créature *f*; (*animal*) bête *f*

**croak** [kroʊk] I. *vi* ❶ (*make deep, rough sound*) croasser ❷ *inf* (*die*) crever II. *vt* (*speak with rough voice*) dire d'une voix rauque III. *n* (*person*) croassement *m*; (*frog*) coassement *m*

**crockery** [ˈkrɑ·kər·i] *n* poterie *f*

**crocodile** [ˈkrɑ·kə·daɪl] <-(s)> *n* crocodile *m*

**crook** [krʊk] I. *n* ❶ *inf* (*thief*) escroc *m* ❷ (*curve*) courbe *f* II. *vt* plier

**crooked** *adj* ❶ *inf* (*dishonest*) malhonnête ❷ (*not straight*) courbé(e); (*nose*) crochu(e)

**crop** [krɑp] I. *n* ❶ (*plant*) culture *f*; (*cereal*) moisson *f*; (*harvest*) récolte *f* ❷ *fig* (*group*) foule *f* ❸ (*very short hair cut*) coupe *f* de cheveux ras ❹ (*throat pouch*) jabot *m* ❺ (*whip*) cravache *f* II. <-pp-> *vt* ❶ (*plant land with crops*) cultiver ❷ (*cut short*) couper ras

♦ **crop up** *vi inf* survenir

**cross** [krɑs] I. *n* ❶ (*cross*) croix *f* ❷ (*mixture*) croisement *m* ❸ *fig* compromis *m* II. <-er, -est> *adj* maussade III. *vt* ❶ (*go across*) traverser ❷ (*lle across each other: one's arms, legs*) croiser ❸ (*make sign of cross*) **to ~ oneself** se signer ❹ (*oppose*) contrecarrer ❺ (*crossbreed*) croiser ▶ **to ~ sb's mind** venir à l'esprit de qn; **to ~ sb's path** se trouver sur le chemin de qn IV. *vi* ❶ (*intersect*) se croiser ❷ (*go across*) passer

♦ **cross off** *vt*, **cross out** *vt* rayer

♦ **cross over** I. *vi* faire une traversée II. *vt* ❶ (*go across to opposite side*) traverser ❷ (*change sides in disagreement*) **to ~ to sth** passer à qc

**cross-check** *vt* vérifier par recoupement

**cross-country** I. *adj* ❶ (*across countryside*) à travers champs ❷ (*across a country*) à travers le pays ❸ SPORTS (*race*) de cross; **~ skiing** ski *m* de fond

II. *adv* ❶ (*across a country*) à travers le pays ❷ (*across countryside*) à travers champs III. *n* ❶ (*running*) cross *m* ❷ (*ski*) ski *m* de fond

**cross-cultural** *adj* interculturel(le)

**cross-dress** *vi* se travestir

**cross-dresser** *n* travesti(e) *m(f)*

**cross-examine** *vt* soumettre à un contre-interrogatoire

**cross-eyed** *adj* qui louche

**crossing** *n* ❶ (*place to cross*) passage *m*; (*intersection of road and railway*) passage *m* à niveau ❷ (*trip across area*) traversée *f*

**cross-legged** I. *adj* **to be in a ~ position** avoir les jambes croisées II. *adv* les jambes croisées; **to sit ~** être assis en tailleur

**crossroads** *n* carrefour *m*

**crosstown** I. *adj* qui traverse la ville II. *adv* à travers la ville

**crosswalk** *n* passage *m* clouté

**crossword (puzzle)** *n* mots *mpl* croisés

**crouch** [kraʊtʃ] *vi* s'accroupir

**crow**¹ [kroʊ] *n* corneille *f* ▶ **as the ~ flies** à vol d'oiseau

**crow**² [kroʊ] *vi* ❶ (*sound a cock-a-doodle-doo*) faire cocorico ❷ (*cry out happily: a baby*) gazouiller

**crowbar** [ˈkroʊ·bɑr] *n* levier *m*

**crowd** [kraʊd] I. *n* + *sing/pl vb* ❶ (*throng*) foule *f* ❷ *inf* (*particular group of people*) clique *f* ▶ **to follow the ~** *pej* suivre le troupeau II. *vt* ❶ (*take up space*) entasser ❷ (*pressure*) pousser

**crowded** *adj* bondé(e)

**crowd-pleaser** *n* **to be a ~** plaire aux foules

**crown** [kraʊn] I. *n* ❶ (*round ornament*) couronne *f* ❷ (*top part*) sommet *m* II. *vt* couronner

**crucial** [ˈkru·ʃᵊl] *adj* crucial(e)

**crucifix** [ˌkru·sɪ·ˈfɪks] *n* crucifix *m*

**crucifixion** *n* crucifixion *f*

**crucify** [ˈkru·sɪ·faɪ] *vt* crucifier

**crud** [krʌd] *n inf* crasse *f*

**crude** [krud] I. <-r, -st> *adj* ❶ (*rudimentary*) rudimentaire; (*unsophistica-*

ted) grossier(-ère) ② (*vulgar*) vulgaire
II. *n* pétrole *m* brut
**cruel** [kruəl] <-(l)ler, -(l)lest> *adj*
cruel(le); **to be ~ to sb** être cruel envers qn ► **to be ~ to be kind** *prov* qui aime bien châtie bien
**cruelty** *n* cruauté *f*
**cruise** [kruz] I. *n* croisière *f* II. *vi* ① (*ship*) croiser ② (*travel at constant speed: airplane*) planer; (*car*) rouler
**cruise control** *n* contrôle *m* de vitesse
**crumb** [krʌm] *n* CULIN ① (*very small piece*) miette *f* ② (*opposed to crust: bread*) mie *f* ③ *fig* (*small amount*) miettes *fpl*; (*of comfort*) brin *m*
**crumble** ['krʌm·bl] I. *vt* ① (*break into crumbs*) émietter ② (*break into bits: stone*) effriter II. *vi* ① (*break into crumbs*) s'émietter ② *fig* s'effriter
**crumbly** <-ier, -iest> *adj* friable
**crummy** ['krʌm·i] <-ier, -iest> *adj inf* minable
**crumple** ['krʌm·pl] I. *vt* froisser II. *vi* ① (*dented: mudguard*) se plier ② (*wrinkled*) se friper; (*face*) se décomposer ③ (*collapse*) s'effondrer
**crunch** [krʌn(t)ʃ] I. *vt* CULIN croquer II. *vi* ① (*make crushing sound: gravel, snow*) craquer ② CULIN (*crush with the teeth*) **to ~ on sth** croquer dans qc III. *n* ① (*crushing sound: feet, gravel, snow*) craquement *m* ② *inf* (*difficult situation*) situation *f* critique ③ (*sit-up*) exercice *m* abdominal ► **it's ~ time** *inf* c'est l'heure des abdos
**crusade** [kru·'seɪd] I. *n* croisade *f*; **to start a ~ against sth** partir en croisade contre qc II. *vi* **to ~ for/against sth** partir en croisade pour/contre qc
**crush** [krʌʃ] I. *vt* ① (*compress*) écraser ② (*cram*) entasser ③ (*grind*) broyer ④ (*wrinkle: papers, dress*) froisser ⑤ (*shock severely*) anéantir ⑥ *fig* (*suppress: a rebellion, an opposition*) écraser ⑦ *fig* (*ruin: hopes*) détruire II. *vi* ① (*compress*) s'écraser ② (*cram into*) s'entasser ③ (*hurry: crowd*) se presser ④ (*wrinkle*) se froisser III. *n* ① (*crowd of people*) cohue *f* ② *inf* (*temporary in-*

*fatuation*) béguin *m*; **to have a ~ on sb** avoir le béguin pour qn ③ (*crushed ice drink*) granité *m*
**crushing** *adj* écrasant(e); (*news, remark*) percutant(e)
**crust** [krʌst] *n a.* GEO croûte *f*
**crusty** ['krʌs·ti] <-ier, -iest> *adj* ① (*crunchy: bread*) croustillant(e) ② (*grumpy, surly*) hargneux(-euse)
**crutch** [krʌtʃ] *n* ① MED (*walking support*) béquille *f*; **to be on ~es** avoir des béquilles ② (*source of support*) soutien *m*
**cry** [kraɪ] I. *n* ① (*act of shedding tears*) pleurs *mpl* ② (*loud utterance*) cri *m*; **to give a ~** pousser un cri ③ (*appeal*) appel *m*; **~ for help** appel au secours ④ ZOOL (*yelp*) cri *m* II. *vi* pleurer; **to ~ for joy** pleurer de joie ► **it is no use ~ing over spilled milk** ce qui est fait est fait III. *vt* ① (*shed tears*) pleurer ② (*exclaim*) crier ► **to ~ one's eyes out** pleurer à chaudes larmes; **to ~ wolf** crier au loup
◆**cry off** *vi inf* se décommander
◆**cry out** I. *vi* ① (*let out a shout*) pousser des cris ② (*say crying*) s'écrier; **to ~ for sth** réclamer qc à grands cris ► **for crying out loud!** *inf* nom de dieu! II. *vt* crier
**crystal** ['krɪs·təl] I. *n* cristal *m* II. *adj* ① (*crystalline*) *a. fig* cristallin(e) ② (*made of crystal*) en cristal
**crystal clear** *adj* ① (*transparent*) cristallin(e) ② (*obvious*) clair(e)
**CT** *n* ① GEO *abbr of* **Connecticut** ② MED *abbr of* **computerized tomography** scanner *m*; **~ scan** scanographie *f*
**cub** [kʌb] *n* ZOOL petit *m*; **bear ~** ourson *m*; **lion ~** lionceau *m*
**Cuba** ['kju·bə] *n* (l'île *f* de) Cuba
**Cuban** I. *adj* cubain(e) II. *n* Cubain(e) *m(f)*
**cube** [kjub] I. *n* cube *m*; **ice ~** glaçon *m*; **~ root** racine *f* cubique III. *vt* CULIN couper en dés
**cubic** ['kju·bɪk] *adj* cubique; **~ centimeter** centimètre *m* cube; **~ capacity** volume *m*

**cubicle** ['kju·bɪ·kl] n ① (shower) cabine f ② (part of office) box m

**Cub Scout** n louveteau m

**cuckoo** ['ku·ku] I. n ZOOL coucou m II. adj inf cinglé(e); **to go ~** devenir cinglé(e)

**cuckoo clock** n coucou m

**cucumber** ['kju·kʌm·bər] n CULIN concombre m ▸ **to be (as) cool as a ~** inf être d'un calme imperturbable

**cuddle** ['kʌd·l] I. vt câliner II. vi se câliner III. n câlin m; **to give sb a ~** câliner qn

**cuddly** adj mignon(ne)

**cue** [kju] n ① (signal for an actor) réplique f ② SPORTS (stick used in billiards) queue f ▸ (right) **on ~** au bon moment

**cue card** n fiche f mémento

**cuff** [kʌf] I. n ① (end of sleeve) poignet m; (for cuff links) manchette f ② (turned-up pants leg) revers m ③ (slap) gifle f ④ pl, inf (handcuffs) menottes fpl ▸ **off the ~** à l'improviste II. vt ① (slap playfully) gifler ② inf LAW (handcuff) menotter

**cul-de-sac** ['kʌl·də·sæk] <-s> n a. fig impasse f

**culprit** ['kʌl·prɪt] n coupable mf

**cultivate** ['kʌl·t̬ə·veɪt] vt a. fig cultiver

**cultural** adj culturel(le)

**culture** ['kʌl·tʃər] I. n a. BIO culture f II. vt BIO faire une culture de

**cultured** adj cultivé(e); **~ pearl** perle f de culture

**culture shock** n choc m culturel

**cum laude** [,kʊm·'laʊ·deɪ] adj, adv UNIV avec mention

**cunning** ['kʌn·ɪŋ] I. adj (ingenious: person) rusé(e); (plan, device, idea) astucieux(-euse) II. n ingéniosité f

**cup** [kʌp] I. n ① (drinking container) tasse f; **coffee ~** tasse de café; **~ of tea** tasse de thé ② CULIN tasse f (≈ 230 millilitres ou grammes); **a ~ of flour** 230 grammes mpl de farine ③ SPORTS (trophy) coupe f; **world ~** coupe f du monde ④ (bowl-shaped container) coupe f ⑤ (part of bra) bonnet m ⑥ SPORTS (protection) coque f ▸ **not to be one's ~ of**

**tea** inf ne pas être sa tasse de thé II. <-pp-> vt ① (make bowl-shaped) **to ~ one's hands** mettre ses mains en coupe ② (put curved hand around) **to ~ sth in one's hands** entourer qc de ses mains

**cupboard** ['kʌb·ərd] n placard m

**cupful** <-s o cupsful> n tasse f

**curb** [kɜrb] I. vt ① (control: emotion, appetite) refréner; (inflation, expenses) limiter ② (hinder) freiner II. n ① (control) frein m ② (of road) bord m du trottoir

**cure** [kjʊr] I. vt ① MED (heal) a. fig guérir; **to ~ sb of sth** guérir qn de qc ② (eradicate) a. fig éradiquer ③ CULIN (smoke) fumer; (salt) saler; (dry) sécher II. n a. fig remède m

**curfew** ['kɜr·fju] n LAW couvre-feu m

**curiosity** [,kjʊr·i·'a·sə·t̬i] n ① (thirst for knowledge) curiosité f; **out of ~** par curiosité ② (highly unusual object) curiosité f ▸ **~ killed the cat** prov la curiosité est un vilain défaut

**curious** ['kjʊr·i·əs] adj curieux(-euse)

**curl** [kɜrl] I. n ① (loop of hair) boucle f; (tight) frisette f ② (spiral: of smoke) volute f II. vi ① (wave) boucler; (in tight curls) friser ② (wind itself) se recroqueviller; **to ~ around sth** s'enrouler autour de qc III. vt ① (make curly) **to ~ one's hair** boucler ses cheveux; (tightly) friser ses cheveux ② (wrap) enrouler ▸ **to ~ one's lip** faire la moue

**curler** n bigoudi m

**curly** ['kɜr·li] <-ier, -iest> adj bouclé(e); (tightly) frisé(e)

**currant** ['kɜr·ənt] n groseille f

**currency** ['kɜr·ən(t)·si] n ① (money used in a country) devise f ② (acceptance) circulation f; **to gain ~** se répandre

**current** ['kɜr·ənt] I. adj ① (present) actuel(le); (year, research, development) en cours ② (common) courant(e); **in ~ use** d'usage courant ③ FIN (income, expenditure) courant(e) ④ (latest: craze, fashion, issue) dernier(-ère) II. n a. fig courant m

**currently** adv actuellement

**curriculum** [kə·ˈrɪk·jə·ləm] <-s o curricula> n SCHOOL, UNIV programme m d'études

C **curriculum vitae** [kə·ˌrɪk·jə·ləm·ˈvi·taɪ] <-s o curricula vitae> n ECON curriculum vitæ m

**curry**¹ [ˈkɜr·i] n curry m; **chicken ~** poulet m au curry

**curry**² [ˈkɜr·i] vt **to ~ favor with sb** pej s'insinuer auprès de qn

**curse** [kɜrs] I. vi jurer II. vt maudire; **to ~ sb for doing sth** maudire qn d'avoir fait qc III. n ❶ (swear word) juron m ❷ (magic spell) sort m; **to put a ~ on sb** jeter un sort sur qn ❸ fig (very bad thing) malédiction f ❹ (cause of evil) fléau m

**cursed** adj maudit(e)

**cursor** n COMPUT curseur m; **to move the ~** déplacer le curseur

**curt** [kɜrt] <-er, -est> adj pej sec(sèche)

**curtain** [ˈkɜr·tən] n ❶ (material hung at windows) rideau m; **to draw the ~s** tirer les rideaux ❷ fig (screen) écran m; **~ of rain** écran de pluie ❸ THEAT (stage screen) rideau m; **to raise/lower the ~** lever/baisser le rideau ▶ **the final ~** le dernier rappel; **to be ~s for sb** inf être fini pour qn

**curtain call** n THEAT rappel m; **to take a ~** être rappelé

**curtain raiser** n a. fig THEAT lever m du rideau

**curve** [kɜrv] I. n courbe f; (on road) virage m II. vi se courber; **to ~ around sth** (path, road) faire le tour de qc; **to ~ downward/upward** (path) descendre/monter en courbe

**cushion** [ˈkʊʃ·ən] I. n coussin m; **to act as a ~** a. fig amortir les chocs II. vt a. fig amortir; **to ~ sb/sth from sth** protéger qn/qc de qc

**cushy** [ˈkʊʃ·i] <-ier, -iest> adj pej, inf (very easy) pépère; **~ job** planque f; **to have a ~ time** se la couler douce

**custard** [ˈkʌs·tərd] n ≈ flan m

**custodian** [kʌs·ˈtoʊ·di·ən] n a. fig gardien(ne) m(f)

**custody** [ˈkʌs·tə·di] n ❶ LAW (guardianship) garde f; **to award ~ of sb to sb** accorder la garde de qn à qn ❷ LAW (detention) garde f à vue; **to take sb into ~** mettre qn en garde à vue

**custom** [ˈkʌs·təm] I. n SOCIOL (tradition) coutume f; **according to ~** selon l'usage; **to be sb's ~ to +infin** c'est la coutume de qn de +infin; **as is sb's ~** selon la coutume de qn II. adj (fait) sur mesure; **~ suit** costume m sur mesure

**customer** n ECON ❶ (buyer) client(e) m(f) ❷ pej, inf (person) type m ▶ **the ~ is always right** le client a toujours raison

**customer service** n ECON service m clientèle

**custom-made** adj fait(e) sur commande; (clothes) fait(e) sur mesure

**customs** [ˈkʌs·təmz] n pl ECON, FIN douane f; **to pay ~** payer un droit de douane

**customs house** n HIST bureau m de douane

**customs officer** n douanier m

**cut** [kʌt] I. n ❶ (cutting) coupure f; (on object, wood) entaille f ❷ (slice) tranche f; (of meat) morceau m ❸ (wound) coupure f; **deep ~** plaie f profonde ❹ MED incision f ❺ (style: of clothes, hair) coupe f ❻ (share) part f ❼ (decrease) réduction f; (in interest, production) baisse f; (in staff) compression f ❽ pl (decrease in spending) compressions fpl budgétaires ❾ ELEC (interruption) coupure f ❿ CINE, LIT coupure f ⓫ (blow) coup m ⓬ GAMES (cards) coupe f ▶ **to be a ~ above sb/sth** être un cran au-dessus de qn/qc II. adj ❶ (sliced, incised) coupé(e) ❷ (shaped) taillé(e) ❸ (reduced) réduit(e) III. <cut, cut, -tt-> vt ❶ (make an opening, incision) couper; **to ~ open a box** ouvrir une boîte avec des ciseaux; **to ~ sth out of sth** découper qc dans qc ❷ (slice) couper; **to ~ in pieces** couper en morceaux ❸ (shape) tailler; (fingernails, hair, a flower) couper; (grass) tondre; (initials) graver ❹ MED inciser ❺ fig (ties) rompre; **to ~ sb loose** libérer qn ❻ FIN, ECON réduire; (*costs, prices*) diminuer ❼ CINE (*a film*) monter ❽ (*remove*) couper ❾ *inf* SCHOOL, UNIV (*a class*) sécher; (*school*) manquer ❿ TECH (*motor*) couper ⓫ (*have a tooth emerge*) **to ~ one's teeth** faire ses dents; **to ~ one's teeth on sth** se faire les dents sur qc ⓬ (*split card deck: cards*) couper ⓭ (*record: CD*) graver ⓮ *fig* (*stop: sarcasm*) arrêter ▸ **to ~ corners** rogner sur les coûts; **to ~ it** *inf* le faire; **to ~ one's losses** sauver les meubles; **to ~ it** (**a little/bit**) **fine** ne pas se laisser de marge **IV.**<cut, cut, -tt-> *vi* ❶ (*make an incision*) couper; (*in slice*) trancher ❷ (*in class*) ❸ CAMES couper ▸ **to ~ to the chase** aller à l'essentiel; **to ~ loose** couper les ponts; **to ~ both ways** à double tranchant; **to ~ and run** filer

◆**cut across** *vt* ❶ (*cut*) couper à travers ❷ *fig* transcender

◆**cut away** *vt* (*slice off*) enlever (en coupant)

◆**cut back I.** *vt* ❶ (*trim down*) tailler; (*tree*) élaguer ❷ FIN, ECON réduire; (*costs*) diminuer **II.** *vi* ❶ (*turn around*) revenir en arrière ❷ (*save money*) faire des économies

◆**cut down** *vt* ❶ BOT (*a tree*) abattre ❷ (*do less: wastage*) réduire ❸ (*take out part: a film*) couper ❹ FASHION raccourcir ▸ **to cut sb down to size** *inf* remettre qn à sa place

◆**cut in I.** *vi* ❶ (*interrupt*) intervenir; **to ~ on sb** couper la parole à qn ❷ AUTO se rabattre; **to ~ in front of sb** faire une queue de poisson à qn **II.** *vt* ❶ (*divide profits with*) partager les parts avec ❷ *inf* (*include when playing*) **to cut sb in on the deal** donner sa part à qn

◆**cut into** *vt* ❶ (*start cutting*) couper dans ❷ (*hurt*) blesser ❸ (*start using*) entamer; **to ~ one's free time** empiéter sur son temps libre ❹ (*interrupt*) interrompre

◆**cut off** *vt* ❶ (*slice away*) couper ❷ (*stop talking*) **to cut sb off** interrompre qn ❸ TEL, ELEC couper ❹ (*isolate*)

isoler; **to cut oneself off from sb** couper les liens avec qn; **to be ~ from sth** être coupé de qc ❺ AUTO faire une queue de poisson ▸ **to cut sb off without a penny** déshériter qn

◆**cut out I.** *vt* ❶ (*slice out of*) découper; **to ~ dead wood from a bush** tailler du bois mort dans un buisson; **to cut the soft spots out of the vegetables** enlever les parties abîmées des légumes ❷ (*remove from: a book*) découper; **to cut a scene out of a film** couper une séquence dans un film; **to cut sugar out** supprimer le sucre ❸ (*stop*) supprimer; **to ~ smoking** arrêter de fumer ❹ *inf* (*desist*) **cut it out!** ça suffit! ❺ (*block light*) **to ~ the light** empêcher la lumière de passer ❻ (*not include in plans*) **to cut sb out of sth** mettre qn à l'écart de qc ❼ (*exclude*) **to cut sb out of one's will** déshériter qn ▸ **to have one's work ~ for oneself** avoir du pain sur la planche; **to be ~ for sth** être fait pour qc **II.** *vi* ❶ (*stop*) s'arrêter; (*car*) caler ❷ (*pull away quickly*) faire une queue de poisson; **to ~ of traffic** couper à travers la circulation ❸ (*leave quickly*) filer

◆**cut up** *vt* (*slice into pieces*) couper; (*herbs*) hacher

**cutback** *n* réduction *f*

**cute** [kjut] <-r, -st> *adj* mignon(ne)

**cutesy** ['kjut·si] *adj inf* un peu trop mignon(ne)

**cutlery** ['kʌt·lᵊr·i] *n* coutellerie *f*

**cutlet** ['kʌt·lət] *n* ❶ (*cut of meat*) côtelette *f* ❷ (*patty*) croquette *f*

**cutoff I.** *n* embargo *m* **II.** *adj* ❶ (*with a limit*) limite; **~ point** limite *f* ❷ (*isolated*) isolé(e) ❸ FASHION (*short*) raccourci(e) ❹ ELEC **~ switch/button** interrupteur *m*

**cutout I.** *n* ❶ (*shape*) découpage *m* ❷ (*safety device*) disjoncteur *m* **II.** *adj* découpé(e)

**cut-rate** *adj* (*goods*) à prix réduit

**cutthroat** *adj* acharné(e)

**cutting I.** *n* ❶ (*article*) coupure *f* ❷ BOT bouture *f* **II.** *adj* ❶ (*that cuts: blade,* *edge*) tranchant(e) ❷ *fig* (*remark*) blessant(e); (*wind*) cinglant(e)

**cutting-edge** *adj* branché(e)

**CV** [ˌsiˈvi] *n abbr of* **curriculum vitae** CV *m*

**cyberspace** *n* COMPUT cyberespace *m*

**cycle¹** [ˈsaɪ·kl] SPORTS **I.** *n abbr of* **bicycle** vélo *m* **II.** *vi abbr of* **bicycle** faire du vélo

**cycle²** [ˈsaɪ·kl] *n* cycle *m*; **to do sth on a ...** ~ faire qc régulièrement

**cycling** *n* cyclisme *m*

**cyclist** *n* cycliste *mf*

**cylinder** [ˈsɪl·ɪn·dər] *n* ❶ MATH cylin-

dre *m* ❷ TECH joint *m* de culasse; **to be firing on all four ~s** marcher à pleins gaz

**cylindrical** [sɪˈlɪn·drɪk·əl] *adj* cylindrique

**cymbal** [ˈsɪm·bəl] *n* MUS cymbale *f*

**cynical** *adj pej* cynique

**Czech** [tʃek] **I.** *adj* tchèque **II.** *n* ❶ (*person*) Tchèque *mf* ❷ LING tchèque *m; s.a.* **English**

**Czechoslovakia** *n* HIST Tchécoslovaquie *f*

**Czech Republic** *n* la République tchèque

# Dd

**D, d** [di] <-'s> *n* ❶ LING D *m*, d *m*; **D-Day** (le) jour J; **~ as in Delta** (*on telephone*) d comme Désiré ❷ MUS ré *m*

**DA** [ˌdiˈeɪ] *n abbr of* **district attorney** ≈ procureur *m* de la République

**dad** [dæd] *n inf* papa *m;* **mom and ~** maman *f* et papa

**daddy** [ˈdæd·i] *n childspeak, inf* (*father*) papa *m*

**daddy longlegs** *n* ZOOL faucheux *m*

**daffodil** [ˈdæf·ə·dɪl] *n* BOT jonquille *f*

**dagger** [ˈdæg·ər] *n* dague *f*

**daily** [ˈdeɪ·li] **I.** *adj* quotidien(ne); (*rate, wage, allowance*) journalier(-ère); **~ routine** train-train *m* quotidien; **on a ~ basis** tous les jours; **one's ~ bread** *inf* pain *m* quotidien de qn **II.** *adv* quotidiennement **III.** <-ies> *n* PUBL quotidien *m*

**dairy** [ˈder·i] **I.** *n* ❶ (*building for milk production*) crémerie *f* ❷ (*shop*) laiterie *f* **II.** *adj* laitier(-ère)

**dairy products** *n* produits *mpl* laitiers

**daisy** [ˈdeɪ·zi] <-sies> *n* BOT marguerite *f*; (*smaller*) pâquerette *f*

**dam** [dæm] **I.** *n* barrage *m* **II.** <-mm-> *vt* ❶ (*block a river*) **to ~**

**sth** (**up**) [*o to ~* (**up**) **sth**] endiguer qc ❷ (*hold back*) **to ~ up** (*emotions*) contenir

**damage** [ˈdæm·ɪdʒ] **I.** *vt* ❶ (*harm*) endommager ❷ *fig* nuire **II.** *n* ❶ (*physical harm*) dégâts *mpl* ❷ (*harm*) tort *m;* **to do ~ to sb/sth** causer du tort à qn/qc ❸ *pl* LAW dommages *mpl* et intérêts ▸ **what's the ~?** *iron, inf* à combien s'élève la note?

**damage control** *n* **to do ~** limiter les dégâts

**damn** [dæm] **I.** *interj inf* zut!; **~ it!** merde!; **~ you!** tu m'emmerdes! **II.** *adj* fichu(e); **~ fool** crétin *m* **III.** *vt* ❶ (*lay the guilt for*) condamner ❷ (*curse*) maudire ❸ REL damner **IV.** *adv inf* sacrément; **to know ~ well** savoir très bien **V.** *n inf* **to not give a ~ about sb/sth** ne rien avoir à foutre de qn/qc; **it's not worth a ~** ça ne vaut pas un clou

**damned I.** *adj* ❶ *inf* (*cursed*) foutu(e) ❷ REL damné(e) ▸ **I'll be ~ if I do and ~ if I don't** *inf* je suis mal barré de toute façon **II.** *npl* **the ~** les damnés *mpl* **III.** *adv inf* sacrément

**damp** [dæmp] METEO I. *adj* humide II. *n* humidité *f* III. *vt* (*wet*) humecter

**dampen** ['dæm·ən] *vt* ① (*make wet*) humecter ② (*make a good feeling less: enthusiasm*) étouffer ③ (*make a noise softer*) amortir

**dance** [dæn(t)s] I.<-cing> *vi* danser II.<-cing> *vt* danser III. *n* ① (*instance of dancing*) danse *f* ② (*set of steps*) pas *mpl*; **slow** ~ slow ③ (*social function*) soirée *f* dansante ④ (*art form*) danse *f*; **classical/modern** ~ danse classique/moderne

**dancer** *n* danseur, -euse *m, f*

**dancing** *n* danse *f*

**dandelion** ['dæn·də·laɪən] *n* BOT pissenlit *m*

**dandruff** ['dæn·drəf] *n* MED pellicule *f*

**Dane** [deɪn] *n* Danois(e) *m(f)*

**danger** ['deɪn·dʒər] *n* ① (*dangerous situation*) danger *m*; **to be in** ~ être en danger; **to be out of** ~ être hors de danger ② *iron* (*chance*) risque *m*

**dangerous** ['deɪn·dʒ³r·əs] *adj* dangereux(-euse)

**danger zone** *n* zone *f* de danger

**Danish** ['deɪ·nɪʃ] I. *adj* danois(e) II. *n* danois *m; s.a.* **English**

**Danube** ['dæn·jub] *n* GEO Danube *m*

**dare** [deər] I.<daring> *vt* ① (*challenge*) défier ② (*risk doing*) oser ③ (*face the risk: danger, death*) braver ▶ **don't you** ~! tu n'as pas intérêt à faire ça!; **how** ~ **you do this** comment osez-vous faire cela II.<daring> *vi* oser III. *n* (*challenge*) défi *m*

**daredevil** *inf* I. *n* casse-cou *m inv* II. *adj* audacieux(-euse)

**daring** I. *adj* ① (*courageous*) audacieux(-euse) ② (*revealing*) osé(e) II. *n* audace *f*

**dark** [dark] I. *adj* ① (*black*) noir(e) ② (*not light-colored*) foncé(e); **tall,** ~ **and handsome** beau, grand et mat ③ *fig* (*tragic*) sombre; (*prediction*) pessimiste; **to have a** ~ **side** avoir une face cachée ④ (*evil*) méchant(e) ⑤ (*secret*) secret(-ète) II. *n* **the** ~ le noir; **to be afraid of the** ~ avoir peur du noir; **to**

**do sth before** ~ faire qc avant que la nuit tombe (*subj*) ▶ **to be (completely) in the** ~ **about sth** ne rien comprendre du tout à qc

**dark horse** *n* ① (*person with hidden qualities*) ➤ avoir des talents cachés ② SPORTS, POL candidat *m* inattendu

**darkness** *n* pénombre *f*

**darkroom** *n* PHOT chambre *f* noire

**darling** ['dar·lɪŋ] I. *n* ① (*beloved*) amour *m*; **to be the** ~ **of sth** être la coqueluche de qc ② (*form of address*) chéri(e) *m(f)* II. *adj* adorable

**dart** [dart] I. *n* ① (*type of weapon*) flèche *f* ② *pl* (*bar game*) fléchettes *fpl* ③ FASHION pince *f* II. *vi* se précipiter

**dash** [dæʃ] I.<-es> *n* ① (*rush*) précipitation *f*; **mad** ~ course *f* folle ② (*short fast race*) sprint *m* ③ (*little quantity*) goutte *f*; (*salt, pepper*) pincée *f*; (*lemon, oil*) filet *m*; (*drink*) doigt *m* ④ (*punctuation*) tiret *m* ⑤ (*flair*) brio *m* ⑥ (*Morse signal*) trait *m* ⑦ *inf* AUTO (*dashboard*) tableau *m* de bord II. *vi* ① (*hurry*) se précipiter; **to** ~ **around** courir; **to** ~ **out of** sortir en courant de qc ② *form* (*strike against*) se projeter; (*waves*) se briser III. *vt* ① (*destroy, discourage*) anéantir ② *form* (*hit*) heurter; **to be** ~**ed against sth** être projeté sur qc ③ *form* (*throw with force*) projeter

**dashboard** *n* tableau *m* de bord

**data** ['deɪ·tə] *npl* donnée *f*

**database** *n* COMPUT base *f* de données

**data processing** *n* traitement *m* de données

**date**[1] [deɪt] I. *n* ① (*calendar day*) date *f*; **out of** ~ dépassé; **to** ~ jusqu'à présent; **to be up to** ~ être actuel ② (*appointment*) rendez-vous *m*; **to go out on a** ~ sortir avec qn; **to have a** ~ **with sb** avoir un rencard avec qn *inf* ③ (*person*) petit ami (petite amie) *m(f)*; **to find a** ~ se trouver un copain II. *vt* ① (*have a relationship*) sortir avec ② (*give a date*) dater; **your letter** ~**d December 20** ta/votre lettre datée du 20 décembre ③ (*reveal the age*) **that**

**D**

~s her ça ne la rajeunit pas III. *vi* ❶ (*have a relationship*) sortir avec qn ❷ (*go back to: event*) **to ~ from** remonter à ❸ (*show time period*) dater ❹ (*go out of fashion*) être dépassé

**date²** [deɪt] *n* datte *f*

**dated** *adj* dépassé(e)

**dative** ['deɪ.tɪv] I. *n* datif *m;* **to be in the ~** être au datif II. *adj* **~ case** datif *m*

**daughter** ['dɔː.tər] *n* fille *f*

**daughter-in-law** <daughters-in-law> *n* belle-fille *f*

**dawn** [dɔn] *n* ❶ *a. fig* aube *f;* **to go back to the ~ of time** remonter à la nuit des temps ❷ (*daybreak*) aurore *f;* **at ~** à l'aube; **from ~ to dusk** du matin au soir

**day** [deɪ] *n* ❶ (*24 hours*) jour *m,* journée *f;* **four times a ~** quatre fois *f* par jour; **every ~** tous les jours; **have a nice ~!** bonne journée!, bonjour! *Québec;* **during the ~** (dans) la journée ❷ (*particular day*) **that ~** ce jour-là; **(on) the following ~** le lendemain; **from that ~ onwards** dès lors; **Christmas Day** le jour de Noël; **three years ago to the ~** il y a 3 ans jour pour jour ❸ (*imprecise time*) **one of these ~s** un de ces jours; **some ~** un jour ou l'autre; **every other ~** tous les deux jours; **~ in, ~ out** tous les jours que (le bon) Dieu fait ❹ (*period of time*) journée *f;* **during the ~** pendant la journée ❺ (*working hours*) journée *f;* **8-hour ~** journée de 8 heures; **~ off** jour *m* de congé [*o* repos] ❻ (*distance*) **it's three ~s from here by train** c'est à trois journées de train d'ici ❼ *pl, form* (*life*) **his/her ~s are numbered** ses jours *mpl* sont comptés ▶ **~ by ~** jour après jour

**daydream** I. *vi* rêvasser II. *n* rêverie *f*

**daylight** *n* (lumière *f* du) jour *m;* **in broad ~** au grand jour ▶ **to knock the** living **~s out of sb** *inf* tabasser qn; **to scare the** living **~s out of sb** *inf* flanquer la frousse à qn

**daytime** *n* journée *f*

**day-to-day** *adj* quotidien(ne)

**day trip** *n* excursion *f*

**daze** [deɪz] I. *n* **to be in a ~** être abasourdi II. *vt* **to be ~d** être abasourdi

**dazzle** ['dæz.l] I. *vt* éblouir II. *n* éblouissement *m*

**DC** [ˌdiː'siː] *n* ❶ *abbr of* **direct current** courant *m* continu ❷ *abbr of* **District of Columbia** DC *m*

**DE** *n abbr of* **Delaware**

**dead** [ded] I. *adj* ❶ (*no longer alive*) *a. fig* mort(e); **to be shot ~** être abattu; **to be ~ on arrival** (*at the hospital*) être décédé lors du transport (à l'hôpital) ❷ (*broken*) mort(e); **to go ~** ne plus fonctionner ❸ (*numb*) engourdi(e) ❹ (*dull*) monotone; (*eyes*) éteint(e) ❺ (*lacking power, energy*) mort(e) ❻ (*out of bounds: ball*) sorti(e) ❼ (*total*) complètement; (*stop*) complet(-ète) ▶ **over my ~** body il faudra me passer sur le corps; **to be a ~** duck être foutu d'avance; **to be a ~** ringer **for sb** être le sosie de qn; **sb would not be** seen **~ in sth** (*wear*) qn ne porterait jamais (de son vivant) qc; (*go out*) qn n'irait jamais (de son vivant) dans qc II. *n* ❶ *pl* (*dead people*) **the ~** les morts *mpl* ❷ (*realm of those who have died*) (royaume *m* des) morts *mpl;* **to come back from the ~** (*come back to life*) revenir à la vie; (*recover form an illness*) recouvrer la santé ▶ **to do sth in the ~ of** night/ winter faire qc au cœur de la nuit/de l'hiver III. *adv* ❶ *inf* (*totally*) complètement; **~ certain** sûr et certain; **~ ahead** tout droit ❷ *inf* **to be ~ set against sth** être complètement opposé à qc; **to be ~ set on sth** vouloir qc à tout prix ▶ **to stop ~ in one's** tracks stopper net l'avancée de qn

**dead-end** *adj* **~ street** impasse *f;* **~ job** activité *f* sans débouchés

**deadline** *n* date *f* limite; **to meet/to miss a ~** respecter/dépasser la date limite

**deadly** I.<-ier, -iest> *adj* mortel(le); (*look*) tueur(-euse) II.<-ier, -iest> *adv* ❶ (*in a fatal way*) mortellement ❷ (*absolutely*) terriblement

**deaf** [def] **I.** *adj* ❶ *(unable to hear anything)* sourd(e); **to be ~ in one ear** être sourd d'une oreille; **to go ~** devenir sourd ❷ *(hard of hearing)* malentendant(e) ▶ **to turn a ~ ear** faire la sourde oreille; **to fall on ~ ears** tomber dans l'oreille d'un sourd; **to be (as) ~ as a <u>post</u>** être sourd comme un pot **II.** *npl* **the ~** les malentendants *mpl*

**deafen** ['def·ᵊn] *vt* *(to make deaf)* rendre sourd

**deafening** *adj* assourdissant(e)

**deaf-mute** *adj* sourd(e)-muet(te)

**deaf mute** *n* sourd-muet *m*/sourde-muette *f*

**deafness** *n* surdité *f*

**deal** [dil] **I.** *n* ❶ *(agreement)* marché *m* ❷ *(bargain)* affaire *f;* **to make sb a ~** faire faire une affaire à qn ❸ **a (great) ~** beaucoup; **a great ~ of work** beaucoup de travail; **a good ~ of money/stress** pas mal d'argent/de stress ❹ *(passing out of cards)* donne *f* ▶ **what's the <u>big</u> ~?** *inf* où est le problème?; **<u>what's the</u> ~ with that?** *inf* c'est quoi ce truc? **II.** *vi* <dealt, dealt> ❶ *(make business)* faire des affaires; **to ~ in sth** faire du commerce de qc ❷ *(sell drugs)* dealer **III.** *vt* <dealt, dealt> ❶ *(pass out: cards)* distribuer ❷ *(give)* donner; **to ~ sb a blow** porter un coup à qn ❸ *(sell: drugs)* revendre

◆ **deal with** *vt* ❶ *(handle: problem)* se charger de ❷ *(discuss: subject)* traiter de ❸ *(do business: partner)* traiter avec

**dealer** *n* ❶ *(one who sells)* marchand(e) *m(f);* **antique ~** brocanteur, -euse *m, f* ❷ *(drug dealer)* dealer *m* ❸ *(one who deals cards)* donneur *m*

**dealt** [delt] *pt, pp of* **deal**

**dear** [dɪr] **I.** *adj* cher(chère); **to be ~ to sb** être cher à qn; **to do sth for ~ life** faire qc désespérément **II.** *adv* *(cost)* cher **III.** *interj inf* **oh ~ !**, **~ me!** mon Dieu! **IV.** *n* ❶ *(sweet person)* amour *m;* **my ~** mon chéri/ma chérie; *form* mon cher/ma chère; **to be (such) a ~** être (si) gentil; **my ~est** *iron* mon chéri/ma chérie ❷ *inf* *(friendly address)* (mon) chou *m*

**dearly** *adv* cher

**death** [deθ] *n* mort *f;* **to die a natural ~** décéder d'une mort naturelle; **to be put to ~** être mis à mort; **frightened to ~** mort de peur ▶ **to be at ~'s <u>doorstep</u>** être à l'article de la mort; **to ~** *(until one dies)* à mort; *(very much)* à mourir; **to have sb worried to ~** se faire un sang d'encre

**deathbed** *n* lit *m* de mort

**death penalty** *n* **the ~** la peine de mort

**death row** *n* quartier *m* des condamnés à mort; **to be on ~** être dans le couloir de la mort

**debate** [dɪ·'bert] **I.** *n* débat *m* **II.** *vt* débattre **III.** *vi* **to ~ about sth** débattre de qc; **to ~ whether ...** s'interroger si ...

**debit** ['deb·ɪt] **I.** *n* débit *m* **II.** *vt* **to ~ sth from sth** porter qc au débit de qc

**debit card** *n* carte *f* de paiement

**debt** [det] *n* dette *f*, pouf *m* Belgique; **to run up a (huge) ~** s'endetter lourdement; **to be out of ~** être acquitté de ses dettes; **to get heavily into ~** s'endetter lourdement ▶ **to be <u>in</u> ~ to sb** être redevable à qn

**decade** ['dek·erd] *n* décennie *f*

**decaf** ['di·kæf] **I.** *adj inf abbr of* **decaffeinated II.** *n inf* déca *m*

**decaffeinated** [ˌdi·'kæf·ɪ·nert·ɪd] *adj* décaféiné(e)

**decay** [dɪ·'ker] **I.** *n* ❶ *(deterioration)* délabrement *m;* **environmental ~** dégradation *f* de l'environnement; **to fall into ~** se délabrer ❷ *(decline)* a. *fig* déclin *m;* *(of civilization)* décadence *f;* **moral ~** déchéance *f* morale ❸ *(rotting)* décomposition *f* ❹ MED *(dental decay)* carie *f* ❺ PHYS désintégration *f* **II.** *vi* ❶ *(deteriorate)* se détériorer; *(tooth)* se carier; *(food)* pourrir ❷ BIO se décomposer ❸ PHYS se désintégrer **III.** *vt* *(food)* décomposer; *(tooth)* carier

**deceased I.** *n form* **the ~** *(used for one person)* le défunt, la défunte; *(several persons)* les défunt(e)s **II.** *adj form* décédé(e)

**D**

**deceive** [dɪ'siːv] *vt* tromper; **to ~ one-self** se tromper; **to ~ sb into doing sth** tromper qn en faisant qc ▸ **appearances can be deceiving** *prov* les apparences peuvent être trompeuses

**December** [dɪ'sem·bər] *n* décembre *m; s.a.* **April**

**decency** ['diː·sᵊn(t)·si] *n* ① (*social respectability*) décence *f* ② (*goodness*) bonté *f* ③ *pl* (*approved behavior*) convenances *fpl* ④ *pl* (*basic comforts*) commodités *fpl*

**decent** ['diː·sᵊnt] *adj* ① (*socially acceptable*) décent(e) ② (*good*) gentil(le) ③ (*appropriate*) convenable

**deceptive** [dɪ'sep·tɪv] *adj* trompeur(-euse)

**decibel** ['des·ɪ·bel] *n* décibel *m*

**decide** [dɪ'saɪd] **I.** *vi* (*make a choice*) se décider **II.** *vt* décider

**decimal** ['des·ɪ·mᵊl] *n* décimale *f*

**decision** [dɪ'sɪʒ·ᵊn] *n* ① (*choice*) décision *f*; **~ about sth** décision sur qc; **to make a ~** prendre une décision ② LAW décision *f*; **to hand down a ~** rendre une décision de justice

**decisive** [dɪ'saɪ·sɪv] *adj* décisif(-ive); (*person, tone, manner*) décidé(e)

**deck** [dek] **I.** *n* ① (*walking surface of a ship*) pont *m* ② (*level on a bus*) impériale *f*; (*level in stadium*); **upper/lower ~** tribune *f* haute/basse ③ (*roofless porch*) terrasse *f* ④ (*complete set*) **~ of cards** jeu *m* de cartes ⑤ MUS platine *f* ▸ **to clear the ~(s)** tout déblayer; **to hit the ~** *sl* se casser la gueule **II.** *vt* ① (*adorn*) orner; **to be ~ed with flowers** être orné de fleurs ② *sl* (*knock down*) mettre à terre

**declaration** *n* déclaration *f*

**declare** [dɪ'kler] **I.** *vt* déclarer; **to ~ bankruptcy** se déclarer en faillite **II.** *vi* *form* (*decide publicly*) **to ~ for/against sth** se déclarer en faveur de/contre qc

**decline** [dɪ'klaɪn] **I.** *n* ① (*deterioration*) déclin *m* ② (*decrease*) baisse *f*; **to be on the ~** être en baisse **II.** *vi* ① (*diminish*) baisser ② (*refuse*) refuser ③ (*de-*

*teriorate*) être sur le déclin **III.** *vt* décliner; **to ~ to** +*infin* refuser de +*infin*

**decontaminate** [ˌdiː·kən·'tæm·ɪ·neɪt] *vt* ECOL, CHEM décontaminer

**decorate** ['dek·ə·reɪt] *vt* ① (*adorn*) décorer ② (*add new paint*) peindre ③ (*add wallpaper*) tapisser ④ (*give a medal*) décorer

**decoration** *n* ① (*sth that adorns*) décoration *f* ② (*with paint*) peinture *f* ③ (*with wallpaper*) tapisserie *f*

**decorator** *n* décorateur, -trice *m, f*; **interior ~** décorateur *m* d'intérieur

**decrease** ['diː·kriːs] **I.** *vt, vi* baisser **II.** *n* baisse *f*; **to be on the ~** être en baisse

**decree** [dɪ'kriː] **I.** *n form* ① POL décret *m* ② LAW jugement *m* **II.** *vt* ① (*order by decree*) décréter ② LAW ordonner

**dedicate** ['ded·ɪ·keɪt] *vt* ① (*devote: life, time*) consacrer; **to ~ oneself to sth** se consacrer à qc ② (*do in sb's honor*) dédier; **to ~ sth to sb** dédier qc à qn ③ (*sign on: book, record*) dédicacer

**dedication** *n* ① (*devotion*) dévouement *m*; **to show ~ to sth** montrer du dévouement vis-à-vis de qc ② (*statement in sb's honor*) dédicace *f* ③ (*official opening*) consécration *f*

**deduct** [dɪ'dʌkt] *vt* déduire

**deduction** *n* déduction *f*; **to make a ~** tirer une conclusion

**deed** [diːd] *n* ① acte *m*; **~ to a house** acte de propriété; **to do a good ~** faire une bonne action

**deep** [diːp] **I.** *adj* ① (*not shallow*) profond(e); **how ~ is the sea?** quelle est la profondeur de la mer?; **it is 100 feet ~** elle a 30 mètres de profondeur ② (*extending back: stage*) profond(e); (*shelf, strip*) large; (*carpet, snow*) épais(se); **to be 6 inches ~** (*water*) faire 15 cm de profondeur ③ *fig* (*full, intense*) profond(e); (*desire, need*) grand(e); **to take a ~ breath** respirer profondément; **to be in ~ trouble** avoir de gros ennuis ④ *fig* (*profound: aversion, feelings, regret*) profond(e); **to have a ~ understanding of sth** avoir une grande compréhension de qc ⑤ (*absorbed* *by*) **to be ~ in sth** être très absorbé dans qc; **to be ~ in debt** être très endetté ⑥ (*far back*) **the Deep South** le Sud profond; **in the ~ past** il y a très longtemps ⑦ *inf* (*hard to understand*) profond(e); (*knowledge*) approfondi(e) ⑧ (*low in pitch: voice*) grave ⑨ (*dark: color*) intense; **~ red** rouge foncé; **~ blue eyes** yeux *mpl* d'un bleu profond ▶ **to jump in at the ~ end** se jeter à l'eau II. *adv* a. *fig* profondément; **to run ~** être profond; **~ inside** dans mon for intérieur; **~ in my heart** tout au fond de moi; **~ in the forest** au plus profond de la forêt ▶ **still waters run ~** *prov* il faut se méfier de l'eau qui dort

**deep-freeze** *vt* congeler

**deep-fry** *vt* faire cuire dans la friture

**deeply** *adv* profondément; **to ~ regret sth** regretter beaucoup qc; **to be ~ interested in sth** être très intéressé par qc

**deep-sea** *adj* **~ animal** animal *m* pélagique

**deep-six** *vt sl* liquider

**deer** [dɪr] *n* chevreuil *m*

**defamation** *n form* diffamation *f*

**defeat** [dɪ·ˈfiːt] I. *vt* (*person*) battre; (*hopes*) anéantir II. *n* défaite *f*

**defect** [ˈdiː·fekt, *vb*: dɪ·ˈfekt] I. *n* ① (*imperfection*) défaut *m* ② TECH vice *m* ③ MED problème *m*; **heart ~** problème au cœur II. *vi* POL **to ~ from/to a country** s'enfuir de/vers un pays

**defective** [dɪ·ˈfek·tɪv] *adj* (*brakes, appliance*) défectueux(-euse)

**defend** [dɪ·ˈtend] *vt, vi* défendre

**defendant** [dɪ·ˈfen·dənt] *n* LAW défendeur, -deresse *m, f*

**defense** [dɪ·ˈfen(t)s] *n* défense *f*; **~ mechanism** réflexe *m* de défense; **to put up a ~** se défendre

**defense secretary** *n* ministre *mf* de la Défense

**defensive** [dɪ·ˈfen(t)·sɪv] I. *adj* ① (*intended for defense*) défensif(-ive) ② (*quick to challenge*) sur la défensive II. *n* défensive *f*; **to be/go on the ~** être/se mettre sur la défensive

**defiant** *adj* provocateur(-trice); (*stand*) de défi; **to remain ~** faire preuve de provocation; **to be in a ~ mood** être d'humeur provocatrice

**deficient** [dɪ·ˈfɪʃ·ənt] *adj* incomplet(-ète); **to be ~ in sth** manquer de qc

**define** [dɪ·ˈfaɪn] *vt* définir; (*limit, extent*) déterminer; (*eyes, outlines*) dessiner

**definite** [ˈdef·ɪ·nət] I. *adj* ① (*clearly stated*) défini(e); (*plan, amount*) précis(e); (*opinion, taste*) bien arrêté(e) ② (*clear, unambiguous*) net(te); (*reply*) clair(e) et net(te); (*evidence*) évident(e) ③ (*firm*) ferme; (*refusal*) catégorique ④ (*sure*) sûr(sure); **to be ~ about sth** être sûr de qc ⑤ (*undeniable: asset, advantage*) évident(e) II. *n inf* **they are ~s for the party** ils sont sûrs d'être invités à la soirée

**definitely** *adv* ① (*without doubt*) sans aucun doute; **I will ~ be there** je serai là à coup sûr; **I will ~ do it** je le ferai sans faute; **it was ~ him in the car** c'est sûr que c'était lui dans la voiture; **it was ~ the best option** c'était sans aucun doute la meilleure solution ② (*categorically: decided, sure*) absolument

**definition** [ˌdef·ɪ·ˈnɪʃ·ən] *n* définition *f*; **to lack ~** ne pas être net

**definitive** [dɪ·ˈtɪn·ə·tɪv] *adj* ① (*final*) définitif(-ive); (*proof*) irréfutable ② (*best: book*) de référence

**deformed** *adj* malformé(e); **to be born ~** naître avec une malformation

**defrost** [ˌdiː·ˈfrɑst] *vt, vi* (*food*) décongeler; (*refrigerator, windshield*) dégivrer

**defroster** *n* AUTO dégivreur *m*

**degree** [dɪ·ˈgriː] *n* ① (*amount*) a. MATH, METEO degré *m* ② (*extent*) mesure *f*; **to a certain ~** dans une certaine mesure; **by ~s** par étapes ③ (*qualification*) diplôme *m* universitaire; **bachelor's ~** ≈ licence *f*; **master's ~** ≈ maîtrise *f*

**dehydrated** *adj* (*food*) déshydraté(e)

**dehydration** *n* MED déshydratation *f*

**deice** [ˌdiː·ˈaɪs] *vt* dégeler

**Delaware** [ˈdel·ə·wer] *n* le Delaware

**delay** [dɪ'leɪ] I. *vt* retarder II. *vi* tarder III. *n* retard *m*

**delegate** ['del·ɪ·gət, *vb:* 'del·ɪ·geɪt] I. *n* délégué(e) *m(f)* II. *vt* déléguer; **to ~ sb to (do) sth** déléguer qn pour (faire) qc III. *vi* déléguer

**D**

**delegation** *n* délégation *f*

**delete** [dɪ'li:t] I. *vt* ❶ (*cross out*) rayer ❷ COMPUT (*file, letter*) effacer II. *vi* COMPUT effacer III. *n* COMPUT (*delete key*) touche *f* d'effacement

**deli** ['del·i] *n inf abbr of* **delicatessen**

**deliberate** [dɪ'lɪb·ə·rət, *vb:* dɪ'lɪb·ə·reɪt] I. *adj* (*act, movement*) délibéré(e); (*decision*) voulu(e); **it was ~** cela a été fait exprès II. *vi form* délibérer III. *vt form* délibérer de

**deliberately** *adv* intentionnellement

**delicacy** ['del·ɪ·kə·si] *n* ❶ (*fine food*) mets *m* raffiné ❷ (*fragility*) délicatesse *f* ❸ (*sensitivity*) sensibilité *f*

**delicate** ['del·ɪ·kət] *adj* ❶ (*fragile*) délicat(e) ❷ (*highly sensitive: instrument*) fragile ❸ (*fine: balance*) précaire

**delicatessen** [ˌdel·ɪ·kə·'tes·ᵊn] *n* épicerie *f* fine

**delicious** [dɪ'lɪʃ·əs] *adj* délicieux(-euse)

**delight** [dɪ'laɪt] I. *n* délice *m;* **to do sth with ~** faire qc avec plaisir; **to take ~ in sth** prendre plaisir à qc II. *vt* enchanter

**delighted** *adj* ravi(e)

**delightful** *adj* (*people*) charmant(e); (*evening, place*) délicieux(-euse)

**delirious** [dɪ'lɪr·i·əs] *adj* ❶ MED (*affected by delirium*) **to be ~** délirer ❷ (*ecstatic*) délirant(e); **to be ~ with joy** être délirant de joie

**deliver** [dɪ'lɪv·ər] I. *vt* ❶ (*distribute to addressee: goods*) livrer; (*newspaper, mail*) distribuer ❷ (*recite: lecture, speech*) faire; (*verdict*) prononcer ❸ (*direct: a blow*) porter; (*a ball*) lancer ❹ (*give birth to*) **to ~ a baby** mettre un enfant au monde ❺ (*produce: promise*) tenir ❻ (*hand over*) remettre ❼ (*rescue*) délivrer ❽ POL (*a vote*) obtenir ▸ **to ~ the goods** *inf* tenir ses promesses II. *vi* ❶ (*make a delivery*) livrer; (*mail-*

*man*) distribuer le courrier ❷ *fig* tenir ses promesses

**delivery** [dɪ'lɪv·ᵊr·i] *n* ❶ (*act of distributing goods*) livraison *f;* (*of newspaper, mail*) distribution *f;* **on ~** à la livraison; **to take ~ of sth** se faire livrer qc ❷ (*manner of speaking*) élocution *f* ❸ (*birth*) accouchement *m* ❹ SPORTS lancer *m*

**delivery room** *n* salle *f* d'accouchement

**delivery van** *n* camionnette *f* de livraison

**deluxe** [dɪ'lʌks] *adj* de luxe

**demand** [dɪ'mænd] I. *vt* ❶ (*request, require*) demander ❷ (*request forcefully*) exiger; (*payment*) réclamer ❸ (*require*) exiger; (*time, skills*) demander II. *n* ❶ (*request*) demande *f* ❷ (*pressured request*) exigence *f* ❸ ECON (*desire for sth*) demande *f;* **to be in ~** être demandé; **to do sth on ~** faire qc à la demande; **to make a ~ that ...** exiger que +*subj;* **to meet a ~ for sth** satisfaire le besoin de qc ❹ LAW réclamation *f;* **to receive a ~ for payment** recevoir un avis de paiement

**demanding** *adj* exigeant(e); (*task, job*) astreignant(e)

**demeaning** *adj* avilissant(e)

**democracy** [dɪ'mɑ·krə·si] *n* démocratie *f*

**democrat** ['dem·ə·kræt] *n* démocrate *mf*

**democratic** *adj* démocratique

**democratization** *n* démocratisation *f*

**demolish** [dɪ'mɑ·lɪʃ] *vt* démolir

**demon** ['di·mən] I. *n* (*evil spirit*) démon *m* ▸ **to work like a ~** *inf* travailler comme un fou II. *adj inf* démoniaque

**demoniacal** *adj* démoniaque

**demonstrate** ['dem·ən·streɪt] I. *vt* (*show clearly*) démontrer; (*enthusiasm, knowledge*) montrer II. *vi* **to ~ against/in support of sth** manifester contre/en faveur de qc

**demonstration** *n* ❶ (*act of showing*) démonstration *f;* **as a ~ of sth** en signe de qc; **to give sb a ~ of sth** faire la dé-

**D**

monstration de qc à qn ❷ (*march or parade*) manifestation *f*

**demonstrator** *n* ❶ (*person who demonstrates a product*) démonstrateur, -trice *m, f* ❷ (*person who takes part in protest*) manifestant(e) *m(f)*

**demote** [dɪ'moʊt] *vt* MIL rétrograder

**den** [den] *n* ❶ (*lair*) tanière *f* ❷ (*room in house*) antre *m* ❸ *iron* (*place for committing crime*) repaire *m*

**denial** [dɪ'naɪ·əl] *n* ❶ (*act of refuting*) déni *m* ❷ (*refusal*) dénégation *f*

**denim** ['den·ɪm] *n* ❶ (*thick cotton cloth*) denim *m* ❷ *inf* (*clothes made of denim*) jean *m*

**Denmark** ['den·mark] *n* le Danemark

**dense** [den(t)s] <-r, -st> *adj* ❶ (*thick, compact: book, crowd, fog*) dense ❷ *fig, inf* (*stupid*) limité(e)

**density** ['den(t)·sə·t̬i] *n* densité *f*

**dent** [dent] I. *n* ❶ (*a hollow made by pressure*) bosse *f* ❷ *fig* (*adverse effect*) blessure *f* II. *vt* ❶ (*put a dent in*) cabosser ❷ *fig* (*have adverse effect on*) **to ~ sb's confidence** entacher la confiance de qn

**dental** ['den·t̬əl] *adj* dentaire

**dentist** *n* dentiste *mf*

**dentistry** ['den·t̬ɪ·stri] *n* médecine *f* dentaire

**dentures** ['den(t̬)·ʃərz] *npl* denture *f;* **to wear ~** porter un dentier

**deny** [dɪ'naɪ] *vt* (*accusation*) dénier; (*family*) renier; **to ~ that ...** renier que ...; **to ~ doing sth** dénier avoir fait qc

**deodorant** [di·'oʊ·dər·ənt] *n* déodorant *m*

**depart** [dɪ'part] I. *vi* (*person, train, ship*) partir; (*plane*) décoller; **to ~ from sth** partir de qc; *fig* s'écarter de qc II. *vt* quitter

**departed** I. *adj* défunt(e) II. *n pl* **the ~** le/la défunt(e)

**department** *n* ❶ (*section*) département *m;* (*of an organization*) service *m* ❷ ADMIN, POL département *m* ministériel; **Department of Transportation**

ministère *m* des Transports ❸ *fig, inf* (*domain*) domaine *m*

**department store** *n* grand magasin *m*

**departure** [dɪ'part·ʃər] *n* ❶ (*act of vehicle leaving*) départ *m* ❷ (*deviation*) déviation *f* ❸ (*new undertaking*) changement *m*

**depend** [dɪ'pend] *vi* ❶ (*rely on*) **to ~ on sb/sth** dépendre de qn/qc; **to be ~ doing sth** dépendre du fait que qn/qc fait/fasse (*subj*) qc ❷ (*rely (on)*) **to ~ on sb/ sth** compter sur qn/qc

**dependability** [dɪ‚pen·də·'bɪl·ə·t̬i] *n* fiabilité *f*

**dependent** I. *adj* ❶ (*contingent*) **to be ~ on sth** dépendre de qc ❷ (*in need of*) dépendant(e); **to be ~ on sth** être dépendant de qc; **to be ~ on drugs** être accro à la drogue II. *n* personne *f* à charge

**deplete** [dɪ'plit] *vt* vider; **to ~ one's bank account** *iron* épuiser son compte en banque

**deplorable** *adj* déplorable

**deploy** [dɪ'plɔɪ] *vt* (*one's resources, troops*) déployer; (*an argument*) exposer

**deployment** *n* déploiement *m*

**deport** [dɪ'pɔrt] *vt* déporter

**deportee** [‚di·pɔr·'ti] *n* déporté(e) *m(f)*

**deposit** [dɪ'paz·ɪt] I. *vt* ❶ (*put*) déposer; **to ~ money in(to) one's account** déposer de l'argent sur un compte ❷ (*pay as security*) **to ~ sth with sb** verser qc à qn II. *n* ❶ (*sediment*) dépôt *m* ❷ (*payment made as first installment*) provision *f* ❸ (*security*) caution *f;* (*on a bottle/can*) consigne *f*

**deprecation** *n a. form* dépréciation *f*

**depress** [dɪ'pres] *vt* ❶ (*sadden*) désoler ❷ (*reduce or lower in amount: prices*) déprécier; (*the economy*) décourager ❸ *form* (*press down: a button, a pedal*) appuyer sur

**depressed** *adj* ❶ (*sad*) déprimé(e); **to be ~ about sth** être déprimé par qc ❷ (*affected by depression: market*) en déclin *m*

**depressing** *adj* déprimant(e)

**D**

**depression** *n* dépression *f*

**deprive** [dɪˈpraɪv] *vt* priver; **to ~ sb of sth** priver qn de qc; **to ~ sb of sleep** empêcher qn de dormir

**depth** [depθ] *n a. fig* profondeur *f;* **in ~** en profondeur; **with great ~ of feeling** avec une grande sensibilité

**deputy** [ˈdep·jə·t̬i] I. *n* député(e) *m(f);* **to act as sb's ~** agir en tant que représentant de qn II. *adj inv* suppléant(e); **~ manager** gérant *m* adjoint

**derailment** *n* ❶ *(accident)* déraillement *m* ❷ *fig* dérapage *m*

**deranged** *adj* dérangé(e)

**derby** [ˈdɜr·bi] *n* ❶ *(horserace)* course *f* hippique; **the Kentucky Derby** le Derby du Kentucky ❷ *(race)* course *f* ❸ *(hat)* chapeau *m* melon

**derelict** [ˈder·ə·lɪkt] I. *adj (building)* délabré(e); *(site)* en ruine *f* II. *n form* épave *f*

**derive** [dɪˈraɪv] I. *vt* **to ~ sth from sth** tirer qc de qc II. *vi* **to ~ from sth** *(a word)* dériver de qc; *(custom)* venir de qc

**descend** [dɪˈsend] I. *vi* ❶ *(go down)* descendre ❷ *(fall: darkness)* tomber ❸ *(deteriorate)* **to ~ into sth** tomber en qc ❹ *(lower oneself)* s'abaisser ❺ **~ from sb/sth** provenir de qn/qc II. *vt* descendre

**descendant** [dɪˈsen·dənt] *n* descendant(e) *m(f)*

**descent** [dɪˈsent] *n* ❶ *(movement)* descente *f* ❷ *fig (decline)* déclin *m* ❸ *(ancestry)* descendance *f*

**describe** [dɪˈskraɪb] *vt* décrire; **to ~ sb as sth** qualifier qn de qc

**description** [dɪˈskrɪp·ʃən] *n* description *f; **of every ~** en tout genre

**descriptive** [dɪˈskrɪp·tɪv] *adj* descriptif(-ive); *(statistics)* parlant(e)

**desert**[1] [dɪˈzɜrt] I. *vi* déserter II. *vt* ❶ *(run away from duty: the army, one's post)* déserter ❷ *(abandon)* abandonner

**desert**[2] [ˈdez·ərt] *n a. fig* désert *m*

**deserter** *n* déserteur *m*

**deserve** [dɪˈzɜrv] *vt* mériter

**design** [dɪˈzaɪn] I. *vt* ❶ *(conceive)* concevoir ❷ *(draw)* dessiner II. *n* ❶ *(planning)* concept *m;* *(plan or drawing)* dessin *m* ❷ *(art of creating designs)* design *m* ❸ *(pattern)* motif *m* ❹ *(intention)* intention *f* III. *adj inv* *(fault, feature)* de style; *(chair, table)* design *inv*

**designated driver** *n* conducteur, -trice *m, f* désigné(e) *(pour ne pas boire d'alcool)*

**designer** I. *n* ❶ *(creator)* désigner *m* ❷ FASHION styliste *mf* ❸ THEAT décorateur, -trice *m, f* II. *adj (furniture)* de créateur; *(clothing)* de marque

**desirable** *adj* ❶ *(sought-after)* souhaitable ❷ *(sexually attractive)* désirable

**desire** [dɪˈzaɪər] I. *vt* désirer; **to ~ that** désirer que +*subj* II. *n* désir *m;* **to express the ~ to** +*infin* exprimer le désir de +*infin*

**desk** [desk] *n* ❶ *(table for writing on)* bureau *m* ❷ *(service counter)* comptoir *m* (de magasin); **to work at the front ~** travailler à l'accueil ❸ *(newspaper office or section)* rédaction *f*

**desktop** [ˈdesk·tap] *n* COMPUT **~ (computer)** ordinateur *m* de table

**desolate** [ˈdes·ᵊl·ət] *adj* désolé(e)

**despair** [dɪˈsper] I. *n* *(feeling of hopelessness)* désespoir *m;* **to be in ~ about sth** être désespéré par qc II. *vi* désespérer; **to ~ of sb/sth** s'affliger de qn/qc

**despairing** *adj pej* désespéré(e)

**desperate** [ˈdes·pᵊr·ət] *adj* ❶ *(risking all on a small chance: attempt, measure, solution)* désespéré(e) ❷ *(serious: situation)* désespéré(e) ❸ *(great)* extrême ❹ *(having great need or desire)* **to be ~ for sth** être prêt à tout pour qc

**desperation** *n* désespoir *m*

**despite** [dɪˈspaɪt] *prep* malgré; **~ having done sth** bien qu'ayant fait qc

**dessert** [dɪˈzɜrt] *n* dessert *m*

**destination** [ˌdes·tɪˈneɪ·ʃən] *n* destination *f*

**destroy** [dɪˈstrɔɪ] *vt a. fig* détruire

**destruction** [dɪˈstrʌk·ʃən] *n* destruction *f;* **to leave a trail of ~** faire des ravages derrière soi

**destructive** [dɪˈstrʌk·tɪv] *adj* destructeur(-trice)

**detach** [dɪˈtætʃ] *vt* détacher

**detached** *adj* ❶ (*separated*) séparé(e) ❷ (*disinterested*) détaché(e); (*impartial*) neutre

**detail** [ˈdiˈteɪl] **I.** *n* détail *m;* **in ~** en détail; **to give ~s about sth** donner des renseignements sur qc; **to go into ~** entrer dans les détails; **to take down ~s** prendre des coordonnées *fpl* **II.** *vt* ❶ (*explain fully*) détailler ❷ (*tell*) mentionner ❸ ART finaliser

**detailed** *adj* détaillé(e)

**detain** [dɪˈteɪn] *vt* ❶ (*hold as prisoner*) détenir ❷ *form* (*delay*) retarder ❸ *form* (*keep waiting*) faire patienter

**detainee** [ˌdiˈteɪˈni] *n* détenu(e) *m(f)*

**detect** [dɪˈtekt] *vt* ❶ (*discover*) découvrir ❷ (*discover presence of*) détecter la présence de ❸ (*sense presence of*) percevoir la présence de

**detective** [dɪˈtek·tɪv] *n* ❶ (*police*) inspecteur *m* de police ❷ (*private*) détective *m* privé

**detention center** *n* ❶ (*jail*) centre *m* de détention ❷ (*for refugees*) centre *m* d'accueil (pour réfugiés politiques); (*for illegal immigrants*) centre *m* de rétention

**detergent** [dɪˈtɜr·dʒ³nt] *n* détergent *m;* (*for clothes*) lessive *f*

**deteriorate** [dɪˈtɪr·i·ə·reɪt] *vi* se détériorer

**determination** *n* ❶ (*resolution*) résolution *f* ❷ (*direction towards an aim*) détermination *f*

**determine** [dɪˈtɜr·mɪn] *vt* ❶ (*decide*) déterminer ❷ (*settle*) régler ❸ (*find out*) établir ❹ (*influence*) dépendre de ❺ LAW (*terminate*) conclure

**determined** *adj* déterminé(e); **to be ~ to do sth** être bien décidé à faire qc

**deterrence** [dɪˈter·³n(t)s] *n* dissuasion *f*

**detest** [dɪˈtest] *vt* détester

**detour** [ˈdiˈtʊr] *n* détour *m;* **to make [*o* take] a ~** faire un détour

**detoxify** [diˈtak·sɪ·faɪ] *vt* désintoxiquer

**deuce** [dus] *n* ❶ (*two on cards or die*) deux ❷ (*score in tennis*) égalité *f*

**devastating** *adj* ❶ (*causing destruction*) dévastateur(-trice) ❷ (*powerful*) puissant(e) ❸ (*with great effect*) ravageur(-euse)

**devastation** *n* ❶ (*destruction*) dévastation *f* ❷ (*being devastated*) désespoir *m*

**develop** [dɪˈvel·əp] **I.** *vi* ❶ (*grow, evolve*) a. *fig* se développer; **to ~ into sth** devenir qc; **to ~ out of sth** croître de qc ❷ (*become apparent*) se manifester; (*event*) se produire; (*illness*) se déclarer; (*feelings*) naître; (*hole*) se former **II.** *vt* ❶ (*grow, expand*) a. *fig* développer ❷ (*acquire*) acquérir; (*infection, habit*) contracter; (*cancer*) développer ❸ (*improve*) développer; (*city*) aménager; (*region*) mettre en valeur; (*symptoms*) présenter; **to ~ sth into sth** transformer qc en qc ❹ (*create*) créer ❺ (*catch*) attraper; **to ~ an allergy to sth** devenir allergique à qc ❻ (*build*) construire ❼ PHOT, MATH développer ❽ MUS élaborer

**developer** *n* ❶ (*sb who develops*) adolescent(e) *m(f)* ❷ (*person that develops land*) promoteur, -trice *m, f* ❸ (*company*) compagnie *f* de construction ❹ PHOT révélateur *m*

**developing** *adj* croissant(e)

**development** *n* ❶ (*process*) développement *m* ❷ (*growth*) croissance *f* économique ❸ (*growth stage*) élaboration *f* ❹ (*new event*) développement *m* ❺ (*progress*) progrès *m;* (*of a product*) élaboration *f* ❻ (*building of*) construction *f* ❼ (*building on: of land*) développement *m* ❽ (*industrialization*) développement *m* industriel ❾ MUS élaboration *f* ❿ GAMES mouvement *m*

**device** [dɪˈvaɪs] *n* ❶ (*mechanism*) machine *f* ❷ (*method*) moyen *m,* **literary/rhetorical ~** procédé *m* littéraire/rhétorique ❸ (*bomb*) engin *m* (explosif) ❹ COMPUT périphérique *m* ▸ **to leave sb**

**D**

to his/their <u>own</u> ~s laisser qn se débrouiller seul

**devil** ['dev·əl] n ① (Satan) **the Devil** le Diable; **to be possessed by the Devil** être possédé par le Démon ② (evil spirit) diable m ③ inf (wicked person) démon m; (mischievous person) diable, -esse m, f ④ inf (person) **handsome ~** beau gosse m; **lucky ~** veinard m ⑤ (difficult thing) **to have a ~ of a time doing sth** avoir de la peine à faire qc ⑥ (feisty energy) **like the ~** comme un possédé ⑦ (indicating surprise) **who/what/where/how the ~...?** qui/que/où/comment diable...? ► **between the ~ and the deep blue <u>sea</u>** entre Charybde et Scylla; **to go to the ~** aller au diable; **to play the ~ with sth** jouer avec le feu en ce qui concerne qc; <u>speak</u> of the ~ en parlant du loup

**devil's advocate** n avocat m du diable

**devious** ['di·vi·əs] adj ① (dishonest) malhonnête ② (winding) détourné(e)

**devote** [dɪ·'vout] vt consacrer; **to ~ sth to sb/sth** consacrer qc à qn/qc; **to ~ oneself to sth** se vouer à qc

**devoted** adj dévoué(e)

**devotion** [dɪ·'vou·ʃən] n ① (loyalty) fidélité f ② (affection) tendresse f ③ (admiration) admiration f ④ (great attachment) dévouement m ⑤ (religious attachment) dévotion f

**devout** [dɪ·'vaut] adj ① (strongly religious) dévot(e) ② (devoted) fervent(e)

**dew** [du] n rosée f

**dexterity** [dek·'ster·ə·ţi] n ① (skillful handling) habileté f ② (mental skill) dextérité f

**diabetes** [daɪə·'bi·ţəs] n diabète m

**diabetic** [daɪə·'be·ţɪk] I. n ① diabétique m II. adj ① (who has diabetes) diabétique ② (for diabetics) pour diabétiques

**diagnose** [daɪəg·'nous] vt diagnostiquer

**diagnosis** [daɪəg·'nou·sɪs] <-ses> n diagnostic m

**diagonal** [daɪ·'æg·ᵊn·ᵊl] I. n diagonale f II. adj diagonal(e)

**diagram** ['daɪə·græm] I. n ① (drawing) schéma m ② (plan) carte f ③ (chart) diagramme m ④ MATH, PHYS figure f II. <-mm-> vt dessiner

**dial** [daɪəl] I. n ① (knob, indicator) bouton m; **radio/television ~** bouton m de fréquence/panneau m de réglage ② (clock face) cadran m ③ (disk on a telephone) cadran m téléphonique II. <-l- o -ll-> vi faire le numéro; **to ~ direct** appeler directement III. <-l- o -ll-> vt (number) composer; (country, person) avoir

**dialect** ['daɪə·lekt] n dialecte m

**dialog, dialogue** ['daɪə·lag] n ① (conversation) discussion f ② LIT, THEAT, POL dialogue m; **to engage in ~** s'engager dans un dialogue

**diameter** [daɪ·'æm·ə·ţər] n ① (line) diamètre m ② (magnifying measurement) grossissement m

**diamond** ['daɪə·mənd] n ① (precious stone) diamant m ② (rhombus) losange m ③ (card with diamond symbol) carreau m ④ (glittering particle) poussière f de diamant ⑤ (tool for cutting glass) machine f à tailler le diamant ⑥ (baseball field) terrain m de base-ball

**diamond anniversary** n noces fpl de diamant

**diaper** ['daɪə·pər] n couche f

**diarrhea, diarrhoea** [daɪə·'riə] n diarrhée f

**diary** ['daɪə·ri] n ① (journal) journal m intime; **to keep a ~** tenir un journal intime ② (planner) agenda m

**dice** [daɪs] I. n ① pl of **die**[1] ② GAMES dés mpl; **to roll the ~** faire rouler les dés ③ (chunk) cube m ► <u>no</u> ~! inf pas question! II. vt couper en dés

**dick** [dɪk] n vulg (penis) bite f ② pej (stupid man) con m

**dictate** ['dɪk·teɪt] I. vi ① (say sth to be written down) dicter ② (command) dicter; **to ~ to sb** imposer à qn II. vt ① (say sth to be written down) dicter ② (command) dicter ③ (make necessary) imposer III. n ordre m

**dictation** n dictée f

**dictator** n ❶ (*ruler*) despote m ❷ (*sb who dictates a text*) a. POL dictateur m

**dictatorship** n dictature f

**dictionary** ['dɪk·ʃ³n·er·i] n dictionnaire m

**did** [dɪd] pt of **do**

**didn't** [dɪd·³nt] = **did not** s. **do**

**die¹** [daɪ] n ❶ <dice> (*cube with spots*) dé m ❷ <dies> TECH matrice f ► **the ~ is cast** les dés mpl sont jetés

**die²** [daɪ] <dying, died> I. vi ❶ (*cease to live*) a. fig, iron mourir; **to ~ of cancer** mourir du cancer; **to ~ of boredom** mourir d'ennui ❷ inf (*desire*) **to be dying to do sth** mourir d'envie de faire qc; **I'm dying for a drink** je meurs de soif ❸ (*stop working*) disparaître; (*light, battery*) s'éteindre; (*car*) s'arrêter ❹ fig (*fade: hope, feelings*) mourir ► **never say ~** il ne faut jamais désespérer; **do or ~!** ça passe ou ça casse!; **sth to ~ for** qc d'irrésistible II. vt to **~ a natural/violent death** mourir d'une mort naturelle/violente

◆**die down** vi baisser; (*wind, emotion*) se calmer; (*sound*) s'éteindre

◆**die off** vi mourir; (*species*) s'éteindre; (*customs*) se perdre

◆**die out** vt s'éteindre

**diesel** ['di·səl] n diesel m

**diet¹** [daɪət] I. n ❶ (*what one eats and drinks*) alimentation f ❷ (*for medical reasons*) diète f ❸ (*to lose weight*) régime m II. adj allégé(e); **~ soda** soda m light III. vi être au régime/à la diète

**diet²** [daɪət] n POL (*legislative assembly*) diète f

**dietary fiber** n fibre f diététique

**differ** ['dɪf·ər] vi ❶ (*be unlike*) **to ~ from sth** différer de qc ❷ (*disagree*) **to ~ with sb** être en désaccord avec qn

**difference** ['dɪf·³r·ən(t)s] n ❶ (*state of being different*) différence f; **to make a big ~** faire une différence considérable; **to not make any ~** ne rien changer; **with a ~** qui sort de l'ordinaire ❷ (*disagreement*) différend m; (*of opinion*) divergence f; **to put aside/to settle one's ~s** mettre de côté/aplanir ses différends

**different** adj ❶ (*not the same*) différent(e) ❷ (*distinct*) distinct(e) ❸ (*unusual*) hors du commun ► **to be as ~ as night and day** être le jour et la nuit

**difficult** ['dɪf·ɪ·kəlt] adj difficile

**difficulty** <-ties> n ❶ (*being difficult*) difficulté f ❷ (*much effort*) peine f; **with ~** avec peine ❸ (*problem*) problème m; **to encounter difficulties** faire face à des problèmes; **to have ~ doing sth** avoir de la peine à faire qc

**dig** [dɪg] I. n ❶ (*poke*) coup m (de coude); **~ in the ribs** coup m dans les côtes ❷ (*critical, sarcastic remark*) pique f; **to take a ~ at sb** lancer une pique à qn ❸ (*act of digging: in garden*) coup m de bêche ❹ (*excavation*) fouilles fpl II. <-gg-, dug, dug> vi ❶ (*turn over ground*) creuser; (*in garden*) bêcher; **to ~ through sth** creuser qc; **to ~ for a bone** creuser pour chercher un os ❷ (*excavate: on a site*) faire des fouilles; **to ~ for sth** chercher qc ❸ (*search*) a. fig fouiller; **to ~ into the past** fouiller dans le passé ► **to ~ in one's heels** s'entêter III. vt ❶ (*move ground: hole, tunnel*) creuser; (*garden*) bêcher ❷ (*excavate: site*) fouiller ❸ (*thrust*) enfoncer; **to ~ one's hands in(to) one's pockets** enfoncer ses mains dans les poches; **to ~ deep into one's pockets** gratter le fond de ses poches ❹ sl (*like*) **I ~ sth** qc me botte ❺ sl (*understand*) piger ► **to ~ one's own grave** creuser sa propre tombe; **to ~ oneself into/out of a hole** se mettre dans une situation délicate/se sortir d'une situation délicate

◆**dig in** I. vi ❶ inf (*eat*) bouffer ❷ MIL se retrancher II. vt **to dig oneself in** camper sur ses positions

**digital television** n télévision f numérique

◆**dig out** vt a. fig déterrer

◆**dig up** vt a. fig déterrer ► **to ~ the dirt on sb** déterrer des informations compromettantes sur qn

**D**

**digest** ['daɪ·dʒest, *vb*: daɪ·'dʒest] **I.** *n* condensé *m* **II.** *vt* ① (*break down*) a. *fig* digérer ② (*assimilate*) assimiler **III.** *vi* digérer

**digestion** *n* digestion *f*

**digger** ['dɪg·ər] *n* ① (*machine*) excavatrice *f*; (*for the garden*) bêche *f* ② (*person*) mineur *m*; **gold** ~ chercheur, -euse *m*, *f* d'or; *fig, pej* (*woman*) poule *f* de luxe

**digit** ['dɪdʒ·ɪt] *n* ① (*number from 0 to 9*) chiffre *m* ② (*finger*) doigt *m* ③ (*toe*) orteil *m*

**digital** *adj* numérique

**dignified** *adj* digne

**dignity** ['dɪg·nə·ti] *n* ① (*respect*) dignité *f* ② (*state worthy of respect*) honneur *m*

**dike¹** [daɪk] *n* (*anti-flood embankment*) digue *f*

**dike²** [daɪk] *n pej, inf s.* **dyke²**

**dilapidated** [dɪ·'læp·ɪ·deɪ·t̪ɪd] *adj* délabré(e)

**dilemma** [dɪ·'lem·ə] *n* dilemme *m*

**dilute** [daɪ·'lut] **I.** *vt* ① (*add liquid*) diluer ② *fig* (*reduce*) édulcorer **II.** *adj* dilué(e)

**dim** [dɪm] **I.**<-mm-> *adj* ① (*not bright*) sombre; (*light*) faible; (*color*) terne ② (*unclear: view*) faible; (*recollection*) vague ③ *fig* (*stupid*) borné(e) ▶ **to take a ~ view of sth** ne pas apprécier qc **II.**<-mm-> *vt* (*lights*) baisser **III.**<-mm-> *vi* (*lights*) baisser

**dime** [daɪm] *n* pièce *f* de dix cents ▶ **a ~ a dozen** treize à la douzaine

**din** [dɪn] **I.** *n* vacarme *m* **II.** *vt* **to ~ sth into sb** faire rentrer qc dans la tête de qn

**dine** [daɪn] *vi form* dîner

**diner** ['daɪ·nər] *n* ① (*person*) dîneur, -euse *m*, *f* ② (*restaurant*) petit restaurant *m*

**dining room** *n* salle *f* à manger

**dinner** ['dɪn·ər] *n* ① (*evening meal*) dîner *m*, café *m* complet *Suisse*, souper *m Belgique, Québec, Suisse* ② (*lunch*) déjeuner *m*

**dinner party** *n* dîner *m*

**dinner table** *n* table *f* (de la salle à manger)

**dinnertime** *n* heure *f* du dîner; **at ~** à l'heure du dîner

**dinosaur** ['daɪ·nə·sɔr] *n* ① (*extinct reptile*) dinosaure *m* ② *fig* (*old-fashioned*) fossile *m*

**dip** [dɪp] **I.** *n* ① (*instance of dipping*) trempage *m* ② (*brief swim*) plongeon *m*; (*brief study*) survol *m* rapide ③ CULIN sauce *f* apéritif ④ (*sudden drop*) chute *f*; (*of a road*) déclivité *f* ⑤ (*liquid*) bain *m*; (*cleaning liquid*) solution *f* nettoyante **II.** *vt* ① (*immerse*) tremper ② (*put into*) **to ~ sth in sth** plonger qc dans qc ③ (*lower*) baisser ④ (*disinfect: sheep*) laver ⑤ (*dye*) teindre **III.** *vi* ① (*drop down: road*) descendre; (*sun*) se coucher ② (*decline: rates, sales*) baisser ③ (*submerge and re-emerge*) plonger ④ (*lower: plane*) piquer

◆**dip into** *vt always sep* puiser dans; **to ~ one's pocket** payer de sa poche; **to ~ one's savings** puiser dans ses économies

**diploma** [dɪ·'plou·mə] *n* (*certificate*) diplôme *m*

**diplomacy** *n* diplomatie *f*

**diplomat** ['dɪp·lə·mæt] *n* diplomate *mf*

**diplomatic** *adj* diplomatique

**Dipper** ['dɪp·ər] *n* ASTR **the Big/Little ~** la Grande/Petite Ourse

**direct** [dɪ·'rekt] **I.** *vt* ① (*control: company*) diriger; (*traffic*) régler ② (*command*) ordonner; **to ~ sb to do sth** donner à qn de faire qc; **as ~ed** selon les instructions ③ (*aim in a direction*) diriger; **to ~ sb/sth to sb/sth** diriger qn/qc vers qn/qc ④ (*address*) adresser; **to ~ a remark toward sb** faire une remarque à l'intention de qn ⑤ CINE réaliser ⑥ THEAT mettre en scène ⑦ MUS diriger **II.** *vi* ① THEAT faire de la mise en scène ② CINE faire de la réalisation **III.** *adj* ① direct(e); (*danger, cause*) immédiat(e); (*refusal*) catégorique; **in ~ sunlight** en plein soleil; **the ~ opposite of sth** tout le contraire de qc

**❷** (*frank*) direct(e); (*person*) franc(he); (*refusal*) net(te) **❸** (*without intermediary*) direct(e) **IV.** *adv* directement; (*broadcast*) en direct

**direct debit** *n* prélèvement *m* automatique

**direction** [dɪ·ˈrek·ʃⁿn] *n* **❶** (*supervision*) direction *f*; **under the ~ of** sous la direction de **❷** CINE, THEAT mise *f* en scène **❸** (*course*) orientation *f* **❹** (*where sb is going to or from*) direction *f* **❺** (*tendency*) sens *m* **❻** *pl* **~s** instructions *fpl*

**directly** *adv* **❶** (*straight, without anyone intervening*) directement **❷** (*exactly*) diamétralement **❸** (*frankly*) franchement **❹** (*immediately*) immédiatement **❺** (*shortly*) tout de suite

**director** *n* **❶** ECON (*manager*) directeur, -trice *m, f* **❷** CINE, THEAT metteur *m* en scène **❸** (*board member*) administrateur, -trice *m, f*; **board of ~s** conseil *m* d'administration

**directory** [dɪ·ˈrek·tⁿr·i] *n* **❶** (*book*) annuaire *m*; **address ~** répertoire *m* d'adresses **❷** COMPUT répertoire *m*

**directory assistance** *n* (service *m* des) renseignements *mpl*

**dirt** [dɜrt] *n* **❶** (*unclean substance*) saleté *f* **❷** (*earth*) terre *f* **❸** (*scandal*) ragots *mpl* **❹** (*bad language*) obscénité *f* ▸ **to eat ~** ramper; **to treat sb like ~** traiter qn comme un chien

**dirty** [ˈdɜr·ti] **I.** <-ier, -iest> *adj* **❶** (*unclean*) sale **❷** (*causing to be dirty*) salissant(e); **to do the ~ work** *fig* faire le sale boulot **❸** (*mean*) sale; **~ tricks campaign** campagne *f* pleine de coups bas **❹** (*lewd: movie, book*) cochon(ne); (*look*) noir(e); (*old man*) lubrique; **~ words** obscénités *fpl*; **~ talk** grossièretés *fpl* **❺** (*not pure: color*) sale; **~ gray color** couleur *f* grisâtre **II.** *adv* *inf* **to play ~** donner des coups bas; **to talk ~** dire des gros mots; (*make explicit comments*) dire des cochonneries **III.** *vt* salir **IV.** *vi* se salir

**disability** [ˌdɪs·ə·ˈbɪl·ə·ti] *n* **❶** (*incapacity*) handicap *m* **❷** (*condition of incapacity*) incapacité *f*

**disable** [dɪ·ˈseɪ·bl̩] *vt* **❶** (*make incapable of functioning*) mettre hors service **❷** MED rendre infirme

**disabled I.** *adj* handicapé(e) **II.** *npl* **the ~** les handicapés *mpl*

**disadvantage** [ˌdɪs·əd·ˈvæn·tɪdʒ] **I.** *n* inconvénient *m*; **social/educational ~** handicap *m* social/scolaire; **to be at a ~** être dans une position désavantageuse; **to be put at a ~** être désavantagé **II.** *vt* désavantager

**disagree** [ˌdɪs·ə·ˈgri] *vi* **❶** (*argue*) ne pas être d'accord **❷** (*argue*) être en désaccord **❸** (*be different*) ne pas concorder **❹** (*have bad effect*) ne pas réussir

**disagreeable** *adj* désagréable

**disagreement** *n* **❶** (*lack of agreement*) désaccord *m* **❷** (*argument*) différend *m*; **~ over sth** dispute *f* à propos de qc **❸** (*discrepancy*) divergence *f*

**disappear** [ˌdɪs·ə·ˈpɪr] *vi* **❶** (*vanish*) disparaître; **to ~ from sight** être perdu de vue **❷** (*become extinct*) disparaître; **to have all but ~ed** *fig* avoir quasiment disparu

**disappearance** *n* disparition *f*

**disappoint** [ˌdɪs·ə·ˈpɔɪnt] *vt* décevoir

**disappointed** *adj* déçu(e); **to be ~ in sb/sth** être déçu par qn /qc

**disappointing** *adj* décevant(e)

**disappointment** *n* **❶** (*dissatisfaction*) déception *f* **❷** (*sth or sb that disappoints*) **to be a ~ to sb** décevoir qn

**disapprove** [ˌdɪs·ə·ˈpruv] *vi* ne pas être d'accord; **to ~ of sth** désapprouver qc

**disarray** [ˌdɪs·ə·ˈreɪ] *n* **❶** (*disorder*) désordre *m* **❷** (*confusion*) confusion *f*; **in a state of ~** en plein désarroi

**disaster** [dɪ·ˈzæs·tər] *n* **❶** (*huge misfortune*) désastre *m*; **~ area** région *f* sinistrée; **natural/global ~** catastrophe *f* naturelle/mondiale; **to avert ~** prévenir les catastrophes **❷** (*failure*) désastre *m*; **to spell ~ for sth** signifier le désastre pour qn

**disastrous** [dɪ·ˈzæs·trəs] *adj* **❶** (*causing disaster*) désastreux(-euse) **❷** (*very unsuccessful*) catastrophique

D

**D**

**disbelief** [,dɪs·bɪ·'lif] *n* incrédulité *f*

**disc** [dɪsk] *n a.* MED disque *m*

**discard** ['dɪ·skard, *vb:* dɪ·'skard] **I.** *n* GAMES défausse *f* **II.** *vt* ❶ (*reject*) se débarrasser de ❷ (*reject card*) écarter **III.** *vi* GAMES se défausser

**disciple** [dɪ·'saɪ·pl] *n* disciple *mf*

**discipline** ['dɪs·ə·plɪn] **I.** *n* discipline *f* **II.** *vt* ❶ (*control*) discipliner ❷ (*punish*) to ~ sb for sth punir qn pour qc

**disc jockey** *n* disc-jockey *m*

**disclaimer** [dɪs·'kleɪ·mər] *n* clause *f* de non-responsabilité; INET disclaimer *m*

**disclose** [dɪs·'klouz] *vt* ❶ (*make public*) divulguer; to ~ that ... révéler que ... ❷ (*uncover*) montrer

**disco** ['dɪs·kou] **I.** *n* ❶ (*place*) discothèque *f* ❷ (*music*) musique *f* disco **II.** *vi* danser le disco

**discomfort** [dɪs·'kʌm(p)·fərt] *n* ❶ (*slight pain*) gêne *f* ❷ (*uneasiness*) malaise *m;* ~ at sth sentiment *m* de malaise face à qc ❸ (*inconvenience*) inconfort *m*

**disconnect** [,dɪs·kə·'nekt] *vt* ❶ (*put out of action: electricity, gas, telephone*) couper ❷ (*break connection of*) débrancher ❸ COMPUT *a. fig* déconnecter ❹ (*separate*) détacher

**disconnected** *adj* ❶ (*cut off*) déconnecté(e); (*from reality*) coupé(e) ❷ (*incoherent*) décousu(e)

**discontinue** [,dɪs·kən·'tɪn·ju] *vt form* ❶ (*cease*) cesser ❷ (*stop making*) interrompre

**discount** ['dɪs·kaʊnt, *vb:* dɪ·'skaʊnt] **I.** *n* remise *f;* to give (sb) a ~ on sth faire une remise (à qn) sur qc; at a ~ à prix réduit **II.** *vt* ❶ (*disregard*) ne pas tenir compte de; (*possibility*) écarter ❷ (*reduce: price*) faire baisser

**discourage** [dɪ·'skɜr·ɪdʒ] *vt* ❶ (*dishearten*) décourager ❷ (*dissuade*) dissuader; to ~ sb from doing sth dissuader qn de faire qc ❸ (*oppose*) déconseiller

**discouraging** *adj* décourageant(e)

**discover** [dɪ·'skʌv·ər] *vt* découvrir; to ~ sb doing sth attraper qn en train de faire qc

**discoverer** *n* découvreur, -euse *m, f*

**discovery** [dɪ·'skʌv·ºr·i] <-ries> *n* découverte *f*

**discreet** [dɪ·'skrit] *adj* discret(-ète)

**discrepancy** [dɪ·'skrep·ºn(t)·si] <-cies> *n form* divergence *f*

**discretion** [dɪ·'skreʃ·ºn] *n* ❶ (*tact*) discrétion *f;* to be the (very) soul of ~ être la discrétion même ❷ (*good judgment*) jugement *m;* the age of ~ LAW l'âge *m* de raison ❸ (*freedom to do sth*) discrétion *f;* at sb's ~ à la discrétion de qn; to leave sth to sb's ~ laisser qc à la discrétion de qn ► ~ is the better part of **valor** *prov* prudence est mère de sûreté *prov*

**discriminate** [dɪ·'skrɪm·ɪ·neɪt] **I.** *vi* ❶ (*see a difference*) distinguer; to ~ between sth and sth faire la distinction entre qc et qc ❷ (*make judgment*) faire de la discrimination; to ~ against sb faire de la discrimination envers qn; to ~ in favor of sb favoriser qn; to be sexually ~d against être victime de discrimination sexuelle **II.** *vt* distinguer

**discriminating** *adj form* (*discerning: person*) averti(e); (*palate, taste*) fin(e)

**discrimination** [dɪ·,skrɪm·ɪ·'neɪ·ʃºn] *n* ❶ (*unfair treatment*) discrimination *f* ❷ (*discernment*) discernement *m*

**discus** ['dɪs·kəs] *n* ❶ (*object which is thrown*) disque *m* ❷ (*event or sport*) the ~ le lancer du disque

**discuss** [dɪ·'skʌs] *vt* discuter de; to ~ how ... discuter comment ...; to ~ doing sth parler de faire qc

**discussion** *n* discussion *f;* ~ group groupe *m* de discussion; to be under ~ être discuté; to hold a ~ tenir une discussion

**disease** [dɪ·'ziz] *n a. fig* maladie *f*

**diseased** *adj a. fig* malade

**disembark** [,dɪs·ɪm·'bark] *vi* débarquer

**disgrace** [dɪs·'greɪs] **I.** *n* ❶ (*loss of honor*) disgrâce *f;* to bring ~ on [*o* upon] sb déshonorer qn ❷ (*shameful thing or person*) honte *f* **II.** *vt* déshonorer

**disgraceful** *adj* honteux(-euse);

(*conduct*) scandaleux(-euse); **it is ~ that** c'est une honte que +*subj*

**disgruntled** [dɪsˈɡrʌn·tld] *adj* mécontent(e)

**disguise** [dɪsˈɡaɪz] **I.** *n* déguisement *m;* **to be in ~** être déguisé **II.** *vt* ❶ (*change appearance*) déguiser; **to ~ oneself** se déguiser ❷ (*hide*) dissimuler

**disgust** [dɪsˈɡʌst] **I.** *n* ❶ (*revulsion*) dégoût *m; **much to sb's ~** au grand dégoût de qn; **to turn away from sth in ~** s'en aller dégoûté de qc ❷ (*indignation*) écœurement *m* **II.** *vt* ❶ (*sicken*) dégoûter ❷ (*revolt*) écœurer; **to be ~ed by sb/sth** être scandalisé par qn/qc; **to be ~ed with oneself** se dégoûter soi-même

**disgusted** *adj* dégoûté(e)

**disgusting** *adj* ❶ (*revolting*) dégoûtant(e) ❷ (*repulsive*) répugnant(e)

**dish** [dɪʃ] **I.** **<-es>** *n* ❶ (*plate*) assiette *f;* (*container*) plat *m;* **oven-proof ~** plat à four ❷ *pl* **the ~es** la vaisselle; **to do the ~es** faire la vaisselle ❸ (*food*) plat *m;* **sweet ~** dessert *m* ❹ (*equipment*) parabole *f;* **satellite ~** antenne *f* satellite **II.** *vt inf* démolir ▸ **to ~ the dirt on sb/sth** faire éclater un scandale sur qn/qc

  ◆ **dish out** *vt* ❶ (*hand out*) prodiguer ❷ (*serve*) servir ▸ **he was really able to dish it out to her** *sl* il a vraiment pu lui passer un savon

  ◆ **dish up** *vt inf* ❶ (*serve*) servir ❷ (*offer*) offrir

**dishcloth** [ˈdɪʃ·klaθ] *n* torchon *m* (à vaisselle)

**dishonest** [dɪˈsa·nɪst] *adj* malhonnête; **morally ~** de mauvaise foi

**dishwasher** *n* ❶ (*machine*) lave-vaisselle *m* ❷ (*person*) plongeur, -euse *m, f*

**disillusioned** *adj* désabusé(e); **to be ~ with sb/sth** perdre ses illusions sur qn/qc

**disintegrate** [dɪˈsɪn·tə·ɡreɪt] *vi a. fig* désintégrer; (*marriage*) dissoudre; (*into chaos*) dégénérer

**disjointed** [dɪsˈdʒɔɪn·tɪd] *adj* décousu(e)

**disk** [dɪsk] *n* COMPUT disque *m;* **hard ~** disque dur; **floppy ~** disquette *f*

**disk drive** *n* unité *f* de disque(tte)s; **hard ~** disque *m* dur; **floppy ~** lecteur *m* de disquettes

**diskette** [dɪsˈket] *n* disquette *f*

**dislike** [dɪˈslaɪk] **I.** *vt* ne pas aimer **II.** *n* ❶ (*aversion*) aversion *f;* **to take a ~ to sb/sth** avoir de l'antipathie pour qn/qc ❷ (*object of aversion*) grief *m*

**dislocate** [dɪˈsloʊ·keɪt] *vt* ❶ (*put out of place*) déplacer ❷ MED luxer ❸ (*disturb*) perturber

**dislodge** [dɪˈsladʒ] *vt* extraire

**dismal** [ˈdɪz·məl] *adj* ❶ (*depressing: outlook*) sinistre, (*expression*) lugubre ❷ *inf* (*awful: failure*) terrible; (*truth*) horrible; (*weather*) épouvantable

**dismiss** [dɪˈsmɪs] *vt* ❶ (*not consider*) déprécier; (*idea, thought*) dénigrer ❷ (*fire from work*) licencier; **to be ~ from one's job** être démis de ses fonctions ❸ (*send away*) congédier; **to ~ sth from sth** ôter qc de qc; **to ~ students after class** laisser partir les étudiants après le cours; **to ~ thoughts from one's mind** chasser des pensées de son esprit ❹ LAW (*appeal*) rejeter; (*court, indictment, charge*) récuser; **to ~ a** (**court**) **case** aboutir à un non-lieu

**dismissal** *n* ❶ (*disregarding*) dévalorisation *f* ❷ (*firing from a job*) licenciement *m;* (*removal from high position*) destitution *f* ❸ (*sending away*) renvoi *m*

**disobedience** [ˌdɪs·ə·ˈbi·di·ən(t)s] *n* désobéissance *f*

**disobedient** *adj* désobéissant(e)

**disobey** [ˌdɪs·ə·ˈbeɪ] **I.** *vt* désobéir à **II.** *vi* désobéir

**disorder** [dɪˈsɔr·dər] *n* ❶ (*lack of order*) désordre *m* ❷ (*disease*) troubles *mpl;* **kidney/mental ~** troubles rénaux/mentaux ❸ (*upheaval*) désordre *m;* **civil ~** révolte *f;* **public ~** émeute *f*

**disorderly** *adj* ❶ (*untidy*) en désordre ❷ (*unruly*) indiscipliné(e); (*conduct*) ivre et incohérent(e)

**D**

**disorganized** [dɪ'sɔːɾ·gə·naɪzd] *adj* désorganisé(e)

**dispenser** *n* distributeur *m*; **soap-/drink/cash** ~ distributeur de savon/de boissons/de billets

**displace** [dɪ'spleɪs] *vt* ① (*force from place*) déplacer ② (*take the place of*) remplacer; **to** ~ **sb as sth** supplanter qn en tant que qc ③ PHYS déplacer

**displaced person** *n* personne *f* déplacée

**display** [dɪ'spleɪ] I. *vt* ① (*arrange*) exposer; (*on a bulletin board*) afficher sur un panneau (d'affichage) ② (*show*) laisser paraître II. *n* ① (*arrangement of things*) étalage *m*; **on** ~ être en vitrine; **firework(s)** ~ feu *m* d'artifice ② (*demonstration*) exposition *f*; (*of affection, anger*) démonstration *f*; (*of love*) témoignage *m* ③ COMPUT écran *m*

**displease** [dɪ'spliːz] *vt* mécontenter; **to be** ~**d by sth** être contrarié par qc

**displeasure** [dɪ'pleʒ·ər] *n* mécontentement *m*; **much to sb's** ~ au grand déplaisir de qn

**disposable** [dɪ'spoʊ·zə·bl] I. *adj* ① (*not meant for recycling*) jetable; *a. fig* (*person*) remplaçable ② ECON (*assets, funds, income*) disponible II. *n pl* (*articles mpl*) jetables *mpl*

**disposal** *n* ① (*getting rid of*) enlèvement *m* ② (*availability*) **to be at sb's** ~ être à la disposition de qn ③ *inf* (*garbage disposal*) broyeur *m* d'ordures

**disprove** [dɪ'spruːv] *vt* réfuter

**disqualification** *n* ① (*process*) disqualification *f* ② (*instance*) exclusion *f* ③ LAW suspension *f*

**disqualify** [dɪ'skwɑ·lə·faɪ] <-ie-> *vt* ① (*debar*) rendre inapte; **to** ~ **sb from sth** rendre qn inapte à qc ② SPORTS, GAMES disqualifier

**disquieting** *adj form* troublant(e)

**disrespect** [ˌdɪs·rɪ·'spekt] *n* incorrection *f*; **to show** ~ manquer de respect; **to show sb** ~ faire preuve *f* d'insolence envers qn; **no** ~ **to sb but ...** malgré tout le respect que l'on doit à qn, ...

**disrespectful** *adj* irrespectueux(-euse); (*gesture*) insolent(e)

**disrupt** [dɪs·'rʌpt] *vt* ① (*interrupt and stop*) interrompre; (*career*) briser ② (*disturb*) perturber

**disruption** *n* ① (*interruption*) interruption *f* ② (*disturbance*) perturbation *f*

**disruptive** *adj* perturbateur(-trice)

**dissatisfaction** [ˌdɪs·sæt·əs·'fæk·ʃən] *n* mécontentement *m*; ~ **with sb/sth** mécontentement vis-à-vis de qn/qc

**dissatisfied** [dɪs·'sæt·əs·faɪd] *adj* mécontent(e); **to be** ~ **with sb/sth** être mécontent de qn/qc

**dissolve** [dɪ'zɑlv] I. *vt* ① (*make become part of a liquid*) (faire) dissoudre; (*melt*) faire fondre ② (*make disappear*) faire disparaître ③ (*break up*) désagréger; (*marriage*) dissoudre II. *vi* ① (*become part of a liquid*) se dissoudre; (*melt*) fondre ② (*disappear*) disparaître; (*tension*) se relâcher ③ (*break up*) **to** ~ **into giggles/laughter** être pris de ricanement/se tordre de rire; **to** ~ **into tears** fondre en larmes

**dissuade** [dɪ'sweɪd] *vt form* dissuader; **to** ~ **sb from doing sth** dissuader qn de faire qc

**distance** ['dɪs·t³n(t)s] I. *n* ① (*space*) *a. fig* distance *f*; **within a** ~ **of ...** dans un rayon de ...; **within walking-/driving** ~ on peut y aller à pied/en voiture ② (*space far away*) lointain *m*; **at a** ~ avec du recul; **in the** ~ au loin ▶ **to go the** ~ tenir la distance; *fig* aller (jusqu')au bout; **to keep one's** ~ garder ses distances; **to keep one's** ~ **from sb/sth** se tenir à distance de qn/qc II. *vt* distancer; **to** ~ **oneself from sb/sth** se distancer de qn/qc; *fig* prendre ses distances par rapport à qn/qc

**distant** ['dɪs·t³nt] *adj* ① (*far away*) éloigné(e); (*shore*) lointain(e); **in the not too** ~ **future** dans un proche avenir; **the dim and** ~ **past** les temps *mpl* anciens; **at some** ~ **point in the future** à (long/court) terme ② (*not closely related: relative*) éloigné(e) ③ (*faint:*

*memory*) lointain(e) ❹ (*aloof: person*) distant(e)

**distaste** [dɪˈsteɪst] *n* répugnance *f;* ~ **for sth** aversion *f* pour qc; **to sb's** ~ au dégoût de qn

**distasteful** *adj* répugnant(e); (*topic*) déplaisant(e)

**distil** <-ll->, **distill** [dɪˈstɪl] *vt a. fig* distiller

**distillery** *n* distillerie *f*

**distinct** [dɪˈstɪŋ(k)t] *adj* ❶ (*obviously different*) distinct(e); **to be ~ from sth** être distinct de qc; **as ~ from sth** par opposition à qc ❷ (*likely: possibility*) réel(le) ❸ (*clear: advantage*) net(te)

**distinctive** *adj* ❶ (*distinguishing: feature*) distinctif(-ive) ❷ (*special: taste*) caractéristique ❸ (*clear*) distinct(e)

**distinguish** [dɪˈstɪŋgwɪʃ] **I.** *vt* distinguer; **to ~ sb/sth from sb/sth** distinguer qn/qc de qn/qc; **to ~ oneself in sth** se distinguer en qc **II.** *vi* faire la distinction

**distinguished** *adj* ❶ (*celebrated*) éminent(e) ❷ (*stylish*) distingué(e)

**distort** [dɪˈstɔrt] *vt* dénaturer; (*facts, truth*) altérer; (*history*) travestir

**distract** [dɪˈstrækt] *vt* distraire; (*attention*) détourner

**distracted** *adj* distrait(e)

**distress** [dɪˈstres] **I.** *n* ❶ (*state of danger*) détresse *f;* **in ~** en détresse ❷ (*suffering*) souffrance *f* ❸ (*sorrow*) affliction *f;* **to be a ~ to sb** être un fardeau pour qn **II.** *vt* ❶ (*upset*) faire de la peine à; **to ~ oneself** s'inquiéter; **to be deeply ~ed** être profondément affligé ❷ (*make look old: jeans*) user

**distressed** *adj* ❶ (*unhappy*) affligé(e) ❷ (*in difficulties*) en détresse ❸ (*made to look old: jeans*) usé(e)

**distribute** [dɪˈstrɪbˌjut] *vt* ❶ (*share*) distribuer; **to ~ sth fairly** partager qc équitablement ❷ (*spread over space*) répartir; **to ~ sth evenly** étaler uniformément; **to be widely ~d** être largement répandu ❸ ECON (*goods, films*) distribuer

**distribution** *n* ❶ (*sharing*) distribu-

tion *f* ❷ (*spreading*) diffusion *f;* (*of resources*) répartition *f;* **equitable ~** partage *m* équitable ❸ ECON (*of goods, movies*) distribution *f*

**distributor** [dɪˈstrɪbˌjəˌtər] *n* ❶ (*person*) distributeur *m;* (*for cars*) concessionnaire *m* ❷ (*device*) distributeur *m;* AUTO delco *m*

**district** [ˈdɪstrɪkt] *n* ❶ (*defined area: in city*) quartier *m;* (*in country*) région *f* ❷ (*administrative sector*) district *m*

**district attorney** *n* ≈ procureur *m* de la République

**District of Columbia** *n* Washington *m*

**distrust** [dɪsˈtrʌst] **I.** *vt* se méfier de **II.** *n* méfiance *f*

**distrustful** *adj* méfiant(e); **to be deeply ~ of sth** être très méfiant envers qc

**disturb** [dɪsˈtɜrb] *vt* ❶ (*bother*) déranger ❷ (*worry*) ennuyer; **to be ~ed that …** être ennuyé que +*subj;* **to be ~ed to** +*infin* être agacé de +*infin* ❸ (*move around*) déranger; (*water*) troubler ▶ **to ~ the peace** troubler l'ordre *m* public

**disturbance** [dɪsˈtɜrbˌbən(t)s] *n* ❶ (*nuisance*) dérangement *m;* **to be a ~** être le désordre ❷ (*public incident*) troubles *mpl;* **to cause a ~** troubler l'ordre public ❸ METEO perturbation *f*

**disturbed** *adj* ❶ (*worried*) inquiet(-ète) ❷ PSYCH perturbé(e)

**disturbing** *adj* (*news*) inquiétant(e); (*film*) choquant(e); **to be ~ to sb** être gênant pour qn; **it is ~ that** c'est pénible que +*subj*

**disused** *adj* non utilisé(e)

**ditch** [dɪtʃ] **I.** <-es> *n* fossé *m* **II.** *vt* ❶ *sl* (*discard, abandon: stolen car*) abandonner; (*proposal, job*) laisser tomber; (*stop dating*) laisser tomber; (*boy friend*) plaquer ❷ *sl* (*skip: class, school*) sécher ❸ (*land on the sea*) **to ~ a plane** faire un amerrissage forcé **III.** *vi* ❶ (*land on the sea*) faire un amerrissage forcé ❷ (*dig*) creuser un fossé

**ditto** [ˈdɪtˌoʊ] *adv* idem; **~ for me** idem pour moi

**dive** [daɪv] **I.** *n* ❶ (*plunge*) *a. fig* plon-

**D**

geon *m* ❷ AVIAT piqué *m* ❸ *sl* (*run-down establishment*) boui-boui *m* ❹ SPORTS **to take a ~** simuler une chute II. *vi* <dived *o* dove, dived> ❶ (*plunge*) *a. fig* plonger; **stocks ~d by 25% to ...** les actions *fpl* ont plongé de 25 % et sont maintenant à ... ❷ (*in air: plane*) descendre en piqué ❸ (*lunge*) **to ~ for sth** se ruer vers qc; **to ~ for cover** plonger à l'abri

**diver** *n* (*person who dives*) plongeur, -euse *m, f*

**diverse** [dɪˈvɜrs] *adj* ❶ (*varied*) divers(e) ❷ (*not alike*) différent(e)

**diversify** [dɪˈvɜr·sɪ·faɪ] <-ie-> I. *vt* diversifier II. *vi* se diversifier

**diversion** [dɪˈvɜr·ʃən] *n* ❶ (*changing of direction*) déviation *f* ❷ (*distraction*) diversion *f* ❸ (*entertainment*) distraction *f*

**divert** [dɪˈvɜrt] *vt* ❶ (*change the direction of*) dévier ❷ (*distract: attention*) détourner ❸ (*entertain*) divertir

**divide** [dɪˈvaɪd] I. *vt* ❶ (*split*) *a. fig* (*cell, group*) diviser ❷ (*share: food, work, time*) partager; **to ~ sth among/with...** partager qc entre/avec... ❸ (*separate: mountain, wall*) séparer ❹ MATH **to ~ six by two** diviser six par deux II. *vi* ❶ (*split*) *a. fig* se diviser; (*road*) bifurquer; (*group*) se séparer; **to ~ into sth** se diviser en qc; **our paths ~d** nos routes *fpl* se sont séparées ❷ MATH **10 ~d by 2** 10 divisé par 2 ▶ **~ and conquer** POL diviser pour régner III. *n* ❶ (*gulf*) gouffre *m* ❷ (*watershed*) ligne *f* de partage des eaux; **the Great Divide** la ligne de partage des Rocheuses

◆**divide up** *vt* partager

**divided** *adj* ❶ (*undecided*) partagé(e) ❷ (*in disagreement*) divisé(e)

**dividend** [ˈdɪv·ɪ·dend] *n* ❶ ECON, MATH dividende *m* ❷ *fig* **your hard work will eventually pay ~s** ton travail finira par payer [*o* porter ses fruits]

**diving** *n* ❶ (*jumping*) plongeon *m* ❷ (*swimming*) **deep-sea ~** plongée *f* sous-marine

**diving board** *n* plongeoir *m*

**division** [dɪˈvɪʒ·ən] *n* ❶ (*splitting up*) partage *m* ❷ (*disagreement*) division *f* ❸ (*border*) ligne *f* de séparation ❹ ECON, MATH, MIL, SPORTS division *f*

**divorce** [dɪˈvɔrs] I. *n* divorce *m* II. *vt* divorcer; **to get ~d from sb** divorcer de qn III. *vi* divorcer

**divorcé** *n* homme *m* divorcé

**divorced** *adj* divorcé(e)

**divorcée** *n* femme *f* divorcée

**divulge** [dɪˈvʌldʒ] *vt* divulguer

**DIY** [ˌdi·aɪˈwaɪ] *n abbr of* **do-it-your-self** bricolage *m*

**dizzy** [ˈdɪz·i] <-ier, -iest> *adj* ❶ (*having a spinning sensation*) pris(e) de vertiges ❷ (*causing a spinning sensation*) vertigineux(-euse)

**dizzying** *adj* (*progress, speeds, heights*) vertigineux(-euse)

**DNA** [ˌdi·en·ˈeɪ] *n abbr of* **deoxyribonucleic acid** ADN *m*

**do**[1] [du] I. <does, did, done> *aux* ❶ (*word used to form questions*) **you have a dog?** avez-vous un chien ? ❷ (*to form negatives*) **Freddy doesn't like olives** Freddy n'aime pas les olives ❸ (*to form negative imperatives*) **don't go!** n'y va pas ! ❹ (*for emphasis*) **I ~ like her** je l'aime vraiment bien; **~ you (now)?** ah, oui, vraiment?!; **~ come to our party!** venez à notre fête, vraiment!; **so you ~ like beer after all** finalement, tu aimes la bière ❺ (*to replace a repeated verb*) **she runs faster than he does** elle court plus vite que lui; **so ~ I** moi aussi; **"I don't smoke." "neither ~ I."** "je ne fume pas." "moi non plus."; **"may I?" "please ~!"** *form* "Puis-je?" "je vous en prie, faites!" ❻ (*in tag questions and replies*) **I saw him yesterday – did you?** je l'ai vu hier – vraiment?; **you like beef, don't you?** tu aimes le bœuf, n'est-ce pas?; **who did that? – I did** qui a fait ça? – moi; **should I come? – no, don't** dois-je venir? – non, surtout pas II. <does, did, done> *vt* ❶ (*carry out*) faire; **to ~ sth again** refaire qc; **to ~ justice to**

**sb/sth** être juste envers qn/qc; **this photo doesn't ~ her justice** cette photo ne l'avantage pas; **what ~ you ~ for a living?** qu'est-ce que tu fais comme travail?; **to ~ everything possible** faire tout son possible; **what is he ~ing …?** que fait-il?; **this just can't be done!** ça ne se fait pas, c'est tout!; **what can I ~ for you?** que puis-je (faire) pour vous?; **to ~ nothing but …** ne faire que …; **don't just stand there, ~ something!** ne reste pas planté là, réagis! ❷ (*undertake*) **what am I supposed to ~ with you/this cake?** qu'est-ce que je suis supposé faire de toi/de ce gâteau? ❸ (*place somewhere*) **what have you done with my coat?** qu'est-ce que tu as fait de mon manteau? ❹ (*adjust*) **can you ~ something with my car?** est-ce que tu peux/vous pouvez faire qc pour ma voiture? ❺ (*help*) **can you ~ anything for my back?** pouvez-vous faire qc pour mon dos?; **this medication does nothing** ce médicament ne fait aucun effet ❻ (*act*) **to ~ sb well** bien agir envers qn ❼ (*deal with*) **if you ~ the dishes, I'll ~ the drying** si tu laves la vaisselle, je l'essuie ❽ (*solve: equation*) calculer; (*crossword puzzle*) faire ❾ (*make neat*) **to ~ the dishes** faire la vaisselle; **to ~ one's nails** faire les ongles; **to get one's hair done** se faire coiffer ❿ (*go at a speed of*) **to ~ … miles/per hour** faire du … miles à l'heure ⓫ (*cover a distance*) **to ~ San Francisco to Boston in four days** faire San Francisco Boston en quatre jours ⓬ (*be satisfactory*) **"I only have bread – will that ~ you?"** "Je n'ai que du pain – ça te va ?" ⓭ (*cook*) faire cuire ⓮ (*cause*) **will you ~ me a favor?** tu veux me faire plaisir ?; **to ~ sb good/harm** faire du bien/du mal à qn; **to ~ the honor of ~ing sth** *form* faire l'honneur de faire qc ⓯ *inf* (*swindle*) arnaquer; **to ~ sb out of sth** escroquer qn de qc ⓰ *inf* (*serve prison time*) **to ~ one's time** faire son temps ▸ **to ~ a number on sb**

*sl* jouer un sale tour à qn; **~ unto** others **as you would have them do unto you** *prov* ne faites pas à autrui ce que vous ne voudriez pas qu'on vous fît; **to ~ it** with **sb** *inf* coucher avec qn III. <does, did, done> *vi* ❶ (*act*) faire; **you did right** tu as bien fait; **~ as you like** fais comme tu veux ❷ (*be satisfactory*) convenir; **that book will ~** ce livre fera l'affaire; **the money will ~** l'argent suffira; **thank you, that will ~** merci, ça me suffit; **this really won't ~!** cela ne peut pas continuer ainsi! ❸ (*manage*) **to ~ well** (*person*) bien s'en tirer; (*business*) bien marcher; **how are you ~ing?** bonjour, ça va ?; **to be ~ing well** bien aller; **you did well to come** tu as bien fait de venir ❹ (*finish with*) **to be done with sb/sth** en avoir terminé [*o* fini] avec qn/qc ❺ *inf* (*going on*) **there's something ~ing in town** il y a de l'activité en ville ▸ **~ or** die **marche ou crève** IV. *n inf* (*party*) fête *f* ▸ **the ~s** and **don'ts** ce qu'il faut faire et ce qu'il ne faut pas faire

◆**do away with** *vt inf* ❶ (*dispose of*) se débarrasser de ❷ (*kill*) liquider

◆**do in** *vt always sep* ❶ *inf* (*kill*) liquider; **to do oneself in** se foutre en l'air ❷ (*make exhausted*) **to be done in** être crevé

◆**do over** *vt* ❶ *inf* (*redo*) refaire ❷ *inf* (*redecorate*) refaire

◆**do up** *vt* ❶ (*dress in an impressive way*) **to be done up** être sur son trente et un; **to do oneself up** se faire beau(belle) ❷ (*wrap*) emballer ❸ (*fasten: buttons*) **to ~ sb's buttons** boutonner qn, fermer; (*zipper*) remonter; (*laces*) nouer; (*hair, shoes*) attacher ❹ (*restore: house*) retaper; (*room*) refaire

◆**do with** *vt* ❶ (*be related to*) **to have to ~ sb** avoir à faire avec qn; **to have to ~ sth** avoir à voir avec qc; **this book has to ~ human behavior** ce livre parle du comportement humain ❷ (*bear*) supporter ❸ *inf* (*need*) **I could ~ a vacation** j'aurais besoin de vacances;

**I could ~ some sleep** un bon somme me ferait du bien ❹ (*finish*) **to be done with** être fini; **to be done with sth** en avoir fini avec qc; **are you done with the book?** as-tu encore besoin du livre?
◆ **do without** *vt* se passer de

**do²** [du] *n sl* coupe *f* (de cheveux)

**do³** [doʊ] *n* MUS do *m*

**DOA** [,di·oʊ·'eɪ] *adj abbr of* **dead on arrival** décédé(e) en cours de transfert à l'hôpital

**dock¹** [dak] **I.** *n* ❶ (*wharf*) dock *m* ❷ (*for receiving ship*) bassin *m;* **dry ~** cale *f* sèche; **in ~** en réparation ❸ (*pier*) jetée *f* **II.** *vi* se mettre à quai; **the ship is ~ing** le bateau arrive à quai **III.** *vt* ❶ NAUT amarrer ❷ AVIAT arrimer

**dock²** [dak] *vt* ❶ (*reduce*) diminuer; **the company ~ed me 15% of my salary** la société a fait une retenue de 15 % sur mon salaire ❷ (*cut off the tail of*) écourter la queue de

**doctor** ['dak·tər] **I.** *n* ❶ (*physician*) médecin *m;* **to go to the ~** aller chez le médecin ❷ (*person with a doctorate*) docteur *mf;* **Doctor of Jurisprudence** docteur en droit; **~'s degree** doctorat *m* ▶ **to be just what the ~ ordered** *iron* c'est justement ce qu'il fallait; **this hot bath is just what the ~ ordered** ce bain chaud, c'est exactement ce dont j'avais besoin **II.** *vt pej* ❶ (*illegally alter: document*) falsifier ❷ (*poison*) frelater ❸ (*to repair*) rafistoler

**doctorate** *n* doctorat *m*

**document** ['da·kjə·mənt] **I.** *n* document *m;* **travel ~s** papiers *mpl* **II.** *vt* **to ~ a file** rassembler de la documentation pour un dossier

**documentary** [,da·kjə·'men·tər·i] **I.** <-ries> *n* documentaire *m* **II.** *adj* ❶ (*factual*) documenté(e) ❷ (*contained in documents: evidence*) écrit(e)

**documentation** *n* ❶ (*evidence*) document *m* ❷ (*information*) documentation *f*

**dodge** [dadʒ] **I.** *vt* esquiver; (*question*) éluder; (*responsibility*) fuir; (*person*) éviter; (*pursuer*) échapper à **II.** *vi*

❶ (*move quickly*) se défiler ❷ SPORTS esquiver **III.** *n* ❶ *inf* (*trick*) combine *f;* **tax ~** magouille *f* fiscale ❷ (*quick movement*) esquive *f*

**does** [dʌz] *3rd pers sing of* **do**

**doesn't** *s.* **does not** *s.* **do**

**dog** [dɔg] **I.** *n* ❶ (*animal*) chien *m;* **hunting/pet ~** chien de chasse/compagnie; **police ~** chien policier ❷ *inf* (*person*) **lucky ~** veinard *m* ❸ *pej* (*ugly female*) cageot *m;* (*nasty male*) rosse *f;* **the** (**dirty**) **~!** quelle peau de vache! ▶ **every ~ has its day** *prov* à chacun son heure; **~ eat ~** *prov* les loups ne se font pas de cadeaux; **to go to the ~s** mal tourner; **to live a ~'s life** mener une vie de chien; **let sleeping ~s lie** *prov* il ne faut pas réveiller l'eau qui dort **II.** <-gg-> *vt* ❶ (*hound*) suivre à la trace; **to ~ sb with questions** harceler qn de questions ❷ (*trail*) **the police ~ged the murderer** la police filait l'assassin

**dog collar** *n* ❶ (*a collar around a dog's neck*) collier *m* ❷ *inf* (*clerical collar*) col *m* de prêtre

**doing** *n* action *f;* **to be (of) sb's ~** être l'œuvre de qn; **is this your ~?** c'est toi qui as fait ça?

**do-it-yourself** *adj* de bricolage; **~ home improvement** rénovation *f* immobilière faite par soi-même

**dole** [doʊl] *vt* **to ~ sth out** distribuer qc

**doll** [dal] *n* ❶ (*toy*) poupée *f* ❷ *inf* (*darling*) petite chérie *f*

**dollar** ['da·lər] *n* dollar *m*, piastre *f Québec*

**dolphin** ['dal·fɪn] *n* dauphin *m*

**dome** [doʊm] *n* ❶ ARCHIT dôme *m* ❷ *sl* (*head*) caboche *f;* (*bald head*) crâne *m* d'œuf

**domestic** [də·'mes·tɪk] **I.** *adj* ❶ (*household: appliances, commitments*) ménager(-ère); (*situation, life, bliss*) familial(e); (*violence, dispute*) conjugal(e); (*fuel*) domestique; **~ worker** employé(e) *m(f)* de maison; **to do ~ work** faire des ménages ❷ (*domesticated: animal*) domestique ❸ ECON, FIN (*not for-*

*eign: market, flight, affairs, trade*) intérieur(e); (*products, economy, currency*) national(e); (*crisis, issue*) de politique intérieure; **gross ~ product** produit *m* national brut. *n* domestique *mf*

**domesticated** *adj* casanier(-ère)

**dominance** ['dɑ·mə·nən(t)s] *n a.* MIL suprématie *f*

**dominate** ['dɑ·mə·neɪt] I. *vt* dominer II. *vi* dominer; (*issue, question*) prédominer

**Dominican Republic** *n* République *f* dominicaine

**donate** ['doʊ·neɪt] I. *vt* donner; (*money*) faire un don de II. *vi* ECON, FIN faire un don

**donation** *n* don *m*

**done** *pp of* do

**donkey** ['dɑŋ·ki] *n* âne *m*

**donor** ['doʊ·nər] *n* donateur, -trice *m, f*; **blood/organ ~** donneur, -euse *m, f* de sang/d'organes

**don't = do not** *s.* do

**donut** ['doʊ·nʌt] *n* beignet *m*, beigne *m Québec*

**doodle** ['du·dl] I. *vi* gribouiller II. *n* gribouillage *m*

**door** [dɔr] *n* ❶ (*movable barrier*) porte *f*; **front ~** porte d'entrée; **sliding/ swing ~** porte coulissante/battante; **revolving ~** porte à tambour ❷ (*doorway*) entrée *f*; **the third ~ on the left** la troisième porte à gauche ▶ **to be knocking on the ~** ne pas être loin du but; **to leave the ~ open to sth** laisser la porte ouverte à qc; **to show sb the ~** *inf* mettre qn à la porte

**doorbell** *n* sonnette *f* de porte

**doorman** <-men> *n* portier *m*

**doormat** *n a. pej* paillasson *m*

**doorstep** *n* pas *m* de porte

**doorway** *n* entrée *f*

**dormant** ['dɔr·mənt] *adj* ❶ (*inactive: volcano*) endormi(e) ❷ BOT, BIO (*not growing*) dormant(e)

**dormitory** ['dɔr·mə·tɔri] <-ries> *n* ❶ (*sleeping quarters*) dortoir *m* ❷ (*for students*) foyer *m* d'étudiants

**dosage** ['doʊ·sɪdʒ] *n* dosage *m*

**dose** [doʊs] I. *n* ❶ (*portion*) dose *f* ❷ *fig* **in small ~s** à petites doses II. *vt* MED traiter

**dot** [dɑt] I. *n a.* TYP point *m;* **at six o'clock on the ~** à six heures précises [*o* pile] II.<-tt-> *vt* ❶ (*mark with a dot*) pointer ❷ (*cover*) parsemer; **to ~ the landscape** être disséminé dans le paysage ▶ **to ~ your i's and cross your i's** mettre les points sur les i

**double** ['dʌb·l] I. *adj* double II. *adv* ❶ (*twice*) deux fois ❷ (*in two*) **to start seeing ~** commencer à voir (en) double; (*to fold, bend*) en deux III. *vt* ❶ (*make twice as much/many*) doubler ❷ (*fold in two*) plier IV. *vi* ❶ (*become twice as much/many*) doubler ❷ (*serve a second purpose*) *a.* THEAT **to ~ as sb/ sth** doubler qn/qc V. *n pl* SPORTS double *m;* **men's/women's/mixed ~s** messieurs/dames/mixte ▶ **or nothing** GAMES quitte ou double; **on the ~** au pas de course

◆**double back** *vi* faire demi-tour

◆**double up** *vi* ❶ (*bend over*) se plier en deux; **to ~ with laughter/pain** être plié de rire/de douleur ❷ (*share room*) partager la même chambre

**double-barreled** *adj* ❶ (*two barrels: shotgun*) à deux canons ❷ (*two purposes*) à double usage

**double bass** <-es> *n* contrebasse *f*

**double bed** *n* lit *m* à deux places

**double-check** *vt* revérifier; **to ~ that ...** bien s'assurer que ...; (*verify in two ways*) vérifier deux fois que ...

**double-cross** I. *vt* doubler II.<-es> *n* double jeu *m*

**double-decker** *n* autobus *m* à impériale

**double dribble** *n* SPORTS reprise *f* de dribble

**double dutch** *n* GAMES *jeu de saut à la corde*

**double feature** *n* programme constitué de deux films principaux

**double-park** I. *vi* se garer en double file II. *vt* garer en double file

**doubles** *npl* SPORTS double *m*

**doubt** [daʊt] I. *n* doute *m;* **to be in ~**

**D**

avoir des doutes; **to cast ~ on sb/sth** mettre qn/qc en doute; **not a shadow of (a) ~** pas l'ombre *f* d'un doute; **no ~** incontestablement; **to have one's ~s about sth** avoir ses doutes quant à qc **II.** *vt* douter de; **to ~ whether** douter que +*subj*

**doubtful** *adj* douteux(-euse); **to be ~ whether** être douteux que +*subj;* **to be ~ about sth** avoir des doutes sur qc

**doubtless** *adv* ① (*without doubt*) sans aucun doute ② (*presumably*) sans doute

**dough** [doʊ] *n* ① CULIN (*mixture to be baked*) pâte *f* ② *sl* (*money*) t(h)une *f*

**doughnut** ['doʊ·nʌt] *n s.* **donut**

**dove**[1] [dʌv] **I.** *n* colombe *f* **II.** *adj* **~ gray** grisâtre

**dove**[2] [doʊv] *pt of* **dive**

**down**[1] [daʊn] **I.** *adv* ① (*with movement*) en bas, vers le bas; **to come** [*o* **go**] **~** descendre; **to fall ~** tomber; **to lie ~** s'allonger; **on the way ~ from Seattle** en venant de Seattle; **to go to Key West/the Gulf** descendre à Key West/sur le Golfe ② (*less intensity*) **prices are ~** les prix *mpl* ont baissé; **to be ~ 12%** être en baisse de 12 %; **the wind died ~** le vent s'apaisa ③ (*position*) en bas; **~ there/here** là-bas/ici; **further ~** plus bas; **~ South** dans le Sud ④ (*temporal*) **~ to here** jusqu'ici; **~ through the ages** de tout temps; **~ to recent times** jusqu'à présent; **from grandfather ~ to granddaughter** du grand-père à la petite-fille ⑤ (*in writing*) **to write/get sth ~** coucher qc par écrit ▶ **to** **come ~ with the flu** attraper la grippe; **to be ~ on one's luck** ne pas avoir de chance; **~ with sb/sth!** à bas qn/qc! **II.** *prep* **to go ~ the stairs** descendre l'escalier; **to fall ~ the stairs** dégringoler les escaliers; **to live ~ the street** habiter plus bas dans la rue; **to go/drive ~ the street** descendre la rue; **her hair reaches ~ her back** ses cheveux lui tombent dans le dos; **to come ~ (through) the centuries** être transmis au fil des siècles **III.** *adj* ① (*de-*

*pressed*) **to feel ~** être déprimé ② COM·PUT, TECH en panne **IV.** *n* (*in football*) **first/second ~** premier/second envoi *m* **V.** *vt* ① (*strike down: opponent*) terrasser ② (*drink quickly*) **to ~ a glass of sth** vider un verre de qc; (*eat quickly*) engloutir ③ (*in football*) **to ~ the ball** sortir la balle du jeu

**down**[2] [daʊn] *n* duvet *m*

**downfall** *n* ① (*fall from power*) effondrement *m* ② (*cause of sb's fall*) ruine *f;* **sth is sb's ~** qc est la ruine de qn

**downhearted** *adj* abattu(e)

**downhill I.** *adv* (*toward the bottom of a hill*) en descendant **II.** *adj* descendant(e); **~ hike** descente *f*

**download** ['daʊn·loʊd] **I.** *vt* COMPUT télécharger (vers l'aval) **II.** *n* COMPUT téléchargement *m*

**down-market** *adj* bon marché

**down payment** *n* acompte *m*

**downpour** *n* averse *f*, drache *f* Belgique

**downright I.** *adj* (*utter*) pur(e); **it is a ~ disgrace** c'est vraiment une honte **II.** *adv* vraiment

**downsize I.** *vt* réduire **II.** *vi* réduire ses effectifs

**downstairs I.** *adv* en bas de l'escalier **II.** *adj* au rez-de-chaussée **III.** *n* rez-de-chaussée *m*

**downstream** *adv* dans le sens du courant

**down-to-earth** *adj* terre à terre *inv*

**downtown I.** *n no art* centre *m* **II.** *adv* dans/vers le centre ville **III.** *adj* du centre ville

**downward(s) I.** *adj* ① (*going down*) descendant(e) ② (*decreasing*) en baisse; **to be on a ~ trend** avoir une tendance à la baisse **II.** *adv* vers le bas; **everyone from management ~** tout le monde de la direction jusqu'au plus petit employé

**doz.** *n abbr of* **dozen** douzaine *f*

**doze** [doʊz] **I.** *vi* somnoler **II.** *n* (*short nap*) somme *m*

**dozen** ['dʌz·ᵊn] *n* (*twelve*) douzaine *f* ▶ **by the ~** à la pelle

**Dr.** *n abbr of* **Doctor** Dr *m*

**drab** [dræb] *adj* <drabber, drabbest> *pej* (*colors, existence*) grisâtre

**draft** [dræft] **I.** *n* ❶ (*air current*) courant *m* d'air ❷ (*preliminary version*) ébauche *f* ❸ MIL (*military conscription*) contingent *m* ❹ SPORTS (*player selection process*) sélection *f* ❺ FIN, ECON (*bank order*) lettre *f* de change ❻ CULIN pression *f*; **beer on ~** bière *f* à la pression ❼ NAUT (*water depth*) tirant *m* d'eau ❽ *form* (*gulp*) ingestion *f* de liquide **II.** *vt* ❶ MIL (*conscript*) recruter ❷ SPORTS (*select: player*) sélectionner ❸ (*prepare a preliminary version*) esquisser; (*plan*) ébaucher **III.** *adj* ❶ CULIN (*in a cask*) (à la) pression ❷ (*used for pulling: animal*) de trait

**draftswoman** <-women> *n* TECH ❶ TECH dessinatrice *f* technique ❷ ART dessinatrice *f*

**drafty** [ˈdræf·ti] *adj* plein(e) de courants d'air

**drag** [dræg] **I.** *n* ❶ PHYS (*force*) résistance *f*; AVIAT traînée *f* ❷ (*impediment*) obstacle *m* ❸ *inf* (*bore*) raseur, -euse *m, f* ❹ *inf* (*puff on cigarette*) taffe *f* ❺ *inf* SOCIOL (*women's clothes worn by a man*) **to be in ~** être habillé en travesti ❻ *sl* (*street*) **the main ~** la rue principale ❼ (*for dredging*) drague *f* ❽ SPORTS *s.* **drag race II.** <-gg-> *vt* ❶ (*pull*) a. *fig* traîner; **to ~ sb out of bed** tirer qn de son lit; **to ~ sb away from sth** arracher qn à/de qc ❷ COMPUT (*icon*) faire glisser; **to ~ and drop** glisser-déposer ❸ (*search: river, lake*) draguer ▸ **to ~ one's feet** [*o* **heels**] traîner les pieds; **to ~ sb's name through the mud** traîner le nom de qn dans la boue **III.** <-gg-> *vi* ❶ (*proceed slowly*) traîner; (*time, speech*) traîner en longueur ❷ *inf* (*puff*) **to ~ on a cigarette** tirer sur une cigarette

◆ **drag on** <-gg-> *vi pej* s'éterniser

◆ **drag out** <-gg-> *vt* faire traîner

**dragon** [ˈdræg·ən] *n* dragon *m*

**dragonfly** [ˈdræg·ən·flaɪ] <-flies> *n* libellule *f*

**drag queen** *n* drag queen *f*

**drag race** *n* course *f* d'accélération

**drain** [dreɪn] **I.** *vt* ❶ (*remove liquid from*) a. BOT, AGR, MED drainer ❷ (*empty*) vider ❸ (*tire out*) épuiser **II.** *vi* ❶ (*become empty*) se vider; (*liquid, water*) s'écouler ❷ BOT, AGR (*permit drainage*) être drainé(e) ❸ (*vanish gradually: energy*) s'épuiser **III.** *n* ❶ TECH (*pipe for removing liquid*) drain *m* ❷ (*constant expenditure*) fuite *f* ❸ *fig* SOCIOL, ECON **brain ~** fuite *f* des cerveaux ❹ MED drain *m* ❺ *pl* (*plumbing system*) canalisation *f* ▸ **to be down the ~** être tombé à l'eau

**drainpipe** [ˈdreɪn·paɪp] *n* TECH collecteur *m*

**drama** [ˈdrɑm·ə] *n* drame *m*

**drama queen** *n pej, sl* comédienne *f*

**dramatic** [drə·ˈmæt̬·ɪk] *adj* dramatique

**dramatization** *n* ❶ THEAT, CINE, TV (*adaptation for stage, screen*) adaptation *f* dramatique ❷ *pej* (*exaggeration of importance*) dramatisation *f*

**drank** [dræŋk] *pt of* **drink**

**drastic** [ˈdræs·tɪk] *adj* ❶ (*severe*) drastique; (*measures, budget cuts*) draconien(ne); (*change*) radical(e); (*action*) énergique; (*rise, change*) dramatique ❷ MED drastique

**draw** [drɔ] **I.** *n* ❶ (*sb/sth attractive*) attraction *f* ❷ (*power to attract attention*) séduction *f* ❸ SPORTS (*drawn contest*) match *m* nul ❹ (*reaction*) **to be quick on the ~** être rapide à dégainer; *fig* saisir au vol **II.** <drew, drawn> *vt* ❶ (*make picture*) dessiner; (*a line*) tirer ❷ (*portray*) représenter; (*a picture*) faire ❸ (*pull*) tirer; **to ~ sb aside** mettre qn à l'écart ❹ (*attract*) attirer; (*cheers*) susciter ❺ (*elicit: a confession*) soutirer; (*a criticism*) provoquer ❻ (*formulate*) faire; (*a conclusion*) tirer ❼ (*extract*) extraire; (*a weapon*) sortir; MED (*blood*) prélever; **to ~ blood** a. *fig* faire saigner ❽ GAMES (*a card*) tirer ❾ (*obtain*) obtenir *inf* ❿ FIN, ECON (*earn*) obtenir; (*a salary*) percevoir ⓫ (*select in lottery*) tirer au sort ⓬ (*obtain water*) puiser; **to ~ sb's bath** tirer un bain pour qn ⑬ CULIN (*get from a cask: beer*) tirer ⑭ FIN, ECON (*write a bill: check*) tirer ⑮ (*inhale: a breath*) prendre; **to ~ breath** *fig* souffler (un peu) ⑯ NAUT (*displace water*) jauger ⑰ SPORTS (*stretch a bow*) bander ▸ **to ~ a blank** faire chou blanc; **to ~ the line at sth** fixer des limites à qc; **to ~ a veil over sth** tirer un voile sur qc *f* **III.** <drew, drawn> *vi* ① ART (*make a picture*) dessiner ② (*move*) se diriger; **to ~ near** s'approcher; (*time*) approcher; **to ~ apart** se séparer; **to ~ away** s'éloigner; (*recoil*) avoir un mouvement de recul; **to ~ ahead of sb/sth** prendre de l'avance sur qn/qc; **to ~ to a close** tirer à sa fin; **to ~ even with sb/sth** égaliser avec qn/qc ③ (*draw lots*) effectuer un tirage au sort

◆**draw in** *vt* ① (*involve*) impliquer ② (*retract: reins*) tirer; (*claws*) rentrer ③ (*inhale*) aspirer

◆**draw off** *vt* retirer; (*a beer*) tirer

◆**draw on I.** *vt* ① (*use*) se servir de ② (*inhale smoke: cigarette, pipe*) tirer sur **II.** *vi* ① (*continue*) s'avancer; (*time*) avancer ② *form* (*approach (in time)*) s'approcher

◆**draw out** *vt* ① (*prolong*) prolonger; (*situation, meeting*) faire traîner; (*meal*) prolonger; (*vowels*) allonger ② (*make talk*) **to draw sth out of sb** faire parler qn au sujet de qc

◆**draw up** *vt* ① (*draft: a document, contract, program*) dresser; (*a plan*) élaborer ② (*pull*) tirer; **to draw oneself up** se dresser

**drawback** ['drɔ·bæk] *n* inconvénient *m*
**drawbridge** *n* pont-levis *m*
**drawer** ['drɔ·ər] *n* tiroir *m;* **chest of ~s** commode *f*
**drawing** *n* ① ART dessin *m* ② (*lottery*) tirage *m*
**drawing board** *n* ART planche *f* à dessin ▸ **back to the ~!** *inf* retour à la case départ!
**drawing room** *n form* salon *m*
**drawn** [drɔn] **I.** *pp of* **draw II.** *adj* (*face*) tiré(e)

**dread** [dred] **I.** *vt* ① (*fear*) craindre ② (*be apprehensive about*) redouter **II.** *n* terreur *f;* **to fill sb with ~** remplir qn d'effroi; **to live/be in ~ of doing sth** vivre/être dans l'angoisse de faire qc

**dreadful** *adj* ① (*terrible: mistake*) terrible; (*accident*) atroce ② (*bad quality*) qui ne vaut rien ③ (*very great: annoyance, bore*) gros(se)
**dreadfully** *adv* ① (*in a terrible manner*) terriblement ② (*poorly*) très faiblement ③ (*extremely*) fortement
**dream** [drim] **I.** *n* rêve *m;* **to have a ~ about sth** rêver de qc ▸ **never in my wildest ~s** même dans mes rêves les plus fous + *neg;* **in your ~s!** tu rêves!; **like a ~** à merveille **II.** *adj* de rêve; **to be (living) in a ~ world** vivre dans un monde imaginaire **III.** <dreamed *o* dreamt, dreamed *o* dreamt> *vi* rêver; **to ~ about** [*o* **of**] **sb/sth** rêver de qn/qc; **~ on!** tu peux toujours y compter!; **to ~ of doing sth** s'imaginer faire qc **IV.** <dreamed *o* dreamt, dreamed *o* dreamt> *vt* ① PSYCH (*experience a dream*) rêver ② (*imagine*) imaginer

◆**dream up** *vt* imaginer

**dreamt** [drem(p)t] *pt, pp of* **dream**
**dreamy** ['dri·mi] *adj* ① (*dreamlike*) surréaliste ② (*fantasizing*) rêveur(-euse) ③ *inf* (*delightful*) fabuleux(-euse)
**dreary** ['drɪr·i] *adj* ennuyeux(-euse)
**drench** [dren(t)ʃ] *vt* asperger; **to be ~ed in sweat** être en nage
**dress** [dres] **I.** *n* ① <-es> (*woman's garment*) robe *f* ② (*clothing*) tenue *f;* **to wear traditional ~** porter le costume traditionnel *m* **II.** *vi* s'habiller **III.** *vt* ① (*put on clothing*) habiller ② CULIN (*salad*) assaisonner; (*poultry*) habiller ③ MED (*treat a wound*) panser ④ (*prepare*) apprêter; (*stone*) tailler; **to ~ sb's hair** (bien) coiffer qn ⑤ (*decorate: shop windows*) décorer

◆**dress down I.** *vi* **to ~ in sth** porter simplement qc **II.** *vt inf* **to dress sb down** passer un savon à qn
◆**dress up I.** *vi* ① FASHION (*wear formal*

*clothing*) (bien) s'habiller ❷ (*wear disguise*) se déguiser **II.** *vt* ❶ FASHION (*put on clothing*) **to dress oneself up** s'habiller; **to be all dressed up** être sur son trente et un ❷ (*embellish: a pizza*) garnir; (*a story*) enjoliver ❹ (*present in a better way*) améliorer la présentation de

**dressing** *n* ❶ FASHION (*wearing clothes*) habillement *m* ❷ CULIN (*sauce*) assaisonnement *m*; **French ~** vinaigrette *f* ❸ MED (*covering for an injury*) pansement *m*

**dressing gown** *n* robe *f* de chambre
**dressing table** *n* coiffeuse *f*
**dress rehearsal** *n* répétition *f* générale
**dress shirt** *n* chemise *f* habillée
**drew** [dru] *pt of* **draw**
**dribble** ['drɪb·l] **I.** *n* ❶ (*saliva*) bave *f* ❷ (*small droplet*) gouttelette *f* ❸ SPORTS drib(b)le *m* **II.** *vi* ❶ (*drool*) baver ❷ (*trickle*) dégouliner ❸ SPORTS drib(b)ler **III.** *vt* ❶ (*cause to flow in drops*) faire (é)goutter ❷ SPORTS (*ball*) drib(b)ler

**dried** [draɪd] **I.** *pt, pp of* **dry II.** *adj* (*having been dried*) séché(e); (*fruit, vegetables*) sec(sèche); (*mushrooms*) déshydraté(e); (*milk*) en poudre

**drift** [drɪft] **I.** *n* ❶ (*slow movement*) mouvement *m*; (*of ship*) dérive *f*; (*of current*) sens *m*; (*of events*) cours *m*; **downward ~** écroulement *m* ❷ METEO (*mass blown together*) amoncellement *m*; (*of sand*) dune *f*; (*of snow*) congère *f*; (*of clouds*) traînée *f* ❸ (*central meaning*) sens *m* général; **to catch sb's ~** comprendre où qn veut en venir ❹ TECH (*tool*) jet *m* (d'extraction) **II.** *vi* ❶ (*be moved*) a. *fig* dériver; (*smoke,* ❶ *voice*) flotter; (*attention*) se relâcher; **to ~ out to sea** dériver sur la mer ❷ (*move aimlessly*) errer; **to ~ away** partir nonchalamment; **to ~ into sth** se laisser aller à qc ❸ METEO (*be piled into drifts: sand*) s'entasser; (*of snow*) former des congères

◆**drift apart** *vi* (*friends*) se perdre de vue
◆**drift off** *vi* s'assoupir; **to ~ to sleep** se laisser gagner par le sommeil

**drill** [drɪl] **I.** *n* ❶ TECH (*tool*) perceuse *f*; **dentist's ~** roulette *f* de dentiste ❷ MIL, SCHOOL (*training*) entraînement *m* ❸ *inf* (*procedure*) **fire ~** exercice *m* d'incendie **II.** *vt* ❶ (*bore: hole*) percer; (*well*) forer ❷ (*teach*) entraîner; **to ~ sth into sb** faire rentrer qc dans la tête de qn **III.** *vi* ❶ (*bore*) forer; **to ~ for oil** faire des forages pétroliers ❷ (*practice*) s'entraîner

**drill instructor** *n* MIL instructeur *m* d'exercices

**drink** [drɪŋk] **I.** *n* ❶ CULIN boisson *f*; **soft ~** boisson sans alcool; **to have no food or ~** ne pas s'alimenter ❷ (*alcoholic beverage*) verre *m* **II.**<drank, drunk> *vi* boire; **to ~ to sb/sth** boire à la santé de qn/à qc; **to not ~ and drive** ne pas conduire sous l'emprise de l'alcool ▶ **to ~ like a fish** boire comme un trou; **I'll ~ to that!** et comment! **III.**<drank, drunk> *vt* boire; **to ~ a toast** porter un toast; **to ~ sb under the table** tenir l'alcool mieux que qn
◆**drink in** *vt* (*words*) boire; (*beauty, moonlight*) se délecter de

**drinkable** *adj* ❶ (*safe to drink*) potable ❷ (*easy to drink*) buvable
**drinker** *n* CULIN ❶ (*person who drinks*) buveur, -euse *m, f* ❷ (*alcoholic*) ivrogne *mf*
**drinking water** *n* eau *f* potable

**drip** [drɪp] **I.**<-pp-> *vi* goutter **II.**<-pp-> *vt* faire (s'é)goutter **III.** *n* ❶ (*drop*) goutte *f* ❷ MED (*feeding*) perfusion *f* ❸ *inf* (*idiot*) benêt *m*
**dripping I.** *adj* ❶ (*experiencing a drip: tap, faucet*) qui goutte ❷ (*drenched*) trempé(e); **to be ~ with sweat** ruisseler de sueur ▶ **to be ~ with sth** être plein de qc **II.** *adv* **to be ~ wet** être complètement trempé **III.** *n pl* jus *m* de viande

**drive** [draɪv] **I.** *n* ❶ (*act of driving*) conduite *f*; **to go for a ~** aller faire un

D

tour en voiture ❷(*distance driven*) trajet *m*; **it's a 5-mile ~ from here** c'est à 8 km d'ici en voiture ❸TECH (*transmission*) propulsion *f*; **front-wheel ~** traction *f* avant; **four-wheel ~** véhicule *m* à quatre roues motrices ❹PSYCH dynamisme *m*; **to lack ~** manquer d'ardeur; **sex ~** appétit *m* sexuel ❺(*campaign*) campagne *f*; **fund-raising ~** campagne de récolte de fonds ❻(*small road*) allée *f* ❼SPORTS (*long hit*) dégagement *m* ❽AGR (*forced march*) conduite *f* ❾COMPUT **hard ~** unité *f* de disque II.<drove, driven> *vt* ❶AUTO conduire; **to ~ 5 miles** rouler 8 km; **to ~ the car into the garage** rentrer la voiture au garage ❷(*urge*) conduire; (*a herd, the economy*) mener; **to ~ sb/sth out of sth** chasser qn/qc de qc ❸(*propel*) entraîner ❹(*impel*) obliger; **to ~ sb to drink/to suicide** pousser qn à la boisson/au suicide ❺(*render*) rendre; **to ~ sb wild** rendre qn complètement fou ❻(*force through blows: nail, wedge*) planter; (*into the ground*) enfoncer; **to ~ a wedge between sb/sth** a. *fig* dresser une barrière entre qn/qc ❼TECH (*provide the power*) fournir l'énergie ❽SPORTS (*hit far*) dégager ▶ **to ~ a hard <u>bargain</u> with sb** attendre beaucoup de qn (en retour) III.<drove, driven> *vi* ❶AUTO (*operate*) conduire; **to ~ into sth** rentrer dans qc ❷(*travel*) se rendre; **to ~ past** passer en voiture; **to ~ away** partir en voiture ❸TECH (*function*) fonctionner; (*to cause to function*) actionner; (*to control*) commander; (*to drill*) forer

♦**drive at** *vt insep* en venir à

♦**drive off** *vi* (*car*) démarrer; (*person*) s'en aller en voiture

♦**drive up** *vi* arriver

**driven** ['drɪvⁿən] I. *pp* of **drive** II. *adj* ❶(*impelled*) animé(e) d'un ardent désir ❷(*propelled*) actionné(e)

**driver** *n* ❶AUTO (*person*) conducteur, -trice *m*, *f*; **bus ~** conducteur d'autobus; **truck/taxi ~** chauffeur *m* de camion/taxi ❷SPORTS (*golf club*) club *m* de dé-

part ❸COMPUT pilote *m* (de périphérique)

**driver('s) license** *n* permis *m* de conduire

**driveway** ['draɪv·weɪ] *n* allée *f*

**driving** I. *n* conduite *f*; **~ while intoxicated** conduite en état d'ivresse II. *adj* ❶AUTO, TECH de conduite ❷(*related to engine*) moteur(-trice) ❸METEO (*driven by the wind: rain*) battant(e); **~ snow** tempête *f* de neige ❹(*powerful*) puissant(e); **the ~ force** *fig* le moteur

**driving test** *n* permis *m* de conduire

**drizzle** ['drɪz·l] I. *n* ❶METEO (*light rain*) bruine *f* ❷CULIN (*small amount of liquid*) pluie *f* II. *vi* METEO bruiner III. *vt* CULIN asperger

**droop** [drup] I. *vi* ❶(*sag*) s'affaisser ❷(*feel depressed*) être déprimé II. *n* affaissement *m*

**drop** [drap] I. *n* ❶(*liquid portion*) a. *fig* goutte *f*; (*of alcohol*) doigt *m*; **to not drink a ~** ne pas boire une goutte d'alcool; **~ by ~** goutte à goutte ❷(*decrease*) baisse *f*; **a ~ in sth** une baisse de qc ❸(*length, vertical distance*) hauteur *f* ❹(*difference in amount*) écart *m* ❺(*fall*) a. *fig* chute *f*; (*from aircraft*) parachutage *m* ❻(*hard candy*) bonbon *m*; **cough ~** pastille *f* contre la toux ❼*inf* (*collection point*) planque *f* ▶ **a ~ in the <u>bucket</u>** une goutte d'eau dans la mer; **at the ~ of a <u>hat</u>** sur le champ II.<-pp-> *vt* ❶(*allow to fall*) lâcher; (*bomb*) larguer; (*anchor*) jeter; (*from airplane*) parachuter; (*by accident*) laisser tomber ❷(*lower*) baisser ❸(*abandon*) abandonner; (*person, friend*) laisser tomber; **to ~ the subject** parler d'autre chose ❹*inf* (*express*) laisser échapper; **to ~ a hint about sth** faire une allusion à qc; **to ~ a word in sb's ear** glisser un mot à l'oreille de qn ❺(*leave out*) laisser; (*scene, word*) sauter; **to ~ the h's** ne pas aspirer les h ❻(*dismiss*) renvoyer ❼(*give a lift*) déposer ❽*inf* (*send*) envoyer ▶ **to ~ one's <u>guard</u>** baisser la garde III.<-pp-> *vi* ❶(*fall*) tomber; (*delib-*

*erately*) se laisser tomber; (*road, plane*) descendre ❷ (*go lower*) baisser ❸ *inf* (*become exhausted, die*) s'écrouler; **to ~ dead** mourir subitement ▸ **to ~ like flies** tomber comme des mouches; **~ dead!** *inf* va te faire voir (ailleurs)!

◆**drop in** *vi inf* **to ~ on sb** (*briefly*) faire un saut chez qn; (*unexpectedly*) passer voir qn

◆**drop off** I. *vt inf* déposer II. *vi* ❶ (*descend*) tomber ❷ (*decrease*) baisser ❸ *inf* (*fall asleep*) s'assoupir; **to ~ to sleep** s'endormir

◆**drop out** *vi* (*give up membership*) se retirer; (*of school*) abandonner

**drop cloth** *n* bâche *f* de protection

**drop-dead** *adv sl* vachement; **she is ~ gorgeous** elle est super belle

**dropout** ['drɑp·aʊt] *n* ❶ (*sb who drops school*) étudiant(e) *qui abandonne ses études* ❷ (*dissenter*) marginal(e) *m(f)*

**drought** [draʊt] *n* sécheresse *f*

**drove**[1] [droʊv] *pt of* **drive**

**drove**[2] [droʊv] *n* ❶ ZOOL troupeau *m* ❷ *pl, inf* (*crowd*) horde *f*; **in ~s** en troupeau

**drown** [draʊn] I. *vt* noyer; **to ~ oneself** se noyer ▸ **like a ~ed rat** *inf* mouillé jusqu'aux os; **to ~ one's sorrows** noyer son chagrin dans l'alcool II. *vi* se noyer

◆**drown out** *vt* étouffer

**drowning** *n* noyade *f*

**drowsy** <-ier, -iest> *adj* somnolent(e)

**drug** [drʌg] I. *n* ❶ (*medicine*) médicament *m* ❷ (*narcotic*) drogue *f* II. <-gg-> *vt* droguer

**drug addict** *n* drogué(e) *m(f)*

**drug addiction** *n* toxicomanie *f*

**drugstore** ['drʌg·stɔr] *n* drugstore *m*

**drum** [drʌm] I. *n* ❶ (*percussion*) tambour *m* ❷ *pl* batterie *f* ❸ (*container*) bidon *m* ❹ (*washing machine part*) tambour *m* ▸ **to bang** [*o* **beat**] **the ~ for sb/sth** rebattre les oreilles avec qn/qc II. <-mm-> *vi* ❶ (*play percussion*) battre du tambour ❷ (*tap*) *a. fig* tambouriner III. *vt* tambouriner; **to ~ one's fingers** tapoter des doigts

◆**drum up** *vt* ❶ (*elicit*) attirer; **to ~ support for sb/sth** encourager le soutien pour qn/qc ❷ (*invent*) imaginer

**drummer** *n* batteur *m*

**drunk** [drʌŋk] I. *pp of* **drink** II. *adj* ❶ (*inebriated*) ivre ❷ (*affected*) grisé(e) III. *n pej* alcoolo *mf*

**drunken** ['drʌŋ·kən] *adj pej* ❶ (*intoxicated*) ivre ❷ (*addicted*) alcoolique ❸ (*showing effects of drink*) d'ivrogne

**dry** [draɪ] I. <-ier, -iest *o* -er, est> *adj* ❶ (*not wet*) sec(sèche); **to go ~** s'assécher ❷ METEO (*climate*) sec(sèche), aride ❸ (*not moist: skin*) sec(sèche) ❹ (*missing water: river, riverbed*) tari(e) ❺ (*not sweet: sherry, martini*) sec(sèche); (*champagne*) brut(e) ❻ (*without fat: toast*) sans beurre ❼ (*sarcastic*) caustique ❽ *pej* (*uninteresting*) plat(e) ❾ (*without alcohol*) sans alcool; (*bar*) qui ne sert pas d'alcool; **~ county** région *f* où l'alcool est prohibé ▸ **to bleed sb ~** saigner qn à blanc; **to be (as) as a bone** *inf* être sec comme les blés; **to run ~** être vidé II. <-ie-> *vt* sécher; (*skin*) dessécher; (*the dishes*) essuyer; (*clothes*) faire sécher; **to ~ oneself** se sécher; **to ~ one's hair** se sécher les cheveux III. <-ie-> *vi* sécher; (*skin*) se dessécher; **to put sth out to ~** mettre qc à sécher

◆**dry up** I. *vi* ❶ (*become dry: lake*) s'assécher; (*river*) se tarir ❷ (*run out: source*) s'assécher; (*goods*) s'épuiser II. *vt* assécher

**dry cleaners** *n* teinturier *m*

**dryer** *n* séchoir *m*; **hair ~** sèche-cheveux *m*; **tumble ~** sèche-linge *m*

**dual** ['du·əl] *adj* double

**dub**[1] [dʌb] <-bb-> *vt* ❶ (*nickname*) surnommer ❷ (*confer knighthood on*) adouber

**dub**[2] [dʌb] <-bb-> *vt* ❶ CINE doubler; **to be ~bed into French** être postsynchronisé en français ❷ MEDIA copier un enregistrement

**dubious** ['du·bɪ·əs] *adj* ❶ *pej* (*doubtful*) douteux(-euse) ❷ (*ambiguous*) suspect(e) ❸ (*hesitating*) hésitant(e)

D

**D**

**duchess** ['dʌtʃ·ɪs] n duchesse f
**duck** [dʌk] I. n canard m ▸ **to take to sth like a ~ to** <u>water</u> inf faire qc avec beaucoup de facilité II. vi ❶ (dip head) baisser la tête subitement; **to ~ under water** plonger subitement sous l'eau ❷ (hide quickly) s'esquiver III. vt ❶ (evasively dip quickly) **to ~ one's head** baisser la tête subitement; **to ~ one's head under water** plonger sa tête subitement sous l'eau ❷ (avoid) esquiver
**duct** [dʌkt] n conduit m
**duct tape** n chatterton m
**dude** [djud] n sl (guy) type m, mec m; **he's one crazy ~** ce mec est cinglé ▸**~, <u>check this out</u>!** eh mec, regarde ça!
**due** [du] I. adj ❶ (owing) dû(due); (debt, tax) exigible; **a bill ~ (on) January 1** un effet payable le 1er janvier; **to be ~ sth** devoir qc; **to fall ~** arriver à échéance ❷ (appropriate) **with (all) ~ respect** sauf votre respect; **with ~ caution** avec la prudence qui convient; **after ~ consideration** après mûre réflexion; **to treat sb with the respect ~ to him/her** se comporter envers qn avec tout le respect qui lui est dû ❸ (expected) **to be ~ to** +infin devoir +infin; **the video is ~ out soon** la vidéo va bientôt sortir; **the baby is ~ in May** le bébé doit arriver en mai II. n ❶ (sth owed) dû m; **to give sb his/her ~** donner à qn ce qui lui revient ❷ pl (fees) droits mpl; (of membership) cotisation f; **to pay ~s** payer ses droits; **to pay one's ~s** (obligations) remplir ses obligations; (debts) payer ses dettes III. adv **~ north** plein nord; **to go ~ west** aller droit vers l'ouest
**duffel bag, duffle bag** n sac m marin
**dug** [dʌg] pt, pp of **dig**
**duke** [duk] n duc m
**dull** [dʌl] I. adj ❶ pej (tedious) monotone ❷ (not bright) terne; (lighting) sombre ❸ (muffled) sourd(e) ❹ (blunt) émoussé(e) II. vt ❶ (make dull) ternir ❷ (alleviate) soulager ❸ (blunt) engour-

dir III. vi ❶ (become dull) se ternir ❷ (become less sharp) s'émousser
**duly** ['du·li] adv ❶ (appropriately) dûment ❷ (punctually) en temps voulu
**dumb** [dʌm] adj ❶ (mute) muet(te); **deaf and ~** sourd(e)-muet(te) ❷ pej, inf (stupid) con(ne); **to act** [o **play**] **~** faire l'innocent
◆**dumb down** vt sl (book, text) simplifier
**dumbstruck** ['dʌm·strʌk] adj stupéfait(e)
**dummy** ['dʌm·i] I. <-mmies> n ❶ (mannequin) mannequin m ❷ (duplicate) faux m ❸ pej (fool) idiot(e) m(f) II. adj ❶ (duplicate) factice ❷ (false) faux(fausse)
**dump** [dʌmp] I. n ❶ (area for garbage) décharge f ❷ (depot) dépôt m ❸ (messy place) dépotoir m ❹ COMPUT vidage m II. vt ❶ (throw away) jeter ❷ (abandon: project) abandonner ❸ sl (end relationship suddenly) larguer ❹ ECON faire du dumping pour ❺ (transfer data) vider
**dumping** n ❶ (disposal of garbage) décharge f ❷ ECON dumping m
**dumpling** ['dʌm·plɪŋ] n quenelle f
**dune** [dun] n dune f
**dungarees** [ˌdʌŋ·gəˈriz] npl salopette f; (work clothes) bleu m de travail
**dungeon** ['dʌn·dʒən] n donjon m
**duplicate** ['du·plɪ·kət, vb: 'du·plɪ·keɪt] I. adj en double; **a ~ key** un double de clé; **a ~ receipt/document** le duplicata d'une quittance/d'un document II. n ❶ (copy) double m; (of cassette tape, object) copie f; LAW duplicata m; **in ~** en double III. vt ❶ (copy) faire un double de; (of document) (photo)copier; (of cassette tape, object) copier; LAW faire un duplicata de ❷ (replicate) reproduire; **nothing can ~ motherhood** fig rien ne peut remplacer la maternité ❸ (repeat) refaire
**durability** [ˌdʊr·ə·ˈbɪl·ə·t̬i] n résistance f
**durable** ['dʊr·ə·bl] adj ❶ (long-lasting) durable ❷ (wear-resistant) résistant(e)
**duration** [dʊ·ˈreɪ·ʃən] n durée f ▸**for**

**the ~** jusqu'à la fin; *(for a very long time)* une éternité

**during** ['dʊr·ɪŋ] *prep* pendant; **~ work** pendant le travail; **~ the week** les jours *mpl* ouvrables; **to work ~ the night** travailler la nuit; **it happened ~ the night** c'est arrivé au cours de la nuit

**dusk** [dʌsk] *n* ❶ *(twilight)* a. fig crépuscule *m*, brunante *f Québec* ❷ *(gloom)* pénombre *f*

**dust** [dʌst] **I.** *n* poussière *f* ▸ **to bite the ~** mordre la poussière; **to throw ~ in the eyes of sb** jeter à qn de la poudre aux yeux; **to wait until the ~ has settled**, **to let the ~ settle** attendre que tout redevienne *(subj)* calme **II.** *vt* ❶ *(clean dust from)* dépoussiérer ❷ *(spread finely)* **to ~ sth with sth** saupoudrer qc de qc; **to ~ sth with insecticide** vaporiser qc d'insecticide **III.** *vi* épousseter

**dust bunny** *n* mouton *m*

**dust cover** *n (for furniture)* housse *f*; *(for books)* jaquette *f*

**duster** ['dʌs·tər] *n* chiffon *m*, patte *f Suisse*

**dustpan** *n* pelle *f* à poussière, ramasse-poussière *m Belgique, Nord*

**dustup** *n inf* ❶ *(physical)* bagarre *f* ❷ *(noisy)* altercation *f*

**dusty** <-ier, -ies> *adj* ❶ *(covered in dust)* poussiéreux(-euse) ❷ *(of grayish color)* cendré(e)

**Dutch** [dʌtʃ] **I.** *adj* néerlandais(e), hollandais(e) **II.** *n* ❶ *(people)* **the ~** les

Néerlandais [o Hollandais] ❷ LING néerlandais *m* **III.** *adv* **to go ~** partager l'addition

**duty** ['du·t̬i] <-ties> *n* ❶ *(obligation)* devoir *m;* **to do one's ~** faire son devoir; **to do sth out of ~** faire qc par devoir ❷ *(task)* fonction *f;* **to report for ~** travailler; **to be on/off ~** reprendre/quitter son travail ❸ *(revenue)* taxe *f;* **customs duties** taxes douanières

**duty-free** [ˌdu·t̬i·'fri] *adj* hors taxe *inv*

**duvet** [du·'veɪ] *n* couette *f*

**dwarf** [dwɔrf] **I.** <-s o -ves> *n (very small person)* nain(e) *m(f)* **II.** *vt* ❶ *(make smaller)* rapetisser ❷ *fig* écraser

**dwell upon** *vt* ❶ *(pay attention to)* s'étendre sur ❷ *(do sth at length)* s'attarder sur

**dye** [daɪ] **I.** *vt* teindre **II.** *n* teinture *f*; *(for hair)* coloration *f*

**dying** *adj* ❶ *(process of death)* mourant(e); **to my ~ day** à ma mort; **sb's ~ words** les dernières paroles *fpl* de qn ❷ *(ceasing)* moribond(e); **the ~ moments of sth** les derniers moments *mpl* de qc

**dyke¹** [daɪk] *n s.* **dike¹**

**dyke²** [daɪk] *n pej, inf (lesbian)* gouine *f*

**dynamic** [daɪ·'næm·ɪk] *adj* dynamique

**dynamite** ['daɪ·nə·maɪt] **I.** *n* dynamite *f* **II.** *vt* dynamiter

**dynasty** ['daɪ·nə·sti] <-ies> *n* dynastie *f*

**dyslexic** [dɪ·'slek·sɪk] *adj* dyslexique

# Ee

**E**

**E, e** [i] <-'s *o* -s> *n* ❶ (*letter*) E *m*, e *m*; **~ as in Echo** (*on telephone*) e comme Eugène ❷ MUS mi *m*

**E.** *n abbr of east* E *m*

**each** [itʃ] **I.** *adj* chaque; **~ one of you** chacun de vous; **~ month** tous les mois *mpl* **II.** *pron* ❶ (*every person*) chacun; **~ of them** chacun d'entre eux; **$70** ~ 70 dollars par personne ❷ (*every thing*) **$10** ~ 10 dollars pièce; **one pound/three of** ~ une livre/trois de chaque

**each other** *reciprocal pron, after verb* l'un l'autre; **made for** ~ faits l'un pour l'autre

**eager** ['iˑɡər] *adj* ❶ (*keen*) avide; **to be ~ for sth** être avide de qc ❷ (*enthusiastic*) enthousiaste ❸ (*impatient*) **with ~ anticipation** avec beaucoup d'impatience; **to be ~ to** +*infin* être impatient de +*infin*

**eagle** ['iˑɡl] *n* aigle *m*

**ear**[1] [ɪr] *n* oreille *f*; **to smile from ~ to ~** sourire jusqu'aux oreilles ▶ **to be up to one's ~s in** <u>debt</u>/<u>work</u> avoir des dettes/du travail jusqu'au cou; **to be all ~s** être tout ouïe; **to have a** <u>good</u> **~ for sth** avoir de l'oreille pour qc; **to go in one ~ and out the other** rentrer par une oreille et sortir par l'autre; **to** <u>play</u> **it by ~** *fig, inf* improviser

**ear**[2] [ɪr] *n* BOT épi *m*

**earache** ['ɪrˑeɪk] *n* mal *m* d'oreille(s)

**earl** [ɜrl] *n* comte *m*

**earlobe** ['ɪrˑloʊb] *n* lobe *m* de l'oreille

**early** ['ɜrˑli] <-ier, -iest> **I.** *adj* ❶ (*at beginning of day*) matinal(e); **the ~ hours** les premières heures *fpl*; **in the ~ morning** de bon matin; **~ riser** lève-tôt *mf* ❷ (*close to beginning of period*) premier(-ère); **in the ~ afternoon** en début d'après-midi; **in the ~ 15th century** au début du XVᵉ siècle; **in an earlier letter** dans une lettre précédente ❸ (*ahead of expected time*) anticipé(e);

**to be** ~ être en avance *fpl* ❹ (*first*) **an ~ edition** une des premières éditions ❺ *form* (*prompt*) **at your earliest convenience** dans les plus brefs délais **II.** *adv* ❶ (*in day*) de bonne heure; **to get up** ~ se lever tôt ❷ (*ahead of time*) en avance; **5 minutes early** avec 5 minutes d'avance ❸ (*close to beginning of period*) au début de; **~ in life** dans la jeunesse; **as ~ as 1803** dès 1803; **what I said earlier** ce que j'ai dit avant ❹ (*prematurely*) prématurément; **to die** ~ mourir jeune

**earn** [ɜrn] *vt* ❶ (*be paid*) gagner; **to ~ a living** gagner sa vie; **to ~ $800 a week** gagner 800 dollars par semaine ❷ *fig* **her painting ~ed her success** sa peinture lui a valu le succès; **to ~ sb nothing but criticism** ne rapporter que des critiques à qn ❸ (*deserve*) mériter

**earnings** ['ɜrˑnɪŋz] *npl* salaire *m*

**earphones** ['ɪrˑfoʊnz] *npl* RADIO, TV (*set*) casque *m*; (*separate*) écouteurs *mpl*

**earpiece** *n* ❶ (*of phone*) écouteur *m* ❷ (*of glasses*) embout *m*

**earring** *n* boucle *f* d'oreille

**earshot** *n* **to be in/out of ~** être à/hors de portée de voix

**earth** [ɜrθ] *n* ❶ terre *f*; (*planet*) Earth la (planète) Terre; **the ~'s atmosphere** l'atmosphère *f* terrestre; **who/where/why on ~ ...** *inf* qui/où/pourquoi donc ... ▶ **to** <u>bring</u> **sb/to** <u>come</u> **back (down) to ~** ramener qn/revenir sur terre; **to** <u>cost</u> **the ~** coûter les yeux de la tête; **to** <u>promise</u> **the ~** promettre la lune

**earthly** ['ɜrθˑli] *adj* ❶ (*concerning life on earth*) terrestre ❷ *inf* (*possible*) **it is of no ~ use to her** ça ne lui est d'aucune utilité

**earthquake** ['ɜrθˑkweɪk] *n* ❶ tremblement *m* de terre ❷ *fig* bouleversement *m*

**E**

**earthshattering** *adj* incroyable

**ease** [iz] **I.** *n* ❶ (*opp: effort*) facilité *f;* **for ~ of use** pour un usage facile; **to do sth with ~** faire qc avec aisance ❷ (*comfort*) aisance *f;* **to feel ill at ~** se sentir mal à l'aise ❸ (*relaxed attitude*) aisance *f;* **to put sb at ~** mettre qn à l'aise ❹ MIL **to stand at ~** se tenir au repos **II.** *vt* (*situation*) améliorer; (*crisis, problem*) atténuer; (*mind*) tranquilliser; (*pain*) adoucir; (*strain*) calmer; (*traffic*) alléger; **to ~ sth into/out of sth** aider qc à entrer dans/à sortir de qc **III.** *vi* s'atténuer; (*tension*) se détendre
**◆ease off, ease up** *vi* (*activity*) diminuer; (*pain*) s'estomper

**easel** ['i·z°l] *n* chevalet *m*

**easily** ['i·zɪ·li] *adv* ❶ (*without difficulty*) facilement; **it's ~ done** c'est facile a fairc; **to win ~** gagner haut la main ❷ (*clearly*) certainement; **to be ~ the best** être de loin le meilleur ❸ (*probably*) probablement

**east** [ist] **I.** *n* ❶ (*cardinal point*) est *m;* **to lie 5 miles to the ~ of sth** être à 5 miles à l'est de qc; **to go/drive to the ~** aller/rouler vers l'est; **farther ~** plus à l'est ❷ GEO est *m;* **in the ~ of France** dans l'est de la France ❸ POL **the East** (les pays *mpl* de) l'Est **II.** *adj* (d')est, oriental(e), est; **~ wind** vent *m* d'est; **~ coast** côte *f* est [o orientale]

**Easter** ['i·stər] *n* REL Pâques *fpl;* **at/ over ~** à Pâques

**Easter Bunny** *n* lapin *m* de Pâques

**Easter egg** *n* œuf *m* de Pâques

**easterly** ['i·star·li] **I.** *adj* ❶ (*in the east*) à l'est ❷ (*toward the east*) vers l'est ❸ (*from east*) de l'est **II.** *<-lies> n* vent *m* d'est

**eastern** ['i·stərn] *adj* d'est; **~ Canada** l'est *m* du Canada; **the ~ part of the country** l'est du pays

**eastward** ['ist·wərd] **I.** *adj* est; **in an ~ direction** en direction de l'est **II.** *adv* s. **eastwards**

**eastwards** ['ist·wərdz] *adv* vers l'est/à l'est

**easy** ['·zi] *<-ier, -iest> adj* ❶ (*simple*)

facile; **within ~ reach** à portée de main; **to be far from ~** être loin d'être facile; **it's ~ to cook/clean** c'est facile à cuisiner/à nettoyer; **he's ~ to annoy** il est vite contrarié; **it's an ~ mistake to make** c'est une faute qu'on fait facilement; **it's as ~ as pie** c'est un jeu d'enfant; **that's easier said than done** *inf* c'est plus facile à dire qu'à faire; **~ money** *inf* argent *m* vite gagné ❷ (*comfortable, carefree*) confortable; (*mind*) tranquille ❸ (*relaxed*) décontracté(e); (*charm*) agréable; **to walk at an ~** marcher d'un pas souple ❹ *pej* (*overly simple*) simplet(te) ▶ **to be on ~ street** *inf* ne pas avoir de problèmes financiers **II.** *adv* avec précaution; **to go ~ on sth** *inf* y aller doucement sur [o avec] qc; **go ~ on coffee!** ralentis un peu sur le café!; **to go ~ on sb** *inf* y aller doucement avec qn ▶ **take things** *inf* n'en fais pas trop; **take it ~!** du calme!; **~ come, ~ go** *inf* vite gagné, vite dépensé **III.** *interj inf* **~ does it!** doucement!

**easy-going** *adj* (*person*) facile à vivre; (*attitude*) complaisant(e)

**eat** [it] **I.** *<ate, eaten> vt* manger; **to ~ breakfast** prendre le petit-déjeuner; **to ~ lunch** déjeuner ▶ **to ~ sb for breakfast** *inf* ne faire qu'une bouchée de qn; **~ your heart out!** *inf* tu vas mourir de jalousie!; **what's ~ing him?** *inf* quelle mouche le pique? **II.** *vi* manger; **let's ~ out** allons au restaurant ▶ **to have sb ~ing out of one's hand** faire faire à qn ce que l'on veut; **to ~ like a horse** manger comme quatre

**eaten** ['i·tən] *pp* of **eat**

**eater** ['i·tər] *n* mangeur, -euse *m, f*

**eatery** ['i·tər·i] *n inf* restau *m*

**eavesdrop** ['ivz·drap] *<-pp-> vi* écouter aux portes; **to ~ on sth/sb** écouter indiscrètement qc/qn

**echo** ['ek·oʊ] **I.** *<-es> n a. fig* écho *m* **II.** *<-es, -ing, -ed> vi* faire écho; **to ~ with sth** retentir de qc **III.** *<-es, ing, -ed> vt* ❶ répéter ❷ *fig* rappeler

**eclipse** [ɪ·'klɪps] **I.** *n* ❶ éclipse *f;* **lunar/**

**solar ~** éclipse de lune/du soleil ❷ *fig* **to be in ~** se faire rare; **to go into ~** disparaître petit à petit **II.** *vt* ❶ éclipser ❷ *fig* cacher; **to ~ sb** surpasser qn

**ecological** [ˌiˑkəˈlaˑdʒɪˑkəl] *adj* écologique

**ecologically** [ˌɪˑkəˈlaˑdʒɪkˑəlˑi] *adv* de façon écologique; **~ friendly** qui respecte l'écologie

**ecology** [iˈkaˑləˑdʒi] *n* écologie *f*

**e-commerce** [ˈiˑkaˑmɜrs] *n* commerce *m* électronique

**economic** [ˌiˑkəˈnaˑmɪk] *adj* économique

**economical** [ˌiˑkəˈnaˑmɪkˑəl] *adj* économe; *pej* avare; **it's not ~** ce n'est pas économique

**economics** [ˌiˑkəˈnaˑmɪks] *npl* ❶ + *sing vb* (*discipline*) économie *f* ❷ + *pl vb* (*matter*) aspects *mpl* économiques

**economist** [ɪˈkaˑnəˑmɪst] *n* économiste *mf*

**economy** [ɪˈkaˑnəˑmi] <-ies> *n* économie *f*; **the state of the ~** la situation économique

**edge** [edʒ] **I.** *n* ❶ (*limit*) *a. fig* bord *m*; (*of table*) rebord *m* ❷ (*cutting part of blade*) tranchant *m*; **to put an ~ on a knife** aiguiser un couteau; **to take the ~ off sth** émousser qc; *fig* adoucir qc ❸ (*sharpness*) acuité *f* ▸ **to be on-edge** être nerveux; **to be on the ~ of one's <u>seat</u>** être tenu en haleine; **to have the ~ over sb/sth** avoir un léger avantage sur qn/qc **II.** <-ging> *vt* ❶ (*border*) border ❷ (*move*) **to ~ one's way into sth** se faufiler dans qc **III.** <-ging> *vi* **to ~ closer** s'approcher lentement; **to ~ forward** s'avancer doucement

**edible** [ˈedˑɪˑbl] *adj* comestible

**edit** [ˈedˑɪt] *vt* ❶ (*correct*) réviser ❷ (*be responsible for publications*) diriger ❸ CINE (*film*) monter ❹ COMPUT (*file*) éditer

**edition** [ɪˈdɪʃˑən] *n* ❶ TYP édition *f*; **hardcover/paperback ~** édition cartonnée/de poche; **limited ~** édition à tirage limité ❷ RADIO, TV diffusion *f* ❸ (*repetition*) **it's the 11th ~ of this tournament** ce tournoi se joue pour la onzième fois ❹ (*copy*) reproduction *f*

**editor** [ˈedˑɪˑtər] *n* ❶ TYP (*of newspaper, magazine*) rédacteur, -trice *m*, *f* en chef; (*of publishing department*) éditeur, -trice *m*, *f* ❷ (*person editing texts: classic texts*) éditeur, -trice *m*, *f*; (*article*) assistant(e) *m(f)* de rédaction ❸ CINE monteur, -euse *m*, *f* ❹ COMPUT éditeur *m*

**editorial** [ˌedˑəˈtɔrˑiˑəl] **I.** *n* éditorial *m* **II.** *adj* de la rédaction; **~ staff** rédaction *f*

**EDT** [ˌiˑdiˈti] *n abbr of* **Eastern Daylight Time** EDT *m* (*heure d'été de l'est de l'Amérique du Nord*)

**educate** [ˈedʒˑʊˑkeɪt] *vt* ❶ (*bring up*) éduquer ❷ (*teach*) instruire; **~d in Canada** qui a fait ses études au Canada ❸ (*train*) former; (*animal*) dresser ❹ (*inform*) **to ~ sb in** [*o* **about**] **sth** informer qn de qc

**educated** [ˈedʒˑʊˑkeɪˑtɪd] *adj* instruit(e); **highly ~** cultivé(e)

**education** [ˌedʒˑʊˑˈkeɪˑʃən] *n* ❶ (*system*) enseignement *m*; **the Department of ~** POL le ministère de l'éducation ❷ (*training*) formation *f* ❸ UNIV sciences *fpl* de l'éducation

**educational** [ˌedʒˑʊˑˈkeɪˑʃənˑəl] *adj* ❶ SCHOOL scolaire; (*film*) éducatif(-ive); (*software*) pédagogique; (*system*) d'enseignement; **his ~ background** son cursus scolaire ❷ (*instructive*) instructif(-ive); **for ~ purposes** dans un but pédagogique ❸ (*raising awareness*) d'information

**eerie** [ˈɪrˑi] <-r, -st>, **eery** <-ier, -iest> *adj* ❶ (*strange*) sinistre ❷ (*mysterious*) surnaturel(le) ❸ (*frightening*) inquiétant(e)

**effect** [ɪˈfekt] **I.** *n* ❶ (*consequence*) effet *m*; **the ~ was to make things worse** ça a eu pour effet de faire empirer les choses; **the ~ this had on the children** l'effet que cela a eu sur les enfants; **to come into ~** (*changes*) prendre effet; (*law*) entrer en vigueur; **to**

take ~ (*change*) entrer en vigueur; (*drug*) commencer à agir; **with imme-diate ~** avec effet immédiat; **did it have any ~?** est-ce que cela eu un ef-fet?; **to no ~** en vain ❷ (*impression*) effet *m*; **for artistic ~** pour faire un effet artistique; **the overall ~** l'effet général ❸ *pl* (*artist's tricks*) effets *mpl*; **sound ~s** bruitage *m* ❹ (*meaning*) **a letter to the ~ that …** une lettre selon laquel-le …; **in ~** en effet ❺ *pl* (*belongings*) **personal ~s** effets *mpl* personnels II. *vt* effectuer; (*merger*) réaliser; (*change*) provoquer

**effective** [ɪˈfek·tɪv] *adj* ❶ (*achieving re-sult: measures, medicine*) efficace; (*person*) compétent(e) ❷ (*operative: law*) en vigueur ❸ (*impressive: dem-onstration, lighting*) impressionnant(e) ❹ (*real: leader*) véritable; (*cost*) effec-tif(-ive)

**efficiency** [ɪˈfɪʃ·ən(t)·si] *n* ❶ (*compe-tence*) bon fonctionnement *m*; (*of a method*) efficacité *f*; (*of a person*) com-pétence *f* ❷ TECH rendement *m*

**efficient** [ɪˈfɪʃ·ənt] *adj* efficace; (*per-son*) compétent(e)

**effort** [ˈef·ərt] *n* ❶ (*work*) effort *m*; **to be worth the ~** valoir la peine; **it's an ~ for him to breathe** ça lui demande un effort de respirer; **she just won't make the ~** elle ne veut pas faire l'ef-fort; **I'll make every ~ to be there** je ferai tout mon possible pour être là ❷ (*attempt*) tentative *f*; **my ~s to com-municate** mes efforts pour communi-quer

**effortless** [ˈef·ərt·ləs] *adj* ❶ (*easy*) fa-cile ❷ (*painless*) sans effort

**e-file** *vt abbr of* **electronically file to ~ sth** (*tax return*) remplir qc en ligne

**e.g.** [ˌiˈdʒi] *abbr of* (**exempli gratia**) **for example** par ex.

**egg** [eg] *n* ❶ œuf *m*; **to lay an ~** pondre un œuf; **beaten/scrambled/fried ~s** œufs battus/brouillés/sur le plat; **hard--bolled/soft-boiled ~** œufs durs/mol-lets ❷ (*female reproductive cells*) ovu-le *m* ▸ **to have ~ on one's <u>face</u>** *inf*

avoir l'air fin; **to put all one's ~s in one <u>basket</u>** mettre tous ses œufs dans le même panier

**eggshell** *n* coquille *f* d'œuf

**egg white** *n* blanc *m* d'œuf

**ego** [ˈiˈgoʊ] *n* <-s> ❶ PSYCH ego *m* ❷ (*self-esteem*) vanité *f*; **to bolster sb's ~** donner de l'assurance *f* à qn

**egoist** [ˈiˈgoʊ·ɪst] *n pej* égoïste *mf*

**ego surfing** *n no art* COMPUT egosurf *m* (*recherche de son nom sur Internet via les moteurs de recherche*)

**egotistic(al)** [ˌiˈgoʊ·tɪs·tɪk·(əl)] *adj pej* égoïste *soutenu*

**eiderdown** [ˈaɪ·dər·daʊn] *n* édredon *m*

**eight** [eɪt] I. *adj* huit; **he is ~** il a huit ans II. *n* (*number*) huit *m*; **~ o'clock** huit heures *fpl*; **it's ~** il est huit heures

**eighteen** [ˌeɪˈtin] *adj* dix-huit; *s.a.* **eight**

**eighth** [eɪtθ] I. *adj* huitième; **~ note** croche *f* II. *n* ❶ (*order*) **the ~** le(la) hui-tième ❷ (*date*) **the ~ of June, June ~** le huit juin ❸ (*equal parts*) **to cut a cake into ~** couper un gâteau en huit III. *adv* (*in lists*) huitièmement

**eightieth** [ˈeɪ·ti·əθ] *adj* quatre-ving-tième, *s.a.* **eighth**

**eighty** [ˈeɪ·ti] I. *adj* quatre-vingts, hui-tante *Suisse*, octante *Belgique, Suisse* II. *n* ❶ (*number*) quatre-vingts *m* ❷ (*age*) **to be in one's eighties** avoir quatre-vingts ans passés ❸ (*decade*) **the eighties** les années *fpl* quatre-vingts; *s.a.* **eight**

**Eire** [ˈer·ə] *n* République *f* d'Irlande

**either** [ˈi·ðər] I. *adj* ❶ (*one of two*) **~ method will work** n'importe la-quelle des deux méthodes marchera; **I didn't see ~ film** je n'ai vu ni l'un ni l'autre de ces films; **~ way it's expen-sive** dans les deux cas, c'est cher ❷ (*both*) **on ~ foot** sur chaque pied II. *pron* **which one? – ~ ~** n'importe lequel; **~ of you can go** l'un ou l'autre peut y aller III. *adv* (*in alter-natives*) **~ … or** soit … soit; **it's good with ~ meat or fish** c'est bon avec de la viande ou du poisson; *after neg* non

plus; **if he doesn't go, I won't go** ~ s'il ne part pas, moi non plus **IV.** *conj* ~ ... **or ...** soit ... soit ...; ~ **buy it or rent it** achetez-le ou (bien) louez-le; **I can** ~ **stay or leave** je peux ou rester ou partir
**eke out** [ik aʊt] *vt* (*money, food*) faire durer; **to** ~ **a living** avoir du mal à joindre les deux bouts
**elastic** [ɪ·ˈlæs·tɪk] **I.** *adj a. fig* élastique **II.** *n* (*band*) élastique *m*
**elbow** [ˈel·boʊ] **I.** *n a. fig* coude *m* ▸ **to give sb the** ~ *inf* plaquer qn **II.** *vt* **to** ~ **sb out of the way** écarter qn de son chemin
**elbow room** *n* ❶ (*space to move*) espace *m* ❷ (*freedom of action*) marge *f* de manœuvre
**e-learning** [ˈiː·ˌlɜː·nɪŋ] *n no pl* e-learning *m*, formation *f* en ligne
**elect** [ɪ·ˈlekt] **I.** *vt* ❶ (*by voting*) élire; **to** ~ **sb as president/to sth** élire qn président/à qc ❷ (*decide*) **to** ~ **to** +*infin* choisir de +*infin* **II.** *n* REL **the** ~ les élus *mpl* **III.** *adj* **the president-**~ le futur président
**election** [ɪ·ˈlek·ʃən] *n* élection *f*
**electric** [ɪ·ˈlek·trɪk] *adj* électrique; (*fence*) électrifié(e); (*atmosphere*) chargé(e) d'électricité; ~ **blanket** couverture *f* chauffante; ~ **shock** MED électrochoc *m*
**electrical** [ɪ·ˈlek·trɪ·kəl] *adj* électrique; ~ **failure** panne *f* d'électricité; ~ **engineer** électrotechnicien(ne) *m(f)*
**electric chair** *n* chaise *f* électrique
**electrician** [ɪ·ˌlek·ˈtrɪʃ·ən] *n* électricien(ne) *m(f)*
**electricity** [ɪ·ˌlek·ˈtrɪs·ə·ti] *n* électricité *f*; **powered by** ~ électrique
**electrocardiogram** [ɪ·ˌlek·troʊ·ˈkar·di·ə·græm] *n* électrocardiogramme *m*
**electrocute** [ɪ·ˈlek·trə·kjut] *vt* électrocuter
**electronic** [ɪ·ˌlek·ˈtra·nɪk] *adj* électronique
**electronics** [ɪ·ˌlek·ˈtra·nɪks] *npl* ❶ + *sing vb* (*science*) électronique *f* ❷ + *pl vb* (*circuits*) circuits *mpl* électroniques

**elegance** [ˈel·ə·gən(t)s] *n* élégance *f*
**elegant** [ˈel·ə·gənt] *adj* élégant(e)
**element** [ˈel·ə·mənt] *n* ❶ *a.* CHEM, MATH élément *m* ❷ ELEC résistance *f* ❸ (*amount*) **an** ~ **of luck** une part de chance ❹ *pl* (*rudiments*) rudiments *mpl* ❺ *pl* METEO **the** ~**s** les éléments *mpl*
**elementary** [ˌel·ə·ˈmen·tər·i] *adj* élémentaire; ~ **education** enseignement *m* primaire
**elementary school** *n* école *f* primaire
**elephant** [ˈel·ɪ·fənt] *n* éléphant *m*
**elevation** [ˌel·ɪ·ˈveɪ·ʃən] *n* ❶ *form* (*height, hill*) hauteur *f*; **an** ~ **of 1000 m** une altitude de 1000 m ❷ ARCHIT élévation *f* ❸ (*rise*) ascension *f*
**elevator** [ˈel·ɪ·veɪ·tər] *n* ❶ (*for people*) ascenseur *m* ❷ (*for freight*) monte-charge *m*
**eleven** [ɪ·ˈlev·ən] **I.** *adj* onze **II.** *n* (*number*) onze *m*; *s.a.* **eight**
**eleventh** [ɪ·ˈlev·ənθ] *adj* onzième; *s.a.* **eighth**
**eligible** [ˈel·ɪdʒ·ə·bl] *adj* éligible; **to be** ~ **for sth** avoir droit à qc; **to be** ~ **to vote** être en droit de voter; **an** ~ **bachelor** un bon parti
**eliminate** [ɪ·ˈlɪm·ɪ·neɪt] *vt* ❶ *a.* ANAT éliminer ❷ (*exclude*) écarter ❸ *inf* (*murder*) supprimer
**elite** [ɪ·ˈliːt] **I.** *n* élite *f* **II.** *adj* d'élite; ~ **university** université d'élite
**else** [els] *adv* ❶ (*in addition*) **everybody** ~ tous les autres; **everything** ~ tout le reste; **someone** ~ quelqu'un d'autre; **anyone** ~ toute autre personne; **why** ~**?** pour quelle autre raison?; **what/who** ~**?** quoi/qui d'autre? ❷ (*different*) **something** ~ autre chose ❸ (*otherwise*) **or** ~ **we could see a film** ou bien nous pourrions voir un film; **do that or** ~**!** fais ça, sinon tu vas voir!
**elsewhere** [ˈels·(h)wer] *adv* ailleurs
**e-mail address** *n* adresse *f* électronique
**emancipated** *adj a.* POL émancipé(e); (*ideas*) libéral(e)

**embark** [em·'bark] I. *vi* s'embarquer II. *vt* embarquer

**embarrass** [em·'ber·əs] *vt* embarrasser

**embarrassed** *adj* embarrassé(e); **I was ~ to ask her** j'étais gêné de lui demander

**embarrassing** *adj* embarrassant(e)

**embarrassment** *n* gêne *f*; **to be an ~ to sb** être une source d'embarras pour qn

**embassy** ['em·bə·si] <-assies> *n* ambassade *f*

**embezzle** [em·'bez·l] <-ling> *vt* (*funds*) détourner

**embrace** [em·'breɪs] I. *vt* ❶ embrasser ❷ *fig* (*idea*) adopter; (*opportunity*) saisir; (*religion*) embrasser II. *n* embrassade *f*; **in your ~** dans tes bras

**embroider** [em·'brɔɪ·dər] I. *vi* broder II. *vt* ❶ broder ❷ *fig* enjoliver

**embryo** ['em·bri·oʊ] *n* embryon *m*

**emerald** ['em·ər·əld] I. *n* ❶ (*stone*) émeraude *f* ❷ (*color*) vert *m* émeraude II. *adj* vert émeraude

**emergency** [ɪ·'mɜr·dʒən(t)·si] I. <-ies> *n a.* MED urgence *f*; **state of ~** POL état *m* d'urgence II. *adj* (*landing*) forcé(e); (*measures*) d'exception; (*exit, brake*) de secours; (*situation*) d'urgence

**emergency brake** *n* AUTO frein *m* à main

**emigrant** ['em·ɪ·grənt] *n* émigrant(e) *m(f)*

**emigrate** ['em·ɪ·greɪt] *vi* émigrer

**emit** [ɪ·'mɪt] <-tt-> *vt* (*radiation, groan*) émettre; (*odor*) répandre; (*rays*) diffuser; (*smoke*) dégager; (*heat, light*) émettre; (*squeal*) laisser échapper

**emoticon** *n* COMPUT émoticone *m*

**emotion** [ɪ·'moʊ·ʃən] *n* ❶ (*affective state*) émotion *f* ❷ (*feeling*) sentiment *m*

**emotional** [ɪ·'moʊ·ʃən·əl] *adj* émotionnel(le); (*ceremony*) émouvant(e); (*decision*) impulsif(-ive); (*reaction*) émotif(-ive); **an ~ person** une personne sensible; **~ blackmail** chantage *m* au sentiment; **to make an ~ appeal to sb** faire appel aux bons sentiments de qn

**emotionless** *adj* impassible

**emperor** ['em·pər·ər] *n* empereur *m*

**emphasis** ['em(p)·fə·sɪs] <-phases> *n* ❶ (*when explaining*) insistance *f*; **to place** [*o* **put**] **great ~ on sth** mettre l'accent *m* sur qc; **the ~ is on ...** l'accent est mis sur... ❷ LING accentuation *f*; **the ~ is on the first syllable** l'accentuation est sur la première syllabe

**emphasize** ['em(p)·fə·saɪz] *vt* ❶ (*insist on*) souligner; (*fact*) insister sur ❷ LING accentuer

**emphatic** [em·'fæt·ɪk] *adj* ❶ (*forcibly expressive*) emphatique; (*assertion*) catégorique ❷ (*strong*) énergique; (*victory*) écrasant(e); (*answer*) net(te); (*refusal*) formel(le)

**empire** ['em·paɪər] *n a. fig* empire *m*

**employ** [em·'plɔɪ] *vt* ❶ (*pay to do work*) employer; **he is ~ed in the travel industry** il travaille dans l'industrie du tourisme ❷ (*use*) utiliser

**employee** ['em·plɔɪ·'i] *n* employé(e) *m(f)*

**employer** [em·'plɔɪ·ər] *n* employeur, -euse *m, f*

**employment** *n* ❶ (*state of having work*) emploi *m*; **~ agency** agence *f* de placement ❷ (*use*) emploi *m*

**empress** ['em·prɪs] *n* impératrice *f*

**emptiness** ['em(p)·tɪ·nəs] *n* vide *m*; (*of speech*) vacuité *f*

**empty** ['em(p)·ti] I. <-ier, -iest> *adj* ❶ (*with nothing inside*) vide; (*stomach*) creux(-euse); **on an ~ stomach** à jeun ❷ AUTO à vide ❸ (*without inhabitants*) inoccupé(e) ❹ CULIN (*calories*) non calorique ❺ (*pointless: gesture*) futile; (*words*) vain(e); (*threat*) en l'air II. <-ies> *n pl* bouteilles *fpl* vides, vidanges *fpl Belgique* III. <-ie-> *vt* vider IV. <-ie-> *vi* ❶ se vider ❷ GEO (*river*) **to ~ into sth** se déverser dans qc

**empty-handed** *adj* ❶ les mains vides ❷ *fig* bredouille

**EMT** *n abbr of* **emergency medical technician** ambulancier, -ère *m, f*, technicien ambulancier, technicienne ambulancière *m, f Québec, Suisse*

**emulate** ['em·jʊ·leɪt] *vt* ① imiter ② COMPUT émuler

**enable** [ɪ·'neɪ·bl] *vt* ① (*give the ability, make possible*) **to ~ sb to** +*infin* donner à qn la possibilité de +*infin* ② COMPUT permettre

**enamor** [ɪ·'næm·ər] *vt* **to be ~ed of sb** être amoureux de qn; **I'm not very ~ed of the idea** *iron* je ne suis pas vraiment fou de l'idée

**enchanted** *adj* enchanté(e)

**enchanting** *adj* charmant(e)

**enchilada** [ˌen·tʃɪ·'la·də] *n* tortilla fourrée servie avec une sauce épicée ▶ **the whole ~** *inf* et tout le tralala

**encl.** *n abbr of* **enclosure, enclosed** PJ *f*

**enclose** [en·'kloʊz] *vt* ① (*surround*) cerner; **to ~ sth with sth** entourer qc de qc ② (*include in same envelope*) joindre

**enclosure** [en·'kloʊ·ʒər] *n* ① (*area*) enceinte *f* ② (*for animals*) enclos *m* ③ (*act of enclosing*) clôture *f* ④ (*enclosed item*) pièce *f* jointe

**encode** [en·'koʊd] *vt* ① (*code*) coder ② LING encoder

**encore** ['an·kɔr] *n* bis *m*

**encounter** [en·'kaʊn·tər] I. *vt* ① (*experience*) rencontrer; **to ~ resistance** trouver de la résistance ② (*meet*) rencontrer à l'improviste II. *n* ① rencontre *f*; (*with enemy*) affrontement *m*; **her ~ with the boss** sa collision avec le patron ② SPORTS confrontation *f*

**encourage** [en·'kɜr·ɪdʒ] *vt* ① (*give confidence to*) encourager; **to ~ sb to** +*infin* encourager qn à +*infin* ② (*support*) favoriser

**encouragement** *n* encouragement *m*; **to give ~ to sth** encourager qn

**encouraging** *adj* stimulant(e); (*sign*) encourageant(e)

**encryption** [ɪn·'krɪp·ʃən] *n* COMPUT cryptage *m*

**encyclopedia** [en·ˌsaɪ·klə·'pi·di·ə] *n* encyclopédie *f*

**encyclopedic** [en·ˌsaɪ·klə·'pi·dɪk] *adj* encyclopédique

**end** [end] I. *n* ① (*finish*) fin *f*; **to come to an end** se terminer; **to put an ~ to sth** mettre fin à qc ② (*last point physically*) bout *m*; SPORTS côté *m*; **at the ~ of the corridor** au bout du couloir ③ (*last point of a range*) extrémité *f*; **at the other ~ of the scale** à l'autre extrême *m* ④ (*involving communication, exchange*) **how are things on your ~?** et pour toi/vous, comment ça se passe? ⑤ (*purpose*) objectif *m*; **to this ~** dans cette intention; **to achieve one's ~s** arriver à ses fins ⑥ (*death*) **sudden/untimely ~** mort *f* soudaine/précoce; **to meet one's ~** trouver la mort ⑦ (*small left over piece*) bout *m* ▶ **to burn the candle at both ~s** brûler la chandelle par les deux bouts; **to reach the ~ of the line** [*o* **road**] arriver en fin de course; **~ of story** un point, c'est tout; **and that's the ~ of the story** et je ne veux plus en entendre parler; **to make ~s meet** joindre les deux bouts; **in the ~** en fin de compte II. *vt* ① (*finish*) finir ② (*bring to a stop*) mettre un terme à III. *vi* ① (*result in*) **to ~ in sth** se terminer en qc ② (*finish*) finir; **to ~ with sth** s'achever par qc

◆ **end up** *vi* **to ~ a rich man** finir par devenir riche; **to ~ homeless** se retrouver à la rue; **to ~ doing sth** finir par faire qc

**endanger** [en·'deɪn·dʒər] *vt* mettre en danger

**ending** ['en·dɪŋ] *n* ① (*last part*) fin *f*; **a happy ~** une belle fin ② LING terminaison *f*

**endless** ['end·ləs] *adj* ① TECH sans fin ② (*infinite*) infini(e) ③ (*going on too long*) interminable

**endorse** [en·'dɔrs] *vt* ① (*declare approval for*) appuyer ② (*promote: product*) approuver ③ FIN (*check*) endosser

**endorsement** *n* ① (*support: of plan*) appui *m* ② (*recommendation*) approbation *f* ③ FIN endossement *m*

**endurance** [en·'dʊr·ən(t)s] *n* endurance *f*; **an ~ record** un record d'endurance; **to irritate sb beyond ~** agacer qn au plus haut point

**endure** [en·'dʊr] I. vt ① (*tolerate*) tolérer ② (*suffer*) endurer II. vi *form* durer

**enemy** ['en·ə·mi] I. n ① ennemi(e) *m(f)* II. adj MIL ennemi(e)

**energetic** [ˌen·ər·'dʒeṭ·ɪk] adj ① (*opp: weak*) énergique ② (*active*) actif(-ive)

**energize** ['en·ər·dʒaɪz] vt ① ELEC alimenter (en courant) ② *fig* stimuler

**energy** ['en·ər·dʒi] <-ies> n a. PHYS énergie *f;* **to be bursting with ~** déborder d'énergie; **to conserve one's ~** économiser ses forces; **to channel all one's energies into sth** concentrer tous ses efforts sur qc

**enforcement** n exécution *f;* (*of regulation*) observation *f;* (*of law*) application *f*

**engage** [en·'geɪdʒ] I. vt ① *form* (*hold interest of*) attirer; (*sb's attention*) éveiller; **to ~ sb in conversation** engager la conversation avec qn ② MIL attaquer ③ TECH activer; (*automatic pilot*) mettre; (*gear*) passer; **to ~ the clutch** embrayer II. vi ① (*interact*) **to ~ with sb** communiquer avec qn; **to ~ with the enemy** MIL attaquer l'ennemi ② TECH (*cogs*) s'engrener

**engaged** adj ① (*occupied*) occupé(e); **to be ~ in doing sth** être en train de faire qc ② (*before wedding*) **~ to be married** fiancé(e); **to get ~ to sb** se fiancer à qn

**engagement** n ① (*appointment*) rendez-vous *m* ② MIL combat *m* ③ (*agreement to marry*) fiançailles *fpl*

**engaging** adj engageant(e)

**engine** ['en·dʒɪn] n ① (*motor*) moteur *m;* **diesel/gasoline ~** moteur diesel/à essence ② AVIAT réacteur *m;* **jet ~** moteur *m* à réaction ③ RAIL locomotive *f*

**engineer** [ˌen·dʒɪ·'nɪr] I. n ① (*person qualified in engineering*) ingénieur *mf* ② a. RAIL mécanicien(ne) *m(f)* ③ RAIL conducteur, -trice *m, f* ④ TECH technicien(ne) *m(f)* ⑤ *fig, pej*

instigateur, -trice *m, f* II. vt ① construire ② *pej* manigancer

**engineering** [ˌen·dʒɪ·'nɪr·ɪŋ] n ingénierie *f*

**England** ['ɪŋ·glənd] n l'Angleterre *f*

**English** ['ɪŋ·glɪʃ] I. adj anglais(e); **~ people** les Anglais *mpl;* **an ~ film** un film en anglais; **an ~ class** un cours d'anglais; **~ speaker** anglophone *mf* II. n ① *pl* (*people*) **the ~** les Anglais *mpl* ② LING anglais *m;* **to translate into ~** traduire en anglais

**enjoy** [en·'dʒɔɪ] vt ① (*get pleasure from*) prendre plaisir à; **I ~ed the meal/coffee** j'ai bien aimé le repas/le café; **to ~ doing sth** aimer faire qc; **to ~ oneself** s'amuser ② (*have as advantage*) jouir de

**enjoyable** adj (*evening*) agréable; (*film, book*) bon(ne)

**enjoyment** n plaisir *m*

**enlarge** [en·'lardʒ] I. vt ① a. PHOT agrandir ② (*expand: territory*) étendre; (*vocabulary*) accroître II. vi s'agrandir

**enlargement** n agrandissement *m*

**enlist** [en·'lɪst] I. vi MIL **to ~ in the army** s'engager dans l'armée II. vt ① MIL recruter; **enlisted men** simples soldats *mpl* ② **to ~ sb's support/help** s'assurer le soutien/l'aide *f* de qn

**enormous** [ɪ·'nɔr·məs] adj énorme

**enough** [ɪ·'nʌf] I. adv suffisamment; **is this hot ~?** est-ce assez chaud?; **it's true ~** ce n'est que trop vrai; **funnily/curiously ~, I ...** le plus drôle/curieux, c'est que ... II. adj suffisant(e); **~ eggs/water** assez d'œufs/d'eau; **that's ~ crying!** ça suffit les pleurs! III. pron **I know ~ about it** j'en sais assez; **I've had ~** (*to eat*) ça me suffit; (*when angry*) j'en ai marre; **that should be ~** cela suffira; **that's ~!** ça suffit!

**enquire** [en·'kwaɪər] s. **inquire**

**enquiry** [en·'kwaɪ·ri] <-ies> n s. **inquiry**

**enraged** adj furieux(-euse)

**enroll** I. vi ① MIL s'engager ② (*register*) **to ~ in a course** s'inscrire à un cours II. vt immatriculer

**E**

**en route** [ˌɑnˈrut] *adv* en route

**ensure** [enˈʃʊr] *vt* garantir; *(security)* assurer; **to ~ everything is ready** s'assurer que tout est prêt

**enter** [ˈentər] **I.** *vt* ① *(go into: room, phase)* entrer dans; **it never ~ed my mind** *fig* ça ne m'a jamais traversé l'esprit ② *(insert)* introduire ③ *(write down)* inscrire; *(payment)* noter; COMPUT *(data)* entrer ④ *(join: college, school)* entrer à; *(navy, firm)* rejoindre; **to ~ the priesthood** entrer dans les ordres ⑤ *(participate: competition, exam)* s'inscrire à; *(race)* s'inscrire pour ⑥ *(make known: bid)* engager; *(claim, counterclaim)* faire; *(plea)* interjeter **II.** *vi* THEAT entrer **III.** *n* COMPUT touche *f* "entrée"; **to press ~** appuyer sur "entrée"

**enter key** *n* COMPUT touche *f* "entrée"

**enterprise** [ˈentərˌpraɪz] *n* ① *(undertaking)* entreprise *f* ② *(initiative)* esprit *m* d'initiative; **to show ~** se montrer entreprenant ③ *(firm)* entreprise *f*

**enterprising** *adj* entreprenant(e)

**entertain** [ˌentərˈteɪn] **I.** *vt* ① *(amuse)* amuser; *(with music, stories)* divertir; *(with activity)* occuper ② *(offer hospitality to guests)* recevoir ③ *(consider: doubts)* concevoir; *(suspicion)* éprouver; *(hope)* nourrir; *(idea)* prendre en considération **II.** *vi* recevoir

**entertainer** [ˌentərˈteɪnər] *n* artiste *mf*

**entertaining** *adj* divertissant(e)

**entertainment** *n* divertissement *m*, fun *m Québec;* **the ~ industry** l'industrie *f* du spectacle

**enthusiasm** [enˈθuziˌæzəm] *n* enthousiasme *m*

**enthusiastic** [enˌθuziˈæstɪk] *adj* enthousiaste; **to be ~ about sth** s'enthousiasmer pour qc

**enticing** *adj* attrayant(e); *(smile)* séduisant(e)

**entire** [enˈtaɪr] *adj* ① *(whole)* tout(e); **an ~ country** un pays entier; **the ~ two hours** les deux heures *fpl* en entier ② *(complete)* complet(-ète)

**entirely** *adv* entièrement; *(agree)* complètement; **~ for sb's benefit** uniquement pour qn

**entirety** [enˈtaɪrəˌti] *n form* intégralité *f*

**entitled** *adj* autorisé(e)

**entrance¹** [ˈentrən(t)s] *n* ① *a.* THEAT entrée *f* ② *(right to enter)* admission *f*

**entrance²** [enˈtræn(t)s] *vt* ravir

**entrance exam(ination)** *n* examen *m* d'entrée

**entrance fee** *n* droits *mpl* d'entrée [*o* d'inscription]

**entrance hall** *n* hall *m* d'entrée

**entrant** [ˈentrənt] *n* participant(e) *m(f)*

**entrée** [ˈɑntreɪ] *n* CULIN plat *m* de résistance

**entrepreneur** [ˌɑntrəprəˈnɜr] *n* entrepreneur *m*

**entrepreneurial** [ˌɑntrəprəˈnɜriˌəl] *adj* entrepreneurial(e)

**entrust** [enˈtrʌst] *vt* **to ~ sth to sb** confier qc à qn; **to ~ sb with sth** charger qn de qc

**entry** [ˈentri] <-ies> *n* ① *(act of entering)* entrée *f* ② *(joining an organization)* adhésion *f* ③ *(recorded item: in dictionary)* entrée *f*; *(in accounts)* écriture *f*; *(in diary)* note *f* ④ *(application, entrant: for exam, competition)* inscription *f*; *(for race)* concurrent(e) *m(f)*

**entry-level** *adj* pour débutant(e)s

**entryway** *n* entrée *f*

**envelope** [ˈenvəˌloʊp] *n* enveloppe *f* ▶ **to push the ~** repousser les limites

**envious** [ˈenviəs] *adj* envieux(-euse); **to be ~ of sb/sth** envier qn/qc

**environment** [enˈvaɪrˀnmənt] *n* environnement *m;* **home ~** environnement familial; **~-friendly** qui respecte l'environnement

**environmental** [enˌvaɪrənˈmenˌtˀl] *adj* environnemental(e); **~ damage** dégâts *mpl* écologiques; **~ impact** effets *mpl* sur l'environnement

**environmentalist** [enˌvaɪrˀnˈmenˌtˀlˌɪst] *n* environnementaliste *mf*

**environmentally friendly** *adj* qui respecte l'environnement

**envision** [ɪn·ˈvɪʒ·ˈən] *vt* prévoir; **to ~ doing sth** prévoir de faire qc

**envy** [ˈen·vi] I. *n* envie *f*; **to feel ~ toward sb** envier qn; **to be the ~ of sb** faire l'envie de qn ►**to be green with ~** être vert de jalousie II.<-ie-> *vt* envier; **to ~ sb sth** envier qc chez qn

**eon** [ˈi·ən] *n* éternité *f*

**epidemic** [ˌep·ə·ˈdem·ɪk] I. *adj* épidémique II. *n* épidémie *f*

**epilog(ue)** [ˈep·ə·lɔg] *n* épilogue *m*

**epiphany** [ɪ·ˈpɪf·ə·ni] *n* révélation *f*

**episode** [ˈep·ə·soʊd] *n* épisode *m*

**epoxy** [ɪ·ˈpak·si] *n* résine *f* époxyde

**equal** [ˈi·kwəl] I. *adj* ❶ *(the same, same in amount: time, terms, share)* égal(e); *(reason, status)* même; **to be ~ to sth** être égal à qc; **~ in volume** de volume égal; **~ pay for ~ work** à travail égal, salaire égal ❷ *(able to do)* **to be ~ to a task** être à la hauteur d'une tâche ►**all <u>things</u> being ~** toutes choses égales par ailleurs II. *n* égal(e) *m(f)*; **to have no ~** ne pas avoir son pareil III. <-l- *o* -ll-> *vt* ❶ MATH être égal à ❷ *(match: amount, record)* égaler

**equality** [ɪ·ˈkwɑl·ə·ti] *n no pl* égalité *f*; **racial ~** égalité raciale; *(European Union)*; **the E~ Act** loi générale sur l'égalité de traitement

**equalize** [ˈi·kwə·laɪz] *vt* égaliser

**equally** [ˈi·kwəl·i] *adv* **~ good** aussi bien; **to contribute ~ to sth** contribuer à qc à part égale; **to divide sth ~** diviser qc en parts égales; **but ~, we know that ...** mais de même, nous savons que ...

**equal opportunity** *n* égalité *f* des chances

**equation** [ɪ·ˈkweɪ·ʒən] *n* équation *f* ►**the other <u>side</u> of the ~** l'autre membre/partie de l'équation

**equator** [ɪ·ˈkweɪ·tər] *n* **the ~** l'équateur *m*

**equip** [ɪ·ˈkwɪp] <-pp-> *vt* ❶ *(fit out)* équiper; **to ~ oneself with sth** s'équiper de qc ❷ *(prepare)* **to ~ sb for sth** préparer qn à qc

**equipment** *n* équipement *m*; **camping ~** matériel *m* de camping

**equivalent** [ɪ·ˈkwɪv·ˈəl·ənt] I. *adj* **~ to sth** équivalent(e) à qc; **to be ~ to doing sth** revenir à faire qc II. *n* équivalent *m*

**erase** [ɪ·ˈreɪs] *vt* ❶ COMPUT, FIN effacer; *(losses)* éliminer ❷ *(blackboard)* effacer

**eraser** [ɪ·ˈreɪs·ər] *n* gomme *f*, efface *f* Québec

**erect** [ɪ·ˈrekt] I. *adj* ❶ *(upright)* droit(e); **to stand ~** se tenir debout ❷ ANAT *(penis)* en érection II. *vt* ❶ *(build)* a. fig ériger ❷ *(put up)* installer

**erection** [ɪ·ˈrek·ʃən] *n* a. ANAT érection *f*

**erosion** [ɪ·ˈroʊ·ʒən] *n* érosion *f*

**erotic** [ɪ·ˈrɑ·tɪk] *adj* érotique

**err** [ɜr] *vi form* commettre une erreur; **to ~ on the side of caution** pécher par excès de prudence ►**to ~ is <u>human</u>** *prov* l'erreur est humaine *prov*

**erratic** [ɪ·ˈræt·ɪk] *adj (quality, performance)* inégal; *(pulse)* irrégulier(-ère); *(personality, behavior)* imprévisible

**error** [ˈer·ər] *n* ❶ *(mistake)* erreur *f*; **to do sth in ~** faire qc par erreur; **the margin of ~** la marge d'erreur ❷ SPORTS faute *f* ►**to see the ~ of one's <u>ways</u>** prendre conscience de ses erreurs

**erupt** [ɪ·ˈrʌpt] *vi* ❶ *(explode: volcano)* entrer en éruption ❷ MED *(teeth)* sortir; *(rash)* apparaître

**eruption** [ɪ·ˈrʌp·ʃən] *n* éruption *f*

**escalator** [ˈes·kə·leɪ·tər] *n* escalator *m*

**escape** [ɪ·ˈskeɪp] I. *vi* ❶ *(flee: prisoner)* s'évader; *(animal)* s'échapper ❷ *(leak: gas)* s'échapper; *(liquid)* fuir ❸ COMPUT **to ~ from a program** quitter une application ►**to ~ with one's <u>life</u>** s'en sortir vivant II. *vt* ❶ *(avoid)* **to ~ sth** échapper à qc; **to ~ the fact that ...** on ne peut pas ignorer le fait que ... ❷ *(fail to be noticed or remembered)* **to ~ sb's attention** échapper à l'attention de qn; **her name ~s me** son nom m'échappe ❸ *(not suppressed)* **a cry ~d them** ils ont laissé échapper un cri III. *n* ❶ *(act of fleeing)* évasion *f* ❷ *(avoidance)* **to have a narrow ~** l'échapper belle ❸ *(accidental outflow)*

**E**

fuite *f* ❹ LAW ~ **clause** clause *f* dérogatoire

**escort** ['es·kɔrt] I. *vt* to ~ **sb** to **safety** escorter qn en lieu sûr II. *n* ❶ (*guard*) escorte *f*; **under police** ~ sous escorte policière ❷ (*social companion*) compagnon *m*, hôtesse *f*

**Eskimo** ['es·kə·mou] <-s> *n* ❶ (*person*) Esquimau(de) *m(f)* ❷ LING eskimo *m*; *s.a.* **English**

**especially** [ɪ·'speʃ·ə·li] *adv* surtout; **he's brought this ~ for you** il a apporté cela spécialement pour toi/vous; **I was ~ happy to meet them** j'étais particulièrement content de les rencontrer

**espionage** ['es·pi·ə·naʒ] *n* espionnage *m*

**espresso** [e·'spres·ou] <-s> *n* express *m*; **two ~s** deux express

**essential** [ɪ·'sen·(t)ʃl] I. *adj* (*component, difference*) essentiel(le) II. *n* pl **the ~s** l'essentiel; **to be reduced to its ~s** être réduit à l'essentiel

**essentially** [ɪ·'sen·(t)ʃl·i] *adv* ❶ (*basically*) en gros ❷ (*mostly*) essentiellement; **to be ~ correct** être correct pour l'essentiel

**EST** [i·es·'ti] *n abbr of* **Eastern Standard Time** EST *m* (*heure de l'est de l'Amérique du Nord*)

**establish** [ɪ·'stæb·lɪʃ] *vt* ❶ (*set up*) établir; (*fellowship, hospital*) fonder ❷ (*find out: facts*) établir ❸ (*demonstrate*) **to ~ one's authority over sb** affirmer son autorité sur qn; **to ~ sb as** faire reconnaître qn en tant que ❹ ADMIN **to ~ residence** élire domicile

**establishment** *n* ❶ (*business*) établissement *m*; **business** ~ maison *f* de commerce; **family** ~ entreprise *f* familiale ❷ (*group*) **the** ~ la classe dominante ❸ (*setting up*) création *f* ❹ (*discovery: of facts*) établissement *m*

**estate** [ɪ·'steɪt] *n* ❶ (*land*) propriété *f* ❷ LAW biens *mpl* ❸ (*the press*) **the fourth** ~ le quatrième pouvoir ❹ (*state*) état *m*; **the holy ~ of matrimony** les liens *mpl* sacrés du mariage

**estimate** ['es·tɪ·mɪt] I. *vt* (*cost, increase*) estimer II. *n* ❶ (*assessment*) estimation *f*; **at a conservative** ~ au bas mot; **at a rough** ~ à vue de nez ❷ (*quote*) devis *m*

**estimated** ['es·tɪ·meɪ·tɪd] *adj* estimé(e); ~ **time of arrival** heure *f* d'arrivée prévue; **it will cost an ~ $1000** le coût est estimé à 1000 dollars

**estuary** ['es·tʃu·er·i] <-ies> *n* estuaire *m*

**etc.** *adv abbr of* **et cetera** etc.

**et cetera** [ɪt·'set·ər·ə] *adv* et cætera

**eternal** [ɪ·'tɜr·nəl] *adj* ❶ (*lasting forever*) éternel(le) ❷ *pej* (*incessant*) constant(e) ▸ **hope springs** ~ *prov* l'espoir fait vivre *prov*; ~ **triangle** ménage *m* à trois

**eternally** [ɪ·'tɜr·nəl·i] *adv* ❶ (*forever*) éternellement ❷ (*incessantly*) constamment

**eternity** [ɪ·'tɜr·nə·ti] *n* éternité *f*; **for all** ~ pour l'éternité

**ethical** ['eθ·ɪk·əl] *adj* éthique

**ethics** ['eθ·ɪks] *n pl + sing vb* éthique *f*; **code of** ~ code de déontologie

**ethnic** ['eθ·nɪk] I. *adj* ethnique; ~ **cleansing** purification *f* ethnique II. *n pej* membre *m* d'une minorité ethnique

**EU** [ˌi·'ju] *n abbr of* **European Union** UE *f*; ~ **countries** pays *mpl* membres de l'UE

**Eucharist** ['ju·kər·ɪst] *n* REL **the** ~ l'Eucharistie *f*

**eulogy** ['ju·lə·dʒi] <-ies> *n* (*high praise*) éloge *m*; (*at funeral*) éloge *m* (funèbre)

**euro** ['jʊr·ou] *n* euro *m*

**euro bailout fund**, **eurozone bailout fund** *n* FIN fonds *m* de secours européen

**Europe** ['jʊr·əp] *n* l'Europe *f*; **Eastern** ~ l'Europe de l'Est

**European** [jʊr·ə·'pi·ən] I. *adj* européen(ne) II. *n* Européen(ne) *m(f)*

**European Union** *n* Union *f* européenne

**evacuate** [ɪ·'væk·ju·eɪt] *vt* évacuer

**evacuation** [ɪˌvæk·ju·'eɪ·ʃn] *n* évacuation *f*

**evade** [ɪ·'veɪd] *vt* (*question*) esquiver;

(*police*) échapper à; (*tax*) éviter; **to ~ capture** éviter d'être pris

**evaluate** [ɪˈvæl·ju·eɪt] *vt* (*calculate value*) évaluer

**evaporate** [ɪˈvæp·ə·reɪt] I. *vt* faire évaporer II. *vi* s'évaporer; *fig* se volatiliser

**even** [ˈiˑvən] I. *adv* ❶ (*used to intensify*) même; **not ~** même pas; **~ as a child, she ...** même lorsqu'elle était enfant, elle ...; **~ you have to admit that ...** même toi, tu dois admettre que ... ❷ (*despite*) **~ if ...** même si ...; **~ so ...** tout de même ...; **~ then he ...** et alors, il ...; **~ though he** bien qu'il +*subj* ❸ *with comparative* **~ more/less/better/worse** encore plus/moins/mieux/pire; **that's ~ better than ...** c'est encore mieux que ... II. *adj* ❶ (*level*) nivelé(e); (*temperature*) constant(e); **~ rows** rangs *mpl* équilibrés; **an ~ surface** une surface plane ❷ (*equal*) égal(e); **an ~ contest** une compétition équilibrée; **to get ~ with sb** se venger de qn; **now you're ~** maintenant vous êtes quittes ❸ (*constant, regular*) régulier(-ère); **to have an ~ temper** être d'une humeur toujours égale ❹ (*fair, of same amount*) équitable; **an ~ distribution of wealth** une distribution équitable des richesses ❺ MATH pair(e); **an ~ page** une page paire III. *vt* ❶ (*make level*) aplanir ❷ (*equalize*) égaliser

**◆even out** I. *vi* (*prices*) s'équilibrer II. *vt* égaliser; (*differences*) réduire

**◆even up** *vt* rééquilibrer

**evening** [ˈiːvˑnɪŋ] *n* soir *m*, (*as period, event*) soirée *f*; **good ~!** bonsoir!; **in the ~** le soir; **that ~** ce soir-là; **the previous ~** la veille au soir; **every Monday ~** tous les lundis soir(s); **(on) Monday ~** lundi dans la soirée, dans la soirée de lundi; **during the ~** dans la soirée; **8 o'clock in the ~** 8 heures du soir; **at the end of the ~** en fin de soirée; **all ~** toute la soirée

**evening class** *n* cours *m* du soir

**evening dress** *n* tenue *f* de soirée

**evenly** [ˈiˑvənˑli] *adv* ❶ (*calmly*) calme-

ment; **to state sth ~** déclarer qc posément ❷ (*equally*) équitablement; **to divide sth ~** partager qc à parts égales; **to be ~ spaced** être espacé de manière régulière

**event** [ɪˈvent] *n* ❶ (*happening*) événement *m*; **a social ~** rencontre *f*; **a sports ~** un événement sportif; **after the ~** après coup ❷ (*case*) cas *m*; **in the ~** en l'occurrence; **in the ~ (that) it rains** au cas où il pleuvrait

**even-tempered** [ˈiˑvənˈtempˑərd] *adj* d'humeur égale

**eventful** [ɪˈventˑfəl] *adj* plein(e) d'événements

**eventual** [ɪˈvenˑtʃʊˑəl] *adj* (*final*) final(e); **the ~ cost will be ...** finalement, le coût total sera de ...

**eventuality** [ɪˌvenˑtʃʊˈælˑəˑt̬i] <-ies> *n* éventualité *f*

**eventually** *adv* ❶ (*finally*) finalement ❷ (*some day*) un de ces jours; **he'll do it ~** il finira bien par le faire

**ever** [ˈevˑər] *adv* ❶ (*on any occasion*) **never ~** jamais; *inf* jamais de la vie; **if you ~ meet her** si jamais tu la rencontres; **have you ~ met her?** est-ce que tu l'as déjà rencontrée?; **did he ~ call you?** est-ce qu'il t'a appelé en fait?; **his fastest ~ race** sa course la plus rapide de toutes; **the biggest ship ever** le plus grand bateau jamais construit ❷ (*always*) toujours; **as ~** comme toujours; **as good as ~** aussi bon que d'habitude; **harder than ever** plus difficile que jamais; **~ since ...** depuis que ...; **~vigilant/-popular** toujours vigilant/populaire ❸ (*for emphasis*) **why ~ did he leave?** pourquoi est-il donc parti?

**every** [ˈevˑri] *adj* ❶ (*each*) **~ child/cat/pencil** chaque enfant *mf*/chat *m*/crayon *m*; **~ time** (à) chaque fois; **not ~ book can be borrowed** les livres ne peuvent pas tous être empruntés; **~ one of them** tous sans exception; **~ second counts** chaque seconde compte; **~ Sunday** chaque dimanche *m*; **in ~ way** à tous points de vue ❷ (*repeated*) **~ other day** un jour sur deux; **~ now**

**and then** [*o again*] de temps en temps ❸ (*used for emphasis*) ~ **single page** chaque page *f;* **you had ~ chance to go** tu as eu toutes les possibilités d'y aller; **her ~ wish** son moindre désir

**everybody** ['ev·ri·ba·di] *indef pron, sing* tout le monde; ~ **but Paul** tous sauf Paul; ~ **who agrees** tous ceux qui sont d'accord; **where's ~ going?** où est-ce que tout le monde va?; ~ **else** tous les autres

**everyday** ['ev·ri·deɪ] *adj* quotidien(ne); ~ **language** langage *m* courant; ~ **life** la vie quotidienne; ~ **topic** sujet *m* banal

**everyone** ['ev·ri·wʌn] *pron s.* **everybody**

**everything** ['ev·ri·θɪŋ] *indef pron, sing* ❶ (*all things*) tout; **is ~ all right?** tout va bien?; ~ **is OK** ça va bien, c'est correct *Québec;* ~ **they drink** tout ce qu'ils boivent; **to do ~ necessary/one can** faire tout le nécessaire/ce qu'on peut; **because of the weather and** ~ à cause du temps et tout ça ❷ (*the most important thing*) **to be ~ to sb** être tout pour qn; **money isn't** ~ ce n'est pas tout d'être riche; **time is** ~ c'est le temps qui compte; *s.a.* **anything**

**everywhere** ['ev·ri·(h)wer] *adv* partout; ~ **else** partout ailleurs; **to look ~ for sth** chercher qc partout; **people arrived from** ~ les gens arrivaient de toutes parts

**evict** [ɪ·'vɪkt] *vt* **to ~ sb from their home** expulser qn de chez lui

**evidence** ['ev·ɪ·dᵊn(t)s] **I.** *n* ❶ LAW (*from witness*) témoignage *m;* (*physical proof*) preuve *f;* **circumstantial ~** preuve indirecte; **fresh ~** nouvelle preuve; **to be used as ~** être utilisé comme preuve ❷ (*indications*) évidence *f;* **to be much in ~** être bien en évidence; **on the ~ of recent events** sur la base de récents événements **II.** *vt form* **to ~ interest in sth** montrer de l'intérêt pour qc

**evident** ['ev·ɪ·dᵊnt] *adj* évident(e)

**evil** ['i·vᵊl] **I.** *adj* mauvais(e); **the ~ eye** le mauvais œil; ~ **spirit(s)** mauvais esprits *mpl;* **to have an ~ tongue** avoir une langue de vipère **II.** *n pej* mal *m;* **social ~** fléau *m* social; **the ~s of the past** les erreurs *fpl* du passé; **good and ~** le bien et le mal; **it's the lesser of two ~s** c'est un moindre mal

**evolution** [ˌev·ə·'lu·ʃᵊn] *n* évolution *f*

**ewe** [ju] *n* brebis *f*

**ex** [eks] <-es> *n inf* (*former spouse*) ex *mf*

**ex-** *in compounds* ancien(ne)

**exact** [ɪg·'zækt] **I.** *adj* exact(e); **to have the ~ change** avoir l'appoint; **the ~ opposite** tout le contraire; ~ **copy** reproduction *f* fidèle **II.** *vt* ❶ exiger; **to ~ revenge on sb** prendre sa revanche sur qn ❷ *pej* extorquer

**exactly** *adv* (*precisely*) exactement; **how ~ did he do that?** comment a-t-il fait au juste?; **I don't ~ agree** je ne suis pas tout à fait d'accord; **not ~** pas vraiment

**exaggerate** [ɪg·'zædʒ·ə·reɪt] **I.** *vt* exagérer; (*situation*) grossir **II.** *vi* exagérer

**exaggerated** [ɪg·'zædʒ·ər·eɪ·t̬ɪd] *adj* exagéré(e)

**exaggeration** [ɪgˌzædʒ·ᵊr·'eɪ·ʃᵊn] *n* exagération *f;* **it's no ~ to say that …** on peut dire sans exagérer que …

**exam** [ɪg·'zæm] *n* examen *m;* **to take/pass an ~** passer/réussir un examen

**examination** [ɪgˌzæm·ɪ·'neɪ·ʃᵊn] *n* examen *m;* **on closer ~** après un examen plus approfondi

**examine** [ɪg·'zæm·ɪn] *vt* ❶ (*test*) examiner; **to ~ sb on sth** interroger qn sur qc ❷ (*study, scan*) étudier ❸ LAW interroger

**example** [ɪg·'zæm·pl] *n* exemple *m;* **for ~** par exemple; **to give sb an ~ of sth** donner à qn un exemple de qc; **to set an ~** donner l'exemple; **to make an ~ of sb** donner qn en exemple

**exasperating** *adj* exaspérant(e)

**excavate** ['ek·skə·veɪt] **I.** *vt* ❶ (*expose by digging*) déterrer; (*site*) fouiller ❷ (*hollow by digging*) creuser **II.** *vi* faire des fouilles *fpl*

**excavation** [ˌek·skə·ˈveɪ·ʃən] *n* ① (*digging in ground*) excavation *f;* (*of tumulus*) dégagement *m;* (*of tunnel*) percée *f* ② *pl* (*by archaeologists*) fouilles *fpl*

**exceed** [ɪk·ˈsid] *vt* dépasser

**exceedingly** *adv form* excessivement

**excel** [ɪk·ˈsel] <-ll-> I. *vi* exceller; **to ~ at chess** exceller aux échecs; **to ~ in French** être excellent en français II. *vt* **to ~ oneself** se surpasser

**excellence** [ˈek·səl·ən(t)s] *n* excellence *f*

**excellent** [ˈek·səl·ənt] *adj* ① excellent(e); **to have ~ taste** avoir un très bon goût ② ~! parfait!

**except** [ɪk·ˈsept] I. *prep* sauf; **~ for sb/ sth** à l'exception de qn/qc; **why would he do it ~ to annoy me?** pourquoi est-ce qu'il le ferait à moins que ce ne soit pour m'embêter? II. *conj* ~ **that** sauf que; **to do nothing ~ wait** ne rien faire si ce n'est attendre

**excepting** *prep, conj* excepté

**exception** [ɪk·ˈsep·ʃən] *n* ① (*special case*) exception *f;* **with the ~ of ...** à l'exception de ...; **with a few ~s** à part quelques exceptions ② (*objection*) **to take ~ to sth** s'élever contre ▶ **the ~ proves the rule** *prov* l'exception confirme la règle *prov*

**exceptional** [ɪk·ˈsep·ʃən·əl] *adj* exceptionnel(le)

**exceptionally** [ɪk·ˈsep·ʃən·əl·i] *adv* exceptionnellement; **to be ~ bright** être particulièrement intelligent

**excerpt** [ˈek·sɜrpt] I. *n* extrait *m* II. *vt* **to be ~ed from sth** être extrait de qc

**excess** [ɪk·ˈses] I. <-es> *n* ① (*overindulgence*) excès *m;* **to do sth to ~** faire qc avec excès ② (*surplus amount*) excédent *m;* **in ~ of $500** qui dépasse $500 II. *adj* excédentaire; **~ production** excédent de production

**excessive** [ɪk·ˈses·ɪv] *adj* excessif(-ive); **~ zeal** excès *m* de zèle

**exchange** [ɪks·ˈtʃeɪndʒ] I. *vt* ① (*trade for the equivalent*) **to ~ sth for sth** échanger qc contre qc; **to ~ addresses** échanger des adresses ② (*interchange*)

interchanger ③ ECON vendre II. *n* ① (*interchange, trade*) échange *m;* **in ~ for sth** en échange de qc ② FIN, ECON change *m;* **foreign ~** devises *fpl* ③ (*discussion*) échange *m* verbal ④ TEL (*telephone*) ~ central *m* téléphonique

**exchange student** *n* étudiant(e) en échange *f*

**excise¹** [ˈek·saɪz] *n* taxe *f*

**excise²** [ek·ˈsaɪz] *vt form* ① exciser ② *fig* supprimer

**excitable** [ɪk·ˈsaɪ·tə·bl] *adj* ① ANAT excitable ② (*person*) nerveux(-euse)

**excite** [ɪk·ˈsaɪt] *vt* ① (*arouse strong feelings in*) exciter; **to ~ an audience** captiver un public ② (*elicit*) susciter; (*passion*) attiser; (*feelings*) provoquer; (*imagination*) stimuler

**excited** [ɪk·ˈsaɪ·tɪd] *adj* ① *a.* ANAT, PHYS excité(e) ② (*happy*) ~**d about an idea** enthousiasmé par une idée; **there is nothing to get ~ about** il n'y a pas de quoi s'exciter; **don't get ~ about it yet** ne te réjouis pas trop vite ③ (*angry*) **don't get ~!** ne t'énerve pas!

**excitement** *n* excitation *f;* **to be in a state of ~** être tout excité

**exciting** *adj* (*match, prospect*) passionnant(e); (*discovery*) sensationnel(le)

**exclaim** [ɪks·ˈkleɪm] I. *vi* s'exclamer; **to ~ in delight** pousser un cri de joie II. *vt* **to ~ that ...** s'écrier que ...

**exclamation** [ˌeks·klə·ˈmeɪ·ʃən] *n* exclamation *f*

**exclamation point** *n* point *m* d'exclamation

**exclude** [ɪks·ˈklud] *vt* exclure

**excluding** *prep* à l'exclusion de; **~ sb/ sth** sans compter qn/qc; **~ taxes** taxes *fpl* non comprises

**exclusive** [ɪks·ˈklu·sɪv] I. *adj* ① (*debarring*) **two things are mutually ~** deux choses s'excluent mutuellement ② (*only, sole, total*) exclusif(-ive) ③ (*reserved for a few: restaurant*) de luxe; **~ to this paper** en exclusivité dans ce journal II. *n* (*in media*) exclusivité *f*

**excruciating** [ɪk·ˈskru·ʃi·eɪ·tɪŋ] *adj* atroce; (*pain*) insupportable

**excursion** [ɪkˈskɜr·ʒ⋅ᵊn] n excursion f, course f Suisse

**excusable** adj excusable

**excuse** [ɪkˈskjuz] I. vt ① (justify) excuser; **to ~ sb's lateness** excuser le retard de qn; **that does not ~ her lying** ça n'excuse pas ses mensonges ② (allow not to attend) **he was ~d from gym** il a été dispensé de sport ▸ **~ me** (calling for attention, apologizing) excuse(z)-moi; (please repeat) pardon; (indignantly) je m'excuse II. n excuse f; **poor ~** mauvaise excuse; **there's no ~ for it** c'est inexcusable; **a poor ~ for a film/teacher** iron un semblant de film/de prof

**exec** [ɪgˈzek] n inf abbr of **executive** cadre m

**execute** [ˈek·sɪ·kjut] vt a. LAW exécuter

**execution** [ˌek·sɪ·kju·ʃᵊn] n exécution f

**executioner** [ˌek·sɪ·kju·ʃᵊn·ər] n bourreau m

**executive** [ɪgˈzek·jə·tɪv] I. n ① (manager) cadre m ② + sing/pl vb POL (power m) exécutif m; (of organization) comité m exécutif II. adj ① POL exécutif(-ive) ② ECON (committee) de direction; (post) de cadre; (decisions) de la direction

**exempt** [ɪgˈzempt] I. vt exempter; **to ~ sb from doing sth** dispenser qn de faire qc II. adj exempt(e); **to be ~ from tax** être exonéré d'impôt

**exemption** [ɪgˈzemp·ʃᵊn] n ① (release) exemption f ② MIL, SCHOOL dispense f ③ FIN **tax** ~ exonération f d'impôt; **~ from taxes** dégrèvement m d'impôts

**exercise** [ˈek·sər·saɪz] I. vt ① (giving physical exercise to: muscles, body) exercer; (dog) sortir; (horse) entraîner ② form (disturb) **to ~ sb's mind** préoccuper qn ③ form (apply: authority) exercer; **to ~ caution** faire preuve de prudence II. vi faire de l'exercice III. n ① (training, workout) exercice m; **to do leg ~s** faire travailler ses jambes ② MIL manœuvres fpl ③ sing (action, achievement) exercice m; **a marketing ~** une opération de marketing

④ (use) usage m ⑤ pl cérémonie f; **the graduation ~s** la remise des diplômes

**exert** [ɪgˈzɜrt] vt ① (apply: control, pressure) exercer; **to ~ (one's) influence** jouer de son influence ② (make an effort) **to ~ oneself** (make an effort) se donner du mal

**exertion** [ɪgˈzɜr·ʃᵊn] n effort m

**exhale** [eks·ˈheɪl] I. vt ① (breathe out) exhaler ② (give off gases, scents) dégager ③ fig respirer II. vi expirer

**exhaust** [ɪgˈzɔst] I. vt ① épuiser; **to ~ oneself** s'épuiser II. n ① (gas) gaz mpl d'échappement ② (pipe) pot m d'échappement

**exhausted** adj épuisé(e)

**exhausting** adj épuisant(e)

**exhaustion** [ɪgˈzɔs·tʃᵊn] n épuisement m

**exhaustive** [ɪgˈzɔ·stɪv] adj (comprehensive) exhaustif(-ive)

**exhaust pipe** n AUTO tuyau m d'échappement

**exhibit** [ɪgˈzɪb·ɪt] I. n ① (display) pièce f exposée ② ART exposition f; **~ of paintings** exposition de peinture ③ LAW pièce f à conviction II. vt ① (show) exposer ② (display: character traits) manifester III. vi ART exposer

**exhibition** [ˌek·sɪ·ˈbɪ·ʃᵊn] n (display) exposition f; **the dinosaur ~** l'exposition sur les dinosaures ▸ **to make an ~ of oneself** pej se donner en spectacle

**exhibitor** [ɪgˈzɪb·ɪ·tər] n exposant(e) m(f)

**exhilarating** [ɪgˈzɪl·ᵊr·eɪ·t̬ɪŋ] adj exaltant(e)

**exhilaration** [ɪgˈzɪl·ᵊr·eɪ·ʃᵊn] n euphorie f

**exist** [ɪgˈzɪst] vi ① (be) exister ② (live) **to ~ on sth** vivre de qc ③ (survive) subsister

**existence** [ɪgˈzɪs·tᵊn(t)s] n ① (being real) existence f; **to be in ~** exister; **to come into ~** naître ② (life) vie f

**existing** adj actuel(le)

**exit** [ˈek·sɪt] I. n ① sortie f; **emergency ~** sortie de secours; **~ visa** visa m de sortie II. vi sortir

**exodus** ['ek·sə·dəs] *n sing* ① (*mass departure*) exode *m* ② REL **Exodus** l'Exode *m*

**exorbitant** [ıg·'zɔr·bə·tʰənt] *adj* exorbitant(e)

**exotic** [ıg·'za·t̬ık] *adj* exotique

**expand** [ık·'spænd] I. *vi* ① (*increase*) augmenter ② (*enlarge: city*) s'étendre; PHYS (*metal, gas*) se dilater; (*business, economy*) se développer; **we're ~ing into electronics** nous nous lançons dans l'électronique II. *vt* ① (*make bigger*) augmenter ② (*elaborate*) développer

**expansion** [ık·'spæn·(t)ʃən] *n* ① (*spreading out*) expansion *f*; (*of gas*) dilatation *f* ② (*growth: of population*) accroissement *m*; (*of business*) développement *m* ③ (*elaboration*) développement *m*

**expatriate** [ek·'sper·tri·eıt] I. *n* expatrié(e) *m(f)* II. *vt* expatrier

**expect** [ık·'spekt] *vt* ① (*think likely*) s'attendre à; **to ~ to** +*infin* s'attendre à +*infin;* **to ~ sb to** +*infin* s'attendre à ce que +*subj;* **to ~ sth from sb** s'attendre à qc de la part de qn ② (*require*) attendre; **to ~ sth from sb** attendre qc de qn; I ~ **you to** +*infin* j'attends de vous que vous +*subj;* **is that too much to ~?** est-ce que c'est trop demander? ③ (*wait for*) attendre; **to be ~ing a baby** attendre un bébé

**expectant** [ık·'spek·tʰənt] *adj* qui est dans l'attente

**expectation** [ˌek·spek·'teı·ʃʰən] *n* attente *f;* **to live up to sb's ~s** répondre aux attentes de qn

**expedition** [ˌek·spı·'dıʃ·ʰən] *n* expédition *f*

**expel** [ık·'spel] <-ll-> *vt* (*pupil*) renvoyer; **to ~ sb from a country** expulser qn d'un pays

**expenditure** [ık·'spen·dı·tʃər] *n* ① (*act of spending*) dépense *f* ② (*money*) ~ **on sth** les dépenses *fpl* pour qc

**expense** [ık·'spen(t)s] *n* ① (*cost*) dépense *f;* **at great ~** à grands frais; **to go to the ~ of sth/doing sth** se mettre en frais pour qc/faire qc; **at sb's ~** aux frais de qn ② *pl* (*money*) frais *mpl;* **to be on ~s** (*meal*) passer dans les frais; (*executive*) avoir ses frais payés ③ (*disadvantage*) **a joke at my ~** une plaisanterie à mes dépens; **at the ~ of his career** au détriment de sa carrière ▶ **all ~s paid** tous frais payés

**expense account** *n* note *f* de frais

**expensive** [ık·'spen(t)·sıv] *adj* cher(chère); **to have ~ tastes** avoir des goûts de luxe

**experience** [ık·'spır·i·ən(t)s] I. *n* expérience *f; from ~* par expérience II. *vt* connaître; (*loss*) subir; (*sensation*) ressentir

**experienced** *adj* expérimenté(e)

**experiment** [ık·'sper·ı·mənt] I. *n* expérience *f;* **to conduct an ~** faire une expérience II. *vi* **to ~ on animals** faire des expériences sur des animaux; **to ~ with sth on sb/qc** expérimenter qc sur qn/qc; **to ~ with drugs** essayer des drogues

**experimental** [ek·ˌsper·ı·'men·tʰəl] *adj* expérimental(e)

**expert** ['ek·spɜrt] I. *n* expert(e) *m(f);* **gardening ~** expert en jardinage; **an ~ at doing sth** un expert dans l'art de faire qc II. *adj* expert(e); **~ at doing sth** expert en qc

**expertise** [ˌek·spɜr·'tiz] *n* ① (*knowledge*) compétence *f* ② (*skill*) habileté *f*

**expiration** [ˌek·spə·'reı·ʃʰən] *n* expiration *f*

**expiration date** *n* date *f* d'expiration

**expire** [ık·'spaıər] *vi* ① (*terminate*) expirer ② *a. fig, form* rendre l'âme

**expiry** [ık·'spaı·ri] *n s.* expiration

**explain** [ık·'spleın] I. *vt* expliquer; **to ~ sth away** trouver des justifications à II. *vi* s'expliquer

**explanation** [ˌek·splə·'neı·ʃʰən] *n* explication *f;* **to give sb an ~ for why ...** expliquer à qn pourquoi ...

**explicit** [ık·'splıs·ıt] *adj* ① (*clear*) **to be ~ about sth** être explicite sur qc ② (*vulgar*) (à caractère) pornographique

**explode** [ık·'sploud] I. *vi* ① (*blow up*)

exploser; (*tire, ball*) éclater; (*engine, plane*) exploser ② (*burst*) exploser; **to ~ with** [*o in*] **anger** exploser de colère; **to ~ into a riot** dégénérer en révolte **II.** *vt* ① (*blow up*) faire exploser; (*tire, ball*) faire éclater ② (*destroy: theory*) démonter; (*myth*) détruire

**exploit** ['ek·splɔɪt] **I.** *vt a. pej* exploiter; (*loophole, change*) profiter de **II.** *n* exploit *m*

**exploitation** [,ek·splɔɪ·'teɪ·ʃən] *n* exploitation *f*

**exploration** [,ek·splɔr·'eɪ·ʃən] *n* ① (*journey*) exploration *f* ② (*examination*) examen *m*; **to carry out an ~ of sth** procéder à l'examen de qc ③ (*searching*) **~ for sth** recherche *f* de qc

**exploratory** [ɪk·'splɔr·ə·tɔr·i] *adj* (*voyage*) d'exploration; (*test*) préparatoire; **~ well** sondage *m*

**explore** [ɪk·'splɔr] **I.** *vt* explorer **II.** *vi* **to ~ for sth** aller à la recherche de qc

**explorer** [ɪk·'splɔr·ər] *n* explorateur, -trice *m, f*

**explosion** [ɪk·'splou·ʒən] *n* explosion *f*

**explosive** [ɪk·'splou·sɪv] **I.** *adj* explosif(-ive) **II.** *n* explosif *m*

**export** [ɪk·'spɔrt] **I.** *vt* exporter; **to ~ sth to Germany** exporter qc vers l'Allemagne **II.** *vi* exporter **III.** *n* exportation *f*; **~ goods** biens *mpl* d'exportation; **~ business** exportation *f*

**exposed** *adj* exposé(e)

**exposition** [,ek·spə·'zɪʃ·ən] *n* exposition *f*

**exposure** [ɪk·'spou·ʒər] *n* ① *a.* PHOT exposition *f* ② MED **to die of ~** mourir de froid ③ (*revelation*) révélation *f* ④ (*media coverage*) couverture *f* ⑤ (*contact*) **~ to** (*people, influence*) fréquentation *f* de; (*radiation*) exposition *f* à

**express** [ɪk·'spres] **I.** *vt* ① (*convey: thoughts, feelings*) exprimer; **to ~ oneself through music** s'exprimer par la musique ② (*send*) **to ~ sth to sb** envoyer qc en express à qn **II.** *adj* ① RAIL express *inv* ② LAW exprès(expresse) ▶**by ~ delivery** en exprès **III.** *n* ① RAIL

express *m* ② (*delivery service*) **by ~** en exprès **IV.** *adv* (*intentional*) exprès

**expression** [ɪk·'spreʃ·ən] *n* expression *f*; **to give ~ to sth** exprimer qc; **to find ~ in sth** se manifester dans qc

**expressionless** [ɪk·'spreʃ·ən·ləs] *adj* inexpressif(-ive)

**expressive** [ɪk·'spres·ɪv] *adj* expressif(-ive)

**expressly** *adv* expressément

**expressway** [ɪk·'spres·weɪ] *n* autoroute *f*

**expulsion** [ɪk·'spʌl·ʃən] *n* expulsion *f*; **~ from a school** renvoi *m* d'une école

**exquisite** ['ek·skwɪ·zɪt] *adj* ① (*delicate*) exquis(e) ② (*intense*) vif(vive)

**extend** [ɪk·'stend] **I.** *vi* ① **to ~ for/ beyond sth** s'étendre sur/au-delà de qc ② *fig* **to ~ to sth/doing sth** aller jusqu'à qc/faire qc; **the restrictions ~ to residents** les restrictions s'appliquent aussi aux résidents **II.** *vt* ① (*increase*) étendre ② (*prolong*) prolonger ③ (*stretch*) étendre; (*neck*) tendre ④ (*offer*) **to ~ sth to sb** offrir qc à qn; **to ~ a warm welcome to sb** accueillir qn chaleureusement

**extension** [ɪk·'sten·(t)ʃən] *n* ① (*increase*) augmentation *f*; (*of scope, role*) extension *f*; (*of opportunities*) augmentation *f* ② (*continuation*) prolongement *m* ③ (*lengthening of deadline*) prolongation *f* ④ (*added piece*) (unité *f* d')extension *f* ⑤ TEL poste *m*

**extension cord** *n* ELEC rallonge *f*

**extensive** [ɪk·'sten(t)·sɪv] *adj* vaste; (*coverage*) large; (*research*) approfondi(e); (*repairs*) important(e); (*damage*) considérable

**extent** [ɪk·'stent] *n* étendue *f*; **to an ~** jusqu'à un point; **to some ~** dans une certaine mesure; **to a greater ~** en grande partie; **to the ~ that** dans la mesure où; **to what ~?** dans quelle mesure?

**exterior** [ɪk·'stɪr·i·ər] **I.** *n* extérieur *m*; **on the ~** à l'extérieur **II.** *adj* extérieur(e)

**external** [ɪk·'stɜr·nəl] *adj* ① (*exterior,*

*foreign*) extérieur(e); **~ to sth** étranger à qc ❷ (*on surface, skin*) *a.* MED, COMPUT externe; **for ~ use only** à usage externe exclusivement

**extinct** [ɪkˈstɪŋkt] *adj* éteint(e); **to become ~** disparaître

**extinguish** [ɪkˈstɪŋ·gwɪʃ] *vt* éteindre

**extort** [ɪkˈstɔrt] *vt* **to ~ money from sb** extorquer de l'argent à qn

**extortion** [ɪkˈstɔr·ʃ°n] *n* extorsion *f*

**extortionate** [ɪkˈstɔr·ʃ°n·ət] *adj pej* exorbitant(e)

**extra** [ˈek·strə] **I.** *adj* supplémentaire; **to have ~ money** avoir de l'argent en plus; **vegetables are ~** les légumes ne sont pas compris **II.** *adv* ❶ (*more*) en plus ❷ (*very*) **~ thick/strong** super épais/extra fort **III.** *n* ❶ ECON supplément *m* ❷ AUTO option *f* ❸ CINE figurant(e) *m(f)* **IV.** *pron* **to pay ~** payer plus

**extract** [*ek*·ˈstrækt, *vb:* ɪk·ˈstrækt] **I.** *n* extrait *m* **II.** *vt* ❶ extraire; **to ~ sth from sth** extraire qc de qc ❷ *fig* **to ~ a confession from sb** arracher un aveu à qn; **to ~ a piece of information from sb** tirer une information de qn

**extraction** [ɪk·ˈstræk·ʃ°n] *n* ❶ (*removal*) extraction *f* ❷ (*origin*) origine *f*

**extramarital** [ˌek·strə·ˈmer·ə·t̬°l] *adj* extraconjugal(e)

**extraordinary** [ɪk·ˈstrɔr·dən·er·i] *adj* extraordinaire

**extraterrestrial** [ˌek·strə·tə·ˈres·tri·əl] **I.** *adj* extraterrestre **II.** *n* extraterrestre *mf*

**extravagance** [ɪk·ˈstræv·ə·gən(t)s] *n* extravagance *f*

**extravagant** [ɪk·ˈstræv·ə·gənt] *adj* ❶ (*exaggerated*) extravagant(e); (*claims, demands*) immodéré(e) ❷ (*luxurious*) luxueux(-euse); **~ tastes** goûts *mpl* de luxe

**extreme** [ɪk·ˈstrim] **I.** *adj a.* METEO extrême; (*pain*) intense; (*pleasure*) immense, (*happiness*) suprême, **the ~ right** l'extrême droite; **isn't that a little ~?** ce n'est pas un peu excessif? **II.** *n* ❶ (*limit*) extrême *m;* **to go from one ~**

**to the other** passer d'un extrême à l'autre; **to go to ~s** pousser les choses à l'extrême ❷ (*utmost*) **in the ~** à l'extrême

**extremely** *adv* extrêmement; (*dull*) horriblement; (*sorry*) infiniment

**extroverted** *adj* extraverti(e)

**eye** [aɪ] **I.** *n* ❶ ANAT œil *m;* **to blink one's ~s** cligner des yeux *mpl;* **her ~s flashed with anger** ses yeux jetaient des éclairs de colère ❷ (*hole*) trou *m;* (*of needle*) chas *m* ❸ METEO centre *m* d'une dépression; (*of hurricane*) œil *m* ❹ (*bud on potato*) œil *m* ▸ **to have ~s in the back of one's head** *inf* avoir des yeux dans le dos; **that's a sight for sore ~s** c'est agréable à regarder; **to have ~s bigger than one's stomach** *iron* avoir les yeux plus gros que le ventre; **to be at the ~ of the storm** être au cœur de la tempête; **an ~ for an ~, a tooth for a tooth** *prov* œil pour œil, dent pour dent *prov;* **not to be able to take one's ~s off sb/sth** *inf* ne pas lâcher qn/qc du regard; **a black ~** un œil au beurre noir; **as far as the ~ can see** à perte de vue; **to keep one's ~s peeled** [*o* **open**] *inf* ouvrir l'œil; **to do sth with one's ~s open** *inf* faire qc en connaissance de cause; **with one's ~s shut** *inf* les yeux fermés; (*right*) **before sb's very ~s** juste sous les yeux de qn; **not to believe one's ~s** ne pas en croire ses yeux; **to keep an ~ on sb/sth** *inf* surveiller qn/qc; **to keep an ~ out for sb/sth** *inf* essayer de repérer qn/qc; **to see ~ to ~ on sth** avoir la même opinion sur qc; **to set ~s on sb/sth** *inf* jeter un œil sur qn/qc; **in** [*o* **to**] **sb's ~s** aux yeux de qn **II.**<-d, -d, -ing> *vt* ❶ (*look at carefully*) observer; (*warily*) examiner ❷ *inf* (*look with longing*) reluquer ❸ **to be brown-/green-~d** avoir les yeux bruns/verts

**eyebrow** *n* sourcil *m;* **to pluck/raise one's ~s** s'épiler/froncer les sourcils

**eye contact** *n* échange *m* de regards; **to make ~ with sb** regarder qn dans les yeux

**eyeglass** n ❶ pl lunettes fpl ❷ (monocle) monocle m

**eyeglass case** n étui m à lunettes

**eyelash** <-es> n cil m

**eyelid** n paupière f

**eyeliner** n eye-liner m

**eye-opener** n révélation f

**eye-popping** adj inv, fig, inf truculent(e)

**eye shadow** n fard m à paupières

**eyesight** n vue f

**eyesore** n horreur f

**eyestrain** n fatigue f oculaire

**eye test** n examen m de la vue

**eyetooth** <-teeth> n canine f supérieure ▸ **to give one's eyeteeth for sth** donner n'importe quoi pour qc

**eyewitness** <-es> n témoin m oculaire

**F**

# Ff

**F, f** [ef] <-'s o -s> n ❶ (letter) F m, f m; **~ as in Foxtrot** (on telephone) f comme François ❷ MUS fa m

**f** n abbr of **feminine** f

**F** n abbr of **Fahrenheit** F

**fabric** ['fæb·rɪk] n ❶ FASHION tissu m ❷ (structure) a. fig structure f; **the ~ of everyday life** les réalités fpl de la vie

**fabricate** ['fæb·rɪ·keɪt] vt ❶ (invent) inventer ❷ (manufacture) fabriquer

**fabulous** ['fæb·jə·ləs] adj fabuleux(-euse); (sum) astronomique; (city, character) légendaire

**face** [feɪs] I. n ❶ ANAT a. fig visage m; **to lie ~ down** être allongé sur le ventre; **to tell sth to sb's ~** dire qc à qn en face ❷ (expression) mine f; **you should have seen her ~** tu aurais vu sa tête; **to make ~s at sb** faire des grimaces fpl à qn ❸ (surface) surface f; (of building) façade f; (of mountain) versant m; (of clock) cadran m; **the cards were ~ up** les cartes étaient à l'endroit ❹ (appearance) face f; **loss of ~** humiliation f ❺ (image) image f ▸ **to disappear off the ~ of the earth** disparaître de la surface de la terre; **in ~ of sth** face à qc; (despite) en dépit de qc; **on the ~ of it** à première vue II. vt ❶ (turn toward: person, audience) faire face à; (room, house) donner sur; **the house facing ours** la maison en face de la nô-

tre; **to ~ the front** regarder devant soi ❷ (confront: problems, danger) faire face à; (rival, team) affronter; **to ~ the facts** regarder les choses en face; **let's ~ it, it's too big** soyons francs, c'est trop grand; **to be ~d with sth** se trouver confronté à qc ❸ (run the risk) risquer ❹ ARCHIT **to ~ sth with sth** revêtir qc de qc ▸ **to ~ the music** inf faire front III. vi **to ~ toward sth** se tourner vers qc; **to ~ south** (person) regarder vers le sud; (house) être exposé au sud; **about ~!** demi-tour!

**facecloth** n ≈ gant m de toilette, débarbouillette f Québec, lavette f Suisse

**facelift** n lifting m; **to have a ~** se faire faire un lifting

**facility** [fə·'sɪl·ə·t̬i] <-ies> n ❶ (skill) facilité f; **to have a ~ for sth** avoir un don pour qc ❷ (building) établissement m; **training/recycling ~** centre m de formation/recyclage; **manufacturing ~** usine f ❸ pl (equipment) équipement m ❹ pl, inf (restroom) vécés mpl

**fact** [fækt] n fait m; **hard ~s** des faits mpl; **a statement of ~** une constatation; **~ and fiction** le réel et l'imaginaire m ▸ **the ~s of life** inf les choses fpl de la vie; **in ~** [o **as a matter of ~**] en fait

**fact-check** vt (article) vérifier

**fact-checker** *n* vérificateur, -trice *m, f*
**factor** ['fæk·tər] *n* facteur *m;* **the hu-man** ~ le facteur humain
**factory** ['fæk·t⁹r·i] <-ies> *n* usine *f;* **shoe** ~ fabrique *f* de chaussures
**factual** ['fæk·tʃu·əl] *adj* factuel(le); (*account, information*) basé(e) sur les faits
**faculty** ['fæk·ªl·ti] <-ies> *n* ❶ (*teaching staff*) corps *m* enseignant ❷ UNIV faculté *f* ❸ (*ability*) faculté *f;* **mental faculties** capacités *fpl* intellectuelles
**fade** [feɪd] I. *n* CINE fondu *m* II. *vi* ❶ (*wither: flower*) se faner ❷ (*lose color*) se décolorer; (*color*) se ternir; (*inscription*) s'effacer ❸ (*disappear*) *a. fig* disparaître; (*light*) baisser; (*echo*) s'évanouir; (*popularity*) baisser; (*hope*) s'amenuiser; (*smile, memory*) s'effacer; **to** ~ **from sight** s'estomper III. *vt* ❶ (*wither: flower*) faner ❷ (*cause to lose color*) décolorer ❸ CINE fondre; **to** ~ **one scene into another** enchaîner deux scènes
◆ **fade away** *vi* (*sound, light*) s'affaiblir; (*person*) dépérir
◆ **fade in** CINE, TV I. *vi* faire une ouverture en fondu II. *vt* faire apparaître en fondu
◆ **fade out** CINE, TV I. *vi* faire une fermeture en fondu II. *vt* faire disparaître en fondu
**fag** [fæg] *n pej, vulg* (*male homosexual*) pédé *m*
**fail** [feɪl] I. *vi* ❶ (*not succeed: person, plan*) échouer; **to** ~ **in sth** échouer à qc; **he** ~**ed to beat the record** il n'a pas réussi à battre le record; **to be doomed to** ~ être voué à l'échec ❷ (*to not do sth one should do*) **to** ~ **to** +*infin* (*by neglect*) négliger de +*infin;* **to** ~ **to appreciate sth** ne pas être capable de comprendre qc; **the parcel** ~**ed to arrive** le paquet n'est pas arrivé ❸ *a.* SCHOOL, UNIV (*not pass a test*) être recalé(e); **to** ~ **in literature** sécher en littérature ❹ TECH, AUTO (*brakes*) lâcher; (*engine, power steering*) ne pas répondre; (*power*) être coupé ❺ MED (*kidneys, heart*) lâcher; (*health*) se détériorer; **to**

**be** ~**ing fast** (*person*) faiblir de jour en jour ❻ FIN, COM (*go bankrupt*) faire faillite ❼ AGR, BOT (*not grow*) ne rien donner ▶ **if all else** ~**s** en dernier recours II. *vt* ❶ (*not pass: exam, interview*) être recalé(e) à; (*driving test*) rater; **to** ~ **geography** être recalé en géographie ❷ (*not let pass: student, candidate*) recaler ❸ (*not help sb when needed*) faire défaut à; **your courage** ~**s you** le courage te/vous manque; **you've never** ~**ed me** tu ne m'as jamais déçu III. *n* (*unsuccessful result*) échec *m* ▶ **without** ~ (*definitely*) sans faute; (*always, without exception*) chaque fois
**failing** I. *adj* défaillant(e); **he is in** ~ **health** sa santé se détériore; **to have** ~ **eyesight** avoir la vue qui baisse II. *n* faiblesse *f;* **the play has one big** ~ la pièce pèche sur un point III. *prep* à défaut de; ~ **that** à défaut
**failure** ['feɪl·jər] *n* ❶ (*being unsuccessful*) échec *m;* **to end in** ~ se solder par un échec ❷ (*unsuccessful person*) raté(e) *m(f);* **he was a** ~ **as a leader** en tant que leader, il était décevant ❸ (*not doing sth*) **his** ~ **to inform us** le fait qu'il ne nous a pas informés; ~ **to follow the instructions will result ...** le non-respect des instructions entraînera ...; ~ **to render assistance** non-assistance *f* à personne en danger ❹ TECH, ELEC (*breakdown*) défaillance *f;* **electrical** ~ panne *f* de courant ❺ MED insuffisance *f* ❻ COM **business** ~**s** les faillites *fpl* d'entreprise
**faint** [feɪnt] I. *adj* ❶ (*not strong or clear: sound, murmur*) faible; (*light, odor, mark, smile*) léger(-ère); (*memory, idea*) vague *m* ❷ (*slight: resemblance, possibility, suspicion*) léger(-ère); (*chance*) minime; **he did not make the** ~**est attempt to apologize** il n'a même pas essayé de s'excuser; **to not have the** ~**est** (**idea**) ... *inf* ne pas avoir la moindre idée ... ❸ (*weak*) faible; **to feel** ~ se sentir défaillir II. *vi* s'évanouir III. *n* évanouissement *m*
**fair**[1] [fer] I. *adj* ❶ (*just and equal for all:*

**F**

*price, society, trial, wage)* juste; (*deal)* équitable; (*competition)* loyal(e); **he had his ~ share** il a eu sa part ➋ *(reasonable: comment, point, question)* légitime; (*in accordance with rules: fight, contest)* en règle; **it's not ~ that** ce n'est pas juste que +*subj;* **that was ~ enough** c'était légitime; **it's only ~ that** c'est normal que +*subj; I think it's ~ to say that …* je crois qu'il convient de dire que …; **to be ~, …** il faut être juste, … ➌ *(quite large: amount, number, size)* assez grand(e); **it cost a ~ amount** ça a coûté pas mal d'argent ➍ *(reasonably good: chance, possibility, prospect)* bon(ne); **to have a ~ idea of sth** savoir à peu près qc ➎ *(average)* ~ **(to middling)** moyen(ne) ➏ *(light or blond in color: hair)* blond(e); (*skin, complexion)* clair(e) ➐ METEO *(clear and dry: weather)* agréable ▸ **to give sb a ~ shake** *inf* donner toutes ses chances à qn; **~'s ~** *inf* sois juste **II.** *adv (in an honest way)* **to play ~** jouer franc jeu ▸ **~ and square** dans les règles; (*in the centre of the target)* en plein dans le mille

**fair²** [fer] *n* ➊ *(county fair)* foire *f;* (*for entertainment)* fête *f* foraine ➋ ECON salon *m;* **local crafts ~** exposition-vente *f* artisanale ➌ AGR foire *f*

**fairground** *n* champ *m* de foire

**fairly** *adv* ➊ *(quite, rather)* relativement ➋ *(in a fair way: treat, deal with, share out)* équitablement; (*win, fight)* honorablement

**fair trade** *n* commerce *m* équitable; **~ goods** produits *mpl* du commerce équitable

**fairway** *n (in golf)* fairway *m*

**fairy** ['fer·i] <-ries> *n (imaginary creature)* fée *f*

**fairy tale I.** *n* ➊ *(for children)* conte *m* de fée ➋ *pej* histoires *fpl* **II.** *adj* **fairy-tale** de conte de fée; **a ~ wedding** un mariage de conte de fée

**faith** [feɪθ] *n* ➊ *(confidence, trust)* confiance *f;* **to have ~ in sb/sth** avoir confiance en qn/qc ➋ *(belief)* foi *f;* **to**

**keep the ~** garder la foi; **to lose one's ~** perdre la foi ▸ **in good ~** de bonne foi

**faithful I.** *adj* fidèle; (*service, support)* loyal(e) **II.** *n pl* **the ~** les fidèles *mpl*

**faithfully** *adv* fidèlement

**fake** [feɪk] **I.** *n* ➊ *(counterfeit object)* faux *m* ➋ *(impostor)* imposteur *m* **II.** *adj* faux(fausse); **~ leather** cuir *m* synthétique **III.** *vt* ➊ *(make a counterfeit copy: signature)* contrefaire; (*calculations)* falsifier ➋ *(pretend to feel or experience)* feindre; **to ~ it** faire semblant **IV.** *vi* faire semblant

**fall** [fɔl] <fell, fallen> **I.** *vi* ➊ *(drop down from a height)* tomber; **to ~ to one's death** faire une chute mortelle; **to ~ to one's knees** tomber à genoux; **to ~ down the stairs** tomber dans les escaliers; **to ~ flat** s'étaler; *fig* tomber à plat *inf;* **to ~ flat on one's face** s'étaler de tout son long *inf;* (*be unsuccessful)* échouer complètement; (*thing, scheme)* rater complètement ➋ *(land: a bomb, missile)* tomber; **the blame fell on me** *fig* la faute est tombée sur moi; **the stress ~s on the first syllable** LING l'accent est sur la première syllabe ➌ *(become lower, decrease: demand, numbers, prices)* baisser; (*dramatically)* chuter; **to ~ by 10%** chuter de 10 %; **to ~ below a figure/level** tomber en dessous d'un chiffre/niveau; **to ~ in sb's estimation** baisser dans l'estime de qn ➍ *(be defeated or overthrown: city, government, dictator)* tomber; **to ~ from power** être déchu; **to ~ to sb** tomber aux mains de qn; (*in an election)* passer aux mains de qn ➎ SPORTS *(in cricket: wicket)* tomber ➏ REL *(do wrong, sin)* pécher ➐ *(happen at a particular time)* tomber; **to ~ on a Monday/Wednesday** tomber un lundi/mercredi ➑ *(happen: night, darkness)* tomber ➒ *(belong)* rentrer; **to ~ into a category/class** rentrer dans une catégorie/classe; **to ~ within sth** rentrer dans qc; **to ~ outside sth** tomber en dehors de qc ➓ *(hang down: hair, cloth,* *fabric*) tomber ⑪ (*become*) **to ~ asleep** s'endormir; **to ~ ill** tomber malade; **to ~ silent** devenir silencieux; **to ~ prey to sb/sth** devenir la proie de qn/qc ⑫ (*enter a particular state*) **to ~ in love with sb/sth** tomber amoureux de qn/ qc; **to ~ out of favor with sb** tomber en disgrâce auprès de qn; **to ~ under the influence of sb/sth** tomber sous l'influence de qn/qc; **to ~ under the spell of sb/sth** tomber sous le charme de qn/qc ▸ **to ~ on deaf ears** (*cries, pleas, shouts*) ne pas être entendu; **to ~ into the hands of sb** tomber aux mains de qn; **to ~ in line with sth** suivre qc; **to ~ into place** (*fit together*) concorder; (*become clear*) devenir clair; **to ~ short** ne pas être tout à fait à la hauteur **II.** *n* ❶ (*act of falling*) chute *f;* **to break sb's ~** amortir la chute de qn ❷ (*downward movement: of a leaf, of the curtain*) chute *f;* (*of a level, popularity*) baisse *f;* (*of the tide*) descente *f* ❸ (*defeat: of a government, city*) chute *f;* (*of a castle*) prise *f* ❹ (*autumn*) automne *m* ❺ *pl* (*waterfall*) chutes *fpl* ▸ **to take a ~ for sb** porter le chapeau à la place de qn **III.** *adj* (*of autumn*) d'automne

◆**fall apart** *vi* a. *fig* se désintégrer; (*building*) tomber en ruine; (*person*) s'effondrer

◆**fall away** *vi* ❶ (*become detached: plaster, rock*) tomber ❷ (*slope downward: land, ground*) descendre ❸ (*disappear: negative factor, feeling*) disparaître; (*supporters*) partir

◆**fall back** *vi* ❶ (*move backwards: crowd*) reculer ❷ MIL (*retreat: army*) se replier

◆**fall behind I.** *vi* (*become slower, achieve less: child, company, country*) prendre du retard; (*fail to do sth on time*) avoir du retard; **to ~ on** (*work*) prendre du retard dans; (*rent*) prendre du retard dans le paiement de **II.** *vt* ❶ (*become slower than*) prendre du retard sur ❷ (*fail to keep to sth*) **to ~ schedule** prendre du retard ❸ SPORTS

(*have fewer points than*) passer derrière

◆**fall down I.** *vi* ❶ (*from upright position: person, object*) tomber ❷ (*collapse: a building, structure*) s'effondrer ❸ (*be unsatisfactory: plan, policy*) ne plus tenir; **to ~ on the job** *inf* ne pas faire du bon boulot **II.** *vt* (*hole, stairs*) tomber dans; **to ~ a cliff** tomber d'une falaise

◆**fall for** *vt inf* ❶ (*be attracted to*) tomber amoureux de ❷ (*be deceived by*) se laisser prendre à; **and I fell for it!** et je suis tombé dans le panneau!

◆**fall in** *vi* ❶ (*drop in the water*) tomber ❷ (*collapse: the roof, ceiling*) s'effondrer ❸ MIL (*form a line: soldiers, squad, company*) former les rangs; **to ~ behind sb** se mettre en rang derrière qn

◆**fall off I.** *vi* ❶ (*become detached*) tomber ❷ (*decrease*) baisser **II.** *vt* (*of table, roof*) tomber de; **to ~ a horse/ bicycle** faire une chute de cheval/de vélo

◆**fall on** *vt* ❶ (*descend onto*) tomber sur ❷ (*attack*) se jeter sur ❸ (*eat or seize greedily*) **to ~ food** se jeter sur la nourriture

◆**fall out** *vi* ❶ (*drop out*) tomber; **her hair started to ~** elle a commencé à perdre ses cheveux ❷ *inf* (*quarrel*) se brouiller ❸ MIL (*move out of line: soldiers, squad, company*) rompre les rangs ❹ (*happen, turn out: things, events*) se passer

◆**fall over I.** *vi* ❶ (*drop to the ground*) tomber par terre ❷ (*drop on its side*) se renverser **II.** *vt* ❶ (*trip*) trébucher sur; **to ~ one's own feet** trébucher ❷ *inf* (*be very eager*) **to ~ oneself to** +*infin* se démener pour +*infin*

◆**fall through I.** *vi* (*plan*) tomber à l'eau; (*sale, agreement*) échouer **II.** *vt* (*gap, hole*) tomber dans

◆**fall to** *vt* ❶ *form* (*be responsible*) incomber à; **it falls to me to tell you …** il m'incombe de vous dire … ❷ (*fail*) **to ~ pieces** se désintégrer; (*person*) s'effondrer; (*building*) tomber en ruine

**F**

**F**

**fallen** ['fɔl·ən] adj ❶ (*lying on the ground: apple, leaf*) tombé(e); (*tree*) abattu(e); **~ leaves** feuilles *fpl* mortes ❷ (*overthrown: politician, dictator*) déchu(e); REL (*angel*) déchu(e)

**false** [fɔls] I. adj a. fig faux(fausse); **a ~ imprisonment** une détention arbitraire; **a ~ bottom** un double fond II. adv **to play sb ~** trahir qn

**falsify** ['fɔl·sɪ·faɪ] vt falsifier

**fame** [feɪm] n ❶ (*being famous*) célébrité *f*; **to win ~** devenir célèbre; **her claim to ~** son titre de gloire ❷ (*reputation*) renommée *f*

**familiar** [fə·'mɪl·jər] I. adj ❶ (*well-known to oneself*) familier(-ère) ❷ (*acquainted*) **to be ~ with sb/sth** connaître qn/qc; **his face is ~** son visage ne m'est pas inconnu; **is the name ~?** ce nom vous dit quelque chose? ❸ (*friendly and informal*) familier(-ère); **to be on ~ terms with sb** bien s'entendre avec qn II. n démon *m* familier

**family** ['fæm·əl·i] n ❶ <-lies> + *sing/pl vb* (*group*) famille *f* ❷ (*relations, family members*) famille *f*; **to be ~** être de la famille; **to be (like) one of the ~** faire partie de la famille; **to run in the ~** être de famille; **to start a ~** avoir des enfants; **do you have ~?** (*children*) vous avez des enfants?; (*relatives*) vous avez de la famille?

**family doctor** n médecin *m* de famille

**family name** n nom *m* de famille

**family tree** n arbre *m* généalogique

**famine** ['fæm·ɪn] n famine *f*

**famished** ['fæm·ɪʃt] adj inf **to be ~** être affamé

**famous** ['feɪ·məs] adj célèbre ▸ **~ last words!** inf tu parles!

**famously** adv ❶ (*as is well-known*) **he ~ replied...** sa réponse, restée célèbre, a été ... ❷ inf (*excellently*) à merveille

**fan**[1] [fæn] I. n ❶ (*hand-held cooling device*) éventail *m* ❷ (*electrical cooling device*) ventilateur *m* II. <-nn-> vt ❶ (*cool with a fan*) éventer ❷ (*cause to burn better: amber, flame*) attiser ❸ fig (*fears, passions*) attiser

**fan**[2] [fæn] n (*admirer*) fan *mf*; **to be a ~ of sb/sth** être un fan de qn/qc; (*very much*) adorer qn/qc

**fanatic** [fə·'næt·ɪk] n ❶ pej (*obsessed believer*) fanatique *mf* ❷ (*enthusiast*) mordu(e) *m(f)*

**fan club** n fan-club *m*

**fancy** ['fæn(t)·si] I. <-ie-> vt ❶ (*imagine*) s'imaginer; **~ that!** tu t'imagines!; **~ meeting you here!** quelle surprise de te/vous voir ici! ❷ (*want, like*) avoir envie de; **I didn't ~ walking home** ça ne me disait rien de rentrer à pied II. n ❶ (*liking*) **to take a ~ to sb/sth** s'enticher de qn/qc ❷ (*imagination*) imagination *f* ❸ <-cies> (*whimsical idea*) fantaisie *f*; **an idle ~** une lubie III. adj <-ier, -iest> ❶ (*elaborate: decoration, frills*) fantaisie inv; (*sauce, cocktail, camera*) sophistiqué(e); **we'll make dinner, nothing ~** nous préparerons le repas, rien de compliqué ❷ fig (*phrases, talk*) recherché(e); **~ footwork** inf manœuvres *fpl* habiles ❸ (*whimsical: ideas, notions*) fantaisiste ❹ inf (*expensive: hotel, place, shop*) chic inv; **~ car** voiture *f* de luxe

**fancy-free** adj **to be footloose and ~** être libre comme l'air

**fantastic** [fæn·'tæs·tɪk] adj ❶ (*unreal, magical: animal, figure*) fantastique ❷ inf (*wonderful: offer, opportunity, time*) fantastique ❸ (*extremely large: amount, size, sum*) colossal(e) ❹ (*unbelievable, bizarre: coincidence*) incroyable

**fanzine** ['fæn·zin] n fanzine *m*

**FAQ** n COMPUT abbr of **frequently asked question** FAQ *f*

**far** [far] <farther, farthest *o* further, furthest> I. adv ❶ (*a long distance*) a. fig loin; **how ~ is Miami from here?** Miami est à quelle distance d'ici?; **as ~ as the bridge** jusqu'au pont; **~ and wide** partout; **~ away** loin; **~ from sth** loin de qc; **not ~ off** non loin; **you can only go so ~** il y a forcément une limite; **~ from it** au contraire; **~ from rich/empty** loin d'être riche/vide; **as**

~ **as the eye can see** à perte de vue ❷ (*distant in time*) ~ **away** loin dans le passé; **sth is not ~ off** qc n'est pas loin; **it goes as ~ back as …** cela remonte jusqu'à …; **so ~** jusqu'à présent ❸ (*in progress, degree*) **to get as ~ as doing sth** arriver à faire qc; **to not get very ~ with sth** ne pas aller très loin dans qc; **to not get very ~ with sb** ne pas parvenir à grand-chose avec qn ❹ (*much*) ~ **better/nicer/warmer** bien mieux/plus joli/plus chaud; **to be ~ too** being être beaucoup trop qc ❺ (*connecting adverbial phrase*) **as ~ as** autant que; **as ~ as I can see** d'après ce que je peux en juger; **as ~ as I know** pour au tant que je sache *subj*; **as ~ as she/he is concerned** en ce qui la/le concerne ▶ **by** ~ de loin; ~ **and away** de loin; **he will go** ~ il ira loin; **so ~ so good** jusqu'à présent c'est bien; **to go too** ~ aller trop loin; **worse by** ~ bien pire II. *adj* ❶ (*at great distance*) lointain(e); **in the ~ distance** au loin ❷ (*more distant*) **on the ~ end/side** à l'autre bout/de l'autre côté; **the ~ wall of the room** le mur du fond ❸ (*extreme*) **the ~ left/right of a party** l'extrême gauche/droite d'un parti ▶ **to be a ~ cry from sb/sth** n'avoir rien à voir avec qn/qc

**fare** [fer] I. *n* ❶ (*price for trip*) tarif *m*; (*bus*) prix *m* du ticket; (*train, plane*) prix du billet; **one-way/round-trip ~** tarif aller/aller retour ❷ (*traveler in a taxi*) client(e) *m(f)* ❸ (*food of a specified type*) cuisine *f* II. *vi* (*get on*) **to ~ well/badly** bien/mal s'en sortir

**Far East** *n* **the ~** l'Extrême-Orient *m*

**farewell** [ˌfer·'wel] I. *interj form* adieu! II. *n* adieu *m*; **to say one's ~s to sb** dire adieu à qn III. *adj* d'adieu

**far-fetched** *adj fig* tiré(e) par les cheveux

**farm** [farm] I. *n* ferme *f* II. *adj* de ferme III. *vt* exploiter; **to ~ beef cattle** faire de l'élevage de bovins IV. *vi* être agriculteur(-trice)

**farmer** *n* agriculteur, -trice *m, f*, habi-

tant(e) *m(f) Québec;* **cattle ~** éleveur de bétail

**farmhouse** I. <-s> *n* ferme *f* II. *adj* de ferme

**farming** *n* agriculture *f;* **cattle ~** élevage *m* de bétail

**far-off** *adj* (*place,*) éloigné(e); (*country, time*) lointain(e)

**far-sighted** *adj* ❶ (*shrewdly anticipating the future: person*) prévoyant(e); (*decision*) avisé(e); (*policy*) à long terme ❷ (*unable to see objects close up: person*) hypermétrope

**fart** [fart] *inf* I. *n* ❶ (*gas from bowels*) pet *m* ❷ *pej* (*annoying person*) **he's an old ~** il est barbant II. *vi* péter

**farther** ['far·ðər] I. *adv comp of far* ❶ (*at/to a greater distance*) ~ **away from sth** plus loin que qc; ~ **down/up sth** plus bas/haut que qc; ~ **east/west** plus à l'est/l'ouest; ~ **on** plus loin ❷ (*at/to more advanced point*) ~ **back** plus loin en arrière; ~ **back in time** plus loin dans le passé ❸ (*additional*) *s.* **further** II. *adj comp of far* (*more distant*) plus éloigné(e); **the ~ end** le côté le plus éloigné

**farthest** ['far·ðɪst] I. *adv superl of far* (*to/at greatest distance: go, come*) **the ~ along** [*o* **away**] le plus loin; **the ~ east/west** le plus à l'est/ouest II. *adj superl of far* (*most distant*) le/la plus éloigné(e)

**fascinate** ['fæs·ə·neɪt] *vt* fasciner

**fascinating** *adj* fascinant(e)

**fascism, Fascism** ['fæʃ·ɪ·zəm] *n* fascisme *m*

**fashion** ['fæʃ·ən] I. *n* ❶ (*popular style*) mode *f;* **to be in ~** être à la mode; **to be out of ~** être démodé; **to go out of ~** se démoder; **the latest ~** la dernière mode ❷ *pl* (*newly designed clothes*) créations *fpl* de mode; **the spring ~s** les créations de printemps ❸ (*industry*) mode *f* ❹ (*manner: friendly, peculiar, stupid*) manière *f* II. *adj* de mode III. *vt form* ❶ (*make using hands*) **to ~ sth out of sth** fabriquer qc en qc ❷ *fig* (*create*) créer

**F**

**fashionable** *adj* à la mode; *(area, night-club, restaurant)* branché(e)

**fast¹** [fæst] **I.** <-er, -est> *adj* ❶ *(opp: slow)* rapide; **to be a ~ runner** courir vite ❷ *(ahead of the time: clock)* en avance ❸ *(firmly attached)* ferme ❹ *(immoral)* frivole ❺ PHOT *(film)* très sensible **II.** *adv* ❶ *(quickly)* vite; **how ~ is that car?** quelle est la vitesse de cette voiture? ❷ *(firmly)* ferme; **stuck ~** bel et bien coincé; **to hold ~ to sth** s'accrocher à qc ❸ *(deeply: asleep)* profondément

**fast²** [fæst] **I.** *vi* jeûner **II.** *n* jeûne *m*

**fasten** ['fæsᵊn] **I.** *vt* ❶ *(attach)* attacher ❷ *(fix)* fixer; *(coat)* boutonner ❸ *(close)* (bien) fermer **II.** *vi* ❶ *(do up)* s'attacher ❷ *(close)* se fermer
 ◆ **fasten down** *vt* fixer
 ◆ **fasten on I.** *vt a. fig* s'accrocher à **II.** *vi a. fig* **to ~ to sth/sb** s'accrocher à qn/qc
 ◆ **fasten up I.** *vt* fermer **II.** *vi* se fermer

**fastener** *n* fermeture *f*

**fast food** *n* fast-food *m*

**fast-forward I.** *n* avance *f* rapide **II.** *vt* faire avancer **III.** *vi* avancer

**fast lane** *n* voie *f* de gauche; **to live life in the ~** *fig* vivre la grande vie

**fat** [fæt] **I.** <fatter, fattest> *adj* ❶ *(fleshy)* gros(se); **to get ~** grossir ❷ *(containing fat)* gras(se) ❸ *(thick)* épais(se) ❹ *(large: check, fee, profits)* gros(se) ❺ *iron* sacré(e) **II.** *n* ❶ *(body tissue)* graisse *f* ❷ *(meat tissue)* gras *m* ❸ *(for cooking, in food)* matière *f* grasse ► **to live off the ~ of the land** vivre comme un coq en pâte

**fatal** ['feɪtᵊl] *adj* fatal(e); **it would be ~ to stop now** ça serait catastrophique de s'arrêter maintenant

**fatality** [fəˈtæl·ə·t̮i] <-ties> *n* fatalité *f*

**fatally** *adv* fatalement

**fate** [feɪt] *n sing* destin *m;* **to leave sb to their ~** abandonner qn à son sort

**fated** *adj* destiné(e); **it was ~ that ...** il était écrit que ...

**fat-free** *adj* sans matière graisse

**father** ['fɑ·ðər] **I.** *n* père *m;* **Father Eric** le père Eric **II.** *vt* *(child)* engendrer

**father-in-law** <fathers-in-law> *n* beau-père *m*, beaux-pères *mpl*

**fattening** *adj* **to be ~** faire grossir

**fatty** ['fæt̮·i] **I.** *adj* gras(se); *(tissue)* graisseux(-euse) **II.** <fatties> *n pej, inf* petit gros *m*, petite grosse *f*

**faucet** ['fɔ·sɪt] *n* robinet *m*

**fault** [fɔlt] *n* ❶ *(guilt, mistake)* faute *f;* **the ~ lies with sb/sth** la responsabilité incombe à qn/qc; **through no ~ of sb's own** sans être de la faute de qn; **to be at ~** être dans son tort; **to find ~ with sb/sth** avoir qc à redire à qn/qc ❷ *(character weakness, defect)* défaut *m* ❸ *(crack in earth's surface)* faille *f* ❹ SPORTS faute *f* **II.** *vt* avoir qc à redire à; **you can't ~ his argument/ pronunciation** tu ne peux rien trouver à redire à son argument/sa pronunciation

**faultless** *adj* impeccable

**faulty** *adj* ❶ *(having a defect: product)* défectueux(-euse) ❷ *(mistaken, misleading)* incorrect(e)

**faux pas** [ˌfoʊˈpɑ] *n* impair *m*

**favor** ['feɪ·vər] **I.** *n* ❶ *(approval)* faveur *f;* **to be in ~ of sth** être en faveur de [*o* pour] qc; **to decide in ~ of sth** décider en la faveur de qc; **to be/fall out of ~ with sb** être/tomber en disgrâce auprès de qn; **to win sb's ~** gagner la faveur de qn; **to have sth in one's ~** qc est en sa faveur ❷ *(helpful act)* service *m* **II.** *vt* ❶ *(prefer)* préférer; *(method, solution)* être pour; **to ~ doing sth** préférer faire qc ❷ *(give advantage or benefit to)* favoriser ❸ *(show partiality toward)* favoriser ❹ *inf (look like)* ressembler à

**favorable** *adj* favorable; **to take a ~ view of sth** voir qc sous un jour favorable

**favorably** *adv* *(review)* favorablement; **to look ~ on an application** donner une opinion favorable à une candidature; **it compares ~ with the other**

**one** il/elle est pratiquement aussi bien que l'autre

**favorite** ['feɪ·vᵊr·ɪt] **I.** *adj* préféré(e) **II.** *n* préféré(e) *mf*; sports favori(te) *m(f)*

**fax** [fæks] **I.** *n* (*message*) fax *m*; (*machine*) fax, télécopieur *m Québec* **II.** *vt* faxer *m*

**FBI** [ˌef·biˑˈaɪ] *n abbr of* **Federal Bureau of Investigation** police *f* judiciaire fédérale

**fear** [fɪr] **I.** *n* ❶ (*state of being afraid*) peur *f*; **to live in ~** vivre dans la peur; **for ~ of doing sth** par crainte de faire qc; **for ~ that** par crainte que +*subj*; **to strike ~ into sb** terrifier qn; **without ~ or favor** équitablement ❷ (*worry*) inquiétude *f*; **no ~!** pas question!; **there's no ~ of that happening** il n'y a pas de risque que ça arrive **II.** *vt* avoir peur de; **I ~ you are wrong** j'ai bien peur que tu te trompes *subj*

**fearful** *adj* ❶ (*anxious*) craintif(-ive); **to be ~ of sth** avoir peur de qc; **to be ~ that** être inquiet que +*subj*; **to be ~ of doing sth** avoir peur de faire qc ❷ (*terrible*) affreux(-euse)

**feast** [fist] **I.** *n* ❶ (*meal*) *a. fig* festin *m* ❷ (*holiday*) jour *m* férié ❸ REL fête *f* **II.** *vi* **to ~ on sth** se délecter de qc **III.** *vt* régaler ▸ **to ~ one's** <u>eyes</u> **on sth** se délecter à la vue de qc

**feat** [fit] *n* exploit *m*; **~ of skill** tour *m* d'adresse; **~ of engineering** performance *f* technique

**feather** ['feð·ᵊr] *n* plume *f* ▸ **to be a ~ in sb's** <u>cap</u> être quelque chose dont qn peut être fier; **as** <u>light</u> **as a ~** aussi léger qu'une plume

**feature** ['fiˑtʃᵊr] **I.** *n* ❶ (*distinguishing attribute*) particularité *f*; **a distinguishing ~** un signe particulier; **a useful ~ of the new software/model** une caractéristique utile du nouveau logiciel/modèle ❷ *pl* (*facial attributes*) traits *mpl* (du visage) ❸ PUBL article *m*; **a ~ on sth** un document exclusif sur qc ❹ RADIO, TV reportage *m* ❺ CINE (*film*) long métrage *m* **II.** *vt* ❶ (*have as aspect, attribute: magazine*) présenter;

(*hotel*) offrir; **she's ~d on the program** on parle d'elle dans l'émission ❷ (*have as performer, star*) avoir pour vedette **III.** *vi* figurer; **to ~ in sth** apparaître dans qc

**February** ['feb·ruˑerˑi] *n* février *m*; *s.a.* **April**

**fecal** ['fiˑkᵊl] *adj* fécal

**federal** ['fed·ᵊrˑᵊl] *adj* fédéral(e)

**federal court** *n* cour *f* fédérale

**fed up** *adj inf* **to be ~ with sb/sth** en avoir marre de qn/qc

**fee** [fi] *n* (*of doctor, lawyer, artist*) honoraires *mpl*; **membership ~** cotisation *f*; **admission ~** droits *mpl* d'entrée

**feeble** ['fiˑbl] *adj* faible; (*excuse*) faible; (*joke*) mauvais(e)

**feed** [fid] <**fed**> **I.** *n* ❶ (*food*) nourriture *f*; **cattle ~** aliments *mpl* pour bétail ❷ *inf* (*meal*) repas *m* ❸ TECH approvisionnement *m* **II.** *vt* ❶ (*give food to, provide food for*) nourrir; **to ~ the cat** donner à manger au chat; **to ~ sth to sb** donner qc à manger à qn ❷ (*supply: machine*) alimenter; (*fire, meter, someone*) approvisionner; **to ~ sth into the computer** entrer qc dans l'ordinateur ❸ (*give*) fournir; **to ~ sth to sb** fournir qc à qn **III.** *vi* manger

◆**feed on** *vt* ❶ (*eat*) se nourrir de ❷ (*exploit*) **they ~ people's fears** ils tirent profit des craintes des gens

◆**feed up** *vt* (*animals*) engraisser; **you need feeding up** tu as besoin de manger

**feedback** ['fid·bæk] *n a. fig* réaction *f*; (*in sound system*) retour *m*

**feeding bottle** *n* biberon *m*

**feel** [fil] **I.** *n* ❶ (*texture, act of touching*) toucher *m* ❷ (*impression*) impression *f*; **a ~ of mystery** un parfum de mystère ❸ (*natural talent*) sens *m* inné **II.** <**felt, felt**> *vi* ❶ (*have a sensation or emotion*) se sentir; **to ~ hot/cold** avoir chaud/froid; **to ~ hungry/thirsty** avoir faim/soif; **I ~ unhappy about the idea** l'idée ne m'enchante pas; **to ~ like sth/doing sth** avoir envie de qc/faire qc; **how do you ~ about sth?**

qu'est-ce que vous pensez de qc? ②(*seem*) paraître; **everything ~s different** tout semble différent; **it ~s as if I'd never been away** c'est comme si je n'étais jamais parti ③(*use hands to search*) **to ~ around somewhere** tâtonner autour de soi quelque part III.<felt, felt> *vt* ①(*be physically aware of: pain, pressure, touch*) sentir ②(*experience: loneliness, shame*) ressentir ③(*touch*) toucher; **to ~ your way somewhere** avancer à tâtons quelque part ④(*think, believe*) penser; **she ~s that nobody listens to her** elle a l'impression que personne ne l'écoute

◆**feel for** *vt* avoir de la compassion pour

**feeling** *n* ①(*emotion, sensation*) sentiment *m*; **to hurt sb's ~s** blesser qn dans ses sentiments; **to play with ~** jouer avec émotion ②(*impression, air*) impression *f*; **to get the ~ that ...** avoir l'impression que ...; **I had a ~ he'd win** j'avais comme l'idée qu'il gagnerait ③(*opinion*) opinion *f* ④(*physical sensation*) sensation *f* ⑤(*natural talent*) sens *m* inné

**feet** [fi:t] *n pl of* **foot**

**fell**¹ [fel] *pt of* **fall**

**fell**² [fel] *vt* (*tree*) abattre; (*person*) assommer

**fellow** ['fel·oʊ] I. *n* ①*inf* (*guy*) type *m* ②*inf* (*boyfriend*) mec *m* ③(*comrade*) camarade *mf* ④*UNIV* (*research fellow*) assistant(e) *m(f)* de recherche ⑤*UNIV* (*professor*) professeur *mf* ⑥(*member*) membre *mf* II. *adj* **~ sufferer** compagnon *m* d'infortune; **~ student** camarade *mf*; **my ~ passengers** les autres passagers *mpl*

**fellow citizen** *n* concitoyen(ne) *m(f)*

**felt**¹ [felt] *pt, pp of* **feel**

**felt**² [felt] I. *n* feutre *f* II. *adj* en feutre

**felt-tip (pen)** [,felt·'tɪp (pen)] *n* (stylo *m*) feutre *m*

**female** ['fi·meɪl] I. *adj* ①(*related to females*) féminin(e); *BIO, ZOOL* femelle;

**~ teachers** enseignantes *fpl* ②*TECH* femelle II. *n a. pej* femelle *f*

**feminine** ['fem·ə·nɪn] I. *adj a. LING* féminin(e) II. *n LING* **the ~** le féminin

**feminist** I. *n* féministe *mf* II. *adj* féministe

**fence** [fen(t)s] I. *n* ①(*barrier*) barrière *f* ②*SPORTS* obstacle *m* ③*inf* (*receiver of stolen goods*) receleur, -euse *m, f* ▸ **to sit on the ~** ne pas se mouiller II. *vi* ①*SPORTS* faire de l'escrime ②*form* se dérober; **to ~ with sb** esquiver qn III. *vt* ①(*close off*) clôturer ②(*sell: stolen goods*) écouler

**fencer** *n* escrimeur, -euse *m, f*

**fencing** *n* ①*SPORTS* escrime *f* ②(*barrier*) clôture *f*

**fender** ['fen·dər] *n AUTO* aile *f*

**ferocious** [fə·'roʊ·ʃəs] *adj* ①(*cruel*) féroce ②(*extreme: heat, temper*) terrible

**ferry** ['fer·i] <-ies> I. *n* ferry *m*; (*smaller*) bac *m*, traversier *m Québec* II. *vt* **to ~ sb somewhere** transporter qn quelque part

**fertile** ['fɜr·t̬ə¹l] *adj* fertile

**fertilize** ['fɜr·t̬ə·laɪz] *vt* ①(*make able to produce much*) fertiliser ②(*impregnate*) féconder

**fertilizer** *n* engrais *m*

**fest** [fest] *n inf* fête *f*

**festival** ['fes·tɪ·vᵊl] *n* ①(*special event*) festival *m* ②(*religious day or period*) fête *f*

**festive** ['fes·tɪv] *adj* festif(-ive); **the ~ season** les fêtes *fpl* de fin d'année

**festivity** [fes·'tɪv·ə·t̬i] <-ies> *n* ①*pl* festivités *fpl* ②(*festiveness*) fête *f*

**fetch** [fetʃ] *vt* ①(*bring back: stick, object*) aller chercher ②(*be sold for*) rapporter; (*price*) remporter

**fetching** *adj iron* charmant(e)

**fetish** ['fet̬·ɪʃ] *n a. PSYCH* fétiche *m*

**fetus** ['fi·t̬əs] *n* fœtus *m*

**fever** ['fi·vər] *n* fièvre *f*

**feverish** *adj a. MED* fébrile

**few** [fju] I.<fewer, fewest> *adj* peu de; **one of the ~ friends** l'un des rares amis; **there are two too ~** il en manque deux; **not ~er than 100 people**

pas moins de 100 personnes; **to be ~ and far between** être rare II. *pron* peu; **~ of us** peu d'entre nous III. *n* **a ~** quelques un(e)s; **a ~ of us** certains d'entre nous; **quite a ~ people** pas mal de gens; **the ~** la minorité; **the happy ~** les heureux élus *mpl;* **the ~ who have the book** les rares personnes *fpl* à avoir le livre

**fiberglass** *n* fibre *f* de verre

**fiber optic cable** *n* câble *m* en fibres optiques

**fiber optics** *n sing* fibre *f* optique

**fiction** ['fɪk·ʃən] *n* fiction *f*

**fictitious** [fɪk·'tɪʃ·əs] *adj* ① *(fictional)* fictif(-ive) ② *(imaginary)* imaginaire

**fiddle** ['fɪd·l] I. *vi* ① *inf (play the violin)* jouer du violon ② *(fidget with/finger aimlessly)* **to ~ with sth** tripoter qc II. *n inf* violon *m*

**fidget** ['fɪdʒ·ɪt] I. *vi* ① *(be impatient)* s'agiter ② *(be nervous)* s'énerver II. *n* **to be a ~** ne pas tenir en place

**fidgety** *adj* agité(e)

**field** [fild] I. *n* ① *(open land)* a. MIL, ELEC, COMPUT champ *m* ② *(sphere of activity)* domaine *m* ③ SPORTS *(ground)* terrain *m* ④ *(contestants in competition)* concurrents *mpl* II. *vt* SPORTS ① *(return: ball)* attraper et relancer; *fig (questions)* répondre à ② *(send: team)* faire jouer

**fielder** *n* SPORTS joueur, -euse *m, f* de champ

**fierce** [fɪrs] *adj* <-er, -est> ① *(untamed: animal)* féroce ② *(powerful, extreme, violent: love, discussion)* véhément(e); *(expression, competition, combat)* féroce

**fifteen** [ˌfɪf·'tin] *adj* quinze; *s.a.* **eight**

**fifteenth** *adj* quinzième; *s.a.* **eighth**

**fifth** [fɪfθ] *adj* cinquième; *s.a.* **eighth**

**fiftieth** ['fɪf·ti·əθ] *adj* cinquantième; *s.a.* **eighth**

**fifty** ['fɪf·ti] *adj* cinquante; *s.a.* **eight**, **eighty**

**fifty-fifty** *adj* **a ~ chance** cinquante pour cent de chances

**fig** [fɪg] *n* figue *f*

**fight** [faɪt] I. <fought, fought> *vi* ① *(exchange blows)* se battre ② *(wage war, do battle)* combattre; **to ~ with/against sb** se battre avec/contre qn ③ *(dispute, quarrel bitterly)* **to ~ over sth** se disputer pour qc ④ *(struggle to overcome sth)* **to ~ for sth** se battre pour qc; **to ~ against sth** lutter contre qc II. *vt* *(enemy, crime)* combattre; *(person)* se battre contre; *(a case, an action)* défendre; **to ~ an election** POL mener une campagne électorale III. *n* ① *(violent confrontation)* bagarre *f;* **to get into a ~ with sb** se bagarrer avec qn ② *(quarrel)* dispute *f* ③ *(battle)* combat *m* ④ *(struggle, campaign)* lutte *f;* **there's no ~ left in him** il ne se bat plus; **to put up a good ~** bien se défendre ⑤ SPORTS combat *m*

◆**fight back** I. *vi* se défendre; **to ~ against cancer** se battre contre le cancer II. *vt* ① *(fight)* combattre ② *fig (tears)* refouler

◆**fight off** *vt* ① *(repel, repulse)* repousser ② *(resist)* battre

**fighter** *n* ① *(person withstanding problems)* battant(e) *m(f)* ② *(person who fights)* combattant(e) *m(f)* ③ *(military plane)* chasseur *m*

**fighting** I. *n* combats *mpl* II. *adj* combatif(-ive)

**figuratively** *adv* au figuré; **~ speaking** au sens figuré

**figure** ['fɪg·jər] I. *n* ① *(outline of body)* silhouette *f;* **to have a good ~** avoir un beau corps; **to watch one's ~** garder la ligne ② *(personality)* personnalité *f,* **a leading ~ in the movement** un personnage important dans le mouvement ③ *(digit)* chiffre *m;* **to be good with ~s** être bon en calcul ④ *pl (bookkeeping, economic data)* chiffres *mpl* ⑤ *(diagram, representation)* figure *f* II. *vt* penser III. *vi* *(appear)* figurer

◆**figure out** *vt* ① *(understand)* (arriver à) comprendre ② *(work out)* calculer

**file**[1] [faɪl] I. *n* ① *(binder for ordering documents)* classeur *m* ② *(dossier)* dos-

**F**

sier *m*, farde *f Belgique*, fiche *f Suisse*
❸ COMPUT fichier *m* ❹ (*column, queue, row*) file *f*; **in (single)** ~ en file indienne II. *vt* ❶ (*arrange: data*) classer ❷ LAW (*petition*) déposer ❸ PUBL (*report*) envoyer III. *vi* ❶ (*officially register request*) **to ~ for sth** faire une demande de qc; **to ~ for bankruptcy** déposer le bilan ❷ (*move in line*) marcher en rang; **to ~ in/out** entrer/sortir en rang

**file²** [faɪl] I. *n* lime *f* II. *vt* limer

**file cabinet** *n* armoire *f* de classement

**file clerk** *n* documentaliste *mf*

**filename** *n* COMPUT nom *m* de fichier

**filet** [fɪˈleɪ] I. *n* filet *m* II. *vt* (*meat*) désosser; (*fish*) découper en filets

**filing cabinet** *n* armoire *f* de classement

**fill** [fɪl] I. *vt* ❶ (*make full*) remplir ❷ (*appoint to: post*) pourvoir ❸ (*occupy: post*) occuper ❹ (*seal: a hole*) boucher; (*a tooth*) plomber ❺ (*make person feel*) **to ~ sb with** (*joy, excitement, disgust, anger*) remplir de ❻ (*fulfill: prescription, order*) remplir II. *vi* se remplir

◆**fill in** I. *vt* ❶ (*seal opening: a hole*) boucher ❷ (*complete: form*) remplir; **~ your name and address** notez votre nom et votre adresse ❸ (*inform, give the facts*) **to fill sb in on the details** mettre qn au courant des détails II. *vi* **to ~ for sb** remplacer qn

◆**fill out** I. *vt* remplir II. *vi* prendre du poids

◆**fill up** I. *vt* remplir; **I need to ~ my car** j'ai besoin de faire le plein d'essence II. *vi* **to ~ with sth** se remplir de qc

**fillet** [ˈfɪl·ɪt] *s.* **filet**

**filling** I. *n* ❶ (*for cushion, toy*) rembourrage *m* ❷ (*for tooth*) plombage *m* ❸ CULIN farce *f*; (*for sandwich*) garniture *f* II. *adj* (*food*) nourrissant(e)

**filling station** *n* station-service *f*

**film** [fɪlm] I. *n* film *m*; (*for camera*) pellicule *f* II. *vt, vi* filmer

**film star** *n* vedette *f* de cinéma

**filter** [ˈfɪl·tər] I. *n* filtre *m* II. *vt* filtrer; (*coffee*) faire passer III. *vi* filtrer

◆**filter out** *vt a. fig* filtrer

◆**filter through** *vi* (*light*) passer à travers; (*news, reports*) filtrer

**filthy** I. *adj* sale II. *adv inf* **to be ~ rich** être bourré de fric

**fin** [fɪn] *n* ❶ ZOOL nageoire *f* ❷ TECH aileron *m*

**final** [ˈfaɪ·nəl] I. *adj* ❶ (*last*) final(e) ❷ (*decisive*) définitif(-ive) ❸ (*irrevocable*) irrévocable; **and that's ~!** c'est mon dernier mot! II. *n* ❶ SPORTS finale *f* ❷ *pl* SCHOOL les examens *mpl* de fin d'année scolaire

**finalist** [ˈfaɪ·nəl·ɪst] *n* finaliste *mf*

**finalize** [ˈfaɪ·nə·laɪz] *vt* mettre au point; (*deal*) conclure

**finally** [ˈfaɪ·nəl·i] *adv* ❶ (*at long last, eventually*) finalement ❷ (*expressing relief or impatience*) enfin ❸ (*in conclusion, to conclude*) pour finir ❹ (*conclusively, irrevocably*) définitivement

**finance** [ˈfaɪ·næn(t)s] I. *vt* financer II. *n* ❶ (*cash flow*) finance *f* ❷ *pl* (*capital, funds*) finances *fpl*

**financial** *adj* financier(-ère)

**find** [faɪnd] I. <found, found> *vt* trouver; **to ~ sb/sth (to be) sth** trouver que qn/qc est qc; **I ~ it's best to go early** je trouve qu'il vaut mieux y aller tôt; **to ~ oneself alone/somewhere** se retrouver seul/quelque part; **to ~ sb guilty/innocent** déclarer qn coupable/innocent; **to be nowhere to be found** être introuvable ▸ **to ~ fault with sb/sth** trouver qc à redire à qn/qc II. *vi* LAW **to ~ for/against sb** se prononcer en faveur de/contre qn III. *n* trouvaille *f*; **~ function** COMPUT fonction *f* "recherche"

◆**find out** I. *vt* ❶ (*uncover, detect, discover*) découvrir ❷ (*enquire*) essayer de savoir ❸ (*show to be guilty*) **to find sb out** attraper qn; **don't get found out** ne te fais pas prendre II. *vi* apprendre; **to ~ about sth** apprendre à propos de qc

**finder** *n* personne *f* qui trouve

**finding** *n* ❶ (*discovery*) découverte *f* ❷ *pl* (*conclusion*) conclusions *fpl*

**fine¹** [faɪn] I. *adj* ① (*admirable, excellent: example, food*) excellent(e); (*wine, dish*) fin(e) ② (*acceptable, satisfactory*) bien *inv*; (*that's*) ~! c'est bien!; **everything's** ~ tout va bien ③ (*thin, light*) fin(e) ④ (*cloudless: weather*) beau(belle) ⑤ (*distinguished*) raffiné(e) ⑥ (*subtle: distinction, nuance*) subtil(e); **there's a ~ line between sth and sth** il n'y a qu'un pas de qc à qc II. *adv* ① (*acceptable, satisfactorily*) bien; **to feel ~** se sentir bien; **to suit sb** ~ convenir parfaitement à qn ② (*in fine parts*) finement ▶ **that's cutting it a bit** ~ c'est un peu juste

**fine²** [faɪn] I. *n* amende *f* II. *vt* **to ~ sb for sth** LAW condamner qn à une amende pour qc; (*for breaking rule*) faire payer une amende à qn pour qc

**fine art** *n* beaux-arts *mpl*

**finger** ['fɪŋ·gər] I. *n a. fig* doigt *m;* **to point a ~ at sb/sth** *a. fig* montrer qn/qc du doigt ▶ **to not lay a ~ on sb** ne pas toucher qn; **to not lift a ~** ne pas lever le petit doigt II. *vt* ① (*handle, touch*) toucher ② (*play with*) tripoter ③ *inf* (*reveal to police*) balancer

**fingernail** *n* ongle *m*

**fingerprint** I. *n* ① ANAT, LAW empreinte *f* digitale ② (*dirty mark*) trace *f* de doigt II. *vt* prendre les empreintes digitales de

**fingertip** *n* bout *m* du doigt

**finicky** ['fɪn·ɪ·ki] *adj pej* tatillon(ne)

**finish** ['fɪn·ɪʃ] I. *vi* ① (*cease, conclude*) se terminer ② (*stop talking*) finir (de parler) ③ SPORTS finir II. *vt* finir; **to ~ doing sth** finir de faire qc III. *n* ① SPORTS arrivée *f* ② (*conclusion of process*) fin *f* ③ (*quality*) fini *m;* (*on furniture*) finition *f*

◆**finish off** I. *vt* ① (*conclude*) finir ② (*eat/drink*) finir ③ *inf* (*beat or make somebody fatigued*) achever ④ *inf* (*kill*) achever II. *vi* finir

◆**finish up** *vt, vi* finir; **to ~ doing sth** se retrouver à faire qc

◆**finish with** *vt* en finir avec; **I haven't finished with that yet** j'ai encore besoin de ça

**finished** *adj* ① (*through, used up*) fini(e); **to be ~ with sth** en avoir fini avec qc ② (*final, accomplished*) final(e)

**fir** [fɜr] *n* sapin *m*

**fire** [faɪər] I. *n* ① (*element*) feu *m;* ~! au feu!; **to catch** ~ prendre feu ② (*burning*) incendie *m;* **to be on** ~ être en feu; **to set sth on** ~ mettre le feu à qc ③ (*shots*) coups *mpl* de feu; ~! feu!; **to cease** ~ cesser le feu; **to open** ~ **on sb** ouvrir le feu sur qn; **to come under** ~ **for sth** *fig* être sous les feux de la critique pour qc ▶ **to play with** ~ jouer avec le feu II. *vt* ① (*set off: rocket*) lancer; (*shot*) tirer; **to ~ a gun at sb/sth** décharger une arme sur qn/qc ② (*dismiss: worker*) licencier ③ (*excite*) **to ~ sb's imagination** stimuler l'imagination de qn ④ *fig* (*direct*) **to ~ questions at sb** mitrailler qn de questions ⑤ (*bake: pot*) cuire III. *vi* tirer; **to ~ at sb/sth** tirer sur qn/qc

◆**fire away** *vi* ① (*shoot*) tirer ② *inf* ~! vas-y!

◆**fire off** *vt* ① (*shoot*) tirer ② (*send*) envoyer

**firearm** *n* arme *f* à feu

**firebomb** I. *n* bombe *f* incendiaire II. *vt* lancer une bombe incendiaire sur

**firecracker** *n* pétard *m*

**fire department** *n* (sapeurs-)pompiers *mpl*, service *m* du feu *Suisse*

**fire eater** *n* cracheur *m* de feu

**fire engine** *n* voiture *f* de pompiers

**fire escape** *n* escalier *m* de secours

**fire extinguisher** *n* extincteur *m*

**firefighter** *n* (sapeur-)pompier *m*

**fire hydrant** *n* borne *f* d'incendie, hydrant *m Suisse*, hydrante *f Suisse*

**fireman** <-men> *n* pompier *m*

**fireplace** *n* cheminée *f*

**firepower** *n* puissance *f* de feu *sans pl*

**fireproof** *adj* résistant(e) aux températures élevées

**fire station** *n* caserne *f* des pompiers

**firestorm** *n* incendie *m* dévastateur

**fire truck** *n* camion *m* de pompier(s)

**firewoman** <-women> *n* femme *f* pompier

**F**

**firewood** *n* bois *m* de chauffage
**firm**¹ [fɜrm] **I.** *adj* ❶ (*hard*) ferme ❷ (*steady*) *a.* fig (*table, basis*) solide ❸ (*resolute*) ferme **II.** *adv* ferme; **to stand ~** *a.* fig rester ferme **III.** *vt* **to ~ (up) sth** raffermir qc **IV.** *vi* **to ~ (up)** se raffermir
**firm**² [fɜrm] *n* entreprise *f;* law **~** cabinet *m* d'avocats
**first** [fɜrst] **I.** *adj* premier(-ère); **for the ~ time** pour la première fois; **to do sth ~thing** faire qc en premier ▶ **in the ~ place** primo; **to not know the ~ thing about sth** ne pas avoir la moindre idée de qc; **~ things ~** une chose après l'autre; **~ and foremost** tout d'abord **II.** *adv* en premier; **it ~ happened on Sunday** c'est arrivé la première fois dimanche; **~ of all** *inf* tout d'abord; **at ~** d'abord; **~ come ~ served** *inf* les premiers arrivés sont les premiers servis **III.** *n* ❶ (*coming before*) premier, -ère *m, f;* **that's the ~ I've heard of that** c'est la première fois que j'en entends parler; **a ~ for sb** une première pour qn ❷ (*beginning*) commencement *m;* **from the very ~** au tout début ❸ (*date*) **the ~ of June** le premier juin ❹ auto première *f* **IV.** *pron* le premier/la première; *s.a.* **eighth**
**first aid** *n* premiers secours *mpl*
**first aid kit** *n* kit *m* de secours
**first-class** *adj* (*hotel, ticket*) de première classe; (*merchandise*) de première qualité; (*restaurant*) excellent(e); (*mail*) (au tarif) rapide
**firsthand** *adj, adv* de première main
**firstly** *adv* premièrement
**first name** *n* prénom *m*
**first night** *n* première *f*
**first-rate** *adj* de première classe
**fiscal year** *n* FIN année *f* fiscale
**fish** [fɪʃ] **I.** <-(es)> *n* ❶ zool poisson *m* ❷ CULIN poisson *m* ▶ **there are plenty more ~ in the sea** un de perdu, dix de retrouvés; (*like*) **a ~ out of water** (comme) un poisson hors de l'eau **II.** *vi* (*catch fish*) pêcher **III.** *vt* pêcher; (*body*) repêcher; **to ~ the sea/a lake**

pêcher en mer/dans un lac; **to ~ sb/sth (out) from sth** sortir qn/qc de qc
**fishbowl** *n* bocal *m* à poissons
**fisherman** <-men> *n* pêcheur *m*
**fishing** **I.** *n* pêche *f* **II.** *adj* de pêche
**fish stick** *n* bâtonnet *m* de poisson pané
**fishy** [ˈfɪʃ·i] <-ier, -iest> *adj* ❶ (*tasting like fish*) qui a un goût de poisson ❷ *inf* (*dubious*) louche
**fist** [fɪst] *n* poing *m*
**fit**¹ [fɪt] **I.** <-tter, -ttest> *adj* ❶ (*suitable*) bon(ne); **~ to eat** qui se mange, mangeable; **a meal ~ for a king** un repas digne d'un roi; **~ for human consumption** bon à la consommation; **to see ~ to** +*infin* juger nécessaire de +*infin;* **as you see ~** comme bon vous semble ❷ (*having skills*) capable; **to be not ~ to** +*infin* ne pas être capable de +*infin* ❸ (*ready, prepared*) prêt(e) ❹ (*healthy through physical training*) en forme ▶ **to be (as) ~ as a fiddle** *inf* être en pleine forme **II.** <fitting, - *o* -tt-> *vt* ❶ (*be correct size for*) aller à ❷ (*position/shape as required*) adapter ❸ (*match: description*) correspondre à; **music to ~ the occasion** de la musique qui convient à l'occasion; **the theory doesn't ~ the facts** la théorie ne colle pas aux faits **III.** *vi* <fitting, - *o* -tt-> ❶ (*be correct size*) aller ❷ (*be appropriate*) s'adapter **IV.** *n* coupe *f;* **the dress is a perfect ~** la robe est à la bonne taille
♦ **fit in I.** *vi* ❶ (*fit*) aller; **we will all ~** il y aura de la place pour tout le monde ❷ (*match*) **to ~ with sth** correspondre à qc ❸ (*with group, background*) s'intégrer **II.** *vt* (*find room for*) **to fit sb/sth in somewhere** caser qn/qc quelque part *inf*
♦ **fit together** *vi* s'adapter
**fit**² [fɪt] *n a.* fig crise *f;* (*of anger*) accès *m;* **in ~s of laughter** dans un fou rire; **in ~s and starts** par crises; **he'll have a ~** il va faire une crise
**fitness** *n* ❶ (*competence, suitability*) aptitude *f* ❷ (*good condition, health*) forme *f*

**fitted** ['fɪt·ɪd] adj (*garment*) ajusté(e); (*wardrobe*) encastré(e); ~ **carpet** moquette f; ~ **sheet** drap m housse

**fitting** I. n ❶ pl (*fixtures*) installations fpl ❷ (*for clothes*) essayage m II. adj approprié(e)

**five** [faɪv] adj cinq; *s.a.* **eight**

**fiver** n *inf* billet m de cinq

**fix** [fɪks] I. vt ❶ (*decide, arrange: date, price*) fixer ❷ (*repair: bicycle, roof, leak*) réparer; **to ~ one's hair** arranger ses cheveux mpl ❸ *inf* (*prepare: food, meal*) préparer ❹ (*arrange dishonestly: race, election*) truquer ❺ (*place*) poser; **to ~ sth on sth** fixer qc à qc; **to ~ the blame on sb** repousser la faute sur qn; **to ~ one's attention/eyes on sth** fixer son attention/les yeux sur qc ❻ *inf* (*sterilize: animal*) couper ❼ TECH fixer II. vi **to be ~ing to do sth** *inf* prévoir de faire qc III. n ❶ *sing, inf* (*dilemma, embarrassment*) pépin m; **to be in a ~** être dans le pétrin ❷ *inf* (*dosage of narcotics*) dose f
◆ **fix on** vt a. *inf* fixer
◆ **fix up** vt ❶ (*supply with*) **to fix sb up** trouver ce qu'il faut à qn; **to fix sb up with sth** trouver qn pour qn ❷ (*arrange, organize*) arranger ❸ (*repair, make*) remettre en état

**fixation** [fɪk·'seɪ·ʃən] n fixation f; ~ **with sb/sth** une fixation sur qn/qc

**fixed** adj fixe; (*expression, smile, stare*) figé(e); (*appointment*) fixé(e); ~**-term contract** contrat m à durée déterminée

**fixings** npl *inf* CULIN garniture f

**fixture** ['fɪks·tʃər] n (*immovable object*) équipement m ▸ **to be a permanent ~** faire partie des meubles

**fizzle (out)** ['fɪz·l (aʊt)] vi (*plan, film, match*) partir en eau de boudin

**FL** n *abbr of* **Florida**

**flag¹** [flæg] I. n ❶ (*national symbol*) a. COMPUT drapeau m ❷ NAUT pavillon m II.<-gg-> vt ❶ (*mark*) marquer ❷ *fig* signaler III.<-gg-> vi faiblir; (*conversation*) languir; (*party, film, player*) faiblir
◆ **flag down** vt (*taxi*) héler; (*driver, car*) arrêter

**flag²** [flæg] I. n dalle f II. vt daller

**flagpole** n hampe f

**flair** [fler] n flair m; **to have a ~ for sth** avoir du flair pour qc

**flake** [fleɪk] I. vi (*skin*) peler; (*paint, wood*) s'écailler II. n ❶ (*peeling*) pellicule f; (*of paint, metal*) écaille f; (*of chocolate, wood*) copeau m; (*of snow, cereal*) flocon m ❷ *inf* (*unusual person*) fou, folle m, f
◆ **flake out** vi *inf* s'endormir d'épuisement

**flame** [fleɪm] I. n ❶ a. *fig* (*fire*) flamme f ❷ *inf* COMPUT message m incendiaire II. vi ❶ (*blaze, burn*) a. *fig* flamber ❷ (*glare*) flamboyer III. vt *inf* COMPUT envoyer des messages incendiaires à

**flan** [flæn] n flan m

**flannel** ['flæn·əl] n flanelle f; ~**s** pantalon m de flanelle

**flap** [flæp] I.<-pp-> vt **to ~ sth** agiter qc; **to ~ one's wings** battre des ailes II.<-pp-> vi ❶ (*fly by waving wings*) battre des ailes ❷ (*vibrate, flutter*) battre ❸ *inf* (*become excited*) s'affoler III. n ❶ (*flutter*) battement m ❷ (*fold*) rabat m ❸ (*hinged part*) rabat m; (*on wing*) volet m de freinage ❹ *inf* (*fluster, panic*) affolement m; **to be in a ~** s'affoler

**flare** [fler] I. n ❶ (*blaze, burst of flame*) flamme f ❷ (*signal*) signal m ❸ (*widening*) évasement m ❹ pl FASHION pantalon m à pattes d'éléphant II. vi ❶ (*burn up*) a. *fig* s'enflammer; **tempers ~d** le ton est monté ❷ (*widen, broaden*) s'évaser; (*nostrils*) se dilater III. vt évaser; (*nostrils*) dilater; **~d skirt** une jupe évasée

**flash** [flæʃ] I. vt ❶ (*shine briefly*) a. *fig* (*smile, look*) lancer; (*signal*) envoyer; **to ~ one's headlights** faire un appel de phares; **to ~ a mirror at sb** faire miroiter un miroir en direction de qn ❷ (*show quickly*) montrer rapidement ❸ (*communicate*) **to ~ news** faire un flash d'informations II. vi ❶ (*shine briefly*) a. *fig* briller; (*headlights*) clignoter; (*eyes*) jeter des éclairs

**F**

**②** (*move swiftly*) **to ~ by/past** filer/ passer comme un éclair **③** inf (*expose oneself*) s'exhiber **III.** n **①** (*burst of light*) éclair m; **a ~ of lightning** un éclair; **in a ~** en un rien de temps **②** PHOT a. fig flash m **③** RADIO, TV, PUBL flash m

**flashlight** n lampe f torche

**flashy** <-ier, -iest> adj pej, inf tape- à-l'œil

**flask** [flæsk] n flacon m

**flat** [flæt] **I.** adj **①** <-ter, -test> (*smooth and level*) a. ANAT, MED plat(e) **②** <-ter, -test> (*boring*) plat(e) **③** (*stale: beer, soda pop*) qui n'a plus de bulles **④** AUTO (*tire*) à plat **⑤** (*absolute: refusal*) clair(e) et net(te) **⑥** COM (*rate*) forfaitaire; (*fee*) fixe **⑦** MUS bémol; pej faux(fausse); **A ~** la m bémol **II.** adv **①** (*in a position*) à plat; **to lie ~** être allongé à l'horizontale **②** inf (*absolutely*) **he turned me down ~** il m'a repoussé nettement **③** inf (*exactly*) exactement; **in five minutes ~** dans exactement cinq minutes ▸ **to fall ~** (*joke*) tomber à plat; (*plan, attempt*) échouer; (*performance*) manquer ses effets **III.** n **①** (*level surface: of a sword, a knife*) côté m plat **②** MUS bémol

**flat rate I.** n forfait m; INET, TEL forfait m illimité **II.** adj forfaitaire; TEL, INET illimité(e)

**flatter** vt flatter

**flattering** adj flatteur(-euse)

**flattery** ['flæt·ər·i] n flatterie f

**flavor** ['fleɪ·vər] **I.** n **①** CULIN (*taste*) goût m; (*of ice cream*) parfum m; (*of tea*) arôme m **②** (*characteristic, quality*) note f **II.** vt CULIN assaisonner; (*sweet dish*) parfumer

**flavoring** n arôme m

**flea** [fli] n puce f

**flea market** n marché m aux puces

**fled** [flɛd] pp of **flee**

**fledg(e)ling** ['flɛdʒ·lɪŋ] **I.** n oisillon m **II.** adj (*business, industry, state*) qui débute

**flee** [fli] <fled> vt, vi fuir

**fleeting** adj fugitif(-ive)

**flesh** [flɛʃ] n chair f ▸ **in the ~** en chair et en os

**flesh-colored** adj (de) couleur chair

**flew** [flu] pp, pt of **fly**

**flex** [flɛks] **I.** vt, vi fléchir **II.** n (*electrical cord*) câble m

**flexibility** [ˌflɛk·sə·ˈbɪl·ə·t̬i] n flexibilité f

**flexible** ['flɛk·sə·bl] adj flexible

**flextime** ['flɛks·taɪm] n horaire m à la carte

**flick** [flɪk] **I.** vt (*jerk*) **to ~ sth** donner une tape à qc **II.** n (*hit*) petit coup m; **with a ~ of the wrist** d'un mouvement du poignet

**flight** [flaɪt] n **①** (*act of flying*) vol m **②** (*escape*) a. fig ECON fuite f; **to take ~** prendre la fuite **③** (*series*) (*of stairs*) escalier m ▸ **a ~ of fancy** un rêve fou

**flight attendant** n (*woman*) hôtesse f de l'air; (*man*) steward m

**flimsy** ['flɪm·zi] <-ier, -iest> adj **①** (*light and thin: dress, blouse*) léger(-ère) **②** (*easily broken: construction, structure*) peu solide **③** (*lacking seriousness: excuse*) faible

**fling** [flɪŋ] <flung> **I.** vt a. fig jeter; (*ball*) lancer; **I flung the money back at them** je leur ai renvoyé l'argent à la figure **II.** n **①** (*good time*) bon temps m **②** (*affair*) aventure m
  ♦ **fling off** vt se défaire de

**flip** [flɪp] <-pp-> **I.** vt (*turn over*) **to ~ sth** (**over**) retourner qc; **to ~ a coin** lancer une pièce; **to ~ a switch** pousser un bouton **II.** vi **①** (*turn quickly*) **to ~ over** tourner **②** inf (*go crazy*) péter les plombs **III.** n salto m

**flip-flop** ['flɪp·flap] n **①** FASHION **~s** tongs fpl **②** inf (*reversal of opinion*) retournement m de veste

**flipper** n **①** ZOOL aileron m **②** (*swimming aid*) palme f

**flirt** [flɜrt] **I.** n dragueur, -euse m, f **II.** vi flirter; **to ~ with the idea of doing sth** fig flirter avec l'idée de faire qc

**flirtatious** adj flirteur(-euse)

**float** [floʊt] **I.** vi **①** (*on water, air*) a. fig flotter; (*boat*) être à flot; **to ~ to the**

surface remonter à la surface; **balloons** ~ed by des ballons flottaient en l'air; **music/the smell of cooking** ~ed through the window de la musique/une odeur de cuisine sortait de la fenêtre ❷ (*move aimlessly*) errer ❸ ECON (*fluctuate in exchange rate*) flotter **II.** *vt* ❶ (*keep afloat*) faire flotter; (*boat*) mettre à flot ❷ ECON, FIN (*offer on the stock market*) introduire en bourse ❸ (*put forward: idea, plan*) lancer ❹ FIN (*currency*) laisser flotter **III.** *n* ❶ (*buoyant device*) flotteur *m*; (*on fishing line*) bouchon *m* ❷ (*decorated parade vehicle*) char *m*

**flock** [flak] **I.** *n* ❶ (*group*) troupeau *m*; (*of birds*) volée *f*; (*of people*) foule *f* ❷ REL ouailles *fpl* **II.** *vi* s'attrouper; **people ~ed to hear him** les gens s'attroupaient pour l'entendre

**flood** [flʌd] **I.** *vt* ❶ (*overflow*) a. *fig* inonder; (*person*) submerger; **a river ~s its banks** une rivière sort de son lit ❷ AGR, ECOL (*valley*) irriguer ❸ AUTO (*engine*) noyer **II.** *vi* être inondé; (*river*) déborder; (*people*) affluer **III.** *n* ❶ (*overflow*) inondation *f*; **in ~** en décrue; **~s of light** des flots de lumière ❷ (*outpouring*) flot *m*; (*of mail, calls*) déluge *m*; (*of products*) invasion *f*; **~s of tears** des torrents *mpl* de larmes ❸ REL **the Flood** le Déluge

**floodgates** *n pl* **to open the ~** ouvrir les vannes

**floodlight I.** *n* projecteur *m* **II.**<irr> *vt* éclairer aux projecteurs

**floodplain** *n* plaine *f* inondable

**floodwater** *n* crues *fpl*; **the ~ of the Nile** les crues du Nil

**floor** [flɔr] **I.** *n* ❶ (*surface*) sol *m*; (*wooden*) plancher *m* ❷ (*level of a building*) étage *m*; **ground-~ apartment** appartement *m* de plein pied; **first ~** rez-de-chaussée *m* ❸ GEO (*bottom of ocean*) fond *m*; (*of forest*) sol *m* ❹ ECON, POL (*place of formal discussion*) **the ~** le parquet; **to have the ~** avoir la parole ► **to go through the ~** (*prices*) toucher le plancher; **to take the ~** prendre la

parole; (*stand up and start dancing*) aller sur la piste de danse **II.** *vt* ❶ (*make floor out of sth*) **to ~ a room** poser un revêtement de sol dans une pièce; (*with wood*) parqueter une pièce ❷ (*knock down*) terrasser ❸ (*shock*) désarçonner

**floorboard** *n* lame *f* de parquet

**flop** [flap] <-pp-> **I.** *vi* ❶ (*fall*) tomber; (*on seat*) s'affaler ❷ (*fail*) faire un bide **II.** *n inf* flop *m*; **to be a ~** être un bide

**floppy** <-ier, -iest> *adj* (*hat, hair*) mou(molle); (*ears*) pendant(e)

**Florida** ['flɔ·rɪd·ə] *n* Floride *f*

**florist** ['flɔr·ɪst] *n* fleuriste *mf*

**floss** [flas] **I.** *n* (*dental*) ~ fil *m* dentaire **II.** *vt, vi* **to ~** (*one's teeth*) se passer du fil dentaire

**flour** [flaʊər] **I.** *n* farine *f* **II.** *vt* **to ~ sth** saupoudrer qc de farine

**flourishing** *adj* florissant(e)

**flow** [floʊ] **I.** *vi* a. *fig* couler; (*stream, blood*) circuler; (*air*) passer; (*drinks*) couler à flots; **to ~ from sth** découler de qc; **the river ~s through the town** la rivière traverse la ville **II.** *n sing* écoulement *m*; (*of people, words*) flot *m*; (*of capital, tide*) flux *m*; (*of traffic*) affluence *f*; (*of data*) flux *m* ► **to go with the ~** suivre le courant; **to go against the ~** aller à contre-courant

**flower** ['flaʊ·ər] **I.** *n* fleur *f*; **to be in ~** être en fleur **II.** *vi a. fig* fleurir

**flowerpot** *n* pot *m* de fleurs

**flown** [floʊn] *pp* of **fly**

**flu** [flu] *n* grippe *f*

**fluctuate** ['flʌk·tʃu·eɪt] *vi* fluctuer

**fluent** *adj* éloquent(e), **to be ~ in Portuguese** parler couramment le portugais

**fluffy** <-ier, -iest> *adj* ❶ (*of or like fluff*) duveteux(-euse); (*clothes*) moelleux(-euse) ❷ CULIN mousseux(-euse)

**fluid** ['flu·ɪd] **I.** *n* fluide *m* **II.** *adj* fluide

**flung** [flʌŋ] *pp, pt* of **fling**

**flush**[1] [flʌʃ] **I.** *vi* ❶ (*blush*) rougir ❷ (*operate toilet*) tirer la chasse d'eau; **the toilet didn't ~** la chasse d'eau n'a pas fonctionné **II.** *vt* ❶ (*cleanse*) **to ~ the toilet** tirer la chasse; **to ~ sth**

**F**

**down the toilet** jeter qc dans les toilettes ❷ *(redden)* faire rougir **III.** *n* ❶ *(reddening)* rougeur *m* ❷ *(rush: of anger, emotion)* accès *m;* *(of pleasure, enthusiasm)* élan *m* ❸ *(cleansing device)* chasse *f* d'eau

**flush²** *adj* ❶ *(level or flat)* de niveau ❷ *inf (rich)* qui a des sous

**fluster** ['flʌs·tər] **I.** *vt* **to ~ sb** rendre qn nerveux **II.** *n* nervosité *f;* **to be in a ~** être agité

**flute** [flut] *n* MUS flûte *f*

**flux** [flʌks] *n* flux *m;* **to be in a state of ~** être en mouvement perpétuel

**fly¹** [flaɪ] <flew, flown> **I.** *vi* ❶ *(travel in air)* voler; **to ~ over the Pacific** survoler le Pacifique ❷ *(travel by plane)* voyager en avion; **to ~ to Canada** aller au Canada en avion; **to ~ into/out of Miami** aller à/partir de Miami en avion ❸ *(move quickly: arrows, glass, stones)* voler; **he sent me ~ing** il m'a fait faire un vol plané; **he sent the vase ~ing** il a envoyé le vase en l'air ❹ *(hurry)* foncer; **he flew downstairs** il a foncé en bas; **to ~ into a temper** piquer une colère; **the weeks flew by** *fig* les semaines sont passées comme un souffle ❺ *(wave: flag, hair)* voler ▸ **to ~ in the face of logic/reason** dépasser toute logique/l'entendement; **sb flies off the handle** la moutarde monte au nez de qn **II.** *vt* ❶ *(pilot: plane)* piloter; **to ~ passengers/supplies to a country** transporter des passagers/des approvisionnements par avion vers un pays ❷ *(make move through air: kite)* faire voler; **to ~ the UN flag** faire flotter le drapeau des Nations Unies **III.** *n (zipper)* braguette *f*

◆ **fly away** *vi* s'envoler

◆ **fly in I.** *vi* arriver en avion **II.** *vt (aid, troops)* acheminer par avion

◆ **fly out** *vi* **to ~ to somewhere** s'envoler quelque part

**fly²** *n (small winged insect)* mouche *f* ▸ **sb wouldn't harm a ~** qn ne ferait pas de mal à une mouche; **to drop like flies** *inf* tomber comme des mouches;

**~ in the ointment** un cheveu dans la soupe; **on the ~** *inf* en vitesse

**flying I.** *n* vol *m;* **to be afraid of ~** avoir peur de l'avion **II.** *adj* ❶ *(able to move: insect)* volant(e) ❷ *(moving in the air: glass, object)* qui vole ❸ *(hurried: visit)* éclair *inv* ❹ *(related to flight: accident)* d'avion; *(lesson)* de pilotage; *(jacket)* de pilote

**flyover** *n* MIL défilé *m* aérien

**FM** [ˌef·'em] *n abbr of* **frequency modulation** FM *f*

**foam** [foʊm] **I.** *n* mousse *f;* **shaving ~** mousse à raser **II.** *vi* écumer; *(soap)* mousser; **to ~ at the mouth** *(horse)* avoir de l'écume aux lèvres; *(person)* écumer de rage

**focal point** *n* ❶ *(focus)* foyer *m* ❷ *(central point)* point *m* central

**focus** ['foʊ·kəs] <-es *o* foci> **I.** *n* ❶ *(center: of interest, attention)* centre *m;* *(of unrest, discontent)* foyer *m* ❷ PHYS *(converging point)* a. *fig* foyer *m;* **to be in ~** être net; **to be out of ~** être flou; **to bring sth into ~** mettre qc au point ❸ MED foyer *m* **II.** <-s- *o* -ss-> *vi* ❶ *(see clearly)* régler; **to ~ on sth** regarder fixement qc ❷ *(concentrate)* **to ~ on sth** focaliser sur qc; **try and ~ on the exam/the details** essaie de te concentrer sur l'examen/les détails **III.** *vt* ❶ *(concentrate)* concentrer; **to ~ one's attention on sth** focaliser son attention sur qc ❷ *(bring into focus)* focaliser; *(lens)* mettre au point; **to ~ a camera** faire la mise au point

**fog** [fɔg] **I.** *n a. fig* brouillard *m;* **to be in a ~** être dans le brouillard **II.** <-gg-> *vt fig (obscure)* brouiller

◆ **fog up** *vi (glasses, window)* s'embuer

**foggy** ['fɑ·gi] <-ier, -iest> *adj* brumeux(-euse) ▸ **to not have the foggiest (idea)** *impers* ne pas (en) avoir la moindre idée

**foil¹** [fɔɪl] *n* ❶ *(wrap)* papier *m* d'aluminium ❷ *fig* repoussoir *m*

**foil²** [fɔɪl] *vt* faire échouer; *(plan)* contrecarrer

**foil**³ [fɔɪl] *n* SPORTS fleuret *m*

**fold**¹ [fould] *n* ❶ (*sheep pen*) parc *m* à moutons ❷ *fig* (*home*) **the ~** le bercail

**fold**² [fould] **I.** *vt* ❶ (*bend over upon self*) plier; (*wings*) replier ❷ (*wrap*) envelopper; **to ~ one's arms** croiser les bras; **to ~ one's hands** joindre les mains ❸ CULIN **to ~ sth into sth** incorporer peu à peu qc dans qc **II.** *vi* ❶ (*bend over upon self*) se plier ❷ (*fail or go bankrupt: business*) mettre la clé sous le paillasson; (*play*) quitter l'affiche **III.** *n* pli *m*

♦**fold up I.** *vt* plier **II.** *vi* se plier

**folder** *n* ❶ (*cover, holder*) chemise *f* ❷ COMPUT classeur *m* ❸ (*leaflet*) prospectus *m*

**folding** *adj* pliant(e)

**foliage** ['fou·li·ɪdʒ] *n* feuillage *m*

**folk song** *n* chanson *f* folk

**follow** ['fa·lou] **I.** *vt* ❶ (*come, go after*) *a. fig* suivre ❷ (*adhere to: instructions, example*) suivre; (*leader*) être le disciple de; (*team*) être supporter de ❸ (*practice, carry out: diet*) suivre; (*career*) poursuivre; (*profession*) exercer ❹ (*understand, watch closely*) suivre ▶**to ~ one's <u>nose</u>** *inf* y aller au pif; **to ~ <u>suit</u>** faire de même **II.** *vi* ❶ (*take same route*) suivre ❷ (*come/happen next*) suivre; **what's to ~?** qu'est-ce qu'il y a après? ❸ (*result*) s'ensuivre; **that doesn't ~** ce n'est pas logique

♦**follow through I.** *vt* mener à terme **II.** *vi* aller jusqu'au bout

♦**follow up I.** *vt* (*lead, suggestion*) donner suite à; (*patient*) suivre; **they followed up their success with a new record** après leur succès ils ont battu un nouveau record **II.** *vi* **to ~ on a question** ajouter quelque chose sur un point

**fond** [fand] <-er, -est> *adj* ❶ (*liking*) **to be ~ of sb/sth** aimer beaucoup qn/qc ❷ (*loving, tender: memories, gesture*) bon; (*gesture*) tendre ❸ (*foolish: hope*) naïf(naïve)

**font** [fant] *n* TYP, COMPUT police *f* de caractères

**food** [fud] *n* nourriture *f*; **do we have enough ~?** est-ce qu'il a assez à manger?; **dairy ~s** produits *mpl* laitiers; **Italian ~** la cuisine italienne ▶**~ for <u>thought</u>** matière *f* à penser

**food poisoning** *n* intoxication *f* alimentaire

**food processor** *n* robot *m*

**food stamps** *npl* bons *mpl* d'alimentation

**fool** [ful] **I.** *n* ❶ (*silly person*) idiot(e) *m(f)*; **to make a ~ of sb** tourner qn en ridicule ❷ (*jester*) fou *m* **II.** *vt* duper; **you can't ~ me!** tu ne peux rien me cacher!; **you could have ~ed me!** tu plaisantes! **III.** *vi* **to ~ around** faire l'imbécile **IV.** *adj* stupide

**foolish** *adj* bête

**foot** [fut] **I.** <feet> *n* ❶ (*of person, object*) pied *m*; (*of animal*) patte *f*; **on ~** à pied; **to get to one's feet** se lever ❷ (*unit*) pied *m* ❸ (*lower part*) pied *m*; **at the ~ of the bed** au pied du lit; **at the ~ of the page** au bas de la page ▶**to be <u>back</u> on one's feet** être de nouveau sur pieds; **to have one ~ in the <u>grave</u>** avoir un pied dans la tombe; **to have both feet on the <u>ground</u>** avoir les deux pieds sur terre; **to get off on the <u>right</u>/<u>wrong</u> ~** bien/mal commencer; **to <u>put</u> one's ~ in one's mouth** mettre les pieds dans le plat **II.** *vt* **to ~ the bill** payer la facture

**football** ['fut·bɔl] *n* ❶ football *m* américain ❷ (*ball*) ballon *f* de football

**footbridge** *n* passerelle *f*

**footing** *n* ❶ (*grip*) **to lose one's ~** perdre pied ❷ (*basis*) pied *m*; **on an equal ~** sur un pied d'égalité

**footnote** *n* note *f* (de bas de page)

**footpath** *n* sentier *m*

**footprint** *n* empreinte *f* de pied

**footstep** *n* pas *m* ▶**to <u>follow</u> in sb's ~s** suivre les traces de qn

**for** [fɔr] **I.** *prep* ❶ pour ❷ (*to give to*) pour; **open the door ~ me** ouvre-moi la porte; **to ask/look ~ oneself** demander/regarder (par) soi-même ❸ (*as*

**F**

**F**

*purpose*) ~ **sale/rent** à vendre/louer; **it's time** ~ **lunch/bed** c'est l'heure du déjeuner/de se coucher; **to invite sb** ~ **lunch** inviter qn à déjeuner; **to go** ~ **a walk** aller se promener; **what** ~? pour quoi faire?; **what's that** ~? à quoi ça sert?; **it's** ~ **cutting cheese** c'est pour couper le fromage; ~ **this to be possible** pour que cela soit possible *subj;* **to look** ~ **a way to** +*infin* chercher un moyen de +*infin* ❹ (*to acquire*) **eager** ~ **power/affection** avide de pouvoir/ assoiffé d'affection; **to search** ~ **sth** chercher qc; **to ask/hope** ~ **news** demander/espérer des nouvelles; **to apply** ~ **a job** faire une demande d'emploi; **to shout** ~ **help** appeler à l'aide; **to give sth** ~ **sth else** échanger qc contre qc d'autre ❺ (*toward*) **the train** ~ **Boston** le train pour Boston; **to run** ~ **safety** se sauver en courant; **to reach** ~ **sth** rattraper qc ❻ (*distance of*) **to walk** ~ **8 miles** faire 8 miles à pied ❼ (*amount of time*) ~ **now** pour l'instant; ~ **a while/a time** pendant un moment/un certain temps; **to last** ~ **hours** durer des heures; **I haven't been there** ~ **three years** je n'y ai pas été depuis trois ans; **not** ~ **another 3 months** pas avant 3 mois ❽ (*on date of*) **to plan sth/have sth finished** ~ **Sunday** organiser/avoir fini qc pour dimanche; **to set the wedding** ~ **May 4** fixer le mariage au 4 mai ❾ (*in support of*) **is he** ~ **or against it?** est-il pour ou contre?; **to fight** ~ **sth** lutter en faveur de qc ❿ (*employed by*) **to work** ~ **sb/a company** travailler chez qn/pour une firme ⓫ (*the task of*) **it's** ~ **him to** +*infin* c'est à lui de +*infin* ⓬ (*in substitution*) **the substitute** ~ **the teacher** le remplaçant du professeur; **say hello** ~ **me** dis/dites bonjour de ma part; **to work/feel** ~ **sb** travailler à la place de/ compatir avec qn ⓭ (*as price of*) **a check** ~ **$100** un chèque de 100$; **I paid $10** ~ **it** je l'ai payé 10 dollars ⓮ (*concerning*) **as** ~ **me/that** quant à moi/cela; **two are enough** ~ **me** deux

me suffiront; **too hard** ~ **me** trop dur pour moi; **sorry** ~ **doing sth** désolé d'avoir fait qc *subj* ⓯ (*in reference to*) **to make it easy/hard** ~ **sb** (**to do sth**) faciliter/compliquer la tâche à qn ⓰ (*as cause*) **excuse me** ~ **being late** excuse-/excusez-moi d'être en retard; **as the reason** ~ **one's behavior** comme raison de son comportement; **in prison** ~ **fraud** en prison pour fraude; ~ **lack of sth** par manque de qc ⓱ (*as reason*) **to do sth** ~ **love** faire qc par amour; ~ **fear of doing sth** de peur de faire qc; **to cry** ~ **joy** pleurer de joie ⓲ (*despite*) ~ **all that/her money** malgré tout/ tout son argent; ~ **all I know** autant que je sache *subj* ⓳ (*as*) ~ **example** par exemple; **he** ~ **one** lui par exemple ▸ **he's in** ~ **it!** ça va être sa fête!; **that's kids** ~ **you!** c'est typique des gosses! **II.** *conj form* car

**forbid** [fər·ˈbɪd] <forbad(e), forbid(den)> *vt* interdire; **to** ~ **sb from doing sth, to** ~ **sb to do sth** interdire à qn de faire qc ▸ **God** ~ jamais de la vie!

**forbid(den) I.** *adj* interdit(e) **II.** *pp of* **forbid**

**force** [fɔrs] **I.** *n a.* PHYS force *f;* **to be in** ~ être en vigueur; **to come in** ~ arriver en masse; **by sheer** ~ **of numbers** par la force du nombre; **by** ~ **of habit** par habitude; **the** ~ **of sb's personality** le force de caractère de qn; **the police** ~ la police **II.** *vt* forcer; **to** ~ **sb/oneself to** +*infin* forcer qn/se forcer à +*infin;* **to** ~ **one's way** se frayer un chemin; **to** ~ **sth into a suitcase** tasser qc dans une valise; **to** ~ **a smile** faire un sourire forcé; **to** ~ **oneself on sb** s'imposer à qn; **to** ~ **sb into doing sth** forcer qn à faire qc; **the changes were** ~**d on us** on nous a imposé les changements; **to** ~ **a confession out of sb** obtenir une confession par la force ▸ **to** ~ **sb's hand** forcer la main de qn; **to** ~ **an issue** forcer une décision

**forced** *adj* forcé(e)

**forceful** *adj* énergique

**forearm** *n* avant-bras *m*

**forecast** <forecast *o* forecasted>
I. *n* ❶ (*prediction*) pronostics *mpl*
❷ (*weather prediction*) prévisions *fpl*
météo II. *vt* prévoir

**foreclosure** *n* saisie *f*

**forefather** *n* ancêtre *mf*

**foreground** I. *n* premier plan *m; to put
oneself in the* ~ se mettre en avant
II. *vt* **to** ~ **sth** mettre qc en avant

**forehand** I. *n* coup *m* droit II. *adj* SPORTS
~ **shot** coup *m* droit

**forehead** *n* front *m*

**foreign** ['fɔr·ɪn] *adj* ❶ (*from another
country*) étranger(-ère); ~ **exchange**
change *m* ❷ (*involving other countries:
trade, policy*) extérieur(e); (*travel, correspondent*) à l'étranger; ~ **relations**
relations *fpl* avec l'étranger ❸ *fig* (*not
known*) étranger(-ère); **to be** ~ **to sb**
être étranger à qn ❹ (*not belonging:
body*) étranger(-ère)

**foreigner** *n* étranger, -ère *m, f*

**foremost** I. *adj* plus important(e); **to be
one of the** ~ **authorities on** être l'une
des autorités les plus en vue II. *adv* de
loin; **first and** ~ avant tout

**forename** *n* prénom *m*

**foresee** *irr vt* prévoir

**forest** ['fɔr·ɪst] *n a. fig* forêt *f*

**forester** *n* garde *m* forestier

**forestry** ['fɔr·ɪ·stri] *n* sylviculture *f*

**forever** [fər'ev·ər] *adv* toujours; **to take**
~ **to** +*infin inf* prendre des heures pour
+*infin*

**foreword** *n* avant-propos *m*

**forgave** [fɔr'geɪv] *pt of* **forgive**

**forge** [fɔrdʒ] I. *vt* ❶ (*make illegal copy:
document*) falsifier; (*painting*) contrefaire; ~**d documents** des faux *mpl*
❷ (*heat and shape: metal*) forger ❸ *fig*
(*form with effort*) forger; (*career*) se forger II. *vi* foncer; **to** ~ **into the lead**
prendre la tête III. *n* forge *f*

**forgery** ['fɔr·dʒə·ri] <-ies> *n* contrefaçon *f*

**forget** [fər'get] <forgot, forgotten>
I. *vt* oublier; **to** ~ **to** +*infin* oublier de
+*infin;* **to** ~ **doing sth** oublier avoir fait
qc; ~ **it!** laisse tomber!; **to** ~ **oneself**

*form* se laisser aller; **and don't** ~
**it!** et tâche de ne pas l'oublier! II. *vi* oublier; **to** ~ **about sb/sth** oublier qn/qc;
**to** ~ **about doing sth** oublier de faire
qc; **you can** ~ **about that vacation** ne
compte plus sur les vacances

**forgetful** *adj* ❶ (*unable to remember
things*) distrait(e) ❷ *form* (*oblivious*) ou-
blieux(-euse); **to be** ~ **of sth** négliger qc

**forgive** [fər'gɪv] <forgave, forgiven>
I. *vt* ❶ (*cease to blame*) pardonner; **to**
~ **sb/oneself for doing sth** pardonner
qn/se pardonner d'avoir fait qc; ~ **me if
I interrupt** excusez-moi de vous interrompre; ~ **my ignorance/language**
excuse mon ignorance/mon langage
❷ *form* (*not ask for payment*) **to** ~ **sb
sth** faire grâce à qn de qc II. *vi* pardonner

**forgot** [fər'gɑt] *pt of* **forget**

**forgotten** *pt of* **forget**

**fork** [fɔrk] I. *n* ❶ (*eating tool*) fourchette *f* ❷ (*garden tool*) fourche *f* ❸ (*Y-
-shaped division*) embranchement *m*
❹ *pl* (*support of bicycle*) fourche *f* II. *vt*
(*till: garden*) fourcher III. *vi* bifurquer;
**to** ~ **left/right** bifurquer à gauche/
droite

**forked** *adj* fourchu(e) ▸ **to speak with
a** <u>tongue</u> mentir

**forklift** *n* chariot *m* élévateur

**form** [fɔrm] I. *n* ❶ (*type, variety*) forme *f;* **in the** ~ **of sth** sous la forme de
qc; **to take the** ~ **of sth** prendre la forme de qc ❷ (*outward shape*) *a.* LING forme *f;* **in the** ~ **of sth** dans la forme de
qc; **to** ~ **take** ~ prendre forme ❸ CHEM
(*physical state*) forme *f;* **in liquid/so-
lid** ~ sous forme liquide/solide ❹ (*document*) formulaire *m* ❺ (*condition*)
forme *f;* **to be in good/excellent** ~
être en bonne/excellente forme ▸ **in
any (way,) shape or** ~ en aucune façon; **true to** ~ comme d'habitude II. *vt*
❶ (*make the shape of*) former; **to** ~ **sth
into an object** modeler un objet en qc;
**I** ~**ed the ideas into a book** j'ai transformé les idées en un livre ❷ (*develop
in the mind: opinion*) former; **to** ~ **the**

**F**

**impression** donner l'impression ❸ (*set up: committee, group*) former; (*friendship*) nouer ❹ LING (*use*) former ❺ *form* (*influence*) former; **to ~ sb/sb's character** former qn/le caractère de qn ❻ (*constitute*) constituer; **to ~ part of sth** faire partie de qc **III.** *vi* se former; **to ~ into groups of six** former des groupes de six

**formal** ['fɔr·məl] *adj* ❶ (*proper, well-organized*) formel(le); **he had no ~ training** il n'a pas eu de formation professionnelle ❷ (*special, ceremonious: occasion, address, behavior*) formel(le); (*language*) soutenu(e) ❸ (*official*) officiel(le) ❹ (*connected with artistic form*) formel(le)

**formality** [fɔ·'mæl·ə·t̮i] <-ties> *n* formalité *f*

**formalize** ['fɔr·mə·laɪz] *vt* formaliser

**format** ['fɔr·mæt] **I.** *n* format *m* **II.** <-tt-> *vt* COMPUT formater

**formation** [fɔr·'meɪ·ʃᵊn] *n* formation *f*; **in** (**close**) **~** en rangs serrés

**former** *adj* ❶ (*first*) premier(-ère) ❷ (*earlier, older*) ancien(ne); (*existence, era*) antérieur(e)

**formerly** *adv* avant; (*long ago*) anciennement; **~ known as sb** (*in former times*) auparavant connu sous le nom de qn

**formula** ['fɔr·mju·lə] <-s *o* -lae> *n* ❶ (*mathematical rule*) formule *f* ❷ COM (*recipe for product*) formule *f* ❸ (*plan*) formule *f* ❹ (*form of words*) tournure *f* ❺ (*baby food*) lait *m* en poudre

**fort** [fɔrt] *n* fort *m* ▸ **to hold the ~** garder la boutique

**forth** [fɔrθ] *adv form* en avant; **go/set ~** se mettre en route; **back and ~** d'avant en arrière; **to pace back and ~** aller et venir; **from that day ~** dorénavant

**forthcoming** *adj* ❶ (*happening soon*) prochain(e) ❷ (*coming out soon: film, book*) qui va sortir ❸ (*ready, available*) disponible; **no money was ~** l'argent n'arrivait pas ❹ (*ready to give information*) expansif(-ive); **to not be ~ about sth** ne pas être très bavard sur qc

**forthright** *adj* franc(he)

**fortieth** ['fɔr·t̮i·əθ] *adj* quarantième; *s.a.* **eighth**

**fortnight** ['fɔrt·naɪt] *n sing* quinzaine *f*

**fortunate** ['fɔr·t̮ᵊn·ət] *adj* chanceux(-euse); **to be ~ to do** [*o* **be doing**] **sth** avoir la chance de faire qc; **it is ~** (**for him**) **that** il a de la chance que +*subj*

**fortunately** *adv* heureusement

**fortune** ['fɔr·t̮ʃən] *n* ❶ (*a lot of money*) fortune *f*; **to be worth a ~** valoir une fortune; **to cost a ~** coûter une fortune; **to make a/one's ~** faire fortune; **to seek one's ~** chercher fortune ❷ *form* (*luck*) chance *f*; **to have the good ~ to** +*infin* avoir la chance de +*infin*; **to read/tell sb's ~** dire la bonne aventure à qn ❸ *pl* (*what happens to sb*) destin *m*

**fortune cookie** *n petit gâteau surprise servi en fin de repas*

**fortune teller** *n* diseur, -euse *m, f* de bonne aventure

**forty** ['fɔr·t̮i] *adj* quarante ▸ **to have ~ winks** *inf* piquer un somme; *s.a.* **eight, eighty**

**forward** ['fɔr·wərd] **I.** *adv* ❶ *a. fig* (*toward the front*) en avant; (*position*) à l'avant; **to lean ~** se pencher en avant; **to go ~** avancer; **to run ~** avancer en courant; **to push oneself ~** se mettre en avant ❷ *form* (*onwards in time*) **from that day ~** à compter de ce jour **II.** *adj* ❶ (*front: position*) avant *inv* ❷ (*toward the front*) en avant ❸ (*advanced*) avancé(e); **~ planning** la planification ❹ FIN à terme ❺ *pej* (*too bold and self-confident*) effronté(e) **III.** *n* SPORTS avant *m* **IV.** *vt* ❶ (*send to new address: mail*) faire suivre ❷ *form* COM (*send*) expédier; **to ~ sb sth** expédier qc à qn ❸ *form* (*help to progress*) encourager

**forwarding address** *n* adresse *f* de réexpédition

**forwards** *adv s.* **forward**

**foster** ['fɑ·stər] **I.** *vt* ❶ (*look after: children*) garder ❷ (*place with a new fami-*

*ly*) placer ❸ (*encourage*) encourager; **to ~ sth in sb** stimuler qc chez qn II. *adj* adoptif(-ive)

**fought** [fɔt] *pt, pp of* **fight**

**foul** [faʊl] I. *adj* ❶ (*dirty and disgusting*) infect(e); (*air*) vicié(e); (*taste, smell*) infect(e) ❷ (*highly unpleasant: mood*) infâme; **the weather was ~** il faisait un temps horrible II. *n* SPORTS coup *m* bas *f* III. *vt* ❶ (*pollute*) polluer ❷ (*make dirty*) souiller ❸ SPORTS (*player*) commettre une faute contre

**foul-mouthed** *adj* grossier(-ère)

**found**[1] [faʊnd] *pt, pp of* **find**

**found**[2] [faʊnd] *vt* (*create*) fonder

**found**[3] [faʊnd] *vt* (*melt*) fondre

**foundation** [faʊn·deɪ·ʃən] *n* ❶ *pl* (*base of a building*) fondation *f*; **~ stone** première pierre *f* ❷ *fig* (*basis*) base *f*; **to lay the ~(s) of sth** poser les bases de qc ❸ (*evidence to support sth*) fondement *m*; **to have no ~** n'avoir aucun fondement ❹ (*organization, establishment*) fondation *f* ❺ (*base make-up*) fond *m* de teint

**founder**[1] *n* fondateur, -trice *m, f*

**founder**[2] *vi* ❶ (*sink*) sombrer ❷ *fig* (*fail*) échouer

**fountain** [ˈfaʊn·tⁿn] *n* ❶ (*man-made water jet*) fontaine *f* ❷ (*spray*) a. *fig* jet *m*

**fountain pen** *n* stylo *m* à encre

**four** [fɔr] I. *adj* quatre II. *n* quatre *m* ▸ **to be on all ~s** être à quatre pattes; *s.a.* **eight**

**four-door** (*car*) *n* voiture *f* quatre portes

**fourteen** [ˌfɔrˈtin] *adj* quatorze; *s.a.* **eight**

**fourteenth** *adj* quatorzième; *s.a.* **eighth**

**fourth** [fɔrθ] I. *adj* quatrième II. *n* (*quarter*) quart *m*; *s.a.* **eighth**

**four-wheel drive** *n* quatre roues motrices *m*

**fox** [faks] I. *n* ❶ (*animal*) renard *m* ❷ *inf* (*cunning person*) **an old ~** un vieux renard ❸ *inf* (*sexy woman*) fille *f* sexy II. *vt* ❶ (*mystify*) laisser perplexe ❷ (*trick*) **to ~ sb into doing sth** berner qn en faisant qc

**foyer** [ˈfɔɪ·ər] *n* entrée *f*; THEAT foyer *m*

**fraction** [ˈfræk·ʃən] *n* fraction *f*; **by a ~** d'une fraction; **a ~ of a second** une fraction de seconde

**fracture** [ˈfræk·tʃər] I. *vt* ❶ MED (*break*) fracturer ❷ (*cause a crack in*) fissurer ❸ *fig* (*destroy: accord*) rompre II. *vi* se fracturer III. *n a. fig* MED fracture *f*

**fragile** [ˈfrædʒ·ᵊl] *adj* fragile

**fragment** [ˈfræg·mənt, *vb:* ˈfræg·ment] I. *n a. fig* fragment *m* II. *vi a. fig* se fragmenter III. *vt a. fig* fragmenter

**frame** [freɪm] I. *n* ❶ (*for picture*) a. COMPUT cadre *m* ❷ (*enclosure: of door, window*) châssis *m* ❸ *pl* (*rim on eyeglasses*) monture *f* ❹ (*structure*) charpente *f*; (*for tent*) armature *f*; (*for cycle*) cadre *m* ❺ (*body*) ossature *f* ❻ (*section of film*) image *f* ❼ (*for plants*) châssis *m* ❽ *fig* **~ of mind** état *m* d'esprit; **~ of reference** système *m* de référence II. *vt* ❶ (*put in a frame*) encadrer; **to ~ the face** mettre le visage en valeur ❷ (*put into words*) formuler; (*regulations*) concevoir ❸ *inf* (*falsely incriminate*) monter un coup contre

**frame-up** *n inf* coup *m* monté

**framework** *n fig* cadre *m*

**France** [fræn(t)s] *n* la France

**frank**[1] [fræŋk] I. *adj* franc(he) II. *vt* affranchir

**frank**[2] [fræŋk] *n inf abbr of* **frankfurter** saucisse *f* de Francfort

**frankencorn** [ˈfræŋ·kⁿn·kɔːn] *n no pl, pej, inf* maïs *m* transgénique

**frankfurter** [ˈfræŋk·fɜr·tər] *n* saucisse *f* de Francfort

**frantic** [ˈfræn·tɪk] *adj* ❶ (*wild and desperate*) fou(folle) ❷ (*hurried and confused*) effréné(e)

**fraud** [frɔd] *n* ❶ LAW (*obtaining money by deceit*) fraude *f* ❷ (*thing intended to deceive*) imposture *f* ❸ (*deceiver*) imposteur *m*

**fray**[1] [freɪ] *vi* ❶ (*become worn*) s'effilocher ❷ *fig* **tempers ~** les gens s'énervent

**fray²** [freɪ] *n* **to enter the ~** entrer dans l'arène

**freak** [friːk] I. *n* ❶ (*abnormal thing*) phénomène *m* ❷ (*abnormal person, animal*) monstre *m*; *fig* phénomène *m* de foire ❸ (*fanatical enthusiast*) fana *mf* II. *adj* anormal(e) III. *vi* **to ~ (out)** devenir fou(folle)

**freckle** ['frek·l] *n pl* tache *f* de rousseur

**free** [fri] I. <-r, -est> *adj* ❶ (*not tied up or restricted*) *a. fig* (*person, country, elections*) libre; **to set sb/sth ~** libérer qn/qc; **to break ~ of sth** se libérer de qc; **to be ~ from sth** être libéré de qc; **to be ~ to** +*infin* être libre de +*infin*; **feel ~ to** +*infin* n'hésite pas à +*infin*; **to leave sb ~ to** +*infin* laisser qn libre de +*infin*; **to go into a ~ fall** FIN partir en chute libre ❷ (*costing nothing: sample*) gratuit(e); **to be ~ of tax** être exonéré de taxes ❸ (*not occupied: seat*) libre; **I'm leaving Monday ~** je ne prévois rien lundi ❹ (*without*) **~ of** [*o from*] **sth** sans; **~ of disease/prejudice** dépourvu de toute maladie/de tout préjugé; **~ of commitments** libéré de tout engagement; **sugar-~** sans sucre ❺ (*giving in large amounts*) généreux(-euse); **to be ~ with one's advice** être prodigue en conseils ❻ (*not strict: translation*) libre ▶ **to be as ~ as a bird** être libre comme l'air; **there's no such thing as a ~ lunch** c'est ce qui s'appelle renvoyer l'ascenseur II. *adv* ❶ (*in freedom*) en (toute) liberté ❷ (*costing nothing*) gratuitement; **~ of charge** gratuit; **for ~** *inf* gratuitement III. *vt* ❶ (*release*) **to ~ sb/sth from sth** libérer qn/qc de qc ❷ (*relieve*) **to ~ sb/sth from sth** soulager qn/qc de qc; **to ~ sb from a contract** dégager qn d'un contrat ❸ (*make available*) **to ~ sth for sth** libérer qc pour qc; **to ~ up a week to** +*infin* prendre une semaine (de libre) pour +*infin*; **to ~ sb to** +*infin* laisser du temps à qn pour +*infin*

**freedom** ['fri·dəm] *n* liberté *f*; **to have the ~ to** +*infin* avoir la liberté de +*infin*; **~ of information** libre accès *m* à

l'information; **to give sb the ~ to do sth** donner carte blanche à qn pour faire qc

**free kick** *n* SPORTS coup *m* franc

**freelance** I. *n* free-lance *mf*, travailleur *m* autonome *Québec* II. *adj* free-lance *inv*, autonome *Québec* III. *adv* en free-lance IV. *vi* travailler en free-lance

**freely** *adv* ❶ (*unrestrictedly*) librement ❷ (*without obstruction*) sans contrainte ❸ (*frankly*) franchement ❹ (*generously*) généreusement

**free-range** *adj* fermier(-ère)

**free speech** *n* liberté *f* d'expression

**freestyle** I. *n* SPORTS nage *f* libre II. *adj* libre

**freeware** *n* COMPUT logiciel *m* gratuit, gratuiciel *m Québec*

**freeway** *n* autoroute *f*

**freewheeling** *adj* (*person*) insouciant(e)

**free will** *n* libre arbitre *m*; **to do sth of one's own ~** faire qc de son propre chef

**freeze** [friz] <froze, frozen> I. *vi* ❶ (*become solid*) geler; **to ~ solid** durcir sous l'action du gel ❷ (*get cold*) geler; **to ~ to death** mourir de froid ❸ *impers* (*be below freezing point*) **it ~s** il gèle ❹ *fig* se figer; **~! ne bougez plus!** II. *vt* ❶ (*turn to ice*) geler; (*food*) congeler ❷ *fig* glacer ❸ CINE **to ~ an image** faire un arrêt sur image ❹ FIN (*pay*) geler; (*account*) bloquer ❺ (*anesthetize*) insensibiliser ❻ COMPUT figer ▶ **to make sb's blood ~** glacer le sang de qn III. *n* ❶ METEO gel *m*; **big ~** fortes gelées *fpl* ❷ ECON (*stoppage: of price, wage*) gel *m*

**freezer** *n* congélateur *m*; **~ compartment** freezer *m*

**freezing** I. *adj* glacial(e); (*person*) gelé(e) II. *n* congélation *f*; **to be above/below ~** être au-dessus/au-dessous de zéro

**freight** [freɪt] I. *n inv* ❶ (*goods*) fret *m* ❷ (*transportation*) transport *m* ❸ (*charge*) fret *m* ❹ RAIL train *m* de marchandises II. *adj* (*price*) de marchandises; (*charges*) de fret; (*company*, *service*) de transport **III.** *adv* (*by freight system*) **to send sth ~** expédier qc en régime ordinaire **IV.** *vt* ❶ (*transport*) affréter ❷ (*load*) *a. fig* charger

**freighter** *n* ❶ (*ship*) cargo *m* ❷ (*plane*) avion-cargo *m*

**French** [fren(t)ʃ] **I.** *adj* français(e); **~ team** équipe *f* de France; **~ speaker** francophone *mf* **II.** *n* ❶ (*people*) **the ~** les Français *mpl* ❷ LING français *m*; **excuse my ~!** passez-moi l'expression!; *s.a.* **English**

**French bread** *n* pain *m* blanc

**French fries** *npl* (pommes) frites *fpl*, patates *fpl* frites *Québec*

**French kiss** *n* patin *m* *inf*

**Frenchman** <-men> *n* Français *m*

**French toast** *n* pain *m* perdu

**French window** *n* porte-fenêtre *f*

**Frenchwoman** <-women> *n* Française *f*

**frequency** ['fri·kwən(t)·si] <-ies> *n* fréquence *f*; **low/high ~** basse/haute fréquence; **to happen with increasing ~** arriver de plus en plus fréquemment

**frequent** ['fri·kwənt] **I.** *adj* ❶ (*happening often*) fréquent(e); (*expression*) courant(e) ❷ (*regular*) habituel(le); **a ~ flyer** un passager fidélisé **II.** *vt* fréquenter

**fresh** [freʃ] *adj* ❶ (*new*) frais(fraîche); **to make a ~ start** repartir à zéro; **~ in sb's mind** tout frais dans la mémoire de qc ❷ (*unused*) nouveau(-elle); (*shirt*) propre ❸ (*recently made*) frais(fraîche); **~ from New York** nouvellement arrivé de New York; **~ from the oven/factory** qui sort du four/de l'usine; **~ off the presses** qui vient de paraître ❹ (*clean, cool, not stale*) frais(fraîche); (*air*) pur(e); **to get a breath of ~ air** s'oxygéner ❺ METEO frais(fraîche) ❻ (*not tired*) frais(fraîche) et net(te) ❼ *inf* (*disrespectful*) effronté(e); **to get ~ with** (*teacher*) être insolent avec; (*woman*) prendre des libertés avec ▸ **to be ~ out of sth** être en panne de qc

**freshen** ['freʃ·ən] **I.** *vt* ❶ (*make newer*) rafraîchir ❷ (*refill*) **to ~ sb's drink**

remplir à nouveau le verre de qn **II.** *vi* METEO se rafraîchir

**friction** ['frɪk·ʃən] *n* friction *f*; (*between two things*) frottement *m*; (*between two people*) désaccord *m*

**Friday** ['fraɪ·deɪ] *n* vendredi *m*; **on ~s** le vendredi; **every ~** tous les vendredis; **this** (**coming**) **~** ce vendredi; **a week from ~** vendredi en huit; **every other ~** un vendredi sur deux

**fridge** [frɪdʒ] *n* frigo *m*

**fried egg** *n* œuf *m* au plat

**friend** [frend] *n* ❶ (*person*) ami(e) *m(f)*; **childhood ~** ami d'enfance; **the best of ~s** les meilleurs amis du monde; **my old ~ the taxman** *iron* mon cher ami le fisc; **to be just good ~s** être ami avec qn; **to be just good ~s** être bons amis, sans plus; **to be a** (**good**) **~ to sb** être un véritable ami pour qn; **to make ~s with sb** se lier d'amitié avec qn ❷ (*supporter*) ami *m* ▸ **with ~s like him/her, who needs enemies?** Dieu me garde de mes amis; mes ennemis, je m'en charge!; **a ~ in need is a ~ indeed** *prov* c'est dans le besoin qu'on reconnaît ses vrais amis *prov*; **what are ~s for?** c'est à ça que servent les amis!

**friendly** <-ier, -iest> *adj* ❶ (*showing friendship*) amical(e); (*attitude*) aimable; (*pet*) affectueux(-euse); **not very ~** pas très gentil; **they became ~ on vacation** ils sont devenus amis en vacances; **to be on ~ terms with sb** être en bons termes avec qn; **to get too ~ with sb** se montrer trop familier avec qn ❷ (*pleasant: neighborhood, school*) sympathique; (*reception*) accueillant(e) ❸ (*not competitive*) **a ~ nation** un pays ami

**friendly fire** *n* MIL tirs *mpl* amis

**friendship** *n* amitié *f*; **to form a ~ with sb** se lier d'amitié avec qn; **to strike up a ~ with sb** se prendre d'amitié pour qn; **to hold out the hand of ~ to sb** tendre la main à qn

**fright** [fraɪt] *n* ❶ *sing* (*feeling*) peur *f* ❷ (*awful experience*) frayeur *f*; **to give**

sb a ~ effrayer qn ▶ **to get the ~ of
one's life** avoir la peur de sa vie

**frighten** ['fraɪ·tⁿn] I. *vt* effrayer; **to ~ sb
to death** faire mourir qn de peur II. *vi*
prendre peur; **to ~ easily** s'effrayer
pour un rien

**frightful** *adj* épouvantable

**frigid** ['frɪdʒ·ɪd] *adj* ❶ MED frigide ❷ GEO
glacial(e) ❸ (*unfriendly*) froid(e)

**fringe** [frɪn(d)ʒ] I. *n* ❶ (*edging*) bordure *f* ❷ *fig* (*outer edge*) périphérie *f*; (*of
society*) marge *f*; (*of bushes*) lisière *f*;
**~ groups** groupes *mpl* politiques en
marge II. *vt* franger III. *adj* alterna-
tif(-ive)

**fringe benefits** *n pl* avantages *mpl* sociaux

**frisk** [frɪsk] I. *vi* gambader II. *vt* fouiller

**fro** [froʊ] *adv* **to go to and ~** faire des
va-et-vient

**frock** [frak] *n inf* robe *f*

**frog** [frɔɡ] *n* grenouille *f* ▶ **to have a ~
in one's throat** avoir un chat dans la
gorge

**from** [fram] *prep* ❶ de ❷ (*as starting
point*) **where is he ~?** d'où est-il?; **to
fly ~ New York to Tokyo** aller de New
York à Tokyo (en avion); **shirts ~ $5**
des chemises à partir de 5 dollars
❸ (*temporal*) **~ time to time** de temps
en temps; **~ his childhood** depuis son
enfance; **~ the age of 7 upward** dès
l'âge de 7 ans; **~ that date on(ward)** à
partir de cette date ❹ (*at distance to*)
**100 feet ~ the river** à 100 pieds du
fleuve ❺ (*source, origin*) **a card ~
Dad/Mexico** une carte de papa/du
Mexique; **to drink ~ a cup/the bottle**
boire dans une tasse/à la bouteille;
**translated ~ the English** traduit de
l'anglais; **~ "War and Peace"** extrait
[*o* tiré] de "Guerre et Paix"; **tell her ~
me** dites-lui de ma part ❻ (*in reference
to*) **~ what I heard** d'après ce que j'ai
entendu (dire); **~ my point of view** a.
*fig* de mon point de vue; **to judge ~ appearances** juger selon les apparences;
**different ~ the others** différent des
autres ❼ (*caused by*) **~ experience** par

expérience; **weak ~ hunger** affaibli par
la faim ❻ (*expressing removal, separation*) **to steal/take sth ~ sb** voler/
prendre qc à qn; **to tell good ~ evil** distinguer le bien du mal; **to shade sth ~
the sun** protéger qc du soleil; **4 sub-
tracted ~ 7 equals 3** MATH 4 ôté de 7
égalent 3 ▶ **~ bad to worse** de mal en
pis

**front** [frʌnt] I. *n* ❶ *sing* (*side: of machine*) avant *m*; (*of building*) façade *f*; (*of
shop*) devanture *f*; (*of document*) recto *m*; **lying on his ~** allongé(e) sur le
ventre ❷ (*area: of building, vehicle*) devant *m*; (*of crowd, audience*) premiers
rangs *mpl*; **at the ~ of the procession**
en tête du cortège ❸ PUBL (*outside cover: of magazine, book*) couverture *f*; (*of
paper*) recto *m* ❹ (*ahead of sb/sth*) **to
be two points in ~** mener par deux
points ❺ (*facing*) **in ~ of sb/sth** en
face de qn/qc; **in ~ of witnesses** en
présence de témoins ❻ (*appearance*) façade *f*; **to put on a bold ~** faire bonne
contenance; **to be a ~ for sth** n'être
qu'une couverture pour qc ❼ (*area of
activity*) côté *m*; **on the work ~** sur le
plan du travail ❽ MIL, POL, METEO
front *m*; **at the ~** MIL au front ❾ *inf* (*impudence*) effronterie *f* ▶ **to pay up** =
payer d'avance II. *adj* ❶ (*in front*) de
devant; (*leg, teeth*) de devant; (*wheel*)
avant; (*view*) de face; (*seat*) au premier
rang; (*in car*) à l'avant; **~ office** réception *f*; **on the ~ cover** en couverture
❷ *fig* de façade III. *vt* ❶ *passive* (*past
facade on*) **to be ~ed with sth** être recouvert de qc ❷ (*be head of*) diriger;
(*group*) être à la tête de ❸ TV présenter
IV. *vi* (*face*) **to ~ south** être exposé
au sud; **to ~ onto sth** donner sur qc
❷ *fig* **to ~ for sb/sth** servir de couverture à qn/qc

**front door** *n* porte *f* d'entrée

**front page** *n* première page *f*

**front runner** *n* favori *m*

**front yard** *n* jardin *m* de devant

**frost** [frast] I. *n* ❶ (*ice crystals*) givre *m*
❷ (*period*) gelée *f* ❸ (*temperature*)

**gel** *m* **II.** *vt* **❶** (*cover with frost*) givrer **❷** CULIN glacer

**frostbite** ['fros(t)·baɪt] *n* gelure *f*

**frosty** ['frɒ·sti] <-ier, -iest> *adj* **❶** (*cold: air*) glacial(e); (*earth*) gelé(e); (*window*) couvert(e) de givre **❷** *fig* glacial(e)

**froth** [frɒθ] **I.** *n inv* écume *f* **II.** *vi* écumer; (*beer*) mousser; **to ~ at the mouth** *fig, inf* écumer de rage **III.** *vt* **to ~ sth** (**up**) faire mousser qc

**frown** [fraʊn] **I.** *vi* froncer les sourcils; **to ~ on sth** *fig* voir qc d'un mauvais œil **II.** *n* froncement *m* de sourcils

**froze** [frouz] *pt of* **freeze**

**frozen I.** *pp of* **freeze II.** *adj* **❶** (*covered with ice*) gelé(e) **❷** (*deep-frozen*) congelé(e); **~ foods** surgelés *mpl* **❸** (*cold*) glacé(e) **❹** FIN bloqué(e)

**fruit** [frut] **I.** *n* **❶** BOT fruit *m;* **to be in ~** porter des fruits **❷** *fig* (*results*) fruits *mpl* **II.** *vi* porter des fruits

**fruitcake** *n* **❶** CULIN cake *m* **❷** *inf* (*person*) cinglé(e) *m(f)*

**fruit cocktail** *n* macédoine *f* de fruits

**frustrate** ['frʌs·treɪt] <-ting> *vt* **❶** (*annoy*) énerver **❷** (*foil*) contrecarrer

**frustrated** *adj* frustré(e); (*effort*) vain(e)

**frustration** *n* frustration *f*

**fry¹** [fraɪ] <-ie-> **I.** *vt* faire frire **II.** *vi* **❶** (*be cooked*) frire **❷** *inf* (*get burned*) griller

**fry²** [fraɪ] *n* fretin *m*

**frying pan** *n* poêle *f* (à frire) ▶ **out of the ~, into the** fire de mal en pis

**ft.** *n abbr of* **foot** *or* **feet** pied *m*

**fuck** [fʌk] *vulg* **I.** *vt* **❶** (*have sex with*) baiser **❷** *impers* (*damn*) **~ it!** merde!; **~ you!** je t'emmerde! **II.** *vi* baiser **III.** *n* **❶** (*act*) baise *f* **❷** (*person*) **a good/bad ~** un bon/mauvais coup **❸** (*used as an expletive*) **what the ~ are you doing?** qu'est-ce que tu fous, bordel de merde? **❹** (*intensifier*) **will you go there? – the – I will!** tu va y aller? – tu déconnes ou quoi!; **to not give a ~** n'en avoir rien à foutre **IV.** *interj* **~!** bordel de merde!

**fucker** *n vulg* (*stupid person*) connard, connasse *m, f*

**fucking** *vulg* **I.** *adj* de merde; **why won't this ~ thing work?** pourquoi est-ce que ce putain de truc ne marche pas?; **what a ~ idiot!** quel idiot fini! **II.** *adv* **I know ~ well what happened** je sais ce qui s'est passé, putain

**fuel** ['fju·əl] **I.** *n* **❶** (*power source*) combustible *m* **❷** (*petrol*) carburant *m* ▶ **to add ~ to the** fire jeter de l'huile sur le feu **II.** <*-l-* *o* *-ll-*> *vt a. fig* alimenter; (*hatred*) attiser; (*doubts*) nourrir; **to be ~ed by sth** marcher à qc

**fulfillment** *n* (*of task*) accomplissement *m;* (*of ambition*) réalisation *f;* **personal ~** épanouissement *m* personnel

**full** [fʊl] **I.** <-er, -est> *adj* **❶** (*opp: empty*) plein(e); (*person*) rassasié(e); (*room*) comble; (*disk*) saturé(e); **~ to the brim** rempli à ras bord; **to be ~ of praise for sb/sth** ne pas tarir d'éloges sur qn/qc; **to talk with one's mouth ~** parler la bouche pleine; **to do sth on a ~ stomach** faire qc le ventre plein **❷** (*no spaces left: list, hotel*) complet(-ète) **❸** (*complete*) complet(-ète); (*text*) intégral(e); (*day*) bien rempli(e); (*explanation*) détaillé(e); (*member*) à part entière; (*professor*) titulaire; **I have a very ~ week ahead** je vais avoir une semaine très chargée; **~ details of the offer** toutes les précisions sur la promotion; **to be in ~ swing** battre son plein; **to come to a ~ stop** s'arrêter complètement; **we waited a ~ hour** on attendu toute une heure; **in ~ view of sb** sous les yeux de qn; **to be ~ of sth** ne parler que de qc; **to be ~ of oneself** être très satisfait de soi **❹** (*maximum*) plein(e); **at ~ volume** à plein volume; **at ~ blast** à fond; **at ~ speed** à toute vitesse; **~ steam ahead!** NAUT en avant toutes! **❺** (*rounded: face, cheeks*) rond(e); (*lips*) charnu(e); (*figure*) fort(e); (*skirt*) ample ▶ **to be ~ of beans** (*badly mistaken*) se gourer complètement; **things have come ~** circle la boucle est bouclée **II.** *adv* complètement; **~ in the face** en plein visage;

**F**

**F**

I know ~ well that ... je sais parfaitement que ... III. *n* in ~ intégralement; **name in** ~ nom et prénoms

**fullback** *n* SPORTS arrière *m*

**full-grown** *adj* adulte

**full moon** *n* pleine lune *f*

**full-time** I. *adj* à plein temps; **it's a ~ job doing that** *fig* ça occupe du matin au soir II. *adv* à plein temps

**fully** ['fʊl·i] *adv* ❶ (*completely*) entièrement; (*open*) complètement; (*appreciate*) pleinement; (*understand*) parfaitement; (*study*) à fond; (*explain*) en détail; (*load*) au maximum ❷ (*at least*) au moins; **~ three hours** trois bonnes heures

**fume** [fjum] *vi* a. *fig* fulminer; **to ~ at sth** fulminer contre qc

**fun** [fʌn] I. *n* amusement *m;* **for** ~ pour s'amuser; **have** ~! amusez-vous bien!; **you're no** ~! tu n'es pas marrant!; **to make** ~ **of sb** se moquer de qn II. *adj* drôle; **to be** ~ être amusant

**functional** *adj* ❶ (*serving a function*) a. MED fonctionnel(le) ❷ (*operational, working*) opérationnel(le)

**fund** [fʌnd] I. *n* fonds *m;* **pension** ~ caisse *f* de retraite; **to be short of** ~**s** être à court de capitaux II. *vt* financer

**fundamental** [ˌfʌn·də·'men·t̬əl] *adj* fondamental(e); (*need*) vital(e); (*principle*) premier(-ère); (*question, concern*) principal(e); (*importance, error*) capital(e); **to learn the** ~**s** apprendre les principes de base

**funeral** ['fju·nəˌrəl] *n* funérailles *fpl;* **to attend a** ~ assister à un enterrement

**funeral home** *n* entreprise *f* de pompes funèbres, salon *m* funéraire [*o* mortuaire] *Québec*

**funeral parlor** *n s.* **funeral home**

**funnel** ['fʌn·əl] I. *n* ❶ (*implement*) entonnoir *m* ❷ (*chimney*) cheminée *f* II. <-l- *o* -ll-> *vt* a. *fig* verser; (*attention*) canaliser; (*goods, information*) faire passer III. *vi* (*people*) s'engouffrer; (*liquid, gases*) passer

**funny** ['fʌn·i] <-ier, -iest> *adj* ❶ (*amusing*) drôle; (*joke*) bon(ne) ❷ (*odd, pe-*

*culiar*) curieux(-euse); (*thing*) bizarre; (*feeling*) étrange; (*idea*) drôle; **it feels ~ being back here** ça fait bizarre d'être de retour ici ❸ (*dishonest*) malhonnête; (*business*) louche ❹ (*not working or feeling well*) **to feel** ~ ne pas se sentir bien; **sth acts** ~ qc se met à ne plus bien marcher ❺ *inf* **don't try anything** ~ ne fais pas le malin

**fur** [fɜr] *n* ❶ (*animal hair*) poils *mpl* ❷ (*clothing*) fourrure *f* ❸ *pl* (*in hunting*) peaux *fpl* ▶ **the** ~ **the flies** il y a du grabuge

**furious** ['fjʊr·i·əs] *adj* ❶ (*very angry*) furieux(-euse); **to be** ~ **with sb** être en colère contre qn ❷ (*intense, violent: argument, storm*) violent(e); **at a** ~ **pace** au pas de charge

**furnish** ['fɜr·nɪʃ] *vt* ❶ (*supply*) fournir; **to** ~ **sb with sth** fournir qc à qn ❷ (*provide furniture*) meubler; **to be** ~**ed with sth** être équipé en qc

**furniture** ['fɜr·nɪ·tʃər] *n* meubles *mpl;* **piece of** ~ meuble *m*

**furor** ['fjʊrˌɔr] *n* (*outcry*) colère *f;* **to cause a** ~ déclencher la fureur

**furry** ['fɜr·i] <-ier, -iest> *adj* ❶ (*covered with fur*) à poil ❷ (*looking like fur: toy*) en peluche

**further** ['fɜr·ðər] I. *adj comp of* **far** ❶ (*additional*) supplémentaire; **on** ~ **examination** après examen ultérieur; **until** ~ **notice** jusqu'à nouvel ordre ❷ (*greater distance*) a. *fig* plus éloigné(e) II. *adv comp of* **far** ❶ (*greater extent*) plus loin; ~ **away** plus loin; **we didn't get much** ~ nous ne sommes pas allés plus loin; **he wouldn't go any** ~ il refusait d'aller plus loin; **to look** ~ **ahead** regarder vers l'avenir ❷ (*greater distance*) plus loin; ~ **along the coast** plus loin sur la côte ❸ (*more*) de plus; **I have nothing** ~ **to say on this matter** je n'ai rien à ajouter à ce sujet III. *vt* faire avancer; (*cause, interest*) servir; (*training, research*) poursuivre; (*career*) faire avancer

**furthermore** *adv* en outre

**furthest** ['fɜr·ðɪst] I. *adj superl of* **far** *a.*

*fig* le(la) plus éloigné(e) **II.** *adv superl of* **far** *a. fig* le plus loin; **to be ~ north** être plus au nord; **$500 is the ~ I can go** 500 dollars est mon dernier prix

**fuse** [fjuz] **I.** *n* ❶ (*electrical safety device*) fusible *m;* **to blow a ~** faire sauter un plomb ❷ (*ignition device, detonator*) détonateur *m* ❸ (*string*) mèche *f* ▸ **to have a short ~** ne pas avoir de patience; **to blow one's ~** péter les plombs **II.** *vi* ❶ (*melt*) fondre; **to ~ together** s'unifier ❷ (*connect*) *a. fig* fusionner **III.** *vt* ❶ (*melt*) fondre ❷ (*connect*) faire fusionner

**fuse box** <-xes> *n* boîte *f* à fusibles

**fuselage** ['fju·sə·laʒ] *n* fuselage *m*

**fuss** [fʌs] **I.** *n* ❶ (*trouble*) histoires *f;* **to make a ~ about sth** faire des histoires pour qc ❷ (*attentiveness*) attentions *fpl;* **to make a ~ over sb** être aux petits soins pour qn **II.** *vi* ❶ (*make a fuss*) faire des histoires ❷ (*worry*) **to ~ over sb/sth** s'en faire énormément au sujet de qn/qc ❸ (*be agitated*) s'agiter ❹ (*show attention*) **to ~ over sb** être aux petits soins pour qn

**fussy** ['fʌs·i] <-ier, -iest> *adj* ❶ *pej* (*picky*) méticuleux( euse); **to be a ~**

**eater** être difficile sur la nourriture ❷ (*upset: baby*) qui fait ses caprices ❸ *pej* (*over decorated*) surchargé(e) ❹ (*needing much care: job*) minutieux(-euse)

**futile** ['fju·təl] *adj* ❶ (*vain*) vain(e) ❷ (*unimportant*) futile; **to prove ~** se révéler dérisoire

**future** ['fju·tʃər] **I.** *n* ❶ (*the time to come*) avenir *m;* **what the ~ will bring** ce que l'avenir nous réserve; **in the ~** à l'avenir ❷ (*prospects*) avenir *m;* **to face an uncertain ~** affronter des lendemains incertains ❸ LING futur *m;* **to be in the ~** (*tense*) être au futur ❹ *pl* FIN marchés *mpl* à terme **II.** *adj* futur(e); (*events*) à venir; **at some ~ date** à une date ultérieure

**fuze** [fjuz] **I.** *n* (*ignition device, detonator*) détonateur *m;* (*string*) mèche *f* **II.** *vt* (*bomb*) amorcer

**fuzzy** *adj* ❶ (*unclear: image*) flou(e); (*sound, reception*) brouillé(e) ❷ *fig* (*confused*) confus(e) ❸ (*frizzy: hair*) crépu(e); **peaches have ~ skin** les pêches ont des peaux duveteuses

**FYI** *abbr of* **for your information** pour (votre) information

# Gg

**G, g** [dʒi] <-'s o -s> n G m, g m; ~ **as in Golf** (on telephone) g comme Gaston
**g** n ① abbr of **gram** g m ②<-'s> PHYS abbr of **gravity** g m
**G**[1] n MUS sol m
**G**[2] I.<-'s> n inf ($1000) mille dollars mpl II. adj inv abbr of **General Audiences** (movie) tout public; **rated ~** classé tout public
**GA** n abbr of **Georgia**
**gadget** ['gædʒ·ɪt] n gadget m
**gaff(e)** [gæf] n gaffe f
**gage** [geɪdʒ] s. **gauge**
**gain** [geɪn] I. n ①(profit) gain m, profit m ②(increase) augmentation f; **weight ~** prise f de poids ③FIN hausse f; **to make ~s** être en hausse ④(advantage) gain m II. vt ①(obtain) obtenir; (confidence, respect, sympathy) gagner; (experience, knowledge, reputation) acquérir; (victory, success) remporter; **to ~ freedom/independence** conquérir sa liberté/son indépendance; **to ~ access to sth** accéder à qc; **to ~ acceptance** être accepté; **to ~ control of sth** prendre le contrôle de qc; **to ~ insight into sth** avoir un aperçu de qc ②(increase) gagner; **to ~ altitude** gagner de l'altitude; **to ~ weight/velocity** prendre du poids/de la vitesse; **to ~ momentum** prendre de l'ampleur; **to ~ strength** prendre des forces; **to ~ ground** gagner du terrain; (progress) progresser; **to ~ ground on sb** (catch up) rattraper qn ③(reach: destination) atteindre ▶**to ~ a** <u>foothold</u> prendre pied; **to ~ the upper** <u>hand</u> prendre le dessus; **nothing ventured, nothing ~ed** prov qui ne risque rien n'a rien prov III. vi ①(benefit) **to ~ by sth** bénéficier de qc; **to ~ by doing sth** gagner à faire qc ②(increase: prices, numbers) augmenter; **to ~ in popularity** gagner en popularité; **to ~ in num-**

**bers/height** devenir plus nombreux/plus grand; **to ~ in weight** prendre du poids ③(catch up) **to ~ on sb/sth** rattraper qn/qc
**gala** ['geɪ·lə] n (social event) gala m; **a ~ night** une nuit de gala
**galactic** [gə·'læk·tɪk] adj inv galactique
**gale** [geɪl] n ①(wind) vent m violent; **~-force winds** vents mpl forts ②fig éclat m; **~s of laughter** éclats de rire
**gallant** adv ①(with charm) galamment ②(bravely) vaillamment
**gallery** ['gæl·ər·i] <-ies> n galerie f ▶**to play to the ~** épater la galerie
**gallon** ['gæl·ən] n ①(unit) gallon m (≈ 3,79 litres aux États-Unis) ②(lots) **~s of sth** litres mpl de qc
**gallop** ['gæl·əp] I. vi a. fig (horse) galoper; (rider) aller au galop; **to ~ away** partir au galop; (to be in a hurry) descendre la rue à toute allure II. vt (cause to gallop: a horse) faire galoper III. n sing galop m; **at a ~** au galop; **to break into a ~** se mettre au galop
**galore** [gə·'lɔr] adj inv à profusion
**gamble** ['gæm·bl] I. n risque m II. vi ①(bet) jouer (de l'argent); **to ~ at cards/on horses** jouer aux cartes/aux courses; **to ~ on the stock market** jouer en bourse ②(take a risk hoping) **to ~ on sb/sth** compter sur qn/qc; **to ~ on doing sth** compter faire qc III. vt jouer; **to ~ everything on sth** fig miser sur qc
**gambler** n joueur, -euse m, f
**gambling** n jeu m
**game**[1] [geɪm] I. n ①(play, amusement) jeu m; **to be just a ~ to sb** a. fig n'être qu'un jeu pour qn ②(contest: board game, chess) partie f; (baseball, football) match m; (tennis) jeu m; **~ over** fin f de partie; **to play a good ~** faire un bon match ③SPORTS (skill level) jeu m; **to be off one's ~** ne pas être en forme;

to be on one's ~ bien jouer ④ *pej (dishonest plan)* jeu *m;* **to play ~s with sb** jouer avec qn; **to beat sb at their own ~** battre qn à son propre jeu ⑤ *pl (organized)* jeux *mpl;* **the Olympic Games** les Jeux olympiques ▶ **to play the ~** jouer le jeu; **to give the ~ away** vendre la mèche; **~ over!** fin de la partie!; **what's your ~?** où veux-tu en venir? II. *adj inf* ① *(willing)* partant(e); **to be ~ to** +*infin* être partant pour +*infin* ② *(lame: leg)* estropié(e)

**game²** [geɪm] *n* ZOOL, CULIN gibier *m*

**game plan** *n* stratégie *f*

**game show** *n* jeu *m* télévisé

**gammon** ['gæm·ən] *n (ham)* jambon *m*

**gang** [gæŋ] I. *n* ① *(organized group)* bande *f;* *(of workers)* équipe *f* ② *pej (criminal group)* gang *m* ③ *inf (group of friends)* bande *f* II. *vi pej* **to ~ up on sb** se liguer contre qn; **to ~ up with sb** s'allier à qn

**gangway** ['gæŋ·weɪ] I. *n* NAUT, AVIAT passerelle *f* II. *interj inf* ~! laissez passer!

**gap** [gæp] *n* ① *(opening)* trou *m;* *(in text)* blanc *m;* *(in teeth)* écart *m;* *(in trees, clouds)* trouée *f;* *(in knowledge)* lacune *f* ② *(space)* espace *m* ③ *fig* créneau *m;* *(emotional)* vide *m;* **to fill a ~** combler un vide ④ *(break in time)* intervalle *m* ⑤ *(difference)* écart *m;* **the generation ~** le fossé des générations; **to bridge/close the ~ between sth** réduire l'écart entre qc

**garage** [gə·'rɑːʒ] I. *n* ① *(place to house a vehicle)* garage *m;* **one-car ~** garage à une place ② *(auto repair shop, dealer)* garage *m* II. *vt* rentrer (dans le garage)

**garbage** ['gɑr·bɪdʒ] *n* ① *(household trash)* ordures *fpl;* **to take out the ~** sortir les poubelles ② *pej (nonsense, useless ideas)* âneries *fpl* ▶ **~ in, ~ out** COMPUT qualité des entrées = qualité des sorties

**garbage can** *n* poubelle *f*

**garbage collector** *n* éboueur *m*

**garbage dump** *n* dépôt *m* d'ordures

**garbage man** *n inf* éboueur *m*

**garden** ['gɑr·dən] I. *n* jardin *m;* **flow-er ~** jardin d'agrément; **vegetable ~** jardin potager; **~ hose** tuyau *m* d'arrosage II. *vi* jardiner

**garden center** *n* jardinerie *f*

**gardener** *n* jardinier, -ère *m, f*

**gardening** *n* jardinage *m*

**gargle** ['gɑr·gl] I. *vi* se gargariser II. *n* gargarisme *m*

**garlic** ['gɑr·lɪk] I. *n* ail *m* II. *adj (sauce, bread)* à l'ail; *(smell, breath)* d'ail

**garment** ['gɑr·mənt] *n form* vêtement *m;* **~ industry** industrie *f* du vêtement

**garter snake** *n* couleuvre *f* rayée

**gas** [gæs] I. <-es *o* -sses> *n* ① *(not a liquid or solid, fuel)* gaz *m* ② *inf* MED anesthésie *f* ③ MIL gaz *m* de combat; **~ mask** masque *m* à gaz ④ *inf (fuel)* essence *f;* **to get ~** prendre de l'essence; **to step on the ~** appuyer sur l'accélérateur ⑤ *inf* **a ~** une bonne rigolade ⑥ *(flatulence)* gaz *mpl* II. <-ss-> *vt (by accident)* asphyxier; *(deliberately)* gazer

**gas chamber** *n* chambre *f* à gaz

**gas cooker** *n* ① *(stove)* gazinière *f* ② *(small device)* réchaud *m* à gaz

**gash** [gæʃ] I. <-shes> *n* ① *(deep cut, wound)* entaille *f;* *(on face)* balafre *f* II. *vt* entailler; *(face)* balafrer

**gas mask** *n* masque *m* à gaz

**gasoline** ['gæs·əl·in] *n* essence *f;* **unleaded ~** essence *f* sans plomb

**gasp** [gæsp] I. *vi* haleter; **to ~ for air** haleter II. *vt* **to ~ (out) sth** dire qc d'une voix haletante III. *n* sursaut *m*

**gas pipe** *n* conduite *f* de gaz

**gas pump** *n* pompe *f* à essence

**gas station** *n* station-service *f*

**gas station operator** *n* pompiste *m*

**gassy** ['gæs·i] <-ier, -iest> *adj* très gazeux(-euse)

**gastroenteritis** [,gæs·trou·,en·tə·'raɪ·tɪs] *n* MED gastroentérite *f*

**gasworks** *n* + *sing vb* usine *f* à gaz

**gate** [geɪt] *n* ① *(entrance barrier: of field)* barrière *f;* *(of garden, property)* portail *m;* **safety ~** portail de sécurité; RAIL barrière automatique ② *(for horses)*

**G**

**starting** ~ starting-gate *m* ❸ (*number of paying customers*) entrées *fpl* ❹ AVIAT porte *f* ❺ NAUT vanne *f*

**gatekeeper** *n* gardien(ne) *m(f)*; RAIL garde-barrière *mf*

**gate receipts** *n* entrées *fpl*

**gateway** *n* ❶ (*entrance*) entrée *f* ❷ (*means of access*) porte *f* ❸ COMPUT passerelle *f*

**gather** ['gæð·ər] I. *vt* ❶ (*collect together: things, information*) rassembler; (*berries, herbs, flowers*) cueillir; (*by asking: intelligence*) recueillir; **to ~ one's thoughts** rassembler ses idées ❷ (*pull nearer*) **to ~ sb in one's arms** serrer qn dans ses bras; **to ~ a sheet around oneself** s'enrouler dans un drap ❸ FASHION (*fabric*) froncer ❹ (*increase*) **to ~ speed** prendre de la vitesse ❺ (*accumulate*) **to ~ courage** rassembler son courage; **to ~ one's strength** reprendre des forces ❻ (*infer*) conclure; (*from other people*) comprendre II. *vi* ❶ (*people*) se rassembler; (*clouds*) s'amasser; (*storm*) se préparer

**gathering** I. *n* rassemblement *m*; **a social/family ~** une réunion informelle/de famille II. *adj* (*darkness, speed*) croissant(e); (*storm*) menaçant(e)

**gauge** [geɪdʒ] I. *n* ❶ (*size*) calibre *m* ❷ RAIL écartement *m* ❸ (*instrument*) jauge *f* II. *vt* évaluer

**gauze** [gɔz] *n* gaze *f*

**gave** [geɪv] *pt of* **give**

**gawk** [gɔk] *vi inf* rester bouche bée; **to ~ at sb/sth** regarder qn/qc bouche bée

**gay** [geɪ] I. *adj* ❶ (*homosexual*) gay *inv*, homo *inf* ❷ (*cheerful, lighthearted*) gai(e) II. *n* gay *m*, homo *m inf*

**gaze** [geɪz] I. *vi* regarder fixement; **to ~ around oneself** regarder autour de soi II. *n* regard *m*; **to be exposed to the public ~** être exposé au regard du public

**GB** [,dʒi·'bi] *n* ❶ COMPUT *abbr of* **gigabyte** Go *m* ❷ *abbr of* **Great Britain** GB *f*

**gear** [gɪr] I. *n* ❶ AUTO (*speed*) vitesse *f*; **in first/second ~** en première/secon-

de; **to be in neutral ~** être au point mort; **to change** [*o* shift] **~s** changer de vitesse ❷ (*mechanism*) mécanisme *m* ❸ TECH (*set of parts*) **~(s)** engrenage *m* ❹ (*toothed wheel*) roue *f* dentée ❺ *inf* (*equipment*) attirail *m* ❻ *inf* (*clothes*) tenue *f* ❼ *inf* (*belongings*) affaires *fpl* ► **to ~ shift into high** ~ passer au plein régime II. *vi* TECH s'engrener III. *vt* ❶ TECH engrener ❷ *fig* **to ~ sth to sth** adapter qc à qc; **to be ~ed for sth** être préparé pour qc

**gearbox** <-xes> *n* boîte *f* de vitesses

**gearshift** *n* ❶ (*lever*) levier *m* de vitesses ❷ (*action*) changement *m* de vitesses

**GED** [,dʒi·i·'di] *n abbr of* **general equivalency diploma** ≈ DAEU *m*

**gee** [dʒi] *interj inf* ouah

**gelatin(e)** ['dʒəl·ə·tin] *n* gélatine *f*

**gem** [dʒem] *n* ❶ (*jewel*) pierre *f* précieuse ❷ (*precious, helpful person*) perle *f*

**Gemini** ['dʒem·ɪ·naɪ] *n* Gémeaux *mpl*; *s.a.* **Aquarius**

**gender** ['dʒen·dər] *n* ❶ (*sexual identity*) sexe *m* ❷ LING genre *m*

**gene** [dʒin] *n* gène *m*

**general** ['dʒen·ər·əl] I. *adj* général(e); **in ~** en général II. *n* MIL général *m*; **major ~** général *m* de division

**general anesthetic** *n* anesthésie *f* générale

**general delivery** *n* poste *f* restante

**general election** *n* élections *fpl* législatives

**generalization** *n* généralisation *f*

**generally** ['dʒen·ər·əl·i] *adv* ❶ (*usually*) généralement ❷ (*mostly*) dans l'ensemble ❸ (*in a general sense*) **speaking ...** d'une manière générale ... ❹ (*widely, extensively*) généralement; **to be ~ available** être disponible pour tout le monde; **it is ~ believed that ...** il est courant de croire que ...

**general practitioner** *n* médecin *m* généraliste

**general strike** *n* grève *f* générale

**generate** ['dʒen·ər·eɪt] *vt* ❶ (*produce:*

*energy*) produire ❷ *fig* (*cause to arise*) engendrer; (*reaction, feeling*) susciter; (*ideas, interest*) faire naître ❸ LING générer ❹ ECON générer ❺ MATH engendrer

**generation** [ˌdʒen·ə·ˈreɪ·ʃ°n] I. *n* ❶ (*set of people born in the same time span*) *a. fig* génération *f*; **for ~s** pendant des générations et des générations ❷ (*production*) production *f* II. *n in compounds* **first- and second-~ immigrants** immigrés *mpl* de la première et de la seconde génération

**generator** *n* ❶ (*dynamo*) dynamo *f*; (*bigger*) groupe *m* électrogène ❷ *form* (*producer*) générateur, -trice *m, f*

**generic** [dʒə·ˈner·ɪk] I. *adj* (*brand, term*) générique II. *n* ❶ MED médicament *m* générique ❷ COM produit *m* générique

**generous** [ˈdʒen·ər·əs] *adj* généreux(-euse); **a ~ tip** un gros pourboire; **to be ~ in defeat** ne pas être mauvais perdant; **to be ~ with sth** ne pas être avare de qc

**genetic** [dʒɪ·ˈnet·ɪk] *adj* génétique

**geneticist** [dʒɪ·ˈnet·ə·sɪst] *n* généticien(ne) *m(f)*

**genitalia** [ˌdʒen·ɪ·ˈteɪ·li·ə] *npl form*, **genitals** *npl* parties *fpl* génitales

**genius** [ˈdʒi·ni·əs] *n* génie *m*; **a stroke of ~** un coup de génie

**genocide** [ˈdʒen·ə·saɪd] *n* génocide *m*

**gent** [dʒent] *n iron, inf* gentleman *m*

**gentle** [ˈdʒen·tl] *adj* ❶ (*kind, calm*) doux(douce) ❷ (*subtle: hint, persuasion, reminder*) discret(-ète) ❸ (*moderate: breeze, exercise*) doux(douce) ❹ (*high-born*) **to be of ~ birth** être bien né

**gentleman** <-men> *n* ❶ (*polite, well--behaved man*) gentleman *m* ❷ (*polite term of reference*) monsieur *m* ❸ (*male audience members*) **ladies and ~** mesdames et messieurs ❹ (*man of high social class*) gentilhomme *m*

**genuine** [ˈdʒen·ju·ɪn] *adj* ❶ (*not fake*) authentique; **the ~ article** *inf* le vrai de vrai ❷ (*real, sincere*) sincère; **in ~ surprise** avec un air de surprise réelle

**genus** [ˈdʒi·nəs] <-nera> *n* BIO genre *m*

**geography** [dʒi·ˈa·grə·fi] *n* géographie *f*

**geologist** *n* géologue *mf*

**geology** [dʒi·ˈa·lə·dʒi] *n* géologie *f*

**Georgia** [ˈdʒɔr·dʒə] *n* la Géorgie

**germ** [dʒɜrm] *n* ❶ (*embryo*) *a. fig* germe *m* ❷ MED microbe *m*

**German** [ˈdʒɜr·mən] I. *adj* allemand(e); **~ speaker** germanophone *mf* II. *n* ❶ (*person*) Allemand(e) *m(f)* ❷ LING allemand *m; s.a.* **English**

**German measles** *n* rubéole *f*

**German shepherd** *n* berger *m* allemand

**Germany** [ˈdʒɜr·mə·ni] *n* l'Allemagne *f*; **Federal Republic of ~** République *f* fédérale d'Allemagne

**germ warfare** *n* guerre *f* bactériologique

**gesture** [ˈdʒes·tʃər] I. *n* geste *m* II. *vi* exprimer par gestes III. *vt* **to ~ sb to** +*infin* faire le geste à qn de +*infin*

**get** [get] I. <got, got *o* gotten> *vt inf* ❶ (*obtain*) obtenir; (*offer*) offrir; **to ~ sth for sb**, **to ~ sb sth** obtenir qc pour qn, offrir qc à qn; **to ~ a glimpse of sb/sth** apercevoir qn/qc; **to ~ the impression that ...** avoir l'impression que ...; **to ~ time off** prendre du temps libre ❷ (*receive*) recevoir; **to ~ a surprise** avoir une surprise; **to ~ a radio station** capter une station de radio ❸ (*find: idea, job*) trouver ❹ (*catch*) attraper; **to ~ one's plane/bus** avoir son avion/bus ❺ (*fetch*) aller chercher ❻ (*buy*) acheter; **to ~ sth for sb** acheter qc à qn ❼ *inf* (*hear, understand*) piger; **to ~ it** piger; **to ~ sb/sth wrong** mal capter qn/qc ❽ (*prepare: lunch, dinner*) préparer ❾ *inf* (*confuse*) embrouiller ❿ *inf* (*irk*) ennuyer ⓫ *inf* (*strike*) toucher ⓬ *inf* (*notice*) remarquer ⓭ *inf* (*deal with*) **to ~ the door** aller à la porte; **to ~ the telephone** répondre au téléphone ⓮ (*cause to be*) **to ~ sb to do sth** faire faire qc à qn; **to ~ sb ready** préparer qn; **to ~ sth finished/typed** finir/taper qc; **to ~ sth somewhere** faire passer qc quelque part ▶ **to ~ cracking** *inf*

G

s'y mettre; **to ~ going** *inf* y aller **II.** *vi* ① (*become*) devenir; **to ~ upset** se fâcher; **to ~ used to sth** s'habituer à qc; **to ~ to be sth** devenir qc; **to ~ to like sth** commencer à aimer qc; **to ~ married** se marier ② (*have opportunity*) **to ~ to** +*infin* avoir l'occasion de +*infin* ③ (*travel*) prendre; **to ~ home** rentrer chez soi

◆**get about** *vi* se déplacer

◆**get across I.** *vt* faire traverser; (*a message*) faire passer **II.** *vi* ① (*go across*) traverser ② (*communicate*) **to ~ to sb/sth** communiquer avec qn/qc

◆**get ahead** *vi* ① (*go ahead*) avancer; **to ~ in sth** prendre de l'avance dans qc ② (*take the lead*) prendre la tête

◆**get along** *vi* ① (*progress*) avancer; **how are you getting along?** comment ça va? ② (*be on good terms*) s'entendre bien; **to ~ with sb** s'entendre avec qn ③ (*go*) s'en aller

◆**get around I.** *vt* contourner **II.** *vi* circuler

◆**get at** *vt insep, inf* ① (*suggest*) **to ~ sth** en venir à qc ② (*influence illegally*) suborner ③ (*reach*) atteindre

◆**get away** *vi* s'en aller

◆**get back I.** *vt* récupérer **II.** *vi* revenir

◆**get by** *vi* ① (*manage*) se débrouiller; **to ~ on sth** s'en sortir avec qc ② (*pass*) passer

◆**get down I.** *vt* ① (*fetch down*) descendre ② (*disturb*) **to get sb down** déprimer qn, déforcer qn *Belgique* ③ (*write down*) noter ④ (*swallow*) avaler **II.** *vi* ① (*go down*) descendre ② (*bend down*) se baisser; **to ~ on one's knees** s'agenouiller; **to ~ on the ground** se mettre par terre ③ (*begin to do sth*) **to ~ to sth** se mettre à qc

◆**get in I.** *vt* ① (*bring inside*) rentrer ② *inf* (*find time for*) **to get sb in** caser qn ③ (*say*) placer; **to get a word in** placer un mot **II.** *vi* ① (*become elected*) se faire élire ② (*enter*) entrer ③ (*find time for*) **to ~ sth** [*o* **to get sth in**] trouver du temps pour faire qc ④ (*arrive*) arriver; **to ~ from work** rentrer du travail

◆**get into** *vt* ① (*involve, become interested in*) se mettre à; **to ~ the habit of doing sth** prendre l'habitude de faire qc; **to get sb into trouble** mettre qn dans le pétrin ② (*enter*) entrer dans; **to ~ a school** rentrer dans une école; **to ~ a car** monter dans une voiture, embarquer dans une voiture *Québec*

◆**get off I.** *vi* ① (*exit*) descendre ② (*depart*) partir ③ *sl* (*have an orgasm*) prendre son pied **II.** *vt* ① (*exit*) descendre de ② (*remove from*) **to get sth off sth** enlever qc de qc ③ (*send*) envoyer ④ (*avoid punishment*) **to get sb off sth** dispenser qn de qc

◆**get on I.** *vi* ① (*experience good relationship*) s'entendre ② (*manage*) s'en sortir ③ (*continue*) continuer ④ (*get older*) se faire vieux(vieille) ⑤ (*get late*) se faire tard **II.** *vt always sep, inf* **to get it on with sb** s'envoyer en l'air avec qn

◆**get out I.** *vt* ① (*exit*) sortir ② (*remove*) retirer **II.** *vi* ① (*leave*) sortir ② (*stop*) **to ~ of sth** arrêter qc ③ (*avoid*) **to ~ of doing sth** éviter de faire qc

◆**get over** *vt* ① (*recover from*) **to ~ sth** (*illness, shock*) se remettre de qc; (*difficulty*) surmonter qc ② (*forget about*) oublier ③ (*to go across*) franchir

◆**get through I.** *vi* ① (*make understand*) **to ~ to sb** faire comprendre à qn ② (*succeed in contacting*) avoir la communication; **to ~ to sb/sth** avoir qn/qc (en ligne) **II.** *vt* ① (*make understood*) faire comprendre ② (*survive*) surmonter ③ (*finish*) finir ④ (*succeed*) réussir ⑤ (*get communication*) communiquer; **to get a message through** faire passer un message

◆**get to** *vt* ① (*begin*) commencer ② (*make emotional*) **to ~ sb** remuer les tripes à qn

◆**get together I.** *vi* se rassembler **II.** *vt* rassembler

◆**get up I.** *vt* ① (*organize*) organiser ② (*cause*) **to ~ the strength/courage to** +*infin* rassembler ses forces/son courage pour +*infin* ③ (*wake up*) **to**

**get sb up** réveiller qn ④(*move up*) monter ⑤(*climb*) **to ~ the ladder/a tree** monter à l'échelle/sur un arbre ⑥ *inf* (*dress*) **to get sb/oneself up like sth** déguiser/se déguiser en qc II. *vi* ①(*wake up, stand up*) se lever ②(*climb*) monter

**getaway** ['geṭ·ə·weɪ] *n inf* fuite *f;* **to make a ~** filer; **~ car** voiture *f* en fuite

**get-together** *n inf* réunion *f*

**getup** *n inf* accoutrement *m*

**ghastly** ['gæst·li] <-ier, -iest> *adj inf* horrible

**gherkin** ['gɜr·kɪn] *n* cornichon *m*

**ghost** [goʊst] I. *n* ①(*spirit*) fantôme *m* ②(*memory*) ombre *f* ▶ **a ~ of a chance** une once de chance; **to give up the ~** rendre l'âme II. *vt* écrire; **to ~ a book** servir de nègre à l'auteur d'un livre III. *vi* servir de nègre

**ghostly** <-ier, -iest> *adj* spectral(e)

**GI** [,dʒi·'aɪ] *n* MIL GI *m* (*soldat américain*)

**giant** [dʒaɪənt] I. *n* géant *m* II. *adj* de géant

**giddy** ['gɪd·i] <-ier, -iest> *adj s.* **dizzy**

**gift** [gɪft] *n* ①(*present*) cadeau *m;* **to be a ~ from the gods** être un don du ciel ②*inf* (*sth easily obtained*) gâteau *m* ③(*talent*) don *m;* **to have the ~ of gab** *inf* avoir la langue bien pendue

**gift certificate** *n* chèque-cadeau *m*

**gifted** *adj* doué(e); (*child*) surdoué(e)

**gig** [gɪg] I. *n inf* concert *m;* **to have a ~** jouer sur scène II. *vi* <-gg-> donner un concert

**gigantic** [dʒaɪ·'gæn·t̬ɪk] *adj* gigantesque

**giggle** ['gɪg·l] I. *vi* rire bêtement II. *n* ①(*laugh*) petit rire *m* nerveux ②*pl* (*laugh attack*) fou rire *m;* **to get (a fit of) the ~s** avoir le fou rire

**gimmick** ['gɪm·ɪk] *n pej* ①(*trick*) truc *m* ②(*attention-getter*) astuce *f*

**gimmicky** *adj pej* qui relève du gadget

**gin**[1] [dʒɪn] *n* gin *m;* **~ and tonic** gin tonic *m*

**gin**[2] [dʒɪn] *n* (*trap*) piège *m*

**gin**[3] [dʒɪn] *n inf* GAMES **~ rummy** gin rami *m*

**ginger** ['dʒɪn·dʒər] I. *n* ①(*root spice*) gingembre *m* ②(*reddish-yellow*) roux *m* II. *adj* roux(rousse)

**gingerbread** *n* ≈ pain *m* d'épice, ≈ couque *f Belgique*

**gip** [dʒɪp] *s.* **gyp**

**Gipsy** ['dʒɪp·si] *n s.* **Gypsy**

**giraffe** [dʒə·'ræf] <-(s)> *n* girafe *f*

**girl** [gɜrl] *n* fille *f*

**girlfriend** *n* petite amie *f*, blonde *f Québec*

**Girl Scout** *n* éclaireuse *f*

**gist** [dʒɪst] *n* substance *f;* **to give sb the ~ of sth** résumer qc pour qn; **to get the ~ of sth** comprendre l'essentiel de qc

**give** [gɪv] I. *vt* <gave, given> ①(*hand over, offer, provide*) a. *fig* donner; **to ~ sth to sb** [*o* **to ~ sb sth**] donner qc à qn; **to ~ sb the creeps** donner la chair de poule à qn; **to ~ one's life to sth** sacrifier sa vie pour qc; **to ~ sb a smile** faire un sourire à qn; **to ~ sb trouble** créer des problèmes à qn; **to ~ sth a push** pousser qn; **to ~ sb a call** passer un coup de téléphone à qn; **to ~ sth a go** essayer qc; **to ~ sb pleasure** procurer de la joie à qn; **to ~ sb/sth a bad name** faire une mauvaise réputation à qn/qc; **to ~ (it) one's all** [*o* **best**] donner de son mieux; **don't ~ me that!** ne me raconte pas d'histoires!; **~ me a break!** laisse-moi tranquille!; **to not ~ a damn** *inf* s'en foutre complètement ②(*pass on*) a. TEL **to ~ sb sth** passer qc à qn ▶ **to ~ a dog a bad name** *prov* qui veut noyer son chien l'accuse de la rage *prov*; **to not ~ much for sth** ne pas donner cher pour qc II. *vi* <gave, given> ①(*offer*) donner; **to ~ as good as one gets** rendre coup pour coup; **to ~ of one's best** faire de son mieux ②(*alter in shape*) se détendre ▶ **it is better to ~ than to receive** *prov* il y a plus de bonheur à donner qu'à recevoir

◆**give away** *vt* ①(*offer for free*) distribuer ②(*form: bring to altar*) conduire à l'autel ③(*reveal*) révéler; **to give the**

**game** away vendre la mèche; **to give sb away** dénoncer qn

◆**give back** *vt* rendre

◆**give in** *vi* céder; **to ~ to sb/sth** céder à qn/qc

◆**give off** *vt* émettre; (*heat, smell*) dégager

◆**give out** I. *vi* ❶(*run out*) s'épuiser ❷(*stop working*) lâcher II. *vt* ❶(*distribute*) distribuer ❷(*announce*) annoncer ❸(*produce: noise*) émettre

◆**give up** I. *vt* ❶(*resign*) abandonner ❷(*quit*) **to ~ doing sth** arrêter de faire qc ❸(*hand over*) **to ~ sth to sb** remettre qc à qn II. *vi* ❶(*surrender*) se rendre ❷(*cease trying to guess*) donner sa langue au chat *inf*

**give-and-take** *n* concessions *fpl*

**given** ['gɪv·ən] I. *n* **to take it as a ~ that ...** être sûr que ... II. *adj* (*time, place*) donné(e); **to be ~ to doing sth** être enclin à faire qc III. *prep* étant donné IV. *pp of* **give**

**giver** ['gɪv·ər] *n* donneur, -euse *m, f*

**glacier** ['gleɪ·ʃər] *n* glacier *m*

**glad** [glæd] <gladder, gladdest> *adj* content(e)

**gladly** *adv* avec plaisir

**glamorize** *vt* rendre attrayant

**glamorous** *adj* glamour *inv*

**glamourize** *vt s.* **glamorize**

**glamourous** *adj s.* **glamorous**

**glance** [glæn(t)s] I. *n* ❶ coup *m* d'œil; **at a ~** d'un coup d'œil; **at first ~** au premier coup d'œil II. *vi* ❶(*look cursorily*) **to ~ at sb/sth** jeter un coup d'œil sur qn/qc; **to ~ up** lever les yeux; **to ~ around** jeter un coup d'œil autour de soi ❷(*shine*) étinceler

◆**glance off** I. *vi* ricocher II. *vt* ricocher sur

**glare** [gler] I. *n* ❶ (*mean look*) regard *m* furieux ❷(*bright reflection*) éclat *m* de lumière ❸*fig* **to be in the** (**full**)/**in a ~ of publicity** être sous les feux des projecteurs II. *vi* ❶(*look*) **to ~ at sb** lancer un regard furieux à qn ❷(*shine overly brightly*) briller avec éclat

**glaring** *adj* ❶(*that which blinds*) éblouissant(e) ❷(*obvious*) flagrant(e); (*weakness*) manifeste

**glass** [glæs] *n* ❶(*hard transparent material*) verre *m*; **pane of ~** vitre *f* ❷(*holder for drinks, drink in a glass*) verre *m* ❸(*glassware*) verrerie *f* ❹(*mirror*) **looking ~** miroir *m*

**glasses** *n* ❶ *pl* (*device to improve vision*) lunettes *fpl* ❷ *pl* (*binoculars*) jumelles *fpl*

**glass fiber** *n s.* **fiberglass**

**glassful** *n* verre *m*

**glazier** *n* vitrier *m*

**glee club** *s.* **singing club**

**glide** [glaɪd] I. *vi* ❶(*move smoothly*) glisser ❷(*fly*) planer II. *n* (*sliding movement*) glissé *m*

**glider** *n* planeur *m*

**gliding** *n* vol *m*

**glimmer** ['glɪm·ər] *n* lueur *f*

**glimpse** [glɪm(p)s] I. *vt* apercevoir II. *n* aperçu *m*; **to catch a ~ of sb/sth** entrevoir qn/qc

**glint** [glɪnt] I. *vi* luire II. *n* trait *m* de lumière

**glisten** ['glɪs·ən] *vi* scintiller

**glitch** [glɪtʃ] *n inf* pépin *m*

**gloat** [gloʊt] *vi* exulter; **to ~ over** [*o* **about**] **sth** jubiler à l'idée de qc

**global** ['gloʊ·bəl] *adj* ❶(*worldwide*) mondial(e); **~ warming** réchauffement *m* de la planète ❷(*total*) d'ensemble ❸(*complete*) complet, -ète ► **to go ~** *inf* se mondialiser

**globe** [gloʊb] *n* ❶(*round map of world*) globe *m* ❷(*ball-shaped object*) sphère *f*

**globetrotter** ['gloʊb·ˌtra·tər] *n* globetrotter *mf*

**gloomy** ['glu·mi] <-ier, -iest> *adj* ❶(*dismal*) lugubre ❷(*dark*) sombre

**glorify** ['glɔr·ə·faɪ] <-ie-> *vt a.* REL glorifier

**glorious** ['glɔr·i·əs] *adj* ❶(*honorable, illustrious*) *a. iron* glorieux(-euse) ❷(*splendid*) splendide

**glory** ['glɔr·i] I. *n a.* REL gloire *f* II. <-ie-> *vi* exulter de joie

**glossary** ['gla·s<sup>a</sup>r·i] <-ries> n glossaire m

**glossy** ['gla·si] I.<-ier, -iest> adj ❶ (shiny) a. TYP brillant(e) m ❷ (only superficially attractive) a. pej miroitant(e) II.<-ssies> n PHOT cliché m sur papier glacé

**glove** [glʌv] I. n FASHION gant m ▶ to **fit like a** ~ aller comme un gant II. vt ganter

**glove box**, n AUTO boîte f à gants

**glow** [gloʊ] I. n ❶ (radiance of light) lueur f; (of colors) éclat m ❷ (radiance of heat) rougeoiement m ❸ fig (of pride) élan m II. vi ❶ (illuminate or look radiant) rayonner ❷ (be red and hot) rougeoyer

**glowworm** n ZOOL ver m luisant

**glucose** ['glu·koʊs] n CHEM, CULIN, MED glucose m

**glue** [glu] I. n colle f; to stick to sb like ~ coller qn comme de la glue II. vt coller; to be ~d to sth fig être collé à qc; to keep one's eyes ~d to sb/sth rester les yeux fixés sur qn/qc
◆ **glue down** vt a. inf coller

**glue stick** n bâtonnet m de colle

**gluten** ['glu·t<sup>a</sup>n] n CULIN gluten m

**gluten intolerance** n intolérance f au gluten

**gnarled** [nɑrld] adj noueux(-euse)

**gnaw** [nɔ] I. vi a. fig ronger; to ~ on sth/at sb ronger qc/qn II. vt a. fig ronger

**gnome** [noʊm] n LIT (elf) gnome m; garden ~ nain m de jardin

**go** [goʊ] I.<went, gone> vi ❶ a. TECH aller; to ~ home aller à la maison; to ~ badly/well aller mal/bien; to ~ from bad to worse aller de mal en pis ❷ (travel, leave) partir; to ~ on a cruise/vacation/a trip partir en croisière/vacances/voyage ❸ (do) to ~ doing sth aller faire qc ❹ (become) devenir; to ~ wrong se tromper ❺ (exist) être; to ~ hungry/thirsty avoir faim/soif ❻ (pass) passer ❼ (begin) commencer; ready, set, ~! attention, prêts, partez! ❽ ECON (be sold) être vendu; to ~

**like hot cakes** partir comme des petits pains; to ~ **for sth** coûter qc ❾ (serve, contribute) **to ~ to sth** contribuer à qc; (be allotted: money) être alloué pour qc ❿ (be told/sung) **the story ~es that ...** on dit que ... ⓫ (fail) péricliter; MED (die) mourir II.<went, gone> vt faire ▶ **to ~ a long way** aller un long chemin; to ~ **it alone** le faire tout seul III.<-es> n ❶ (turn) élan m ❷ (attempt) essai m; **all in one ~** en un (seul) coup ❸ (a success) succès m; **to be no** ~ ne pas être un succès ❹ (energy) énergie f ▶ **to be on the** ~ être très pris

◆ **go about** vt ❶ (undertake) se mettre à ❷ (be busy: one's business, work) vaquer à

◆ **go after** vt to ~ **sb/sth** courir après qn/qc

◆ **go against** vt to ~ **sb/sth** aller à l'encontre de qn/qc

◆ **go ahead** vi avancer; (begin) commencer

◆ **go along** vi avancer

◆ **go around** I. vi ❶ (visit) **to ~ to sb's** faire un tour chez qn ❷ (rotate) **to ~ tourner** ❸ (suffice for all) (not) enough to ~ ne pas être suffisant ❹ (be in circulation) circuler; **to ~ that ...** le bruit court que ... II. vt **to ~ sth** faire le tour de qc

◆ **go at** vt to ~ **sb/sth** s'attaquer à qn/qc

◆ **go away** vi partir; **to ~ from sth** s'éloigner de qc

◆ **go back** vi ❶ (return, date back) revenir en arrière ❷ (move backwards) reculer

◆ **go beyond** vt aller au-delà de

◆ **go by** I. vi passer; **to ~ sb's house** passer chez qn II. vt ❶ (be guided by) **to ~ sth** être conduit par qc ❷ (be known by) **to ~ the name of sb** être inscrit sous le nom de qn

◆ **go down** vi ❶ (get down) descendre; ASTR (set) se coucher; NAUT (sink) sombrer ❷ (collapse) a. COMPUT s'effondrer; TECH tomber en panne ❸ (decrease) a.

**G**

FIN baisser; (*in size*) diminuer ④ (*lose, be defeated*) perdre

◆ **go for** *vi* ① (*try to achieve*) **to ~ sth** essayer d'avoir qc ② (*attack*) **to ~ sb** s'en prendre à qn; **to ~ the jugular** sauter dessus à qn ③ (*sell for*) **to ~** être vendu pour ④ (*be true for*) **to ~ sb/sth** être valable pour qn/qc ⑤ *inf* (*like*) **to ~ sb/sth** avoir le béguin pour qn/qc

◆ **go in** *vi* ① (*enter*) entrer ② TECH (*connect*) se connecter à

◆ **go into** *vt* ① (*enter*) entrer dans; **to ~ action/effect** entrer en action/vigueur; **to ~ detail** entrer dans les détails ② MED (*begin*) **to ~ a coma/trance** tomber dans le coma/en transe ③ (*begin career in: business, production*) se lancer dans ④ (*crash into*) rentrer dans

◆ **go off** I. *vi* ① (*explode*) exploser ② TECH, ELEC (*make sound*) retentir; (*alarm clock*) sonner ③ *inf* (*happen*) arriver; **to ~ badly/well/smoothly** se passer mal/bien/sans problème ④ (*leave*) partir ⑤ (*fall asleep*) s'endormir II. *vt* **to ~ the subject** s'écarter du sujet

◆ **go on** I. *vi* ① (*happen*) se passer ② (*go further, continue*) continuer ③ (*elapse: time*) passer ④ (*move on, proceed*) avancer II. *vt* **to have very little to ~** pouvoir se baser sur peu de choses

◆ **go out** *vi* ① (*socialize*) sortir ② (*date*) **to ~ with sb** sortir avec qn ③ ELEC, TECH (*stop working*) s'éteindre ④ (*become unfashionable*) se démoder ⑤ RADIO, TV (*be sent out*) être diffusé

◆ **go over** I. *vi* **to ~ badly/well** être mal/bien accueilli II. *vt* ① (*examine*) vérifier ② (*rehearse*) revoir ③ (*cross: border, river, street*) traverser ④ (*exceed: budget, limit*) dépasser

◆ **go through** *vt* ① (*undergo*) a. MED, PSYCH **~ sth** passer par qc ② (*be routed through*) **to ~ sb/sth** passer par chez qn/qc ③ POL, ADMIN passer ④ (*examine*) **to ~ sth** examiner qc

◆ **go together** *vi* ① (*harmonize*) **to ~ with sth** aller (bien) avec qc ② (*date*)

sortir ensemble

◆ **go under** I. *vi* ① NAUT (*sink*) sombrer ② ECON (*fail*) chuter ③ (*become unconscious*) s'évanouir II. *vt* aller sous qc

◆ **go up** *vi* ① (*move higher, travel northwards*) monter ② (*increase*) a. FIN, ECON augmenter ③ (*approach*) **to ~ to sb/sth** s'approcher de qn/qc ④ (*burn up*) a. *fig* s'enflammer

◆ **go with** *vt* ① (*date*) **to ~ sb** sortir avec qn ② (*be associated with*) **to ~ sth** être associé à qc ③ (*agree with*) **to ~ sth** être d'accord pour qc; **to ~ sb on sth** être d'accord avec qn sur qc

◆ **go without** *vt, vi* **to ~ (sth)** faire (qc) sans

**go-ahead** *n* carte *f* blanche

**goal** [goʊl] *n* a. SPORTS but *m*

**goalie** *inf*, **goalkeeper** *n* SPORTS gardien(ne) *m(f)* de but

**goat** [goʊt] *n* ① ZOOL, BIO chèvre *f* ② (*scapegoat*) bouc *m* émissaire

**goatee** [goʊ·'ti] *n* bouc *m*

**go-between** *n* intermédiaire *m*

**god** [gad] *n* REL a. *fig* dieu *m*

**godchild** *n* filleul(e) *m(f)*

**goddaughter** *n* filleule *f*

**goddess** <-es> *n* REL a. *fig* déesse *f*

**godfather** *n* REL a. *fig* parrain *m*

**godmother** *n* REL marraine *f*

**godparent** *n* REL parrain *m* et marraine *f*

**godsend** *n inf* cadeau *m* du ciel

**godson** *n* REL filleul *m*

**goes** 3ʳᵈ *pers sing of* go

**go-getter** *n* homme, femme *m*, *f* d'action

**goggles** *npl* lunettes *fpl* protectrices

**going** I. *n* ① (*act of leaving*) départ *m*; **comings and ~s** allées *fpl* et venues *fpl* ② (*conditions*) conditions *fpl*; **while the ~ is good** tant que les conditions sont bonnes ③ (*progress*) progression *f* II. *adj* ① (*available*) disponible ② (*in action*) en marche; **to get sth ~** mettre qc en marche ③ (*current*) qui marche III. *vi aux* **to be ~ to +** *infin* être sur le point de + *infin*

**goings-on** *npl* ① (*unusual events*) choses *fpl* extraordinaires ❷ (*activities*) affaires *fpl*

**gold** [goʊld] **I.** *n* ❶ *no indef art* (*metal or color*) or *m* ❷ *no indef art* (*golden object*) objet *m* en or ▸ **to have a heart of** ~ avoir un cœur en or **II.** *adj* ❶ (*made of gold: ring, tooth, watch*) en or; (*medal, record, coin*) d'or ❷ <more ~, most ~> (*gold-colored*) doré(e), or *inv* ▸ **not all that glitters is** ~ *prov* tout ce qui brille n'est pas or *prov*

**gold coin** *n* pièce *f* en or

**gold digger** *n* ❶ MIN (*gold miner*) chercheur, -euse *m, f* d'or ❷ *fig, pej* (*sb looking for material gain*) personne *f* vénale

**golden** *adj* ❶ (*made of gold*) en or ❷ (*concerning gold*) d'or ❸ <more ~, most ~> (*gold-colored*) doré(e) ❹ (*very good: memory*) en or ▸ **silence is** ~ *prov* le silence est d'or *prov*

**golden handshake** *n inf* parachute *m* doré

**goldfish** <-(es)> *n* BIO poisson *m* rouge

**gold medal** *n* SPORTS médaille *f* d'or

**goldmine** *n* mine *f* d'or

**golf** [gɑlf] **I.** *n* golf *m* **II.** *vi* jouer au golf

**golf ball** *n* SPORTS balle *f* de golf

**golf club** *n* SPORTS club *m* de golf

**golf course** *n* SPORTS terrain *m* de golf

**golfer** *n* SPORTS golfeur, -euse *m, f*

**golf links** *npl* SPORTS *s.* **golf course**

**gone** [gɑn] **I.** *pp of* **go II.** *adj* ❶ (*no longer there*) parti(e) ❷ (*beyond hope*) sans appel ❸ (*dead*) disparu(e) ❹ *inf* (*pregnant*) en cloque

**good** [gʊd] **I.** <better, best> *adj* bon(ne); **to be** ~ **with one's hands** être adroit de ses mains; **to have (got) it** ~ *inf* avoir (eu) de la chance; **to be/sound too** ~ **to be true** être/paraître trop beau pour être vrai; **to be** ~ **for business** ECON être bon pour les affaires; **to make sth** ~ (*pay for*) payer qc; (*do successfully*) réussir qc; **to be as** ~ **as new** être comme neuf; **the** ~ **old days** le bon vieux temps **II.** *n* bien *m*; **to be up to no** ~ n'avoir rien de bon en tête; **to do sb** ~ **to** +*infin* faire du bien

à qn de +*infin*; **for one's own** ~ pour son bien ▸ **for** ~ définitivement **III.** *interj* ❶ (*said to express approval*) bien ❷ (*said to express surprise or shock*) ~ **God!** mon Dieu! ❸ (*said as greeting*) ~ **evening!** bonsoir!; ~ **morning!** bonjour! ❹ (*said to express agreement*) **very** ~! d'accord!

**goodbye I.** *interj* au revoir! **II.** *n* au revoir *m*; **to say** ~ **to sb** dire au revoir à qn; **to say** ~ **to sth** dire adieu à qc

**good-for-nothing I.** *n pej* bon(ne) *m(f)* à rien **II.** *adj pej* bon(ne) à rien

**Good Friday** *n* REL Vendredi *m* saint

**good-humored** *adj* de bonne humeur

**good-looking I.** <more ~, most ~ o better-looking, best-looking> *adj* beau(belle) **II.** *n* belle allure *f*

**good-natured** *adj* ❶ (*having pleasant character*) d'un bon naturel ❷ (*not malicious*) bienveillant(e)

**goodness I.** *n* ❶ (*moral virtue or kindness*) bonté *f* ❷ CULIN (*healthful qualities*) qualités *fpl* nutritives ❸ (*said for emphasis*) **for** ~' **sake** pour l'amour de Dieu; ~ **knows ...** Dieu sait ...; **honest to** ~ de vrai **II.** *interj* (**my**) ~ (**me**)! mon Dieu!

**goods** *npl* ❶ (*freight*) marchandises *fpl* ❷ ECON, LAW (*wares, personal belongings*) biens *mpl* ▸ **to deliver the** ~ y arriver

**good-sized** *adj* assez grand(e)

**good-tempered** *adj irr* aimable

**goodwill** *n* ❶ (*willingness*) bonne volonté *f* ❷ ECON incorporels *mpl*

**goody I.** <-dies> *n* CULIN friandise *f* **II.** *interj childspeak* bien

**goof** [guf] **I.** *vi inf* faire des conneries **II.** *n inf* ❶ (*mistake*) connerie *f* ❷ (*silly person*) imbécile *mf*
  ◆ **goof up** *vt inf* foutre

**goofy** <goofier, goofiest> *adj inf* bête comme ses pieds

**goose** [gus] *n* oie *f*

**gooseberry** ['gus·ber·i] <-ries> *n* groseille *f*

**goose bumps** *npl* chair *f* de poule

**gorge** [gɔrdʒ] **I.** *n* ❶ GEO (*wide ravine*)

**G**

gorge f ❷ (*contents of stomach*) bile f ❸ *inf* (*large feast*) gueuleton m II. *vi* to ~ on sth se gaver de qc III. *vt* to ~ oneself on sth se gaver de qc

**gorgeous** *adj* a. fig merveilleux(-euse)

**gorilla** [gə·ˈrɪl·ə] n ZOOL, BIO a. fig gorille m

**gorse** [gɔrs] n BOT, BIO genêt m

**gory** [ˈgɔr·i] <-rier, -riest> *adj* a. fig, iron sanglant(e)

**gospel** [ˈgas·pᵊl] n ❶ REL **Gospel** Évangile m ❷ MUS gospel m ❸ fig (*principle*) évangile m

**gossip** [ˈga·səp] I. n ❶ (*rumor*) potins mpl ❷ pej (*person who gossips*) commère f II. *vi* cancaner; to ~ about sb faire des commérages sur qn

**gossip column** n PUBL échos mpl

**got** [gat] pt, pp of **get**

**gotten** [ˈga·tᵊn] pp of **got**

**gourmet** [ˈgʊr·meɪ] CULIN I. n gourmet m II. *adj* (*restaurant*) gastronome

**gourmet food store** n CULIN épicerie f fine

**Gov.** n ❶ abbr of **governor** gouverneur m ❷ abbr of **government** gouvernement m

**government** [ˈgʌv·ərn·mənt] n POL, ADMIN gouvernement m; ~ **policy** police f d'État

**GP** [ˌdʒi·ˈpi] n MED abbr of **general practitioner** généraliste mf

**GPS** [ˈdʒi·ˌpiː·es] abbr of **global navigation system** inf GPS m

**grab** [græb] I. n to make a ~ for/at sth essayer de saisir qc ▶ to be up for ~ s être à prendre II. <-bb-> *vt* ❶ (*snatch, take hold of*) a. LAW saisir ❷ inf (*get, acquire: a meal*) prendre ❸ (*take advantage of: a chance*) saisir ❹ inf how does sth ~ you? comment tu trouves/vous trouvez qc? III. <-bb-> *vi* to ~ at sth se saisir de qc; to ~ at sb s'agripper à qn

**grace** [greɪs] I. n a. REL grâce f II. *vt form* ❶ (*honor*) honorer ❷ (*make beautiful*) rendre grâce à

**graceful** *adj* gracieux(-euse)

**gracious** [ˈgreɪ·ʃəs] I. *adj* ❶ (*courteous*) affable ❷ (*elegant*) gracieux(-euse)

❸ REL plein(e) de grâce II. *interj* **goodness** ~! mon Dieu!

**grade** [greɪd] I. n ❶ (*rank*) rang m; (*on scale*) échelon m ❷ (*type, quality*) qualité f ❸ SCHOOL (*level in school*) classe f ❹ SCHOOL, UNIV (*mark in school*) note f ❺ (*level*) niveau m ❻ GEO (*gradient, slope*) pente f ▶ to **make the** ~ se montrer à la hauteur II. *vt* ❶ SCHOOL, UNIV (*evaluate*) noter ❷ (*categorize*) classer ❸ (*reduce slope*) niveler

**grade school** n SCHOOL école f primaire

**gradual** [ˈgrædʒ·u·əl] *adj* ❶ (*not sudden*) graduel(le) ❷ (*not steep*) doux(douce)

**gradually** *adv* graduellement

**graduate** [ˈgrædʒ·u·ət, vb: ˈgrædʒ·u·eɪt] I. n ❶ UNIV diplômé(e) m(f) ❷ SCHOOL bachelier, -ère m, f II. *vi* UNIV obtenir son diplôme; SCHOOL avoir son bac(calauréat); to ~ **from sth to sth** passer de qc à qc III. *vt* ❶ SCHOOL, UNIV (*award degree*) remettre un diplôme à ❷ (*arrange in a series, mark out*) graduer

**graduation** [ˌgrædʒ·u·ˈeɪ·ʃᵊn] n ❶ SCHOOL, UNIV (*completion of schooling*) remise f des diplômes f ❷ (*promotion*) promotion f ❸ (*marks of calibration*) graduation f

**grain** [greɪn] I. n ❶ a. AGR, CULIN, PHOT a. fig grain m; a ~ **of truth** un brin de vérité ❷ (*direction of fibers: of wood*) veinure f; (*of meat*) fibre f ▶ to take sth with a ~ of **salt** ne pas prendre qc au pied de la lettre; to **go against the** ~ être contre nature II. *vt* ❶ (*granulate*) grener ❷ (*texturize*) greneler

**gram** [græm] n gramme m

**grammar** [ˈgræm·ər] n grammaire f

**grammar school** n ≈ école f primaire

**grammatical** [grə·ˈmæt·ɪ·kᵊl] *adj* LING grammatical(e)

**grand** [grænd] I. *adj* a. inf grand(e); **the Grand Canyon** le Grand Canyon; to **make a ~ entrance** faire une grande entrée m II. n ❶ inv, inf (*one thousand dollars*) mille dollars mpl ❷ MUS s. **grand piano**

**grandchild** <-children> *n* petit-fils *m*, petite-fille *f*

**granddaughter** *n* petite-fille *f*

**grandfather** *n* grand-père *m*

**grandma** *n inf* mamie *f*

**grandmother** *n* grand-mère *f*

**grandpa** *n inf* papi *m*

**grandparent** *n* grands-parents *mpl*

**grand piano** *n* MUS piano *m* à queue

**grandson** *n* petit-fils *m*

**grandstand** *n* SPORTS premières tribunes *fpl*

**grand sum, grand total** *n* FIN somme *f* totale

**granite** ['græn·ɪt] *n* MIN granit *m*

**grannie, granny** ['græn·i] < -nies> *n inf s.* **grandmother** mamie *f*

**grant** [grænt] I. *n* ❶ (*money for education*) bourse *f* ❷ (*from authority*) subvention *f* II. *vt* ❶ (*allow*) **to ~ sb sth** accorder qc à qn ❷ (*transfer legally*) **to ~ sb sth** céder qc à qn ❸ *form* (*consent to fulfill*) **to ~ sb sth** concéder qc à qn; **to ~ sb a request** accéder à la demande de qn ❹ (*admit to*) reconnaître; **to ~ that ...** admettre que ... ▶ **to take sth for ~ed** considérer qc comme allant de soi

**granulated** ['græn·jə·leɪ·tɪd] *adj* (*sugar*) cristallisé(e)

**grape** [greɪp] *n* raisin *m*

**grapefruit** <-s> *n* pamplemousse *m*

**grapevine** *n* vigne *f* ▶ **sb heard on the ~ that ...** qn a entendu dire que ...

**graph** [græf] *n* graphique *m* II. *vt* dessiner sous forme de graphique

**graphic** *adj* ❶ (*using a graph*) graphique ❷ (*vividly descriptive*) vivant(e)

**graphic design** *n* conception *f* graphique

**graphics** *npl* ❶ (*drawings*) graphique *m* ❷ (*representation*) art *m* graphique

**grasp** [græsp] I. *n* ❶ (*grip*) prise *f* ❷ (*attainability*) portée *f*; **to be within sb's ~** être à la portée de qn ❸ (*understanding*) compréhension *f*; **to have a good ~ of a subject** bien maîtriser un sujet; **to lose one's ~** (*person*) perdre son emprise II. *vt* ❶ (*take firm hold*)

empoigner; **to ~ sb by the arm/hand** saisir qn par le bras/la main ❷ (*understand*) saisir III. *vi* **to ~ at sth** essayer de saisir qc; **to ~ at the chance** saisir l'occasion

**grass** [græs] I. *n* ❶ <-es> (*genus of plant*) herbe *f* ❷ (*green plant*) herbe *f sans pl* ❸ (*lawn*) gazon *m* ❹ *inf* (*marijuana*) herbe *f* ▶ **the ~ is (always) greener on the other side (of the fence)** *prov* on n'est jamais content de ce qu'on a II. *vt* mettre en herbe

**grasshopper** *n* sauterelle *f* ▶ **to be knee-high to a ~** être haut comme trois pommes

**grass snake** *n* couleuvre *f*

**grate¹** [greɪt] *n* ❶ (*grid in fireplace*) grille *f* de foyer ❷ (*fireplace*) foyer *m*

**grate²** [greɪt] I. *vi* ❶ (*annoy: noise*) agacer; **to ~ on sb** taper sur les nerfs de qn ❷ (*rub together*) grincer II. *vt* (*shred*) râper

**grateful** *adj* reconnaissant(e)

**grater** *n* râpe *f*

**gratifying** *adj* agréable

**grating** I. *n* grille *f* II. *adj* grinçant(e)

**gratis** ['græt·əs] I. *adj* gratuit(e) II. *adv* gratuitement

**gratitude** ['græt·ə·tud] *n form* gratitude *f*

**gratuity** [grə·'tu·ə·ti] <-ties> *n form* pourboire *m*

**grave¹** [greɪv] *n* (*burial place*) tombe *f*

**grave²** [greɪv] *adj* ❶ (*seriously bad*) grave ❷ (*serious*) sérieux(-euse) ❸ (*worrying*) inquiétant(e) ❹ (*momentous*) capital(e) ❺ (*solemn: music*) solennel(le)

**gravel** ['græv·əl] I. *n* ❶ (*small stones*) gravier *m* ❷ MED calcul *m* II. *vt* gravillonner

**gravestone** *n* pierre *f* tombale

**graveyard** *n* cimetière *m*

**gravity** ['græv·ə·ti] *n* gravité *f*

**gravy** ['greɪ·vi] *n* ❶ (*meat juices*) jus *m* de viande ❷ *inf* (*easy money*) bénéf *m*

**gray** [greɪ] *adj* gris(e); **to go |o turn| ~** grisonner

**graying** *adj* grisonnant(e)

G

**graze¹** [greɪz] **I.** *n* égratignure *f* **II.** *vt* ① *(injure surface skin)* écorcher; **to ~ one's knee/elbow** s'égratigner le genou/coude ② *(touch lightly)* effleurer

**graze²** [greɪz] **I.** *vi* ① *(eat grass: cattle, sheep)* paître ② *inf (eat frequent small meals)* grignoter **II.** *vt (cattle, sheep, herds)* faire paître

**grease** [gris] **I.** *n* graisse *f* **II.** *vt* graisser ▶ **like ~d lightning** en quatrième vitesse; **to ~ sb's palm** graisser la patte à qn

**greaseproof paper** *n* papier *m* sulfurisé

**greasy** ['gri·si] *n* gras(se)

**great** [greɪt] **I.** *n* grand(e) **II.** *adj* ① *(very big, famous and important)* grand(e); **a ~ deal of time/money** beaucoup de temps/d'argent; **a ~ many people** beaucoup de gens *mpl* ② *(wonderful)* merveilleux(-euse); **the ~ thing about sb/sth is that …** le grand avantage de qn/qc est que …; **to be ~ at doing sth** *inf* être doué pour faire qc; **~!** *iron, inf* génial! ③ *(very healthy)* en pleine forme ④ *(for emphasis)* **~ big** énorme ⑤ *(good)* excellent(e); *(organizer)* de première

**Great Britain** *n* la Grande-Bretagne

**greater** *n* agglomération *f*; **Greater Los Angeles** l'agglomération de Los Angeles; **the ~ metropolitan area** la grande agglomération

**great-grandchild** *n* arrière-petit-fils *m*, arrière-petite-fille *f*

**great-grandparents** *n pl* arrière--grands-parents *mpl*

**Great Lakes** *n* les Grands Lacs *mpl*

**greatly** *adv form* très

**greatness** *n* grandeur *f*

**Great Wall of China** *n* la grande Muraille de Chine

**Greece** [gris] *n* la Grèce

**greed** [grid] *n (desire for more)* avidité *f*

**greediness** *n s.* greed

**greedy** *adj* ① *(wanting food)* gourmand(e) ② *(wanting too much)* avide; **~ for money/power** avide d'argent/de pouvoir

**Greek** [grik] **I.** *adj* grec(que) **II.** *n* ① *(person)* Grec, Grecque *m, f* ② LING

grec *m;* **ancient ~** grec ancien ▶ **it's all ~ to me** pour moi c'est du chinois; *s.a.* **English**

**green** [grin] **I.** *adj* ① *(color)* vert(e) ② *(ecological: product, policies, issues)* écologique; *(person, vote, party)* écologiste ▶ **it makes him ~ with envy** ça le fait pâlir d'envie **II.** *n* ① *(color)* vert *m* ② *pl (green vegetables)* légumes *mpl* verts ③ *(member of Green Party)* écologiste *mf* ④ *(area of grass)* espace *m* vert ⑤ SPORTS green *m; s.a.* **blue**

**greenback** *n inf* billet *m* vert

**greenbelt** *n* zone *f* verte

**green card** *n* carte *f* de séjour

**greenhouse** *n* serre *f*

**green thumb** *n fig* **to have a ~** avoir la main verte

**greet** [grit] *vt* ① *(welcome by word or gesture)* saluer ② *(receive)* accueillir ③ *(become noticeable to)* attendre

**greeting** *n* ① *(welcome)* salut *m;* **to send one's ~s to sb** envoyer ses salutations à qn ② *pl (goodwill)* vœux *mpl;* **to exchange ~s** échanger des vœux ③ *(receiving)* accueil *m*

**greeting card** *n* carte *f* de vœux

**grenade** [grə·'neɪd] *n* grenade *f*

**grew** [gru] *pt of* grow

**grey** [greɪ] *adj s.* gray

**greyhound** *n* lévrier *m*

**grey matter** *n inf* matière *f* grise

**grid** [grɪd] *n* ① *(pattern)* quadrillage *m* ② *(grating)* grille *f* ③ *(electricity network)* **power ~** réseau *m* électrique ④ SPORTS **starting ~** ligne *f* de départ

**gridlock** *n* embouteillage *m*

**grief** [grif] *n* ① *(extreme sadness)* chagrin *m* ② *(trouble)* **to give sb ~** causer des ennuis à qn ▶ **good ~!** *inf* ciel!

**grievance** ['gri·və(n)t)s] *n* ① *(complaint)* doléance *f*; **to file a ~** déposer une plainte ② *(sense of injustice)* grief *m*

**grill** [grɪl] **I.** *n* ① *(part of cooker)* gril *m* ② *(informal restaurant)* grill *m* ③ *(food)* grillade *f* **II.** *vt* ① *(cook)* faire griller ② *inf (interrogate)* cuisiner

**grim** [grɪm] *adj* ❶(*very serious*) grave; **to be ~-faced** avoir une mine sévère ❷(*unpleasant*) désagréable ❸(*horrible*) terrible; **~ outlook** perspective *f* effroyable ▸**to hang on like ~ death** (*person*) se cramponner de toutes ses forces

**grin** [grɪn] **I.** *n* sourire *m* **II.** *vi* faire un large sourire ▸**to ~ and bear it** garder le sourire

**grind** [graɪnd] **I.** *n inf* ❶(*tiring work*) corvée *f*; **the daily ~** le train-train quotidien ❷(*sound*) grincement *m* ❸(*dance*) déhanchement *m* **II.** <ground, ground> *vt* ❶(*mill: corn, pepper, coffee*) moudre; (*meat*) hacher ❷(*crush*) écraser ❸(*make noise*) grincer ❹(*sharpen*) aiguiser ❺(*polish*) polir **III.** *vi* ❶(*move noisily*) grincer; **to ~ to a halt** s'immobiliser ❷*inf* (*dance*) se déhancher
    ♦**grind down** *vt* ❶(*file*) polir ❷(*mill*) moudre ❸(*wear*) user ▸**to ~ sb down** avoir qn à l'usure; (*oppress*) accabler qn
    ♦**grind out** *vt* ❶(*produce continuously*) produire régulièrement ❷(*produce in a boring manner*) rabâcher ❸(*extinguish: cigarette*) écraser

**grindstone** *n* pierre *f* à aiguiser ▸**to keep one's nose to the ~** travailler sans relâche

**grip** [grɪp] **I.** *n* ❶(*hold*) prise *f* ❷(*way of holding*) adhérence *f* ❸(*bag*) sac *m* de voyage ▸**to come to ~s with sth** s'attaquer à qc; **to get a ~ on oneself** se ressaisir; **to be in the ~ of sth** être en proie à qc **II.** <-pp-> *vt* ❶(*hold firmly*) empoigner ❷(*overwhelm*) **to be ~ped by emotion** être saisi par l'émotion ❸(*interest deeply*) captiver **III.** *vi* adhérer

**gristle** ['grɪs·l] *n* nerfs *mpl*

**grit** [grɪt] **I.** *n* ❶(*small stones*) gravillon *m* ❷(*courage*) cran *m* **II.** <-tt-> *vt* ❶(*press together*) *a. fig* **to ~ one's teeth** serrer les dents ❷(*cover*) sabler

**grizzly** **I.** <-ier, iest> *adj* grisonnant(e) **II.** <-zzlies> *n* grizzli *m*

**groan** [groʊn] **I.** *n* gémissement *m* **II.** *vi*

❶(*make a noise: floorboards, hinges*) grincer; (*people*) gémir ❷*inf* (*complain*) grogner

**grocer** ['groʊ·sər] *n* épicier, -ère *m, f*

**grocery** ['groʊ·sər·i] <-ies> *n* épicerie *f*

**groggy** ['grɔ·gi] <-ier -iest> *adj* groggy *inv*

**groin** [grɔɪn] *n* ❶ANAT aine *f* ❷(*male sex organs*) testicules *mpl*

**groom** [grum] **I.** *n* ❶(*person caring for horses*) palefrenier *m* ❷(*bridegroom*) marié *m* **II.** *vt* ❶(*clean: animal*) faire la toilette de; (*horse*) panser ❷(*prepare*) préparer

**groove** [gruv] *n* ❶(*long narrow indentation*) rainure *f* ❷MUS sillon *m* ▸**to get into a ~** devenir routinier

**groovy** <-ier, -iest> *adj inf* épatant(e)

**gross** [groʊs] **I.** *adj* ❶*form* LAW grave; **~ negligence** faute *f* lourde ❷(*very fat*) obèse ❸(*extremely offensive*) vulgaire ❹(*revolting*) dégueulasse ❺(*total*) total(e) ❻FIN (*pay, amount, income*) brut(e) **II.** *vt* FIN **to ~ $2000** gagner 2000 dollars brut

**grotesque** [groʊ·ˈtesk] **I.** *n* ART, LIT grotesque *m* **II.** *adj* grotesque

**grouchy** <-ier, -iest> *adj* grognon

**ground¹** [graʊnd] **I.** *n* ❶(*the Earth's surface*) terre *f*; **above ~** en surface; MIN à la surface; **below ~** sous terre; MIN au jour ❷(*bottom of the sea*) fond *m* de la mer ❸(*soil*) sol *m* ❹(*large area of land*) domaine *m*; **parade ~** MIL terrain *m* de manœuvres ❺(*area of knowledge*) domaine *m*; **we found some common ~** nous avons trouvé un terrain d'entente; **to be on safe ~** reposer sur des bases solides ❻(*reason*) raison *f*; **~s for divorce** motifs *mpl* de divorce; **on the ~s that ...** à cause de ...; **on what ~s ?** à quel titre ? ❼ELEC. prise *f* de terre; **~ wire** fil *m* neutre **II.** *vt* ❶(*base*) baser; **to be ~ed in sth** être basé sur qc ❷AVIAT (*unable to fly*) empêcher de voler; (*forbid*) interdire de vol; **to be ~ed** rester au sol ❸(*run aground: ship*) échouer ❹(*unable to move*) **to be ~ed** être incapable de bouger; *inf* (*teenager*) être consigné ⑤ ELEC mettre à la masse **III.** *vi* (*ship*) échouer

**ground²** [graʊnd] **I.** *pt of* **grind II.** *adj* moulu(e); (*meat*) haché(e) **III.** *n pl* sédiment *m;* **coffee ~s** marc *m* de café

**ground beef** *n* hachis *m* de bœuf

**groundbreaking** *adj* novateur(-trice)

**ground cloth** *n* tapis *m* de sol

**ground crew** *n* équipage *m* non navigant

**ground floor** *n* rez-de-chaussée *m inv* ► **to go in on the ~** être là depuis le début

**ground frost** *n* gelée blanche

**groundhog** *n* marmotte *f* d'Amérique

**groundless** *adj* sans fondement

**ground personnel** *n* personnel *m* non navigant

**ground sheet** *n s.* **ground cloth**

**groundskeeper** *n* gardien(ne) *m(f)* de parc

**groundwork** *n* travail *m* préparatoire; **to lay the ~ for sth** préparer le terrain pour qc

**ground zero** *n* ① **Ground Zero** Ground Zero *m* ② PHYS point *m* zéro

**group** [gruːp] **I.** *n* ① (*several together*) groupe *m* ② (*specially assembled*) réunion *f* ③ (*category*) classe *f* ④ (*business association*) groupement *m* ⑤ (*musicians*) formation *f* **II.** *vt* grouper **III.** *vi* se grouper; **to ~ together around sb** se rassembler autour de qn

**group ticket** *n* billet *m* de groupe

**grow** [groʊ] <grew, grown> **I.** *vi* ① BIO, AGR (*increase in size: trees, plants, hair*) pousser; (*child, animal*) grandir ② (*increase*) croître; **to ~ by 2 %** augmenter de 2 % ③ (*flourish*) se développer ④ (*develop*) développer ⑤ (*become, get*) devenir; **to ~ wiser** s'assagir; **to ~ worse** empirer; **to ~ to like sth** finir par aimer qc **II.** *vt* ① (*cultivate: tomatoes, corn*) cultiver; (*flowers*) faire pousser ② (*let grow: a beard, moustache*) se laisser pousser ③ ECON (*develop*) développer ► **money doesn't ~ on**

**trees** l'argent ne pousse pas sur les arbres

◆**grow into** *vt* devenir; **to ~ a shirt** pouvoir porter une chemise à présent

◆**grow up** *vi* ① (*become adult*) devenir adulte; **when I ~ I'm going to be a ...** quand je serai grand, je serai ... ② (*develop*) développer ► **~, will you!** grandis, veux-tu!

**growl** [graʊl] **I.** *n* ① (*low throaty sound: of a dog*) grognement *m* ② (*rumble: of stomach*) gargouillement *m* ③ *fig* grondement *m* **II.** *vi* (*dog*) grogner; (*person*) gronder; **to ~ out sth** grommeler qc

**grown** [groʊn] **I.** *pp of* **grow II.** *adj* grand(e); **a ~ man** un homme adulte; **to be fully ~** avoir fini de grandir

**grown-up I.** *n* adulte *mf* **II.** *adj* adulte

**growth** [groʊθ] *n* ① (*increase in size*) croissance *f* ② (*stage of growing*) développement *m;* **this plant has reached full ~** cette plante est arrivée à maturité ③ (*increase*) essor *m;* **rate of ~** taux *m* d'expansion ④ ECON (*development*) croissance *f* ⑤ (*increase in importance*) expansion *f* ⑥ (*growing part of plant*) pousse *f* ⑦ (*facial hair*) **to have three days' ~ on one's chin** avoir une barbe de trois jours ⑧ (*caused by disease*) tumeur *f*

**gruel(l)ing** *adj* épuisant(e)

**gruesome** ['gruː·səm] *adj* horrible

**grumble** ['grʌm·bl] **I.** *n* (*complaint*) grognement *m* **II.** *vi* grommeler; **to ~ about sb/sth** trouver à redire à qn/qc

**grumpy** ['grʌm·pi] *adj inf* ① (*bad tempered*) grincheux(-euse), gringe *Suisse* ② (*temporarily annoyed*) grognon

**grunt** [grʌnt] **I.** *n* grognement *m* **II.** *vi* grogner

**GU** *n s.* **Guam**

**Guam** [gwam] *n* Guam *f sans art*

**guarantee** [ˌger·ᵊn·'ti] **I.** *n* ① (*promise*) promesse *f* ② (*promise of repair, replacement*) garantie *f* ③ (*document*) contrat *m* de garantie ④ (*certainty*) sûreté *f* ⑤ (*person, institution*) garant(e) *m(f)* ⑥ (*responsibility for sb's debt*) caution f ❼ (*item given as security*) gage m II. vt ❶ (*promise*) **to ~ sb sth** garantir qc à qn ❷ (*promise to correct faults*) protéger; **to be ~d for three years** être assuré pendant trois ans ❸ (*make certain*) **to ~ that …** garantir que … ❹ (*take responsibility for sb's debt*) se porter garant de

**guaranteed** *adj* garanti(e)

**guard** [gard] I. n ❶ (*person*) garde m; **prison ~** gardien(ne) m(f) de prison; **to be on ~** être de faction ❷ (*defensive stance*) position f de défense; **to be on one's ~** être sur ses gardes; **to be caught off (one's) ~** tromper la vigilance de qn; *fig* être pris au dépourvu; **to drop one's ~** ne plus être méfiant ❸ (*protective device*) dispositif m de sécurité; **face ~** masque m protecteur; **fire~** garde-feu m II. vt garder; **to ~ sb/ sth against sb/sth** protéger qn/qc de qn/qc

**guard dog** n chien m de garde

**guard duty** n garde f

**guardian** ['gar·di·ən] n ❶ (*responsible person*) tuteur, -trice m, f ❷ *form* (*protector*) protecteur, -trice m, f; **to be the ~ of sth** être le gardien de qc

**guardian angel** n a. *fig* ange m gardien

**guardrail** n barrière f de sécurité

**guess** [ges] I. n supposition f; **a lucky ~** un coup de chance; **Mike's ~ is that …** d'après Mike …; **to take a ~** deviner; **to take a wild ~** risquer une hypothèse ▶ **it's anybody's** [*o* **anyone's**] **~** Dieu seul le sait II. vi ❶ (*conjecture*) deviner, taper à *pouf Belgique* ❷ (*believe, suppose*) supposer ▶ **to keep sb ~ing** laisser qn dans l'ignorance III. vt ❶ (*conjecture*) deviner ❷ (*estimate*) évaluer ❸ (*suppose*) supposer ▶ **~ what?** tu sais quoi?

**guessing game** n a. *fig* devinettes *fpl*

**guesstimate** *inf* I. n calcul m au pifomètre II. vt **to ~ sth** estimer qc au pifomètre

**guest** [gest] I. n ❶ (*invited or paid-for person*) invité(e) m(f); **paying ~** (*renter*) hôte mf payant(e); (*lodger*) pen-

sionnaire mf ❷ (*in tourism/hotel customer*) client(e) m(f) ❸ (*guesthouse customer*) invité(e) m(f) ▶ **be my ~** fais/faites comme chez toi/vous II. vi **to ~ on a show/an album** être invité à une émission/sur un album

**guesthouse** n pension f de famille

**guestroom** n chambre f d'amis

**guest worker** n travailleur, -euse m, f immigré(e)

**guidance** ['gar·dən(t)s] n ❶ (*help and advice*) conseil m ❷ (*direction*) direction f ❸ (*steering system: system*) guidage m

**guide** [gard] I. n ❶ (*person, book*) a. *fig* guide m ❷ (*indication*) indication f; **as a rough ~** à peu près II. vt a. *fig* guider; **to be ~d by one's emotions** suivre son instinct

**guidebook** n guide m

**guided** *adj* ❶ (*led by a guide*) guidé(e) ❷ (*automatically steered*) téléguidé(e)

**guide dog** n chien m d'aveugle

**guideline** n directive f

**guiding light** n *fig* soutien m

**guild** [gɪld] n guilde f

**guilder** n florin m

**guillotine** ['gɪl·ə·tin] n *HIST* guillotine f

**guilt** [gɪlt] n ❶ (*shame for wrongdoing*) mauvaise conscience f; **feelings of ~** sentiments *mpl* de culpabilité ❷ (*responsibility for crime*) culpabilité f

**guilty** ['gɪl·t̬i] <-ier, -iest> *adj* coupable; (*secret*) inavouable; **to have a ~ conscience** avoir mauvaise conscience; **innocent until proven ~** présumé innocent

**guinea pig** n ❶ *ZOOL* cochon m d'Inde ❷ *fig* cobaye m

**guitar** [gɪ·'tar] n guitare f

**guitarist** n guitariste mf

**gulf** [gʌlf] n ❶ (*area of sea*) golfe m ❷ (*chasm*) a. *fig* gouffre m; **we have to bridge the ~** nous devons calmer notre différend

**Gulf of Mexico** n le Golfe du Mexique

**gull¹** [gʌl] n mouette f; *s.a.* seagull

**gull²** [gʌl] vt duper

**gullible** ['gʌl·ə·bl] *adj* crédule

G

**gully** <-llies> n ❶ (*narrow gorge*) petit ravin m ❷ (*channel*) couloir m

**gum¹** [gʌm] n ❶ (*a sweet*) chewing ~ chewing-gum m ❷ (*soft sticky substance*) gomme f ❸ (*glue*) colle f ❹ BOT gommier m
◆ **gum up** vt **to ~ the works** bousiller le travail

**gum²** [gʌm] **I.** n ANAT gencive f **II.** <-mm-> vt mâchonner

**gumbo** ['gʌm·boʊ] n CULIN gombo m

**gun** [gʌn] **I.** n ❶ (*weapon*) arme f à feu ❷ (*handgun*) revolver m ❸ SPORTS pistolet m; **to wait for the starting ~** attendre le signal de départ ❹ (*device*) pistolet m ❺ (*person*) bandit m armé ▸ **to do sth with ~s blazing** faire qc avec détermination; **to jump the ~** SPORTS partir avant le départ; **to stick to one's ~s** ne pas en démordre **II.** <-nn-> vt inf accélérer
◆ **gun for** vt ❶ (*pursue*) en avoir après ❷ (*strive for*) vouloir à tout prix

**gunfight** n affrontement m de coups de feu

**gunfire** n ❶ (*gunfight*) fusillade f ❷ (*shots*) coups m de feu ❸ MIL canonnade f

**gunman** <-men> n malfaiteur m armé

**gunpoint** n **at ~** sous la menace d'une arme

**gunpowder** n poudre f à canon

**gunshot** n coup m de feu

**gust** [gʌst] **I.** n (*of wind*) rafale f **II.** vi souffler par rafales

**gusty** <-ier -iest> adj de grand vent

**gut** [gʌt] **I.** n ❶ (*intestine*) intestin m; **a ~ feeling** une intuition; **a ~ reaction** une réaction viscérale ❷ (*animal intestine*) boyau m ❸ pl (*bowels*) entrailles fpl ❹ (*belly*) ~(s) ventre m ❺ pl (*courage*) cran m; (*strength of character*) avoir un fort caractère; **it takes ~s** il faut du cran **II.** <-tt-> vt ❶ (*remove the innards*) vider ❷ (*destroy*) ravager

**gutter** ['gʌt̬·ər] n ❶ (*drainage channel: at the roadside*) caniveau m; (*on the roof*) gouttière f ❷ fig **to end up in the ~** finir sous les ponts

**guy** [gaɪ] n inf ❶ (*man*) type m ❷ pl (*people*) ami(e)s pl; **hi ~s!** salut les gars! ❸ (*rope to brace a tent*) **~ cord** corde f de tente

**guzzle** ['gʌz̬·l] inf **I.** vt ❶ (*eat*) a. fig bouffer ❷ (*drink*) siffler **II.** vi (*food*) s'empiffrer; (*drink*) se pinter

**gym** [dʒɪm] n ❶ abbr of **gymnasium** ❷ abbr of **physical education**

**gymnasium** [dʒɪmˈneɪ·zi·əm] n gymnase m, halle f de gymnastique Suisse

**gymnast** ['dʒɪm·næst] n gymnaste mf

**gymnastics** npl (*physical exercises*) gymnastique f

**gym shoes** n chaussures fpl de sport

**gym shorts** n short m (de sport)

**gynecologist** n gynécologue mf

**gyp** [dʒɪp] sl **I.** <-pp-> vt arnaquer **II.** n arnaque f

**Gypsy** ['dʒɪp·si] <-sies> n (*from Spain*) gitan(e) m(f); (*from Eastern Europe*) tzigane mf

# Hh

**H, h** [eɪtʃ] <-'s> *n* H *m*, h *m*; **~ as in Hotel** (*on telephone*) h comme Henri

**habit** ['hæb·ɪt] *n* ① (*repeated action*) habitude *f*; **to be in the ~ of doing sth** avoir l'habitude de faire qc; **to do sth out of** (**force of**) **~** faire qc par habitude; **to get into the ~ of doing sth** prendre l'habitude de faire qc; **to make a ~ of sth** prendre l'habitude de qc ② *inf* (*drug addiction*) accoutumance *f*; **to have a heroin ~** *pej* être accro à l'héroïne ③ (*special clothing*) habit *m*; **riding ~** tenue *f* d'équitation

**habitual** [hə·'bɪtʃ·u·əl] *adj* ① (*occurring often, as a habit*) habituel(le); **to become ~** devenir une habitude ② (*usual*) d'usage ③ (*act by force of habit*) a. *pej* invétéré(e)

**hack¹** [hæk] **I.** *n* ① (*cut*) entaille *f* ② (*blow*) coup *m* **II.** *vt* ① (*chop wildly/violently*) tailler; **to ~ sb to death** lacérer qn à mort ② SPORTS (*in soccer*) donner un coup de pied à ③ *inf* (*cope with difficult situation*) **to not be able to ~ it** ne pas pouvoir s'en sortir **III.** *vi* **to ~ at sth** taillader qc; **to ~ off sth** trancher qc

**hack²** [hæk] COMPUT **I.** *vt* pirater **II.** *vi* faire du piratage (informatique) **III.** *n* piratage *m* (informatique)

**hack³** [hæk] **I.** *vi* se promener à cheval **II.** *n* ① (*horse*) cheval *m* ② *inf* (*taxicab*) taxi *m* ③ *pej* (*bad journalist*) gratte-papier *m*

**had** [həd, *stressed:* hæd] *pt*, *pp of* have

**haddock** ['hæd·ək] *inv n* aiglefin *m*

**hadn't** ['hæd·ənt] = **had not** *s.* have

**haggle** ['hæg·l] **I.** *vi* marchander **II.** *vt* **to ~ sth down** marchander qc

**hail¹** [heɪl] **I.** *n* grêle *f*; **a ~ of abuse** une flopée d'injures; **a ~ of insults/stones** une volée d'insultes/de pierres **II.** *vi* grêler

**hail²** [heɪl] *vt* (*a taxi*) héler; (*person*) saluer

**hair** [her] *n* ① (*locks on head*) cheveux *mpl*; **to have one's ~ cut** se faire couper les cheveux ② (*single hair*) cheveu *m* ③ (*single locks on head and body*) poil *m* ④ (*furry covering on plant*) duvet *m* ▶ **that'll put ~s on your** <u>chest</u> *iron*, *inf* ça te rendra plus viril; **to** <u>make</u> **sb's ~ stand on end** *inf* faire dresser les cheveux sur la tête de qn

**hairbrush** *n* brosse *f* à cheveux

**hair conditioner** *n* après-shampoing *m*

**hair curler** *n* bigoudi *m*

**haircut** *n* ① (*cut*) coupe *f* de cheveux ② (*hairstyle*) coiffure *f*

**hairdo** <-s> *n iron*, *inf* coiffure *f*

**hairdresser** *n* coiffeur, -euse *m*, *f*

**hairdressing salon** *n* salon *m* de coiffure

**hair dryer** *n* sèche-cheveux *m*, foehn *m* *Suisse*

**hairpiece** *n* mèche *f* postiche

**hairpin** *n* épingle *f* à cheveux

**hair-raising** *adj inf* effrayant(e)

**hairsplitting I.** *n* chicane *f* **II.** *adj pej* subtil(e)

**hairspray** *n* laque *f*; **a can of ~** une bombe de laque

**hairstyle** *n* coiffure *f*

**hairy** ['her·i] *adj* ① (*having much hair*) poilu(e) ② *inf* (*desperate, alarmingly dangerous*) périlleux(-euse) ③ (*pleasantly risky/scary*) effrayant(e)

**half** [hæf] **I.** <-halves> *n* ① (*equal part, fifty per cent*) moitié *f*; **in ~** en deux; **~ an hour/a dozen** une demi-heure/demi-douzaine; **~ the audience** la moitié du public; **~ (of) the time** la moitié du temps; **at ~ past nine** à neuf heures et demie ② SPORTS mi-temps *f*; **first/second ~** première/seconde mi-temps ▶ **to go halves on sth** partager qc; **in ~**

a <u>second</u> en moins d'une seconde **II.** *adj* demi(e); **two and a ~ cups** deux tasses et demie; **~ man, ~ beast** mi-homme, mi-animal; **the second ~ century** la seconde moitié du siècle **III.** *adv* à moitié; **~ asleep/naked** à moitié endormi/nu; **to be ~ right** ne pas avoir tout à fait tort; **to be not ~ bad** ne pas être si mauvais que ça; **~ as tall again** moitié moins grand

**half-and-half** *n* CULIN *produit laitier contenant autant de crème que de lait*

**half-dollar** *n* demi-dollar *m*

**half-dozen** *n* demi-douzaine *f*

**halfhearted** *adj* sans enthousiasme; *(attempt)* hésitant(e)

**half-mast** *n* **at ~** à mi-mât; **to fly a flag at ~** monter son pavillon en berne; **to lower to ~** descendre à mi-mollet

**half-moon** *n* demi-lune *f;* **~ shaped** en forme de demi-lune

**half-price I.** *n* demi-tarif *m* **II.** *adj, adv* (à) demi-tarif *inv*

**half-staff** *n s.* **half-mast**

**halftime** *n* SPORTS mi-temps *f;* **at ~** à la mi-temps; **~ score** score *m* à la mi-temps

**halfway I.** *adj* milieu *m;* **~ point** point *m* à mi-chemin **II.** *adv* ❶ *(in the middle of a point)* à mi-chemin; **~ down** à mi-hauteur; **~ through** à mi-terme; **~ through the year** au milieu de l'année; **~ up** à mi-côté; **to meet sb ~** rencontrer qn à mi-chemin; *fig* trouver un compromis ❷ *(partly)* à peu près

**half-yearly I.** *adj* semestriel(le) **II.** *adv* tous les six mois

**hall** [hɔːl] *n* ❶ *(corridor)* couloir *m* ❷ *(room by front door)* entrée *f;* *(of public building, hotel)* hall *m*, allée *f* Suisse ❸ *(large public room)* salle *f*, aula *f* Suisse ❹ UNIV, SCHOOL réfectoire *m;* **residence ~** résidence *f* universitaire ❺ *(large country house)* manoir *m*

**hallmark** ['hɔːlˌmɑːrk] *n* ECON marque *f;* **to bear all the ~s of sb/sth** *fig* avoir toutes les caractéristiques de qn/qc

**Halloween, Hallowe'en** *n* Halloween *m*

**hallucinate** [həˈluːsɪˌneɪt] *vi* avoir des hallucinations

**halo** ['heɪˌloʊ] <-s *o* -es> *n* ❶ *(light)* auréole *f* ❷ *fig* nimbe *m* ❸ *(light circle on moon)* halo *m*

**halt** [hɔːlt] **I.** *n* arrêt *m;* **to bring sth to a ~** faire marquer un temps d'arrêt à qc; **to come to a ~** s'interrompre momentanément **II.** *vt* arrêter **III.** *vi* faire halte

**halter top** *n* dos-nu *m*

**halve** [hæv] *vt* ❶ *(lessen by 50 per cent)* diminuer de moitié ❷ *(cut in two equal pieces)* diviser en deux

**ham** [hæm] *n* ❶ *(cured pork meat)* jambon *m* ❷ *pej (person who overacts)* **what a ~!** quel cabotin! ❸ *(non-professional radio operator)* **~ radio operator** radioamateur *m*

**hamburger** ['hæmˌbɜːrɡər] *n* CULIN hamburger *m*

**hammer** ['hæmˌər] **I.** *n* ❶ *(tool)* marteau *m* ❷ *(part of modern gun)* chien *m* **II.** *vt* ❶ *(hit with tool)* marteler; **to ~ a nail into sth** enfoncer un clou dans qc ❷ *inf (beat easily in sports)* **to ~ sb** battre qn à plates coutures; **to ~ sb to a pulp** réduire qn en bouillie ❸ FIN, ECON écraser ❹ *(condemn, disapprove of)* massacrer **III.** *vi* marteler; **to ~ on a door** frapper vigoureusement à une porte

◆**hammer in** *vt* enfoncer à coups de marteau

◆**hammer out** *vt* ❶ *(shape by beating)* étendre sous le marteau ❷ *(find solution after difficulties)* élaborer; *(a settlement)* mettre au point

**hammock** ['hæmˌək] *n* hamac *m*

**hamper**[1] ['hæmˌpər] *vt* ❶ *(restrict ability to achieve)* **to ~ sth** gêner qc; **to ~ sb** empêtrer qn ❷ *(disturb)* embarrasser ❸ *(limit extent of activity)* entraver

**hamper**[2] ['hæmˌpər] *n* ❶ *(basket for dirty linen)* manne *f* ❷ *(large picnic basket)* panier *m* à pique-nique

**hamster** ['hæm(p)ˌstər] *n* hamster *m*

**hamstring** ['hæmˌstrɪŋ] **I.** *n* tendon *m*

du jarret; **strained** ~ tendon *m* déchiré II.<irr> *vt* couper les jarrets à

**hand** [hænd] I. *n* ❶ (*limb joined to arm*) main *f;* **to do sth by** ~ faire qc à la main; **to shake** ~**s with sb** serrer la main de qn; **to take sb by the** ~ prendre qn par la main; (**get your**) ~**s off!** ne me touche pas!; **to keep one's** ~**s off sb** ne pas toucher qn; ~ **in** ~ main dans la main; ~**s up!** hauts les mains! ❷ (*responsibility, control*) **to have sth well in** ~ avoir qc bien en main; **to get out of** ~ échapper au contrôle; **to have a** ~ **in sth** être impliqué dans qc; **to be out of one's** ~**s** ne rien pouvoir y faire; **to be in good** ~**s** être en de bonnes mains; **to fall into the wrong** ~**s** tomber entre de mauvaises mains; **to put sth into the** ~**s of sb/sth** confier qc à qn; **to get sb/sth off one's** ~**s** se débarrasser de qn/qc ❸ (*reach*) **to keep sth close at** ~ garder qc à portée de (la) main; **on** ~ (*available to use*) à disposition ❹ **in** [*o* **at**] ~ (*in progress*) en cours; **the job at** ~ le travail en cours; **the problem in** ~ le problème en question ❺ (*pointer on clock/watch*) aiguille *f;* **the big/little** ~ la grande/petite aiguille ❻ GAMES (*assortment of cards*) jeu *m;* (*section/round of card game*) partie *f* ❼ (*manual worker*) ouvrier, -ère *m, f* ❽ *pl* (*sailor*) équipage *m;* **all** ~**s on deck!** tout le monde sur le pont! ❾ (*skillful person*) personne *f* habile; **to be an old** ~ **at sth** être un expert en qc ❿ (*assistance with work*) aide *f;* **to give sb a** ~ donner un coup de main à qn ⓫ **to give sb a big** ~ (*clap performer enthusiastically*) applaudir vivement qn ⓬ (*measurement of horse's height*) paume *f* ⓭ (*handwriting, penmanship*) signature *f* ▶ **a bird in the** ~ (*is worth two in the bush*) un tiens vaut mieux que deux tu l'auras; **to be** ~ **in glove** être de mèche; **to make/lose money over fist** s'enrichir/perdre de l'argent rapidement; **I only have one pair of** ~**s** je n'ai que deux mains; **to have time on one's** ~**s** avoir du temps libre;

**to have one's** ~**s full** avoir du pain sur la planche; **on the one** ~ **... on the other** (~) ... d'une part ... d'autre part ...; **to ask for sb's** ~ **in marriage** *form* demander la main de qn; **to go in** ~ **with sth** aller de pair avec qc II. *vt* **to** ~ **sb sth** passer qc à qn ▶ **to** ~ **sb a line, to** ~ **a line to sb** *pej, inf* donner un tuyau à qn

◆**hand back** *vt* (*give back, return to*) repasser; **to hand sb sth back** [*o* **to hand sth back to sb**] rendre qc à qn

◆**hand down** *vt* ❶ (*pass on within family*) transmettre; **to hand sth down from one generation to another** transmettre qc de génération en génération ❷ (*make decision public*) prononcer

◆**hand in** *vt* remettre

◆**hand on** *vt* ❶ (*pass through family*) transmettre ❷ (*pass on*) passer

◆**hand out** *vt* ❶ (*distribute to group equally: roles, samples*) distribuer ❷ (*give, distribute*) donner

◆**hand over** *vt* **to** ~ **sth to sb** (*check*) remettre qc à qn

**handbag** *n* sac *m* à main, sacoche *f Belgique*

**handbook** *n* guide *m;* **student** ~ manuel *m* de l'étudiant

**hand brake** *n* frein *m* à main

**handcuff** I. *vt* passer les menottes à; **to** ~ **sb to sb/sth** attacher qn à qn/qc avec des menottes II. *n pl* ~**s** menottes *fpl*

**handful** *n* ❶ (*quantity holdable in hand*) poignée *f* ❷ (*small number, small quantity*) petit nombre *m;* **the** ~ **of sb(s)/sth(s), who/that ...** les quelques personnes/choses qui ... ❸ (*person hard to manage*) **to be a bit of a** ~ donner un peu de fil à retordre ❹ *iron* (*a lot*) **quite a** ~ presque une poignée

**hand grenade** *n* grenade *f* à main

**handgun** *n* revolver *m*

**handicap** ['hæ·dɪ·kæp] I. *n a. fig* handicap *m* II.<-pp-> *vt* handicaper

**handicapped** *adj* handicapé(e)

**handkerchief** <-s> *n* mouchoir *m*

**handle** ['hæn·dl] I. *n* ❶ (*handgrip to*

*move objects*) manche *m;* **pot ~** queue *f* de casserole; **door ~** poignée *f* de porte, clenche *f Belgique* ❷ *inf* (*name with highborn connotations*) titre *m* II. *vt* ❶ (*feel/grasp an object*) toucher ❷ (*move/transport sth*) manipuler ❸ (*deal with, direct, manage*) prendre en main; **to ~ a job** s'occuper d'un travail ❹ (*discuss, write about, portray*) traiter ❺ (*operate dangerous/difficult object*) manœuvrer ❻ (*deal in, trade in*) négocier III. *vi* + *adv/prep* **to ~ well** être (facilement) maniable; **~ with care!** fragile!

**handlebars** *npl* guidon *m*

**hand luggage** *n* bagage *m* à main

**handmade** *adj* fait(e) (à la) main

**hand-me-down** *n* vêtement *m* usagé

**hand-picked** *adj* trié(e) sur le volet

**handrail** *n* main *f* courante

**handshake** *n* poignée *f* de main

**handsome** *adj* ❶ (*traditionally attractive looking*) beau(belle) ❷ (*impressive/majestic looking*) imposant(e) ❸ (*larger than expected: sum*) considérable ❹ (*well-meaning/gracious*) bon(ne); **a ~ apology** une bonne excuse

**handstand** *n* poirier *m*

**hand to hand** *adv* (*to fight*) corps à corps

**hand-to-hand** *adj* **~ combat** combat *m* corps à corps

**hand to mouth** *adv* **to live (from) ~** *a. fig* vivre au jour le jour

**handwriting** *n* écriture *f*

**handwritten** *adj* écrit(e) à la main

**handy** *adj* ❶ (*useful*) pratique; **to come in ~** être utile ❷ (*nearby*) à portée de main ❸ (*skillful*) adroit

**handyman** <-men> *n* homme *m* à tout faire

**hang** [hæŋ] I. <hung *o* hanged, hung *o* hanged> *vi* ❶ (*be suspended: from hook*) être accroché; (*from above*) être suspendu ❷ (*droop, fall: clothes, curtain, hair*) tomber; (*arm*) pendre ❸ (*bend over*) se pencher ❹ (*die by execution*) être pendu ❺ (*float:*

*smoke, smell*) flotter II. <hung *o* hanged, hung *o* hanged> *vt* ❶ (*attach: from hook*) accrocher; (*from above*) suspendre; (*laundry*) étendre; (*wallpaper*) poser ❷ *passive* (*decorate*) **to be hung with sth** être orné de qc ❸ (*droop*) **to ~ one's head** baisser la tête ❹ (*execute through suspension*) pendre ❺ *inf* (*make a left/right turn*) **to ~ a left/right** virer à gauche/droite III. *n* (*clothes' hanging*) tombé *m* ▸ **to get the ~ of sth** *fig, inf* piger qc

**hang about, hang around** I. *vi* ❶ (*waste time*) traîner ❷ *inf* (*wait*) poireauter III. *vt* **to ~ sb** traîner avec qn

◆**hang back** *vi* ❶ (*remain behind*) rester en arrière ❷ (*hesitate*) hésiter

◆**hang on** I. *vi* ❶ (*wait briefly*) patienter; **~!** *TEL* ne quitte/quittez pas! ❷ (*hold on to*) *a. fig* se cramponner; **to ~ to sth** ne pas lâcher qc ❸ *inf* (*remain firm*) tenir bon II. *vt* ❶ (*fasten onto*) se cramponner à ❷ (*rely on, depend on*) dépendre de ❸ **to ~ sb's (every) word** (*listen very carefully*) être pendu aux lèvres de qn

◆**hang out** I. *vt* pendre (au dehors); (*the laundry*) étendre; (*a flag*) sortir II. *vi* ❶ *inf* (*spend time*) traîner ❷ *inf* (*hang loosely*) dépasser

◆**hang together** *vi* se tenir

◆**hang up** I. *vi* raccrocher; **to ~ on sb** raccrocher au nez de qn II. *vt a. fig* accrocher

**hanger** *n* cintre *m*

**hang-gliding** *n* deltaplane *m*

**hangover** *n* ❶ (*sickness after excessive alcohol*) gueule *f* de bois ❷ *pej* (*things from the past*) débris *mpl*

**hankie, hanky** *n inf abbr of* **handkerchief**

**Hanukkah** ['haːnəˌkə] *n* Hanoukka *f*

**happen** ['hæpˑ³n] I. *vi* arriver; **to ~ to sb** arriver à qn; **whatever ~s** quoi qu'il arrive; **to ~ again** se reproduire II. *vt* **~s that …** il se trouve que …; **to ~ to do sth** faire qc par hasard

**happily** *adv* ❶ (*contentedly, fortunate-*

*ly*) heureux(-euse) ② (*willingly*) de bon cœur

**happiness** *n* bonheur *m*

**happy** ['hæp·i] <-ier, -iest *o* more ~, most ~> *adj* heureux(-euse); **in happier times** dans des temps meilleurs; **to be ~ about sb/sth** être content de qn/qc; **a ~ birthday** un joyeux anniversaire

**happy hour** *n* happy hour *m o f*

**harass** [hə·'ræs] *vt* harceler

**harbor** ['har·bər] **I.** *n* port *m* **II.** *vt* ① (*cling to negative ideas: resentment, suspicions*) nourrir ② (*keep in hiding*) donner asile à

**hard** [hard] **I.** *adj* ① (*firm, rigid*) a. *fig* dur(e); **~ left/right** extrême gauche/droite *f* ② (*difficult, complex*) difficile; **to be ~ of hearing** être dur d'oreille; **to give sb a ~ time** donner du fil à retordre à qn; **to learn the ~ way** apprendre à ses dépens; **to do sth the ~ way** ne pas prendre le plus court chemin (pour faire qc) ③ (*harsh, intense: fight, winter, work*) rude; **to be a ~ worker** travailler dur; **to have a ~ time** en baver; **to give sb a ~ time** mener la vie dure à qn ④ (*strong*) a. *fig* (*drink, liquor*) fort(e); (*drugs*) dur(e) ⑤ (*reliable: facts, evidence*) tangible ⑥ (*containing much lime: water*) calcaire ▸ **to drive a bargain** en demander beaucoup; **no ~ feelings!** sans rancune!; **~ luck!** pas de chance!; **to be as ~ as nails** être un dur; **to play ~ to get** se faire désirer **II.** *adv* ① (*solid, rigid*) dur ② (*energetically, vigorously: play, study, try, work*) sérieusement; (*press, pull*) fort ③ (*painfully, severely*) durement ▸ **to follow ~ on the heels of sth** suivre qc de très près

**hardback I.** *n* livre *m* relié **II.** *adj* (*edition*) relié(e)

**hard-boiled** *adj* ① (*cooked*) **~ egg** œuf *m* dur ② *fig, inf* dur(e) à cuire

**hard-core** *adj* ART, MUS hardcore *inv*

**hard currency** *n* devise *f* forte

**hard disk** *n* COMPUT disque *m* dur

**harden I.** *vt* ① (*make firmer/more solid*) durcir ② (*make tougher*) endurcir **II.** *vi* ① (*become firmer/more solid*) durcir ② (*become less flexible/conciliatory*) s'endurcir

**hard labor** *n* travaux *mpl* forcés

**hard-liner** *n* POL pur *m* et dur *m*

**hardly** *adv* à peine; **~ ever/anybody** presque jamais/personne

**hard-nosed** *adj inf* dur(e)

**hard-on** *n vulg* trique *f*

**hardware** *n* ① (*things for house/garden*) articles *mpl* de quincaillerie ② COMPUT hardware *m*, matériel *m*

**hardware store** *n* quincaillerie *f*

**hard-wearing** *adj* résistant(e)

**hard-working** *adj* travailleur(-euse)

**hare** [her] <-(s)> *n* lièvre *m*

**harm** [harm] **I.** *n* mal *m;* **there's no ~ in asking** il n'y a pas de mal à demander **II.** *vt* ① (*hurt*) faire du mal à ② (*damage*) endommager

**harmful** *adj* nuisible

**harmless** *adj* ① (*causing no harm*) inoffensif(-ive) ② (*banal*) anodin(e)

**harmony** ['har·mə·ni] *n* harmonie *f;* **in ~** en harmonie

**harsh** [harʃ] *adj* rude; (*colors*) cru(e); (*voice*) perçant(e)

**harvest** ['har·vɪst] **I.** *n* a. *fig* récolte *f* **II.** *vt* récolter **III.** *vi* faire la récolte

**harvest festival** *n* fête *f* des moissons

**has** [hæz] *3rd pers sing of* **have**

**has-been** *n pej, inf* has been *m inv*

**hash browns** *npl* pommes *fpl* de terre sautées

**hasn't** = **has not** *s.* **have**

**hassle** ['hæs·l] **I.** *n inf* ① (*bother*) emmerdement *m* ② (*argument, dispute*) engueulade *f* **II.** *vt inf* emmerder

**haste** [heɪst] *n* (*hurried action*) hâte *f;* **to make ~** se hâter ▸ **~ makes waste** *prov* qui va piano va sano *prov*

**hasty** *adj* ① (*fast, quick, hurried*) rapide ② (*rashly, badly thought out: decisions, conclusions*) précipité(e)

**hat** [hæt] *n* chapeau *m*

**hatch¹** [hætʃ] *n* écoutille *f* ▸ **down the ~!** *sl* cul sec!

**hatch²** [hætʃ] **I.** *vi* éclore **II.** *vt* ① (*cause egg split allowing birth*) faire éclore

**②** (*devise in secret: plan*) mijoter **III.** *n* couvée *f*

**hatch³** [hætʃ] *vt* ART hachurer

**hate** [heɪt] **I.** *n* haine *f*; **to feel ~ for sb** éprouver de la haine pour qn **II.** *vt* haïr; **to ~ doing sth/to do sth** détester faire qc

**hateful** *adj* haineux(-euse)

**hat stand** *n* portemanteau *m*

**hat trick** *n* SPORTS hat trick *m* (*le fait de marquer trois buts dans un match*)

**haul** [hɔl] **I.** *vt* **①** (*pull with effort*) tirer, haler *Québec* **②** (*tow*) remorquer **③** (*transport goods*) transporter par camion **II.** *n* **①** (*distance*) trajet *m* **②** (*quantity caught*) prise *f*; (*of stolen goods*) butin *m*; (*of drugs*) saisie *f*

**haunt** [hɔnt] **I.** *vt* hanter **II.** *n* repaire *m*

**haunted** *adj* **①** (*frequented by ghosts*) hanté(e) **②** (*troubled, suffering: look, eyes*) tourmenté(e)

**have** [hæv] <has, had, had> *aux, vt* avoir; **to ~ to** +*infin* devoir +*infin*; **has he/~ you ...?** est-ce qu'il a/tu as ...?; **to ~ sth to do** avoir qc à faire; **to ~ sth ready** avoir qc de prêt; **to ~ a talk with sb** avoir une discussion avec qn ▸ **to ~ the time** avoir le temps; **to ~ it in for sb** *inf* avoir qn dans le collimateur; **to have had it** *inf* (*be broken*) être foutu; **to ~ had it with sb/sth** *inf* en avoir marre de qn/qc

◆ **have on** *vt* **①** (*wear: clothes*) porter **②** (*carry*) porter; **to have sth on oneself** porter qc sur soi **③** (*possess information*) **to have sth on sb/sth** avoir qc sur qn/qc

◆ **have out** *vt* **①** *inf* (*remove*) retirer **②** *inf* (*argue, discuss strongly*) **to have it out with sb** s'expliquer avec qn

◆ **have over** *vt* recevoir

**have-nots** *npl* sans-le-sou *mpl*

**haven't** ['hævənt] = **have + not** *s.* **have**

**Hawaii** [həˈwaɪˑi] *n* Hawaï *m sans art*

**Hawaiian I.** *adj* hawaïen(ne) **II.** *n* **①** (*person*) Hawaïen(ne) *m(f)* **②** LING hawaïen *m*; *s.a.* **English**

**hawk** [hɔk] **I.** *n a. fig a.* POL faucon *m* **II.** *vt* colporter **III.** *vi* faire du colportage

**hay** [heɪ] *n* foin *m* ▸ **to make ~ while the sun shines** battre le fer pendant qu'il est chaud; **to hit the ~** *inf* se mettre au pieu

**hay fever** *n* rhume *m* des foins

**haystack** *n* tas *m* de foin ▸ **a needle in a ~** une aiguille dans une botte de foin

**hazardous** *adj* **①** (*uncertain*) hasardeux(-euse) **②** (*risky*) risqué(e) **③** (*dangerous*) dangereux(-euse)

**haze** [heɪz] **I.** *n a. fig* brume *f* **II.** *vt* **to ~ sb** bizuter qn

**hazelnut** [ ] **I.** *n* noisette *f* **II.** *adj* noisette *inv*

**hazy** <-ier, -iest> *adj a. fig* brumeux(-euse)

**he** [hi] *pers pron* **①** (*male person or animal*) il; **~'s** [*o* = **is**] **my father** c'est mon père; **here ~ comes** le voilà **②** (*unspecified sex*) **~ who ...** *form* celui qui ... **③** REL (*God*) **He answered my prayer** Il a exaucé ma prière

**head** [hed] **I.** *n* **①** *a. fig* tête *f*; **to need a clear ~ to** +*infin* avoir besoin d'avoir la tête reposée pour +*infin*; **to put ideas into sb's ~** mettre des idées dans la tête de qn; **to use one's ~** se creuser la tête; **at the ~ of the table** en bout de table **②** (*person in charge*) chef *m*; SCHOOL directeur, -trice *m, f* **③** (*coin face*) côté *m* pile **④** (*water source*) source *f* **⑤** (*beer foam*) mousse *f* ▸ **to have one's ~ in the clouds** avoir la tête dans les nuages; **to have a good ~ for numbers** avoir la bosse des maths; **to be ~ over heels in love** être fou amoureux; **to have a good ~ on one's shoulders** avoir la tête bien posée sur ses épaules; **to be ~ and shoulders above sb** avoir plus d'une tête d'avance sur qn; **~s or tails?** pile ou face?; **to keep one's ~ above water** garder la tête hors de l'eau; **to keep a cool ~** garder la tête froide; **to go to sb's ~** (*fame, success*) monter à la tête de qn **II.** *vt* **①** (*lead*) être à la tête de **②** SPORTS **to ~ the ball** faire une tête **III.** *vi* aller; **to ~ home** aller à la maison **IV.** adj principal(e)

◆**head back** vi retourner; **to ~ home/ to camp** retourner à la maison/au camp

◆**head for** vt ❶ (go toward) se diriger vers; **to ~ the exit** aller vers la sortie ❷ fig **to ~ disaster** aller au désastre

◆**head off I.** vt ❶ (get in front of sb) aller au devant de qn; (turn sb aside) se détourner de qn ❷ fig (avoid) éviter **II.** vi **to ~ toward/to sth** garder le cap sur qc

◆**head up** vt diriger

**headache** ['hedˌeɪk] n a. fig maux mpl de tête

**headband** n bandeau m

**headlamp** n s. **headlight**

**headlight** n phare m

**headline I.** n gros titre m; **the ~s** la une des journaux **II.** vt **to ~ sth** mettre qc à la une

**headmaster** n directeur m

**headmistress** <-es> n directrice f

**head office** n centrale f

**head of state** <heads of state> n chef m d'État

**head-on I.** adj de front; (collision) frontal(e) **II.** adv de plein fouet

**headphones** npl écouteurs mpl

**headquarters** npl + sing/pl vb MIL quartier m général; (of companies) maison f mère; (of the police) direction f

**headrest** n appuie-tête m

**head restraint** n appuie-tête m

**headroom** n hauteur f sous plafond

**headscarf** <-scarves> n foulard m

**headset** n casque m

**head start** n avance f

**head waiter** n maître m d'hôtel

**headway** n **to make ~** faire des progrès

**heal** [hil] **I.** vt ❶ (give treatment) guérir ❷ fig **to ~ differences** régler des différends **II.** vi guérir; (wound, injury) panser

**health** [helθ] n a. fig a. ECON santé f; **for ~ reasons** pour des raisons de santé; **to drink to sb's ~** boire à la santé de qn

**health food** n alimentation f diététique

**health food store** n magasin m d'alimentation diététique

**health insurance** n assurance-maladie f

**health spa** n station f thermale

**healthy** <-ier, -iest> adj (person) en bonne santé; (body, food, economy) sain(e)

**heap** [hip] **I.** n tas m **II.** vt entasser

**hear** [hɪr] <heard, heard> vt, vi ❶ (perceive with ears) entendre ❷ (be told about) entendre dire

**heard** [hɜrd] pt, pp of **hear**

**hearing** n ❶ (ability to hear) ouïe f; **to be hard of ~** être dur d'oreille ❷ LAW (official examination) audition f

**hearing aid** n appareil m

**heart** [hart] n a. fig cœur m; **to have a weak** [o bad] **~** être cardiaque; **to break sb's ~** briser le cœur de qn; **to be at the ~ of sth** être au cœur de qc; **to get to the ~ of the matter** aller au cœur des choses ▶ **from the bottom of the/one's ~** du fond de/de son cœur; **to one's ~'s content** à cœur joie; **to put one's ~ and soul into sth** mettre tout son cœur et toute son âme dans qc; **with all one's ~** de tout cœur; **to die of a broken ~** mourir d'amour; **to have one's ~ set on sth** se consacrer de tout cœur à qc; **to know by ~** savoir par cœur; **to not have the ~ to +** infin ne pas avoir le cœur à + infin

**heart attack** n crise f cardiaque

**heartbreaking** adj déchirant(e)

**heartbroken** adj **to be ~** avoir le cœur brisé

**heartburn** n brûlures fpl d'estomac

**heartthrob** n inf idole f

**heartwarming** adj encourageant(e)

**heat** [hit] **I.** n ❶ (warmth, high temperature) chaleur f; **to turn up/down the ~** monter/baisser le chauffage; **to cook sth on high/low** faire cuire qc à feu vif/doux ❷ (emotional state) feu m; **in the ~ of the moment/argument** dans le feu de l'action/la discussion ❸ (sports race) éliminatoire f ❹ (breeding time) chaleur f; **to be in ~** être en chaleur ▶ **to put the ~ on sb**

faire pression sur qn; **to take the ~ off (of)** sb servir de bouclier à qn **II.** *vt, vi* chauffer

◆**heat up I.** *vt* chauffer **II.** *vi* s'échauffer; (*situation*) s'intensifier

**heated** *adj* ❶(*made warm: pool*) chauffé(e); (*blanket*) chauffant(e) ❷(*emotional: debate*) passionné(e)

**heater** *n* radiateur *m*; **water ~** chauffe-eau *m inv*

**heather** ['heð·ər] *n* bruyère *f*

**heat wave** *n* vague *f* de chaleur

**heaven** ['hev·ən] *n* paradis *m*; **to go to ~** aller au ciel; **it's ~** *inf* c'est le paradis; **to be ~ on earth** être le paradis sur terre; **to be in ~** être aux anges ▶**what/where/when/who/why in ~'s name** que/où/quand/qui/pourquoi diable; **for ~'s sake!** bon sang!; **good ~s!** bonté divine!; **it stinks to high ~** ça schlingue; **~ forbid** Dieu m'en/nous en garde; **thank ~s** Dieu merci

**heavenly**<-ier, -iest> *adj* ❶(*of heaven: body*) céleste ❷(*pleasure-giving*) divin(e)

**heaven-sent** *n* manne *f*

**heavy** ['hev·i] **I.** *adj* <-ier, -iest> ❶(*weighing a lot: object, food*) lourd(e); **to do ~ lifting/carrying** soulever/porter des choses lourdes; **how ~ is it?** combien ça pèse? ❷(*hard, difficult: work, breathing*) pénible; (*schedule, day*) chargé(e); (*book, film*) difficile; (*pitch*) lourd(e) ❸(*intense, strong: rainfall, accent*) fort(e); (*blow*) violent(e); (*cold*) gros(se); (*sleep*) profond(e) ❹(*abundant: applause, frost, gale*) fort(e); (*crop, investment*) gros(se); (*period*) abondant(e) ❺(*not delicate, coarse: features*) grossier(-ère); (*step, style*) lourd(e) ❻(*severe: fine, sea*) gros(se); (*casualties, losses*) lourd(e) ❼(*oppressive: responsibility, sky, perfume*) lourd(e); (*smell*) fort(e) ❽(*excessive: drinker, smoker*) gros(se); **to be a ~ sleeper** avoir le sommeil lourd ❾(*large, thick: beard, clouds, shoes*) gros(se) ▶**to do sth**

**with a ~ hand** faire qc en utilisant la manière forte **II.** *adv* **to weigh ~** peser lourd; **to be ~-going** être ardu **III.** *n* <-ies> *inf* dur(e) *m(f)*

**heavyweight I.** *adj* ❶(*in boxing*) poids lourd *inv* ❷(*particularly heavy cloth*) lourd(e) **II.** *n* poids *m* lourd

**Hebrew** [hiˈbru] **I.** *n* hébreu *m; s.a.* **English II.** *adj* hébreu

**hectic** ['hek·tɪk] *adj* (*week*) mouvementé(e); (*pace*) effréné(e)

**he'd** [hid] **I.** = **he had/he would** *s.* **have/will**

**hedge** [hedʒ] **I.** *n* ❶(*line of bushes*) haie *f* ❷(*protection*) barrière *f* **II.** *vi* se réserver **III.** *vt passive* **to be ~d with sth** être entouré de qc ▶**to ~ one's bets** se couvrir

**hedgehog** *n* hérisson *m*

**heel** [hil] **I.** *n* ❶(*back of foot, sock, shoe*) talon *m* ❷(*back of the hand*) paume *f* ❸*pej, inf* (*unfair person*) peau *f* de vache ▶**to be hard on sb's ~s** être sur les talons de qn; **to take to one's ~s** prendre ses jambes à son cou; **to turn on one's ~s** tourner les talons **II.** *interj* au pied! **III.** *vt* refaire le talon de

**height** [haɪt] *n* ❶(*top to bottom: of a person*) taille *f*; (*of a thing*) hauteur *f* ❷*pl* (*high places*) **to be afraid of ~s** avoir le vertige; **to scale (new) ~s** atteindre un (nouveau) record ❸(*hill*) ~**s** hauteurs *fpl* ❹*fig* (*strongest point*) sommet *m*; (*of career, glory*) apogée *m*; (*of folly, stupidity, kindness*) comble *m*; **to be at the ~ of fashion** être du dernier cri; **to attain great ~s** atteindre les hautes sphères

**heir** [er] *n* héritier *m*; **to be (the) ~ to sth** hériter de qc

**heiress** ['er·ɪs] *n* héritière *f*; **to be (the) ~ to sth** hériter de qc

**heirloom** ['er·lum] *n* héritage *m*; **the table is a family ~** la table est un meuble de famille

**heist** [haɪst] *n inf* casse *m*; **jewelry ~** le casse d'une bijouterie

**held** [held] **I.** *adj* **hand-~** portable; **a**

**firmly-~ opinion** une opinion tenace; **a long-~ view** un point de vue de longue date II. *pt, pp of* hold

**helicopter** ['hel·ɪ·kap·tər] *n* hélicoptère *m*

**hell** [hel] I. *n* ❶ (*Devil's residence*) *a. fig* enfer *m;* **~ on earth** l'enfer; **to go through ~** vivre l'horreur; **to make sb's life ~** *inf* rendre la vie impossible à qn ❷ *inf* (*very much*) **it's cold as ~** il fait un froid de canard; **it's hot as ~** il fait une chaleur d'enfer; **I suffered like ~** j'ai souffert comme c'est pas permis; **a ~ of a decision/performance** une sacrée décision/performance ▶**to not have a <u>chance</u> in ~** n'avoir aucune chance; **come ~ or high <u>water</u>** *inf* quoi qu'il arrive; **to have been to ~ and <u>back</u>** avoir vécu l'enfer; **to <u>annoy</u> the ~ out of sb** *inf* énerver qn au plus haut point; **to <u>be</u> ~** être atroce; **to <u>beat</u> the ~ out of sb** passer qn à tabac; **to <u>do</u> sth for the ~ of it** faire qc pour le plaisir; **to <u>give</u> sb ~ for sth** engueuler qn comme du poisson pourri à cause de qc; **go to ~!** *vulg* va te faire voir!; **there will be ~ to <u>pay</u>** *inf* ça va barder II. *interj* **what the ~ are you doing?** mais qu'est-ce que tu fous? ▶**~'s <u>bells</u>** bon sang; **to work <u>like</u> ~** *vulg* travailler comme un dingue; **the ~ you <u>do</u>!** *inf* c'est ça!; **to <u>hope</u> to ~** *inf* espérer vraiment; **<u>what</u> the ~!** *vulg* et puis merde!

**he'll** [hil] = **he will** *s.* will

**hello** [hə·'loʊ] I.<-s> *n* bonjour *m* II. *interj* ❶ (*said in greeting*) bonjour! ❷ (*beginning of phone call*) allo ❸ (*to attract attention*) il y a quelqu'un? ❹ (*surprise*) tiens!

**helmet** ['hel·mət] *n* casque *m*

**help** [help] I. *vi* aider; **that doesn't ~** cela n'avance à rien II. *vt* ❶ (*assist*) aider ❷ (*ease*) **to ~ the pain** soulager la douleur ❸ (*prevent*) **I can't ~ it** je n'y peux rien; **it can't be ~ed** on n'y peut rien; **she can't ~ being famous** ce n'est pas de sa faute si elle est célèbre; **to not be able to ~ (doing) sth** ne pas pouvoir s'empêcher de faire qc; **she**

**couldn't ~ but +**infin elle n'a pas pu s'empêcher de +infin ❹ (*serve*) servir; **to ~ oneself to sth** se servir de qc ❺ *inf* (*steal*) **to ~ oneself to sth** se servir de qc III. *n* ❶ (*assistance*) aide *f;* **to be a ~** (*things*) servir; (*people*) aider ❷ (*sb employed for small jobs*) aide *f;* **to have ~** [*o* hired ~] **come in** avoir une femme de ménage ▶**every little bit ~s** les petits ruisseaux font les grandes rivières IV. *interj* **~!** au secours!; **so ~ me God** je jure que c'est la vérité

◆**help out** I. *vt* aider II. *vi* donner un coup de main

**helper** *n* assistant(e) *m(f)*

**helpful** *adj* ❶ (*willing to help*) serviable ❷ (*useful*) utile

**helping** I. *n* ❶ (*portion: food*) portion *f* ❷ *fig* part *f* II. *adj* **to give sb a ~ hand** donner un coup de main à qn

**helpless** *adj* démuni(e); **to be ~ against sb/sth** être impuissant face à qn/qc

**helpline** ['help·laɪn] *n* assistance *f* téléphonique

**hem** [hem] I. *n* ourlet *m;* **to take up the ~ of a skirt** raccourcir une jupe II.<-mm-> *vt* faire un ourlet à

**hemisphere** ['hem·ɪ·sfɪr] *n* hémisphère *m*

**hen** [hen] *n* poule *f*

**hencoop** ['hen·kup], **henhouse** *n* poulailler *m*

**heptathlon** [hep·'tæθ·lɑn] *n* heptathlon *m*

**her** [hɜr] I. *poss adj* (*of a she*) son, sa *m, f,* ses *pl; s.a.* **my** II. *pers pron* ❶ (*she*) elle; **it's ~** c'est elle ❷ *objective pron direct* la, l' + *vowel; indirect* lui; *after prep* elle; **I saw ~** je l'ai vue; **he told ~ that ...** il lui a dit que ...; **he'll give sth to ~** il va lui donner qc; **it's for ~** c'est pour elle; **it's from ~** c'est d'elle, c'est de sa part

**herb** [hɜrb] *n* herbe *f;* **dried/fresh ~s** fines herbes sèches/fraîches

**herd** [hɜrd] I. *n* ❶ (*large group of animals*) troupeau *m;* (*of deer*) harde *f;* (*of whales*) banc *m* ❷ *pej* (*group of peo-*

*H*

**H**

ple) troupeau *m* **II.** *vt* (*animals*) mener **III.** *vi* vivre en troupeau

**here** [hɪr] **I.** *adv* ❶ (*in, at, to this place*) ici; **give it ~** *inf* donne-le-/-la moi; **~ and there** ça et là ❷ (*indicating presence*) **Paul is ~** Paul est là; **~ you are** te voilà; **~'s sb/sth** voici qn/qc ❸ (*now*) **~, I am referring to sth** là, je veux parler de qc; **we can stop ~** on peut s'arrêter là; **where do we go from ~?** qu'est-ce qu'on fait maintenant?; **~ goes!** allons-y!; **~ we go!** nous voilà!, c'est parti!; **~ we go again!** et c'est reparti! ▸ **~ today (and) gone tomorrow** c'est un vrai courant d'air **II.** *interj* hé!; **~, take it!** tiens, prends-le!; (*at roll-call*) présent!

**hereby** *adv form* par la présente; **the undersigned ~ declares ...** le soussigné déclare ...

**heredity** [hə·ˈred·ɪ·ti] *n* hérédité *f*

**heritage** [ˈher·ɪ·t̬ɪdʒ] *n* héritage *m*

**hero** [ˈhɪr·oʊ] <-es> *n* ❶ (*brave man, main character*) héros *m* ❷ (*sb greatly admired*) idole *f* ❸ (*sandwich*) long sandwich avec de la viande, du fromage et des crudités

**heroin** [ˈher·oʊ·ɪn] *n* héroïne *f*

**heroine** [ˈher·oʊ·ɪn] *n* héroïne *f*

**heroism** [ˈher·oʊ·ɪ·z³m] *n* héroïsme *m*; **act of ~** acte *m* héroïque

**heron** [ˈher·ən] <-(s)> *n* héron *m*

**herring** [ˈher·ɪŋ] <-(s)> *n* hareng *m*

**hers** [hɜrz] *poss pron* (*belonging to her*) le sien, la sienne, les sien(ne)s; **this glass is ~** ce verre est à elle; **a book of ~** (l')un de ses livres

**herself** [hər·ˈself] *pers pron* ❶ *reflexive* se, s' + *vowel*; **she hurt ~** elle s'est blessée ❷ *emphatic* elle-même ❸ *after prep* elle(-même); **she's proud of ~** elle est fière d'elle; **she lives by ~** elle vit seule

**he's** [hiz] ❶ = **he is** *s.* **he** ❷ = **he has** *s.* **have**

**hesitate** [ˈhez·ɪ·teɪt] *vi* hésiter

**hesitation** *n* hésitation *f*; **to have no ~ in doing sth** *form* ne pas hésiter à faire qc

**heterosexual** [ˌhet̬·ə·roʊ·ˈsek·ʃu·əl] **I.** *n*

hétérosexuel(le) *m(f)* **II.** *adj* hétérosexuel(le)

**HEV** [ˌeɪtʃ·iː·ˈviː] *n abbr of* **hybrid electric vehicle** véhicule *m* électrique hybride

**hexagon** [ˈhek·sə·gən] *n* hexagone *m*

**hexagonal** *adv* hexagonal(e)

**hey** [heɪ] *interj inf* ❶ (*said to attract attention*) hep! ❷ (*expressing surprise*) oh!

**hi** [haɪ] *interj* salut!

**HI** *n abbr of* Hawaii

**hibernate** [ˈhaɪ·bər·neɪt] *vi* hiberner

**hid** [hɪd] *vt, vi s.* hide

**hidden** [ˈhɪd·ən] **I.** *pp of* hide **II.** *adj* ❶ (*out of sight: feelings, talent*) caché(e); **~ agenda** programme *m* secret ❷ ECON (*assets, reserves*) latent(e)

**hide¹** [haɪd] <hid, hidden> **I.** *vi* se cacher **II.** *vt* cacher; **to ~ sth from sb** cacher qc à qn

◆ **hide away I.** *vt* **to hide sth away** cacher qc **II.** *vi* se cacher

◆ **hide out** *vi* se cacher

**hide²** [haɪd] *n* peau *f*; **calf ~** veau *m* ▸ **to save one's ~** sauver sa peau

**hide-and-seek** [ˌhaɪd·n·ˈsik] *n* cache-cache *m inv*; **to play ~** jouer à cache-cache

**high** [haɪ] **I.** *adj* ❶ (*elevated*) haut(e); (*forehead*) large; **100 feet ~ and 10 feet wide** 30 mètres de haut et 3 mètres de large; **shoulder-/waist-~** à hauteur d'épaule/à la taille ❷ (*above average*) élevé(e); (*technology, opinion, quality*) haut(e); (*hopes*) grand(e); (*explosives*) de forte puissance; (*color*) vif(vive); (*caliber*) gros(se); **to be full of ~ praise for sb/sth** ne pas tarir d'éloges sur qn/qc ❸ MED élevé(e); (*fever*) fort(e); **to suffer from ~ blood pressure** avoir de la tension ❹ (*important, eminent: priest*) grand(e); (*treason, rank*) haut(e); **to have friends in ~ places** avoir des amis bien placés; **to be ~ and mighty** *pej* prendre de(s) grands airs ❺ (*noble: ideals, character*) noble; **to have ~ principles** avoir des principes ❻ (*intoxicated by drugs*) shooté(e);

**to be (as) ~ as a kite** être complètement défoncé ❼ *(euphoric)* **to be ~** être sur un petit nuage ❽ *(of high frequency, shrill)* haut(e) ▶ **to be in ~ spirits** être de bonne humeur; **to leave sb ~ and dry** planter qn là *inf;* **to stink to ~ heaven** *(stink)* sentir la mort; *(be very suspicious)* sentir le soufre; **come hell or ~ water** qu'il vente ou qu'il pleuve; **to be ~ time to** +*infin* être grand temps de +*infin* **II.** *adv a. fig* haut; **the sea/tide runs ~** la mer/la marée monte vite ▶ **to hold one's head ~** garder la tête haute; **to live ~ on the hog** vivre comme un pacha; **to search for sth ~ and low** chercher qc dans tous les coins **III.** *n* ❶ *(high(est) point/level/amount)* sommet *m;* **an all-time ~** un niveau jamais atteint; **~s and lows** des hausses *fpl* et des baisses *fpl; fig* des hauts *mpl* et des bas *mpl* ❷ *(euphoria caused by drugs)* **to be on a ~** planer ❸ *(heaven)* **from on ~** du ciel

**high court** *n* LAW *s.* **supreme court**

**high-fiber** *adj* riche en fibres

**high heels** *n* talons *mpl* aiguilles

**highjack** *vt s.* **hijack**

**highlight I.** *n* ❶ *(most interesting part)* meilleur moment *m* ❷ *pl (bright tint in hair)* mèches *fpl* **II.** *vt* ❶ *(draw attention)* souligner ❷ *(mark with pen)* surligner ❸ *(tint: hair)* faire des mèches dans

**highlighter** *n* surligneur *m*

**highly** *adv* hautement; **~-skilled** très doué(e); **to speak ~ of someone** dire beaucoup de bien de qn

**high-performance** *adj* de haute performance

**high point** *n* point *m* culminant

**high-pressure I.** *adj* ❶ TECH à haute pression ❷ ECON **~ sales techniques** techniques *fpl* de vente à l'arrachée **II.** *vt Am* mettre sous pression

**high pressure** *n* haute pression *f*

**high-rise I.** *n* tour *f* **II.** *adj* **a ~ building** une tour

**high school** *n* lycée *m*

**high season** *n* haute saison *f*

**high society** *n* haute société *f*

**high-speed train** *n* train *m* à grande vitesse

**high-spirited** *adj* ❶ *(cheerful, lively)* vif(vive) ❷ *(fiery)* fougueux(-euse)

**high-tension** *adj (cable)* à haute tension

**high tension** *n* haute tension *f*

**high tide** *n* ❶ GEO marée *f* haute ❷ *fig* point *m* culminant

**highway** *n* autoroute *f*

**hijack** I. *vt* détourner II. *n* détournement *m*

**hijacker** *n* pirate *mf* (de l'air)

**hijacking** *n* détournement *m*

**hike** [haɪk] I. *n* ❶ *(long walk with backpack)* randonnée *f* ❷ *inf (increase)* augmentation *f* II. *vt, vi* augmenter

**hiker** *n* randonneur, -euse *m, f*

**hiking** *n* randonnée *f*

**hilarious** [hɪ·ˈleɪ·i·əs] *adj* ❶ *(very amusing)* hilarant(e) ❷ *(noisy and amusing)* délirant(e)

**hill** [hɪl] *n* ❶ *(small mountain) a. fig* colline *f* ❷ *(hillside)* coteau *m* ❸ *(steep slope)* côte *f* ▶ **to be over the ~** *inf* se faire vieux; **sth ain't worth a ~ of beans** *inf* ne pas valoir un haricot

**hillside** *n* flanc *m* de la colline

**hilltop I.** *n* sommet *m* de la colline **II.** *adj* au sommet d'une colline

**hilly** <-ier, -iest> *adj* vallonné(e)

**him** [hɪm] *pers pron* ❶ *(he)* lui; **it's ~** c'est lui ❷ *objective pron: direct* le, l' *vowel; indirect, after prep* lui; **I saw ~** je l'ai vu; **she told ~ that ...** elle lui a dit que ...; **he'll give sth to ~** il va lui donner qc; **it's for ~** c'est pour lui; **it's from ~** c'est de lui, c'est de sa part ▶ **everything comes to ~ who waits** *prov* tout vient à point à qui sait attendre *prov*

**Himalayas** [ˌhɪm·ə·ˈleɪ·əz] *npl* **the ~** l'Himalaya *m*

**himself** [hɪm·ˈself] *pers pron* ❶ *reflexive* se, s' *+ vowel;* **he hurt ~** il s'est blessé ❷ *(emphatic)* lui-même ❸ *after prep* lui(-même); **he's proud of** ~ il est fier de lui; **he lives by** ~ il vit seul

**hindrance** ['hɪn·drən(t)s] *n* obstacle *m*

**hindsight** ['haɪnd·saɪt] *n* recul *m*; **in** ~, **with** (**the benefit of**) ~ avec du recul

**hint** [hɪnt] **I.** *n* ① (*practical tip*) conseil *m*; **a helpful** ~ un truc ② (*slight amount*) soupçon *m* ③ (*allusion*) allusion *f*; **to drop a** ~ faire une allusion; **to be unable to take a** ~ ne pas comprendre vite **II.** *vi* **to** ~ **at sth** faire une allusion à qc **III.** *vt* **to** ~ **sth to sb** insinuer qc à qn

**hip¹** [hɪp] *n* hanche *f* ▶ **to shoot from the** ~ *inf* dégainer en tirant

**hip²** [hɪp] **I.** *adj inf* branché(e) **II.** *interj* ~ ~ **hooray!** hip hip hip! hourra!

**hip³** [hɪp] *n* (*rose hip*) églantine *f*

**hippo** ['hɪp·oʊ] *n inf* hippopotame *m*

**hippopotamus** [ˌhɪp·ə·'pɑ·t̬ə·məs] <-es *o* -mi> *n* hippopotame *m*

**hire** [haɪr] **I.** *n* ① (*act of hiring*) location *f* ② (*of employee*) embauche *f* **II.** *vt* ① (*employ*) embaucher ② (*rent*) louer

 ◆ **hire out** *vt* louer; **to** ~ **sth by the hour** louer qc à l'heure; **to hire oneself out as sth** offrir ses services en tant que qc

**his** [hɪz] **I.** *poss adj* (*of a he*) son, sa, ses *pl*; **he lost** ~ **head** il a perdu la tête; *s.a.* **my II.** *poss pron* (*belonging to him*) le sien, la sienne, les sien(ne)s; **a friend of** ~ un ami à lui; **this glass is** ~ ce verre est à lui; *s.a.* **hers**

**Hispanic** [hɪs·'pæn·ɪk] **I.** *adj* ① (*related to Spanish-speaking countries*) latino-américain(e) ② (*related to Spain*) hispanique **II.** *n* Latino-américain(e) *m(f)*

**hiss** [hɪs] **I.** *vt, vi* siffler **II.** *n* sifflement *m*

**historic(al)** *adj* historique

**history** ['hɪs·t̬ər·i] *n* histoire *f*

**hit** [hɪt] **I.** *n* ① (*blow, stroke*) *a. fig* coup *m*; **to take a direct** ~ (*be bombed*) être frappé ② SPORTS coup *m*; (*in fencing*) touche *f*; **to score a** ~ toucher ③ (*success*) succès *m*; ~ **film** un film à succès ④ (*successful song*) tube *m* ⑤ *inf* (*murder*) meurtre *m* **II.** <-tt-, hit,

hit> *vt* ① (*strike*) *a. fig* frapper; **to** ~ **one's head** se cogner la tête; **I don't know what** ~ **him** je ne sais pas ce qu'il lui est arrivé ② (*crash into: tree, car*) percuter ③ (*reach*) *a. fig* atteindre; **to** ~ **rock bottom** avoir le moral au plus bas; **to be** ~ (*be shot*) être touché ④ SPORTS (*a ball*) frapper; (*person*) toucher ⑤ (*affect negatively*) toucher ⑥ (*arrive at*) arriver à ⑦ (*encounter, come up against: iceberg*) heurter; **to** ~ **a bad streak** prendre un mauvais tour; **to** ~ **a lot of resistance** rencontrer beaucoup de résistance; **to** ~ **a traffic jam** tomber sur un bouchon ⑧ *inf* (*attack, kill*) buter ⑨ (*press: key, button*) appuyer sur ▶ **to** ~ **the deck** s'aplatir au sol; **to** ~ **the hay** *inf* aller au pieu; **to** ~ **home** frapper les esprits; **to** ~ **the jackpot** toucher le jackpot; **to** ~ **the nail on the head** tomber juste; **to** ~ **the road** s'en aller; **to** ~ **the roof** être furieux; **to** ~ **one's stride** trouver son rythme **III.** *vi* ① (*strike*) frapper ② (*collide*) entrer en collision ③ (*attack*) attaquer

 ◆ **hit back** *vi* riposter

 ◆ **hit off** *vt always sep* **to hit it off with sb** bien s'entendre avec qn

 ◆ **hit on** *vt* ① *sl* (*show sexual interest*) draguer ② (*think of*) trouver, tomber sur

**hit-and-run** [ˌhɪt·ᵊn·'rʌn] **I.** *n* ① (*accident*) délit *m* de fuite ② MIL ~ **warfare** guerre *f* éclair **II.** *adj* ~ **accident** délit *m* de fuite

**hitch** [hɪtʃ] **I.** *n* ① (*temporary difficulty or obstacle*) anicroche *f*; **without a** ~ sans accroc ② (*knot*) nœud *m* **II.** *vt* ① (*fasten*) **to** ~ **sth to sth** attacher qc à qc ② *inf* (*hitchhike*) **to** ~ **a lift** faire du stop ③ *sl* (*to marry*) **to get** ~**ed** se caser **III.** *vi inf* faire du stop

 ◆ **hitch up** *vt* remonter

**hitcher** *n s.* **hitchhiker**

**hitchhike** *vi* faire de l'auto-stop, faire du pouce *Québec*

**hitchhiker** *n* auto-stoppeur, -euse *m, f*

**hitchhiking** *n* auto-stop *m*

**hi-tech** [ˌhaɪ·'tek] *adj* hi-tech *inv*

**hit man** ['hɪt·mæn] <-men> *n* tueur *m*

**HIV** [ˌeɪtʃ·aɪ·'vi] *n abbr of* **human im-munodeficiency virus** VIH *m*

**hive** [haɪv] *n* ruche *f*

**hoarse** [hɔrs] *adj* enroué(e)

**hoax** [hoʊks] **I.** *n* canular *m;* **a bomb ~** une fausse alerte à la bombe **II.** *vt* faire un canular à; **to ~ sb into thinking sth** faire croire qc à qn

**hobble** ['ha·bl] **I.** *vi* boiter **II.** *vt* entraver

**hobby** ['ha·bi] <-bbies> *n* passe--temps *m inv*

**hockey** ['ha·ki] *n* hockey *m*

**hoe** [hoʊ] *n* houe *f*

**hog** [hɔg] **I.** *n* porc *m* châtré **II.** <-gg-> *vt inf* s'accaparer

**hoist** [hɔɪst] *vt* (*raise or haul up*) remon-ter; (*a flag*) hisser ► **to ~ a few** s'en-voyer quelques verres

**hold** [hoʊld] **I.** *n* ➊ (*grasp, grip*) *a.* sports prise *f*; **to get a ~ of sb/sth** (*find*) trouver qn/qc; **to lose ~ of sth** lâcher qc; **to take ~ of sb/sth** saisir qn/qc ➋ (*intentional delay*) suspens *m;* **to be on ~** tel être en attente; **to put sth on ~** mettre qc en suspens; **to put sb on ~** faire attendre qn ➌ (*control, controlling force*) emprise *f* ➍ naut, aviat soute *f* ► **no ~s barred** sans rete-nue **II.** <held, held> *vt* ➊ (*grasp*) tenir; **to ~ hands** se tenir la main; **to ~ sb in one's arms** prendre qn dans ses bras; **to ~ sb/sth tight** serrer qn/qc (dans ses bras) ➋ (*keep*) maintenir; **to ~ one's head high** garder la tête haute; **to ~ the lead** maintenir la tête; **to ~ sb to his/her word** obliger qn à tenir sa promesse ➌ (*retain: interest, attention*) retenir; (*room*) réserver; law détenir; **to ~ sb prisoner/hostage** retenir qn pri-sonnier/en otage ➍ (*maintain*) mainte-nir; **to ~ the road** tenir la route ➎ (*de-lay, stop*) retarder; **~ it!** arrête(z) tout!; **to ~ one's fire** mil *a. fig* arrêter les hos-tilités; **to ~ sb's phone calls** suspendre les appels ➏ (*hold back*) retenir; **to ~ one's breath** retenir sa respiration; *fig* mettre sa main au feu ➐ (*contain*) contenir; **to ~ no interest** ne présenter

aucun intérêt; **what the future ~s** ce que réserve l'avenir ➑ (*possess, own*) avoir; (*majority, shares, record*) déte-nir ➒ (*conduct: negotiations*) mener; (*conversation, conference*) tenir; (*par-ty, tournament*) organiser; **the election is being held on Tuesday** l'élection aura lieu mardi ➓ (*believe*) considérer; **sb is held in great respect** qn est tenu en grand respect; **to ~ sb responsible for sth** tenir qn pour responsable de qc ► **to ~ all the cards** avoir toutes les car-tes en main; **~ your horses!** du calme!, doucement!; **to ~ the key to sth** avoir la clé de qc; **~ the line!** ne quittez pas!, gardez la ligne! *Québec;* **to ~ one's own** tenir bon; **~ your tongue!** tais--toi!; **sth ~s water** qc se tient **III.** *vi* ➊ (*remain*) *a. fig* tenir; **~ tight!** tins/te-nez bon!; **to ~ still** ne pas bouger; **to ~ true** être vrai **II.** *vi* ➋ (*continue*) durer; (*weather*) se maintenir ➌ (*believe*) croi-re ➍ (*contain, promise*) **what the fu-ture ~s** ce que le futur réserve

◆**hold against** *vt* **to hold it against sb** en vouloir à qn

◆**hold back I.** *vt* retenir; (*tears, anger*) contenir; **to ~ information** ne pas dé-voiler des informations ► **there's no holding me (back)** rien ne peut me re-tenir **II.** *vi* se retenir; **to ~ from doing sth** se retenir de faire qc

◆**hold down** *vt* maintenir; (*person*) maîtriser; (*job*) garder

◆**hold forth** *vi pej* **to ~ about sth** dis-serter sur qc

◆**hold in** *vt* retenir

◆**hold off I.** *vt* ➊ (*keep distant*) tenir à distance ➋ (*postpone, delay*) remettre à plus tard **II.** *vi* ➊ (*postpone, delay*) différer; **the rain has held off** il n'a pas plu; **to ~ (on) doing sth** attendre pour faire qc ➋ (*keep distant*) se tenir à dis-tance

◆**hold on** *vi* ➊ (*affix, attach*) maintenir ➋ (*keep going*) **to ~ (tight)** tenir bon ➌ (*wait*) attendre

◆**hold onto** *vt* ➊ (*grasp*) *a. fig* s'accro-cher à ➋ (*keep, not throw away*) garder

**H**

**H**

◆**hold out** I. vt ❶ (*stretch out*) tendre ❷ (*offer*) offrir II. vi ❶ (*resist*) tenir bon ❷ (*continue: supplies*) durer ❸ (*not do/tell*) **to ~ on sb** cacher qc à qn ❹ (*insist*) **to ~ for sth** s'obstiner à demander qc

◆**hold out for** vt (*hope*) espérer

◆**hold over** vt ❶ (*extend*) prolonger ❷ (*defer*) **to hold sth over until Monday** remettre qc à lundi

◆**hold to** vt s'en tenir à

◆**hold together** I. vi tenir ensemble II. vt maintenir ensemble

◆**hold up** I. vt ❶ (*support*) soutenir ❷ (*put in the air, raise*) lever; **to be held up by (means of)/with sth** être maintenu par qc ❸ (*delay*) retarder ❹ (*rob*) attaquer ❺ (*offer as example*) **to hold sb up as sth** présenter qn comme qc; **to hold sth up to ridicule** considérer comme ridicule II. vi ❶ (*exist as true*) (se) tenir ❷ (*get along*) s'entendre

◆**hold with** vt être d'accord avec

**holdall** ['hoʊld-ɔl] n fourre-tout m inv

**holder** n ❶ (*device for holding objects*) support m ❷ (*owner*) détenteur, -trice m, f; **office-~** propriétaire mf

**holdup** n ❶ (*act of robbing*) hold-up m ❷ (*delay*) retard m

**hole** [hoʊl] I. n ❶ (*hollow space, cavity*) trou m ❷ (*animal's burrow: of fox, rabbit*) terrier m ❸ SPORTS trou m ❹ inf (*unpleasant place*) trou m ❺ inf (*difficult situation*) **to be in the ~** être dans la mouise II. vt ❶ (*make holes, perforate*) trouer ❷ SPORTS (*hit a ball into a hole in golf*) **to ~ a ball** lancer une balle dans le trou

◆**hole up** vi inf se terrer

**holiday** ['hɑl-ə-deɪ] n jour m férié

**Holland** ['hɑl-ənd] n la Hollande

**hollow** ['hɑl-oʊ] I. adj a. fig, pej creux(-euse); (*promise*) vain(e); (*laughter*) faux(fausse) II. n creux m III. vt GEO **to ~ (out) sth, to ~ sth (out)** creuser qc IV. adv creux; **to feel ~** avoir un creux

**holly** ['hɑl-i] n houx m

**holocaust** ['hɑ-lə-kɑst] n holocauste m; **the Holocaust** l'holocauste

**holy** ['hoʊ-li] <-ier, -iest> adj a. fig saint(e); **to be a ~ terror** être une sacrée terreur

**Holy Communion** n sainte communion f

**home** [hoʊm] I. n maison f; **to make oneself at ~** se mettre à l'aise, faire comme chez soi II. adv ❶ (*at or to one's place*) à la maison ❷ (*one's country*) au pays ❸ (*understanding*) **to bring sth ~ to sb** faire comprendre qc à qn ▸**until the cows come ~** jusqu'à la saint-glinglin; **sth is nothing to write ~ about** qc n'est rien d'important III. adj a. SPORTS local(e)

**home address** n adresse f (personnelle)

**home banking** n banque f à domicile

**homeland** n pays m natal

**homeless** I. adj sans abri II. n + pl vb **the ~** les sans-abri mpl inv

**home loan** n FIN hypothèque f

**home-made** adj fait(e) maison

**homeopathy** [hoʊ-mi-'ɑ-pə-θi] n homéopathie f

**homeowner** n propriétaire mf

**home run** n (*in baseball*) coup m de circuit

**homesick** adj **to feel ~** avoir le mal du pays

**homework** n ❶ (*work after school*) devoirs mpl ❷ (*paid work done at home*) travail m à domicile

**homicide** ['hɑ-mə-saɪd] n form LAW homicide m

**homosexual** [hoʊ-moʊ-'sek-ʃʊ-əl] adj homosexuel(le)

**homosexuality** n homosexualité f

**honest** ['ɑ-nɪst] adj honnête

**honestly** I. adv ❶ (*truthfully, with honesty*) honnêtement ❷ (*with certainty*) franchement II. interj vraiment!

**honesty** ['ɑ-nɪ-sti] n honnêteté f; **in all ~** en toute honnêteté

**honey** ['hʌn-i] n ❶ (*sweet liquid from bees*) miel m ❷ (*pleasant person*) personne f délicieuse; (*excellent or good* *thing*) délice *m* ③ (*darling, dear*) chéri(e) *m(f)*

**honeybee** *n* abeille *f*

**honeycomb** I. *n* rayon *m* (de miel) II. *adj* en nid-d'abeilles

**honeymoon** I. *n* (*post-marriage vacation*) lune *f* de miel II. *vi* être en lune de miel

**honor** ['a·nər] I. *n* honneur *m*; **His/Your Honor** LAW Son/Votre Honneur II. *vt* honorer

**honorable** I. *adj a.* POL honorable II. *n* (*aristocrat*) noble *mf*

**honorary** ['a·nə·rer·i] *adj a.* UNIV honorifique

**hood**¹ [hʊd] *n* ① (*covering for head*) capuche *f* ② AUTO capot *m*

**hood**² [hʊd] *n inf* gangster *m*

**hood**³ [hʊd] *n inf abbr of* **neighborhood** quartier *m*

**hoof** [hʊf] I. <hooves *o* hoofs> *n* (*hard covering on animal's foot*) sabot *m* II. *vi* **to ~ it** traîner ses savates

**hook** [hʊk] I. *n* (*curved device*) *a.* SPORTS crochet *m*; (*for coats*) patère *f*; (*for fish*) hameçon *m* ▶ **by ~ or by crook** par tous les moyens; **~, line and sinker** complètement II. *vt* accrocher; (*a fish*) hameçonner; **to ~ sth to sth** accrocher qc à qc III. *vi* s'agrafer

♦**hook up** I. *vt* ① (*connect, link up*) raccorder; (*computers*) connecter ② *sl* (*cause to meet*) donner rendard à II. *vi* ① (*connect*) se raccorder ② *sl* (*meet*) se donner rendard; (*meet for sex*); **to ~ with sb** avoir un rendez-vous coquin avec qn

**hooked** *adj* ① (*curved like a hook*) crochu(e) ② (*addicted to, dependent on*) accroché(e)

**hooker**¹ *n sl* pute *f*

**hooker**² *n* SPORTS crochet *m*

**hooligan** ['huː·lɪ·gən] *n* hooligan *m*

**hoops** *npl sl* SPORTS basket *m*

**hoot** [hut] I. *vi* ① (*make an owl's sound*) hululer ② (*make a sound*) mugir; (*train*) siffler; (*with horn*) klaxonner ③ (*shout in disapproval*) huer; **to ~ with laughter** se tordre de rire II. *vt*

① (*make a sound*) **to ~ one's horn** klaxonner ② (*boo*) huer III. *n* ① (*owl's sound*) hululement *m* ② (*whistle*) mugissement *m*; (*of train*) sifflement *m*; (*of horn*) coup *m* de klaxon ③ (*shout*) huée *f*; **~s of laughter** hurlements *mpl* de rire ▶ **to not give a ~ about sth** *inf* ne rien en avoir à faire de qc

**hop**¹ [hap] <-pp-> I. *vi* sauter; **to ~ in a car** grimper dans une voiture II. *n* ① (*hopping movement*) saut *m* ② *inf* (*informal dance*) sauterie *f* ③ (*short journey*) saut *m*

**hop**² [hap] *n* (*vine with flower clusters*) houblon *m*; **~s** le houblon

**hope** [hoʊp] I. *n* espoir *m* II. *vi* espérer; **to ~ for sth** espérer qc III. *vt* espérer; **I ~ not** j'espère que non; **to ~ to** +*infin* espérer +*infin*

**hopeful** I. *adj* plein d'espoir II. *n* espoir *m*

**hopefully** *adv* plein d'espoir

**hopeless** *adj* désespéré(e)

**hopelessly** *adv* désespérément

**hopping mad** *adj inf* furax

**horizon** [hə·ˈraɪ·zⁿn] *n a. fig* horizon *m*

**horizontal** I. *adj* horizontal(e) II. *n* MATH horizontale *f*

**hormone** ['hɔr·moʊn] *n* hormone *f*

**horn** [hɔrn] *n* ① ZOOL corne *f* ② (*material*) corne *f* ③ (*receptacle, shape*) corne *f* ④ (*honk*) klaxon *m* ⑤ MUS cor *m* ▶ **to take the bull by the ~s** prendre le taureau par les cornes

**hornet** ['hɔr·nɪt] *n* frelon *m*

**horny** <-ier, -iest> *adj* ① (*made of horn*) en corne ② *inf* (*sexually excited, lustful*) chaud(e)

**horoscope** ['hɔr·ə·skoʊp] *n* horoscope *m*

**horrible** ['hɔr·ə·bl] *adj* horrible

**horrid** ['hɔr·ɪd] *adj* atroce

**horrific** [hɔ·ˈrɪf·ɪk] *adj* horrifiant(e)

**horrify** ['hɔr·ɪ·faɪ] <-ied> *vt* horrifier

**horror** ['hɔr·ər] *n* horreur *f*; **to one's ~** à sa grande horreur

**horror-stricken, horror-struck** *adj* frappé(e) d'horreur

**horse** [hɔrs] *n* ① ZOOL cheval *m* ② SPORTS

H

**pommel** ~ cheval m d'arçons ▶ **~-and--buggy** d'un autre temps; **to put the cart before the** ~ mettre la charrue devant les bœufs; **to hear sth straight from the ~'s mouth** apprendre qc de source sûre; **you can lead a** ~ **to water, but you can't make him drink** prov on ne fait pas boire un âne qui n'a pas soif prov; **to beat a dead** ~ perdre son temps; **to be on one's high** ~ prendre de(s) grands airs; **to get on one's high** ~ monter sur ses grands chevaux; **to back the wrong** ~ miser sur le mauvais cheval; **hold your ~s!** inf du calme!

**horseback I.** n on ~ à cheval; **police on** ~ police f montée **II.** adj ~ **riding** équitation f; **a** ~ **rider** un cavalier **III.** adv à cheval

**horse chestnut** n marron m d'Inde

**horseplay** n tohu-bohu m

**horsepower** inv n cheval-vapeur m

**horse race** n course f de chevaux

**horseracing** n hippisme m

**horseshit** vulg **I.** n (nonsense) connerie f; **what a load of** ~! quel ramassis de conneries! **II.** interj c'est que des conneries!

**horseshoe** n fer m à cheval

**horse-trading** n pej marchandage m

**horticulture** [ˈhɔr·tə·kʌl·tʃər] n horticulture f

**hose**[1] [hoʊz] n tuyau m

**hose**[2] [hoʊz] n s. **hosiery**

**hosiery** [ˈhoʊ·ʒər·i] n bas mpl

**hospice** [ˈha·spɪs] n MED hospice m

**hospitable** adj hospitalier(-ère)

**hospital** [ˈha·spɪ·t̬əl] n hôpital m; ~ **staff/bill** le personnel/tarif hospitalier; **to spend time in the** ~ être hospitalisé

**hospitality** [ˌha·spɪ·ˈtæl·ə·t̬i] n hospitalité f

**hospitalize** [ˈhas·pɪ·t̬əl·aɪz] vt hospitaliser

**host**[1] [hoʊst] **I.** n ① (organizer of an event) hôte, -esse m, f; (in hotel) hôtelier, -ère m, f; **to play** ~ **to sth** accueillir qc ② TV animateur, -trice m, f ③ BIO,

COMPUT hôte m ④ COMPUT serveur m **II.** adj ① (hosting: family, city) d'accueil ② COMPUT serveur **III.** vt ① (act as a host to: party) organiser ② TV animer

**host**[2] [hoʊst] n sing multitude f

**host**[3] [hoʊst] n REL hostie f

**hostage** [ˈha·stɪdʒ] n otage m

**hostel** [ˈha·stəl] n foyer m; **youth** ~ auberge f de jeunesse

**hostess** [ˈhoʊ·stɪs] n hôtesse f

**hostile** [ˈha·stəl] adj (climate) hostile; (aircraft) ennemi(e)

**hot** [hat] <-ter, -test> adj ① (very warm) chaud(e); **it's** ~ il fait chaud ② (spicy) fort(e) ③ (dangerous) brûlant(e); **to be too** ~ **to handle** être un sujet brûlant ④ inf (sexually attractive) chaud(e) ⑤ (exciting: music, news, party) chaud(e) ⑥ inf (skillful) **to be** ~ **at sth** être fort en qc ▶ **to get into** ~ **water** se fourrer dans le pétrin

**hot dog** n ① (sausage in a roll) hot--dog m ② inf (showoff) frimeur, -euse m, f

**hotel** [hoʊ·ˈtel] n hôtel m

**hotel accommodation** n hébergement m à l'hôtel

**hotel bill** n note f d'hôtel

**hotel register** n registre m de l'hôtel

**hotel staff** n personnel m hôtelier

**hotheaded** adj irascible

**hotline** n ① POL téléphone m rouge ② TEL hotline f

**hot plate** n plaque f chauffante

**hotshot** n inf as m

**hot spot** n ① inf boîte f de nuit ② COMPUT point m chaud

**hot stuff** n (sexy woman, man) canon m

**hot-tempered** adj irascible

**hot-water bottle** n bouillotte f

**hound** [haʊnd] **I.** n chien m de chasse **II.** vt pourchasser

**hour** [aʊr] n heure f; **to be paid by the** ~ être payé à l'heure; **for ~s** pendant des heures; **every** ~ **on the** ~ toutes les heures; **business ~s** fpl d'ouverture; **an** ~ **away** à une heure de distance ▶ **sb's** ~ **has come** l'heure de qn est venue

**hourglass** n sablier m
**hour hand** n grande aiguille f
**hourly** adv toutes les heures
**house** [haʊs] **I.** n ❶ (building) maison f ❷ POL chambre f ❸ THEAT salle f; **to play to a full ~** jouer devant une salle pleine ❹ MUS house f ▶ **to put** [o **set**] **one's ~ in order** mettre de l'ordre dans ses propres affaires **II.** vt ❶ (give place to live) héberger ❷ (contain) contenir
**houseboat** n péniche f
**housebroken** adj propre
**household** **I.** n ménage m **II.** adj ménager(-ère)
**householder** n ❶ (owner) propriétaire mf de maison ❷ (tenant) locataire, -trice m, f
**househusband** n homme m au foyer
**housekeeper** n intendant(e) m(f)
**houseplant** n plante f d'appartement
**housewarming** n crémaillère f; **~ party** pendaison f de crémaillère; **to have a ~** pendre la crémaillère
**housewife** <-wives> n femme f au foyer
**housework** n travaux mpl ménagers
**housing development** n lotissement m
**housing shortage** n manque m de logements
**hover** ['hʌv·ər] vi ❶ (stay in air) planer; (helicopter) effectuer un vol stationnaire ❷ (wait near) guetter; **to ~ around sb** rôder autour de qn ❸ fig (hesitate) hésiter; **to ~ between sth and sth** osciller entre qc et qc
**hovercraft** <-(s)> n aéroglisseur m
**hoverport** n port m pour aéroglisseurs
**how** [haʊ] **I.** adv ❶ (in what way) comment; **to know ~ to** +infin savoir +infin; **~ come?** [o **so**] comment ça? ❷ (asking about condition) comment; **~ are you?** comment vas-tu/allez-vous? ❸ (exclamation) comme, que; **~ nice!** comme c'est gentil!; **~ kind of her!** comme c'est gentil de sa part! ❹ (that) que; **he told me ~ he had seen her there** il m'a dit qu'il l'avait vue là-bas ▶ **~ do you do?** bonjour!, enchanté; form; s.a. **many, much, long,**

**old, far II.** n comment m; **to know the ~(s) and why(s) of sth** savoir le pourquoi et le comment de qc
**however** [haʊ·'ev·ər] **I.** adv ❶ (in whatever way) de quelque manière que +subj ❷ (to whatever extent) si … que +subj; **~ hard I try** j'ai beau essayer; **~ much it rains** même s'il pleut des cordes **II.** conj ❶ (in whichever way) cependant ❷ (nevertheless) néanmoins
**howl** [haʊl] **I.** vi ❶ (cry) hurler ❷ inf (laugh) hurler de rire **II.** n hurlements mpl
◆**howl down** vt huer
**HQ** [ˌeɪtʃ·'kjuː] n abbr of **headquarters** QG m
**hr.** n abbr of **hour** h
**HTML** [ˌeɪtʃ·tiː·em·'el] n abbr of **Hypertext Markup Language** COMPUT HTML m
**hub** [hʌb] n ❶ (middle part of a wheel) moyeu m ❷ fig milieu m
**hubcap** ['hʌb·kæp] n enjoliveur m
**huddle** ['hʌd·l] **I.** vi ❶ (gather) se blottir ❷ (in football) se rassembler sur le terrain (pour élaborer une tactique) **II.** n ❶ (gathering: of things) fouillis m; (of persons) petit groupe m ❷ (in football) rassemblement des joueurs sur le terrain pour élaborer une tactique
◆**huddle down** vi se blottir
◆**huddle together** vi se serrer l'un contre l'autre/les uns contre les autres
◆**huddle up** vi ❶ (crowd) se blottir l'un contre l'autre; **to ~ against sb/sth** se blottir contre qn/qc ❷ (in football) se rassembler sur le terrain (pour élaborer une tactique)
**hug** [hʌg] **I.** <-gg-> vt ❶ (hold close to body) embrasser ❷ fig (cling firmly to) se tenir à **II.** vi s'embrasser **III.** n accolade f; **to give sb a ~** embrasser qn
**huge** [hjudʒ] adj énorme
**hum** [hʌm] <-mm-> **I.** vi ❶ (make a low continuous sound) a. fig (bee) bourdonner; (machine) vrombir; (person) fredonner ❷ (be full of activity) bourdonner d'activité **II.** vt fredonner **III.** n (of insect) bourdonnement m; (of ma-

**H**

*chinery, plane*) vrombissement *m;* (*of voices*) bruit *m* sourd; (*of melody*) fredonnement *m*

**human** ['hju·mən] *adj* humain(e)

**humane** [hju·'meɪn] *adj* humain(e)

**humanitarian** [hju·ˌmæn·ə·'ter·i·ən] I. *n* philanthrope *mf* II. *adj* humanitaire

**humanly** *adv* humainement

**human rights** *npl* droits *mpl* de l'homme

**humid** ['hju·mɪd] *adj* humide

**humidity** [hju·'mɪd·ə·ti] *n* humidité *f*

**humiliate** [hju·'mɪl·i·eɪt] *vt* humilier

**humiliation** *n* humiliation *f*

**humor** ['hju·mər] *n* ❶ (*capacity for amusement*) humour *m;* **sense of ~** sens *m* de l'humour ❷ (*something amusing*) humour *m* ❸ (*mood*) humeur *f*

**humorous** *adj* humoristique

**hump** [hʌmp] I. *n* bosse *f* ▸ **to be over the ~** avoir passé le cap II. *vt sl* (*have sex with*) sauter III. *vi sl* baiser *vulg*

**hundred** ['hʌn·drəd] <-(s)> *adj* cent; *s.a.* **eight, eighty**

**hundredth** *adj* centième; *s.a.* **eighth**

**hung** [hʌŋ] I. *pt, pp of* **hang** II. *adj* suspendu(e)

**Hungarian** I. *adj* hongrois(e) II. *n* ❶ (*person*) Hongrois(e) *m(f)* ❷ LING hongrois *m; s.a.* **English**

**Hungary** ['hʌŋ·gᵊr·i] *n* la Hongrie

**hunger** ['hʌŋ·gər] *n* ❶ (*pain from lack of food*) faim *f* ❷ (*desire*) soif *f;* **~ for knowledge** soif *f* de savoir

**hunger strike** *n* une grève de la faim

**hung jury** *n* jury *m* dans l'impasse

**hungry** ['hʌŋ·gri] <-ier, -iest> *adj* ❶ (*desiring food*) affamé(e); **to go ~** être affamé ❷ (*want badly*) assoiffé(e); **to be ~ for sth** être assoiffé de qc

**hunk** [hʌŋk] *n* ❶ (*large, thick piece*) gros morceau *m* ❷ *inf* (*attractive man*) canon *m*

**hunt** [hʌnt] I. *vt* ❶ (*chase to kill*) chasser ❷ (*search for*) rechercher II. *vi* ❶ (*chase to kill*) chasser ❷ (*search*) rechercher; **to ~ through sth** fouiller dans qc; **to ~ high and low for sb/sth**

remuer ciel et terre pour trouver qn/qc III. *n* ❶ (*hunting action, place*) chasse *f* ❷ (*search*) recherche *f;* **to be on the ~ for sb** rechercher qn; **to be on the ~ for sth** être en quête de qc ❸ (*association of hunters*) amicale *f* de chasseurs

**hunter** *n* ❶ (*one that hunts*) chasseur, -euse *m, f* ❷ (*hunting dog*) chien *m* de chasse

**hunting** *n* chasse *f*

**hunting license** *n* permis *m* de chasse

**hunting season** *n* saison *f* de la chasse

**hurdle** ['hɜr·dl] I. *n* ❶ (*obstacle, impediment*) obstacle *m* ❷ *pl* (*hurdle race*) course *f* de haies ❸ (*fence*) haie *f* II. *vi* faire une course de haies III. *vt* ❶ (*jump over*) sauter ❷ *fig* franchir

**hurdler** *n* coureur *m* de haies

**hurdle race** *n* course *f* de haies

**hurrah** [hə·'rɑ], **hurray** *interj* hourra!

**hurricane** ['hɜr·ɪ·keɪn] *n* ouragan *m;* **~ force wind** cyclone *m*

**hurricane warning** *n* avis *m* de tempête

**hurried** *adj* ❶ (*fast*) rapide ❷ (*neglected, dashed off*) bâclé(e) ❸ (*sooner or faster than intended*) précipité(e)

**hurry** ['hɜr·i] <-ied> I. *vi* se dépêcher II. *vt* presser III. *n* précipitation *f;* **to do sth in a ~** faire qc à toute allure; **to leave in a ~** partir précipitamment

◆**hurry along** I. *vi* se dépêcher II. *vt* presser

◆**hurry away, hurry off** I. *vi* filer II. *vt* (*person*) emmener en toute hâte; (*things*) emporter en toute hâte

◆**hurry on** I. *vi* s'empresser II. *vt* presser

◆**hurry up** I. *vi* se dépêcher II. *vt* **to hurry sb up** faire se presser qn; **to hurry sth up** activer qc

**hurt** [hɜrt] I. <hurt, hurt> *vi* faire mal II. *vt* ❶ (*cause pain: person, animal*) blesser ❷ (*harm, damage: sb's feelings, pride*) heurter; **to ~ sb** blesser qn; **to ~ sth** abîmer qc III. *adj* blessé(e) IV. *n* ❶ (*pain*) douleur *f* ❷ (*injury*) blessure *f* ❸ (*offense*) offense *f*

**hurtful** *adj* blessant(e)

**hurtle** ['hɜr·tl̩] I. *vi* foncer; **to ~ down** descendre à toute vitesse II. *vt* précipiter

**husband** ['hʌz·bənd] I. *n* mari *m* II. *vt* (*money*) bien gérer

**hush** [hʌʃ] I. *n* silence *m* II. *interj* chut! III. *vi* se taire IV. *vt* ➊ (*make quiet*) faire taire ➋ (*soothe*) calmer
♦ **hush up** *vt pej* étouffer

**husky**[1] ['hʌs·ki] <-ier, -iest> *adj* ➊ (*low, rough*) rauque; (*voice*) enroué(e) ➋ (*big, strong*) robuste

**husky**[2] ['hʌs·ki] *n* husky *m* (sibérien)

**hustle** ['hʌs·l̩] I. *vt* ➊ (*push*) pousser; **to ~ sb away** emmener qn de force ➋ (*hurry*) presser ➌ (*jostle*) bousculer ➍ *inf* (*urge*) pousser II. *vi* ➊ (*hurry*) se presser ➋ *inf* (*practice prostitution*) faire le trottoir ➌ *inf* (*swindle*) arnaquer III. *n* ➊ (*activity*) **~ (and bustle)** effervescence *f* ➋ *inf* (*swindle*) arnaque *f*

**hustler** *n inf* ➊ (*swindler*) escroc *m* ➋ (*prostitute*) tapineuse *f*

**hut** [hʌt] *n* ➊ (*small dwelling place*) cabane *f* ➋ (*garden shelter*) abri *m* de jardin ➌ (*temporary building*) baraque *f* ➍ (*mountain shelter*) refuge *m*

**hutch** [hʌtʃ] *n* ➊ (*box for animals*) cage *f*; (*for rabbits*) clapier *m* ➋ *pej* (*hut*) bicoque *f* ➌ (*cabinet, for dishes*) dressoir *m*

**hybrid** ['haɪ·brɪd] *n* ➊ BOT, ZOOL hybride *m* ➋ (*something mixed*) croisement *m* ➌ AUTO hybride, véhicule *m* hybride; **~ powertrain** système de propulsion hybride; **~ electric vehicle** véhicule électrique hybride

**hydraulics** *n + sing vb* hydraulique *f*

**hydroelectric** [,haɪ·droʊ·ɪˈlek·trɪk] *adj* hydroélectrique

**hydrogen** ['haɪ·drə·dʒən] *n* hydrogène *m*

**hygiene** ['haɪ·dʒin] *n* hygiène *f*

**hygienic** [,haɪ·dʒen·ɪk] *adj* hygiénique

**hymn** [hɪm] *n* hymne *m*

**hymnal, hymnbook** *n* livre *m* de cantiques

**hype** [haɪp] I. *n* battage *m* publicitaire II. *vt* faire du battage publicitaire pour

**hyperlink** *n* COMPUT hyperlien *m*

**hypermarket** *n* hypermarché *m*

**hypertext** I. *n* COMPUT hypertexte *m* II. *adj* COMPUT hypertextuel(le)

**hyphen** ['haɪ·fən] *n* ➊ (*short line between two words*) trait *m* d'union ➋ (*short line at the end of a line*) tiret *m*

**hypnosis** [hɪpˈnoʊ·sɪs] *n* hypnose *f*

**hypnotherapy** [,hɪp·noʊ·ˈθer·ə·pi] *n* hypnothérapie *f*

**hypnotist** *n* hypnotiseur, -euse *m, f*

**hypnotize** ['hɪp·nə·taɪz] *vt* hypnotiser

**hypocrite** ['hɪp·ə·krɪt] *n* hypocrite *mf*

**hypothetical** [,haɪ·poʊ·ˈθet·ɪk·əl] *adj* hypothétique; (*question*) théorique

**hysterical** *adj* surexcité(e)

**H**

# I i

**I, i** [aɪ] <-'s> *n* I *m*, i *m*; **~ as in India** i comme Irma

**I** *pers pron* (*1st person sing*) je, j' + *vowel*; **she and ~** elle et moi

**IA** *n abbr of* **Iowa**

**ibid.** [ɪ·ˈbɪd] *adv abbr of* **ibidem** (**in the same place**) ibid.

**ice** [aɪs] **I.** *n* ❶ (*frozen water*) glace *f*; (*on road*) verglas *m*; **to put sth on ~** (*food, drink*) mettre qc à rafraîchir ❷ (*ice cube*) glaçons *mpl* ❸ (*Italian ice*) glace *f* ▸ **to put sth on ~** geler qc; **to break the ~** rompre la glace; **to be skating on thin ~** avancer sur un terrain glissant **II.** *vt* glacer

**ice age** *n* période *f* glaciaire

**ice ax** *n* piolet *m*

**iceberg** *n* iceberg *m*

**iceberg lettuce** *n* laitue *f* iceberg

**icebox** *n* ❶ (*cooler*) glacière *f* ❷ (*refrigerator*) réfrigérateur *m*

**icebreaker** *n* brise-glace *m*

**icecap** *n* calotte *f* glaciaire

**ice cream** *n* crème *f* glacée

**ice-cream parlor** *n* glacier *m*

**ice cube** *n* glaçon *m*

**iced** *adj* ❶ (*covered with ice*) glacé(e) ❷ (*cold: coffee, tea*) glacé(e); (*water*) avec des glaçons ❸ (*covered with icing: cake*) glacé(e)

**ice hockey** *n* hockey *m* sur glace

**ice pack** *n* ❶ (*for swelling*) vessie *f* de glace ❷ (*sea ice*) mer *f* de glace

**ice-skate** *vi* patiner (sur la glace)

**ice skating** *n* patinage *m* sur glace

**icicle** [ˈaɪ·sɪ·kl] *n* ❶ (*directed upwards*) glaçon *m* en forme de stalagmite ❷ (*directed downwards*) glaçon *m* en forme de stalactite

**icing** *n* glaçage *m* ▸ **to be the ~ on the cake** *pej* être la cinquième roue du carrosse; (*unexpected extra*) être la cerise sur le gâteau

**icon** [ˈaɪ·kɑn] *n* ❶ REL, COMPUT icône *f* ❷ (*idol*) idole *f*

**ICU** [ˌaɪ·siˈju] *n abbr of* **intensive care unit** service *m* de soins intensifs

**icy** [ˈaɪ·si] *adj* ❶ (*covered with ice*) glacé(e); (*road*) verglacé(e); (*ground*) gelé(e) ❷ (*very cold: wind*) glacial(e); (*feet, water*) glacé(e) ❸ *fig* (*unfriendly: look, stare*) glacial(e)

**I'd** [aɪd] = **I would** *s.* **would**

**ID**[1] [ˌaɪ·ˈdi] *inf* **I.** *n abbr of* **identification** pièce *f* d'identité **II.** *vt* ❶ *abbr of* **identify** identifier ❷ (*check age of*) vérifier les papiers d'identité de

**ID**[2] *n abbr of* **Idaho**

**Idaho** [ˈaɪ·də·hoʊ] *n* l'Idaho *m*

**ID card** *n* carte *f* d'identité

**idea** [aɪ·ˈdi·ə] *n* ❶ (*notion, opinion, suggestion, plan*) idée *f* ❷ (*conception*) conception *f*; **to not be sb's ~ of sth** ne pas être ce que qn appelle qc ❸ (*impression*) impression *f* ❹ (*purpose*) **the ~ behind sth** le but de qc ▸ **to not have the slightest ~** ne pas avoir la moindre idée

**ideal** [aɪ·ˈdi·əl] **I.** *adj* idéal(e) **II.** *n* idéal *m*

**ideally** *adv* idéalement

**identification** [aɪ·ˌden·tə·fɪ·ˈkeɪ·ʃ°n] *n* ❶ (*determination*) identification *f* ❷ (*proof of identity*) pièce *f* d'identité

**identification papers** *npl* papiers *mpl* d'identité

**identify** [aɪ·ˈden·tə·faɪ] <-ied> **I.** *vt* identifier; (*car, house*) reconnaître; **to ~ oneself** décliner son identité; **to ~ oneself with sth** se reconnaître dans qc **II.** *vi* s'identifier; **to ~ with sb** s'identifier à qn; **to be ~ied with sth** être assimilé à qc

**identical** [aɪ·ˈden·tə·kl] *adj* identique; **~ twins** vrais jumeaux *mpl*

**identity** [aɪ·ˈden·tə·ti] *n* identité *f*

**idiom** [ˈɪd·i·əm] *n* LING ❶ (*fixed phrase*)

expression *f* idiomatique ❷ (*language*) idiome *m*

**idiomatic** [ˌɪd·i·əˈmæt·ɪk] *adj* idiomatique

**idiot** [ˈɪd·i·ət] *n* idiot(e) *m(f)*

**idiotic** *adj* bête

**idle** [ˈaɪ·dl] I. *adj* ❶ (*lazy, doing nothing*) oisif(-ive); **to lie ~** rester inactif ❷ (*not working or acting: person*) inactif(-ive); (*period*) d'inactivité ❸ (*with nothing to do: person*) désœuvré(e); (*factory, machine*) à l'arrêt ❹ (*pointless, without purpose*) inutile; (*threat, talk*) en l'air; (*rumors, fear*) sans fondement; (*curiosity*) simple ❺ FIN (*capital*) improductif(-ive) II. *vi* ❶ (*willingly do nothing*) paresser ❷ (*having nothing to do*) être inactif ❸ (*engine, machine*) tourner au ralenti; (*computer, disk drive, screen*) être en veille

**idolize** [ˈaɪ·dəlˌaɪz] *vt* idolâtrer

**if** [ɪf] I. *conj* ❶ si ❷ (*supposing that*) **~ it snows** s'il neige; **~ not** sinon; **as ~ it were true** comme si c'était vrai ❸ (*every time that*) **~ he needs me, I'll help him** s'il a besoin de moi, je l'aiderai ❹ (*whether*) **I wonder ~ he'll come** je me demande s'il viendra ❺ (*although*) **even ~** même si II. *n* si *m inv*; **no ~ s, ands or buts!** pas de si ni de mais!

**igloo** [ˈɪg·lu] *n* igloo *m*

**ignition** [ɪgˈnɪʃ·ən] *n* ❶ AUTO allumage *m*; **to turn the ~** (**on**) démarrer ❷ AVIAT mise *f* à feu

**ignition key** *n* clé *f* de contact

**ignition switch** *n* contact *m* de démarrage

**ignorance** [ˈɪg·nər·ən(t)s] *n* ignorance *f*

**ignorant** *adj* ignorant(e)

**ignore** [ɪgˈnɔr] *vt* ignorer

**IL** *n abbr of* **Illinois**

**ill** [ɪl] I. *adj* ❶ (*sick*) malade; **to feel ~** ne pas se sentir bien ❷ (*bad, harmful*) mauvais(e); (*effects*) néfaste; **~ fortune** malchance *f* II. *adv* mal; **I can ~ afford sth** je peux difficilement me permettre qc III. *n* ❶ (*problem*) mal *m*; **the ~s of society** les maux *mpl* de la société ❷ *pl* (*sick people*) **the ~** les malades *mpl*

❸ (*evil*) mal *m*; **to wish sb ~** souhaiter du mal à qn

**I'll** [aɪl] = **I will** s. **will**

**ill-conceived** *adj* mal préparé(e)

**illegal** [ɪˈli·gəl] *adj* ❶ (*forbidden by law*) illégal(e) ❷ (*forbidden by law or rules*) illicite

**illegal immigrant** *n* immigré *m* clandestin

**illegible** [ɪˈledʒ·ə·bl] *adj* illisible

**illegitimate** [ˌɪl·ɪˈdʒɪt·ə·mət] *adj* ❶ (*not lawful*) illégitime *m* ❷ (*unauthorized*) illicite

**Illinois** [ˌɪl·ɪˈnɔɪ] *n* l'Illinois *m*

**illiterate** [ɪˈlɪt·ər·ət] I. *adj* ❶ (*unable to read or write*) analphabète ❷ (*uncultured, uneducated: person*) inculte; (*style*) incorrect(e) ❸ *pej* (*ignorant*) ignorant(e) II. *n* analphabète *mf*

**ill-mannered** *adj* (*person*) mal élevé(e); (*behavior*) grossier(-ère)

**illness** *n* maladie *f*

**illogical** [ɪˈla·dʒɪ·kəl] *adj* illogique

**ill-timed** *adj* inopportun(e)

**illuminate** [ɪˈlu·məˌneɪt] *vt* ❶ (*light up*) éclairer ❷ (*decorate with lights*) illuminer ❸ ART (*manuscript*) enluminer ❹ *fig* (*clarify*) éclairer

**illumination** *n* ❶ *form* (*lighting*) éclairage *m*; (*of building*) illumination *f* ❷ *pl* (*light decoration*) illuminations *fpl* ❸ (*of books, manuscripts*) enluminure *f* ❹ *fig* (*clarification*) éclaircissement *m*

**illusion** [ɪˈlu·ʒən] *n* illusion *f*; **to have no ~s about sth** ne pas se faire d'illusions sur qc

**illustrate** [ˈɪl·əˌstreɪt] *vt* illustrer

**illustration** *n* ❶ (*drawing*) illustration *f* ❷ (*example*) exemple *m*

**illustrious** [ɪˈlʌs·tri·əs] *adj* illustre

**I'm** [aɪm] = **I am** s. **am**

**image** [ˈɪm·ɪdʒ] *n* ❶ (*likeness*) ressemblance *f*; **it is the spitting ~ of him** c'est lui tout craché ❷ (*picture*) image *f*; **reverse** [*o* **mirror**] **~** image inverse ❸ (*reputation*) image *f* de marque

**imagery** [ˈɪm·ɪdʒ·ər·i] *n* imagerie *f*

**imagination** [ɪˌmædʒ·ɪˈneɪ·ʃən] *n* ima-

gination *f*; **not by any stretch of the ~**
pas même en rêve; **to capture sb's ~**
passionner qn; **to leave nothing to
the ~** *inf* ne rien laisser deviner

**imaginative** [ɪ·ˈmædʒ·ɪ·nə·ṭɪv] *adj* in-
génieux(-euse)

**imagine** [ɪ·ˈmædʒ·ɪn] *vt* imaginer;
**~ that!** tu penses!

**imitate** [ˈɪm·ɪ·təɾt] *vt* imiter

**imitation** I. *n* ❶ (*mimicry*) mimique *f*;
(*of voices*) imitation *f* ❷ (*copy*) copie *f*
II. *adj* faux(fausse); **~ leather** skaï *m*

**immaculate** [ɪ·ˈmæk·jʊ·lət] *adj* ❶ REL,
LIT immaculé(e) ❷ (*flawless*) impeccable

**immature** [ˌɪm·ə·ˈtʊr] *adj* ❶ (*not developed: people, animals*) immature;
(*sexually*) sans expérience ❷ *pej* (*childish*) immature

**immaturity** *n* immaturité *f*

**immediate** [ɪ·ˈmi·di·ɪt] *adj* ❶ (*without
delay*) immédiat(e); (*danger*) immi-
nent(e); **to take ~ effect/action** prendre effet/agir immédiatement ❷ (*nearest*) proche; (*area, vicinity*) immé-
diat(e); **the ~ family** les proches
parents *mpl* ❸ (*direct: cause*) direct(e)

**immediately** I. *adv* ❶ (*at once*) immédiatement; **~ after** aussitôt après
❷ (*closely*) **~ after sth** juste après qc
II. *conj* dès que

**immense** [ɪ·ˈmen(t)s] *adj* immense;
(*importance*) considérable

**immensely** *adv* énormément

**immersion heater** *n* chauffe-eau *m*
électrique

**immigrant** [ˈɪm·ɪ·grənt] *n* immigrant(e)
*m(f)*; **~ family** famille *f* immigrée

**immigrate** [ˈɪm·ɪ·greɪt] *vi* immigrer

**immigration** *n* ❶ immigration *f* ❷ (*government agency*) services *mpl* de l'immigration

**immoral** [ɪ·ˈmɔr·əl] *adj* immoral(e)

**immortal** [ɪ·ˈmɔr·ṭəl] I. *adj* ❶ (*undying*)
immortel(le) ❷ (*unforgettable*) éter-
nel(le) II. *n* immortel(le) *m(f)*

**immune** [ɪ·ˈmjun] *adj* ❶ MED (*person*)
immunisé(e); (*system, deficiency, reaction*) immunitaire ❷ (*not vulnerable*)

insensible; **~ to criticism** imperméable
à la critique ❸ (*protected, exempt*) **to
be ~ from sth** être à l'abri de qc; (*taxation*) être exonéré de qc

**immunity** [ɪ·ˈmju·nə·ṭi] *n* MED, LAW immunité *f*

**immunize** [ˈɪm·jə·naɪz] *vt* immuniser

**impact** [ˈɪm·pækt] I. *n a. fig* impact *m*
II. *vt* ❶ (*hit*) heurter ❷ (*affect*) avoir
une incidence [*o* un impact] sur III. *vi*
**to ~ on sb/sth** avoir un impact sur qn/
qc

**impaired** *adj* (*vision, mobility*) ré-
duit(e); **hearing-~ person** personne *f*
malentendante

**impartial** [ɪm·ˈpar·ʃəl] *adj* impartial(e)

**impassable** *adj a. fig* infranchissable

**impatience** [ɪm·ˈpeɪ·ʃən(t)s] *n* impatience *f*

**impatient** *adj* impatient(e)

**impeach** [ɪm·ˈpitʃ] *vt* POL, LAW mettre en
accusation; **to ~ sb for sth** limoger qn
pour qc

**impeachment** *n* ❶ LAW mise *f* en accusation ❷ POL (*of president*) impeachment *m*

**impending** [ɪm·ˈpend·ɪŋ] *adj* immi-
nent(e)

**imperative** [ɪm·ˈper·ə·ṭɪv] I. *adj a.* LING
impératif(-ive); **it is ~ that** il est indispensable que +*subj* II. *n* ❶ (*essential
thing*) impératif *m* ❷ LING **the ~** l'impératif *m*

**imperfect** [ɪm·ˈpɜr·fɪkt] I. *adj* ❶ (*not
perfect*) imparfait(e) ❷ (*flawed*) défec-
tueux(-euse) ❸ (*not sufficient*) insuffi-
sant(e) ❹ (*not finished*) inachevé(e)
II. *n* LING **the ~** l'imparfait *m*

**imperfection** *n* ❶ (*flaw*) défaut *m*
❷ (*lack of perfection*) imperfection *f*

**imperial** [ɪm·ˈpɪr·i·əl] *adj* impérial(e)

**imperialistic** *adj* impérialiste

**impersonal** [ˌɪm·ˈpɜr·sən·əl] *adj* ❶ PSYCH
détaché(e) ❷ LING impersonnel(le)

**impersonate** [ɪm·ˈpɜr·sən·eɪt] *vt*
❶ (*imitate*) imiter ❷ (*pretend to be*) se
faire passer pour

**impersonator** *n* ❶ THEAT imitateur, -tri-
ce *m, f* ❷ LAW imposteur *m*

**impertinent** [ɪmˈpɜr·t̬ə·n·ənt] *adj* impertinent(e)

**impetuous** [ɪmˈpetʃ·u·əs] *adj* impétueux(-euse); (*action*) impulsif(-ive)

**implant** [ˈɪm·plænt, *vb:* ɪmˈplænt] I. *n* implant *m* II. *vt* **①** MED greffer **②** PSYCH inculquer

**implausible** [ɪmˈplɔ·zə·bl̩] *adj* peu plausible

**implement** [ˈɪm·plɪ·mənt] I. *n* **①** (*tool*) instrument *m*; **farming ~s** outillage *m* agricole **②** (*small tool*) ustensile *m*; **writing ~** de quoi écrire II. *vt* **①** (*put into effect*) exécuter; (*plan, law, agreement*) mettre en application **②** COMPUT implémenter

**implicate** [ˈɪm·plɪ·keɪt] *vt* impliquer

**implication** *n* implication *f*; **by ~** implicitement

**implore** [ɪmˈplɔr] *vt* implorer; **to ~ sb to** +*infin* supplier qn de +*infin*

**imploring** *adj* implorant(e)

**imply** [ɪmˈplaɪ] <-ie-> *vt* **①** (*suggest*) sous-entendre **②** (*mean*) impliquer

**impolite** [ˌɪm·pəˈlaɪt] *adj* impoli(e)

**impoliteness** *n* **①** (*lack of good manners*) impolitesse *f* **②** (*rudeness*) grossièreté *f*

**import** [ˈɪm·pɔrt, *vb:* ɪmˈpɔrt] I. *n* **①** (*non-domestic product*) importation *f* **②** (*significance*) importance *f* II. *vt* importer

**importance** [ɪmˈpɔr·t̬ən(t)s] *n* importance *f*

**important** *adj* **①** (*significant*) important(e); (*event*) capital(e) **②** (*influential: person*) influent(e)

**importantly** *adv* d'un air important

**impose** [ɪmˈpoʊz] I. *vt* imposer; **to ~ sth on sb** infliger qc à qn; **to ~ a tax on sth** taxer qc II. *vi* s'imposer; **to ~ on sb's patience/hospitality** abuser de la patience/de l'hospitalité de qn

**imposing** *adj* imposant(e)

**imposition** [ˌɪm·pəˈzɪʃ·ən] *n* imposition *f*; **it's an ~ on me** c'est abuser de ma bonté

**impossibility** [ɪm·pɑ·sə·ˈbɪl·ə·t̬i] *n* impossibilité *f*

**impossible** [ɪmˈpɑ·sə·bl̩] I. *adj* a. *fig* impossible; (*problem*) insoluble II. *n* **the ~** l'impossible *m*

**imposter, impostor** [ɪmˈpɑ·stər] *n* imposteur *m*

**impotent** *adj* **①** MED impuissant(e) **②** *fig* faible

**impound** [ɪmˈpaʊnd] *vt* **①** (*stolen goods*) confisquer **②** (*dog, car*) mettre à la fourrière

**impoverish** [ɪmˈpɑ·vər·ɪʃ] *vt* appauvrir

**impractical** [ɪmˈpræk·tɪ·kəl] *adj* **①** (*not sensible, unrealistic: plan, idea*) irréaliste **②** (*not adapted for use or action*) pas pratique; (*high heels*) importable **③** (*not skilled: person*) qui manque d'esprit pratique **④** (*impracticable*) impraticable

**imprecise** [ˌɪm·prɪˈsaɪs] *adj* imprécis(e)

**impress** [ɪmˈpres] I. *vt* **①** (*affect*) impressionner; **I'm not ~ed by that** ça me laisse froid **②** (*make realize*) **to ~ sth on sb** faire comprendre qc à qn **③** (*stamp*) imprimer II. *vi* faire impression

**impression** [ɪmˈpreʃ·ən] *n* **①** (*idea*) impression *f*; **to be under** [*o* **to have**] **the ~ that …** avoir l'impression que … **②** (*effect*) impression *f*; **to make an ~ on sb** faire de l'effet à qn **③** (*imitation*) imitation *f* **④** (*imprint*) empreinte *f* **⑤** TYP tirage *m*

**impressionable** *adj* influençable; **~ age** âge *m* où l'on se laisse influencer

**impressive** [ɪmˈpres·ɪv] *adj* (*causing awe*) impressionnant(e); (*striking*) saisissant(e)

**imprison** [ɪmˈprɪz·ən] *vt* emprisonner

**imprisonment** *n* emprisonnement *m*, collocation *f Belgique*

**improbability** *n* invraisemblance *f*

**improbable** [ɪmˈprɑ·bə·bl̩] *adj* improbable; **an ~ excuse** une excuse invraisemblable; **it is ~ that he will come** il est peu probable qu'il vienne

**improper** [ɪmˈprɑ·pər] *adj* **①** (*not suitable*) impropre **②** (*not correct*) incorrect(e); (*use*) abusif(-ive); **to make ~**

**use of sth** faire mauvais usage de qc ❸ (*indecent*) indécent(e)

**improve** [ɪmˈpruv] I. *vt* (*make better*) améliorer II. *vi* ❶ (*become better*) s'améliorer; (*wine*) se bonifier ❷ (*make more perfect*) **to ~ on sth** perfectionner qc

**improvement** *n* ❶ (*act, measure*) amélioration *f*; (*of machine*) perfectionnement *m*; **to be an ~ on sb/sth** être supérieur à qn/qc ❷ (*state*) progrès *m*; (*of illness*) amélioration *f* ❸ (*increase in value*) revalorisation *f*

**improvisation** *n* improvisation *f*

**improvise** [ˈɪm·prə·vaɪz] I. *vt* improviser; **to ~ a speech** faire un discours impromptu II. *vi* improviser

**impudence** [ˈɪm·pjə·dⁿ(t)s] *n* impudence *f*

**impudent** *adj* impertinent(e)

**impulse** [ˈɪm·pʌls] *n* ❶ (*urge*) élan *m*; **to do sth on (an) ~** faire qc sur un coup de tête ❷ ELEC, PHYS impulsion *f* ❸ ANAT influx *m* nerveux ❹ (*motive*) **the ~ behind sth** la raison qui se cache derrière qc

**impulsive** [ɪmˈpʌl·sɪv] *adj* impulsif(-ive)

**impunity** [ɪmˈpju·nə·t̬i] *n* impunité *f*

**impurity** <-ies> *n* impureté *f*

**in**[1] [ɪn] I. *prep* ❶ (*inside, into*) dans; **to be ~ bed** être au lit; **~ town/jail** en ville/prison; **~ France/Burgundy/Tokyo/Cyprus** en France/Bourgogne/à Tokyo/Chypre; **~ Peru/the West Indies/the Languedoc** au Pérou/aux Antilles/dans le Languedoc ❷ (*within*) **~ sb's face/the picture** sur le visage de qn/l'image; **~ the snow/sun** sous la neige/au soleil; **the best ~ France/town** le meilleur de France/la ville ❸ (*position of*) **~ the beginning/end** au début/à la fin; **right ~ the middle** en plein milieu ❹ (*during*) **~ the twenties** dans les années vingt; **to be ~ one's thirties** avoir la trentaine; **~ those days** à cette époque-là; **~ May/spring** en mai/au printemps; **~ the afternoon** (dans) l'après-midi; **at 11 ~ the morning** à 11 h du matin ❺ (*at later time*) **~ a week/three hours** dans une semaine/trois heures; **~ (the) future** à l'avenir ❻ (*within a period*) **to do sth ~ 4 hours** faire qc en 4 heures ❼ (*for*) **he hasn't done that ~ years/a week** il n'a pas fait ça depuis des années/de toute une semaine ❽ (*in situation, state, manner of*) **~ fashion** à la mode; **~ search of sb/sth** à la recherche de qn/qc; **~ this way** de cette manière; **to be ~ a hurry** être pressé; **~ alphabetical order** par ordre alphabétique; **written ~ black and white** écrit noir sur blanc; **~ a suit and tie** en costume-cravate ❾ (*concerning, with respect to*) **deaf ~ one ear** sourd d'une oreille; **to be interested ~ sth** s'intéresser à qc; **to have faith ~ God** croire en Dieu; **to have confidence ~ sb** avoir confiance en qn; **to have a say ~ the matter** avoir voix au chapitre; **change ~ attitude** changement *m* d'attitude; **rise ~ prices** augmentation *f* des prix ❿ (*by*) **~ saying sth** en disant qc ⓫ (*taking the form of*) **to speak ~ French** parler (en) français; **~ the form of a request** sous la forme d'une demande ⓬ (*made of*) **~ wood/stone** en bois/pierre ⓭ (*sound of*) **~ a whisper** en chuchotant; **to speak ~ a loud/low voice** parler à voix haute/basse ⓮ (*aspect of*) **2 feet ~ length/high** 2 pieds de long/haut; **~ every respect** à tous points de vue ⓯ (*ratio*) **two ~ six** deux sur six; **once ~ ten years** une fois tous les dix ans; **10 ~ number** au nombre de 10; **~ part** en partie ⓰ (*substitution of*) **~ sb's place** à la place de qn; **~ lieu of sth** en guise de qc ⓱ (*as consequence of*) **~ return/reply** en échange/réponse ▸ **heaven's name!** au nom du Ciel!; **~ all** (*all together*) en tout; **all ~ all** en général II. *adv* (*at a place*) **to be ~** être là; (*at home*) être à la maison; (*in jail*) être en prison ▸ **to be ~ for sth** *inf* être bon pour qc; **~ on sth** au courant de qc; *s.a.* **in between** III. *adj* (*popular*) dans le vent; **to be ~**

être à la mode; *s.a.* **out** IV. *n* **the ~s and outs** les tenants *mpl* et les aboutissants *mpl*

**in²** [ɪn] *n abbr of* **inch** pouce *m*

**IN** *n abbr of* **Indiana**

**inability** [ˌɪn·ə·ˈbɪl·ə·t̬i] *n* incapacité *f*

**inaccessible** [ˌɪn·æk·ˈses·ə·bl] *adj* inaccessible

**inaccuracy** [ɪn·ˈæk·jə·rə·si] <-ies> *n* inexactitude *f*

**inaccurate** [ɪn·ˈæk·jə·rət] *adj* inexact(e)

**inactive** [ɪn·ˈæk·tɪv] *adj* inactif(-ive)

**inadequacy** [ɪn·ˈæd·ɪ·kwə·si] <-ies> *n* ❶ (*insufficiency*) insuffisance *f* ❷ (*defect*) imperfection *f*

**inadequate** [ɪn·ˈæd·ɪ·kwət] *adj* inadéquat(e); (*knowledge, funds*) insuffisant(e); **to feel ~** ne pas se sentir à la hauteur

**inadmissible** [ˌɪn·əd·ˈmɪs·ə·bl] *adj* inadmissible; **~ evidence** preuves *fpl* irrecevables

**inadvertent** [ˌɪn·əd·ˈvɜr·t̬ənt] *adj* commis(e) par inadvertance

**inadvisable** [ˌɪn·əd·ˈvaɪ·zə·bl] *adj* inopportun(e); **it is ~ to** +*infin* il est déconseillé de +*infin*

**inanimate** [ɪn·ˈæn·ɪ·mət] *adj* inanimé(e)

**inappropriate** [ˌɪn·ə·ˈproʊ·pri·ət] *adj* inapproprié(e)

**inarticulate** [ˌɪn·ar·ˈtɪk·jʊ·lət] *adj* ❶ (*unable to express oneself*) **to be ~** être incapable de s'exprimer ❷ (*unclear*) incompréhensible

**inattentive** [ˌɪn·ə·ˈten·t̬ɪv] *adj* inattentif(-ive)

**inaudible** [ɪn·ˈɔ·də·bl] *adj* inaudible

**inauguration** *n* ❶ (*induction into office: of president*) investiture *f* ❷ (*opening: of building*) inauguration *f*

**in between** I. *prep* entre II. *adv* entre les deux

**in box** *n* COMPUT boîte *f* de réception

**incalculable** [ɪn·ˈkæl·kjə·lə·bl] *adj* incalculable, (*value*) inestimable

**incandescent** [ˌɪn·ken·ˈdes·ənt] *adj* incandescent(e)

**incapable** [ɪn·ˈkeɪ·pə·bl] *adj* incapable

**incense¹** [ˈɪn·sen(t)s] *n* encens *m*

**incense²** [ɪn·ˈsen(t)s] *vt* mettre en colère

**incentive** [ɪn·ˈsen·t̬ɪv] *n* ❶ FIN, ECON prime *f* ❷ (*cause for action*) motivation *f;* **to give an ~** motiver

**inch** [ɪn(t)ʃ] I. <-es> *n* pouce *m;* **every ~** chaque centimètre ▶ **to not give** [*o* **move**] **an ~** ne pas bouger d'un pouce; **~ by** petit à petit II. *vi + directional adv* **to ~ along** [*o* **forward**] avancer à petits pas III. *vt* **to ~ one-self/sth forward** s'avancer/faire avancer qc d'un pouce

**incident** *n* incident *m*

**incidental** *adj* ❶ (*minor*) secondaire; **~ expenses** faux frais *mpl* ❷ (*occurring by chance*) accidentel(le) ❸ (*happening as a consequence*) **to be ~ to sth** accompagner qc

**incidentally** *adv* ❶ (*by the way*) à propos ❷ (*accidentally*) incidemment

**incinerator** *n* incinérateur *m*

**incision** [ɪn·ˈsɪʒ·ən] *n* MED incision *f*

**incite** [ɪn·ˈsaɪt] *vt* inciter, instiguer *Belgique*

**inclination** [ˌɪn·klɪ·ˈneɪ·ʃən] *n* ❶ (*tendency*) tendance *f* ❷ (*liking*) penchant *m* ❸ (*slope*) inclinaison *f*

**incline** [ˈɪn·klaɪn, *vb:* ɪn·ˈklaɪn] I. *n* pente *f* II. *vi* ❶ (*tend*) **to ~ to(ward) sth** tendre vers qc ❷ (*lean*) pencher III. *vt* ❶ (*encourage*) **to ~ sb to** +*infin* porter qn à +*infin* ❷ (*make lean*) incliner; **to ~ one's head** baisser la tête

**inclined** *adj* enclin(e)

**include** [ɪn·ˈklud] *vt* comprendre

**including** *prep* (y) compris; **not ~ tax** taxe *f* non comprise; **up to and ~ June 6th** jusqu'au 6 juin inclus

**inclusion** [ɪn·ˈklu·ʒən] *n* inclusion *f*

**inclusive** [ɪn·ˈklu·sɪv] *adj* ❶ (*including*) compris(e); **all-~** tout compris ❷ (*for all people, diverse*) **~ policy** politique *f* non discriminatoire

**incoherent** [ˌɪn·koʊ·ˈhɪr·ənt] *adj* incohérent(e)

**income** [ˈɪn·kʌm] *n* revenu *m*

**income tax** *n* impôt *m* sur le revenu

**incoming** *adj* ❶ (*arriving*) qui arrive; (*call*) de l'extérieur ❷ (*new*) nouveau(-elle) ❸ (*recently elected*) entrant(e)

**incomparable** [ɪnˈkam·pʰr·ə·bl] *adj* incomparable

**incompatible** [ˌɪn·kəmˈpæt·ə·bl] *adj* incompatible

**incompetent** I. *adj* incompétent(e) II. *n pej* incapable *mf*

**incomplete** [ˌɪn·kəmˈplit] *adj* ❶ (*not complete*) incomplet(-ète) ❷ (*not finished*) inachevé(e)

**incomprehensible** [ˌɪn·kam·prɪ·ˈhen(t)·sə·bl] *adj* incompréhensible

**inconceivable** [ˌɪn·kənˈsi·və·bl] *adj* inconcevable

**inconclusive** [ˌɪn·kənˈklu·sɪv] *adj* peu concluant(e)

**inconsequential** *adj* sans conséquence

**inconsiderate** [ˌɪn·kənˈsɪd·ᵊr·ət] *adj* inconsidéré(e); **to be ~ to sb** manquer d'égards envers qn

**inconsistency** [ˌɪn·kənˈsɪs·tᵊn(t)·si] <-ies> *n* inconsistance *f*

**inconsistent** *adj* inconsistant(e)

**inconsolable** [ˌɪn·kənˈsoʊ·lə·bl] *adj* inconsolable

**inconspicuous** [ˌɪn·kənˈspɪk·ju·əs] *adj* discret(-ète); **to try to look ~** essayer de passer inaperçu

**inconvenience** [ˌɪn·kənˈvi·ni·ən(t)s] I. *n* désagrément *m* II. *vt* déranger

**inconvenient** *adj* inopportun(e)

**incorporated** *adj* ECON (*company*) à responsabilité limitée

**incorporation** *n* ❶ (*integration*) incorporation *f* ❷ LAW, ECON constitution *f* en société

**incorrect** [ˌɪn·kəˈrekt] *adj* ❶ (*not correct*) incorrect(e); **to prove ~** s'avérer inexact ❷ *fig* déplacé(e)

**incorruptible** [ˌɪn·kəˈrʌp·tə·bl] *adj* incorruptible

**increase** [ˈɪn·kris, *vb:* ɪnˈkris] I. *n* ❶ (*in quantity*) augmentation *f*; **tax ~** hausse *f* de l'impôt ❷ (*in quality*) intensification *f* II. *vt*, *vi* augmenter; **to ~ threefold/tenfold** tripler/décupler

**increasing** *adj* croissant(e)

**incredible** [ɪnˈkred·ɪ·bl] *adj* incroyable

**incur** [ɪnˈkɜr] <-rr-> *vt* encourir; (*losses*) subir; (*debt*) contracter; (*sb's anger*) s'attirer

**incurable** [ɪnˈkjʊr·ə·bl] *adj* incurable

**indebted** [ɪnˈdet·ɪd] *adj* ❶ (*obliged*) **~ to sb for sth** redevable à qn de qc ❷ FIN endetté(e)

**indecent** *adj* indécent(e)

**indecision** [ˌɪn·dɪˈsɪʒ·ᵊn] *n* indécision *f*

**indecisive** [ˌɪn·dɪˈsaɪ·sɪv] *adj* indécis(e)

**indeed** [ɪnˈdid] *adv* ❶ (*as was suspected*) en effet ❷ (*emphasizing*) vraiment

**indefinite** [ɪnˈdef·ə·nət] *adj* indéfini(e)

**indefinitely** *adv* indéfiniment

**independence** [ˌɪn·dɪˈpen·dən(t)s] *n* indépendance *f*

**independent** I. *adj* a. LING indépendant(e) II. *n* POL **an Independent** un(e) non-inscrit(e)

**in-depth** [ˈɪn·depθ] *adj* approfondi(e)

**indescribable** [ˌɪn·dɪˈskraɪ·bə·bl] *adj* indescriptible

**indestructible** [ˌɪn·dɪˈstrʌk·tə·bl] *adj* indestructible; (*toy*) incassable

**index** [ˈɪn·deks] I. *n* ❶ <-es> (*alphabetical list*) index *m* ❷ <-ices *o* -es> ECON, MATH indice *m*; **cost-of-living ~** indice officiel du coût de la vie ❸ <-ices *o* -es> (*indication*) indice *m* ❹ REL **the Index** l'Index *m* II. *vt* a. ECON indexer

**index card** *n* fiche *f*

**index finger** *n* index *m*

**Indian** I. *adj* ❶ (*of/from India*) indien(ne), de l'Inde ❷ (*of/from Native Americans*) a. *pej* indien(ne) II. *n* ❶ (*from India*) Indien(ne) *m(f)* ❷ (*Native American*) a. *pej* Indien(ne) *m(f)*

**Indiana** [ˌɪn·diˈæn·ə] *n* l'Indiana *m*

**indicate** [ˈɪn·dɪ·keɪt] *vt* indiquer

**indication** *n* a. MED indication *f*; **there is every/no ~ that ...** tout/rien ne porte à croire que ...

**indicative** [ɪnˈdɪk·ə·tɪv] I. *adj* a. LING indicatif(-ive) II. *n* LING indicatif *m*

**indicator** *n* a. TECH indicateur *m*

**indices** [ˈɪn·dɪ·siz] *n pl of* **index**

**indict** [ɪnˈdaɪt] *vt* LAW **to ~ sb on sth** inculper qn de qc

**indifference** [ɪnˈdɪf·ər·ən(t)s] *n* indifférence *f*

**indifferent** *adj* ❶ (*not interested*) indifférent(e) ❷ (*not good or bad*) médiocre

**indigenous** [ɪnˈdɪdʒ·ɪ·nəs] *adj* indigène

**indigestible** [ˌɪn·dɪ·ˈdʒəs·tə·bl] *adj* inassimilable

**indigestion** [ˌɪn·dɪ·ˈdʒəs·tʃ²n] *n* indigestion *f*

**indignant** [ɪnˈdɪg·nənt] *adj* indigné(e)

**indignation** *n* ❶ *no indef art* indignation *f* ❷ (*humiliating occurrence*) **to suffer ~** endurer des humiliations

**indignity** [ɪnˈdɪg·nə·t̬i] *n* humiliation *f*

**indirect** [ˌɪn·dɪ·ˈrekt] *adj* a. LING indirect(e); **by ~ means** de manière détournée

**indiscreet** [ˌɪn·dɪ·ˈskrit] *adj* indiscret(-ète)

**indiscretion** [ˌɪn·dɪ·ˈskreʃ·²n] *n* indiscrétion *f*

**indiscriminate** [ˌɪn·dɪ·ˈskrɪm·ɪ·nət] *adj* ❶ (*without criteria*) sans distinction; (*revenge*) aveugle ❷ (*uncritical*) dépourvu(e) d'esprit critique ❸ (*random*) général(e)

**indispensable** [ˌɪn·dɪ·ˈspen(t)·sə·bl] *adj* indispensable

**indistinct** [ˌɪn·dɪ·ˈstɪŋ(k)t] *adj* indistinct(e)

**indistinguishable** [ˌɪn·dɪ·ˈstɪŋ·gwɪ·ʃə·bl] *adj* indiscernable

**individual** [ˌɪn·dɪ·ˈvɪdʒ·u·əl] **I.** *n* individu *m* **II.** *adj* (*case*) individuel(le); (*attention*) particulier(-ère); (*needs, style*) personnel(le)

**individualistic** *adj* individualiste

**indoctrinate** [ɪnˈdak·trɪ·neɪt] *vt* endoctriner

**indoor** [ˈɪn·ˈdɔr] *adj* d'intérieur; (*sports*) en salle; (*pool, tennis court*) couvert(e)

**indoors** *adv* à l'intérieur

**induce** [ɪnˈdus] *vt* ❶ (*persuade*) inciter ❷ (*cause*) provoquer

**induction** [ɪnˈdʌk·ʃ²n] *n* range [*o* **stove**] plaque [*o* **table**] *f* à induction

**indulge** [ɪnˈdʌldʒ] **I.** *vt* ❶ (*allow to enjoy: one's passion, desire*) céder à; **to ~ oneself in sth** s'accorder qc ❷ (*spoil*) gâter; **to ~ oneself** se faire plaisir **II.** *vi* se laisser tenter; **to ~ in sth** (*allow oneself*) s'offrir qc; (*to become involved in*) se livrer à qc

**indulgent** *adj* **to be ~ toward sb/sth** être indulgent envers qn/qc

**industrial** [ɪnˈdʌs·tri·əl] *adj* industriel(le)

**industrialization** *n* industrialisation *f*

**industrialize** [ɪnˈdʌs·tri·ə·laɪz] **I.** *vt* industrialiser **II.** *vi* s'industrialiser

**industrial park** *n* zone *f* industrielle

**industry** [ˈɪn·də·stri] *n* industrie *f*; **computer/electricity ~** industrie électronique/électrique

**inebriated** [ɪˈni·bri·eɪ·t̬ɪd] *adj* enivré(e)

**inedible** [ɪnˈed·ɪ·bl] *adj* ❶ (*not for eating*) non comestible ❷ *pej* (*unfit to be eaten*) immangeable

**ineffective** [ˌɪn·ɪ·ˈfek·tɪv] *adj* inefficace

**ineffectual** [ˌɪn·ɪ·ˈfek·tʃu·əl] *adj form* inefficace; (*efforts*) vain(e); **to be ~ at doing sth** ne pas être capable de faire qc

**inefficient** *adj* non rentable; (*person, organization*) incompétent(e)

**ineligible** [ɪnˈel·ɪ·dʒə·bl] *adj* inéligible; **to be ~ to +infin** ne pas avoir le droit de +*infin*; **to be ~ for sth** ne pas avoir droit à qc

**inept** [ɪˈnept] *adj* ❶ (*clumsy*) inepte ❷ (*unskilled*) inapte; **to be socially ~** être socialement inadapté

**inequality** [ˌɪn·ɪ·ˈkwa·lə·t̬i] *n* inégalité *f*

**inescapable** [ˌɪn·ɪ·ˈskeɪ·pə·bl] *adj* inéluctable

**inevitable** [ɪnˈev·ɪ·t̬ə·bl] **I.** *adj* inévitable **II.** *n no indef art* **the ~** l'inévitable *m*

**inexact** [ˌɪn·ɪg·ˈzækt] *adj* inexact(e)

**inexcusable** [ˌɪn·ɪk·ˈskju·zə·bl] *adj* inexcusable

**inexhaustible** [ˌɪn·ɪg·ˈzɔ·stə·bl] *adj* inexhaustible

**inexpensive** [ˌɪn·ɪkˈspen(t)·sɪv] *adj* bon marché

**inexperienced** *adj* inexpérimenté(e)

**inexplicable** [ˌɪn· əkˈspli·kə·bl] I. *adj* inexplicable II. *n no indef art* **the ~** l'inexplicable *m*

**infallible** [ɪn·ˈfæl·ə·bl] *adj* infaillible

**infamous** [ˈɪn·fə·məs] *adj* ① (*with bad reputation*) tristement célèbre ② (*horrible*) infâme

**infancy** [ˈɪn·fən(t)·si] *n a. fig* enfance *f*

**infant** *n* enfant *m;* **newborn ~** nouveau-né *m*

**infantile** [ˈɪn·fən·taɪl] *adj pej* infantile

**infantry** [ˈɪn·fən·tri] *n* MIL **the ~** + *sing/ pl vb* l'infanterie *f*

**infatuated** [ɪn·ˈfætʃ·u·eɪ·tɪd] *adj* **to be ~ with sb/sth** être entiché de qn/qc; **to become ~ with sb/sth** s'enticher de qn/qc

**infect** [ɪn·ˈfekt] *vt* ① (*contaminate*) *a. fig, pej* contaminer; **to ~ sb with sth** transmettre qc à qn; **to become ~ed** s'infecter ② (*pass on sth desirable: one's laugh, good humor*) communiquer; **to ~ sb with sth** communiquer qc à qn

**infection** *n* MED infection *f*

**infectious** *adj a.* MED contagieux(-euse)

**inferior** [ɪn·ˈfɪr·ɪ·ər] I. *adj* inférieur(e) II. *n* subalterne *mf*

**inferiority complex** *n* complexe *m* d'infériorité

**inferno** [ɪn·ˈfɜr·noʊ] *n* brasier *m*

**infertile** [ɪn·ˈfɜr·t̬ə l] *adj* ① MED (*man, woman*) stérile ② AGR (*land*) infertile

**infest** [ɪn·ˈfest] *vt a. fig* infester

**infidelity** [ˌɪn·fə·ˈdel·ə·t̬i] <-ies> *n* infidélité *f*

**infinite** [ˈɪn·fə·nɪt] I. *adj a.* MATH infini(e) II. *n* **the Infinite** l'infini *m*

**infinitive** [ɪn·ˈfɪn·ə·t̬ɪv] LING I. *n* infinitif *m* II. *adj* infinitif(-ive)

**infinity** [ɪn·ˈfɪn·ə·t̬i] *n* ① (*in distance, extent*) *a.* MATH infini *m* ② (*state, huge amount*) infinitude *f*

**infirm** [ɪn·ˈfɜrm] *adj* infirme

**infirmary** [ɪn·ˈfɜr·mˀə·ri] *n* MED ① (*hospi-tal*) hôpital *m* ② (*sick room*) infirmerie *f*

**inflame** [ɪn·ˈfleɪm] *vt* ① (*provoke, inten-sify: emotions, feelings*) enflammer ② (*stir up*) **to ~ sb** mettre qn en colère

**inflammable** [ɪn·ˈflæm·ə·bl] *adj* ① (*burning easily*) inflammable ② *fig* explosif(-ive)

**inflammation** [ˌɪn·flə·ˈmeɪ·ʃən] *n* MED inflammation *f*

**inflammatory** [ɪn·ˈflæm·ə·tɔr·i] *adj* ① MED (*disease, arthritis*) inflammatoire ② (*language, statement, speech*) incen-diaire

**inflatable** [ɪn·ˈfleɪ·t̬ə·bl] I. *adj* gonflable II. *n* pneumatique *m*

**inflate** [ɪn·ˈfleɪt] I. *vt a.* ECON gonfler II. *vi* se gonfler

**inflated** *adj a.* ECON gonflé(e) ② *pej, form* LING enflé(e)

**inflation** [ɪn·ˈfleɪ·ʃən] *n* ① FIN, ECON infla-tion *f* ② (*of balloon, ball*) gonflement *m*

**inflationary** *adj* FIN inflationniste

**inflexible** [ɪn·ˈflek·sə·bl] *adj* (*person*) inflexible; (*object*) rigide

**influence** [ˈɪn·flu·ən(t)s] I. *n* influence *f;* **to be an ~ on sb/sth** avoir de l'in-fluence sur qn/qc ▸ **to be under the ~** (*drunk*) être sous l'effet de l'alcool; **driving under the ~** conduire en état d'ivresse II. *vt* influencer

**influential** *adj* influent(e)

**influenza** [ˌɪn·flu·ˈen·zə] *n form* MED grippe *f*

**influx** [ˈɪn·flʌks] *n* influx *m*

**inform** [ɪn·ˈfɔrm] *vt* informer; **to ~ the police** alerter la police; **to ~ sb what/ when/where/whether ...** dire à qn ce que/quand/où/si ...

**informal** *adj* informel(le); (*meeting, in-vitation*) non officiel(le); (*manner, style*) simple; (*atmosphere, clothes*) décontracté(e); (*party, dinner*) sans cérémonie; (*announcement, talks*) officieux(-euse)

**informant** [ɪn·ˈfɔr·mənt] *n* informateur, -trice *m, f*

**information** [ˌɪn·fər·ˈmeɪ·ʃən] *n* infor-mation *f*

**information science** n informatique f

**information superhighway** n autoroute f de l'information

**information technology** n technologie f de l'information

**informative** [ɪnˈfɔr·mə·t̬ɪv] adj informatif(-ive)

**informer** n délateur, -trice m, f

**infrared** [ˈɪn·frəˈred] adj infrarouge

**infrastructure** [ˈɪn·frəˌstrʌk·tʃər] n infrastructure f

**infrequent** [ɪnˈfri·kwənt] adj rare

**infuriate** [ɪnˈfjʊr·iˌeɪt] vt to ~ sb rendre qn furieux

**infusion** [ɪnˈfju·ʒən] n ❶ ECON (*input*) investissement m ❷ MED (*of blood, plasma*) perfusion f ❸ (*brewed drink*) infusion f

**ingratitude** [ɪnˈɡræt̬·əˌtud] n ingratitude f

**ingredient** [ɪnˈgri·di·ənt] n ❶ (*in recipe*) ingrédient m ❷ (*component*) composant m

**inhabit** [ɪnˈhæb·ɪt] vt habiter (dans)

**inhabitable** adj habitable

**inhabitant** [ɪnˈhæb·ɪ·t̬ənt] n habitant(e) m(f)

**inhale** [ɪnˈheɪl] vt, vi inhaler

**inherit** [ɪnˈher·ɪt] I. vt a. fig to ~ sth from sb hériter (de) qc de qn II. vi hériter

**inheritance** [ɪnˈher·ɪ·t̬ən(t)s] n a. LAW héritage m

**inhibition** n a. PSYCH inhibition f

**inhospitable** [ɪnˈha·spɪ·t̬ə·bl] adj inhospitalier(-ère)

**inhuman** [ɪnˈhju·mən] adj ❶ a. fig, pej (*cruel*) inhumain(e) ❷ (*non-human*) inhumain(e)

**inhumane** [ˌɪn·hjuˈmeɪn] adj (*cruel*) inhumain(e)

**initial** [ɪˈnɪʃ·əl] I. adj initial(e) II. n initiale f III. <-l- o -ll-> vt parapher

**initially** adv initialement

**initiation** [ɪ·ˌnɪʃ·iˈeɪ·ʃən] n initiation f

**initiative** [ɪˈnɪʃ·ə·t̬ɪv] n initiative f; to show ~ montrer de l'initiative

**inject** [ɪnˈdʒekt] vt MED, ECON injecter

**injection** n ECON, MED injection f

**injure** [ˈɪn·dʒər] vt ❶ (*wound*) blesser

❷ (*damage*) endommager ❸ form (*do wrong to*) causer du tort à

**injured** adj blessé(e)

**injury** [ˈɪn·dʒɚ·i] <-ries> n blessure f

**injustice** [ɪnˈdʒʌs·tɪs] n injustice f

**ink** [ɪŋk] I. n ART, BIO, TYP encre f II. vt ❶ TYP encrer ❷ fig, inf (*sign*) signer

**ink-jet printer** n imprimante f à jet d'encre

**inland** [ˈɪn·lənd] I. adj intérieur(e) II. adv (*go, travel*) vers l'intérieur; (*live*) dans les terres

**in-laws** [ˈɪn·lɔz] npl belle-famille f

**inlet** [ˈɪn·let] n GEO bras m de rivière

**inmate** [ˈɪn·meɪt] n pensionnaire mf

**inn** [ɪn] n auberge f

**inner** [ˈɪn·ər] adj ❶ (*inside, internal*) a. PSYCH intérieur(e) ❷ (*personal*) intime

**inner city** n quartiers mpl défavorisés

**inner-city** adj des quartiers défavorisés; ~ areas quartiers mpl défavorisés

**innermost** adj le/la/les plus intime(s); in sb's ~ being dans le for intérieur de qn; the ~ circle le cœur

**inner tube** n chambre f à air

**innocence** [ˈɪn·ə·sn̩(t)s] n innocence f

**innocent** I. adj innocent(e); (*substance*) inoffensif(-ive); to be ~ of sth être dépourvu de qc II. n innocent(e) m(f)

**innovation** n innovation f

**innuendo** [ˌɪn·juˈen·dou] <-es> n insinuation f; sexual ~ avances fpl sexuelles

**inoculate** [ɪˈna·kjəˌleɪt] vt inoculer

**inoculation** n inoculation f

**inoffensive** [ˌɪn·əˈfen(t)·sɪv] adj inoffensif(-ive)

**inoperable** [ˌɪn·ɑ·pər·ə·bl] adj ❶ MED (*not treatable*) inopérable ❷ (*not functioning*) inopérant(e)

**inordinate** [ɪˈnɔr·dən·ɪt] adj form immodéré(e)

**inpatient** [ˈɪn·peɪ·ʃənt] n patient(e) m(f) hospitalisé(e)

**input** [ˈɪn·pʊt] I. n ❶ no indef art (*resource put into a system*) apport m ❷ (*contribution*) contribution f ❸ ELEC (*place, device*) entrée f; (*power supply*) puissance f d'alimentation ❹ COMPUT saisie *f* (de données) **II.** <-tt-, put *o* putted> *vt* COMPUT entrer

**inquest** ['ɪn·kwest] *n a.* COM *a. fig* enquête *f*

**inquire** [ɪn·'kwaɪr] **I.** *vi* ❶ (*ask for information*) **to ~ about sth** se renseigner sur qc ❷ (*investigate*) **to ~ into a matter** faire des recherches sur un sujet **II.** *vt* demander; **to ~ whether/when ...** demander si/quand ...

**inquiry** [ɪn·'kwaɪ·ri] <-ies> *n* ❶ (*investigation of facts*) recherches *fpl*; **to make inquiries into sth** se renseigner sur qc ❷ LAW investigation *f*; **to hold an ~** faire une enquête

**inquisitive** [ɪn·'kwɪz·ə·t̬ɪv] *adj* curieux(-euse)

**insane** [ɪn·'seɪn] *adj* ❶ MED malsain(e) ❷ *inf* (*crazy*) fou(folle)

**insanitary** [ɪn·'sæn·ɪ·ter·i] *adj* malsain(e)

**insatiable** [ɪn·'seɪ·ʃə·bl] *adj* insatiable

**inscription** [ɪn·'skrɪp·ʃən] *n* ❶ (*handwritten dedication in book*) dédicace *f* ❷ (*inscribed words*) inscription *f*

**insect** ['ɪn·sekt] *n* insecte *m*

**insecticide** [ɪn·'sek·tɪ·saɪd] *n* insecticide *m*

**insecure** [ˌɪn·sɪ·'kjʊr] *adj* ❶ (*lacking confidence*) **to be ~** manquer d'assurance ❷ (*unstable*) instable; (*job, future*) précaire ❸ (*not firm or fixed*) peu solide ❹ (*unsafe: computer system*) vulnérable

**insecurity** [ˌɪn·sɪ·'kjʊr·ə·t̬i] *n* ❶ insécurité *f* ❷ (*lack of self-confidence*) manque *m* d'assurance ❸ (*precariousness*) précarité *f*

**insensitive** [ɪn·'sen(t)·sə·t̬ɪv] *adj a. pej* insensible

**inseparable** [ɪn·'sep·ər·ə·bl] *adj* ❶ (*emotionally close*) stoïque ❷ (*connected*) *a.* LING inséparable

**insert** ['ɪn·sɜrt, *vb:* ɪn·'sɜrt] **I.** *n* ❶ (*in newspaper, book*) insertion *f* ❷ (*in shoe, clothing*) incrustation *f* **II.** *vt* insérer

**inside** [ɪn·'saɪd] **I.** *adj inv, a. fig* (*internal*) intérieur(e); **~ information** infor-

mations *fpl* de première main; **~ joke** plaisanterie *f* maison; **~ job** coup *m* monté de l'intérieur; **~ story** vérité *f* **II.** *n* ❶ (*internal part or side*) intérieur *m*; **to turn sth ~ out** retourner qc; *fig* mettre qc sens dessus dessous; **to know a place ~ out** connaître un endroit comme sa poche ❷ (*one's feelings, sense of right*) for *m* intérieur ❸ *pl, inf* (*of person*) entrailles *fpl*; (*of machine, appliance*) système *m* interne **III.** *prep* (*within*) à l'intérieur de; **from ~ sth** de l'intérieur de qc; **~ of sth** *inf* à l'intérieur de qc; **to play/go ~ the house** jouer/entrer dans la maison **IV.** *adv* ❶ (*within something*) à l'intérieur; **to go ~** entrer ❷ *inf* (*in jail*) en taule ❸ (*internally*) intérieurement; *s.a.* **outside**

**insider** *n* initié(e) *m(f)*

**insight** ['ɪn·saɪt] *n* ❶ *no indef art* (*perception*) perspicacité *f*; **to have ~ into sth** avoir connaissance de qc ❷ (*instance*) aperçu *m*; **to gain ~ into sb/sth** pouvoir se faire une idée de qn/qc; **to give sb ~ into sb/sth** éclairer qn sur qn/qc

**insignificant** *adj* insignifiant(e)

**insist** [ɪn·'sɪst] *vt, vi* insister

**insistence** [ɪn·'sɪs·t̬ən(t)s] *n no indef art* insistance *f*

**insistent** *adj* insistant(e)

**insole** ['ɪn·soʊl] *n* semelle *f* (intérieure)

**insolent** *adj* insolent(e)

**insoluble** [ɪn·'sal·jə·bl] *adj* CHEM insoluble

**insomnia** [ɪn·'sam·ni·ə] *n no indef art* insomnie *f*

**inspect** [ɪn·'spekt] *vt* ❶ (*examine carefully*) *a.* MIL inspecter ❷ (*examine officially*) contrôler

**inspection** *n* inspection *f*; **on closer ~** vu de plus près

**inspector** *n* inspecteur, -trice *m, f*; **ticket ~** contrôleur *m*

**inspiration** [ˌɪn(t)·spə·'reɪ·ʃən] *n* inspiration *f*

**inspire** [ɪn·'spaɪr] *vt a.* MED inspirer

**install** [ɪn·'stɔl] *vt a.* CONSTR, COMPUT, TECH

installer; **to ~ carpeting** poser la moquette

**installation** [ˌɪn·stə·ˈleɪ·ʃən] n ❶ *no indef art* CONSTR installation f ❷ MIL (*place, facility*) site m ❸ (*into an office or position*) institution f ❹ ART forme f

**installment** n ❶ COM acompte m; **to be paid in monthly ~s** être payé par mensualités; **to pay for sth in ~s** payer qc par traites ❷ RADIO, TV (*episode*) épisode m

**installment plan** n COM contrat m de vente à crédit

**instance** [ˈɪn·stən(t)s] I. n ❶ (*particular case*) cas m ❷ **for ~** (*for example*) par exemple ❸ *form* **in the first ~** (*at first*) en premier lieu; **in the second ~** (*later*) en second lieu ❹ *form* (*urging, request, order*) instance f; **to do sth at sb's ~** faire qc à l'instance de qn II. vt *form* **to ~ sth** statuer qc en exemple

**instant** I. adj a. CULIN instantané(e) II. n instant m; **to do sth** (*right*) **this ~** faire qc tout de suite; **not for an ~** pas une seule fois

**instantly** adv immédiatement

**instant replay** n répétition f immédiate; (*in slow motion*) ralenti m

**instead of** [ɪn·ˈsted əv] prep **~ sb/sth** à la place de qn/qc; **~ doing sth ,** au lieu de faire qc

**instinct** [ˈɪn(t)·stɪŋ(k)t] n instinct m; **business/political ~s** sens m des affaires/pour la politique

**instinctive** adj instinctif(-ive)

**institute** [ˈɪn(t)·stɪ·tut] I. n institut m II. vt instituer

**institution** n a. inf institution f

**instruct** [ɪn·ˈstrʌkt] vt ❶ (*teach*) **to ~ sb in sth** instruire qn en qc ❷ (*direct, order formally*) **to ~ sb to +infin** donner l'ordre à qn de +infin

**instruction** n instruction f; **to give sb ~s** donner des instructions à qn; **sb ~s are to +infin** qn a pour instruction de +infin

**instruction book, instruction manual** n livret m d'utilisation

**instruction pamphlet** n notice f (explicative)

**instructive** adj instructif(-ive)

**instructor** n ❶ (*teacher of a skill*) moniteur, -trice m, f ❷ UNIV (*teacher*) professeur mf

**instrument** [ˈɪn(t)·strə·mənt] n a. fig instrument m

**instrumental** I. adj ❶ (*relating to tools*) a. MUS instrumental(e) ❷ (*greatly influential*) **to be ~ to sth** aider à qc; **to be ~ in doing sth** aider à faire qc II. n instrumental m

**insubstantial** [ˌɪn·səb·ˈstæn·(t)ʃəl] adj ❶ (*lacking substance*) formel(le) ❷ (*lacking significance*) négligeable ❸ *form* (*not real*) imaginaire

**insufficiency** [ˌɪn·sə·ˈfɪʃ·ᵊn(t)·si] n insuffisance f

**insufficient** adj insuffisant(e); **to release sb for ~ evidence** relaxer qn pour manque de preuves; **~ funds** FIN défaut m de provision

**insular** [ˈɪn(t)·sə·lər] adj ❶ GEO (*of an island*) insulaire ❷ pej (*narrow-minded*) borné(e)

**insulate** [ˈɪn(t)·sə·leɪt] vt isoler

**insulating** adj isolant(e)

**insulation** n ❶ (*protective covering*) isolant m ❷ (*from outside influences*) isolation f

**insult¹** [ɪn·ˈsʌlt] vt insulter

**insult²** [ˈɪn·sʌlt] n a. fig insulte f ▸ **to add ~ to injury** et pour comble

**insurance** [ɪn·ˈʃʊr·ᵊn(t)s] n ❶ *no indef art* (*financial protection*) assurance f ❷ *no indef art* (*payment by insurance company*) montant m de l'assurance ❸ *no indef art* (*profession*) assurances fpl ❹ *no indef art* (*premium*) prime f d'assurance ❺ (*protective measure*) mesure f de protection

**insurance coverage** n couverture f d'assurance

**insurance policy** <-ies> n police f d'assurance

**insure** [ɪn·ˈʃʊr] vt assurer

**insured** I. adj assuré(e) II. n form LAW **the ~** l'assuré m

**insurer** n ① (agent) assureur m ② (company) assurance f

**intact** [ɪnˈtækt] adj a. fig intact(e)

**integrated** adj ① (included) intégré(e) ② HIST (desegregated: school, education) de déségrégation raciale

**integrated circuit** n circuit m intégré

**intellectual** [ˌɪn·təˈlˈek·tʃu·əl] I. n intellectuel(le) m(f) II. adj intellectuel(le)

**intelligence** [ɪnˈtel·ɪ·dʒ³n(t)s] n ① (brain power) a. COMPUT intelligence f ② + sing/pl vb (inside information) informations fpl ③ (government or espionage agency) service m de renseignements

**intelligence service** n service m de renseignements

**intelligent** adj intelligent(e)

**intend** [ɪnˈtend] vt ① (aim for, plan) avoir l'intention; **to ~ to** +infin avoir l'intention de +infin; **what I ~ is ...** mon intention est ...; **to be ~ed as sth** être censé être qc ② (earmark, destine) **to be ~ed for sb/sth** être destiné à qn/qc; **to be ~ed to** +infin être destiné à +infin

**intended** I. adj ① (intentional) intentionnel(le) ② (planned) prévu(e); (mistake, effect) voulu(e) II. n sing, a. iron, inf fiancé(e) m(f)

**intense** [ɪnˈten(t)s] adj ① (extreme, strong) intense; (pain, excitement) vif(vive); (feeling, interest) profond(e) ② (passionate: person) véhément(e)

**intensify** [ɪnˈten(t)·sɪ·faɪ] I. vt intensifier; (the pressure) augmenter II. vi s'accroître

**intensity** [ɪnˈten(t)·sə·t̬i] n intensité f

**intensive** adj intensif(-ive); (analysis) serré(e)

**intensive care (unit)** n MED (service m des) soins mpl intensifs

**intent** [ɪnˈtent] I. n ① (intention) intention f; **for all ~s and purposes** pratiquement ② LAW préméditation f II. adj ① (concentrated, occupied) absorbé(e); **to be ~ on sb/sth** être tout entier à qn/qc ② (determined) **to be/seem ~ on sth** être/sembler résolu à qc

**intention** [ɪnˈten·(t)ʃ³n] n intention f; **to have no ~ of doing sth** n'avoir nullement l'intention de faire qc

**intentional** adj intentionnel(le)

**interactive** adj interactif(-ive)

**intercept** [ˌɪn·tərˈsept] vt intercepter

**interception** n interception f

**interchange** [ˌɪn·tərˈtʃeɪndʒ] I. n ① form (exchange) échange m ② (on highway) échangeur m (d'autoroute) II. vt échanger III. vi alterner

**interchangeable** adj interchangeable

**intercity** [ˌɪn·tərˈsɪt̬·i] adj interurbain(e)

**intercom** [ˌɪn·tərˈkam] n interphone m

**intercourse** [ˈɪn·tərˌkɔrs] n ① (relationship) rapports mpl; **sexual ~** relations fpl sexuelles ② form fréquentation f

**interest** [ˈɪn·trɪst] I. n ① (curiosity) intérêt m; **to take an ~ in sth** s'intéresser à qc; **to lose ~ in sb/sth** se désintéresser de qn/qc; **to be of ~** être intéressant ② (hobby) centre m d'intérêt; **to pursue one's own ~s** poursuivre ses propres buts ③ (profit, advantage) intérêt m; **to be in sb's ~** être dans l'intérêt de qn ④ FIN (on borrowed money) intérêt m; **rate of ~, ~ rate** taux m d'intérêts ⑤ FIN (stake) intérêt m; **to have an ~ in sb/sth** être intéressé par qn/qc II. vt intéresser; **to ~ sb in sth** susciter l'intérêt de qn pour qc

**interested** adj ① (arousing interest) intéressé(e); **to be ~ in sb/sth** être intéressé par qn/qc; **I am ~ to know more about it** cela m'intéresse d'en savoir plus ② (concerned, involved) intéressé(e); **the ~ parties** les parties fpl concernées

**interesting** adj a. iron intéressant(e)

**interfere** [ˌɪn·tərˈfɪr] vi ① (become involved) **to ~ in sth** se mêler de qc; (private life, relationship) s'immiscer dans qc ② (hinder) **to ~ with sth** gêner qc ③ (disturb) **to ~ with sb/sth** contrarier qn/qc ④ (handle without permission) **to ~ in/with sth** toucher à qc

⑤ RADIO, TECH (*disturb*) **to ~ with sth** perturber qc

**interference** [ˌɪn·tərˈfɪr·ᵊn(t)s] n ❶ (*interfering*) ingérence f; (*in privacy*) intrusion f ❷ RADIO, TECH interférences fpl ❸ SPORTS obstruction f

**interior** [ɪnˈtɪr·i·ər] I. *adj inv* intérieur(e); (*decorator, scene*) d'intérieur II. n ❶ (*inside*) intérieur m ❷ POL (*domestic affairs*) **Department of the Interior** ministère m de l'Intérieur

**interior design** n architecture f d'intérieur

**interior designer** n architecte mf d'intérieur

**intermediary** [ˌɪn·tərˈmi·di·ər·i] <-ries-> I. n intermédiaire mf; **through an ~** par un intermédiaire II. *adj* intermédiaire

**intermediate** [ˌɪn·tərˈmi·di·ət] *adj* intermédiaire; **~ course** cours m de niveau moyen

**intermission** [ˌɪn·tərˈmɪʃ·ᵊn] n ❶ interruption f; **without ~** sans arrêt ❷ THEAT, MUS entracte m; **before/during ~** avant/pendant la pause

**intermittent** [ˌɪn·tərˈmɪt·ᵊnt] *adj* intermittent(e); **she made ~ movie appearances** elle a fait quelques apparitions dans des films

**intern** [ɪnˈtɜrn] I. vt MIL interner II. vi UNIV, SCHOOL **to ~ with a company** faire un stage dans une entreprise III. n ❶ MED interne mf ❷ (*trainee*) stagiaire mf

**internal** *adj* intérieur(e); (*affairs, bleeding, investigation*) interne

**Internal Revenue Service** n ≈ fisc m (*service des impôts*)

**international** [ˌɪn·tərˈnæʃ·ᵊn·ᵊl] I. *adj* international(e) II. n (*communist organization, song*) **the International** l'Internationale f

**Internet** [ˈɪn·tər·net] I. *adj* Internet *inv* II. n Internet m; **the ~** l'Internet m; **to access the ~** accéder à Internet

**Internet access** n accès m Internet

**Internet café** n cybercafé m

**internship** n ❶ MED internat m ❷ (*as trainee*) stage m

**interphone** [ˌɪn·tərˈfoʊn] n s. **intercom**

**interplay** [ˈɪn·tərˌpleɪ] n interaction f

**Interpol** [ˈɪn·tərˌpɑl] n *no art abbr of* **International Criminal Police Commission** Interpol m

**interpret** [ɪnˈtɜr·prət] I. vt interpréter II. vi faire l'interprète

**interpretation** n a. THEAT, LIT interprétation f; **to be open to ~** être sujet à interprétation

**interpreter** n ❶ LIT, THEAT interprète mf ❷ (*oral translator*) interprète mf ❸ (*type of computer program*) interprète m

**interrogate** [ɪnˈter·ə·ɡeɪt] vt ❶ (*cross-question*) questionner ❷ (*get data from computer*) consulter

**interrogation** n interrogation f; **under ~** en train de subir un interrogatoire

**interrogative** [ˌɪn·tərˈrɑ·ɡə·tɪv] I. n LING interrogatif m II. *adj* ❶ (*having questioning form*) interrogatif(·trice) ❷ LING (*pronoun*) interrogatif(·ive)

**interrupt** [ˌɪn·tərˈrʌpt] vt interrompre; **will you stop ~ing me!** arrête de me couper la parole

**interruption** n interruption f; **~ in the flow of food** rupture f dans la chaîne alimentaire; **without ~** sans arrêt

**intersection** n ❶ (*crossing of lines*) intersection f ❷ (*crossroads*) croisement m, carrefour m

**interval** [ˈɪn·tər·vᵊl] n ❶ (*period*) intervalle m; **at five minute ~s** à cinq minutes d'intervalle ❷ METEO période f; **sunny ~s** éclaircies fpl ensoleillées ❸ MUS, MATH intervalle m

**intervene** [ˌɪn·tərˈvin] vi ❶ intervenir; **to ~ on sb's behalf** intervenir au nom de qn ❷ (*meddle unhelpfully*) interférer ❸ (*come to pass between*) s'écouler

**intervening** *adj inv* intermédiaire; **in the ~ period** entre-temps

**intervention** [ˌɪn·tərˈven·(t)ʃᵊn] n intervention f

**interview** [ˈɪn·tərˌvju] I. n ❶ (*for job*)

entretien *m* ❷ PUBL, RADIO, TV interview *f* **II.** *vt* ❶ *(for job)* faire passer un entretien à ❷ PUBL, RADIO, TV interviewer **III.** *vi* ❶ *(for job)* faire passer des entretiens ❷ PUBL, RADIO, TV faire une interview

**interviewee** [ˌɪn·tər·vjuˈi] *n* ❶ *(for job)* candidat(e) *m(f)* ❷ PUBL, RADIO, TV interviewé(e) *m(f)*

**interviewer** *n* ❶ PUBL, RADIO, TV interviewer *m* ❷ *(for job)* directeur, -trice *m, f* du personnel

**intestinal** *adj* intestinal(e)

**intestine** [ɪn·ˈtes·tɪn] *n* MED intestin *m*

**intimate¹** [ˈɪn·tə·mət] **I.** *adj* ❶ *(close)* intime; ~ **circle** cercle *m* d'intimes ❷ *(very detailed)* approfondi(e) **II.** *n* intime *mf*

**intimate²** [ˈɪn·tə·meɪt] *vt* signifier

**intimidate** [ɪn·ˈtɪ·mɪ·deɪt] *vt* intimider; **to ~ sb into doing sth** décourager qn de faire qc

**intimidating** *adj* intimidant(e)

**intimidation** *n* intimidation *f*

**into** [ˈɪn·tə] *prep* ❶ dans ❷ *(movement to inside)* **to come/go ~ a place** entrer dans un lieu; **to put sth ~ it/place** mettre qc dedans/en place; **to get/let sb ~ a car** monter/faire monter qn en voiture ❸ *(movement toward)* **to walk** [*o* **drive**] ~ **a tree** percuter un arbre; **to run** [*o* **bump**] ~ **sb/sth** tomber sur qn/qc ❹ *(through time of)* **to work late ~ the night** travailler tard dans la nuit ❺ *(change to)* **to put sth ~ English** traduire qc en anglais; **to change bills ~ coins** changer des billets contre des pièces ❻ *(begin)* **to burst ~ tears/ laughter** éclater en sanglots/de rire; **to get ~ the habit of doing sth** prendre l'habitude de faire qc ❼ *(make smaller)* **to cut sth ~ two/slices** couper qc en deux/tranches; **3 goes ~ 6 twice** 6 divisé par 3 donne 2 ❽ *inf (interested in)* **to be ~ sb/sth** être dingue de qn/qc

**intolerable** *adj* intolérable; **an ~ place to live in** un lieu où il est insupportable de vivre

**intolerant** *adj* intolérant(e); **lactose/alcohol ~** MED intolérant au lactose/à l'alcool

**intoxicating** *adj* a. *fig* enivrant(e); **an ~ drink** une boisson alcoolisée

**intoxication** *n* ❶ a. *fig* ivresse *f* ❷ MED intoxication *f*

**intransitive** [ɪn·ˈtræn(t)·sə·tɪv] LING **I.** *adj* intransitif(-ive) **II.** *n* intransitif *m*

**intricacy** [ˈɪn·trɪ·kə·si] <-cies> *n* complexité *f*

**intricate** [ˈɪn·trɪ·kət] *adj* ❶ *(complicated)* compliqué(e) ❷ *(complex)* complexe

**intrigue** [ˈɪn·trig, *vb:* ɪn·ˈtrig] **I.** *n* intrigue *f*; ~ **against sb/sth** machination *f* contre qn/qc **II.** *vt* éveiller la curiosité de; **to be ~d by sth** être intrigué par qc **III.** *vi* intriguer

**intriguing** *adj* mystérieux(-euse)

**introduce** [ˌɪn·trə·ˈdus] *vt* ❶ *(acquaint)* **to ~ sb to sb** présenter qn à qn; **to ~ oneself** se présenter ❷ *(raise interest in subject)* **to ~ sb to sth** faire connaître qc à qn ❸ *(bring in)* introduire; *(law, controls)* établir; *(products)* lancer ❹ *(insert)* introduire ❺ *(announce)* présenter

**introduction** [ˌɪn·trə·ˈdʌk·ʃən] *n* ❶ *(making first acquaintance)* présentation *f*; **letter of ~** lettre *f* de recommandation; **to serve as an ~ to sth** servir d'introduction à qc ❷ *(establishment)* introduction *f*; ~ **into the market** lancement *m* sur le marché ❸ MED *(insertion)* introduction *f* ❹ *(preliminary section)* introduction *f*

**introductory** [ˌɪn·trə·ˈdʌk·tə·ri] *adj* d'introduction; *(price)* de lancement

**intrude** [ɪn·ˈtrud] **I.** *vi* ❶ *(go where shouldn't be)* s'ingérer; **to ~ on sb** faire intrusion auprès de qn ❷ *(meddle)* s'immiscer **II.** *vt* ❶ *(force in)* imposer ❷ GEO pénétrer

**intruder** *n* ❶ *(unwelcome visitor)* importun *m* ❷ LAW *(burglar, thief)* intrus(e) *m(f)*

**intrusion** [ɪn·ˈtru·ʒən] *n* a. GEO intrusion *f*

**intrusive** [ɪn·ˈtru·sɪv] *adj* importun(e)

**invade** [ɪnˈveɪd] *vt a. fig* envahir; **to ~ sb's privacy** porter atteinte à la vie privée de qn

**invalid¹** [ˈɪn·və·lɪd] **I.** *n* invalide *mf* **II.** *adj* invalide

**invalid²** [ɪnˈvæl·ɪd] *adj* ❶ *(not legally binding)* non valide ❷ *(unsound)* nul(le) et non avenu(e)

**invaluable** [ɪnˈvæl·ju·ə·bl] *adj* inestimable

**invariable** [ɪnˈver·i·ə·bl] *adj* invariable

**invasion** [ɪnˈveɪ·ʒən] *n* ❶ MIL invasion *f* ❷ *(interference: of privacy)* intrusion *f*

**invent** [ɪnˈvent] *vt* inventer

**invention** *n* invention *f*; **power(s) of ~** force *f* d'imagination

**inventive** *adj* inventif(-ive)

**inventor** *n* inventeur, -trice *m, f*

**inventory** [ˈɪn·vən·tɔr·i] <-ies> *n* inventaire *m; (stock)* stock *m;* **to take ~** faire l'inventaire; *fig* recenser

**invertebrate** [ɪnˈvɜr·tə·brɪt] **I.** *adj* invertébré(e) **II.** *n* ZOOL invertébré *m*

**invest** [ɪnˈvest] **I.** *vt* investir; **to ~ time and effort in sth** investir du temps et des efforts dans qc **II.** *vi* investir; **to ~ in sth** investir dans qc

**investigate** [ɪnˈves·tɪ·ɡeɪt] *vt (a case, crime)* enquêter sur; **to ~ how/ whether/why …** rechercher comment/si/pourquoi …

**investigation** *n* enquête *f*

**investigative** *adj* investigateur(-trice); **~ journalism** journalisme *m* d'investigation

**investigator** *n* enquêteur, -trice *m, f*

**investment** [ɪnˈves(t)·mənt] *n* investissement *m*

**investment fund** *n* fonds *mpl* d'investissement

**investment trust** *n* société *f* d'investissement

**investor** *n* investisseur *m*

**invigorating** *adj* ❶ *(giving strength)* revigorant(e) ❷ *fig (stimulating, heartening)* stimulant(e)

**invincible** [ɪnˈvɪn(t)·sə·bl] *adj* invincible; **~ will** volonté *f* de fer

**invisible** [ɪnˈvɪz·ə·bl] *adj a.* ECON invisible; **~ ink** encre *f* sympathique

**invitation** [ɪn·vɪˈteɪ·ʃən] *n* invitation *f*; **~ to sth** invitation à qc

**invite** [ˈɪn·vaɪt, *vb:* ɪnˈvaɪt] **I.** *n inf* invitation *f* **II.** *vt* ❶ *(request to attend)* inviter; **to ~ sb for/to sth** inviter qn à qc ❷ *(formally request)* solliciter ❸ *(provoke, tempt reaction)* encourager; **to ~ criticism** encourager la critique

**inviting** *adj* ❶ *(attractive: look, prospect)* attirant(e) ❷ *(tempting)* tentant(e)

**invoice** [ˈɪn·vɔɪs] **I.** *vt (goods)* facturer; *(a client)* envoyer une facture à **II.** *n* facture *f*

**involuntary** [ɪnˈvɑ·lən·ter·i] *adj* involontaire

**involve** [ɪnˈvɑlv] *vt* ❶ *(concern, affect)* impliquer ❷ *(include, number among)* inclure ❸ *(entail, necessitate)* nécessiter

**involved** *adj* ❶ *(complicated: story)* embrouillé(e) ❷ *(connected with, mixed up in)* impliqué(e); **to be ~ in sth** être mêlé à qc

**involvement** *n* ❶ *(commitment)* engagement *m* ❷ *(participation)* participation *f*

**inward** [ˈɪn·wərd] **I.** *adj* ❶ *(toward center)* intérieur(e) ❷ *(personal, private: life)* intime; *(doubts, reservations)* profond(e) **II.** *adv* ❶ *(toward center)* vers l'intérieur ❷ *(toward the mind)* à l'intérieur

**inwardly** *adv* intérieurement

**inwards** *adv s.* **inward** II.

**in-your-face** *adj inf* cru(e)

**IOU** [ˌaɪ·oʊˈju] *n a. fig, inf abbr of* **I owe you** reconnaissance *f* de dette

**Iowa** [ˈaɪə·wə] *n* l'Iowa *m*

**IQ** [ˌaɪˈkju] *n abbr of* **intelligence quotient** QI *m*

**IRA** [ˌaɪ·ɑrˈeɪ] *n abbr of* **Irish Republican Army** IRA *f*

**Iran** [ɪˈræn] *n* l'Iran *m*

**Iranian** [ɪˈreɪ·ni·ən] **I.** *adj* iranien(ne) **II.** *n* Iranien(ne) *m(f)*

**Iraq** [ɪˈræk] *n* l'Irak *m*

**Iraqi I.** *adj* irakien(ne) **II.** *n* Irakien(ne) *m(f)*

**irate** [aɪˈreɪt] *adj* furieux(-euse)

**Ireland** [ˈaɪrˌlənd] *n* l'Irlande *f*; Republic of ~ République *f* d'Irlande

**Irish** [ˈaɪˌrɪʃ] **I.** *adj* irlandais(e) **II.** *n* ❶ (*people*) **the** ~ les Irlandais ❷ LING irlandais *m*; *s.a.* **English**

**Irishman** *n* Irlandais *m*

**Irishwoman** *n* Irlandaise *f*

**iron** [ˈaɪ·ərn] **I.** *adj* (*discipline, will*) de fer **II.** *n* ❶ (*metal*) fer *m* ❷ (*for pressing clothes*) fer *m* à repasser; **steam** ~ fer *m* à vapeur ❸ SPORTS (*golf club*) fer *m* ▸ **to have many** ~**s in the fire** avoir plusieurs cordes à son arc **III.** *vt* (*shirt, blouse*) repasser; **to** ~ **sth out** *fig* (*disagreements, problems*) arranger qc **IV.** *vi* repasser

**Iron Age** *n* l'âge *m* de fer

**Iron Curtain** *n* HIST rideau *m* de fer

**iron fist** *n s.* **iron hand** ▸ **an** ~ **in a velvet glove** une main de fer dans un gant de velours *prov*

**iron hand** *n* main *f* de fer; **to rule with an** ~ gouverner qc d'une main de fer

**ironic, ironical** *adj* ironique

**ironing** *n* repassage *m*

**ironing board** *n* table *f* à repasser

**ironware** *n* ferronnerie *f*

**irony** [ˈaɪ·rən·i] *n* ironie *f*

**irrational** [ɪˈræʃ·ən·əl] *adj* irrationnel(le)

**irrecoverable** [ˌɪr·ɪˈkʌv·ər·ə·bl] *adj* irrécouvrable; **a financial loss** une perte financière irrécupérable

**irregular** [ɪˈreg·jə·lər] **I.** *adj* ❶ *a.* LING, MIL irrégulier(-ère) ❷ *form* (*abnormal, peculiar: behavior, habits*) désordonné(e) **II.** *n* MIL (*unofficial soldier*) soldat *m* irrégulier

**irregularity** <-ies> *n* irrégularité *f*

**irrelevant** *adj* non pertinent(e)

**irreparable** [ɪˈrep·ər·ə·bl] *adj* irréparable

**irreplaceable** [ˌɪr·ɪˈpleɪ·sə·bl] *adj* irremplaçable

**irresistible** [ˌɪr·ɪˈzɪs·tə·bl] *adj* irrésistible

**irresponsible** [ˌɪr·ɪˈspan(t)·sə·bl] *adj* irresponsable

**irreverent** [ɪˈrev·ər·ənt] *adj* irrévérencieux(-euse)

**irreversible** [ˌɪr·ɪˈvɜr·sə·bl] *adj* irréversible; (*decision*) irrévocable

**irrigation** *n* ❶ AGR irrigation *f* ❷ MED (*washing*) lavage *m*

**irritable** [ˈɪr·ɪ·tə·bl] *adj* irritable

**irritate** [ˈɪr·ɪ·teɪt] *vt a.* MED irriter

**irritation** *n a.* MED irritation *f*

**IRS** [ˌaɪ·arˈes] *n abbr of* **Internal Revenue Service** ≈fisc *m*

**is** [ɪz] *3ʳᵈ pers sing of* **be**

**ISDN** *n* TEL *abbr of* **Integrated Services Digital Network** RNIS *m*

**Islam** [ɪzˈlam] *n no art* l'Islam *m*

**Islamic** [ɪzˈla·mɪk] *adj* islamique

**island** [ˈaɪ·lənd] *n a. fig* île *f*

**islander** *n* insulaire *mf*

**isn't** [ˈɪz·ənt] = **is not** *s.* **be**

**isolate** [ˈaɪ·sə·leɪt] *vt* isoler

**isolated** *adj* isolé(e)

**isolation** *n* isolement *m*

**isolation unit** *n* salle *f* de quarantaine

**isosceles triangle** [aɪˈsa·sˌəl·iz·ˌtraɪ·æŋ·gl] *n* MATH triangle *m* isocèle

**Israel** [ˈɪz·ri·əl] *n* Israël *m sans art*

**Israeli I.** *adj* israélien(ne) **II.** *n* Israélien(ne) *m(f)*

**Israelite** [ˈɪz·ri·ə·laɪt] *n* Israélite *mf*

**issue** [ˈɪʃ·u] **I.** *n* ❶ (*problem, topic*) question *f*; **at** ~ (*in discussion, controversial*) controversé(e); **to take** ~ **with sb over sth** *form* prendre le contre-pied de qn sur qc ❷ (*single publication*) numéro *m* ❸ FIN, ECON (*distribution of stock, stamps*) émission *f* **II.** *vt* ❶ (*put out*) délivrer; **to** ~ **an arrest warrant** diffuser un avis de recherche ❷ (*make public: bank notes, statement*) émettre; (*communiqué, newsletter*) rendre public **III.** *vi* **to** ~ **from sth** *form* sortir de qc

**it** [ɪt] **I.** *dem pron* ce, c' + *vowel*; **who was** ~**?** qui était-ce?; ~ **is ...** c'est ..., ça est ... *Belgique*; ~ **all** tout cela **II.** *pers pron* il, elle **III.** *impers pron* il; **what time is** ~**?** quelle heure est-il?;

~'s **cold**, ~'s **snowing** il fait froid, il neige; ~ **seems that ...** il semble que ... **IV.** *objective pron* ❶ *(direct object)* le, la, l' + *vowel;* **I can do** ~ je peux le/la faire ❷ *(indirect object)* lui; **give** ~ **something to eat** donne-lui à manger ❸ *(prepositional object)* **I heard about** ~ j'en ai entendu parler; **I'm afraid of** ~ j'en ai peur; **I went to** ~ j'y suis allé; **think of** ~ pensez-y ❹ *(non-specific object)* en; **to have** ~ **in for sb** en avoir après qn ▸ **that's** ~**!** ça y est!; *(in anger)* ça suffit!; **this is** ~**!** nous y sommes!

**IT** [ˌaɪˈti] *n* COMPUT *abbr of* **Information Technology** informatique *f*

**Italian** [ɪˈtæl·jən] **I.** *adj* italien(ne) **II.** *n* ❶ *(person)* Italien(ne) *m(f)* ❷ LING italien *m; s.a.* **English**

**italic** [ɪˈtæl·ɪk] **I.** *adj* italique; ~ **type** caractère *m* en italique **II.** *n pl* COMPUT, TYP italiques *mpl;* **in** ~ **s** en italique

**italicize** [ɪˈtæl·ɪ·saɪz] *vt* TYP **to** ~ **sth** mettre qc en italique

**Italy** [ˈɪt·ªl·i] *n* l'Italie *f*

**itch** [ɪtʃ] **I.** *vi a. inf* démanger **II.** *n* démangeaison *f*

**itchy** <-ier, -iest> *adj* irritant(e)

**item** [ˈaɪ·təm] *n* ❶ *(point, thing)* a. COM-PUT article *m;* ~ **by** ~ point par point; **news** ~ nouvelle *f* ❷ *inf (couple in relationship)* couple *m*

**itemize** [ˈaɪ·təm·aɪz] *vt* **to** ~ **sth** présenter qc point par point

**itinerary** [aɪˈtɪn·ər·er·i] <-ies> *n* itinéraire *m*

**it'll** [ˈɪt·l] = **it will** *s.* **be**

**its** [ɪts] *poss adj (of sth)* son, sa, ses *pl;* **the cat hurt** ~ **head** le chat s'est blessé à la tête

**it's** [ɪts] = **it is** *s.* **be**

**itself** [ɪtˈself] *reflex pron* ❶ *after verbs* se, s' + *vowel* ❷ *(specifically)* lui-même, elle-même; **the plan in** ~ le plan en soi; **the door closes by** ~ la porte se ferme toute seule; *s.a.* **myself**

**I've** [aɪv] = **I have** *s.* **have**

**ivory** [ˈaɪ·vər·i] <-ies> **I.** *n* ❶ *(from elephants' tusks)* ivoire *m* ❷ *pl (ivory goods)* ivoirerie *f* ❸ *pl, iron, inf (keys of piano)* touches *fpl* de piano **II.** *adj* ❶ *(substance)* en ivoire ❷ *(color)* ivoire *inv*

**ivy** [ˈaɪ·vi] <-ies> *n* lierre *m*

# J j

**J, j** [dʒeɪ] <-'s o -s> n J, j m; **~ as in Juliet** (on telephone) j comme Joseph

**jab** [dʒæb] **I.** n ① (shove) coup m ② SPORTS direct m **II.** <-bb-> vt ① (poke or prick) planter ② (plug) prise f ② (push) **to ~ sth in(to) sth** donner des coups de qc dans qc **III.** <-bb-> vi ① SPORTS **to ~ at sb** lancer un direct à qn ② (thrust at) **to ~ at sb/sth with sth** donner un coup de qc à qn/qc

**jack** [dʒæk] n ① TECH vérin m ② AUTO cric m ③ (card) valet m ④ (plug) prise f ⑤ (in lawn bowling) cochonnet m ⑥ sl (nothing) **to not know ~ about sth** savoir que dalle sur qc
♦**jack off** vt, vi vulg s. **jerk off**
♦**jack up** vt ① (raise: car, truck) soulever ② fig, inf (prices, rent) faire grimper

**jackass** ['dʒæk·æs] n ① ZOOL âne m ② inf (idiot) crétin(e) m(f)

**jacket** ['dʒæk·ɪt] n ① FASHION veste f ② (of book) couverture f ③ MUS pochette f

**jacket potato** n pomme de terre f en robe des champs

**jackpot** ['dʒæk·pɑt] n jackpot m; **to hit the ~** ramasser le gros lot; fig, inf décrocher la timbale

**Jacuzzi®** [dʒə·'ku·zi] n jacuzzi® m

**jaded** ['dʒeɪd·ɪd] adj **to be ~ with sth** être las de qc

**jagged** ['dʒæg·ɪd] adj déchiqueté(e); (coastline) découpé(e); (rock) pointu(e); (speech, cut) irrégulier(-ère)

**jail** [dʒeɪl] **I.** n prison f; **to put sb in ~** incarcérer qn **II.** vt emprisonner; **to ~ sb for three months** condamner qn à trois mois de prison

**jailbreak** ['dʒeɪl·breɪk] n évasion f (de prison); **to attempt a ~** faire une tentative d'évasion

**jailer** ['dʒeɪ·lər], **jailor** ['dʒeɪ·lər] n gardien(ne) m(f) de prison

**jam¹** [dʒæm] n confiture f

**jam²** [dʒæm] **I.** n ① inf (awkward situation) pétrin m ② (crowd) cohue f; **traffic ~** AUTO embouteillage m ③ (in machine) bourrage m ④ MUS bœuf m **II.** <-mm-> vt ① (cause to become stuck) coincer; (machine, mechanism) bloquer ② (cram) **to ~ sth into sth** fourrer qc dans qc ③ RADIO brouiller **III.** <-mm-> vi ① (become stuck) se coincer; (brakes, photocopier) se bloquer ② (play music) faire des improvisations collectives de jazz

**jam-packed** [ˌdʒæm·'pækt] adj inf bondé(e); **to be ~ (with people)** être plein à craquer

**janitor** ['dʒæn·ə·tər] n concierge mf

**January** ['dʒæn·ju·er·i] n janvier m; s.a. **April**

**Japan** [dʒə·'pæn] n le Japon

**Japanese** [ˌdʒæp·ə·n·'iz] **I.** adj japonais(e) **II.** n ① (person) Japonais(e) m(f) ② LING japonais m; s.a. **English**

**jar¹** [dʒɑr] n ① (container) jarre f; (of jam) pot m ② (amount) pot m

**jar²** [dʒɑr] **I.** <-rr-> vt ébranler; (person) choquer; **to ~ one's elbow** se cogner le coude **II.** <-rr-> vi ① (cause feelings) **to ~ on sb** froisser qn ② (make a sound) rendre un son discordant ③ (be unsuitable: effect) ne pas être à sa place; **to ~ with sth** jurer avec qc **III.** n secousse f

**javelin** ['dʒæv·əl·ɪn] n javelot m

**jaw** [dʒɔ] **I.** n ① ANAT mâchoire f ② pl (mouth) gueule f **II.** vi inf papoter; **to ~ at sb** faire un sermon à qn

**jawbreaker** ['dʒɔ·ˌbreɪ·kər] n ① (sweet) bonbon m dur ② sl (tongue twister) mot m imprononçable

**jazz** [dʒæz] n ① MUS jazz m ② pej, inf (nonsense) baratin m ▸ **and all that ~** pej, inf et tout le tremblement
♦**jazz up** vt inf ① MUS adapter pour le jazz ② (brighten or enliven) égayer; **to**

**~ food with spices** relever la nourriture avec des épices

**jazzy** ['dʒæz·i] <-ier, -iest> *adj* ❶MUS jazzy *inv* ❷*inf* (*flashy*) voyant(e)

**jealous** ['dʒel·əs] *adj* ❶(*envious*) jaloux(-ouse) ❷(*protective*) **to keep a ~ watch over sb** surveiller qn d'un œil jaloux

**jealousy** ['dʒel·ə·si] <-ies> *n* jalousie *f*

**jeans** [dʒinz] *npl* jean(s) *m*

**jeer** [dʒɪr] I. *vt* huer II. *vi* railler; **to ~ at sb** se moquer de qn III. *n* raillerie *f*

**jelly** ['dʒel·i] <-ies> *n* gelée *f*; (*jam*) confiture *f*

**jellyfish** ['dʒel·i·fɪʃ] <-es> *n* ❶ZOOL méduse *f* ❷*inf* (*person*) lopette *f*

**jeopardize** ['dʒep·ər·daɪz] *vt* mettre en danger

**jerk** [dʒɜrk] I. *n* ❶(*movement*) secousse *f*; (*pull*) coup *m* sec ❷*inf* (*stupid person*) pauvre crétin(e) *m(f)* ❸SPORTS épaulé-jeté *m* II. *vi* tressaillir; **to ~ to a halt** s'arrêter brusquement III. *vt* ❶(*move*) donner une secousse à ❷SPORTS (*weight*) faire un épaulé-jeté ▶ **to ~ sb's chain** *sl* casser les pieds à qn
 ◆ **jerk around** *vt* abuser
 ◆ **jerk off** *vi vulg* se branler

**jerky** ['dʒɜr·ki] I. <-ier, -iest> *adj* saccadé(e) II. *n* **beef ~** du bœuf séché en lanières

**jersey** ['dʒɜr·zi] *n* ❶(*garment*) tricot *m* ❷SPORTS maillot *m* ❸(*cloth*) jersey *m*

**Jesus** ['dʒi·zəs] I. *n no art* Jésus *m*; **~ Christ** Jésus-Christ *m* II. *interj vulg* **~ (Christ)!** nom de Dieu!

**jet¹** [dʒet] I. *n* ❶(*plane*) avion *m* à réaction ❷(*stream*) jet *m* ❸(*hole*) gicleur *m* II. <-tt-> *vi* ❶(*fly*) **to be ~ting in from Paris** arriver de Paris en avion; **to be ~ting off to New York** s'envoler pour New York ❷(*spurt*) gicler

**jet²** [dʒet] *n* (*stone*) jais *m*

**jet fighter** *n* chasseur *m* à réaction

**jet lag** *n* décalage *m* horaire

**jet-propelled** [‚dʒet·prə·'peld] *adj* à réaction

**jet set** ['dʒet·set] *n inf* **the ~** le [*o* la] jet-set

**jetty** ['dʒet·i] *n* ❶(*pier*) embarcadère *m* ❷(*breakwater*) jetée *f*

**Jew** [dʒu] *n* Juif *m*, Juive *f*

**jewel** ['dʒu·əl] *n* ❶(*stone*) pierre *f* précieuse ❷(*watch part*) rubis *m* ❸ *a. fig* joyau *m* ▶ **the crown ~s** les joyaux *mpl* de la couronne

**jewel(l)er** ['dʒu·ə·lər] *n* bijoutier, -ière *m, f*; **~'s** (*shop*) bijouterie *f*

**jewelry** ['dʒu·əl·ri] *n* bijouterie *f*

**Jewish** ['dʒu·ɪʃ] *adj* juif(juive)

**jiffy** ['dʒɪf·i] *n inf* **in a ~** en un clin d'œil; **she'll be back in a ~** elle revient tout de suite

**jigsaw (puzzle)** *n a. fig* puzzle *m*

**jingle** ['dʒɪŋ·gl] I. *vi* tinter II. *vt* faire tinter III. *n* ❶(*noise*) tintement *m* ❷(*in advertisements*) jingle *m*

**jinx** [dʒɪŋks] I. *n* porte-malheur *m*; **to break the ~** échapper à la guigne; **to put a ~ on sb/sth** jeter un sort à qn/qc II. *vt* porter malheur à; **to be ~ed** avoir la guigne

**job** [dʒab] *n* ❶(*work*) emploi *m*; **to get a ~** trouver un travail; **his ~ at the factory** son boulot *m* à l'usine ❷(*piece of work*) tâche *f*; **to do a good ~ of sth** se surpasser dans qc ❸(*duty*) travail *m* ▶ **to do the ~** *inf* faire l'affaire

**job counselor** *n* conseiller, -ère *m, f* de l'emploi

**job-hunt** *vi* **to be ~ing** être à la recherche d'un emploi

**job interview** *n* entretien *m* d'embauche

**jobseeker** *n* demandeur, -euse *m, f* d'emploi

**jock** [dʒak] *n sl* sportif *m*

**jockey** ['dʒa·ki] I. *n* jockey *m* II. *vi* **to ~ for sth** intriguer pour obtenir qc; **to ~ for position** jouer des coudes

**jockstrap** ['dʒak·stræp] *n* slip *m* à coquille

**Joe Blow** [‚dʒoʊ·'bloʊ] *n no art, inf* Monsieur Tout-le-monde

**jog** [dʒag] I. *n* ❶(*pace*) petit trot *m* ❷(*run*) jogging *m* ❸(*knock*) pous-

sée f II.<-gg-> vi faire du jogging
III.<-gg-> vt secouer; **to ~ sb's elbow**
pousser le coude de qn ► **to ~ sb's
memory** rafraîchir la mémoire de qn
◆ **jog along** vi ❶ inf (advance slowly)
aller cahin-caha ❷ fig aller tant bien que
mal

**jogger** ['dʒɑ.ər] n joggeur, -euse m, f
**jogging** ['dʒɑg.ɪŋ] n jogging m
**john** [dʒɑn] n sl ❶ (bathroom) cabinets
mpl ❷ (prostitute's client) micheton m
**John Doe** n Monsieur m Untel
**join** [dʒɔɪn] I. vt ❶ (connect) joindre;
(using glue, screws) assembler; (towns,
roads) relier; **to ~ hands** se donner la
main; **to ~ (together) in marriage** unir
par le mariage ❷ (go and be with) rejoindre; (in a car, on a walk) rattraper;
**to ~ sb in doing sth** se joindre à qn
pour qc ❸ (reach, touch: river, road) rejoindre ❹ (become a member of: club,
party) adhérer à; (sect, company) entrer dans; **to ~ the army** s'engager dans
l'armée; **to ~ forces with sb** s'unir
à qn ❺ (get involved in) s'inscrire à
► **~ the club!** bienvenue au club! II. vi
❶ (connect) se joindre ❷ (become a
member) adhérer III. n raccord m
**joint** [dʒɔɪnt] I. adj commun(e); **it was
a ~ effort** ce furent des efforts conju-
gués II. n ❶ ANAT articulation f; (in
wood) assemblage m; (in pipe) jointure f ❷ (meat) rôti m ❸ inf (place) endroit m ❹ inf (nightclub) boîte f
(de nuit) ❺ inf (marijuana cigarette)
joint m
**joint account** n compte m joint
**jointly** ['dʒɔɪnt.li] adv conjointement
**joint venture** n coentreprise f
**joke** [dʒoʊk] I. n ❶ (sth funny) plaisanterie f; **to tell a ~** raconter une blague;
**to play a ~ on sb** jouer un tour à qn;
**the ~'s on her** c'est à elle de rire jaune
❷ inf (sth very easy) **this is a ~** ça, c'est
de la tarte; **it's no ~ being a farmer** ce
n'est pas drôle d'être fermier ❸ inf (ridiculous thing or person) risée f; **he's a
complete ~!** ce qu'il est drôle! II. vi
plaisanter; **to ~ about sth** se moquer de

qc; **you must be joking!** tu veux/vous
voulez rire!
**joker** ['dʒoʊ.kər] n ❶ (one who jokes)
blagueur, -euse m, f ❷ inf (foolish person) imbécile mf ❸ (card) joker m
► **he's the ~ in the deck** avec lui c'est
le grand inconnu
**joking** ['dʒoʊk.ɪŋ] I. adj de plaisanterie; **it's no ~ matter** il n'y a pas de quoi
rire II. n plaisanterie f
**jokingly** adv en plaisantant
**jolly** ['dʒɑ.li] I. <-ier, -iest> adj ❶ (happy) joyeux(-euse) ❷ (cheerful) jovial(e)
II. <-ies> n pl, sl **to get one's jollies**
prendre son pied
**jostle** ['dʒɑ.sl] I. vt bousculer II. vi se
bousculer; **to ~ for position** jouer des
coudes pour obtenir un poste
**journal** ['dʒɜr.nəl] n ❶ (periodical) revue f; **quarterly ~** revue trimestrielle
❷ (newspaper, diary) journal m
**journalism** ['dʒɜr.nəl.ɪ.zəm] n journalisme m
**journalist** ['dʒɜr.nəl.ɪst] n journaliste
mf; **freelance ~** pigiste mf
**journey** ['dʒɜr.ni] I. n ❶ (trip) a. fig voyage m; (period in movement) trajet m
II. vi voyager
**joy** [dʒɔɪ] n ❶ (gladness) joie f; **to jump
for ~** sauter de joie; **the ~ of winning/
singing** le plaisir de gagner/chanter
❷ (source of pleasure) plaisir m; **to be
sb's pride and ~** être la fierté de qn
**joyful** ['dʒɔɪ.fəl] adj joyeux(-euse)
**joyous** ['dʒɔɪ.əs] adj joyeux(-euse)
**joy ride** ['dʒɔɪ.raɪd] n sl virée f
**joy rider** n chauffard dans une voiture
volée
**joystick** ['dʒɔɪ.stɪk] n ❶ AVIAT levier m
de commande ❷ COMPUT joystick m,
manette f de jeu
**Jr.** n abbr of **Junior** junior m
**jubilant** ['dʒu.bɪ.lənt] adj enchanté(e)
**jubilation** [ˌdʒu.bɪ.'leɪ.ʃən] n jubilation f
**jubilee** ['dʒu.bɪ.li] n jubilé m
**Judaism** ['dʒu.deɪ.ɪ.zəm] n judaïsme m
**judge** [dʒʌdʒ] I. n juge m; (in contest)
arbitre m; **to be a good ~ of character**
savoir bien juger les gens; **I'll be the ~**

**of that!** c'est moi qui en jugerai! II. *vi* ❶ (*decide*) juger; **to ~ by** [*o* **from**] **sth** juger d'après qc ❷ LAW rendre un jugement III. *vt* ❶ (*decide*) juger; (*contest*) arbitrer ❷ (*estimate*) estimer ❸ (*assess*) évaluer, juger ▸ **you can't ~ a book by its cover** *prov* il ne faut pas se fier aux apparences

**judg(e)ment** ['dʒʌdʒ·mənt] *n* ❶ LAW jugement *m* ❷ (*opinion*) avis *m* ❸ (*discernment*) appréciation *f*; **use your ~** c'est à toi/vous de juger

**judgmental** [dʒʌdʒ·'mən·t̬əl] *adj* critique

**judo** ['dʒu·doʊ] *n* judo *m*

**jug** [dʒʌg] *n* (*container*) cruche *f*

**juggernaut** ['dʒʌg·ər·nɔt] *n* poids *m* lourd

**juggle** ['dʒʌg·l] *a. fig* I. *vt* jongler avec II. *vi* **to ~ with sth** jongler avec qc

**juggler** ['dʒʌg·lər] *n* jongleur, -euse *m, f*

**juice** [dʒus] *n* ❶ *a. fig* jus *m* ❷ (*bodily liquid*) suc *m*

**juicy** ['dʒu·si] <-ier, -iest> *adj* juteux(-euse)

**jukebox** ['dʒuk·baks] *n* juke-box *m*

**July** [dʒu·'laɪ] *n* juillet *m*; *s.a.* **April**

**jumbo** ['dʒʌm·boʊ] I. *adj* géant(e) II. *n inf* jumbo-jet *m*

**jump** [dʒʌmp] I. *vi* ❶ (*leap*) sauter; **to ~ up** se lever d'un bond; **to ~ forward/ across** faire un bond en avant/franchir d'un bond; **to ~ in** (*car*) sauter dans; **to ~ on** (*bus, train*) sauter dans; (*bicycle, horse*) sauter sur ❷ (*jerk*) sursauter; **to make sb ~** faire sursauter qn ❸ (*increase suddenly*) faire un bond ❹ (*skip*) sauter; **to ~ from one thing to another** passer d'un seul coup d'une chose à une autre ▸ **to ~ to conclusions** tirer des conclusions trop hâtives; **to ~ for joy** bondir de joie; **to go ~ in the lake** *inf* aller se faire voir II. *vt* ❶ (*leap across or over*) sauter par-dessus ❷ (*attack*) **to ~ sb** sauter sur qn ❸ (*skip*) sauter; (*forfeit*) **to ~ bail** se soustraire à la justice ▸ **to ~ the gun** agir prématurément; **to ~ ship** déserter le navire III. *n* ❶ (*leap*) saut *m*

❷ (*hurdle*) obstacle *m* ❸ (*step*) pas *m* ❹ (*head start*) avance *f*; **to get a ~ on sb** devancer qn

◆**jump around** *vi* sautiller

◆**jump at** *vt* **to ~ an opportunity** sauter sur une occasion

**jumper** ['dʒʌm·pər] *n* ❶ (*person or animal*) sauteur, -euse *m, f* ❷ (*pinafore dress*) robe-tablier *f*

**jumper cables** *n pl* câbles *mpl* de démarrage

**jumping jack** *n* pantin *m* articulé

**jumpy** ['dʒʌm·pi] <-ier, -iest> *adj inf* nerveux(-euse)

**junction** ['dʒʌŋ(k)·ʃən] *n* (*roads*) intersection *f*; (*for trains*) nœud *m* ferroviaire

**juncture** ['dʒʌŋ(k)·tʃər] *n form* **at this ~** à ce moment précis    **J**

**June** [dʒun] *n* juin *m*; *s.a.* **April**

**jungle** ['dʒʌŋ·gl] *n* jungle *f* ▸ **it's a ~ out there** c'est un panier de crabes là--dehors

**junior** ['dʒu·njər] I. *adj* ❶ (*younger*) junior ❷ SPORTS minime ❸ (*lower in rank*) subalterne; **~ partner** jeune associé *m* II. *n* ❶ (*son*) junior *m* ❷ (*low-ranking person*) subordonné(e) *m(f)* ❸ UNIV étudiant(e) *m(f)* de troisième année

**junior college** *n* université *f* de premier cycle

**junior high school** *n* ≈ collège *m*

**junk**[1] [dʒʌŋk] I. *n* ❶ (*jumble*) brocante *f*; **~ shop** bric-à-brac *m* ❷ (*rubbish*) vieilleries *fpl*; **the ~ on TV** les navets *mpl* à la télé ❸ *sl* (*narcotics*) came *f* II. *vt inf* balancer

**junk**[2] [dʒʌŋk] *n* (*vessel*) jonque *f*

**junk food** *n* nourriture *f* industrielle

**junkie** ['dʒʌŋ·ki] *n inf* ❶ (*drug addict*) camé(e) *m(f)* ❷ (*addict*) accro *mf*

**junk mail** *n* réclame *f*

**junkyard** *n* décharge *f*

**jurisdiction** [ˌdʒʊr·ɪs·'dɪk·ʃən] *n* juridiction *f*

**juror** ['dʒʊr·ər] *n* juré(e) *m(f)*

**jury** ['dʒʊr·i] *n* jury *m*

**just** [dʒʌst] I. *adv* ❶ (*at that moment*) juste; **to be ~ doing sth** être juste en train de faire qc; **he ~ left** il vient de partir; **~ then** juste à ce moment-là; **~ last Friday** pas plus tard que vendredi dernier; **~ as he finished** il venait justement de finir ②(*only*) juste; **he ~ smiled** il n'a fait que sourire; **~ sit down** assieds-toi/asseyez-vous donc; **~ for fun** juste pour s'amuser; (*not*) **~ anybody** (pas) n'importe qui ③(*barely*) tout juste; **~ in time** juste à temps; **~ about** tout juste ④(*very*) vraiment ▶**it's ~ my luck** c'est bien ma chance; **it's ~ one of those things** *prov* ce sont des choses qui arrivent; **~ as well!** heureusement! II. *adj* (*fair*) juste; (*cause*)

légitime; (*reward*) mérité(e) ▶**to get one's deserts** avoir ce qu'on mérite

**justice** ['dʒʌs·tɪs] *n* ① *a.* LAW justice *f* ②(*judge*) juge *mf* ▶**to do sb** mettre qn en valeur

**justification** [ˌdʒʌs·tə·fɪ·'keɪ·ʃ°n] *n* justification *f*

**justify** ['dʒʌs·tɪ·faɪ] *vt* justifier; **to ~ sb's faith** mériter la confiance de qn

**justly** ['dʒʌst·li] *adv* avec raison

**juvenile** ['dʒu·və·n°l] *adj* ①*form* (*young*) juvénile; (*delinquent*) jeune; **~ court** tribunal *m* pour enfants ②*pej* (*childish*) puéril(e)

---

# Kk

**K, k** [keɪ] <-'s> *n* K, k *m;* **~ as in Kilo** (*on telephone*) k comme Kléber

**K** *n* COMPUT *abbr of* **kilobyte** Ko *m*

**kangaroo** [ˌkæŋ·gə·'ru] <-(s)> *n* kangourou *m*

**Kansas** ['kæn·zəs] *n* le Kansas

**karate** [kə·'ra·ţi] *n* karaté *m*

**karate chop** *n* coup porté avec le tranchant de la main

**karma** ['kar·mə] *n* karma *m*

**kayak** ['kaɪ·æk] *n* kayak *m*

**KB** [ˌkeɪ·'bi] *n* COMPUT *abbr of* **kilobyte** Ko *m*

**keel** [kil] *n* NAUT quille *f*

**keen** [kin] *adj* ①(*eager*) enthousiaste; **to be ~ on doing sth** (*want to do it*) tenir à faire qc; (*do it a lot*) adorer faire qc ②(*perceptive: mind, eye*) vif(vive); (*hearing, awareness*) fin(e); (*eyesight*) perçant(e) ③(*extreme: interest, desire*) vif(vive); (*competition*) acharné(e) ④(*biting*) mordant(e)

**keep** [kip] I. *n* ①(*living costs*) frais *mpl* de logement; **to earn one's ~** gagner sa vie ②(*tower*) donjon *m* ▶**for ~s** pour

de bon II.<kept, kept> *vt* ①(*not let go of: property*) garder; (*visitor*) retenir; **to ~ information from sb** cacher des informations à qn; **~ this to yourself** gardez ça pour toi/gardez ça pour vous ②(*store*) ranger; **to ~ the plant by a window** placer la plante près d'une fenêtre; **I ~ a bottle in the fridge** j'ai une bouteille au frigo ③(*maintain in a given state*) **to ~ sb/sth under control** maîtriser qn/qc; **to ~ sb under observation** garder qn en observation; **to ~ one's eyes fixed on sb/sth** garder ses yeux rivés sur qn/qc; **to ~ food warm** garder un plat au chaud; **to ~ sb waiting** faire attendre qn ④(*look after*) **to ~ house** tenir la maison; **to ~ animals** avoir des animaux; **to ~ a mistress** entretenir une maîtresse ⑤(*respect: promise*) tenir; (*appointment*) se rendre à ⑥(*write regularly: record, diary*) tenir; **to ~ a record of sth** prendre qc en note ⑦(*for security*) **to ~ watch over sth** surveiller qc; **to ~ guard** monter la garde ⑧(*prevent*) **to ~ sb from doing sth** empêcher qn de faire qc

❾ (*help or force to continue*) **to ~ sb talking** retenir qn de parler; **we have enough oil to ~ us going for a month** on a assez de fioul pour tenir un mois ▸ **to ~ one's hands to oneself** garder ses distances III.<kept, kept> *vi* ❶ (*stay fresh*) se conserver ❷ (*stay*) ~ **calm** garder son calme; **to ~ right** rester sur la droite; **to ~ warm** se protéger du froid; **to ~ quiet** rester tranquille ❸ (*continue*) **to ~ doing sth** continuer à faire qc; **I ~ going somehow** je me maintiens; **he ~s pestering me** il n'arrête pas de me harceler

◆**keep away** I. *vi* **to ~ from sb/sth** ne pas s'approcher de qn/qc II. *vt* **to keep sb/sth away from sb/sth** tenir qn/qc à l'écart de qn/qc

◆**keep back** I. *vi* (*stay away*) ne pas s'approcher; **to ~ from sb/sth** garder ses distances de qn/qc II. *vt* ❶ (*hold away*) **to keep sb/sth back from sb/sth** empêcher qn/qc de s'approcher de qn/qc ❷ (*retain: money*) retenir; (*information*) cacher

◆**keep down** *vt* ❶ (*repress: costs, speed, level*) empêcher d'augmenter; (*protesters, workers*) contrôler; (*one's voice*) baisser ❷ (*not vomit*) **to keep sth down** se retenir de rendre qc

◆**keep in** *vt* **to keep one's emotions in** retenir ses émotions

◆**keep off** *vt* ❶ (*stay off*) rester à l'écart de; '**~ the grass**' 'pelouse interdite' ❷ *fig* **to ~ a topic** éviter d'aborder un sujet ❸ **to keep sb/sth off sth** tenir qn/qc à l'écart de qc

◆**keep on** I. *vi* **to ~ doing sth** continuer à faire qc II. *vt* (*clothes, workers*) garder

◆**keep on at** *vt inf* **to ~ sb about sth** harceler qn au sujet de qc

◆**keep out** I. *vi* rester (en) dehors; **to ~ of sth** ne pas se mêler de qc II. *vt always sep* empêcher d'entrer

◆**keep up** *vt* **to ~ appearances** garder les apparences

◆**keep up with** *vt* (*runner, driver*) aller à la même vitesse que; (*other students*) arriver à suivre ▸ **to ~ the Joneses** faire aussi bien que les voisins

**keeper** ['ki·pər] *n* (*of animals, in soccer*) gardien(ne) *m(f)*

**keeping** ['kip·ɪŋ] *n* ❶ (*guarding*) garde *mf* ❷ (*respecting*) **to be in/not in ~ with** (*policy, philosophy*) correspondre/ne pas correspondre à; (*aims, principles*) être en accord/désaccord avec; (*period, style*) s'harmoniser/détonner avec

**kennel** ['ken·əl] I. *n* ❶ (*dog shelter*) niche *f* ❷ *pl* + *sing/pl verb* (*boarding for dogs*) chenil *m* II. *vt* **to ~ a dog** mettre un chien dans un chenil

**Kentucky** [kən·'tʌk·i] *n* le Kentucky

**Kentucky Derby** *n* **the ~** le Derby du Kentucky

**kept** [kept] I. *pt, pp of* **keep** II. *adj* entretenu(e)

**kerosene** ['ker·ə·sin] *n* pétrole *m*; (*for jet engines*) kérosène *m*

**ketchup** ['ketʃ·əp] *n* ketchup *m*

**kettle** ['ket·l] *n* bouilloire *f* ▸ **to be a different ~ of fish** être une autre paire de manches

**key** [ki] I. *n* ❶ (*locking device*) clé *f*, clef *f* ❷ (*essential point*) **the ~ to sth** la clé de qc ❸ (*list of symbols*) légende *f*; **answer ~** solutions *fpl* ❹ MUS ton *m*; **in the ~ of C major** en do majeur; **off ~** faux ❺ COMPUT touche *f*, piton *m Québec*; **SHIFT ~** touche "majuscule" II. *adj* (*factor, question, figure*) clé, clef; **sth is ~** qc est essentiel III. *vt* ❶ (*adapt*) **to ~ sth to sb** adapter qc à qn ❷ (*vandalize*) **to ~ a car** érafler une voiture avec une clé

◆**key in** *vt* saisir; **to ~ in a password** taper un code

◆**key up** *vt* **to be keyed up** être excité

**keyboard** ['ki·bɔrd] I. *n* MUS, COMPUT clavier *m*; **to play the ~** jouer du synthétiseur II. *vt* saisir

**keyhole** ['ki·hoʊl] *n* trou *m* de serrure

**key ring** *n* porte-clé *m*

**keystroke** *n* frappe *f*

**keyword** *n* ❶ (*cipher*) code *m* ❷ (*important word*) mot-clé *m*

**kg** *n abbr of* **kilogram** kg *m*

**kick** [kɪk] **I.** *n* ❶ (*blow with foot*) coup *m* de pied ❷ (*excited feeling*) **to get a ~ out of sth** prendre plaisir à qc; **to do sth for ~s** faire qc pour s'amuser ❸ (*gun jerk*) recul *m* ❹ (*strong effect*) coup *m* **II.** *vt* donner un coup de pied dans; **to ~ oneself** s'en vouloir; **to ~ the ball into the net** envoyer le ballon au but ▸ **to ~ the bucket** casser sa pipe; **to ~ the habit** *sl* décrocher

◆**kick around I.** *vi inf* traîner **II.** *vt* (*ball*) taper dans; **to kick an idea around** *inf* tourner et retourner une idée

◆**kick back I.** *vt* renvoyer (avec le pied) **II.** *vi inf* se la couler douce

◆**kick in I.** *vt inf* contribuer **II.** *vi* (*system, mechanism*) se déclencher

◆**kick off I.** *vi* donner le coup d'envoi **II.** *vt* **to kick sth off with sth** enlever qc d'un coup de pied

◆**kick out** *vt* **to kick sb/sth out** jeter qc/qn dehors; **to be kicked out of school** être renvoyé de l'école

◆**kick up** *vt* ❶ **to ~ dust** faire voler la poussière ❷ *fig* **to ~ a fuss** faire des histoires

**kid** [kɪd] **I.** *n* ❶ (*child*) gosse *mf* ❷ (*young person*) gamin(e) *m(f)*; **~ sister** petite sœur *f*; **~ brother** petit frère *m* ❸ (*young goat*) chevreau *m*, chevrette *f* ❹ (*goatskin*) chevreau *m* ▸ **to treat sb with ~ gloves** prendre des gants avec qn **II.** <-dd-> *vi* raconter des blagues; **no ~ding** sans rire **III.** *vt* faire marcher; **to ~ oneself** se faire des illusions

**kidnap** [ˈkɪd·næp] <-pp-> *vt* kidnapper

**kidnapper** [ˈkɪd·næp·ər] *n* kidnappeur, -euse *m, f*

**kidnapping** [ˈkɪd·næp·ɪŋ] *n* enlèvement *m*

**kidney** [ˈkɪd·ni] *n* ❶ ANAT rein *m* ❷ (*food*) rognon *m*

**kidney bean** *n* haricot *m* rouge

**kill** [kɪl] **I.** *n* mise *f* à mort ▸ **to be in on the ~** assister au dénouement; **to go in for the ~** descendre dans l'arène **II.** *vi*

tuer **III.** *vt* ❶ (*cause to die*) tuer; **to ~ oneself** se suicider; **to ~ oneself trying** *inf* se tuer à essayer; **my back/knee is ~ing me** mon dos/genou me fait atrocement souffrir ❷ (*destroy*) supprimer ▸ **to ~ two birds with one stone** *prov* faire d'une pierre deux coups; **to ~ time** tuer le temps

◆**kill off** *vt* ❶ exterminer ❷ *fig* éliminer

**killer** [ˈkɪl·ər] *n* ❶ (*murderer*) tueur, -euse *m, f*; **to be a ~** (*disease, drug*) être meurtrier ❷ *fig* **to be a ~** (*joke*) être à mourir de rire; (*ruthless person*) être impitoyable

**killer bee** *n* abeille *f* tueuse

**killer whale** *n* orque *f*

**kilo** [ˈkiˌloʊ] *n* kilo *m*

**kilogram** [ˈkɪlˌoʊˌɡræm] *n* kilogramme *m*

**kilometer** [kɪˈlɑ·məˌtər] *n* kilomètre *m*

**kilt** [kɪlt] *n* kilt *m*

**kin** [kɪn] *n* parents *mpl*; **his next of ~** son plus proche parent

**kind**¹ [kaɪnd] *adj* gentil(le), fin(e) *Québec*; **with ~ regards** cordialement

**kind**² [kaɪnd] **I.** *n* ❶ (*group*) genre *m*; **the first of its ~** le premier de sa catégorie; **all ~s of** toutes sortes de; **it's some ~ of insect/map** c'est une espèce d'insecte/de carte; **what ~ of car/book is it?** quel genre de voiture/livre est-ce? ❷ (*payment*) **to pay sb in ~** payer qn en nature ❸ (*similarly*) **to answer in ~** renvoyer l'ascenseur **II.** *adv inf* **~ of difficult/angry** plutôt difficile/coléreux; **I'd ~ of hoped she'd come** en fait, j'espérais qu'elle viendrait

**kindergarten** [ˈkɪn·dərˌɡar·tⁿn] *n* école *f* maternelle

**kindly** [ˈkaɪnd·li] **I.** *adj* (*person*) aimable; (*smile, voice*) doux(douce); **to be a ~ soul** être la gentillesse même **II.** *adv* gentiment; **to not take ~ to sb/sth** ne pas apprécier qn/qc

**kindness** [ˈkaɪnd·nəs] *n* ❶ (*manner*) gentillesse *f* ❷ <-es> (*kind act*) petite *f* attention

**king** [kɪŋ] *n* roi *m*

**kingdom** ['kɪŋ·dəm] *n* ❶ (*country*) royaume *m* ❷ (*domain*) **animal/ plant** ~ règne *m* animal/végétal

**kingdom come** *n inf* ❶ (*next world*) **to blow sb up to** ~ envoyer qn dans l'autre monde ❷ (*end of time*) **till** ~ jusqu'à la fin des siècles

**kingfisher** ['kɪŋ.fɪʃ.ər] *n* martin-pêcheur *m*

**king-size** ['kɪŋ·saɪz] *adj* (*bed, duvet*) très grand(e); (*package, bottle*) géant(e)

**kiosk** ['ki·ask] *n* kiosque *m*

**kipper** ['kɪp·ər] *n* hareng *m* fumé

**kiss** [kɪs] **I.** *n* bise *f*, baise *f Belgique*; **love and** ~**es** (*in a letter*) grosses bises *fpl*; **to blow sb a** ~ envoyer un baiser à qn **II.** *vi* s'embrasser **III.** *vt* donner un baiser à, donner un bec *Belgique, Québec, Suisse*; **to** ~ **sb goodnight/goodbye** embrasser qn en lui souhaitant bonne nuit/disant au revoir; **to** ~ **sth goodbye** *inf* pouvoir dire adieu à qc

**kit** [kɪt] *n* ❶ (*set*) trousse *f*; (*for activity*) nécessaire *m*; **tool** ~ kit *m* ❷ (*components*) pièces *fpl* détachées

**kitchen** ['kɪtʃ·ɪn] *n* cuisine *f*

**kitchenette** [ˌkɪtʃ·ɪ·'net] *n* kitchenette *f*

**kitchen sink** *n* évier *m* ▶ **everything but the** ~ tout sauf les murs

**kitchen unit** *n* élément *m* de cuisine

**kite** [kaɪt] *n* cerf-volant *m*; **to fly a** ~ faire voler un cerf-volant

**kitten** ['kɪt·ᵊn] *n* chaton *m*

**kitty**[1] ['kɪt·i] *n childspeak* (*cat*) minou *m*

**kitty**[2] ['kɪt·i] *n* (*fund*) caisse *f*

**kiwi** ['ki·wi] *n* ❶ (*bird*) kiwi *m* ❷ CULIN ~ (**fruit**) kiwi *m* ❸ *inf* (*New Zealander*) Néo-Zélandais(e) *m(f)*

**KKK** [ˌkeɪ·keɪ·'keɪ] *n abbr of* **Ku Klux Klan**

**knack** [næk] *n* (*skill*) tour *m* de main; **to have a** ~ **for** (**doing**) **sth** avoir le don pour faire qc

**knee** [ni] **I.** *n* genou *m*; **to get down on one's** ~**s** se mettre à genoux; **on your** ~**s!** à genoux ! ▶ **to bring sb to his/ their** ~**s** forcer qn à capituler **II.** *vt* donner un coup de genou à

**kneecap I.** *n* rotule *f* **II.** <-pp-> *vt* **to** ~ **sb** tirer dans le genou de qn

**kneel** [nil] <knelt *o* -ed, knelt *o* -ed> *vi* **to** ~ (**down**) s'agenouiller; **she was** ~**ing** elle était à genoux

**knelt** [nelt] *pt of* **kneel**

**knew** [nu] *pt of* **know**

**knickknack** ['nɪk·næk] *n inf* bibelot *m*

**knife** [naɪf] <knives> **I.** *n* couteau *m*; **forks and knives** couverts *mpl* ▶ **to be under the** ~ MED être sur le billard **II.** *vt* poignarder; **to get** ~**d** recevoir un coup de couteau

**knight** [naɪt] **I.** *n* ❶ (*man*) chevalier *m* ❷ (*chess figure*) cavalier *m* ▶ ~ **in shining armor** prince *m* charmant **II.** *vt* faire chevalier

**knit** [nɪt] **I.** *n* tricot *m* **II.** <knit *o* -ted, knit *o* -ted> *vi* ❶ (*connect wool*) tricoter ❷ (*mend: bones*) se souder ❸ (*join*) lier **III.** *vt* ❶ (*make with wool*) tricoter; ~ **skirt** jupe *f* en tricot ❷ (*furrow*) **to** ~ **one's brows** froncer les sourcils

◆ **knit together I.** *vi* ❶ (*join*) se réunir ❷ (*mend*) se souder **II.** *vt* ❶ (*join by knitting*) **to knit two together** tricoter deux mailles ensemble ❷ (*join*) unir

**knitting** ['nɪt·ɪŋ] *n* ❶ (*action*) tricotage *m* ❷ (*material*) tricot *m*

**knitwear** ['nɪt·wer] *n* tricots *mpl*

**knob** [nab] *n* (*of door, drawer, bedpost, switch*) bouton *m*

**knock** [nak] **I.** *n* coup *m* **II.** *vi a.* TECH cogner; **to** ~ **at the door** frapper à la porte; **my knees are** ~**ing** mes genoux s'entrechoquaient **III.** *vt* ❶ (*hit*) frapper; **to** ~ **sb/sth to the ground** faire tomber qn/qc par terre; **to** ~ **sb senseless** [*o* silly] sonner qn ❷ *inf* (*criticize*) dire du mal de; **I'm not** ~**ing the idea** je ne rejette pas cette idée ▶ **to** ~ (**some**) **sense into sb** apprendre à vivre à qn; **to** ~ **sb's socks off** *sl* en mettre plein la vue à qn; **to** ~ **sb dead** *sl* épater qn

◆ **knock around I.** *vi inf* ❶ traîner ❷ *fig* bourlinguer **II.** *vt always sep* **to knock sb/sth around** tabasser qn/ malmener qc

**K**

◆**knock back** *vt inf* ❶(*return: ball*) renvoyer ❷*inf* (*cost*) **to knock sb back $5** coûter 5 dollars à qn ❸*inf* (*drink*) siffler

◆**knock down** *vt* ❶(*cause to fall*) renverser ❷(*hit: object*) abattre; (*person*) jeter à terre ❸(*sell at auction*) **to knock sth down to sb** adjuger qc à qn ❹(*reduce: seller*) solder; (*buyer*) faire baisser ❺(*demolish: door*) défoncer; (*building*) détruire ❻*fig* **to ~ every argument** démonter tous les arguments ❼*sl* (*earn*) toucher

◆**knock off** *vt* ❶(*cause to fall off*) **to knock sb/sth off sth** faire tomber qn/qc de qc ❷*inf* (*reduce*) **to knock 10% off the price** faire un rabais de 10% sur le prix ❸*inf* (*rob: a bank*) piquer ❹*inf* (*murder*) liquider ❺(*produce easily: job*) expédier; (*book, article*) bâcler

▶**knock it off!** ça suffit!

◆**knock out** *vt* ❶(*stun*) assommer; (*drink, drugs*) endormir ❷(*remove*) retirer; (*teeth*) casser ❸(*eliminate*) a. SPORTS éliminer ❹*inf* (*produce*) débiter ❺*inf* (*work hard*) **to knock oneself out doing sth** se tuer à faire qc ❻*fig* **to knock sb out** couper le sifflet à qn

◆**knock over** *vt* renverser

◆**knock together** *vt* ❶(*hit together*) entrechoquer ❷*inf* (*produce quickly*) bricoler en vitesse; (*meal*) improviser ❸*fig* **to knock heads together** secouer un bon coup

◆**knock up** *vt sl* (*impregnate*) engrosser

**knockdown** ['nak·daʊn] *adj* ❶(*cheap: price*) sacrifié(e) ❷(*easily dismantled*) démontable

**knocker** ['nak·ər] *n* ❶(*on door*) heurtoir *m* ❷*pl, sl* (*breasts*) nichons *mpl*

**knockout** ['nak·aʊt] **I.** *n* ❶SPORTS K.-O. *m* ❷(*attractive person or thing*) merveille *f* **II.** *adj* foudroyant(e); (*idea*) époustouflant(e); **~ blow** coup *m* de grâce

**knockout drops** *npl* soporifique *m*

**knot** [nat] **I.** *n* ❶(*tied rope*) nœud *m* ❷(*small group*) noyau *m* ❸NAUT

nœud *m* ▶**sb's stomach is in ~s** qn a l'estomac noué **II.**<-tt-> *vt* nouer; **to ~ a tie** faire un nœud de cravate; **to ~ sth together** nouer qc ensemble **III.**<-tt-> *vi* (*muscles, stomach*) se nouer

**know** [noʊ] **I.**<knew, known> *vt* ❶(*have knowledge*) savoir; (*facts*) connaître; **to ~ a bit of French** savoir un peu parler français; **she ~s all about them** (*has heard about*) elle sait tout d'eux; **to not ~ the first thing about sth/sb** ne pas savoir la moindre chose sur qc/qn; **if you ~ what I mean** si tu vois/vous voyez ce que je veux dire ❷(*be familiar with: person, date, price, name, details*) connaître; **to ~ sb by name/sight** connaître qn de nom/vue; **she ~s all about it** (*is an expert on*) elle sait tout là-dessus; **~ing her, …** telle que je la connais, …; **to get to ~ sb/sth** faire la connaissance de qn/apprendre qc; **to ~ a place like the back of one's hand** connaître un lieu comme le fond de sa poche ❸(*experience*) **to have ~n wealth** avoir connu la richesse ❹(*recognize*) **to ~ sb/sth by sth** reconnaître qn/qc à qc ❺(*differentiate*) **to ~ sth/sb from sth/sb** distinguer qc/qn de qc/qn ▶**you ~ something?** [o **what**] *inf* tu sais/vous savez quoi? **II.**<knew, known> *vi* ❶savoir; **as far as I ~** autant que je sache; **how should I ~?** comment le saurais-je?; **to ~ better than sb** mieux s'y connaître que qn ❷*inf* (*understand*) **you ~** tu vois/vous voyez III.**n to be in the ~ about sth** être au courant de qc

**knowingly** ['noʊ·ɪŋ·li] *adv* sciemment

**knowledge** ['na·lɪdʒ] *n no indef art* connaissance *f*; **to have no ~ of sth** tout ignorer de qc; **a working ~** des connaissances pratiques; **to my ~** à ma connaissance; **not to my ~** pas que je sache

**knowledgeable** ['na·lɪdʒ·ə·bl] *adj* bien informé(e)

**known** [noʊn] **I.** *pp of* **know** **II.** *adj* (*criminal, admirer*) connu(e); **to make**

sth ~ faire connaître qc; **he's better ~ as** il est plus connu comme; **to make oneself ~ to sb** se faire connaître de qn

**knuckle** ['nʌk·l] n ① ANAT articulation f ② CULIN jarret m

**KO** [ˌkeɪ·'oʊ] n abbr of **knockout** K.-O. m

**Korea** [kə·'riː·ə] n la Corée; **North/ South ~** la Corée du Nord/Sud

**Korean** [kə·'riː·ən] I. adj coréen(ne) II. n ① (person) Coréen(ne) m(f) ② LING coréen m; s.a. **English**

**kosher** ['koʊ·ʃər] adj ① REL casher inv

② inf (legitimate) O.-K.; **not quite ~** pas très catholique

**KS** n abbr of **Kansas**

**kudos** ['kuː·doʊs] npl prestige m

**Ku Klux Klan** ['kuː·klʌks·'klæn] n no indef art **the ~** le Ku Klux Klan

**Kurd** [kɜrd] n Kurde mf

**Kurdish** [ˌkɜrd·ɪʃ] I. adj kurde II. n kurde m; s.a. **English**

**Kuwait** [kʊ·'weɪt] n le Koweït [o Kuwait]

**Kuwaiti** [kʊ·'wər·ti] I. adj koweïtien(ne) II. n Koweïtien(ne) m(f)

**KY** n abbr of **Kentucky**

---

# L l

**L, l** [el] <-s> n L m, l m; **~ as in Lima** (on telephone) l comme Louis

**l** n abbr of **liter** l m

**L** adj abbr of **large** L

**LA** [ˌel·'eɪ] n ① abbr of **Los Angeles** LA ② abbr of **Louisiana** la Louisiane

**lab** [læb] n abbr of **laboratory** labo m

**label** ['leɪ·b<sup></sup>l] I. n a. COMPUT étiquette f ② (brand name) marque f; **designer ~** griffe f ③ MUS label m II. vt <-l- o -ll->, vt a. fig étiqueter

**labor** ['leɪ·bər] I. n ① (work) a. MED travail m ② (workers) main-d'œuvre f II. vi ① (work hard) travailler dur ② (do with effort) peiner; **to ~ for sth** se donner de la peine pour qc ③ PSYCH **to ~ under the delusion** [o **illusion**] **that …** se faire des illusions sur le fait que …, s'imaginer que … III. vt s'étendre sur ▶ **to ~ a point** insister lourdement sur un point

**laboratory** ['læb·rə·ˌtɔr·i] <-ies> n laboratoire m

**labor camp** n camp m de travaux forcés

**labor dispute** n conflit m social

**labor force** n ① (population) actifs mpl ② (employees) effectif m

**labor-intensive** adj qui exige un travail intensif

**labor market** n marché m de l'emploi

**labor pains** npl MED douleurs fpl de l'accouchement

**Labrador** ['læb·rə·dər] n GEO le Labrador

**Labrador retriever** ['læb·rə·dər rɪ·'triː·vər] n ZOOL labrador m

**lace** [leɪs] I. n ① (cloth) dentelle f ② (edging) bordure f ③ (tie for shoe) lacet m II. vt ① (fasten) lacer ② (add) ajouter; **to ~ a drink** corser une boisson ▶ **lace up l.** vt lacer II. vi se lacer

**laceration** n lacération f

**lace-ups** npl chaussures fpl à lacets

**lack** [læk] I. n manque m II. vt manquer de

**lackadaisical** [ˌlæk·ə·'deɪ·zɪ·k<sup></sup>l] adj indolent(e)

**lackluster** ['læk·ˌlʌs·tər] adj terne

**lactose** ['læk·toʊs] n lactose m

**lad** [læd] n inf gars m

**ladder** ['læd·ər] n a. fig (device) échelle f

**laden** ['leɪ·d<sup></sup>n] adj chargé(e)

**ladies' man** n homme m à femmes

**ladies' room** n toilettes fpl pour dames

**ladle** ['leɪ·dl] I. *n* louche *f*, poche *f Suisse* II. *vt* to ~ (out) (*soup*) servir

**lady** ['leɪ·di] <-ies> *n* ❶ (*woman*) dame *f*; **ladies and gentlemen!** mesdames et messieurs! ❷ (*title*) lady *f*

**ladybug** *n* coccinelle *f*

**laid** [leɪd] *pt, pp of* **lay**

**laid-back** [ˌleɪd·'bæk] *adj* décontracté(e)

**lain** [leɪn] *pp of* **lie**

**lake** [leɪk] *n* lac *m*

**lamb** [læm] I. *n* a. *fig* agneau *m* II. *vi* agneler

**lambaste** [læm·'beɪst] *vt* vilipender *form*

**lambswool** *n* laine *f* d'agneau

**lame** [leɪm] *adj* ❶ (*injured*) estropié(e) ❷ (*weak, stupid: excuse*) piètre; (*joke*) vaseux(-euse)

**lame duck** *n* POL candidat(e) sortant(e) *m*

**lamp** [læmp] *n* lampe *f*

**lamppost** *n* réverbère *m*

**lampshade** *n* abat-jour *m inv*

**LAN** [læn] *n* COMPUT *abbr of* **local area network** réseau *m* local; **~ party** lan party *f*

**land** [lænd] I. *n* ❶ a. AGR terre *f* ❷ (*area of ground*) terrain *m* ❸ (*nation*) pays *m* II. *vi* ❶ AVIAT atterrir ❷ NAUT débarquer ❸ (*end up*) a. SPORTS retomber III. *vt* ❶ (*bring onto land: plane*) faire atterrir; (*boat*) faire accoster ❷ (*unload*) décharger ❸ (*obtain: contract*) décrocher; (*fish*) prendre; (*job*) dégoter

**landing** *n* ❶ ARCHIT palier *m* ❷ AVIAT atterrissage *m* ❸ NAUT débarquement *m*

**landlady** *n* propriétaire *f*

**landlord** *n* propriétaire *m*

**landmass** *n* masse *f* continentale

**landowner** *n* propriétaire *mf* foncier(-ère)

**landscape** ['læn(d)·skeɪp] I. *n* ❶ GEO paysage *m* ❷ COMPUT mode *m* de paysage II. *vt* (*garden*) aménager

**landslide** *n* ❶ GEO glissement *m* de terrain ❷ POL raz-de-marée *m* électoral

**lane** [leɪn] *n* ❶ (*street*) ruelle *f* ❷ AUTO (*marked strip*) voie *f* ❸ SPORTS

couloir *m* ❹ (*route*) **air ~** couloir aérien; **shipping ~** route *f* de navigation

**language** ['læŋ·gwɪdʒ] *n* ❶ (*system of communication*) langage *m*; **foul ~** grossièretés *fpl* ❷ (*idiom of a cultural community*) langue *f* ▶ **to speak the same ~** parler la même langue; *fig* être sur la même longueur d'onde

**language arts** *n* maîtrise *f* de la langue

**lanky** *adj* dégingandé(e)

**lantern** ['læn·tərn] *n* ❶ (*light in a container*) lanterne *f*; **paper ~** lampion *m* ❷ ARCHIT lanterneau *m*

**lap¹** [læp] *n* giron *m* ▶ **to live in the ~ of luxury** vivre dans le grand luxe

**lap²** [læp] SPORTS I. *n* tour *m* de piste II. <-pp-> *vt* to ~ **sb** prendre un tour d'avance sur qn III. *vi* (*complete one circuit*) boucler un circuit

**lap³** [læp] <-pp-> I. *vt* ❶ (*drink*) laper ❷ (*wrap*) enrouler II. *vi* (*hit gently*) to ~ **against sth** clapoter contre qc

◆**lap up** *vt* ❶ (*drink*) laper ❷ *inf* (*accept eagerly*) s'empresser d'accepter

**lapse** [læps] I. *n* ❶ (*period*) intervalle *m*; (*of time*) laps *m* ❷ (*temporary failure*) faute *f*; (*of judgment*) erreur *f*; (*of memory*) trou *m*; (*in behavior*) écart *m*; (*concentration, standards*) baisse *f* II. *vi* ❶ (*make worse*) faire une erreur; (*standards, concentration*) baisser ❷ (*end*) se périmer; (*contract*) expirer; (*subscription*) prendre fin ❸ (*revert to*) to ~ **into sth** tomber dans qc; **to ~ into silence** se taire

**laptop** ['læp·tap] *n* portable *m*

**larch** [lartʃ] *n* mélèze *m*

**lard** [lard] I. *n* saindoux *m* II. *vt* larder; **to ~ sth with sth** *fig* truffer qc de qc

**larder** *n* garde-manger *m inv*

**large** [lardʒ] I. *adj* ❶ (*great: number*) grand(e); (*audience*) nombreux(-euse); **to grow ~r** s'agrandir ❷ (*fat*) gros(se); **to get ~r** grossir ❸ (*of wide range*) **a ~ amount of work** beaucoup de travail; **~-than-expected** plus important que prévu; **~st-ever** le plus grand qu'il soit ▶ **to be ~r than life** se faire remarquer

**II.** *n* **to be at ~** être en liberté **III.** *adv* **by and ~** en gros

**largely** *adv* en grande partie

**large-scale** *adj* ❶ (*in large proportions*) à grande échelle ❷ (*extensive*) grand(e); (*emergency aid*) de grande envergure

**lark** [lɑːk] *n* alouette *f*

**larva** ['lɑː·və] <-vae> *n* larve *f*

**lasagna** [lə·'zɑː·njə] *n*, *n* lasagnes *fpl*

**laser** ['leɪ·zər] *n* laser *m*

**laser printer** *n* imprimante *f* laser

**lash¹** [læʃ] <-shes> *n* cil *m*; *s.a.* **eyelash**

**lash²** [læʃ] **I.** <-shes> *n* ❶ (*whip*) fouet *m* ❷ (*flexible part of a whip*) lanière *f* ❸ (*stroke of a whip*) coup *m* de fouet ❹ *fig* (*criticism*) **to feel the full ~ of sb's tongue** ressentir les paroles acerbes de qn **II.** *vt* ❶ (*whip*) fouetter ❷ (*criticize*) s'en prendre à ❸ (*attach*) attacher; **to ~ sb/sth to sth** attacher qn/qc à qc; **to ~ sth together** ligoter qc ❹ (*drive*) **to ~ sb into sth** mettre qn dans un état de qc **III.** *vi* ❶ (*beat*) fouetter; **to ~ at sth** frapper qc d'un grand coup de fouet; **to ~ against the windows** fouetter les vitres ❷ (*move violently*) **to ~ around** se débattre

◆ **lash out** *vi* ❶ (*attack physically*) envoyer des coups; **to ~ at sb with sth** donner un grand coup à qn avec qc ❷ (*attack verbally*) **to ~ at sb** bombarder qn de paroles blessantes; **to ~ against sb** critiquer qn avec violence; *pej* descendre qn en flammes

**last¹** [læst] **I.** *n* **the ~** le(la) dernier(-ère); **that's the ~ I saw of her** je ne l'ai jamais revue; **to never hear the ~ of it** ne jamais finir d'en entendre parler; **the next to ~** l'avant-dernier *m* ▸ **to the ~** jusqu'au bout **II.** *adj* dernier(-ère); **for the ~ 2 years** depuis 2 ans; **the day before ~** avant-hier ▸ **to be on one's legs** être à bout; ECON être au bord de la faillite; **to be the ~ straw** être la goutte d'eau qui fait déborder le vase **III.** *adv* ❶ (*most recently*) la dernière fois ❷ (*coming after everyone/everything*) en dernier; **to arrive ~** arriver dernier(-ère) ❸ (*finally*) finalement ▸ **at** (**long**) **~** enfin; **~ but not least** enfin et surtout

**last²** [læst] **I.** *vi* ❶ (*continue*) durer ❷ (*remain good*) se maintenir ❸ (*be enough*) être suffisant ❹ (*to endure*) endurer **II.** *vt* **to ~** (*sb*) **a lifetime** en avoir pour la vie

**last-ditch** *adj*, **last-gasp** *adj* ultime

**lasting** *adj* continu(e); (*damage*) permanent(e); (*peace*) durable

**lastly** *adv* en dernier lieu

**last-minute** *adj* de dernière minute

**last name** *n* nom *m* de famille

**latch** [lætʃ] **I.** *n* loquet *m* **II.** *vt* ❶ (*close*) fermer au loquet ❷ TECH verrouiller

**late** [leɪt] **I.** *adj* ❶ (*after appointed time*) en retard; (*arrival, frost*) tardif(-ive) ❷ (*delayed*) retardé(e) ❸ (*advanced time*) tard; **~ nineteenth-century** la fin du dix-neuvième siècle; **to be in one's ~ twenties** être proche de la trentaine ❹ (*deceased*) feu(e) ❺ (*recent*) récent(e) **II.** *adv* ❶ (*after usual time*) en retard; **too little, too ~** trop peu, trop tard ❷ (*at an advanced time*) **~ in the day/at night** vers la fin de la journée/tard dans la nuit; **~ in life** pas plus tard que; **of ~** récemment

**latecomer** ['leɪt·ˌkʌm·ər] *n* retardataire *mf*

**lately** *adv* (*recently*) dernièrement; **until ~** jusqu'à récemment

**later** ['leɪ·tər] **I.** *adj comp of* **late** ❶ (*at future time*) ultérieur(e) ❷ (*not punctual*) plus tard **II.** *adv comp of* **late** ensuite; **no ~ than nine o'clock** à neuf heures au plus tard; **~ on** un peu plus tard; **see you ~ !** à plus tard!

**late show** *n* TV programme *m* de fin de soirée

**latest** ['leɪ·tɪst] **I.** *adj superl of* **late** (*most recent*) **the ~ ...** le(la) tout(e) dernier(-ère) ... **II.** *n* **at the** (**very**) **~** au plus tard; **to know the ~** connaître la dernière; **the ~ we can stay is two o'clock** on peut rester jusqu'à deux heures maximum [*o* au plus tard]

**Latin** ['læt.ən] I. *adj* **❶** LING, GEO latin(e) **❷** (*of Latin America*) latino-américain(e) II. *n* **❶** Latin(e) *m(f)* **❷** (*Latin American*) Latino-Américain(e) *m(f)* **❸** LING latin *m; s.a.* **English**

**Latina** [lə'ti·na] I. *adj* latino II. *n* Latino *f*

**Latin America** *n* l'Amérique *f* latine

**Latin American** I. *adj* latino-américain(e) II. *n* Latino-Américain(e) *m(f)*

**Latino** [lə'ti·nou] I. *adj* latino II. *n* Latino *mf*

**latter** ['læt̮·ər] *adj* **❶** (*second of two*) second(e) **❷** (*near the end*) dernier(-ère)

**laugh** [læf] I. *n* **❶** (*sound expressing amusement*) rire *m* **❷** *inf* (*an amusing activity*) blague *f* ▸ **to** ~ **do sth for a** ~ faire qc pour rire II. *vi* **❶** (*express amusement*) rire; **to** ~ **out loud** s'esclaffer **❷** *inf* (*scorn*) **to** ~ **at sb/sth** se moquer de qn/qc ▸ **he who** ~**s last** ~**s longest** *prov* rira bien qui rira le dernier *prov*
♦ **laugh off** *vt* tourner en plaisanterie ▸ **to laugh one's head off** *inf* être mort de rire

**laughable** *adj* comique

**laughing** I. *n* rires *mpl* II. *adj* rieur(-euse); **this is no** ~ **matter** il n'y a pas de quoi rire

**laughter** ['læf·tər] *n* rire *m* ▸ ~ **is the best medicine** *prov* le rire est le meilleur des remèdes *prov*

**launch¹** [lɔn(t)ʃ] *n* (*boat*) vedette *f*

**launch²** I. *n* a. *fig* lancement *m* II. *vt* **❶** (*send out*) lancer; **to** ~ **a boat** mettre un bateau à l'eau **❷** (*begin something: attack*) déclencher; (*campaign*) lancer; (*product*) promouvoir
♦ **launch into** *vt* se lancer dans; **to** ~ **a passionate speech** se jeter dans un discours passionné

**launch pad** *n* **❶** (*starting area*) plateforme *f* de lancement **❷** (*starting point*) point *m* de départ

**Laundromat®** ['lɔn·drou·mæt] *n* laverie *f* (automatique)

**laundry** ['lɔn·dri] *n* **❶** (*dirty clothes*) linge *m* (sale); **to do the** ~ faire la lessive **❷** (*freshly washed clothes*) linge *m* pro-

pre **❸** (*place for washing clothes*) blanchisserie *f*, buanderie *f Québec*

**laundry basket** *n* panier *m* à linge

**lavatory** ['læv·ə·tɔr·i] *n* toilettes *fpl*

**law** [lɔ] *n* **❶** (*rule, set of rules*) loi *f*; **the first** ~ **of sth** la première règle de qc; ~ **and order** ordre *m* public; **to be against the** ~ être contraire à la loi; **to take the** ~ **into one's own hands** faire justice soi-même **❷** (*legislation*) droit *m* **❸** *inf* (*police*) police *f* **❹** (*court*) justice *f* **❺** (*scientific principle*) loi *f*; ~ **of averages** loi des probabilités ▸ **the** ~ **of the jungle** la loi de la jungle

**law court** *n* tribunal *m*

**law enforcement** *n* application *f* de la loi

**lawn¹** [lɔn] *n* (*grass*) pelouse *f*

**lawn²** [lɔn] *n* (*textile*) linon *m*

**lawnmower** *n* tondeuse *f*

**lawn tennis** *n form* tennis *m* sur gazon

**lawn tractor** *n* tracteur *m* à gazon

**lawsuit** *n* procès *m*

**lawyer** ['lɔ·jər] *n* avocat(e) *m(f)*

**laxative** ['læk·sə·t̮ɪv] I. *n* laxatif *m* II. *adj* laxatif(-ive)

**lay** [leɪ] I. <laid, laid> *vt* **❶** (*place, arrange*) poser; **to** ~ **the blame on sb** donner la faute à qn **❷** (*install*) mettre; (*cable, carpet, pipes*) poser **❸** (*render*) **to** ~ **sth bare** mettre qc à nu; **to** ~ **sb/ sth open to ridicule** ridiculiser qn/qc **❹** (*hatch: egg*) pondre **❺** FIN (*wager*) parier ▸ **to** ~ **hands on sb** lever la main sur qn; REL faire l'imposition des mains à qn II. <laid, laid> *vi* pondre III. *n* configuration *f*
♦ **lay aside** *vt* a. *fig* mettre de côté
♦ **lay down** *vt* **❶** (*place on a surface*) déposer **❷** (*relinquish*) quitter **❸** (*decide on*) convenir **❹** (*establish: rule, principle*) établir; **to** ~ **the law** dicter sa loi
♦ **lay into** *vt* **❶** *inf* (*assault*) rosser **❷** *inf* (*attack verbally*) tuer **❸** (*eat heartily*) dévorer
♦ **lay off** I. *vt* **❶** (*fire*) licencier; (*temporarily*) mettre au chômage technique

② inf (stop) arrêter ③ inf (leave alone) ficher la paix à II. vi arrêter; ~! arrête!

◆**lay out** vt ① (organize) planifier ② (spread out) étaler ③ (prepare for burial) exposer ④ inf (render unconscious) liquider; **to lay sb out cold** refroidir qn ⑤ inf (spend lots of money) **to lay money out on sth** mettre beaucoup de fric dans qc ⑥ (explain) **to lay sth out for sb** exposer qc à qn

◆**lay up** vt ① (build up a stock) stocker ② inf (be put out of action) **to be laid up (in bed) with sth** être cloué au lit avec qc

**lay²** [leɪ] adj ① (not professional) profane ② (not of the clergy) laïc(laïque)

**lay³** [leɪ] pt of **lie**

**layabout** n inf flemmard(e) m(f)

**layer** I. n ① (uniform level of substance) couche f ② fig (level) niveau m ③ (laying hen) pondeuse f II. vt ① (arrange into layers) **to ~ sth with sth** faire des couches de qc et de qc ② (cut into layers) dégrader III. vi faire des couches

**layer cake** n gâteau composé de quatre couches de crème

**layoff** n licenciement m

**layout** n ① (design, plan) plan m ② TYP mise f en page

**layover** n (stopover) halte f; (of plane) escale f

**lazy** ['leɪ·zi] <-ier, -iest> adj ① pej (not showing energy) paresseux(-euse) ② (tranquil) tranquille

**lb.** n abbr of **pound** livre f

**LCD** [ˌel·siˈdi] I. adj abbr of **liquid crystal display** à cristaux liquides II. n abbr of **liquid crystal display** affichage m à cristaux liquides

**lead¹** [lid] I. <led, led> vt ① (be in charge of) diriger; (a discussion, an investigation) mener ② (be the leader of) mener ③ (guide) mener; **to ~ the way** montrer le chemin ④ (cause to have/do sth) **to ~ sb into/to problems** causer des problèmes à qn; **to ~ sb to believe** amener qn à croire; **to ~ sb astray** détourner qn du droit chemin ⑤ COM,

SPORTS (be ahead of) **to ~ sb** être en avance sur qn ⑥ (live a particular way) **to ~ a life of luxury** mener une vie de luxe II. <led, led> vi ① (direct) mener; **to ~ to/into/onto sth** mener à/à l'intérieur de/sur qc ② (guide) guider ③ (be ahead) mener ④ fig (cause to develop, happen) **to ~ to sth** aboutir à qc ⑤ GAMES jouer le premier III. n ① (front position) tête f ② (advantage) avance f ③ (example) exemple m ④ (clue) indice m ⑤ (leading role) rôle m principal ⑥ (connecting wire) câble m ⑦ GAMES **to have the ~** jouer le premier

◆**lead away** I. vt ① (take away: prisoner) emmener ② fig éloigner du sujet II. vi fig s'éloigner du sujet

◆**lead off** I. vt ① (start) commencer ② (take away) emmener II. vi commencer

◆**lead on** I. vi avancer II. vt pej **to lead sb on** tromper qn

**lead²** [led] n ① (metallic substance) plomb m ② (pencil filling) mine f de crayon

**leader** ['li·dər] n ① (decision maker) a. POL leader m ② MUS (conductor) chef m d'orchestre

**leadership** n ① (leading position, action) direction f ② (leaders) dirigeants mpl ③ ECON leadership m

**lead-free** ['led·fri] adj sans plomb

**leading¹** ['lid·ɪŋ] adj leader

**leading²** ['led·ɪŋ] n baguettes fpl de plomb

**leading-edge** adj (technology) de pointe

**lead poisoning** n intoxication f par le plomb

**lead singer** n première voix f

**lead story** n PUBL article m leader

**lead time** n temps m de procuration

**lead-up** n prélude m

**leaf** [lif] <leaves> n ① a. BOT, TECH feuille f ② (table part) rallonge f ▶ **to turn over a new ~** tourner la page

**leaflet** ['li·flət] I. n prospectus m II. vt, vi distribuer des prospectus

**leafy** ['li·fi] <-ier, iest> adj vert(e)

**league** [liɡ] n ❶ a. sports ligue f ❷ fig (*group with similar level*) groupe m homogène; **to be/not be in the same ~ as sb/sth** être/ne pas être de force égale avec qn/qc ▶ **to be out of sb's ~** inf ne pas être pour qn

**leak** [lik] I. n a. fig fuite f II. vi ❶ (*let escape*) fuir ❷ (*let enter*) laisser filtrer; **to ~ like a sieve** être une vraie passoire III. vt ❶ (*let escape*) laisser passer ❷ fig **to ~ sth to sb** divulguer qc à qn

**leaky** <-ier, -iest> adj qui fuit

**lean¹** [lin] I. vi ❶ (*be inclined*) pencher; **to ~ against sth** s'appuyer contre qc ❷ fig (*tend toward*) pencher pour; **to ~ to the left/right** avoir des tendances de gauche/droite II. vt appuyer; **to ~ sth against sth** appuyer qc contre qc
◆ **lean on** vi **to ~ sb** ❶ (*rely on*) se reposer sur qn ❷ inf (*exert pressure*) faire pression sur qn
◆ **lean over** I. vt se pencher vers II. vi **to ~ to sb** se pencher vers qn

**lean²** [lin] adj maigre

**leap** [lip] I. <leaped, leaped o leapt, leapt> vi sauter; **to ~ with joy** sauter de joie II. <leaped, leaped o leapt, leapt> vt sauter par-dessus; (*horse*) faire sauter III. n a. fig bond m; **to take a ~** bondir; fig faire un bond ▶ **to do sth by ~s and bounds** faire qc rapidement
◆ **leap out** vi sauter à l'œil
◆ **leap up** vi ❶ (*jump up*) sauter en l'air ❷ (*rise quickly*) faire un bond en avant

**leap year** n année f bissextile

**learn** [lɜrn] vt, vi apprendre ▶ **to ~ sth by heart** apprendre qc par cœur

**learner** n apprenant(e) m(f); (*pupil*) élève mf

**learning disability** n <-ies> troubles mpl d'apprentissage

**learnt** [lɜrnt] pt, pp of learn

**leaseholder** n preneur, -euse m, f à bail

**leash** [liʃ] n laisse f ▶ **to be (kept) on a short ~** inf ne pas avoir beaucoup de libertés

**least** [list] I. adv moins; **~ of all** moins que tout II. adj moindre III. n le moins; **at ~** au moins; **not in the ~** pas du tout;

**to say the ~** le moins qu'on puisse dire; **it's the ~ I can do** c'est la moindre des choses

**leather** [ˈlɛð·ər] n cuir m

**leave¹** [liv] I. <left, left> vt ❶ (*let*) laisser; **to ~ sb sth** laisser qc à qn; **to ~ sb/ sth be** laisser qn/qc tranquille; **to ~ sb alone** laisser qn tranquille ❷ (*depart from: home, wife, work*) quitter ▶ **to ~ a lot to be desired** laisser beaucoup à désirer; **to ~ sb in the lurch** laisser qn dans l'incertitude; **to ~ sb cold** laisser qn froid; **to ~ it at that** en rester là II. <left, left> vi partir III. n départ m; **to take (one's) ~ of sb** prendre congé de qn
◆ **leave behind** vt a. fig laisser (derrière soi)
◆ **leave off** vt (*omit*) **to leave sb/sth off** laisser qn/qc
◆ **leave on** vt ❶ (*keep on*) garder ❷ (*machine*) laisser en marche
◆ **leave out** vt ❶ (*omit*) omettre ❷ (*leave outside*) laisser dehors
◆ **leave over** vt **to be left over from sth** rester de qc

**leave²** [liv] n ❶ (*permission, consent*) permission f ❷ (*vacation time*) congé m

**lecture** [ˈlɛk·tʃər] I. n ❶ (*formal speech*) discours m ❷ (*educational talk*) conférence f ❸ univ cours m magistral ❹ pej (*preaching*) sermon m ❺ (*advice*) conseil m II. vi tenir une conférence III. vt **to ~ sb on sth** ❶ (*give a speech*) tenir un discours à qn sur qc ❷ (*reprove*) faire la morale à qn sur qc ❸ (*advise*) donner un bon conseil à qn sur qc

**lecturer** n ❶ (*person giving talks*) conférencier, -ère m, f ❷ (*teacher*) chargé(e) m(f) de cours

**led** [lɛd] pt, pp of lead

**LED** [ˌɛl·iˈdi] n s. **light-emitting diode** diode f électroluminescente

**ledge** [lɛdʒ] n rebord m

**leek** [lik] n poireau m

**leery** [ˈlɪr·i] adj méfiant(e); **to be ~ of sb/sth** se méfier de qn/qc

**left¹** [lɛft] I. n ❶ (*direction opposite right*) gauche f ❷ (*left side*) côté m gauche; **on/to the** ~ à gauche ❸ (*political grouping*) **the** ~ la gauche ❹ *inf s.* **left-hander** II. *adj* gauche III. *adv* à gauche

**left²** [left] *pt, pp of* **leave**

**left-hand** *adj* gauche

**left-handed** *adj* ❶ (*regularly using left hand*) gaucher(-ère) ❷ (*for left hand use*) pour gaucher(-ère)

**left-hander** *n* gaucher, -ère *m, f*

**leftover** ['left‧oʊ‧vər] I. *adj* ~ **food** un reste de nourriture II. *n pl* restes *mpl*

**left wing** *n* POL aile *f* gauche

**left-wing** *adj* POL gauchiste

**leg** [leg] *n* ❶ (*limb*) jambe *f* ❷ (*clothing part*) jambe *f* ❸ (*segment of a competition*) manche *f* ▸ **to pull sb's** ~ faire marcher qn

**legal¹** ['li‧gəl] *adj* (*lawful*) légal(e)

**legal²** ['li‧gəl] *adj* (*paper*) au format US "legal"

**legalize** ['li‧gəl‧aɪz] *vt* légaliser

**legally** ['li‧gəl‧i] *adv* légalement

**legal tender** *n* monnaie *f* légale

**lemon** ['lem‧ən] *n* ❶ (*fruit*) citron *m* ❷ (*color*) jaune *m* citron ❸ *inf* (*car*) tacot *m*

**lemonade** [‧lem‧ə‧'neɪd] *n* limonade *f*

**lemon peel, lemon rind** *n* écorce *f* de citron

**lemon squeezer** *n* presse-citron *m*

**lend** [lend] <lent, lent> *vt* ❶ (*give for a short time*) prêter ❷ (*impart, grant*) **to** ~ **sb/sth sth** donner qc à qn/qc; **to** ~ **weight to an argument** donner du poids à un argument ❸ (*accommodate*) **to** ~ **oneself to sth** se prêter à qc ▸ **to** ~ **an ear** prêter l'oreille; **to** ~ **a hand to sb** donner un coup de main à qn

**length** [leŋ(k)θ] *n* (*measurement*) longueur *f*; **to be x feet in** ~ faire x pieds de long ▸ **to go to great** ~**s to** +*infin* remuer terre et ciel pour +*infin*

**lengthen** ['leŋ(k)‧θən] I. *vt* ❶ (*cause time extension*) prolonger ❷ (*make longer*) rallonger; **to be** ~**ed** (*vowels*) être allongé II. *vi* s'allonger

**lengthy** <-ier, -iest> *adj* long(ue); (*discussion*) interminable

**lenient** *adj* indulgent(e)

**lens** [lenz] <-ses> *n* lentille *f*; (*of glasses*) verre *m*

**lent** [lent] *pt of* **lend**

**Lent** [lent] *n no art* carême *m*

**lentil** ['lent‧əl] *n* BOT lentille *f*

**Leo** ['li‧oʊ] *n* Lion *m*; *s.a.* **Aquarius**

**leopard** ['lep‧ərd] *n* léopard *m*

**leotard** ['li‧ə‧tard] *n* ❶ SPORTS justaucorps *m* ❷ (*fashion*) maillot *m*

**lesbian** ['lez‧bi‧ən] I. *n* lesbienne *f* II. *adj* lesbien(ne)

**less** [les] I. *adj comp of* **little** moins de; **sth of** ~ **value** qc de moindre valeur II. *adv* moins; **no more, no** ~ ni plus ni moins; **to see sb** ~ voir qn moins souvent; **not him, much** ~ **her** pas lui, encore moins elle III. *pron* moins; ~ **and** ~ de moins en moins; **to have** ~ **than sb** avoir moins que qn; **to cost** ~ **than sth** coûter moins cher que qc ▸ **in** ~ **than no time** en un rien de temps IV. *prep* ~ **5%** moins 5%

**lesser** ['les‧ər] *adj* moindre; **to a** ~ **extent** dans une moindre mesure; **the** ~ **of two evils** le moindre mal

**lesser-known** *adj* moins connu(e)

**lesson** ['les‧ən] *n* ❶ (*teaching period*) cours *m* ❷ (*useful experience*) leçon *f*; **to teach sb a** ~ donner une leçon à qn

**let** [let] *vt* ❶ (*give permission*) laisser; **to** ~ **sb** +*infin* laisser qn +*infin* ❷ (*allow*) laisser; ~ **him be!** laisse-le tranquille!; **to** ~ **sb know sth** faire savoir à qn; **to** ~ **sth pass** laisser passer qc ❸ (*in suggestions*) ~**'s go** on y va; ~ **us pray** prions ❹ (*filler while thinking*) ~**'s see** voyons; ~ **me think** attends/attendez (un moment) ❺ (*expressing defiance*) ~ **sb** +*infin* laisser +*infin*; ~ **it rain** laisse faire ❻ (*giving a command*) **to** ~ **sb do sth** faire que qn fasse qc *subj* ❼ MATH **to** ~ **sth be sth** supposer que qc est qc ▸ ~ **alone** et encore moins; **to** ~ **fly** balancer

◆**let down** I. *vt* ❶ (*lower: window*) baisser; (*object*) faire descendre; (*hair*) détacher ❷ (*fail, disappoint*) décevoir; (*car*) lâcher ❸ (*leave: person*) laisser tomber ④ FASHION rallonger **II.** *vi* descendre

◆**let in** *vt* laisser entrer; **to let oneself in the house** ouvrir la porte ▸ **to let oneself in for** sth mettre les pieds dans qc; **to let sb in on sth** mettre qn au courant de qc

◆**let off** *vt* ① (*punish only mildly*) **to let sb off** faire grâce à qn ② (*fire: a bomb*) faire exploser; (*fireworks*) tirer; (*a gun*) décharger ▸ **to ~ steam** *inf* se défouler

◆**let on** *vi inf* ① (*divulge*) dire; **to ~ that ...** laisser entendre que ...; (*show*) laisser paraître que ... ② (*claim, pretend*) prétendre

◆**let out I.** *vi* (*end*) finir **II.** *vt* ① (*release*) laisser sortir; (*a burp, air, a cry, a chuckle*) laisser échapper; (*secret*) divulguer ② FASHION (*make wider: a dress*) élargir ③ (*rent*) louer

◆**let up I.** *vi* ① (*become weaker or stop*) cesser; (*rain*) se calmer; (*the fog*) disparaître ② (*go easy on*) **to ~ on sb** pardonner qc à qn ③ (*release*) **to ~ on sth** relâcher qc II. *vt* faire se relever

**lethal** ['li·θəl] *adj* ① (*able to cause death*) létal(e) ② (*extremely dangerous*) *a. fig* mortel(le); **~ weapon** arme *f* meurtrière

**letter** ['let·ər] **I.** *n* lettre *f* ▸ **to the ~** à la lettre **II.** *adj* (*paper*) lettre (*format US*)

**letter-size** *adj* au format US lettre

**lettuce** ['let̬·ɪs] *n* laitue *f*

**levee¹** ['lev·i] *n* (*embankment*) levée *f*

**levee²** ['lev·i] *n* (*formal reception*) réception *f* officielle

**level** ['lev·əl] **I.** *adj* ① (*horizontal, flat*) plat(e); (*spoon*) rase; (*flight*) horizontal(e) ② (*having the same height, amount*) **to be ~ with sth** être au niveau de qc ③ (*steady*) égal(e); **to keep a ~ head** garder la tête au clair; **in a ~ tone** sur un ton calme **II.** *adv* droit; **to draw ~ with sth** arriver à la même hauteur que qc **III.** *n* ① niveau *m*; **ground ~** rez-de-chaussée *m*; **above sea ~** au-dessus du niveau de la mer; **at the local/national/regional ~**

au niveau local/national/régional ② (*amount, rate: of alcohol, inflation*) taux *m* **IV.** *vt* ① (*make level*) niveler ② (*smooth and flatten*) aplanir ③ (*demolish completely: building, town*) raser ④ (*point*) **to ~ sth at sb** (*a gun, pistol, rifle*) diriger qc sur qn **V.** *vi inf* **to ~ with sb** parler franchement avec qn

◆**level off** *vi*, **level out I.** *vi* ① (*cease to fall or rise*) se stabiliser ② (*cease to slope*) s'aplanir **II.** *vt* égaliser

**level-headed** *adj* réfléchi(e)

**lever** ['lev·ər] **I.** *n* ① (*bar controlling a machine*) levier *m* ② (*device moving heavy object*) pince-monseigneur *f* ③ *fig* (*use of threat*) moyen *m* de pression **II.** *vt* + *adv/prep* **to ~ sth (up)** soulever qc avec un levier

**leverage** ['lev·ərɪdʒ] **I.** *n* ① (*action of using lever*) *a.* ECON, FIN effet *m* de levier ② *fig* influence *f* **II.** *vt* faire croître par effet de levier; **to ~ sth across sth** réaliser une levée de fonds via qc

**liable** ['laɪ·ə·bl] *adj* ① (*prone*) enclin(e) ② LAW responsable

**liar** ['laɪ·ər] *n* menteur, -euse *m, f*

**libel** ['laɪ·bəl] **I.** *n* LAW, PUBL diffamation *f* **II.** *vt* LAW, PUBL diffamer

**liberal** ['lɪb·ər·əl] **I.** *adj* ① (*tolerating lifestyles or beliefs*) *a.* POL libéral(e) ② (*generous*) généreux(-euse) *a.* ECON, POL ③ (*not strict: interpretation*) libre **II.** *n* libéral(e) *m(f)*

**liberal arts** *n* **the ~** les arts *mpl* libéraux

**liberate** ['lɪb·ər·eɪt] *vt* ① (*free*) libérer ② *fig, iron, inf* (*steal*) voler

**liberation** *n* libération *f*; **~ from sb/sth** émancipation *f* de qn/qc

**libertarian** [,lɪb·ər·ter·i·ən] *adj, n* libertaire *mf*

**liberty** ['lɪb·ər·t̬i] *n form* liberté *f*; **to be at ~** être libre

**Libra** ['li·brə] *n* Balance *f*; *s.a.* **Aquarius**

**librarian** [laɪ·brer·i·ən] *n* bibliothécaire *mf*

**library** ['laɪ·brer·i] <-ies> *n* ① (*books or media collection*) bibliothèque *f* ② (*serial publication*) collection *f* ▸ **a walk-**

**ing ~** (*person*) une encyclopédie vivante

**library card** *n* carte *f* de bibliothèque

**license** ['laɪ·sᵊn(t)s] **I.** *n* ❶(*document*) permis *m* ❷(*maker's permission*) licence *f*; **under ~** sous autorisation ❸*form* (*freedom*) licence *f*; **to have ~ to** +*infin* avoir l'autorisation de +*infin* **II.** *vt* **to ~ sb to** +*infin* donner à qn une licence pour +*infin*

**licensed** *adj* sous licence; **to be ~ to** +*infin* avoir une licence pour +*infin*

**license plate** *n* plaque *f* d'immatriculation

**lick** [lɪk] **I.** *n* ❶(*running of tongue over sth*) lèchement *m* ❷(*small quantity or layer: of color*) touche *f* ❸MUS (*brief phrase in music*) **a few ~s** quelques notes **II.** *vt* ❶(*move tongue across sth*) lécher ❷*fig* (*lightly touch*) **flames** ► **(at) sb/sth** des flammes *fpl* effleurent qn/qc ❸*inf* (*defeat without difficulty*) écraser ❹*inf* (*strike sb repeatedly*) tabasser ► **to ~ sb's boots** lécher les bottes de qn

**licorice** ['lɪk·ər·ɪs] *n* réglisse *f*

**lid** [lɪd] *n* ❶(*removable covering*) couvercle *m* ❷(*eyelid*) paupière *f* ► **to blow the ~ off sth** lever le secret sur qc; **to keep the ~ on sth** garder le secret sur qc; **to put a ~ on sth** (*stop*) mettre un point final à qc

**lie¹** [laɪ] **I.**<-y-> *vi* mentir ► **to ~ through one's teeth** mentir comme un arracheur de dents **II.**<-y-> *vt* **to ~ one's way somewhere** s'en sortir par un mensonge **III.**<lies> *n* mensonge *m;* **to be a pack of ~s** n'être que mensonge

**lie²** [laɪ] <-y-, lay, lain> *vi* ❶(*be horizontally positioned*) être couché; **to ~ flat** être posé à plat ❷(*exist, be positioned*) être; **to ~ off the coast** ne pas être loin de la côte; **to ~ in ruins** être en ruine ❸*form* (*be buried somewhere*) reposer ❹(*be responsibility of*) **to ~ with sb/sth** incomber à qn/qc ► **to ~ heavily on one's mind** rester assis sur ses positions

◆**lie around** *vi* traîner

◆**lie back** *vi* se pencher en arrière

◆**lie down** *vi* se coucher ► **to ~ on the job** se la couler douce; **to take sth lying down** prendre qc sur soi

**Lieut.** *n abbr of* **Lieutenant** Lt *m*

**life** [laɪf] <lives> *n* vie *f*; **to be full of ~** être plein de vie ► **to be a matter of ~ and death** être une question de vie ou de mort; **to be the man/woman in sb's ~** *inf* être l'homme/la femme de la vie de qn; **to take sb's ~** mettre fin aux jours de qn; **to take one's (own) ~** mettre fin à ses jours; **not on your ~!** *inf* certainement pas!; **that's ~!** c'est la vie!

**lifeboat** *n* bateau *m* de sauvetage

**lifeguard** *n* maître nageur *m*

**life insurance** *n* assurance *f* vie

**life jacket** *n* gilet *m* de sauvetage

**lifelike** *adj* fidèle à la réalité

**life-or-death** *adj* (*situation*) de vie ou de mort; (*struggle*) à mort

**life preserver** *n* ❶(*life jacket*) gilet *m* de sauvetage ❷(*lifesaver*) bouée *f* de sauvetage

**life raft** *n* radeau *m*

**lifesaver** *n* ❶(*rescuer*) sauveteur, -euse *m, f* ❷(*flotation device*) bouée *f* de sauvetage ❸(*very good thing*) planche *f* de salut

**life sentence** *n* peine *f* d'emprisonnement à vie

**lifestyle** *n* style *m* de vie

**lifetime** *n* ❶(*time one is alive*) vie *f*; **in sb's ~** de la vie de qn; **to happen once in a ~** n'arriver qu'une seule fois dans la vie; **to seem like a ~** sembler durer une éternité ❷(*time sth exists, functions*) durée *f* de vie

**lift** [lɪft] **I.** *n* ❶(*device for lifting: for goods*) monte-charge *m inv*; (*for skiers*) téléski *m* ❷(*upward motion*) **to give sth a ~** soulever qc ❸(*car ride*) **to give sb a ~** prendre qn en voiture ❹*fig* (*positive feeling*) **to give sb a ~** donner du courage à qn; (*cheer up*) donner le moral à qn ❺(*rise, increase*) augmentation *f* ❻(*upward force*) poussée *f*

**⑦** AVIAT portance f II. *vi* se lever; (*fog*) se dissiper III. *vt* ① (*move upward*) lever; (*weights*) soulever ② *fig* (*raise*) élever; **to ~ one's eyes** lever les yeux au ciel; **to ~ one's voice** élever la voix ③ *fig* (*make entertaining and interesting*) relever ④ (*make tighter*) lifter; **to ~ one's face** se faire faire un lifting du visage ⑤ (*unearth*) récolter ⑥ (*move by air*) soulever en l'air ⑦ (*stop: a ban, restrictions*) lever ⑧ *inf* (*steal*) piquer; (*plagiarize*) copier ⑨ (*remove from*) enlever ▶ **to not ~ a finger** ne pas lever le petit doigt
◆ **lift off** *vi* décoller
◆ **lift up** *vt* soulever ▶ **to ~ one's head** lever la tête; **to ~ one's voice** élever la voix

**liftoff** *n* AVIAT, TECH décollage *m*

**light¹** [laɪt] I. *adj* ① *a. fig* CULIN léger(-ère) ② (*not intense, strong: breeze, rain*) petit(e); **to be a ~ sleeper** avoir le sommeil léger ▶ **to be as ~ as a feather** être léger comme une plume II. *adv* légèrement ▶ **to get off ~** s'enlever facilement; **to travel ~** voyager avec peu de bagages III. *n pl* conclusions *fpl*

**light²** [laɪt] I. *n* ① (*energy, source of brightness, lamp*) *a. fig* lumière *f*; **to cast ~ on sth** jeter la lumière sur qc ② (*brightness*) lueur *f*; **to do sth by the ~ of sth** faire qc à la lumière de qc ③ (*daytime*) lumière *f* du jour; **first ~** premières lueurs *fpl* ④ (*way of perceiving*) jour *m* ⑤ (*flame for igniting*) feu *m* ⑥ *pl* (*person's abilities, standards*) facultés *fpl* ▶ **to bring sth to ~** faire la lumière sur qc; **to come to ~** éclater au grand jour; **in ~ of sth** compte tenu de qc II. *adj* clair(e) III. *vt* <lit, lit *o* lighted, lighted> ① (*illuminate*) *a. fig* éclairer ② (*start burning: a cigarette, pipe*) allumer IV. *vi* <lit, lit *o* lighted, lighted> s'allumer
◆ **light up** I. *vt* ① (*make illuminated*) éclairer ② (*ignite*) allumer II. *vi* ① (*become bright*) *a. fig* s'éclairer ② (*start smoking tobacco*) allumer une cigarette

**light bulb** *n* ampoule *f* électrique

**lighten¹** I. *vi* s'éclairer; (*sky*) s'éclaircir II. *vt* éclairer; (*color*) éclaircir

**lighten²** I. *vt* ① (*make less heavy*) alléger ② *fig* (*make more bearable, easier*) soulager ③ (*make less tense, serious*) **to ~ sb's mood** dérider qn II. *vi* se relâcher

**lighter** ['laɪ·tər] *n* briquet *m*

**light-headed** *adj* ① (*faint*) étourdi(e) ② (*silly and ebullient*) écervelé(e)

**light-hearted** *adj* ① (*person*) de bonne humeur; (*atmosphere*) joyeux(-euse); (*speech, remark*) léger(-ère)

**lighthouse** *n* phare *m*

**lighting** *n* éclairage *m*

**lightly** *adv* légèrement; **to sleep ~** avoir le sommeil léger; **to not take sth ~** ne pas prendre qc à la légère

**lightning** ['laɪt·nɪŋ] *n* foudre *f*; **a flash of ~** un éclair *f*; **to be quick as ~** être aussi rapide que l'éclair

**lightning rod** *n* ① (*safety device*) paratonnerre *m* ② *fig* (*lightning conductor*) souffre-douleur *m inv*

**lightweight** I. *adj* ① (*of light weight*) léger(-ère) ② (*sport*) poids léger *inv* ③ *fig, pej* (*not influential: person*) qui manque d'envergure II. *n* ① (*class of competitors*) poids *mpl* légers ② (*competitor*) poids *m* léger ③ (*person lacking importance*) personne *f* manquant d'envergure

**likable** ['laɪ·kə·bl] *adj* sympathique

**like¹** [laɪk] I. *vt* aimer; **to ~ doing sth** aimer faire qc; **sb would ~ sth** qn aimerait qc II. *vi* vouloir; **if you ~** si tu veux/ vous voulez III. *n pl* préférences *fpl*; **sb's ~s and dislikes** ce que qn aime et n'aime pas

**like²** [laɪk] I. *adj inv* semblable; **to be of ~ mind** être du même avis II. *prep* ① (*similar to*) **to be ~ sb/qc** être semblable à qn/qc; **to look ~ sth** ressembler à qc; **what was it ~?** comment était-ce? ② (*in the manner of*) comme; **to work ~ crazy** travailler comme un fou ③ (*such as*) tel(le) que; **there is nothing ~ sth** il n'y a rien de tel que qc

►~ **father,** ~ son tel père, tel fils III. *conj* comme; **he doesn't do it** ~ **I do** il ne le fait pas comme moi IV. *n* semblable *mf*; **toys, games, and the** ~ des jouets, des jeux et autres choses du même genre V. *adv sl* **it was,** ~, **really bad** c'était, comment dire, vraiment mauvais

**likeable** ['laɪ.kə.bl] *adj s.* likable

**likelihood** ['laɪ.klɪ.hʊd] *n* probabilité *f*

**likely** ['laɪ.kli] I. <-ier, -iest *o* more ~, most ~> *adj* ❶ (*probable*) probable ❷ (*promising*) prometteur(·euse) ► **a** ~ **story!** qu'est-ce que c'est que ces salades? II. <more ~, most ~> *adv* probablement ► **not** ~! jamais de la vie!

**like-minded** *adj* sympathisant(e)

**likeness** <-es> *n* ❶ (*looking similar*) ressemblance *f*; **a family** ~ un air de famille ❷ (*representation*) représentation *f* ❸ (*portrait*) portrait *m*

**likewise** ['laɪk.waɪz] *adv* ❶ (*in a similar way*) pareillement ❷ *inf* (*me too*) moi aussi ❸ (*introducing similar point*) de même

**liking** ['laɪ.kɪŋ] *n* penchant *m*; **to be to sb's** ~ être au goût de qn

**lilac** ['laɪ.lək] I. *n* lilas *m* II. *adj* lilas *inv*

**Lilliputian** [ˌlɪl·ə·'pju·ʃ°n] *adj iron* lilliputien(ne)

**lily** ['lɪl·i] <-lies> *n* lys *m*

**lima bean** ['laɪ·mə bin] *n* haricot *m* de Lima

**limb** [lɪm] *n* ❶ (*tree part*) branche *f* ❷ (*body part*) membre *m* ► **to be/go out on a** ~ **to** +*infin* être dans une situation difficile pour +*infin*

**lime¹** [laɪm] I. *n* ❶ (*green citrus fruit*) citron *m* vert ❷ (*juice from lime fruit*) citronnade *f* ❸ (*citrus fruit tree*) limettier *m* II. *adj* ❶ (*light yellowish-green*) citron vert *inv* ❷ CULIN au citron vert

**lime²** [laɪm] I. *n* (*white deposit*) chaux *f* II. *vt* chauler

**limit** ['lɪm·ɪt] I. *n* limite *f*; **to put a** ~ **on sth** limiter qc; **to do sth within** ~ **s** faire qc dans les limites II. *vt* limiter

**limp¹** [lɪmp] I. *vi* boiter II. *n* boitement *m*

**limp²** [lɪmp] *adj* ❶ (*floppy, loose*) mou(molle) ❷ *fig* (*exhausted*) crevé(e) ❸ *fig* (*lacking forcefulness*) faible

**line¹** [laɪn] <-ning> *vt* (*cover*) doubler ► **to** ~ **one's pockets with sth** se mettre de l'argent plein les poches avec qc

**line²** [laɪn] I. *n* ❶ (*mark*) a. TYP, COMPUT, TEL ligne *f*; (*of poem*) vers *m*; **hold the** ~! ne quitte/quittez pas!, garde/gardez la ligne! *Québec;* **to be/stay on the** ~ être/rester en ligne ❷ (*drawn line*) trait *m* ❸ (*row*) file *f*; (*of trees*) rangée *f*; **front** ~ ligne *f* de front; **to be in a** ~ être aligné; **to stand in** ~ faire la queue ❹ (*path without curves, arcs*) ligne *f* droite ❺ (*chronological succession: of disasters*) succession *f*; (*of family*) lignée *f* ❻ (*cord*) corde *f*; (*for fishing*) ligne *f* ❼ *pl* (*general idea*) fil *m* rouge; **along the** ~ **s of sth** du même genre que qc ► **to be out of** ~ ne pas être en accord; **to drop sb a** ~ *inf* écrire une petite bafouille à qn; **in** ~ **with sb/sth** en accord avec qn/qc II. <-ning> *vt* **to** ~ **sth** faire des lignes sur qc; **to** ~ **the route** border la route; **along the** ~ **d** se ranger

◆ **line up** I. *vt* ❶ (*put in a row facing*) aligner ❷ (*plan, organize*) planifier ❸ (*rally, organize against*) **to line sb/ sth up against sb/sth** dresser qn/qc contre qn/qc II. *vi* ❶ (*stand in a row*) se mettre en ligne ❷ (*wait one behind another*) faire la queue ❸ (*rally, organize against*) **to** ~ **against/behind sb/ sth** se mettre contre/derrière qn

**linen** ['lɪn·ɪn] *n* ❶ (*cloth*) linge *m*; **bed** ~ **s** draps *mpl* ❷ (*flax*) lin *m*

**line-up** *n* ❶ (*selection*) sélection *f*; **we've got a** ~ **of guests on our show** nous avons une longue liste d'invités notre programme ❷ (*row*) file *f* ❸ (*identification of criminal*) alignement *m* pour la revue; **police** ~ séance *f* d'identification

**lingerie** [ˌlan·ʒə·'reɪ] *n* lingerie *f*

**lining** ['laɪ·nɪŋ] *n* doublure *f*

**link** [lɪŋk] I. *n* ❶ (*ring in a chain*) maillon *m* ❷ (*connection between two* *units*) *a.* COMPUT lien *m*; **rail ~** liaison *f* ferroviaire ▶ **to be the weak ~** être le maillon faible (de la chaîne) II. *vt* ❶ (*connect*) **to ~ things together** relier des choses entre elles ❷ (*associate*) **to ~ sth to sth** associer qc à qc ❸ (*clasp*) **to ~ hands** se donner la main III. *vi* coïncider

**lint** [lɪnt] *n* fibres *fpl* de coton

**lion** [laɪən] *n* ❶ ZOOL lion *m* ❷ (*celebrated person*) monstre *m* ▶ **the ~'s share** la part du lion

**lioness** [laɪə·'nes] <-sses> *n* lionne *f*

**lip** [lɪp] *n* ❶ lèvre *f* ❷ (*rim*) bord *m* ❸ *inf* (*impudent speech*) **any more of your ~ and ...** si tu fais encore de l'insolent, ... ▶ **to lick one's ~s** se lécher les babines

**lip-read** *vt, vi* lire sur les lèvres

**lipstick** *n* tube *m* de rouge à lèvres

**liquefy** ['lɪk·wə·faɪ] <-ie-> I. *vt* ❶ CHEM liquéfier ❷ FIN devenir plus liquide II. *vi* se liquéfier

**liqueur** [lɪ·'kɜr] *n* liqueur *f*

**liquid** ['lɪk·wɪd] I. *n* liquide *m* II. *adj a.* FIN liquide

**liquidize** ['lɪk·wɪ·daɪz] *vt* liquéfier

**liquify** *vt s.* **liquefy**

**liquor** ['lɪk·ər] *n* spiritueux *m;* **he cannot hold his ~** il ne tient pas l'alcool

**lisp** [lɪsp] I. *n* zézaiement *m; to have* **a ~** zozoter II. *vi* avoir un cheveu sur la langue III. *vt* dire en zozotant

**list¹** [lɪst] I. *n* (*itemized record*) liste *f;* **price ~** tarifs *mpl; ~ of stocks* FIN cote *f* II. *vt* ❶ (*make a list*) répertorier; **to ~ sth in alphabetical order** classer qc par ordre alphabétique ❷ (*enumerate*) énumérer ❸ FIN coter

**list²** [lɪst] I. *vi* NAUT **to ~ to port/starboard** prendre de la gîte à bâbord/tribord II. *n* NAUT gîte *f*

**listen** ['lɪs·ən] I. *vi* **to ~ to sb/sth** écouter qn/qc; **to ~ to reason** écouter la voix de la raison II. *n inf* **it's worth a ~** cela vaut la peine d'être écouté

♦ **listen in** *vi* ❶ RADIO écouter ❷ (*listen to private conversation*) **to ~ on sth** écouter qc discrètement

**listener** ['lɪs·ən·ər] *n* auditeur, -trice *m, f*

**lit¹** [lɪt] *pt, pp of* **light**

**lit²** [lɪt] *n abbr of* **literature** litt.

**liter** ['li·tər] *n* litre *m*

**literacy** ['lɪt·ər·ə·si] *n* ❶ (*ability to read and write*) degré *m* d'alphabétisation ❷ (*ability to understand*) **computer ~** compréhension *f* de l'informatique

**literally** *adv* littéralement; **to take sth ~** prendre qc au pied de la lettre

**literature** ['lɪt·ər·ə·tʃər] *n* ❶ (*written artistic works*) littérature *f* ❷ (*specialized texts, promotional material*) documentation *f*

**lithograph** ['lɪθ·ə·græf] I. *n* lithographie *f* II. *vt* lithographier

**litter** ['lɪt·ər] I. *n* ❶ (*refuse*) détritus *mpl* ❷ ZOOL portée *f* ❸ (*for cats*) litière *f* ❹ MED civière *f* II. *vt* **to be ~ed with sth** être recouvert de qc; **his dirty clothes ~ed the floor** ses vêtements sales jonchaient le sol

**litterbug** *n inf* porc *m*

**little** ['lɪt·l] I. *adj* ❶ (*small*) petit(e); **a ~ house** une maisonnette ❷ (*young*) **the ~ ones** les petits *mpl* ❸ (*brief*) **for a ~ while** pendant un court instant; **to have a ~ word with sb** échanger deux mots avec qn ❹ (*not enough*) peu de ❺ (*unimportant: problem*) léger(·ère) ❻ (*weak: smile*) petit(e) II. *pron* peu; **as ~ as possible** le moins possible; **to know ~** ne pas savoir grand-chose; **to have ~ to say** n'avoir presque rien à dire III. *adv* peu; **~ by ~** peu à peu; **a ~ more than a minute ago** il y a à peine une minute; **as ~ as possible** le moins possible; **a ~-known place** un endroit méconnu; **~ did I think that ...** j'étais loin de penser que ...

**live¹** [laɪv] I. *adj* ❶ (*living*) vivant(e); **real ~** en chair et en os ❷ RADIO, TV en direct; **to give a ~ performance** jouer en public ❸ (*carrying electrical power*) conducteur(·trice) ❹ MIL amorcé(e) ❺ (*burning*) ardent(e) II. *adv* ❶ RADIO, TV en direct ❷ MUS en public

**live²** [lɪv] I. *vi* ❶ (*be alive*) vivre; **the right to ~** le droit à la vie; **as long as sb**

~**s** tant qu'il y aura de la vie ② (*reside*) habiter; **to ~ together/apart** vivre ensemble/séparés ▶ **we ~ and learn** on apprend à tout âge; **to ~ and let ~** faire preuve de tolérance; **to ~ to regret sth** passer sa vie à regretter qc II. *vt* vivre; **to ~ a life of luxury** mener une vie de luxe; **to ~ life to the fullest** profiter pleinement de la vie; **to ~ one's own life** vivre sa vie ▶ **to ~ a lie** vivre dans le mensonge; **to ~ and breathe sth** ne vivre que pour qc

◆**live down** *vt* (*one's past*) faire oublier; (*failure, mistake*) chercher à effacer

◆**live off, live on** *vt* **to ~ sth** vivre de qc; **to ~ sb** vivre aux crochets de qn; **his brother lives off his inheritance** son frère vit de son héritage ▶ **to ~ the fat of the land** vivre comme un coq en pâte

◆**live out** *vi* ① (*live*) **to ~ one's life** passer sa vie ② (*fulfill: one's destiny*) décider de; (*one's dreams, fantasies*) réaliser

◆**live through** *vt* survivre à

◆**live up to** *vt* (*expectations*) répondre à; (*promises*) tenir; (*reputation*) faire honneur à; (*principles*) vivre selon; **to ~ a standard** être à la hauteur

**livelihood** ['laɪv·li·hʊd] *n* moyens *mpl* d'existence; **to earn one's ~** gagner sa vie; **to lose one's ~** perdre son gagne-pain

**lively** ['laɪv·li] *adj* ① (*full of life and energy*) vif(vive); (*person*) plein(e) d'entrain; (*manner, nature*) pétulant(e); (*party, conversation*) animé(e); (*imagination*) fertile; (*example, expression*) percutant(e) ② (*lifelike*) vivant(e) ③ (*bright*) éclatant(e)

**liver**[1] ['lɪv·ər] *n* foie *m*

**liver**[2] ['lɪv·ər] *n* **clean ~** personne *f* vertueuse; **fast ~** noceur *m*

**liverwurst** ['lɪv·ər·wɜrst] *n* saucisse *f* de foie

**livestock** ['laɪv·stak] I. *n* + *sing vb* bétail *m* II. *adj* (*breeder, breeding*) de cheptel; (*fair*) aux bestiaux

**living** ['lɪv·ɪŋ] I. *n* ① (*livelihood*) vie *f*; **I paint for a ~** je vis de ma peinture ② (*way of life*) vie *f*; **standard of ~** niveau *m* de vie; **to make a good ~** bien gagner sa vie ③ + *pl vb* (*people who are still alive*) **the ~** les vivants *mpl* II. *adj* ① (*alive*) vivant(e); **does he have any ~ grandparents?** ses grands-parents sont-ils toujours en vie? ② (*existent: language, legend*) vivant(e); (*tradition*) vivace ③ (*exact: image*) exact(e); **to be the ~ embodiment of sb/sth** être la personnification même de qn/qc ▶ **to scare the ~ daylights out of sb** faire une peur bleue à qn

**living conditions** *npl* conditions *fpl* de vie

**living quarters** *npl* ① (*housing*) logement(s) *m(pl)* ② MIL quartier *m*

**living room** *n* séjour *m*, vivoir *m* Qué bec

**living will** *n* testament *m* de vie

**lizard** ['lɪz·ərd] *n* lézard *m*

**load** [loʊd] I. *n* ① (*amount carried*) charge *f*; **a ship with a full ~ of passengers** un paquebot rempli de passagers ② (*burden*) poids *m*; **that's a ~ off sb's mind** qn a l'esprit soulagé ③ (*amount of work*) **to lighten the ~** rendre la vie plus facile; **to share the ~** partager la besogne ④ *inf* (*lots*) **a ~ of sth** un tas de qc ▶ **get a ~ of this!** *inf* regarde/écoute un peu ça! II. *vt* ① AUTO, COMPUT, MIL charger ② (*burden*) **to ~ sb with sth** accabler qn de qc ③ TECH (*film , software*) charger; (*camera*) armer; (*cassette*) insérer ▶ **to ~ the dice** piper les dés III. *vi* se charger; (*truck*) prendre un chargement

◆**load down** *vt* ① (*load*) **to load sb/ sth down with sth** charger qn/qc de qc ② (*overload*) surcharger; **to be loaded down with presents** crouler sous les cadeaux

◆**load up** I. *vt* charger II. *vi* faire le chargement

**loaded** *adj* ① (*filled with live ammunition*) chargé(e) ② (*not objective: question*) insidieux(-euse); **to be ~ in favor**

L

of sb/sth avoir un parti pris pour qn/qc ❸ GAMES ~ dice dés *mpl* pipés ❹ *inf* cousu(e) d'or ❺ *inf* (*drunk*) to be ~ être plein

**loaf**[1] [loʊf] <loaves> *n* pain *m*

**loaf**[2] *vi* traînasser

**loan** [loʊn] I. *vt* prêter; to ~ sth to sb, to ~ sb sth prêter qc à qn II. *n* ❶ (*borrowed money*) emprunt *m* ❷ (*act of lending*) prêt *m*; the book I want is out on ~ le livre que je veux a été emprunté

**lobby** ['la·bi] I. <-bbies> *n* ❶ ARCHIT entrée *f*; (*of hotel*) hall *m*; (*of theater*) foyer *m* ❷ (*influential group*) lobby *m* II. <-ie-> *vi* exercer une pression; to ~ to have sth done faire pression pour obtenir qc III. <-ie-> *vt* faire pression sur

**lobbyist** *n* membre *m* d'un groupe de pression

**lobster** ['lab·stər] *n* homard *m*

**local** ['loʊ·kəl] I. *adj* local(e); (*accent, dialect, politician*) régional(e); (*hero*) national(e); (*police*) municipal(e) II. *n* ❶ *pl* (*inhabitant of a place*) habitants *mpl* de la région ❷ (*bus*) bus *m* urbain ❸ (*local branch of a trade union*) branche *f* syndicale locale

**local anesthetic** *n* anesthésie *f* locale

**local area network** *n* COMPUT réseau *m* local

**local call** *n* communication *f* locale

**local news** *n* + *sing vb* informations *fpl* locales

**local time** *n* heure *f* locale

**loch** [lak] *n* loch *m*

**lock**[1] [lak] I. *n* ❶ (*fastening device*) serrure *f* ❷ (*unit of a canal*) écluse *f* ❸ (*wrestling hold*) clef *f*; to hold sb in a body ~ immobiliser qn avec son corps ▶~, stock and <u>barrel</u> dans sa totalité; to be under ~ and <u>key</u> être enfermé à clef II. *vt* ❶ (*fasten with a lock*) fermer à clef, barrer *Québec* ❷ (*confine safely*) enfermer ❸ (*be held fast*) to be ~ed être bloqué; (*be jammed*) être coincé ▶to ~ <u>horns</u> over sth se disputer pour qc III. *vi* se bloquer

◆**lock away** *vt* ❶ (*secure behind a lock*) mettre en sécurité ❷ (*confine in prison or hospital*) enfermer ❸ (*confine somewhere free of disruption*) to lock oneself away s'isoler

◆**lock on** *vi*, **lock onto** *vi* MIL accrocher

◆**lock out** *vt* ❶ (*prevent entrance by locking all doors*) enfermer dehors; she locked herself out of her car elle a laissé les clefs de sa voiture à l'intérieur ❷ ECON priver de travail

◆**lock up** I. *vt* ❶ (*lock away*) mettre sous clef; (*documents*) mettre en sûreté ❷ (*confine in prison or mental hospital*) enfermer II. *vi* fermer

**lock**[2] [lak] *n* mèche *f* de cheveux

**locker** ['la·kər] *n* casier *m*

**locksmith** ['lak·smɪθ] *n* serrurier *m*

**locomotive** [ˌloʊ·kə·'moʊ·tɪv] I. *n* locomotive *f* II. *adj* locomotif(-ive)

**lodge** [ladʒ] I. *vi* ❶ (*become stuck*) se loger ❷ (*stay in a rented room*) loger II. *vt* ❶ LAW to ~ a complaint porter plainte; to ~ a protest protester ❷ (*make become stuck*) loger ❸ (*accommodate*) loger III. *n* ❶ (*inn*) pavillon *m*; hunting/ski ~ gîte *m* ❷ (*guard's house*) loge *f* ❸ (*beaver's lair*) hutte *f*

**lodging** *n* ~(s) logement *m*; board and ~ pension *f* complète

**loft** [laft] I. *n* (*raised area, living space*) loft *m* II. *vt* lancer haut

**log**[1] [lɔg] I. *n* (*piece of wood*) rondin *m*; (*for fire*) bûche *f* ▶to <u>sleep like a</u> ~ dormir comme une souche II. <-gg-> *vt* (*tree*) débiter; (*forest*) décimer

**log**[2] [lɔg] I. *n* registre *m*; ~ (book) NAUT journal *m* de bord; AUTO carnet *m* de route; AVIAT carnet *m* de vol II. *vt* enregistrer III. *vi* COMPUT to ~ into sth se connecter à qc

**log**[3] *n abbr of* **logarithm** logarithme *m*

**logical** *adj* logique

**loiter** ['lɔɪ·tər] *vi* ❶ (*linger*) flâner ❷ (*hang around*) traîner

**lollipop** ['la·li·pap] *n* sucette *f*, suçon *m* *Québec*

**loneliness** ['loʊn·lɪ·nəs] *n* solitude *f*

**lonely** ['loʊn·li] <-ier, -iest *o* more ~, most ~> *adj* ❶ *(unhappy because alone)* seul(e) ❷ *(solitary)* solitaire ❸ *(isolated)* isolé(e); *(street)* peu fréquenté(e)

**loner** ['loʊn·ər] *n* solitaire *mf*

**long**¹ [lɔŋ] I. *adj* long(ue); **to have come a ~ way** revenir de loin; **to have a ~ way to go** avoir du chemin à faire ► **in the ~ run** à la longue; **to be a ~ shot** être un coup à tenter; **~ time no see!** *inf* voilà un revenant!; **to be ~ in the tooth** ne plus être de la première jeunesse. II. *adv* ❶ *(a long time)* depuis longtemps; **~ ago** il y a longtemps; **~ after/before** bien après/avant; **before ~** avant bien longtemps; **at ~ last** enfin; **~ live the king!** longue vie au roi! ❷ *(for the whole duration)* **all day/night ~** toute la journée/nuit; **as ~ as sb lives** aussi longtemps que qn est en vie ❸ *((but) only if)* **as ~ as ... ** seulement si ... ❹ *(no more)* **to no ~er** +*infin* ne plus +*infin* ❺ *(goodbye)* **so ~** à bientôt

**long**² [lɔŋ] *vi* avoir envie; **to ~ for sb/sth** désirer qn/qc

**long-distance** I. *adj* ❶ *(going a long way: flight)* long-courrier; *(train)* grande ligne ❷ *(separated by a great distance)* à distance; *(call)* longue distance ❸ SPORTS *(race, runner)* de fond II. *adv* **to call ~** faire un appel longue distance; **to travel ~** faire un long voyage

**longevity** [lɔŋ·ˈdʒev·ə·t̬i] *n* longévité *f*

**long-haired** *adj pej* aux cheveux longs; *(animals)* aux poils longs

**longish** *adj inf* assez long(ue)

**long jump** *n* SPORTS **the ~** le saut en longueur

**long-range** *adj* ❶ *(across a long distance)* longue portée ❷ *(long-term)* à long terme

**long-sighted** *adj* prévoyant(e)

**long-suffering** *adj* d'une patience à toute épreuve

**long-term** *adj* ❶ *(effective on a longer period)* à long terme ❷ *(lasting long)* (de) longue durée

**long wave** I. *n* grandes ondes *fpl* II. *adj* longues ondes *inv*

**long-winded** *adj* prolixe

**look** [lʊk] I. *n* ❶ *(act of looking, examining)* regard *m;* **to have a ~ at sth** jeter un coup d'œil à qc ❷ *(appearance, expression)* air *m;* **to have the ~ of sb/sth** avoir l'air de qn/qc; **by the ~ of things** selon toute apparence; **sb's good ~s** le physique de qn ❸ *(act of searching)* **to take a ~ for sb/sth** chercher qn/qc ❹ *(specified style)* look *m* ► **if ~s could kill** si les yeux pouvaient tuer II. *interj* regarde(z)! III. *vi* ❶ *(use one's sight)* **to ~ at sb/sth** regarder qn/qc; **to ~ sb up and down** regarder qn des pieds à la tête; **to be not much to ~ at** ne pas en valoir la peine; **to ~ the other way** regarder dans l'autre direction ❷ + *adj or n (appear, seem, resemble)* avoir l'air; **to ~ one's age** faire son âge; **to ~ one's best** être à son avantage; **to ~ like sb/sth** ressembler à qn/qc ❸ *(hope)* **to ~ to do sth** espérer faire qc; **to ~ ahead** se tourner vers l'avenir ❹ *(pay attention)* faire attention ❺ *(regard, consider)* **to ~ at sth** considérer qc ❻ *(examine, study, evaluate)* **to ~ at sth** examiner qc ❼ *(face a particular direction)* **to ~ north** faire face au nord ► **don't ~ a gift horse in the mouth** *prov* à cheval donné on ne regarde pas à la bride *prov*

◆**look after** *vt* s'occuper de; **to ~ oneself** prendre soin de soi; **to ~ one's interests** veiller sur ses propres intérêts

◆**look ahead** *vi* regarder devant soi

◆**look around** *vi* ❶ *(turn around to look)* se retourner ❷ *(look in all directions)* regarder autour de soi ❸ *(search)* **to ~ for sb/sth** chercher qn/qc II. *vt* *(inspect)* faire le tour de; *(house)* visiter

◆**look away** *vi* regarder ailleurs; **to ~ from sth** détourner les yeux de qc

◆**look back** *vi* regarder derrière soi; **to ~ on sth** revenir sur qc; **to never ~** ne jamais regarder en arrière

◆**look down** *vi* ❶ *(from above)* regar-

L

der en bas ❷ (*lower one's eyes*) baisser les yeux ❸ (*hate*) **to ~ on sb/sth** mépriser qn/qc

◆**look for** *vt* ❶ (*seek*) chercher ❷ (*expect*) s'attendre à

◆**look forward** *vi* ❶ (*anticipate pleasurably*) **to ~ to sth** attendre qc avec impatience; **to ~ to seeing sb** être impatient de voir qn ❷ *form* (*anticipate with specified feelings*) **to ~ to sth** espérer qc

◆**look into** *vi* ❶ (*investigate*) examiner; (*reasons*) étudier ❷ (*predict*) envisager

◆**look on** *vt* considérer

◆**look out** *vi* ❶ (*face a particular direction*) **to ~ on sth** regarder qc ❷ (*watch out, be careful*) **to ~ for sb/sth** se méfier de qn/qc ❸ (*look for*) **to ~ for sb/ sth** rechercher qn/qc; **to ~ for number one** penser à ses propres intérêts

◆**look over** *vt* jeter un coup d'œil à

◆**look through** *vt* ❶ (*look*) regarder ❷ (*examine*) examiner ❸ (*peruse*) parcourir ❹ (*not acknowledge sb*) **to look (straight) through sb** ne pas reconnaître qn

◆**look to** *vt* ❶ (*take care*) faire attention à ❷ (*expect*) **to ~ sb/sth for sth** se tourner vers qn/qc pour qc ❸ (*count on*) compter sur

◆**look up** I. *vt* ❶ (*consult a reference work*) chercher ❷ (*look for and visit*) aller voir II. *vi* ❶ *a. fig* (*raise one's eyes upward*) **to ~ at sb/sth** lever les yeux vers qn/qc ❷ (*improve*) s'améliorer ❸ (*see as role model*) **to ~ to sb** avoir de l'admiration pour qn

**look-alike** *n* sosie *m*

**lookout** *n* ❶ (*observation post*) guet *m* ❷ (*person set as a guard*) guetteur, -euse *m, f* ❸ (*act of keeping watch*) **to be on the ~ for sb/sth** être à la recherche de qn/qc; **to keep a ~ for sth** guetter qc

**loon** *n* ZOOL plongeon *m*

**loop** [lup] I. *n* ❶ (*curve*) *a.* COMPUT boucle *f* ❷ ELEC circuit *m* fermé II. *vi* former

une boucle III. *vt* **to ~ sth** faire une boucle avec qc

**loophole** ['lup·hʊl] *n* échappatoire *f*

**loose** [lus] I. *adj* ❶ (*not tight: knot, rope, screw*) desserré(e); (*clothing*) ample; (*skin*) relâché(e); **~ connection** mauvais contact *m* ❷ (*partly detached, not confined*) détaché(e); **to get ~** se détacher; **~ sheet of paper** feuille *f* de papier séparée ❸ (*release*) **to let sth ~** lâcher qc ❹ (*not exact*) vague; (*translation*) approximatif(-ive) ❺ (*not strict or controlled: discipline, style*) relâché(e) ❻ (*sexually immoral*) amoral(e); **~ morals** mœurs *fpl* relâchées II. *adv* **to hang ~** pendre ► **hang ~!** reste calme! III. *n* **to be on the ~** être en cavale IV. *vt form* lâcher

**loosely** *adv* ❶ (*not fixed*) lâchement; **to hang ~** pendre ❷ (*not tightly*) sans serrer; (*tied, wrapped*) mal ❸ (*not exactly*) approximativement ❹ (*not strictly*) de façon relâchée; **~ organized society** société *f* désorganisée

**loosen** ['lu·sən] I. *vt* ❶ (*untie*) défaire ❷ (*unfasten*) desserrer ❸ (*weaken*) relâcher; **to ~ sb's tongue** délier la langue de qn; **to ~ ties with sb/sth** distendre ses liens avec qn/qc II. *vi* ❶ *a. fig* (*unfasten*) se desserrer ❷ (*relax*) se détendre

**lord** [lɔrd] *n* ❶ (*god*) **the Lord** le Seigneur ❷ (*powerful man*) seigneur *m;* **drug ~** parrain *m* de la drogue ❸ (*British nobleman*) lord *m;* **~ of the manor** châtelain *m*

**lose** [luz] <lost, lost> I. *vt* perdre; **to ~ one's life** perdre la vie; **to ~ no time in doing sth** ne pas perdre de temps à faire qc ► **to ~ face** perdre la face; **to ~ heart** perdre courage; **to have lost one's marbles** *iron* perdre la tête; **to have nothing ~** n'avoir rien à perdre; **to ~ sight of sth** perdre qc de vue; **to ~ sleep over sth** s'en faire pour qc; **to ~ touch with sb** perdre le contact avec qn; **to ~ track of sb/sth** perdre la trace de qn/qc II. *vi* perdre; **to ~ to sb/ sth** se faire battre par qn/qc

**loser** n ❶ (*defeated person, group*) perdant(e) m(f) ❷ pej (*unsuccessful person*) loser m

**losing** adj perdant(e); (*battle*) perdu(e) d'avance

**loss** [las] <-es> n perte f; **to be at a ~ to** +*infin* être embarrassé pour +*infin*

**lost** [last] I. pt, pp of **lose** II. adj (*soul*) en peine; (*opportunity*) manqué(e); **to be ~** être perdu(e); **to get ~** s'égarer ▸ **a cause** une cause perdue

**lost and found** n objets mpl trouvés

**lot** [lat] n ❶ (*much/many*) **a ~/~s** beaucoup; **a ~ of people/rain** beaucoup de gens/pluie; **to feel a ~ better** se sentir beaucoup mieux ❷ (*plot of land*) terrain m; **building ~** lotissement m; **parking ~** parking m ❸ (*group of people*) groupe m ❹ (*everything*) **the whole ~** le tout ❺ (*fate*) sort m ❻ (*share in a lottery*) lot m; **to draw ~s** tirer au sort ❼ (*unit in an auction*) lot m

**lottery** ['la·tər·i] <-ies> n loterie f

**loud** [laʊd] I. adj ❶ (*very audible*) fort(e); **~ and clear** clair et précis ❷ pej (*garish*) criard(e) ❸ pej (*aggressively noisy*) bruyant(e) II. adv bruyamment; (*to laugh out, to speak*) fort

**loudmouth** n inf grande gueule f

**loudspeaker** n ❶ (*part of PA system*) haut-parleur m ❷ (*radio, stereo speaker*) enceinte f

**Louisiana** [lu·i·zi·'æn·ə] n la Louisiane

**lounge** [laʊndʒ] I. n salon m II. vi ❶ (*recline in a relaxed way*) se prélasser ❷ (*be, stand idly*) paresser

**lousy** <-ier, -iest> adj pej, inf ❶ (*of poor quality*) nul(le); **to feel ~** se sentir mal foutu ❷ (*meager*) **a ~ $5** 5 malheureux dollars ❸ (*infested with lice*) pouilleux(-euse)

**love** [lʌv] I. vt ❶ aimer ❷ (*greatly like*) **to ~ to** +*infin* adorer +*infin*; **I'd ~ it if you could come** ça me ferait vraiment plaisir que tu viennes subj II. n ❶ (*strong affection or passion*) amour m; **~ at first sight** coup m de foudre; **to be in ~ with sb** être amou-

reux de qn; **to make ~ to sb** faire l'amour à qn; **to fall in ~ with sb** tomber amoureux de qn ❷ SPORTS zéro m; **forty-~** quarante zéro ▸ **there is no ~ lost between the two** ils ne peuvent pas s'encadrer

**love-hate relationship** n relation f houleuse

**love letter** n lettre f d'amour

**love life** n inf vie f amoureuse

**lovely** ['lʌv·li] <-lier, -iest> adj beau(belle)

**lovemaking** n amour m (physique); **to be good at ~** bien savoir faire l'amour

**lover** n ❶ (*for a woman*) amant m; (*for a man*) maîtresse f; **to be/become ~s** être/devenir amants; **her live-in ~** le partenaire avec qui elle vit ❷ (*sb who loves sth*) amoureux, -euse m, f; **a nature/an opera ~** un amoureux de la nature/l'opéra

**love seat** n fauteuil m pour deux

**lovesick** adj **to be ~** avoir un chagrin d'amour

**love song** n chanson f d'amour

**love story** n histoire f d'amour

**loving** adj tendre; **~ care** affection f

**low** [loʊ] I. adj <-er, -est> ❶ (*not high or tall, not great: altitude, wall*) bas(se); (*neckline*) plongeant(e) ❷ (*small in number*) faible; **to be ~ in cholesterol** être peu riche en cholestérol; **to be ~ in calories** être hypocalorique; **to be ~ in funds** avoir peu de réserves ❸ (*reduced in quantity: level*) bas(se); **to be ~ on sth** n'avoir presque plus de qc ❹ (*intensity: frequency, sound, voice*) bas(se); (*light*) faible ❺ (*poor, not of high quality*) mauvais(e); **to hold sth in ~ regard** mésestimer qc ❻ (*lowly, not important*) **to be a ~ priority** ne pas être une priorité ❼ (*unfair, mean*) **a ~ trick** un coup bas ❽ (*sad, dejected*) **in ~ spirits** abattu(e); **to feel ~** ne pas avoir le moral II. <-er, -est> adv bas; **to fly ~** voler bas; **to be cut ~** (*dress, blouse*) être très décolleté; **to turn the music ~er** baisser la musique III. n ❶ (*low level*) **record ~** baisse f record; **to reach an**

**all-time ~** atteindre son niveau le plus bas ❷(*difficult moment*) **the highs and ~s** les hauts *mpl* et les bas ❸ METEO zone *f* de basse pression
**low-calorie** *adj* hypocalorique
**low-cut** *adj* décolleté(e)
**lower¹** ['ləʊ·ər] *vt* ❶(*let down, haul down*) baisser; (*landing gear, lifeboat*) descendre; (*sails, mast*) amener; **to ~ oneself to** +*infin* s'abaisser pour +*infin* ❷(*reduce, decrease*) *a. fig* baisser; **to ~ one's expectations** ne pas attendre trop ❸(*diminish*) rabaisser ❹(*demean, degrade*) **to ~ oneself to** +*infin* s'abaisser à +*infin*
**lower²** [laʊr] *vi* se couvrir; **~ing sky** ciel *m* menaçant; **to ~ at sb** jeter un regard menaçant à qn
**lower³** ['ləʊ·ər] *adj* inférieur(e); **in the ~ back** dans le bas du dos
**lower case, lower-case letter** *n* TYP minuscule *f*
**low-fat** *adj* allégé(e)
**low-necked** *adj* décolleté(e)
**low season** *n* basse saison *f*
**low tide, low water** *n* marée *f* basse
**lox** *n* saumon *m* fumé
**loyalty** ['lɔɪ·əl·t̬i] <-ties> *n* loyauté *f*; **sb's ~ to sth** la loyauté de qn envers qc; **to have divided loyalties** être partagé
**loyalty card** *n* carte *f* de fidélité
**lozenge** ['la·zəndʒ] *n* losange *m*; **throat/cough ~s** pastille *f* pour la gorge/toux
**Ltd.** ['lɪm·ə·t̬ɪd] *n abbr of* **limited** ≈ SARL *f*
**luck** [lʌk] *n* ❶((*good*) *fortune*) chance *f*; **to bring sb ~** porter chance à qn; **to be in ~** avoir de la chance; **to be out of ~** ne pas avoir de chance; **to be down on one's ~** avoir la guigne; **to be the ~ of the draw** être une question de chance; **with** (**any**) **~** avec un peu de chance; **as ~ would have it ...** le hasard a voulu que ...; **no such ~!** *inf* tu parles!; **don't do that; it's bad ~** ne fais pas ça, ça porte malheur ❷(*success*) chance *f*; **to wish sb good ~ in sth** souhaiter bonne chance à qn pour qc; **did you**

**have any ~ opening that bottle?** est-ce que tu as réussi à ouvrir cette bouteille?
**lucky** <-ier, -iest> *adj* ❶(*have luck: person*) chanceux(-euse); **to be ~ at games/in love** avoir de la chance au jeu/en amour; **it is ~ that ...** heureusement que ...; **to make a ~ guess** deviner au hasard ❷(*bringing good fortune: number*) porte-bonheur *inv*; **~ day** jour *m* de chance
**luggage** ['lʌg·ɪdʒ] *n* bagages *mpl*; **hand ~** bagage à main
**luggage rack** *n* ❶(*on train, bus*) porte-bagages *m* ❷(*on car roof*) galerie *f*
**lukewarm** [ˌluk·'wɔrm] *adj a. fig* tiède; **to be ~ about an idea** ne pas être très chaud pour une idée
**lullaby** ['lʌl·ə·baɪ] *n* berceuse *f*
**luminous** ['lu·mə·nəs] *adj* ❶(*visible in darkness*) fluorescent(e) ❷(*brilliant*) sensationnel(le)
**lump** [lʌmp] **I.** *n* ❶(*solid mass of a substance:* of coal, sugar) morceau *m*; (*of clay*) motte *f*; (*in cooking*) grumeau *m* ❷(*abnormal growth*) grosseur *f* ❸ *inf* (*oaf*) empoté(e) *m(f)*; **fat ~** gros tas *m* **II.** *vt* ❶(*combine*) regrouper; **to ~ all the people in the same group** mettre tout le monde dans le même groupe; *fig* mettre tout le monde dans le même panier ❷(*endure*) **if you don't like it, you can ~ it** si ça ne te plaît pas c'est pareil
**lump sum** *n* somme *f* forfaitaire; **~ payment** versement *m* unique; **to pay in a ~** payer en une fois
**lumpy** <-ier, -iest> *adj* (*sauce, gravy*) grumeleux(-euse); (*surface*) irrégulier(-ère)
**lunatic** ['lu·nə·t̬ɪk] **I.** *n* ❶(*mentally ill person*) fou, folle *m, f* ❷ POL **the ~ fringe** les extrémistes *mpl* ❸ *sl* (*crazy person*) dingue *mf* **II.** *adj* dingue
**lunch** [lʌn(t)ʃ] **I.** *n* déjeuner *m*, dîner *m* Belgique, Québec; **buffet ~** buffet *m*; **to be out to ~** être parti déjeuner ▸ **to be out to ~** être dérangé **II.** *vi* déjeuner, dîner *Belgique, Québec*; **to ~ on sand-**

**wiches** manger des sandwichs au déjeuner

**lunch break** *n* pause *f* de midi

**luncheon** ['lʌn·(t)ʃən] *n form* déjeuner *m*

**luncheon meat** *n* pâté *m* de viande

**lunch hour** *n s.* **lunch break**

**lunchtime I.** *n* heure *f* du déjeuner; **to do sth by ~** faire qc d'ici midi **II.** *adj* (*concert*) de midi

**lung** [lʌŋ] *n* poumon *m* ▶ **to shout at the top of one's ~s** crier à pleins poumons

**lung cancer** *n* cancer *m* du poumon

**lurch** [lɜrtʃ] **I.** *vi* (*crowd, person*) tituber; (*train, ship*) tanguer; (*car*) faire une embardée **II.** *n* embardée *f* ▶ **to leave sb in the ~** laisser qn en plan

**luscious** ['lʌʃ·əs] *adj* ❶ (*richly sweet: fruit, wine*) gorgé(e) de sucre ❷ (*delicious*) succulent(e) ❸ *inf* (*voluptuous: girl, lips*) pulpeux(-euse); (*curves*) généreux(-euse) ❹ (*fertile: landscape, land*) riche

**Luxembourg** ['lʌk·səm·bɜrg] *n* ❶ (*province*) (la province de) Luxembourg ❷ (*country*) le Luxembourg ❸ (*capital*) Luxembourg(-ville) *m*

**Luxembourger** *n* Luxembourgeois(e) *m(f)*

**luxurious** [lʌg·'ʒʊr·i·əs] *adj* luxueux (-euse); (*tastes*) de luxe; **to take a ~ bath** se prélasser dans un bain

**luxury** ['lʌk·ʃər·i] **I.** <-ies> *n pl* luxe *m*; **to buy oneself little luxuries** se faire des petits plaisirs **II.** *adj* (*goods*) de luxe

**lying** ['laɪ·ɪŋ] **I.** *present participle of* **lie** **II.** *n* (*place to lie*) couche *f* **III.** *adj* menteur(-euse)

# Mm

**M**

**M, m** [em] <-'s> *n* M *m*, m *m;* **~ as in Mike** (*on telephone*) m comme Marcel

**M I.** *n abbr of* **male** homme *m* **II.** *adj abbr of* **medium** M

**m I.** *n* ❶ *abbr of* **meter** m m ❷ *abbr of* **mile** mile m ❸ *abbr of* **million** million m ❹ *abbr of* **minute(s)** min *f* ❺ *abbr of* **masculine** masculin *m* **II.** *adj abbr of* **married** marié(e)

**ma** [ma] *n inf* ❶ (*mother*) maman *f* ❷ (*old woman*) madame *f*

**MA** [,em·'eɪ] *n* ❶ *abbr of* **Master of Arts** ≈ maîtrise *f* de lettres ❷ *abbr of* **Massachusetts**

**macadamia nut** [,mæk·ə·'deɪ·mi·ə nʌt] *n* noix *f* de macadamia

**macaroni** [,mæk·ə·'roʊ·ni] *n* macaroni *m*

**macaroni and cheese** *n* macaronis *mpl* au fromage

**machete** [mə·'(t)ʃeţ·i] *n* machette *f*

**machine** [mə·'ʃin] **I.** *n* ❶ (*mechanical device*) a. *pej* machine *f* ❷ (*washing machine*) machine *f* (à laver) ❸ (*vending machine*) distributeur *m* ❹ *inf* (*automobile, motorcycle*) engin *m* ❺ (*controlling system*) appareil *m*; **the party ~** la machine du parti **II.** *vt* ❶ (*operate on a machine: tool, part*) usiner ❷ (*saw: hem*) coudre

**machine gun** *n* mitrailleuse *f*

**machine-made** *adj* fabriqué(e) à la machine

**machine-readable** *adj* COMPUT lisible par ordinateur

**machinery** [mə·'ʃi·nər·i] *n* ❶ (*machines*) machines *fpl* ❷ (*working parts of machine*) mécanisme *m* ❸ (*working parts of organization*) rouages *mpl*

**machine-washable** *adj* lavable en machine

**mackerel** ['mæk·rᵊl] <-(s)> n maquereau m

**mad** [mæd] adj ❶<-er, -est> inf (angry) furieux(-euse); **don't get ~ at me** ne te fâche pas contre moi ❷<-er, -est> a. inf (insane, frantic) fou(folle); (animal) enragé(e); **to go ~** devenir fou; **to drive sb ~** rendre qn fou; **I ran/searched like ~** j'ai couru/cherché comme un fou ❸<-er, -est> inf (enthusiastic) dingue; **to be ~ about sb/sth** être dingue de qn/qc; **the fans went ~** c'était la folie parmi les fans

**madam** ['mæd·əm] n ❶ form (polite form of address) madame f ❷ (head of brothel) mère f maquerelle

**maddening** adj exaspérant(e)

**made** [meɪd] I. pp, pt of **make** II. adj **~ in ...** fabriqué à ...; **well-~** bien fait(e)

**made-up** adj ❶ (wearing make-up) maquillé(e) ❷ (untrue) faux(fausse) ❸ (invented) inventé(e) ❹ (made in advance) tout(e) fait(e)

**madly** adv ❶ (frantically) comme un(e) fou(folle); **to behave ~** avoir un comportement de fou ❷ (very much, intensely) follement

**madness** n folie f

**mag** [mæg] n sl abbr of **magazine** magazine m

**magazine** ['mæg·ə·zin] n ❶ (publication) magazine m ❷ MIL magasin m

**magic** ['mædʒ·ɪk] I. n ❶ magie f II. adj magique; (show) de magie

**magical** adj magique; (evening, surroundings) fabuleux(se)

**magician** [mə·'dʒɪʃ·ᵊn] n magicien(ne) m(f)

**magistrate** ['mædʒ·ɪ·streɪt] n magistrat(e) m(f)

**magnet** ['mæg·nət] n (metal) aimant m; **to be a ~ for sb/sth** fig exercer une attirance sur qn/qc

**magnetic** adj a. fig magnétique; **~ person** personne f qui a du magnétisme; **~ north** pôle m magnétique

**magnificent** adj magnifique

**magnify** ['mæg·nɪ·faɪ] vt ❶ (make bigger) grossir ❷ (make worse) aggraver

**magnifying glass** n loupe f

**magnitude** ['mæg·nɪ·tud] n ❶ (great size) a. fig ampleur f ❷ ASTR magnitude f

**magpie** ['mæg·paɪ] n ❶ (bird) pie f ❷ pej (collector) quelqu'un qui ne jette rien

**mahogany** [mə·'hag·ə·ni] n acajou m

**maid** [meɪd] n domestique f

**maiden name** n nom m de jeune fille

**maid of honor** n demoiselle f d'honneur

**mail¹** [meɪl] I. n a. COMPUT courrier m; **by ~** par la poste II. vt expédier

**mail²** [meɪl] n (armor) maille f

**mailbox** n boîte f aux lettres; COMPUT boîte f (aux lettres) électronique

**mailing list** n fichier m d'adresses

**mailman** n facteur m

**main** [meɪn] I. adj principal(e); **that's the ~ thing** c'est l'essentiel II. n TECH conduite f

**Maine** [meɪn] I. n le Maine II. adj du Maine

**mainframe** ['meɪn·freɪm] n COMPUT ❶ (computer) macroordinateur m ❷ (central unit) unité f centrale

**mainland** ['meɪn·lənd] n **the ~** le continent; **~ Europe** l'Europe f continentale

**mainly** adv ❶ (primarily) principalement ❷ (mostly) surtout

**main road** n route f principale

**main street** n rue f principale

**maintain** [meɪn·'teɪn] vt ❶ (keep: order) maintenir; **to ~ contact/silence** garder contact/le silence ❷ (preserve: machine) entretenir ❸ (provide for) entretenir ❹ (assert) soutenir; (one's innocence) clamer

**maintenance** ['meɪn·tᵊn·ən(t)s] n ❶ (keeping) maintien m ❷ (preservation: of buildings, machines) entretien m

**maize** [meɪz] n maïs m

**majestic** adj majestueux(-euse)

**majesty** ['mædʒ·ə·sti] n ❶ (tremendous beauty) splendeur f ❷ (title for royalty)

majesté *f*; **Her/His/Your Majesty** Sa/
Votre Majesté

**major** ['meɪ·dʒər] I. *adj* majeur(e); **A ~
MUS** la *m* majeur II. *n* ① MIL major *m*
② (*primary subject*) matière *f* principale ③ (*student studying a subject*) **to be
a history ~** avoir histoire comme matière principale III. *vi* **to ~ in history** faire
histoire en matière principale

**majority** [mə'dʒɔr·ə·t̬i] *n* majorité *f*;
**the vast ~ of children** la grande majorité des enfants

**major-league** [ˌmeɪ·dʒər·'liːg] *adj*
① SPORTS de la ligue majeure ② *inf*
(*large, important*) faisant partie de la
crème de la crème

**make** [meɪk] I.<made, made> *vt*
① (*do*) faire; **to ~ time** trouver du
temps; **to ~ sth (out) of sth** faire qc à
partir de qc; **made of plastic/paper** en
plastic/papier; **to show what one's
(really) made of** *fig* montrer de quoi
qn est fait; **to ~ a decision** prendre une
décision ② (*create, change*) **to ~ sb cu-
rious/sick** rendre qn curieux/malade;
**they made her vice-president** ils
l'ont nommée vice-présidente; **that
made the situation worse** ça a fait
empirer les choses; **to ~ oneself
heard/understood** se faire entendre/
comprendre; **to ~ oneself known to
sb** se présenter à qn ③ (*earn, get: money, enemies*) se faire; **to ~ friends** se
faire des ami(e)s; **to ~ a living** gagner sa
vie ④ (*force, cause*) **to ~ sb/sth do sth**
faire faire qc à qn; **to ~ sb change their
mind** faire changer qn d'avis; **it ~s me
feel sick** ça me rend malade ⑤ *inf* (*get
to, reach*) **to ~ it** y arriver; **I can't ~ it
tomorrow** demain je ne peux pas; **to ~
it to sth** arriver à qc; **I made the team**
j'ai été accepté dans l'équipe ⑥ (*calculate, decide*) **we'll ~ it Friday/$30** di-
sons vendredi/30 dollars ▸ **to ~ sb's
day** faire plaisir à qn; **to ~ sense** avoir
du sens; **to ~ sense of sth** arriver à
comprendre qc; **to ~ or break sth** décider du sort de qn/qc; **to be made
of money** rouler sur l'or II. *vi* **to ~ do**

with sth faire avec qc III. *n* marque *f*
▸ **to be on the ~** *pej* en vouloir

◆**make for** *vt* ① (*head for*) se diriger
vers ② (*result in*) conduire à

◆**make of** *vt* ① (*understand, think of*)
**to make sth of sb/sth** penser qc de
qn/qc; **what do you ~ it?** qu'est-ce que
tu en penses?; **can you make anything of it?** tu y comprends quelque
chose? ② (*consider important*) **to
make too much of sb/sth** accorder
trop d'importance à qn/qc ▸ **do you
want to make something of it?** *inf* tu
as quelque chose à redire?

◆**make off** *vi inf* se tirer; **to ~ with sth**
partir avec qc

◆**make out** I. *vi inf* ① (*succeed, cope*)
s'en sortir; **how are you making out?**
tu t'en sors? ② (*succeed sexually*) **to ~
with sb** se faire qn II. *vt* ① *inf* (*claim*)
prétendre; **to make sb/sth out to be
sth** faire passer qn/qc pour qc; **she
makes herself out to be a genius** elle
se fait passer pour un génie ② (*understand with difficulty*) distinguer; (*writing*) déchiffrer; *fig* discerner; **to make
sb out** ③ (*write: a
check*) faire; **the check's made out to
me** le chèque est à mon nom ▸ **to ~ a
case for sth** présenter des arguments
pour qc

◆**make over** *vt* ① LAW (*transfer ownership*) céder ② (*alter, convert*) **to ~ sth
into sth** transformer qc en qc ③ (*redo,
alter*) reprendre

◆**make up** I. *vt* ① (*compensate*) compenser; (*a deficit, loss*) combler; (*the
time, ground*) rattraper; **I'll make it up
to you** je tâcherai de me rattraper
② (*complete: a sum, team*) compléter;
**to ~ the difference** payer la différence
③ (*settle*) arranger; (*a dispute*) régler;
**to make it up** se réconcilier ④ (*comprise*) composer; **to ~ the majority of
sth** former la majorité de qc; **to be
made up of** (*people*) être composé de;
(*things*) contenir ⑤ (*put makeup on*)
maquiller ⑥ (*invent*) inventer ⑦ (*prepare*) préparer ⑧ PUBL mettre en pages

**M**

**⑨** SCHOOL **to ~ an exam** rattraper un examen ▸ **to ~ one's mind** se décider **II.** *vi* **①** (*be friends again*) se réconcilier **②** (*put on makeup*) se maquiller
◆ **make up for** *vt* compenser; (*disappointment*) rattraper; **to ~ lost time** rattraper le temps perdu

**make-believe** *n* illusion *f*

**makeover** *n* **①** (*beauty treatment*) soin *m* de beauté **②** (*redecoration*) transformation *f*

**maker** *n* **①** (*manufacturer*) fabricant(e) *m(f)*; (*of a film*) réalisateur, -trice *m, f* **②** (*God*) **to** <u>meet</u> **one's Maker** rencontrer son Créateur

**makeshift I.** *adj* de fortune **II.** *n* solution *f* provisoire

**makeup** *n* **①** (*constitution*) constitution *f* **②** (*character*) caractère *m* **③** (*cosmetics*) maquillage *m*; **to put on ~** se maquiller

**makeup artist** *n* maquilleur, -euse *m, f*

**makeup remover** *n* démaquillant *m*

**M** **malaria** [məˈler·i·ə] *n* malaria *f*

**male** [meɪl] **I.** *adj* (*animal*) mâle; (*person*) masculin(e); **the ~ lead** l'acteur *m* principal **II.** *n* **①** (*person*) homme *m*; (*animal*) mâle *m*; ~~**dominated** (*society*) dominé par les hommes; (*profession*) essentiellement masculin **②** (*animal*) mâle *m*

**malfunction** [ˌmælˈfʌŋ(k)·ʃən] **I.** *vi* *form* mal fonctionner **II.** *n* défaillance *f*

**malicious** *adj* **①** (*bad: person*) malveillant(e) **②** LAW délictueux(-euse); **~ wounding** blessures *fpl* volontaires

**malignancy** [məˈlɪg·nən(t)·si] *n* **①** MED malignité *f* **②** *fig* malveillance *f*

**malignant** *adj* **①** MED malin(-igne) **②** *fig* malveillant(e)

**mall** [mɔl] *n* centre *m* commercial

**malnutrition** [ˌmæl·nuˈtrɪ·ʃən] *n* malnutrition *f*

**malpractice** [ˌmælˈpræk·tɪs] *n* faute *f* professionnelle; **medical ~** faute *f* médicale

**malt** [mɔlt] **I.** *n* **①** (*grain*) malt *m* **②** (*ice cream drink*) boisson *f* à l'orgeat accompagnée de crème glacée **③** *s.* **malt whiskey II.** *vt* malter

**Malta** [ˈmɔl·tə] *n* Malte *f*

**malt whiskey** *n* (whisky *m*) pur malt *m*

**mammal** [ˈmæm·əl] *n* mammifère *m*

**man** [mæn] <men> **I.** *n* **①** (*male human*) homme *m;* **she married a Greek ~** elle a épousé un Grec **②** (*human race*) l'homme *m* **③** (*object in games*) pion *m* ▸ **a ~-to-~ talk** une discussion entre hommes; **the ~ in the** <u>street</u> l'homme de la rue **II.** *vt* <-nn-> prendre la responsabilité de; **to ~ a ship** être membre de l'équipage d'un navire **III.** *interj* *inf* **~, that was good!** ouah, c'était cool!

**manage** [ˈmæn·ɪdʒ] **I.** *vt* **①** (*accomplish*) **to ~ to** +*infin* arriver à +*infin*; **how did you ~ that?** comment tu as fait? **②** (*deal with*) *a.* ECON gérer **II.** *vi* (*cope*) s'en tirer; (*achieve aim*) réussir

**management** *n* ECON gestion *f*; (*managers*) la direction; **~ skills** compétences *fpl* en gestion

**management studies** *n* études *fpl* en gestion d'entreprise

**manager** *n* **①** (*person with control function*) directeur, -trice *m, f*, manager *m* **②** (*of store, project*) gérant(e) *m(f)* **③** (*of artist*) manager *m* **④** SPORTS entraîneur, -euse *m, f*

**managerial** *adj* directorial(e); **~ position** poste *m* de cadre; **~ skills** qualités *fpl* de gestionnaire

**mandarin** [ˈmæn·dər·ɪn] *n* (*fruit*) mandarine *f*

**Mandarin** [ˈmæn·dər·ɪn] *n* LING mandarin *m*

**mandatory** [ˈmæn·də·tɔr·i] *adj* obligatoire

**mandolin** [ˈmæn·dəl·ɪn] *n* mandoline *f*

**man-eater** *n* **①** ZOOL mangeur *m* d'hommes **②** *fig, inf* mangeuse *f* d'hommes

**manhunt** [ˈmæn·hʌnt] *n* chasse *f* à l'homme

**maniac** [ˈmeɪ·ni·æk] *n* **①** PSYCH fou, folle *m, f*, maniaque *mf* **②** *inf* (*fan*) fou, folle *m, f;* **football ~** fou de football

**manifesto** [ˌmæn·ɪˈfest·oʊ] <-sto(e)s> *n* manifeste *m*

**manipulate** [məˈnɪp·jə·leɪt] *vt* **①** *pej*

(*influence unfairly*) manipuler; (*statistics, figures*) trafiquer ❷ (*control with hands*) manœuvrer ❸ (*treat body with hands*) manipuler

**manipulative** *adj pej* manipulateur(-trice)

**mankind** [ˌmænˈkaɪnd] *n* humanité *f*

**manly** <-ier, -iest> *adj* viril(e)

**man-made** *adj* artificiel(le); (*fibers*) synthétique

**mannequin** [ˈmæn·ɪ·kɪn] *n* mannequin *mf*

**manner** [ˈmæn·ər] *n* ❶ (*style*) manière; **in a ~ of speaking** en quelque sorte ❷ *pl* (*social behavior*) manières *fpl*; **that's bad ~s** ce n'est pas des manières ❸ (*way of behaving*) façon *f* d'être ❹ *form* (*kind, type*) sorte *f*; **all ~ of ...** toutes sortes de ...

**manor** [ˈmæn·ər], **manor house** *n* manoir *m*

**manpower** [ˈmæn·paʊər] *n* main-d'œuvre *f*

**mansion** [ˈmæn·(t)ʃ°n] *n* manoir *m*

**manslaughter** [ˈmæn·slɔ·tər] *n* homicide *m* involontaire

**mantelpiece** [ˈmæn·t°l·pis] *n* dessus *m* de cheminée

**manual** [ˈmæn·ju·əl] **I.** *adj* manuel(le) **II.** *n* (*book*) manuel *m*

**manufacture** [ˌmæn·jə·ˈfæk·tʃər] **I.** *vt* ❶ (*produce*) manufacturer ❷ (*fabricate: excuse, story*) fabriquer **II.** *n* fabrication *f*

**manufacturer** *n* fabricant *m*; (*of cars*) constructeur *m*

**manure** [məˈnʊr] *n* engrais *m*

**manuscript** [ˈmæn·jə·skrɪpt] *n* manuscrit *m*

**many** [ˈmen·i] <more, most> **I.** *adj* beaucoup de; **his ~ books** ses nombreux livres; **how ~ glasses?** combien de verres?; **too/so ~ people** trop/tellement de gens; **one chair too ~** une chaise en trop; **as ~ words/letters as** autant de mots/lettres que; **~ times** [*o* **a time**] souvent ▶ **~ happy returns!** joyeux anniversaire! **II.** *pron* beaucoup; **I've read so/too ~** j'en ai tant/trop lu;

**one too ~** un de trop; **I saw ~ more** j'en ai vu bien d'autres; *s.a.* **much III.** *n* **the ~** la masse

**map** [mæp] **I.** *n* ❶ (*representation: of a country*) carte *f*; (*of a town, building, subway*) plan *m* ❷ RAIL carte *f* du réseau ❸ (*outline*) schéma *m* ❹ (*stars*) planisphère *m* ▶ **to put sth on the ~** faire connaître qc **II.** <-pp-> *vt* (*region*) dresser une carte de

**maple** [ˈmeɪ·pl] *n* ❶ (*tree*) érable *m* ❷ (*wood*) (bois *m* d')érable *m*

**marathon** [ˈmer·ə·θən] **I.** *n* marathon *m* **II.** *adj* ❶ (*related to a marathon: race*) de marathon ❷ *fig* marathon *inv*

**marble** [ˈmar·bl] **I.** *n* ❶ (*stone*) marbre *m* ❷ (*for games*) bille *f*; **~s** (*game*) les billes ▶ **to lose** one's **~s** *inf* perdre la boule **II.** *vt* marbrer

**march** [martʃ] **I.** <-ches> *n* ❶ MIL, MUS marche *f*; **to be on the ~** être en marche ❷ (*political action*) manifestation *f* **II.** *vi* ❶ MIL marcher en rang; **forward ~!** en avant toute! ❷ (*walk with determination*) marcher d'un pas décidé; **he ~ed up to me** il a marché sur moi ❸ (*to express opinions*) manifester; **to ~ against animal cruelty** défiler contre la cruauté envers les animaux **III.** *vt* **to ~ sb off** emmener qn

**March** [martʃ] *n* mars *m*; *s.a.* **April**

**margarine** [ˈmar·dʒər·ɪn] *n* margarine *f*

**margin** [ˈmar·dʒɪn] *n* ❶ TYP marge *f* ❷ (*periphery of an area*) bord *m* ❸ *a.* SOCIOL, ECON marge *f*; **to win by a narrow ~** gagner de justesse

**marijuana** [ˌmer·ɪˈwa·nə] *n* marihuana *f*, marijuana *f*

**marina** [məˈri·nə] *n* port *m* de plaisance

**marinate** [ˈmer·ɪ·neɪt] *vt* mariner

**marine** [məˈrin] *adj* ❶ (*concerning sea life*) marin(e) ❷ (*concerning shipping matters*) maritime ❸ (*concerning naval operations*) naval(e)

**Marine** *n* MIL (*member of the U.S. Marine Corps*) marine *m*

M

**Marine Corps** *n* MIL corps *m* de la marine américaine

**marital** ['mer·ɪ·t̬ᵊl] *adj* matrimonial(e); (*infidelity*) conjugal(e)

**marital status** *n* form situation *f* de famille

**mark¹** [mark] **I.** *n* ❶(*spot, stain*) tache *f* ❷(*scratch*) marque *f* ❸(*feature*) trait *m*; **the ~ of genius** le signe du génie; **as a ~ of sth** en signe de qc ❹(*written sign, signal*) marque *f*; **punctuation ~** signe *m* de ponctuation; **question ~** point *m* d'interrogation ❺(*specified point*) **it costs around the $50 ~** ça coûte autour de 50 dollars ❻(*target*) cible *f*; **to hit the ~** toucher le but ❼SPORTS ligne *f* de départ; **on your ~s!** à vos marques! ▶**to be quick/slow off the ~** avoir l'esprit vif/lent **II.** *vt* ❶(*stain, spoil: clothes*) tacher; (*body*) faire des marques sur; (*wood, glass*) marquer ❷(*show by sign or writing: name, price*) indiquer; (*distance, direction*) marquer; **the site is ~ed by a plaque** une plaque signale le site ❸(*constitute*) caractériser; (*beginning, end*) indiquer; (*time, a turning point*) marquer ❹(*celebrate: occasion*) marquer; **they marked the anniversary with demonstrations** l'anniversaire a été commémoré avec des manifestations ❺(*clearly identify*) **to ~ sb as sth** repérer qn comme étant qc ❻SPORTS marquer ❼COMPUT surligner ▶(**you**) **~ my words!** faites bien attention à ce que je vous dis! **III.** *vi* (*stain*) tacher

◆**mark down** *vt* (*reduce: prices*) baisser; **to be marked down** (*shares*) s'inscrire à la baisse

◆**mark off** *vt* ❶(*divide: land*) délimiter; (*intervals*) marquer ❷(*cross off*) rayer

◆**mark out** *vt* distinguer

◆**mark up** *vt* (*increase*) augmenter

**mark²** [mark] *n* HIST (*currency*) mark *m*

**marker** *n* ❶(*sign, symbol*) a. fig marque *f* ❷(*sign to indicate position*) balise *f* ❸COMPUT marqueur *m* ❹(*pen*) marqueur *m* ❺SPORTS marqueur, -euse *m, f*

**market** ['mar·kɪt] **I.** *n* marché *m*; **to be in the ~ for sth** être acheteur de qc; **to put a house on the ~** mettre une maison en vente; **there's a good ~ for sth** il y a une grosse demande pour qc **II.** *vt* commercialiser; **you need to ~ yourself better** il faut que tu saches te vendre *subj*

**marketplace** *n* ❶(*place for market*) place *f* du marché ❷(*commercial arena*) arène *f* commerciale

**market research** *n* étude *f* de marché

**market share** *n* part *f* de marché

**markup** *n* (*profit*) marge *f* bénéficiaire; (*increase*) majoration *f*

**marmalade** ['mar·mᵊl·eɪd] *n* confiture *f* d'oranges

**marquee** [mar·'ki] *n* auvent *m*

**marriage** ['mer·ɪdʒ] *n* a. fig mariage *m*; **related by ~** parents par alliance

**marriage ceremony** *n* cérémonie *f* du mariage

**marriage certificate** *n* acte *m* de mariage

**marriage license** *n* certificat *m* de mariage

**married** **I.** *n* pl marié(e) **II.** *adj* ❶(*concerning marriage: couple*) marié(e); (*life*) conjugal(e) ❷(*very involved*) **to be ~ to sth** être marié avec qc

**marry** ['mer·i] **I.** *vt* ❶(*wed officially*) épouser, marier Belgique, Nord, Québec; **to get married to sb** se marier avec qn ❷(*officiate at ceremony*) marier ❸(*organize wedding of*) marier ❹fig (*associate*) marier **II.** *vi* se marier ▶**to ~ into money** faire un mariage d'argent

**marsh** [marʃ] <-shes> *n* marais *m*

**marshy** ['mar·ʃi] <-ier, -iest> *adj* marécageux(-euse)

**martial** ['mar·ʃᵊl] *adj* martial(e)

**martial law** *n* loi *f* martiale

**martini** [mar·'ti·ni] *n* martini *m*

**marvelous** *adj* merveilleux(-euse); **to feel ~** se sentir extraordinairement bien

**Maryland** ['mer·ə·lənd] I. *n* le Maryland II. *adj* du Maryland

**mascara** [mæs·'ker·ə] *n* mascara *m*

**masculine** ['mæs·kjə·lɪn] I. *adj* masculin(e); LING masculin II. *n* masculin *m*

**mash** [mæʃ] *vt* écraser (en purée); **to ~ potatoes** passer les pommes de terre

**mashed potatoes** *n* purée *f* de pommes de terre

**mask** [mæsk] I. *n a. fig* masque *m*; **as a ~ for sth** pour dissimuler qc II. *vt* masquer

**masochist** *n* masochiste *mf*

**masquerade** [,mæs·kə·'reɪd] I. *n* mascarade *f* II. *vi* **to ~ as sth** se déguiser en qc

**mass** [mæs] I. *n* ❶ *(formless quantity, quantity of matter)* a. PHYS masse *f*; *(of persons)* foule *f* ❷ *(large quantity)* grande quantité *f*; *(of contradictions)* multitude *f*; *(of the people, population)* majorité *f*; **~es of sth** des tonnes *fpl* de qc; **~es of people** des tas *mpl* de gens II. *vi* s'amonceler; *(troops, demonstrators)* se masser III. *adj (large)* massif(-ive); *(widespread)* de masse

**Massachusetts** [,mæs·ə·'tʃu·sɪts] I. *n* le Massachusetts II. *adj* du Massachusetts

**massacre** ['mæs·ə·kər] I. *n* ❶ *(killing of many people)* massacre *m* ❷ *(loss or defeat)* hécatombe *f* II. *vt* a. fig massacrer

**massage** ['mə·sa(d)ʒ] I. *n* massage *m* II. *vt* ❶ *(rub)* masser ❷ *(modify: figures)* fignoler

**massage parlor** *n* salon *m* de massage

**massive** ['mæs·ɪv] *adj* ❶ *(heavy, solid: rock)* massif(-ive) ❷ *(huge: amount)* énorme ❸ *(severe: attack, stroke)* foudroyant(e)

**mass media** *n* + *sing/pl vb* **the ~** les mass medias *mpl*

**mass-produce** *vt* produire en série

**mast** [mæst] *n* ❶ NAUT mât *m* ❷ *(flag pole)* **at half~** ➤ en berne ❸ RADIO, TV pylône *m*

**master** I. *n* ❶ *(person in control)* maître(sse) *m(f)* ❷ *(competent person)* maître *m* ❸ *(original for making copies)* master *m* ➤ **to be one's own ~** être son propre maître II. *vt* ❶ *(have knowledge, control of)* maîtriser ❷ *(overcome)* surmonter

**master bedroom** *n* chambre *f* principale

**masterful** *adj* ❶ *(authoritative)* magistral(e) ❷ *(skillful)* compétent(e) ❸ *(dominating)* plein(e) d'autorité

**master key** *n* passe-partout *m*

**mastermind** I. *n* ❶ *(expert)* spécialiste *mf* ❷ *(planner, organizer)* cerveau *m* II. *vt* orchestrer

**masterpiece** *n* chef-d'œuvre *m*

**mastery** ['mæs·tər·i] *n* maîtrise *f*

**mat** [mæt] *n* ❶ *(floor protection)* tapis *m*; **beach** ~ natte *f* ❷ *(doormat)* paillasson *m* ❸ *(protection for furniture)* housse *f*; *(decorative)* napperon *m*; **(place)** ~ set *m* de table ❹ *(covering)* revêtement *m*

**match¹** [mætʃ] <-tches> *n* allumette *f*

**match²** [mætʃ] I. *n* ❶ *(one of a pair)* pendant *m* ❷ *(partner)* **to be a good ~ for sb** bien aller avec qn; **to make a good ~** être un bon parti ❸ *(competitor)* adversaire *mf* (valable); **to be no ~ for sb** ne pas faire le poids avec qn ❹ *(same color)* quelque chose d'assorti; **to be a good ~ for sth** être bien coordonné avec qc ❺ SPORTS match *m* II. *vi (clothes, colors)* être assortis; *(blood types)* correspondre; *(pieces of evidence)* être pareil; **two socks that ~** deux chaussettes *fpl* qui vont ensemble III. *vt* ❶ *(be a match for: clothes)* être assorti à; *(blood type, piece of evidence, specification, need)* correspondre à ❷ *(find a match for: clothes)* trouver quelque chose d'assorti à; *(blood type, piece of evidence)* faire correspondre à; *(specification, need)* satisfaire; **to ~ skills to jobs** adapter les compétences aux métiers ❸ *(equal: rival)* égaler ; *(achievement)* être à la hauteur de; *(achievement)* égaler; **we'll ~ your salary** vous recevrez le même salaire

**matchbox** <-xes> *n* boîte *f* d'allumettes

**matching** *adj* correspondant(e); FASHION assorti(e)

**M**

**match point** n SPORTS balle f de match

**matchstick** n allumette f

**mate¹** [meɪt] I. n ❶ (*sexual partner*) compagnon, compagne m, f ❷ BIO partenaire mf ❸ (*assistant*) aide mf ❹ inf (*friend*) copain, copine m, f; (*school*) camarade mf; (*at work*) collègue mf II. vi s'accoupler III. vt to ~ sth with sth accoupler qc avec qc

**mate²** [meɪt] I. n GAMES mat m II. vt faire échec et mat à

**material** [mə·'tɪr·i·əl] I. n ❶ (*for making things, doing jobs*) a. fig matériau m; raw ~s matières fpl premières ❷ (*cloth*) tissu m ❸ (*documentation, sources*) matière f ❹ pl (*equipment*) matériel m; writing ~s fournitures fpl de bureau II. adj ❶ (*relating to the physical*) matériel(le) ❷ (*important*) essentiel(le)

**maternal** [mə·'tɜr·nᵊl] adj maternel(le)

**maternity** n maternité f

**math** [mæθ] n abbr of **mathematics** maths fpl

**mathematical** adj mathématique

**mathematician** n mathématicien(ne) m(f)

**mathematics** [ˌmæθ·ə·'mæt·ɪks] n + sing vb mathématiques fpl

**matinee** [ˌmæt·ᵊn·'eɪ] n matinée f; (*in the afternoon*) séance f; a ~ **performance** une matinée

**matriculation** n UNIV inscription f

**matt** [mæt], **matte** adj mat(e)

**matter** ['mæt·ər] I. n ❶ a. fig (*substance*) matière f ❷ (*subject*) sujet m ❸ (*affair*) affaire f; as a ~ of fact en fait; for that ~ d'ailleurs; in this ~ à cet égard; a ~ of taste/opinion une question de goût/point de vue; a ~ of minutes une affaire de quelques minutes; in a ~ of seconds dans une poignée de secondes; the truth of the ~ le fin mot de l'histoire ❹ pl (*the situation*) choses fpl; to make ~s worse pour ne pas arranger les choses; to take ~s into one's own hands prendre les choses en mains ❺ (*problem*) the ~ le problème; what's the ~ (with

you)? qu'est-ce qui ne va pas? ❻ (*importance*) no ~ what peu importe ce que +subj; no ~ who/what/where qui/quoi/où que ce soit subj; no ~ how de n'importe quelle manière II. vi importer; it doesn't ~ if … cela n'a pas d'importance si …; it ~s that il importe que +subj

**matter-of-fact** adj ❶ (*straightforward*) terre-à-terre inv ❷ (*emotionless: style*) prosaïque

**mattress** ['mæt·rəs] n matelas m

**mature** [mə·'tʊr] I. adj ❶ (*adult or full grown*) mûr(e); (*animal*) adulte; (*tree*) adulte ❷ (*experienced: person, attitude*) mûr(e); (*work*) de maturité ❸ form (*very thoughtful*) réfléchi(e) ❹ (*payable*) arrivé(e) à terme II. vi ❶ (*become physically adult*) devenir adulte ❷ (*develop fully*) mûrir; (*wine*) vieillir ❸ (*become payable*) arriver à terme III. vt ❶ CULIN affiner ❷ (*make more adult*) faire mûrir

**maturity** n ❶ (*result of becoming mature*) maturité f ❷ FIN échéance f

**max** [mæks] n abbr of **maximum** max m

**maximize** vt ❶ (*extend*) maximiser ❷ COMPUT (*window*) agrandir

**maximum** ['mæk·sɪ·məm] I. <-ima o -imums> n maximum m II. adj maximum inv; ~ **temperatures** températures fpl maximales

**may** [meɪ] <3ʳᵈ pers sing may, might, might> aux ❶ form (*be allowed*) ~ I come in? puis-je entrer ? ❷ (*possibility*) I ~ go/finish je pourrais partir/finir; she ~ well return il se pourrait bien qu'elle revienne ▸ be that as it ~ quoi qu'il en soit

**May** [meɪ] n (*month*) mai m; s.a. **April**

**maybe** adv ❶ (*perhaps*) peut-être ❷ (*approximately*) environ ❸ (*suggestion*) ~ **we should stop** on devrait peut-être s'arrêter

**mayor** [meɪər] n maire m, maïeur(e) m(f) Belgique, président(e) m(f) Suisse (*dans les cantons de Valais et de Neuchâtel*)

**maypole** ['meɪ·poʊl] *n* mât de fête du *1er* Mai

**maze** [meɪz] *n* dédale *m*

**MD** [ˌem·'di] *n* ❶ *abbr of* **Doctor of Medicine** Docteur *m* en Médecine ❷ *abbr of* **Maryland**

**me** [mi] *objective pron* me, m' + *vowel*, moi *tonic form;* **it's ~** c'est moi; **look at ~** regarde/regardez-moi; **he told ~ that ...** il m'a dit que ...; **older than ~** plus vieux que moi

**ME** *n abbr of* **Maine**

**meadow** ['med·oʊ] *n* pré *m*

**meal¹** [mil] *n* repas *m*

**meal²** [mil] *n* ❶ (*coarsely ground grain*) semoule *f* ❷ (*flour*) farine *f*

**mean¹** [min] *adj* ❶ (*unkind, aggressive*) méchant(e); **to have a ~ streak** avoir un côté mauvais; **to play a ~ trick on sb** jouer un sale tour à qn ❷ (*miserly*) avare ❸ (*wretched*) misérable; **the ~ streets** les bas quartiers *mpl* ❹ *fig* (*poor*) pauvre ❺ *inf* (*excellent*) excellent(e) ▶ **to be no ~ feat** ne pas être une mince affaire

**mean²** [min] <meant, meant> *vt* ❶ (*express meaning*) signifier; **it ~s "hello" in Arabic** ça veut dire "salut" en arabe; **what do you ~ by that?** qu'est-ce que tu veux dire?; **I ~ that** je suis sérieux ❷ (*refer to*) parler de; **do you ~ me?** tu veux dire moi? ❸ (*result in*) impliquer; **this ~s war** c'est la guerre ❹ (*have significance*) **it ~s a lot to me** c'est important pour moi ❺ (*intend, suppose*) **to ~ to +infin** avoir l'intention de +*infin;* **I didn't ~ to upset you** je ne voulais pas te faire de peine; **to be ~t to be sth** être destiné à qc; **to ~ well** avoir de bonnes intentions

**mean³** [min] **I.** *n* ❶ (*middle*) milieu *m* ❷ MATH moyenne *f* **II.** *adj* moyen(ne)

**meaning** *n* ❶ (*signification*) signification *f;* **do you get my ~?** tu vois ce que je veux dire? ❷ (*interpretation*) interprétation *f* ❸ (*significance, value*) sens *m;* **to have a special ~ for sb** être particulièrement important pour qn ▶ **what is the ~ of this?** qu'est-ce que cela veut dire?

**meaningful** *adj* ❶ (*important or serious*) pertinent(e); (*relationship*) sérieux(-euse) ❷ (*implying something*) entendu(e) ❸ (*worthwhile*) sérieux(-euse)

**meaningless** *adj* ❶ (*without sense*) dépourvu(e) de sens ❷ (*with little importance*) insignifiant(e) ❸ (*vague*) vague

**means** *n* ❶ (*method*) moyen *m* ❷ *pl* (*income*) moyens *mpl;* **a person of ~** une personne qui a les moyens ▶ **a ~ to an end** un moyen de parvenir à ses fins; **the end justifies the ~** *prov* la fin justifie les moyens *prov;* **by all ~** certainement; **by no ~** en aucun cas

**meant** [ment] *pt, pp of* **mean**

**meantime** *n* **for the ~** pour l'instant; **in the ~** pendant ce temps(-là)

**meanwhile** *adv* entre-temps

**measles** ['miz·lz] *n* + *sing vb* rougeole *f*

**measure** ['meʒ·ər] **I.** *n* ❶ (*measurement, unit, system*) mesure *f* ❷ (*set amount, portion*) mesure *f;* (*alcohol*) dose *f* ❸ (*instrument*) mètre *m;* (*ruler*) règle *f;* (*container*) verre *m* doseur ❹ (*degree*) part *f;* **a ~ of success** un certain succès ❺ (*proof, indication*) preuve *f* ❻ *fig* (*plan, action*) mesure *f* ▶ **for good ~** en plus **II.** *vt* ❶ (*judge size*) mesurer ❷ (*stating size*) mesurer ❸ *fig* (*consider: one's strength*) mesurer; (*one's words*) peser ❹ (*judge*) juger **III.** *vi* mesurer

**measurement** *n* ❶ (*measuring*) mesure *f* ❷ *pl* (*size details*) mensurations *fpl;* **to take sb's ~s** prendre les mesures de qn

**measuring cup** *n* verre *m* mesureur

**meat** [mit] *n* ❶ (*flesh of animals*) viande *f* ❷ *pl* (*flesh of person*) chair *f* ❸ (*edible parts: of fish*) chair *f;* (*of fruit*) chair *f* ❹ (*subject matter*) substance *f*

**meatball** *n* boulette *f* de viande

**meatloaf** *n* gâteau *m* de viande

**mechanic** [mɪ·'kæn·ɪk] *n* mécanicien(ne) *m(f)*

**M**

**mechanical** *adj* ➊ (*relating to machines: failure, problem, reliability*) mécanique; ~ **engineering** la mécanique ➋ (*technical*) technique ➌ (*by machine*) mécanisé(e) ➍ (*machine-like*) machinal(e)

**mechanism** ['mek·ə·nɪ·z³m] *n* ➊ (*working parts*) mécanisme *m* ➋ (*method*) procédé *m;* **defense** ~ système *m* de défense

**medal** ['med·³l] *n* médaille *f*

**meddle** ['med·l] *vi* intervenir; **to** ~ **in sth** se mêler de qc; **to** ~ **with sth** fourrer son nez dans qc

**media** ['mi·di·ə] I. *n* **the** ~ les médias *mpl* II. *adj* des médias; (*coverage*) médiatique; ~ **studies** études *fpl* de communication

**mediate** ['mi·di·eɪt] I. *vi* **to** ~ **between sb and sb** servir de médiateur entre qn et qn II. *vt* arbitrer; (*settlement*) négocier

**mediator** *n* médiateur, -trice *m, f*

**medic** ['med·ɪk] *n inf* toubib *m*

**medical** ['med·ɪ·k³l] I. *adj* médical(e); **to seek** ~ **advice** demander conseil à un médecin II. *n inf* visite *f* médicale

**medication** [ˌmed·ɪ·ˈkeɪ·ʃ³n] <-(s)> *n* médication *f;* **to be taking** ~ **for sth** suivre un traitement pour qc

**medicinal** *adj* médicinal(e); (*properties*) thérapeutique; ~ **drug** médicament *m*

**medicine** ['med·ɪ·sən] *n* ➊ (*drug*) médicament *m* ➋ (*science, practice*) médecine *f;* **herbal** ~ phytothérapie *f* ▸ **to give sb a taste of their own** ~ rendre la monnaie de sa pièce à qn

**medieval** [ˌmi·di·ˈvəl] *adj a. pej* moyenâgeux(-euse); (*literature*) du Moyen-Âge

**meditate** ['med·ɪ·teɪt] *vi* méditer

**Mediterranean** [ˌmed·ɪ·tə·ˈreɪ·ni·ən] I. *adj* méditerranéen(ne) II. *n* ➊ **the** ~ la Méditerranée ➋ (*person*) méditerranéen(ne) *m(f)*

**Mediterranean Sea** *n* mer *f* Méditerranée

**medium** ['mi·di·əm] I. *adj* ➊ (*average*) moyen(ne) ➋ CULIN (*steak*) à point

➌ (*size*) medium *inv* II. *n* ➊ <-s *o* media> (*a means*) moyen *m* ➋ (*middle state, midpoint*) milieu *m;* **to find a happy** ~ trouver le juste milieu ➌ (*art material, form*) matériau *m* ➍ PUBL, TV média *m;* **advertising** ~ organe *m* de publicité; **print** ~ presse *f* écrite ➎ <-s> (*spiritualist*) médium *m* ➏ (*environment*) milieu *m* ➐ COMPUT support *m*

**medium-dry** *adj* demi-sec(demi-sèche)

**meet** [mit] <met, met> I. *vt* ➊ (*encounter*) rencontrer; (*an enemy*) affronter; **to** ~ **sb face to face** se trouver nez à nez avec qn ➋ (*by arrangement*) retrouver ➌ (*make the acquaintance of*) faire la connaissance de ➍ (*fulfill: standard, need*) répondre à; (*costs*) prendre en charge; (*deadline*) respecter; (*obligation*) remplir; (*challenge*) relever ➎ (*counter: accusation*) recevoir ▸ **there's more to this than** ~**s the eye** c'est moins simple que ça en a l'air; **to make ends** ~ joindre les deux bouts; **to** ~ **sb halfway** couper la poire en deux II. *vi* ➊ (*encounter*) se rencontrer ➋ (*assemble*) se réunir ➌ SPORTS, MIL s'affronter ➍ (*get acquainted*) faire connaissance ➎ (*join*) se rejoindre; (*eyes*) se rencontrer; **we met in Paris** on s'est connus à Paris III. *n* rencontre *f*
◆ **meet with** *vt* rencontrer; (*failure*) essuyer; (*success*) remporter; (*reaction*) être reçu avec

**meeting** *n* ➊ (*organized gathering*) réunion *f,* épluchette *f Québec* ➋ (*act of coming together*) rencontre *f;* **a** ~ **of minds** une entente profonde

**megabyte** ['meg·ə·baɪt] *n* COMPUT méga-octet *m*

**melody** ['mel·ə·di] <-odies> *n* mélodie *f*

**melon** ['mel·ən] *n* melon *m*

**melt** [melt] I. *vi* fondre II. *vt a. fig* fondre

**member** ['mem·bər] *n* membre *m*

**membership** I. *n* ➊ + *sing/pl vb* (*people*) membres *mpl* ➋ (*state of belonging*) adhésion *f* II. *adj* d'adhésion; **annual** ~ **fee** cotisations *fpl* annuelles

**membership card** *n* carte *f* d'adhérent

**memo** ['mem·oʊ] *n abbr of* **memorandum** mémo *m*

**memo pad** *n* bloc-notes *m*

**memorabilia** [ˌmem·ə·rə·ˈbɪl·i·ə] *n pl* souvenirs *mpl*

**memorable** ['mem·ˈr·ə·bl] *adj* mémorable

**memorial** [mə·ˈmɔr·i·əl] *n* mémorial *m*; **as a ~ to sb** à la mémoire de qn

**memorize** ['mem·ə·ˌraɪz] *vt* ❶ *(commit to memory)* mémoriser ❷ *(learn by heart)* apprendre par cœur

**memory** ['mem·ˈr·i] *n* ❶ *(ability to remember)* mémoire *f*; **from ~** de mémoire; **to commit sth to ~** apprendre qc par cœur; **in ~ of sb/sth** en souvenir de qn/qc; **if my ~ serves me right** si ma mémoire est bonne ❷ *(remembered event)* souvenir *m* ❸ COMPUT mémoire *f*

**memory capacity** *n* COMPUT capacité *f* de mémoire

**men** [men] *n pl of* **man**

**menacing** *adj* menaçant(e)

**mend** [mend] I. *n* raccommodage *m* ❷ *inf* **to be on the ~** aller mieux II. *vt* ❶ *(repair)* réparer; *(socks)* repriser ❷ *(improve)* corriger ▸ **to ~ fences with sb** *prov* se réconcilier avec qn; **to ~ one's ways** s'amender III. *vi a. fig* se remettre; *(wound)* guérir

**men's room** ['menz·ˌrum] *n* toilettes *fpl* pour hommes

**mental** ['men·t̬ᵊl] *adj* ❶ *(related to the mind: age, health)* mental(e) ❷ *inf (crazy)* fou(folle)

**mentally** *adv* mentalement; **~ stable** équilibré(e)

**mention** ['men·(t)ʃᵊn] I. *n* mention *f*; **no ~ was made of sb/sth** il n'a pas été fait mention de qn/qc II. *vt* mentionner; **to ~ sth in passing** signaler qc en passant; **don't ~ it!** il n'y a pas de quoi!; **not to ~ ...** sans parler de ...

**menu** ['men·ju] *n* CULIN, COMPUT menu *m*; **what's on the ~ for today?** *fig* qu'est ce qu'il y a au programme aujourd'hui?

**meow** [mi·ˈaʊ] I. *n* miaulement *m* II. *vi* miauler

**merchandise** ['mɜr·tʃᵊn·daɪz] *n form* marchandises *fpl*

**merchant** ['mɜr·tʃənt] I. *n* ❶ *(trader)* négociant(e) *m(f)* ❷ *(retailer)* commerçant(e) *m(f)* II. *adj* marchand(e)

**mercy** ['mɜr·si] *n* pitié *f*; REL miséricorde *f*; **to have ~ on sb** avoir pitié de qn; **to show no ~** ne montrer aucune compassion; **to be at the ~ of sb** être à la merci de qn; **to plead for ~** demander grâce

**merge** [mɜrdʒ] I. *vi* ❶ *(join)* se (re)joindre ❷ ECON fusionner ❸ *(fade)* **to ~ into sth** se fondre dans qc ❹ *(blend)* **to ~ into/with sth** se mêler à qc II. *vt* ❶ *(unify)* unifier ❷ ECON fusionner

**merger** *n* ECON fusion *f*

**merit** ['mer·ɪt] I. *n* ❶ *(virtue)* valeur *f* ❷ *(advantage)* mérite *m*; **to consider each case on its own ~s** juger au cas par cas II. *vt form* mériter

**mermaid** ['mɜr·meɪd] *n* sirène *f*

**merry** ['mer·i] *adj* ❶ *(happy)* joyeux(-euse); **Merry Christmas** Joyeux Noël ❷ *inf (slightly drunk)* pompette

**merry-go-round** *n* manège *m*

**mesmerize** ['mez·mᵊr·aɪz] *vt* hypnotiser

**mess** [mes] I. *n* ❶ *(not neat)* bazar *m*, margaille *f Belgique;* **to be (in) a ~** être en fouillis; **to make a ~** faire un chantier ❷ *(dirty)* **to make a ~ on sth** salir qc ❸ *(trouble)* **to get oneself into a ~** se mettre dans de beaux draps; **to make a ~ of sth** massacrer qc ❹ *(animal excrement)* crotte *f* ❺ *(officers' eating hall)* mess *m* II. *vt inf* ❶ *(make messy)* **to ~ sth (up)** mettre du désordre dans qc ❷ *(screw up)* **to ~ sth (up)** gâcher qc III. *vi (screw up)* faire du travail bâclé

**message** ['mes·ɪdʒ] *n a.* COMPUT message *m*

**messenger** ['mes·ɪn·dʒər] *n* messager, -ère *m, f*; *(in offices)* coursier, -ère *m, f*

**messy** ['mes·i] <-ier, -iest> *adj*

M

① (*not neat: room*) désordonné(e); (*presentation*) brouillon(ne); (*clothes*) débraillé(e) ② (*dirty*) sale ③ *fig* **it's a ~ business** c'est une sale embrouille

**met** [met] *pt of* **meet**

**metabolism** [məˈtæb·əl·ɪ·zªm] *n* métabolisme *m*

**metal** [ˈmet·ªl] *n* ① (*iron, steel, etc.*) métal *m* ② MUS heavy metal *m*

**metaphor** [ˈmet·ə·fɔr] *n* métaphore *f*

**meter**[1] [ˈmi·tər] I. *n* compteur *m*; (**parking**) ~ parcmètre *m* II. *vt* (*gas, water*) mesurer au compteur

**meter**[2] [ˈmi·tər] *n* ① (*unit of measurement*) mètre *m* ② (*poetic rhythm*) mesure *f*

**method** [ˈmeθ·əd] *n* méthode *f* ▶ **there's a ~ to his madness** il n'est pas aussi fou qu'il en a l'air

**methodology** [ˌmeθ·ə·ˈda·lə·dʒi] *n* méthodologie *f*

**metric system** [ˈmetrɪk ˈsɪs·təm] *n* système *m* métrique

**Mexican** I. *adj* mexicain(e) II. *n* Mexicain(e) *m(f)*

**Mexico** [ˈmek·sɪ·kou] *n* le Mexique

**mezzanine** [ˈmez·ə·nin] *n* ~ (**floor**) mezzanine *f*

**MI** *n abbr of* **Michigan**

**MIA** [ˌem·aɪ·ˈeɪ] *abbr of* **missing in action** (*soldier*) porté disparu

**mice** [maɪs] *n pl of* **mouse**

**Michigan** [ˈmɪʃ·ɪ·ɡən] I. *n* le Michigan II. *adj* du Michigan

**microbrewery** *n* petite brasserie *f*, microbrasserie *f Québec*

**microchip** *n* puce *f* (électronique)

**microclimate** *n* microclimat *m*

**microorganism** *n* micro-organisme *m*

**microphone** [ˈmaɪ·krə·foun] *n* microphone *m*

**microscope** [ˈmaɪ·krə·skoup] *n* microscope *m*

**microscopic** *adj* microscopique

**microwave** [ˈmaɪ·krou·weɪv] I. *n* ① (*oven*) micro-ondes *m* ② (*short wave*) micro-onde *f* II. *vt* faire cuire au micro-ondes

**microwave oven** *n* four *m* à micro-ondes

**midday** [ˌmɪd·ˈdeɪ] *n* midi *m inv, sans art*

**middle** [mɪd·l] I. *n sing* ① a. *fig* (*centre*) milieu *m*; **to be in the ~ of doing sth** être en train de faire qc; **in the ~ of nowhere** *pej* en pleine pampa ② *inf* (*waist*) taille *f* II. *adj* ① (*in the middle*) du milieu; **to be in one's ~ forties** avoir autour de quarante-cinq ans ② (*intermediate*) moyen(ne)

**middle age** *n* ≈ cinquantaine *f*

**middle-aged** *adj* d'une cinquantaine d'années

**Middle Ages** *n* **the ~** le Moyen-Âge

**middle-class** *adj* de classe moyenne

**middle class, middle classes** *npl* **the ~** classe *f* moyenne; *pej* la bourgeoisie; **the upper/lower ~** la haute bourgeoisie/bourgeoisie

**Middle East** *n* **the ~** le Moyen-Orient

**middleman** <-men> *n* intermédiaire *m*

**middle name** *n* deuxième prénom *m*

**middle-of-the-road** *adj* ① (*moderate*) modéré(e) ② *pej* (*boring*) moyen(ne)

**midge** [mɪdʒ] *n pl, a. fig* moustique *m*

**midlife crisis** *n* crise *f* de la quarantaine

**midnight** I. *n* minuit *m* II. *adj* de minuit ▶ **to burn the ~ oil** travailler jusque tard dans la nuit

**midsummer** *n* ① (*middle part of summer*) cœur *m* de l'été; **in ~** en plein été ② (*solstice*) solstice *m* d'été

**midterm** *n* ① POL (*middle of period of office*) milieu *m* de mandat; **~ election/poll** élection *f*/sondage *m* en cours de mandat ② UNIV, SCHOOL (*middle of a term*) milieu *m* de trimestre

**midway** I. *adv* à mi-chemin II. *n* champ *m* de foire

**midwife** <-wives> *n* sage-femme *f*

**midwinter** *n* ① (*middle of winter*) milieu *m* de l'hiver ② (*solstice*) solstice *m* d'hiver

**might**[1] [maɪt] I. *pt of* **may** II. *aux* ① (*expressing possibility*) **sb/sth ~** *+infin* qn/qc pourrait *+infin*; **sb/sth ~ have done sth** qn/qc aurait pu faire qc; **it ~**

**M**

**have been ...** ça aurait pu être ...; **are you coming? - I ~** est-ce que tu viens? - Peut-être ②(*reproachfully*) **~ I know ...?** est-ce que je pourrais savoir ...?; **you ~ have known that ...** tu aurais dû te douter que ... ③*form* (*politely make suggestion*) **~ I suggest ...?** pourrais-je suggérer ...? ▸**you ~ as well** do sth tant qu'à faire, tu devrais faire qc

**might²** [maɪt] *n* ①(*authority*) pouvoir *m* ②MIL (*strength*) force *f*

**mighty** I.<-ier, -iest> *adj* puissant(e) II. *adv inf* sacrément

**migraine** ['maɪ·ɡreɪn] <-(s)> *n* migraine *f*

**migrant** ['maɪ·ɡrənt] I. *n* migrant(e) *m(f)*; ZOOL oiseau *m* migrateur II. *adj* (*worker*) migrant(e)

**mike** [maɪk] *n inf abbr of* **microphone** micro *m*

**milage** *n s.* **mileage**

**mild** [maɪld] <-er, -est> *adj* ①(*not severe or intense: annoyance, shock*) petit(e); (*climate, day*) modéré(e); (*asthma, infection*) sans gravité; (*cigarette, criticism, increase*) léger(·ère); (*curry, flavor*) doux(douce) ②(*in character*) doux(douce); **to be of a ~ disposition** avoir bon caractère

**mildly** *adv* ①(*gently*) gentiment ②(*slightly*) légèrement ▸**to put it ~** c'est le moins qu'on puisse dire

**mile** [maɪl] *n* mile *m* (*équivalent à 1609 mètres*); **for ~s and ~s** sur des kilomètres ▸**to be ~s away** être à des lieues

**mileage** ['maɪ·lɪdʒ] *n* ①(*traveling expenses*) frais *mpl* de déplacement ②(*distance traveled*) distance *f* parcourue en miles; **it gets good ~** il/elle ne consomme pas beaucoup

**military** ['mɪl·ɪ·ter·i] I. *n* **the ~** l'armée *f* II. *adj* militaire

**military academy** *n* école *f* militaire

**milk** [mɪlk] I. *n* lait *m*; **whole ~** lait entier; **skim ~** lait écrémé ▸**it's no use crying over spilled ~** ce qui est arrivé est arrivé II. *vt* ①(*extract milk*) traire ②(*take money from*) soutirer de l'ar-

gent à ③(*exploit: story, situation*) tirer avantage de

**milk chocolate** *n* chocolat *m* au lait

**milkman** <-men> *n* laitier *m*

**milkshake** *n* milk-shake *m*; **strawberry ~** milk-shake à la fraise

**milky** <-ier, -iest> *adj* laiteux(-euse)

**Milky Way** *n* **the ~** la voie lactée

**mill** [mɪl] I. *n* ①(*building or machine*) moulin *m* ②(*factory*) usine *f* II. *vt* ①(*grind*) mouliner ②(*shape: metal*) travailler III. *vi* **to ~ (around)** fourmiller

**millennium** [mɪˈlen·i·əm] <-s *o* -ennia> *n* millénaire *m*

**miller** *n* meunier, -ère *m, f*

**milligram** *n* milligramme *m*

**milliliter** *n* millilitre *m*

**million** ['mɪl·jən] <-(s)> *n* ①(*a thousand thousand*) million *m* ②*inf* (*countless number*) millier *m*; **a ~ times** des milliers de fois; **to be one in a ~** être unique ③(*money*) million *m* ▸**to feel like a ~ bucks** se sentir merveilleusement bien

**millionaire** [ˌmɪl·jəˈner] *n* millionnaire *mf*

**mince** [mɪn(t)s] I. *vt* hacher ▸**to not ~ words** ne pas mâcher ses mots II. *vi* marcher à petits pas

**mincer** *n* hachoir *m*

**mind** [maɪnd] I. *n* ①(*brain*) esprit *m*; **to have a good ~** être intelligent ②(*thought, memory*) esprit *m*; **to bring sth to ~** se rappeler qc; **bear in ~ that ...** n'oubliez pas que ...; **it slipped my ~** ça m'est sorti de l'esprit ③(*intention*) esprit *m*; **to have sth in ~** avoir qc en tête; **I have half a ~ to +infin** ça me démange de +*infin* ④(*conscious-ness*) esprits *mpl*; **to be out of one's ~** avoir perdu la raison; **there's something on my ~** je suis préoccupé; **to take one's ~ off sth** oublier qc; **I can't keep my ~ off food/her** je n'arrête pas de penser à la nourriture/à elle ⑤(*sing (opinion)*) avis *m*; **to change one's ~** changer d'avis ⑥(*intelligent person*) esprit *m* ▸**in one's ~'s eye**

dans son esprit; **to be in two ~s about sth** être partagé au sujet de qc **II.** *vt* **①** (*be careful of*) faire attention à; **don't ~ me** ne fais pas attention à moi **②** (*take care of*) garder **③** (*concern oneself*) s'occuper de; **to ~ one's business** s'occuper de ses affaires **④** (*object*) **I wouldn't ~ sth** j'aimerais bien qc; **I wouldn't mind having a cup of coffee/a shower** ça me dirait bien de prendre un café/une douche; **would you ~ doing sth?** pourriez-vous faire qc?; **I don't ~ doing sth** ça ne me dérange pas de faire qc; **if you don't ~ me saying so, ...** si je peux me permettre de le dire, ... **⑤** (*obey*) obéir à ▶ **to ~ one's P's** and **Q's** se tenir **III.** *vi* **do you ~ if ...?** est-ce que cela vous ennuie si ...?; **if you don't ~** si cela ne vous ennuie pas; **I don't ~!** ça m'est égal!; **do you ~!** je vous demande pardon!; **never ~!** ça ne fait rien!

**mind-boggling** *adj fig* époustouflant(e)

**M** **mindless** *adj* **①** (*unaware*) inconscient(e); (*violence*) gratuit(e) **②** (*stupid, simple*) stupide; (*activity*) abrutissant(e)

**mind reader** *n fig* voyant(e) *m(f)*

**mine¹** [maɪn] *poss pron* (*belonging to me*) le mien, la mienne; **this glass is ~** ce verre est à moi; **a colleague of ~** un de mes collègues; *s.a.* **hers**

**mine²** [maɪn] **I.** *n* MIN *a. fig* mine *f* **II.** *vt* MIN (*coal, iron*) extraire; (*area*) exploiter

**mine³** [maɪn] **I.** *n* MIL mine *f*; **to clear an area of ~s** déminer une zone **II.** *vt* miner

**mine detector** *n* détecteur *m* de mines

**minefield** *n a. fig* champ *m* de mines

**miner** *n* mineur *m*

**mineral** ['mɪn·ªr·ªl] **I.** *n* CHEM minéral *m* **II.** *adj* minéral(e); **~ ore** minerai *m*

**mineral water** *n* eau *f* minérale

**mingle** ['mɪŋ·gl] **I.** *vt* **①** (*mix*) mélanger; **to be ~d with sth** être mélangé avec qc **②** *fig* mêler; **to be ~d with sadness/a noise** être mêlé de tristesse/à un bruit **II.** *vi* **①** (*mix*) se mélanger; **to ~**

**with sth** se mélanger à qc **②** (*in group*) se mêler

**miniature** ['mɪn·i·ə·tʃər] **I.** *adj* miniature **II.** *n* miniature *f*

**minibus** ['mɪn·i·bʌs] *n* minibus *m*

**minimal** ['mɪn·ɪ·mªl] *adj* minimal(e)

**minimize** ['mɪn·ɪ·maɪz] *vt* minimiser

**minimum** ['mɪn·ɪ·məm] **I.**<-s *o* minima> *n* minimum *m* **II.** *adj* minimum *inv*

**mining** *n* exploitation *f* minière

**miniskirt** ['mɪn·i·skɜrt] *n* minijupe *f*

**minister** ['mɪn·ɪ·stər] **I.** *n* **①** REL pasteur *m* **②** POL ministre *mf* **II.** *vi* **to ~ to sb** servir qn

**ministry** ['mɪn·ɪ·stri] <-ies> *n a.* POL, REL ministère *m*

**minivan** ['mɪn·i·væn] *n* monospace *m*

**Minnesota** [ˌmɪn·ɪ·'soʊ·t̬ə] **I.** *n* le Minnesota **II.** *adj* du Minnesota

**minor** ['maɪ·nər] **I.** *adj* mineur(e) **II.** *n* mineur(e) *m(f)*

**minority** [maɪ·'nɔr·ə·t̬i] **I.**<-ities> *n* minorité *f*; **to be in the ~** être minoritaire **II.** *adj* minoritaire

**mint¹** [mɪnt] *n* **①** *a.* BOT menthe *f* **②** (*candy*) bonbon *m* à la menthe

**mint²** [mɪnt] **I.** *n* **①** (*coin factory*) Hôtel *m* de la Monnaie **②** *inf* (*sum of money*) fortune *f* **II.** *vt* (*coin*) frapper; (*stamp*) estamper; (*usage*) lancer **III.** *adj* neuf(neuve)

**minus** ['maɪ·nəs] **I.** *prep a.* MATH moins; **he left ~ his coat/wallet** *inf* il est parti sans son manteau/son portefeuille **II.** *adj* **①** MATH négatif(·ive) **②** *fig* (*quantity*) négligeable **III.** *n* moins *m*; *s.a.* **plus**

**minute¹** ['mɪn·ɪt] **I.** *n* **①** (*sixty seconds*) minute *f*; **just a ~!** une minute!; **the ~ I arrived** dès que je suis arrivé **②** *pl* (*record*) procès-verbal *m* **II.** *vt* noter dans le procès-verbal

**minute²** [maɪ·'nut] *adj* minuscule; **in ~ detail** dans le moindre détail

**minute hand** *n* petite aiguille *f*

**miracle** ['mɪr·ə·kl] *n* miracle *m*; **a ~ drug/cure** un médicament/traitement miracle

**miraculous** [mɪˈræk·jə·ləs] *adj* miraculeux(-euse)

**mirror** [ˈmɪr·ər] I. *n* a. *fig* miroir *m;* (**rear-view**) ~ rétroviseur *m;* (**side**) ~ rétroviseur *m* extérieur II. *vt* refléter

**misbehave** *vi* a. *fig* mal se comporter, se méconduire *Belgique*

**misc.** [ˌmɪs·əlˈeɪ·nɪ·əs] *abbr of* **miscellaneous** divers(e)

**miscalculation** *n* a. *fig* mauvais calcul *m*

**miscarriage** *n* ❶ MED fausse couche *f* ❷ LAW ~ **of justice** erreur *f* judiciaire

**miscarry** <-ied, -ying> *vi* ❶ MED faire une fausse couche ❷ (*go wrong*) échouer

**miscellaneous** [ˌmɪs·əlˈeɪ·nɪ·əs] *adj* divers(e)

**mischief** *n* bêtises *fpl;* **to make** ~ semer la zizanie

**miscount** I. *n* erreur *f* de calcul II. *vt* mal compter

**misdemeanor** [ˌmɪs·dɪˈmiˈnər] *n* délit *m*

**miser** [ˈmaɪ·zər] *n* avare *mf*

**miserable** [ˈmɪz·ər·ə·bl] *adj* ❶ (*unhappy*) malheureux(-euse); **to feel** ~ avoir le cafard; **to make life** ~ **for sb** rendre la vie insupportable à qn ❷ (*poor, wretched*) misérable ❸ (*unpleasant: day, weather, conditions*) épouvantable; (*performance, failure*) lamentable ❹ (*small: pay*) misérable

**misery** [ˈmɪz·ər·i] *n* ❶ (*suffering*) souffrance *f;* **to put sb out of their** ~ abréger les souffrances de qn ❷ (*distress: of war*) misère *f* ❸ (*sadness*) tristesse *f* ❹ (*person*) grincheux, ·euse *m, f*

**misfit** [ˈmɪs·fɪt] *n* marginal(e) *m(f)*

**misfortune** *n* ❶ (*bad luck*) malchance *f* ❷ (*mishap*) malheur *m*

**mishap** *n form* incident *m*

**misinterpretation** *n* mauvaise interprétation *f;* **open to** ~ qui prête à confusion

**misjudge** *vt* se tromper sur

**misjudgment** *n* erreur *f* de jugement

**mislead** *vt irr* ❶ (*by accident*) induire en erreur ❷ (*persuade*) tromper; **to** ~ **sb into believing sth** faire croire à tort qc

à qn; **to let oneself be misled** se laisser duper

**misleading** *adj* trompeur(-euse)

**misplace** *vt form* égarer

**misprint** *n* coquille *f*

**mispronounce** *vt* mal prononcer

**misread** *vt irr* ❶ (*read badly*) mal lire ❷ *fig* mal interpréter

**misrepresent** *vt* (*facts*) déformer; **to** ~ **sb as sth** faire passer à tort qn pour qc

**miss**[1] [mɪs] *n* (*form of address*) mademoiselle *f;* **Miss Italy** Miss Italie

**miss**[2] [mɪs] I. <-sses> *n* ❶ (*not hit*) coup *m* manqué ❷ (*failure: film, record*) flop *m inf* II. *vi* ❶ (*not hit sth*) a. SPORTS rater ❷ (*misfire*) avoir des ratés III. *vt* ❶ (*not hit, not catch: target, bus, train*) rater; **the bullet just** ~**ed me** la balle m'a manqué de peu ❷ (*not meet: deadline*) dépasser ❸ (*avoid*) échapper à ❹ (*not see: page*) sauter; (*stop*) rater ❺ (*not hear*) ne pas entendre; **sorry I** ~**ed that …** excuse-moi je n'ai pas compris … ❻ (*be absent: school, class*) manquer ❼ (*not take advantage: opportunity, offer*) laisser passer ❽ (*regret absence*) **she** ~**es them** ils lui manquent; **did you** ~ **me?** est-ce que je t'ai manqué?; **I** ~ **driving** ça me manque de conduire ❾ (*notice loss*) **I'm** ~**ing my wedding ring** je ne trouve plus mon alliance ▸ **to** ~ **the boat** rater le coche; **to** ~ **the point** n'avoir pas compris

◆**miss out** I. *vt* ❶ (*omit*) omettre ❷ (*overlook*) oublier II. *vi* rater quelque chose; **to be missing out on sth** ne pas profiter de qc

**missile** [ˈmɪs·əl] *n* (*weapon*) missile *m*

**missing** [ˈmɪs·ɪŋ] *adj* ❶ (*lost or stolen*) disparu(e); **to go** ~ disparaître; **to report sb** ~ signaler la disparition de qn ❷ (*not confirmed as alive*) disparu(e); **to be** ~ **in action** être porté disparu ❸ (*absent, not present*) a. *fig* absent(e) ❹ (*left out*) manquant(e)

**mission** [ˈmɪʃ·ən] *n* mission *f*

**Mississippi** *n* le Mississippi

**Missouri** [mɪˈzʊr·i] I. *n* le Missouri II. *adj* du Missouri

**M**

**misspell** *vt irr* mal orthographier

**misspelling** *n* faute *f* d'orthographe

**mist** [mɪst] *n* brume *f*

**mistake** [mɪˈsteɪk] **I.** *n* erreur *f*; **careless ~** faute *f* d'étourderie; **my ~** je me suis trompé; **spelling/typing ~** faute d'orthographe/de frappe ▶ **make no ~ about it** tu peux en être sûr **II.** *vt irr* **you can't ~ it, there's not mistaking it** tu ne peux pas le rater; **I mistook you for your brother** je t'ai pris pour ton frère

**mistaken I.** *pp of* **mistake II.** *adj* **to be ~ about sb/sth** se tromper à propos de qn/qc; **if I'm not ~** si je ne m'abuse; **it was a case of ~ identity** il y avait erreur sur la personne

**mister** [ˈmɪs·tər] *n* monsieur *m*

**mistook** [mɪˈstʊk] *pt of* **mistake**

**mistreat** *vt* maltraiter

**mistress** [ˈmɪs·trɪs] *n a. pej* maîtresse *f*

**mistrust** [ˌmɪsˈtrʌst] **I.** *n* méfiance *f* **II.** *vt* se méfier de

**mistrustful** *adj* méfiant(e)

**misty** [ˈmɪs·ti] <-ier, -iest> *adj* ❶ *(slightly foggy)* brumeux(-euse) ❷ *(unclear: eyes)* embué(e); **to be ~-eyed** être tout ému ❸ *(vague)* vague

**misunderstand I.** *vt irr* mal comprendre; **to be misunderstood** être incompris; **don't ~ me!** comprenez-moi bien! **II.** *vi irr* mal comprendre

**misunderstanding** *n* ❶ *(misinterpretation)* erreur *f* d'interprétation ❷ *(quarrel)* malentendu *m* ❸ *(difficulty in communication)* quiproquo *m*

**mitten** [ˈmɪt·ən] *n* ❶ *(with bare fingers)* moufle *f* ❷ *(fingerless)* mitaine *f*

**mix** [mɪks] **I.** *n* ❶ *(combination)* mélange *m* ❷ *(pre-mixed ingredients)* préparation *f* ❸ MUS mixage *m* **II.** *vi* ❶ *(combine)* se mélanger ❷ *(make contact with people)* être sociable; **the people you ~ with** les gens que tu fréquentes **III.** *vt* ❶ *(put ingredients together: dough, drink, paint)* mélanger; **to ~ sth into sth** mélanger qc à qc; **to ~ sth with sth** mélanger qc et qc ❷ MUS mixer

♦ **mix in** *vt* incorporer

♦ **mix up** *vt* ❶ *(confuse)* confondre; **I mix you up with your brother** je te confonds avec ton frère ❷ *(put in wrong order)* mélanger ❸ *(combine ingredients: dough)* mélanger ❹ *(associate)* **to get mixed up in sth** être mêlé à qc

**mixed** *adj* ❶ *(assorted: vegetables, flavors)* assorti(e) ❷ *(involving opposites: marriage)* mixte ❸ *(bathing)* mixte; **people of ~ race** des métis *mpl* ❸ *(positive and negative: reactions, reviews)* mitigé(e); **to be a ~ blessing** avoir du bon et du mauvais; **to have ~ feelings about sth** être partagé au sujet de qc

**mixture** [ˈmɪks·tʃər] *n* ❶ *(combination)* mélange *m* ❷ *(combined substances)* préparation *f*

**mix-up** *n* ❶ *(confusion)* confusion *f* ❷ *(misunderstanding)* malentendu *m*

**mo.** [moʊ] *n abbr of* **month** mois *m*

**MMR** [ˌem·em·ˈar] *n* MED *abbr of* **measles, mumps and rubella** ROR *f*

**MN** [ˌem·ˈen] *n abbr of* **Minnesota**

**MO** [ˌem·ˈoʊ] *n* ❶ *abbr of* **modus operandi** mode *m* opératoire ❷ *abbr of* **Missouri**

**moan** [moʊn] **I.** *n* ❶ *(sound of pain)* gémissement *m* ❷ *(complaint)* plainte *f* **II.** *vi* ❶ *(make a sound: person, wind)* gémir ❷ *(complain)* se plaindre

**mobile¹** [ˈmoʊ·bəl] *adj* mobile; **to be ~** *(able to walk)* pouvoir marcher

**mobile²** [ˈmoʊ·bil] *n* ART mobile *m*

**mobility** [moʊˈbɪl·ə·ti] *n* mobilité *f*

**mobilization** *n* mobilisation *f*

**mobster** [ˈmab·stər] *n inf* truand *m*

**mock** [mak] **I.** *adj* ❶ *(not real)* faux(fausse) *m* ❷ *(imitated: emotion)* simulé(e) **II.** *vi* **to ~ at sb** se moquer de qn **III.** *vt* ❶ *(ridicule)* se moquer de ❷ *(ridicule by imitation)* **to ~ sb/sth** parodier qn/qc

**model** [ˈma·dəl] **I.** *n* ❶ *(representation)* maquette *f* ❷ *(example, creation, version)* a. ART modèle *m* ❸ *(mannequin)* mannequin *mf* **II.** *adj* ❶ *(ideal)* modèle ❷ *(small: car, aircraft, figures)* miniature **III.** <-ll-> *vt* ❶ *(produce)* a. fig modeler; **to ~ sth in clay** modeler qc en argile; **to ~ sth on sth** modeler qc sur qc; **to ~ oneself on sb** prendre qn pour modèle ② (*show: clothes*) présenter **IV.** *vi* ① (*show clothes*) être mannequin ② (*pose*) poser (comme modèle)

**modem** ['moʊ·dəm] *n* COMPUT modem *m*

**moderate¹** ['ma·dər·ət] **I.** *n* POL modéré(e) *m(f)* **II.** *adj* ① (*neither great nor small: size, ability*) moyen(ne) ② (*avoiding extremes*) a. POL modéré(e); (*climate*) tempéré(e)

**moderate²** ['ma·dər·ɑɪt] **I.** *vt* ① (*make less extreme*) modérer ② (*control: examination, debate*) être le modérateur pour **II.** *vi* se modérer

**moderation** *n* modération *f*; **in ~** avec modération

**moderator** *n* ① (*chairman*) président(e) *m(f)* ② (*mediator*) médiateur, -trice *m, f*

**modern** ['ma·dərn] *adj* moderne; **~ children** les enfants d'aujourd'hui

**modernize** ['ma·dər·nɑɪz] **I.** *vt* moderniser **II.** *vi* se moderniser

**modest** ['ma·dɪst] *adj* ① (*not boastful, not large*) modeste ② (*not provocative: person*) pudique; (*garment*) convenable

**modular** ['ma·dʒə·lər] *adj* modulaire

**module** ['ma·dʒul] *n* module *m*

**moist** [mɔɪst] *adj* humide; (*cake*) moelleux(-euse)

**moisten** ['mɔɪ·sən] **I.** *vt* (*cloth*) humidifier; (*skin*) hydrater **II.** *vi* (*eyes*) s'embuer

**moisture** ['mɔɪs·tʃər] *n* humidité *f*

**moisturizer** *n* crème *f* hydratante

**molar** ['moʊ·lər] **I.** *n* molaire *f* **II.** *adj* molaire

**mold¹** [moʊld] *n* BIO moisissure *f*

**mold²** [moʊld] **I.** *n* moule *m* **II.** *vt* (*clay*) mouler; (*character*) former

**mole¹** [moʊl] *n* (*animal, spy*) taupe *f*

**mole²** [moʊl] *n* ANAT grain *m* de beauté

**molehill** ['moʊl·hɪl] *n* taupinière *f*

**molest** [mə·'lest] *vt* ① (*attack*) agresser ② (*attack sexually*) agresser sexuellement

**moment** ['moʊ·mənt] *n* ① (*time*) moment *m;* **it'll just take a few ~s** ça ne sera pas long; **not for a ~** pas un instant; **at any ~** d'un moment à l'autre; **the ~ I arrive/arrived** dès que j'arriverai/je suis arrivé; **the play had its ~s** il y a eu de bons moments dans la pièce ② *form* (*importance*) importance *f*

**momentary** ['moʊ·mən·ter·i] *adj* momentané(e)

**momentum** [moʊ·'men·təm] *n* a. *fig* élan *m;* **to gain ~** prendre de l'élan; **to lose ~** être en perte de vitesse

**mommy** ['ma·mi] <-mies> *n inf* maman *f*

**monarch** ['ma·nərk] *n* monarque *mf*

**monarchy** <-chies> *n* monarchie *f*

**monastery** ['ma·nə·ster·i] <-ries> *n* monastère *m*

**Monday** ['mʌn·di] *n* lundi *m; s.a.* **Friday**

**money** ['mʌn·i] *n* argent *m;* **I paid good ~ for this** j'ai payé pour ça; **the ~'s good** c'est bien payé; **to get one's ~'s worth** en avoir pour son argent; **to put ~ into sth** investir dans qc; **to put ~ on sth** parier sur qc ▶ **put your ~ where your mouth is** passez à la caisse; **~ doesn't grow on trees** *prov* l'argent ne tombe pas du ciel *prov;* **to have ~ to burn** avoir de l'argent à jeter par la fenêtre; **~ talks** *prov* l'argent est roi *prov*

**money order** *n* mandat *m* postal

**monitor** ['ma·nə·tər] **I.** *n* ① (*screen*) moniteur *m* ② (*apparatus*) appareil *m* de contrôle ③ (*observer*) observateur, -trice *m, f* **II.** *vt* ① (*check, observe*) contrôler ② (*watch*) surveiller ③ (*listen to*) écouter; (*a conversation*) suivre

**monk** [mʌŋk] *n* moine *m*

**monkey** ['mʌŋ·ki] **I.** *n* singe *m* **II.** *vi inf* **to ~ around** faire des singeries; **to ~ with sth** jouer avec qc

**monkey business** *n inf* (*trickery*) magouilles *fpl;* (*games*) bêtises *fpl*

**mono** ['ma·noʊ] *n inf* MED *abbr of* (*infectious*) **mononucleosis** mononucléose *f* (infectieuse)

**M**

**monopolize** [mə·'na·pə·laɪz] *vt* monopoliser

**monotonous** *adj* monotone

**monsoon** [man·'sun] *n* mousson *f*

**monster** ['man(t)·stər] I. *n* monstre *m* II. *adj inf* monstre

**monstrous** ['man(t)·strəs] *adj* monstrueux(-euse)

**Montana** *n* le Montana

**month** [mʌn(t)θ] *n* mois *m;* **the sixth of the ~** le six du mois; **a ~'s notice/ salary** un mois de préavis/de salaire

**monthly** I. *adj* mensuel(le) II. *adv* mensuellement III. *n* mensuel *m*

**monument** ['man·jə·mənt] *n* monument *m;* **a ~ to their perseverance** *fig* un témoignage de leur persévérance

**monumental** *adj* monumental(e)

**mood¹** [mud] *n* ❶ (*feeling*) humeur *f;* **in a good/bad ~** de bonne/mauvaise humeur; **to be in a talkative ~** être loquace; **to be in no ~ to** +*infin* form ne pas être d'humeur à +*infin* ❷ (*atmosphere*) ambiance *f;* **to lighten the ~** détendre l'atmosphère

**mood²** [mud] *n* LING mode *m*

**moody** ['mu·di] <-dier, -diest> *adj* lunatique, capricieux(-euse)

**moon** [mun] I. *n* lune *f* ▶ **to be over the ~ about sth** être au ciel avec qc; **to promise sb the ~** promettre la lune à qn II. *vt sl* montrer son derrière à

**moonlight** I. *n* clair *m* de lune II. *vi* <-ghted> *inf* travailler au noir

**moonlit** *adj* éclairé(e) par la lune

**moor¹** [mʊr] *n* (*open area*) lande *f*

**moor²** [mʊr] *vt* NAUT amarrer

**mooring** ['mʊr·ɪŋ] *n* NAUT mouillage *m;* **~s** amarres *fpl*

**moose** [mus] *n* élan *m*

**mop** [map] I. *n* ❶ ((*floor*) *mop*) balai *m* à laver; (*sponge*) ~ balai-éponge *m* ❷ (*mop of hair*) tignasse *f* II. <-pp-> *vt* ❶ (*clean with mop*) essuyer; **to ~ the floor** passer la serpillière ❷ (*wipe sweat from*) s'essuyer; **to ~ one's forehead** s'éponger le front

**moped** *n* mobylette® *f*

**moral** ['mɔr·əl] I. *adj* moral(e); **he has**

**no ~ fiber** il n'a pas de caractère II. *n* ❶ (*moral message*) morale *f* ❷ *pl* (*standards*) moralité *f*

**morale** [mə·'ræl] *n* moral *m*

**moral support** *n* soutien *m* moral

**more** [mɔr] I. *adj comp of* **much, many** plus de; **is there any ~ wine?** y a-t-il encore du vin?; **some ~ wine** encore un peu de vin; **a few ~ nuts** quelques noix de plus; **~ and ~ questions** de plus en plus de questions II. *adv comp of* **much, many** plus; **once ~** une fois de plus; **never ~** plus jamais; **to see ~ of sb** voir qn plus souvent; **~ than 10** plus de 10; **~ than ever** plus que jamais; **the ~ you try** plus tu essaies III. *pron comp of* **much, many** plus; **~ and ~** de plus en plus; **to have ~ than sb** en avoir plus que qn; **to cost ~ than sth** coûter plus cher que qc; **the ~ you eat, the ~ you get fat** plus on mange, plus on grossit; **do you need ~?** tu en veux encore?; **what ~ does he want?** qu'est-ce qu'il veut de plus?; **there is nothing ~ to do** il n'y a plus rien à faire ▶ **all the ~** d'autant plus; **all the ~ so because** d'autant plus que; **~ or less** plus ou moins

**moreover** [mɔr·'oʊ·vər] *adv form* de plus

**morgue** [mɔrg] *n* ❶ (*place for corpses*) morgue *f* ❷ *fig* (*boring atmosphere*) **to be a ~** être mortel ❸ (*archives*) archives *fpl*

**morning** ['mɔr·nɪŋ] *n* ❶ (*begin of a day*) matin *m;* **good ~!** bonjour!; **in the ~** le matin; **on Sunday ~** dimanche matin; **I'll come in the ~** je viendrai dans la matinée; **early in the ~** de bon matin; **6/11 o'clock in the ~** six/onze heures du matin ❷ (*as unit of time*) matinée *f,* avant-midi *m* (*en Belgique et féminin au Québec*)

**morning sickness** *n* nausées *fpl*

**moron** ['mɔr·an] *n pej, inf* débile *mf*

**mortal** ['mɔr·t̬əl] I. *adj* mortel(le) II. *n* mortel, -le *m, f*

**mortality** [mɔr·'tæl·ə·t̬i] *n* mortalité *f*

**mortgage** ['mɔr·gɪdʒ] I. *n* crédit *m* immobilier II. *vt* hypothéquer

**mortuary** ['mɔr·tʃu·er·i] *n* mortuaire *m*

**mosaic** [mou·'zeɪ·ɪk] *n* mosaïque *f*

**Moslem** ['maz·lem] *adj, n* s. **Muslim**

**mosque** [mask] *n* mosquée *f*

**mosquito** [məˈski·tou] <-es *o* -s> *n* moustique *m*, brûlot *m Québec*

**moss** [mas] <-es> *n* mousse *f*

**most** [moust] I. *adj superl of* **many, much** le plus de; **for the ~ part** en majeure partie; **~ people** la plupart des gens II. *adv superl of* **many, much** le plus; **a ~ beautiful evening** une merveilleuse soirée; **what I want** ~ ce que je désire le plus; **~ of all** par-dessus tout; **~ likely** très probablement III. *pron superl of* **many, much** ~ **of them/the time** la plupart d'entre eux/du temps; **~ of the wine** la plus grande partie du vin; **at the very ~** au grand maximum; **to make the ~ of sth/oneself** tirer le meilleur parti de qc/soi-même; **the ~ you can have is ...** on peut avoir tout au plus ...

**mostly** *adv* ❶ (*usually*) la plupart du temps ❷ (*nearly all*) pour la plupart ❸ (*in the majority*) principalement

**motel** [mou·'tel] *n* motel *m*

**moth** [maθ] *n* mite *f*

**mothball** I. *n* boule *f* de naphtaline II. *vt* ❶ (*store*) mettre en réserve ❷ (*stop*) geler

**moth-eaten** *adj* mité(e)

**mother** ['mʌð·ər] I. *n* ❶ (*female parent*) mère *f* ❷ *vulg s.* **motherfucker** II. *vt* materner III. *adj* mère

**motherboard** *n* COMPUT carte *f* mère

**motherfucker** *n vulg* (*man*) connard *m*; (*woman*) salope *f*; (*thing*) saloperie *f*

**motherhood** *n* maternité *f*

**mother-in-law** <mothers-> *n* belle-mère *f*

**motherly** *adj* maternel(le)

**mother tongue** *n* langue *f* maternelle

**motion** ['mou·ʃən] I. *n* ❶ (*movement*) mouvement *m*; **in slow ~** au ralenti; **to put sth in ~** mettre qc en marche ❷ (*formal suggestion at meeting*) motion *f* ► **to set the wheels in ~** lancer le processus; **to go through the ~s** faire semblant II. *vt* **to ~ sb to** +*infin* faire signe à qn de +*infin*; **to ~ sb in** faire signe à qn d'entrer III. *vi* **to ~ to sb** faire signe à qn

**motionless** *adj* immobile

**motion picture** *n form* film *m*

**motivate** ['mou·tə·veɪt] *vt* motiver; **to ~ sb to** +*infin* inciter qn à +*infin*; **racially ~d crime** crimes *mpl* racistes

**motivation** *n* motivation *f*

**motive** ['mou·tɪv] I. *n* motif *m*; (*for the murder*) mobile *m* II. *adj* moteur(-trice)

**motor** ['mou·tər] I. *n* (*engine*) *a. fig* moteur *m* II. *adj* moteur(-trice)

**motorbike** *n inf* moto *f*

**motorboat** *n* bateau *m* à moteur

**motorcycle** *n form* motocyclette *f*

**motorcycling** *n* motocyclisme *m*

**motorcyclist** *n* motocycliste *mf*

**motor home** *n* camping-car *m*

**motorist** *n* automobiliste *mf*

**motor vehicle** *n* véhicule *m* motorisé

**motto** ['ma·tou] *n* <-s *o* -es> devise *f*

**mound** [maund] *n* ❶ (*of objects*) tas *m* ❷ (*small hill*) monceau *m*; **burial ~** tumulus *m*

**mount**[1] [maunt] *n* mont *m*

**mount**[2] [maunt] I. *n* ❶ (*backing, setting frame*) marie-louise *f*; (*of a gem*) monture *f* ❷ (*support*) support *m* ❸ (*horse*) monture *f* II. *vt* (*get on: bicycle*) monter sur; (*ladder*) grimper à; (*stairs*) monter ❷ (*organize: an attack, a campaign*) lancer; (*an operation, a squadron*) monter ❸ (*fasten for display: a gem, painting*) monter ❹ (*set*) **to ~ guard over sth** surveiller qc III. *vi* ❶ (*climb*) *a. fig* monter ❷ SPORTS se mettre en selle ❸ (*increase*) augmenter

**mountain** ['maun·tʰən] *n* montagne *f* ► **to make a ~ out of a molehill** faire tout un plat de pas grand chose

**mountain bike** *n* vélo *m* tout terrain

**mountaineer** *n* (*climber*) alpiniste *mf*

**mountaineering** *n* alpinisme *m*

**mountainous** *adj* ❶ (*rocky*) montagneux(-euse) ❷ NAUT (*wave*) immense

**M**

**mountain range** n GEO chaîne f de montagnes

**mourn** [mɔːn] I. vi **to ~ for sb/sth** pleurer qn/qc II. vt pleurer

**mourner** n proche mf du défunt; **the ~s** le cortège funèbre

**mouse** [maʊs] <mice> n ❶(small rodent) a. pej souris f ❷(shy person) timide mf ❸COMPUT souris f

**mouse hole** n trou m de souris

**mouse pad** n tapis m de souris

**mousetrap** n piège m à souris

**moustache** [ˈmʌs·tæʃ] n moustache f

**mouth**[1] [maʊθ] n ❶ANAT bouche f; (of an animal) gueule f; **to keep one's ~ shut** se taire; **to make sb's ~ water** faire saliver qn ❷(opening) ouverture f; (of a bottle) goulot m; (of a cave, volcano) bouche f; (of a river) embouchure f ▸ **to have a big ~** inf être une grande gueule; **to shoot one's ~ off about sth** inf crier qc sur les toits

**mouth**[2] [maʊð] vt ❶(utter) proférer ❷(mime) articuler sans son

**mouthful** n ❶(amount of food) bouchée f ❷(amount of drink) gorgée f ❸inf (unpronounceable word) **to be a ~** être difficile à prononcer

**mouth organ** n harmonica m

**mouthpiece** n ❶TEL, MUS (of a telephone) microphone m; (of a musical instrument, pipe) embout m ❷SPORTS protège-dents m ❸POL porte-parole m

**mouth-to-mouth** I. adj bouche à bouche inv; **~ resuscitation** bouche à bouche m II. n bouche à bouche m

**mouthwash** n bain m de bouche

**move** [muːv] I. n ❶(movement) mouvement m; **to be on the ~** (traveling) être parti; (working) être en déplacement ❷(act) action f; (in game) coup m; **a good/bad ~** une bonne/mauvaise décision ❸(change: of home, premises) déménagement m; (of job) changement m ▸ **to get a ~ on** se grouiller II. vi ❶(position) bouger; (on wheels) rouler; **to ~ out of the way** s'écarter du chemin ❷(walk, run) se déplacer ❸inf (intensive use) **he can**

really **~**! (runner) il court bien!; (dancer) il bouge bien! ❹(act) agir; (in games) avancer ❺(develop) bouger ❻(change: to new home, premises) déménager; (to new job) être muté; **we're moving into e-commerce** nous nous lançons dans le commerce électronique ❼(change attitude) faire des concessions ❽inf (leave) partir ❾(be bought) se vendre ❿(frequent) **to ~ in exalted circles** fréquenter des gens bien placés ⓫form (suggest) **to ~ for an adjournment** proposer l'ajournement III. vt ❶(to new position: object) bouger; (passengers, troops) transporter; **~ the vase to the right/over there** mets le vase à droite/là-bas ❷(to new time: meeting) déplacer; (patient) déplacer le rendez-vous de ❸(to new address) déménager; (to new job) muter; **we ~d her to sales** nous l'avons transférée à la vente ❹(cause movements in: arms, legs) bouger; (branches) agiter; (machinery) faire bouger ❺(cause emotions) toucher; **to be ~d to tears** être ému aux larmes ❻(persuade) persuader; **what ~d you to write the book?** qu'est-ce qui vous a poussé à écrire le livre? ❼(suggest at meeting) proposer ▸ **to ~ heaven and earth** remuer ciel et terre; **to ~ mountains** soulever des montagnes

♦**move along** I. vt faire circuler II. vi ❶(walk further on) avancer ❷(run further on) courir ❸(drive further on) continuer à rouler ❹(make room) faire de la place ❺(develop) avancer

♦**move around** I. vi ❶(not stay still) bouger ❷(go around) circuler ❸(travel) voyager ❹(change address) déménager ❺(change jobs) changer d'emploi II. vt changer de place

♦**move away** I. vi ❶(move house) déménager; **to ~ from one city to another** déménager d'une ville à l'autre ❷(change) **to ~ from a market/field** quitter un marché/un domaine II. vt always sep **to move a chair/sb's arm**

**away** déplacer une chaise/pousser le bras de qn
◆**move back** I. *vt* faire revenir II. *vi* redéménager
◆**move down** I. *vi* baisser II. *vt* SCHOOL **to move sb down** rétrograder qn; **to move sb down a grade** faire descendre d'une classe
◆**move in** I. *vi* ❶ (*into a house, an office*) emménager; **to ~ with a friend** emménager avec un ami ❷ (*intervene: police, troops*) intervenir ❸ (*advance to attack*) **to ~ on sb** avancer sur qn II. *vt* faire entrer
◆**move off** *vi* ❶ (*walk*) partir; (*parade, protesters*) se mettre en mouvement ❷ (*run*) s'élancer ❸ (*drive*) démarrer ❹ (*fly*) décoller
◆**move on** I. *vi* ❶ (*continue a trip*) reprendre la route; (*traffic*) se remettre en mouvement ❷ (*walk*) avancer ❸ (*be ordered away*) circuler ❹ (*to new stage*) passer à autre chose; (*in career*) monter dans la hiérarchie; **to ~ to higher things** passer à quelque chose de mieux ❺ (*develop*) changer ❻ (*pass: time*) passer ❼ (*change subject*) continuer; **to ~ to sth** passer à qc II. *vt* (*ask to leave*) faire circuler ❷ (*force to leave*) faire partir
◆**move out** I. *vi* ❶ (*to new home, office*) déménager; (*leave home*) quitter la maison; **to ~ of sth** quitter qc ❷ (*retreat*) se retirer II. *vt* sortir; (*person*) faire partir; (*furniture*) déménager
◆**move over** *vi* ❶ (*make room*) se pousser ❷ (*switch to*) **to ~ to sth** passer à qc ❸ (*leave position*) laisser sa place II. *vt* (*move aside*) mettre de côté
◆**move up** I. *vi* ❶ (*go up, rise*) monter ❷ SCHOOL passer (dans une classe supérieure) ❸ (*make room*) faire de la place ❹ (*have promotion*) avoir de l'avancement ❺ (*increase*) augmenter II. *vt* ❶ (*go upward*) monter ❷ SCHOOL passer ❸ (*give promotion*) promouvoir
**movement** ['muːv·mənt] *n* ❶ (*motion, group*) a. MED, MUS mouvement *m* ❷ FIN fluctuation *f*; **an upward ~ in share prices** une tendance à la hausse des ac-

tions ❸ (*tendency*) tendance *f*; **a ~ toward/against sth** un mouvement vers/contre qc
**mover** *n* (*removal man*) déménageur *m*
**movie** ['muː·vi] *n* (*film*) film *m*; **the ~s** le cinéma
**movie camera** *n* caméra *f*
**movie star** *n* vedette *f* de cinéma
**movie theater** *n* cinéma *m*
**moving** I. *adj* ❶ (*that moves: vehicle*) en mouvement; (*part*) mobile ❷ (*motivating*) moteur(-trice); **the ~ drive** l'énergie *f* ❸ (*touching*) émouvant(e) II. *n* déménagement *m*
**mow** [moʊ] <mowed, mown *o* mowed> I. *vi* (*cut grass, grain*) tondre II. *vt* tondre; (*a field*) faucher
**mower** *n* ❶ (*lawn cutter*) tondeuse *f* à gazon ❷ (*on a farm*) faucheuse *f*
**mown** [moʊn] *pp of* **mow**
**MP** [ˌem·'piː] *n* ❶ *abbr of* **Military Police** police *f* militaire ❷ *Can abbr of* **Member of Parliament** député(e) *m(f)*
**mpg** *n abbr of* **miles per gallon** miles *mpl* au gallon
**mph** [ˌem·piː·'eɪtʃ] *abbr of* **miles per hour** miles par heure *mpl*
**Mr.** ['mɪs·tər] *n abbr of* **Mister** (*title for man*) M.; **~ Big** le grand chef; **~ Right** l'homme *m* idéal ▶**no more ~ Nice Guy** finies les politesses
**Mrs.** ['mɪs·ɪz] *n abbr of* **Mistress** ❶ (*woman*) Mme ❷ (*representative*) Madame *f*
**MS** [ˌem·'es] *n* ❶ *abbr of* **Master of Science** ≈ maîtrise *f* de sciences ❷ *abbr of* **Mississippi**
**Ms.** [mɪz] *n abbr of* **Miss** terme d'adresse pour une femme qui évite la distinction entre Miss et Mrs.
**MS** [ˌem·'es] *n* ❶ *abbr of* **Master of Science** ≈ maîtrise *f* de sciences ❷ *abbr of* **Mississippi**
**MST** *n abbr of* **Mountain Standard Time** heure *f* des Montagnes Rocheuses
**MT** *n abbr of* **Montana**
**Mt.** *n abbr of* **Mount, Mountain** Mt. *m*

**M**

**much** [mʌtʃ] <more, most> I. *adj* beaucoup de; **you don't need ~ water** il ne faut pas beaucoup d'eau; **how ~ milk?** quelle quantité de lait?; **too/so ~ water** trop/tellement d'eau; **as ~ water as** autant d'eau que; **three times as ~ water** trois fois plus d'eau II. *adv* très; **~ better** beaucoup mieux; **thank you very ~** merci beaucoup; **I don't use it ~** je ne m'en sers pas beaucoup; **a ~-deserved rest/shower** un repos/une douche bien mérité(e); **to my astonishment** à mon grand étonnement; **not him, ~ less her** pas lui, encore moins elle; *s.a.* many III. *pron* beaucoup de; **not ~ of the money is left** il ne reste pas grand-chose de l'argent; **~ of the day** une bonne partie de la journée; **too ~** trop; **you earn twice as ~ as I do** tu gagnes deux fois plus que moi

**mucky** <-ier, -iest> *adj* ❶ (*dirty*) sale ❷ (*obscene*) cochon(ne)

**mud** [mʌd] *n* boue *f* ▶ **to drag sb's name through the ~** traîner le nom de qn dans la boue

**muddle** ['mʌd·l] *n* ❶ (*confused situation*) embrouille *f;* **we're in a ~** on est dans le pétrin ❷ (*messy state*) désordre *m* ❸ (*mental confusion*) **to be in a ~** être perdu

**muddy** I. *vt* ❶ (*make dirty*) salir ❷ (*confuse*) embrouiller ▶ **to ~ the waters** brouiller les pistes II. <-ier, -iest> *adj* sale; (*ground*) boueux(-euse)

**mudguard** *n* (*of a car*) pare-boue *m;* (*of a bicycle*) garde-boue *m*

**mudpack** *n* masque *m* à l'argile

**muffin** ['mʌf·ɪn] *n* CULIN muffin *m* (*petit gâteau*)

**mug** [mʌg] I. *n* ❶ (*drinking vessel*) grande tasse *f* ❷ *pej* (*face*) tronche *f* II. <-gg-> *vt* agresser

**mugger** *n* agresseur, -euse *m, f*

**muggy** <-ier, -iest> *adv* lourd, fade *Belgique;* **it's ~** il fait lourd

**mule¹** [mjul] *n* (*donkey*) *a. pej* mule *f*

**mule²** [mjul] *n* ❶ (*woman's shoe*) mule *f* ❷ (*house shoe*) pantoufle *f*

**multicolored** *adj* multicolore

**multidisciplinary** *adj* multidisciplinaire

**multimillionaire** *n* multimillionnaire *mf*

**multinational** I. *adj* multinational(e) II. *n* multinationale *f*

**multiplayer** ['mʌl·tiˌpleɪ·ər] *adj* (*computer game*) multijoueur(-euse)

**multiple** ['mʌl·tə·pl] *adj* multiple

**multiple-choice** *adj* à choix multiple

**multiplication** [ˌmʌl·tə·plɪ·'keɪ·ʃən] *n* multiplication *f*

**multiply** ['mʌl·tə·plaɪ] I. *vt* multiplier II. *vi* se multiplier

**mum** [mʌm] *n* **~'s the word!** *inf* chut!

**mumble** ['mʌm·bl] *vt, vi* marmonner

**mummy** ['mʌm·i] <-mies> *n* momie *f*

**mumps** [mʌmps] *n + sing vb* MED oreillons *mpl*

**mural** ['mjʊr·əl] *n* fresque *f*

**murder** ['mɜr·dər] I. *n* (*killing*) meurtre *m;* (*emphasizing premeditation*) assassinat *m;* **attempted ~** tentative *f* de meurtre ▶ **to be ~** être tuant; **to get away with ~** tout se permettre II. *vt* ❶ (*kill*) assassiner ❷ *fig* massacrer

**murderer** *n* meurtrier, -ère *m, f*

**murky** ['mɜr·ki] <-ier, -iest> *adj a. fig* obscur(e); (*water*) trouble; (*day, weather*) couvert(e); **it's a ~ business** c'est louche

**murmur** ['mɜr·mər] I. *vi* murmurer; **to ~ to oneself** marmonner dans sa barbe II. *vt* murmurer III. *n* murmure *m;* **without a ~** sans broncher

**muscle** ['mʌs·l] *n* ❶ ANAT muscle *m;* **to not move a ~** ne pas bouger d'un poil ❷ *fig* (*influence*) pouvoir *m;* **to flex one's ~s** se faire les muscles ◆ **muscle in** *vi* s'imposer; **to ~ on sth** s'imposer dans qc

**muscular** ['mʌs·kjə·lər] *adj* ❶ (*relating to muscles*) musculaire ❷ (*strong*) musclé(e)

**muscular dystrophy** *n* myopathie *f*

**museum** [mju·'zi·əm] *n* musée *m*

**mushroom** ['mʌʃ·rum] I. *n a. fig* champignon *m* II. *vi* pousser comme des champignons

**music** ['mju·zɪk] *n inv* musique *f;* **rock ~** rock 'n' roll *m;* **that's ~ to my ears** ça fait plaisir à entendre

**musical** ['mju·zɪ·kəl] **I.** *adj* musical(e); **a ~ instrument** un instrument de musique **II.** *n* comédie *f* musicale

**music box** *n* boîte *f* à musique

**musician** [mju·'zɪ·ʃən] *n* musicien(ne) *m(f)*

**music stand** *n* pupitre *m*

**Muslim** ['mʌz·ləm] **I.** *n* musulman(ne) *m(f)* **II.** *adj* musulman(ne)

**mussel** ['mʌs·əl] *n* moule *f*

**must** [mʌst] **I.** *aux* devoir; **you ~ go now** il faut que tu partes maintenant *subj;* **he ~ be late** il doit être en retard; **you simply ~ come** tu dois venir absolument *subj* **II.** *n inf* must *m*

**mustache** ['mʌs·tæʃ] *n* moustache *f*

**mustard** ['mʌs·tərd] *n inv* ❶ (*plant, paste*) moutarde *f* ❷ (*color*) moutarde *m* ▸ **to cut the ~** faire le poids

**mustn't** ['mʌs·ənt] = **must not** *s.* **must**

**must-see** *adj inf* à ne pas manquer; **this is the ~ movie of the year** c'est le film de l'année qu'il faut voir

**mutilate** ['mju·tə·leɪt] *vt a. fig* mutiler

**mutiny** ['mju·tɪ·ni] **I.** *n* mutinerie *f* **II.** *vi* se mutiner

**mutton** ['mʌt·ən] *n inv* mouton *m*

**mutual** ['mju·tʃu·əl] *adj* mutuel(le); (*friend*) commun(e); (*feeling*) réciproque

**mutual fund** *n* fonds *m* commun de placement

**mutually** *adv* mutuellement

**MVP** *n abbr of* **most valuable player** meilleur(e) joueur, -euse *m, f*

**my** [maɪ] *poss adj* mon *m,* ma *f;* **this car is ~ own** cette voiture est à moi; **I hurt ~ foot/head** je me suis blessé le pied/à la tête

**myself** [maɪ·'self] *reflex pron* ❶ *after verbs* me, m' + *vowel;* **I injured/corrected ~** je me suis blessé/corrigé; **I always enjoy ~** je m'amuse toujours; **I bought ~ a bag** je me suis acheté un sac ❷ (*I or me*) moi-même; **I'll do it ~** je le ferai moi-même; **I did it all by ~** je l'ai fait tout seul; **I prefer Mozart, ~** personnellement je préfère Mozart ❸ *after prep* **I said to ~ ...** je me suis dit ...; **I am ashamed at ~** j'ai honte; **I live by ~** je vis seul

**mysterious** [mɪ·'stɪr·i·əs] *adj* mystérieux(-euse)

**mystery** ['mɪs·tər·i] <-ies> *n* mystère *m*

**myth** [mɪθ] *n a. pej* mythe *m*

**mythology** [mɪ·'θa·lə·dʒi] *n* mythologie *f*

**M**

# Nn

**N, n** [en] <-'s> n N m, n m; **~ as in November** (*on telephone*) n comme Nicolas

**N** n ❶ abbr of **north** N m ❷ abbr of **newton** N m

**n** n ❶ MATH abbr of **n** n m ❷ abbr of **noun** n m ❸ abbr of **neuter** N m

**NA, N/A** abbr of **not applicable** sans rapport

**nag¹** [næg] I. <-gg-> vi faire des remarques incessantes; **to ~ at sb** harceler qn II. <-gg-> vt harceler; **to ~ sb to do/ about doing sth** harceler qn pour qu'il(elle) fasse qc +subj III. n inf (*person*) râleur, -euse m, f

**nag²** [næg] n (*horse*) bourrin m

**nail** [neɪl] I. n ❶ (*metal fastener*) clou m ❷ ANAT (*finger/toe end*) ongle m ▸ **to be a ~ in sb's/sth's coffin** être un autre coup funeste pour qn/à qc II. vt ❶ (*fasten*) **to ~ sth to sth** clouer qc à qc ❷ inf (*catch*) épingler

**nail-biting** adj à suspense

**nailbrush** n brosse f à ongles

**nail clippers** npl coupe-ongles m

**nail file** n lime f à ongles

**nail polish** n vernis m à ongles

**nail scissors** n ciseaux mpl à ongles

**naive, naïve** [na·'iv] adj pej naïf(-ive); **to make the ~ assumption that...** avoir la naïveté de supposer que ...

**naked** ['neɪ·kɪd] adj ❶ (*uncovered*) a. fig nu(e); **stark ~** inf nu comme un verre; **to the ~ eye** à l'œil nu ❷ (*not hidden*) flagrant(e); (*ambition*) non dissimulé(e)

**name** [neɪm] I. n ❶ (*what one is called*) nom m; **full ~** nom et prénom; **first ~** prénom m; **last ~** nom de famille; **what's your ~?** comment t'appelles-tu?; **to call sb ~s** injurier qn; **in the ~ of sb/sth** au nom de qn/qc ❷ (*reputation*) réputation f; **to make a ~ for oneself** se faire une réputation ▸ **to be**

**the ~ of the game** être tout ce qui compte; **to take sb's ~ in vain** parler de qn II. vt ❶ (*call*) nommer; (*child, file, product*) appeler; **to be ~d after/ for sb** recevoir le nom de qn; **sb ~d Jones** un nommé Jones ❷ (*appoint*) nommer ❸ (*list*) citer ❹ (*specify*) désigner; (*time, conditions, price*) fixer

**name-calling** npl injures fpl

**nameplate** n médaillon m

**nanny** ['næn·i] n nurse f

**nap¹** [næp] I. n sieste f II. <-pp-> vi faire une sieste; **to be caught ~ping** être pris au dépourvu

**nap²** [næp] inv n (*on fabric*) poil m

**napkin** ['næp·kɪn] n serviette f

**narc** [nark] n sl (*police officer*) agent m de la police des stups

**narcotic** [nar·'kɑt·ɪk] I. n ❶ LAW (*illegal drug*) stupéfiant m ❷ MED (*drug causing sleepiness*) narcotique m II. adj ❶ LAW (*illegal*) de stupéfiant ❷ MED (*sleep-inducing*) narcotique

**narrate** ['ner·eɪt] vt raconter

**narration** [ner·'eɪ·ʃᵊn] n narration f

**narrator** ['ner·eɪ·t̬ər] n narrateur, -trice m, f

**narrow** ['ner·oʊ] I. <-er, -est> adj a. fig étroit(e); (*victory*) de justesse; **to make a ~ escape** l'échapper belle II. vi ❶ (*become narrow*) se rétrécir ❷ fig (*gap*) se réduire III. vt ❶ (*make narrow*) rétrécir ❷ fig (*gap*) réduire; (*possibilities*) limiter

**narrowly** adv ❶ (*just*) de peu ❷ (*closely*) de près ❸ (*in a limited way*) étroitement

**narrow-minded** adj (*person*) à l'esprit étroit; (*opinions, views*) étroit(e)

**nasty** ['næs·ti] <-ier, -iest> adj ❶ (*unpleasant*) désagréable ❷ (*spiteful*) méchant(e) ❸ (*bad, serious: accident, habit*) vilain(e) ❹ (*morally bad*) ignoble

**nation** [neɪ·ʃᵊn] n ❶ (*country, state*) nation *f*; **to serve the ~** servir l'État ❷(*people living in a state*) peuple *m*; **the whole ~** le pays entier ❸(*ethnic group or tribe*) nation *f*

**national** ['næʃ·ᵊn·ᵊl] I.*adj* national(e) II.*n pl* ressortissant(e) *m(f)*

**national anthem** *n* hymne *m* national

**nationality** [ˌnæʃ·ᵊn·ˈæl·ə·ti] <-ties> *n* nationalité *f*

**national park** *n* parc *m* national

**nationwide** I.*adv* à l'échelle nationale; (*opinion*) national(e) II.*adj* au niveau national; (*be known*) dans tout le pays

**native** ['neɪ·t̬ɪv] I.*adj* ❶(*born in or local to place*) natif(-ive); (*plant*) aborigène ❷(*of place of origin*) de naissance; (*country*) d'origine ❸(*indigenous, primitive*) indigène; (*village*) primitif(-ive) ❹(*local, traditional*) du pays ❺(*original*) natif(-ive); (*language*) maternel(le) ❻(*innate aptitude*) naturel(le); (*talent*) inné(e) II.*n* ❶(*born, living in a place*) autochtone *mf*; **to be a ~ of New England** être originaire de la Nouvelle-Angleterre; **to speak English like a ~** parler l'anglais comme un natif ❷*pej* (*indigene*) indigène *mf*

**Native American** I.*n* Amérindien(ne) *m(f)* II.*adj* amérindien(ne)

**native speaker** *n* locuteur, -trice *m, f* natif(-ive); **to be an English ~** être de langue maternelle anglaise

**NATO** ['neɪ·t̬oʊ] *n no art abbr of* **North Atlantic Treaty Organization** OTAN *f*

**natural** ['nætʃ·ɚ·əl] I.*adj* naturel(le); (*state*) primitif(-ive); (*parents*) biologique; **it's only ~ that** il est tout à fait naturel que +*subj*; **to be a ~ leader** être né pour être un meneur II.*n inf* talent *m*; **to be a ~ for sth** être doué pour qc; **as a singer, she's a ~** c'est une chanteuse née

**natural childbirth** *n* accouchement *m* naturel

**natural disaster** *n* catastrophe *f* naturelle

**natural gas** *n* gaz *m* naturel

**natural history** *n* histoire *f* naturelle

**naturalist** I.*n* naturaliste *mf* II.*adj* naturaliste

**naturally** *adv* naturellement; **it comes ~ to her** c'est inné chez elle

**natural resources** *npl* ressources *fpl* naturelles

**natural science** *n* sciences *fpl* naturelles

**natural selection** *n* sélection *f* naturelle

**nature** ['neɪ·tʃɚ] *n* ❶*no art* (*the environment, natural forces*) nature *f* ❷(*essential qualities, temperament*) nature *f*; **things of this ~** les choses *fpl* de ce genre; **it's in her ~ to do that** c'est dans son tempérament de faire ça

**nature conservation** *n* protection *f* de la nature

**nature lover** *n* amoureux, -euse *m, f* de la nature

**nature preserve** *n* réserve *f* naturelle

**nature trail** *n* sentier *m* (aménagé)

**naught** [nɔt] *pron* **to be (all) for ~** être en vain; **to come to ~** n'aboutir à rien

**naughty** ['nɔ·t̬i] <-ier, -iest> *adj* ❶(*badly behaved, mischievous*) *a. iron* vilain(e) ❷(*wicked*) méchant(e) ❸*iron, inf* (*sexually stimulating*) cochon(ne)

**nauseous** ['nɔ·ʃəs] *adj* nauséeux(-euse); **to be** [*o feel*] **~** avoir des nausées

**nautical** ['nɔ·t̬ɪ·kᵊl] *adj* nautique

**nautical mile** *n* mil(l)e *m* nautique

**naval** ['neɪ·vᵊl] *adj* naval(e); (*officer*) de marine

**navel** ['neɪ·vᵊl] *n* nombril *m* ▸**to contemplate one's ~** se regarder le nombril

**navigate** ['næv·ɪ·geɪt] I.*vt* ❶NAUT naviguer; **to ~ the ocean/a river** naviguer sur l'océan/une rivière ❷(*steer, pilot*) gouverner ❸(*manage to get through*) **to ~ one's way to the door** se frayer un chemin jusqu'à la porte ❹COMPUT **to ~ the Internet** naviguer sur Internet II.*vi* ❶NAUT, AVIAT naviguer ❷AUTO diriger

**navigation** [ˌnæv·ɪ·ˈgeɪ·ʃᵊn] *n no pl* (*navigating*) navigation *f*; **~ system** système de navigation

N

**navigator** ['næv·ɪ·geɪ·tər] n ❶ NAUT navigateur, ·trice m, f ❷ AUTO copilote m

**navy** ['neɪ·vi] I. <-vies> n ❶ (military fleet) **the Navy** la Marine ❷ (color) marine II. adj bleu marine inv

**NB** [ˌen·'bi] adv abbr of **nota bene** NB

**NBA** [ˌen·bi·'eɪ] n abbr of **National Basketball Association** NBA f

**NC** n abbr of **North Carolina**

**ND** [ˌen·'di] n abbr of **North Dakota**

**NE** [ˌen·'i] ❶ abbr of **Nebraska** ❷ abbr of **New England** ❸ abbr of **northeast** N-E f

**near** [nɪr] I. adj ❶ (over distance) proche; **the ~est place** l'endroit m le plus proche ❷ (in time) proche; **in the ~ future** dans un proche avenir ❸ (dear) proche; **a ~ and dear friend** un ami intime ❹ (similar) proche; (portrait) ressemblant(e); **the ~est thing** ce qui se rapproche le plus de qc ❺ (not quite) **to the ~est dollar** à un dollar près; **to have a ~ accident** frôler l'accident II. adv ❶ (in space or time) près; **to be ~** (building) être à proximité; (event) être imminent; **how ~ is the post office?** à quelle distance se trouve la poste?; **~ at hand** à portée de (la) main; **to come ~er to sb/sth** se rapprocher de qn/qc; **we're getting ~ Easter** nous approchons de Pâques ❷ (almost) presque; **a ~ perfect murder** un meurtre presque parfait; **as ~ as I can guess** autant que je puisse deviner subj ❸ **~ to** (person) proche de; (building, town) près de; **to be ~ to tears** fig être au bord des larmes; **to be ~ to doing sth** être sur le point de faire qc III. prep ❶ (in proximity to) **~ sb/ sth** près de qn/qc; **~ the house** aux abords de la maison; **~ the end/top of the page** vers la fin/le haut de la page; **to be nowhere ~ sth** être loin de qc; **we're nowhere ~ an agreement** nous sommes loin de trouver un accord ❷ (almost) **it's ~/nowhere ~ midnight** il est presque/loin d'être minuit; **it's ~ Christmas** Noël approche; **it's nowhere ~ enough** c'est loin de suffi-

re ❸ (like) **nowhere ~ the truth** à mille lieues de la vérité IV. vt s'approcher de; **it's ~ing completion** c'est presque terminé; **to be ~ing one's goal** toucher au but

**nearby** [ˌnɪr·'baɪ] I. adj proche; **there are a few shops ~** il y a quelques magasins tout près d'ici II. adv à proximité; **is it ~?** est-ce que c'est près d'ici?

**Near East** n **the ~** le Proche-Orient

**nearly** ['nɪr·li] adv presque; **not ~ enough** loin d'être suffisant; **to not be ~ as bad as sth** être loin d'être aussi mauvais que qc; **he very ~ lost his life** il a failli perdre la vie

**near miss** <-es> n ❶ (attack) coup raté de peu ❷ (accident) accident m évité de justesse; **to have a ~** y échapper de justesse; **that was a ~** il s'en est fallu de peu ❸ fig **that was a ~ for him** il a raté le gros lot de peu

**nearsighted** adj myope

**nearsightedness** n myopie f

**neat** [nit] adj ❶ (orderly, well-ordered) ordonné(e); (room) bien rangé(e); (handwriting, appearance) soigné(e); (beard) bien soigné(e); **~ and tidy** propre et bien rangé ❷ (skillful) adroit(e); (solution) bien formulé(e) ❸ (undiluted, pure: gin, whiskey) sec(sèche) ❹ inf (good: bike) super inv; (guy) formidable

**Nebraska** [nə·'bræs·kə] n le Nebraska

**necessarily** ['nes·ə·ser·əl·i] adv ❶ (as a necessary result) nécessairement ❷ (inevitably, therefore) inévitablement ❸ (perforce) forcément; **I don't ~ have to believe him** je ne suis pas forcé de le croire

**necessary** ['nes·ə·ser·i] adj nécessaire; **to make the ~ arrangements** prendre les dispositions utiles; **a ~ evil** un mal nécessaire; **it is ~ for him to do it** il faut qu'il le fasse +subj; **it is not ~ to +infin** ce n'est pas la peine de +infin; **to do what is ~** faire ce qu'il faut; **if ~** au besoin

**necessity** [nə·'ses·ə·t̬i] <-ties> n ❶ (the fact of being necessary) nécessité *f*; **a case of absolute ~** un cas de force majeure ❷ *(need)* besoin *m*; **when the ~ arises** quand le besoin se fait sentir; **~ for sb to** +*infin* besoin pour qn de +*infin* ❸ *(basic need)* besoin *m*; **to be a ~** être indispensable; **the bare necessities** le strict nécessaire ▶ **~ is the mother of invention** *prov* la nécessité rend ingénieux

**neck** [nek] **I.** *n* ❶ *(body part)* cou *m* ❷ *(nape)* nuque *f* ❸ *(area below head)* encolure *f* ❹ *(cut of meat)* collier *m* ❺ *(long thin object part: of a bottle)* goulot *m*; *(of a vase)* col *m*; *(of a violin)* manche *m* ❻ *(distance in horse racing)* **by a ~** d'une encolure ▶ **in this ~ of the woods** *inf* dans le coin; **to be up to one's ~ in sth** *inf* être complètement impliqué dans qc; **to be breathing down sb's ~** être tout près de qn; **to finish and ~ and ~** arriver au coude à coude; **to stick one's ~ out** prendre des risques **II.** *vi inf* ❶ *(kiss)* se bécoter ❷ *(caress)* se peloter

**necklace** *n* collier *m*
**neckline** *n* encolure *f*; **low ~** décolleté *m*
**necktie** *n* cravate *f*
**nectar** ['nek·tər] *n* nectar *m*
**need** [niːd] **I.** *n* ❶ *(want, requirement, lack)* besoin *m*; **to be badly in ~ of sth** avoir grandement besoin de qc; **to meet sb's ~s** subvenir aux besoins de qn; **as the ~ arises** quand la nécessité se fera sentir; **if ~ be** en cas de besoin; **there's no ~ to buy it** il n'est pas nécessaire de l'acheter; **there's no ~ to shout!** tu n'as pas besoin de crier! ❷ *(emergency, crisis)* difficulté *f*; **in his hour of ~ his friend was there** dans les moments difficiles, son ami était là **II.** *vt* ❶ *(require)* avoir besoin de; **I ~ time to think about it** il me faut du temps pour y réfléchir; **you'll be ~ing your sunglasses today!** tu devras porter tes lunettes aujourd'hui!; **I ~ sb to help me** j'ai besoin que qn m'aide ❷ *(must, have to)* **to ~ to** +*infin* être obligé de +*infin*; **he ~s to improve** il

faut qu'il s'améliore; **they didn't ~ to wait long** ils n'ont pas eu à attendre longtemps; **they ~ to be tested** ils doivent être testés ▶ **that's all we ~!** *iron* il ne manquait plus que ça! **III.** *aux* ~ **I attend the conference?** faut-il vraiment que j'assiste à la conférence?; **you ~n't worry** *inf* tu n'as pas à t'inquiéter; **to ~ not** +*infin* ne pas avoir à +*infin*; **you ~n't have done all this work** il n'était pas nécessaire de faire tout ce travail

**needle** ['niː·dl] **I.** *n* aiguille *f* ▶ **to look** [*o* **search**] **for a ~ in a haystack** chercher une aiguille dans une botte de foin; **to be on pins and ~s** être sur des charbons ardents **II.** *vt* ❶ *inf (annoy)* agacer ❷ *(prick)* piquer

**needless** *adj* superflu(e); **~ to say …** inutile de dire …
**needy** ['niː·di] **I.**<-ier, -iest> *adj* nécessiteux(-euse) **II.** *npl* **the ~** les nécessiteux *mpl*

**negative** ['neg·ə·tɪv] **I.** *adj* ❶ *(denoting denial, refusal)* *a.* ELEC négatif(-ive) ❷ *(expressing negation: clause)* de nullité ❸ *(pessimistic)* négatif(-ive) **II.** *n* ❶ *(rejection, refusal)* réponse *f* négative; **in the ~** par la négative ❷ *(photographic image)* négatif *m* **III.** *vt* ❶ *form (say no to)* dire non à ❷ *(reject, decline)* rejeter ❸ *(contradict)* contredire **IV.** *interj* négatif!

**neglect** [nɪ'glekt] **I.** *vt* négliger; *(garden, building)* laisser à l'abandon; *(duties)* oublier; *(opportunity)* laisser échapper; **to ~ to** +*infin* omettre de +*infin* **II.** *n* ❶ *(not caring)* négligence *f* ❷ *(poor state)* manque *m* d'entretien; **to be in a state of ~** être à l'abandon
**neglected** *adv* négligé(e); *(building)* mal entretenu(e); *(child)* délaissé(e); **to feel ~** se sentir délaissé
**negligence** ['neg·lɪ·dʒən(t)s] *n* négligence *f*
**negotiate** [nɪ'goʊ·ʃi·eɪt] **I.** *vt* ❶ *(discuss, bargain)* négocier; **to be ~d** à débattre ❷ *(travel through: obstacle)* franchir; *(sharp curve)* négocier ❸ *(sur-*

*mount or solve: problems, difficulties*) surmonter **II.** *vi* négocier; **to ~ with sb** être en pourparlers avec qn; **to ~ for peace with sb** entreprendre des pourparlers pour la paix avec qn

**negotiation** [nɪ·ˌgoʊ·ʃi·ˈeɪ·ʃᵊn] *n* négociation *f;* **to be in ~ with sb** être en pourparlers avec qn

**negotiator** *n* négociateur, -trice *m, f*

**neigh** [neɪ] **I.** *n* hennissement *m* **II.** *vi* hennir

**neighbor** [ˈneɪ·bər] **I.** *n* ❶ (*person living next door*) voisin(e) *m(f)* ❷ (*adjacent country*) pays *m* limitrophe ❸ (*fellow citizen*) prochain *m* ▶ **love your ~ as you love yourself** aime ton prochain comme toi-même **II.** *vi* **to ~ on sth** être adjacent à qc

**neighborhood** [ˈneɪ·bər·hʊd] *n* ❶ (*district*) quartier *m;* **the library is in my ~** la bibliothèque est près de chez moi; **~ shops** commerces *mpl* de proximité ❷ (*people of the district*) voisinage *m* ❸ (*vicinity*) environs *mpl;* **in the ~ of sth** *fig* aux alentours de qc

N

**neither** [ˈni·ðər] **I.** *pron* aucun (des deux); **which one? – ~ (of them)** lequel? – ni l'un ni l'autre **II.** *adv* ni; **~ ... nor ...** ni ... ni ... ▶ **sth is ~ here nor there** qc importe peu **III.** *conj* non plus; **if he won't eat, ~ will I** s'il ne mange pas, moi non plus **IV.** *adj* aucun des deux; **in ~ case** ni dans un cas ni dans l'autre; **~ book is good** ces deux livres ne sont bons ni l'un ni l'autre

**neon** [ˈni·an] *n* néon *m*

**neo-Nazi** **I.** *n* néonazi(e) *m(f)* **II.** *adj* néonazi(e)

**nephew** [ˈnef·ju] *n* neveu *m*

**nerd** [nɜrd] *n inf* nul(le) *m(f)*

**nerve** [nɜrv] *n* ❶ ANAT nerf *m;* **~ ending** terminaison *f* nerveuse ❷ *pl* (*worry*) nerfs *mpl;* **to be a bundle of ~s** être un paquet de nerfs; **to get on sb's ~s** *inf* taper sur les nerfs de qn ❸ *inf* (*audacity*) culot *m;* **to have the ~ to** *+infin* avoir le culot de *+infin* ❹ (*courage*) courage *m;* **to lose one's ~** perdre son sang-froid ▶ **~s of steel** nerfs d'acier; **to hit a (raw) ~** toucher la corde sensible

**nervous** [ˈnɜr·vəs] *adj* ❶ (*agitated, excited*) nerveux(-euse); **to be a ~ wreck** être à bout de nerfs ❷ (*tense, anxious*) angoissé(e); **to make sb ~** rendre qn nerveux; **to feel ~** avoir les nerfs en boule; **to be ~ about doing sth** avoir peur de faire qc ❸ (*timid*) timide; **to make sb ~** mettre qn mal à l'aise; **to be ~** (*for performance, test*) avoir le trac ❹ MED nerveux(-euse)

**nervous breakdown** *n* dépression *f* nerveuse

**nervousness** *n* ❶ (*nervous condition*) nervosité *f* ❷ (*fearfulness, anxiety*) trac *m*

**nest** [nest] **I.** *n* ❶ (*animal's home*) nid *m* ❷ (*set*) jeu *m* **II.** *vi* se nicher

**net¹** [net] **I.** *n* ❶ *a. fig* filet *m* ❷ (*material*) tulle *f* **II.** <-tt-> *vt* ❶ (*catch: fish*) attraper; (*criminals*) arrêter ❷ SPORTS (*hit into a net*) **to ~ a goal** marquer un but

**net²** [net] **I.** *adj* ❶ (*after deduction*) net(te) ❷ (*final*) final(e) **II.** *vt* (*profit*) rapporter net; (*income*) gagner net

**Net** [net] *n* COMPUT **the ~** le Net; **~ surfer** internaute *mf*

**Netherlands** [ˈneð·ər·ləndz] *n* **the ~** les Pays-Bas *mpl*

**netiquette** [ˈnet·ɪ·ket] *n* COMPUT étiquette *f* de réseau, nétiquette *f*

**netspeak** [ˈnet·spik] *n* COMPUT cyberjargon *m*

**netting** [ˈnet̬·ɪŋ] *n* ❶ (*material*) filets *mpl* ❷ SPORTS (*netted structure*) treillis *m* métallique

**nettle** [ˈnet̬·l] **I.** *n* ortie *f* **II.** *vt* agacer

**network** [ˈnet·wɜrk] **I.** *n* ❶ (*system*) réseau *m* ❷ (*number, variety*) ensemble *m* ❸ (*group of broadcasting stations*) chaînes *fpl* **II.** *vt* ❶ (*link together*) relier; COMPUT, TECH connecter ❷ (*broadcast*) diffuser **III.** *vi* tisser un réseau de relations

**networking** *n* ❶ COMPUT (*work*) travail *m* en réseau ❷ COMPUT (*connecting*) mise *f* en réseau ❸ (*making* *contacts*) établissement *m* d'un réseau de contacts

**neurotic** [nʊ·'ra·tɪk] I. *n* névrosé(e) *m(f)* II. *adj* névrosé(e)

**neuter** ['nu·tər] I. *adj* neutre II. *vt* (*males*) castrer; (*females*) stériliser

**neutral** ['nu·trəl] I. *adj* ❶ (*impartial*) neutre ❷ (*unemotional*) de marbre II. *n* ❶ (*nonaligned country*) pays *m* neutre ❷ AUTO point *m* mort

**neutrality** [nu·'træl·ə·ți] *n* neutralité *f*

**neutralize** ['nu·trə·laɪz] *vt* neutraliser

**Nevada** [nə·'væd·ə] *n* le Nevada

**never** ['nev·ər] *adv* jamais; **~ in all my life** jamais de la vie; **~ again!** plus jamais!; **~ ever** plus jamais; **he ~ told me that!** *inf* il ne me l'a jamais dit! ▶ **~ mind** ça ne fait rien; **~ mind that/ him** ne fais pas attention à ça/lui

**never-ending** *adj* interminable

**nevertheless** [ˌnev·ər·ðə·'les] *adv* néanmoins

**new** [nu] I. *adj* ❶ (*just made*) neuf(neuve); **brand ~** tout neuf ❷ (*latest, replacing former one*) nouveau(-elle); **~ blood** *fig* sang *m* nouveau; **to feel like a ~ man/woman** se sentir revivre; **I'm ~ around here** je suis nouveau ici; **I'm ~ to the Internet/this job** Internet/ce boulot est nouveau pour moi; **everything is so ~ to me** tout est si nouveau pour moi; **we're ~ to Chicago** nous venons d'arriver à Chicago ▶ **what's ~?** quoi de neuf? II. *adv* récemment

**newbie** *n sl* COMPUT newbie *m*, internaute *mf* novice

**newcomer** *n* ❶ (*freshly arrived person*) nouveau, -elle venu(e) *m* ❷ (*beginner*) débutant(e) *m(f)*

**New England** *n* la Nouvelle-Angleterre

**newfangled** *adj pej* dernier cri *inv*

**newfound** *adj* tout(e) nouveau(-elle)

**New Hampshire** *n* le New Hampshire

**newish** ['nu·ɪʃ] *adj inf* assez neuf(neuve)

**New Jersey** *n* le New Jersey

**newly** *adv* ❶ (*recently*) récemment; **~ married** jeune marié ❷ (*freshly, once* *again*) de frais; **~ painted** fraîchement peint

**newlywed** *n* jeune marié(e) *m(f)*

**New Mexico** *n* le Nouveau-Mexique

**news** [nuz] *n* ❶ (*fresh information*) nouvelle(s) *fpl*; **to be in the ~** faire parler de soi; **financial/sports ~** chronique *f* sportive/financière; **to break the ~ to sb** annoncer la nouvelle à qc; **to have ~ for sb** avoir du nouveau pour qn; **that's ~ to me** je ne savais pas ❷ TV, RADIO (*program*) **the ~** informations *fpl*; **on the ~** aux informations ▶ **no ~ is good ~** *prov* pas de nouvelles, bonnes nouvelles *prov*

**news agency** *n* agence *f* de presse

**newscast** *n* informations *fpl*

**news flash** *n* flash *m* d'information

**news item** *n* ❶ point *m* d'information ❷ COMPUT article *m* de forum

**newsletter** *n* bulletin *m*

**news magazine** *n* magazine *m* d'actualités

**newspaper** *n* journal *m;* **daily ~** quotidien *m*

**newsreel** *n* actualités *fpl* (filmées)

**newsroom** *n* salle *f* de rédaction

**newsstand** *n* kiosque *m*

**newsworthy** *adj* d'un intérêt médiatique

**New Year** *n* nouvel an *m;* **Happy New Year!** bonne année!

**New York** I. *n* New York II. *adj* new-yorkais(e)

**New Yorker** *n* New-yorkais(e) *m(f)*

**next** [nekst] I. *adj* ❶ (*after this one*) prochain(e); **you're ~** c'est votre tour; **who's ~?** à qui le tour? ❷ (*following*) suivant(e); **the ~ day** le lendemain; **in the ~ two days/ten minutes** d'ici deux jours/dix minutes ❸ (*in series, space: house*) voisin(e); **on the ~ floor up/down** à l'étage du dessus/dessous; **at the ~ table** à la table d'à-côté; **I need the ~ size up/down** il me faut une taille au-dessus/au-dessous II. *adv* ❶ (*afterward*) ensuite; **David left ~** David est parti après ❷ (*in a moment*) maintenant; **~, add the eggs** mainte-

**N**

nant, incorporer les œufs ❸ (*second*) après; **the ~ oldest is John** c'est John qui est ensuite le plus âgé ❹ (*again*) la prochaine fois; **when I ~ come** quand je reviendrai **III. pron the ~** le(la) prochain(e); **the ~ to leave was David** ensuite, c'est David qui est parti; **from one minute to the ~** d'une minute à l'autre

**next door** *adv* à côté; **the woman/ man ~** la dame/le monsieur d'à-côté; **to go ~** aller chez les voisins

**next-door** *adj* d'à-côté; **~ neighbor** voisin *m* d'à-côté

**next of kin** *n* plus proche parent *m*

**next to** *adv* ❶ (*beside*) à côté de; **~ the skin** à même la peau ❷ (*second to*) **~ last** avant-dernier; **~ Bach, I like Mozart best** après Bach, c'est Mozart que je préfère ❸ (*almost*) presque; **to cost ~ nothing** coûter trois fois rien; **it takes ~ no time** c'est très rapide

**NFL** [ˌen·ef·'el] *n abbr of* **National Football League** Ligue *f* nationale de football américain

**N** **NH** [ˌen·'eɪtʃ] *n abbr of* **New Hampshire**

**NHL** [ˌen·eɪtʃ·'el] *n abbr of* **National Hockey League** LNH *f*

**nib** [nɪb] *n* plume *f*

**nibble** ['nɪb·l] **I.** *n* morceau *m* **II.** *vt* ❶ (*eat with small bites*) grignoter, gruger *Québec* ❷ (*peck at sensually*) mordiller **III.** *vi* ❶ (*snack lightly*) grignoter ❷ *fig* (*show interest in*) **to ~ at an offer** se montrer tenté par une offre ❸ (*deplete slowly*) **to ~ away at sth** grignoter doucement qc

**nice** [naɪs] *adj* ❶ (*pleasant, agreeable*) agréable; **~ weather** beau temps *m*; **far ~r** beaucoup plus beau; **~ to meet you!** enchanté de faire votre connaissance! ❷ (*kind, friendly*) gentil(le); **a ~ guy** un bon gars; **it was ~ of you to call** c'est gentil d'avoir appelé ❸ (*beautiful*) joli(e) ❹ (*socially approved: person, accent*) sympathique ❺ *iron* (*unpleasant, bad, awkward*) joli(e); **what a ~ thing to say to your brother** c'est

gentil de dire ça à ton frère ❻ (*fine, subtle*) subtil(e)

**nicely** *adv* ❶ (*well*) bien ❷ (*politely*) poliment

**niche** [nɪtʃ, niʃ] *n* ❶ (*in wall*) niche *f* ❷ (*suitable position*) créneau *m* ▶**to find one's ~** trouver sa voie

**nick** [nɪk] **I.** *n* ❶ (*cut*) entaille *f* ❷ (*chip, dent*) ébréchure *f* ▶**in the ~ of time** juste à temps **II.** *vt* ❶ (*cut*) entailler; **to ~ oneself** se couper ❷ (*chip, dent*) ébrécher ❸ *inf* (*charge unfairly, trick*) rouler

**nickel** ['nɪk·l] *n* ❶ (*metallic element*) nickel *m* ❷ (*coin*) pièce *f* de cinq cents

**nickname** ['nɪk·neɪm] **I.** *n* surnom *m* **II.** *vt* surnommer

**nicotine** ['nɪk·ə·tin] *n* nicotine *f*

**nicotine patch** *n* patch *m* de nicotine

**niece** [nis] *n* nièce *f*

**niggling** *adj* tatillon(ne); (*doubt*) obsédant(e)

**night** [naɪt] **I.** *n* ❶ (*end of day*) soir *m*; **10 (o'clock) at ~** 10 heures du soir; **the ~ before** la veille au soir ❷ (*opp: day*) nuit *f*; **good ~!** bonne nuit!; **last ~** cette nuit, la nuit dernière; (*evening*) hier soir; **open at ~** ouvert la nuit; **during the ~** au cours de la nuit; **far into the ~** tard dans la nuit; **at dead of ~** en pleine nuit; **the Arabian Nights** les Mille et Une Nuits *fpl*; **to work ~s** travailler de nuit ❸ (*evening spent for activity*) soirée *f*; **a girls' ~ out** une soirée entre filles **II.** *adj* de nuit

**nightcap** *n* ❶ (*drink*) boisson généralement alcoolisée prise avant de se coucher ❷ (*cap*) bonnet *m* de nuit

**nightclothes** *npl* vêtements *mpl* de nuit

**nightclub** *n* boîte *f* de nuit

**nightfall** *n* tombée *f* du jour [*o* de la nuit], brunante *f Québec*

**nightgown** *n* chemise *f* de nuit

**nightie** *n inf* chemise *f* de nuit

**nightingale** ['naɪ·tən·gəɪl] *n* rossignol *m*

**nightlife** *n* vie *f* nocturne

**night-light** *n* veilleuse *f*

**nightly I.** adj ❶ (done each night) de tous les soirs ❷ (nocturnal) nocturne **II.** adv tous les soirs

**nightmare** n cauchemar m; **~ scenario** scénario m catastrophe

**night owl** n inf oiseau m de nuit

**night school** n cours mpl du soir

**night shift** n équipe f de nuit; **to work the ~** être de nuit

**nightshirt** n chemise f de nuit

**nightspot** n inf boîte f de nuit

**nighttime** n nuit f

**night watchman** n veilleur m de nuit

**nil** [nɪl] n néant m

**Nile** [naɪl] n **the ~** le Nil

**NIMBY** ['nɪm·bi] n pej abbr of **not in my back yard** riverain(e) m(f) contestataire

**nine** [naɪn] **I.** adj neuf inv; s.a. **eight II.** n neuf m inv ► **be dressed to the ~s** inf être sur son trente et un

**9-11, 9/11** [,naɪn·ɪ·'lev·ən] n no art le 11 septembre

**nineteen** [,naɪn·'tin] adj dix-neuf inv; s.a. **eight**

**nineteenth** adj dix-neuvième; s.a. **eighth**

**ninetieth** adj quatre-vingt-dixième; s.a. **eighth**

**ninety** ['naɪn· t̬i] adj quatre-vingt-dix inv, nonante Belgique, Suisse; s.a. **eight, eighty**

**ninth** [naɪn(t)θ] **I.** adj neuvième **II.** n ❶ (position) neuvième mf ❷ (fraction) neuvième m ❸ (date) **the ~ of February** le neuf février; s.a. **eighth**

**nip¹** [nɪp] **I.** <-pp-> vt ❶ (bite) mordre; **to ~ sth off** couper qc avec les dents ❷ (pinch) pincer ► **to ~ sth in the bud** étouffer qc dans l'œuf **II.** n ❶ (pinch) pincement m ❷ (bite) morsure f ❸ (feeling of cold) **there's a ~ in the air** il fait frisquet

**nip²** [nɪp] n inf goutte f

**nipple** ['nɪp·l] n ❶ (part of breast) mamelon m ❷ (teat for bottle) tétine f

**nippy** ['nɪp·i] <-ier, -iest> adj inf (chilly) frisquet(te)

**nit** [nɪt] n ZOOL lente f

**nitpicking I.** adj pej, inf tatillon(ne) **II.** n pej, inf chipotage m

**nitrate** ['naɪ·treɪt] n nitrate m

**nitrogen** ['naɪ·trə·dʒən] n azote m

**nitty-gritty** [,nɪt̬·ɪ·'grɪt̬·i] n inf **the ~** la dure réalité; **to get down to the ~** passer aux choses sérieuses

**NJ** [,en·'dʒeɪ] n abbr of **New Jersey**

**NM** [,en·'em] n abbr of **New Mexico**

**no** [noʊ] **I.** adj ❶ (not any) **to have ~ time/money** ne pas avoir le temps/d'argent; **to be ~ friend/genius** ne pas être un ami/génie; **to be of ~ importance/interest** n'avoir aucune importance/aucun intérêt; **~ doctor would do it** aucun médecin ne le ferait; **there is ~ way of getting out** il est impossible de sortir; **I'm in ~ mood for excuses** je ne suis pas d'humeur à écouter vos excuses; **there's ~ hurry** ça ne presse pas ❷ (prohibition) **~ smoking/entry** défense de fumer/d'entrer; **~ parking** stationnement m interdit ► **by ~ means** aucunement; **in ~ time** en un rien de temps; **~ way!** pas question! **II.** adv I **~ longer work** je ne travaille plus; **it was ~ easy task** ce n'était pas (une) chose facile; **~ more than 30** pas plus de 30 ► **~ less** rien que ça inf **III.** <-es o -s> n non m inv; **to not take ~ for an answer** insister **IV.** interj non!; **oh ~!** oh non!

**nobility** [noʊ·'bɪl·ə·t̬i] n noblesse f

**noble** ['noʊ·bl] **I.** adj ❶ (aristocratic, honorable) noble ❷ (exalted: ideas) grand(e) **II.** n noble mf

**nobleman** <-men> n noble m

**nobody** ['noʊ·bə·di] **I.** pron indef pron, sing personne; **~ spoke** personne n'a parlé; **~ but me** personne sauf moi **II.** n inf zéro m; **those people are nobodies** ces gens sont des moins que rien

**nocturnal** [nak·'tɜr·nəl] adj form nocturne

**nod** [nad] **I.** n signe m de la tête ► **to give sb the ~** donner le feu vert à qn **II.** <-dd-> vt **to ~ one's head** dire oui d'un signe de la tête; **to ~ (one's)**

**agreement** donner son accord d'un signe de tête III.<-dd-> *vi* **to ~ to** [*o at*] **sb** saluer qn d'un signe de tête
◆ **nod off** <-dd-> *vi inf* s'endormir

**no-go area** *n* MIL zone *f* interdite

**noise** [nɔɪz] *n* ❶(*unpleasant sounds*) bruit *m* ❷(*sound*) bruit *m;* **a clink-ing/rattling ~** un tintement/cliquetis ❸ELEC interférence *f* ▶**to make ~ about doing sth** *inf* laisser entendre que qn fait qc

**noiseless** *adj* silencieux(-euse)

**noise pollution** *n* nuisances *fpl* sonores

**noisily** *adv* bruyamment

**noisy** ['nɔɪ·zi] <-ier, -iest> *adj* bruyant(e); **to be ~** (*person*) faire du bruit

**nomad** ['noʊ·mæd] *n* nomade *mf*

**nomadic** [noʊ·'mæd·ɪk] *adj* nomade; (*existence*) de nomade

**no man's land** *n fig* no man's land *m inv*

**nominate** ['na·mə·neɪt] *vt* ❶(*propose*) proposer; (*for award*) nominer; **to ~ sb for a post** désigner qn à un poste ❷(*appoint*) nommer

**nomination** [ˌna·mə·'neɪ·ʃən] *n* ❶(*proposal*) proposition *f;* **an Oscar ~** une nomination pour l'oscar ❷(*appointment*) nomination *f*

**nominative** ['na·mə·nə·tɪv] I.*n* nominatif *m* II.*adj* nominatif(-ive)

**nominee** [ˌna·mə·'ni] *n* nominé *m*

**nonaggression** *n* non-agression *f;* **~ pact** pacte *m* de non-agression

**nonalcoholic** *adj* non alcoolisé(e)

**nonchalant** [ˌnan·ʃə·'lant] *adj* nonchalant(e)

**noncombatant** *adj* non-combattant(e)

**noncombustible** *adj* non combustible

**noncommissioned officer** *n* sous-officier *m*

**noncommittal** *adj* qui n'engage à rien; **to be ~** ne pas s'engager

**nonconformist** I.*n* non-conformiste *mf* II.*adj* non-conformiste

**noncooperation** *n* non coopération *f*

**nondescript** *adj* (*color*) indéfinissable; (*person*) quelconque

**none** [nʌn] I.*pron* ❶(*nobody*) person-

ne; **~ other than sb** nul autre que qn ❷(*not any*) aucun(e); **~ of the wine** pas une goutte de vin; **~ of the cake** pas un morceau du gâteau; **~ of that!** ça suffit! ❸*pl* (*not any*) **~** (**at all**) pas un seul; **~ of them** aucun d'entre eux; **~ of my letters arrived** aucune de mes lettres n'est arrivée ▶**it's ~ of your business** ce ne sont pas tes affaires II.*adv* ❶(*not at all*) **he looks ~ the better** il n'a pas du tout l'air d'aller mieux ❷(*not very*) **it's ~ too soon/sure** ce n'est pas trop tôt/si sûr ▶**to be ~ the wiser** ne pas être plus avancé; **to be ~ the worse** ne pas être le pire

**nonentity** [na·'nen·tə·ti] *n* (*person*) personne *f* insignifiante; (*thing*) chose *f* insignifiante

**non-essential** I.*adj* non essentiel(le) II.*n pl* **~s** accessoires *mpl*

**nonetheless** *adv* néanmoins

**nonevent** *n* ratage *m*

**nonexistence** *n* non-existence *f*

**nonexistent** *adj* inexistant(e)

**nonfiction** *n* ouvrages *mpl* généraux

**nonflammable** *adj* (*material*) ininflammable

**noninfectious** *adj* non contagieux (-euse)

**nonnegotiable** *adj* non négociable

**no-no** *n inf* **that's a** (**definite**) **~** ça ne se fait pas

**nonpolluting** *adj* non polluant(e)

**nonproductive** *adj* non productif(-ive)

**nonprofit** *adj* à but non lucratif

**nonproliferation** I.*n* POL non-prolifération *f* II.*adj* POL de non-prolifération

**nonrefundable** *adj* non remboursable

**nonresident** *n* non-résident(e) *m(f)*

**nonreturnable** *adj* non consigné(e)

**nonsense** I.*n* absurdité *f;* **it is ~ to say that ...** il est absurde de dire que ...; **what's all this ~?** qu'est-ce que c'est que ces bêtises? II.*interj* **~!** quelle bêtise!

**nonsensical** *adj* absurde

**nonsmoker** *n* non-fumeur, -euse *m, f*

**nonsmoking** *adj* non-fumeurs *inv*

**nonstarter** *n inf* **to be a ~** être voué à l'échec

**nonstick** *adj* anti-adhérent(e); **~ pan** poêle *f* antiadhésive

**nonstop** I.*adj* ❶(*without stopping*) sans arrêt; (*flight*) sans escale; (*train*) direct(e) ❷(*uninterrupted*) ininterrompu(e) II.*adv* non-stop

**nontaxable** *adj* non imposable

**nontoxic** *adj* non toxique

**nonverbal** *adj* non verbal(e)

**nonviolent** *adj* non-violent(e)

**noob** [nu:b] *n* COMPUT, INET débutant(e) *m(f)*

**noodle**¹ ['nu·dl] *n pl* nouilles *fpl*; **~ soup** soupe *f* au vermicelle

**noodle**² ['nu·dl] *n inf* ❶(*idiot*) nouille *f* ❷(*head*) caboche *f*

**noodle**³ ['nu·dl] *vi inf* MUS jouer quelques notes

**noon** [nun] *n* midi *m*; **at/around ~/** vers midi

**no one** ['noʊ·wʌn] *pron s.* **nobody**

**noose** [nus] *n* nœud *m*

**nope** [noʊp] *adv inf* non

**nor** [nɔr] *conj* ❶(*and also not*) **~ do I/ we** moi/nous non plus; **it's not funny, ~** (**is it**) c'est ni drôle, ni intelligent; **I can not speak German, ~ can I write it** je ne parle pas l'allemand et je ne l'écris pas non plus ❷(*not either*) ni; *s.a.* **neither**

**norm** [nɔrm] *n* norme *f*

**normal** ['nɔr·məl] I.*adj* ❶(*conforming to standards*) normal(e); **in the ~ way** normalement ❷(*usual: doctor*) habituel(le); **as** (**is**) **~** comme d'habitude; **in ~ circumstances** en temps normal II.*n* normale *f*; **to return to ~** revenir à la normale

**normalize** ['nɔr·məl·aɪz] I.*vt* régulariser II.*vi* se régulariser

**normally** ['nɔr·məl·i] *adv* normalement

**north** [nɔrθ] I.*n* ❶(*cardinal point*) nord *m*; **to the ~ of sth** au nord de qc; **to go/drive to the ~** aller/rouler vers le nord; **further ~** plus au nord ❷GEO nord *m*; **in the ~ of France** dans le nord de la France II.*adj* nord *inv;*

**~ wind** vent *m* du nord; **~ coast** côte *f* nord; **a ~ wall** un mur exposé au nord III.*adv* au nord; (*travel*) vers le nord

**North America** *n* l'Amérique *f* du Nord

**North American** I.*n* Nord-américain(e) *m(f)* II.*adj* nord-américain(e)

**North Carolina** *n* la Caroline du Nord

**North Dakota** *n* le Dakota du Nord

**northeast** I.*n* nord-est *m*; *s.a.* **north** II.*adj* nord-est *inv; s.a.* **north** III.*adv* au nord-est; (*travel*) vers le nord-est; *s.a.* **north**

**northeasterly** *adj* nord-est; *s.a.* **northerly**

**northeastern** *adj* du nord-est

**northerly** *adj* ❶(*of or in the northern part*) au nord; **~ part/coast** partie *f/* côte *f* nord ❷(*toward the north: direction*) vers le nord ❸(*from the north: wind*) du nord

**northern** ['nɔr·ðərn] *adj* du nord, septentrional; **~ hemisphere** hémisphère *m* nord; **the ~ part of the country** le nord du pays

**northerner** *n* ❶(*native, inhabitant*) habitant(e) *m(f)* du nord; (*of American North*) habitant(e) *m(f)* du nord des États-Unis ❷HIST nordiste *mf*

**Northern Ireland** *n* Irlande *f* du Nord

**northern lights** *n* l'aurore *f* boréale

**northernmost** *adj* le plus au nord

**North Korea** *n* la Corée du Nord

**North Pole** *n* **the ~** le pôle Nord

**North Sea** *n* **the ~** la mer du Nord

**northward** I.*adj* au nord II.*adv* vers le nord

**northwest** I.*n* nord-ouest *m inv; s.a.* **north** II.*adj* nord-ouest, *s.a.* **north** III.*adv* au nord-ouest; (*travel*) vers le nord-ouest; *s.a.* **north**

**northwesterly** *adj* nord-ouest *inv; s.a.* **northerly**

**northwestern** *adj* du nord-ouest *inv*

**Norway** ['nɔr·weɪ] *n* la Norvège

**Norwegian** [nɔr·'wi·dʒən] I.*adj* norvégien(ne) II.*n* ❶(*person*) Norvégien(ne) *m(f)* ❷LING norvégien *m; s.a.* **English**

**nose** [noʊz] I.*n* nez *m*; **to have a**

**N**

**runny ~** avoir le nez qui coule; **to blow one's ~** se moucher le nez ▶ **to keep one's ~ to the <u>grindstone</u>** *inf* travailler sans relâche; **to keep one's ~ <u>clean</u>** *inf* se tenir à carreau; **to <u>have</u> a (good) ~ for sth** avoir du nez pour qc; **to <u>have</u> one's ~ in sth** avoir le nez dans qc; **to <u>keep</u> one's ~ out of sth** *inf* ne pas se mêler de qc; **<u>under</u> sb's ~** sous le nez de qn **II.** *vi* ❶ (*move*) **to ~ forward** s'avancer ❷ *inf* (*search*) **to ~ into sth** fouiller dans qc **III.** *vt* **to ~ one's way forward/in/out/up** s'avancer/entrer/sortir/monter lentement; **to ~ its way through sth** progresser dans qc
◆**nose around** *vi inf* fouiner
◆**nose out I.** *vt* découvrir **II.** *vi* avancer prudemment

**nosebleed** *n* saignement *m* de nez; **to have a ~** saigner du nez

**nosedive I.** *n* ❶ AVIAT piqué *m;* **to go into a ~** descendre en piqué ❷ FIN chute *f* libre **II.** *vi* ❶ AVIAT descendre en piqué ❷ FIN faire une chute libre

**nose ring** *n* anneau *m* de nez

**nosey** <-ier, -iest> *adj s.* nosy

**nosh** [nɑʃ] **I.** *n inf* (*food*) bouffe *f* **II.** *vi inf* (*eat*) bouffer

**nostalgia** [nɔ·ˈstæl·dʒə] *n* nostalgie *f*

**nostalgic** [nɔ·ˈstæl·dʒɪk] *adj* nostalgique

**nostril** [ˈnɑ·strəl] *n* narine *f;* (*of a horse*) naseau *m*

**nosy** [ˈnoʊ·zi] <-ier, -iest> *adj pej* curieux(-euse)

**not** [nɑt] *adv* ❶ (*expressing the opposite*) ne … pas; **he's ~ here** il n'est pas ici; **it's red, ~ blue** c'est rouge, pas bleu; **of course ~** bien sûr que non; **~ so fast** pas si vite; **I hope ~** j'espère que non; **whether it rains or ~** qu'il pleuve ou pas; **~ that I know** que je sache; **~ at all** (pas) du tout; **thanks – ~ at all** merci – de rien; **~ including sth** sans compter qc; **~ to mention that …** sans parler de … ❷ (*in tags*) **isn't it?/ won't they?/don't you?** n'est-ce pas? ❸ (*less than*) **~ a minute later** à peine une minute plus tard; **to be ~ a mile away** être à un mille à peine ❹ (*express-*

*ing an opposite*) pas; **~ much** pas beaucoup; **~ that …** ce n'est pas que …; **~ I** pas moi

**notably** *adv* ❶ (*particularly*) notamment; **most ~** plus particulièrement ❷ (*in a noticeable way*) remarquablement

**notary** [ˈnoʊ·tər·i], **notary public** <-ies> *n* notaire *m*

**note** [noʊt] **I.** *n* ❶ (*short informal letter*) mot *m* ❷ (*reminder*) note *f;* **to make/take ~ of sth** noter qc ❸ LIT commentaire *m* ❹ MUS note *f* ❺ (*piece of paper money*) billet *m* ❻ (*quality*) **a ~ of despair** une note de désespoir ❼ *form* (*important*) **of ~** d'importance ▶ **to <u>strike</u> the right ~** être tout à fait dans la note **II.** *vt form* ❶ (*write down*) noter ❷ (*mention, observe*) remarquer

**notebook** *n* ❶ (*book*) carnet *m* ❷ (*laptop*) notebook *m*

**noted** *adj* célèbre; **to be ~ for sth** être célèbre pour qc; **to be ~ as an expert** être connu en tant qu'expert

**notepad** *n* bloc-notes *m*

**notepaper** *n* papier *m* à lettres

**noteworthy** <-ier, -iest> *adj form* notable; **nothing/sth ~** rien/quelque chose de remarquable

**nothing** [ˈnʌθ·ɪŋ] **I.** *indef pron, sing* ❶ (*not anything*) rien; **~ happened** rien ne s'est passé; **~ new** rien de neuf; **next to ~** presque rien; **~ came of it** cela n'a rien donné; **~ doing!** rien à faire!; **good for ~** bon à rien; **to make ~ of it** ne rien y comprendre; **~ much** pas grand-chose; **that's ~!** ce n'est rien du tout!; **time means ~ to me** le temps ne compte pas pour moi ❸ (*only*) **~ but sth** seulement qc; **he is ~ if not strict** il est strict avant tout ▶ **~ <u>ventured</u>, ~ gained** *prov* qui ne risque rien n'a rien *prov; it* has ~ **to <u>do</u> with me** ça ne me regarde pas **II.** *adv* it's ~ **less than sth** ce n'est ni plus ni moins que qc; **it's ~ short of great/madness** c'est ni plus ni moins génial/de la folie; **it's ~ more than a joke** ça n'est rien de plus qu'une plaisanterie; **he's ~ like me** il ne me ressemble pas du tout **III.** *n* ① (*nonexistence*) rien *m* ② MATH, SPORTS zéro *m*; **three to ~** trois à zéro [*o* rien] ③ (*person*) nullité *f*; *s.a.* **anything, something**

**notice** ['nou·t̬ɪs] **I.** *n* ① (*announcement: in paper*) annonce *f*; (*for birth, marriage*) avis *m*; (*on board*) affiche *f* ② (*attention*) attention *f*; **to escape sb's ~** échapper à l'attention de qn; **to take ~ of sb/sth** faire attention à qn/qc ③ (*warning*) avis *m*; **to give sb (due) ~ of sth** avertir [*o* prévenir] qn de qc; **on short ~** avec un court préavis; **at a moment's ~** immédiatement; **until further ~** jusqu'à nouvel ordre ④ (*when ending contract*) a. LAW avis *m*; **to give (one's) ~** donner sa démission; **to be given (one's) ~** être licencié; **to give an employee two weeks' ~** donner un préavis de deux semaines à un employé **II.** *vt* remarquer; **to ~ sb/ sth do sth** remarquer que qn/qc fait qc

**noticeable** *adj* perceptible

**notification** [ˌnou·t̬ə·fɪ·ˈkeɪ·ʃən] *n* notification *f*; **to get ~ of sth** être informé de qc

**notify** ['nou·t̬ə·faɪ] <-ie-> *vt* notifier; **to ~ sb of [*o* about] sth** aviser qn de qc

**notion** ['nou·ʃən] *n* idée *f*; **to have no ~ of sth** n'avoir aucune idée de qc

**notorious** [nou·ˈtɔr·ɪ·əs] *adj* notoire; **to be ~ for sth** être tristement célèbre pour qc

**notwithstanding** [ˌnat·wɪθ·ˈstæn·dɪŋ] *form* **I.** *prep* en dépit de **II.** *adv* néanmoins

**nougat** ['nu·gət] *n* nougat *m*

**nought** [nɔt] *pron s.* **naught**

**noun** [naʊn] *n* nom *m*

**nourish** ['nɜr·ɪʃ] *vt* (*feed*) nourrir

**nourishing** ['nɜr·ɪʃ·ɪŋ] *adj* nourrissant(e)

**novel¹** ['na·vəl] *n* roman *m*

**novel²** ['na·vəl] *adj* nouveau(-elle); (*idea, concept*) original(e)

**novelist** ['na·vəl·ɪst] *n* romancier, -ère *m, f*

**novelty** ['na·vəl·t̬i] <-ies> *n* ① (*newness, originality*) nouveauté *f* ② (*trinket*) fantaisie *f*; **~ bracelet** bracelet *m* fantaisie

**November** [nou·ˈvem·bər] *n* novembre *m*; *s.a.* **April**

**novice** ['na·vɪs] **I.** *n* ① (*inexperienced person*) apprenti(e) *m(f)* ② REL novice *mf* **II.** *adj* ① (*inexperienced*) débutant(e); (*pilot*) inexpérimenté(e) ② REL novice

**now** [naʊ] **I.** *adv* ① (*at the present time, shortly*) maintenant; **she's coming ~** elle vient tout de suite, elle arrive; **I'll call her (right) ~** je vais l'appeler immédiatement; **I'm shaving right ~** je suis en train de me raser; **he'll call any time ~** il doit appeler incessamment sous peu; **she called just ~** elle vient d'appeler juste à l'instant; **before ~** auparavant; **as of ~** dès à présent ② (*in narrative*) **she was an adult ~** elle était alors adulte; **by ~ she was very angry** à ce moment-là, elle était très en colère ③ (*involving the listener*) **~, you need good equipment** écoute, il te faut un bon équipement; **~ don't interrupt me!** ne m'interromps (donc) pas!; **~ that changes everything!** ah, voilà qui change tout!; **be careful ~!** fais attention!; **~, ~** voyons, voyons; (*warning*) allons, allons; **~ then, who's next?** bon, à qui le tour? ▶ (**every**) **~ and then** de temps en temps; (**it's**) **~ or never** (c'est) maintenant ou jamais; **~ you're/we're talking!** à la bonne heure! **II.** *conj* **~ (that)** … maintenant que … **III.** *adj inf* actuel(le)

**nowadays** ['naʊ·ə·deɪz] *adv* de nos jours

**nowhere** ['nou·(h)wer] **I.** *adv* a. *fig* nulle part; **to appear out of ~** sortir de nulle part; **he is ~ to be found** on ne le trouve nulle part; **to be getting ~** ne pas y arriver; **to get sb ~** ne mener qn nulle part; **to be ~ near a place** être

N

loin d'un endroit **II.** *adj inf* qui ne mène à rien

**noxious** ['nak·ʃəs] *adj form* nocif(-ive)

**nozzle** ['na·zl] *n* embout *m; (of hose)* jet *m; (of a gas pump)* pistolet *m; (of a vacuum cleaner)* suceur *m*

**nuance** ['nu·an(t)s] *n* nuance *f*

**nubile** ['nu·bɪl] *adj* nubile

**nuclear** ['nu·kli·ər] *adj* nucléaire ▸ **to go ~** *inf* exploser

**nuclear-free zone** *n* zone *f* anti-nucléaire

**nuclear nonproliferation treaty** *n* traité *m* de non-prolifération des armes nucléaires

**nucleus** ['nu·kli·əs] <-ei *o* -es> *n* noyau *m*

**nude** [nud] **I.** *adj* nu(e) **II.** *n* ⓵ ART nu *m* ⓶ *(naked)* **in the ~** tout nu

**nudge** [nʌdʒ] **I.** *vt* ⓵ *(push with the elbow)* pousser du coude ⓶ *(push gently)* pousser ⓷ *(persuade sb into sth)* **to ~ sb into sth** pousser qn dans qc; **to ~ sb into doing sth** pousser qn à faire qc ⓸ *(approach)* approcher; **to be nudging fifty** approcher les cinquante ans **II.** *n* coup *m* de coude; **to give sb a ~** donner un coup de coude à qn; *(encourage)* pousser qn

**nudist** ['nu·dɪst] *n* nudiste *mf*

**nudity** ['nu·də·t̬i] *n* nudité *f*

**nugget** ['nʌg·ɪt] *n* ⓵ *(formed lump)* pépite *f* ⓶ CULIN nugget *m (boulette de viande panée)* ⓷ *iron (interesting information)* bribe *f*

**nuisance** ['nu·sᵊn(t)s] *n* ⓵ *(annoyance)* ennui *m;* **she's a ~** elle est pénible; **what a ~!** que c'est embêtant!; **to make a ~ of oneself** embêter le monde ⓶ LAW dommage *m;* **public ~** atteinte *f* (portée) à l'ordre public

**nuke** [nuk] *sl* **I.** *vt* ⓵ MIL atomiser ⓶ *(cook in microwave)* passer au four à micro-ondes **II.** *n* bombe *f* nucléaire

**nullify** ['nʌl·ɪ·faɪ] <-ie-> *vt* annuler

**numb** [nʌm] **I.** *adj* ⓵ *(deprived of sensation)* engourdi(e); *(nerve)* insensible; **go ~** s'engourdir ⓶ *fig* hébété(e); **I felt ~ after hearing the news** je suis tombé sous le choc quand j'ai entendu la nouvelle **II.** *vt* ⓵ *(deprive of sensations: limbs)* engourdir ⓶ *(desensitize)* désensibiliser ⓷ *(lessen: pain)* endormir

**number** ['nʌm·bər] **I.** *n* ⓵ *(arithmetical unit)* nombre *m* ⓶ *(written symbol)* chiffre *m* ⓷ *(on numbered item: telephone, page, bus)* numéro *m* ⓸ *(individual item: sketch, magazine)* numéro *m;* **he was driving a classy little ~** il conduisait une voiture superbe; **she wore a little red ~** elle portait une petite robe rouge ⓹ *(amount)* nombre *m;* **any ~ of friends/books** de nombreux amis/livres; **in large/huge/enormous ~s** en très grand nombre; **by (sheer) force of ~s** par le nombre; **to be few in ~** être peu nombreux ▸ **to look out for ~ one** prendre soin de soi; **to be (the) ~ one** être le meilleur; **there's safety in ~s** *prov* plus on est nombreux, moins on court de risques; **to have sb's ~** connaître qn **II.** *vt* ⓵ *(assign a number to)* numéroter ⓶ *(be sth in number)* compter; **to be ~ed amongst sth** compter parmi qc

**numbering** *n* comptage *m*

**numbness** *n* ⓵ *(being numb)* engourdissement *m* ⓶ *(lack of emotional feeling)* insensibilité *f*

**numbskull** ['nʌm·skʌl] *n pej s.* **numskull**

**numeracy** ['nu·mᵊr·ə·si] *n* MATH calcul *m*

**numeral** ['nu·mᵊr·ᵊl] *n* chiffre *m*

**numerical** [nu·'mer·ɪ·kl] *adj* numérique

**numeric keypad** *n* COMPUT touches *fpl* numériques

**numerous** ['nu·mᵊr·əs] *adj* nombreux(-euse)

**numskull** ['nʌm·skʌl] *n pej* nigaud(e) *m(f)*

**nun** [nʌn] *n* religieuse *f*

**nurse** [nɜrs] **I.** *n* infirmier, -ère *m, f* **II.** *vt* ⓵ *(care for)* soigner; **to ~ sb back to health** faire recouvrer la santé à qn ⓶ *(treat: an injury, a bad cold)* guérir ⓷ *(harbor: feeling)* nourrir ⓸ *(nurture: fire)* entretenir ⓹ *(breast-feed)* allaiter

⑥(*drink*) siroter ⑦(*hold carefully*) bercer III. *vi* téter

**nursery** ['nɜr·sᵊr·i] <-ies> *n* ❶(*day nursery*) crèche *f* ❷(*bedroom for infants*) chambre *f* d'enfants ❸BOT pépinière *f*

**nursery rhyme** *n* comptine *f*

**nursery school** *n* maternelle *f*, école *f* gardienne *Belgique*

**nursing** I. *n* ❶(*profession*) profession *f* d'infirmière ❷(*practice*) soins *mpl* ❸(*breast-feeding*) allaitement *m* II. *adj* ❶(*concerning nursing: profession*) d'infirmier(-ère); (*department*) des soins; (*staff*) soignant(e) ❷(*breast-feeding*) qui allaite

**nurture** ['nɜr·tʃər] I. *vt* form ❶(*feed*) nourrir ❷(*encourage, harbor*) nourrir ❸(*educate*) éduquer II. *n* (*upbringing*) éducation *f*

**nut** [nʌt] *n* ❶(*hard edible fruit*) noix *f*; (*of hazel*) noisette *f* ❷TECH écrou *m* ❸*inf* (*crazy person*) cinglé(e) *m(f)* ❹(*enthusiast*) dingue *mf* ❺*inf* (*person's head*) caboche *f* ▸ **the ~s and bolts** of sth les détails *mpl* pratiques de qc; **to be a hard** [*o* **tough**] **~ to crack** (*person*) être peu commode; (*problem*) être un problème difficile à résoudre

**nutcracker** *n* casse-noix *m inv*

**nutmeg** *n* CULIN ❶(*hard fruit*) noix *f*

muscade ❷(*warm, aromatic spice*) muscade *f*

**nutrient** ['nu·tri·ənt] I. *n* aliment *m* II. *adj* nutritif(-ive)

**nutrition** [nu·'trɪ·ʃᵊn] *n* nutrition *f*

**nutritional** *adj* nutritionnel(le); (*value*) nutritif(-ive)

**nutritionist** *n* nutritionniste *mf*

**nutritious** [nu·'trɪ·ʃəs] *adj* nutritif(-ive)

**nuts** [nʌts] I. *npl vulg* (*testicles*) couilles *fpl* II. *adj sl* cinglé(e); **to go ~** piquer une crise; **to be ~ about sb/sth** être dingue de qn/qc

**nutshell** ['nʌt·ʃel] *n* coque *f* de noix ▸ **in a ~** en bref

**nutty** ['nʌt·i] <-ier, -iest> *adj* ❶(*full of nuts*) aux noix; (*chocolate*) aux noisettes ❷(*like nuts: taste*) de noix; (*like hazelnut*) de noisette ❸*inf* (*crazy, eccentric*) dingue; (*as*) **~ as a fruitcake** complètement barjot

**NV** [ˌen·'vi] *n abbr of* **Nevada**

**NY** [ˌen·'waɪ] *n abbr of* **New York**

**nylon** ['naɪ·lan] I. *n* nylon *m* II. *adj* en nylon; (*thread*) de nylon

**nymph** [nɪm(p)f] *n* nymphe *f*

**nympho** ['nɪm(p)·foʊ] *n inf* nympho *f*

**nymphomaniac** [ˌnɪm(p)·foʊ·'meɪ·ni·æk] I. *n* nymphomane *f* II. *adj* nymphomane

N

# Oo

**O, o** [oʊ] <-'s> n ❶ (*letter*) O m, o m;
**~ as in Oscar** (*on telephone*) o comme
Oscar ❷ (*zero*) zéro m

**oak** [oʊk] n ❶ (*tree*) chêne m ❷ (*wood*)
chêne m ► **great** [*o mighty*] **~s from
little acorns grow** *prov* les petits ruisseaux font les grandes rivières *prov*

**oar** [ɔr] n rame f

**oasis** [oʊˈeɪˌsɪs] <-ses> n oasis f

**oath** [oʊθ] n ❶ LAW serment m; **under ~** sous serment; **to take an ~**
prêter serment ❷ (*swearword*) juron m

**obedience** [oʊˈbiːdiˌən(t)s] n obéis-
sance f

**obedient** [oʊˈbiːdiˌənt] adj obéis-
sant(e)

**obesity** [oʊˈbiːsəˌti] n obésité f

**obey** [oʊˈbeɪ] I. vt obéir à; (*law*) se
conformer à II. vi obéir

**object** [ˈabˌdʒɪkt, vb: əbˈdʒɛkt] I. n
❶ (*thing*) a. fig objet m ❷ (*purpose,
goal*) but m; **money is no ~** peu importe le prix; **with this ~ in mind** à cette
fin ❸ form (*subject*) objet m; **the ~ of
his desire** l'objet de son désir ❹ (*of
verb*) complément m d'objet II. vi faire
objection III. vt objecter; **to ~ that ...**
faire valoir que ...

**objection** [əbˈdʒɛkˌʃən] n objection f;
**to raise an ~ to sth** soulever une objection à qc

**objective** [əbˈdʒɛkˌtɪv] I. n objectif m
II. adj objectif(-ive)

**objectively** adv objectivement

**obligation** [ˌaˌbləˈɡeɪˌʃən] n obligation f

**oblige** [əˈblaɪdʒ] I. vt ❶ (*compel*) obliger; **to ~ sb to** +*infin* obliger qn à +*infin* ❷ (*perform a service for*) rendre service à; **~ him by shutting the door**
faites-lui le plaisir de fermer la porte; **to
be ~d to sb** être reconnaissant à qn; **I'd
be ~d if you'd leave now** je vous sau-
rai gré de partir immédiatement; **much**

**~d** merci beaucoup II. vi **to be happy
to ~** être empressé à rendre service

**oblong** [ˈabˌlɔŋ] I. n rectangle m II. adj
MATH oblong(ue)

**obnoxious** [əbˈnakˌʃəs] adj pej
odieux(-euse)

**OBO, obo** adv COM abbr of **or best offer**
à débattre

**obscene** [əbˈsin] adj ❶ (*indecent*) obscène ❷ (*shocking*) scandaleux(-euse)

**obscenity** [əbˈsenˌəˌti] <-ties> n
❶ (*obscene behavior*) obscénité f
❷ (*swear word*) obscénité f ❸ (*offensive situation*) infamie f

**obscure** [əbˈskjʊr] I.<-r, -st> adj
❶ (*not well known*) obscur(e); (*author*)
inconnu(e); (*village*) ignoré(e) ❷ (*difficult to understand*) incompréhensible;
(*text*) obscur(e) II. vt ❶ (*make indistinct*) obscurcir ❷ fig **to ~ sth from sb**
cacher qc à qn

**observant** [əbˈzɜrˌvᵊnt] adj (*alert*) ob-
servateur(-trice)

**observation** [ˌabˌzərˈveɪˌʃᵊn] n a. LAW,
MED observation f; **to keep sb in the
hospital for ~** garder qn en observation
à l'hôpital; **under ~** en observation

**observation tower** n belvédère m

**observation ward** n station f d'observation

**observatory** [əbˈzɜrˌvəˌbɔrˌi] n observatoire m

**observe** [əbˈzɜrv] vt, vi a. form observer; **to ~ sb do(ing) sth** observer qn en
train de faire qc; **to ~ the speed limit**
respecter la limitation de vitesse

**observer** n (*watcher*) observateur, -tri-
ce m, f

**obsess** [əbˈses] vt obséder

**obsessed** adj obsédé(e)

**obsession** [əbˈsefˌᵊn] n a. MED obsession f

**obsessive** [əbˈsesˌɪv] I. adj (*secrecy*)
obsessionnel(le); (*type*) obsessif(-ive); **to**

**be ~ about sth** être obsédé par qc **II.** *n* obsessionnel(le) *m(f)*

**obsolete** ['ab·sə²·lit] *adj* désuet(e); (*word, technique*) obsolète; (*design, form*) démodé(e); (*method*) dépassé(e)

**obstacle** ['ab·stə·kl] *n* obstacle *m*

**obstinate** ['ab·stə·nət] *adj* (*person, refusal*) obstiné(e); (*blockage*) tenace; (*cold, pain, problem*) persistant(e)

**obstruct** [əb·'strʌkt] *vt* ❶ *a.* MED (*intestines, path*) obstruer; (*progress, traffic*) bloquer ❷ LAW, SPORTS faire obstruction à

**obstruction** [əb·'strʌk·ʃ°n] *n a.* LAW, SPORTS obstruction *f*

**obtain** [əb·'teɪn] **I.** *vt form* obtenir; **to ~ sth from sb** obtenir qc de qn **II.** *vi form* être en vigueur; **the rules that ~ed** les lois *fpl* en vigueur

**obtainable** *adj* disponible

**obvious** ['ab·vi·əs] **I.** *adj* évident(e); (*stain*) voyant(e); **to make sth ~ to sb** rendre qc clair et distinct pour qn **II.** *n* évidence *f*; **to state the ~** enfoncer des portes ouvertes

**obviously I.** *adv* manifestement **II.** *interj* évidemment!

**occasion** [ə·'keɪ·ʒ°n] **I.** *n* occasion *f*; **on ~** à l'occasion; **on rare ~s** rarement **II.** *vt form* **to ~ sb sth** occasionner qc à qn

**occasional** *adj* occasionnel(le); **to pay an ~ visit** faire une visite de temps en temps

**occasionally** *adv* de temps en temps

**occupancy rate** *n* taux *m* d'occupation

**occupant** ['a·kjə·pənt] *n form* occupant(e) *m(f)*

**occupation** ['a·kjə·'peɪ·ʃ°n] *n a. form a.* MIL occupation *f*

**occupied** *adj* occupé(e)

**occupier** *n* occupant(e) *m(f)*

**occupy** ['a·kju·paɪ] *vt a. form* occuper; **to ~ oneself** s'occuper; **to ~ one's mind** s'occuper l'esprit; **to ~ one's time** occuper son temps; **~ing forces** les forces *fpl* occupantes

**occur** [ə·'kɜːr] <-rr-> *vi* ❶ (*take place*: *event, accident*) avoir lieu; (*change, explosion, mistake*) se produire; (*symp-*

*tom*) apparaître; (*problem, opportunity*) se présenter ❷ (*be found*) se trouver ❸ (*come to mind*) **it ~s to me that ...** il me semble que ...; **it ~ed to me to +*infin*** il m'est venu à l'idée de +*infin*

**occurrence** [ə·'kɜːr·ən(t)s] *n* ❶ (*event*) fait *m* ❷ (*incidence*) incidence *f*

**ocean** ['oʊ·ʃ°n] *n* océan *m*; **~s of sth** des montagnes *fpl* de qc

**o'clock** [ə·'klak] *adv* **it's 2 ~** il est deux heures

**octagon** ['ak·tə·gan] *n* octogone *m*

**October** [ak·'toʊ·bər] *n* octobre *m*; *s.a.* **April**

**octopus** ['ak·tə·pəs] <-es *o* -pi> *n* octopode *m*

**OD** [‚oʊ·'di] *abbr of* **overdose I.** *n* OD *f* **II.** *vi* <-ing, -ed> **to ~ on sth** *a. fig* faire une overdose de qc; (*food*) forcer sur qc

**odd** [ad] *adj* <-er, -est> ❶ (*strange*) bizarre ❷ (*not even: number*) impair(e) ❸ (*and more*) et quelques; **50 ~ people** une cinquantaine de personnes ❹ (*occasional*) occasionnel(le); **to have the ~ drink or two** prendre un verre de temps en temps; **at ~ times** de temps en temps; **~ jobs** petits travaux *mpl* ❺ (*unmatched: glove, sock*) dépareillé(e) ▸ **to feel like the ~ <u>man</u> out** ne pas se sentir à sa place

**oddly** *adv* bizarrement; **~ enough** bizarrement

**odds** *npl* (*probability*) chances *fpl*; (*for betting*) cote *f*; **to give long ~ on/ against sth** donner toutes les chances/ ne donner presque aucune chance à qc; **to lengthen/shorten the ~** accroître/ amincir les chances; **against all (the) ~** contre toute espérance ▸ **to be at ~ with sb/sth** être en désaccord avec qn/qc; **~ and ends** bric-à-brac *m*

**odds-on** [‚adz·'an] *adj* **the ~ favorite** le grand favori

**odometer** [oʊ·'da·mə·tər] *n* odomètre *m*

**odorless** *adj form* inodore

**of** [əv, *stressed:* av] *prep* ❶ (*belonging to*) de; **the end ~ the film/play** la fin du film/de la pièce; **the works ~**

O

Twain les œuvres de Twain; **a friend ~ mine/theirs** un de mes/leurs amis; **a drawing ~ Paul's** (*he owns it*) un dessin (appertenant) à Paul; (*he drew it*) un dessin fait par Paul; **a drawing ~ Paul** (*he is on it*) un portrait de Paul ❷ (*describing*) **a man ~ courage/no importance** un homme courageux/sans importance; **a city ~ wide avenues** une ville aux larges avenues; **80 years ~ age** âgé de 80 ans; **it's kind ~ him** c'est gentil à lui [*o* est *sa part*]; **this idiot ~ a plumber** cet imbécile de plombier ❸ (*dates and time*) **the 4th ~ May/in May ~ 2007** le 4 mai/en mai 2007; **ten/a quarter ~ two** deux heures moins dix/le quart ❹ (*nature, content*) **a ring ~ gold** une bague en or; **to smell/taste ~ cheese** sentir le/avoir un goût de fromage; **~ itself, it's not important** en soi, ce n'est pas important; **it happened ~ itself** c'est arrivé tout seul ❺ (*among*) **one ~ the best** un des meilleurs; **I know two ~ them** je connais deux d'entre eux; **there are five ~ them** ils sont (à) cinq; **two ~ the five** deux sur les cinq; **you ~ all people** toi entre tous; **today ~ all days** aujourd'hui justement

**off** [af] **I.** *prep* ❶ (*apart from*) **the top is ~ the jar** le couvercle n'est pas sur le bocal; **just ~ Cape Cod** juste au large de Cape Cod; **the mill is ~ the road** le moulin est à l'écart de la route ❷ (*away from*) **her street is ~ the main road** sa rue part de la route principale; **to take sth ~ the shelf/wall** prendre qc sur l'étagère/enlever qc du mur; **keep ~ the grass** pelouse interdite; **to go ~ the air** RADIO quitter l'antenne ❸ (*down from*) **to fall/jump ~ a ladder** tomber/sauter d'une échelle; **to get ~ the train** descendre du train ❹ (*from*) **to eat ~ a plate** manger dans une assiette; **to wipe the water ~ the bench** essuyer l'eau qui est sur le banc; **to take $10 ~ the price** faire une réduction de 10 dollars ❺ (*stop liking*) **to be ~ drugs** être désintoxiqué **II.** *adv* ❶ (*not on*) **to switch/turn sth ~** éteindre/arrêter qc; **it's ~ between them** *fig* c'est fini entre eux ❷ (*away*) **the town is 5 miles ~ to the east** la ville est à 5 miles vers l'est; **not far/a way's ~** pas très loin/à quelque distance; **to drive/run ~** partir/partir en courant; **it's time I was ~** il est temps que je m'en aille *subj* ❸ (*removed*) **the lid's ~** le couvercle n'est pas dessus; **with one's coat ~** sans manteau ❹ (*free from work*) **to get ~ at 4:00 p.m.** sortir du travail à 16 h; **to get a day ~** avoir un jour de congé; **to take time/an afternoon ~** prendre des congés/prendre son après-midi ❺ (*completely*) **to kill ~** anéantir; **to pay sth ~** finir de payer qc ❻ COM **5% ~** 5% de rabais ❼ (*until gone*) **to walk ~ one's dinner** faire une promenade digestive; **to work ~ the calories** brûler les calories ▶**~ and on, on and ~** de temps en temps; **it rained ~ and on** il pleuvait par intermittence **III.** *adj inv* ❶ (*not on: light*) éteint(e); (*faucet*) fermé(e); (*water, electricity*) coupé(e); (*concert*) annulé(e); (*engagement*) rompu(e) ❷ (*bad: day*) mauvais(e) ❸ (*free from work*) **to be ~ at 5 p.m.** terminer à 17h; **I'm ~ on Mondays** je ne suis pas là le lundi ❹ (*provided for*) **to be well/not well ~** être aisé/dans la gêne ❺ (*rude*) **to go ~ on sb** *inf* engueuler qn **IV.** *vt inf* (*kill*) buter

**off-chance** *n* **on the ~** à tout hasard

**off-color** *adj* obscène

**offend** [ə·'fend] **I.** *vi* LAW commettre un délit **II.** *vt* (*upset sb's feelings*) offenser

**offender** *n* LAW délinquant(e) *m(f)*

**offense** [ə·'fen(t)s] *n* ❶ LAW (*crime*) délit *m* ❷ (*upset feelings*) offense *f*; **to cause ~ to sb** offenser qn; **to take ~ at sth** s'offenser de qc; **no ~ (intended)** je ne voulais pas t'offenser ❸ (*attack*) attaque *f* ❹ SPORTS offensive *f*; **to be on ~** jouer en attaque

**offensive** [ə·'fen(t)·sɪv] **I.** *adj* ❶ (*causing offense: remark, smell*) offensant(e); (*language*) insultant(e); (*joke*) injurieux(-euse) ❷ (*attack*) offensif(-ive)

**II.** *n* MIL offensive *f*; **to launch an ~** lancer une offensive

**offer** ['ɑ·fər] **I.** *vt* ❶ (*give*) offrir; **to ~ sb sth** offrir qc à qn; **to ~ congratulations** adresser des félicitations ❷ (*give choice of having*) **to ~ sb sth** proposer qc à qn; **to ~ a choice** donner un choix ❸ (*volunteer*) **to ~ to** +*infin* proposer de +*infin*; **to ~ a suggestion** faire une suggestion ❹ (*provide: information, excuse, reward*) donner; **to have much to ~** avoir beaucoup à donner; **to ~ resistance** offrir de la résistance; **to ~ a glimpse** donner un coup d'œil ❺ (*bid*) faire une offre de ❻ (*sell*) proposer; **to be ~ed for sale** être mis en vente **II.** *vi* (*opportunity*) se présenter **III.** *n a.* ECON offre *f*; **to make sb an ~ they can't refuse** faire à qn une offre qui ne se refuse pas

**offhand** [ˌɑfˈhænd] **I.** *adj* désinvolte **II.** *adv* de but en blanc

**office** ['ɑ·fɪs] *n* ❶ (*room for working*) bureau *m*; **a doctor's ~** un cabinet médical ❷ (*authoritative position*) fonction *f*; **to hold ~** être au pouvoir; (*governor, mayor*) être en fonction; **to be out of ~** ne plus être au pouvoir; **to come into ~** arriver au pouvoir

**office building** *n* complexe *m* de bureaux

**office equipment** *n* équipement *m* de bureau

**office hours** *npl* heures *fpl* de bureau

**officer** *n* ❶ (*person in army, police*) officier *m* ❷ (*civil servant*) fonctionnaire *mf* ❸ (*manager*) responsable *mf*

**office staff** *n* personnel *m* de bureau

**office supplies** *npl* fournitures *fpl* de bureau

**office worker** *n* employé(e) *m(f)* de bureau

**official** [ə·ˈfɪʃ·əl] **I.** *n* ❶ (*responsible person*) officiel(le) *m(f)* ❷ (*referee*) arbitre *mf* **II.** *adj* officiel(le)

**officially** *adv* officiellement

**off-key I.** *adv* MUS faux; **to sing ~** chanter faux **II.** *adj* ❶ (*out of tune*) qui sonne faux ❷ *fig* (*inopportune*) qui tombe mal

**off-limits** *adj* interdit(e) d'accès

**offline** *adj* COMPUT hors-ligne; **to be ~** être déconnecté; **to go ~** se déconnecter

**off-peak** *adj* en basse saison; (*call*) aux heures creuses; **~ hours** heures *fpl* creuses

**off peak** *adv* ❶ (*outside peak hours*) aux heures creuses ❷ (*off season*) en basse saison; **to go on vacation when it's ~** partir en vacances [en] hors saison

**off-putting** *adj* ❶ (*disconcerting*) peu engageant(e) ❷ (*extremely unpleasant*) désagréable

**off-season** *n* hors saison *f*

**offshore I.** *adj* ❶ (*at sea*) au large; (*nearer to coast: fishing, waters*) côtier(-ère) ❷ (*blowing toward the sea: wind*) de terre ❸ (*related to oil extracting: drilling, company*) offshore *inv* ❹ COM, POL (*abroad*) extraterritorial(e) **II.** *adv* au large

**offside(s)** SPORTS **I.** *adj* hors-jeu *inv*; **~ position** position *f* de hors-jeu; **~ rule** règle *f* du hors-jeu **II.** *adv* hors-jeu **III.** *n* hors-jeu *m inv*

**offspring** <offspring> *n* (*young animal, child*) progéniture *f*

**off-white** *n* blanc *m* cassé

**often** ['ɑ·fən] *adv* souvent; **it's not ~ that ...** ce n'est pas souvent que ...; **how ~** combien de fois; **as ~ as not** la plupart du temps

**oh** [oʊ] **I.** *interj* oh!; **~ dear!** mon dieu!; **~ really?** ah oui? **II.** *n* oh *m*

**OH** [ˌoʊ·ˈeɪtʃ] *n abbr of* **Ohio**

**Ohio** [oʊ·ˈhaɪ·oʊ] *n* l'Ohio *m*

**oil** [ɔɪl] **I.** *n* ❶ (*lubricant, for cooking*) huile *f*; **to change the ~** faire la vidange; (*corn*) ~ huile de maïs; **to cook with ~** cuisiner à l'huile ❷ (*petroleum*) pétrole *m* ❸ *pl* (*oil-based colors*) **~s** huiles *fpl* ▸ **to mix like ~ and water** être complètement différent, s'entendre mal **II.** *vt* huiler

**oil change** *n* AUTO vidange *f*

**oil company** *n* compagnie *f* pétrolière

O

**oil field** n champ m pétrolifère

**oil-fired** adj ~ **heating system** chauffage m central au mazout

**oil level** n TECH niveau m d'huile

**oil painting** n peinture f à l'huile

**oil pipeline** n oléoduc m

**oil-producing** adj producteur(-trice) de pétrole

**oil production** n production f pétrolifère

**oilskin** n toile f cirée

**oil slick** n nappe f de pétrole

**oil tanker** n NAUT pétrolier m

**oil well** n puits m de pétrole

**oily** ['ɔɪ·li] <-ier, -iest> adj ❶ (oil-like) huileux(-euse) ❷ (soaked in oil, greasy) graisseux(-euse) ❸ (unpleasantly polite) visqueux(-euse) form

**ointment** ['ɔɪnt·mənt] n MED onguent m

**OK**[1], **okay** [ˌoʊ·'keɪ] inf I. adj ❶ (fine) O.K.; **to be** ~ aller bien; **that's** ~ c'est bon; **is it** ~ **for me to go now?** est-ce que je peux m'en aller maintenant?; **to be an** ~ **guy** être un mec bien; **to be** ~ **for money/work** avoir assez d'argent/de travail ❷ (not bad) pas mal II. interj O.K.!, d'accord! III. <OKed, okayed> vt approuver IV. n accord m; **to get the** ~ avoir l'accord; **to give the** ~ donner son accord V. adv bien; **to go** ~ aller bien

**OK**[2] n abbr of **Oklahoma**

**Oklahoma** [ˌoʊ·klə·'hoʊ·mə] n l'Oklahoma m

**old** [oʊld] I. adj <-er, -est> ❶ (not young, new) vieux(vieille); **to grow** ~**er** vieillir ❷ (denoting an age) âgé(e); **how** ~ **is she?** quel âge a-t-elle?; **she is six years** ~ elle a six ans; **to be** ~ **enough to** +infin être assez grand pour +infin ❸ (former) ancien(ne) ❹ (long known: friend) de longue date ❺ (expression of affection) **poor** ~ **Julie's cat died** le pauvre petit chat de Julie est mort ▸ **in the** (**good**) ~ **days** dans le bon vieux temps; **to be as** ~ **as the hills** être aussi vieux que Mathusalem II. n (elderly people) **the** ~ pl les personnes fpl âgées

**old age** n vieillesse f; **in one's** ~ sur ses vieux jours

**old-fashioned** adj pej ❶ (out: clothes, views) démodé(e) ❷ (traditional) d'autrefois

**old people's home** n maison f de retraite

**olive** ['a·lɪv] I. n ❶ (fruit) olive f ❷ (tree) olivier m ❸ (wood) (bois m d')olivier m ❹ (color) vert m olive II. adj olive inv; (skin) mat(e)

**Olympic** [oʊ·'lɪm·pɪk] adj (champion, flame, stadium) olympique

**omelet(te)** ['am·lət] n omelette f

**ominous** ['a·mə·nəs] adj ❶ (announcing sth bad) de mauvais augure ❷ (threatening) menaçant(e)

**omission** [oʊ·'mɪʃ·ən] n omission f

**omit** [oʊ·'mɪt] <-tt-> vt omettre

**on** [ɔn] I. prep ❶ (in contact with top) sur; **a table with a glass** ~ **it** une table avec un verre dessus; ~ **the ground** par terre ❷ (in contact with) **a fly** ~ **the wall/ceiling** une mouche sur le mur/au plafond; **a cut** ~ **one's finger** une coupure au doigt; **to hang** ~ **a branch** pendre à une branche; **to put sth** ~ **sb's shoulder/finger** mettre qc sur l'épaule/au doigt de qn; **to be** ~ **the plane** être dans l'avion; **I have the money** ~ **me** j'ai l'argent sur moi ❸ (by means of) **to go there** ~ **the train/bus** y aller en train/bus; ~ **foot** à pied; **to keep a dog** ~ **a leash** tenir un chien en laisse ❹ (source of) **to run** ~ **gas** fonctionner au gaz; **to live** ~ **$2,000 a month** vivre avec 2 000 dollars par mois ❺ MED **to be** ~ **drugs** se droguer; **to be** ~ **cortisone** être sous cortisone ❻ (spatial) ~ **the right/left** à droite/gauche; ~ **the corner/back of sth** au coin/dos de qc; **a house** ~ **the river** une maison au bord du fleuve; **a house/to live** ~ **Main Street** une maison dans/habiter Main Street ❼ (temporal) ~ **Sunday/Fridays** dimanche/le vendredi; ~ **May the 4th** le 4 mai; ~ **the evening of May the 4th** le soir du 4 mai; ~ **his birthday** le jour de son anniversaire

⑧ (*at time of*) **to leave ~ time** partir à l'heure; **to stop ~ the way** s'arrêter en route; **~ arriving there** en arrivant là-bas; **to finish ~ schedule** finir comme prévu ⑨ (*about*) **a lecture ~ Shakespeare** un cours sur Shakespeare; **my views ~ the economy** mon point de vue sur l'économie; **I agree with you ~ this** je suis d'accord avec toi sur ça; **to compliment sb ~ sth** féliciter qn pour qc; **to be there ~ business** être là pour affaires ⑩ (*through medium of*) **~ TV** à la télé; **~ video** en [*o* sur] vidéo; **~ CD** sur CD; **to speak ~ the radio/phone** parler à la radio/au téléphone; **to work ~ a computer** travailler sur un ordinateur; **to play sth ~ the flute** jouer qc à la flûte ⑪ (*involvement*) **to work ~ a project** travailler sur un projet; **two ~ each side** deux de chaque côté ⑫ (*against*) **an attack/to turn ~ sb** une attaque/se retourner contre qn ⑬ (*payments*) **to buy sth ~ credit** acheter qc à crédit; **this is ~ me** *inf* c'est ma tournée ⑭ (*progress*) **to be ~ page 10** en être à la page 10 ⑮ (*for*) **to spend $10 ~ sth** dépenser 10 dollars pour qc ⑯ (*connected to*) **to be ~ the phone** (*have one*) avoir le téléphone; (*talking*) être au téléphone **II.** *adv* ① (*wearing*) **to have nothing ~** être nu; **I put a hat ~** j'ai mis un chapeau ② (*forward*) **to go/move ~** continuer/avancer; **from that day ~** à partir de ce jour-là ③ (*aboard*) **to get ~** monter ④ (*on duty*) **de service ► ~ and off** par intermittence; **~ and ~** continuellement **III.** *adj* ① (*not off: light*) allumé(e); (*faucet, water, gas*) ouvert(e); (*electricity*) branché(e); **to be ~** (*machine*) être en marche; **the top is ~** le couvercle est mis; **the concert is still ~** (*not cancelled*) le concert n'est pas annulé; (*not over*) le concert n'est pas fini ② (*happening*) **is the wedding still ~?** est-ce que le mariage va bien avoir lieu?; **what's ~?** (*films, TV*) qu'est-ce qu'il y a à la télé/au cinéma?; **you're ~!** THEAT, TV c'est à toi/vous! **► you're ~!** *inf* d'accord!; *s.a.* **off, onto**

**on-again, off-again** *adj inf* (*relationship, plan*) en dents de scie

**once** [wʌn(t)s] **I.** *adv* ① (*a single time*) une fois; **~ a week** une fois par semaine; **~ and for all** une fois pour toutes; **~ upon a time there was ...** il était une fois ...; **he was on time for ~** pour une fois, il était à l'heure ② (*formerly*) autrefois **► ~ bitten twice shy** *prov* chat échaudé craint l'eau froide *prov* **II.** *conj* (*as soon as*) une fois que; **but ~ I arrived, ...** mais une fois arrivé, ... **► at ~** (*immediately*) tout de suite; **all at ~** soudain

**oncoming** [ˈɒnˌkʌmˌɪŋ] *adj* (*vehicle*) venant en sens inverse

**one** [wʌn] **I.** *n* un *m* **► in ~s and twos** par petits groupes; **to be ... and ...** (**all**) **in ~** être à la fois ... et ... **II.** *adj* ① *numeral* un(e); **~ hundred** cent; **as ~ man** comme un seul homme; **~ man in** [*o* **out of**] **two** un homme sur deux; **a ~-bedroom apartment** un deux-pièces ② *indef* un(e); **we'll meet ~ day** on se verra un de ces jours; **~ winter night** par une nuit d'hiver ③ (*sole, single*) seul(e); **her ~ and only hope** son seul et unique espoir ④ (*same*) même; **they're ~ and the same person** c'est une seule et même personne; *s.a.* **eight III.** *pron* ① *impers pron* on; **what ~ can do** ce qu'on peut faire; **~'s** son(sa); **to wash ~'s face** se laver le visage ② *indef pron* (*particular thing, person*) un(e); **~ Mr. Smith** un certain M. Smith; **~ of them** l'un d'entre eux; **do you have ~?** est-ce que tu en as un?; **not ~** pas un; **~ by ~** un par un; **no ~** personne; **each ~** chacun ③ *dem pron* **this ~** celui(celle)-là; **which ~?** lequel(laquelle)?; **any ~** n'importe lequel(laquelle); **to be the only ~** être le(la) seul(e); **the thinner ~** le(la) plus mince; **the little ~s** les petits *mpl*; **the ~ who ...** celui(celle) qui ... **► I for ~** moi, pour ma part

**one-night stand** *n* ① (*performance*) représentation *f* exceptionnelle ② (*sexual* *relationship*) aventure *f* sans lendemain

**oneself** [wʌn·'self] *reflex pron* ❶ *after verbs* se, s' + *vowel*, soi *tonic form;* **to deceive/express ~** se tromper/s'exprimer ❷ (*same person*) soi-même; *s.a.* **myself**

**one-time** *adj* ❶ (*former*) ancien(ne) ❷ (*happening only once*) d'une fois

**one-way** *adj a. fig* à sens unique

**ongoing** ['ɑn·gou·ɪŋ] *adj* ❶ (*happening now*) en cours; **~ state of affairs** l'état *m* actuel des choses ❷ (*continuing*) continuel(le); (*process*) continu(e); **to have an ~ relationship** avoir une relation suivie

**onion** ['ʌn·jən] *n* oignon *m*

**online** *adj, adv* COMPUT en ligne; **to go ~** se connecter

**online store** *n* cyberboutique *f*

**onlooker** ['ɑn·lʊk·ər] *n* spectateur, -trice *m, f*

**only** ['oun·li] I. *adj* seul(e); (*son, child*) unique; **the ~ way of doing sth** la seule façon de faire qc; **I'm not the ~ one** il n'y a pas que moi; **the ~ thing is ...** seulement ... II. *adv* seulement; **not ~ ... but also** non seulement ... mais aussi; **he has ~ two** il n'en a que deux; **it's ~ too true** ce n'est que trop vrai; **~ Paul can do it** seul Paul peut le faire; **I've ~ just eaten** je viens juste de manger III. *conj* (*but*) seulement; **it's lovely, ~ it's too big** c'est mignon mais trop grand

**onset** ['ɑn·set] *n* début *m*

**on-the-job training** *n* formation *f* en entreprise [*o* sur le tas]

**onto, on to** ['ɑn·tu] *prep* ❶ (*in direction of*) sur; **to climb ~ a bike** enfourcher un vélo; **to step ~ the sidewalk** monter sur le trottoir ❷ (*connection*) **to be ~ sth** être sur une piste

**onward** ['ɑn·wərd] I. *adj* en avant; **the ~ march of time** la marche du temps II. *adv* en avant; **from tomorrow ~** à partir de demain; **from this time ~** désormais

**OPEC** ['ou·pek] *n abbr of* **Organization**

**of Petroleum Exporting Countries** OPEP *f*

**open** ['ou·pən] I. *n* ❶ (*outdoors, outside*) (**out**) **in the ~** dehors; (*in the country*) en plein air; **to sleep out in the ~** dormir à la belle étoile; **to get sth** (**out**) **in the ~** *fig* mettre qc au grand jour ❷ SPORTS **the French Open** l'open *m* de France; (*in tennis*) le tournoi de Roland Garros II. *adj* ❶ (*unclosed, not closed*) *a. fig* (*room, box, arms*) ouvert(e); (*letter*) décacheté(e); (*legs*) écarté(e); **half ~** entrouvert(e); **to push sth ~** ouvrir qc; **with eyes wide ~** les yeux *mpl* grand ouverts; *fig* en connaissance de cause ❷ (*undecided: problem, question*) non résolu(e); (*result*) indécis(e); **to keep one's options ~** envisager toutes les possibilités; **to leave the date ~** ne pas fixer de date ❸ (*available, possible*) **~ to sb** (*course, club*) ouvert(e) à qn; **~ to the public** ouvert(e) au public ❹ (*open-minded*) ouvert(e); **to be ~ to sth** être ouvert à qc; **to have an ~ mind** avoir l'esprit large ❺ (*not closed in, unrestricted*) libre; (*view, road*) dégagé(e); (*field*) sans enclos; (*ticket*) open *inv;* **the ~ road** la grand-route; **on the ~ sea** en haute mer; **~ space** espace *m* libre; **~ spaces** grands espaces *mpl;* **to sleep in the ~ air** dormir à la belle étoile ❻ (*uncovered, exposed*) découvert(e); (*drain*) à ciel ouvert; **to be ~ to sth** être exposé à qc ❼ (*public: scandal*) public(-que) ❽ (*frank: person*) franc(he); (*conflict*) ouvert(e) ❾ SPORTS (*game*) ouvert(e); (*tournament*) open *inv* ❿ (*still available: job*) vacant(e) ⓫ (*likely to be affected by*) **to be ~ to sth** être exposé à qc; **to be ~ to question** être contestable; **to be ~ to criticism** s'exposer à la critique ⓬ ECON (*check*) en blanc ▶ **it's ~ house** c'est une journée portes ouvertes III. *vi* ❶ (*change from closed*) s'ouvrir; **~ wide!** ouvre(z) grand! ❷ (*give access*) **to ~ onto/into sth** donner sur qc ❸ (*ready for service*) ouvrir ❹ (*start*) commencer ❺ (*become visible*) éclore

**IV.** *vt* ❶ (*change from closed*) ouvrir; (*legs*) écarter; (*pores*) dilater; **to ~ one's eyes** entrouvrir les yeux; *fig* être vigilant; **to ~ the door to sth** *fig* être réceptif à qc ❷ (*remove fastening*) ouvrir; (*bottle*) déboucher ❸ (*start service*) ouvrir ❹ (*inaugurate*) inaugurer ❺ (*start, set up*) commencer; (*negotiations, debate*) engager; **to ~ fire** ouvrir le feu ❻ (*reveal*) révéler; **to ~ one's heart to sb** ouvrir son cœur à qn ❼ (*make available to public*) ouvrir (au public)

◆**open up** **I.** *vi* ❶ (*open*) *a. fig* s'ouvrir; **to ~ to sb** s'ouvrir à qn ❷ (*start a business*) ouvrir ❸ (*shoot*) ouvrir le feu **II.** *vt a. fig* ouvrir

**open-air** *adj* (*concert, market*) en plein air; (*swimming pool*) découvert(e)

**open-ended** *adj* (*question, discussion*) ouvert(e); (*commitment, offer*) flexible; (*contract, credit*) à durée indéterminée; (*period*) indéterminé(e); (*situation*) flou(e)

**opener** *n* ❶ (*device: for bottles*) décapsuleur *m*; (*for cans*) ouvre-boîtes *m inv*; **a letter ~** un coupe-papier ❷ (*event*) premier numéro *m*

**open house** *n* journée *f* portes ouvertes

**opening** **I.** *n* ❶ (*gap, hole*) ouverture *f*; (*breach*) brèche *f* ❷ (*opportunity*) occasion *f*; (*of work*) poste *m* ❸ (*beginning, introduction*) début *m* ❹ (*start, first performance*) ouverture *f*; (*ceremony, exhibition*) inauguration *f* **II.** *adj* d'ouverture; (*ceremony*) d'inauguration

**opening bid** *n* première mise *f* à prix

**opening day** *n* SPORTS jour *m* de la première rencontre (de la saison)

**opening hours** *n* heures *fpl* d'ouverture

**opening night** *n* THEAT première *f*

**openly** *adv* ❶ (*frankly, honestly*) franchement ❷ (*publicly*) publiquement

**open-minded** *adj* ❶ (*accessible to new ideas*) qui a l'esprit large; **to be ~** avoir l'esprit large ❷ (*unprejudiced*) sans préjugés

**open sandwich** *n* canapé *m*

**opera** ['a·pᵊr·ə] *n* opéra *m*

**opera house** *n* opéra *m*

**operate** ['a·pᵊr·eɪt] **I.** *vi* ❶ (*work, run: machine, system*) fonctionner ❷ (*perform surgery*) opérer ❸ (*be in effect: drug, forces*) faire effet ❹ COM, MIL opérer **II.** *vt* ❶ (*work, run: a machine, system*) faire fonctionner ❷ (*run, manage: store, business*) gérer; (*factory*) diriger; (*farm*) exploiter

**operation** [ˌa·pə·'reɪ·ʃᵊn] *n* ❶ (*way of working*) fonctionnement *m* ❷ (*functioning state*) **to be in ~** être en marche; **to come into ~** (*machines*) commencer à fonctionner; (*system, rules*) entrer en application ❸ MIL, MATH, COM opération *f* ❹ (*surgery*) opération *f*

**operator** ['a·pər·eɪ·t̬ər] *n* ❶ (*person*) opérateur, -trice *m, f* ❷ TEL standardiste *mf* ❸ (*company*) opérateur *m*

**opinion** [ə·'pɪn·jən] *n* ❶ (*belief, assessment*) opinion *f*; **it is my ~ that ...** je pense que ... ❷ (*view*) avis *m*; **in my ~** à mon avis; **to be of the ~ that ...** estimer que ...; **to have a high/bad ~ of sb/sth** estimer/mésestimer qn/qc; **it's just a matter of ~** c'est juste une question de point de vue

**opinion poll** *n* sondage *m* d'opinion

**opponent** [ə·'pou·nənt] *n* ❶ POL opposant(e) *m(f)* ❷ SPORTS adversaire *mf*

**opportune** [ˌa·pər·'tun] *adj* opportun(e); **at an ~ moment** au moment voulu

**opportunistic** [ˌa·pər·tu·'nɪs·tɪk] *adj* opportuniste

**opportunity** [ˌa·pər·'tu·nə·t̬i] <-ties> *n* ❶ (*convenient occasion*) occasion *f*; **an ~ to do sth** une occasion pour faire qc; **at every ~** aussi souvent que possible; **to take the ~ to** +*infin* saisir l'occasion de +*infin* ❷ (*chance for advancement*) opportunité *f*

**oppose** [ə·'pouz] *vt* s'opposer à

**opposed** *adj* opposé(e); **to be ~ to sth** être hostile à qc

**opposing** *adj* opposé(e); (*team*) adverse; (*opinion*) contraire

**opposite** ['a·pə·zɪt] **I.** *n* contraire *m*;

O

**quite the ~!** bien au contraire! ► **~s at-tract** les contraires s'attirent II. *adj* ① (*absolutely different: tendency, character*) opposé(e); (*opinion*) contraire ② (*on the other side*) opposé(e); **the ~ side of the street** l'autre côté de la rue ③ (*facing*) d'en face; **see ~ page** voir page ci-contre III. *adv* (*facing*) en face de IV. *prep* en face de; **to sit ~ one another** être assis face à face

**opposition** [ˌɑ·pə·ˈzɪ·ʃ°n] *n* ① (*resistance*) opposition *f;* **~ to sth** opposition à qc ② POL opposition *f* ③ (*contrast*) contraste *m* ④ (*opposing team*) adversaire *mf*

**oppressive** [ə·ˈpres·ɪv] *adj* ① (*burdensome*) oppressif(-ive); (*regime*) tyrannique ② (*close, stifling*) suffocant(e); (*heat*) étouffant(e)

**optician** [ɑp·ˈtɪʃ·ən] *n* opticien(ne) *m(f)*

**optimal** [ˈɑp·tɪ·məl] *adj* optimal(e)

**optimism** [ˈɑp·tə·mɪ·z°m] *n* optimisme *m*

**optimist** [ˈɑp·tə·mɪst] *n* optimiste *mf*

**optimistic** *adj* optimiste

**optimum** [ˈɑp·tə·məm] I. *n* optimum *m* II. *adj* (*choice*) optimal(e)

**option** [ˈɑp·ʃ°n] *n* ① (*choice*) option *f* ② (*possibility*) choix *m;* **to have the ~ of doing sth** pouvoir choisir de faire qc; **I have no ~ but to pay** je n'ai pas d'autre alternative que de payer ③ (*right to buy or sell*) option *f* ④ COMPUT option *f*

**optional** *adj* facultatif(-ive)

**or** [ɔr] *conj* ou; **either ... ~ ...** ou (bien) ... ou (bien) ...; **to ask whether ~ not sb is coming** demander si oui ou non qn vient; **I can't read ~ write** je ne sais ni lire ni écrire; **sb/sth ~ other** je ne sais qui/quoi; **somewhere/sometime ~ other** quelque part/tôt ou tard; **come here ~ else!** viens/venez ici, sinon tu vas/vous allez voir!; *s.a.* **either**

**OR** [ˌoʊ·ˈɑr] *n abbr of* **Oregon**

**oral** [ˈɔr·əl] *adj* ① (*spoken*) oral(e) ② (*related to the mouth*) buccal(e); (*contraceptive*) oral(e); (*medication*) par voie orale

**orange** [ˈɔr·ɪndʒ] I. *adj* orange *inv* II. *n*

① (*fruit*) orange *f* ② (*color*) orange *m; s.a.* **blue**

**orangeade** [ɔr·ɪndʒ·ˈeɪd] *n* orangeade *f*

**orange juice** *n* jus *m* d'orange

**orangoutang, orangutan** [ɔ·ˈræŋ·ə·tæn] *n* orang-outan *m*

**orbit** [ˈɔr·bɪt] I. *n* ① (*planet course*) orbite *f* ② (*sphere of activity, interest*) domaine *m* ③ ANAT orbite *f* II. *vi* être en orbite III. *vt* ① (*encircle, travel in circular path*) décrire une orbite autour de ② (*put into orbit*) placer en orbite

**orchard** [ˈɔr·tʃərd] *n* verger *m*

**orchestra** [ˈɔr·kɪ·strə] *n* orchestre *m*

**orchestra pit** *n* fosse *f* d'orchestre

**orchid** [ˈɔr·kɪd] *n* orchidée *f*

**ordeal** [ɔr·ˈdil] *n* épreuve *f*

**order** [ˈɔr·dər] I. *n* ① (*tidiness*) ordre *m;* **to put sth in ~** ranger qc; **to put one's affairs in ~** mettre ses affaires en ordre ② (*particular sequence*) ordre *m;* **in reverse ~** à l'envers; **to be in/out of ~** être en ordre/en désordre ③ (*command*) ordre *m;* **on sb's ~s** sur l'ordre de qn; **to take ~s from sb** être aux ordres de qn ④ (*working condition*) **in working/running ~** en état de marche; **to be out of ~** être hors service ⑤ (*state of peaceful harmony*) ordre *m;* **to restore ~ to a country** rétablir l'ordre dans un pays ⑥ (*all right*) **to be in ~** être en règle; **that is perfectly in ~** aucune objection; **a celebration is in ~** rien ne s'oppose à une fête ⑦ (*purpose*) **in ~ to** +*infin* afin de +*infin;* **in ~ for you to succeed ...** pour réussir ...; **in ~ that everyone can see** pour que tout le monde puisse voir (*subj*) ⑧ (*social class, rank*) classe *f* ⑨ (*request to supply goods*) commande *f;* **to put in an ~** passer (une) commande; **made to ~** fait sur commande ⑩ (*kind*) genre *m;* **of the highest ~** de premier ordre ⑪ (*system, constitution*) ordre *m* ⑫ REL (*fraternity, brotherhood*) ordre *m* ⑬ MATH degré *m* ⑭ (*procedure rules*) **~ of procedure** règlement *m* intérieur ► **the ~ of the day** l'ordre du jour II. *vt* ① (*command*) ordonner; **to ~ sb to**

+*infin* donner à qn l'ordre de +*infin*; **I was ~ed to leave** on m'a ordonné de partir ❷ (*request goods or a service*) commander ❸ (*arrange*) arranger; **to ~ one's thoughts** reprendre ses esprits; **to ~ sth into groups** classer qc par groupes ❹ (*ordain, decide*) **to ~ that ...** décréter que ... ❺ (*arrange according to procedure*) régler **III.** *vi* commander

◆ **order around** *vt always sep* **to order sb around** donner des ordres à qn

**order form** *n* bon *m* de commande

**orderly I.** *adj* ❶ (*methodically arranged*) méthodique ❷ (*tidy*) ordonné(e); (*room*) en ordre ❸ (*well behaved, not unruly*) discipliné(e); **in an ~ fashion** dans le calme **II.** *n* ❶ (*hospital attendant*) aide-infirmier, -ère *m, f* ❷ MIL planton *m*

**ordinarily** *adv* normalement

**ordinary** ['ɔr·dən·er·i] **I.** *n* ❶ (*normal state*) ordinaire *m*; **out of the ~** qui sort de l'ordinaire; **nothing out of the ~** rien d'inhabituel ❷ (*judge*) juge *m* ❸ REL ordinaire *m* **II.** *adj* ordinaire; (*clothes*) de tous les jours; **in the ~ way** en temps normal; **she's no ~ teacher** elle n'est pas une enseignante comme les autres

**ordnance** ['ɔrd·nən(t)s] *n* MIL ordonnance *f*

**oregano** [ə·'reg·ə·noʊ] *n* origan *m*

**Oregon** ['ɔr·ɪ·gən] *n* l'Oregon *m*

**organ** ['ɔr·gən] *n* ❶ MUS orgue *f* ❷ (*body part*) organe *m*

**organ donor** *n* donneur, -euse *m, f* d'organe

**organ grinder** *n* ❶ (*musician*) joueur, -euse *m, f* d'orgue de Barbarie ❷ *fig* responsable *mf*

**organic** [ɔr·'gæn·ɪk] *adj* ❶ (*related to living substance*) organique ❷ (*not artificial: fruit, agriculture*) biologique; **~ fruit** fruit *m* bio; **~ farming methods** méthode de production biologique; **~ label** label bio; **~ supermarket** supermarché bio ❸ (*fundamental*) fon-

damental(e) ❹ (*systematic*) systématique

**organism** ['ɔr·gən·ɪ·zᵊm] *n* organisme *m*

**organist** ['ɔr·gən·ɪst] *n* organiste *mf*

**organization** [ˌɔr·gən·ɪ·'zei·ʃᵊn] *n* ❶ (*act of organizing*) organisation *f* ❷ (*group*) organisation *f* ❸ (*association*) association *f* ❹ (*tidiness*) ordre *m*

**organize** ['ɔr·gən·aɪz] **I.** *vt* ❶ (*arrange*) organiser; (*a meal*) s'occuper de; **to get ~d** s'organiser ❷ (*bring in a trade union*) syndiquer **II.** *vi* ❶ (*get arranged*) s'organiser ❷ (*form a trade union*) se syndiquer

**orgasm** ['ɔr·gæz·ᵊm] **I.** *n* orgasme *m* **II.** *vi* avoir un orgasme

**Orient** ['ɔr·i·ənt] *n* **the ~** l'Orient *m*

**oriental** [ɔr·i·'en·tᵊl] **I.** *n* Oriental(e) *m(f)* **II.** *adj* oriental(e); (*carpet*) d'Orient

**orientation** [ɔr·i·en·'tei·ʃᵊn] *n* orientation *f*

**origin** ['ɔr·ə·dʒɪn] *n* origine *f*

**original I.** *n* ❶ (*not a copy or imitation*) original *m* ❷ (*unusual person*) original(e) *m(f)* **II.** *adj* ❶ (*initial: sin*) originel(le) ❷ (*new, novel, unique*) original(e) ❸ (*not copied or imitated, firsthand: painting*) authentique; (*manuscript*) original(e)

**originality** [ə·ˌrɪdʒ·ɪ·'næl·ə·t̬i] *n* originalité *f*

**originally** *adv* ❶ (*first condition*) à l'origine ❷ (*at source*) au départ

**ornament** ['ɔr·nə·mənt] **I.** *n* ❶ (*decoration, adornment*) ornement *m* ❷ (*small object*) bibelot *m* ❸ MUS fioriture *f* **II.** *vt* ornementer

**ornithology** [ɔr·nə·'θɑ·lə·dʒi] *n* ornithologie *f*

**orphan** ['ɔr·fᵊn] **I.** *n* orphelin(e) *m(f)* **II.** *vt* **to be ~ed** devenir orphelin

**orphanage** ['ɔr·fᵊn·ɪdʒ] *n* orphelinat *m*

**orthodontist** [ɔr·θoʊ·'dɑn·t̬ɪst] *n* orthodontiste *mf*

**orthodox** ['ɔr·θə·dɑks] *adj* ❶ (*religiously accepted, conventional*) orthodoxe

**O**

**②** (*unoriginal, conventional*) conformiste **③** (*strictly religious*) intégriste

**orthopedist** n orthopédiste mf

**Oscar** ['ɑ·skər] n oscar m

**ostracize** ['a·strə·saɪz] vt **①** (*socially exclude*) frapper d'ostracisme **②** (*banish*) mettre en quarantaine

**ostrich** ['a·strɪtʃ] n **①** (*bird*) autruche f **②** pej (*person*) personne pratiquant la "*politique de l'autruche*"

**other** ['ʌð·ər] I. adj autre; **the ~ woman/man** l'autre mf; **the ~ day** l'autre jour m; **every ~ day/week** un jour/une semaine sur deux; **any ~ questions?** pas d'autres questions? II. pron **①** (*different ones*) autre; **the ~s** les autres mpl à fpl; **none ~ than Paul** nul autre que Paul; **each ~** l'un l'autre; **some eat, ~s drink** les uns mangent, d'autres boivent **②** sing (*either/or*) **to choose one or the ~** choisir l'un ou l'autre; **to not have one without the ~** ne pas avoir l'un sans l'autre **③** (*being vague*) **sb/sth or ~** quelqu'un/quelque chose III. adv **~ adv** autrement; **somehow or ~** d'une manière ou d'une autre

**O**

**other than** prep (*besides*) **~ sb/sth à** part qn/qc; **he can't do anything ~ pay** il ne peut que payer; **no choice ~ to stay** pas d'autre choix que de rester; **it's anything ~ perfect** c'est tout sauf parfait

**otherwise** ['ʌð·ər·waɪz] I. adj form autre II. adv **①** (*differently*) autrement; **married or ~** marié ou non; **Samantha, ~ known as Sam** Samantha, que l'on connaît également sous le nom de Sam **②** (*in other respects*) par ailleurs III. conj sinon

**ouch** [aʊtʃ] interj aïe!

**ought** [ɔt] aux **①** (*have as a duty, should*) **he ~ to tell her** il devrait lui dire **②** (*had better*) **we ~ to do sth** il vaudrait mieux que nous fassions qc (*subj*) **③** (*be wise or advisable*) **you ~ not to do that** tu ne devrais pas faire cela

**ounce** [aʊn(t)s] n once f ▶ **not an ~ of**

**sth** pas du tout de qc, pas une brique de qc *Suisse*

**our** [aʊər] poss adj notre mf, nos pl; s.a. **my**

**ours** [aʊərz] poss pron (*belonging to us*) le , la nôtre; **a book of ~** un de nos livres; **this table is ~** cette table est à nous

**ourselves** [aʊər·'selvz] poss pron **①** after verbs nous; **we hurt ~** nous nous sommes blessés **②** (*we or us*) nous-mêmes; s.a. **myself**

**out** [aʊt] I. vt révéler l'homosexualité de II. prep inf s. **out of** III. adv **①** (*not inside*) dehors; **to go ~** sortir; **get ~!** dehors!; **to find one's way ~** trouver la sortie **②** (*outside*) dehors; **keep ~!** défense d'entrer!; **to eat ~** aller au restaurant **③** (*distant, away*) loin; **ten miles ~** à dix miles; **~ at sea** au large; **she's ~ in front** être loin devant; **~ in California/the country** en Californie/à la campagne; **to go ~ to the West Coast** partir pour la côte ouest; **the tide is going ~** la mer se retire **④** (*remove*) **to cross ~ words** rayer des mots; **to get a stain ~** enlever une tache; **to put ~ a fire** éteindre un feu **⑤** (*available*) **the best one that's ~** le meilleur sur le marché **⑥** (*unconscious*) **to knock sb ~** assommer qn; **to pass ~** s'évanouir; **to be ~ cold** être assommé **⑦** (*completely*) **burnt ~** entièrement brûlé; **to be tired ~** être épuisé **⑧** (*emerge*) **to come ~** se révéler **⑨** (*come to an end, conclude*) **to go ~** passer de mode ▶ **~ and about** (*on the road*) de sortie; (*healthy*) sur pied; **~ with it!** dis/dites-le donc!; s.a. **inside, in** IV. adj **①** (*absent, not present*) sorti(e) **②** (*released, published: film, novel*) sorti(e) **③** (*revealed: news*) rendu(e) public(-que) **④** BOT (*flower*) en fleur **⑤** (*visible*) **the sun/moon is ~** le soleil/la lune brille **⑥** (*finished*) fini(e); **before the week is ~** avant la fin de la semaine **⑦** (*not working: fire, light*) éteint(e); (*workers*) en grève ❽ *inf* (*in existence*) **to be** ~ (*person*) exister; (*object*) être sur le marché ❾ (*unconscious, tired*) K.-O. *inv* ❿ SPORTS (*ball*) sortie(e); (*player*) éliminé(e); *fig* sur la touche ⓫ (*not allowed*) **that's** ~ c'est hors de question ⓬ (*unfashionable*) passé(e) de mode ▸ **to be** ~ **for sth** +*infin* chercher à faire qc ▸ +*infin* **V.** *n* échappatoire *f*; **to be looking for an** ~ chercher une issue ▸ **to be on the** ~ **s with sb** être brouillé avec qn

**out-and-out** *adj* complet(-ète); (*liar*) fini(e)

**outboard** *n* ❶ (*motor for boat*) moteur *m* hors-bord ❷ (*boat with outboard motor*) hors-bord *m inv*

**outboard motor** *n* moteur *m* hors-bord

**outbreak** *n* ❶ (*sudden start: of war*) déclenchement *m;* (*of spots, of violence*) éruption *f;* (*of fever*) accès *m;* (*of hives*) crise *f* ❷ (*epidemic*) épidémie *f*

**outburst** *n* accès *m*

**outcome** *n* résultat *m;* (*of an election*) issue *f*

**outcry** <-ries> *n* tollé *m;* **a public** ~ une clameur de protestation

**outdated** *adj* ❶ (*old*) désuet(-ète); (*word*) vieilli(e) ❷ (*out of fashion*) démodé(e)

**outdo** *vt irr* surpasser

**outdoor** *adj* extérieur(e); (*swimming pool*) découvert(e); (*sports, activity*) de plein air

**outdoors** *n* dehors *m;* **the great** ~ la pleine nature

**outer** ['aʊ·tər] *adj* extérieur(e); **the** ~ **suburbs** la grande banlieue

**outermost** *adj* le (la) plus à l'extérieur, le (la) plus éloigné(e)

**outfit** *n* ❶ (*set of clothes*) tenue *f* ❷ *inf* (*company*) boîte *f*

**outgoing** *adj* ❶ (*sociable*) sociable ❷ (*extroverted*) extraverti(e) ❸ (*leaving*) sortant(e)

**outgrow** *vt irr* ❶ (*grow too big for: clothes, cradle*) devenir trop grand pour; **to** ~ **sth** (*a habit, taste, interest*) passer l'âge de faire qc; **to** ~ **all that** dé-

passer tout ça ❷ (*grow too fast*) grandir plus vite que ❸ (*become bigger or faster than*) dépasser

**outhouse** *n* ❶ (*outdoor toilet*) toilettes *fpl* extérieures ❷ (*small separate building*) dépendance *f*

**outing** *n* ❶ (*walk*) sortie *f;* **family** ~ sortie en famille ❷ (*revelation of homosexuality*) outing *m* (*le fait de révéler l'homosexualité d'une personne*)

**outlaw** **I.** *n* hors-la-loi *m inv* **II.** *vt* ❶ (*ban*) interdire ❷ (*make illegal*) déclarer illégal(e)

**outlet** *n* ❶ (*exit*) sortie *f;* (*of a river*) embouchure *f* ❷ (*means of expression*) exutoire *m* ❸ (*store or business*) point *m* de vente ❹ ELEC prise *f* de courant

**outline** **I.** *n* ❶ (*general plan*) plan *m;* **the main** ~ les grandes lignes *fpl* ❷ (*rough plan*) ébauche *f* ❸ (*description of main points*) synthèse *f* ❹ ART (*contour*) contour *m* ❺ (*summary*) résumé *m* **II.** *vt* ❶ (*draw outer line of*) esquisser; **to be** ~ **d against the horizon** se dessiner à l'horizon ❷ (*summarize*) résumer

**outlook** *n* ❶ (*future prospect*) perspective *f;* **the weather** ~ les prévisions *fpl* météorologiques ❷ (*general view, attitude*) attitude *f*

**outnumber** *vt* être supérieur en nombre à; **to be** ~ **ed** être en minorité

**out of** *prep* ❶ (*toward outside from*) hors de, en dehors de; **to jump** ~ **bed** sauter (hors) du lit; **to take sth** ~ **a box** prendre qc dans une boîte; **to look/ lean** ~ **the window** regarder par/se pencher à la fenêtre ❷ (*outside from*) ~ **sight/reach** hors de vue/d'atteinte; **to drink** ~ **a glass** boire dans un verre ❸ (*away from*) **to be** ~ **town/the office** ne pas être en ville/au bureau; **to get** ~ **the rain** se mettre à l'abri de la pluie; ~ **the way!** pousse-toi/poussez-vous! ❹ (*without*) **to be** ~ **sth** ne plus avoir qc; **to be** ~ **money/work** être à court d'argent/sans emploi; ~ **breath** hors d'haleine; ~ **order** en panne

**⑤** (*from*) **made ~ wood** fait en bois; **to copy sth ~ a file** copier qc dans un fichier; **to get sth ~ sb** soutirer qc à qn **⑥** (*because of*) **to do sth ~ politeness** faire qc par politesse **⑦** **in 3 cases ~ 10** dans 3 cas sur 10 ▶ **to be ~ it** *inf* être à côté de ses pompes; (*drunk, drugged*) être dans les vapes; **to be ~ one's <u>mind</u>** avoir perdu la tête; **~ this <u>world</u>** (*excellent*) divin

**out-of-bounds I.** *adj* hors limites *inv* **II.** *adv* en dehors des limites

**out-of-date** *adj* **①** (*existing after a fixed date*) périmé(e) **②** (*worthless*) caduc(-que) **③** (*no more in use*) obsolète **④** (*not in use for long time*) désuet(-ète); (*word*) vieilli(e) **⑤** (*out of fashion*) démodé(e)

**out-of-the-way** *adj* à l'écart

**outplay** *vt* SPORTS jouer mieux que

**outpost** *n* **①** MIL (*guards to prevent attack*) avant-poste *m* **②** (*base to prevent attack*) camp *m* volant **③** (*distant branch or settlement*) bastion *m*

**output** *n* **①** ECON (*amount produced*) rendement *m;* **total ~** productivité *f* globale **②** (*production*) production *f* **③** (*power, energy*) puissance *f* **④** COMPUT sortie *f*

**outrageous** [aʊtˈreɪˈdʒəs] *adj* **①** (*cruel*) atroce **②** (*shocking, exaggerated*) scandaleux(-euse) **③** (*bold*) scandaleux(-euse)

**outset** *n* commencement *m;* **at the ~** au départ; **from the ~** dès le début

**outside I.** *adj* **①** (*external: door*) extérieur(e) **②** (*not belonging to sth: call, world, help*) extérieur(e); **my ~ interests** mes centres *mpl* d'intérêts **③** (*not likely: possibility, chance*) faible **④** (*highest: estimate*) maximum **⑤** AUTO **~ lane** voie *f* de gauche **II.** *n* **①** (*external part or side*) *a. fig* extérieur *m;* **on/from the ~** à/vu de l'extérieur **②** (*at most*) **at the (very) ~** tout au plus **③** AUTO **to pass on the ~** dépasser par la gauche **III.** *prep* **①** (*not within*) à l'extérieur de; **from ~ sth** de l'extérieur de qc; **to play/go ~ the house** jouer en

dehors de/sortir de la maison; **experts from ~ the company/school** des experts externes à l'entreprise/l'école **②** (*next to*) **~ sb's window** sous la fenêtre de qn; **to wait ~ the door** attendre devant la porte **③** (*not during*) **~ business hours** en dehors des heures de travail **IV.** *adv* **①** (*outdoors*) dehors, à la porte *Belgique;* **to go ~** sortir **②** (*not inside*) à l'extérieur **③** (*beyond*) au-delà **④** (*except for*) excepté; **~ of us/Paris** à part nous/Paris; *s.a.* **inside**

**outsider** *n* **①** (*stranger*) étranger, -ère *m, f* **②** (*not belonging to a group, office*) intervenant(e) *m(f)* extérieur **③** (*outcast*) exclu(e) *m(f)*

**outskirts** *npl* périphérie *f*

**outspoken** *adj* franc(he)

**outstanding** *adj* **①** (*excellent, extraordinary*) exceptionnel(le) **②** (*of special note, remarkable*) remarquable **③** (*noticeable: feature, incident*) marquant(e) **④** (*remaining: debt, amount*) impayé(e); (*sick day*) à prendre; (*assignment*) inachevé(e); (*issues, business*) en suspens; (*invoice*) en souffrance; (*problems*) non résolu(e)

**outturn** *n* rendement *m*

**outward I.** *adj* **①** (*exterior, external*) extérieur(e); **to all ~ appearances** selon toute apparence **②** (*going out*) vers l'extérieur; **the ~ journey** l'aller *m* **③** (*apparent, superficial*) apparent(e) **II.** *adv* vers l'extérieur

**outwardly** *adv* apparemment

**outwards** *adv s.* **outward**

**oval** [ˈoʊ·vəl] **I.** *n* ovale *m* **II.** *adj* ovale

**oven** [ˈʌv·ən] *n* four *m*

**oven glove** *n* gant *m* à four

**ovenproof** *adj* résistant(e) aux hautes températures

**oven-ready** *adj* prêt(e) à mettre au four

**over** [ˈoʊ·vər] **I.** *prep* **①** (*above*) sur; **the bridge ~ the highway** le pont traversant l'autoroute; **to fly ~ the sea** survoler la mer; **4 ~ 12 equals one third** MATH 4 sur 12 équivalent à un tiers **②** (*on*) **to hit sb ~ the head** frapper qn à la tête; **to drive ~ sth** écraser qc (en voiture); **to spread a cloth ~ it/the table** mettre une nappe dessus/sur la table ❸(*across*) **view ~ the valley** vue *f* sur la vallée; **to go ~ the bridge** traverser le pont; **it rained all ~ the Midwest** il a plu sur tout le Midwest; **famous all ~ the world** connu dans le monde entier; **to look ~ a house** visiter une maison; **to look ~ sb's shoulder** regarder par-dessus l'épaule de qn; **to jump ~ the fence** sauter la barrière ❹(*during*) **~ (the) winter** pendant l'hiver; **~ the years** au fil des années; **~ time** avec le temps; **~ a two-year period** sur une période de deux ans ❺(*more than*) **~ 95°F** au dessus de 95°F; **~ $50** plus de 50 dollars; **to speak for ~ an hour** parler plus d'une heure; **to be ~ an amount** dépasser une somme; **~ and above that** en plus de ça; **children ~ 14** les enfants *mpl* de plus de 14 ans; **to value sth ~ money** préférer qc à l'argent ❻(*through*) **to hear sth ~ the noise** entendre qc par-dessus le bruit; **what came ~ him?** qu'est-ce qui lui a pris? ❼(*in superiority to*) **to rule ~ the Romans** régner sur les Romains; **to have command ~ sth** avoir le commandement de qc; **to have an advantage ~ sb** avoir un avantage sur qn ❽(*about*) **~ sth** au sujet de qc; **to puzzle ~ a question** tenter de résoudre une question ❾(*for checking*) **to watch ~ a child** surveiller un enfant; **to look/go ~ a text** jeter un coup d'œil sur/parcourir un texte ❿(*past*) **to be ~ the worst** avoir le pire derrière soi; *s.a.* **under II.** *adv* ❶(*at a distance*) **it's ~ here/there** c'est ici/là-bas ❷(*moving across*) **to come ~ here** venir (par) ici; **to go ~ there** aller là-bas; **to pass/hand sth ~ here** faire passer/remettre qc; **he swam ~ to me** il m'a rejoint à la nage; **call her ~** appelle-la; **he went ~ to the enemy** *fig* il est passé à l'ennemi ❸(*on a visit*) **come ~ tonight** passe(z) ce soir ❹(*moving above: go, jump*) par-dessus; **to fly ~** passer dans le ciel ❺(*downward*) **to fall ~** tomber;

**to knock sth ~** faire tomber qc ❻(*another way up*) **to turn the page/pancake ~** tourner la page/crêpe ❼(*completely*) **to look for sb all ~** chercher qn partout; **to turn sth ~ and ~** tourner et retourner qc dans tous les sens; **to talk/think sth ~** discuter de/bien réfléchir à qc ❽(*again*) **I repeated it ~ and ~** je n'ai cessé de le répéter; **to do sth all ~** refaire qc entièrement ❾(*more*) **children 14 and ~** les enfants *mpl* de 14 ans et plus; **if there's any left ~** s'il en reste ❿(*sb's turn*) **"~"** RADIO, AVIAT "à vous"; **~ and out!** terminé! **III.** *adj inv* ❶(*finished*) fini(e); **it's all ~** tout est fini; **the snow is ~** il a cessé de neiger ❷(*remaining*) de reste; **there are three left ~** il en reste encore trois

**overall** I. *n pl* salopette *f* II. *adj* (*results*) global(e); **~ winner** grand gagnant *m;* (*commander, pattern*) général(e) III. *adv* dans l'ensemble

**overbalance** *vi* se déséquilibrer

**overboard** *adv* par-dessus bord; **to fall ~** tomber par-dessus bord; **man ~!** un homme à la mer! ▸ **to go ~** s'emballer

**overbook** *vt* surbooker

**overcast** *adj* (*sky*) chargé(e); (*weather*) couvert(e)

**overcharge** I. *vt* faire payer trop cher à II. *vi* demander trop

**overcoat** *n* pardessus *m*

**overcome** <irr> I. *vt* (*obstacle, fear, problems*) surmonter; (*one's enemies*) vaincre; **to ~ temptation** résister à la tentation; **to be ~ with sth** (*fear, emotion*) être gagné par qc II. *vi* vaincre; **we shall ~!** nous vaincrons!

**overconfident** *adj* trop sûr(e) de soi

**overcrowded** *adj* (*room, train*) bondé(e); (*prison, city*) surpeuplé(e); (*class*) surchargé(e)

**overdo** *vt* ❶(*exaggerate*) exagérer; **don't ~ it!** (*irony, salt*) n'en rajoute pas!; (*work*) n'en fais pas trop! ❷(*use too much*) exagérer sur ❸(*cook too long*) cuire trop longtemps

**overdone** *adj* ❶(*exaggerated: make-*

O

-up) exagéré(e) ② (*cooked too long*) trop cuit(e)

**overdose** I. *n* overdose *f*; **to die of an ~** mourir d'une overdose II. *vi* **to ~ on sth** être en overdose de qc; *fig* faire une overdose de qc

**overdraft** *n* FIN découvert *m* bancaire

**overdraw** *irr* I. *vi* mettre son compte à découvert II. *vt* **to ~ sth** mettre qc à découvert

**overdue** *adj* (*work, book*) en retard; (*bill*) impayé(e)

**overestimate** I. *n* surestimation *f* II. *vt* surestimer

**overexcited** *adj* surexcité(e)

**overflow** I. *n* ① (*of liquid*) débordement *m* ② (*pipe*) trop-plein *m* ③ (*surplus*) surplus *m* II. *vi a. fig* déborder; **to ~ with sth** déborder de qc; **to be full to ~ing** être plein à craquer *inf* III. *vt fig* inonder

**overgrown** *adj* ① (*too full of plants*) envahi(e); **to be ~ with sth** être envahi par qc ② *pej* (*immature*) attardé(e)

**overhaul** I. *n* révision *f* II. *vt* ① (*examine and repair*) réviser ② *fig* remanier

**overhead** I. *n* ① (*costs of running business*) frais *mpl* généraux ② *inf* (*projector*) rétroprojecteur *m* ③ (*transparency*) transparent *m* II. *adj* ① (*above head level: railroad*) aérien(ne); **~ lighting** éclairage *m* au plafond; **~ volley** balle *f* haute ② (*concerning running business: costs*) courant(e) ③ (*taken from above*) en l'air III. *adv* en l'air

**overhear** *irr* I. *vt* **to ~ sth** entendre qc par hasard; **to ~ sb** entendre ce que dit qn; **to ~ sb saying sth** entendre qn dire qc II. *vi* entendre

**overheat** I. *vt a. fig* surchauffer II. *vi* ① (*get too hot*) chauffer trop; (*engine*) chauffer ② *fig* s'échauffer ③ FIN (*economy*) être en surchauffe

**overjoyed** *adj* fou(folle) de joie

**overkill** *n* it's ~ c'est exagéré; **media ~** matraquage *m* médiatique

**overland** *adj, adv* par (la) route

**overload** I. *n* ① (*too much demand for electricity*) surtension *f* ② (*excess*) sur-

charge *f* II.<irr> *vt a. fig* surcharger; (*roads*) encombrer

**overlook** I. *n* (*viewpoint*) aperçu *m* II. *vt* ① (*have a view of*) donner sur ② (*not notice, forget*) négliger ③ (*ignore, disregard*) laisser passer

**overnight** I. *adj* ① (*during the night: trip, convoy*) de nuit ② (*for one night: stay*) d'une nuit; SPORTS (*leader*) du jour ③ (*sudden: celebrity, sensation*) du jour au lendemain ④ (*for next-day delivery*) ~ **delivery** livraison *f* en 24 h II. *adv* ① (*for a night*) une nuit; **to stay ~ with sb** passer la nuit chez qn ② (*during the night*) toute la nuit ③ (*very quickly*) du jour au lendemain III. *n* nuit *f*

**overpass** *n* CONSTR (*for roads*) autopont *m*; (*for railroad line*) pont *m* ferroviaire

**overpay** *irr vt, vi* surpayer

**overpopulated** *adj* surpeuplé(e)

**overpowering** *adj* bouleversant(e)

**overrated** *adj* surestimé(e)

**overreact** *vi* **to ~ to sth** réagir à outrance à qc

**overreaction** *n* réaction *f* excessive

**overriding** *adj* primordial(e)

**overrun** I. *n* ① (*extension, invasion*) invasion *f* ② (*exceeding allowed time, cost*) dépassement *m*; **cost ~** dépassement du coût estimé II.<overran, overrun> *vt* ① (*occupy, invade*) envahir; **to be ~ with sth** être envahi par qc; (*be infested*) être infesté de qc; (*be filled*) être inondé de qc ② (*take, use too much: one's time, budget*) dépasser ③ (*run, extend over*) dépasser III.<overran, overrun> *vi* ① (*exceed allotted time*) durer plus longtemps que prévu ② (*exceed allotted money*) dépasser le budget prévu; **to ~ on costs** dépasser les frais

**overseas** I. *adj* ① (*across the sea: colony, person*) d'outre-mer; (*trade, aid*) extérieur(e) ② (*related to a foreign country: trip*) à l'étranger; (*student*) étranger(-ère) II. *adv* ① (*abroad*) à l'étranger ② (*across the sea*) outre-mer

**overshadow** *vt* ❶ (*cast a shadow over*) ombrager ❷ *fig* **to ~ sb/sth** (*cast gloom over*) jeter une ombre sur qn/qc; (*appear more important*) faire de l'ombre à qn/qc; **to be ~ed by sb** être éclipsé par qn

**oversight** *n* ❶ (*failure to notice sth*) oubli *m* ❷ (*surveillance*) surveillance *f*

**oversleep** *irr vi* se réveiller en retard

**overspend** I. *vi* dépenser trop II. *vt* dépasser

**overstaffed** *adj* en sureffectif

**overstay** *vt* **to ~ a visa** dépasser la durée de validité pour un visa; **I've ~ed my welcome** j'ai abusé de votre/son hospitalité

**overstep** *vt irr* dépasser ▸**to ~ the <u>mark</u>** dépasser les bornes

**overtake** *irr* I. *vt* ❶ (*go past, become greater: a car, a country, a competitor*) dépasser ❷ (*exceed: an amount, a level*) dépasser ❸ (*happen*) rattraper; **to be ~n by events** être rattrapé par les événements; **to be ~n by grief** être pris de chagrin; **to ~ sb** s'emparer de qn II. *vi* AUTO dépasser

**over-the-counter** *adj* FIN, MED en vente libre

**overthrow** I.<irr> *vt* renverser II. *n* ❶ (*removal from power*) renversement *m* ❷ SPORTS (*ball thrown too far*) hors-jeu *m inv*

**overtime** *n* ❶ (*extra work*) heures *fpl* supplémentaires ❷ SPORTS prolongations *fpl*

**overture** ['oʊ·vər·tʃər] *n a. fig* ouverture *f*

**overturn** I. *vi* basculer; (*car*) se renverser; (*boat*) chavirer II. *vt a. fig* renverser; (*boat*) faire chavirer

**overview** *n* vue *f* d'ensemble

**overweight** *adj* trop lourd(e); (*person*) trop gros(se); **to be 20 pounds ~** peser 20 livres de trop

**overwhelming** *adj* (*majority, argument, victory*) écrasant(e); (*support*) massif(-ive); (*grief, heat*) accablant(e); (*joy*) immense; (*desire, need*) irrésistible

**overwork** I. *vt* (*person, body*) surmener; (*machine, idea*) utiliser à outrance II. *vi* se surmener III. *n* surmenage *m*

**ow** [aʊ] *interj* aïe!

**owe** [oʊ] *vt a. fig* devoir; **to ~ sb sth** devoir qc à qn

**owing** *adj* dû(due)

**owl** [aʊl] *n* chouette *f*

**own** [oʊn] I. *pron* **my** ~ le(la) mien(ne); **it is my ~** c'est à moi; **to have problems of one's ~** avoir ses propres problèmes; **a room of one's ~** une chambre à soi ▸**to <u>come</u> into one's ~** révéler ses qualités; **(all) <u>on</u> one's ~** (tout) seul II. *adj* propre; **in one's ~ time** (*outside working hours*) en dehors des heures de travail de qn III. *vt* posséder; **as if they ~ed the place** comme s'ils étaient chez eux

**owner** *n* propriétaire *mf*

**ownership** ['oʊ·nər·ʃɪp] *n* propriété *f*

**ox** [aks] <oxen> *n* bœuf *m*

**oxidize** ['ak·sɪ·daɪz] I. *vi* s'oxyder II. *vt* oxyder

**oxygen** ['ak·sɪ·dʒən] *n* oxygène *m*

**oyster** ['ɔɪ·stər] *n* huître *f*

**oz.** *n s. ounce* once *f*

**ozone** ['oʊ·zoʊn] *n* ❶ CHEM ozone *m* ❷ *inf* (*clean air*) air *m* pur

**ozone layer** *n* couche *f* d'ozone

O

# Pp

**P, p** [piː] <-'s> *n* P *m*, p *m*; ~ **as in Papa** (*on telephone*) p comme Pierre ▸ **to mind one's ~'s and Q's** faire attention à ce que l'on dit

**PA** [ˌpiːˈeɪ] *n* ❶ *abbr of* **Pennsylvania** ❷ (*loudspeaker*) *abbr of* **public-address system** ❸ (*assistant to a superior*) *abbr of* **personal assistant**

**pa** *n inf* (*father*) papa *m*

**p.a.** *adv abbr of* **per annum** par an

**pace** [peɪs] **I.** *n* ❶ (*step*) pas *m*; **a few ~s away from sb/sth** à deux pas de qn/qc ❷ (*speed*) pas *m*; **to force** [*o* **up**] **the ~** forcer l'allure; **to set the ~** donner l'allure; **to keep up the ~** maintenir la cadence; **at sb's own ~** à son (propre) rythme; **to keep ~ with sb/sth** *a. fig* suivre le rythme de qn/qc ▸ **to put sb/sth through his/its ~s** mettre qn/qc à l'épreuve **II.** <pacing> *vt* **to ~ sth** (**off**) arpenter qc **III.** *vi* marcher; **to ~ up and down** marcher de long en large

**pacemaker** ['peɪsˌmeɪkər] *n* ❶ SPORTS (*speed setter*) meneur, -euse *m, f* ❷ (*heart rhythm regulator*) stimulateur *m* cardiaque

**Pacific I.** *n* **the ~** le Pacifique **II.** *adj* pacifique

**Pacific Ocean** *n* océan *m* Pacifique

**pacifist I.** *n* pacifiste *mf* **II.** *adj* pacifiste

**pack** [pæk] **I.** *n* ❶ (*box: of cigarettes*) paquet *m*; (*of beer*) pack *m* ❷ (*group*) groupe *m*; (*of wolves, dogs*) meute *f* ❸ *pej* (*group, set*) tas *m*; **nothing but a ~ of lies** rien qu'un tissu de mensonges ❹ SPORTS mêlée *f* ❺ MIL patrouille *f* ❻ (*complete set*) ~ **of cards** jeu *m* de cartes ❼ (*rucksack*) sac *m* à dos ❽ (*beauty treatment*) masque *m* **II.** *vi* ❶ (*prepare travel luggage*) faire ses bagages ❷ (*cram*) s'entasser; **to ~ into a room** s'entasser dans une pièce

❸ (*compress*) se tasser ❹ *inf* (*carry a gun*) **are you ~ing?** est-ce que tu portes un revolver? ▸ **to send sb ~ing** envoyer promener qn **III.** *vt* ❶ (*put into*) ranger dans une valise; **to ~ one's bags** *a. fig* faire ses valises; **did you ~ the camera?** tu as pris l'appareil photo?; **to ~ a lot into a suitcase** mettre plein de choses dans une valise ❷ (*wrap*) emballer; (*for sale*) conditionner ❸ (*fill*) **to ~ sth with sth** remplir qc de qc; **to be ~ed with tourists** être rempli de touristes ❹ (*cram*) entasser; **to be ~ed like sardines** être serrés comme des sardines ❺ (*compress*) tasser ❻ (*have force*) **to ~ power** avoir de la puissance; **to ~ a punch** *a. fig* avoir du punch ❼ *inf* (*carry*) **to be ~ing a pistol** porter un flingue

◆**pack in** *vt* ❶ (*attract an audience*) **they're packing them in** ils attirent un monde fou ❷ (*cram in*) entasser ❸ (*stop*) **to ~ sth** plaquer qc ▸ **to pack it in** laisser tomber

◆**pack off** *vt inf* expédier

◆**pack up I.** *vt* ❶ (*pack: for mailing, storage*) emballer; (*for travel*) rassembler; **to ~ one's belongings** faire ses valises ❷ *inf* (*finish*) laisser tomber; **to pack it up and go home** rentrer chez soi **II.** *vi* ❶ (*pack and go*) plier bagage ❷ *inf* (*stop: work*) arrêter de bosser

**package** ['pækɪdʒ] **I.** *n* ❶ (*packet*) paquet *m* ❷ (*set*) ensemble *m* **II.** *vt* ❶ (*pack*) emballer; (*for sale*) conditionner ❷ *fig* présenter

**package deal** *n* contrat *m* forfaitaire

**package tour** *n*, **package vacation** *n* voyage *m* à forfait

**packaging** *n* ❶ (*wrapping materials*) conditionnement *m* ❷ (*the wrapping of goods*) emballage *m* ❸ (*presentation*) packaging *m*

**packet** ['pæk·ɪt] *n* a. *inf* paquet *m;* **soup in a ~** soupe *f* en sachet
**packing** *n* ❶ (*putting things into cases*) emballage *m* ❷ (*protective wrapping*) conditionnement *m* ❸ COMPUT compression *f*
**pact** [pækt] *n* pacte *m*
**pad** [pæd] I. *n* ❶ (*piece of material, rubber*) tampon *m;* **cotton wool ~** coton *m;* **scouring ~** tampon à récurer; **ink ~** tampon encreur; (**sanitary**) **~** serviette *f* périodique ❷ (*protection*) coussinet *m;* SPORTS protection *f;* **knee ~** genouillère *f* ❸ FASHION **shoulder ~** épaulette *f* ❹ (*book of blank paper*) bloc *m* ❺ (*sole of an animal*) coussinet *m* ❻ (*takeoff and landing area*) piste *f;* **launch ~** rampe *f* de lancement ❼ *inf* (*house or apartment*) piaule *f* ❽ (*water lily leaf*) feuille *f* de nénuphar II.<-dd-> *vt* matelasser
**padded** *adj* matelassé(e); (*cell*) capitonné(e); (*bra*) rembourré(e); **~ shoulders** épaulettes *fpl*
**padding** *n* ❶ (*material*) rembourrage *m* ❷ (*protecting material*) protections *fpl* ❸ (*adding information*) remplissage *m*
**paddle¹** ['pæd·l] I. *n* ❶ (*oar*) pagaie *f* ❷ NAUT pale *f* II. *vt* ❶ (*row*) pagayer ❷ *inf* (*spank*) donner la fessée à ▶ **to ~ one's own canoe** diriger seul sa barque III. *vi* (*row*) pagayer
**paddle²** ['pæd·l] I. *n* promenade *f* dans l'eau; **to go for a ~** aller barboter dans l'eau II. *vi* patauger
**paddling pool** *n* pataugeoire *f*
**padlock** ['pæd·lɑk] I. *n* cadenas *m* II. *vt* cadenasser
**page¹** [peɪdʒ] *n* ❶ (*one sheet of paper*) a. *fig* page *f;* **front ~** première page *f* ❷ COMPUT page *f;* **home ~** (*on site*) page *f* d'accueil; (*individual*) page *f* personnelle; **to visit a ~** aller voir une page
**page²** [peɪdʒ] I. *n* (*attendant*) page *m* II. *vt* ❶ (*over loudspeaker*) appeler ❷ (*by pager*) envoyer un message à
**pageant** ['pædʒ·ənt] *n* ❶ (*historical show*) reconstitution *f* historique

❷ (*show*) spectacle *m* pompeux; **beauty ~** concours *m* de beauté
**pager** *n* alphapage® *m*
**paid** [peɪd] I. *pt, pp* of **pay** II. *adj* **~ vacation** congés *mpl* payés
**pain** [peɪn] I. *n* ❶ (*physical suffering*) douleur *f;* **to be in ~** souffrir; **to double up in ~** se tordre de douleur ❷ (*mental suffering*) souffrance *f* ❸ *pl* (*great care*) peine *f;* **to go to** [*o* **take**] **great ~s to** +*infin* se donner beaucoup de peine pour +*infin* ▶ **to be a ~** (**in the neck**) *inf* être casse-pieds II. *vt* **it ~s sb to** +*infin* cela fait de la peine à qn de +*infin*
**painful** *adj* ❶ (*causing physical pain*) douloureux(-euse); (*death*) pénible ❷ (*upsetting, embarrassing*) pénible
**painkiller** *n* analgésique *m*
**painless** *adj* ❶ (*not painful*) indolore ❷ *fig* facile
**painstaking** ['peɪnz·teɪ·kɪŋ] *adj* méticuleux(-euse)
**paint** [peɪnt] I. *n* a. *pej* peinture *f;* **oil ~s** couleurs à l'huile II. *vi* peindre III. *vt* ❶ (*put color on*) peindre ❷ *pej* (*apply make-up*) peinturlurer ❸ (*conceal with paint*) **to ~ sth out** [*o* **over**], **to ~ out** [*o* **over**] **sth** couvrir qc de peinture ❹ (*describe*) dépeindre; **to ~ a grim/rosy picture of sth** dresser un portrait sombre/rose de qc ▶ **to ~ the town red** faire la fête
**paintbrush** *n* pinceau *m*
**painter¹** *n* peintre *mf*
**painter²** *n* amarre *f*
**painting** *n* ❶ (*activity*) peinture *f* ❷ (*picture*) tableau *m*
**paint stripper** *n* décapant *m*
**pair** [per] *n* ❶ (*two*) paire *f;* **a ~ of pants** un pantalon; **in ~s** par deux ❷ (*couple*) couple *m;* **you're a fine ~!** vous faites la paire! ▶ **I've only got one ~ of hands** je n'ai que deux mains
◆ **pair off** I. *vi* former un couple; **to ~ with sb** se mettre avec qn II. *vt* **to pair sb off with sb** mettre qn avec qn
**pajamas** [pə·ˈdʒɑ·məz] *npl* pyjama *m*
**Pakistan** ['pæk·ɪ·stæn] *n* le Pakistan

P

**Pakistani I.** *adj* pakistanais(e) **II.** *n* Pakistanais(e) *m(f)*

**palace** ['pæl·əs] *n* palais *m*

**pale** [peɪl] **I.** *adj* pâle **II.** *vi* blêmir; **to ~ in comparison with sth** ne pas soutenir la comparaison avec qc; **to ~ into insignificance** perdre toute importance

**Palestine** ['pæl·ə·staɪn] *n* la Palestine

**Palestinian I.** *adj* palestinien(ne) **II.** *n* Palestinien(ne) *m(f)*

**palm** [pam] **I.** *n* paume *f*; **to read sb's ~** lire les lignes de la main de qn **II.** *vt* dissimuler (dans sa main)

◆ **palm off** *vt* **to palm sth off on sb** refiler qc à qn; **to palm sth off as sth** faire passer qc pour qc

**palm (tree)** *n* palmier *m*; **~ leaf** feuille *f* de palmier

**paltry** ['pɔl·tri] <-ier, -iest> *adj* ① (*small and worth little*) dérisoire ② (*of poor quality*) misérable

**pamphlet** ['pæm·flɪt] *n* pamphlet *m*

**pan¹** [pæn] **I.** *n* ① (*saucepan*) casserole *f*; **frying ~** poêle *f* ② (*container for oven*) plat *m*; (*for cakes*) moule *m* **II.** *vt inf* (*criticize*) démolir **III.** *vi* **to ~ for gold** faire de l'orpaillage

◆ **pan out** *vi* (*happen*) se passer; **to ~ all right** s'arranger

**pan²** [pæn] CINE **I.** *vi* faire un panoramique **II.** *vt* (*camera*) panoramiquer

**pancake** ['pæn·keɪk] *n* crêpe *f*

**panda** ['pæn·də] *n* panda *m*

**pandemonium** [ˌpæn·də·'mou·ni·əm] *n* charivari *m*

**pane** [peɪn] *n* vitre *f*

**panic** ['pæn·ɪk] **I.** *n* panique *f* **II.** <-ck-> *vi* ① (*lose control*) **to ~ about sth** paniquer à cause de qc ② (*cause quick thoughtless action*) s'affoler **III.** *vt* affoler; **to ~ sb into doing sth** précipiter qn à faire qc **IV.** *adj* (*decision, measures*) dicté par la panique; **~ buying** stockage *m*; **~ selling** vente *d'actions* effectuée sous l'effet de la panique

**panic attack** *n* PSYCH crise *f* de panique

**panorama** [ˌpæn·ə·'ræm·ə] *n* panorama *m*

**pansy** ['pæn·zi] <-sies> *n* ① (*small garden flower*) pensée *f* ② *pej, sl* (*effeminate man*) tapette *f*; (*wimp*) mauviette *f*

**pant** [pænt] **I.** *vi* haleter; **to ~ for breath** chercher son souffle **II.** *vt* dire en haletant **III.** *n* halètement *m*

**panties** ['pæn·t̬iz] *npl* culotte *f*

**pantomime** ['pæn·tə·maɪm] *n* pantomime *f*

**pantry** ['pæn·tri] <-tries> *n* placard *m* à provisions

**pants** *npl* FASHION pantalon *m* ▶ **to beat the ~ off sb** *inf* flanquer une rossée à qn; **to scare the ~ off sb** *inf* faire une peur bleue à qn; **to be caught with one's ~ down** *inf* être pris au dépourvu

**pantyhose** *npl* collant *m*

**panty liner** *n* protège-slip *m*

**paper** ['peɪ·pər] **I.** *n* ① (*writing material*) papier *m*; **to commit sth to ~** coucher qc par écrit; **on ~** en théorie ② (*newspaper*) journal *m*; **daily ~** quotidien *m* ③ UNIV (*by student*) exposé *m*; (*at conference, in review*) papier *m* ④ (*official documents in general*) document *m*; **~s** pièces *fpl*; (*for identity*) papiers *mpl* (d'identité) ⑤ (*wallpaper*) papier *m* peint **II.** *vt* tapisser

**paperback** *n* livre *m* de poche; **~ edition** édition *f* de poche

**paper bag** *n* sac *m* en papier

**paper boy** *n* livreur *m* de journaux

**paper clip** *n* trombone *m*

**paper cup** *n* gobelet *m* en papier

**paperweight** *n* presse-papiers *m*

**paperwork** *n* paperasserie *f*

**papier-mâché** [ˌpeɪ·pər·mə·'ʃeɪ] *n* carton-pâte *m*

**paprika** [pæp·'ri·kə] *n* paprika *m*

**par** [par] **I.** *n* ① (*equality*) **to be on (a) ~ with sb** être au même niveau que qn; **below ~** en dessous de la moyenne; **to feel up to ~** se sentir bien ② FIN **~ value** valeur *f* nominale; **at/above/below ~** au niveau/au-dessus/au-dessous du pair ③ (*in golf*) par *m* ▶ **that's ~ the course** *pej* c'est ce à quoi il faut s'attendre **II.** *vt* (*in golf: hole, course*) faire un par

**parachute** ['per·ə·ʃut] I. *n* parachute *m* II. *vi* descendre en parachute III. *vt* (*person*) parachuter; (*things*) larguer par parachute

**parade** [pə·'reɪd] I. *n* ❶ (*procession*) parade *f* ❷ (*military procession*) défilé *m;* **to be on ~** être à l'exercice ❸ (*inspection of soldiers*) revue *f* II. *vi* défiler III. *vt* ❶ (*exhibit*) afficher ❷ (*show off*) faire étalage de; *fig, pej* étaler; **to ~ one's knowledge** faire étalage de ses connaissances

**paradise** ['per·ə·daɪs] *n* paradis *m*

**paradox** ['per·ə·daks] <-xes> *n* paradoxe *m;* **it is a ~ that** il est paradoxal que +*subj*

**paragraph** ['per·ə·græf] *n* paragraphe *m*

**parallel** ['per·ə·lel] I. *n* ❶ MATH parallèle *f* ❷ *fig* (*comparison*) parallèle *m;* **to draw a ~** établir un parallèle; **without ~** sans pareil ❸ GEO (*degree of latitude*) parallèle *m* ❹ ELEC **in ~** en dérivation II. *adj a. fig* parallèle III. *vt* ❶ (*be parallel to*) *a.* MATH être parallèle à ❷ (*be similar to*) être analogue à ❸ (*be equal to*) égaler IV. *adv* **to run ~ to sth** être parallèle à qc

**parallel bars** *npl* SPORTS barres *fpl* parallèles

**Paralympic Games** *n* Jeux *mpl* Paralympiques

**Paralympics** [ˌpær·ə·'lɪm·pɪks] *n* Paralympiques *mpl*

**paralysis** [pə·'ræl·ə·sɪs] <-yses> *n* paralysie *f*

**paralytic** [ˌper·ə·'lɪt·ɪk] I. *adj* ❶ (*with paralysis*) paralytique ❷ *inf* (*completely drunk and incapable*) ivre mort(e) II. *n* paralytique *mf*

**paralyze** ['per·əl·aɪz] *vt* ❶ (*render immobile, powerless*) paralyser ❷ (*stupefy*) stupéfier; **to be ~d with fear** être transi de peur

**paramedic** [ˌper·ə·'med·ɪk] *n* auxiliaire *mf* médical(e)

**paramount** ['per·ə·maʊnt] *adj form* suprême; (*importance*) crucial(e)

**paranoid** ['per·ə·nɔɪd] I. *adj* paranoïaque; **don't be so ~!** arrête ta parano! II. *n* paranoïaque *mf*

**paratrooper** *n* parachutiste *mf*

**parboil** ['par·bɔɪl] *vt* faire cuire à demi

**parcel** ['par·səl] I. *n* ❶ (*small package*) colis *m* ❷ (*objects sent in paper*) paquet *m* ❸ (*area of land*) parcelle *f* II. <-l-, -ll-> *vt* empaqueter

**parcel post** *n* service *m* des colis postaux

**pardon** ['par·dən] I. *vt* ❶ (*excuse*) pardonner; **~ the interruption** veuillez pardonner cette interruption ❷ LAW (*prisoner*) gracier II. *interj* ❶ (*said to excuse oneself*) **~ me!** excusez-moi! ❷ (*request to repeat*) **~?** comment? III. *n* ❶ LAW pardon *m* ❷ *form* (*said to request repetition*) **I beg your ~?** pardon?; **I beg your ~!** je vous demande pardon!

**parent** ['per·ənt] *n* père *m*, mère *f;* **~s** parents *mpl;* **single ~** parent *m* célibataire

**parental** *adj* (*authority*) parental(e); (*guidance*) des parents

**parenthesis** [pə·'ren(t)·θə·sɪs] <-theses> *n pl* parenthèse *f*

**parenthood** *n* condition *f* des parents

**parish** ['per·ɪʃ] *n* paroisse *f*

**park** [park] I. *n* parc *m* II. *vt* ❶ AUTO garer ❷ *inf* (*deposit*) déposer ❸ *inf* (*sit down*) **to ~ oneself** s'installer III. *vi* se garer

**park-and-ride** *n* parking *m* relais

**parking** *n* ❶ AUTO stationnement *m* ❷ (*space to park*) place *f*

**parking area** *n* aire *f* de stationnement

**parking lot** *n* parking *m*, stationnement *m Québec*

**parking meter** *n* parcmètre *m*

**parking space** *n* place *f* de stationnement

**parking ticket** *n* contravention *f*

**park ranger** *n* gardien *m* de parc

**parkway** *n* grande voie *f* de communication

**parliament** ['par·lə·mənt] *n* parlement *m*

**parrot** ['per·ət] I. *n* perroquet *m* II. *vt*

*pej* répéter comme un perroquet; **to ~ sb** répéter ce que dit qn

**parsley** ['par·sli] *n* persil *m*

**parsnip** ['par·snɪp] *n* panais *m*

**part** [part] **I.** *n* ❶ (*not the whole*) partie *f*; **the best ~ of the day** le meilleur moment de la journée; **~ of growing up is ...** grandir ça veut dire aussi ...; **in large ~** en majeure partie; **for the most ~** pour la plupart ❷ (*component of machine*) pièce *f* ❸ (*area, region*) région *f*; **in these ~s** par ici ❹ (*measure*) mesure *f* ❺ (*role, involvement*) participation *f*; **to want no ~ in sth** ne pas vouloir se mêler de qc; **for my ~** en ce qui me concerne ❻ (*episode in media serial*) épisode *m* ❼ CINE, THEAT (*character*) rôle *m*; MUS partie *f* ❽ (*parting of hair*) raie *f*, ligne *f* des cheveux *Belgique* ▸ **to become ~ of the <u>furniture</u>** faire partie du décor; **to be ~ and <u>parcel</u> of sth** faire partie intégrante de qc; **to <u>dress</u> the ~** s'habiller de façon appropriée **II.** *adv* en partie; **~ Irish, ~ American** un peu irlandais un peu américain **III.** *vt* ❶ (*divide, separate*) séparer; (*curtains*) entrouvrir; **to ~ company from sb** se séparer de qn; **to ~ one's hair** se faire une raie ❷ (*move apart*) écarter **IV.** *vi* se diviser; (*curtains*) s'entrouvrir; (*people*) se quitter; **to ~ from sb/sth** quitter qn/qc; **to ~ with sb/sth** se séparer de qn/qc; **to ~ on good/bad terms** partir en bons/mauvais termes; **to ~ with one's money** *inf* débourser de l'argent

**partial** ['par·ʃəl] *adj* ❶ (*only in part*) partiel(le) ❷ (*biased*) partial(e) ❸ (*fond of*) **to be ~ to sth** avoir un faible pour qc

**partially** *adv* partiellement; (*cooked*) en partie; **to be ~ blind** être malvoyant

**participant** [par·tɪs·ə·pənt] *n* participant(e) *m(f)*

**participate** [par·tɪs·ə·peɪt] *vi* participer; **to ~ in sth** prendre part à qc

**participation** *n* participation *f*

**participle** ['par·tɪ·sɪ·pl] *n* participe *m*

**particle** ['par·tə·kl] *n* ❶ (*small amount of matter*) particule *f* ❷ (*the tiniest quantity*) quantité *f* infime

**particular** [pər·tɪk·jə·lər] **I.** *adj* ❶ (*indicating sth individual*) particulier(-ère); (*reason*) précis(e); **that ~ day** ce jour-là; **this passage is of ~ interest** ce passage est particulièrement intéressant; **in ~** en particulier; **nothing (in) ~** rien de spécial ❷ (*demanding, fussy, meticulous*) exigeant(e); **to be very ~ about sth** être très tatillon au sujet de qc; **to be ~ about one's appearance** soigner sa tenue **II.** *n pl, form* détails *mpl*

**particularly** *adv* particulièrement

**particulate filter** *n* filtre *m* à particules; **diesel ~** filtre *m* à particules diesel

**parting** ['par·tɪŋ] *n* séparation *f*; **~ words** mots *mpl* d'adieu

**partition** [par·tɪʃ·ən] **I.** *n* ❶ (*structural division in building*) cloison *f* ❷ COMPUT partition *f* ❸ (*division: of country*) partition *f* **II.** *vt* ❶ (*divide buildings, rooms*) cloisonner; **to ~ sth off** séparer qc par une cloison ❷ (*divide countries into nations*) diviser

**partly** ['part·li] *adv* en partie

**partner** ['part·nər] **I.** *n* ❶ (*part owner of company*) associé(e) *m(f)* ❷ (*accomplice*) complice *mf*; **~ in crime** complice ❸ (*in a couple*) compagnon, compagne *m, f* ❹ (*in game, project*) partenaire *mf* **II.** *vt* (*for game, dance, project*) être le/la partenaire de

**partnership** ['part·nər·ʃɪp] *n* ❶ *no pl* (*condition*) partenariat *m* ❷ (*relationship*) **domestic ~** PACS *m*

**part of speech** *n* partie *f* de discours

**part payment** *n* règlement *m* partiel

**part-time** *adj, adv* à temps partiel

**party** ['par·ti] **I.** *n* <-ties> ❶ (*social gathering*) fête *f* ❷ (*evening gathering*) soirée *f* ❸ (*reception*) réception *f* ❹ (*political group*) parti *m* ❺ (*group of visitors*) groupe *m* ❻ (*side in lawsuit, contract*) partie *f*; **the guilty ~ hasn't been found** le coupable en question n'a pas été trouvé; **to be a ~ to a crime** être complice d'un crime **II.** <-ie-> *vi* faire la fête

**P**

**pass** [pæs] I. <-es> n ❶ (*mountain road*) col m ❷ SPORTS (*transfer of a ball*) passe f ❸ (*movement*) ~ **of the hand** geste m de la main ❹ (*sexual advances, overture*) avance f; **to make a ~ at sb** faire des avances à qn ❺ (*authorization permitting entry*) laissez-passer m inv; (*for public transport*) titre m de transport; **bus ~** abonnement m pour le bus ❻ SCHOOL (*permit to leave class*) permission f ❼ (*predicament, difficult state*) passe f II. vt ❶ (*go past*) passer devant; AUTO dépasser ❷ (*exceed: certain point*) dépasser ❸ (*hand to*) **to ~ sth to sb** passer qc à qn; **to ~ sth around** faire passer qc ❹ (*accept*) approuver; (*student*) faire passer ❺ SPORTS (*transfer to another player*) passer ❻ (*be successful in: exam, test*) réussir ❼ (*occupy*) passer; **to ~ the time** passer le temps ❽ POL (*officially approve: bill, law*) adopter ❾ (*utter, pronounce*) émettre; (*a comment, remark*) faire; **to ~ judgment on sb/sth** émettre un jugement sur qn/qc ❿ form MED (*excrete*) **to ~ urine** [*o water*] uriner; **to ~ feces** aller à la selle; **to ~ gas** inf péter ⓫ **to ~ the buck to sb/sth** pej, inf rejeter la responsabilité sur qn/qc III. vi ❶ (*move by, go away*) passer; **to ~ unnoticed** passer inaperçu; **to ~ across** sth traverser qc ❷ (*overtake*) dépasser ❸ (*transfer*) **to ~ from sth to sth** passer de qc à qc; **to ~ from generation to generation** passer de génération en génération ❹ SPORTS (*transfer ball*) faire une passe ❺ SCHOOL (*qualify*) être reçu(e) ❻ (*obtain majority approval: motion, resolution*) passer ❼ (*elapse: hours, evening, day*) passer; **to ~ on a question** passer sur une question ❾ (*enter*) passer; **to let a comment ~** laisser passer un commentaire; **to ~ into** sth passer dans qc ❿ (*take place*) se passer ⓫ (*disappear*) disparaître

◆**pass away** I. vi ❶ (*die*) décéder ❷ (*gradually fade*) disparaître II. vt (*time, hours*) passer

◆**pass by** I. vi ❶ (*elapse*) passer; **time passes by** le temps s'écoule ❷ (*go past*) passer (à côté) II. vt passer devant; **life passes sb by** qn passe à côté de la vie

◆**pass down** vt passer; (*songs, traditions*) transmettre; **to pass sth down from sb to sb** passer qc de qn à qn

◆**pass off** vt **to pass sth/sb off as sb/ sth** faire passer qn/qc pour qn/qc; **pass oneself off as sb/sth** se faire passer pour qn/qc

◆**pass on** I. vi (*die of natural cause*) décéder II. vt ❶ (*give after getting: information, virus, tips*) transmettre; **to pass sth on to sb** transmettre qc à qn ❷ (*hand down: stories, traditions, clothes*) transmettre ❸ ECON (*costs*) répercuter; **to be passed on to sb** se répercuter sur qn ❹ (*give to next person*) faire passer

◆**pass out** I. vi (*become unconscious*) perdre connaissance II. vt (*distribute*) distribuer

◆**pass over** vt **to pass sb over** ignorer qn; **to ~ sth** passer qc sous silence; **to be passed over for promotion** ne pas se faire accorder de promotion

◆**pass through** I. vt a. fig traverser II. vi passer; (*bullet*) traverser

◆**pass up** vt laisser passer

**passage** ['pæsɪdʒ] n ❶ (*act or process of moving through*) a. fig passage m; ~ **of time** écoulement m du temps ❷ (*journey*) voyage m; NAUT traversée f ❸ (*corridor*) passage m ❹ (*path*) corridor m ❺ (*duct*) a. MED conduit m ❻ LIT, MUS (*excerpt*) passage m ❼ (*transition*) passage m ❽ POL (*of a bill*) adoption f

**passageway** n passage m

**passbook** n livret m de caisse d'épargne

**passenger** ['pæsˑ ᵊnˑdʒər] n passager, -ère m, f; (*in public transportation*) voyageur, -euse m, f

**passenger train** n train m de voyageurs

**passer-by** <passers-by> n passant(e) m(f)

**passing** I. adj ❶ (*going past*) qui passe; **with each ~ day** à chaque jour qui pas-

P

se ❷ (*brief, fleeting, short-lived*) passager(-ère); (*glance*) furtif(-ive) ❸ (*unimportant, casual: remark, thought*) en passant **II.** n ❶ (*passage*) passage m; (*of time*) écoulement m ❷ SPORTS (*ball transfer skill*) passe f ❸ (*end*) mort f; *fig* fin f

**passing place** n voie f de dédoublement

**passion** ['pæʃ·ən] n passion f; **to have a ~ for sth** avoir la passion de qc; **to have a ~ for sb** aimer qn passionnément; **to have a ~ for doing sth** adorer faire qc; **crime of ~** crime m passionnel; **to hate sb/sth with a ~** avoir horreur de qn/qc

**passionate** ['pæʃ·ə·nɪt] adj passionné(e); (*relationship, drama*) passionnel(le)

**passive** ['pæs·ɪv] **I.** n LING passif m **II.** adj a. LING passif(-ive); **the ~ voice** la forme passive

**passport** ['pæs·pɔrt] n passeport m

**password** n a. COMPUT mot m de passe

**past** [pæst] **I.** n a. LING passé m; **to be a thing of the ~** appartenir au passé; **sb with a ~** qn au passé chargé **II.** adj ❶ (*being now over*) passé(e); **the ~ week** la semaine dernière ❷ LING **~ tense** temps m du passé; **simple ~** prétérit m; **~ perfect** plus-que-parfait m; **~ participle** participe m passé ❸ (*bygone*) révolu(e); **in years ~** [o **~ years**] autrefois ❹ (*former*) ancien(ne); **Eve's ~ husband** l'ex-mari m d'Eve **III.** prep ❶ (*temporal*) plus de; **ten/a quarter ~ two** deux heures dix/et quart; **it's ~ 2 o'clock** il est 2 h passées; **to be ~ thirty** avoir plus de trente ans ❷ (*spatial*) plus loin que; **it's just ~ sth** c'est juste un peu plus loin que qc ❸ (*after*) **when we've gotten ~ the exams** après les examens; **he's ~ that** *iron, pej* il a passé l'âge ❹ (*beyond*) au-delà de; **to be ~ the expiration date** être en périmé; **I'm ~ caring** ça m'est égal; **I wouldn't put it ~ them** ils en sont bien capables **IV.** adv devant; **to run/swim ~** passer en courant/à la nage

**pasta** ['pas·tə] n pâtes fpl

**paste**[1] [peɪst] **I.** n ❶ (*sticky mixture*) pâte f ❷ (*adhesive substance*) colle f ❸ CULIN (*mixture*) pâte f; **tomato ~** concentré m de tomates; **anchovy ~** pâte d'anchois ❹ (*glass in jewelry*) pâte f de verre **II.** vt ❶ (*fasten, fix*) coller ❷ COMPUT (*insert into document*) coller; **to cut and ~** couper-coller

**paste**[2] [peɪst] vt *inf* (*beat easily, thrash*) donner une raclée à

**pasteurize** ['pæs·tʃə·raɪz] vt pasteuriser

**pastime** ['pæs·taɪm] n passe-temps m

**pastry** ['peɪ·stri] <-ries> n ❶ CULIN (*cake dough*) pâte f ❷ CULIN (*cake*) pâtisserie f

**pastry chef** n pâtissier, -ière m, f

**pastureland** n pâturages mpl

**pasty** ['peɪ·sti] <-ier, -iest> adj *pej* pâteux(-euse); (*skin, complexion*) terreux(-euse)

**pat**[1] [pæt] **I.** <-tt-> vt (*tap*) tapoter; **to ~ sb on the back** *fig* féliciter qn **II.** n ❶ (*gentle stroke, pat*) petite tape f; **to give sb/sth a ~** donner une petite tape à qn/qc ❷ (*little quantity: of butter*) plaquette f

**pat**[2] [pæt] **I.** adv **to have an answer down ~** avoir une réponse toute prête **II.** adj facile; **~ answer** réponse f toute prête

**patch** [pætʃ] **I.** n ❶ (*repair piece*) pièce f; (*for tire*) rustine f ❷ MED (*piece of fabric*) patch m ❸ (*cover for eye*) cache m ❹ (*small area*) pièce f; **~ of fog** nappe f de brouillard; **~ of ice** plaque f de gel; **a ~ of blue sky** un morceau de ciel bleu ❺ *inf* (*phase*) période f; **to go through a bad ~** passer par un moment difficile ❻ COMPUT (*software update*) rustine® f **II.** vt (*cover, reinforce, sew up*) rapiécer; **to ~ a tire** poser une rustine à une roue

◆**patch up** vt ❶ (*renovate, restore, mend*) rafistoler ❷ *fig* (*settle: differences*) régler; **they've patched things up between them** ils se sont raccommodés

**patchy** ['pætʃ·i] <-ier, -iest> adj (quality, performance) inégal(e)

**paternal** [pə·'tɜr·n³l] adj paternel(le)

**paternity** [pə·'tɜr·nə·t̮i] n a. fig, form paternité f

**paternity leave** n congé m de paternité

**path** [pæθ] n ❶ (footway, trail) a. COMPUT chemin m; (of a garden) allée f; **to clear a** ~ dégager une voie ❷ (direction) trajet m; (of a bullet, missile) trajectoire f; (of a storm) passage m; **to block somebody's** ~ bloquer le passage de qn ❸ fig voie f; **the** ~ **of his career** son itinéraire m de carrière; ~ **success** chemin m de la gloire

**pathetic** [pə·'θet̮·ɪk] adj ❶ (sad) pathétique ❷ (not good) lamentable

**pathological** adj (liar) pathologique

**pathway** ['pæθ·weɪ] n a. fig sentier m

**patience** ['peɪ·ʃ³n(t)s] n patience f; **to lose one's** ~ perdre patience; **to try sb's** ~ mettre la patience de qn à l'épreuve

**patient** I. adj patient(e); **to be** ~ **with sb** être patient avec qn II. n MED patient(e) m(f)

**patio** ['pæt̮·i·oʊ] <-s> n patio m

**patriotic** adj patriotique; (person) patriote

**patriotism** n patriotisme m

**patrol** [pə·'troʊl] I. <-ll-> vi patrouiller II. <-ll-> vt patrouiller dans III. n patrouille f

**patrol car** n voiture f de police

**patrolman** n agent m de police (en patrouille)

**patronizing** adj pej condescendant(e)

**pattern** I. n ❶ (identifiable structure) schéma m; ~**s of activity/behavior** modes mpl d'activité/de comportement ❷ ART (design, motif) motif m; **chevron** ~ chevron m ❸ FASHION (paper guide for dressmaking) patron m ❹ (sample of textiles, paper) échantillon m ❺ (example, model, norm) modèle m II. vt ❶ (model) modeler ❷ (decorate) orner

**pause** [pɔz] I. n pause f ▸ **to give sb** ~ **form** donner à réfléchir à qn II. vi faire une pause; **to** ~ **for thought** prendre une pause pour réfléchir

**pave** [peɪv] vt a. fig paver; **to be** ~**d with sth** être pavé de qc; **to** ~ **the way for sth** ouvrir la voie à qc

**pavement** n chaussée f

**pavilion** [pə·'vɪl·jən] n pavillon m

**paw** [pɔ] I. n a. iron, a. inf patte f II. vt ❶ (strike with the paw) donner un coup de patte à ❷ pej, inf (touch in an offensive way) tripoter III. vi donner des coups de pattes

**pawn**[1] I. vt **to** ~ **sth** mettre qc en gage II. n gage m; **to be in** ~ être en gage

**pawn**[2] n GAMES a. fig pion m

**pawnbroker** n prêteur, -euse m, f sur gages

**pawnshop** n mont-de-piété m

**pay** [peɪ] I. <paid, paid> vt ❶ (give money) payer, **to** ~ **sb for sth** payer qn pour qc; **to** ~ **cash** payer en liquide; **to** ~ **a refund** effectuer un remboursement; **to** ~ **sb to** +infin payer qn pour +infin; **to** ~ **a salary** verser un salaire; **to** ~ **a loan** rembourser un prêt; **to** ~ **one's way** payer sa part; **to** ~ **ten dollars an hour** payer dix dollars de l'heure; **to** ~ **the price** fig payer le prix ❷ (benefit, be worthwhile, repay) rapporter; **to** ~ **dividends** fig porter ses fruits ❸ (give) **to** ~ **attention to sb/sth** prêter attention à qn/qc; **to** ~ **sb a compliment** faire un compliment à qn; **to** ~ **homage to sb/sth** rendre hommage à qn/qc; **to** ~ **one's respects to sb** présenter ses respects à qn II. <paid, paid> vi ❶ (settle, recompense) payer; **to** ~ **by cash** payer en liquide; **to** ~ **by check/credit card** payer par chèque/carte de crédit ❷ (suffer) payer; **to** ~ **with one's life** fig payer de sa vie ❸ (benefit, be worthwhile) rapporter; **it** ~**s to** +infin ça rapporte de +infin; **it doesn't** ~ **to** +infin ce n'est pas rentable de +infin ▸ **to** ~ **through the nose for sth** inf payer le prix fort pour qc III. n paie f; **to be in the** ~ **of sb/sth** être à la solde de qn/qc

◆**pay back** vt ❶ (return money) rem-

P

bourser; **to pay sb sth back** rembourser qc à qn ❷ (*get revenge*) **to pay sb back for sth** faire payer qc à qn
◆ **pay off I.** *vt* ❶ (*repay: debt, creditor*) rembourser ❷ (*pay before laying off*) licencier **II.** *vi fig* payer
◆ **pay out I.** *vt* ❶ (*expend, spend money*) payer ❷ (*unwind: rope*) laisser filer **II.** *vi* payer
◆ **pay up** *vi* payer

**payable** *adj* payable; ~ **to sb/sth** à la charge de qn/qc; **to make a check ~ to sb/sth** faire un chèque à l'ordre de qn/qc

**pay dirt** *n* ❶ MIN filon *m* ❷ *inf* (*discovery*) **to hit ~** découvrir un filon

**payee** [peɪˈiː] *n* bénéficiaire *mf*

**payer** *n* payeur, -euse *m, f*

**paying** *adj* ❶ (*who pays*) payant(e) ❷ (*profitable*) rentable; **a ~ proposition** une bonne affaire

**payment** *n* ❶ (*sum paid*) paiement *m* ❷ (*repayment*) remboursement *m*; **30 easy ~s** 30 versements *mpl* par traites ❸ (*reward*) récompense *f*

**payoff** *n* ❶ (*full payment*) indemnités *fpl* (de départ) ❷ *inf* (*positive result*) fruit *m* ❸ (*profit on a bet*) récompense *f* ❹ *inf* (*bribe*) pot-de-vin *m*; **to receive a ~ from sb** percevoir un pot-de-vin de qn

**pay-per-click** *n* COMPUT pay-per-click *m inv*

**pay-per-view** *n* TV pay-per-view *m* (*paiement à la séance*)

**payslip** *n* feuille *f* de paie

**pay-TV** *n* télévision *f* à la carte

**PC** [ˌpiˈsi] **I.** *n* COMPUT *abbr of* **Personal Computer** PC *m* **II.** *adj abbr of* **politically correct** politiquement correct(e)

**PE** [ˌpiˈi] *n abbr of* **physical education** EPS *f*

**pea** [pi] *n* petit pois *m* ▶ **to be like two ~s in a pod** se ressembler comme deux gouttes d'eau

**peace** [pis] *n a. fig* paix *f*; ~ **activist** activiste *mf* pacifiste; **to make ~** faire la paix; **to rest in ~** reposer en paix; **to be at ~ with the world** ne pas avoir le

moindre souci; **to keep/disturb the ~** veiller à/troubler l'ordre public; **to make one's ~ with sb** faire la paix avec qn; **to leave sb/sth in ~** laisser qn/qc en paix ▶ **to hold one's ~** garder le silence

**peacekeeping I.** *n* pacification *f* **II.** *adj* de pacification; ~ **force** force *f* de maintien de la paix

**peacetime** *n* temps *m* de paix

**peach** [pitʃ] **I.** <-es> *n* ❶ (*sweet, yellow fruit*) pêche *f*; ~ **tree** pêcher *m* ❷ *inf* (*nice thing*) chou(te) *m(f)*; **a ~ of an idea** une super idée **II.** *adj* (*color*) pêche *inv*

**peacock** [ˈpiˌkak] *n* paon *m*

**peak** [pik] **I.** *n* ❶ (*mountain top*) pic *m*; **to reach the ~** atteindre le sommet ❷ (*climax*) sommet *m*; (*in a period*) moment *m* le plus fort; (*of a trend*) apogée *f* **II.** *vi* (*sb's career*) être à son sommet; (*athlete*) atteindre un record; (*figures, rates, production*) atteindre son niveau maximum **III.** *adj* ❶ (*the busiest*) ~ **hours** heures *fpl* de pointe ❷ (*the best, highest: speed, capacity*) maximal(e); (*demand*) record; (*season*) haut(e); **in ~ condition** dans le meilleur état; **during ~ periods** pendant les périodes de pointe

**peanut** [ˈpiˌnʌt] *n* cacahuète *f*, pinotte *f* Québec; ~ **oil/butter** huile *f*/beurre *m* de cacahuètes ▶ **to pay ~s** payer des clopinettes

**pear** [per] *n* poire *f*; ~ **tree** poirier *m*

**pearl** [pɜrl] *n a. fig* perle *f*; **to be a (real) ~** être une perle (fine); ~ **necklace** collier *m* de perles; **cultured ~s** perles de culture; ~ **button** bouton *m* de nacre; ~**s of wisdom** *fig* propos *mpl* édifiants

**peasant** [ˈpezˈənt] *n* paysan(ne) *m(f)*

**peat moss** *n* sphaigne *f*

**pebble** [ˈpebˌl] *n* galet *m*

**peck** [pek] **I.** *n* ❶ (*bite made by a beak*) coup *m* de bec ❷ (*quick kiss*) bécot *m* **II.** *vt* ❶ (*bite with a beak*) becqueter ❷ (*strike with beak*) donner un coup de bec à; **to ~ holes in sth** faire des trous à coups de bec dans qc ❸ (*kiss quickly*)

**P**

bécoter **III.** *vi* **❶** (*bite with one's beak*) becqueter; **to ~ at sth** becqueter qc **❷** (*nibble*) picorer; **to ~ at one's food** *inf* picorer sa nourriture

**peckish** ['pek·ɪʃ] *adj* irascible

**peculiar** [pɪ·kjul·jər] *adj* **❶** (*strange, unusual*) étrange **❷** (*belonging to, special*) particulier(-ère); **of ~ interest** d'un intérêt particulier

**peculiarly** *adv* **❶** (*strangely*) étrangement **❷** (*belonging to, especially*) particulièrement

**pedal** ['ped·əl] **I.** *n* pédale *f* **II.** <-l-, -ll-> *vi* pédaler **III.** *vt* **to ~ a bike** faire du vélo

**pedal boat** *n* pédalo *m*

**pedestal** ['ped·ɪ·stəl] *n* piédestal *m* ▶ **to knock sb off his/her ~** faire tomber qn de son piédestal

**pedestrian I.** *n* piéton(ne) *m(f)* **II.** *adj* **❶** (*for walkers*) piéton(ne) **❷** *form* (*uninteresting, dull*) prosaïque

**pedestrian crossing** *n* passage *m* piéton

**pediatric** [ˌpi·di·'æt·rɪk] *adj* pédiatrique

**pediatrician** *n* MED pédiatre *mf*

**pedigree** ['ped·ɪ·gri] *n* **❶** (*genealogy: of an animal*) pedigree *m;* (*of a person*) ascendance *f;* **~ dog** chien *m* de race **❷** (*educational, professional background*) antécédents *mpl* **❸** (*history, background*) histoire *f*

**pee** [pi] *inf* **I.** *n* pipi *m;* **to take a ~** faire pipi; **to go ~** *childspeak* aller faire pipi **II.** *vi* faire pipi **III.** *vt* (*one's pants*) mouiller

**peek** [pik] **I.** *n* coup *m* d'œil **II.** *vi* jeter un coup d'œil furtif

**peel** [pil] **I.** *n* pelure *f* **II.** *vt* peler; (*fruit, vegetables*) éplucher; **to ~ wallpaper** décoller le papier peint; **to ~ the wrapping from sth** enlever l'emballage de qc ▶ **to keep one's eyes ~ed for sth** *inf* faire gaffe à qc **III.** *vi* (*skin*) peler; (*paint*) s'écailler; (*wallpaper*) se décoller

◆ **peel off I.** *vt* enlever; **to ~ an adhesive strip** décoller un ruban adhésif; **to peel the paper off sth** enlever le papier de qc; **to ~ wallpaper** décoller le papier peint **II.** *vi* **❶** (*come off*) se décoller **❷** (*veer away: car, motorcycle*) s'écarter

**peeler** *n* éplucheur *m*

**peelings** *npl* épluchures *fpl*

**peep**[1] [pip] **I.** *n* **❶** (*answer, utterance*) bruit *m;* **to not raise a ~** ne pas souffler mot; **to not give a ~** ne pas broncher *inf;* **one more ~ out of you** encore un mot de ta/votre part **❷** (*tiny bird sound*) pépiement *m;* **to make a ~** pépier **II.** *vi* pépier

**peep**[2] [pip] **I.** *n* coup *m* d'œil; **to have a ~ at sth** regarder furtivement qc; **to get a ~ at sth** voir qc rapidement **II.** *vi* **❶** (*look quickly, look secretly*) **to ~ at sb/sth** jeter un coup d'œil sur qn/qc; **to ~ into/through sth** jeter un coup d'œil à l'intérieur de/à travers qc **❷** (*appear, come partly out*) sortir

**peep show** *n* peep-show *m*

**peer**[1] [pɪr] *vi* regarder; **to ~ into the distance** scruter au loin

**peer**[2] [pɪr] *n* pair *m;* **~ group** pairs *mpl*

**peg** [peg] **I.** *n* (*small hook*) piquet *m;* (*for clothes*) pince *f* à linge; (*of a violin, guitar*) cheville *f* ▶ **to take** [*o* **bring**] **sb/sth down a ~ or two** remettre qn/qc à sa place **II.** <-gg-> *vt* **❶** (*fasten*) fixer (avec des piquets) **❷** COM (*hold at certain level*) maintenir **❸** *inf* (*categorize*) cataloguer

**Pekin(g)ese** [ˌpi·kɪŋ·'iz] **I.** <-(s)> *n* pékinois *m* **II.** *adj* **~ dog** chien *m* pékinois

**pelican** ['pel·ɪ·kən] *n* pélican *m*

**pelt**[1] [pelt] *n* **❶** (*animal skin*) peau *f* **❷** (*fur*) fourrure *f*

**pelt**[2] [pelt] **I.** *vt* **to ~ sb with sth** bombarder qn de qc; **to ~ sb with insults** couvrir qn d'insultes **II.** *vi* **❶** *impers* (*rain heavily*) **it's ~ing down** il pleut des cordes **❷** (*run, hurry*) courir à toutes jambes; **to ~ across the yard** traverser la cour à toutes jambes **III.** *n* **at full ~** à toute vitesse

**pen**[1] [pen] **I.** *n* **❶** (*writing utensil*) stylo *m;* **to put ~ to paper** écrire; **to write in ~** écrire au stylo **❷** (*quill*) plume *f*

P

▶ **the ~ is <u>mightier</u> than the sword** *prov* la plume est plus tranchante que l'épée II. <-nn-> *vt* (*letter*) écrire

**pen²** [pen] **I.** *n* parc *m*; **pig ~** porcherie *f* II. <-nn-> *vt* parquer

**penalize** ['pi·nəl·aız] *vt* sanctionner

**penalty** ['pen·əl·ti] <-ties> *n* ❶ LAW peine *f* ❷ (*punishment*) pénalité *f* ❸ (*disadvantage*) inconvénient *m* ❹ (*fine, extra charge*) amende *f* ❺ SPORTS penalty *m*

**pencil** ['pen(t)·səl] **I.** *n* ❶ (*writing utensil*) crayon *m*; **in ~** au crayon ❷ (*thin line: of light*) trait *m*; **~-thin** mince comme un fil II. <-l-, -ll-> *vt* écrire au crayon

**pencil case** *n* trousse *f*

**pencil pusher** *n pej, inf* rond-de-cuir *m*

**pencil sharpener** *n* taille-crayon *m*

**pencil skirt** *n* jupe *f* droite

**pendant** ['pen·dənt] *n* pendentif *m*

**penetrate** ['pen·ə·treıt] *vt* pénétrer

**penguin** ['peŋ·gwın] *n* pingouin *m*

**penicillin** [ˌpen·ı·'sıl·ın] *n* pénicilline *f*

**peninsula** [pə·'nın(t)·sə·lə] *n* péninsule *f*

**penis** ['pi·nıs] <-nises *o* -nes> *n* pénis *m*

**penknife** ['pen·naıf] <-knives> *n* canif *m*

**Pennsylvania** [ˌpen(t)·səl·'veı·njə] *n* la Pennsylvanie

**penny** ['pen·i] <-ies> *n* ❶ (*value*) penny *m*; **I don't have a ~ to my name** je suis sans le sou ❷ (*coin*) cent *m* ▶ **a ~ for your <u>thoughts</u>!** à quoi penses-tu?; **to cost (sb) a <u>pretty</u> ~** coûter à qn une jolie somme

**pen pal** *n* correspondant(e) *m(f)*

**pension** ['pen·(t)ʃən] *n* ❶ (*retirement money*) retraite *f*; **to draw** [*o* **collect**] **a ~** toucher une retraite; **to live on a ~** vivre de sa retraite ❷ (*payment*) pension *f*

◆ **pension off** *vt* **to ~ sb, to pension sb off** mettre qn à la retraite

**pensioner** *n* retraité(e) *m(f)*, bénéficiaire *mf* d'une retraite *Suisse*

**pension fund** *n* assurance *f* vieillesse

**pension plan** *n* plan *m* de retraite

**pentagon** ['pen·tə·gan] *n* pentagone *m*; **the Pentagon** le Pentagone

**people** ['pi·pl] **I.** *npl* ❶ (*persons*) gens *mpl o fpl*; **married ~** les gens mariés; **divorced ~** les divorcés; **homeless ~** les sans-abri ❷ (*persons comprising a nation*) peuple *m* ❸ *pl* (*ordinary citizens*) **the ~** le peuple ❹ *pl inf* (*family*) famille *f*; (*associates*) collaborateurs *mpl* II. *vt* **to be ~d by sth** être peuplé de qc

**pepper** ['pep·ər] **I.** *n* ❶ (*hot spice*) poivre *m* ❷ (*vegetable*) **bell ~** poivron *m* II. *vt* ❶ (*add pepper to*) poivrer ❷ (*pelt*) **to ~ sb/sth with sth** assaillir qn/qc de qc; **to ~ sb with bullets** cribler qn de balles; **to be ~ed with sth** être émaillé de qc; **to be ~ed with mistakes** être truffé de fautes

**pepper mill** *n* moulin *m* à poivre

**peppermint** *n* ❶ (*mint plant*) menthe *f* (poivrée) ❷ (*candy*) bonbon *m* à la menthe

**pep talk** *n* **to give (sb) a ~** encourager qn

**per** [pɜr] *prep* par; **$5 ~ pound/hour** 5 dollars la livre/l'heure; **100 miles ~ hour** 160 km à l'heure; **~ cent** pour cent

**per capita** *adj, adv* (*income*) par habitant

**perceivable** *adj* perceptible

**per cent, percent** [pər·'sent] **I.** *n* pour cent *m* II. *adv* pour cent

**perception** [pər·'sep·ʃən] *n* perception *f*

**perch¹** [pɜrtʃ] **I.** <-es> *n* perchoir *m* II. *vi* se percher III. *vt* percher; **to be ~ed somewhere** être perché quelque part; **to ~ oneself on sth** se jucher sur qc

**perch²** [pɜrtʃ] <-(es)> *n* (*fish*) perche *f*

**percussion** [pər·'kʌʃ·ən] **I.** *n* percussion *f*; **to be on ~** être aux percussions II. *adj* (*instrument*) à percussion; (*player, solo*) de percussion

**perfect¹** ['pɜr·fıkt] **I.** *adj* ❶ (*ideal*) parfait(e); **to have a ~ right to +***infin* avoir parfaitement le droit de +*infin*

❷ (*absolute*) véritable; (*silence*) complet(-ète) II. *n* LING parfait *m*

**perfect²** [pɜr·ˈfekt] *vt* perfectionner

**perfection** [pər·ˈfek·ʃən] *n* perfection *f*

**perfectly** *adv* ❶ (*very well*) parfaitement ❷ (*completely*) complètement ❸ (*extremely*) extrêmement

**perforate** [ˈpɜr·fər·eɪt] *vt* perforer

**perform** [pər·ˈfɔrm] I. *vt* ❶ (*act, sing or play in public*) interpréter; (*a play*) jouer; (*a trick, dance*) exécuter ❷ (*do, accomplish*) accomplir; (*function, task*) remplir; (*operation*) procéder à II. *vi* ❶ (*give an artistic performance*) jouer ❷ (*operate, give results: system, machine*) fonctionner; **to ~ well/poorly** (*car, camera, worker*) faire une bonne/mauvaise performance; (*player*) bien/mal jouer; (*company*) avoir de bons/mauvais résultats; **how did she ~ under pressure?** comment a-t-elle travaillé sous la pression?

**performance** [pər·ˈfɔr·mən(t)s] *n* ❶ (*execution on stage, staging*) représentation *f*; (*of an artist, actor*) interprétation *f* ❷ (*show of ability, quality*) a. SPORTS performance *f*; **her ~ on the exams** ses résultats *mpl* aux examens; **we're paid based on ~** nous sommes payés au résultat ❸ (*accomplishing*) exécution *f*; **~ test** test *m* de qualité ❹ *inf* (*fuss*) cirque *m*

**performer** *n* interprète *mf*

**perfume** [ˈpɜr·fjum] I. *n* parfum *m* II. *vt* parfumer

**perhaps** [pər·ˈhæps] *adv* peut-être

**perimeter** [pə·ˈrɪm·ɪ·tər] *n* ❶ (*edge, border*) bordure *f* ❷ (*length of edge*) périmètre *m*

**period** [ˈpɪr·i·əd] I. *n* ❶ (*length of time*) a. GEO, ECON période *f* ❷ (*interval of time*) intervalle *m*; **he's had ~s of unemployment** il a eu des périodes de chômage ❸ (*lesson, class session*) classe *f* ❹ (*distinct stage*) époque *f* ❺ (*menstruation*) règles *fpl*; **to get/have one's ~** avoir ses règles ❻ LING point *m* II. *adj* (*furniture, instruments, drama*) d'époque

**periodic** *adj* périodique

**perishable** *adj* périssable

**perk¹** [pɜrk] *n* (*benefit*) avantage *m*

**perk²** [pɜrk] *vt inf* (*make in percolator, percolate*) passer

◆**perk up** I. *vi* ❶ (*become more lively*) s'animer ❷ (*cheer up*) se ragaillardir ❸ (*increase, recover*) augmenter ❹ (*twitch: ears*) se dresser II. *vt* ❶ (*cheer up*) ranimer ❷ (*make more interesting*) relever ❸ (*cause increase in*) augmenter ❹ (*raise*) a. *fig* relever; **to ~ one's ears** dresser l'oreille

**perm** [pɜrm] I. *n abbr of* **permanent** permanente *f* II. *vt* **to ~ sb's hair** faire une permanente à qn; **to get one's hair ~ed** se faire faire une permanente

**permanent** I. *adj* permanent(e); (*change, closure*) définitif(-ive); (*position*) fixe; (*ink*) indélébile II. *n* permanente *f*

**permission** [pər·ˈmɪʃ·ən] *n* permission *f*; **to ask for ~** demander la permission; **to give ~** donner la permission; **to need ~ from sb to** +*infin* avoir besoin de l'autorisation de qn pour +*infin*

**permit** [ˈpɜr·mɪt, *vb:* pər·ˈmɪt] I. *n* permis *m* II.<-tt-> *vt* permettre; **to ~ sb to** +*infin* autoriser qn à +*infin*; **to ~ oneself sth** se permettre qc III. *vi* permettre; **weather ~ting** si le temps le permet; **if time ~s ...** s'il y a le temps ...

**perpendicular** [ˌpɜr·pən·ˈdɪk·ju·lər] I. *adj* ❶ (*at a 90° angle*) **to be ~ to sth** être perpendiculaire à qc ❷ (*very steep*) abrupt(e) II. *n* perpendiculaire *f*

**perplexed** *adj* perplexe; **to be ~ by sth** être intrigué par qc

**persecute** [ˈpɜr·sɪ·kjut] *vt* ❶ (*subject to hostility*) persécuter ❷ (*harass*) harceler

**persecution** *n* persécution *f*

**persevere** [ˌpɜr·sə·ˈvɪr] *vi* **to ~ in** (**doing**) **sth** persévérer à faire qc

**persist** [pər·ˈsɪst] *vi* ❶ (*continue*) continuer; (*cold, heat, rain*) persister; (*habit, tradition*) perdurer ❷ (*continue despite difficulty*) persister; **to ~ in doing sth** persister à faire qc

P

**persistent** *adj* **①** (*long lasting*) persistant(e); (*difficulties*) perpétuel(le); (*rumor*) ancré(e) **②** (*continuous, constant*) continuel(le); (*demands, rain*) constant(e) **③** (*determined, persevering*) déterminé(e); **to be ~ in sth** être persévérant dans qc

**persnickety** [pər·'snɪk·ə·t̬i] *adj pej* **①** (*overly exact or fussy*) **to be ~ about sth** être pointilleux à propos de qc **②** (*needing extra care*) minutieux(-euse)

**person** ['pɜr·sᵊn] <-s *o* people> *n* personne *f*; **book ~** bibliophile *mf*; **cat/dog ~** amateur *m* de chat/chien; **people ~** personne *f* sociable; **~ of principle** individu *m* à principes; **homeless ~** sans-abri *mf*; **in ~** en personne; **per ~** par personne **②** LING personne *f*

**personal** *adj* **①** (*of a particular person, individual*) personnel(le); (*estate, property*) privé(e); **~ data** coordonnées *fpl* **②** (*direct, done in person: service*) personnel(le); **to give sb/sth ~ attention** s'occuper personnellement de qn/qc; **I like the ~ touch** j'aime bien le côté humain **③** (*private*) privé(e); (*letter*) personnel(le); **~ diary** journal *m* intime **④** (*offensive*) offensant(e); **to get ~** devenir offensant; **(it's) nothing ~!** rien de personnel! **⑤** (*bodily, physical*) physique; (*hygiene*) intime; **his ~ appearance** son apparence *f* **⑥** (*human*) humain(e)

**personal ad** *n* petite annonce *f* personnelle

**personal assistant** *n* assistant(e) *m(f)*

**personal computer** *n* ordinateur *m* personnel

**personality** <-ties> *n* personnalité *f*

**personalize** ['pɜr·sᵊn·ᵊl·aɪz] *vt* (*gift, approach*) personnaliser

**personally** *adv* personnellement; **I didn't mean that ~** je ne visais personne

**personnel** [ˌpɜr·sᵊn·'el] *n* **①** *pl* (*staff, employees*) personnel *m* **②** (*human resources department*) ressources *fpl* humaines

**perspective** [pər·'spek·tɪv] *n* **①** (*viewpoint*) perspective *f*; **to get sth in ~** placer qc dans son contexte; **from a(n) historical ~** d'un point de vue historique; **~ on sth** point *m* de vue sur qc **②** (*method of representation*) perspective *f*; **in ~** en perspective; **out of ~** hors de la perspective

**perspiration** [ˌpɜr·spə·'reɪ·ʃᵊn] *n* transpiration *f*; **dripping with ~** en nage

**perspire** [pər·'spaɪər] *vi* transpirer

**persuade** [pər·'sweɪd] *vt* persuader; **to ~ sb to +infin** convaincre qn de +infin

**persuasion** *n* **①** (*act of convincing*) persuasion *f* **②** (*conviction*) croyance *f*; **to be of (the) Catholic/Protestant ~** être de confession catholique/protestante; **parties of every ~** des partis *mpl* de toutes tendances

**persuasive** *adj* persuasif(-ive); **~ powers** pouvoirs *mpl* de persuasion

**pertinent** ['pɜr·tᵊn·ᵊnt] *adj form* pertinent(e); **to be ~ to sth** avoir un rapport avec qc

**perverse** [pər·'vɜrs] *adj pej* **①** (*deliberately unreasonable, harmful*) pervers(e); (*interest*) malsain(e); (*pride*) mal placé(e) **②** (*sexually deviant*) pervers(e)

**perversion** *n pej* **①** (*abnormal behavior*) perversion *f* **②** (*corruption*) corruption *f*; (*of the truth*) déformation *f*

**pervert** ['pɜr·vɜrt] **I.** *n pej* **①** (*extreme sexual deviant*) pervers(e) *m(f)* **②** (*creepy person*) sale type *m* **II.** *vt* **to ~ sb** pervertir qn; **to ~ sth** déformer qc

**pessimism** ['pes·ə·mɪ·zᵊm] *n* pessimisme *m*

**pessimist** *n* pessimiste *mf*

**pessimistic** *adj* pessimiste

**pest** [pest] *n* **①** (*animal*) animal *m* nuisible; (*insect*) insecte *m* nuisible **②** *inf* (*annoying person*) casse-pieds *mf inv*

**pester** *vt* **to ~ sb for sth** harceler qn pour obtenir qc

**pesticide** ['pes·tə·saɪd] *n* pesticide *m*

**pet** [pet] **I.** *n* **①** (*house animal*) animal *m* domestique **②** *pej* (*favorite person*) chouchou(te) *m(f)* **③** *inf* (*nice or thoughtful person*) ange *m* **II.** *adj*

P

**❶** (*concerning domestic animals: cat*) domestique **❷** (*favorite*) favori(te); **~ peeve** bête *f* noire III. *vt* **❶** (*treat well*) chouchouter **❷** (*cuddle*) peloter

**petal** ['pet·əl] *n* pétale *m*

**peter** ['pi·tər] *vi* **to ~ out** (*food*) s'épuiser; (*trail, track, path*) disparaître; (*conversation, interest*) tarir

**petite** [pə·'tit] *adj* menu(e); **~ clothing** vêtement *m* pour femmes menues

**petition** [pə·'tɪʃ·°n] I. *n* **❶** (*signed document*) pétition *f* **❷** LAW demande *f*; **to file a ~** faire une demande II. *vi* **❶** (*start a petition*) **to ~ about sth** pétitionner pour qc **❷** (*request formally*) **to ~ for sth** faire une requête pour qc; **to ~ for divorce** demander le divorce III. *vt* adresser une pétition à

**petroleum** [pə·'trou·li·əm] *n* pétrole *m*

**petticoat** ['pet·ɪ·kout] *n* jupon *m*

**petty** ['pet·i] <-ier, -iest> *adj pej* **❶** (*trivial*) insignifiant(e) **❷** (*narrow-minded*) mesquin(e) **❸** (*minor*) mineur(e)

**pew** [pju] *n* banc *m* (d'église)

**phantom** ['fæn·təm] I. *n* fantôme *m* II. *adj* fantôme

**pharmaceutic(al)** *adj* pharmaceutique

**pharmacist** *n* pharmacien(ne) *m(f)*

**pharmacy** ['far·mə·si] <-cies> *n* pharmacie *f*

**phase** [feɪz] I. *n* phase *f*; **to go through a ~** faire sa crise; **in ~** en phase; **out of ~** déphasé II. *vt* échelonner; **to be ~d** être échelonné

&#9670;**phase in** *vt* introduire progressivement

&#9670;**phase out** *vt* retirer progressivement; (*production*) stopper progressivement; **to phase sb out** se débarrasser de qn

**PhD** [ˌpi·eɪtʃ·'di] *n abbr of* **Doctor of Philosophy** doctorat *m*; **a ~ in sth** un doctorat en qc; **to be a ~** être titulaire d'un doctorat

**pheasant** ['fez·°nt] <-(s)> *n* faisan *m*

**phenomenal** *adj* phénoménal(e)

**phenomenon** [fə·'na·mə·nan] <phenomena *o* -s> *n* phénomène *m*

**philistine** ['fɪl·ɪ·stin] *n pej* philistin *m*

**philosopher** *n* philosophe *mf*

**philosophic(al)** *adj* **❶** (*concerning philosophy*) philosophique **❷** (*calm*) philosophe

**philosophy** [fɪ·'la·sə·fi] *n* philosophie *f*

**phish** [fɪʃ] *vi* INET hameçonner

**phobia** ['fou·bi·ə] *n* phobie *f*

**phoenix** ['fi·nɪks] *n* phénix *m*; **to rise from the ashes like a ~** renaître de ses cendres tel un phénix

**phone** [foun] I. *n* téléphone *m*; **to answer the ~** répondre au téléphone; **to hang up the ~** raccrocher le téléphone; **to be on the ~** être au téléphone; **~ call/line** appel *m*/ligne *f* téléphonique II. *vi* téléphoner; **he ~d for a pizza** il a commandé une pizza par téléphone III. *vt* téléphoner à

&#9670;**phone back** *vt, vi* rappeler

&#9670;**phone in** *vi* téléphoner; **to ~ sick** téléphoner pour prévenir qu'on est malade

&#9670;**phone up** *vt* téléphoner à

**phone booth** *n* cabine *f* téléphonique

**phonetic** [fou·'net·ɪk] *adj* phonétique

**phosphorescent** *adj* phosphorescent(e)

**photo** ['fou·tou] <-s> *n inf abbr of* **photograph** photo *f*

**photo album** *n* album *m* photos

**photocopier** *n* photocopieur *m*

**photocopy** ['fou·tou·ka·pi] I. *n* <-ies> *n* photocopie *f* II. *vt* photocopier

**P**

**photo finish** *n* SPORTS photo-finish *f*

**photograph** ['fou·tou·græf] I. *n* photo(graphie) *f* II. *vt* photographier III. *vi* **to ~ well** être bien en photo

**photograph album** *n form* PHOT *s.* **photo album**

**photographer** *n* photographe *mf*

**photographic** *adj* photographique

**photography** [fə·'ta·grə·fi] *n* photographie *f*

**photojournalism** *n* photojournalisme *m*

**photojournalist** *n* reporter *mf* photographe

**photosynthesis** *n* photosynthèse *f*

**phrase** [freɪz] I. *n* **❶** (*words not forming sentence*) locution *f*; **verb/noun ~** syntagme *m* verbal/nominal **❷** (*idioma-*

*tic expression*) expression f ❸ MUS phrase f II. vt formuler

**phrase book** n guide m de conversation

**physical** I. adj physique II. n MED visite f médicale

**physical education** n éducation f physique

**physical science** n sciences fpl physiques

**physical therapy** n kinésithérapie f

**physician** [fɪ·ˈzɪʃ·ᵊn] n (*doctor*) médecin m

**physicist** [ˈfɪz·ɪ·sɪst] n ❶ (*scientist*) physicien(ne) m(f) ❷ (*student*) étudiant(e) m(f) en sciences physiques

**physics** [ˈfɪz·ɪks] n + sing vb physique f

**physiotherapist** n kinésithérapeute mf

**physiotherapy** [ˌfɪz·i·oʊ·ˈθer·ə·pi] n kinésithérapie f

**pianist** [ˈpi·ᵊn·ɪst] n pianiste mf

**piano**¹ [pi·ˈæn·oʊ] <-s> n (*instrument*) piano m

**piano**² [ˈpja·noʊ] adv (*softly*) piano

**pic** n sl ❶ (*film*) film m ❷ (*picture*) image f ❸ (*photo*) photo f

**pick**¹ [pɪk] I. vt ❶ (*select*) choisir; (*team*) sélectionner; (*winner*) désigner ❷ (*harvest*) cueillir; (*mushrooms*) ramasser ❸ (*remove: scab*) gratter; **to ~ one's nose** se curer le nez; **to ~ sth clean** décortiquer qc ❹ (*steal*) voler; **to ~ a lock** crocheter une serrure; **to ~ sb's pocket** faire les poches de qn ▸ **to ~ sb's brain** inf demander conseil à qn; **to ~ a fight with sb** chercher la bagarre avec qn II. vi choisir; **to ~ and choose among sb/sth** faire son choix parmi qn/qc III. n ❶ (*selection*) **to take one's ~** faire son choix ❷ inf (*the best*) **the ~** (*person*) la crème; (*of thing*) le meilleur; **to have one's ~ of sth** avoir le choix de qc

◆**pick off** vt ❶ (*shoot*) abattre ❷ (*remove*) enlever

◆**pick on** vt ❶ (*bully*) embêter ❷ (*criticize*) s'en prendre à

◆**pick out** vt ❶ (*select*) choisir ❷ (*recognize*) reconnaître ❸ (*manage to see*) distinguer ❹ (*highlight*) **to be picked**

**out** être mis en évidence ❺ (*play*) **to ~ a tune on an instrument** pianoter un air sur un instrument

◆**pick over** vt trier

◆**pick up** I. vt ❶ (*lift up: sth dropped*) relever; (*weight*) soulever; (*pen*) prendre; **to ~ the phone** prendre le téléphone; **to pick oneself up** a. fig se relever ❷ (*gather*) ramasser ❸ (*tidy: books, toys, a room*) ranger ❹ (*stop for, collect: thing, person*) aller chercher; **to ~ passengers** prendre des passagers; (*survivor*) recueillir ❺ (*learn*) apprendre; **to ~ a little French** apprendre quelques mots de français; **to ~ the tune** trouver l'air ❻ (*collect: news*) relever; (*idea*) chercher; (*a prize*) récolter ❼ (*buy*) acheter ❽ (*pay*) **to ~ the tab** [o **check**] inf casquer ❾ (*catch: illness*) attraper ❿ inf (*arrest*) arrêter ⓫ sl (*make acquaintance for sex*) ramasser ⓬ (*detect: broadcast, signal*) capter; (*radio signal*) intercepter; (*scent*) détecter; (*plane, ship*) repérer ⓭ (*continue, resume*) reprendre II. vi ❶ (*improve: condition*) s'améliorer; (*business*) reprendre; (*person*) se rétablir ❷ (*continue, increase*) reprendre

◆**pick up on** vt inf (*notice: a mistake*) relever

**pick**² [pɪk] n (*tool*) pioche f; **ice ~** pic m à glace

**picket** [ˈpɪk·ɪt] I. n ❶ (*strike*) piquet m de grève; (*at demonstration*) cordon m de manifestants ❷ (*striker*) gréviste mf en faction; (*demonstrator*) manifestant(e) m(f) ❸ (*pointed stake for fence*) piquet m II. vt ❶ (*demonstrate: factory*) former un piquet de grève face à; (*the White House*) former un cordon de protestation face à ❷ (*blockade*) clôturer de piquets III. vi faire le piquet de grève

**picket line** n piquet m de grève; **to cross a ~** traverser un piquet de grève

**pickle** [ˈpɪk·l] I. n (*preserved vegetable*) pickles mpl (*condiment de légumes conservés dans du vinaigre*) ▸ **to be** (**caught**) **in a** (*pretty*) **~** inf être dans le

P

pétrin **II.** *vt* to ~ **sth** conserver qc dans du vinaigre

**pickled** *adj* ❶ (*conserved in vinegar*) au vinaigre ❷ *fig, inf* (*drunk*) bourré(e)

**pickpocket** ['pɪk.pa.kɪt] *n* pick-pocket *m*

**pickup** *n* ❶ *s.* pickup truck ❷ *inf* (*acceleration power*) reprise *f* ❸ (*improvement*) amélioration *f* ❹ *inf* (*casual partner*) partenaire *mf* de rencontre ❺ *inf* (*hitchhiker*) passager, -ère *m, f* pris(e) en route ❻ *inf* (*collection*) ramassage *m* ❼ (*part of phonograph*) lecteur *m*

**pickup truck** *n* camionnette *f*

**picnic** ['pɪk.nɪk] **I.** *n* pique-nique *m* ▸ to be **no** ~ *inf* ne pas être une partie de plaisir **II.**<-ck-> *vi* pique-niquer

**picture** ['pɪk.tʃər] **I.** *n* ❶ (*visual image*) image *f* ❷ (*photograph*) photo *f*; to take a ~ of **sb/sth** prendre une photo de qn/qc ❸ (*painting*) tableau *m*; (*drawing*) dessin *m* ❹ (*movie*) motion ~ film *m* ❺ (*mental image, image on TV*) image *f* ❻ (*account, depiction*) tableau *m*; to paint a ~ of **sth** peindre le portrait de qc ▸ to **get** the ~ *inf* piger; to **leave sb out of** the ~ laisser qn sur la touche **II.** *vt* ❶ (*represent*) représenter ❷ (*imagine*) to ~ **oneself** s'imaginer; to ~ **sb doing sth** s'imaginer qn en train de faire qc ❸ (*describe*) dépeindre

**picture book** *n* livre *m* illustré

**picture frame** *n* cadre *m*

**picture gallery** *n* galerie *f* de photos

**picturesque** [ˌpɪk.tʃə'resk] *adj* pittoresque

**pie** [paɪ] *n* CULIN (*savory*) tourte *f*; (*sweet*) tarte *f* (recouverte de pâte) ▸ ~ **in the sky** *inf* des châteaux *mpl* en Espagne; **easy as** ~ *inf* simple comme bonjour

**piece** [pis] *n* ❶ (*bit*) morceau *m*; (*land*) parcelle *f*; (*glass, pottery*) fragment *m*; in ~**s** en morceaux; in one ~ en un seul morceau; *fig* (*person*) intact(e) ❷ (*item, one of set*) a ~ **of paper** une feuille de papier; a ~ **of furniture** un meuble; a ~ **of advice** un conseil; a ~

of **evidence** une preuve; a ~ **of information** une information; a ~ **of news** une nouvelle ❸ (*unit in game: chess*) pièce *f* ❹ (*work: written, musical*) morceau *m*; (*painted, drawn, sculpted*) pièce *f*; a good ~ **of work** du bon travail ❺ (*coin*) pièce *f*; a **10-cent** ~ une pièce de 10 cents ❻ *vulg* (*woman*) meuf *f* ▸ to be a ~ of **cake** *inf* être du gâteau; to want a ~ of the **cake** vouloir une part du gâteau; to **give sb** a ~ of **sb's mind** *inf* dire ses quatre vérités à qn; to **pick up** the ~**s** recoller les morceaux

**pie chart** *n* MATH camembert *m*

**pier** [pɪr] *n* ❶ (*boardwalk*) jetée *f* ❷ ARCHIT (*pillar: in church*) pilier *m*; (*in foundations*) pile *f*

**pierce** [pɪrs] **I.** *vt* ❶ (*make a hole in*) *a. fig* percer ❷ (*go through*) transpercer **II.** *vi a. fig* to ~ **into sth** percer qc; to ~ **through sth** transpercer qc

**piercing I.** *adj* ❶ (*biting: cold, rain, wind*) glacial(e) ❷ (*sharp, penetrating: eyes, look*) perçant(e); (*reply, wit*) mordant(e) ❸ (*loud*) perçant(e) **II.** *n* piercing *m*

**pig** [pɪg] *n* ❶ (*animal*) cochon *m*; **wild** ~ sanglier *m* ❷ *inf* (*overeater*) to **make a** (**real**) ~ **of oneself** se goinfrer; a **greedy** ~ un goinfreur ❸ *pej, inf* (*swinish person*) porc *m* ❹ *pej, sl* (*police officer*) poulet *m* ▸ to **buy a** ~ **in a poke** acheter les yeux fermés

◆ **pig out** *vi inf* se goinfrer; to ~ **on sth** se goinfrer de qc; to be pigged out être goinfré

**pigeon** ['pɪdʒ.ən] *n* pigeon *m*

**pigeonhole I.** *n* ❶ (*compartment*) casier *m* ❷ (*category*) to put into ~**s** (*people*) cataloguer; (*things*) étiqueter **II.** *vt* ❶ (*place in compartment*) classer ❷ (*categorize: people*) cataloguer; (*things*) étiqueter ❸ (*put off*) remettre à plus tard

**piggyback I.** *n* to **give sb a** ~ (**ride**) porter qn sur le dos **II.** *adv* sur le dos

**piggy bank** *n* tirelire *f* (en forme de cochon)

**P**

**pigheaded** *adj pej* têtu(e) comme une mule

**piglet** ['pɪg·lɪt] *n* porcelet *m*

**pigment** ['pɪg·mənt] *n* pigment *m*

**pigsty** *n a. fig, pej* porcherie *f*, boiton *m* Suisse

**pigtail** ['pɪg·teɪl] *n* natte *f*

**pile¹** [paɪl] I. *n* ❶ (*heap*) pile *f*; **to have ~s of sth** *inf* avoir un tas de qc ❷ *inf* (*fortune*) fric *m*; **to make a ~ of money** *inf* faire un tas de fric ❸ (*big building*) édifice *m* II. *vt* entasser; (*objects*) empiler; **to ~ sth (high)** empiler qc; **to be ~d high with sth** être couvert de piles de qc

◆**pile in** *vi* s'entasser

◆**pile on** *vt* ❶ (*heap*) amonceler ❷ (*exaggerate*) exagérer; **to pile it on** *inf* exagérer

◆**pile up** I. *vi* s'accumuler II. *vt* accumuler

**pile²** [paɪl] *n* ARCHIT pieu *m*

**pile³** [paɪl] *n* poil *m*

**piles** *npl inf* hémorroïdes *fpl*

**pile-up** *n* ❶ *inf* (*car crash*) carambolage *m* ❷ (*accumulation*) accumulation *f*

**pilgrimage** *n a. fig* pèlerinage *m*

**pill** [pɪl] *n* ❶ (*medicinal tablet*) pilule *f* ❷ (*contraceptive tablet*) **the ~** la pilule; **to be on the ~** prendre la pilule ▶ **to be a bitter [*o* hard] ~ to swallow** être dur à avaler

**pillar** ['pɪl·ər] *n a. fig* pilier *m*; **~ of flame/smoke** colonne *f* de feu/fumée; **a ~ of the community** *fig* un pilier de la communauté

**pillow** ['pɪl·oʊ] *n* oreiller *m*, coussin *m* Belgique

**pillowcase, pillow cover, pillowslip** *n* taie *f* d'oreiller

**pilot** ['paɪ·lət] I. *n a.* TEL pilote *m* II. *vt* ❶ (*guide*) piloter; (*person*) guider ❷ (*test*) tester

**pilot boat** *n* bateau-pilote *m*

**pilot lamp** *n* témoin *m*

**pilot light** *n* ❶ (*small flame igniting heating*) veilleuse *f* ❷ *s.* **pilot lamp**

**pilot's license** *n* brevet *m* de pilote

**pimp** [pɪmp] I. *n* maquereau *m* II. *vi* être proxénète

**pimple** ['pɪm·pl] *n* bouton *m*

**PIN** [pɪn] *n abbr of* **personal identification number** code *m* confidentiel

**pin** [pɪn] I. *n* ❶ (*needle*) épingle *f*; **safety ~** épingle de nourrice ❷ MIL (*safety device on grenade*) goupille *f* ❸ (*ornamental object for clothing*) épingle *f* ❹ (*brooch*) broche *f* ❺ SPORTS (*bowling*) ~ quille *f* ❻ *pl, inf* (*legs*) gambettes *fpl* ▶ **you could hear a ~ drop** *fig* on entendait les mouches voler; **to be on ~s and needles** être tout excité II. <-nn-> *vt* ❶ (*fasten with pin*) épingler; **to ~ a medal on sb** accrocher une médaille sur qn ❷ (*immobilize*) bloquer; **~ned to the floor** coincé(e) contre le sol ❸ (*defeat in wrestling*) plaquer au sol ❹ *inf* (*accuse*) **to ~ the blame on sb** attribuer la responsabilité à qn

◆**pin down** *vt* ❶ (*define clearly*) identifier; **it's hard to ~ exactly what I felt** c'est difficile de définir exactement ce que j'ai ressenti ❷ (*pressure sb to decide*) coincer; **to ~ sb to sth** coincer qn sur qc ❸ (*restrict sb's movement*) coincer ❹ (*fasten with pin*) accrocher

◆**pin up** *vt* (*on wall*) punaiser; **~ one's hair** attacher ses cheveux

**pinch** [pɪn(t)ʃ] I. *vt* ❶ (*nip, tweak*) pincer ❷ (*grip hard*) serrer; **these shoes ~ my feet** ces chaussures me font mal aux pieds ❸ *sl* (*steal*) piquer II. *vi* serrer; (*boots, shoes, slippers*) blesser III. *n* ❶ (*nip*) pincement *m*; **to give sb a ~ on the cheek** pincer qn à la joue ❷ (*small quantity*) pincée *f* ▶ **in a ~** si besoin est; **to feel the ~** être en difficulté

**pine¹** [paɪn] *n* ❶ (*tree*) pin *m* ❷ (*wood*) (bois *m* de) pin *m*

**pine²** [paɪn] *vi* se languir; **to ~ for sb/sth** languir après qn/qc

**pineapple** ['paɪ·næp·l] *n* ananas *m*

**pine cone** *n* pomme *f* de pin, pive *f* Suisse

**Ping-Pong®** *n inf* ping-pong *m*

**pink**[1] [pɪŋk] **I.** n **1** (*color*) rose m **2** BOT œillet m **II.** adj rose; **to turn ~** rosir; (*person, face*) rougir ► **to see ~ elephants** iron avoir des hallucinations; *s.a.* **blue**

**pink**[2] [pɪŋk] vt denteler

**pinkie** n inf petit doigt m

**pinpoint** ['pɪn·pɔɪnt] **I.** vt **1** (*give exactly: location*) localiser; (*time*) déterminer **2** fig (*identify*) mettre le doigt sur **II.** adj **with ~ accuracy** avec extrême précision **III.** n point m

**pinstripe** ['pɪn·straɪp] n petite rayure f; **to wear ~s** porter un costume à fines rayures; **~(d) shirt** chemise f à fines rayures

**pint** [paɪnt] n pinte f

**pintsize, pintsized** adj inf petit format

**pinup** n pin up f inv; (*male*) star f (masculine)

**pioneer** [ˌpaɪ·ə·ˈnɪr] **I.** n pionnier, -ière m, f **II.** adj pionnier(-ère) **III.** vt être le pionnier pour

**pip** [pɪp] n BOT pépin m

**pipe** [paɪp] **I.** n **1 a.** TECH (*industrial tube*) tuyau m **2** (*for smoking*) pipe f **3** MUS (*wind instrument*) pipeau m; (*in organ*) tuyau m **4** (*sound: of bird*) chant m ► **put that in your ~ and smoke it** inf mets-toi bien ça dans le crâne **II.** vt **1** (*transport using cylinders*) **to ~ sth** acheminer qc par canalisation **2** (*sing, speak shrilly: bird*) pépier; (*of person*) dire d'une voix aiguë **3** MUS jouer (du pipeau/de la cornemuse)

◆ **pipe down** vi inf **1** (*be quiet*) la mettre en veilleuse **2** (*be quieter*) baisser le ton

◆ **pipe up** vi se faire entendre

**pipe bomb** n bombe f fabriquée à partir d'un tube

**pipeline** ['paɪp·laɪn] n pipeline m; **in the ~** fig en préparation

**piper** ['paɪ·pər] n flûtiste mf

**piracy** ['paɪ·rə·si] n piraterie f; COM piratage m

**pirate** ['paɪ·rət] **I.** n pirate mf **II.** adj (*copy, video*) pirate **III.** vt pirater

**Pisces** ['paɪ·siz] n Poissons mpl; *s.a.* **Aquarius**

**piss** [pɪs] vulg **I.** n pisse f; **to go take a ~** aller pisser **II.** vi pisser

**pissed** adj inf furax

**pistachio** [pɪ·ˈstæʃ·iˌoʊ] <-s> n pistache f

**pistol** ['pɪs·təl] n pistolet m

**piston** ['pɪs·tən] n TECH piston m

**pit**[1] [pɪt] **I.** n **1** (*hole in ground*) fosse f **2** (*mine*) mine f **3** (*hollow, depression*) creux m **4** (*pockmark*) marque f **5** (*lowest part*) **in the ~ of one's stomach** dans le creux de l'estomac **6** THEAT, MUS (*area of seating*) parterre m; **orchestra ~** fosse f d'orchestre **7** (*in motor racing*) stand m ► **to be the ~s** inf être nul **II.** vt **1** (*make holes in*) creuser un trou **2** (*place in opposition*) **to ~ sb against sb** opposer qn contre qn

**pit**[2] [pɪt] **I.** n noyau m **II.** <-tt-> vt dénoyauter

**pita** ['pi·ʈə], **pita bread** n pita m

**pitch**[1] [pɪtʃ] **I.** n **1** SPORTS (*baseball*) pitch m **2** MUS, LING (*tone depth, height*) tonalité f; **perfect ~** oreille f absolue **3** (*persuasive talk*) **sales ~** baratin m **4** (*slope in roofs*) inclinaison f ► **to be at a fever ~** être très excité **II.** vt **1** (*hurl*) lancer **2** (*in baseball*) pitcher **3** (*put up*) dresser; **to ~ camp** établir un camp **4** (*try to promote*) **to ~ sth to sb/sth** promouvoir qc à qn/qc **5** (*aim*) **to ~ sth to** (*consumers, market*) s'adresser à; (*audience*) adapter qc pour **6** MUS (*note*) donner; **to ~ one's voice higher/ lower** hausser/baisser le ton de la voix **III.** vi **1** (*in baseball*) tomber **2** (*suddenly thrust*) tomber; **to ~ forward** tomber en avant **3** (*slope*) être en pente

◆ **pitch in** vi inf s'y mettre

**pitch**[2] [pɪtʃ] n (*bitumen*) brai m

**pitch-black** adj, **pitch-dark** adj (*dark*) noir(e) comme dans un four

**pitfall** ['pɪt·fɔl] n écueil m

**pity** ['pɪt·i] **I.** n **1** (*compassion*) pitié f; **out of ~** par pitié; **to take ~ on sb/sth**

**P**

prendre qn/qc en pitié ❷ (*unfortunate matter*) **it's a ~!** c'est dommage!; **what a ~!** quel dommage! II.<-ies, -ied> *vt* avoir de la peine pour

**pixel** [ˈpɪk·səl] *n* COMPUT pixel *m*

**pixelate, pixellate** [ˈpɪk·sə·leɪt] *vt* COMPUT pixéliser

**pizza** [ˈpiːt·sə] *n* pizza *f*

**pizzeria** *n* pizzeria *f*

**place** [pleɪs] I. *n* ❶ (*location, area*) endroit *m; form* (*of birth, death, work*) lieu *m; ~* **of refuge** refuge *m* ❷ (*residence, commercial location*) adresse *f;* (*dwelling*) résidence *f;* (*house*) maison *f;* (*apartment*) appartement *m;* **at Paul's ~** chez Paul; **a little ~ in Corsica** un petit village en Corse; **~ of residence** domicile *m* ❸ (*appropriate setting*) endroit *m;* **it's not the ~/no ~ to** +*infin* ce n'est pas l'endroit/un endroit pour +*infin* ❹ (*position*) place *f;* **to lose one's ~** perdre sa place; **in ~ of sb/sth** à la place de qn/qc; **out of ~** déplacé(e); **to be in ~** être en place; **in the first/second** ~ en premier/second lieu; **to take first/second** ~ se placer premier/second; **people in high ~s** des gens *mpl* haut placés ❺ (*square*) place *f* ❻ MATH **to three decimal ~s** avec trois décimales ❼ (*seat*) place *f;* **to change ~s with sb** changer de place avec qn; **to save sb a ~** garder une place à qn; **to have a ~ in a class** être admis à suivre un cours ❽ *inf* (*indefinite location*) **any ~** n'importe où; **some ~** quelque part; **every ~** partout; **no ~** nulle part ► **all over the ~** partout, the **film was all over the ~** le film était complètement incohérent; **to go ~s** *inf* (*become successful*) faire son chemin II. *vt* ❶ (*position, put*) placer; **to ~ an advertisement in the newspaper** mettre une annonce dans le journal ❷ (*situate*) situer; **to be well-~d** être bien situé ❸ (*impose*) **to ~ an embargo on sb/sth** frapper qn/qc d'embargo; **to ~ a limit on sth** fixer une limite à qc ❹ (*ascribe*) **to ~ the blame on sb** jeter le blâme sur qn; **to ~ one's hopes**

**on sb/sth** mettre tous ses espoirs en qn/qc; **to ~ emphasis on sth** *a. fig* mettre l'accent sur qc; **to ~ one's faith** [*o* **trust**] **in sb/sth** faire confiance à qn/qc ❺ (*arrange for*) **to ~ an order for sth** passer une commande de qc; **to ~ a bet** faire un pari ❻ (*appoint to a position*) **to ~ sb in charge of sth** charger qn de qc; **to ~ sb under arrest** arrêter qn ❼ (*classify*) placer; **~d first/ second** classé premier/second; **to ~ sth above** [*o* **before**] **sth** faire passer qc avant qc; **to ~ sb's face** se souvenir de qn

**place mat** *n* set *m* de table

**place name** *n* nom *m* de lieu

**plagiarize** [ˈpleɪ·dʒə·raɪz] *vt, vi* plagier

**plain** [pleɪn] I. *adj* ❶ (*clear, obvious*) clair(e); **in ~ language** en langage clair; **it's ~ (to see) that ...** il est clair que ... ❷ (*unflavored: yogurt, bagel*) nature *inv* ❸ (*uncomplicated: clothing, envelope*) très simple; **~ and simple** pur(e) et simple ❹ (*mere, pure: truth, torture*) pur(e) ❺ (*one color: fabric*) uni(e) ❻ (*unattractive*) sans attrait II. *adv* ❶ (*clearly*) clairement ❷ *inf* (*downright*) vraiment III. *n* ❶ GEO plaine *f;* **the ~s** la prairie ❷ (*knitting stitch*) maille *f*

**plainly** *adv* ❶ (*simply*) simplement ❷ (*clearly*) clairement ❸ (*obviously*) franchement ❹ (*undeniably*) indéniablement

**plainspoken** *adj* **to be ~** être franc

**plait** [plæt] I. *n* tresse *f* II. *vt* tresser

**plan** [plæn] I. *n* ❶ (*detailed idea, program*) plan *m;* **the ~ is to surprise them** l'idée *f* est de les surprendre; **to go according to ~** se dérouler comme prévu; **to make ~s for sth** planifier qc ❷ (*vague intention, aim*) projet *m;* **I have other ~s** je suis occupé ❸ FIN, ECON (*insurance policy*) plan *m* II.<-nn-> *vt* ❶ (*work out in detail*) planifier; **to ~ to do sth** projeter de faire qc ❷ (*design, make a plan*) faire le plan de III. *vi* faire des projets; **we need to ~ ahead** nous

devons prévoir à l'avance; **to ~ for retirement** prévoir sa retraite
♦ **plan on** vt to ~ doing sth avoir le projet de faire qc
**plane¹** [pleɪn] n (aircraft) avion m
**plane²** [pleɪn] I. n ❶(level surface) niveau m ❷MATH plan m ❸(level of thought, intellect) niveau m II. adj a. MATH plat(e)
**plane³** [pleɪn] I. n (tool) rabot m II. vt raboter
**plane⁴** [pleɪn] n BOT ~ (**tree**) platane m
**plane crash** n catastrophe f aérienne
**planet** ['plæn·ɪt] n planète f
**planetarium** [,plæn·ɪ·'ter·i·əm] <-s o -ria> n planétarium m
**plank** [plæŋk] n ❶(long board) planche f ❷(important element) point m
**planner** n planificateur, -trice m, f; **city ~** urbaniste mf
**planning** n planification f; **city ~** urbanisme m
**plant** [plænt] I. n ❶BIO plante f ❷(factory) usine f ❸(machinery for companies) équipement m ❹(informer) taupe f ❺sing (object placed to mislead) objet destiné à faire prendre quelqu'un II. vt a. fig planter; (bomb) poser; (spy) infiltrer; (colony, idea) implanter; **to ~ drugs on sb** placer de la drogue pour faire prendre qn; **to ~ doubts about sth** semer des doutes sur qc
**plantation** [plæn·'teɪ·[ə]n] n plantation f
**plaque** [plæk] n ❶(plate identifying building) plaque f ❷MED (on teeth) plaque f dentaire; (in arteries) athérome m
**plasma** ['plæz·mə] n no pl MED, PHYS, ASTRON plasma m; **~ screen** écran m plasma
**plaster** ['plæs·tər] I. n a. MED plâtre m II. vt a. inf plâtrer; **~ed with slogans/ posters** couvert(e) de slogans/d'affiches
**plaster cast** n a. ART plâtre m
**plastered** adj inf bourré(e)
**plastic** ['plæs·tɪk] I. n ❶(material) plastique m ❷inf (credit card) **to pay with ~** payer par carte de crédit II. adj ❶(made from plastic) en plastique ❷ pej (artificial: food) synthétique; (smile) artificiel(le) ❸ART (malleable) plastique

**plastic explosive** n explosif m au plastic
**plastic surgery** n chirurgie f esthétique
**plate** [pleɪt] I. n ❶(serving dish) assiette f ❷(portion of food) **a ~ of pasta** une assiette de pâtes ❸(cutlery) (**silver**) ~ argenterie f ❹(panel, sheet) plaque f ❺(sign) a. AUTO, TYP plaque f ❻TYP (picture in book) planche f ❼GEO (on earth's crust) plaque f ▶ **to have a lot on one's ~** en avoir par-dessus la tête II. vt (with gold, silver) plaquer
**plateful** n assiette f
**plate warmer** n chauffe-assiettes m
**platform** ['plæt·fɔrm] n ❶(raised surface) plateforme f ❷RAIL quai m ❸(stage) estrade f; **to be a ~ for sth** fig être une tribune pour qc ❹ pl s. **platform shoes**
**platform shoes** npl chaussures fpl à semelles compensées
**platinum** ['plæt·nəm] n platine m
**platonic** [plə·'tɑ·nɪk] adj platonique
**plausible** ['plɔ·zə·bl] adj plausible
**play** [pleɪ] I. n ❶(games) jeu m; **to be at ~** être en train de jouer ❷(theatrical piece) pièce f de théâtre; **one-act ~** pièce en un acte ❸(freedom to move) jeu m ▶ **to bring sth into ~** faire rentrer qc en jeu; **to come into ~** rentrer en jeu II. vi jouer; (radio) marcher; **to ~ to a full house** jouer à guichets fermés ▶ **to ~ to the gallery** amuser la galerie; **to ~ into sb's hands** faire le jeu de qn III. vt ❶GAMES jouer; **to ~ bridge/cards/golf** jouer au bridge/aux cartes/au golf; **to ~ host to sb/sth** accueillir qn/qc; **to ~ Germany** SPORTS jouer contre l'Allemagne; **to ~ a slot machine** jouer à une machine à sous; **to ~ the stock market** jouer en Bourse; **to ~ a joke on sb** faire une blague à qn; **to ~ a trick on sb** jouer un tour à qn ❷(perform: symphony, role) interpréter; (flute, guitar) jouer de; **they were ~ing Mozart** (orchestra) ils jouaient Mozart; (radio station) ils pas-

**P**

saient du Mozart; **to ~ a CD** mettre un CD; **to ~ a concert** donner un concert; **to ~ a vital role in sth** *fig* jouer un rôle fondamental dans qc ► **to ~ second <u>fiddle</u> to sb/sth** être dans l'ombre de qn/qc; **to ~ the <u>field</u>** avoir plusieurs amants; **to ~ <u>it</u> cool** rester calme; **to ~ <u>it</u> safe** rester prudent; **to ~ <u>hard</u> to get** se laisser désirer; **to ~ <u>hardball</u>** ne pas être tendre; **to ~ <u>havoc</u> with sth** chambouler qc; **to ~ <u>hooky</u>** faire l'école buissonnière; **to ~ a <u>hunch</u>** agir par intuition; **to ~ <u>possum</u>** (*pretend to be asleep*) faire semblant de dormir; (*pretend to be ignorant or unaware*) faire l'innocent; **to ~ sb for a <u>sucker</u>** prendre qn pour un idiot; **to ~ <u>dumb</u>** faire le con

◆ **play along** *vi* ❶ MUS **to ~ with sb** accompagner qn ❷ (*pretend to agree with*) **to ~ with sb/sth** marcher avec qn/qc

◆ **play down** *vt* minimiser

◆ **play off** I. *vi* SPORTS **to ~ for third place** jouer pour la troisième place du podium II. *vt* **to play sb off against sb** monter qn contre qn

◆ **play on** I. *vt* (*exploit*) **to ~ sb's feelings/weakness** exploiter les sentiments/la faiblesse de qn II. *vi* (*keep playing*) continuer de jouer

◆ **play out** I. *vt* ❶ (*act out: fantasies*) réaliser; (*scene, scenario*) jouer ❷ (*follow assigned or fated role: destiny*) suivre II. *vi* (*occur*) **the tragedy played out in New York** la tragédie s'est déroulée à New York

◆ **play up** *vt* exagérer

◆ **play up to** *vt* **to ~ sb** flatter qn

**playboy** *n pej* play-boy *m*

**player** *n* ❶ (*participant, performer*) joueur, -euse *m, f;* **soccer ~** footballeur *m;* **tennis ~** joueur de tennis; **flute ~** flûtiste *mf* ❷ (*stage actor*) acteur, -trice *m, f* ❸ (*device*) lecteur *m;* (*for CDs*) platine *f;* **DVD ~** lecteur de DVD

**playful** *adj* (*person, animal*) joueur(-euse), jouette *Belgique;* (*mood, nature, remark*) enjoué(e)

**playground** *n* (*for children*) cour *f* de récréation

**playgroup** *n* jardin *m* d'enfants

**playing card** *n* carte *f* à jouer

**playing field** *n* terrain *m* de sports

**playmate** ['pleɪ·meɪt] *n* (*childhood playfellow*) copain, copine *m, f*

**playoff** *n* match *m* pour départager deux équipes

**playpen** ['pleɪ·pen] *n* parc *m* (pour bébé)

**playroom** *n* salle *f* de jeu

**playwright** *n* dramaturge *mf*

**plaza** ['pla·za] *n* place *f*

**plead** [plid] <pleaded, pleaded> I. *vi* ❶ (*implore, beg*) implorer; **to ~ for forgiveness/mercy** implorer le pardon/la grâce; **to ~ with sb to** +*infin* implorer qn de +*infin* ❷ + *adj* (*answer to a charge in court*) plaider II. *vt* ❶ (*argue or represent in court: insanity*) plaider; **to ~ sb's case** plaider la cause de qn ❷ (*claim as a pretext: ignorance*) invoquer ❸ (*argue for: a cause*) défendre

**pleasant** ['plez·ᵊnt] *adj* (*weather, person*) agréable

**please** [pliz] I. *vt* faire plaisir à; **to be hard to ~** être difficile à contenter; **~ yourself** *inf* fais comme tu voudras II. *vi* ❶ (*be agreeable*) faire plaisir; **eager to ~** désireux(-euse) de plaire ❷ (*think fit, wish*) **if you ~** s'il te/vous plaît; **to do as one ~s** faire à sa guise; **do whatever you ~** fais comme tu veux ► **~ God!** si Dieu le veut! III. *interj* ❶ (*with a request*) s'il te/vous plaît; **~ close the gate** merci de fermer la porte ❷ (*said to accept sth politely*) **yes, ~** oui je veux bien

**pleased** *adj* content(e); **to be ~ with oneself** être content de soi; **I am ~ to inform you that ...** j'ai le plaisir de vous informer que ...; **~ to meet you** enchanté ► **to be as ~ as punch about sth** être content comme tout à propos de qc

**pleasing** *adj* (*agreeable: manner*) agréable; (*news*) qui fait plaisir

**pleasurable** *adj* agréable

**pleasure** ['pleʒ·ər] *n* plaisir *m*; **it's a ~** je vous en prie; **to take ~ in sth/in doing sth** prendre plaisir à qc/faire qc

**pleasure boat** *n* bateau *m* de plaisance

**pleat** [plit] *n* pli *m*

**plentiful** *adj* (*supply*) abondant(e); **the cherries are ~ this year** il y a des quantités de cerises cette année

**plenty** ['plen·ṭi] **I.** *n* (*abundance*) abondance *f* **II.** *adv* bien assez; **it's ~ big** c'est assez grand; **~ good/bad** *inf* très bon/mauvais **III.** *pron* **~ of money/ time** beaucoup d'argent/de temps; **there was ~ of room** il y avait plein de place; **to have ~** en avoir bien assez

**pliers** [plaɪərz] *npl* pince *f*; **a pair of ~** une pince

**plonk** [plɑŋk] *n, vt s.* **plunk**

**plot** [plat] **I.** *n* ① (*conspiracy, secret plan*) complot *m* ② (*story line*) intrigue *f* ③ (*small piece of land*) parcelle *f*; **garden ~** jardin *m*; **vegetable ~** potager *m* ▶ **the ~ thickens** *iron* les choses *fpl* se compliquent **II.** <-tt-> *vt* ① (*conspire*) comploter ② (*create: story line*) écrire ③ (*present or represent graphically: curve*) tracer ④ MIL (*position*) pointer **III.** <-tt-> *vi* comploter

**plow** [plaʊ] **I.** *n* charrue *f* **II.** *vt* ① (*till*) labourer ② *fig* **to ~ one's way through sth** (*move through*) avancer péniblement dans qc; (*finish off*) réussir à finir qc **III.** *vi* ① (*till ground*) labourer ② (*advance*) **to ~ through a crowd** foncer à travers une foule; **to ~ through a book/job** peiner sur un livre/une tâche

◆**plow into** *vt* **to ~ into a wall** entrer en plein dans un mur

**plowshare** *n* soc *m* de charrue

**pluck** [plʌk] *vt* ① (*remove by picking away*) cueillir ② (*remove quickly*) arracher ③ (*remove hair, feathers*) arracher; (*chicken*) plumer; **to ~ one's eyebrows** s'épiler les sourcils ④ (*sound: strings of instrument*) pincer ⑤ (*pull at*) tirer sur ⑥ (*remove from a situation*) **to ~ sb from sth** sortir qn de qc

**plug** [plʌg] **I.** *n* ① (*connector, socket*) prise *f* de courant; (*for peripheral, phone*) fiche *f*; **to pull the ~ on sth** débrancher qc; *fig* stopper qc ② (*stopper*) bonde *f* ③ *inf* (*publicity*) pub *f*; **to give a book a ~** faire la promotion d'un livre ④ AUTO **spark ~** bougie *f* ⑤ ARCHIT **wall ~** cheville *f* ⑥ (*wad: of tobacco*) chique *f* **II.**<-gg-> *vt* ① (*stop up, close: hole*) boucher; (*leak*) arrêter ② *inf* (*publicize*) faire du battage pour ③ *inf* (*shoot*) flinguer

◆**plug along** *vi*, **plug away** *vi* travailler dur

◆**plug in I.** *vt* brancher **II.** *vi* se brancher

**plughole** ['plʌg·hoʊl] *n* trou *m* d'écoulement

**plug-in** *n* COMPUT module *m* d'extension, plugiciel *m*

**plum** [plʌm] **I.** *n* ① (*fruit*) prune *f* ② (*exceptionally good opportunity*) affaire *f* **II.** *adj* ① (*purplish-red color*) prune *inv* ② (*exceptionally good or favorable: job, part*) en or

**plumber** *n* plombier *m*

**plumbing** *n* plomberie *f*; **~ fixture** installation *f* de plomberie

**plummet** ['plʌm·ɪt] *vi* tomber à la verticale; (*prices, profits*) s'effondrer; (*confidence*) tomber à zéro

**plump** [plʌmp] **I.** *adj* ① (*rounded, slightly fat: chicken*) dodu(e); **~ and juicy grapes** des gros raisins *mpl* juteux ② (*fat*) potelé(e); **pleasingly ~** aux formes généreuses **II.** *vt* **to ~ (up)** (*pillows*) remettre en forme

**plunge** [plʌndʒ] **I.** *n* ① (*sharp decline*) chute *f* ② (*swim*) plongeon *m* ▶ **to take the ~** se jeter à l'eau **II.** *vi* ① (*fall suddenly or dramatically*) plonger; *fig* (*prices, profits*) s'effondrer; **to ~ to one's death** faire une chute mortelle ② (*leap*) **to ~ into sth** plonger dans qc ③ (*enter suddenly, dash*) **to ~ into** se précipiter dans ④ (*begin abruptly*) **to ~ in** se lancer; **to ~ into sth** se lancer dans qc **III.** *vt* ① (*immerse*) **to ~ sth into sth** plonger qc dans qc; **to ~ a knife into sb/sth** planter un couteau

P

dans qn/qc ❷(*cause to experience abruptly*) **to ~ sb/sth into sth** plonger qn/qc dans qc

**plunk** [plʌŋk] **I.** *n inf* bruit *m* sourd **II.** *vt inf* poser bruyamment; **to ~ oneself down on sth** s'affaler sur qc

**pluperfect** ['plu·,pɜr·fɪkt] **I.** *adj* LING au plus-que-parfait **II.** *n* LING **the ~** le plus-que-parfait

**plural** ['plʊr·əl] **I.** *n* pluriel *m; in the ~* au pluriel **II.** *adj* ❶LING pluriel(le) ❷(*pluralistic*) pluraliste

**plus** [plʌs] **I.** *prep* (*and*) *a.* MATH plus **II.** *adj* ❶(*more*) plus; **to have 200 ~** en avoir plus de 200 ❷(*having a positive charge*) positif(-ive) **III.** *n* ❶(*sign*) plus *m; a. fig* atout *m; s.a.* **minus**

**plush** [plʌʃ] **I.** *adj* ❶(*luxurious, expensive: restaurant*) de luxe ❷(*made of plush: upholstery*) en peluche **II.** *n* peluche *f*

**plutonium** [plu·'toʊ·ni·əm] *n* plutonium *m*

**plywood** ['plaɪ·wʊd] *n* contre-plaqué *m*

**pm** *adv*, **p.m.** *adv abbr of* **post meridiem** ❶(*in the afternoon*) de l'après-midi ❷(*in the evening*) du soir

**PM** [,pi·'em] *n* ❶ *abbr of* **postmortem** autopsie *f* ❷ *abbr of* **Prime Minister** Premier ministre *m*

**pneumonia** [nu·'moʊ·njə] *n* MED pneumonie *f*

**poach**[1] [poʊtʃ] *vt* pocher

**poach**[2] [poʊtʃ] **I.** *vt* ❶(*catch illegally*) **to ~ animals/game** braconner des animaux/du gibier ❷(*appropriate unfairly or dishonestly: ideas*) s'approprier ❸(*lure away*) débaucher **II.** *vi* ❶(*catch illegally*) braconner ❷(*encroach*) empiéter

**pocket** ['pak·ɪt] **I.** *n* poche *f*; **air ~** trou *m* d'air; **out-of-~ expenses** frais *mpl* ▸ **to have deep ~s** avoir beaucoup d'argent; **to pay for sth out of one's own ~** payer qc de sa poche; **to have sb in one's ~** (*back*) ~ un dans sa poche; **to line one's ~s** se remplir les poches **II.** *adj* de poche **III.** *vt*

empocher; **to ~ one's change** prendre la monnaie

**pocketbook** *n* ❶(*woman's handbag*) sac *m* à main ❷(*wallet, ability to pay*) portefeuille *m* ❸(*paperback book*) livre *m* de poche

**pocketknife** <-knives> *n* couteau *m* de poche

**pocket money** *n* argent *m* de poche

**pod** [pad] *n* (*K-cup*) **coffee ~** dosette *f*

**podcasting** *n* podcasting *m*

**podiatry** [pə·'daɪ·ə·tri] *n* podologie *f*

**podium** ['poʊ·di·əm] <-dia> *n* podium *m*

**poem** [poʊəm] *n* poème *m*

**poet** [poʊət] *n* poète *m*

**poetic** [poʊ·'et·ɪk] *adj* poétique; **it's ~ justice** c'est un juste retour des choses

**poetry** ['poʊə·tri] *n* poésie *f;* **~ in motion** la grâce personnifiée

**point** [pɔɪnt] **I.** *n* ❶(*sharp end*) pointe *f* ❷(*promontory*) promontoire *m; rocky ~* promontoire rocheux ❸(*particular place*) endroit *m* ❹(*intersection*) point *m* ❺(*particular time*) moment *m;* (*in a process*) point *m;* **to be at the ~ of death** être à l'article de la mort; **at this ~ in time** à ce stade; **at the ~ where she leaves the house** au moment où elle quitte la maison; **~ of no return** point *m* de non-retour; **to do sth up to a ~** faire qc jusqu'à un certain point ❻(*sth expressed, main idea*) point *m;* **that's a good ~** ça, c'est un point intéressant; **to drive home a ~** insister sur un point; **to be beside the ~** être hors sujet; **to get to the ~** aller à l'essentiel; **to get the ~ of sth** saisir qc; **to miss the ~ of sth** ne pas comprendre qc; **to make one's ~** dire ce qu'on a à dire; **to prove one's ~** démontrer qu'on a raison; **to see sb's ~** voir ce que qn veut dire ❼(*purpose*) intérêt *m;* **no/little ~ (in)** doing sth pas/peu d'intérêt à faire qc; **what's the ~ of sth/of doing sth?** quel est l'intérêt de qc/de faire qc? ❽(*aspect*) **weak/strong ~** point *m* faible/fort ❾(*unit of counting or scoring*) point *m*

**⑩**MATH virgule *f;* **two ~ three** deux virgule trois **⑪**(*dot*) point *m* **⑫***pl* (*toes of ballet shoes*) pointes *fpl* ▸ **a case in ~** un bon exemple; **to make a ~ of doing sth** tenir absolument à faire qc **II.***vi* **①**(*show with one's finger*) **to ~ at sb/ sth** montrer qn/qc du doigt **②**(*use as evidence or proof*) **to ~ to sth** attirer l'attention sur qc **③**(*indicate*) **to ~ to sth** indiquer qc; **everything ~s to you as the murderer** tout vous désigne comme étant le meurtrier **④**COMPUT **to ~ to an icon** pointer sur une icône **III.***vt* **①**(*aim*) **to ~ sth at sb/sth** diriger qc sur qn/qc; **to ~ a finger at sb** pointer le doigt vers qn; **to ~ the finger at sb** montrer du doigt **②**(*direct, show position or direction*) **to ~ sb in the right direction** montrer le chemin à qn; **to ~ sb/sth toward sth** diriger qn/qc vers qn/qc; **to ~ the way to sth** indiquer la direction de qc; *fig* montrer la voie à suivre pour qc

◆**point out** *vt* **①**(*show*) montrer **②**(*say*) **to ~ that ...** faire remarquer que ...

◆**point up** *vt form* souligner

**point-blank** **I.***adv* **①**(*at very close range*) à bout portant **②**(*bluntly, directly*) de but en blanc **II.***adj* **①**(*very close, not far away*) **to shoot sb/sth at ~ range** tirer à bout portant sur qn/qc **②**(*blunt, direct*) de but en blanc; **~ question** question *f* à brûle-pourpoint

**pointed** *adj* **①**(*tapering to a point, having a point*) pointu(e) **②**(*penetrating*) lourd(e) de sous-entendus

**pointless** *adj* **it's ~** ça n'a pas de sens; **it's ~ to go now** ça ne sert à rien d'y aller maintenant

**point of view** *n* point *m* de vue

**poison** ['pɔɪ-zⁿn] **I.***n* poison *m;* **to take ~** s'empoisonner ▸ **one man's meat is another man's ~** *prov* le malheur des uns fait le bonheur des autres *prov* **II.***vt* **①**(*give poison to*) a. *fig* empoisonner; (*mind*) corrompre **②**(*put poison in: water, drink*) empoisonner

**poison gas** *n* gaz *m* toxique

**poisonous** *adj* **①**(*containing poison: mushroom, plant*) vénéneux(-euse); (*snake*) venimeux(-euse); (*gas*) toxique **②**(*excessively malicious, malignant*) pernicieux(-euse); (*atmosphere*) nocif(-ive)

**poker¹** *n* (*card game*) poker *m*

**poker²** *n* (*tool*) tisonnier *m*

**Poland** ['poʊ-lənd] *n* la Pologne

**polar** ['poʊ-lər] *adj* **①**GEO polaire **②**(*complete*) **~ opposites** opposés *mpl* complets

**polar bear** *n* ours *m* blanc

**Polaris** *n* étoile *f* polaire

**Pole** [poʊl] *n* (*person*) Polonais(e) *m(f)*

**pole¹** [poʊl] *n* **①**(*for tent*) mât *m;* (*for skiing*) bâton *m;* **fishing ~** canne *f* à pêche

**pole²** [poʊl] *n* **①**(*axis of rotation*) pôle *m* **②**(*one of two opposed positions*) antipode *m;* **to be ~s apart** être aux antipodes l'un de l'autre

**pole dancer** *n* danseuse, dans un club ou bar érotique, qui se sert d'une barre verticale allant du sol au plafond

**pole dancing** *n* danse autour d'une barre verticale allant du sol au plafond dans un club ou bar érotique

**police** [pə-'lis] **I.***n pl* **the ~** (*in town*) la police; (*outside towns*) la gendarmerie; **~ department** service *m* de police **II.***vt* **①**(*officially control and guard*) maintenir l'ordre dans **②**(*control and regulate*) contrôler; **to ~ oneself** se faire la police **③**MIL contrôler

**police car** *n* voiture *f* de police

**police dog** *n* chien *m* policier

**police escort** *n* escorte *f* policière

**police force** *n* **①**(*body of police*) forces *fpl* de l'ordre **②**(*administrative unit*) **the ~** la police

**police lineup** *n* séance *f* d'identification

**policeman** <-men> *n* policier *m*

**police officer** *n* agent *mf* de police

**police raid** *n* raid *m* de la police

**police station** *n* poste *m* de police

**policewoman** <-women> *n* femme *f* policier

P

**policy**[1] ['pa·lə·si] <-cies> n a. POL politique f

**policy**[2] ['pa·lə·si] <-cies> n (insurance) police f d'assurance

**policyholder** n assuré(e) m(f)

**policymaker** n décideur m

**polio** [,pou·li·ou] n polio f

**poliomyelitis** [,pou·li·ou·,maiə·'lai·təs] n poliomyélite f

**polish** ['pa·lɪʃ] I. n ❶ (substance to polish things) cirage m; **furniture ~** cire f; **nail ~** vernis m à ongles; **shoe ~** cirage à chaussures ❷ (act of polishing sth) **to give sth a ~** faire briller qc; **to give one's shoes a ~** cirer ses chaussures ❸ (sophisticated or refined style) raffinement m II. vt a. fig polir; (shoes, floor, furniture) cirer; (silver, brass) astiquer; (nails) vernir; **to ~ one's French** perfectionner son français
♦ **polish off** vt ❶ (finish completely) finir ❷ (defeat easily) achever
♦ **polish up** vt ❶ (polish to a shine) faire briller ❷ (improve, brush up) perfectionner

**Polish** ['pou·lɪʃ] I. adj polonais(e) II. n LING polonais m; s.a. **English**

**polite** [pə·'laɪt] adj ❶ (courteous) poli(e); **to make ~ conversation** bavarder poliment ❷ (refined, cultured) raffiné(e); **~ society** bonne société f

**politely** adv poliment

**politeness** n politesse f

**political** adj politique

**politically** adv **to resolve sth ~** résoudre qc politiquement; **~ correct** politiquement correct

**politician** n politicien(ne) m(f)

**politics** n + sing vb politique f; **to talk ~** parler politique; **to be into ~** faire de la politique; **to go into ~** se lancer dans la politique

**poll** [poʊl] I. n ❶ (public survey) sondage m ❷ **the ~s** pl (voting places) les urnes fpl ❸ (number of votes cast) voix fpl II. vt ❶ (record the opinion) interroger ❷ (receive) **to ~ votes** obtenir des voix

**pollen** ['pa·lən] n pollen m

**pollutant** [pəl·'u·tənt] n polluant m

**pollute** [pə·'lut] vt ❶ (contaminate, make impure) polluer ❷ fig (destroy the purity, wholesomeness) corrompre

**polluter** n pollueur, -euse m, f

**pollution** n pollution f

**polo** ['pou·lou] n SPORTS, FASHION polo m

**polyester** [,pa·li·'es·tər] n CHEM polyester m; **~ shirt/pants** chemise f/pantalon m en polyester

**polystyrene** [,pa·lɪ·'stai·rin] n polystyrène m

**polytechnic** [,pa·lɪ·'tek·nɪk] n ≈ Institut m universitaire de technologie

**pompous** ['pam·pəs] adj pej pompeux(-euse)

**poncho** ['pan·tʃou] n poncho m

**pond** [pand] n ❶ (still water) mare f; (larger) étang m; **duck ~** mare aux canards ❷ iron (ocean, Atlantic ocean) **the ~** l'Océan m

**pony** ['pou·ni] n poney m

**ponytail** n queue f de cheval

**poodle** ['pu·dl] n ZOOL caniche m

**pool**[1] [pul] I. n ❶ (body of liquid) mare f; (of water, rain, blood, light) flaque f ❷ (construction built to hold water) bassin m ❸ SPORTS **swimming ~** piscine f II. vt mettre en commun

**pool**[2] [pul] I. n ❶ (common fund) fonds m commun ❷ (common supply) réservoir m; (for cars) parc m; (of contacts) réseau m; **a ~ of talent** un vivier de talents ❸ SPORTS billard m américain ❹ (total money staked in gambling) cagnotte f II. vt ❶ (combine in a common fund) **to ~ sth** mettre qc en commun ❷ (share) partager

**pooper-scooper** ['pu·pər,sku·pər] n ramasse-crottes m inv

**poor** [pʊr] I. adj ❶ (lacking money) pauvre ❷ (of inadequate quality) mauvais(e); **to be ~ at sth** être mauvais à qc; **to be a ~ excuse for sth** être une mauvaise excuse pour qc; **to have ~ eyesight** avoir une mauvaise vue; **to be in ~ health** être en mauvaise santé; **a ~ memory** une mauvaise mémoire ❸ (deserving of pity) pauvre ❹ iron

**P**

(*humble*) humble **II.** *n* the ~ *pl* les pauvres *mpl*

**poorly I.** *adv* ① (*in a manner resulting from poverty*) pauvrement ② (*inadequately, badly*) mal; ~ **dressed** mal habillé; **to think ~ of sb/sth** avoir une mauvaise opinion de qn/qc **II.** *adj* souffrant(e); **to feel ~** être malade

**pop¹** [pɑp] **I.** *n* ① (*noise*) pan *m* ② *inf* (*drink*) boisson *f* gazeuse **II.** *vi* ① (*make a sound: cork*) sauter; (*balloon, gun*) éclater; (*ears*) se déboucher ② (*bulge: eyes*) écarquiller **III.** *vt* ① (*make a sound: cork*) faire sauter; (*balloon*) faire éclater ② (*put*) mettre; **to ~ sth in your mouth** fourrer qc dans sa bouche ③ *inf* (*take: pills*) prendre **IV.** *adv* **to go ~** exploser

◆**pop in** *vi* (*to shop*) entrer rapidement; (*to friend's house*) passer

◆**pop off** *vi inf* (*talk angrily*) **to ~ about sth** pester contre qc

◆**pop up** *vi* surgir

**pop²** [pɑp] *n* (*father*) papa *m*

**pop³** [pɑp] **I.** *adj* ① (*popular: culture*) pop *inv* ② MUS (*concert, singer*) pop *inv* ③ *pej* de quatre sous; ~ **psychology** psychologie *f* à bon marché **II.** *n* MUS pop *f*

**popcorn** ['pɑp·kɔrn] *n* pop-corn *m*

**pope** [poʊp] *n* ① (*bishop of Rome*) pape *m* ② (*Orthodox priest*) pope *m*

**popper** ['pɑ·pər] *n* (*for corn*) machine *f* à pop-corn

**poppy** ['pɑ·pi] <-ppies> *n* coquelicot *m*; (*for drugs*) pavot *m*

**Popsicle®** *n* esquimau® *m* (glacé)

**pop star** *n* vedette *f* de la chanson

**popular** ['pɑ·pjə·lər] *adj* ① (*liked, understood by many people*) populaire; (*brand*) courant(e); **to be ~** être apprécié de tous; **you won't be ~ if you say that** ça va ne pas te rendre populaire de dire ça ② (*widespread*) étendu(e); **a ~ misconception** une idée fausse largement répandue ③ (*of or by the people: culture, tradition*) populaire; (*feeling*) du peuple

**popularity** [ˌpɑ·pjə·'ler·ə·ti] *n* popularité *f*

**population** *n* population *f*

**population explosion** *n* explosion *f* démographique

**pop-up window** *n* COMPUT incrustation *f*

**porcelain** ['pɔr·sə¹·ɪn] *n* porcelaine *f*

**porch** [pɔrtʃ] *n* ① (*roofed part: of a house, church*) marquise *f* ② (*of a hotel*) véranda *f*

**porcupine** ['pɔr·kjə·paɪn] *n* porc-épic *m*

**pork** [pɔrk] *n* porc *m*

**porn** [pɔrn] *n inf* porno *m*

**pornographic** *adj* ① (*containing pornography*) pornographique ② (*obscene*) obscène

**pornography** [pɔr·'nɑ·grə·fi] *n* pornographie *f*

**porpoise** ['pɔr·pəs] *n* marsouin *m*

**porridge** ['pɔr·ɪdʒ] *n* bouillie *f* d'avoine

**port¹** [pɔrt] *n* (*harbor*) port *m*; ~ **of call** NAUT escale *f*; *fig* halte *f*; **to come into ~** entrer dans le port; **to leave ~** lever l'ancre ▸ **any ~ in a storm** nécessité fait loi *prov*

**port²** [pɔrt] AVIAT, NAUT **I.** *n* bâbord *m*; **to turn to ~** virer à bâbord **II.** *adj* **the ~ side** à bâbord

**port³** [pɔrt] COMPUT **I.** *n* port *m* **II.** *vt* transférer

**port⁴** [pɔrt] *n* (*wine*) porto *m*

**portable** ['pɔr·tə·bl] *adj* portatif(-ive); ~ **radio** poste *m* portatif; ~ **computer** ordinateur *m* portable; ~ **telephone** téléphone *m* portable, cellulaire *m Québec*, Natel® *m Suisse*

**portal** ['pɔː·tə¹] *n* INET portail *m*; **web** [*o* **Internet**] ~ portail *m* web [*o* Internet]

**porter** ['pɔr·tər] *n* ① (*person who carries*) porteur *m*; **hotel ~** portier *m* ② (*train attendant*) employé(e) *m(f)* des wagons-lits

**portfolio** [pɔrt·'foʊ·li·oʊ] *n* ① (*case*) serviette *f* ② (*examples of drawings, designs*) portfolio *m* ③ FIN, POL portefeuille *m*

**portion** ['pɔr·ʃ°n] **I.** *n* ① (*part*) partie *f*; **to accept one's ~ of the blame** accep-

P

ter sa part de responsabilité ❷ CULIN portion *f* **II.** *vt* to ~ sth (out) [*o* to ~ (out) sth] partager qc; to ~ sth (out) among ... répartir qc entre ...

**portrait** [ˈpɔrt‧rɪt] *n* a. *fig* portrait *m*

**portraitist, portrait painter** *n* portraitiste *mf*

**portray** [pɔrˈtreɪ] *vt* dépeindre; **he's ~ed as a monster** il est présenté comme un monstre; **the actor ~ing the king** l'acteur qui incarne le roi

**Portugal** [ˈpɔr‧tʃə‧gəl] *n* le Portugal

**Portuguese** [ˌpɔr‧tʃəˈgiz] **I.** *adj* portugais(e) **II.** *n* ❶ (*person*) Portugais(e) *m(f)* ❷ LING portugais *m; s.a.* **English**

**pose** [poʊz] **I.** *vi* ❶ (*assume a position: person*) poser ❷ (*pretend to be*) to ~ as sb/sth se faire passer pour qn/qc ❸ (*behave in an affected manner*) se donner des airs **II.** *vt* ❶ (*cause*) poser; (*difficulty*) soulever; (*threat*) présenter ❷ (*ask: question*) poser; to ~ questions questionner **III.** *n* ❶ (*bodily position*) pose *f;* to strike a ~ poser pour la galerie ❷ (*pretense*) affectation *f*

**poser**[1] *n pej* (*pretentious person*) poseur, -euse *m, f*

**poser**[2] *n* (*problem*) question *f* difficile

**posh** [pɑʃ] *adj inf* chic *inv*

**position** [pəˈzɪʃ‧ən] **I.** *n* ❶ (*place*) place *f;* to be in a different ~ être dans une position différente ❷ (*location*) situation *f;* in/into ~ en place; to get in ~ être en place ❸ SPORTS, MIL position *f* ❹ (*place in order*) place *f* ❺ (*job*) emploi *m;* ~ of responsibility/of trust poste *m* à responsabilité/de confiance ❻ (*situation*) situation *f;* to be in the ~ of having to ~ se trouver dans la situation de devoir +*infin;* to be in no ~ to help/criticize être mal placé pour aider/critiquer ❼ *form* (*opinion*) position *f;* John's ~ is that ... d'après Jean, ...; to take the ~ that ... adopter le point de vue que ... **II.** *vt* ❶ (*locate*) mettre en position; (*troops*) poster ❷ (*put in place: object*) mettre en place; (*village*) situer; to ~ oneself on sth se mettre sur qc

**positive** [ˈpɑ‧zə‧tɪv] *adj* ❶ (*certain*) certain(e); (*evidence*) concret(-ète); to be ~ about sth être sûr de qc ❷ (*giving cause for hope: attitude, response*) positif(-ive); (*criticism*) constructif(-ive); to think ~ voir les choses de façon positive ❸ MED, MATH, ELEC positif(-ive) ❹ (*complete: miracle, outrage*) véritable

**positively** *adv* ❶ (*in the affirmative: reply*) positivement ❷ (*in a good way: react*) positivement; **more ~** de façon plus positive ❸ *inf* (*completely*) absolument; **you're ~ certain?** tu es absolument certain?; **they ~ hate him** ils le détestent franchement

**possess** [pəˈzes] *vt* a. *fig* posséder; **what ~ed you?** qu'est-ce qui t'/vous a pris?; **to be ~ed by anger/ambition** être possédé par la colère/l'ambition

**possession** *n* ❶ (*having*) possession *f;* **it's** [*o* **I have it**] **in my ~** c'est en ma possession; **to come into ~ of sth** *form* acquérir qc ❷ *pl* (*something owned*) biens *mpl* ❸ POL colonie *f*

**possessive** *adj* possessif(-ive)

**possibility** [ˌpɑ‧sə‧ˈbɪl‧ə‧ti] *n* <-ties> (*feasible circumstance or action*) possibilité *f* ❷ *pl* (*potential*) potentiel *m* ❸ (*likelihood*) éventualité *f;* **there is every ~ that** il est fort possible que +*subj;* **is there any ~ that ...?** *form* y a-t-il une possibilité pour que +*subj?*

**possible** [ˈpɑ‧sə‧bl] *adj* ❶ (*that can be done*) possible; **there is no ~ excuse for this** il n'y a aucune excuse possible pour ça; **as soon as/if ~** dès que/si possible ❷ (*that could happen*) éventuel(le)

**possibly** *adv* ❶ (*by any means*) **he did all he ~ could to land the plane** il a fait tout ce qui était dans son possible pour atterrir ❷ (*adding emphasis*) **could you ~ lend me your car?** te/vous serait-il possible de me prêter ta/votre voiture?; **he said he could not ~ go to the reception** il a dit qu'il lui était impossible d'aller à la réception; **I can't ~ accept it** je ne peux vraiment pas accepter ❸ (*perhaps*) peut-être; **very** ~ très probablement

**post¹** [poʊst] **I.** *n* ❶ (*pole*) poteau *m* ❷ (*stake*) pieu *m* ❸ SPORTS poteau *m* **II.** *vt* annoncer ► **to keep sb ~ed** tenir qn au courant

**post²** [poʊst] **I.** *n* ❶ MIL poste *m* ❷ (*job/place where someone works*) poste *m;* **to take up a** ~ entrer en fonction **II.** *vt* poster; **to** ~ **oneself somewhere** se poster quelque part; **to be** ~**ed somewhere** être affecté quelque part ❷ LAW **to** ~ **bail for sb** payer la caution de qn

**post-** *in compounds* post; ~**communism** postcommunisme *m;* ~**communist Russia** la Russie de l'après-communisme; **a** ~**concert dinner** un dîner après le concert

**postage** ['poʊ·stɪdʒ] *n* affranchissement *m*

**postal** ['poʊ·stᵊl] *adj* (*employee*) postal(e) ❷ *sl* **to go** ~ péter les plombs

**postcard** *n* carte *f* postale

**poster** *n* (*announcement*) affiche *f;* (*in home*) poster *m*

**posterity** [pɑ·'ster·ə·ti] *n* postérité *f*

**postgraduate I.** *n* étudiant(e) *m(f)* de troisième cycle **II.** *adj* de troisième cycle

**posthaste** *adv form* en toute hâte

**Post-it®** *n* Post-it® *m*

**postman** <-men> *n* facteur, -trice *m, f*

**postmark I.** *n* cachet *m* de la poste **II.** *vt* oblitérer

**postmodern** *adj* postmoderne

**postmodernism** *n* postmodernisme *m*

**postmortem I.** *n* ❶ MED ~ (**examination**) autopsie *f;* **to carry out a** ~ faire une autopsie ❷ *inf* (*discussion*) synthèse *f* rétrospective **II.** *adj* ❶ (*related to a postmortem*) d'autopsie ❷ (*after death*) post-mortem *inv*

**postnatal** *adj* post-natal(e)

**post office** *n* **the** ~ la Poste

**postoperative** *adj* postopératoire

**postpaid I.** *adj* port payé *inv;* (*envelope, reply card*) affranchi(e) **II.** *adv* en port payé

**postpone** [poʊs(t)·'poʊn] *vt* (*delay*)

différer, postposer *Belgique;* **to** ~ **sth until a later date** renvoyer qc à une date ultérieure; **I've** ~**d traveling** j'ai retardé mon voyage

**postponement** *n* ❶ (*delaying*) délai *m* ❷ (*deferment*) renvoi *m* à une date ultérieure; (*of payment*) retard *m;* (*of a court case*) ajournement *m*

**postscript** ['poʊs(t)·skrɪp] *n* ❶ (*at the end of a letter*) post-scriptum *m inv* ❷ (*at the end of a story, article*) postface *f* ❸ *fig* **to add a** ~ **to sth** dire un mot de plus sur qc

**posture** ['pɑs·tʃər] **I.** *n* ❶ (*habitual position of the body*) posture *f;* **to have good/bad** ~ bien/mal se tenir ❷ (*pose*) pose *f;* **in a very awkward** ~ dans une très fâcheuse posture; **in a kneeling/an upright** ~ (en position) agenouillée/debout; **to adopt a** ~ prendre une pose ❸ (*attitude*) attitude *f* **II.** *vi pej* se donner des airs

**postwar** *adj* d'après-guerre; ~ **era** après--guerre *f*

**pot¹** [pɑt] **I.** *n* ❶ (*container*) pot *m;* (*for cooking*) marmite *f;* ~**s and pans** casseroles *fpl;* **coffee** ~ cafetière *f* ❷ (*amount contained in a pot*) **a** ~ **of coffee** un grand café ❸ *inf* (*common fund*) cagnotte *f* ❹ (*total staked money*) **to win the** ~ gagner la cagnotte ❺ *inf* (*a lot*) ~**s of sth** des tas de qc; ~**s of money** beaucoup d'argent; **to have** ~**s of money** rouler sur l'or ❻ *inf* (*potbelly*) gros ventre *m* ❼ *inf* (*potshot*) **to take a** ~ **at sb/sth** tirer à l'aveuglette sur qn/qc ► **to go to** ~ *inf* (*country, economy, business*) aller à la ruine; (*hopes, plan*) tomber à l'eau **II.** <-tt-> *vt* ❶ (*put in a pot: plants*) mettre qc en pot ❷ (*preserve: food*) mettre qc en conserve ❸ *inf* (*shoot*) buter

**pot²** [pɑt] *n sl* (*marijuana*) herbe *f*

**potato** [pə·'teɪ·toʊ] <-es> *n* pomme *f* de terre; **mashed** ~**es** purée *f* (de pommes de terre)

**potato chips** *npl* chips *fpl*

**potato peeler** *n* économe *m*

**potent** *adj* puissant(e); (*motive, argument*) convaincant(e); (*drink*) très fort(e); (*force, spell, temptation*) profond(e); MED viril(e)

**potential** I. *adj* potentiel(le) II. *n* potentiel *m*; **to achieve one's ~** atteindre son maximum; **to have considerable ~** offrir des possibilités considérables

**potentially** *adv* potentiellement

**pothole** ['pat‧hoʊl] *n* **①** (*hole in road surface*) nid *m* de poule **②** (*underground hole*) caverne *f*

**potion** ['poʊ‧ʃən] *n* **①** (*drink*) breuvage *m*; **love/magic ~** philtre *m* d'amour/magique **②** *pej* (*medicine*) potion *f*

**pot roast** *n* rôti *m* à la cocotte

**potted** ['pa‧tɪd] *adj* (*plant*) en pot; (*food*) en conserve; **~ meat** terrine *f*

**potter** ['pa‧tər] *n* potier *m*

**pottery** ['pa‧tər‧i] *n* poterie *f*

**potty** ['pa‧ti] <-ties> *n* pot *m* de bébé

**pouch** [paʊtʃ] *n* **①** (*a small bag*) petit sac *m*; **tobacco ~** blague *f* à tabac **②** (*animal's pocket*) poche *f*

**poultry** ['poʊl‧tri] *n* **①** *pl* (*birds*) volaille *f* **②** (*meat*) volaille *f*

**pound¹** [paʊnd] *n* (*unit of weight, currency*) livre *f*; **ten ~s sterling** dix livres sterling

**pound²** [paʊnd] I. *vt* **①** (*hit repeatedly*) frapper; **the waves ~ed the ship** les vagues fouettaient le navire **②** (*crush: spices*) piler; **to ~ to pieces** réduire en miettes **③** (*beat*) battre **④** (*bombard*) a. *fig* pilonner; **to ~ sb with questions** assaillir qn de questions **⑤** (*walk along*) **to ~ the pavement** battre le trottoir; **to ~ the beat** patrouiller **⑥** (*instill*) **to ~ sth into sb's head** faire rentrer qc dans la tête de qn II. *vi* **①** (*beat on noisily*) frapper; **to ~ on a table** frapper fort sur une table; **to ~ on a wall** cogner sur un mur; **to ~ away at sth** taper sur qc à tour de bras; **to ~ away at the keyboard** taper sur le clavier comme un forcené **②** (*throb*) battre fort; (*heart*) battre vite; **my head is ~ing**

j'ai des élancements dans la tête **③** (*walk/run noisily*) marcher/courir d'un pas pesant

**pound³** [paʊnd] *n* (*place for stray animals, cars*) fourrière *f*

**pour** [pɔr] I. *vt* **①** (*cause to flow*) verser **②** (*serve*) servir; **to ~ sb sth** servir qc à qn **③** *fig* déverser; **the company ~ed a lot of money into the project** la société a investi beaucoup d'argent dans le projet ▸ **to ~ money down the drain** jeter l'argent par les fenêtres; **to ~ cold water on sth** se montrer peu enthousiaste pour qc II. *vi* **①** (*fill a glass or cup*) verser **②** (*flow in large amounts*) couler à flots; (*smoke*) s'échapper; **water ~ed through the hole** l'eau *f* coulait à travers le trou; **the crowd ~ed into the theater** la foule entrait en masse dans le théâtre III. *n* (*rain*) **it's ~ing** il pleut à verse

◆**pour in** I. *vi* se déverser; (*letters, messages, reports*) arriver par milliers II. *vt* verser; (*money*) investir

◆**pour out** I. *vt* **①** (*serve from a container: drinks*) verser **②** (*recount*) déverser; **to ~ one's problems/ thoughts to sb** déballer ses problèmes/ pensées à qn **③** (*cause to flow quickly*) répandre II. *vi* se déverser

**pout** [paʊt] I. *vi* faire la moue II. *vt* **to ~ one's lips** faire la moue III. *n* moue *f*

**poverty** ['pa‧vər‧ti] *n* pauvreté *f*; **to live in** (**abject**) **~** vivre dans le (plus grand) besoin; **~ of sth** *form* pénurie de qc *f*; **he has such a ~ of intelligence** il est dénué d'intelligence

**poverty line** *n* seuil *m* de pauvreté; **to live below the ~** vivre en dessous du seuil de pauvreté

**poverty-stricken** *adj* frappé(e) par la misère

**POW** [,pi‧oʊ‧'dʌb‧l‧ju] *n abbr of* **prisoner of war** prisonnier, -ère *m*, *f* de guerre

**powder** ['paʊ‧dər] I. *n* **①** poudre *f*; **curry ~** curry *m* en poudre **②** (*make-up*) poudre *f* **③** (*snow*) poudreuse *f* II. *vt* saupoudrer; **to ~ one's nose** a.

**P**

*iron* se poudrer le nez; **to be ~ed with sth** être saupoudré de qc

**powdered** *adj* ❶(*in powder form*) en poudre; (*coffee*) instantané(e) ❷(*covered with powder*) poudré(e)

**powdered sugar** *n* sucre *m* glace

**powder room** *n* toilettes *fpl* pour dames

**power** [pauər] **I.** *n* ❶(*ability to control*) pouvoir *m*; **to be in sb's ~** être à la merci de qn ❷(*political control*) pouvoir *m* ❸(*country, organization, person*) puissance *f* ❹(*right*) pouvoir *m*; **it is within sb's ~ to ~ +***infin* c'est dans les compétences *fpl* de qn de +*infin* ❺(*ability: of concentration, persuasion*) pouvoir *m*; **to do everything in one's ~** faire tout ce qui est en son pouvoir ❻(*strength*) puissance *f*; **~ walking** marche *f* en force ❼(*electricity*) énergie *f*; **~ failure** panne *f* d'alimentation; **~ switch** interrupteur *m* général; **~ drill** perceuse *f* électrique ❽(*magnifying strength*) agrandissement *m* ❾(*value of magnifying strength*) grossissement *m* ❿MATH puissance *f*; **three to the second ~** trois puissance deux ▶**more ~ to** <u>you</u>! tant mieux pour vous!; **the ~s that** <u>be</u> les autorités *fpl* **II.** *vi* (*move*) **to ~ along the track** foncer sur la piste **III.** *vt* (*engine, rocket*) propulser; **nuclear-~ed** nucléaire

**powerboat** *n* hors-bord *m inv*

**power brakes** *npl* AUTO servofreins *mpl*

**power cable** *n* câble *m* d'alimentation

**powerful** *adj* ❶(*influential, mighty*) puissant(e) ❷(*having great physical strength*) vigoureux(-euse); (*arms, legs, muscles, swimmer*) puissant(e) ❸(*having a great effect: wind, storm*) violent(e); (*bite, ideas*) profond(e); (*drug, voice*) fort(e); (*explosion, medicine, incentive*) puissant(e); (*evidence, argument*) solide ❹(*affecting the emotions: drama, literature, music*) puissant(e); (*language, painting, emotions*) fort(e) ❺(*able to perform very well: car, computer, motor*) performant(e); (*light*) intense; (*memory*) puissant(e)

**powerfully** *adv* ❶(*effectively*) efficacement ❷(*using great force*) puissamment ❸(*greatly: influenced*) fortement

**powerless** *adj* impuissant(e); **to be ~ to +***infin* ne pas pouvoir +*infin*; **to be ~ against sb/sth** être impuissant face à qn/qc

**power line** *n* ❶ELEC ligne *f* électrique ❷(*high voltage electrical line*) ligne *f* (à) haute tension

**power of attorney** *n* procuration *f*

**power outage** *n* coupure *f* de courant

**power plant** *n* centrale *f* électrique; **coal-fired/nuclear ~** centrale thermique au charbon/nucléaire

**power station** *n s.* **power plant**

**power steering** *n* AUTO direction *f* assistée

**pp.** *n abbr of* **pages** pp. *fpl*

**PR** [piː'ɑr] *n* ❶*abbr of* **public relations** relations *fpl* publiques *m* ❷*abbr of* **Puerto Rico** ❸*abbr of* **proportional representation** représentation *f* proportionnelle

**practical** ['præktɪkəl] *adj* ❶(*not theoretical*) pratique; **for all ~ purposes** à toutes fins utiles ❷(*realistic: person, solution*) pratique; **it is ~ to do sth** qc est faisable ❸(*good at solving problems*) bricoleur(euse) ❹(*suitable*) fonctionnel(le) ❺*inf* (*virtual*) quasi-

**practically** *adv* pratiquement; **~ speaking** concrètement (parlant); **~ impossible** (*almost*) pratiquement impossible; (*in a practical manner*) impossible sur le plan pratique

**practice** ['præktɪs] **I.** *n* ❶(*action, performance*) pratique *f*; **I've had a lot of ~** j'ai eu beaucoup d'entraînement ❷(*normal procedure*) pratique *f*; **to make a ~ of sth** prendre l'habitude de qc ❸(*training session*) entraînement *m*; **ballet/music ~** exercices *mpl* de danse/de musique; **to be out of ~** être rouillé ❹(*business: of a doctor, lawyer*) cabinet *m* ▶**~ makes perfect** c'est en forgeant qu'on devient forgeron *prov* **II.** *vt* ❶(*do, carry out*) pratiquer; (*good hygiene*) avoir ❷(*improve skill*) s'exercer à; (*one's backhand*)

**P**

améliorer; (*flute, one's French*) travailler; **to ~ doing sth** s'entraîner à faire qc ❸(*work in: dentistry, law, medicine*) exercer ►**to ~ what one preaches** mettre en pratique ses propres préceptes III.*vi* ❶(*train*) s'exercer ❷SPORTS s'entraîner ❸(*work in a profession*) exercer

**practicing** *adj* (*Catholic*) pratiquant(e); (*doctor*) en exercice

**praise** [preɪz] I.*vt* ❶(*express approval*) faire l'éloge de; (*child*) féliciter; **he ~d the work of the firefighters** il a rendu hommage au travail des pompiers; **to ~ sb/sth to the skies** porter qn/qc aux nues ❷(*worship*) exalter; (*God*) louer II.*n* ❶(*expression of approval*) éloge *m*; **to sing the ~s of sb/sth** chanter les louanges de qn/qc; **in ~ of sb/sth** en l'honneur de qn/qc ❷*form* (*worship*) louange *f*; **to give ~ to God/the Lord** glorifier Dieu/le Seigneur

**prank** [præŋk] *n* canular *m*; **to play a ~ on sb** jouer un tour à qn

**prawn** [prɔːn] *n* crevette *f* rose

**pray** [preɪ] I.*vt, vi* prier II.*adv form* **~, do come in!** veuillez entrer, je vous en (en) prie!

**prayer** [preə] *n* prière *f*; **to not have a ~ of doing sth** n'avoir que de maigres espoirs de faire qc

**prayer rug** *n* tapis *m* de prière

**praying mantis** ['preɪ·ɪŋ·'mæn·tɪs] *n* mante *f* religieuse

**pre-** *in compounds* pré; **~revolutionary France** la France d'avant la révolution; **a ~term meeting** une réunion avant le début du trimestre

**preach** [pritʃ] I.*vi* ❶(*give a sermon*) faire un sermon; **to ~ to sb** prêcher qn ❷*pej* (*lecture*) **to ~ to sb** sermonner qn ►**to ~ to the converted** prêcher un converti II.*vt* prêcher; **to ~ a sermon** faire un sermon; **to ~ patience/restraint** exhorter à la patience/à la modération

**preacher** *n* pasteur *mf*

**precarious** [prɪˈker·i·əs] *adj* précaire

**precaution** [prɪˈkɔ·ʃⁿn] *n* précaution *f*;

**to take ~(s) against sth** prendre des mesures *fpl* contre qc

**precautionary** *adj* préventif(-ive)

**precede** [prɪˈsid] *vt* précéder

**precedent** *n* précédent *m*; **to break with ~** couper d'avec le passé; **to set a ~** créer un précédent

**preceding** *adj* précédent(e); (*decade*) dernier(-ère); (*year*) d'avant; **the ~ day** la veille

**precinct** ['pri·sɪŋ(k)t] *n* ❶(*police or fire service district*) quartier *m* de sécurité ❷(*electoral district*) circonscription *f* électorale ❸(*boundary*) enceinte *f*; **within the ~s of sth** dans l'enceinte de qc; **the ~s of sth** les environs *mpl* de qc

**precious** ['preʃ·əs] I.*adj* ❶(*of great value*) précieux(-euse); **to be ~ to sb** être cher à qn ❷*pej* (*affected*) affecté(e); (*person*) compassé(e) II.*adv inf* **~ few** très peu; **to be ~ little help** n'être d'aucun secours

**precipice** ['pres·ə·pɪs] *n* ❶(*steep side*) précipice *m* ❷*fig* (*dangerous situation*) gouffre *m*; **to stand at the edge of the ~** être au bord du précipice

**precipitation** *n* précipitation *f*

**precise** [prɪˈsaɪs] *adj* ❶(*accurate, exact*) précis(e); (*pronunciation*) clair(e); (*observation*) détaillé(e); (*tone of voice*) juste; (*work*) soigné(e) ❷(*careful: movement*) précis(e); **to be ~ about doing sth** être minutieux en faisant qc

**precisely** *adv* ❶(*exactly*) précisément; **at ~ midnight** à minuit précis ❷(*just*) juste; **to do ~ the opposite** faire tout le contraire; **to do ~ that** faire précisément cela ❸(*carefully: work*) avec rigueur

**precision** [prɪˈsɪʒ·ⁿn] *n* précision *f*; **with mathematical ~** avec une rigueur mathématique; **with great ~** avec (un) grand soin; **~ timing** chronométrage *m* de précision

**precocious** [prɪˈkoʊ·ʃəs] *adj* ❶(*developing early: maturity, talent, skill*) précoce ② *pej* (*maturing too early*) prématuré(e)

**preconfigured** *adj inv* a ~ **computer** un ordinateur préconfiguré

**predator** ['pre·də·tər] *n* (*animal*) prédateur *m*; (*bird*) rapace *m*

**predecessor** ['pred·ə·ses·ər] *n* prédécesseur *mf*

**predict** [prɪ·'dɪkt] *vt* prédire

**predictable** *adj* ① (*able to be predicted*) prévisible ② *pej* (*not very original*) banal(e)

**prediction** *n* prédiction *f*

**predominantly** *adv* (*European, hostile*) majoritairement; **horses figure ~ in his paintings** il a peint surtout des chevaux

**preeminence** *n form* prééminence *f*; **America's ~ in this sport** la primauté des États-Unis dans ce sport; **sb's intellectual ~** la supériorité intellectuelle de qn

**preeminent** *adj form* prééminent(e); (*artist, scientist, sportsman*) éminent(e)

**preempt** *vt form* ① (*act before: person*) devancer; (*action, choice*) anticiper ② (*to have a legal right*) avoir une priorité légale sur ③ (*to use one's legal right*) exercer son droit de préemption sur

**preemption** *n* ① (*prior action*) action *f* préventive; **war of ~** MIL guerre *f* d'assaut ② (*right of appropriation before others*) droit *m* de préemption ③ ECON marché *m* préférentiel

**preemptive** *adj* préventif(ive)

**preexist** *vt* préexister à

**preexisting** *adj* (*condition*) préexistant(e)

**prefab** ['pri·fæb] *inf* I. *n* préfabriqué *m* II. *adj* en préfabriqué

**preface** ['pre·fɪs] I. *n* (*introduction*) préface *f*; (*of a report*) préliminaire *m*; (*of a speech*) introduction *f* II. *vt form* ① (*write a preface to*) préfacer ② (*introduce*) **to ~ sth with sth** faire précéder qc de qc

**prefect** ['pri·fekt] *n* (*official*) préfet *m*

**prefer** [prɪ·'fɜr] <-rr-> *vt* ① (*like better*) préférer; **to ~ sth to sth** préférer qc à qc; **sb would ~ that** qn aimerait mieux que +*subj* ② LAW **to ~ charges against sb** porter plainte contre qn

**preferable** ['pref·ər·ə·bl] *adj* préférable

**preferably** *adv* de préférence

**preference** ['pref·ər·ən(t)s] *n* (*liking better, preferred thing*) préférence *f*; **in ~ to doing sth** plutôt que de faire qc

**preferential** *adj* (*treatment*) préférentiel(le)

**prefix** ['pri·fɪks] <-es> *n* LING préfixe *m*

**pregnancy** ['preg·nən(t)·si] *n* grossesse *f*; (*in animals*) gestation *f*

**pregnant** *adj* ① MED (*woman*) enceinte; **to get sb ~** mettre qn enceinte ② (*meaningful*) lourd(e) de sens

**prejudge** [,pri·'dʒʌdʒ] *vt pej* **to ~ sb** avoir des préjugés sur qn; **to ~ sth** préjuger de qc

**prejudice** ['predʒ·ə·dɪs] I. *n* ① (*preconceived opinion*) préjugé *m* ② (*bias*) parti *m* pris; **without ~ to sth** sans porter atteinte à qc II. *vt* porter atteinte à; (*chances*) compromettre; (*cause, outcome, result*) préjuger de; LAW (*case*) entraver le déroulement de; (*witness, jury*) influencer

**prejudiced** *adj pej* (*attitude, judgment, opinion*) préconçu(e); (*witness*) partial(e)

**preliminary** [prɪ·'lɪm·ə·ner·i] I. *adj* (*selection, stage, study, talk*) préliminaire; SPORTS (*heat*) éliminatoire II. <-ries> *n* ① (*introduction*) préliminaire *m*; **as a ~** en (guise d')introduction ② SPORTS épreuve *f* éliminatoire ③ *form* (*exam*) examen *m* préparatoire; (*with quota selection*) concours *m* d'entrée ④ *pl* PUBL sélection *f*

**premarital** [,pri·'mer·ə·t̬əl] *adj* avant le mariage

**premature** [,pri·mə·'tʊr] *adj* prématuré(e)

**premier** [prɪ·'mɪr] *adj* le(la) plus important(e)

**premium quality** *n* qualité *f* supérieure

**preoccupied** *adj* **to be ~** être préoccu-

**P**

pé; **to be ~ with sb/sth** se faire du souci pour qn/qc

**prepaid** [ˌpriːˈpeɪd] *adj* prépayé(e);
(*envelope, postcard*) préaffranchi(e);
(*charge*) réglé(e) d'avance

**preparation** [ˌpre·pə·ˈreɪ·ʃ°n] I. *n*
❶ (*getting ready*) préparation *f*
❷ (*substance*) préparation *f* ❸ *pl*
(*measures*) préparatifs *mpl;* **to make
(one's) ~ for sth/to +** *infin* se préparer à qc/à + *infin* II. *adj* (*stage*) préparatoire; (*time*) de préparation

**prepare** [prɪ·ˈper] I. *vt* préparer; **to ~
+** *infin* s'apprêter à + *infin;* **to ~ sb for
sth/to +** *infin* préparer qn à qc/à + *infin*
II. *vi* **to ~ for sth** se préparer à qc

**prepay** [ˌpriːˈpeɪ] *vt irr* payer d'avance

**preposition** [ˌpre·pə·ˈzɪʃ·°n] *n* préposition *f*

**preposterous** [prɪ·ˈpɑ·stər·əs] *adj* ex-
travagant(e); (*accusation*) absurde;
(*idea*) farfelu(e)

**preschool** I. *n* maternelle *f* II. *adj* pré-
scolaire

**prescribe** [prɪ·ˈskraɪb] *vt* ❶ (*give as
treatment*) **to ~ sth for sb** prescrire qc
à qn; **to be ~d sth** se faire prescrire qc
❷ (*recommend*) recommander ❸ *form*
(*allocate*) allouer ❹ (*order*) dicter; **as
~d by law** comme dicté par la loi; **in-
ternationally ~d standards** normes
*fpl* internationales

**prescription** [prɪ·ˈskrɪp·ʃ°n] *n* ❶ (*doctor's order*) ordonnance *f* ❷ *form* (*rule*)
prescription *f*

**presence** [ˈprez·°n(t)s] *n* présence *f*
► **to make one's ~ felt** se faire remarquer

**present**[1] [ˈprez·°nt] I. *n* **the ~** le présent; **at ~** à présent, à cette heure *Belgique* II. *adj* ❶ (*current*) actuel(le); **at
the ~ moment/time** en ce moment
❷ LING **~ tense** (temps *m*) présent *m*
❸ (*in attendance, existing*) présent(e);
**~ company excepted** à l'exception
des personnes ici présentes

**present**[2] [ˈprez·°nt, *vb:* prɪ·ˈzent] I. *n*
(*gift*) cadeau *m;* **to get sth as a ~** avoir
qc en cadeau; **to give sth to sb as a ~**

offrir qc à qn II. *vt* ❶ (*give*) présenter;
**to ~ sb with a challenge** mettre qn au
défi; **to ~ sb with (the) facts** exposer
les faits à qn; **to ~ sth to sb, to ~ sb
with sth** (*gift*) offrir qc à qn; (*award,
medal, report*) remettre qc à qn
❷ (*offer*) offrir; **to ~ a sharp contrast
to sth** offrir un contraste net avec qc
❸ (*exhibit*) exposer; (*paper, report*)
présenter ❹ (*introduce*) présenter
❺ (*host*) présenter ❻ (*perform:
concert, show*) donner ❼ (*deliver: bill*)
remettre ❽ (*bring before court*) exposer

**presentation** [ˌprez·°n·ˈter·ʃ°n] *n*
❶ (*act of presenting*) présentation *f;* (*of
a theory*) exposition *f;* (*of a dissertation, thesis*) soutenance *f;* **to give a ~
on sth** faire un exposé sur qc ❷ (*act of
giving: of a medal, gift*) remise *f*

**presently** [ˈprez·°nt·li] *adv* ❶ (*soon*)
bientôt ❷ (*now*) à présent

**preservative** *n* conservateur *m;* **free of
artificial ~s** sans conservateur

**preserve** [prɪ·ˈzɜrv] I. *vt* ❶ (*maintain,
keep*) conserver; (*peace, status quo*)
maintenir ❷ (*protect*) préserver II. *n*
❶ (*specially conserved fruit*) conserve *f;* **apricot/strawberry ~s** conserves d'abricots/de fraises ❷ (*domain,
responsibility*) domaine *m;* **to regard
sth as one's ~** considérer qc comme
étant à soi ❸ (*reserve*) réserve *f;* **na-
ture/wildlife ~** réserve naturelle/sau-
vage

**preserved** *adj* ❶ (*maintained*) bien
conservé(e); (*building*) en bon état; **to
be poorly ~** être mal entretenu ❷ CULIN
en conserve; **~ food** conserves *fpl*

**presidency** *n* présidence *f;* **during
his ~** au cours de son mandat de président

**president** [ˈprez·ɪ·dᵊnt] *n* président(e)
*m(f);* **Mr. President** M. le Président;
**Madam President** Madame la Présidente

**presidential** *adj* (*of president*) prési-
dentiel(le)

**press** [pres] I. *n* ❶ TYP *printing* **~** presse *f* (typographique) ❷ *pl* (*media*) pres-

se *f;* ~ **reports** reportages *mpl;* **to leak sth to the** ~ divulguer qc à la presse ❸ (*push*) pression *f;* **to give sth a** ~ appuyer sur qc ❹ (*ironing action*) repassage *m;* **to give sth a** ~ donner un coup de fer (à repasser) à qc ❺ (*instrument for pressing*) presse *f;* **garlic** ~ presse-ail *m* ▸ **freedom of the** ~ liberté *f* de la presse **II.** *vt* ❶ (*push*) appuyer sur; **to** ~ **sth into a hole** pousser qc dans un trou; **he** ~**ed his leg against mine** il a pressé sa jambe contre la mienne ❷ (*squeeze*) serrer ❸ (*extract juice from*) presser ❹ (*iron*) repasser ❺ (*force, insist*) faire pression sur; **to** ~ **sb for an answer/decision** presser qn de répondre/prendre une décision ❻ LAW **to** ~ **charges against sb/sth** engager des poursuites contre qn/qc ▸ **to** ~ **one's luck** forcer la chance **III.** *vi* ❶ (*push*) appuyer; **to** ~ **against sth** presser contre qc ❷ (*be urgent*) presser; **time is** ~**ing** le temps presse

**pressing** *adj* pressant(e); (*issue, matter*) urgent(e)

**press photographer** *n* photographe *mf* de presse

**press release** *n* communiqué *m* de presse

**pressure** ['preʃ·ər] **I.** *n* ❶ (*force*) pression *f;* **to apply** ~ faire pression ❷ (*stress*) pression *f* ❸ (*influence*) pression *f;* **to be under** ~ **to** +*infin* être contraint de +*infin;* **to do sth under** ~ **from sb** faire qc sous la pression de qn ❹ METEO, PHYS pression *f* **II.** *vt* **to** ~ **sb to** +*infin* contraindre qn à +*infin*

**pressure cabin** *n* cabine *f* pressurisée

**pressure cooker** *n* autocuiseur *m*

**pressure group** *n* groupe *m* de pression

**pressure washer** *n* nettoyeur *m* haute pression

**pressurize** ['preʃ·ə·raɪz] *vt* (*control air pressure*) pressuriser

**presumably** [prɪ·'zu·mə·bli] *adv* sans doute

**presume** [prɪ·'zum] **I.** *vt* présumer; ~**d dead** présumé mort **II.** *vi* être impor-

tun; **to** ~ **to** +*infin* se permettre de +*infin;* **to** ~ **on sb/sth** abuser de qn/qc

**pretax** *adj* avant impôt

**pretend** [prɪ·'tend] **I.** *vt* ❶ (*feign*) faire semblant ❷ (*claim*) prétendre; **to** ~ **to be sb** se faire passer pour qn; **I don't** ~ **to be an expert** je ne prétends pas être un expert **II.** *vi* ❶ (*feign*) faire semblant; **I was just** ~**ing!** c'était juste pour rire! ❷ *form* (*claim*) **to** ~ **to sth** prétendre à qc

**pretty** ['prɪṭ·i] **I.** *adj* <-ier, -iest> joli(e) ▸ **to not be just a** ~ **face** en avoir dans le crâne; **a** ~ **penny** une coquette somme **II.** *adv* assez; **to be** ~ **certain** être presque certain; ~ **nearly finished** presque terminé; ~ **much** à peu près ▸ **to be sitting** ~ avoir le bon filon

**pretzel** ['pret·sᵊl] *n* bretzel *m*

**prevail** [prɪ·'veɪl] *vi* ❶ (*triumph*) l'emporter ❷ (*be widespread*) prédominer

**prevent** [prɪ·'vent] *vt* ❶ (*keep from happening*) empêcher; (*disaster*) éviter; **to** ~ **sb/sth from doing sth** empêcher qn/qc de faire qc ❷ MED prévenir

**prevention** *n* prévention *f;* **Society for the** ~ **of Cruelty to Animals** société *f* protectrice des animaux ▸ **an ounce of** ~ **is worth a pound of cure** *prov* mieux vaut prévenir que guérir *prov*

**preview** ['pri·vju] **I.** *n* ❶ (*show*) avant-première *f* ❷ (*exhibition*) vernissage *m* ❸ (*trailer*) bande-annonce *f* **II.** *vt* visionner

**previous** ['pri·vi·əs] *adj* précédent(e); **on the** ~ **day** la veille; **the** ~ **evening** la veille au soir; **no** ~ **experience required** aucune expérience requise; **the** ~ **summer** l'été *m* dernier

**previously** *adv* ❶ (*beforehand*) avant ❷ (*formerly*) par le passé

**prey** [preɪ] *n* proie *f* ▸ **to fall** ~ **to sb/ sth** devenir la proie de qn/qc

**price** [praɪs] **I.** *n* prix *m;* ~ **tag** étiquette *f;* **to name one's** ~ donner son prix; **to fetch a** ~ atteindre une somme; **to put a** ~ **on sth** évaluer qc ▸ **to set a** ~ **on sb's head** mettre la tête de qn à prix; **to pay the** [*o* **a heavy**] ~ payer le

**P**

prix; **at any ~** à n'importe quel prix; **what ~ sth?** que devient qc? II. *vt* ❶(*mark with price tag*) mettre le prix sur; **to be ~d at one dollar** coûter un dollar ❷(*set value*) fixer le prix de; **to be reasonably ~d** avoir un prix raisonnable; (*restaurant*) être abordable ❸(*inquire about cost*) demander le prix de ►**to ~ oneself out of the market** ne plus pouvoir suivre la concurrence du marché

**priceless** *adj* inestimable

**pricey** ['praɪ·si] <pricier, priciest> *adj inf* chérot

**prick** [prɪk] I. *n* ❶(*sharp pain*) piqûre *f* ❷*vulg* (*penis*) bite *f* ❸*vulg* (*jerk*) sale con *m* II. *vt* piquer; (*balloon*) crever; **to ~ (one's) sth** (se) piquer qc ►**to ~ the balloon** tout gâcher

**prickly** <-ier, -iest> *adj* ❶(*thorny*) épineux(-euse) ❷(*tingling: sensation*) de picotement ❸*inf* (*easily offended*) irritable

**pride** [praɪd] I. *n* ❶(*proud feeling*) fierté *f*; **to take ~ in sb/sth** être fier de qn/qc; **to take ~ in one's appearance** être soucieux de son apparence ❷(*self-respect*) orgueil *m*; **to have too much ~ to** +*infin* être trop orgueilleux pour +*infin*; **to hurt sb's ~** blesser qn dans son orgueil; **to swallow one's ~** ravaler son orgueil ❸(*animal group*) bande *f* ►**to be one's ~ and joy** être la fierté de qn II. *vt* **to ~ oneself on doing sth** être fier de faire qc; **~ oneself on being sth** ne pas cacher son orgueil d'être qc

**priest** [prist] *n* prêtre *m*

**prima donna** [pri·mə·'da·nə] *n* ❶(*number one singer*) prima donna *f inv* ❷*pej* **to behave like a ~** se prendre pour une star

**primarily** *adv* essentiellement

**primary** ['praɪ·mer·i] I. *adj* principal(e); (*color, election, school*) primaire; (*meaning, importance*) premier(-ère) II. <-ies> *n POL* primaire *f*

**prime minister** *n* premier ministre *m*

**prime number** *n* nombre *m* premier

**prime time** *n* heures *fpl* de grande écoute

**primitive** ['prɪm·ɪ·tɪv] *adj* primitif(-ive)

**primrose** ['prɪm·roʊz] *n* primevère *f*

**prince** [prɪn(t)s] *n* prince *m*

**princess** ['prɪn(t)·sɪs] *n* princesse *f*

**principal** ['prɪn(t)·sə·pəl] I. *adj* (*main*) principal(e) II. *n* ❶(*high school director*) directeur, -trice *m*, *f*, préfet, -ète *m*, *f Belgique* ❷(*sum of money*) capital *m*

**principle** ['prɪn(t)·sə·pl] I. *n* principe *m* II. *adj* (*person*) qui a des principes

**print** [prɪnt] I. *n* ❶(*printed lettering or writing*) caractères *mpl* ❷(*printed text*) texte *m* ❸(*photo*) épreuve *f* ❹(*fingerprint*) empreinte *f* ❺(*pattern on fabric*) imprimé *m* ❻(*engraving*) gravure *f* ►**to appear in ~** être publié; **to be in/out of ~** être en stock/épuisé II. *vt* ❶(*produce, reproduce*) imprimer; (*special issue, copies*) tirer; **to be ~ed in hardback** être édité en version reliée ❷(*write*) écrire en lettres d'imprimerie ❸*PHOT* tirer III. *vi* ❶(*produce*) imprimer; **to be ~ing** être sous presse ❷(*write in unjoined letters*) écrire en lettres d'imprimerie

**printer** *n* ❶(*person*) imprimeur *m* ❷*COMPUT* imprimante *f*

**printout** *n COMPUT* sortie *f* d'imprimante

**prior**[1] ['praɪər] *form* I. *adj* (*earlier*) précédent(e); (*approval*) préalable; (*arrest, conviction*) antérieur(e); **to have a ~ engagement** avoir d'autres engagements; **without ~ notice** sans préavis II. *adv* (*before*) **~ to sth** avant qc; **~ to doing sth** avant de faire qc

**prior**[2] ['praɪər] *n REL* (*officer below abbot*) prieur *m*

**priority** [praɪ·'ɔr·ə·ti] I. *n* priorité *f*; **to have a high ~** être d'une grande importance; **to have ~ over sb** avoir la préséance sur qn; **to get one's priorities straight** savoir ce qui est important II. *adj* prioritaire; (*task*) prioritaire; **to get ~ treatment** être traité en priorité

**prism** ['prɪz·əm] *n* prisme *m*

**prison** ['prɪz·ən] *n* ❶(*jail*) prison *f*; **to**

P

**put sb in(to)** ~ emprisonner qn; **~ life** vie *f* carcérale ❷(*time in jail*) réclusion *f*

**prison cell** *n* cellule *f* (de prison)

**prisoner** *n* prisonnier, -ère *m, f*; **to hold sb ~** détenir qn

**privacy** ['praɪ·və·si] *n* intimité *f*; **to want some ~** désirer être seul

**private** ['praɪ·vət] **I.** *adj* ❶(*not public*) privé(e) ❷(*personal: opinion, papers*) personnel(le) ❸(*confidential*) confidentiel(le); **their ~ joke** une plaisanterie entre eux ❹(*not open to the public*) privé(e); (*ceremony, funeral*) célébré(e) dans l'intimité ❺(*for private use*) privé(e); (*tutoring, lesson*) particulier(-ère) ❻(*not state-run*) privé(e) ❼(*secluded*) retiré(e) ❽(*not social*) réservé(e) ❾(*undisturbed*) tranquille **II.** *n* ❶(*privacy*) intimité *f*; **to speak to sb in ~** parler à qn en particulier ❷(*lowest-ranking army soldier*) soldat *m* de deuxième classe ❸ *pl, inf*(*genitals*) parties *fpl* intimes

**private life** *n* vie *f* privée

**privately** *adv* ❶(*in private, not publicly*) en privé; (*celebrate*) dans l'intimité; **to speak ~ with sb** parler à qn en particulier ❷(*secretly*) en secret ❸(*personally*) à titre personnel; (*benefit*) personnellement ❹(*by private individuals, not publicly*) **~-owned business** commerce *m* appartenant au secteur privé

**privatization** *n* privatisation *f*

**privatize** ['praɪ·və·taɪz] *vt* privatiser

**privilege** ['prɪv·əl·ɪdʒ] **I.** *n* ❶(*special right or advantage*) privilège *m*; **diplomatic ~** immunité *f* diplomatique ❷(*honor*) honneur *m* **II.** *vt* **to be ~d to** +*infin* avoir le privilège de +*infin*

**privileged** *adj* ❶(*special, having some privileges*) privilégié(e) ❷(*confidential: information*) privé(e)

**prize¹** [praɪz] **I.** *n* ❶(*thing to be won*) prix *m*; (*in the lottery*) lot *m* ❷(*reward*) récompense *f* **II.** *adj* ❶(*first-rate*) de premier ordre ❷(*prize-winning*) primé(e) **III.** *vt* priser; **sb's ~d**

**possession** le bien le plus prisé de qn; **to ~ sth highly** faire grand cas de qc

**prize²** [praɪz] *vt* s. **pry²**

**prize money** *n* SPORTS prix *m* en argent

**prizewinner** *n* (*of a game*) gagnant(e) *m(f)*; (*of an exam*) lauréat(e) *m(f)*

**pro¹** [proʊ] **I.** *n* pour *m*; **the ~s of sth** les avantages *mpl* de qc; **the ~s and cons of sth** le pour et le contre de qc **II.** *prep* pour; **to be ~-European** être pro-européen; **he has always been ~ sport** il a toujours été pour l'activité sportive **III.** *adj* (*vote*) pour **IV.** *adv* pour; **to debate ~ and con** débattre du pour et du contre

**pro²** [proʊ] *n inf* pro *mf*

**probability** [ˌprɑ·bə·ˈbɪl·ə·t̬i] *n* probabilité *f*

**probable** ['prɑ·bə·bl] *adj* vraisemblable; **it is ~ that** il est probable que +*subj*

**problem** ['prɑ·bləm] *n* problème *m*; **to pose a ~ for sb** créer un problème à qn

**procedure** [prə·ˈsi·dʒər] *n* procédure *f*

**proceed** [proʊ·ˈsid] *vi form* ❶(*progress*) continuer; **to ~ with sth** poursuivre qc; **to ~ with a lawsuit** intenter un procès; **to ~ against sb** poursuivre qn en justice ❷(*come from*) **to ~ from sth** provenir de qc ❸(*continue walking, driving*) avancer ❹(*continue: debate, work*) se poursuivre ❺(*start, begin*) commencer; **to ~ with sth** commencer (avec) qc; **to ~ to** +*infin* se mettre à +*infin*

**proceeds** *n pl* bénéfices *mpl*

**process¹** ['prɑ·ses] **I.** *n* ❶(*series of actions, steps*) processus *m*; **a long and painful ~** un travail long et pénible; **to be in the ~ of doing sth** être en train de faire qc ❷LAW, ADMIN procédure *f* ❸(*method*) procédé *m* ▸**in the ~** en même temps **II.** *vt* ❶(*act upon, treat*) traiter; (*raw materials*) transformer ❷COMPUT traiter ❸PHOT développer

**process²** [proʊ·ˈses] *vi form* défiler (en procession)

**procession** [prə·ˈseʃ·ən] *n* ❶*a. fig* cortège *m*; (*of cars*) file *f*; **a nonstop ~ of**

**visitors** un défilé interminable de visiteurs ② REL procession *f*

**processor** *n* COMPUT processeur *m*

**procrastinate** [prouˈkræs·tə·neɪt] *vi* atermoyer

**proctor** *n* SCHOOL, UNIV (*exam supervisor*) surveillant(e) *m(f)* (d'examen)

**prodigy** [ˈpra·də·dʒi] *n* prodige *m;* **child ~** enfant *mf* prodige

**produce** [ˈpra·dus, *vb:* prəˈdus] **I.** *n* ① (*agricultural products*) produits *mpl;* **~ section** rayon *m* des produits frais ② *fig* produit *m* **II.** *vt* ① (*create*) produire; (*effect*) provoquer; (*illusion*) créer; (*meal*) confectionner; (*odor*) dégager; (*report*) rédiger ② (*manufacture*) fabriquer ③ (*give birth to: offspring*) donner naissance à ④ (*bring before the public: film, program*) produire; (*opera, play*) mettre en scène; (*book*) préparer; **a beautifully ~d biography** une biographie merveilleusement présentée ⑤ (*direct a recording*) procéder à l'enregistrement de ⑥ (*bring into view, show*) montrer; (*gun, knife, weapon*) sortir; (*ticket, identification*) présenter; (*alibi*) fournir ⑦ (*cause, bring about*) entraîner; (*hysteria, uncertainty*) provoquer; (*results*) produire ⑧ (*result in, yield*) rapporter ⑨ ELEC (*a spark*) faire jaillir

**producer** *n* producteur, -trice *m, f;* (*of a play*) metteur *m* en scène

**product** [ˈpra·dʌkt] *n a. fig* produit *m*

**production** *n* ① (*manufacturing process*) fabrication *f;* **to go into ~** entrer en production ② (*manufacturing yield, quantity produced*) production *f* ③ CINE, TV, RADIO (*act of producing*) production *f* ④ THEAT (*version*) mise *f* en scène; (*show*) production *f* ⑤ MUS production *f* ⑥ *form* (*presentation*) présentation *f*

**production manager** *n* directeur, -trice *m, f* de (la) production

**productive** *adj* ① (*producing*) productif(-ive); (*land, soil*) fertile ② (*accomplishing much*) fécond(e); (*conversation, meeting*) fructueux(-euse)

**Prof.** [praf] *n abbr of* **Professor** Prof. *m*

**profession** [prəˈfeʃ·ᵊn] *n* profession *f*

**professional I.** *adj* professionnel(le); **he looks ~!** il a l'air d'être du métier! **II.** *n* professionnel(le) *m(f)*

**professionalism** *n* professionnalisme *m*

**professor** [prəˈfes·ər] *n* professeur *mf*

**proficient** *adj* compétent(e); **to be ~ at/in sth** être compétent dans

**profile** [ˈprou·faɪl] **I.** *n* ① (*outline*) profil *m* ② (*portrayal*) portrait *m* ③ (*public image*) **to raise sb's/sth's ~** mieux faire connaître qn/qc; **in a high~ position** dans une position en vue ▸ **to keep a low ~** adopter un profil bas **II.** *vt* ① (*describe*) faire le portrait de ② (*draw a profile of*) dessiner le profil de

**profit** [ˈpra·fɪt] **I.** *n* profit *m;* FIN bénéfice *m;* **to sell sth at a ~** vendre qc à profit **II.** *vi* **to ~ from/by sth** tirer profit de qc **III.** *vt* profiter à

**profitable** [ˈpra·fɪt·ə·bl] *adj* ① (*producing a profit: business*) rentable; (*investment*) lucratif(-ive) ② (*advantageous, beneficial*) avantageux(-euse); **to make ~ use of one's time** bien profiter de son temps

**profiteering** *n pej* affairisme *m*

**profit margin** *n* marge *f* bénéficiaire

**profit sharing** *n* participation *f* aux bénéfices

**profit taking** *n* FIN prise *f* de bénéfices

**profound** [prəˈfaund] *adj* profond(e); (*knowledge*) approfondi(e)

**program** [ˈprou·græm] **I.** *n* ① (*broadcast*) émission *f* ② (*presentation, guide, list of events*) programme *m* ③ (*plan*) programme *m;* **modernization ~** plan *m* de modernisation ④ COMPUT (*computer instructions*) programme *m* **II.** <-mm-> *vt* programmer

**programmable** *adj* programmable

**programmer** *n* ① COMPUT, RADIO, TECH (*person*) programmeur, -euse *m, f* ② (*device*) programmateur *m*

**programming** *n a.* COMPUT programmation *f*

**progress** [ˈpra·gres, *vb:* prəˈgres] **I.** *n* ① progrès *mpl;* **the patient is making ~**

l'état *m* du patient s'améliore; **to be in ~** être en cours; **to make slow ~** avancer lentement; **the slow ~ of the inquiry** la lenteur de l'enquête; **to make ~ toward sth** avancer vers qc; **to give sb a ~ report** présenter un bilan à qn II. *vi* progresser; **to ~ to sth** passer à qc; **to ~ toward sth** s'acheminer vers qc

**progressive** [prə·'gres·ɪv] I. *adj* ❶ *a.* LING progressif(-ive) ❷ *(favoring social progress)* progressiste II. *n* ❶ *(advocate of social reform)* progressiste *mf* ❷ LING **the ~** la forme progressive

**prohibit** [prou·'hɪb·ɪt] *vt (forbid)* interdire; **to ~ sb from doing sth** interdire à qn de faire qc; **to be ~ed by law** être prohibé par la loi

**prohibition** [ˌprou·(h)ɪ·'bɪʃ·ən] *n* ❶ *(ban)* interdiction *f* ❷ LAW, HIST **Prohibition** la prohibition

**project** ['prɑ·dʒekt, *vb:* prə·'dʒekt] I. *n* projet *m* II. *vt* ❶ *(forecast: costs, timetable)* prévoir; **to be ~ed to +** *infin* être projeté de + *infin;* **the ~ed increase** l'augmentation *f* prévue ❷ *(send out)* projeter; **to ~ one's voice** faire entendre sa voix ❸ CINE *(show on screen)* **to ~ sth onto screen** projeter qc sur qc ❹ PSYCH **to ~ sth onto sb/sth** projeter qc sur qn/qc; **to ~ oneself onto sb** se projeter sur qn III. *vi (protrude)* avancer; **~ing teeth** dents *fpl* en avant

**projectile** [prə·'dʒek·təl] *n* projectile *m*

**projector** [prə·'dʒek·tər] *n* projecteur *m*

**prolong** [prou·'lɔŋ] *vt* prolonger

**prom** [prɑm] *n (formal school dance)* bal *m* des lycéens

**promenade** [ˌprɑ·mə·'neɪd] I. *n a.* form promenade *f* II. *vi* se promener

**promiscuous** [prə·'mɪs·kju·əs] *adj pej* aux nombreux(-euses) partenaires sexuel(le)s

**promise** ['prɑ·mɪs] I. *vt* promettre; **to ~ sb sth** promettre qc à qn; **to ~ oneself sth** se promettre qc; **it's true, I ~ you** c'est vrai, je t'assure II. *vi* promettre III. *n* ❶ *(pledge)* promesse *f;* **~s, ~s!** ce ne sont que des promesses de Gas-

con! ❷ *(potential)* espoir *m;* **to show ~** être très prometteur; **to fulfill one's (early) ~** répondre à tous les espoirs

**promising** *adj (career, work)* prometteur(-euse); *(musician)* qui promet; **to get off to a ~ start** bien démarrer

**promote** [prə·'mout] *vt* promouvoir; **to ~ sb to sth** promouvoir qn au rang de qc; **to ~ a new book** faire la promotion d'un nouveau livre

**promoter** *n* promoteur, -trice *m, f*

**promotion** *n a.* COM promotion *f*

**promotional material** *n* matériel *m* publicitaire

**prompt** [prɑm(p)t] I. *vt* ❶ *(spur)* encourager; **what ~ed you to write to me?** qu'est-ce qui vous a poussé à m'écrire? ❷ THEAT *(remind of lines)* souffler le texte à II. *adj (quick)* prompt(e); *(action, delivery)* rapide; **to be ~ in doing sth** être prompt à faire qc III. *n* ❶ COMPUT message *m* ❷ THEAT *(words)* **to give sb a ~** souffler son texte à qn

**promptly** *adv* ❶ *(quickly)* promptement ❷ *inf (immediately afterward)* tout de suite

**pronoun** ['prou·naun] *n* LING pronom *m*

**pronounce** [prə·'naun(t)s] *vt* ❶ LING *(speak)* prononcer ❷ *(declare)* déclarer; **to ~ sb man and wife** déclarer qn mari et femme

**pronounced** *adj* prononcé(e)

**pronunciation** [prə·ˌnʌn(t)·si·'eɪ·ʃən] *n* prononciation *f*

**proof** [pruf] I. *n* ❶ *(facts establishing truth)* ❷ *a.* LAW, MATH preuve *f* ❷ *(test)* épreuve *f* ❸ TYP, PHOT *(first printing)* épreuve *f* ❹ *(degree of strength: of alcohol)* la proportion d'alcool pur dans les spiritueux II. *adj (impervious)* imperméable; **burglar~** à l'épreuve des cambriolages; **child-~** qui résiste aux enfants III. *adj* imprégner

**proofread** <proofread> TYP, PUBL I. *vt* corriger II. *vi* faire des corrections

**propaganda** [ˌprɑ·pə·'gæn·də] *n no indef art, pej* propagande *f;* **~ war/film** guerre *f*/film *m* de propagande

P

**propeller** *n* hélice *f*

**proper** ['prɑ·pər] I. *adj* ❶ (*true: meal, tool*) vrai(e); **they don't have ~ classrooms** ils n'ont pas de véritables salles de classe ❷ (*suitable, correct: method, training, place*) convenable; **the ~ time for sth** le moment qui convient pour qc ❸ (*socially respectable*) respectable; **to be ~ to** +*infin* être bien pour +*infin;* **it's right and ~ for him to do that** c'est tout à fait normal qu'il le fasse ❹ *form* (*itself*) même; **the city ~** la ville proprement dite II. *adv* (*completely*) vraiment

**properly** *adv* ❶ (*correctly*) correctement; **pronounce the word ~** prononce le mot comme il faut ❷ (*suitably*) convenablement

**property** ['prɑ·pər·ti] *n* ❶ (*possession*) bien *m;* **is this your ~?** est-ce que cela vous appartient? ❷ *LAW* (*right to possession*) propriété *f* ❸ (*buildings and land*) biens *mpl* immobiliers ❹ (*house*) propriété *f* ❺ <-ties> (*attribute*) propriété *f* ❻ <-ties> *THEAT* (*prop*) accessoire *m*

**property tax** *n* impôt *m* foncier

**prophecy** ['prɑ·fə·si] <-ies> *n* prophétie *f*

**P** **prophet** ['prɑ·fɪt] *n a.* *REL* prophète *m*

**proportion** [prə·'pɔr·ʃən] *n* ❶ (*comparative part*) proportion *f* ❷ (*quantifiable relationship*) **to increase in ~ to sth** augmenter en proportion de qc; **in ~ to sb's income** proportionnellement au revenu de qn ❸ (*relative importance*) **to have/keep a sense of ~** avoir/garder le sens de la mesure; **to keep things in ~** relativiser les choses; **retaliation in ~ to the attack** riposte *f* proportionnelle à l'attaque; **to be in/out of ~ to sth** être proportionné/disproportionné par rapport à qc ❹ *pl* (*size, dimensions*) proportions *fpl;* **building of gigantic ~s** bâtiment *m* aux proportions énormes

**proportional** *adj* proportionnel(le); **to be ~ to sth** être proportionnel à qc

**proposal** *n* proposition *f;* **marriage ~** demande *f* en mariage

**propose** [prə·'pouz] I. *vt* ❶ (*suggest*) proposer; **to ~ doing sth** proposer de faire qc; **to ~ a toast** porter un toast ❷ (*intend*) projeter; **to ~ to do/ doing sth** projeter de faire qc II. *vi* **to ~ to sb** faire une demande en mariage à qn

**proposition** [ˌprɑ·pə·'zɪʃ·ən] I. *n* proposition *f;* **the business is a worthwhile ~** c'est une affaire rentable II. *vt* faire une proposition à

**proprietor** *n* propriétaire *mf*

**prose** [prouz] *n no indef art* *LIT* prose *f*

**prosecute** ['prɑ·sɪ·kjut] I. *vt a.* *LAW* poursuivre II. *vi* engager des poursuites judiciaires

**prosecuting** *adj* de l'accusation; **the ~ attorney** l'accusation *f*

**prosecution** *n* ❶ *LAW* (*court proceedings*) poursuites *fpl;* **to face ~** s'exposer à des poursuites ❷ *LAW* (*the prosecuting party*) **the ~** l'accusation *f;* **witness for the ~** témoin *m* à charge

**prosecutor** *n* *LAW* accusateur, -trice *m, f*

**prospect** ['prɑ·spekt] I. *n* ❶ (*likely future*) perspective *f;* **I find that a troubling ~** je trouve cette éventualité préoccupante ❷ (*chance of sth*) chance *f;* **there is no ~ of that happening** il n'y a aucun risque que ça arrive *subj* ❸ (*potential customer*) client(e) *m(f)* potentiel(le) ❹ (*potential associate*) **the new ~s** (*for team, membership*) les possibles candidats *mpl* ❺ (*view*) vue *f* II. *vi* *MIN* prospecter; **to ~ for gold** prospecter de l'or

**prospective** *adj* (*member, player*) futur(e); (*employer*) éventuel(le)

**prospector** *n* *MIN* prospecteur *m;* **gold ~** chercheur *m* d'or

**prospectus** [prə·'spek·təs] *n* prospectus *m*

**prosper** ['prɑ·spər] *vi* prospérer

**prosperity** [prɑ·'sper·ə·ti] *n* prospérité *f*

**prosperous** *adj* (*business, economy*) prospère

**prostitute** ['prɑ·stə·tut] I. *n* prostitué(e)

*m(f)* II. *vt* prostituer; **to ~ oneself** se prostituer

**prostitution** *n* prostitution *f*

**protect** [prə'tekt] *vt* protéger; (*interests*) préserver

**protection** *n* protection *f*

**protection factor** *n* facteur *m* de protection

**protective** *adj* ❶ (*affording protection*) de protection; **~ custody** détention *f* préventive ❷ (*wishing to protect*) protecteur(-trice); **to be ~ of sb/sth** être soucieux de qn/qch

**protector** *n* ❶ (*sb who protects sth*) a. HIST protecteur, -trice *m, f* ❷ (*device*) protection *f*

**protein** ['prou·tin] *n* protéine *f*

**protest** ['prou·test] I. *n* protestation *f*; **to do sth in ~ of sth** faire qc pour protester contre qc II. *vi* protester; **to ~ about sb/sth** émettre une objection sur qn/qc; (*demonstrators*) manifester contre qn/qc III. *vt* ❶ (*solemnly affirm*) assurer; **to ~ one's innocence** protester de son innocence ❷ (*show dissent*) protester contre

**Protestant** ['pra·tə·stənt] *n* REL protestant(e) *m(f)*; **the ~ church** l'Eglise *f* protestante

**protester** *n* protestataire *mf*

**protest march** *n* marche *f* de protestation

**protrude** [prou·'trud] *vi* saillir; **to ~ from sth** saillir de qc

**proud** [praud] I. *adj* (*pleased and satisfied*) fier(fière); **as ~ as a peacock** fier comme un coq II. *adv* **to do sb ~** faire honneur à qn

**prove** [pruv] <proved, proven o proved> I. *vt* prouver; **to ~ a point** démontrer qu'on a raison; **to ~ oneself (to be) sth** montrer qu'on est qc II. *vi* s'avérer; **to ~ (to be) impossible** s'avérer impossible

**proven** ['pru·vən] I. *pp of* **prove** II. *adj* (*remedy*) efficace; **a impossibility** une impossibilité prouvée

**proverb** ['pra·vɜrb] *n* proverbe *m*

**provide** [prə·'vaɪd] *vt* ❶ (*supply, make available: food, money, instructions*) fournir; (*security, access*) offrir; (*education*) assurer; (*answer*) donner; **to ~ sth for sb/sth, to ~ sb/sth with sth** apporter qc à qn/qc; **to ~ oneself with sth** (*equip*) se procurer qc ❷ *form* LAW prévoir

**provided** (**that**) *conj* pourvu que +*subj*; **he'll get it ~ he pays for it** il l'aura à condition de le payer

**provider** [prə·(ʊ)·'vaɪ·dər] *n* TEL, INET fournisseur *m*; **Internet** |**service**| **~** fournisseur *m* de services Internet

**province** ['pra·vɪn(t)s] *n* ❶ (*area*) province *f* ❷ (*branch of a subject*) domaine *m*

**provision** [prə·'vɪʒ·ən] *n* ❶ (*act of providing*) **to be responsible for the ~ of food/bedding** assurer l'approvisionnement *m* de nourriture/l'équipement *m* en literie ❷ *pl* (*food*) provisions *fpl* ❸ (*preparation, prior arrangement*) disposition *fpl* ❹ (*stipulation in a document*) disposition *f*

**provisional** *adj* provisoire

**provocative** [prə·'va·kə·tɪv] *adj* provocant(e)

**provoke** [prə·'vouk] *vt* provoquer

**prowl** [praul] I. *n* tour *m* à la recherche d'une proie; **to be on the ~** rôder II. *vt* rôder dans III. *vi* rôder

**proximity** [prak·'sɪ·mə·ti] *n form* proximité *f*; **to be in** (**close**) **~ to sb/sth** être très proche de qn/qch

**prudent** ['pru·dənt] *adj* prudent(e)

**prune**[1] [prun] *n* (*dried plum*) prune *f*

**prune**[2] [prun] *vt* ❶ BOT (*trim: tree, shrub*) **to ~ sth** (**down**) tailler qc ❷ (*make smaller: article*) raccourcir; (*costs, budget*) tailler dans

**pruning shears** *npl* sécateur *m*

**pry**[1] [praɪ] <pries, pried> *vi* être indiscret(-ète); **to ~ into sth** fouiner dans qc

**pry**[2] [praɪ] *vt* **to ~ sth off** [*o to ~ off sth*] retirer qc à l'aide d'un levier; **to ~ sth open** ouvrir qc à l'aide d'un levier; **to ~ sth out of sb** arracher qc à qn

**PS** [ˌpi·'es] *n abbr of* **postscript** PS *m*

P

**pseudonym** ['su·də·nım] n pseudonyme m

**psychiatric** adj psychiatrique

**psychiatrist** n psychiatre mf

**psychiatry** [sai·'kai·ə·tri] n psychiatrie f

**psychic** ['sai·kık] I. n voyant(e) m(f) II. adj ❶ (concerning occult powers) parapsychologique ❷ (of the mind) psychique; **to be ~** avoir des dons de voyance

**psychical** adj s. **psychic**

**psychological** adj psychologique

**psychologist** n psychologue mf

**psychology** [sai·'ka·lə·dʒi] <-ies> n psychologie f

**PT** n SCHOOL abbr of **physical training** EPS f

**pt** n ❶ abbr of **part** partie f ❷ abbr of **pint** pinte f ❸ abbr of **point** point m

**PTA** n abbr of **Parent Teacher Association** association f de parents d'élèves

**pub** [pʌb] n inf (bar) pub m

**pub.** [pʌb] n ❶ abbr of **publication** ❷ abbr of **publisher**

**puberty** ['pju·bər·ţi] n puberté f

**pubic** ['pju·bık] adj pubien(ne)

**public** ['pʌb·lık] I. adj public(-que); **in the ~ interest** dans l'intérêt général; **at ~ expense** aux frais du contribuable; **to go ~ with sth** rendre qc public II. n + sing/pl vb public m; **in ~** en public

**public-address system** n système m de haut-parleurs

**publication** [ˌpʌb·lɪ·'keɪ·ʃən] n publication f

**public domain** n domaine m public

**public enemy** n ennemi m public; **~ number one** ennemi public numéro un

**public health service** n service m de la santé publique

**public holiday** n jour m férié

**publicity** [pʌb·'lɪ·sə·ţi] I. n publicité f II. adj publicitaire

**publicize** ['pʌb·lɪ·saɪz] vt (event) annoncer; **don't ~ it** ne le crie pas sur les toits; **her much-~d divorce** son divorce dont les médias ont beaucoup parlé

**publicly** adv publiquement; **a ~ funded project** un projet subventionné par les fonds publics

**public property** n propriété f de l'État; **her life is ~** fig sa vie intéresse tout le monde

**public school** n école f publique

**public telephone** n téléphone m public

**public transportation** n transports mpl publics

**publish** ['pʌb·lɪʃ] vt publier

**publisher** n ❶ (publishing company) maison f d'édition ❷ (position in publishing) éditeur, -trice m, f

**publishing** n no art édition f

**pudding** ['pʊd·ɪŋ] n (creamy dessert) pudding m

**puddle** ['pʌd·l] n flaque f d'eau

**pudgy** ['pʌdʒ·i] <pudgier, pudgiest> adj trapu(e)

**Puerto Rican** I. adj portoricain(e) II. n Portoricain(e) m(f)

**Puerto Rico** [ˌpwer·ţə·'ri·koʊ] n Porto Rico

**puff** [pʌf] I. n ❶ inf (blast: of air, smoke) bouffée f; **to vanish in a ~ of smoke** s'évanouir dans un nuage de fumée ❷ (light pastry) chou m à la crème ❸ (stuffed quilt) édredon m; s.a. **eiderdown** ❹ pej, inf (praising writing, speech) pub f II. vi ❶ (blow) souffler; (steam engine) lancer des bouffées de vapeur ❷ (breathe forcefully) haleter ❸ (smoke) **to ~ on** [o at] **a cigar** tirer sur un cigare III. vt ❶ (blow) souffler; ❷ (smoke: a cigar, cigarette) tirer sur ❸ pej (praise over-enthusiastically) faire mousser inf

◆ **puff out** I. vt ❶ (cause to swell) gonfler ❷ (emit) **to ~ smoke** envoyer des bouffées de fumée II. vi (swell) se gonfler

◆ **puff up** I. vt gonfler; **to be puffed up with pride** être bouffi d'orgueil II. vi gonfler; (eyes) enfler

**puff pastry** n pâte f feuilletée

**puffy** <-ier, -iest> adj bouffi(e)

**puke** [pjuk] inf I. vt **to ~ sth** (**up**) [o to ~ (**up**) **sth**] vomir qc II. vi vomir; **to**

**make sb (want to) ~** donner à qn envie de vomir

**pull** [pʊl] I. vt ❶ (*exert force, tug, draw*) tirer; (*rope*) tirer sur; **to ~ sth open** ouvrir qc; **to ~ sth across a river** faire traverser la rivière à qc en tirant; **to ~ sb to one side** tirer qn sur le côté; **to ~ the trigger** appuyer sur la gâchette ❷ (*extract*) extraire; (*tooth, weeds*) arracher; (*cork*) enlever; (*gun, knife*) sortir; **to ~ sth out of sth** sortir qc de qc; **to ~ sb out of sth** extraire qn de qc; **to ~ a gun/knife on sb** tirer une arme/un couteau pour attaquer qn ❸ MED (*strain: muscle, tendon*) se déchirer ❹ (*attract: audience, crowd*) attirer ▶ **to ~ sb's leg** inf faire marcher qn; **to not ~ one's punches** inf ne pas mâcher ses mots; **to ~ strings** faire marcher ses relations II. vt ❶ (*exert a pulling force*) tirer ❷ (*row*) ramer III. n ❶ (*act of pulling*) coup m; **to give sth a ~** tirer sur qc ❷ (*huge effort*) **winning the election will be a long ~** remporter l'élection sera un travail de longue haleine ❸ (*knob, handle*) poignée f ❹ (*deep inhalation or swig*) **to take a ~ on a cigarette** tirer une bouffée sur une cigarette; **to take a ~ on a bottle** boire une gorgée à la bouteille ❺ inf (*influence*) influence f ❻ inf (*appeal*) attrait m

◆ **pull ahead** vi prendre la tête; **to ~ of sb** prendre de l'avance sur qn

◆ **pull apart** vt ❶ (*break into pieces, dismantle*) **to pull sth apart** démonter qc ❷ (*separate using force*) **to pull sb/sth apart** séparer qn/qc avec force ❸ (*severely criticize*) **to pull sb/sth apart** descendre qn/qc en flammes

◆ **pull away** I. vi ❶ (*depart: train*) partir; (*car*) démarrer ❷ (*increase lead*) prendre de l'avance II. vt (*letter, hand*) retirer; **to pull a child away from the road** écarter un enfant de la chaussée

◆ **pull back** I. vi ❶ (*troops*) **to ~ from sth** se retirer de qc ❷ (*change mind*) changer d'avis II. vt retirer

◆ **pull down** vt ❶ (*move to lower posi-*

*tion*) a. fig (*blinds*) baisser ❷ (*demolish*) démolir ❸ (*weaken*) affaiblir ❹ inf (*earn wages*) toucher

◆ **pull in** I. vi ❶ (*arrive: bus, train*) arriver ❷ AUTO (*park*) s'arrêter II. vt ❶ (*attract in large numbers: fans, a crowd*) attirer ❷ LAW arrêter; **to pull sb in for questioning** appréhender qn pour l'interroger ❸ (*by contracting muscles*) **to pull one's stomach in** rentrer son ventre

◆ **pull off** vt ❶ (*take off: lid, sweater*) enlever ❷ inf (*succeed*) réussir; **we pulled it off!** on a réussi! ❸ (*leave: road*) quitter

◆ **pull out** I. vi ❶ (*leave: bus, train*) partir ❷ (*withdraw*) se retirer; **to ~ of sth** se retirer de qc ❸ (*drive onto a road*) déboîter II. vt ❶ (*take out*) sortir ❷ (*remove: tooth, troops*) retirer; (*plug*) enlever; (*weeds*) déraciner ❸ (*select*) choisir

◆ **pull over** I. vt ❶ (*order to stop: car, driver*) faire s'arrêter (sur le côté) ❷ (*put on or take off garment*) **to pull sth over one's head** passer qc par la tête II. vi AUTO s'arrêter sur le bord de la route

◆ **pull through** I. vi s'en sortir II. vt **to pull sb/sth through** tirer qn/qc d'affaire

◆ **pull together** I. vt ❶ (*regain composure*) **to pull oneself together** se ressaisir ❷ (*organize, set up*) **to pull sth together** rassembler qc II. vi coopérer

◆ **pull up** I. vt ❶ (*raise*) a. fig remonter; (*blinds*) lever; **to ~ a chair** prendre une chaise ❷ (*uproot*) arracher ❸ (*stop*) arrêter II. vi s'arrêter

**pull-down menu** n COMPUT menu m déroulant

**pulley** ['pʊl·i] <-eys> n TECH poulie f

**pullout** I. n ❶ MIL (*withdrawal of soldiers*) retrait m ❷ PUBL (*part of magazine*) encart m publicitaire II. adj (*able to be folded away: bed, table*) dépliable

**pull-tab** n (*of can*) anneau m

**pulpit** ['pʊlp·ɪt] n REL chaire f

**pulse¹** [pʌls] I. n ❶ (*heartbeat*) pouls m

P

②(*single vibration*) pulsation *f* ③(*rhythm*) rythme *m* ▸ **to have one's finger on the ~ of sth** être tout à fait au courant de qc **II.** *vi* battre

**pulse²** [pʌls] *n* CULIN légume *m* sec

**pump¹ I.** *n* pompe *f* **II.** *vt* ①(*use pump on*) pomper; **to ~ money into an industry** injecter de l'argent dans une industrie; **~ed full of heroin** plein d'héroïne; **to ~ sb's stomach** MED faire un lavage d'estomac à qn ②(*interrogate*) tirer les vers du nez à

**pump²** [pʌmp] *n* (*high-heeled shoe*) escarpin *m*

**pumpkin** ['pʌmp·kɪn] *n* citrouille *f*

**pun** [pʌn] **I.** *n* calembour *m* **II.** <-nn-> *vi* faire un jeu de mots

**punch¹** [pʌn(t)ʃ] **I.** *vt* ①(*hit*) **to ~ sb** donner un coup de poing à qn; **to ~ sth** frapper qc d'un coup de poing ②(*press: key, button*) appuyer sur; (*a number*) composer ③ AGR (*drive*) **to ~ cattle/a herd** conduire le bétail/ un troupeau **II.** <-ches> *n* ①(*hit*) coup *m* de poing ②*inf* (*strong effect*) punch *m*

**punch²** [pʌn(t)ʃ] **I.** *vt* ①(*pierce*) percer; (*paper*) perforer; **to ~ holes in sth** faire des trous dans qc ②(*stamp*) poinçonner; (*a ticket*) composter **II.** <-ches> *n* ①(*tool for puncturing*) poinçonneuse *f*; (*for paper*) perforeuse *f*

**punch³** [pʌn(t)ʃ] *n* (*drink*) punch *m*

**punch line** *n* chute *f* (*d'une histoire drôle*)

**punctual** ['pʌŋk·tʃu·əl] *adj* à l'heure; (*person*) ponctuel(le)

**punctuality** *n* ponctualité *f*

**punctuation** *n* ponctuation *f*

**puncture** ['pʌŋk·tʃər] **I.** *vt* ①(*pierce*) perforer; (*tire*) crever; **to ~ a hole in sth** percer un trou dans qc ②MED ponctionner; **a ~d lung** un poumon perforé **II.** *vi* (*burst: tire*) crever **III.** *n* ①(*hole*) perforation *f*; (*in a tire*) crevaison *f*; **to have a ~** crever ②MED ponction *f*; (*of bite, injection*) piqûre *f*; **a ~ wound** une marque de piqûre

**punish** ['pʌn·ɪʃ] *vt* ①(*penalize*) punir;

**to ~ sb with a fine** frapper qn d'une amende ②(*treat badly*) malmener

**punishment** *n* ①(*punishing*) punition *f* ②(*penalty*) sanction *f*; LAW peine *f* ③*inf* (*severe treatment*) **to take a lot of ~** *inf* (*person*) encaisser; (*furniture*) en voir de toutes les couleurs

**punk** [pʌŋk] **I.** *n* ①*inf* (*worthless person*) vaurien *m* ②(*anarchist*) punk *mf* ③MUS **~ rock** punk *m* **II.** *adj* MUS punk *inv*

**punt¹** [pʌnt] SPORTS **I.** *vt* **to ~ the ball** envoyer la balle d'un coup de volée **II.** *vi* envoyer un coup de volée **III.** *n* coup *m* de volée

**punt²** [pʌnt] *n* NAUT (*flat-bottomed boat*) bachot *m*

**punt³** [pʊnt] *n* HIST (*Irish currency*) livre *f* irlandaise

**puny** ['pju·ni] <-nier, -niest> *adj* ①(*thin and weak: person*) chétif(-ive); (*hand, arm*) frêle ②(*with little power*) *a. fig* faible

**pup** [pʌp] **I.** *n* (*baby animal: dog*) chiot *m* **II.** *vi* <-pp-> mettre bas

**pupil¹** ['pju·pəl] *n* (*school child*) élève *mf*

**pupil²** ['pju·pəl] *n* ANAT pupille *f*

**puppet** ['pʌp·ɪt] *n* ①(*doll*) poupée *f*; (*on strings*) marionnette *f* ②*pej* (*one controlled by another*) marionnette *f*

**puppeteer** [pʌp·ə·'tɪr] *n* ①THEAT marionnettiste *mf* ②*pej* manipulateur, -trice *m, f*

**puppet government** *n* gouvernement *m* fantoche

**puppet show** *n* spectacle *m* de marionnettes

**puppy** ['pʌp·i] <-ppies> *n* chiot *m*

**purchase** ['pɜr·tʃəs] **I.** *vt* ①*form* (*buy*) acheter ②*form* FIN (*acquire*) acquérir **II.** *n* *form* ①(*item*) achat *m* ②(*act of buying*) achat *m* ③FIN (*acquiring*) acquisition *f* ④(*hold, grip*) prise *f*

**pure** [pjʊr] *adj* pur(e)

**purée** [pjʊ·'reɪ] **I.** *vt* **to ~ sth** réduire qc en purée **II.** *n* purée *f*

**purely** *adv* purement; **~ by chance** tout à fait par hasard

**purify** ['pjʊr·ə·faɪ] *vt a. fig* purifier

**purity** ['pjʊr·ɪ·ti] *n* pureté *f*

**purple** ['pɜr·pl] **I.** *adj* ❶ (*blue and red mix*) violet(te) ❷ (*red*) pourpre; **to become ~ (in the face)** rougir **II.** *n* ❶ (*blue and red mix*) violet *m* ❷ (*crimson*) pourpre *m*; *s.a.* **blue**

**purpose** ['pɜr·pəs] **I.** *n* (*reason*) but *m*; **to have a strength of ~** être très résolu; **to serve a ~** faire l'affaire; **for that very ~** à cette fin; (*for this reason*) pour cette raison; **for all practical ~s** en fait ▶ **for all intents and ~s** pratiquement, au fond; **on ~** exprès **II.** *vi form* **to ~ to +***infin* se proposer de +*infin*

**purpose-built** *adj* construit(e) spécialement

**purposely** *adv* exprès

**purse** [pɜrs] **I.** *n* ❶ (*handbag*) sac *m* (à main) ❷ SPORTS (*prize money*) prix *m* ❸ (*money: of a person*) moyens *mpl*; **public ~** trésor *m* public ▶ **to hold the ~ strings** tenir les cordons de la bourse **II.** *vt* **to ~ one's lips** pincer les lèvres **III.** *vi* (*lips*) se pincer

**pursue** [pər·'su] *vt* ❶ (*follow*) *a. fig* poursuivre ❷ (*seek to find: dreams, happiness*) rechercher; (*one's aims*) poursuivre ❸ (*continue*) *a. fig* poursuivre; (*course, direction*) suivre; **we won't ~ the matter any further** nous n'allons pas nous étendre sur ce sujet ❹ (*engage in: career, studies*) poursuivre

**pursuer** *n* poursuivant(e) *m(f)*

**pursuit** [pər·'sut] *n* ❶ (*action of pursuing*) poursuite *f*; **to be in (hot) ~ of sb/sth** être aux trousses de qn/qc; **in ~ of happiness** à la recherche du bonheur ❷ (*activity*) activité *f*

**pus** [pʌs] *n* pus *m*

**push** [pʊʃ] **I.** *vt* ❶ (*shove, give a push, forcefully move*) *a. fig* pousser; **to ~ a door open** ouvrir une porte en la poussant; **to ~ sth into sth** fourrer qc dans qc; **to ~ one's way through sth** se frayer un chemin à travers qc; **to ~ sb out of the way** écarter qn du chemin; **to be ~ed** être bousculé ❷ (*persuade*)

pousser; **to ~ sb into doing sth** pousser qn à faire qc ❸ (*force, be demanding: students, workers*) pousser; **to ~ oneself** se forcer; **to ~ one's luck** y aller un peu fort; **to ~ sb too hard** exiger trop de qn ❹ (*press: button, bell*) appuyer sur; **to ~ sth into sth** enfoncer qc dans qc ❺ *inf* (*promote*) faire la pub de; (*plan, system*) préconiser; (*candidate, idea*) soutenir; **to ~ oneself** se mettre en avant ❻ (*approach age*) **to be ~ing 30** approcher de la trentaine ❼ *inf* (*sell: drugs*) revendre **II.** *vi* ❶ (*force movement*) pousser; **~ (***on door***) poussez; to ~ past sb** bousculer qn ❷ (*apply pressure*) *a. fig* faire pression; **~ (***on bell***)** appuyez ❸ (*pass through*) *a.* MIL avancer; **to ~ into/out of sth** entrer/sortir de qc en se frayant un chemin **III.** **<-shes>** *n* ❶ (*shove*) *a. fig* poussée *f*; **to give sb/sth a ~** *a. fig* pousser qn/qc ❷ (*act of pressing*) pression *f*; **at the ~ of a button** à la pression du bouton ❸ (*strong action*) effort *m*; **to make a ~ for sth** faire un effort pour qc ❹ (*help, persuasion*) encouragement *m*; **he needs a bit of a ~** il a besoin d'un petit coup de pouce ▶ **when ~ comes to shove** s'il le faut

◆ **push along** **I.** *vi inf* s'en aller **II.** *vt to* push sth along pousser qc

◆ **push around** *vt inf* **to push sb around** marcher sur les pieds de qn

◆ **push away** *vt* repousser

◆ **push back** *vt a. fig* **to ~ sb/sth** repousser qn/qc

◆ **push down** *vt* ❶ (*knock down*) renverser ❷ (*press down*) appuyer sur; **to push sth down sth** enfoncer qc dans qc ❸ (*lower down*) *a.* ECON faire baisser

◆ **push forward** **I.** *vt* ❶ (*advance*) pousser en avant ❷ (*promote*) **to push sth forward** faire avancer qc ❸ (*call attention to oneself*) **to push oneself forward** se mettre en avant **II.** *vi* avancer

◆ **push in** *vt* ❶ (*insert, break*) enfoncer; **to push one's way in** se frayer un passage ❷ (*force in*) **to push sb in**

P

pousser qn dedans

◆**push off** NAUT I. *vi* pousser au large II. *vt* **to push sth off** pousser qc au large

◆**push on** I. *vi* continuer; **to ~ with sth** continuer qc II. *vt* pousser

◆**push out** *vt* ❶ (*force out*) **to push sb/sth out** pousser qn/qc dehors; **to push sb/sth out of sth** faire sortir qn/qc de qc en le poussant ❷ (*get rid of*) **to push sb out** exclure qn

◆**push over** *vt* **to push sb/sth over** faire tomber qn/qc

◆**push through** I. *vt* ❶ (*have accepted: proposal, measure*) faire passer ❷ (*help to pass through*) **to push sb through sth** faire passer qn à travers qc ❸ (*go through*) se frayer un chemin à travers II. *vi* se frayer un chemin

◆**push up** *vt* ❶ (*move higher*) **to push sb/sth up** relever qn/qc ❷ ECON (*cause increase*) augmenter ▶ **to ~ (the) <u>dai-sies</u>** *iron* manger les pissenlits par la racine

**push-button** *adj* (*telephone*) à touches; (*controls*) à boutons

**push button** *n* bouton *m*

**pushcart** *n* charrette (à bras) *f*

**pushover** *n inf* ❶ (*easy success*) **to be a ~** être du gâteau ❷ (*easily influenced person*) **to be a ~** être facile à convaincre ❸ (*weak person*) **to be a ~ for sth** craquer pour qc

**pushpin** ['puʃ·pɪn] *n* punaise *f*

**pushup** *n* traction *f;* **to do ~s** faire des pompes II. *adj* (*bra*) rembourré(e)

**pushy** ['puʃ·i] *adj pej* ❶ (*domineering*) autoritaire ❷ (*ambitious*) ambitieux(-euse)

**puss** [pus] <-sses> *n inf* ❶ (*cat*) minou *m* ❷ (*girl*) minette *f*

**pussy** ['pus·i] *n* <-ssies> ❶ *inf* (*cat*) minou *m* ❷ *vulg* chatte *f*

**put** [put] <-tt-, put, put> *vt* ❶ (*place*) mettre; **to ~ sth into sth** mettre qc dans qc; (*thrust*) enfoncer qc dans qc; **to ~ some more milk in one's coffee** rajouter du lait dans son café ❷ (*direct*) mettre; **to ~ the emphasis on sth** met-

tre l'accent sur qc; **to ~ pressure on sb** mettre qn sous pression; **to ~ faith in sth** croire en qc; **to ~ a spell on sb** jeter un sort sur qn; **to ~ sb in his place** remettre qn à sa place ❸ (*invest*) placer; **to ~ sth in an account** déposer qc sur un compte; **to ~ money on sth** placer de l'argent sur qc; **to ~ energy/time/money into sth** investir de l'énergie/du temps/de l'argent dans qc ❹ CULIN (*add*) **to ~ sth in sth** ajouter qc à qc ❺ (*cause to be*) mettre; **to ~ sb in a good mood/at ease** mettre qn de bonne humeur/à l'aise; **to ~ sb in prison/in a taxi** mettre qn en prison/dans un taxi; **to ~ sb to shame** faire honte à qn; **to ~ sb on trial** faire passer qn en jugement; **to ~ sb to work** faire travailler qn; **to ~ sb at risk** faire courir un danger à qn ❻ (*present: point of view*) présenter; (*case, problem*) exposer; (*question*) poser; (*arguments*) proposer; (*proposition*) faire; **to ~ sth to a vote** soumettre qc à un vote ❼ (*express*) dire; **to ~ it bluntly** pour parler franc; **to ~ sth on paper** coucher qc sur le papier; **I couldn't have ~ it better (myself)** on ne saurait mieux le formuler; **as sb ~ it** comme qn dit; **how to ~ it** comment dire; **to ~ one's feelings into words** mettre des mots sur ses sentiments ❽ (*value*) **to ~ sth to efficiency before appearance** placer l'efficacité avant l'apparence; **I'd ~ her right at the top** pour moi, c'est la meilleure ❾ (*estimate*) estimer; **to ~ sb/sth at sth** estimer qn/qc à qc ❿ SPORTS **to ~ the shot** lancer le poids

◆**put about** <-tt-> *irr* I. *vt* (*spread rumor*) **to put sth about** faire circuler qc; **to put it about that ...** faire circuler le bruit que ... II. *vi* NAUT virer de bord

◆**put across** *vt irr* **to put sth across** faire comprendre qc; (*idea, message*) faire passer qc; **she puts herself across well** elle sait comment se présenter

◆**put aside** <-tt-> *vt irr* ❶ (*save*) mettre de côté; **to put some money aside** mettre de l'argent de côté; **to ~ some time** se réserver du temps ❷ (*leave ignore: work, problem, differences*) mettre de côté

◆ **put away** <-tt-> *vt irr* ❶ (*save, set aside*) mettre de côté ❷ *inf* (*eat*) engloutir ❸ (*clean up*) ranger ❹ *inf* (*have institutionalized*) **to be ~** (*in an old people's home*) être mis en maison de retraite; (*in prison*) être emprisonné; (*in a hospital*) être interné ❺ *inf* (*kill*) **to put sb away** éliminer ❻ *fig* (*ignore, remove: worries, idea*) écarter ❼ SPORTS (*defeat*) battre

◆ **put back** <-tt-> *vt irr* ❶ (*return to its place*) **to put sth back** remettre qc (à sa place) ❷ (*postpone*) remettre ❸ (*invest*) remettre ❹ (*delay*) retarder ❺ *inf* (*drink*) siffler

◆ **put by** <-tt-> *vt irr* mettre de côté

◆ **put down** <-tt-> *irr* **I.** *vt* ❶ (*set down*) poser; **I couldn't put the book down** je ne pouvais pas lâcher le livre ❷ (*put to bed*) **to put a baby down** coucher un bébé ❸ (*lower, decrease*) baisser ❹ (*pay, give as deposit*) verser ❺ (*write*) inscrire; **to put sth down on paper** coucher qc sur papier; **to put sb down for sth** inscrire qn sur la liste pour qc; **to put one's name down for sth** s'inscrire pour qc; **I put my name down for the camping trip** je me suis inscrit pour la sortie camping; **put me down for $20** je donnerai 20 dollars; **put it down on the bill** ils l'ont mis sur la facture; **I'll put it down in my diary** je vais le noter dans mon agenda ❻ (*attribute*) **to put sth down to sb/sth** mettre qc sur le compte de qn/qc ❼ (*consider*) **to ~ sb as sth** prendre qn pour qc ❽ MIL (*suppress: a rebellion*) réprimer ❾ *inf* (*deride*) humilier ❿ (*have killed*) abattre; (*a dog*) faire piquer ⓫ AVIAT poser **II.** *vi* AVIAT se poser

◆ **put forward** <-tt-> *vt irr* ❶ (*submit, offer*) avancer; (*a candidate, plan*) proposer; **to put oneself forward for promotion** demander une promotion ❷ (*advance*) avancer

◆ **put in** <-tt-> *irr* **I.** *vt* ❶ (*place inside*) mettre (dedans); (*from outside*) rentrer ❷ (*add, insert: ingredient, paragraph*) ajouter ❸ (*plant*) planter ❹ (*install*) (faire) installer ❺ (*appoint*) désigner; (*at election*) élire ❻ FIN (*deposit*) déposer ❼ (*invest, devote*) investir; **to ~ 8 hours' work** faire 8 heures de travail ❽ (*present*) présenter; (*claim*) déposer; (*protest*) formuler; **to ~ a plea** plaider; **to put one's name in for sth** poser sa candidature pour qc; **to put sb in for sth** inscrire qn à qc; (*for exam*) présenter qn à qc ❾ (*make*) **to ~ a (phone) call to sb** passer un coup de fil à qn **II.** *vi* ❶ (*dock*) faire escale ❷ (*apply for*) **to ~ for sth** faire une demande de qc; **to ~ for a job** poser sa candidature pour un travail; **to put sb in for sth** inscrire qn à qc

◆ **put off** <-tt-> *vt irr* ❶ (*postpone, delay*) repousser; **to put sth off for a week** remettre qc à une semaine; **to put sb off** décommander qn ❷ (*dissuade*) dissuader; **to put sb off doing sth** dissuader qn de faire qc ❸ (*repel*) dégoûter; **to put sb off his dinner** couper l'appétit à qn; **her voice puts a lot of people off** sa voix rebute pas mal de gens ▸ **never ~ until tomorrow what you can do today** *prov* il ne faut jamais remettre à demain ce que l'on peut faire le jour même *prov*

◆ **put on** <-tt-> *vt irr* ❶ (*wear*) porter; **to ~ some make-up** se maquiller; **to put clean things on** mettre des vêtements propres, se rappropier *Belgique, Nord* ❷ (*turn on*) allumer; **I'll put the kettle on** je vais faire bouillir de l'eau; **to ~ the brakes** freiner ❸ (*play: CD, movie*) passer; (*play, concert*) monter ❹ (*assume, pretend*) affecter; (*an air, accent*) prendre; **to put it on** faire semblant; (*show off*) crâner; **to ~ an act** jouer la comédie; **to put sb on** faire marcher qn ❺ (*indicate, inform*) **to put sb on to sth** indiquer qc à qn; **to put sb**

**P**

on to (*dentist, shop*) indiquer qn à qn; (*culprit*) mettre qn sur la piste de ⑥ (*increase, add*) augmenter; **to ~ weight/ 10 pounds** prendre du poids/5 kilos; **to ~ speed** prendre de la vitesse; **to put 10% on the price of sth** majorer de 10% le prix de qc ⑦ (*provide: extra trains, flights*) mettre en service; (*dinner party*) offrir; (*TV program*) passer ⑧ (*begin cooking*) **to put the dinner on** se mettre à cuisiner ⑨ (*bet*) **to put sth on sth** miser qc sur qc ⑩ (*hand over to*) **to put sb on the (tele)phone** passer qn; **I'll put you on to your mother** je te passe ta mère ⑪ (*prescribe*) **to put sb on steroids** prescrire des stéroïdes à qn

◆ **put out** <-tt-> *irr* **I.** *vt* ① (*extinguish, turn off*) éteindre; (*gas, water*) fermer ② (*take outside*) sortir; **to ~ the trash** sortir les poubelles ③ (*issue: announcement, warning*) faire passer ④ (*broadcast*) diffuser ⑤ (*produce*) produire ⑥ (*extend*) étendre; (*new shoots*) déployer; **to ~ one's hand** tendre la main ⑦ (*disconcert*) contrarier; **to be ~ by sth** être déconcerté par qc ⑧ (*lay out for ready use: uniform, tools*) préparer; (*silverware, plates*) placer; **to put sth out for sb/sth** sortir qc à qn/ qc ⑨ (*make unconscious*) endormir **II.** *vi* ① NAUT (*set sail*) quitter le port ② *inf* (*offer sex*) **to ~ for sb** coucher avec qn

◆ **put over** <-tt-> *vt irr* ① (*make understood*) **to put sth over** faire comprendre qc ② (*postpone*) remettre à plus tard ③ *inf* **to put <u>one</u> over on sb** avoir qn

◆ **put through** <-tt-> *vt irr* ① TEL (*connect*) **to put sb through** mettre qn en ligne; **to put sb through to sb** passer qn à qn ② (*implement*) **to put sth through** mener qc à bien; (*proposal*) faire accepter qc; (*deal*) conclure qc; **to put a bill through Congress** faire accepter un projet de loi par le Congrès ③ (*make endure*) **to put sb through sth** faire subir qc à qn; **to put sb**

**through hell** faire souffrir le martyre à qn; **he really put me through it** il m'en a fait baver ④ (*support financially*) **to put sb through college** payer l'université à qn; **to put oneself through college** se payer l'université

◆ **put together** <-tt-> *vt irr* ① (*assemble: pieces*) assembler; (*radio, band, model*) monter; (*facts*) reconstituer ② (*place near*) **to put two things together** mettre deux choses côte à côte; *fig* rapprocher deux choses ③ (*connect*) **to put clues/facts together** rapprocher des indices/des faits; **to put two sets of figures together** comparer deux séries de chiffres ④ MATH (*add*) **to put 10 and 15 together** additionner 10 et 15 ⑤ CULIN (*mix*) mélanger ⑥ (*prepare, organize: plan, strategy*) élaborer; (*book, program*) faire; (*team*) rassembler; (*legal case*) constituer ⑦ (*create: dinner*) improviser ▸ **to put two and two together** *prov* tirer ses conclusions

◆ **put up** <-tt-> *irr* **I.** *vt* ① (*raise*) lever; **to ~ one's hand** lever la main; (*satellite*) placer en orbite ② (*build, install*) ériger; (*tent*) dresser; (*shelves*) poser; (*wallpaper*) poser ③ (*give shelter*) **to put sb up** (**for the night**) héberger qn (pour la nuit) ④ (*submit, present*) présenter; **to ~ a struggle** opposer une résistance; **to put sb up as sth** proposer qn comme qc; **to put sb up for election** proposer qn à une élection; **to put sth up for sale/rent** mettre qc en vente/location; **to be ~ for sale/auction** être en vente/aux enchères; **to put sb up to doing sth** *inf* pousser qn à faire qc ⑤ (*provide: money*) fournir ⑥ (*display: poster*) accrocher; (*notice*) afficher; (*sign*) mettre **II.** *vi* (*lodge*) **to ~ at sb's place/in a hotel** loger chez qn/à l'hôtel; **to ~ at sb's place/in a hotel for the night** passer la nuit chez qn/à l'hôtel

◆ **put up with** <-tt-> *vt irr, inf* **to ~ with sb/sth** supporter qn/qc

**putdown** *n inf* réplique *f* bien envoyée

**putoff** *n inf* excuse *f*
**put-on** *n inf* **it's a ~** c'est du cinéma
**putt** [pʌt] SPORTS **I.** *vt, vi* putter **II.** *n*
putt *m*
**putting green** *n* SPORTS green *m*
**put-up** *adj inf* **~ job** coup *m* monté
**put-upon** *adj inf* **to feel ~** se sentir exploité
**puzzle** ['pʌz·l] **I.** *vt* intriguer **II.** *vi* **to ~ about** [*o* **over**] **sth** chercher à comprendre qc **III.** *n* ❶(*analytical game*) devinette *f* ❷(*mechanical game*) casse-tête *m* ❸(*jigsaw puzzle*) puzzle *m*, casse-tête *m Québec* ❹(*mystery*) mystère *m*

**puzzled** *adj* ❶(*worried*) perplexe; **we are ~ about what to do now** nous ne savons que faire maintenant ❷(*surprised*) surpris(e)
**puzzling** *adj* déroutant(e)
**pylon** ['paɪ·lan] *n* pylône *m*
**pyramid** ['pɪr·ə·mɪd] *n* pyramide *f*
**pyramid scheme** *n* ECON, FIN système *m* pyramidale
**Pyrex®** ['paɪ·reks] **I.** *n* pyrex® *m* **II.** *adj* en pyrex
**pyromaniac** *n* pyromane *mf*
**python** ['paɪ·θən] <-(ons)> *n* python *m*

**Q, q** [kju] <-'s> *n* Q *m*, q *m*; **~ as in Quebec** (*on telephone*) q comme Quintal
**Q** *n abbr of* **Queen** reine *f*
**QR code** *n abbr of* **Quick Response** INET code *m* QR
**qtr.** *n abbr of* **quarter** quart *m*
**quadrant** ['kwa·drənt] *n* ❶(*quarter of circle*) quart *m* de cercle ❷(*quarter of plane surface*) quart *m*
**quadriceps** [ˌkwa·drɪ·'seps] *n* ANAT quadriceps *m*
**quadruple** ['kwa·drʊ·pl] **I.** *vt, vi* quadrupler **II.** *adj* quadruple
**qualification** [ˌkwa·lɪ·fɪ·'keɪ·ʃən] *n* ❶(*credentials, skills*) qualification *f* ❷(*document, exam*) diplôme *m* ❸(*the act of qualifying*) obtention *f* d'un diplôme ❹(*limiting criteria*) réserve *f* ❺(*condition*) condition *f* ❻SPORTS, LING qualification *f*
**qualified** *adj* ❶(*competent*) qualifié(e) ❷(*trained*) diplômé(e); **I'm not ~ to answer that question** je ne suis pas compétent pour répondre à cette question ❸(*limited*) mitigé(e)

**qualify** ['kwa·lɪ·faɪ] <-ie-> **I.** *vt* ❶(*give credentials, make eligible*) qualifier ❷(*add reservations to*) nuancer ❸LING qualifier ❹(*give the right*) donner droit à ❺(*describe*) **to ~ sb/sth as sth** qualifier qn/qc de qc **II.** *vi* ❶SPORTS se qualifier ❷(*meet standards*) **to ~ for sth** remplir les conditions requises pour qc; **it hardly qualifies as sth** on ne peut pas appeler ça qc ❸(*be eligible*) **to ~ for sth** avoir droit à qc ❹(*have qualifications*) être qualifié
**quality** ['kwa·lə·ti] <-ies> *n* qualité *f*; **she has managerial qualities** c'est une bonne gestionnaire **II.** *adj* de qualité
**quality control** *n* contrôle *m* qualité
**quality time** *n* moments privilégiés passés avec quelqu'un
**quantity** ['kwan·tə·ti] <-ies> *n* quantité *f*; **a ~ of cotton wool** du coton
**quarantine** ['kwɔr·ən·tin] **I.** *n* quarantaine *f* **II.** *vt* **to ~ sb/an animal** mettre qn/un animal en quarantaine
**quarrel** ['kwɔr·əl] **I.** *n* dispute *f*; **to have a ~** se disputer **II.** <-ll-> *vi* se disputer

**quarry** ['kwɔr·i] I. n ❶ (*mine*) carrière f ❷ *fig* proie f II. <-ie-> vt ❶ (*extract: mineral*) extraire ❷ (*cut into: hillside*) creuser

**quart** [kwɔrt] n 0,946 litres

**quarter** ['kwɔr·tər] I. n ❶ (*one fourth*) quart m ❷ (*25-cent coin*) pièce f de 25 cents; (*sum*) 25 cents mpl ❸ (*15 minutes*) **a ~ to three** trois heures moins le quart; **a ~ past** [*o* **after**] **three** trois heures et quart ❹ (*1/4 of year, school term*) trimestre m ❺ SPORTS (*period*) quart-temps m ❻ (*neighborhood*) quartier m; **the French Quarter** le quartier français ❼ pl (*unspecified group or person*) milieu m; **there have been protests from some ~s** il y a eu des protestations de la part de certains ❽ (*area of compass*) quart m II. vt ❶ (*cut into four*) **to ~ sth** couper qc en quatre ❷ *passive* (*give housing*) **to be ~ed** être cantonné III. adj quart de; **a ~ pound** ≈ 100 grammes

**quarterfinal** n quart m de finale; **in the ~s** aux quarts de finale

**quarterly** ['kwɔr·tər·li] I. adv par trimestre II. adj (*magazine*) trimestriel(le)

**quartertone** n MUS quart m de ton

**quartz** [kwɔrts] n quartz m

**quay** [ki] n quai m

**queen** [kwin] I. n ❶ (*female monarch*) a. *fig* reine f ❷ GAMES dame f ❸ *pej* (*gay man*) folle f II. vt GAMES damer

**queer** [kwɪr] I. <-er, -est> adj ❶ (*strange: ideas*) bizarre ❷ *pej* (*homosexual*) pédé II. n *pej* (*a homosexual*) pédé m

**query** ['kwɪr·i] I. <-ies> n ❶ (*question*) question f ❷ COMPUT requête f II. <-ie-> vt (*ask*) demander

**question** ['kwes·tʃən] I. n ❶ (*inquiry*) a. SCHOOL, UNIV question f; **to ask sb a ~** poser une question à qn ❷ LING interrogation f ❸ (*doubt*) **without ~** sans aucun doute; **to be beyond ~** ne pas faire de doute; **it's open to ~** cela se discute; **to call sth into ~** mettre qc en doute ❹ (*issue*) question f; **to be a ~ of time/money** être une question de temps/d'argent; **to be out of the ~** être hors de question; **the time/place in ~** le moment/lieu en question II. vt ❶ (*ask*) questionner ❷ (*interrogate*) a. SCHOOL interroger ❸ (*doubt: ability, facts, findings*) mettre en doute; **I'd ~ whether that's true** je me pose la question de savoir si c'est vrai

**questionable** adj discutable

**question mark** n point m d'interrogation

**questionnaire** [ˌkwes·tʃə·'ner] n questionnaire m

**queue** [kju] I. n COMPUT file f d'attente II. vi COMPUT être en file d'attente

**quick** [kwɪk] I. <-er, -est> adj ❶ (*fast*) rapide; **to grab a ~ drink** s'en jeter un petit; **to grab a ~ sandwich** manger un sandwich sur le pouce; **to give sb a ~ call** passer un petit coup de fil à qn; **the ~ est way** le chemin le plus rapide; **to have a ~ temper** s'emporter facilement; **to be a ~ learner** apprendre vite ❷ (*bright*) vif(vive); **~ thinking** rapidité f d'esprit II. <-er, -est> adv inf vite; **as ~ as possible** aussi vite que possible; **to get rich ~** s'enrichir rapidement III. interj vite! IV. n (*edge of digit*) **to bite/cut nails to the ~** se ronger/se couper les ongles jusqu'au sang

**quick-frozen** adj surgelé(e)

**quickly** adv vite; **the report was ~ written** le rapport a été écrit rapidement

**quickness** n rapidité f

**quicksand** ['kwɪk·sænd] n sables mpl mouvants

**quick-witted** adj vif(vive)

**quiet** [kwaɪət] I. n ❶ (*silence*) silence m ❷ (*piece*) calme m II. adj ❶ (*not loud*) doux(douce); (*voice*) bas(se) ❷ (*silent*) tranquille; **be ~** tais-toi; **to keep ~** se tenir tranquille; **to keep sb ~** (*with activity*) tenir qn tranquille; (*with bribe*) faire taire qn ❸ (*secret: arrangement*) caché(e); **to keep sth ~, keep ~ about sth** garder qc pour soi; **to have a ~ word with sb** glisser discrètement un mot à l'oreille de qn ❹ (*not showy*) simple; (*wedding*) inti-

**Q**

me; (*clothes*) sobre ⑤(*calm*) calme;
**they're a ~ couple** c'est un couple discret; **to have a ~ night in** passer une
soirée tranquille à la maison
◆**quiet down I.** *vi* ❶(*become quiet*)
se taire ❷(*become calm*) se calmer
**II.** *vt* ❶(*make quiet*) calmer ❷(*make
calm* (*down*)) apaiser

**quietly** *adv* ❶(*silently*) silencieusement ❷(*behaving well: play*) sagement
❸(*speaking*) doucement ❹(*peacefully*) paisiblement ❺(*discreetly*) discrètement; **to be ~ confident** être calme et
sûr de soi

**quilt** [kwɪlt] **I.** *n* édredon *m;* **continental ~** couette *f* **II.** *vt* piquer

**quince** [kwɪn(t)s] *n* coing *m*

**quit** [kwɪt] **I.** *vt* ❶(*leave*) *a.* COMPUT quitter; **to ~ one's job** démissionner
❷(*stop*) abandonner; **~ bothering me**
arrête de m'embêter **II.** *vi* ❶(*give up*)
abandonner ❷(*resign*) démissionner

**quite** [kwaɪt] *adv* ❶(*fairly*) assez; **~ a
lot of money/letters** vraiment beau
coup d'argent/de lettres ❷(*completely*) complètement; (*different*) tout à fait;
**it's ~ simple** c'est très simple ❸(*exactly*) tout à fait; **he didn't ~ succeed** il

n'a pas vraiment réussi; **~ the opposite**
plutôt le contraire ❹(*really*) véritable;
**it was ~ a struggle** c'était vraiment difficile; **it's been ~ a day!** quelle journée!; **he's ~ the hero, isn't he?** *iron*
c'est tout à fait un héros, n'est-ce pas?

**quits** [kwɪts] *adj* **to call it ~** en rester là
de jeu

**quiz** [kwɪz] **I.<-es>** *n* ❶(*short test*)
contrôle-surprise *m* ❷(*contest*) jeu-
-concours *m* **II.** *vt* questionner

**quiz-show host** *n* animateur, -trice *m, f*
de jeu

**quota** [ˈkwoʊ·tə] *n* ❶(*allowance*) quota *m;* (*export, import*) contingent *m*
❷(*allotment*) dose *f*

**quotation** [kwoʊˈteɪ·ʃ³n] *n* ❶(*passage*) citation *f* ❷ FIN cotation *f*

**quotation marks** *npl* guillemets *mpl*

**quote** [kwoʊt] **I.** *n* ❶ *inf* (*quotation*) citation *f* ❷ *pl, inf* (*punctuation marks*)
guillemets *mpl* ❸ *inf* (*estimate*) devis *m* ▸ **~ ... unquote** je cite ... fin de
citation **II.** *vt* ❶(*repeat verbatim*) citer;
**the press ~d him as saying sth** selon
les journaux, il aurait dit qc ❷(*give;
price*) établir ❸ FIN **to be ~d on the
Stock Exchange** être coté en Bourse
**III.** *vi* citer

**Q**

# Rr

**R, r** [ar] <-'s o -s> n R m, r m; **~ as in Romeo** r comme Raoul

**r** [ar] ELEC abbr of **resistance** résistance f

**R** [ar] **I.** n SPORTS abbr of **run** point m **II.** adj CINE abbr of **restricted** interdit(e) aux moins de dix-sept ans

**R.** [ar] n abbr of **River** rivière f

**rabbi** ['ræb·aɪ] n rabbin m

**rabbit** ['ræb·ɪt] n lapin m

**rabies** ['reɪ·biz] n + sing vb la rage

**race¹** [reɪs] **I.** n ❶ SPORTS **a 100-meter ~** un cent mètres ❷ (contest) course f ▶ **a ~ against time** une course contre la montre **II.** vi ❶ (compete) courir; **to ~ against sb** faire la course avec qn ❷ (rush) aller à toute allure; (heart, engine) s'emballer; **to ~ along/past** aller/passer à toute vitesse ❸ (hurry) se dépêcher; **to ~ for a bus** se dépêcher pour attraper un bus **III.** vt ❶ (compete with) faire la course avec ❷ (enter for races: horse, dog) faire courir ❸ (rev up: engine) emballer ❹ (transport) emmener à toute vitesse

**race²** [reɪs] n (ethnicity) race f

**race³** [reɪs] n GEO canal m

**race car** n voiture f de course

**race car driver** n pilote mf automobile

**racecourse** n champ m de courses

**racehorse** n cheval m de course

**race riot** n émeute f raciale

**racial** ['reɪ·ʃ°l] adj racial(e)

**racial conflict** n conflit m racial

**racial profiling** n contrôle n au faciès

**racing** n ❶ (act of racing) course f ❷ (races: horses) les courses fpl; (cars, cycles) la course f

**racing bicycle, racing bike** n inf vélo m de course

**racism** ['reɪ·sɪ·z°m] n racisme m

**racist** **I.** n raciste mf **II.** adj raciste

**rack** [ræk] **I.** n ❶ (frame, shelf) étagère f; (for the oven) grille f; (for dishes) égouttoir m; (in dishwasher) panier m;

(for billiard balls) triangle m ❷ (joint) **~ of lamb** carré m d'agneau ❸ (for torture) chevalet m de torture ❹ sl (bed) pieu m **II.** vt (hurt) torturer ▶ **to ~ one's brains** se creuser la tête

**racket** ['ræk·ɪt] n ❶ SPORTS raquette f ❷ inf (noise) vacarme m ❸ (dishonest practice) racket m

**racquetball** n jeu m de paume

**radar gun** n pistolet-radar m

**radial** ['reɪ·di·əl] adj radial(e)

**radiation** n (light) irradiation f; (heat) rayonnement m; (waves) radiation f

**radiator** ['reɪ·di·eɪ·t̬ər] n radiateur m

**radical** ['ræd·ɪ·k°l] **I.** n ❶ (person) radical(e) m(f) ❷ CHEM radical m **II.** adj radical(e)

**radio** ['reɪ·di·oʊ] **I.** n ❶ (broadcasting) radio f; **on the ~** à la radio ❷ (device) (poste m de) radio f **II.** vt (call) contacter par radio; (send) envoyer par radio **III.** vi envoyer un message par radio

**radioactive** [ˌreɪ·di·oʊ·'æk·tɪv] adj radioactif(-ive)

**radioactivity** n radioactivité f

**radio alarm clock** n radio-réveil m

**radio cassette recorder** n radiocassette m

**radio contact** n contact m radio

**radiography** [ˌreɪ·di·'a·grə·fi] n radiographie f

**radiologist** n radiologue mf

**radio station** n station f de radio; **local ~** radio f locale

**radish** ['ræd·ɪʃ] <-es> n radis m

**radius** ['reɪ·di·əs] <-dii o -es> n ❶ (half of diameter) rayon m; **everything within a ~ of 5 miles** |o **within a five mile ~**| tout dans un rayon de 5 miles ❷ ANAT radius m

**raffle** ['ræf·l] **I.** n tombola f **II.** vt mettre en tombola

**raft** [ræft] **I.** n ❶ (flat vessel) radeau m ❷ inf (a lot) **a ~ of sth** une montagne de qc **II.** *vi* **to ~ across/down the riv-er** traverser/descendre la rivière en radeau

**rag** [ræg] **I.** *n* ❶ (*cloth*) lambeau *m;* (*for dusting*) chiffon *m* à épousseter ❷ *pl* (*old clothes*) guenilles *fpl* ❸ *pej, sl* (*newspaper*) torchon *m* ❹ (*ragtime music*) ragtime *m* ▶ **to be on the ~** *sl* avoir ses ragnagnas **II.** <-gg-> *vt inf* (*tease*) taquiner

**rage** [reɪdʒ] **I.** *n* (*anger*) colère *f;* **to be in a ~** être furieux ▶ **to be all the ~** faire fureur **II.** *vi* ❶ (*express fury*) **to ~ at sb/sth** fulminer contre qn/qc ❷ (*continue: battle*) faire rage; (*epidemic*) sévir ❸ (*wind*) souffler en tempête; (*sea*) être démonté(e)

**ragged** *adj* ❶ (*torn*) en lambeaux; (*clothes*) en haillons ❷ (*wearing rags: children*) en guenilles; (*appearance*) négligé(e) ❸ (*disorderly*) désordonné(e) ❹ (*rough*) dentelé(e); (*coastline*) découpé(e) ❺ (*irregular*) irrégulier(-ère)

**raging** *adj* ❶ (*angry*) furieux(-euse) ❷ METEO violent(e); (*sea*) démonté(e) ❸ (*burning fiercely*) ardent(e); **a ~ inferno** un véritable brasier ❹ (*severe*) fort(e)

**raid** [reɪd] **I.** *n* ❶ (*attack*) raid *m* ❷ (*robbery*) hold-up *m inv* ❸ (*search*) descente *f* **II.** *vt* ❶ (*attack*) lancer un raid contre ❷ (*search*) faire une descente dans ❸ (*rob*) attaquer; **to ~ the fridge** *fig, inf* faire une razzia dans le frigo

**raider** [reɪ·dər] *n* ❶ (*attacker*) attaquant *m* ❷ (*robber*) cambrioleur, -euse *m, f* ❸ *pej* (*investor*) **corporate ~** prédateur

**rail**[1] [reɪl] *n* ❶ (*for trains*) rail *m;* **by ~** en train; **to go off the ~s** sortir des rails; *fig* s'écarter du droit chemin ❷ (*fence*) barre *f;* (*on track*) corde *f;* (*for protection*) garde-fou *m* ❸ (*to hang things*) tringle *f*

**rail**[2] [reɪl] *vi* (*criticize*) **to ~ at sb** râler sur qn; **to ~ against sb/sth** râler contre qn/qc

**railroad I.** *n* ❶ (*track*) voie *f* ferrée ❷ (*system*) chemin *m* de fer; **the**

French **~** les chemins *mpl* de fer français **II.** *vt inf* ❶ (*force to do*) imposer; **to ~ sb into doing sth** forcer qn à faire qc ❷ (*convict unfairly*) déclarer coupable à tort

**railroad car** *n* voiture *f* wagon

**railroad crossing** *n* passage *m* à niveau

**railroad network** *n* réseau *m* ferroviaire

**railway** *n* service *m* des trains

**rain** [reɪn] **I.** *n* ❶ (*precipitation*) pluie *f* ❷ *pl* (*season*) saison *f* des pluies ▶ (**come) ~ or shine** qu'il pleuve ou qu'il vente **II.** *vi* pleuvoir **III.** *vt fig* **to ~ blows/questions on sb** faire pleuvoir les coups/les questions sur qn ▶ **it's ~ing cats and dogs** il pleut des cordes ◆ **rain out** *vt* **to be rained out** être annulé à cause de la pluie

**rainbow** [reɪn·boʊ] *n a. fig* arc-en--ciel *m*

**rain check** *n* bon de réduction différé pour l'achat d'un article qui n'est plus disponible; **I'll take a ~** ça sera pour une autre fois

**raincoat** *n* imperméable *m*

**raindrop** *n* goutte *f* de pluie

**rainfall** *n* ❶ (*period*) chute *f* de pluie ❷ (*quantity*) pluviosité *f*

**rain forest** *n* forêt *m* tropicale

**rain ga(u)ge** *n* pluviomètre *m*

**rainy** <-ier, -iest> *adj* pluvieux(-euse); (*season*) des pluies

**raise** [reɪz] **I.** *n* augmentation *f* **II.** *vt* ❶ (*lift up*) lever; (*flag*) hisser; (*one's eyebrows*) froncer ❷ (*cause to rise*) soulever ❸ (*rouse*) réveiller; **to ~ sb from the dead** relever qn d'entre les morts ❹ (*stir up: dust*) soulever ❺ (*increase*) augmenter; **to ~ one's voice** hausser le ton ❻ (*in gambling*) **to ~ sb $10** faire une relance de 10 dollars à qn ❼ MATH élever ❽ (*improve*) améliorer; (*standard of living*) augmenter ❾ (*promote*) promouvoir ❿ (*arouse: laugh, murmur, cheer*) provoquer; (*doubts*) semer; (*fears*) engendrer; (*havoc*) causer; (*hopes*) faire naître; (*suspicions*) éveiller ⓫ (*introduce: issue, question*) soulever; **I'll ~ this with him** je lui en par-

**R**

lerai ⑫(*collect: funds*) rassembler; (*money*) se procurer ⑬*form* (*build: monument*) ériger ⑭(*bring up: children, family*) élever ⑮(*cultivate*) cultiver; (*cattle*) élever ⑯(*end: siege*) lever ⑰(*contact*) joindre ▸ **to ~ eyebrows** (*decision*) faire grincer des dents; **to ~ the roof** faire un bruit de tonnerre

**raisin** ['reɪ·zⁿn] *n* raisin *m* sec

**rake¹** [reɪk] *n* (*immoral man*) débauché *m*

**rake²** [reɪk] *n* (*slope*) inclinaison *f*

**rake³** [reɪk] **I.** *n* (*tool*) râteau *m* **II.** *vt* ratisser

 ◆**rake in** *vt* ①(*mix*) remuer à la pelle ②*inf* (*gain: money, profits, awards*) rafler; **to rake it in** remuer le fric à la pelle

 ◆**rake up** *vt* ①(*gather: leaves*) ramasser ②(*refer to: memories*) remuer

**rally¹** ['ræl·i] <-ies> *n* (*in racing*) rallye *m*

**rally²** ['ræl·i] **I.**<-ies> *n* ①(*improvement*) amélioration *f*; FIN remontée *f* ②(*in tennis*) échange *m* **II.**<-ie-> *vi* (*improve*) aller mieux; **stocks rallied** les cours ont remonté

**rally³** ['ræl·i] **I.**<-ies> *n* (*gathering*) rassemblement *m* **II.**<-ie-> *vt* **to ~ sb against/in favor of sth** rallier qn contre/à la cause de qc

 ◆**rally around I.** *vt* venir à l'aide de **II.** *vi* se rallier

**ram** [ræm] **I.** *n* (*male sheep*) bélier *m* **II.**<-mm-> *vt* (*door*) défoncer; (*car*) emboutir

**ramble** ['ræm·bl] **I.** *n* randonnée *f* **II.** *vi* ①(*hike*) se balader ②(*meander*) déambuler ③(*talk with digressions*) divaguer

**rambler** *n* ①(*walker*) randonneur, -euse *m, f* ②BOT rosier *m* grimpant

**ramp** [ræmp] *n* ①(*incline*) rampe *f* ②AVIAT passerelle *f*

**ran** [ræn] *pt of* **run**

**ranch** [ræntʃ] <-es> *n* ranch *m*

**rancid** ['ræn(t)·sɪd] *adj* rance; **to go ~** rancir

**R & B** [ˌar·ən(d)·'bi] *n abbr of* **rhythm and blues** R & B *m*

**random** ['ræn·dəm] **I.** *n* **at ~** au hasard **II.** *adj* fait(e) au hasard; (*sample*) prélevé(e) au hasard; (*attack, crime*) aveugle; (*error*) aléatoire

**random access memory** *n* COMPUT mémoire *f* vive

**randy** ['ræn·di] <-ier, -iest> *adj* en chaleur

**rang** [ræŋ] *pt of* **ring**

**range** [reɪndʒ] **I.** *n* ①(*distance covered: of a weapon*) portée *f*; (*of a plane*) rayon *m* d'action; (*of action*) champ *m*; **at a ~ of** à une distance de; **at long ~** à longue portée; **at close ~** à bout portant; **within one's ~** à sa portée; **out of ~** hors de portée ②(*length of time*) **in the long/short ~** à long/court terme ③(*scope: of vision, hearing*) champ *m*; (*of voice*) étendue *f*; (*of ability*) répertoire *m*; **to be out of ~** être hors d'atteinte ④(*spread, selection: of products, colors*) gamme *f*; (*products, sizes, patterns*) choix *m*; (*of temperatures*) écart *m*; (*of prices, jobs, possibilities*) éventail *m*; (*of fashion*) collection *f*; **a full ~ of sth** un assortiment complet de qc; **that is beyond my price ~** cela dépasse ma gamme de prix ⑤(*sphere, domain: of activity*) champ *m*; (*of knowledge*) étendue *f*; (*of influence, research*) domaine *m* ⑥(*row: of buildings*) rangée *f*; (*of mountains*) chaîne *f* ⑦SPORTS (**shooting**) ~ champ *m* de tir; **driving ~** (*in golf*) practice *m* ⑧(*stove*) fourneau *m* ⑨(*feeding land*) prairie *f* **II.** *vi* ①(*vary*) varier; **to ~ from sth to sth** aller de qc à qc ②(*wander*) errer ③(*travel*) parcourir ④(*be placed in row*) s'aligner ⑤(*deal with*) **to ~ over sth** couvrir qc ⑥(*cover distance*) **to ~ over sth** avoir une portée de qc; (*eyes*) parcourir qc **III.** *vt* s'aligner; **to ~ oneself against sb/sth** s'aligner contre qn/qc

**range finder** *n* télémètre *m*

**ranger** *n* garde *m* forestier; **park ~** gardien *m* de parc national

**rank¹** [ræŋk] **I.** *n* ①(*position*) rang *m*; **the top ~s of government** les hautes sphères *fpl* du pouvoir; **to pull ~** profiter de son statut ② MIL rang *m*; **to close ~s** *a. fig* serrer les rangs; **to join the ~s** rejoindre les rangs de l'armée ③ (*members of group*) rang *m*; **the ~s of race car drivers** les rangs *mpl* de coureurs automobiles ④ (*row or line*) rangée *f* II. *vi* se classer; **to ~ above sb** être supérieur à qn; **to ~ as sb/sth** être reconnu comme qn/qc III. *vt* classer; **to ~ sb among sb/sth** compter qn parmi qn/qc; **to ~ sth among sth** classer qc comme qc

**rank²** [ræŋk] *adj* ① (*absolute*) parfait(e) ② (*growing thickly: plant*) luxuriant(e) ③ (*overgrown*) envahi(e) ④ (*smelling unpleasant*) nauséabond(e)

**rank-and-file** *adj* ① MIL de l'infanterie ② (*belonging to majority*) de la base

**ransom** ['ræn(t)·sᵊm] I. *n* rançon *f*; **to be held for ~** *fig* avoir le couteau sous la gorge ▸ a **king's ~** une somme fabuleuse II. *vt* racheter

**rape** [reɪp] I. *n* ① (*sexual attack*) viol *m* ② BOT colza *m* II. *vt* violer

**rapid** ['ræp·ɪd] I. *adj* rapide II. *n pl* rapides *mpl*

**rapid transit** *n* réseau *m* de transport rapide

**rap session** *n sl* **to have a ~** tailler une bavette

**rare** [rer] *adj* ① (*uncommon*) rare ② (*undercooked*) saignant(e) ③ (*thin*) raréfié(e)

**rarely** ['rer·li] *adv* rarement

**rarity** ['rer·ə·t̬i] <-ies> *n* rareté *f*; **to be something of a ~** ne pas être fréquent

**rascal** ['ræs·kᵊl] *n* polisson(ne) *m(f)*

**rash** [ræʃ] I. *n* irritation *f* II. *adj* irréfléchi(e); **in a ~ moment** dans un moment d'égarement; **that was ~ of you** c'était risqué de ta part

**rasher** *n* tranche *f* de bacon

**raspberry** ['ræz·ˌber·i] <-ies> *n* ① (*fruit*) framboise *f* ② (*plant*) framboisier *m*

**rat** [ræt] I. *n* ① (*rodent*) rat *m* ② *inf* (*bad person*) ordure *f* II. <-tt-> *vt inf* **to ~ on sb** balancer qn

**rate** [reɪt] I. *n* ① (*ratio*) taux *m* ② (*speed*) **~ (of speed)** vitesse *f*; **at a fast ~** à toute vitesse; **at a slow ~** doucement ③ (*charge*) taux *m* ④ (*proportion*) taux *m* ▸ **at this ~** à ce compte-là; **at any ~** en tout cas II. *vt* ① (*consider*) considérer; **a highly ~d journalist** un journaliste très estimé ② (*evaluate*) évaluer ③ (*rank, classify*) classer ④ FIN évaluer ⑤ *inf* (*deserve*) mériter III. *vi* se classer; **to ~ as sth** être considéré comme qc

**rather** ['ræð·ər] *adv* ① (*preferably*) plutôt; **~ than** +*infin* plutôt que de +*infin*; **I'd ~ not** je ne préfère pas ② (*more exactly*) plus exactement; **~ ... than ...** plutôt ... que ... ③ (*very*) assez; **he answered the telephone ~ sleepily** il a répondu au téléphone quelque peu endormi

**ratify** ['ræt̬·ə·faɪ] <-ie-> *vt* ratifier

**rating** *n* ① (*evaluation*) estimation *f* ② (*performance class*) cote *f* de qualité ③ *pl* (*number of viewers*) audimat® *m*

**ratio** ['reɪ·ʃi·oʊ] <-os> *n* proportion *f*; **the ~ of nurses to patients** le nombre d'infirmières par malade

**ration** ['ræʃ·ᵊn] I. *n* ration *f* II. *vt* rationner

**rational** *adj* logique; (*explanation*) rationnel(le)

**rationale** [ˌræʃ·ə·'næl] *n* raisonnement *m*

**rat race** *n inf* foire *f* d'empoigne

**rattle** ['ræt̬·l] I. *n* ① (*noise*) bruit *m*; (*of keys, coins*) cliquetis *m* ② (*toy*) hochet *m* ③ (*of rattlesnake*) sonnettes *fpl* II. <-ling, -led> *vi* (*make noises*) faire du bruit; **to ~ along** rouler dans un bruit de ferraille III. <-ling, -led> *vt* ① (*bang together*) agiter ② (*make nervous*) déranger; **to get ~d** paniquer

**rattlesnake** ['ræt̬·l·sneɪk] *n* serpent *m* à sonnette

**ratty** ['ræt̬·i] <-ier, -iest> *adj inf* grincheux(-euse)

**rave** [reɪv] I. *n* ① *pl* (*praise*) éloges *mpl* ② *inf* (*party*) rave *f* ③ (*music*) **~ (music)** rave *f* II. *adj inf* élogieux(-euse)

**R**

**III.**vi ❶(*talk wildly*) délirer; **to ~ about sb/sth** divaguer à propos de qn/qc ❷(*address angrily*) tempêter; **to ~ against sb/sth** s'emporter contre qn/qc ❸(*praise*) s'extasier; **to ~ about sb/sth** faire l'éloge de qn/qc ❹(*attend rave party*) aller à une rave

**raven** ['rei·v°n] *n* corbeau *m*

**ravine** [rə·'vin] *n* ravin *m*

**raving** ['rei·vɪŋ] **I.***n* délire *m* **II.**adj ❶(*acting wildly*) furieux(-euse) ❷(*extreme*) délirant(e); (*success*) fou(folle); **to be a ~ beauty** être d'une grande beauté

**ravioli** [ˌræv·i·'ou·li] *n* raviolis *mpl*

**raw** [rɔ] **I.***n* **in the ~** (*unrefined*) tel qu'il/telle qu'elle est; (*naked*) dans le plus simple appareil **II.**adj ❶(*unprocessed*) brut(e); **~ material** *a.* fig matière *f* première ❷(*uncooked*) cru(e) ❸(*inexperienced: beginner*) total(e); **a ~ recruit** un bleu ❹(*unrestrained*) sans frein; (*energy*) sans retenue ❺MED (*sore*) à vif ❻(*chilly: weather*) âpre ❼(*brutal*) cru(e) ► **to get a ~ deal** se faire avoir; **to touch a ~ nerve** piquer au vif

**ray** [rei] *n* ❶(*of light*) rayon *m* ❷(*radiation*) radiation *f* ❸(*in science fiction*) rayon *m* laser; **~ gun** fusil *m* à rayons laser ❹(*trace: of hope, optimism*) lueur *f* ❺(*fish*) raie *f*

**razor** ['rei·zər] **I.***n* rasoir *m* **II.**vt raser

**razor blade** *n* lame *f* de rasoir

**razor sharp, razor-sharp** adj ❶(*very sharp*) tranchant(e) comme un rasoir ❷(*clear: mind*) acéré(e)

**RC** [ˌɑr·'si] **I.***n abbr of* **Red Cross** Croix-Rouge *f* **II.**adj abbr of **Roman Catholic** catholique

**Rd.** *n abbr of* **road** r. *f*

**re** [ri] *prep* concernant

**RE** [ˌɑr·'i] *n abbr of* **real estate** immobilier *m*

**reach** [ritʃ] **I.**<-es> *n* ❶(*accessibility*) portée *f*; **within easy ~ of schools and boutiques** avec écoles et boutiques à proximité; **to be out of ~** (*too far*) être hors de portée; (*too expensive*) être in-

abordable; (*impossible*) être du domaine du rêve ❷(*arm length*) rayon *m* d'action; SPORTS allonge *f* ❸*pl* (*area, expanse*) étendue *f*; **the upper/lower ~es of the Amazon** la haute/basse Amazone; **the farthest ~es of the universe** le fin fond de l'univers ❹(*sphere of action*) champ *m* d'action **II.**vt ❶(*arrive at*) atteindre; (*Italy, New York*) arriver à; (*destination*) arriver à; (*person*) parvenir à ❷(*come to: agreement*) aboutir à; (*conclusion*) arriver à; (*decision*) prendre; (*level, point, situation, stage*) atteindre ❸(*stretch for*) atteindre; **to ~ one's hand out** tendre sa main ❹(*contact: colleague*) joindre; (*market, public*) toucher ❺(*understand*) comprendre ❻(*pass*) passer **III.**vi s'étendre; **to ~ for sth** (étendre le bras pour) saisir qc; **to ~ over for sth** tendre le bras pour prendre qc ► **to ~ for the stars** essayer d'attraper la lune ◆**reach out** vi ❶(*with arm*) tendre le bras ❷(*communicate*) communiquer; **to ~ to sb** aller vers qn

**react** [ri·'ækt] *vi a.* MED, CHEM réagir

**reaction** [ri·'æk·ʃ°n] *n* ❶(*response*) *a.* MED, PHYS, CHEM réaction *f* ❷*pl* (*physical reflexes*) réflexes *mpl* ❸*form* POL réaction *f*

**reactionary** [ri·'æk·ʃ°n·er·i] POL **I.**adj réactionnaire **II.**<-ies> *n* réactionnaire *mf*

**reactor** [ri·'æk·tər] *n* PHYS réacteur *m*; **nuclear ~** réacteur nucléaire; **fusion ~** réacteur à fusion; **fission ~** réacteur à fission

**read**[1] [red] adj lu(e); **little/widely ~** (*magazine*) peu/très lu; (*student*) peu/très cultivé(e)

**read**[2] [rid] **I.***n* lecture *f*; **it's a good ~** ça se laisse lire **II.**<read, read> vt ❶(*book, magazine, newspaper*) lire ❷(*music*) lire; **to ~ sb's lips** lire sur les lèvres de qn ❸(*recite*) lire à voix haute; **to ~ sth back to sb** relire qc à qn ❹(*interpret: situation*) analyser; **to ~ sth in sb's face** lire qc sur le visage de qn; **to ~ sb's mind, to ~ sb like a book** *inf* lire dans les pensées de qn ❺ (*note information*) relever ❻ *inf* (*hear and understand*) recevoir ❼ PUBL corriger ❽ (*show information*) indiquer ▸ **~ my lips!** écoute bien ce que je te dis!; **to ~ sb the riot act** faire une sommation à qn **III.** <read, read> *vi* ❶ (*in books, magazines*) lire ❷ (*recite*) lire à voix haute ❸ (*have effect*) **to ~ well** se lire bien ▸ **to ~ between the lines** lire entre les lignes

◆ **read out** *vt* ❶ (*read aloud*) lire à voix haute ❷ COMPUT afficher

◆ **read over, read through** *vt* parcourir

◆ **read up** *vi* **to ~ on sb/sth** lire sur qn/qc

**reader** *n* ❶ (*person who reads*) lecteur, -trice *m, f* ❷ (*book of excerpts: at school*) livre *m* de lecture; (*at college*) recueil *m* de textes ❸ (*device*) lecteur *m*

**readily** ['red·ɪ·li] *adv* ❶ (*willingly*) volontiers ❷ (*easily*) facilement

**readiness** *n* ❶ (*willingness*) bonne volonté *f;* **sb's ~ to** + *infin* le désir de qn de + *infin* ❷ (*quickness*) empressement *m* ❸ (*preparedness*) **to be in ~ for sth** être prêt pour qc

**reading I.** *n* ❶ (*activity*) lecture *f* ❷ (*material*) lecture *f;* **to make (for) good bedtime ~** être un bon livre de chevet ❸ (*recital*) lecture *f* ❹ (*interpretation*) interprétation *f* ❺ TECH relevé *m* **II.** *adj* (*speed*) de lecture; **to have a ~ knowledge of English** savoir lire l'anglais

**read-only memory** *n* COMPUT mémoire *f* morte

**ready** ['red·i] **I.** <-ier, -iest> *adj* ❶ (*prepared*) prêt(e); **to get ~ for sth** se préparer pour qc; **to be ~ and waiting, to be ~, willing and able** être fin prêt; **to be ~ to** + *infin* être disposé à + *infin*; **to be ~ with an excuse** avoir une excuse toute prête ❷ (*quick*) prêt(e); (*mind*) vif(vive); **~ cash** argent *m* liquide; **to have a ~ reply to every question** avoir réponse à tout ▸ **~, set, go!**

SPORTS à vos marques, prêts, partez! **II.** <-ies> *n* **at the ~** (*prepared*) prêt(e) **III.** <-ie-> *vt* préparer

**real** [ril] **I.** *adj* ❶ (*actual*) vrai(e); (*threat*) véritable; (*costs*) réel(le); **in ~ terms** FIN en valeur absolue ❷ (*genuine, considerable*) véritable; (*gentleman, problem*) vrai(e); (*food*) traditionnel(le) ❸ (*main*) vrai(e) ▸ **to be the ~ McCoy** [*o* **thing**] *inf* être du vrai de vrai **II.** *adv inf* (*very, really*) vachement

**real estate agent** *n* agent *m* immobilier

**realistic** *adj a.* ART, LIT réaliste

**reality show** *n* reality show *m*

**reality television** *n*, **reality TV** téléréalité *f*

**realize** ['ri·ə·laɪz] *vt* ❶ (*know: fact, situation*) réaliser; **sorry, I never ~d** désolé, je ne me rendais pas compte; **I ~ you're in a hurry** je me rends compte que vous êtes pressé ❷ (*achieve: hopes, dreams*) réaliser ❸ FIN (*assets*) réaliser; (*price*) rapporter

**really** ['ri·li] **I.** *adv* vraiment **II.** *interj* ❶ (*surprise*) c'est vrai? ❷ (*annoyance*) vraiment!

**realtor** ['ri·əl·tər] *n* agent *m* immobilier

**rear¹** [rɪr] **I.** *adj* arrière; **the ~ door/entrance** la porte/l'entrée *f* de derrière **II.** *n* ❶ (*back part*) **the ~** l'arrière *m;* **to bring up the ~** fermer la marche ❷ *inf* (*buttocks*) derrière *m;* **to be a pain in the ~** être un enquiquineur

**rear²** [rɪr] **I.** *vt* ❶ (*bring up*) élever ❷ (*raise*) lever; **this issue/inflation is ~ing its ugly head again** ce problème/cette inflation point de nouveau à l'horizon ❸ *form* (*build*) dresser **II.** *vi* ❶ (*raise: horse*) se dresser ❷ (*extend high*) s'élever

**rear admiral** *n* contre-amiral *m*

**rear end** *n* ❶ (*back part*) train *m* arrière ❷ *inf* (*buttocks*) derrière *m*

**rearrange** [ˌri·ə·'reɪndʒ] *vt* réarranger; (*skirt*) réajuster; (*schedule*) modifier; **to ~ the order of sth** remettre de l'ordre dans qc

**rearview mirror** *n* rétroviseur *m*

**R**

**rear-wheel drive** *n* roues *fpl* arrières motrices; (*in car*) traction *f* arrière

**reason** ['riːzᵊn] **I.** *n* ❶ (*ground*) raison *f*; **the ~ why ...** la raison pour laquelle ...; **the ~ for sth** la raison de qc; **sb's ~ for doing sth** la raison pour laquelle qn fait qc; **by ~ of sth** pour cause de qc ❷ (*judgment*) raison *f*; **within ~** tout en restant raisonnable; **to be beyond all ~** dépasser la raison; **it stands to ~ that ...** il va sans dire que ... ❸ (*sanity*) raison *f*; **to lose all ~** perdre toute sa raison **II.** *vt* **to ~ that ...** calculer que ...; **to ~ sth out** résoudre qc; **to ~ out that ...** déduire que ... **III.** *vi* raisonner; **to ~ with** discuter avec

**reasonable** *adj* raisonnable; **beyond a ~ doubt** sans l'ombre d'un doute

**reasonably** *adv* ❶ (*with reason*) raisonnablement ❷ (*acceptably*) assez; **~ priced** à un prix raisonnable

**reasoning** *n* raisonnement *m*

**reassure** [ˌriːəˈʃʊr] *vt* rassurer

**reassuring** *adj* rassurant(e)

**rebate** ['riːbeɪt] *n* ❶ (*refund*) remboursement *m* ❷ (*discount*) rabais *m*

**rebel** ['rebᵊl, *vb:* rɪˈbel] **I.** *n a. fig* rebelle *mf* **II.** <-ll-> *vi a. fig* se rebeller

**rebellion** [rɪˈbeljən] *n* rébellion *f*

**rebellious** *adj* rebelle

**reboot** [ˌriːˈbuːt] COMPUT **I.** *vt, vi* redémarrer **II.** *n* redémarrage *m*

**rebuild** [ˌriːˈbɪld] *vt irr, a. fig* reconstruire; (*engine*) remonter

**receding** *adj* (*chin*) fuyant(e); **~ hairline** front *m* dégarni

**receipt** [rɪˈsiːt] *n* ❶ (*document*) reçu *m*; (*for rent*) quittance *f* de loyer; (*at checkout*) ticket *m* de caisse ❷ *pl* (*income*) recettes *fpl* ❸ (*act of receiving*) réception *f*; **payable on** [*o* **upon**] **~** payable à la réception

**receive** [rɪˈsiːv] *vt* ❶ (*get, hear, see*) *a.* TECH recevoir; **to ~ recognition** être reconnu ❷ (*endure*) subir; (*a rebuke*) essuyer; **to ~ a long sentence** être condamné à une peine de longue durée ❸ (*greet*) accueillir ❹ *form* (*accommodate*) recevoir ❺ (*admit to member-*

*ship*) admettre ❻ LAW (*stolen goods*) receler; **guilty of receiving** coupable de recel ▶ **it is more** <u>blessed</u> **to give than to ~** *prov* donner est plus doux que recevoir

**receiver** *n* ❶ TECH récepteur *m*; (*on telephone*) combiné *m* ❷ (*bankruptcy official*) administrateur *m* judiciaire ❸ LAW (*of stolen goods*) receleur, -euse *m, f*

**recent** ['riːsᵊnt] *adj* récent(e); **in ~ times** ces derniers temps

**recently** *adv* récemment

**reception** [rɪˈsepʃᵊn] *n* ❶ (*welcome*) accueil *m*; **the idea got a chilly/ warm ~** l'idée a été mal/bien accueillie ❷ RADIO, TV réception *f* ❸ (*social event*) réception *f* ❹ (*area in hotel, building*) réception *f*

**reception desk** *n* réception *f*

**receptionist** *n* réceptionniste *mf*

**recession** [rɪˈseʃᵊn] *n* ECON récession *f*; **to be in/go into ~** être en/entrer en récession

**recharge** [ˌriːˈtʃɑːrdʒ] **I.** *vt* recharger ▶ **to ~ one's** <u>batteries</u> recharger ses accus **II.** *vi* se recharger

**rechargeable** *adj* rechargeable

**recipe** ['resəpi] *n* recette *f*; **the ~ for success** la meilleure formule pour réussir ▶ **to be a ~ for** <u>disaster</u> mener (tout) droit à la catastrophe

**recipient** [rɪˈsɪpiənt] *n* (*of welfare, money*) bénéficiaire *mf*; (*of mail, gift*) destinataire *mf*; (*of an award*) lauréat(e) *m(f)*; (*of a transplant*) receveur, -euse *m, f*

**recital** [rɪˈsaɪtᵊl] *n* ❶ MUS récital *m* ❷ (*description*) énoncé *m*

**reckless** ['rekləs] *adj* ❶ (*careless*) imprudent(e) ❷ (*rash*) inconscient(e)

**reckon** ['rekᵊn] **I.** *vt* ❶ (*calculate*) calculer ❷ (*consider*) penser **II.** *vi inf* (*presume*) **could you help me with this? – I ~ so.** pourrais-tu m'aider pour cela? – oui, je crois bien.

◆**reckon in** *vt* tenir compte de

◆**reckon on** *vt insep* ❶ (*count on*) compter sur ❷ (*expect*) s'attendre à; **to ~ doing sth** compter faire qc

◆**reckon up** *vt* calculer
◆**reckon with** *vt insep* ❶ (*take account of*) compter avec ❷ (*expect*) s'attendre à
◆**reckon without** *vt insep* ne pas prévoir

**reckoning** *n* ❶ (*calculating, estimating*) calculs *mpl* ❷ (*avenging, punishing*) règlement *m* de compte

**reclaim** [rɪ·ˈkleɪm] *vt* ❶ (*claim back*) récupérer ❷ (*make usable: land*) assainir ❸ *form* (*reform*) guérir

**recline** [rɪ·ˈklaɪn] **I.** *vi* ❶ (*lean back*) s'allonger ❷ (*be horizontal*) être étendu(e) **II.** *vt* (*head, arm*) appuyer; (*seat*) incliner

**recliner** *n* chaise *f* longue

**recognition** [ˌrek·əg·ˈnɪʃ·ən] *n* reconnaissance *f*; **to change beyond ~** devenir méconnaissable; **to achieve ~** être (publiquement) reconnu; **there's a growing ~ that ...** il est de plus en plus reconnu que ...

**recognizable** *adj* reconnaissable

**recognize** [ˈrek·əg·naɪz] *vt* ❶ (*know again*) reconnaître ❷ (*appreciate*) être reconnaissant(e) pour ❸ (*acknowledge*) reconnaître

**recognized** *adj* reconnu(e)

**recollect** [ˌrek·ə·ˈlekt] **I.** *vt* se rappeler **II.** *vi* se souvenir

**recommend** [ˌrek·ə·ˈmend] *vt* recommander; **it is not ~ed** ce n'est pas conseillé

**recommendable** *adj* recommandable

**recommendation** [ˌrek·ə·mən·ˈdeɪ·ʃən] *n* ❶ (*suggestion*) recommandation *f* ❷ (*advice*) conseil *m* ❸ (*letter of reference*) recommandation *f*; **to write sb a ~** écrire une lettre de recommandation à qn

**reconsider** [ˌri·kən·ˈsɪd·ər] *vt, vi* reconsidérer; **I think you should ~** je crois que vous devriez y repenser

**reconstruct** [ˌri·kən·ˈstrʌkt] *vt* ❶ (*rebuild*) reconstruire ❷ (*re-create*) recréer ❸ (*reorganize*) restructurer ❹ (*assemble evidence*) reconstituer ❺ (*simulate crime*) procéder à une reconstitution de

**record¹** [ˈrek·ərd] **I.** *n* ❶ (*account*) rapport *m*; LAW enregistrement *m*; (*of proceedings*) procès-verbal *m*; **to set the ~ straight** mettre les choses au clair; **to say sth on/off the ~** dire qc officiellement/officieusement; **strictly off the ~** en toute confidentialité ❷ (*note*) note *f*; **to keep a ~ of sth** noter qc; **to leave a ~ of sth** laisser une trace de qc; **there is no ~ of your complaint** il n'y a pas de trace de votre réclamation ❸ (*file*) dossier *m*; **public ~s** archives *fpl* ❹ (*personal history*) antécédents *mpl*; **to have a good/bad ~** avoir (une) bonne/mauvaise réputation; **criminal ~** casier *m* (judiciaire); **to have a clean ~** avoir un passé sans tache ❺ (*achievements*) résultats *mpl*; **safety ~** résultats *mpl* en matière de sécurité ❻ (*recording*) enregistrement *m* ❼ (*music album*) disque *m* ❽ (*achievement*) a. SPORTS record *m* ❾ COMPUT article *m* **II.** *adj* (*unbeaten*) record *inv*; **in ~ time** en un temps record

**record²** [rɪ·ˈkɔrd] **I.** *vt* ❶ (*music, voice*) enregistrer ❷ (*write about: event*) rapporter; LAW prendre acte de ❸ (*register*) indiquer **II.** *vi* ❶ (*person, machine*) enregistrer; (*sound*) s'enregistrer

**recorded** *adj* enregistré(e); (*computer file*) sauvegardé(e)

**recorder** *n* ❶ (*tape*) magnétophone *m* ❷ (*video*) magnétoscope *m* ❸ (*instrument*) flûte *f* à bec

**record holder** *n* détenteur, -trice *m*, *f* de record

**recording** *n* (*material, process*) enregistrement *m*

**recover** [rɪ·ˈkʌv·ər] **I.** *vt* ❶ (*get back: property*) récupérer; (*balance, composure*) retrouver; (*consciousness*) reprendre; (*health*) recouvrer; (*strength*) récupérer ❷ LAW se faire attribuer; (*damages, compensation*) obtenir **II.** *vi* ❶ (*regain health*) récupérer ❷ (*return to normal*) se rétablir

**recovery** [rɪ·ˈkʌv·ər·i] <-ies> *n* ❶ MED

R

rétablissement *m;* **the rate of ~** le taux de guérison; **to make a full/quick/slow ~ from sth** guérir complètement/rapidement/lentement de qc ② ECON *(of a company, market)* reprise *f;* *(of stock, prices)* remontée *f* ③ *(getting back)* récupération *f;* *(of cost)* récupération *f;* *(of damages)* indemnisation *f;* *(of debts)* recouvrement *m*

**re-create** ['ri:kri·eɪt] *vt* recréer

**recreation** *n* ① *(activity)* récréation *f* ② *(process)* divertissement *m*

**recreational** *adj* de loisir

**recreational drug** *n* drogue *f* récréative

**recreational vehicle** *n* camping-car *m*

**recreation area** *n* terrain *m* de jeux

**recreation center** *n* salle *f* polyvalente

**rectangular** [rek·'tæŋ·gjə·lər] *adj* rectangulaire

**rector** ['rek·tər] *n* ① REL *(of parish)* recteur *m* ② *(of primary school)* directeur, -trice *m, f;* *(of secondary school)* proviseur *mf;* *(of college)* président(e) *m(f)*

**recurring** *adj* récurrent(e)

**recycle** [ri:·'saɪ·kl] *vt* recycler

**recycling** I. *n* recyclage *m* II. *adj* de recyclage

**red** [red] I. *adj* rouge; *(hair)* roux(rousse) ▸ **not one ~ cent** *sl* pas un sou II. *n* ① *(color)* rouge *m;* *(hair)* roux *m;* **to turn ~** *(from dye)* devenir rouge; *(with embarrassment)* rougir ② POL rouge *mf* ▸ **in the ~** à découvert; *s.a.* blue

**red blood cell** *n* globule *m* rouge

**Red Cross** *n* **the ~** la Croix-Rouge

**red deer** *n inv* cerf *m* (commun)

**reddish** ['red·ɪʃ] *adj* rougeâtre; *(hair)* tirant sur le roux

**redecorate** [ˌri:·'dek·ər·eɪt] I. *vt* redécorer II. *vi* refaire la décoration

**redefine** [ˌri:·dɪ·'faɪn] *vt* redéfinir

**redevelop** [ˌri:·dɪ·'vel·əp] *vt* réaménager

**redevelopment** *n* réaménagement *m*

**red-faced** *adj* embarrassé(e)

**red-haired** *adj* roux(rousse)

**red-handed** *adj* **to catch sb ~** (sur)prendre qn la main dans le sac

**redhead** *n* roux, rousse *m, f*

**redheaded** *adj* ① *(with red hair)* roux(rousse) ② ZOOL à tête rouge

**red herring** *n* faux problème *m*

**red-hot** *adj* ① *(heated)* chauffé(e) au rouge; *(extremely hot)* brûlant(e) ② *fig* ardent(e); *(exciting)* chaud(e) ③ *inf (fresh)* de dernière minute

**redirect** [ˌri:·dɪ·'rekt] *vt (visitor)* réorienter; *(energy)* canaliser; *(letter)* réexpédier; *(mail)* faire suivre; *(on internet)* rediriger

**red light** *n* feu *m* rouge

**red-light district** *n* quartier *m* chaud

**redness** ['red·nəs] *n* rougeur *f*

**red pepper** *n* ① *(vegetable)* poivron *m* rouge ② *(spice)* paprika *m*

**Red Sea** *n* **the ~** la Mer Rouge

**red tape** *n fig* paperasserie *f*

**reduce** [rɪ·'du:s] I. *vt* ① *(make less)* réduire; *(speed)* modérer; *(taxes)* diminuer ② *(make cheaper)* solder; *(price)* baisser ③ MIL dégrader ④ *(cook down)* réduire ⑤ *(force)* réduire; **~d to tears** en larmes; **to be ~d to doing sth** (en) être réduit à faire qc II. *vi (sauce)* réduire

**reduced** *adj* ① *(made cheaper)* soldé(e); *(fare, wage)* réduit(e) ② *(diminished)* réduit(e)

**reduced-sugar** *adj inv* à teneur en sucre réduite

**reduction** [rɪ·'dʌk·ʃən] *n* réduction *f;* *(in traffic)* diminution *f;* *(in wages)* baisse *f*

**redundant** [rɪ·'dʌn·dənt] *adj* ① *(superfluous)* excessif(-ive) ② LING redondant(e)

**reed** [ri:d] *n* ① BOT roseau *m* ② MUS anche *f*

**reef¹** [ri:f] *n* GEO récif *m*

**reef²** [ri:f] I. *n* NAUT ris *m* II. *vt* **to ~ the sails** ar(r)iser les voiles

**reel** [ri:l] I. *n* ① *(spool)* rouleau *m;* *(for film)* pellicule *f;* *(bobbin)* bobine *f* ② *(for winding)* dévidoir *m;* *(for fishing line)* moulinet *m* ③ *(dance)* contredanse *f* II. *vi* ① *(move unsteadily)* tituber; **to ~ back** s'écarter en titubant; **to send sb ~ing** envoyer qn valser ② *(become dizzy)* être pris(e)

de vertige; **the news left me ~ing**
*fig* la nouvelle m'a abasourdi ③ (*re-coil*) être éjecté(e) ④ (*whirl around*)
tourbillonner ⑤ (*dance*) danser un
quadrille

**reelect** [ˌriːɪˈlekt] *vt* réélire
**reelection** *n* réélection *f*
**reenter** [ˌriːˈentər] I. *vt* ① (*go in again*)
rentrer dans ② (*begin again with: poli-tics*) revenir à; (*college*) réintégrer
③ COMPUT retaper; (*data*) saisir de nou-veau II. *vi* rentrer
**reentry** [ˌriːˈentri] <-ies> *n* ① (*entering again*) rentrée *f* ② (*new enrollment*)
réinscription *f*
**ref** [ref] *n* inf abbr of **referee** arbitre *mf*
**ref.** [ref] *n* abbr of **reference** (*code*)
réf. *f*
**refectory** [rɪˈfektəri] <-ies> *n* (*at insti-tution*) cantine *f*; (*at college*) restau-rant *m* universitaire
**refer** [rɪˈfɜːr] <-rr-> *vt* ① (*direct*) ren-voyer; (*to a hospital, doctor*) envoyer;
**to ~ sb** (*back*) **to sb/sth** (r)envoyer
à qc/qn ② (*pass, send on: a problem,
matter*) soumettre; **to ~ sth back to
sth** (*a decision, dispute*) remettre qc à
qc ③ (*consult, turn to*) **to ~ to sb/sth**
consulter qn/qc
**referee** [ˌrefəˈriː] I. *n* ① SPORTS arbitre
*mf* ② (*for employment*) référence *f*
II. <-d-> *vt, vi* SPORTS arbitrer
**reference** [ˈrefərən(t)s] I. *n* ① (*allu-sion*) référence *f*; **with ~ to ...** à propos
de ce que ...; **in ~ to sb/sth** à propos
de qn/qc ② (*responsibilities*) **terms
of ~** mandat *m* ③ (*consultation*) **with-out ~ to sb** sans passer par qn ④ (*in
text*) renvoi *m* ⑤ (*recommendation*)
référence *f*; **letter of ~** lettre *f* de réfé-rence II. *vt* (*book, article, study*) faire
référence à
**reference book** *n* ouvrage *m* de réfé-rence
**reference number** *n* numéro *m* de ré-férence
**refill** [ˈriːfɪl, *vb*: ˌriːˈfɪl] I. *n* recharge *f*; **do
you want a ~?** tu en veux un autre?
II. *vt* recharger

**refine** [rɪˈfaɪn] *vt* ① (*purify*) raffiner
② (*polish*) affiner
**refined** *adj* ① (*purified*) raffiné(e);
(*metal*) purifié(e) ② (*taste, palate*) so-phistiqué(e) ③ (*manners*) raffiné(e)
**refinery** [rɪˈfaɪnəri] <-ies> *n* raffine-rie *f*
**reflect** [rɪˈflekt] I. *vt* ① (*throw back:
heat*) renvoyer; (*light*) réfléchir ② (*mir-ror, reveal*) refléter; (*image*) ren-voyer II. *vi* ① (*contemplate*) réfléchir
② (*show quality*) **the results ~ well
on him** les résultats sont tout à son hon-neur; **to ~ badly on sb/sth** jeter le dis-crédit sur qn/qc
**reflection** [rɪˈflekʃən] *n* ① (*reflecting*)
réflexion *f*; **sound ~** retour *m* du son
② (*mirror image*) reflet *m* ③ (*thought*)
réflexion *f*; **on ~** à la réflexion ④ (*criti-cism*) atteinte *f*; **to be no ~ on sth** ne
pas porter atteinte à qc
**reflector** *n* réflecteur *m*
**reflex** [ˈriːfleks] <-es> I. *n* réflexe *m*
II. *adj* réflexe
**refrain**[1] [rɪˈfreɪn] *vi* s'abstenir
**refrain**[2] [rɪˈfreɪn] *n a.* MUS refrain *m*
**refresh** [rɪˈfreʃ] *vt* ① (*enliven*) se déten-dre; (*memory*) rafraîchir ② (*cool*) rafraî-chir ③ (*refill*) **to ~ sb's drink** remplir à
nouveau le verre de qn ④ COMPUT
(*screen*) réactualiser
**refresher (course)** [rɪˈfreʃər (kɔːrs)] *n*
cours *m* de révision
**refreshing** *adj* ① (*cooling*) rafraîchis-sant(e) ② (*unusual: idea*) vivifiant(e);
**it's ~ to** +*infin* ça fait du bien de +*infin*
**refreshment** *n* ① *form* (*rest*) repos *m*
② *form* (*eating and drinking*) une colla-tion ③ *pl* (*food and drink*) un buffet
**refrigerate** [rɪˈfrɪdʒəreɪt] *vt* réfrigérer
**refrigeration** *n* réfrigération *f*
**refrigerator** *n* réfrigérateur *m*
**refuel** [ˌriːˈfjuːəl] <-l- *o* -ll-> I. *vi* se ravi-tailler en carburant II. *vt* ① (*fill again*)
ravitailler en carburant ② *fig* (*debate,
controversy*) alimenter; (*hopes, desire*)
ranimer
**refuge** [ˈrefjuːdʒ] *n a. fig* refuge *m*; **to
take ~ in sth** chercher refuge dans qc

**R**

**refugee** [ˌref·jʊˈdʒi] n réfugié(e) m(f)

**refugee camp** n camp m de réfugiés

**refund** [ˈriːfʌnd, vb: riːˈfʌnd] I. n remboursement m II. vt rembourser

**refusal** [rɪˈfjuːzⁿl] n (rejection) refus m; (of an application) rejet m

**refuse**¹ [rɪˈfjuːz] I. vi refuser II. vt refuser; (consent) ne pas accorder; (offer) rejeter

**refuse**² [ˈref·juːs] n déchets mpl

**regain** [rɪˈgeɪn] vt recouvrer; (consciousness, control) reprendre; (lost ground, territory) regagner

**regard** [rɪˈgɑːrd] I. n ❶(consideration) considération f; **without ~ for sth** sans tenir compte de qc; (esteem) estime f; **to hold sb/sth in low ~** ne pas porter qn/qc très haut dans son estime; **to hold sb/sth in high ~** avoir beaucoup d'estime pour qn/qc; **(give my) ~s to your sister** transmettez mes amitiés à votre sœur ❸(gaze) regard m ❹(aspect) **in this ~** à cet égard ❺(concerning) **with ~ to sb/sth** en tenant compte de qc II. vt ❶(consider) considérer; **a highly ~ed doctor** un docteur hautement estimé ❷(concern) regarder; **as ~s the house/your son** en ce qui concerne la maison/votre fils

**regarding** prep concernant

**regardless** adv tout de même

**regardless of** prep (sex, class) sans distinction de; (difficulty, expense) sans se soucier de

**regime, régime** [rəˈʒiːm] n régime m

**region** [ˈriːdʒⁿn] n région f

**regional** adj ❶(of regions) régional(e) ❷(local) local(e)

**register** [ˈredʒ·ɪ·stər] I. n ❶(list) registre m ❷(cash drawer) caisse f enregistreuse ❸LING registre m II. vt ❶(record) inscrire; (birth, death) déclarer; (car) immatriculer; (trademark, invention) déposer ❷TECH enregistrer III. vi ❶(record officially) **to ~ as sth** s'inscrire comme qc; **to ~ as unemployed** s'inscrire au chômage; **to ~ for a course** s'inscrire à un cours ❷TECH s'enregistrer

**registered** adj ❶(recorded) enregistré(e); (patent) déposé(e) ❷(qualified: practioner, nurse) agréé(e); (official) diplômé(e) d'état; (voter) inscrit(e) sur les listes

**registered mail** n envoi m (en) recommandé

**registration** [ˌredʒ·ɪ·ˈstreɪ·ʃⁿn] n ❶(action of registering) a. SCHOOL, UNIV inscription f; (of births, deaths) déclaration f; (at hotel) enregistrement m ❷(for vehicles) immatriculation f

**registration fee** n cotisation f; (for club) droits mpl d'inscription

**registration number** n numéro m d'immatriculation

**registry** [ˈredʒ·ɪ·stri] <-ies> n enregistrement m; **bridal ~** liste f de mariage

**regret** [rɪˈgret] I.<-tt-> vt regretter II.<-tt-> vi regretter; **I ~ to inform you that …** form je suis désolé de devoir vous annoncer que … III. n regret m

**regretful** adj désolé(e); (feeling) de regret; (smile) navré(e); **to be ~ about sth** avoir des regrets à propos de qc

**regretfully** adv avec regret

**regrettable** adj regrettable

**regular** [ˈreg·jə·lər] I. adj ❶(steady, periodic) régulier(-ère); (reader) fidèle; **on a ~ basis** régulièrement; **a ~ customer** un(e) habitué(e) ❷(normal) normal(e); (procedure, doctor) habituel(le); (size) standard inv; (gas) ordinaire ❸MATH symétrique ❹(correct) régulier(-ère) inf ❺LING régulier(-ère) ❻inf (real) vrai(e); **a ~ guy** un type sympa II. n ❶(visitor) habitué(e) m(f) ❷MIL **a ~ (soldier)** un soldat de l'armée régulière

**regularity** [ˌreg·jə·ˈler·ə·t̮i] n régularité f

**regularly** adv régulièrement

**regulate** [ˈreg·jə·leɪt] vt ❶(administer) réglementer ❷(adjust) régler

**regulation** [ˌreg·jə·ˈleɪ·ʃⁿn] n ❶(rule) règlement m; (health, safety) norme f; **the rules and ~s** le règlement ❷ADMIN réglementa-

tion *f* ③ (*action: of a machine*) réglage *m* II. *adj* réglementaire

**regulator** *n* régulateur, -trice *m, f;* ADMIN
contrôleur, -euse *m, f*

**rehab** ['riˈhæb] *inf* I. *n abbr of* **rehabili-**
**tation** désintox *f inv;* **to go into** ~ faire
une cure de désintox II. <-bb-> *vt abbr*
*of* **rehabilitate** ① (*socially*) réinsérer
② (*restore*) réhabiliter

**rehabilitation center** *n* (*for criminals*)
centre *m* de réinsertion; (*for addicts*)
centre *m* de désintoxication

**rehearsal** [rɪˈhɜr.səl] *n* ① THEAT répétition *f* ② MIL exercice *m*

**rehearse** [rɪˈhɜrs] *vt* (*a play, scene*) répéter; (*lines*) réciter; (*arguments*) ressasser

**reign** [reɪn] I. *vi* régner II. *n* règne *m*

**reimburse** [ˌri·ɪmˈbɜrs] *vt* rembourser

**rein** [reɪn] *n* (*for horse riding*) rêne *f;*
(*for horse driving*) guide *f* ▸ **to give sb**
**free** ~ donner carte blanche à qn; **to**
**keep a tight** ~ **on sb/sth** garder le
contrôle sur qn/qc

**reindeer** ['reɪn·dɪr] *n inv* renne *m*

**reinforce** [ˌri·ɪnˈfɔrs] *vt* ① (*streng-*
*then*) renforcer; (*argument, demand*)
appuyer ② (*increase: troops*) renforcer

**reinforcement** *n* ① (*of building*) armature *f* ② *pl* (*fresh troops*) *a. fig* renforts
*mpl*

**reject** ['ri·dʒɛkt, *vb:* rɪˈdʒɛkt] I. *n*
① (*product*) rebut *m* ② (*person*) lais-
sé(e)-pour-compte *m(f)* II. *vt* ① (*de-*
*cline*) rejeter; (*application, article*) refuser ② LAW (*bill, complaint*) rejeter;
(*claim, authority*) contester ③ MED (*re-*
*sist transplant*) rejeter ④ TECH (*of pro-*
*ducts*) mettre au rebut

**rejection** [rɪˈdʒɛk·ʃən] *n a.* MED rejet *m;*
**a** ~ **letter** une lettre de refus

**rejoice** [rɪˈdʒɔɪs] *vi* **to** ~ **at** [*o* **in**] **sth** se
réjouir de qc

**rejuvenate** [riˈdʒu·və·neɪt] *vt* ① (*re-*
*store youth*) rajeunir ② (*invigorate*) revigorer ③ (*modernize*) rajeunir

**relapse** [rɪˈlæps] I. *n* rechute *f* II. *vi* re-
chuter; **to** ~ **into alcoholism/drug**

**abuse** retomber dans l'alcoolisme/la
toxicomanie

**relate** [rɪˈleɪt] I. *vt* ① (*establish connec-*
*tion*) relier; **I couldn't** ~ **the two ca-**
**ses** je n'arrivais pas à faire le rapprochement entre ces deux cas ② (*tell*) relater
II. *vi* ① (*concern*) **to** ~ **to sb/sth** se
rapporter à qn/qc ② **to** ~ **to sb** (*feel*
*sympathy with*) communiquer avec qn;
(*identify with*) s'identifier à qn

**related** *adj* ① (*physically linked*) relié(e);
② (*having common element*) lié(e);
(*subjects*) connexe ③ (*of same family*)
parent(e) ④ (*of same species*) apparen-
té(e)

**relating to** *prep* concernant

**relation** [rɪˈleɪ·ʃən] *n* ① (*link*) relation *f;*
**to bear no** ~ **to sb/sth** n'avoir aucun
rapport avec qn/qc ② (*relative*) pa-
rent(e) *m(f)* ③ *pl* (*dealings between*
*people*) relations *fpl;* **have sexual** ~**s**
**with sb** avoir des rapports sexuels avec
qn

**relationship** *n* ① (*link*) relation *f*
② (*family connection*) lien *m* de parenté ③ (*between people*) relation *f;* **to be**
**in a** ~ **with sb** être avec qn

**relative** ['rel·ə·tɪv] I. *adj* ① (*connected*
*to*) lié(e) ② (*in comparison*) relatif(-ive)
II. *n* parent(e) *m(f)*

**relatively** *adv* relativement; ~ **speaking**
comparativement

**relax** [rɪˈlæks] I. *vi* se détendre II. *vt* relâcher

**relaxation** [ˌri·lækˈseɪ·ʃən] *n* ① (*recrea-*
*tion*) relaxation *f;* **for** ~ pour se détendre ② (*of rules, standards*) assouplisse-
ment *m*

**relaxed** *adj* décontracté(e)

**relaxing** *adj* relaxant(e); (*day*) de détente

**relay** ['ri·leɪ] I. *n* ① SPORTS (*race*) course *f*
de relais ② (*group*) relais *m* II. *vt* relayer

**release** [rɪˈlis] I. *vt* ① (*free*) libérer
② LAW libérer, **to** ~ **sb on parole/pro-**
**bation** mettre qn en liberté condition-
nelle/surveillée ③ (*free from suffering*)
délivrer ④ (*move something*) dégager;

**R**

(*brake*) lâcher ⑤ PHOT (*shutter*) déclencher ⑥ (*detonate*) lâcher ⑦ (*allow to escape: gas, steam*) relâcher ⑧ (*weaken: grip*) relâcher ⑨ (*make public*) publier ⑩ (*publish*) sortir **II.** n ① (*act of setting free*) libération *f*; (*from prison*) sortie *f*; (*from bad feeling*) délivrance *f* ② (*act of unfastening*) déblocage *m;* (*of handbrake*) desserrage *m* ③ (*handle, knob*) manette *f* de déblocage; (*of brake, clutch*) desserrage *m* ④ (*allowing use of: funds, goods*) déblocage *m* ⑤ (*relaxation*) relâchement *m;* (*of tension*) diminution *f* ⑥ (*escape of gases*) échappement *m* ⑦ (*making public*) publication *f* ⑧ (*public relations info*) communiqué *m* ⑨ (*new CD, film*) sortie *f*

**relegate** ['rel·ə·geɪt] *vt* reléguer

**relent** [rɪ·'lent] *vi* (*person*) se radoucir; (*wind, rain*) se calmer

**relentless** *adj* implacable; (*pressure, criticism*) incessant(e)

**relevant** *adj* ① (*appropriate*) pertinent(e); (*documents*) d'intérêt; (*evidence*) approprié(e) ② (*important*) important(e)

**reliability** [rɪ·ˌlaɪ·ə·'bɪl·ə·t̬i] *n* ① (*dependability*) fiabilité *f* ② (*trustworthiness*) confiance *f*

**reliable** [rɪ·'laɪ·ə·bl] *adj* ① (*dependable*) fiable ② (*credible*) sûr(e); (*evidence*) solide; (*figures, testimony*) fiable ③ (*trustworthy*) de confiance

**reliance** [rɪ·'laɪ·ən(t)s] *n* (*dependence*) ~ **on sb/sth** dépendance *f* de qn/de qc

**reliant** *adj* **to be** ~ **on sth** to +*infin* dépendre de qn/qc pour +*infin*

**relief** [rɪ·'lif] **I.** *n* ① (*after something bad*) soulagement *m;* **to feel an incredible sense of** ~ se sentir vraiment soulagé ② (*help*) aide *f;* **to be on** ~ (*on welfare*) bénéficier d'aides sociales; **tax** ~ dégrèvement *m* fiscal ③ (*replacement*) substitut *m* ④ MIL (*rescue*) libération *f* ⑤ ART, GEO relief *m* **II.** *adj* (*substitute*) de remplacement

**relief worker** *n* ① (*substitute*) sup-

pléant(e) *m(f)* ② (*humanitarian*) travailleur, -euse *m, f* humanitaire

**relieve** [rɪ·'liv] *vt* ① (*take worries from*) soulager ② (*substitute for*) remplacer ③ MIL (*city*) libérer ④ (*alleviate: famine*) lutter contre; (*symptoms*) soulager; (*boredom*) dissiper; (*anxiety*) calmer; (*pressure*) atténuer; (*tension*) diminuer ⑤ (*take away*) **to** ~ **sb of sth** débarrasser qn de qc; *iron* délester qn de qc ⑥ *inf* (*urinate, defecate*) **to** ~ **oneself** se soulager

**religion** [rɪ·'lɪdʒ·ən] *n a. fig* religion *f*

**religious** [rɪ·'lɪdʒ·əs] *adj* ① (*of religion*) religieux(-euse) ② (*meticulous*) scrupuleux(-euse)

**relish** ['rel·ɪʃ] **I.** *n* ① (*enjoyment*) plaisir *m* ② (*sauce*) condiment *m* **II.** *vt* aimer; **to** ~ **the thought that ...** se réjouir à la pensée que ...

**relive** [ˌri·'lɪv] *vt* revivre

**reluctance** [rɪ·'lʌk·t̬ən(t)s] *n* réticence *f*

**reluctant** *adj* réticent(e); **a** ~ **hero** un héros malgré lui

**rely** [rɪ·'laɪ] <-ie-> *vi* ① (*trust*) **to** ~ **on sb/sth** compter sur qn/qc ② (*depend on*) **to** ~ (**up**)**on sb/sth** dépendre de qn/qc

**remain** [rɪ·'meɪn] *vi* rester; **to** ~ **anonymous** garder l'anonymat; **to** ~ **silent** garder le silence; **that** ~ **s to be seen** cela reste à voir

**remaining** *adj* qui reste; **our only** ~ **hope** notre dernier espoir *m*

**remains** *npl* ① (*leftovers*) restes *mpl* ② HIST vestiges *mpl* ③ *form* (*corpse*) dépouille *f*

**remand** [rɪ·'mænd] **I.** *vt* renvoyer; **to** ~ **sb into custody** placer qn en détention provisoire **II.** *n* renvoi *m;* **to be held on** ~ être en détention préventive

**remark** [rɪ·'mark] **I.** *vt* faire remarquer **II.** *n* remarque *f*

**remarkable** *adj* remarquable

**remarkably** *adv* remarquablement

**remedy** ['rem·ə·di] **I.** <-ies> *n* ① (*treatment*) remède *m* ② (*legal redress*) recours *m* (légal) **II.** *vt* remédier à

**remember** [rɪ·'mem·bər] **I.** *vt* se souvenir de; **a night to ~** une nuit inoubliable II. *vi* se souvenir ▸ **you** ~ *inf* vous savez

**remind** [rɪ·ˈmaɪnd] *vt* rappeler; **to ~ sb of sb/sth** faire penser qn à qn/qc; **that ~s me!** je me souviens!

**reminder** *n* ❶(*making someone remember*) aide-mémoire *m inv* ❷(*something awakening memories*) rappel *m* ❸(*collection notice*) rappel *m*

**remorseful** *adj* repentant(e)

**remote** [rɪ·ˈmoʊt] <-er, -est *o* more ~, most ~> *adj* ❶(*distant in place*) lointain(e) ❷(*far from towns*) isolé(e) ❸(*distant in time*) éloigné(e) ❹(*standoffish*) distant(e) ❺(*unlikely: likelihood*) infime

**remote control** *n* télécommande *f*

**remote-controlled** *adj* télécommandé(e); (*television*) avec télécommande

**removal** [rɪ·ˈmuːvəl] *n* ❶(*dismissal*) éviction *f* ❷(*act of removing: of people*) déplacement *m;* (*of objects*) enlèvement *m;* (*of words, entries*) retrait *m*

**remove** [rɪ·ˈmuv] *vt* ❶(*take away*) enlever; (*entry, name*) rayer; (*word, film, handcuffs*) retirer; (*troublemaker, spectators*) faire sortir; (*ban*) lever; (*difficulty*) écarter; (*makeup, stain*) ôter; (*stitches*) enlever ❷(*take off: clothes*) retirer; (*tie*) enlever ❸(*dismiss: from job*) renvoyer; (*from office*) destituer ❹*fig* (*doubts, fears*) effacer

**remover** *n* **makeup ~** démaquillant *m;* **stain ~** détachant *m;* **nail-polish ~** dissolvant *m*

**renaissance** [ˌren·ə·ˈsɑn(t)s] *n* ❶(*revival*) renaissance *f* ❷HIST **the Renaissance** la Renaissance

**rename** [ˌri·ˈneɪm] *vt* renommer

**rend** [rend] <rent *o* -ed> *vt form* ❶(*tear*) déchirer ❷(*split*) diviser

**rendezvous** [ˈrɑn·deɪ·vu] I. *n inv* ❶(*meeting*) rendez-vous *m* ❷(*meeting place*) lieu *m* de rendez-vous II. *vi* se rencontrer; **to ~ with sb** retrouver qn

**renew** [rɪ·ˈnu] *vt* ❶(*begin again: promise, agreement*) renouveler; (*attack*) relancer; (*friendship, relationship*) re-

nouer; (*subscription*) renouveler ❷(*replace*) changer

**renewable** *adj* renouvelable

**renewed** *adj* renouvelé(e); (*relationship*) renoué(e); **to receive ~ support** avoir un regain de soutien

**renovate** [ˈren·ə·veɪt] *vt* rénover

**renowned** *adj* réputé(e)

**rent¹** [rent] I. *n* (*rip*) déchirure *f* II. *pt, pp* of **rend**

**rent²** [rent] I. *n* loyer *m;* **for ~** à louer II. *vt* louer

 ◆ **rent out** *vt* louer

**rental** I. *n* location *f* II. *adj* de location

**rent-free** *adj* gratuit(e)

**reopen** [ri·ˈoʊ·pən] I. *vt* rouvrir II. *vi* se rouvrir

**reorder** [ˌri·ˈɔr·dər] I. *n* nouvelle commande *f* II. *vt* ❶(*order again*) commander à nouveau ❷(*rearrange*) réorganiser

**reorganize** [ri·ˈɔr·gən·aɪz] I. *vt* réorganiser II. *vi* se réorganiser

**rep** [rep] *n inf* ❶(*salesperson*) *abbr of* **representative** VRP *mf* ❷*abbr of* **repertory company** compagnie *f* théâtrale de répertoire ❸*abbr of* **reputation** réput *f*

**repair** [rɪ·ˈper] I. *vt* ❶(*restore*) réparer; (*road*) rénover ❷(*set right*) réparer II. *vi* **to ~ somewhere** se rendre quelque part III. *n* ❶(*mending*) réparation *f;* **beyond ~** irréparable ❷(*state*) état *m;* **to be in good/bad ~** être en bon/mauvais état

**repair kit** *n* kit *m* de réparation

**repairman** <-men> *n* ❶(*for house*) réparateur *m* ❷(*for cars*) garagiste *m*

**repair shop** *n* atelier *m* de réparation

**repay** [rɪ·ˈpeɪ] *irr vt* ❶(*pay back*) rembourser; (*debt, loan*) s'acquitter de ❷(*reward for kindness*) récompenser

**repayable** *adj* remboursable

**repayment** *n* remboursement *m*

**repeat** [rɪ·ˈpit] I. *vt* ❶(*say again*) répéter ❷(*recite*) réciter ❸(*do again*) refaire ❹SCHOOL (*class, year*) redoubler, doubler *Belgique* ❺COM, ECON (*order*) renouveler ❻**to ~ itself** (*incident*) se

**R**

répéter; **to ~ oneself** se répéter **II.** *vi* ❶ (*reoccur*) se répéter ❷ *inf* (*give indigestion*) **to ~ on sb** donner des renvois à qn **III.** *n* ❶ (*recurrence*) répétition *f* ❷ TV rediffusion *f* **IV.** *adj* récurrent(e)

**repeated** *adj* répété(e)

**repeatedly** *adv* à plusieurs reprises

**repeat offender** *n* récidiviste *mf*

**repel** [rɪ·ˈpel] <-ll-> *vt* ❶ (*ward off*) parer ❷ MIL (*attack*) repousser ❸ (*force apart*) repousser ❹ (*disgust*) dégoûter

**repellent** [rɪ·ˈpel·ənt] **I.** *n* ❶ (*for insects*) insecticide *m;* **mosquito ~** lotion *f* antimoustique ❷ (*impervious substance*) (**water**) **~** enduit *m* hydrofuge **II.** *adj* repoussant(e)

**repetition** [ˌrep·ə·ˈtɪʃ·ən] *n* répétition *f;* **this book is full of ~** ce livre se répète sans arrêt

**replace** [rɪ·ˈpleɪs] *vt* ❶ (*take place of*) remplacer ❷ (*put back*) replacer; **to ~ the receiver** raccrocher ❸ (*substitute*) remplacer

**replacement** **I.** *n* remplacement *m* **II.** *adj* de remplacement

**replay** [ˈriː·pleɪ, *vb:* ˌriː·ˈpleɪ] **I.** *n* ❶ SPORTS (*replayed match*) nouvelle rencontre *f* ❷ (*replaying recording*) répétition *f* **II.** *vt* (*melody, match*) rejouer; (*recording*) repasser

**reply** [rɪ·ˈplaɪ] **I.**<-ie-> *vi* ❶ (*respond*) répondre ❷ (*react*) répliquer **II.**<-ies> *n* ❶ (*response*) réponse *f* ❷ (*reaction*) riposte *f*

**report** [rɪ·ˈpɔrt] **I.** *n* ❶ (*account*) rapport *m;* (*shorter*) compte rendu *m* ❷ TV, RADIO reportage *m;* **weather ~** bulletin *m* météo(rologique) ❸ LAW procès-verbal *m* ❹ SCHOOL (*evaluation*) bulletin *m* ❺ (*unproven claim*) rumeur *f;* **there have been ~s of fighting** on nous a rapporté qu'il y avait des batailles ❻ *form* (*explosion*) détonation *f* **II.** *vt* ❶ (*give account of: casualties, facts*) rapporter; TV, RADIO faire un reportage sur; **he is ~ed to be living in Egypt** il paraît qu'il vit en Egypte ❷ (*make public*) annoncer ❸ (*inform*) signaler; **to be ~ed missing** être porté disparu

❹ (*denounce*) dénoncer; (*fault*) signaler ❺ POL rapporter **III.** *vi* ❶ (*write report*) faire un rapport; **to ~ on sth to sb** faire un rapport à qn sur qc ❷ (*in journalism*) faire un reportage; **~ing from New York, our correspondent ...** de New York, notre correspondant ... ❸ (*present oneself formally*) se présenter; **to ~ for duty** prendre son service

**report card** *n* bulletin *m* scolaire

**reported** *adj* ❶ (*so-called*) soi-disant(e) ❷ (*known*) connu(e)

**reportedly** *adv* à ce qu'on dit

**reporter** *n* journaliste *mf*

**repossess** [ˌriː·pə·ˈzes] *vt* saisir

**represent** [ˌrep·rɪ·ˈzent] *vt* ❶ (*show, symbolize, be spokesperson of*) représenter ❷ (*be: progress, loss*) représenter ❸ (*claim as*) **to ~ sth as sth** présenter qc comme qc

**representative** **I.** *adj* a. POL représentatif(-ive) **II.** *n* ❶ (*person representing another*) a. ECON, POL représentant(e) *m(f);* **elected ~** élu *m* ❷ (*Congressman*) député(e) *m(f)*

**repression** *n* répression *f;* PSYCH refoulement *m*

**repressive** *adj* répressif(-ive)

**reproach** [rɪ·ˈproʊtʃ] **I.** *vt* faire des reproches; **to ~ sb for doing sth** reprocher à qn d'avoir fait qc **II.** *n* reproche *m;* **to be above ~** être au-dessus de tout reproche

**reproachful** *adj* réprobateur(-trice)

**reprocessing plant** *n* ECOL, TECH usine *f* de retraitement

**reproduce** [ˌriː·prə·ˈdus] **I.** *vi* se reproduire **II.** *vt* reproduire

**reproduction** [ˌriː·prə·ˈdʌk·ʃən] *n* reproduction *f*

**reproductive** [ˌriː·prə·ˈdʌk·tɪv] *adj* reproducteur(-trice)

**reptile** [ˈrep·taɪl] *n* reptile *m*

**republic** [rɪ·ˈpʌb·lɪk] *n* république *f*

**republican** **I.** *n* républicain(e) *m(f)* **II.** *adj* républicain(e)

**repulsive** *adj* répulsif(-ive)

**reputable** *adj* convenable

**reputation** [ˌrep·jə·ˈteɪ·ʃən] *n* réputation f; **to have a ~ for sth** être connu pour qc; **to know sb/sth by ~** connaître qn/qc de nom

**request** [rɪ·ˈkwest] **I.** n ❶ (*act of asking*) demande f ❷ (*formally asking*) sollicitation f ❸ RADIO demande f **II.** vt ❶ (*ask for: help, information*) demander; **to ~ sb to** +*infin* prier qn de +*infin* ❷ RADIO demander

**requiem** [ˈrek·wi·əm] n a. MUS requiem m inv

**require** [rɪ·ˈkwaɪər] vt ❶ (*need*) nécessiter; **~d reading** ouvrage m incontournable ❷ (*demand*) demander; **to be ~d of sb** être requis de qn ❸ (*officially order*) **to be ~d to** +*infin* être prié de +*infin* ❹ form (*wish to have*) désirer

**requirement** n exigence f; **to meet the ~s of sb/sth** répondre aux besoins de qn/qc

**resale value** n valeur f de rachat

**reschedule** [ˌriː·ˈsked·ʒ·ul] vt (*meeting, program*) reprogrammer; (*date*) reporter; (*debt*) rééchelonner

**rescue** [ˈres·kju] **I.** vt sauver; (*hostage, prisoner*) libérer **II.** n sauvetage m; (*of a hostage, prisoner*) libération f; **to come to sb's ~** venir à la rescousse de qn; ECON; **~ company** holding m

**rescue package** n FIN, POL plan m de sauvetage

**research** [rɪ·ˈsɜrtʃ] **I.** n ❶ (*investigation*) recherche f ❷ (*texts*) travaux mpl **II.** vi faire de la recherche **III.** vt étudier

**researcher** n UNIV chercheur m; (*for news shows*) documentaliste mf

**resemblance** [rɪ·ˈzem·blən(t)s] n ressemblance f; **family ~** air m de famille; **to bear a ~ to** avoir des ressemblances avec qn/qc

**resemble** [rɪ·ˈzem·bl] vt ressembler à, tirer sur *Belgique, Nord*

**resent** [rɪ·ˈzent] vt (*person*) en vouloir à; (*situation, attitude*) avoir du ressentiment contre; **to ~ doing** [o **having to do**] **sth** être mécontent d'avoir à faire qc

**resentful** adj mécontent(e)

**resentment** n rancœur f; **to feel (a) ~ against sb** être en colère après qn

**reservation** [ˌrez·ər·ˈveɪ·ʃ·ən] n ❶ (*hesitation, doubt*) réserve f ❷ (*booking*) réservation f ❸ (*area of land*) réserve f

**reserve** [rɪ·ˈzɜrv] **I.** n ❶ a. form réserve f; **to put sth on ~** mettre qc de côté ❷ SPORTS remplaçant(e) m(f) ❸ MIL (*army*) ~ réserve f **II.** vt ❶ (*keep: leftovers, rest*) garder ❷ (*save*) **to ~ sth for sb/sth** mettre qc de côté pour qn/qc; **to ~ the right to** +*infin* se réserver le droit de +*infin* ❸ (*make reservation: room, seat, ticket*) réserver

**reserved** adj réservé(e)

**reservoir** [ˈre·zərv·wɔr] n a. fig réservoir m

**residence** [ˈrez·ɪ·d·ən(t)s] n a. form résidence f; **to take up ~** emménager

**resident** **I.** n a. POL résident(e) m(f); **~ parking** stationnement m réservé aux riverains **II.** adj ❶ (*staying at*) domicilié(e) ❷ (*living on site*) sur place

**resident alien** n résident(e) m(f) étranger(-ère)

**residential** adj résidentiel(le); (*staff*) à demeure

**resign** [rɪ·ˈzaɪn] **I.** vi démissionner **II.** vt ❶ (*leave: post, position*) abandonner ❷ (*accept unwillingly*) **to ~ oneself to sth/doing sth** se résigner à qc/à faire qc

**resignation** [ˌrez·ɪg·ˈneɪ·ʃ·ən] n ❶ (*official letter*) (lettre f de) démission f ❷ (*act of resigning*) démission f ❸ (*acceptance*) résignation f

**resigned** adj résigné(e)

**resilient** adj ❶ (*able to survive setbacks*) résistant(e) ❷ (*able to keep shape*) élastique

**resist** [rɪ·ˈzɪst] **I.** vt ❶ (*withstand*) résister à ❷ (*refuse to accept*) s'opposer à **II.** vi résister

**resistance** [rɪ·ˈzɪs·tən(t)s] n résistance f ▶ **the path of least ~** la solution de facilité

**resistant** adj résistant(e); **to be ~ to sth** être résistant à qc

**resolution** n résolution f

**resort** [rɪˈzɔrt] I. n ❶ (for vacation) villégiature f; **ski ~** station f de ski; **vacation ~** lieu m de vacances ❷ (measure) **as a last ~** en dernier recours II. vi **to ~ to sth/doing sth** recourir à qc/finir par faire qc

**resource center** n centre m de documentation

**resourceful** adj (person) ingénieux (-euse)

**respect** [rɪˈspekt] I. n ❶ (esteem, consideration) respect m; **to command** ~ susciter le respect; **out of ~ for sb/sth** par respect pour qn/qc ❷ pl, form (polite greetings) **to pay one's ~s to sb** présenter ses hommages à qn ▸ in **many/some** ~s à beaucoup d'égards/à certains égards II. vt respecter; **to ~ oneself** s'estimer

**respectable** adj respectable; (area, person, behavior) décent(e); **to make oneself** ~ se rendre présentable

**respected** adj respecté(e)

**respectful** adj respectueux(-euse)

**respectively** adv respectivement

**respirator** [ˈres·pə·reɪ·tər] n MED respirateur m

**respiratory system** n système m respiratoire

**respond** [rɪˈspand] I. vt répondre II. vi ❶ (answer) **to ~ to sth** répondre à qc ❷ (react) réagir

**response** [rɪˈspan(t)s] n réponse f; **to meet with a bad/good ~** être bien/mal accueilli

**responsibility** [rɪˌspan(t)·sə·ˈbɪl·ə·ti] n responsabilité f; **whose ~ is this?** qui est le responsable de ceci?

**responsible** [rɪˈspan(t)·sə·bl] adj (person) responsable; (job, task) à responsabilité; **to hold sb/sth ~ for sth** tenir qn/qc (pour) responsable de qc

**responsibly** adv de façon responsable

**responsive** [rɪˈspan(t)·sɪv] adj a. MED réceptif(-ive)

**rest** [rest] I. vt ❶ (repose) reposer ❷ (support) reposer; **to ~ sth against/on sth** appuyer qc contre/sur qc II. vi ❶ (cease activity) se reposer ❷ form (be

responsibility of) incomber; **the matter ~s with them** la question dépend d'eux ❸ (be supported) reposer; **to ~ on sth** s'appuyer sur qc ❹ (depend) **to ~ on sb/sth** s'appuyer sur qn/qc ▸ **to ~ on one's laurels** se reposer sur ses lauriers; **you can ~ assured that ...** vous pouvez être assuré(s) que ... III. n ❶ (repose) repos m; (at work) pause f; **give it a ~!** inf laisse tomber! ❷ MUS pause f ❸ (support) support m ❹ + sing/pl verb (remainder) **the ~** le reste; **the ~ of the people/books** les autres personnes/livres ▸ **to come to ~** s'arrêter; **at ~** (not moving) au repos; (dead) mort

**rest area** n aire f de repos

**restaurant** [ˈres·tə·rant] n restaurant m

**restful** adj tranquille; (place) de repos; (atmosphere) reposant(e)

**rest home** n maison f de repos

**resting place** n abri m; **sb's final** [o last] ~ la dernière demeure de qn

**restless** adj ❶ (fidgety) agité(e) ❷ (impatient) impatient(e); **to get ~** s'impatienter; (start making trouble) s'agiter ❸ (wakeful) troublé(e); (night) agité(e)

**restoration** n ❶ (act of restoring) restauration f ❷ (reestablishment) rétablissement m ❸ (return to owner) remise f

**restore** [rɪˈstɔr] vt ❶ (to original state) restaurer ❷ (to former state) ramener; COMPUT réafficher; **to ~ sb to health** rendre la santé à qn ❸ (reestablish) rétablir ❹ (return to owner) restituer

**restrain** [rɪˈstreɪn] vt ❶ (physically hold back: troublemaker) retenir; **to ~ sb from doing sth** empêcher qn de faire qc ❷ (keep under control: dog, horse) maîtriser; (inflation) contenir

**restraint** [rɪˈstreɪnt] n ❶ (self-control) mesure f ❷ (restriction) contrainte f; (on press) limitation f; (on imports) restriction f

**restrict** [rɪˈstrɪkt] vt ❶ (limit) restreindre; **to ~ oneself to sth** se limiter à qc ❷ (confine) limiter à un endroit

**restricted** adj ❶ (limited) restreint(e);

(*view*) limité(e) ❷ (*confined*) limité(e) ❸ (*secret: information*) confidentiel(le); (*zone*) secret(-ète); ~ **area** zone *f* interdite

**restriction** *n* ❶ (*limit*) restriction *f*; (*of speed*) limitation *f* ❷ (*limitation*) limitation *f*

**restrictive** *adj* restrictif(-ive)

**restroom** ['rest·rum] *n* toilettes *fpl*

**rest stop** *n* aire *f* de repos

**result** [rɪ·'zʌlt] I. *n* ❶ (*consequence*) résultat *m*; **as a ~ of sth** par suite de qc; **as a ~** en conséquence ❷ MATH résultat *m* II. *vi* résulter; **to ~ in sth** avoir qc pour résultat; **to ~ in sb('s) doing sth** avoir pour résultat que qn fait qc

**resumé** ['rez·ʊ·meɪ] *n* ❶ (*work history*) curriculum (vitæ) *m*, CV *m* ❷ (*summary*) résumé *m*

**resumption** [rɪ·'zʌm(p)·ʃən] *n* reprise *f*

**resurrect** [ˌrez·ə·'rekt] *vt* ❶ *a.* REL (*bring back to life*) ressusciter ❷ (*revive*) ranimer; (*idea*) faire revivre

**resuscitate** [rɪ·'sʌs·ə·teɪt] *vt* (*revive*) ranimer; (*from unconsciousness*) ressusciter

**retail price** *n* prix *m* de détail

**retake** ['riː·teɪk, *vb:* ˌriː·'teɪk] I. *n* CINE prise *f* II. *vt irr* ❶ (*take again: territory*) reprendre ❷ (*regain: title*) regagner ❸ (*film again*) refaire ❹ (*rewrite: test, exam*) repasser ❺ (*capture again: criminal*) rattraper

**retch** [retʃ] *vi* avoir la nausée

**rethink** [ˌriː·'θɪŋk] *irr* I. *vt* repenser II. *vi* reconsidérer

**retina** ['ret·ə·n·ə] <-s *o* -nae> *n* ANAT rétine *f*

**retire** [rɪ·'taɪər] I. *vi* ❶ (*stop working*) prendre sa retraite; **to ~ from business** se retirer des affaires ❷ (*stop competing*) se retirer; **to ~ from sth** abandonner qc ❸ *form* (*withdraw*) se retirer ❹ *form* (*go to bed*) se coucher III. *vt* ❶ (*cause to stop working*) **to ~ sb from sth** mettre qn à la retraite de qc ❷ *a.* MIL (*pull back*) replier

**retired** *adj* retraité(e)

**retiree** *n* retraité(e) *m(f)*

**retirement** *n* retraite *f*; **to go into ~** partir en retraite; **to come out of ~** reprendre sa carrière

**retirement age** *n* âge *m* de la retraite

**retiring** *adj* réservé(e)

**retreat** [rɪ·'triːt] I. *vi* ❶ MIL *a. fig* battre en retraite ❷ (*move backward*) reculer ❸ (*withdraw*) se retirer II. *n* ❶ MIL retraite *f*; **to beat a (hasty) ~** *a. fig* battre (rapidement) en retraite ❷ (*from opinion, position*) revirement *m* ❸ (*safe place*) abri *m*; **country ~** maison *f* de campagne ❹ (*period of seclusion*) retraite *f*

**retriever** *n* chien *m* d'arrêt

**retrofit** ['ret·roʊ·fɪt] *vt irr* TECH **to ~ sth with sth** moderniser qc avec qc

**retrospect** ['ret·rə·spekt] *n* **in ~** rétrospectivement

**return** [rɪ·'tɜrn] I. *n* ❶ (*coming, going back*) retour *m*; **~ to work** reprise *f* du travail ❷ (*giving back*) retour *m*; (*of money*) remboursement *m*; (*of stolen items*) restitution *f* ❸ (*sending back*) renvoi *m* ❹ (*recompense*) récompense *f* ❺ (*profit*) bénéfice *m* ❻ (*in tennis, etc*) renvoi *m*; **~ of serve** retour *m* de service ❼ *pl* POL résultats *mpl* électoraux ❽ *pl* (*returned goods*) rendus *mpl* ❾ COMPUT touche *f* "retour" ► **in ~ for sth** en retour de qc II. *vi* ❶ (*go back*) retourner ❷ (*come back: person, symptoms*) revenir; **to ~ home** rentrer III. *vt* ❶ (*give back*) rendre; **to ~ merchandise** retourner des marchandises; **to ~ sb's love** aimer qn en retour; **to ~ a call** rappeler ❷ (*place back*) remettre ❸ FIN rapporter ❹ *form* LAW (*verdict*) déclarer; (*judgment*) prononcer ❺ SPORTS renvoyer

**return match** *n* match *m* retour

**return ticket** *n* billet *m* de retour

**reunification** [ˌri·ju·nə·fɪ·'keɪ·ʃən] *n* réunification *f*

**reunion** [ˌri·'ju·njən] *n* ❶ (*meeting*) réunion *f* ❷ (*of group members*) assemblée *f* ❸ *form* (*bringing together*) retrouvailles *fpl*

**reunite** [ˌri·ju·'naɪt] *vt* réunir; (*after ar-*

R

*gument*) réconcilier; **to be ~d with sb** retrouver qn

**reusable** *adj* réutilisable

**reuse** [ˌriːˈjuːz] *vt* réutiliser

**reveal** [rɪˈviːl] *vt* révéler

**revenge** [rɪˈvendʒ] **I.** *n* vengeance *f*; **to take (one's) ~ on sb for sth** se venger sur qn pour qc ▸ **~ is <u>sweet</u>** *prov* la vengeance est douce **II.** *vt* (*avenge*) venger

**revenue** [ˈrevˌəˌnu] *n* ❶ (*income*) revenu *m*; **tax ~** recettes *fpl* fiscales ❷ *pl* (*instances of income*) recettes *fpl*

**reverend** [ˈrevˌərˌənd] **I.** *adj* vénérable **II.** *n* révérend *m*

**reversal** *n* ❶ (*change to opposite*) revirement *m* ❷ (*turning other way*) renversement *m*; (*of roles*) inversion *f* ❸ (*misfortune*) revers *m* ❹ LAW annulation *f*

**reverse** [rɪˈvɜːrs] **I.** *vt* ❶ (*change to opposite, exchange*) inverser; (*trend, situation*) renverser; **to ~ the charges** TEL demander une communication en PCV ❷ (*turn the other way*) retourner ❸ LAW (*judgment*) annuler **II.** *vi* faire marche arrière **III.** *n* ❶ (*opposite*) contraire *m*; **to do sth in ~** faire qc en sens inverse ❷ AUTO (*backward gear*) marche *f* arrière ❸ (*misfortune*) échec *m* ❹ (*back side*) revers *m*; (*of a coin*) envers *m*; (*of a document*) verso *m* **IV.** *adj* contraire; (*direction*) opposé(e); (*order*) inverse; **the ~ side** (*of paper*) le verso; (*of garment*) l'envers *m*

**reversible** *adj* ❶ FASHION réversible ❷ (*not permanent: decision*) révocable; (*operation*) réversible

**review** [rɪˈvjuː] **I.** *vt* ❶ (*consider*) revoir ❷ (*reconsider*) reconsidérer ❸ (*revise*) réviser; (*notes*) revoir ❹ (*study again*) réviser ❺ (*write about*) faire la critique de ❻ MIL faire passer en revue **II.** *n* ❶ (*examination*) examen *m*; (*of a situation*) bilan *m*; **to be under ~** être en cours de révision ❷ (*reconsideration*) révision *f*; **to come up for ~** devoir être révisé ❸ (*criticism*) critique *f* ❹ (*periodical*)

revue *f* ❺ MIL revue *f* ❻ THEAT *s.* revue ❼ SCHOOL, UNIV révision *f*

**reviewer** *n* critique *mf*

**revise** [rɪˈvaɪz] *vt* ❶ (*rewrite: text*) réviser ❷ (*reconsider*) revoir; (*opinion*) changer

**revision** [rɪˈvɪʒˌən] *n* révision *f*; **for ~** à revoir

**revitalize** [riːˈvaɪˌtʰˌəlˌaɪz] *vt* ranimer; (*trade*) relancer

**revive** [rɪˈvaɪv] **I.** *vt* ❶ MED (*patient*) réanimer ❷ (*give life to: tired person*) ranimer; (*hopes, interest*) faire renaître; (*economy, custom, fashion*) relancer ❸ THEAT (*present again*) remonter **II.** *vi* ❶ MED reprendre connaissance ❷ (*be restored: tired person*) retrouver ses esprits; (*hopes, interest*) renaître; (*economy, business*) reprendre; (*custom, fashion*) revenir

**revoke** [rɪˈvoʊk] *vt* LAW révoquer; (*order*) annuler; (*license*) retirer

**revolting** *adj* révoltant(e); **to taste ~** avoir un goût infâme

**revolution** [ˌrevˌəˈluːʃˌən] *n* ❶ (*revolt*) révolution *f* ❷ *a. fig* (*change*) révolution *f* ❸ (*rotation*) tour *m*

**revolutionary** [ˌrevˌəˈluːʃˌənˌerˌi] **I.** <-ies> *n* révolutionnaire *mf* **II.** *adj* révolutionnaire

**revolving** *adj* en rotation

**revue** [rɪˈvjuː] *n* revue *f*

**reward** [rɪˈwɔːrd] **I.** *n* récompense *f*; **the ~(s) of sth** les fruits *mpl* de qc **II.** *vt* ❶ (*give a reward*) récompenser ❷ (*repay*) rémunérer

**rewarding** *adj* gratifiant(e)

**rewind** [ˌriːˈwaɪnd] *irr* **I.** *vt* rembobiner; (*watch*) remonter **II.** *vi* (*wind back*) rembobiner **III.** *n* rembobinage *m*

**rewrite** [ˈriːˌraɪt, *vb:* ˌriːˈraɪt] **I.** *n* nouvelle version *f* **II.** *vt irr* LIT réécrire

**rheumatism** [ˈruːmˌəˌtɪˌzᵊm] *n* MED rhumatisme *m*

**rhinestone** *n* faux diamant *m*

**rhino** *inf*, **rhinoceros** [raɪˈnɑːsˌərˌəs] <-(es)> *n* rhinocéros *m*

**Rhode Island** [ˌroʊdˈaɪˌlˌənd] **I.** *n* le Rhode Island **II.** *n* du Rhode Island

R

**rhubarb** ['ru·barb] *n* rhubarbe *f*

**rhyme** [raɪm] **I.** *n* ❶ (*similar sound*) rime *f*; **in** ~ en vers ❷ (*ode*) comptine *f* ► **without** ~ **or reason** sans rime ni raison **II.** *vt* faire rimer **III.** *vi* rimer

**rhythm** ['rɪð·ᵊm] *n* (*beat*) rythme *m*

**RI** [‚ar·'aɪ] *n abbr of* **Rhode Island**

**rib** [rɪb] **I.** *n* ❶ (*bone*) côte *f* ❷ (*cut of meat*) côte *f* ❸ (*in structure*) armature *f*; (*in umbrella*) baleine *f* ❹ (*stripe*) côtes *fpl* **II.**<-bb-> *vt inf* taquiner

**ribbon** ['rɪb·ᵊn] *n* ❶ (*long strip*) ruban *m* ❷ (*of medal*) galon *m*

**rice** [raɪs] **I.** *n* riz *m* **II.** *vt* (*potatoes*) réduire en purée

**rice pudding** *n* gâteau *m* de riz

**rich** [rɪtʃ] **I.**<-er, -est> *adj* ❶ (*wealthy*) *a.* GEO riche; **to get** ~ *inf* s'enrichir ❷ AGR (*harvest*) abondant(e) ❸ (*opulent*) somptueux(-euse) ❹ (*plenty*) to be ~ **in sth** être riche en qc; **vitamin-**~ vitaminé(e) ❺ (*intense*) riche; (*color*) onctueux(-euse) ❻ (*fatty: meal, dessert*) riche ❼ *sl* (*laughable*) un peu fort (de café) **II.** *n* ❶ **the** ~ *pl* les riches *mpl* ❷ *pl* les richesses *fpl*

**ricochet** ['rɪk·ə·ʃeɪ] **I.** *vi* ricocher **II.** *n* ricochet *m*

**rid** [rɪd] <rid *o* ridded, rid *o* ridded> *vt* **to** ~ **sb/sth of sth** débarrasser qn/qc de qc/; **to get** ~ **of sb/sth** se débarrasser de qn/qc

**ridden** ['rɪd·ᵊn] **I.** *pp of* **ride II.** *adj* **guilt-/crime-/debt-**~ rongé par la culpabilité/le crime/la doute

**riddle¹** ['rɪd·l] *n* (*puzzle*) énigme *f*

**riddle²** ['rɪd·l] **I.** *n* crible *m* **II.** *vt* ❶ (*perforate*) cribler; **to be** ~**d with** (*holes, mice, mistakes*) être infesté de ❷ (*put through sieve*) passer au crible

**ride** [raɪd] **I.** <rode, ridden> *vt* ❶ (*sit on*) **to** ~ **a bike/horse** monter à vélo/cheval; **to be riding a bike/motorcycle** être à vélo/en moto ❷ (*go in vehicle: a bike, Ferris wheel*) monter sur; (*a bus, train, car*) monter dans ❸ (*sail: rapids, canoe, raft*) prendre ❹ (*travel: distance*) faire ❺ (*surf: waves*) chevaucher ❻ *inf* (*pressure*) **to** ~ **sb** être sur le

dos de qn **II.**<rode, ridden> *vi* ❶ (*ride a horse*) monter à cheval ❷ (*travel*) aller à dos d'animal; **he was riding on a donkey** il était sur le âne; **you can** ~ **across Paris on your bike** tu peux traverser Paris à bicyclette ► **to** ~ **roughshod over sb** fouler qn aux pieds; **sth is riding on sth** qc dépend de qc **III.** *n* ❶ (*trip, journey*) trajet *m*; (*on a bike*) tour *m*; (*on horse*) promenade *f*; **to give sb a** ~ emmener qn (en voiture) ❷ (*at amusement park*) tour *m* ► **to take sb for a** ~ *inf* faire marcher qn

 ◆ **ride out** *vt a. fig* surmonter

 ◆ **ride up** *vi* remonter

**rider** *n* ❶ (*on horse*) cavalier, -ère *m, f*; (*on bike*) cycliste *mf*; (*on motorcycle*) motocycliste *mf* ❷ (*amendment*) annexe *f* ❸ (*addition to statement*) clause *f* additionnelle

**ridge** [rɪdʒ] *n* ❶ GEO crête *f* ❷ METEO (*of pressure*) ligne *f* ❸ (*of roof*) arête *f* ❹ (*on surface*) nervure *f*

**ridicule** ['rɪd·ɪ·kjul] **I.** *n* ridicule *m* **II.** *vt* ridiculiser

**ridiculous** *adj* ridicule; **don't be** ~! ne dis pas n'importe quoi!

**riding** ['raɪ·dɪŋ] *n* équitation *f*

**rifle¹** ['raɪ·fl] *n* (*weapon*) fusil *m*

**rifle²** ['raɪ·fl] *vt, vi* (*steal*) fouiller

**rig** [rɪg] **I.**<-gg-> *vt* ❶ (*falsify result: election*) truquer; (*market*) manipuler ❷ (*equip with mast: yacht*) gréer **II.** *n* ❶ (*in oil industry*) derrick *m* ❷ (*truck*) semi-remorque *m* ❸ (*sail assembly*) gréement *m* ❹ *inf* (*clothing*) tenue *f*

**rigging** *n* ❶ (*manipulation of results*) trucage *m* ❷ (*ropes on ships*) gréement *m*

**right** [raɪt] **I.** *adj* ❶ (*morally good, justified: policy, attitude*) bon(ne); (*distribution, punishment*) juste; **to do the** ~ **thing** bien agir; **it's just not** ~ ce n'est pas normal; **to stay on the** ~ **side of the law** rester dans la légalité ❷ (*true, correct: answer, method, suspicion*) bon(ne); **to be** ~ **about sth** avoir raison à propos de qc; **42, that can't be** ~ 42, ce n'est pas possible; **that's** ~, 42 c'est

**R**

bien ça, 42 ③ (*best, appropriate*) bon(ne); **the ~ way to do things** la manière convenable de faire les choses; **to be in the ~ place at the ~ time** être là où il faut au bon moment ④ (*direction*) droit(e); **to make a ~ turn** tourner à droite ⑤ (*well*) bien; **to not be** (**quite**) **~ in the head** *inf* ne pas avoir toute sa tête ⑥ (*in correct state*) **to set sth ~** redresser qc **II.** n ① (*civil privilege*) droit m ② (*lawfulness*) bien m; **I'm in the ~** j'ai raison ③ pl (*copyright*) droits mpl; **all ~s reserved** tous droits réservés ④ (*right side*) droite f; **on the ~** à droite; **to make a ~** tourner à droite ⑤ SPORTS droit m **III.** adv ① (*correctly: answer*) correctement ② (*well: work*) bien; **she doesn't dress/talk ~** elle ne sait pas s'habiller/parler ③ (*in rightward direction*) à droite ④ (*directly*) exactement; **to be ~ behind sb** être juste derrière qn; (*encourage*) soutenir qn **IV.** vt ① (*rectify: mistake*) rectifier; (*situation*) redresser ② (*set upright*) redresser **V.** interj ① (*in agreement*) d'accord! ② (*attracting attention*) bon! ③ inf (*requesting confirmation*) n'est-ce pas?

**right-angled** adj à angle droit

**right-hand** adj droit(e); **on the ~ side** du côté droit

**right-handed** adj droitier(-ère)

**rightly** adv correctement; **quite ~** à juste titre

**right of way** <rights of way> n ① (*footpath*) passage m ② (*on road*) **to have the ~** avoir la priorité; **to yield the ~** céder le passage

**right-wing** adj POL (*attitudes, party*) de droite

**rigorous** ['rɪg⋅ər⋅əs] adj rigoureux(-euse)

**rind** [raɪnd] n (*of lemon*) zeste m; (*of bacon*) couenne f; (*of cheese*) croûte f, couenne f Suisse

**ring¹** [rɪŋ] **I.** n ① (*circle*) anneau m; (*drawn*) cercle m ② (*stain*) tache f; (*under eyes*) cerne f ③ (*clique, group of people: of drugs, spies*) cercle m; (*of spies, criminals*) réseau m

④ (*jewelry*) bague f; **wedding ~** alliance f ⑤ (*arena: in boxing*) ring m; (*in circus*) arène f ▶ **to run ~s around sb** battre qn à plate(s) couture(s) **II.** vt ① (*encircle*) encercler ② (*mark: bird*) baguer

**ring²** [rɪŋ] **I.** n ① (*sound*) sonnerie f ② (*telephone call*) coup m de fil ③ (*quality*) accent m **II.** <rang, rung> vt (*bell*) faire sonner; (*alarm*) déclencher ▶ **that ~s a bell** inf ça me dit quelque chose **III.** <rang, rung> vi ① (*telephone, bell*) sonner; (*ears*) tinter; **to ~ at the door** sonner à la porte ② (*resound*) **to ~ with laughter/applause** résonner de rires/d'applaudissements ▶ **to ~ true** sonner juste

◆ **ring in** vt **to ~ the New Year** fêter le Nouvel An

◆ **ring out** vt **to ~ the old Year** sonner la fin de l'année

**ring tone** n sonnerie f

◆ **ring up** vt ① (*key in sale*) enregistrer ② fig (*achieve*) réaliser

**ringleader** n meneur, -euse m, f

**ringside** **I.** n premier rang m **II.** adj ① (*seats*) du premier rang ② fig (*view*) de premier plan

**ringtone** n tonalité f de la sonnerie

**rink** [rɪŋk] n (*for ice skating*) patinoire f; (*for roller skating*) piste f

**rinse** [rɪn(t)s] **I.** vt, vi rincer **II.** n rinçage m; **to give sth a ~** rincer qc

**riot** [raɪət] **I.** n ① (*disturbances*) émeute f ▶ **to be a ~** inf être tordant **II.** vi se soulever; fig faire un scandale **III.** adv **to run ~** fig se déchaîner; (*imagination*) s'emballer

**rioting** n émeutes fpl

**rip** [rɪp] **I.** n accroc m **II.** <-pp-> vi ① se déchirer ② (*move quickly*) aller à toute allure ▶ **to let ~** se déchaîner **III.** <-pp-> vt déchirer; **to ~ sth apart** mettre qc en pièces; **to ~ sth open** ouvrir qc en le déchirant; **to ~ sth out** arracher qc

◆ **rip off** vt ① (*remove quickly: cover*) déchirer; (*clothes*) enlever à toute vitesse ❷ *sl* (*overcharge*) arnaquer ❸ *sl* (*steal*) piquer

♦ **rip up** *vt* (*pull apart fast*) déchirer

**RIP** [ˌɑr·aɪˈpi] *abbr of* **rest in peace** qu'il/elle repose en paix

**ripe** [raɪp] *adj* ❶ (*fully developed: fruit*) mûr(e); (*cheese*) fait(e) ❷ (*ready*) prêt(e); **a ~ old age** un âge avancé; **at the ~ old age of 16** *iron* au grand âge de 16 ans

**ripen** [ˈraɪ·pᵊn] I. *vt* faire mûrir II. *vi* mûrir

**rip-off** *n sl* arnaque *f*

**rise** [raɪz] I. *n* ❶ (*in status, power*) montée *f* ❷ (*increase*) hausse *f* ▸ **to give ~ to sth** donner lieu à qc; **to give ~ to hopes** faire naître l'espoir II. <rose, risen> *vi* ❶ (*move upward: person in chair or bed*) se lever; (*smoke*) s'élever; **to ~ to the bait** mordre à l'hameçon ❷ (*in status*) s'élever; **to ~ to power** arriver au pouvoir; **to ~ to the challenge** relever le défi; **to ~ to the occasion** se montrer à la hauteur de la situation; **to ~ to fame** devenir célèbre ❸ (*become higher: road, river*) monter; (*temperature, prices*) augmenter; (*hopes*) grandir; (*dough*) lever ❹ (*be higher: trees, buildings*) s'élever ❺ THEAT (*curtain*) se lever ❻ (*become visible: moon, sun*) se lever; (*river*) monter ❼ REL ▸ **to ~ from the dead** ressusciter d'entre les morts ❽ (*rebel*) se soulever

**risen** [ˈrɪz·ᵊn] *pp of* **rise**

**risk** [rɪsk] I. *n* risque *m;* **fire/safety ~** risque d'incendie/pour la sécurité; **to be at ~** être en danger II. *vt* risquer; **to ~ life and limb** *fig* risquer sa peau

**risk-free** *adj* sans risque

**risky** [ˈrɪs·ki] <-ier, -iest> *adj* risqué(e)

**ritual** [ˈrɪtʃ·u·əl] I. *n* rituel *m* II. *adj* rituel(le)

**rival** [ˈraɪ·vᵊl] I. *n* rival(e) *m(f)* II. *adj* rival(e) III. <-l- *o* -ll-> *vt* rivaliser avec; **to ~ sb in sth** rivaliser avec qn en qc

**river** [ˈrɪv·ər] I. *n* ❶ (*stream*) rivière *f;* (*flowing to ocean*) fleuve *m* ❷ *fig* (*of tears*) flot *m* ▸ **down ~** en aval; **up ~** en amont II. *adj* fluvial(e)

**riverbed** *n* lit *m* de la rivière

**RN** [ˌɑrˈen] *n abbr of* **registered nurse** infirmière *f* diplômée d'État

**road** [roʊd] *n* ❶ (*linking places*) route *f;* **dirt ~** chemin *m* de terre; **on the ~** (*when driving*) sur la route; (*traveling*) sur les routes, en tour ❷ (*in residential area*) rue *f* ▸ **to come to the end of the ~** arriver en fin de parcours; **all ~s lead to Rome** *prov* tous les chemins mènent à Rome *prov;* **some years down the ~** d'ici quelques années; **to get sth on the ~** *inf* commencer qc; **let's hit the ~!** *inf* en route!

**road accident** *n* accident *m* de la route

**roadblock** *n* barrage *m* routier

**roadkill** *n* animal *m* écrasé

**road map** *n* carte *f* routière

**road rage** *n* furie *f* au volant, agressivité *f* des automobilistes

**road show** *n* tournée *f*

**roadside** I. *n* bord *m* de la route II. *adj* au bord de la route

**road sign** *n* panneau *m* de signalisation

**road transportation** *n* transports *mpl* routiers

**roadwork** *n* ❶ (*maintenance*) travaux *mpl* d'entretien du réseau routier ❷ (*construction*) construction *f* des routes

**roar** [rɔr] I. *vi* hurler; (*lion*) rugir; (*engine*) gronder II. *n* ❶ (*growl*) rugissement *m* ❷ (*loud noise*) grondement *m*

**roast** [roʊst] I. *vt* ❶ rôtir; (*coffee*) torréfier ❷ *inf* (*poke fun at*) ridiculiser II. *vi* griller III. *n* rôti *m* IV. *adj* rôti(e); (*coffee*) torréfié(e); (*potato*) rôti(e)

**roast beef** *n* rosbif *m*

**rob** [rab] <-bb-> *vt* ❶ (*burglarize*) voler; (*a bank*) dévaliser ❷ (*defraud*) escroquer ❸ (*deprive*) priver ▸ **to ~ Peter to pay Paul** *prov* déshabiller (saint) Pierre pour habiller (saint) Paul *prov*

**robber** [ˈra·bər] *n* voleur, -euse *m, f*

**robbery** [ˈra·bər·i] <-ies> *n* ❶ (*crime*) cambriolage *m* ❷ (*instance of burglary*) vol *m*

**robe** [roʊb] *n* ❶ (*formal*) robe *f* de soirée ❷ (*dressing gown*) robe *f* de chambre

**R**

**robin** ['ra·bɪn] n rouge-gorge m

**robot** ['rou·bat] n ① (machine) robot m ② fig, pej (person) automate m

**rock¹** [rak] n ① (substance) roche f ② (stone) rocher m; (smaller) pierre f; **to be solid as a ~** être solide comme un roc ③ fig, inf (diamond) diam m ▸ **on the ~s** (experiencing difficulties) en pleine débâcle; (with ice) avec des glaçons

**rock²** [rak] I. vt ① (swing) balancer; (a baby) bercer ② (shake: person, house) secouer ▸ **to ~ the boat** sl faire des vagues II. vi ① (sway) se balancer; **to ~ back and forth** se balancer d'avant en arrière ② (dance) danser le rock'n'roll III. n MUS rock m

**rock climbing** n varappe f

**rocket** ['ra·kɪt] I. n ① (vehicle, firework) a. MIL fusée f II. vi **to ~ (up)** monter en flèche; **to ~ sth** atteindre rapidement qc III. vt attaquer à la roquette

**rock garden** n rocaille f

**rocking** ['rak·ɪŋ] n balancement m

**rocking chair** n rocking-chair m, berçante f Québec

**rock 'n' roll** n rock and roll m

**rocky¹** ['ra·ki] <-ier, -iest> adj rocheux(-euse)

**rocky²** ['ra·ki] <-ier, -iest> adj ① (weak) patraque ② inf (doomed) chancelant(e)

**Rocky Mountains** n les Montagnes fpl Rocheuses

**rod** [rad] n ① (thin bar: of wood) baguette f; (of metal) tige f; (for support) tringle f; (for punishment) a. fig canne f ② (fishing rod) canne f à pêche

**rode** [roud] pt of ride

**rodeo** ['rou·di·ou] <-s> n rodéo m

**roe¹** [rou] n (fish eggs) œufs mpl de poisson

**roe²** [rou] <-(s)> n (deer) chevreuil m

**role model** n modèle m

**roll** [roul] I. vt ① (push circular object) faire rouler; (dice) jeter ② (move in circles) rouler; **to ~ one's eyes/one's r's** rouler les yeux/les r ③ (shape: into cylinder) enrouler; (into ball) rouler en boule; **to be many things all ~ed into one** être plusieurs choses à la fois ④ (make: cigarette) rouler ⑤ (flatten, compress: grass) passer au rouleau; (metal) laminer II. vi ① (move around axis) rouler; (car) faire un tonneau; (eyes) rouler ② (sway) onduler; (ship) tanguer ③ (be in operation) tourner ④ **make noise** (thunder) gronder ▸ **to be ~ing in the aisles** se tordre de rire; **to get the ball ~ing** mettre les choses en route; **to ~ with the punches** sl encaisser les coups III. n ① (movement) roulement m; (in gymnastics) roulade f; (by plane) looping m; **to be on a ~** fig être bien parti ② (cylinder) rouleau m; (of fat) bourrelet m; **a ~ of film** une pellicule ③ (noise: of drum, thunder) roulement m ④ (names) liste f; **to call (the) ~** faire l'appel ⑤ (bread) petit pain m

♦ **roll back** I. vt ① ECON (costs, priced) baisser ② (return to last state) faire reculer II. vi ECON reculer

♦ **roll in** vi ① (stagger into) rappliquer ② inf (arrive: money, customers) crouler sous l'argent ▸ **to be rolling in it** être plein aux as

♦ **roll on** I. vi continuer; (time) s'écouler II. vt ① (apply with roller) appliquer au rouleau ② (put on) enfiler

♦ **roll out** I. vt ① (flatten) aplatir à l'aide d'un rouleau; (pastry) étendre au rouleau ② (make available: product) sortir ③ (unroll) a. fig (red carpet) dérouler II. vi sortir; **to ~ of bed** sortir du lit

♦ **roll over** vi se retourner; (car) capoter

♦ **roll up** I. vi inf se pointer II. vt ① (coil: string) enrouler ② (fold up) a. fig (sleeves) retrousser

**roll bar** n AUTO arceau m de sécurité

**roller** ['rou·lər] n rouleau m; (for roads) rouleau m compresseur; (for metal) laminoir m; (for hair) bigoudi m

**roller coaster** n montagnes fpl russes ▸ **to be on an emotional ~** passer par des hauts et des bas

**roller-skate** *vi* faire du patin à roulettes

**rolling pin** *n* rouleau *m* (à pâtisserie)

**roll-neck** ['roʊl·nek] *n* col *m* roulé

**roly-poly** [ˌroʊ·liˈpoʊ·li] *adj inf* grassouillet(te)

**ROM** [ram] *n* COMPUT *abbr of* **read only memory** ROM *m*

**Roman** ['roʊ·mən] **I.** *adj* romain(e) **II.** *n* Romain(e) *m(f)*

**Roman Catholic I.** *n* catholique *mf* **II.** *adj* catholique

**romance** [roʊˈmæn(t)s] *n* ❶ (*love affair*) liaison *f* ❷ (*love story*) roman *m* d'amour; LIT roman *m* de chevalerie ❸ (*glamour*) charme *m*

**Roman numeral** *n* chiffre *m* romain

**romantic** [roʊˈmæn·tɪk] **I.** *adj* ❶ (*concerning love*) a. LIT, ART romantique ❷ (*unrealistic*) romanesque **II.** *n* romantique *mf*

**Rome** [roʊm] *n* Rome ► **when in ~, do as the <u>Romans</u> (do)** *prov* à Rome, faites comme les Romains *prov*

**roof** [ruf] **I.** *n* toit *m*; (*of a cave, mouth*) voûte *f* ► **to hit the ~** sortir de ses gonds **II.** *vt* couvrir; **to ~ sth in** recouvrir qc

**roof garden** *n* jardin *m* sur le toit

**roof rack** *n* galerie *f* (de voiture)

**rook** [rʊk] *n* ❶ (*chess piece*) tour *f* ❷ (*bird*) freux *m*

**rookie** ['rʊk·i] *n inf* ❶ MIL a. *fig* recrue *f*; (*cop*) flic *m* débutant ❷ SPORTS débutant(e) *m(f)*

**room** [rum] **I.** *n* ❶ (*in house*) pièce *f*, place *f* Belgique, Nord; (*bedroom*) chambre *f*; (*classroom, meeting room*) salle *f*; (*for work*) bureau *m*; **~ and board** pension *f* complète ❷ (*people in room*) assemblée *f* ❸ (*space*) place *f* ❹ (*possibility*) marge *f*; **to have ~ for improvement** pouvoir mieux faire **II.** *vi* **to ~ with sb** (*share room*) partager une chambre avec qn **III.** *adj* **two-~ apartment** deux-pièces *m*

**roomie** ['rum·i] *n inf* s. **roommate**

**roommate** *n* (*person sharing room*) camarade *mf* de chambre; (*sharing apartment*) colocataire, -trice *m, f*

**room service** *n* service *m* de chambre

**roomy** ['rum·i] <-ier, -iest> *adj* spacieux(-euse)

**rooster** *n* coq *m*

**root** [rut] **I.** *n* ❶ a. *fig* racine *f*; **to put** [*o* **set**] **down ~s** *fig* s'enraciner; **the ~ of all evil** la source de tous les maux; **to lie at the ~ of a problem** être à l'origine d'un problème ❷ MATH racine *f* ❸ pl (*ancestry*) racines *fpl* **II.** *vt* enraciner **III.** *vi* (*establish roots*) s'enraciner

♦**root for** *vt inf* (*cheer on*) soutenir

**root vegetable** *n* légume *m* à racine comestible

**rope** [roʊp] **I.** *n* ❶ (*solid cord*) corde *f* ❷ (*of garlic, onions*) tresse *f* ❸ pl (*in boxing ring*) corde *f* ❹ pl, *fig* (*method of working*) **to learn the ~s** apprendre les ficelles; **to show sb the ~s** mettre qn au courant ► **to be at the end of one's ~** être au bout du rouleau **II.** *vt* ❶ (*fasten*) attacher ❷ SPORTS **to ~ sb** (*together*) encorder qn

**rope ladder** *n* échelle *f* de corde

**ropewalker** *n* THEAT funambule *mf*

**rose**[1] [roʊz] **I.** *n* ❶ BOT rose *f* ❷ (*color*) rose *m* ❸ ARCHIT rosace *f* ❹ (*on watering can*) pomme *f* **II.** *adj* rose; *s.a.* **blue**

**rose**[2] [roʊz] *pt of* **rise**

**rosebud** *n* bouton *m* de rose

**rose hip** *n* églantine *f*

**rosemary** ['roʊz·mer·i] *n* romarin *m*

**roster** ['ra·stər] *n* rota *m*

**rosy** ['roʊ·zi] <-ier, -iest> *adj* ❶ (*colored*) rose ❷ *fig* **to look ~** être prometteur

**rot** [rat] **I.** *n* ❶ (*decay*) pourriture *f* ❷ *fig* (*something bad*) ineptie *f*; (*nonsense*) bêtises *fpl* **II.** <-tt-> *vi* ❶ (*decay*) pourrir ❷ *fig* **to leave sb to ~** laisser dépérir qn **III.** *vt* décomposer

**rotate** ['roʊ·teɪt] **I.** *vt* ❶ (*turn around*) faire tourner ❷ (*alternate*) alterner; **to ~ duties** remplir des fonctions à tour de rôle **II.** *vi* **to ~ around sth** tourner autour de qc

**rotation** *n* ❶ (*action of rotating*) rotation *f*; **~s per minute** tours/minutes

R

*mpl* ❷ (*taking turns*) roulement *m*; **in ~** à tour de rôle

**rotor** ['rou·tər] *n* rotor *m*

**rotten** ['rɑ·t̬ən] *adj* ❶ (*decaying*) pourri(e) ❷ (*mean, nasty*) méchant(e) ❸ (*not good*) infect(e); **to feel ~** (*ill*) se sentir mal en point; (*guilty*) se sentir mal

**rough** [rʌf] **I.** *adj* ❶ (*uneven: surface, material*) rugueux(-euse); (*ground, road*) raboteux(-euse) ❷ (*poorly made*) brut(e) ❸ (*unmelodic*) rauque; (*accent*) rude ❹ (*imprecise: guess, estimate*) approximatif(-ive); (*work*) gros(se); **a ~ drawing** une ébauche ❺ (*harsh*) brutal(e) ❻ (*stormy: sea*) agité(e); (*weather*) mauvais(e) ❼ (*difficult*) difficile; (*justice*) sommaire; **to be ~ on sb** *inf* être dur avec qn **II.** *n* ❶ (*in golf*) rough *m* ❷ (*unfinished*) **a diamond in the ~** diamant *m* brut; (*person*) brute *f* au cœur tendre ❸ (*sketch*) ébauche *f* **III.** *vt* (*beat up*) **to ~ sb up** malmener qn ▸ **to ~ it** *inf* vivre à la dure

**roughly** *adv* ❶ (*approximately*) grossièrement; (*calculate*) approximativement; **~ speaking** en général ❷ (*aggressively*) rudement

**roughness** *n* ❶ (*quality of surface*) rugosité *f*; (*of the ground*) inégalité *f* ❷ (*unfairness*) brutalité *f*; (*of a game*) violence *f*

**round** [raund] **I.** *n* ❶ (*shape*) rond *m* ❷ (*work: of a guard*) ronde *f*; (*of a postman*) tournée *f*; **to make the ~s** (*illness, story*) circuler ❸ SPORTS (*of golf*) partie *f*; (*in a championship*) manche *f*; (*in horse jumping*) parcours *m* ❹ (*unit: of bread*) tranche *f*; (*of ammunition*) cartouche *f*; **a ~ of applause** des applaudissements *mpl* ❺ (*series: of drinks*) tournée *f*; (*of voting*) tour *m*; (*of applications, interviews*) série *f* ❻ MUS canon *m* **II.** *adj* ❶ (*shape*) rond(e) ❷ *fig* (*vowel*) arrondi(e); (*number*) rond(e); **~ sum** somme *f* rondelette **III.** *adv* **to go ~ and ~** tourner en rond; **all year ~** tout au long de l'année **IV.** *prep s.* **around V.** *vt*

❶ (*form into curve*) arrondir ❷ (*move*) contourner; (*bend*) prendre; (*cape*) doubler ❸ (*number*) arrondir

◆**round down** *vt* arrondir au chiffre inférieur

◆**round off** *vt* terminer

◆**round out** *vt* parfaire

◆**round up** *vt* ❶ (*increase: number*) arrondir au chiffre supérieur ❷ (*gather*) rassembler

**roundabout** *adj* indirect(e); **to take a ~ route** faire un détour; **to ask sb in a ~ way** demander à qn de manière détournée

**roundtable, roundtable conference, roundtable discussion** *n* table *f* ronde

**round-the-clock I.** *adj* de jour et de nuit **II.** *adv* vingt-quatre heures sur vingt-quatre

**round-trip** *adj* (*ticket, fare*) aller-retour *m*

**rousing** *adj* (*cheer, welcome*) enthousiaste; (*speech, chant*) vibrant(e)

**rout** [raut] **I.** *vt a. fig* mettre en déroute **II.** *n* déroute *f*

**route** [rut] **I.** *n* ❶ (*way*) itinéraire *m* ❷ (*delivery path*) tournée *f*; **to have a delivery ~** avoir un itinéraire de livraison; **to have a paper ~** distribuer les journaux ❸ (*road*) route *f* ❹ *fig* voie *f* **II.** *vt* faire passer

**routine** [ru·ˈtin] **I.** *n* ❶ (*habit*) routine *f*; **to do sth as a matter of ~** faire qc systématiquement; **daily ~** train-train *m* quotidien ❷ THEAT numéro *m* ❸ COMPUT routine *f* **II.** *adj* ❶ (*regular*) ordinaire; (*medical case*) banal(e); (*check-up*) de routine; (*inquiry, inspection*) d'usage ❷ *pej* (*uninspiring*) routinier(-ère)

**roving** ['rou·vɪŋ] *adj* (*animal, thieves*) errant(e); (*ambassador, musician*) itinérant(e); **to have a ~ eye** ne pas avoir les yeux dans sa poche

**row¹** [rou] *n* (*of trees, houses*) rangée *f*; (*of seats, people*) rang *m*; (*of cars*) file *f*; **in a ~** en rang; **in a ~** d'affilée

**row²** [rau] **I.** *vi* ramer; SPORTS faire de l'aviron; **to ~ across the lake** traverser le lac à la rame **II.** *vt* **to ~ the boat to sth** ramer vers qc; **to ~ sb/sth** transporter qn/qc en canot; **to ~ sb across the lake** ramener qn en canot sur le lac **III.** *n* rame *f;* **to go for a ~** faire un tour de canot

**rowboat** ['rou·bout] *n* canot *m* (à rames)

**rowing** *n* aviron *m*

**royal** ['rɔɪəl] **I.** *adj* ❶ *(of a monarch)* a. *fig* royal(e); **Your/His/Her ~ Highness** Votre/Son Altesse ❷ *inf (big)* gros(se); **he's a ~ pain in the ass** c'est un emmerdeur de première **II.** *n inf* membre *m* de la famille royale

**rpm** [ˌar·piˈem] *n abbr of* **revolutions per minute** tr/min *m*

**RSVP** *abbr of* **répondez s'il vous plaît** RSVP

**rub** [rʌb] **I.** *n* frottement *m* **II.** <-bb-> *vt* frotter; *(body)* frictionner; *(one's eyes, hands)* se frotter ▸ **to ~** **elbows** [*o* **shoulders**] **with sb** *inf* côtoyer qn; **to ~ sb the wrong way** prendre qn à rebrousse-poil **III.** <-bb-> *vi* se frotter; **these shoes ~ against my heel** ces chaussures qui frottent au talon

◆**rub down** *vt* ❶ *(prepare for decoration)* nettoyer; **to rub sth down with sandpaper** poncer qc avec du papier de verre ❷ *(dry)* essuyer (en frottant)

◆**rub in** *vt* ❶ *(spread on skin)* faire pénétrer ❷ *inf (keep reminding)* rappeler sans cesse

◆**rub off I.** *vi* ❶ *(become clean)* s'effacer; *(mark)* partir ❷ *(affect)* **to ~ on sb** déteindre sur qn **II.** *vt* effacer

◆**rub out** *vt* ❶ *(erase)* effacer ❷ *sl (murder)* éliminer

**rubber** ['rʌb·ər] **I.** *n* ❶ *(elastic substance)* caoutchouc *m* ❷ *sl (condom)* capote *f* ❸ *pl (waterproof shoes)* bottes *fpl* en caoutchouc ❹ *(in bridge)* partie *f* **II.** *adj* en caoutchouc

**rubber band** *n* élastique *m*

**rubber boat** *n* bateau *m* pneumatique

**rubbernecker** ['rʌb·ərˌnek·ər] *n sl* badaud(e) *m(f)*

**rubber-stamp** *vt pej* approuver

**rubber tree** *n* arbre *m* à gomme

**rubbery** ['rʌb·əˈr·i] <-ier, -iest> *adj* ❶ *(rubber-like)* caoutchouteux(-euse) ❷ *inf (weak)* mou(molle)

**rubbing alcohol** *n* alcool *m* à 90°

**rubbish** ['rʌb·ɪʃ] *n* ❶ *inf (waste)* déchets *mpl* ❷ *inf (nonsense)* bêtises *fpl* ❸ *inf (junk, something worthless)* camelote *f*

**rubble** ['rʌb·l] *n* ❶ *(smashed rock)* gravats *mpl* ❷ *(from demolished building)* décombres *mpl* ❸ *fig* **to reduce sth to ~** réduire qc en poussière

**rubdown** *n* friction *f;* **to give sb a ~** frictionner qn

**rubella** [ru·ˈbel·ə] *n* MED rubéole *f*

**ruby** ['ru·bi] **I.** <-ies> *n* rubis *m* **II.** *adj* ❶ *(colored)* (couleur) rubis *inv* ❷ *(made of stones: necklace, bracelet)* de rubis

**rucksack** ['rʌk·sæk] *n* sac *m* à dos

**ruction** ['rʌk·ʃən] *n inf* grabuge *m*

**rudder** ['rʌd·ər] *n* gouvernail *m*

**rude** [rud] *adj* ❶ *(impolite)* impoli(e) ❷ *(coarse)* grossier(-ère) ❸ *(sudden)* soudain(e); *(shock)* rude; **I had a ~ awakening** j'ai perdu mes illusions

**rug** [rʌg] *n* carpette *f* ▸ **to pull the ~ (out) from under sb's feet** couper l'herbe sous les pieds de qn

**rugby** ['rʌg·bi] *n* rugby *m;* **a ~ team/ ball** une équipe/balle de rugby

**rugged** ['rʌg·ɪd] *adj* ❶ *(uneven: cliff, mountains)* découpé(e); *(country, coast, bank)* accidenté(e); *(ground)* rocailleux(-euse) ❷ *(tough: individual, face)* rude ❸ *(solid: vehicle, constitution)* robuste

**ruin** ['ru·ɪn] **I.** *vt* ❶ *(destroy)* a. *fig (reputation, country)* ruiner; *(dress)* abîmer ❷ *(spoil: day, plan, house)* gâcher; *(child)* gâter ❸ *(impoverish)* ruiner **II.** *n* ruine *f;* **to be in/fall into ~(s)** être/tomber en ruine; **to be on the road to ~** aller à la ruine

**rule** [rul] **I.** *n* ❶ *(instruction)* règle *f;* **to play by the ~s** jouer d'après les règles; **the school ~s** le règlement scolaire ❷ *(control)* autorité *f* ❸ *(ruler)* règle *f*

**R**

▸as a ~ of **thumb** en général; **as a general** ~ en règle générale **II.** vt ❶ (*govern*) gouverner ❷ (*control*) mener ❸ (*draw: line*) tirer; (*paper*) tracer des lignes sur ❹ (*decide*) décider; LAW déclarer ▸**to ~ the roost** faire la loi **III.** vi ❶ (*control*) régner ❷ sl (*be great*) **skateboarding/rap ~s!** c'est trop cool le skate/rap!

◆**rule off** vt tirer

◆**rule out** vt exclure; **to ~ doing sth** décider de ne pas faire qc

**rule book** n the ~ le règlement

**ruler** n ❶ (*person in power*) dirigeant(e) m(f) ❷ (*for measuring*) règle f

**rum** [rʌm] n rhum m

**rumble** ['rʌm·bl] **I.** n grondement m **II.** vi gronder; (*stomach*) gargouiller

**rummy** ['rʌm·i] n rami m

**rumor** ['ru·mər] **I.** n rumeur f; **to spread** [o *circulate*] **the ~ that …** faire circuler la rumeur que …; **~ has it that …** le bruit court que … **II.** vt sb is ~ed to be/do/doing sth la rumeur dit que qn serait qc/ferait qc

**run** [rʌn] **I.** n ❶ (*jog*) course f; **to go for a ~** (aller) courir; **to make a ~ for it** foncer ❷ (*excursion*) tour m ❸ (*journey*) trajet m; (*bombing*) ~ MIL sortie f ❹ (*series*) série f; (*of cards*) suite f; **to have a ~ of good/bad luck** être en veine/dans la déveine ❺ (*period*) période f; (*of events*) cours m; **in the long ~** à la longue; **in the short ~** à court terme ❻ (*production*) lot m; **a** (**print**) **~ of 5000** un tirage à 5000 exemplaires ❼ (*demand*) ruée f; **a ~ on sth** une forte demande de qc ❽ (*type*) genre m; **the common ~ of movies/students** les films/étudiants ordinaires ❾ (*trend*) a. fig tendance f ❿ (*enclosed area: for animals*) enclos m; (*for skiing*) piste f ⓫ (*freedom*) **to have the ~ of sth** avoir qc à son entière disposition ⓬ SPORTS point m ⓭ (*hole*) maille f filée; **to have a ~ in one's stockings** avoir une échelle dans ses bas ⓮ (*leak: of ink, paint*) bavure f ▸**to give sb/sth a ~ for their money** donner du fil à retordre à qn/

qc; **to have the ~s** inf avoir la courante **II.** <-nn-, ran, run> vi ❶ (*move fast using feet*) courir; **to ~ at sb** foncer sur qn; **to come ~ning toward sb** venir vers qn en courant; **to ~ up/down the street** monter/descendre la rue en courant; **to ~ for help/the bus** courir pour chercher de l'aide/attraper le bus; **to ~ in place/for cover** courir sur place/à l'abri; **don't come ~ning to me** fig ne viens pas pleurer chez moi ❷ (*operate*) fonctionner; (*wheel, engine*) tourner; **to ~ on diesel** rouler au diesel; **we're ~ning on time** nous sommes dans les temps ❸ (*go, leave*) filer; **I have to ~** je dois filer ❹ (*flee*) fuir ❺ (*last*) durer; **to ~ for two years** (*play*) être à l'affiche pendant deux ans; (*TV series*) passer pendant deux ans; (*contract*) être valable deux ans ❻ (*flow: water, nose*) couler; (*eyes*) pleurer; (*ink, paint*) baver; (*color*) déteindre; **emotions ran high** les émotions étaient fortes ❼ POL se porter candidat; **to ~ for president** être candidat à la présidence; **to ~ against sb** se présenter contre qn ❽ + adj (*become*) être; **to ~ short of sth** être à court de qc; **to ~ low on sth** être bientôt plus avoir de qc ❾ (*stockings, tights*) filer ❿ (*follow route*) passer; **the river ~s through Burgundy** la rivière coule à travers la Bourgogne ⓫ SPORTS faire du jogging ▸**to ~ around in circles** (*be busy*) se mettre en quatre; **to ~ in the family** être de famille **III.** <-nn-, ran, run> vt ❶ (*by moving feet: race, distance*) courir ❷ (*enter in race*) courir; **to ~ a horse** faire courir un cheval; **to ~ a candidate** présenter un candidat ❸ (*drive*) conduire; **to ~ sb home/to the train station** conduire qn à la maison/à la gare ❹ (*pass*) faire passer; **to ~ one's hand through one's hair** se passer la main dans les cheveux; **to ~ a vacuum cleaner over a rug** passer l'aspirateur sur un tapis ❺ (*operate*) faire fonctionner; (*a car*) entretenir; (*train*) faire circuler; (*motor, program*) faire tourner ❻ (*manage, govern*) gérer; (*company, government*) diriger; (*household, store, hotel*) tenir; **to be too expensive to ~** être trop cher ❼ (*let flow: bath, tap, water*) faire couler ❽ (*tell*) **to ~ sth by sb** soumettre qc à qn ❾ (*issue: an article*) publier; (*series, a film*) passer ❿ (*smuggle*) faire passer ⓫ (*not heed*) **to ~ a red light** passer au (feu) rouge ⓬ (*incur: danger, risk*) courir ⓭ (*have: temperature, a deficit*) avoir; (*test*) effectuer ▶ **to ~ oneself into the <u>ground</u>** s'épuiser; **to ~ the <u>show</u>** faire la loi; **to ~ sb <u>ragged</u>** éreinter qn

◆**run across** *vt, vi* traverser
◆**run after** *vt* poursuivre
◆**run along** *vi* (*leave*) partir; **~ now!** vas-y maintenant!
◆**run around** *vi* ❶ (*bustle*) courir dans tous les sens ❷ (*run freely*) **to ~ in the street** courir dans la rue ❸ *inf* (*have affair*) **to ~ with sb** sortir avec qn
◆**run away** *vi* s'enfuir; **to ~ with the idea that ...** aller s'imaginer que ...
◆**run down** I. *vt inf* ❶ (*criticize*) dénigrer ❷ (*reduce: production, inventory*) réduire (progressivement) ❸ (*hit: car, person*) renverser; (*boat*) heurter ❹ (*exhaust*) décharger; **to ~ oneself down** se vider ❺ (*find*) découvrir II. *vi* ❶ (*lose power: clock*) s'arrêter; (*battery*) se décharger ❷ (*deteriorate*) se détériorer
◆**run in** *vt sl* (*arrest*) arrêter
◆**run into** *vt* ❶ (*meet by chance*) rencontrer par hasard ❷ AUTO entrer en collision avec ❸ (*reach*) atteindre; **the cost will ~ the millions** les coûts s'élèveront à plusieurs millions; **to ~ debt** s'endetter
◆**run off** I. *vi* ❶ *inf* (*leave*) s'enfuir ❷ (*elope*) **to ~ with sb** s'enfuir avec qn ❸ *inf* (*steal*) **to ~ with sth** se tirer avec qc ❹ (*drain*) s'écouler II. *vt* ❶ (*reproduce*) tirer des exemplaires de; **to ~ a copy** faire une copie ❷ (*write quickly*) pondre ❸ (*chase away*) chasser ❹ (*drain*) laisser s'écouler
◆**run on** *vi* ❶ (*continue*) se poursuivre

❷ (*continue talking*) parler sans s'arrêter; **to ~ for another hour** ne plus s'arrêter de parler pendant une heure; **to ~ and on for three pages** continuer sur trois pages
◆**run out** *vi* ❶ (*contract*) expirer ❷ (*be short of*) **to ~ of sth** se trouver à court de qc; **to ~ of patience** perdre patience ❸ *inf* (*abandon*) **to ~ on sb** abandonner qn
◆**run over** I. *vt* ❶ (*injure: person*) renverser ❷ (*read again*) revoir ❸ (*exceed*) excéder II. *vi a. fig* déborder
◆**run through** I. *vt* ❶ (*rehearse: speech, act*) répéter ❷ (*read or repeat quickly*) repasser sur ❸ (*pervade*) traverser ❹ (*spend*) venir à bout de II. *vi* passer en courant

**runabout** *n* petite voiture *f*
**runaround** *n inf* **to give sb the ~** faire tourner qn en bourrique
**runaway** I. *adj* ❶ (*out of control: train, car*) fou(folle); (*horse*) emballé(e) ❷ (*escaping: from an institution*) en fuite; (*from home*) fugueur(-euse) ❸ (*enormous: success*) immense; (*inflation*) galopant(e) II. *n* fugueur, -euse *m, f*; (*from prison*) fugitif, -ive *m, f*
**rundown** I. *n* (*report, summary*) résumé *m* II. *adj* ❶ (*dilapidated*) décrépit(e); (*facilities*) défectueux(-euse) ❷ (*worn out*) à bout
**rung** [rʌŋ] I. *pp of* **ring** II. *n* ❶ (*ladder step*) échelon *m* ❷ *fig* (*level*) niveau *m*
**run-in** *n inf* dispute *f*
**runner** ['rʌn·ər] *n* ❶ (*person that runs*) coureur, -euse *m, f* ❷ (*racing horse*) cheval *m* partant ❸ (*messenger*) messager *m* ❹ (*smuggler*) trafiquant(e) *m(f)* ❺ (*blade of skate*) patin *m* ❻ (*rod to slide on*) glissière *f* ❼ BOT rejeton *m* ❽ (*long rug*) tapis *m*
**runner-up** <runners-up> *n* second(e) gagnant(e) *m(f)*
**running** I. *n* ❶ (*action of a runner*) course *f* ❷ (*operation*) fonctionnement *m;* **the day-to-day ~ of the business** l'organisation *f* quotidienne d'une

**R**

compagnie ▸ **to be in/out of the ~** être/ne pas être dans la course **II.** *adj* ❶ (*consecutive*) de suite ❷ (*ongoing*) permanent(e); (*commentary*) simultané(e) ❸ (*operating*) en marche ❹ (*flowing*) courant(e)

**running costs** *npl* coûts *mpl* d'entretien

**runny** ['rʌn·i] <-ier, -iest> *adj* coulant(e); (*nose*) qui coule; (*sauce*) liquide

**runoff** *n* ❶ (*rainfall*) eaux *fpl* de ruissellement ❷ (*second election*) deuxième tour *m* ❸ (*extra competition*) épreuve supplémentaire pour départager des ex-æquo

**run-up** *n* ❶ (*running approach*) course *f* ❷ (*sudden increase: in price, demand, value*) flambée *f* ❸ (*prelude, final stage*) dernière étape *f*; **the ~ to sth** le compte à rebours avant qc

**runway** *n* piste *f*

**rupture** ['rʌp·tʃər] **I.** *n* ❶ (*act of bursting*) rupture *f* ❷ (*hernia*) hernie *f* **II.** *vt* rompre **III.** *vi* se rompre; (*blood vessel*) éclater

**rural** ['rʊr·əl] *adj* rural(e)

**rush¹** [rʌʃ] *n* BOT jonc *m*

**rush²** [rʌʃ] **I.** *n* ❶ (*hurry*) précipitation *f*; **to be in a ~** être pressé; **to leave in a ~** partir précipitamment ❷ (*charge, attack*) ruée *f* ❸ (*surge*) afflux *m*; (*of air*) bouffée *f*; (*of dizziness*) soudaine vague *f*; **~ of excitement** montée *f* d'adrénaline ❹ (*mass migration*) ruée *f*; **gold ~** ruée vers l'or ❺ SPORTS course *f* **II.** *vi* ❶ (*hurry*) se précipiter; **to ~ in/out** se ruer dedans/dehors; **to ~ around** courir dans tous les sens; **to ~**

up to sb arriver en courant vers qn ❷ (*do prematurely*) **to ~ into sth** se lancer aveuglément dans qc; **to ~ to conclusions** tirer des conclusions trop vite ❸ SPORTS attaquer **III.** *vt* ❶ (*hurry*) faire à la hâte ❷ (*transport*) emmener d'urgence ❸ (*pressure: person*) bousculer; (*job*) faire très vite; **to ~ sb into doing sth** pousser qn à faire qc ❹ (*attack*) prendre d'assaut; (*person*) attaquer

**rush hour** *n* heure *f* de pointe

**rush job** *n* travail *m* urgent

**Russia** ['rʌʃ·ə] *n* la Russie

**Russian I.** *adj* russe **II.** *n* ❶ (*person*) Russe *mf* ❷ LING russe *m*; *s.a.* **English**

**rust** [rʌst] **I.** *n* ❶ (*corrosion*) rouille *f* ❷ (*color*) couleur *f* rouille **II.** *vi* **to ~ (away/through)** se rouiller **III.** *vt* rouiller

**rust-colored** *adj* (de couleur) rouille *inv*; (*hair*) roux

**rustler** *n* (*cattle thief*) voleur, -euse *m, f* de bétail

**rusty** ['rʌs·ti] <-ier, -iest> *adj* rouillé(e)

**rut** [rʌt] *n* ❶ (*track*) sillon *m* ❷ ZOOL rut *m* ▸ **to be (stuck) in/get out of a ~** s'enfoncer dans le/sortir du train-train

**ruthless** ['ruθ·ləs] *adj* sans pitié; (*ambition*) ravageur(-euse); (*behavior*) cruel(le); (*decision, dictator, plan*) impitoyable; **to be ~ in doing sth** (*cruel*) faire qc de manière cruelle; (*severe*) être sans pitié pour faire qc

**RV** [ar·'vi] *n abbr of* **recreational vehicle** camping-car *m*

**rye** [raɪ] *n* seigle *m*

# Ss

**S, s** [ɛs] <-'s> *n* s *m*, S *m inv*; **~ as in Sierra** s comme Suzanne

**S I.** *n* ❶ *abbr of* **south** S *m* ❷ *abbr of* **satisfactory II.** *adj* ❶ *abbr of* **south, southern** sud *inv* ❷ *abbr of* **small** S

**s** *inv abbr of* **second** s *f*

**sabbatical** [sə-'bæt̬·ɪ·kəl] **I.** *n* congé *m* sabbatique; **to be on ~** être en congé sabbatique **II.** *adj* sabbatique

**sabotage** ['sæb·ə·taʒ] **I.** *n* sabotage *m* **II.** *vt* saboter

**sachet** [sæ-'ʃeɪ] *n* sachet *m*

**sack¹** [sæk] **I.** *n* ❶ (*bag*) sac *m* ❷ *inf* (*bed*) **to hit the ~** se pieuter ❸ *sl* (*dismissal from job*) **to get the ~** se faire virer; **to give sb the ~** virer qn **II.** *vt* virer

**sack²** [sæk] **I.** *n* (*pillaging*) pillage *m* **II.** *vt* mettre à sac

**sacred** ['seɪ·krɪd] *adj* sacré(e)

**sacrifice** ['sæk·rə·faɪs] **I.** *n a. fig* sacrifice *m* ▸ **to make the ultimate ~** faire le sacrifice suprême **II.** *vt a. fig* sacrifier; **to ~ sb to the gods** donner qn en sacrifice aux dieux **III.** *vi* **to ~ to sb** sacrifier à qn

**sad** [sæd] *adj* ❶ (*unhappy, sorrowful*) triste; **to make sb ~** attrister qn ❷ (*deplorable, shameful*) navrant(e) ▸ **~ to say** malheureusement

**sadden** ['sæd·ən] *vt* attrister

**saddle** ['sæd·l] **I.** *n a.* CULIN selle *f* ▸ **to be in the ~** (*riding*) être en selle; (*in charge*) tenir les rênes **II.** *vt* ❶ (*put saddle on: horse*) seller ❷ *inf* (*burden*) **to ~ sb with sth** mettre qc sur les bras de qn; **to ~ oneself with debts** s'encombrer de dettes

**sadness** *n* tristesse *f*

**safari** [sə-'fɑr·i] *n* safari *m*

**safe** [seɪf] **I.** *adj* ❶ (*out of danger*) en sécurité; **to not be ~** être en danger; **to be ~ from sb/sth** être protégé contre qn/qc ❷ (*not harmed: person*) hors de danger; (*object*) intact(e); **~ and sound** sain et sauf ❸ (*secure*) sûr(e); **to feel ~**

se sentir en sécurité; **to keep sth in a ~ place** conserver qc dans un lieu sûr ❹ (*not dangerous: streets*) sûr(e); (*roof, building*) solide; (*meat, product*) sans danger; **to not be ~** être dangereux ❺ (*not taking risks, not risky*) sûr(e); (*choice, driver*) prudent(e); (*method, contraceptive*) sans risque; **to not be ~** être dangereux; **it is ~ to say that ...** je peux dire sans prendre de risque que ...; **to be ~ with sb** ne rien risquer avec qn; **it is a ~ bet that ...** il y a fort à parier que ... ▸ **to be on the ~ side** par précaution; **to play it ~** ne pas prendre de risques **II.** *n* coffre-fort *m*

**safecracker** *n* perceur *m* de coffres-forts

**safe deposit box** *n* coffre *m*

**safe house** *n* ❶ (*for spies, terrorists*) lieu *m* sûr ❷ (*for battered women*) foyer *m* pour femmes battues

**safekeeping** *n* sécurité *f*; **in ~** en lieu sûr; **to give sth to sb for ~** confier qc à la garde de qn

**safe sex** *n* rapports *mpl* sexuels protégés

**safety** ['seɪf·ti] *n* sécurité *f*; **to be concerned for sb's ~** s'inquiéter du sort de qn ▸ **there's ~ in numbers** *prov* plus on est nombreux, moins on court de risques

**safety belt** *n* ceinture *f* de sécurité

**safety lock** *n* verrouillage *m* de sécurité

**safety measures** *npl* mesures *fpl* de sécurité

**safety pin** *n* épingle *f* de nourrice

**safety regulations** *npl* réglementation *f* sur la sécurité

**Sagittarius** [ˌsædʒ·ə·'ter·i·əs] *n no art* Sagittaire *m; s.a.* **Aquarius**

**said** [sed] **I.** *pp, pt of* **say II.** *adj inv* cité(e)

**sail** [seɪl] **I.** *n* ❶ (*fabric*) voile *f* ❷ (*voyage*) traversée *f* (en bateau); **to set ~** prendre la mer ❸ (*windmill blade*) aile *f* **II.** *vi* ❶ (*travel on sailboat*) faire

**S**

de la voile ② (*ship, tanker*) naviguer; **to ~ around the world** faire le tour du monde en voile ③ (*start voyage*) prendre la mer ④ (*move smoothly*) voler; **to ~ by** [*o* past] passer ⑤ *inf* (*attack*) **to ~ into sb** attaquer qn ⑥ (*do easily*) **to ~ through sth** réussir qc sans problèmes **III.** *vt* ① (*navigate*) manœuvrer; (*ship*) commander ② (*travel by ship: seas*) parcourir

**sailboard** *n* planche *f* à voile
**sailboat** *n* voilier *m*
**sailing** *n* ① (*traveling on water*) navigation *f* ② (*sport*) voile *f* ③ (*departure from port*) appareillage *m*
**sailor** *n* marin *m*
**saint** [seɪnt] *n a. fig* saint(e) *m(f)*; **Saint Peter** Saint-Pierre *m*; **to be no ~** ne pas être un saint
**sake¹** [seɪk] *n* ① (*purpose*) **for the ~ of sth** [*o* for sth's ~] pour qc; **for the ~ of peace** pour avoir la paix ② (*benefit*) **for the ~ of sb** [*o* for sb's ~] pour le bien de qn ▶ **for God's** [*o* **heaven's**] ~ *pej, inf* pour l'amour de Dieu
**sake²** ['sɑ·ki], **saki** *n* (*Japanese rice drink*) saké *m*
**salad** ['sæl·əd] *n* salade *f*
**salad dressing** *n* vinaigrette *f*; (*creamy*) sauce *f* pour salade
**salami** [sə·'lɑ·mi] *n* salami *m*
**salaried** *adj* salarié(e); (*job*) rémunéré(e); **a ~ employee** un salarié; **~ staff** salariés *mpl*
**salary** ['sæl·ə·ri] *n* salaire *m*
**salary cap** *n* plafond *m* des salaires
**sale** [seɪl] *n* ① (*act of selling*) vente *f*; **for ~** à vendre, à remettre *Belgique*; **on ~** en vente ② *pl* (*amount sold*) chiffre *m* d'affaires ③ (*special selling event*) soldes *mpl*
**sale price** *n* prix *m* de vente
**sales associate** *n* conseiller, -ère *m, f* clientèle
**salesclerk** *n* vendeur, -euse *m, f*
**sales department** *n* service *m* des ventes
**salesgirl** *a. pej s.* **saleslady**
**saleslady** *n* vendeuse *f*

**salesman** *n* ① (*in shop*) vendeur *m* ② (*representative*) représentant *m*
**salesperson** *n* ① (*in shop*) vendeur, -euse *m, f* ② (*representative*) représentant(e) *m(f)*
**sales receipt** *n* reçu *m*
**saleswoman** *n* ① (*in shop*) vendeuse *f* ② (*representative*) représentante *f*
**saliva** [sə·'laɪ·və] *n* salive *f*
**salmon** ['sæm·ən] *n* saumon *m*
**salmonella** [ˌsæl·mə·'nel·ə] *n* salmonelle *f*
**salmonella poisoning** *n* salmonellose *f*
**salon** [se·'lɑn] *n* salon *m*; **hair/beauty ~** salon de coiffure/beauté; **literary ~** salon littéraire
**saloon** [sə·'lun] *n* ① (*bar*) bar *m* ② HIST saloon *m*
**salt** [sɔlt] **I.** *n a. fig* sel *m* ▶ **to take sth with a grain of ~** ne pas prendre qc au pied de la lettre; **to rub ~ in the/sb's wound** remuer le couteau dans la plaie **II.** *vt* saler **III.** *adj* (*air, water*) salé(e); (*cod, pork, beef*) salé(e)
**salt-and-pepper** *adj* poivre et sel *inv*
**salt cellar** *n* salière *f*
**saltwater I.** *n* ① (*seawater*) eau *f* de mer ② (*water with salt*) eau *f* salée **II.** *adj* ① (*consisting of saltwater: lake*) d'eau salée ② (*living in seawater: fish*) d'eau de mer
**salty** *adj a. fig* salé(e)
**salvation** [sæl·'veɪ·ʃən] *n a.* REL salut *m*
**Salvation Army** *n* Armée *f* du Salut
**same** [seɪm] **I.** *adj, pron* même; **~ difference** c'est du pareil au même; **the ~ again** encore un(e) autre; **at the ~ time** au même moment; (**the**) **~ to you** vous de même ▶ **to be one and the ~** une seule et même chose; **by the ~ token** de même **II.** *adv* **to think/do the ~** penser/faire de même; **the ~ as** de la même façon que; **~ as usual** comme d'habitude
**sample** ['sæm·pl] **I.** *n* ① (*small representative unit*) échantillon *m*; MED prélèvement *m* ② (*music extract*) sample *m* **II.** *vt* ① (*try*) essayer; (*taste*)

goûter ❷ (*survey*) sonder ❸ MED prélever ❹ MUS sampler

**sanction** ['sæŋ(k)·f°n] **I.** *n* sanction *f* **II.** *vt* sanctionner

**sand** [sænd] **I.** *n* ❶ (*granular substance*) sable *m* ❷ *pl* (*large expanse of sand*) banc *m* de sable **II.** *vt* sabler **III.** *adj* de sable

**sandal** ['sæn·d°l] *n* sandale *f*

**sandbag I.** *n* sac *m* de sable **II.** <-gg-> *vt* renforcer avec des sacs de sable

**sandbank, sandbar** *n* banc *m* de sable

**sandbox** *n* bac *m* à sable

**sandcastle** *n* château *m* de sable

**sandpaper I.** *n* papier *m* de verre **II.** *vt* poncer

**sandpit** *n* sablière *f*

**sandwich** ['sæn(d)·wɪtʃ] **I.** <-es> *n* sandwich *m* **II.** *adj* en sandwich; **a ~ cookie** un biscuit fourré **III.** *vt* coincer; **to be ~ed** être pris en sandwich

**sandwich shop** *n* sandwicherie *f*

**sandy** <-ier, -iest> *adj* ❶ (*containing sand*) sableux(-euse) ❷ (*in texture*) de sable ❸ (*in color*) sable

**sang** [sæŋ] *pt of* **sing**

**sanitary** ['sæn·ɪ·ter·i] *adj* sanitaire; (*pad, towel*) hygiénique

**sanitation** [,sæn·ɪ·'ter·f°n] *n* hygiène *f*

**sank** [sæŋk] *pt of* **sink**

**Santa Claus** ['sæn·tə·,klɔz] *n* le père Noël

**sarcasm** ['sar·kæz·°m] *n* sarcasme *m*

**sarcastic** [sar·'kæs·tɪk] *adj* sarcastique

**sardine** [sar·'din] *n* sardine *f* ▸ **to be packed (in) like ~s** être serrés comme des sardines

**SARS** [saz] *n no art* MED *abbr of* **severe acute respiratory syndrome** SARS *m*

**SASE** *n abbr of* **self-addressed stamped envelope** enveloppe *f* (libellée) au nom et à l'adresse de l'expéditeur

**sassy** *adj* effronté(e)

**sat** [sæt] *pt, pp of* **sit**

**satchel** ['sætʃ·°l] *n* sacoche *f*

**satellite** ['sæt·°l·aɪt] **I.** *n* satellite *m* **II.** *adj* satellite

**satellite dish** *n* parabole *f*

**satire** ['sæt·aɪər] *n* satire *f*

**satisfaction** [,sæt·ɪs·'fæk·f°n] *n* ❶ (*state of being satisfied*) satisfaction *f* ❷ (*of a debt*) acquittement *m* ❸ (*compensation*) réparation *f*

**satisfactory** [,sæt·ɪs·'fæk·t°r·i] *adj* satisfaisant(e)

**satisfy** ['sæt·ɪs·faɪ] <-ie-> **I.** *vt* ❶ (*meet desires: hunger, curiosity, need*) satisfaire ❷ (*fulfill: demand, requirement, condition*) satisfaire à ❸ (*convince*) convaincre; **to be satisfied as to sth** être convaincu de qc ❹ (*pay off: debt*) s'acquitter de **II.** *vi* donner satisfaction

**satisfying** *adj* satisfaisant(e)

**saturate** ['sætʃ·ər·eɪt] *vt* ❶ (*soak*) imprégner; **to be ~d with sth** être imprégné de qc ❷ (*fill to capacity*) saturer; **to be ~d with sth** être saturé de qc

**Saturday** ['sæt·ər·deɪ] *n* samedi *m*; *s.a.* **Friday**

**sauce** [sɔs] *n* ❶ (*liquid*) sauce *f* ❷ *inf* (*impudence, backtalk*) culot *m*

**sauceboat** *n* saucière *f*

**saucepan** *n* casserole *f*

**saucer** ['sɔ·sər] *n* soucoupe *f*, sous-tasse *f Belgique, Suisse*

**saucy** ['sɔ·si] <-ier, -iest> *adj inf* (*impudent*) culotté(e)

**Saudi Arabia** [,sɑʊ·di·ə·'reɪ·bi·ə] *n* l'Arabie *f* saoudite

**Saudi (Arabian) I.** *adj* saoudien(ne) **II.** *n* Saoudien(ne) *m(f)*

**sauna** ['sɑʊ·nə] *n* sauna *m*

**sausage** ['sɔ·sɪdʒ] *n* saucisse *f*; (*dried*) saucisson *m*

**sausage meat** *n* chair *f* à saucisse

**sausage roll** *n* ≈ friand *m*

**save**[1] [seɪv] **I.** *vt* ❶ (*rescue*) sauver; **to ~ sb from sth** protéger qn de qc; **to ~ sb from falling** empêcher qn de tomber ❷ (*reserve*) réserver; **to ~ sb a seat/ spot** garder un siège/une place pour qn ❸ (*keep for future use*) mettre de côté; (*money*) épargner ❹ (*collect: coins, stamps*) collectionner ❺ (*not waste*) économiser; **to ~ one's strength** ménager ses forces; **to ~ time** gagner du temps ❻ (*prevent from doing*) épargner

S

**7** COMPUT sauvegarder; **to ~ sth as ...** enregistrer qc sous ... **8** SPORTS (*a goal*) arrêter ► **to ~ one's breath** économiser sa salive **II.** *vi* économiser **III.** *n* SPORTS arrêt *m*

**save²** [seɪv] **I.** *prep* excepté; **all ~ the youngest** tous à l'exception du plus jeune **II.** *conj form* ~ **that ...** excepté que ...

**saving I.** *n* **1** (*economy*) économie *f* **2** *pl* (*saved money*) économies *fpl* **II.** *prep* sauf

**savings account** *n* compte *m* (d')épargne

**savings bank** *n* caisse *f* d'épargne

**savory I.** *adj* **1** (*appetizing*) savoureux(-euse) **2** (*salty*) salé(e) **3** (*spicy*) épicé(e) **4** (*socially acceptable*) recommandable **II.** *n* canapé *m*

**saw¹** [sɔ] *pt of* **see**

**saw²** [sɔ] **I.** *n* scie *f* **II.** *vt, vi* <-ed, sawn *o* -ed> scier

**saw³** [sɔ] *n* (*trite saying*) dicton *m*

**sawdust** ['sɔ·dʌst] *n* sciure *f*

**sawn** [sɔn] *pp of* **saw**

**saxophone** ['sæk·sə·foʊn] *n* saxophone *m*

**say** [seɪ] **I.** <said, said> *vt* **1** (*express*) dire; **to ~ sth about sb/sth** dire qc à propos de qn/qc; **to have nothing to ~ to sb** n'avoir rien à dire à qn; (**let's**) **~ ...** disons que ... **2** (*show: watch, sign, instructions*) indiquer **3** (*recite: poem, prayer*) réciter; **to ~ grace** dire ses grâces ► **to ~ the least** c'est le moins que l'on puisse dire (*subj*); **~ no more!** n'en dites pas davantage!; **to ~ nothing of sth** sans parler de qc; **you can ~ that again!** *sl* tu veux répéter!; **you don't ~!** c'est pas possible! **II.** <said, said> *vi* dire ► **that is to ~** c'est-à-dire; **I'll ~!** *inf* et comment! **III.** *n* parole *f;* **to have one's ~** dire son mot; **to have a ~ in sth** avoir son mot à dire dans qc

**saying** *n* **1** (*act of saying*) adage *m;* **it goes without ~** cela va sans dire **2** (*proverb*) proverbe *m;* **as the ~ goes**

comme dit le proverbe; (*what people say*) comme on dit

**SC** *n abbr of* **South Carolina**

**scab** [skæb] *n* **1** (*on a wound*) croûte *f* **2** BOT teigne *f* **3** ZOOL gale *f* **4** *pej* (*strikebreaker*) jaune *mf*

**scaffolding** *n* échafaudage *m*

**scald** [skɔld] **I.** *vt* **1** (*burn*) ébouillanter **2** (*heat*) faire chauffer (sans bouillir) **II.** *n* MED brûlure *f*

**scalding** *adj* bouillant(e); **~ hot** brûlant(e)

**scale¹** [skeɪl] **I.** *n* **1** ZOOL écaille *f* **2** (*flake of skin*) squame *f* **3** (*mineral coating*) calcaire *m;* (*of a boiler, coffee machine, iron*) tartre *m* **II.** *vt* détartrer

**scale²** [skeɪl] **I.** *n* **1** (*system of gradations*) *a.* ECON échelle *f;* (*of thermometer*) graduation *f;* **a sliding ~** une échelle mobile **2** (*for weighing*) balance *f;* **a bathroom ~** un pèse-personne **3** (*great size*) étendue *f;* **advantages of ~** les avantages *mpl* du commerce de grande envergure **4** MUS gamme *f* ► **to tip the ~s** faire pencher la balance **II.** *vt* escalader **III.** *vi* ECON être en (phase d')expansion

♦ **scale down I.** *vt* réduire **II.** *vi* ECON être en perte de vitesse

♦ **scale up I.** *vt* augmenter **II.** *vi* être en augmentation

**scalp** [skælp] **I.** *n* **1** (*on head*) cuir *m* chevelu **2** HIST scalp *m* **3** *fig* **to take a ~** remporter une victoire écrasante **II.** *vt* **1** HIST (*cut off scalp*) scalper **2** *inf* (*resell at inflated price*) revendre au marché noir **3** *iron, inf* (*defeat*) filer une déculottée

**scalpel** ['skæl·pəl] *n* MED scalpel *m*

**scalper** ['skælp·ər] *n* revendeur, -euse *m, f* au marché noir

**scaly** ['skeɪ·li] <-ier, -iest> *adj* écailleux(-euse)

**scam** [skæm] *n inf* arnaque *f*

**scandal** ['skæn·dᵊl] *n* **1** (*shocking incident*) scandale *m* **2** (*gossip*) ragot *m;* **to spread ~** colporter une rumeur

**scandalous** *adv* **1** (*shocking*) scan-

daleux(-euse) ②(*disgraceful*) hon-
teux(-euse)
**Scandinavia** [ˌskæn·dɪ·'neɪ·vi·ə] *n* la
Scandinavie
**Scandinavian I.** *adj* scandinave **II.** *n*
Scandinave *mf*
**scapegoat** ['skeɪp·goʊt] *n* bouc *m*
émissaire
**scar** [skar] **I.** *n* ①MED (*mark on skin*) cicatrice *f*; (*from a blade*) balafre *f*; ~ **tissue** tissu *m* cicatriciel ②(*mark of damage*) stigmate *m* ③PSYCH (*emotional,
psychological*) traumatisme *m* ④GEO
écueil *m* **II.**<-rr-> *vt* MED **to be ~red
by sth** garder les traces de qc; **to be
~red for life** être marqué à vie
**III.**<-rr-> *vi* **to ~ (over)** se cicatriser
**scarcely** *adv* ①(*barely*) à peine ②(*certainly not*) pas du tout
**scare** [sker] **I.** *vt* effrayer; **to ~ sb into/
out of doing sth** forcer qn à faire/à ne
pas faire qc sous la menace; **to ~ the
life** [*o inf* **shit**] **out of sb** terroriser qn
**II.** *vi* prendre peur **III.** *n* ①(*sudden
fright*) frayeur *f* ②(*public panic*) panique *f*; **bomb ~** alerte *f* à la bombe
**scarecrow** ['sker·kroʊ] *n* épouvantail *m*
**scarf¹** [skarf] <scarves *o* -s> *n*
①(*headscarf*) foulard *m* ②(*protecting
from cold*) écharpe *f*
**scarf²** [skarf] *vt sl* bouffer; **to ~ sth
(down/up)** (tout) bouffer qc
**scarlet** ['skar·lət] **I.** *n* écarlate *f* **II.** *adj*
écarlate
**scarlet fever** *n* MED scarlatine *f*
**scary** ['sker·i] <-ier, -iest> *adj* ef-
frayant(e)
**scattered** *adj* ①(*strewn about*) éparpil-
lé(e) ②(*widely separated*) dispersé(e)
③(*sporadic*) rare
**scavenger** *n* ZOOL charognard(e) *m(f)*
**scene** [sin] *n* ①THEAT, CINE *a. fig* scène *f*;
**the ~ is set in France** l'action se déroule en France ②(*place*) lieu *m*; (*of
operations*) théâtre *m*; **on the ~** sur les
lieux ③(*view*) vue *f* ④THEAT (*scenery
set*) décor *m* ⑤(*milieu, area*) scène *f*;
**to be/not be sb's ~** *inf* être/ne pas
être le genre de qn ⑥(*fuss*) scène *f* ▶ **to**

**be/do sth behind the ~s** être/faire qc
dans les/en coulisses
**scenery** ['si·nə·ri] *n* ①(*landscape*) paysage *m* ②THEAT, CINE décor *m* ▶ **a change of ~** un changement de décor
**scenic** ['si·nɪk] *adj* ①(*picturesque: landscape*) pittoresque; (*route*) panoramique ②THEAT de scène
**scent** [sent] **I.** *n* ①(*aroma*) odeur *f*
②(*perfume*) parfum *m* ③(*animal's
mark*) marque *f* olfactive ▶ **to throw
sb off the ~** lancer qn sur une fausse
piste **II.** *vt* ①(*smell*) flairer ②(*detect*)
pressentir ③(*apply perfume*) parfumer
**sceptical** *adj s.* **skeptical**
**schedule** ['skedʒ·ul] **I.** *n* ①(*timetable*)
emploi *m* du temps; (*of a bus, train*) horaire *m*; **flight ~** plan *m* de vol ②(*plan*)
**according to ~** selon les prévisions *fpl*
③FIN programme *m* **II.** *vt* ①(*plan*) prévoir ②(*arrange*) programmer
**scheduled** *adj* prévu(e); (*flight, service*)
régulier(-ère)
**schizophrenic I.** *adj* PSYCH, MED ①(*person*) schizophrène ②(*behavior*) schi-
zoïde **II.** *n* PSYCH, MED schizophrène *mf*
**scholar** ['ska·lər] *n* UNIV ①(*academic*)
universitaire *mf* ②(*educated person*)
érudit(e) *m(f)* ③(*holder of scholarship*) boursier, -ère *m, f*
**scholarship** *n* ①(*academic achievement*) érudition *f* ②(*financial award*)
bourse *f*
**scholastic** [skə·'læs·tɪk] *adj* scolaire
**school¹** [skul] **I.** *n* ①(*institution*) école *f* ②(*premises of school*) école *f*
③(*school session*) cours *m* ④ I *sing/
pl vb* (*all students and staff*) école *f*; **the
whole ~** toute l'école ⑤(*college, academy*) école *f* ⑥(*division of university*)
année *f* ⑦ART, SOCIOL, PHILOS école *f*
**II.** *vt* dresser **III.** *adj* scolaire
**school²** [skul] *n* (*of fish*) banc *m*
**schoolboy** *n* élève *m*; (*of elementary
age*) écolier *m*; (*up to age 16*) collé-
gien *m*; (*from grades 7 through 12*) ly-
céen *m*
**schoolchild** <-ren> *n* écolier, -ère *m, f*
**school district** *n* secteur *m* scolaire

S

**schoolgirl** n élève f; (of elementary age) écolière f; (up to age 16) collégienne f; (from grades 7 through 12) lycéenne f

**schoolmaster** n maître m d'école

**schoolmate** n camarade mf de classe

**schoolroom** n salle f de classe

**schoolteacher** n enseignant(e) m(f)

**science** [saɪən(t)s] I. n science f II. adj scientifique

**science fiction** I. n LIT, CINE science-fiction f II. adj de science-fiction

**scientific** [ˌsaɪən·ˈtɪ·fɪk] adj scientifique

**scientist** [ˈsaɪən·tɪst] n scientifique mf

**scissors** [ˈsɪz·ərz] npl ❶(tool) ciseaux mpl ❷SPORTS ~ **kick** ciseau m

**scold** [skoʊld] vt gronder

**scone** [skoʊn] n petit pain sucré servi avec du beurre

**scoop** [skup] I. n ❶(food utensil) cuillère f; **measuring ~** mesure f ❷(amount held by scoop) mesure f; (of ice-cream) boule f ❸ inf (piece of news) exclusivité f II. vt ❶(pick up) a. fig to ~ (up) sth ramasser qc (à la pelle/à la cuillère) ❷(make a hole) enlever; to ~ sth out creuser ❸(measure) doser ❹PUBL, TV, RADIO présenter en exclusivité

**scooter** [ˈsku·tər] n ❶(child's toy) trottinette f ❷(motorcycle) scooter m

**score** [skɔr] I. n SPORTS score m II. vt ❶SPORTS (basket, goal) mettre; (points) marquer ❷inf (get, buy) dégoter III. vi SPORTS marquer un point

**scorekeeper** n marqueur, -euse m, f

**scorer** n ❶(in soccer) tireur, -euse m, f; (in basketball) marqueur, -euse m, f ❷s. **scorekeeper**

**Scorpio** [ˈskɔr·pi·oʊ] n Scorpion m; s.a. **Aquarius**

**scorpion** [ˈskɔr·pi·ən] n scorpion m

**Scot** [skat] I. adj écossais(e); ~s **pine** pin m sylvestre II. n (person) Écossais m

**Scotch** [skatʃ] I. n scotch m II. adj écossais(e)

**Scotch tape®** n Scotch® m

**Scotland** [ˈskat·lənd] n l'Écosse f

**Scotsman** <-men> n Écossais m

**Scotswoman** <-women> n Écossaise f

**Scottish** [ˈska·tɪʃ] I. adj écossais(e) II. n pl **the** ~ les Écossais mpl

**scouring pad** n éponge f métallique

**scramble** [ˈskræm·bl] I.<-ling> vi ❶(climb) grimper; **to ~ up/down a hill** escalader/descendre une pente; **to ~ through** se frayer un passage ❷(rush) se précipiter; **to ~ for sth** se ruer vers qc; **to ~ up a ladder** monter une échelle à toute vitesse ❸(struggle) **to ~ for sth** se battre pour qc II.<-ling> vt (eggs) brouiller III. n ❶(climbing) escalade f ❷(rush, struggle) bousculade f; **the ~ for the door** la ruée vers la porte

**scrambled eggs** n œufs mpl brouillés

**scrap¹** [skræp] I. n ❶(small piece) morceau m; (of paper, cloth) bout m; (of information) bribe f; **not a ~ of evidence** pas la moindre preuve ❷pl (leftovers) restes mpl ❸(metal) ferraille f II.<-pp-> vt ❶(get rid of) se débarrasser de ❷fig (plan) abandonner ❸(use for scrap metal) apporter à la casse

**scrap²** [skræp] I. n inf (fight) empoignade f II.<-pp-> vi s'empoigner; **to ~ over sth with sb** s'empoigner pour qc avec qn

**scrape** [skreɪp] I. vt gratter; (one's shoes) frotter; (one's knee) s'écorcher; (car) érafler ▸ **to ~ (together) a living** s'en sortir tout juste II. vi ❶(make scraping sound) grincer ❷(scratch) gratter ❸(rub against) frotter III. n ❶(sound) grincement m ❷(act of scraping) grattement m ❸(graze on skin) égratignure f

**scrapheap** n tas m de ferraille

**scratch** [skrætʃ] I. n ❶(cut on skin) égratignure f, griffe f Belgique ❷(beginning state) début m; **to start (over) from ~** (tout) recommencer depuis le début II. adj improvisé(e) III. vt ❶(cut slightly) égratigner ❷(relieve itch) gratter ❸(erase, remove) effacer; inf (cancel) annuler ❹(write hastily) griffonner ▸ **to ~ the surface of sth** effleurer qc

**IV.** *vi* ❶ (*scrape surface*) gratter ❷ (*in billiards*) blouser une boule

**scratch paper** *n* (feuille *f* de) brouillon *m*

**scratch ticket** *n* carte *f* à gratter

**scratchy** <-ier, -iest> *adj* ❶ (*with scratches: record*) rayé(e) ❷ (*irritating to skin*) irritant(e)

**scrawl** [skrɔːl] **I.** *vt, vi* gribouiller **II.** *n* gribouillage *m*

**scream** [skriːm] **I.** *n* ❶ (*cry*) hurlement *m* ❷ (*of engine*) crissement *m* ❸ *inf* (*something funny*) grosse blague *f*; **to be a ~** être à mourir de rire **II.** *vi* hurler; **to ~ for help** crier à l'aide; **to ~ about sth** se mettre en rage à cause de qc **III.** *vt* hurler; **to ~ one's head off** *inf* s'époumoner

**screen** [skriːn] **I.** *n* ❶ TV, COMPUT écran *m* ❷ (*for privacy*) cloison *f*; (*decorative*) paravent *m*; (*for protection*) écran *m* ❸ *fig* (*of troops*) camouflage *m* ❹ (*for window*) moustiquaire *f* ❺ (*sieve*) passoire *f* **II.** *vt* ❶ (*hide*) cacher; **to ~ sth from view** dissimuler qc ❷ (*protect*) protéger ❸ (*examine*) examiner; **to ~ one's calls** filtrer les appels ❹ TV passer à l'écran; CINE projeter ❺ (*put through sieve*) passer à la passoire

◆ **screen off** *vt* cloisonner

**screening** *n* ❶ CINE projection *f* ❷ TV diffusion *f* ❸ (*test*) *a.* MED examen *m*

**screen saver** *n* économiseur *m* d'écran

**screenwriter** *n* scénariste *mf*

**screw** [skruː] **I.** *n* ❶ (*pin*) vis *f* ❷ (*turn*) rotation *f*; **to give sth a ~** (*with fingers*) tourner qc; (*with screwdriver*) visser qc ❸ (*propeller*) hélice *f* ▸ **to have a ~ <u>loose</u>** *inf* ne pas tourner rond **II.** *vt* ❶ (*fasten*) visser; (*by twisting*) serrer ❷ *inf* (*cheat*) entuber ❸ *vulg* baiser ▸ **to have one's <u>head</u> ~ed on right** *inf* avoir la tête bien sur les épaules **III.** *vi* ❶ (*move in curve*) se visser ❷ *vulg* baiser

◆ **screw around** *vi* ❶ *sl* (*act stupidly*) glandouiller ❷ *vulg* (*be sexually promiscuous*) coucher à droite à gauche

◆ **screw down** *vt* visser

◆ **screw off I.** *vt* dévisser **II.** *vi* se dévisser

◆ **screw up I.** *vt inf* (*mess up*) foutre en l'air **II.** *vi* se visser

**screwdriver** *n* tournevis *m*

**screw top** *n* fermeture *f* à vis

**script** [skrɪpt] **I.** *n* ❶ (*written text: of film*) script *m*; (*of play*) texte *m* ❷ (*style of writing*) script *m* ❸ COMPUT script *m* **II.** *vt* écrire le script de

**scroll bar** *n* COMPUT barre *f* de défilement

**scrounge** [skraʊndʒ] *inf* **I.** *vt* **to ~ sth off sb** taper qc à qn **II.** *vi* **to ~ off sb** taxer qn **III.** *n pej* resquille *f*

**scrub¹** [skrʌb] <-bb-> **I.** *vt* ❶ (*clean by rubbing*) frotter ❷ *sl* (*cancel*) rayer **II.** *vi* frotter **III.** *n* **to give sth a (good) ~** astiquer qc

**scrub²** [skrʌb] *n* ❶ (*short trees, bushes*) buissons *mpl* ❷ (*area covered with bushes*) broussaille *f*

**scrubbing brush, scrub brush** *n* brosse *f*

**scruffy** <-ier, -iest> *adj* mal entretenu(e)

**scuba diving** *n* plongée *f*

**scuffle** ['skʌf·l] **I.** *n* bagarre *f*, margaille *f* *Belgique* **II.** *vi* se bagarrer

**sculpt** [skʌlpt] *vt, vi* sculpter

**sculptor** *n* sculpteur, -euse *m, f*

**sculpture** ['skʌlp·tʃər] **I.** *n* sculpture *f* **II.** *vt, vi s.* **sculpt**

**scum** [skʌm] *n* ❶ (*on liquid*) mousse *f* ❷ *fig, pej* (*worthless people*) rebut *m*

**scythe** [saɪð] **I.** *n* faux *f* **II.** *vt* faucher

**SD** *n abbr of* **South Dakota**

**sea** [siː] *n a. fig* mer *f*; **to be at ~** être au large; **by ~** par voie maritime; **the open ~** le large

**seacoast** *n* côte *f*

**seafood** *n* fruits *mpl* de mer

**seafront** *n sing* front *m* de mer

**seagull** *n* mouette *f*

**seal¹** [siːl] *n* phoque *m*

**seal²** [siːl] **I.** *n* ❶ (*wax mark*) sceau *m* ❷ (*stamp*) cachet *m* ❸ (*to prevent opening*) cachet *m*; (*on door*) fermoir *m* ❹ (*airtight or watertight joint*) joint *m* ▸ **sb's ~ of <u>approval</u>** l'approba-

S

tion f de qn **II.** vt ❶ (put seal on) cacheter ❷ (make airtight, watertight) colmater ❸ (close: border, port) fermer ❹ (finalize: deal, agreement) conclure
◆ **seal off** vi sceller

**sea level** n niveau m de la mer

**sea lion** n otarie f

**seam** [siːm] **I.** n ❶ (in fabric) couture f; (hem) ourlet m ❷ (junction) jointure f; (welded) soudure f ❸ NAUT joint m ❹ (between rocks) veine f ▶ **to be bursting at the ~s** être plein à craquer **II.** vt (stitch together) coudre

**seaport** n port m maritime

**search** [sɜːtʃ] **I.** <-es> n ❶ (act of searching) recherches fpl ❷ (by police: of a building) perquisition f; (of a person) fouille f ❸ COMPUT recherche f **II.** vi ❶ (make a search) faire des recherches; **to ~ for sb/sth** chercher qn/qc; **to ~ through sth** fouiller qc ❷ COMPUT effectuer une recherche **III.** vt ❶ (seek) chercher ❷ (look in) fouiller; (place, street) ratisser ❸ COMPUT rechercher; (directory, file) rechercher dans ❹ (examine carefully: conscience, heart) examiner; (face, memory) scruter ▶ **~ me!** inf (je n'en ai) pas la moindre idée!
◆ **search out** vt chercher

**search engine** n COMPUT moteur m de recherche

**search function** n COMPUT fonction f de recherche

**searchlight** n projecteur m

**search party** <-ies> n expédition f de secours

**search warrant** n mandat m de perquisition

**seashell** n coquillage m

**seashore** n ❶ (beach) plage f ❷ (land near sea) littoral m

**seasick** adj **to be ~** avoir le mal de mer

**seasickness** n mal m de mer

**seaside** n bord m de mer

**season** ['siːzən] **I.** n ❶ (period of year) saison f; **the holiday ~** la période des vacances ❷ (period of plenty) **asparagus/strawberry ~** saison f des asperges/fraises; **sth is in ~** c'est la saison de qc ❸ SPORTS saison f **II.** vt ❶ (add salt, pepper) assaisonner ❷ (dry out: wood) faire sécher **III.** vi (wood) sécher

**seasonal** adj ❶ (of time of year) saisonnier(-ère) ❷ (grown in a season) de saison

**seasoning** n ❶ (salt, pepper) assaisonnement m ❷ (herb, spice) condiment m ❸ (drying out) séchage m

**season ticket** n ❶ THEAT, SPORTS abonnement m ❷ AUTO carte f d'abonnement

**seat** [siːt] **I.** n ❶ (furniture) siège m; **to save a ~ for sb** garder une place à qn ❷ THEAT fauteuil m ❸ (sing (part: of a chair) siège m; (of slacks, pants) fond m ❹ (buttocks) fesses fpl ❺ POL siège m ❻ (location of government) **county ~** chef-lieu m ❼ (country residence) résidence f; **a country ~** un château ❽ (style of riding) assiette f ▶ **by the ~ of one's pants** par intuition **II.** vt ❶ (sit down) asseoir ❷ (offer a seat) placer ❸ (have enough seats for) **the hall ~s 250 guests** le hall peut contenir 250 invités à table

**seat belt** n ceinture f de sécurité

**seating** n capacité f d'accueil; **the restaurant has ~ for 60** le restaurant peut servir 60 couverts

**seating arrangements** npl plan m de table

**seaweed** n algues fpl

**seaworthy** adj (boat) en état de naviguer

**sec.** [sek] n abbr of **second** seconde f

**secluded** [sɪˈkluːd.ɪd] adj retiré(e)

**second**[1] ['sek.ənd] **I.** adj ❶ (after first) deuxième; **every ~ week/year** tous les quinze jours/deux ans ❷ (after winner) second(e) ❸ (in importance, size) deuxième; **to be ~ only to sb/sth** être juste derrière qn/qc; **to be ~ to none** être le meilleur ❹ (another: car, chance) deuxième; **to have ~ thoughts about sth** ne plus être sûr de qc **II.** n ❶ no art (second gear) seconde f ❷ pl (extra helping) supplément m; **anyone for ~s?** est-ce que qn en veut encore? ❸ (*flawed item*) article *m* de deuxième choix ❹ (*in a duel*) témoin *m* ❺ (*in boxing*) soigneur *m* III. *vt* (*support*) appuyer; I ~ **that** je suis d'accord IV. *adv* deuxième

**second²** ['sek·ᵊnd] *n* seconde *f*

**secondary** ['sek·ən·der·i] *adj* secondaire

**secondary school** *n* école d'enseignement secondaire, école *f* secondaire *Québec*

**second best** *adj* to settle for ~ se rabattre sur un deuxième choix

**second class** I. *n* deuxième classe *f* II. *adv* ❶ (*in second class: travel*) en deuxième classe ❷ (*by second-class mail: send*) en courrier ordinaire

**second-class** *adj* ❶ (*in second class: ticket, train car*) de deuxième classe ❷ (*inferior: service, treatment*) de deuxième rang

**second cousin** *n* cousin(e) *m(f)* au second degré

**second floor** *n* (*floor above ground*) premier étage *m*

**second-hand** I. *adj* ❶ (*clothes, shop*) d'occasion ❷ (*received indirectly: news*) de seconde main II. *adv* ❶ (*used: buy*) d'occasion ❷ (*from third party: hear*) d'un tiers

**second language** *n* seconde langue *f*

**secondly** *adv* deuxièmement

**second-rate** *adj* de deuxième rang

**secrecy** ['si·krə·si] *n* ❶ (*act*) secret *m;* **in ~ of** sth en secret ❷ (*characteristic*) discrétion *f*

**secret** ['si·krət] I. *n* secret *m; to make no ~ of* sth ne pas cacher qc II. *adj* ❶ (*known to few*) secret(-ète); **to keep** sth ~ **from** sb cacher qc à qn ❷ (*hidden: door*) dérobé(e)

**secretary** ['sek·rə·ter·i] <-ies> *n* ❶ (*office assistant*) secrétaire *mf* ❷ **company** ~ secrétaire *mf* général(e) ❸ (*head of government department*) **Secretary of State** secrétaire *mf* d'État

**secretary-general** <secretaries-general> *n* secrétaire *mf* général(e)

**secretive** ['si·krə·t̬ɪv] *adj* (*behavior*) secret(-ète); (*person*) cachottier(-ère)

**sect** [sekt] *n* secte *f*

**section** ['sek·ʃ°n] I. *n* ❶ (*part*) partie *f;* (*of a road, railroad*) tronçon *m;* (*of a document*) chapitre *m;* (*of an orange*) quartier *m;* (*of a newspaper*) pages *fpl* ❷ (*department*) service *m* ❸ MUS **the brass** ~ les cuivres *mpl* ❹ (*military unit*) groupe *m* ❺ (*surgical cut*) section *f* II. *vt* sectionner; **to be ~ed into subject areas** être divisé en domaines

**sector** ['sek·tər] *n* secteur *m*

**secure** [sɪ·ˈkjʊr] I. *adj* <-rer, -est *o* more ~, most ~> ❶ (*safe: base, ladder*) sûr(e); **financially** ~ sans risques financiers ❷ (*unworried*) en sécurité; ~ **in the knowledge that …** sûr que … ❸ (*guarded*) protégé(e) II. *vt* ❶ (*obtain: release, loan*) obtenir ❷ (*make safe: doors, windows*) bien fermer; (*position*) assurer; (*house*) protéger ❸ (*fasten: seatbelt*) attacher ❹ (*guarantee: loan*) garantir ❺ (*protect*) protéger

**security** [sɪ·ˈkjʊr·ə·t̬i] <-ies> *n* ❶ no art (*measures*) sécurité *f* ❷ no art (*personnel*) service *m* de sécurité ❸ (*safety*) sécurité *f* ❹ *sing* (*payment guarantee*) garantie *f* ❺ *pl* (*investments*) valeurs *fpl* (boursières)

**security blanket** *n* doudou *m*

**security guard** *n* gardien(ne) *m(f)*

**sedan** [sɪ·ˈdæn] *n* berline *f*

**sedative** ['sed·ə·t̬ɪv] I. *adj* sédatif(-ive) II. *n* sédatif *m*

**seduce** [sɪ·ˈdus] *vt* séduire; **to be ~d into doing sth** se laisser convaincre de faire qc

**seduction** [sɪ·ˈdʌk·ʃ°n] *n* ❶ (*persuasion into sex*) séduction *f* ❷ (*something seductive*) ~(**s**) charme *m*

**seductive** [sɪ·ˈdʌk·tɪv] *adj* ❶ (*sexy*) séducteur(-trice) ❷ (*attractive: argument*) séduisant(e)

**see¹** [si] *n* diocèse *m;* **the Holy See** le Saint-Siège

**see²** [si] <saw, seen> I. *vt* ❶ (*perceive with eyes*) voir ❷ (*watch: play, page,*

**S**

*sights*) voir ❸ (*view: house for sale*) voir ❹ (*meet socially*) voir; ~ **you!** *inf* à bientôt ❺ (*accompany*) raccompagner; **I'll ~ you to the door** je t'accompagne jusqu'à la porte ❻ (*have relationship with*) sortir avec ❼ (*understand*) voir; **to ~ reason** entendre raison ❽ (*envision: chance, possibility*) voir; **I saw it coming** je m'y attendais ❾ (*ensure*) **to ~ that …** s'assurer que … ▶ **I will ~ him in hell first** plutôt mourir; **to ~ the last of sb/sth** se débarrasser de qn/qc; **to ~ the light** (*understand*) comprendre; (*be converted*) avoir une révélation II. *vi a. fig* voir; **to ~ into the future** lire dans l'avenir; **as far as the eye can ~** à perte de vue; **wait and ~** on verra; **as far as I can ~** d'après ce que je comprends ▶ **to not ~ eye to eye with sb** ne pas être d'accord avec qn; **~ing is believing** *prov* il faut le voir pour le croire *prov*

◆ **see about** *vt infs*'occuper de ▶ **we'll soon ~ that!** c'est ce qu'on verra!

◆ **see in** I. *vi* voir à l'intérieur II. *vt* ❶ (*perceive*) trouver ❷ (*welcome*) faire entrer

◆ **see off** *vt* **to see sb off** accompagner qn

◆ **see out** *vt* ❶ (*escort to door*) accompagner; **I'll see myself out** inutile de me raccompagner ❷ (*last until end of*) **to ~ the winter** passer l'hiver

◆ **see through** *vt* ❶ (*look through*) voir à travers ❷ (*not be deceived by: lies*) déceler ❸ (*support*) aider ❹ (*continue to end*) faire jusqu'au bout

◆ **see to** *vt* ❶ (*attend to*) s'occuper de ❷ *inf* (*repair*) réparer ❸ (*ensure*) **to ~ it that** faire en sorte que +*subj*

**seed** [sid] I. *n* ❶ AGR graine *f*; (*of fruit*) pépin *m*; **to sow ~s** semer des graines ❷ *fig* (*beginning*) germe *m*; **it sowed the ~s of doubt in her mind** ça a semé le doute dans son esprit ❸ SPORTS tête *f* de série II. *vt* ❶ (*sow with seeds*) ensemencer ❷ (*start*) germer ❸ (*remove seeds from*) épépiner ❹ SPORTS **to be ~ed** être classé

**seed money** *n* capital *m* de départ

**seek** [sik] <sought> I. *vt* ❶ (*look for*) chercher ❷ (*strive for: happiness, revenge*) rechercher; (*asylum, fortune*) chercher; (*justice, damages*) demander ❸ (*ask for: advice, permission*) demander II. *vi* ❶ (*search*) chercher; ~ **and you shall find** quand on cherche on trouve ❷ *form* (*attempt*) **to ~ to** +*infin* essayer de +*infin*

**seem** [sim] *vi* ❶ (*appear to be*) sembler ❷ (*appear*) **it ~s as if …** on dirait que …; **so it ~s** on dirait; **it ~s like months since I started** j'ai l'impression que ça fait des mois que j'ai commencé

**seemingly** *adv* apparemment

**seen** [sin] *pp* of **see**

**seep** [sip] *vi* filtrer; **to ~ into sth** s'infiltrer dans qc

**seesaw** I. *n* ❶ (*at playground*) bascule *f* ❷ *fig* va-et-vient *m inv* II. *vi* ❶ (*at playground*) jouer à la bascule ❷ (*move back and forth*) balancer ❸ (*rise and fall*) osciller ❹ *fig* être en dents de scie

**see-through** *adj* transparent(e)

**segregate** ['seg·rə·geɪt] *vt* ❶ (*isolate*) isoler ❷ (*separate*) séparer; (*racially*) faire subir une ségrégation à

**seize** [siz] *vt* ❶ (*grasp*) saisir; **to ~ hold of sth** saisir qc ❷ (*capture*) capturer; (*hostage, power*) prendre; (*city, territory*) s'emparer de ❸ (*confiscate: drugs*) saisir

◆ **seize up** *vi* (*machine, program*) se bloquer; (*engine*) se gripper

**seizure** ['si·ʒər] *n* ❶ (*seizing: of power, territory*) prise *f*; (*of drugs, property*) saisie *f* ❷ MED crise *f*

**seldom** ['sel·dəm] *adv* rarement

**select** [sə·'lekt] I. *vt* ❶ (*choose*) choisir ❷ SPORTS, COMPUT sélectionner II. *vi* choisir III. *adj* ❶ (*exclusive*) sélect(e) ❷ (*chosen*) choisi(e)

**selection** *n* ❶ (*choosing*) choix *m* ❷ (*range*) sélection *f* ❸ (*extracts*) morceaux *mpl* choisis

**selective** *adj* sélectif(-ive); ~ **breeding**

élevage *m* par sélection; ~ **entry** sélection *f* à l'entrée

**selective service** *n* MIL service *m* militaire obligatoire

**self** [self] *n* ❶ <selves> **to find one's true ~** trouver sa véritable personnalité; **to be (like) one's old ~** être de nouveau soi-même ❷ *form* PSYCH **the ~** le moi

**self-addressed** *n* ~ **stamped envelope** enveloppe *f* (libellée) au nom et à l'adresse de l'expéditeur

**self-adhesive** *adj* autocollant(e)

**self-appointed** *adj* autoproclamé(e)

**self-assured** *adj* sûr(e) de soi

**self-centered** *adj* égocentrique

**self-confidence** *n* confiance *f* en soi

**self-conscious** *adj* embarrassé(e)

**self-contained** *adj* ❶ (*independent: apartment*) indépendant(e) ❷ (*self-sufficient*) autosuffisant(e) ❸ (*reserved*) indépendant(e)

**self-control** *n* sang-froid *m*

**self-defense** *n* ❶ (*protection*) légitime défense *f* ❷ (*skill*) autodéfense *f*

**self-employed** I. *adj* indépendant(e) II. *n pl* **the ~** les libéraux *mpl*

**self-explanatory** *adj* qui s'explique de soi-même

**self-fulfilling** *adj* qui se réalise tout seul; ~ **prophecy** prédiction *f* qui se réalise

**self-fulfillment** *n* ❶ épanouissement *m* de soi

**selfie** ['sel·fiː] *n* TEL, INET selfie *m*

**self-important** *adj* suffisant(e)

**self-indulgent** *adj* complaisant(e)

**self-interest** *n* intérêt *m* personnel

**selfish** ['sel·fɪʃ] *adj* égoïste

**selfishness** *n* égoïsme *m*

**self-possessed** *adj* posé(e)

**self-reliant** *adj* indépendant(e)

**self-respect** *n* dignité *f*; **to take away sb's ~** avilir qn

**self-satisfied** *adj* content(e) de soi; **to look ~** avoir l'air suffisant

**self-service** I. *n* libre-service *m* II. *adj* en libre service; **a ~ Laundromat** une laverie automatique; **a ~ restaurant** un self-service

**self-sufficient** *adj* autosuffisant(e); **to be a ~ type** être du genre indépendant

**self-willed** *adj* volontaire

**self-winding watch** *n* montre *f* automatique

**sell** [sel] I. *n* vente *f*; **hard/soft ~** vente agressive/non agressive II. <sold, sold> *vt* vendre, remettre *Belgique* ▸ **to ~ sb down the river** lâcher qn; **he sold himself short** il n'a pas su se vendre à sa juste valeur III. *vi* <sold, sold> se vendre ▸ **to ~ like hotcakes** se vendre comme des petits pains

◆ **sell off** *vt* liquider; **to sell sth off at half price** brader qc à moitié prix

◆ **sell out** I. *vi* ❶ (*sell everything*) vendre jusqu'à épuisement des stocks; **to ~ of merchandise/a brand** liquider des marchandises/une marque ❷ (*betray cause*) **to ~ on sb** vendre qn II. *vt* ❶ (*have none left*) **to be sold out** être épuisé; **tickets are sold out for tonight** ce soir, on joue à guichets fermés ❷ *inf* (*betray*) vendre

**seller** *n* ❶ (*person selling*) vendeur, -euse *m, f* ❷ (*popular product*) produit *m* qui se vend bien

**sell-out** *n* ❶ (*no tickets left*) **this play was a total ~** cette pièce a été jouée à guichets fermés ❷ (*betrayal*) trahison *f*

**selves** [selvz] *n pl of* **self**

**semen** ['siː·mən] *n* semence *f*

**semester** [sə·'mes·tər] *n* semestre *m*

**semi** ['sem·i] *n inf* ❶ *s*. **semitrailer** ❷ *inf* SPORTS *s*. **semifinal**

**semicircle** *n* demi-cercle *m*

**semicolon** *n* point-virgule *m*

**semiconscious** *adj* **to be ~** être à moitié conscient

**semidetached** *adj* (*house*) jumelé(e)

**semifinal** *n* SPORTS demi-finale *f*

**semifinalist** *n* SPORTS demi-finaliste *mf*

**seminar** ['sem·ə·nar] *n* ❶ UNIV séminaire *m* ❷ (*workshop*) stage *m*

**semiprecious** *adj* (*stone*) semi-précieux(-euse)

**semitrailer** *n* semi-remorque *m*

**semitropical** *adj s*. **subtropical**

S

**semi-vegetarian** *n* semi-végétarien(ne) *m(f)*

**semolina** [ˌsem·ə·ˈli·nə] *n* semoule *f*

**send** [send] <sent, sent> I. *vt* ❶COM (*dispatch*) envoyer ❷(*cause to happen*) envoyer ❸(*cause to feel*) **to ~ sb into a panic** faire paniquer qn ► **to ~ sb packing** *inf* envoyer qn promener II. *vi* (*transmit*) réaliser une transmission

◆ **send away** I. *vi* **to ~ for sth** demander qc par courrier II. *vt* ❶(*dismiss*) renvoyer ❷(*cause to go*) **to send sb away to some place** expédier qn quelque part

◆ **send back** *vt* renvoyer

◆ **send for** *vt* ❶(*summon*) envoyer chercher ❷(*request*) demander par courrier

◆ **send in** *vt* ❶(*submit*) soumettre ❷(*send*) envoyer ❸COM (*order*) placer ❹(*let enter*) faire entrer ❺MIL (*reinforcements*) envoyer

◆ **send off** I. *vt* ❶(*post*) expédier; (*letter*) poster ❷SPORTS expulser II. *vi* s. **send away**

◆ **send on** *vt* renvoyer; (*a letter*) faire suivre

◆ **send out** *vt* ❶(*emit*) émettre ❷(*mail*) expédier ❸(*dispatch*) détacher

◆ **send up** *vt* ❶(*drive up*) faire monter; (*a rocket*) lancer ❷*inf* (*put in prison*) incarcérer ❸*inf* (*make parody of*) caricaturer

**sender** *n* expéditeur, -trice *m, f*; **'return to ~'** 'retour à l'envoyeur'

**sendoff** *n* **to give sb a ~** dire au revoir à qn

**send-up** *n* *inf* caricature *f*

**senile** ['si·naɪl] *adj* sénile

**senior** ['si·njər] I. *adj* ❶(*older*) aîné(e); **John B. O'Malley ~** John B. O'Malley père ❷SCHOOL, UNIV (*student*) de dernière année; **the ~ boys/girls** les grand(e)s ❸(*high-ranking*) supérieur(e); (*employee*) de grade supérieur; **to be ~ to sb** être au-dessus de qn; (*longer in service*) avoir plus d'ancien-

neté que qn ❹(*related to the elderly*) du troisième âge II. *n* ❶(*older person*) aîné(e) *m(f)*; **to be two years sb's ~** avoir deux ans de plus que qn ❷(*person of higher rank*) supérieur(e) *m(f)* ❸(*student of graduating class*) SCHOOL élève *mf* de dernière année; UNIV étudiant(e) *m(f)* de dernière année ❹(*elderly person*) personne *f* du troisième âge

**senior high** (**school**) *n* lycée *m*

**sensation** [sen·ˈseɪ·ʃən] *n* ❶sensation *f* ❷(*feeling*) impression *f* ❸(*strong excitement*) sensation *f*

**sensational** *adj* ❶(*causing excitement*) sensationnel(le) ❷PUBL (*newspaper*) à sensation; (*disclosure*) qui fait sensation

**sense** [sen(t)s] I. *n* ❶MED, BIO sens *m*; **the ~ of smell** l'odorat *m*; **the ~ of taste** le goût; **the ~ of touch** le toucher; **the ~ of hearing** l'ouïe *f*; **the ~ of sight** la vue ❷(*common sense*) sens *m* ❸ *pl* (*good judgment*) raison *f*; **to bring sb to his/her ~s** ramener qn à la raison ❹(*meaning*) sens *m* ❺(*way*) sens *m* ► **what's the ~ in doing sth?** à quoi cela sert-il de faire qc ?; **sth doesn't make** (**any**) **~** qc ne rime à rien; **to make** (**good**) **~** se tenir II. *vt* sentir

**senseless** *adj* ❶(*foolish, pointless*) insensé(e); (*killing*) gratuit(e); **it is ~ to** +*infin* ça n'a aucun sens de +*infin* ❷MED (*unconscious*) inanimé(e)

**sensible** ['sen(t)·sə·bl] *adj* raisonnable

**sensibly** *adv* ❶(*rationally*) raisonnablement ❷(*suitably*) correctement

**sensitive** ['sen(t)·sə·tɪv] *adj* ❶(*understanding*) compréhensif(-ive); **to be ~ to sth** être sensible à qc ❷(*touchy*) sensible

**sensor** ['sen(t)·sər] *n* TECH, ELEC capteur *m*

**sent** [sent] *pp, pt of* **send**

**sentence** ['sen·tən(t)s] I. *n* ❶LING phrase *f* ❷LAW condamnation *f*; **to serve a ~** purger une peine II. *vt* **to ~ sb to sth** condamner qn à qc

**sentimental** *adj a. pej* sentimental(e)

**sentry** ['sen·tri] *n* sentinelle *f*; **to stand ~** être en faction

**separate** ['sep·ə·ɪt, *vb:* 'sep·ə·ɪeɪt] **I.** *adj* **①** *(not joined physically)* séparé(e); **a ~ piece of paper** une feuille à part **②** *(distinct)* distinct(e) **③** *(different)* différent(e) **II.** *vt* séparer ▸ **to ~ the men from the boys** différencier les hommes des garçons **III.** *vi* se séparer

**separated** *adj* séparé(e)

**separation** *n* séparation *f*

**September** [sep·'tem·bər] *n* septembre *m; s.a.* **April**

**septic** ['sep·tɪk] *adj* infecté(e)

**septic tank** *n* fosse *f* septique

**sequel** ['si·kwəl] *n* **①** *(continued story)* suite *f*; **the ~ to sth** la suite de qc **②** *(consequence)* conséquence *f*

**sequence** ['si·kwən(t)s] *n* **①** *(order)* suite *f* **②** *(part of film)* séquence *f*

**sequin** ['si·kwɪn] *n* paillette *f*

**sergeant** ['sar·dʒənt] *n* **①** MIL sergent *m* **②** *(policeman)* brigadier *m*

**serial** ['sɪr·i·əl] **I.** *n* feuilleton *m* **II.** *adj* en série

**series** ['sɪr·iz] *inv n* série *f*

**serious** ['sɪr·i·əs] *adj* **①** *(not funny, sincere)* sérieux(-euse); **to be ~ about doing sth** envisager sérieusement de faire qc **②** *(solemn)* grave **③** *inf* *(substantial)* important(e); **to have some ~ difficulty** avoir de grosses difficultés; **~ money** beaucoup d'argent **④** *inf* *(extremely good)* excellent(e)

**seriously** *adv* **①** *(sincerely)* sérieusement; *(wounded)* grièvement; **to take sb/sth ~** prendre qn/qc au sérieux **②** *inf* *(really)* vraiment **③** *inf* *(very, extremely)* très

**seriousness** *n* **①** *(truthfulness)* sérieux *m;* **in all ~** sérieusement **②** *(grave nature)* gravité *f*

**sermon** ['sɜr·mən] *n a. pej* sermon *m*

**serpent** ['sɜr·pənt] *n* serpent *m*

**serrated** ['ser·eɪ·tɪd] *adj* en dents de scie

**servant** ['sɜr·vənt] *n* **①** *(in household)* serviteur, servante *m, f* **②** *(government employee)* employé(e) *m(f);* **a public ~** un(e) employé(e) de la fonction publique

**serve** [sɜrv] **I.** *vt* **①** *(help customer)* servir **②** *(provide for guests)* servir **③** *(work for, give service to)* être au service de **④** *(complete time period)* servir; **to ~ 10 years** *(in military)* servir 10 ans dans l'armée; *(in jail)* faire 10 ans de prison; **to ~ one year as director** exercer sa fonction de directeur pendant un an **⑤** *(help achieve needs)* servir à; **to ~ the purpose** faire l'affaire **⑥** *(in public transportation: region, town)* desservir **⑦** *(in tennis)* servir **⑧** *(formally deliver)* **to ~ sb with sth** délivrer qc à qn ▸ **to ~ sb right** être bien fait pour qn **II.** *vi a.* SPORTS servir; **to ~ as +*infin*** servir à +*infin* **III.** *n* SPORTS service *m*

♦ **serve up** *vt* servir

**server** ['sɜr·vər] *n* **①** *(tableware)* service *m* **②** *(waiter)* serveur, -euse *m, f* **③** COMPUT serveur *m* **④** *(in tennis)* serveur, -euse *m, f*

**service** ['sɜr·vɪs] **I.** *n* **①** *(set)* service *m* **②** *(assistance)* service *m; out of ~* hors service; **to be of ~ to sb** être utile à qn **③** REL service **④** TECH entretien *m;* AUTO révision *f* **⑤** MIL *(military service)* ▸ **to be in ~** être en service; **to be at sb's ~** être au service de qn **II.** *vt* entretenir; *(car)* réviser

**service area** *n* **①** *(along highway)* aire *f* de services **②** TEL, RADIO zone *f* d'émission

**service charge** *n* service *m*

**service entrance** *n* porte *f* de service

**service road** *n* voie *f* d'accès

**service station** *n* station-service *f*

**serving** ['sɜr·vɪŋ] *n* portion *f*

**servo** ['sɜr·voʊ] *n* AUTO, TECH **①** *abbr of* **servomechanism** servomécanisme *m* **②** *abbr of* **servomotor** servomoteur *m* **③** *inf* *(service station)* station-service *f*

**session** ['seʃ·ən] *n* **①** *(formal sitting, meeting)* a. COMPUT session *f* **②** *(period for specific activity)* séance *f;* **re-**

cording ~ session d'enregistrement ③ (*period for classes*) cours *m* ④ UNIV année *f* universitaire

**set** [set] I. *n* ① (*scenery on stage*) scène *f*; (*in film, on TV*) plateau *m* ② ANAT **the ~ of sb's jaw** la dentition de qn ③ (*hair arrangement*) mise *f* en plis ④ (*group, collection: of keys, tools*) jeu *m*; (*of stamps, numbers, books*) série *f*; (*of gems, sheets*) parure *f*; **chess ~** jeu *m* d'échec ⑤ (*group of people*) groupe *m* ⑥ MATH (*group*) ensemble *m* ⑦ (*television*) poste *m* ⑧ SPORTS (*game*) set *m* ⑨ (*at concert, show*) partie *f* II. *adj* ① (*ready, prepared*) prêt(e); **to get ~** se tenir prêt ② (*fixed*) fixe; (*expression, face, smile*) figé(e); (*date, opinion, idea*) arrêté(e) ③ (*resolute*) résolu(e); **to be ~ on doing sth** être résolu à faire qc ④ (*assigned*) obligatoire; (*book, subject*) au programme; (*task*) assigné(e) ▶ **to be ~ in one's ways** avoir ses petites habitudes III. <-tt-, set, set> *vt* ① (*place, put somewhere*) poser ② (*locate*) *a.* CINE, LIT, THEAT situer; **the scene is ~ in sth** l'action se déroule dans qc ③ (*cause to be*) mettre; **to ~ sth on fire** mettre le feu à qc; **to ~ sb loose/free** lâcher/libérer qn ④ (*adjust: clock, timer*) régler; **to ~ the alarm for 7.00 A.M.** mettre le réveil à 7 heures ⑤ (*prepare: stage*) préparer; (*trap*) tendre; **to ~ the table** mettre la table ⑥ (*establish, fix: limit, price, date*) fixer; **to ~ an example for sb** donner un exemple à qn; **to ~ a record** établir un record ⑦ (*place in normal position*) remettre; **to ~ a broken bone** réduire une fracture ⑧ (*arrange*) **to ~ sb's hair** faire une mise en plis à qn ⑨ (*adorn: jewel*) sertir ⑩ TYP (*lay out*) composer ⑪ (*cause to start*) **to ~ sb to +*infin*** mettre qn à +*infin;* **to ~ sb to work** mettre qn au travail ⑫ (*provide with music*) **to ~ sth to music** mettre qc en musique ▶ **to ~ one's heart on doing sth** avoir bon espoir de faire qc; **to ~ one's mind to sth** (*concentrate on*) s'appliquer à qc; (*be*

*determined*) s'attaquer à qc; **to ~ sail for some place** mettre les voiles pour un endroit; **to ~ the stage for sth** (*conditions are right*) réunir toutes les conditions pour qc; (*make likely to happen*) préparer le terrain pour qc IV. <-tt-, set, set> *vi* ① (*go down, sink: sun*) se coucher ② (*become firm*) durcir; (*jelly, cement, dye*) prendre; (*bone*) se ressouder

◆ **set about** *vt* **to ~ doing sth** se mettre à faire qc

◆ **set against** *vt* **to set sth against sth** ① (*offset*) déduire qc de qc ② (*compare*) comparer qc à qc ③ (*use as compensation*) contrebalancer qc par qc ④ (*make opposed*) dresser qn contre qn/qc; **to be dead ~ sb/sth** être résolument opposé à qn/qc

◆ **set apart** *vt* ① (*distinguish*) distinguer ② (*reserve*) mettre de côté; **to ~ a day for doing sth** se réserver un jour pour faire qc

◆ **set aside** *vt* ① (*reserve*) *a. fig* **to set sth aside** mettre qc de côté; (*time*) réserver qc ② (*declare invalid*) annuler ③ (*reject*) rejeter

◆ **set back** *vt* ① (*delay*) retarder ② (*place away from*) mettre en retrait de ③ *inf* (*cost*) **to set sb back** coûter à qn

◆ **set down** *vt* ① (*place on something*) déposer ② (*land*) poser ③ (*drop off*) déposer ④ (*write down*) inscrire

◆ **set in** *vi* survenir

◆ **set off** I. *vi* se mettre en route; **to ~ on sth** partir pour qc II. *vt* ① (*detonate*) déclencher ② (*cause to do, start*) **to set sb off doing sth** faire faire qc à qn ③ (*enhance*) rehausser

◆ **set out** I. *vt a. fig* exposer II. *vi* ① (*begin journey*) se mettre en route; **to ~ for somewhere** partir pour quelque part ② (*have intention, aim*) **to ~ to +*infin*** avoir l'intention de +*infin*

◆ **set to** *vi* ① (*start working, dealing with*) **to ~ work** se mettre au travail ② *inf* (*begin fighting*) **to ~ with sb** en venir aux mains avec qn

◆ **set up** vt ❶ (*put in position or view*) dresser; (*camp*) établir; **to set sth up again** relever qc ❷ (*establish*) créer; **to set sb up in business** lancer qn dans les affaires ❸ (*organize*) organiser ❹ **to set oneself up as sth** (*claim to be*) s'établir comme qc; (*pose as*) se poser en qc ❺ (*provide*) **to set sb up with sth** approvisionner qn en qc ❻ inf (*deceive, frame*) piéger

**setback** n revers m

**setting** n ❶ (*location, scenery*) cadre m ❷ (*position*) réglage m ❸ (*frame for jewel*) monture f ❹ TYP (*layout*) composition f ❺ MUS arrangement m

**settle** ['set·l] I. vi ❶ (*get comfortable*) s'installer ❷ (*calm down*) se calmer ❸ (*end dispute*) se régler ❹ (*pay*) régler; **to ~ with sb** régler qn ❺ (*live permanently*) s'établir ❻ (*accumulate*) se déposer ❼ (*land, alight*) se poser ❽ (*sink down*) s'affaisser II. vt ❶ (*calm down*) calmer; **this will ~ your stomach** cela va apaiser tes/vos nausées ❷ (*decide*) décider de ❸ (*resolve: details, crisis*) régler ❹ (*pay*) régler ❺ (*colonize*) coloniser

◆ **settle down** vi ❶ (*get comfortable*) s'installer ❷ (*adjust to new situation*) **to ~ in sth** s'adapter à qc ❸ (*calm down*) se calmer ❹ (*start quiet life*) se ranger

◆ **settle for** vt accepter

◆ **settle in** vi s'installer

◆ **settle on** vt décider de; **to ~ a date** s'entendre sur une date

◆ **settle up** vi régler

**settled** adj ❶ (*comfortable*) installé(e) ❷ (*calm*) stable ❸ (*established*) rangé(e) ❹ (*fixed: idea*) fixe

**settlement** n ❶ (*agreement*) arrangement m; **to reach a ~** trouver un arrangement ❷ FIN, ECON (*payment*) règlement m ❸ LAW (*property arrangement*) constitution f ❹ (*colony*) colonie f ❺ (*colonization*) colonisation f ❻ (*sinking*) affaissement m

**settler** n colon m

**setup** n ❶ (*way things are arranged*) si-tuation f ❷ (*arrangement*) arrangement m ❸ inf (*conspiracy*) coup m monté

**seven** ['sev·ən] adj sept; s.a. **eight**

**seventeen** [ˌsev·ən·'tin] adj dix-sept; s.a. **eight**

**seventh** adj septième ▸ **to be in ~ heaven** être au septième ciel; s.a. **eighth**

**seventy** ['sev·ən·ṭi] adj soixante-dix, septante *Belgique, Suisse*; s.a. **eight**

**sever** ['sev·ər] vt ❶ (*cut*) a. fig **to ~ sth from sth** sectionner qc de qc ❷ (*put an end*) a. fig rompre

**several** ['sev·ər·əl] I. adj ❶ (*some*) ~ **times** plusieurs fois ❷ (*separate*) différent(e); **the ~ interests of each** les divers intérêts mpl de chacun II. pron **we've got ~** nous en avons plusieurs; **~ of us** plusieurs d'entre nous

**severe** [sə·'vɪr] <-r, -st> adj sévère; (*illness, wound*) grave; (*winter, weather, test*) rigoureux(-euse); (*headache, injury, pain*) violent(e)

**sew** [soʊ] <sewed, sewn o sewed> I. vt coudre II. vi coudre

◆ **sew up** vt ❶ (*repair by sewing*) recoudre ❷ (*stitch*) suturer ❸ fig, inf (*arrange*) conclure

**sewage** ['su·ɪdʒ] n eaux fpl usées

**sewer** ['soʊ·ər] n égout m

**sewing** n couture f

**sewn** [soʊn] pp of **sew**

**sex** [seks] I. <-es> n ❶ (*gender*) sexe m; **members of the male/female** ~ membres mpl de la gente masculine/féminine ❷ (*erotic stimulation*) sexe m; **casual ~** rapports sexuels de rencontre; **group ~** partouze f inf; **to have ~** avoir des rapports sexuels ❸ (*reproduction: people*) rapports mpl sexuels; (*animals*) accouplement m II. vt **to ~ sb/an animal** déterminer le sexe de qn/d'un animal

**sex life** n vie f sexuelle

**sex offender** n délinquant(e) m(f) sexuel(le)

**sextet** [sek·'stet] n sextuor m

**sexual** ['sek·ʃu·əl] adj sexuel(le)

**S**

**sexuality** [ˌsek·ʃu·ˈæl·ə·t̬i] *n* sexualité *f*

**sexually** *adv* sexuellement

**shabby** [ˈʃæb·i] <-ier, -iest> *adj* miteux(-euse); (*excuse*) minable

**shack** [ʃæk] I. *n* cabane *f* II. *vi sl* to ~ **up together** vivre ensemble

**shade** [ʃeɪd] I. *n* ❶ (*area without sunlight*) a. *fig* ombre *f* ❷ (*for lamp*) abat-jour *m* ❸ *pl* (*blinds*) store *m* ❹ (*variation*) a. *fig* nuance *f* ❺ (*a little*) soupçon *m*; **a ~ under/over sth** un peu plus de/moins de qc ❻ *pl, sl* (*sunglasses*) lunettes *fpl* noires II. *vt* ❶ (*protect from sunlight*) ombrager; (*eyes*) protéger; **to be ~d by a tree** être à l'ombre d'un arbre ❷ ART (*darken parts*) ombrer ❸ (*decrease*) baisser progressivement III. *vi* ❶ (*change color*) se dégrader ❷ (*be indistinguishable*) **to ~ into sth** se confondre avec qc ❸ (*decrease*) baisser

**shadow** [ˈʃæd·oʊ] I. *n* ❶ (*darker space*) a. *fig* ombre *f* ❷ (*darkness*) obscurité *f* ❸ *pl* (*under the eyes*) cernes *fpl* ❹ (*trace*) ombre *f*; **the ~ of (a) doubt** l'ombre d'un doute ▶ **to be a ~ of one's former self** n'être plus que l'ombre de soi-même II. *vt* ❶ (*create shaded area*) assombrir ❷ (*bring darkness*) ombrager ❸ (*follow*) suivre; (*trail*) filer III. *adj* fantôme

**shady** [ˈʃeɪ·di] <-ier, -iest> *adj* ❶ (*protected from light*) ombragé(e) ❷ *inf* (*dubious*) louche; **a ~ character** un drôle de caractère

**shake** [ʃeɪk] I. *n* ❶ (*movement*) secousse *f*; **a ~ of one's head** un hochement de la tête ❷ *pl, inf* (*shivering*) tremblote *f*; **to get the ~s** avoir la tremblote ❸ *inf* (*milk shake*) milk-shake *m* ❹ *inf* (*chance*) chance *f*; **to give sb a fair ~** donner une vraie chance à qn II. <shook, shaken> *vt* ❶ (*move back and forth*) secouer; **to ~ one's fist at sb** montrer le poing à qn; **to ~ hands with sb, to ~ sb by the hand** serrer la main à qn ❷ (*unsettle*) secouer ▶ **to ~ a leg** *inf* se secouer; **more than you can ~ a stick at** *sl* plus que nécessaire III. <shook, shaken> *vi* trembler; **~ well before using** bien agiter avant emploi ▶ **to ~ like a leaf** trembler comme une feuille

◆**shake off** *vt* ❶ (*wiggle to remove*) secouer ❷ (*eliminate*) se débarrasser de; **to ~ one's shackles** *fig* se libérer de ses chaînes

◆**shake out** *vt* secouer

◆**shake up** *vt* ❶ (*agitate*) secouer ❷ (*upset*) bouleverser

**shaken** I. *pp of* **shake** II. *adj* secoué(e)

**shakeup** *n inf* bouleversement *m*

**shakily** [ˈʃeɪk·ɪ·li] *adv* ❶ (*not stable*) branlant(e) ❷ (*uncertainly*) mal assuré(e); **to walk ~** marcher d'un pas mal assuré

**shaky** <-ier, -iest> *adj* ❶ (*trembling, not smooth: voice, writing, hand*) tremblotant(e); **to be ~ on one's feet** ne pas bien tenir sur ses jambes ❷ (*not clear: memory, knowledge*) vacillant(e) ❸ (*upset*) secoué(e) ❹ (*not stable: chair, building*) branlant(e); (*person*) faible; (*economy*) instable; **to be on ~ ground** être sur un terrain glissant

**shall** [ʃæl] *aux* ❶ (*future*) **I ~ do ...** je ferai ... ❷ (*ought to, must*) **you ~ obey** tu devras obéir ❸ (*be mandatory*) **it ~ be unlawful** il est interdit

**shallow** [ˈʃæl·oʊ] *adj* ❶ (*not deep*) peu profond(e) ❷ (*superficial*) superficiel(le)

**shambles** *n + sing vb, inf* pagaille *f*

**shame** [ʃeɪm] I. *n* ❶ (*humiliation*) a. *iron* honte *f*; **to feel a deep sense of ~** éprouver un profond ressentiment; **to put sb to ~** faire honte à qn; **it's a crying ~ that** c'est une honte que +*subj* ❷ (*disappointment*) dommage *m* II. *vt* ❶ (*discredit*) discréditer ❷ (*force*) **to ~ sb/sth into doing sth** obliger qn/qc à faire qc

**shameful** *adj* honteux(-euse)

**shameless** *adj* ❶ (*unashamed*) éhonté(e) ❷ (*insolent*) effronté(e) ❸ (*without decency*) sans pudeur

**shampoo** [ʃæm·ˈpu] I. *n* shampooing *m* II. *vt* shampooiner

**shandy** [ˈʃæn·di] <-ies> *n* panaché *m*

S

**shape** [ʃeɪp] **I.** *n* ❶(*outline*) forme *f*; **out of ~** déformé(e); **to lose ~** se déformer; **to take ~** prendre forme; **in any way, ~ or form** de quelque façon que ce soit; **in all ~s and sizes** *fig* de toutes sortes ❷(*condition*) forme *f*; **to get into ~** mettre en forme; **to get back into ~** retrouver la forme; **to whip sb/ sth into ~** remettre qn/qc sur pied **II.** *vt* ❶(*form*) modeler; (*wood, stone*) tailler ❷*fig* former

**share** [ʃer] **I.** *n* ❶(*part*) part *f*; **to have one's (fair) ~ of sth** avoir sa part de qc ❷(*partial ownership*) action *f* **II.** *vt* partager; **to ~ a birthday** avoir son anniversaire le même jour; **to ~ (common) characteristics** avoir des caractéristiques communes **III.** *vi* partager ► **~ and ~ alike** à chacun sa part

**shareholder** *n* actionnaire *mf*

**shark** [ʃɑrk] <-(s)> *n* requin *m*

**sharp** [ʃɑrp] **I.** *adj* ❶(*pointed*) tranchant(e); (*pencil*) bien taillé(e) ❷(*angular: features, corner*) anguleux(-euse); (*nose, teeth*) pointu(e); (*edge, angle*) aigu(ë) ❸(*stabbing: pain*) violent(e) ❹*fig* (*biting: critic, word, attack*) cinglant(e); (*look, eyes*) perçant(e); (*rebuke, reprimand*) sévère; (*tongue*) acéré(e) ❺(*piquant*) épicé(e) ❻(*not honest*) ~ **practice** pratique *f* malhonnête ❼(*very cold*) pénétrant(e) ❽(*sudden*) brusque; (*abrupt*) abrupt(e); (*deterioration, drop*) soudain(e) ❾(*marked*) marqué(e); ~ **left/right** virage *m* à gauche/ droite; **to make a ~ left** tourner à gauche toute ❿(*vivid*) net(te); **to bring into ~ focus** mettre au point ⓫(*perceptive: mind*) vif(vive); (*question*) perspicace; **to keep a ~ eye out for sth** avoir l'œil pour qc ⓬*inf* (*trendy*) stylé(e) ⓭MUS **C ~ do** *m* dièse **II.** *adv* **at twelve o'clock ~** à midi pile **III.** *n* MUS dièse *m*

**sharpen** *vt* ❶(*knife*) aiguiser; (*pencil*) tailler ❷(*strengthen*) aiguiser; (*debate, pain, fear*) aviver; (*skills*) affiner ❸(*make vivid: picture, image*) rendre

plus net(te) ❹(*senses, eyes, ears*) affiner

**sharpener** *n* (*for pencil*) taille- -crayon *m*; (*for knife*) aiguisoir *m*

**sharp-tempered** *adj* coléreux(-euse)

**shatter I.** *vt* briser en morceaux **II.** *vi* se briser en morceaux

**shattering** *adj* épuisant(e)

**shave** [ʃeɪv] **I.** *n* rasage *m* ► **to be a close ~** être juste **II.** *vi* se raser **III.** *vt* ❶(*remove body hair*) raser; **to ~ one's legs** se raser les jambes ❷(*decrease price*) réduire

**shaven** *adj* rasé(e); ~ **head** crâne *m* rasé

**shaver** *n* rasoir *m*

**shaving I.** *adj* ~ **cream/foam** crème/ mousse à raser; ~ **brush** blaireau *m* **II.** *n* rasage *m*

**shawl** [ʃɔl] *n* châle *m*

**she** [ʃi] **I.** *pers pron* (*female person, animal*) elle; ~'**s my mother** c'est ma mère; **here ~ comes** la voilà; **her baby is a ~** son bébé est une fille; ~ **who ... form** celle qui ... **II.** *prefix* **a ~-cat** une chatte; **a ~-devil** une diablesse

**shebang** [ʃɪ'bæŋ] *n sl* **the whole ~** tout le fourbi

**shed** [ʃed] *n* abri *m*

**sheep** [ʃip] *n* mouton *m*; (*ewe*) brebis *f*

**sheet** [ʃit] *n a.* COMPUT feuille *f*

**shelf** [ʃelf] <-ves> *n* ❶(*for storage*) étagère *f*, tablar(d) *m Suisse* ❷(*rock*) rebord *m* ❸ECON **off the ~** sous forme de stock

**shelf life** *n* durée *f* de conservation avant vente

**shell** [ʃel] **I.** *n* ❶(*exterior: of mollusk*) coquille *f*; (*of crab, turtle*) carapace *f*; (*of nut, egg*) coque *f* ❷(*rigid exterior*) enveloppe *f* protectrice ❸(*basic structure: of building, boat*) carcasse *f* ❹(*gun explosives*) cartouche *f*; (*artillery*) obus *m* ❺(*racing boat*) canot *m* de compétition ► **to come out of one's ~** sortir de sa coquille; **to crawl into one's ~** se glisser à l'intérieur de sa coquille; *fig* se renfermer sur soi-même **II.** *vt* ❶(*remove shell: nuts*) décortiquer; (*peas*) écosser ❷(*fire*) bombarder

**S**

III. *vi* to ~ **easily** bien se décortiquer
◆**shell out** *inf* I. *vt* casquer II. *vi* to ~ **for sb/sth** raquer pour qn/qc
**shellfish** *n* crustacé *m*
**shell-shocked** *adj* traumatisé(e)
**shelter** ['ʃel·tər] I. *n* ① (*building*) refuge *m*; (*from rain, bombs*) abri *m* ② (*protection*) refuge *m* ③ *fig* **tax ~** échappatoire *f* fiscale II. *vi* ① (*find protection*) s'abriter; to ~ **from sth** s'abriter de qc ② (*be refugee*) se réfugier III. *vt* ① (*protect: from weather*) abriter; *fig* (*from truth*) protéger ② (*give refuge: fugitive*) accueillir
**sheltered** *adj* ① (*against weather*) abrité(e) ② *fig* (*overprotected*) **to be ~** vivre dans un cocon
**sheriff** ['ʃer·ɪf] *n* shérif *m*
**shield** [ʃild] I. *n* ① (*defense*) bouclier *m*; **protective ~** plaque *f* de protection ② (*protective layer*) protection *f* ③ (*coat of arms*) blason *m* ④ (*with logo*) écusson *m* ⑤ (*police badge*) plaque *f* II. *vt* protéger
**shift** [ʃɪft] I. *vt* ① (*rearrange*) changer de place; (*blame*) rejeter; to ~ **one's ground** changer d'avis ② AUTO (*gears, lanes*) changer de; to ~ **gears** *fig* passer à autre chose II. *vi* ① (*rearrange position*) changer de place; (*wind*) tourner ② AUTO to ~ **into reverse/first gear** passer en marche arrière/en première ③ *inf* (*move over*) to ~ (**over**) se pousser III. *n* ① (*alteration*) modification *f* ② (*period of work*) poste *m*, durée *f* de travail d'une équipe; to **work in ~s** faire les postes ③ (*people working a shift*) équipe *f*
**shine** [ʃaɪn] I. *n* éclat *m* ▶ **rain or ~** par tous les temps; to **take a ~ to sb** s'amouracher de qn II. <-ed *o* shone, -ed *o* shone> *vi* ① (*emit, reflect light*) briller; (*brightly*) étinceler; (*light*) illuminer ② (*excel*) être une lumière; to ~ **at sth** exceller en qc ③ (*be obvious*) transparaître III. <-ed *o* shone, -ed *o* shone> *vt* ① (*point light*) braquer une lumière sur ② (*polish*) faire reluire; (*shoes*) faire briller

◆**shine out** *vi* (*easily seen*) to ~ **of sb** émaner de qn
**shingles** *n* + *sing/pl verb* MED zona *m*
**shin splints** *npl* inflammation *f* du tibia
**shiny** <-ier, -iest> *adj* brillant(e); (*metal*) luisant(e)
**ship** [ʃɪp] I. *n* bateau *m*; (*merchant*) cargo *m*; (*passenger*) paquebot *m*; (*sailing*) voilier *m*; to **board a ~** embarquer II. <-pp-> *vt* ① (*send by boat*) expédier par bateau; (*freight*) charger ② (*transport*) transporter
◆**ship out** *vt* envoyer par bateau
**shipper** *n* expéditeur, -trice *m, f*
**shipping company** *n* compagnie *f* de navigation
**shipshape** ['ʃɪp·ʃeɪp] *adj inf* bien rangé(e)
**shipwreck** I. *n* ① (*accident*) naufrage *m* ② (*remains*) épave *f* II. *vt* ① (*sink*) faire couler; to **be ~ed** faire naufrage ② *fig* ruiner
**shipyard** *n* chantier *m* maritime
**shirker** *n pej* flemmard(e) *m(f)*
**shirt** [ʃɜrt] *n* chemise *f* ▶ to **give sb the ~ off one's** <u>back</u> *sl* donner à qn jusqu'à sa dernière chemise
**shirtsleeve** *n* manche *f* de chemise; to **be in ~s** être en bras de chemise ▶ to **roll up one's ~s** remonter ses manches
**shit** [ʃɪt] *vulg* I. *n inf* ① (*excrement*) merde *f*; to **take a ~** chier ② *fig* (*nonsense*) connerie *f* ③ (*trouble*) **don't take (any) ~ from him!** ne te laisse pas faire par lui!; to **be in deep ~** être dans la merde ④ (*care*) to **not give a ~ about anything** se foutre de tout ⑤ (*things*) saloperies *fpl* ⑥ (*cannabis*) shit *m* ⑦ (*as intensifier*) to **beat the ~ out of sb** taper qn comme un fou; to **scare the ~ out of sb** flanquer la frousse à qn ▶ to **have ~ for** <u>brains</u> être con comme un balai; **when the ~ hits the** <u>fan</u> quand la merde nous tombera dessus; <u>no</u> ~! merde alors! II. *interj* merde! III. <-tt-, shit *o* shat, shit *o* shat> *vi* chier IV. <-tt-, shit *o* shat, shit *o* shat> *vt* to ~ **oneself** chier dans son froc; to ~ **bricks** se chier dessus

**shitty** ['ʃɪt·i] <-ier, -iest> *adj vulg* ❶ (*bad, worthless*) merdique ❷ (*contemptible*) dégueulasse ❸ (*dirty*) dégueulasse ❹ (*sick*) **to feel ~** se sentir mal

**shiver** ['ʃɪv·ər] I. *n* ❶ (*tremble*) frisson *m;* **to send ~s (up and) down sb's spine** donner des sueurs froides à qn ❷ *pl* (*state*) tremblement *m;* **to give sb the ~s** *fig* faire peur à qn II. *vi* frissonner; **to ~ with cold/like a leaf** trembler de froid/comme une feuille

**shivery** <-ier, -iest> *adj* frissonnant(e); **to feel ~** se sentir fiévreux

**shock**[1] [ʃɑk] I. *n* ❶ *inf* (*electric shock*) décharge *f* ❷ (*unpleasant surprise*) choc *m;* **to get a ~** être surpris ❸ (*health condition*) état *m* de choc; **to suffer from ~** souffrir d'un traumatisme ❹ (*jarring*) secousse *f* II. *vt* choquer

**shock**[2] [ʃɑk] *n* (*of hair*) tignasse *f*

**shock absorber** *n* amortisseur *m*

**shocking** *adj* ❶ (*scandalous*) choquant(e) ❷ (*very bad*) atroce; (*accident*) terrible; (*crime*) odieux(-euse); (*weather, conditions*) épouvantable ❸ (*causing distress: news, scene*) bouleversant(e); (*truth*) terrible ❹ (*surprising*) étonnant(e)

**shockproof** *adj* ❶ (*not damageable*) résistant(e) aux chocs ❷ (*insulated*) isolé(e)

**shock wave** *n* onde *f* de choc

**shoddy** <-ier, -iest> *adj* ❶ (*poorly produced*) de mauvaise qualité ❷ (*disrespectful*) méprisable

**shoe** [ʃu] I. *n* ❶ (*for foot*) chaussure *f,* soulier *m Québec;* **to put on/take off ~s** se chausser/se déchausser ❷ (*horseshoe*) fer *m* ▶ **if I were in your ~s** *inf* si j'étais à votre place; **to fill sb's ~s** prendre la place de qn II. <shod, shod *o* shodden> *vt* (*horse*) ferrer

**shoelace** *n* lacet *m* de chaussure; **to tie one's ~s** lacer ses chaussures

**shoe polish** *n* cirage *m*

**shoeshine man** *n* cireur *m* de chaussures

**shoe size** *n* pointure *f*

**shoe store** *n* magasin *m* de chaussures

**shone** [ʃoʊn] *pt, pp of* **shine**

**shoo** [ʃu] I. *interj inf* ouste! II. *vi inf* (*drive away*) chasser

**shook** [ʃʊk] *n pt of* **shake**

**shoot** [ʃut] I. *n* ❶ (*hunt*) partie *f* de chasse ❷ CINE tournage *m* ❸ PHOT séance *f* photo ❹ BOT pousse *f* II. <shot, shot> *vi* ❶ (*fire bullet*) tirer; **to ~ at sb/sth** tirer sur qn/qc ❷ CINE tourner ❸ PHOT prendre des photos ❹ (*move rapidly*) filer; **to ~ ahead of sb** passer devant qn; **to ~ to fame** devenir célèbre du jour au lendemain ❺ *inf* (*aim*) **to ~ for sth** viser qc ❻ BOT pousser ❼ SPORTS tirer ▶ BOT **to ~ from the hip** *sl* parler sans réfléchir; **to ~ for the moon** demander la lune III. <shot, shot> *vt* ❶ (*discharge weapon: person*) tirer sur; (*animal*) chasser; **to ~ sb dead** tuer qn; **he was shot** on lui a tiré dessus ❷ (*film*) tourner ❸ (*photograph*) photographier ❹ SPORTS (*goal, basket*) marquer; **to ~ pool** faire une partie de billard ❺ *inf* (*inject: heroin*) se piquer à ▶ **to ~ the breeze** *sl* parler de la pluie et du beau temps; **to ~ oneself in the foot** se causer du tort à soi même IV. *interj* mince alors!

◆**shoot down** *vt* ❶ (*kill: person*) descendre ❷ (*bring down: airplane*) abattre ❸ *fig, inf* (*refute: suggestion, proposal*) descendre

◆**shoot off** I. *vt* (*gun*) décharger ▶ **to shoot one's mouth off** *inf* ne pas s'empêcher d'ouvrir son bec II. *vi* partir en trombe

◆**shoot out** I. *vi* (*flame, water*) jaillir; (*person, car*) partir en trombe II. *vt* **to shoot it out** *inf* avoir un règlement de compte

◆**shoot up** I. *vi* ❶ (*grow rapidly*) pousser vite ❷ (*increase rapidly*) monter en flèche; (*rocket, skyscraper*) s'élever ❸ *inf* (*inject*) se shooter II. *vt* (*person*) tirer sur; (*building*) mitrailler; **to be shot up** recevoir des balles

**shooting** I. *n* ❶ (*act, killing*) fusillade *f*

**S**

**②** (*gunfire*) tirs *mpl* **③** (*hunting*) chasse *f* **④** (*sport*) tir *m* **⑤** CINE tournage *m* **⑥** PHOT séance *f* photo II. *adj* (*pain*) lancinant(e)

**shooting star** *n a. fig* étoile *f* filante

**shop** [ʃap] I. *n* **①** (*store, boutique*) magasin *m;* **to set up ~ as a baker** ouvrir une boulangerie **②** (*manufacturing area*) atelier *m* ▸ **to talk** ~ parler travail II. <-pp-> *vi* faire ses courses; **to go ~ping** aller faire les courses

**shopkeeper** *n* commerçant(e) *m(f)*

**shoplifter** *n* voleur, -euse *m, f* à l'étalage

**shoplifting** *n* vol *m* à l'étalage

**shopper** *n* personne *f* qui fait ses courses

**shopping** *n* **①** (*purchasing*) courses *fpl,* magasinage *m Québec;* (*Christmas*) achats *mpl;* **to go on a ~ spree** dévaliser les magasins **②** (*items purchased*) achats *mpl*

**shopping bag** *n* sac *m* à provisions

**shopping cart** *n* chariot *m* de supermarché

**shopping mall** *n* (*indoor*) grand centre *m* commercial; (*outdoor*) rue *f* commerçante

**shop window** *n* vitrine *f*

**shopworn** *adj* **①** (*from use as display*) défraîchi(e) **②** (*tedious*) rassis(rassie)

**shore** [ʃɔr] *n* **①** (*coast*) côte *f* **②** (*beach*) plage *f;* **from** (**the**) ~ du bord de la mer; **on** ~ sur le rivage II. *vt a. fig* **to** ~ **sth** (**up**) étayer qc

**short** [ʃɔrt] I. *adj* **①** (*not long*) court(e) **②** (*not tall*) petit(e) **③** (*not far: distance*) pas très loin; **at** ~ **range** à courte portée **④** (*brief*) bref(brève); (*memory*) court(e); **on** ~ **notice** dans un bref délai; ~ **and sweet** aussi rapide qu'un éclair **⑤** (*not enough*) **to be ~ on sth, to be in ~ supply of sth** manquer de qc; **to be ~ of breath** être essoufflé; **to be ~** (**of cash**) être sur la corde raide **⑥** (*rude*) **to be ~ with sb** manquer de patience avec qn; (*angry*); **to have a ~ temper** [*o* **fuse**] s'emporter facilement ▸ **to get the ~ end of the stick** en pâ-

tir; **to make ~ work of sb** ne faire qu'une bouchée de qn; **to make ~ work of sth** se dépêcher de faire qc II. *n* **①** CINE (*genre*) court métrage *m* **②** *inf* ELEC court-circuit *m* III. *adv* (*stop*) net; **to stop ~ of doing sth** se retenir de faire qc; **to cut sb ~** couper la parole à qn; **to run ~ of sth** se trouver à court de qc ▸ **in** ~ en bref; **for** ~ pour faire court

**shortage** ['ʃɔr·tɪdʒ] *n* pénurie *f*

**shortcake** *n* (*biscuit*) gâteau *m* sablé; **strawberry ~** tarte *f* sablée aux fraises

**shortchange** *vt* **①** (*not give enough change*) ne pas rendre assez de monnaie à **②** *inf* (*treat unfairly*) **to be ~d** être dupé

**short circuit** *n* court-circuit *m*

**short-circuit** I. *vi* se mettre en court-circuit II. *vt* ELEC *a. fig* court-circuiter

**short cut** *n* **①** (*direct path*) *a.* COMPUT raccourci *m* **②** *fig* solution *f* de facilité

**shorten** ['ʃɔr·tᵊn] I. *vt* raccourcir; (*story*) abréger II. *vi* **①** (*make shorter*) raccourcir **②** (*reduce odds*) s'affaiblir

**short-handed** *adj* **to be ~** être en sous-effectif

**shortlist** *vt* sélectionner

**short-lived** *adj* (*happiness*) de courte durée

**shortly** *adv* peu de temps

**shorts** *npl* **①** (*short pants*) short *m;* **a pair of ~** un short **②** (*men's underwear*) caleçon *m*

**short-sighted** *adj* **①** (*of eyesight*) myope **②** (*not prudent*) imprévoyant(e)

**short-sleeved** *adj* à manches courtes

**short-staffed** *adj* **to be ~** être en sous-effectif

**short story** *n* nouvelle *f*

**short-tempered** *adj* coléreux(-euse)

**short-term** *adj* (*loan, policy, memory*) à court terme

**short-term parking** *n* parking *m* de courte durée

**short wave** *n* ondes *fpl* courtes

**short-wave** *adj* ~ **signal** signal *m* en ondes courtes; ~ **radio/receiver** radio *f*/récepteur *m* à ondes courtes

**shot¹** [ʃat] **I.** *n* ① (*firing of weapon*) coup *m* (de feu) ② (*ammunition*) plomb *m* ③ SPORTS (*attempt at scoring*) tir *m* ④ (*throw*) lancement *m* ⑤ (*photograph*) photo *f* ⑥ CINE plan *m*; **to get a ~ of sth** filmer qc ⑦ *inf* MED piqûre *f*; (*of heroin*) shoot *m* ⑧ *inf* (*try*) essai *m*; **to give sth one's best ~** faire de son mieux ⑨ (*of whiskey, vodka*) petit verre *m* ▶ **~ in the arm** un coup de pouce; **to take a ~ in the dark** *inf* répondre au pif **II.** *pp, pt of* **shoot**

**shot²** [ʃat] *adj* ① (*woven to show colors: silk*) à reflets; **to be ~ with silver** avoir des reflets argentés ② *inf* (*worn out*) foutu(e)

**shotgun** *n* fusil *m* de chasse

**shot put** *n* SPORTS **the ~** le lancer du poids

**should** [ʃʊd] *aux* ① (*showing obligation*) I/you ~ je/tu devrais; **to insist that one ~ do sth** insister pour que qn fasse qc (*subj*) ② (*asking for advice*) ~ I …? est-ce que je dois …? ③ (*might*) **for fear that sb/sth ~ …** si jamais qn/qc …; **if I ~ fall** au cas où je tomberais

**shoulder** ['ʃoʊl·dər] **I.** *n* ① (*body part*) épaule *f* ② FASHION épaulette *f*; **padded ~s** épaulettes *fpl* ③ CULIN épaule *f* ④ (*side of a road*) accotement *m*; **hard ~** bande *f* d'arrêt d'urgence ⑤ (*shoulder-like part: of a mountain*) crête *f* ▶ **a ~ to cry on** une épaule pour pleurer; **~ to ~** côte à côte **II.** *vt* ① (*place on shoulders*) porter sur ses épaules ② *fig* (*accept: responsibility*) endosser ③ (*move one's shoulders*) pousser de l'épaule; **to ~ one's way** se frayer un chemin à coups d'épaules

**shoulder bag** *n* sac *m* à bandoulière

**shoulder pad** *n* épaulette *f*

**shoulder strap** *n* (*of dress*) bretelle *f*; (*of bag*) bandoulière *f*

**shout** [ʃaʊt] **I.** *n* (*loud cry*) cri *m* ▶ **to give sb a ~** *inf* engueuler qn; (*phone*) passer un coup de fil à qn **II.** *vi* **to ~ at sb** crier après qn; **to ~ for help** crier à l'aide ▶ **to give sb sth to ~ about** donner à qn l'occasion de se réjouir **III.** *vt*

(*slogan, warning*) crier

◆**shout down** *vt* faire taire qn en criant plus fort

◆**shout out** *vt* crier

**shouting** *n* cris *mpl*; **within ~ distance of sth** à portée de voix de qc; *fig* tout près de qc

**shouting match** *n* engueulade *f*

**shove** [ʃʌv] **I.** *n* poussée *f* **II.** *vt* pousser; **to ~ sb/sth aside** pousser qn/qc de côté; **to ~ sb around** bousculer qn; **to ~ one's way through sth** se frayer un chemin dans qc en poussant **III.** *vi* pousser; **to ~ along/over** se pousser

◆**shove off** *vi* ① *inf* (*go away*) se casser ② (*in boat*) pousser au large

**shovel** ['ʃʌv·əl] **I.** *n* ① (*tool*) pelle *f* ② (*quantity*) pelletée *f* **II.** <-l- *o* -ll-> *vt* pelleter **III.** <-l- *o* -ll-> *vi* se goinfrer

**show** [ʃoʊ] **I.** *n* ① (*demonstration*) démonstration *f* ② (*false demonstration*) semblant *m*; **just for ~** pour impressionner ③ (*exhibition: of fashion*) défilé *m*; (*of photographs*) exposition *f* ④ (*play*) spectacle *m*; (*concert*) concert *m* ⑤ TV émission *f* ⑥ CINE séance *f* ⑦ *inf* (*business*) affaires *fpl* ▶ **on a ~ of hands** à main levée; **let's get the ~ on the road** *inf* au boulot **II.** <showed, shown> *vt* ① (*display: flag, way*) montrer; **to ~ signs of sth** donner des signes de qc; **to ~ sb around a place** faire visiter un endroit à qn; **to ~ sb how to** +*infin* montrer à qn comment +*infin* ② (*express: bias, enthusiasm*) montrer; (*courage, initiative*) faire preuve de ③ (*record*) enregistrer; (*statistics*) montrer; (*profit, loss*) faire apparaître ④ (*escort*) raccompagner; **to ~ sb to the door** raccompagner qn jusqu'à la porte ⑤ (*project: movie, TV drama*) passer ▶ **to ~ sb the door** virer qn; **he has nothing to ~ for his efforts** il n'a pas été récompensé pour ses efforts; **that will ~ him/them** *inf* ça lui/leur apprendra **III.** <showed, shown> *vi* ① (*be visible*) se voir ② *sl* (*arrive*) arriver ③ (*be shown: film*) passer

**S**

◆ **show in** *vt* faire entrer

◆ **show off** I. *vt* exhiber II. *vi* frimer

◆ **show out** *vt* raccompagner

◆ **show up** I. *vi* ❶ (*appear*) ressortir ❷ *inf* (*arrive*) venir II. *vt* ❶ (*expose*) **to show sb up as** (**being**) **sth** révéler qn comme qc ❷ (*embarrass*) faire honte à

**show biz** *n inf abbr of* **show business** showbiz *m*

**show business** *n* show-business *m*

**showcase** I. *n* vitrine *f* II. *vt* présenter; (*talent*) exposer

**shower** ['ʃaʊər] I. *n* ❶ (*brief fall: of rain, snow, hail*) averse *f*; (*of stones*) volée *f*; (*of sparks*) pluie *f*; **thunder ~** averse orageuse ❷ (*large amount*) **to bring a ~ of praise upon sb** encenser qn ❸ (*for washing*) douche *f* ❹ (*party*) enterrement de vie de jeune fille ou fête organisée pour la naissance d'un bébé II. *vt* ❶ (*cover*) *a. fig* couvrir; **to ~ sb with sth** couvrir qn de qc ❷ (*spray*) verser; (*missiles*) pilonner III. *vi* ❶ (*take a shower*) prendre une douche ❷ *fig* **to ~ over sb/sth** pleuvoir sur qn/qc

**shower gel** *n* gel *m* douche

**shower stall** *n* cabine *f* de douche

**showery** ['ʃaʊər·i] *adj* pluvieux(-euse)

**show jumping** *n* concours *m* de saut d'obstacles

**shown** [ʃoʊn] *pp of* **show**

**showoff** *n* vantard(e) *m(f)*

**show room** *n* salle *f* d'exposition

**shrank** [ʃræŋk] *pt of* **shrink**

**shrapnel** ['ʃræp·nəl] *n* éclat *m* d'obus

**shredder** ['ʃred·ər] *n* déchiqueteuse *f*

**shrimp** [ʃrɪmp] *n* ❶ <-(s)> (*crustacean*) crevette *f* ❷ *pej, sl* (*short person*) nabot(e) *m(f)*

**shrink** [ʃrɪŋk] I. *n sl* psy *mf* II. <shrank *o* shrunk, shrunk *o* shrunken> *vt* (*sweater*) faire rétrécir; (*costs*) réduire III. <shrank *o* shrunk, shrunk *o* shrunken> *vi* ❶ (*become smaller: sweater*) rétrécir; (*number, audience*) se réduire; (*profits*) chuter ❷ (*be reluctant to*) **to ~ from doing sth** être réticent à faire qc

◆ **shrivel up** *vi* (*fruit*) se flétrir ▶**to want to ~ and die** vouloir disparaître

**shrub** [ʃrʌb] *n* arbuste *m*

**shrug** [ʃrʌg] I. *n* haussement *m* d'épaules II. <-gg-> *vt* **to ~ one's shoulders** hausser les épaules; *fig* s'en ficher III. <-gg-> *vi* hausser les épaules

◆ **shrug off** *vt* ❶ (*dismiss*) ignorer ❷ (*get rid of*) faire fi de

**shrunk** [ʃrʌŋk] *pp, pt of* **shrink**

**shuffle** ['ʃʌf·l] I. *n* ❶ (*of feet*) traînement *m* de pieds ❷ (*of cards*) **to give the cards a ~** battre les cartes ❸ (*rearrangement*) **to give one's papers a ~** remettre de l'ordre dans ses papiers ❹ (*shakeup*) **cabinet ~** remaniement *m* ministériel; **management ~** changement *m* de directeurs II. *vt* ❶ (*drag*) **to ~ one's feet** traîner les pieds ❷ (*mix*) brasser; (*cards*) battre ❸ (*move around*) déplacer III. *vi* ❶ (*mix cards*) mélanger ❷ (*drag one's feet*) traîner les pieds ❸ *fig* **to ~ along** traîner

**shut** [ʃʌt] I. *adj* (*door*) fermé(e); (*curtains*) tiré(e); **to slam a door ~** claquer une porte II. <-tt-, shut, shut> *vt* fermer; (*book*) refermer; **to ~ one's ears to sth** ne pas vouloir entendre qc III. <-tt-, shut, shut> *vi* ❶ (*close*) se fermer ❷ (*stop operating*) fermer

◆ **shut away** *vt* enfermer

◆ **shut down** I. *vt* fermer II. *vi* (*factory*) fermer; (*engine*) s'arrêter

◆ **shut in** *vt* enfermer

◆ **shut off** *vt* ❶ (*isolate*) couper ❷ (*turn off: engine*) couper ❸ (*stop sending: aid*) stopper; (*signals*) arrêter

◆ **shut out** *vt* ❶ (*block out: light*) bloquer; (*memory*) effacer ❷ (*exclude*) exclure; (*of power*) évincer ❸ sports écarter

◆ **shut up** I. *vt* ❶ (*confine*) enfermer ❷ *inf* (*cause to stop talking*) faire taire; **to shut sb up for good** refroidir qn II. *vi infse* taire

**shutdown** *n* fermeture *f*

**shutter** *n* ❶ phot déclencheur *m* ❷ (*window cover*) volet *m*

**shuttle** ['ʃʌt·l] I. *n* ❶ (*transportation*) navette *f*; **air ~ service** service *m* de vol régulier ❷ (*space shuttle*) navette *f* spatiale ❸ (*on sewing machine*) canette *f* II. *vt* véhiculer III. *vi* faire la navette

**shuttle bus** *n* navette *f*

**shuttle flight** *n* vol *m* régulier

**shuttle service** *n* service *m* de navette

**shy** [ʃaɪ] I. <-er *o* -ier, -est *o* -iest> *adj* ❶ (*timid: person, smile*) timide; (*child, animal*) craintif(-ive); **to be ~ of people** craindre les gens ❷ (*lacking*) manquer de; **we are \$50 ~** il nous manque 50 dollars II. <-ie-> *vi* (*horse*) se cabrer

◆**shy away** *vi* **to ~ from doing sth** éviter de faire qc

**shyness** *n* timidité *f*; (*of animals*) caractère *m* craintif

**sick** [sɪk] I. <-er, -est> *adj* ❶ (*ill*) *a. fig* malade; **to get** [*o* form **fall**] **~** tomber malade; **to feel ~** se sentir mal; **to call in ~**, se faire porter malade ❷ (*nauseous*) **to be** [*o* get] **~** vomir; **to feel ~** avoir mal au cœur ❸ *inf* (*disgusted*) écœuré(e) ❹ *inf* (*fed up*) **to be ~ of sb/sth** en avoir marre de qn/qc; **to be ~ and tired of sth** en avoir assez de qc ❺ *inf* (*cruel, tasteless*) malsain(e) ▶**~ as a dog** malade comme un chien; **to be worried ~** *inf* être malade d'inquiétude II. *n pl* **the ~** les malades *mpl*

**sickening** *adj* ❶ (*disgusting*) écœurant(e) ❷ (*annoying*) insoutenable

**sick leave** ['sɪk·liːv] *n* MED **to be on ~** être en congé de maladie

**sickness** *n* ❶ (*illness*) maladie *f* ❷ (*vomiting*) vomissements *mpl* ❸ *fig* (*disgust*) écœurement *m*

**sick pay** *n* ADMIN, MED indemnité *f* de maladie

**side** [saɪd] *n* ❶ (*surface*) côté *m*; (*of record*) face *f*; (*of mountain*) flanc *m*; **the right ~** l'endroit *m*; **the wrong ~** l'envers *m*; **at sb's ~** aux côtés de qn; **~ by** côté *f* à côte ❷ (*edge*) bord *m*; **on all ~s** de tous les côtés ❸ (*left or right half*) moitié *f* ❹ (*direction*) côté *m*; **from ~ to ~** d'un côté à l'autre ❺ (*opposing group*) côté *m*; **to take ~s** prendre parti; **to take sb's ~** prendre

parti pour qn; **to be on the other ~** être dans l'autre camp ❻ (*aspect*) aspect *m*; (*of story*) version *f* ❼ (*team*) équipe *f* ❽ (*of the family*) côté *m* ▶**the other ~ of the coin** le revers de la médaille; **on the ~** à côté; (*served separately*) en accompagnement

**sideboard** ['saɪd·bɔrd] *n* buffet *m*

**sideburns** ['saɪd·bɜrnz] *npl* favoris *mpl*

**side dish** *n* CULIN garniture *f*

**side effect** *n* MED effet *m* secondaire

**sideline** I. *n* ❶ SPORTS ligne *f* de touche; **on the ~s** *a. fig* sur la touche ❷ (*secondary activity*) activité *f* secondaire II. *vt inf* ❶ (*keep from playing*) remplacer ❷ (*ignore opinions of*) mettre sur la touche

**side road** *n* route *f* secondaire

**sidestep** <-pp-> I. *vt* éviter II. *vi* faire un pas de côté

**side street** *n* petite rue *f*

**sidewalk** *n* trottoir *m*

**sieve** [sɪv] I. *n* tamis *m* II. *vt* tamiser

**sigh** [saɪ] I. *n* soupir *m* II. *vi* ❶ (*emit a breath*) soupirer ❷ *fig, form* (*long for*) **to ~ for sb** regretter qn

**sight** [saɪt] I. *n* ❶ (*faculty of seeing*) vue *f* ❷ (*act of seeing*) vue *f*; **at first ~** à première vue; **to catch ~ of sb/sth** apercevoir qn/qc; **get out of my ~!** *inf* hors de ma vue ! ❸ (*view*) vue *f* ❹ (*range of vision*) vue *f*; **to be out of one's ~** être hors de vue de qn; *fig* être éloigné de qn; **within ~ of sth** en vue de qc ❺ *pl* (*attractions*) attractions *fpl* touristiques ❻ (*gun's aiming device*) mire *f* ▶**to be a ~ for sore eyes** *inf* être un spectacle réjouissant; **~ unseen** sans regarder; **to set one's ~s on sb/sth** avoir l'œil sur qn/qc II. *vt* (*see*) apercevoir

**sightseeing** ['saɪt·siː·ɪŋ] *n* tourisme *m*

**sign** [saɪn] I. *n* ❶ (*signpost*) panneau *m* ❷ (*signboard*) enseigne *f* ❸ (*gesture*) geste *m*; **to make a ~ to sb** faire un signe à qn ❹ (*symbol*) signe *m* ❺ (*indication*) indication *f*; **the first ~ of spring** les premiers signes du printemps II. *vt* ❶ (*write signature on*) signer ❷ (*ges-*

*ticulate*) faire signe **III.** *vi* ❶ (*write signature*) signer ❷ (*gesticulate*) faire un signe; **to ~ to sb that ...** indiquer à qn par un signe que ...

◆ **sign in I.** *vi* signer en arrivant **II.** *vt* **sign sb in** signer pour faire entrer qn

◆ **sign off** *vi* ❶ (*end*) terminer ❷ (*end a letter*) finir une lettre

◆ **sign on I.** *vi* **to ~ as sth** s'engager comme qc; **to ~ with a company** se faire embaucher dans une entreprise **II.** *vt* engager

◆ **sign out I.** *vi* signer à la sortie **II.** *vt* (*record departure*) noter le départ de

◆ **sign up I.** *vi a.* MIL s'engager; **to ~ for sth** s'inscrire à qc **II.** *vt* **to sign sb up for sth** inscrire qn à qc

**signal** ['sɪɡ·nəl] **I.** *n* ❶ (*particular gesture*) *a.* COMPUT signal *m*; **to give sb the ~ to** *+infin* faire signe à qn de *+infin* ❷ (*indication*) signe *m*; **to be a ~ that ...** indiquer que ... ❸ AUTO clignotant *m* **II.** <-l- *o* -ll-> *vt* ❶ (*indicate*) signaler; **to ~ that ...** indiquer que ... ❷ (*gesticulate*) faire signe **III.** <-l- *o* -ll-> *vi* faire des signaux

**signal(l)er** *n* RAIL aiguilleur, -euse *m, f*
**signal light** *n* lampe *f* témoin
**signal tower** *n* RAIL poste *m* d'aiguillage
**signature** ['sɪɡ·nə·tʃər] *n* signature *f*
**significance** [sɪɡ·'nɪf·ə·kən(t)s] *n* ❶ (*importance*) importance *f* ❷ (*meaning*) signification *f*
**significant** *adj* ❶ (*considerable*) considérable ❷ (*important*) important(e) ❸ (*meaningful*) significatif(-ive)
**signpost** *n* ❶ (*post*) poteau *m* indicateur ❷ *fig* indication *f*
**silence** ['saɪ·lən(t)s] **I.** *n* silence *m* ► **~ is golden** *prov* le silence est d'or *prov* **II.** *vt* réduire au silence
**silent** ['saɪ·lənt] *adj* silencieux(-euse); **~ film** *m* muet
**silently** *adv* silencieusement
**silent partner** *n* ECON associé(e) *m(f)* commanditaire
**silhouette** [ˌsɪl·u·'et] **I.** *n* silhouette *f* **II.** *vt* **to be ~d against sth** se profiler sur qc

**silk** [sɪlk] *n* soie *f*
**silly** ['sɪl·i] <-ier, -iest> **I.** *adj* bête; **to look ~** avoir l'air ridicule **II.** *n* bêta *m*
**silo** ['saɪ·loʊ] *n* silo *m*
**silver** ['sɪl·vər] **I.** *n* ❶ (*precious metal*) argent *m* ❷ (*coins*) pièces *fpl* d'argent ❸ (*cutlery*) **the ~** l'argenterie *f* **II.** *adj* ❶ (*made of silver*) en argent ❷ (*silver-colored*) argenté(e) **III.** *vt* argenter
**silver wedding anniversary** *n* noces *fpl* d'argent
**similar** ['sɪm·ə·lər] *adj* semblable
**similarity** [ˌsɪm·ə·'ler·ə·t̬i] *n* ressemblance *f*
**simmer** ['sɪm·ər] **I.** *vi* CULIN mijoter **II.** *vt* faire mijoter **III.** *n* **to keep at a ~** cuire à petit feu

◆ **simmer down** *vi inf* se calmer

**simple** ['sɪm·pl] <-r, -st *o* more ~, most ~> *adj* ❶ (*not complex*) simple ❷ (*foolish*) bête
**simplify** ['sɪm·plə·faɪ] *vt* simplifier
**simply** ['sɪm·pli] *adv* ❶ (*not complexly*) simplement ❷ (*absolutely*) absolument
**simultaneous** [ˌsaɪ·məl·'teɪ·njəs] *adj* simultané(e)
**sin** [sɪn] **I.** *n* péché *m* **II.** <-nn-> *vi* pécher
**since** [sɪn(t)s] **I.** *adv* ❶ (*from that point on*) depuis; **ever ~** depuis lors ❷ (*ago*) **long ~** il y a longtemps **II.** *prep* depuis; **how long has it been ~ the crime?** à quand remonte le crime? **III.** *conj* ❶ (*from time that*) depuis que; **it's been a week now ~ I came back** cela fait maintenant une semaine que je suis revenu ❷ (*because*) puisque
**sincere** [sɪn·'sɪr] *adj* sincère
**sincerely** *adv* ❶ (*in sincere manner*) sincèrement ❷ (*closing letters*) **~ (yours)** veuillez agréer, Madame/Monsieur, mes respectueuses salutations
**sing** <sang *o* sung, sung> **I.** *vi* ❶ (*make music: bird, person*) chanter ❷ (*make high-pitched noise: kettle*) siffler; (*wind*) hurler ❸ (*be filled with ringing*) bourdonner **II.** *vt* chanter; **to ~ tenor/soprano** avoir une voix de ténor/de soprano ► **to ~ another tune** chanter sur

un autre ton; (*change what you think*) changer d'avis

◆ **sing out** I. *vi* ❶ (*sing loudly*) chanter à tue-tête ❷ *inf* (*call out*) gueuler II. *vt inf* gueuler

**sing.** LING *abbr of* **singular**

**singer** ['sɪŋ·ər] *n* chanteur, -euse *m, f*

**singer-songwriter** *n* compositeur, -trice *m, f* interprète

**singing** *n* chant *m*

**singing club** *n* chorale *f*

**singing telegram** *n* télégramme *m* chanté

**single** ['sɪŋ·gl] I. *adj* ❶ (*one*) seul(e); **not a ~ word** pas un mot; **every ~ day** tous les jours ❷ (*for one person: bed*) à une place; (*room*) simple ❸ ECON (*currency, price, market*) unique ❹ (*unmarried*) célibataire; (*parent*) isolé(e) II. *n* ❶ (*one-dollar bill*) billet *m* d'un dollar ❷ (*record*) single *m* ❸ (*single room*) chambre *f* individuelle ❹ *pl* SPORTS simple *m* III. *vi* SPORTS jouer en simple

◆ **single out** *vt* identifier

**single file** *n* **in ~** en file indienne

**single-handed** I. *adj* sans aide II. *adv* tout seul

**single-lens reflex** (**camera**) *n* PHOT appareil *m* photo reflex

**single-minded** *adj* tenace

**single-parent family** <-ies> *n* famille *f* monoparentale

**singleton** ['sɪŋ·gl·tən] *n* célibataire *mf*

**singsong** I. *n* **to speak in a ~** parler d'une voix chantante II. *adj* chantant(e)

**singular** ['sɪŋ·gjə·lər] I. *adj* ❶ LING au singulier ❷ (*extraordinary*) singulier(-ère) II. *n* LING singulier *m*

**sinister** ['sɪn·ɪ·stər] *adj* ❶ (*scary*) épouvantable ❷ *inf* (*ominous*) sinistre

**sink** [sɪŋk] <sank *o* sunk, sunk> I. *n* (*in kitchen*) évier *m*; (*in bathroom*) lavabo *m* II. *vi* ❶ (*not float*) couler ❷ (*go downward: to the bottom*) sombrer ❸ (*drop down*) s'effondrer; **to ~ to one's knees** tomber à genoux ❹ (*decrease: prices, interest rate*) diminuer ❺ (*become softer: voice*) s'adoucir ❻ (*become sadder: heart*) s'assombrir

❼ (*decline: in sb's estimation*) baisser ❽ (*deteriorate: health*) s'aggraver; **to ~ into a coma** tomber dans le coma ► "**~ or** **swim**" "marche ou crève" III. *vt* ❶ (*cause to submerge*) plonger ❷ (*ruin*) ruiner ❸ MIN (*well*) forer ❹ SPORTS battre (à plate couture) ❺ (*lower: voice*) réduire

◆ **sink back** *vi* ❶ (*lean back*) s'affaler ❷ (*return to bad habits*) **to ~ into sth** replonger dans qc

◆ **sink down** *vi* ❶ (*descend: aircraft*) effectuer une descente ❷ (*drop to ground*) s'effondrer ❸ (*sit*) s'asseoir

◆ **sink in** I. *vi* ❶ (*go into surface*) s'enfoncer ❷ (*be absorbed: liquid*) pénétrer ❸ (*be understood*) rentrer (dans la tête de qn) II. *vt* ❶ (*eat*) **to sink one's teeth into sth** planter ses crocs dans qc ❷ (*invest*) **to sink one's money into sth** placer son argent dans qc

**sinkhole** *n* gouffre *m*

**sinking** I. *adj* ❶ (*not floating*) qui coule ❷ (*sad: feeling*) angoissant(e) ❸ (*declining*) en baisse II. *n* (*of ship*) naufrage *m*; (*by torpedoes*) torpillage *m*

**sinner** ['sɪn·ər] *n* pécheur, pécheresse *m, f*

**sip** [sɪp] I. *n* petite gorgée *f*; **to have** [*o* **take**] **a ~** boire une gorgée II. <-pp-> *vt* boire à petites gorgées; (*alcohol*) siroter III. <-pp-> *vi* boire à petites gorgées

**sir** [sɜr] *n* Monsieur *m*; **yes ~** oui Monsieur; MIL oui mon commandant; **no ~** *inf* certainement pas

**siren** ['saɪ·rən] *n* sirène *f*

**sissy** ['sɪs·i] *pej* I. <-ies> *n* <-ier, -iest> *inf* poule *f* mouillée II. *adj* *inf* de nana

**sister** ['sɪs·tər] I. *n* ❶ (*woman, girl*) sœur *f* ❷ (*nun*) **Sister Catherine** sœur Catherine II. *adj* (*city, university, school*) jumelé(e); **~ company** société *f* apparentée

**sister-in-law** <:sisters-in-law:> *n* belle--sœur *f*

**sit** [sɪt] <-tt, sat, sat> I. *vi* ❶ (*be seated*) être assis; (*for a portrait*) poser; (*bird*) être perché ❷ (*take sitting position*)

S

s'asseoir; "~"! (*to a dog*) "assis!" ❸ (*be in session: assembly, court*) siéger ❹ (*be placed, not moved*) se trouver; **to ~ still** se tenir tranquille ❺ *inf* (*babysit*) s'occuper de ❻ (*on nest: bird*) couver ❼ (*be agreeable*) plaire; **that doesn't ~ well with me** ça ne me convient pas ▶ **to ~ on the fence** tergiverser; **to be ~ting pretty** être bien loti II. *vt* ❶ (*put on seat*) asseoir ❷ (*place*) placer

◆**sit around** *vi* ne rien faire

◆**sit back** *vi* ❶ (*lean back*) se caler dans sa chaise ❷ (*do nothing*) ne rien faire ❸ (*relax*) se détendre

◆**sit down** I. *vi* s'asseoir II. *vt* asseoir

◆**sit in** *vi* ❶ (*attend*) **to ~ on sth** assister à qc ❷ (*represent*) **to ~ for sb** remplacer qn ❸ (*participate in sit-in*) occuper les locaux ❹ (*feel heavy: sb's stomach*) rester sur

◆**sit on** *vt* ❶ (*not deal with*) ne pas s'occuper de ❷ (*keep secret*) garder secret ❸ *inf* (*rebuke*) rembarrer ❹ (*put end to: idea, scheme*) mettre un terme à

◆**sit out** I. *vi* ❶ (*sit outside*) s'asseoir dehors ❷ (*not dance*) faire tapisserie II. *vt* ❶ (*not take part in*) ne pas prendre part à ❷ (*sit until the end*) rester jusqu'à la fin de

◆**sit through** *vt* rester jusqu'au bout de

◆**sit up** I. *vi* ❶ (*sit erect*) se redresser; **to ~ straight** se tenir droit ❷ (*not go to bed*) veiller; **to ~ waiting for sb** attendre qn ❸ *inf* (*pay attention*) faire attention II. *vt* redresser

**sitcom** ['sɪt·kam] *n inf abbr of* **situation comedy** sitcom *f*

**site** [saɪt] I. *n* ❶ (*place*) site *m*; (*of building*) emplacement *m*; (*of a battle*) champ *m*; (*of recent events*) lieux *mpl* ❷ (*building land*) chantier *m*; **archaeological ~** site *m* archéologique ❸ COMPUT site II. *vt* construire

**sitting room** *n* salon *m*

**situated** *adj* ❶ (*located*) situé(e); **to be ~ near ...** se situer près de ... ❷ (*in a state*) **to be ~ for sth** bien convenir pour qc

**situation** [ˌsɪtʃ·u·'eɪ·ʃ°n] *n* situation *f*

**six** [sɪks] I. *adj* six ▶ **to be ~ feet under iron** être à six pieds sous terre II.<-es> *n* six *m*; *s.a.* **eight**

**six-pack** *n* pack *m* de six (unités)

**sixteen** [sɪk·'stin] *adj* seize; *s.a.* **eight**

**sixth** *adj* sixième; *s.a.* **eighth**

**sixtieth** *adj* soixantième; *s.a.* **eighth**

**sixty** ['sɪk·sti] *adj* soixante; *s.a.* **eight, eighty**

**sizable** *adj* considérable

**size**[1] [saɪz] I. *n* ❶ TECH apprêt *m* ❷ (*glue*) colle *f* II. *vt* ❶ TECH apprêter ❷ (*glue*) encoller

**size**[2] [saɪz] I. *n* (*of person, clothes*) taille *f*; (*of building, room*) dimension *f*; (*of country, area*) étendue *f*; (*of paper, books*) format *m*; (*of an amount, bill, debt*) montant *m*; (*of problems*) importance *f*; **to double in ~** doubler de volume; **to take** [*o* **wear**] **~ 10** (*of clothing*) faire du 42; **to take** [*o* **wear**] **~ 8½** (*of shoes*) chausser du 40 II. *vt* classer

◆**size up** *vt* évaluer; (*problem*) mesurer (l'ampleur de)

**sizeable** *s.* **sizable**

**skate**[1] [skeɪt] *n* (*fish*) raie *f*

**skate**[2] [skeɪt] I. *n* ❶ (*ice skate*) patin *m* à glace ❷ (*roller skate*) patin *m* à roulettes ❸ (*skateboard*) planche *f* à roulettes, skate-board *m* II. *vi* ❶ (*on ice*) patiner ❷ (*on roller skates*) faire du patin à roulettes; (*on Rollerblades*®) faire du roller; (*on skateboard*) faire du skate-board ❸ *inf* (*not act responsibly*) **to ~ over an issue** esquiver une question ▶ **to be skating on thin ice** s'aventurer sur un terrain glissant

**skateboard** ['skeɪt·bɔrd] *n* planche *f* à roulettes, skate-board *m*

**skateboarder** *n* skateur, -euse *m, f*

**skater** *n* ❶ (*on ice skates*) patineur, -euse *m, f* ❷ (*on a skateboard*) skater, -euse *m, f*

**skating rink** *n* ❶ (*for ice-skating*) patinoire f ② (*for roller-skating*) piste f de patin à roulettes

**skeleton** ['skel·ə·tᵊn] n ① (*bone system*) a. *fig* squelette m ② (*framework: of boat, plane*) carcasse f; (*of building*) charpente f ③ (*sketch: of book, report*) ébauche f ▸ **to have ~s in the closet** cacher un cadavre dans son placard

**skeptic** ['skep·tɪk] n sceptique mf

**skeptical** adj sceptique

**skepticism** ['skep·tɪ·sɪ·zᵊm] n scepticisme m

**sketch** [sketʃ] I. n ① (*drawing*) esquisse f ② (*outline*) croquis m ③ (*first draft*) ébauche f ④ (*summary*) résumé m ⑤ (*comedy scene*) sketch m II. vt esquisser

**sketchpad** n carnet m de croquis

**sketchy** ['sketʃ·i] <-ier, -iest> adj ① (*vague*) rapide; (*idea*) vague ② (*incomplete*) insuffisant(e) ③ (*not realized*) ébauché(e)

**skewer** ['skju·ər] I. n ① (*for cubed meat*) brochette f ② (*for roast*) broche f II. vt ① (*fasten: meat*) mettre à la broche ② (*pierce*) embrocher

**ski** [ski] I. n ski m II. vi skier

**ski boot** n chaussure f de ski

**skid** [skɪd] I. <-dd-> vi ① (*slide while driving*) déraper; **to ~ to a halt** s'arrêter en dérapage ② (*slide*) **to ~ along/across sth** passer/traverser qc en glissant II. n ① (*slide while driving*) dérapage m ② (*spinning*) virage m en boucle ③ AVIAT patin m (d'atterrissage)

**skier** ['ski·ər] n skieur, -euse m, f

**ski goggles** npl lunettes fpl de ski

**skiing** n de ski

**ski instructor** n moniteur, -trice m, f de ski

**ski jump** n ① (*event*) saut m à ski ② (*runway*) tremplin m pour le saut à ski

**skill** [skɪl] n ① expertise f ② (*ability*) talent m ③ (*technique*) technique f

**skim milk** n lait m écrémé

**skin** [skɪn] I. n ① (*of person, fruit*) peau f ② (*animal hide*) cuir m; (*of lion, zebra*) peau ③ (*covering: of aircraft,*

*ship*) habillage m ▸ **it's no ~ off sb's back** cela ne fera pas de mal à qn; **to get under sb's ~** (*irritate, annoy*) taper sur les nerfs de qn II. <-nn-> vt ① (*remove skin: fruit, vegetables*) peler; (*animal*) dépouiller ② (*wound*) faire une écorchure à ③ *fig* **to ~ sb alive** écorcher vif qn

**skinny** ['skɪn·i] <-ier, -iest> adj maigrelet(te)

**skinny-dip** <-pp-> vi *inf* se baigner nu

**skin rash** n éruption f cutanée

**skintight** [skɪn·'taɪt] adj moulant(e)

**skip** [skɪp] I. n saut m II. <-pp-> vt a. *fig* sauter; (*stones*) faire ricocher; **to ~ rope** sauter à la corde ▸ **to ~ it** *inf* laisser tomber III. <-pp-> vi ① (*take light steps*) sautiller ② (*jump, leave out*) sauter ③ *inf* (*go quickly*) faire un saut

**ski pole** n bâton m de ski

**skipper** ['skɪp·ər] I. n ① NAUT, SPORTS capitaine m ② AVIAT commandant m ③ (*form of address*) chef m II. vt avoir la responsabilité de; (*ship, aircraft*) commander; (*team*) diriger

**skip rope** n corde f à sauter

**ski rack** n porte-skis m inv

**ski resort** n station f de ski

**skirt** [skɜrt] I. n ① (*garment*) jupe f ② *pej, sl* (*women*) minette f II. vt ① (*go around: path*) contourner ② (*avoid: issue, question*) esquiver

**ski run** n piste f de ski

**skit** [skɪt] n (*about person*) pastiche m; (*about thing*) parodie f

**skittle** ['skɪt·l] n ① pl (*game*) jeu m de quilles ② (*pin*) quille f

**ski vacation** n vacances fpl au ski

**skull** [skʌl] n crâne m

**sky** [skaɪ] <-ies> n ① (*expanse overhead*) ciel m ② pl (*the heavens*) les cieux mpl ▸ **the ~'s the limit** sans limites

**sky-blue** I. adj bleu ciel inv II. n bleu ciel m

**skydiving** n saut m en parachute

**sky-high** I. adj (*extremely high*) très haut(e) II. adv très haut; **to go ~** (*prices*) s'envoler

S

**skyjack** *vt* (*flight, plane*) détourner

**skylight** ['skaɪ·laɪt] *n* lucarne *f*

**skyline** ['skaɪ·laɪn] *n* ❶ (*of city rooftops*) silhouette *f* ❷ (*horizon*) horizon *m*

**skype** [skaɪp] *vi, vt* TEL, INET skyper

**skyscraper** *n* gratte-ciel *m*

**slack**¹ [slæk] **I.** *adj* ❶ (*not taut*) a. *pej* lâche; **to get** ~ se relâcher ❷ (*not busy: demand, business*) calme **II.** *n* mou *m*; **to take up the** ~ tendre la corde; *fig* relancer le marché **III.** *vi* (*become loose*) a. *fig* se relâcher **IV.** *vt* ❶ (*loosen*) desserrer ❷ (*reduce*) ralentir

**slack**² *n* (*coat dust*) poussier *m*

**slacken I.** *vt* ❶ (*make less tight: reins, rope*) desserrer ❷ (*reduce: one's pace, speed*) ralentir; (*vigilance*) relâcher **II.** *vi* se relâcher

◆**slacken off I.** *vi* se relâcher **II.** *vt* relâcher

**slacks** *npl* pantalon *m*

**slag** [slæg] *n* (*from coal*) scories *fpl*

**slam**¹ [slæm] **I.** <-mm-> *vt* ❶ (*close noisily*) claquer ❷ *inf* (*criticize severely*) descendre en flamme ❸ (*hit hard*) **to** ~ **sth into sth** cogner qc contre qc ❹ (*put down violently*) **to** ~ **down sth, to** ~ **sth down** balancer qc **II.** <-mm-> *vi* ❶ (*shut noisily*) claquer ❷ (*hit hard*) **to** ~ **against sth** cogner contre qc; **to** ~ **into sth** cogner qc **III.** *n* bruit *m* de choc

**slam**² [slæm] *n* ❶ SPORTS, GAMES chelem *m* ❷ LIT slam *m*

**slander** ['slæn·dər] **I.** *n* LAW diffamation *f* **II.** *vt* diffamer

**slanderous** ['slæn·dər·əs] *adj* diffamatoire

**slanted** *adj* (*roof*) incliné(e); (*writing*) penché(e)

**slap** [slæp] **I.** *n* ❶ (*with open hand*) tape *f*; **to give sb a** ~ **in the face** donner une claque à qn ❷ (*noise*) coup *m* ▶**a** ~ **on the** <u>wrist</u> un avertissement; **to be a** ~ **in the** <u>face</u> **for sb** faire l'effet d'une claque à qn **II.** <-pp-> *vt* ❶ (*hit with open hand*) taper; **to** ~ **sb on the back** taper qn dans le dos; (*in congratu-*

*lation*) taper qn sur l'épaule ❷ (*strike*) **to** ~ **sth against sth** cogner qc contre qc **III.** *vi* (*make slapping noise*) claquer; **to** ~ **against sth** taper contre qc **IV.** *adv inf* directement

◆**slap down** *vt* ❶ (*put down with slap*) balancer ❷ (*silence rudely*) engueuler

◆**slap on** *vt* ❶ *inf* (*put on quickly*) tartiner ❷ *inf* (*impose*) **to slap sth on sb** refiler qc à qn

**slapdash** ['slæp·dæʃ] *adj pej, inf* bâclé(e)

**slash** [slæʃ] **I.** *n* ❶ (*cut*) entaille *f* ❷ (*swinging blow*) grand coup *m* ❸ FASHION (*decorative opening*) fente *f* ❹ (*punctuation mark*) barre *f* oblique **II.** *vt* ❶ (*cut*) taillader; (*one's wrists*) s'entailler ❷ (*reduce*) réduire ❸ *fig* **to** ~ **one's way through sth** se tailler un chemin à travers qc **III.** *vi* (*with knife*) **to** ~ **at sth** frapper qc

**slate** [sleɪt] **I.** *n* ❶ (*rock, stone, blackboard*) ardoise *f* ❷ POL liste *f* électorale ▶**to have a** <u>clean</u> ~ avoir les mains propres; **to wipe the** ~ <u>clean</u> faire table rase **II.** *vt* ❶ (*cover with slate: a roof*) couvrir d'ardoises ❷ POL **to be** ~**d for sth** être inscrit pour qc

**slaughter** ['slɔ·tər] **I.** *vt* a. *fig* abattre **II.** *n* ❶ (*killing for food*) abattage *m* ❷ (*cruel killing*) a. *fig* massacre *m*

**slave** [sleɪv] **I.** *n* a. *fig* esclave *mf* **II.** <-ving> *vi* travailler comme un esclave; **to** ~ **at sth** s'échiner à qc

**sleazy** ['sli·zi] <-ier, -iest> *adj* miteux(-euse)

**sledge** [sledʒ] *n* traîneau *m*, glisse *f* Suisse

**sleep** [slip] **I.** *n* sommeil *m*; **to get** [*o* **go**] **to** ~ s'endormir; **to put sb/an animal to** ~ endormir qn/un animal **II.** <slept, slept> *vi* dormir; ~ **tight!** dors/dormez bien! ▶**to** ~ **like a** <u>log</u>, <u>rock</u> *inf* dormir comme une marmotte **III.** *vt* **to** ~ **four/ten** dormir à quatre/dix

◆**sleep around** *vi inf* (*be promiscuous*) coucher

◆**sleep in** vi ❶ (*stay in bed*) dormir tard ❷ (*sleep in employer's house*) être hébergé(e)

◆**sleep off** vt faire la grasse matinée

◆**sleep out** vi découcher

◆**sleep through** I. vt **to ~ noise/a storm** ne pas être réveillé par le bruit/ une tempête; **to ~ a film/lecture** dormir pendant un film/un cours II. vi dormir comme une souche

◆**sleep together** vi dormir ensemble

**sleeper** n ❶ (*person*) dormeur, -euse m, f; **to be a heavy/light ~** avoir le sommeil profond/léger ❷ (*train*) wagon-lit m

**sleeper cell** n MIL, POL cellule f dormante

**sleeping** adj endormi(e)

**sleeping accommodation(s)** n hébergement m

**sleeping bag** n sac m de couchage

**sleeping car** n wagon-lit m

**sleeping pill** n somnifère m

**sleepless** adj insomniaque; **a ~ night** une nuit blanche

**sleepwalk** vi être somnambule

**sleepwalker** n somnambule mf

**sleepy** ['sliˑpi] <-ier, -iest> adj ❶ (*drowsy*) somnolent(e) ❷ (*very quiet: town, afternoon*) tranquille

**sleet** [slit] I. n neige f fondue II. vi it is ~ing il tombe de la neige fondue

**sleeve** [sliv] n ❶ (*of shirt, jacket*) a. fig manche f ❷ (*tube-shaped cover*) manchon m ❸ (*cover for record*) pochette f de disque

**sleeveless** adj sans manches

**sleigh** [sleɪ] n traîneau m

**slender** ['slenˑdər] adj mince

**slept** [slept] pt, pp of **sleep**

**slice** [slaɪs] I. n ❶ (*thin piece: of bread, meat, lemon*) tranche f; (*of cake, pizza*) morceau m ❷ (*part: of the profits, a market*) part f ❸ SPORTS balle f coupée II. vt ❶ (*cut in slices*) couper en tranches ❷ SPORTS (*the ball*) couper III. vi **to ~ easily** se couper facilement

◆**slice off** vt trancher

◆**slice up** vt couper (en tranches)

**sliced** adj coupé(e); (*bread*) en tranches

**slide** [slaɪd] I. <slid, slid> vi ❶ (*glide smoothly*) glisser ❷ (*move quietly*) **to ~ somewhere** se glisser quelque part ❸ (*decline*) se dégrader; **to let sth/ things ~** laisser faire qc/les choses II. <slid, slid> vt pousser III. n ❶ (*act of sliding*) glissade f ❷ (*at playground*) toboggan m ❸ (*on ice*) patinoire f ❹ GEO glissement m ❺ PHOT diapositive f ❻ (*glass for microscope*) porte- -objet m ❼ MUS mouvement m

**slide projector** n projecteur m de diapositives

**slide show** n (*professional*) diaporama m; (*private*) séance f diapos

**sliding** adj coulissant(e)

**slight** [slaɪt] I. <-er, -est> adj ❶ (*small: chance, possibility*) infime, **the ~est thing/idea** la moindre chose/idée ❷ (*not noticeable or serious*) insignifiant(e) ❸ (*slim, delicate*) frêle ❹ (*lightweight*) léger(-ère) II. n (*snub*) offense f III. vt offenser

**slightly** adv un peu

**slim** [slɪm] <-mm-> I. adj ❶ (*attractively thin*) mince ❷ (*not thick*) léger(-ère) ❸ (*slight: chance, possibility*) maigre II. vi **to ~** (**down**) maigrir

**slimy** ['slaɪˑmi] <-ier, -iest> adj a. pej visqueux(-euse)

**sling** [slɪŋ] I. n ❶ (*for broken arm*) écharpe f ❷ (*for baby*) écharpe f porte- -bébé ❸ (*carrying strap*) bandoulière f II. <slung, slung> vt ❶ (*hang*) suspendre; **to ~ sth over one's shoulder** mettre qc en bandoulière ❷ (*throw*) jeter ❸ inf (*put carelessly*) balancer

**slingshot** ['slɪŋˑʃɑt] n fronde f

**slip**[1] [slɪp] n ❶ (*piece: of paper*) bout m; (*official*) bordereau f; **a pay ~** un bulletin de paie ❷ BOT bouture f

**slip**[2] [slɪp] I. <-pp-> vi ❶ (*slide*) glisser; **to ~ through one's fingers** filer entre les doigts ❷ (*move quietly*) se glisser; **to ~ into one's jeans** enfiler son jean; **to ~ into a coma** sombrer dans le coma ❸ (*let out*) **to let sth ~** laisser échapper qc; (*concentration*) relâcher qc ❹ (*de-*

*cline*) baisser ⑤ (*make mistake*) faire une erreur **II.** <-pp-> *vt* ① (*put smoothly*) glisser; **to ~ sb money** glisser de l'argent à qn; **to ~ a shirt on** enfiler une chemise ② (*escape from*) s'échapper; **to ~ sb's mind** échapper à qn **III.** *n* ① (*act of sliding*) glissement *m* ② (*fall*) *a.* *fig* chute *f* ③ (*stumble*) faux pas *m* ④ (*mistake*) erreur *f*; **a ~ of the tongue** un lapsus ⑤ (*petticoat*) combinaison *f*

◆**slip away** *vi* s'éclipser

◆**slip by** *vi* filer; (*time*) passer

◆**slip down** *vi* ① (*fall down*) glisser ② (*be swallowed easily*) descendre tout(e) seul(e)

◆**slip in I.** *vt* glisser **II.** *vi* se glisser

◆**slip off I.** *vi* ① (*leave quietly*) s'éclipser ② (*fall off*) reculer **II.** *vt* ① (*fall from*) glisser de ② (*take off*) enlever

◆**slip on** *vt* (*clothing*) passer

◆**slip out** *vi* ① (*go out*) s'éclipser ② (*escape*) s'échapper; **it slipped out** *fig* cela m'a échappé

◆**slip up** *vi* *inf* se tromper

**slipcover** *n* housse *f*

**slip-on I.** *adj* **~ shoes** mocassins *mpl* **II.** *n* ① (*sweater*) pull *m* ② *pl* (*shoes*) mocassins *mpl*

**slippery** ['slɪp.ər.i] <-ier, -iest> *adj* ① (*not giving firm hold*) glissant(e) ② (*untrustworthy*) douteux(-euse)

**slit** [slɪt] **I.** <-tt-, slit, slit> *vt* couper en deux; **to ~ one's wrists** s'entailler les veines; **to ~ sb's throat** couper la gorge à qn **II.** *n* fente *f*

**slob** [slɑb] *n* *pej*, *inf* cochon(ne) *m(f)*

**slogan** ['sloʊ.gən] *n* slogan *m*

**slope** [sloʊp] **I.** *n* pente *f*; **ski ~** piste *f* de ski **II.** *vi* ① (*be on slope*) **to ~ down** être en pente; **to ~ up** monter ② (*lean*) pencher **III.** *vt* incliner

**sloping** *adj* (*roof, ground*) en pente; (*shoulders*) tombant(e)

**sloppiness** *n* négligence *f*

**sloppy** <-ier, -iest> *adj* ① (*careless*) négligé(e) ② *iron* (*overly sentimental*) à l'eau de rose ③ (*too wet*) trempé(e); (*food*) en bouillie

**slot** [slɑt] **I.** *n* ① (*narrow opening*) fente *f* ② COMPUT fenêtre *f* ③ TV tranche *f* horaire **II.** <-tt-> *vt* (*put into slot*) **to ~ sth in** insérer qc

**slot machine** *n* distributeur *m* automatique

**slow** [sloʊ] **I.** *adj* *a.* *fig* lent(e); **to be 10 minutes ~** (*clock, watch*) retarder de 10 minutes **II.** *vt*, *vi* ralentir

◆**slow down** *vt*, *vi* ralentir

**slowdown** *n* ECON ralentissement *m*

**slowly** *adv* lentement

**slow motion** CINE **I.** *n* ralenti *m*; **in ~** au ralenti **II.** *adj* lent(e)

**slowpoke** *n* *inf* lambin, -e *m, f*

**slow train** *n* omnibus *m*

**SLR** (**camera**) *n* PHOT *abbr of* single- -lens reflex (**camera**) appareil *m* photo reflex

**sluggish** *adj* ① (*not active*) paresseux(-euse) ② FIN (*trading*) stagnant(e)

**slum** [slʌm] **I.** *n* SOCIOL quartier *m* pauvre **II.** <-mm-> *vi* *inf* zoner **III.** <-mm-> *vt* **to ~ it** *iron* zoner

**slumber** ['slʌm.bər] **I.** *n* sommeil *m* **II.** *vi* dormir

**slumlord** *n* marchand(e) *m(f)* de sommeil

**slump** [slʌmp] **I.** *n* ECON ① (*sudden decline*) effondrement *m* ② (*recession*) crise *f* **II.** *vi* *a.* FIN s'effondrer

**slur** [slɜr] **I.** *n* insulte *f* **II.** <-rr-> *vt* (*pronounce unclearly*) mal articuler

**slush** [slʌʃ] *n* ① (*melting snow*) neige *f* fondue ② *pej* LING sensiblerie *f*

**slushy** <-ier, -iest> *adj* ① (*melting*) détrempé(e) par la neige ② (*overly sentimental*) d'une sentimentalité excessive

**sly** [slaɪ] *adj* <-ier *o* -er, -iest *o* -est> rusé(e); (*smile*) espiègle; (*humor*) coquin(e); **on the ~** en cachette

**smack** [smæk] **I.** *vt* ① (*slap*) frapper ② (*slap noisily*) claquer **II.** *n* ① *inf* (*slap*) claque *f* ② *inf* (*noisy kiss*) smack *m*; **a ~ on the lips/cheek** un bisou sur la bouche/joue ③ (*loud noise*) claquement *m* **III.** *adv* en plein; **~ in the middle** au beau milieu

**small** [smɔl] **I.** *adj* ① (*not large*) petit(e)

**②** (*young*) petit(e) **③** (*insignificant*) tout(e) petit(e); **to be no ~ matter** ne pas être une mince affaire; **~ wonder that …** *iron* ce n'est guère étonnant que … +*subj* **④** (*on limited scale*) peu considérable; **in a ~ way** modestement **⑤** TYP, LIT **a ~ letter** une minuscule; **with a ~ 'c'** avec un c minuscule ▶ **it's a ~ world!** *prov* le monde est petit *prov* II. *n* **the ~ of the back** la chute des reins

**small ad** *n* petite annonce *f*

**small change** *n* petite monnaie *f*

**small-minded** *adj* étroit(e) d'esprit

**smallpox** *n* variole *f*

**small print** *n* texte *m* en petits caractères

**small-scale** *adj* réduit(e)

**small talk** *n* bavardages *mpl* sans importance

**smalltime** *adj* insignifiant(e)

**smart** [smart] I. *adj* **①** (*clever*) intelligent(e); **to make a ~ move** prendre une sage décision; **to be ~ with sb** *pej* faire le malin avec qn **②** (*stylish*) élégant(e) **③** (*quick*) vif(vive); **to do sth at a ~ pace** faire qc à un rythme soutenu II. *vi* **①** (*graze*) brûler; (*eyes*) piquer III. *n* **①** (*pain*) douleur *f* cuisante **②** *pl, sl* (*intelligence*) jugeote *f*

**smart aleck** *n inf* petit(e) malin(e) *m(f)*

**smarten** ['smarˑtᵊn] I. *vt* **to ~ sth up** arranger qc; **to ~ oneself up** (*improve one's appearance*) se faire beau II. *vi* **to ~ up** (*person*) se faire beau

**smartphone, smart phone** ['smaːtˑfəʊn] *n* smartphone *m*

**smash** [smæʃ] I. *n* **①** (*noise*) fracas *m* **②** (*blow*) coup *m* **③** (*collision*) accident *m* **④** SPORTS smash *m* **⑤** *inf* (*success*) gros succès *m* II. *vt* **①** (*shatter*) briser; (*violently*) fracasser **②** (*strike*) **to ~ sth against sth** heurter qc contre qc avec violence **③** (*destroy: opponent, army*) écraser **④** SPORTS (*a record*) pulvériser; **to ~ the ball** faire un smash **⑤** PHYS (*atom*) pulvériser III. *vi* **①** (*shatter*) éclater; **to ~ into pieces** éclater en morceaux **②** (*strike against*) se heurter violemment; **to ~ into/ through sth** s'écraser violemment contre qc

◆**smash in** *vt* défoncer; **to smash sb's face in** casser la figure à qn

◆**smash up** *vt* démolir

**smashing** *adj inf* (*success*) énorme

**smashup** *n* destruction *f* complète

**smear** [smɪr] I. *vt* **①** (*spread messily*) barbouiller; **to ~ sth with sth** enduire qc de qc **②** (*destroy by criticizing: reputation, name*) salir II. *n* **①** (*blotch*) tâche *f* **②** (*public accusations*) diffamation *f*

**smell** [smel] <-ed *o* smelt, -ed *o* smelt> I. *n* **①** (*sense of smell*) odorat *m* **②** (*odor*) odeur *f*; **the ~ of roses** le parfum des roses **③** (*bad odor*) puanteur *f* **④** (*sniff*) **to give sth a ~** sentir qc ▶ **the** (*sweet*) **~ of success** la griserie du succès II. *vi* **①** (*sniff*) sentir **②** (*give off odor*) sentir; **sweet-~ing** qui sent bon; **to ~ of sth** sentir qc **③** *pej* (*have bad smell*) sentir mauvais; **to ~ of money** *fig* puer le fric III. *vt a. fig* sentir ▶ **to ~ a rat** se douter de qc

**smelly** ['smelˑi] <-ier, -iest> *adj pej* malodorant(e)

**smelt**[1] [smelt] *pt, pp of* **smell**

**smelt**[2] [smelt] *vt* (*metal*) fondre

**smelt**[3] [smelt] <-(s)> *n* ZOOL éperlan *m*

**smile** [smaɪl] I. *n* sourire *m*; **to be all ~s** être tout sourire II. *vi* **①** (*produce smile*) sourire; **to ~ in the face of adversity** garder le sourire **②** (*approve*) **to ~ on sb/sth** sourire à qn/qc III. *vt* sourire; **to ~ a sad smile** avoir un sourire triste

**smiling** *adj* souriant(e)

**smog** [smɒg] *n* smog *m*

**smoke** [sməʊk] I. *n* **①** (*dirty air*) fumée *f* **②** *inf* (*cigarette*) cigarette *f* ▶ **where there's ~, there's fire** *prov* il n'y a pas de fumée sans feu *prov*; **to go up in ~** partir en fumée II. *vt* **①** (*use tobacco*) fumer **②** (*cure: meat, sausage*) fumer III. *vi* fumer

◆**smoke out** *vt* enfumer

**smoke bomb** *n* bombe *f* fumigène

**smoked** *adj* fumé(e)

**smoke detector** *n* détecteur *m* de fumée

**smoked salmon** *n* saumon *m* fumé

**smokeless** *adj* sans fumée

**smoker** *n* ❶ (*person*) fumeur, -euse *m, f* ❷ (*in train*) compartiment *m* fumeur ❸ (*device*) fumeur *m*

**smoke screen** *n* ❶ MIL écran *m* de fumée ❷ (*concealment*) rideau *m* de fumée

**smokestack** *n* cheminée *f*

**smoking** *n* tabagisme *m*; **to quit ~** arrêter la cigarette

**smoky** ['smou·ki] <-ier, -iest> *adj* ❶ (*filled with smoke*) enfumé(e) ❷ (*producing smoke*) qui fume ❸ (*appearing smoke-like*) noirci(e) par la fumée ❹ (*tasting of smoke*) qui a un goût de fumée

**smooch** [smutʃ] I. *n* **to have a ~** se bécoter II. *vi* se bécoter

**smooth** [smuð] I. *adj* ❶ (*not rough*) lisse; (*skin*) doux(douce) ❷ (*well-mixed, not lumpy*) homogène ❸ (*calm: sea, ride*) calme ❹ (*without problems*) sans problèmes; (*flight*) calme ❺ (*not harsh: wine, brandy*) moelleux(-euse) ❻ (*polished*) doux(douce); **to be a ~ talker** être un beau parleur II. *vt* ❶ (*make smooth*) lisser; (*sheet*) défroisser ❷ (*rub even*) égaliser ❸ (*make less difficult*) **to ~ the way for sb** faciliter les choses pour qn; **to ~ the path to sth** ouvrir la voie vers qc

◆ **smooth down** *vt* lisser

◆ **smooth over** *vt* aplanir

**smoothie** *n* ❶ (*juice drink*) cocktail non alcoolisé à base de fruits, de jus de fruit, de yaourt et servi avec des glaçons ❷ *pej* charmeur, -euse *m, f*

**SMS** [ˌes·em·'es] TEL, INET I. *n abbr of* **short message service** (*service, message*) SMS *m* II. *vt inf* **to ~ sb** envoyer un SMS [*o* texto] à

**smug** [smʌg] <-gg-> *adj* suffisant(e)

**smuggle** ['smʌg·l] *vt* LAW faire passer

**smuggler** *n* contrebandier, -ère *m, f*

**snack** [snæk] I. *n* casse-croûte *m* II. *vi* grignoter

**snack bar** *n* snack-bar *m*, casse-croûte *m* Québec

**snag** [snæg] I. *n* ❶ (*damage to fabric*) accroc *m* ❷ *fig* (*problem*) obstacle *m* caché; **there's a ~** il y a un hic II. <-gg-> *vt* ❶ (*catch and pull*) faire un accroc ❷ (*cause problems*) causer des problèmes ❸ *inf* (*catch*) saisir III. <-gg-> *vi* **to ~ on sth** accrocher à qc

**snail** [sneɪl] *n* escargot *m*

**snake** [sneɪk] I. *n* serpent *m* II. *vi* serpenter

**snakeskin** *n* peau *f* de serpent

**snap** [snæp] I. *n* ❶ (*sound*) claquement *m* ❷ (*photograph*) instantané *m* ❸ (*for fastening clothes*) bouton-pression *m* ❹ METEO **a cold ~** une vague de froid ▸ **in a ~** en un clin d'œil II. <-pp-> *vt* ❶ (*break in two*) casser; (*a ruler*) briser; **to ~ sth off** [*o* **to ~ off sth**] arracher qc ❷ (*make snapping sound*) faire claquer; **to ~ one's fingers** faire claquer ses doigts; **to ~ sth shut** fermer qc brusquement ❸ (*photograph*) prendre; **to ~ sb doing sth** prendre qn en photo en train de faire qc ❹ (*say sharply*) dire sèchement ▸ **to ~ one's fingers at sb** narguer qn III. <-pp-> *vi* ❶ (*make sound*) claquer ❷ (*break suddenly*) se casser ❸ (*spring into position*) **to ~ back** revenir brusquement; **to ~ shut** se fermer avec un bruit sec ❹ (*bite*) **to ~ at sb/sth** essayer de mordre qn/happer qc ❺ (*speak sharply*) parler sèchement; **to ~ at sb** s'adresser à qn d'un ton sec; **to ~** (**back**) **that ...** répliquer sèchement que ... ▸ **~ to it!** la ferme! IV. *adj* hâtif(-ive)

◆ **snap out** I. *vt* (*order*) donner d'un ton sec II. *vi inf* **~ of it!** secoue-toi!

◆ **snap up** *vt* ❶ (*seize*) saisir ❷ (*buy*) rafler

**snarl**[1] [snarl] I. *n* ❶ (*growl*) grognement *m*; (*by person*) grondement *m* ❷ (*sound*) ronronnement *m* II. *vi* grogner; **to ~ at sb** gronder contre qn

**snarl²** [snɑrl] I. n ❶ (*in hair*) enchevêtrement m ❷ (*traffic jam*) embouteillage m II. vi (*become tangled*) s'emmêler

**snatch** [snætʃ] I. <-es> n ❶ (*sudden grab*) mouvement m vif ❷ (*theft*) vol m à l'arraché ❸ (*fragment*) fragment m; (*of conversation*) bribe f; (*of time*) courte période f; **a few ~es of music** quelques notes fpl de musique ❹ vulg (*vulva*) chatte f II. vt ❶ (*grab quickly*) saisir; **to ~ sth out of sb's hand** arracher qc de la main de qn ❷ (*steal*) voler ❸ (*kidnap*) kidnapper ❹ (*take advantage of*) saisir ❺ SPORTS arracher de justesse III. vi saisir brusquement; **to ~ at sth** essayer de saisir qc

◆ **snatch away** vt arracher; **to snatch sth away from sb** arracher qc des mains de qn

◆ **snatch up** vt ramasser vivement

**snazzy** ['snæz·i] <-ier, -iest> adj inf chouette

**sneakers** n pl baskets fpl, espadrilles fpl Québec

**sneak preview** n avant-première f

**sneak thief** n chipeur, -euse m, f

**sneaky** <-ier, -iest> adj sournois(e)

**sneeze** [sniz] I. n éternuement m II. vi éternuer ▸ **not to be ~d at** ne pas être à dédaigner

**snicker** ['snɪk·ər] I. n ricanement m II. vi ricaner

**sniff** [snɪf] I. n reniflement m; **to catch a ~ of sth** sentir qc II. vi ❶ (*inhale sharply*) renifler ❷ (*show disdain*) renifler avec dédain; **to ~ at sth** dédaigner qc III. vt renifler

◆ **sniff out** vt ❶ (*locate by smelling*) détecter ❷ fig (*discover*) déterrer

**snigger** ['snɪg·ər] s. **snicker**

**snip** [snɪp] I. n ❶ (*cut*) entaille f; **to give sth a ~** donner un coup de ciseaux à qc ❷ (*small piece: of cloth*) bout m; (*of information*) bribe f II. vt couper

**sniper** n MIL tireur m embusqué, sniper m

**snooze** [snuz] inf I. vi faire un somme II. n petit somme m; **to take a ~** faire un (petit) somme

**snore** [snɔr] MED I. vi ronfler II. n ronflement m

**snorkel** ['snɔr·kəl] SPORTS I. n tuba m II. <-l- o -ll-> vi faire de la plongée avec un tuba

**snot** [snɑt] n vulg (*mucus*) morve f

**snout** [snaʊt] n ❶ BIO museau m; (*of a pig*) groin m ❷ sl ANAT pif m

**snow** [snoʊ] I. n ❶ METEO neige f ❷ TV (*static*) neige f ❸ sl (*cocaine*) neige f II. vi neiger III. vt sl embobiner; **to ~ sb into believing sth** faire croire qc à qn

◆ **snow in** vt **to be snowed in** être bloqué par la neige

◆ **snow under** vt **to be snowed under with sth** être submergé de qc

**snowball** I. n boule f de neige II. vi lancer des boules de neige; fig faire boule de neige

**snowboard** I. n snowboard m II. vi faire du snowboard

**snowcapped** adj enneigé(e)

**snow chains** npl AUTO chaînes fpl à neige

**snowdrift** n congère f, banc m de neige Québec, menée f Suisse

**snowflake** n flocon m de neige

**snow line** n neiges fpl éternelles

**snowman** n bonhomme m de neige

**snowmobile** n motoneige m

**snowplow** n chasse-neige m

**snowstorm** n tempête f de neige

**snow tire** n AUTO pneu m neige

**snowy** <-ier, -iest> adj ❶ METEO (*typically with snow: region, country*) neigeux(-euse) ❷ (*covered with snow: street, highway, field*) enneigé(e) ❸ (*with much snow: day, winter*) de neige; (*month, season*) des neiges ❹ ART (*pure white*) blanc(he) comme neige

**snub** [snʌb] I. <-bb-> vt snober II. n rebuffade f

**snug** [snʌg] adj <-gg-> ❶ (*cozy*) confortable ❷ (*warm*) douillet(te) ❸ FASHION (*tight*) ajusté(e) ❹ (*adequate: income, wage*) confortable

**snuggle** ['snʌg·l] I. vi se blottir II. vt blottir

S

**so** [soʊ] **I.** adv ❶ (in same way) ainsi; ~ **to speak** pour ainsi dire ❷ (also) ~ **did/do/have/am I** moi aussi ❸ (like that) ~ **they say** c'est ce qu'on dit; **is that** ~? vraiment?; **I hope/think** ~ je l'espère/le pense ❹ (to such degree) tellement; ~ **late** si tard; ~ **many books** tant de livres; **to be** ~ **kind as to** +infin avoir la gentillesse de +infin ❺ (as a result) ~ **that he did sth** de sorte [o si bien] qu'il a fait qc ▶~ **long!** à un de ces jours!; ~ **long as** (if) dans la mesure où; **and** ~ **on** [o **forth**] et ainsi de suite; **or** ~ à peu près; *s.a.* **far, much, many II.** conj ❶ (therefore) donc ❷ (in order that) ~ ... **pour** ... +infin; ~ **that** ... pour que ... +subj ❸ (summing up) alors; ~ **what?** et alors?; ~ **now,** ... et maintenant, ...; ~, **I was saying** ... j'étais donc en train de dire ...; ~ **(then) he told me** ... et alors il m'a dit ...; ~ **that's why!** ah! c'est pour ça!

**soak** [soʊk] **I.** n ❶ (time under water) immersion f; **to give sth a** ~ faire tremper qc ❷ sl (heavy drinker) poivrot(e) m(f) **II.** vt ❶ CULIN (set in water) faire tremper ❷ (make wet) tremper ❸ sl (overcharge) faire casquer **III.** vi ❶ (let sit in water: beans, peas) tremper ❷ sl (drink heavily) boire comme un trou
◆**soak in** I. vi ❶ (become absorbed) pénétrer ❷ (become understood) piger inf **II.** vt a. fig s'imprégner de qc
◆**soak off** vt faire partir en laissant tremper
◆**soak up** vt a. fig absorber; (the atmosphere) s'imprégner de

**soaking I.** n trempage m; **to give sth a** ~ laisser tremper qc **II.** adj ~ (wet) trempé(e)

**soap** [soʊp] **I.** n ❶ (for washing) savon m; **a bar/piece of** ~ une savonnette ❷ TV (soap opera) feuilleton m ▶~ **soft** inf flatteries fpl **II.** vt savonner

**soap dispenser** n distributeur m de savon (liquide)

**soap opera** n TV soap-opéra m

**sober** ['soʊ·bər] **I.** adj ❶ CULIN (not drunk) sobre ❷ (serious: mood) sérieux(-euse) ❸ (calm) calme ❹ (moderate: person) posé(e) ❺ (plain: clothes, color) sobre ❻ (simple: truth) simple **II.** vt calmer **III.** vi se calmer
◆**sober up I.** vi ❶ (become less drunk) se dégriser ❷ (become serious) se calmer **II.** vt ❶ (make less drunk) dégriser ❷ (make serious) calmer

**so-called** adj soi-disant(e)

**soccer** ['sa·kər] n football m

**sociable** ['soʊ·ʃə·bl] adj ❶ (fond of mixing socially) sociable; **to not feel very** ~ ne pas être d'humeur à côtoyer du monde ❷ (friendly) amical(e); **to do sth just to be** ~ faire qc par politesse

**social** ['soʊ·ʃəl] SOCIOL **I.** adj social(e) **II.** n soirée f

**socialize** ['soʊ·ʃə·laɪz] **I.** vi ❶ SOCIOL (have human contact) fréquenter des gens ❷ fig (talk: student) bavarder **II.** vt socialiser

**social worker** n assistant(e) m(f) social(e)

**society** [sə·'saɪ·ə·t̬i] n société f

**sociopolitical** adj sociopolitique

**sock**¹ [sak] <-s o sox> n (for foot) chaussette f; **ankle** ~s socquettes fpl ▶**to knock sb's** ~s **off** inf épater qn

**sock**² [sak] inf **I.** vt ❶ (hit) mettre une beigne à; **to** ~ **sb in the eye** mettre un coquard à qn ❷ fig **to be** ~**ed with sth** être sonné par qc **II.** n beigne f

**socket** ['sa·kɪt] n ❶ (energy source) prise f de courant; (for light bulb) douille f ❷ (cavity) cavité f

**soda** ['soʊ·də] n CULIN ❶ (seltzer) eau f de Seltz ❷ (soft drink) soda m ❸ (sodium) soude f

**sofa** ['soʊ·fə] n sofa m

**sofa bed** n canapé-lit m

**soft** [saft] adj ❶ (not hard: ground, sand) mou(molle); (pillow, chair) mœlleux(-euse); (wood, rock) tendre; (contact lenses) souple ❷ (melted: ice cream, butter) ramolli(e) ❸ (smooth: cloth, skin, hair) doux(douce); (leather) souple; **a** ~ **landing** un atterrissage en dou-

ceur ④ (*weak: muscles*) mou(molle)
⑤ (*mild: climate, drug*) doux(douce)
⑥ (*not glaring: color, light*) doux(douce); (*blue*) tendre ⑦ (*quiet: music, sound, words*) doux(douce) ⑧ (*lenient*) indulgent(e); (*heart*) tendre; **to be ~ on sb/sth** se montrer indulgent envers qn/qc ⑨ (*easy*) facile ⑩ (*not refined: outline, plan*) flou(e)
▶ **to be ~ in the** <u>head</u> *pej* être débile; **to have a ~** <u>spot</u> **for sb** avoir un faible pour qn

**soft-boiled** *adj* CULIN (*egg*) mollet
**soft drink** *n* boisson *f* non alcoolisée
**soften I.** *vi* ① (*let get soft: butter, ice cream*) se ramollir; (*skin, color*) s'adoucir; (*leather*) s'assouplir ② (*become less severe*) s'attendrir **II.** *vt* ① (*make soft: butter, margarine*) ramollir; (*skin*) adoucir, (*leather*) assouplir ② (*make more pleasant: a sound, color*) adoucir ③ (*make emotional*) attendrir ④ (*make easier to bear: pain, effect, anger*) atténuer; (*blow*) amortir
♦ **soften up I.** *vt* ① (*make softer*) ramollir ② (*persuade*) amadouer ③ MIL (*weaken*) amoindrir **II.** *vi* se ramollir
**softheaded** *adj* bête
**softhearted** *adj* au cœur tendre
**softly** *adv* doucement
**software** ['saf(t)·wer] *n* COMPUT logiciel *m*
**soggy** ['sa·gi] <-ier, -iest> *adj* ① (*wet and soft*) trempé(e); (*field, ground*) détrempé(e) ② (*rainy: weather, atmosphere*) lourd(e) ③ (*mushy*) ramolli(e)
**soil**[1] [sɔɪl] **I.** *vt* *form* ① (*make dirty*) souiller; (*clothing*) salir ② *fig* (*ruin: reputation*) entacher **II.** *vi* se salir
**soil**[2] [sɔɪl] *n a. fig* AGR, BOT sol *m*
**solar** ['sou·lər] *adj* solaire; (*car*) à énergie solaire; (*light*) du soleil
**solar energy** *n* ECOL, ELEC énergie *f* solaire
**sold** [sould] *pt, pp of* **sell**
**soldier** ['soul·dʒər] MIL **I.** *n a. fig* soldat *m* **II.** *vi* servir dans l'armée
**sold-out** *adj* (*book, products*) épuisé(e); (*concert*) complet(-ète)

**sole**[1] [soul] *adj* ① (*only*) unique ② (*exclusive: right*) exclusif(-ive)
**sole**[2] [soul] *n* (*of foot*) plante *f* du pied; (*of shoe*) semelle *f*
**sole**[3] [soul] *n* (*fish*) sole *f*
**solely** ['sou·li] *adv* uniquement
**solicitor** *n* ① POL (*lawyer for city*) ≈ juriste *mf* ② *Can* LAW (*lawyer*) avocat(e) *m(f)*
**solid** ['sa·lɪd] **I.** *adj* ① (*strong, hard, stable*) solide ② (*not hollow*) plein(e); (*silver, gold*) massif(-ive); (*crowd, mass*) compact(e) ③ (*not liquid*) solide ④ (*true: facts, reasons, meal*) solide ⑤ (*without interruption*) sans interruption; (*wall, line*) continu(e); **four ~ hours** quatre heures d'affilée ⑥ (*unanimous: approval*) unanime *fig* (*healthy, reliable: boy, democrat, relationship*) solide **II.** *adv* ① (*completely*) complètement ② (*continuously*) d'affilée **III.** *n* ① (*solid object, substance*) solide *m* ② *pl* CULIN aliments *mpl* solides
**solidarity** [ˌsa·lə·ˈder·ə·t̬i] *n* solidarité *f*
**solid-state** *adj* PHYS relatif(-ive) aux substances solides; (*conductor, device*) semi-conducteur(-trice); **~ physics** physique *f* des solides
**solitary** ['sa·lə·ter·i] **I.** *adj* ① (*single*) seul(e); ZOOL solitaire ② (*isolated*) isolé(e); **to go for a ~ stroll/walk** se promener en solitaire ③ (*secluded, remote*) retiré(e) **II.** *n* ① *inf* (*isolation in prison*) isolement *m* cellulaire ② (*hermit*) ermite *m*
**solitary confinement** *n* isolement *m* cellulaire
**solitude** ['sa·lə·tud] *n* solitude *f*
**soluble** ['sal·jə·bl] *adj* soluble
**solution** [sə·ˈlu·ʃən] *n* solution *f*
**solve** [salv] *vt* résoudre
**some** [sʌm] **I.** *indef adj* ① *pl* (*several*) quelques; **~ people think ...** il y a des gens qui pensent ... ② (*imprecise*) (*at*) **~ place** quelque part; (*at*) **~ time** à un moment quelconque; **~ other time** une autre fois; **~ time ago** il y a quelques temps ③ (*a little*) un peu; **to ~ extent** dans une certaine mesure **II.** *indef pron*

**S**

**①** pl (several) quelques-un(e)s; ~ like it, others don't certains l'aiment, d'autres pas **②** sing (part of it) en **III.** adv environ; ~ more nuts/wine encore quelques noix/un peu de vin

**somebody** ['sʌm·ˌba·di] indef pron (some person) quelqu'un; ~ or other je ne sais qui; s.a. anybody, nobody

**somehow** ['sʌm·haʊ] adv **①** (through unknown methods) d'une façon ou d'une autre **②** (for unclear reason) pour une raison ou une autre **③** (come what may) coûte que coûte

**someone** ['sʌm·wʌn] pron s. somebody

**someplace** ['sʌm·pleɪs] adv quelque part

**somersault** ['sʌm·ər·sɔlt] **I.** n **①** (movement) a. fig culbute f **②** SPORTS saut m périlleux **II.** vi **①** (make movement) faire des culbutes; (vehicle, car) faire des tonneaux **②** SPORTS faire un saut périlleux

**something** ['sʌm(p)·θɪŋ] **I.** indef pron, sing **①** (some object, concept) quelque chose; ~ or other je ne sais quoi **②** (about) ... or ~ inf ... ou quelque chose comme ça; five foot ~ cinq pieds et quelques; his name is Paul ~ il s'appelle Paul Machin-Chose **II.** n a little ~ un petit quelque chose; a certain ~ un je-ne-sais-quoi **III.** adv (about) un peu; ~ over $100 un peu plus de 100 dollars; ~ around $10 dans les 10 dollars; s.a. anything, nothing

**sometime** ['sʌm·taɪm] **I.** adv un jour ou l'autre **II.** adj ancien(ne)

**sometimes** adv quelquefois

**somewhat** ['sʌm·(h)wat] adv quelque peu; to feel ~ better se sentir un peu mieux

**somewhere** ['sʌm·(h)wer] adv **①** (non-specified place) quelque part; ~ else autre part; (to other place) ailleurs; fig quelque part; to get ~ aboutir **②** (roughly) environ

**son** [sʌn] n **①** (male offspring) a. fig fils m **②** (form of address to boy) fiston m **③** (boy) gars m

**sonar** ['soʊ·nar] n abbr of sound navigation and ranging sonar m

**song** [sɔŋ] n **①** (musical form) chanson f **②** (action of singing) chant m; to burst into ~ se mettre à chanter **③** (of bird) chant m

**song and dance** n inf **①** THEAT spectacle m de chant et de danse **②** (untrue tale) histoires fpl; to give a ~ about sb/sth faire toute une histoire de qc/à propos de qn

**songbook** n recueil m de chansons

**sonic** ['sa·nɪk] adj sonique; (wave) sonore

**sonic boom** n bang m supersonique

**son-in-law** <sons-in-law o -s> n beau-fils m

**son of a bitch** <sons of bitches> n vulg fils m de pute

**soon** [sun] adv **①** (shortly) peu de temps; ~ after sth peu après qc; how ~ dans combien de temps; as ~ as dès que **②** (rapidly) rapidement

**sooner** ['sun·ər] adv comp of soon plus tôt; ~ or later tôt ou tard; the ~ the better le plus tôt sera le mieux; no ~ said than done c'est plus vite dit que fait

**soot** [sʊt] n suie f

**soothing** adj **①** (calming) reposant(e); (comment, smile) apaisant(e) **②** (relieving pain) calmant(e) **③** (relaxing: ointment, balm, massage) apaisant(e)

**sophisticated** [sə·ˈfɪs·tə·keɪ·tɪd] adj sophistiqué(e); (taste) raffiné(e); (style) recherché(e)

**sopping** ['sa·pɪŋ] adj inf trempé(e); to be ~ wet être tout trempé

**soppy** ['sa·pi] <-ier, -iest> adj inf fleur bleue inv

**sore** [sɔr] **I.** adj **①** (painful) douloureux(-euse); to have a ~ throat avoir mal à la gorge **②** fig (touchy) a ~ point un sujet délicat **③** inf (angry) en rogne; ~ loser mauvais perdant m **④** (severe, urgent) to be in ~ need of sth avoir grand besoin de qc ▶ to stick out like a ~ **thumb** (thing) être criard; (person) se faire remarquer **II.** *n* **①** MED plaie *f* **②** *fig* blessure *f*

**sorrow** ['sar·oʊ] *n* chagrin *m;* *(of a book, film, music)* tristesse *f;* **to feel ~ over sth** être chagriné par qc

**sorry** ['sar·i] <-ier, -iest> **I.** *adj* **①** *(apologizing)* désolé(e); **to feel ~ for oneself** s'apitoyer sur son sort **②** *(regretful)* **to say ~** s'excuser **③** *(said before refusing)* désolé(e); **④** *(poor in quality)* piteux(-euse); *(choice)* malheureux(-euse); *(sight)* triste **II.** *interj* **①** *(in apology)* ~! désolé(e)! **②** *(before refusing)* non, désolé(e) **③** *(requesting repetition)* ~? pardon?

**sort** [sɔrt] **I.** *n* **①** *(type)* sorte *f;* **some ~ of sth** un genre de qc; **nothing of the ~** rien de la sorte; **something of the ~** quelque chose comme ça; **all ~s of people** des gens de tous les milieux; **that's my ~ of thing** c'est le genre de chose que j'aime **②** *inf (type of person)* **to be a friendly ~** être un brave type/ une brave fille; **to not be the ~ to +** *infin* ne pas être du genre à +*infin* **③** *inf (in a way)* **~ of** à peu près; **to be ~ of embarrassing** être plutôt gênant **④** COMPUT tri *m* ▸ **to be out of ~s** être mal en point **II.** *vt* **①** *(select)* a. COMPUT trier **②** *(clean up)* ranger **III.** *vi* trier; **to ~ through sth** faire le tri dans qc

  ♦ **sort out** *vt* **①** *(select)* trier; **to ~ sth from sth** séparer qc de qc **②** *(organize, clean up)* ranger; *(files)* classer; *(papers, desk)* mettre de l'ordre dans **③** *(fix)* arranger **④** *(resolve: problem)* régler; *(difficulties)* aplanir; *(priorities)* établir; **to ~ whether/what/who ...** essayer de savoir si/ce que/qui

**so-so** *inf* **I.** *adj* moyen(ne) **II.** *adv* comme ci, comme ça

**soul** [soʊl] *n* **①** *(spirit)* âme *f* **②** *(profound feelings)* âme *f* **③** *(person)* âme *f* **④** MUS soul *f* **⑤** *(essence)* cœur *m;* **to be the ~ of discretion/ honesty** être la discrétion/l'honnêteté personnifiée

**soul mate** *n* âme *f* sœur

**sound¹** [saʊnd] **I.** *n* **①** *(tone)* son *m;* **to**

**like the ~ of one's own voice** aimer s'entendre parler **②** *(noise)* bruit *m;* **knocking ~** cognement *m* **③** PHYS son *m* **④** MUS son *m* **⑤** *(idea expressed in words)* **I don't like the ~ of it** cela ne me dit rien qui ne vaille **II.** *vi* **①** *(resonate: bell)* sonner; *(alarm, siren)* retentir **②** LING sonner; **it ~s better** cela sonne mieux **③** *(appear)* sembler; **to ~ as though ...** on dirait que ...; **to ~ nice** avoir l'air bien; **it ~s like Bach** on dirait du Bach **III.** *vt* **①** *(make ring: bell)* sonner; *(alarm)* donner; *(buzzer)* déclencher; *(gong)* faire sonner; *(siren)* faire retentir; **to ~ the (car) horn** klaxonner **②** *(pronounce)* prononcer **③** *fig (give signal)* **to ~ the retreat** MIL sonner la retraite

**sound²** [saʊnd] **I.** *adj* **①** *(healthy: person)* en bonne santé; *(body)* sain(e); **to be of ~ mind** être sain d'esprit **②** *(in good condition)* en bon état **③** *(trustworthy)* solide; *(advice)* judicieux(-euse); *(investment, method)* sûr(e); *(reasoning)* valable; *(view)* sensé(e); **environmentally ~** bon pour l'environnement **④** *(thorough)* complet(-ète); *(defeat)* total(e), *(knowledge)* approfondi(e); *(sleep)* profond(e) **II.** *adv* **to be ~ asleep** être profondément endormi

**sound³** [saʊnd] *vt* **①** NAUT sonder **②** MED *(person)* ausculter

  ♦ **sound out** *vt* sonder

**sound⁴** *n* **①** *(sea channel)* bras *m* de mer **②** *(sea surrounded by land)* détroit *m*

**soundboard** *n* MUS table *f* d'harmonie

**sound box** *n* caisse *f* de résonance

**sound effects** *npl* effets *mpl* sonores

**sound engineer** *n* ingénieur *mf* du son

**sounding board** *n* MUS table *f* d'harmonie

**soundproof I.** *adj* insonorisé(e) **II.** *vt* insonoriser

**sound system** *n* sono *f*

**soup** [sup] *n* soupe *f;* *(thinner soup)* potage *m;* **clear ~** bouillon *m*

**soupspoon** *n* cuillère *f* à soupe

S

**sour** [saʊər] **I.** *adj* ❶ (*bitter*) aigre; **to go ~** devenir aigre; (*milk*) tourner ❷ *fig* aigri(e); **to go ~** mal tourner ▶ **to be just ~ grapes** être déçu **II.** *n* **whiskey ~** whisky *m* citron **III.** *vt* ❶ CULIN (*give bitter taste*) faire tourner ❷ *fig* aigrir **IV.** *vi* ❶ CULIN (*become bitter*) tourner ❷ *fig* s'aigrir

**source** [sɔrs] **I.** *n* a. *fig* source *f;* **to have one's ~ in sth** avoir son origine dans qc; **to track down the ~ of sth** tracer la provenance de qc **II.** *vt* ❶ (*state origin*) **to be ~d from sth** provenir de qc ❷ (*obtain from other business*) se procurer

**sour cream** *n* crème *f* aigre

**south** [saʊθ] **I.** *n* ❶ (*cardinal point*) sud *m* ❷ GEO sud *m;* **in the ~ of France** dans le midi de la France; **the South** les États *mpl* du Sud **II.** *adj* (*side, coast*) sud *inv;* **~ wind** vent *m* du sud; **in ~ Paris** dans le sud de Paris **III.** *adv* au sud; (*travel*) vers le sud; **a window facing ~** une fenêtre exposée au sud

**South Africa** *n* l'Afrique *f* du Sud

**South African** **I.** *adj* sud-africain(e) **II.** *n* Sud-africain(e) *m(f)*

**South America** *n* l'Amérique *f* du Sud

**South American** **I.** *adj* sud-américain(e) **II.** *n* Sud-américain(e) *m(f)*

**South Carolina** *n* la Caroline-du-Sud

**South Dakota** *n* le Dakota-du-Sud

**south-east** **I.** *n* sud-est *m* **II.** *adj* du sud--est **III.** *adv* au sud-est; (*travel*) vers le sud-est; *s.a.* **south**

**southeasterly** *adj* du sud-est

**southeastern** *adj* du sud-est

**southeastward(s)** *adv* vers le sud-est

**southerly** [ˈsʌðərli] **I.** *adj* (*toward the south*) vers le sud; **the most ~ place** l'endroit *m* le plus au sud **II.** *adv* sud **III.** <-ies> *n* sud *m*

**southern** *adj* du sud; (*from south of France*) du midi; **~ California** le sud de la Californie

**southerner** *n* ❶ (*native, inhabitant*) habitant(e) *m(f)* du sud; (*of American South*) habitant(e) *m(f)* du sud des États-Unis ❷ HIST sudiste *mf*

**Southern Hemisphere** *n* hémisphère *m* sud

**southern lights** *npl* aurore *f* australe

**South Korea** *n* la Corée du Sud

**South Korean** **I.** *adj* sud-coréen(e) **II.** *n* Coréen(ne) *m(f)* du Sud

**South Pole** *n* le pôle Sud

**southwest** **I.** *n* sud-ouest *m* **II.** *adj* du sud-ouest **III.** *adv* au sud-ouest; (*travel*) vers le sud-ouest; *s.a.* **south**

**southwesterly** **I.** *adj* du sud-ouest **II.** *adv* vers le sud-ouest

**southwestern** *adj* du sud-ouest

**southwestward(s)** *adv* vers le sud-ouest

**souvenir** [ˌsuːvəˈnɪr] *n* souvenir *m*

**Soviet** [ˈsoʊviˌet] **I.** *n* HIST soviet *m* **II.** *adj* soviétique

**Soviet Union** *n* HIST l'Union *f* soviétique

**sow** [soʊ] <sowed, sown *o* sowed> *vt,* *vi* a. *fig* semer

**sown** [soʊn] *pp of* **sow**

**soy** [sɔɪ] *n,* **soya** [ˈsɔɪ·ə] *n* soja *m*

**soybean** *n* graine *f* de soja

**soymilk** *n* lait *m* de soja

**soy sauce** *n* sauce *f* soja

**spa** [spɑ] *n* station *f* thermale; **day ~** centre *m* de spa

**space** [speɪs] **I.** *n* ❶ (*area, gap*) a. COMPUT, TYP espace *m;* **a blank ~** un blanc; **empty ~** vide *m* ❷ (*room*) place *f;* **open ~** espaces *mpl* verts; **wide open ~** grands espaces *mpl;* **to take up ~** prendre de la place; **to stare into ~** regarder dans le vide ❸ (*interval of time*) période *f;* **in the ~ of one hour** en l'espace d'une heure ❹ (*outer space*) espace *m;* **in ~** dans l'espace; **to go into ~** aller dans l'espace **II.** *vt* espacer

**space blanket** *n* couverture *f* thermique

**space center** *n* centre *m* spatial

**spacecraft** <-> *n* vaisseau *m* spatial

**space flight** *n* voyage *m* spatial

**space lab, space laboratory** *n* laboratoire *m* spatial

**space-saving** *adj* peu encombrant(e)

**spaceship** *n* vaisseau *m* spatial

**space shuttle** *n* navette *f* spatiale

**space station** *n* station *f* spatiale

**space suit** *n* scaphandre *m*

**space tourism** *n* tourisme *m* spatial

**space travel** *n* voyage *m* dans l'espace

**space traveler** *n* astronaute *mf*

**space walk** *n* sortie *f* dans l'espace

**spacing** ['speɪs·ɪŋ] *n* espacement *m*; **single/double ~** simple/double interligne *m*

**spacious** ['speɪ·ʃəs] *adj* spacieux(-euse)

**spade** [speɪd] *n* ❶ (*garden tool*) bêche *f* ❷ (*playing card*) pique *m* ▶ **to** call **a ~ a ~** appeler un chat un chat; **in ~s** *inf* à fond

**spaghetti** [spə·'geṭ·i] *n* spaghettis *mpl*

**spaghetti Western** *n* western *m* spaghetti

**Spain** [speɪn] *n* l'Espagne *f*

**spam** [spæm] *n* *no pl, sl* INET spam *m*; **~ filter** filtre *m* anti-spam, pourriel *m* *Québec*

**spambot** ['spæm·bɒt] *n* COMPUT spambot *m*

**Spanglish** ['spæŋ·lɪʃ] *n* spanglish *m* (*langue hybride mêlant l'anglais et l'espagnol*); *s.a.* **English**

**Spaniard** ['spæn·jərd] *n* Espagnol(e) *m(f)*

**Spanish** ['spæn·ɪʃ] I. *adj* espagnol(e); **~ speaker** hispanophone *mf* II. *n* ❶ (*people*) **the ~** les Espagnols *mpl* ❷ LING espagnol *m*; *s.a.* **English**

**spank** [spæŋk] I. *vt* fesser II. *n* fessée *f*; **to give sb a ~** donner la fessée à qn

**spare** [sper] I. *vt* ❶ (*be merciful to*) épargner ❷ (*refrain from doing*) épargner; (*efforts, strength*) ménager; **to ~ no expense** ne pas regarder à la dépense ❸ (*do without*) se passer de; **to ~ (the) time** avoir le temps; **to not have time to ~** ne pas avoir le temps; **to ~ sb a moment** accorder une minute à qn ▶ **to have sth** to **~** avoir qc de réserve II. *adj* ❶ (*reserve: key, clothes*) de rechange ❷ (*available: seat, room, cash*) disponible; **to have a ~ minute** avoir une minute ❸ (*simple*) dépouillé(e) III. *n* ❶ (*reserve item*) pièce *f* de rechange; (*tire*) roue *f* de secours ❷ (*in bowling*) spare *m*

**spareribs** *npl* travers *mpl* de porc

**spare time** *n* temps *m* libre; **in my ~** à mes heures perdues

**spare tire** *n* ❶ AUTO roue *f* de secours ❷ *fig, iron* (*undesired fat at waist*) bouée *f*

**spark** [spark] I. *n* ❶ (*from fire*) a. *fig* étincelle *f* ❷ (*small amount*) étincelle *f* II. *vt* a. *fig* déclencher; **to ~ sth in sb** déclencher qc en qn; **to ~ sb into action** pousser qn à l'action III. *vi* jeter des étincelles

**sparkler** *n* ❶ (*firework*) bougie *f* magique ❷ *inf* (*diamond*) diam *m*

**sparkling** *adj* a. *fig* étincelant(e); (*drink*) pétillant(e), spitant(e) *Belgique*

**spark plug** *n* bougie *f*

**sparrow** ['spær·oʊ] *n* moineau *m*

**sparrow hawk** *n* ['spær·oʊ·hɔk] *n* épervier *m*

**Spartan** ['spar·tᵊn] *adj* spartiate

**spat¹** [spæt] *pt, pp of* **spit**

**spat²** [spæt] I. *n* (*brief argument*) prise *f* de bec II. <-tt-> *vi* avoir une prise de bec

**speak** [spik] <spoke, spoken> I. *vi* ❶ (*articulate*) parler; **to ~ to sb about sth** parler de qc à qn; **to ~ for/against sth** être en faveur/opposé à qc; **the facts ~ for themselves** les faits parlent d'eux-mêmes; **to ~ in a whisper** chuchoter; **~ only when you're spoken to!** tu réponds quand on te parle! ❷ (*from specified point of view*) **geographically ~ing** d'un point de vue géographique; **~ing of sth** à propos de qc; **so to ~** pour ainsi dire ❸ (*make formal speech*) faire un discours; **to ~ in public** parler en public ❹ (*communicate on phone*) être à l'appareil ▶ **actions ~ louder than words** *prov* les actes sont plus éloquents que les paroles II. *vt* ❶ (*say*) dire; (*language*) parler; **to ~ the truth** dire la vérité; **to ~ one's mind** donner son opinion ❷ (*reveal*) révéler

◆ **speak out** *vi* prendre la parole; **to ~**

**against sth** dénoncer qc
♦ **speak up** *vi* parler fort; **to ~ for sth** parler en faveur de qn
**speaker** *n* ❶ *(of a specific language)* interlocuteur, -trice *m, f* ❷ *(orator)* orateur, -trice *m, f* ❸ *(chairperson of legislature)* **the Speaker** le(la) président(e) de la Chambre des représentants ❹ *(loudspeaker)* haut-parleur *m* ❺ COMPUT enceinte *f*
**speaking** I. *n* parler *m*; **public ~** art *m* oratoire II. *adj a. fig* parlant(e); **to be no longer on ~ terms with sb** ne plus adresser la parole à qn; **English-~** de langue anglaise
**spear** [spɪr] I. *n* ❶ *(weapon)* lance *f* ❷ *(of asparagus)* pointe *f* II. *vt* **to ~ sb/sth** transpercer qn/qc d'un coup de lance
**spearmint** ['spɪr·mɪnt] I. *n* menthe *f* II. *adj* à la menthe
**spec** [spek] *n inf abbr of* **specifications** caractéristiques *fpl*
**special** ['speʃ·ᵊl] I. *adj* spécial(e); *(attention, treatment, diet)* particulier(-ère); *(clinic, committee, school)* spécialisé(e); **to be ~ to sb** compter pour qn; **nothing ~** *inf* rien de spécial II. *n* ❶ *(TV program, show)* programme *m* spécial ❷ CULIN plat *m* du jour ❸ *pl (sale items)* offres *fpl* spéciales ❹ RAIL train *m* spécial
**special education** *n* éducation *f* spécialisée
**special effects** *npl* effets *mpl* spéciaux
**specialist** I. *n* spécialiste *mf*; **a heart ~** un(e) cardiologue II. *adj* spécialisé(e)
**specialize** ['speʃ·ə·laɪz] *vi* se spécialiser
**specially** *adv* ❶ *(specifically)* spécialement ❷ *(in particular)* particulièrement
**specialty** ['speʃ·ᵊl·ti] <-ies> *n* spécialité *f*
**species** ['spi·fiz] *inv n* espèce *f*; **to be a rare ~** *fig, iron, inf* être un drôle d'oiseau
**specific** [spə·'sɪf·ɪk] *adj* ❶ *(distinguishing)* spécifique; **to be ~ to sth** être spécifique à qc ❷ *(clearly defined: date, details, knowledge)* précis(e)

**specifically** *adv* ❶ *(expressly)* spécifiquement ❷ *(clearly)* expressément
**specification** [ˌspes·ə·fɪ·'keɪ·ʃᵊn] *n* spécification *f*; **~s** caractéristiques *fpl*
**specimen** ['spes·ə·mən] *n* ❶ *(example)* spécimen *m*; **a fine ~** *inf* un beau spécimen; **a poor ~** *inf* un sale type ❷ *(sample)* échantillon *m*; MED *(urine, blood)* prélèvement *m*
**spectacles** *n pl* lunettes *fpl*
**spectacular** [spek·'tæk·jə·lər] I. *adj* spectaculaire II. *n* grand spectacle *m*
**spectator** [spek·'teɪ·t̬ər] *n* spectateur, -trice *m, f*
**speech** [spitʃ] <-es> *n* ❶ *(act of speaking)* parole *f*; **to be slow in ~** parler lentement ❷ *(lines spoken by actor)* texte *m* ❸ *(public talk)* discours *m*
**speechless** *adj* muet(te); **to leave sb ~** laisser qn sans voix
**speechwriter** *n* rédacteur, -trice *m, f* de discours
**speed** [spid] I. *n* ❶ *(velocity)* vitesse *f*; **cruising ~** vitesse de croisière; **(at) full ~** à toute vitesse; **at lightning ~** à la vitesse de l'éclair; **the ~ of light/sound** la vitesse de la lumière/du son ❷ *fig (quickness)* rapidité *f* ❸ *(gear on bicycle)* vitesse *f* ❹ *sl (amphetamine)* amphète *f* ▸ **to be up to ~** aller à toute vitesse; **to bring sb up to ~** tenir qn au courant de qc II. <-ed *o* sped, -ed *o* sped> *vi* ❶ *(hasten)* se dépêcher ❷ *(exceed speed limit)* aller trop vite III. <-ed *o* sped, -ed *o* sped> *vt* accélérer; *(person)* presser
♦ **speed up** I. *vt* accélérer; *(person)* presser II. *vi* ❶ *(gather momentum)* aller plus vite ❷ *(accelerate activity)* accélérer
**speedboat** *n* hors-bord *m*
**speed bump** *n* ralentisseur *m*
**speed dating** *n no art* speed dating *m*
**speeding** *n* excès *m* de vitesse
**speed limit** *n* limite *f* de vitesse
**speedometer** [spi·'da·mə·t̬ər] *n* compteur *m* de vitesse
**speedup** *n* accélération *f*
**speedy** ['spi·di] <-ier, -iest> *adj* rapide

**spell¹** [spel] *n* (*in magic*) formule *f* magique; **to cast** [*o* **put**] **a ~ on sb** jeter un sort à qn; **to be under sb's ~** *fig* être sous le charme de qn

**spell²** [spel] **I.** *n* période *f*; **cold ~** vague *f* de froid; **sunny ~** éclaircie *f*; **to have dizzy ~s** avoir des étourdissements **II.** *vt* <-ed, -ed> (*take turns*) remplacer

**spell³** [spel] <-ed, -ed> **I.** *vt* ① (*form using letters*) épeler; **how do you ~ ...** comment écrit-on ... ② (*signify*) signifier; **N O ~ s no** N O fait no **II.** *vi* connaître l'orthographe; **I can't ~** je suis nul en orthographe

◆**spell out** *vt* ① (*spell*) épeler ② (*explain*) expliquer clairement ▸ **do I have to spell it out for you?** *inf* tu veux que je te fasse un dessin? (*subj*)

**spell checker** *n* COMPUT correcteur *m* orthographique

**spelling** *n* orthographe *f*

**spelling bee** *n* concours *m* d'orthographe

**spend** [spend] <spent, spent> **I.** *vt* ① (*pay out: money*) dépenser ② (*pass: time, night*) passer **II.** *vi* dépenser de l'argent

**spending money** *n* argent *m* de poche

**spent** [spent] **I.** *pp, pt of* **spend II.** *adj* (*used*) usagé(e); (*bullet*) perdu(e)

**sperm** [spɜrm] <-(s)> *n* ① (*male reproductive cell*) spermatozoïde *m* ② (*semen*) sperme *m*

**spice** [spaɪs] **I.** *n* ① CULIN épice *f* ② (*excitement*) piment *m* **II.** *vt* ① (*add flavor to*) épicer ② (*add excitement to*) pimenter

**spick-and-span** [ˌspɪk·ən·ˈspæn] *adj inf* impeccable; **to keep a kitchen ~** avoir une cuisine d'une propreté impeccable

**spicy** <-ier, -iest> *adj* ① (*seasoned*) épicé(e) ② (*sensational*) croustillant(e)

**spider** [ˈspaɪ·dər] *n* araignée *f*

**spider web** *n* toile *f* d'araignée

**spiffy** [ˈspɪf·i] *adj inf* chic *inv*

**spike** [spaɪk] **I.** *n* ① (*pointed object*) pointe *f* ② (*cleat on shoes*) crampon *m* ③ *pl* (*cleats*) pointes *fpl* ④ *pl* (*high-heeled shoes*) talons *mpl* aiguilles **II.** *vt* ① (*pierce with spike*) percer avec une pointe ② *inf* (*put end to*) stopper ③ *inf* (*add alcohol*) relever

**spiky** [ˈspaɪ·ki] <-ier, -iest> *adj* ① (*having sharp points*) piquant(e); (*hair*) en brosse ② (*irritable*) irritable

**spill** [spɪl] **I.** *n* ① (*act of spilling*) déversement *m*; **to wipe up a ~** essuyer qc qui s'est renversé ② *inf* (*fall*) chute *f*; **to take a ~ on sth** tomber de qc **II.** <-ed *o* spilt, -ed *o* spilt> *vt* renverser ▸ **to ~ the beans** vendre la mèche **III.** <-ed *o* spilt, -ed *o* spilt> *vi* ① (*flow*) couler ② (*spread*) **to ~ into sth** se déverser dans qc

**spilt** [spɪlt] *pp, pt of* **spill**

**spin** [spɪn] **I.** *n* ① (*rotation*) tournoiement *m*; (*of wheel*) tour *m*; (*of dancer*) pirouette *f*; **to go into a ~** descendre en vrille; **to put ~ on a ball** donner de l'effet à une balle ② (*spin-dry*) essorage *m*; **to give sth a ~** essorer qc ③ *inf* (*trip*) tour *m*; **to go for a ~** aller faire un tour ④ (*method of considering*) perspective *f*; **to put a positive ~ on sth** montrer qc sous un jour favorable **II.** <-nn-, spun, spun> *vi* ① (*rotate*) tourner; (*dancer, top*) tournoyer; **my head is ~ning** j'ai la tête qui tourne ② *inf* (*drive*) conduire; **to ~ out of control** faire un tête-à-queue ③ (*make thread*) filer **III.** <-nn-, spun, spun> *vt* ① (*rotate*) faire tourner; **to ~ a coin** jouer à pile ou face ② (*make thread out of*) filer ③ (*spin-dry: clothes*) essorer ▸ **it makes my head ~** ça me fait tourner la tête

◆**spin out I.** *vi* faire un tête-à-queue **II.** *vt* faire durer

**spinach** [ˈspɪn·ɪtʃ] *n* épinards *mpl*

**spinal cord** *n* moelle *f* épinière

**spine** [spaɪn] *n* ① (*spinal column*) colonne *f* vertébrale ② (*spike*) épine *f* ③ (*part of book*) dos *m* ▸ **to send shivers (up and) down one's ~** donner froid dans le dos

**spinning top** *n* toupie *f*

S

**spinoff** *n* ❶ ECON scission *f* ❷ (*byproduct*) produit *m* ❸ (*derived work*) retombée *f*

**spiral** ['spaɪ·rəl] I. *n* spirale *f* II. *adj* en spirale III. <-l- *o* -ll-> *vi* ❶ (*move in spiral*) tourner en spirale; (*smoke*) faire des volutes; (*leaf, plane*) vriller; **to ~ downward** descendre en spirale ❷ (*increase*) **to ~ upward** monter en flèche ❸ (*decrease*) **to ~ downward** chuter

**spire** [spaɪər] *n* (*of church*) flèche *f*

**spirit** ['spɪr·ɪt] I. *n* ❶ (*nature*) esprit *m* ❷ (*mood*) esprit *m*; **to be in high/low ~s** être de bonne/mauvaise humeur; **to break sb's ~** casser le moral de qn ❸ (*courage*) courage *m* ❹ (*character*) caractère *m*; **to be young in ~** être jeune de caractère ❺ (*soul*) esprit *m*; **the Holy Spirit** le Saint-Esprit; **to be with sb in ~** être avec qn par la pensée ❻ (*ghost*) esprit *m* ❼ *pl* (*alcoholic drink*) spiritueux *m* II. *vt* **to ~ sth away** faire disparaître qc discrètement

**spirited** *adj* (*discussion*) animé(e); (*reply*) vif(vive)

**spiritual** ['spɪr·ɪ·tʃu·əl] I. *adj* spirituel(le) II. *n* MUS negro-spiritual *m*

**spit¹** [spɪt] *n* ❶ (*for roasting*) broche *f* ❷ (*point of land*) pointe *f* (de terre)

**spit²** [spɪt] I. *n* *inf* crachat *m*; **it needs ~ and polish** ça a besoin d'être lustré II. <spat *o* spit, spat *o* spit> *vi* ❶ (*expel saliva*) cracher ❷ (*crackle*) crépiter III. <spat *o* spit, spat *o* spit> *vt* **to ~ nails** voir rouge

◆ **spit out** *vt* cracher; **to spit it out** *inf* cracher ce qu'on a à dire

◆ **spit up** *vi* (*baby*) faire son rot

**spite** [spaɪt] I. *n* ❶ (*desire to hurt*) méchanceté *f* ❷ (*despite*) **in ~ of sth** malgré qc; **in ~ of oneself** malgré soi II. *vt* contrarier

**spiteful** *adj* méchant(e)

**spitting image** *n* **to be the ~ of sb** être (tout) le portrait craché de qn

**splash** [splæʃ] I. *n* ❶ (*sound*) plouf *m* ❷ (*small amount*) touche *f* ▸ **to make a ~** faire sensation II. *vt* ❶ (*scatter liquid*) éclabousser, gicler *Suisse*; **to ~**

one's face with water s'asperger le visage avec de l'eau ❷ (*print prominently*) être à la une de; **to be ~ed across the front page** s'étaler en première page III. *vi* (*spread via splashes*) **to ~ onto sth** éclabousser qc

◆ **splash down** *vi* AVIAT amerrir

**splendid** ['splen·dɪd] *adj* ❶ (*magnificent*) splendide ❷ (*fine*) fantastique

**splendor** ['splen·dər] *n* ❶ (*grandness*) splendeur *f* ❷ *pl* (*beautiful things*) merveilles *fpl*

**splint** [splɪnt] I. *n* MED attelle *f* II. *vt* mettre une attelle à

**splinter** I. *n* (*of wood*) écharde *f*; (*of glass*) éclat *m* II. *vi* (*split*) faire éclater; **to ~ into small groups** éclater en petits groupes

**split** [splɪt] I. *n* ❶ (*crack*) fissure *f* ❷ (*tear*) déchirure *f* ❸ (*division*) scission *f* ❹ (*end of relationship*) rupture *f* ❺ (*share*) part *f* ❻ (*in gymnastics*) grand écart *m* II. <split, split> *vt* ❶ (*cut*) fendre; **to ~ one's head open** s'ouvrir le crâne ❷ (*tear*) déchirer ❸ (*divide*) diviser; (*money, shares*) partager ❹ (*cause division: party*) diviser ▸ **to ~ the difference** couper la poire en deux; **to ~ hairs** couper les cheveux en quatre III. <split, split> *vi* ❶ (*crack*) se fendre; (*material, dress*) se déchirer; **to ~ down the middle** se fendre au milieu ❷ (*divide*) se scinder; **to ~ from sth** se désolidariser de qc ❸ *sl* (*leave*) filer

◆ **split off** I. *vt* détacher II. *vi* ❶ (*become detached*) se détacher ❷ (*separate*) **to ~ from sth** se séparer de qc

◆ **split up** I. *vt* partager; **to ~ the work** se répartir le travail II. *vi* se séparer

**split personality** *n* PSYCH dédoublement *m* de la personnalité

**split second** *n* fraction *f* de seconde

**split-up** *n* séparation *f*

**spoil** [spɔɪl] I. *n pl* **~s** butin *m* II. <-ed *o* spoilt, -ed *o* spoilt> *vt* ❶ (*ruin: child*) gâter; (*landscape, party*) gâcher ❷ (*treat well*) gâter; **to be ~ed for choice** avoir l'embarras du choix;

**~ yourself!** fais-toi plaisir! **III.** <-ed *o* spoilt, -ed *o* spoilt> *vi* s'abîmer

**spoiled** *adj* (*child*) gâté(e)

**spoilsport** *n inf* rabat-joie *mf*

**spoilt** *pp, pt of* **spoil**

**spoke**[1] [spoʊk] *n* rayon *m*

**spoke**[2] [spoʊk] *pt of* **speak**

**spoken** *pp of* **speak**

**spokesperson** *n* porte-parole *m inv*

**sponge** [spʌndʒ] **I.** *n* ❶ (*for washing*) éponge *f* ❷ (*cake*) gâteau *m* mousseline **II.** *vt* ❶ (*clean by rubbing*) frotter à l'éponge ❷ (*absorb liquid*) **to ~ sth up** éponger qc
◆ **sponge down, sponge off** *vt* nettoyer avec une éponge
◆ **sponge on** *vt pej, inf* vivre aux crochets de

**sponge cake** *n* gâteau *m* mousseline

**sponger** *n pej* pique-assiette *mf*

**sponsor** ['spɑn(t)sər] **I.** *n* ❶ ECON, SPORTS sponsor *m* ❷ (*supporter*) parrain, marraine *m, f* **II.** *vt* parrainer; (*athlete, team, event*) sponsoriser

**spontaneity** [ˌspɑn·t²n·'eɪ·ə·t̬i] *n* spontanéité *f*

**spontaneous** [spɑn·'teɪ·ni·əs] *adj* spontané(e)

**spooky** <-ier, -iest> *adj inf* sinistre

**spoon** [spun] **I.** *n* ❶ (*utensil*) cuillère *f* ❷ (*amount held in spoon*) cuillerée *f* **II.** *vt* **to ~ sth into sth** verser qc dans qc à la cuillère

**spoonful** <-s *o* spoonsful> *n* cuillerée *f*

**sporadic** [spə·'ræd·ɪk] *adj* (*gunfire*) sporadique; (*showers*) épars(e)

**sport** [spɔrt] **I.** *n* ❶ (*athletic activity*) sport *m*; **to play ~s** faire du sport ❷ (*fun*) amusement *m*; **to do sth for ~** faire qc pour s'amuser ❸ (*form of address*) **how are you doing, ~?** salut mon vieux, ça va? ▸ **to be a bad ~** *inf* être mauvais perdant **II.** *vt* (*wear*) arborer

**sporting** *adj* SPORTS sportif(-ive)

**sports car** *n* voiture *f* de sport

**sports coat** *n* blouson *m*

**sportsman** *n* sportif *m*

**sportsmanship** *n* esprit *m* sportif

**sportswear** *n* vêtements *mpl* de sport

**sportswoman** *n* sportive *f*

**sportswriter** *n* chroniqueur, -euse *m, f* sportif

**sporty** <-ier, -iest> *adj* ❶ (*athletic*) sportif(-ive) ❷ (*flashy: car*) de sport

**spot** [spɑt] **I.** *n* ❶ (*mark: of blood, grease*) tache; (*on skin*) bouton *m* ❷ FASHION (*pattern*) pois *m* ❸ (*place*) endroit *m* ❹ (*part of show*) séquence *f*; (*commercial*) spot *m* (de publicité) ❺ *inf* (*spotlight*) rayon *m* lumineux ▸ **to put sb on the ~** mettre qn sur la sellette **II.** <-tt-> *vi* (*cause spots*) tacher **III.** <-tt-> *vt* (*see*) apercevoir; **to ~ why/what ...** entrevoir pourquoi/ce que ...

**spot-check** *vt* contrôler à l'improviste

**spotless** *adj* ❶ (*clean*) impeccable ❷ (*unblemished*) immaculé(e)

**spotlight I.** *n* ❶ (*beam of light*) rayon *m* lumineux ❷ THEAT, CINE projecteur *m* ▸ **to be in/out of the ~** être/ne pas être en vue **II.** <-ed *o* spotlit, -ed *o* spotlit> *vt* mettre en lumière

**spotted** *adj* (*dog*) tacheté(e); **to be ~ with sth** être taché de qc

**spotty** ['spɑ·t̬i] <-ier, -iest> *adj* (*sales*) frauduleux(-euse); (*progress*) malhonnête

**spouse** [spaʊs] *n* ❶ (*husband*) époux *m* ❷ (*wife*) épouse *f*

**sprain** [spreɪn] **I.** *n* foulure *f* **II.** *vt* se fouler

**sprang** [spræŋ] *pt of* **spring**

**spray**[1] [spreɪ] **I.** *n* ❶ (*mist: of perfume, water*) pulvérisation *m*; (*of saltwater*) embruns *mpl*; (*of bullets*) salve *f* ❷ (*container: of perfume*) vaporisateur *m*; (*for hair, paint*) bombe *f* **II.** *vt* (*perfume, product*) vaporiser; (*water*) arroser; **to ~ sb with sth** asperger qn de qc **III.** *vi* gicler

**spray**[2] [spreɪ] *n* inflorescence *f*; (*of flowers*) gerbe *f*

**spread** [spred] **I.** *n* ❶ (*act of spreading*) déploiement *m* ❷ (*range*) gamme *f*; (*of opinion*) diffusion *f* ❸ (*article*) publication *f* ❹ (*ranch*) ranch *m* ❺ *inf* (*meal*)

**S**

banquet *m* II. <spread, spread> *vi*
**❶** (*propagate*) se propager; **to ~ like**
**wildfire** se répandre comme une traînée de poudre **❷** (*stretch*) s'étirer **❸** (*cover surface*) s'étendre
III. <spread, spread> *vt* **❶** (*cause to*
*expand*) déployer; (*one's legs*) allonger;
(*virus, disease*) répandre; (*panic*) semer; (*culture*) développer **❷** (*cover*
*with*) étaler; **to ~ toast with jam** tartiner un toast avec de la confiture **❸** (*dis-*
*tribute*) distribuer **❹** (*tell others: rumor,*
*lies*) répandre; (*the word*) faire passer

**spreadsheet** *n* COMPUT **❶** (*software*) tableur *m* **❷** (*work screen*) feuille *f* de
calcul

**spree** [spri] *n* **killing ~** folie *f* meurtrière; **to go (out) on a shopping ~**
aller dévaliser les boutiques

**spring** [sprɪŋ] I. *n* **❶** (*season*) printemps *m* **❷** (*curved device*) ressort *m*
**❸** (*elasticity*) élasticité *f*; **to have a ~**
**in one's step** avoir le pas souple
**❹** (*source of water*) source *f*
II. <sprang *o* sprung, sprung> *vi*
**❶** (*move quickly*) se précipiter; **to ~ to**
**one's feet** bondir sur ses pieds **❷** (*ap-*
*pear: to mind*) surgir III. <sprang *o*
sprung, sprung> *vt* (*produce*) **to ~ sth**
**on sb** faire qc à qn par surprise IV. *adj*
(*supported by springs*) à ressort(s)

**springboard** *n* tremplin *m*

**spring break** *n* UNIV vacances *fpl* de
printemps

**spring-cleaning** *n* nettoyage *m* de printemps

**spring roll** *n* rouleau *m* de printemps

**springtime** *n* printemps *m*

**springy** ['sprɪŋ·i] <-ier, -iest> *adj* prin-
tanier(-ère)

**sprinkle** ['sprɪŋ·kl] I. *vt* arroser II. *n* (*of*
*rain, snow*) averse *f*; (*of salt, flour*) pincée *f*

**sprinkler** *n* **❶** (*for lawn*) arroseur *m*
**❷** (*for field*) canon *m* (à eau)

**sprinkling** *n* **❶** (*light covering*) fine
couche *f* **❷** (*small amount*) pincée *f*

**sprint** [sprɪnt] SPORTS I. *n* course *f* de vitesse II. *vi* pratiquer la course de vitesse

**sprout** [spraʊt] I. *n* **❶** (*of plant*) pousse *f*; (*of seeds, bulb*) germe *m* **❷** *pl*
(*Brussels sprouts*) choux *mpl* de
Bruxelles; (*soybean sprouts*) pousses
*fpl* de (graines de) soja; (*alfalfa sprouts*)
pousses *fpl* de luzerne II. *vi* **❶** (*grow*)
pousser; (*seed, bulb*) germer **❷** *fig* germer III. *vt* (*shoots, hair*) faire; (*mous-*
*tache*) se laisser pousser

**sprung** [sprʌŋ] *pp, pt of* **spring**

**spud** [spʌd] *n inf* patate *f*

**spun** [spʌn] *pp, pt of* **spin**

**spunky** ['spʌŋk·i] *adj inf* plein(e) d'audace

**spy** [spaɪ] I. *n* espion(ne) *m(f)* II. *vi* **to ~**
**on sb/sth** espionner qn/qc III. *vt* remarquer

**spyware** ['spaɪ·wer] *n* logiciel *m* espion

**squad** [skwad] *n* **❶** (*group*) groupe *m*
(d'élite) **❷** (*sports team*) équipe *f* sportive **❸** (*military unit*) escouade *f*

**squadron** ['skwa·drən] *n* **❶** MIL esca-
dron *m* **❷** AVIAT, NAUT escadrille *f*

**square** [skwer] I. *n* **❶** (*geometric*
*shape*) carré *m* **❷** (*part of town*) square *m* **❸** (*marked space*) case *f*; **to go**
**back to ~** revenir à la case dé-
part **❹** (*tool*) équerre *f* **❺** *inf* (*boring*
*person*) ringard(e) *m(f)* **❻** (*number ti-*
*mes itself*) carré *m* II. *adj* **❶** <-r, -st>
(*square-shaped*) carré(e) **❷** <-r, -st>
(*short and solid*) carré(e); **❸** MATH car-
ré(e); **5 ~ miles** 5 miles *mpl* carrés
**❹** (*right-angled: corner*) à angle droit
**❺** (*owing nothing*) quitte **❻** SPORTS à
égalité **❼** <-r, -st> *inf* (*on the same*
*level*) équilibré(e) **❽** <-r, -st> (*straight*)
droit(e); **to be ~ with sb** être honnête
avec qn **❾** (*arranged, in order*) **to get**
**sth ~** arranger qc **❿** <-r, -st> *inf* (*old-*
*fashioned*) ringard(e) III. *vt* **❶** (*align*)
aligner; (*one's shoulders*) redresser
**❷** *inf* (*settle*) arranger; (*a matter*) régler **❸** (*multiply by itself*) élever au carré **❹** SPORTS égaliser IV. *adv* droit; **~ in**
**the middle** en plein milieu

**square root** *n* racine *f* carrée

**squash**[1] [skwaʃ] *n* (*vegetable*) courge *f*

**squash**[2] [skwaʃ] I. *n* **❶** (*dense pack*) en-

tassement *m* ② (*racket game*) squash *m*
II. *vt* ① (*crush*) écraser ② (*make feel stupid*) écraser ③ *fig* (*rumor*) étouffer
**squashy** <-ier, -iest> *adj* mou(molle)
**squatter** ['skwaṭ·ər] *n* (*of house*) squatter, -euse *m, f;* (*of land*) exploitant(e) *m(f)* illégitime
**squeak** [skwik] I. *n* grincement *m* II. *vi* (*mouse, door, hinge*) couiner
**squeaky-clean** *adj* irréprochable
**squeegee** ['skwi·dʒi] I. *n* raclette *f* II. *vt* éponger
**squeeze** [skwiz] I. *n* ① (*pressing action*) compression *f* ② (*obtained by squeezing*) pression *f;* **to give sth a ~** presser qc ③ ECON (*on spending*) restriction *f;* (*on jobs*) limitation *f* ④ *fig, sl* amoureux, -euse *m, f* II. *vt* ① (*firmly press*) presser; (*cloth*) essorer; (*sb's hand*) serrer; (*trigger, doll*) appuyer sur ② (*force into*) entasser; **to ~ sth into sth** faire entrer qc dans qc; **to ~ one's way through** se frayer un passage ③ (*extort*) soutirer; **to ~ money out of sb** extorquer de l'argent à qn ④ *fig* (*put pressure on*) faire pression sur ⑤ ECON (*wages*) bloquer
**squid** [skwid] <-(s)> *n* cal(a)mar *m*
**squint** [skwint] I. *vi* ① MED loucher ② (*partly close eyes*) plisser les yeux II. *n* ① MED strabisme *m* ② *inf* (*quick look*) **to have a ~ at sth** donner un coup d'œil à qc
**squirrel** ['skwɜr·əl] *n* écureuil *m*
**squirt** [skwɜrt] I. *vt* ① (*make flow out*) faire gicler; (*perfume, deodorant*) vaporiser ② (*shower off*) asperger II. *vi* jaillir III. *n* ① (*amount*) pulvérisation *f* ② *pej* (*young person*) salaud *m*
**Sr.** *n* Sr *m*
**St.** *n* ① *abbr of* **saint** St *m* ② *abbr of* **street** rue *f*
**stab** [stæb] I.<-bb-> *vt* poignarder; **to ~ sb with sth** donner un coup de qc dans qc II.<-bb-> *vi a. fig* **to ~ at sb/ sth** porter un coup de couteau à qn/qc III. *n* ① (*with pointed object*) coup *m* de couteau; **to make a ~ at sth with sth** porter un coup de qc à qc ② (*sud-

den pain*) élancement *m;* (*of jealousy*) accès *m* ③ *fig* (*attack*) coup *m* ► **to take a ~ at doing sth** s'essayer à faire qc
**stabbing** I. *n* coup *m* de couteau II. *adj* (*pain*) lancinant(e)
**stability** [stə·'bɪl·ə·ṭi] *n* stabilité *f*
**stabilize** ['steɪ·bə·laɪz] I. *vt* stabiliser II. *vi* se stabiliser
**stable**[1] ['steɪ·bl] <-r, -st *o* more stable, most stable> *adj* ① (*firm*) *a. fig* stable ② PSYCH (*well-balanced*) équilibré(e)
**stable**[2] ['steɪ·bl] I. *n* écurie *f* II. *vt* (*horse*) loger
**stack** [stæk] I. *vt* ① (*arrange in pile*) empiler ② (*fill*) remplir ③ AVIAT (*airplane*) mettre en attente ④ *pej* (*preselect*) favoriser II. *n* ① (*pile*) pile *f* ② *inf* (*large amount*) tas *m;* **to have ~s of them** en avoir des tas ③ **the ~s** *pl* (*in library*) rayons *mpl*
**stadium** ['steɪ·di·əm] <-s *o* -dia> *n* stade *m*
**staff** [stæf] I. *n* ① (*employees*) personnel *m;* **editorial ~** rédaction *f* ② MIL (*group of officers*) état-major *m* ③ (*stick*) bâton *m* ④ (*flagpole*) mât *m* ⑤ MUS (*stave*) portée *f* II. *vt* (*provide personnel*) pourvoir en personnel; **to be ~ed by sb** être composé de qn III. *adj* du personnel
**stag** [stæg] I. *n* (*male deer*) cerf *m* II. *adv* en célibataire
**stage** [steɪdʒ] I. *n* ① (*period in process*) stade *m* ② (*section: of trip, race*) étape *f* ③ (*in theater*) scène *f;* **to set the ~** préparer le terrain ④ **the ~** (*theatrical profession*) le théâtre ⑤ (*scene of action*) scène *f;* **the political ~** la scène politique II. *vt* ① (*produce on stage*) mettre en scène ② (*organize*) monter
**stagger** ['stæg·ər] I. *vi* chanceler; **to ~ to bed** aller au lit d'un pas chancelant; **to ~ under the weight of sth** *fig* chanceler sous le poids de qc II. *vt* ① (*astonish*) stupéfier ② (*arrange at differing times*) échelonner III. *n* pas *m* chancelant
**staggering** *adj* renversant(e)

S

**stagnant** ['stæg·nənt] *adj a. fig* stagnant(e)

**stain** [steɪn] I. *vt* ① (*discolor*) tacher ② (*dye*) teindre ③ *fig* (*blemish*) ternir II. *vi* se tacher III. *n* ① (*discoloration*) tache *f* ② (*dyestuff*) teinture *f* ③ *fig* (*blemish*) atteinte *f*

**stainless** *adj a. fig* sans tache

**stair** [ster] *n* ① (*step in staircase*) marche *f* ② *pl* (*set of steps*) escalier *m*; **a flight of ~ s** un escalier

**staircase** *n* escalier *m*; **a spiral ~** un escalier en colimaçon; **a secret ~** un escalier dérobé

**stake¹** [steɪk] I. *n* ① (*sharpened stick*) piquet *m*; (*wooden*) pieu *m* ② (*execution by burning*) *a. fig* **the ~** le bûcher; **to be burned at the ~** mourir sur le bûcher ▶ **to pull up ~ s** déménager II. *vt* ① (*fasten to stake*) fixer à l'aide de piquets; (*plants*) tuteurer ② LAW **to ~ a claim** faire valoir ses droits

**stake²** [steɪk] *n* ① (*share*) intérêt *m* ② (*amount at risk*) enjeu *m*; GAMES mise *f*; **to be at ~** être en jeu ③ SPORTS (*horserace*) course *f* ④ *inf* (*competitive activity*) course *f*

**stakeout** *n inf* surveillance *f*

**stale** [steɪl] *adj* ① (*not fresh*) pas frais(fraîche); (*bread*) rassis(e); (*air*) vicié(e) ② (*old*) usé(e); **to get ~** s'user ③ (*out of date*) périmé(e)

**stalk¹** [stɔk] *n* (*stem*) tige *f*; (*supporting flower*) pédoncule *m*

**stalk²** [stɔk] I. *vt* traquer II. *vi* **to ~ in/out** entrer/sortir d'un air arrogant

**stalker** ['stɔː·kər] *n* ① (*hunter*) chasseur, -euse *m, f* ② (*of people*) stalker *m*

**stalking-horse** *n fig* prétexte *m*

**stall** [stɔl] I. *n* ① (*for animal*) stalle *f* ② (*compartment in room*) cabine *f*; **shower ~** cabine de douche ③ (*seat in church*) (*choir*) **~ s** stalle *f* ④ (*vendor booth*) stand *m* ⑤ AUTO (*loss of power*) calage *m* II. *vi* ① (*stop running: motor, vehicle*) caler ② *inf* (*delay*) essayer de gagner du temps III. *vt* ① (*cause to stop running: car, motor*) caler ② *inf* (*keep waiting*) faire poireauter ③ (*delay*) repousser

**stamina** ['stæm·ə·nə] *n* résistance *f*

**stammer** ['stæm·ər] I. *vt, vi* bégayer II. *n* bégaiement *m*; **to have a ~** bégayer

**stamp** [stæmp] I. *n* ① (*postage stamp*) timbre *m* ② (*implement*) tampon *m*; **rubber ~** tampon ③ (*official mark*) cachet *m*; (*on metal*) poinçon *m* ④ (*characteristic*) marque *f* ⑤ COM (*coupon*) bon *m*; **food ~** bon alimentaire ⑥ (*with foot*) battement *m* de pied II. *vt* ① (*place postage on*) timbrer ② (*mark with*) tamponner; (*metal*) poinçonner ③ *fig* **to ~ oneself on sth** laisser sa marque sur qc; **to ~ sb/sth as** (**being**) **sb/sth** étiqueter qn/qc comme qn/qc ④ (*with foot*) trépigner III. *vi* trépigner

**stamp collection** *n* collection *f* de timbres

**stampede** [stæm·'pid] I. *n* ruée *f* II. *vi* se ruer III. *vt* ① (*cause to flee*) jeter la panique ② (*force into action*) **to ~ sb into doing sth** pousser qn à faire qc

**stand** [stænd] I. *n* ① (*position*) *a. fig* position *f*; **to make a ~ against sth** s'opposer à qc ② (*standstill*) arrêt *m* ③ (*for spectators*) tribune *f* ④ (*support*) support *m* ⑤ (*stall, booth*) stand *m*; **a news ~** un kiosque à journaux ⑥ (*for vehicles*) station *f* ⑦ (*small table*) petite table *f* ⑧ (*site of performance*) stand *m* ⑨ (*sexual encounter*) **a one-night ~** une histoire sans lendemain ⑩ **the ~** (*witness box*) barre *f* (des témoins) ⑪ (*group of plants*) bouquet *m* II. <**stood, stood**> *vi* ① (*be upright*) se tenir debout; **to ~ tall** se tenir droit; **to ~ (up)** se lever; **to ~ at attention** MIL se mettre au garde-à-vous ② (*be located*) se trouver; **to ~ somewhere** (*mountain, church*) se dresser quelque part; **to ~ in sb's way** barrer le passage à qn ③ (*have a position*) *a. fig* se tenir; **to ~ on an issue** avoir un point de vue sur un sujet; **to ~ on one's own two feet**

ne dépendre que de soi; **to ~ still** se tenir immobile; **to ~ guard** se tenir sur ses gardes ❹ (*be in specified state*) être; **to ~ motionless/alone** rester immobile/seul; **to ~ to lose sth** risquer de perdre qc; **to ~ to gain sth** avoir des chances de gagner qc; **to ~ five feet tall** faire un mètre cinquante (de haut) ❺ (*remain upright*) tenir; **to ~ to reason** aller sans dire ❻ (*remain motionless*) reposer; (*tea*) infuser; **to let sth ~** laisser reposer qc **III.** <stood, stood> *vt* ❶ (*place upright*) placer; **to ~ sth on its head** faire tenir qc sur sa tête; **to ~ sth against sth** mettre qc contre qc ❷ (*bear*) supporter; **to not be able to ~ doing sth** ne pas supporter de faire qc ❸ (*pay for*) payer ❹ LAW (*undergo*) **to ~ trial for sth** passer en jugement pour qc ▶ **to ~ a <u>chance</u> of doing sth** *inf* avoir de bonnes chances de faire qc

◆ **stand around** *vi* se tenir là

◆ **stand aside** *vi* a. *fig* s'écarter

◆ **stand back** *vi* ❶ (*stay back*) être en retrait ❷ (*move back*) reculer ❸ *fig* prendre du recul

◆ **stand by** **I.** *vi* ❶ (*observe*) se tenir là ❷ (*be ready to take action*) se tenir prêt; **to ~ for sth** se parer à qc ❸ (*wait*) attendre **II.** *vt* soutenir; (*decision*) maintenir; (*one's word, promise*) tenir

◆ **stand down** *vi* (*resign*) se retirer

◆ **stand for** *vt* ❶ (*represent*) signifier ❷ (*tolerate*) supporter

◆ **stand in** *vi* **to ~ for sb** remplacer qn

◆ **stand out** *vi* ❶ (*project from*) ressortir ❷ (*be noticeable, better*) se détacher ❸ (*be opposed to*) **to ~ against sth** résister à qc

◆ **stand up** **I.** *vi* ❶ (*assume upright position*) se lever; **to ~ straight** se tenir droit ❷ (*be standing*) se tenir debout ❸ (*be accepted as true*) se tenir **II.** *vt* ❶ (*put straight*) redresser ❷ *inf* poser un lapin à

**standalone** *n* COMPUT poste *m* autonome

**standard** ['stæn·dərd] **I.** *n* ❶ (*level of quality*) niveau *m* ❷ (*basis for evalua-*

*tion*) norme *f* ❸ (*flag*) étendard *m* ❹ (*basis of currency: gold, silver*) étalon *m* ❺ (*well-known piece of music*) standard *m* **II.** *adj* ❶ (*normal, not special: language, size, procedures*) standard *inv* ❷ (*classic: book, song*) classique ❸ (*average, acceptable: procedure, practice*) ordinaire

**standardize** ['stæn·dər·daɪz] *vt* standardiser

**standby** **I.** *n* ❶ (*reserve*) réserve *f*; **to be (put) on ~** être en attente ❷ (*substitute*) remplaçant(e) *m(f)*; **to be (put) on ~** se tenir prêt ❸ *no pl* (*readiness*) **on ~** en veilleuse; ELEC en veille [*o* stand-by]; **~ mode** mode *m* veille ❹ (*backup*) réserve *f* ❺ (*plane ticket*) billet *m* stand-by ❻ (*traveler*) passager, -ère *m, f* [*on*] stand-by **II.** *adj* de réserve **III.** *adv* en attente, AVIAT, TOURIST **to fly ~** voyager en standby

**stand-in** *n* remplaçant(e) *m(f)*

**standing** **I.** *n* ❶ (*position*) rang *m* ❷ (*duration*) durée *f* **II.** *adj* ❶ (*upright*) debout *inv* ❷ (*permanent*) fixe ❸ (*stagnant*) stagnant(e) ❹ (*not reaped*) sur pied

**standpoint** ['stæn(d)·pɔɪnt] *n* point *m* de vue

**standstill** ['stæn(d)·stɪl] *n* arrêt *m;* **to be at a ~** être immobile; **to come to a ~** s'immobiliser

**standup comedy** *n* stand up comedy *m* (*spectacle comique solo*)

**stank** [stæŋk] *pt of* **stink**

**staple¹** ['steɪ·pl] **I.** *n* ❶ (*main product*) produit *m* de base ❷ (*basic food*) aliment *m* de base ❸ (*important component*) élément *m* principal **II.** *adj* de base

**staple²** ['steɪ·pl] **I.** *n* (*for attaching*) agrafe *f* **II.** *vt* agrafer

**stapler** *n* agrafeuse *f*

**star** [star] **I.** *n* ❶ (*heavenly body*) a. *fig* étoile *f* ❷ (*famous performer*) star *f* ❸ (*asterisk*) astérisque *m* ▶ **to <u>see</u> ~s** voir trente-six chandelles **II.** <-rr-> *vi* THEAT, CINE **to ~ in a film** être la vedette

S

d'un film; ~**ring Johnny Depp** avec Johnny Depp dans le rôle principal **III.** <-rr-> vt ❶ THEAT, CINE avoir en vedette ❷ (*mark with asterisk*) marquer d'un astérisque **IV.** adj ❶ (*outstanding*) de premier ordre ❷ (*in ratings*) **a four-~ hotel** un hôtel quatre étoiles ❸ THEAT, CINE, MUS vedette

**starboard** ['star·bərd] n tribord m

**stare** [ster] **I.** vi regarder fixement; **to ~ at sb/sth** fixer qn/qc du regard **II.** vt to **~ sb in the face/eyes** dévisager qn/regarder qn dans le blanc des yeux **III.** n regard m

**staring** ['ster·ɪŋ] adj (*eyes*) fixe

**star-studded** adj ❶ (*full of stars*) étoilé(e) ❷ fig prestigieux(-euse)

**start** [start] **I.** vi ❶ (*begin*) commencer; **to ~ anew** [o (**all over**) **again**] recommencer à zéro; **... to ~ with ...** commencer ...; **to ~ with, ...** tout d'abord; **don't ~!** inf ne commence pas! ❷ (*begin journey*) partir ❸ (*begin operating: vehicle, motor*) démarrer ❹ (*make sudden movement*) sursauter ❺ SPORTS prendre le départ **II.** vt ❶ (*begin*) commencer; (*a family*) fonder; **to ~ doing sth** commencer à faire qc ❷ (*set in motion: conversation*) entamer; (*fight, trouble, war*) déclencher; (*trend, fashion, rumor*) lancer; (*meeting*) débuter; (*fire*) allumer ❸ TECH (*set in operation: machine*) mettre en marche; (*motor, car*) démarrer ❹ COM (*establish*) lancer ❺ inf (*cause to do*) **to ~ sb/sth doing sth** faire faire qc à qn/qc ❻ COMPUT démarrer **III.** n ❶ (*beginning*) commencement m; **to get off to a good/bad ~** prendre un bon/mauvais départ; **to make a late/early ~** commencer tard/de bonne heure; **to make a fresh/good ~** recommencer/bien commencer; **to give sb a ~ in sth** lancer qn dans qc; **from ~ to finish** du début à la fin; **a false ~** un faux départ ❷ SPORTS (*beginning place*) départ m ❸ (*beginning time*) départ m ❹ (*beginning advantage*) avance f; **to have a good ~ in life** avoir bien débuté dans la

vie ❺ (*sudden movement*) sursaut m; **to give sb a ~** faire sursauter qn

◆ **start back** vi ❶ (*be startled*) faire un bond en arrière ❷ (*begin return*) prendre le chemin du retour

◆ **start off I.** vi ❶ (*begin activity*) commencer; **to ~ by doing sth** commencer en faisant qc ❷ (*begin journey*) se mettre en route **II.** vt **to start sth off** commencer qc; **to start sb off on sth** lancer qn sur qc

◆ **start out** vi ❶ (*begin journey*) se mettre en route ❷ (*begin process, career*) commencer; (*company, business*) se lancer; **to ~ as/doing sth** débuter comme/en faisant qc

◆ **start over** vi recommencer

◆ **start up I.** vt ❶ (*organize, implement: business, company*) lancer; (*restaurant, club*) ouvrir ❷ (*turn on: engine*) démarrer **II.** vi ❶ (*begin undertaking*) se lancer ❷ (*begin running: motor, vehicle*) démarrer

**start button** n COMPUT bouton m "démarrer"

**starter** n ❶ SPORTS (*in competition*) partant(e) m(f) ❷ SPORTS (*in race*) starter m ❸ inf CULIN (*appetizer*) entrée f ▶ **for ~s** inf tout d'abord

**starting** adj de départ

**startle** ['star·tl̩] vt effrayer

**startling** adj effrayant(e)

**starvation** [star·'veɪ·ʃ°n] **I.** n famine f **II.** adj (*diet*) draconien(ne); (*wages*) de misère

**starve** [starv] **I.** vi ❶ (*die*) souffrir de la faim; **to ~** (**to death**) mourir de faim ❷ fig (*feel deprived*) **to be ~ing for sth** manquer de qc **II.** vt ❶ (*let die*) faire mourir de faim; **to ~ oneself** (**to death**) se laisser mourir de faim ❷ fig (*deprive*) **to be ~d for sth** être privé de qc

**state** [steɪt] **I.** n ❶ (*condition*) a. fig état m; **~ of mind** état d'esprit; **solid/liquid ~** CHEM état solide/liquide ❷ (*nation*) état m; **the State** l'État; **affairs of ~** affaires fpl d'État ❸ (*dignified rank*) rang m; **to do sth in ~** faire qc en grande pompe **II.** *adj* ❶ (*national*) a. fig d'État ❷ (*of American states*) de l'État; **the ~ line** la frontière (entre les États) ❸ (*owned by government*) national(e); (*industry*) du secteur public ❹ (*governmental*) public(-que); (*document*) officiel(le) ❺ (*showing ceremony*) officiel(le); (*funeral*) national(e) **III.** *vt* ❶ (*declare*) **to ~ (that)** … déclarer que … ❷ (*express*) formuler; (*opinion, reference*) donner; (*problem, condition*) poser; **as ~ d in my letter** comme je l'ai mentionné plus haut ❸ (*specify*) spécifier; (*conditions*) fixer

**State Department** *n* **the ~** le ministère des Affaires étrangères

**statement** ['steɪt·mənt] *n* ❶ (*act of expressing*) a. fig déclaration *f* ❷ (*description*) exposé *m* ❸ (*bank statement*) relevé *m* de compte

**state-of-the-art** *adj* dernier cri *inv*; (*technology*) de pointe

**States** *n pl, inf* **the ~** les États-Unis *mpl*

**state trooper** *n* gendarme *m*

**station** ['steɪ·ʃ°n] **I.** *n* ❶ (*train stop*) gare *f*; **subway ~** station *f* de métro ❷ (*building*) poste *m*; **police ~** poste de police; **gas** [*o* **service**] **~** station-service *f* ❸ RADIO, TV station *f* ❹ (*position*) poste *m*; **to man one's ~** se rendre à son poste ❺ (*social position*) position *f*; **one's ~ in life** sa situation sociale **II.** *vt* MIL (*troops*) poster

**stationary** ['steɪ·ʃə·ner·i] *adj* immobile; (*prices*) stationnaire; **a ~ bicycle** un vélo d'appartement

**stationery** ['steɪ·ʃə·ner·i] *n* ❶ (*paper and envelopes*) fournitures *fpl* de bureau ❷ (*office supplies*) matériel *m* de bureau

**stationery store** *n* papeterie *f*

**station wagon** *n* break *m*

**statistical** *adj* statistique

**statistics** [stə·'tɪs·tɪks] *npl* ❶ + *sing vb* (*science*) statistique *f* ❷ + *pl vb* (*numerical data*) statistiques *fpl*

**statue** ['stætʃ·u] *n* statue *f*

**status** ['stæ·təs] *n* statut *m*

**status quo** *n* statu quo *m*

**status symbol** *n* signe *m* extérieur de richesse

**stay**[1] [steɪ] *n* NAUT étai *m*

**stay**[2] [steɪ] **I.** *vi* ❶ (*remain present*) rester; **to ~ put** *inf* ne pas bouger; **to be here to ~** être entré dans les mœurs ❷ (*remain temporarily*) séjourner; **to ~ overnight** passer la nuit ❸ (*remain*) rester; **to ~ within budget** COM ne pas dépasser le budget **II.** *vt* ❶ (*assuage*) arrêter; (*hunger, thirst*) apaiser; (*order, execution*) suspendre ❷ (*endure*) tenir; **to ~ the course** tenir bon ❸ (*remain temporarily*) **to ~ the night/week somewhere** passer la nuit/la semaine quelque part **III.** *n* ❶ (*visit*) séjour *m*; **an overnight ~** une nuit ❷ LAW (*stop*) suspension *f*

◆ **stay at** *vt inf* persévérer dans

◆ **stay away** *vi* **to ~ from sth** ne pas s'approcher de qc; **to ~ in droves** ne pas venir en nombre

◆ **stay behind** *vi* rester

◆ **stay down** *vi* ❶ (*not be vomited*) **nothing I eat stays down** je rends tout ce que je mange ❷ (*remain underwater*) rester sous l'eau

◆ **stay in** *vi* rester à la maison

◆ **stay on** *vi* ❶ (*remain longer*) rester plus longtemps ❷ (*remain in place*) rester en place

◆ **stay out** *vi* ❶ (*not come home*) rester dehors; **to ~ all night** sortir toute la nuit; **to ~ late/past midnight** rentrer tard/après minuit ❷ (*continue strike*) rester en grève

◆ **stay up** *vi* rester debout

**steady I.** <-ier, -iest> *adj* ❶ (*stable*) stable ❷ (*regular*) régulier(-ère); (*temperature*) constant(e); (*breathing, pulse*) stable; **a ~ boyfriend/girlfriend** un(e) petit(e) ami(e) ❸ (*controlled*) posé(e); (*nerves*) solide; **a ~ hand** une main sûre **II.** <-ie-> *vt* (*things*) maintenir; (*people*) calmer; **to ~ oneself** se ressaisir; **to ~ one's nerves** calmer ses nerfs **III.** *adv* **to go ~ with sb** sortir avec qn

**steak** [steɪk] *n* steak *m*

**steal** [stil] **I.** *n inf* affaire *f*; **to be a ~** être

S

donné II.<stole, stolen> vt ❶(take illegally) a. fig voler; (sb's heart) prendre ❷(do secretly) to ~ a glance at sb/sth jeter un coup d'œil à qn/qc ▸ to ~ the **show** ravir la vedette; to ~ sb's **thunder** couper l'herbe sous le pied à qn III.<stole, stolen> vi ❶(take illegally) voler ❷(move secretly) to ~ in/out entrer/sortir à pas feutrés

**steam** [stim] I. n vapeur f ▸ to **let** off ~ se défouler; to **pick** up ~ s'y mettre; to **run** out of ~ s'essouffler II. vi ❶(produce steam) fumer ❷(move using steam) fonctionner à la vapeur ❸(become steamy) s'embuer III. vt cuire à la vapeur; to ~ open a letter ouvrir une lettre à la vapeur
   ◆**steam up** vt embuer ▸ to **get** steamed up about sth inf s'énerver à cause de qc

**steam engine** n moteur m à vapeur
**steamy** <-ier, -iest> adj ❶(full of steam) plein(e) de vapeur ❷(very humid) humide ❸ inf (erotic) torride
**steel** [stil] I. n ❶(metal) acier m ❷(knife sharpener) aiguisoir m ❸ fig **nerves of** ~ nerfs mpl d'acier II. vt to ~ oneself to +infin s'armer de courage pour +infin
**steep¹** [stip] adj ❶(sloping) raide; (hill) escarpé(e); (climb) abrupt(e); (dive) à pic ❷(expensive) élevé(e)
**steep²** [stip] I. vt ❶(soak) faire tremper ❷CULIN faire macérer ❸ fig to be ~ed in sth être imprégné de qc; to **have** hands ~ed in blood avoir les mains couvertes de sang II. vi ❶(let soak) faire tremper ❷CULIN macérer
**steeple** ['sti·pl] n clocher m
**steer¹** [stɪr] I. vt ❶(direct) conduire ❷(direct toward) to ~ a course toward sth faire route vers qc ❸(guide) guider; (discussion) diriger ❹ fig to ~ a **middle course between sth** trouver un compromis entre qc II. vi ❶(direct vehicle) conduire ❷(direct toward) se diriger ▸ to ~ **clear of sb/sth** éviter qn/qc; (stay away from) se tenir à l'écart de qn/qc

**steer²** [stɪr] n (ox) bœuf m
**steering wheel** n volant m
**stellar** ['stel·ər] adj ❶ASTR stellaire ❷ inf (good) exceptionnel(le)
**step** [step] I. n ❶(movement of foot) pas m; a spring in one's ~ d'un pas léger; to retrace one's ~s retourner sur ses pas; to watch one's ~ faire attention où l'on met ses pieds; fig faire attention à ce que l'on fait; to be out of ~ with sb/sth être déphasé par rapport à qn/qc; to be in ~ with sb/sth être en accord avec qn/qc ❷(stair) marche f; **wooden** ~s escaliers mpl en bois; **watch your** ~! attention à la marche! ❸(stage in process) pas m; every ~ of the way continuellement; to be a ~ **ahead of sb** devancer qn; a ~ in the right/wrong direction une bonne/mauvaise mesure; to be a ~ up être une promotion ❹(measure) mesure f; to take ~s to +infin prendre des mesures pour +infin ❺MUS ton m II. <-pp-> vi marcher; to ~ somewhere aller quelque part; to ~ out of line faire un faux pas
   ◆**step aside** vi s'écarter
   ◆**step back** vi to ~ from sth se retirer de qc
   ◆**step down** I. vi to ~ from sth se retirer de qc II. vt ELEC dévolter
   ◆**step in** vi intervenir
   ◆**step up** vt augmenter
**stepbrother** n beau-frère m
**stepfamily** n + sing/pl vb famille f recomposée
**stepladder** n escabeau m
**stereo** ['ster·i·oʊ] I. n ❶(type of transmission) stéréo f; in ~ en stéréo ❷(hi-fi unit) chaîne f; car ~ autoradio m II. adj s. stereophonic stéréo inv
**stereotype** ['ster·i·ə·taɪp] I. n stéréotype m II. vt stéréotyper
**sterile** ['ster·əl] adj a. fig stérile
**sterilize** vt MED stériliser
**sterling** ['stɜr·lɪŋ] I. n sterling m II. adj ❶(sterling silver) d'argent fin(e) ❷(of high quality) fin(e); (person) admirable
**stern¹** [stɜrn] adj (harsh, grim) sévère

S

**stern²** [stɜrn] *n* NAUT poupe *f*

**stew** [stu] I. *n* ❶ CULIN ragoût *m* ❷ *inf* (*agitated state*) **to be in a ~ about sth** être dans tous ses états à propos de qc II. *vt* faire mijoter III. *vi* ❶ (*simmer slowly*) mijoter ❷ *inf* (*be angry*) **to ~ about sth** être en pelote à propos de qc

**stick¹** [stɪk] *n* ❶ (*piece of wood*) bâton *m*; (*for walking*) canne *f* ❷ (*of cinnamon, chalk, dynamite*) bâton *m*; (*of butter*) morceau *m* ❸ CULIN tige *f*; (*of celery*) branche *f* ❹ MUS (*for conducting*) baguette *f* ❺ AUTO levier *m* de vitesses ❻ *inf* (*remote area*) **the ~s** la cambrousse; **to live out in the ~s** vivre dans un coin perdu ▶ **to get the short end of the ~** comprendre de travers

**stick²** [stɪk] <stuck, stuck> I. *vi* ❶ (*fix by adhesion*) coller ❷ (*endure*) rester; **to ~ in sb's mind** rester gravé dans la mémoire de qn; **to make sth ~** faire rentrer qc ❸ (*jam*) se coincer II. *vt* ❶ (*affix*) coller ❷ (*put, insert*) mettre; **to ~ sth into sth** enfoncer qc dans qc; **to ~ a knife into sb** poignarder qn ❸ *inf* (*not be able to do*) **to be stuck** être coincé; **to be stuck on sth** ne pas arriver à faire qc; **to be stuck with sb** ne pas pouvoir se débarrasser de qn

◆**stick around** *vi inf* ❶ (*wait*) attendre ❷ (*stay*) rester; **~!** reste là!

◆**stick in** *vt* ❶ (*put in*) mettre ❷ (*fix in*) coller ❸ (*pierce*) enfoncer

◆**stick out** I. *vt* tendre; **to ~ one's tongue** tirer la langue ▶ **to stick it out** *inf* tenir le coup II. *vi* ❶ (*protrude*) dépasser; (*ears*) être décollé ❷ (*be obvious*) se voir

◆**stick together** I. *vt* coller II. *vi* ❶ (*adhere*) être collé ❷ (*not separate*) rester ensemble ❸ (*remain loyal*) se soutenir

◆**stick up** I. *vt inf* ❶ (*put higher*) lever ❷ (*commit armed robbery*) braquer; **stick 'em up!** les mains en l'air! II. *vi* se dresser; **to ~ out of sth** sortir de qc

◆**stick up for** *vt* défendre

**sticker** ['stɪkər] *n* ❶ (*adhesive label*) étiquette *f* adhésive; **price ~** étiquette de prix ❷ (*adhesive decoration*) autocollant *m* ❸ (*persistent person*) acharné(e) *m(f)*

**sticker price** *n* prix *m* affiché

**stick-on** *adj* autocollant(e)

**stickup** *n sl* braquage *m*

**sticky** ['stɪki] <-ier, -iest> *adj* ❶ (*adhesive*) collant(e) ❷ (*adhesive and wet*) gluant(e) ❸ (*sweaty*) poisseux(-euse) ❹ (*unpleasant*) difficile

**stiff¹** [stɪf] *n sl* (*dead body*) cadavre *m*

**stiff²** *adj* ❶ (*hard*) raide; (*dough*) dur(e); **to be bored ~** *inf* s'ennuyer à cent sous de l'heure ❷ (*tense*) *a. fig* tendu(e) ❸ (*strong: alcohol, wind*) fort(e) ❹ (*severe: sentence, penalty*) sévère; (*welcome*) froid(e)

**stigmatize** ['stɪg·mə·taɪz] *vt* stigmatiser

**still¹** [stɪl] I. *n* calme *m* II. *adj* ❶ (*not moving*) immobile ❷ (*peaceful*) calme ❸ (*silent*) silencieux(-euse) ❹ (*not carbonated: drink*) non gazeux (-euse); **~ water** eau *f* plate III. *adv* sans bouger; **to stand ~** ne pas bouger; **to sit ~** rester tranquille IV. *vt* calmer

**still²** [stɪl] *adv* ❶ (*continuing situation*) encore ❷ (*nevertheless*) encore ❸ (*to greater degree*) encore; **and all** malgré tout ❸ (*to greater degree*) encore; **better ~** encore mieux

**still³** [stɪl] *n* (*for distilling*) alambic *m*

**stimulate** ['stɪm·jə·leɪt] *vt a.* ECON, MED stimuler; (*conversation*) animer

**sting** [stɪŋ] I. *n* ❶ BIO, ZOOL (*part of insect*) dard *m*; (*of scorpion*) aiguillon *m* ❷ (*injury by insect, plant*) piqûre *f* ❸ (*pain*) brûlure *f* ❹ *sl* (*cleverly organized theft*) escroquerie *f* ❺ *sl* (*police operation*) coup *m* monté II. <stung, stung> *vt, vi* piquer

**stinging nettle** [ˌstɪn·ɪŋ·ˈneṭ·l] *n* ortie *f*

**stingy** ['stɪn·dʒi] <-ier, -iest> *adj inf* radin(e)

**stink** [stɪŋk] I. *n* ❶ (*unpleasant smell*) puanteur *f* ❷ *inf* (*trouble*) raffut *m* II. <stank o stunk, stunk> *vi* ❶ *a. inf* (*smell*) **to ~ of sth** puer qc ❷ *sl* (*be bad*) être pourri(e) *vulg*; **to ~ at sth** être nul(le) en qc

**S**

**stinker** *n pej, sl* saleté *f;* **you little ~!** espèce d'ordure!

**stir** [stɜr] **I.** *n* ❶ *(agitation)* **to give sth a ~** remuer qc ❷ *(excitement)* **to cause a ~** faire du bruit **II.** <-rr-> *vt* ❶ *(agitate)* remuer ❷ *(arouse: person)* émouvoir; *(imagination)* stimuler; *(memory)* réveiller; *(fire)* attiser; **to ~ (up) trouble** chercher des noises **III.** *vi* bouger

**stir-fry** ['stɜrˌfraɪ] **I.** <-fries> *n* sauté *m* **II.** <-ie-> *vt* faire sauter

**stitch** [stɪtʃ] **I.** <-es> *n* FASHION, MED point *m* ▶ **to be in ~es** être plié de rire **II.** *vt, vi* coudre

**stock** [stak] **I.** *n* ❶ *(reserves)* réserves *fpl* ❷ COM, ECON *(merchandise in shop)* stock *m;* **to be out of ~** être en rupture de stock ❸ FIN *(share in company)* action *f* ❹ *(farm animals)* bétail *m* ❺ SOCIOL *(line of descent)* origine *f;* ZOOL, BIO *(breeding line)* souche *f* ❻ *(popularity)* réputation *f* ❼ *(broth, bouillon)* bouillon *m* **II.** *adj* *(standard: expression)* commun(e); *(character)* stéréotypé(e) **III.** *vt* COM, ECON ❶ *(keep in supply)* stocker ❷ *(supply with merchandise: store)* approvisionner ❸ *(fill: shelves)* remplir

**stockbroker** ['stakˌbroʊkər] *n* agent *m* de change

**stock car** *n* stock-car *m*

**stock-car racing** *n* course *f* de stock-car

**stock certificate** *n* titre *m* d'action(s)

**stock dividend** *n* dividende *f* en actions; **~ share** action *f* gratuite

**stock exchange** *n* Bourse *f*

**stocking** ['stɑ·kɪŋ] *n* bas *m*

**stock issue** *n* émission *f* des actions

**stock market** *n* marché *m* boursier

**stockpile** ['stak·paɪl] **I.** *n* réserves *fpl* **II.** *vt* faire des réserves de

**stoke** [stoʊk] *vt a. fig* entretenir

**stole¹** [stoʊl] *pt of* **steal**

**stole²** [stoʊl] *n* FASHION, REL étole *f*

**stolen I.** *pp of* **steal II.** *adj* volé(e)

**stomach** ['stʌm·ək] **I.** *n* ANAT ❶ *(digestive organ)* estomac *m;* **to have no ~ for sth** *fig* ne pas avoir le cœur de faire qc ❷ *(abdomen)* ventre *m* **II.** *vt inf* supporter; **to be hard to ~** être difficile à avaler

**stomachache** *n* maux *mpl* d'estomac

**stomping ground** *n* lieu *m* de prédilection

**stone** [stoʊn] **I.** *n* ❶ GEO pierre *f* ❷ *(piece of rock, jewel)* pierre *f;* *(smaller)* caillou *m;* **to be a ~'s throw (away)** être à deux pas ❸ MED *(in kidney, gallbladder)* calcul *m* ❹ *(seed of fruit)* noyau *m* ▶ **to leave no ~ unturned** faire absolument tout ce que l'on peut **II.** *adj* ❶ CONSTR *(made of stone: floor, wall, statue)* en pierre; GEO pierreux(-euse) ❷ *(stoneware: jug)* en grès **III.** *adv* ❶ *(like a stone)* **~ hard** dur(e) comme de la pierre ❷ *inf (completely)* complètement **IV.** *vt* ❶ *(throw stones at)* lancer des cailloux sur; **to ~ sb to death** lapider qn (à mort) ❷ *(remove the kernels)* dénoyauter

**Stone Age** *n* **the ~** l'âge *m* de pierre

**stoned** *adj sl* défoncé(e)

**stony-faced** *adj* (au visage) impassible

**stood** [stʊd] *pt, pp of* **stand**

**stool** [stul] *n* ❶ *(seat)* tabouret *m* ❷ MED *(feces)* selles *fpl*

**stop** [stap] **I.** *n* ❶ *(break in activity)* arrêt *m;* **to come to a ~** s'arrêter; **to put a ~ to sth** mettre fin à qc ❷ *(halting place)* arrêt *m* ❸ LING *(period)* point *m;* *(in telegram)* stop *m* ❹ MUS *(on organ)* jeu *m* **II.** <-pp-> *vt* ❶ *(put halt to: bleeding, leak)* arrêter; **to ~ sb from doing sth** empêcher qn de faire qc ❷ *(refuse payment: payment, production)* cesser; **to a ~ (payment on) a check** faire opposition sur un chèque ❸ *(turn off: mechanism, tape recorder)* arrêter ❹ *(block: ball, punch)* arrêter; *(gap, hole)* boucher; *(one's ears)* se boucher **III.** <-pp-> *vi* ❶ *(halt, cease)* s'arrêter; **to ~ doing sth** arrêter de faire qc; **to ~ at nothing** n'arrêter devant rien

◆ **stop by** *vi* passer

◆ **stop in** *vi* rester chez soi

◆ **stop off** *vi* s'arrêter

◆**stop over** *vi* s'arrêter

◆**stop up** *vt* (*hole, gap*) boucher

**stop-and-go** *adj* (*traffic*) qui avance mal

**stopgap I.** *n* bouche-trou *m* **II.** *adj* provisoire

**stoplight** *n* feu *m* rouge

**stopover** *n* (*by plane*) escale *f*; (*by car, train*) halte *f*

**stop sign** *n* stop *m*

**stopwatch** *n* chronomètre *m*

**storage** ['stɔr·ɪdʒ] *n* a. COMPUT stockage *m*; **to put sth into ~** entreposer qc; (*furniture*) mettre qc en garde-meubles

**storage space** *n* rangement *m*

**store** [stɔr] **I.** *n* ❶ (*shop*) magasin *m* ❷ (*supply*) provision *f*; **in ~** en réserve; **what is in ~ for sb** ce que réserve l'avenir à qn ❸ (*warehouse, storehouse*) entrepôt *m*; **in ~** en dépôt **II.** *vt* COMPUT mémoriser

**store card** *n* carte *f* de paiement [*o* de fidélité]

**storm** [stɔrm] **I.** *n* ❶ METEO *a. fig* tempête *f* ❷ MIL assaut *m*; **to take sth by ~** *a. fig* prendre qc d'assaut **II.** *vi* ❶ METEO tempêter ❷ (*speak angrily*) fulminer **III.** *vt a.* MIL prendre d'assaut

**stormy** ['stɔr·mi] <-ier, -iest> *adj a. fig* orageux(-euse)

**story** ['stɔr·i] <-ies> *n* ❶ (*tale*) histoire *f*; **sb's side of the ~** la version de qn; **or so the ~ goes** d'après ce que l'on raconte ❷ (*news report*) reportage *m* ❸ (*lie*) histoires *fpl* ❹ (*floor in building*) étage *m* ▶ **it's the ~ of my life** c'est tout à fait moi, **it's the same old ~** c'est toujours la même histoire

**stove** [stoʊv] *n* ❶ (*heater*) poêle *m* ❷ (*for cooking*) cuisinière *f*; **induction ~** plaque [*o* table] *f* à induction

**stowaway** *n* passager, -ère *m, f* clandestin(e)

**straggler** *n* traînard(e) *m(f)*

**straight** [streɪt] **I.** *n* ❶ SPORTS (*part of race track*) ligne *f* droite ❷ *inf* (*not homosexual*) hétéro *mf* **II.** *adj* ❶ (*without bend*) droit(e); (*hair*) raide; (*route*) direct(e) ❷ (*honest*) honnête; (*answer*)

franc(he); **to be ~ with sb** être direct avec qn ❸ *inf* (*not homosexual*) hétéro *inv* ❹ (*plain*) simple; **a ~ gin** un gin sec ❺ (*clear*) clair(e) ❻ (*serious*) sérieux(-euse) ❼ *sl* (*not drunk or high*) clean **III.** *adv* ❶ droit; **~ ahead** droit devant ❷ (*at once*) directement; **to get ~ to the point** aller droit au but ❸ *inf* (*honestly*) directement; **to tell it to sb ~** dire carrément à qn ❹ (*clearly: see*) clairement; **to think ~** voir clair

**straightaway** *adv* directement

**straighten** *vt* ❶ (*make straight*) redresser; **to ~ one's hair** se raidir les cheveux ❷ (*make tidy: tie*) ajuster

◆**straighten out I.** *vi* (*become straight*) devenir droit **II.** *vt* ❶ (*make straight*) redresser ❷ (*make neat*) arranger ❸ *fig* arranger; (*problems*) résoudre

◆**straighten up I.** *vi* se redresser **II.** *vt* ❶ (*stand up straight*) redresser; **to ~ one's body** se redresser ❷ (*make neat*) mettre de l'ordre dans; (*room*) ranger

**straightforward** *adj* ❶ (*honest*) franc(franche) ❷ (*easy*) simple

**strain**[1] [streɪn] **I.** *n* ❶ (*pressure*) *a.* PHYS tension *f*; **to put a ~ on sb/sth** exercer une pression sur qn/qc ❷ (*pulled muscle*) entorse *f*; **back ~** tour *m* de reins **II.** *vi* **to ~ to** +*infin* peiner pour +*infin* **III.** *vt* ❶ MED, SPORTS se fouler; (*muscle, ligament*) se froisser; **to ~ one's back** se faire un tour de reins ❷ (*pressure*) mettre à rude épreuve; **to ~ oneself** se surmener; **to ~ one's ears** tendre l'oreille ❸ (*filter liquid out: coffee*) faire passer; (*vegetables*) égoutter

**strain**[2] [streɪn] *n* ❶ (*line of breed*) espèce *f* ▶ (*type*) sorte *f* ❸ (*inherited characteristic*) disposition *f*; (*of humor*) propension *f*

**strait** [streɪt] *n* ❶ GEO détroit *m* ❷ *pl* (*bad situation*) situation *f* difficile; **to be in dire ~s** être en grande difficulté

**strait-laced** ['streɪt·leɪst] *adj* collet monté *inv*

**strange** [streɪndʒ] *adj* ❶ (*odd, bizarre*) étrange; **it's ~ that ...** c'est bizarre

**S**

que … +*subj*; **~r things have happened** tout peut arriver ② (*not known*) étranger(-ère); (*face*) inconnu(e)

**strangely** *adv* bizarrement; **~ enough** chose *f* étrange

**stranger** *n* ① (*unknown person*) inconnu(e) *m(f)* ② (*from another place*) étranger, -ère *m, f*; **to be a ~** ne pas être d'ici; **to be a ~ to sth** ne rien connaître à qc; **no ~ to sth, …** habitué à qc, …

**strangle** ['stræŋ·gl] *vt* ① (*squeeze neck: person*) étrangler; (*thing*) asphyxier ② *fig* (*scream*) étouffer

**strap** [stræp] **I.** *n* ① (*for fastening*) sangle *f*; (*of watch*) bracelet *m*; (*of shoe*) lanière *f*; (*of bra, top*) bretelle *f* ③ (*loop for hanging*) poignée *f* **II.** <-pp-> *vt* to **~ sb/sth to sth** attacher qn/qc à qc

**strapless** *adj* sans bretelles

**strategy** ['stræt̬·ə·dʒi] <-ies> *n* stratégie *f*

**straw** [strɔ] *n* ① (*grain stalk*) paille *f*; **to draw ~s** tirer à la courte paille ② (*for drinking*) paille *f* ► **to be the ~ that breaks the camel's back** [*o* **to be the last ~**] être la goutte d'eau qui fait déborder le vase; **to grasp at ~s** se raccrocher à de faux espoirs

**strawberry** ['strɔ·beri] <-ies> *n* fraise *f*

**straw-colored** *adj* jaune paille

**straw vote** *n* sondage *m* d'opinion

**streak** [strik] **I.** *n* ① (*mark, smear*) trace *f*; **dirty ~s** traces *fpl* ② (*in hair*) mèche *f* ③ (*strip*) filet *m*; (*of light*) trait *m*; **~ of lightning** éclair *m* ④ (*tendency*) tendance *f* ⑤ (*run of fortune*) **lucky ~** période *f* de chance; **to be on a winning ~** être dans une bonne passe **II.** *vt* strier; **to have one's hair ~ed** se faire des mèches; **to be ~ed with black** être veiné de noir **III.** *vi* to **~ off/out/past** passer/sortir/passer à toute allure

**streaker** *n* personne qui court nu lors d'événements publics

**streaky** <-ier, -iest> *adj* strié(e)

**stream** [strim] **I.** *n* ① (*small river*) ruisseau *m* ② (*current*) *a. fig* courant *m* ③ (*flow*) *a. fig* flot *m* **II.** *vi* ① (*flow*) *a. fig* ruisseler; (*nose, eyes*) couler; **to ~** **down one's face** dégouliner sur son visage ② (*move in numbers*) **people ~ in/out/away** des flots de gens entrent/sortent/partent ③ (*shine, spread: light, sun*) entrer à flots **III.** *vt* (*blood, tears*) ruisseler de

**streamer** *n* banderole *f*

**streaming** ['stri:·mɪŋ] *n* INET streaming *m*

**streamline** ['strim·laɪn] *vt* ① (*make aerodynamic*) caréner ② (*improve efficiency*) rationaliser

**street** [strit] *n* rue *f*; **at 24 Oak Street** au 24 de la Oak Street; **on Oak Street** dans la Oak Street; **to take to the ~s** descendre dans les rues ► **the man on** [*o* **in**] **the ~** l'homme *m* de la rue

**streetcar** *n* tramway *m*

**street cred** *n sl* **to have ~** être branché

**streetwise** *adj* conscient(e) des dangers de la rue

**strength** [streŋ(k)θ] *n* ① (*effort, good quality*) *a. fig* force *f*; **to be back to full ~** retrouver ses forces; **to draw ~ from sth** tirer sa force de qc; **on the ~ of sth** en vertu de qc ② (*number*) nombre *m*; **at full ~** au grand complet; **to be below ~** être en sous-effectif

**strengthen** ['streŋ(k)·θən] **I.** *vt* renforcer; (*wall*) fortifier; (*muscles*) développer ► **to ~ one's grip on sth** renforcer son emprise sur qc **II.** *vi* ① (*become strong: muscles*) se renforcer ② FIN (*stock market, prices*) se raffermir

**stress** [stres] **I.** *n* ① (*mental strain*) tension *f*; **to be under ~** être tendu ② MED stress *m* ③ (*emphasis*) insistance *f* ④ LING accent *m* tonique **II.** *vt* ① (*emphasize*) insister ② (*pronounce forcibly*) accentuer ③ *inf* (*cause distress*) **to ~ sb out** stresser qn

**stressful** *adj* stressant(e)

**stress test** *n* test *m* de résistance; MED test *m* d'effort

**stretch** [stretʃ] **I.** <-es> *n* ① (*elasticity*) élasticité *f* ② (*muscle extension*) étirement *m* ③ GEO étendue *f*; (*of land*) bande *f*; (*of road*) section *f* ④ (*period*) période *f*; **to do a ten-year ~ behind**

**bars** passer dix ans derrière les barreaux ⑤(*effort*) effort *m*; **by no ~ of the imagination** même en faisant un gros effort d'imagination ⑥SPORTS ligne *f* droite II. *adj* (*fabric, jeans*) extensible; **a ~ limo** une limousine III. *vi* ①(*become longer, wider: rubber, elastic*) s'étendre; (*clothes*) se détendre ②(*extend muscles*) s'étirer ③(*need time*) se prolonger; **to ~ into June/ next year** se prolonger jusqu'en juin/ jusqu'à l'année prochaine; **to ~ back to last August/1987** remonter à août dernier/ 1987 ④(*cover area*) s'étendre; **to ~ for 25 miles** s'étendre sur 25 miles ⑤(*go beyond*) **to be fully ~ed** être à la limite de ses capacités IV. *vt* ①(*extend*) étirer; (*hand, arm*) tendre ②(*extend by pulling: elastic band*) tendre; (*clothes*) détendre ③(*demand a lot of*) a. *fig* mettre à rude épreuve; (*limits*) outrepasser; **to ~ oneself beyond one's means** vivre au-dessus de ses moyens ④SPORTS **to ~ one's lead** s'avancer en tête ⑤(*go beyond*) forcer; **to ~ it a bit** y aller un peu fort

**stretcher** *n* brancard *m*

**strict** [strɪkt] *adj* ①(*harsh*) strict(e); (*penalty, morals*) sévère ②(*requiring conformity*) strict(e); (*censorship, control*) rigoureux(-euse); (*deadline, time limit*) de rigueur; (*guideline*) astreignant(e); (*order*) formel(le) ③(*complete: secrecy*) absolu(e); (*sense*) précis(e); **in ~est confidence** en toute confidence ④(*conforming: vegetarian*) vrai(e)

**strictly** *adv* ①(*severely*) strictement ②(*exactly*) exactement; (*forbidden, defined*) strictement; **~ speaking** à proprement parler

**stride** [straɪd] I. *vi* ①(*walk*) marcher à grandes enjambées; **to ~ in/out** entrer/sortir à grands pas ②*fig* **to ~ forward** progresser à grands pas II. *n* ①(*long step*) enjambée *f*; **to break one's ~** casser la cadence ②*fig* (*progress*) **to make ~s in sth** faire d'énormes progrès en qc ▶**to break sb's ~**

faire perdre la cadence à qn; **to hit one's ~** prendre sa vitesse de croisière; **to take sth in ~** faire qc sans le moindre effort

**strike** [straɪk] I. *n* ①(*protest action*) grève *f* ②(*sudden attack*) attaque *f*; **air ~** raid *m* ③(*blow*) coup *m* ④(*discovery*) découverte *f* ⑤(*in baseball*) strike *m* *fig* (*warning*) avertissement *m*; **a ~ against sb** un coup porté contre qn II.<struck, struck> *vt* ①(*hit hard*) frapper ②(*collide with*) tamponner ③(*ignite: a match*) craquer ④(*achieve: deal, bargain*) parvenir à; (*a balance*) trouver; **to ~ it rich** faire fortune ⑤(*generate harmony*) **to ~ a chord with sb** être sur la même longueur d'onde que qn ⑥(*coins, medallion*) frapper ⑦<struck, struck *o* stricken> (*cause feelings of*) **to ~ fear into sb** remplir qn d'effroi ⑧<struck, struck *o* stricken> (*cause memories*) **to ~ a chord** se rappeler de qc ⑨<struck, struck *o* stricken> (*create atmosphere*) **to ~ a note of warning** donner l'alerte ⑩(*discover deposit of*) découvrir; (*gold*) remporter; **to ~ oil** atteindre une nappe pétrolifère ⑪**to ~ a pose** poser; *fig* faire des manières ⑫<struck, struck *o* stricken> (*cause suffering*) frapper durement; **an earthquake struck Los Angeles** un tremblement de terre a sévi à Los Angeles ⑬(*clock*) sonner ⑭(*engender thought*) marquer ⑮(*remove*) démonter; (*name from list*) rayer ▶**to ~ a blow against sb** infliger un coup à qn III.<struck, struck> *vi* ①(*hit hard*) frapper fort ②(*attack*) attaquer ③(*stop working as protest*) se mettre en grève ④(*clock*) sonner ▶**to ~ home** frapper juste

◆**strike back** *vi* rendre un coup; **to ~ at sb** répliquer à qn

◆**strike down** *vt* abattre; **to be struck down by a disease** être terrassé par une maladie

◆**strike from** *vt* (*name*) rayer; **to strike sb from the register** rayer qn du registre

S

◆ **strike out I.** vt (in baseball) éliminer sur trois prises **II.** vi ❶ (start out) recommencer ❷ (attack) **to ~ at sb** frapper qn; (criticize) attaquer qn ❸ (fail to hit ball) manquer la balle

◆ **strike up I.** vt ❶ (start) commencer; (conversation) entamer; (relationship) se lancer dans ❷ (start music) se mettre à jouer; (song) entonner **II.** vi commencer

**strikebreaker** n briseur, -euse m, f de grève

**striker** n ❶ (strike participant) gréviste mf ❷ (in soccer) buteur m

**striking** adj ❶ (noticeable) saisissant(e); (beauty, similarity) frappant(e); (feature, personality) saillant(e); (result) étonnant(e) ❷ (good-looking) magnifique

▶ **within ~ distance** à portée de la main; (close to achieving results) à deux doigts de qc

**string** [strɪŋ] **I.** n ❶ (twine) ficelle f ❷ (on guitar, violin) corde f ❸ pl (orchestral section) cordes fpl ❹ (chain: of pearls) collier m ❺ fig (sequence) série f; (of names) suite f ❻ COMPUT suite f; **search ~** chaîne f de recherche ▶ **to pull ~s** tirer les ficelles **II.** <strung, strung> vt ❶ (attach strings to: racket, guitar) corder ❷ (thread onto string) enfiler

◆ **string along** inf **I.** vi **to ~ with sb** accompagner qn **II.** vt ❶ (keep uncertain) faire poireauter ❷ (trick) faire marcher

◆ **string out I.** vi s'espacer **II.** vt ❶ (prolong) faire traîner; **to be strung out over a distance** s'échelonner sur une distance ❷ fig **to be strung out** (be nervous, tense) être à plat; **to be strung out on sth** (be addicted) être accro à qc

◆ **string up** vt ❶ (hang) suspendre ❷ inf (execute) pendre ❸ inf (penalize) punir

**stringent** ['strɪn·dʒənt] adj ❶ (rigorous) rigoureux(-euse); (condition) strict(e); (measure) énergique ❷ (tight) sévère

**strip** [strɪp] **I.** vt ❶ (lay bare) enlever; (a tree of fruit) défruiter ❷ (unclothe) déshabiller ❸ (dismantle) défaire **II.** vi se déshabiller **III.** n ❶ (long narrow piece) bande f; (of metal) lame f; (of land) bande f ❷ (striptease) strip-tease m ❸ (commercial road) voie f ❹ (comic strip) bande f dessinée

**stripe** [straɪp] n ❶ (colored band) rayure f ❷ MIL galon m

**striped** adj à raies; (shirt) à rayures

**strip mall** n zone f commerçante

**strip-mining** n extraction f à ciel ouvert

**stripper** n ❶ (female) strip-teaseuse f; (male) strip-teaseur m ❷ (solvent) décapant m

**strip search** n fouille f d'une personne dévêtue

**strip-search** vt faire déshabiller qn pour le fouiller

**strive** [straɪv] <strove, striven o strived> vi **to ~ to** +infin s'efforcer de +infin; **~ as we may** quels que soient nos efforts (subj); **to ~ for sth** essayer d'obtenir qc

**strode** [stroʊd] pt of **stride**

**stroke** [stroʊk] **I.** n ❶ (gentle caress) caresse f ❷ (blow) coup m ❸ MED attaque f ❹ (bit, sign, sound: of luck, fate) coup m; (of a pen) trait m; **a ~ of genius** un trait de génie; **at the ~ of midnight** sur le coup de minuit ❺ form (lash with whip) coup m de fouet ❻ (swimming method) nage f **II.** vt ❶ (move hand over) caresser ❷ (hit smoothly: ball) frapper

**stroll** [stroʊl] **I.** n petite promenade f **II.** vi flâner

**strong** [strɔŋ] **I.** adj ❶ (powerful: person, wind, currency) fort(e); (defense, country, athlete) puissant(e) ❷ (concentrated: coffee, alcohol) fort(e); (medicine) puissant(e); (competition) serré(e) ❸ (sturdy, durable) solide ❹ (healthy) vigoureux(-euse); (constitution) robuste ❺ (intense: desire) fort(e); (will, influence) grand(e) ❻ (deep-rooted) tenace; (antipathy) grand(e); (bias, fear, opinion) fort(e);

(*bond*) extraordinaire; **she is a ~ person** elle a du ressort ❼ (*very likely*) fort(e); (*chance*) grand(e) ❽ (*having number*) **they were 200 ~** ils/elles étaient au nombre de deux cents ❾ (*marked*) marqué(e); **to have a ~ accent** avoir un fort accent ❿ (*bright: color*) vif(vive), ⓫ (*pungent*) fort(e); (*flavor*) relevé(e); (*language*) grossier(-ère) II. *adv* **to** <u>come</u> **on ~** draguer; **to be still** <u>going</u> **~** se porter toujours bien

**strongly** *adv* ❶ (*solidly*) a. *fig* solidement; **~ built** de constitution robuste ❷ (*powerfully*) fortement; (*establish, believe*) fermement; (*advise*) vivement; (*condemn, criticize*) sévèrement; (*disapprove*) profondément; (*deny*) vigoureusement

**strong-minded** *adj* résolu(e)

**struck** [strʌk] *pt, pp of* **strike**

**struggle** ['strʌɡ·l] I. *n* ❶ (*great effort*) lutte *f*; **without a ~** sans résistance ❷ (*skirmish*) conflit *m* II. *vi* ❶ (*exert oneself*) lutter; **to ~ to one's feet** se lever avec difficulté; **to ~ to** +*infin* avoir de la difficulté à +*infin* ❷ (*fight*) se débattre; **to ~ with sb/sth** être aux prises avec qn/qc; *fig* avoir des difficultés avec qn/qc ❸ (*resist*) résister

**strung** [strʌŋ] *pt, pp of* **string**

**stub** [stʌb] I. *n* ❶ (*of ticket*) bout *m* ❷ (*of cigarette*) mégot *m* ❸ (*short pencil*) bout *m* de crayon II. <-bb-> *vt* **to ~ one's toes** se cogner le pied

**stubborn** ['stʌb·ərn] *adj* têtu(e); (*problem, stain*) tenace

**stuck** [stʌk] *pt, pp of* **stick**

**stuck-up** *adj inf* prétentieux(-euse)

**stud**¹ [stʌd] *n* ❶ (*male horse*) étalon *m* ❷ (*stable*) haras *m* ❸ *inf* (*man*) tombeur *m*

**stud**² [stʌd] *n* ❶ CONSTR (*post*) montant *m* ❷ (*small metal item*) clou *m* pour ornement ❸ (*on dress shirt*) bouton *m* de chemise ❹ *pl* (*for driving in snow*) chaînes *fpl*

**student** ['stu·d⁰nt] *n* SCHOOL élève *mf*; UNIV étudiant(e) *m(f)*

**student teacher** *n* professeur *mf* stagiaire

**studio** ['stu·di·ou] <-s> *n* ❶ (*atelier*) atelier *m* ❷ (*firm*) studio *m* ❸ (*room for recording*) studio *m* (d'enregistrement) ❹ (*one-room apartment*) studio *m*

**studio apartment** *n* studio *m*

**study** ['stʌd·i] I. *vt* étudier II. *vi* faire des études III. <-ies> *n* ❶ (*investigation*) étude *f* ❷ (*academic investigation*) recherche *f* ❸ *pl* (*learning*) études *fpl* ❹ (*room*) bureau *m* (de travail) ❺ (*literary treatment*) étude *f* de texte

**study hall** *n* salle *f* d'étude

**stuff** [stʌf] I. *n* ❶ *inf* (*thing*) truc *m* ❷ (*things*) trucs *mpl*; **to write good ~** bien écrire ❸ (*belongings*) affaires *fpl* ❹ (*basic characteristics*) essence *f* ❺ (*one's knowledge*) **to know one's ~** s'y connaître ❻ (*material*) étoffe *f* ❼ *inf* (*drugs*) came *f* II. *vt* ❶ (*fill*) a. *fig* remplir; (*cushion*) rembourrer; (*animals*) empailler; **to ~ sth into sth** fourrer qc dans qc ❷ *inf* (*eat greedily*) **to ~ oneself** [*o sl* **one's face**] s'empiffrer ❸ CULIN farcir III. *vi* se goinfrer

**stuffed animal** *n* peluche *f*

**stuffing** *n* ❶ (*padding*) rembourrage *m* ❷ CULIN farce *f*

**stuffy** *adj* ❶ (*stodgy*) collet monté *inv* ❷ (*unventilated: room*) mal ventilé(e) ❸ MED **~ nose** nez *m* bouché

**stumble** ['stʌm·bl] I. *n* faux pas *m* II. *vi* ❶ (*trip*) trébucher; **to ~ in/out** entrer/ sortir en trébuchant ❷ (*falter during talking*) **to ~ over sth** buter sur qc

**stumbling block** *n* obstacle *m*

**stump** [stʌmp] I. *n* ❶ (*of tree*) souche *f* ❷ (*of arm, leg*) moignon *m* II. *vt* déconcerter; **to be ~ ed by sth** être incapable de répondre à qc III. *vi* ❶ POL faire campagne ❷ (*walk heavily*) **to ~ in/out** entrer/sortir à pas lourds; **to ~ into sth** entrer à pas lourds dans qc

**stun** [stʌn] <-nn-> *vt* ❶ (*shock*) stupéfier; **~ned silence** silence *m* surprenant ❷ (*make unconscious*) assommer

**stung** [stʌŋ] *pp, pt of* **sting**

**stun gun** n pistolet m hypodermique

**stunk** [stʌŋk] pt, pp of **stink**

**stunned** adj surpris(e)

**stunning** adj ❶(upsetting) bouleversant(e) ❷(dazzling) sensationnel(le); (dress) magnifique

**stupid** ['stu·pɪd] inf I.<-er, -est o more ~, most ~> adj stupide II. n idiot(e) m(f)

**stupidity** [stu·'pɪd·ə·t̬i] n stupidité f

**stutter** ['stʌt̬·ər] I. vt, vi bégayer II. n bégaiement m

**style** [staɪl] I. n ❶(way of expression) style m; **in ~** en grande pompe; **to do things in ~** faire les choses bien ❷(fashion) mode f; **in ~** à la mode; **the latest ~** les dernières tendances fpl; **to go out of ~** passer de mode ❸fig, inf genre m; **to not be sb's ~** ne pas être le genre de qn II. vt dessiner; **elegantly ~d jackets** vestes fpl élégamment coupées; **to ~ hair** se coiffer (les cheveux)

**stylish** ['staɪ·lɪʃ] adj approv ❶(chic, smart) élégant(e); (fashionable) qui a du style, à la mode ❷(polished) raffiné(e)

**stylishly** ['staɪ·lɪʃ·li] adv approv (chic, smartly) avec élégance; (fashionably) à la mode

**stylist** n styliste mf; **hair ~** coiffeur m visagiste

**stylistic** adj stylistique

**sub** [sʌb] I. n ❶inf abbr of **substitute** ❷inf abbr of **submarine** ❸inf abbr of **submarine sandwich** ≈ sandwich m baguette II.<-bb-> vi inf abbr of **substitute** faire un remplacement; **to ~ for sb** remplacer qn

**subconscious** I. n subconscient m II. adj subconscient(e); **~ mind** subconscient m

**subcontractor** n sous-traitant m

**subject** ['sʌb·dʒɪkt] I. n ❶(topic) sujet m; **~ matter** sujet; **to be on the ~ of sb/sth** être à propos de qn/qc ❷SCHOOL, UNIV matière f II. adj ❶(dominated) soumis(e) ❷(exposed to negative factor) sujet(te); **to be ~ to**

sth être sujet à qc ▶**- to sth** sous réserve de qc; **~ to payment** moyennant paiement III. vt assujettir; **to ~ oneself to danger** s'exposer à un danger

**subjective** [səb·'dʒek·tɪv] adj subjectif(-ive)

**submarine** I. n sous-marin m II. adj sous-marin(e)

**submarine sandwich** n petit pain de forme allongée, généralement garni de fromage, de charcuterie en tranche, de tomates, de feuilles de salade, de moutarde et de rondelles d'oignon

**submission** [səb·'mɪʃ·ᵊn] n soumission f; **to force/frighten sb into ~** soumettre qn par la force/la terreur; **to starve sb into ~** réduire qn à la famine

**subscribe** [səb·'skraɪb] I. vt verser II. vi ❶**to ~ to sth** (magazine, newspaper) s'abonner à qc ❷(believe in) **to ~ to sth** souscrire à qc

**subscriber** n abonné(e) m(f)

**subsequent** adj (following) ultérieur(e); **~ to sth** ultérieur à qc ❷(resulting) consécutif(-ive); **~ to sth** suite à qc

**subsequently** adv par la suite

**subside** [səb·'saɪd] vi ❶(abate) diminuer ❷(cave in) s'affaisser

**subsidiary** [səb·'sɪd·i·ər·i] I. adj subsidiaire; (reason) accessoires; **~ company** filiale f II.<-ies> n ECON filiale f

**subsidize** ['sʌb·sə·daɪz] vt subventionner

**subsidy** ['sʌb·sə·di] <-ies> n subvention f

**subsistence** n form subsistance f

**subsistence level** n minimum m vital; **to live at ~ level** avoir tout juste de quoi vivre

**substance** ['sʌb·stᵊn(t)s] n a. fig substance f

**substandard** adj de qualité inférieure; **~ quality** qualité f médiocre

**substantial** [səb·'stæn(t)·ʃᵊl] adj ❶(important) substantiel(le) ❷(real, general) tangible; **to be in ~ agreement** être d'accord dans l'ensemble

**substantially** adv considérablement

**substitute** ['sʌb·stə·tut] I. n ❶ (equivalent) produit m de substitution; **a ~ for sth** un succédané de qc; **there's no ~ for sb/sth** rien ne peut remplacer qn/qc ❷ (replacement worker) remplaçant(e) m(f) II. vt remplacer; **~ black for white** [o white with black] remplacer le blanc par le noir III. vi **to ~ for sb/sth** remplacer qn/qc

**substitute teacher** n remplaçant(e) m(f)

**substitution** n ❶ (replacing) remplacement m ❷ LAW substitution f

**subtitle** I. n sous-titre m II. vt sous-titrer

**subtle** ['sʌt·l] adj subtil(e)

**subtotal** n sous-total m

**subtract** [səb·'trækt] vt **to ~ sth from sth** soustraire qc de qc

**subtraction** n soustraction f

**subtropical** adj subtropical(e)

**suburb** ['sʌb·ɜrb] n banlieue f, quartier m périphérique Suisse; **the ~s** la banlieue

**suburban** [sə·'bɜr·bən] adj de banlieue; **~ commuters** banlieusards mpl

**subway** n RAIL métro m

**succeed** [sək·'sid] I. vi ❶ (achieve purpose) réussir; **the plan ~ed** le plan a marché ❷ (follow) **to ~ to sth** succéder à qc ▸ **if at first you don't ~, then try, try again** prov il faut persévérer dans l'effort II. vt **to ~ sb as sth** succéder à qn en tant que qc; **to ~ sb in sth** succéder à qn à qc

**success** [sək·'ses] n succès m; **a ~ rate** un taux de réussite; **to be a great ~** avoir beaucoup de succès; **to achieve ~** obtenir du succès; **to enjoy ~** remporter du succès

**successful** adj qui a du succès; (book, film, artist) à succès; (business, season) prospère; (harvest, marriage, participant) heureux(-euse); (plan, career) couronné(e) de succès; **to be ~** avoir du succès

**succession** [sək·'seʃ·ən] n succession f; **in ~** successivement

**successive** [sək·'ses·ɪv] adj successif(-ive)

**successor** n successeur mf; **~ to the throne** héritier m du trône

**succulent** adj succulent(e)

**succumb** [sə·'kʌm] vi form succomber; **to ~ to sb/sth** succomber à qn/qc

**such** [sʌtʃ] I. adj tel(le); **there is no ~ thing as ...** ... n'existe pas; **in ~ a situation** dans une situation pareille; **or some ~ remark** ou une remarque dans le genre II. pron **~ is life** ainsi va la vie; **as ~** en tant que tel(le); **to be recognized as ~** être reconnu comme tel III. adv si; **~ great weather/a good book** un si beau temps/bon livre; **to have ~ a good time** si bien s'amuser **such and such** adj inf tel(le); **to arrive at ~ a time** arriver à telle heure

**suck** [sʌk] I. vt ❶ (drink in: water, air) aspirer ❷ (draw into mouth: lollipop, thumb) sucer; (breast) téter ❸ (strongly move) entraîner; **to be ~ed into sth** fig être entraîné dans qc ▸ **to ~ sb dry** sucer jusqu'à la moelle II. vi ❶ (draw into mouth) sucer; (baby) téter; **to ~ on sth** sucer qc; (one's pipe) tirer sur ❷ (pump) aspirer ❸ sl (be bad) faire chier; **this film ~s** ce film est chiant III. n tétée f

◆**suck in** vt ❶ (draw: air, liquid) aspirer; (cheeks) creuser ❷ fig **to get sucked in** se laisser entraîner

◆**suck up** I. vi inf faire de la lèche; **to ~ to sb** cirer les pompes à qn II. vt aspirer; (water) pomper

**sudden** ['sʌd·ən] adj soudain(e); **to put a ~ stop to sth** mettre brusquement un terme à qc; **all of a ~** inf tout d'un coup

**suddenly** adv soudainement

**sue** [su] <suing> I. vt **to ~ sb for sth** poursuivre qn (en justice) pour qc II. vi engager une procédure judiciaire; **to ~ for sth** engager des poursuites pour qc; **to ~ for divorce** entamer une procédure de divorce

**suede** [sweɪd] n daim m

**suffer** ['sʌf·ər] I. vi ❶ (feel pain) souffrir; **to ~ from sth** souffrir de qc ❷ (expe-

S

*rience*) subir; **to ~ from sth** subir les conséquences de qc; **the economy ~ed from the strike** l'économie a souffert des conséquences de la grève ❸ (*be punished*) **to ~ for sth** payer pour qc **II.** *vt* ❶ (*experience*) subir; (*a defeat, setback*) essuyer ❷ MED souffrir de ❸ (*tolerate*) souffrir

**suffering** *n* souffrance *f*

**sufficient** *adj* suffisant(e); **to be ~ for sb/sth** suffire pour qn/qc

**suffocate** ['sʌf·ə·keɪt] *a. fig* **I.** *vi* suffoquer **II.** *vt a. fig* étouffer

**suffocating** *adj a. fig* étouffant(e)

**sugar** ['ʃʊg·ər] **I.** *n* ❶ (*sweetener*) sucre *m;* **powdered ~** sucre en poudre; **brown ~** sucre roux ❷ *inf* (*term of affection*) mon chéri, ma chérie *m, f* ❸ (*showing annoyance*) zut **II.** *vt* sucrer

**sugar bowl** *n* sucrier *m*

**sugarcoat** *vt* dragéifier

**sugarcoated** *adj* ❶ (*with layer of sweetener*) dragéifié(e); **a ~ almond** une dragée ❷ *fig, pej* (*pleasant*) mielleux(-euse)

**sugar-free** *adj* sans sucre

**sugary** ['ʃʊg·ər·i] <-ier, -iest> *adj* ❶ (*made of sugar*) sucré(e) ❷ *fig, pej* (*insincerely kind*) mielleux(-euse)

**suggest** [səg·'dʒest] *vt* ❶ (*propose*) suggérer ❷ (*show*) laisser supposer ❸ (*come to mind*) **to ~ itself** (*idea, inspiration*) venir à l'esprit

**suggestion** [səg·'dʒes·tʃ'n] *n* ❶ (*proposal*) suggestion *f;* **at sb's ~** sur le conseil de qn ❷ (*small amount*) soupçon *m* ❸ PSYCH (*insinuation*) suggestion *f*

**suggestion box** *n* boîte *f* à idées

**suicide** ['su·ə·saɪd] **I.** *n* ❶ (*act*) *a. fig* suicide *m;* **to commit ~** se suicider ❷ (*person*) suicidé(e) *m(f)* **II.** *vi* se suicider

**suit** [sut] **I.** *vt* ❶ (*be convenient*) convenir à; **~ yourself** comme tu voudras ❷ (*be appropriate*) **to ~ sb** convenir (parfaitement) à qn ❸ (*look nice*) aller (bien) à **II.** *vi* convenir; **if it ~s** si cela te(vous) convient **III.** *n* ❶ (*formal clo-*

*thing*) costume *m;* (*for women*) tailleur *m* ❷ (*sports garment*) combinaison *f;* **bathing ~** maillot *m* de bain ❸ LAW poursuite *f;* **to file ~** engager des poursuites ❹ (*in cards*) couleur *f;* **to follow ~** *fig* faire de même

**suitable** ['su·tə·bl] *adj* adéquat(e); (*clothes, answer*) approprié(e); **to be ~ for sb** convenir à qn

**suitcase** ['sut·keɪs] *n* valise *f*

**sulk** [sʌlk] **I.** *vi* bouder **II.** *n* bouderie *f*

**sulky** ['sʌlk·i] <-ier, -iest> *adj* bouder(-euse)

**sullen** ['sʌl·ən] *adj* ❶ (*person*) renfrogné(e) ❷ *fig* (*sky, clouds*) maussade

**sultana** [sʌl·'tæn·ə] *n* ❶ (*grape, raisin*) raisins *mpl* de Smyrne ❷ (*wife of sultan*) sultane *f*

**sultry** ['sʌl·tri] <-ier, -iest> *adj* ❶ (*humid: weather*) lourd ❷ (*sexy*) sensuel(le)

**sum** [sʌm] **I.** *n* ❶ (*amount*) somme *f* ❷ MATH (*after adding*) somme *f* ❸ *no indef art* MATH (*total*) montant *m;* **in ~** en somme **II.** <-mm-> *vt* ❶ (*add*) additionner ❷ (*summarize*) **to ~ sth up/to ~ up sth** faire le résumé de qc; **to ~ sth up as sth** résumer qc comme étant qc

**summarize** ['sʌm·ə·raɪz] **I.** *vi* faire un résumé **II.** *vt* résumer

**summary** ['sʌm·ə'·r·i] **I.** *n* résumé *m;* **in ~** en résumé **II.** *adj* sommaire

**summer** ['sʌm·ər] **I.** *n* été *m* **II.** *adj* d'été **III.** *vi* (*person*) passer l'été; (*animals, plants*) estiver

**summer school** *n* SCHOOL cours *mpl* d'été; UNIV université *f* d'été

**summertime** *n* été *m*

**summer vacation** *n* vacances *fpl* d'été; SCHOOL, UNIV grandes vacances *fpl*

**summit** ['sʌm·ɪt] *n a. fig* sommet *m;* **~ meeting** rencontre *f* au sommet

**sun** [sʌn] **I.** *n* soleil *m* ▶ **to do/try everything under the ~** faire/essayer tout ce qui est possible d'imaginer; **nothing new under the ~** rien de nouveau sous le soleil **II.** <-nn-> *vt* **to ~ oneself** prendre un bain de soleil

**sunbaked** *adj* brûlé(e) par le soleil

**sunbathe** *vi* prendre un bain de soleil
**sunbed** *n* s. **tanning bed**
**sunblock** *n* protection *f* solaire
**sunburn** *n* coup *m* de soleil
**sunburned, sunburnt** *adj* **to be/get ~** avoir/attraper un coup de soleil
**sundae** ['sʌn·di] *n* sundae *m*
**Sunday** ['sʌn·deɪ] *n* dimanche *m*; *s.a.* **Friday**
**sun deck** *n* ❶ (*on boat*) pont *m* supérieur ❷ (*balcony*) terrasse *f*
**sundial** *n* cadran *m* solaire
**sundown** *n* coucher *m* du soleil
**sunflower** *n* tournesol *m*
**sung** [sʌŋ] *pp of* **sing**
**sunglasses** ['sʌn·ˌglæs·ɪz] *npl* lunettes *fpl* de soleil
**sun hat** *n* chapeau *m* de soleil
**sunk** [sʌŋk] *pp of* **sink**
**sunlight** *n no indef art* soleil *m*
**sunlit** ['sʌn·lɪt] *adj* ensoleillé(e)
**sunny** ['sʌn·i] <-ier, -iest> *adj* ❶ (*not overcast*) ensoleillé(e); **~ intervals** éclaircies *fpl*; **the ~ side of sth** *a. fig* le bon côté de qc ❷ (*happy*) radieux(-euse); **to have a ~ disposition** être d'un naturel enjoué ❸ **eggs ~ side up** œufs *mpl* sur le plat
**sun porch** *n* véranda *f*
**sunrise** ['sʌn·raɪz] *n* lever *m* du soleil
**sunroof** *n* toit *m* ouvrant
**sunscreen** *n* écran *m* solaire
**sunset** ['sʌn·set] *n* coucher *m* du soleil; **at ~** au soleil couchant
**sunshade** *n* ❶ (*beach umbrella*) ombrelle *f* ❷ (*awning*) parasol *m*
**sunshine** *n* ❶ *no indef art* (*light, heat of sun*) soleil *m* ❷ *fig* (*cheerfulness*) brin *m* de soleil; **to bring ~ into sb's life** être un rayon de soleil dans la vie de qn
**sunstroke** *n* insolation *f*
**suntan** *n* bronzage *m*; **to get a ~** bronzer
**suntan cream, suntan lotion** *n* crème *f* à bronzer
**suntanned** *adj* bronzé(e)
**sunup** *n* lever *m* du soleil
**super¹** ['su·pər] *adj, adv inf* super *inv*

**super²** ['su·pər] *n abbr of* **superintendent**
**superb** [sə·'pɜrb] *adj* superbe
**superduper** *adj sl* génial(e)
**superficial** [ˌsu·pər·'fɪʃ·əl] *adj a. fig* superficiel(le)
**superfluous** [su·'pɜr·flu·əs] *adj* superflu(e)
**superglue** *n* superglu *f*
**superintendent** *n* ❶ (*person in charge*) responsable *mf*; (*in a department*) chef *mf* de service; (*in a shop*) chef *mf* de rayon ❷ (*janitor*) intendant(e) *m(f)*; (*of building*) concierge *mf*
**superior** [sə·'pɪr·i·ər] **I.** *adj a. pej* supérieur(e) **II.** *n* supérieur(e) *m(f)*
**superiority** [sə·ˌpɪr·i·'ɔr·ə·t̬i] *n* supériorité *f*
**supermarket** *n* supermarché *m*
**supersonic** [ˌsu·pər·'sɑ·nɪk] *adj* AVIAT supersonique
**superstar** *n* superstar *f*
**superstitious** *adj* superstitieux(-euse)
**superstore** *n* hypermarché *m*
**supervision** *n* surveillance *f*
**supervisor** *n* ❶ (*person in charge*) chef *mf*; (*in department*) chef *mf* de service; (*in shop*) chef *mf* de rayon ❷ (*teacher*) directeur, -trice *m, f*
**supper** ['sʌp·ər] *n* souper *m*
**suppertime** *n no indef art* heure *f* du souper
**supplier** [sə·'plaɪ·ər] *n* fournisseur *m*
**supply** [sə·'plaɪ] **I.** <-ie-, ying> *vt* fournir; **to ~ sb/sth with food** approvisionner qn/qc en nourriture **II.** *n* ❶ (*provision*) provision *f*; **electricity/water ~** alimentation *f* en électricité/eau; **food supplies** vivres *mpl* ❷ *pl* (*equipment*) matériel *m*; (*of office*) fournitures *fpl* ❸ *no indef art* ECON (*availability*) offre *f* ❹ (*action of providing*) approvisionnement *m*
**support** [sə·'pɔrt] **I.** *vt* ❶ (*hold up*) *a. fig* maintenir ❷ (*bear: load, roof*) supporter ❸ (*provide with money*) entretenir; **a family to ~** une famille à charge; **to ~ oneself** gagner sa vie ❹ (*help*) soutenir; **to ~ a friend** apporter son soutien à

**S**

un ami ⑤ (*encourage: political party*) soutenir ⑥ SPORTS supporter ⑦ (*show to be true: theory*) appuyer II. n ① (*act of supporting*) appui m ② (*supporting object*) support m ③ (*garment*) maintien m; **knee ~** genouillère f ④ (*help*) soutien m ⑤ no indef art (*provision of necessities*) subvention f ⑥ (*proof of truth*) appui m; **to lend ~ to sth** prêter son appui à qc

**supporter** n ① (*encouraging person: of an idea, right*) défenseur mf; (*of a campaign, party*) partisan(e) m(f) ② (*of building, structure*) support m ③ SPORTS (*fan*) supporter m; (*athletic supporter*) coquille f

**supporting** adj CINE **a ~ role** un second rôle; **a ~ act** une première partie

**supportive** adj (*person*) **to be ~** être d'un grand soutien; **to be ~ of sb/sth** soutenir qn/qc

**suppose** [sə·'pouz] vt ① (*think*) croire ② (*introduce hypothesis*) supposer; **I ~ so** je suppose que oui; **~ (that) we do sth** et si on faisait qc

**supreme** [sə·'prim] I. adj suprême II. adv a. fig **to reign ~** régner en maître absolu

**supreme court** n cour f suprême, ≈ tribunal m fédéral *Suisse*; **the Supreme Court** la Cour suprême

**surcharge** ['sɜr·tʃɑrdʒ] I. n supplément m; (*on tax bill*) surtaxe f II. vt surtaxer; **to be ~d for sth** payer un supplément pour qc

**S** **sure** [ʃʊr] I. adj sûr(e); **to be/feel ~ (that)** … être certain que …; **to make ~ (that)** … s'assurer que …; **to be ~ about sth** être sûr de qc; **to be ~ to** +*infin* être certain de +*infin;* **a ~ sign of sth** un signe certain de qc; **~ thing!** *inf* bien sûr! II.<-r, -st> adv inf vraiment; **~ I will!** bien sûr!; **for ~** à coup sûr; **~ enough** en effet; **oh ~!** bien sûr! ▸**as ~ as I'm** standing/sitting **here** aussi sûr que deux et deux font quatre

**surely** ['ʃʊr·li] adv ① (*certainly*) sûrement ② (*showing astonishment*) tout

de même ③ (*confidently*) avec assurance ④ (*yes, certainly*) bien sûr

**surf** [sɜrf] I. n surf m II. vi ① SPORTS (*ride waves*) faire du surf; (*windsurf*) faire de la planche à voile ② COMPUT surfer III. vt COMPUT naviguer sur

**surface** ['sɜr·fɪs] I. n ① (*part, top*) surface f; **to bring sth to the ~** (*above ground*) déterrer qc; (*above water level*) faire remonter qc ② (*appearance*) apparence f; **to scratch the ~ of sth** creuser qc ③ SPORTS surface f II. vi ① (*come to top*) faire surface ② fig (*become obvious*) apparaître ③ fig (*get out of bed*) faire surface III. vt revêtir IV. adj ① (*above the ground: worker*) de surface ② (*on top of water: fleet*) de surface ③ (*superficial*) superficiel(le)

**surfboard** n SPORTS ① (*for riding waves*) planche f de surf ② (*windsurfboard*) planche f à voile

**surfer** n ① (*person*) a. COMPUT surfeur, -euse m, f ② (*windsurfer*) véliplanchiste mf

**surgeon** ['sɜr·dʒən] n MED chirurgien(ne) m(f)

**surgery** ['sɜr·dʒər·i] n MED ① no indef art (*medical specialty*) chirurgie f ② (*operation*) opération f; **you'll need ~** il faudra t'opérer ③ (*operating room*) bloc m opératoire

**surgical** ['sɜr·dʒɪ·kəl] adj ① MED chirurgical(e) ② fig (*precise*) scientifique

**surname** ['sɜr·neɪm] n nom m de famille

**surplus** ['sɜr·pləs] I. adj ① (*extra*) en trop ② ECON excédentaire II. n ① (*extra amount*) surplus m ② (*in production*) excédent m

**surprise** [sər·'praɪz] I. n surprise f; **to come as a ~ to sb** surprendre qn; **~! ~!** inf ô surprise; iron, inf évidemment II. vt surprendre III. adj surprise

**surprised** adj surpris(e)

**surprising** adj surprenant(e)

**surprisingly** adv étonnamment; **~, no one complained** chose surprenante, personne ne s'est plaint

**surreal** [sə·'ri·əl] adj surréaliste

**surrender** [sə·'ren·dər] I. *vi* to ~ to sb/ sth se rendre à qn/qc; *fig* se livrer à qn/ qc II. *vt form* to ~ sth to sb remettre qc à qn III. *n* ❶ (*act of admitting defeat*) reddition *f*; MIL capitulation *f* ❷ *form* (*giving up*) remise *f*

**surround** [sə·'raund] I. *vt* ❶ (*enclose*) entourer ❷ (*encircle*) encercler II. *n* ❶ (*border*) encadrement *m*; (*of fireplace, window, door*) chambranle *m* ❷ *pl, fig* (*of an area*) environs *mpl*

**surrounding** *adj* (*area*) environnant(e)

**surroundings** *npl* ❶ (*environment*) environnement *m*; **in sb's natural ~** dans le milieu naturel de qn ❷ (*surrounding area: of city*) environs *mpl*

**survey** ['sɜr·veɪ, *vb:* sər·'veɪ] I. *n* ❶ (*study*) étude *f*; (*for market research*) enquête *f*; (*of opinions*) sondage *m* ❷ (*inspection*) inspection *f* ❸ (*description*) tour *m* d'horizon ❹ GEO (*measuring and mapping*) relevé *m* II. *vt* ❶ (*study*) étudier ❷ (*investigate: person*) sonder; (*needs*) enquêter sur ❸ (*look at*) scruter ❹ (*examine*) inspecter; (*house*) faire l'expertise de ❺ GEO relever

**survival** [sər·'vaɪ·vəl] *n* ❶ *no indef art* (*not dying*) survie *f* ❷ *no indef art* (*continuing*) vestige *m*

**survive** [sər·'vaɪv] I. *vi a. fig* survivre; **to ~ on sth** vivre de qc; **I'm surviving** *inf* je m'en sors II. *vt a. fig* survivre à; (*accident, illness*) réchapper à

**survivor** *n* survivant(e) *m(f)*

**suspect** ['sʌs·pekt, *vb:* sə·'spekt] I. *adj* suspect(e) II. *n* suspect(e) *m(f)* III. *vt* ❶ (*think likely*) soupçonner; **I ~ so** j'imagine que oui; **I ~ not** je ne pense pas ❷ (*consider guilty*) soupçonner ❸ (*doubt*) douter de

**suspenders** *npl* bretelles *fpl*

**suspense** [sə·'spen(t)s] *n* suspense *m*; **to keep sb in ~** faire languir qn

**suspension** [sə·'spen·(t)ʃən] *n* ❶ *no indef art* (*temporary stopping*) a. SPORTS suspension *f*; **to be under ~** être suspendu ❷ CHEM suspension *f* ❸ AUTO, TECH (*part of vehicle*) suspension *f*

**suspension bridge** *n* CONSTR pont *m* suspendu

**suspicion** [sə·'spɪʃ·ən] *n* ❶ (*belief*) soupçon *m* ❷ *no indef art* (*believing to be guilty*) soupçon *m*; **to be under ~** être soupçonné ❸ *no indef art* (*mistrust*) méfiance *f* ❹ (*small amount*) soupçon *m*

**suspicious** [sə·'spɪʃ·əs] *adj* ❶ (*causing suspicion: death, circumstances*) suspect(e) ❷ (*having suspicions*) soupçonneux(-euse); **to be ~ about sth** avoir des soupçons sur qc ❸ (*having doubts*) **to be ~ about sth** avoir des doutes sur qc ❹ (*lacking trust*) méfiant(e); **to be ~** se méfier

**sustain** [sə·'steɪn] *vt* ❶ *form* (*suffer: defeat, loss*) subir; **she ~ed severe injuries** elle a été grièvement blessée ❷ (*maintain: life*) maintenir ❸ (*support*) soutenir ❹ LAW (*uphold: objection*) retenir ❺ MUS (*note*) faire durer

**sustainability** *n* ❶ (*ability to be maintained*) capacité *f* de maintien ❷ ECOL, ECON, POL viabilité *f*

**sustainable** *adj* ❶ (*maintainable*) viable; (*development*) durable; (*argument*) valable ❷ ECOL (*resources*) renouvelable; **~ development** développement *m* durable

**sustained** *adj* (*work, applause*) soutenu(e)

**sustaining** *adj* ❶ CULIN (*nourishing*) nourrissant(e) ❷ MUS **~ pedal** pédale *f* de soutien

**suture** ['su·tʃər] MED I. *n* suture *f* II. *vt* suturer

**swab** [swab] I. *n* ❶ MED (*pad for cleaning wound*) compresse *f* ❷ MED (*specimen, sample*) prélèvement *m* II. <-bb-> *vt* ❶ MED (*clean*) nettoyer ❷ NAUT (*mop*) lessiver

**swallow¹** ['swa·loʊ] I. *n* ❶ (*with throat*) déglutition *f* ❷ (*amount swallowed: of drink*) gorgée *f*; (*of food*) cuillerée *f* II. *vt* ❶ (*food, drink*) avaler ❷ (*engulf*) engloutir ❸ *fig, inf* (*believe unquestioningly*) avaler; **to ~ the bait** mordre à l'hameçon; **I find it hard to ~** j'ai

**S**

mal à l'avaler ❹ (*leave unsaid: disappointment, anger, pride*) ravaler **III.** *vi* avaler

◆**swallow down** *vt* ❶ (*swallow*) avaler ❷ (*gulp down*) engloutir

**swallow²** ['swɑ·ləʊ] *n* zool hirondelle *f*

**swam** [swæm] *pt of* **swim**

**swamp** [swɒmp] **I.** *n* ❶ (*area of wet ground*) marécage *m*, savane *f* Québec ❷ *no indef art* (*wetlands*) marais *m* **II.** *vt a. fig* inonder

**swan** [swɒn] *n* zool cygne *m*

**swan song** *n* chant *m* du cygne

**swap** [swɒp] **I.** <-pp-> *vt* échanger **II.** <-pp-> *vi* échanger **III.** *n* ❶ (*exchange*) échange *m* ❷ (*thing to be exchanged*) objet *m* de l'échange

**swap meet** *n* bourse *f* pour objets usagés

**swarm** [swɔrm] **I.** *n* ❶ zool, bio (*of flying insects*) essaim *m* ❷ *fig* (*of people*) nuée *f* **II.** *vi* ❶ zool, bio (*form large group*) essaimer ❷ *fig* (*move in large group*) envahir; **to be ~ing with sth** grouiller de qc

**swath(e)** [sweɪð] **I.** *vt* envelopper **II.** *n* ❶ (*long strip*) andain *m* ❷ *fig* **a large ~ of time** une longue période

**sway** [sweɪ] **I.** *vi* se balancer **II.** *vt* (*persuade*) influencer

**swear** [swer] <swore, sworn> **I.** *vi* ❶ (*curse*) dire des jurons ❷ (*state as truth*) jurer ❸ (*take oath*) prêter serment; **to ~ on the Bible** jurer sur la Bible; **I wouldn't/couldn't ~ to it** *inf* je ne le jurerais pas **II.** *vt* ❶ (*curse*) jurer ❷ (*promise*) jurer; **to ~ sb to secrecy** faire jurer le secret à qn

◆**swear by** *vt inf* jurer par

◆**swear in** *vt* faire prêter serment à

**swear word** *n* gros mot *m*, sacre *m* Québec

**sweat** [swet] **I.** *n* ❶ *no indef art* (*perspiration*) transpiration *f*; **to be dripping with ~** être ruisselant de sueur ❷ *pl* fashion survêtement *m* ▸**to break out a ~** avoir des sueurs froides; **no ~!** pas de problème!; **to work oneself ~ about sth** se faire du souci à

propos de qc **II.** *vi* ❶ (*perspire*) transpirer ❷ *fig* (*work hard*) suer ▸ **to ~ like a pig** *inf* transpirer comme une vache; **to let sb ~** *inf* laisser qn mariner **III.** *vt* ❶ (*overwork: person*) faire trimer ❷ (*cook gently: onions*) faire revenir ▸**to ~ buckets** être en nage; **don't ~ it!** *sl* ne t'embête pas avec ça!

◆**sweat out** *vt* **to sweat it out** ❶ (*do physical exercise*) se défouler ❷ (*suffer while waiting*) prendre son mal en patience

**sweater** *n* pull *m*

**sweatpants** *npl* bas *m* de survêtement

**sweatshirt** ['swet·ʃɜrt] *n* sweat(-shirt) *m*

**sweatsuit** *n*, **sweat suit** *n* survêtement *m*

**sweaty** ['swet·i] <-ier, -iest> *adj* ❶ (*covered in perspiration*) en sueur; (*palms, hands*) moite ❷ (*causing perspiration: afternoon*) moite

**Swede** [swid] *n* Suédois(e) *m(f)*

**Sweden** ['swi·dᵊn] *n* la Suède

**Swedish I.** *adj* suédois(e) **II.** *n* ling suédois *m; s.a.* **English**

**sweep** [swip] **I.** *n* ❶ (*clean with broom*) coup *m* de balai ❷ (*chimney sweep*) ramoneur *m* ❸ (*movement*) large mouvement *m*; **with a ~ of the hand** d'un geste large ❹ (*area*) étendue *f* ❺ (*curve*) courbe *f* ❻ (*range*) *a. fig* étendue *f* ❼ (*search*) recherche *f* ▸**to make a clean ~** (*start afresh*) faire table rase; (*win everything*) tout rafler **II.** <swept, swept> *vt* ❶ (*clean: floor, chimney*) balayer ❷ (*take in powerful manner*) emporter ❸ *inf* (*win*) remporter ▸**to ~ sth under the carpet** [*o* **rug**] faire comme si qc n'existait pas **III.** <swept, swept> *vi* ❶ (*clean*) balayer ❷ (*move*) **to ~ past sb** passer fièrement devant qn; **to ~ into power** être propulsé au pouvoir ❸ (*look around*) scruter

◆**sweep aside** *vt* ❶ (*cause to move*) repousser ❷ *fig* (*dismiss*) rejeter

◆**sweep away** *vt* ❶ (*remove*) repousser; (*objections*) rejeter ❷ (*carry away*) *a. fig* emporter

◆**sweep out** I. *vt* balayer II. *vi* sortir fièrement

◆**sweep up** *vt* ❶ (*clean up with broom*) balayer ❷ (*gather*) ramasser; **to ~ a baby** prendre un bébé dans ses bras

**sweeper** *n* ❶ (*for streets*) balayeuse *f*; (*for carpet*) balai *m* ❷ (*person*) balayeur, -euse *m, f*

**sweet** [swit] I. <-er, -est> *adj* ❶ (*containing sugar*) sucré(e) ❷ (*having nice taste, smell*) doux(douce); (*perfume*) suave ❸ (*not dry: wine*) doux(douce) ❹ *fig* (*pleasant: sound, temper*) doux(douce); **short and ~** bref(brève) ❹ *fig* (*endearing*) mignon(ne); (*kind*) gentil(le); **~ dreams!** fais de beaux rêves! ▶ **to take one's time** prendre tout son temps II. *n* bonbon *m*, boule *f Belgique*

**sweet-and-sour** *adj* CULIN aigre-doux(douce)

**sweet corn** *n* CULIN maïs *m*

**sweeten** ['swi·tⁿn] *vt* ❶ (*make sweet*) sucrer; *fig* adoucir ❷ (*make more acceptable*) édulcorer

**sweetener** *n* ❶ (*artificial sweet substance*) sucrette® *f* ❷ *fig* pot-de-vin *m*

**sweetheart** *n* ❶ (*kind person*) amour *m* ❷ (*term of endearment*) mon cœur

**sweetie** *n inf* **my ~** mon chou

**sweet potato** *n* patate *f* douce

**sweet spot** *n fig, inf* SPORTS centre *m* du cordage (*zone de frappe optimale pour une raquette*)

**sweet-talk** *vt inf* baratiner; **to ~ sb** faire du baratin à qn

**sweet tooth** *n fig, inf* **to have a ~** adorer les sucreries

**swell** [swel] I. <swelled, swollen *o* swelled> *vt a. fig* gonfler II. <swelled, swollen *o* swelled> *vi* ❶ (*get bigger*) se gonfler; (*wood*) gonfler; (*ankle, arm*) enfler; (*sea*) se soulever ❷ (*get louder*) monter III. *n no indef art* ❶ (*increase in sound*) crescendo *m* ❷ (*movement of sea*) houle *f*

**swelling** *n* ❶ MED (*lump*) grosseur *f*

❷ *no indef art* (*inflammation*) inflammation *f*

**sweltering** *adj* (*heat*) écrasant(e)

**swept** [swept] *pt, pp of* **sweep**

**swerve** [swɜrv] I. *vi* ❶ AUTO (*change direction suddenly*) faire un écart ❷ *fig* (*not uphold*) départir II. *n* (*change of direction*) écart *m*

**swift**[1] [swɪft] *adj* (*fast*) rapide

**swift**[2] [swɪft] *n* (*bird*) martinet *m*

**swiftly** *adv* rapidement

**swig** [swɪg] *inf* I. <-gg-> *vt* descendre II. *n* coup *m*; **to take a ~** descendre

**swim** [swɪm] I. <-mm-, swam, swum> *vi* ❶ (*in water*) nager; **to ~ across sth** traverser qc à la nage ❷ (*float in liquid*) baigner ❸ (*be full of water*) baigner ❹ (*whirl*) sembler tourbillonner; **to make sb's head ~** faire tourner la tête de qn II. <-mm-, swam, swum> *vt* ❶ (*cross*) traverser à la nage ❷ (*do*) **to ~ a few strokes** faire quelques brasses; **to ~ the butterfly stroke** faire la nage papillon III. *n* baignade *f*; **to go for a ~** aller nager ▶ **to be in the ~** être dans le coup

**swimmer** *n* nageur, -euse *m, f*

**swimming** *n* ❶ (*act*) nage *f* ❷ SPORTS natation *f*

**swimming pool** *n* piscine *f*

**swimming trunks** *n* caleçon *m* de bain

**swimsuit** *n* maillot *m* de bain

**swindle** ['swɪn·dl] I. *n* escroquerie *f* II. *vt* escroquer

**swine** [swaɪn] <-> *n a. pej* porc *m*

**swine flu** *no pl*, **swine influenza** *n no pl* grippe *f* A

**swing** [swɪŋ] I. *n* ❶ (*movement*) balancement *m* ❷ (*punch*) volée *f* ❸ (*hanging seat*) balançoire *f* ❹ (*sharp change*) revirement *m*; **mood ~** saute *f* d'humeur ❺ (*quick trip*) voyage *m* éclair ❻ (*music*) swing *m* ❼ (*of baseball bat, golf club*) swing *m* ▶ **to get (back) into the ~ of things** *inf* se remettre dans le bain; **to be in full ~** battre son plein II. <swung, swung> *vi* ❶ (*move back and forth*) se balancer ❷ (*move circularly*) **to ~ (around)** se retourner ❸ (*at-*

S

*tempt to hit*) **to ~ at** sb **with** sth essayer de frapper qn avec qc ❹ (*alter, change loyalty*) virer; **to ~ between** sth **and** sth balancer entre qc et qc ❺ (*stop by shortly*) **to ~ by** somewhere passer quelque part ❻ *sl* MUS (*be exciting*) balancer ▶ **to ~ into action** se mettre au boulot III. <swung, swung> vt ❶ (*move back and forth*) balancer ❷ (*turn around*) tourner; (*lift*) envoyer ❸ *inf* (*influence successfully*) arranger; **to ~ it** arranger les choses ▶ **to ~ the balance** faire pencher la balance

**Swiss** [swɪs] I. *adj* suisse II. *n* Suisse *mf*

**Swiss army knife** *n* couteau *m* suisse

**switch** [swɪtʃ] I. <-es> *n* ❶ (*control button*) interrupteur *m* ❷ (*substitution*) remplacement *m* ❸ (*change*) revirement *m* ❹ RAIL aiguillage *m* II. *vi* changer; **to ~ (over) to** sth passer à qc; **to ~ from** sth **to** sth passer de qc à qc III. *vt* ❶ (*change*) changer de; **to ~ one's attention to** sth reporter son attention sur qc ❷ (*adjust settings*) régler; (*current*) commuter ❸ (*exchange*) échanger

◆ **switch off** I. *vt* éteindre II. *vi* ❶ (*turn off*) éteindre ❷ *inf* (*lose attention*) décrocher

◆ **switch on** I. *vt* ❶ (*turn on: light, TV, appliance*) allumer; (*water, gas, tap*) ouvrir ❷ (*use*) **to ~ the charm** faire du charme II. *vi* s'allumer

**switchblade** ['swɪtʃ·bleɪd] *n* couteau *m* à cran d'arrêt

**switchboard operator** *n* standardiste *mf*

**switch knife** *n* couteau *m* à cran d'arrêt

**Switzerland** ['swɪt·sər·lənd] *n* la Suisse

**swivel chair** *n* chaise *f* pivotante

**swollen** ['swoʊ·lən] I. *pp of* **swell** II. *adj* ❶ (*puffy*) enflé(e) ❷ (*fuller than usual: river*) en crue

**swop** [swap] <-pp-> *vt, vi Can s.* **swap** I., II.

**sword** [sɔrd] *n* épée *f*

**swore** [swɔr] *pt of* **swear**

**sworn** [swɔrn] I. *pp of* **swear** II. *adj inv* sous serment; **~ enemy** ennemi *m* juré

**swum** [swʌm] *pp of* **swim**

**swung** [swʌŋ] *pt, pp of* **swing**

**syllable** ['sɪl·ə·bl] *n a. fig* syllabe *f*

**symbol** ['sɪm·bəl] *n* symbole *m*

**symbolism** ['sɪm·bəl·ɪ·zᵊm] *n* symbolisme *m*

**symbolize** ['sɪm·bə·laɪz] *vt* symboliser

**symmetrical** [sɪ·'met·rɪk·əl] *adj* symétrique

**sympathetic** [ˌsɪm·pə·'θeṭ·ɪk] *adj* ❶ (*understanding*) compatissant(e); **to be ~ about** sth avoir de la compassion pour qc ❷ POL (*supporting*) solidaire; **to be ~ toward** sb/sth être solidaire de qn/qc

**sympathize** ['sɪm·pə·θaɪz] *vi* ❶ (*show understanding*) compatir; **to ~ with** sb **over** sth avoir de la compassion pour qn concernant qc ❷ (*agree with*) être d'accord

**sympathy** ['sɪm·pə·θi] <-ies> *n* ❶ (*compassion*) compassion *f*; **please accept my sympathies** veuillez croire à toute ma sympathie ❷ (*feeling of agreement*) solidarité *f*; **to be in ~ with** sb/sth être solidaire de qn/qc

**symphony** ['sɪm(p)·fə·ni] *n* symphonie *f*

**symptom** ['sɪm(p)·təm] *n* ❶ (*sign of disease*) symptôme *m* ❷ (*indicator, sign*) indice *m*

**synagogue** ['sɪn·ə·gɔg] *n* synagogue *f*

**sync(h)** [sɪŋk] *inf* I. *n* synchro *f* II. *vt* synchroniser

**synchronize** ['sɪŋ·krə·naɪz] I. *vt* synchroniser; **to ~ watches** régler nos montres sur la même heure II. *vi* être synchrone

**synthesizer** *n* synthétiseur *m*

**synthetic** [sɪn·'θeṭ·ɪk] *adj* ❶ (*man-made*) synthétique; (*product, sweeteners*) de synthèse; (*flavorings*) artificiel(le) ❷ (*fake*) artificiel(le)

**syringe** [sə·'rɪndʒ] *n* ❶ (*sucking out liquid*) seringue *f* ❷ (*spraying in liquid*) poire *f*

**syrup** ['sɪr·əp] *n* sirop *m*

**system** ['sɪs·təm] *n a.* COMPUT, MATH système *m*; **computer ~** système informatique ► **to get sth out of one's ~** *inf* se débarrasser de qc

**systematic** [ˌsɪs·tə·ˈmæt̬·ɪk] *adj* systématique

# Tt

**T, t** [ti] <-'s *o* -s> *n* ❶ T *m*, t *m*; **~ as in Tango** (*on telephone*) t comme Thérèse ❷ *inf* **it fits him to a ~** ça lui va comme un gant

**t** *n abbr of* **ton** t

**table** [ˈteɪ·bl] *n* ❶ (*piece of furniture*) table *f*; **to set the ~** mettre la table ❷ (*group of people*) tablée *f* ❸ (*collection of information*) a. COMPUT tableau *m* ► **to do sth under the ~** (*illegally*) faire qc sous le manteau; **to turn the ~s on sb** prendre sa revanche sur qn

**tablecloth** *n* nappe *f*

**table manners** *n* bonnes manières *fpl*

**tablespoon** *n* cuiller *f* à soupe, cuiller *f* à table *Québec*; **~ of sugar** cuiller *f* à soupe de sucre

**tablet** [ˈtæb·lɪt] *n* ❶ (*pill*) comprimé *m* ❷ (*with inscription*) plaque *f* commémorative ❸ (*pad of paper*) bloc *m*; (*writing pad*) bloc-note *m* ❹ (*computer*) tablette *f* [tactile]

**3-D, three-'D** *adj inf abbr of* **three-dimensional** 3D; **~ printer** imprimante *f* 3D

**table tennis** *n* tennis *m* de table

**table wine** *n* vin *m* de table

**tabloid** [ˈtæb·lɔɪd] *n* tabloïd *m*; **the ~s** la presse à scandale

**tack** [tæk] **I.** *n* ❶ (*thumbtack*) punaise *f* ❷ (*short nail*) clou *m* ❸ (*approach*) tactique *f* **II.** *vt* (*nail down*) clouer; (*with a thumbtack*) punaiser

**tackle** [ˈtæk·l] **I.** *vt* ❶ (*to get ball*) intercepter ❷ (*deal with: person*) aborder; (*job*) s'attaquer à; (*problem*) aborder; **to ~ sb about sth** aborder qn au sujet de qc **II.** *n* ❶ SPORTS interception *f*; (*by*

bringing player down) plaquage *m* ❷ (*gear*) équipement *m*; **fishing ~** articles *mpl* de pêche

**tacky** [ˈtæk·i] <-ier, -iest> *adj* ❶ (*sticky*) collant(e) ❷ *pej, inf* (*in bad taste*) plouc

**tactful** *adj* plein(e) de tact

**tactic** [ˈtæk·tɪk] *n* ❶ (*approach*) stratégie *f* ❷ *pl* MIL tactique *f*

**tactical** *adj* ❶ (*with a plan*) tactique ❷ MIL stratégique

**tactician** [tæk·ˈtɪʃ·ən] *n* tacticien(ne) *m(f)*

**tactless** *adj* **to be ~** être dépourvu de tact

**tadpole** [ˈtæd·poʊl] *n* têtard *m*

**tag** [tæg] **I.** *n* ❶ (*label*) étiquette *f*; (*of metal*) plaque *f* ❷ (*children's game*) jeu *m* du chat perché ❸ (*phrase*) citation *f* **II.** <-gg-> *vt* ❶ (*label*) a. *fig* étiqueter ❷ (*touch*) toucher ❸ (*fine*) mettre une contravention à

♦ **tag along** *vi inf* suivre

♦ **tag on** *vt* rajouter

**tail** [teɪl] **I.** *n* ❶ (*on animal*) queue *f* ❷ (*rear*) postérieur *m* ❸ AVIAT queue *f* ❹ (*side of a coin*) face *f*; **heads or ~s?** – **~s** pile ou face? – pile ❺ *inf* (*buttocks*) derrière *m* ❻ *inf* (*spy*) fileur *m* ► **I can't make head or ~ of it** je n'y comprends rien; **heads I win, ~s you lose** face je gagne, pile tu perds **II.** *vt* pister; **to be ~ed** être suivi

♦ **tail off** *vt* diminuer; (*sound*) baisser

**tailback** *n* SPORTS demi-arrière *m*

**tailor** [ˈteɪ·lər] **I.** *n* tailleur *m* **II.** *vt* ❶ (*make clothes*) confectionner ❷ (*adapt*) adapter ❸ (*design*) **to ~ sth to sb's needs** faire qc sur mesure pour qn

T

**tailor-made** *adj* ❶ (*custom-made*) fait(e) sur mesure ❷ (*perfect*) parfait(e)
**take** [teɪk] **I.** *n* ❶ (*receipts*) recette *f* ❷ (*filming*) prise *f* de vue ❸ (*view*) position *f*; **what's your ~ on this?** quel est ton/votre avis là-dessus? **II.** <took, taken> *vt* ❶ (*hold and move*) prendre; **to take sth from a shelf/the kitchen** prendre qc sur une étagère/dans la cuisine; **she took everything out of her bag** elle a tout sorti de son sac; **to take sb's hand** prendre la main de qn ❷ (*so as to have with one*) prendre; (*to a different place: person*) emmener; (*things*) emporter; **she always ~s her camera** elle prend toujours son appareil photo; **can you ~ me to the station?** tu peux m'emmener à la gare? ❸ (*bring: guest, friend*) prendre; (*present, letter*) apporter ❹ (*accept: job, responsibility, payment*) prendre; (*cash, applicant*) accepter; (*advice*) suivre; **do you ~ this woman …?** consentez-vous à prendre cette femme …?; **I can't ~ the pressure/the boredom** je ne supporte pas le stress/l'ennui ❺ (*use for travel: train, bus, route*) prendre ❻ (*eat or drink: medicine, sugar*) prendre ❼ (*hold: people*) (pouvoir) contenir; (*traffic*) recevoir ❽ (*require: skills, patience, effort*) demander; (*time*) prendre; **it ~s 10 minutes** ça prend 10 minutes; **it took courage to admit it** il fallait du courage pour l'admettre ❾ (*win, capture: city, position*) s'emparer de; (*prisoners*) capturer ❿ (*as a record: letter, notes, photos*) prendre ⓫ (*expressing thoughts, understanding*) **I ~ it you're coming** vous venez, n'est-ce pas?; **~ my children, for example** regardez mes enfants, par exemple ⓬ (*use*) **take the chance** [*o* **opportunity**] **to** +*infin* saisir l'occasion de +*infin;* **~ the time to think about it** prendre le temps d'y penser; **to ~ a size 14** faire du 42 ⓭ (*study: subject*) faire ⓮ (*with specific objects*) **to ~ a walk** se promener; **to ~ office** entrer en fonction; **to ~ an interest in sb/sth** s'intéresser à

qn/qc; **to ~ an exam** passer un examen ▶ **not to ~ no for an answer** ne pas se contenter d'un non; **point ~n** très juste; **~ my word for it** croyez-moi; **~ it from me** croyez-moi sur parole **III.** <took, taken> *vi* (*have effect*) prendre

◆**take aback** *vt* surprendre
◆**take after** *vi* ressembler à
◆**take along** *vt* emmener
◆**take apart I.** *vt* ❶ (*disassemble*) défaire; (*machine*) démonter ❷ (*analyze*) disséquer ❸ (*destroy: person, team, book*) démolir **II.** *vi* se démonter
◆**take away I.** *vt* ❶ (*remove*) prendre; **two coffees to ~** deux cafés à emporter ❷ (*deprive of*) retirer ❸ (*bring away with*) éloigner ❹ (*make leave: death*) enlever; (*business*) éloigner de chez soi ❺ (*lessen: pain*) diminuer ❻ (*subtract from*) soustraire ▶ **to take sb's breath away** couper le souffle de qn **II.** *vi* (*detract from*) **to ~ from the beauty of sth** rendre qc moins beau
◆**take back** *vt* ❶ (*return to original place: borrowed book, faulty goods*) rapporter ❷ (*accept back*) reprendre ❸ (*accompany a person*) raccompagner ❹ (*let return: spouse*) se remettre avec; (*employee*) reprendre ❺ (*retract*) rétracter ❻ (*carry to a past time*) remonter à; **it takes you back, doesn't it?** ça te ramène dans le passé, n'est-ce pas?
◆**take down** *vt* ❶ (*bring lower*) descendre ❷ (*remove from high place*) déchoir ❸ (*remove*) enlever ❹ (*disassemble*) désassembler; (*scaffolding*) démonter ❺ (*write*) noter ❻ *inf* (*depress*) démoraliser
◆**take in** *vt* ❶ (*bring inside: visitor*) faire entrer; (*washing, shopping*) rentrer ❷ (*accommodate*) héberger; (*for rent*) prendre ❸ (*admit: orphan, stray cat*) recueillir; (*student*) recevoir ❹ (*bring to police: lost property*) rapporter; (*criminal*) se faire emmener ❺ (*deceive*) tromper; **to be taken in by sb/sth** être trompé par qn/qc ❻ (*go to see*) **to ~ a movie** aller au cinéma ❼ (*mentally: de-*

*tails*) absorber; (*sb's death*) accepter; **to ~ the scenery** se remplir du paysage ⑧(*include*) inclure ⑨(*narrow: trousers, skirt*) rétrécir ⑩(*do at home*) **to ~ typing/sewing** faire de la saisie/ de la couture à domicile

◆**take off** I. *vt* ❶(*undress: clothes*) enlever; (*hat, glasses*) retirer ❷(*withdraw: product from market*) retirer; (*player from field*) faire sortir; (*program, film*) retirer; **to take sb off drugs** faire décrocher qn de la drogue; **to take sb off a list** éliminer qn d'une liste; **to take a detective off a case** retirer une enquête à un détective; **to take sb off a diet** ne plus faire suivre de régime à qn ❸(*leave*) **to take oneself off** partir à toute hâte ❹(*not work*) **to take a day/a week off** (*work*) prendre un jour/une semaine (de congé) ❺(*subtract*) déduire; **I'll take 10% off for you** je vous fais une réduction de 10% II. *vi* ❶(*leave the ground: plane*) décoller; (*bird*) s'envoler ❷ *inf* (*leave*) déguerpir ❸ *inf* (*flee*) filer ❹(*have success: project*) se développer; (*idea*) prendre; (*style, new product*) se répandre; **his business is really taking off in Japan** son affaire est en plein essor au Japon

◆**take on** I. *vt* ❶(*start on: job, challenge*) prendre ❷(*acquire: quality, appearance*) prendre ❸(*put to work*) recruter ❹(*oppose: enemy, rival*) s'attaquer à; SPORTS (*team*) jouer contre; (*boxer*) boxer contre ❺(*stop for loading: fuel*) faire le plein de; (*goods*) charger; (*passengers*) embarquer II. *vi* s'en faire

◆**take out** *vt* ❶(*remove*) enlever; (*teeth*) extraire; (*item from drawer, bag*) sortir ❷(*bring outside: chairs, washing*) sortir ❸ CULIN emporter; **pizzas to ~** pizzas à emporter ❹(*entertain: children, friend*) sortir; (*client*) inviter; **to take sb out to dinner** inviter qn à dîner ❺ *inf* (*kill*) éliminer ❻(*destroy*) anéantir ❼(*arrange to get*) se procurer; (*license*) obtenir ❽(*borrow*)

emprunter ❾(*vent*) **to take one's anger/frustration out on sb** se défouler de sa colère/frustration sur qn; **to take it out on sb** se défouler sur qn

◆**take over** I. *vt* ❶(*buy out: company*) racheter ❷(*take charge of: country*) prendre le contrôle; (*ministry, post, responsibility*) reprendre; **her job's taken over her life** son travail envahit sa vie ❸(*assume: debts*) reconnaître II. *vi* (*as government*) prendre le pouvoir; (*as leader, manager*) prendre les rênes; **I'm tired of driving, you ~** je suis fatigué de conduire, tu me remplaces; **to ~ as captain** devenir capitaine; **to ~ from sb** remplacer qn

◆**take to** *vi* ❶(*start to like: person*) se mettre à aimer; (*hobby, activity*) prendre goût à ❷(*begin as a habit*) **to ~ doing sth** se mettre à faire qc ❸(*go to: forest, hills*) se réfugier dans ▶**to ~ one's bed** s'aliter; **to ~ sth like a duck to water** mordre à qc

◆**take up** *vt* ❶(*bring up*) faire monter ❷(*pick up*) ramasser; (*arms*) prendre ❸(*start doing: post*) commencer; (*hobby, language*) se mettre à ❹(*keep busy*) **to be taken up with sb/sth** être absorbé par qn/qc ❺(*discuss*) discuter; (*matter, question*) aborder; **to take a problem up with sb** parler d'un problème avec qn ❻(*accept: challenge*) relever; (*offer*) accepter; (*opportunity*) saisir; (*case*) se charger de; **to take sb up on an invitation** accepter l'invitation de qn ❼(*adopt: attitude*) adopter; (*habit*) prendre ❽(*continue: anecdote, explanation*) reprendre ❾(*join in: song, slogan*) reprendre (en chœur) ❿(*occupy: time, energy*) prendre ⓫(*shorten: coat, dress, pants*) raccourcir ⓬(*ask for*) **to ~ a collection** faire une collecte ⓭(*query*) **to take sb up on sth** reprendre qn sur qc

**taken** I. *pp* of **take** II. *adj* **to be ~ with an idea/painting** être séduit par une idée/un tableau

**takeoff** *n* AVIAT décollage *m*

**takeover** *n* rachat *m*

**takeover bid** n offre f publique d'achat
**tale** [teɪl] n ❶(*story*) histoire f ❷LIT conte m ❸(*true story*) récit m
**talent** ['tæl·ənt] n talent m; **a ~ for writing/annoying people** le don d'écrire/d'embêter tout le monde
**talented** adj talentueux(-euse)
**Taliban** ['tæl·ə·bæn] n Taliban m
**talk** [tɔk] I. n ❶(*discussion*) discussion f; **there's ~ of a new school** on parle d'une nouvelle école; **~s about peace** pourparlers mpl de paix ❷(*conversation*) conversation f; **to have a ~ with sb** avoir une conversation avec qn ❸(*private*) entretien m ❹(*lecture*) exposé m ❺(*things said*) paroles fpl; **you're all ~** pej tout ce que tu fais c'est parler; **to make small ~** parler de choses et d'autres II. vi ❶(*speak*) parler; **everybody's ~ing** tout le monde fait des commentaires; **to ~ to oneself** se parler à soi-même; **to ~ about a job** parler d'un travail ❷(*speak privately*) s'entretenir ▸ **to ~ dirty to sb** parler crûment à qn III. vt ❶(*speak: English, Arabic*) parler; **to ~ sb into/out of doing sth** convaincre qn de faire qc/de ne pas faire qc ❷*inf* (*discuss*) discuter; **we're ~ing big changes** il s'agit de grands changements
♦ **talk back** vi **to ~ to sb** répondre à qn
♦ **talk over** vt parler de
♦ **talk through** vt ❶(*discuss*) débattre de ❷(*reassure*) rassurer
**talkative** ['tɔ·kə·t̬ɪv] adj loquace
**talking point** n sujet m de discussion
**talk show** n talk-show m
**tall** [tɔl] adj grand(e); (*grass, building*) haut(e); **to grow ~(er)** grandir; **to be over six feet ~** faire plus de 1,80 m ▸ **that's a ~ order** c'est beaucoup demander; **a ~ tale** une histoire incroyable
**talon** ['tæl·ən] n ❶(*claw*) serre f ❷*fig* griffe f
**tame** [teɪm] I. adj ❶(*domesticated: animals*) apprivoisé(e); *fig* docile ❷(*un-*

*exciting, dull*) plat(e) ❸(*cultivated*) cultivé(e) II. vt apprivoiser, dompter
**tampon** ['tæm·pan] n tampon m
**tan¹** [tæn] I.<-nn-> vi bronzer II.<-nn-> vt ❶(*by sunlight*) bronzer ❷(*to make into leather*) tanner III. n bronzage m; **to get a ~** bronzer IV. adj fauve
**tan²** [tæn] n MATH abbr of **tangent** tg f
**tandem** ['tæn·dəm] n tandem m
**tangent** ['tæn·dʒənt] n MATH a. fig tangente f; **to go off on a ~** partir sur un autre sujet
**tangerine** [ˌtæn·dʒə·'rin] I. n mandarine f II. adj mandarine inv
**tangle** ['tæŋ·gl] I. n ❶(*mass of entwined threads*) enchevêtrement m ❷*pej* (*confusion, muddle*) embrouille f; **in a ~** embrouillé(e) II. vt emmêler; **I got ~d (up) in the ropes** je me suis pris dans les cordes; **a ~d plot** *fig* une intrigue compliquée III. vi ❶(*knot up*) s'emmêler ❷(*quarrel*) s'accrocher; **don't ~ with her** ne te frotte pas à elle
**tank** [tæŋk] n ❶(*container for storage*) a. AUTO réservoir m; **fish ~** aquarium m ❷(*container for fluid, gas*) citerne f ❸MIL tank m
**tanker** ['tæŋ·kər] n ❶(*boat*) navire-citerne m ❷(*truck*) camion-citerne m
**tank top** n débardeur m
**tanned** adj bronzé(e)
**tanning bed** n solarium m
**tantalizing** adj tentant(e); (*smell*) alléchant(e)
**tantrum** ['tæn·trəm] n caprice m; **temper ~** colère f; **to have [o throw] a ~** faire un caprice
**tap¹** [tæp] I. n ❶(*for water*) robinet m; **to turn the ~ on/off** ouvrir/fermer le robinet; **beer on ~** bière f à la pression ❷(*directly available*) **on ~** disponible II.<-pp-> vt ❶TEL **to ~ a phone** placer un téléphone sur écoute ❷(*make use of, utilize*) exploiter ❸(*let out via tap*) faire couler III. vi **to ~ into sth** exploiter qc; **to ~ into the market** tirer profit du marché
**tap²** [tæp] I. n ❶(*light knock*) tape f

**②** (*tap-dancing*) claquettes *fpl* **II.** *adj* de claquettes **III.** <-pp-> *vt* (*strike lightly*) tapoter; **to ~ sb on the shoulder** taper sur l'épaule de qn **IV.** <-pp-> *vi* **to ~ one's foot on the floor** taper du pied sur le sol

**tap dance** ['tæp·dæn(t)s] *n* claquettes *fpl*

**tape** [teɪp] **I.** *n* **①** (*strip*) ruban *m* **②** (*adhesive strip*) ruban *m* adhésif; **Scotch ~**® scotch® *m* **③** (*material for fastening*) courroie *f* **④** (*tape measure*) mètre *m* ruban **⑤** (*for recording*) bande *f* magnétique; **video/audio ~** cassette *f* vidéo/audio **II.** *vt* **①** (*fasten with tape*) **to ~ sth** (**up**) scotcher qc **②** (*record*) enregistrer

**tape measure** *n* mètre *m* ruban
**tape recorder** *n* magnétophone *m*
**tape recording** *n* enregistrement *m*
**tapered** *adj* FASHION (*trousers, skirt*) en fuseau; (*skirt*) près du corps; AVIAT (*wing*) fuselé(e)
**tap water** *n* eau *f* du robinet
**tar** [tar] **I.** *n* goudron *m* ▶ **to beat the ~ out of sb** *inf* tabasser qn **II.** <-rr-> *vt* goudronner ▶ **to be ~red with the same brush** être mis dans le même panier
**target** ['tar·gɪt] **I.** *n* **①** (*mark aimed at*) a. *fig* cible *f* **②** (*objective*) objectif *m*; **to be on ~** être en train d'atteindre son objectif; **to set oneself a ~** se fixer un objectif (à atteindre) **II.** *vt* **①** (*aim at*) viser; (*market, group*) cibler **②** (*direct*) diriger **III.** *adj* (*market, audience*) visé(e); **~ date** date *f* ciblée
**tariff** ['ter·ɪf] *n* droit *m* de douane
**tarmac** ['tar·mæk] *n* AVIAT piste *f*
**tarnish** ['tar·nɪʃ] **I.** *vi* se ternir **II.** *vt* a. *fig* ternir **III.** *n* ternissure *f*
**tarp** *n* bâche *f*
**tart** [tart] **I.** *n* (*type of pastry*) tarte *f* **II.** *adj* **①** (*sharp, acid in taste*) acide **②** *fig* acerbe; (*wit*) caustique
**tartan** ['tar·t<sup>ə</sup>n] **I.** *n* tartan *m* **II.** *adj* écossais(e)
**tartar(e) sauce** *n* sauce *f* tartare
**task** [tæsk] **I.** *n* tâche *f*; **to take sb to ~**

réprimander qn **II.** *vt passive* **to be ~ed with sth** être chargé de qc
**task force** *n* **①** (*unit for special operation*) corps *m* expéditionnaire **②** (*group for particular purpose*) groupe *m* de travail
**taste** [teɪst] **I.** *n* **①** (*sensation*) goût *m*; **sense of ~** goût *m* **②** (*small portion of food*) bouchée *f* **③** (*liking, fondness*) goût *m*; **to have expensive ~s** avoir des goûts de luxe **④** (*aesthetic quality, discernment*) goût *m*; **to have (good) ~** avoir bon goût; **it's a matter of (personal) ~** c'est une question de goût **⑤** (*short encounter, experience*) aperçu *m*; **to have a ~ of victory/freedom** goûter à la victoire/à la liberté; **to give sb a ~ of army life** faire goûter la vie militaire à qn **⑥** *fig* **to have a ~ of sth** avoir un avant-goût de qc **II.** *vt* a. *fig* goûter à **III.** *vi* + *adj* **to ~ bitter/salty/sweet** avoir un goût amer/salé/sucré; **to ~ like sth** avoir le même goût que qc
**taste bud** ['teɪs·bʌd] *n* papille *f* (gustative)
**tasteful** *adj* de bon goût
**tasteless** *adj* **①** (*without flavor*) fade **②** *pej* (*showing bad taste, unstylish*) de mauvais goût
**tasty** *adj* appétissant(e); **to be ~** être appétissant, goûter *Belgique, Québec*
**tattletale** ['tæt·l·teɪl] *n* concierge *mf* *péj*
**tattoo** [tæt·'u] **I.** *n* **①** (*marking on skin*) tatouage *m* **②** MIL retraite *f* **II.** *vt* tatouer
**taught** [tɒt] *pt, pp* of **teach**
**taunt** [tɒnt] **I.** *vt* railler **II.** *n* raillerie *f*
**Taurus** ['tɔr·əs] *n* Taureau *m*; *s.a.* **Aquarius**
**tax** [tæks] **I.** <-es> *n* (*levy by government: direct*) impôt *m*; (*indirect*) taxe *f*; **income ~** impôt sur le revenu **II.** *vt* **①** (*levy a tax on*) taxer; (*person*) imposer; **to be ~ed lightly/heavily** être légèrement/lourdement taxé [o imposé] **②** (*make demands on, strain*) **to ~ sb's/sb's patience** mettre qn/la patience de qn à l'épreuve; **to ~ sb's memory** faire appel à la mémoire de qn

❸ (*accuse*) **to ~ sb with sth** taxer qn de qc; **to ~ sb with doing sth** accuser qn de faire qc

**taxation** [tæk·'seɪ·ʃən] *n* ❶ (*levying*) imposition *f* ❷ (*money*) impôts *mpl*

**tax-deductible** *adj* déductible des impôts

**tax evasion** *n* fraude *f* fiscale

**tax-exempt** *adj* exonéré(e) d'impôts

**taxi** ['tæk·si] I. *n* taxi *m* II. *vi* rouler

**taxicab** ['tæk·si·kæb] *n* s. **taxi**

**taxi driver** *n* chauffeur *m* de taxi

**taxing** ['tæks·ɪŋ] *adj* pénible

**taxi stand** *n* station *f* de taxis

**taxpayer** *n* contribuable *mf*

**tax return** *n* déclaration *f* d'impôts; **to file one's ~** remplir sa feuille d'impôts

**tax shelter** *n* abri *m* fiscal

**TB** [ˌti·'bi] *n abbr of* **tuberculosis** tuberculose *f*

**tbs., tbsp.** *n* ❶ *abbr of* **tablespoon** ❷ *abbr of* **tablespoonful** cuillerée *f* à soupe

**tea** [ti] *n* ❶ (*plant*) thé *m* ❷ (*drink*) thé *m*; **mint ~** thé à la menthe ❸ (*cup of tea*) thé *m*

**tea bag** *n* sachet *m* de thé, poche *f* de thé *Québec*

**teach** [titʃ] <taught, taught> I. *vt* SCHOOL (*subject, students*) enseigner; **to ~ sb to fish** apprendre à pêcher à qn; **to ~ school** enseigner; **to ~ oneself sth** apprendre qc tout seul; **to ~ sb that ...** apprendre à qn que ... ▶ **that'll ~ you a lesson** ça t'apprendra II. *vi* enseigner

**teacher** ['ti·tʃər] *n* (*in elementary education*) instituteur, -trice *m, f*; (*in secondary education*) professeur *mf*; **the ~s** les enseignants *mpl*; **substitute ~** remplaçant(e) *m(f)*

**teacher's pet** *n* chouchou(te) *m(f)* (du professeur)

**teacher training** *n* formation *f* pédagogique

**teaching** *n* ❶ (*instruction, profession*) l'enseignement *m* ❷ *pl* (*doctrine, precept*) enseignements *mpl*

**teaching assistant** *n* étudiant(e) *m(f)* chargé(e) de cours

**teacup** *n* tasse *f* à thé

**teakettle** *n* bouilloire *f*

**team** [tim] I. *n + sing/pl vb* ❶ (*group*) équipe *f* ❷ (*set of working animals*) attelage *m* II. *vt* (*combine*) associer; **to ~ sth with sth** assortir qc à qc

**teammate** *n* coéquipier, -ère *m, f*

**team spirit** *n* esprit *m* d'équipe

**teapot** *n* théière *f*

**tear¹** [tɪr] *n* larme *f*; **to be in ~s** être en larmes; **to burst into ~s** éclater en sanglots; **to have ~s in one's eyes** avoir les larmes aux yeux; **to reduce sb to ~s** faire pleurer qn

**tear²** [ter] I. *n* déchirure *f*; **there's a ~ in your shirt** ta chemise est déchirée II. <tore, torn> *vt* ❶ (*rip, pull apart*) *a. fig* déchirer; **to ~ a hole in sth** faire un trou dans qc (en le déchirant); **to ~ sb/ sth to shreds** *fig* mettre qn/qc en pièces ❷ *fig* **to be torn between X and Y** être déchiré entre X et Y III. <tore, torn> *vi* ❶ (*rip, come asunder*) se déchirer ❷ (*rush wildly*) foncer; **to ~ down the stairs** dévaler l'escalier

◆ **tear apart** *vt* ❶ (*rip wildly: package, machine*) mettre en pièces ❷ (*divide: party, family*) déchirer ❸ (*criticize, attack: physically*) démolir; (*in writing*) descendre en flammes ❹ (*search thoroughly, ransack*) mettre sens dessus dessous en cherchant

◆ **tear at** *vt* ❶ (*rip: wrapping*) déchirer ❷ (*attack: prey*) s'attaquer à; (*person*) griffer; **to ~ each other's throats** (*physically*) se prendre à la gorge; (*in writing, speech*) s'agresser

◆ **tear away** *vt* arracher; **to tear sb away from sb/sth** arracher qn à qn/ qc; **to tear oneself away** s'arracher

◆ **tear down** *vt* (*poster*) arracher; (*building*) détruire; **to ~ the barriers between communities** *fig* faire tomber les barrières qui séparent les communautés

◆ **tear into** *vt inf* ❶ (*attack*) foncer dans ❷ (*criticize: employee*) s'en prendre à; (*film, book*) attaquer

◆ **tear off** *vt* détacher; (*roughly*) arracher; **to ~ one's clothes** se déshabiller prestement

◆**tear open** *vt* déchirer

◆**tear out** *vt* ❶ (*rip*) arracher ❷ *fig* **to tear one's hair out over sth** s'arracher les cheveux pour qc

◆**tear up** *vt* ❶ (*rip into small pieces*) *a. fig* déchirer; (*agreement*) jeter à la poubelle ❷ (*damage, destroy*) détruire; **to ~ a flowerbed** arracher les fleurs d'une plate-bande

**teardrop** *n* larme *f*

**tearful** *adj* (*parent*) en larmes; **~ letters/reunions** lettres *fpl*/retrouvailles *fpl* pleines de larmes

**tear gas** *n* gaz *m* lacrymogène

**tearjerker** *n inf* mélo *m*

**tease** [tiz] I. *vt* ❶ (*make fun of*) taquiner ❷ (*provoke sexually*) allumer ❸ (*backcomb: hair*) crêper II. *vi* plaisanter III. *n* ❶ *inf* (*playful person*) taquin(e) *m(f)* ❷ *pej* (*flirt*) allumeur, -euse *m, f*

**teaser** *n* ❶ (*playful person*) taquin(e) *m(f)* ❷ *pej* (*flirt*) allumeur, -euse *m, f* ❸ (*introductory advertisement*) pilote *m* ❹ *inf* (*difficult question, task*) colle *f*

**teaspoon** *n* cuillère *f* à café, cuillère *f* à thé *Québec*

**teaspoonful** *n* cuillerée *f* à café

**technical** ['tek·nɪ·kᵊl] *adj* technique

**technical college** *n* ≈ établissement *m* d'enseignement technique

**technician** [tek·'nɪʃ·ᵊn] *n* technicien(ne) *m(f)*

**technique** [tek·'nik] *n* technique *f*

**technological** *adj* technologique

**technology** [tek·'na·lə·dʒi] *n* technologie *f*

**teddy bear** *n* ours *m* en peluche

**tedious** ['ti·di·əs] *adj* ennuyeux(-euse)

**tee** [ti] *n* tee *m*

◆**tee off** I. *vi* ❶ SPORTS commencer le jeu ❷ *fig, inf* (*start*) démarrer II. *vt inf* énerver

**teen** [tin] *n* adolescent(e) *m(f)*; **to be in one's ~** être un adolescent

**teenager** ['tin·eɪ·dʒər] *n* adolescent(e) *m(f)*

**teensy-weensy, teeny-weeny** [ˌti·ni·'wi·ni] *adj inf* minuscule

**tee shirt** ['ti·ʃɜrt] *n* tee-shirt *m*

**teeth** [tiθ] *n pl of* **tooth**

**teethe** [tið] *vi* faire ses dents

**teetotaler** *n* personne qui ne boit jamais d'alcool

**telecast** ['tel·ɪ·kæst] *n* émission *f* de télévision

**telecommunications** ['tel·ɪ·kə·ˌmju·nɪ·'keɪ·ʃᵊnz] *npl* télécommunications *fpl*

**telecommuting** ['tel·ɪ·kə·ˌmju·tɪŋ] *n* COMPUT télétravail *m*

**telephone** ['tel·ə·foʊn] I. *n* téléphone *m*; **by ~** par téléphone; **on the ~** au téléphone; **to pick up the ~** prendre le téléphone; **~ bill** facture *f* de téléphone II. *vt* appeler III. *vi* téléphoner

**telephone book** *n* annuaire *m*

**telephone booth** *n* cabine *f* téléphonique

**telephone call** *n* appel *m* téléphonique; **to make a ~** passer un appel

**telephone directory** *n* s. **telephone book**

**telephone number** *n* numéro *m* de téléphone

**telephoto lens** ['tel·ə·foʊ·ˌtoʊ 'lens] *n* téléobjectif *m*

**telescope** ['tel·ə·skoʊp] I. *n* télescope *m* II. *vt* ❶ (*make shorter*) télescoper ❷ *fig* condenser III. *vi* se télescoper

**televise** ['tel·ə·vaɪz] *vt* téléviser

**television** ['tel·ə·vɪʒ·ᵊn] *n* télévision *f*; **on ~** à la télévision

**television camera** *n* caméra *f* de télévision

**television network** *n* réseau *m* de télévision

**television program** *n* programme *m* de télévision

**television station** *n* chaîne *f* de télévision

**television studio** *n* studio *m* de télévision

**tell** [tel] I. <told, told> *vt* ❶ (*giving information*) dire; **to ~ sb about** [*o of*] **sth** parler de qc à qn; **to ~ sb (that)** ... dire à qn que ...; **we were told that** ...

**T**

on nous a dit que ...; **to ~ sb what happened/where sth is** dire à qn ce qui s'est passé/où se trouve qc; **to ~ sb about a change/a meeting** informer qn d'un changement/d'une réunion; **don't ~ anyone** ne le dis à personne; **your house ~s people a lot about you** ta/votre maison en dit long sur toi/vous; **to ~ the future** prédire l'avenir ② (*narrate: story*) raconter; **to ~ sb (about) what happened** raconter à qn ce qui s'est passé ③ (*command*) **to ~ sb to** +*infin* dire à qn de +*infin;* **do as you're told** *inf* fais ce qu'on te dit ④ (*make out*) discerner; **I can ~ if it's good** je sais tout de suite si c'est bon; **to ~ the difference** faire la différence; **you can never ~** on ne peut jamais savoir ⑤ (*count*) compter; **all told** en tout ▶**I'll ~ you what** tu sais quoi; **that would be ~ing** *inf* ça c'est mon affaire; **I told you so** je te l'avais bien dit; **what did I ~ you?** *inf* je te l'avais bien dit II. <told, told> *vi* dire; **will she ~?** est-ce qu'elle va rapporter?

◆**tell apart** *vt* différencier

◆**tell off** *vt* (*child*) gronder; (*employee*) faire des reproches à; **to tell sb off about sth** faire une remarque à qn à propos de qc

**temp** [temp] *inf* I. *n* intérimaire *mf;* **to do ~ work** faire de l'intérim II. *vi* travailler en intérim

**temper** ['tem·pər] I. *n* ① (*angry state*) colère *f;* **to lose one's ~** se mettre en colère ② (*characteristic mood*) humeur *f;* **to have a very bad ~** avoir très mauvais caractère II. *vt* ① *form* (*moderate*) tempérer; **to ~ with sth** tempérer par qc ② (*make malleable*) tremper

**temperamental** *adj* ① *pej* (*easily irritated*) capricieux(-euse) ② (*characteristic*) inné(e)

**temperature** ['tem·pər·ə·tʃər] *n a. fig* température *f;* **to have a ~** avoir de la température; **to take sb's ~** prendre la température de qn; **a rise/fall in ~** une augmentation/baisse de température

**template** ['tem·plɪt] *n* COMPUT modèle *m*

**temple**[1] ['tem·pl] *n* (*monument*) temple *m*

**temple**[2] ['tem·pl] *n* BIO tempe *f*

**temporarily** ['tem·pər·er·ə̩l·i] *adv* temporairement

**temporary** ['tem·pər·er·i] *adj* temporaire; (*job, worker*) intérimaire; (*solution, building*) provisoire

**tempt** [tempt] *vt* tenter; **to ~ sb into doing sth** inciter qn à faire qc

**temptation** [temp·'tei·ʃən] *n* tentation *f;* **to resist the ~ to** +*infin* résister à la tentation de +*infin*

**tempting** *adj* tentant(e)

**ten** [ten] *adj* dix *inv; s.a.* **eight**

**tenant** ['ten·ənt] *n* locataire *mf*

**tend**[1] [tend] *vi* (*be likely*) **to ~ to** +*infin* avoir tendance à +*infin;* **it ~s to happen that** il arrive souvent que +*subj*

**tend**[2] [tend] I. *vt* (*care for*) s'occuper de II. *vi* **to ~ to sth** s'occuper de qc

**tendency** ['ten·dən(t)·si] <-ies> *n* tendance *f*

**tender**[1] ['ten·dər] *adj* ① (*not tough*) *a. fig* (*kiss, heart, material*) tendre ② (*easily damaged by cold*) délicat(e) ③ (*painful*) sensible

**tender**[2] ['ten·dər] I. *n* ① (*bid*) offre *f* ② FIN **legal ~** monnaie *f* légale II. *vt form* offrir; (*resignation, apologies*) présenter III. *vi* faire une soumission

**tenderness** *n* ① (*feeling*) tendresse *f* ② (*pain*) sensibilité *f*

**tendon** ['ten·dən] *n* tendon *m*

**tenfold** ['ten·foʊld] I. *adj* décuple II. *adv* au décuple

**Tennessee** *n* le Tennessee

**tennis** ['ten·ɪs] *n* tennis *m*

**tennis court** *n* court *m* de tennis

**tennis elbow** *n* synovite *f* du coude

**tennis racket** *n* raquette *f* de tennis

**tenor**[1] ['ten·ər] *n* ténor *m*

**tenor**[2] ['ten·ər] *n form* (*gist*) teneur *f*

**tense**[1] [ten(t)s] I. *adj a. fig* tendu(e); (*muscles*) contracté(e) II. *vt* tendre III. *vi* se tendre

**tense²** [ten(t)s] *n* LING temps *m*

**tension** ['ten(t)·ʃ°n] *n a. fig* tension *f*

**tent** [tent] *n* tente *f*

**tentacle** ['ten·tə·kl] *n a. fig, pej* tentacule *f*

**tentative** ['ten·tə·tɪv] *adj* ❶ (*provisional*) provisoire ❷ (*hesitant*) timide

**tentatively** *adv* ❶ (*provisionally*) provisoirement ❷ (*hesitatingly*) timidement

**tenth** [ten(t)θ] *adj* dixième; *s.a.* **eighth**

**tepid** ['tep·ɪd] *adj a. fig* tiède

**terabyte** ['ter·ə·baɪt] *n* COMPUT téraoctet *m*

**term** [tɜrm] **I.** *n* ❶ (*word*) terme *m* ❷ (*period*) terme *m*; UNIV, SCHOOL trimestre *m*; ~ **of office** mandat *m*; ~ **of imprisonment** durée *f* d'emprisonnement; **to carry a baby to** ~ MED porter un bébé à terme; **in the long/short** ~ à long/court terme ❸ *pl* (*conditions*) conditions *fpl*; **in** ~**s of sth** en termes de qc ► **to come to** ~**s with** (arriver à) accepter ❹ *vt* désigner

**terminal** ['tɜr·mɪ·n°l] **I.** *adj* ❶ (*at the end*) terminal(e); (*patient, illness*) incurable ❷ *fig, inf* (*boredom*) mortel(le) **II.** *n* ❶ (*end of route, station*) terminal *m*; (*at airport*) aérogare *f* ❷ ELEC borne *f* ❸ COMPUT terminal *m*

**terminate** ['tɜr·mɪ·neɪt] *form* **I.** *vt* terminer; (*project, contract*) mettre un terme à **II.** *vi* se terminer

**terminology** [ˌtɜr·mɪ·'na·lə·dʒi] *n* terminologie *f*

**terrace** ['ter·əs] **I.** *n* (*level, patio, porch*) terrasse *f* **II.** *vt* disposer en terrasses

**terrain** [te·'reɪn] *n* terrain *m*

**terrible** ['ter·ə·bl] *adj* (*crime, struggle, experience*) horrible; (*weather, film*) affreux(-euse); **a** ~ **mistake** une terrible erreur; **she looked** ~ (*ill*) elle avait une mine affreuse; (*badly dressed*) elle était très mal habillée

**terribly** *adv* ❶ (*badly: hurt, bleed*) terriblement ❷ *inf* (*extremely*) extrêmement; **it didn't go** ~ **well** ça ne s'est pas vraiment bien passé

**terrific** [tə·'rɪf·ɪk] *adj inf* ❶ (*excellent: party*) génial(e); **to feel** ~ se sentir en

pleine forme; **you look** ~ **in that dress** tu es superbe dans cette robe ❷ (*astounding*) incroyable

**terrified** *adj* terrifié(e)

**terrify** ['ter·ə·faɪ] <-ie-> *vt* terrifier

**terrifying** *adj* terrifiant(e)

**territory** ['ter·ə·br·i] <-ies> *n* ❶ (*land*) *a. fig* territoire *m* ❷ (*field of activity, knowledge*) *a. fig* domaine *m*

**terror** ['ter·ər] *n a. inf* terreur *f*; **to have a** ~ **of sth** avoir la terreur de qc

**terrorism** ['ter·°r·ɪ·z°m] *n* terrorisme *m*

**terrorist** **I.** *n* terroriste *mf* **II.** *adj* terroriste

**test** [test] **I.** *n* ❶ (*examination*) test *m*; SCHOOL examen *m*; **aptitude/IQ** ~ test d'aptitude/de QI; ~ **of skill** épreuve *f* d'adresse; **safety** ~ test de sécurité; **I am taking my driving** ~ **tomorrow** je passe mon permis de conduire) demain ❷ (*scientific examination*) examen *m*; **blood** ~ analyse *f* de sang; **pregnancy** ~ test *m* de grossesse; **to do/run a** ~ faire une analyse ❸ (*challenge*) épreuve *f*; **to put sth to the** ~ mettre qc à l'épreuve **II.** *vt* ❶ (*examine knowledge of*) ❷ (*examine for efficiency: machine*) essayer; (*system*) tester; **to** ~ (**out**) **a theory/an idea** mettre une théorie/une idée à l'essai ❸ (*examine*) analyser; **to** ~ **sb's blood** faire une analyse de sang à qn; **to** ~ **sb's hearing** examiner l'ouïe de qn; **to** ~ **sb/sth for sth** faire subir à qn/qc un examen de qc ❹ (*measure*) mesurer; **to** ~ **the presence of sth** analyser la présence de qc ❺ (*try with senses: by touching*) toucher; (*by tasting*) goûter ❻ (*try to the limit*) **to** ~ **sb/sth** mettre qn/qc à l'épreuve **III.** *vi* (*to* ~ *positive/negative*) avoir des analyses positives/négatives; **to** ~ **for** (*disease, antibodies*) faire des examens pour détecter; (*chemical*) faire des analyses à la recherche de

**testament** ['tes·tə·mənt] *n form, a. fig* testament *m*; **to be** (**a**) ~ **to sth** être le témoignage de qc; **the New/Old Tes-**

T

**tament** l'Ancien/le Nouveau Testament

**test case** n LAW cas m qui fait jurisprudence

**test drive** n essai m sur route

**test-drive** vt essayer un véhicule

**testicle** ['tes·tɪ·kl] n testicule m

**testify** ['tes·tɪ·faɪ] <-ie-> I. vi témoigner; **to ~ to sth** attester qc II. vt témoigner

**testimony** ['tes·tɪ·moʊ·ni] <-ies> n a. fig témoignage m; **to be ~ to** [o of ] **sth** être le témoignage de qc

**test pilot** n pilote m d'essai

**test tube** n éprouvette f

**test-tube baby** n bébé m éprouvette

**tetanus** ['tet·ᵊn·əs] n tétanos m

**Texan** I. n Texan(ne) m(f) II. adj texan(ne)

**Texas** ['tek·səs] n le Texas

**text** [tekst] n ❶ texte m ❷ (textbook) manuel m

**textbook** I. n manuel m II. adj ❶ (demonstration) exemplaire ❷ (usual) typique

**textile** ['tek·staɪl] n pl textile m

**texture** ['teks·tʃər] n ❶ (feel) texture f ❷ (impression given) velouté m

**Thai** I. adj ❶ (of Thailand) thaïlandais(e) ❷ LING thaï(e) II. n ❶ (person) Thaïlandais(e) m(f) ❷ LING thaï m; s.a. **English**

**Thailand** ['taɪ·lənd] n la Thaïlande

**Thames** [temz] n **the ~** (**River**) la Tamise

**than** [ðæn] conj que; **she is taller ~ he** (**is**) [o him] elle est plus grande que lui; **no sooner sb has done sth, ~ ...** à peine qn a-t-il fait qc que ...; s.a. **more, less, other**

**thank** [θæŋk] vt remercier; **to ~ sb for doing sth** remercier qn d'avoir fait qc; **I'll ~ you to** +infin tu vas prier de +infin ▶ **~ goodness!** Dieu merci!

**thankful** adj ❶ (pleased) ravi(e) ❷ (grateful) reconnaissant(e); **I'm just ~ it's over** je suis surtout content que ce soit fini subj

**thankless** adj ingrat(e)

**thanks** I. n pl remerciements mpl; **to give ~ to sb** remercier qn; **thanks to sb** grâce à qn II. interj merci!; **~ a lot/ bunch** a. iron je te remercie

**thank you** n merci m; **~ very much** merci beaucoup; **~ letter** lettre f de remerciement

**that** [ðæt] I. dem pron, pl: those ❶ (sth shown) cela, ça, ce; **read ~** lis/lisez ça; **what's ~?** qu'est-ce que c'est (que ça)?; **~'s why ...** c'est pourquoi ...; **~'s what I want** c'est ce que je veux; **after ~, he retired** après ça, il est parti à la retraite; **~'s a shame** c'est dommage ❷ (countable) celui-là, celle-là; **those** ceux-là, celles-là ▶ **well, ~'s ~** et voilà; **he said he was sorry and all ~** il a dit qu'il était désolé et tout ça; **~'s it** (good idea) voilà; (I've had enough) ça suffit comme ça II. dem adj, pl: those ce, cette m, f, cet + vowel m; **~ dog/child/ man** ce chien/cet enfant/cet homme; **~ bottle/road/letter** cette bouteille/ route/lettre; **those people** ces gens(-là) mpl; **~ car of yours** ta/votre voiture f; **~ car you saw** la voiture que tu as/ vous avez vue; (on) **~ Monday** ce lundi-là III. adv ❶ (showing an amount or degree) **it's ~ big/high** c'est grand/ haut comme ça; **why does it cost ~ much?** pourquoi est-ce que ça coûte autant? ❷ (so) tellement; **it's not ~ far/ warm** ce n'est pas si loin/chaud que ça; s.a. **this** IV. rel pron ❶ subject qui; **the man ~ told me ...** l'homme qui m'a dit ...; **the day ~ he arrived** le jour où il est arrivé ❷ object que, qu' + vowel; **the package ~ I sent** le paquet que j'ai envoyé; **the box ~ he told me about** la boîte dont il m'a parlé; **the day ~ I met you** le jour où je t'ai rencontré V. conj que, qu' + vowel; **I said ~ I'd come** j'ai dit que je viendrais; **so ~ I can go** de façon à ce que je puisse partir subj; **given ~ he's gone** étant donné qu'il est parti

**thatch** [θætʃ] I. n ❶ (straw, roof) chaume m ❷ fig (of hair) touffe f II. vt **to ~ sth** couvrir qc de chaume

**thaw** [θɔ] I. n a. fig amélioration f II. vi

❶ (*unfreeze: snow, ice*) fondre; (*food*) se décongeler ❷ (*become friendlier*) se dérider **III.** *vt* (*snow, ice*) faire fondre; (*food*) décongeler

**the** [ðə, *stressed, before vowel* ði] *def art* le, la *m, f,* l' *m o f* + *vowel,* les *pl;* of [o from] ~ **garden** du jardin; of [o from] ~ **window** de la fenêtre; of [o from] ~ **rooms** des chambres; **at** [o to] ~ **office** au bureau; **at** [o to] ~ **window** à la fenêtre; **at** [o to] ~ **hotel** à l'hôtel; **at** [o to] ~ **doors** aux portes; **to play** ~ **flute** jouer de la flûte; **Charles** ~ **Seventh** Charles sept; **I'll do it in** ~ **winter** je le ferai cet hiver; **the Martins** les Martin *mpl;* **THE James Martin** le fameux James Martin; ~ **more one tries,** ~ **less one succeeds** plus on essaie, moins on réussit; ~ **sooner** ~ **better** plus tôt sera le mieux; **all** ~ **better** tant mieux; **the hottest day** le jour le plus chaud

**theater** ['θiˑəˑtər] *n* ❶ (*building*) théâtre *m* ❷ (*place where movies are shown*) salle *f* de cinéma; **at the** ~ au cinéma ❸ (*lecture theater*) amphithéâtre *m* ❹ (*dramatic art*) théâtre *m*

**theatergoer** *n* amateur, ‑trice *m, f* de théâtre

**theatre** *n s.* **theater**

**theft** [θeft] *n* vol *m*

**their** [ðer] *poss adj* leur(s); *s.a.* **my**

**theirs** [ðerz] *poss pron* (*belonging to them*) le leur, la leur; **they aren't our bags, they are** ~ ce ne sont pas nos sacs, ce sont les leurs; **this house is** ~ cette maison est la leur; **a book of** ~ (l')un de leurs livres; **this table is** ~ cette table est à eux/elles

**them** [ðem] *pers pron pl* ❶ (*they*) eux, elles; **older than** ~ plus âgé qu'eux/elles; **if I were** ~ si j'étais eux/elles ❷ *objective pron as direct,* leur *indirect,* eux, elles *after prep;* **look at** ~ regarde/regardez-les; **I saw** ~ je les ai vus; **he told** ~ **that ...** il leur a dit que ...; **he'll give sth to** ~ il va leur donner qc; **it's for** ~ c'est pour eux; **I ate all of** ~ je les ai tous mangés; **all of** ~ **went** (*people*)

ils y sont tous allés; (*objects on sale*) tout est parti; **I ate some of** ~ j'en ai mangé quelques uns; **some of** ~ **went** il y en a qui y sont allés

**theme** [θim] *n a.* MUS thème *m*

**theme music** *n* générique *m*

**themselves** [ðəmˑ'selvz] *reflex pron* ❶ *after verbs* se, s' + *vowel;* **the girls hurt** ~ les filles se sont blessées ❷ (*they or them*) eux-mêmes *mpl,* elles-mêmes *fpl; s.a.* **myself**

**then** [ðen] **I.** *adv* ❶ (*afterward*) puis, ensuite; **what** ~? et après?; ~ **the door opened** et puis la porte s'est ouverte; **there and** ~ ici et maintenant ❷ (*at that time*) alors; **I was younger** ~ j'étais plus jeune en ce temps là; **why did you leave** ~? pourquoi est-ce que tu es parti à ce moment-là?; **I'll do it by** ~ je l'aurai fait d'ici là; **before** ~ auparavant; **until** ~ jusqu'alors; **since** ~ depuis (ce moment-là); (**every**) **now and** ~ de temps à autre ❸ (*logical then*) alors; **but** ~ **she's a painter** mais bon bien sûr, elle est peintre; ~ **I'll leave** dans ce cas je m'en vais; ~ **why did you leave?** alors pourquoi est-ce que tu es/vous êtes parti(s)?; ~ **he must be there** alors il doit être là; **OK** ~, **let's go** c'est bon, on y va **II.** *adj* d'alors; **the** ~ **king** le roi de l'époque

**theology** [θiˑ'aˑləˑdʒi] <‑ies> *n* théologie *f*

**theoretical** [ˌθiˑəˑ'reṭˑɪˑkəl] *adj* théorique

**theoretically** *adv* théoriquement; ~ **he'll have finished** en principe, il aura terminé

**theory** ['θiˑəˑri] <‑ies> *n* théorie *f*

**therapeutic** [ˌθerˑəˑ'pjuˑṭɪk] *adj* thérapeutique

**therapist** *n* thérapeute *mf*

**therapy** ['θerˑəˑpi] <‑ies> *n* thérapie *f*

**there** [ðer] **I.** *adv* ❶ (*in, at, to place/position*) *a. fig* là; **in** ~ là-dedans; **over** ~ là-bas; **up** ~ là-haut; **we went** ~ nous sommes allés là-bas; **to get** ~ *a. fig* y arriver; ~ **you are!** te/vous voilà!; (*giving sth*) voilà; **I don't agree with you** ~ je ne suis pas d'accord avec toi/vous sur ce point-là ❷ (*indicating existence*) ~ **is/are ...** il y a un ... ▸ **to be not all** ~ avoir un grain; ~ **and then** directement; ~ **you go again** ça recommence; **I've been** ~ je sais ce que c'est **II.** *interj* ❶ (*expressing sympathy*) ~ ~ allez, allez! ❷ (*expressing satisfaction, annoyance*) voilà!

**thereabouts** *adv* ❶ (*place*) par là ❷ (*time, amount*) à peu près

**thereafter** *adv* par la suite; **shortly** ~ peu de temps après

**thereby** *adv form* de cette façon

**therefore** *adv* par conséquent

**therein** *adv form* (*inside*) à l'intérieur; (*in document*) ci-inclus

**thermal** ['θɜrm·əl] *adj* thermique; (*bath, springs*) thermal(e); (*underwear*) en Thermolactyl®

**thermometer** [θər·'ma·mə·ṭər] *n* thermomètre *m*

**Thermos® bottle** ['θɜr·məs-] *n* thermos *m o f*

**thermostat** ['θɜr·mə·stæt] *n* thermostat *m*

**thesaurus** [θɪ·'sɔr·əs] <-es *o form* -ri> *n* dictionnaire *m* des synonymes

**these** [ðiz] *pl of* **this**

**thesis** ['θi·sɪs] <-ses> *n* thèse *f*

**they** [ðeɪ] *pers pron* ❶ (*3rd person pl*) ils *mpl*, elles *fpl*; ~ **'re** [*o* ~ **are**] **my parents/sisters** ce sont mes parents/sœurs; **your shoes?** ~ **are here** tes chaussures? elles sont ici; **to be as rich as** ~ **are** être aussi riche qu'eux/elles ❷ *inf* (*he or she*) **somebody just called: what do** ~ **want?** on a sonné: qu'est-ce qu'elle/il veut? ❸ (*people in general*) on; ~ **say that ...** ils disent que ...

**they'll** [ðeɪl] = **they will** *s.* **will**

**they're** [ðer] = **they are** *s.* **be**

**they've** [ðeɪv] = **they have** *s.* **have**

**thick** [θɪk] **I.** *n inf* **to be in the** ~ **of sth** être en plein qc ▸ **through** ~ **and thin** contre vents et marées **II.** *adj* ❶ (*not thin*) épais(se); **sth 2 inches** ~ qc d'une épaisseur de 2 pouces ❷ (*dense*) épais(se); **it was** ~ **with people/insects** *fig* ça grouillait de monde/d'insectes ❸ (*extreme: accent*) fort(e) ❹ *pej, inf* (*mentally slow*) bête; **get it into your** ~ **head that ...** fais bien rentrer dans ta petite tête que ...

**thicken** ['θɪk·ən] **I.** *vt* épaissir **II.** *vi* ❶ (*become denser*) *a. fig* s'épaissir; **the plot** ~**s** *fig* les choses se compliquent ❷ (*become more numerous*) grossir ❸ (*become wider*) grossir

**thief** [θif, *pl:* θivz] <thieves> *n* voleur, -euse *m, f*

**thigh** [θaɪ] *n* cuisse *f*

**thimble** ['θɪm·bl] *n* dé *m* à coudre

**thin** [θɪn] <-nn-> **I.** *adj* ❶ (*lean*) *a. fig* mince ❷ (*narrow: layer*) fin(e); (*slice, line*) mince ❸ (*sparse: population*) clairsemé(e); (*crowd*) épars(e) ❹ (*not dense*) fin(e); (*mist*) léger(-ère) ❺ (*very fluid*) peu épais(se) ❻ (*feeble*) faible; (*smile*) léger(-ère) ❼ (*lacking oxygen: air*) pauvre en oxygène ▸ **out of** ~ **air** comme par magie; **to disappear into** ~ **air** disparaître comme par magie; **to be** ~**-skinned** être susceptible; **to wear** ~ s'épuiser **II.** <-nn-> *vt* ❶ (*make more liquid*) délayer ❷ (*remove some*) éclaircir **III.** *vi* (*crowd*) se disperser; (*hair*) se raréfier

**thing** [θɪŋ] *n* ❶ (*object*) chose *f*; *inf* machin *m*; **the** ~**s on the table are dirty** les affaires sur la table sont sales ❷ (*abstract use*) chose *f*; *inf* truc *m*; **to do a lot of** ~**s** faire beaucoup de choses; **it's a good** ~ **I had the car** heureusement que j'avais la voiture; **it was a dangerous** ~ **to do** c'était dangereux; **the** ~ **to remember is ...** ce qu'il faut se rappeler c'est; **to do sth first** ~ **in the morning** faire qc de bon matin; **it's been one** ~ **after another** les choses se sont enchaînées les unes derrière les autres; **to forget the whole** ~ tout oublier; **and another** ~ et en plus; **the only** ~ **is** (*that*)... le seul problème est que ...; **how are** ~**s going?** comment ça va?; **there isn't a** ~ **left** il n'y a plus rien; **all** ~**s considered** quoi qu'il en soit; **for one ~** tout d'abord ③ (*the best*) **it was the real ~** c'était pour de vrai ④ (*person, animal*) créature *f;* **the poor ~** le pauvre; **you lucky ~** petit chanceux ▸ **it's just <u>one</u> of those ~s** il y a des jours comme ça; **to do one's <u>own</u>** ~ *inf* faire ses trucs; **to <u>have</u> a ~ about sth** *inf* avoir un problème avec qc; **to <u>make</u> a big ~ out of sth** *inf* faire tout un plat de qc

**thingamabob** ['θɪŋ·ə·mə·ˌbab], **thing-amajig** ['θɪŋ·ə·mə·ˌdʒɪg] *n inf* machin *m*

**think** [θɪŋk] <thought, thought> **I.** *vi* ① (*use one's mind*) penser; **to ~ aloud** [*o* **out loud**] penser tout haut; **to ~ to oneself** se dire; **to ~ for oneself** penser indépendamment; **just ~!** imagine! ② (*consider a question*) réfléchir; **to ~ about sth/how to** +*infin* réfléchir à qc/à comment +*infin;* **about it** pensez-y/pensez-y ③ (*believe, imagine*) croire; **I think so** oui, je crois bien; **I don't ~ so** je ne crois pas ▸ (**you can**) **~ again!** tu te trompes lourdement!; **to ~ <u>big</u>** voir grand **II.** *vt* ① (*use one's mind, have ideas*) penser; **I can't ~ how to do it** je ne vois pas comment faire ② (*believe*) croire; **I ~ he's Irish** je crois qu'il est irlandais; **I ~ she's coming** je pense qu'elle viendra; **who would have thought (that) she'd win** qui aurait dit qu'elle gagnerait; **who does she ~ she is?** elle se prend pour qui? ③ (*consider*) juger; **I thought him a good player** je pensais que c'était un bon joueur; **to not ~ much of sb/sth** ne pas avoir une bonne opinion de qn/qc; **to ~ nothing of sth** ne pas être impressionné par qc ④ (*remember*) **to ~ to** +*infin* penser à +*infin;* **can you ~ where you saw it last?** pouvez-vous vous rappeler quand vous l'avez vu pour la dernière fois?

◆**think ahead** *vi* réfléchir à deux fois

◆**think back** *vi* se souvenir; **to ~ to sth** repenser à qc

◆**think out** *vt* ① (*consider: problem, situation*) réfléchir sérieusement à

② (*plan*) préparer avec soin

◆**think over** *vt* réfléchir à; **I've been thinking things over** j'ai pensé et repensé

◆**think through** *vt* bien réfléchir à

◆**think up** *vt* inf inventer

**thinking I.** *n* ① (*using thought, reasoning*) réflexion *f* ② (*opinions*) opinion *f* **II.** *adj* (*person*) qui réfléchit

**third** [θɜrd] **I.** *n* ① (*3rd day of month*) trois *m* ② (*after second*) troisième *mf* ③ (*fraction*) tiers *m* ④ MUS tierce *f* **II.** *adj* troisième; *s.a.* **eighth**

**thirdly** *adv* troisièmement

**third-rate** *adj* de très mauvaise qualité

**Third World** *n* **the ~** le Tiers-Monde

**thirst** [θɜrst] *n* soif *f;* **a ~ for adventure** *fig* une soif d'aventure

**thirsty** <-ier, -iest> *adj* **to be ~** avoir soif; **to be ~ for sth** *fig* avoir soif de qc

**thirteen** [θɜr·'tin] *adj* treize *inv; s.a.* **eight**

**thirteenth** [θɜr·'tinθ] *adj* treizième; *s.a.* **eighth**

**thirtieth** ['θɜr·ti·əθ] *adj* trentième; *s.a.* **eighth**

**thirty** ['θɜr·ti] *adj* trente *inv; s.a.* **eight**

**this** [ðɪs] **I.** *dem pron* ① (*sth shown*) ceci, ce; **what is ~?** qu'est ce (que c'est)?; **~ is Paul** voilà Paul; **~ is difficult** c'est difficile; **~ is where I live** voilà où j'habite ② (*countable*) **~ (one)** celui-ci *m,* celle-ci *f;* **these (ones)** ceux-ci *mpl,* celles-ci *fpl* **II.** *dem adj* ce *m,* cette *f,* cet *m* + *vowel;* **~ time** cette fois(-ci); **I have ~ pain in my leg** *inf* j'ai une douleur dans la jambe **III.** *adv* **to be ~ high** être haut comme ça; **~ far** jusque là; **is it always ~ loud?** est-ce que c'est toujours aussi fort?; *s.a.* **that**

**thistle** ['θɪs·l] *n* chardon *m*

**thorn** [θɔrn] *n* épine *f* ▸ **to be a ~ in sb's <u>side</u>** être une épine dans le pied de qn

**thorough** ['θɜr·ou] *adj* ① (*complete*) complet(-ète) ② (*detailed*) détaillé(e) ③ (*careful*) minutieux(-euse)

**thoroughfare** *n form* voie *f* publique

T

**thoroughly** *adv* ❶ (*in detail*) en détail ❷ (*completely*) complètement

**those** [ðoʊz] *pl of* **that**

**though** [ðoʊ] I. *conj* bien que +*subj*; **even ~** I'm tired, tired **~ I am** même si je suis fatigué ►**as ~** comme si; **it looks as ~ it's raining** il semble qu'il pleuve; *s.a.* **although** II. *adv* pourtant; **it's still delicious, ~** c'est quand même délicieux

**thought** [θɔt] I. *pp, pt of* **think** II. *n* ❶ (*thinking*) pensée *f*; **to give food for ~** donner matière à réflexion; **current economic ~** tendance *f* actuelle en économie ❷ (*idea*) idée *f*; **it was a nice ~** c'était gentil; **~s of my children** des pensées *fpl* au sujet de mes enfants; **I have no ~(s)** of retiring je n'ai aucune intention de partir à la retraite; **what are your ~s on this?** qu'en pensez-vous? ►**a penny for your ~s** *prov* à quoi penses-tu/pensez-vous?

**thoughtful** *adj* ❶ (*mentally occupied*) pensif(-ive) ❷ (*sensible: approach*) réfléchi(e); (*article*) bien pensé(e) ❸ (*considerate*) prévenant

**thoughtless** *adj* ❶ (*without thinking*) irréfléchi(e) ❷ (*inconsiderate*) indifférent(e)

**thought-provoking** *adj* qui donne matière à réflexion

**thousand** ['θaʊ·zənd] I. *n* ❶ (*1000*) mille *m inv* ❷ (*quantity*) millier *m*; **~s of sth** des milliers *mpl* de qc II. *adj* mille *inv*; *s.a.* **eight**

**thousandth** *adj* millième; *s.a.* **eighth**

**thread** [θred] I. *n* ❶ (*for sewing*) fil *m* ❷ (*groove of screw*) filet *m* II. *vt* ❶ (*pass a thread: needle*) passer un fil dans ❷ (*string: beads*) enfiler ❸ (*insert: tape, film*) introduire

**threat** [θret] *n a. fig* menace *f*; **to pose a ~ to sth** menacer qc

**threaten** ['θret·ən] I. *vt* ❶ (*take hostile action*) menacer ❷ (*be a danger*) constituer une menace pour II. *vi* menacer; **to ~ to** +*infin* menacer de +*infin*

**threatening** *adj* (*behavior*) menaçant(e)

**three** [θri] *adj* trois *inv*; *s.a.* **eight**

**three-D** *adj inf* en 3D

**three-dimensional** *adj* en trois dimensions

**three-piece** *adj* ❶ (*three items*) en trois morceaux; **~ suit** (*costume m*) trois-pièces *m* ❷ (*three people*) à trois; **~ band** trio *m*

**three-quarter** *adj* trois-quarts

**threshold** ['θreʃ·(h)oʊld] *n* ❶ (*doorway*) pas *m* de la porte ❷ (*beginning: of life*) début *m*; (*of a century*) aube *f* ❸ (*limit*) seuil *m*; **pain ~** seuil de tolérance à la douleur

**threw** [θru] *pt of* **throw**

**thrifty** ['θrɪf·ti] <-ier, -iest> *adj* économe

**thrill** [θrɪl] I. *n* ❶ (*feeling*) sensation *f*; (*of emotion*) tressaillement *m* ❷ (*exciting experience*) sensation *f* forte; **it's a real ~ to meet her** c'est vraiment bien de la rencontrer II. *vt* (*crowd*) électriser; **to be ~ed to do sth/with sth** être ravi de faire qc/de qc; **I'm ~ed with my present** je suis enchanté de mon cadeau III. *vi form* **to ~ to sth** vibrer à qc

**thriller** ['θrɪl·ər] *n* ❶ (*novel*) roman *m* à suspens ❷ (*film*) thriller *m*

**thrilling** *adj* (*experience*) palpitant(e); (*story*) passionnant(e)

**thriving** *adj* florissant(e); (*company*) qui prospère; (*children*) bien portant(e)

**throat** [θroʊt] *n* gorge *f*; **to clear one's ~** s'éclaircir la voix ►**to be at each other's ~s** s'étriper; **to force sth down sb's ~** imposer qc à qn

**throb** [θrɑb] I. *n* (*of a heart*) pulsation *f*; (*of pain*) élancement *m* II. <-bb-> *vi* battre fort; (*pulse, heart*) battre à grands coups; **~ bing pain** douleur *f* lancinante

**throne** [θroʊn] *n* trône *m*

**throttle** ['θrɑ·t̬l] I. *n* ❶ (*speed pedal*) accélérateur *m* ❷ (*speed*) **at full ~** à plein gaz II. <-ll-> *vt* ❶ (*in engine: engine*) réduire ❷ (*strangle*) étrangler

**through** [θru] I. *prep* ❶ (*across*) à travers; **to go ~ sth** traverser qc; **to look ~ the hole** regarder par le trou ❷ (*spa-*

*tial*) à travers; **to walk/drive ~ a town** traverser une ville (à pied/en voiture); **she came ~ the door** elle est entrée par la porte; **to go ~ customs** passer la douane ⑤ (*temporal*) **~ the week** pendant la semaine; **all ~ my life** toute ma vie ④ (*up until*) jusqu'à; **open Monday ~ Friday** ouvert du lundi au vendredi ⑤ (*divided by*) à travers; **~ the noise** par-dessus le bruit ⑥ (*in two pieces*) **to cut ~ the rope** couper la corde ⑦ (*by means of*) par; **~ the mail** par la poste; **~ hard work** grâce à un dur travail; **I heard about it ~ a friend** j'en ai entendu parler par un ami II. *adv* ① (*to a destination*) à travers; **to let sb/get ~** laisser passer qn/passer ② TEL **to get ~** contacter son correspondant; **I'm putting you ~** je vous passe votre correspondant ③ (*from beginning to end*) d'un bout à l'autre; **halfway ~** en plein milieu ▸ **~ and ~** complètement III. *adj inv* ① (*finished*) terminé(e); **we are ~** c'est fini entre nous; **I'm ~ with the scissors** je n'ai plus besoin des ciseaux ② (*direct*) direct(e) ③ (*from one side to another*) de transit; **~ traffic** circulation *f* dans la ville

**throughout** [θruːˈaʊt] I. *prep* ① (*spatial*) à travers; **~ the town** dans toute la ville ② (*temporal*) **~ his stay** pendant tout son séjour II. *adv* ① (*spatial*) partout ② (*temporal*) tout le temps

**throughway** *n* autoroute *f*

**throw** [θrəʊ] I. *n* ① (*act of throwing*) jet *m;* **a ~ of the dice** un jet de dés ② SPORTS lancer *m;* (*in wrestling, martial arts*) mise *f* à terre ③ (*cover*) jeté *m* de lit/de canapé ④ (*fall from a horse*) chute *f* (de cheval) II. <threw, thrown> *vi* lancer III. <threw, thrown> *vt* ① (*propel*) jeter; (*carefully*) lancer; (*violently*) projeter; (*kiss*) envoyer; (*punch*) donner; **~ your coats on the bed** jetez vos manteaux sur le lit; **to ~ oneself on sb's mercy** *fig* s'abandonner à la merci de qn; **she threw herself at him** *fig* elle s'est pendue à lui; **the difficulties life ~s at us** les difficultés que la vie

met sur notre chemin ② (*cause to fall: horse rider*) faire tomber; (*wrestler*) mettre à terre; **~n from his horse** jeté à terre par son cheval ③ (*dedicate*) **to ~ oneself into sth** se lancer à corps perdu dans qc ④ (*form on a wheel*) tourner; (*pottery*) façonner ⑤ (*turn on: switch*) appuyer sur ⑥ (*have*) **to ~ a tantrum** faire un caprice; **to ~ a fit** piquer une crise de nerfs ⑦ (*give: party*) organiser ⑧ (*confuse*) déconcerter ⑨ (*cast*) **to ~ light on sth** *a. fig* éclairer qc; **to ~ suspicion on sb** *fig* faire peser des soupçons sur qn ⑩ (*put in a particular state*) **to ~ everything into chaos/confusion** tout faire basculer dans le chaos/la confusion; **to ~ a window/door open** ouvrir une fenêtre/une porte d'un grand coup ▸ **to ~ the book at sb** accuser qn de tous les crimes; **to ~ caution to the wind** oublier toute prudence

◆**throw away** *vt* ① (*discard*) jeter ② (*discard temporarily*) se débarrasser de ③ (*waste*) gaspiller ④ (*speak casually*) laisser tomber

◆**throw back** *vt* ① (*return: ball*) renvoyer; (*fish*) remettre à l'eau; (*one's head, veil*) rejeter en arrière ② (*open: curtains*) retirer ③ (*drink quickly*) boire cul sec ④ (*reflect: light*) réfléchir ⑤ (*delay: schedule*) retarder ⑥ (*in retort: words*) relancer à la figure; **she threw his failure back at him** elle lui a renvoyé ses échecs à la figure

◆**throw down** *vt* ① (*throw from above*) jeter ② (*deposit*) déposer ③ (*eat or drink quickly*) ingurgiter ▸ **to ~ the gauntlet** jeter le gant

◆**throw in** *vt* ① (*put into*) jeter dans ② (*include in price*) donner en plus ③ (*add: quotation, remark*) ajouter ④ SPORTS (*ball*) remettre en touche ▸ **to ~ the towel** jeter l'éponge

◆**throw off** *vt* ① (*remove*) enlever; (*coat*) ôter ② (*make loose*) déséquilibrer ③ (*escape*) semer ④ (*rid oneself of*) se débarrasser de; (*idea*) se défaire de; (*cold*) se sortir de; (*bad mood*) quit-

**T**

ter ⑤ (*write quickly*) écrire au pied levé ⑥ (*radiate: energy*) évacuer ► **to ~ one's shackles** jeter ses chaînes

◆ **throw on** *vt* ① (*place on*) ajouter ② (*put on: clothes*) enfiler

◆ **throw out** *vt* ① (*fling outside*) mettre à la porte ② (*get rid of*) jeter ③ (*reject: case, proposal*) rejeter

◆ **throw together** *vt* ① *inf* (*make quickly: ideas, elements*) rassembler; (*meal*) préparer rapidement ② (*cause to meet*) **misfortune had thrown them together** le malheur les a fait se rencontrer

◆ **throw up** I. *vt* ① (*project upward*) jeter en l'air; (*cloud of dust, smoke, lava*) projeter; **to ~ one's hands in despair** lever les bras en l'air de désespoir ② (*vomit*) vomir ③ (*build quickly*) construire à la hâte ④ (*reveal: question, discoveries*) dégager II. *vi inf* vomir

**throwaway** *adj* ① (*disposable*) jetable ② (*spoken as if unimportant*) dit(e) en passant

**throwback** *n pej* retour *m* en arrière; **he's a ~ to the Victorian age** c'est un survivant de l'époque victorienne

**thrown** *pp of* **throw**

**thru** [θru] *inf s.* **through**

**thrush** [θrʌʃ] *n* ZOOL grive *f*

**thrust** [θrʌst] I. <-, -> *vt* ① (*shove*) pousser; **to ~ sth into sth** enfoncer qc dans qc; **to ~ a letter under sb's nose** brandir une lettre sous le nez de qn; **to ~ sb/sth aside** pousser qn/qc sur le côté ② (*impel*) **to ~ sth on sb** imposer qc à qn II. *n* ① (*lunge*) *a. fig* coup *m* ② (*gist*) idée *f* principale; **the main ~ of sth** l'idée directrice de qc ③ TECH poussée *f*

**thruway** ['θru·weɪ] *n inf s.* **throughway**

**thug** [θʌg] *n* casseur *m*

**thumb** [θʌm] I. *n* pouce *m* ► **to be all ~s** être bien maladroit; **to have a green ~** avoir la main verte; **to give the ~s up/down** to sth accepter/rejeter qc; **to twiddle one's ~** se tourner les pouces; **~s up!** *inf* bravo! II. *vt*

① (*press*) appuyer sur ② (*hitchhike*) **to ~ a ride** faire de l'auto-stop ③ (*turn over: book*) feuilleter ► **to ~ one's nose at sb** *inf* faire un pied de nez à qn III. *vi* (*turn over*) **to ~ through sth** feuilleter qc

**thumbnail** ['θʌm·neɪl] *n* ongle *m* du pouce

**thumbnail sketch** *n* (*description*) portrait *m* rapide

**thumbprint** *n* ① (*impression*) empreinte *f* du pouce ② *fig* empreinte *f*

**thumbtack** *n* punaise *f*

**thump** [θʌmp] I. *vt* cogner; (*door*) cogner à; (*table*) taper sur II. *vi* (*heart*) battre très fort III. *n* ① (*blow*) coup *m* de poing ② (*deadened sound*) bruit *m* sourd

**thunder** ['θʌn·dər] I. *n* ① METEO tonnerre *m*; **clap of ~** coup *m* de tonnerre ② (*booming sound*) grondement *m* ③ (*aggressive voice or sound*) rugissement *m* ④ (*criticism*) foudres *fpl* II. *vi* ① (*make loud rumbling noise*) tonner ② (*declaim*) hurler; **to ~ against sth** fulminer contre qc III. *vt* hurler

**thunderbolt** *n fig* coup *m* de tonnerre

**thunderclap** *n* coup *m* de tonnerre

**thundercloud** *n pl* nuage *m* orageux

**thunderhead** *n* METEO sommet *m* de cumulonimbus

**thunderous** ['θʌn·də·r·əs] *adj* (*applause*) frénétique

**thunderstorm** *n* orage *m*

**Thursday** ['θɜrz·deɪ] *n* jeudi *m; s.a.* **Friday**

**thus** [ðʌs] *adv* ainsi; **~ far** jusque-là

**thyme** [taɪm] *n* thym *m*

**tiara** [tɪ·'er·ə] *n* tiare *f*

**Tibet** [tɪ·'bet] *n* le Tibet

**tick**[1] [tɪk] *n* ZOOL tique *f*

**tick**[2] I. *n* (*quick clicking sound*) cliquetis *m* II. *vi* (*make a clicking sound: clock*) faire tic tac; **hours ~ed away** les heures *fpl* se sont écoulées ► **what makes sb ~** ce qui se passe dans la tête de qn

◆ **tick off** *vt inf* (*exasperate*) emmerder

**ticket** ['tɪk·ɪt] *n* ① (*paper, card*) billet *m*;

(*of subway, bus*) ticket *m* ② (*receipt*) ticket *m* ③ (*price tag*) étiquette *f* ④ AU-TO contravention *f* ⑤ POL programme *m* électoral; **to run on a Democratic ~** se présenter sur une liste démocrate

**tickle** ['tɪk·l] I. *vi* chatouiller; (*itchy clothes*) gratter II. *vt* ① (*touch lightly*) *a. fig* chatouiller ② (*amuse*) amuser; **to ~ sb's fancy** amuser qn III. *n* ① (*sensation of tingling*) chatouillement *m* ② (*light touch*) chatouille *f*; **to give sb a ~** chatouiller qn

**ticklish** *adj* ① (*sensitive to tickling*) chatouilleux(-euse) ② (*awkward*) délicat(e)

**tidal** ['taɪ·dəl] *adj* (*system*) des marées

**tidal wave** *n a. fig* raz *m* de marée

**tide** [taɪd] *n* ① (*fall and rise of sea*) marée *f*; **the ~ goes out/comes in** la mer se retire/monte ② (*main trend of opinion*) courant *m* (de pensée); **to go against the ~** aller à contre-courant

**tidy** ['taɪ·di] I. <-ier, -iest> *adj* ① (*in order: room, desk*) bien rangé(e); (*person*) net(te) ② *inf* (*considerable*) coquet(te) II. *vt* (*room*) ranger; **~ up this mess!** fais disparaître ce chantier! III. *vi* ranger; **to ~ up before guests arrive** mettre de l'ordre avant que les invités n'arrivent

**tie** [taɪ] I. *n* ① (*necktie*) cravate *f* ② (*cord*) lien *m* ③ (*relation*) lien *m*; **family ~s** liens familiaux ④ (*equal ranking: after game*) **there was a ~** il y a eu match nul; (*after race*) ils sont arrivés en même temps; **there was a ~ for third place** il y a eu deux troisièmes ex æquo II. <-y-, -d, -d> *vi* ① (*fasten*) faire un nœud ② (*come equal in ranking*) être à égalité; **to ~ with sb/sth** être à égalité avec qn/qc III. <-y-, -d, -d> *vt* ① (*fasten together*) lier; (*hair, horse*) attacher; (*knot*) faire; (*laces, tie*) nouer; **to ~ a ribbon in a bow** nouer un ruban ② (*restrict, limit, link*) **to ~ sb by/to sth** lier qn par/à qc; **to be ~d to a supplier** dépendre d'un fournisseur

◆**tie back** *vt* (*hair*) nouer en arrière

◆**tie down** *vt* ① (*tie*) attacher ② *fig* **to be tied down** être coincé; **to tie sb down to sth** *inf* coincer qn sur qc

◆**tie up** *vt* ① (*bind*) attacher; (*package*) faire ② (*delay*) **to be tied up by sth** être retenu par qc ③ **to be tied up** (*be busy*) être occupé ④ FIN, ECON (*money*) immobiliser; **to be tied up in sth** être placé dans qc ⑤ (*conclude: piece of business, details*) boucler

**tier** [tɪr] *n* (*row*) rang *m*; (*level*) échelon *m*

**tie tack** *n* épingle *f* de cravate

**tiger** ['taɪ·gər] *n* ZOOL tigre *m*

**tight** [taɪt] I. *adj* ① (*firm: knot, trousers*) serré(e); (*grip*) ferme; (*shoes*) étroit(e) ② (*close: formation, groups*) serré(e) ③ (*stretched tautly*) tendu(e); **a ~ blouse** un chemisier serré ④ (*closely integrated: circle*) fermé(e) ⑤ (*difficult: bend*) étroit(e); (*budget*) restreint(e); **money is ~** le budget est juste ⑥ *inf* (*drunk*) bourré(e) ⑦ *inf* (*mean*) radin(e) ▸ **in a ~ corner** dans une situation difficile II. *adv* (*firmly*) fermement; **hold (on) ~** tiens-toi bien ▸ **sleep ~** dors bien

**tighten** I. *vt* ① (*make tighter*) serrer; (*rope*) tendre ② *fig* (*one's control*) renforcer; (*credit*) resserrer; (*security, regulations*) renforcer; **to ~ one's grip on power** s'accrocher au pouvoir ▸ **to ~ one's belt** se serrer la ceinture; **to ~ the screw** serrer la vis II. *vi* se resserrer; (*rope*) se tendre

**tight-fisted** *adj pej, inf* radin(e)

**tightrope** ['taɪt·roʊp] *n* câble *m*; **to walk a ~** faire un numéro d'équilibre

**tights** [taɪts] *npl* ① (*opaque pantyhose*) collant *m* opaque ② (*for dancing*) justaucorps *m*

**tightwad** ['taɪt·wad] *n pej, inf* radin(e) *m(f)*

**tigress** ['taɪ·grɪs] *n* ZOOL *a. fig* tigresse *f*

**tile** [taɪl] I. *n* ① (*for walls, floors*) carreau *m*; **the ~s** le carrelage ② (*roof tile*) tuile *f* II. *vt* carreler

**till**[1] [tɪl] I. *prep* jusqu'à II. *conj* jusqu'à ce que +*subj*

**till**[2] [tɪl] *n* tiroir-caisse *m*

**till**[3] [tɪl] *vt* travailler

**tiller** ['tɪl·ər] *n* NAUT barre *f*

**tilt** [tɪlt] **I.** *n* ❶ (*position*) inclinaison *f* ❷ (*movement of opinion*) inclination *f* **II.** *vt* incliner; **to ~ sth back** pencher qc vers l'arrière ▶ **to ~ the <u>balance</u> in favor of sb/sth** faire pencher la balance en faveur de qn/qc **III.** *vi* s'incliner; *fig* pencher; **to ~ toward sb/sth** s'incliner vers qn/qc; *fig* pencher pour qn/qc; **to ~ back** être penché en arrière

**timber** ['tɪm·bər] *n* ❶ (*trees*) arbres *mpl* ❷ (*lumber*) bois *m* de construction ❸ (*large beam*) poutre *f*

**timberline** ['tɪm·bər·laɪn] *n* limite *f* des arbres

**time** [taɪm] **I.** *n* ❶ (*chronological dimension*) temps *m*; **in the course of ~** avec le temps; **for a short/long period of ~** pour une courte/longue période; **to kill ~** tuer le temps ❷ (*period of time*) temps *m*; **most of the ~** la plupart du temps; **all the ~** tout le temps; **a long ~ ago** il y a longtemps; **it takes a long/short ~** ça prend beaucoup/peu de temps; **for the ~ being** pour le moment; **in no ~** (*at all*) en moins de rien ❸ (*point in time: in schedule, day*) moment *m*; (*on clock*) heure *f*; **what ~ is it?** quelle heure est-il? **arrival/departure ~** heure *f* d'arrivée/de départ; **the best ~ of day** le meilleur moment de la journée; **at all ~s** toujours; **at the ~ I didn't understand** sur le moment je n'ai pas compris; **the right/wrong ~** (*for doing sth*) le bon/mauvais moment (pour faire qc); **at any ~** à n'importe quelle heure; **at the present** [*o* **at this**] ~ à cette heure; **at the same ~** *a. fig* en même temps; **from ~ to ~** de temps en temps; **it's (about)** ~ il est l'heure; **it's about ~, too!** il est grand temps!; **ahead of ~** en avance; **by the ~ she finds them** d'ici à ce qu'elle les trouve; **by the ~ she'd found them** le temps qu'elle les trouve ❹ (*experience*) **my ~ in Alaska** la période de ma vie en Alaska; **my ~ as a teacher** la période où j'ai été enseignant; **to have a good ~** passer un bon moment; **I had a**

**hard ~ finding them** j'ai eu du mal à les trouver; **to give sb a hard ~** *inf* en faire voir à qn (de toutes les couleurs) ❺ (*opportunity, leisure*) temps *m*; **to have ~ for sth/to +*infin*** avoir du temps pour qc/le temps de *+infin*; **he took the ~ to talk to me** il a pris le temps de me parler; **to take ~ out from sth to do sth** prendre du temps sur qc pour qc; **to take one's ~** prendre son temps ❻ (*incident*) fois *f*; **each ~** chaque fois; **for the hundredth ~** pour la centième fois; **to hit the target the first ~** atteindre la cible du premier coup; **~ after ~** à de nombreuses reprises ❼ (*epoch*) temps *m*; **at that ~, I lived in Miami** en ce temps-là, je vivais à Miami; **at the ~ of sth** à l'époque de qc; **in medieval ~s** au Moyen Âge; **in modern ~s** dans les temps modernes; **the old ~s** le bon vieux temps; **to be ahead of one's ~** être en avance sur son temps ❽ *pl* MATH (*when measuring*) **three ~s six** trois fois six; **three ~s faster** trois fois plus vite ❾ SPORTS temps *m* ❿ MUS mesure *f* ⓫ ECON **double ~** double salaire *m* ▶ **to <u>do</u>/<u>serve</u> ~** *inf* faire de la taule; **to have ~ on one's <u>hands</u>** ne pas savoir du temps à perdre **II.** *vt* ❶ (*measure time of: runner*) chronométrer; (*trip*) mesurer la durée de ❷ (*choose best moment for: wedding, meeting, comment*) choisir le meilleur moment pour

**time bomb** *n a. fig* bombe *f* à retardement

**time capsule** *n* capsule *f* témoin

**time-consuming** *adj* long(ue)

**time limit** *n* (*for applications*) date *f* limite; (*for test, visit*) heure *f* limite

**timely** *adj* <-ier, -iest> (*arrival*) à temps; (*remark*) opportun(e)

**time machine** *n* machine *f* à remonter le temps

**time-out** *n* ❶ (*during game*) temps *m* mort ❷ (*break*) pause *f*

**timepiece** *n* montre *f*; (*clock*) horloge *f*

**timer** ['taɪm·ər] *n* minuterie *f*

**time span** *n* durée *f*

**timetable** n (schedule) emploi m du temps; (of transportation) horaire m; (for negotiations) calendrier m

**time zone** n fuseau m horaire

**timid** ['tɪm·ɪd] adj ❶ (easily frightened) farouche ❷ (shy) timide

**timing** ['taɪm·ɪŋ] n ❶ (time control) timing m; **the ~ of the strike/visit** le moment choisi pour la grève/la visite; **he showed bad ~** il a mal choisi son moment ❷ (rhythm) sens m du rythme

**tin** [tɪn] n ❶ (metal) étain m ❷ (tinplate) fer-blanc m ❸ (container) boîte f ❹ (pan for baking) moule m

**tin can** n boîte f de conserve

**tinfoil** n papier m d'aluminium

**tingle** ['tɪŋ·gl] I. vi picoter; (with excitement) avoir des frissons II. n picotement m; (with excitement) frisson m

**tinsel** ['tɪn(t)·səl] n ❶ (decoration) guirlandes fpl ❷ (something showy) clinquant m

**tint** [tɪnt] I. n ❶ (hue) teinte f ❷ (dye) colorant m II. vt teinter; **~ed glass** verre m fumé

**tiny** ['taɪ·ni] adj <-ier, -iest> tout(e) petit(e); **a ~ bit hard** un petit peu dur

**tip¹** [tɪp] I. n (end part: of sth pointed) pointe f; (of sth rounded) bout m ▶ **on the ~ of one's tongue** sur le bout de la langue; **the ~ of the iceberg** la partie visible de l'iceberg II. <-pp-> vt **to be ~ped with sth** avoir un embout de qc

**tip²** [tɪp] I. <-pp-> vt ❶ (cause to tilt) incliner; **to ~ the scales** fig faire pencher la balance ❷ (touch) effleurer II. <-pp-> vi s'incliner; **to ~ to one side** s'incliner sur le côté

◆**tip over** I. vt renverser II. vi se renverser

◆**tip up** I. vt incliner II. vi s'incliner

**tip³** I. n ❶ (money) pourboire m ❷ (hint) tuyau m II. <-pp-> vt (give money) donner un pourboire à

◆**tip off** vt inf donner des tuyaux à; (police) donner des informations à

**tip-off** n inf tuyau m

**tipsy** ['tɪp·si] adj <-ier, -iest> pompette inf

**tiptoe** ['tɪp·toʊ] I. n **on ~(s)** sur la pointe des pieds II. vi marcher sur la pointe des pieds

**tip-top** adj inf excellent(e)

**tire¹** [taɪər] n AUTO pneu m; **front/winter ~** pneu avant/d'hiver; **spare ~** roue f de secours

**tire²** [taɪər] I. vt fatiguer; **to ~ sb out** mettre qn à plat II. vi se fatiguer; **to ~ of sth** se lasser de qc

**tired** adj ❶ (weary) fatigué(e); **to be ~ of sth** en avoir assez de qc; **to get ~ of sth** se lasser de qc; **to be sick and ~ of sth** en avoir par-dessus la tête de qc ❷ (unoriginal: excuse) rebattu(e)

**tiredness** n fatigue f

**tire gauge** n AUTO manomètre m

**tireless** adj infatigable

**tire pressure** n AUTO pression f des pneus

**tiresome** ['taɪər·səm] adj pej pénible

**tiring** ['taɪr·ɪŋ] adj fatigant(e)

**tissue** ['tɪʃ·u] n ❶ (soft paper) papier m de soie ❷ (for wiping noses) mouchoir m en papier ❸ (cells) tissu m ❹ (complex layer) tissu m ▶ **a ~ of lies** un tissu de mensonges

**tit¹** [tɪt] n vulg nichon m

**tit²** n **~ for tat** un prêté pour un rendu

**titanium** [taɪ·ˈteɪ·ni·əm] n titane m

**title** ['taɪ·t̬l] I. n ❶ (name, position, right) titre m; **job ~** intitulé m du poste ❷ pl (credits of a film) générique m II. vt intituler

**title page** n page f de titre

**title role** n rôle-titre m

**TN** n abbr of **Tennessee**

**to** [tu] I. prep ❶ à ❷ (direction, location) **~ France/Alaska** en France/Alaska; **~ Japan/Peru** au Japon/Pérou; **~ Boston/Oslo** à Boston/Oslo; **~ town** en ville; **~ the dentist/my parents'** chez le dentiste/mes parents; **~ the left/right** à gauche/droite; **~ the north/south** au nord/sud; **I go ~ school/church** je vais à l'école/l'église; **close ~ sth** près de qc; **to fasten sth ~ the wall** fixer qc au mur; **come ~ dinner** venez dîner ❸ (before) **a quar-**

**ter** ~ **five** cinq heures moins le quart; **still four days** ~ **Christmas** encore quatre jours avant Noël ④ (*until*) **I count** ~ **10** je compte jusqu'à 10; ~ **date** jusqu'à ce jour ⑤ (*between*) **from 10** ~ **25** de 10 à 25 ⑥ (*with indirect objects*) **I'm talking** ~ **sb** je parle à qn; **it belongs** ~ **me** cela m'appartient; **listen** ~ **your mother** écoute ta mère ⑦ (*toward*) **he is kind/mean** ~ **sb** il est gentil/méchant avec qn ⑧ (*expressing a relation*) **it's important** ~ **me** c'est important pour moi; **what's it** ~ **them?** *inf* qu'est-ce que ça peut leur faire?; **how many euros** ~ **the dollar?** combien d'euros pour un dollar?; **3 goals** ~ **1** 3 buts à 1; **the odds are 3** ~ **1** la cote est à 3 contre 1 ⑨ (*expressing a reaction*) **much** ~ **my surprise** à ma grande surprise; **to sway** ~ **the rhythm** onduler au rythme de la musique; **sb/sth changes** ~ **sth** qn/qc se change en qc ⑩ (*by*) **known** ~ **sb** connu de qn ⑪ (*expressing a connection*) **the top** ~ **this jar** le couvercle de ce bocal; **secretary** ~ **the boss** secrétaire *mf* du patron; **I had the house** ~ **myself** j'ai eu la maison à moi tout seul ▸ **that's all there is** ~ **it** ce n'est pas plus compliqué que ça; **there's nothing** ~ **it** ce n'est pas difficile; *s.a.* **at, from** II. *infinitive particle* ① *not translated* (*infinitive*) **to** ~ **do/walk/put** faire/marcher/mettre ② (*in commands, wishes*) **I told/asked him** ~ **eat** je lui ai dit/demandé de manger; **he wants** ~ **listen/go there** il veut écouter/y aller; **he wants me** ~ **tell him a story** il veut que je lui raconte une histoire ③ (*after interrog. words*) **I know what** ~ **do/where** ~ **go/how** ~ **say it** je sais quoi faire/où aller/comment le dire ④ (*expressing purpose*) ~ **do sth** pour faire qc; **I write books** ~ **make money** j'écris des livres pour gagner de l'argent; **he comes** ~ **see me** il vient me voir ⑤ (*introducing a complement*) **too tired/rich enough** ~ **+**infin* trop fatigué/assez riche pour **+**infin*; **the last** ~

**leave** le dernier à partir ⑥ (*in impersonal statements*) **it is easy** ~ **+**infin* il est facile de **+**infin*; **sth is easy** ~ **do** qc est facile à faire ⑦ (*in ellipsis*) **he doesn't want** ~ **drink, but I want** ~ il ne veut pas boire, mais moi oui; **I shouldn't, but I want** ~ je ne devrais pas, mais je voudrais bien; **it's hard to explain, but I'll try** ~ c'est difficile à expliquer mais je vais essayer III. *adv* ~ **and fro** ça et là; **to go** ~ **and fro** aller et venir

**toad** [toʊd] *n* ① ZOOL crapaud *m* ② *fig* crapule *f*

**toadstool** *n* champignon *m* vénéneux

**toast** [toʊst] I. *n* ① (*bread*) pain *m* grillé; **a piece of** ~ un toast ② (*act of drinking*) toast *m*; **to drink a** ~ **to sb/sth** porter un toast à qn/qc ▸ **to be** ~ *sl* être foutu II. *vt* ① (*cook over heat*) faire griller ② (*warm up: feet*) se chauffer ③ (*drink to health*) porter un toast à

**toaster** *n* grille-pain *m*

**tobacco** [təˈbæk·oʊ] *n* tabac *m*

**to-be** [təˈbi] *adj* futur(e); **bride-**~ future mariée *f*; **mother-**~ future maman *f*

**toboggan** [təˈbɑˈgən] I. *n* luge *f* II. *vi* faire de la luge

**today** [təˈdeɪ] *adv* ① (*present day*) aujourd'hui; **early** ~ ce matin de bonne heure; **a week from** ~ aujourd'hui en huit ② (*nowadays*) de nos jours

**toddler** *n* enfant *m* en âge de marcher

**to-do list** *n* liste *f* de ce qui est à faire

**toe** [toʊ] I. *n* ① (*part of foot*) orteil *m* ② (*part of shoe, sock*) bout *m* ▸ **to keep sb on his/her** ~**s** maintenir qn en alerte II. *vt* **to** ~ **the line** se mettre au pas

**toenail** *n* ongle *m* de pied

**toffee** [ˈtɑ·fi] *n* caramel *m*

**together** [təˈɡed·ər] I. *adv* ensemble; **she's richer than all of us put** ~ elle est plus riche que nous tous réunis; **to bring people closer** ~ *a. fig* rapprocher les gens ▸ **to get it** ~ *inf* être tout à fait prêt II. *adj inf* équilibré(e)

**toilet** [ˈtɔɪ·lət] *n* toilettes *fpl*, cour *f Belgique*; **to flush the** ~ tirer la chasse d'eau

**toilet paper** *n* papier *m* hygiénique
**toiletries** ['tɔɪ·lɪ·triz] *npl* articles *mpl* de toilette
**token** ['toʊ·kən] I. *n* ❶ (*sign*) signe *m* ❷ (*money substitute*) jeton *m* ▸ **by the** <u>**same**</u> ~ pareillement II. *adj* symbolique; **to make a ~ gesture** faire un geste pour la forme; **the ~ man** l'homme *m* de service
**told** [toʊld] *pt, pp of* **tell** ▸ <u>**all**</u> ~ **en** tout
**tolerance** ['tal·ər·ᵊn(t)s] *n a. fig* tolérance *f*
**tolerant** *adj* tolérant(e)
**tolerate** ['tal·ər·eɪt] *vt a. fig* tolérer
**toll**¹ [toʊl] *n* ❶ (*road charge*) péage *m*; **~ truck** ~ péage *m* de transit poids lourds ❷ (*phone charge*) tarification *f* interurbaine ❸ (*damage*) bilan *m* ▸ **to take its ~ on sb** laisser une empreinte sur qn
**toll**² [toʊl] *vt, vi* sonner
**tollbooth** *n* cabine *f* de péage
**toll-free** *adj* (*call*) gratuit(e)
**toll road** <-roads> *n* route *f* à péage
**tomato** [tə·'meɪ·t̬oʊ] <-oes> *n* tomate *f*
**tomato soup** *n* soupe *f* à la tomate
**tomb** [tum] *n* ❶ (*stone memorial*) tombe *f* ❷ (*burial chamber*) tombeau *m*
**tomboy** ['tam·bɔɪ] *n* garçon *m* manqué
**tombstone** ['tum·stoʊn] *n* pierre *f* tombale
**tomcat** ['tam·kæt] *n* matou *m*
**tomorrow** [tə·'mar·oʊ] I. *adv* demain; **see you ~!** à demain! II. *n* demain *m*; **the day after ~** après-demain; **a week from ~** demain en huit
**ton** [tʌn] < (*s*)> *n* tonne *f*; **~s of sth** *inf* des tonnes de qc
**tone** [toʊn] I. *n* ❶ (*sound*) ton *m*; (*of instrument*) timbre *m*; **in a resigned ~ of voice** avec un ton de voix résigné ❷ (*style*) ton *m*; **to lower the ~ of the neighborhood** faire baisser le standing du quartier ❸ (*shade of color*) ton *m* ❹ (*healthy condition*) tonicité *f*; **muscle ~** tonus *m* musculaire ❺ (*telephone noise*) tonalité *f*; **dial ~** tonalité *f* II. *vt* (*firm muscles*) tonifier
♦ **tone down** *vt a. fig* adoucir

**tone-deaf** *adj* **to be ~** ne pas avoir d'oreille
**toner** ['toʊ·nər] *n* ❶ (*cosmetic*) tonique *m* ❷ COMPUT, PHOT toner *m*
**tongs** [tɔŋz] *n* pince *f*; **a pair of ~** une pince
**tongue** [tʌŋ] *n* ❶ (*mouth part*) *a. fig* langue *f*; **to bite one's ~** se mordre la langue; **to stick one's ~ out at sb** tirer la langue à qn ❷ (*tongue-shaped object: of a land*) langue *f*; (*of a shoe*) languette *f* ❸ (*language*) langue *f* ▸ **to be on the** <u>**tip**</u> **of one's ~** être sur le bout de la langue; **to say sth ~ in** <u>**cheek**</u> dire qc ironiquement
**tongue-tied** *adj* muet(te)
**tongue twister** *n* mot *m*/phrase *f* difficile à dire
**tonic**¹ ['ta·nɪk] *n* tonique *m*
**tonic**² ['ta·nɪk], **tonic water** *n* tonique *m*
**tonight** [tə·'naɪt] *adv* ❶ (*evening*) ce soir ❷ (*night*) cette nuit
**tonsillitis** [,tan(t)·sə·'laɪ·t̬ɪs] *n* angine *f*
**tonsils** ['tan(t)·sᵊlz] *npl* MED amygdales *fpl*
**too** [tu] *adv* ❶ (*overly*) trop; **to be ~ good to be true** être trop beau pour être vrai; **~ much water** trop d'eau; **~ many children** trop d'enfants ❷ (*very*) très; **I'm not ~ happy about it** je n'en suis pas vraiment content; **not to be ~ sure** ne pas être très sûr ❸ (*also*) aussi; **me ~!** *inf* moi aussi! ❹ (*moreover*) de plus
**took** [tʊk] *pt of* **take**
**tool** [tul] I. *n* ❶ (*implement*) *a. fig* outil *m* ❷ (*instrument*) instrument *m* ❸ COMPUT outil *m* II. *vt* ciseler III. *vi inf* rouler pépère
**toolbox**, *n* caisse *f* à outils
**tool kit** *n* trousse *f* à outils
**tooth** [tuθ] <teeth> *n* ❶ ANAT dent *f*; **to bare one's teeth** montrer les dents; **to grind/grit one's teeth** grincer/serrer les dents; **to have a ~ out [*o* pulled]** se faire arracher une dent ❷ *pl* (*tooth-like projection*) dent *f*; **~ of a comb/saw** dent de peigne/scie ▸ **to** <u>**sink**</u> **one's**

**T**

**teeth into sth** se mettre à fond dans qc;
**to go through sth with a fine-~(ed)
comb** passer qc au peigne fin
**toothache** *n* mal *m* de dent; **to have
a ~** avoir mal aux dents
**toothbrush** *n* brosse *f* à dents
**toothpaste** *n* dentifrice *m*
**toothpick** *n* cure-dent *m*
**top**¹ [tap] *n s.* **spinning top**
**top**² [tap] **I.** *n* ❶ (*highest part*) haut *m*;
(*of a tree, mountain*) sommet *m*; **from
~ to bottom** de haut en bas; **at the ~
of the picture** en haut de l'image; **at the
~ of my list** au sommet de ma liste
❷ (*upper surface*) dessus *m*; **on ~ of
sth** au-dessus de qc ❸ (*highest rank*)
sommet *m*; **to be at the ~** être au sommet; **to be at the ~ of the class** être
le premier de la classe ❹ (*clothing*)
haut *m* ❺ (*head end*) bout *m* ❻ (*lid*)
couvercle *m*; (*of pen*) capuchon *m*
❼ (*in addition to*) **on ~ of sth** en plus
de qc ▸ **to say sth off the ~ of one's
<u>head</u>** *inf* dire qc au pied levé; **to feel
on ~ of the <u>world</u>** être aux anges; **to
be on ~ of things** bien gérer la situation **II.** *adj* ❶ (*highest, upper*) du haut;
(*floor, layer*) dernier(-ère); **in the ~
right-hand corner** dans l'angle en haut
à droite ❷ (*best, most important: scien-
tists, executives*) de pointe; (*hotels*)
meilleur(e); (*prize*) premier(-ère); (*company*) coté(e); **she wants the ~ job**
elle veut le poste de chef ❸ (*maximum*)
maximal(e); **at ~ speed** à vitesse maximale **III.** <-pp-> *vt* ❶ (*be at the highest
place: list, ratings*) être en tête de
❷ (*place on top of*) couvrir; **a fence
~ped with barbed wire** une clôture
surmontée de barbelés; **to ~ a dessert
with whipped cream** garnir un dessert de crème fouettée ❸ (*surpass: record, performance*) surpasser ❹ (*exceed, be taller*) dépasser
◆**top off** *vt* ❶ CULIN garnir ❷ (*conclude
satisfactorily*) couronner ❸ (*fill up
again*) remplir
**top hat** *n* chapeau *m* haut-de-forme
**top-heavy** *adj pej* mal équilibré(e)

**topic** ['ta·pɪk] *n* sujet *m*
**topical** *adj* d'actualité; **to be highly ~**
être d'une actualité brûlante
**topless I.** *adj* (*person*) aux seins nus;
(*beach*) seins nus **II.** *adv* seins nus; **to
go ~** faire du seins nus
**topography** [tə·'pa·grə·fi] *n* topogra-
phie *f*
**topping** ['ta·pɪŋ] *n* garniture *f*
**topple** ['ta·pl] **I.** *vt* ❶ (*knock over*) faire
tomber ❷ POL renverser **II.** *vi a. fig* basculer
◆**topple over I.** *vt* ❶ (*let fall down*)
faire tomber ❷ (*fall over*) culbuter sur;
**to ~ a cliff** tomber d'une falaise **II.** *vi*
tomber
**top-secret** *adj* top secret(-ète)
**torch** [tɔrtʃ] <-es> **I.** *n* ❶ (*burning stick*)
flambeau *m* ❷ *s.* **blowtorch II.** *vt inf*
mettre le feu à
**tore** [tɔr] *pt of* **tear**
**torn** [tɔrn] *pp of* **tear**
**tornado** [tɔr·'neɪ·doʊ] *n* <-s *o* -es> tornade *f*
**torpedo** [tɔr·'pi·doʊ] MIL, NAUT
**I.** <-es> *n* torpille *f* **II.** *vt* torpiller
**torrential** *adj* torrentiel(le)
**torso** ['tɔr·soʊ] *n* torse *m*
**tortoise** ['tɔr·təs] *n* tortue *f*
**tortoiseshell** *n* écaille *f* de tortue
**torture** ['tɔr·tʃər] **I.** *n a. fig* torture *f* **II.** *vt
a. fig* torturer
**toss** [tas] **I.** *n* ❶ (*throw*) lancer *m*; **to
win/lose the ~** gagner/perdre à pile
ou face ❷ (*movement*) **with a ~ of
his/her head** d'un mouvement de la
tête **II.** *vt* ❶ (*throw*) lancer; (*salad*) mélanger ❷ (*flip in air*) jeter en l'air; **to ~ a
coin** jouer à pile ou face ❸ (*disturb:
boat*) ballotter; (*branches*) agiter **III.** *vi*
(*decide via a coin toss*) **to ~ for sth**
jouer qc à pile ou face ▸ **to ~ and <u>turn</u>**
se remuer dans tous les sens
◆**toss off** *vt* (*letter*) expédier
◆**toss out** *vt* (*trash*) jeter; (*idea, question*) proposer
**toss-up** *n inf* coup *m* à pile ou face; **it's
a ~ between sth and sth** entre qc et
qc, ça revient au même

**total** ['toʊ·t<sup>ə</sup>l] **I.** n total m; **in ~** au total **II.** adj ❶ (complete) total(e) ❷ (absolute) complet(-ète); (stranger) parfait(e) **III.** vt <-l- o -ll-> ❶ (add up) faire la somme de ❷ (add up to) totaliser un montant de ❸ inf (damage, kill: car) démolir; (person) bousiller

**totally** adv totalement

**totem pole** n mât m totémique

**toucan** ['tu·kæn] n toucan m

**touch** [tʌtʃ] **I.** n ❶ (ability to feel, sense) toucher m; **to the ~** au toucher; **I felt a ~ on my hand** j'ai senti qu'on touchait ma main; **with a ~ of the button** à la pression du bouton ❷ (communication) **to lose ~ with sb** perdre qn de vue; **to be/keep in ~ with sb** être/rester en contact avec qn; **to be in/out of ~ with sth** être/ne pas être au courant de qc ❸ (skill) style m; **to lose one's ~** perdre la main; **personal ~** touche f personnelle ❹ (small amount) pointe f; (of garlic) pointe f; **there was a ~ of irony in his voice** il y avait une pointe d'ironie dans sa voix ❺ SPORTS touche f ▸ **to be a soft ~** inf être une bonne poire **II.** vt ❶ (feel with fingers) toucher; **I ~ed him on the arm** j'ai touché son bras; **her feet never ~ed the ground** elle n'a jamais posé un pied à terre ❷ (come in contact with) a. fig toucher à; **they can't ~ the drug barons** ils ne peuvent pas toucher aux barons de la drogue ❸ (eat, drink) toucher; **she won't ~ meat** elle ne mange jamais de viande ❹ (move emotionally) toucher ❺ (rival in quality) égaler; **you can't ~ real coffee** rien ne vaut le vrai café ❻ (concern) toucher ▸ **to ~ base with sb** prendre des nouvelles de qn; **to not ~ sb/sth with a ten-foot pole** ne pas toucher à qn/qc pour tout l'or du monde; **to ~ bottom** toucher le fond **III.** vi ❶ (feel with fingers) toucher ❷ (come in contact) se toucher

◆ **touch down** vi AVIAT atterrir; SPORTS marquer un essai

◆ **touch off** vt a. fig déclencher

◆ **touch on** vt aborder

◆ **touch up** vt (improve) retoucher

**touchdown** n ❶ (landing) atterrissage m ❷ SPORTS essai m

**touching** adj touchant(e)

**touchscreen** n COMPUT écran m tactile

**touch-tone** adj (telephone) à touches

**touchy** ['tʌtʃ·i] <-ier, -iest> adj inf (person) susceptible; (problem, situation) délicat(e)

**tough** [tʌf] **I.** adj ❶ (hard-wearing: material, covering) solide ❷ (hard to eat) dur(e) ❸ (hard to deal with: exam, examiner, game, conditions) dur(e); **a ~ area to grow up in** une zone où il est difficile de grandir; **she had a pretty ~ time** elle a eu un moment difficile ❹ (resilient: soldiers, players, plants) costaud(e) ❺ inf (unfortunate) dur(e); **to be ~ on sb** être dur avec qn **II.** n inf dur(e) m(f) **III.** vt inf **to ~ it out** tenir bon

**toughen** ['tʌf·<sup>ə</sup>n] vt ❶ (make stronger) endurcir; (sanctions, laws) renforcer ❷ (make hard to cut) durcir

**toupee** [tu·'peɪ] n postiche m

**tour** [tʊr] **I.** n ❶ (long trip) voyage m ❷ (short trip) visite f; **guided ~** visite guidée ❸ (trip for performance) tournée f; **to be on ~** être en tournée ❹ (spell of duty) tournée f; **to be/go on ~** faire sa tournée **II.** vt ❶ (visit) visiter ❷ (perform in) **to ~ Canada** être en tournée au Canada **III.** vi ❶ (travel) voyager ❷ (perform) être en tournée

**tourism** ['tʊr·ɪ·zəm] n tourisme m

**tourist** n touriste mf

**tourist trap** n inf piège m à touristes

**tourist visa** n visa m de tourisme

**tournament** ['tɜr·nə·mənt] n tournoi m

**tout** [taʊt] vt (promote) promouvoir; **to ~ sth as sth** présenter qc comme étant qc

**tow** [toʊ] **I.** n remorquage m; **to be in ~** être remorqué **II.** vt remorquer; **to ~ a car away** (for illegal parking) emmener une voiture à la fourrière

**toward(s)** [tɔrd(z)] prep ❶ (in direction of) vers; **moves ~ democracy** fig des

T

changements *mpl* vers la démocratie ❷(*directed at*) envers; **to feel sympathy ~ sb** ressentir de la compassion pour qn ❸(*for*) pour ❹(*around: time, stage*) vers

**towel** [taʊəl] **I.** *n* serviette *f*, drap *m Belgique* **II.** *vt* <-ll-> essuyer

**tower** [taʊər] **I.** *n* tour *f* ▸ **a ~ of strength** un roc **II.** *vi* s'élever
◆**tower above, tower over** *vi* s'élever au-dessus de

**town** [taʊn] *n* ville *f*; **to be in ~** être en ville; **to be out of ~** (*person*) être en déplacement ▸**to have a night on the ~** s'éclater en ville; **to go to ~ on sth** *inf* mettre le paquet pour qc

**town hall** *n* POL mairie *f*, maison *f* communale *Belgique*

**townhouse** *n* ❶(*residence*) maison *f* de ville ❷(*row house*) maison *f* mitoyenne

**townie** *n inf* citadin(e) *m(f)*

**tow truck** *n* remorqueuse *f*

**toxic** ['tɑk·sɪk] *adj* toxique

**toy** [tɔɪ] **I.** *n* jouet *m* **II.** *vt* **to ~ with** ❶(*play with*) *a.* *fig* jouer avec ❷(*consider: idea*) caresser

**trace** [treɪs] **I.** *n* ❶(*sign*) trace *f*; **to disappear without a ~** disparaître sans laisser de traces ❷(*search*) enregistrement *m* ❸(*slight amount: of drugs*) trace *f*; (*of emotion*) signe *m*; **a ~ of a smile** un sourire esquissé **II.** *vt* ❶(*locate*) retrouver; **to ~ sb to somewhere** remonter la piste de qn jusqu'à quelque part ❷(*track back*) rechercher; (*call*) établir l'origine de; **to ~ sth to sth** établir le lien entre qc et qc ❸(*describe*) retracer ❹(*copy*) décalquer ❺(*draw outlines*) tracer

**track** [træk] **I.** *n* ❶(*path*) chemin *m* ❷(*rails*) voie *f* ferrée ❸ *pl* (*mark*) traces *fpl* ❹(*path followed*) *a.* *fig* piste *f*; **on sb's ~** sur la piste de qn ❺(*path taken by sth*) trajectoire *f* ❻(*career path*) voie *f* ❼SPORTS (*for running*) piste *f*; (*horseracing venue*) champ *m* de course; (*car racing venue*) circuit *m* automobile ❽(*on record*) piste *f*; (*song*)

morceau *m* ▸ **to cover one's ~s** brouiller les pistes; **to keep ~ of changes/ the situation** suivre les changements/ la situation; **to lose ~ of sb** perdre qn de vue; **I've lost ~ of my accounts** je ne sais plus où j'en suis dans mes comptes; **to be on the wrong ~** faire fausse route; **to be on the wrong side of the ~s** *inf* être du mauvais côté de la barrière **II.** *vt* ❶(*pursue: animal*) pister; (*fugitive*) traquer ❷(*follow the path: airplane, missile*) suivre la trajectoire de ❸(*trace*) rechercher **III.** *vi* ❶CINE faire un travel(l)ing ❷(*follow a course*) **to ~ across sth** se déplacer à travers qc
◆**track down** *vt* (*relative*) retrouver; (*article*) dénicher

**track and field** *n* SPORTS épreuves *fpl* d'athlétisme

**track meet** *n* SPORTS compétition *f* sportive

**track record** *n* résultats *mpl*; **she has a good ~ in sales** elle a de bons résultats dans les ventes

**traction** ['træk·ʃ°n] *n* traction *f*; **to be in ~** être en extension

**tractor** *n* tracteur *m*

**trade** [treɪd] **I.** *n* ❶(*buying and selling*) commerce *m*; **balance of ~** balance *f* commerciale; **~ is picking up** les affaires *fpl* reprennent ❷(*type of business*) commerce *m*; **fur ~** commerce *m* des peaux ❸(*occupation*) métier *m*; **to be a carpenter by ~** être charpentier de métier ❹(*swap*) échange *m* **II.** *vi* ❶(*do business*) faire du commerce; **to ~ in sth** faire le commerce de qc ❷(*be bought and sold*) s'échanger **III.** *vt* ❶(*swap*) échanger; (*places*) changer de; **to ~ sth for sth** échanger qc contre qc ❷(*buy and sell*) faire le commerce de
◆**trade in** *vt* échanger; **I traded my car in for a Peugeot** j'ai acheté une Peugeot avec reprise de mon ancienne voiture

**trade fair** *n* COM foire *f*

**trademark** *n* ❶(*identification*) marque *f*; **registered ~** marque déposée

**②** *fig* (*feature*) **sth is sb's** ~ qc est la signature de qn

**tradeoff** *n* **①** (*offsetting balance*) marché *m* **②** (*compromise*) compromis *m*

**trade secret** *n* secret *m* de fabrication; *fig* truc *m* de professionnel

**tradesman** <tradesmen> *n* (*small business*) commerçant *m;* (*bigger business*) négociant *m*

**trading** *n* commerce *m;* FIN transactions *fpl*

**tradition** [trə·'dɪʃ·³n] *n* tradition *f*

**traditional** *adj* traditionnel(le)

**traditionalist** I. *n* traditionaliste *mf* II. *adj* traditionaliste

**traffic** ['træf·ɪk] I. *n* **①** (*vehicle movement*) trafic *m;* (*for cars*) circulation *f;* **heavy ~** circulation dense; **to get stuck in ~** être bloqué par la circulation; **passenger/commercial ~** transport *m* des passagers/marchandises **②** *pej* (*trade, dealings*) trafic *m* II. <trafficked, trafficked> *vi pej* (*trade illegally*) **to ~ in sth** faire du trafic de qc

**traffic jam** *n* embouteillage *m*

**tragedy** ['trædʒ·ə·di] *n* **①** (*literary genre*) tragédie *f* **②** <-ies> (*event*) drame *m*

**tragic** ['trædʒ·ɪk] *adj* tragique

**trail** [treɪl] I. *n* **①** (*path*) chemin *m* **②** (*track*) piste *f* **③** (*trace*) traînée *f;* **to leave a ~** laisser une trace; **to leave a ~ of destruction** tout détruire sur son passage II. *vt* **①** (*follow*) suivre **②** (*drag*) traîner; (*car*) remorquer III. *vi* **①** (*be dragged*) traîner **②** SPORTS **to ~ behind sb/sth** être à la traîne derrière qn/qc

◆ **trail away, trail off** *vi* s'estomper

**trailblazing** *adj* innovateur(-trice), d'avant-garde

**trailer** *n* **①** (*wheeled container*) remorque *f* **②** (*for vacationing*) caravane *f* **③** (*advertisement*) bande *f* annonce

**trailer park** *n* village *m* de mobile homes

**train** [treɪn] I. *n* **①** (*railroad*) train *m;* (*in subway*) métro *m;* **to be on a ~** être dans un train **②** (*series*) série *f;* **my ~ of**

**thought** le fil de ma pensée **③** (*procession*) file *f* **④** (*part of dress*) traîne *f* II. *vi* **①** MIL, SPORTS s'entraîner **②** (*for a job*) être formé; **I'm ~ing to be a teacher** je suis une formation pour devenir professeur III. *vt* **①** (*teach*) former; (*animal*) dresser; **to ~ sb to** +*infin* former qn à +*infin* **②** MIL, SPORTS entraîner **③** BOT (*plant*) faire pousser

**train crash** *n* accident *m* ferroviaire

**trained** *adj* **①** (*educated: staff*) formé(e); (*animal*) dressé(e) **②** (*expert*) diplômé(e); (*dancer*) professionnel(le)

**trainee** [treɪ·'ni] *n* (*in office jobs*) stagiaire *mf;* (*in handicraft, mechanics*) apprenti(e) *m(f)*

**trainer** *n* **①** (*sb who trains others*) formateur, -trice *m, f* **②** SPORTS entraîneur, -euse *m, f*

**training** *n* **①** (*education*) formation *f* **②** SPORTS, MIL entraînement *m*

**training camp** *n* **①** SPORTS stage *m* d'entraînement **②** MIL camp *m* d'entraînement

**traitor** *n* traître, -esse *m, f*

**trajectory** [trə·'dʒek·tər·i] *n* trajectoire *f*

**tram** [træm] *n* tramway *m*

**tramp** [træmp] I. *vi* (*walk heavily*) marcher lourdement II. *vt* parcourir à pied III. *n* **①** (*stomping sound*) bruit *m* sourd **②** (*poor person*) clochard(e) *m(f)* **③** *pej* (*promiscuous woman*) traînée *f*

**trample** ['træm·pl] I. *vt* piétiner; **to ~ sth underfoot** fouler qc aux pieds II. *vi* **to ~ on** [*o* **over**] **sth** **①** (*walk on*) piétiner qc **②** (*despise*) bafouer qc

**trampoline** ['træm·pə·lin] *n* trampoline *m*

**tranquil** ['træn·kwɪl] *adj form* **①** (*calm*) tranquille **②** (*serene*) serein(e)

**tranquility** *n form* tranquillité *f*

**tranquilizer** *n* tranquillisant *m;* **to be on ~s** être sous calmants

**transaction** [træn·'zæk·ʃ³n] *n* COM transaction *f*

**transfer** [træn(t)s·'fɜr] I. <-rr-> *vt* **①** (*move, sell*) transférer **②** (*change ownership of: house, property*) céder; (*power*) transmettre **③** (*relocate: em-*

T

*ployee*) muter; (*factory, office*) transférer; (*work*) relocaliser ④ TEL mettre en ligne; **I'm ~ring you now** je vous passe votre correspondant II. *vi* changer; (*when traveling*) faire la correspondance; (*to new job*) être muté; SPORTS (*to new team*) être transféré III. *n* ① (*process of moving*) transfert *m;* **bank ~** virement *m* ② LAW (*of house, property*) cession *f;* FIN (*of a title*) transmission *f;* (*of power*) passation *f* ③ (*to new job*) mutation *f;* SPORTS transfert *m* ④ (*distributing*) transmission *f* ⑤ (*when traveling*) correspondance *f;* (*ticket*) billet *m* avec correspondance ⑥ (*pattern: on skin*) décalcomanie *f;* (*on a t-shirt*) transfert *m*

**transform** [træn(t)sˈfɔrm] *vt* transformer

**transformation** *n* transformation *f*

**transformer** *n* ELEC transformateur *m*

**transfusion** *n* transfusion *f*

**transistor** [trænˈzɪs·tər] *n* transistor *m*

**transit** [ˈtræn(t)·sɪt] *n* transit *m*

**transition** [trænˈzɪʃ·ən] *n* transition *f*

**transitional** *adj* transitoire; (*government*) de transition

**translate** [trænˈsleɪt] I. *vt* ① (*adapt into other language: written*) traduire; (*oral*) interpréter ② (*adapt*) adapter ③ (*decipher to mean*) interpréter II. *vi* se traduire

**translation** *n* traduction *f*

**translator** *n* traducteur, -trice *m, f*

**transmission** [trænˈsmɪʃ·ən] *n* ① (*act of broadcasting*) a. COMPUT transmission *f* ② MED contagion *f;* (*of a disease*) transmission *f* ③ AUTO boîte *f* de vitesses

**transmit** [træˈsmɪt] <-tt-> I. *vt* transmettre II. *vi* émettre

**transmitter** *n* émetteur *m*

**transparency** [trænˈsper·ən(t)·si] *n* ① (*see-through quality*) a. fig transparence *f* ② <-ies> (*slide: for OHP*) transparent *m*

**transparent** *adj* transparent(e)

**transplant** [trænˈsplænt] I. *vt* transplanter II. *n* ① (*act of transplanting*) transplantation *f;* **kidney ~** greffe *f* de

rein ② (*transplanted organ*) organe *m* greffé

**transport**¹ [trænˈspɔrt] *vt* transporter

**transport**² [ˈtræn(t)·spɔrt] *n* ① (*act of conveyance*) transport *m* ② (*vehicle*) moyen *m* de transport

**transportation** *n* ① (*act of transporting*) transport *m;* **public ~** transports *mpl* en commun ② (*means of transport*) moyen *m* de transport

**trap** [træp] I. *n* ① (*device for catching*) piège *m;* **to fall into the ~** tomber dans le piège ② inf (*mouth*) gueule *f* ③ (*curve in a pipe*) siphon *m* II. *vt* <-pp-> ① (*catch in a trap*) prendre au piège ② (*not permit to escape: water, heat*) retenir

**trapdoor** [ˈtræp·dɔr] *n* THEAT trappe *f*

**trapeze** [træpˈiz] *n* trapèze *m;* **~ artist** trapéziste *mf*

**trash** [træʃ] I. *n* ① (*rubbish*) ordures *fpl;* **to take the ~ out** sortir les poubelles ② pej, inf (*worthless people*) racaille *f* ③ pej, inf (*low-quality goods*) pacotille *f;* (*nonsense*) connerie *f* II. *vt* inf ① (*wreck*) saccager ② (*criticize excessively*) dénigrer

**trash can** [ˈtræʃ·kæn] *n* poubelle *f*

**trashy** [ˈtræʃ·i] *adj* pej, inf minable *f*

**trauma** [ˈtrɔ·mə] *n* traumatisme *m*

**traumatic** [trɔˈmæt·ɪk] *adj* traumatisant(e)

**traumatize** [ˈtrɔ·mə·taɪz] *vt* traumatiser

**travel** [ˈtræv·əl] I. *vi* ① (*make a trip*) voyager; **to ~ to Europe** partir en voyage pour l'Europe; **the wine doesn't ~** le vin ne supporte pas le voyage ② (*move: driver, vehicle*) rouler; (*light, sound*) se déplacer II. *vt* parcourir III. *n* ① (*act of traveling*) voyages *mpl;* **a ~ book** un récit de voyage ② *pl* (*trips*) les voyages *mpl;* **have you seen Robert on your ~s?** as-tu vu Robert au cours de tes déplacements?

**travel agency** *n* agence *f* de voyages

**travel agent** *n* agent *mf* de voyages

**traveler** *n* voyageur, -euse *m, f*

**traveler's check** *n* chèque *m* de voyage

**traveling** I. *adj* (*mobile*) ambulant(e)

**II.** *n (as a tourist)* les voyages *mpl*; *(for business)* déplacement *m*
**travel insurance** *n* assurance *f* voyage
**travel sickness** *n* mal *m* des transports
**traverse** ['træv·ərs] *vt* traverser
**tray** [treɪ] *n* ❶ *(for carrying)* plateau *m*, cabaret *m Québec* ❷ *(container for papers)* corbeille *f* ❸ *(drawer)* tiroir *m*
**treacherous** ['tretʃ·ər·əs] *adj* traître
**tread** [tred] **I.**<trod, trodden *o* trod> *vi* marcher; **to ~ carefully** *fig* avancer prudemment **II.** *vt (set one's foot on)* marcher sur; *(path)* parcourir; *(floor, grapes)* fouler; **to ~ sth down** écraser qc **III.** *n* ❶ *(manner of walking)* pas *m* ❷ *(step)* giron *m* ❸ *(part of tire)* chape *f*
**treason** ['tri·zən] *n* trahison *f*
**treasure** ['treʒ·ər] **I.** *n a. fig* trésor *m* **II.** *vt* chérir; *(memory, moment)* chérir; *(gift)* tenir beaucoup à
**treasure hunt** *n* chasse *f* au trésor
**treasurer** *n* trésorier, -ère *m, f*
**treasury** ['treʒ·ər·i] <-ies> *n* ❶ *(place, funds)* trésorerie *f* ❷ *(government department)* **the Treasury** le ministère des Finances
**Treasury Secretary** *n* ministre *m* des Finances
**treat** [trit] **I.** *vt* ❶ *(behave toward)* traiter; **to ~ badly** maltraiter; **they ~ it as a joke** ils le prennent comme une plaisanterie ❷ *(cure, deal with)* traiter; **to be ~ed for shock/depression** être soigné pour choc/dépression ❸ *(pay for)* inviter; **to ~ sb to sth** offrir qc à qn; **to ~ oneself to sth** s'offrir qc **II.** *vi* traiter **III.** *n (indulgence)* plaisir *m*; *(to eat or drink)* gourmandise *f*; **it was a special ~** c'était une gâterie particulière; **it's my ~** c'est moi qui offre
**treatment** *n a. fig* traitement *m*; **the inhuman ~ of refugees** le traitement inhumain des réfugiés; **hospital/laser ~** traitement hospitalier/laser
**treaty** ['tri·ti] <-ies> *n* traité *m*
**treble** ['treb·l] **I.** *adj* soprano *inv* **II.** *n* ❶ MUS soprano *m* ❷ *(sound range)* aigus *mpl*

**treble clef** *n* clé *f* de sol
**tree** [tri] *n* arbre *m*; **sth doesn't grow on ~s** qc ne tombe pas du ciel
**tree line** *n s.* timberline
**trek** [trek] **I.**<-kk-> *vi* faire de la randonnée; **to ~ in to the office** *fig* se traîner au bureau **II.** *n* randonnée *f*; **a ~ into town** *fig* une expédition en ville
**tremble** ['trem·bl] *vi* trembler; **to ~ with sth** trembler de qc
**tremendous** [trɪ·'men·dəs] *adj* ❶ *(enormous)* énorme ❷ *inf (extremely good)* génial(e)
**tremor** ['trem·ər] *n* tremblement *m*
**trench coat** *n* trench-coat *m*
**trend** [trend] *n* ❶ *(tendency)* tendance *f*; **there's a ~ toward/away from sth** il y a une tendance vers/contre qc ❷ *(popular style)* mode *f*; **to set a new ~** lancer une nouvelle mode
**trendsetter** ['trend·ˌset·ər] *n* lanceur, -euse *m, f* de mode
**trendy** ['tren·di] **I.**<-ier, -iest> *adj* à la mode **II.**<-ies> *n* branché(e) *m(f)*
**trespass** ['tres·pəs] <-es> **I.** *n* violation *f* de propriété *f* **II.** *vi* **to ~ on sb's land** s'introduire sans autorisation sur les terres de qn
**trespasser** *n* intrus(e) *m(f)*; **~s will be prosecuted** défense *f* d'entrer sous peine de poursuites
**trial** [traɪəl] *n* ❶ *(judicial process)* procès *m*; **to go on ~** passer en jugement; **to put sb on ~** faire passer qn devant les tribunaux; **to get a fair ~** *fig* avoir un procès équitable; **~ by media** procès médiatique ❷ *(experimental test)* essai *m*; **by ~ and error** par expériences successives ❸ *(source of problems)* épreuve *f*; **~s and tribulations** tribulations *fpl* ❹ *(competition)* épreuve *f*
**trial run** *n* essai *m*
**triangle** ['traɪ·æŋ·gl] *n* MATH, MUS triangle *m*
**triangular** [traɪ·'æŋ·gjə·lər] *adj* triangulaire
**tribal** ['traɪ·bəl] *adj* tribal(e)
**tribe** [traɪb] *n a. pej* tribu *f*
**tribunal** [traɪ·'bju·nəl] *n* tribunal *m*

T

**tributary** ['trɪb·jə·ter·i] <-ies> n GEO affluent m

**tribute** ['trɪb·jut] n ❶ (*token of respect*) hommage m; **to pay ~ to sb/sth** rendre hommage à qn/qc ❷ (*money, goods paid*) tribut m

**trick** [trɪk] I. n ❶ (*ruse, joke*) tour m; **magic ~** tour m de magie; **to play a ~ on sb** jouer un tour à qn; **a dirty ~** pej un sale tour; **~ of the light** illusion f d'optique ❷ (*technique for doing sth*) truc m; **that will do the ~** ça fera l'affaire; **the ~s of the trade** les ficelles fpl du métier; **to use every ~ in the book** ne reculer devant rien ❸ (*round of cards played*) pli m II. adj (*question*) piège III. vt ❶ (*deceive*) duper; **to ~ sb into doing sth** ruser pour amener qn à faire qc ❷ (*swindle*) rouler

**trickle** ['trɪk·l] I. vi ❶ (*flow slowly*) couler lentement ❷ (*come in small amounts*) **to ~ in/out** (*people*) entrer/sortir petit à petit; **information ~d through** l'information a filtré II. vt faire couler goutte à goutte III. n (*slow flow*) filet m; **a ~ of information/requests** fig une petite quantité d'informations/de demandes

**tricky** ['trɪk·i] <-ier, -iest> adj ❶ (*awkward: question, problem*) compliqué(e); (*task*) difficile ❷ pej (*deceitful*) malin(-igne)

**tricycle** ['traɪ·sɪ·kl] n tricycle m

**trifle** ['traɪ·fl] n ❶ (*insignificant thing*) broutille f ❷ (*small amount*) bagatelle f

**trigger** ['trɪg·ər] I. n ❶ (*gun part*) gâchette f; **to pull the ~** appuyer sur la gâchette ❷ (*precipitating incident*) **to be a ~ for sth** être le déclencheur de qc II. vt **to ~ sth (off)** [o **to ~ (off) sth**] déclencher qc

**trike** [traɪk] n inf abbr of **tricycle** tricycle m

**trillion** ['trɪl·jən] n ❶ (1,000,000,000,000) billion m ❷ (*any very large number*) **~s of sth** des millions mpl de qc

**trilogy** ['trɪl·ə·dʒi] <-ies> n trilogie f

**trim** [trɪm] I. n ❶ (*cut: at salon*) coupe f d'entretien; (*for hedge*) taille f ❷ (*decorative edge*) garniture f ❸ (*on car: inside*) revêtement m; (*outside*) finitions fpl II. adj ❶ (*neat*) soigné(e); (*lawn*) net(te) ❷ (*attractively thin*) mince III. <-mm-> vt ❶ (*cut*) tailler; **to ~ one's beard** se tailler la barbe; **my hair needs ~ming** mes cheveux ont besoin d'une coupe d'entretien ❷ (*decorate*) orner; (*tree*) décorer ❸ (*reduce*) réduire

♦ **trim away** vt élaguer

♦ **trim down** vt réduire

♦ **trim off** vt tailler aux ciseaux; **we managed to trim $50 off the cost** fig on a réussi à faire baisser le coût de 50 dollars

**trio** ['tri·oʊ] n a. MUS trio m

**trip** [trɪp] I. n ❶ (*journey*) voyage m; **business ~** voyage d'affaires; **round ~** aller-retour m; (*shorter*) excursion f; **to go on a ~** faire une excursion ❸ inf (*hallucination*) trip m II. <-pp-> vi ❶ (*stumble*) trébucher ❷ (*be on drug*) faire un trip ▸ **to ~ off the tongue** (*name*) se dire aisément; (*cliché*) couler aisément III. <-pp-> vt (*activate*) déclencher

♦ **trip over** vi trébucher; **to ~ sth** trébucher sur qc

♦ **trip up** I. vt ❶ (*cause to stumble*) faire trébucher ❷ (*cause to fail*) jouer un mauvais tour à qn II. vi ❶ (*fall*) trébucher ❷ (*make a mistake*) **to ~ on sth** buter sur qc

**triple** ['trɪp·l] I. adj triple II. adv trois fois III. vt, vi tripler

**triplet** ['trɪp·lət] n triplé(e) m(f)

**tripod** ['traɪ·pɑd] n tripode m

**triumph** ['traɪ·ʌm(p)f] I. n (*great success*) triomphe m; **to return in ~** faire un retour triomphal II. vi **to ~ over sb/sth** triompher de qn/qc

**triumphant** adj triomphant(e); (*success*) retentissant(e)

**trivia** ['trɪv·i·ə] npl futilités fpl

**trivial** adj ❶ (*unimportant*) insignifiant(e) ❷ (*petty*) banal(e) ❸ (*easy*) simple

**trod** [trad] *pt, pp of* **tread**

**trodden** ['trad·ᵊn] *pp of* **tread**

**trolley** ['tra·li] *n* tramway *m*

**trombone** [tram·'boʊn] *n* trombone *m*

**troop** [trup] **I.** *n* troupe *f* **II.** *vi* (*move in large numbers*) **to ~ down the road** descendre la rue en groupe

**trophy** ['troʊ·fi] *<-ies>* *n* trophée *m*

**tropic** ['tra·pɪk] *n* tropique *m;* **~ of Can-cer** Tropique du Cancer

**tropical** *adj* tropical(e)

**trot** [trat] **I.** *n* ❶ (*horse's gait*) trot *m* ❷ *pl, inf* (*diarrhea*) courante *f* **II.** <-tt-> *vi* ❶ (*move at a trot*) trotter; (*horse*) aller au trot ❷ (*go busily*) filer ❸ *fig* **to ~ through a speech** débiter un discours

♦ **trot off** *vi* s'éloigner (au trot)

♦ **trot out** *vt* (*examples, excuses*) ressortir

**trouble** ['trʌb·l] **I.** *n* ❶ (*difficulty*) ennui *m;* **without too much ~** sans grosse difficulté; **to have ~ doing sth** avoir du mal à faire qc; **to be in ~** avoir des ennuis; **the ~ with sb/sth is that ...** l'ennui avec qn/qc, c'est que ...; **to cause sb ~** causer des ennuis à qn; **to be no ~ at all** ne poser aucun problème; **to take the ~ to +*infin*** se donner la peine de +*infin* ❷ (*problem*) problèmes *mpl;* **to tell sb one's ~s** confier ses problèmes à qn ❸ (*malfunction*) ennuis *mpl;* **knee ~** problème *m* de genou; **to have back ~** avoir mal au dos; **stomach ~** troubles *mpl* digestifs; **car ~** problèmes *mpl* de voiture ❹ (*conflicts, arguments*) troubles *mpl;* **at the first sign of ~** aux premiers signes de troubles; **to look for ~** chercher les ennuis; **to stay out of ~** éviter les ennuis **II.** *vt* ❶ *form* (*cause inconvenience*) déranger; **can I ~ you to stand up?** puis-je vous demander de vous lever? ❷ (*cause worry to*) inquiéter ❸ (*cause problems to*) ennuyer; **my back's troubling me** j'ai des problèmes de dos **III.** *vi* (*make an effort*) se déranger; **to ~ to +*infin*** se donner la peine de +*infin*

**troubled** *adj* ❶ (*suffering troubles: marriage, relationship*) orageux(-euse); (*situation, times*) agité(e) ❷ (*feeling worried*) inquiet(-ète)

**troublemaker** *n* fauteur, -trice *m, f* de troubles

**troubleshooter** *n* médiateur, -trice *m, f*

**troublesome** *adj* ❶ (*difficult*) pénible ❷ (*embarrassing*) gênant(e)

**trough** [trɔf] *n* ❶ (*receptacle*) auge *f;* **drinking ~** abreuvoir *m* ❷ (*low point between two crests*) creux *m* ❸ (*low pressure area*) dépression *f*

**troupe** [trup] *n* THEAT troupe *f*

**trousers** ['traʊ·zərz] *npl* (**pair of**) **~** pantalon *m*

**trout** [traʊt] *n* <-(s)> truite *f*

**truant** ['tru·ənt] *n* élève *mf* absentéiste

**truce** [trus] *n* trêve *f*

**truck** [trʌk] **I.** *n* camion *m;* (*long-distance*) poids *m* lourd **II.** *vt* acheminer par camion

**truck driver, trucker** *n* camionneur *m;* (*long-distance*) routier *m*

**true** [tru] **I.** *adj* ❶ (*not false*) vrai(e); **to ring ~** sonner vrai; **to be ~ of sb/sth** être vrai pour qn/qc; **to turn out to be ~** se révéler vrai; **to hold ~ for sb/sth** être de même pour qn/qc ❷ (*genuine*) véritable; **to come ~** se réaliser; **a ~ artist** un véritable artiste; **to discover sb's ~ colors** découvrir le véritable visage de qn; **in the ~ sense of a word** dans le vrai sens du terme ❸ (*faithful*) fidèle; **to be/remain ~ to sb/sth** être/rester fidèle à qn/qc; **to form, be ~ ...** fidèle à lui même, ... ❹ (*positioned accurately*) exact(e) **II.** *adv* droit **III.** *n* **to be out of ~** ne pas être d'aplomb

**truffle** ['trʌf·l] *n* truffe *f*

**truly** ['tru·li] *adv* ❶ (*accurately*) vraiment ❷ (*genuinely*) véritablement ❸ (*sincerely*) sincèrement; **yours ~** avec toutes mes salutations; **yours ~ had to pay** *inf* c'est moi qui ai dû payer

**trump** [trʌmp] **I.** *n* **~(s)** atout *m;* **to play a ~/~s** jouer un atout/l'atout **II.** *vt* **to ~ sb/sth** couper qn/qc avec l'atout; *fig* l'emporter sur qn/qc

T

**trumpet** ['trʌm·pət] I. *n* trompette *f* ► **to blow one's own ~** se lancer des fleurs II. *vi* (*elephants*) barrir III. *vt pej* claironner

**trumpeter** *n* trompettiste *mf*

**trunk** [trʌŋk] *n* ❶(*stem, part of body*) tronc *m* ❷(*elephant's nose*) trompe *f* ❸(*large strong case*) malle *f* ❹(*in car*) coffre *m*

**trust** [trʌst] I. *n* ❶(*belief in reliability*) confiance *f;* **to place one's ~ in sb/sth** faire confiance à qn/qc ❷(*responsibility*) charge *f;* **to have sth in ~** avoir la charge de qc; **position of ~** poste *m* à responsabilité ❸(*organization*) fondation *f* ❹ ECON trust *m* II. *vt* ❶(*place trust in*) faire confiance à; **to ~ sb to** +*infin* faire confiance à qn pour +*infin* ❷(*place reliance on*) se fier à; **to ~ sb to, to ~ sb with sth** confier qc à qn; **~ them to win/get lost** *iron* évidemment, ils allaient gagner/se perdre ❸(*hope*) **to ~ that …** espérer que … III. *vi* **to ~ in sb/sth** se fier à qn/qc; **to ~ to luck** s'en remettre à la chance

**trusted** *adj* de confiance

**trust fund** *n* fonds *m* en fidéicommis

**trusting** *adj* confiant(e)

**trustworthy** ['trʌst·ˌwɜr·ði] *adj* (*person*) digne de confiance; (*data, information*) fiable

**trusty** <-ier, -iest> *adj* fidèle

**truth** [truθ] *n* vérité *f;* **the ~ about sb/sth** la vérité sur qn/qc; **in ~** en vérité; **to tell you the ~** pour ne rien te/vous cacher; **there is no ~ in these accusations** il n'y a rien de vrai dans ces accusations

**truthful** *adj* sincère

**truthfully** *adv* sincèrement

**try** [traɪ] I. *n a.* SPORTS essai *m;* **to have a ~ at sth, to give sth a ~** essayer qc II. <-ie-> *vi* ❶(*attempt*) essayer; **to ~ and** +*infin inf* essayer de +*infin;* **to ~ for sth** essayer d'obtenir qc ❷(*make an effort*) faire un effort III. <-ie-> *vt* ❶(*attempt to do sth*) essayer; **to ~** +*infin* essayer de +*infin;* **to ~ doing sth** faire qc pour voir; **to ~ one's luck**

tenter sa chance; **I tried my best** j'ai fait de mon mieux ❷(*test*) essayer; **~ this sauce** goûte cette sauce; **~ the supermarket** va voir au supermarché ❸(*judge*) juger ❹(*cause annoyance*) mettre à l'épreuve ❺(*put on trial*) juger

◆**try on** *vt* (*clothes*) essayer; **to try sth on for size** essayer qc pour voir si c'est la bonne taille

◆**try out** I. *vt* (*computer, idea, person*) essayer II. *vi* SPORTS **to ~ for a team** se présenter à une équipe

**trying** *adj* pénible

**tryout** *n* essai *m*

**tsetse fly** ['tset·si·ˌflaɪ] *n* mouche *f* tsé-tsé

**T-shirt** ['ti·ʃɜrt] *n* t-shirt *m*

**tub** [tʌb] *n* ❶(*container: large*) bac *m;* (*small*) pot *m* ❷(*bathtub*) baignoire *f*

**tubby** ['tʌb·i] <-ier, -iest> *adj inf* rondelet(te)

**tube** [tub] *n* ❶(*cylinder*) tube *m;* (*bigger diameter*) tuyau *m* ❷(*container*) tube *m* ❸(*bodily structure*) tube *m;* **bronchial ~s** bronches *fpl;* **to have one's ~s tied** se faire ligaturer les trompes ❹ *inf* (*television*) **the ~** la télé ► **to go down the ~(s)** *inf* se casser la gueule

**tuberculosis** [tu·ˌbɜr·kjəˈloʊ·sɪs] *n* tuberculose *f*

**tuck** [tʌk] I. *n* ❶(*narrow fold*) pli *m* ❷ *inf* (*surgery: to reduce fat*) liposuccion *f;* (*to reduce flesh*) couture *f;* **to have a tummy ~** *inf* se faire liposucer le ventre II. *vt* ranger; **to be ~ed away** être mis de côté; **to ~ sth in** rentrer qc; **to ~ sth into sth** rentrer qc dans qc

◆**tuck in** I. *vt* (*sheet, child*) border II. *vi inf* (*eat*) bouffer

◆**tuck up** *vt* border

**Tuesday** ['tuz·deɪ] *n* mardi *m;* **Shrove ~** mardi gras; *s.a.* **Friday**

**tuft** [tʌft] *n* touffe *f*

**tug** [tʌg] I. *n* ❶(*pull*) petit coup *m;* **to feel a ~ at one's sleeve** sentir que quelqu'un vous tire par la manche ❷(*boat*) remorqueur *m* II. <-gg-> *vt* tirer sur III. <-gg-> *vi* **to ~ at sth** tirer qc

**tuition** [tuˈɪʃ.ən] *n* ➊ (*school/college fee*) frais *mpl* de scolarité ➋ *form* (*teaching*) enseignement *m;* **private ~** cours *mpl* privés

**tulip** [ˈtuː.lɪp] *n* tulipe *f*

**tumble** [ˈtʌm.bl] I. *n a. fig* chute *f* II. *vi* ➊ (*fall*) tomber (par terre) ➋ (*move*) **the ball ~d down the path** le ballon a roulé le long de l'allée ➌ (*decrease: price*) chuter

  ◆ **tumble down** *vi* s'écrouler; **the rain came tumbling down** un déluge de pluie est tombé

**tumbledown** *adj* en ruine

**tumbler** [ˈtʌm.blər] *n* gobelet *m*

**tummy** [ˈtʌm.i] <-ies> *n childspeak, inf* ventre *m*

**tumor** [ˈtuː.mər] *n* tumeur *f;* **brain ~** tumeur au cerveau

**tuna** [ˈtuː.nə] *n* thon *m*

**tune** [tuːn] I. *n* ➊ (*melody*) air *m* ➋ (*pitch*) accord *m;* **to be in ~** être accordé; **to be out of ~** être désaccordé ▸ **to change one's ~** changer de ton; **to be in/out of ~ with sth** être en accord/désaccord avec qc II. *vt* ➊ MUS accorder ➋ TECH régler; **to be ~d to the local news** être branché sur la chaîne d'informations locales

  ◆ **tune in, tune into** *vt* ➊ RADIO, TV **to ~ to sth** se brancher sur qc; **~ again next week** à la semaine prochaine sur la même longueur d'ondes ➋ *fig, inf* se brancher sur

  ◆ **tune up** I. *vi* MUS s'accorder II. *vt* ➊ AUTO, TECH mettre au point; (*engine*) régler ➋ MUS accorder

**tuner** *n* ➊ (*radio*) tuner *m* ➋ MUS accordeur, -euse *m, f*

**Tunisia** [tuˈniː.ʒə] *n* la Tunisie

**Tunisian** I. *adj* tunisien(ne) II. *n* Tunisien(ne) *m(f)*

**tunnel** [ˈtʌn.əl] I. *n* ➊ (*passage*) tunnel *m* ➋ ZOOL, BIO galerie *f* ▸ **the light at the end of the ~** la lumière au bout du tunnel II. *vi* **to ~ through/under**

sth creuser un tunnel dans/sous qc III. *vt* creuser un tunnel dans; **to ~ one's way out of a prison** s'évader de prison en creusant un tunnel

**turbocharged** *adj* turbo *inv*

**turbulence** [ˈtɜr.bjə.lən(t)s] *n a. fig* turbulence *f*

**turbulent** *adj* turbulent(e)

**turf** [tɜrf] I. *n* ➊ (*grassy earth*) gazon *m* ➋ SPORTS (*ground*) terrain *m* ➌ (*territory*) territoire *m* II. *vt* BOT gazonner

**Turk** [tɜrk] *n* (*person*) Turc, Turque *m, f*

**turkey** [ˈtɜr.ki] *n* ➊ ZOOL, CULIN dinde *f* ➋ *pej, inf* (*failure*) bide *m* ➌ *inf* (*silly person*) con(ne) *m(f)*

**Turkey** [ˈtɜr.ki] *n* la Turquie

**Turkish** [ˈtɜr.kɪʃ] I. *adj* turc(que) II. *n* turc *m; s.a.* **English**

**turn** [tɜrn] I. *n* ➊ (*change of direction: road*) tournant *m;* **to take a ~** tourner; **a left/right ~** un tournant à gauche/à droite ➋ (*rotation*) tour *m* ➌ (*walk*) tour *m* ➍ (*changing point*) tournant *m;* **a ~ of fate** un caprice du destin ➎ (*changing condition*) tournure *f;* **to take a ~ for the worse** s'aggraver; **to take a ~ for the better** s'améliorer ➏ (*allotted time*) tour *m;* **to be sb's ~ to** +*infin* être le tour de qn de +*infin;* **to take ~s doing sth** faire qc à tour de rôle; **to wait one's ~** attendre son tour; **in ~** à tour de rôle; **to speak out of ~** parler mal à propos ➐ (*shape*) tournure *f* ➑ (*service*) tour *m* ➒ MED crise *f* ➓ (*stage performance*) numéro *m* ▸ **at every ~** à tout bout de champ II. *vi* ➊ (*rotate*) tourner ➋ (*turn around*) se retourner; AUTO faire demi-tour; **to ~ to(ward) sb/sth** se tourner vers qn/qc ➌ (*switch direction*) tourner; (*tide*) changer; **to ~ left** tourner à gauche; **to ~ around the corner** tourner au coin de la rue; **my mind ~ed to food** *fig* je me suis mis à penser au repas; **talk ~ed to politics** la conversation est passée à la politique; **to ~ to religion/drugs** se tourner vers la religion/la drogue; **who can I ~ to?** vers qui puis-je me tourner? ➍ (*become*) devenir; **to ~ cold** com-

T

mencer à faire froid; **to ~ green** verdir; **to ~ seven** ❹ (*child*) venir d'avoir sept ans ❺ BOT, BIO (*leaves*) jaunir **III.** *vt* ❶ (*rotate: page, handle*) tourner; **to ~ somersaults** faire des sauts périlleux ❷ (*cause to rotate*) faire tourner ❸ (*turn round*) retourner; **to ~ sth upside down** retourner qc ❹ (*switch direction*) tourner; **to ~ the corner** tourner au coin de la rue; *fig* passer le cap ❺ (*direct*) *a. fig* diriger; **to ~ one's anger on sb** reporter sa colère sur qn ❻ (*transform*) **to ~ sb/sth into sth** transformer qn/qc en qc; **to ~ water blue** donner à l'eau une couleur bleue ❼ (*sprain*) tordre; **to ~ one's ankle** se fouler la cheville ❽ (*feel nauseated*) **to ~ one's stomach** soulever le cœur ❾ (*shape*) tourner ▸**to ~ one's back on sb** tourner le dos à qn; **to ~ the other cheek** tendre l'autre joue; **to ~ a blind eye to sth** fermer les yeux sur qc; **to ~ sb's head** faire tourner la tête à qn; **to ~ the tables** inverser les rôles; **to ~ sth upside down** mettre qc sens dessus dessous

◆**turn against** *vt* se retourner contre

◆**turn around I.** *vt* ❶ (*twist*) retourner ❷ (*turn back: ship, plane*) faire faire demi-tour à ❸ (*reverse: situation*) renverser ❹ (*improve: business*) remettre sur pied **II.** *vi* ❶ (*twist*) tourner; (*person*) se retourner; **you can't just ~ and cancel the wedding** tu/vous ne peux/pouvez pas changer d'avis comme ça et annuler le mariage ❷ (*turn back: ship, plane*) faire demi-tour ❸ (*reverse*) se renverser ❹ (*improve*) se remettre sur pied

◆**turn away I.** *vi* se détourner **II.** *vt* ❶ (*to face the opposite way*) détourner ❷ (*refuse entry*) refuser

◆**turn back I.** *vi* ❶ (*return*) faire demi-tour ❷ (*change plans*) tourner bride; **you can't ~ now** tu/vous ne peux/pouvez pas faire marche arrière maintenant **II.** *vt* ❶ (*send back*) renvoyer ❷ (*fold*) replier ▸**to ~ the clock** revenir en arrière

◆**turn down** *vt* ❶ (*reject*) refuser ❷ (*reduce*) baisser ❸ (*fold*) rabattre

◆**turn in I.** *vt* ❶ (*submit: assignment*) remettre; **to ~ a superb performance** produire une performance exceptionnelle ❷ *inf* (*hand to the police*) livrer ❸ (*give up*) remettre; (*weapons*) rendre **II.** *vi inf* aller se pieuter

◆**turn into I.** *vi* (*change*) se transformer en; **it turned into a fiasco** ça s'est transformé en fiasco **II.** *vt* **to turn sb/ sth into sth** (*by magic, work*) transformer qn/qc en qc

◆**turn off I.** *vt* ❶ ELEC, TECH (*electric device*) éteindre; (*car engine*) arrêter ❷ (*stop the flow: gas, water, tap*) fermer ❸ (*leave your path: road*) quitter ❹ *inf* (*sexually unappealing*) rebuter **II.** *vi* (*leave your path*) **to ~ at sth** tourner à qc ❷ (*no longer pay attention*) décrocher

◆**turn on I.** *vt* ❶ ELEC, TECH (*electric device*) allumer ❷ (*start the flow: gas, tap, water*) ouvrir ❸ *inf* (*excite sexually*) exciter ❹ *inf* (*attract*) brancher ❺ (*attack*) s'attaquer à ❻ (*be dependent on*) reposer sur **II.** *vi* s'allumer

◆**turn out I.** *vi* ❶ (*end up*) finir; **it'll ~ all right** ça va bien se passer; **as things turned out, I was right** en l'occurrence, j'avais raison ❷ (*prove to be*) se révéler; **she turned out to be a great dancer** elle s'est révélée être une grande danseuse; **she turned out to be my aunt** il s'est avéré qu'elle était ma tante ❸ (*go to*) **to ~ for sth** se rendre à qc; **to ~ to vote** se rendre aux urnes **II.** *vt* ❶ (*switch off: electric device*) éteindre ❷ (*stop the flow: gas*) fermer ❸ (*empty: pockets*) vider ❹ (*produce: product*) produire; (*graduates, linguists*) former

◆**turn over I.** *vi* ❶ (*face different direction*) se retourner ❷ (*turn page*) tourner la page ❸ (*start: engine*) tourner **II.** *vt* ❶ (*change the side*) *a. fig* retourner; (*page*) tourner ❷ (*cause to operate: car engine*) faire tourner ❸ (*give in*) remettre ❹ (*hand over:*

*control*) remettre ⑤ (*consider: idea*) réfléchir à; **I've been turning things over** j'ai bien réfléchi ⑥ (*be lucrative: business*) rapporter ⑦ (*cheat*) rouler ⑧ (*change function*) **to turn sth over to sth** transformer qc en qc ▸ **to ~ a new leaf** tourner la page

♦ **turn up** I. *vi* ① (*arrive*) arriver; **when the job turned up, I took it** quand le job s'est présenté, je l'ai pris ② (*be found*) resurgir ③ (*face upward*) pointer vers le haut II. *vt* ① (*increase: volume, gas*) augmenter; (*radio*) mettre plus fort ② (*shorten clothing*) relever ③ (*reveal*) révéler ④ (*find*) trouver

**turnaround** *n* ① (*sudden change*) volte-face *f inv*; (*for business, economy*) redressement *m* ② (*waiting time*) rotation *f*

**turning point** *n* tournant *m*

**turnip** ['tɜr·nɪp] *n* navet *m*

**turnoff** *n* ① (*in road*) embranchement *m* ② *inf* (*sexually unappealing*) **to be a real ~** être vraiment repoussant

**turn-on** *n inf* (*sexually appealing*) **to be a real ~** être excitant

**turnout** *n* ① (*amount of people*) assistance *f* ② (*amount of people who vote*) nombre *m* de votants

**turnover** *n* ① (*rate of employee renewal*) rotation *f* du personnel ② (*total earnings*) chiffre *m* d'affaires ③ (*rate of stock renewal*) écoulement *m* des marchandises ④ CULIN chausson *m*, gosette *f* Belgique

**turnstile** ['tɜrn·staɪl] *n* SPORTS tourniquet *m*

**turntable** ['tɜrn·teɪbl] *n* (*for records*) platine *f*

**turquoise** ['tɜr·kwɔɪz] I. *n* ① (*stone*) turquoise *f* ② (*color*) turquoise *m* II. *adj* ① (*made of this stone*) en turquoise(s) ② (*colored*) turquoise *inv*

**turret** ['tɜr·ɪt] *n* tourelle *f*

**turtle** ['tɜr·tl] <-(s)> *n* tortue *f*

**turtleneck** *n* col *m* roulé

**tusk** [tʌsk] *n* ZOOL défense *f*

**tutor** ['tu·tər] I. *n* ① (*person helping students*) directeur, -trice *m, f* d'études

② (*private teacher*) professeur *m* particulier ③ (*assistant lecturer*) assistant(e) *m(f)* II. *vt* donner des cours à III. *vi* donner des cours

**tutorial** [tu·'tɔr·i·əl] *n* SCHOOL, UNIV travaux *mpl* dirigés

**TV** [ˌti·'vi] *n* TV, ELEC *abbr of* **television** télé *f*

**TV guide** *n* programme *m* télé

**tweezers** ['twi·zərz] *npl* pince *f* à épiler; **a pair of ~** une pince à épiler

**twelfth** [twelfθ] *adj* douzième; *s.a.* **eighth**

**twelve** [twelv] *adj* douze *inv*; *s.a.* **eight**

**twentieth** ['twen·ti·əθ] *adj* vingtième; *s.a.* **eighth**

**twenty** ['twen·ti] *adj* vingt *inv*; *s.a.* **eight, eighty**

**24/7** *n* expression américaine (*prononcée "twenty-four, seven"*) à la mode qui signifie 24 heures sur 24 et 7 jours sur 7, c.-à-d. en permanence, constamment

**twice** [twaɪs] *adv* deux fois; **~ as often/ fast** deux fois plus souvent/plus vite

**twiddle** ['twɪd·l] I. *vt* tripoter ▸ **to ~ one's thumbs** se tourner les pouces II. *vi* **to ~ with sth** tripoter qc

**twig** [twɪg] *n a. pej* brindille *f*

**twilight** ['twaɪ·laɪt] *n* (*opp: dawn*) *a. fig* crépuscule *m; s.a.* **dusk**

**twin** [twɪn] I. *n a. fig* jumeau, jumelle *m, f* II. *adj a. fig* MED, BIO jumeau(jumelle); **a ~ brother** un frère jumeau III. *vt* <-nn-> jumeler

**twinkle** ['twɪŋ·kl] I. *vi* scintiller; (*eyes*) pétiller II. *n* scintillement *m*; (*eyes*) pétillement *m*; **to have a ~ in one's eye** avoir une étincelle dans le regard

**twist** [twɪst] I. *vt* ① (*turn: metal, cloth*) tordre; (*handle, lid*) tourner; **to ~ one's ankle** se fouler la cheville; **I ~ed the top off the jar** j'ai dévissé le couvercle du pot; **to ~ sth out of shape** déformer qc en le tordant; **he ~ed his face into an ugly smile** *fig* son visage se déforma en un vilain sourire ② (*wind around*) enrouler; **to ~ sth together** (*strands, hands*) entrelacer qc ③ (*manipulate:*

T

*words*) déformer; **to ~ sth into sth** transformer qc en qc ❹ *inf* (*cheat*) rouler ▶ **to ~ sb's arm** forcer la main à qn; **to ~ sb around one's little finger** mener qn par le bout du nez **II.** *vi* ❶ (*turn around*) se (re)tourner ❷ (*squirm around*) s'enrouler; **to ~ and turn** s'agiter dans tous les sens ❸ (*contort*) *a.* MED se tordre ❹ (*curve: path*) serpenter; **to ~ and turn** faire des zigzags ❺ (*change*) se transformer ❻ (*dance*) twister **III.** *n* ❶ (*turn*) tour *m*; **with a ~ of sth** d'un tour de qc ❷ (*rotation*) rotation *f*; MED entorse *f* ❸ (*action*) torsion *f* ❹ (*sharp curve*) tournant *m*; **~s and turns** tours *mpl* et détours *mpl* ❺ (*changing point*) tournant *m*; **to take a new ~** prendre un nouveau tournant *f*; **to give sth a ~** donner une nouvelle tournure à qc; **a surprise ~ to the story** une tournure surprenante dans l'histoire ❼ (*curl: hair*) torsade *f*; (*lemon*) zeste *m*; (*ribbon*) tortillon *m*; (*thread*) torsade *f* ❽ (*dance*) twist *m*; **to do the ~** danser le twist

**twisted** *adj a. fig* tordu(e); (*ankle*) foulé(e); (*path, river*) tortueux(-euse)

**twister** *n* ❶ METEO *s.* **tornado** ❷ *pej, inf* (*swindler*) escroc *mf*

**twitch** [twɪtʃ] **I.** *vi* ❶ (*nervous movement: muscle*) se contracter; (*person*) avoir un tic ❷ (*move nervously*) s'agiter **II.** *vt* ❶ (*jerk*) contracter; (*nose, tail*) remuer ❷ (*tug quickly*) tirer d'un coup sec; **to ~ sth out of sth** arracher qc de qc **III.** <-es> *n* ❶ (*small spasm*) tic *m* ❷ (*quick pull*) coup *m* sec

**twitter** [ˈtwɪ·tər] *vi* ❶ (*chirp*) gazouiller ❷ (*talk rapidly*) **to ~ away** parler vite ❸ TEL, INET twitter

**two** [tu] **I.** *adj* deux; **to be ~ of** être de la même espèce; **to have ~ of sth** avoir qc en double ▶ **that makes ~ of us** *inf* on est deux **II.** *n* deux *m* ▶ **~'s company, three's a crowd** *prov* nous serions mieux seuls plutôt qu'à trois; **to put ~ and ~ together** *inf* tirer ses conclusions; **it takes ~ to tango** *prov*

chacun a sa part de responsabilité; *s.a.* **eight**

**two-dimensional** *adj* ❶ (*flat*) bidimensionnel(le) ❷ *fig, pej* superficiel(le)

**two-faced** *adj* hypocrite

**twofold I.** *adv* doublement **II.** *adj* double

**two-part** *adj* en deux parties

**two-piece I.** *n* FASHION ❶ (*jacket and pants*) (costume *m*) deux-pièces *m* ❷ (*bikini*) (maillot *m*) deux-pièces *m* **II.** *adj* deux pièces

**two-seater** *n* AUTO voiture *f* à deux places

**twosome** *n* couple *m*

**two-way** *adj* à double sens; (*exchange*) bilatéral(e); **~ radio** poste *m* émetteur-récepteur

**TX** *n abbr of* **Texas**

**tycoon** [taɪˈkun] *n* FIN magnat *m*

**type** [taɪp] **I.** *n* ❶ (*sort*) type *m*; **people of every ~** gens *mpl* de toutes sortes; **do you like that ~ of thing?** tu aimes/vous aimez ce genre de choses? ❷ BIO espèce *f*; **blood ~** groupe *m* sanguin ❸ (*sort of person*) genre *m*; **he's not the ~ to forget** il n'est pas du genre à oublier; **he's not my ~** il n'est pas mon genre ❹ TYP, PUBL caractère *m*; **in large/small ~** en gros/petits caractères **II.** *vt* ❶ (*write: typewriter*) taper; (*computer*) saisir ❷ (*categorize*) classifier **III.** *vi* (*typewriter*) taper (à la machine)

◆ **type out, type up** *vt* (*typewriter*) taper (à la machine); (*computer*) saisir

**typewriter** [ˈtaɪp·ˌraɪ·tər] *n* machine *f* à écrire, dactylographe *m* Québec

**typewritten** *adj* dactylographié(e)

**typhoon** [taɪˈfun] *n* METEO typhon *m*

**typical** [ˈtɪp·ɪ·kəl] **I.** *adj* typique; **the ~ American** l'Américain *m* type; **it is ~ of him/her** c'est bien lui/elle **II.** *interj inf* **~!** ça ne m'étonne pas!

**typically** *adv* ❶ (*characteristically*) typiquement ❷ (*usually*) généralement

**typify** [ˈtɪp·ɪ·faɪ] <-ie-> *vt* ❶ (*be characteristic of*) être caractéristique de ❷ (*embody*) être le type même de

**typing** *n* dactylographie *f;* ~ **speed/error** vitesse *f*/erreur *f* de frappe

**typist** *n* dactylo *mf*

**typo** *n* (*error*) coquille *f*

**tyrant** ['taɪ·rənt] *n a. fig* tyran *m*

# Uu

**U, u** [ju] <-'s> *n* U *m,* u *m;* ~ **as in Uniform** (*on telephone*) u comme Ur-sule

**U** [ju] *n inf abbr of* **university** universi-té *f*

**udder** ['ʌd·ər] *n* mamelle *f*

**UFO** [ˌju·ef·'oʊ] <(')s> *n abbr of* **un-identified flying object** ovni *m*

**ugly** ['ʌg·lɪ] <-ier, iest> *adj* ❶ *pej* (*not attractive*) laid(e); ~ **duckling** vilain pe-tit canard *m* ❷ (*angry: look, word, wound*) vilain(e) ❸ (*violent*) terrible; (*incident*) regrettable; **to turn** ~ mal tourner ❹ (*unpleasant*) déplaisant(e) ❺ (*threatening*) menaçant(e)

**UK** [ju·'keɪ] *n abbr of* **United Kingdom the** ~ le Royaume-Uni

**ulcer** ['ʌl·sər] *n* MED ulcère *m*

**ulterior** [ʌl·'tɪr·i·ər] *adj* ultérieur(e); ~ **motive** arrière-pensée *f*

**ultimate** ['ʌl·tə·mɪt] I. *adj* ❶ (*best*) su-prême ❷ (*final*) final(e); **the** ~ **purpose** le but ultime ❸ (*fundamental*) fonda-mental(e) ❹ (*furthest*) le(la) plus éloi-gné(e) II. *n* summum *m;* **the** ~ **in sth** le summum de qc

**ultimately** *adv* finalement

**ultimatum** [ˌʌl·tə·'meɪ·təm] <ultimata *o* -tums> *n* ultimatum *m*

**ultrasound** *n* ❶ (*sound, vibrations*) ul-trasons *mpl* ❷ (*scan*) échographie *f*

**ultraviolet** I. *n* ASTR, PHYS ultraviolet *m* II. *adj* ultraviolet(te); (*treatment*) aux ultraviolets

**umbilical cord** [ʌm·'bɪl·ɪ·kl kɔrd] *n* cor-don *m* ombilical

**umbrella** [ʌm·'brel·ə] *n* ❶ (*covering*) *a. fig* parapluie *m;* (*for sun*) ombrelle *f;* (*on the beach*) parasol *m* ❷ (*protec-tion*) protection *f;* **under the** ~ **of sth** sous les auspices de qc

**umpire** ['ʌm·paɪər] SPORTS I. *n* arbitre *mf* II. *vt* arbitrer

**umpteen** ['ʌm(p)·tin] *adj, pron inf* des tas de

**umpteenth** *adj* énième

**UN** [ju·'en] *n abbr of* **United Nations the** ~ l'ONU *f*

**unable** [ʌn·'eɪ·bl] *adj* **to be** ~ **to do sth** (*attend, reach*) ne pas pouvoir faire qc; (*swim, read*) ne pas savoir faire qc; (*in-capable*) être incapable de faire qc

**unabridged** [ˌʌn·ə·'brɪdʒd] *adj* inté-gral(e)

**unacceptable** [ˌʌn·ək·'sep·tə·bl] *adj* ❶ (*not good enough*) inacceptable; **sth is** ~ **to sb** qn ne peut pas accepter qc ❷ (*intolerable*) inadmissible

**unaccompanied** [ˌʌn·ə·'kʌm·pə·nid] *adj* (*passenger*) non accompagné(e); (*voice, violin*) sans accompagnement

**unaccounted for** [ˌʌn·ə·'kaʊn·tɪd·ˌfɔr] *adj* manquant(e); **to be** ~ manquer

**unadventurous** [ˌʌn·əd·'ven·tʃər·əs] *adj* peu audacieux( euse)

**unafraid** [ˌʌn·ə·'freɪd] *adj* sans peur; **to be** ~ **of sb/sth** ne pas avoir peur de qn/qc

**unanimous** [ju·'næn·ə·məs] *adj* unani-me

**unanimously** *adv* à l'unanimité

**unappealing** [ˌʌn·ə·'pilɪŋ] *adj* peu at-trayant(e)

**unapproachable** [ˌʌn·ə·'prou·tʃə·bl] *adj* ❶ (*protected from entering*) inac-cessible ❷ (*not friendly*) inabordable

**unattached** [ˌʌn·əˈtætʃt] *adj* libre; (*journalist, worker*) indépendant(e)

**unattended** [ˌʌn·əˈten·dɪd] *adj* sans surveillance

**unattractive** [ˌʌn·əˈtræk·tɪv] *adj* ❶ (*quite ugly*) peu attrayant(e) ❷ (*unpleasant*) déplaisant(e)

**unauthorized** [ʌnˈɑ·θə·raɪzd] *adj* non autorisé(e)

**unavailable** [ˌʌn·əˈveɪ·lə·bl] *adj* indisponible; **she's ~** elle n'est pas libre

**unavoidable** [ˌʌn·əˈvɔɪ·də·bl] *adj* inévitable

**unaware** [ˌʌn·əˈwer] *adj* **to be ~ of sth** ne pas être conscient de qc; (*not informed*) ignorer qc

**unawares** *adv* inconsciemment; (*to take, catch*) au dépourvu

**unbearable** [ʌnˈber·ə·bl] *adj* insupportable

**unbearably** *adv* incroyablement

**unbeatable** [ʌnˈbi·tə·bl] *adj* imbattable

**unbeaten** [ʌnˈbi·tən] *adj* SPORTS (*team, person*) invaincu(e); (*record*) qui n'a pas encore été battu(e)

**unbelievable** [ˌʌn·bɪˈli·və·bl] *adj* incroyable

**unbleached** [ʌnˈblitʃt] *adj* écru(e); (*paper, cloth*) sans chlore; (*flour*) non traité(e)

**unbreakable** [ʌnˈbreɪ·kə·bl] *adj* ❶ (*unable to be broken*) incassable ❷ (*that must be kept: rule*) inviolable; (*promise*) sacré(e) ❸ SPORTS (*record*) imbattable

**unbroken** [ʌnˈbroʊ·kən] *adj* ❶ (*not broken or damaged*) intact(e) ❷ (*continuous*) ininterrompu(e) ❸ (*not surpassed: record*) qui n'a pas été battu(e) ❹ (*uncultivated: land*) vierge

**unbutton** [ʌnˈbʌt·ən] *vt* déboutonner

**uncalled-for** [ʌnˈkɔld·fɔr] *adj pej* déplacé(e)

**uncanny** [ʌnˈkæn·ɪ] *adj* <-ier, -iest> étrange; (*likeness*) troublant(e)

**uncertain** [ʌnˈsɜr·tən] *adj* ❶ (*unsure*) incertain(e); **to be ~ of sth** n'être pas sûr de qc ❷ (*unknown, not defined: future*) incertain(e); **in no ~ terms** en des termes clairs ❸ (*volatile*) changeant(e); (*temper*) versatile; (*weather*) variable; (*person*) inconstant(e)

**uncertainty** <-ies> *n* incertitude *f*

**unchanged** [ʌnˈtʃeɪndʒd] *adj* inchangé(e)

**uncharacteristic** [ʌnˌker·ɪk·tə·ˈrɪs·tɪk] *adj* inhabituel(le)

**uncivilized** [ʌnˈsɪv·əl·aɪzd] *adj* ❶ (*not civilized*) barbare ❷ (*not polite: behavior, argument*) incorrect(e); (*hour*) indu(e)

**uncle** [ˈʌŋ·kl] *n* oncle *m*

**unclear** [ʌnˈklɪr] *adj* incertain(e); **to be ~ about sth** ne pas être sûr de qc; **it is ~ (as to) whether/what …** on ne sait pas encore si/ce que …

**uncomfortable** [ʌnˈkʌm(p)·fər·tə·bl] *adj* (*shoes, chair*) inconfortable; (*silence, situation*) gênant(e); **to feel ~ about sth** être mal à l'aise à propos de qc; (*embarrassed*) se sentir gêné par qc

**uncommon** [ʌnˈkam·ən] *adj* rare

**unconcerned** [ˌʌn·kənˈsɜrnd] *adj* indifférent(e)

**unconditional** [ˌʌn·kənˈdɪʃ·ən·əl] *adj* sans condition(s)

**unconfirmed** [ˌʌn·kənˈfɜrmd] *adj* non confirmé(e)

**unconnected** [ˌʌn·kəˈnek·tɪd] *adj* sans rapport

**unconscious** [ʌnˈkan·(t)ʃəs] **I.** *adj a. fig* inconscient(e); **to knock sb ~** assommer qn; **the ~ mind** l'inconscient *m*; **to be ~ of sth** *form* ne pas avoir conscience de qc **II.** *n* PSYCH **the ~** l'inconscient *m*

**unconsciously** *adv* inconsciemment

**unconsciousness** *n* MED inconscience *f*

**unconstitutional** [ˌʌn·ˌkan·(t)·stə·ˈtuʃ·ən·əl] *adj* inconstitutionnel(le)

**uncontrollable** *adj* incontrôlable

**uncontrolled** [ˌʌn·kənˈtroʊld] *adj* incontrôlé(e)

**unconvincing** [ˌʌn·kənˈvɪn(t)·sɪŋ] *adj* peu convaincant(e)

**uncooked** [ʌnˈkʊkt] *adj* pas cuit(e)

**uncooperative** [ʌn·kou·'a·pər·ə·t̬ɪv] *adj pej* peu coopératif(-ive)

**uncoordinated** [ʌn·kou·'ɔr·dən·eɪ·t̬ɪd] *adj pej* non coordonné(e); **to be ~** (*person*) manquer de coordination

**uncover** [ʌn·'kʌv·ər] *vt* ❶ (*lay bare*) découvrir ❷ (*expose*) dévoiler

**undecided** [ʌn·dɪ·'saɪ·dɪd] *adj* indécis(e); **to be ~ whether/when ...** ne pas savoir encore si/quand ...

**undeniable** [ʌn·dɪ·'naɪ·ə·bl] *adj* indéniable

**under** ['ʌn·dər] I. *prep* ❶ (*below*) sous; **~ the table/water** sous la table/l'eau; **~ it** dessous; **~ there** là-dessous ❷ (*supporting*) sous; **to break ~ the weight** céder sous le poids ❸ (*less than*) moins de ❹ (*governed by*) sous; **~ the communists** sous le régime des communistes; **I am ~ orders to say nothing** j'ai reçu l'ordre de ne rien dire ❺ (*in state of*) ~ **these conditions** dans ces conditions; **~ the circumstances** vu les circonstances; **~ repair/observation** en réparation/observation ❻ (*in category of*) par; **to classify the books ~ author** classer les livres par auteur ❼ (*according to*) d'après; **the treaty conformément au traité ► to be ~ way** être en route; *s.a.* **over** II. *adv* ❶ au-dessous, en dessous; **to get out from ~** *a. fig* remonter à la surface ❷ *inf* (*unconscious*) **to go ~** tomber dans les pommes

**underachiever** [ʌn·dər·ə·'tʃiv] *n* SCHOOL élève *mf* aux résultats décevants

**underage** [ʌn·dər·'eɪdʒ] *adj* mineur(e)

**undercharge** ['ʌn·dər·tʃardʒ] *vt* ne pas faire payer assez à; **to ~ sb by ten dollars** faire payer dix dollars de moins à qn

**underdeveloped** [ʌn·dər·dɪ·'vel·əpt] *adj* sous-développé(e)

**underdog** ['ʌn·dər·dɔg] *n* opprimé(e) *m(f)*

**underdone** [ʌn·dər·'dʌn] *adj* pas assez cuit(e); (*steak*) saignant(e)

**underestimate** [ʌn·dər·'es·tə·meɪt] *vt* sous-estimer

**undergo** [ʌn·dər·'gou] *irr vt* subir; (*treatment*) suivre

**undergrad** ['ʌn·dər·græd] *n inf* étudiant(e) *m(f)* (de premier cycle)

**undergraduate** [ʌn·dər·'grædʒ·u·ət] *n* étudiant(e) *m(f)* (de premier cycle); **~ program** programme *m* de premier cycle

**underground** ['ʌn·dər·graund] I. *adj* ❶ (*below earth surface*) souterrain(e) ❷ (*clandestine*) clandestin(e) ❸ ART, MUS underground *inv* II. *adv* ❶ (*beneath the ground*) sous terre ❷ (*secretly*) clandestinement; **to go ~** entrer dans la clandestinité III. *n* ❶ (*clandestine movement*) **the ~** le mouvement clandestin ❷ (*alternative group*) mouvement underground

**underhanded** I. *adj* ❶ (*secret*) sournois(e) ❷ (*with arm below shoulder*) par-dessous II. *adv* ❶ (*secretly*) sournoisement ❷ (*below shoulder*) par-dessous

**undermine** [ʌn·dər·'maɪn] *vt a. fig* saper

**underneath** [ʌn·dər·'niθ] I. *prep* sous, au-dessous de II. *adv* (en) dessous; *s.a.* **under** III. *n* dessous *m*

**underpaid** [ʌn·dər·'peɪd] *adj* sous-payé(e)

**underpants** ['ʌn·dər·pænts] *npl* slip *m*

**underpass** ['ʌn·dər·pæs] <-es> *n* passage *m* souterrain

**undersecretary** ['ʌn·dər·sek·rə·ter·i] *n* sous-secrétaire *mf*

**understand** [ʌn·dər·'stænd] *irr* I. *vt* ❶ (*perceive meaning*) comprendre; **to make oneself understood** se faire comprendre; **to ~ one another** se comprendre; **the problem as I ~ it** si je comprends bien le problème ❷ (*believe, infer*) **it is understood that ...** il est entendu que ...; **I ~ that you're leaving** j'ai cru comprendre que tu partais/vous partiez II. *vi* comprendre; **to ~ about sb/sth** comprendre qn/qc; **am I to ~ from this that ...?** dois-je comprendre par là que ...?; **I ~ from the letter that ...** j'ai cru comprendre en lisant la lettre que ...

U

**understandable** *adj* compréhensible

**understanding** I. *n* ① (*comprehension*) compréhension *f*; **to be beyond all ~** être incompréhensible; **my ~ was that ...** j'ai compris que ...; **to have no ~ of sth** ne rien comprendre à qc; **to show great ~** être très compréhensif ② (*interpretation*) interprétation *f* ③ (*agreement*) entente *f*; **to do sth on the ~ that** faire qc à la condition que +*subj* II. *adj* compréhensif(-ive)

**understatement** *n* litote *f*; **it's the ~ of the year** c'est le moins qu'on puisse dire

**understood** [ʌn·dər·'stʊd] *pt, pp of* **understand**

**undertaker** *n* (*funeral director*) entrepreneur, -euse *m, f* des pompes funèbres

**underwater** ['ʌn·dər·'wɔː·tər] I. *adj* sous-marin(e) II. *adv* sous l'eau

**underwear** ['ʌn·dər·wer] *n* sous-vêtements *mpl*

**underwhelming** *adj inf* peu emballant(e); (*disappointing*) décevant(e)

**undesirable** [ʌn·dɪ·'zaɪ·rə·bl] I. *adj pej* indésirable II. *n pl, pej* indésirable *mf*

**undetected** [ʌn·dɪ·'tek·tɪd] *adj* non décelé(e); **to go ~** passer inaperçu(e)

**undid** [ʌn·'dɪd] *pt of* **undo**

**undiscovered** [ʌn·dɪ·'skʌv·ərd] *adj* inconnu(e)

**undo** [ʌn·'du] *irr vt* ① (*unfasten: buttons, laces*) défaire ② (*cancel, wipe out*) annuler

**undone** [ʌn·'dʌn] I. *pp of* **undo** II. *adj* ① (*not fastened*) défait(e); **to come ~** se défaire ② (*uncompleted*) inachevé(e)

**undoubtedly** *adv* indubitablement

**undress** [ʌn·'dres] I. *vt a. fig* déshabiller II. *vi* se déshabiller

**undressed** *adj* déshabillé(e); **to get ~** se déshabiller

**unearth** [ʌn·'ɜrθ] *vt* ① (*dig up*) déterrer ② *fig* (*truth*) découvrir; (*person*) dénicher

**unease** [ʌn·'iz] *n* malaise *m*

**uneasy** *adj* <-ier, -iest> ① (*ill at ease*) mal à l'aise; (*silence*) gêné(e); **to feel ~**

**about sb/sth** se sentir gêné par rapport à qn/qc ② (*apprehensive*) inquiet(-ète) ③ (*difficult: relationship, compromise*) difficile

**unemployed** [ʌn·ɪm·'plɔɪd] I. *n* **the ~** *pl* les chômeurs *mpl* II. *adj* au chômage

**unemployment** [ʌn·ɪm·'plɔɪ·mənt] *n* chômage *m*

**unemployment benefits** *n pl* allocation *f* (de) chômage

**unenforceable** [ʌn·ɪn·'fɔr·sə·bl] *adj* inapplicable

**unequivocal** [ʌn·ɪ·'kwɪv·ə·kəl] *adj* sans équivoque; (*success*) incontestable

**unethical** [ʌn·'eθ·ɪ·kəl] *adj* contraire à l'éthique

**uneven** [ʌn·'i·vən] *adj* ① (*not flat or level*) a. MED irrégulier(-ère) ② (*unequal*) inégal(e)

**unexpected** [ʌn·ɪk·'spek·tɪd] I. *adj* inattendu(e) II. *n* **the ~** l'inattendu *m*

**unfair** [ʌn·'fer] *adj* injuste

**unfaithful** [ʌn·'feɪθ·fəl] *adj* infidèle

**unfamiliar** [ʌn·fə·'mɪl·jər] *adj* ① (*new: sound, face, place*) peu familier(-ère); (*ideas, situation*) inhabituel(le) ② (*unacquainted*) **to be ~ with sth** mal connaître qc

**unfathomable** [ʌn·'fæð·ə·mə·bl] *adj a. fig* insondable; **for some ~ reason...** pour on ne sait trop quelle raison...

**unfit** [ʌn·'fɪt] *adj* <-tt-> ① (*unhealthy*) **to be ~ to travel/work** ne pas être en état de voyager/travailler ② *pej* (*without requisite qualities*) inapte; **to be ~ for work** être inapte au travail ③ (*unsuitable*) impropre; **to be ~ for consumption** être impropre à la consommation; **~ for publication/habitation** impubliable/inhabitable

**unfold** [ʌn·'foʊld] I. *vt* ① (*open out*) ouvrir ② *form* (*make known*) dévoiler II. *vi* ① (*develop*) se dérouler ② (*become revealed*) se révéler ③ (*become unfolded*) s'ouvrir

**unforeseeable** [ʌn·fɔr·'si·ə·bl] *adj* imprévisible

**unforgettable** [ʌn·fər·'geṭ·ə·bl] *adj* inoubliable

U

**unforgivable** [ʌnˈfər·ɡɪv·ə·bl] *adj pej* impardonnable

**unfortunate** [ʌnˈfɔr·tʃən·ət] I. *adj* ① (*luckless*) malchanceux(-euse) ② *pej, form* (*regrettable*) fâcheux(-euse) II. *n* pauvre *mf*

**unfortunately** *adv* malheureusement

**unfriendly** [ʌnˈfrend·li] *adj* <-ier, -iest> (*person*) peu sympathique; (*tone, attitude*) peu amical(e); (*glance, reception*) froid(e); **environmentally** ~ nuisible à l'environnement

**unfurnished** [ʌnˈfər·nɪʃt] *adj* non meublé(e)

**ungrateful** [ʌnˈɡreɪt·fəl] *adj* ingrat(e)

**unhappy** [ʌnˈhæp·i] *adj* <-ier, -iest> ① (*sad, unfortunate*) malheureux(-euse); (*face*) triste; **to make sb** ~ rendre qn malheureux ② (*worried*) inquiet(-ète); **to be** ~ **about doing sth** ne pas aimer faire qc

**unhealthy** [ʌnˈhel·θi] *adj* <-ier, -iest> malsain(e)

**unhurt** [ʌnˈhɜrt] *adj* indemne

**unicorn** [ˈju·nɪ·kɔrn] *n* licorne *f*

**unidentified** [ʌn·aɪˈden·tə·faɪd] *adj* (*unknown*) non identifié(e)

**unification** [ju·nə·fɪˈkeɪ·ʃən] *n* unification *f*

**uniform** [ˈju·nə·fɔrm] I. *n* uniforme *m* II. *adj* uniforme

**unify** [ˈju·nə·faɪ] *vt* unifier

**unimportant** [ʌn·ɪmˈpɔr·tənt] *adj* sans importance

**uninformed** [ʌn·ɪnˈfɔrmd] *adj* mal informé(e); **to be** ~ **about sth** ne pas être au courant de qc

**uninhabited** [ʌn·ɪnˈhæb·ɪ·tɪd] *adj* inhabité(e)

**uninhibited** [ʌn·ɪnˈhɪb·ɪ·tɪd] *adj* ① (*unselfconscious*) sans inhibitions; (*feeling*) non refréné(e) ② (*unrestricted*) déchaîné(e)

**uninstall** [ʌn·ɪnˈstɔl] *vt* COMPUT (*program, software*) désinstaller

**unintended** [ʌn·ɪnˈten·dɪd] *adj* non prévu(e) à cet effet

**unintentional** [ʌn·ɪnˈten·(t)ʃən·əl] *adj* involontaire

**unintentionally** *adv* involontairement

**uninterested** [ʌnˈɪn·trɪs·tɪd] *adj* indifférent(e); **to be** ~ **in sb/sth** être indifférent à qn/qc

**uninteresting** *adj* inintéressant(e)

**union** [ˈju·njən] *n* ① (*act of becoming united*) union *f* ② (*labor union*) syndicat *m* ③ *form* (*marriage*) union *f* ④ (*harmony*) harmonie *f*

**unique** [juˈnik] *adj* unique

**unit** [ˈju·nɪt] *n* ① (*fixed measuring quantity*) a. COM unité *f*; ~ **of measurement** unité de mesure ② (*organized group*) unité *f*; **the family** ~ le noyau familial ③ (*part of larger entity*) section *f* ④ (*mechanical device*) unité *f* ⑤ (*chapter*) unité *f* ⑥ (*apartment*) logement *m*

**unite** [juˈnaɪt] I. *vt* unir II. *vi* a. POL, SOCIOL s'unir

**united** *adj* uni(e); **to be** ~ **against sth** être uni face à qc ▶ ~ **we stand, divided we** **fall** l'union fait la force

**United Kingdom** *n* **the** ~ le Royaume-Uni

**United Nations** *n pl* **the** ~ les Nations *fpl* Unies

**United States** *n* **the** ~ **of America** les États-Unis *mpl* d'Amérique

**unity** [ˈju·nə·ti] *n* unité *f*

**universal** [ˌju·nəˈvɜr·səl] *adj* universel(le)

**universe** [ˈju·nə·vɜrs] *n* **the** ~ l'Univers *m*

**university** [ˌju·nəˈvɜr·sə·ti] <-ies> *n* université *f*

**unjustified** [ʌnˈdʒʌs·tɪ·faɪd] *adj pej* injustifié(e)

**unjustly** *adv pej* ① (*in an unjust manner*) injustement ② (*wrongfully*) à tort

**unkind** [ʌnˈkaɪnd] *adj* ① (*not kind*) peu aimable ② (*not gentle*) rude

**unknown** [ʌnˈnoʊn] I. *adj* inconnu(e); **to be** ~ **to sb/sth** être inconnu de qn/qc II. *n* ① (*sth not known*) **the** ~ l'inconnu *m* ② (*undetermined element*) a. MATH inconnue *f* ③ (*little-known person*) inconnu(e) *m(f)*

**unlawful** [ʌnˈlɔ·fəl] *adj* illégal(e)

**unleaded** [ʌnˈled·ɪd] *adj* sans plomb

U

**unless** [ən·'les] *conj* à moins que +*subj*; **I don't say anything ~ I'm sure** je ne dis rien sans en être sûr; **he won't come ~ he has time** il ne viendra que s'il a le temps; **~ I'm mistaken** si je ne m'abuse

**unlike** [ʌn·'laɪk] *prep* ❶ (*different from*) différent(e) de ❷ (*in contrast to*) contrairement à ❸ (*not characteristic of*) **to be ~ sb/sth** ne pas ressembler à qn/qc

**unlikely** <-ier, -iest> *adj* ❶ (*improbable*) peu probable ❷ (*unconvincing*) invraisemblable

**unlimited** [ʌn·'lɪm·ɪ·ṭɪd] *adj* illimité(e); (*coffee, food*) à volonté

**unload** [ʌn·'loʊd] **I.** *vt* ❶ (*remove the contents*) décharger ❷ *inf* (*get rid of: goods*) refourguer ❸ *fig* (*release: one's heart*) vider **II.** *vi* ❶ AUTO (*discharge contents*) décharger ❷ (*be emptied*) être déchargé(e) ❸ *inf* (*relieve stress*) décompresser ❹ (*hit*) **to ~ on sb/sth** se défouler sur qn/qc

**unlock** [ʌn·'lak] *vt* ❶ (*release a lock*) déverrouiller ❷ (*release*) libérer ❸ (*solve*) résoudre

**unlocked** *adj* **to be ~** ne pas être fermé à clef

**unlucky** [ʌn·'lʌk·i] *adj* ❶ (*unfortunate*) malchanceux(-euse); (*day*) de malchance; (*event*) malencontreux(-euse); **he was ~** il n'a pas eu de chance ❷ (*bringing bad luck*) qui porte malheur; **it is ~ to** +*infin* ça porte malheur de +*infin*

**unmarried** [ʌn·'mer·ɪd] *adj* (*person*) célibataire; (*couple*) non marié(e)

**unmatched** [ʌn·'mætʃt] *adj* sans égal(e)

**unmistakable** [ʌn·mɪ·'steɪ·kə·bl̩] *adj* caractéristique

**unnatural** [ʌn·'nætʃ·ər·əl] *adj* ❶ *pej* (*contrary to nature*) contre nature ❷ (*not normal*) anormal(e) ❸ (*artificial*) artificiel(le) ❹ (*affected*) affecté(e)

**unnecessary** [ʌn·'nes·ə·ser·i] *adj* ❶ (*not necessary*) inutile ❷ (*uncalled for*) injustifié(e)

**unnoticed** [ʌn·'noʊ·ṭɪst] *adj* inaper-

çu(e); **to do sth ~** faire qc sans se faire remarquer

**unobstructed** [ʌn·əb·'strʌk·tɪd] *adj* (*view*) dégagé(e)

**unoccupied** [ʌn·'a·kjə·paɪd] *adj* ❶ (*uninhabited*) inhabité(e) ❷ (*not under military control: territory*) non occupé(e) ❸ (*not taken: chair*) libre

**unofficial** [ʌn·ə·'fɪʃ·əl] *adj* non officiel(le); (*information*) officieux(-euse); (*strike*) sauvage

**unorganized** [ʌn·'ɔr·gən·aɪzd] *adj* qui manque d'organisation

**unpack** [ʌn·'pæk] **I.** *vt* déballer; (*suitcase*) défaire **II.** *vi* défaire ses valises

**unpaid** [ʌn·'peɪd] *adj* ❶ (*not remunerated*) bénévole ❷ (*not paid: job*) non payé(e); (*debt*) impayé(e)

**unpleasant** [ʌn·'plez·ənt] *adj* ❶ (*not pleasing*) désagréable ❷ (*unfriendly*) antipathique

**unplug** [ʌn·'plʌg] <-gg-> *vt* ❶ (*disconnect*) débrancher ❷ (*unstop*) déboucher

**unplugged** [ʌn·'plʌgd] **I.** *adj* (*performance*) acoustique **II.** *adv* en acoustique

**unpopular** [ʌn·'pa·pjə·lər] *adj* impopulaire; **she was ~ with her students** ses élèves ne l'aimaient pas

**unpractical** [ʌn·'præk·tɪ·kəl] *adj* ❶ (*impractical*) peu pratique ❷ (*impossible to implement*) irréalisable

**unprecedented** [ʌn·'pres·ə·den·ṭɪd] *adj* sans précédent

**unpredictable** [ʌn·prɪ·'dɪk·tə·bl̩] *adj* imprévisible

**unqualified** [ʌn·'kwal·ə·faɪd] *adj* ❶ *pej* (*without qualifications*) non qualifié(e) ❷ (*unlimited*) total(e)

**unravel** [ʌn·'ræv·əl] <-l- *o* -ll-> **I.** *vt* ❶ (*unknit*) défaire ❷ (*untangle*) démêler; (*knot*) défaire ❸ (*solve*) résoudre **II.** *vi* se défaire

**unreadable** [ʌn·'ri·də·bl̩] *adj* ❶ (*illegible, badly written*) illisible ❷ (*hard to interpret: expression, face*) impassible

**unreal** [ʌn·'ril] *adj* ❶ (*not real*) irréel(le) ❷ *inf* (*good*) incroyable

**unrealistic** [ˌʌn·ri·ə·ˈlɪs·tɪk] *adj* ❶ (*not realistic*) irréaliste ❷ LIT, THEAT, CINE peu réaliste

**unreasonable** [ʌn·ˈriz·n̩·bl̩] *adj* ❶ (*not showing reason*) déraisonnable ❷ *pej* (*unfair*) irréaliste ; (*price*) exorbitant(e)

**unrefined** [ˌʌn·rɪ·ˈfaɪnd] *adj* ❶ (*not refined: sugar*) non raffiné(e) ; (*oil*) brut(e) ❷ (*not socially polished*) peu raffiné(e)

**unreliable** [ˌʌn·rɪ·ˈlaɪ·ə·bl̩] *adj* peu fiable

**unremarkable** *adj* quelconque

**unreserved** [ˌʌn·rɪ·ˈzɜrvd] *adj* ❶ (*absolute*) absolu(e) ❷ (*not reserved: tickets, seats*) non réservé(e)

**unresponsive** [ˌʌn·rɪ·ˈspan(t)·sɪv] *adj* ❶ (*not conscious: person*) qui ne réagit pas ❷ (*not changing: illness, infection*) réfractaire ; ~ **to treatment** insensible au traitement ❶ (*not sympathetic: person, group*) indifférent(e)

**unrestricted** [ˌʌn·rɪ·ˈstrɪk·tɪd] *adj* non restreint(e) ; (*access*) libre

**unroll** [ʌn·ˈroʊl] I. *vt* dérouler II. *vi* (*become open*) se dérouler

**unsafe** [ʌn·ˈseɪf] *adj* ❶ (*dangerous*) dangereux(-euse) ❷ (*in danger*) en danger

**unsatisfactory** [ʌn·ˌsæt·ɪs·ˈfæk·tə·ri] *adj* peu satisfaisant(e) ; **to be ~** ne pas être satisfaisant ; (*item*) ne pas donner satisfaction

**unsatisfied** [ʌn·ˈsæt·ɪs·faɪd] *adj* ❶ (*not content*) mécontent(e) ❷ (*not convinced*) insatisfait(e) ❸ (*not sated*) non rassasié(e)

**unsaturated** [ʌn·ˈsæt·ʃ·ə·reɪ·tɪd] *adj* CULIN non saturé(e)

**unscathed** [ʌn·ˈskeɪðd] *adj* indemne ; **to escape ~** s'en sortir indemne

**unscheduled** [ʌn·ˈskedʒ·ʊld] *adj* imprévu(e) ; (*train*) supplémentaire

**unscramble** [ʌn·ˈskræm·bl̩] *vt* décoder

**unscrupulous** [ʌn·ˈskru·pjə·ləs] *adj pej* peu scrupuleux(-euse)

**unseen** [ʌn·ˈsin] *adj* invisible ; **to do sth ~** faire qc sans être vu

**unselfish** [ʌn·ˈsel·fɪʃ] *adj* généreux(-euse)

**unsettle** [ʌn·ˈset·l̩] *vt* ❶ (*make nervous*) troubler ❷ (*make unstable*) déstabiliser

**unsettling** *adj* ❶ (*causing nervousness*) troublant(e) ❷ (*causing disruption*) perturbant(e) ❸ COM déstabilisant(e)

**unshakable** [ʌn·ˈʃeɪ·kə·bl̩] *adj* inébranlable

**unshaved, unshaven** [ʌn·ˈʃeɪ·v³n] *adj* pas rasé(e)

**unsightly** [ʌn·ˈsaɪt·li] <-ier, -iest *o* more ~, most ~> *adj* disgracieux(-euse)

**unskilled** [ʌn·ˈskɪld] *adj* non qualifié(e)

**unsociable** [ʌn·ˈsoʊ·ʃə·bl̩] *adj* peu sociable

**unsold** [ʌn·ˈsoʊld] *adj* invendu(e)

**unsolved** [ʌn·ˈsalvd] *adj* non résolu(e)

**unspeakable** [ʌn·ˈspi·kə·bl̩] *adj* ❶ (*not able to be expressed*) indicible ❷ (*too awful: atrocity*) indescriptible

**unstable** [ˌʌn·ˈsteɪ·bl̩] *adj a. fig* instable

**unsubscribe** [ʌn·səb·ˈskraɪb] *vi* se désabonner

**unsuccessful** [ˌʌn·sək·ˈses·fᵊl] *adj* (*attempt, campaign*) infructueux(-euse) ; (*candidate, affair*) malheureux(-euse) ; (*film, business*) sans succès ; **to be ~** (*person, plan*) ne pas réussir ; (*attempt*) échouer

**unsuitable** [ʌn·ˈsu·tə·bl̩] *adj* inapproprié(e) ; **to be ~** ne pas convenir

**unsure** [ʌn·ˈʃʊr] *adj* peu sûr(e) ; **to be ~ about sth** ne pas être (très) sûr de qc

**unsweetened** [ʌn·ˈswi·tᵊnd] *adj* non sucré(e)

**untangle** [ʌn·ˈtæŋ·gl̩] *vt* ❶ (*string, hair*) démêler ❷ *fig* dénouer

**unthinkable** [ʌn·ˈθɪŋ·kə·bl̩] I. *adj* ❶ (*unimaginable*) inimaginable ❷ (*shocking*) impensable II. *n* **the ~** l'impensable *m*

**unthinking** [ʌn·ˈθɪŋ·kɪŋ] *adj* ❶ (*thoughtless*) irréfléchi(e) ❷ (*unintentional*) sans faire exprès

**untie** [ʌn·ˈtaɪ] <-y-> *vt* défaire ; (*boat*) démarrer

**until** [ᵊn·ˈtɪl] I. *prep* jusqu'à ; ~ **then** jusque-là ; ~ **such time as** jusqu'à ce que

**U**

+*subj;* **not ~** pas avant II. *conj* jusqu'à ce que +*subj;* **to not do sth ~** ne pas faire qc avant que +*subj;* **he waited ~ the rain stopped** il a attendu que la pluie cesse *subj;* **we'll wait ~ you've finished** nous attendrons que tu aies/vous ayez fini *subj*

**untimely** [ʌn·'taɪm·li] *adj* ❶ (*premature*) prématuré(e) ❷ (*inopportune*) inopportun(e)

**untouched** [ʌn·'tʌtʃt] *adj* ❶ (*not touched*) **to leave a meal ~** ne pas toucher à un repas ❷ (*unaffected: thing*) intact(e); (*person*) indemne ❸ (*unmentioned: subject*) non traité(e); **to be left ~** ne pas avoir été traité

**untreated** [ʌn·'tri·tɪd] *adj* ❶ (*not treated*) non traité(e) ❷ MED non soigné(e); **to remain ~** (*person*) rester sans soins

**untrue** [ʌn·'tru] *adj* ❶ (*wrong*) faux(fausse) ❷ (*not faithful*) **to be ~** ne pas être fidèle ❸ (*not reliable*) peu fiable

**untrustworthy** [ʌn·'trʌst·ˌwɜr·ði] *adj* (*person*) indigne de confiance; (*report, information*) douteux(-euse)

**unused**[1] [ʌn·'juzd] *adj* ❶ (*not in use*) inutilisé(e) ❷ (*never used: clothes*) neuf(neuve)

**unused**[2] [ʌn·'just] *adj* (*not accustomed*) peu habitué(e); **to be ~ to doing sth** ne pas être habitué à faire qc

**unusual** [ʌn·'ju·ʒu·əl] *adj* ❶ (*uncommon: noise, event*) inhabituel(le); (*case, job*) peu commun(e); **to be ~/ not ~ for sb to do sth** être/ne pas être rare que qn fasse qc (*subj*) ❷ (*interesting: ring, costume, car*) original(e) ❸ (*strange: friends, wish*) bizarre

**unusually** *adv* exceptionnellement; **~ for her, she took the train** elle a exceptionnellement pris le train

**unveil** [ʌn·'veɪl] *vt a.* fig dévoiler

**unwelcome** *adj* (*guests, visit*) importun(e); (*news*) fâcheux(-euse); **to feel ~** ne pas se sentir le bienvenu

**unwell** [ʌn·'wel] *adj* souffrant(e)

**unwilling** [ʌn·'wɪl·ɪŋ] *adj* **to be ~ to** +*infin* ne pas être disposé à +*infin*

**unwillingly** *adv* à contrecœur

**unwind** [ʌn·'waɪnd] *irr* I. *vt* dérouler II. *vi* ❶ (*unroll*) se dérouler ❷ (*relax*) se détendre

**unwise** [ʌn·'waɪz] *adj* (*decision, investment*) peu judicieux(-euse); (*person*) imprudent(e)

**unwrap** [ʌn·'ræp] <-pp-> *vt* (*remove wrapping*) déballer

**unwritten** [ʌn·'rɪt·ᵊn] *adj* ❶ (*not official: rule*) tacite; (*agreement*) verbal(e) ❷ (*not written*) non écrit(e); (*tradition*) oral(e)

**unzip** [ʌn·'zɪp] <-pp-> *vt* ouvrir la fermeture éclair de ❶

**up** [ʌp] I. *adv* ❶ (*movement: to be*) en haut; (*to go*) vers le haut; **on the way ~** en montant; **to look ~** lever les yeux ❷ (*to another point*) **~ North** dans le nord ❸ (*more intensity*) **to be ~** (*river, temperature*) être monté; (*price*) avoir augmenté ❹ (*position: tent*) planté(e); (*flag*) hissé(e); (*curtains, picture*) accroché(e); (*notice*) affiché(e); (*person*) debout *inv* ❺ (*state*) **to be ~ at the top of sth** être en tête de qc; **to feel ~ to sth** se sentir capable de qc ❻ (*limit*) **from the age of 18 ~** à partir de 18 ans; **~ to here** jusqu'ici; **time's ~!** c'est fini! ❼ COMPUT, TECH en service ❽ (*wrong*) **something is ~** quelque chose ne va pas ▸ **things are looking ~** ça va mieux; **~ with sb/sth!** vive qn/qc! II. *prep* ❶ (*higher*) **to go ~ the stairs** monter l'escalier ❷ (*at top of*) **to be/climb ~ a tree** être/grimper dans un arbre ❸ (*along*) **to go/drive ~ the street** remonter la rue (à pied/en voiture) ❹ (*to point of*) **~ until** [*o* till] **midnight/yesterday** [*o* to] jusqu'à minuit/hier ▸ **~ and down sth** aux quatre coins de qc; *s.a.* **down** III. *n* **to be on the ~ and ~** être tout à fait honnête IV. *vi inf* se lever brusquement; **to ~ and go** se tirer V. *vt inf* augmenter VI. *adj* ❶ (*toward a higher place*) qui monte ❷ (*under repair*) en travaux ❸ (*healthy*) en forme; **to be ~ and about** [*o* around] être sur pied ❹ (*rea-*

U

*dy)* **to be ~ for doing sth** être partant pour faire qc

**upbringing** ['ʌp,brɪŋ-ɪŋ] *n* éducation *f*

**upcoming** ['ʌp-,kʌm-ɪŋ] *adj* prochain(e)

**update** ['ʌp-deɪt, *vb:* ʌp-'deɪt] I. *n. a.* COMPUT mise *f* à jour II. *vt* ❶ (*bring up to date*) *a.* COMPUT mettre à jour ❷ (*give latest information*) **to ~ sb on sth** mettre qn au courant de qc

**upgrade**[1] [ʌp-'greɪd] *vt* ❶ (*improve quality*) améliorer ❷ COMPUT (*expand: computer, system*) optimiser; (*software*) installer la nouvelle version de ❸ (*raise in rank: worker*) promouvoir; (*job*) revaloriser; (*passenger*) surclasser

**upgrade**[2] ['ʌp-greɪd] *n* ❶ (*slope*) montée *f*; **to be on the ~** (*prices*) augmenter; (*business*) reprendre ❷ COMPUT, TECH (*expansion*) extension *f* ❸ COMPUT, TECH (*updated version*) nouvelle version *f* ❹ (*raise in class: passenger*) surclassement *m*

**upheaval** [ʌp-'hi·vᵊl] *n* ❶ (*change*) bouleversement *m* ❷ GEO soulèvement *m*

**uphill** [ʌp-'hɪl] I. *adv* **to go ~** monter II. *adj* ❶ (*sloping upward*) qui monte ❷ (*difficult*) difficile; (*struggle*) ardu(e)

**uphold** [ʌp-'hould] *vt irr* ❶ (*support*) soutenir; (*law*) faire respecter ❷ LAW (*verdict*) confirmer

**upholster** [ʌp-'houl·stər] *vt* ❶ (*pad*) rembourrer ❷ (*cover*) tapisser

**upholstery** [ʌp-'houl·stᵊr·i] *n* ❶ (*padding*) rembourrage *m* ❷ (*covering*) revêtement *m* ❸ (*art of upholstering*) tapisserie *f*

**upkeep** ['ʌp·kip] *n* ❶ (*maintain*) entretien *m* ❷ (*cost of maintaining*) frais *mpl* d'entretien ❸ (*of people*) charge *f*

**upload** ['ʌp·loud] INET I. *vt* télécharger II. *n* upload *m*, téléchargement *m* montant

**upon** [ə·'pan] *prep form* ❶ (*on top of*) sur; **~ this** là-dessus ❷ (*around*) **a ring ~ his finger** une bague à son doigt ❸ (*hanging on*) **to hang ~ the wall** être accroché au mur ❹ (*at time of*) **~ sb's arrival** dès l'arrivée de qn ▶ **once ~ a time** il était une fois; *s.a.* **on**

**upper** ['ʌp·ər] I. *adj* ❶ (*further up*) supérieur(e) ❷ GEO (*northern*) **the ~ Midwest** le Middle West du Nord II. *n* ❶ (*part of shoe*) empeigne *f* ❷ *inf* (*drugs*) amphète *f*

**upper case** *n* TYP majuscule *f*

**upper class** *n* aristocratie *f*

**upper-class** *adj* aristocratique

**upright** ['ʌp·raɪt] I. *adj, adv a. fig* droit(e) II. *n* ❶ (*piano*) piano *m* droit ❷ (*perpendicular*) montant *m*

**uproot** [ʌp-'rut] *vt a. fig* déraciner

**upscale** [ʌp·'skeɪl] *adj* haut de gamme

**upset**[1] [ʌp·'set] I. *vt irr* ❶ (*make unhappy: remark, friend*) faire de la peine à; (*event, scene*) bouleverser ❷ (*overturn*) renverser; (*boat, canoe*) faire chavirer ❸ (*throw into disorder: plans, schedule*) bouleverser; (*balance*) rompre ❹ (*cause pain: stomach*) déranger II. *adj* ❶ (*unhappy*) bouleversé(e); **to be/feel ~ about sth** être/se sentir bouleversé par qc; **don't be ~** ne t'en fais/vous en faites pas ❷ *inf* (*bilious*) dérangé(e); **to have an ~ stomach** être dérangé

**upset**[2] ['ʌp·set] *n* ❶ (*upheaval*) bouleversement *m* ❷ (*unhappy feeling*) peine *f*; **to cause sb ~(s)** faire de la peine à qn ❸ SPORTS revers *m* ❹ MED **to have a stomach ~** avoir l'estomac dérangé

**upside down** [ʌp·saɪd·'daun] I. *adj* ❶ (*reversed*) à l'envers ❷ (*chaotic: room, plans*) sens dessus dessous II. *adv* ❶ (*in inverted position*) à l'envers; **to turn sth ~** retourner qc ❷ (*in disorder*) *a. fig* **to turn sth ~** mettre qc sens dessus dessous; **to turn sb ~** bouleverser la vie qn

**upstairs** [ʌp·'sterz] I. *adj* d'en haut; (*room*) à l'étage II. *adv* en haut; (*room*) à l'étage; **to live ~ from sb** vivre au-dessus de chez qn III. *n* **the ~** l'étage *m*

**upstate** ['ʌp·steɪt] I. *adj* du nord; **~ New York** nord *m* de l'État de New York II. *adv* (*to go*) vers le nord; (*to live*) dans le nord

**upstream** [ʌp·'strim] I. *adj* amont *inv* II. *adv* en amont

U

**uptake** ['ʌp·teɪk] *n* (*level of absorption*) assimilation *f* ▸ **to be quick on the ~** *inf* saisir vite; **to be slow on the ~** *inf* être long à la détente

**uptight** [ʌp·'taɪt] *adj inf* tendu(e); **to get ~ about sth** s'énerver à propos de qc

**up-to-date** *adj* ❶ (*contemporary*) actuel(le) ❷ (*latest*) récent(e); **~ news on sth** dernières nouvelles *fpl* de qc ❸ (*updated*) à jour ❹ (*informed*) au courant; **to bring sth ~** mettre qc à jour

**upward** ['ʌp·wərd] **I.** *adj* qui monte; (*movement, mobility*) ascendant(e); (*trend*) à la hausse **II.** *adv* ❶ (*to a higher position*) vers le haut; **to put sth face ~** mettre qc à l'endroit; **to lie face ~** être couché sur le dos ❷ (*more than*) au-dessus; **$100 and ~** cent dollars et plus; **from $1/eight ~** à partir d'un dollar/de huit ans

**uranium** [jʊ·'reɪ·ni·əm] *n* CHEM uranium *m*

**urban** ['ɜr·bən] *adj* urbain(e); **~ areas** zones *fpl* urbaines; **~ decay** dégradation *f* urbaine

**urban myth** *n* légende *f* urbaine

**uremia** [jʊ·'ri·mi·ə] *n* MED urémie *f*

**urge** [ɜrdʒ] **I.** *n* ❶ (*strong desire*) forte envie *f*; **to have an ~ to** +*infin* avoir très envie de +*infin*; **to feel an irresistible ~** avoir un besoin irrésistible ❷ (*compulsion*) impulsion *f* **II.** *vt* ❶ (*push*) pousser ❷ (*encourage*) encourager; **to ~ sb to** +*infin* presser qn de +*infin* ❸ (*seriously recommend*) conseiller vivement; (*caution*) recommander; (*peace*) appeler à; **to urge self-discipline on** [*o* **upon**] **sb** inciter qn à la discipline

◆**urge on** *vt* (*friend*) encourager; **to urge sb on to** +*infin* pousser qn à +*infin*

**urgency** ['ɜr·dʒən(t)·si] *n* ❶ (*top priority*) urgence *f*; **a matter of ~** une affaire urgente ❷ (*insistence*) insistance *f*

**urgent** ['ɜr·dʒənt] *adj* ❶ (*imperative: appeal, plea*) urgent(e); (*need*) pressant(e) ❷ (*insistent*) insistant(e)

**urgently** *adv* ❶ (*very necessarily*) d'urgence ❷ (*insistently*) avec insistance

**urinal** ['jʊr·ən·əl] *n* urinoir *m*

**urinate** ['jʊr·ə·neɪt] *vi* uriner

**urine** ['jʊr·ɪn] *n* urine *f*

**urn** [ɜrn] *n* ❶ (*vase*) urne *f* ❷ (*drink container*) fontaine *f*; **tea/coffee ~** fontaine à thé/café

**Ursa Major** [ˌɜr·sə·'meɪ·dʒər] *n* ASTR la Grande Ourse

**us** [ʌs] *pers pron* (*1st person pl*) nous; **it's ~** c'est nous; **older than ~** plus vieux que nous; **look at ~** regarde/regardez-nous; **he saw ~** il nous a vus; **he gave it to ~** il nous l'a donné; **all/both of ~** nous tous/tous les deux

**US** *n*, **U.S.** [ju·'es] *n abbr of* **United States** USA *mpl*

**USA** [ˌju·es·'eɪ] *n abbr of* **United States of America** USA *mpl*

**USB** [ju·es·'bi:] *n abbr of* **Universal Serial Bus** COMPUT USB *m*; **~** [**flash**] **drive** clé *f* USB

**use¹** [jus] *n* ❶ (*using*) emploi *m*; **in ~** en service; **to make ~ of sth** se servir de qc ❷ (*possibility of applying*) usage *m*; **external ~ only** à usage externe; **to have the ~ of sth** pouvoir se servir de qc ❸ (*usefulness*) utilité *f*; **to be of ~ to sb** être utile à qn; **to be no ~ doing sth** être inutile de faire qc; **I'm no ~ at history** *inf* je suis nul en histoire; **can I be of any ~ to you?** puis-je vous être utile?; **what's the ~ of that/doing sth?** à quoi bon tout ça/faire qc? ❹ (*consumption*) usage *m*; (*of drugs*) consommation *f*; **ready for ~** prêt(e) à l'emploi ❺ LING usage *m* ❻ (*custom*) coutume *f*

**use²** [juz] **I.** *vt* ❶ (*make use of sth*) utiliser; (*tool, machine*) se servir de; (*blackmail, violence*) faire usage de; **I could ~ some help** *inf* j'ai besoin d'aide ❷ (*consume*) consommer ❸ (*form*) (*treat in stated way*) traiter ❹ *pej* (*exploit: people*) utiliser **II.** *vt aux* **I ~d to do sth** je faisais qc; **it ~d to be calm** c'était calme; **there ~d to be a market here** il y avait un marché ici

◆**use up** *vt* ❶ (*use*) consommer; (*mon-*

*ey*) dépenser ❷ (*tire*) épuiser; **to be used up** être épuisé

**used¹** [juzd] *adj* ❶ (*already been used*) usé(e); ❷ (*second-hand*) d'occasion; ~ **car** voiture *f* d'occasion

**used²** [just] *adj* (*familiar with*) habitué(e); **to be ~ to sth** être habitué à qc; **to be ~ to doing sth** avoir l'habitude de faire qc; **to become ~ to sth** s'habituer à qc; **I'm not ~ to big cities/living alone** je n'ai pas l'habitude des grandes villes/de vivre seul

**useful** *adj* utile; **to be ~ to sb/sth** être utile à qn/qc; **to be ~ with sth** *inf* savoir se servir de qc

**usefulness** *n* utilité *f*

**useless** *adj* ❶ (*futile*) inutile ❷ (*unusable*) inutilisable ❸ *inf* (*incompetent*) nul(le)

**user** ['ju·zər] *n* ❶ (*person who uses sth*) utilisateur, -trice *m, f*; (*of gas, electricity*) usager, -ère *m, f* ❷ COMPUT utilisateur, -trice *m, f* ❸ *inf* (*addict*) consommateur, -trice *m, f*; **drug ~s** consommateurs *mpl* de drogue

**user-friendly** *adj* COMPUT convivial(e)

**user interface** *n* COMPUT interface *f* (utilisateur)

**user name** *n* COMPUT nom *m* d'utilisateur

**USMC** [ˌju·es·ˈem·si] *n abbr of* **United States Marine Corps** corps *m* des marines des États-Unis

**USN** [ˌju·es·ˈen] *n abbr of* **United States Navy** marine *f* des États-Unis

**USPS** [ˌju·es·ˈpi·es] *n abbr of* **United States Postal Service** services *mpl* postaux américains

**usual** ['ju·ʒu·əl] I. *adj* habituel(le); **as ~** comme d'habitude; **to be ~ to** +*infin* être d'usage de +*infin* II. *n* **the ~** *inf* comme d'habitude

**usually** ['ju·ʒu·əl·i] *adv* d'habitude

**UT** *n abbr of* Utah

**Utah** ['ju·tɑ] I. *n* l'Utah *m* II. *adj* de l'Utah

**utility** [ju·ˈtɪl·ə·t̬i] <-ies> I. *n* ❶ *form* (*usefulness*) utilité *f* ❷ (*public service*) (**public**) **~** service *m* public ❸ COMPUT utilitaire *m* II. *adj* ❶ (*useful*) utilitaire ❷ (*functional*) fonctionnel(le)

**utilize** ['ju·t̬ə·laɪz] *vt* utiliser

**utmost** ['ʌt·moʊst] I. *adj* extrême; **with the ~ caution** avec la plus grande précaution; **a matter of ~ importance** une affaire de première importance II. *n* **the ~** l'extrême *m*; **to offer the ~ in performance** offrir le maximum en matière de performance; **to try one's ~** essayer tout son possible

**utopian** *adj* utopique

**utter¹** ['ʌt̬·ər] *adj* complet(-ète); **to be ~ nonsense** être absolument nonsense; **~ madness** pure folie *f*; **an ~ waste of time** une pure perte de temps

**utter²** ['ʌt̬·ər] *vt* (*make a sound: word, name*) prononcer; (*sound*) émettre; (*cry, grunt*) pousser

**utterly** *adv* ❶ (*completely*) complètement; **to be ~ convinced that ...** être tout à fait convaincu que ... ❷ (*absolutely*) absolument

**U-turn** ['ju·tɜrn] *n* ❶ AUTO demi-tour *m* ❷ *fig* volte-face *f*

**U**

# V v

**V, v** [viː] <-'s o -s> n V m, v m; **~ as in Victor** (on telephone) v comme Victor

**V** n ① abbr of **volume** v ② abbr of **volt** V m

**VA** n abbr of **Virginia**

**vacancy** ['veɪ·kən(t)·si] <-ies> n ① (available room) chambre f à louer ② (employment opportunity) poste m vacant ③ (lack of expression) vide m

**vacant** ['veɪ·kənt] adj ① (empty) vide ② (unoccupied: room) inoccupé(e) ③ (expressionless) vide

**vacate** ['veɪ·keɪt] vt form quitter

**vacation** [veɪ·'keɪ·ʃən] I. n ① vacances fpl; **to take a ~** prendre des vacances; **on ~** en vacances, vacances fpl; **summer ~** les vacances d'été ② (paid time off work) congés mpl payés II. vi passer des vacances

**vaccinate** ['væk·sə·neɪt] vt MED vacciner

**vaccination** [ˌvæk·sə·'neɪ·ʃən] n MED vaccination f

**vaccine** ['væk·'sin] n MED vaccin m

**vacuum** ['væk·jum] I. n ① (space) a. fig vide m; **to fill/leave a ~** remplir/laisser un vide ② (vacuum cleaner) aspirateur m II. vt (carpet) passer l'aspirateur sur; (room) passer l'aspirateur dans

**vacuum cleaner** n aspirateur m

**vagina** [və·'dʒaɪ·nə] n ANAT vagin m

**vaginal** ['vædʒ·ə·n·əl] adj ANAT vaginal(e)

**vagrant** ['veɪ·grənt] n vagabond(e) m(f)

**vague** [veɪg] adj ① (imprecise) vague ② (absent-minded) distrait(e) ③ (uncertain, unsure) confus(e)

**vaguely** adv ① (faintly: remember) vaguement ② (distractedly: say, smile) d'un air distrait; (move) distraitement

**vain** [veɪn] adj ① pej (conceited) vaniteux(-euse) ② (futile) vain(e); **in ~** en vain

**valedictorian** [ˌvæl·ə·dɪk·tɔ·ri·ən] n SCHOOL major mf de la promotion (qui prononce le discours de fin d'année)

**valentine** ['væl·ən·taɪn] n ① (card) carte de vœux pour la Saint-Valentin ② (sweetheart) Valentin(e) m(f)

**valet parking** n voiturier m

**valiantly** adv vaillamment

**valid** ['væl·ɪd] adj ① (acceptable) valable; (license) en règle; (passport, ticket) valide ② (worthwhile) pertinent(e)

**valley** ['væl·i] n vallée f

**valuable** I. adj a. fig précieux(-euse) II. n pl objets mpl de valeur

**value** ['væl·ju] I. n ① (importance, worth) valeur f; **to place a high ~ on sth** attacher une grande importance à qc ② (possible price) valeur f; **the ~ of sth falls/rises** qc perd/prend de la valeur ③ (ethical standard) valeur f; **basic ~s** les grandes valeurs II. vt estimer

**valued** adj estimé(e)

**valve** [vælv] n ① (control) soupape f ② (part of organs) valvule f ③ (instrument part) piston m

**vampire** ['væm·paɪər] n vampire m

**van** [væn] n ① (passenger vehicle) camionnette f ② (commercial vehicle) véhicule m de fonction

**vandal** ['væn·dəl] n vandale mf

**vandalism** ['væn·dəl·ɪ·zəm] n vandalisme m

**vandalize** ['væn·dəl·aɪz] vt saccager

**vanilla** [və·'nɪl·ə] I. n BOT vanille f II. adj (ice cream, yogurt) à la vanille

**vanish** ['væn·ɪʃ] vi disparaître; **to ~ into thin air** se volatiliser

**vanity** ['væn·ə·ti] n vanité f

**vantage point** n point m de vue; **from the ~ of sb/sth** du point de vue de qn/qc

**vapor** ['veɪ·pər] n vapeur f; **water ~** vapeur d'eau

**vaporize** ['veɪ·pə·raɪz] I. vt vaporiser II. vi s'évaporer

**vapor pressure** n pression f de la vapeur

**vapor trail** n traînée f blanche

**variable** ['ver·i·ə·bl] adj, n variable f

**variation** [ˌver·i·'eɪ·ʃ⁰n] n a. MUS variation f; **~s on a theme** variations sur un thème

**varied** adj varié(e); (career) mouvementé(e); (group) hétérogène

**variety** [və·'raɪə· t̮i] n (diversity) variété f; **a ~ of styles** divers styles mpl; **in a ~ of ways** de plusieurs manières; **for a ~ of reasons** pour diverses raisons

**variety show** n spectacle m de variétés

**various** ['ver·i·əs] adj divers(e)

**variously** adv diversement

**varnish** ['var·nɪʃ] I. n vernis m II. vt vernir

**vary** ['ver·i] <-ie-> I. vi varier; (opinions) diverger; **to ~ from sth** différer de qc; **to ~ from sth to sth** varier de qc à qc II. vt varier; **to ~ one's route** changer de route

**varying** adj variable

**vase** [veɪs] n vase m

**vast** [væst] adj (country, fortune, majority) vaste; **a ~ difference/amount of money** une énorme différence/somme d'argent

**Vatican** ['væt̮·ɪ·kən] n **the ~** le Vatican

**vault** [vɔlt] I. n ① (type of arch) voûte f ② (secure room) salle f des coffres ③ (safe) coffre-fort m ④ (chamber) caveau m; **family ~** caveau familial ⑤ (jump) saut m II. vt ① (jump) sauter ② (promote very fast) propulser III. vi sauter

**VCR** [ˌvi·si·'ar] n abbr of video cassette recorder magnétoscope m

**veal** [vil] n (viande f de) veau m

**veg** [vedʒ] vi infto ~ (out) glander

**vegan** ['vi·gən] I. n végétalien(ne) m(f) II. adj végétalien(ne)

**vegetable** ['vedʒ·tə·bl] I. n a. pej légume m; **~ soup** soupe f de légumes; **early ~s** primeurs fpl II. adj végétal(e); (soup, dish) de légumes

**vegetable garden** n potager m

**vegetable oil** n huile f végétale

**vegetarian** [ˌvedʒ·ə·'ter·i·ən] I. n végétarien(ne) m(f) II. adj végétarien(ne); **~ diet** régime m végétarien

**vegetation** [ˌvedʒ·ə·'teɪ·ʃ⁰n] n végétation f

**vehicle** ['vi·ə·kl] n form, a. fig véhicule m

**vehicular** [vi·'hɪk·jə·lər] adj form véhiculaire; **~ traffic** circulation f routière; **~ manslaughter** le fait de tuer qn avec une voiture

**veil** [veɪl] I. n a. fig voile m; **~ of secrecy** fig voile de mystère II. vt ① passive (cover by veil) **to be ~ed** être voilé ② (cover) voiler

**vein** [veɪn] n ① (blood vessel) a. MIN veine f ② (for plant sap) nervure f ③ (style) veine f ④ (frame of mind) humeur f

**velvet** ['vel·vɪt] n velours m

**vending machine** n distributeur m automatique

**vendor** ['ven·dər] n marchand(e) m(f)

**venetian blind** n store m vénitien

**vengeance** ['ven·dʒ⁰n(t)s] n vengeance f; **with a ~** de plus belle

**venison** ['ven·ɪ·s⁰n] n chevreuil m

**venom** ['ven·əm] n a. fig venin m

**venomous** ['ven·ə·məs] adj fig, pej venimeux(-euse)

**ventilate** ['ven·t̮ə·leɪt] vt (oxygenate) aérer

**ventilation** [ˌven·t̮ə·'leɪ·ʃ⁰n] n aération f

**ventilator** ['ven·t̮ə·leɪ·t̮ər] n ventilateur m

**ventriloquist** [ven·'trɪl·ə·kwɪst] n ventriloque mf

**venture** ['ven·tʃər] I. n entreprise f; **my first ~ into journalism** ma première incursion f dans le journalisme II. vt ① (dare to express: explanation) hasarder; **to ~ an opinion** se hasarder à donner une opinion ② (put at risk) risquer; **to ~ to** +infin se risquer à +infin ▶ **nothing ~d, nothing gained** prov qui ne risque rien n'a rien prov III. vi s'aventurer; **to ~ into sth** s'aventurer dans qc; **to ~ out in sth** se risquer à sortir dans qc

**venue** ['ven·ju] n ① (place) lieu m de

**V**

rencontre; (*in hall*) salle *f*; (*for match*) terrain *m* ② LAW prétoire *m*

**Venus** ['vi·nəs] *n* Vénus *f*

**verb** [vɜrb] *n* verbe *m*

**verbal** ['vɜr·bəl] *adj a.* LING verbal(e)

**verdict** ['vɜr·dɪkt] *n* verdict *m*; **guilty ~** verdict de culpabilité; **to deliver a ~** rendre un verdict; **what's your ~?** quel est ton verdict?

**verge** [vɜrdʒ] *n* (*brink*) **to be on the ~ of tears** être au bord des larmes; **to be on the ~ of resigning/leaving sb** être sur le point de démissionner/quitter qn

**verge on** *vt* friser; **to ~ the ridiculous** friser le ridicule

**verification** [ˌver·ə·fɪ·'keɪ·[ə]n] *n* vérification *f*

**verify** ['ver·ə·faɪ] <-ie-> *vt* vérifier

**Vermont** [vər·'mɑnt] **I.** *n* le Vermont **II.** *adj* du Vermont

**versatile** ['vɜr·sə·t[ə]l] *adj* (*tool, actor*) polyvalent(e); (*mind*) souple

**versatility** [ˌvɜr·sə·'tɪl·ə·t̬i] *n* polyvalence *f*

**verse** [vɜrs] *n* ① (*poetry*) vers *m*; (*of song*) couplet *m*; **in ~** en vers ② REL verset *m*

**version** ['vɜr·ʒ[ə]n] *n* version *f*

**versus** ['vɜr·səs] *prep* ① (*in comparison*) par opposition [*o* rapport] à ② SPORTS, LAW contre

**vertebra** ['vɜr·t̬ə·brə] <-brae> *n* vertèbre *f*

**vertebrate** ['vɜr·t̬ə·brɪt] **I.** *n* vertébré *m* **II.** *adj* vertébré(e)

**vertical** ['vɜr·t̬ə·k[ə]l] *adj* vertical(e)

**vertigo** ['vɜr·t̬ə·goʊ] *n* vertige *m*

**very** ['ver·i] **I.** *adv* ① (*extremely*) très; **to be ~ hungry** avoir très faim ② (*to a great degree*) **~ much** beaucoup; **we're ~ much in love** nous sommes très amoureux ③ (*expression of emphasis*) **the ~ best** tout ce qu'il y a de mieux; **the ~ first/last** le tout premier/dernier; **to do the ~ best one can** vraiment faire tout son possible; **at the ~ most/least** tout au plus/au moins; **it's my ~ own** c'est le mien ▶ **~ well** très bien **II.** *adj* même; **this ~**

**house** cette maison *f* même; **to the ~ end** jusqu'au bout; **from the ~ beginning** depuis le tout début; **the ~ thought of sth** la seule pensée de qc

**vessel** ['ves·əl] *n* ① *form* (*boat*) vaisseau *m* ② *form* (*container*) récipient *m* ③ ANAT, BOT vaisseau *m*

**vest**[1] [vest] *n* ① (*sleeveless garment*) gilet *m* ② SPORTS maillot *m*

**vest**[2] [vest] *vt form* investir; **by the authority ~ed in me** en vertu de l'autorité dont je suis investi

**vet**[1] [vet] *n inf* (*animal doctor*) vétérinaire *mf*

**vet**[2] [vet] *n inf* (*veteran*) vétéran *m*

**vet**[3] [vet] *vt* <-tt-> examiner; **to be ~ed by sb/sth** recevoir l'approbation de qn/qc

**veteran** ['vet̬·ər·ən] **I.** *n* ① (*person with experience*) vétéran *m* ② MIL ancien combattant *m* **II.** *adj* (*very experienced*) aguerri(e)

**veterinarian** [ˌvet̬·ər·ɪ·'ner·i·ən] *n* vétérinaire *mf*

**veterinary** ['vet̬·ər·ɪ·ner·i] *adj* vétérinaire

**VFW** [ˌvi·ef·'dʌb·l·ju] *abbr of* **Veterans of Foreign Wars** vétérans *mpl* ayant combattu à l'étranger

**VHF** [ˌvi·eɪtʃ·'ef] *adj abbr of* **very high frequency** RADIO, TV VHF *inv*

**VI** *n abbr of* **Virgin Islands**

**via** [vaɪə] *prep* ① (*through*) par; **~ New York** via New York ② (*using*) **~ the bridge** en empruntant le pont; **~ courier** par courrier

**vibe** [vaɪb] *npl inf* ① (*general atmosphere*) ambiance *f*; **I'm getting good/bad ~s about sth** je sens/je ne sens pas qc ② *pl* MUS *s.* **vibraphone**

**vibrant** ['vaɪ·brənt] *adj* ① (*lively: person*) vibrant(e) ② (*bustling*) animé(e) ③ (*bright: color, light*) vif(vive) ④ (*strong: voice, sound*) sonore

**vibraphone** ['vaɪ·brə·foʊn] *n* MUS vibraphone *m*

**vibrate** ['vaɪ·breɪt] **I.** *vi* ① (*shake quickly*) vibrer ② (*continue to be heard: sound*) retentir **II.** *vt* faire vibrer

V

**vibration** [vaɪ·ˈbreɪ·ʃᵊn] *n* vibration *f*
**vice** [vaɪs] *n* vice *m*
**vice president** *n* vice-président(e) *m(f)*
**vice versa** [ˌvaɪ·sə·ˈvɜr·sə] *adv* vice versa
**vicinity** [və·ˈsɪn·ə·t̬i] *n* voisinage *m;* **in the ~ of sth** dans les alentours de qc; **in the immediate ~** à proximité
**vicious** [ˈvɪʃ·əs] *adj* ① (*malicious*) malveillant(e); (*gossip*) méchant(e) ② (*cruel*) violent(e) ③ (*able to cause pain*) pervers(e); (*animal*) méchant(e)
**vicious circle** *n* cercle *m* vicieux
**victim** [ˈvɪk·tɪm] *n* (*of crime, illness*) victime *f;* (*of disaster*) sinistré(e) *m(f)*
**victimize** [ˈvɪk·tə·maɪz] *vt* persécuter; **to be ~d** être victime de persécutions
**Victorian** [vɪk·ˈtɔr·i·ən] **I.** *adj* victorien(ne) **II.** *n* Victorien(ne) *m(f)*
**victorious** [vɪk·ˈtɔr·i·əs] *adj* victorieux(-euse); (*team*) vainqueur
**victory** [ˈvɪk·tᵊr·i] *n* victoire *f;* **to lead sb to ~** mener qn à la victoire; **to win a ~ in sth** sortir victorieux de qc
**video** [ˈvɪd·i·oʊ] *n* ① (*movie*) vidéo *f;* **to come out on ~** sortir en vidéo ② (*tape*) cassette vidéo *f* ③ (*recorded footage*) film *m* vidéo ④ (*of song*) clip vidéo *m*
**video camera** *n* caméra *f* vidéo
**videocassette** *n* cassette *f* vidéo
**videoconference** *n* visioconférence *f*
**videoconferencing** *n* vidéoconférence *f*
**video game** *n* jeu *m* vidéo
**videotape** **I.** *n* bande *f* vidéo **II.** *vt* enregistrer sur une cassette vidéo
**Vienna** [vi·ˈen·ə] *n* Vienne
**Vietnam**, **Viet Nam** [ˌviet·ˈnam] *n* le Viêt-nam [*o* Vietnam]
**Vietnamese** [vi·ˌet·nə·ˈmiz] **I.** *adj* vietnamien(ne) **II.** *n* ① (*person*) Vietnamien(ne) *m(f)* ② LING vietnamien *m;* *s.a.* **English**
**view** [vju] **I.** *n* ① (*opinion, idea*) opinion *f;* **conflicting ~s** avis *mpl* divergents; **to share sb's ~** partager l'avis de qn; **to have ~s about sb/sth** avoir des opinions sur qn/qc; **to hold strong ~s about sth** avoir des idées arrêtées sur qc; **in sb's ~** d'après qn ② (*sight*) vue *f;* **to block sb's ~** gêner le champ de vision de qn ③ (*ability to see*) vue *f;* **in full ~ of sb** sous les yeux *mpl* de qn; **to come into ~** s'approcher; **to hide sth from ~** cacher qc ►**to have sth in ~** avoir qc en vue; **in ~ of** étant donné; **to be on ~** être exposé; **with a ~ to doing sth** dans le but de faire qc **II.** *vt* ① (*consider*) considérer; **to be ~ed as dangerous/a threat** être considéré comme dangereux/une menace ② (*envisage*) envisager; **to ~ sth with delight** envisager qc avec ravissement ③ (*see, watch: works of art*) voir; (*house*) visiter; (*slide*) visionner
**viewer** *n* ① TV téléspectateur, -trice *m, f* ② (*device for slides*) *a.* COMPUT visionneuse *f*
**viewpoint** *n* point *m* de vue
**vigilant** [ˈvɪdʒ·ɪ·lənt] *adj* vigilant(e); **a ~ eye** un œil attentif
**vigorous** [ˈvɪg·ᵊr·əs] *adj* ① (*energetic*) vigoureux(-euse); (*protest*) ferme ② SPORTS (*exercise*) intensif(-ive) ③ (*flourishing: growth*) fort(e)
**vile** [vaɪl] <-r, -st> *adj* ① (*very bad*) exécrable; (*smell, taste*) infect(e) ② (*morally bad*) vil(e)
**village** [ˈvɪl·ɪdʒ] *n* ① (*settlement*) village *m* ② + *sing/pl vb* (*populace*) village *m*
**villain** [ˈvɪl·ən] *n* ① (*evil person*) scélérat(e) *m(f)* ② (*bad guy*) voyou *m*
**VIN** [ˌvi·aɪ·ˈen] *n abbr of* **vehicle identification number** plaque *f* d'immatriculation du véhicule
**vinaigrette** [ˌvɪn·ə·ˈgret] *n* vinaigrette *f*
**vindictive** [vɪn·ˈdɪk·tɪv] *adj* vindicatif(-ive)
**vine** [vaɪn] *n* ① (*grape plant*) vigne *f* ② (*climbing plant*) plante *f* grimpante
**vinegar** [ˈvɪn·ə·gər] *n* vinaigre *m*
**vineyard** [ˈvɪn·jərd] *n* vignoble *m*
**vintage** [ˈvɪn·t̬ɪdʒ] **I.** *n* ① (*wine*) cru *m;* **the 1983 ~** le cru de 1983 ② (*year*) millésime *m* **II.** *adj* ① CULIN de grand cru; **a ~ year** une grande année ② (*classic quality*) classique ③ (*old: car, clothes*) d'époque

V

**viola** [viˈou·lə] *n* MUS alto *m*

**violate** [ˈvaɪə·leɪt] *vt* ① (*break*) désobéir à ② (*enter illegally*) transgresser; (*a tomb*) profaner ③ (*disturb*) déranger; **to ~ sb's privacy** faire intrusion chez qn ④ *form* (*rape*) violer

**violation** [ˌvaɪə·ˈleɪ·ʃ°n] *n* ① (*act of not respecting*) violation *f*; **in ~ of sth** en violation de qc ② (*act of breaking law*) infraction *f*

**violence** [ˈvaɪə·l°n(t)s] *n* violence *f*

**violent** [ˈvaɪə·l°nt] *adj* ① (*cruel*) violent(e); (*argument*) virulent(e) ② (*very powerful*) fort(e); **to have a ~ temper** être colérique

**violet** [ˈvaɪə·lɪt] I. *n* ① BOT violette *f* ② (*color*) violet *m* II. *adj* violet(te); *s.a.* **blue**

**violin** [ˌvaɪə·ˈlɪn] *n* violon *m*

**violinist** *n* violoniste *mf*

**VIP** [ˌviˈaɪ·ˈpi] I. *n abbr of* **very important person** VIP *mf* II. *adj* VIP *inv*; **to be given ~ treatment** être traité comme une personnalité de marque

**virgin** [ˈvɜr·dʒɪn] I. *n* vierge *f*; (*man*) puceau *m inf* II. *adj* vierge; **pure ~ wool** pure laine *f* vierge

**Virginia** [vərˈdʒɪn·jə] I. *n* la Virginie II. *adj* de Virginie

**Virgin Islands** *n* les îles *fpl* Vierges

**virginity** [vərˈdʒɪn·ə·t̬i] *n* virginité *f*

**Virgo** [ˈvɜr·gou] *n* Vierge *f*; *s.a.* **Aquarius**

**virile** [ˈvɪr·°l] *adj* viril(e)

**virility** [vəˈrɪl·ə·t̬i] *n* virilité *f*

**virtual** [ˈvɜr·tʃu·əl] *adj* ① (*as described*) quasi-; **it's a ~ impossibility** c'est quasiment impossible ② COMPUT virtuel(le)

**virtually** *adv* ① (*nearly*) pratiquement; **~ unknown** quasiment inconnu; **~ the whole town** la quasi-totalité de la ville ② COMPUT virtuellement

**virtuous** [ˈvɜr·tʃu·əs] *adj* (*morally good*) vertueux(-euse)

**virus** [ˈvaɪ·rəs] *n a.* COMPUT virus *m*

**visa** [ˈvi·zə] *n* visa *m*

**vise** [vaɪs] *n* étau *m*

**visibility** [ˌvɪz·ə·ˈbɪl·ə·t̬i] *n* visibilité *f*

**visible** [ˈvɪz·ə·bl] *adj* visible

**vision** [ˈvɪʒ·°n] *n* ① (*sight*) vue *f* ② (*dream, hope*) vision *f*; **to have ~s of doing sth** se voir faire qc; **my ~ for the school/company** mes espoirs *mpl* pour l'école/l'entreprise ③ (*imagination*) perspicacité *f*; **a man of great ~** un homme qui voit loin

**visit** [ˈvɪz·ɪt] I. *n* visite *f*; **to pay a ~ to sb** rendre visite à qn; **a ~ to the library** un tour chez le libraire; **during our ~ to Miami** au cours de notre séjour à Miami II. *vt* (*town, museum*) visiter; (*person*) aller voir; **to ~ sb in the hospital** se rendre auprès de qn à l'hôpital III. *vi* être en visite; **to ~ with sb** aller voir qn

**visitor** [ˈvɪz·ɪ·t̬ər] *n* ① (*guest*) invité(e) *m(f)*; **to have ~s** avoir de la visite ② (*tourist*) visiteur, -euse *m, f*; **to be a frequent ~ to sth** visiter régulièrement qc

**visitor center** *n* centre *m* d'accueil

**visor** [ˈvaɪ·zər] *n* visière *f*

**visual aid** *n* support *m* visuel

**visualize** [ˈvɪʒ·u·ə·laɪz] *vt* visualiser

**vital** [ˈvaɪ·t̬°l] *adj* ① (*necessary: food, medicine*) vital(e); (*information, clue, measure*) capital(e); (*ingredient*) indispensable; **to be ~ to sth** être indispensable à qc; **it is ~ that** il est capital que *+subj* ② *form* (*energetic*) énergique

**vitality** [vaɪˈtæl·ə·t̬i] *n* vitalité *f*

**vital statistics** *n pl* mensurations *fpl*

**vitamin** [ˈvaɪ·t̬ə·mɪn] *n* vitamine *f*

**vivacious** [vɪˈveɪ·ʃəs] *adj* enjoué(e)

**vivid** [ˈvɪv·ɪd] *adj a. fig* vif(vive); (*example, description*) frappant(e); (*memory, picture*) net(te); (*language*) vivant(e)

**vocabulary** [vouˈkæb·jə·ler·i] *n* ① (*words*) vocabulaire *m* ② (*glossary*) lexique *m*

**vocal** [ˈvou·k°l] I. *adj* ① (*related to the voice*) vocal(e) ② (*outspoken*) qui se fait entendre ③ (*articulate*) parler beaucoup II. *n* ~(**s**) chant *m*; **on ~s** au chant

**vocalist** *n* chanteur, -euse *m, f*

**vocation** [vouˈkeɪ·ʃ°n] *n* vocation *f*

**vocational** *adj* professionnel(le)

**vodka** ['vad·kə] *n* vodka *f*

**voice** [vɔɪs] I. *n a.* *fig* voix *f;* **tenor ~** voix de ténor; **his ~ is breaking** sa voix mue; **to keep one's ~ down** parler à voix basse; **to lower/raise one's ~** baisser/hausser le ton; **to lose one's ~** avoir une extinction de voix ► **to give ~ to sth** exprimer qc; **to listen to the ~ of reason** écouter la voix de la raison II. *vt* exprimer

**voicemail** *n* boîte *f* vocale

**voiceover** *n* TV, CINE voix *f* off

**void** [vɔɪd] I. *n a.* *fig* vide *m;* **to fill the ~** combler le vide II. *adj* ❶ (*invalid*) nul(le); **to declare sth ~** annuler qc ❷ (*empty*) vide; **~ of sth** dépourvu(e) de qc III. *vt* ❶ (*declare not valid*) annuler ❷ (*drain away*) évacuer

**VoIP** [vɔɪp] *vt, vi abbr of* **Voice over Internet Protocol** INET communiquer par voip

**vol.** *n abbr of* **volume** vol *m*

**volatile** ['va·lə·t<sup>ə</sup>l] *adj* ❶ (*changeable*) versatile ❷ (*explosive*) explosif(-ive) ❸ (*easily vaporized*) volatile

**volcanic** [val·ˈkæn·ɪk] *adj* volcanique

**volcano** [val·ˈkeɪ·noʊ] <-es *o* -s> *n* volcan *m*

**volition** [voʊ·ˈlɪʃ·<sup>ə</sup>n] *n form* volonté *f;* **to do sth (out) of one's own ~** faire qc de son propre gré

**volley** ['va·li] I. *n* ❶ (*salvo*) volée *f;* (*gunfire*) salve *f* ❷ (*onslaught*) torrent *m* ❸ SPORTS volée *f* II. *vi* SPORTS effectuer une volée III. *vt* SPORTS **to ~ a ball** effectuer une volée

**volleyball** ['va·li·bɔl] *n* volley ball *m*

**volt** [voʊlt] *n* volt *m*

**voltage** ['voʊl·tɪdʒ] *n* voltage *m*

**volume** ['val·jum] *n* ❶ (*sound, measurement*) volume *m;* **to turn the ~ up/down** augmenter/baisser le volume ❷ (*book*) volume *m;* **in ten ~s** en dix volumes ► **to speak ~s about sth** en dire long sur qc

**voluntary** ['va·l<sup>ə</sup>n·ter·i] *adj* ❶ (*of one's free will*) volontaire ❷ (*without payment*) bénévole

**volunteer** [ˌva·lən·ˈtɪr] I. *n* ❶ (*unpaid worker*) bénévole *mf* ❷ (*person willing to do*) volontaire *mf;* **~ helpers** bénévoles *mfpl* II. *vt* **to ~ sb to +infin** proposer à qn de +*infin;* **to ~ help** offrir son aide III. *vi* se porter volontaire; **to ~ to +infin** offrir volontiers ses services pour +*infin;* **to ~ for sth** se proposer pour qc

**vomit** ['va·mɪt] I. *vt, vi* vomir; **to ~ blood** cracher du sang II. *n* vomi *m*

**vote** [voʊt] I. *n* ❶ *a.* POL vote *m,* votation *f Suisse;* **10% of the ~** 10% des voix; **to cast one's ~** voter; **they get my ~** je vote pour eux; **sth gets sb's ~** (*approve*) qn est d'accord avec qc ❷ (*right to elect*) droit *m* de vote II. *vt* (*elect*) voter; **to ~ in an election** voter à une élection; **to ~ on sth** soumettre qc au vote; **to ~ for/against sb/sth** voter pour/contre qn/qc; **to ~ to strike** choisir de se mettre en grève; **to ~ on who/how/when...** voter pour décider qui/comment/quand... ► **to ~ with one's feet** quitter le navire III. *vt* ❶ (*elect*) voter; **to ~ sb into office** faire élire qn à un poste ❷ (*propose*) proposer; **to ~ that** proposer que +*subj* ❸ (*decide to give*) **to ~ sb/sth sth** décider d'accorder qc à qn/qc

◆**vote down** *vt* rejeter

◆**vote in** *vt* (*person*) élire; (*law*) adopter

◆**vote out** *vt* (*person*) ne pas réélire; (*bill*) rejeter

**voter** ['voʊ·t̬ər] *n* électeur, -trice *m, f*

**voting** I. *adj* votant(e) II. *n* vote *m*

**voting booth** *n* isoloir *m*

**vouch** [vaʊtʃ] *vt* **to ~ that ...** garantir que ...

◆**vouch for** *vt* se porter garant de

**voucher** ['vaʊ·tʃər] *n* ❶ (*coupon*) bon *m* ❷ (*receipt*) reçu *m*

**vow** [vaʊ] I. *vt* jurer; **to ~ revenge** jurer de se venger; **to ~ to +infin** jurer de +*infin;* **to ~ that ...** jurer que ... II. *n* vœu *m;* **to take a ~** faire un vœu

**voyage** ['vɔɪ·ɪdʒ] I. *n a.* *fig* voyage *m* II. *vi* voyager; **to ~ across sth** traverser qc

**vs.** ['vɜr·səs] *abbr of* **versus** contre
**VT** *n abbr of* **Vermont**
**vulgar** ['vʌl·gər] *adj a. pej* vulgaire
**vulnerable** ['vʌl·nər·ə·bl] *adj* vulnéra-

ble; (*spot*) faible; **to be ~ to sth** être
sensible à qc
**vulture** ['vʌl·tʃər] *n a. fig* vautour *m*

---

# Ww

**W, w** ['dʌb·l·ju] <-'s> *n* W *m*, w *m*;
**~ as in Whiskey** (*on telephone*) w
comme William
**w** *n abbr of* **watt** W
**W** *n s.* **west, western**
**WA** *n abbr of* **Washington**
**wack** [wæk] *adj sl* bizarroïde
**wacky** ['wæk·i] <-ier, -iest> *adj inf* far-
felu(e)
**waddle** ['wa·dl] *vi* se dandiner
**wade** [weɪd] *vi* ❶ (*cross water*) passer à
gué ❷ (*walk in water*) marcher dans
l'eau
**waders** ['weɪ·dərz] *n pl* (*rubber boots*)
bottes *fpl* de pêcheur
**wafer** ['weɪ·fər] *n* ❶ (*sweet cookie*) gaufrette *f* ❷ REL hostie *f*
**wafer-thin** *adj* mince comme du papier
à cigarette
**waffle**[1] ['wa·fl] *vi inf* parler par circonlo-
cutions
**waffle**[2] ['wa·fl] *n* (*thin cake*) gaufre *f*
**wag**[1] [wæg] I. <-gg-> *vt, vi* remuer II. *n*
(*to and fro movement*) **with a ~ of his
tail** en remuant la queue
**wag**[2] [wæg] *n* (*person*) plaisantin *m*
**wage**[1] [weɪdʒ] *vt form* (*campaign*) mener; **to ~ war** faire la guerre
**wage**[2] [weɪdʒ] *n* **~(s)** salaire *m*
**wage dumping** *n* dumping *m* salarial
**wager** ['weɪ·dʒər] I. *n* pari *m*; **to do
sth for a ~** faire qc pour tenir un
pari II. *vt* ❶ parier ❷ *fig* **to ~ one's
reputation/life** mettre sa main au
feu
**wagon** ['wæg·ən] *n* (*four-wheeled cart*)
chariot *m* ▶ **to be on the ~** *inf* ne plus

boire une goutte d'alcool; **to fall off
the ~** *inf* se remettre à boire
**wagonload** ['wæg·ən·loʊd] *n* wagon *m*
**wail** [weɪl] I. *vi* gémir; (*siren*) hurler; **to
~ over sth** se lamenter sur qc II. *n* gémissement *m*; (*siren*) hurlement *m*
**waist** [weɪst] *n* taille *f*
**waistband** ['weɪs(t)·bænd] *n* ceinture *f*
**waistline** ['weɪs(t)·laɪn] *n* taille *f*
**wait** [weɪt] I. *n* attente *f* ▶ **to lie in ~
for sb** guetter qn II. *vi* ❶ (*stay*) attendre; **to ~ for sb/sth** attendre qn/qc;
**~ and see** attends de voir ❷ (*help*) servir ▶ **~ a little** un instant; **I can't ~ to
do sth** j'ai hâte de faire qc; **to keep sb
~ing** faire attendre qn; **~ and see!** attends voir! III. *vt* ❶ (*await*) attendre
❷ (*help*) servir; **to ~ table(s)** faire le
service ▶ **to ~ one's turn** attendre son
tour
◆ **wait behind** *vi* rester
◆ **wait in** *vi* rester à la maison; **to ~ for
sb** rester à la maison pour attendre qn
◆ **wait on** *vt* ❶ (*serve*) servir ❷ *form*
(*expect*) attendre ▶ **to ~ sb hand and
foot** être aux petits soins avec qn
◆ **wait up** *vi* ❶ (*not go to bed*) ne pas
aller se coucher; **to ~ for sb** attendre qn
❷ (*wait for me*) attendre; **~!** attends-
-moi!
**waiter** ['weɪ·tər] *n* serveur *m*
**waiting room** *n* salle *f* d'attente
**waitress** ['weɪ·trɪs] *n* serveuse *f*
**wake**[1] [weɪk] *n* NAUT *a. fig* sillage *m* ▶ **to
follow in sb's ~** marcher dans le sillage
de qn; **in the ~ of sth** dans le sillage de
qc

**wake²** [weɪk] n (*vigil beside a corpse*) veillée f mortuaire

**wake³** [weɪk] <woke o waked, woken o waked> I. *vi* se réveiller II. *vt* a. *fig* réveiller; **to ~ the dead** réveiller les morts

◆ **wake up** I. *vi* ❶ (*stop sleeping*) a. *fig* se réveiller ❷ (*become aware of*) **to ~ to sth** prendre conscience de qc II. *vt* réveiller; **to wake oneself up** se réveiller

**Wales** [weɪlz] n le pays de Galles

**walk** [wɔːk] I. n ❶ (*going on foot*) marche f; **to be ten minutes' ~ from here** être à dix minutes à pied d'ici ❷ (*gait*) démarche f ❸ (*stroll*) promenade f; **to go for a ~** aller se promener; **to take sb out for a ~** emmener qn en promenade; **to take a ~** faire une promenade ❹ (*promenade*) promenade f ▶ ~ of **life** milieu m; **from all ~s of life** de tous les milieux II. *vt* ❶ (*go on foot*) parcourir (à pied) ❷ (*accompany*) **to ~ sb somewhere** emmener qn quelque part; **to ~ sb home** raccompagner qn à la maison ❸ (*take for a walk: dog*) sortir ❹ (*make move*) faire marcher III. *vi* ❶ (*go on foot*) marcher; **to ~ into/out of a room** entrer dans/quitter une pièce ❷ (*stroll*) se promener ▶ **to be ~ing on air** être sur un nuage; **to ~ the streets** (*wander*) errer dans les rues; (*be a prostitute*) faire le trottoir

◆ **walk away** *vi* ❶ (*leave*) s'en aller; **to ~ from sth** (*house, group*) quitter qc; (*car*) sortir de qc ❷ (*ignore*) **to ~ from sth** éviter qc; **to ~ from sb** s'éloigner de qn ❸ (*escape unhurt*) **to ~ from an accident** sortir indemne d'un accident ❹ *inf* (*win*) **to ~ with sth** (*prize*) remporter qc ❺ *inf* (*steal*) **to ~ with sth** faucher qc

◆ **walk in on** *vt* **to ~ sb** entrer sans prévenir

◆ **walk off** I. *vi* partir II. *vt* **to ~ a meal** prendre l'air pour digérer

◆ **walk on** *vi* THEAT être figurant

◆ **walk out** *vi* ❶ (*leave room*) sortir ❷ (*leave to express dissatisfaction*) par-tir; **her husband walked out** son mari l'a quittée; **the delegation walked out of the meeting** la délégation a quitté la réunion ❸ (*go on strike*) se mettre en grève

◆ **walk over** I. *vi* s'approcher; **to ~ to sb** s'approcher de qn II. *vt* **to walk (all) over sb** marcher sur les pieds de qn; **don't let him walk (all) over you** *fig* ne te laisse pas marcher sur les pieds

**walker** ['wɔːkər] n ❶ (*person who walks*) marcheur, -euse m, f; **to be a fast/slow ~** marcher vite/lentement ❷ (*person walking for pleasure*) promeneur, -euse m, f ❸ (*support while walking*) déambulateur m ❹ (*support for baby*) trotteur m

**walkie-talkie** [ˌwɔːkiˈtɔːki] n talkie-walkie m

**walking** ['wɔːkɪŋ] I. n ❶ (*act of walking*) marche f ❷ (*stroll*) promenade f II. *adj* ambulant(e); (*encyclopedia*) vivant(e); **to be within ~ distance of sth** être à quelques pas de qc

**walking wounded** *npl* **the ~** les blessés *mpl* légers

**walkout** ['wɔːkaʊt] n ❶ (*strike*) grève f surprise; **to stage a ~** faire la grève ❷ (*sudden departure*) départ m en signe de protestation

**walkway** ['wɔːkweɪ] n passage m (pour piétons)

**wall** [wɔːl] I. n ❶ (*division structure*) a. *fig* mur m; **the Great Wall of China** la Grande Muraille de Chine ❷ (*climbing wall, natural structure*) paroi f ❸ AUTO flanc m ❹ ANAT paroi f ▶ **to have one's <u>back</u> to the ~** être dos au mur; **to hit a <u>brick</u> ~** se heurter au mur; **to be a <u>fly</u> on the ~** être une petite souris; **to be like beating/hitting one's <u>head</u> against a brick ~** être à se taper la tête contre les murs; **to <u>drive</u> sb up the ~** rendre qn fou; **<u>off</u> the ~** *inf* dingue II. *vt* **to ~ off** séparer par un mur; **to ~ up** murer

**wall chart** ['wɔːltʃɑːt] n panneau m mural

**wallet** ['wɑːlɪt] n portefeuille m

W

**wallpaper** ['wɔl·peɪ·pər] I. *n* papier *m* peint II. *vt* tapisser

**wall-to-wall** [ˌwɔl·tə·'wɔl] *adj* ❶ ~ **carpet** moquette *f* ❷ *fig* ~ **coverage** couverture *f* (médiatique) complète

**walnut** ['wɔl·nʌt] *n* ❶ (*nut*) noix *f* ❷ (*tree*) noyer *m*

**walrus** ['wɔl·rəs] <- *o* walruses> *n* morse *m*

**waltz** [wɔlts] <watzes> I. *n* valse *f* II. *vi* valser; **to ~ into a room** faire irruption dans une pièce

**wand** [wand] *n* (*magician's stick*) baguette *f*; **to wave one's magic ~** donner un coup de baguette magique

**wander** ['wan·dər] I. *vt* ❶ (*walk through*) se balader dans ❷ (*roam: the streets*) traîner dans; (*world*) courir II. *vi* ❶ (*walk*) **to ~ (around)** se promener au hasard; **to ~ off** partir ❷ (*roam*) errer; **to ~ through the streets** traîner dans les rues ❸ (*not concentrate*) s'égarer; **to ~ off the point** s'écarter du sujet; **his mind is ~ing** il divague III. *n inf* balade *f*

**wane** [weɪn] I. *vi* décroître II. *n no indef art* **to be on the ~** décroître

**want** [wɔnt] I. *n* ❶ (*need*) besoin *m*; **to be in ~ of sth** avoir besoin de qc ❷ *no indef art* (*lack*) manque *m*; **for ~ of sth** faute de qc; **for ~ of anything better** faute de mieux II. *vt* ❶ (*wish*) vouloir; **to ~ to do sth** vouloir faire qc; **to ~ sb to do sth** vouloir que qn fasse qc +*subj*; **to ~ sth done** vouloir que qc soit fait; **I just don't ~ to know!** je ne veux pas savoir!; **you're not ~ed here** tu n'es pas le bienvenu ici ❷ (*feel like*) avoir envie; **to ~ (to do) sth** avoir envie de (faire) qc ❸ (*wish to speak to*) demander; **to be ~ed for murder/by the police** être recherché pour meurtre/par la police ❹ (*desire sexually*) désirer ❺ (*need*) avoir besoin de; **your car ~s cleaning** ta voiture a besoin d'être lavée; **to ~ \$200** demander 200 dollars
◆ **want in** *vi inf* vouloir entrer; **to ~ (on a deal)** vouloir être sur un coup
◆ **want out** *vi inf* (*from a room*) vouloir

sortir; (*from an arrangement*) vouloir retirer ses cartes du jeu

**want ad** ['wɔnt·ˌæd] *n inf* petite annonce *f*

**wanting** ['wan·tɪŋ] *adj* **to be ~ in sth** manquer de qc; **to be found ~** laisser à désirer

**war** [wɔr] *n no indef art* guerre *f*; **to be at ~** être en guerre; **~ hero** héros *m* de guerre; **to declare ~ on sb/sth** *a. fig* déclarer la guerre à qn/qc; **to wage ~ against sb/sth** faire la guerre contre qn/qc; *fig* être en guerre contre qn/qc; **price/trade ~** guerre des prix/commerciale

**war crime** *n* crime *m* de guerre

**war criminal** *n* criminel(le) *m(f)* de guerre

**war cry** *n a. fig* cri *m* de guerre

**ward** [wɔrd] *n* ❶ (*part of hospital*) salle *f* (d'hôpital); **emergency/maternity ~** salle d'urgence/de maternité ❷ (*political area*) circonscription *f* électorale ❸ (*child*) pupille *mf*
◆ **ward off** *vt* écarter

**warden** ['wɔr·dən] *n* ❶ (*supervisor*) gardien(ne) *m(f)*; **traffic ~** contractuel(le) *m(f)* ❷ (*prison head*) directeur, -trice *m, f*

**wardrobe** ['wɔr·droʊb] *n* ❶ (*armoire*) armoire *f* ❷ *no indef art* (*collection*) garde-robe *f* ❸ (*department*) costumes *mpl*

**warehouse** ['wer·haʊs] *n* entrepôt *m*

**warfare** ['wɔr·fer] *n no indef art* guerre *f*

**warhead** ['wɔr·hed] *n* ogive *f*

**warm** [wɔrm] I. *adj* ❶ (*quite hot*) chaud(e); **I'm ~** j'ai chaud; **it's ~** il fait chaud; **to get ~** se réchauffer; **to keep ~** ne pas prendre froid; **to keep sth ~** garder qc au chaud ❷ (*not hot enough*) tiède ❸ (*showing feeling: greeting, welcome*) chaleureux(-euse); (*support*) enthousiaste ❹ (*suggesting heat: colors, atmosphere*) chaud(e) ❺ (*close in guessing*) **to be ~** être chaud ▶ **cold hands, ~ heart** mains froides, cœur chaud *prov;* **to keep sb's seat ~ (for sb)** *inf* garder la place de qn

**W**

au chaud **II.** *vt a. fig* réchauffer **III.** *vi* chauffer

◆ **warm toward** *vt* **to ~ sb** ressentir de la sympathie pour qn; **to ~ sth** se laisser séduire par qc

◆ **warm up I.** *vi* ❶ (*become hot*) se réchauffer ❷ (*begin to function properly: engine, machine*) chauffer ❸ (*limber up*) s'échauffer ❹ (*animate: party, atmosphere*) chauffer; (*debate*) s'échauffer **II.** *vt* ❶ (*make hot*) réchauffer ❷ (*start: engine*) faire chauffer ❸ (*animate*) faire chauffer

**warm-blooded** [ˌwɔrm·ˈblʌd·ɪd] *adj* à sang chaud

**warm front** *n* front *m* chaud

**warm-hearted** [ˌwɔrm·ˈhar·t̬ɪd] *adj* chaleureux(-euse)

**warmly** *adv* (*to recommend, be dressed*) chaudement; (*to welcome*) chaleureusement

**warmth** [wɔrm(p)θ] *n no indef art, a. fig* chaleur *f*

**warm-up** *n* échauffement *m*

**warn** [wɔrn] *vt* avertir; **I'm ~ing you!** je te/vous préviens!; **to ~ sb against/about sth** mettre qn en garde contre qc; **to ~ sb to do sth** conseiller à qn de faire qc; **to have been ~ed** avoir été prévenu

**warning** [ˈwɔrn·ɪŋ] *n* ❶ *no indef art* (*notifying*) avertissement *m*; **without ~** sans prévenir ❷ (*written notification*) avis *m* ❸ (*threat*) alerte *f* ❹ AUTO **~ lights** feux *mpl* de détresse; **~ sign** panneau *m* avertisseur ❺ *no indef art* (*advice*) conseil *m*, **a word of ~** un conseil ❻ (*caution*) avertissement *m* ❼ *fig* signe *m* annonciateur

**war paint** [ˈwɔr·peɪnt] *n* peinture *f* de guerre; **to put on the ~** *inf* se peinturlurer

**warpath** [ˈwɔr·pæθ] *n no indef art, fig, inf* **to be on the ~** (*aggressive*) être sur le sentier de la guerre; (*bad-tempered*) être d'humeur massacrante

**warped** [wɔrpt] *adj a. fig* tordu(e)

**warrant** [ˈwɔr·ᵊnt] **I.** *n* (*official document*) mandat *m*; **search ~** mandat de

perquisition **II.** *vt* ❶ (*justify*) justifier ❷ (*guarantee*) garantir

**warranty** [ˈwɔr·ᵊn·t̬i] *n* garantie *f*

**warrior** [ˈwɔr·jər] *n* guerrier, -ère *m, f*

**warship** [ˈwɔr·ʃɪp] *n* navire *m* de guerre

**wart** [wɔrt] *n* (*growth*) verrue *f* ▸ **~s and all** *inf* avec ses défauts

**wartime** [ˈwɔr·taɪm] *n no indef art* temps *m* de guerre

**wary** [ˈwer·i] <-ier, -iest> *adj* prudent(e); **to be ~ of sb/sth** se méfier de qn/qc

**was** [wɑz] *pt of* **be**

**wash** [wɑʃ] **I.** *n* ❶ (*cleaning with water*) **to have a ~** se laver ❷ **the ~** (*clothes for cleaning*) le linge sale; **to be in the ~** être au sale ❸ (*thin paint layer*) lavis *m* ▸ **it'll all come out in the ~** *inf* ça finira par s'arranger **II.** *vt* ❶ (*clean with water*) laver; **to ~ a car** nettoyer une voiture; **to ~ one's hair/hands** se laver les cheveux/les mains ❷ (*clean*) nettoyer ❸ (*dilute*) laver ❹ (*carry away*) laver; **to be ~ed downstream** être emporté par le courant ▸ **to ~ one's hands of sth** se laver les mains de qc; **to ~ one's dirty linen in public** laver son linge sale en public **III.** *vi* ❶ (*clean oneself*) se laver ❷ (*bathe*) baigner; **to ~ along the rocks** (*sea, wave*) balayer les falaises ▸ **that won't ~ with me** ça ne marche pas avec moi

◆ **wash away I.** *vi* partir au lavage **II.** *vt* ❶ (*remove by flow of water*) faire partir au lavage ❷ (*carry away*) emporter ❸ (*remove*) laver; **to wash one's sins away** se laver de ses péchés

◆ **wash down** *vt* ❶ (*swallow with liquid*) faire descendre ❷ (*clean with water*) laver à grande eau

◆ **wash off I.** *vi* partir au lavage **II.** *vt* faire partir au lavage

◆ **wash out I.** *vi* partir au lavage **II.** *vt* ❶ (*clean inside*) rincer ❷ (*wash quickly*) **to wash sth out** passer qc sous l'eau ❸ (*postpone*) **to be washed out** être annulé à cause de la pluie ❹ (*erode*) éroder

◆ **wash up I.** *vi* ❶ *s.* **wash** ❷ (*clean*

**W**

*face and hands*) se débarbouiller ❸ (*be deposited by sea*) échouer **II.** *vt* ❶ (*deposit on beach*) rejeter ❷ (*to clean*) **to ~ the dishes** laver la vaisselle ❸ *fig* **to be all washed up** être fini

**washable** [ˈwɒʃ·ə·bl] *adj* lavable

**washbasin** [ˈwɒʃˌbeɪ·sᵊn] *n* lavabo *m*

**washcloth** [ˈwɒʃ·klɑθ] *n* ≈ gant *m* de toilette

**washed-out** [ˌwɒʃt·ˈaʊt] *adj* ❶ (*bleached*) délavé(e) ❷ (*tired*) lessivé(e)

**washer** [ˈwɒʃ·ər] *n* ❶ *s.* **washing machine** ❷ (*plastic ring*) joint *m*

**washing** [ˈwɒ·ʃɪŋ] *n no indef art* ❶ (*act of cleaning clothes*) lessive *f;* **to do the ~** faire la lessive ❷ (*clothes*) linge *m;* **to hang out the ~** étendre le linge

**washing machine** *n* machine *f* à laver

**Washington** [ˈwɒ·ʃɪŋ·tən] **I.** *n* (*state*) l'Etat *m* de Washington **II.** *adj* du Washington

**Washington** (**D.C.**) [ˈwɒ·ʃɪŋ·tən] *n* Washington

**washout** [ˈwɒʃ·aʊt] *n inf* catastrophe *f*

**washroom** [ˈwɒʃ·rum] *n* toilettes *fpl*

**wasn't** [wɑ·zᵊnt] = **was not** *s.* **be**

**wasp** [wɑsp] *n* guêpe *f*

**waste** [weɪst] **I.** *n* ❶ (*misuse*) gaspillage *m;* **it's a ~ of money** c'est de l'argent gaspillé; **it's a ~ of time** c'est une perte de temps; **it was a ~ of energy/food** c'était un gaspillage d'énergie/de nourriture; **what a ~!** quel gâchis! ❷ *no indef art* (*unwanted matter*) déchets *mpl;* **to go to ~** être gaspillé ❸ (*desert*) ~(s) désert *m* **II.** *vt* ❶ gaspiller; (*time*) perdre; **to ~ no time in doing sth** ne pas perdre son temps à faire qc; **the meal was ~d on him** il n'a pas su apprécier le repas; **a ~d afternoon/chance** un après-midi gâché/une opportunité gâchée ❷ *inf* (*kill*) tuer ❸ (*destroy: muscles, body*) atrophier **III.** *vi* **~ not, want** not *prov* qui épargne gagne

◆ **waste away** *vi* dépérir

**wastebasket** [ˈweɪs(t)·bæs·kət] *n* poubelle *f*

**waste disposal** *n* ~ (**unit**) broyeur *m* à ordures

**wasteful** [ˈweɪs(t)·fᵊl] *adj* **to be ~ of sth** être du gaspillage de qc; **~ expenditure** dépenses *fpl* inutiles

**wasteland** [ˈweɪs(t)·lænd] *n* terre *f* en friche; *fig* désert *m*

**waste product** *n* déchet *m*

**watch** [wɒtʃ] **I.** *n* ❶ (*clock*) montre *f* ❷ (*act of observation*) surveillance *f;* **to be under** (**close**) **~** être sous (haute) surveillance; **to keep** (**a**) **close ~ on/over sb/sth** surveiller qn/qc de près; **to keep ~** faire le guet ❸ (*guard(s)*) garde *f;* **to keep ~** monter la garde ❹ METEO (*alert*) **hurricane/tornado ~** alerte *f* ouragan/de tornade **II.** *vt* ❶ (*look at*) regarder; **to ~ a movie/TV** regarder un film/la télé ❷ (*observe*) observer; (*suspects*) surveiller; **to ~ sb do sth** regarder qn faire qc; **to ~ sb/sth like a hawk** surveiller qn/qc de près ❸ (*take care of: children*) surveiller ❹ (*be careful about*) faire attention à; (*one's weight*) surveiller; **to ~ every penny** compter chaque sou; **~ it!** (*fais/faites*) attention!; **to ~ the world go by** regarder passer la foule **III.** *vi* ❶ (*look at*) regarder; **to ~ as sb/sth does sth** regarder comment qn/qc fait qc ❷ (*be on alert*) guetter

◆ **watch out** *vi* faire attention; **~!** (*fais/faites*) attention!; **to ~ for sb/sth** prendre garde à qn/qc; (*watch the approach of*) guetter qn/qc

**watchdog** [ˈwɒtʃ·dɔg] *n* ❶ (*guard dog*) chien *m* de garde ❷ (*keeper of standards: person*) contrôleur, -euse *m, f;* (*organization*) organisme *m* de contrôle

**watchful** [ˈwɒtʃ·fᵊl] *adj* vigilant(e); **to keep a ~ eye on sb/sth** garder un œil attentif sur qn/qc

**watchman** [ˈwɒtʃ·mən] <-men> *n* gar-

**W**

dien(ne) *m(f)*; **night** ~ gardien *m* de nuit

**water** ['wɔ·tər] **I.** *n* ❶ (*liquid*) eau *f*; **bottled** ~ eau en bouteille; **a bottle/glass of** ~ une bouteille/un verre d'eau; **under** ~ sous l'eau; (*flooded*) inondé(e); **running** ~ eau courante; **to keep one's head above** ~ *a. fig* maintenir la tête hors de l'eau; **to tread** ~ *a. fig* faire du sur-place; **to pass** ~ uriner ▸ **to throw out the** <u>baby</u> **with the bath** ~ jeter le bébé avec l'eau du bain; **to be** ~ **under the** <u>bridge</u> être du passé; **to be like a** <u>fish</u> **out of** ~ être complètement dépaysé; **through** <u>hell</u> **and high** ~ contre vents et marées; **to get into** <u>hot</u> ~ se mettre dans le pétrin; **to be in** <u>deep</u> ~ être dans le pétrin; **still** ~**s run** <u>deep</u> il n'est pire eau que l'eau qui dort *prov*; **to** <u>hold</u> ~ tenir debout **II.** *vt* ❶ (*give water to: plants*) arroser; (*cows, horses*) faire boire ❷ (*dilute*) diluer **III.** *vi* ❶ (*produce tears*) pleurer ❷ (*salivate*) saliver

**waterbed** *n* lit *m* à eau

**watercolor** *n* aquarelle *f*

**watercress** ['wɔ·tər·krɛs] *n* cresson *m* de fontaine

**waterfall** ['wɔ·tər·fɔl] *n* cascade *f*

**waterfront** ['wɔ·tər·frʌnt] *n* bord *m* de l'eau

**water heater** *n* chauffe-eau *m*

**watering can** *n* arrosoir *m*

**water lily** *n* nénuphar *m*

**water main** *n* conduite *f* principale d'eau

**watermelon** ['wɔ·tər·mɛl·ən] *n* pastèque *f*

**water meter** *n* compteur *m* d'eau

**water polo** *n* water-polo *m*

**water pressure** *n* pression *f* de l'eau

**waterproof I.** *adj* étanche; (*clothes*) imperméable **II.** *vt* imperméabiliser

**water-repellent** *adj* imperméable

**watershed** *n* ❶ GEO ligne *f* de partage des eaux ❷ *fig* tournant *m* décisif

**water-ski I.** *vi* faire du ski nautique **II.** <-s> *n* ski *m* nautique

**water skiing** *n* ski *m* nautique

**water softener** *n* adoucisseur *m*

**water supply** *n* ❶ (*amount of water*) approvisionnement *m* en eau ❷ (*system*) alimentation *f* en eau

**watertight** ['wɔ·tər·taɪt] *adj* ❶ (*sealed*) étanche ❷ (*unquestionable*) inattaquable

**waterway** ['wɔ·tər·weɪ] *n* voie *f* navigable

**waterworks** ['wɔ·tər·wɜrks] *n pl* ❶ (*water storage*) station *f* hydraulique ❷ *inf* (*organs*) vessie *f* ▸ **to** <u>turn</u> **on the** ~ *pej* se mettre à pleurer comme une Madeleine

**watery** ['wɔ·tər·i] <more, most *o* -ier, -iest> *adj* ❶ (*bland*) fade; (*coffee*) dilué(e); (*soup*) trop clair(e) ❷ (*weak, pale*) délavé(e) ❸ (*full of tears*) mouillé(e)

**watt** [wat] *n* watt *m*

**wattage** ['wa·t̬ɪdʒ] *n* ELEC puissance *f* en watts

**wave** [weɪv] **I.** *n* ❶ (*surge of water*) *a. fig* vague *f*; ~ **of strikes/enthusiasm** vague de grèves/d'enthousiasme; **to make** ~**s** créer des remous ❷ (*hand movement*) signe *m* (de la main); **with a** ~ **of sb's hand** d'un signe de la main ❸ PHYS onde *f*; **long/medium/short** ~ onde longue/moyenne/courte ❹ (*hairstyle*) cran *m* **II.** *vi* ❶ (*make hand movement*) faire un signe (de la main); **to** ~ **at/to sb/sth** faire un signe de la main à qn/qc ❷ (*move from side to side*) ondoyer; (*flag*) flotter **III.** *vt* ❶ (*move to signal*) faire un signe (de la main); **to** ~ **hello to sb** saluer qn d'un geste; **to** ~ **goodbye to sb** dire au revoir à qn d'un geste; **to** ~ **one's hand** faire un signe de la main; **he** ~**d me forward** il m'a fait signe d'avancer; **to** ~ **goodbye to sth** *fig* dire adieu à qc ❷ (*move side to side: wand, flag*) agiter

◆ **wave aside** *vt fig* écarter

◆ **wave down** *vt* faire signe de s'arrêter à

◆ **wave on** *vt* faire signe de continuer à

**wavelength** *n a. fig* longueur *f* d'ondes;

**W**

**to be on the same ~** être sur la même longueur d'ondes

**wavy** ['weɪ·vi] <-ier, -iest> *adj* onduleux(-euse); *(hair)* ondulé(e)

**wax** [wæks] I. *n* cire *f;* *(in ears)* cérumen *m* II. *vt* ❶ *(polish)* cirer ❷ *(remove hair from)* épiler ▶ **to ~ and wane** croître et décroître

**waxwork** ['wæks·wɜrk] *n* figure *f* en cire

**way** [weɪ] I. *n* ❶ *(route, path)* chemin *m;* **the ~ to the station** le chemin de la gare; **the ~ to success** *fig* le chemin de la gloire; **to make one's ~ somewhere** se rendre quelque part; **to go the wrong ~** faire fausse route; **to be on the ~** être sur le chemin; **the ~ back** le retour; **on the ~** sur le chemin de qc; **to be on the ~ back** être sur le chemin du retour; **on the ~ home** en rentrant; **a baby is on the ~** un bébé est en route; **to lose one's ~** se perdre; **to find one's ~ into/out of sth** trouver l'entrée/la sortie de qc; **to find one's ~ through sth** se frayer un chemin à travers qc; **to find a ~ around a problem** trouver une solution à un problème; **to be out of the ~** être isolé; *fig* être exceptionnel; **to be under ~** être en route; **to lead the ~** *a. fig* montrer le chemin; **by ~ of sth** via qc; **by the ~** chemin faisant; *fig* à propos; **to be under ~** être en route; **to give ~** ❶ *(agree)* céder; *(fall down)* céder ❷ *(facing direction)* direction *f;* **it's the other ~ around** c'est dans l'autre sens; *fig* c'est le contraire; **both ~s** dans les deux sens; **to put sth the right ~ up** mettre qc dans le bon sens; **this ~** par ici ❸ *(respect)* égard *m;* **in that ~** à cet égard; **in many ~s** à bien des égards; **in a ~** dans une certaine mesure; **in a big/small ~** sur une grande/petite échelle ❹ *(state)* état *m;* **to be in a good/bad ~** *(person)* être bien/mal; *(thing)* être en bon/mauvais état ❺ *(distance)* distance *f;* **all the ~** *(the whole distance)* tout le long du chemin; *(completely)* jusqu'au bout; **all the ~ here** jusqu'ici; **to go all the**

**~ with sb** *inf* aller jusqu'au bout avec qn; **to be a long ~ off** *(remote)* être loin; *(event)* être assez loin; **to have a ~ to go** avoir du chemin à parcourir ❻ *(manner)* façon *f;* **this ~** de cette façon; **in no ~** en aucune façon; **~ of life** mode *m* de vie; **in one's own ~** à sa façon; **sb's ~s** les habitudes *fpl* de qn; **the ~ to do sth** la manière de faire qc; **her ~ of doing sth** sa façon de faire qc; **by ~ of sth** en guise de qc; **to get one's own ~** arriver à ses fins; **to have a ~ with sb** savoir s'y prendre avec qn; **either ~** quoiqu'il arrive; **to be in the family ~** être enceinte; **no ~!** *inf* *(impossible)* impossible!; *(definitely no!)* pas question!; **in no ~** en aucun cas; **there's no ~ we can finish on time** on ne finira jamais à temps ❼ *(space for movement)* **to be in sb's ~** barrer le passage à qn; **to be in the ~** gêner le passage; *fig* gêner; **to get out of the/sb's ~** s'écarter du chemin/du chemin de qn ▶ **that's the ~ the cookie crumbles** *prov* c'est la vie; **where there's a will, there's a ~** *prov* vouloir c'est pouvoir *prov;* **to see/find out which ~ the wind blows** voir d'où vient le vent; **to have come a long ~** revenir de loin; **to go a long ~** faciliter les choses; **to go out of one's/the ~** se donner du mal; **you can't have it both ~s** tu/vous dois/devez choisir II. *adv* *inf* bien; **to be ~ ahead of sb/sth** *inf* être bien en avance sur qn/qc

**wayside** ['weɪ·saɪd] *n* *(roadside)* bord *m* de la route ▶ **to fall by the ~** abandonner en route

**wazoo** [wɑ·'zu] *n sl* **up** *[o* out*]* **the ~** à revendre

**we** [wi] *pers pron* nous; **as ~ say** comme on dit

**weak** [wik] *adj* ❶ *(not strong)* *a. fig* faible; *(chin)* fuyant(e); **a ~ link** *[o* spot*]* *fig* un point faible; **the film is ~ on plot** le film manque d'action; **to have a ~ heart** avoir le cœur fragile; **to be/go ~ at the knees** avoir les jambes comme du coton ❷ (*light: drink, coffee*) léger(-ère)

**weaken** ['wiˑkən] I. *vi* ❶ (*become less strong*) s'affaiblir ❷ (*become less resolute*) faiblir II. *vt* affaiblir

**weakling** ['wiˑklɪŋ] *n pej* personne *f* chétive

**weakly** *adv* ❶ (*without strength*) faiblement ❷ (*unconvincingly*) mollement

**weakness** ['wikˑnəs] <-es> *n* ❶ (*being irresolute*) faiblesse *f* ❷ (*area of vulnerability*) faiblesse *f* ❸ (*strong liking*) faible *m*; **to have a ~ for sth** avoir un faible pour qc

**wealth** [welθ] *n* ❶ (*money*) richesse *f* ❷ (*large amount*) abondance *f*

**wealthy** ['welθi] <-ier, -iest> *adj* riche II. *n* **the ~** les riches *mpl*

**weapon** ['wepˑən] *n a. fig* arme *f*

**weaponry** ['wepˑənˑri] *n* armement *m*

**wear** [wer] <wore, worn> I. *n* ❶ (*clothing*) vêtements *mpl*; **men's** ~ (*clothing*) vêtements pour hommes ❷ (*amount of use*) usure *f*; **to show signs of ~** commencer à s'user; **~ and tear** usure *f*; **to be the worse for ~** être ivre II. *vt* ❶ (*have on body*) *a. fig* porter ❷ (*make a hole*) user; **to ~ holes in sth** trouer qc ▶ **to ~ the pants** porter la culotte III. *vi* s'user; **to ~ thin** être usé; *fig* être à bout

◆ **wear away** I. *vi irr* s'user II. *vt* user

◆ **wear down** *vt irr*; *a. fig* user; **to ~ sb's resistance** épuiser la résistance de qn

◆ **wear off** I. *vi irr* s'effacer; (*pain*) disparaître; (*effect*) cesser; (*anesthetic*) cesser de faire effet II. *vt* effacer

◆ **wear on** *vi irr* (*day, night*) s'avancer

◆ **wear out** I. *vi irr* s'user; *fig* s'épuiser II. *vt* user; *fig* épuiser

**weary** ['wɪrˑi] <-ier, -iest> *adj* ❶ (*very tired*) fatigué(e) ❷ (*bored*) las(se); **to be/grow ~ of sth** se lasser de qc ❸ (*tiring*) fatigant(e)

**weasel** ['wiˑzᵊl] *n* belette *f*

**weather** ['weðˑər] I. *n* temps *m*; **~ permitting** si le temps le permet; **what's the ~ like?** quel temps fait-il? ▶ **to be under the ~** être patraque II. *vi* s'alté-

rer; (*rocks*) s'éroder; (*with patina*) se patiner III. *vt* altérer; (*rock*) éroder ▶ **to ~ the storm** surmonter la crise

**weather forecast** *n* météo *f*

**weatherman** ['weðˑərˑmæn] *n* présentateur *m* météo

**weave** [wiv] I. <wove *o* weaved, woven> *vt* ❶ (*produce cloth*) tisser; **to ~ sth into sth** tisser qc en qc ❷ (*intertwine things*) tresser ❸ (*make a whole*) tramer ❹ (*move in twisting*) **to ~ one's way through sth** se faufiler à travers qc II. <wove *o* weaved, woven> *vi* ❶ (*produce cloth*) tisser ❷ (*intertwine*) tresser ❸ (*move by twisting*) **to ~ between sth** se faufiler entre qc III. *n* ❶ (*way of making cloth*) tissage *m* ❷ (*way of intertwining*) tressage *m*

**web** [web] *n* ❶ (*trap*) toile *f*; **spider ~** toile d'araignée ❷ (*network*) tissu *m* ❸ (*tissue for birds*) palmure *f*

**Web, WEB** [web] I. *n* COMPUT Web *m*; **the (World Wide) ~** la Toile, le Web II. *adj inv* COMPUT Web

**webcam** *n* COMPUT webcam *f*

**webpage** *n* COMPUT page *f* Web [*o* sur la toile]

**web portal** *n* INET portail *m* Internet

**website** *n* COMPUT site *m* (sur) Internet

**wed** [wed] <wedded, wedded *o* wed, wed> *form* I. *vt* épouser II. *vi* se marier

**we'd** [wid] ❶ = **we had** *s.* **have** ❷ = **we would** *s.* **will**

**wedded** ['wedˑɪd] I. *pt, pp* de **wed** II. *adj* marié(e); **lawful ~ wife** *form* légitime épouse *f*

**wedding** ['wedˑɪŋ] *n* mariage *m*

**wedge** [wedʒ] I. *n* ❶ (*for door*) cale *f* ❷ (*piece*) morceau *m* II. *vt* (*jam into*) caler

**Wednesday** ['wenzˑdeɪ] *n* mercredi *m*; **Ash ~** mercredi des Cendres; *s.a.* **Friday**

**wee** [wi] I. *adj inf* minuscule; **a ~ bit** un tout petit peu ▶ **in the ~ hours of the morning** aux premières heures du matin II. *n inf* pipi *m*; **to have a ~** faire pipi III. *vi inf* faire pipi

**weed** [wid] I. *n* ❶ (*wild plant*) mauvaise

**W**

herbe *f* ❷ *inf* (*marijuana*) herbe *f* ► **to grow** like a ~ pousser comme de la mauvaise herbe II. *vt, vi* désherber

**weed killer** ['wid·kɪl·ər] *n* désherbant *m*

**weedy** ['wi·di] <-ier, iest> *adj* ❶ (*full of weeds*) envahi(e) par les mauvaises herbes ❷ (*underdeveloped*) dépourvu(e) d'intérêt

**week** [wik] *n* semaine *f*; **a few ~s ago** il y a quelques semaines; **last ~** la semaine dernière; **once a ~** une fois par semaine; **during the ~** pendant la semaine ► **~ in, ~ out, ~ after ~** semaine après semaine; **~ by ~, ~ from ~ to ~** d'une semaine à l'autre

**weekday** ['wik·deɪ] *n* jour *m* de la semaine; **on ~s** les jours de la semaine

**weekend** *n* week-end *m*; **on the ~(s)** le week-end

**weekly** I. *adj* hebdomadaire II. *adv* une fois par semaine III. *n* hebdomadaire *m*

**weeknight** *n* soir *m* de la semaine

**weenie** ['wi·ni] *n* ❶ *inf* (*hot dog*) saucisse *f* de Francfort ❷ *sl* (*penis*) zizi *m*

**weep** [wip] I. *vi* <wept, wept> **to ~ over sb/sth** pleurer sur qn/qc II. *vt* <wept, wept> **to ~ tears of joy** verser des larmes de joie

**weigh** [weɪ] I. *vi* peser II. *vt* ❶ (*measure weight*) peser; **to ~ oneself** se peser; **to be weighed down by sth** plier sous le poids de qc; *fig* être accablé de qc ❷ (*consider carefully*) **to ~ one's words** peser ses mots ❸ NAUT **to ~ anchor** lever l'ancre

♦ **weigh in** *vi* ❶ (*be weighed*) se faire peser ❷ *inf* (*intervene*) intervenir

♦ **weigh out** *vt* peser

♦ **weigh up** *vt* ❶ (*calculate and compare*) évaluer ❷ (*judge, assess*) juger

**weight** [weɪt] I. *n* ❶ (*heaviness*) poids *m*; **to put on** [*o* **gain**] **~** prendre du poids ❷ (*metal piece*) poids *m*; **to lift ~s** lever des poids ❸ (*value*) poids *m*; **to attach ~ to sth** attacher de l'importance à qc ► **to take the ~ off one's feet** se reposer; **to be a ~ off sb's mind** être un soulagement pour qn II. *vt* ❶ (*hold*) lester; **to ~ sth down**

maintenir qc avec un poids ❷ *fig* pondérer; **to be ~ed in favor of sb/sth** peser en faveur de qn/qc; **to be ~ed against sb** être défavorable à qn

**weightless** ['weɪt·lɪs] *adj* en état d'apesanteur

**weightlifter** ['weɪt·lɪf·tər] *n* haltérophile *mf*

**weightlifting** ['weɪt·lɪf·tɪŋ] *n* haltérophilie *f*

**weighty** ['weɪ·ti] <-ier, -iest> *adj* ❶ (*heavy*) lourd(e) ❷ (*important*) important(e); (*issue*) sérieux(-euse)

**weird** [wɪrd] *adj* bizarre

**welcome** ['wel·kəm] I. *vt* accueillir II. *n a. fig* accueil *m*; **to outstay one's ~** abuser de l'hospitalité de qn III. *adj* bienvenu(e); **to make sb ~** faire bon accueil à qn ► **you're ~!** de rien!, bienvenue! *Québec*; **to be ~ to (do) sth** pouvoir faire qc IV. *interj* bienvenue!; **~ home!** bienvenue à la maison!; **~ back!** heureux de te/vous revoir!

**weld** [weld] I. *vt a. fig* souder II. *n* soudure *f*

**welfare** ['wel·fer] *n* ❶ (*state of wellness*) bien-être *m* ❷ (*state aid or relief*) aide *f* sociale; **~ system** système *m* d'aides sociales; **to be on ~** toucher l'aide sociale

**we'll** [wil] = **we will** *s.* **will**

**well¹** [wel] I. <better, best> *adj* **to be/ feel/get ~** aller bien; **all is ~** tout va bien; **to look ~** avoir l'air d'aller bien II. <better, best> *adv* ❶ (*in a good manner*) bien ❷ (*thoroughly*) bien; **to be pretty ~** aller plutôt bien; **to be pretty ~ paid** être plutôt bien payé; **~ below** (**sth**) bien en dessous (de qc) ❸ (*justifiably*) **I can't very ~ ask him** je ne peux pas raisonnablement lui demander ► **as ~** aussi; **as ~ as** ainsi que III. *interj* (*exclamation*) eh bien!; **~, ~!** eh bien!; **oh ~!** oh!; **very ~!** très bien!

**well²** [wel] *n* puits *m*; **oil ~** puits de pétrole

**well-behaved** *adj* sage

**well-being** *n* bien-être *m*

**well-done** *adj* (*meat*) à point

**well-dressed** *adj* bien habillé(e)
**well-educated** *adj* cultivé(e)
**well-fed** *adj* bien nourri(e)
**well-known** *adj* connu(e)
**well-made** *adj* bien fait(e)
**well-meaning** *adj* bien intentionné(e)
**well-off** I. *adj* (*wealthy*) riche II. *npl*
the ~ les nantis *mpl*
**well-organized** *adj* bien organisé(e)
**well-paid** *adj* bien payé(e)
**well-read** *adj* ❶ (*knowledgeable*) culti-
vé(e) ❷ (*read frequently*) très lu(e)
**well-to-do** *adj inf* riche
**well-wisher** *n* supporter *m*
**Welsh** [welʃ] I. *adj* gallois(e) II. *n*
❶ (*people*) **the ~** les Gallois *mpl* ❷ LING
gallois *m; s.a.* **English**
**Welshman** ['welʃ·mən] <-men> *n* gallois *m*
**Welshwoman** ['welʃ·wʊ·mən] <-wom-
en> *n* galloise *f*
**went** [went] *pt of* **go**
**wept** [wept] *pt, pp of* **weep**
**were** [wɜr] *pt of* **be**
**we're** [wɪr] = **we are** *s.* **be**
**weren't** [wɜrnt] = **were not** *s.* **be**
**werewolf** ['wer·wʊlf] <-wolves> *n*
loup-garou *m*
**west** [west] I. *n* ❶ (*cardinal point*)
ouest *m*; **in the ~ of France** dans
l'ouest de la France; **to lie 5 miles to
the ~ of sth** être à 5 miles à l'ouest de
qc; **to go/drive to the ~** aller/rouler
vers l'ouest; **farther ~** plus à l'ouest
❷ POL occident *m* ▶ **to go ~** (*thing*)
être fichu [*o* perdu]; (*person*) passer
l'arme à gauche II. *adj* GEO ouest *inv*;
~ **wind** vent *m* d'ouest; ~ **coast** côte *f*
ouest
**westbound** ['west·baʊnd] *adj, adv* en
direction de l'ouest
**westerly** ['wes·tər·li] *adj* ❶ (*of western
part*) à l'ouest; ~ **part** partie *f* ouest
❷ (*toward the west*) vers l'ouest; ~ **direction** direction *f* ouest ❸ (*from the
west*) d'ouest
**western** ['wes·tərn] I. *adj* ❶ GEO de
l'ouest; ~ **Canada** l'ouest *m* du Canada
❷ POL occidental(e) II. *n* CINE western *m*

**westerner** ['wes·tərn·ər] *n* occiden-
tal(e) *m(f)*
**westernize** ['wes·tər·naɪz] *vt* occiden-
taliser
**West Germany** *n* HIST l'Allemagne *f* de
l'Ouest
**West Virginia** *n* la Virginie-Occidentale
**wet** [wet] I. <wetter, wettest> *adj*
❶ (*soaked*) mouillé(e); **to get ~** se
mouiller; **to get sth ~** mouiller qc; **to
get one's hands ~** se mouiller les
mains ❷ (*damp*) *a.* METEO humide;
(*weather*) pluvieux(-euse); (*day*) de
pluie; (*season*) des pluies; **it's ~** il pleut
▶ **to be ~ behind the ears** être encore
jeune II. <-tt-, wet, wet *o* -tt-, wet-
ted, wetted> *vt* ❶ (*make damp*)
mouiller ❷ (*urinate on*) **to ~ the bed**
mouiller le lit; **to ~ one's pants** mouiller sa culotte
**wet dream** *n* pollution *f* nocturne
**we've** [wiv] = **we have** *s.* **have**
**whale** [(h)weɪl] *n* baleine *f* ▶ **to have a
~ of a time** drôlement bien s'amuser
**whaling** *n* chasse *f* à la baleine
**wharf** [(h)wɔrf] <-ves> *n* quai *m*
**what** [(h)wʌt] I. *interrog adj* quel(le);
~ **kind of book?** quel genre de livre?;
~ **time is it?** quelle heure est-il?;
~ **schools is he talking about?** de
quelles écoles parle-t-il?; ~ **one does
he like?** lequel, laquelle aime-t-il?;
~ **ones does he like?** lesquels, lesquel-
les aime-t-il? II. *pron* ❶ *interrog* que,
qu' + *vowel*, quoi *tonic form*; ~ **can I
do?** que puis-je faire?; · **'s up?** *inf*
qu'est-ce qui se passe?; ~ **for?** pourquoi?; ~ **does he look like?** à quoi res-
semble-t-il?; ~**'s his name?** comment
s'appelle-t-il?; ~ **about Paul?** et Paul?;
~ **about a walk?** et si on faisait une balade?; ~ **if it snows?** *inf* et s'il neige?
❷ *rel use* ce + *rel pron*; ~ **I like is ~ he
says/is talking about** ce qui me plaît,
c'est ce qu'il dit/ce dont il parle; ~ **'s
more** qui plus est; **he knows ~'s ~!** il
s'y connaît! III. (*exclamation*) ~ **an
idiot!** quel idiot!; ~ **a fool I am!** que
suis-je bête! IV. *interj* ~! quoi!; **so ~?** et

W

alors?; **is he coming, or ~?** il arrive ou quoi?

**whatever** [(h)wʌtˈev·ər] I. *pron* ~ **you do** quoi que tu fasses *subj;* **take ~ you want** prends ce que tu veux II. *adj, adv* quel que soit; **give me ~ money you have** donne-moi tout ce que tu as comme argent III. *interj sl* ça m'est bien égal!

**what's-his-name** [ˈ(h)wʌt·sɪz·neɪm] *n* machin *m*

**whatsoever** [ˌ(h)wʌt·sou·ˈev·ər] *adv* **nothing ~** absolument rien; **no reason ~** pas la moindre raison

**wheat** [(h)wit] *n* blé *m*

**wheat germ** *n* germes *mpl* de blé

**wheel** [(h)wil] I. *n* ❶ (*circular object*) roue *f;* **on ~s** sur des roues ❷ AUTO volant *m;* **to be at the ~** être au volant ❸ NAUT gouvernail *m* ❹ *pl, inf* (*car*) bagnole *f* ▸ **to set the ~s in motion** mettre les choses en route; **to be a big ~** *inf* être un gros bonnet II. *vt* pousser ▸ **to ~ sth out** faire ressortir qc ◆ **wheel around** *vi* se retourner

**wheelbarrow** [ˈ(h)wil·ber·ou] *n* brouette *f*

**wheelchair** [ˈ(h)wil·tʃer] *n* fauteuil *m* roulant

**wheeling** [ˈ(h)wil·ɪŋ] *n* ~ **and dealing** *inf* brassage *m* d'affaires

**wheeze** [(h)wiz] <-zing> *vi* respirer avec peine

**when** [(h)wen] I. *adv* quand; **since ~?** depuis quand? II. *conj* ❶ (*at which time*) quand; ~ **you arrive, call me** appelle-moi quand tu arrives; **in the days ~ ...** à l'époque où ... ❷ (*during the time*) lorsque; ~ **singing that song** en chantant cette chanson ❸ (*every time*) chaque fois que; ~ (*considering that*) **how can I listen ~ I can't hear?** comment écouter si je n'entends rien? ❺ (*although*) **he's buying it ~ he could borrow it** il l'achète alors qu'il pourrait l'emprunter

**whenever** ~ [(h)wen·ˈev·ər] I. *adv* **I can do it tomorrow or** ~ je peux le faire demain ou n'importe quand; ~ **did I**

say that? (mais) quand donc ai-je dit cela? II. *conj* ❶ (*every time*) quand; ~ **I can** chaque fois que je peux ❷ (*at any time*) **he can come ~ he wants** il peut venir quand il veut

**where** [(h)wer] I. *adv* où; ~ **is he going?** où va-t-il?; ~ **did you get that idea?** d'où te/vous vient cette idée? II. *conj* (*là*) où; ~ **I'll tell him ~ to go** je lui dirai où il faut aller; **the box ~ he puts his things** la boîte dans laquelle il met ses affaires; **this is ~ my pen was found** c'est là qu'on a trouvé mon stylo

**whereabouts** [ˈ(h)wer·ə·bauts] I. *adv inf* où II. *n* **sb/sth's exact ~** le lieu exact où se trouve qn/qc

**whereas** [(h)wer·ˈæz] *conj* ❶ (*while*) alors que ❷ LAW attendu que

**whereby** [(h)wer·ˈbaɪ] *adv* par quoi

**whereupon** [ˈ(h)wer·ə·pan] *conj* (*directly after which*) après quoi

**wherever** [ˌ(h)wer·ˈev·ər] I. *adv* **... or ~** ... ou Dieu sait où; ~ **did she find that?** mais où donc a-t-elle trouvé ça? II. *conj* ❶ (*in every place*) ~ **there is sth** partout où il y a qc ❷ (*in any place*) ~ **he likes** où il veut

**whet** [(h)wet] <-tt-> *vt* (*increase*) stimuler

**whether** [ˈ(h)weð·ər] *conj* ❶ (*if*) si ❷ (*all the same*) que +*subj;* ~ **it rains or not** qu'il pleuve ou non

**which** [(h)wɪtʃ] I. *interrog adj* quel(le); ~ **one?** lequel, laquelle?; ~ **ones?** lesquel(le)s?; ~ **games do you play?** à quels jeux joues-tu? II. *pron* ❶ *interrog* ~ **is his?** lequel, laquelle est à lui? ❷ *rel use* **the book ~ I read** le livre que j'ai lu; **the book of ~ I'm speaking** le livre dont je parle; **she agreed, ~ surprised me** elle était d'accord, ce qui m'a surpris

**whichever** [(h)wɪtʃ·ˈev·ər] I. *pron* celui (celle) qui; **take ~ you like best** prends celui que tu préfères; **at 3 or 4 o'clock, ~ works for you** à 3 ou 4 heures, suivant ce qui t'/vous arrange II. *adj* ❶ (*any*) n'importe quel(le); **take**

W

~ **book you want** choisis le livre que tu veux ❷ (*no matter which*) quel(le) que soit; ~ **way I take** quel que soit le chemin que je prenne; ~ **you choose, I'll take it** quel que soit celui que tu choisisses, je le prendrai

**while** [(h)waɪl] **I.** *n* moment *m;* **quite a** ~ assez longtemps; **once in a** ~ de temps en temps; **I'm staying in Boston for a** ~ je reste à Boston pour quelque temps **II.** *conj* ❶ (*during which time*) pendant que; **I was dreaming ~ I was doing sth** je rêvais en faisant qc ❷ (*although*) ~ **I agree with you** bien que je sois d'accord avec toi ❸ (*however*) **my wife's a vegetarian, ~ I eat meat** ma femme est végétarienne alors que je mange de la viande

**whim** [wɪm] *n* caprice *m;* **to do sth on a** ~ faire qc sur un coup de tête

**whimper** ['(h)wɪm·pər] **I.** *vi* gémir; (*child*) geindre **II.** *n* gémissement *m*

**whine** [(h)waɪn] **I.** <*-ning*> *vi* ❶ (*make noise: animal*) gémir ❷ (*cry, complain*) pleurnicher **II.** *n* plainte *f*

**whip** [(h)wɪp] **I.** *n* ❶ (*lash*) fouet *m;* **to crack a** ~ faire claquer le fouet ❷ POL chef *mf* de file **II.** <*-pp-*> *vt* ❶ (*lash with a whip*) fouetter ❷ (*force fiercely*) forcer ❸ (*beat into a froth*) fouetter ❹ *inf* (*defeat*) battre à plate(s) couture(s) **III.** <*-pp-*> *vi fig* **to ~ across sth** traverser qc à toute allure
◆ **whip out** *vt* (*take out quickly*) sortir rapidement
◆ **whip up** *vt* ❶ (*encourage: enthusiasm*) susciter; *pej* stimuler ❷ *inf* (*make quickly*) préparer en quatrième vitesse ❸ (*beat into a froth*) battre

**whiplash** ['(h)wɪp·læʃ] *n* MED lésion *f* des cervicales

**whipped cream** *n* crème *f* fouettée

**whipping cream** *n* crème *f* fraîche

**whirlpool** ['(h)wɜrl·pul] *n* ❶ (*in sea*) remous *m* ❷ (*Jacuzzi®*) baignoire *f* à remous

**whirlwind** ['(h)wɜrl·wɪnd] **I.** *n* tourbillon *m* de vent **II.** *adj* enivrant(e); **a ~ tour** une visite éclair

**whisk** [(h)wɪsk] **I.** *vt* ❶ (*flick*) effleurer ❷ (*whip rapidly: cream*) fouetter; (*eggs*) battre ❸ (*take*) **to ~ sth away/off the table** enlever rapidement qc de la table **II.** *n* CULIN fouet *m*

**whisker** ['(h)wɪs·kər] *n pl* (*on people*) favoris *mpl;* (*on cat*) moustaches *fpl*
▶ **by a** ~ d'un poil

**whiskey** ['(h)wɪs·ki] *n* whisky *m*

**whisper** ['(h)wɪs·pər] **I.** *vi* chuchoter **II.** *vt* ❶ (*speak softly*) chuchoter ❷ (*gossip*) **to ~ that …** faire courir le bruit que … **III.** *n* ❶ (*soft speech*) murmure *m;* **to say sth in a ~** dire qc tout bas ❷ (*rumor*) rumeur *f*

**whistle** ['(h)wɪs·l] **I.** <*-ling*> *vt, vi* siffler **II.** *n* ❶ (*sound*) sifflement *m* ❷ (*device*) sifflet *m;* **to blow a ~** donner un coup de sifflet ▶ **to blow the ~ on sb/sth** dénoncer qn/qc

**whistleblower** ['(h)wɪs·l·bloʊ·ər] *n* dénonciateur, -trice *m, f*

**white** [(h)waɪt] **I.** *adj* blanc(he) ▶ **~r than ~** plus blanc que neige; **to turn ~ with fear** pâlir de peur **II.** *n* ❶ (*color, of egg, eye*) blanc *m* ❷ (*person*) Blanc, Blanche *m, f; s.a.* **blue**

**whiteboard** *n* tableau *m* blanc

**white hat** *n* COMPUT chapeau *m* blanc (*qui explore les systèmes informatiques sans intentions malhonnêtes*)

**White House** *n* **the ~** la Maison-Blanche

**white lie** *n* pieux mensonge *m*

**white-out** *n* ❶ (*blizzard*) blizzard *m* ❷ (*liquid to cover mistakes*) blanc *m* correcteur

**whitewash** ['(h)waɪt·waʃ] **I.** *n* ❶ (*solution*) blanc *m* de chaux ❷ (*cover-up*) blanchiment *m* **II.** *vt* ❶ (*cover in white solution*) blanchir à la chaux ❷ *pej* (*conceal negative side*) blanchir

**Whit Monday** [,(h)wɪt·'mʌn·deɪ] *n* lundi *m* de Pentecôte

**Whitsun** ['(h)wɪt·sᵊn] **I.** *n* les fêtes *fpl* de Pentecôte **II.** *adj* de Pentecôte

**Whit Sunday** [,(h)wɪt·'sʌn·deɪ] *n* dimanche *m* de Pentecôte

**whiz** [(h)wɪz] *inf* **I.** *n* ❶ (*expert*) as *m;*

**W**

**a ~ at sth** un as de qc ❷ (*noise*) sifflement *m* ❸ *sl* (*act of urinating*) **to take a ~** pisser II. *vi* **to ~ along/past** passer à toute allure; **to ~ through sth** (*list, newspaper*) survoler qc

**whiz kid** *n* jeune prodige *mf*

**who** [hu] *interrog or rel pron* qui; *s.a.* **whom, whose**

**whoa** [(h)woʊ] *interj* ❶ (*command to stop a horse*) ho! ❷ *fig, inf* (*used to stop something*) doucement! ❸ *inf* (*expression of surprise or disbelief*) pas possible!

**whodun(n)it** [ˌhuˈdʌn·ɪt] *n inf:* film ou roman policier

**whoever** [huˈev·ər] *pron* quiconque

**whole** [hoʊl] I. *adj* ❶ (*entire*) entier(-ère); **~ milk** lait *m* entier; **the ~ thing** le tout ❷ (*intact*) entier(-ère) ❸ *inf* **it's a ~ lot better** c'est vraiment beaucoup mieux ▸ **the ~ enchilada** *inf* toute la panoplie; **the ~ shebang** *inf* tout le bataclan; **to go (the) ~ hog,** **to go the ~ nine yards** *inf* aller jusqu'au bout II. *n* ❶ (*complete thing*) totalité *f;* **as a ~** dans sa totalité; **on the ~** dans l'ensemble ❷ **the ~** le tout

**whole-hearted** [ˌhoʊlˈhar·tɪd] *adj* sans réserve; (*thanks*) qui viennent du cœur

**wholesale** [ˈhoʊl·seɪl] I. *n* vente *f* en gros II. *adj* ❶ (*sales in bulk*) de gros ❷ (*on a large scale: slaughter*) en série; (*reform*) en masse III. *adv* ❶ (*by bulk*) en gros ❷ (*in bulk*) en bloc

**wholesaler** [ˈhoʊl·seɪ·lər] *n* grossiste *mf*

**wholesome** [ˈhoʊl·səm] *adj* salubre; (*life*) sain(e); (*advice*) salutaire

**who'll** [hul] = **who will** *s.* **will**

**wholly** [ˈhoʊ·li] *adv* tout à fait; (*convinced*) entièrement; (*different*) complètement

**whom** [hum] *form interrog or rel pron* **~ did he see?** qui a-t-il vu?; **those ~ I love** ceux que j'aime; **the person of ~ I spoke** la personne dont j'ai parlé

**whooping cough** [ˈhu·pɪŋ·kɔf] *n* coqueluche *f*

**whoops** [(h)wʊps] *interj inf* houp-là!

**whopper** [(h)ˈwɑ·pər] *n iron* ❶ (*huge thing*) monstre *m* ❷ (*blatant lie*) énormité *f*

**whopping** [(h)ˈwɑ·pɪŋ] *adj inf* énorme; **a ~ lie** un mensonge monumental

**whore** [hɔr] *n inf* putain *f*

**who's** [huz] ❶ = **who is** *s.* **is** ❷ = **who has** *s.* **has**

**whose** [huz] I. *poss adj* **~ book is this?** à qui est ce livre?; **~ son is he?** de qui est-il le fils?; **~ car did you take?** tu/vous as/avez pris la voiture de qui?; **the girl ~ brother I saw** la fille dont j'ai vu le frère II. *poss pron* **~ is this pen?** à qui est ce stylo?; **~ can I borrow?** lequel est-ce que je peux emprunter?

**why** [(h)waɪ] I. *conj* pourquoi; **~ not?** pourquoi pas?; **~ not ring her?** pourquoi ne pas l'appeler? II. *n* **the ~s and wherefores (of sth)** le pourquoi et comment (de qc) III. *interj* tiens!

**WI** *n abbr of* **Wisconsin**

**wick** [wɪk] *n* mèche *f*

**wicked** [ˈwɪk·ɪd] *adj* ❶ (*evil, cruel: person*) méchant(e); (*action, plan*) mauvais(e); (*lie*) affreux(-euse) ❷ (*unpleasant: wind*) affreux(-euse) ❸ (*playfully malicious: smile, sense of humor*) malicieux(-euse) ❹ *sl* (*fun*) super *inv*

**wicker** [ˈwɪk·ər] I. *n* osier *m* II. *adj* en osier

**wide** [waɪd] I. <-r, -st> *adj* ❶ (*broad*) large; **to be two feet ~** faire deux pieds de large ❷ (*very big*) immense; (*gap*) considérable ❸ (*very open*) grand(e) ouvert(e); (*eyes*) écarquillé(e) ❹ (*varied*) ample; (*experience, range*) étendu(e) ❺ (*extensive*) vaste; (*support*) considérable II.<-r, -st> *adv* très; **to open ~** ouvrir en grand; **to be ~ open** être grand ouvert

**wide-awake** *adj* bien éveillé(e)

**wide-eyed** *adj* ❶ (*with wide-open eyes*) **to be ~** avoir les yeux grands ouverts ❷ (*innocent: child*) innocent(e)

**widely** *adv* ❶ (*broadly*) largement; **~ spaced** très espacé ❷ (*extensively: known, admired, used*) très; (*thought, believed*) communément; (*accepted*) généralement ③ (*considerably: vary*) énormément

**widen** ['waɪ·d³n] I. *vt* élargir; (*discussion*) étendre II. *vi* s'élargir

**widescreen** *adj* TV grand écran *inv*

**widespread** ['waɪd·spred] *adj* répandu(e); (*rioting, support*) général(e)

**widow** ['wɪd·oʊ] I. *n* veuve *f* II. *vt* laisser veuf(veuve); **to be ~ed** être veuf

**widower** ['wɪd·oʊ·ər] *n* veuf *m*

**width** [wɪdθ] *n* largeur *f*; **20 feet in ~** 20 pieds de large

**wield** [wiːld] *vt* ① (*hold*) manier ② (*use: influence, power*) exercer

**wife** [waɪf] <**wives**> *n* épouse *f*; **to live together as man and ~** vivre maritalement

**Wi-Fi®** ['waɪ·faɪ] *n no pl abbr of* **Wireless Fidelity** INET wifi *m*

**wig** [wɪg] *n* perruque *f*

**wiggle** ['wɪg·l] I. *vt* remuer II. *vi* se déhancher III. *n* ① (*movement*) déhanchement *m* ② (*line*) trait *m* ondulé

**wild** [waɪld] I. *adj* ① (*untamed: animal, flower*) sauvage ② (*unrestrained: person*) dissipé(e); (*country*) sauvage; (*life*) dissolu(e); (*party, talk*) délirant(e); (*weather, conditions*) très mauvais(e); (*wind*) violent(e); (*sea*) agité(e) ③ (*enthusiastic*) fou(folle); **to be ~ about sth** être un fana de qc; **he's not ~ about the idea** il n'est pas emballé par l'idée ④ (*not accurate: punch, shot*) au hasard ⑤ *inf* (*angry*) fou(folle); **to go ~** devenir fou de rage; **to drive sb ~** rendre qn fou ⑥ (*messy: hair*) sauvage ⑦ *inf* (*wonderful*) génial(e) ▶ **beyond sb's ~est** <u>dreams</u> au-delà des rêves les plus fous de qn II. *adv* sauvage; **to grow/live ~** pousser/vivre à l'état sauvage ▶ **to** <u>run</u> **~** se déchaîner III. *n* ① (*natural environment*) nature *f*; **in the ~** à l'état sauvage ② *pl* (*remote places*) régions *fpl* reculées; **in the ~s of Africa** au fin fond de l'Afrique

**wildcard** *n* ① *a.* COMPUT joker *m* ② SPORTS (*extra team or player*) athlète *mf* invité(e) à jouer

**wilderness** ['wɪl·dər·nəs] *n* ① (*unpopu-* lated) désert *m* ② (*overgrown area*) jungle *f*

**wildfire** ['waɪld·faɪər] *n* feu *m* de forêt ▶ **to** <u>spread</u> **like ~** se répandre comme une traînée de poudre

**wild goose chase** *n* (*hopeless search*) fausse piste *f*

**wildlife** ['waɪld·laɪf] *n* faune *f* et flore *f*

**wildly** *adv* ① (*in uncontrolled way*) frénétiquement; (*vary*) sensiblement ② (*haphazardly*) au hasard; (*to guess*) à tout hasard ③ *inf* (*very*) extrêmement

**will¹** [wɪl] <**would, would**> *aux* ① (*expressing future*) **I/we ~** [*o* **I'll/we'll**] **do sth** je ferai/nous ferons qc; **you won't be late, ~ you?** tu/vous ne seras/serez pas en retard, n'est-ce pas?; **she won't pay – yes, she ~!** elle ne paiera pas – si, elle paiera! ② (*polite form*) **~ you please follow me?** voulez-vous me suivre, s'il vous plaît? ③ (*wish, agree*) vouloir; **say what you ~** dis/dites ce que tu/vous veux/voulez; **the engine won't start** le moteur ne veut pas démarrer ④ (*emphatic*) **a drama ~ happen** on ne pourra éviter un drame; **I ~ succeed despite you** je réussirai malgré toi/vous ⑤ (*explaining a procedure*) **they'll give you an anesthetic** on vous fera une anesthésie ⑥ (*conjecture*) devoir; **that ~ be the doctor** cela doit être le médecin

**will²** [wɪl] I. *n* ① (*faculty*) volonté *f*; **strength of ~** force *f* de caractère; **against sb's ~** contre la volonté de qn; **to lose the ~ to live** perdre la raison de vivre ② LAW testament *m* ▶ **where there's a ~, there's a** <u>way</u> *prov* quand on veut on peut II. *vt* ① (*make happen*) **to ~ sb to do sth** faire faire qc à qn; **to ~ sb to win/live** souhaiter de toutes ses forces que qn gagne/vive +*subj* ② (*bequeath*) léguer

**willing** ['wɪl·ɪŋ] *adj* ① (*not opposed*) disposé(e); **to be ~ to do sth** être prêt à faire qc; **to be ready and ~** être volontiers disponible ② (*enthusiastic*) enthousiaste

**W**

**willingly** *adv* ❶ (*gladly*) volontiers ❷ (*voluntarily*) volontairement

**willingness** *n* (*readiness*) bonne volonté *f*; **~ to do sth** désir *m* de faire qc

**willow** ['wɪl·oʊ], **willow tree** *n* BOT saule *m*

**willpower** ['wɪl·paʊər] *n* volonté *f*; **by sheer ~** par pure force de caractère

**wilt** [wɪlt] *vi* ❶ (*droop: plants*) se faner ❷ (*feel weak: person*) se sentir faible ❸ (*lose confidence*) se dégonfler

**wimp** [wɪmp] *n inf* lavette *f*

◆**wimp out** *vi inf* se dégonfler

**win** [wɪn] I. *n* ❶ POL, SPORTS victoire *f* ❷ (*bet*) pari *m* gagnant II. <won, won> *vt* gagner; (*contract, scholarship*) décrocher; (*popularity*) acquérir; (*reputation*) se faire; (*sb's heart*) conquérir III. <won, won> *vi* gagner; **to ~ by two lengths** l'emporter de deux longueurs ▶ **to ~ hands down** gagner les doigts dans le nez; **~ or lose** quoi qu'il arrive; **you ~!** soit! tu as gagné!

◆**win back** *vt* (*territory, love*) reconquérir; (*voters*) récupérer; (*esteem*) regagner

◆**win over** *vt* ❶ (*change mind of*) convaincre ❷ (*gain support of*) gagner à sa cause

**wince** [wɪn(t)s] *vi* grimacer

**wind**[1] [wɪnd] I. *n* ❶ (*current of air*) vent *m*; **breath of ~** courant *m* d'air; **gust of ~** rafale *f* de vent ❷ (*breath*) souffle *m*; **to knock the ~ out of sb** couper le souffle à qn ❸ MUS **the ~s** les instruments *mpl* à vent ❹ (*meaningless words*) n'importe quoi ❺ (*gas*) **to break ~** lâcher un vent ▶ **to get ~ of sth** avoir vent de qc; **to go/run like the ~** aller/filer comme le vent II. *vt* (*hurt*) couper le souffle à

**wind**[2] [waɪnd] <wound, wound> I. *vt* ❶ (*wrap around: film*) rembobiner; (*yarn*) enrouler ❷ (*turn: handle*) tourner II. *vi* serpenter

◆**wind down** I. *vt* ❶ (*lower*) baisser ❷ (*reduce*) réduire II. *vi* ❶ (*become less active*) être en perte de vitesse; (*party, meeting*) tirer à sa fin ❷ (*relax*) se détendre

◆**wind up** I. *vt* ❶ (*bring to an end*) terminer; (*debate, meeting*) clore; (*affairs*) conclure ❷ (*raise*) monter ❸ (*tension a spring*) remonter II. *vi* ❶ (*end*) se terminer ❷ *inf* (*end up*) se retrouver; **to ~ doing sth** finir par faire qc

**windfall** ['wɪn(d)·fɔl] *n* ❶ (*fruit*) fruit *m* tombé ❷ *fig* aubaine *f*

**wind farm** *n* centrale *f* éolienne

**winding** ['waɪn·dɪŋ] *adj* sinueux(-euse)

**wind instrument** ['wɪnd ˈɪn·strə·mənt] *n* instrument *m* à vent

**windmill** ['wɪn(d)·mɪl] *n* moulin *m* à vent

**window** ['wɪn·doʊ] *n* ❶ (*glass*) fenêtre *f*; (*of store*) vitrine *f*; (*of vehicle*) vitre *f*; **at the ~** à la fenêtre; **in the ~** par la fenêtre; (*in store*) en vitrine ❷ (*stained glass*) vitrail *m* ❸ COMPUT fenêtre *f* ❹ (*time period*) créneau *m* ▶ **to go out the ~** *inf* s'envoler

**window cleaner** *n* ❶ (*person*) laveur, -euse *m, f* de carreaux ❷ (*product*) produit *m* à nettoyer les vitres

**window dressing** *n* ❶ (*in shop*) étalage *m* ❷ *pej* (*show*) façade *f*

**windowpane** *n* vitre *f*

**window shopping** *n* lèche-vitrines *m*; **to go ~** faire du lèche-vitrines

**wind power** *n* énergie *f* éolienne

**windshield** ['wɪn(d)·ʃild] *n* pare-brise *m*

**windshield wiper** *n* essuie-glace *m*

**windsurfer** ['wɪn(d)·sɜrf·ər] *n* véliplanchiste *mf*

**windsurfing** ['wɪn(d)·sɜrf·ɪŋ] *n* planche *f* à voile

**windy** ['wɪn·di] <-ier, -iest> *adj* venteux(-euse); **it was a ~ day** [*o* **it was ~**] il y avait beaucoup de vent

**wine** [waɪn] CULIN I. *n* vin *m* II. *vt* **to ~ and dine** faire un dîner bien arrosé

**wine bottle** *n* bouteille *f* de vin

**wine cellar** *n* cave *f* à vins

**wine cooler** *n* ❶ (*drink*) consommation préparée à base de vin, de jus de fruit et parfois d'eau gazeuse ❷ (*container*) seau *m* à glace

**wine glass** <-es> *n* verre *m* à vin

**wine list** *n* carte *f* des vins

**winery** ['waɪ·n°r·i] <-ies> *n* établissement *m* vinicole

**wine tasting** *n* dégustation *f* de vins

**wing** [wɪŋ] I. *n* ❶ ZOOL aile *f*; **on the ~** en vol ❷ AVIAT aile *f* ❸ POL aile *f*; **the left/right ~** le parti de gauche/droite ❹ SPORTS aile *f*; (*player*) ailier *m* ❺ ARCHIT aile *f*; **the west ~ of the house** l'aile ouest de la maison ❻ *pl* THEAT coulisses *fpl* ▸ **to take sb under one's ~** prendre qn sous son aile II. *vt* (*travel fast*) **to ~ one's way** voler ▸ **to ~ it** *inf* improviser

**winger** ['wɪŋ·ər] *n* SPORTS ailier *m*

**wing nut** *n* TECH écrou *m* à ailettes

**wingspan** ['wɪŋ·spæn] *n* envergure *f*

**wink** [wɪŋk] I. *n* clin *m* d'œil ▸ **not to sleep a ~** ne pas fermer l'œil (de la nuit); **in a ~** en un clin d'œil II. *vi* ❶ (*close one eye*) faire un clin d'œil ❷ (*flash: light*) clignoter

**winner** ['wɪn·ər] *n* ❶ (*person who wins*) gagnant(e) *m(f)*; **to back a ~** *a. fig* miser sur un gagnant; **everyone's a ~!** tout le monde gagne! ❷ *inf* SPORTS but *m* de la victoire

**winning** ['wɪn·ɪŋ] I. *adj* ❶ (*that wins*) gagnant(e); **to be on a ~ streak** (*team*) accumuler les victoires ❷ (*charming*) adorable; **with his/her ~ ways** avec sa grâce irrésistible ❸ (*achieving victory*) victoire *f*; **~ isn't everything** la réussite n'est pas tout ❷ *pl* (*money*) gains *mpl*

**winter** ['wɪn·tər] I. *n* hiver *m*; **in (the) ~** en hiver II. *vi* hiberner

**winter sports** *npl* sports *mpl* d'hiver

**wintry** ['wɪn·tri] *adj* ❶ (*typical of winter*) hivernal(e) ❷ (*unfriendly*) froid(e)

**wipe** [waɪp] I. *n* ❶ (*act of wiping*) coup *m* de torchon ❷ (*tissue*) lingette *f* II. *vt* ❶ (*remove dirt by rubbing*) essuyer; **to ~ one's nose** se moucher; **to ~ one's bottom** s'essuyer; **to ~ sth clean** nettoyer qc; **to ~ sth away/off** faire partir qc ❷ (*erase: disk, tape*) effacer ▸ **to ~ sth off the map** rayer qc de la carte; **to ~ the smile off sb's face** faire perdre le sourire à qn III. *vi* essuyer

◆**wipe down** *vt* essuyer

◆**wipe off** *vt* (*erase*) effacer

◆**wipe out** I. *vt* ❶ (*clean inside of*) essuyer ❷ (*destroy: population*) exterminer ❸ (*cancel*) effacer ❹ *inf* (*tire out*) pomper ❺ *inf* (*economically*) ruiner II. *vi inf* AUTO déraper

◆**wipe up** *vt, vi* essuyer

**wire** [waɪər] I. *n* ❶ (*metal thread*) fil *m* métallique ❷ ELEC fil *m* ▸ **to get one's ~s crossed** s'embrouiller; **to get in under the ~** *inf* arriver de justesse; **down to the ~** *inf* jusqu'à la dernière minute II. *vt* ❶ (*fasten with wire*) attacher ❷ ELEC (*building*) faire l'installation électrique de ❸ (*equip with microphone*) **to be ~d** (*person, room*) être équipé de micros cachés; **to be ~d for sound** avoir un micro sur soi

**wire cutters** *npl* cisailles *fpl*

**wireless** ['waɪər·ləs] I. *n* (*radio*) TSF *f* II. *adj* a. TEL sans fil

**wireless communication** *n* téléphonie *f* mobile

**wiretapping** ['waɪər·ˌtæp·ɪŋ] *n* écoute *f* téléphonique

**wiring** ['waɪər·ɪŋ] *n* ELEC ❶ (*system*) circuit *m* électrique ❷ (*installation*) installation *f* électrique

**Wisconsin** [wɪ·'skɑn(t)·sən] I. *n* le Wisconsin II. *adj* du Wisconsin

**wisdom** ['wɪz·dəm] *n no indef art* sagesse *f*

**wisdom tooth** <- teeth> *n* dent *f* de sagesse

**wise** [waɪz] I. *adj* ❶ (*having knowledge*) sage; (*advice, choice*) judicieux(-euse); (*words*) de sagesse; **is that ~?** est-ce bien raisonnable? ❷ *inf* (*aware*) **nobody will be the ~r** personne n'en saura rien; **I'm none the ~r** je ne suis pas plus avancé II. *vi* **to ~ up to sth** réaliser qc III. *vt* **to ~ sb up about sb/sth** mettre qn au parfum sur qn/qc

**W**

**wise guy** n pej, inf petit malin m
**wisely** adv sagement
**wish** [wɪʃ] I. <-es> n ❶ (desire) souhait m; **against my ~es** contre ma volonté; **to have no ~ to do sth** n'avoir aucune envie de faire qc ❷ (magic wish) vœu m; **to make a ~ that** faire le vœu que +subj ❸ pl (greetings, at end of letter) amitiés fpl; **good/best ~es** mes amitiés II. vt ❶ (feel a desire) **I ~ she knew/I had a camera** si seulement elle savait/j'avais un appareil photo; **I ~ I hadn't told you** j'aurais mieux fait de ne rien te/vous dire ❷ form (want) vouloir ❸ (make a wish) **to ~ (that)** faire le vœu que +subj ❹ (express good wishes) souhaiter; **to ~ sb well** souhaiter à qn que tout aille bien III. vi vouloir; **if you ~** si tu/vous veux/voulez; **to ~ for sth** souhaiter qc; **you couldn't ~ for better weather** on ne pouvait pas espérer meilleur temps
**wishful** ['wɪʃ·fᵊl] adj **it is ~ thinking** c'est prendre ses désirs pour des réalités
**wisp** [wɪsp] n (of hair) mèche f; (of straw) brin m; (of smoke) filet m
**wispy** ['wɪs·pi] <-ier, -iest> adj fin(e)
**wistful** ['wɪs(t)·fᵊl] adj nostalgique
**wit** [wɪt] I. n ❶ (humor) esprit m ❷ (person) personne f vive d'esprit ❸ pl (intelligence) esprit m; **battle of ~s** joute f d'esprit; **to have one's ~s about one** avoir toute sa présence d'esprit II. adv form **to ~** à savoir
**witch** [wɪtʃ] <-es> n a. pej sorcière f
**witchcraft** ['wɪtʃ·kræft] n sorcellerie f
**witch doctor** ['wɪtʃ·dak·tər] n guérisseur, -euse m, f
**witch-hunt** n chasse f aux sorcières
**with** [wɪð] prep ❶ (accompanied by) avec; **he'll be ~ you in a second** il est à vous dans une seconde; **fries ~** ketchup CULIN des frites fpl au ketchup ❷ (by means of) **to take sth ~ the fingers/both hands** prendre qc avec les doigts/à deux mains ❸ (having) **the man ~ the hat/the loud voice** l'homme m au chapeau/qui parle fort; **a computer ~ an external modem** un

ordinateur avec un modem externe; **children ~ eczema** les enfants mpl qui ont de l'eczéma; **~ no hesitation at all** sans la moindre hésitation ❹ (dealing with) **to be ~ Fiat** travailler chez Fiat; **we're ~ the same bank** nous travaillons avec la même banque ❺ (on one's person) **to have sth ~ one** avoir qc sur soi; **he took the key ~ him** il a emporté les clés ❻ (manner) **to welcome sb ~ open arms** accueillir qn à bras ouverts; **~ a smile** en souriant; **~ one's own eyes** de ses propres yeux; **~ tears in one's eyes** les larmes fpl aux yeux; **to sleep ~ the window open** dormir la fenêtre ouverte ❼ (in addition to) **and ~ that, he went out** et là-dessus [o sur ce] il sortit ❽ (caused by) **to cry ~ rage** pleurer de rage; **to turn red ~ anger** devenir rouge de colère; **to be infected ~ a virus** être contaminé par un virus ❾ (full of) **black ~ flies** noir de mouches; **to fill up ~ fuel** faire le plein de carburant ❿ (presenting a situation) **it's the same ~ me** c'est pareil pour moi; **~ the situation being what it is** la situation étant ce qu'elle est; **~ five minutes to go** les cinq dernières minutes ⓫ (opposing) **a war ~ Italy** une guerre contre l'Italie; **to be angry ~ sb** être en colère contre qn ⓬ (supporting) **to be ~ sb** être avec qn; **he's ~ us** il est des nôtres ⓭ (concerning) **to be pleased ~ sth** être content de qc; **what's the matter ~ him?** qu'est-ce qu'il a? ⓮ (understanding) **I'm not ~ you** inf je ne te/vous suis pas; **to be ~ it** inf être dans le coup
**withdraw** [wɪð·'drɔ] irr I. vt retirer II. vi se retirer; **to ~ in favor of sb** se désister en faveur de qn; **to ~ into a fantasy world** se replier dans un monde imaginaire
**withdrawal** [wɪð·'drɔ·ᵊl] n ❶ (removal) a. FIN retrait m; **~ symptoms** état m de manque ❷ PSYCH repli m sur soi
**wither** ['wɪð·ər] I. vi ❶ (become dry: plant) se dessécher; (flower) se faner ❷ (lose vitality) dépérir; (beauty) se fa-

**W**

ner ❸ *fig* **to ~ (away)** (*hope*) s'évanouir ❹ MED (*limb*) s'atrophier **II.** *vt* (*make dry*) dessécher; (*flower*) faner

**withering** ['wɪð·ər·ɪŋ] *adj* ❶ (*dry*) desséchant(e); (*heat*) accablant(e) ❷ (*contemptuous: look, remark*) méprisant(e); (*scorn*) cinglant(e)

**withhold** [wɪð·'hould] *vt irr* ❶ (*not give: help, permission*) refuser; (*evidence, information*) cacher ❷ (*not pay: benefits, rent*) suspendre

**within** [wɪð·'ɪn] **I.** *prep* ❶ (*inside of*) à l'intérieur de; **~ the country** à l'intérieur des frontières du pays; **~ the party** au sein du parti ❷ (*in limit of*) **~ sight** en vue; **~ hearing/easy reach** à portée de voix/de main ❸ (*in less than*) **~ one hour** en l'espace d'une heure; **~ 3 days** sous 3 jours; **~ 2 miles of sth** à moins de 2 miles de qc ❹ (*not exceeding*) **~ the law** dans le cadre de la loi; **to be ~ budget** être dans le budget **II.** *adv* dedans, à l'intérieur; **from ~** de l'intérieur

**without** [wɪð·'ðaut] *prep* sans; **~ a warning** sans crier gare; **to be ~ a job** ne pas avoir de travail; **to do ~ sth** se passer de qc; **~ saying a word/explaining** sans dire mot/explications

**withstand** [wɪð·'stænd] *irr vt* résister à

**witness** ['wɪt·nəs] **I.** *n* ❶ (*person who sees*) témoin *mf*; **to ~ to sth** témoigner de qc; **to take the ~ stand** aller à la barre (des témoins) ❷ *form* (*testimony*) témoignage *m*; **to bear ~ to sth** porter témoignage de qc **II.** *vt* ❶ (*see*) *a. fig* être témoin de; **it's dangerous, ~ the number of accidents** c'est dangereux, regarde le nombre d'accidents ❷ (*countersign: document, signature*) certifier

**witty** ['wɪt·i] <-ier, -iest> *adj* plein(e) d'esprit

**wizard** ['wɪz·ərd] *n* ❶ (*magician*) magicien(ne) *m(f)* ❷ (*expert*) génie *m*; **computer/financial ~** génie de l'informatique/des finances ❸ COMPUT assistant *m*

**w/o** *prep abbr of* **without** sans

**wobble** ['wa·bl] **I.** *vi* vaciller; (*chair, ta*

*ble*) branler; (*person*) être chancelant(e); (*voice, building*) trembler **II.** *vt* faire trembler **III.** *n* ❶ (*movement*) vacillement *m* ❷ (*sound*) tremblement *m*

**wobbly** ['wa·bli] <-ier, -iest> *adj* ❶ (*unsteady*) *a. fig* branlant(e); **to feel ~** se sentir faible ❷ (*sound: note, voice*) tremblant(e)

**wok** [wak] *n* wok *m*

**woke** [wouk] *pt of* **wake**

**woken** ['wou·kən] *pp of* **wake**

**wolf** [wulf] **I.** <wolves> *n* loup *m*; **~ cub** louveteau *m* ▸ **a ~ in sheep's clothing** un loup déguisé en brebis; **to cry ~** crier au loup; **to throw sb to the wolves** jeter qn dans la fosse aux lions **II.** *vt inf* **to ~ sth (down)** engloutir qc

**woman** ['wum·ən] <women> *n* (*female*) femme *f*; **a ~ candidate** une candidate; **a ~ president** une présidente; **a ~ driver** une conductrice; **the women's movement** le mouvement des femmes; **women's studies** études *fpl* féminines ▸ **a ~'s place is in the home** la place de la femme est derrière les fourneaux

**womb** [wum] *n* utérus *m*

**won**[1] [wʌn] *pt, pp of* **win**

**won**[2] [wʌn] *n* won *m*

**wonder** ['wʌn·dər] **I.** *vt* ❶ (*ask oneself*) se demander; **to ~ who/when/if** se demander qui/quand/si; **it makes you ~** cela donne à réfléchir; **I ~ if I could ask you a favor?** est-ce que je peux te/vous demander une faveur? ❷ (*feel surprise*) **to ~ that** s'étonner que +*subj* **II.** *vi* ❶ (*ask oneself*) se demander; **to ~ about sb/sth** se poser des questions sur qn/qc; **to ~ about doing sth** songer à faire qc ❷ (*feel surprise*) **to ~ at sb/sth** s'étonner de qn/qc **III.** *n* ❶ (*feeling*) étonnement *m*; **to fill sb with ~** émerveiller qn; **in ~** avec émerveillement ❷ (*marvel*) merveille *f*; **~ drug** remède *m* miracle ▸ **to do ~s** faire des miracles

**wonderful** ['wʌn·dər·fəl] *adj* merveilleux(-euse); **to feel ~** se sentir en pleine forme

**W**

**wonderland** ['wʌn·dər·lænd] *n* pays *m* des merveilles

**won't** [wəʊnt] = **will not** *s.* **will**

**woo** [wu] *vt* courtiser

**wood** [wʊd] *n* ❶ (*material*) bois *m*; **oak** ~ (bois de) chêne *m* ❷ *pl* (*group of trees*) bois *m*; **in the** ~**s** dans les bois ❸ (*golf club*) bois *m* ▶ **he can't see the** ~ **for the trees** les arbres lui cachent la forêt; **to knock on** ~ toucher du bois; **not to be out of the** ~**s** ne pas être tiré d'affaire

**wooded** ['wʊd·ɪd] *adj* boisé(e)

**wooden** ['wʊd·ən] *adj* ❶ (*made of wood*) en bois; (*leg*) de bois ❷ (*awkward*) gauche; (*smile*) forcé(e)

**woodland** ['wʊd·lənd] *n* région *f* boisée; ~ **plant/animal** plante *f*/animal *m* des bois

**woodpecker** ['wʊd·pek·ər] *n* ZOOL pivert *m*

**woodwind** ['wʊd·wɪnd] MUS I. *n* the ~**s** les bois *mpl* II. *adj* ~ **instrument** instrument *m* à vent

**woodwork** ['wʊd·wɜrk] *n* (*parts of building*) charpente *f* ▶ **to come out of the** ~ ressortir d'on ne sait où

**woodworm** ['wʊd·wɜrm] *inv n* (*larva*) ver *m* à bois

**woody** ['wʊd·i] <-ier, -iest> *adj* ❶ (*texture*) ligneux(-euse) ❷ (*taste*) boisé(e)

**wool** [wʊl] *n* laine *f* ▶ **to pull the** ~ **over sb's eyes** voiler la face de qn

**woolen** ['wʊl·ən] *adj* en laine

**word** [wɜrd] I. *n* ❶ LING mot *m*; **rude** ~**s** gros mots; **in a** ~ en un mot; **in other** ~**s** en d'autres termes; **to not breathe a** ~ **of sth** ne rien dire à propos de qc; **not to know a** ~ **of French** ne pas connaître un mot de français; ~ **for** ~ mot pour mot; **to be too ridiculous for** ~**s** être d'un ridicule sans nom ❷ (*speech, conversation*) **to have a** ~ **with sb** parler un instant à qn; **to say a few** ~**s about sth** dire quelques mots à propos de qc ❸ *no art* (*news*) nouvelles *fpl*; **to have** ~ **from sb/sth** avoir des nouvelles de qn/qc; **to get** ~ **of sth** apprendre qc; **the good** ~ *inf* la

bonne nouvelle; (**the**) ~ **is out** (**that**) … on a appris que … ❹ (*order*) ordre *m*; **to give the** ~ donner l'ordre; **a** ~ **of advice** un conseil ❺ (*promise*) promesse *f*; **to keep/give one's** ~ tenir/donner sa parole; **a man of his** ~ un homme de parole ❻ *pl* MUS paroles *fpl* ▶ **by** ~ **of mouth** de vive voix; **to put** ~**s in(to) sb's mouth** faire dire à qn ce que qn ne veut pas dire; **to take the** ~**s out of sb's mouth** enlever les mots de la bouche à qn; **to put in a good** ~ **for sb/sth** (**with sb**) glisser (à qn) un mot en faveur de qn/qc; **sb cannot get a** ~ **in edgewise** *inf* qn ne peut pas en placer une; **to take sb's** ~ **for it** croire qn sur parole; **my** ~! ma parole! II. *vt* formuler

**word count** *n* nombre *m* de mots

**wording** *n* formulation *f*

**word processing** *n* COMPUT traitement *m* de texte

**word processor** *n* COMPUT logiciel *m* de traitement de texte

**wordy** ['wɜr·di] <-ier, iest> *adj* verbeux(-euse)

**wore** [wɔr] *pt of* **wear**

**work** [wɜrk] I. *n* ❶ (*useful activity*) travail *m*; **to be at** ~ être au travail; **it's hard** ~ **doing sth** c'est dur de faire qc; **to put a lot of** ~ **into sth** beaucoup travailler sur qc; **it needs more** ~ (*essay*) il faut retravailler ça; **to do some** ~ **on the car/house** faire quelques réparations sur la voiture/dans la maison ❷ (*employment*) emploi *m*; **to be in** ~ travailler; **to be out of** ~ être sans emploi; **to get** ~ **as a translator** trouver un emploi en tant que traducteur ❸ (*place*) travail *m*; **to be at** ~ être au travail; **to leave for** ~ partir travailler ❹ (*sth produced by sb*) travail *m*; **to be sb's** ~ être l'œuvre *f* de qn; **the** ~ **of professional thieves/a craftsman** l'œuvre de voleurs professionnels/d'un artisan; ~**s of art in bronze** œuvres *fpl* d'art en bronze ❺ *pl*, + *sing/pl vb* (*factory*) usine *f* ❻ *pl* (*working parts*) *a. fig* rouages *mpl* ❼ *pl*, *inf* (*everything*) **the**

~s la totale ► **to have one's ~ cut out for oneself** peiner à faire qc II. vi ➊ (*be busy, do job*) travailler; **to ~ for peace** œuvrer pour la paix ➋ (*function*) marcher; **to ~ on batteries** fonctionner avec des piles ➌ (*have effect*) faire effet; **to ~ against sb/sth** agir contre qn/qc; **to ~ for sb** agir en faveur de qn; **to ~ both ways** agir dans les deux sens ➍ (*make progress toward sth*) **to ~ free** se libérer; **to ~ loose** se desserrer ► **to ~ like a charm** fonctionner comme un charme III. vt ➊ (*make sb work*) faire travailler; **to ~ oneself to death** se tuer au travail ➋ (*do work*) travailler; **to ~ long hours** travailler de longues heures; **to ~ overtime** faire des heures supplémentaires ➌ (*operate*) faire fonctionner; **to be ~ed by sth** être actionné par qc ➍ (*achieve*) **to ~ sth free** parvenir à dégager qc; **to ~ sth loose** desserrer qc; **to ~ one's way through the crowd** se frayer un chemin à travers la foule ➎ (*bring about*) opérer; **to ~ it/things (out) so that ...** faire de sorte que ... ➏ (*shape*) travailler ➐ (*exploit*) exploiter ► **to ~ one's fingers to the bone** se saigner aux quatre veines

◆ **work in** vt ➊ (*mix in*) incorporer ➋ (*include*) introduire

◆ **work off** vt évacuer; (*one's anger*) passer; **to ~ some fat** perdre du poids

◆ **work out** I. vt ➊ (*calculate*) calculer; **to ~ the total** faire le total ➋ (*reason*) résoudre; (*solution, answer*) trouver; **we can work things out** on peut arranger les choses ➌ (*decide*) décider ➍ (*understand*) comprendre II. vi ➊ (*give a result*) **to ~ to $10** revenir à 10 dollars ➋ (*be a success*) marcher; **to ~ well/badly** bien/mal se passer; **how are things working out?** comment ça va? ➌ (*do exercise*) s'entraîner

◆ **work up** vt ➊ (*upset*) **to work sb up into a rage** mettre qn en rage; **to get worked up** se mettre dans tous ses états ➋ (*develop*) développer; **to ~ an appetite** s'ouvrir l'appétit; **to ~ enthu-** siasm/interest **for sth** s'enthousiasmer pour/s'intéresser à qc

**workaholic** [ˌwɜr·kə·ˈhal·ɪk] n bourreau m de travail

**workaround** n solution f de rechange; (*temporary*) solution f intermédiaire

**workbench** n établi m

**workbook** n livre m d'exercices

**workday** n journée f de travail

**worker** [ˈwɜr·kər] n ➊ (*employee*) travailleur, -euse m, f; **office ~** employé m de bureau ➋ (*manual worker*) ouvrier, -ère m, f; **construction ~** ouvrier du bâtiment ➌ (*person who works hard*) travailleur, -euse m, f ➍ ZOOL ouvrière f; **~ bee** abeille f ouvrière

**workforce** [ˈwɜrk·fɔrs] n + sing/pl vb ➊ (*industry*) **the ~** la main-d'œuvre ➋ (*company*) personnel m

**working** adj ➊ (*employed*) qui travaille; (*population*) actif(-ive); **~ people** ouvriers mpl ➋ (*pertaining to work*) de travail; (*lunch*) d'affaires ➌ (*functioning*) qui fonctionne; **to be in good ~ order** être en bon état de fonctionnement; **to have a ~ knowledge of English** avoir des bases d'anglais

**working-class** adj ouvrier(-ère)

**workload** [ˈwɜrk·loʊd] n charge f de travail

**workman** [ˈwɜrk·mən] <-men> n ouvrier m

**workmanship** n travail m; **fine ~** beau travail

**workout** [ˈwɜrk·aʊt] n séance f d'entraînement

**work permit** n permis m de travail

**workplace** [ˈwɜrk·pleɪs] n lieu m de travail; **in the ~** sur le lieu de travail

**workshop** [ˈwɜrk·ʃap] n atelier m

**workstation** n COMPUT poste m de travail

**world** [wɜrld] n ➊ GEO monde m; **the ~'s population** la population mondiale; **~ Cup** Coupe f du monde; **~ record** record m mondial; **to come into the ~** venir au monde ➋ (*defined group*) monde m; **the Muslim/English-speaking ~** le monde musul- **W**

man/anglophone; **the ~ of fashion** le monde de la mode ►**to be a man/woman of the ~** être un homme/une femme d'expérience; **the ~ is sb's oyster** le monde appartient à qn; **to live in a ~ of one's own** vivre dans son monde; **to mean the ~ to sb** être tout pour qn; **to be out of this ~** inf être super; **to think the ~ of sb** adorer qn

**World Bank** [ˌwɜrld·ˈbæŋk] n Banque f mondiale

**world-class** adj de niveau mondial

**world-famous** adj de renommée internationale

**worldly** [ˈwɜrld·li] adj ❶ (of practical matters: success, goods) matériel(le) ❷ (materialistic) matérialiste ❸ (having experience) avisé(e)

**worldwide** I. adj mondial(e) II. adv (all over the world) à travers le monde

**worm** [wɜrm] I. n a. COMPUT ver m II. vt ❶ (treat for worms) **to ~ a cat** traiter un chat contre les vers ❷ (squeeze through) **to ~ one's way through sth** se faufiler à travers qc ❸ (gain trust slowly) **to ~ oneself into sth** s'insinuer dans qc

**worn** [wɔrn] I. pp of **wear** II. adj usé(e); (stone, statue) abîmé(e); (person) las(se)

**worn-out** [ˌwɔrn·ˈaʊt] adj ❶ (exhausted) épuisé(e) ❷ (used up) complètement usé(e)

**worried** [ˈwɜr·id] adj inquiet(-ète); **to be ~ about sb/sth** s'inquiéter de qn/qc; **I'm ~ he'll leave** j'ai peur qu'il ne parte; **to be ~ to death about sb/sth** être mort d'inquiétude pour qn/qc; **to be ~ sick** être fou d'inquiétude

**worry** [ˈwɜr·i] I. n <-ies> (concern) souci m II. vt <-ie-, -ing> (preoccupy, concern) inquiéter; **it worries me that she can't sleep** cela m'inquiète qu'elle ne puisse pas dormir ►**don't you ~ your pretty little head** iron, inf ne te tracasse pas la tête III. vi <-ie-, -ing> vi (be concerned) **to ~ about sth** s'inquiéter pour qc; **there's nothing to ~**

about il n'y a pas de quoi s'inquiéter; **not to ~** inf ce n'est pas grave

**worrying** adj inquiétant(e)

**worse** [wɜrs] I. adj comp of **bad** ❶ (not as good) pire; **to be ~ at English than sb** (else) être plus mauvais en anglais que qn (d'autre); **to be even ~ than ...** être encore pire que ...; **to be a lot ~** être bien pire; **there's nothing ~ than sth** il n'y a rien de pire que qc; **to make sth ~** empirer qc; **to get ~ and ~** iron empirer; **to make matters ~, he ...** pour envenimer la situation, il ... ❷ (sicker) **to be ~** aller plus mal ►**to be none the ~ for sth** ne pas être trop affecté par qc II. adv comp of **badly** plus mal; **you could do ~ than do sth** ce ne serait pas si mal si tu faisais qc III. n pire m; **to change for the ~** changer en mal; **to have seen ~** avoir vu pire

**worsen** [ˈwɜr·sən] vt, vi empirer

**worship** [ˈwɜr·ʃɪp] I. vt <-p- o -pp-> REL vouer un culte à II. vi <-p- o -pp-> pratiquer (sa religion); **to ~ in a church/mosque** aller à l'église/la mosquée III. n a. fig culte m; **place of ~** lieu m de culte; **act of ~** acte m de dévotion

**worshiper,** n ❶ REL fidèle mf ❷ fig adorateur, -trice m, f

**worst** [wɜrst] I. adj superl of **bad** (least good) **the ~ ...** le pire ...; **my ~ mistake** ma plus grave erreur; **the ~ thing** la pire des choses; **my ~ enemy** mon pire ennemi; **the ~ student** le plus mauvais étudiant II. adv superl of **badly** le plus mal; **to be the ~ affected** être le plus touché III. n (most terrible thing) **the ~** le pire; **at ~** au pire; **~ of all** pire que tout; **the ~ is over** le pire est passé ►**if worse comes to ~** dans le pire des cas

**worth** [wɜrθ] I. n valeur f; **two dollars' ~ of apples** pour deux dollars de pommes; **I got my money's ~** j'en ai eu pour mon argent II. adj **to be ~ $2** valoir 2 dollars; **sth is ~ a lot to me** j'attache un grand prix à qc; **it's ~ seeing** ça vaut la peine d'être vu; **it's not ~ changing** ça ne vaut pas la peine de

W

changer; **it's ~ a try** ça vaut la peine d'essayer ▸ **to be ~ one's** weight **in gold** valoir son pesant d'or; **for all one is ~** de toutes ses forces

**worthless** ['wɜrθ·ləs] *adj* qui ne vaut rien; **to feel ~** se sentir bon à rien

**worthwhile** [ˌwɜrθ·'(h)waɪl] *adj* (*activity, talks*) qui en vaut la peine; **to be (very) ~** en valoir vraiment la peine

**worthy** ['wɜr·ði] I.<-ier, -iest> *adj* digne; (*cause*) noble; **to be ~ of sb/sth** être digne de qn/qc II.<-ies> *n iron* notable *m*

**would** [wʊd] *aux* ① *pt of* **will** ② (*in indirect speech*) **he said he ~ come** il a dit qu'il viendrait; **I thought I ~ have arrived on time** j'ai cru que j'arriverais à l'heure ③ (*conditional*) **I ~ come if I had time** je viendrais si j'avais du temps; **it ~ have been hard to drive** cela aurait été difficile de rouler ④ (*implied condition*) **it ~ be a pleasure** ce serait avec plaisir; **my mother ~ know** ma mère le saurait ⑤ (*desires and preferences*) **I'd like some water** j'aimerais un peu d'eau; **~ you mind …?** auriez-vous l'obligeance …? ⑥ (*I wish*) **they'd go** j'aimerais qu'ils partent; **I ~ rather do sth** je préférerais faire qc ⑥ (*regularity in past*) **as a child, I ~ work from 6 to 6** enfant, je travaillais de 6 heures à 18 heures ⑦ (*characteristic behavior*) **she ~ say that, ~n't she?** c'est ce qu'elle dirait, non?; **she ~ never do that** elle ne ferait jamais une telle chose ⑧ (*offering polite advice*) **I ~ come early if I were you** j'arriverais tôt si j'étais vous; **I ~n't go on Thursday** je ne partirais pas jeudi (à ta/votre place) ⑨ (*asking motives*) **why ~ he do that?** pourquoi ferait-il une telle chose?

**would-be** ['wʊd·bi] *adj* soi-disant(e)

**wouldn't** ['wʊdᵊnt] — **would not** *s.* **would**

**wound**[1] [waʊnd] *pt, pp of* **wind**

**wound**[2] [wund] I. *n a. fig* blessure *f* II. *vt a. fig* blesser

**wounded** ['wund·ɪd] I. *adj a. fig* blessé(e) II. *npl* MED **the ~** les blessés *mpl*

**woven** ['woʊv·ᵊn] I. *pp of* **weave** II. *adj* tissé(e)

**wow** [waʊ] I. *interj inf* ouah! II. *vt inf* (*impress*) emballer

**wrap** [ræp] I. *n* ① (*piece of clothing*) châle *m* ② (*wrapping*) emballage *m*; **plastic ~** emballage en plastique ▸ **to** keep **sth under ~s** garder qc secret; **it's a ~** ça y est, c'est fini II. *vt* <-pp-> emballer

◆**wrap up** I. *vt* ① (*completely cover*) envelopper ② (*dress warmly: child*) emballer; **to wrap oneself up** s'emmitoufler ③ (*involve*) **to be wrapped up in sth** être absorbé par qc ④ *inf* (*finish well*) conclure II. *vi* (*dress heavily*) s'emmitoufler

**wrapper** ['ræp·ər] *n* emballage *m*

**wrapping paper** *n* papier *m* d'emballage

**wreak** [rik] <-ed, -ed *o* wrought, wrought> *vt form* (*damage*) entraîner; (*vengeance*) assouvir; **to ~ havoc** faire des ravages

**wreath** [riθ] <-s> *n* couronne *f*

**wreck** [rek] I. *vt* ① (*damage*) démolir ② (*cause to be ruined: chances, hopes*) ruiner; (*lives, career, friendship*) briser II. *n* ① (*crashed vehicle*) épave *f* ② (*sinking*) naufrage *m* ③ *inf* (*sick person*) loque *f* ④ (*car, machine*) tas *m* de ferraille

**wreckage** ['rek·ɪdʒ] *n* ① (*damaged pieces*) débris *mpl* ② (*wreck*) épave *f*

**wren** [ren] *n* troglodyte *m*

**wrench** [ren(t)ʃ] I. *vt* ① (*twist out*) arracher; **to ~ sth from/out of sth** arracher qc de qc; **to ~ sth free** libérer qc d'un mouvement brusque ② (*injure*) se tordre; **to ~ one's foot** se faire une entorse au pied ③ (*take*) **to ~ sth from sb** arracher qc à qn II. *n* ① (*tool*) clef *f* ② (*painful departure*) déchirement *m*

**wrestle** ['res·l] SPORTS I.<-ling> *vt* (*fight*) lutter; **to ~ sb to the ground** jeter qn au sol II.<-ling> *vi* ① (*fight*) lut-

**W**

ter ② (*deal with: problem, computer*) se débattre avec

**wrestler** ['res·l·ər] *n* ① (*athlete*) lutteur, -euse *m, f* ② (*show performer*) catcheur, -euse *m, f*

**wrestling** ['res·l·ɪŋ] *n* ① (*sport*) lutte *f* ② (*show*) catch *m*

**wretched** ['retʃ·ɪd] *adj* ① (*unhappy, depressed*) **to feel/look** ~ se sentir/avoir l'air mal ② (*of poor quality, miserable*) lamentable

**wriggle** ['rɪg·l] I. <-ling> *vi* ① (*squirm*) se tortiller; (*person*) s'agiter ② (*move by twisting*) **to** ~ **through/under sth** se faufiler à travers/sous qc II. <-ling> *vt* (*toes*) remuer

**wring** [rɪŋ] <wrung, wrung> *vt* ① (*twist to squeeze out*) tordre; (*shirt*) essorer; **to** ~ **sb's/sth's neck** *a. fig* tordre le cou à qn/qc; **to** ~ **the water out of sth** tordre qc pour l'essorer ② (*obtain*) **to** ~ **information from sb** arracher des renseignements à qn

**wrinkle** ['rɪŋ·kl] I. *n* (*material*) pli *m*; (*face*) ride *f* ▶ **to** iron **out the** ~**s** aplanir les difficultés II. <-ling> *vi* (*form folds: material*) se froisser; (*face, skin*) se rider III. <-ling> *vt* (*put folds in: material*) froisser; (*face*) rider ▶ **to** ~ **one's** brow froncer les sourcils

**wrinkled** ['rɪŋ·kld], **wrinkly** ['rɪŋ·kli] *adj* (*clothes*) froissé(e); (*skin*) ridé(e)

**wrist** [rɪst] *n* poignet *m*

**wristwatch** ['rɪs(t)·watʃ] *n* montre-bracelet *f*

**write** [raɪt] <wrote, written, writing> I. *vt* ① (*mark*) écrire; (*check*) remplir; (*essay, commentary*) rédiger ② (*write to*) écrire à ▶ **to be nothing to** ~ home **about** n'être rien de bouleversant II. *vi* (*mark letters*) écrire; **to learn (how) to read and** ~ apprendre à lire et à écrire; **to** ~ **for a living** vivre de sa plume

♦**write back** I. *vt* répondre II. *vi* répondre

♦**write down** *vt* noter; **to** ~ **ideas** mettre ses idées par écrit

♦**write in** I. *vi* écrire II. *vt* (*insert*) insérer

♦**write off** I. *vt* ① (*give up*) faire une croix sur ② (*lose interest*) se désintéresser de ③ (*damage*) démolir ④ FIN amortir II. *vi* - **for sth** demander qc par courrier

♦**write out** *vt* ① (*put into writing*) écrire ② (*fill out*) **to write a check (out) to sb** faire un chèque à qn ③ (*remove: character*) rayer; **to write sb out of one's will** rayer qn de son testament

♦**write up** *vt* ① (*put in written form*) écrire ② (*critique*) **to** ~ **a film** écrire un article sur un film; **to be written up favorably** faire l'objet de critiques élogieuses ③ LAW faire un rapport sur

**write-protected** *adj* COMPUT protégé(e) contre l'écriture

**writer** ['raɪ·tər] *n* ① (*professional who writes*) écrivain *m*; **she is a** ~ elle est écrivain ② COMPUT (*of CD-ROM, DVD*) graveur *m*

**write-up** ['raɪt·ʌp] *n* critique *f*

**writing** ['raɪ·tɪŋ] *n* ① (*handwriting*) écriture *f* ② (*anything written*) écrit *m*; **in** ~ par écrit ③ *pl* LIT, THEAT, PUBL œuvre *f*; **women's** ~ **in the 19th century** la littérature féminine au 19ᵉ siècle ④ (*creation of a written work*) écriture *f*

**written** ['rɪt·ᵊn] I. *pp of* **write** II. *adj* écrit(e); ~ **exam** examen *m* écrit ▶ **to be** ~ **all over one's** face se lire sur le visage de qn; **to be** ~ **in the** stars être écrit; **the** ~ word l'écrit *m*

**wrong** [rɔŋ] I. *adj* ① (*not right*) faux(fausse); **to be** ~ (**about sb/sth**) avoir tort (à propos de qn/qc); **to be plainly** ~ avoir complètement tort; **to prove sb** ~ prouver le contraire à qn ② (*not appropriate*) mauvais(e); **he's the** ~ **person for the job** ce n'est pas la bonne personne pour le travail; **to go** ~ aller mal; **there's something** ~ il y a quelque chose qui ne tourne pas rond; **what is** ~ **with him?** qu'est-ce qui ne va pas avec lui?; **what's** ~ **with doing this?** quel mal y a-t-il à faire cela? ③ (*morally reprehensible*) mal; **it is** ~ **of sb to so sth** c'est mal de sa part de qn de faire qc; **to do sth ~** faire qc de mal ❹ (*not functioning correctly*) **to be ~** (*watch*) ne pas être à l'heure ▸ **to get up out of the ~ side of the <u>bed</u>** se lever du mauvais pied; **to fall into the ~ <u>hands</u>** tomber dans de mauvaises mains; **to go down the ~ <u>way</u>** être avalé de travers; **to have sth on the ~ <u>way</u> around** avoir qc à l'envers II. *adv* mal; **to get sb/sth ~** mal comprendre qn/qc; **to go ~** (*plan*) ne pas marcher III. *n* ❶ (*moral reprehensibility*) mal *m;* **to do sb no ~** ne faire aucun mal à qn; **to know right from ~** distinguer le bien du mal ❷ (*unfair actions*) tort *m;* **to do sb ~** faire du tort à qn ❸ (*unjust action*) injustice *f;* **to suffer a ~** être victime d'une injustice ▸ **to be <u>in</u> the ~**

(*not right*) avoir tort; LAW être dans son tort IV. *vt form* ❶ (*treat unjustly*) léser ❷ (*judge character unjustly*) être injuste envers

**wrongful** ['rɒŋ·fᵊl] *adj* injustifié(e)

**wrongly** ['rɒŋ·li] *adv* ❶ (*unfairly*) à tort ❷ (*incorrectly*) mal

**wrote** [roʊt] *pt of* **write**

**wrung** [rʌŋ] *pt, pp of* **wring**

**wry** [raɪ] <wrier, wriest *o* wryer, wryest> *adj* ironique

**wt.** [weɪt] *n abbr of* **weight** p. *m*

**WV** *n abbr of* **West Virginia**

**WWW** *n abbr of* **World Wide Web** COMPUT TAM *f*

**WY** *n abbr of* **Wyoming**

**Wyoming** [waɪˈoʊ·mɪŋ] I. *n* le Wyoming II. *adj* du Wyoming

**X, x** [eks] <-'s> I. *n* ❶ a. MATH X *m*, x *m*; **~ as in X-ray** (*on telephone*) x comme Xavier ❷ (*used in place of name*) **Mr. ~** M. X ❸ (*symbol for kiss*) bisou *m* ❹ (*cross symbol*) croix *f* II. *vt* (*delete*) **to ~ sth out** rayer qc

**xenophobia** [ˌzen·ə·ˈfoʊ·bi·ə] *n* xénophobie *f*

**Xerox®** ['zɪr·aks] I. *n* (*photocopy*) photocopie *f* II. *vt* (*photocopy*) photocopier; **a ~ed copy of the document** une photocopie du document

**Xmas** ['krɪs·məs] *inf abbr of* **Christmas** Noël *m*

**X-ray** I. *n* ❶ PHYS rayon *m* X ❷ MED radio(graphie) *f;* **to have an ~** passer une radio(graphie) ❸ (*picture*) radio *f* II. *vt* MED radiographier

**xylophone** ['zaɪ·lə·foʊn] *n* xylophone *m*

X

# Yy

**Y, y** [waɪ] <-'s> *n* a. MATH Y *m*, y *m;* ~ **as in Yankee** (*on telephone*) y comme Yvonne

**yacht** [jɒt] *n* yacht *m*

**yachting** *n* (*sailing*) navigation *f* de plaisance

**yak** [jæk] I. *n* ZOOL, BIO ya(c)k *m* II. *vi inf* papoter

**yank** [jæŋk] I. *vt inf* ① (*pull hard*) tirer d'un coup sec ② (*remove forcefully*) a. *fig* arracher; (*tooth*) arracher d'un coup sec II. *n inf* (*hard pull*) coup *m* sec; **to give sth a ~** donner un coup sec à qc

**Yankee** ['jæŋ·ki] I. *n inf* ① (*American*) Ricain(e) *m(f)* ② HIST (*person from northern US*) nordiste *mf* ③ (*person from New England*) Yankee *mf* II. *adj inf* ricain(e)

**yap** [jæp] <-pp-> *vi* a. *pej* japper

**yard¹** [jɑrd] *n* (*3 feet*) yard *m* (*0,914 m*)

**yard²** [jɑrd] *n* ① (*lawn*) jardin *m* ② (*work area*) chantier *m*

**yardstick** ['jɑrd·stɪk] *n* ① (*measuring stick*) étalon *m* ② (*standard for comparison*) critère *m*

**yawn** [jɔn] I. *vi* (*show tiredness: person*) bâiller II. *n* ① (*sign of tiredness*) bâillement *m* ② *inf* (*boring thing*) **to be a ~** être ennuyeux à mourir

**yd.** [jɑrd] *n abbr of* **yard(s)** yard *m*

**yeah** [jeə] *adv inf* (*yes*) ouais; **oh ~?** ah ouais?

**year** [jɪr] *n* ① (*twelve months*) année *f;* **the ~** (*that*) … [*o* **when** …] l'année où …; **all ~ round** toute l'année; **the thing/person of the ~** la chose/personne de l'année; **I'm six ~s old** j'ai six ans ② (*a long time*) année *f;* **for ~s** depuis des années; **over the ~s** à travers les années; **~ in, ~ out** année après année ③ SCHOOL classe *f;* **academic ~** année *f* universitaire, année *f* académique *Belgique, Québec, Suisse;* **school ~** année scolaire ► **to take ~s off sb** rajeunir qn

**yearbook** ['jɪr·bʊk] *n* PUBL annuaire *m*

**year-long** ['jɪr·lɔŋ] *adj* d'une année

**yearly** I. *adj* (*happening every year*) annuel(le) II. *adv* (*every year*) annuellement

**yearn** [jɜrn] *vi* **to ~ for sth** désirer qc ardemment; **to ~ to do sth** brûler de faire qc

**yearning** *n* désir *m; a* **~ for sth** un désir de qc

**yeast** [jist] *n* levure *f*

**yell** [jel] I. *n* hurlement *m* II. *vi* hurler; **to ~ at sb** hurler après qn; **to ~ for sb/sth** appeler qn/qc en hurlant III. *vt* hurler; **to ~ sth at sb** hurler qc à qn

**yellow** ['jel·oʊ] I. *adj* ① (*color*) jaune; **golden ~** jaune d'or; **to turn ~** jaunir ② *pej* (*cowardly*) lâche II. *n* jaune *m* III. *vt, vi* jaunir; *s.a.* **blue**

**Yellow Pages®** *n* pages *fpl* jaunes

**yelp** [jelp] I. *vi, vt* glapir II. *n* (*high--pitched cry*) glapissement *m*

**yep** [jep] *adv inf* (*yes*) ouais

**yes** [jes] I. *adv* ① (*affirmative*) oui; **~, ma'am** oui, madame ② (*contradicting a negative*) si II. <yeses> *n* (*statement in favor*) oui *m*

**yes man** ['jes·mæn] <-men> *n pej* béni--oui-oui *m inv*

**yesterday** ['jes·tər·deɪ] *adv* hier; **the day before ~** avant-hier; **late ~** hier dans la soirée; **~ morning/evening** [*o* **night**] hier matin/(au) soir ► **I wasn't born ~!** je ne suis pas né de la dernière pluie!

**yet** [jet] I. *adv* ① (*till now*) (**as**) **~** jusqu'à présent; **to have not ~ done sth** n'avoir toujours pas fait qc; **the fastest ~** le plus rapide jusqu'à présent ② (*already*) **not ~** pas encore; **don't go** (**just**) **~** ne pars pas déjà ③ (*still*) **she's young ~** elle est encore jeune ④ (*even*)

**~ more beautiful/wine** encore plus beau/de vin II. *conj* pourtant, néanmoins; **incredible, ~ it's true** c'est incroyable mais vrai

**yew** [juː] *n* if *m*

**Yiddish** ['jɪd·ɪʃ] I. *adj* yiddish *inv* II. *n* yiddish *m; s.a.* **English**

**yield** [jiːld] I. *n* rendement *m* II. *vt* ❶ (*provide*) *a. fig* rapporter; (*results*) donner ❷ (*give up*) céder III. *vi* ❶ (*bend: material*) céder ❷ (*let other cars go first*) céder la priorité ❸ (*surrender*) se rendre ❹ (*give way*) céder; **to ~ to pressure** céder à la pression

**yodel** ['jou·dəl] MUS I. *vt, vi* (*sing*) iodler II. *n* (*yodeled song*) tyrolienne *f*

**yoga** ['jou·gə] *n* (*exercises*) yoga *m;* **to do ~** faire du yoga

**yog(h)urt** ['jou·gərt] *n* yaourt *m*

**yoke** [jouk] I. *n* ❶ AGR *a. fig* joug *m* ❷ FASHION empiècement *m* II. *vt* ❶ (*fit with yoke: animal*) atteler ❷ (*combine*) **to ~ sb/sth together** unir qn/qc

**yolk** [jouk] *n* jaune *m*

**you** [juː] *pers pron* ❶ (*2ⁿᵈ person sing*) tu *subject pron,* te *objective pron,* t' *+ vowel,* toi *tonic form;* **I see ~** je te vois; **do ~ see me?** me vois-tu?; **I love ~** je t'aime; **it's for ~** c'est pour toi; **older than ~** plus âgé que toi; **if I were ~** si j'étais toi ❷ (*2nd person pl or polite form*) vous; **older than ~** plus âgé que vous; **all of ~** vous tous; **~ men** vous, les hommes ❸ (*indefinite person*) **~ never know** on ne sait jamais; **it makes ~ mad** ça rend fou

**you'll** [juːl] = **you will** *s.* **will**

**young** [jʌŋ] I. *adj* jeune; **~ people** les jeunes *mpl;* **sb's ~er brother** le frère cadet de qn; **you're only ~ once!** on n'est jeune qu'une fois!; **to be ~ at**

**heart** être jeune de cœur II. *n pl* **the ~** ❶ (*young people*) les jeunes *mpl* ❷ ZOOL, BIO les petits *mpl*

**your** [jʊr] *poss adj* ❶ (*one owner*) ton *m,* ta *f,* tes *pl* ❷ (*several owners or polite form*) votre *mf,* vos *pl* ❸ (*indefinite owner*) **it depends on ~ age** ça dépend de l'âge qu'on a; *s.a.* **my**

**you're** [jʊr] = **you are** *s.* **be**

**yours** [jʊrz] *poss pron* ❶ (*belonging to you*) le tien, la tienne; **this glass is ~** ce verre est à toi ❷ *pl or sing polite form* (*belonging to you*) le vôtre, la vôtre; **this glass is ~** ce verre est à vous; *s.a.* **hers, ours**

**yourself** [jʊr·'self] *reflex pron* ❶ *after verbs* (*one person*) te, t' *+ vowel;* (*polite form*) vous ❷ (*you*) toi-même; (*polite form*) vous-même; *s.* **myself**

**youth** [juːθ] *n* ❶ (*period when young*) jeunesse *f* ❷ (*young man*) jeune homme *m* ❸ (*young people*) **the ~** les jeunes *mpl*

**youthful** ['juːθ·fəl] *adj* ❶ (*young*) jeune ❷ (*young-looking*) jeune; **to look ~** avoir l'air jeune ❸ (*typical of the young*) de jeunesse; (*enthusiasm*) juvénile

**youth hostel** *n* auberge *f* de jeunesse

**you've** [juːv] = **you have** *s.* **have**

**yo-yo®** ['jou·jou] I. *n* (*toy*) yo-yo *m inv* II. *vi* fluctuer

**yr.¹** *pron abbr of* **your** ton, ta

**yr.²** *n abbr of* **year** année *f*

**yuck** [jʌk] *interj inf* berk!

**yucky** ['jʌk·i] <-ier, -iest> *adj* dégoûtant(e)

**yum** [jʌm] *interj inf* miam-miam!

**yummy** ['jʌm·i] <-ier, -iest> *adj inf* ❶ (*delicious*) délicieux(-euse) ❷ (*sexy*) sexy *inv*

**Y**

# Zz

**Z, z** [zi] <-'s> n Z m, z m; **~ as in Zulu** (*on telephone*) z comme Zoé ►**to know sth from <u>A</u> to ~** connaître qc de A à Z; **to <u>catch</u>/get some ~'s** *inf* se pieuter

**zap** [zæp] **I.**<-pp-> vt inf ❶ (*destroy: object*) détruire; (*person*) éliminer ❷ (*send fast*) expédier ❸ CULIN (*in the microwave*) passer au micro-ondes **II.**<-pp-> vi ❶ inf (*go*) foncer; **to ~ through sth** se dépêcher de faire qc ❷ inf TV **to ~ between channels** zapper d'une chaîne à l'autre

**zebra** ['zi·brə] <-(bras)> n zèbre m

**zero** ['zɪr·oʊ] **I.** adj ❶ (*number*) zéro ❷ (*nil*) nul(le); **~ hour** MIL heure f H; **~ growth** croissance f nulle **II.** vi ❶ MIL **to ~ in on** régler le tir sur ❷ (*focus on*) **to ~ in on** cibler

**zero-energy** adj à consommation énergétique nulle

**zero tolerance** n tolérance f zéro

**zigzag** ['zɪg·zæg] **I.** n (*crooked line*) zigzag m **II.** adj (*crooked*) en zigzag **III.**<-gg-> vi zigzaguer

**zilch** [zɪltʃ] n inf zéro m

**zillionaire** n inf multimilliardaire mf

**zinc** [zɪŋk] n no indef art zinc m

**zip** [zɪp] inf **I.** n ❶ (*vigor*) punch m ❷ (*ZIP code*) code m postal **II.** pron (*nothing*) que dalle; **to know ~ about**

sth ne rien savoir de qc **III.**<-pp-> vt **to ~ a bag** fermer un sac **IV.**<-pp-> vi (*go quickly*) **to ~ somewhere** passer quelque part

◆**zip up I.** vt ❶ (*close*) fermer ❷ COMPUT zipper **II.** vi (*close with a zip*) se fermer avec une fermeture éclair

**zip code, ZIP code** n ≈ code m postal

**zipper** n fermeture f éclair®

**zippy** ['zɪp·i] <-ier, -iest> adj inf plein(e) de punch; (*car*) nerveux(-euse)

**zodiac** ['zoʊ·di·æk] n zodiaque m

**zombie** ['zam·bi] n a. pej zombie m

**zone** [zoʊn] **I.** n zone f; **combat ~** zone de combat; **time ~** fuseau m horaire; **no-parking ~** stationnement m interdit **II.** vt réserver

**zoo** [zu] n zoo m

**zoological** [ˌzoʊ·ə·'la·dʒɪ·kəl] adj zoologique

**zoom** [zum] **I.** n PHOT zoom m; **~ lens** zoom m **II.** vi inf ❶ inf (*move very fast*) passer à toute vitesse; **to ~ past** passer très vite ❷ (*increase dramatically*) monter en flèche ❸ PHOT, CINE zoomer

◆**zoom in** vi CINE, PHOT faire un zoom avant; **to ~ on sth** fig faire un zoom avant sur qc

**zucchini** [zu·'ki·ni] <-(s)> n CULIN courgette f

# Annexes
## Appendices

# Verbes français
## French verbs

Pour des raisons d'économie de place dans la partie dictionnaire, certains verbes sont suivis d'un chiffre entre chevrons qui renvoie à un des 14 tableaux de conjugaison à utiliser comme modèle.

To save space in the main part of the dictionary, some verbs are followed by angle brackets which contain a number referring to one of the 14 model verbs.

### 1 chanter

| présent | imparfait | futur simple | passé simple |
|---|---|---|---|
| je chante | je chantais | je chanterai | je chantai |
| tu chantes | tu chantais | tu chanteras | tu chantas |
| il/elle chante | il/elle chantait | il/elle chantera | il/elle chanta |
| nous chantons | nous chantions | nous chanterons | nous chantâmes |
| vous chantez | vous chantiez | vous chanterez | vous chantâtes |
| ils/elles chantent | ils/elles chantaient | ils/elles chanteront | ils/elles chantèrent |

| conditionnel présent | subjonctif présent | subjonctif imparfait |
|---|---|---|
| je chanterais | que je chante | que je chantasse |
| tu chanterais | que tu chantes | que tu chantasses |
| il/elle chanterait | qu'il/elle chante | qu'il/elle chantât |
| nous chanterions | que nous chantions | que nous chantassions |
| vous chanteriez | que vous chantiez | que vous chantassiez |
| ils/elles chanteraient | qu'ils/elles chantent | qu'ils/elles chantassent |

| participe présent | participe passé | impératif présent | impératif passé |
|---|---|---|---|
| chantant | chanté | chante | aie chanté |
| | | chantons | ayons chanté |
| | | chantez | ayez chanté |

## 2 commencer

| présent | imparfait | futur simple | passé simple |
|---------|-----------|--------------|--------------|
| je commence | je commençais | je commencerai | je commençai |
| tu commences | tu commençais | ... | tu commenças |
| il/elle commence | il/elle commençait | | il/elle commença |
| nous commençons | nous commencions | | nous commençâmes |
| vous commencez | vous commenciez | | vous commençâtes |
| ils/elles commencent | ils/elles commençaient | | ils/elles commencèrent |

| conditionnel présent | subjonctif présent | subjonctif imparfait |
|----------------------|--------------------|-----------------------|
| je commencerais | que je commence | que je commençasse |
| ... | que tu commences | que tu commençasses |
| | qu'il/elle commence | qu'il/elle commençât |
| | que nous commencions | que nous commençassions |
| | que vous commenciez | que vous commençassiez |
| | qu'ils/elles commencent | qu'ils/elles commençassent |

| participe présent | participe passé | impératif présent | impératif passé |
|-------------------|-----------------|-------------------|-----------------|
| commençant | commencé | commence | aie commencé |
| | | commençons | ayons commencé |
| | | commencez | ayez commencé |

## 2a changer

| présent | imparfait | futur simple | passé simple |
|---|---|---|---|
| je change | je changeais | je changerai ... | je changeai |
| tu changes | tu changeais | | tu changeas |
| il/elle change | il/elle changeait | | il/elle changea |
| nous changeons | nous changions | | nous changeâmes |
| vous changez | vous changiez | | vous changeâtes |
| ils/elles changent | ils/elles changeaient | | ils/elles changèrent |

| conditionnel présent | subjonctif présent | subjonctif imparfait |
|---|---|---|
| je changerais ... | que je change | que je changeasse |
| | que tu changes | que tu changeasses |
| | qu'il/elle change | qu'il/elle changeât |
| | que nous changions | que nous changeassions |
| | que vous changiez | que vous changeassiez |
| | qu'ils/elles changent | qu'ils/elles changeassent |

| participe présent | participe passé | impératif présent | impératif passé |
|---|---|---|---|
| changeant | changé | change | aie changé |
| | | changeons | ayons changé |
| | | changez | ayez changé |

### 3 rejeter

| présent | imparfait | futur simple | passé simple |
|---|---|---|---|
| je rejette | je rejetais ... | je rejetterai ... | je rejetai ... |
| tu rejettes | | | |
| il/elle rejette | | | |
| nous rejetons | | | |
| vous rejetez | | | |
| ils/elles rejettent | | | |

| conditionnel présent | subjonctif présent | subjonctif imparfait | |
|---|---|---|---|
| je rejetterais ... | que je rejette | que je rejetasse ... | |
| | que tu rejettes | | |
| | qu'il/elle rejette | | |
| | que nous rejetions | | |
| | que vous rejetiez | | |
| | qu'ils/elles rejettent | | |

| participe présent | participe passé | impératif présent | impératif passé |
|---|---|---|---|
| rejetant | rejeté | rejette | aie rejeté |
| | | rejetons | ayons rejeté |
| | | rejetez | ayez rejeté |

## 4 peler

| présent | imparfait | futur simple | passé simple |
|---|---|---|---|
| je pèle | je pelais ... | je pèlerai | je pelai ... |
| tu pèles | | tu pèleras | |
| il/elle pèle | | il/elle pèlera | |
| nous pelons | | nous pèlerons | |
| vous pelez | | vous pèlerez | |
| ils/elles pèlent | | ils/elles pèleront | |

| conditionnel présent | subjonctif présent | subjonctif imparfait | |
|---|---|---|---|
| je pèlerais | que je pèle | que je pelasse ... | |
| tu pèlerais | que tu pèles | | |
| il/elle pèlerait | qu'il/elle pèle | | |
| nous pèlerions | que nous pelions | | |
| vous pèleriez | que vous peliez | | |
| ils/elles pèle-raient | qu'ils/elles pè-lent | | |

| participe présent | participe passé | impératif présent | impératif passé |
|---|---|---|---|
| pelant | pelé | pèle | aie pelé |
| | | pelons | ayons pelé |
| | | pelez | ayez pelé |

## 5 préférer

| présent | imparfait | futur simple | passé simple |
|---|---|---|---|
| je préfère | je préférais ... | je préférerai ... | je préférai ... |
| tu préfères | | | |
| il/elle préfère | | | |
| nous préférons | | | |
| vous préférez | | | |
| ils/elles préfè-rent | | | |

| conditionnel présent | subjonctif présent | subjonctif imparfait |
|---|---|---|
| je préférerais ... | que je préfère | que je préférasse ... |
| | que tu préfères | |
| | qu'il/elle préfère | |
| | que nous préfé-rions | |
| | que vous préfé-riez | |
| | qu'ils/elles pré-fèrent | |

| participe présent | participe passé | impératif présent | impératif passé |
|---|---|---|---|
| préférant | préféré | préfère | aie préféré |
| | | préférons | ayons préféré |
| | | préférez | ayez préféré |

## 6 appuyer

| présent | imparfait | futur simple | passé simple |
|---|---|---|---|
| j'appuie | j'appuyais ... | j'appuierai ... | j'appuyai ... |
| tu appuies | | | |
| il/elle appuie | | | |
| nous appuyons | | | |
| vous appuyez | | | |
| ils/elles appuient | | | |

| conditionnel présent | subjonctif présent | subjonctif imparfait |
|---|---|---|
| j'appuierais ... | que j'appuie | que j'appuyasse ... |
| | que tu appuies | |
| | qu'il/elle appuie | |
| | que nous appuyions | |
| | que vous appuyiez | |
| | qu'ils/elles appuient | |

| participe présent | participe passé | impératif présent | impératif passé |
|---|---|---|---|
| appuyant | appuyé | appuie | aie appuyé |
| | | appuyons | ayons appuyé |
| | | appuyez | ayez appuyé |

**7 essayer**

| présent | imparfait | futur simple | passé simple |
|---------|-----------|--------------|--------------|
| j'essaie/essaye<br>tu essaies/es-<br>sayes<br>il/elle essaie/es-<br>saye<br>nous essayons<br>vous essayez<br>ils/elles es-<br>saient/essayent | j'essayais … | j'essaierai/es-<br>sayerai … | j'essayai … |

| conditionnel présent | subjonctif présent | subjonctif imparfait |
|----------------------|--------------------|-----------------------|
| j'essaierais/es-<br>sayerais … | que j'essaie/es-<br>saye<br>que tu essaies/<br>essayes<br>qu'il/elle essaie/<br>essaye<br>que nous es-<br>sayions<br>que vous es-<br>sayiez<br>qu'ils/elles es-<br>saient/essayent | que j'essayasse … |

| participe présent | participe passé | impératif présent | impératif passé |
|-------------------|-----------------|-------------------|-----------------|
| essayant | essayé | essaie/essaye<br>essayons<br>essayez | aie essayé<br>ayons essayé<br>ayez essayé |

## 8 agir

| présent | imparfait | futur simple | passé simple |
|---|---|---|---|
| j'agis | j'agissais | j'agirai | j'agis |
| tu agis | tu agissais | tu agiras | tu agis |
| il/elle agit | il/elle agissait | il/elle agira | il/elle agit |
| nous agissons | nous agissions | nous agirons | nous agîmes |
| vous agissez | vous agissiez | vous agirez | vous agîtes |
| ils/elles agissent | ils/elles agissaient | ils/elles agiront | ils/elles agirent |

| conditionnel présent | subjonctif présent | subjonctif imparfait |
|---|---|---|
| j'agirais ... | que j'agisse | que j'agisse |
| | que tu agisses | que tu agisses |
| | qu'il/elle agisse | qu'il/elle agît |
| | que nous agissions | que nous agissions |
| | que vous agissiez | que vous agissiez |
| | qu'ils/elles agissent | qu'ils/elles agissent |

| participe présent | participe passé | impératif présent | impératif passé |
|---|---|---|---|
| agissant | agi | agis | aie agi |
| | | agissons | ayons agi |
| | | agissez | ayez agi |

## 9 devenir

| présent | imparfait | futur simple | passé simple |
|---|---|---|---|
| je deviens | je devenais ... | je deviendrai | je devins |
| tu deviens | | tu deviendras | tu devins |
| il/elle devient | | il/elle deviendra | il/elle devint |
| nous devenons | | nous deviendrons | nous devînmes |
| vous devenez | | vous deviendrez | vous devîntes |
| ils/elles deviennent | | ils/elles deviendront | ils/elles devinrent |

| conditionnel présent | subjonctif présent | subjonctif imparfait |
|---|---|---|
| je deviendrais ... | que je devienne | que je devinsse |
| | que tu deviennes | que tu devinsses |
| | qu'il/elle devienne | qu'il/elle devînt |
| | que nous devenions | que nous devinssions |
| | que vous deveniez | que vous devinssiez |
| | qu'ils/elles deviennent | qu'ils/elles devinssent |

| participe présent | participe passé | impératif présent | impératif passé |
|---|---|---|---|
| devenant | devenu | deviens | sois devenu |
| | | devenons | soyons devenus |
| | | devenez | soyez devenus |

## 10 sortir

| présent | imparfait | futur simple | passé simple |
|---|---|---|---|
| je sors | je sortais ... | je sortirai ... | je sortis... |
| tu sors | | | |
| il/elle sort | | | |
| nous sortons | | | |
| vous sortez | | | |
| ils/elles sortent | | | |

| conditionnel présent | subjonctif présent | subjonctif imparfait |
|---|---|---|
| je sortirais ... | que je sorte | que je sortisse ... |
| | que tu sortes | |
| | qu'il/elle sorte | |
| | que nous sortions | |
| | que vous sortiez | |
| | qu'ils/elles sortent | |

| participe présent | participe passé | impératif présent | impératif passé |
|---|---|---|---|
| sortant | sorti | sors | sois sorti |
| | | sortons | soyons sortis |
| | | sortez | soyez sortis |

## 11 ouvrir

| présent | imparfait | futur simple | passé simple |
|---|---|---|---|
| j'ouvre | j'ouvrais ... | j'ouvrirai ... | j'ouvris ... |
| tu ouvres | | | |
| il/elle ouvre | | | |
| nous ouvrons | | | |
| vous ouvrez | | | |
| ils/elles ouvrent | | | |

| conditionnel présent | subjonctif présent | subjonctif imparfait |
|---|---|---|
| j'ouvrirais ... | que j'ouvre | que j'ouvrisse ... |
| | que tu ouvres | |
| | qu'il/elle ouvre | |
| | que nous ou-vrions | |
| | que vous ouvriez | |
| | qu'ils/elles ou-vrent | |

| participe présent | participe passé | impératif présent | impératif passé |
|---|---|---|---|
| ouvrant | ouvert | ouvre | aie ouvert |
| | | ouvrons | ayons ouvert |
| | | ouvrez | ayez ouvert |

## 12 apercevoir

| présent | imparfait | futur simple | passé simple |
|---------|-----------|--------------|--------------|
| j'aperçois | j'apercevais … | j'apercevrai … | j'aperçus |
| tu aperçois | | | tu aperçus |
| il/elle aperçoit | | | il/elle aperçut |
| nous apercevons | | | nous aperçûmes |
| vous apercevez | | | vous aperçûtes |
| ils/elles aperçoivent | | | ils/elles aperçurent |

| conditionnel présent | subjonctif présent | subjonctif imparfait |
|----------------------|--------------------|-----------------------|
| j'apercevrais … | que j'aperçoive | que j'aperçusse |
| | que tu aperçoives | que tu aperçusses |
| | qu'il/elle aperçoive | qu'il/elle aperçût |
| | que nous apercevions | que nous aperçussions |
| | que vous aperceviez | que vous aperçussiez |
| | qu'ils/elles aperçoivent | qu'ils/elles aperçussent |

| participe présent | participe passé | impératif présent | impératif passé |
|-------------------|-----------------|-------------------|-----------------|
| apercevant | aperçu | aperçois | aie aperçu |
| | | apercevons | ayons aperçu |
| | | apercevez | ayez aperçu |

## 13 comprendre

| présent | imparfait | futur simple | passé simple |
|---|---|---|---|
| je comprends | je comprenais | je comprendrai | je compris |
| tu comprends | tu comprenais | tu comprendras | tu compris |
| il/elle comprend | il/elle comprenait | il/elle comprendra | il/elle comprit |
| nous comprenons | nous comprenions | nous comprendrons | nous comprîmes |
| vous comprenez | vous compreniez | vous comprendrez | vous comprîtes |
| ils/elles comprennent | ils/elles comprenaient | ils/elles comprendront | ils/elles comprirent |

| conditionnel présent | subjonctif présent | subjonctif imparfait |
|---|---|---|
| je comprendrais ... | que je comprenne | que je comprisse |
| | que tu comprennes | que tu comprisses |
| | qu'il/elle comprenne | qu'il/elle comprît |
| | que nous comprenions | que nous comprissions |
| | que vous compreniez | que vous comprissiez |
| | qu'ils/elles comprennent | qu'ils/elles comprissent |

| participe présent | participe passé | impératif présent | impératif passé |
|---|---|---|---|
| comprenant | compris | comprends | aie compris |
| | | comprenons | ayons compris |
| | | comprenez | ayez compris |

## 14 vendre

| présent | imparfait | futur simple | passé simple |
|---|---|---|---|
| je vends | je vendais | je vendrai ... | je vendis |
| tu vends | tu vendais | | tu vendis |
| il/elle vend | il/elle vendait | | il/elle vendit |
| nous vendons | nous vendions | | nous vendîmes |
| vous vendez | vous vendiez | | vous vendîtes |
| ils/elles vendent | ils/elles vendaient | | ils/elles vendirent |

| conditionnel présent | subjonctif présent | subjonctif imparfait |
|---|---|---|
| je vendrais ... | que je vende | que je vendisse ... |
| | que tu vendes | |
| | qu'il/elle vende | |
| | que nous vendions | |
| | que vous vendiez | |
| | qu'ils/elles vendent | |

| participe présent | participe passé | impératif présent | impératif passé |
|---|---|---|---|
| vendant | vendu | vends | aie vendu |
| | | vendons | ayons vendu |
| | | vendez | ayez vendu |

# Verbes français irréguliers
## French irregular verbs

| Infinitif | Présent | Imparfait | Futur | Passé simple | Subjonctif présent | Subjonctif imparfait | Part. présent | Part. passé |
|---|---|---|---|---|---|---|---|---|
| accroître | j'accrois | j'accroissais | j'accroîtrai | j'accrus | que j'accroisse | que j'accrusse | accroissant | accru, e |
| | nous accroissons | nous accroissions | nous accroîtrons | nous accrûmes | que nous accroissions | que nous accrussions | | |
| | ils accroissent | ils accroissaient | ils accroîtront | ils accrurent | qu'ils accroissent | qu'ils accrussent | | |
| acquérir | j'acquiers | j'acquérais | j'acquerrai | j'acquis | que j'acquière | que j'acquisse | acquérant | acquis, e |
| | il acquiert | il acquérait | il acquerra | il acquit | qu'il acquière | qu'il acquît | | |
| | nous acquérons | nous acquérions | nous acquerrons | nous acquîmes | que nous acquérions | que nous acquissions | | |
| | ils acquièrent | ils acquéraient | ils acquerront | ils acquirent | qu'ils acquièrent | qu'ils acquissent | | |

| Infinitif | Présent | Imparfait | Futur | Passé simple | Subjonctif présent | Subjonctif imparfait | Part. présent | Part. passé |
|---|---|---|---|---|---|---|---|---|
| aller | je vais | j'allais | j'irai | j'allai | que j'aille | que j'allasse | allant | allé, e |
| | tu vas | tu allais | tu iras | tu allas | que tu ailles | que tu allasses | | |
| | il va | il allait | il ira | il alla | qu'il aille | qu'il allât | | |
| | nous allons | nous allions | nous irons | nous allâmes | que nous allions | que nous allassions | | |
| | vous allez | vous alliez | vous irez | vous allâtes | que vous alliez | que vous allassiez | | |
| | ils vont | ils allaient | ils iront | ils allèrent | qu'ils aillent | qu'ils allassent | | |
| asseoir | j'assieds | j'asseyais | j'assiérai | j'assis | que j'asseye | que j'assisse | asseyant o assoyant | assis, e |
| | il assied | il asseyait | il assiéra | il assit | qu'il asseye | qu'il assît | | |
| | nous asseyons | nous asseyions | nous assiérons | nous assîmes | que nous asseyions | que nous assissions | | |
| | ils asseyent | ils asseyaient | ils assiéront | ils assirent | qu'ils asseyent | qu'ils assissent | | |
| | o j'assois | o j'assoyais | o j'assoirai | | o que j'assoie | | | |
| | il assoit | il assoyait | il assoira | | qu'il assoie | | | |
| | nous assoyons | nous assoyions | nous assoirons | | que nous assoyions | | | |
| | ils assoient | ils assoyaient | ils assoiront | | qu'ils assoient | | | |

| Infinitif | Présent | Imparfait | Futur | Passé simple | Subjonctif présent | Subjonctif imparfait | Part. présent | Part. passé |
|---|---|---|---|---|---|---|---|---|
| avoir | j'ai | j'avais | j'aurai | j'eus | que j'aie | que j'eusse | ayant | eu, e |
| | tu as | tu avais | tu auras | tu eus | que tu aies | que tu eusses | | |
| | il a | il avait | il aura | il eut | qu'il ait | qu'il eût | | |
| | nous avons | nous avions | nous aurons | nous eûmes | que nous ayons | que nous eussions | | |
| | vous avez | vous aviez | vous aurez | vous eûtes | que vous ayez | que vous eussiez | | |
| | ils ont | ils avaient | ils auront | ils eurent | qu'ils aient | qu'ils eussent | | |
| battre | je bats | je battais | je battrai | je battis | que je batte | que je battisse | battant | battu, e |
| | il bat | il battait | il battra | il battit | qu'il batte | qu'il battît | | |
| | nous battons | nous battions | nous battrons | nous battîmes | que nous battions | que nous battissions | | |
| | ils battent | ils battaient | ils battront | ils battirent | qu'ils battent | qu'ils battissent | | |
| boire | je bois | je buvais | je boirai | je bus | que je boive | que je busse | buvant | bu, e |
| | il boit | il buvait | il boira | il but | qu'il boive | qu'il bût | | |
| | nous buvons | nous buvions | nous boirons | nous bûmes | que nous buvions | que nous bussions | | |
| | ils boivent | ils buvaient | ils boiront | ils burent | qu'ils boivent | qu'ils bussent | | |

| Infinitif | Présent | Imparfait | Futur | Passé simple | Subjonctif présent | Subjonctif imparfait | Part. présent | Part. passé |
|---|---|---|---|---|---|---|---|---|
| bouillir | je bous | je bouillais | je bouillirai | je bouillis | que je bouille | que je bouillisse | bouillant | bouilli, e |
| | nous bouillons | nous bouillions | nous bouillirons | nous bouillîmes | que nous bouillions | que nous bouillissions | | |
| | ils bouillent | ils bouillaient | ils bouilliront | ils bouillirent | qu'ils bouillent | qu'ils bouillissent | | |
| clore | je clos | - | je clorai | - | que je close | - | closant | clos, e |
| | il clôt | | il clora | | qu'il close | | | |
| | nous closons | | nous clorons | | que nous closions | | | |
| | ils closent | | ils cloront | | qu'ils closent | | | |
| conclure | je conclus | je concluais | je conclurai | je conclus | que je conclue | que je conclusse | concluant | conclu, e |
| conduire | je conduis | je conduisais | je conduirai | je conduisis | que je conduise | que je conduisisse | conduisant | conduit, e |
| coudre | je couds | je cousais | je coudrai | je cousis | que je couse | que je cousisse | cousant | cousu, e |
| | il coud | il cousait | il coudra | il cousit | qu'il couse | qu'il cousît | | |
| | nous cousons | nous cousions | nous coudrons | nous cousîmes | que nous cousions | que nous cousissions | | |
| | ils cousent | ils cousaient | ils coudront | ils cousirent | qu'ils cousent | qu'ils cousissent | | |

| Infinitif | Présent | Imparfait | Futur | Passé simple | Subjonctif présent | Subjonctif imparfait | Part. présent | Part. passé |
|---|---|---|---|---|---|---|---|---|
| courir | je cours | je courais | je courrai | je courus | que je coure | que je courusse | courant | couru, e |
| | il court | il courait | il courra | il courut | qu'il coure | qu'il courût | | |
| | nous courons | nous courions | nous courrons | nous courûmes | que nous courions | que nous courussions | | |
| | ils courent | ils couraient | ils courront | ils coururent | qu'ils courent | qu'ils courussent | | |
| craindre | je crains | je craignais | je craindrai | je craignis | que je craigne | que je craignisse | craignant | craint, e |
| | nous craignons | nous craignions | nous craindrons | nous craignîmes | que nous craignions | que nous craignissions | | |
| | ils craignent | ils craignaient | ils craindront | ils craignirent | qu'ils craignent | qu'ils craignissent | | |
| croire | je crois | je croyais | je croirai | je crus | que je croie | que je crusse | croyant | cru, e |
| | il croit | il croyait | il croira | il crut | qu'il croie | qu'il crût | | |
| | nous croyons | nous croyions | nous croirons | nous crûmes | que nous croyions | que nous crussions | | |
| | ils croient | ils croyaient | ils croiront | ils crurent | qu'ils croient | qu'ils crussent | | |

| Infinitif | Présent | Imparfait | Futur | Passé simple | Subjonctif présent | Subjonctif imparfait | Part. présent | Part. passé |
|---|---|---|---|---|---|---|---|---|
| croître | je croîs | je croissais | je croîtrai | je crûs | que je croisse | que je crûsse | croissant | crû, crue, cru(e)s |
| | nous croissons | nous croissions | nous croîtrons | nous crûmes | que nous croissions | que nous crûssions | | |
| | ils croissent | ils croissaient | ils croîtront | ils crûrent | qu'ils croissent | qu'ils crûssent | | |
| cueillir | je cueille | je cueillais | je cueillerai | je cueillis | que je cueille | que je cueillisse | cueillant | cueilli, e |
| | il cueille | il cueillait | il cueillera | il cueillit | qu'il cueille | qu'il cueillît | | |
| | nous cueillons | nous cueillions | nous cueillerons | nous cueillîmes | que nous cueillions | que nous cueillissions | | |
| | ils cueillent | ils cueillaient | ils cueilleront | ils cueillirent | qu'ils cueillent | qu'ils cueillissent | | |
| défaillir | je défaille | je défaillais | je défaillirai | je défaillis | que je défaille | que je défaillisse | défaillant | défailli |
| devoir | je dois | je devais | je devrai | je dus | que je doive | que je dusse | devant | dû, due, du(e)s |
| | il doit | il devait | il devra | il dut | qu'il doive | qu'il dût | | |
| | nous devons | nous devions | nous devrons | nous dûmes | que nous devions | que nous dussions | | |
| | ils doivent | ils devaient | ils devront | ils durent | qu'ils doivent | qu'ils dussent | | |

| Infinitif | Présent | Imparfait | Futur | Passé simple | Subjonctif présent | Subjonctif imparfait | Part. présent | Part. passé |
|---|---|---|---|---|---|---|---|---|
| dire | je dis | je disais | je dirai | je dis | que je dise | que je disse | disant | dit, e |
| | nous disons | nous disions | nous dirons | nous dîmes | que nous disions | que nous dissions | | |
| | vous dites | vous disiez | vous direz | vous dîtes | que vous disiez | que vous dissiez | | |
| | ils disent | ils disaient | ils diront | ils dirent | qu'ils disent | qu'ils dissent | | |
| dormir | je dors | je dormais | je dormirai | je dormis | que je dorme | que je dormisse | dormant | dormi |
| | nous dormons | nous dormions | nous dormirons | nous dormîmes | que nous dormions | que nous dormissions | | |
| | ils dorment | ils dormaient | ils dormiront | ils dormirent | qu'ils dorment | qu'ils dormissent | | |
| écrire | j'écris | j'écrivais | j'écrirai | j'écrivis | que j'écrive | que j'écrivisse | écrivant | écrit, e |
| | il écrit | il écrivait | il écrira | il écrivit | qu'il écrive | qu'il écrivît | | |
| | nous écrivons | nous écrivions | nous écrirons | nous écrivîmes | que nous écrivions | que nous écrivissions | | |
| | ils écrivent | ils écrivaient | ils écriront | ils écrivirent | qu'ils écrivent | qu'ils écrivissent | | |
| émouvoir see mouvoir, exception: | | | | | | | | ému, e |

| Infinitif | Présent | Imparfait | Futur | Passé simple | Subjonctif présent | Subjonctif imparfait | Part. présent | Part. passé |
|---|---|---|---|---|---|---|---|---|
| envoyer | j'envoie | j'envoyais | j'enverrai | j'envoyai | que j'envoie | que j'envoyasse | envoyant | envoyé, e |
| | nous envoyons | nous envoyions | nous enverrons | nous envoyâmes | que nous envoyions | que nous envoyassions | | |
| | ils envoient | ils envoyaient | ils enverront | ils envoyèrent | qu'ils envoient | qu'ils envoyassent | | |
| être | je suis | j'étais | je serai | je fus | que je sois | que je fusse | étant | été |
| | tu es | tu étais | tu seras | tu fus | que tu sois | que tu fusses | | |
| | il est | il était | il sera | il fut | qu'il soit | qu'il fût | | |
| | nous sommes | nous étions | nous serons | nous fûmes | que nous soyons | que nous fussions | | |
| | vous êtes | vous étiez | vous serez | vous fûtes | que vous soyez | que vous fussiez | | |
| | ils sont | ils étaient | ils seront | ils furent | qu'ils soient | qu'ils fussent | | |
| exclure | j'exclus | j'excluais | j'exclurai | j'exclus | que j'exclue | que j'exclusse | excluant | exclu, e |
| | il exclut | il excluait | il exclura | il exclut | qu'il exclue | qu'il exclût | | |
| | nous excluons | nous excluions | nous exclurons | nous exclûmes | que nous excluions | que nous exclussions | | |
| | ils excluent | ils excluaient | ils excluront | ils exclurent | qu'ils excluent | qu'ils exclussent | | |

| Infinitif | Présent | Imparfait | Futur | Passé simple | Subjonctif présent | Subjonctif imparfait | Part. présent | Part. passé |
|---|---|---|---|---|---|---|---|---|
| extraire | j'extrais | j'extrayais | j'extrairai | - | que j'extraie | - | extrayant | extrait, e |
| | nous extrayons | nous extrayions | nous extrairons | | que nous extrayions | | | |
| | ils extraient | ils extrayaient | ils extrairont | | qu'ils extraient | | | |
| faillir | je faillis | je faillissais | je faillirai | je faillis | que je faillisse | que je faillisse | faillissant o faillant | failli |
| | nous faillissons | nous faillissions | nous faillirons | nous faillîmes | que nous faillissions | que nous faillissions | | |
| | ils faillissent | ils faillissaient | ils failliront | ils faillirent | qu'ils faillissent | qu'ils faillissent | | |
| | | o je faillais | o je faudrai | | o que je faille | | | |
| | | nous faillions | nous faudrons | | que nous faillions | | | |
| | | ils faillaient | ils faudront | | qu'ils faillent | | | |
| faire | je fais | je faisais | je ferai | je fis | que je fasse | que je fisse | faisant | fait, e |
| | tu fais | tu faisais | tu feras | tu fis | que tu fasses | que tu fisses | | |
| | il fait | il faisait | il fera | il fit | qu'il fasse | qu'il fît | | |
| | nous faisons | nous faisions | nous ferons | nous fîmes | que nous fassions | que nous fissions | | |
| | vous faites | vous faisiez | vous ferez | vous fîtes | que vous fassiez | que vous fissiez | | |
| | ils font | ils faisaient | ils feront | ils firent | qu'ils fassent | qu'ils fissent | | |

| Infinitif | Présent | Imparfait | Futur | Passé simple | Subjonctif présent | Subjonctif imparfait | Part. présent | Part. passé |
|---|---|---|---|---|---|---|---|---|
| falloir | il faut | il fallait | il faudra | il fallut | qu'il faille | qu'il fallût | – | fallu |
| frire | je fris | – | je frirai | – | – | – | – | frit, e |
| | nous/vous/ils | | nous frirons | | | | | |
| | – | | ils friront | | | | | |
| fuir | je fuis | je fuyais | je fuirai | je fuis | que je fuie | que je fuisse | fuyant | fui, e |
| | il fuit | il fuyait | il fuira | il fuit | qu'il fuie | qu'il fuît | | |
| | nous fuyons | nous fuyions | nous fuirons | nous fuîmes | que nous fuyions | que nous fuissions | | |
| | ils fuient | ils fuya ent | ils fuiront | ils fuirent | qu'ils fuient | qu'ils fuissent | | |
| haïr | je hais | je haïssais | je haïrai | je haïs | que je haïsse | que je haïsse | haïssant | haï, e |
| | il hait | il haïssait | il haïra | il haït | qu'il haïsse | qu'il haït | | |
| | nous haïssons | nous haïssions | nous haïrons | nous haïmes | que nous haïssions | que nous haïssions | | |
| | ils haïssent | ils haïssaient | ils haïront | ils haïrent | qu'ils haïssent | qu'ils haïssent | | |

| Infinitif | Présent | Imparfait | Futur | Passé simple | Subjonctif présent | Subjonctif imparfait | Part. présent | Part. passé |
|---|---|---|---|---|---|---|---|---|
| joindre | je joins | je joignais | je joindrai | je joignis | que je joigne | que je joignisse | joignant | joint, e |
| | il joint | il joignait | il joindra | il joignit | qu'il joigne | qu'il joignît | | |
| | nous joignons | nous joignions | nous joindrons | nous joignîmes | que nous joignions | que nous joignissions | | |
| | ils joignent | ils joignaient | ils joindront | ils joignirent | qu'ils joignent | qu'ils joignissent | | |
| lire | je lis | je lisais | je lirai | je lus | que je lise | que je lusse | lisant | lu, e |
| | il lit | il lisait | il lira | il lut | qu'il lise | qu'il lût | | |
| | nous lisons | nous lisions | nous lirons | nous lûmes | que nous lisions | que nous lussions | | |
| | ils lisent | ils lisaient | ils liront | ils lurent | qu'ils lisent | qu'ils lussent | | |
| mettre | je mets | je mettais | je mettrai | je mis | que je mette | que je misse | mettant | mis, e |
| | il met | il mettait | il mettra | il mit | qu'il mette | qu'il mît | | |
| | nous mettons | nous mettions | nous mettrons | nous mîmes | que nous mettions | que nous missions | | |
| | ils mettent | ils mettaient | ils mettront | ils mirent | qu'ils mettent | qu'ils missent | | |

| Infinitif | Présent | Imparfait | Futur | Passé simple | Subjonctif présent | Subjonctif imparfait | Part. présent | Part. passé |
|---|---|---|---|---|---|---|---|---|
| moudre | je mouds | je moulais | je moudrai | je moulus | que je moule | que je moulusse | moulant | moulu, e |
| | il moud | il moulait | il moudra | il moulut | qu'il moule | qu'il moulût | | |
| | nous moulons | nous moulions | nous moudrons | nous moulûmes | que nous moulions | que nous moulussions | | |
| | ils moulent | ils moulaient | ils moudront | ils moulurent | qu'ils moulent | qu'ils moulussent | | |
| mourir | je meurs | je mourais | je mourrai | je mourus | que je meure | que je mourusse | mourant | mort, e |
| | il meurt | il mourait | il mourra | il mourut | qu'il meure | qu'il mourût | | |
| | nous mourons | nous mourions | nous mourrons | nous mourûmes | que nous mourions | que nous mourussions | | |
| | ils meurent | ils mouraient | ils mourront | ils moururent | qu'ils meurent | qu'ils mourussent | | |
| mouvoir | je meus | je mouvais | je mouvrai | je mus | que je meuve | que je musse | mouvant | mû, mue, mu(e)s |
| | il meut | il mouvait | il mouvra | il mut | qu'il meuve | qu'il mût | | |
| | nous mouvons | nous mouvions | nous mouvrons | nous mûmes | que nous mouvions | que nous mussions | | |
| | ils meuvent | ils mouvaient | ils mouvront | ils murent | qu'ils meuvent | qu'ils mussent | | |

| Infinitif | Présent | Imparfait | Futur | Passé simple | Subjonctif présent | Subjonctif imparfait | Part. présent | Part. passé |
|---|---|---|---|---|---|---|---|---|
| naître | je nais | je naissais | je naîtrai | je naquis | que je naisse | que je naquisse | naissant | né, e |
| | il naît | il naissait | il naîtra | il naquit | qu'il naisse | qu'il naquît | | |
| | nous naissons | nous naissions | nous naîtrons | nous naquîmes | que nous naissions | que nous naquissions | | |
| | ils naissent | ils naissaient | ils naîtront | ils naquirent | qu'ils naissent | qu'ils naquissent | | |
| nuire | je nuis | je nuisais | je nuirai | je nuisis | que je nuise | que je nuisisse | nuisant | nui |
| | nous nuisons | nous nuisions | nous nuirons | nous nuisîmes | que nous nuisions | que nous nuisissions | | |
| | ils nuisent | ils nuisaient | ils nuiront | ils nuisirent | qu'ils nuisent | qu'ils nuisissent | | |
| paraître | je parais | je paraissais | je paraîtrai | je parus | que je paraisse | que je parusse | paraissant | paru, e |
| | il paraît | il paraissait | il paraîtra | il parut | qu'il paraisse | qu'il parût | | |
| | nous paraissons | nous paraissions | nous paraîtrons | nous parûmes | que nous paraissions | que nous parussions | | |
| | ils paraissent | ils paraissaient | ils paraîtront | ils parurent | qu'ils paraissent | qu'ils parussent | | |

| Infinitif | Présent | Imparfait | Futur | Passé simple | Subjonctif présent | Subjonctif imparfait | Part. présent | Part. passé |
|---|---|---|---|---|---|---|---|---|
| peindre | je peins | je peignais | je peindrai | je peignis | que je peigne | que je peignisse | peignant | peint, e |
| | nous peignons | nous peignions | nous peindrons | nous peignîmes | que nous peignions | que nous peignissions | | |
| | ils peignent | ils peignaient | ils peindront | ils peignirent | qu'ils peignent | qu'ils peignissent | | |
| plaindre | je plains | je plaignais | je plaindrai | je plaignis | que je plaigne | que je plaignisse | plaignant | plaint, e |
| | il plaint | il plaignait | il plaindra | il plaignit | qu'il plaigne | qu'il plaignît | | |
| | nous plaignons | nous plaignions | nous plaindrons | nous plaignîmes | que nous plaignions | que nous plaignissions | | |
| | ils plaignent | ils plaignaient | ils plaindront | ils plaignirent | qu'ils plaignent | qu'ils plaignissent | | |
| plaire | je plais | je plaisais | je plairai | je plus | que je plaise | que je plusse | plaisant | plu |
| | il plaît | il plaisait | il plaira | il plut | qu'il plaise | qu'il plût | | |
| pleuvoir | il pleut | il pleuvait | il pleuvra | il plut | qu'il pleuve | qu'il plût | pleuvant | plu |
| *fig* | ils pleuvent | ils pleuvaient | ils pleuvront | ils plurent | qu'ils pleuvent | qu'ils plussent | | |

| Infinitif | Présent | Imparfait | Futur | Passé simple | Subjonctif présent | Subjonctif imparfait | Part. présent | Part. passé |
|---|---|---|---|---|---|---|---|---|
| pouvoir | je peux | je pouvais | je pourrai | je pus | que je puisse | que je pusse | pouvant | pu |
| | il peut | il pouvait | il pourra | il put | qu'il puisse | qu'il pût | | |
| | nous pouvons | nous pouvions | nous pourrons | nous pûmes | que nous puissions | que nous pussions | | |
| | ils peuvent | ils pouvaient | ils pourront | ils purent | qu'ils puissent | qu'ils pussent | | |
| prédire | je prédis | je prédisais | je prédirai | je prédis | que je prédise | que je prédisse | prédisant | prédit, e |
| | il prédit | il prédisait | il prédira | il prédit | qu'il prédise | qu'il prédît | | |
| | nous prédisons | nous prédisions | nous prédirons | nous prédîmes | que nous prédisions | que nous prédisions | | |
| prévoir see voir, exception: | | | je prévoirai | | | | | |
| résoudre | je résous | je résolvais | je résoudrai | je résolus | que je résolve | que je résolusse | résolvant | résolu, e |
| | il résout | il résolvait | il résoudra | il résolut | qu'il résolve | qu'il résolût | | |
| | nous résolvons | nous résolvions | nous résoudrons | nous résolûmes | que nous résolvions | que nous résolussions | | |
| | ils résolvent | ils résolvaient | ils résoudront | ils résolurent | qu'ils résolvent | qu'ils résolussent | | |

| Infinitif | Présent | Imparfait | Futur | Passé simple | Subjonctif présent | Subjonctif imparfait | Part. présent | Part. passé |
|---|---|---|---|---|---|---|---|---|
| rire | je ris | je riais | je rirai | je ris | que je rie | que je risse | riant | ri |
|  | il rit | il riait | il rira | il rit | qu'il rie | qu'il rît |  |  |
|  | nous rions | nous riions | nous rirons | nous rîmes | que nous riions | que nous rissions |  |  |
|  | ils rient | ils riaient | ils riront | ils rirent | qu'ils rient | qu'ils rissent |  |  |
| rompre | je romps | je rompais | je romprai | je rompis | que je rompe | que je rompisse | rompant | rompu, e |
|  | il rompt | il rompait | il rompra | il rompit | qu'il rompe | qu'il rompît |  |  |
|  | nous rompons | nous rompions | nous romprons | nous rompîmes | que nous rompions | que nous rompissions |  |  |
|  | ils rompent | ils rompaient | ils rompront | ils rompirent | qu'ils rompent | qu'ils rompissent |  |  |
| savoir | je sais | je savais | je saurai | je sus | que je sache | que je susse | sachant | su, e |
|  | il sait | il savait | il saura | il sut | qu'il sache | qu'il sût |  |  |
|  | nous savons | nous savions | nous saurons | nous sûmes | que nous sachions | que nous sussions |  |  |
|  | ils savent | ils savaient | ils sauront | ils surent | qu'ils sachent | qu'ils sussent |  |  |

| Infinitif | Présent | Imparfait | Futur | Passé simple | Subjonctif présent | Subjonctif imparfait | Part. présent | Part. passé |
|---|---|---|---|---|---|---|---|---|
| servir | je sers | je servais | je servirai | je servis | que je serve | que je servisse | servant | servi, e |
| | il sert | il servait | il servira | il servit | qu'il serve | qu'il servît | | |
| | nous servons | nous servions | nous servirons | nous servîmes | que nous servions | que nous servissions | | |
| | ils servent | ils servaient | ils serviront | ils servirent | qu'ils servent | qu'ils servissent | | |
| suffire | je suffis | je suffisais | je suffirai | je suffis | que je suffise | que je suffisse | suffisant | suffi |
| | nous suffisons | nous suffisions | nous suffirons | nous suffîmes | que nous suffisions | que nous suffissions | | |
| | ils suffisent | ils suffisaient | ils suffiront | ils suffirent | qu'ils suffisent | qu'ils suffissent | | |
| suivre | je suis | je suivais | je suivrai | je suivis | que je suive | que je suivisse | suivant | suivi, e |
| | il suit | il suivait | il suivra | il suivit | qu'il suive | qu'il suivît | | |
| | nous suivons | nous suivions | nous suivrons | nous suivîmes | que nous suivions | que nous suivissions | | |
| | ils suivent | ils suivaient | ils suivront | ils suivirent | qu'ils suivent | qu'ils suivissent | | |

| Infinitif | Présent | Imparfait | Futur | Passé simple | Subjonctif présent | Subjonctif imparfait | Part. présent | Part. passé |
|---|---|---|---|---|---|---|---|---|
| taire | je tais | je taisais | je tairai | je tus | que je taise | que je tusse | taisant | tu, e |
| | il tait | il taisait | il taira | il tut | qu'il taise | qu'il tût | | |
| | nous taisons | nous taisions | nous tairons | nous tûmes | que nous taisions | que nous tussions | | |
| | ils taisent | ils taisaient | ils tairont | ils turent | qu'ils taisent | qu'ils tussent | | |
| teindre | je teins | je teignais | je teindrai | je teignis | que je teigne | que je teignisse | teignant | teint, e |
| | il teint | il teignait | il teindra | il teignit | qu'il teigne | qu'il teignît | | |
| | nous teignons | nous teignions | nous teindrons | nous teignîmes | que nous teignions | que nous teignissions | | |
| | ils teignent | ils teignaient | ils teindront | ils teignirent | qu'ils teignent | qu'ils teignissent | | |
| traduire | je traduis | je traduisais | je traduirai | je traduisis | que je traduise | que je traduisisse | traduisant | traduit, e |
| | il traduit | il traduisait | il traduira | il traduisit | qu'il traduise | qu'il traduisît | | |
| | nous traduisons | nous traduisions | nous traduirons | nous traduisîmes | que nous traduisions | que nous traduisissions | | |
| | ils traduisent | ils traduisaient | ils traduiront | ils traduisirent | qu'ils traduisent | qu'ils traduisissent | | |

| Infinitif | Présent | Imparfait | Futur | Passé simple | Subjonctif présent | Subjonctif imparfait | Part. présent | Part. passé |
|---|---|---|---|---|---|---|---|---|
| traire | je trais | je trayais | je trairai | – | que je traie | – | trayant | trait, e |
| | il trait | il trayait | il traira | | qu'il traie | | | |
| | nous trayons | nous trayions | nous trairons | | que nous trayions | | | |
| | ils traient | ils trayaient | ils trairont | | qu'ils traient | | | |
| | | | | | | | | |
| vaincre | je vaincs | je vainquais | je vaincrai | je vainquis | que je vainque | que je vainquisse | vainquant | vaincu, e |
| | il vainc | il vainquait | il vaincra | il vainquit | qu'il vainque | qu'il vainquît | | |
| | nous vainquons | nous vainquions | nous vaincrons | nous vainquîmes | que nous vainquions | que nous vainquissions | | |
| | ils vainquent | ils vainquaient | ils vaincront | ils vainquirent | qu'ils vainquent | qu'ils vainquissent | | |
| | | | | | | | | |
| valoir | je vaux | je valais | je vaudrai | je valus | que je vaille | que je valusse | valant | valu, e |
| | il vaut | il valait | il vaudra | il valut | qu'il vaille | qu'il valût | | |
| | nous valons | nous valions | nous vaudrons | nous valûmes | que nous valions | que nous valussions | | |
| | ils valent | ils valaient | ils vaudront | ils valurent | qu'ils vaillent | qu'ils valussent | | |

| Infinitif | Présent | Imparfait | Futur | Passé simple | Subjonctif présent | Subjonctif imparfait | Part. présent | Part. passé |
|---|---|---|---|---|---|---|---|---|
| vêtir | je vêts | je vêtais | je vêtirai | je vêtis | que je vête | que je vêtisse | vêtant | vêtu, e |
| | il vêt | il vêtait | il vêtira | il vêtit | qu'il vête | qu'il vêtît | | |
| | nous vêtons | nous vêtions | nous vêtirons | nous vêtîmes | que nous vêtions | que nous vêtissions | | |
| | ils vêtent | ils vêtaient | ils vêtiront | ils vêtirent | qu'ils vêtent | qu'ils vêtissent | | |
| vivre | je vis | je vivais | je vivrai | je vécus | que je vive | que je vécusse | vivant | vécu, e |
| | il vit | il vivait | il vivra | il vécut | qu'il vive | qu'il vécût | | |
| | nous vivons | nous vivions | nous vivrons | nous vécûmes | que nous vivions | que nous vécussions | | |
| | ils vivent | ils vivaient | ils vivront | ils vécurent | qu'ils vivent | qu'ils vécussent | | |
| voir | je vois | je voyais | je verrai | je vis | que je voie | que je visse | voyant | vu, e |
| | il voit | il voyait | il verra | il vit | qu'il voie | qu'il vît | | |
| | nous voyons | nous voyions | nous verrons | nous vîmes | que nous voyions | que nous vissions | | |
| | ils voient | ils voyaient | ils verront | ils virent | qu'ils voient | qu'ils vissent | | |

| Infinitif | Présent | Imparfait | Futur | Passé simple | Subjonctif présent | Subjonctif imparfait | Part. présent | Part. passé |
|---|---|---|---|---|---|---|---|---|
| vouloir | je veux | je voulais | je voudrai | je voulus | que je veuille | que je voulusse | voulant | voulu, e |
| | il veut | il voulait | il voudra | il voulut | qu'il veuille | qu'il voulût | | |
| | nous voulons | nous voulions | nous voudrons | nous voulûmes | que nous voulions | que nous voulussions | | |
| | ils veulent | ils voulaient | ils voudront | ils voulurent | qu'ils veuillent | qu'ils voulussent | | |

# Verbes anglais irréguliers
## English irregular verbs

| Infinitive | Past | Past Participle |
|---|---|---|
| arise | arose | arisen |
| awake | awoke | awaked, awoken |
| be | was *sing*, were *pl* | been |
| bear | bore | borne, born |
| beat | beat | beaten |
| become | became | become |
| begin | began | begun |
| behold | beheld | beheld |
| bend | bent | bent |
| bet | bet, betted | bet, betted |
| bid | bade, bid | bid, bidden |
| bind | bound | bound |
| bite | bit | bitten |
| bleed | bled | bled |
| blow | blew | blown |
| break | broke | broken |
| breed | bred | bred |
| bring | brought | brought |
| build | built | built |
| burn | burned, burnt | burned, burnt |
| burst | burst | burst |
| buy | bought | bought |
| can | could | – |
| cast | cast | cast |
| catch | caught | caught |
| choose | chose | chosen |
| cling | clung | clung |

| Infinitive | Past | Past Participle |
|---|---|---|
| come | came | come |
| cost | cost, costed | cost, costed |
| creep | crept | crept |
| cut | cut | cut |
| deal | dealt | dealt |
| dig | dug | dug |
| dive | dived, dove | dived |
| do | did | done |
| draw | drew | drawn |
| dream | dreamed, dreamt | dreamed, dreamt |
| drink | drank | drunk |
| drive | drove | driven |
| dwell | dwelt, dwelled | dwelt, dwelled |
| eat | ate | eaten |
| fall | fell | fallen |
| feed | fed | fed |
| feel | felt | felt |
| fight | fought | fought |
| find | found | found |
| flee | fled | fled |
| fling | flung | flung |
| fly | flew | flown |
| forbid | forbade, forbad | forbidden, forbid |
| forget | forgot | forgotten |
| freeze | froze | frozen |
| get | got | gotten, got |
| give | gave | given |
| go | went | gone |
| grind | ground | ground |
| grow | grew | grown |
| hang | hung, LAW hanged | hung, LAW hanged |
| have | had | had |

| Infinitive | Past | Past Participle |
|---|---|---|
| hear | heard | heard |
| hide | hid | hidden |
| hit | hit | hit |
| hold | held | held |
| hurt | hurt | hurt |
| keep | kept | kept |
| kneel | knelt, kneeled | knelt, kneeled |
| know | knew | known |
| lay | laid | laid |
| lead | led | led |
| leap | leaped, leapt | leaped, leapt |
| learn | learned, learnt | learned, learnt |
| leave | left | left |
| lend | lent | lent |
| let | let | let |
| lie | lay | lain |
| light | lighted, lit | lighted, lit |
| lose | lost | lost |
| make | made | made |
| may | might | – |
| mean | meant | meant |
| meet | met | met |
| mistake | mistook | mistaken |
| mow | mowed | mown, mowed |
| pay | paid | paid |
| put | put | put |
| quit | quit, quitted | quit, quitted |
| read [rid] | read [red] | read [red] |
| rend | rent, rended | rent, rended |
| rid | rid, ridded | rid, ridded |
| ride | rode | ridden |
| ring | rang | rung |

| Infinitive | Past | Past Participle |
|---|---|---|
| rise | rose | risen |
| run | ran | run |
| saw | sawed | sawed, sawn |
| say | said | said |
| see | saw | seen |
| seek | sought | sought |
| sell | sold | sold |
| send | sent | sent |
| set | set | set |
| sew | sewed | sewn, sewed |
| shake | shook | shaken |
| shave | shaved | shaved, shaven |
| shine | shone, shined | shone, shined |
| shit | shit, *iron* shat | shit, *iron* shat |
| shoe | shod | shod, shodden |
| shoot | shot | shot |
| show | showed | shown, showed |
| shrink | shrank, shrunk | shrunk, shrunken |
| shut | shut | shut |
| sing | sang, sung | sung |
| sink | sank, sunk | sunk |
| sit | sat | sat |
| sleep | slept | slept |
| slide | slid | slid |
| sling | slung | slung |
| slit | slit | slit |
| smell | smelled, smelt | smelled, smelt |
| sow | sowed | sown, sowed |
| speak | spoke | spoken |
| speed | sped, speeded | sped, speeded |
| spell | spelled, spelt | spelled, spelt |
| spend | spent | spent |

| Infinitive | Past | Past Participle |
|---|---|---|
| spill | spilled, spilt | spilled, spilt |
| spin | spun | spun |
| spit | spat, spit | spat, spit |
| split | split | split |
| spoil | spoiled, spoilt | spoiled, spoilt |
| spread | spread | spread |
| spring | sprang, sprung | sprung |
| stand | stood | stood |
| steal | stole | stolen |
| stick | stuck | stuck |
| sting | stung | stung |
| stink | stank, stunk | stunk |
| stride | strode | stridden |
| strike | struck | struck |
| string | strung | strung |
| strive | strove | striven, strived |
| swear | swore | sworn |
| sweep | swept | swept |
| swell | swelled | swollen, swelled |
| swim | swam | swum |
| swing | swung | swung |
| take | took | taken |
| teach | taught | taught |
| tear | tore | torn |
| tell | told | told |
| think | thought | thought |
| throw | threw | thrown |
| thrust | thrust | thrust |
| tread | trod | trodden, trod |
| wake | woke, waked | waked, woken |
| wear | wore | worn |
| weave | wove | woven |

| Infinitive | Past | Past Participle |
|------------|------|-----------------|
| weep | wept | wept |
| win | won | won |
| wind | wound | wound |
| wring | wrung | wrung |
| write | wrote | written |

# Les nombres
# Numerals

## Les nombres cardinaux
### Cardinal numbers

| | | |
|---|---|---|
| zéro | 0 | zero |
| un, une | 1 | one |
| deux | 2 | two |
| trois | 3 | three |
| quatre | 4 | four |
| cinq | 5 | five |
| six | 6 | six |
| sept | 7 | seven |
| huit | 8 | eight |
| neuf | 9 | nine |
| dix | 10 | ten |
| onze | 11 | eleven |
| douze | 12 | twelve |
| treize | 13 | thirteen |
| quatorze | 14 | fourteen |
| quinze | 15 | fifteen |
| seize | 16 | sixteen |
| dix-sept | 17 | seventeen |
| dix-huit | 18 | eighteen |
| dix-neuf | 19 | nineteen |
| vingt | 20 | twenty |
| vingt et un | 21 | twenty-one |
| vingt-deux | 22 | twenty-two |
| vingt-trois | 23 | twenty-three |
| vingt-quatre | 24 | twenty-four |
| vingt-cinq | 25 | twenty-five |

| trente | 30 | thirty |
|--------|----|--------|
| trente et un | 31 | thirty-one |
| trente-deux | 32 | thirty-two |
| trente-trois | 33 | thirty-three |
| quarante | 40 | forty |
| quarante et un | 41 | forty-one |
| quarante-deux | 42 | forty-two |
| cinquante | 50 | fifty |
| cinquante et un | 51 | fifty-one |
| cinquante-deux | 52 | fifty-two |
| soixante | 60 | sixty |
| soixante et un | 61 | sixty-one |
| soixante-deux | 62 | sixty-two |
| soixante-dix | 70 | seventy |
| soixante et onze | 71 | seventy-one |
| soixante-douze | 72 | seventy-two |
| soixante-quinze | 75 | seventy-five |
| soixante-dix-neuf | 79 | seventy-nine |
| quatre-vingt(s) | 80 | eighty |
| quatre-vingt-un | 81 | eighty-one |
| quatre-vingt-deux | 82 | eighty-two |
| quatre-vingt-cinq | 85 | eighty-five |
| quatre-vingt-dix | 90 | ninety |
| quatre-vingt-onze | 91 | ninety-one |
| quatre-vingt-douze | 92 | ninety-two |
| quatre-vingt-dix-neuf | 99 | ninety-nine |
| cent | 100 | one hundred |
| cent un | 101 | one hundred and one |
| cent deux | 102 | one hundred and two |
| cent dix | 110 | one hundred and ten |
| cent vingt | 120 | one hundred and twenty |
| cent quatre-vingt-dix-neuf | 199 | one hundred and ninety-nine |

| deux cents | 200 | two hundred |
| deux cent un | 201 | two hundred and one |
| deux cent vingt-deux | 222 | two hundred and twenty-two |
| trois cents | 300 | three hundred |
| quatre cents | 400 | four hundred |
| cinq cents | 500 | five hundred |
| six cents | 600 | six hundred |
| sept cents | 700 | seven hundred |
| huit cents | 800 | eight hundred |
| neuf cents | 900 | nine hundred |
| mille | 1000 | one thousand |
| mille un | 1001 | one thousand and one |
| mille dix | 1010 | one thousand and ten |
| mille cent | 1100 | one thousand one hundred |
| deux mille | 2000 | two thousand |
| dix mille | 10000 | ten thousand |
| cent mille | 100000 | one hundred thousand |
| un million | 1000000 | one million |
| deux millions | 2000000 | two million |
| deux millions cinq cent mille | 2500000 | two million, five hundred thousand |
| un milliard | 1000000000 | one billion |
| mille milliard | 1000000000000 | one thousand billion |

## Les nombres ordinaux

## Ordinal numbers

| premier, ère | 1er, 1ère | 1st | first |
|---|---|---|---|
| second, e deuxième | 2nd, 2nde, 2e | 2nd | second |
| troisième | 3e | 3rd | third |
| quatrième | 4e | 4th | fourth |
| cinquième | 5e | 5th | fifth |
| sixième | 6e | 6th | sixth |
| septième | 7e | 7th | seventh |
| huitième | 8e | 8th | eighth |
| neuvième | 9e | 9th | ninth |
| dixième | 10e | 10th | tenth |
| onzième | 11e | 11th | eleventh |
| douzième | 12e | 12th | twelfth |
| treizième | 13e | 13th | thirteenth |
| quatorzième | 14e | 14th | fourteenth |
| quinzième | 15e | 15th | fifteenth |
| seizième | 16e | 16th | sixteenth |
| dix-septième | 17e | 17th | seventeenth |
| dix-huitième | 18e | 18th | eighteenth |
| dix-neuvième | 19e | 19th | nineteenth |
| vingtième | 20e | 20th | twentieth |
| vingt et unième | 21e | 21st | twenty-first |
| vingt-deuxième | 22e | 22nd | twenty-second |
| vingt-troisième | 23e | 23rd | twenty-third |
| trentième | 30e | 30th | thirtieth |
| trente et unième | 31e | 31st | thirty-first |
| trente-deuxième | 32e | 32nd | thirty-second |
| quarantième | 40e | 40th | fortieth |
| cinquantième | 50e | 50th | fiftieth |
| soixantième | 60e | 60th | sixtieth |
| soixante-dixième | 70e | 70th | seventieth |

| soixante et onzième | 71ᵉ | 71st | seventy-first |
|---|---|---|---|
| soixante-douzième | 72ᵉ | 72nd | seventy-second |
| soixante-dix-neu-vième | 79ᵉ | 79th | seventy-ninth |
| quatre-vingtième | 80ᵉ | 80th | eightieth |
| quatre-vingt-unième | 81ᵉ | 81st | eighty-first |
| quatre-vingt-deuxième | 82ᵉ | 82nd | eighty-second |
| quatre-vingt-dixième | 90ᵉ | 90th | ninetieth |
| quatre-vingt-onzième | 91ᵉ | 91st | ninety-first |
| quatre-vingt-dix-neu-vième | 99ᵉ | 99th | ninety-ninth |
| centième | 100ᵉ | 100th | one hundredth |
| cent unième | 101ᵉ | 101st | one hundred and first |
| cent dixième | 110ᵉ | 110th | one hundred and tenth |
| cent quatre-vingt-quinzième | 195ᵉ | 195th | one hundred and ninety-fifth |
| deux(-)centième | 200ᵉ | 200th | two hundredth |
| trois(-)centième | 300ᵉ | 300th | three hundredth |
| cinq(-)centième | 500ᵉ | 500th | five hundredth |
| millième | 1000ᵉ | 1000th | one thousandth |
| deux(-)millième | 2 000ᵉ | 2 000th | two thousandth |
| millionième | 1000 000ᵉ | 1000 000th | one millionth |
| dix(-)millionième | 10 000 000ᵉ | 10 000 000th | ten millionth |

# Les fractions

## Fractional numbers

| | | |
|---|---|---|
| un demi | $^1/_2$ | one half |
| un tiers | $^1/_3$ | one third |
| un quart | $^1/_4$ | one quarter |
| un cinquième | $^1/_5$ | one fifth |
| un dixième | $^1/_{10}$ | one tenth |
| un centième | $^1/_{100}$ | one hundredth |
| un millième | $^1/_{1000}$ | one thousandth |
| un millionième | $^1/_{1000\,000}$ | one millionth |
| deux tiers | $^2/_3$ | two thirds |
| trois quarts | $^3/_4$ | three quarters |
| deux cinquièmes | $^2/_5$ | two fifths |
| trois dixièmes | $^3/_{10}$ | three tenths |
| | | |
| un et demi | $1^1/_2$ | one and a half |
| deux et demi | $2^1/_2$ | two and a half |
| cinq trois huitièmes | $5^3/_8$ | five and three eighths |
| un virgule un | 1,1 | one point one |

# Poids, mesures et températures
# Weights, measures and temperatures

## Système décimal
## Decimal system

| giga | 1 000 000 000 | G | giga |
|---|---|---|---|
| méga | 1 000 000 | M | mega |
| hectokilo | 100 000 | hk | hectokilo |
| myria | 10 000 | ma | myria |
| kilo | 1000 | k | kilo |
| hecto | 100 | h | hecto |
| déca | 10 | da | deca |
| déci | 0,1 | d | deci |
| centi | 0,01 | c | centi |
| milli | 0,001 | m | milli |
| décimilli | 0,0001 | dm | decimilli |
| centimilli | 0,00001 | cm | centimilli |
| micro | 0,000001 | μ | micro |

### Tableaux de conversion

Le système impérial de mesures existe encore aux États-Unis; en Grande Bretagne, le système métrique est officiellement adopté, mais l'ancien système demeure la référence pour beaucoup de personnes. Il en est de même pour l'échelle Fahrenheit des températures. Seules les mesures impériales encore en usage courant figurent dans ces tableaux. En multipliant une mesure métrique par le facteur de conversion en gras, on obtient la mesure impériale correspondante; inversement une mesure impériale divisée par le même facteur donnera la mesure métrique.

### Conversion tables

Only U. S. Customary units still in common use are given here. To convert a metric measurement to U. S. Customary measures, multiply by the conversion factor in bold. Likewise dividing a U. S. Customary measurement by the same factor will give the metric equivalent. Note that the decimal comma is used throughout rather than the decimal point.

## Mesures métriques
Metric measurement

## Mesures impériales
U. S. Customary Measures

| mille marin | 1852 m | – | nautical mile | | | |
|---|---|---|---|---|---|---|
| kilomètre | 1000 m | km | kilometer | 0,62 | mile (= 1760 yards) | m, mi |
| hectomètre | 100 m | hm | hectometer | | | |
| décamètre | 10 m | dam | decameter | | | |
| mètre | 1 m | m | meter | 1,09 | yard (= 3 feet) | yd |
| | | | | 3,28 | foot (= 12 inches) | ft |
| décimètre | 0,1 m | dm | decimeter | | | |
| centimètre | 0,01 m | cm | centimeter | 0,39 | inch | in |
| millimètre | 0,001 m | mm | millimeter | | | |
| micron | 0,000 001 m | µ | micron | | | |
| millimicron | 0,000 000 001 m | mµ | millimicron | | | |
| Angstrœm | 0,000 000 0001 m | Å | angstrom | | | |

### Mesures de surface
Surface measure

| kilomètre carré | 1 000 000 m² | km² | square kilometer | 0,386 | square mile (= 640 acres) | sq. m., sq. mi. |
|---|---|---|---|---|---|---|
| hectomètre carré | 10 000 m² | hm² | square hectometer | 2,47 | acre (= 4840 square yards) | a. |
| hectare | | ha | hectare | | | |
| décamètre carré | 100 m² | dam² | square decameter | | | |
| are | | a | are | | | |
| mètre carré | 1 m² | m² | square meter | 1.196 | square yard (9 square feet) | sq. yd |
| | | | | 10,76 | square feet (= 144 square inches) | sq. ft |

| décimètre carré | 0,01 m² | dm² | square decimeter | | | |
| centimètre carré | 0,0001 m² | cm² | square centimeter | 0,155 | square inch | sq. in. |
| millimètre carré | 0,000 001 m² | mm² | square millimeter | | | |

## Mesures de volume

Volume and capacity

| kilomètre cube | 1 000 000 000 m³ | km³ | cubic kilometer | | | |
| mètre cube | 1 m³ | m³ | cubic meter | 1,308 | cubic yard (= 27 cubic feet) | cu. yd |
| stère | | st | stere | 35,32 | cubic foot (= 1728 cubic inches) | cu. ft |
| hectolitre | 0,1 m³ | hl | hectoliter | | | |
| décalitre | 0,01 m³ | dal | decaliter | | | |
| décimètre cube | 0,001 m³ | dm³ | cubic decimeter | 0,26 | gallon | gal |
| litre | | l | liter | 2,1 | pint | pt |
| décilitre | 0,0001 m³ | dl | deciliter | | | |
| centilitre | 0,00001 m³ | cl | centiliter | 0,352 | fluid ounce | fl. oz |
| | | | | 0,338 | | |
| centimètre cube | 0,000 001 m³ | cm³ | cubic centimeter | 0,061 | cubic inch | cu. in. |
| millilitre | 0,000 001 m³ | ml | milliliter | | | |
| millimètre cube | 0,000 000 001 m³ | mm³ | cubic millimeter | | | |

## Poids
### Weight

| tonne | 1000 kg | t | tonne | 1,1 | [short] ton (= 2000 pounds) | t. |
|---|---|---|---|---|---|---|
| quintal | 100 kg | q | quintal | | | |
| kilogramme | 1000 g | kg | kilogram | 2,2 | pound (= 16 ounces) | lb |
| hecto-gramme | 100 g | hg | hectogram | | | |
| déca-gramme | 10 g | dag | decagram | | | |
| gramme | 1 g | g | gram | 0,035 | ounce | oz |
| carat | 0,2 g | – | carat | | | |
| déci-gramme | 0,1 g | dg | decigram | | | |
| centi-gramme | 0,01 g | cg | centigram | | | |
| milli-gramme | 0,001 g | mg | milligram | | | |
| micro-gramme | 0,000 001 g | µg | microgram | | | |

## Températures: Fahrenheit et Celsius

## Temperatures: Fahrenheit and Celsius

Pour convertir une température Celsius en degrés Fahrenheit, il faut multiplier par 1,8 et ajouter 32; par exemple 100 °C (point d'ébullition de l'eau) × 1,8 = 180; 180 + 32 = 212° F.

To convert a temperature from degrees Celsius to Fahrenheit, multiply by 1.8 and add 32; e.g. 100 °C (boiling point of water) × 1.8 = 180; 180 + 32 = 212° F.

Pour convertir une température Fahrenheit en degrés Celsius, il faut soustraire 32 et diviser par 1,8; par exemple 212° F (point d'ébullition de l'eau) – 32 = 180; 180 ÷ 1,8 = 100 °C.

To convert a temperature from degrees Fahrenheit to Celsius, deduct 32 and divide by 1.8; e.g. 212° F (boiling point of water) – 32 = 180; 180/1.8 = 100 °C.

|  |  | Fahrenheit | Celsius |
|---|---|---|---|
| point de congélation de l'eau | freezing point of water | 32° | 0° |
| point d'ébullition de l'eau | boiling point of water | 212° | 100° |
| un jour extrêmement froid | an extremely cold day | –40° | –40° |
| un jour froid | a cold day | 14° | –10° |
| un jour frais | a cool day | 50° | 10° |
| un jour doux | a mild day | 68° | 20° |
| un jour de chaleur | a warm day | 86° | 30° |
| un jour extrêmement chaud | a very hot day | 104° | 40° |
| la température normale du corps humain | normal body temperature | 98.6° | 37° |

## Symboles et abréviations

| | | |
|---|---|---|
| ► | bloc phraséolo-gique | idiom block |
| = | contraction | contraction |
| ≈ | correspond à | equivalent to |
| — | changement d'interlocuteur | change of speaker |
| ® | marque déposée | trademark |
| ◆ | verbe à particule | phrasal verb |
| *1st pers* | première personne | first person |
| *3rd pers* | troisième personne | third person |
| *a.* | aussi | also |
| *abr de, abbr of* | abréviation de | abbreviation of |
| *adj* | adjectif | adjective |
| ADMIN | administration | administration |
| *adv* | adverbe | adverb |
| AGR | agriculture | agriculture |
| ANAT | anatomie | anatomy |
| *app* | apposition | apposition |
| ARCHIT | architecture | architecture |
| *art* | article | article |
| ART | beaux-arts | art |
| ASTR | astronomie, astrologie | astronomy, astrology |
| AUTO | automobile, moyens de transport | automobile, transport |
| *aux* | auxiliaire | auxiliary verb |
| AVIAT | aviation, espace | aviation, aerospace, space technology |
| *Belgique* | belgicisme | Belgian-French word |
| BIO | biologie | biology |
| BOT | botanique | botany |
| *Can* | anglais canadien | Canadian English |
| CHEM | chimie | chemistry |
| CHEMDFER | chemin de fer | railways |
| *child-speak* | langage enfantin | children's language |
| CHIM | chimie | chemistry |
| CINE | cinéma | cinema, film |
| COM | commerce | commerce |
| *comp* | comparatif | comparative |
| *compl* | complément | complement |
| COMPUT | informatique | computing |
| *cond* | conditionnel | conditional |
| *conj* | conjonction | conjunction |
| CONSTR | construction | construction |

## Symbols and Abbreviations

| | | |
|---|---|---|
| COUT | couture | sewing |
| CULIN | art culinaire | culinary, art of cooking |
| DANCE | danse | dance |
| *déf, def* | défini | definite |
| *défec* | verbe défectif | defective verb |
| *dém* | démonstratif | demonstrative |
| *dét, det* | déterminant | determiner |
| *dim* | diminutif | diminutive |
| ECOL | écologie | ecology |
| ECOLE | école | school |
| ECON | économie, industrie | economics |
| ELEC | électricité, électronique | electricity, electronics |
| *enfantin* | langage enfantin | children's language |
| *f* | féminin | feminine |
| FASHION | mode, couture | fashion, sewing |
| *fém* | féminin | feminine |
| *fig* | figuré | figurative |
| FIN | finances, bourse, impôts | finance, banking, stock exchange |
| *form* | langage formel | formal language |
| *fpl* | féminin pluriel | feminine plural |
| *fut* | futur | future |
| GAMES | jeux | games |
| *gén* | généralement | generally |
| GEO | géographie, géologie | geography, geology |
| HIST | histoire, historique | history, historical |
| *imparf* | imparfait | imperfect |
| *imper* | impératif | imperative |
| *impers* | impersonnel | impersonal |
| *indéf, indef* | indéfini | indefinite |
| *indic* | indicatif | indicative |
| INET | Internet | internet |
| *inf* | langage informel | informal language |
| *infin* | infinitif | infinitive |
| INFORM | informatique | computing |
| *insep* | inséparable | inseparable |
| *interj* | interjection | interjection |
| *interrog* | interrogatif | interrogative |
| *inv* | invariable | invariable |
| *iron* | ironique, humoristique | ironic, humorous |
| *irr* | irrégulier | irregular |
| JEUX | jeux | games |

| | | |
|---|---|---|
| JUR | juridique | law |
| LAW | juridique | law |
| LING | linguistique, grammaire | linguistics, grammar |
| LIT | littérature, poésie | literature, poetry |
| *loc* | locution | phrase |
| *m* | masculin | masculine |
| *m of* | masculin ou féminin | masculine or feminine |
| *masc* | masculin | masculine |
| *mf* | masculin et féminin | masculine and feminine |
| *mfpl* | masculin et féminin pluriel | masculine and feminine plural |
| MATH | mathématiques, géométrie | mathematics, geometry |
| MED | médecine, pharmacie | medicine, pharmacology |
| MEDIA | média | media |
| METEO | météorologie | meteorology, weather |
| *Midi* | du Midi | southern of France |
| MIL | militaire | military |
| MIN | industrie minière | mining |
| *mpl* | masculin pluriel | masculine plural |
| MUS | musique | music |
| *n* | substantif | noun |
| NAUT | navigation | nautical, naval |
| *nég, neg* | négation | negation |
| *Nord* | du Nord | northern of France |
| *num* | numéral | numeral |
| *opp* | opposé, antonyme | opposite, antonym |
| *part passé* | participe passé | past participle |
| *part prés* | participe présent | present participle |
| *péj, pej* | péjoratif | pejorative, disapproving |
| *pers* | personnel, personne | personal, person |
| PHILOS | philosophie | philosophy |
| PHOT | photographie | photography |
| PHYS | physique | physics |
| *pl* | pluriel | plural |
| POL | politique | politics |
| *poss* | possessif | possessive |
| *pp* | participe passé | past participle |
| *prép, prep* | préposition | preposition |
| *prés* | présent | present |
| PRESSE | presse | publishing, journalism |
| *pron* | pronom | pronoun |
| *prov* | proverbe | proverb |
| PSYCH | psychologie, psychiatrie | psychology, psychiatry |
| *pt* | temps du passé | past tense |
| PUBL | presse | publishing, journalism |
| *qc* | quelque chose | something |
| *qn* | quelqu'un | somebody |
| *Québec* | québécisme | French-Canadianism |
| RADIO | radio | radio |
| RAIL | chemin de fer | railways |
| *reg* | régulier | regular |
| *rel* | relatif | relative |
| REL | religion | religion |
| *s.* | voir | see |
| *sb* | quelqu'un | somebody |
| SCHOOL | école | school |
| *sep* | séparable | separable |
| *sing* | singulier | singular |
| *sing/pl vb* | verbe singulier ou pluriel | singular or plural verb |
| *sl* | argot américain | American slang |
| SOCIOL | sociologie | sociology |
| *soutenu* | soutenu | formal language |
| SPORT, SPORTS | sport | sports |
| sth | quelque chose | something |
| *subj* | subjonctif | subjunctive |
| *subst* | substantif | noun |
| *Suisse* | helvétisme | Swiss expression |
| *superl* | superlatif | superlative |
| TECH | technique | technical |
| TEL | télécommunications | telecommunications |
| THEAT | théâtre | theatre |
| TV | télévision | television |
| TYP | typographie | typography, printing, graphic arts |
| UNIV | université | university |
| *v.* | voir | see |
| *vb* | verbe | verb |
| *vi* | verbe intransitif | intransitive verb |
| *vpr* | verbe pronominal | reflexive verb |
| *vt* | verbe transitif | transitive verb |
| *vulg* | langage vulgaire | vulgar language |
| ZOOL | zoologie | zoology |

## FREE E-DICTIONARY DOWNLOADING INSTRUCTIONS

1. To download your FREE e-dictionary visit:
   www.barronsbooks.com/pocket424/

2. Please have the printed book in front of you. You will be asked two security questions. For example, "what is the first headword on page 361?"

3. Follow the prompts.

This e-dictionary can be read on any desktop or laptop with Windows or Mac operating systems. It is not compatible with Tablets or Smartphones.

## SYSTEM REQUIREMENTS

| Windows: | Mac: |
| --- | --- |
| Windows 8.1 | Mac OS 10.7 and above |
| Max 50 MB hard drive space* | Max 70 MB hard drive space* |

\* with all 4 dictionaries